WILKINSON'S

ROAD TRAFFIC
OFFENCES

WILKINSON'S
ROAD TRAFFIC OFFENCES

Twentieth Edition

VOLUME 2

Prepared by PAUL H. NIEKIRK, M.A.
of Gray's Inn, Barrister

General Editor
PETER WALLIS
District Judge (Magistrates' Courts)
Recorder of the Crown Court

Sweet & Maxwell

AUSTRALIA
LBC Information Services
Sydney

CANADA AND USA
Carswell
Toronto

NEW ZEALAND
Brooker's
Auckland

SINGAPORE AND MALAYSIA
Sweet & Maxwell Asia
Singapore and Kuala Lumpur

Published by
Sweet & Maxwell Limited of
100 Avenue Road
London NW3 3PF
(http://www.sweetandmaxwell.co.uk)

Typeset by Servis Filmsetting Ltd, Manchester
Printed and bound in Great Britain by Clays Ltd, St Ives plc

No natural forests were destroyed to make this product;
only farmed timber was used and replanted.

A CIP catalogue record for this book is available from the British Library.

ISBN 0 421 82580 4

Twentieth Edition 2001

ISBN 0-421-82580-4

9 780421 825802 >

Contents

Table of Cases

All entries are tabled to paragraph number.

Table of Statutes

*All entries are tabled to paragraph number. Page numbers in **bold** type indicate where the entry is reproduced.*

Table of Statutes

Table of Statutes

Table of Statutes

Table of Statutes

Table of Statutes

Table of Statutes

Table of Statutes

Table of Statutes

Table of Statutes

Table of Statutes

Table of Statutes

Table of Statutes

Table of Statutes

Table of Statutes

Table of Statutes

Table of Statutes

Table of Statutes

Table of Statutes

Table of Statutes

Table of Statutes

Table of Statutes

Table of Statutes

Table of Statutes

Table of Statutes

Table of Statutes

Table of Statutes

Table of Statutes

Table of Statutory Instruments

Table of Statutory Instruments

Table of Statutory Instruments

Table of Statutory Instruments

Table of Statutory Instruments

Table of Statutory Instruments

Table of Statutory Instruments

Table of Statutory Instruments

Table of Statutory Instruments

Table of Statutory Instruments

Table of Statutory Instruments

Table of Statutory Instruments

Table of Statutory Instruments

Table of Statutory Instruments

Table of Statutory Instruments

Table of European Provisions

*All entries are tabled to paragraph number. Page numbers in **bold** type indicate where the entry is reproduced.*

Table of European Provisions

Table of European Provisions

Table of European Provisions

Table of European Provisions

Table of European Provisions

Regulations

Table of European Provisions

Table of European Provisions

Table of European Provisions

Table of European Provisions

Table of International Conventions and Agreements

*All entries are tabled to paragraph number. Page numbers in **bold** type indicate where the entry is reproduced.*

Table of International Conventions and Agreements

Table of International Conventions and Agreements

Section A

Statutes

Chronological List*

* For the alphabetical list of statutes, see p. 5 below.

Statutes

Statutes

Alphabetical List

Statutes

Statutes

The Town Police Clauses Act 1847

(10 & 11 Vict. c. 89)

An Act for consolidating in one Act certain provisions usually contained in Acts for regulating the police of towns. **A1.01**

[22nd July 1847]

*   *   *

38. What vehicles to be deemed hackney carriages

Every wheeled carriage, whatever may be its form or construction, used in standing or plying for hire in any street within the prescribed distance, and every carriage standing upon any street within the prescribed distance, having thereon any numbered plate required by this or the special Act to be fixed upon a hackney carriage, or having thereon any plate resembling or intended to resemble any such plate as aforesaid, shall be deemed to be a hackney carriage within the meaning of this Act; and in all proceedings at law or otherwise the term *"hackney carriage"* shall be sufficient to describe any such carriage: **A1.02**

Provided always, that no stage coach used for the purpose of standing or plying for passengers to be carried for hire at separate fares, and duly licensed for that purpose, and having thereon the proper numbered plates required by law to be placed on such stage coaches, shall be deemed to be a hackney carriage within the meaning of this Act.

[The definition of "hackney carriage" in this Act is incorporated by reference into section 80 of the Local Government (Miscellaneous Provisions) Act 1976 (q.v.).] **A1.03**

*   *   *

The Metropolitan Public Carriage Act 1869

(32 & 33 Vict. c. 115)

A2.01   An Act for amending the law relating to hackney and stage carriages within the Metropolitan Police District.

[11th August 1869]

*   *   *

2. Limits of Act

A2.02   The limits of this Act shall be the metropolitan police district, and the city of London . . .

A2.03   *[Section 2 is printed as amended by the Statute Law (Repeals) Act 1989.]*

*   *   *

4. Interpretation

A2.04   In this Act "*stage carriage*" shall mean any carriage for the conveyance of passengers which plies for hire in any public street, road, or place within the limits of this Act, and in which the passengers or any of them are charged to pay separate and distinct or at the rate of separate and distinct fares for their respective places or seats therein.

"*Hackney carriage*" shall mean any carriage for the conveyance of passengers which plies for hire within the limits of this Act, and is [neither a stage carriage nor a tramcar].

["*London cab order*" shall mean an order made by Transport for London.]

["*Prescribed*" shall mean prescribed by London cab order.]

[Any power to make a London cab order under this Act includes power to vary or revoke a previous such order.]

A2.05   *[Section 4 has been amended by the Greater London Authority Act 1999, s.253 and Sched. 20, para.5(1) and (2).*
The definition of "hackney carriage" in this Act is incorporated by reference into section 80 of the Local Government (Miscellaneous Provisions) Act 1976 (q.v.). It is printed as amended by the Transport and Works Act 1992, s.62(1).]

The Criminal Law Act 1967

(1967 c. 58)

An Act to amend the law in England and Wales by abolishing the division of crimes into felonies and misdemeanours and to amend and simplify the law in respect of matters arising from or related to that division or the abolition of it . . . and for purposes connected therewith. **A3.01**

[21st July 1967]

*   *   *

6. Trial of offences

(1) *[Plea on indictment; failure to plead.]* **A3.02**

(2) *[Alternative verdicts on indictment for murder.]*

(3) Where, on a person's trial on indictment for any offence except treason or murder, the jury find him not guilty of the offence specifically charged in the indictment, but the allegations in the indictment amount to or include (expressly or by implication) an allegation of another offence falling within the jurisdiction of the court of trial, the jury may find him guilty of that other offence or of an offence of which he could be found guilty on an indictment specifically charging that other offence.

(4) For purposes of subsection (3) above any allegation of an offence shall be taken as including an allegation of attempting to commit that offence; and where a person is charged on indictment with attempting to commit an offence or with any assault or other act preliminary to an offence, but not with the completed offence, then (subject to the discretion of the court to discharge the jury with a view to the preferment of an indictment for the completed offence) he may be convicted of the offence charged notwithstanding that he is shown to be guilty of the completed offence.

(5) Where a person arraigned on an indictment pleads not guilty of an offence charged in the indictment but guilty of some other offence of which he might be found guilty on that charge, and he is convicted on that plea of guilty without trial for the offence of which he has pleaded not guilty, then (whether or not the two offences are separately charged in distinct counts) his conviction of the one offence shall be an acquittal of the other.

(6) *[Abolition of proceedings by criminal information.]*

(7) Subsections (1) to (3) above shall apply to an indictment containing more than one count as if each count were a separate indictment.

[Section 6(3) is expressly saved by the Road Traffic Offenders Act 1988, s.24(1).] **A3.03**

*   *   *

The Criminal Appeal Act 1968

(1968 c. 19)

A4.01 An Act to consolidate certain enactments relating to appeals in criminal cases to the criminal division of the Court of Appeal, and thence to the House of Lords.

[8th May 1968]

*   *   *

PART I

APPEAL TO COURT OF APPEAL IN CRIMINAL CASES

*   *   *

Appeal against sentence

9. Appeal against sentence following conviction on indictment

A4.02 [(1)] A person who has been convicted of an offence on indictment may appeal to the Court of Appeal against any sentence (not being a sentence fixed by law) passed on him for the offence, whether passed on his conviction or in subsequent proceedings.

[(2) A person who on conviction on indictment has also been convicted of a summary offence under section 41 of the Criminal Justice Act 1988 [*q.v.*], (power of Crown Court to deal with summary offence where person committed for either way offence) may appeal to the Court of Appeal against any sentence passed on him for the summary offence (whether on his conviction or in subsequent proceedings) under subsection (7) of that section.]

A4.03 [*Section 9 is printed as amended by the Criminal Justice Act 1988, s.170(1) and Sched. 15, paras 20 and 21.*

With effect from a date (or dates to be announced, section 9 will be further amended by the Crime and Disorder Act 1998, ss.119, 121(2) and Sched. 8, para.12, so as to insert after the words "for either way offence)" in section 9(2) the words "or paragraph 6 of Schedule 3 to the Crime and Disorder Act 1998 (power of Crown Court to deal with summary offence where person sent for trial for indictable-only offence)". This amendment was brought into force in respect of specified areas only on January 4, 1999 by the Crime and Disorder Act 1998 (Commencement No. 2 and Transitional Provisions) Order 1998 (S.I. 1998 No. 2327; not reproduced in this work), art.4(2)(c), for the purpose of sending any person for trial under section 51 of that Act from any area specified in Schedule 2 to the order. The areas specified in Schedule 2 to the order are: the petty sessional areas of Bromley, Croydon, and Sutton; and the petty sessional divisions of Aberconwy, Arfon, Blackburn, Darwen and Ribble Valley, Burnley and Pendle, Colwyn, Corby, Daventry, Dyffryn Clwyd, Eifionydd and Pwllheli, Gateshead, Kettering, Meirionnydd, Newcastle under Lyme and Pirehill North, Newcastle upon Tyne, Northampton, Rhuddlan, Staffordshire Moorlands, Stoke on Trent, Towcester, Wellingborough, and Yns Mon/Anglesey.]

10. Appeal against sentence in other cases dealt with at [the Crown Court]

A4.04 (1) This section has effect for providing rights of appeal against sentence when a person is dealt with by [the Crown Court] (otherwise than on appeal from a magistrates' court) for an offence of which he was not convicted on indictment.

(2) The proceedings from which an appeal against sentence lies under this section are those where an offender convicted of an offence by a magistrates' court—

- (a) is committed by the court to be dealt with for his offence [before the Crown Court]; or
- [(b) having been made the subject of an order for conditional discharge or a community order within the meaning of [the Powers of Criminal Courts (Sentencing) Act 2000] . . . or given a suspended sentence, appears or is brought before the Crown Court to be further dealt with for his offence] [; or
- [(c) having been released under Part II of the Criminal Justice Act 1991 after serving part of a sentence of imprisonment or detention imposed for the offence, is ordered by the Crown Court to be returned to prison or detention.]

(3) An offender dealt with for an offence [before the Crown Court] in a proceeding to which subsection (2) of this section applies may appeal to the Court of Appeal against sentence in any of the following cases:—

- (a) where either for that offence alone or for that offence and other offences for which sentence is passed in the same proceeding, he is sentenced to imprisonment [or to [detention in a young offender institution]] for a term of six months or more; or
- (b) where the sentence is one which the court convicting him had not power to pass; or
- (c) where the court in dealing with him for the offence makes in respect of him—
    - (i) a recommendation for deportation; or
    - (ii) an order disqualifying him for holding or obtaining a licence to drive a motor vehicle under [Part III of the Road Traffic Act 1988]; or
    - (iii) an order under [section 119 of the Powers of Criminal Courts (Sentencing) Act 2000] (orders as to existing suspended sentence when person subject to the sentence is again convicted) [; or
    - [(iv) a banning order under section 14A of the Football Spectators Act 1989; or]
    - [(v) a declaration of relevance under the Football Spectators Act 1989;]
    - (vi), (vii) *[Repealed.]*
- [(cc) where the court makes such an order with regard to him as is mentioned in section [116(2) or (4) of the Powers of Criminal Courts (Sentencing) Act 2000].]
- [(d) *[Repealed.]*]

(4) For purposes of subsection (3)(a) of this section [and section 11 of this Act], any two or more sentences are to be treated as passed in the same proceeding, if—

- (a) they are passed on the same day; or
- (b) they are passed on different days but the court in passing any one of them states that it is treating that one together with the other or others as substantially one sentence;

and consecutive terms of imprisonment [or detention] and terms which are wholly or partly concurrent are to be treated as a single term.

[(5) *[Omitted.]*]

[Section 10 is printed as amended by the Courts Act 1971, s.56(1) and Sched. 8, para.57(1); the Road   **A4.05**
Traffic Act 1972, s.205(2) and Sched. 10, para.3; the Criminal Justice Act 1972, s.64(1) and Sched. 5; the Powers of Criminal Courts Act 1973, s.56(1) and Sched. 5, para.28; the Interpretation Act 1978, s.17(2)(a); the Criminal Justice Act 1982, s.77 and Sched. 14, para.23; the Criminal Justice Act 1988, ss.123 and 170(1) and (2), Sched. 8, paras 1 and 2, Sched. 15, paras 20 and 22, and Sched. 16; the Football Spectators Act 1989, ss.15(7) and 23(3)(a); the Criminal Justice Act 1991, s.100 and Sched. 11, para.3; the Crime and Disorder Act 1998, ss.119, 120(2), Sched. 8, para.13, and Sched. 10; the

Access to Justice Act 1999, s.58(4)–(7); the Powers of Criminal Courts (Sentencing) Act 2000, s.165(1) and Sched. 9, para.28; the Football (Disorder) Act 2000, s.1(2), (3), Sched. 2, para. 1, and Sched. 3.

With effect from a date to be announced, the following words will be inserted into section 10(2)(b) after the words "conditional discharge" by the Youth Justice and Criminal Evidence Act 1999, s.67(1) and Sched. 4, para.4(1) and (2):

[, a referral order within the meaning of Part I of the Youth Justice and Criminal Evidence Act 1999 (referral to youth offender panel)].]

11. Supplementary provisions as to appeal against sentence

A4.06   (1) [Subject to subsection (1A) below, an] appeal against sentence, whether under section 9 or under section 10 of this Act, lies only with the leave of the Court of Appeal.

[(1A) If the judge who passed the sentence grants a certificate that the case is fit for appeal under section 9 or 10 of this Act, an appeal lies under this section without the leave of the Court of Appeal.]

(2) Where [the Crown Court], in dealing with an offender either on his conviction on indictment or in a proceeding to which section 10(2) of this Act applies, has passed on him two or more sentences in the same proceeding (which expression has the same meaning in this subsection as it has for the purposes of section 10), being sentences against which an appeal lies under section 9[(1)] or section 10, an appeal or application for leave to appeal against any one of those sentences shall be treated as an appeal or application in respect of both or all of them.

[(2A) Where following conviction on indictment a person has been convicted under section 41 of the Criminal Justice Act 1988 [*q.v.*] of a summary offence an appeal or application for leave to appeal against any sentence for the offence triable either way shall be treated also as an appeal or application in respect of any sentence for the summary offence and an appeal or application for leave to appeal against any sentence for the summary offence shall be treated also as an appeal or application in respect of the offence triable either way.]

[(2B) If the appellant or applicant was convicted on indictment of two or more offences triable either way, the references to the offence triable either way in subsection (2A) above are to be construed, in relation to any summary offence of which he was convicted under section 41 of the Criminal Justice Act 1988 following the conviction on indictment, as references to the offence triable either way specified in the notice relating to that summary offence which was given under subsection (2) of that section.]

(3) On an appeal against sentence the Court of Appeal, if they consider that the appellant should be sentenced differently for an offence for which he was dealt with by the court below may—

(a) quash any sentence or order which is the subject of the appeal; and

(b) in place of it pass such sentence or make such order as they think appropriate for the case and as the court below had power to pass or make when dealing with him for the offence;

but the Court shall so exercise their powers under this subsection that, taking the case as a whole, the appellant is not more severely dealt with on appeal than he was dealt with by the court below.

[(4) The power of the Court of Appeal under subsection (3) of this section to pass a sentence which the court below had power to pass for an offence shall, notwithstanding that the court below made no order under [section 119(1) of the Powers of Criminal Courts (Sentencing) Act 2000 in respect of a] suspended sentence previously passed on the appellant for another offence, include power to deal with him in respect of that sentence where the court below made no order in respect of it.]

[(5) The fact that an appeal is pending against an interim hospital order under [the Mental Health Act 1983] shall not affect the power of the court below to renew or terminate the order or to deal with the appellant on its termination; and where the Court of Appeal quash such an order but do not pass any sentence or make any other order in its place the Court may [, subject to section 25 of the Criminal Justice and Public Order Act 1994,] direct the appellant to be kept in custody or released on bail pending his being dealt with by the court below.]

(6) Where the Court of Appeal make an interim hospital order by virtue of subsection (3) of this section—

(a) the power of renewing or terminating it and of dealing with the appellant on its termination shall be exercisable by the court below and not by the Court of Appeal; and

(b) the court below shall be treated for the purposes of [section [38(7)] of the said Act of 1983] (absconding offenders) as the court that made the order.

[Section 11 is printed as amended by the Courts Act 1971, s.56(1) and Sched. 8, para.57(1); the   **A4.07**
Criminal Justice Act 1982, s.29(2)(a); the Mental Health (Amendment) Act 1982, s.65(1) and Sched. 3, para.37; the Mental Health Act 1983, s.148 and Sched. 4, para.23; and the Criminal Justice Act 1988, s.170(1) and Sched. 15, paras 20, 23 and 24; the Criminal Justice and Public Order Act 1994, s.168(2) and Sched. 10, para.20; the Powers of Criminal Courts (Sentencing) Act 2000, s.165(1) and Sched. 9, para. 29.

The Criminal Justice and Public Order Act 1994, s.25 (to which reference is made in this section), precludes the grant of bail to certain persons charged with or convicted of homicide or rape.]

*   *   *

PART III

MISCELLANEOUS AND GENERAL

*   *   *

50. Meaning of "sentence"

[(1) In this Act "*sentence*", in relation to an offence, includes any order made by a court   **A4.08**
when dealing with an offender including, in particular—

(a) a hospital order under Part III of the Mental Health Act 1983, with or without a restriction order;

(b) an interim hospital order under that Part;

[(bb) a hospital direction and a limitation direction under that Part;]

(c) a recommendation for deportation;

(cc) *[repealed.]*

(d) a confiscation order under the [Drug Trafficking Act 1994] other than one made by the High Court;

(e) a confiscation order under Part VI of the Criminal Justice Act 1988;

(f) an order varying a confiscation order of a kind which is included by virtue of paragraph (d) or (e) above;

(g) an order made by the Crown Court varying a confiscation order which was made by the High Court by virtue of [section 19 of the Act of 1994]; and

(h) a declaration of relevance under . . . the Football Spectators Act 1989.]

[(1A) [Section 14 of the Powers of Criminal Courts (Sentencing) Act 2000] (under which a conviction of an offence for which . . . an order for conditional or absolute discharge is made is deemed not to be a conviction except for certain purposes) shall not prevent an appeal under this Act, whether against conviction or otherwise.]

(2) Any power of the criminal division of the Court of Appeal to pass a sentence includes a power to make a recommendation for deportation in cases where the court from which the appeal lies had power to make such a recommendation.

[(3) An order under section 17 of the Access to Justice Act 1999 is not a sentence for the purposes of this Act.]

A4.09   *[Section 50 is printed as amended by the Criminal Justice Act 1982, s.66(1); the Mental Health (Amendment) Act 1982, s.65(1) and Sched. 3, para.40; the Mental Health Act 1983, s.148(1) and Sched. 4, para.23; the Football Spectators Act 1989, s.23(3)(b); the Criminal Justice Act 1991, ss.100, 101(2), Sched. 11, para.4, and Sched. 13; the Criminal Justice Act 1993, s.79(13) and Sched. 5, para.1; the Drug Trafficking Act 1994, s.65(1) and Sched. 1, para.2; the Crime (Sentences) Act 1997, s.55(1) and Sched. 4, para.6(1); the Powers of Criminal Courts (Sentencing) Act 2000, s.165(1) and Sched. 9, para.30; the Football (Disorder) Act 2000, s.1(3) and Sched. 3; and (with effect from April 2, 2001) the Access to Justice Act 1999, s.24 and Sched. 4, para.3 (see the Access to Justice Act 1999 (Commencement No. 7, Transitional Provisions and Savings) Order 2001 (S.I. 2001 No. 916; not reproduced in this work), arts 1(2) and 3(a)(ii)).*

The definition of "sentence" above has been expressly incorporated into section 35(6) of the Criminal Justice Act 1988 (q.v.).]

51. Interpretation

A4.10   (1) In this Act, except where the context otherwise requires—

"*appeal*", where used in Part I or II of this Act, means appeal under that Part, and "*appellant*" has a corresponding meaning and in Part I includes a person who has given notice of application for leave to appeal;

"*the court of trial*", in relation to an appeal, means the court from which the appeal lies;

"*the defendant*", in Part II of this Act, means, in relation to an appeal, the person who was the appellant before the criminal division of the Court of Appeal, and references to the prosecutor shall be construed accordingly;

. . .

["*the judge of the court of trial*" means, where the Crown Court comprises justices of the peace, the judge presiding;]

. . .

"*under disability*" has the meaning assigned to it by section 4 of the Criminal Procedure (Insanity) Act 1964 (unfitness to plead); and

. . .

(2) Any expression used in this Act which is defined in [section 145(1) [and (1AA)] of the Mental Health Act 1983] has the same meaning in this Act as in that Act.

(2A) *[Omitted.]*

(3) *[Repealed.]*

[Section 51 is printed as amended (so far as is relevant) by the Courts Act 1971, s.56(1) and Sched. 8, para.57(3); the Immigration Act 1971, s.34(1) and Sched. 6; the Supreme Court Act 1981, s.152(4) and Sched. 7; the Mental Health Act 1983, s.148(1) and Sched. 4, para.23; the Health Act 1999 (Supplementary, Consequential, etc., Provisions) Order 2000 (S.I. 2000 No. 90; not reproduced in this work), art.3(2) and Sched. 2, para.1.]

*   *   *

The Theft Act 1968

(1968 c. 60)

A5.01 An Act to revise the law of England and Wales as to theft and similar or associated offences
. . .

[26th July 1968]

*   *   *

12. Taking motor vehicle or other conveyance without authority

A5.02 (1) Subject to subsections (5) and (6) below, a person shall be guilty of an offence if, without having the consent of the owner or other lawful authority, he takes any conveyance for his own or another's use or, knowing that any conveyance has been taken without such authority, drives it or allows himself to be carried in or on it.

(2) A person guilty of an offence under subsection (1) above shall [be liable on summary conviction to a fine not exceeding level 5 on the standard scale, to imprisonment for a term not exceeding six months, or to both].

(3) *[Repealed.]*

(4) If on the trial of an indictment for theft the jury are not satisfied that the accused committed theft, but it is proved that the accused committed an offence under subsection (1) above, the jury may find him guilty of the offence under subsection (1) [and if he is found guilty of it, he shall be liable as he would have been liable under subsection (2) above on summary conviction].

(5) Subsection (1) above shall not apply in relation to pedal cycles; but, subject to subsection (6) below, a person who, without having the consent of the owner or other lawful authority, takes a pedal cycle for his own or another's use, or rides a pedal cycle knowing it to have been taken without such authority, shall on summary conviction be liable to a fine not exceeding [level 3 on the standard scale].

(6) A person does not commit an offence under this section by anything done in the belief that he has lawful authority to do it or that he would have the owner's consent if the owner knew of his doing it and the circumstances of it.

(7) For the purposes of this section—

(a) "*conveyance*" means any conveyance constructed or adapted for the carriage of a person or persons whether by land, water or air, except that it does not include a conveyance constructed or adapted for use only under the control of a person not carried in or on it, and "*drive*" shall be construed accordingly; and

(b) "*owner*", in relation to a conveyance which is the subject of a hiring agreement or hire-purchase agreement, means the person in possession of the conveyance under that agreement.

A5.03 *[Section 12 is printed as amended by the Criminal Justice Act 1982, ss.38, 46; the Police and Criminal Evidence Act 1984, s.119(2) and Sched. 7, Pt I; the Criminal Justice Act 1988, s.37(1).*

If a magistrates' court grants bail to a person charged with or convicted of an offence under section 12 or section 12A of this Act, the prosecution (provided that objection was taken to the application for bail) may appeal to a judge of the Crown Court against the order granting bail under the Bail (Amendment) Act 1993, s.1 (not reproduced in this work).

An offence under section 12(5) of taking or riding a pedal cycle without the owner's consent may be recorded in national police records; see the National Police Records (Recordable Offences) Regulations 2000 (S.I. 2000 No. 1139; not reproduced in this work).]

[12A. Aggravated vehicle-taking

(1) Subject to subsection (3) below, a person is guilty of aggravated taking of a vehicle if—   **A5.04**

   (a) he commits an offence under section 12(1) above (in this section referred to as a "*basic offence*") in relation to a mechanically propelled vehicle; and

   (b) it is proved that, at any time after the vehicle was unlawfully taken (whether by him or another) and before it was recovered, the vehicle was driven, or injury or damage was caused, in one or more of the circumstances set out in paragraphs (a) to (d) of subsection (2) below.

(2) The circumstances referred to in subsection (1)(b) above are—

   (a) that the vehicle was driven dangerously on a road or other public place;

   (b) that, owing to the driving of the vehicle, an accident occurred by which injury was caused to any person;

   (c) that, owing to the driving of the vehicle, an accident occurred by which damage was caused to any property, other than the vehicle;

   (d) that damage was caused to the vehicle.

(3) A person is not guilty of an offence under this section if he proves that, as regards any such proven driving, injury or damage as is referred to in subsection (1)(b) above, either—

   (a) the driving, accident or damage referred to in subsection (2) above occurred before he committed the basic offence; or

   (b) he was neither in nor on nor in the immediate vicinity of the vehicle when that driving, accident or damage occurred.

(4) A person guilty of an offence under this section shall be liable on conviction on indictment to imprisonment for a term not exceeding two years or, if it is proved that, in circumstances falling within subsection (2)(b) above, the accident caused the death of the person concerned, five years.

(5) If a person who is charged with an offence under this section is found not guilty of that offence but it is proved that he committed a basic offence, he may be convicted of the basic offence.

(6) If by virtue of subsection (5) above a person is convicted of a basic offence before the Crown Court, that court shall have the same powers and duties as a magistrates' court would have had on convicting him of such an offence.

(7) For the purposes of this section a vehicle is driven dangerously if—

   (a) it is driven in a way which falls far below what would be expected of a competent and careful driver; and

   (b) it would be obvious to a competent and careful driver that driving the vehicle in that way would be dangerous.

(8) For the purposes of this section a vehicle is recovered when it is restored to its owner or to other lawful possession or custody; and in this subsection "*owner*" has the same meaning as in section 12 above.]

A5.05   *[Section 12A was inserted by the Aggravated Vehicle-Taking Act 1992, s.1. As to bail, see the note to section 12 of this Act above.]*

*   *   *

25. Going equipped for stealing, etc.

A5.06   (1) A person shall be guilty of an offence if, when not at his place of abode, he has with him any article for use in the course of or in connection with any burglary, theft or cheat.

(2) A person guilty of an offence under this section shall on conviction on indictment be liable to a term of imprisonment for a term not exceeding three years.

(3) Where a person is charged with an offence under this section, proof that he had with him any article made or adapted for use in committing a burglary, theft or cheat shall be evidence that he had it with him for such use.

(4) Any person may arrest without warrant anyone who is or whom he, with reasonable cause, suspects to be, committing an offence under this section.

(5) For the purposes of this section an offence under section 12(1) of this Act of taking a conveyance shall be treated as theft and *"cheat"* means an offence under section 15 of this Act.

*   *   *

The Transport Act 1968

(1968 c. 73)

An Act to make further provision with respect to transport and related matters.

[25th October 1968]

A6.01

Visiting forces, etc.   Part VI of the Transport Act 1968 (the only Part of the Act reproduced in this work) does not apply to a person or vehicle in the service of a visiting force or headquarters (as defined); see the Visiting Forces and International Headquarters (Application of Law) Order 1999 (S.I. 1999 No. 1736; not reproduced in this work), art.8(1)(a).

ARRANGEMENT OF SECTIONS

A6.02

*   *   *

PART VI

DRIVERS' HOURS

Section

A6.03

*   *   *

PART VI

DRIVERS' HOURS

95. Vehicles and drivers subject to control under Part VI

(1), (1A) *[Omitted.]*

A6.04

(2) This Part of this Act applies to—

  (a) passenger vehicles, that is to say—

   (i) public service vehicles; and

   (ii) motor vehicles (other than public service vehicles) constructed or adapted to carry more than twelve passengers;

(b) goods vehicles, that is to say—

   (i) heavy locomotives, light locomotives, motor tractors and any motor vehicle so constructed that a trailer may by partial superimposition be attached to the vehicle in such a manner as to cause a substantial part of the weight of the trailer to be borne by the vehicle; and

   (ii) motor vehicles (except those mentioned in paragraph (a) of this subsection) constructed or adapted to carry goods other than the effects of passengers.

[(c) vehicles not falling within paragraph (a) and (b) of this subsection which—

   (i) are vehicles within the meaning given by Article 1 of Council Regulation (EEC) No. 3820/85 of 29th December 1985 on the harmonisation of certain social legislation relating to road transport; and

   (ii) are not referred to in Article 4 of that Regulation.]

(3) This Part of this Act applies to any such person as follows (in this Part of this Act referred to as "*a driver*"), that is to say—

(a) a person who drives a vehicle to which this Part of this Act applies in the course of his employment (in this Part of this Act referred to as "*an employee-driver*"); and

(b) a person who drives such a vehicle for the purposes of a trade or business carried on by him (in this Part of this Act referred to as "*an owner-driver*");

and in this Part of this Act references to driving by any person are references to his driving as aforesaid.

A6.05   *[Section 95 is printed as amended by the Community Drivers' Hours and Recording Equipment (Amendment) Regulations 1998 (S.I. 1998 No. 2006; not reproduced in this work).]*

96. Permitted driving time and periods of duty

A6.06   (1) Subject to the provisions of this section, a driver shall not on any working day drive a vehicle or vehicles to which this Part of this Act applies for periods amounting in the aggregate to more than ten hours.

(2) Subject to the provisions of this section, if on any working day a driver has been on duty for a period of, or for periods amounting in the aggregate to, five and a half hours and—

(a) there has not been during that period, or during or between any of those periods, an interval of not less than half an hour in which he was able to obtain rest and refreshment; and

(b) the end of that period, or of the last of those periods, does not mark the end of that working day,

there shall at the end of that period, or of the last of those periods, be such an interval as aforesaid.

(3) Subject to the provisions of this section, the working day of a driver—

(a) except where paragraph (b) or (c) of this subsection applies, shall not exceed eleven hours;

(b) if during that day he is off duty for a period which is, or periods which taken together are, not less than the time by which his working day exceeds eleven hours, shall not exceed twelve and a half hours;

(c) if during that day—

(i) all the time when he is driving vehicles to which this Part of this Act applies is spent in driving one or more express carriages or contract carriages, and

(ii) he is able for a period of not less than four hours to obtain rest and refreshment,

shall not exceed fourteen hours.

(4) Subject to the provisions of this section, there shall be, between any two successive working days of a driver, an interval for rest which—

(a) subject to paragraph (b) of this subsection, shall not be of less than eleven hours;

(b) if during both those days all or the greater part of the time when he is driving vehicles to which this Part of this Act applies is spent in driving one or more passenger vehicles, may, on one occasion in each working week, be of less than eleven hours but not of less than nine and a half hours;

and for the purposes of this Part of this Act a period of time shall not be treated, in the case of an employee-driver, as not being an interval for rest by reason only that he may be called upon to report for duty if required.

(5) Subject to the provisions of this section a driver shall not be on duty in any working week for periods amounting in the aggregate to more than sixty hours.

(6) Subject to the provisions of this section, there shall be, in the case of each working week of a driver, a period of not less than twenty-four hours for which he is off duty, being a period either falling wholly in that week or beginning in that week and ending in the next week; but—

(a) where the requirements of the foregoing provisions of this subsection have been satisfied in the case of any week by reference to a period ending in the next week, no part of that period (except any part after the expiration of the first twenty-four hours of it) shall be taken into account for the purpose of satisfying those requirements in the case of the next week; and

(b) those requirements need not be satisfied in the case of any working week of a driver who on each working day falling wholly or partly in that week drives one or more stage carriages if that week is immediately preceded by a week in the case of which those requirements have been satisfied as respects that driver or during which he has not at any time been on duty.

(7) If in the case of the working week of any driver the following requirement is satisfied, that is to say, that, in each of the periods of twenty-four hours beginning at midnight which make up that week, the driver does not drive a vehicle to which this Part of this Act applies for a period of, or periods amounting in the aggregate to, more than four hours, the foregoing provisions of this section shall not apply to him in that week, except that the provisions of subsections (1), (2) and (3) shall nevertheless have effect in relation to the whole of any working day falling partly in that week and partly in a working week in the case of which that requirement is not satisfied.

(8) If on any working day a driver does not drive any vehicle to which this Part of this Act applies—

(a) subsections (2) and (3) of this section shall not apply to that day, and

(b) the period or periods of duty attributable to that day for the purposes of subsection (5) of this section shall, if amounting to more than eleven hours, be treated as amounting to eleven hours only.

(9) For the purposes of subsections (1) and (7) of this section no account shall be taken of any time spent driving a vehicle elsewhere than on a road if the vehicle is being so driven in the course of operations of agriculture or forestry.

(10) For the purposes of enabling drivers to deal with cases of emergency or otherwise to meet a special need, the [Secretary of State for the Environment, Transport and the Regions] may by regulations—

  (a) create exemptions from all or any of the requirements of subsections (1) to (6) of this section in such cases and subject to such conditions as may be specified in the regulations;

  (b) empower the traffic [commissioner] for any area, subject to the provisions of the regulations—

    (i) to dispense with the observance of all or any of those requirements (either generally or in such circumstances or to such extent as the [commissioner thinks] fit) in any particular case for which provision is not made under paragraph (a) of this subsection;

    (ii) to grant a certificate (which, for the purposes of any proceedings under this Part of this Act, shall be conclusive evidence of the facts therein stated) that any particular case falls or fell within any exemption created under the said paragraph (a);

and regulations under this subsection may enable any dispensation under paragraph (b)(i) of this subsection to be granted retrospectively and provide for a document purporting to be a certificate granted by virtue of paragraph (b)(ii) of this subsection to be accepted in evidence without further proof.

(11) If any of the requirements of [the domestic drivers' hours code] is contravened in the case of any driver—

  (a) that driver; and

  (b) any other person (being that driver's employer or a person to whose orders that driver was subject) who caused or permitted the contravention;

shall be liable on summary conviction to a fine not exceeding [level 4 on the standard scale]; but a person shall not be liable to be convicted under this subsection if he proves to the court—

    (i) that the contravention was due to unavoidable delay in the completion of a journey arising out of circumstances which he could not reasonably have foreseen; or

    (ii) in the case of a person charged under paragraph (b) of this subsection, that the contravention was due to the fact that the driver had for any particular period or periods driven or been on duty otherwise than in the employment of that person or, as the case may be, otherwise than in the employment in which he is subject to the orders of that person, and that the person charged was not, and could not reasonably have become, aware of that fact.

[(11A) Where, in the case of a driver . . . of a motor vehicle, there is in Great Britain a contravention of any requirement of [the applicable Community rules] as to period of driving, or distance driven, or periods on or off duty, then the offender and any other person (being the offender's employer or a person to whose orders the offender was subject) who caused or permitted the contravention shall be liable on summary conviction to a fine not exceeding [level 4 on the standard scale].]

[(11B) But a person shall not be liable to be convicted under subsection (11A) if—

  (a) he proves the matters specified in paragraph (i) of subsection (11); or

  (b) being charged as the offender's employer or a person to whose orders the offender was subject, he proves the matters specified in paragraph (ii) of that subsection.]

(12) The [Secretary of State for the Environment, Transport and the Regions] may by order—

(a) direct that subsection (1) of this section shall have effect with the substitution for the reference to ten hours of a reference to nine hours, either generally or with such exceptions as may be specified in the order;

(b) direct that paragraph (a) of subsection (3) of this section shall have effect with the substitution for the reference to eleven hours of a reference to any shorter period, or remove, modify or add to the provisions of that subsection containing exceptions to the said paragraph (a);

(c) remove, modify or add to any of the requirements of subsections (1), (4), (5) or (6) of this section or any of the exemptions provided for by subsections (7), (8) and (9) thereof;

and any order under this subsection may contain such transitional and supplementary provisions as the [Secretary of State for the Environment, Transport and the Regions] thinks necessary or expedient, including provisions amending any definition in section 103 of this Act which is relevant to any of the provisions affected by the order.

[(13) In this Part of this Act *"the domestic drivers' hours code"* means the provisions of subsections (1) to (6) of this section as for the time being in force (and, in particular, as modified, added to or substituted by or under any instrument in force under section 95(1) of this Act or subsection (10) or (12) of this section).]

[Section 96 is printed as amended by the Secretary of State for the Environment Order 1970 (S.I. 1970   **A6.07**
No. 1681); the European Communities Act 1972, s.4 and Sched. 4, para.9(2); the Road Traffic (Drivers' Ages and Hours of Work) Act 1976, s.2(1); the Secretary of State for Transport Order 1976 (S.I. 1976 No. 1775); the Transport Act 1978, s.10; the Minister of Transport Order 1979 (S.I. 1979 No. 571); the Transfer of Functions (Transport) Order 1981 (S.I. 1981 No. 238); the Criminal Justice Act 1982, ss.38 and 46(1); the Transport Act 1985, s.3 and Sched. 2, Pt II, para.1(2); the Community Drivers' Hours and Recording Equipment Regulations 1986 (S.I. 1986 No. 1457), reg.2; the Secretary of State for the Environment, Transport and the Regions Order 1997 (S.I. 1997 No. 2971).

For modifications of subs (9), above, in relation to drivers engaged in quarrying operations or on building construction and civil engineering work, see the Drivers' Hours (Goods Vehicles) (Modifications) Order 1970 (S.I. 1970 No. 257) below.

The text of section 96 as it applies to the drivers of passenger vehicles is modified by the Drivers' Hours (Passenger and Goods Vehicles) (Modifications) Order 1971 (S.I. 1971 No. 818); and the text as so modified is set out as an appendix to S.I. 1971 No. 818 below. The text of section 96 as it applies to the drivers of goods vehicles is modified by the Drivers' Hours (Goods Vehicles) (Modifications) Order 1986 (S.I. 1986 No. 1459); and the text as so modified is set out as an appendix to S.I. 1986 No. 1459 (q.v.).

Temporary, short-term, exemptions from section 96(1) in cases of emergency and special need are outside the scope of this work but are noted from time to time in Wilkinson's Road Traffic Law Bulletin.

Section 95(1) of this Act, as amended, inter alia, empowers the Secretary of State to make regulations substituting, adapting, etc., the provisions of this Part of this Act to take account of the operation of any Community provision.]

[97. Installation and use of recording equipment

[(1) No person shall use, or cause or permit to be used, a vehicle to which this section   **A6.08**
applies—

[(a) unless there is in the vehicle recording equipment which—

(i) has been installed in accordance with the Community Recording Equipment Regulation;

(ii) complies with Annexes I and II to that Regulation; and

(iii) is being used as provided by [Articles 13 to 15] of that Regulation] [,or] [(b) in which there is recording equipment which has been repaired (whether before or after installation) otherwise than in accordance with the Community Recording Equipment Regulation;]

and any person who contravenes this subsection shall be liable on summary conviction to a fine not exceeding [level 5] on the standard scale.]

[(1A) A person shall not be liable to be convicted under subsection (1) of this section if he proves to the court that he neither knew nor ought to have known that the recording equipment had not been installed or repaired, as the case may be, in accordance with the Community Recording Equipment Regulation.]

(2) A person shall not be liable to be convicted under subsection (1)[(a)] of this section if he proves to the court that the vehicle in question was proceeding to a place where recording equipment which would comply with the requirements of Annexes I and II of the Community Recording Equipment Regulation was to be installed in the vehicle in accordance with that Regulation.

(3) A person shall not be liable to be convicted under subsection (1)[(a)] of this section by reason of the recording equipment installed in the vehicle in question not being in working order if he proves to the court that—

(a) it had not become reasonably practicable for the equipment to be repaired by an approved fitter or workshop; and

(b) the requirements of [Article 16(2)] of the Community Recording Equipment Regulation were being complied with.

(4) A person shall not be liable to be convicted under subsection (1)[(a)] of this section by reason of any seal on the recording equipment installed in the vehicle in question not being intact if he proves to the court that—

(a) the breaking or removal of the seal could not have been avoided;

(b) it had not become reasonably practicable for the seal to be replaced by an approved fitter or workshop; and

(c) in all other respects the equipment was being used as provided by [Articles 13 to 15] of the Community Recording Equipment Regulation.

(5) For the purposes of this section recording equipment is used as provided by [Articles 13 to 15] of the Community Recording Equipment Regulation if, and only if, the circumstances of its use are such that each requirement of those Articles is complied with.

(6) This section applies at any time to any vehicle to which this Part of this Act applies if, at that time, Article 3 of the Community Recording Equipment Regulation requires recording equipment to be installed and used in that vehicle; and in this section and sections 97A and 97B of the Act any expression which is also used in that Regulation has the same meaning as in that Regulation.

(7) In this Part of this Act—

["*the Community Recording Equipment Regulation*" means Council Regulation (EEC) No. 3821/85 on recording equipment in road transport [*q.v.*] as it has effect in accordance with—

(a) Commission Regulation (EEC) No. 3314/90;

(b) Commission Regulation (EEC) No. 3688/92; and

(c) Commission Regulation (EC) No. 2479/95;

and as read with the Community Drivers' Hours and Recording Equipment (Exemptions and Supplementary Provisions) Regulations 1986 [*S.I. 1986 No. 1456* (*q.v.*)];]

"*recording equipment*" means equipment for recording information as to the use of a vehicle.]

[*Section 97 was substituted by the Passenger and Goods Vehicles (Recording Equipment) Regulations 1979 (S.I. 1979 No. 1746) and is printed as subsequently amended by the Passenger and Goods Vehicles (Recording Equipment) (Amendment) Regulations 1984 (S.I. 1984 No. 144), reg.2(2); the Criminal Justice Act 1982, ss.39(2), 46(1) and Sched. 3; the Community Drivers' Hours and Recording Equipment Regulations 1986 (S.I. 1986 No. 1457), reg.3; the Passenger and Goods Vehicles (Recording Equipment) Regulations 1989 (S.I. 1989 No. 2121); the Passenger and Goods Vehicles (Recording Equipment) Regulations 1996 (S.I. 1996 No. 941; not reproduced in this work).]*   **A6.09**

[97A. Provisions supplementary to section 97

(1) If an employed [driver] of a vehicle to which section 97 of this Act applies fails—   **A6.10**

  (a) without reasonable excuse to return any record sheet which relates to him to his employer within twenty-one days of completing it; or

  (b) where he has two or more employers by whom he is employed as a [driver] of such a vehicle, to notify each of them of the name and address of the other or others of them,

he shall be liable on summary conviction to a fine not exceeding [level 4 on the standard scale].

(2) If the employer of [drivers] of a vehicle to which section 97 of this Act applies fails without reasonable excuse to secure that they comply with subsection (1)(a) of this section, he shall be liable on summary conviction to a fine not exceeding [level 4 on the standard scale].

(3) Where a [driver] of a vehicle to which section 97 of this Act applies has two or more employers by whom he is employed as a [driver] of such a vehicle, subsection (1)(a) and subsection (2) of this section shall apply as if any reference to his employer, or any reference which is to be construed as such a reference, were a reference to such of those employers as was the first to employ him in that capacity.]

[*Section 97A was inserted by the Passenger and Goods Vehicles (Recording Equipment) Regulations 1979 (S.I. 1979 No. 1746) and is printed as subsequently amended by the Criminal Justice Act 1982, ss.39(2), 46(1), and Sched. 3; the Community Drivers' Hours and Recording Equipment Regulations 1986 (S.I. 1986 No. 1457), reg.3.]*   **A6.11**

[97AA. Forgery, etc., of seals on recording equipment

(1) A person who, with intent to deceive, forges, alters or uses any seal on recording equipment installed in, or designed for installation in, a vehicle to which section 97 of this Act applies, shall be guilty of an offence.   **A6.12**

(2) A person guilty of an offence under subsection (1) above shall be liable—

  (a) on conviction on indictment, to imprisonment for a term not exceeding two years, or

  (b) on summary conviction, to a fine not exceeding the statutory maximum.

(3) In the application of this section to England and Wales a person "*forges*" a seal if he makes a false seal in order that it may be used as genuine.]

[*Section 97AA was inserted by the Passenger and Goods Vehicles (Recording Equipment) Regulations 1989 (S.I. 1989 No. 2121).]*   **A6.13**

[97B. Records, etc., produced by equipment may be used in evidence

A6.14   (1) Where recording equipment is installed in a vehicle to which this Part of this Act applies, any record produced by means of the equipment shall, in any proceedings under this Part of this Act, be evidence . . . of the matters appearing from the record.

(2) Any entry made on a record sheet by a [driver] for the purposes of [Article 15(2) or (5) or 16(2)] of the Community Recording Equipment Regulation shall, in any proceedings under this Part of this Act, be evidence . . . of the matters appearing from that entry.]

A6.15   *[Section 97B was inserted by the Passenger and Goods Vehicles (Recording Equipment) Regulations 1979 (S.I. 1979 No. 1746) and is printed as subsequently amended by the Community Drivers' Hours and Recording Equipment Regulations 1986 (S.I. 1986 No. 1457), reg.3.*
Words relating exclusively and expressly to Scotland in section 97(1) and (2) have been omitted.]

98. Written records

A6.16   (1) *[Power to make regulations regarding keeping records and maintaining registers.]*

(2) *[Power to include supplementary and incidental provisions in regulations.]*

[(2A) The requirements of regulations made under this section shall not apply as respects the driving of a vehicle to which section 97 of this Act applies and in relation to which subsection (1)(b) of that section has come into force.]

(3) *[Dispensations from requirements imposed by this section.]*

(4) Any person who contravenes any regulations made under this section [or any requirement as to [books, records or documents]] of [the applicable Community rules] shall be liable on summary conviction to a fine not exceeding [level 4 on the standard scale]; but the employer of an employee-driver shall not be liable to be convicted under this sub-section by reason of contravening any such regulation whereby he is required to cause any records to be kept if he proves to the court that he has given proper instructions to his employees with respect to the keeping of the records and has from time to time taken reasonable steps to secure that those instructions are being carried out.

[(4A) A person shall not be liable to be convicted under subsection (4) of this section by reason of contravening any regulation made under this section if he proves to the court that, if the vehicle in question had been such a vehicle as is mentioned in subsection (2A) of this section, there would have been no contravention of the provisions of this Part of this Act so far as they relate to the use of such vehicles.]

(5) Any entry made by an employee-driver for the purposes of regulations under this section [or of [the applicable Community rules]] shall, in any proceedings under this Part of this Act, be admissible in evidence against his employer.

A6.17   *[Section 98 is printed as amended by the European Communities Act 1972, s.4, and Sched. 4, para.9; the Road Traffic (Drivers' Ages and Hours of Work) Act 1976, s.2(1); the Passenger and Goods Vehicles (Recording Equipment) Regulations 1979 (S.I. 1979 No. 1746); the Criminal Justice Act 1982, ss.38, 46(1).*
The reference in section 98(2A) to section 97(1)(b) refers to that provision before it was amended by the Passenger and Goods Vehicles (Recording Equipment) Regulations 1989 (S.I. 1989 No. 2121), which redesignated section 97(1)(b) as section 97(1)(a)(ii); see §14.214 in Vol. 1.
The Drivers' Hours (Goods Vehicles) (Keeping of Records) Regulations 1987 (S.I. 1987 No. 1421) (q.v.) were made under section 98.]

99. Inspection of records and other documents

A6.18   (1) An officer may, on production if so required of his authority, require any person to produce, and permit him to inspect and copy—

(a) any book or register which that person is required by regulations under section 98 of this Act to carry or have in his possession for the purpose of making in it any entry required by those regulations or which is required under those regulations to be carried on any vehicle of which that person is the driver;

(b) any . . . , book or register which that person is required by regulations under section . . . 98 of this Act to preserve;

[(bb) any record sheet which that person is required by [Article 14(2)] of the Community Recording Equipment Regulation to retain or by [Article 15(7)] of that Regulation to be able to produce;]

(c) if that person is the owner of a vehicle to which this Part of this Act applies, any other document of that person which the officer may reasonably require to inspect for the purpose of ascertaining whether the provisions of this Part of this Act or of regulations made thereunder have been complied with;

[(d) any . . . book, register or document required by [the applicable Community rules] or which the officer may reasonably require to inspect for the purpose of ascertaining whether the requirements of [the applicable Community rules] have been complied with;]

and that record [sheet], book, register or document shall, if the officer so requires by notice in writing served on that person, be produced at the office of the traffic [commissioner] specified in the notice within such time (not being less than ten days) from the service of the notice as may be so specified.

(2) An officer may, on production if so required of his authority—

[(a) at any time, enter any vehicle to which this Part of this Act applies and inspect that vehicle and any recording equipment installed in it and inspect and copy any record sheet on the vehicle on which a record has been produced by means of the equipment or an entry has been made;]

(b) at any time which is reasonable having regard to the circumstances of the case, enter any premises on which he has reason to believe that such a vehicle is kept or that any such [record sheets], books, registers or other documents as are mentioned in subsection (1) of this section are to be found, and inspect any such vehicle, and inspect and copy any such record [sheet], book, register, or document which he finds there.

(3) For the purpose of exercising his powers under subsection (2)(a) and, in respect of a document carried on, or by the driver of, a vehicle, under subsection (1) (a) [or (d)] of this section, an officer may detain the vehicle in question during such time as is required for the exercise of that power.

(4) Any person who—

(a) fails to comply with any requirement under subsection (1) of this section; or

(b) obstructs an officer in the exercise of his powers under subsection (2) or (3) of this section,

shall be liable on summary conviction to a fine not exceeding [level 3 on the standard scale].

[(4A) A person shall not be liable to be convicted under subsection (4) of this section by reason of failing to comply with any requirement under subsection 6(1)(a) or (b) of this section if he proves to the court that, if the vehicle in question had been such a vehicle as is mentioned in section 98(2A) of this Act, there would have been no contravention of the provisions of this Part of this Act so far as they relate to the use of such vehicles.]

(5) Any person who makes, or causes to be made, [any record or entry on a record sheet kept or carried for the purposes of the Community Recording Equipment Regulation or] under section 97 of this Act or any entry in a [book, register or document kept or carried] for the purposes of regulations under section 98 thereof [or [the applicable Community rules]] which he knows to be false or, with intent to deceive, alters or causes to be altered any such record or entry shall be liable—

    (a) on summary conviction, to a fine not exceeding [the prescribed sum];

    (b) on conviction on indictment, to imprisonment for a term not exceeding two years.

(6) If an officer has reason to believe that an offence under subsection (5) of this section has been committed in respect of any record or document inspected by him under this section, he may seize that record or document; and where a record or document is seized as aforesaid and within six months of the date on which it was seized no person has been charged since that date with an offence in relation to that record or document under that subsection and the record or document has not been returned to the person from whom it was taken, a magistrates' court shall, on an application made for the purpose by that person or by an officer, make such order respecting the disposal of the record or document and award such costs as the justice of the case may require.

(7) *[Applies to Scotland.]*

(8) In this section *"officer"* means [an examiner appointed under section 66A of the Road Traffic Act 1988] and any person authorised for the purposes of this section by the traffic [commissioner] for any area.

(9) The powers conferred by this section on an officer as defined in subsection (8) of this section shall be exercisable also by a police constable, who shall not, if wearing uniform, be required to produce any authority.

(10) In this section references to the inspection and copying of any record produced by means of equipment installed for the purposes of section 97 of this Act in a vehicle include references to the application to the record of any process for eliciting the information recorded thereby and to taking down the information elicited from it.

A6.19   *[Section 99 is printed as amended by the European Communities Act 1972, s.4 and Sched. 4, para.9; the Road Traffic Act 1972, s.203(1), and Sched. 7; the Road Traffic (Drivers' Ages and Hours of Work) Act 1976, s.2(1); the Interpretation Act 1978, s.17(2)(a); the Passenger and Goods Vehicles (Recording Equipment) Regulations 1979 (S.I. 1979 No. 1746); the Magistrates' Courts Act 1980, s.32(2); the Criminal Justice Act 1982, ss.38, 46(1); the Transport Act 1985, s.3(5) and Sched. 2, Pt II, para.1(4); the Community Drivers' Hours and Recording Equipment Regulations 1986 (S.I. 1986 No. 1457), reg.3; the Road Traffic Act 1991, s.48 and Sched. 4, para.2.*

     As to the "prescribed sum", see the Magistrates' Courts Act 1980, s.32(9) below.]

A6.20   **[99A. Power to prohibit driving of vehicle**

    (1) If—

        (a) the driver of a UK vehicle obstructs an authorised person in the exercise of his powers under subsection (2) or (3) of section 99 of this Act or fails to comply with any requirement made by an authorised person under subsection (1) of that section,

        (b) it appears to an authorised person that, in relation to a UK vehicle or its driver, there has been a contravention of any of the provisions of—

            (i) sections 96 to 98 of this Act and any orders or regulations under those sections, or

            (ii) the applicable Community rules,

or that there will be such a contravention if the vehicle is driven on a road, or

(c) it appears to an authorised person that an offence under section 99(5) of this Act has been committed in respect of a UK vehicle or its driver,

the authorised person may prohibit the driving of the vehicle on a road either for a specified period or without limitation of time.

(2) Where an authorised person prohibits the driving of a vehicle under this section, he may also direct the driver to remove the vehicle (and, if it is a motor vehicle drawing a trailer, also to remove the trailer) to such place and subject to such conditions as are specified in the direction; and the prohibition shall not apply to the removal of the vehicle in accordance with that direction.

(3) On imposing a prohibition under subsection (1) of this section, the authorised person shall give notice in writing of the prohibition to the driver of the vehicle, specifying the circumstances (as mentioned in paragraph (a), (b) or (c) of that subsection) in consequence of which the prohibition is imposed and stating whether it is imposed only for a specified period (and if so specifying the period) or without limitation of time.

(4) Any direction under subsection (2) of this section may be given—

(a) in the notice under subsection (3) of this section, or

(b) in a separate notice in writing given to the driver of the vehicle.

(5) In this section—

"*authorised person*" means—

(a) an examiner appointed by the Secretary of State under section 66A of the Road Traffic Act 1988, or

(b) a constable authorised to act for the purposes of this section by or on behalf of a chief officer of police;

"*UK vehicle*" means a vehicle registered under the Vehicle Excise and Registration Act 1994.]

[Section 99A was inserted by the Transport Act 2000, s.266, with effect from February 1, 2001 (see the Transport Act 2001 (Commencement No. 3) Order 2001 (S.I. 2001 No. 57; not reproduced in this work)) (the subsequent amendment of S.I. 2001 No. 57 by the Transport Act 2000 (Commencement No. 3) (Amendment) Order 2001 (S.I. 2001 No. 115; not reproduced in this volume) does not affect the insertion of section 99A).]   **A6.21**

99B. Duration and removal of prohibition   A6.22

(1) Subject to any exemption granted under subsection (2) of this section, a prohibition under subsection (1) of section 99A of this Act shall come into force as soon as notice of it has been given in accordance with subsection (3) of that section and shall continue in force—

(a) until it is removed under subsection (3) of this section, or

(b) in the case of a prohibition imposed for a specified period, until it is removed under that subsection or that period expires, whichever first occurs.

(2) Where notice of a prohibition has been given under section 99A(3) of this Act in respect of a vehicle, an exemption in writing for the use of the vehicle in such manner, subject to such conditions and for such purposes as may be specified in the exemption may be granted by any authorised person.

(3) A prohibition under section 99A(1) of this Act may be removed by any authorised person, if he is satisfied that appropriate action has been taken to remove or remedy the

circumstances (as mentioned in paragraph (a), (b) or (c) of section 99A(1) of this Act) in consequence of which the prohibition was imposed; and on doing so the authorised person shall give notice in writing of the removal of the prohibition to the driver of the vehicle.

(4) In this section, "*authorised person*" has the same meaning as in section 99A of this Act.]

A6.23   *[Section 99B was inserted by the Transport Act 2000, s.266, with effect from February 1, 2001 (see the Transport Act 2001 (Commencement No. 3) Order 2001 (S.I. 2001 No. 57; not reproduced in this work)) (the subsequent amendment of S.I. 2001 No. 57 by the Transport Act 2000 (Commencement No. 3) (Amendment) Order 2001 (S.I. 2001 No. 115; not reproduced in this volume) does not affect the insertion of section 99B).]*

A6.24   **[99C. Failure to comply with prohibition**

Any person who—

    (a) drives a vehicle on a road in contravention of a prohibition imposed under section 99A(1) of this Act,

    (b) causes or permits a vehicle to be driven on a road in contravention of such a prohibition, or

    (c) refuses or fails to comply within a reasonable time with a direction given under section 99A(2) of this Act,

shall be guilty of an offence and liable on summary conviction to a fine not exceeding level 5 on the standard scale.]

A6.25   *[Section 99C was inserted by the Transport Act 2000, s.266, with effect from February 1, 2001 (see the Transport Act 2001 (Commencement No. 3) Order 2001 (S.I. 2001 No. 57; not reproduced in this work)) (the subsequent amendment of S.I. 2001 No. 57 by the Transport Act 2000 (Commencement No. 3) (Amendment) Order 2001 (S.I. 2001 No. 115; not reproduced in this work) does not affect the insertion of section 99C).]*

*　　　*　　　*

A6.26   **102. Application to the Crown and exemption for police and fire brigade**

(1) Subject to subsection (2) of this section, this Part of this Act shall apply to vehicles and persons in the public service of the Crown.

(2) This Part of this Act shall not apply in the case of motor vehicles owned by the Secretary of State for Defence and used for naval, military or air force purposes or in the case of vehicles so used while being driven by persons for the time being subject to the orders of a member of the armed forces of the Crown.

[(3) Where an offence under this Part of this Act is alleged to have been committed in connection with a vehicle in the public service of the Crown, proceedings may be brought in respect of the offence against a person nominated for the purpose on behalf of the Crown; and, subject to subsection (3A) below, where any such offence is committed any person so nominated shall also be guilty of the offence as well as any person actually responsible for the offence (but without prejudice to proceedings against any person so responsible).]

[(3A) Where a person is convicted of an offence by virtue of subsection (3) above—

    (a) no order may be made on his conviction save an order imposing a fine,

    (b) payment of any fine imposed on him in respect of that offence may not be enforced against him, and

    (c) apart from the imposition of any such fine, the conviction shall be disregarded for all purposes other than any appeal (whether by way of case stated or otherwise).]

(4) This Part of this Act shall not apply in the case of motor vehicles while being used for police or fire brigade purposes.

[Section 102 is printed as amended by the Road Traffic (Consequential Provisions) Act 1988, s.4 and Sched. 3, para 6(6).]   **A6.27**

[102A. Exclusion of application to tramcars and trolley vehicles

(1) This Part of this Act and section 255 of the Road Traffic Act 1960 in its application thereto shall not apply to tramcars or trolley vehicles operated under statutory powers.   **A.6.28**

(2) In this section *"operated under statutory powers"* means, in relation to tramcars or trolley vehicles, that their use is authorised or regulated by special Act of Parliament or by an order having the force of an Act.

(3) Subsection (1) above shall have effect subject to any such Act or order as is mentioned in subsection (2) above, and any such Act or order may apply to tramcars or trolley vehicles to which it relates any of the provisions excluded by the said subsection (1).]

[Section 102A was inserted by the Road Traffic (Consequential Provisions) Act 1988, s.4 and Sched. 3, para.6(7).]   **A6.29**

103. Interpretation, supplementary provisions, etc., for Part VI

(1) In this Part of this Act—

"agriculture" has the meaning assigned by section 109(3) of the Agriculture Act 1947 [*q.v.*]   **A6.30**
    . . . ;

[*"the applicable Community rules"* means any directly applicable Community provision for the time being in force about the driving of road vehicles;]

[*"the Community Recording Equipment Regulation"* has the meaning given by section 97(7) of this Act;]

[*"the domestic drivers' hours code"* has the meaning given by section 96(13) of this Act;]

"driver", *"employee-driver"* and *"owner-driver"* have the meaning assigned by section 95(3) of this Act;

"employer", in relation to an employee-driver, means the employer of that driver in the employment by virtue of which that driver is an employee-driver;

. . .

"prescribed" means prescribed by regulations made by the [Secretary of State for the Environment, Transport and the Regions];

[*"recording equipment"* has the meaning given by section 97(7) of this Act;]

[*"record sheet"* includes a temporary sheet attached to a record sheet in accordance with [Article 16(2) of the Community Recording Equipment Regulation;]]

[*"relevant Community provision"* means any Community provision for the time being in force about the driving of road vehicles, whether directly applicable or not;]

"working day" in relation to any driver, means—

  (a) any period during which he is on duty and which does not fall to be aggregated with any other such period by virtue of paragraph (b) of this definition; and

  (b) where a period during which he is on duty is not followed by an interval for rest of not less than eleven hours or (where permitted by virtue of section 96(4)(b) of this Act) of not less than nine and a half hours, the aggregate of that period and each successive such period until there is such an interval as aforesaid, together with any interval or intervals between periods so aggregated;

["*working week*" means, subject to subsection (5) of this section, a week beginning at midnight between Sunday and Monday;]

and any expression not defined above which is also used in the [Road Traffic Act 1988] has the same meaning as in that Act.

(2) For the purposes of this Part of this Act a director of a company shall be deemed to be employed by it.

(3) In this Part of this Act references to a person driving a vehicle are references to his being at the driving controls of the vehicle for the purpose of controlling its movement, whether it is in motion or is stationary with the engine running.

(4) In this Part of this Act references to a driver on duty are references—

(a) in the case of an employee-driver, to his being on duty (whether for the purpose of driving a vehicle to which this Part of this Act applies or for other purposes) in the employment by virtue of which he is an employee-driver, or in any other employment under the person who is his employer in the first-mentioned employment; and

(b) in the case of an owner-driver, to his driving a vehicle to which this Part of this Act applies for the purposes of a trade or business carried on by him or being otherwise engaged in work for the purposes of that trade or business, being work in connection with such a vehicle or the load carried thereby.

(5) The traffic [commissioner] for any area may, on the application of an owner-driver or of the employer of an employee-driver, from time to time direct that a week beginning at midnight between two days other than [Sunday and Monday] shall be, or be deemed to have been, a working week in relation to that owner-driver or employee-driver; but where by virtue of any such direction a new working week begins before the expiration of a previous working week then, without prejudice to the application of the provisions of this Part of this Act in relation to the new working week, those provisions shall continue to apply in relation to the previous working week until its expiration.

(6) In [section] 98(2)(e) of this Act "*a small goods vehicle*" means a goods vehicle which has a plated weight of the prescribed description not exceeding [3500 kilograms] or (not having a plated weight) has an unladen weight not exceeding [1525 kilograms]; but the [Secretary of State for the Environment, Transport and the Regions] may by regulations direct that the foregoing provisions of this subsection shall have effect, in relation to either or both of those sections—

(a) with the substitution for either of the weights there specified of such other weight as may be specified in the regulations;

(b) with the substitution for either of those weights or for any other weight for the time being specified as aforesaid of a weight expressed in terms of the metric system, being a weight which is equivalent to that for which it is substituted or does not differ from it by more than 5 per cent thereof.

[(7) An offence under this Part of this Act may be treated for the purpose of conferring jurisdiction on a court (but without prejudice to any jurisdiction it may have apart from this subsection) as having been committed in any of the following places, that is to say—

(a) the place where the person charged with the offence was driving when evidence of the offence first came to the attention of a constable or vehicle examiner;

(b) the place where that person resides or is believed to reside or be at the time when the proceedings are commenced; or

(c) the place where at that time that person or, in the case of an employee-driver, that person's employer or, in the case of an owner-driver, the person for whom he was driving, has his place or principal place of business or his operating centre for the vehicle in question.

In this subsection "*vehicle examiner*" means an officer within the meaning of section 99 of this Act.]

(8) The enactments specified in Schedule 11 to this Act shall have effect subject to the amendments there specified.

(9) Any order made under section 166(2) of this Act appointing a day for the purposes of any of the provisions of this Part of this Act may contain such transitional provisions as the [Secretary of State for the Environment, Transport and the Regions] thinks necessary or expedient as respects the application of any particular provision of this Part of this Act to a working week or working day falling partly before and partly after the date on which that provision comes into operation.

[Section 103 is printed as amended by the Road Traffic (Drivers' Ages and Hours of Work) Act 1976, **A6.31** *ss.2(1) and 3; the Interpretation Act 1978, s.17(2)(a); the Minister of Transport Order 1979 (S.I. 1979 No. 571); the Passenger and Goods Vehicles (Recording Equipment) Regulations 1979 (S.I. 1979 No. 1746); the Transfer of Functions (Transport) Order 1981 (S.I. 1981 No. 238); the Road Traffic Acts 1960 and 1972, Road Traffic Regulation Act 1967, and Transport Act 1968 (Metrication) Regulations 1981 (S.I. 1981 No. 1373); the Transport Act 1985, ss.3(5) and 139(3), Sched. 2, Pt II, para.1(5), Sched. 8; the Community Drivers' Hours and Recording Equipment Regulations 1986 (S.I. 1986 No. 1457), reg.3; the Drivers' Hours (Harmonisation with Community Rules) Regulations 1986 (S.I. 1986 No. 1458), reg.3; the Secretary of State for the Environment, Transport and the Regions Order 1997 (S.I. 1997 No. 2971).*

In the definition of "agriculture", words relating expressly and exclusively to Scotland have been omitted. The term "agriculture" is defined in section 109(3) of the Agriculture Act 1947 as follows:

"*agriculture*" includes horticulture, fruit growing, seed growing, dairy farming and live-stock breeding and keeping, the use of land as grazing land, meadow land, osier land, market gardens and nursery grounds, and the use of land for woodlands where that use is ancillary to the farming of land for other agricultural purposes, and "*agricultural*" shall be construed accordingly;

The definition of "working day" has been modified in its application to the drivers of passenger vehicles and goods vehicles; see further the Drivers' Hours (Passenger and Goods Vehicles) (Modifications) Order 1971 (S.I. 1971 No. 818) and the Drivers' Hours (Goods Vehicles) (Modifications) Order 1986 (S.I. 1986 No. 1459) below.

The amendments to subsection (6) effected by the Road Traffic Acts 1960 and 1972, Road Traffic Regulation Act 1967, and Transport Act 1968 (Metrication) Regulations (S.I. 1981 No. 1373) (namely "3500 kilograms" for "3 tons" and "1525 kilograms" for "30 hundredweight") were expressed specifically to apply to section 98(2) of this Act.]

*   *   *

The Chronically Sick and Disabled Persons Act 1970

(1970 c. 44)

A7.01   An Act to make further provision with respect to the welfare of chronically sick and disabled persons; and for connected purposes.

[29th May 1970]

*   *   *

20. Use of invalid carriages on highways

A7.02   (1) In the case of a vehicle which is an invalid carriage complying with the prescribed requirements and which is being used in accordance with the prescribed conditions—

(a) no statutory provision prohibiting or restricting the use of footways shall prohibit or restrict the use of that vehicle on a footway;

(b) if the vehicle is mechanically propelled, it shall be treated for the purposes of the [Road Traffic Regulation Act [1984] and [the Road Traffic Act 1988 [, except section 22A of that Act (causing danger to road users by interfering with motor vehicles, etc.),] and the Road Traffic Offenders Act 1988]] as not being a motor vehicle [and sections 1 to 4, 163, 170 and 181 of the Road Traffic Act 1988 shall not apply to it]; and

(c) whether or not the vehicle is mechanically propelled, it shall be exempted from the requirements of [section 83 of the said Act of 1988].

(2) In this section—

"*footway*" means a way which is a footway, footpath or bridleway within the meaning of [the Highways Act 1980] . . . ;

"*invalid carriage*" means a vehicle, whether mechanically propelled or not, constructed or adapted for use for the carriage of one person, being a person suffering from some physical defect or disability;

"*prescribed*" means prescribed by regulations made by the [Secretary of State for the Environment, Transport and the Regions];

"*statutory provision*" means a provision contained in, or having effect under, any enactment.

(3) [Omitted.]

A7.03   *[Section 20 is printed as amended by the Secretary of State for the Environment Order 1970 (S.I. 1970 No. 1681); the Road Traffic Act 1972, s.203(1) and Sched. 7; the Secretary of State for Transport Order 1976 (S.I. 1976 No. 1775); the Minister of Transport Order 1979 (S.I. 1979 No. 571); the Highways Act 1980, s.343(2) and Sched. 24, para.19; the Transfer of Functions (Transport) Order 1981 (S.I. 1981 No. 238); the Road Traffic Regulation Act 1984, s.146(a) and Sched. 13, para.10; the Road Traffic (Consequential Provisions) Act 1988, s.4 and Sched. 3, para.7; the Road Traffic Act 1991, s.48 and Sched. 4, para.3(a) and (b); the Secretary of State for the Environment, Transport and the Regions Order 1997 (S.I. 1997 No. 2971).*

Words relating expressly and exclusively to Scotland have been omitted from the definition of "footway".

The Use of Invalid Carriages on Highways Regulations 1988 (S.I. 1988 No. 2268) (q.v.) have been made under this section.]

21. Badges for display on motor vehicles used by disabled persons

(1)–(3) *[Omitted.]*   **A7.04**

[(4A) A badge issued under this section may be displayed only in such circumstances and in such manner as may be prescribed.]

[(4B) A person who drives a motor vehicle on a road (within the meaning of the Road Traffic Act 1988) at a time when a badge of a form prescribed under this section is displayed on the vehicle is guilty of an offence unless the badge is issued under this section and displayed in accordance with regulations made under it.]

[(4C) A person guilty of an offence under subsection (4B) above shall be liable on summary conviction to a fine not exceeding level 3 on the standard scale.]

(5)–(7E) *[Omitted.]*

(8) The local authorities for the purposes of this section shall be the common council of the City of London, the council of a county . . . [or metropolitan district] in England . . . or of a London borough [, the council of a Welsh county or county borough] . . .; and in this section "*motor vehicle*" has the same meaning as in the Road Traffic Regulation Act [1984].

(9) *[Omitted.]*

[Subsection (8) is printed as amended by the Local Government Act 1972, s.272(1) and Sched. 30; the   **A7.05**
Road Traffic Regulation Act 1984, s.146(a) and Sched. 13, para.11; the Local Government Act 1985, s.8 and Sched. 5, Pt I, para.1; the Road Traffic Act 1991, s.35(1) and (4); the Local Government (Wales) Act 1994, s.22(4) and Sched. 10, para.8 (see also ibid., s.66(8) and Sched. 18).

Words relating expressly and exclusively to Scotland have been omitted from subsection (8) above.

The Disabled Persons (Badges for Motor Vehicles) (England) Regulations 2000 (S.I. 2000 No. 682 below) and the Disabled Persons (Badges for Motor Vehicles) (Wales) Regulations 2000 (S.I. 2000 No. 1786 below) have been made under this section and the Local Authorities' Traffic Orders (Exemptions for Disabled Persons) (England) Regulations 2000 (S.I. 2000 No. 683 below) and the Local Authorities' Traffic Orders (Exemptions for Disabled Persons) (Wales) Regulations 2000 (S.I. 2000 No. 1785 below) have been made in part under this section.]

*   *   *

The Road Traffic (Foreign Vehicles) Act 1972

(1972 c. 27)

A8.01   An Act to make provision, in relation to foreign goods vehicles and foreign public service vehicles, for securing the observance of certain statutory provisions relating to road traffic; and for purposes connected with those matters.

[11th May 1972]

A8.02   *Visiting forces, etc.*   Visiting forces and headquarters (as defined), members of such forces or headquarters, and persons employed by such forces are exempt from the operation of the 1972 Act to the extent that, by virtue of any rule of law whereby enactments do not bind the Crown, such forces, headquarters, members or persons would have been so exempt if the forces or headquarters had been part of the home forces; see the Visiting Forces and International Headquarters (Application of Law) Order 1999 (S.I. 1999 No. 1736; not reproduced in this work), art.12(1) and Sched. 5.

ARRANGEMENT OF SECTIONS

A8.04   1. Power in certain cases to prohibit driving of foreign vehicle

(1) The provisions of this section shall have effect with respect to any foreign goods vehicle or foreign public service vehicle where—

(a) an examiner [or an authorised inspector] exercises, in relation to the vehicle or its driver, any functions of the examiner [or authorised inspector] under an enactment [or instrument] specified in the first column of Schedule 1 to this Act, or [any functions of the authorised inspecting officer under a Community instrument specified in that column, or]

(b) an authorised person exercises, in relation to the vehicle, any functions of that person under [sections 78 and 79 of the Road Traffic Act 1988] (weighing of motor vehicles).

(2) If in any such case as is mentioned in subsection (1)(a) of this section—

(a) the driver obstructs the examiner [or authorised inspector] in the exercise of his functions under the enactment [or instrument] in question, or refuses, neglects or otherwise fails to comply with any requirement made by the examiner [or authorised inspector] under that enactment [or instrument], or

(b) it appears to the examiner [or authorised inspector] that, in relation to the vehicle or its driver, there has been a contravention of any of the enactments or instruments specified in the first column of Schedule 2 to this Act, or that there will be such a contravention if the vehicle is driven on a road,

the examiner [or authorised inspector] may prohibit the driving of the vehicle on a road, either absolutely or for a specified purpose, and either for a specified period or without any limitation of time.

(3) If in any such case as is mentioned in subsection (1)(b) of this section—

(a) the driver obstructs the authorised person in the exercise of his functions under [the said sections 78 and 79], or refuses, neglects or otherwise fails to comply with any requirement made by the authorised person under [those sections], or

(b) it appears to the authorised person that any limit of weight applicable to the vehicle by virtue of regulations made under [section 41 of the Road Traffic Act 1988] has been exceeded, or will be exceeded if the vehicle is driven on a road,

the authorised person may prohibit the driving of the vehicle on a road, either absolutely or for a specified purpose.

(4) Where an examiner [or an authorised inspector] or an authorised person prohibits the driving of a vehicle under this section, he may also direct the driver to remove the vehicle (and, if it is a motor vehicle drawing a trailer, also to remove the trailer) to such place and subject to such conditions as are specified in the direction; and the prohibition shall not apply to the removal of the vehicle in accordance with that direction.

(5) Where a prohibition is imposed under subsection (2) or subsection (3) of this section, the examiner [or authorised inspector] or authorised person shall forthwith give notice in writing of the prohibition to the driver of the vehicle, specifying the circumstances (as mentioned in paragraph (a) or paragraph (b) of either of those subsections) in consequence of which the prohibition is imposed, and—

(a) stating whether the prohibition is on all driving of the vehicle or only on driving it for a specified purpose (and, if the latter, specifying the purpose), and

(b) where the prohibition is imposed under subsection (2) of this section, also stating whether it is imposed only for a specified period (and, if so, specifying the period) or without limitation of time;

and any direction under subsection (4) of this section may be given either in that notice or in a separate notice in writing given to the driver of the vehicle.

[(6) In the case of a goods vehicle—

(a) a prohibition under subsection (2)(b) above, by reference to a supposed contravention of [section 40A of the Road Traffic Act 1988 (using vehicle in dangerous condition, etc.) or regulations under section 41 of that Act (construction, weight, equipment, etc., of motor vehicles and trailers),] may be imposed with a direction making it irremovable unless and until the vehicle has been inspected at an official testing station;

(b) a prohibition imposed under subsection (3) above may be against driving the vehicle on a road until the weight has been reduced and official notification has been given to whoever is for the time being in charge of the vehicle that it is permitted to proceed.]

[(7) Official notification for the purposes of subsection (6)(b) above must be in writing and be given by an authorised person and may be withheld until the vehicle has been weighed or re-weighed in order to satisfy the person giving the notification that the weight has been sufficiently reduced.]

A8.05

[Section 1 is printed as amended by the Transport Act 1978, s.9(1) and Sched. 3, para.8; the Transport Act 1982, s.10(4); the Road Transport (International Passenger Services) Regulations 1984 (S.I. 1984 No. 748), reg.22; the Road Traffic Act 1991, s.4 and Sched. 4, para.6; the Public Service Vehicles (Community Licences) Regulations 1999 (S.I. 1999 No. 1322), reg.13(1) below.

The references to "authorised inspector" in this section were inserted by the Transport Act 1982, s.10(4), and will take effect from a date to be announced. Until such date, the text of section 1 should be read as if such references were omitted.]

2. Provisions supplementary to section 1

A8.06

(1) Subject to any exemption granted under subsection (2) of this section, a prohibition under section 1 of this Act shall come into force as soon as notice of it has been given in accordance with subsection (5) of that section, and shall continue in force until it is removed under the following provisions of this section (or, in the case of a prohibition imposed only for a specified period, shall continue in force until either it is removed under this section or that period expires, whichever first occurs).

(2) Where notice of a prohibition has been given under subsection (5) of section 1 of this Act in respect of a vehicle, an exemption in writing for the use of the vehicle in such manner, subject to such conditions and for such purpose as may be specified in the exemption may be granted—

(a) in the case of a prohibition under subsection (2) of that section, by any examiner [or authorised inspector], or

(b) in the case of a prohibition under subsection (3) of that section, by any authorised person.

(3) A prohibition under subsection (2) of section 1 of this Act may be removed by any examiner [or authorised inspector], and a prohibition under subsection (3) of that section may be removed by any authorised person, if he is satisfied that appropriate action has been taken to remove or remedy the circumstances (as mentioned in paragraph (a) or paragraph (b) of either of those subsections) in consequence of which the prohibition was imposed; and on doing so the examiner [or authorised inspector] or authorised person shall forthwith give notice in writing of the removal of the prohibition to the driver of the vehicle.

[(3A) If the prohibition under section 1 of this Act has been imposed with a direction under subsection (6)(a) of that section, the prohibition shall not then be removed under subsection (3) above unless and until the vehicle has been inspected at an official testing station.]

[(3B) In the case of vehicles brought to an official testing station for inspection with a view to removal of a prohibition, [section [72A] of the Road Traffic Act 1988] (fees for inspection) applies.]

(4) In the exercise of his functions under section 1 of this Act or under this section an examiner [or an authorised inspector] shall act in accordance with any general directions given by the Secretary of State; and (without prejudice to the preceding provisions of this subsection) an examiner [or an authorised inspector], in exercising his functions under subsection (2) of this section, shall act in accordance with any directions given by the Secretary of State with respect to the exercise of those functions in any particular case.

[Section 2 is printed as amended by the Transport Act 1978, s.9(1) and Sched. 3, para.9; the Transport
Act 1982, s.10(4); the Road Traffic (Consequential Provisions) Act 1988, s.4 and Sched. 3, para.9(2);
the Road Traffic Act 1991, s.48 and Sched. 4, para.7.

The references to "authorised inspector" were inserted by the Transport Act 1982, s.10(4), and will take
effect from a date to be announced. Until such date, the text of section 2 should be read as if such references
were omitted.]

3. Enforcement provisions

(1) Any person who—

  (a) drives a vehicle on a road in contravention of a prohibition imposed under section 1
  of this Act, or

  (b) causes or permits a vehicle to be driven on a road in contravention of such a prohibition, or

  (c) refuses, neglects or otherwise fails to comply within a reasonable time with a direction given under subsection (4) of that section,

shall be guilty of an offence and shall be liable on summary conviction to a fine not exceeding [level 5 on the standard scale].

(2) *[Repealed.]*

(3) Where a constable in uniform has reasonable cause to suspect the driver of a vehicle
of having committed an offence under subsection (1) of this section, the constable may
detain the vehicle, and for that purpose may give a direction, specifying an appropriate
person and directing the vehicle to be removed by that person to such place and subject to
such conditions as are specified in the direction; and the prohibition shall not apply to the
removal of the vehicle in accordance with that direction.

(4) Where under subsection (3) of this section a constable—

  (a) detains a motor vehicle drawing a trailer, or

  (b) detains a trailer drawn by a motor vehicle,

then, for the purpose of securing the removal of the trailer, he may also (in a case falling
within paragraph (a) of this subsection) detain the trailer or (in a case falling within paragraph (b) of this subsection) detain the motor vehicle; and a direction under subsection (3)
of this section may require both the motor vehicle and the trailer to be removed to the place
specified in the direction.

(5) A vehicle which, in accordance with a direction given under subsection (3) of this
section, is removed to a place specified in the direction shall be detained in that place, or in
any other place to which it is removed in accordance with a further direction given under
that subsection, until a constable (or, if that place is in the occupation of the Secretary of
State, the Secretary of State) authorises the vehicle to be released on being satisfied—

  (a) that the prohibition (if any) imposed in respect of the vehicle under section 1 of
  this Act has been removed, or that no such prohibition was imposed, or

  (b) that appropriate arrangements have been made for removing or remedying the circumstances in consequence of which any such prohibition was imposed, or

  (c) that the vehicle will be taken forthwith to a place from which it will be taken out of
  Great Britain, or

  (d) in the case of a vehicle detained under subsection (4) of this section, that (in the
  case of a motor vehicle) the purpose for which it was detained has been fulfilled or
  (in the case of a trailer) it is no longer necessary to detain it for the purpose of safe-
  guarding the trailer or its load.

(6) Any person who—

    (a) drives a vehicle in accordance with a direction given under this section, or

    (b) is in charge of a place at which a vehicle is detained under subsection (5) of this section,

shall not be liable for any damage to, or loss in respect of, the vehicle or its load unless it is shown that he did not take reasonable care of the vehicle while driving it or, as the case may be, did not, while the vehicle was detained in that place, take reasonable care of the vehicle or (if the vehicle was detained there with its load) did not take reasonable care of its load.

(7) In this section *"appropriate person"*—

    (a) in relation to a direction to remove a motor vehicle, other than a motor vehicle drawing a trailer, means a person licensed to drive vehicles of the class to which the vehicle belongs, and

    (b) in relation to a direction to remove a trailer, or to remove a motor vehicle drawing a trailer, means a person licensed to drive vehicles of a class which, when the direction is complied with, will include the motor vehicle drawing the trailer in accordance with that direction.

A8.09   *[Section 3 is printed as amended by the Criminal Justice Act 1982, ss.37, 39(2), 46, and Sched. 3; the Police and Criminal Evidence Act 1984, s.119(2) and Sched. 7.]*

4. Production of certain documents

A8.10   (1) Subsection (3) of this section shall have effect in relation to a vehicle where it appears to an examiner that the vehicle—

    (a) is a foreign goods vehicle within the meaning of regulations for the time being in force under [section 57(6) of the Goods Vehicles (Licensing of Operators) Act 1995] (which enables certain provisions of that Act to be modified in their application to vehicles brought temporarily into Great Britain), and

    (b) is being used, or has been brought into Great Britain for the purpose of being used, in such circumstances as, by virtue of [section 2(1)] of that Act as modified by the regulations, to require a document of a description specified in the regulations to be carried on it.

(2) The next following subsection shall also have effect in relation to a vehicle where it appears to an examiner that the vehicle—

    (a) is a foreign public service vehicle, and

    (b) is being used, or has been brought into Great Britain for the purpose of being used, in such circumstances as, by virtue of [section 12(1) of the Public Passenger Vehicles Act 1981 as modified by regulations for the time being in force under section 60(1)(m) of that Act] (which enables certain provisions of that Act to be modified in their application to public service vehicles [registered outside Great Britain]), to require a document of a description specified in the regulations to be carried on it.

(3) In the circumstances mentioned in subsection (1) or subsection (2) of this section, the examiner, on production if so required of his authority,—

    (a) may require the driver of the vehicle to produce a document of the description in question and to permit the examiner to inspect and copy it, and

    (b) may detain the vehicle for such time as is requisite for the purpose of inspecting and copying the document;

and, if the driver refuses or fails to comply with any such requirement (including any case where he does so by reason that no such document is carried on the vehicle), the examiner may prohibit the driving of the vehicle on a road, either absolutely or for a specified purpose, and either for a specified period or without limitation of time.

(4) In subsections (4) and (5) of section 1 and in section 2 and 3 of this Act any reference to a prohibition imposed under section 1, or under subsection (2) of section 1, of this Act shall be construed as including a reference to a prohibition imposed under this section; and, in relation to a prohibition imposed under this section, so much of section 1(5) or of section 2(3) of this Act as relates to the circumstances in consequence of which the prohibition was imposed shall be read subject to the appropriate modifications.

[Section 4 is printed as amended by the Transport Act 1980, s.43(1) and Sched. 5, Pt II; the Public   **A8.11**
Passenger Vehicles Act 1981, s.88(2) and Sched. 7, para.16; the Goods Vehicles (Licensing of Operators)
Act 1995, s.60(1) and Sched. 7, para.5(1).]

5, 6. *[Repealed.]*   **A8.12**

7. Interpretation and transitional provisions

(1) In this Act, except in so far as the context otherwise requires, the following ex-   **A8.13**
pressions have the meanings hereby assigned to them respectively, that is to say—

"*authorised person*" means a person (whether an examiner or not) authorised to exercise the powers of [section 78 of the Road Traffic Act 1988] with respect to the weighing of motor vehicles and trailers;

"*drivers*"—

(a) in relation to a motor vehicle, includes any person who is in charge of the vehicle and, if a separate person acts as steersman, includes that person as well as any other person in charge of the vehicle or engaged in the driving of it, and

(b) in relation to a trailer, means any person who (in accordance with the preceding paragraph) is the driver of the motor vehicle by which the trailer is drawn;

"*examiner*" means [an examiner appointed under section 66A of the Road Traffic Act 1988, or a constable authorised to act for the purposes of this Act by or on behalf of a chief officer of police];

"*foreign goods vehicle*" (except in section 4 of this Act) means a goods vehicle which has been brought into Great Britain and which, if a motor vehicle, is not registered in the United Kingdom or, if a trailer, is drawn by a motor vehicle not registered in the United Kingdom which has been brought into Great Britain;

"*foreign public service vehicle*" means a public service vehicle which has been brought into Great Britain and is not registered in the United Kingdom;

"*goods vehicle*" means a motor vehicle constructed or adapted for use for the carriage or haulage of goods or burden of any description, or a trailer so constructed or adapted;

["*official testing station*" means a station maintained by the Secretary of State under [section [72A] of the Road Traffic Act 1988] [or premises designated by him under section 10(12) of the Transport Act 1982];]

"*public service vehicle*" shall be construed in accordance with [the Public Passenger Vehicles Act 1981];

"*road*" means any highway and any other road to which the public has access, and includes bridges over which a road passes.

[(1A) References in any provision of this Act to an authorised inspector are references to a person authorised by the Secretary of State under section 8 of the Transport Act 1982 to exercise the function to which that provision relates.]

(2) In this Act any reference to driving a vehicle shall, in relation to a trailer, be construed as a reference to driving the motor vehicle by which the trailer is drawn.

(3) In this Act any reference to a motor vehicle drawing a trailer, or to a motor vehicle by which a trailer is drawn, shall be construed as a reference to a motor vehicle to which a trailer is attached for the purpose of being drawn by it; and where, for the purpose of being drawn by a motor vehicle, two or more trailers (one of which is attached to the motor vehicle) are attached to each other, the motor vehicle shall for the purposes of this Act be treated as drawing each of those trailers.

(4) For the purposes of this Act a motor vehicle which does not for the time being have exhibited on it a licence or trade plates [issued under the Vehicle Excise and Registration Act 1994 shall] be presumed, unless the contrary is proved, not to be registered in the United Kingdom.

(5) Where, in accordance with subsection (4) of this section, a motor vehicle is presumed not to be registered in the United Kingdom, but is subsequently proved to have been so registered, anything which—

(a) has been done in relation to the vehicle, or in relation to a trailer drawn by it, by a person relying in good faith on that presumption and purporting to act by virtue of any provision of this Act, and

(b) would have been lawfully done by virtue of that provision if the vehicle had not been registered in the United Kingdom,

shall be treated as having been lawfully done by virtue of that provision.

(6) Any reference in any provision of this Act to regulations made under an enactment specified in that provision shall be construed as including a reference to any regulations which, by virtue of that or any other enactment, have effect, or are to be treated, as if made under the enactment so specified.

(7) *[Repealed.]*

A8.14   *[Section 7 is printed as amended by the Road Traffic Act 1974, s.24(3) and Sched. 7; the Transport Act 1978, s.9(1) and Sched. 3, para.10; the Transport Act 1980, s.43(1) and Sched. 5, Pt II; the Public Passenger Vehicles Act 1981, s.88(2) and Sched. 7, para.17; the Transport Act 1982, s.74(1) and Sched. 5, para.17(2); the Road Traffic (Consequential Provisions) Act 1988, s.4 and Sched. 3, para.9(3); the Road Traffic Act 1991, s.48 and Sched. 4, para.8(a) and (b); the Vehicle Excise and Registration Act 1994, s.63 and Sched. 3, para.5.*

The reference in the definition of "official testing station" to premises designated under section 10(2) of the Transport Act 1982 and section 7(1A) above were inserted by ibid., s.74(1) and Sched. 5, para.17(2), with effect from a date to be announced. Until such date, the text of section 7 should be read as if that reference and section 7(1A) were omitted.]

A8.15   **8. Short title, commencement and extent**   *[Omitted.]*

Section 1   SCHEDULE 1

[PROVISIONS] CONFERRING FUNCTIONS ON EXAMINERS

A8.16   *Provisions*   *Function conferred*

. . .

[Section 99 of the Transport Act 1968.]   [To inspect and copy record sheets, books, registers and other documents required to be carried on goods vehicles and

[Section 67 of the Road Traffic Act 1988.]

public service vehicles, to inspect recording equipment and to inspect and copy record sheets on which records have been produced by such equipment or entries have been made.]

To test the condition of motor vehicles on roads.

[Section 68 of the Road Traffic Act 1988.]

To inspect . . . vehicles to secure proper maintenance.

[Regulation 16 of the Road Transport (International Passenger Services) Regulations 1984.]

[To require the production of, and to inspect, copy and mark, documents required to be kept or carried on certain passenger vehicles.]

[Article 3A(3) of Council Regulation (EEC) No. 684/92 of 16 March 1992 on common rules for the international carriage of passengers by coach and bus [*q.v.*], as amended by Council Regulation (E.C.) No. 11/98 of 11 December 1997.]

[To require the production of a certain document which is required to be kept on board certain passenger vehicles.]

[Regulation 7 of the Road Transport (Passenger Vehicles Cabotage) Regulations 1999 [*S.I. 1999 No. 3413 below*].

[To require the production of certain documents which are required to be kept on board certain passenger vehicles.]

[*Schedule 1 is printed as amended by the Passenger and Goods Vehicles (Recording Equipment) Regulations 1979 (S.I. 1979 No. 1746), reg.3; the Transport Act 1980, s.43(1) and Sched. 5, Pt II; the Public Passenger Vehicles Act 1981, s.88(2) and Sched. 7, para.18; the Road Transport (International Passenger Services) Regulations 1984 (S.I. 1984 No. 748), reg.22; the Road Traffic (Consequential Provisions) Act 1988, s.4 and Sched. 3, para.9(4); the Road Traffic Act 1991, s.83 and Sched. 8; the Public Service Vehicles (Community Licences) Regulations 1999 (S.I. 1999 No. 1322), reg.13(2) below; the Road Transport (Passenger Vehicles Cabotage) Regulations 1999 (S.I. 1999 No. 3413), reg.10(1)(a) below.]* **A8.17**

Section 1

SCHEDULE 2

PROVISIONS RELATING TO VEHICLES AND THEIR DRIVERS

Provisions	*Effect*	**A8.18**
[Section 2 of the Goods Vehicles (Licensing of Operators) Act 1995].	To require users of certain goods vehicles to hold operators' licences unless exempted from doing so.	
Regulations under [section 57(2)(d) of the Goods Vehicles (Licensing of Operators) Act 1995].	To require goods vehicles to be identified by plates, marks etc.	
Sections 96 to 98 of the Transport Act 1968 and regulations and orders made under those sections [and [the applicable Community rules] within the meaning of Part VI of that Act].	To limit driving time and periods of duty of drivers of goods and public service vehicles and to require the installation of recording equipment in, and the keeping of records on, such vehicles.	
Any order under section 100 of the Transport Act 1968.	To give effect to international agreements relating to vehicles used on international journeys.	

[Regulations under section 41 of the Road Traffic Act 1988.]	To regulate the construction, weight, equipment and use of motor vehicles and trailers on roads.
Sections 68 to 73 and 76 to 79 of the Road Traffic Act 1972 and regulations made under those sections.	*To require vehicles to carry front and rear lamps, headlamps and reflectors, to regulate their position, character and use and to make special provision for vehicles carrying overhanging or projecting loads and vehicles towing and being towed.*
[Regulation 19 of the Road Transport (International Passenger Services) Regulations 1984.]	[To impose penalties for contravention of certain requirements relating to international passenger services.]
[Section 40A of the Road Traffic Act 1988.	To create offence of using motor vehicle or trailer in dangerous condition etc.]
[Regulations 3 and 7 of the Public Service Vehicles (Community Licences) Regulations 1999 [*S.I. 1999 No. 1322 below*].]	[To impose a penalty for contravention of certain requirements relating to international passenger services.]
[Regulations 3, 4 and 7 of the Road Transport (Passenger Vehicles Cabotage) Regulations 1999 [*S.I. 1999 No. 3413 below*].]	[To impose penalties for contravention of certain requirements relating to national passenger services by a carrier registered in a foreign member State.]

[Schedule 2 is printed as amended by the European Communities Act 1972, s.4(1) and Sched. 4, para.9(4); the Road Traffic (Drivers' Ages and Hours of Work) Act 1976, s.2(3); the Road Transport (International Passenger Services) Regulations 1984 (S.I. 1984 No. 748), reg.22; the Road Traffic (Consequential Provisions) Act 1988, ss.3(1) and 4, Sched. 1, Pt I, and Sched. 3, para.9(5); the Road Traffic Act 1991, s.48 and Sched. 4, para.9; the Goods Vehicles (Licensing of Operators) Act 1995, s.60(1) and Sched. 7, para.6; the Public Service Vehicles (Community Licences) Regulations 1999 (S.I. 1999 No. 1322), reg.13(3) below; the Road Transport (Passenger Vehicles Cabotage) Regulations 1999 (S.I. 1999 No. 3413), reg.10(1)(b) below.

The words printed in italics have lapsed.]

The Health and Safety at Work, etc., Act 1974

(1974 c. 37)

An Act to make further provision for securing the health, safety and welfare of persons at work, for protecting others against risks to health or safety in connection with the activities of persons at work, for controlling the keeping and use and preventing the unlawful acquisition, possession and use of dangerous substances . . . and for connected purposes. **A9.01**

[31st July 1974]

ARRANGEMENT OF SECTIONS

PART I

HEALTH, SAFETY AND WELFARE IN CONNECTION WITH WORK, AND CONTROL OF DANGEROUS SUBSTANCES AND CERTAIN EMISSIONS INTO THE ATMOSPHERE

Preliminary

*   *   *

PART I

HEALTH, SAFETY AND WELFARE IN CONNECTION WITH WORK, AND CONTROL OF
DANGEROUS SUBSTANCES AND CERTAIN EMISSIONS INTO THE ATMOSPHERE

Preliminary

1. Preliminary

A9.03

(1) The provisions of this Part shall have effect with a view to—

(a) securing the health, safety and welfare of persons at work;

(b) protecting persons other than persons at work against risks to health or safety arising out of or in connection with the activities of persons at work;

(c) controlling the keeping and use of explosive or highly flammable or otherwise dangerous substances, and generally preventing the unlawful acquisition, possession and use of such substances; . . .

(2) The provisions of this Part relating to the making of health and safety regulations . . . and the preparation and approval of codes of practice shall in particular have effect with a view to enabling the enactments specified in the third column of Schedule 1 and the regulations, orders and other instruments in force under those enactments to be progressively replaced by a system of regulations and approved codes of practice operating in combination with the other provisions of this Part and designed to maintain or improve the standards of health, safety and welfare established by or under those enactments.

(3) For the purposes of this Part risks arising out of or in connection with the activities of persons at work shall be treated as including risks attributable to the manner of conducting an undertaking, the plant or substances used for the purposes of an undertaking and the condition of premises so used or any part of them.

(4) References in this Part to the general purposes of this Part are references to the purposes mentioned in subsection (1) above.

[Section 1 is printed as amended by the Employment Protection Act 1975, ss.116, 125(3), Sched. 15, para.1, and Sched. 18; the Environmental Protection Act 1990, s.162(2) and Sched. 16, Pt I.]   **A9.04**

General duties

2. General duties of employers to their employees   *[Omitted.]*   **A9.05**

3. General duties of employers and self-employed to persons other than their employees   *[Omitted.]*

4. General duties of persons concerned with premises to persons other than their employees   *[Omitted.]*

5. General duty of persons in control of certain premises in relation to harmful emissions into atmosphere   *[Repealed.]*

6. General duties of manufacturers, etc., as regards articles and substances for use at work   *[Omitted.]*

7. General duties of employees at work   *[Omitted.]*

8. Duty not to interfere with or misuse things provided pursuant to certain provisions   *[Omitted.]*

9. Duty not to charge employees for things done or provided pursuant to certain specific requirements   *[Omitted.]*

The Health and Safety Commission and the Health and Safety Executive

10. Establishment of the Commission and the Executive

(1) There shall be two bodies corporate to be called the Health and Safety Commission   **A9.06**
and the Health and Safety Executive which shall be constituted in accordance with the following provisions of this section.

(2) The Health and Safety Commission (hereafter in this Act referred to as "*the Commission*") shall consist of a chairman appointed by the Secretary of State and not less than six nor more than nine other members appointed by the Secretary of State in accordance with subsection (3) below.

(3), (4)   *[Omitted.]*

(5) The Health and Safety Executive (hereafter in this Act referred to as "*the Executive*" shall consist of three persons of whom one shall be appointed by the Commission with the approval of the Secretary of State to be the director of the Executive and the others shall be appointed by the Commission with the like approval after consultation with the said director.

(6)–(8)   *[Omitted.]*

11. General functions of the Commission and the Executive   *[Omitted.]*

12. Control of the Commission by the Secretary of State   *[Omitted.]*

13. Other powers of the Commission   *[Omitted.]*

14. Power of the Commission to direct investigations and inquiries
[Omitted.]

Health and safety regulations and approved codes of practice

15. Health and safety regulations

[(1) Subject to the provisions of section 50, the Secretary of State, the Minister of Agriculture, Fisheries and Food or the Secretary of State and that Minister acting jointly shall have power to make regulations under this section for any of the general purposes of this Part (and regulations so made are in this Part referred to as *"health and safety regulations"*).]

(2) Without prejudice to the generality of the preceding subsection, health and safety regulations may for any of the general purposes of this Part make provision for any of the purposes mentioned in Schedule 3.

(3) Health and safety regulations—

   (a) may repeal or modify any of the existing statutory provisions;

   (b) may exclude or modify in relation to any specified class of case any of the provisions of sections 2 to 9 or any of the existing statutory provisions;

   (c) may make a specified authority or class of authorities responsible, to such extent as may be specified, for the enforcement of any of the relevant statutory provisions.

(4) Health and safety regulations—

   (a) may impose requirements by reference to the approval of the Commission or any other specified body or person;

   (b) may provide for references in the regulations to any specified document to operate as references to that document as revised or re-issued from time to time.

(5) Health and safety regulations—

   (a) may provide (either unconditionally or subject to conditions, and with or without limit of time) for exemptions from any requirement or prohibition imposed by or under any of the relevant statutory provisions;

   (b) may enable exemptions from any requirement or prohibition imposed by or under any of the relevant statutory provisions to be granted (either unconditionally or subject to conditions, and with or without limit of time) by any specified person or by any person authorised in that behalf by a specified authority.

(6) Health and safety regulations—

   (a) may specify the persons or classes of persons who, in the event of a contravention of a requirement or prohibition imposed by or under the regulations, are to be guilty of an offence, whether in addition to or to the exclusion of other persons or classes of persons;

   (b) may provide for any specified defence to be available in proceedings for any offence under the relevant statutory provisions either generally or in specified circumstances;

(c) may exclude proceedings on indictment in relation to offences consisting of a contravention of a requirement or prohibition imposed by or under any of the existing statutory provisions, sections 2 to 9 or health and safety regulations;

(d) may restrict the punishments [(other than the maximum fine on conviction on indictment)] which can be imposed in respect of any such offence as is mentioned in paragraph (c) above.

(e) *[Relates to offshore safety only.]*

(7) Without prejudice to section 35, health and safety regulations may make provision for enabling offences under any of the relevant statutory provisions to be treated as having been committed at any specified place for the purpose of bringing any such offence within the field of responsibility of any enforcing authority or conferring jurisdiction on any court to entertain proceedings for any such offence.

(8) Health and safety regulations may take the form of regulations applying to particular circumstances only or to a particular case only (for example, regulations applying to particular premises only).

(9) If an Order in Council is made under section 84(3) providing that this section shall apply to or in relation to persons, premises or work outside Great Britain then, notwithstanding the Order, health and safety regulations shall not apply to or in relation to aircraft in flight, vessels, hovercraft or offshore installations outside Great Britain or persons at work outside Great Britain in connection with submarine cables or submarine pipelines except in so far as the regulations expressly so provide.

(10) In this section "*specified*" means specified in health and safety regulations.

[Section 15 is printed as amended by the Employment Protection Act 1975, s.116 and Sched. 15, **A9.09**
para.6; and by the Criminal Law Act 1977, s.65(4) and Sched. 12.
The Carriage of Dangerous Goods (Classification, Packaging and Labelling) and Use of Transportable Pressure Receptacles Regulations 1996 (S.I. 1996 No. 2092), the Carriage of Explosives by Road Regulations 1996 (S.I. 1996 No. 2093), the Carriage of Dangerous Goods by Road (Driver Training) Regulations 1996 (S.I. 1996 No. 2094), and the Carriage of Dangerous Goods by Road Regulations 1996 (S.I. 1996 No. 2095), have been made in part under this section. These regulations are not reproduced in this work.]

16. Approval of codes of practice by the Commission

(1) For the purpose of providing practical guidance with respect to the requirements of **A9.10**
any provision of sections 2 to 7 or of health and safety regulations or of any of the existing statutory provisions, the Commission may, subject to the following subsection . . . —

(a) approve and issue such codes of practice (whether prepared by it or not) as in its opinion are suitable for that purpose;

(b) approve such codes of practice issued or proposed to be issued otherwise than by the Commission as in its opinion are suitable for that purpose.

(2) *[Consultation prior to issue of code and approval of Secretary of State.]*

(3) *[Notice of approval of code.]*

(4) *[Revision of code.]*

(5), (6) *[Withdrawal of code.]*

(7) References in this Part to an approved code of practice are references to that code as it has effect for the time being by virtue of any revision of the whole or any part of it approved under this section.

(8) The power of the Commission under subsection (1)(b) above to approve a code of practice issued or proposed to be issued otherwise than by the Commission shall include power to approve a part of such a code of practice; and accordingly in this Part "code of practice" may be read as including a part of such a code of practice.

A9.11   *[Section 16 is printed as amended by the Employment Protection Act 1975, ss.116, 125(3), Sched. 15, para.7, and Sched. 18.]*

17. Use of approved codes of practice in criminal proceedings

A9.12   (1) A failure on the part of any person to observe any provision of an approved code of practice shall not of itself render him liable to any civil or criminal proceedings; but where in any criminal proceedings a party is alleged to have committed an offence by reason of a contravention of any requirement or prohibition imposed by or under any such provision as is mentioned in section 16(1) being a provision for which there was an approved code of practice at the time of the alleged contravention, the following subsection shall have effect with respect to that code in relation to those proceedings.

(2) Any provision of the code of practice which appears to the court to be relevant to the requirement or prohibition alleged to have been contravened shall be admissible in evidence in the proceedings; and if it is proved that there was at any material time a failure to observe any provision of the code which appears to the court to be relevant to any matter which it is necessary for the prosecution to prove in order to establish a contravention of that requirement or prohibition, that matter shall be taken as proved unless the court is satisfied that the requirement or prohibition was in respect of that matter complied with otherwise than by way of observance of that provision of the code.

(3) In any criminal proceedings—

(a) a document purporting to be a notice issued by the Commission under section 16 shall be taken to be such a notice unless the contrary is proved; and

(b) a code of practice which appears to the court to be the subject of such a notice shall be taken to be the subject of that notice unless the contrary is proved.

Enforcement

A9.13   **18. Authorities responsible for enforcement of the relevant statutory provisions**   *[Omitted.]*

19. Appointment of inspectors   *[Omitted.]*

20. Powers of inspectors   *[Omitted.]*

21. Improvement notices   *[Omitted.]*

22. Prohibition notices   *[Omitted.]*

23. Provisions supplementary to sections 21 and 22   *[Omitted.]*

24. Appeal against improvement or prohibition notices   *[Omitted.]*

25. Power to deal with imminent danger   *[Omitted.]*

25A. Power of customs officer to detain articles and substances   *[Omitted.]*

26. Power of enforcing authorities to indemnify their inspectors
[Omitted.]

Obtaining and disclosure of information

27. Obtaining of information by the Commission, the Executive, enforcing authorities, etc.   *[Omitted.]*

27A. Information communicated by the Commissioners of Customs and Excise   *[Omitted.]*

28. Restrictions on disclosure of information   *[Omitted.]*

29–32.   *[Repealed by the Employment Protection Act 1975.]*

Provisions as to offences

33. Offences

(1) It is an offence for a person—

A9.14

(a) to fail to discharge a duty to which he is subject by virtue of sections 2 to 7;

(b) to contravene section 8 or 9;

(c) to contravene any health and safety regulations . . . or any requirement or prohibition imposed under any such regulations (including any requirement or prohibition to which he is subject by virtue of the terms of or any condition or restriction attached to any licence, approval, exemption or other authority issued, given or granted under the regulations);

(d) to contravene any requirement imposed by or under regulations under section 14 or intentionally to obstruct any person in the exercise of his powers under that subsection;

(e) to contravene any requirement imposed by an inspector under section 20 or 25;

(f) to prevent or attempt to prevent any other person from appearing before an inspector or from answering any question to which an inspector may by virtue of section 20(2) require an answer;

(g) to contravene any requirement or prohibition imposed by an improvement notice or a prohibition notice (including any such notice as modified on appeal);

(h) intentionally to obstruct an inspector in the exercise or performance of his powers or duties [or to obstruct a customs officer in the exercise of his powers under section 25A];

(i) to contravene any requirement imposed by a notice under section 27(1);

(j) to use or disclose any information in contravention of section 27(4) or 28;

(k) to make a statement which he knows to be false or recklessly to make a statement which is false where the statement is made—

(i) in purported compliance with a requirement to furnish any information imposed by or under any of the relevant statutory provisions; or

(ii) for the purpose of obtaining the issue of a document under any of the relevant statutory provisions to himself or another person;

(l) intentionally to make a false entry in any register, book, notice or other document required by or under any of the relevant statutory provisions to be kept, served or given or, with intent to deceive, to make use of any such entry which he knows to be false;

(m) with intent to deceive, to . . . use a document issued or authorised to be issued under any of the relevant statutory provisions or required for any purpose thereunder or to make or have in his possession a document so closely resembling any such document as to be calculated to deceive;

(n) falsely to pretend to be an inspector;

(o) to fail to comply with an order made by a court under section 42.

(1A) *[Penalty for breach of duty under sections 2–6.]*

(2) A person guilty of an offence under paragraph (d), (f), (h) or of subsection (1) above, or of an offence under paragraph (e) of that subsection consisting of contravening a requirement imposed by an inspector under section 20, shall be liable on summary conviction to a fine not exceeding [level 5 on the standard scale].

(2A) *[Penalty for breach of section 33(1)(g) or (o).]*

(3) Subject to any provision made by virtue of section 15(6)(d) [or (e)] or by virtue of paragraph 2(2) of Schedule 3, a person guilty of [an offence under subsection (1) above not falling within subsection (1A), (2) or (2A) above], or of an offence under any of the existing statutory provisions, being an offence for which no other penalty is specified, shall be liable—

(a) on summary conviction, to a fine not exceeding [the prescribed sum];

(b) on conviction on indictment—

(i) if the offence is one to which this sub-paragraph applies, to imprisonment for a term not exceeding two years, or a fine, or both;

(ii) if the offence is not one to which the preceding sub-paragraph applies, to a fine.

(4) Subsection (3)(b)(i) above applies to the following offences—

(a) an offence consisting of contravening any of the relevant statutory provisions by doing otherwise than under the authority of a licence issued by the Executive . . . something for the doing of which such a licence is necessary under the relevant statutory provisions;

(b) an offence consisting of contravening a term of or a condition or restriction attached to any such licence as is mentioned in the preceding paragraph;

(c) an offence consisting of acquiring or attempting to acquire, possessing or using an explosive article or substance (within the meaning of any of the relevant statutory provisions) in contravention of any of the relevant statutory provisions;

(d) *[Repealed.]*

(e) an offence under subsection (1)(j) above.

(5), (6) *[Repealed.]*

A9.15   *[Section 33 is printed as amended by the Employment Protection Act 1975, ss.116, 125(3), Sched. 15, para.11, and Sched. 18; the Criminal Law Act 1977, ss.15(1), 30(1) and (2), 31, and Scheds 1 and 6; the Magistrates' Courts Act 1980, s.32(2) and (9); the Forgery and Counterfeiting Act 1981, s.30 and Schedule, Pt I; the Criminal Justice Act 1982, s.46; the Consumer Protection Act 1987, s.36 and Sched. 3, para.6; the Offshore Safety Act 1992, s.4.*

Sections 33–42 of the 1974 Act do not apply to visiting forces and headquarters (as defined), members of such forces or headquarters, and persons employed by such forces to the extent that, by virtue of any rule of law whereby enactments do not bind the Crown, such forces, headquarters, members or persons would have been so exempt if the forces or headquarters had been part of the home forces; see the Visiting Forces and International Headquarters (Application of Law) Order 1999 (S.I. 1999 No. 1736; not reproduced in this work), art.12(1) and Sched. 5.]

34. Extension of time for bringing summary proceedings

(1) Where— **A9.16**

(a) a special report on any matter to which section 14 of this Act applies is made by virtue of subsection (2)(a) of that section; or

(b) a report is made by the person holding an inquiry into any such matter by virtue of subsection (2)(b) of that section; or

(c) a coroner's inquest is held touching the death of any person whose death may have been caused by an accident which happened while he was at work or by a disease which he contracted or probably contracted at work or by any accident, act or omission which occurred in connection with the work of any person whatsoever; or

(d) *[applies to Scotland]*;

and it appears from the report or, in a case falling within paragraph (c) above, from the proceedings at the inquest, that any of the relevant statutory provisions was contravened at a time which is material in relation to the subject-matter of the report, inquest or inquiry, summary proceedings against any person liable to be proceeded against in respect of the contravention may be commenced at any time within three months of the making of the report or, in a case falling within paragraph (c) above, within three months of the conclusion of the inquest.

(2) Where an offence under any of the relevant statutory provisions is committed by reason of a failure to do something at or within a time fixed by or under any of those provisions, the offence shall be deemed to continue until that thing is done.

(3) Summary proceedings for an offence to which this subsection applies may be commenced at any time within six months from the date on which there comes to the knowledge of a responsible enforcing authority evidence sufficient in the opinion of that authority to justify a prosecution for that offence; and for the purposes of this subsection—

(a) a certificate of an enforcing authority stating that such evidence came to its knowledge on a specified date shall be conclusive evidence of that fact; and

(b) a document purporting to be such a certificate and to be signed by or on behalf of the enforcing authority in question shall be presumed to be such a certificate unless the contrary is proved.

(4) The preceding subsection applies to any offence under any of the relevant statutory provisions which a person commits by virtue of any provision or requirement to which he is subject as the designer, manufacturer, importer or supplier of any thing; and in that subsection *"responsible enforcing authority"* means an enforcing authority within whose field of responsibility the offence in question lies, whether by virtue of section 35 or otherwise.

(5), (6) *[Apply to Scotland.]*

[Words relating exclusively to Scotland have been omitted from section 34(1). **A9.17**
As to the application of section 34 to visiting forces, etc., see the note to section 33 above.]

35. Venue

An offence under any of the relevant statutory provisions committed in connection with **A9.18**
any plant or substance may, if necessary for the purpose of bringing the offence within the field of responsibility of any enforcing authority or conferring jurisdiction on any court to entertain proceedings for the offence, be treated as having been committed at the place where that plant or substance is for the time being.

[As to the application of section 35 to visiting forces, etc., see the note to section 33 above.] **A9.19**

36. Offences due to fault of other person

A9.20

(1) Where the commission by any person of an offence under any of the relevant statutory provisions is due to the act or default of some other person, that other person shall be guilty of the offence, and a person may be charged with and convicted of the offence by virtue of this subsection whether or not proceedings are taken against the first-mentioned person.

(2) Where there would be or have been the commission of an offence under section 33 by the Crown but for the circumstance that that section does not bind the Crown, and that fact is due to the act or default of a person other than the Crown, that person shall be guilty of the offence which, but for that circumstance, the Crown would be committing or would have committed, and may be charged with and convicted of that offence accordingly.

(3) The preceding provisions of this section are subject to any provision made by virtue of section 15(6).

A9.21

[As to the application of section 36 to visiting forces, etc., see the note to section 33 above.]

37. Offences by bodies corporate

A9.22

(1) Where an offence under any of the relevant statutory provisions committed by a body corporate is proved to have been committed with the consent or connivance of, or to have been attributable to any neglect on the part of, any director, manager, secretary or other similar officer of the body corporate or a person who was purporting to act in any such capacity, he as well as the body corporate shall be guilty of that offence and shall be liable to be proceeded against and punished accordingly.

(2) Where the affairs of a body corporate are managed by its members, the preceding subsection shall apply in relation to the acts and defaults of a member in connection with his functions of management as if he were a director of the body corporate.

A9.23

[As to the application of section 37 to visiting forces, etc., see the note to section 33 above.]

38. Restriction on institution of proceedings in England and Wales

A9.24

Proceedings for an offence under any of the relevant statutory provisions shall not, in England and Wales, be instituted except by an inspector or [the Environment Agency or] by or with the consent of the Director of Public Prosecutions.

A9.25

[Section 38 is printed as amended by the Environment Act 1995, s.120 and Sched.22, para.30(7). As to the application of section 38 to visiting forces, etc., see the note to section 33 above.]

39. Prosecutions by inspectors

A9.26

(1) An inspector, if authorised in that behalf by the enforcing authority which appointed him, may, although not of counsel or a solicitor, prosecute before a magistrates' court proceedings for an offence under any of the relevant statutory provisions.

(2) This section shall not apply to Scotland.

A9.27

[As to the application of section 39 to visiting forces, etc., see the note to section 33 above.]

40. Onus of proving limits of what is practicable, etc.

A9.28

In any proceedings for an offence under any of the relevant statutory provisions consisting of a failure to comply with a duty or requirement to do something so far as is practicable or so far as is reasonably practicable, or to use the best practicable means to do something, it shall be for the accused to prove (as the case may be) that it was not practicable or not reasonably practicable to do more than was in fact done to satisfy the duty or requirement, or that there was no better practicable means than was in fact used to satisfy the duty or requirement.

[As to the application of section 40 to visiting forces, etc., see the note to section 33 above.]   **A9.29**

41. Evidence

(1) Where an entry is required by any of the relevant statutory provisions to be made in any register or other record, the entry, if made, shall, as against the person by or on whose behalf it was made, be admissible as evidence . . . of the facts stated therein.   **A9.30**

(2) Where an entry which is so required to be so made with respect to the observance of any of the relevant statutory provisions has not been made, that fact shall be admissible as evidence . . . that that provision has not been observed.

[Words relating expressly and exclusively to Scotland have been omitted from section 41. As to the application of section 41 to visiting forces, etc., see the note to section 33 above.]   **A9.31**

42. Power of court to order cause of offence to be remedied or, in certain cases, forfeiture

(1) Where a person is convicted of an offence under any of the relevant statutory provisions in respect of any matters which appear to the court to be matters which it is in his power to remedy, the court may, in addition to or instead of imposing any punishment, order him, within such time as may be fixed by the order, to take such steps as may be specified in the order for remedying the said matters.   **A9.32**

(2) The time fixed by an order under subsection (1) above may be extended or further extended by order of the court on an application made before the end of that time as originally fixed or as extended under this subsection, as the case may be.

(3) Where a person is ordered under subsection (1) above to remedy any matters, that person shall not be liable under any of the relevant statutory provisions in respect of those matters in so far as they continue during the time fixed by the order or any further time allowed under subsection (2) above.

(4) Subject to the following subsection, the court by or before which a person is convicted of an offence such as is mentioned in section 33(4)(c) in respect of any such explosive article or substance as is there mentioned may order the article or substance in question to be forfeited and either destroyed or dealt with in such other manner as the court may order.

(5) The court shall not order anything to be forfeited under the preceding subsection where a person claiming to be the owner of or otherwise interested in it applies to be heard by the court, unless an opportunity has been given to him to show cause why the order should not be made.

[As to the application of section 42 to visiting forces, etc., see the note to section 33 above.]   **A9.33**

Financial provisions

43. Financial provisions   *[Omitted.]*   **A9.34**

Miscellaneous and supplementary

44. Appeals in connection with licensing provisions in the relevant statutory provisions   *[Omitted.]*

45. Default powers   *[Omitted.]*

46. Service of notices   *[Omitted.]*

47. Civil liability   *[Omitted.]*

48. Application to Crown

A9.35   (1) Subject to the provisions of this section, the provisions of this Part, except sections 21 to 25 and 33 to 42, and of regulations made under this Part shall bind the Crown.

(2) Although they do not bind the Crown, sections 33 to 42 shall apply to persons in the public service of the Crown as they apply to other persons.

(3) For the purposes of this Part and regulations made thereunder persons in the service of the Crown shall be treated as employees of the Crown whether or not they would be so treated apart from this subsection.

(4) Without prejudice to section 15(5), the Secretary of State may, to the extent that it appears to him requisite or expedient to do so in the interests of the safety of the State or the safe custody of persons lawfully detained, by order exempt the Crown either generally or in particular respects from all or any of the provisions of this Part which would, by virtue of subsection (1) above, bind the Crown.

(5) The power to make orders under this section shall be exercisable by statutory instrument, and any such order may be varied or revoked by a subsequent order.

(6) Nothing in this section shall authorise proceedings to be brought against Her Majesty in her private capacity, and this subsection shall be construed as if section 38(3) of the Crown Proceedings Act 1947 (interpretation of references in that Act to Her Majesty in her private capacity) were contained in this Act.

A9.36   **49. Adaptation of enactments to metric units or appropriate metric units** *[Omitted.]*

50. Regulations under the relevant statutory provisions   *[Omitted.]*

51. Exclusion of application to domestic employment   *[Omitted.]*

51A. Application of Part to police   *[Omitted.]*

A9.37   **52. Meaning of work and at work**

(1) For the purposes of this Part—

   (a) "*work*" means work as an employee or as a self-employed person;

   (b) an employee is at work throughout the time when he is in the course of his employment, but not otherwise; . . .

   [(bb) a person holding the office of constable is at work throughout the time when he is on duty, but not otherwise; and]

   (c) a self-employed person is at work throughout such time as he devotes to work as a self-employed person;

and, subject to the following subsection, the expressions "*work*" and "*at work*", in whatever context, shall be construed accordingly.

(2) Regulations made under this subsection may—

   (a) extend the meaning of "*work*" and "*at work*" for the purposes of this Part; and

   (b) in that connection provide for any of the relevant statutory provisions to have effect subject to such adaptations as may be specified in the regulations.

(3) *[Exercise of regulation-making power.]*

(4) *[Repealed by the Employment Protection Act 1975.]*

[Section 52 is printed as amended by the Employment Protection Act 1975; the Police (Health and **A9.38**
Safety) Act 1997, s.2.]

53. General interpretation of Part I

(1) In this Part, unless the context otherwise requires—   **A9.39**

. . .

"*article for use at work*" means—

    (a) any plant designed for use or operation (whether exclusively or not) by persons at work, and

    (b) any article designed for use as a component in any such plant;

["*article of fairground equipment*" means any fairground equipment or any article designed for use as a component in any such equipment;]

"*code of practice*" (without prejudice to section 16(8)) includes a standard, a specification and any other documentary form of practical guidance;

"*the Commission*" has the meaning assigned by section 10(2);

"*conditional sale agreement*" means an agreement for the sale of goods under which the purchase price or part of it is payable by instalments, and the property in the goods is to remain in the seller (notwithstanding that the buyer is to be in possession of the goods) until such conditions as to the payment of instalments or otherwise as may be specified in the agreement are fulfilled;

"*contract of employment*" means a contract of employment or apprenticeship (whether express or implied and, if express, whether oral or in writing);

"*credit-sale agreement*" means an agreement for the sale of goods, under which the purchase price or part of it is payable by instalments, but which is not a conditional sale agreement;

["*customs officer*" means an officer within the meaning of the Customs and Excise Management Act 1979;]

"*domestic premises*" means premises occupied as a private dwelling (including any garden, yard, garage, outhouse or other appurtenance of such premises which is not used in common by the occupants of more than one such dwelling), and "*non-domestic premises*" shall be construed accordingly;

"*employee*" means an individual who works under a contract of employment [or is treated by section 51A as being an employee], and related expressions shall be construed accordingly;

"*enforcing authority*" has the meaning assigned by section 18(7);

"*the Executive*" has the meaning assigned by section 10(5);

"*the existing statutory provisions*" means the following provisions while and to the extent that they remain in force, namely the provisions of the Acts mentioned in Schedule 1 which are specified in the third column of that Schedule and of the regulations, orders or other instruments of a legislative character made or having effect under any provision so specified;

. . .

["*fairground equipment*" means any fairground ride, any similar plant which is designed to be in motion for entertainment purposes with members of the public on or inside it or any plant which is designed to be used by members of the public for entertainment purposes either as a slide or for bouncing upon, and in this definition the reference to plant which is designed to be in motion with members of the public on or inside it includes a reference to swings, dodgems and other plant which is designed to be in motion wholly or partly under the control of, or to be put in motion by, a member of the public;]

"*the general purposes of this Part*" has the meaning assigned by section 1;

"*health and safety regulations*" has the meaning assigned by section 15(1);

"*hire-purchase agreement*" means an agreement other than a conditional sale agreement, under which—

(a) goods are bailed . . . in return for periodical payments by the person to whom they are bailed . . . ; and

(b) the property in the goods will pass to that person if the terms of the agreement are complied with and one or more of the following occurs:

  (i) the exercise of an option to purchase by that person;

  (ii) the doing of any other specified act by any party to the agreement;

  (iii) the happening of any other event;

and "*hire-purchase*" shall be construed accordingly;

"*improvement notice*" means a notice under section 21;

"*inspector*" means an inspector appointed under section 19;

. . .

"*local authority*" means—

(a) in relation to England . . ., a county council; . . . a district council, a London borough council, the Common Council of the City of London, the Sub-Treasurer of the Inner Temple or the Under-Treasurer of the Middle Temple,

[(*aa*) in relation to Wales, a county council or a county borough council.]

(b) [*applies to Scotland.*];

["*micro-organism*" includes any microscopic biological entity which is capable of replication;]

"*offshore installation*" means any installation which is intended for underwater exploitation of mineral resources or exploration with a view to such exploitation;

"*personal injury*" includes any disease and any impairment of a person's physical or mental condition;

"*plant*" includes any machinery, equipment or appliance;

"*premises*" includes any place and, in particular, includes—

(a) any vehicle, vessel, aircraft or hovercraft,

(b) any installation on land (including the foreshore and other land intermittently covered by water), any offshore installation, and any other installation (whether floating, or resting on the seabed or the subsoil thereof, or resting on other land covered with water or the subsoil thereof), and

(c) any tent or movable structure;

"*prescribed*" means prescribed by regulations made by the Secretary of State;

"*prohibition notice*" means a notice under section 22;

. . .

"*the relevant statutory provisions*" means—

(a) the provisions of this Part and of any health and safety regulations . . . ; and

(b) the existing statutory provisions;

"*self-employed person*" means an individual who works for gain or reward otherwise than under a contract of employment, whether or not he himself employs others;

"*substance*" means any natural or artificial substance [(including micro-organisms)], whether in solid or liquid form or in the form of a gas or vapour;

"*substance for use at work*" means any substance intended for use (whether exclusively or not) by persons at work;

"*supply*", where the reference is to supplying articles or substances, means supplying them by way of sale, lease, hire or hire-purchase, whether as principal or agent for another.

(2)–(6) *[Repealed.]*

[Section 53 is printed as amended by the Employment Protection Act 1975, ss. 116, 125(3), Sched. 15, para.18, and Sched. 18; the Local Government Act 1985, s.102(2) and Sched. 17; the Consumer Protection Act 1987, s.36 and Sched. 3, para.7; the Local Government (Wales) Act 1994, s.22(3) and Sched. 9, para.9; the Police (Health and Safety) Act 1997, s.6(1).   **A9.40**

In the definition of "hire-purchase agreement", words relating expressly and exclusively to Scotland have been omitted.]

54. Application of Part I to Isles of Scilly   *[Omitted.]*   **A9.41**

*   *   *

PART IV

MISCELLANEOUS AND GENERAL

*   *   *

80. General power to repeal or modify Acts and instruments

(1) Regulations made under this subsection may repeal or modify any provision to which   **A9.42** this subsection applies if it appears to the authority making the regulations that the repeal or, as the case may be, the modification of that provision is expedient in consequence of or in connection with any provision made by or under Part I.

(2) Subsection (1) above applies to any provision, not being among the relevant statutory provisions, which—

(a) is contained in this Act or in any other Act passed before or in the same Session as this Act; or

(b) is contained in any regulations, order or other instrument of a legislative character which was made under an Act before the passing of this Act; or

(c) applies, excludes or for any other purpose refers to any of the relevant statutory provisions and is contained in any Act not falling within paragraph (a) above or in any regulations, order or other instrument of a legislative character which is made under an Act but does not fall within paragraph (b) above.

(2A) *[Applies to employment legislation.]*

(3) Without prejudice to the generality of subsection (1) above, the modifications which may be made by regulations thereunder include modifications relating to the enforcement of provisions to which this section applies (including the appointment of persons for the purpose of such enforcement, and the powers of persons so appointed).

[(4) The power to make regulations under subsection (1) above shall be exercisable by the Secretary of State, the Minister of Agriculture, Fisheries and Food or the Secretary of State and that Minister acting jointly; but the authority who is to exercise the power shall, before exercising it, consult such bodies as appear to him to be appropriate.]

[(5) In this section "*the relevant statutory provisions*" has the same meaning as in Part I.]

A9.43   [*Section 80 is printed as amended by the Employment Protection Act 1975, s.116 and Sched. 15, para.19.*]

A9.44   **81. Expenses and receipts**   [*Omitted.*]

82. General provisions as to interpretation and regulations

A9.45   (1) In this Act—

(a) "*Act*" includes a provisional order confirmed by an Act;

(b) "*contravention*" includes failure to comply, and "*contravene*" has a corresponding meaning;

(c) "*modifications*" includes additions, omissions and amendments, and related expressions shall be construed accordingly;

(d) any reference to a Part, section or Schedule not otherwise identified is a reference to that Part or section of, or Schedule to, this Act.

(2) Except in so far as the context otherwise requires, any reference in this Act to an enactment is a reference to it as amended, and includes a reference to it as applied, by or under any other enactment, including this Act.

(3) Any power conferred by Part I or II or this Part to make regulations—

(a) includes power to make different provision by the regulations for different circumstances or cases and to include in the regulations such incidental, supplemental and transitional provisions as the authority making the regulations considers appropriate in connection with the regulations; and

(b) shall be exercisable by statutory instrument, which shall be subject to annulment in pursuance of a resolution of either House of Parliament.

A9.46   **83. Minor and consequential amendments, and repeals**   [*Omitted.*]

84. Extent, and application of Act   [*Omitted.*]

85. Short title and commencement   [*Omitted.*]

SCHEDULES

*   *   *

SCHEDULE 3   Section 15

Subject-Matter of Health and Safety Regulations

A9.47   **1.**—(1) Regulating or prohibiting—

(a) the manufacture, supply or use of any plant;

(b) the manufacture, supply, keeping or use of any substance;

(c) the carrying on of any process or the carrying out of any operation.

(2) Imposing requirements with respect to the design, construction, guarding, siting,

installation, commissioning, examination, repair, maintenance, alteration, adjustment, dismantling, testing or inspection of any plant.

(3) Imposing requirements with respect to the marking of any plant or of any articles used or designed for use as components in any plant, and in that connection regulating or restricting the use of specified markings.

(4) Imposing requirements with respect to the testing, labelling or examination of any substance.

(5) Imposing requirements with respect to the carrying out of research in connection with any activity mentioned in sub-paragraphs (1) to (4) above.

2.—(1) Prohibiting the importation into the United Kingdom or the landing or unloading there of articles or substances of any specified description, whether absolutely or unless conditions imposed by or under the regulations are complied with.

(2) Specifying, in a case where an act or omission in relation to such an importation, landing or unloading as is mentioned in the preceding sub-paragraph constitutes an offence under a provision of this Act and of [the Customs and Excise Acts 1979], the Act under which the offence is to be punished.

3.—(1) Prohibiting or regulating the transport of articles or substances of any specified description.   **A9.48**

(2) Imposing requirements with respect to the manner and means of transporting articles or substances of any specified description, including requirements with respect to the construction, testing and marking of containers and means of transport and the packaging and labelling of articles or substances in connection with their transport.

4.—(1) Prohibiting the carrying on of any specified activity or the doing of any specified thing except under the authority and in accordance with the terms and conditions of a licence, or except with the consent or approval of the specified authority.

(2) Providing for the grant, renewal, variation, transfer and revocation of licences (including the variation and revocation of conditions attached to licences).

5. Requiring any person, premises or thing to be registered in any specified circumstances or as a condition of the carrying on of any specified activity or the doing of any specified thing.   **A9.49**

6.—(1) Requiring, in specified circumstances, the appointment (whether in a specified capacity or not) of persons (or persons with specified qualifications or experience, or both) to perform specified functions, and imposing duties or conferring powers on persons appointed (whether in pursuance of the regulations or not) to perform specified functions.

(2) Restricting the performance of specified functions to persons possessing specified qualifications or experience.

7. Regulating or prohibiting the employment in specified circumstances of all persons or any class of persons.   **A9.50**

8.—(1) Requiring the making of arrangements for securing the health of persons at work or other persons, including arrangements for medical examinations and health surveys.

(2) Requiring the making of arrangements for monitoring the atmospheric or other conditions in which persons work.

A9.51   **9.** Imposing requirements with respect to any matter affecting the conditions in which persons work, including in particular such matters as the structural condition and stability of premises, the means of access to and egress from premises, cleanliness, temperature, lighting, ventilation, overcrowding, noise, vibrations, ionising and other radiations, dust and fumes.

     10. Securing the provision of specified welfare facilities for persons at work, including in particular such things as an adequate water supply, sanitary conveniences, washing and bathing facilities, ambulance and first-aid arrangements, cloakroom accommodation, sitting facilities and refreshment facilities.

A9.52   **11.** Imposing requirements with respect to the provision and use in specified circumstances of protective clothing or equipment, including affording protection against the weather.

     12. Requiring in specified circumstances the taking of specified precautions in connection with the risk of fire.

A9.53   **13.**—(1) Prohibiting or imposing requirements in connection with the emission into the atmosphere of any specified gas, smoke or dust or any other specified substance whatsoever.

     (2) Prohibiting or imposing requirements in connection with the emission of noise, vibrations or any ionising or other radiations.

     (3) Imposing requirements with respect to the monitoring of any such emission as is mentioned in the preceding sub-paragraphs.

     14. Imposing requirements with respect to the instruction, training and supervision of persons at work.

A9.54   **15.**—(1) Requiring, in specified circumstances, specified matters to be notified in a specified manner to specified persons.

     (2) Empowering inspectors in specified circumstances to require persons to submit written particulars of measures proposed to be taken to achieve compliance with any of the relevant statutory provisions.

     16. Imposing requirements with respect to the keeping and preservation of records and other documents, including plans and maps.

A9.55   **17.** Imposing requirements with respect to the management of animals.

     18. The following purposes as regards premises of any specified description where persons work, namely—

         (a) requiring precautions to be taken against dangers to which the premises or persons therein are or may be exposed by reason of conditions (including natural conditions) existing in the vicinity;

         (b) securing that persons in the premises leave them in specified circumstances.

A9.56   **19.** Conferring, in specified circumstances involving a risk of fire or explosion, power to search a person or any article which a person has with him for the purpose of ascertaining whether he has in his possession any article of a specified kind likely in those circumstances to cause a fire or explosion, and power to seize and dispose of any article of that kind found on such a search.

     20. Restricting, prohibiting or requiring the doing of any specified thing where any accident or other occurrence of a specified kind has occurred.

A9.57   **21.** As regards cases of any specified class, being a class such that the variety in the circumstances of particular cases within it calls for the making of special provision for particular cases, any of the following purposes, namely—

(a) conferring on employers or other persons power to make rules or give directions with respect to matters affecting health or safety;

(b) requiring employers or other persons to make rules with respect to any such matters;

(c) empowering specified persons to require employers or other persons either to make rules with respect to any such matters or to modify any such rules previously made by virtue of this paragraph; and

(d) making admissible in evidence without further proof, in such circumstances and subject to such conditions as may be specified, documents which purport to be copies of rules or rules of any specified class made under this paragraph.

22. Conferring on any local or public authority power to make byelaws with respect to any specified matter, specifying the authority or person by whom any byelaws made in the exercise of that power need to be confirmed, and generally providing for the procedure to be followed in connection with the making of any such byelaws.

Interpretation

23.—(1) In this Schedule "*specified*" means specified in health and safety regulations.   **A9.58**

(2) It is hereby declared that the mention in this Schedule of a purpose that falls within any more general purpose mentioned therein is without prejudice to the generality of the more general purpose.

[Schedule 3 is printed as amended by the Customs and Excise Management Act 1979, s.177(1) and   **A9.59**
Sched. 4, para.12.

The Carriage of Dangerous Goods (Classification, Packaging and Labelling) and Use of Transportable Pressure Receptacles Regulations 1996 (S.I. 1996 No. 2092), the Carriage of Explosives by Road Regulations 1996 (S.I. 1996 No. 2093), the Carriage of Dangerous Goods by Road (Driver Training) Regulations 1996 (S.I. 1996 No. 2094), and the Carriage of Dangerous Goods by Road Regulations 1996 (S.I. 1996 No. 2095) were made in part under this Schedule. These regulations are not reproduced in this work.]

*   *   *

The International Road Haulage Permits Act 1975

(1975 c. 46)

A10.01 An Act to make further provision with respect to the forgery, carriage and production of licences, permits, authorisations and other documents relating to the international carriage of goods by road; and for purposes connected therewith.

[1st August 1975]

1. Carriage on United Kingdom vehicles, and production, of international road haulage permits

A10.02 (1) The Secretary of State may by regulations made by statutory instrument provide that—

(a) a goods vehicle registered in the United Kingdom, or

(b) a trailer drawn by a vehicle registered in the United Kingdom, or

(c) an unattached trailer which is for the time being in the United Kingdom,

may not be used on a journey to which the regulations apply, being a journey—

(i) for or in connection with the carriage or haulage of goods either for hire or reward or for or in connection with any trade or business carried on by the user of the vehicle, and

(ii) either between a place in the United Kingdom and a place outside the United Kingdom or, if the journey passes through any part of the United Kingdom, between places both of which are outside the United Kingdom,

unless a document of a description specified in the regulations is carried on the vehicle or, in the case of a trailer, is carried either on the vehicle drawing it or by a person in charge of it.

(2) If it appears to an examiner that a goods vehicle registered in the United Kingdom or a trailer is being used in such circumstances that, by virtue of regulations under subsection (1) above, a document of a description specified in the regulations is required to be carried as mentioned in that subsection he may, on production if so required of his authority,—

(a) require the driver of the goods vehicle concerned or, in the case of a trailer, the driver of the vehicle drawing it or the person in charge of it to produce a document of the description in question and to permit the examiner to inspect and copy it,

(b) detain the goods vehicle or trailer concerned for such time as is requisite for the purpose of inspecting and copying the document,

(c) at any time which is reasonable having regard to the circumstances of the case enter any premises on which he has reason to believe that there is kept a vehicle (whether a goods vehicle or a trailer) which is being used on a journey to which regulations under subsection (1) above apply, and

(d) at any time which is reasonable having regard to the circumstances of the case enter any premises in which he has reason to believe that any document of a description specified in regulations under subsection (1) above is to be found and inspect and copy any such document which he finds there.

(3) If, without reasonable excuse, any person uses a goods vehicle or trailer in contravention of regulations under subsection (1) above he shall be liable on summary conviction to a fine not exceeding [level 4 on the standard scale].

(4) If the driver of a goods vehicle which is being used in such circumstances as are specified in subsection (2) above or the person in charge of, or the driver of a vehicle drawing, a trailer which is being so used—

    (a) without reasonable excuse refuses or fails to comply with a requirement under subsection (2) above, or

    (b) wilfully obstructs an examiner in the exercise of his powers under that subsection,

he shall be liable on summary conviction to a fine not exceeding [level 3 on the standard scale].

(5) If any person (other than a person specified in subsection (4) above) wilfully obstructs an examiner in the exercise of his powers under paragraph (d) of subsection (2) above, he shall be liable on summary conviction to a fine not exceeding [level 3 on the standard scale].

(6) For the purposes of this section a motor vehicle which for the time being has exhibited on it a licence or trade plates [issued under the Vehicle Excise and Registration Act 1994 shall] be presumed, unless the contrary is proved, to be registered in the United Kingdom.

(7) [*Need for consultation before regulations made.*]

(8) Any reference in this section to a person using a vehicle (whether a goods vehicle or a trailer) shall be construed as if this section were included in [the Goods Vehicles (Licensing of Operators) Act 1995] . . .

(9) In this section—

"*examiner*" means an examiner appointed under . . . [. . . [section 66A] of the Road Traffic Act 1988] . . . ;

"*goods vehicle*" means a motor vehicle constructed or adapted for use for the carriage of goods or burden of any description;

"*trailer*" means a trailer so constructed or adapted;

and for the purposes of this subsection "*motor vehicle*" and "*trailer*" have the same meaning as [in the Road Traffic Act 1988] . . .

[Section 1 is printed as amended by the Criminal Justice Act 1982, ss.37, 38 and 46; the Road Traffic (Consequential Provisions) Act 1988, s.4 and Sched. 3, para.13; the Road Traffic Act 1991, ss.48, 83, Sched. 4, para.10, and Sched. 8; the Vehicle Excise and Registration Act 1994, s.63 and Sched. 3, para.8; the Goods Vehicles (Licensing of Operators) Act 1995, s.60(1) and Sched. 7, para.7.   **A10.03**

References to Northern Ireland legislation have been omitted from the text of section 1(8) and (9).]

2. Power to prohibit vehicle or trailer being taken out of the United Kingdom

(1) If it appears to an examiner:—   **A10.04**

    (a) that a goods vehicle or a trailer is being used in such circumstances as are specified in subsection (2) of section 1 above, and

    (b) that, without reasonable excuse, the driver of the goods vehicle or, as the case may require, the person in charge of, or the driver of a vehicle drawing, the trailer has refused or failed to comply with a requirement under that subsection,

the examiner may prohibit the removal of the goods vehicle or trailer out of the United Kingdom, either absolutely or for a specified purpose, and either for a specified period or without limitation of time.

(2) Where an examiner prohibits the removal of a goods vehicle or trailer out of the United Kingdom under subsection (1) above, he shall forthwith give notice in writing of the prohibition to the driver of the goods vehicle or, as the case may require, to the person in charge of, or the driver of the vehicle drawing, the trailer, specifying—

    (a) the circumstances in consequence of which the prohibition is imposed,

    (b) whether the prohibition applies absolutely or for a specified purpose, and

    (c) whether the prohibition is for a specified period or without limit of time,

and the prohibition under subsection (1) above shall come into force as soon as notice thereof is given under this subsection.

(3) Where an examiner is satisfied, with respect to a goods vehicle or trailer to which a prohibition under subsection (1) above relates,—

    (a) that the goods vehicle or trailer is being used on a journey to which regulations under section 1(1) above do not apply, or

    (b) that there is carried on the goods vehicle or, in the case of a trailer, on the vehicle drawing it or by a person in charge of it a document of a description specified in those regulations,

he may remove the prohibition and, where he does so, shall forthwith give notice in writing of the removal of the prohibition to the driver of the goods vehicle or, as the case may require, to the person in charge of, or the driver of the vehicle drawing, the trailer and the prohibition shall cease to have effect on the giving of that notice.

(4) Unless the person to whom a notice is given under subsection (2) or subsection (3) above is the person using the vehicle concerned, as soon as practicable after such a notice has been given, the examiner who gave it shall take steps to bring the contents of the notice to the attention of the person using the vehicle.

(5) In the exercise of his functions under this section, an examiner shall act in accordance with any general directions given by the Secretary of State.

(6) Any person who, without reasonable excuse,—

    (a) removes a goods vehicle or trailer out of the United Kingdom in contravention of a prohibition under subsection (1) above, or

    (b) causes or permits a goods vehicle or trailer to be removed out of the United Kingdom in contravention of such a prohibition,

shall be guilty of an offence and liable on summary conviction to a fine not exceeding [level 4 on the standard scale].

(7) Subsections (8) and (9) of section 1 above shall apply in relation to this section as they apply in relation to that.

A10.05   *[Section 2 is printed as amended by the Criminal Justice Act 1982, ss.37, 38 and 46.]*

A10.06   **3.**   *[Repealed by the Goods Vehicles (Licensing of Operators) Act 1995.]*

    4, 5.   *[Omitted.]*

The Local Government (Miscellaneous Provisions) Act 1976

(1976 c. 57)

An Act to make amendments for England and Wales of provisions of the law which relates to local authorities or highways and is commonly amended by local Acts . . .

A11.01

[15th November 1976]

ARRANGEMENT OF SECTIONS

PART I

GENERAL

*   *   *

Supplemental

Section

44. Interpretation, etc., of Part I

A11.02

PART II

HACKNEY CARRIAGES AND PRIVATE HIRE VEHICLES

PART I

GENERAL

*   *   *

Supplemental

A11.03   **44. Interpretation, etc., of Part I**

(1), (1A), (1B), (2) *[Omitted.]*

(3) When an offence under this Part of this Act (including an offence under byelaws made by virtue of section 12 of this Act) which has been committed by a body corporate is proved to have been committed with the consent or connivance of, or to be attributable to any neglect on the part of, any director, manager, secretary or other similar officer of the body corporate or any person who was purporting to act in any such capacity, he as well as the body corporate shall be guilty of that offence and be liable to be proceeded against and punished accordingly.

Where the affairs of a body corporate are managed by its members the preceding provisions of this subsection shall apply in relation to the acts and defaults of a member in connection with his functions of management as if he were a director of the body corporate.

(4)–(6) *[Omitted.]*

A11.04   *[Section 44(3) is expressly applied to offences under Part II of this Act by section 72(2).]*

PART II

HACKNEY CARRIAGES AND PRIVATE HIRE VEHICLES

45. Application of Part II

A11.05   (1) The provisions of this Part of this Act, except this section, shall come into force in accordance with the following provisions of this section.

(2) If the Act of 1847 is in force in the area of a district council, the council may resolve that the provisions of this Part of this Act, other than this section, are to apply to the relevant area; and if the council do so resolve those provisions shall come into force in the relevant area on the day specified in that behalf in the resolution (which must not be before the expiration of the period of one month beginning with the day on which the resolution is passed).

In this subsection "*the relevant area*", in relation to a council, means—

(a) if the Act of 1847 is in force throughout the area of the council, that area; and

(b) if the Act of 1847 is in force for part only of the area of the council, that part of that area.

(3) A council shall not pass a resolution in pursuance of the foregoing subsection unless they have—

   (a) published in two consecutive weeks, in a local newspaper circulating in their area, notice of their intention to pass the resolution; and

   (b) served a copy of the notice, not later than the date on which it is first published in pursuance of the foregoing paragraph, on the council of each parish or community which would be affected by the resolution or, in the case of such a parish which has no parish council, on the chairman of the parish meeting.

(4) If after a council has passed a resolution in pursuance of subsection (2) of this section the Act of 1847 comes into force for any part of the area of the council for which it was not in force when the council passed the resolution, the council may pass a resolution in accordance with the foregoing provisions of this section in respect of that part as if that part were included in the relevant area for the purposes of subsection (2) of this section.

46. Vehicle drivers' and operators' licences

(1) Except as authorised by this Part of this Act—   **A11.06**

   (a) no person being the proprietor of any vehicle, not being a hackney carriage [or London cab] in respect of which a vehicle licence is in force, shall use or permit the same to be used in a controlled district as a private hire vehicle without having for such a vehicle a current licence under section 48 of this Act;

   (b) no person shall in a controlled district act as driver of any private hire vehicle without having a current licence under section 51 of this Act;

   (c) no person being the proprietor of a private hire vehicle licensed under this Part of this Act shall employ as the driver thereof for the purpose of any hiring any person who does not have a current licence under the said section 51;

   (d) no person shall in a controlled district operate any vehicle as a private hire vehicle without having a current licence under section 55 of this Act;

   (e) no person licensed under the said section 55 shall in a controlled district operate any vehicle as a private hire vehicle—

      (i) if for the vehicle a current licence under the said section 48 is not in force, or

      (ii) if the driver does not have a current licence under the said section 51.

(2) If any person knowingly contravenes the provisions of this section he shall be guilty of an offence.

[Section 46 is printed as amended by the Transport Act 1985, s.139(2) and Sched. 7, para.17(1).]   **A11.07**

47. Licensing of hackney carriages   *[Omitted.]*   **A11.08**

48. Licensing of private hire vehicles

(1)–(4) *[Omitted.]*

(5) Where a district council grant under this section a vehicle licence in respect of a   **A11.09** private hire vehicle they shall issue a plate or disc identifying that vehicle as a private hire vehicle in respect of which a vehicle licence has been granted.

(6) (a) Subject to the provisions of this Part of this Act, no person shall use or permit to be used in a controlled district as a private hire vehicle a vehicle in respect of which a licence has been granted under this section unless the plate or disc issued in accordance with subsection (5) of this section is exhibited on the vehicle in such manner as the district council shall prescribe by condition attached to the grant of the licence.

(b) If any person without reasonable excuse contravenes the provisions of this subsection he shall be guilty of an offence.

(7) *[Omitted.]*

A11.10   *[Section 48 has been applied to applications for vehicle licences made at any time before April 1, 2000 to the council of a "wholly excluded district" (i.e. a district the whole of which ceased on that date to be within the metropolitan police district) or the council of a "partially excluded district" (i.e. a district part of which ceased on that date to be within the metropolitan police district) to which Part II of this Act did not apply before March 13, 2000, see article 4(3) of the Greater London Authority Act 1999 (Hackney Carriages and Private Hire Vehicles) (Transitional and Consequential Provisions) Order 2000 (S.I. 2000 No. 412; not reproduced in this work).]*

49. Transfer of hackney carriages and private hire vehicles

A11.11   (1) If the proprietor of a hackney carriage or of a private hire vehicle in respect of which a vehicle licence has been granted by a district council transfers his interest in the hackney carriage or private hire vehicle to a person other than the proprietor whose name is specified in the licence, he shall within fourteen days after such transfer give notice in writing thereof to the district council specifying the name and address of the person to whom the hackney carriage or private hire vehicle has been transferred.

(2) If a proprietor without reasonable excuse fails to give notice to a district council as provided by subsection (1) of this section he shall be guilty of an offence.

50. Provisions as to proprietors

A11.12   (1) Without prejudice to the provisions of section 68 of this Act, the proprietor of any hackney carriage or of any private hire vehicle licensed by a district council shall present such hackney carriage or private hire vehicle for inspection and testing by or on behalf of the council within such period and at such place within the area of the council as they may by notice reasonably require:
   Provided that a district council shall not under the provisions of this subsection require a proprietor to present the same hackney carriage or private hire vehicle for inspection and testing on more than three separate occasions during any one period of twelve months.

(2) The proprietor of any hackney carriage or private hire vehicle—

   (a) licensed by a district council under the Act of 1847 or under this Part of this Act; or

   (b) in respect of which an application for a licence has been made to a district council under the Act of 1847 or under this Part of this Act;

shall, within such period as the district council may by notice reasonably require, state in writing the address of every place where such hackney carriage or private hire vehicle is kept when not in use, and shall if the district council so require afford to them such facilities as may be reasonably necessary to enable them to cause such hackney carriage or private hire vehicle to be inspected and tested there.

(3) Without prejudice to the provisions of [section 170 of the Act of 1988], the proprietor of a hackney carriage or of a private hire vehicle licensed by a district council shall report to them as soon as reasonably practicable, and in any case within seventy-two hours of the occurrence thereof, any accident to such hackney carriage or private hire vehicle causing damage materially affecting the safety, performance or appearance of the hackney carriage or private hire vehicle or the comfort or convenience of persons carried therein.

(4) The proprietor of any hackney carriage or of any private hire vehicle licensed by a district council shall at the request of any authorised officer of the council produce for

inspection the vehicle licence for such hackney carriage or private hire vehicle and the certificate of the policy of insurance or security required by [Part VI of the Act of 1988] in respect of such hackney carriage or private hire vehicle.

(5) If any person without reasonable excuse contravenes the provisions of this section, he shall be guilty of an offence.

[Section 50 is printed as amended by the Road Traffic (Consequential Provisions) Act 1988, s.4 and   **A11.13**
Sched. 3, para.16(2).]

51. Licensing of drivers of private hire vehicles   *[Omitted.]*   **A11.14**

52. Appeals in respect of drivers' licences   *[Omitted.]*

53. Drivers' licences for hackney carriages and private hire vehicles

(1) (a) Every licence granted by a district council under the provisions of this Part of this   **A11.15**
Act to any person to drive a private hire vehicle shall remain in force for three years from the date of such licence or for such lesser period as the district council may specify in such licence.

(b) Notwithstanding the provisions of the Public Health Act 1875 and the Town Police Clauses Act 1889, every licence granted by a district council under the provisions of the Act of 1847 to any person to drive a hackney carriage shall remain in force for three years from the date of such licence or for such lesser period as they may specify in such licence.

(2) Notwithstanding the provisions of the Act of 1847, a district council may demand and recover for the grant to any person of a licence to drive a hackney carriage, or a private hire vehicle, as the case may be, such a fee as they consider reasonable with a view to recovering the costs of issue and administration and may remit the whole or part of the fee in respect of a private hire vehicle in any case in which they think it appropriate to do so.

(3) The driver of any hackney carriage or of any private hire vehicle licensed by a district council shall at the request of any authorised officer of the council or of any constable produce for inspection his driver's licence either forthwith or—

   (a) in the case of a request by an authorised officer, at the principal offices of the council before the expiration of the period of five days beginning with the day following that on which the request is made;

   (b) in the case of a request by a constable, before the expiration of the period aforesaid at any police station which is within the area of the council and is nominated by the driver when the request is made.

(4) If any person without reasonable excuse contravenes the provisions of this section, he shall be guilty of an offence.

54. Issue of drivers' badges

(1) When granting a driver's licence under section 51 of this Act a district council shall   **A11.16**
issue a driver's badge in such a form as may from time to time be prescribed by them.

(2) (a) A driver shall at all times when acting in accordance with the driver's licence granted to him wear such badge in such position and manner as to be plainly and distinctly visible.

(b) If any person without reasonable excuse contravenes the provisions of this subsection, he shall be guilty of an offence.

A11.17   **55. Licensing of operators of private hire vehicles**   *[Omitted.]*

56. Operators of private hire vehicles

A11.18   (1) For the purposes of this Part of this Act every contract for the hire of a private hire vehicle licensed under this Part of this Act shall be deemed to be made with the operator who accepted the booking for that vehicle whether or not he himself provided the vehicle.

(2) Every person to whom a licence in force under section 55 of this Act has been granted by a district council shall keep a record in such form as the council may, by condition attached to the grant of the licence, prescribe and shall enter therein, before the commencement of each journey, such particulars of every booking of a private hire vehicle invited or accepted by him, whether by accepting the same from the hirer or by undertaking it at the request of another operator, as the district council may by condition prescribe and shall produce such record on request to any authorised officer of the council or to any constable for inspection.

(3) Every person to whom a licence in force under section 55 of this Act has been granted by a district council shall keep such records as the council may, by condition attached to the grant of the licence, prescribe of the particulars of any private hire vehicle operated by him and shall produce the same on request to any authorised officer of the council or to any constable for inspection.

(4) A person to whom a licence in force under section 55 of this Act has been granted by a district council shall produce the licence on request to any authorised officer of the council or any constable for inspection.

(5) If any person without reasonable excuse contravenes the provisions of this section, he shall be guilty of an offence.

A11.19   **57. Power to require applicants to submit information**

(1) A district council may require any applicant for a licence under the Act of 1847 or under this Part of this Act to submit to them such information as they may reasonably consider necessary to enable them to determine whether the licence should be granted and whether conditions should be attached to any such licence.

(2) Without prejudice to the generality of the foregoing subsection—

    (a) a district council may require an applicant for a driver's licence in respect of a hackney carriage or a private hire vehicle—

        (i) to produce a certificate signed by a registered medical practitioner to the effect that he is physically fit to be the driver of a hackney carriage or a private hire vehicle; and

        (ii) whether or not such a certificate has been produced, to submit to examination by a registered medical practitioner selected by the district council as to his physical fitness to be the driver of a hackney carriage or a private hire vehicle;

    (b) a district council may require an applicant for an operator's licence to submit to them such information as to—

        (i) the name and address of the applicant;

        (ii) the address or addresses whether within the area of the council or not from which he intends to carry on business in connection with private hire vehicles licensed under this Part of this Act;

        (iii) any trade or business activities he has carried on before making the application;

        (iv) any previous application he has made for an operator's licence;

(v) the revocation or suspension of any operator's licence previously held by him;

(vi) any convictions recorded against the applicant;

as they may reasonably consider necessary to enable them to determine whether to grant such licence;

(c) in addition to the information specified in paragraph (b) of this subsection, a district council may require an applicant for an operator's licence to submit to them—

(i) if the applicant is or has been a director or secretary of a company, information as to any convictions recorded against that company at any relevant time; any trade or business activities carried on by that company; any previous application made by that company for an operator's licence; and any revocation or suspension of an operator's licence previously held by that company;

(ii) if the applicant is a company, information as to any convictions recorded against a director or secretary of that company; any trade or business activities carried on by any such director or secretary; any previous application made by any such director or secretary for an operator's licence; and any revocation or suspension of an operator's licence previously held by such director or secretary;

(iii) if the applicant proposes to operate the vehicle in partnership with any other person, information as to any convictions recorded against that person; any trade or business activities carried on by that person; any previous application made by that person for an operator's licence; and any revocation or suspension of an operator's licence previously held by him.

(3) If any person knowingly or recklessly makes a false statement or omits any material particular in giving information under this section, he shall be guilty of an offence.

58. Return of identification plate or disc on revocation or expiry of licence, etc.

(1) On—   **A11.20**

(a) the revocation or expiry of a vehicle licence in relation to a hackney carriage or private hire vehicle; or

(b) the suspension of a licence under section 68 of this Act;

a district council may by notice require the proprietor of that hackney carriage or private hire vehicle licensed by them to return to them within seven days after the service on him of that notice the plate or disc which—

(a) in the case of a hackney carriage, is required to be affixed to the carriage as mentioned in section 38 of the Act of 1847; and

(b) in the case of a private hire vehicle, was issued for the vehicle under section 48(5) of this Act.

(2) If any proprietor fails without reasonable excuse to comply with the terms of a notice under subsection (1) of this section—

(a) he shall be guilty of an offence and liable on summary conviction to a fine not exceeding [level 3 on the standard scale] and to a daily fine not exceeding ten pounds; and

(b) any authorised officer of the council or constable shall be entitled to remove and retain the said plate or disc from the said hackney carriage or private hire vehicle.

[Section 58 is printed as amended by the Criminal Justice Act 1982, ss.38 and 46.]   **A11.21**

A11.22   **59. Qualifications for drivers of hackney carriages**   *[Omitted.]*

60. Suspension and revocation of vehicle licences   *[Omitted.]*

61. Suspension and revocation of drivers' licences

A11.23   (1) *[Omitted.]*

(2) (a) Where a district council suspend, revoke or refuse to renew any licence under this section they shall give to the driver notice of the grounds on which the licence has been suspended or revoked or on which they have refused to renew such licence within fourteen days of such suspension, revocation or refusal and the driver shall on demand return to the district council the driver's badge issued to him in accordance with section 54 of this Act.

(b) If any person without reasonable excuse contravenes the provisions of this section he shall be guilty of an offence and liable on summary conviction to a fine not exceeding [level 1 on the standard scale].

(3) *[Omitted.]*

A11.24   *[Section 61 is printed as amended by the Criminal Justice Act 1982, ss.38 and 46.]*

A11.25   **62. Suspension and revocation of operators' licences**   *[Omitted.]*

63. Stands for hackney carriages   *[Omitted.]*

A11.26   **64. Prohibition of other vehicles on hackney carriage stands**

(1) No person shall cause or permit any vehicle other than a hackney carriage to wait on any stand for hackney carriages during any period for which that stand has been appointed, or is deemed to have been appointed, by a district council under the provisions of section 63 of this Act.

(2) Notice of the prohibition in this section shall be indicated by such traffic signs as may be prescribed or authorised for the purpose by the Secretary of State in pursuance of his powers under [section 64 of the Road Traffic Regulation Act 1984].

(3) If any person without reasonable excuse contravenes the provisions of this section, he shall be guilty of an offence.

(4) In any proceedings under this section against the driver of a public service vehicle it shall be a defence to show that, by reason of obstruction to traffic or for other compelling reason, he caused his vehicle to wait on a stand or part thereof and that he caused or permitted his vehicle so to wait only for so long as was reasonably necessary for the taking up or setting down of passengers.

A11.27   *[Section 64 is printed as amended by the Road Traffic Regulation Act 1984, s.146(a) and Sched. 13, para.36.]*

A11.28   **65. Fixing of fares for hackney carriages**   *[Omitted.]*

66. Fares for long journeys   *[Omitted.]*

67. Hackney carriages used for private hire   *[Omitted.]*

68. Fitness of hackney carriages and private hire vehicles

A11.29   Any authorised officer of the council in question or any constable shall have power at all reasonable times to inspect and test, for the purpose of ascertaining its fitness, any hackney carriage or private hire vehicle licensed by a district council, or any taximeter affixed to such a vehicle, and if he is not satisfied as to the fitness of the hackney carriage or private hire vehicle or as to the accuracy of its taximeter he may by notice in writing require the proprietor of the hackney carriage or private hire vehicle to make it or its taximeter available for further inspection and testing at such reasonable time and place as may be specified in the notice and suspend the vehicle licence until such time as such authorised officer or constable is so satisfied:

Provided that, if the authorised officer or constable is not so satisfied before the expiration of a period of two months, the said licence shall, by virtue of this section, be deemed to have been revoked and subsections (2) and (3) of section 60 of this Act shall apply with any necessary modifications.

69. Prolongation of journeys   *[Omitted.]*   **A11.30**

70. Fees for vehicle and operators' licences   *[Omitted.]*

71. Taximeters   *[Omitted.]*

72. Offences due to fault of other person

(1) Where an offence by any person under this Part of this Act is due to the act or default   **A11.31** of another person, then, whether proceedings are taken against the first-mentioned person or not, that other person may be charged with and convicted of that offence, and shall be liable on conviction to the same punishment as might have been imposed on the first-mentioned person if he had been convicted of the offence.

(2) Section 44(3) of this Act shall apply to an offence under this Part of this Act as it applies to an offence under Part I of this Act.

73. Obstruction of authorised officers   **A11.32**

(1) Any person who—

(a) wilfully obstructs an authorised officer or constable acting in pursuance of this Part of this Act or the Act of 1847; or

(b) without reasonable excuse fails to comply with any requirement properly made to him by such officer or constable under this Part of this Act; or

(c) without reasonable cause fails to give such an officer or constable so acting any other assistance or information which he may reasonably require of such person for the purpose of the performance of his functions under this Part of this Act or the Act of 1847;

shall be guilty of an offence.

(2) If any person, in giving any such information as is mentioned in the preceding subsection, makes any statement which he knows to be false, he shall be guilty of an offence.

74. Saving for certain businesses

Where any provision of this Part of this Act coming into operation on [the relevant day]   **A11.33** requires the licensing of a person carrying on any business, or of any vehicle used by a person in connection with any business, it shall be lawful for any person who—

(a) immediately before that day was carrying on that business; and

(b) had before that day duly applied for the licence required by that provision;

to continue to carry on that business until he is informed of the decision with regard to his application and, if the decision is adverse, during such further time as is provided under section 77 of this Act.

[In this section *"the relevant day"* means —

(a) in relation to a district the whole or part of which ceased to be within the metropolitan police district by virtue of the coming into force of section 323 of the Greater London Authority Act 1999 (alteration of the metropolitan police district), 1st April 2000;

(b) in any other case, a day fixed by resolution under section 45 of this Act.]

A11.34   *[Section 74 has been amended by article 7(1) and (2) of the Greater London Authority Act 1999 (Hackney Carriages and Private Hire Vehicles) (Transitional and Consequential Provisions) Order 2000 (S.I. 2000 No. 412; not reproduced in this work).]*

75. Saving for certain vehicles, etc.

A11.35   (1) Nothing in this Part of this Act shall—

(a) apply to a vehicle used for bringing passengers or goods within a controlled district in pursuance of a contract for the hire of the vehicle made outside the district if the vehicle is not made available for hire within the district;

(b) apply to a vehicle used only for carrying passengers for hire or reward under a contract for the hire of the vehicle for a period of not less than seven days;

(c) apply to a vehicle while it is being used in connection with a funeral or a vehicle used wholly or mainly, by a person carrying on the business of a funeral director, for the purpose of funerals;

[(cc) apply to a vehicle while it is being used in connection with a wedding;]

(d) require the display of any plate, disc or notice in or on any private hire vehicle licensed by a council under this Part of this Act during such period that such vehicle is used for carrying passengers for hire or reward—

    (i) . . .

    (ii) under a contract for the hire of the vehicle for a period of not less than 24 hours.

(2) Paragraphs (a), (b) and (c) of section 46(1) of this Act shall not apply to the use or driving of a vehicle or to the employment of a driver of a vehicle while the vehicle is used as a private hire vehicle in a controlled district if a licence issued under section 48 of this Act by the council whose area consists of or includes another controlled district is then in force for the vehicle and a driver's licence issued by such a council is then in force for the driver of the vehicle.

(2A) *[Applies to Scotland.]*

[(2B) Paragraphs (a), (b) and (c) of section 46(1) of this Act shall not apply to the use or driving of a vehicle, or to the employment of a driver of a vehicle, if—

(a) a London PHV licence issued under section 7 of the Private Hire Vehicles (London) Act 1998 is in force in relation to that vehicle; and

(b) the driver of the vehicle holds a London PHV driver's licence issued under section 13 of that Act.]

(3) Where a licence under section 48 of this Act is in force for a vehicle, the council which issued the licence may, by a notice in writing given to the proprietor of the vehicle, provide that paragraph (a) of subsection (6) of that section shall not apply to the vehicle on any occasion specified in the notice or shall not so apply while the notice is carried in the

vehicle; and on any occasion on which by virtue of this subsection that paragraph does not apply to a vehicle section 54(2)(a) of this Act shall not apply to the driver of the vehicle.

[Section 75 is printed as amended by the Transport Act 1985, s.139(2) and Sched. 7, para.17(2); and as prospectively amended by the Private Hire Vehicles (London) Act 1998, ss.39(1), 40(2) and Sched. 1, para.1.   **A11.36**

Until the prospective amendment effected by the 1998 Act takes effect, this section should be read as if section 75(2B) had not been enacted.]

76. Penalties

Any person who commits an offence against any of the provisions of this Part of this Act in respect of which no penalty is expressly provided shall be liable on summary conviction to a fine not exceeding [level 3 on the standard scale].   **A11.37**

[Section 76 is printed as amended by the Criminal Justice Act 1982, ss.38 and 46.]   **A11.38**

77. Appeals (against decisions of district councils)   *[Omitted.]*   **A11.39**

78. Application of provisions of Act of 1936   *[Omitted.]*

79. Authentication of licences   *[Omitted.]*

80. Interpretation of Part II

(1) In this Part of this Act, unless the subject or context otherwise requires—   **A11.40**
"*the Act of 1847*" means the provisions of the Town Police Clauses Act 1847 with respect to hackney carriages;
"*the Act of 1936*" means the Public Health Act 1936;
. . .
"*authorised officer*" means any officer of a district council authorised in writing by the council for the purposes of this Part of this Act;
"*contravene*" includes fail to comply;
["*controlled district*" means any area for which this Part of this Act is in force by virtue of—
  (a) a resolution passed by a district council under section 45 of this Act; or
  (b) section 255(4) of the Greater London Authority Act 1999;]
"*daily fine*" means a fine for each day during which an offence continues after conviction thereof;
"*the district*", in relation to a district council in whose area the provisions of this Part of this Act are in force, means—
  (a) if those provisions are in force throughout the area of the council, that area; and
  (b) if those provisions are in force for part only of the area of the council, that part of that area;
"*driver's badge*" means, in relation to the driver of a hackney carriage, any badge issued by a district council under byelaws made under section 68 of the Act of 1847 and, in relation to the driver of a private hire vehicle, any badge issued by a district council under section 54 of this Act;
"*driver's licence*" means, in relation to the driver of a hackney carriage, a licence under section 46 of the Act of 1847 and, in relation to the driver of a private hire vehicle, a licence under section 51 of this Act;
"*hackney carriage*" has the same meaning as in the Act of 1847 [*q.v.*];

"*hackney carriage byelaws*" means the byelaws for the time being in force in the controlled district in question relating to hackney carriages;

["*London cab*" means a vehicle which is a hackney carriage within the meaning of the Metropolitan Public Carriage Act 1869 [*q.v.*];]

"*operate*" means in the course of business to make provision for the invitation or acceptance of bookings for a private hire vehicle;

"*operator's licence*" means a licence under section 55 of this Act;

"*private hire vehicle*" means a motor vehicle constructed or adapted to seat [fewer than nine passengers], other than a hackney carriage or public service vehicle [or a London cab] [or tramcar], which is provided for hire with the services of a driver for the purpose of carrying passengers;

"*proprietor*" includes a part-proprietor and, in relation to a vehicle which is the subject of a hiring agreement or hire-purchase agreement, means the person in possession of the vehicle under that agreement;

"*public service vehicle*" has the same meaning as in [the Public Passenger Vehicles Act 1981];

"*taximeter*" means any device for calculating the fare to be charged in respect of any journey in a hackney carriage or private hire vehicle by reference to the distance travelled or time elapsed since the start of the journey, or a combination of both; and

"*vehicle licence*" means in relation to a hackney carriage a licence under sections 37 to 45 of the Act of 1847 [in relation to a London cab a licence under section 6 of the Metropolitan Public Carriage Act 1869] and in relation to a private hire vehicle means a licence under section 48 of this Act.

(2) In this Part of this Act references to a licence, in connection with a controlled district, are references to a licence issued by the council whose area consists of or includes that district, and "*licensed*" shall be construed accordingly.

(3) Except where the context otherwise requires, any reference in this Part of this Act to any enactment shall be construed as a reference to that enactment as applied, extended, amended or varied by, or by virtue of, any subsequent enactment including this Act.

[(4) In this Part of this Act, except where the context otherwise requires, references to a district council shall, in relation to Wales, be construed as references to a county council or county borough council.]

A11.41

[Section 80 is printed as amended by the Transport Act 1980, s.43(1) and Sched. 5, Pt II; the Public Passenger Vehicles Act 1981, s.88(2) and Sched. 7, para.20; the Transport Act 1985, s.139(2) and Sched. 7, para.17(3); the Road Traffic (Consequential Provisions) Act 1988, s.3(1) and Sched. 1, Pt I; the Transport and Works Act 1992, s.62(3); the Local Government Reorganisation (Wales) (Consequential Amendments No. 3) Order 1996 (S.I. 1996 No. 3071; not reproduced in this work); the Greater London Authority Act 1999 (Hackney Carriages and Private Hire Vehicles) (Transitional and Consequential Provisions) Order 2000 (S.I. 2000 No. 412; not reproduced in this work), art.7(1) and (3).]

*   *   *

The Refuse Disposal (Amenity) Act 1978

(1978 c. 3)

An Act to consolidate certain enactments relating to abandoned vehicles and other refuse.   **A12.01**
[23rd March 1978]

*   *   *

3. Removal of abandoned vehicles

(1) Where it appears to a local authority that a motor vehicle in their area is abandoned   **A12.02**
without lawful authority on any land in the open air or on any other land forming part of
a highway, it shall be the duty of the authority, subject to the following provisions of this
section, to remove the vehicle.

(2) Where it appears to a local authority that the land on which a motor vehicle is abandoned as aforesaid is occupied by any person, the authority shall give him notice . . . that
they propose to remove the vehicle in pursuance of subsection (1) above but shall not be
entitled to remove it if he objects to the proposal . . . within the prescribed period.

(3) A local authority shall not be required by virtue of subsection (1) above to remove a
vehicle situated otherwise than on a carriageway within the meaning of [the Highways Act
1980] if it appears to them that the cost of its removal to the nearest convenient carriageway within the meaning of that Act would be unreasonably high.

(4) *[Repealed.]*

(5) Where in pursuance of this section a local authority propose to remove a vehicle
which in their opinion is in such a condition that it ought to be destroyed they shall, not less
than the prescribed period before removing it, cause to be affixed to the vehicle a notice
stating that the authority propose to remove it for destruction on the expiration of that
period.

[(6) Any vehicle removed under this section by the council of a London borough whose
area is included in the area of a London waste disposal authority, or by the council of a
metropolitan district whose area is included in the area of the Greater Manchester Waste
Disposal Authority or the Merseyside Waste Disposal Authority, shall be delivered by them
to the authority in question in accordance with such arrangements (including arrangements
as to the sharing of any expenses incurred or sums received by the council and the authority under this Act) as may be agreed between the council and the authority or, in default of
agreement, as may be determined by arbitration.]

(7) Any vehicle removed by the council of [a non-metropolitan district in England]
under this section shall be delivered by them to the county council in accordance with such
arrangements (including arrangements as to the sharing of any expenses incurred or sums
received by the district council and the county council under this Act) as may be agreed
between the district council and the county council or, in default of agreement, as may be
determined by arbitration.

(8) While a vehicle, other than a vehicle to which a notice was affixed in accordance with
subsection (5) above, is in the custody of a local authority [, a London waste disposal
authority, the Greater Manchester Waste Disposal Authority, the Merseyside Waste

Disposal Authority] . . . or the council of a county in England in pursuance of this section, it shall be the duty of that body to take such steps as are reasonably necessary for the safe custody of the vehicle.

(9) Subsections (5) and (6) of section 1 above shall apply to the duties imposed by subsections (1) and (2) above as if—

    (a) for any reference to the duty imposed by that section there were substituted a reference to the duties aforesaid; and

    (b) for any reference to a local authority within the meaning of that section there were substituted a reference to a local authority within the meaning of this section.

[(10) In this section and section 5 the area of the Greater Manchester Waste Disposal Authority is the metropolitan county of Greater Manchester excluding the metropolitan district of Wigan.]

A12.03   *[Section 3 is printed as amended by the Local Government, Planning and Land Act 1980, s.194 and Sched. 34, Pt III; the Highways Act 1980, s.343(2) and Sched. 24, para.30; the Roads (Scotland) Act 1984, s.156(3) and Sched. 11; the Local Government Act 1985, ss.9 and 102, and Sched. 6, para.4(3), and Sched. 17; the Waste Regulation and Disposal (Authorities) Order 1985 (S.I. 1985 No. 1884; not reproduced in this work).*

Section 3 is expressly applied by the Road Traffic Regulation Act 1984, s.104 (q.v.), the Motor Vehicles (Tests) Regulations 1981 (S.I. 1981 No. 1694), reg.6(2) (q.v.), and the Goods Vehicles (Plating and Testing) Regulations 1988 (S.I. 1988 No. 1478), reg.44(1).

The provisions of section 3 in their application to land within airports at Bristol, Coventry, Gloucester/ Cheltenham, Liverpool, London Luton, Manchester and Southend have been modified by the Airports (Designation) (Removal and Disposal of Vehicles) Order 1990 (S.I. 1990 No. 54), as amended by the Airports (Designation) (Removal and Disposal) (Amendment) Order 1993 (S.I. 1993 No. 2117) (not reproduced in this work) so as to confer on the airport operators the functions exercisable under section 3 by local authorities.]

*　　*　　*　　*

11. Interpretation

A12.04   (1) In this Act, unless the contrary intention appears, the following expressions have the following meanings, that is to say—

"*the Common Council*" means the Common Council of the City of London;

. . .

"*licence*" means, in relation to a vehicle, a licence issued for the vehicle under [the Vehicle Excise and Registration Act 1994];

"*local authority*" means—

    (a) in relation to England, a district council, London borough council or the Common Council;

    (b) *[applies to Scotland]*; and

    (c) in relation to Wales, a [county council or county borough council];

["*London waste disposal authority*" means an authority established by Parts II, III, IV or V of Schedule 1 to the Waste Regulation and Disposal (Authorities) Order 1985;]

"*motor vehicle*" means a mechanically propelled vehicle intended or adapted for use on roads, whether or not it is in a fit state for such use, and includes any trailer intended or adapted for use as an attachment to such a vehicle, any chassis or body, with or without wheels, appearing to have formed part of such a vehicle or trailer and anything attached to such a vehicle or trailer;

"*owner*", in relation to a motor vehicle which is the subject of a hiring agreement or hire-purchase agreement, includes the person entitled to possession of the vehicle under the agreement;

"*prescribed*" means prescribed by regulations made by the Secretary of State;

"*the relevant date*" has the meaning given to it by section 13(3) below.

(2) Any reference in this Act to an enactment is a reference to it as amended or applied by or under any other enactment, including this Act.

[Section 11 is printed as amended by the Waste Regulation and Disposal (Authorities) Order 1985 (S.I. **A12.05**
1985 No. 1884; not reproduced in this work); the Vehicle Excise and Registration Act 1994, s.63 and Sched. 3, para.12; the Local Government (Wales) Act 1994, s.22(3) and Sched. 9, para.11.
A definition relating exclusively and expressly to Scotland has been omitted from section 11(1).]

*   *   *

The Interpretation Act 1978

(1978 c. 30)

A13.01   An Act to consolidate the Interpretation Act 1889 and certain other enactments relating to the construction and operation of Acts of Parliament and other instruments, with amendments to give effect to recommendations of the Law Commission and the Scottish Law Commission.

[20th July 1978]

*   *   *

5. Definitions

A13.02   In any Act, unless the contrary intention appears, words and expressions listed in Schedule 1 to this Act are to be construed according to that Schedule.

*   *   *

7. References to service by post

A13.03   Where an Act authorises or requires any document to be served by post (whether the expression "*serve*" or the expression "*give*" or "*send*" or any other expression is used) then, unless the contrary intention appears, the service is deemed to be effected by properly addressing, pre-paying and posting a letter containing the document and, unless the contrary is proved, to have been effected at the time at which the letter would be delivered in the ordinary course of post.

*   *   *

SCHEDULE 1

WORDS AND EXPRESSIONS DEFINED

*   *   *

A13.04   ["*The standard scale*", with reference to a fine or penalty for an offence triable only summarily,—

    (a) in relation to England and Wales, has the meaning given by section 37 of the Criminal Justice Act 1982 [*q.v.*];

    (b) *[applies to Scotland]*

    (c) *[applies to Northern Ireland]*]

*   *   *

["*Statutory maximum*", with reference to a fine or penalty on summary conviction for an offence,—

    (a) in relation to England and Wales, means the prescribed sum within the meaning of section 32 of the Magistrates' Courts Act 1980 [*q.v.*];

    (b) *[applies to Scotland]*

(c)   *[applies to Northern Ireland]*]

*   *   *

[The definitions of "the standard scale" and "statutory maximum" were added to Schedule 1 by the   **A13.05**
Criminal Justice Act 1988, s.170(1) and Sched. 15, para.58.]

*   *   *

The Transport Act 1980

(1980 c. 34)

A14.01 An Act to . . . prohibit the display of certain roof-signs on vehicles other than taxis; . . . and for connected purposes.

[30th June 1980]

*   *   *

64. Roof-signs on vehicles other than taxis

A14.02 (1) There shall not, in any part of England and Wales outside the metropolitan police district and the City of London, be displayed on or above the roof of any vehicle which is used for carrying passengers for hire or reward but which is not a taxi—

 (a) any sign which consists of or includes the word "taxi" or "cab", whether in the singular or plural, or "hire", or any word of similar meaning or appearance to any of those words, whether alone or as part of another word; or

 (b) any sign, notice, mark, illumination or other feature which may suggest that the vehicle is a taxi.

 (2) Any person who knowingly—

 (a) drives a vehicle in respect of which subsection (1) is contravened; or

 (b) causes or permits that subsection to be contravened in respect of any vehicle,

shall be liable on summary conviction to a fine not exceeding [level 3 on the standard scale].

 (3) In this section "*taxi*" means a vehicle licensed under section 37 of the Town Police Clauses Act 1847, section 6 of the Metropolitan Carriage Act 1869, [section 10 of the Civic Government (Scotland) Act 1982] or any similar local enactment.

A14.03 *[Section 64 is printed as amended by the Criminal Justice Act 1982, s.46(1); the Transport Act 1985, s.139(2) and Sched. 7, para.20.*
The definition of "taxi" is incorporated by reference into the Road Traffic Act 1988, s.47(3) (q.v.).]

*   *   *

The Magistrates' Courts Act 1980

(1980 c. 43)

An Act to consolidate certain enactments relating to the jurisdiction of, and the practice and procedure before, magistrates' courts . . . A15.01

[1st August 1980]

*　　　*　　　*

11. Non-appearance of accused: general provisions

(1) Subject to the provisions of this Act, where at the time and place appointed for the trial or adjourned trial of an information the prosecutor appears but the accused does not, the court may proceed in his absence. **A15.02**

(2) Where a summons has been issued, the court shall not begin to try the information in the absence of the accused unless either it is proved to the satisfaction of the court, on oath or in such other manner as may be prescribed, that the summons was served on the accused within what appears to the court to be a reasonable time before the trial or adjourned trial or the accused has appeared on a previous occasion to answer the information.

(3) A magistrates' court shall not in a person's absence sentence him to imprisonment or detention in a detention centre or make [a [detention and training order] or] an order under [section 119 of the Powers of Criminal Courts (Sentencing) Act 2000] that a suspended sentence passed on him shall take effect.

(4) A magistrates' court shall not in a person's absence impose any disqualification on him, except on resumption of the hearing after an adjournment under section 10(3) above; and where a trial is adjourned in pursuance of this subsection the notice required by section 10(2) above shall include notice of the reason for the adjournment.

[Section 11 is printed as amended by the Criminal Justice and Public Order Act 1994, s.168(2) and **A15.03** *Sched. 10, para.39; the Crime and Disorder Act 1998, ss.119, 121(2) and Sched. 8, para.39; the Powers of Criminal Courts (Sentencing) Act 2000, s.165(1) and Sched. 9, para.61.*

References in any enactment to a "detention centre" (as in section 11(3) above) are treated as if they are references to a young offender institution; see the Criminal Justice Act 1988, s.123(6) and Sched. 8, para.1.

With effect from a date to be announced under the Criminal Justice and Court Services Act 2000, s.80(2), the words "or detention in a detention centre" in section 11(3) will be repealed by the 2000 Act, s.74 and Sched. 7, paras 58 and 59 (and see also ibid., s.75 and Sched. 8).]

[12. Non-appearance of accused: plea of guilty

(1) This section shall apply where— **A15.04**

  (a) a summons has been issued requiring a person to appear before a magistrates' court, other than a youth court, to answer to an information for a summary offence, not being—

    (i) an offence for which the accused is liable to be sentenced to be imprisoned for a term exceeding three months; or

    (ii) an offence specified in an order made by the Secretary of State by statutory instrument; and

(b) the [justices' chief executive for] the court is notified by or on behalf of the prosecutor that the documents mentioned in subsection (3) below have been served upon the accused with the summons.

(2) The reference in subsection (1)(a) above to the issue of a summons requiring a person to appear before a magistrates' court other than a youth court includes a reference to the issue of a summons requiring a person who has attained the age of 16 at the time when it is issued to appear before a youth court.

(3) The documents referred to in subsection (1)(b) above are—

(a) a notice containing such statement of the effect of this section as may be prescribed;

[(b) either of the following, namely—

   (i) a concise statement of such facts relating to the charge will be placed before the court by the prosecutor if the accused pleads guilty without appearing before the court, or

   (ii) a copy of such written statement or statements complying with subsections (2)(a) and (b) and (3) of section 9 of the Criminal Justice Act 1967 (proof by written statement) as will be so placed in those circumstances; and]

(c) if any information relating to the accused will or may, in those circumstances be placed before the court by or on behalf of the prosecutor, a notice containing or describing that information.

(4) Where the [justices' chief executive for] the court receives a notification in writing purporting to be given by the accused or by a legal representative acting on his behalf that the accused desires to plead guilty without appearing before the court—

(a) the [justices' chief executive for] the court shall inform the prosecutor of the receipt of the notification; and

(b) the following provisions of this section shall apply.

(5) If at the time and place appointed for the trial or adjourned trial of the information—

(a) the accused does not appear; and

(b) it is proved to the satisfaction of the court, on oath or in such manner as may be prescribed, that the documents mentioned in subsection (3) above have been served upon the accused with the summons,

the court may, subject to section 11(3) and (4) above and subsections (6) to (8) below, proceed to hear and dispose of the case in the absence of the accused, whether or not the prosecutor is also absent, in like manner as if both parties had appeared and the accused had pleaded guilty.

(6) If at any time before the hearing the [justices' chief executive for] the court receives an indication in writing purporting to be given by or on behalf of the accused that he wishes to withdraw the notification—

(a) the [justices' chief executive for] the court shall inform the prosecutor of the withdrawal; and

(b) the court shall deal with the information as if the notification had not been given.

(7) Before accepting the plea of guilty and convicting the accused under subsection (5) above, the court shall cause the following to be read out before the court by the clerk of the court, namely—

[(a) in a cause where a statement of facts as mentioned in subsection (3)(b)(i) above was served on the accused with the summons, that statement;]

[(aa) in a case where a statement or statements as mentioned in subsection (3)(b)(ii) above was served on the accused with the summons and the court does not otherwise direct, that statement or those statements;]

(b) any information contained in a notice so served, and information described in such a notice and produced by or on behalf of the prosecutor;

(c) the notification under subsection (4) above; and

(d) any submission received with the notification which the accused wishes to be brought to the attention of the court with a view to mitigation of sentence.

[(7A) Where the court gives a direction under subsection (7)(aa) above the court shall cause an account to be given orally before the court by the clerk of the court of so much of any statement as is not read aloud.]

[(7B) Whether or not a direction under paragraph (aa) of subsection (7) above is given in relation to any statement served as mentioned in that paragraph the court need not cause to be read out the declaration required by section 9(2)(b) of the Criminal Justice Act 1967.]

(8) If the court proceeds under subsection (5) above to hear and dispose of the case in the absence of the accused, the court shall not permit—

(a) any other statement with respect to any facts relating to the offence charged; or

(b) any other information relating to the accused,

to be made or placed before the court by or on behalf of the prosecutor except on a resumption of the trial after an adjournment under section 10(3) above.

(9) If the court decides not to proceed under subsection (5) above to hear and dispose of the case in the absence of the accused, it shall adjourn or further adjourn the trial for the purpose of dealing with the information as if the notification under subsection (4) above had not been given.

(10) In relation to an adjournment on the occasion of the accused's conviction in his absence under subsection (5) above or to an adjournment required by subsection (9) above, the notice required by section 10(2) above shall include notice of the reason for the adjournment.

(11) No notice shall be required by section 10(2) above in relation to an adjournment—

(a) which is for not more than 4 weeks; and

(b) the purpose of which is to enable the court to proceed under subsection (5) above at a later time.

(12) No order shall be made under subsection (1) above unless a draft of the order has been laid before and approved by the resolution of each House of Parliament.

(13) Any such document as is mentioned in subsection (3) above may be served in Scotland with a summons which is so served under the Summary Jurisdiction (Process) Act 1881.]

[Section 12 is printed as substituted by the Criminal Justice and Public Order Act 1994, s.45 and Sched. 5, para.1; the Magistrates' Courts (Procedure) Act 1998, s.45 and Sched. 5, para.1; and (with effect from April 1, 2001) the Access to Justice Act 1999, s.90(1) and Sched. 13 (paras 95 and 97) (see the Access to Justice Act 1999 (Commencement No. 7, Transitional Provisions and Savings) Order 2001 (S.I. 2001 No. 916; not reproduced in this work), arts 1(2) and 2(a)(ii)). **A15.05**

Reference is made in section 12 to the Criminal Justice Act 1967, s.9(2)(a), (b) and (3), which is not reproduced in this work; section 9(2)(a) requires the statement to be signed; section 9(2)(b) requires the statement to contain a declaration that it is true; and section 9(3) requires a statement made by a person under 18 years to give his age, a statement made by a person who cannot write to be accompanied by a declaration that it has been read out before it was signed, and a statement referring to an exhibit to be accompanied by such (when served) or by information as to its availability for inspection.]

[12A. Application of section 12 where accused appears

A15.06   (1) Where the clerk of the court has received such a notification as is mentioned in subsection (4) of section 12 above but the accused nevertheless appears before the court at the time and place appointed for the trial or adjourned trial, the court may, if he consents, proceed under subsection (5) of that section as if he were absent.

(2) Where the clerk of the court has not received such a notification and the accused appears before the court at that time and place and informs the court that he desires to plead guilty, the court may, if he consents, proceed under section 12(5) above as if he were absent and the clerk had received such a notification.

(3) For the purposes of subsections (1) and (2) above, subsections (6) to (11) of section 12 above shall apply with the modifications mentioned in subsection (4) or, as the case may be, subsection (5) below.

(4) The modifications for the purposes of subsection (1) above are that—

(a) before accepting the plea of guilty and convicting the accused under subsection (5) of section 12 above, the court shall afford the accused an opportunity to make an oral submission with a view to mitigation of sentence; and

(b) where he makes such a submission, subsection (7)(d) of that section shall not apply.

(5) The modifications for the purposes of subsection (2) above are that—

(a) subsection (6) of section 12 above shall apply as if any reference to the notification under subsection (4) of that section were a reference to the consent under subsection (2) above;

(b) subsection (7)(c) and (d) of that section shall not apply; and

(c) before accepting the plea of guilty and convicting the accused under subsection (5) of that section, the court shall afford the accused an opportunity to make an oral submission with a view to mitigation of sentence.]

A15.07   *[Section 12A was inserted by the Criminal Justice and Public Order Act 1994, s.45 and Sched. 5, para.2.]*

13. Non-appearance of accused: issue of warrant

A15.08   (1) Subject to the provisions of this section, where the court, instead of proceeding in the absence of the accused, adjourns or further adjourns the trial, the court may . . . issue a warrant for his arrest.

(2) Where a summons has been issued, the court shall not issue a warrant under this section [unless the condition in subsection (2A) below or that in subsection (2B) below is fulfilled].

[(2A) The condition in this subsection is that it is proved to the satisfaction of the court, on oath or in such other manner as may be prescribed, that the summons was served on the accused within what appears to the court to be a reasonable time before the trial or adjourned trial.]

[(2B) The condition in this subsection is that—

(a) the adjournment now being made is a second or subsequent adjournment of the trial,

(b) the accused was present on the last (or only) occasion when the trial was adjourned, and

(c) on that occasion the court determined the time for the hearing at which the adjournment is now being made.]

[(3) A warrant for the arrest of any person who has attained the age of 18 shall not be issued under this section unless—

(a) the information has been substantiated on oath and the offence to which the warrant relates is punishable with imprisonment, or

(b) the court, having convicted the accused, proposes to impose a disqualification on him.]

[(3A) A warrant for the arrest of any person who has not attained the age of 18 shall not be issued under this section unless—

(a) the information has been substantiated on oath, or

(b) the court, having convicted the accused, proposes to impose a disqualification on him.]

[(4) This section shall not apply to an adjournment on the occasion of the accused's conviction in his absence under subsection (5) of section 12 above or to an adjournment required by subsection (9) of that section.]

(5) Where the court adjourns the trial—

(a) after having, either on that or on a previous occasion, received any evidence or convicted the accused without hearing evidence on his pleading guilty under section 9(3) above; or

(b) after having on a previous occasion convicted the accused without hearing evidence on his pleading guilty under section [12(5)] above,

the court shall not issue a warrant under this section unless it thinks it undesirable, by reason of the gravity if the offence, to continue the trial in the absence of the accused.

[Section 13 is printed as amended by the Criminal Justice Act 1991, s.68 and Sched. 8, para.6(1)(a);   **A15.09**
the Criminal Justice and Public Order Act 1994, s.45 and Sched. 5, para.3(2) and (3); the Criminal
Procedure and Investigations Act 1996, s.48(1)–(3); the Magistrates' Courts (Procedure) Act 1998, s.3.]

*   *   *

32. Penalties on summary conviction for offences triable either way

(1) *[Omitted.]*   **A15.10**

(2) For any offence triable either way which is not listed in Schedule 1 to this Act, being an offence under a relevant enactment, the maximum fine which may be imposed on summary conviction shall by virtue of this subsection be the prescribed sum unless the offence is one for which by virtue of an enactment other than this subsection a larger fine may be imposed on summary conviction.

(3)–(8) *[Omitted.]*

(9) In this section—

"fine" includes a pecuniary penalty but does not include a pecuniary forfeiture or pecuniary compensation;

"the prescribed sum" means [£5,000] or such sum as is for the time being substituted in this definition by an order in force under section 143(1) below;

"relevant enactment" means an enactment contained in the Criminal Law Act 1977 or in any Act passed before, or in the same Session as, that Act.

[Section 32 is printed as amended by the Criminal Justice Act 1991, s.17(2)(c).   **A15.11**
The definition of the "prescribed sum" in this section has been incorporated by reference into the
Interpretation Act 1978, Sched. 1 (q.v.).

None of the offences listed in Schedule 1 to this Act (to which section 32(2) refers) is a road traffic offence.]

*   *   *

148. "Magistrates' court"

A15.12   (1) In this Act the expression *"magistrates' court"* means any justice or justices of the peace acting under any enactment or by virtue of his or their commission or under the common law.

(2) *[Omitted.]*

A15.13   *[The definition in subsection (1) is incorporated by reference into the Public Passenger Vehicles Act 1981, s.82 below.]*

*   *   *

The Highways Act 1980

(1980 c. 66)

An Act to consolidate the Highways Acts 1959 to 1971 and related enactments, with amendments to give effect to recommendations of the Law Commission. **A16.01**

[13th November 1980]

*   *   *

137. Penalty for wilful obstruction

(1) If a person, without lawful authority or excuse, in any way wilfully obstructs the free passage along a highway he is guilty of an offence and liable to a fine not exceeding [level 3 on the standard scale]. **A16.02**

(2) *[Repealed.]*

[Section 137 is printed as amended by the Criminal Justice Act 1982, ss.38, 46(1); the Police and Criminal Evidence Act 1984, s.119(2) and Sched. 7, Pt I. **A16.03**

As to the application of the fixed penalty procedure to offences under section 137, see the Road Traffic Offenders Act 1988, Sched. 3 below. Offences under section 137(1) have been designated as fixed penalty parking offences by the Schedule to the Fixed Penalty Order 2000 (S.I. 2000 No. 2792) below.]

*   *   *

329. Further provision as to interpretation

(1) In this Act, except where the context otherwise requires— **A16.04**

. . .

"*bridge*" does not include a culvert, but, save as aforesaid, means a bridge or viaduct which is part of a highway, and includes the abutments and any other part of a bridge but not the highway carried thereby;

"*bridleway*" means a highway over which the public have the following, but no other, rights of way, that is to say, a right of way on foot and a right of way on horseback or leading a horse, with or without a right to drive animals of any description along the highway;

. . .

"*carriageway*" means a way constituting or comprised in a highway, being a way (other than a cycle track) over which the public have a right of way for the passage of vehicles;

. . .

"*cycle track*" means a way constituting or comprised in a highway, being a way over which the public have the following, but no other, rights of way, that is to say, a right of way on pedal cycles [(other than pedal cycles which are motor vehicles within the meaning of [the Road Traffic Act 1988])] with or without a right of way on foot;

. . .

"*footpath*" means a highway over which the public have a right of way on foot only, not being a footway;

"*footway*" means a way comprised in a highway which also comprises a carriageway, being a way over which the public have a right of way on foot only;

. . .

"*the Minister*", subject to subsection (5) below, means as respects England, the [Secretary of State for the Environment, Transport and the Regions] and as respects Wales, the Secretary of State; and in section 258 of, and paragraphs 7, 8(1) and (3), 14, 15(1) and (3), 18(2), 19 and 21 of Schedule 1 to, this Act, references to the Minister and the Secretary of State acting jointly are to be construed, as respects Wales, as references to the Secretary of State acting alone;

. . .

"*proposed highway*" means land on which, in accordance with plans made by a highway authority, that authority are for the time being constructing or intending to construct a highway shown in the plans;

"*special road*" means a highway, or a proposed highway, which is a special road in accordance with section 16 above;

. . .

"*statutory undertakers*" means persons authorised by any enactment to carry on any of the following undertakings:—

  (a) a railway, tramway, road transport, water transport, canal, inland navigation, dock, harbour, pier or lighthouse undertaking, or

  (b) an undertaking for the supply of . . . or hydraulic power,

and "*statutory undertaking*" is to be construed accordingly;

["*street*" has the same meaning as in Part III of the New Roads and Street Works Act 1991;]

. . .

"*trunk road*" means a highway, or a proposed highway, which is a trunk road by virtue of section 10(1) or section 19 above or by virtue of an order or direction under section 10 above or under any other enactment;

. . .

(2)–(5) *[Omitted.]*

A16.05 *[Only selected definitions from section 329(1) are set out above.*
The definition of "cycle track" is printed as amended by the Cycle Tracks Act 1984, s.1(1) and the Road Traffic (Consequential Provisions) Act 1988, s.4 and Sched. 3, para.21(2).
The definition of "the Minister" is printed as amended by the Transfer of Functions (Transport) Order 1981 (S.I. 1981 No. 238); the Secretary of State for the Environment, Transport and the Regions Order 1997 (S.I. 1997 No. 2971).
The definition of "statutory undertakers" is printed as amended by the Gas Act 1986, s.67(4) and Sched. 9, Pt I; by the Gas Act 1995, s.16(1) and Sched. 4, para.2(1)(xxix), a public gas transporter is deemed to be a statutory undertaker for the purpose of the Highways Act 1980. The definition has also been amended by the Water Act 1989, s.190(3) and Sched. 27, Pt I; by ibid., s.190(1) and Sched. 25, para.1(1) and (2)(xxv), the National Rivers Authority, every water undertaker and every sewerage undertaker is deemed to be a statutory undertaker, and its undertaking a statutory undertaking, for the purposes of the Highways Act 1980. The definition was further amended by the Electricity Act 1989, s.112(4) and Sched. 18; by ibid., ss.3(7) and 112(1) and Sched. 16, paras 2(4)(d) and 38, a person who holds a licence under section 6 of the Act (licence authorising supply of electricity) and who is entitled to exercise any power conferred by paragraph 1 of Schedule 4 to the Electricity Act 1989 (street works, etc.) is deemed to be a statutory undertaker, and his undertaking a statutory undertaking, for the purposes of the Highways Act 1980.
The definition of "street" is printed as substituted by the New Roads and Street Works Act 1991, s.168(1) and Sched. 8, Pt I, para.15(1) and (2).

That term is defined for the purposes of Part III of the 1991 Act by section 48 which, so far as material, reads as follows:

(1) In this Part a "*street*" means the whole or any part of the following, irrespective of whether it is a thoroughfare—

    (a) any highway, road, lane, footway, alley or passage,

    (b) any square or court, and

    (c) any land laid out as a way whether it is for the time being formed as a way or not.

Where a street passes over a bridge or through a tunnel, references in this Part to the street include that bridge or tunnel.

(2) The provisions of this Part apply to a street which is not a maintainable highway subject to such exceptions and adaptations as may be prescribed.

(3) *[Meaning of "street works".]*

(4) *[Meaning of "undertaker".]*

(5) *[Meaning of references to the undertaker in relation to apparatus in a street.]*

Section 10 of this Act (to which reference is made in the definition of "trunk road" in section 329(1)) provides that all highways which were trunk roads under the earlier legislation should continue to be trunk roads and section 19 provides that a special road to be provided under a scheme will (unless otherwise provided in the scheme) become a trunk road.

Subsection (5) of section 329 relates to functions in relation to part of a particular road (as to which, see further the Transfer of Functions (Transport) Order 1981 (S.I. 1981 No. 238), art.3(1)) and the National Assembly for Wales (Transfer of Functions) Order 1999 (S.I. 1999 No. 672; not reproduced in this work), art.2 and Sched. 1.]

*   *   *

SCHEDULE 4

CLASSES OF TRAFFIC FOR PURPOSES OF SPECIAL ROADS

Class I:

Heavy and light locomotives, motor tractors, heavy motor cars, motor cars and motor   **A16.06**
cycles whereof the cylinder capacity of the engine is not less than 50 cubic centimetres, and trailers drawn thereby, which comply with general regulations as to construction and use made, or having effect as if made, under [section 41 of the Road Traffic Act 1988] and in the case of which the following conditions are satisfied:—

    (i) that the whole weight of the vehicle is transmitted to the road surface by means of wheels;

    (ii) that all wheels of the vehicle are equipped with pneumatic tyres;

    (iii) that the vehicle is not controlled by a pedestrian;

    (iv) that the vehicle is not a vehicle chargeable with duty under [paragraph 4(3) of Schedule 1 to the Vehicle Excise and Registration Act 1994]; and

    (v) in the case of a motor vehicle, that it is so constructed as to be capable of attaining a speed of 25 miles per hour on the level under its own power, when unladen and not drawing a trailer.

Class II:

Motor vehicles and trailers the use of which for or in connection with the conveyance of abnormal indivisible loads is authorised by order made, or having effect as if made, by the Minister under [section 44(1) of the Road Traffic Act 1988].

Motor vehicles and trailers constructed for naval, military, air force or other defence purposes, the use of which is authorised by order made, or having effect as if made, by the Minister under [section 44(1) of the Road Traffic Act 1988].

Motor vehicles and trailers, to which any of the following Articles of the Motor Vehicles (Authorisation of Special Types) General Order 1973, namely Article 16 (which relates to vehicles for moving excavated material), Article 17 (which relates inter alia to vehicles constructed for use outside the United Kingdom) and Article 21 (which relates to engineering plant) relate and which are authorised to be used by any of those Articles of the said order or by any other [order made, or having effect as if made, under section 44(1) of the Road Traffic Act 1988], the said motor vehicles being vehicles in respect of which the following condition is satisfied, that is to say, that the vehicle is so constructed as to be capable of attaining a speed of 25 miles per hour on the level under its own power, when unladen and not drawing a trailer.

Class III:
Motor vehicles controlled by pedestrians.

Class IV:
All motor vehicles (other than invalid carriages and motor cycles whereof the cylinder capacity of the engine is less than 50 cubic centimetres) not comprised in Class I, Class II or Class III.

Class V:
Vehicles drawn by animals.

Class VI:
Vehicles (other than pedal cycles, perambulators, push-chairs and other forms of baby carriages) drawn or propelled by pedestrians.

Class VII:
Pedal cycles.

Class VIII:
Animals ridden, led or driven.

Class IX:
Pedestrians, perambulators, push-chairs and other forms of baby carriages and dogs held on a lead.

Class X:
Motor cycles whereof the cylinder capacity of the engine is less than 50 cubic centimetres.

Class XI:
Invalid carriages.

In this Schedule any expression defined for the purposes of [the Road Traffic Act 1988] has the same meaning as in that Act and the expression "*abnormal indivisible load*" has the same meaning as in the Motor Vehicles (Authorisation of Special Types) General Order 1973.

A16.07   *[Schedule 4 is printed as amended by the Road Traffic (Consequential Provisions) Act 1988, s.4 and Sched. 3, para.21(3); the Vehicle Excise and Registration Act 1994, s.64 and Sched. 4, para.4.*

Schedule 4 refers to the Motor Vehicles (Authorisation of Special Types) General Order 1973 (S.I. 1973 No. 1101). This order was, however, revoked and replaced on November 1, 1979 by the Motor Vehicles (Authorisation of Special Types) General Order 1979 (S.I. 1979 No. 1198). The provisions in the 1979 Order which relate to vehicles for moving excavated material, vehicles constructed for use outside the United Kingdom, and engineering plant, are articles 15, 16 and 19, respectively (see below); the term "abnormal indivisible load" is defined in article 3(1) of the 1979 Order (q.v.).

For the Vehicle Excise and Registration Act 1994, Sched. 1, para.4(3), and the Road Traffic Act 1988, s.44(1), see below.]

The Public Passenger Vehicles Act 1981

(1981 c. 14)

An Act to consolidate certain enactments relating to public passenger vehicles.

[15th April 1981]

A17.01

Visiting forces, etc.   Visiting forces and headquarters (as defined), members of such forces or headquarters, and persons employed by such forces are exempt from the operation of the 1981 Act to the extent that, by virtue of any rule of law whereby enactments do not bind the Crown, such forces, headquarters, members or persons would have been so exempt if the forces or headquarters had been part of the home forces; see the Visiting Forces and International Headquarters (Application of Law) Order 1999 (S.I. 1999 No. 1736; not reproduced in this work), art. 12(1) and Sched. 5.

A17.02

ARRANGEMENT OF SECTIONS

PART I

PRELIMINARY

Definition and classification of public service vehicles

PART II

GENERAL PROVISIONS RELATING TO PUBLIC SERVICE VEHICLES

Fitness of public service vehicles

Public service vehicle operators' licences

*   *   *

PART IV

MODIFICATION OF REQUIREMENTS OF PART II IN RELATION TO CERTAIN VEHICLES AND AREAS

Fare-paying passengers on school buses

*   *   *

PART V

MISCELLANEOUS AND SUPPLEMENTARY

*   *   *

SCHEDULES

*   *   *

PART I

PRELIMINARY

Definition and classification of public service vehicles

1. Definition of "public service vehicle"

(1) Subject to the provisions of this section, in this Act *"public service vehicle"* means a   **A17.04**
motor vehicle (other than a tramcar) which—

  (a) being a vehicle adapted to carry more than eight passengers, is used for carrying passengers for hire or reward; or

  (b) being a vehicle not so adapted, is used for carrying passengers for hire or reward at separate fares in the course of a business of carrying passengers.

(2) For the purposes of subsection (1) above a vehicle "is used" as mentioned in paragraph (a) or (b) of that subsection if it is being so used or if it has been used as mentioned in that paragraph and that use has not been permanently discontinued.

(3) A vehicle carrying passengers at separate fares in the course of a business of carrying passengers, but doing so in circumstances in which the conditions set out in Part I, . . . or III of Schedule 1 to this Act are fulfilled, shall be treated as not being a public service vehicle unless it is adapted to carry more than eight passengers.

(4) For the purposes of this section a journey made by a vehicle in the course of which one or more passengers are carried at separate fares shall not be treated as made in the course of a business of carrying passengers if—

  (a) the fare or aggregate of the fares paid in respect of the journey does not exceed the amount of the running costs of the vehicle for the journey; and

  (b) the arrangements for the payment of fares by the passenger or passengers so carried were made before the journey began;

and for the purposes of paragraph (a) above the running costs of a vehicle for a journey shall be taken to include an appropriate amount in respect of depreciation and general wear.

(5) For the purposes of this section, . . . and Schedule 1 to this Act—

(a) a vehicle is to be treated as carrying passengers for hire or reward if payment is made for, or for matters which include, the carrying of passengers, irrespective of the person to whom the payment is made and, in the case of a transaction effected by or on behalf of a member of any association of persons (whether incorporated or not) on the one hand and the association or another member thereof on the other hand, notwithstanding any rule of law as to such transactions;

(b) a payment made for the carrying of a passenger shall be treated as a fare notwithstanding that it is made in consideration of other matters in addition to the journey and irrespective of the person by or to whom it is made;

(c) a payment shall be treated as made for the carrying of a passenger if made in consideration of a person's being given a right to be carried, whether for one or more journeys and whether or not the right is exercised.

(6) Where a fare is paid for the carriage of a passenger on a journey by air, no part of that fare shall be treated for the purposes of subsection (5) above as paid in consideration of the carriage of the passenger by road by reason of the fact that, in case of mechanical failure, bad weather or other circumstances outside the operator's control, part of that journey may be made by road.

A17.05   *[Section 1 is printed as amended by the Transport Act 1985, s.139(3) and Sched. 8.]*

A17.06   **2.** *[Repealed.]*

*   *   *

PART II

GENERAL PROVISIONS RELATING TO PUBLIC SERVICE VEHICLES

Fitness of public service vehicles

6. Certificate of initial fitness (or equivalent) required for use as public service vehicles

A17.07   (1) A public service vehicle adapted to carry more than eight passengers shall not be used on a road unless—

(a) [an examiner appointed under section 66A of the Road Traffic Act 1988] [or an authorised inspector] has issued a certificate (in this Act referred to as a "*certificate of initial fitness*") that the prescribed conditions as to fitness are fulfilled in respect of the vehicle; or

(b) a certificate under section 10 of this Act has been issued in respect of the vehicle; or

(c) there has been issued in respect of the vehicle a certificate under section 47 of the Road Traffic Act 1972 [or sections 55 to 58 of the Road Traffic Act 1988 [*q.v.*]] (type approval) of a kind which by virtue of regulations is to be treated as the equivalent of a certificate of initial fitness.

[(1A) *[Omitted.]*]

(2) Subject to section 68(3) of this Act, if a vehicle is used in contravention of subsection

(1) above, the operator of the vehicle shall be liable on summary conviction to a fine not exceeding [level 4 on the standard scale].

[Section 6 is printed as amended by the Criminal Justice Act 1982, ss.37 and 46; the Road Traffic (Consequential Provisions) Act 1988, s.4 and Sched. 3, para.22; the Road Traffic Act 1991, s.48 and Sched. 4, para.14. The words "or an authorised inspector" in section 6(1)(a) printed inside square brackets were added by the Transport Act 1982, s.10(3), as amended by the Road Traffic Act 1991, s.48 and Sched. 4, para.19(1) and (2), and will take effect from a date to be announced. Section 6(1A) was added by the Transport Act 1982, s.10(8), and will also take effect from a date to be announced.   **A17.08**

The application of ss.6, 12, 18 and 22 of this Act to certain vehicles is excluded (and in some cases a modified version of s.12 is applied) by the Road Transport (International Passenger Services) Regulations 1984 (S.I. 1984 No. 748), regs 4–12 (inclusive) (q.v.).]

7. Certifying officers and public service vehicle examiners   *[Repealed.]*   **A17.09**

8. Powers of, and facilities for, inspection of public service vehicles

(1), (1A), (2) *[Repealed.]*   **A17.10**

(3) The Secretary of State may—

   (a) provide and maintain stations where inspections of public service vehicles . . . may be carried out;

   (b) designate premises as stations where such inspections may be carried out; and

   (c) provide and maintain apparatus for the carrying out of such inspections;

and in this Act "*official PSV testing station*" means a station provided, or any premises for the time being designated, under this subsection.

[Section 8 is printed as amended by the Road Traffic Act 1991, ss.11, 83 and Sched. 8.]   **A17.11**

9. Power to prohibit driving of unfit public service vehicles   *[Repealed.]*   **A17.12**

9A. Extensions of sections 8 and 9 to certain passenger vehicles other than public service vehicles

(1) Section 8 of this Act shall apply . . . to any motor vehicle (other than a tramcar) which is adapted to carry more than eight passengers but is not a public service vehicle as it applies to a public service vehicle.   **A17.13**

(2) *[Repealed.]*

[Section 9A was inserted by the Transport Act 1985, s.33, and is printed as amended by the Road Traffic Act 1991, s.83 and Sched. 8.]   **A17.14**

10. Approval of type vehicle and effect thereof   *[Omitted.]*   **A17.15**

11. Modification of section 6 in relation to experimental vehicles

(1) Where it appears to the Secretary of State expedient to do so for the purpose of the making of tests or trials of a vehicle or its equipment, he may by order made in respect of that vehicle for the purposes of section 6 of this Act dispense with such of the prescribed conditions as to fitness referred to in subsection (1)(a) of that section as are specified in the order.   **A17.16**

(2) While such an order is in force in respect of a vehicle, section 6 of this Act shall have effect in relation to the vehicle as if the prescribed conditions as to fitness referred to in subsection (1)(a) of that section did not include such of those conditions as are dispensed with by the order.

(3) An order under this section shall specify the period for which it is to continue in force, and may contain, or authorise the imposition of, requirements, restrictions or prohibitions relating to the construction, equipment or use of the vehicle to which the order relates.

(4) Where an order under this section in respect of a vehicle is revoked or otherwise ceases to have effect, any certificate of initial fitness issued under section 6 of this Act in respect of the vehicle while the order was in force shall, for the purposes of that section as regards any use of the vehicle after the order has ceased to have effect, be deemed never to have been issued.

Public service vehicle operators' licences

12. PSV operators' licences

A17.17   [(1) A public vehicle shall not be used on a road for carrying passengers for hire or reward except under a PSV operator's licence granted in accordance with the following provision of this Part of this Act.]

(2)–(4) *[Omitted.]*

(5) Subject to section 68(3) of this Act, if a vehicle is used in contravention of subsection (1) above, the operator of the vehicle shall be liable on summary conviction to a fine not exceeding [level 4 on the standard scale].

A17.18   *[Section 12 is printed as amended by the Criminal Justice Act 1982, ss.37 and 46; the Transport Act 1985, s.1(3) and Sched. 1, para.4.*

For section 68(3) of this Act, see below.

The application of this section to certain vehicles is excluded (or a modified version of the section is applied); see further the notes to section 6 of this Act.]

*   *   *

16. Conditions attached to licences

A17.19   (1) [Subject to subsection (1A) below and section 12(7) of the Transport Act 1985] [a traffic commissioner] on granting a PSV operator's licence shall attach to it one or more conditions specifying the maximum number of vehicles (being vehicles having their operating centre in the area of [that commissioner]) which the holder of the licence may at any one time use under the licence.

[(1A) In the case of a restricted licence, the number specified as the maximum in any condition imposed under subsection (1) above shall not, except in any prescribed case or class of case, exceed two.]

(2) Conditions attached under subsection (1) above to a PSV operator's licence may specify different maximum numbers for different descriptions of vehicle.

(3) [A traffic commissioner] may (whether at the time when the licence is granted or at any time thereafter) attach to a PSV operator's licence granted by [him] such conditions or additional conditions as [he thinks] fit for restricting or regulating the use of vehicles under the licence, being conditions of any prescribed description.

(4) Without prejudice to the generality of the power to prescribe descriptions of conditions for the purposes of subsection (3) above, the descriptions which may be so prescribed include conditions for regulating the places at which vehicles being used under a PSV operator's licence may stop to take up or set down passengers.

(5), (6) *[Variation of operator's licence by traffic commissioner.]*

(6A), (6B) *[Consideration by traffic commissioner of undertakings given for purposes of section 16(6).]*

(7) Subject to section 68(3) of this Act, if a condition attached to a PSV operator's licence is contravened, the holder of the licence shall be liable on summary conviction to a fine not exceeding [level 3 on the standard scale].

(8) Compliance with any condition attached to a PSV operator's licence . . . [(other than a condition so attached under subsection (1A) above)] may be temporarily dispensed with by the traffic [commissioner] by whom the licence was granted if [he is] satisfied that compliance with the condition would be unduly onerous by reason of circumstances not foreseen when the condition was attached or, if the condition has been altered, when it was last altered.

(9) It is hereby declared that the conditions attached under subsection (1) [or (1A)] above to a PSV operator's licence granted by the traffic [commissioner] for any area do not affect the use by the holder of the licence of a vehicle—

(a) under a PSV operator's licence granted to him by the traffic [commissioner] for another area; or

(b) in circumstances such that another person falls to be treated as the operator of the vehicle (for example, by virtue of regulations under section 81(1)(a) of this Act).

[Section 16 is printed as amended by the Criminal Justice Act 1982, ss.37 and 46; the Transport Act   **A17.20**
1985, ss.3(5), 24(1), 139(2) and (3), Sched. 2, Pt II, para.4(7), Sched. 7, para.21(4), and Sched. 8. For sections 68(3) and 81(1)(a) of this Act, see below.

The Public Service Vehicles (Operators' Licences) Regulations 1995 (S.I. 1995 No. 2908) below were in part made under this section.]

[16A. Conditions as to matters required to be notified

(1) On issuing a standard licence, a traffic commissioner shall attach to it the following   **A17.21**
conditions, namely—

(a) a condition requiring the licence-holder to inform the commissioner of any event which could affect the fulfilment by the licence-holder of any of the requirements of section 14(1) of this Act, and to do so within 28 days of the event; and

(b) a condition requiring the licence-holder to inform the commissioner of any event which could affect the fulfilment by a relevant transport manager of the requirements mentioned in section 14(1)(a) or (c) of this Act, and to do so within 28 days of the event coming to the licence-holder's knowledge.

(2) In subsection (1)(b) above the reference to a "*relevant transport manager*" is a reference to any transport manager employed by the licence-holder who is relied on by the licence-holder to fulfil the requirements of section 14(1)(c) of this Act.

(3) Any person who contravenes any condition attached under this section to a licence of which he is the holder is guilty of an offence and liable on summary conviction to a fine not exceeding level 4 on the standard scale.]

[Section 16A was inserted by the Public Service Vehicles Operators (Qualifications) Regulations 1999   **A17.22**
(S.I. 1999 No. 2431; not reproduced in this work).

The requirements in section 14(1) (to which reference is made in the text of section 16A) are: (a) the requirement to be of good repute; (b) the requirement to be of appropriate financial standing; and (c) the requirement as to professional competence.]

17. Revocation, suspension, etc., of licences   *[Omitted.]*   **A17.23**

[17A. Assessors to assist traffic commissioners   *[Omitted.]*]

18. Duty to exhibit operator's disc

A17.24   (1) Where a vehicle is being used in circumstances such that a PSV operator's licence is required, there shall be fixed and exhibited on the vehicle in the prescribed manner an operator's disc issued under this section showing particulars of the operator of the vehicle and of the PSV operator's licence under which the vehicle is being used.

[(2) A traffic commissioner on granting a PSV operator's licence shall supply the person to whom the licence is granted—

    (a) with a number of operators' discs equal to the maximum number of vehicles that he may use under the licence in accordance with the condition or conditions attached to the licence under section 16(1) of this Act; or

    (b) with such lesser number of operators' discs as he may request.]

[(2A) Where, in the case of any PSV operator's licence, the maximum number referred to in subsection (2)(a) above is increased on the variation of one or more of the conditions there referred to, the traffic commissioner on making the variation shall supply the holder of the licence

    (a) with such number of additional operators' discs as will bring the total number of operators' discs held by him in respect of the licence to that maximum number, or

    (b) with such lesser number of additional operators' discs as he may request.]

[(2B) Where the number of operators' discs currently held in respect of a PSV operator's licence is less than the maximum number referred to in subsection (2)(a) above, the traffic commissioner by whom the licence was granted shall on the application of the holder of the licence supply him with such number of additional operators' discs as is mentioned in subsection (2A)(a) or (b) above.]

[(2C) Where, in accordance with regulations under subsection (3)(aa) below, all the operators' discs held in respect of a PSV operator's licence expire at the same time, the traffic commissioner by whom the licence was granted shall supply the holder of the licence with a number of new operators' discs equal to the number of discs that have expired.]

(3) Regulations may make provision—

    (a) as to the form of operators' discs and the particulars to be shown on them;

    [(aa) as to the expiry of operators' discs;]

    (b) with respect to the custody and production of operators' discs;

    (c) for the issue of new operators' discs in place of those lost, destroyed or defaced;

    (d) for the return of operators' discs [on their expiry or otherwise ceasing to have effect] on the revocation or [termination] of a PSV operator's licence or in the event of a variation of one or more conditions attached to a licence under section 16(1) of this Act having the effect of reducing the maximum number of vehicles which may be used under the licence[;]

    [(e) for the voluntary return of operators' discs by the holder of a PSV operator's licence.]

(4) Subject to section 68(3) of this Act, if a vehicle is used in contravention of subsection (1) above, the operator of the vehicle shall be liable on summary conviction to a fine not exceeding [level 3 on the standard scale].

A17.25   *[Section 18 is printed as amended by the Criminal Justice Act 1982, ss.37 and 46; the Transport Act 1985, ss.3(5), 24(2), and Sched. 2, Pt II, para.4(9); the Deregulation and Contracting Out Act 1994, ss.63 and 68 and Sched. 14, para.6.*

The Public Service Vehicles (Operators' Licences) Regulations 1995 (S.I. 1995 No. 2908) below were in part made under this section.

For section 68(3) of this Act, see below.
The application of this section to certain vehicles is excluded; see further the notes to section 6 of this Act.
The text of section 18(1) in its application to an operator who is a partnership is modified by the Operation of Public Service Vehicles (Partnership) Regulations 1986 (S.I. 1986 No. 1628), Schedule, Pt I (not reproduced in this work) so that the firm's name is disclosed on the disc.]

19. Duty to inform traffic commissioners of relevant convictions, etc.

(1) A person who has applied for a PSV operator's licence shall forthwith notify the traffic [commissioner] to whom the application was made if, in the interval between the making of the application and the date on which it is disposed of, a relevant conviction occurs of the applicant, or any employee or agent of his, or of any person proposed to be engaged as transport manager whose repute and competence are relied on in connection with the application.   **A17.26**

(2) It shall be the duty of the holder of a PSV operator's licence to give notice in writing to the traffic [commissioner] by whom the licence was granted of—

(a) any relevant conviction of the holder; and

(b) any relevant conviction of any officer, employee or agent of the holder for an offence committed in the course of the holder's road passenger transport business,

and to do so within 28 days of the conviction in the case of a conviction of the holder or his transport manager and within 28 days of the conviction coming to the holder's knowledge in any other case.

(3) It shall be the duty of the holder of a PSV operator's licence within 28 days of the occurrence of—

(a) the bankruptcy or liquidation of the holder, or the sequestration of his estate [or the making of an administration order under [Part II of the Insolvency Act 1986] in relation to the holder] or the appointment of a receiver, manager or trustee of his road passenger transport business; or

(b) any change in the identity of the transport manager of the holder's road passenger transport business,

to give notice in writing of that event to the traffic [commissioner] by whom the licence was granted.

(4) [A traffic commissioner] on granting or varying a PSV operator's licence, or at any time thereafter, may require the holder of the licence to inform [him] forthwith or within a time specified by [him] of any material change specified by [him] in any of [the holder's] circumstances which were relevant to the grant or variation of the licence.

(5) Subject to section 68(1) of this Act, a person who fails to comply with subsection (1), (2) or (3) above or with any requirement under subsection (4) above shall be liable on summary conviction to a fine not exceeding [level 3 on the standard scale].

[Section 19 is printed as amended by the Criminal Justice Act 1982, ss.37 and 46; the Insolvency Act 1985, s.235(1) and Sched. 8, para.34; the Transport Act 1985, s.3(5) and Sched. 2, Pt II, para.4(10); the Insolvency Act 1986, s.439(2) and Sched. 14.   **A17.27**
For section 68(1) of this Act, see below.
The text of section 19(1)–(3) in its application to an operator which is a partnership is modified by the Operation of Public Service Vehicles (Partnership) Regulations 1986 (S.I. 1986 No. 1628), Schedule, Pt I (not reproduced in this work) so as (inter alia) to require a relevant conviction of any partner, employee or agent to be notified under subsection (1) and subsection (2) and so as to require dissolution of the partnership to be given under subsection (3).]

20. Duty to give traffic commissioners information about vehicles

A17.28

(1) It shall be the duty of the holder of a PSV operator's licence, on the happening to any public service vehicle owned by him of any failure or damage of a nature calculated to affect the safety of occupants of the public service vehicle or of persons using the road, to report the matter as soon as is practicable to the [Secretary of State].

(2) It shall be the duty of the holder of a PSV operator's licence, on any alteration otherwise than by replacement of parts being made in the structure or fixed equipment of any public service vehicle owned by him, to give notice of the alteration as soon as is practicable to the [Secretary of State].

(3) The traffic [commissioner] by whom a PSV operator's licence was granted may—

    (a) require the holder of the licence to supply [him] forthwith or within a specified time with such information as [he] may reasonably require about the public service vehicles owned by [the holder] and normally kept at an operating centre within the area of [that commissioner], and to keep up to date information supplied by [the holder] under this paragraph; or

    (b) require the holder or former holder of the licence to supply [him] forthwith or within a specified time with such information as [he] may reasonably require about the public service vehicles owned by [the holder or former holder] at any material time specified by [him] which were at that time normally kept at an operating centre within the area of [that commissioner].

In this subsection *"material time"* means a time when the PSV operator's licence in question was in force.

(4) Subject to section 68(1) of this Act, a person who fails to comply with the provisions of subsection (1) or (2) above or with any requirement under subsection (3) above shall be liable on summary conviction to a fine not exceeding [level 3 on the standard scale].

(5) A person who in purporting to comply with any requirement under subsection (3) above supplies any information which he knows to be false or does not believe to be true shall be liable on summary conviction to a fine not exceeding [level 4 on the standard scale].

(6) *[Repealed.]*

A17.29

[Section 20 is printed as amended by the Criminal Justice Act 1982, ss.37 and 46; the Transport Act 1985, ss.3(5) and 29, Sched. 2, Pt II, para.4(11); the Road Traffic Act 1991, s.83 and Sched. 8.

Section 20 has also been prospectively amended with effect from a date to be announced by the Transport Act 1982, s.10, and the Road Traffic Act 1991, s.48 and Sched. 4, para.19.

For section 68(1) of this Act, see below.]

A17.30   **21. Certificates of qualification**   *[Omitted.]*

Drivers' licences

A17.31   **22. Drivers' licences**   *[Repealed.]*

23. Appeals to courts of summary jurisdiction in connection with drivers' licences   *[Repealed.]*

23A. Northern Ireland drivers' licences   *[Repealed.]*

Regulation of conduct, etc., of drivers, inspectors, conductors and passengers

24. Regulation of conduct of drivers, inspectors and conductors

(1) Regulations may make provision for regulating the conduct, when acting as such, of—   **A17.32**

    (a) . . . drivers of public service vehicles, and

    (b) inspectors and conductors of such vehicles [, and]

    [(c) drivers, inspectors and conductors of tramcars.]

(2) Subject to section 68(1) of this Act, if a person to whom regulations having effect by virtue of this section apply contravenes, or fails to comply with, any of the provisions of the regulations, he shall be liable on summary conviction to a fine not exceeding [level 2 on the standard scale] and, in the case of an offence by a person acting as driver [of a public service vehicle], the court by which he is convicted may, if it thinks fit, cause particulars of the conviction to be endorsed upon the licence granted to that person under [Part III of the Road Traffic Act 1988] [or, as the case may be, the counterpart (if any) of his Community licence (within the meaning of that Part)].

(3) The person who has the custody of the licence shall, if so required by the convicting court, produce the licence within a reasonable time for the purpose of endorsement, and, subject to section 68(1) of this Act, if he fails to do so, shall be liable on summary conviction to a fine not exceeding [level 3 on the standard scale].

(4) In this section and in section 25 of this Act "*inspector*", in relation to a public service vehicle, means a person authorised to act as an inspector by the holder of the PSV operator's licence under which the vehicle is being used.

[(5) Notwithstanding section 1(1) of this Act, in this section and in sections 25 and 26 of this Act "*public service vehicle*" shall be construed as meaning a public service vehicle being used on a road for carrying passengers for hire or reward.]

[Section 24 is printed as amended by the Criminal Justice Act 1982, ss.37 and 46; the Road Traffic   **A17.33**
(Driver Licensing and Information Systems) Act 1989, ss.7, 16, 24(2) and (4), Sched. 3, para.2(a), (b)
and (c), and Sched. 6; the Transport and Works Act 1992, s.61(1), (2)(a) and (b); the Driving Licences
(Community Driving Licence) Regulations 1996 (S.I. 1996 No. 1974), reg.5 and Sched. 4 (not repro-
duced in this work).

For section 68(1) of this Act, see below.

The Public Service Vehicles (Conduct of Drivers, Inspectors, Conductors and Passengers) Regulations
1990 (S.I. 1990 No. 1020) (q.v.) were made in part under this section.

Community driving licence. *In relation to driving licences which came into force after May 31,*   **A17.34**
1990 (after December 31, 1990 for Northern Ireland driving licences) only, paragraph 2(b) of Schedule 3
to the Road Traffic (Driver Licensing and Information Systems) Act 1989 (which amended section 24(2)
of the Public Passenger Vehicles Act 1981) was itself amended by the Driving Licences (Community
Driving Licence) Regulations 1990 (S.I. 1990 No. 144) on April 1, 1990 so that the following amend-
ments take effect (in respect of such licences):

    (i) *the words "the counterpart of" are inserted in section 24(2) after the words "endorsed upon"*
    (paragraph 2(b)(i) of Schedule 3, as substituted);

    (ii) *the words "and its counterpart" are inserted in section 24(3) after the words "custody of the*
    licence" (paragraph 2(bb)(i) of Schedule 3, as inserted); and

    (iii) *the word "them" is substituted in section 24(3) for the second reference to the words "the licence"*
    (paragraph 2(bb)(ii) of Schedule 3, as inserted).]

25. Regulation of conduct of passengers

(1) *[Regulation-making power.]*   **A17.35**

(2) *[Repealed.]*

(3) Subject to section 68(1) of this Act, if a person contravenes, or fails to comply with, a provision of regulations having effect by virtue of this section, he shall be liable on summary conviction to a fine not exceeding [level 3 on the standard scale].

(4) *[Applies to Scotland.]*

A17.36   *[Section 25 is printed as amended (so far as relevant to this work) by the Criminal Justice Act 1982, ss.37 and 46; the Police and Criminal Evidence Act 1984, s.119(2) and Sched. 7, Pt I.*

The Public Service Vehicles (Conduct of Drivers, Inspectors, Conductors and Passengers) Regulations 1990 (S.I. 1990 No. 1020) (q.v.) have effect in part as if made under this section.

For section 68(1) of this Act, see below.]

26. Control of number of passengers

A17.37   (1) *[Regulation-making power.]*

(2) Subject to section 68(1) and (3) of this Act, if a person contravenes, or fails to comply with, a provision of regulations having effect by virtue of this section, he shall be liable on summary conviction to a fine not exceeding [level 2 on the standard scale].

A17.38   *[Section 26 is printed as amended by the Criminal Justice Act 1982, ss.37, 39(1), 46, and Sched. 2. For section 68(1) and (3) of this Act, see below.*

The Public Service Vehicles (Carrying Capacity) Regulations 1984 (S.I. 1984 No. 1406) (not reproduced in this work) were made in part under this section.]

*   *   *

PART IV

MODIFICATION OF REQUIREMENTS OF PART II IN RELATION TO CERTAIN VEHICLES AND AREAS

Fare-paying passengers on school buses

46. Fare-paying passengers on school buses

A17.39   (1) Subject to subsection (2) below, a local education authority may—

     (a) use a school bus, when it is being used to provide free school transport, to carry as fare-paying passengers persons other than those for whom the free school transport is provided;

     (b) use a school bus belonging to the authority, when it is not being used to provide free school transport, to provide a local . . . service;

and sections 6, 8, 9, [and 12(1)] of this Act shall not apply to a school bus belonging to a local education authority in the course of its use by the authority in accordance with this subsection.

(2) Subsection (1) above does not affect the duties of a local education authority in relation to the provision of free school transport or authorise a local education authority to make any charge for the carriage of a pupil on a journey which he is required to make in the course of his education at a school maintained by such an authority.

(3) In this section—

"*free school transport*" means transport provided by a local education authority in pursuance of arrangements under section 55(1) of the Education Act 1944 for the purpose of facilitating the attendance of [persons] at a place of education;

. . .

"*school bus*", in relation to a local education authority, means a motor vehicle which is used by that authority to provide free school transport.

(4) *[Applies to Scotland.]*

[Section 46 is printed as amended by the Transport Act 1985, ss.1(3) and 139(3), Sched. 1, para.6, **A17.40**
and Sched. 8; the Road Traffic (Driver Licensing and Information Systems) Act 1989, s.7 and Sched. 3,
para.3; the Further and Higher Education Act 1992, s.93(1) and Sched. 8, para.90.]

*   *   *

PART V

MISCELLANEOUS AND SUPPLEMENTARY

*   *   *

60. General power to make regulations for purposes of Act

(1), (1A) *[Omitted.]*   **A17.41**

(2) In this Act "*prescribed*" means prescribed by regulations and "*regulations*" means regulations made [by the Secretary of State].

(3) *[Repealed.]*

[Section 60 is printed as amended by the Transport Act 1985, s.134(2)(c) and (d). **A17.42**
The Community Bus Regulations 1986 (S.I. 1986 No. 1245; not reproduced in this work), the Minibus
and Other Section 19 Permit Buses Regulations 1987 (S.I. 1987 No. 1230; not reproduced in this work),
the Public Service Vehicles (Conduct of Drivers, Inspectors, Conductors and Passengers) Regulations 1990
(S.I. 1990 No. 1020) (q.v.), the Public Service Vehicles (Operators' Licences) Regulations 1995 (S.I. 1995
No. 2908) (q.v.), and the Public Service Vehicles (Operators' Licences) (Fees) Regulations 1995 (S.I. 1995
No. 2909) (not reproduced in this work) were made in part under this section.]

*   *   *

Provisions relating to offences and legal proceedings

65. Forgery and misuse of documents

(1) This section applies to the following documents and other things, namely—   **A17.43**

  (a) a licence under Part II . . . of this Act;

  (b) a certificate of initial fitness under section 6 of this Act;

[(bb) a notice removing a prohibition under section 9 of this Act;]

  (c) a certificate under section 10 of this Act that a vehicle conforms to a type vehicle;

  (d) an operator's disc under section 18 of this Act;

  (e) a certificate under section 21 of this Act as to the repute, financial standing or professional competence of any person;

[(ea) a control document issued under Article 6 of Council Regulation (EC) No. 12/98 of 11 December 1997;]

  (f) *[repealed.]*

(2) A person who, with intent to deceive—

  (a) forges or alters, or uses or lends to, or allows to be used by, any other person, a document or other thing to which this section applies; or

(b) makes or has in his possession any document or other thing so closely resembling a document or other thing to which this section applies as to be calculated to deceive,

shall be liable—

    (i) on conviction on indictment, to imprisonment for a term not exceeding two years;

    (ii) on summary conviction, to a fine not exceeding the statutory maximum.

(3) In the application of this section to England and Wales—

["*forges*" means makes a false document or other thing in order that it may be used as genuine]; . . .

(4) *[Repealed.]*

A17.44   *[Section 65 is printed as amended by the Forgery and Counterfeiting Act 1981, s.12; the Transport Act 1985, s.139(3) and Sched. 8; the Road Traffic Act 1991, s.83 and Sched. 8; the Statute Law (Repeals) Act 1993, s.1(1) and Sched. 1, Pt XIV, group 2; the Road Transport (Passenger Vehicles Cabotage) Regulations 1999 (S.I. 1999 No. 3413), reg.10(2) and (3) below.*

    As to references in sections 65(1)(a) and 66(a) to a licence under any Part of this Act, see the Road Transport (International Passenger Services) Regulations 1984 (S.I. 1984 No. 748), reg.21 below.]

66. False statements to obtain licence, etc.

A17.45   A person who knowingly makes a false statement for the purpose of—

    (a) obtaining the grant of a licence under Part II . . . of this Act to himself or any other person, obtaining the variation of such licence, preventing the grant or variation of any such licence or procuring the imposition of a condition or limitation in relation to any such licence;

    (b) obtaining the issue of a certificate of initial fitness under section 6 of this Act;

    (c) obtaining the issue of a certificate under section 10 of this Act that a vehicle conforms to a type vehicle;

    (d) obtaining the issue of an operator's disc under section 18 of this Act; . . .

    (e) obtaining the issue of a certificate under section 21 of this Act as to the repute, financial standing or professional competence of any person; [or]

    [(f) obtaining the issue of a control document under Article 6 of Council Regulation (EC) No. 12/98 of 11 December 1997;]

shall be liable on summary conviction to a fine not exceeding [level 4 on the standard scale].

A17.46   *[Section 66 is printed as amended by the Criminal Justice Act 1982, ss.37 and 46; the Transport Act 1985, s.139(3) and Sched. 8; the Road Transport (Passenger Vehicles Cabotage) Regulations 1999 (S.I. 1999 No. 3413), reg.10(2) and (4) below.*

    See further the note to section 65.]

A17.47   **66A. Issue of false documents**   *[Omitted.]*

A17.48   **67. Penalty for breach of regulations**

Subject to section 68(1) of this Act, if a person acts in contravention of, or fails to comply with, any regulations made by the Secretary of State under this Act . . . and contravention thereof, or failure to comply therewith, is not made an offence under any other provision of this Act, he shall for each offence be liable on summary conviction to a fine not exceeding [level 2 on the standard scale].

A17.49   *[Section 67 is printed as amended by the Criminal Justice Act 1982, ss.37 and 46; the Transport Act 1985, s.139(3) and Sched. 8.]*

68. Defences available to persons charged with certain offences

(1) It shall be a defence for a person charged with an offence under any of the provisions   **A17.50**
of this Act mentioned in subsection (2) below to prove that there was a reasonable excuse
for the act or omission in respect of which he is charged.

(2) The provisions referred to in subsection (1) above are—

(a) sections 19(5), 20(4), 24(2) and (3), 25(3), 26(2), . . . 67 and 70(3); . . .

(b) *[repealed.]*

(3) It shall be a defence for a person charged with an offence under any of the provisions
of this Act mentioned in subsection (4) below to prove that he took all reasonable precautions and exercised all due diligence to avoid the commission of any offence under that
provision.

(4) The provisions referred to in subsection (3) above are—

(a) sections 6(2), . . . 12(5), 16(7), 18(4), 26(2), [and 27(2)]; . . .

(b) *[repealed.]*

[Section 68 is printed as amended by the Transport Act 1985, ss.1(3) and 139(3), Sched. 1, para.11,   **A17.51**
and Sched. 8; the Road Traffic (Driver Licensing and Information Systems) Act 1989, s.16 and Sched. 6;
the Road Traffic Act 1991, s.83 and Sched. 8.]

69. Restriction on institution in England and Wales of proceedings under Part II

(1) Subject to the provisions of this section proceedings for an offence under Part II . . .   **A17.52**
of this Act shall not, in England and Wales, be instituted except by or on behalf of the
Director of Public Prosecutions or by a person authorised in that behalf by [a traffic com-
missioner], a chief officer of police, or the council of a county or district.

(2) Subsection (1) above shall not apply to proceedings for the breach of regulations
having effect by virtue of section 25 or 26 of this Act.

(3) Subsection (1) above shall not prevent the institution by or on behalf of the Secretary
of State of proceedings for an offence under section 27 of this Act.

[Section 69 is printed as amended by the Transport Act 1985, ss.3(5) and 139(3), Sched. 2, Pt II,   **A17.53**
para.4(19), and Sched. 8.]

70. Duty to give information as to identity of driver in certain cases

(1) Where the driver of a vehicle is alleged to be guilty of an offence under Part II . . . of   **A17.54**
this Act—

(a) the person keeping the vehicle shall give such information as to the identity of
the driver as he may be required to give by or on behalf of a chief officer of police,
and

(b) any other person shall if required as aforesaid give any information which it is in
his power to give and may lead to the identification of the driver.

(2) A person who fails to comply with the requirement of paragraph (a) of subsection (1)
above shall, unless he shows to the satisfaction of the court that he did not know and could
not with reasonable diligence ascertain who the driver of the vehicle was, be liable on
summary conviction to a fine not exceeding [level 3 on the standard scale].

(3) Subject to section 68(1) of this Act, a person who fails to comply with the requirement of paragraph (b) of subsection (1) above shall be liable on summary conviction to a
fine not exceeding [level 3 on the standard scale].

A17.55   *[Section 70 is printed as amended by the Criminal Justice Act 1982, s.38(1), (6) and (8) (it being assumed that the section 70 offence, being a re-enactment of an offence in the Road Traffic Act 1960, was a summary offence created not later than July 29, 1977 and hence within the scope of section 38(1) of the 1982 Act); the Transport Act 1985, s.139(3) and Sched. 8.]*

*   *   *

71. Evidence by certificate

A17.56   (1) In any proceedings in England or Wales for an offence under Part II . . . of this Act a certificate in the prescribed form, purporting to be signed by a constable and certifying that the person specified in the certificate stated to the constable—

  (a) that a particular motor vehicle was being driven or used by, or belonged to, that person on a particular occasion; or

  (b) that a particular motor vehicle on a particular occasion was used by or belonged to a firm in which that person also stated that he was at the time of the statement a partner; or

  (c) that a particular motor vehicle on a particular occasion was used by or belonged to a company of which that person also stated that he was at the time of the statement a director, officer or employee,

shall be admissible as evidence for the purpose of determining by whom the vehicle was being driven or used or to whom it belonged, as the case may be, on that occasion.

(2) Nothing in subsection (1) above shall be deemed to make a certificate admissible as evidence in proceedings for an offence except in a case where and to the like extent to which oral evidence to the like effect would have been admissible in those proceedings.

(3) Nothing in subsection (1) above shall be deemed to make a certificate admissible as evidence in proceedings for an offence—

  (a) unless a copy thereof has, not less than seven days before the hearing or trial, been served in the prescribed manner on the person charged with the offence; or

  (b) if that person, not later than three days before the hearing or trial or within such further time as the court may in special circumstances allow, serves a notice in the prescribed form and manner on the prosecutor requiring attendance at the trial of the person who signed the certificate.

(4) In this section *"prescribed"* means prescribed by rules made by the Secretary of State by statutory instrument.

A17.57   *[Section 71 is printed as amended by the Transport Act 1985, s.139(3) and Sched. 8.*

No rules have been prescribed under section 71(3). This section re-enacts the Road Traffic Act 1960, s.242, without, however, repealing it. Hence the Evidence by Certificate Rules 1961 (S.I. 1961 No. 248), as amended, rr. 2, 3 and Schedule, made under the 1960 Act may not, strictly, be applicable under section 71; cf the Interpretation Act 1978, s.17(2)(b) (which applies where an Act "repeals and re-enacts a previous enactment").]

72. Proof in summary proceedings of identity of driver of vehicle

A17.58   Where on a summary trial in England or Wales of an information for an offence under Part II . . . of this Act—

  (a) it is proved to the satisfaction of the court, on oath or in a manner prescribed by rules made under [section 144 of the Magistrates' Courts Act 1980], that a requirement under subsection (1) of section 70 of this Act to give information as to the identity of the driver of a particular vehicle on the particular occasion to which the information relates has been served on the accused by post; and

(b) a statement in writing is produced to the court purporting to be signed by the accused that the accused was the driver of that vehicle on that occasion,

the court may accept that statement as evidence that the accused was the driver of that vehicle on the occasion.

[Section 72 is printed as amended by the Magistrates' Courts Act 1980, s.154(2) and Sched. 8, para.5 **A17.59** *(which came into operation after this Act had received the royal assent but before this Act came into operation); the Transport Act 1985, s.139(3) and Sched. 8.]*

73. Time within which summary proceedings for certain offences may be commenced

Summary proceedings for an offence under section 65 or 66 of this Act may be brought **A17.60** within a period of six months from the date on which evidence sufficient in the opinion of the prosecutor to warrant the proceedings came to his knowledge; but no such proceedings shall be brought by virtue of this section more than three years after the commission of the offence.

For the purposes of this section a certificate by or on behalf of the prosecutor and stating the date on which such evidence as aforesaid came to his knowledge shall be conclusive evidence of that fact; and a certificate stating that matter and purporting to be so signed shall be deemed to be so signed unless the contrary is proved.

74. Offences by companies

(1) Where an offence under Part II . . . of this Act committed by a company is proved **A17.61** to have been committed with the consent or connivance of, or to be attributable to any neglect on the part of, any director, manager, secretary or other similar officer of the company, or any person who was purporting to act in any such capacity, he, as well as the company, shall be guilty of that offence and be liable to be proceeded against and punished accordingly.

(2) Where the affairs of a company are managed by its members, subsection (1) above shall apply in relation to the acts and defaults of a member in connection with his functions of management as if he were a director of the company.

[Section 74 is printed as amended by the Transport Act 1985, s.139(3) and Sched. 8.] **A17.62**

*　　　*　　　*

81. Interpretation of references to the operator of a vehicle or service

(1) For the purposes of this Act— **A17.63**

(a) regulations may make provision as to the person who is to be regarded as the operator of a vehicle which is made available by one holder of a PSV operator's licence to another under a hiring arrangement; and

(b) where regulations under paragraph (a) above do not apply, the operator of a vehicle is—

(i) the driver, if he owns the vehicle; and
(ii) in any other case, the person for whom the driver works (whether under a contract of employment or any other description of contract personally to do work).

(2) *[Repealed.]*

[Section 81 is printed as amended by the Transport Act 1985, s.1(3) and Sched. 1, para.12.] **A17.64**

82. General interpretation provisions

A17.65   (1) In this Act, unless the context otherwise requires—

"*certificate of initial fitness*" has the meaning given by section 6;

. . .

"*company*" means a body corporate;

. . .

"*contravention*", in relation to any condition or provision, includes a failure to comply with the condition or provision, and "contravene" shall be construed accordingly;

"*director*", in relation to a company, includes any person who occupies the position of a director, by whatever name called;

"*driver*", where a separate person acts as steersman of a motor vehicle, includes that person as well as any other person engaged in the driving of the vehicle, and "*drive*" shall be construed accordingly;

. . .

"*fares*" include sums payable in respect of a contract ticket or a season ticket;

"*international operation*" means a passenger transport operation starting or terminating in the United Kingdom and involving an international journey by the vehicle concerned, whether or not any driver leaves or enters the United Kingdom with that vehicle;

"*local authority*" means—

(a) in relation to England and Wales, any local authority within the meaning of the Local Government Act 1972;

(b) *[applies to Scotland.]*

["*local service*" has the same meaning as in the Transport Act 1985;]

"*magistrates' court*" [has the same meaning] as in the Magistrates' Courts Act 1980;

"*modification*" includes addition, omission and alteration, and related expressions shall be construed accordingly;

"*motor vehicle*" means a mechanically propelled vehicle intended or adapted for use on roads;

"*national operation*" means a passenger transport operation wholly within the United Kingdom;

"*official PSV testing station*" has the meaning given by section 8(3);

"*operating centre*", in relation to a vehicle, means the base or centre at which the vehicle is normally kept;

"*operator*" has the meaning given by section 81;

"*owner*", in relation to a vehicle which is the subject of an agreement for hire, hire-purchase, conditional sale or loan, means the person in possession of the vehicle under that agreement, and references to owning a vehicle shall be construed accordingly;

"*prescribed*" has the meaning given by section 60(2);

["*prescribed testing authority*" means such person authorised by the Secretary of State under section 8 of the Transport Act 1982 to carry on a vehicle testing business within the meaning of Part II of that Act as may be prescribed;]

"*PSV operator's licence*" means a PSV operator's licence granted under the provisions of Part II of this Act;

"*public service vehicle*" has the meaning given by section 1;

"*relevant conviction*" means a conviction (other than a spent conviction) of any offence prescribed for the purposes of this Act, or an offence under the law of Northern Ireland, or of a country or territory outside the United Kingdom, corresponding to an offence so prescribed;

"*restricted licence*" means such a PSV operator's licence as is mentioned in section 13(3);

"*road*" means any highway and any other road to which the public has access, and includes bridges over which a road passes;

. . .

"*standard licence*" means a PSV operator's licence which is not a restricted licence;

"*statutory provision*" means a provision contained in an Act or in subordinate legislation within the meaning of the Interpretation Act 1978;

["*traffic commissioner*" means the person appointed to be the commissioner for a traffic area constituted for the purposes of this Act;]

"*tramcar*" includes any carriage used on any road by virtue of an order made under the Light Railways Act 1896;

"*transport manager*", in relation to a business, means an individual who, either alone or jointly with one or more other persons, has continuous and effective responsibility for the management of the road passenger transport operations of the business;

. . .

[(1A) References in any provision of this Act to an authorised inspector are references to an authorised inspector under section 8 of the Transport Act 1982 and, where the function to which that provision relates is one of those specified in section 9 of that Act (testing and surveillance functions), are limited to an authorised inspector authorised under section 8 to exercise that function.]

(2) Any reference in this Act to a Community instrument or to a particular provision of such an instrument—

(a) is a reference to that instrument or provision as amended from time to time, and

(b) if that instrument or provision is replaced, with or without modification, shall be construed as a reference to the instrument or provision replacing it.

[(3) In this Act—

(a) any reference to a county shall be construed in relation to Wales as including a reference to a county borough;

(b) any reference to a county council shall be construed in relation to Wales as including a reference to a county borough council; and

(c) section 17(4) and (5) of the Local Government (Wales) Act 1994 (references to counties and districts to be construed generally in relation to Wales as references to counties and county boroughs) shall not apply.]

[Section 82 is printed as amended by the Transport Act 1982, s.74(1) and Sched. 5, para.23; the **A17.66**
Transport Act 1985, ss.1(3), 3(5) and 139(3), Sched. 1, para.13, Sched. 2, Pt II, para.4(20), and Sched. 8; the Road Traffic Act 1991, s.83 and Sched. 8; the Local Government (Wales) Act 1994, s.22(1) and Sched. 7, para.36; the Access to Justice Act 1999, s.76(2) and Sched. 10, paras 33 and 37.

The definition of "prescribed testing authority" (in section 82(1)) and section 82(1A), which were inserted by the Transport Act 1982, s.74(1) and Sched. 5, para.23, will take effect from a date or dates to be announced.

The term "local authority" is defined for the purposes of the Local Government Act 1972 by ibid., s.270(1) (as amended by the Local Government Act 1985, s.102(2) and Sched. 17; the Local Government (Wales) Act 1994, s.1(5)) as "a county council, . . . a district council, a London borough council or a parish [council but, in relation to Wales, means a county council, county borough council or community council]".]

A17.67 **83. Construction of references in other Acts, etc., to public service vehicles, licensing authorities, etc.**

(1) A provision of an Act other than this Act or of an instrument having effect under an enactment not repealed by this Act which (however expressed) defines "*public service vehicle*" . . . by reference to the Road Traffic Act 1930 or the Road Traffic Act 1960 shall have effect as if it provided that that expression should be construed in like manner as if it were contained in this Act.

(2) *[Repealed.]*

A17.68 *[Section 83 is printed as amended by the Transport Act 1985, ss.1(3) and 139(3), Sched. 1, para.14, and Sched. 8.]*

* * *

SCHEDULE 1

PUBLIC SERVICE VEHICLES: CONDITIONS AFFECTING STATUS FOR CLASSIFICATION

PART I

SHARING OF TAXIS AND HIRE-CARS

A17.69 **1.** The making of the agreement for the payment of separate fares must not have been initiated by the driver or by the owner of the vehicle, by any person who has made the vehicle available under any arrangement, or by any person who receives any remuneration in respect of the arrangements for the journey.

A17.70 **2.**—(1) The journey must be made without previous advertisement to the public of facilities for its being made by passengers to be carried at separate fares, except where the local authorities concerned have approved the arrangements under which the journey is made as designed to meet the social and welfare needs of one or more communities, and their approvals remain in force.

(2) In relation to a journey the local authorities concerned for the purposes of this paragraph are those in whose area any part of the journey is to be made; and in this sub-paragraph "*local authority*" means—

    (a) in relation to England and Wales, [the council of a county, metropolitan district or London borough and the Common Council of the City of London];

    (b) *[applies to Scotland.]*

A17.71 **3.** *[Repealed.]*

PART II

PARTIES OF OVERSEAS VISITORS

4. *[Repealed.]*

PART III

ALTERNATIVE CONDITIONS AFFECTING STATUS FOR CLASSIFICATION

A17.72 **5.** Arrangements for the bringing together of all the passengers for the purpose of making the journey must have been made otherwise than by, or by a person acting on behalf of—

(a) the holder of the PSV operator's licence under which the vehicle is to be used, if such a licence is in force,

(b) the driver or the owner of the vehicle or any person who has made the vehicle available under any arrangement, if no such licence is in force,

and otherwise than by any person who receives any remuneration in respect of the arrangements.

6. The journey must be made without previous advertisement to the public of the arrangements therefor.

7. All passengers must, in the case of a journey to a particular destination, be carried to, **A17.73** or to the vicinity of, that destination, or, in the case of a tour, be carried for the greater part of the journey.

8. No differentiation of fares for the journey on the basis of distance or of time must be made.

PART IV

SUPPLEMENTARY

9. For the purposes of paragraphs 2 and 6 above no account shall be taken of any such **A17.74** advertisement as follows, that is to say—

(a) a notice displayed or announcement made—

   (i) at or in any place of worship for the information of persons attending that place of worship;

   (ii) at or in any place of work for the information of persons who work there; or

   (iii) by any club or other voluntary association at or in any premises occupied or used by the club or association;

(b) a notice contained in any periodical published for the information of, and circulating wholly or mainly among—

   (i) persons who attend or might reasonably be expected to attend a particular place of worship or a place of worship in a particular place; or

   (ii) persons who work at a particular place of work or at any of two or more particular places of work; or

   (iii) the members of a club or other voluntary association.

[Schedule 1 is printed as amended by the Local Government Act 1985, s.8(1) and Sched. 5, para.3(7); **A17.75**
the Transport Act 1985, s.139(2) and (3), Sched. 7, para.21(12), and Sched. 8.]

SCHEDULE 2

TRAFFIC COMMISSIONERS   **A17.76**

[Omitted.]

SCHEDULE 3   Sections 14(2) and 17(6)

SUPPLEMENTARY PROVISION AS TO QUALIFICATIONS FOR PSV OPERATOR'S LICENCE

Good repute

1.—(1) In determining whether an individual is of good repute, [a traffic commissioner] **A17.77** shall have regard to all the relevant evidence and in particular to—

(a) relevant convictions of his and of his employees and agents; and

(b) such other information as the [commissioner] may have as to his previous conduct, in whatever capacity, in relation to the operation of vehicles of any description in the course of a business.

(2) In determining whether a company is of good repute, [a traffic commissioner] shall have regard to all the relevant evidence and in particular to—

(a) relevant convictions of the company and its officers, employees and agents; and

(b) such other information as the [commissioner] may have as to previous conduct of—

(i) the company's officers, employees and agents in relation to the operation of vehicles of any description in the course of any business carried on by the company; and

(ii) each of the company's directors, in whatever capacity, in relation to the operation of vehicles of any description in the course of any other business.

[(3) A traffic commissioner shall determine that an individual is not of good repute if he has—

(a) more than one conviction of a serious offence; or

(b) been convicted of road transport offences.]

[(4) For the purposes of sub-paragraph (3)(a) above a "*serious offence*" is—

(a) an offence under the law in force in any part of the United Kingdom for which a sentence of imprisonment for a term exceeding three months, a fine exceeding level 4 on the standard scale or a community service order for more than sixty hours was imposed; and

(b) any corresponding offence under the law of a country or territory outside the United Kingdom for which a corresponding punishment was imposed.]

[(5) For the purposes of sub-paragraph (3)(b) above a *road transport offence* is—

(a) an offence under the law of any part of the United Kingdom relating to road transport including in particular—

(i) an offence relating to drivers' hours of work or rest periods, the weights or dimensions of commercial vehicles, road or vehicle safety or the protection of the environment; and

(ii) any other offence concerning professional liability; or

(b) any corresponding offence under the law of a country or territory outside the United Kingdom.]

[(6) In sub-paragraph (4)(a) above "*a sentence of imprisonment*" includes any form of custodial sentence or order other than one under the enactments relating to mental health and "*a community service order*" means an order under [section 46 of the Powers of Criminal Courts (Sentencing) Act 2000] or the Community Service by Offenders (Scotland) Act 1978.]

[(7) In sub-paragraphs (4)(a) and (5)(a) above references to an offence under the law in force in any part of the United Kingdom include a reference to a civil offence (wherever committed) within the meaning of the Army Act 1955, the Air Force Act 1955 or the Naval Discipline Act 1957.]

[(8) For the purposes of sub-paragraph (3) above spent convictions shall be disregarded; and a traffic commissioner may also disregard an offence if such time as he considers appropriate has elapsed since the date of the conviction.]

[(9) Sub-paragraph (3) above is without prejudice to the power of a traffic commissioner to determine that an individual is not of good repute for reasons other than convictions of the kind there mentioned.]

[(10) In this paragraph references to an individual include references to a transport manager as well as to an individual who is an applicant for, or the holder of, a PSV operator's licence.]

Appropriate financial standing

2.   *[Omitted.]*   **A17.78**

Professional competence

3–7.   *[Omitted.]*

Persons engaged in road passenger transport before 1st January 1978

8–10.   *[Omitted.]*

[Schedule 3 is printed as amended by the Transport Act 1985, s.3(5) and Sched. 2, Pt II,   **A17.79** *para.4(21)(a); the Public Service Vehicle Operators (Qualifications) Regulations 1990 (S.I. 1990 No. 1851); the Public Service Vehicle Operators (Qualifications) Regulations 1999 (S.I. 1999 No. 2431; not reproduced in this work); and the Powers of Criminal Courts (Sentencing) Act 2000, s.165(1) and Sched. 9, para.81.*

Provisions from paragraph 1 are incorporated by reference into the Public Service Vehicles (Operators' Licences) Regulations 1995 (S.I. 1995 No. 2908), Schedule below.]

*   *   *

The Criminal Attempts Act 1981

(1981 c. 47)

A18.01   An Act to amend the law of England and Wales . . . and . . . to repeal the provisions of section 4 of the Vagrancy Act 1824 which apply to suspected persons and reputed thieves; to make provision against unauthorised interference with vehicles . . .

[27th July 1981]

*   *   *

PART II

SUSPECTED PERSONS, ETC.

8. Abolition of offence of loitering, etc., with intent

A18.02   The provisions of section 4 of the Vagrancy Act 1824 which apply to suspected persons and reputed thieves frequenting or loitering about the places described in that section with the intent there specified shall cease to have effect.

A18.03   *[In the Vagrancy Act 1824, s.4, the words from "every suspected person" to "arrestable offence" were formally repealed by section 10 of and Part II of the Schedule to this Act.]*

9. Interference with vehicles

A18.04   (1) A person is guilty of the offence of vehicle interference if he interferes with a motor vehicle or trailer or with anything carried in or on a motor vehicle or trailer with the intention that an offence specified in subsection (2) below shall be committed by himself or some other person.

(2) The offences mentioned in subsection (1) above are—

(a) theft of the motor vehicle or trailer or part of it;

(b) theft of anything carried in or on the motor vehicle or trailer; and

(c) an offence under section 12(1) of the Theft Act 1968 (taking and driving away without consent);

and, if it is shown that a person accused of an offence under this section intended that one of those offences should be committed, it is immaterial that it cannot be shown which it was.

(3) A person guilty of an offence under this section shall be liable on summary conviction to imprisonment for a term not exceeding three months or to a fine not exceeding [level 4 in the standard scale] or to both.

(4) *[Repealed.]*

A18.05   (5) In this section "*motor vehicle*" and "*trailer*" have the meanings assigned to them by [section 185(1) of the Road Traffic Act 1988 [*q.v.*]].

[Section 9 is printed as amended by the Criminal Justice Act 1982, s.46(1); the Police and Criminal Evidence Act 1984, s.119(2) and Sched. 7, Pt I; the Road Traffic (Consequential Provisions) Act 1988, s.4 and Sched. 3, para.23.]

*   *   *

The Criminal Justice Act 1982

(1982 c. 48)

An Act to make further provision as to the sentencing and treatment of offenders (including provision as to . . . the standardisation of fines and of certain other sums specified in enactments relating to the powers of criminal courts) . . .

A19.01

[28th October 1982]

*   *   *

Introduction of standard scale of fines

A19.02

37. The standard scale of fines for summary offences

(1) There shall be a standard scale of fines for summary offences, which shall be known as *"the standard scale"*.

[(2) The standard scale is shown below—

Level on the scale	Amount of fine
1	£200
2	£500
3	£1,000
4	£2,500
5	£5,000.]

(3) Where any enactment (whether contained in an Act passed before or after this Act) provides—

(a) that a person convicted of a summary offence shall be liable on conviction to a fine or a maximum fine by reference to a specified level on the standard scale; or

(b) confers power by subordinate instrument to make a person liable on conviction of a summary offence (whether or not created by the instrument) to a fine or maximum fine by reference to a specified level on the standard scale,

it is to be construed as referring to the standard scale for which this section provides as that standard scale has effect from time to time by virtue either of this section or of an order under section 143 of the Magistrates' Courts Act 1980.

A19.03

[Section 37 is printed as amended by the Criminal Justice Act 1991, s.17(1). For the level of fines immediately before October 1, 1992 (when the above levels of fines were introduced), see the Criminal Penalties, etc. (Increase) Order 1984 (S.I. 1984 No. 447).]

*   *   *

The Road Traffic Regulation Act 1984

(1984 c. 27)

A20.01 An Act to consolidate the Road Traffic Regulation Act 1967 and certain related enactments, with amendments to give effect to recommendations of the Law Commission and the Scottish Law Commission.

[26th June 1984]

A20.02 *General note.* All the functions of a Minister of the Crown under the Road Traffic Regulation Act 1984 exercisable in relation to Wales (except where otherwise indicated in notes below) have been transferred to the National Assembly for Wales by the National Assembly for Wales (Transfer of Functions) Order 1999 (S.I. 1999 No. 672; not reproduced in this work), art.2 and Sched. 1.

All proceedings under this Act (except those under sections 35A(2), 43(5) and (12), 47(3), 52(1), 108(3), 115(1) and (2), 116(1) and 129(3)) are specified by the Prosecution of Offences Act 1985 (Specified Proceedings) Order 1999 (S.I. 1999 No. 904) below as being proceedings the conduct of which the Director of Public Prosecutions is not required to take over from the police under the Prosecution of Offences Act 1985, s.3(3)(a).

ARRANGEMENT OF SECTIONS

*　　　*　　　*

PART I

GENERAL PROVISIONS FOR TRAFFIC REGULATION

Outside Greater London

Temporary suspension

*　　　*　　　*

PART II

Traffic Regulation in Special Cases

*   *   *

PART III

Crossings and Playgrounds

Pedestrian crossings

School crossings

*   *   *

PART IV

Parking Places

Provision of off-street parking, and parking on roads without payment

*   *   *

Parking on highways for payment

*   *   *

*   *   *

Special parking provisions

*   *   *

PART V

TRAFFIC SIGNS

Section

*   *   *

PART VI

SPEED LIMITS

Section

*   *   *

PART VIII

CONTROL AND ENFORCEMENT

Removal or immobilisation of vehicles

Section

PART I

GENERAL PROVISIONS FOR TRAFFIC REGULATION

Outside Greater London

*   *   *

5. Contravention of traffic regulation order

A20.04   (1) A person who contravenes a traffic regulation order, or who uses a vehicle, or causes or permits a vehicle to be used in contravention of a traffic regulation order, shall be guilty of an offence.

A20.05   (2) *[Repealed by the New Roads and Street Works Act 1991, s.168(2) and Sched. 9.]*

[The term "traffic regulation order" is defined as an order under section 1 of this Act by ibid., s.1(1). For the possible disapplication of section 5 above, see the Road Traffic Act 1991, Sched. 3, para.2(4) below.

For the mode of trial of and punishment for offences under section 5, see the Road Traffic Offenders Act 1988, Sched. 2, Pt I below.]

In Greater London

6. Orders similar to traffic regulation orders

A20.06   (1) [The traffic authority for a road in Greater London may make an order under this section for controlling or regulating vehicular and other traffic (including pedestrians). Provision may, in particular, be made—]

(a) for any of the purposes, or with respect to any of the matters, mentioned in Schedule 1 to this Act, and

(b) for any other purpose which is a purpose mentioned in any of paragraphs [(a) to (g)] of section 1(1) of this Act.

(2) *[Power to make orders in respect of roads for which the Secretary of State is responsible.]*

(3) Any order under this section may be made so as to apply—

[(a) to the whole area of a local authority, or to particular parts of that area, or to particular places or streets or parts of streets in that area;]

(b) throughout the day, or during particular periods;

(c) on special occasions only, or at special times only;

(d) to traffic of any class;

(e) subject to such exceptions as may be specified in the order or determined in a manner provided for by it.

(4) *[Repealed.]*

(5) No order under this section shall contain any provision for regulating the speed of vehicles on roads.

(6) In this section, in section 7 of this Act and in Schedule 1 to this Act "*street*" includes any highway, any bridge carrying a highway and any lane, mews, footway, square, court, alley or passage whether a thoroughfare or not . . .

A20.07

[Section 6 is printed as amended by the Local Government Act 1985, s.8(1) and Sched. 5, para.4(3); the New Roads and Street Works Act 1991, s.168(1) and (2), Sched. 8, para.21, and Sched. 9; the Environment Act 1995, s.120(1) and Sched. 22, para.36(2).

As to the application of section 6 to tramcars and trolley vehicles (other than duobuses), see the Tramcars and Trolley Vehicles (Modification of Enactments) Regulations 1992 (S.I. 1992 No. 1217) (q.v.), regs 3, 5 and 11.

Sections 6–8 of this Act do not apply to any person or vehicle in the service of a visiting force or head-quarters (as defined); see the Visiting Forces and International Headquarters (Application of Law) Order 1999 (S.I. 1999 No. 1736; not reproduced in this work), art.8(1) and (2)(a).

As to the enforcement of prohibitions imposed under the London Local Authorities Act 1995 (c. x) in respect of parts of roads in special parking areas within the borough of a participating council, see the notes to section 8 below.

As to the penalty charges payable under the London Local Authorities Act 1996 (c. ix), see the notes to section 8 below.]

7. Supplementary provisions as to orders under section 6

(1) Any order under section 6 of this Act may make provision for identifying any part of   **A20.08** any road to which, or any time at which or period during which, any provision contained in the order is for the time being to apply by means of a traffic sign of a type or character specified in the order (being a type prescribed or character authorised under section 64 of this Act) and for the time being lawfully in place; and, for the purposes of any order so made, any such traffic sign placed on or near a street shall be deemed to be lawfully in place unless the contrary is proved.

(2) Any such order which imposes any restriction on the use by vehicles of streets in Greater London, or the waiting of vehicles in such streets, may include provision with respect to the issue and display of certificates or other means of identification of vehicles which are excepted from the restriction, whether generally or in particular circumstances or at particular times.

(3) Any such order may also include provision with respect to the issue, display and oper-ation of devices . . . for indicating the time at which a vehicle arrived at, and the time at which it ought to leave, any place in a street in which waiting is restricted by the order, or one or other of those times, and for treating the indications given by any such device as evi-dence of such facts and for such purposes as may be prescribed by the order.

(4) Any such order may provide for the suspension or modification, so long as the order remains in force, of any provisions of any Acts (whether public general or local or private, and including provisions contained in this Act), byelaws or regulations dealing with the same subject matter as the order, or of any Acts conferring power to make byelaws or reg-ulations dealing with the same subject matter, so far as such provisions apply to any place or street to which the order applies.

(5) *[Prohibition on appeals against decisions relating to road service licences in certain circumstances.]*

(6) *[Duty to consult before making order under section 6.]*

(7) *[Definition for purposes of section 7(5).]*

[Section 7 is printed as amended by the Deregulation (Parking Equipment) Order 1996 (S.I. 1996 No.   **A20.09** *1553) (q.v.), art.2(1)(a) and Schedule.*

As to visiting forces, etc., see the note to section 6 above.]

8. Contravention of order under section 6

(1) Any person who acts in contravention of, or fails to comply with, an order under   **A20.10** section 6 of this Act shall be guilty of an offence.

[(1A) Subsection (1) above does not apply in relation to any order under section 6 of this Act so far as it designates any parking places.]

(2) *[Repealed by the New Roads and Street Works Act 1991, s.168(2) and Sched. 9.]*

A20.11   *[Section 8 is printed as amended by the Road Traffic Act 1991, s.65(2), in respect of designated London boroughs. In areas in respect of which that amendment is not in force, the text of section 8 should be read as if section 8(1A) were omitted.*

The reference to "designated London boroughs" is a reference to those London boroughs which have been so designated in commencement orders to the Road Traffic Act 1991. The commencement orders are listed below, together with the dates on which they brought provisions into force. The designated London boroughs are also listed below, with an indication of the commencement order appropriate to each.

A20.12   ***Commencement orders.*** *The Road Traffic Act 1991 (Commencement No. 1) Order 1991 (S.I. 1991 No. 2054) (October 1, 1991); the Road Traffic Act 1991 (Commencement No. 2) Order 1992 (S.I. 1992 No. 199) (March 2, and April 1, 1992); the Road Traffic Act 1991 (Commencement No. 3) Order 1992 (S.I. 1992 No. 421) (April 1, 1992); the Road Traffic Act 1991 (Commencement No. 4 and Transitional Provisions) Order 1992 (S.I. 1992 No. 1286) (July 1, 1992); the Road Traffic Act 1991 (Commencement No. 5 and Transitional Provisions) Order 1992 (S.I. 1992 No. 2010) (September 1, 1992); the Road Traffic Act 1991 (Commencement No. 6 and Transitional Provisions) Order 1993 (S.I. 1993 No. 1461) (July 5, 1993); the Road Traffic Act 1991 (Commencement No. 6 and Transitional Provisions) (Amendment) Order 1993 (S.I. 1993 No. 1686) (July 5, 1993); the Road Traffic Act 1991 (Commencement No. 7 and Transitional Provisions) Order 1993 (S.I. 1993 No. 2229) (October 4, 1993); the Road Traffic Act 1991 (Commencement No. 8 and Transitional Provisions) Order 1993 (S.I. 1993 No. 2803) (December 6, 1993); the Road Traffic Act 1991 (Commencement No. 9 and Transitional Provisions) Order 1993 (S.I. 1993 No. 3238) (January 31, 1994); the Road Traffic Act 1991 (Commencement No. 10 and Transitional Provisions) Order 1994 (S.I. 1994 No. 81) (April 5, 1994); the Road Traffic Act 1991 (Commencement No. 11 and Transitional Provisions) Order 1994 (S.I. 1994 No. 1482) (July 4, 1994); and the Road Traffic Act 1991 (Commencement No. 12 and Transitional Provisions) Order 1994 (S.I. 1994 No. 1484) (July 4, 1997).*

A20.13   ***Designated London boroughs***

Barking and Dagenham (S.I. 1994 No. 1482)
Barnet (S.I. 1994 No. 1482)
Bexley (S.I. 1994 No. 1484)
Brent (S.I. 1994 No. 1482)
Bromley (S.I. 1993 No. 2229)
Camden (S.I. 1993 No. 2803)
Croydon (S.I. 1994 No. 1482)
Ealing (S.I. 1994 No. 1482)
Enfield (S.I. 1994 No. 1482)
Greenwich (S.I. 1994 No. 1482)
Hackney (S.I. 1993 No. 2803)
Hammersmith and Fulham (S.I. 1993 No. 2229)
Haringey (S.I. 1994 No. 1482)
Harrow (S.I. 1994 No. 1482)
Havering (S.I. 1994 No. 1482)
Hillingdon (S.I. 1994 No. 1482)
Hounslow (S.I. 1993 No. 2803)
Islington (S.I. 1994 No. 1482)
Kensington and Chelsea (royal borough) (S.I. 1994 No. 1482)
Kingston upon Thames (royal borough) (S.I. 1994 No. 1482)
Lambeth (S.I. 1994 No. 1482)

Lewisham (S.I. 1993 No. 2229)
Merton (S.I. 1994 No. 1482)
Newham (S.I. 1994 No. 1482)
Redbridge (S.I. 1994 No. 1482)
Richmond upon Thames (S.I. 1993 No. 3238, S.I. 1994 No. 81)
Southwark (S.I. 1994 No. 81)
Sutton (S.I. 1994 No. 1482)
Tower Hamlets (S.I. 1994 No. 1482)
Waltham Forest (S.I. 1994 No. 1482)
Wandsworth (S.I. 1993 No. 1461)
Westminster (city) (S.I. 1994 No. 1482)

For the possible disapplication of section 8, see the Road Traffic Act 1991, s.76(3)(a).

For the mode of trial of and punishment for offences under section 8, see the Road Traffic Offenders Act 1988, Sched. 2, Pt I.

A driver of a vehicle may not cause it to stop on part of a road in London in a special parking area within the limits of a crossing or a crossing controlled area and this prohibition is enforceable as if it had been imposed by an order under section 6 of this Act; see the London Local Authorities Act 1995 (c. x), s.4(1), (2) (not reproduced in this work). Similarly, a prohibition under section 5(3) of the 1995 Act (not reproduced in this work) on the waiting of vehicles in a prohibited zone (as defined) during any period when parking is restricted in the designated parking place in respect of which the prohibited zone exists, and a special temporary waiting prohibition within a special parking area under section 9 of the 1995 Act (not reproduced in this work), are enforceable as if they had been imposed under an order under section 6 of this Act.

Penalty charges may be payable for bus lane offences committed in London by non-compliance with a traffic order made under section 6; see the London Local Authorities Act 1996 (c. ix), Pt II (ss.3–9), as amended by the London Local Authorities Act 2000 (c. vii), s.48 and Sched. 2, para.1 (not reproduced in this work).

As to visiting forces, etc., see the notes to section 6 above.]

Experimental traffic schemes

9. Experimental traffic orders   *[Omitted.]*   **A20.14**

10. Supplementary provisions as to experimental traffic orders   *[Omitted.]*

11. Contravention of experimental traffic order

[(1)] Any person who acts in contravention of, or fails to comply with, an experimental traffic order shall be guilty of an offence.   **A20.15**

[(2) This section does not apply in relation to any experimental traffic order so far as it designates any parking places in Greater London.]

[Section 11 is printed as amended by the Road Traffic Act 1991, s.65(3), in respect of designated   **A20.16** *London boroughs. In areas in respect of which that amendment is not in force, the text of section 11 is the text of section 11(1) as set out above.*

For the designated London boroughs, see the note to section 8 above.

For the possible disapplication of section 11, see the Road Traffic Act 1991, s.76(3)(b), and Sched. 3, para.2(4).

For the mode of trial of and punishment for offences under section 11, see the Road Traffic Offenders Act 1988, Sched. 2, Pt I.

Penalty charges may be payable for bus lane offences committed in London by non-compliance with an experimental traffic order under section 9; see the London Local Authorities Act 1996 (c. ix), Pt II (ss.3–9), as amended by the London Local Authorities Act 2000 (c. vii), s.48 and Sched. 2, para.1 (not reproduced in this work).]

A20.17   **12. Experimental traffic schemes in Greater London**   *[Repealed.]*

A20.18   **13. Contravention of regulations under section 12**   *[Repealed.]*

Temporary suspension

A20.19   **13A. Temporary suspension of provisions under section 6 or 9 order**
[Omitted.]

PART II

Traffic Regulation in Special Cases

A20.20   **[14. Temporary prohibition or restriction on roads**

(1) If the traffic authority for a road are satisfied that traffic on the road should be restricted or prohibited—

    (a) because works are being or are proposed to be executed on or near the road; or

    (b) because of the likelihood of danger to the public, or of serious damage to the road, which is not attributable to such works; or

    (c) for the purpose of enabling the duty imposed by section 89(1)(a) or (2) of the Environmental Protection Act 1990 (litter clearing and cleaning) to be discharged,

the authority may by order restrict or prohibit temporarily the use of that road, or of any part of it, by vehicles, or vehicles of any class, or by pedestrians, to such extent and subject to such conditions or exceptions as they may consider necessary.

    [(1A) *[Applies to Scotland.]*]

(2) The traffic authority for a road may at any time by notice restrict or prohibit temporarily the use of the road, or of any part of it, by vehicles, or vehicles of any class, or by pedestrians, where it appears to them that it is—

    (a) necessary or expedient for the reason mentioned in paragraph (a) or the purpose mentioned in paragraph (c) of subsection (1) above; or

    (b) necessary for the reason mentioned in paragraph (b) of that subsection,

that the restriction or prohibition should come into force without delay.

(3) When considering the making of an order or the issue of a notice under the foregoing provisions an authority shall have regard to the existence of alternative routes suitable for the traffic which will be affected by the order or notice.

(4) The provision that may be made by an order or notice under the foregoing provisions is—

    (a) any such provision as is mentioned in section 2(1), (2) or (3) or 4(1) of this Act; or

    (b) any provision restricting the speed of vehicles;

but no such order or notice shall be made or issued with respect to any road which would have the effect of preventing at any time access for pedestrians to any premises situated on or adjacent to the road, or to any other premises accessible for pedestrians from, and only from, the road.

(5) Where any such order or notice is made or issued by an authority (in this subsection referred to as the "*initiating authority*") any such provision as is mentioned in subsection (4) above may be made as respects any alternative road—

    (a) if that authority is the traffic authority for the alternative road, by an order made by the initiating authority or by that notice;

(b) if the initiating authority is not the traffic authority for the alternative road, by an order made by the initiating authority with the consent of the traffic authority for the alternative road.

(6) Section 3(1) and (2) of this Act shall apply to the provisions that may be made under subsection (5) above as they apply to the provisions of a traffic regulation order.

(7) An order or notice made or issued under this section may—

(a) suspend any statutory provision to which this subsection applies; or

(b) for either of the reasons or for the purpose mentioned in subsection (1) above suspend any such provision without imposing any such restriction or prohibition as is mentioned in subsection (1) or (2) above.

(8) Subsection (7) above applies to—

(a) any statutory provision of a description which could have been contained in an order or notice under this section;

(b) an order under section 32(1)(b), 35, 45, 46 or 49 of this Act or any such order as is mentioned in paragraph 11(1) of Schedule 10 to this Act; and

(c) an order under section 6 of this Act so far as it designates any parking places in Greater London.

(9) In this section "*alternative road*", in relation to a road as respects which an order is made under subsection (1) or a notice is issued under subsection (2) above, means a road which—

(a) provides an alternative route for traffic diverted from the first-mentioned road or from any other alternative road; or

(b) is capable of providing such an alternative route apart from any statutory provision authorised by subsection (7) above to be suspended by an order made or notice issued by virtue of subsection (5) above.]

[Section 14 (and also section 15) was substituted by the Road Traffic (Temporary Restrictions) Act **A20.21** *1991, s.1(1) and Sched. 1.*

As to the application of section 14 to tramcars and trolley vehicles (other than duobuses), see the Tramcars and Trolley Vehicles (Modification of Enactments) Regulations 1992 (S.I. 1992 No. 1217) (q.v.), regs 4 and 6 (for transitional provisions, see ibid., regs 15 and 16). As to the application of section 14 to trams, see also the Leeds Supertram Act 1993 (c. xv), s.4(4).

As to the transfer of functions of a Minister of the Crown under section 14(1), (2), (3) and (5) which are exercisable in Scotland in relation to the imposition of speed limits to the Scottish Ministers, see the Scotland Act 1998 (Transfer of Functions to the Scottish Ministers etc.) Order 1999 (S.I. 1999 No. 1750; not reproduced in this work), art.2 and Sched. 1.]

15. Duration of orders and notices under section 14   *[Omitted.]*   **A20.22**

16. Supplementary provisions as to orders and notices under section 14

(1) A person who contravenes, or who uses or permits the use of a vehicle in contraven-   **A20.23** tion of, a restriction or prohibition imposed under section 14 of this Act shall be guilty of an offence.

(2), (2A) *[Regulation-making power.]*

(3), (4) *[Repealed by the New Roads and Street Works Act 1991, s.168(2) and Sched. 9.]*

[The Road Traffic (Temporary Restrictions) Procedure Regulations 1992 (S.I. 1992 No. 1215) (not **A20.24** *reproduced in this work) have been made under this section.*

As to notice of intended prosecution of certain offences under section 16(1), see the Road Traffic Offenders Act 1988, Sched. 1, para.1A below.

As to the disapplication of section 16(1) in relation to designated special parking areas, see the Road Traffic Act 1991, Sched. 3, para.2(4)(ba) below.

For the mode of trial of and punishment for offences under section 16, see the Road Traffic Offenders Act 1988, Sched. 2, Pt I.

As to the transfer of functions of a Minister of the Crown under section 16(2) and (2A) which are exercisable in Scotland in relation to the imposition of speed limits to the Scottish Ministers, see the Scotland Act 1998 (Transfer of Functions to the Scottish Ministers etc.) Order 1999 (S.I. 1999 No. 1750; not reproduced in this work), art.2 and Sched. 1.]

[16A. Prohibition or restriction on roads in connection with certain events

A20.25   (1) In this section *"relevant event"* means any sporting event, social event or entertainment which is held on a road.

(2) If the traffic authority for a road are satisfied that traffic on the road should be restricted or prohibited for the purpose of—

     (a) facilitating the holding of a relevant event,

     (b) enabling members of the public to watch a relevant event, or

     (c) reducing the disruption to traffic likely to be caused by a relevant event,

the authority may by order restrict or prohibit temporarily the use of that road, or any part of it, by vehicles of any class or by pedestrians, to such extent and subject to such conditions or exceptions as they may consider necessary or expedient.

(3) Before making an order under this section the authority shall satisfy themselves that it is not reasonably practicable for the event to be held otherwise than on a road.

(4) An order under this section—

     (a) may not be made in relation to any race or trial falling within subsection (1) of section 12 of the Road Traffic Act 1988 (motor racing on public ways);

     (b) may not be made in relation to any competition or trial falling within subsection (1) of section 13 of that Act (regulation of motoring events on public ways) unless the competition or trial is authorised by or under regulations under that section; and

     (c) may not be made in relation to any race or trial falling within subsection (1) of section 31 of that Act (regulation of cycle racing on public ways) unless the race or trial is authorised by or under regulations made under that section.

(5) An order under this section may relate to the road on which the relevant event is to be held or to any other road.

(6) In the case of a road for which the Secretary of State is the traffic authority, the power to make an order under this section is also exercisable, with his consent, by the local traffic authority or by any local traffic authority which is the traffic authority for any other road to which the order relates.

(7) In the case of a road for which a local traffic authority is the traffic authority, the power to make an order under this section is also exercisable, with the consent of that local traffic authority, by a local traffic authority which is the traffic authority for any other road to which the order relates.

(8) When considering the making of an order under this section, an authority shall have regard to the safety and convenience of alternative routes suitable for the traffic which will be affected by the order.

(9) The provision that may be made by an order under this section is—

(a) any such provision as is mentioned in section 2(1), (2) or (3) or 4(1) of this Act;

(b) any provision restricting the speed of vehicles; or

(c) any provision restricting or prohibiting—
  (i) the riding of horses, or
  (ii) the leading or driving of horses, cattle, sheep or other animals,

but no such order shall be made with respect to any road which would have the effect of preventing at any time access for pedestrians to any premises situated on or adjacent to the road, or to any other premises accessible for pedestrians from, and only from, the road.

(10) An order under this section may—

(a) suspend any statutory provision to which this subsection applies; or

(b) for any of the purposes mentioned in subsection (2) above, suspend any such provision without imposing any such restriction or prohibition as is mentioned in that subsection.

(11) Subsection (10) above applies to—

(a) any statutory provision of a description which could have been contained in an order under this section;

(b) an order under section 32(1)(b), 35, 45, 46 or 49 of this Act or any such order as is mentioned in paragraph 11(1) of Schedule 10 to this Act; and

(c) an order under section 6 of this Act so far as it designates any parking places in Greater London.]

[Section 16A was inserted by the Road Traffic Regulation (Special Events) Act 1994, s.1(1).]   **A20.26**

[16B. Restrictions on orders under section 16A

(1) An order under section 16A of this Act shall not continue in force for a period of   **A20.27**
more than three days beginning with the day on which it comes into force unless—

(a) the order is made by the Secretary of State as the traffic authority for the road concerned; or

(b) before the order is made, he has agreed that it should continue in force for a longer period.

(2) Where an order under section 16A of this Act has not ceased to be in force and the relevant event to which it relates has not ended, the Secretary of State may, subject to subsections (4) and (5) below, from time to time direct that the order shall continue in force for a further period not exceeding three days beginning with the day on which it would otherwise cease to be in force.

(3) A direction under subsection (2) above may relate to all the roads to which the order under section 16A of this Act relates or only to specified roads.

(4) Where an order under section 16A of this Act relates only to roads for which the Secretary of State is not himself the traffic authority, he shall not give a direction under subsection (2) above except at the request of the traffic authority for any road to which the order relates.

(5) Where an order under section 16A of this Act relates to any road for which the Secretary of State is not himself the traffic authority, he shall not give a direction under subsection (2) above affecting that road except with the consent of the traffic authority for that road.

(6) Where an order has been made under section 16A of this Act in any calendar year, no further order may be made under that section in that year so as to affect any length of road affected by the previous order, unless the further order—

    (a)　is made by the Secretary of State as the traffic authority for the road concerned; or

    (b)　is made with his consent.

(7) For the purposes of subsection (6) above, a length of road is affected by an order under section 16A of this Act if the order contains provisions—

    (a)　prohibiting or restricting traffic on that length of road; or

    (b)　suspending any statutory provision applying to traffic on that length of road.]

A20.28　　　*[Section 16B was inserted by the Road Traffic Regulation (Special Events) Act 1994, s.1(1).]*

[16C. Supplementary provisions as to orders under section 16A

A20.29　　　(1) A person who contravenes, or who uses or permits the use of a vehicle in contravention of, a restriction or prohibition imposed by an order under section 16A of this Act shall be guilty of an offence.

(2), (3) *[Regulations as to procedure for making orders under section 16A.]*]

A20.30　　　*[Section 16C was inserted by the Road Traffic Regulation (Special Events) Act 1994, s.1(1).]*

17. Traffic regulation on special roads

A20.31　　　[(1) A special road shall not be used except by traffic of a class authorised to do so—

    (a)　in England and Wales, by a scheme made, or having effect as if made, under section 16 of the Highways Act 1980 or by virtue of paragraph 3 of Schedule 23 to that Act, or

    (b)　*[applies to Scotland.]*]

(2) The Secretary of State may make regulations with respect to the use of special roads. [Such regulations may, in particular—

    (a)　regulate the manner in which and the conditions subject to which special roads may be used by traffic authorised to do so;]

    (b)　authorise, or enable such authority as may be specified in the regulations to authorise, the use of special roads on occasion or in an emergency or for the purpose of crossing, or for the purpose of securing access to premises abutting on or adjacent to the roads, by traffic other than that described in paragraph (a) above; . . .

    (c)　relax, or enable any authority so specified to relax, any prohibition or restriction imposed by the regulations.

    [(d)　include provisions having effect in such places, at such times, in such manner or in such circumstances as may for the time being be indicated by traffic signs in accordance with the regulations.]

(3) Regulations made under subsection (2) above may make provision with respect to special roads generally, or may make different provision with respect to special roads provided for the use of different classes of traffic, or may make provision with respect to any particular special road.

    [(3A)　*[Applies to Scotland.]*]

(4) If a person uses a special road in contravention of this section or of regulations under subsection (2) above, he shall be guilty of an offence.

[(5) The provisions of this section and of any regulations under subsection (2) above do not apply in relation to a road, or part of a road, until the date declared by the traffic authority, by notice published in the prescribed manner, to be the date on which the road or part is open for use as a special road.

This does not prevent the making of regulations under subsection (2) above before that date, so as to come into force in relation to that road or part on that date.]

(6) In this section "*use*", in relation to a road, includes crossing . . .

[Section 17 is printed as amended by the New Roads and Street Works Act 1991, s.168(1) and (2), **A20.32**
Sched. 8, Pt II, para.28(1)–(5), and Sched. 9; the Road Traffic Act 1991, ss.48, 83, Sched. 4, para.25, and Sched. 8.

Words in section 17(1) relating expressly and exclusively to Scotland have been omitted.

The Motorways Traffic (England and Wales) Regulations 1982 (S.I. 1982 No. 1163) (q.v.) have effect as if made under this section.

As to notice of intended prosecution of certain offences under section 17(4), see the Road Traffic Offenders Act 1988, Sched. 1, para.1A below.

For the application of the fixed penalty procedure to offences under subsection (4), see the Road Traffic Offenders Act 1988, Pt III and Sched. 3 below.

As to the admissibility of evidence of speeding in respect of offences under section 17(4), see section 20 of the Road Traffic Offenders Act 1988.

As exceptions to the transfer of functions to the National Assembly for Wales of functions of a Minister of the Crown exercisable in relation to Wales (see the General note at p. 122 above), the functions under section 17(2) and (3) with respect to special roads generally have been expressly excluded from that transfer; see the National Assembly for Wales (Transfer of Functions) Order 1999 (S.I. 1999 No. 672; not reproduced in this work), art.2 and Sched. 1.

As to the transfer of the function of the Secretary of State under section 17(2) and (5) which is exercisable in Scotland in relation to the making of regulations with respect to any particular special road to the Scottish Ministers, see the Scotland Act 1998 (Transfer of Functions to the Scottish Ministers etc.) Order 1999 (S.I. 1999 No. 1750; not reproduced in this work), art.2 and Sched. 1. As to the exercise of other functions under section 17(2) only after consultation with the Scottish Ministers, see S.I. 1999 No. 1750, art.4 and Sched. 3.]

17A. Further provisions as to special roads   *[Omitted.]*   **A20.33**

*   *   *

PART III

CROSSINGS AND PLAYGROUNDS

Pedestrian crossings

23. Powers of local authorities with respect to pedestrian crossings on roads   **A20.34**
other than trunk roads   *[Omitted.]*

24. Pedestrian crossings on trunk roads   *[Omitted.]*

25. Pedestrian crossing regulations

(1) The Secretary of State may make regulations with respect to the precedence of veh-   **A20.35**
icles and pedestrians respectively, and generally with respect to the movement of traffic (including pedestrians), at and in the vicinity of crossings.

(2)–(4) *[Omitted.]*

(5) A person who contravenes any regulations made under this section shall be guilty of an offence.

(6) In this section "*crossing*" means a crossing for pedestrians established—

    (a) by a local authority under section 23 of this Act, or

    (b) by the Secretary of State in the discharge of the duty imposed on him by section 24 of this Act,

and (in either case) indicated in accordance with the regulations having effect as respects that crossing; and, for the purposes of a prosecution for a contravention of the provisions of a regulation having effect as respects a crossing, the crossing shall be deemed to be so established and indicated unless the contrary is proved.

A20.36   *[The Zebra, Pelican and Puffin Crossings and General Directions 1997 (S.I. 1997 No. 2400) (q.v.) have been made in part under this section.*

See also paragaph 9(2) of Schedule 10 to this Act below.

For the application of the fixed penalty procedure to offences under subsection (5) (except offences in respect of moving motor vehicles), see the Road Traffic Offenders Act 1988, Pt III, and Sched. 3 below.

A driver of a vehicle may not at any time cause it to stop on any part of a road in a special parking area designated by an order under section 76(1) of the Road Traffic Act 1991 in the borough of a participating council (i.e. the common council of the City of London, and the council of any London borough other than Tower Hamlets) within the limits of a crossing established under section 25 of the 1984 Act or a crossing controlled area (i.e. any area of carriageway in the vicinity of a crossing, the presence and limits of which are duly indicated in accordance with regulations under section 25) (London Local Authorities Act 1995 (c. x), s.4(2), as amended by the London Local Authorities Act 2000 (c. vii), s.48 and Sched. 2, para.1, and as read together with the 1995 Act, ss.2, 4(1) and 4(6)). Penalty charges may be imposed in respect of contraventions of section 4(2) and, where a driver causes a vehicle to stop in contravention of section 4(2), he is not liable to prosecution for an offence under section 25 of the 1984 Act unless the case falls within section 4(4)(a)(i), (ii) or (iii) of the 1995 Act; those provisions provide that no penalty charge is payable under section 4(2) by the driver of a vehicle who causes it to stop where (i) by reason of that stopping the vehicle is removed by (or under arrangements made by) a constable or traffic warden under regulations under section 99 of the 1984 Act; or (ii) a notice is given to the driver under section 54(2) or (4) of the Road Traffic Offenders Act 1988 in respect of the offence under section 25 of the 1984 Act; or (iii) notice of an intention to prosecute the driver in respect of such an offence is given by the commissioner of police to the council of the appropriate borough within 14 days, beginning with the day on which the vehicle stopped.

As an exception to the transfer of functions to the National Assembly for Wales of functions of a Minister of the Crown exercisable in relation to Wales (see the General note at p. 122 above), the functions under section 25 (other than section 25(4) together with the other provisions of section 25 so far as relating thereto) have been expressly excluded from that transfer; see the National Assembly for Wales (Transfer of Functions) Order 1999 (S.I. 1999 No. 672; not reproduced in this work), art.2 and Sched. 1.

As to the exercise of functions of the Secretary of State under section 25(1) which are exercisable in relation to Scotland only after consultation with the Scottish Ministers, see the Scotland Act 1998 (Transfer of Functions to the Scottish Ministers etc.) Order 1999 (S.I. 1999 No. 1750; not reproduced in this work), art.4 and Sched. 3.]

School crossings

A20.37   **26. Arrangements for school crossing patrols**   *[Omitted.]*

    27.   *[Repealed]*

28. Stopping of vehicles at school crossings

(1) When . . . a vehicle is approaching a place in a road where [a person is] crossing or   **A20.38**
seeking to cross the road, a school crossing patrol wearing a uniform approved by the
Secretary of State shall have power, by exhibiting a prescribed sign, to require the person
driving or propelling the vehicle to stop it.

(2) When a person has been required under subsection (1) above to stop a vehicle—

  (a) he shall cause the vehicle to stop before reaching the place where the [person is]
  crossing or seeking to cross and so as not to stop or impede [his] crossing, and

  (b) the vehicle shall not be put in motion again so as to reach the place in question so
  long as the sign continues to be exhibited.

(3) A person who fails to comply with paragraph (a) of subsection (2) above, or who
causes a vehicle to be put in motion in contravention of paragraph (b) of that subsection,
shall be guilty of an offence.

(4) In this section—

  (a) "*prescribed sign*" means a sign of a size, colour and type prescribed by regulations
  made by the Secretary of State or, if authorisation is given by the Secretary of
  State for the use of signs of a description not so prescribed, a sign of that description;

  (b) "*school crossing patrol*" means a person authorised to patrol in accordance with
  arrangements under section 26 of this Act;

and regulations under paragraph (a) above may provide for the attachment of reflectors to
signs or for the illumination of signs.

(5) For the purposes of this section—

  (a) where it is proved that a sign was exhibited by a school crossing patrol, it shall be
  presumed, unless the contrary is proved, to be of a size, colour and type prescribed,
  or of a description authorised, under subsection (4)(b) above, and, if it was exhibited in circumstances in which it was required by the regulations to be illuminated,
  to have been illuminated in the prescribed manner; [and]

  (b) where it is proved that a school crossing patrol was wearing a uniform, the uniform
  shall be presumed, unless the contrary is proved, to be a uniform approved by the
  Secretary of State; . . .

[The Traffic Signs (Welsh and English Language Provisions) Regulations and General Directions 1985   **A20.39**
(S.I. 1985 No. 713) and the Traffic Signs Regulations and General Directions 1994 (S.I. 1994 No.
1519) below, were made in part under this section; the Transport Act 2000, s.270(1) and (3) (with effect
from January 30, 2001; see the Transport Act 2001 (Commencement No. 3) Order 2001 (S.I. 2001 No.
57; not reproduced in this work) and also the 2001 Act, s.274 and Sched. 31, Pt V(2).

As an exception to the transfer of functions to the National Assembly for Wales of functions of a
Minister of the Crown exercisable in relation to Wales (see the General note at p. 122 above), the func-
tions under section 28 have been expressly excluded from that transfer; see the National Assembly for
Wales (Transfer of Functions) Order 1999 (S.I. 1999 No. 672; not reproduced in this work), art.2
and Sched. 1.

As to the transfer of the function of the Secretary of State under section 28(4)(a) which is exercisable in
Scotland of authorising the use of signs of a description not prescribed by regulations under section 28(4)(a)
to the Scottish Ministers, see the Scotland Act 1998 (Transfer of Functions to the Scottish Ministers etc.)
Order 1999 (S.I. 1999 No. 1750; not reproduced in this work), art.2 and Sched. 1.]

*   *   *

PART IV

PARKING PLACES

Provision of off-street parking, and parking on roads without payment

A20.40   **32. Power of local authorities to provide parking places**   *[Omitted.]*

33. Additional powers of local authorities in connection with off-street parking places   *[Omitted.]*

34. Provision of access to premises through off-street parking places *[Omitted.]*

35. Provision as to use of parking places provided under section 32 or section 33

A20.41   (1) As respects any parking place—

     (a) provided by a local authority under section 32 of this Act, or

     (b) provided under any letting or arrangements made by a local authority under section 33(4) of this Act,

the local authority, subject to Parts I to III of Schedule 9 to this Act, may by order make provisions as to—

     (i) the use of the parking place, and in particular the vehicles or class of vehicles which may be entitled to use it,

     (ii) the conditions on which it may be used,

     (iii) the charges to be paid in connection with its use (where it is an off-street one), and

     (iv) the removal from it of a vehicle left there in contravention of the order and the safe custody of the vehicle,

[and the power under paragraph (iii) to make provision as to the payment of charges shall include power to make provision requiring those charges, or any part of them, to be paid by means of the hire or purchase in advance, or the use, of parking devices in accordance with the order].

(2) Where under section 34 of this Act a means of access to any premises has been provided by a local authority through an off-street parking place, then, subject to Parts I to III of Schedule 9 to this Act and to the provisions of any agreement made by the local authority under subsection (3) of section 34 and to any rights granted by them under that subsection, the authority may by an order under subsection (1) above make provision as to the use of the parking place as the means of access and, in particular, as to the vehicles or class of vehicles which may be entitled to use the means of access and as to the conditions on which the means of access may be used.

(3) An order under subsection (1) above may provide for a specified apparatus or device to be used—

     (a) as a means to indicate—

       (i) the time at which a vehicle arrived at, and the time at which it ought to leave, a parking place or one or other of those times, or

       (ii) the charges paid or payable in respect of a vehicle in an off-street parking place; or

     (b) as a means to collect any such charges,

and may make provision regulating the use of any such apparatus or device . . .

[(3A) An order under subsection (1) above may also provide—

(a) for regulating the issue, use and surrender of parking devices;

(b) for requiring vehicles to display parking devices when left in any parking place in respect of which the parking devices may be used;

(c) without prejudice to the generality of paragraph (b) above, for regulating the manner in which parking devices are to be displayed or operated;

(d) for prescribing the use, and the manner of use, of apparatus . . . designed to be used in connection with parking devices;

(e) for treating—

(i) the indication given by a parking device, or

(ii) the display or the failure to display a parking device on or in any vehicle left in any parking place,

as evidence (and, in Scotland, as sufficient evidence) of such facts as may be provided by the order;

(f) for the refund, in such circumstances and in such manner as may be prescribed in the order, of the whole or part of the amount of any charge paid in advance in respect of a parking device;

(g) for the payment of a deposit in respect of the issue of a parking device and for the repayment of the whole or any part of any such deposit.]

[(3B) In this section and in section 35A below "*parking device*" means either a card, disc, token, meter, permit, stamp or other similar device, whether used in a vehicle or not . . . which being used either by itself, or in conjunction with any such apparatus as is referred to in subsection (3A)(d) above—

(a) indicates, or causes to be indicated, the payment of a charge, and—

(i) the period in respect of which it has been paid and the time of the beginning or end of the period, or

(ii) whether or not the period for which it has been paid or any further period has elapsed, or

(iii) the period for which the vehicle in relation to which the parking device is used is permitted to park in the parking place, and the time of the beginning or end of the period, or

(iv) whether or not the period for which the vehicle in relation to which the parking device is used is permitted to park in the parking place or any further period has elapsed; or

(b) operates apparatus controlling the entry of vehicles to or their exit from the parking place, or enables that apparatus to be operated;

or any other device of any such description as may from time to time be prescribed for the purposes of this section and section 35A below by order made by the Secretary of State . . .]

[(3C) An order under subsection (3B) above which revokes or amends a previous order under that subsection may make such saving and transitional provision as appears to the Secretary of State to be necessary or expedient.]

[(3D) The power to make orders under subsection (3B) above is exercisable by statutory instrument which shall be subject to annulment in pursuance of a resolution of either House of Parliament.]

(4)–(9) *[Repealed.]*

[*Section 35 is printed as amended by the Road Traffic (Consequential Provisions) Act 1988, s.3*   **A20.42**
and Sched. 1; the Parking Act 1989, s.1; the Road Traffic Act 1991, ss.44(2), 83 and Sched. 8;

the Deregulation (Parking Equipment) Order 1996 (S.I. 1996 No. 1553), art.2(1)(a) and Schedule (not reproduced in this work).

    The amendments effected by the Parking Act 1989, s.1, are stated by section 1(5) not to affect the validity of orders under subsection (1) above which were made before May 16, 1990.]

[35A. Offences and proceedings in connection with parking places provided under section 32 or section 33

A20.43   (1) In the event of any contravention of, or non-compliance with, a provision of an order under section 35(1) above, the person responsible shall be guilty of an offence.

    (2) A person who, with intent to defraud—

       (a) interferes with any such apparatus or device mentioned in section 35(3) above as is by an order under section 35(1) above to be used for the collection of charges at an off-street parking place, or operates or attempts to operate it by the insertion of objects other than current coins or bank notes of the appropriate denomination, or the appropriate credit or debit cards, or

       (b) interferes with any such apparatus as is mentioned in section 35(3A)(d) above or with a parking device, or operates or attempts to operate any such apparatus or any parking device otherwise than in the manner prescribed, or

       (c) displays a parking device otherwise than in the manner prescribed,

shall be guilty of an offence.

    (3) An order under section 35(1) above may include provision—

       (a) for determining the person responsible for any contravention of or non-compliance with the order;

       (b) for treating—

          (i) the indications given by any such apparatus or device as is mentioned in section 35(3) above used in pursuance of the order, or

          (ii) the indications given by any such apparatus as is mentioned in section 35(3A)(d) above used in pursuance of the order, or any tickets issued by it, or the absence of any such ticket from a vehicle left in a parking place,

       as evidence . . . of such facts and for such purposes as may be provided by the order;

       (c) for applying with any appropriate adaptations any of the provisions of subsections (4) to (6) of section 47 of this Act.

    (4) *[Repealed.]*

    (5) While a vehicle is within a parking place, it shall not be lawful for the driver or conductor of the vehicle, or for any person employed in connection with it, to ply for hire or accept passengers for hire; and if a person acts in contravention of this subsection he shall be guilty of an offence.

    (6) In this section—

"*credit card*" means a card or similar thing issued by any person, use of which enables the holder to defer the payment by him of the charge for parking a vehicle; and

"*debit card*" means a card or similar thing issued by any person, use of which by the holder causes the charge for parking a vehicle to be paid by the electronic transfer of funds from any current account of his at a bank or other institution providing banking services.]

A20.44   *[Section 35A was inserted by the Parking Act 1989, s.2, and is printed as subsequently amended by the Deregulation (Parking Equipment) Order 1996 (S.I. 1996 No. 1553), art.2(1)(a) and Schedule (not reproduced in this work).*

Words in section 35A(3)(b) relating specifically and exclusively to Scotland have been omitted.

As to the possible disapplication of section 35A(1), see Schedule 3, paragraph 1(4), to the Road Traffic Act 1991 below.

As to the conduct of proceedings under section 35A(2), see the General note at p. 122 above.

For the application of the fixed penalty procedure to offences under subsection (1), see the Road Traffic Offenders Act 1988, Pt III and Sched. 3 below.]

[35B. Display of information

(1) The Secretary of State may make regulations requiring local authorities to display at off-street parking places provided by them under section 32 above such information about parking there as is specified in the regulations.   **A20.45**

(2) Regulations under this section may also—

  (a) require the display of any orders under section 35(1) above relating to the parking place;

  (b) specify the manner in which the information and orders are to be displayed;

  (c) exempt local authorities, in specified circumstances or subject to specified conditions, from the requirement to display information and orders, or to display them in the specified manner; and

  (d) provide, in relation to a parking place at which a local authority fails to comply with the regulations or with any specified provision of the regulations, that, except in any specified circumstances, any order under section 35(1) above shall be of no effect in its application to that parking place in so far as it requires the payment of any charge in connection with use of the parking place—

    (i) while the failure to comply continues, and

    (ii) as respects vehicles parked there when the failure to comply was remedied, during a specified period thereafter.

(3) Regulations under this section may make different provision for different circumstances and for different descriptions of parking place, and may exempt specified descriptions of parking place from any provision of the regulations.

(4) In any proceedings for contravention of, or non-compliance with, an order under section 35(1) above relating to an off-street parking place, it shall be assumed, unless the contrary is shown, that any relevant regulations under this section were complied with at all material times.]

[Section 35B was inserted by the Parking Act 1989, s.3.]   **A20.46**

35C. Variation of charges at off-street parking places by notice   *[Omitted.]*   **A20.47**

*   *   *

Parking on highways for payment

45. Designation of paying parking places on highways   *[Omitted.]*

46. Charges at, and regulation of, designated parking places

(1) Subject to Parts I to III of Schedule 9 to this Act the authority by whom a designation order is made [with respect to any parking place outside Greater London] shall by order prescribe any charges to be paid for vehicles left in a parking place designated by the order; and any such charge may be prescribed either—   **A20.48**

(a) as an amount (in this Act referred to as an "*initial charge*") payable in respect of an initial period and an amount (in this Act referred to as an "*excess charge*") payable, in addition to an initial charge, in respect of any excess over an initial period, or

(b) as an amount payable regardless of the period for which a vehicle is left.

[(1A) *[Prescription of charges by order.]*]

(2) The authority by whom a designation order is made may, subject to Parts I to III of Schedule 9 to this Act, by order make such provision as may appear to that authority to be necessary or expedient for regulating or restricting the use of any parking place designated by the order, or otherwise for or in connection with the operation of such a parking place, and in particular (but without prejudice to the generality of the foregoing words) provision—

(a) for regulating the time at which and the method by which any charge is to be paid and for requiring the use of apparatus (in this Act referred to as a "*parking meter*") . . ., being apparatus designed either—

(i) to indicate whether any charge has been paid and whether the period for which it has been paid or any further period has elapsed, or

(ii) to indicate the time and to issue tickets indicating the payment of a charge and the period in respect of which it has been paid;

(b) for treating the indications given by a parking meter or any ticket issued by it, or the absence of any such ticket from a vehicle left in a parking place, as evidence (and, in Scotland, sufficient evidence) of such facts as may be provided by the order;

[(c) for prohibiting the insertion in a parking meter of coins or bank notes additional to those inserted by way of payment of any charge, or for prohibiting the insertion or re-insertion in a parking meter of a credit or debit card additional to the original insertion of such a card.]

(d)–(k) *[Omitted.]*

(3) *[Periodical inspection of parking meters.]*

(4) *[Periodical inspection of apparatus.]*

[(5) In this section and in section 47 below, "*credit card*" and "*debit card*" have the meanings given by section 35A(6) above [*q.v.*].]

A20.49   *[Section 46 is printed as amended by the Parking Act 1989, s.4 and Schedule, para. 2; the Road Traffic Act 1991, s.64(1) and (2); the Deregulation (Parking Equipment) Order 1996 (S.I. 1996 No. 1553), art.2(1)(a) and Schedule (not reproduced in this work).*

The words printed within square brackets in section 46(1) (inserted by section 64(1) of the 1991 Act) have effect in designated London boroughs (as to which, see the note to section 8 above.]

A20.50   **46A. Variation of charges at designated parking places by notice**   *[Omitted.]*

47. Offences relating to designated parking places

A20.51   (1) A person who—

(a) being the driver of a vehicle, leaves the vehicle in a designated parking place otherwise than as authorised by or under an order relating to the parking place, or leaves the vehicle in a designated parking place for longer after the excess charge has been incurred than the time so authorised, or fails duly to pay any charge payable under section 45 of this Act, or contravenes or fails to comply with any provision of an order relating to the parking place as to the manner in which vehicles shall stand in, or be driven in or out of, the parking place, or

(b) whether being the driver of a vehicle or not, otherwise contravenes or fails to comply with any order relating to designated parking places,

shall, subject to section 48 of this Act, be guilty of an offence [; but this subsection does not apply in relation to any designated parking place in Greater London].

(2) In relation to an offence under paragraph (a) of subsection (1) above of leaving a vehicle for longer after the excess charge has been incurred than the time authorised by an order relating to the parking place, or failing duly to pay any charge payable under section 45 of this Act, the reference in that paragraph to the driver of a vehicle shall be construed as a reference to the person driving the vehicle at the time when it was left in the parking place.

(3) A person who, with intent to defraud, interferes with a parking meter, or operates or attempts to operate a parking meter by the insertion of objects other than current coins [or bank notes of the appropriate denomination, or the appropriate credit or debit cards], shall be guilty of an offence.

(4) Where, in any proceedings in England or Wales for an offence under this section of failing to pay any charge, it is proved that the amount which has become due, or any part of that amount, has not been duly paid, the court shall order the payment of the sum not paid; and any sum ordered to be paid by virtue of this subsection shall be recoverable as a penalty.

(5) *[Repealed.]*

(6) Where in any proceedings for an offence under this section of failing to pay an excess charge it is not proved that the excess charge had become due, but it is proved that an initial charge has not been paid, the defendant may be convicted of an offence under this section of failing to pay an initial charge.

(7) *[Repealed.]*

[Section 47 is printed as amended by the Road Traffic (Consequential Provisions) Act 1988, s.3   **A20.52**
and Sched. 1; the Parking Act 1989, s.4 and Schedule, para.3; the Road Traffic Act 1991, s.65(1); the Deregulation (Parking Equipment) Order 1996 (S.I. 1996 No. 1553), art.2(1)(a) and Schedule (not reproduced in this work).

The words printed within square brackets in section 47(1) (inserted by section 65(1) of the 1991 Act) have effect in designated London boroughs (as to which, see the note to section 8, above).

For the possible disapplication of section 47(1), see Schedule 3, paragraph 1(4) to the Road Traffic Act 1991.

As to the conduct of proceedings under section 47(3), see the General note at p. 122 above.

For the application of the fixed penalty procedure to offences under section 47(1), see the Road Traffic Offenders Act 1988, Pt III and Sched. 3 below.]

48. Acceptance of payment as bar to proceedings under section 47

(1) Where a parking meter relating to the space in which a vehicle is left in a designated   **A20.53**
parking place indicates that the period for which payment was made for the vehicle by an initial charge has expired, but the authority by whom the parking place is controlled are satisfied that the initial charge was not paid, acceptance by the authority of payment of the excess charge shall be a bar to proceedings for an offence under section 47(1)(a) of this Act of failing to pay the initial charge.

(2) Where in the case of any vehicle—

(a) an authorisation by way of such a certificate, other means of identification or device as is referred to in section 4(2), 4(3), 7(2) or 7(3) of this Act, or such a permit or token as is referred to in section 46(2)(i) of this Act [*q.v.*], has been issued with respect to the vehicle, and

(b) the authority by whom a designated parking place is controlled are satisfied that, in accordance with the terms on which the authorisation was issued, a charge has become payable and has not been paid in respect of any period for which the vehicle has been left in that parking place,

acceptance by that authority of payment of the amount of that charge shall be a bar to proceedings for an offence under section 47(1)(a) of this Act of failing duly to pay the charge.

49. Supplementary provisions as to designation orders and designated parking places

A20.54

(1) Where under a designation order vehicles may not be left at all times in the designated parking place—

(a) the parking place shall for the purposes of sections 46 and 47 of this Act be treated, as respects any time during which vehicles may not be left there in pursuance of the order, as if it were not designated by the order; and

(b) any vehicle left in the parking place which remains there at the beginning of a period during which vehicles may be left there in pursuance of the order shall, for the purposes of those sections, be treated as if it had been left there at the beginning of that period, but without prejudice to any rights or liabilities in respect of anything done or omitted at any time before the beginning, or after the end, of that period.

(2) *[Revocation of designation as a parking place.]*

(3) *[Repealed.]*

(4) Subject to Parts I to III of Schedule 9 to this Act, the authority by whom a parking place is designated under section 45 of this Act may by order empower the local authority, the chief officer of police or any other person specified by or under the order to provide for the moving, in case of emergency, of vehicles left in the parking place; to suspend the use of the parking place or any part of it on such occasions or in such circumstances as may be determined by or under the order; and to provide for the temporary removal of any parking meters installed at the parking place.

[(4A) A constable, or a person acting under the instructions (whether general or specific) of the chief officer of police, may suspend the use of a parking place designated under section 45 of this Act for not more than 7 days in order to prevent or mitigate congestion or obstruction of traffic, or danger to or from traffic, in consequence of extraordinary circumstances.]

(5) *[Acquisition of parking meters, etc.]*

(6) *[Exercise of powers by order.]*

A20.55

[Section 49 is printed as amended by the Road Traffic Act 1991, s.48 and Sched. 4, para.27; the Local Government (Wales) Act 1994, s.22(1) and Sched. 7, para.38(4).]

A20.56 **50.**   *[Repealed.]*

[51. Parking devices for designated parking places

A20.57

(1) Any power of a local authority to make charges under section 45 of this Act for vehicles left in a designated parking place shall include power to require those charges, or any part of them, to be paid by means of the hire or purchase in advance, or the use, of parking devices in accordance with any relevant provision of an order under section 46 of this Act.

(2) Any power of a local authority to make orders under section 46(2) of this Act shall include power by any such order to make provision—

(a) for regulating the issue, use and surrender of parking devices;

(b) for requiring vehicles to display parking devices when left in any parking place in respect of which the parking devices may be used;

(c) without prejudice to the generality of paragraph (b) above, for regulating the manner in which parking devices are to be displayed or operated;

(d) for prescribing the use, and the manner of use, of apparatus. . . designed to be used in connection with parking devices;

(e) for treating—

(i) the indications given by a parking device; or

(ii) the display or the failure to display a parking device on or in any vehicle left in any parking place,

as evidence . . . of such facts as may be provided by the order;

(f) for the refund, in such circumstances and in such manner as may be prescribed in the order, of the whole or part of the amount of any charge paid in advance in respect of a parking device;

(g) for the payment of a deposit in respect of the issue of a parking device and for the repayment of the whole or part of any such deposit.

(3) For the purposes of subsection (2) above—

(a) the references to parking meters in section 46(2)(b) and (c) of this Act shall include references to the apparatus referred to in subsection (2)(d) above; and

(b) the reference in section 46(2)(c) of this Act to the insertion in a parking meter of coins [or banknotes] additional to those inserted by way of payment of any charge [or to the insertion or re-insertion in a parking meter of a credit or debit card additional to the original insertion of such a card] shall include (so far as is appropriate) a reference to insertions or re-insertions in any such apparatus of parking devices additional to the original insertion of those devices.

(4) [In this section and in section 52 below *"parking device"* means either] a card, disc, token, meter, permit, stamp or other similar device, whether used in a vehicle or not . . . which, being used either by itself, or in conjunction with any such apparatus as is referred to in subsection (2)(d) above, indicates, or causes to be indicated, the payment of a charge, and—

(a) the period in respect of which it has been paid and the time of the beginning or end of the period; or

(b) whether [or not] the period for which it has been paid or any further period has elapsed [; or]

[(c) the period for which the vehicle in relation to which the parking device is used is permitted to park in the parking place, and the time of the beginning or end of the period; or]

[(d) whether or not the period for which the vehicle in relation to which the parking device is used is permitted to park in the parking place or any further period has elapsed;]

[or any other device of any such description as may from time to time be prescribed for the purposes of this section and section 52 below by order made by the Secretary of State . . .]

(4A) *[Saving and transitional provisions in orders.]*

(4B) *[Exercise of order-making power.]*

(5), (6) *[Repealed.]*

A20.58   *[Section 51 is printed as substituted by the Road Traffic Regulation (Parking) Act 1986, s.2(1), and as subsequently amended by the Parking Act 1989, s.4 and Schedule, para.4; the Road Traffic Act 1991, s.48 and Sched. 4, para.28; the Deregulation (Parking Equipment) Order 1996 (S.I. 1996 No. 1553), art.2(1)(a) and Schedule (not reproduced in this work).*

Words relating specifically and exclusively to Scotland have been omitted from section 51(2)(e).]

52. Offences and proceedings in connection with parking devices and associated apparatus

A20.59   (1) A person who, with intent to defraud,—

(a) interferes with any apparatus referred to in section 51(2)(d) of this Act or with a parking device, or operates or attempts to operate any such apparatus or any parking device otherwise than in the manner prescribed, or

(b) displays a parking device otherwise than in the manner prescribed,

shall be guilty of an offence.

(2) *[Repealed.]*

(3) In section 48(1) of this Act the reference to a parking meter relating to the space in which a vehicle is left in a designated parking place shall include references to—

(a) any such apparatus as is referred to in section 51(2)(d) of this Act which relates to the space in which a vehicle is so left, and

(b) to a parking device used in respect of a vehicle left in a space in a designated parking place.

A20.60   *[Section 52 is printed as amended by the Road Traffic (Consequential Provisions) Act 1988, s.3 and Sched. 1; the Deregulation (Parking Equipment) Order 1996 (S.I. 1996 No. 1553), art.2(1)(a) and Schedule (not reproduced in this work).*

As to the conduct of the proceedings under section 52(1), see the General note at p. 122 above.]

*   *   *

Special parking provisions

61. Loading areas

A20.61   (1) If it appears to [the council of a county, metropolitan district or London borough or the Common Council of the City of London] that any land in their area which is not part of a highway has been set apart by the occupier of the land for use as a place where vehicles may be driven and parked for the purpose of being loaded or unloaded in connection with a trade or business carried on or in the vicinity of the land, the council may, subject to Part III of Schedule 9 to this Act, by an order made with the consent of the owner and the occupier of the land—

(a) designate the land as an area to which the following provisions of this section apply (in this section referred to as a "*loading area*"), and

(b) specify the trade or business in question.

(2) A council which has made an order in pursuance of subsection (1) above—

(a) may vary the order by a subsequent order made with the consent of the owner and the occupier of the land to which the order relates;

(b) may revoke the order by a subsequent order made with the consent of the owner and the occupier of the loading area in question; and

(c) shall revoke the order by a subsequent order if requested in writing to do so by the owner and the occupier of the loading area in question.

(3) An order in pursuance of subsection (1) or (2)(a) above may contain provisions prohibiting the parking, in the loading area to which the order relates, of vehicles of such kinds as are specified in the order, except authorised vehicles, at all times or at times so specified, and may make different provision in pursuance of the preceding provisions of this subsection for different parts of the area; and in this subsection "*authorised vehicle*", in relation to a loading area, means a goods vehicle (as defined by [section 192(1) of the Road Traffic Act 1988]) which is in the area for the purpose of being loaded or unloaded in connection with the trade or business specified in the order designating the area.

(4) Where an order has been made by a council in pursuance of subsection (1) above and, by virtue of paragraph 22(1)(e) of Schedule 9 to this Act, traffic signs are required to be placed on the loading area to which the order relates, a person authorised in that behalf by the council may enter on the loading area for the purpose of placing any such traffic signs and for the purpose of maintaining or removing the signs.

(5) A person who, without reasonable excuse, causes a vehicle to be in any part of a loading area at a time when the parking of it there is prohibited by an order made in pursuance of subsection (1) above shall be guilty of an offence.

(6) References in subsections (2) to (5) above to an order made in pursuance of subsection (1) above include, in the case of such an order which has been varied in pursuance of subsection (2)(a) of this section, references to the order as so varied.

(7) Subsections (3) to (5) of section 44 of the Local Government (Miscellaneous Provisions) Act 1976 (which contain ancillary provisions for the purposes of Part I of that Act) shall have effect as if this section were included in that Part of that Act.

(8) In this section "*owner*", in relation to any land, means a person who, either on his own account or as agent or trustee for another person, is receiving the rackrent of the land or would be entitled to receive it if the land were let at a rackrent; and any reference to a traffic sign, in relation to any land which is not a road, includes a reference to any object, device, line or mark which would be a traffic sign (as defined by section 64 of this Act) if the land were a road.

[Section 61 is printed as amended by the Local Government Act 1985, s.8(1) and Sched. 5, Pt I, para.4(25); the Road Traffic (Consequential Provisions) Act 1988, s.4 and Sched. 3, para.25(2).   **A20.62**

As to the disapplication of section 61(5) in relation to designated parking areas, see the Road Traffic Act 1991, Sched. 3, para.2(4)(bb) below.]

*   *   *

PART V

TRAFFIC SIGNS

64. General provisions as to traffic signs

(1) In this Act "*traffic sign*" means any object or device (whether fixed or portable) for conveying, to traffic on roads or any specified class of traffic, warnings, information, requirements, restrictions or prohibitions of any description—   **A20.63**

(a) specified by regulations made by the Ministers acting jointly, or

(b) authorised by the Secretary of State,

and any line or mark on a road for so conveying such warnings, information, requirements, restrictions or prohibitions.

(2) Traffic signs shall be of the size, colour and type prescribed by regulations made as mentioned in subsection (1)(a) above except where the Secretary of State authorises the erection or retention of a sign of another character; and for the purposes of this subsection illumination, whether by lighting or by the use of reflectors or reflecting material, or the absence of such illumination, shall be part of the type or character of a sign.

(3) Regulations under this section may be made so as to apply either generally or in such circumstances only as may be specified in the regulations.

(4) Except as provided by this Act, no traffic sign shall be placed on or near a road except—

    (a) a notice in respect of the use of a bridge;

    (b) a traffic sign placed, in pursuance of powers conferred by a special Act of Parliament or order having the force of an Act, by the owners or operators of a tramway, light railway or trolley vehicle undertaking, a dock undertaking or a harbour undertaking; or

    (c) a traffic sign placed on any land—

        (i) by a person authorised under the following provisions of this Act to place the sign on a [road], and

        (ii) for a purpose for which he is authorised to place it on a [road].

(5) Regulations under this section, or any authorisation under subsection (2) above, may provide that [section 36 of the Road Traffic Act 1988] (drivers to comply with traffic directions) shall apply to signs of a type specified in that behalf by the regulations or, as the case may be, to the sign to which the authorisation relates.

(6) References in any enactment (including any enactment contained in this Act) to the erection or placing of traffic signs shall include references to the display of traffic signs in any manner, whether or not involving fixing or placing.

A20.64   *[Section 64 is printed as amended by the Road Traffic (Consequential Provisions) Act 1988, s.4 and Sched. 3, para.25(3); the New Roads and Street Works Act 1991, s.168(1) and Sched. 8, Pt II, para.47.*

As an exception to the transfer of functions to the National Assembly for Wales of functions of a Minister of the Crown exercisable in relation to Wales (see the General note at p. 122 above), the functions under section 64 (other than so far as section 64 confers the power to (i) prescribe a variant of any sign of a type prescribed by "the Ministers" and carrying words in English, being a variant identical with a sign of that type except for the substitution or addition of words in Welsh (and any increase in size needed to accommodate the substituted or added words); and (ii) authorise signs not otherwise prescribed) have been expressly excluded from that transfer; see the National Assembly for Wales (Transfer of Functions) Order 1999 (S.I. 1999 No. 672; not reproduced in this work), art.2 and Sched. 1.

As to the transfer of functions of the Secretary of State under section 64(1)(b) and (2) which are exercisable in relation to Scotland to the Scottish Ministers, see the Scotland Act 1998 (Transfer of Functions to the Scottish Ministers etc.) Order 1999 (S.I. 1999 No. 1750; not reproduced in this work), art.2 and Sched. 1. As to the exercise of functions of the Secretary of State under section 64(1)(a) which are exercisable in relation to Scotland only after consultation with the Scottish Ministers, see S.I. 1999 No. 1750, art.4 and Sched. 3.

The functions under section 64 which are exercisable jointly by the Secretaries of State charged with general responsibility under this Act in relation to England, Wales and Scotland, respectively, have been transferred to the Secretary of State with effect from December 27, 1999; see the Transfer of Functions (Road Traffic) Order 1999 (S.I. 1999 No. 3143; not reproduced in this work).

The Traffic Signs (Welsh and English Language Provisions) Regulations and General Directions 1985 (S.I. 1985 No. 713), and the Traffic Signs Regulations and General Directions 1994 (S.I. 1994 No. 1519), the Zebra, Pelican and Puffin Crossings Regulations and General Directions 1997 (S.I. 1997 No.

2400), and the Traffic Signs (Temporary Obstructions) Regulations 1997 (S.I. 1997 No. 3053) (q.v.) were made in part under this section.]

*   *   *

PART VI

SPEED LIMITS

81. General speed limit for restricted roads

(1) It shall not be lawful for a person to drive a motor vehicle on a restricted road at a speed exceeding 30 miles per hour.   **A20.65**

(2) The Ministers acting jointly may by order made by statutory instrument and approved by a resolution of each House of Parliament increase or reduce the rate of speed fixed by subsection (1) above, either as originally enacted or as varied under this subsection.

[Provision is made for the application of section 81 to directions in orders made under the Road Traffic Act 1934, s.1, by Sched. 10, para.14, to this Act (q.v.).   **A20.66**

As an exception to the transfer of functions to the National Assembly for Wales of functions of a Minister of the Crown exercisable in relation to Wales (see the General note at p. 122 above), the functions under section 81 have been expressly excluded from that transfer; see the National Assembly for Wales (Transfer of Functions) Order 1999 (S.I. 1999 No. 672; not reproduced in this work), art.2 and Sched. 1. The functions of the Ministers under section 81(2) are, however, exercisable only after consultation with the National Assembly; see S.I. 1999 No. 672, art.5(1) and Sched. 2.

As to the exercise of functions of the Ministers under section 81(2) which are exercisable in relation to Scotland only after consultation with the Scottish Ministers, see the Scotland Act 1998 (Transfer of Functions to the Scottish Ministers etc.) Order 1999 (S.I. 1999 No. 1750; not reproduced in this work), art.4 and Sched. 3.

The functions under section 81(2) which are exercisable jointly by the Secretaries of State charged with general responsibility under this Act in relation to England, Wales and Scotland, respectively, have been transferred to the Secretary of State with effect from December 27, 1999; see the Transfer of Functions (Road Traffic) Order 1999 (S.I. 1999 No. 3143; not reproduced in this work).]

82. What roads are restricted roads

(1) Subject to the provisions of this section and of section 84(3) of this Act, a road is a restricted road for the purposes of section 81 of this Act [if—   **A20.67**

   (a) in England and Wales, there is provided on it a system of street lighting furnished by means of lamps placed not more than 200 yards apart;

   (b) *[applies to Scotland.]*]

(2) [The traffic authority for a road may direct]

   (a) that [the road] which is a restricted road for the purposes of section 81 of this Act shall cease to be a restricted road for those purposes, or

   (b) that [the road] which is not a restricted road for those purposes shall become a restricted road for those purposes.

[(3) A special road is not a restricted road for the purposes of section 81 on or after the date declared by the traffic authority, by notice published in the prescribed manner, to be the date on which the special road, or the relevant part of the special road, is open for use as a special road.]

[Section 82 is printed as amended by the New Roads and Street Works Act 1991, s.168(1) and Sched. 8, Pt II, para.59(1)–(4).   **A20.68**

As to the transfer of functions of a Minister of the Crown under section 82(1)(b), (2) and (3) which are exercisable in relation to Scotland to the Scottish Ministers, see the Scotland Act 1998 (Transfer of Functions to the Scottish Ministers etc.) Order 1999 (S.I. 1999 No. 1750; not reproduced in this work), art.2 and Sched. 1.

Certain roads may be deemed to be roads subject to a direction under section 82(2)(a) by Sched. 10, para.16, to this Act (q.v.).]

83. Provisions as to directions under section 82(2)

A20.69   (1) [A direction under section 82(2) by the Secretary of State shall be given] by means of an order made by the Secretary of State after giving public notice of his intention to make an order.

[(2) A direction under section 82(2) by a local traffic authority shall be given by means of an order made by the authority.]

(3) Section 68(1)(c) of this Act shall apply to any order made under subsection (2) above.

A20.70   *[Section 83 is printed as amended by the New Roads and Street Works Act 1991, s.168(1) and Sched. 8, Pt II, para.60(1)–(3).*

As to the transfer of functions of the Secretary of State under section 83(1) which are exercisable in relation to Scotland to the Scottish Ministers, see the Scotland Act 1998 (Transfer of Functions to the Scottish Ministers etc.) Order 1999 (S.I. 1999 No. 1750; not reproduced in this work), art.2 and Sched. 1.]

84. Speed limits on roads other than restricted roads

A20.71   [(1) An order made under this subsection as respects any road may prohibit—

    (a) the driving of motor vehicles on that road at a speed exceeding that specified in the order,

    (b) the driving of motor vehicles on that road at a speed exceeding that specified in the order during periods specified in the order, or

    (c) the driving of motor vehicles on that road at a speed exceeding the speed for the time being indicated by traffic signs in accordance with the order.]

[(1A) An order made by virtue of subsection (1)(c) above may—

    (a) make provision restricting the speeds that may be indicated by traffic signs or the periods during which the indications may be given, and

    (b) provide for the indications to be given only in such circumstances as may be determined by or under the order;

but any such order must comply with regulations made under subsection (1B) below, except where the Secretary of State authorises otherwise in a particular case.]

[(1B) The Secretary of State may make regulations governing the provision which may be made by orders of local authorities under subsection (1)(c) above, and any such regulations may in particular—

    (a) prescribe the circumstances in which speed limits may have effect by virtue of an order,

    (b) prescribe the speed limits which may be specified in an order, and

    (c) make transitional provision and different provision for different cases.]

[(2) The power to make an order under subsection (1) is exercisable by the traffic authority, who shall before exercising it in any case give public notice of their intention to do so.]

(3) While an order [made by virtue of subsection (1)(a)] above is in force as respects a road, that road shall not be a restricted road for the purposes of section 81 of this Act.

(4) This section does not apply to any part of a special road which is open for use as a special road.

(5) Section 68(1)(c) of this Act shall apply to any order made under subsection (1) above.

[(6) Any reference in a local Act to roads subject to a speed limit shall, unless the contrary intention appears, be treated as not including a reference to roads subject to a speed limit imposed only by virtue of subsection (1)(b) or (c) above.]

[Section 84 is printed as amended by the New Roads and Street Works Act 1991, s.168(1) and Sched. **A20.72**
8, Pt II, para.61; the Road Traffic Act 1991, s.45(1)–(4).

Orders made before July 1, 1992 under section 84 do not apply to tramcars or trolley vehicles (other than duobuses): the Tramcars and Trolley Vehicles (Modification of Enactments) Regulations 1992 (S.I. 1992 No. 1217), reg.15 (q.v.). The application of such orders to duobuses is regulated by ibid., reg.16 (q.v.).

Certain speed limits which were in force before November 1, 1962 are deemed by Sched. 10, para.15, to this Act (q.v.) to have been imposed by orders under section 84(1).

The consent of the Secretary of State (under paragraph 13 or 14 of Schedule 9 to this Act) to the making of orders under section 84(1) which contain provisions applying a speed limit of 20 miles per hour to any road has been dispensed with after June 16, 1999 by the Road Traffic Regulation Act 1984 (Amendment) Order 1999 (S.I. 1999 No. 1608; not reproduced in this work).

As to the transfer of functions of the Secretary of State under section 84(1), (1A) and (1B) which are exercisable in relation to Scotland to the Scottish Ministers, see the Scotland Act 1998 (Transfer of Functions to the Scottish Ministers etc.) Order 1999 (S.I. 1999 No. 1750; not reproduced in this work), art.2 and Sched. 1.]

85. Traffic signs for indicating speed restrictions

(1) For the purpose of securing that adequate guidance is given to drivers of motor vehi- **A20.73**
cles as to whether any, and if so what, limit of speed is to be observed on any road, it shall be the duty of the Secretary of State, [in the case of a road for which he is the traffic authority, to] erect and maintain . . . traffic signs in such positions as may be requisite for that purpose.

(2) [In the case of any other road, it is the duty of the local traffic authority—]

    (a) to erect and maintain . . . traffic signs in such positions as may be requisite in order to give effect to general or other directions given by the Secretary of State for the purpose mentioned in subsection (1) above, and

    (b) to alter or remove traffic signs as may be requisite in order to give effect to such directions, either in consequence of the making of an order by the Secretary of State or otherwise.

(3) If a [local traffic authority] makes default in executing any works required for the performance of the duty imposed on them by subsection (2) above, the Secretary of State may himself execute the works; and the expense incurred by him in doing so shall be recoverable by him from the local authority and, in England or Wales, shall be so recoverable summarily as a civil debt.

(4) [Where no such system of street or carriageway lighting as is mentioned in section 82(1) is provided on a road], but a limit of speed is to be observed on the road, a person shall not be convicted of driving a motor vehicle on the road at a speed exceeding the limit unless the limit is indicated by means of such traffic signs as are mentioned in subsection (1) or subsection (2) above.

(5) In any proceedings for a contravention of section 81 of this Act, where the proceedings relate to driving on a road provided with [such a system of street or carriageway lighting], evidence of the absence of traffic signs displayed in pursuance of this section to indicate that the road is not a restricted road for the purposes of that section shall be evidence that the road is a restricted road for those purposes.

(6) Where by regulations made under section 17(2) of this Act a limit of speed is to be observed then, if it is to be observed—

    (a) on all special roads, or

    (b) on all special roads provided for the use of particular classes of traffic, or

    (c) on all special roads other than special roads of such description as may be specified in the regulations, or

    (d) as mentioned in paragraph (a), (b) or (c) above except for such lengths of special road as may be so specified,

this section shall not apply in relation to that limit (but without prejudice to its application in relation to any lower limit of maximum speed or, as the case may be, any higher limit of minimum speed, required by any such regulations to be observed on any specified length of any specified special road).

(7) The power to give general directions under subsection (2) above shall be exercisable by statutory instrument.

A20.74   *[Section 85 is printed as amended by the New Roads and Street Works Act 1991, s.168(1) and Sched. 8, Pt II, para.62(1)–(6); the Road Traffic Act 1991, ss.48, 83, Sched. 4, para.30, and Sched. 8.*

As an exception to the transfer of functions to the National Assembly for Wales of functions of a Minister of the Crown exercisable in relation to Wales (see the General note at p. 122 above), the function under section 85(2) (so far as it relates to the giving of general directions) has been expressly excluded from that transfer; see the National Assembly for Wales (Transfer of Functions) Order 1999 (S.I. 1999 No. 672; not reproduced in this work), art.2 and Sched. 1.

As to the transfer of functions of the Secretary of State under section 85(1) and (3) which are exercisable in relation to Scotland to the Scottish Ministers, and the function under section 85(2) of giving directions other than general directions, see the Scotland Act 1998 (Transfer of Functions to the Scottish Ministers etc.) Order 1999 (S.I. 1999 No. 1750; not reproduced in this work), art.2 and Sched. 1. As to the exercise of function of the Secretary of State of giving general directions with respect to traffic signs to indicate speed limits under section 85(2)(a) which are exercisable in relation to Scotland only after consultation with the Scottish Ministers, see S.I. 1999 No. 1750; not reproduced in this work), art.4 and Sched. 3.]

86. Speed limits for particular classes of vehicles

A20.75   (1) It shall not be lawful for a person to drive a motor vehicle of any class on a road at a speed greater than the speed specified in Schedule 6 to this Act as the maximum speed in relation to a vehicle of that class.

(2), (3) *[Omitted.]*

(4) *[Repealed by the New Roads and Street Works Act 1991, s.168(1) and (2), Sched. 8, Pt II, para.63, and Sched. 9.]*

(5), (6) *[Omitted.]*

A20.76   *[As an exception to the transfer of functions to the National Assembly for Wales of functions of a Minister of the Crown exercisable in relation to Wales (see the General note at p. 122 above), the functions under section 86 have been expressly excluded from that transfer; see the National Assembly for Wales (Transfer of Functions) Order 1999 (S.I. 1999 No. 672; not reproduced in this work), art.2 and Sched. 1.*

As to the exercise of functions of a Minister of the Crown under section 86(2) which are exercisable in relation to Scotland only after consultation with the Scottish Ministers, see the Scotland Act 1998 (Transfer of Functions to the Scottish Ministers etc.) Order 1999 (S.I. 1999 No. 1750; not reproduced in this work), art.4 and Sched. 3.]

87. Exemption of fire brigade, ambulance and police vehicles for speed limits

No statutory provisions imposing a speed limit on motor vehicles shall apply to any **A20.77** vehicle on an occasion when it is being used for fire brigade, ambulance or police purposes, if the observance of that provision would be likely to hinder the use of the vehicle for the purpose for which it is being used on that occasion.

88. Temporary speed limits

(1) Where it appears to the Secretary of State desirable to do so in the interests of safety **A20.78** or for the purpose of facilitating the movement of traffic, he may, after giving public notice of his intention to do so, by order prohibit, for a period not exceeding 18 months, the driving of motor vehicles—

    (a) on all roads, or on all roads in any area specified in the order, or on all roads of any class so specified, or on all roads other than roads of any class so specified, or on any road so specified, at a speed greater than that specified in the order, or

    (b) on any road specified in the order, at a speed less than the speed specified in the order, subject to such exceptions as may be so specified.

(2) Any prohibition imposed by an order under subsection (1) above may be so imposed either generally, or at times, on days or during periods specified in the order; but the provisions of any such order shall not, except in so far as may be provided by the order, affect the provisions of sections 81 to 84 of this Act.

(3) For the purposes of an order under subsection (1)(a) above, roads may be classified by reference to any circumstances appearing to the Secretary of State to be suitable for the purpose, including their character, the nature of the traffic to which they are suited or the traffic signs provided on them.

(4) The provisions of any order under subsection (1) above may be continued, either indefinitely or for a specified period, by an order of the Secretary of State made by statutory instrument, which shall be subject to annulment in pursuance of a resolution of either House of Parliament.

(5) Where by virtue of an order under this section a speed limit is to be observed, then—

    (a) if it is to be observed on all roads, on all roads of any class specified in the order or on all roads other than roads of any class so specified, section 85 of this Act shall not apply in relation to that limit;

    (b) if it is to be observed on all roads in any area and, at all points where roads lead into the area, is indicated as respects the area as a whole by means of such traffic signs as are mentioned in subsection (1) or subsection (2) of section 85 of this Act, the limit shall, for the purposes of subsection (4) of that section, be taken as so indicated with respect to all roads in the area.

(6) This section does not apply to any part of a special road which is open for use as a special road.

(7) If a person drives a motor vehicle on a road in contravention of an order under subsection (1)(b) above, he shall be guilty of an offence; but a person shall not be liable to be

convicted of so driving solely on the evidence of one witness to the effect that, in the opinion of the witness, he was driving the vehicle at a speed less than that specified in the order.

A20.79   *[As to the admissibility of evidence of speeding in respect of offences under section 88(7), see section 20 of the Road Traffic Offenders Act 1988 below.*

As an exception to the transfer of functions to the National Assembly for Wales of functions of a Minister of the Crown exercisable in relation to Wales (see the General note at p. 122 above), the functions under section 88 have been expressly excluded from that transfer; see the National Assembly for Wales (Transfer of Functions) Order 1999 (S.I. 1999 No. 672; not reproduced in this work), art.2 and Sched. 1.

As to the exercise of functions of the Secretary of State under section 88(1) and (4) which are exercisable in relation to Scotland only after consultation with the Scottish Ministers, see the Scotland Act 1998 (Transfer of Functions to the Scottish Ministers etc.) Order 1999 (S.I. 1999 No. 1750; not reproduced in this work), art.4 and Sched. 3.

As to notice of intended prosecution of offences under section 88(7), see the Road Traffic Offenders Act 1988, Sched. 1, para.1A below.

For the application of the fixed penalty procedure to offences under subsection (7), see the Road Traffic Offenders Act 1988, Pt III and Sched. 3 below.]

89. Speeding offences generally

A20.80   (1) A person who drives a motor vehicle on a road at a speed exceeding a limit imposed by or under any enactment to which this section applies shall be guilty of an offence.

(2) A person prosecuted for such an offence shall not be liable to be convicted solely on the evidence of one witness to the effect that, in the opinion of the witness, the person prosecuted was driving the vehicle at a speed exceeding a specified limit.

(3) The enactments to which this section applies are—

   (a) any enactment contained in this Act except section 17(2);

   (b) section 2 of the Parks Regulation (Amendment) Act 1926; and

   (c) any enactment not contained in this Act, but passed after 1st September 1960, whether before or after the passing of this Act.

(4) If a person who employs other persons to drive motor vehicles on roads publishes or issues any time-table or schedule, or gives any directions, under which any journey, or any stage or part of any journey, is to be completed within some specified time, and it is not practicable in the circumstances of the case for that journey (or that stage or part of it) to be completed in the specified time without the commission of such an offence as is mentioned in subsection (1) above, the publication or issue of the time-table or schedule, or the giving of the directions, may be produced as prima facie evidence that the employer procured or (as the case may be) incited the persons employed by him to drive the vehicles to commit such an offence.

A20.81   *[As to the admissibility of evidence of speeding in respect of offences under section 89(1), see section 20 of the Road Traffic Offenders Act 1988 below.*

As to notice of intended prosecution of offences under section 89(1), see the Road Traffic Offenders Act 1988, Sched. 1, para.1A below.

For the application of the fixed penalty procedure to offences under subsection (1), see the Road Traffic Offenders Act 1988, Pt III and Sched. 3 below.]

A20.82   **90, 91.**   *[Repealed.]*

*　　　*　　　*

PART VIII

CONTROL AND ENFORCEMENT

*   *   *

98.   *[Repealed.]*

Removal or immobilisation of vehicles

99. Removal of vehicles illegally, obstructively or dangerously parked, or abandoned or broken down

(1), (2) *[Power to make regulations for removal of vehicles.]*   A20.83

(3) *[Notice to occupier of land where vehicle is.]*

(4) *[Notice of intention to remove vehicle for destruction.]*

(5) In this section "*vehicle*" means any vehicle, whether or not it is in a fit state for use on roads, and includes any chassis or body, with or without wheels, appearing to have formed part of such a vehicle, and any load carried by, and anything attached to, such a vehicle.

[(6) *[Interpretation of section 99.]*]

[Section 99(6) (not reproduced) was inserted by the Road Traffic Act 1991, s.48 and Sched. 4, para.32.   A20.84
The definition in section 99(5) has been incorporated by reference into the Removal and Disposal of Vehicles (Loading Areas) Regulations 1986 (S.I. 1986 No. 184), reg.2 (q.v.), and the Removal and Disposal of Vehicles Regulations 1986 (S.I. 1986 No. 183), reg.2 (q.v.).
As an exception to the transfer of functions to the National Assembly for Wales of functions of a Minister of the Crown exercisable in relation to Wales (see the General note at p. 122 above), the functions under section 99 have been expressly excluded from that transfer; see the National Assembly for Wales (Transfer of Functions) Order 1999 (S.I. 1999 No. 672; not reproduced in this work), art.2 and Sched. 1.]

100. Interim disposal of vehicles removed under section 99   *[Omitted.]*   A20.85

101. Ultimate disposal of vehicles abandoned and removable under this Act   *[Omitted.]*

102. Charges for removal, storage and disposal of vehicles   *[Omitted.]*

103. Supplementary provisions as to removal of vehicles   *[Omitted.]*

104. Immobilisation of vehicles illegally parked

(1) Subject to sections 105 and 106 of this Act, where a constable finds on a road a   A20.86
vehicle which has been permitted to remain at rest there in contravention of any prohibition or restriction imposed by or under any enactment, he may—

  (a) fix an immobilisation device to the vehicle while it remains in the place in which he finds it; or

  (b) move it from that place to another place on the same or another road and fix an immobilisation device to it in that other place;

or authorise another person to take under his direction any action he could himself take by virtue of paragraph (a) or (b) above.

(2) On any occasion when an immobilisation device is fixed to a vehicle in accordance with this section the constable or other person fixing the device shall also affix to the vehicle a notice—

    (a) indicating that such a device has been fixed to the vehicle and warning that no attempt should be made to drive it or otherwise put it in motion until it has been released from that device;

    (b) specifying the steps to be taken in order to secure its release; and

    (c) giving such other information as may be prescribed.

(3) A vehicle to which an immobilisation device has been fixed in accordance with this section may only be released from that device by or under the direction of a [person authorised to give such a direction by the chief officer of police within whose area the vehicle in question was found].

(4) Subject to subsection (3) above, a vehicle to which an immobilisation device has been fixed in accordance with this section shall be released from that device on payment in any manner specified in the notice affixed to the vehicle under subsection (2) above of such charge in respect of the release as may be prescribed.

(5) A notice affixed to a vehicle under this section shall not be removed or interfered with except by or under the authority of the person in charge of the vehicle or the person by whom it was put in the place where it was found by the constable; and any person contravening this subsection shall be guilty of an offence.

(6) Any person who, without being authorised to do so in accordance with this section, removes or attempts to remove an immobilisation device fixed to a vehicle in accordance with this section shall be guilty of an offence.

(7) Where a vehicle is moved in accordance with this section before an immobilisation device is fixed to it, any power of removal under regulations for the time being in force under section 99 of this Act which was exercisable in relation to that vehicle immediately before it was so moved shall continue to be exercisable in relation to that vehicle while it remains in the place to which it was so moved.

(8) In relation to any vehicle which is removed in pursuance of any such regulations or under section 3 of the Refuse Disposal (Amenity) Act 1978 [*q.v.*] (duty of local authority to remove abandoned vehicles) from a place to which it was moved in accordance with this section, references in the definition of "person responsible" in section 102(8) of this Act and section 5 of the said Act of 1978 mentioned above (recovery from person responsible of charges and expenses in respect of vehicles removed) to the place from which the vehicle was removed shall be read as references to the place in which it was immediately before it was moved in accordance with this section.

(9) In this section "*immobilisation device*" means any device or appliance designed or adapted to be fixed to a vehicle for the purpose of preventing it from being driven or otherwise put in motion, being a device or appliance of a type approved by the Secretary of State for use for that purpose in accordance with this section.

(10) *[Repealed.]*

(11), (12) *[Omitted.]*

[(12A) For the purposes of this section, the suspension under section 13A or 49 of this Act of the use of a parking place is a restriction imposed under this Act.]

A20.87   *[Section 104 is printed as amended by the Road Traffic Act 1991, ss.48, 83, Sched. 4, paras 34(1) and (2), 35, and Sched. 8.*

Section 106 (to which section 104 is subject) states that sections 104 and 105 only extend to such areas as the Secretary of State specifies. The only known orders having effect under section 106 are the Immobilisation of Vehicles Illegally Parked (London Boroughs of Camden, Kensington and Chelsea, and Westminster, and the City of London) Order 1986 (S.I. 1986 No. 1225) and the Immobilisation of Vehicles Illegally Parked (London Borough of Hammersmith and Fulham) Order 1989 (S.I. 1989 No. 1746; not reproduced in this work). However, sections 104–106 of this Act have been applied to Crown roads in the royal parks (Hyde Park, Kensington Gardens, Regent's Park, St James's Park and Green Park in Greater London) as they apply in relation to other roads to which the public has access; Crown Roads (Royal Parks) (Application of Road Traffic Enactments) Order 1987 (S.I. 1987 No. 363), art.5 (not reproduced in this work).

The following immobilisation devices have been approved:

the "Wheelok 'P'"	*Immobilisation Devices (Approval) Order 1983*
the "Bulldog Model 11 T"	*Immobilisation Devices (Approval) Order 1983*
the "Wheelok Model P II"	*Immobilisation Devices (Approval) Order 1986*
the "Claw"	*Immobilisation Devices (Approval) Order 1987*
the "Prest On"	*Immobilisation Device Approval 1993*
the TMP "Professional" Wheel Clamp	*Immobilisation Device Approval 1997*
the TMP "Secura" Wheel Clamp	*Immobilisation Device Approval 1998*
the TMP "HGV" Wheel Clamp	*Immobilisation Device (No. 2) Approval 1998*

Neither the orders nor the approvals are published as statutory instruments. The 1983 order was dated April 22, 1983; the 1986 order was dated June 30, 1986; the 1987 order was dated November 2, 1987; the 1993 approval was dated October 2, 1993; the 1997 approval was dated January 29, 1997; the 1998 approval and the 1998 (No. 2) approval were both dated November 5, 1998.

As an exception to the transfer of functions to the National Assembly for Wales of functions of a Minister of the Crown exercisable in relation to Wales (see the General note at p. 122 above), the functions under section 104 have been expressly excluded from that transfer; see the National Assembly for Wales (Transfer of Functions) Order 1999 (S.I. 1999 No. 672; not reproduced in this work), art.2 and Sched. 1.

The Vehicles (Charges for Release from Immobilisation Devices) Regulations 1992 (S.I. 1992 No. 386; not reproduced in this work) prescribe the charge for release from an immobilisation device under section 104(4).]

105. Exemptions from section 104

(1) Subject to the following provisions of this section, section 104(1) of this Act shall not apply in relation to a vehicle found by a constable in the circumstances mentioned in that subsection if either— **A20.88**

(a) a current disabled person's badge is displayed on the vehicle; or

(b) the vehicle is in a meter bay within a parking place designated by a designation order.

(2) The exemption under subsection (1)(b) above shall not apply in the case of any vehicle [found otherwise than in Greater London] if—

(a) the meter bay in which it was found was not authorised for use as such at the time when it was left there (referred to below in this section as the time of parking); or

(b) an initial charge was not duly paid at the time of parking; or

(c) there has been since that time any contravention in relation to the relevant parking meter of any provision made by virtue of section 46(2)(c) of this Act; or

(d) more than two hours have elapsed since the end of any period for which an initial charge was duly paid at the time of parking or (as the case may be) since the end of any unexpired time in respect of another vehicle available on the relevant parking meter at the time of parking.

[(2A) The exemption under subsection (1)(b) above shall not apply in the case of any vehicle found in Greater London if the meter bay in which it was found was not authorised for use as such at the time when it was left there.]

(3) For the purposes of [subsections (2)(a) and (2A)] above, a meter bay in a parking place designated by a designation order is not authorised for use as such at any time when—

(a) by virtue of section 49(1)(a) of this Act the parking place is treated for the purposes of sections 46 and 47 of this Act as if it were not designated by that order; or

(b) the use of the parking place or of any part of it that consists of or includes that particular meter bay is suspended . . .

(4) In relation to any vehicle found in a meter bay within a parking place designated by a designation order, references in subsection (2) above to an initial charge are references to an initial charge payable in respect of that vehicle under section 45 or 50 of this Act.

(5) In any case where section 104(1) of this Act would apply in relation to a vehicle but for subsection (1)(a) above, the person guilty of contravening the prohibition or restriction mentioned in section 104(1) is also guilty of an offence under this subsection if the conditions mentioned in subsection (6) below are met.

(6) Those conditions are that at the time when the contravention occurred—

(a) the vehicle was not being used [in accordance with regulations under] section 21 of the Chronically Sick and Disabled Persons Act 1970 (badges for display on motor vehicles used by disabled persons); and

(b) he was not using the vehicle in circumstances falling within section [117(1)(b)] of this Act.

(7) In this section, "*meter bay*" means a parking space equipped with a parking meter; and the references in subsection (2) above to the relevant parking meter are references to the parking meter relating to the meter bay in which the vehicle in question was found.

A20.89   *[Section 105 is printed as amended by the Road Traffic Act 1991, ss.48, 81, 83, Sched. 4 (para.36(1)–(3)), Sched. 7 (para.6), and Sched. 8.*

As an exception to the transfer of functions to the National Assembly for Wales of functions of a Minister of the Crown exercisable in relation to Wales (see the General note at p. 122 above), the functions under section 105 have been expressly excluded from that transfer; see the National Assembly for Wales (Transfer of Functions) Order 1999 (S.I. 1999 No. 672; not reproduced in this work), art.2 and Sched. 1.]

A20.90   **106.** *[Initial experimental period for immobilisation of vehicles.]*

[106A. Immobilisation of vehicles in London

A20.91   (1) Sections 104 and 105 of this Act shall extend throughout Greater London if the Secretary of State makes an order to that effect.

(2) If such an order is made, section 106 of this Act shall cease to apply in relation to Greater London when the order comes into force.

(3) *[Amends section 106 before any order under subsection (2) above takes effect.]*

(4) *[Orders to be made by statutory instruments.]*]

A20.92   *[Section 106A was inserted by the Road Traffic Act 1991, s.75.]*

Enforcement of excess parking charges

107. Liability of vehicle owner in respect of excess parking charge

(1) This section applies where—   A20.93

  (a) an excess charge has been incurred in pursuance of an order under sections 45 and 46 of this Act;

  (b) notice of the incurring of the excess charge has been given or affixed as provided in the order; and

  (c) the excess charge has not been duly paid in accordance with the order;

and in the following provisions of this Part of this Act "*the excess charge offence*" means the offence under section 47 of this Act of failing duly to pay the excess charge.

(2) Subject to the following provisions of this section—

  (a) for the purposes of the institution of proceedings in respect of the excess charge offence against any person as being the owner of the vehicle at the relevant time, and

  (b) in any proceedings in respect of the excess charge offence brought against any person as being the owner of the vehicle at the relevant time,

it shall be conclusively presumed (notwithstanding that that person may not be an individual) that he was the driver of the vehicle at the time and, accordingly, that acts or omissions of the driver of the vehicle at that time were his acts or omissions.

(3) Subsection (2) above shall not apply in relation to any person unless, within the period of 6 months beginning on the day on which the notice of the incurring of the excess charge was given or affixed as mentioned in subsection (1)(b) above, a notice under section 108 of this Act has been served on him—

  (a) by or on behalf of the authority which is the local authority for the purposes of sections 45 and 46 of this Act in relation to the parking place concerned, or

  (b) by or on behalf of the chief officer of police.

(4) If the person on whom a notice under section 108 of this Act is served in accordance with subsection (3) above was not the owner of the vehicle at the relevant time, subsection (2) above shall not apply in relation to him if he furnishes a statutory statement of ownership to that effect in compliance with the notice.

(5) The presumption in subsection (2) above shall not apply in any proceedings brought against any person as being the owner of the vehicle at the relevant time if, in those proceedings, it is proved—

  (a) that at the relevant time the vehicle was in the possession of some other person without the consent of the accused, or

  (b) that the accused was not the owner of the vehicle at the relevant time and that he has a reasonable excuse for failing to comply with the notice under section 108 of this Act served on him in accordance with subsection (3) above.

108. Notice in respect of excess parking   A20.94

(1) A notice under this section shall be in the prescribed form, shall give particulars of the excess charge and shall provide that unless the excess charge is paid before the expiry of the appropriate period, the person on whom the notice is served—

  (a) is required, before the expiry of that period, to furnish to the authority or chief officer of police by or on behalf of whom the notice was served a statutory statement of ownership (as defined in Part I of Schedule 8 to this Act), and

(b) is invited, before the expiry of that period, to furnish to that authority or chief officer of police a statutory statement of facts (as defined in Part II of that Schedule).

(2) If, in any case where—

(a) a notice under this section has been served on any person, and

(b) the excess charge specified in the notice is not paid within the appropriate period,

the person so served fails without reasonable excuse to comply with the notice by furnishing a statutory statement of ownership he shall be guilty of an offence.

(3) If, in compliance with or in response to a notice under this section, any person furnishes a statement which is false in a material particular, and does so recklessly or knowing it to be false in that particular, he shall be guilty of an offence.

(4) Where a notice under this section has been served on any person in respect of any excess charge—

(a) payment of the charge by any person before the date on which proceedings are begun for the excess charge offence, or, as the case may be, for an offence under subsection (2) above in respect of a failure to comply with the notice, shall discharge the liability of that or any other person (under this or any other enactment) for the excess charge offence or, as the case may be, for the offence under subsection (2) above;

(b) conviction of any person of the excess charge offence shall discharge the liability of any other person (under this or any other enactment) for that offence and the liability of any person for an offence under subsection (2) above in respect of a failure to comply with the notice; and

(c) conviction of the person so served of an offence under subsection (2) above in respect of a failure to comply with the notice shall discharge the liability of any person for the excess charge offence;

but, except as provided by this subsection, nothing in section 107 of this Act or this section shall affect the liability of any person for the excess charge offence.

A20.95   *[As to the conduct of proceedings under section 108(3), see the General note at p. 122 above.]*

109. Modifications of sections 107 and 108 in relation to hired vehicles

A20.96   (1) This section shall apply where—

(a) a notice under section 108 of this Act has been served on a vehicle-hire firm, and

(b) at the relevant time the vehicle in respect of which the notice was served was let to another person by the vehicle-hire firm under a hiring agreement to which this section applies.

(2) Where this section applies, it shall be a sufficient compliance with the notice served on the vehicle-hire firm if the firm furnishes to the chief officer of police or local authority by or on behalf of whom the notice was served a statement in the prescribed form, signed by or on behalf of the vehicle-hire firm, stating that at the relevant time the vehicle concerned was hired under a hiring agreement to which this section applies, together with—

(a) a copy of that hiring agreement, and

(b) a copy of a statement of liability in the prescribed form, signed by the hirer under that hiring agreement;

and accordingly, in relation to the vehicle-hire firm on whom the notice was served, the reference in section 108(2) of this Act to a statutory statement of ownership shall be construed as a reference to a statement under this subsection together with the documents specified in paragraphs (a) and (b) above.

(3) If, in a case where this section applies, the vehicle-hire firm has complied with the notice served on the firm by furnishing the statement and copies of the documents specified in subsection (2) above, then sections 107 and 108 of this Act shall have effect as if in those provisions—

(a) any reference to the owner of the vehicle were a reference to the hirer under the hiring agreement, and

(b) any reference to a statutory statement of ownership were a reference to a statutory statement of hiring.

(4) Where, in compliance with a notice under section 108 of this Act, a vehicle-hire firm has furnished copies of a hiring agreement and statement of liability as mentioned in subsection (2) above, a person authorised in that behalf by the chief officer of police or local authority to whom the documents are furnished may, at any reasonable time within 6 months after service of that notice, and on production of his authority, require the production by the firm of the originals of those documents; and if, without reasonable excuse, a vehicle-hire firm fails to produce the original of a document when required to do so under this subsection, the firm shall be treated as not having complied with the notice under section 108 of this Act.

(5) This section applies to a hiring agreement, under the terms of which the vehicle concerned is let to the hirer for a fixed period of less than 6 months (whether or not that period is capable of extension by agreement between the parties or otherwise); and any reference in this section to the currency of the hiring agreement includes a reference to any period during which, with the consent of the vehicle-hire firm, the hirer continues in possession of the vehicle as hirer, after the expiry of the fixed period specified in the agreement, but otherwise on terms and conditions specified in it.

(6) In this section "*statement of liability*" means a statement made by the hirer under a hiring agreement to which this section applies to the effect that the hirer acknowledges that he will be liable, as the owner of the vehicle, in respect of any excess charge which, during the currency of the hiring agreement, may be incurred with respect to the vehicle in pursuance of an order under sections 45 and 46 of this Act.

(7) In this section—

"*hiring agreement*" refers only to an agreement which contains such particulars as may be prescribed and does not include a hire-purchase agreement within the meaning of the Consumer Credit Act 1974, and

"*vehicle-hire firm*" means any person engaged in hiring vehicles in the course of a business.

[*The term "hire-purchase agreement" (see section 109(7) above) is defined by the Consumer Credit Act*   **A20.97**
1974, s.189(1), as follows:

"*hire-purchase agreement*" means an agreement, other than a conditional sale agreement, under which—

(a) goods are bailed . . . in return for periodical payments by the person to whom they are bailed . . ., and

(b) the property in the goods will pass to that person if the terms of the agreement are complied with and one or more of the following occurs—

(i) the exercise of an option to purchase by that person,

(ii) the doing of any other specified act by any party to the agreement,

(iii) the happening of any other specified event;

The following definition appears in ibid., s.189(1):

"*conditional sale agreement*" means an agreement for the sale of goods or land under which the purchase price or part of it is payable by instalments, and the property in the goods or land is to remain in the seller (notwithstanding that the buyer is to be in possession of the goods or land) until such conditions as to the payment of instalments or otherwise as may be specified in the agreement are fulfilled;]]

110. Time for bringing, and evidence in, proceedings for certain offences

A20.98   (1) Proceedings in England and Wales for an offence under section 108(3) of this Act may be brought within a period of six months from the date on which evidence sufficient in the opinion of the prosecutor to warrant the proceedings came to his knowledge; but no such proceedings shall be brought by virtue of this section more than 3 years after the commission of the offence.

(2) *[Applies to Scotland.]*

(3) For the purposes of subsections (1) and (2) above a certificate signed by or on behalf of the prosecutor or, as the case may be, the Lord Advocate or the local authority, and stating the date on which evidence such as is mentioned in the subsection in question came to his or their knowledge, shall be conclusive evidence of that fact; and a certificate stating that matter and purporting to be so signed shall be deemed to be so signed unless the contrary is proved.

(4) Where any person is charged with the offence of failing to pay an excess charge, and the prosecutor produces to the court any of the statutory statements in Schedule 8 to this Act or a copy of a statement of liability (within the meaning of section 109 of this Act) purporting—

(a) to have been furnished in compliance with or in response to a notice under section 108 of this Act, and

(b) to have been signed by the accused,

the statement shall be presumed, unless the contrary is proved, to have been signed by the accused and shall be evidence . . . in the proceedings of any facts stated in it tending to show that the accused was the owner, the hirer or the driver of the vehicle concerned at a particular time.

A20.99   *[Words relating exclusively and expressly to Scotland have been omitted from section 110(4).]*

A20.100   111. Supplementary provisions as to excess charges

(1) The provisions of Schedule 8 to this Act shall have effect for the purposes of sections 107 to 109 of this Act (in this section referred to as "*the specified sections*").

(2) In the specified sections—

"*appropriate period*", in relation to a notice under section 108 of this Act, means the period of 14 days from the date on which the notice is served, or such longer period as may be specified in the notice or as may be allowed by the chief officer of police or authority by or on behalf of whom the notice is served;

"*driver*", in relation to an excess charge and in relation to an offence of failing duly to pay such a charge, means the person driving the vehicle at the time when it is alleged to have been left in the parking place concerned;

"*relevant time*", in relation to an excess charge, means the time when the vehicle was left in the parking place concerned, notwithstanding that the period in respect of which the excess charge was incurred did not begin at that time.

(3) For the purposes of the specified sections the owner of a vehicle shall be taken to be the person by whom the vehicle is kept; and for the purpose of determining, in the course of any proceedings brought by virtue of the specified sections, who was the owner of the vehicle at any time, it shall be presumed that the owner was the person who was the registered keeper of the vehicle at that time.

(4) Notwithstanding the presumption in subsection (3) above, it shall be open to the defence in any proceedings to prove that the person who was the registered keeper of a vehicle at a particular time was not the person by whom the vehicle was kept at that time, and it shall be open to the prosecution to prove that the vehicle was kept by some other person at that time.

(5) A notice under section 108 of this Act may be served on any person—

(a) by delivering it to him or by leaving it at his proper address, or

(b) by sending it to him by post;

and, where the person on whom such a notice is to be served is a body corporate, it shall be duly served if it is served on the secretary or clerk of that body.

(6) For the purposes of subsection (5) above and of section 7 of the Interpretation Act 1978 (references to service by post) in its application to that subsection, the proper address of any person on whom such a notice is to be served—

(a) shall, in the case of the secretary or clerk of a body corporate, be that of the registered or principal office of that body or the registered address of the person who is the registered keeper of the vehicle concerned at the time of service, and

(b) shall in any other case be the last known address of the person to be served.

(7) References in this section to the person who was or is the registered keeper of a vehicle at any time are references to the person in whose name the vehicle was or is at that time registered under [the Vehicle Excise and Registration Act 1994]; and, in relation to any such person, the reference in subsection (6)(a) above to that person's registered address is a reference to the address recorded in the record kept under that Act with respect to that vehicle as being that person's address.

(8) For the purposes of sections 1(2) and 2(1) of the Magistrates' Courts Act 1980 (power to issue summons or warrant and jurisdiction to try offences), any offence under subsection (2) of section 108 of this Act shall be treated as committed at any address which at the time of service of the notice under that section to which the offence relates was the accused's proper address (in accordance with subsection (6) above) for the service of any such notice as well as at the address to which any statutory statement furnished in response to that notice is required to be returned in accordance with the notice.

[Section 111 is printed as amended by the Vehicle Excise and Registration Act 1994, s.63 and Sched. 3, para.18(1).]   **A20.101**

PART IX

FURTHER PROVISIONS AS TO ENFORCEMENT

General provisions

112. Information as to identity of driver or rider

(1) This section applies to any offence under any of the foregoing provisions of this Act except—   **A20.102**

   (a) sections 43, 52, 88(7), 104, 105 and 108;

   (b) the provisions of subsection (2) or (3) of section 108 as modified by subsections (2) and (3) of section 109; and

   (c) section [35A(5)] in its application to England and Wales.

(2) Where the driver of a vehicle is alleged to be guilty of an offence to which this section applies—

   (a) the person keeping the vehicle shall give such information as to the identity of the driver as he may be required to give—

      (i) by or on behalf of a chief officer of police, or

     (ii) in the case of an offence under section [35A(1)] or against section 47 of this Act, by or on behalf of a chief officer of police or, in writing, by or on behalf of the local authority for the parking place in question; and

   (b) any other person shall, if required as mentioned in paragraph (a) above, give any information which it is in his power to give and which may lead to the identification of the driver.

(3) In subsection (2) above, references to the driver of a vehicle include references to a person riding a bicycle or tricycle (not being a motor vehicle); and—

   (a) *[Repealed.]*

   (b) in relation to an offence under section 61(5) of this Act, subsection (2)(a) above shall have effect as if, for subparagraphs (i) and (ii), there were substituted the words "by a notice in writing given to him by a local authority in whose area the loading area in question is situated",

and in subsection (2)(a) above, as modified by paragraph (b) of this subsection, "*local authority*" means any of the following, that is to say, a county council, . . . a district council, a London borough council and the Common Council of the City of London.

(4) Except as provided by subsection (5) below, a person who fails to comply with the requirements of subsection (2)(a) above shall be guilty of an offence unless he shows to the satisfaction of the court that he did not know, and could not with reasonable diligence have ascertained, who was the driver of the vehicle or, as the case may be, the rider of the bicycle or tricycle; and a person who fails to comply with the requirements of subsection (2)(b) above shall be guilty of an offence.

(5) *[Applies to Scotland.]*

[Section 112 is printed as amended by the Local Government Act 1985, s.102(2) and Sched. 17; the Parking Act 1989, s.4 and Schedule, para.6.]

113.   *[Repealed.]*

114.   *[Repealed.]*

115. Mishandling of parking documents and related offences

[(1) A person shall be guilty of an offence who, with intent to deceive—

   (a) uses, or lends to, or allows to be used by, any other person,—

      (i) any parking device or apparatus designed to be used in connection with parking devices;

     (ii) any ticket issued by a parking meter, parking device or apparatus designed to be used in connection with parking devices;

(iii) any authorisation by way of such a certificate, other means of identification or device as is referred to in any of sections 4(2), 4(3), 7(2) and 7(3) of this Act; or

(iv) any such permit or token as is referred to in section 46(2)(i) of this Act;

(b) makes or has in his possession anything so closely resembling any such thing as is mentioned in paragraph (a) above as to be calculated to deceive; or

(c) *[applies to Scotland.]*]

(2) A person who knowingly makes a false statement for the purpose of procuring the grant or issue to himself or any other person of any such authorisation as is mentioned in subsection (1) above shall be guilty of an offence.

(2A) *[Repealed.]*

(3) *[Applies to Scotland.]*

A20.106

[Section 115 is printed as amended by the Road Traffic Regulation (Parking) Act 1986, s.2(2); the Deregulation (Parking Equipment) Order 1996 (S.I. 1996 No. 1553), art.2(1)(a) and Schedule (not reproduced in this work).

As to the conduct of proceedings under section 115(1) and (2), see the General note to this Act at p. 122 above.]

116. Provisions supplementary to section 115

A20.107

(1) If any person authorised in that behalf by or under a designation order has reasonable cause to believe that a document or article carried on a vehicle, or by the driver or person in charge of a vehicle, is a document or article in relation to which an offence has been committed under subsection (1) of section 115 of this Act (so far as that subsection relates to such authorisations as are referred to in it) or under subsection (2) of that section, he may detain that document or article, and may for that purpose require the driver or person in charge of the vehicle to deliver up the document or article; and if the driver or person in charge of the vehicle fails to comply with that requirement, he shall be guilty of an offence.

(2) When a document or article has been detained under subsection (1) above and—

(a) at any time after the expiry of 6 months from the date when that detention began no person has been charged since that date with an offence in relation to the document or article under subsection (1) or (2) of section 115 of this Act, and

(b) the document or article has not been returned to the person to whom the authorisation in question was issued or to the person who at that date was the driver or person in charge of the vehicle,

then, on an application made for the purpose to a magistrates' court . . ., the court shall make such order respecting disposal of the document or article and award such costs . . . as the justice of the case may require.

(3) Any of the following, but no other, persons shall be entitled to make an application under subsection (2) above with respect to a document or article, that is to say—

(a) the person to whom the authorisation was issued;

(b) the person who, at the date when the detention of the document or article began, was the driver or person in charge of the vehicle; and

(c) the person for the time being having possession of the document or article.

A20.108

[Words relating exclusively and expressly to Scotland in section 116(2) have been omitted. As to the conduct of proceedings under section 116(1), see the General note at p. 122 above.]

A20.109   **117. Wrongful use of disabled person's badge**

[(1) A person who at any time acts in contravention of, or fails to comply with, any provision of an order under this Act relating to the parking of motor vehicles is also guilty of an offence under this section if at that time—

    (a) there was displayed on the motor vehicle in question a badge of a form prescribed under section 21 of the Chronically Sick and Disabled Persons Act 1970, and

    (b) he was using the vehicle in circumstances where a disabled person's concession would be available to a disabled person's vehicle,

but he shall not be guilty of an offence under this section if the badge was issued under that section and displayed in accordance with regulations made under it.]

    (2) *[Repealed.]*

    (3) In this section—

    . . .

"disabled person's concession" means—

    (a) an exemption from an order under this Act given by reference to disabled persons' vehicles; or

    (b) a provision made in any order under this Act for the use of a parking place by disabled persons' vehicles.

A20.110   *[Section 117 is printed as amended by the Road Traffic Act 1991, ss.35(6), 83, and Sched. 8.*

Disabled persons' badges are in the form prescribed in the Schedule to the Disabled Persons (Badges for Motor Vehicles) (England) Regulations 2000 (S.I. 2000 No. 682; not reproduced in this work) and in the Schedule to the Disabled Persons (Badges for Motor Vehicles) (Wales) Regulations 2000 (S.I. 2000 No. 1786; not reproduced in this work) which were made under the Chronically Sick and Disabled Persons Act 1970, s.21. (q.v.).]

A20.111   **118.**   *[Repealed.]*

        119.   *[Applies to Scotland.]*

        120, 121.   *[Repealed.]*

PART X

GENERAL AND SUPPLEMENTARY PROVISIONS

*   *   *

[121A. Traffic authorities

A20.112   (1) The Secretary of State is the traffic authority—

    (a) for every highway in England and Wales for which he is the highway authority within the meaning of the Highways Act 1980, and

    (b) *[applies to Scotland.]*

    [(1A) Transport for London is the traffic authority for every GLA road.]

    (2) In Greater London, the council of the London borough or the Common Council of the City of London are the traffic authority for all roads in the borough or, as the case may

be, in the City [which are not GLA roads and] for which the Secretary of State is not the traffic authority.

(3) In England and Wales outside Greater London, the council of the county or metropolitan district are the traffic authority for all roads in the county or, as the case may be, the district for which the Secretary of State is not the traffic authority.

(4) [*Applies to Scotland.*]

(5) In this Act "*local traffic authority*" means a traffic authority other than the Secretary of State.]

[*Section 121A was inserted by the New Roads and Street Works Act 1991, s.168(1) and Sched. 8, Pt II, para.70; the Greater London Authority Act 1999, s.271 (which, inter alia, inserted section 121(1A)).*   **A20.113**
A different section 121A(1A) has been inserted by the Scotland Act 1998 (Consequential Modifications) (No. 2) Order 1999 (S.I. 1999 No. 1820), art.2(3) and Sched. 2, Pt 1, para.73; this provision reads:

(1A) The Scottish Ministers are the traffic authority for every road in Scotland for which they are the roads authority within the meaning of the Roads (Scotland) Act 1984.]

**121B. London borough council exercising powers so as to affect another   A20.114
traffic authority's roads**   [*Omitted.*]

121C. Functions of GLA under this Act to be exercised by the Mayor
[*Omitted.*]

*   *   *

130. Application of Act to Crown

(1) Subject to the provisions of this section and section 132 of this Act, the provisions of   **A20.115**
this Act specified in subsection (2) below shall apply to vehicles and persons in the public service of the Crown.

(2) The provisions referred to in subsection (1) above are—

(a) sections 1 to 5, 9 [to 16C], 21 to 26, 38, 42, 45 to 51, 52 . . . (3), 58 to 60, 62 to 67, 69 to 71, [76 to 90], 99, 100, 104, 105, 125 and 126;

(b) except in relation to vehicles and persons in the armed forces of the Crown when on duty, sections 6 to 8; and

(c) . . .

(3) In relation to vehicles used for naval, military or air force purposes, while being driven by persons for the time being subject to the orders of a member of the armed forces of the Crown, the Secretary of State may by regulations vary the provisions of any statutory provision imposing a speed limit on motor vehicles; but regulations under this subsection may provide that any variation made by the regulations shall have effect subject to such conditions as may be specified in the regulations.

(4) [*Repealed.*]

(5) [*Repealed.*]

[*Section 130 is printed as amended by the Road Traffic (Consequential Provisions) Act 1988, s.3(1) and   **A20.116**
Sched. 1, Pt I; the New Roads and Street Works Act 1991, s.168(1) and Sched. 8, Pt II, para.74; the Road Traffic Regulation (Special Events) Act 1994, s.3(1) and Schedule, para.3; the Deregulation (Parking Equipment) Order 1996 (S.I. 1996 No. 1553), art.2(1)(a) and Schedule (not reproduced in this work).*
Section 132 of this Act (to which this section is subject) makes special provision regarding certain Crown roads.]

As to the effect of section 130(3) in relation to vehicles used for the purposes of a visiting force or head-quarters (as defined), when being driven by a person subject to the orders of a member of such a force or head-quarters, see the Visiting Forces and International Headquarters (Application of Law) Order 1999 (S.I. 1999 No. 1736; not reproduced in this work), art.8(3).

As an exception to the transfer of functions to the National Assembly for Wales of functions of a Minister of the Crown exercisable in relation to Wales (see the General note at p. 122 above), the functions under section 130 have been expressly excluded from that transfer; see the National Assembly for Wales (Transfer of Functions) Order 1999 (S.I. 1999 No. 672; not reproduced in this work), art.2 and Sched. 1.]

*   *   *

136. Meaning of "motor vehicle" and other expressions relating to vehicles

A20.117   (1) In this Act, subject to section 20 of the Chronically Sick and Disabled Persons Act 1970 (which makes special provision with respect to invalid carriages), "*motor vehicle*" means a mechanically propelled vehicle intended or adapted for use on roads and "*trailer*" means a vehicle drawn by a motor vehicle.

(2) In this Act "*motor car*" means a mechanically propelled vehicle, not being a motor cycle or an invalid carriage, which is constructed itself to carry a load or passengers and of which the weight unladen—

  (a) if it is constructed solely for the carriage of passengers and their effects, is adapted to carry not more than 7 passengers exclusive of the driver, and is fitted with tyres of such type as may be specified in regulations made by the Secretary of State, does not exceed 3050 kilograms;

  (b) if it is constructed or adapted for use for the conveyance of goods or burden of any description, does not exceed 3050 kilograms (or 3500 kilograms if the vehicle carries a container or containers for holding, for the purposes of its propulsion, any fuel which is wholly gaseous at 17.5 degrees Celsius under a pressure of 1.013 bar or plant and materials for producing such fuel); or

  (c) in a case falling within neither of the foregoing paragraphs, does not exceed 2540 kilograms.

(3) In this Act "*heavy motor car*" means a mechanically propelled vehicle, not being a motor car, which is constructed itself to carry a load or passengers and of which the weight unladen exceeds 2540 kilograms.

(4) In this Act (except for the purposes of [sections 57 and 63]) "*motor cycle*" means a mechanically propelled vehicle (not being an invalid carriage) with fewer than 4 wheels, of which the weight unladen does not exceed 410 kilograms.

(5) In this Act "*invalid carriage*" means a mechanically propelled vehicle of which the weight unladen does not exceed 254 kilograms and which is specially designed and con-structed, and not merely adapted, for the use of a person suffering from some physical default or disability and is used solely by such a person.

(6) In this Act "*motor tractor*" means a mechanically propelled vehicle which is not con-structed itself to carry a load, other than excepted articles, and of which the weight unladen does not exceed 7370 kilograms.

(7) In this Act "*light locomotive*" and "*heavy locomotive*" mean a mechanically propelled vehicle which is not constructed itself to carry a load, other than excepted articles, and of which the weight unladen—

  (a) in the case of a light locomotive, exceeds 7370 but does not exceed 11690 kilo-grams, and

  (b) in the case of a heavy locomotive, exceeds 11690 kilograms.

(8) In subsections (6) and (7) above *"excepted articles"* means any of the following, that is to say, water, fuel, accumulators and other equipment used for the purpose of propulsion, loose tools and loose equipment.

[*As an exception to the transfer of functions to the National Assembly for Wales of functions of a Minister*   **A20.118**
of the Crown exercisable in relation to Wales (see the General note at p. 122 above), the functions under section 136 have been expressly excluded from that transfer; see the National Assembly for Wales (Transfer of Functions) Order 1999 (S.I. 1999 No. 672; not reproduced in this work), art.2 and Sched. 1.
     Section 136 is printed as amended by the Transport Act 2000, s.271(1) and (3) (with effect from February 1, 2001; see the Transport Act 2001 (Commencement No. 3) Order 2001 (S.I. 2001 No. 57; not reproduced in this work).]

137. Supplementary provisions relating to section 136

(1) A side-car attached to a motor vehicle shall, if it complies with such conditions as   **A20.119**
may be specified in regulations made by the Secretary of State, be regarded as forming part of the vehicle to which it is attached and not as being a trailer.

(2) For the purposes of section 136 of this Act, in a case where a motor vehicle is so constructed that a trailer may by partial superimposition be attached to the vehicle in such a manner as to cause a substantial part of the weight of the trailer to be borne by the vehicle, that vehicle shall be deemed to be a vehicle itself constructed to carry a load.

(3) For the purposes of that section, in the case of a motor vehicle fitted with a crane, dynamo, welding plant or other special appliance or apparatus which is a permanent or essentially permanent fixture, the appliance or apparatus shall not be deemed to constitute a load or goods or burden of any description, but shall be deemed to form part of the vehicle.

(4) The Secretary of State may by regulations vary any of the maximum or minimum weights specified in section 136 of this Act; and such regulations may have effect—

(a) either generally or in the case of vehicles of any class specified in the regulations, and

(b) either for the purposes of this Act and of all regulations made under it or for such of those purposes as may be so specified.

(5) Nothing in section 86 of this Act shall be construed as limiting the powers conferred by subsection (4) above.

[*As an exception to the transfer of functions to the National Assembly for Wales of functions of a*   **A20.120**
Minister of the Crown exercisable in relation to Wales (see the General note at p. 122 above), the functions under section 137 have been expressly excluded from that transfer; see the National Assembly for Wales (Transfer of Functions) Order 1999 (S.I. 1999 No. 672; not reproduced in this work), art.2 and Sched. 1.]

138. Meaning of "heavy commercial vehicle"

(1) Subject to subsections (4) to (7) below, in this Act *"heavy commercial vehicle"* means any   **A20.121**
goods vehicle which has an operating weight exceeding 7.5 tonnes.

(2) The operating weight of a goods vehicle for the purposes of this section is—

(a) in the case of a motor vehicle not drawing a trailer, or in the case of a trailer, its maximum laden weight;

(b) in the case of an articulated vehicle, its maximum laden weight (if it has one) and otherwise the aggregate maximum laden weight of all the individual vehicles forming part of that articulated vehicle; and

(c) in the case of a motor vehicle (other than an articulated vehicle) drawing one or more trailers, the aggregate maximum laden weight of the motor vehicle and the trailer or trailers attached to it.

(3) In this section—

"*articulated vehicle*" means a motor vehicle with a trailer so attached to it as to be partially superimposed upon it;

"*goods vehicle*" means a motor vehicle constructed or adapted for use for the carriage of goods or burden of any description, or a trailer so constructed or adapted;

"*trailer*" means any vehicle other than a motor vehicle;

and references to the maximum laden weight of a vehicle are references to the total laden weight which must not be exceeded in the case of that vehicle if it is to be used in Great Britain without contravening any regulations for the time being in force under [section 41 of the Road Traffic Act 1988] (construction and use regulations).

(4) The Secretary of State may by regulations amend subsections (1) and (2) above (whether as originally enacted or as previously amended under this subsection)—

(a) by substituting weights of a different description for any of the weights there mentioned, or

(b) in the case of subsection (1) above, by substituting a weight of a different description or amount, or a weight different both in description and amount, for the weight there mentioned.

(5) Different regulations may be made under subsection (4) above for the purposes of different provisions of this Act and as respects different classes of vehicles or as respects the same class of vehicles in different circumstances and as respects different times of the day or night and as respects roads in different localities.

(6) Regulations made under subsection (4) above shall not so amend subsection (1) above that there is any case in which a goods vehicle whose operating weight (ascertained in accordance with subsection (2) above as originally enacted) does not exceed 7.5 tonnes is a heavy commercial vehicle for any of the purposes of this Act.

(7), (8) *[Repealed by the Statute Law (Repeals) Act 1993, s.1(1) and Sched. 1, Pt XV, group 1.]*

A20.122   *[Section 138 is printed as amended by the Road Traffic (Consequential Provisions) Act 1988, s.4 and Sched. 3, para.25(8).*

As an exception to the transfer of functions to the National Assembly for Wales of functions of a Minister of the Crown exercisable in relation to Wales (see the General note at p. 122 above), the functions under section 138 have been expressly excluded from that transfer; see the National Assembly for Wales (Transfer of Functions) Order 1999 (S.I. 1999 No. 672; not reproduced in this work), art.2 and Sched. 1.]

A20.123   139. Hovercraft   *[Omitted.]*

140. Certain vehicles not to be treated as motor vehicles

A20.124   (1) For the purposes of this Act—

(a) a mechanically propelled vehicle which is an implement for cutting grass, is controlled by a pedestrian and is not capable of being used or adapted for any other purpose;

(b) any other mechanically propelled vehicle controlled by a pedestrian which may be specified by regulations made by the Secretary of State for the purposes of this section and of [section 189 of the Road Traffic Act 1988]; and

(c) an electrically assisted pedal cycle of such class as may be prescribed by regulations so made,

shall be treated as not being a motor vehicle.

(2) In this section "*controlled by a pedestrian*" means that the vehicle either—

(a) is constructed or adapted for use only under such control, or

(b) is constructed or adapted for use either under such control or under the control of a person carried on it, but is not for the time being in use under, or proceeding under, the control of a person carried on it.

[*Section 140 is printed as amended by the Road Traffic (Consequential Provisions) Act 1988, s.4 and Sched. 3, para.25(9).*   **A20.125**

As an exception to the transfer of functions to the National Assembly for Wales of functions of a Minister of the Crown exercisable in relation to Wales (see the General note at p. 122 above), the functions under section 140 have been expressly excluded from that transfer; see the National Assembly for Wales (Transfer of Functions) Order 1999 (S.I. 1999 No. 672; not reproduced in this work), art.2 and Sched. 1.]

141.   [*Repealed.*]   **A20.126**

[141A. Tramcars and trolley vehicles: regulations

(1) The Secretary of State may by regulations provide that such of the provisions mentioned in subsection (2) below as are specified in the regulations shall not apply, or shall apply with modifications—   **A20.127**

(a) to all tramcars or to tramcars of any specified class, or

(b) to all trolley vehicles or to trolley vehicles of any specified class.

(2) The provisions referred to in subsection (1) above are the provisions of sections 1 to 14, [16A to 16C,] 18 and 81 to 89 of this Act.

(3) Regulations under this section—

(a) may make different provision for different cases,

(b) may include such transitional provisions as appear to the Secretary of State to be necessary or expedient, and

(c) may make such amendments to any special Act as appear to the Secretary of State to be necessary or expedient in consequence of the regulations or in consequence of the application to any tramcars or trolley vehicles of any of the provisions mentioned in subsection (2) above.

(4) In this section—

"*special Act*" means a local Act of Parliament passed before the commencement of this section which authorises or regulates the use of tramcars or trolley vehicles;

"*tramcar*" includes any carriage used on any road by virtue of an order under the Light Railways Act 1896; and

"*trolley vehicle*" means a mechanically propelled vehicle adapted for use on roads without rails under power transmitted to it from some external source (whether or not there is in addition a source of power on board the vehicle).]

[*Section 141A was inserted by the Road Traffic Act 1991, s.46(1), and is printed as subsequently amended by the Road Traffic Regulation (Special Events) Act 1994, s.3(1) and Schedule, para.4.*   **A20.128**

As an exception to the transfer of functions to the National Assembly for Wales of functions of a Minister of the Crown exercisable in relation to Wales (see the General note at p. 122 above), the functions under section 141A have been expressly excluded from that transfer; see the National Assembly for Wales (Transfer of Functions) Order 1999 (S.I. 1999 No. 672; not reproduced in this work), art.2 and Sched. 1.]

142. General interpretation of Act

A20.129

(1) In this Act, except where the context otherwise requires, the following expressions have the meanings hereby assigned to them respectively, that is to say—

"*bridge authority*" means the authority or person responsible for the maintenance of a bridge;

"*bridleway*" means a way over which the public have the following, but no other, rights of way, that is to say, a right of way on foot and a right of way on horseback or leading a horse, with or without a right to drive animals of any description along the way;

["*credit card*" and "*debit card*" have the meanings given by section 35A(6) [*q.v.*] of this Act;]

"*designation order*" means an order under section 45 of this Act (including any order so made by virtue of section 50(1) of this Act) and "*designated parking place*" means a parking place designated by a designation order;

"*disabled person's badge*" means any badge issued, or having effect as if issued, under any regulations for the time being in force under section 21 of the Chronically Sick and Disabled Persons Act 1970;

"*disabled person's vehicle*" means a vehicle lawfully displaying a disabled person's badge;

"*driver*" where a separate person acts as steersman of a motor vehicle, includes that person as well as any other person engaged in the driving of the vehicle, and "*drive*" and "*driving*" shall be construed accordingly;

"*excess charge*" has the meaning assigned to it by section 46(1) of this Act [*q.v.*];

"*experimental traffic order*" has the meaning assigned to it by section 9(1) of this Act;

except in section 71(2) of this Act, "*footpath*" means a way over which the public has a right of way on foot only;

["*GLA road*" (subject to section (4) below) has the same meaning as in the Highways Act 1980 (see sections 329(1) and 14D(1) of that Act);]

["*GLA side road*" shall be construed in accordance with section 124A(9) of this Act;]

. . .

"*initial charge*" has the meaning assigned to it by section 46(1) of this Act [*q.v.*];

. . .

"*magistrates' court*" [has the same meaning] as in the Magistrates' Courts Act 1980 [*q.v.*];

"*the Ministers*" means the Secretaries of State charged with general responsibility under this Act in relation to England, Wales and Scotland respectively;

["*off-street parking accommodation*" means parking accommodation for motor vehicles off the highway . . . ;]

subject to section 111(3) and (4) of, and paragraph 11(2) and (3) of Schedule 12 to, this Act, "*owner*", in relation to a vehicle which is subject to a hiring agreement or hire-purchase agreement, means the person in possession of the vehicle under that agreement;

"*parking device*" has the meaning assigned to it by [section 35(3B) [*q.v.*] or, as the case may be,] section 51(4) [*q.v.*] of this Act;

"*parking meter*" has the meaning assigned to it by section 46(2)(a) of this Act [*q.v.*];

"*prescribed*" means prescribed by regulations made by the Secretary of State;

"*public service vehicle*" [has the same meaning] as in the Public Passenger Vehicles Act 1981 [*q.v.*];

["*road*"—

(a) in England and Wales, means any length of highway or of any other road to which the public has access, and includes bridges over which a road passes, and

(b) [*applies to Scotland.*];]

["*special road*", in England and Wales, has the same meaning as in the Highways Act 1980 . . . ;]

"*statutory*", in relation to any prohibition, restriction, requirement or provision, means contained in, or having effect under, any enactment (including any enactment contained in this Act);

"*street parking place*" and "*off-street parking place*" refer respectively to parking places on land which does, and on land which does not, form part of a road;

["*traffic authority*" and "*local traffic authority*" have the meanings given by section 121A of this Act;]

"*traffic sign*" has the meaning assigned to it by section 64(1) of this Act [*q.v.*]; and

"*traffic regulation order*" has the meaning assigned to it by section 1 of this Act.

["*trunk road*" has the same meaning as in the Highways Act 1980 (see section 329(1) of that Act) [*q.v.*]]

[(1A) In this Act—

(a) any reference to a county shall be construed in relation to Wales as including a reference to a county borough;

(b) any reference to a county council shall be construed in relation to Wales as including a reference to a county borough council; and

(c) section 17(4) and (5) of the Local Government (Wales) Act 1994 (references to counties and districts to be construed generally in relation to Wales as references to counties and county boroughs) shall not apply.]

(2) Any reference in this Act to a tricycle shall be construed as including a reference to a cycle which is not a motor vehicle and has 4 or more wheels.

(3) References in this Act to a class of vehicles or traffic (other than the references in section 17) shall be construed as references to a class defined or described by reference to any characteristics of the vehicles or traffic or to any other circumstances whatsoever.

[(4) Any reference in this Act to a GLA road includes a reference to a GLA side road.]

[Section 142 is printed as amended by the Roads (Scotland) Act 1984, s.156(1) and (3), Sched. 9, **A20.130**
para.93(44), and Sched. 11; the Local Government Act 1985, ss.8(1) and 102(2), Sched. 5, para.4(37), and Sched. 17; the Transport Act 1985, s.1(3) and Sched. 1, para.15(4); the Parking Act 1989, s.4 and Schedule, para.8; the New Roads and Street Works Act 1991, s.168(1) and Sched. 8, Pt II, para.78; the Local Government (Wales) Act 1994, s.22(1) and Sched. 7, para.38(10); the Access to Justice Act 1999, s.76(2) and Sched. 10, para.38; the Greater London Authority Act 1999, s.294(1), (3) and (4).
Words relating expressly and exclusively to Scotland have been omitted from the definitions.]

143. Saving for law of nuisance *[Omitted.]* **A20.131**

144. Transitional provisions and savings

(1) The transitional provisions and savings in Schedule 10 to this Act shall have effect. **A20.132**

(2) The enactment in this Act of the provisions specified in the first column of Schedule 11 to this Act (being re-enactments, with or without modifications, of provisions contained in the instruments specified in the corresponding entries in the second column of that Schedule, which were instruments made in the exercise of powers conferred by Acts of Parliament) shall be without prejudice to the validity of those re-enacted provisions; and any question as to their validity shall be determined as if the re-enacted provisions were contained in instruments made in the exercise of those powers.

* * *

Section 86

SCHEDULE 6

Speed Limits for Vehicles of Certain Classes

PART I

Vehicles Fitted with Pneumatic Tyres on All Wheels
(see application provisions below the following Table)

Table

A20.133

1	2	3		
Item No	Class of Vehicle	Maximum speed (in miles per hour) while vehicle is being driven on:		
		(a) Motorway	(b) Dual carriageway road not being a motorway	(c) Other road
1	A passenger vehicle, motor caravan or dual-purpose vehicle not drawing a trailer being a vehicle with an unladen weight exceeding 3·05 tonnes or adapted to carry more than 8 passengers: (i) if not exceeding 12 metres in overall length (ii) if exceeding 12 metres in overall length	70 60	60 60	50 50
2	An invalid carriage	not applicable	20	20
3	A passenger vehicle, motor caravan, car-derived van or dual-purpose vehicle drawing one trailer	[60]	[60]	50
4	A passenger vehicle, motor caravan, car-derived van or dual-purpose vehicle drawing more than one trailer	40	20	20
5	(1) A goods vehicle having a maximum laden weight not exceeding 7·5 tonnes and which is not— (a) an articulated vehicle, or (b) drawing a trailer, or (c) a car-derived van (2) A goods vehicle which is— (a) (i) an articulated vehicle having a maximum laden weight not exceeding 7·5 tonnes, or (ii) a motor vehicle, other than a car-derived van, which is drawing one trailer where the aggregate maximum laden weight of the motor vehicle and the trailer does not exceed 7·5 tonnes (b) (i) an articulated vehicle having a maximum laden weight exceeding 7·5	70 60	60 [60]	50 50

[continued on next page

1	2	3		
Item No	*Class of Vehicle*	*Maximum speed (in miles per hour) while vehicle is being driven on:*		
		(a) Motorway	(b) Dual carriageway road not being a motorway	(c) Other road
5— cont.	(2) (b) (i)—*cont.* tonnes, (ii) a motor vehicle having a maximum laden weight exceeding 7·5 tonnes and not drawing a trailer, or (iii) a motor vehicle drawing one trailer where the aggregate maximum laden weight of the motor vehicle and the trailer exceeds 7·5 tonnes (c) a motor vehicle, other than a car-derived van, drawing more than one trailer	60 40	50 20	40 20
6	A motor tractor (other than an industrial tractor), a light locomotive or a heavy locomotive— (a) if the provisions about springs and wings as specified in paragraph 3 of Part IV of this Schedule are complied with and the vehicle is not drawing a trailer, or if those provisions are complied with and the vehicle is drawing one trailer which also complies with those provisions (b) in any other case	40 20	30 20	30 20
7	A works truck	18	18	18
8	An industrial tractor	not applicable	18	18
[9	An agricultural motor vehicle	40	40	40]

Application

This Part applies only to motor vehicles, not being track-laying vehicles, every wheel of which is fitted with a pneumatic tyre and to such vehicles drawing one or more trailers, not being track-laying vehicles, every wheel of which is fitted with a pneumatic tyre.   **A20.134**

[Schedule 6, Part I, is printed as amended by the Motor Vehicles (Variation of Speed Limits) Regulations 1986 (S.I. 1986 No. 1175; not reproduced in this work).   **A20.135**
As an exception to the transfer of functions to the National Assembly for Wales of functions of a Minister of the Crown exercisable in relation to Wales (see the General note at p. 122 above), the functions under Schedule 6 as a whole have been expressly excluded from that transfer; see the National Assembly for Wales (Transfer of Functions) Order 1999 (S.I. 1999 No. 672; not reproduced in this work), art.2 and Sched. 1.]

PART II

VEHICLES (OTHER THAN TRACK-LAYING VEHICLES) NOT FITTED WITH PNEUMATIC TYRES ON
ALL WHEELS
(see application provisions below the following Table)

TABLE

A20.136

1	2	3
Item No	Class of Vehicle	Maximum speed (in miles per hour) while vehicle is being driven on a road
1	A motor vehicle, or in the case of a motor vehicle drawing one or more trailers, the combination, where— (a) every wheel is fitted with a resilient tyre, or (b) at least one wheel is fitted with a resilient tyre and every wheel which is not fitted with a resilient tyre is fitted with a pneumatic tyre	20
2	A motor vehicle, or in the case of a motor vehicle drawing one or more trailers, the combination, where any wheel is not fitted with either a pneumatic tyre or a resilient tyre	5

A20.137   *Application*

This Part does not apply to—

    (a) a motor vehicle which is a track-laying vehicle; or

    (b) a motor vehicle which is not a track-laying vehicle but which is drawing one or more trailers any one of which is a track-laying vehicle.

A20.138   *[See the note to Part I of this Schedule.]*

PART III

TRACK-LAYING VEHICLES
(see application provisions below the following Table)

TABLE

A20.139

1	2	3
Item No	Class of Vehicle	Maximum speed (in miles per hour) while vehicle is being driven on a road
1	A motor vehicle, being a track-laying vehicle which is fitted with— (a) springs between its frame and its weight-carrying rollers, and (b) resilient material between the rim of its weight-carrying rollers and the surface of the road, and which is not drawing a trailer	20

[continued on next page

1	2	3
Item No	*Class of Vehicle*	*Maximum speed (in miles per hour) while vehicle is being driven on a road*
2	A vehicle specified in item 1 above drawing one or more trailers each one of which is either— (a) a track-laying vehicle fitted with springs and resilient material as mentioned in that item, or (b) not a track-laying vehicle and each wheel of which is fitted with either a pneumatic tyre or a resilient tyre	20
3	A vehicle specified in item 1 above drawing one or more trailers any one of which is either— (a) a track-laying vehicle not fitted with springs and resilient material as mentioned in that item, or (b) not a track-laying vehicle and at least one wheel of which is not fitted with either a pneumatic tyre or a resilient tyre	5
4	A motor vehicle being a track-laying vehicle which is not fitted with springs and resilient material as mentioned in item 1 above, whether drawing a trailer or not	5
5	A motor vehicle not being a track-laying vehicle, which is drawing one or more trailers any one or more of which is a track-laying vehicle— (a) if every wheel of the motor vehicle and of any non-track-laying trailer is fitted with a pneumatic tyre or with a resilient tyre, and every trailer which is a track-laying vehicle is fitted with springs and resilient material as mentioned in item 1 (b) in any other case	20 5

Application

This Part applies to—   **A20.140**

    (a) a motor vehicle which is a track-laying vehicle, and

    (b) a motor vehicle of any description which is drawing one or more trailers any one or more of which is a track-laying vehicle.

[See the note to Part II of this Schedule]   **A20.141**

PART IV

APPLICATION AND INTERPRETATION

1. This Schedule does not apply to a vehicle which is being used for the purpose of   **A20.142**
experiments or trials under section 6 of the Road Improvement Act 1925 or section 283 of
the Highways Act 1980.

2. In this Schedule—

["*agricultural motor vehicle*",] "*articulated vehicle*", "*dual-purpose vehicle*", "*industrial tractor*",
"*passenger vehicle*", "*pneumatic tyre*", "*track-laying*", "*wheel*" and "*works truck*" have the same
meanings as are respectively given to those expressions in [Regulation 3(2) of the Road
Vehicles (Construction and Use) Regulations 1986] [*S.I. 1986 No. 1078 (q.v.)*];

"*car-derived van*" means a goods vehicle which is constructed or adapted as a derivative of a passenger vehicle and which has a maximum laden weight not exceeding 2 tonnes;

"*construction and use requirements*" has the same meaning as in [section 41(7) of the Road Traffic Act 1988];

"*dual-carriageway road*" means a road part of which consists of a central reservation to separate a carriageway to be used by vehicles proceeding in one direction from a carriageway to be used by vehicles proceeding in the opposite direction;

"*goods vehicle*" has the same meaning as in [section 192(1) of the Road Traffic Act 1988];

"*maximum laden weight*" in relation to a vehicle or a combination of vehicles means—

(a) in the case of a vehicle, or combination of vehicles, in respect of which a gross weight not to be exceeded in Great Britain is specified in construction and use requirements, that weight;

(b) in the case of any vehicle, or combination of vehicles, in respect of which no such weight is specified in construction and use requirements, the weight which the vehicle, or combination of vehicles, is designed or adapted not to exceed when in normal use and travelling on a road laden;

"*motor caravan*" has the same meaning as in [Regulation 2(1) of the Motor Vehicles (Type Approval) (Great Britain) Regulations 1984] [*S.I. 1984 No. 981 (q.v.)*];

"*motorway*" has the same meaning as in Regulation 3(1) of the Motorways Traffic (England and Wales) Regulations 1982 [*S.I. 1982 No. 1163 (q.v.)*], as regards England and Wales . . .; and

"*resilient tyre*" means a tyre, not being a pneumatic tyre, which is soft or elastic.

A20.143   **3.** The specification as regards springs and wings mentioned in item 6 of Part I of this Schedule is that the vehicle—

(i) is equipped with suitable and sufficient springs between each wheel and the frame of the vehicle, and

(ii) unless adequate protection is afforded by the body of the vehicle, is provided with wings or other similar fittings to catch, so far as practicable, mud or water thrown up by the rotation of the wheels.

4. A vehicle falling in two or more classes specified in Part I, II or III of this Schedule shall be treated as falling within the class for which the lower or lowest speed limit is specified.

A20.144   *[Schedule 6, Part IV, is printed as amended by the Interpretation Act 1978, ss.17(2)(a) and 23; the Motor Vehicles (Variation of Speed Limits) Regulations 1986 (S.I. 1986 No. 1175; not reproduced in this work); the Road Traffic (Consequential Provisions) Act 1988, s.4 and Sched. 3, para.25(10).*

Words in the definition of "motorway" relating expressly and exclusively to Scotland have been omitted.

See also section 144(2) above and the note to Part I of this Schedule.]

SCHEDULE 7

A20.145   *[Repealed.]*

Section 111   SCHEDULE 8

Statutory Statements (Excess Charges)

PART I

STATUTORY STATEMENT OF OWNERSHIP OR HIRING

1. For the purposes of the specified sections, a statutory statement of ownership is a statement in the prescribed form, signed by the person furnishing it and stating—   **A20.146**

  (a) whether he was the owner of the vehicle at the relevant time; and

  (b) if he was not the owner of the vehicle at the relevant time, whether he ceased to be the owner before, or became the owner after, the relevant time, and, if the information is in his possession, the name and address of the person to whom, and the date on which, he disposed of the vehicle or, as the case may be, the name and address of the person from whom, and the date on which, he acquired it.

2. For the purposes of the specified sections, a statutory statement of hiring is a statement in the prescribed form, signed by the person furnishing it, being the person by whom a statement of liability was signed and stating—

  (a) where at the relevant time the vehicle was let to him under the hiring agreement to which the statement of liability refers; and

  (b) if it was not, the date on which he returned the vehicle to the possession of the vehicle-hire firm concerned.

PART II

STATUTORY STATEMENT OF FACTS

3. For the purposes of the specified sections, a statutory statement of facts is a statement which is in the prescribed form and which—   **A20.147**

  (a) states that the person furnishing it was not the driver of the vehicle at the relevant time;

  (b) states the name and address at the time when the statement is furnished of the person who was the driver of the vehicle at the relevant time; and

  (c) is signed both by the person furnishing it and by the person stated to be the driver of the vehicle at the relevant time.

PART III

INTERPRETATION

4. In this Schedule "*the specified sections*" has the meaning assigned to it by subsection (1) of section 111 of this Act.   **A20.148**

5. Subsections (2) to (4) of that section shall have effect for the purposes of Parts I and II of this Schedule as they have effect for the purposes of the specified sections.

6. In paragraph 2 above "*statement of liability*", "*hiring agreement*" and "*vehicle-hire firm*" have the same meanings as in section 109 of this Act.

[Paragraph 3 of Schedule 8 will come into operation on a date to be appointed under section 145(2). Until such date, paragraph 20(2) of Schedule 10 has effect; see Schedule 10, paragraph 20(1) below.]   **A20.149**

SCHEDULE 9

SPECIAL PROVISIONS AS TO CERTAIN ORDERS

[Omitted.]   **A20.150**

SCHEDULE 10

TRANSITIONAL PROVISIONS AND SAVINGS

*   *   *

Pedestrian crossings

9.—(1) *[Omitted.]*

A20.151 (2) Section 25(6) of this Act shall apply in relation to a crossing established, or having effect as if established—

(a) by a local authority under section 21 of the 1967 Act (whether as that section had effect at any time before the commencement of the said Act of 1980 or as it had effect by virtue of that Act), or

(b) by a Minister under section 22 of the 1967 Act,

as it applies in relation to a crossing established by a local authority under section 23 or by the Secretary of State under section 24 of this Act.

*   *   *

Speed limits

A20.152 **14.**—(1) A direction in an order made under section 1 of the Road Traffic Act 1934 that a length of road is to be deemed to be, or not to be, a road in a built-up area, if—

(a) by virtue of paragraph 10 of Schedule 8 to the 1967 Act it had effect as a direction that that length of road was to become, or (as the case may be) was to cease to be, a restricted road for the purposes of section 71 of that Act, and

(b) the direction continues so to have effect immediately before the commencement of this Act,

shall have the like effect for the purposes of section 81 of this Act [*q.v.*].

(2) Any reference in any provision of an Act, or of any instrument (other than such an order as is mentioned in sub-paragraph (1) above) made under an enactment repealed by the Road Traffic Act 1960, to a road in a built-up area, if the provision is in force immediately before the commencement of this Act, shall be construed as a reference to a restricted road for the purposes of section 81 of this Act.

A20.153 **15.** Any limit of speed which was in force on 1st November 1962 by virtue of any direction, order or regulation given or made by an authority under section 19(2), 26 or 34 of the Road Traffic Act 1960, if—

(a) by virtue of paragraph 12 of Schedule 8 to the 1967 Act it was deemed to have been imposed by an order made by that authority under section 74(1) of the 1967 Act, and

(b) it continues to be in force immediately before the commencement of this Act,

shall be deemed to have been imposed by an order made by that authority under section 84(1) of this Act and may be revoked or varied accordingly.

A20.154 **16.**—(1) This paragraph applies to any road which—

(a) would have become a restricted road for the purposes of section 71 of the 1967 Act on 1st November 1982 as a result of the repeal of section 72(2) of the 1967 Act by section 61 of the Transport Act 1982; but

(b) by reason of section 61(2) of that Act was taken to have ceased to be a restricted road before that day by virtue of a direction duly given under section 72(3) of the 1967 Act and still in force at the beginning of that day; and

(c) did not become a restricted road at any time between the beginning of that day and the commencement of this Act.

(2) At the commencement of this Act, any road to which this paragraph applies shall be treated as if it were the subject of a direction duly given under section 82(2)(a) of this Act [*q.v.*].

(3) Nothing in sub-paragraph (2) above prevents a direction under section 82(2)(b) of this Act being given in respect of any road to which this paragraph applies.

*   *   *

Statutory statement of facts

20.—(1) Sub-paragraph (2) below shall have effect until the coming into operation of   **A20.155**
paragraph 3 of Schedule 8 to this Act [*q.v.*] as if that sub-paragraph were contained in Part II of Schedule 8.

(2) For the purposes of sections 107 to 109 of this Act, a statutory statement of facts is a statement which is in the prescribed form and which either—

(a) states that the person furnishing it was the driver of the vehicle at the relevant time and is signed by him; or

(b) states that that person was not the driver of the vehicle at the relevant time, states the name and address at the time the statement is furnished of the person who was the driver of the vehicle at the relevant time and is signed both by the person furnishing it and by the person stated to be the driver of the vehicle at the relevant time.

SCHEDULE 11

PROVISIONS OF THIS ACT AND INSTRUMENTS REFERRED TO IN SECTION 144(2)

Provisions of Act	*Instruments*	
1. Sections 99 to 102 and 103(3).	The Removal and Disposal of Vehicles (Alteration of Enactments) Order 1967 (S.I. 1967 No. 1900).	**A20.156**
2. Schedule 6.	The Motor Vehicles (Variation of Speed Limits) Regulations 1984 (S.I. 1984 No 325).	

*   *   *

The Police and Criminal Evidence Act 1984

(1984 c. 60)

A21.01   An Act to make further provision in relation to the powers and duties of the police . . .

[31st October 1984]

ARRANGEMENT OF PARTS

A21.02   Part

*   *   *

PART I

POWERS TO STOP AND SEARCH

1. Power of constable to stop and search persons, vehicles, etc.

A21.03   (1) A constable may exercise any power conferred by this section—

(a) in any place to which at the time when he proposes to exercise the power the public or any section of the public has access, on payment or otherwise, as of right or by virtue of express or implied permission; or

(b) in any other place to which people have ready access at the time when he proposes to exercise the power but which is not a dwelling.

(2) Subject to subsections (3) to (5) below, a constable—

(a) may search—

(i) any person or vehicle;

(ii) anything which is in or on a vehicle,

for stolen or prohibited articles [or any article to which subsection (8A) below applies]; and

(b) may detain a person or vehicle for the purpose of such a search.

(3) This section does not give a constable power to search a person or vehicle or anything in or on a vehicle unless he has reasonable grounds for suspecting that he will find stolen or prohibited articles [or any article to which subsection (8A) below applies].

(4) *[Omitted.]*

(5) If a vehicle is in a garden or yard occupied with and used for the purposes of a dwelling or on other land so occupied and used, a constable may not search the vehicle or anything in or on it in the exercise of the power conferred by this section unless he has reasonable grounds for believing—

(a) that the person in charge of the vehicle does not reside in the dwelling; and

(b) that the vehicle is not in the place in question with the express or implied permission of a person who resides in the dwelling.

(6) If in the course of such a search a constable discovers an article which he has reasonable grounds for suspecting to be a stolen or prohibited article [or an article to which subsection (8A) below applies], he may seize it.

(7) An article is prohibited for the purposes of this Part of this Act if it is—

(a) an offensive weapon; or

(b) an article—

(i) made or adapted for use in the course of or in connection with an offence to which this sub-paragraph applies; or

(ii) intended by the person having it with him for such use by him or by some other person.

(8) The offences to which subsection (7)(b)(i) above applies are—

(a) burglary;

(b) theft;

(c) offences under section 12 of the Theft Act 1968 (taking motor vehicle or other conveyance without authority); and

(d) offences under section 15 of that Act (obtaining property by deception).

[(8A) *[Applies to offence of having article with blade or point in public place.]*]

(9) In this Part of this Act "*offensive weapon*" means any article—

(a) made or adapted for use for causing injury to persons; or

(b) intended by the person having it with him for such use by him or by some other person.

[Section 1 is printed as amended by the Criminal Justice Act 1988, s.140(1).   **A21.04**
Guidance on the exercise of powers requiring reasonable grounds of suspicion (e.g. as in section 1(3)) is given in the code of practice for the exercise by police officers of statutory powers to stop and search (Code A (1999) under this Act), paras 1.6 to 1.7A. These paragraphs read as follows (they are reproduced by kind permission of the Stationery Office):

1.6   Whether a reasonable ground for suspicion exists will depend on the circumstances in each case, but there must be some objective basis for it. An officer will need to consider the nature of the article suspected of being carried in the context of other factors such as the time and the place, and the behaviour of the person concerned or those with him. Reasonable suspicion may exist, for example, where information has been received such as a description of an article being carried or of a suspected offender; a person is seen acting covertly or warily or attempting to hide something; or a person is carrying a certain type of article at an unusual time or in a place where a number of burglaries or thefts are known to have taken place recently. But the decision to stop and search must be based on all the facts which bear on the likelihood that an article of a certain kind will be found.

1.6A For example, reasonable suspicion may be based upon reliable information or intelligence which indicates that members of a particular group or gang, or their associates, habitually carry knives unlawfully or weapons or controlled drugs.

1.7 Subject to the provision in paragraph 1.7AA below, reasonable suspicion can never be supported on the basis of personal factors alone without supporting intelligence or information. For example, a person's colour, age, hairstyle or manner of dress, or the fact that he is known to have a previous conviction for possession of an unlawful article, cannot be used alone or in combination with each other as the sole basis on which to search that person. Nor may it be founded on the basis of stereotyped images of certain persons or groups as more likely to be committing offences.

1.7AA However, where there is reliable information or intelligence that members of a group or gang who habitually carry knives unlawfully or weapons or controlled drugs, and wear a distinctive item of clothing or other means of identification to indicate membership of it, the members may be identified by means of that distinctive item of clothing or other means of identification.

1.7A Where a police officer has reasonable grounds to suspect that a person is in innocent possession of a stolen or prohibited article or other item for which he is empowered to search, the power of stop and search exists notwithstanding that there would be no power of arrest. However every effort should be made to secure the person's co-operation in the production of the article before resorting to the use of force.]

2. Provisions relating to search under section 1 and other powers

A21.05   (1) A constable who detains a person or vehicle in the exercise—

(a) of the power conferred by section 1 above; or

(b) of any other power—

    (i) to search a person without first arresting him; or
    (ii) to search a vehicle without making an arrest,

need not conduct a search if it appears to him subsequently—

    (i) that no search is required; or
    (ii) that a search is impracticable.

(2) If a constable contemplates a search, other than a search of an unattended vehicle, in the exercise—

(a) of the power conferred by section 1 above; or

(b) of any other power, except the power conferred by section 6 below and the power conferred by section 27(2) of the Aviation Security Act 1982—

    (i) to search a person without first arresting him; or
    (ii) to search a vehicle without making an arrest,

it shall be his duty, subject to subsection (4) below, to take reasonable steps before he commences the search to bring to the attention of the appropriate person—

(i) if the constable is not in uniform, documentary evidence that he is a constable; and

(ii) whether he is in uniform or not, the matters specified in subsection (3) below;

and the constable shall not commence the search until he has performed that duty.

(3) The matters referred to in subsection (2)(ii) above are—

(a) the constable's name and the name of the police station to which he is attached;

(b) the object of the proposed search;

(c) the constable's grounds for proposing to make it; and

(d) the effect of section 3(7) or (8) below, as may be appropriate.

(4) A constable need not bring the effect of section 3(7) or (8) below to the attention of the appropriate person if it appears to the constable that it will not be practicable to make the record in section 3(1) below.

(5) In this section "*the appropriate person*" means—

(a) if the constable proposes to search a person, that person; and

(b) if he proposes to search a vehicle, or anything in or on a vehicle, the person in charge of the vehicle.

(6) On completing a search of an unattended vehicle or anything in or on such a vehicle in the exercise of any such power as is mentioned in subsection (2) above a constable shall leave a notice—

(a) stating that he has searched it;

(b) giving the name of the police station to which he is attached;

(c) stating that an application for compensation for any damage caused by the search may be made to that police station; and

(d) stating the effect of section 3(8) below.

(7) The constable shall leave the notice inside the vehicle unless it is not reasonably practicable to do so without damaging the vehicle.

(8) The time for which a person or vehicle may be detained for the purposes of such a search is such time as is reasonably required to permit a search to be carried out either at the place where the person or vehicle was first detained or nearby.

(9) Neither the power conferred by section 1 above nor any other power to detain and search a person without first arresting him or to detain and search a vehicle without making an arrest is to be construed—

(a) as authorising a constable to require a person to remove any of his clothing in public other than an outer coat, jacket or gloves; or

(b) as authorising a constable not in uniform to stop a vehicle.

(10) This section and section 1 above apply to vessels, aircraft and hovercraft as they apply to vehicles.

3. Duty to make records concerning searches

(1) Where a constable has carried out a search in the exercise of any such power as is mentioned in section 2(1) above, other than a search—   **A21.06**

(a) under section 6 below; or

(b) under section 27(2) of the Aviation Security Act 1982,

he shall make a record of it in writing unless it is not practicable to do so.

(2)–(6) *[Omitted.]*

(7) If a constable who conducted a search of a person made a record of it, the person who was searched shall be entitled to a copy of the record if he asks for one before the end of the period specified in subsection (9) below.

(8) If—

(a) the owner of a vehicle which has been searched or the person who was in charge of the vehicle at the time when it was searched asks for a copy of the record of the search before the end of the period specified in subsection (9) below; and

(b) the constable who conducted the search made a record of it,

the person who made the request shall be entitled to a copy.

(9) The period mentioned in subsections (7) and (8) above is the period of 12 months beginning with the date on which the search was made.

(10) The requirements imposed by this section with regard to records of searches of vehicles shall apply also to records of searches of vessels, aircraft and hovercraft.

4. Road checks

A21.07   (1) This section shall have effect in relation to the conduct of road checks by police officers for the purpose of ascertaining whether a vehicle is carrying—

(a) a person who has committed an offence other than a road traffic offence or a [vehicle] excise offence;

(b) a person who is a witness to such an offence;

(c) a person intending to commit such an offence; or

(d) a person who is unlawfully at large.

(2) For the purposes of this section a road check consists of the exercise in a locality of the power conferred by [section 163 of the Road Traffic Act 1988] in such a way as to stop during the period for which its exercise in that way in that locality continues all vehicles or vehicles selected by any criterion.

(3) Subject to subsection (5) below, there may only be such a road check if a police officer of the rank of superintendent or above authorises it in writing.

(4) An officer may only authorise a road check under subsection (3) above—

(a) for the purpose specified in subsection (1)(a) above, if he has reasonable grounds—

(i) for believing that the offence is a serious arrestable offence; and

(ii) for suspecting that the person is, or is about to be, in the locality in which vehicles would be stopped if the road check were authorised;

(b) for the purpose specified in subsection (1)(b) above, if he has reasonable grounds for believing that the offence is a serious arrestable offence;

(c) for the purpose specified in subsection (1)(c) above, if he has reasonable grounds—

(i) for believing that the offence would be a serious arrestable offence; and

(ii) for suspecting that the person is, or is about to be, in the locality in which vehicles would be stopped if the road check were authorised;

(d) for the purpose specified in subsection (1)(d) above, if he has reasonable grounds for suspecting that the person is, or is about to be, in that locality.

(5) An officer below the rank of superintendent may authorise such a road check if it appears to him that it is required as a matter of urgency for one of the purposes specified in subsection (1) above.

(6) If an authorisation is given under subsection (5) above, it shall be the duty of the officer who gives it—

(a) to make a written record of the time at which he gives it; and

(b) to cause an officer of the rank of superintendent or above to be informed that it has been given.

(7) The duties imposed by subsection (6) above shall be performed as soon as it is practicable to do so.

(8) An officer to whom a report is made under subsection (6) above may, in writing, authorise the road check to continue.

(9) If such an officer considers that the road check should not continue, he shall record in writing—

(a) the fact that it took place; and

(b) the purpose for which it took place.

(10) An officer giving an authorisation under this section shall specify the locality in which vehicles are to be stopped.

(11) An officer giving an authorisation under this section, other than an authorisation under subsection (5) above—

(a) shall specify a period, not exceeding seven days, during which the road check may continue; and

(b) may direct that the road check—

(i) shall be continuous; or
(ii) shall be conducted at specified times,

during that period.

(12) If it appears to an officer of the rank of superintendent or above that a road check ought to continue beyond the period for which it has been authorised he may, from time to time, in writing specify a further period, not exceeding seven days, during which it may continue.

(13) Every written authorisation shall specify—

(a) the name of the officer giving it;

(b) the purpose of the road check; and

(c) the locality in which vehicles are to be stopped.

(14) The duties to specify the purposes of a road check imposed by subsections (9) and (13) above include duties to specify any relevant serious arrestable offence.

(15) Where a vehicle is stopped in a road check, the person in charge of the vehicle at the time when it is stopped shall be entitled to obtain a written statement of the purpose of the road check if he applies for such a statement not later than the end of the period of twelve months from the day on which the vehicle was stopped.

(16) Nothing in this section affects the exercise by police officers of any power to stop vehicles for purposes other than those specified in subsection (1) above.

[Section 4 is printed as amended by the Road Traffic (Consequential Provisions) Act 1988, s.4 and   **A21.08**
Sched. 3, para.27(1); the Vehicle Excise and Registration Act 1994, s.63 and Sched. 3, para.19.
"Serious arrestable offences" are described in section 116 of and Schedule 5 to this Act (q.v.).]

*   *   *

6. Statutory undertakers, etc.

(1) A constable employed by statutory undertakers may stop, detain and search any   **A21.09**
vehicle before it leaves a goods area included in the premises of the statutory undertakers.

[(1A) Without prejudice to any powers under subsection (1) above, a constable employed by the British Railways Board may stop, detain and search any vehicle before it leaves a goods area which is included in the premises of any successor of the British Railways Board and is used wholly or mainly for the purposes of a relevant undertaking.]

(2) In this section *"goods area"* means any area used wholly or mainly for the storage or handling of goods[; and *"successor of the British Railways Board"* and *"relevant undertaking"* have the same meaning as in the Railways Act 1993 (Consequential Modifications) Order 1999].

A21.10   (3), (4) *[Omitted.]*

[Section 6 is printed as amended by the Railways Act 1993 (Consequential Modifications) (No. 2) Order 1999 (S.I. 1999 No. 1998; not reproduced in this work), art.5. The definitions to which reference is made in section 6(2) may be found in S.I. 1999 No. 1998, art.2(1).

The application to section 6(1) of the code of practice for the exercise by police officers of statutory powers of stop and search is expressly excluded by paragraph 1.4(ii) of Code A (1999) under this Act.]

7. Part I—supplementary

(1), (2) *[Omitted.]*

A21.11   (3) In this Part of this Act *"statutory undertakers"* means persons authorised by any enactment to carry on any railway, light railway, road transport, water transport, canal, inland navigation, dock or harbour undertaking.

*   *   *

PART III

ARREST

24. Arrest without warrant for arrestable offences

A21.12   (1) The powers of summary arrest conferred by the following subsections shall apply—

    (a) to offences for which the sentence is fixed by law;

    (b) to offences for which a person of 21 years of age or over (not previously convicted) may be sentenced to imprisonment for a term of five years (or might be so sentenced but for the restrictions imposed by section 33 of the Magistrates' Courts Act 1980); and

    (c) to the offences to which subsection (2) below applies, and in this Act *"arrestable offence"* means any such offence.

(2) The offences to which this subsection applies are—

    (a) *[certain customs and excise offences;]*

    (b) *[certain offences under the official secrets legislation;]*

  [(bb) *[certain offences under the official secrets legislation;]]*

    (c) *[certain offences under the Sexual Offences Act 1956;]*

    (d) offences under section 12(1) (taking motor vehicle or other conveyance without authority, etc.) or 25(1) (going equipped for stealing, etc.) of the Theft Act 1968;

    (e) *[offences under the Football (Offences) Act 1991;]*

    (f) *[offences under the Obscene Publications Act 1959, s.2;]*

    (g) *[offences under the Protection of Children Act 1978, s.1;]*

    (h) *[offences under the Criminal Justice and Public Order Act 1994, s.166;]*

    (i) *[offences under the Public Order Act 1986, s.19;]*

    (j) *[offences under the Criminal Justice and Public Order Act 1994, s.167;]*

(k) *[offences under the Prevention of Crime Act 1953, s.1(1);]*

(l) *[offences under the Criminal Justice Act 1988, s.139(1);]*

(m) *[offences under the Criminal Justice Act 1988, s.139A(1), (2);]*

(n) *[offences of harassment under the Protection from Harassment Act 1997, s.2;]*

(o) *[offences of failing to comply with requirement to remove mask, etc., under the Criminal Justice and Public Order Act 1994, s.60(8)(b);]*

(p) *[racially-aggravated harassment under the Crime and Disorder Act 1998, s.32(1)(a);]*

(q) *[offences of failing to comply with requirements imposed by or under banning order or notice under the Football Spectators Act 1989, s.21B;]*

(r) *[repealed.]*

(3) Without prejudice to section 2 of the Criminal Attempts Act 1981, the powers of summary arrest conferred by the following subsections shall also apply to the offences of—

(a) conspiring to commit any of the offences mentioned in subsection (2) above;

(b) attempting to commit any such offence [other than an offence under section 12(1) of the Theft Act 1968];

(c) inciting, aiding, abetting, counselling or procuring the commission of any such offence;

and such offences are also arrestable offences for the purposes of this Act.

(4) Any person may arrest without a warrant—

(a) anyone who is in the act of committing an arrestable offence;

(b) anyone whom he has reasonable grounds for suspecting to be committing such an offence.

(5) Where an arrestable offence has been committed, any person may arrest without a warrant—

(a) anyone who is guilty of the offence;

(b) anyone whom he has reasonable grounds for suspecting to be guilty of it.

(6) Where a constable has reasonable grounds for suspecting that an arrestable offence has been committed, he may arrest without a warrant anyone whom he has reasonable grounds for suspecting to be guilty of the offence.

(7) A constable may arrest without a warrant—

(a) anyone who is about to commit an arrestable offence;

(b) anyone whom he has reasonable grounds for suspecting to be about to commit an arrestable offence.

[Section 24 is printed as amended by the Criminal Justice Act 1988, s.170(1) and (2) and Sched. 15,　　**A21.13**
para.98, and Sched. 16; the Crime and Disorder Act 1998, ss.27(1), 32(2) and 84(2); the Football (Offences and Disorder) Act 1999, s.8(3); the Football (Disorder) Act 2000, s.1(2) and Sched. 2, para.2.

With effect from a date to be announced under the Criminal Justice and Court Services Act 2000, s.80(2), the numeral "18" will be substituted in section 24(1)(b) for the numeral "21" by the 2000 Act, s.74 and Sched.7, paras 76 and 77.

Section 33 of the Magistrates' Courts Act 1980 (to which section 24(1)(b) refers) restricts the sentence which a court may impose in relation to certain criminal damage offences.

For the Theft Act 1968, ss.12 and 25, see below.]

25. General arrest conditions

(1) Where a constable has reasonable grounds for suspecting that any offence which is　　**A21.14**
not an arrestable offence has been committed or attempted, or is being committed or

attempted, he may arrest the relevant person if it appears to him that service of a summons is impracticable or inappropriate because any of the general arrest conditions is satisfied.

(2) In this section "*the relevant person*" means any person whom the constable has reasonable grounds to suspect of having committed or having attempted to commit the offence or of being in the course of committing or attempting to commit it.

(3) The general arrest conditions are—

(a) that the name of the relevant person is unknown to, and cannot be readily ascertained by, the constable;

(b) that the constable has reasonable grounds for doubting whether a name furnished by the relevant person as his name is his real name;

(c) that—

(i) the relevant person has failed to furnish a satisfactory address for service; or

(ii) the constable has reasonable grounds for doubting whether an address furnished by the relevant person is a satisfactory address for service;

(d) that the constable has reasonable grounds for believing that arrest is necessary to prevent the relevant person—

(i) causing physical injury to himself or any other person;

(ii) suffering physical injury;

(iii) causing loss of or damage to property;

(iv) committing an offence against public decency; or

(v) causing an unlawful obstruction of the highway;

(e) that the constable has reasonable grounds for believing that arrest is necessary to protect a child or other vulnerable person from the relevant person.

(4) For the purposes of subsection (3) above an address is a satisfactory address for service if it appears to the constable—

(a) that the relevant person will be at it for a sufficiently long period for it to be possible to serve him with a summons; or

(b) that some other person specified by the relevant person will accept service of a summons for the relevant person at it.

(5) Nothing in subsection (3)(d) above authorises the arrest of a person under sub-paragraph (iv) of that paragraph except where members of the public going about their normal business cannot reasonably be expected to avoid the person to be arrested.

(6) This section shall not prejudice any power of arrest conferred apart from this section.

26. Repeal of statutory powers of arrest without warrant or order

A21.15   (1) Subject to subsection (2) below, so much of any Act (including a local Act) passed before this Act as enables a constable—

(a) to arrest a person for an offence without a warrant; or

(b) to arrest a person otherwise than for an offence without a warrant or an order of a court,

shall cease to have effect.

(2) Nothing in subsection (1) above affects the enactments specified in Schedule 2 to this Act.

[The enactments originally listed in Schedule 2 to this Act included sections 5(5), 7 and 10 of the Road Traffic Act 1972; reference to these provisions in Schedule 2 was repealed by the Road Traffic (Consequential Provisions) Act 1988, s.3(1) and Sched. 1, Pt I.]   **A21.16**

*   *   *

31. Arrest for further offence

Where—   **A21.17**

(a) a person—

(i) has been arrested for an offence; and

(ii) is at a police station in consequence of that arrest; and

(b) it appears to a constable that, if he were released from that arrest, he would be liable to arrest for some other offence,

he shall be arrested for that other offence.

*   *   *

PART IV

DETENTION

Detention—conditions and duration

34. Limitations on police detention

(1) A person arrested for an offence shall not be kept in police detention except in accordance with the provisions of this Part of this Act.   **A21.18**

(2) Subject to subsection (3) below, if at any time a custody officer—

(a) becomes aware, in relation to any person in police detention, that the grounds for the detention of that person have ceased to apply; and

(b) is not aware of any other grounds on which the continued detention of that person could be justified under the provisions of this Part of this Act,

it shall be the duty of the custody officer, subject to subsection (4) below, to order his immediate release from custody.

(3) No person in police detention shall be released except on the authority of a custody officer at the police station where his detention was authorised or, if it was authorised at more than one station, a custody officer at the station where it was last authorised.

(4) A person who appears to the custody officer to have been unlawfully at large when he was arrested is not to be released under subsection (2) above.

(5) A person whose release is ordered under subsection (2) above shall be released without bail unless it appears to the custody officer—

(a) that there is need for further investigation of any matter in connection with which he was detained at any time during the period of his detention; or

(b) that proceedings may be taken against him in respect of any such matter,

and, if it so appears, he shall be released on bail.

(6) For the purposes of this Part of this Act a person arrested under [section 6(5) of the Road Traffic Act 1988] is arrested for an offence.

[(7) For the purposes of this Part of this Act a person who returns to a police station to answer to bail or is arrested under section 46A below shall be treated as arrested for an offence and the offence in connection with which he was granted bail shall be deemed to be that offence.]

A21.19   *[Section 34 is printed as amended by the Road Traffic (Consequential Provisions) Act 1988, s.4 and Sched. 3, para.27(2); the Criminal Justice and Public Order Act 1994, s.29(1) and (3).]*

35. Designated police stations

A21.20   (1) The chief officer of police for each police area shall designate the police stations in his area which, subject to section 30(3) and (5) above, are to be the stations in that area to be used for the purpose of detaining arrested persons.

(2), (3) *[Omitted.]*

(4) In this Act "*designated police station*" means a police station for the time being designated under this section.

36. Custody officers at police stations

A21.21   (1) One or more custody officers shall be appointed for each designated police station.

(2) A custody officer for a designated police station shall be appointed—

(a) by the chief officer of police for the area in which the designated police station is situated; or

(b) by such other police officer as the chief officer of police for that area may direct.

(3) No officer may be appointed a custody officer unless he is of at least the rank of sergeant.

(4) An officer of any rank may perform the functions of a custody officer at a designated police station if a custody officer is not readily available to perform them.

(5) Subject to the following provisions of this section and to section 39(2) below, none of the functions of a custody officer in relation to a person shall be performed by an officer who at the time when the function falls to be performed is involved in the investigation of an offence for which that person is in police detention at that time.

(6) Nothing in subsection (5) above is to be taken to prevent a custody officer—

(a) performing any function assigned to custody officers—
(i) by this Act; or
(ii) by a code of practice issued under this Act;

(b) carrying out the duty imposed on custody officers by section 39 below;

(c) doing anything in connection with the identification of a suspect; or

(d) doing anything under [sections 7 and 8 of the Road Traffic Act 1988].

(7) Where an arrested person is taken to a police station which is not a designated police station, the functions in relation to him which at a designated police station would be the functions of a custody officer shall be performed—

(a) by an officer who is not involved in the investigation of an offence for which he is in police detention, if such an officer is readily available; and

(b) if no such officer is readily available, by the officer who took him to the station or any other officer.

(8) References to a custody officer in the following provisions of this Act include refer-

ences to an officer other than a custody officer who is performing the functions of a custody officer by virtue of subsection (4) or (7) above.

(9) Where by virtue of subsection (7) above an officer of a force maintained by a police authority who took an arrested person to a police station is to perform the functions of a custody officer in relation to him, the officer shall inform an officer who—

(a) is attached to a designated police station; and

(b) is of at least the rank of inspector,

that he is to do so.

(10) The duty imposed by subsection (9) above shall be performed as soon as it is practicable to perform it.

[*Section 36 is printed as amended by the Road Traffic (Consequential Provisions) Act 1988, s.4 and Sched. 3, para.27(3).*]   **A21.22**

37. Duties of custody officer before charge

(1) Where—   **A21.23**

(a) a person is arrested for an offence—

(i) without a warrant; or

(ii) under a warrant not endorsed for bail, . . .

the custody officer at each police station where he is detained after his arrest shall determine whether he has before him sufficient evidence to charge that person with the offence for which he was arrested and may detain him at the police station for such period as is necessary to enable him to do so.

(2) If the custody officer determines that he does not have such evidence before him, the person arrested shall be released either on bail or without bail, unless the custody officer has reasonable grounds for believing that his detention without being charged is necessary to secure or preserve evidence relating to an offence for which he is under arrest or to obtain evidence by questioning him.

(3) If the custody officer has reasonable grounds for so believing, he may authorise the person arrested to be kept in police detention.

(4)–(6) [*Written record of grounds for detention.*]

(7) Subject to section 41(7) below, if the custody officer determines that he has before him sufficient evidence to charge the person arrested with the offence for which he was arrested, the person arrested—

(a) shall be charged; or

(b) shall be released without charge, either on bail or without bail.

(8) Where—

(a) a person is released under subsection (7)(b) above; and

(b) at the time of his release a decision whether he should be prosecuted for the offence for which he was arrested has not been taken,

it shall be the duty of the custody officer so to inform him.

(9) If the person arrested is not in a fit state to be dealt with under subsection (7) above, he may be kept in police detention until he is.

(10) [*Duty under section 37(1) to be performed as soon as practicable.*]

(11)–(14) [*Repealed.*]

(15) *[Definitions.]*

A21.24   *[Section 37 is printed as amended by the Criminal Justice Act 1991, s.101(2) and Sched. 13; the Criminal Justice and Public Order Act 1994, s.29(1) and (4)(a), s.168(3) and Sched. 11.]*

A21.25   **38. Duties of custody officer after charge**   *[Omitted.]*

39. Responsibilities in relation to persons detained

A21.26   (1) Subject to subsections (2) and (4) below, it shall be the duty of the custody officer at a police station to ensure—

(a) that all persons in police detention at that station are treated in accordance with this Act and any code of practice issued under it and relating to the treatment of persons in police detention; and

(b) that all matters relating to such persons which are required by this Act or by such codes of practice to be recorded are recorded in the custody records relating to such persons.

(2) If the custody officer, in accordance with any code of practice issued under this Act, transfers or permits the transfer of a person in police detention—

(a) to the custody of a police officer investigating an offence for which that person is in police detention; or

(b) to the custody of an officer who has charge of that person outside the police station,

the custody officer shall cease in relation to that person to be subject to the duty inposed on him by subsection (1)(a) above; and it shall be the duty of the officer to whom the transfer is made to ensure that he is treated in accordance with the provisions of this Act and of any such codes of practice as are mentioned in subsection (1) above.

(3) If the person detained is subsequently returned to the custody of the custody officer, it shall be the duty of the officer investigating the offence to report to the custody officer as to the manner in which this section and the codes of practice have been complied with while that person was in his custody.

(4) If an arrested juvenile is [moved to local authority accommodation] under section 38(6) above, the custody officer shall cease in relation to that person to be subject to the duty imposed on him by subsection (1) above.

(5) *[Repealed.]*

(6) Where—

(a) an officer of higher rank than the custody officer gives directions relating to a person in police detention; and

(b) the directions are at variance—

(i) with any decision made or action taken by the custody officer in the performance of a duty imposed on him under this Part of this Act; or

(ii) with any decision or action which would but for the directions have been made or taken by him in the performance of such a duty,

the custody officer shall refer the matter at once to an officer of the rank of superintendent or above who is responsible for the police station for which the custody officer is acting as custody officer.

A21.27   *[Section 39 is printed as amended by the Children Act 1989, s.108(5) and (7), Sched. 13, para.54, and Sched. 15.]*

40. Review of police detention   *[Omitted.]*

41. Limits on period of detention without charge

(1) Subject to the following provisions of this section and to sections 42 and 43 below, a
person shall not be kept in police detention for more than 24 hours without being charged.

(2) The time from which the period of detention of a person is to be calculated (in this
Act referred to as "*the relevant time*")—

    (a) in the case of a person to whom this paragraph applies, shall be—

        (i) the time at which that person arrives at the relevant police station, or
        (ii) the time 24 hours after the time of that person's arrest,

    whichever is the earlier;

    (b) in the case of a person arrested outside England and Wales, shall be—

        (i) the time at which that person arrives at the first police station to which he is
taken in the police area in England and Wales in which the offence for which
he was arrested is being investigated; or
        (ii) the time 24 hours after the time of that person's entry into England and
Wales,

    whichever is the earlier;

    (c) in the case of a person who—

        (i) attends voluntarily at a police station; or
        (ii) accompanies a constable to a police station without having been arrested,

    and is arrested at the police station, the time of his arrest;

    (d) in any other case, except where subsection (5) below applies, shall be the time at
which the person arrested arrives at the first police station to which he is taken after
his arrest.

(3) Subsection (2)(a) above applies to a person if—

    (a) his arrest is sought in one police area in England and Wales;

    (b) he is arrested in another police area; and

    (c) he is not questioned in the area in which he is arrested in order to obtain evidence
in relation to an offence for which he is arrested;

and in sub-paragraph (i) of that paragraph "*the relevant police station*" means the first police
station to which he is taken in the police area in which his arrest was sought.

(4) Subsection (2) above shall have effect in relation to a person arrested under section 31
above as if every reference in it to his arrest or his being arrested were a reference to his
arrest or his being arrested for the offence for which he was originally arrested.

(5) If—

    (a) a person is in police detention in a police area in England and Wales ("*the first area*");
and

    (b) his arrest for an offence is sought in some other police area in England and Wales
("*the second area*"); and

    (c) he is taken to the second area for the purposes of investigating that offence, without
being questioned in the first area in order to obtain evidence in relation to it,

the relevant time shall be—

        (i) the time 24 hours after he leaves the place where he is detained in the first
area; or

(ii) the time at which he arrives at the first police station to which he is taken in the second area,

whichever is the earlier.

(6) When a person who is in police detention is removed to hospital because he is in need of medical treatment, any time during which he is being questioned in hospital or on the way there or back by a police officer for the purpose of obtaining evidence relating to an offence shall be included in any period which falls to be calculated for the purposes of this Part of this Act, but any other time while he is in hospital or on his way back shall not be so included.

(7) Subject to subsection (8) below, a person who at the expiry of 24 hours after the relevant time is in police detention and has not been charged shall be released at that time either on bail or without bail.

(8) Subsection (7) above does not apply to a person whose detention for more than 24 hours after the relevant time has been authorised or is otherwise permitted in accordance with section 42 or 43 below.

(9) A person released under subsection (7) above shall not be re-arrested without a warrant for the offence for which he was previously arrested unless new evidence justifying a further arrest has come to light since his release [; but this subsection does not prevent an arrest under section 46A below].

A21.30   *[Section 41 is printed as amended by the Criminal Justice and Public Order Act 1994, s.29(1) and (4)(b).]*

*   *   *

A21.31   **46A. Power of arrest for failure to answer police bail**   *[Omitted.]*

PART V

QUESTIONING AND TREATMENT OF PERSONS BY POLICE

*   *   *

56. Right to have someone informed when arrested

A21.32   (1) Where a person has been arrested and is being held in custody in a police station or other premises, he shall be entitled, if he so requests, to have one friend or relative or other person who is known to him or who is likely to take an interest in his welfare told, as soon as is practicable except to the extent that delay is permitted by this section, that he has been arrested and is being detained there.

(2) Delay is only permitted—

(a) in the case of a person who is in police detention for a serious arrestable offence; and

(b) if an officer of at least the rank of superintendent authorises it.

(3) In any case the person in custody must be permitted to exercise the right conferred by subsection (1) above within 36 hours from the relevant time, as defined in section 41(2) above.

(4) An officer may give an authorisation under subsection (2) above orally or in writing but, if he gives it orally, he shall confirm it in writing as soon as is practicable.

(5) [Subject to subsection (5A) below] an officer may only authorise delay where he has reasonable grounds for believing that telling the named person of the arrest—

(a) will lead to interference with or harm to evidence connected with a serious arrestable offence or interference with or physical injury to other persons; or

(b) will lead to the alerting of other persons suspected of having committed such an offence but not yet arrested for it; or

(c) will hinder the recovery of any property obtained as a result of such an offence.

[(5A) *[Applies to drug trafficking offences.]*]

(6) If a delay is authorised—

(a) the detained person shall be told the reason for it; and

(b) the reason shall be noted on his custody record.

(7) The duties imposed by subsection (6) above shall be performed as soon as is practicable.

(8) The rights conferred by this section on a person detained at a police station or other premises are exercisable whenever he is transferred from one place to another; and this section applies to each subsequent occasion on which they are exercisable as it applies to the first such occasion.

(9) There may be no further delay in permitting the exercise of the right conferred by subsection (1) above once the reason for authorising delay ceases to subsist.

(10), (11) *[Apply to terrorism provisions.]*

[Section 56 is printed as amended by the Drug Trafficking Offences Act 1986, s.32(1).]   **A21.33**

57. Additional rights of children and young persons

[Amends the Children and Young Persons Act 1933, s.34.]   **A21.34**

58. Access to legal advice

(1) A person arrested and held in custody in a police station or other premises shall be entitled, if he so requests, to consult a solicitor privately at any time.   **A21.35**

(2) Subject to subsection (3) below, a request under subsection (1) above and the time at which it was made shall be recorded in the custody record.

(3) Such a request need not be recorded in the custody record of a person who makes it at a time while he is at a court after being charged with an offence.

(4) If a person makes such a request, he must be permitted to consult a solicitor as soon as is practicable except to the extent that delay is permitted by this section.

(5) In any case he must be permitted to consult a solicitor within 36 hours from the relevant time, as defined in section 41(2) above.

(6) Delay in compliance with a request is only permitted—

(a) in the case of a person who is in police detention for a serious arrestable offence; and

(b) if an officer of at least the rank of superintendent authorises it.

(7) An officer may give an authorisation under subsection (6) above orally or in writing, but, if he gives it orally, he shall confirm it in writing as soon as is practicable.

(8) [Subject to subsection (8A) below] an officer may only authorise delay where he has

reasonable grounds for believing that the exercise of the right conferred by subsection (1) above at the time when the person detained desires to exercise it—

(a) will lead to interference with or harm to evidence connected with a serious arrestable offence or interference with or physical injury to other persons; or

(b) will lead to the alerting of other persons suspected of having committed such an offence but not yet arrested for it; or

(c) will hinder the recovery of any property obtained as a result of such an offence.

[(8A) *[Applies to drug trafficking offences.]*]

(9) If delay is authorised—

(a) the detained person shall be told the reason for it; and

(b) the reason shall be noted on his custody record.

(10) The duties imposed by subsection (9) above shall be performed as soon as is practicable.

(11) There may be no further delay in permitting the exercise of the right conferred by subsection (1) above once the reason for authorising delay ceases to subsist.

[(12) Nothing in this section applies to a person arrested or detained under the terrorism provisions.]

A21.36   *[Section 58 is printed as amended by the Drug Trafficking Offences Act 1986, s.32(2); the Terrorism Act 2000, s.125(1) and Sched. 5, para.5(1) and (6).*
The term "serious arrestable offence" is defined in section 116 below.]

* * *

PART VIII

Evidence in Criminal Proceedings—General

* * *

Miscellaneous

78. Exclusion of unfair evidence

A21.37   (1) In any proceedings the court may refuse to allow evidence on which the prosecution proposes to rely to be given if it appears to the court that, having regard to all the circumstances, including the circumstances in which the evidence was obtained, the admission of the evidence would have such an adverse effect on the fairness of the proceedings that the court ought not to admit it.

(2) Nothing in this section shall prejudice any rule of law requiring a court to exclude evidence.

[(3) This section shall not apply in the case of proceedings before a magistrates' court inquiring into an offence as examining justices.]

A21.38   *[Section 78 is printed as amended by the Criminal Procedure and Investigations Act 1996, s.47 and Sched. 1, para.26.]*

79. Time for taking accused's evidence

A21.39   If at the trial of any person for an offence—

(a) the defence intends to call two or more witnesses to the facts of the case; and

(b) those witnesses include the accused,

the accused shall be called before the other witness or witnesses unless the court in its discretion otherwise directs.

*   *   *

PART VIII Supplementary

82. Part VIII—interpretation

(1) In this Part of this Act—   **A21.40**

"*Confession*" includes any statement wholly or partly adverse to the person who made it, whether made to a person in authority or not and whether made in words or otherwise;

"*court-martial*" means a court-martial constituted under the Army Act 1955, the Air Force Act 1955 or the Naval Discipline Act 1957 or a disciplinary court constituted under [section 52G] of the said Act of 1957;

"*proceedings*" means criminal proceedings, including—

(a) proceedings in the United Kingdom or elsewhere before a court-martial constituted under the Army Act 1955 [, the Air Force Act 1955 or the Naval Discipline Act 1957];

(b) proceedings in the United Kingdom or elsewhere before the Courts-Martial Appeal Court—

(i) on an appeal from a court-martial so constituted . . .; or

(ii) on a reference under section 34 of the Courts-Martial (Appeals) Act 1968; and

(c) proceedings before a Standing Civilian Court; and

"*Service court*" means a court-martial or a Standing Civilian Court.

(2) In this Part of this Act references to conviction before a Service court are [references to a finding of guilty which is, or falls to be treated as, the finding of the court; and] "*convicted*" shall be construed accordingly.

(3) Nothing in this Part of this Act shall prejudice any power of a court to exclude evidence (whether by preventing questions from being put or otherwise) at its discretion.

[Section 82 is printed as amended by the Armed Forces Act 1996, ss.5, 35, Sched. 6 (paras 14, 104, 105   **A21.41**
and 107) and Sched. 7 (Pt I).

With effect from a date to be announced under the Youth Justice and Criminal Evidence Act 1999, s.68(4), the following amendments will be effected by ibid., s.67(3) and Sched. 6, to section 82(1):

(i) in paragraph (a) of the definition of "proceedings", the words after "court-martial" will be repealed; and

(ii) in paragraph (b)(i) of the definition of "proceedings", the words "so constituted" will be repealed.]

PART XI

MISCELLANEOUS AND SUPPLEMENTARY

*   *   *

116. Meaning of "serious arrestable offence"

(1) This section has effect for determining whether an offence is a serious arrestable   **A21.42**
offence for the purpose of this Act.

(2) The following arrestable offences are always serious—

(a) an offence (whether at common law or under any enactment) specified in Part I of Schedule 5 to this Act; and

(b) an offence under an enactment specified in Part II of that Schedule; [and]

[(c) *[applies to drug trafficking offences.]*]

(3) Subject to [subsection (4)] below, any other arrestable offence is serious only if its commission—

(a) has led to any of the consequences specified in subsection (6) below; or

(b) is intended or is likely to lead to any of those consequences.

(4) An arrestable offence which consists of making a threat is serious if carrying out the threat would be likely to lead to any of the consequences specified in subsection (6) below.

(5) *[Repealed.]*

(6) The consequences mentioned in subsections (3) and (4) above are

(a) serious harm to the security of the State or to public order;

(b) serious interference with the administration of justice or with the investigation of offences or of a particular offence;

(c) the death of any person;

(d) serious injury to any person;

(e) substantial financial gain to any person; and

(f) serious financial loss to any person.

(7) Loss is serious for the purposes of this section if, having regard to all the circumstances, it is serious for the person who suffers it.

(8) In this section "*injury*" includes any disease and any impairment of a person's physical or mental condition.

A21.43   *[Section 116 is printed as amended by the Prevention of Terrorism (Temporary Provisions) Act 1989, s.25(1) and Sched. 8, para.6(1) and (7); the Drug Trafficking Act 1994, ss.65(1) and 67(1), Sched. 1, para.9, and Sched. 3; the Terrorism Act 2000, s.125(1) and Sched. 5, para.5(1) and (11).*
The term "arrestable offence" is defined in section 24(1) of this Act (q.v.).]

*   *   *

SCHEDULE 5

SERIOUS ARRESTABLE OFFENCES

PART I

OFFENCES MENTIONED IN SECTION 116(2)(a)

*   *   *

PART II

OFFENCES MENTIONED IN SECTION 116(2)(b)

Explosive Substances Act 1883 (c. 3)

A21.44   **1.** *[Omitted.]*

Sexual Offences Act 1956 (c. 69)

2. *[Omitted.]*

Firearms Act 1968 (c. 27)

3–5. *[Omitted.]*

6. *[Repealed.]*

Taking of Hostages Act 1982 (c. 28)

7. *[Omitted.]*

Aviation Security Act 1982 (c. 36)

8. *[Omitted.]*

A21.45

[Criminal Justice Act 1988 (c. 33)]

9. *[Omitted.]*

[Road Traffic Act 1988 (c. 52)

[Section 1 (causing death by [dangerous] driving).]
[Section 3A (causing death by careless driving when under the influence of drink or drugs)]]

[Aviation and Maritime Security Act 1990 (c. 31)

11–13. *[Omitted.]]*

A21.46

[Channel Tunnel (Security) Order 1994 (S.I. 1994 No. 570)

14, 15. *[Omitted.]]*

[Protection of Children Act 1978 (c. 37)

14. *[Omitted.]]*

[Obscene Publications Act 1959 (c. 66)

15. *[Omitted.]]*

[Schedule 5 is printed as amended (so far as relevant to this work) by the Criminal Justice Act 1988, s.170(1) and Sched. 15, para.102; the Road Traffic (Consequential Provisions) Act 1988, ss.3(1) and 4, and Sched. 1, Pt I, and Sched. 3, para.27(5); the Road Traffic Act 1991, s.48 and Sched. 4, para.39(a) and (b).

A21.47

Textual amendments which are not relevant to this work have resulted in two items being numbered as "14" and two other items as "15" in Part II of this Schedule (see the Channel Tunnel (Security) Order 1994 (S.I. 1994 No. 570) (not reproduced in this work) and the Criminal Justice and Public Order Act 1994, s.85 (not reproduced in this work)).]

*   *   *

The Prosecution of Offences Act 1985

(1985 c. 23)

A22.01 An Act to provide for the establishment of a Crown Prosecution Service for England and Wales; to make provision as to costs in criminal cases . . . .

[23rd May 1985]

ARRANGEMENT OF SECTIONS

*   *   *

PART I

THE CROWN PROSECUTION SERVICE

Constitution and functions of Service

*   *   *

PART I

THE CROWN PROSECUTION SERVICE

Constitution and functions of Service

*   *   *

3. Functions of the Director

(1), (2) *[Omitted.]*

(3) In this section—

. . .

"police force" means any police force maintained by a police authority under [the Police Act 1996] [, the National Crime Squad] and any other body of constables for the time being specified by order made by the Secretary of State for the purposes of this section;

. . .

[The definition of "police force" in subsection (3) is incorporated by reference into section 17 (q.v.). The definition is printed as amended by the Police Act 1996, s.103 and Sched. 7, para.39; the Police Act 1997, s.134(1) and Sched. 9, para.48.]

*   *   *

PART II

COSTS IN CRIMINAL CASES

Award of costs out of central funds

16. Defence costs

(1) Where—

   (a) an information laid before a justice of the peace for any area, charging any person with an offence, is not proceeded with;

   (b) a magistrates' court inquiring into an indictable offence as examining justices determines not to commit the accused for trial;

   (c) a magistrates' court dealing summarily with an offence dismisses the information;

that court or, in a case falling within paragraph (a) above, a magistrates' court for that area, may make an order in favour of the accused for a payment to be made out of central funds in respect of his costs (a "defendant's costs order").

(2) Where—

   (a) any person is not tried for an offence for which he has been indicted or committed for trial; or

[(aa) *[Relates to complex cases of serious fraud.]*]

   (b) any person is tried on indictment and acquitted on any count in the indictment;

the Crown Court may make a defendant's costs order in favour of the accused.

(3) Where a person convicted of an offence by a magistrates' court appeals to the Crown Court under section 108 of the Magistrates' Courts Act 1980 (right of appeal against conviction of sentence), and, in consequence of the decision on appeal—

   (a) his conviction is set aside; or

   (b) a less severe punishment is awarded;

the Crown Court may make a defendant's costs order in favour of the accused.

  (4) Where the Court of Appeal—

   (a) allows an appeal under Part I of the Criminal Appeal Act 1968 against—

     (i) conviction;
     (ii) a verdict of not guilty by reason of insanity; or
     [(iii) a finding under the Criminal Procedure (Insanity) Act 1964 that the appellant is under a disability, or that he did the act or made the omission charged against him;] or

  [(aa) directs under section 8(1B) of the Criminal Appeal Act 1968 the entry of a judgment and verdict of acquittal;]

   (b) on an appeal under that Part against conviction—

     (i) substitutes a verdict of guilty of another offence;
     (ii) in a case where a special verdict has been found, orders a different conclusion on the effect of that verdict to be recorded; or
     (iii) is of the opinion that the case falls within paragraph (a) or (b) of section 6(1) of that Act (cases where the court substitutes a finding of insanity or unfitness to plead); or

   (c) on an appeal under that Part against sentence, exercises its power under section 11(3) of that Act (powers where the court considers that the appellant should be sentenced differently for an offence for which he was dealt with by the court below);

the court may make a defendant's costs order in favour of the accused.

  [(4A) *[Relates to complex cases of serious fraud.]*]

  (5) Where—

   (a) any proceedings in a criminal cause or matter are determined before a Divisional Court of the Queen's Bench Division;

   (b) the House of Lords determines an appeal, or application for leave to appeal, from such a Divisional Court in a criminal cause or matter;

   (c) the Court of Appeal determines an application for leave to appeal to the House of Lords under Part II of the Criminal Appeal Act 1968; or

   (d) the House of Lords determines an appeal, or application for leave to appeal, under Part II of that Act;

the court may make a defendant's costs order in favour of the accused.

  (6) A defendant's costs order shall, subject to the following provisions of this section, be for the payment out of central funds, to the person in whose favour the order is made, of such amount as the court considers reasonably sufficient to compensate him for any expenses properly incurred by him in the proceedings.

  (7) Where a court makes a defendant's costs order but is of the opinion that there are circumstances which make it inappropriate that the person in whose favour the order is made should recover the full amount mentioned in subsection (6) above, the court shall—

   (a) assess what amount would, in its opinion, be just and reasonable; and

   (b) specify that amount in the order.

  (8) *[Repealed.]*

(9) Subject to subsection (7) above, the amount to be paid out of central funds in pursuance of a defendant's costs order shall—

(a) be specified in the order, in any case where the court considers it appropriate for the amount to be so specified and the person in whose favour the order is made agrees the amount; and

(b) in any other case, be determined in accordance with regulations made by the Lord Chancellor for the purposes of this section.

(10) Subsection (6) above shall have effect, in relation to any case falling within subsection (1)(a) or (2)(a) above, as if for the words "in the proceedings" there were substituted the words "in or about the defence".

(11) Where a person ordered to be retried is acquitted at his retrial, the costs which may be ordered to be paid out of central funds under this section shall include—

(a) any costs which, at the original trial, could have been ordered to be so paid under this section if he had been acquitted; and

(b) if no order was made under this section in respect of his expenses on appeal, any sums for the payment of which such an order could have been made.

(12) *[Meaning of "relevant transfer provision".]*

[Section 16 is printed as amended by the Criminal Justice Act 1988, s.170(1) and Sched. 15,   **A22.06**
para.103; the Legal Aid Act 1988, s.45(2) and Sched. 6; the Criminal Procedure (Insanity and Unfitness to Plead) Act 1991, s.7 and Sched. 3, para.7.]

17. Prosecution costs

(1) Subject to subsection (2) below, the court may—   **A22.07**

(a) in any proceedings in respect of an indictable offence; and

(b) in any proceedings before a Divisional Court of the Queen's Bench Division or the House of Lords in respect of a summary offence;

order the payment out of central funds of such amount as the court considers reasonably sufficient to compensate the prosecutor for any expenses properly incurred by him in the proceedings.

(2) No order under this section may be made in favour of—

(a) a public authority; or

(b) a person acting—

(i) on behalf of a public authority; or
(ii) in his capacity as an official appointed by such an authority.

(3) Where a court makes an order under this section but is of the opinion that there are circumstances which make it inappropriate that the prosecution should recover the full amount mentioned in subsection (1) above, the court shall—

(a) assess what amount would, in its opinion, be just and reasonable; and

(b) specify that amount in the order.

(4) Subject to subsection (3) above, the amount to be paid out of central funds in pursuance of an order under this section shall—

(a) be specified in the order, in any case where the court considers it appropriate for the amount to be so specified and the prosecutor agrees the amount; and

(b) in any other case be determined in accordance with regulations made by the Lord Chancellor for the purposes of this section.

(5) Where the conduct of proceedings to which subsection (1) above applies is taken over by the Crown Prosecution Service, that subsection shall have effect as if it referred to the prosecutor who had the conduct of the proceedings before the intervention of the Service and to expenses incurred by him up to the time of intervention.

(6) In this section "*public authority*" means—

    (a) a police force within the meaning of section 3 of this Act;

    (b) the Crown Prosecution Service or any other government department;

    (c) a local authority or other authority or body constituted for purposes of—

        (i) the public service or of local government; or

        (ii) carrying on under national ownership any industry or undertaking or part of an industry or undertaking; or

    (d) any other authority or body whose members are appointed by Her Majesty or by any Minister of the Crown or government department or whose revenues consist wholly or mainly of money provided by Parliament.

Award of costs against accused

18. Award of costs against accused

A22.08   (1) Where—

    (a) any person is convicted of an offence before a magistrates' court;

    (b) the Crown Court dismisses an appeal against such a conviction or against the sentence imposed on that conviction; or

    (c) any person is convicted of an offence before the Crown Court;

the court may make such order as to the costs to be paid by the accused to the prosecutor as it considers just and reasonable.

(2) Where the Court of Appeal dismisses—

    (a) an appeal or application for leave to appeal under Part I of the Criminal Appeal Act 1968; or

    (b) an application by the accused for leave to appeal to the House of Lords under Part II of this Act;

    [(c) *[relates to complex cases of serious fraud.]*]

it may make such order as to the costs to be paid by the accused, to such person as may be named in the order, as it considers just and reasonable.

(3) The amount to be paid by the accused in pursuance of an order under this section shall be specified in the order.

(4) Where any person is convicted of an offence before a magistrates' court and—

    (a) under the conviction the court orders payment of any sum as a fine, penalty, forfeiture or compensation; and

    (b) the sum so ordered to be paid does not exceed £5;

the court shall not order the accused to pay any costs under this section unless in the particular circumstances of the case it considers it right to do so.

(5) Where any person under [the age of eighteen] is convicted of an offence before a magistrates' court, the amount of any costs ordered to be paid by the accused under this section shall not exceed the amount of any fine imposed on him.

(6) Costs ordered to be paid under subsection (2) above may include the reasonable costs of any transcript of a record of proceedings made in accordance with rules of court made for the purposes of section 32 of the Criminal Appeal Act 1968.

Other awards

19. Provisions for orders as to costs in other circumstances

(1)–(3A) *[Regulation-making powers.]*   **A22.10**

(4) The Court of Appeal may order the payment out of central funds of such sums as appear to it to be reasonably sufficient to compensate an appellant who is not in custody and who appears before it on, or in connection with, his appeal under Part I of the Criminal Appeal Act 1968.

(5) *[Regulation-making powers.]*

19A. Costs against legal representatives, etc.   *[Omitted.]*   **A22.11**

Supplemental

20. Regulations   *[Omitted.]*

21. Interpretation, etc.

(1) In this Part—   **A22.12**

["*accused*" and "*appellant*", in a case where section 44A of the Criminal Appeal Act 1968 (death of convicted person) applies, include the person approved under that section;]

"*defendant's costs order*" has the meaning given in section 16 of this Act;

. . .

["*legally assisted person*", in relation to any proceedings, means a person to whom [a right to representation funded by the Legal Services Commission as part of the Criminal Defence Service] has been granted for the purposes of the proceedings;]

"*proceedings*" includes—

    (a) proceedings in any court below; and

    (b) in relation to the determination of an appeal by any court, any application made to that court for leave to bring the appeal; and

"*witness*" means any person properly attending to give evidence, whether or not he gives evidence or is called at the instance of one of the parties or of the court, but does not include a person attending as a witness to character only unless the court has certified that the interests of justice required his attendance.

(2) Except as provided by or under this Part no costs shall be allowed on the hearing or determination of, or of any proceedings preliminary or incidental to, an appeal to the Court of Appeal under Part I of the Criminal Appeal Act 1968.

(3) Subject to rules of court made under section 53(1) of the Supreme Court Act 1981 (power by rules to distribute business of Court of Appeal between its civil and criminal divisions), the jurisdiction of the Court of Appeal under this Part, or under regulations made under this Part, shall be exercised by the criminal division of that Court; and references in this Part to the Court of Appeal shall be construed as references to that division.

(4) For the purposes of sections 16 and 17 of this Act, the costs of any party to proceedings shall be taken to include the expense of compensating any witness for the expense, trouble or loss of time, properly incurred in or incidental to his attendance.

[(4A) Where one party to any proceedings is a legally assisted person then—

   (a) for the purposes of sections 16 and 17 of this Act, his costs shall be taken not to include [the cost of representation funded for him by the Legal Services Commission as part of the Criminal Defence Service;] and

   (b) for the purposes of sections 18[, 19 and 19A of this Act, his costs shall be taken to include the cost of representation funded for him by the Legal Services Commission as part of the Criminal Defence Service].]

(5) Where, in any proceedings in a criminal cause or matter or in either of the cases mentioned in subsection (6) below, an interpreter is required because of the accused's lack of English, the expenses properly incurred on his employment shall not be treated as costs of any party to the proceedings.

(6) The cases are—

   (a) where an information charging the accused with an offence is laid before a justice of the peace . . . but not proceeded with and the expenses are incurred on the employment of the interpreter for the proceedings on the information; and

   (b) where the accused is committed for trial but not tried and the expenses are incurred on the employment of the interpreter for the proceedings in the Crown Court.

A22.13   *[Section 21 is printed as amended by the Legal Aid Act 1988, ss.45(2) and (4), Sched. 5, paras 14 and 15, and Sched. 6; the Criminal Appeal Act 1995, s.29(1) and Sched. 2, para.15; the Access to Justice Act 1999, s.106 and Sched.15, Pt V(3); and also (with effect from April 2, 2001) by the 1999 Act, s.24 and Sched. 4, paras 27 and 30 (see the Access to Justice Act 1999 (Commencement No. 7, Transitional Provisions and Savings) Order 2001 (S.I. 2001 No. 916; not reproduced in this work), arts 1(2) and 3(a)(ii)).*

    In section 21(4A)(a), the word "include" has been retained editorially although it was formally repealed by the Access to Justice Act 1999, s.24 and Sched. 4, paras 27 and 30(1) and (3)(a).]

*   *   *

The Transport Act 1985

(1985 c. 67)

An Act to amend the law relating to road passenger transport . . .

[30th October 1985]

ARRANGEMENT OF SECTIONS

PART I

GENERAL PROVISIONS RELATING TO ROAD PASSENGER TRANSPORT

*　　　*　　　*

Meaning of "local service"

Section

PART II

Regulation of Road Passenger Transport in London

London local service licences

Section

. . . .

34. London local services
35. London local service licences
36. London bus services under the control of London Regional Transport

. . . .

38. Conditions attached to licences
39. Grant of licences for certain excursions or tours

. . . .

*   *   *

PART VI

Miscellaneous and General

Section

. . . .

Provisions supplementary to Parts I and II

. . . .

127. Offences and legal proceedings

. . . .

General supplementary provisions

. . . .

137. Interpretation

. . . .

SCHEDULES

Schedule 1—Amendments consequential on the abolition of road service licensing

. . . .

Schedule 7—Minor and consequential amendments

. . . .

*   *   *

PART I

General Provisions relating to Road Passenger Transport

*   *   *

Meaning of "local service"

2. Local services

A23.03   (1) In this Act "*local service*" means a service, using one or more public service vehicles, for the carriage of passengers by road at separate fares other than one—

     (a) which is excluded by subsection (4) below; or

(b) in relation to which (except in an emergency) one or both of the conditions mentioned in subsection (2) below are met with respect to every passenger using the service.

(2) The conditions are that—

(a) the place where he is set down is fifteen miles or more, measured in a straight line, from the place where he was taken up;

(b) some point on the route between those places is fifteen miles or more, measured in a straight line, from either of those places.

(3) Where a service consists of one or more parts with respect to which one or both of the conditions are met, and one or more parts with respect to which neither of them is met, each of those parts shall be treated as a separate service for the purposes of subsection (1) above.

(4) A service shall not be regarded for the purposes of this Act as a local service if—

(a) the conditions set out in Part III of Schedule 1 to the 1981 Act (trips organised privately by persons acting independently of vehicle operators, etc.) are met in respect of each journey made by the vehicles used in providing the service; or

(b) every vehicle used in providing the service is so used under a permit granted under section 19 of this Act.

(5) Subsections (5)(b), (c) and (6) of section 1 of the 1981 Act (meaning of "fares") shall apply for the purposes of this section.

* * *

Taxis and hire cars

* * *

11. Advance booking of taxis and hire cars at separate fares

(1) Where the conditions mentioned in subsection (2) below are met, a licensed taxi or licensed hire car may be used for the carriage of passengers for hire or reward at separate fares without thereby— **A23.04**

(a) becoming a public service vehicle for the purposes of the 1981 Act or any related enactment; or

(b) ceasing (otherwise than by virtue of any provision made under section 13 of this Act) to be subject to the taxi code or (as the case may be) the hire car code.

(2) The conditions are that—

(a) all the passengers carried on the occasion in question booked their journeys in advance; and

(b) each of them consented, when booking his journey, to sharing the use of the vehicle on that occasion with others on the basis that a separate fare would be payable by each passenger for his own journey on that occasion.

12. Use of taxis in providing local services

(1) Where the holder of a taxi licence— **A23.05**

(a) applies to the appropriate traffic commissioner for a restricted PSV operator's licence to be granted to him under Part II of the 1981 Act; and

(b) states in his application that he proposes to use one or more licensed taxis to provide a local service;

section 14 of the 1981 Act (conditions to be met before grant of PSV operator's licence) shall not apply and the commissioner shall grant the application.

(2) In this section "*special licence*" means a restricted PSV operator's licence granted by virtue of this section.

(3) *[Repealed.]*

(4) Without prejudice to his powers to attach other conditions under section 16 of the 1981 Act, any traffic commissioner granting a special licence shall attach to it, under that section, the conditions mentioned in subsection (5) below.

(5) The conditions are—

    (a) that every vehicle used under the licence shall be one for which the holder of the licence has a taxi licence; and

    (b) that no vehicle shall be used under the licence otherwise than for the purpose of providing a local service with one or more stopping places within the area of the authority which granted the taxi licence of the vehicle in question.

(6) In subsection (5)(b) above "*local service*" does not include an excursion or tour.

(7) The maximum number of vehicles which the holder of a special licence may at any one time use under the licence shall be the number of vehicles for which (for the time being) he holds taxi licences; and a condition to that effect shall be attached to every special licence under section 16(1) of the 1981 Act.

(8) Section 1(2) of the 1981 Act (vehicle used as public service vehicle to be treated as such until that use is permanently discontinued) shall not apply to any use of a licensed taxi for the provision of a local service under a special licence.

(9) At any time when a licensed taxi is being so used it shall carry such documents, plates and marks, in such manner as may be prescribed.

(10) Such provisions in the taxi code as may be prescribed shall apply in relation to a licensed taxi at any time when it is being so used; and any such provision may be so applied subject to such modifications as may be prescribed.

(11) For the purposes of section 12(3) of the 1981 Act (which provides that where two or more PSV operators' licences are held they must be granted by traffic commissioners for different traffic areas), special licences shall be disregarded.

(12) A person may hold more than one special licence but shall not at the same time hold more than one such licence granted by the traffic commissioner for a particular traffic area.

(13) The following provisions shall not apply in relation to special licences or (as the case may be) the use of vehicles under such licences—

    (a) sections 16(1A) and (2), 17(3)(d), 18 to 20 . . . and 26 of the 1981 Act; and

    (b) section 26(5) and (6) of this Act;

and for the purposes of section 12 of that Act this section shall be treated as if it were in Part II of that Act.

A23.06   *[Section 12 is printed as amended by the Road Traffic (Driver Licensing and Information Systems) Act 1989, s.16 and Sched. 6; by the Deregulation and Contracting Out Act 1994, s.68 and Sched. 14, para.8.*

    The text of section 12(12) in its application to the holder of a special licence who is in a partnership is modified by the Operation of Public Service Vehicles (Partnership) Regulations 1986 (S.I. 1986 No. 1628), Schedule, Pt II (not reproduced in this work).]

13. Provisions supplementary to sections 10 to 12

(1), (2) *[Power to make orders modifying taxi code and hire car code.]*   A23.07

(3) In this section, and in sections 10 to 12 of this Act—

"*licensed taxi*" means—

   (a) in England and Wales, a vehicle licensed under—

      (i) section 37 of the Town Police Clauses Act 1847; or
      (ii) section 6 of the Metropolitan Public Carriage Act 1869;

     or under any similar enactment; and

   (b) *[applies to Scotland.]*

"*London taxi area*" means the area to which the Metropolitan Public Carriage Act 1869 applies;

"*licensed hire car*" means a vehicle which is licensed under section 48 of the Local Government (Miscellaneous Provisions) Act 1976 [or section 7 of the Private Hire Vehicles (London) Act 1998 [*q.v.*]];

"*hire car code*", in relation to a licensed hire car used as mentioned in section 11 of this Act, means those provisions made by or under any enactment which would apply if it were hired by a single passenger for his exclusive use;

"*related enactment*", in relation to the 1981 Act, means any statutory provision (whenever passed or made) relating to public service vehicles in which public service vehicle is defined directly or indirectly by reference to the provisions of the 1981 Act;

"*taxi code*", in relation to any licensed taxi used as mentioned in section 10, 11 or 12 of this Act, means—

   (a) in England and Wales, those provisions made by or under any enactment which would apply if the vehicle were plying for hire and were hired by a single passenger for his exclusive use; and

   (b) *[applies to Scotland.]*

"*taxi licence*" means a licence under section 6 of the Metropolitan Public Carriage Act 1869, section 37 of the Town Police Clauses Act 1847 or any similar enactment, or a taxi licence under section 10 of the Civic Government (Scotland) Act 1982.

(4) *[Scope of orders under section 13(1).]*

[Section 13 is printed as prospectively amended by the Private Hire Vehicles (London) Act 1998, ss.39(1), 40(2) and Sched. 1, para.4. Until that prospective amendment has taken effect, the definition of "licensed hire car" in section 13(3) should be read as if the reference to the 1998 Act (set within square brackets) were omitted.]   A23.08

*   *   *

Modification of PSV requirements in relation to vehicles used for certain purposes

18. Exemption from PSV operator and driver licensing requirements of vehicles used under permits

[(1)] [Section 12(1)] of the 1981 Act (licensing of operators . . . in relation to the use of   A23.09
public service vehicles for the carriage of passengers) shall not apply—

   (a) to the use of any vehicle under a permit granted under section 19 of this Act, if and so long as the requirements under subsection (2) of that section are met; [or]

   (b) to the use of any vehicle under a permit granted under section 22 of this Act; . . .]

   (c) *[repealed.]*

[(2) Where a holder of a licence under Part III of the Road Traffic Act 1988 was first granted a licence under that Part before 1st January 1997, he may drive any small bus at a time when it is being used as mentioned in paragraph (a) or (b) of subsection (1) above, notwithstanding that his licence under that Part does not authorise him to drive a small bus when it is being so used.

(3) Where—

    (a) a holder of a licence under Part III of the Road Traffic Act 1988 was first granted a licence under that Part on or after 1st January 1997, or

    (b) a Community licence holder is authorised by virtue of section 99A(1) of that Act to drive in Great Britain a motor vehicle of any class,

he may drive any small bus to which subsection (4) below applies at a time when it is being used as mentioned in paragraph (a) or (b) of subsection (1) above, notwithstanding that he is not authorised by his licence under that Part or by virtue of that section (as the case may be) to drive such a bus.

(4) This subsection applies to any small bus which, when laden with the heaviest load which it is constructed to carry, weighs—

    (a) not more than 3.5 tonnes, excluding any part of that weight which is attributable to specialised equipment intended for the carriage of disabled passengers, and

    (b) not more than 4.25 tonnes otherwise.

(5) In this section—

"*Community licence*" has the same meaning as in Part III of the Road Traffic Act 1988,

and

"*small bus*" has the same meaning as in sections 19 to 21 of this Act.]

A23.10   *[Section 18 is printed as amended by the Road Traffic (Driver Licensing and Information Systems) Act 1989, ss.7, 16, Sched. 3, para.4(a)–(c), and Sched. 6; the Driving Licences (Community Driving Licence) Regulations 1996 (S.I. 1996 No. 1974), reg.4 and Sched. 3, para.1 (not reproduced in this work).]*

19. Permits in relation to use of buses by educational and other bodies

A23.11   (1) In this section and sections 20 and 21 of this Act—

"*bus*" means a vehicle which is adapted to carry more than eight passengers;

"*large bus*" means a vehicle which is adapted to carry more than sixteen passengers;

"*small bus*" means a vehicle which is adapted to carry more than eight but not more than sixteen passengers; and

"*permit*" means a permit granted under this section in relation to the use of a bus for carrying passengers for hire or reward.

(2) The requirements that must be met in relation to the use of a bus under a permit for the exemption under section [18(1)(a)] of this Act to apply are that the bus—

    (a) is being used by a body to whom a permit has been granted under this section;

    (b) is not being used for the carriage of members of the general public nor with a view to profit nor incidentally to an activity which is itself carried on with a view to profit;

    (c) is being used in every respect in accordance with any conditions attached to the permit; and

    (d) is not being used in contravention of any provision of regulations made under section 21 of this Act.

(3) A permit in relation to the use of a small bus may be granted by a body designated by an order under subsection (7) below either to itself or to any other body to whom, in accordance with the order, it is entitled to grant a permit.

(4) A permit in relation to the use of a small bus may be granted by a traffic commissioner to any body appearing to him to be eligible in accordance with subsection (8) below and to be carrying on in his area an activity which makes it so eligible.

(5) A permit in relation to the use of a large bus may be granted by a traffic commissioner to any body which assists and co-ordinates the activities of bodies within his area which appear to him to be concerned with—

(a) education;

(b) religion;

(c) social welfare; or

(d) other activities of benefit to the community.

(6) A traffic commissioner shall not grant a permit in relation to the use of a large bus unless satisfied that there will be adequate facilities or arrangements for maintaining any bus used under the permit in a fit and serviceable condition.

(7) The Secretary of State may by order designate for the purpose of this section bodies appearing to him to be eligible in accordance with subsection (8) below and, with respect to any body designated by it, any such order—

(a) shall specify the classes of body to whom the designated body may grant permits;

(b) may impose restrictions with respect to the grant of permits by the designated body and, in particular, may provide that no permit may be granted, either generally or in such cases as may be specified in the order, unless there are attached to the permit such conditions as may be so specified; and

(c) may require the body to make returns with regard to the permits granted by it.

(8) A body is eligible in accordance with this subsection if it is concerned with—

(a) education;

(b) religion;

(c) social welfare;

(d) recreation; or

(e) other activities of benefit to the community.

(9) A body may hold more than one permit but may not use more than one bus at any one time under the same permit.

[An editorial emendation has been made to the text of section 19(2) so that the original reference to   **A23.12**
"section 18(a)" now reads "section 18(1)(a)" following the amendments effected to that provision.

The functions of the Secretary of State exercisable under section 19(7) in relation to Wales have been transferred to the National Assembly for Wales by the National Assembly for Wales (Transfer of Functions) Order 1999 (S.I. 1999 No. 672; not reproduced in this work), art.2 and Sched 1.

As to the transfer of functions of the Secretary of State under section 19(7) which are exercisable in relation to Scotland to the Scottish Ministers, see the Scotland Act 1998 (Transfer of Functions to the Scottish Ministers etc.) Order 1999 (S.I. 1999 No. 1750; not reproduced in this work), art.2 and Sched. 1.

For the bodies designated for the purposes of section 19(7), see the Section 19 Minibus (Designated Bodies) Order 1987 (S.I. 1987 No. 1229), as amended (not reproduced in this work).]

20. Further provision with respect to permits under section 19   **A23.13**
[Omitted.]

A23.14   **21. Permits under section 19: regulations**

(1) Regulations may prescribe—

(a) the conditions to be fulfilled by any person driving a bus while it is being used under a permit;

(b) the conditions as to fitness which are to be fulfilled by any small bus used under a permit;

(c) the form of permits; and

(d) the documents, plates and marks to be carried by any bus while it is being used under a permit and the manner and position in which they are to be carried.

(2) Where regulations are made by virtue of subsection (1)(b) above, section 6 of the 1981 Act (certificate of initial fitness for public service vehicles) shall not apply in relation to any small bus subject to the regulations.

(3) Regulations under this section may contain such transitional provisions as the Secretary of State thinks fit.

A23.15   *[The Minibus and Other Section 19 Permit Buses Regulations 1987 (S.I. 1987 No. 1230; not reproduced in this work) have been made in part under section 21.]*

22. Community bus permits

A23.16   (1) In this section and section 23 of this Act—

"community bus service" means a local service provided—

(a) by a body concerned for the social and welfare needs of one or more communities;

(b) without a view to profit, either on the part of that body or of anyone else; and

(c) by means of a vehicle adapted to carry more than eight but not more than sixteen passengers; and

"community bus permit" means a permit granted under this section in relation to the use of a public service vehicle—

(a) in providing a community bus service; or

(b) in providing a community bus service and (other than in the course of a local service) carrying passengers for hire or reward where the carriage of those passengers will directly assist the provision of the community bus service by providing financial support for it.

(2)–(4) *[Omitted.]*

23. Further provisions with respect to community bus permits

A23.17   (1)–(4) *[Omitted.]*

(5) Subject to section 68(3) of the 1981 Act (as applied by section 127(4) of this Act), if a condition attached to a community bus permit is contravened, the holder of the permit shall be liable on summary conviction to a fine not exceeding level 3 on the standard scale.

(6), (7) *[Omitted.]*

A23.18   *[The Community Bus Regulations 1986 (S.I. 1986 No. 1245; not reproduced in this work) have been made in part under section 23.]*

*   *   *

Further amendments with respect to PSV operators' licences

*   *   *

30. Plying for hire by large public service vehicles

(1) A public service vehicle which is adapted to carry more than eight passengers shall not be used on a road in plying for hire as a whole.   **A23.19**

(2) Subject to section 68(3) of the 1981 Act (as applied by section 127(4) of this Act), if a vehicle is used in contravention of subsection (1) above, the operator of the vehicle shall be liable on summary conviction to a fine not exceeding level 3 on the standard scale.

*   *   *

PART II

REGULATION OF ROAD PASSENGER TRANSPORT IN LONDON

Note to Part II. Part II of this Act (sections 34–46) has been prospectively repealed by the Greater London Authority Act 1999, s.423 and Sched. 34, Pt II below. At April 1, 2001, no date had been announced for its repeal, but article 3(3) of the Regulation of Bus Services in Greater London (Transitional Provisions) Order 2000 (S.I. 2000 No. 1462; not reproduced in this work), states that it will be repealed immediately after the end of the transitional period (as defined). By article 2 of S.I. 2000 No. 1462, the "transitional period" is defined as the period which begins with July 3, 2000 and ends with the last day on which a London local service licence granted under the 1985 Act ceases to be in force.   **A23.20**

London local service licences

34. London local services

(1) In this Act "*London local service*" means (subject to subsection (3) below) a local service with one or more stopping places in London.   **A23.21**

(2) In this Part of this Act—

  (a) "*bus service*" means a local service other than an excursion or tour; and

  (b) "*London bus service*" means a London local service other than an excursion or tour.

(3) Where a local service is or is to be provided both inside and outside London, any part of the service which is or is to be provided outside London shall be treated as a separate service for the purposes of this Act if there is any stopping place for that part of the service outside London.

[As to the prospective repeal of all the provisions in Part II of this Act, see the note to Part II above.]   **A23.22**

35. London local service licences

(1) Subject to subsection (2) below and to section 36 of this Act, a London local service shall not be provided except under a London local service licence granted in accordance with the following provisions of this Part of this Act.   **A23.23**

(2) A London local service licence is not required for the provision by any person under an agreement with the Railways Board [, or the Director of Passenger Rail Franchising, of any service secured by the Board or, as the case may be, the Director of Rail Franchising under section 4A of the 1962 Act (provision of road passenger transport services)].

(3) The traffic commissioner for the Metropolitan Traffic Area (referred to below in this Part of this Act as the metropolitan traffic commissioner) shall be responsible for granting London local service licences.

(4) Subject to subsection (5) below and to section 38(4) of this Act, a London local service licence shall be of no effect at any time at which the holder does not also hold—

    (a) a PSV operator's licence granted by the metropolitan traffic commissioner or by the traffic commissioner for any other traffic area . . .; or

    (b) a permit under section 22 of this Act.

(5) Subsection (4) above does not apply to a London local service licence held by a local education authority.

(6) Subject to section 68(3) of the 1981 Act (as applied by section 127(4) of this Act), if a London local service is provided in contravention of subsection (1) above, the operator of the service shall be liable on summary conviction to a fine not exceeding level 3 on the standard scale.

A23.24

[Section 35 is printed as amended by the Railways Act 1993 (Consequential Modifications) (No. 2) Order 1994 (S.I. 1994 No. 1649; not reproduced in this work); the Statute Law (Repeals) Act 1995, s.1(1) and Sched. 1, Pt V, group 2.

As to the prospective repeal of all the provisions in Part II of this Act, see the note to Part II above.

Pending the repeal of Part II, section 35 has effect (after July 2, 2000) as if subsections (1), (2) and (6) were omitted; see the Regulation of Bus Services in Greater London (Transitional Provisions) Order 2000 (S.I. 2000 No. 1462; not reproduced in this work), art.3(1)(a).

See further section 39(4) of this Act below.]

36. London bus services under the control of London Regional Transport

A23.25

(1) A London local service licence is not required for the provision of a London bus service—

    (a) by London Regional Transport or any subsidiary of theirs; or

    (b) by any other person in pursuance of any agreement entered into by London Regional Transport by virtue of [section 3(2) or (2A)(a)] of the London Regional Transport Act 1984 (referred to below in this section as the 1984 Act).

(2)–(7) *[Omitted.]*

A23.26

[Section 36 is printed as amended by the London Regional Transport Act 1996, s.4(2)(c).

As to the prospective repeal of all the provisions in Part II of this Act, see the note to Part II above.

Pending the repeal of Part II as a whole, Part II has effect (after July 2, 2000) as if section 36 were omitted; see the Regulation of Bus Services in Greater London (Transitional Provisions) Order 2000 (S.I. 2000 No. 1462; not reproduced in this work), art.3(1)(b).]

A23.27 ### 37. Grant of licences   *[Omitted.]*

38. Conditions attached to licences

(1)–(6) *[Omitted.]*

A23.28

(7) Subject to section 68(3) of the 1981 Act (as applied by section 127(4) of this Act), if a condition attached under this section to a London local service licence is contravened, the holder of the licence shall be liable on summary conviction to a fine not exceeding level 3 on the standard scale.

A23.29

[As to the prospective repeal of all the provisions in Part II of this Act, see the note to Part II above.]

39. Grant of licences for certain excursions or tours

(1) This section applies where, in the case of any application for a London local service   **A23.30**
licence, the metropolitan traffic commissioner is satisfied that the service which the applicant proposes to provide under the licence ("the proposed service") would be an excursion
or tour and is also satisfied either—

 (a) that the proposed service would not compete directly with any authorised London
      bus service; or

 (b) that the proposed service would operate only to enable passengers to attend special
      events.

(2) In subsection (1)(a) above, "*authorised London bus service*" means—

 (a) any London bus service for which a London local service licence has been granted;
      and

 (b) any London bus service which, by virtue of section 36(1) of this Act, does not
      require a London local service licence.

(3) In any case to which this section applies, sections 35, 37 and 38 of this Act shall apply
subject to the modifications provided by the following provisions of this section.

(4) Section 35(4) of this Act shall not prevent a London local service licence granted in
pursuance of this section from having effect for the purposes of the provision of a service
by means of a vehicle whose operator holds any such licence or permit as is there mentioned . . .

(5)–(10) *[Omitted.]*

[Section 39 is printed as amended by the Statute Law (Repeals) Act 1995, s.1(1) and Sched. 1, Pt V,   **A23.31**
group 2.
As to the prospective repeal of all the provisions in Part II of this Act, see the note to Part II above.]

*   *   *

PART VI

MISCELLANEOUS AND GENERAL

*   *   *

Provisions supplementary to Parts I and II

*   *   *

127. Offences and legal proceedings

(1) Section 65 of the 1981 Act (forgery and misuse of documents) shall apply to the fol-   **A23.32**
lowing documents, namely—

 (a) a permit under section 19 or 22 of this Act; and

 (b) a London local service licence.

(2) Section 66 of that Act (false statements to obtain licence, etc.) shall apply in relation
to a false statement for the purpose of obtaining the grant of any such permit or licence as
it applies in relation to a false statement for the purposes there mentioned.

(3) Section 67 of that Act (penalty for breach of regulations under that Act) shall have
effect as if Parts I and II of this Act were contained in that Act.

(4) The defence provided by section 68(3) of that Act (that the person charged took all reasonable precautions and exercised all due diligence to avoid the commission of an offence under certain provisions of that Act) shall apply in relation to an offence under any of the following provisions of this Act, that is to say, sections 23(5), 30(2), 35(6) and 37(7).

(5) The provisions of that Act mentioned in subsection (6) below shall apply in relation to an offence, or (as the case may be) in relation to proceedings for an offence, under Part I or II of this Act as they apply in relation to an offence, or in relation to proceedings for an offence, under Part II of that Act.

(6) Those provisions are—

section 69 (restrictions on institution in England or Wales of proceedings for an offence under Part II);

section 70 (duty to give information as to identity of driver in certain cases);

section 71 (evidence of certificate in proceedings in England or Wales for an offence under Part II);

section 72 (proof in summary proceedings in England and Wales of identity of driver of vehicle); and

section 74 (offences under Part II committed by companies).

(7) *[Applies to Scotland.]*

General supplementary provisions

*　　　*　　　*

137. Interpretation

　　(1) In this Act, unless the context otherwise requires—

"*the 1962 Act*" means the Transport Act 1962;

"*the 1972 Act*" means the Local Government Act 1972;

"*the 1968 Act*" means the Transport Act 1968;

"*the 1981 Act*" means the Public Passenger Vehicles Act 1981;

"*body*" means a body of persons, whether corporate or unincorporate;

. . .

"*excursion or tour*" means a service for the carriage of passengers by road at separate fares on which the passengers travel together on a journey, with or without breaks, from one or more places to one or more other places and back;

. . .

"*local service*" has the meaning given by section 2 of this Act;

"*London*" means the administrative area of Greater London as for the time being constituted;

"*London local service*" has the meaning given by section 34(1) of this Act;

. . .

"*prescribed*" means prescribed by regulations;

. . .

"*regulations*" means regulations made by the Secretary of State;

. . .

"*social services functions*" means functions which are social services functions for the purposes of the Local Authority Social Services Act 1970;

. . .

"*stopping place*" means, in relation to any service or part of a service, a point at which passengers are (or, in the case of a proposed service, are proposed to be) taken up or set down in the course of that service or part;

. . .

"*traffic area*" means a traffic area constituted for the purposes of the 1981 Act, and section 80 of that Act shall apply to references in this Act to the Metropolitan Traffic Area;

. . .

and the expressions listed in subsection (2) below have the same meaning as in the 1981 Act.

(2) Those expressions are—

"*company*";

"*contravention*";

"*fares*";

"*modification*";

"*operator*" (in references to the operator of a vehicle);

"*operating centre*";

"*PSV operator's licence*";

"*public service vehicle*";

"*road*";

"*statutory provision*"; and

"*traffic commissioner*".

[(2A) In this Act—

  (a) any reference to a county shall be construed in relation to Wales as including a reference to a county borough;

  (b) any reference to a county council shall be construed in relation to Wales as including a reference to a county borough council; and

  (c) section 17(4) and (5) of the Local Government (Wales) Act 1994 (references to counties and districts to be construed generally in relation to Wales as references to counties and county boroughs) shall not apply.]

(3) References in this Act to a vehicle's being used for carrying passengers for hire or reward shall be read in accordance with section 1(5) of the 1981 Act.

(4)–(6) *[Omitted.]*

(7) For the purposes of this Act the operator of a passenger transport service of any description is the person, or each of the persons, providing the service; and for those purposes the operator of a vehicle being used on a road for the carriage of passengers for hire or reward at separate fares shall be taken to be providing the service by means of the vehicle unless he proves that the service is or forms part of a service provided not by himself but by one or more other persons.

(8) *[Omitted.]*

[*Section 137 is printed as amended by the New Roads and Street Works Act 1991, s.168(1) and (2), Sched. 8, Pt IV, para.117(1) and (3), and Sched. 9; the Statute Law (Repeals) Act 1993, s.1(1) and Sched. 1, Pt XIV, group 2; the Local Government (Wales) Act 1994, s.22(1) and Sched. 7, para.39(10).*   **A23.34**

Only selected definitions in section 137(1) are reproduced.

As to the Local Authority Social Services Act 1970, see the note to the Community Drivers' Hours and Recording Equipment (Exemptions and Supplementary Provisions) Regulations 1986 (S.I. 1986 No. 1456), Schedule, para.2 below.

The Public Service Vehicles (Conduct of Drivers, Inspectors, Conductors and Passengers) Regulations 1990 (S.I. 1990 No. 1020) (q.v.) were made in part under section 137.]

* * *

SCHEDULE 1

AMENDMENTS CONSEQUENTIAL ON THE ABOLITION OF ROAD SERVICE LICENSING

* * *

A23.35   **16.**—(1) Subject to any provision made by or under this Act, in any enactment or instrument passed or made before the commencement of section 1 of this Act—

(a) any reference to a stage carriage service shall be construed as a reference to a local service;

(b) any reference to an express carriage service shall be construed as a reference to any service for the carriage of passengers for hire or reward at separate fares which is neither a local service nor one provided by a vehicle to which sub-paragraph (2) below applies;

(c) any reference to a stage carriage shall be construed as a reference to a public service vehicle being used in the provision of a local service;

(d) any reference to any express carriage shall be construed as a reference to a public service vehicle being used to carry passengers for hire or reward at separate fares other than one being used in the provision of a local service; and

(e) any reference to a contract shall be construed as a reference to a public service vehicle being used to carry passengers for hire or reward otherwise than at separate fares.

(2) When used in circumstances in which the conditions set out in Part III of Schedule I to the 1981 Act are fulfilled, a public service vehicle carrying passengers at separate fares shall be treated, for the purposes of any enactment or instrument to which paragraph (d) or (e) of sub-paragraph (1) above applies, as being used to carry passengers otherwise than at separate fares.

A23.36   *[Although section 1(3) of the Act was brought into operation on January 6, 1986 (see the Transport Act 1985 (Commencement No. 1) Order 1985 (S.I. 1985 No. 1887), art.3(1) and Schedule) for limited purposes ("to the extent necessary for the bringing into force of the provisions of Schedule 1 brought into force by this Order"), it is thought that "commencement" of section 1 (see paragraph 16(1) above) is the date when that section was brought fully into operation (i.e. October 26, 1986) (see the Transport Act 1985 (Commencement) (No. 6) Order 1986 (S.I. 1986 No. 1794)).]*

* * *

SCHEDULE 7

MINOR AND CONSEQUENTIAL AMENDMENTS

General

A23.37   **1.** In England and Wales, the provisions made by or under any enactment which apply to motor vehicles used—

(a) to carry passengers under a contract express or implied for the use of the vehicle as a whole at or for a fixed or agreed rate or sum; and

(b) to ply for hire for such use;

shall apply to motor vehicles adapted to carry less than nine passengers as they apply to motor vehicles adapted to carry less than eight passengers.

*　　　*　　　*

The Criminal Justice Act 1988

(1988 c. 33)

A24.01 An Act . . . to amend the law with regard to the jurisdiction and powers of criminal courts . . . and for connected purposes.

[29th July 1988]

*   *   *

PART IV

REVIEWS OF SENTENCING

35. Scope of Part IV

A24.02 (1) A case to which this Part of this Act applies may be referred to the Court of Appeal under section 36 below.

(2) Subject to Rules of Court, the jurisdiction of the Court of Appeal under section 36 below shall be exercised by the criminal division of the Court, and references to the Court of Appeal in this Part of this Act shall be construed as references to that division.

(3) This Part of this Act applies to any case [—

(a) of a description specified in an order under this section; or

(b) in which sentence is passed on a person—

(i) for an offence triable only on indictment; or

(ii) for an offence of a description specified in an order under this section]

(4) The Secretary of State may by order made by statutory instrument provide that this Part of this Act shall apply to any case [of a description specified in the order or to any case] in which sentence is passed on a person for an offence triable either way of a description specified in the order.

(5) A statutory instrument containing an order under this section shall be subject to annulment in pursuance of a resolution of either House of Parliament.

(6) In this Part of this Act "*sentence*" has the same meaning as in the Criminal Appeal Act 1968, except that it does not include an interim hospital order under Part III of the Mental Health Act 1983, and "sentencing" shall be construed accordingly.

(7)–(11) *[Apply to Northern Ireland.]*

A24.03 *[Section 35 is printed as amended by the Criminal Justice and Public Order Act 1994, s.168(1) and Sched. 9, para.34.*

The term "sentence" is defined in section 50 of the Criminal Appeal Act 1968 (q.v.) for the purposes of that Act.]

36. Reviews of sentencing

A24.04 (1) If it appears to the Attorney General—

(a) that the sentencing of a person in a proceeding in the Crown Court has been unduly lenient; and

(b) that the case is one to which this Part of this Act applies, he may, with the leave of the Court of Appeal, refer the case to them for them to review the sentencing of that person; and on such a reference the Court of Appeal may—

    (i) quash any sentence passed on him in the proceeding; and

    (ii) in place of it pass such sentence as they think appropriate for the case and as the court below had power to pass when dealing with him.

(2) Without prejudice to the generality of subsection (1) above, the condition specified in paragraph (a) of that subsection may be satisfied if it appears to the Attorney General that the judge erred in law as to his powers of sentencing [or failed to impose a sentence required by [section 109(2), 110(2) or 111(2) of the Powers of Criminal Courts (Sentencing) Act 2000]].

(3) For the purposes of this Part of this Act any two or more sentences are to be treated as passed in the same proceeding if they would be so treated for the purposes of section 10 of the Criminal Appeal Act 1968 [*q.v.*].

(4) No judge shall sit as a member of the Court of Appeal on the hearing of, or shall determine any application in proceedings incidental or preliminary to, a reference under this section of a sentence passed by himself.

(5) Where the Court of Appeal have concluded their review of a case referred to them under this section the Attorney General or the person to whose sentencing the reference relates may refer a point of law involved in any sentence passed on that person in the proceeding to the House of Lords for their opinion, and the House shall consider the point and give their opinion on it accordingly, and either remit the case to the Court of Appeal to be dealt with or deal with it themselves; and section 35(1) of the Criminal Appeal Act 1968 (composition of House for appeals) shall apply also in relation to any proceedings of the House under this section.

(6) A reference under subsection (5) above shall be made only with the leave of the Court of Appeal or the House of Lords; and leave shall not be granted unless it is certified by the Court of Appeal that the point of law is of general public importance and it appears to the Court of Appeal or the House of Lords (as the case may be) that the point is one which ought to be considered by that House.

(7) For the purpose of dealing with a case under this section the House of Lords may exercise any powers of the Court of Appeal.

(8) The supplementary provisions contained in Schedule 3 to this Act shall have effect.

(9) *[Applies to Northern Ireland.]*

[Section 36 is printed as amended by the Crime (Sentences) Act 1997, s.55(1) and Sched. 4, para.13;   **A24.05**
the Powers of Criminal Courts (Sentencing) Act 2000, s.165(1) and Sched. 9, para.102.]

PART V

JURISDICTION, IMPRISONMENT, FINES, ETC

Jurisdiction

*   *   *

40. Power to join in indictment count for common assault, etc.

(1) A count charging a person with a summary offence to which this section applies may   **A24.06**
be included in an indictment if the charge—

    (a) is founded on the same facts or evidence as a count charging an indictable offence; or

(b) is part of a series of offences of the same or similar character as an indictable offence which is also charged,

but only if (in either case) the facts or evidence relating to the offence were disclosed [to a magistrates' court inquiring into the offence as examining justices] [or are disclosed by material which, in pursuance of regulations made under paragraph 1 of Schedule 3 to the Crime and Disorder Act 1998 (procedure where person sent for trial under section 51), has been served on the person charged].

(2) Where a count charging an offence to which this section applies is included in an indictment, the offence shall be tried in the same manner as if it were an indictable offence; but the Crown Court may only deal with the offender in respect of it in a manner in which a magistrates' court could have dealt with him.

(3) The offences to which this section applies are—

    (a) common assault;

    [(aa) an offence under section 90(1) of the Criminal Justice Act 1991 (assaulting a prisoner custody officer);]

    [(ab) an offence under section 13(1) of the Criminal Justice and Public Order Act 1994 (assaulting a secure training custody officer);]

    (b) an offence under section 12(1) of the Theft Act 1968 [*q.v.*] (taking motor vehicle or other conveyance without authority, etc.);

    (c) an offence under [section 103(1)(b) of the Road Traffic Act 1988] [*q.v.*] (driving a motor vehicle while disqualified);

    (d) an offence mentioned in the first column of Schedule 2 to the Magistrates' Courts Act 1980 (criminal damage, etc.) which would otherwise be triable only summarily by virtue of section 22(2) of that Act; and

    (e) any summary offence specified under subsection (4) below.

(4) The Secretary of State may by order made by statutory instrument specify for the purposes of this section any summary offence which is punishable with imprisonment or involves obligatory or discretionary disqualification from driving.

(5) *[Statutory instruments subject to negative resolution procedure.]*

A24.07   *[Section 40 is printed as amended by the Road Traffic (Consequential Provisions) Act 1988, s.4 and Sched. 3, para.39; the Criminal Justice and Public Order Act 1994, s.168(1) and Sched. 9, para.35; the Crime and Disorder Act 1998, s.119 and Sched. 8, para.66.*

    The words "to a magistrates' court inquiring into the offence as examining justices" within square brackets in section 40(1) were inserted in place of the words "in an examination or deposition taken before a justice in the presence of the person charged" on March 8, 1997 by the Criminal Procedure and Investigations Act 1996, s.47 and Sched. 1, para.34, in relation to any alleged offence in relation to which Part I of the 1996 Act applies; see the Criminal Procedure and Investigations Act 1996 (Commencement) (Section 65 and Schedules 1 and 2) Order 1997 (S.I. 1997 No. 683).]

41. Power of Crown Court to deal with summary offence where person committed for either way offence

A24.08   (1) Where a magistrates' court commits a person to the Crown Court for trial on indictment for an offence triable either way or a number of such offences, it may also commit him for trial for any summary offence with which he is charged and which—

    (a) is punishable with imprisonment or involves obligatory or discretionary disqualification from driving; and

    (b) arises out of circumstances which appear to the court to be the same as or connected with those giving rise to the offence, or one of the offences, triable either way, whether or not evidence relating to that summary offence appears on the depositions or written statements in the case; and the trial of the information charging the summary offence shall then be treated as if the magistrates' court had adjourned it under section 10 of the Magistrates' Courts Act 1980 and had not fixed the time and place for its resumption.

(2) Where a magistrates' court commits a person to the Crown Court for trial on indictment for a number of offences triable either way and exercises the power conferred by subsection (1) above in respect of a summary offence, the magistrates' court shall give the Crown Court and the person who is committed for trial a notice stating which of the offences triable either way appears to the court to arise out of circumstances which are the same as or connected with those giving rise to the summary offence.

(3) A magistrates' court's decision to exercise the power conferred by subsection (1) above shall not be subject to appeal or liable to be questioned in any court.

(4) The committal of a person under this section in respect of an offence to which section 40 above applies shall not preclude the exercise in relation to the offence of the power conferred by that section; but where he is tried on indictment for such an offence, the functions of the Crown Court under this section in relation to the offence shall cease.

(5) If he is convicted on the indictment, the Crown Court shall consider whether the conditions specified in subsection (1) above were satisfied.

(6) If it considers that they were satisfied, it shall state to him the substance of the summary offence and ask him whether he pleads guilty or not guilty.

(7) If he pleads guilty, the Crown Court shall convict him, but may deal with him in respect of that offence only in a manner in which a magistrates' court could have dealt with him.

(8) If he does not plead guilty, the powers of the Crown Court shall cease in respect of the offence except as provided by subsection (9) below.

(9) If the prosecution inform the Court that they would not desire to submit evidence on the charge relating to the summary offence, the Court shall dismiss it.

(10) The Crown Court shall inform the clerk of the magistrates' court of the outcome of any proceedings under this section.

(11) Where the Court of Appeal allows an appeal against conviction of an offence triable either way which arose out of circumstances which were the same as or connected with those giving rise to a summary offence of which the appellant was convicted under this section—

(a) it shall set aside his conviction of the summary offence and give the clerk of the magistrates' court notice that it has done so; and

(b) it may direct that no further proceedings in relation to the offence are to be undertaken;

and the proceedings before the Crown Court in relation to the offence shall thereafter be disregarded for all purposes.

(12) A notice under subsection (11) above shall include particulars of any direction given under paragraph (b) of that subsection in relation to the offence.

(13) *[Repealed by the Access to Justice Act 1999.]*

[Section 41 is printed as amended (with effect from April 1, 2001) by the Access to Justice Act 1999,   **A24.09**
s.106 and Sched. 15, Pt V(7) (see the Access to Justice Act 1999 (Commencement No. 7, Transitional

Provisions and Savings) Order 2001 (S.I. 2001 No. 916; not reproduced in this work), arts 1(2) and 2(c)(ii)).]

*   *   *

SCHEDULE 3

Section 36

REVIEWS OF SENTENCING—SUPPLEMENTARY

A24.10   **1.** Notice of an application for leave to refer a case to the Court of Appeal under section 36 above shall be given within 28 days from the day on which the sentence, or the last of the sentences, in the case was passed.

2. If the registrar of criminal appeals is given notice of a reference or application to the Court of Appeal under section 36 above, he shall—

(a) take all necessary steps for obtaining a hearing of the reference or application; and

(b) obtain and lay before the Court in proper form all documents, exhibits and other things which appear necessary for the proper determination of the reference or application.

A24.11   **3.** Rules of court may enable a person to whose sentencing such a reference or application relates to obtain from the registrar any documents or things, including copies or reproductions of documents, required for the reference or application and may authorise the registrar to make charges for them in accordance with scales and rates fixed from time to time by the Treasury.

4. An application to the Court of Appeal for leave to refer a case to the House of Lords under section 36(5) above shall be made within the period of 14 days beginning with the date on which the Court of Appeal conclude their review of the case; and an application to the House of Lords for leave shall be made within the period of 14 days beginning with the date on which the Court of Appeal conclude their review or refuse leave to refer the case to the House of Lords.

A24.12   **5.** The time during which a person whose case has been referred for review under section 36 above is in custody pending its review and pending any reference to the House of Lords under subsection (5) of that section shall be reckoned as part of the term of any sentence to which he is for the time being subject.

6. Except as provided by paragraphs 7 and 8 below, a person whose sentencing is the subject of a reference to the Court of Appeal under section 36 above shall be entitled to be present, if he wishes it, on the hearing of the reference, although he may be in custody.

A24.13   **7.** A person in custody shall not be entitled to be present—

(a) on an application by the Attorney General for leave to refer a case; or

(b) on any proceedings preliminary or incidental to a reference,

unless the Court of Appeal give him leave to be present.

8. The power of the Court of Appeal to pass sentence on a person may be exercised although he is not present.

A24.14   **9.** A person whose sentencing is the subject of a reference to the House of Lords under section 36(5) above and who is detained pending the hearing of that reference shall not be entitled to be present on the hearing of the reference or of any proceeding preliminary or incidental thereto except where an order of the House authorises him to be present, or where the House or the Court of Appeal, as the case may be, give him leave to be present.

10. The term of any sentence passed by the Court of Appeal or House of Lords under section 36 above shall, unless they otherwise direct, begin to run from the time when it would have begun to run if passed in the proceeding in relation to which the reference was made.

11. When on a reference to the Court of Appeal under section 36 above or a reference to the House of Lords under subsection (5) of that section the person whose sentencing is the subject of the reference appears by counsel for the purpose of presenting any argument to the Court or the House, he shall be entitled to his costs, that is to say to the payment out of central funds of such funds as are reasonably sufficient to compensate him for expenses properly incurred by him for the purpose of being represented on the reference; and any amount recoverable under this paragraph shall be ascertained, as soon as practicable, by the registrar of criminal appeals or, as the case may be, such officer as may be prescribed by order of the House of Lords.   **A24.15**

12. *[Applies to Northern Ireland.]*

*   *   *

The Road Traffic Act 1988

(1988 c. 52)

A25.01 An Act to consolidate certain enactments relating to road traffic with amendments to give effect to recommendations of the Law Commission and the Scottish Law Commission.

[15th November 1988]

ARRANGEMENT OF SECTIONS

PART I

PRINCIPAL ROAD SAFETY PROVISIONS

Driving offences

Section

PART III

LICENSING OF DRIVERS OF VEHICLES

PART IV

LICENSING OF DRIVERS OF LARGE GOODS VEHICLES AND PASSENGER-CARRYING VEHICLES

PART V

DRIVING INSTRUCTION

Instructors to be registered or licensed

Registration

Licences

Appeals

Examinations and tests

Disabled persons: emergency control certificates, etc.

General and supplemental

PART VI

PART VII

MISCELLANEOUS AND GENERAL

PART 1

Principal Road Safety Provisions

Driving offences

[1. Causing death by dangerous driving

A25.03   A person who causes the death of another person by driving a mechanically propelled vehicle dangerously on a road or other public place is guilty of an offence.]

A25.04   *[Section 1 is printed as substituted by the Road Traffic Act 1991, s.1.*

The offence under section 1 is expressly excluded from the application of the Criminal Justice Act 1982, s.32 (early release of prisoners); see Part II of Schedule 1 to that Act, as amended by the Road Traffic (Consequential Provisions) Act 1988, s.4 and Sched. 3, para.24.

An offence under section 1 is designated as a "serious arrestable offence" by the Police and Criminal Evidence Act 1984, s.116(2) and Sched. 5, Pt II, as amended by the Road Traffic (Consequential Provisions) Act 1988, s.4 and Sched. 3, para.27(5).

As to alternative charges to a charge under section 1, see the Road Traffic Offenders Act 1988, s.24(1) below.

The offence under section 1 being punishable by a term of imprisonment of five years or more, if a magistrates' court grants bail to a person charged with or convicted of an offence under this section, the prosecution (provided objection was taken to the application for bail) may appeal to a judge of the Crown Court against the order granting bail under the Bail (Amendment) Act 1993, s.1 (not reproduced in this work).

Subject to (in particular) the Powers of Criminal Courts (Sentencing) Act 2000, s.79 (general restrictions on imposing discretionary custodial sentences) and s.80 (length of discretionary custodial sentences), where a person aged at least 14 but under 18 is convicted of an offence under this section and the court is of the opinion that none of the other methods in which the case may legally be dealt with is suitable, it may sentence the offender to be detained for such period (not exceeding the maximum term of imprisonment with which the offence is punishable in the case of a person aged 21 or over) as may be specified, and that person will be detained in such place and under such conditions as the Secretary of State may direct or arrange; see the 2000 Act, ss.91(2)(a), (3), (4) and 92(1).]

[2. Dangerous driving

A25.05   A person who drives a mechanically propelled vehicle dangerously on a road or other public place is guilty of an offence.]

A25.06   *[Section 2 is printed as substituted by the Road Traffic Act 1991, s.1.*

As to alternative charges to a charge under section 2, see the Road Traffic Offenders Act 1988, s.24(1) below.]

[2A. Meaning of dangerous driving

A25.07   (1) For the purposes of sections 1 and 2 above a person is to be regarded as driving dangerously if (and, subject to subsection (2) below, only if)—

(a) the way he drives falls far below what would be expected of a competent and careful driver, and

(b) it would be obvious to a competent and careful driver that driving in that way would be dangerous.

(2) A person is also to be regarded as driving dangerously for the purposes of sections 1 and 2 above if it would be obvious to a competent and careful driver that driving the vehicle in its current state would be dangerous.

(3) In subsections (1) and (2) above "*dangerous*" refers to danger either of injury to any person or of serious damage to property; and in determining for the purposes of those sub-

sections what would be expected of, or obvious to, a competent and careful driver in a particular case, regard shall be had not only to the circumstances of which he could be expected to be aware but also to any circumstances shown to have been within the knowledge of the accused.

(4) In determining for the purposes of subsection (2) above the state of a vehicle, regard may be had to anything attached to or carried on or in it and to the manner in which it is attached or carried.]

[Section 2A was inserted by the Road Traffic Act 1991, s.1.]   **A25.08**

[3. Careless, and inconsiderate, driving

If a person drives a mechanically propelled vehicle on a road or other public place   **A25.09**
without due care and attention, or without reasonable consideration for other persons using the road or place, he is guilty of an offence.]

[Section 3 is printed as substituted by the Road Traffic Act 1991, s.2.]   **A25.10**

[3A. Causing death by careless driving when under the influence of drink or drugs

(1) If a person causes the death of another person by driving a mechanically propelled   **A25.11**
vehicle on a road or other public place without due care and attention, or without reasonable consideration for other persons using the road or place, and—

   (a) he is, at the time when he is driving, unfit to drive through drink or drugs, or

   (b) he has consumed so much alcohol that the proportion of it in his breath, blood or urine at that time exceeds the prescribed limit, or

   (c) he is, within 18 hours after that time, required to provide a specimen in pursuance of section 7 of this Act, but without reasonable excuse fails to provide it,

he is guilty of an offence.

(2) For the purposes of this section a person shall be taken to be unfit to drive at any time when his ability to drive properly is impaired.

(3) Subsection (1)(b) and (c) above shall not apply in relation to a person driving a mechanically propelled vehicle other than a motor vehicle.]

[Section 3A was inserted by the Road Traffic Act 1991, s.3.
As to alternative charges to a charge under section 3A, see the Road Traffic Offenders Act 1988, s.24(1)   **A25.12**
below.
Subject to (in particular) the Powers of Criminal Courts (Sentencing) Act 2000, s.79 (general restrictions on imposing discretionary custodial sentences) and s.80 (length of discretionary custodial sentences), where a person aged at least 14 but under 18 is convicted of an offence under this section and the court is of the opinion that none of the other methods in which the case may legally be dealt with is suitable, it may sentence the offender to be detained for such period (not exceeding the maximum term of imprisonment with which the offence is punishable in the case of a person aged 21 or over) as may be specified, and that person will be detained in such place and under such conditions as the Secretary of State may direct or arrange; see the 2000 Act, ss.91(2)(b), (3), (4) and 92(1).]

Motor vehicles: drink and drugs

4. Driving, or being in charge, when under influence of drink or drugs

(1) A person who, when driving or attempting to drive a [mechanically propelled vehicle]   **A25.13**
on a road or other public place, is unfit to drive through drink or drugs is guilty of an offence.

(2) Without prejudice to subsection (1) above, a person who, when in charge of a [mechanically propelled vehicle] which is on a road or other public place, is unfit to drive through drink or drugs is guilty of an offence.

(3) For the purposes of subsection (2) above, a person shall be deemed not to have been in charge of a [mechanically propelled vehicle] if he proves that at the material time the circumstances were such that there was no likelihood of his driving it so long as he remained unfit to drive through drink or drugs.

(4) The court may, in determining whether there was such a likelihood as is mentioned in subsection (3) above, disregard any injury to him and any damage to the vehicle.

(5) For the purposes of this section, a person shall be taken to be unfit to drive if his ability to drive properly is for the time being impaired.

(6) A constable may arrest a person without warrant if he has reasonable cause to suspect that person is or has been committing an offence under this section.

(7) For the purpose of arresting a person under the power conferred by subsection (6) above, a constable may enter (if need be by force) any place where that person is or where the constable, with reasonable cause, suspects him to be.

(8) Subsection (7) above does not extend to Scotland, and nothing in that subsection affects any rule of law in Scotland concerning the right of a constable to enter any premises for any purpose.

A25.14   *[Section 4 is printed as amended by the Road Traffic Act 1991, s.4.*

As to alternative charges to a charge under section 4(1), see the Road Traffic Offenders Act 1988, s.24(1) below.

As to the application of sections 4–11 to tramcars and other guided vehicles, see section 192A below.

The code of practice for the identification of persons by police officers does not affect any procedure under sections 4–11 of this Act; see paragraph 1.15(i) of Code D (1995) under the Police and Criminal Evidence Act 1984.]

5. Driving or being in charge of a motor vehicle with alcohol concentration above prescribed limit

A25.15   (1) If a person—

    (a)   drives or attempts to drive a motor vehicle on a road or other public place, or

    (b)   is in charge of a motor vehicle on a road or other public place,

after consuming so much alcohol that the proportion of it in his breath, blood or urine exceeds the prescribed limit he is guilty of an offence.

(2) It is a defence for a person charged with an offence under subsection (1)(b) above to prove that at the time he is alleged to have committed the offence the circumstances were such that there was no likelihood of his driving the vehicle whilst the proportion of alcohol in his breath, blood or urine remained likely to exceed the prescribed limit.

(3) The court may, in determining whether there was such a likelihood as is mentioned in subsection (2) above, disregard any injury to him and any damage to the vehicle.

A25.16   *[As to alternative charges to a charge under section 5(1), see the Road Traffic Offenders Act 1988, s.24(1) below.*

See also the notes to section 4 above.]

6. Breath tests

A25.17   (1) Where a constable in uniform has reasonable cause to suspect—

(a) that a person driving or attempting to drive or in charge of a motor vehicle on a road or other public place has alcohol in his body or has committed a traffic offence whilst the vehicle was in motion, or

(b) that a person has been driving or attempting to drive or been in charge of a motor vehicle on a road or other public place with alcohol in his body and that that person still has alcohol in his body, or

(c) that a person has been driving or attempting to drive or been in charge of a motor vehicle on a road or other public place and has committed a traffic offence whilst the vehicle was in motion,

he may, subject to section 9 of this Act, require him to provide a specimen of breath for a breath test.

(2) If an accident occurs owing to the presence of a motor vehicle on a road or other public place, a constable may, subject to section 9 of this Act, require any person who he has reasonable cause to believe was driving or attempting to drive or in charge of the vehicle at the time of the accident to provide a specimen of breath for a breath test.

(3) A person may be required under subsection (1) or subsection (2) above to provide a specimen either at or near the place where the requirement is made or, if the requirement is made under subsection (2) above and the constable making the requirement thinks fit, at a police station specified by the constable.

(4) A person who, without reasonable excuse, fails to provide a specimen of breath when required to do so in pursuance of this section is guilty of an offence.

(5) A constable may arrest a person without warrant if—

(a) as a result of a breath test he has reasonable cause to suspect that the proportion of alcohol in that person's breath or blood exceeds the prescribed limit, or

(b) that person has failed to provide a specimen of breath for a breath test when required to do so in pursuance of this section and the constable has reasonable cause to suspect that he has alcohol in his body,

but a person shall not be arrested by virtue of this subsection when he is at a hospital as a patient.

(6) A constable may, for the purpose of requiring a person to provide a specimen of breath under subsection (2) above in a case where he has reasonable cause to suspect that the accident involved injury to another person or of arresting him in such a case under subsection (5) above, enter (if need be by force) any place where that person is or where the constable, with reasonable cause, suspects him to be.

(7) Subsection (6) above does not extend to Scotland, and nothing in that subsection shall affect any rule of law in Scotland concerning the right of a constable to enter any premises for any purpose.

(8) In this section "*traffic offence*" means an offence under—

(a) any provision of Part II of the Public Passenger Vehicles Act 1981 [*q.v.*],

(b) any provision of the Road Traffic Regulation Act 1984 [*q.v.*],

(c) any provision of the Road Traffic Offenders Act 1988 [*q.v.*] except Part III, or

(d) any provision of this Act except Part V.

[Offences of failing to supply a specimen under section 6 and any other offences of which persons may have been convicted in the same proceedings may be recorded in national police records; see the National Police Records (Recordable Offences) Regulations 2000 (S.I. 2000 No. 1139; not reproduced in this work). See also the notes to section 4 above.]   **A25.18**

7. Provision of specimens for analysis

A25.19   (1) In the course of an investigation into whether a person has committed an offence under [section 3A, 4] or 5 of this Act a constable may, subject to the following provisions of this section and section 9 of this Act, require him—

    (a) to provide two specimens of breath for analysis by means of a device of a type approved by the Secretary of State, or

    (b) to provide a specimen of blood or urine for a laboratory test.

    (2) A requirement under this section to provide specimens of breath can only be made at a police station.

    (3) A requirement under this section to provide a specimen of blood or urine can only be made at a police station or at a hospital; and it cannot be made at a police station unless—

    (a) the constable making the requirement has reasonable cause to believe that for medical reasons a specimen of breath cannot be provided or should not be required, or

    (b) at the time the requirement is made a device or a reliable device of the type mentioned in subsection (1)(a) above is not available at the police station or it is then for any other reason not practicable to use such a device there, or

    [(bb) a device of the type mentioned in subsection (1)(a) above has been used at the police station but the constable who required the specimens of breath has reasonable cause to believe that the device has not produced a reliable indication of the proportion of alcohol in the breath of the person concerned, or]

    (c) the suspected offence is one under [section 3A, 4] of this Act and the constable making the requirement has been advised by a medical practitioner that the condition of the person required to provide the specimen might be due to some drug;

but may then be made notwithstanding that the person required to provide the specimen has already provided or been required to provide two specimens of breath.

    (4) If the provision of a specimen other than a specimen of breath may be required in pursuance of this section the question whether it is to be a specimen of blood or a specimen of urine shall be decided by the constable making the requirement, but if a medical practitioner is of the opinion that for medical reasons a specimen of blood cannot or should not be taken the specimen shall be a specimen of urine.

    (5) A specimen of urine shall be provided within one hour of the requirement for its provision being made and after the provision of a previous specimen of urine.

    (6) A person who, without reasonable excuse, fails to provide a specimen when required to do so in pursuance of this section is guilty of an offence.

    (7) A constable must, on requiring any person to provide a specimen in pursuance of this section, warn him that a failure to provide it may render him liable to prosecution.

A25.20   *[Section 7 is printed as amended by the Road Traffic Act 1991, s.48 and Sched. 4, para. 42(a) and (b); the Criminal Procedure and Investigations Act 1996, s.63(1).*

In section 7, section 7(3)(bb) applies only where it is proposed to make a requirement mentioned in section 7(3) after the day appointed under section 63(4) of the Criminal Procedure and Investigations Act 1996; see ibid., s.63(3). The Criminal Procedure and Investigations Act 1996 (Appointed Day No. 3) Order 1997 (S.I. 1997 No. 682) designated April 1, 1997 as the appointed day for the purposes of section 63(4) of the 1996 Act.

The breath analysis devices approved under section 7(1)(a) are:

Camic Datamaster[1]	effective March 1, 1998 (see the Breath Analysis Devices Approval 1998, dated February 2, 1998)
Lion Intoxilyzer 6000UK[2]	effective March 1, 1998 (see the Breath Analysis Devices Approval 1998, dated February 2, 1998)
Intoximeter EC/IR[3]	effective March 1, 1998 (see the Breath Analysis Devices (No. 2) Approval 1998, dated February 25, 1998)
Lion Intoxilyzer 6000 UK[4]	effective June 1, 1998 (see the Breath Analysis Devices (No. 3) Approval 1998, dated May 22, 1998)
Lion Intoxilyzer 6000 UK[5]	effective November 2, 1999 (see the Breath Analysis Devices Approval 1999, dated October 25, 1999)

[1] comprising the Camic Datamaster, the Camic gas system and software version 31-10-95
[2] comprising the Lion Intoxilyzer 6000UK, the Lion Intoxilyzer 6000UK gas delivery system type A or type C and software version 2.33
[3] comprising the Lion Intoxilyzer EC/IR, the Lion Intoxilyzer EC/IR gas delivery system and software version EC/IR–UK 5.23
[4] comprising the Lion Intoxilyzer 6000UK, the Lion Intoxilyzer 6000UK gas delivery system type B and software version 2.33
[5] comprising the Lion Intoxilyzer 6000UK, the Lion Intoxilyzer 6000UK gas delivery system type A, B and C and software version 2.34

In the code of practice for the detention, treatment and questioning of persons by police officers it is stated that procedures under section 7 of this Act do not constitute interviewing for the purpose of the code; see paragraph 11.1A of Code C (1995) under the Police and Criminal Evidence Act 1984.
See also the notes to section 4 above.]

8. Choice of specimens of breath

(1) Subject to subsection (2) below, of any two specimens of breath provided by any person in pursuance of section 7 of this Act that with the lower proportion of alcohol in the breath shall be used and the other shall be disregarded. **A25.21**

(2) If the specimen with the lower proportion of alcohol contains no more than 50 microgrammes of alcohol in 100 millilitres of breath, the person who provided it may claim that it should be replaced by such specimen as may be required under section 7(4) of this Act and, if he then provides such a specimen, neither specimen of breath shall be used.

(3) The Secretary of State may by regulations substitute another proportion of alcohol in the breath for that specified in subsection (2) above.

[See the notes to section 4 above.] **A25.22**

9. Protection for hospital patients

(1) While a person is at a hospital as a patient he shall not be required to provide a specimen of breath for a breath test or to provide a specimen for a laboratory test unless the medical practitioner in immediate charge of his case has been notified of the proposal to make the requirement; and— **A25.23**

(a) if the requirement is then made, it shall be for the provision of a specimen at the hospital, but

(b) if the medical practitioner objects on the ground specified in subsection (2) below, the requirement shall not be made.

(2) The ground on which the medical practitioner may object is that the requirement of the provision of a specimen or, in the case of a specimen of blood or urine, the warning required under section 7(7) of this Act, would be prejudicial to the proper care and treatment of the patient.

A25.24   *[See the notes to section 4 above.]*

10. Detention of persons affected by alcohol or a drug

A25.25   (1) Subject to subsections (2) and (3) below, a person required to provide a specimen of breath, blood or urine may afterwards be detained at a police station until it appears to the constable that, were that person then driving or attempting to drive a [mechanically propelled vehicle] on a road, he would not be committing an offence under section 4 or 5 of this Act.

(2) A person shall not be detained in pursuance of this section if it appears to a constable that there is no likelihood of his driving or attempting to drive a [mechanically propelled vehicle] whilst his ability to drive properly is impaired or whilst the proportion of alcohol in his breath, blood or urine exceeds the prescribed limit.

(3) A constable must consult a medical practitioner on any question arising under this section whether a person's ability to drive properly is or might be impaired through drugs and must act on the medical practitioner's advice.

A25.26   *[Section 10 is printed as amended by the Road Traffic Act 1991, s.48 and Sched. 4, para.43. See also the notes to section 4 above.]*

11. Interpretation of sections [3A] to 10

A25.27   (1) The following provisions apply for the interpretation of sections [3A] to 10 of this Act.

(2) In those sections—

"*breath test*" means a preliminary test for the purpose of obtaining, by means of a device of a type approved by the Secretary of State, an indication whether the proportion of alcohol in a person's breath or blood is likely to exceed the prescribed limit,

"*drug*" includes any intoxicant other than alcohol,

"*fail*" includes refuse,

"*hospital*" means an institution which provides medical or surgical treatment for in-patients or out-patients,

"*the prescribed limit*" means, as the case may require—

(a) 35 microgrammes of alcohol in 100 millilitres of breath,

(b) 80 milligrammes of alcohol in 100 millilitres of blood, or

(c) 107 milligrammes of alcohol in 100 millilitres of urine, or such other proportion as may be prescribed by regulations made by the Secretary of State.

(3) A person does not provide a specimen of breath for a breath test or for analysis unless the specimen—

(a) is sufficient to enable the test or the analysis to be carried out, and

(b) is provided in such a way as to enable the objective of the test or analysis to be satisfactorily achieved.

(4) A person provides a specimen of blood if and only if he consents to its being taken by a medical practitioner and it is so taken.

[Section 11 is printed as amended by the Road Traffic Act 1991, s.48 and Sched. 4, para.44.   **A25.28**
The devices which have been approved for use in England and Wales under section 11(2) are:

Alcotest 80	(see the Breath Test Device (Approval) (No. 1) Order 1968)
Alcotest 80A	(see the Breath Test Device (Approval) (No. 1) Order 1975)
Alcolyser	(see the Breath Test Device (Approval) (No. 1) Order 1979)
Alcolmeter	(see the Breath Test Device (Approval) (No. 2) Order 1979)
Alert	(see the Breath Test Device (Approval) (No. 1) Order 1980)
Lion Alcometer S–L2A	(see the Breath Test Device (Approval) Order 1987)
Draeger Alcotest 7410	(see the Breath Test Device (Approval) 1993)
Lion Alcolmeter SL–400 (UK) (INDICATING DISPLAY FORM)	(see the Breath Test Device (No. 2) (Approval) 1993)
Lion Alcolmeter SL–400A (INDICATING DISPLAY FORM)	(see the Breath Test Device (Approval) 1997)
Alcosensor IV UK	(see the Breath Test Device Approval 1999 (effective October 15, 1999))
Lion Alcolmeter SL–400A (INDICATING DISPLAY FORM) software version 3.31	(see the Breath Test Device (Approval) 2000)

See further the notes to section 4 above.]

Motor racing and motoring events on public ways

12. Motor racing on public ways

(1) A person who promotes or takes part in a race or trial of speed between motor vehicles on a public way is guilty of an offence.   **A25.29**

(2) In this section "*public way*" means, in England and Wales, a [highway] . . .

[Section 12 is printed as amended by the Road Traffic Act 1991, s.48 and Sched. 4, para.45.   **A25.30**
Words relating exclusively and expressly to Scotland have been omitted from section 12(2).]

13. Regulation of motoring events on public ways

(1) A person who promotes or takes part in a competition or trial (other than a race or trial of speed) involving the use of motor vehicles on a public way is guilty of an offence unless the competition or trial—   **A25.31**

(a) is authorised, and

(b) is conducted in accordance with any conditions imposed,

by or under regulations under this section.

(2) The Secretary of State may by regulations authorise, or provide for authorising, the holding of competitions or trials (other than races or trials of speed) involving the use of motor vehicles on public ways either—

(a) generally, or

(b) as regards any area, or as regards any class or description of competition or trial or any particular competition or trial,

subject to such conditions, including conditions requiring the payment of fees, as may be imposed by or under the regulations.

(3) Regulations under this section may—

(a) prescribe the procedure to be followed, and the particulars to be given, in connection with applications for authorisation under the regulations, and

(b) make different provision for different classes or descriptions of competition or trial.

(4) In this section "*public way*" means, in England and Wales, a [highway] . . .

A25.32 *[Section 13 is printed as amended by the Road Traffic Act 1991, s.48 and Sched. 4, para.46.*

The functions of the Secretary of State exercisable under section 13(2) in relation to Wales have been transferred to the National Assembly for Wales by the National Assembly for Wales (Transfer of Functions) Order 1999 (S.I. 1999 No. 672; not reproduced in this work), art.2 and Sched. 1.

As to the transfer of functions of the Secretary of State under section 13(2) which are exercisable in relation to Scotland to the Scottish Ministers, see the Scotland Act 1998 (Transfer of Functions to the Scottish Ministers etc.) Order 1999 (S.I. 1999 No. 1750; not reproduced in this work), art.2 and Sched. 1.

Words relating exclusively and expressly to Scotland have been omitted from section 13(4).]

[13A. Disapplication of sections 1 to 3 for authorised motoring events

A25.33 (1) A person shall not be guilty of an offence under sections 1, 2 or 3 of this Act by virtue of driving a vehicle in a public place other than a road if he shows that he was driving in accordance with an authorisation for a motoring event given under regulations made by the Secretary of State.

(2) Regulations under this section may in particular—

(a) prescribe the persons by whom, and limit the circumstances in which and the places in respect of which, authorisations may be given under the regulations;

(b) specify conditions which must be included among those incorporated in authorisations;

(c) provide for authorisations to cease to have effect in prescribed circumstances;

(d) provide for the procedure to be followed, the particulars to be given, and the amount (or the persons who are to determine the amount) of any fees to be paid, in connection with applications for authorisations;

(e) make different provisions for different cases.]

A25.34 *[Section 13A was inserted by the Road Traffic Act 1991, s.5.*

The functions of the Secretary of State exercisable under section 13A in relation for Wales have been transferred to the National Assembly for Wales by the National Assembly for Wales (Transfer of Functions) Order 1999 (S.I. 1999 No. 672; not reproduced in this work), art.2 and Sched. 1.

As to the transfer of functions of the Secretary of State under section 13A(1) which are exercisable in relation to Scotland to the Scottish Ministers, see the Scotland Act 1998 (Transfer of Functions to the Scottish Ministers etc.) Order 1999 (S.I. 1999 No. 1750; not reproduced in this work), art.2 and Sched. 1.

The bodies which may authorise off-road events under section 13A are specified in the Motor Vehicles (Off Road Events) Regulations 1995 (S.I. 1995 No. 1371) (not reproduced in this work).]

Protective measures: seat belts, helmets, etc.

14. Seat belts: adults

(1) The Secretary of State may make regulations requiring, subject to such exceptions as may be prescribed, persons who are driving or riding in motor vehicles on a road to wear seat belts of such description as may be prescribed.   **A25.35**

(2) Regulations under this section—

  (a) may make different provision in relation to different classes of vehicles, different descriptions of persons and different circumstances,

  [(aa) may, for the purpose of implementing the seat belt Directive, authorise the wearing of a seat belt approved under the law of a member State other than the United Kingdom,]

  (b) shall include exceptions for—

    (i) the users of vehicles constructed or adapted for the delivery of goods or mail to consumers or [addressees], as the case may be, while engaged in making local rounds of deliveries,

    (ii) the drivers of vehicles while performing a manoeuvre which includes reversing,

    (iii) any person holding a valid certificate signed by a medical practitioner to the effect that it is inadvisable on medical grounds for him to wear a seat belt,

  [(bb) shall, for the purpose of implementing the seat belt Directive, include an exception for any person holding a certificate to the like effect as that mentioned in paragraph (b)(iii) above which was issued in a member State other than the United Kingdom and which, under the law of that State, is valid for purposes corresponding to those of this section,]

  (c) may make any prescribed exceptions subject to such conditions as may be prescribed, and

  (d) may prescribe cases in which a fee of a prescribed amount may be charged on an application for any certificate required as a condition of any prescribed exception.

(3) A person who drives or rides in a motor vehicle in contravention of regulations under this section is guilty of an offence; but, notwithstanding any enactment or rule of law, no person other than the person actually committing the contravention is guilty of an offence by reason of the contravention.

(4) If the holder of any such certificate as is referred to in subsection (2)(b) [or (bb)] above is informed by a constable that he may be prosecuted for any offence under subsection (3) above, he is not in proceedings for that offence entitled to rely on the exception afforded to him by the certificate unless—

  (a) it is produced to the constable at the time he is so informed, or

  (b) it is produced—

    (i) within seven days after the date on which he is so informed, or

    (ii) as soon as is reasonably practicable,

  at such police station as he may have specified to the constable, or

  (c) where it is not produced at such police station, it is not reasonably practicable for it to be produced there before the day on which the proceedings are commenced.

(5) For the purposes of subsection (4) above, the laying of the information . . . shall be treated as the commencement of the proceedings.

(6) Regulations under this section requiring the wearing of seat belts by persons riding in motor vehicles shall not apply to children under the age of fourteen years.

[(7) In this section, "*the seat belt Directive*" means the Directive of the Council of the European Communities, dated 16th December 1991, (No. 91/671/EEC) on the approximation of the laws of the member States relating to compulsory use of safety belts in vehicles of less than 3.5 tonnes *[O.J. No. L373, December 31, 1991, p. 26]*.]

A25.36　　*[Section 14 is printed as amended by the Road Traffic Act 1991, s.48 and Sched. 4, para.47; the Road Traffic Act 1988 (Amendment) Regulations 1992 (S.I. 1992 No. 3105; not reproduced in this work), reg.2.*

Words relating exclusively and expressly to Scotland have been omitted from section 14(5).

The fixed penalty procedure applies to offences under section 14; see the Road Traffic Offenders Act 1988, Sched. 3.

The Motor Vehicles (Wearing of Seat Belts) Regulations 1993 (S.I. 1993 No. 176) (q.v.) have been made (in part) under section 14.]

15. Restriction on carrying children not wearing seat belts in motor vehicles

A25.37　　(1) Except as provided by regulations, where a child under the age of fourteen years is in the front of a motor vehicle, a person must not without reasonable excuse drive the vehicle on a road unless the child is wearing a seat belt in conformity with regulations.

(2) It is an offence for a person to drive a motor vehicle in contravention of subsection (1) above.

(3) Except as provided by regulations, where a child under the age of fourteen years is in the rear of a motor vehicle and any seat belt is fitted in the rear of that vehicle, a person must not without reasonable excuse drive the vehicle on a road unless the child is wearing a seat belt in conformity with regulations.

[(3A) Except as provided by regulations, where—

(a) a child who is under the age of 12 years and less than 150 centimetres in height is in the rear of a passenger car,

(b) no seat belt is fitted in the rear of the passenger car, and

(c) a seat in the front of the passenger car is provided with a seat belt but is not occupied by any person,

a person must not without reasonable excuse drive the passenger car on a road.]

(4) It is an offence for a person to drive a motor vehicle in contravention of subsection (3) [or (3A)] above.

(5) Provision may be made by regulations—

(a) excepting from the prohibition in subsection (1) [, (3) or (3A)] above children of any prescribed description, vehicles of a prescribed class or the driving of vehicles in such circumstances as may be prescribed,

(b) defining in relation to any class of vehicle what part of the vehicle is to be regarded as the front of the vehicle for the purposes of subsection (1) [or (3A)] above or as the rear of the vehicle for the purposes of subsection (3) [or (3A)] above,

(c) prescribing for the purposes of subsection (1) or (3) above the descriptions of seat belt to be worn by children of any prescribed description and the manner in which such seat belt is to be fixed and used.

[(5A) Without prejudice to the generality of subsection (5) above, regulations made by virtue of paragraph (c) of that subsection may, for the purpose of implementing the seat belt Directive,—

(a) make different provision in relation to different vehicles and different circumstances,

(b) authorise the wearing of a seat belt approved under the law of any member State other than the United Kingdom.]

[(6) Regulations made for the purposes of subsection (3) or (3A) above—

(a) shall include an exemption for any child holding a valid certificate signed by a medical practitioner to the effect that it is inadvisable on medical grounds for him to wear a seat belt, and

(b) shall, for the purpose of implementing the seat belt Directive, include an exemption for any child holding a certificate to the like effect which was issued in any member State other than the United Kingdom and which, under the law of that State, is valid for purposes corresponding to those of this section,

but such regulations may, for the purpose of implementing that Directive, make either of those exemptions subject to such conditions as may be prescribed.]

(7) If the driver of a motor vehicle is informed by a constable that he may be prosecuted for an offence under subsection (4) above, he is not in proceedings for that offence entitled to rely on an exception afforded to a child by a certificate referred to in subsection (6) above unless—

(a) it is produced to the constable at the time he is so informed, or

(b) it is produced—

(i) within seven days after the date on which he is so informed, or
(ii) as soon as is reasonably practicable,

at such police station as he may have specified to the constable, or

(c) where it is not produced at such police station, it is not reasonably practicable for it to be produced there before the day on which the proceedings are commenced.

(8) For the purposes of subsection (7) above, the laying of the information . . . shall be treated as the commencement of the proceedings.

(9) In this section—

["*maximum laden weight*" has the meaning given by Part IV of Schedule 6 to the Road Traffic Regulation Act 1984 [*q.v.*],]

["*passenger car*" means a motor vehicle which—

(a) is constructed or adapted for use for the carriage of passengers and is not a goods vehicle,

(b) has no more than eight seats in addition to the driver's seat,

(c) has four or more wheels,

(d) has a maximum design speed exceeding 25 kilometres per hour, and

(e) has a maximum laden weight not exceeding 3.5 tonnes,]

"*regulations*" means regulations made by the Secretary of State under this section, . . .

"*seat belt*" includes any description of restraining device for a child and any reference to wearing a seat belt is to be construed accordingly.

["*the seat belt Directive*" has the same meaning as in section 14.]

(10) [*Repealed.*]

[*Section 15 is printed as amended by the Road Traffic Act 1991, s.83 and Sched. 8; the Road Traffic*   **A25.38**
Act 1988 (Amendment) Regulations 1992 (S.I. 1992 No. 3105; not reproduced in this work), reg.3.
Words relating exclusively and expressly to Scotland have been omitted from section 15(8).
The fixed penalty procedure applies to offences under section 15(2) and section 15(4); see the Road Traffic Offenders Act 1988, Sched. 3.

The Motor Vehicles (Wearing of Seat Belts by Children in Front Seats) Regulations 1993 (S.I. 1993 No. 31) (q.v.) were made under section 15 and the Motor Vehicles (Wearing of Seat Belts) Regulations 1993 (S.I. 1993 No. 176) (q.v.) were made in part under section 15.]

[15A. Safety equipment for children in motor vehicles

A25.39   (1), (2) *[Power to make regulations prescribing types of equipment recommended as conducive to safety.]*

(3) Except in such circumstances as may be prescribed, if a person sells, or offers for sale, equipment of any description for which a type is prescribed under this section as equipment which is so conducive and that equipment—

     (a) is not of a type so prescribed, or

     (b) is sold or offered for sale in contravention of regulations under this section,

he is, subject to subsection (5) below, guilty of an offence.

(4) Except in such circumstances as may be prescribed, if a person sells, or offers for sale, equipment of any description for which a type is prescribed under this section as equipment conducive to the safety in the event of accident—

     (a) of children not of a class prescribed in relation to equipment of that type, or

     (b) of children in motor vehicles not of a class prescribed in relation to equipment of that type,

he is, subject to subsection (5) below, guilty of an offence.

(5) A person shall not be convicted of an offence under this section in respect of the sale or offer for sale of equipment if he proves that it was sold or, as the case may be, offered for sale for export from Great Britain.

(6) The provisions of Schedule 1 to this Act shall have effect in relation to contraventions of this section.

(7) Regulations under this section may make different provision in relation to different circumstances.

(8) This section applies to equipment of any description for use in a motor vehicle consisting of—

     (a) a restraining device for a child or for a carry-cot, or

     (b) equipment designed for use by a child in conjunction with any description of restraining device.

(9) References in this section to selling or offering for sale include respectively references to letting on hire and offering to let on hire.]

A25.40   *[Section 15A was inserted by the Motor Vehicles (Safety Equipment for Children) Act 1991, s.1.]*

16. Wearing of protective headgear

A25.41   (1) The Secretary of State may make regulations requiring, subject to such exceptions as may be specified in the regulations, persons driving or riding (otherwise than in side-cars) on motor cycles of any class specified in the regulations to wear protective headgear of such description as may be so specified.

(2) A requirement imposed by regulations under this section shall not apply to any follower of the Sikh religion while he is wearing a turban.

(3) Regulations under this section may make different provision in relation to different circumstances.

(4) A person who drives or rides on a motor cycle in contravention of regulations under this section is guilty of an offence; but notwithstanding any enactment or rule of law no person other than the person actually committing the contravention is guilty of an offence by reason of the contravention unless the person actually committing the contravention is a child under the age of sixteen years.

[The fixed penalty procedure applies to offences under section 16; see the Road Traffic Offenders Act 1988, **A25.42** *Sched. 3.*

The Motor Cycles (Protective Helmets) Regulations 1998 (S.I. 1998 No. 1807) (q.v.) have effect as if made in part under section 16.]

17. Protective helmets for motor cyclists

(1) The Secretary of State may make regulations prescribing (by reference to shape, con-   **A25.43** struction or any other quality) types of helmet recommended as affording protection to persons on or in motor cycles, or motor cycles of different classes, from injury in the event of accident.

(2) If a person sells, or offers for sale, a helmet as a helmet for affording such protection and the helmet is neither—

   (a) of a type prescribed under this section, nor

   (b) of a type authorised under regulations made under this section and sold or offered for sale subject to any conditions specified in the authorisation,

subject to subsection (3) below, he is guilty of an offence.

(3) A person shall not be convicted of an offence under this section in respect of the sale or offer for sale of a helmet if he proves that it was sold or, as the case may be, offered for sale for export from Great Britain.

(4) The provisions of Schedule 1 to this Act shall have effect in relation to contraventions of this section.

(5) In this section and that Schedule "*helmet*" includes any head-dress, and references in this section to selling or offering for sale include respectively references to letting on hire and offering to let on hire.

[As to the institution of proceedings under section 17, see the Road Traffic Offenders Act 1988, s.4(1)   **A25.44** *below.*

Proceedings under section 17(2) are specified by the Prosecution of Offences Act 1985 (Specified Proceedings) Order 1999 (S.I. 1999 No. 904) below as being proceedings the conduct of which the Director of Public Prosecutions is not required to take over from the police under the Prosecution of Offences Act 1985, s.3(3)(a).

The Motor Cycles (Protective Helmets) Regulations 1998 (S.I. 1998 No. 1807) (q.v.) have effect as if made in part under this section.]

18. Authorisation of head-worn appliances for use on motor cycles

(1) The Secretary of State may make regulations prescribing (by reference to shape, con-   **A25.45** struction or any other quality) types of appliance of any description to which this section applies as authorised for use by persons driving or riding (otherwise than in side-cars) on motor cycles of any class specified in the regulations.

(2) Regulations under this section—

   (a) may impose restrictions or requirements with respect to the circumstances in which appliances of any type prescribed by the regulations may be used, and

   (b) may make different provision in relation to different circumstances.

(3) If a person driving or riding on a motor cycle on a road uses an appliance of any description for which a type is prescribed under this section and that appliance—

(a) is not of a type so prescribed, or

(b) is otherwise used in contravention of regulations under this section,

he is guilty of an offence.

(4) If a person sells, or offers for sale, an appliance of any such description as authorised for use by persons on or in motor cycles, or motor cycles of any class, and that appliance is not of a type prescribed under this section as authorised for such use, he is, subject to subsection (5) below, guilty of an offence.

(5) A person shall not be convicted of an offence under this section in respect of the sale or offer for sale of an appliance if he proves that it was sold or, as the case may be, offered for sale for export from Great Britain.

(6) The provisions of Schedule 1 to this Act shall have effect in relation to contraventions of subsection (4) above.

(7) This section applies to appliances of any description designed or adapted for use—

(a) with any headgear, or

(b) by being attached to or placed upon the head,

(as, for example, eye protectors or earphones).

(8) References in this section to selling or offering for sale include respectively references to letting on hire and offering to let on hire.

A25.46   *[As to the institution of proceedings under section 18, see the Road Traffic Offenders Act 1988, s.4(1).*

Proceedings under section 18(3) are specified by the Prosecution of Offences Act 1985 (Specified Proceedings) Order 1999 (S.I. 1999 No. 904) below as being proceedings the conduct of which the Director of Public Prosecutions is not required to take over from the police under the Prosecution of Offences Act 1985, s.3(3)(a).

The Motor Cycle (Eye Protectors) Regulations 1999 (S.I. 1999 No. 535) (q.v.) have been made under section 18.]

Stopping on verges, etc., or in dangerous positions, etc.

19. Prohibition of parking of HGVs on verges, central reservations and footways

A25.47   (1) Subject to subsection (2) below, a person who parks a heavy commercial vehicle (as defined in section 20 of this Act) wholly or partly—

(a) on the verge of a road, or

(b) on any land situated between two carriageways and which is not a footway, or

(c) on a footway,

is guilty of an offence.

(2) A person shall not be convicted of an offence under this section in respect of a vehicle if he proves to the satisfaction of the court—

(a) that it was parked in accordance with permission given by a constable in uniform, or

(b) that it was parked in contravention of this section for the purpose of saving life or extinguishing fire or meeting any other like emergency, or

(c) that it was parked in contravention of this section but the conditions specified in subsection (3) below were satisfied.

(3) The conditions mentioned in subsection (2)(c) above are—

(a) that the vehicle was parked on the verge of a road or on a footway for the purpose of loading or unloading, and

(b) that the loading or unloading of the vehicle could not have been satisfactorily performed if it had not been parked on the footway or verge, and

(c) that the vehicle was not left unattended at any time while it was so parked.

(4) In this section *"carriageway"* and *"footway"*, in relation to England and Wales, have the same meanings as in the Highways Act 1980.

[As to the possible disapplication of section 19, see Sched. 3, para.2(4), to the Road Traffic Act 1991 **A25.48**
below.

The fixed penalty procedure applies to offences under section 19; see the Road Traffic Offenders Act 1988, Sched. 3 below. Offences under section 19 have been designated as fixed penalty parking offences by the Fixed Penalty Order 2000 (S.I. 2000 No. 2792).

The terms "carriageway" and "footway" are defined in section 329(1) of the Highways Act 1980 (q.v.).]

19A.   *[Repealed.]*

20. Definition of "heavy commercial vehicle" for the purposes of section 19

(1) In section 19 of this Act, *"heavy commercial vehicle"* means any goods vehicle which has   **A25.49**
an operating weight exceeding 7.5 tonnes.

(2) The operating weight of a goods vehicle for the purposes of this section is—

(a) in the case of a motor vehicle not drawing a trailer or in the case of a trailer, its maximum laden weight,

(b) in the case of an articulated vehicle, its maximum laden weight (if it has one) and otherwise the aggregate maximum laden weight of all the individual vehicles forming part of that articulated vehicle, and

(c) in the case of a motor vehicle (other than an articulated vehicle) drawing one or more trailers, the aggregate maximum laden weight of the motor vehicle and the trailer or trailers attached to it.

(3) In this section *"articulated vehicle"* means a motor vehicle with a trailer so attached to it as to be partially superimposed upon it; and references to the maximum laden weight of a vehicle are references to the total laden weight which must not be exceeded in the case of that vehicle if it is to be used in Great Britain without contravening any regulations for the time being in force under section 41 of this Act.

(4) In this section, and in the definition of *"goods vehicle"* in section 192 of this Act as it applies for the purposes of this section, *"trailer"* means any vehicle other than a motor vehicle.

(5) The Secretary of State may by regulations amend subsections (1) and (2) above (whether as originally enacted or as previously amended under this subsection)—

(a) by substituting weights of a different description for any of the weights there mentioned, or

(b) in the case of subsection (1) above, by substituting a weight of a different description or amount, or a weight different both in description and amount, for the weight there mentioned.

(6) Different regulations may be made under subsection (5) above as respects different classes of vehicles or as respects the same class of vehicles in different circumstances and as respects different times of the day or night and as respects different localities.

(7) Regulations under subsection (5) above shall not so amend subsection (1) above that there is any case in which a goods vehicle whose operating weight (ascertained in accordance with subsection (2) above as originally enacted) does not exceed 7.5 tonnes is a heavy commercial vehicle for any of the purposes of section 19 of this Act.

21. Prohibition of driving or parking on cycle tracks

A25.50   (1) Subject to the provisions of this section, any person who without lawful authority, drives or parks a motor vehicle wholly or partly on a cycle track is guilty of an offence.

(2) A person shall not be convicted of an offence under subsection (1) above with respect to a vehicle if he proves to the satisfaction of the court—

    (a) that the vehicle was driven or (as the case may be) parked in contravention of that subsection for the purpose of saving life, or extinguishing fire or meeting any other like emergency, or

    (b) that the vehicle was owned or operated by a highway authority or by a person discharging functions on behalf of a highway authority and was driven or (as the case may be) parked in contravention of that subsection in connection with the carrying out by or on behalf of that authority of any of the following, that is, the cleansing, maintenance or improvement of, or the maintenance or alteration of any structure or other work situated in, the cycle track or its verges, or

    (c) that the vehicle was owned or operated by statutory undertakers and was driven or (as the case may be) parked in contravention of that subsection in connection with the carrying out by those undertakers of any works in relation to any apparatus belonging to or used by them for the purpose of their undertaking.

(3) In this section—

    (a) "*cycle track*" and other expressions used in this section and in the Highways Act 1980 have the same meaning as in that Act,

    (b) in subsection (2)(c) above "*statutory undertakers*" means any body who are statutory undertakers within the meaning of the Highways Act 1980, any sewerage authority within the meaning of that Act or the operator of a telecommunications code system (as defined by paragraph 1(1) of Schedule 4 to the Telecommunications Act 1984 [*q.v.*]), and in relation to any such sewerage authority "*apparatus*" includes sewers or sewerage disposal works.

(4) This section does not extend to Scotland.

A25.51   *[As to the possible disapplication of section 21, see the Road Traffic Act 1991, Sched. 3, para.2(4) below.*

    The terms "cycle track" and "statutory undertakers" are defined in section 329(1) of the Highways Act 1980 (q.v.). The definition of "sewerage authority" which was formerly included in the Highways Act 1980, s.329(1), was repealed by the Water Act 1989.

    A public gas transporter is deemed by the Gas Act 1995, s.16(1) and Sched. 4, para.2(1)(xxxvii), to be a statutory undertaker for the purposes of section 21.]

22. Leaving vehicles in dangerous positions

A25.52   If a person in charge of a vehicle causes or permits the vehicle or a trailer drawn by it to remain at rest on a road in such a position or in such condition or in such circumstances as to [involve a danger of injury] to other persons using the road, he is guilty of an offence.

A25.53   *[Section 22 is printed as amended by the Road Traffic Act 1991, s.48 and Sched. 4, para.48.*

    The fixed penalty procedure applies to offences under section 22; see the Road Traffic Offenders Act 1988, Sched. 3 below.]

[22A. Causing danger to other road-users

(1) A person is guilty of an offence if he intentionally and without lawful authority or   **A25.54** reasonable cause—

    (a) causes anything to be on or over a road, or

    (b) interferes with a motor vehicle, trailer or cycle, or

    (c) interferes (directly or indirectly) with traffic equipment,

in such circumstances that it would be obvious to a reasonable person that to do so would be dangerous.

(2) In subsection (1) above "*dangerous*" refers to danger either of injury to any person while on or near a road, or of serious damage to property on or near a road; and in determining for the purposes of that subsection what would be obvious to a reasonable person in a particular case, regard shall be had not only to the circumstances of which he could be expected to be aware but also to any circumstances shown to have been within the knowledge of the accused.

(3) In subsection (1) above "*traffic equipment*" means—

    (a) anything lawfully placed on or near a road by a highway authority;

    (b) a traffic sign lawfully placed on or near a road by a person other than a highway authority;

    (c) any fence, barrier or light lawfully placed on or near a road—

        (i) in pursuance of section 174 of the Highways Act 1980, . . . or section 65 of the New Roads and Street Works Act 1991 (which provide for guarding, lighting and signing in streets where works are undertaken), or

        (ii) by a constable or a person acting under the instructions (whether general or specific) of a chief officer of police.

(4) For the purposes of subsection (3) above anything placed on or near a road shall unless the contrary is proved be deemed to have been lawfully placed there.

(5) In this section "*road*" does not include a footpath or bridleway.

(6) This section does not extend to Scotland.]

[Section 22A was inserted by the Road Traffic Act 1991, s.6, and is printed as amended by the New   **A25.55** *Roads and Street Works Act 1991, s.168(1) and Sched. 8, Pt IV, para.121(1) and (2).*
The offence under section 22A being punishable on indictment by a term of imprisonment of five years or more, if a magistrates' court grants bail to a person charged with or convicted of an offence under this section, the prosecution (provided objection was taken to the application for bail) may appeal to a judge of the Crown Court against the order granting bail under the Bail (Amendment) Act 1993, s.1 (not reproduced in this work).]

Other restrictions in interests of safety

23. Restriction of carriage of persons on motor cycles

(1) Not more than one person in addition to the driver may be carried on a [motor bicycle].   **A25.56**

(2) No person in addition to the driver may be carried on a [motor bicycle] otherwise than sitting astride the motor cycle and on a proper seat securely fixed to the motor cycle behind the driver's seat.

(3) If a person is carried on a motor cycle in contravention of this section, the driver of the motor cycle is guilty of an offence.

[Section 23 is printed as amended by the Road Traffic (Driver Licensing and Information Systems) Act   **A25.57** *1989, s.7 and Sched. 3, para.6.*

The fixed penalty procedure applies to offences under section 23; see the Road Traffic Offenders Act 1988, Sched. 3 below.]

24. Restriction of carriage of persons on bicycles

A25.58 (1) Not more than one person may be carried on a road on a bicycle not propelled by mechanical power unless it is constructed or adapted for the carriage of more than one person.

(2) In this section—

(a) references to a person carried on a bicycle include references to a person riding the bicycle, and

(b) "*road*" includes bridleway.

(3) If a person is carried on a bicycle in contravention of subsection (1) above, each of the persons carried is guilty of an offence.

A25.59 *[For the application of the fixed penalty procedure to carrying more than one person on a pedal cycle contrary to section 24, see the Road Traffic Offences Act 1988, Pt III and Sched. 3.*

Proceedings under section 24(3) are specified by the Prosecution of Offences Act 1985 (Specified Proceedings) Order 1999 (S.I. 1999 No. 904) below as being proceedings the conduct of which the Director of Public Prosecutions is not required to take over from the police under the Prosecution of Offences Act 1985, s.3(3)(a).]

25. Tampering with motor vehicles

A25.60 If, while a motor vehicle is on a road or on a parking place provided by a local authority, a person—

(a) gets on to the vehicle, or

(b) tampers with the brake or other part of its mechanism,

without lawful authority or reasonable cause he is guilty of an offence.

A25.61 *[Offences under section 25 and any other offences of which persons may have been convicted in the same proceedings may be recorded in national police records; see the National Police Records (Recordable Offences) Regulations 2000 (S.I. 2000 No. 1139) (not reproduced in this work).]*

26. Holding or getting on to vehicle in order to be towed or carried

A25.62 (1) If, for the purpose of being carried, a person without lawful authority or reasonable cause takes or retains hold of, or gets on to, a motor vehicle or trailer while in motion on a road he is guilty of an offence.

(2) If, for the purpose of being drawn, a person takes or retains hold of a motor vehicle or trailer while in motion on a road he is guilty of an offence.

A25.63 *[Proceedings under section 26(1) and (2) are specified by the Prosecution of Offences Act 1985 (Specified Proceedings) Order 1999 (S.I. 1999 No. 904) below as being proceedings the conduct of which the Director of Public Prosecutions is not required to take over from the police under the Prosecution of Offences Act 1985, s.3(3)(a).]*

27. Control of dogs on roads

A25.64 (1) A person who causes or permits a dog to be on a designated road without the dog being held on a lead is guilty of an offence.

(2) In this section "*designated road*" means a length of road specified by an order in that behalf of the local authority in whose area the length of road is situated.

(3) The powers which under subsection (2) above are exercisable by a local authority in England and Wales are, in the case of a road part of the width of which is in the area of one local authority and part in the area of another, exercisable by either authority with the consent of the other.

(4) An order under this section may provide that subsection (1) above shall apply subject to such limitations or exceptions as may be specified in the order, and (without prejudice to the generality of this subsection) subsection (1) above does not apply to dogs proved—

(a) to be kept for driving or tending sheep or cattle in the course of a trade or business, or

(b) to have been at the material time in use under proper control for sporting purposes.

(5) An order under this section shall not be made except after consultation with the chief officer of police.

(6) The Secretary of State may make regulations—

(a) prescribing the procedure to be followed in connection with the making of orders under this section, and

(b) requiring the authority making such an order to publish in such manner as may be prescribed by the regulations notice of the making and effect of the order.

(7) In this section "*local authority*" means—

(a) in relation to England and Wales, the council of a county, metropolitan district or London borough or the Common Council of the City of London, and

(b) *[applies to Scotland.]*

(8) The power conferred by this section to make an order includes power, exercisable in like manner and subject to the like conditions, to vary or revoke it.

[The functions of the Secretary of State exercisable under section 27(6) in relation to Wales have been   **A25.65** *transferred to the National Assembly for Wales by the National Assembly for Wales (Transfer of Functions) Order 1999 (S.I. 1999 No. 672; not reproduced in this work), art.2 and Sched. 1.*

As to the transfer of functions of the Secretary of State under section 17(6), (2) which are exercisable in relation to Scotland to the Scottish Ministers, see the Scotland Act 1998 (Transfer of Functions to the Scottish Ministers etc.) Order 1999 (S.I. 1999 No. 1750; not reproduced in this work), art.2 and Sched. 1.

As to the institution of proceedings under section 27, see the Road Traffic Offenders Act 1988, s.4(2) below.]

Cycling offences and cycle racing

[28. Dangerous cycling

(1) A person who rides a cycle on a road dangerously is guilty of an offence.   **A25.66**

(2) For the purposes of subsection (1) above a person is to be regarded as riding dangerously if (and only if)—

(a) the way he rides falls far below what would be expected of a competent and careful cyclist, and

(b) it would be obvious to a competent and careful cyclist that riding in that way would be dangerous.

(3) In subsection (2) above "*dangerous*" refers to danger either of injury to any person or of serious damage to property; and in determining for the purposes of that subsection what would be obvious to a competent and careful cyclist in a particular case, regard shall be had not only to the circumstances of which he could be expected to be aware but also to any circumstances shown to have been within the knowledge of the accused.]

A25.67   *[Section 28 is printed as substituted by the Road Traffic Act 1991, s.7.*
As to alternative charges to a charge under section 28, see the Road Traffic Offenders Act 1988, s.24(1)
below.]

29. Careless, and inconsiderate, cycling

A25.68   If a person rides a cycle on a road without due care and attention, or without reasonable
consideration for other persons using the road, he is guilty of an offence.

. . .

A25.69   *[Section 29 is printed as amended by the Road Traffic Act 1991, s.83 and Sched. 8.*
Proceedings under section 29 are specified by the Prosecution of Offences Act 1985 (Specified
Proceedings) Order 1999 (S.I. 1999 No. 904) below as being proceedings the conduct of which the
Director of Public Prosecutions is not required to take over from the police under the Prosecution of Offences
Act 1985, s.3(3)(a).]

30. Cycling when under influence of drink or drugs

A25.70   (1) A person who, when riding a cycle on a road or other public place, is unfit to
ride through drink or drugs (that is to say, is under the influence of drink or a drug to such
an extent as to be incapable of having proper control of the cycle) is guilty of an offence.

(2) *[Applies to Scotland.]*

(3) *[Repealed.]*

A25.71   *[Section 30 is printed as amended by the Road Traffic Act 1991, s.83 and Sched. 8.]*

31. Regulation of cycle racing on public ways

A25.72   (1) A person who promotes or takes part in a race or trial of speed on a public way
between cycles is guilty of an offence, unless the race or trial—

(a) is authorised, and

(b) is conducted in accordance with any conditions imposed,

by or under regulations under this section.

(2) The Secretary of State may by regulations authorise, or provide for authorising, for the
purposes of subsection (1) above, the holding on a public way other than a bridleway—

(a) of races or trials of speed of any class or description, or

(b) of a particular race or trial of speed,

in such cases as may be prescribed and subject to such conditions as may be imposed by or
under the regulations.

(3) Regulations under this section may—

(a) prescribe the procedure to be followed, and the particulars to be given, in connection with applications for authorisation under the regulations, and

(b) make different provision for different classes or descriptions of race or trial.

(4) Without prejudice to any other powers exercisable in that behalf, the chief officer of
police may give directions with respect to the movement of, or the route to be followed by,
vehicular traffic during any period, being directions which it is necessary or expedient to
give in relation to that period to prevent or mitigate—

(a) congestion or obstruction of traffic, or

(b) danger to or from traffic,

in consequence of the holding of a race or trial of speed authorised by or under regulations under this section.

(5) Directions under subsection (4) above may include a direction that any road or part of a road specified in the direction shall be closed during the period to vehicles or to vehicles of a class so specified.

[(6) In this section "*public way*" means, in England and Wales, a highway . . . but does not include a footpath.]

[Section 31 is printed as amended by the Road Traffic Act 1991, s.48 and Sched. 4, para.49.   **A25.73**
Words relating expressly and exclusively to Scotland have been omitted from section 31(6).

The functions of the Secretary of State exercisable under section 31(2) in relation to Wales have been transferred to the National Assembly for Wales by the National Assembly for Wales (Transfer of Functions) Order 1999 (S.I. 1999 No. 672; not reproduced in this work), art.2 and Sched. 1.

As to the transfer of functions of the Secretary of State under section 31(2) which are exercisable in relation to Scotland to the Scottish Ministers, see the Scotland Act 1998 (Transfer of Functions to the Scottish Ministers etc.) Order 1999 (S.I. 1999 No. 1750; not reproduced in this work), art.2 and Sched. 1.

Proceedings under section 31(1) are specified by the Prosecution of Offences Act 1985 (Specified Proceedings) Order 1999 (S.I. 1999 No. 904) below as being proceedings the conduct of which the Director of Public Prosecutions is not required to take over from the police under the Prosecution of Offences Act 1985, s.3(3)(a).]

32. Electrically assisted pedal cycles

(1) An electrically assisted pedal cycle of a class specified in regulations made for the   **A25.74**
purposes of section 189 of this Act and section 140 of the Road Traffic Regulation Act 1984 shall not be driven on a road by a person under the age of fourteen.

(2) A person who—

  (a) drives such a pedal cycle, or

  (b) knowing or suspecting that another person is under the age of fourteen, causes or permits him to drive such a pedal cycle,

in contravention of subsection (1) above is guilty of an offence.

Use of motor vehicles away from roads

33. Control of use of footpaths and bridleways for motor vehicle trials

(1) A person must not promote or take part in a trial of any description between motor   **A25.75**
vehicles on a footpath or bridleway unless the holding of the trial has been authorised under this section by the local authority.

(2) A local authority shall not give an authorisation under this section unless satisfied that consent in writing to the use of any length of footpath or bridleway for the purposes of the trial has been given by the owner and by the occupier of the land over which that length of footpath or bridleway runs, and any such authorisation may be given subject to compliance with such conditions as the authority think fit.

(3) A person who—

  (a) contravenes subsection (1) above, or

  (b) fails to comply with any conditions subject to which an authorisation under this section has been granted,

is guilty of an offence.

(4) The holding of a trial authorised under this section is not affected by any statutory provision prohibiting or restricting the use of footpaths or bridleways or a specified footpath or bridleway; but this section does not prejudice any right or remedy of a person as having any interest in land.

(5) In this section "*local authority*"—

(a) in relation to England and Wales, means the council of a county, metropolitan district or London borough, and

(b) *[applies to Scotland.]*

34. Prohibition of driving motor vehicles elsewhere than on roads

A25.76   (1) Subject to the provisions of this section, if without lawful authority a person drives a motor vehicle—

(a) on to or upon any common land, moorland or land of any other description, not being land forming part of a road, or

(b) on any road being a footpath or bridleway,

he is guilty of an offence.

(2) It is not an offence under this section to drive a motor vehicle on any land within fifteen yards of a road, being a road on which a motor vehicle may lawfully be driven, for the purpose only of parking the vehicle on that land.

(3) A person shall not be convicted of an offence under this section with respect to a vehicle if he proves to the satisfaction of the court that it was driven in contravention of this section for the purpose of saving life or extinguishing fire or meeting any other like emergency.

(4) *[Saving for section 193 of the Law of Property Act 1925 and byelaws and law of trespass.]*

A25.77   *[The fixed penalty procedure applies to offences under section 34; see the Road Traffic Offenders Act 1988, Sched. 3 below.]*

Directions to traffic and to pedestrians and traffic signs

35. Drivers to comply with traffic directions

A25.78   (1) Where a constable is for the time being engaged in the regulation of traffic in a road, a person driving or propelling a vehicle who neglects or refuses—

(a) to stop the vehicle, or

(b) to make it proceed in, or kept to, a particular line of traffic,

when directed to do so by the constable in the execution of his duty is guilty of an offence.

(2) Where—

(a) a traffic survey of any description is being carried out on or in the vicinity of a road, and

(b) a constable gives to a person driving or propelling a vehicle a direction—

(i) to stop the vehicle,

(ii) to make it proceed in, or keep to, a particular line of traffic, or

(iii) to proceed to a particular point on or near the road on which the vehicle is being driven or propelled,

being a direction given for the purposes of the survey (but not a direction requiring any person to provide any information for the purposes of a traffic survey),

the person is guilty of an offence if he neglects or refuses to comply with the direction.

(3) The power to give such a direction as is referred to in subsection (2) above for the purposes of a traffic survey shall be so exercised as not to cause any unreasonable delay to a person who indicates that he is unwilling to provide any information for the purposes of the survey.

[The fixed penalty procedure applies to offences under section 35; see the Road Traffic Offenders Act 1988, Sched. 3 below.]   **A25.79**

36. Drivers to comply with traffic signs

(1) Where a traffic sign, being a sign—   **A25.80**

    (a) of the prescribed size, colour and type, or

    (b) of another character authorised by the Secretary of State under the provisions in that behalf of the Road Traffic Regulation Act 1984,

has been lawfully placed on or near a road, a person driving or propelling a vehicle who fails to comply with the indication given by the sign is guilty of an offence.

(2) A traffic sign shall not be treated for the purposes of this section as having been lawfully placed unless either—

    (a) the indication given by the sign is an indication of a statutory prohibition, restriction or requirement, or

    (b) it is expressly provided by or under any provision of the Traffic Acts that this section shall apply to the sign or to signs of a type of which the sign is one;

and, where the indication mentioned in paragraph (a) of this subsection is of the general nature only of the prohibition, restriction or requirement to which the sign relates, a person shall not be convicted of failure to comply with the indication unless he has failed to comply with the prohibition, restriction or requirement to which the sign relates.

(3) For the purposes of this section a traffic sign placed on or near a road shall be deemed—

    (a) to be of the prescribed size, colour and type, or of another character authorised by the Secretary of State under the provisions in that behalf of the Road Traffic Regulation Act 1984, and

    (b) (subject to subsection (2) above) to have been lawfully so placed,

unless the contrary is proved.

(4) Where a traffic survey of any description is being carried out on or in the vicinity of a road, this section applies to a traffic sign by which a direction is given—

    (a) to stop a vehicle,

    (b) to make it proceed in, or keep to, a particular line of traffic, or

    (c) to proceed to a particular point on or near the road on which the vehicle is being driven or propelled,

being a direction given for the purposes of the survey (but not a direction requiring any person to provide any information for the purposes of the survey).

(5) Regulations made by the [Secretary of State for the Environment, Transport and the Regions], the Secretary of State for Wales and the Secretary of State for Scotland acting jointly may specify any traffic sign for the purposes of column 5 of the entry in Schedule 2 to the Road Traffic Offenders Act 1988 relating to offences under this section (offences committed by failing to comply with certain signs involve discretionary disqualification).

A25.81   *[Section 36 is printed as amended by the Secretary of State for the Environment, Transport and the Regions Order 1997 (S.I. 1997 No. 2971).*

The functions of the Secretary of State for the Environment, Transport and the Regions exercisable under section 36(5) in relation to Wales (so far as exercisable by the Secretary of State for Wales, but only to the extent that functions are exercisable by the National Assembly for Wales under section 64 of the Road Traffic Regulation Act 1984 below) have been transferred to the National Assembly by the National Assembly for Wales (Transfer of Functions) Order 1999 (S.I. 1999 No. 672; not reproduced in this work), art.2 and Sched. 1.

As to the exercise of functions of the Secretary of State for the Environment, Transport and the Regions under section 36(5) which are exercisable in relation to Scotland only after consultation with the Scottish Ministers, see the Scotland Act 1998 (Transfer of Functions to the Scottish Ministers etc.) Order 1999 (S.I. 1999 No. 1750; not reproduced in this work), art.4 and Sched. 3.

Every function of the Secretary of State for the Environment, Transport and the Regions, the Secretary of State for Scotland and the Secretary of State for Wales under section 36(5) has been transferred to the Secretary of State with effect from December 27, 1999; see the Transfer of Functions (Road Traffic) Order 1999 (S.I. 1999 No. 3143; not reproduced in this work).

The fixed penalty procedure applies to offences under section 36; see the Road Traffic Offenders Act 1988, Sched. 3 below.

As to the admissibility of evidence of speeding in respect of offences under section 36(1), see the Road Traffic Offenders Act 1988, s.20 below.

The traffic signs to which this section are applied are prescribed by the Traffic Signs Regulations and General Directions 1994 (S.I. 1994 No. 1519), reg.10(1) (q.v.), and the Traffic Signs (Temporary Obstructions) Regulations 1997 (S.I. 1997 No. 3053), reg.4 (q.v.).

Penalty charges may be payable for bus lane offences committed in London by non-compliance with a traffic sign; see the London Local Authorities Act 1996 (c. ix), Pt II (ss.3–9) (not reproduced in this work).]

37. Directions to pedestrians

A25.82   Where a constable in uniform is for the time being engaged in the regulation of vehicular traffic in a road, a person on foot who proceeds across or along the carriageway in contravention of a direction to stop given by the constable in the execution of his duty, either to persons on foot or to persons on foot and other traffic, is guilty of an offence.

Promotion of road safety

38. The Highway Code

A25.83   (1) The Highway Code shall continue to have effect, subject however to revision in accordance with the following provisions of this section.

(2)–(6) *[Revision and publication of the Highway Code.]*

(7) A failure on the part of a person to observe a provision of the Highway Code shall not of itself render that person liable to criminal proceedings of any kind but any such failure may in any proceedings (whether civil or criminal, and including proceedings for an offence under the Traffic Acts, the Public Passenger Vehicles Act 1981 [*q.v.*] or sections 18 to 23 of the Transport Act 1985 [*q.v.*]) be relied upon by any party to the proceedings as tending to establish or negative any liability which is in question in those proceedings.

(8) In this section "*the Highway Code*" means the code comprising directions for the guidance of persons using roads issued under section 45 of the Road Traffic Act 1930, as from time to time revised under this section or under any previous enactment.

(9) *[Further provision as to the revision of the Highway Code.]*

39. Powers of Secretary of State and local authorities as to giving road safety   **A25.84**
information and training   *[Omitted.]*

40. Powers of Secretary of State to subsidise bodies other than local
authorities for giving road safety information and training   *[Omitted.]*

PART II

CONSTRUCTION AND USE OF VEHICLES AND EQUIPMENT

[Using vehicle in dangerous condition]

[40A. Using vehicle in dangerous condition, etc.

A person is guilty of an offence if he uses, or causes or permits another to use, a motor   **A25.85**
vehicle or trailer on a road when—

(a) the condition of the motor vehicle or trailer, or of its accessories or equipment, or

(b) the purpose for which it is used, or

(c) the number of passengers carried by it, or the manner in which they are carried, or

(d) the weight, position or distribution of its load, or the manner in which it is secured,

is such that the use of the motor vehicle or trailer involves a danger of injury to any person.]

[Section 40A and the italicised heading preceding it were inserted by the Road Traffic Act 1991, s.8(1).   **A25.86**
Section 40A does not apply to tramcars nor to trolley vehicles (other than duobuses): Tramcars and Trolley
Vehicles (Modification of Enactments) Regulations 1992 (S.I. 1992 No. 1217), regs 7, 9 and 11 (q.v.).]

General regulation of construction, use, etc.

41. Regulation of construction, weight, equipment and use of vehicles

(1) The Secretary of State may make regulations generally as to the use of motor veh-   **A25.87**
icles and trailers on roads, their construction and equipment and the conditions under
which they may be so used.

Subsections (2) to (4) below do not affect the generality of this subsection.

(2) *[Particular provisions which may be included in regulations.]*

(3) *[Provisions as to goods vehicles which may be included in regulations.]*

(4) *[Provisions as to lighting equipment and reflectors which may be included in regulations.]*

[(4A) *[Provisions as to speed limiters which may be included in regulations.]*]

(5) *[Power to make different regulations for different classes of vehicles, etc.]*

(6) In framing regulations under this section prescribing a weight of any description
which is not to be exceeded in the case of goods vehicles of a class for which a certificate of
conformity or Minister's approval certificate may be issued under section 57 or 58 of this
Act the Secretary of State must have regard to the design weight of the like description
determined by virtue of section 54 of this Act for vehicles of that class and must secure that
the first-mentioned weight does not exceed the design weight.

(7) In this Part of this Act—

"construction and use requirements" means requirements, whether applicable generally or at
specified times or in specified circumstances, imposed under this section,

"*plated particulars*" means such particulars as are required to be marked on a goods vehicle in pursuance of regulations under this section by means of a plate,

"*plated weights*" means such weights as are required to be so marked.

A25.88   *[The regulations which have effect as if made under section 41 include the Minibus (Conditions of Fitness, Equipment and Use) Regulations 1977 (S.I. 1977 No. 2103), the Community Bus Regulations 1978 (S.I. 1978 No. 1313), the Public Service Vehicles (Conditions of Fitness, Equipment, Use and Certification) Regulations 1981 (S.I. 1981 No. 257) (q.v.), the Road Transport (International Passenger Services) Regulations 1984 (S.I. 1984 No. 748) (q.v.), and the Road Vehicles (Construction and Use) Regulations 1986 (S.I. 1986 No. 1078) (q.v.). The Road Vehicles Lighting Regulations 1989 (S.I. 1989 No. 1796) (q.v.) have been made under this section (read together with section 43), as have the Road Vehicle (Authorised Weight) Regulations 1998 (S.I. 1998 No. 3111) (q.v.).*

Regulations made under section 41 before July 1, 1988 apply to trolley vehicles as if section 193 of and Schedule 4 to the Road Traffic Act 1988 (the combined effect of which excluded the application of specified statutory provisions to certain vehicles, including trolley vehicles) and the corresponding earlier enactments had never been passed: Tramcars and Trolley Vehicles (Modification of Enactments) Regulations 1992 (S.I. 1992 No. 1217), reg.17 (q.v.).]

[41A. Breach of requirement as to brakes, steering-gear or tyres

A25.89   A person who—

  (a) contravenes or fails to comply with a construction and use requirement as to brakes, steering-gear or tyres, or

  (b) uses on a road a motor vehicle or trailer which does not comply with such a requirement, or causes or permits a motor vehicle or trailer to be so used,

is guilty of an offence.]

A25.90   *[Section 41A was inserted by the Road Traffic Act 1991, s.8(2).]*

[41B. Breach of requirement as to weight: goods and passenger vehicles

A25.91   (1) A person who—

  (a) contravenes or fails to comply with a construction and use requirement as to any description of weight applicable to—

    (i) a goods vehicle, or

    (ii) a motor vehicle or trailer adapted to carry more than eight passengers, or

  (b) uses on a road a vehicle which does not comply with such a requirement, or causes or permits a vehicle to be so used,

is guilty of an offence.

(2) In any proceedings for an offence under this section in which there is alleged a contravention of or failure to comply with a construction and use requirement as to any description of weight applicable to a goods vehicle, it shall be a defence to prove either—

  (a) that at the time when the vehicle was being used on the road—

    (i) it was proceeding to a weighbridge which was the nearest available one to the place where the loading of the vehicle was completed for the purpose of being weighed, or

    (ii) it was proceeding from a weighbridge after being weighed to the nearest point at which it was reasonably practicable to reduce the weight to the relevant limit, without causing an obstruction on any road, or

  (b) in a case where the limit of that weight was not exceeded by more than 5 per cent—

(i) that that limit was not exceeded at the time when the loading of the vehicle was originally completed, and

(ii) that since that time no person has made any addition to the load.]

[Section 41B was inserted by the Road Traffic Act 1991, s.8(2).]   A25.92

[42. Breach of other construction and use requirements

A person who—   A25.93

   (a) contravenes or fails to comply with any construction or use requirement other than one within section 41A(a) or 41B(1)(a) of this Act, or

   (b) uses on a road a motor vehicle or trailer which does not comply with such a requirement, or causes or permits a motor vehicle or trailer to be so used,

is guilty of an offence.]

[Section 42 is printed as substituted by the Road Traffic Act 1991, s.8(2).   A25.94

The fixed penalty procedure applies to offences under section 42; see the Road Traffic Offenders Act 1988, Sched. 3 below. Offences under section 42 which consist of causing an unnecessary obstruction of a road in breach of regulation 103 of the Road Vehicles (Construction and Use) Regulations 1986 (S.I. 1986 No. 1087) (q.v.) have been designated as fixed penalty parking offences by the Schedule to the Fixed Penalty Order 2000 (S.I. 2000 No. 2792) (q.v.).

Proceedings under section 42(b) are specified by the Prosecution of Offences Act 1985 (Specified Proceedings) Order 1999 (S.I. 1999 No. 904) below as being proceedings the conduct of which the Director of Public Prosecutions is not required to take over from the police under the Prosecution of Offences Act 1985, s.3(3)(a).]

43. Temporary exemption (contained in regulations) from application of regulations under section 41   *[Omitted.]*

44. Authorisation of use on roads of special vehicles not complying with regulations under section 41

(1) The Secretary of State may by order authorise, subject to such restrictions and con-   A25.95
ditions as may be specified by or under the order, the use on roads—

   (a) of special motor vehicles or trailers, or special types of motor vehicles or trailers, which are constructed either for special purposes or for tests or trials,

   (b) of vehicles or trailers, or types of vehicles or trailers, constructed for use outside the United Kingdom,

   (c) of new or improved types of motor vehicles or trailers, whether wheeled or wheel-less, or of motor vehicles or trailers equipped with new or improved equipment or types of equipment, and

   (d) of vehicles or trailers carrying loads of exceptional dimensions,

[and sections 40A to 42 of this Act shall not apply in relation to] the use of such vehicles, trailers, or types in accordance with the order.

(2) The Secretary of State may by order make provision for securing that, subject to such restrictions and conditions as may be specified by or under the order, regulations under section 41 of this Act shall have effect in their application to such vehicles, trailers and types of vehicles and trailers as are mentioned in subsection (1) above subject to such modifications or exceptions as may be specified in the order.

(3) The powers conferred by this section on the Secretary of State to make orders shall be exercisable by statutory instrument except in the case of orders applying only to specified vehicles or to vehicles of specified persons, but in that excepted case (as in

others) the order may be varied or revoked by subsequent order of the Secretary of State.

A25.96   *[Section 44 is printed as amended by the Road Traffic Act 1991, s.48 and Sched. 4, para.51.*

The orders made by statutory instrument which have effect as if made under section 44 include the Motor Vehicles (Authorisation of Special Types) General Order 1979 (S.I. 1979 No. 1198) (q.v.).]

Tests of vehicles other than goods vehicles to which section 49 applies

45. Tests of satisfactory condition of vehicles

A25.97   (1) This section applies to motor vehicles other than goods vehicles which are required by regulations under section 49 of this Act to be submitted for a vehicle test under that section and has effect for the purpose of ascertaining whether the [following requirements are complied with, namely—

     (a) the prescribed statutory requirements relating to the construction and condition of motor vehicles or their accessories or equipment, and

     (b) the requirement that the condition of motor vehicles should not be such that their use on a road would involve a danger of injury to any person.]

(2) The Secretary of State may by regulations make provision—

     (a) for the examination of vehicles submitted for examination under this section, and

     (b) for the issue, where it is found on such an examination that the requirements mentioned in subsection (1) above are complied with, of a certificate (in this Act referred to as a "*test certificate*") that at the date of the examination the requirements were complied with in relation to the vehicle.

(3) *[Examinations to be carried out by authorised examiners and others.]*

(4) *[Refusal of test certificate.]*

(5) *[Appeal against refusal of test certificate.]*

(6) *[Examination stations and equipment.]*

(7) *[Power to make regulations.]*

(8) In its application to vehicles in which recording equipment is required by Article 3 of the Community Recording Equipment Regulation to be installed and used, this section shall have effect as if any reference to prescribed statutory requirements relating to the construction and condition of motor vehicles or their accessories or equipment included a reference to the prescribed requirements of so much of that Regulation as relates to the installation of recording equipment and the seals to be fixed to such equipment.

A25.98   *[Section 45 is printed as amended by the Road Traffic Act 1991, s.48 and Sched. 4, para.51.*

The following subsections will be inserted into section 45 by the Road Traffic (Vehicle Testing) Act 1999 with effect from a date (or dates) to be announced:

[(6A) *[Courses of instruction relating to examinations under section 45.]*]

[(6B) The Secretary of State shall maintain, or cause to be maintained, records containing such particulars as he thinks fit of—

     (a) vehicles submitted for examination under this section, and

     (b) the carrying out of and the results of the examinations.]

The Motor Vehicles (Tests) Regulations 1981 (S.I. 1981 No. 1694) (q.v.) have effect as if made in part under section 45.]

46. Particular aspects of regulations under section 45   *[Omitted.]*   **A25.99**

[The text of section 46 will be substituted by the Road Traffic (Vehicle Testing) Act 1999 with effect   **A25.100**
*from a date to be announced; in consequence, the following should on such date be substituted for the existing
entry relating to section 46:*

[46. Regulations under section 45 of Road Traffic Act 1988]   *[Omitted.]*

*Section 46A will be inserted by the Road Traffic (Vehicle Testing) Act 1999, s.3, with effect from a date
to be announced; in consequence, the following entry should on such date be inserted after that relating to
section 46:*

[46A. Use of records of vehicle examinations, etc.]   *[Omitted.]]*

[46B. Evidence from records of vehicle examinations   **A25.101**

(1) A statement to which this section applies is admissible in any proceedings as evidence . . . of any fact stated in it with respect to—

   (a) the issue of a test certificate in respect of a vehicle, and

   (b) the date of issue of such a certificate,

to the same extent as oral evidence of that fact is admissible in the proceedings.

(2) This section applies to a statement contained in a document purporting to be—

   (a) a part of the records maintained under section 45(6B) of this Act,

   (b) a copy of a document forming part of those records, or

   (c) a note of any information contained in those records,

and to be authenticated by a person authorised to do so by the Secretary of State.

(3) In this section as it has effect in England and Wales—

"*document*" means anything in which information of any description is recorded;

"*copy*", in relation to a document, means anything onto which information recorded in the document has been copied, by whatever means and whether directly or indirectly; and

"*statement*" means any representation of fact, however made.

(4) *[Applies to Scotland.]*

(5) Nothing in subsection (4) above limits to civil proceedings the reference to proceedings in subsection (1) above.]

[With effect from a date to be announced, section 46B will be inserted by the Road Traffic (Vehicle   **A25.102**
Testing) Act 1999, s.4.
The words omitted from section 46B(1) relate exclusively to Scotland.]]

47. Obligatory test certificates

(1) A person who uses on a road at any time, or causes or permits to be so used, a motor   **A25.103**
vehicle to which this section applies, and as respects which no test certificate has been issued
within the appropriate period before that time, is guilty of an offence.

In this section and section 48 of this Act, the "*appropriate period*" means a period of twelve
months or such shorter period as may be prescribed.

(2) Subject to subsections (3) and (5) below, the motor vehicles to which this section
applies at any time are—

   (a) those first registered [under the Vehicle Excise and Registration Act 1994 or any
   corresponding earlier legislation], not less than three years before that time, and

(b) those which, having a date of manufacture not less than three years before that time, have been used on roads (whether in Great Britain or elsewhere) before being [so registered],

being, in either case, motor vehicles other than goods vehicles which are required by regulations under section 49 of this Act to be submitted for a goods vehicle test.

(3) As respects a vehicle being—

(a) a motor vehicle used for the carriage of passengers and with more than eight seats, excluding the driver's seat, or

(b) a taxi (as defined in section 64(3) of the Transport Act 1980 [*q.v.*]), being a vehicle licensed to ply for hire, or

(c) an ambulance, that is to say, a motor vehicle which is constructed or adapted, and primarily used, for the carriage of persons to a place where they will receive, or from a place where they have received, medical or dental treatment, and which, by reason of design, marking or equipment is readily identifiable as a vehicle so constructed or adapted,

subsection (2)(a) above shall have effect as if for the period there mentioned there were substituted a period of one year.

[(4) For the purposes of subsection (2)(b) above there shall be disregarded—

(a) the use of a vehicle before it is sold or supplied by retail, and

(b) the use of a vehicle to which a motor dealer has assigned a mark under [section 24 of the Vehicle Excise and Registration Act 1994] before it is registered by the Secretary of State under [section 21(2)] of that Act.]

(5) This section does not apply to vehicles of such classes as may be prescribed.

(6) The Secretary of State may by regulations exempt from subsection (1) above the use of vehicles for such purposes as may be prescribed.

(7) The Secretary of State may by regulations exempt from subsection (1) above the use of vehicles in any such area as may be prescribed.

(8) For the purposes of this section the date of manufacture of a vehicle shall be taken to be the last day of the year during which its final assembly is completed, except where after that day modifications are made to the vehicle before it is sold or supplied by retail, and in that excepted case shall be taken to be the last day of the year during which the modifications are completed.

(9) The Secretary of State may by order made by statutory instrument direct that subsection (2) above shall have effect with the substitution, for three years (in both places), of such other period (not being more than ten years) as may be specified in the order.

An order under this subsection shall not have effect unless approved by resolution of each House of Parliament.

A25.104   *[Section 47 is printed as amended by the Finance Act 1994, s.5 and Sched. 2, paras 25 and 29; Vehicle Excise and Registration Act 1994, s.63 and Sched. 3, para.24.*

Proceedings under section 47(1) are specified by the Prosecution of Offences Act 1985 (Specified Proceedings) Order 1999 (S.I. 1999 No. 904) below as being proceedings the conduct of which the Director of Public Prosecutions is not required to take over from the police under the Prosecution of Offences Act 1985, s.3(3)(a).

The Motor Vehicles (Tests) Regulations 1981 (S.I. 1981 No. 1694) have effect as if made in part under section 47.]

48. Supplementary provisions about test certificates

(1) *[Regulations changing length of appropriate period and period under section 47(2).]*   **A25.105**

[(1A) A test certificate issued in respect of a vehicle within the period of one month ending immediately before the date on which section 47 of this Act first applies to the vehicle shall be treated for the purposes of that section as if issued at the end of that period.]

(2) Where—

  (a) within the appropriate period after a test certificate is issued or treated for the purposes of section 47 of this Act as issued, but

  (b) not earlier than one month before the end of that period,

a further test certificate is issued as respects the same vehicle, the further certificate shall be treated for the purposes of that section as if issued at the end of the appropriate period.

(3) Where the particulars contained in a test certificate in accordance with regulations made under section 45 of this Act include a date of expiry falling later, but not more than one month later, than the end of the appropriate period after the date on which it is issued—

  (a) the certificate shall be deemed to have been issued in respect of the same vehicle as an earlier test certificate, and

  (b) the date on which it was issued shall be deemed to have been a date falling within the last month of the appropriate period after the date on which that earlier certificate was issued or treated for the purposes of section 47 of this Act as issued;

and any date of expiry contained in a test certificate shall be deemed to have been entered in accordance with regulations under section 45 of this Act unless the contrary is proved.

(4) The Secretary of State may by regulations make provision for the issue, in such circumstances as may be prescribed, of a certificate of temporary exemption in respect of a public service vehicle adapted to carry more than eight passengers, exempting that vehicle from the provisions of section 47(1) of this Act for such period as may be specified in the certificate.

(5) In relation to any public service vehicle so adapted—

  (a) subsections [(1A),] (2) and (3) above shall have effect as if for "one month" (in [each place]) there were substituted "two months", and

  (b) subsection (3) above shall have effect as if for "last month" there were substituted "last two months".

(6) *[Repealed.]*

[Section 48 is printed as amended by the Road Traffic Act 1991, s.48 and Sched. 4, para.54(1) and   **A25.106**
(3); the Deregulation (Motor Vehicle Tests) Order 1996 (S.I. 1996 No. 1700; not reproduced in this work), art.2.
The term "public service vehicle" is defined in section 1 of the Public Passenger Vehicles Act 1981 (q.v.).]

Tests of certain classes of goods vehicles

49. Tests of satisfactory condition of goods vehicles and determination of plated weights, etc.

(1) The Secretary of State may by regulations make provision for the examination of   **A25.107**
goods vehicles of any prescribed class—

(a) for the purpose of selecting or otherwise determining plated weights or other plated particulars for goods vehicles of that class, or

(b) for the purpose of ascertaining whether any prescribed construction and use requirements (whether relating to plated particulars or not) are complied with in the case of goods vehicles of that class,

[or

(c) for the purpose of ascertaining whether the condition of the vehicle is such that its use on a road would involve a danger of injury to any person,

or for any of these purposes.]

(2) In particular the regulations may make provision—

(a) for the determination, according to criteria or by methods prescribed by or determined under the regulations, of the plated particulars for a goods vehicle (including its plated weights), on an examination of the vehicle for the purpose, and for the issue on such an examination, except as provided by regulations made by virtue of paragraph (c) of this subsection, of a certificate (in this Act referred to as a "*plating certificate*") specifying those particulars,

(b) for the issue, for a goods vehicle which has been found on examination for the purpose to comply with the prescribed construction and use requirements [and the requirement that the condition of the vehicle is not such that its use on a road would involve a danger of injury to any person], of a certificate (in this Act referred to as a "*goods vehicle test certificate*") stating that the vehicle has been found so to comply, and

(c) for the refusal of a goods vehicle test certificate for a goods vehicle which is so found not to comply with those requirements and for requiring a written notification to be given—

(i) of any such refusal, and
(ii) of the grounds of the refusal,

and for the refusal of a plating certificate where a goods vehicle test certificate is refused.

(3) References in subsections (1) and (2) above to construction and use requirements shall be construed—

(a) in relation to an examination of a vehicle solely for the purpose of ascertaining whether it complies with any such requirements, as references to such of those requirements as are applicable to the vehicle at the time of the test, and

(b) in relation to an examination of a vehicle both for that purpose and for the purpose of determining its plated particulars, as references to such of those requirements as will be applicable to the vehicle if a plating certificate is issued for it.

(4) In this Part of this Act—

"*examination for plating*" means an examination under regulations under this section for the purpose of determining plated particulars for a goods vehicle, and

"*goods vehicle test*" means an examination under regulations under this section for the purpose of ascertaining whether any prescribed construction and use requirements [, or the requirement that the condition of the vehicle is not such that its use on a road would involve a danger of injury to any person,] are complied with in the case of a goods vehicle.

(5) In its application to vehicles in which recording equipment is required by Article 3 of the Community Recording Equipment Regulation to be installed and used, this section

shall have effect as if any reference to prescribed construction and use requirements included a reference to prescribed requirements of so much of that Regulation as relates to the installation of recording equipment and the seals to be fixed to such equipment.

[Section 49 is printed as amended by the Road Traffic Act 1991, s.48 and Sched. 4, para.54(1)–(4).   **A25.108**
The Goods Vehicles (Plating and Testing) Regulations 1988 (S.I. 1988 No. 1478) (q.v.) have effect as if made in part under section 49.]

50. Appeals against determinations under section 49   *[Omitted.]*   **A25.109**

51. Particular aspects of regulations under section 49

(1) Without prejudice to the generality of subsection (1) of section 49 of this Act, reg-   **A25.110**
ulations under that section may—

(a), (b) *[Omitted.]*

(c) prescribe the conditions subject to which vehicles will be accepted for such examination and, without prejudice to that—

(i) authorise any person by whom an examination of the vehicle under the regulations or section 50 of this Act is carried out to drive the vehicle, whether on a road or elsewhere, and

(ii) require that a driver of a vehicle examined under those regulations or that section is, except so far as permitted to be absent by the person carrying out the examination, present throughout the whole of the examination and drives the vehicle when directed to do so, and operates the controls in accordance with any directions given to him, by that person,

(d) *[Omitted.]*

(2) Regulations under section 49 of this Act may provide that a person who contravenes or fails to comply with a requirement of regulations imposed by virtue of subsection (1)(c)(ii) above is guilty of an offence.

(3) In this section any reference to the driving of a vehicle is, in relation to a trailer, a reference to the driving of the vehicle by which the trailer is drawn.

52. Supplementary provisions about tests, etc., of goods vehicles   *[Omitted.]*   **A25.111**

53. Obligatory goods vehicle test certificates

(1) If any person at any time on or after the relevant date—   **A25.112**

(a) uses on a road a goods vehicle of a class required by regulations under section 49 of this Act to have been submitted for examination for plating, or

(b) causes or permits to be used on a road a goods vehicle of such a class,

and at that time there is no plating certificate in force for the vehicle, he is guilty of an offence.

In this subsection "*relevant date*", in relation to any goods vehicle, means the date by which it is required by the regulations to be submitted for examination for plating.

(2) If any person at any time on or after the relevant date—

(a) uses on a road a goods vehicle of a class required by regulations under section 49 of this Act to have been submitted for a goods vehicle test, or

(b) causes or permits to be used on a road a goods vehicle of such a class,

and at that time there is no goods vehicle test certificate in force for the vehicle, he is guilty of an offence.

In this subsection *"relevant date"*, in relation to any goods vehicle, means the date by which it is required by the regulations to be submitted for its goods vehicle test.

(3) Any person who—

(a) uses a goods vehicle on a road, or

(b) causes or permits a goods vehicle to be so used,

when an alteration has been made to the vehicle or its equipment which is required by regulations under section 49 of this Act to be, but has not been, notified to the Secretary of State [or the prescribed testing authority] is guilty of an offence.

(4) In any proceedings for an offence under subsection (3) above, it shall be a defence to prove that the alteration was not specified in the relevant plating certificate in accordance with regulations under section 49 of this Act.

(5) The Secretary of State may by regulations—

(a) exempt from all or any of the preceding provisions of this section the use of goods vehicles for such purposes or in such an area as may be prescribed and

(b) make provision for the issue in respect of a vehicle in such circumstances as may be prescribed of a certificate of temporary exemption exempting that vehicle from the provisions of subsection (1) or (2) above for such period as may be specified in the certificate.

A25.113   *[Section 53 is printed as prospectively amended by the Transport Act 1982, s.10(7)(b) (as itself amended by the Road Traffic (Consequential Provisions) Act 1988, s.4 and Sched. 2, Pt I, para.4(4)(b)). The words printed within square brackets in subsection (3) will come into force on a date to be announced; see the Transport Act 1982, s.76(2).*

The Goods Vehicles (Plating and Testing) Regulations 1988 (S.I. 1988 No. 1478) (q.v.) have effect as if made in part under section 53. As to notifiable alterations, see regulation 30; and as to exemptions, see regulation 44.]

Approval of design, construction, equipment and marking of vehicles

54. Type approval requirements

A25.114   (1) Without prejudice to section 41 of this Act, the Secretary of State may by regulations prescribe requirements (in this Part of this Act referred to as *"type approval requirements"*)—

(a) with respect to the design, construction, equipment and marking of vehicles of any class, being requirements which are applicable before, whether or not they are applicable after, vehicles of that class are used on a road,

(b) with respect to the design, construction, equipment and marking of vehicle parts of any class, being requirements which are applicable before, whether or not they are applicable after, vehicle parts of that class are fitted to a vehicle used on a road.

(2) Regulations under this section may provide for the determination, according to criteria or by methods prescribed by or determined under the regulations, of weights of any description which in the opinion of the Secretary of State should not be exceeded in the case of vehicles of any class.

(3) In this Part of this Act references to design weights shall be construed as references to weights determined by virtue of subsection (2) above.

(4) Subject to subsection (5) below, the following provisions of this Act to the end of section 60 apply in relation to parts of vehicles as they apply in relation to vehicles and, accordingly, any reference in those provisions to a vehicle, other than a reference to a goods vehicle, is to be read as including a reference to a vehicle part.

(5) Any provision which relates solely to goods vehicles or design weights does not apply in relation to parts of vehicles, but particular exclusions in those provisions do not affect the generality of this exclusion.

(6) In this Part of this Act, "*the relevant aspects of design, construction, equipment and marking*", in relation to any vehicle, means those aspects of design, construction, equipment and marking which are subject to the type approval requirements or which were used as criteria in determining design weights for that vehicle.

[*The Motor Vehicles (Type Approval for Goods Vehicles) (Great Britain) Regulations 1982 (S.I. 1982 No. 1271) (q.v.), the Motor Vehicles (Type Approval) (Great Britain) Regulations 1984 (S.I. 1984 No. 981) (q.v.), and the Motor Vehicles (Approval) Regulations 2001 (S.I. 2001 No. 25) (q.v.) have effect as if made in part under section 54.*]   **A25.115**

55. Type approval certificates

(1) Where the Secretary of State is satisfied on application made to him by the manu-   **A25.116**
facturer of a vehicle of a class to which regulations under section 54 of this Act apply and after examination of the vehicle—

(a) that the vehicle complies with the relevant type approval requirements, and

(b) that adequate arrangements have been made to secure that other vehicles purporting to conform with that vehicle in the relevant aspects of design, construction, equipment and marking will so conform in all respects or with such variations as may be permitted,

he may approve that vehicle as a type vehicle.

(2) Where the Secretary of State approves a vehicle as a type vehicle he must issue a certificate (in this Part of this Act referred to as a "*type approval certificate*") stating that the vehicle complies with the relevant type approval requirements and specifying—

(a) the permitted variations from the type vehicle, and

(b) the design weights for vehicles so conforming in all respects and for vehicles so conforming with any such variations.

(3) In the following provisions of this section and in sections 56 to 59 of this Act "*conform*" means conform in all respects or with any permitted variation.

(4) Subject to subsection (6) below, a type approval certificate may be issued for a type vehicle where the Secretary of State is satisfied that one or more, but not all, of the relevant type approval requirements are complied with in the case of that vehicle.

(5) A further type approval certificate may be issued by virtue of subsection (4) above on the application of any person—

(a) who manufactures any part of the vehicle, or

(b) by whom the vehicle is finally assembled;

and references in the following provisions of this section and in sections 56 to 59 of this Act to a manufacturer shall be construed accordingly.

(6) The first type approval certificate issued for a type vehicle by virtue of subsection (4) above must specify the design weights for conforming vehicles, and accordingly—

(a) so much of subsection (2) above or section 57(1) to (3) of this Act as requires the Secretary of State or a manufacturer to specify in any certificate under this or that section the design weights or plated weights for a vehicle or as requires the Secretary of State [or the prescribed testing authority] or a manufacturer to mark or secure the marking of the plated weights on a vehicle does not apply to a subsequent type approval certificate issued by virtue of subsection (4) above or to the certificates of conformity issued in consequence of such a type approval certificate, and

(b) so much of section 58(2) of this Act as requires the Secretary of State to specify in any certificate issued by him the design weights and plated weights for a vehicle or to secure that the plated weights are marked on a vehicle does not apply to a Minister's approval certificate issued by virtue of subsection (4) above.

(7) Subsection (6) above does not apply in relation to vehicle parts.

(8) Where the Secretary of State determines on an application under this section not to issue a type approval certificate in respect of a vehicle, he must give to the applicant a written notification of the determination, stating the grounds on which it is based.

A25.117   *[Section 55 is printed as prospectively amended by the Transport Act 1982, s.17(1)(a) (as itself amended by the Road Traffic (Consequential Provisions) Act 1988, s.4 and Sched. 2, Pt I, para.6(1)(b)). The words printed within square brackets in subsection (6) will come into force on a date to be announced; see the Transport Act 1982, s.76(2).*

As to the application of section 55 to parts of vehicles, see section 54(4) and (5) above.]

A25.118   **56. Conditions of, and cancellation or suspension of, type approval certificates**   *[Omitted.]*

57. Certificates of conformity

A25.119   (1) The manufacturer of a type vehicle in respect of which a type approval certificate is in force may issue, in respect of each vehicle manufactured by him which conforms with the type vehicle in such of the relevant aspects of design, construction, equipment and marking as are mentioned in the type approval certificate, a certificate . . . —

(a) stating that it does so conform, and

(b) specifying the design weights for the vehicle,

and must in the case of goods vehicles of such classes as may be prescribed specify in the certificate one or more of the plated weights for the vehicle.

[(1A) In this Part of this Act (except in the expression "*EC certificate of conformity*" and in the definition of that expression in section 85 of this Act) "*certificate of conformity*" means a certificate issued under subsection (1) above.]

(2) *[Specification of plated weights in certificate of conformity.]*

(3) *[Marking of plated weights by means of plate.]*

(4) Any certificate of conformity issued in consequence of any type approval certificate issued by virtue of section 55(4) of this Act shall relate only to the requirement or requirements to which that type approval certificate relates.

(5) *[Inapplicability of subsections (2) and (3) to vehicle parts.]*

A25.120   *[Section 57 is printed as amended by the Motor Vehicles (EC Type Approval) Regulations 1992 (S.I. 1992 No. 3107).*

As to the application of section 57 to parts of vehicles, see section 54(4) and (5) above.

As to the terms "conform" and "manufacturer", see section 55(3) and (5) above; as to the term "goods vehicle", see section 62(3) below.]

58. Minister's approval certificates

A25.121   (1) Where the Secretary of State is satisfied, on application made to him by any person in respect of a vehicle of a class to which regulations under section 54 of this Act apply and after examination of the vehicle, that—

(a) the vehicle complies with the relevant type approval requirements, and

(b) in the case of a goods vehicle, the Secretary of State has sufficient information to enable the plated weights to be ascertained for the vehicle,

he may issue a certificate (in this Part of this Act referred to as a "*Minister's approval certificate*").

(2) *[Content of Minister's approval certificate.]*

(3) Where by virtue of section 57(4) of this Act a certificate of conformity issued in respect of a vehicle relates to one or more, but not all, of the relevant type approval requirements, the Secretary of State may issue in respect of that vehicle a Minister's approval certificate relating to one or more of the other relevant type approval requirements.

(4)–(6) *[Issue of Minister's approval certificate in respect of another vehicle without examination.]*

(7) *[Notice of refusal of Minister's approval certificate.]*

[As to the application of section 58 to parts of vehicles, see section 54(4) and (5) above.   **A25.122**
As to the term "goods vehicle", see section 62(3) below.]

59. Supplementary provisions as to certificates of conformity and Minister's approval certificates

(1) The Secretary of State may by regulations require the prescribed alterations—   **A25.123**

(a) in any of the relevant aspects of design, construction, equipment or marking, or

(b) in any such aspect which affects the plated weight,

made to any vehicle for which a certificate of conformity or a Minister's approval certificate is issued shall, subject to any exemption granted under subsection (2) below, be notified to the Secretary of State [or the prescribed testing authority].

(2) The Secretary of State may by notice in writing given to the manufacturer of vehicles or to the owner of a vehicle for which a Minister's approval certificate is issued—

(a) direct that any specified alteration in any of the aspects mentioned in subsection (1) above to a vehicle to which the direction relates shall be notified to the Secretary of State [or the prescribed testing authority],

(b) exempt a vehicle to which the notice relates from all or any of the requirements of regulations under subsection (1) above, subject to compliance with any conditions specified in the notice.

(3) *[Regulation-making power.]*

(4) A certificate of conformity or a Minister's approval certificate specifying any plated weights shall be treated for the purposes of the provisions of this Part of this Act and any regulations made under them relating to plating certificates (except section 50(1) and (2) of this Act) as a plating certificate.

This subsection does not apply in relation to vehicle parts.

[Section 59 is printed as prospectively amended by the Transport Act 1982, s.10(7) (as itself amended   **A25.124**
by the Road Traffic (Consequential Provisions) Act 1988, s.4 and Sched. 2, Pt I, para.4(4)(d)). The words printed within square brackets in subsections (1) and (2) will come into force on a date to be announced; see the Transport Act 1982, s.76(2).

As to the application of section 59(1) and (2) to parts of vehicles, see section 54(4) and (5) above.

The Motor Vehicles (Type Approval for Goods Vehicles) (Great Britain) Regulations 1982 (S.I. 1982 No. 1271) (q.v.) have effect as if made in part under section 59(1). As to the requirement to notify prescribed alterations, see regulation 10.]

60. Appeals against determinations under sections 54 to 59   *[Omitted.]*   **A25.125**

61. Regulations for the purposes of sections 54 to 60

A25.126

(1)–(3) *[Omitted.]*

(4) Where regulations under this section impose the like requirement as may be imposed by regulations made by virtue of section 51(1)(c)(ii) of this Act, the regulations may provide that a person who contravenes or fails to comply with a requirement so imposed is guilty of an offence.

(5) *[Repealed.]*

A25.127

[Section 61 is printed as amended by the Road Traffic Act 1991, s.83 and Sched. 8.

The Motor Vehicles (Type Approval for Goods Vehicles) (Great Britain) Regulations 1982 (S.I. 1982 No. 1271) (q.v.), the Motor Vehicles (Type Approval) (Great Britain) Regulations 1984 (S.I. 1984 No. 981) (q.v.), and the Motor Vehicles (Approval) Regulations 2001 (S.I. 2001 No. 25) (q.v.) have effect as if made in part under section 61(1).]

62. Other supplementary provisions

A25.128

(1) *[Provision of stations for examination of vehicles.]*

(2) *[Power to make regulations as to recognition of foreign type approval certificates, etc.]*

(3) Except in the case of vehicles of such class as may be prescribed, in sections 57, 58 and 61 of this Act "*goods vehicle*" includes a vehicle which is a chassis for, or will otherwise form part of, a vehicle which when completed will be a goods vehicle.

63. Obligatory type approval certificates, certificates of conformity and Minister's approval certificates

A25.129

(1) If—

    (a) any person at any time on or after the day appointed by regulations made by the Secretary of State in relation to vehicles or vehicle parts of a prescribed class, being vehicles or vehicle parts to which type approval requirements prescribed by those regulations apply—

        (i) uses on a road, or
        (ii) causes or permits to be so used,

    a vehicle of that class or a vehicle to which is fitted a vehicle part of that class, and

    (b) it does not appear from one or more certificates then in force under sections 54 to 58 of this Act that the vehicle or vehicle part complies with those requirements,

he is guilty of an offence.

Different days may be appointed under this subsection in relation to different classes of vehicles or vehicle parts.

[(1A) For the purposes of subsection (1) above a vehicle shall be taken to comply with all relevant type approval requirements if an EC certificate of conformity has effect with respect to the vehicle.]

(2) If a plating certificate—

    (a) has been issued for a goods vehicle to which section 53(1) of this Act or subsection (1) above applies, but

    (b) does not specify a maximum laden weight for the vehicle together with any trailer which may be drawn by it,

any person who on or after the relevant date within the meaning of section 53(1) of this Act or, as the case may be, the day appointed under subsection (1) above uses the vehicle on a road for drawing a trailer, or causes or permits it to be so used, is guilty of an offence.

(3) Any person who—

   (a) uses a vehicle on a road, or

   (b) causes or permits a vehicle to be so used,

when an alteration has been made to the vehicle or its equipment which is required by regulations or directions under section 59 of this Act to be, but has not been, notified to the Secretary of State [or the prescribed testing authority] is guilty of an offence.

(4) In any proceedings for an offence under subsection (3) above, it shall be a defence to prove that the regulations were not or, as the case may be, the alteration was not, specified in the relevant certificate of conformity or Minister's approval certificate in accordance with regulations under section 59(3) of this Act.

[(5) The Secretary of State may make provision for securing that, subject to such restrictions and conditions as may be specified by or under the instrument by which the provision is made—

   (a) the use of vehicles is exempted from all or any of the preceding provisions of this section for purposes specified in the instrument or in such an area as is so specified,

   (b) goods vehicles are exempted from the provisions of subsection (2) above, and

   (c) there are issued in respect of vehicles or vehicle parts, in such circumstances as may be specified in the instrument, certificates of temporary exemption exempting the vehicles or vehicle parts from the provisions of subsection (1) above for such period as may be provided in the certificate.]

[(6) Subject to subsection (7) below, the power conferred by subsection (5) above is exercisable by regulations.]

[(7) That power is exercisable by order in relation to—

   (a) specified vehicles, or

   (b) vehicles of specified persons;

and an order under this subsection may be varied or revoked by a subsequent order of the Secretary of State.]

[Section 63 is printed as amended by the Motor Vehicles (EC Type Approval) Regulations 1992 (S.I.   **A25.130**
1992 No. 3107); the Transport Act 2000, s.264 (with effect from February 1, 2001; see the Transport Act 2001 (Commencement No. 3) Order 2001 (S.I. 2001 No. 57; not reproduced in this work) (the subsequent amendment of S.I. 2001 No. 57 by the Transport Act 2000 (Commencement No. 3) (Amendment) Order 2001 (S.I. 2001 No. 115; not reproduced in this work) does not affect the amendment of section 63); and as prospectively amended by the Transport Act 1982, s.10(7)(c) (as itself amended by the Road Traffic (Consequential Provisions) Act 1988, s.4 and Sched. 2, Pt I, para.4(4)(c)). The words printed within square brackets in subsection (3) will come into force on a date to be announced; see the Transport Act 1982, s.76(2).

As to the disapplication of section 63(1) in respect of the use of certain vehicles, see the Motor Vehicles (Approval) Regulations 2001 (S.I. 2001 No. 25), reg.14(8) below.

The Motor Vehicles (Type Approval) (Great Britain) Regulations 1984 (S.I. 1984 No. 981) (q.v.) and the Motor Vehicles (Approval) Regulations 2001 (S.I. 2001 No. 25) (q.v.) have effect as if made in part under section 63(1).]

[[63A]. Alteration of plated weights for goods vehicles without examination

(1) *[Regulation-making power.]*   **A25.131**

(2) *[Appeal against determination under regulations under this section.]*

(3) *[Amplification of regulation-making power.]*

(4) In this section "*approval certificate*" means a plating certificate and any certificate of conformity or Minister's approval certificate specifying any plated weights.

(5) Any certificate issued in respect of a goods vehicle under regulations made under this section in replacement of an approval certificate of any description mentioned in subsection (4) above—

    (a) shall be in the form appropriate for an approval certificate of that description;

    (b) shall be identical in content with the certificate it replaces, save for any alterations in the plated weights authorised by the regulations; and

    (c) shall be treated for the purposes of this Part of this Act (including this section) and any regulations made under any provision of this Part of this Act as if it were the same certificate as the certificate it replaces;

and any plate so issued in replacement of a plate fixed to the vehicle under [section 57 or 58] of this Act shall, when fixed to the vehicle, be treated as so fixed under that section.]

A25.132   *[Section 63A was inserted by the Transport Act 1982, s.18, and is printed as amended by the Road Traffic (Consequential Provisions) Act 1988, s.4 and Sched. 2, Pt I, para.7.]*

64. Using goods vehicle with unauthorised weights as well as authorised weights marked on it

A25.133   (1) If there is fixed to a goods vehicle a plate containing plated weights of any description—

    (a) determined for that vehicle by virtue of sections 49 to 52 of this Act, or

    (b) specified in a certificate for that vehicle under section 57(1) or (2) or 58(2) or (5) of this Act,

the vehicle shall not, while it is used on a road, be marked with any other weights, except other plated weights, other weights required or authorised to be marked on the vehicle by regulations under section 41 of this Act or weights so authorised for the purposes of this section by regulations made by the Secretary of State and marked in the prescribed manner.

(2) In the event of a contravention of or failure to comply with this section the owner of the vehicle is guilty of an offence.

[64A. Failure to hold EC certificate of conformity for unregistered light passenger vehicle or motor cycle

A25.134   (1) Subject to subsections (2) to (5) below, if a person uses on a road a light passenger vehicle [or a vehicle to which the motorcycle type approval Directive applies]—

    (a) which has not been registered—

        (i) under [section 21 of the Vehicle Excise and Registration Act 1994], or

        (ii) under the law of a member State other than the United Kingdom, and

    (b) in respect of which no EC certificate of conformity has effect,

he is guilty of an offence.

(2) A person shall not be convicted of an offence under this section in respect of [the use of a light passenger vehicle] if he proves—

    (a) that the vehicle was one in respect of which the grant of a licence under [the Vehicle Excise and Registration Act 1994] was not prohibited by [regulation 11 of the Motor Vehicles (EC Type Approval) Regulations 1998 [*S.I. 1998 No. 2051 below*]], or

    (b) in the case of a vehicle in respect of which duty is not chargeable under that Act, that the vehicle was one whose registration under [section 21] of that Act was not prohibited by that regulation.

[(2A) A person shall not be convicted of an offence under this section in respect of the use of a vehicle to which the motorcycle type approval Directive applies if he proves that the vehicle was one in respect of which the grant of a licence or nil licence under the Vehicle Excise and Registration Act 1994 was not prohibited by regulation 16 of the Motor Cycles Etc. (EC Type Approval) Regulations 1999 [*S.I. 1999 No. 2920 below*].]

(3) This section does not apply in relation to a vehicle in respect of which a Minister's approval certificate issued under section 58(1) of this Act or a Department's approval certificate issued under Article 31A(4) of the Road Traffic (Northern Ireland) Order 1981 has effect.

(4) This section does not apply to the use of a vehicle under a trade licence (within the meaning of [the Vehicle Excise and Registration Act 1994) in accordance with regulations made under [section 12(2)] of that Act.

(5) This section does not apply in relation to a vehicle brought temporarily into Great Britain by a person resident outside the United Kingdom.]

[(6) In the application of this section to a vehicle to which the motorcycle type approval Directive applies, any reference to a member State includes a reference to an EEA State.]

[Section 64A was inserted by the Motor Vehicles (EC Type Approval) Regulations 1992 (S.I. 1992   **A25.135**
No. 3107) and is printed as amended by the Interpretation Act 1978, ss.17(2)(a) and 23; the Vehicle Excise and Registration Act 1994, s.63 and Sched. 3, para.24(3); the Motor Cycles Etc. (EC Type Approval) Regulations 1999 (S.I. 1999 No. 2920).
As to the EEA Agreement and the EEA states, see further the note "European Economic Area" to Regulation (EEC) 3820/85 below.]

65. Vehicles and parts not to be sold without required certificate of conformity or Minister's approval certificate

(1) If—   **A25.136**

   (a) any person at any time on or after the day appointed by regulations under section 63(1) of this Act supplies a vehicle or vehicle part of a class to which those regulations apply, and

   (b) it does not appear from one or more certificates in force at that time under sections 54 to 58 of this Act that the vehicle or vehicle part complies with all the relevant type approval requirements prescribed by those regulations,

he is guilty of an offence.

[(1A) For the purposes of subsection (1) above a vehicle shall be taken to comply with all relevant type approval requirements if an EC certificate of conformity has effect with respect to the vehicle.]

(2) In this section references to supply include—

   (a) sell,

   (b) offer to sell or supply, and

   (c) expose for sale.

(3) A person shall not be convicted of an offence under this section in respect of the supply of a vehicle or vehicle part if he proves—

   (a) that it was supplied for export from Great Britain,

   (b) that he had reasonable cause to believe that it would not be used on a road in Great

Britain or, in the case of a vehicle part, that it would not be fitted to a vehicle used on a road in Great Britain or would not be so used or fitted until it had been certified under sections 54 to 58 of this Act, or

(c) that he had reasonable cause to believe that it would only be used for purposes or in any area prescribed by the Secretary of State under section 63(5) of this Act or, in the case of a goods vehicle, under section 53(5) of this Act.

(4) Nothing in subsection (1) above shall affect the validity of a contract or any rights arising under or in relation to a contract.

A25.137   *[Section 65 is printed as amended by the Motor Vehicles (EC Type Approval) Regulations 1992 (S.I. 1992 No. 3107).]*

[65A. Light passenger vehicles [and motor cycles] not to be sold without EC certificate of conformity

A25.138   (1) Subject to subsections (3) to (6) below, any person who supplies a light passenger vehicle [or a vehicle to which the motorcycle type approval Directive applies]—

(a) which has not been registered—

(i) under [section 21 of the Vehicle Excise and Registration Act 1994], or
(ii) under the law of a member State other than the United Kingdom, and

(b) in respect of which no EC certificate of conformity has effect,

is guilty of an offence.

(2) In this section references to supply include—

(a) sell,

(b) offer to sell or supply, and

(c) expose for sale.

(3) A person shall not be convicted of an offence under this section in respect of [the supply of a light passenger vehicle] if he proves—

(a) that the vehicle was one in respect of which the grant of a licence under [the Vehicle Excise and Registration Act 1994] was not prohibited by [regulation 11 of the Motor Vehicles (EC Type Approval) Regulations 1998 [*S.I. 1998 No. 2051 below*]], or

(b) in the case of a vehicle in respect of which duty is not chargeable under that Act, that the vehicle was one whose registration under [section 21] of that Act was not prohibited by that regulation.

[(3A) A person shall not be convicted of an offence under this section in respect of the supply of a vehicle to which the motorcycle type approval Directive applies if he proves that the vehicle was one in respect of which the grant of a licence or nil licence under the Vehicle Excise and Registration Act 1994 was not prohibited by regulation 16 of the Motor Cycles Etc. (EC Type Approval) Regulations 1999 [*S.I. 1999 No. 2920 below*].]

(4) A person shall not be convicted of an offence under this section in respect of the supply of a vehicle if he proves—

(a) that it was supplied for export from the United Kingdom to a country which is not a member State, or

(b) that he had reasonable cause to believe—

(i) that it would not be used on a road in the United Kingdom or any other member State, or
(ii) that it would not be so used until an EC certificate of conformity had been issued in respect of it.

(5) This section does not apply in relation to the supply of a vehicle—

(a) to the Crown for naval, military or air force purposes,

(b) for the purposes of the military forces of any country outside the United Kingdom,

(c) to any public authority in the United Kingdom or any other member State for the purposes of civil defence within the meaning of the Civil Defence Act 1948,

(d) to a police authority for police purposes, or

(e) to any public authority in a member State outside the United Kingdom which has responsibilities for maintaining public order.

(6) This section does not apply in relation to a vehicle in respect of which a Minister's approval certificate issued under section 58(1) of this Act or a Department's approval certificate issued under Article 31A(4) of the Road Traffic (Northern Ireland) Order 1981 has effect.

(7) Nothing in subsection (1) above shall affect the validity of a contract or any rights arising under or in relation to a contract.]

[(8) In the application of this section to a vehicle to which the motorcycle type approval Directive applies, any reference to a member State includes a reference to an EEA State.]

[Section 65A was inserted by the Motor Vehicles (EC Type Approval) Regulations 1992 (S.I. 1992 No. 3107) and is printed as amended by the Interpretation Act 1978, ss.17(2)(a) and 23; the Vehicle Excise and Registration Act 1994, s.63 and Sched. 3, para.24(4); the Motor Cycles Etc. (EC Type Approval) Regulations 1999 (S.I. 1999 No. 2920).   **A25.139**

As to the EEA Agreement and the EEA states, see further the note "European Economic Area" to Regulation (EEC) 3820/85 below.]

Conditions for grant of excise licence

66. Regulations prohibiting the grant of excise licences for certain vehicles except on compliance with certain conditions   *[Omitted.]*

[Vehicle examiners]

[66A. Appointment of examiners

(1) The Secretary of State shall appoint such examiners as he considers necessary for the purpose of carrying out the functions conferred on them by this Part of this Act, [the Goods Vehicles (Licensing of Operators) Act 1995,] the Public Passenger Vehicles Act 1981, the Transport Act 1968 and any other enactment.   **A25.140**

(2) An examiner appointed under this section shall act under the general directions of the Secretary of State.

(3) In this Part of this Act "*vehicle examiner*" means an examiner appointed under this section.]

[Section 66A (and the italicised heading preceding it) was inserted by the Road Traffic Act 1991, s.9(1), and is printed as amended by the Goods Vehicles (Licensing of Operators) Act 1995, s.60(1) and Sched. 7, para.11.   **A25.141**

Persons who on June 30, 1992 were certifying officers, public service vehicle examiners, or examiners under section 68(1) of the Road Traffic Act 1988 are treated as if appointed under section 66A; see the Road Traffic Act 1991 (Commencement No. 4 and Transitional Provisions) Order 1992 (S.I. 1992 No. 1286; not reproduced in this work), art.3.

Examiners appointed under section 66A(1) (together with police constables) are also authorised inspecting officers for the purposes of Regulation (EEC) 684/92 (see the Public Service Vehicles (Community Licences) Regulations 1999 (S.I. 1999 No. 1322), reg.8 below) and Regulation (EC) 12/98 (see the Road Transport (Passenger Vehicles Cabotage) Regulations 1999 (S.I. 1999 No. 3413), reg.8 below).]

Testing vehicles on roads

67. Testing of condition of vehicles on roads

A25.142   (1) An authorised examiner may test a motor vehicle on a road for the purpose of—

[(a) ascertaining whether the following requirements, namely—

(i) the construction and use requirements, and

(ii) the requirement that the condition of the vehicle is not such that its use on a road would involve a danger of injury to any person,

are complied with as respects the vehicle;]

(b) bringing to the notice of the driver any failure to comply with those requirements.

[(2) For the purpose of testing a vehicle under this section the examiner—

(a) may require the driver to comply with his reasonable instructions, and

(b) may drive the vehicle.]

(3) A vehicle shall not be required to stop for a test except by a constable in uniform.

(4) The following persons may act as authorised examiners for the purposes of this section—

(a) [*repealed.*]

(b) a person appointed as an examiner under section [66A] of this Act,

(c) a person appointed to examine and inspect public carriages for the purposes of the Metropolitan Public Carriage Act 1869,

(d) a person appointed to act for the purposes of this section by the Secretary of State,

(e) a constable authorised so to act by or [on behalf of a] chief officer of police, and

(f) a person appointed by the police authority for a police area to act, under the directions of the chief officer of police, for the purposes of this section.

(5) A person mentioned in subsection (4)(a) to (d) and (f) must produce his authority to act for the purposes of this section if required to do so.

(6) On the examiner proceeding to test a vehicle under this section, the driver may, unless the test is required under subsection (7) or (8) below to be carried out forthwith, elect that the test shall be deferred to a time, and carried out at a place, fixed in accordance with Schedule 2 to this Act, and the provisions of that Schedule shall apply accordingly.

(7) Where it appears to a constable that, by reason of an accident having occurred owing to the presence of the vehicle on a road, it is requisite that a test should be carried out forthwith, he may require it to be so carried out and, if he is not to carry it out himself, may require that the vehicle shall not be taken away until the test has been carried out.

(8) Where in the opinion of a constable the vehicle is apparently so defective that it ought not to be allowed to proceed without a test being carried out, he may require the test to be carried out forthwith.

(9) If a person obstructs an authorised examiner acting under this section, or fails to comply with a requirement of this section or Schedule 2 to this Act, he is guilty of an offence.

(10) In this section and in Schedule 2 to this Act—

(a) "*test*" includes "inspect" or "inspection", as the case may require, and

(b) references to a vehicle include references to a trailer drawn by it.

A25.143   [*Section 67 is printed as amended by the Road Traffic Act 1991, ss.10(1)–(5), 83 and Sched. 8.*]

[68. Inspection of public passenger vehicles and goods vehicles

(1) A vehicle examiner—   A25.144

    (a) may at any time, on production if so required of his authority, inspect any vehicle to which this section applies and for that purpose detain the vehicle during such time as is required for the inspection, and

    (b) may at any time which is reasonable having regard to the circumstances of the case enter any premises on which he has reason to believe that such a vehicle is kept.

(2) The power conferred by subsection (1) above to inspect a vehicle includes power to test it and to drive it for the purpose of testing it.

(3) A person who intentionally obstructs an examiner in the exercise of his powers under subsection (1) above is guilty of an offence.

(4) A vehicle examiner or a constable in uniform may at any time require any person in charge of a vehicle to which this section applies and which is stationary on a road to proceed with the vehicle for the purpose of having it inspected under this section to any place where an inspection can be suitably carried out (not being more than five miles from the place where the requirement is made).

(5) A person in charge of a vehicle who refuses or neglects to comply with a requirement made under subsection (4) above is guilty of an offence.

(6) This section applies to—

    (a) goods vehicles,

    (b) public service vehicles, and

    (c) motor vehicles which are not public service vehicles but are adapted to carry more than eight passengers;

but subsection (1)(b) above shall not apply in relation to vehicles within paragraph (c) above or in relation to vehicles used to carry passengers for hire or reward only under permits granted under section 19 or 22 of the Transport Act 1985 (use of vehicles by educational and other bodies or in providing community bus services).]

[Section 68 (and the heading preceding it) is printed as substituted by the Road Traffic Act 1991, s.11.   A25.145
Section 68 has been prospectively amended (from a date to be announced) by the Transport Act 1982, s.10(6), as amended by the Road Traffic (Consequential Provisions) Act 1988, s.4 and Sched. 2, Pt I, para.4; the Road Traffic Act 1991, s.48 and Sched. 4, para.19(3).

Section 68 does not apply to tramcars: Tramcars and Trolley Vehicles (Modification of Enactments) Regulations 1992 (S.I. 1992 No. 1217), reg.7 (q.v.). Section 68 applies to trolley vehicles (other than duobuses) as if section 68(4) were omitted; see S.I. 1992 No. 1217, regs 10 and 11 (q.v.).

Sections 68–74 of this Act do not apply to any person or vehicle in the service of a visiting force or head-quarters (as defined); see the Visiting Forces and International Headquarters (Application of Law) Order 1999 (S.I. 1999 No. 1736; not reproduced in this work), art.8(1) and (2)(b).]

[Prohibition of unfit vehicles]

[69. Power to prohibit driving of unfit vehicles

(1) If on any inspection of a vehicle under section 41, 45, 49, 61, 67, 68 or 77 of this Act   A25.146
it appears to a vehicle examiner that owing to any defects in the vehicle it is, or is likely to become, unfit for service, he may prohibit the driving of the vehicle on a road—

(a) absolutely, or

(b) for one or more specified purposes, or

(c) except for one or more specified purposes.

(2) If on any inspection of a vehicle under any of the enactments mentioned in subsection (1) above it appears to an authorised constable that owing to any defects in the vehicle driving it (or driving it for any particular purpose or purposes or for any except one or more particular purposes) would involve a danger of injury to any person, he may prohibit the driving of the vehicle on a road—

(a) absolutely, or

(b) for one or more specified purposes, or

(c) except for one or more specified purposes.

(3) A prohibition under this section shall come into force as soon as the notice under subsection (6) below has been given if—

(a) it is imposed by an authorised constable, or

(b) in the opinion of the vehicle examiner imposing it the defects in the vehicle in question are such that driving it, or driving it for any purpose within the prohibition, would involve a danger of injury to any person.

(4) Except where subsection (3) applies, a prohibition under this section shall (unless previously removed under section 72 of this Act) come into force at such time not later than ten days from the date of the inspection as seems appropriate to the vehicle examiner imposing the prohibition, having regard to all the circumstances.

(5) A prohibition under this section shall continue in force until it is removed under section 72 of this Act.

(6) A person imposing a prohibition under this section shall forthwith give notice in writing of the prohibition to the person in charge of the vehicle at the time of the inspection—

(a) specifying the defects which occasioned the prohibition;

(b) stating whether the prohibition is on all driving of the vehicle or driving it for one or more specified purposes or driving it except for one or more specified purposes (and, where applicable, specifying the purpose or purposes in question); and

(c) stating whether the prohibition is to come into force immediately or at the end of a specified period.

(7) Where a notice has been given under subsection (6) above, any vehicle examiner or authorised constable may grant an exemption in writing for the use of the vehicle in such manner, subject to such conditions and for such purpose as may be specified in the exemption.

(8) Where such a notice has been given, any vehicle examiner or authorised constable may by endorsement on the notice vary its terms and, in particular, alter the time at which the prohibition is to come into force or suspend it if it has come into force.

(9) In this section "*authorised constable*" means a constable authorised to act for the purposes of this section by or on behalf of a chief officer of police.]

A25.147 *[Section 69 (and the heading preceding it) is printed as substituted by the Road Traffic Act 1991, s.12. Section 69 has been prospectively amended (from a date to be announced) by the Transport Act 1982, s.10(3), as substituted by the Road Traffic Act 1991, s.48 and Sched. 4, para.19(2).*

Section 69 does not apply to tramcars: Tramcars and Trolley Vehicles (Modification of Enactments) Regulations 1992 (S.I. 1992 No. 1217), reg.7 (q.v.).

As to visiting forces, etc., see the notes to section 68 above.]

[69A. Prohibitions conditional on inspection, etc.

(1) Where it appears to the person imposing a prohibition under section 69 of this Act **A25.148**
that the vehicle is adapted to carry more than eight passengers, or is a public service vehicle
not so adapted, the prohibition may be imposed with a direction making it irremovable
unless and until the vehicle has been inspected at an official PSV testing station within the
meaning of the Public Passenger Vehicles Act 1981.

(2) Where it appears to that person that the vehicle is of a class to which regulations
under section 49 of this Act apply, the prohibition may be imposed with a direction making
it irremovable unless and until the vehicle has been inspected at an official testing station.

(3) Where it appears to that person that the vehicle is one to which section 47 of this Act
applies, or would apply if the vehicle had been registered under [the Vehicle Excise and
Registration Act 1994] more than three years earlier, the prohibition may be imposed with
a direction making it irremovable unless and until the vehicle has been inspected, and a test
certificate issued, under section 45 of this Act.

(4) In any other case, the prohibition may be imposed with a direction making it
irremovable unless and until the vehicle has been inspected in accordance with regulations
under section 72 of this Act by a vehicle examiner or authorised constable (within the
meaning of section 69 of this Act).]

[Section 69A was inserted by the Road Traffic Act 1991, s.12, and is printed as amended by the Vehicle **A25.149**
Excise and Registration Act 1994, s.63 and Sched. 3, para.24(1).

Section 69A does not apply to tramcars: Tramcars and Trolley Vehicles (Modification of Enactments)
Regulations 1992 (S.I. 1992 No. 1217), reg.7 (q.v.).

Prohibitions imposed under section 69A may be removed in accordance with the Road Vehicles
(Prohibition) Regulations 1992 (S.I. 1992 No. 1285) (q.v.).

As to visiting forces, etc., see the notes to section 68 above.]

70. Power to prohibit driving of overloaded goods vehicles

(1) Subsections (2) and (3) below apply where a goods vehicle [, or a motor vehicle **A25.150**
adapted to carry more than eight passengers,] has been weighed in pursuance of a
requirement imposed under section 78 of this Act and it appears to—

(a) [a vehicle examiner],

(b) a person authorised with the consent of the Secretary of State to act for the purposes of this subsection by—

(i) a highway authority other than the Secretary of State, or
(ii) a local roads authority in Scotland, or

(c) a constable authorised to act for those purposes by or on behalf of a chief officer
of police,

that the limit imposed by construction and use requirements with respect to any description
of weight which is applicable to that vehicle has been exceeded or would be exceeded if it
were used on a road [or that by reason of excessive overall weight or excessive axle weight
on any axle driving the vehicle would involve a danger of injury to any person].

(2) The person to whom it so appears may, whether or not a notice is given under section
[69(6)] of this Act, give notice in writing to the person in charge of the vehicle prohibiting
the driving of the vehicle on a road until—

(a) that weight is reduced to that limit [or, as the case may be, so that it is no longer
excessive], and

(b) official notification has been given to whoever is for the time being in charge of the
vehicle that it is permitted to proceed.

(3) The person to whom it so appears may also by direction in writing require the person in charge of the vehicle to remove it (and, if it is a motor vehicle drawing a trailer, also remove the trailer) to such place and subject to such conditions as are specified in the direction; and the prohibition shall not apply to the removal of the vehicle or trailer in accordance with that direction.

(4) Official notification for the purposes of subsection (2) above—

    (a) must be in writing and be given by [a vehicle examiner], a person authorised as mentioned in subsection (1) above or a constable authorised as so mentioned, and

    (b) may be withheld until the vehicle has been weighed or reweighed in order to satisfy the person giving the notification that the weight has been sufficiently reduced.

(5) Nothing in this section shall be construed as limiting the power of the Secretary of State to make regulations under section 71(2) of this Act.

A25.151   *[Section 70 is printed as amended by the Road Traffic Act 1991, s.13(1), (2)(a)–(c), (3)(a) and (b), and (4).*

Section 70 does not apply to tramcars: Tramcars and Trolley Vehicles (Modification of Enactments) Regulations 1992 (S.I. 1992 No. 1217), reg.7 (q.v.).

As to visiting forces, etc., see the notes to section 68 above.]

[71. Unfit and overloaded vehicles: offences

A25.152   (1) A person who—

    (a) drives a vehicle in contravention of a prohibition under section 69 or 70 of this Act, or

    (b) causes or permits a vehicle to be driven in contravention of such a prohibition, or

    (c) fails to comply within a reasonable time with a direction under section 70(3) of this Act,

is guilty of an offence.

(2) The Secretary of State may by regulations provide for exceptions from subsection (1) above.]

A25.153   *[Section 71 is printed as substituted by the Road Traffic Act 1991, s.14.*

Section 71 does not apply to tramcars: Tramcars and Trolley Vehicles (Modification of Enactments) Regulations 1992 (S.I. 1992 No. 1217), reg.7 (q.v.).

As to visiting forces, etc., see the notes to section 68 above.

The Road Vehicles (Prohibition) Regulations 1992 (S.I. 1992 No. 1285) which set out exemptions from section 71(1) were made (in part) under section 71(2).]

A25.154   **72. Removal of prohibitions**   *[Omitted.]*

72A. Power to establish official testing stations   *[Omitted.]*

73. Provisions supplementary to sections 69 to 72

A25.155   [(1), (1ZA), (1A), (1B) *[Action on giving notice under section 69(6) or section 70(2)].*]

[(1C) *[Action on giving notice under section 72(7)].*]

(2) *[Repealed.]*

(3) Any reference in sections 69 to 72 of this Act to the driving of a vehicle is, in relation to a trailer, a reference to the driving of the vehicle by which the trailer is drawn.

(4) *[Definitions for purposes of sections 72, 73.]*

[As to visiting forces, etc., see the notes to section 68 above.]   A25.156

Miscellaneous provisions about vehicles and vehicle parts

74. Operator's duty to inspect, and keep records of inspections of, goods vehicles

(1) The Secretary of State may make regulations requiring the operator for the time   A25.157
being of a goods vehicle to which the regulations apply to secure—

  (a) the carrying out by a suitably qualified person (including the operator if so qualified) of an inspection of the vehicle for the purpose of ascertaining whether [the following requirements are complied with, namely—

    (i)] the construction and use requirements with respect to any prescribed matters, being requirements applicable to the vehicle, [and

    (ii) the requirement that the condition of the vehicle is not such that its use on a road would involve a danger of injury to any person], and

  (b) the making and authentication of records of such matters relating to any such inspection as may be prescribed, including records of the action taken to remedy any defects discovered on the inspection,

and providing for the preservation of such records for a prescribed period not exceeding fifteen months and their custody and production during that period.

(2) Regulations under this section may—

  (a) apply to all goods vehicles or to goods vehicles of such classes as may be prescribed,

  (b) require the inspection of goods vehicles under the regulations to be carried out at such times, or before the happening of such events, as may be prescribed, and

  (c) make different provision for different cases.

(3) Any person who contravenes or fails to comply with any provision of regulations under this section is guilty of an offence.

(4) In this section "*the operator*", in relation to a goods vehicle, means the person to whom it belongs or the hirer of it under a hire purchase agreement; but, if he has let it on hire (otherwise than by way of hire-purchase) or lent it to any other person, it means a person of a class prescribed by regulations under this section in relation to any particular class of goods vehicles or, subject to any such regulations, that other person.

[Section 74 is printed as amended by the Road Traffic Act 1991, s.48 and Sched. 4, para.57.   A25.158
As to visiting forces, etc., see the notes to section 68 above.]

75. Vehicles not to be sold in unroadworthy condition or altered so as to be unroadworthy

(1) Subject to the provisions of this section no person shall supply a motor vehicle or   A25.159
trailer in an unroadworthy condition.

(2) In this section references to supply include—

  (a) sell,

  (b) offer to sell or supply, and

  (c) expose for sale.

(3) For the purposes of subsection (1) above a motor vehicle or trailer is in an unroadworthy condition if—

(a) it is in such a condition that the use of it on a road in that condition would be unlawful by virtue of any provision made by regulations under section 41 of this Act as respects—

    (i) brakes, steering gear or tyres, or

    (ii) the construction, weight or equipment of vehicles, or

    (iii) *[repealed.]*

[(b) it is in such a condition that its use on a road would involve a danger of injury to any person.]

(4) Subject to the provisions of this section no person shall alter a motor vehicle or trailer so as to render its condition such that the use of it on a road in that condition

[(a) would be unlawful by virtue of any provision made as respects the construction, weight or equipment of vehicles by regulations under section 41]

[or

(b) would involve a danger of injury to any person.]

(5) A person who supplies or alters a motor vehicle or trailer in contravention of this section, or causes or permits it to be so supplied or altered, is guilty of an offence.

(6) A person shall not be convicted of an offence under this section in respect of the supply or alteration of a motor vehicle or trailer if he proves—

(a) that it was supplied or altered, as the case may be, for export from Great Britain, or

(b) that he had reasonable cause to believe that the vehicle or trailer would not be used on a road in Great Britain, or would not be so used until it had been put into a condition in which it might lawfully be so used, . . .

(c) *[repealed.]*

[(6A) Paragraph (b) of subsection (6) above shall not apply in relation to a person who, in the course of a trade or business—

(a) exposes a vehicle or trailer for sale, unless he also proves that he took all reasonable steps to ensure that any prospective purchaser would be aware that its use in its current condition on a road in Great Britain would be unlawful, or

(b) offers to sell a vehicle or trailer, unless he also proves that he took all reasonable steps to ensure that the person to whom the offer was made was aware of that fact.]

(7) Nothing in the preceding provisions of this section shall affect the validity of a contract or any rights arising under a contract.

(8) *[Repealed.]*

A25.160   *[Section 75 is printed as amended by the Road Traffic Act 1991, ss.16(1)–(5), 83 and Sched. 8. Section 75 does not apply to tramcars: Tramcars and Trolley Vehicles (Modification of Enactments) Regulations 1992 (S.I. 1992 No. 1217), reg.7 (q.v.).]*

76. Fitting and supply of defective or unsuitable vehicle parts

A25.161   (1) If any person—

(a) fits a vehicle part to a vehicle, or

(b) causes or permits a vehicle part to be fitted to a vehicle,

in such circumstances that the use of the vehicle on a road would, by reason of that part being fitted to the vehicle [involve a danger of injury to any person or], constitute a contravention of or failure to comply with any of the construction and use requirements, he is guilty of an offence.

(2) A person shall not be convicted of an offence under subsection (1) above if he proves—

   (a) that the vehicle to which the part was fitted was to be exported from Great Britain, or

   (b) that he had reasonable cause to believe that that vehicle—

      (i) would not be used on a road in Great Britain, or

      (ii) that it would not be so used until it had been put into a condition in which its use [and would not involve a danger of injury to any person] would not constitute a contravention of or a failure to comply with any of the construction and use requirements.

(3) If a person—

   (a) supplies a vehicle part or causes or permits a vehicle part to be supplied, and

   (b) has reasonable cause to believe that the part is to be fitted to a motor vehicle, or to a vehicle of a particular class, or to a particular vehicle,

he is guilty of an offence if that part could not be fitted to a motor vehicle or, as the case may require, to a vehicle of that class or of a class to which the particular vehicle belongs, except in such circumstances that the use of the vehicle on a road would, by reason of that part being fitted to the vehicle, constitute a contravention of or failure to comply with any of the construction and use requirements [or involve a danger of injury to any person].

(4) In this section references to supply include—

   (a) sell, and

   (b) offer to sell or supply.

(5) A person shall not be convicted of an offence under subsection (3) above in respect of the supply of a vehicle part if he proves—

   (a) that the part was supplied for export from Great Britain, or

   (b) that he had reasonable cause to believe that—

      (i) it would not be fitted to a vehicle used on a road in Great Britain, or

      (ii) it would not be so fitted until it had been put into such a condition that it could be fitted otherwise than in such circumstances that the use of the vehicle on a road would, by reason of that part being fitted to the vehicle, constitute a contravention of or failure to comply with any of the construction and use requirements [or involve a danger of injury to any person].

(6) An authorised examiner may at any reasonable hour enter premises where, in the course of a business, vehicle parts are fitted to vehicles or are supplied and test and inspect any vehicle or vehicle part found on those premises for the purpose of ascertaining whether—

   (a) a vehicle part has been fitted to the vehicle in such circumstances that the use of the vehicle on a road would, by reason of that part being fitted to the vehicle, constitute a contravention of or failure to comply with any of the construction and use requirements [or involve a danger of injury to any person], or

   (b) the vehicle part could not be supplied for fitting to a vehicle used on roads in Great Britain without the commission of an offence under subsection (3) above.

(7) For the purpose of testing a motor vehicle and any trailer drawn by it the authorised examiner may drive it and for the purpose of testing a trailer may draw it with a motor vehicle.

(8) Any person who obstructs an authorised examiner acting under subsection (6) or (7) above is guilty of an offence.

(9) In subsections (6) to (8) above "*authorised examiner*" means a person who may act as an authorised examiner for the purposes of section 67 of this Act; and any such person, other than a constable in uniform, shall produce his authority to act for the purpose of subsections (6) and (7) above if required to do so.

(10) Nothing in this section shall affect the validity of a contract or of any rights arising under a contract.

A25.162   *[Section 76 is printed as amended by the Road Traffic Act 1991, s.48 and Sched. 4, para.58(1)–(4). Section 76 does not apply to tramcars: Tramcars and Trolley Vehicles (Modification of Enactments) Regulations 1992 (S.I. 1992 No. 1217), reg.7 (q.v.).]*

77. Testing condition of used vehicles at sale rooms, etc.

A25.163   (1) An authorised examiner may at any reasonable hour enter premises where used motor vehicles or trailers are supplied in the course of a business and test and inspect any used motor vehicle or trailer found on the premises for the purpose of ascertaining whether it is in an unroadworthy condition for the purposes of section 75(1) of this Act.

(2) In this section (except paragraph (d) below) references to supply include—

     (a) sell,

     (b) offer for sale or supply,

     (c) expose for sale, and

     (d) otherwise keep for sale or supply.

(3) An authorised examiner may at any reasonable hour enter premises where vehicles or vehicle parts of a class prescribed for the purposes of section 63 of this Act are supplied in the course of a business and test and inspect any such vehicle or vehicle part for the purpose of ascertaining whether the vehicle or vehicle part complies with the type approval requirements applicable to a vehicle or vehicle part of that class.

(4) For the purpose of testing a motor vehicle and any trailer drawn by it the authorised examiner may drive it and for the purpose of testing a trailer may draw it with a motor vehicle.

(5) A person who obstructs an authorised examiner acting under this section is guilty of an offence.

(6) In this section "*authorised examiner*" means a person who may act as an authorised examiner for the purposes of section 67 of this Act; and any such person, other than a constable in uniform, shall produce his authority to act for the purposes of that section if required to do so.

(7) A motor vehicle or trailer shall be treated for the purposes of this section as used if, but only if, it has previously been sold or supplied by retail.

A25.164   *[Section 77 does not apply to tramcars nor to trolley vehicles (other than duobuses): Tramcars and Trolley Vehicles (Modification of Enactments) Regulations 1992 (S.I. 1992 No. 1217), regs 7, 9 and 11 (q.v.).]*

78. Weighing of motor vehicles

A25.165   (1) Subject to any regulations made by the Secretary of State, an authorised person may, on production of his authority, require the person in charge of a motor vehicle—

     (a) to allow the vehicle or any trailer drawn by it to be weighed, either laden or unladen, and the weight transmitted to the road by any parts of the vehicle or trailer in contact with the road to be tested, and

     (b) for that purpose, to proceed to a weighbridge or other machine for weighing vehicles.

(2) For the purpose of enabling a vehicle or a trailer drawn by it to be weighed or a weight to be tested in accordance with regulations under subsection (1) above, an authorised person may require the person in charge of the vehicle to drive the vehicle or to do any other thing in relation to the vehicle or its load or the trailer or its load which is reasonably required to be done for that purpose.

(3) If a person in charge of a motor vehicle—

(a) refuses or neglects to comply with any requirement under subsection (1) or (2) above, or

(b) obstructs an authorised person in the exercise of his functions under this section,

he is guilty of an offence.

(4) An authorised person may not require the person in charge of the motor vehicle to unload the vehicle or trailer, or to cause or allow it to be unloaded, for the purpose of its being weighed unladen.

(5) *[Regulation-making power.]*

(6) If—

(a) at the time when the requirement is made the vehicle is more than five miles from the weighbridge or other machine, and

(b) the weight is found to be within the limits authorised by law,

the highway authority (in Scotland, roads authority) on whose behalf the requirement is made must pay, in respect of loss occasioned, such amount as in default of agreement may be determined by a single arbitrator (in Scotland, arbiter) agreed upon by the parties or, in default of agreement, appointed by the Secretary of State.

(7) The Secretary of State may by order designate areas in Great Britain where subsection (6) above is to have effect, in such cases as may be specified by the order, with the substitution for five miles of a greater distance so specified.

An order under this subsection shall be made by statutory instrument subject to annulment by a resolution of either House of Parliament.

(8) In this section—

(a) "*road*" includes any land which forms part of a harbour or which is adjacent to a harbour and is occupied wholly or partly for the purposes of harbour operations,

(b) "*authorised person*" means a person authorised by a highway authority (in Scotland, a roads authority) or a constable authorised on behalf of such an authority by a police authority or a chief officer of police,

and in this subsection "*harbour*" and "*harbour operations*" have the meanings given to them by section 57(1) of the Harbours Act 1964.

[Section 78 does not apply to tramcars nor to trolley vehicles (other than duobuses): Tramcars and Trolley Vehicles (Modification of Enactments) Regulations 1992 (S.I. 1992 No. 1217), regs 7, 9 and 11 (q.v.).]   **A25.166**

79. Further provisions relating to weighing of motor vehicles

(1) Where a motor vehicle or trailer is weighed under section 78 of this Act, a certificate   **A25.167**
of weight must be given to the person in charge of the vehicle, and the certificate so given shall exempt the motor vehicle and the trailer, if any, from being weighed so long as it is during the continuance of the same journey carrying the same load.

(2) On production of his authority—

(a) *[repealed.]*

(b) an examiner appointed under section [66A] of this Act, or

(c) any of the Secretary of State's officers authorised by him in that behalf,

may at any time exercise with respect to the weighing of [goods vehicles, public service vehicles, and vehicles which are not public service vehicles but are adapted to carry more than eight passengers] all such powers with respect to the weighing of motor vehicles and trailers as are exercisable under section 78 of this Act by a constable authorised as mentioned in subsection (8) of that section.

(3) The provisions of section 78 of this Act shall apply accordingly in relation to [such vehicles]—

(a) as if references to a constable so authorised included references to such [an] examiner or officer of the Secretary of State, and

(b) as if the reference in subsection (6) to the authority on whose behalf the requirement is made were a reference to the Secretary of State, and

(c) as if the reference in that subsection to the Secretary of State were a reference, in relation to England and Wales, to the Lord Chief Justice of England and, in relation to Scotland, to the Lord President of the Court of Session.

(4) A certificate in the prescribed form which—

(a) purports to be signed by an authorised person (within the meaning of section 78 of this Act) or by a person exercising powers by virtue of subsection (2) above, and

(b) states, in relation to a vehicle identified in the certificate, any weight determined in relation to that vehicle on the occasion of its being brought to a weighbridge or other machine in pursuance of a requirement under section 78(1) of this Act,

shall be evidence . . . of the matter so stated.

(5) If, for the purposes of or in connection with the determination of any weight in relation to a vehicle which is brought to a weighbridge or other machine as mentioned in section 78(1) of this Act, an authorised person (within the meaning of that section) or a person exercising powers by virtue of subsection (2) above—

(a) drives a vehicle or does any other thing in relation to a vehicle or its load or a trailer or its load, or

(b) requires the driver of a vehicle to drive it in a particular manner or to a particular place or to do any other thing in relation to a vehicle or its load or a trailer or its load,

neither he nor any person complying with such a requirement shall be liable for any damage to or loss in respect of the vehicle or its load or the trailer or its load unless it is shown that he acted without reasonable care.

A25.168   *[Section 79 is printed as amended by the Road Traffic Act 1991, ss.48 and 83, Sched. 4, para.59(1)–(3), and Sched. 8.*

Words relating exclusively to Scotland have been omitted from section 79(4).

Section 79 does not apply to tramcars nor to trolley vehicles (other than duobuses): Tramcars and Trolley Vehicles (Modification of Enactments) Regulations 1992 (S.I. 1992 No. 1217), regs 7, 9 and 11 (q.v.).]

80. Approval marks

A25.169   (1) Where any international agreement to which the United Kingdom is a party or a Community obligation provides—

(a) for markings to be applied—

(i) to motor vehicle parts of any description to indicate conformity with a type approved by any country, or

(ii) to a motor vehicle to indicate that the vehicle is fitted with motor vehicle parts of any description and either that the parts conform with a type approved by any country or that the vehicle is such that as so fitted it conforms with a type so approved, and

(b) for motor vehicle parts or, as the case may be, motor vehicles, bearing those markings to be recognised as complying with the requirements imposed by the law of another country,

the Secretary of State may by regulations designate the markings as approval marks, and any markings so designated shall be deemed for the purposes of the Trade Descriptions Act 1968 to be a trade description, whether or not the markings fall within the definition of the expression in section 2 of that Act.

(2) Any person who, without being authorised by the competent authority to apply any approval mark, applies that mark or a mark so nearly resembling it as to be calculated to deceive is guilty of an offence under the Trade Descriptions Act 1968, whether or not he would be guilty of such an offence apart from this subsection.

(3) The conditions subject to which approval of any type may be given on behalf of the United Kingdom or the use of approval marks indicating conformity with a type approved by the United Kingdom may be authorised may include such conditions as to testing or inspection and the payment of fees as the Secretary of State may impose.

(4) In this section—

"*motor vehicle*" means a mechanically propelled vehicle or a vehicle designed or adapted for towing by a mechanically propelled vehicle,

"*motor vehicle part*" means any article made or adapted for use as part of a mechanically propelled vehicle or a vehicle drawn by a mechanically propelled vehicle, or for use as part of the equipment of any such vehicle, shall be treated as including any equipment for the protection of drivers or passengers in or on a motor vehicle notwithstanding that it does not form part of, or of the equipment of, that vehicle, and

"*the competent authority*" means—

(a) as respects any approval marks indicating conformity with a type approved by the United Kingdom, the Secretary of State, and

(b) as respects any approval marks indicating conformity with a type approved by any other country, the authority having power under the law of that country to authorise the use of that mark.

[The Motor Vehicles (Designation of Approval Marks) Regulations 1979 (S.I. 1979 No. 1088) have effect as if made under section 80.   **A25.170**

The Trade Descriptions Act 1968, s.1, makes it an offence for any person in the course of a trade or business to (a) apply a false trade description to any goods, or (b) supply, or offer to supply, any goods to which a false trade description is applied. Under ibid., s.18, the penalty, on summary conviction, is a fine up to the prescribed sum and, on conviction on indictment, a fine and/or imprisonment for up to two years (section 18 has been amended by the Magistrates' Courts Act 1980, s.32(2)). For the statutory defences to charges under the Trade Descriptions Act 1968, see sections 24 and 25 of that Act.]

Pedal cycles and horse-drawn vehicles

81. Regulation of brakes, bells, etc., on pedal cycles

(1)–(4) *[Regulation-making powers.]*   **A25.171**

(5) Regulations under this section as to the use on roads of cycles may prohibit the sale or supply, or the offer of a sale or supply, of a cycle for delivery in such a condition that the

use of it on a road in that condition would be a contravention of the regulations, but no provision made by virtue of this subsection shall affect the validity of any contract or any rights arising under a contract.

(6) If a person sells or supplies or offers to sell or supply a cycle in contravention of any prohibition imposed by regulations made by virtue of subsection (5) above, he is guilty of an offence, unless he proves—

(a) that it was sold, supplied or offered for export from Great Britain, or

(b) that he had reasonable cause to believe that it would not be used on a road in Great Britain, or would not be so used until it had been put into a condition in which it might lawfully be so used.

A25.172   *[The Pedal Cycles (Construction and Use) Regulations 1983 (S.I. 1983 No. 1176) (not reproduced in this work) have effect as if made under section 81.]*

A25.173   **82. Regulation of brakes on horse-drawn vehicles**   *[Omitted.]*

Miscellaneous

83. Offences to do with reflectors and tail lamps

A25.174   A person who sells, or offers or exposes for sale, any appliance adapted for use as a reflector or tail lamp to be carried on a vehicle in accordance with the provisions of this Act or of any regulations made under it, not being an appliance which complies with the construction and use requirements applicable to a class of vehicles for which the appliance is adapted, is guilty of an offence.

A25.175   *[Section 83 does not apply to tramcars: Tramcars and Trolley Vehicles (Modification of Enactments) Regulations 1992 (S.I. 1992 No. 1217), reg.7 (q.v.).]*

A25.176   **84. Appointment of officials and destination of fees**   *[Omitted.]*

85. Interpretation of Part II

A25.177   [(1)] In this Part of this Act—

[*"the Community Recording Equipment Regulation"* means Council Regulation (EEC) No. 3821/85 on recording equipment in road transport [*q.v.*] as it has effect in accordance with—

(a) Commission Regulation (EEC) No. 3314/90;

(b) Commission Regulation (EEC) No. 3688/92; and

(c) Commission Regulation (EC) No. 2479/95;

and as read with the Community Drivers' Hours and Recording Equipment (Exemptions and Supplementary Provisions) Regulations 1986 [*S.I. 1986 No. 1456 (q.v.)*];]

[*"EC certificate of conformity"* means

[(a) in the case of a light passenger vehicle,] any certificate of conformity issued by a manufacturer—

(i) under [regulation 5 of the Motor Vehicles (EC Type Approval) Regulations 1998 [*S.I. 1998 No. 2051 below*], or

(ii) under any provision of the law of a member State other than the United Kingdom giving effect to Article 6 of the light passenger vehicle type approval Directive,

which is expressed to be a certificate for a complete or completed vehicle,] [(b) in the case of a vehicle to which the motorcycle type approval Directive applies, any certificate of conformity issued by a manufacturer under regulation 8(1) of the Motor Cycles Etc. (EC Type Approval) Regulations 1999 [*S.I. 1999 No. 2920 below*] or under any provision of the law of an EEA State other than the United Kingdom giving effect to Article 7(1) of the motorcycle type approval Directive;]

. . .

["*EEA Agreement*" means the Agreement on the European Economic Area signed at Oporto on 2nd May 1992 as adjusted by the Protocol signed at Brussels on 17th March 1993 [*Cm. 2073 and Cm. 2183*];]

["*EEA State*" means a State which is a contracting Party to the EEA Agreement.]

["*light passenger vehicle*" means any motor vehicle which—

(a) has at least four wheels,

(b) is equipped with an internal combustion engine,

(c) is constructed or adapted for use for the carriage of passengers and is not a goods vehicle,

(d) has no more than eight seats in addition to the driver's seat, and

(e) has a maximum design speed exceeding 25 kilometres per hour,

but does not include a quadricycle within the meaning of Article 1(3) of the motorcycle type approval Directive or a vehicle used or intended for use for the purposes of a fire brigade (whether or not one maintained under the Fire Services Act 1947),]

["*the light passenger vehicle type approval Directive*" means Council Directive 70/156/EEC of 6th February 1970 on the approximation of the laws of the member States relating to the type approval of motor vehicles and their trailers as amended by Council Directive 87/403/EEC of 25th June 1987 and Council Directive 92/53/EEC of 18th June 1992,]

["*the motorcycle type approval Directive*" means Council Directive 92/61/EEC of 30th June 1992 relating to the type approval of two or three-wheel motor vehicles,]

"*official testing station*" means a testing station maintained by the Secretary of State under section [72A] of this Act [or premises designated by him under section 10(12) of the Transport Act 1982],

"*prescribed*" means prescribed by regulations made by the Secretary of State,

["*prescribed testing authority*" means such approved testing authority as may be prescribed,]

["*public service vehicle*" has the same meaning as in the Public Passenger Vehicles Act 1981 [*q.v.*],]

"*sold or supplied by retail*" means sold or supplied otherwise than to a person acquiring solely for the purpose of resale or of re-supply for a valuable consideration,

"*tail lamp*" means, in relation to a vehicle, any lamp carried attached to the vehicle for the purpose of showing a red light to the rear in accordance with regulations under section 41 of this Act,

"*traffic area*" has the same meaning as in the Public Passenger Vehicles Act 1981, and

"*vehicle part*" means any article which is a motor vehicle part, within the meaning of section 80 of this Act, and any other article which is made or adapted for use as part of, or as part of the equipment of, a vehicle which is intended or adapted to be used on roads but which is not a motor vehicle within the meaning of that section.

[(2) References in any provision of this Part of this Act to an authorised inspector are references to a person authorised by the Secretary of State under section 8 of the Transport Act 1982 to exercise the function to which that provision relates.]

[*Section 85 is printed as amended by the Interpretation Act 1978, ss.17(2)(a) and 23; the Road Traffic*   **A25.178**
Act 1991, s.48 and Sched. 4, para.61; the Motor Vehicles (EC Type Approval) Regulations 1992 (S.I.

1992 No. 3107); the Goods Vehicles (Licensing of Operators) Act 1995, s.60(1) and Sched. 7, para.13 (see also section 60(2) and Schedule 8, Part I); the Passenger and Goods Vehicles (Recording Equipment) Regulations 1996 (S.I. 1996 No. 941; not reproduced in this work), reg.3; the Motor Cycles Etc. (EC Type Approval) Regulations 1999 (S.I. 1999 No. 2920); and as prospectively amended by the Road Traffic (Consequential Provisions) Act 1988, s.4 and Sched. 2, Pt I, para.17(a)–(c).

The words printed within square brackets at the end of the definition of "official testing station", the definition of "prescribed testing station" and the text of section 85(2) will come into force on a date to be announced; see the Road Traffic (Consequential Provisions) Act 1988, s.8(3), below. The text of section 85 as enacted has prospectively been designated as section 85(1) (although no such textual amendment has been formally effected) following the prospective addition of section 85(2).

Section 8 of the Transport Act 1982 (which has not yet been brought into force) will make provision for private-sector plating and testing by "authorised inspectors".

As to the EEA Agreement and the EEA states, see further the note "European Economic Area" to Regulation (EEC) 3820/85 below.]

86. Index to Part II

A25.179   The expressions listed in the left-hand column below are respectively defined or (as the case may be) fall to be construed in accordance with the provisions of this Part of this Act listed in the right-hand column in relation to those expressions.

Expression	Relevant provision
Certificate of conformity	[Section 57(1A)]
Community Recording Equipment Regulation	Section 85
Construction and use requirements	Section 41(7)
Design weights	Section 54(3)
[EC certificate of conformity	Section 85]
Examination for plating	Section 49(4)
. . .	
Goods vehicle test	Section 49(4)
Goods vehicle test certificate	Section 49(2)(b)
. . .	
[Light passenger vehicle	Section 85]
[Light passenger vehicle type approval Directive	Section 85]
Minister's approval certificate	Section 58(1)
[Motorcycle type Directive	Section 85]
Official testing station	Section 85
Plating certificate	Section 49(2)(a)
Plated particulars	Section 41(7)
Plated weights	Section 41(7)
Prescribed	Section 85
[Public service vehicle	Section 85]
Relevant aspects of design, construction, equipment and marking	Section 54(6)
Sold or supplied by retail	Section 85
Tail lamp	Section 85
Test certificate	Section 45(2)
Traffic area	Section 85
Type approval certificate	Section 55(2)
Type approval requirements	Section 54(1)
[Vehicle examiner	Section 66A]
Vehicle part	Section 85

A25.180

[Section 86 is printed as amended by the Road Traffic Act 1991, ss.48 and 83, Sched. 4, para.62, and Sched. 8; the Motor Vehicles (EC Type Approval) Regulations 1992 (S.I. 1992 No. 3107); the Goods Vehicles (Licensing of Operators) Act 1995, s.60(1) and Sched. 7, para.14 (see also section 60(2) and Schedule 8, Part I).]

PART III

Licensing of Drivers of Vehicles

Part III. With effect from a date to be announced under the Criminal Justice and Court Services Act 2000, s.80, the Secretary of State will be empowered to make any information held by him (in any form) for the purposes of Part III of this Act available to the Police Information Technology Organisation for use by constables; see *ibid.*, s.71(1) and (4).

A25.181

Requirement to hold licence

87. Drivers of motor vehicles to have driving licences

(1) It is an offence for a person to drive on a road a motor vehicle of any class [otherwise than in accordance with] a licence authorising him to drive a motor vehicle of that class.

A25.182

(2) It is an offence for a person to cause or permit another person to drive on a road a motor vehicle of any class [otherwise than in accordance with a licence authorising that other person] to drive a motor vehicle of that class.

[(3) *[Repealed.]*]

[Section 87 is printed as amended by the Road Traffic (Driver Licensing and Information Systems) Act 1989, ss.7 and 16, Sched. 3, para.7, and Sched. 6; the Road Traffic Act 1991, s.17(1) and (2).

A25.183

The following subsections were added to section 87 as it applies to tramcars by the Tramcars and Trolley Vehicles (Modification of Enactments) Regulations 1992 (S.I. 1992 No. 1217), reg.8:

[(3) A licence authorising a person to drive a motor vehicle in category B within the meaning of the Motor Vehicles (Driving Licences) Regulations 1987 [*S.I. 1987 No. 1378, as amended (q.v.)*], shall be regarded as authorising that person to drive a tramcar.]

[(4) Notwithstanding subsection (1) above, a person may drive or cause or permit another person to drive a tramcar if the driver was employed on duties which required the driving of tramcars on a road at any time during the one year period ending immediately before 1st July 1992.]

Proceedings under section 87(2) are specified by the Prosecution of Offences Act 1985 (Specified Proceedings) Order 1999 (S.I. 1999 No. 904) below as being proceedings the conduct of which the Director of Public Prosecutions is not required to take over from the police under the Prosecution of Offences Act 1985, s.3(3)(a).

The fixed penalty procedure applies to offences under section 87(1); see the Road Traffic Offenders Act 1988, Sched. 3 below.]

88. Exceptions

(1) Notwithstanding section 87 of this Act, a person may drive or cause or permit another person to drive a vehicle of any class if—

A25.184

[(a)   the driver has held—
(i) a licence under this Part of this Act to drive vehicles of that or a corresponding class, or

    [(ia) a Community licence to drive vehicles of that or a corresponding class, or]

    (ii) a Northern Ireland licence to drive vehicles of that or a corresponding class, or

    (iii) a British external licence or British Forces licence to drive vehicles of that or a corresponding class, or

    (iv) an exchangeable licence to drive vehicles of that or a corresponding class, and]

[(b) either—

    (i) a qualifying application by the driver for the grant of a licence to drive vehicles of that class for a period which includes that time has been received by the Secretary of State, or]

    [(ii) a licence to drive vehicles of that class granted to him has been revoked or surrendered in pursuance of section 99(2A), (3) or (4) of this Act otherwise than by reason of a current disqualification or of its having been granted in error and he has complied with any requirements imposed on him under section 99(7B) of this Act, and]

(c) any conditions which by virtue of section 97(3) or 98(2) of this Act apply to the driving under the authority of the licence of vehicles of that class are complied with.

[(1A) An application for the grant of a licence to drive vehicles of any class is a qualifying application for the purposes of subsection (1)(b)(i) above if—

(a) the requirements of paragraphs (a), (b) so far as it relates to initial evidence and (c) of section 97(1) of this Act [*q.v.*] have been satisfied;

(b) the applicant—

    (i) is not subject to a current disqualification which is relevant to the licence he applies for, and

    (ii) is not prevented from obtaining it by section 89 of this Act [*q.v.*] [or section 4(1) of or paragraph 6(1) or 9(1) of Schedule 1 to the Road Traffic (New Drivers) Act 1995]; and

(c) the declaration made in pursuance of section 92(1) of this Act [*q.v.*] indicates that he is not suffering from a relevant disability.]

[(1B) A disqualification is relevant to a licence for which a person makes an application if—

(a) in the case of an application made by virtue of any provision of subsection (1)(a) above, the disqualification subsists under or by virtue of any provision of the Road Traffic Acts and relates to vehicles of the class to which his application relates;

[(aa) in the case of an application made by virtue of subsection (1)(a)(i*a*) above, the disqualification subsists under or by virtue of any provision of the law of an EEA State (other than the United Kingdom) and relates to vehicles of the class, or of a class corresponding to the class, to which his application relates;]

(b) in the case of an application made by virtue of subsection (1)(a)(ii) above, the disqualification subsists under or by virtue of any provision of the law of Northern Ireland and relates to vehicles of the class, or of a class corresponding to the class, to which his application relates;

(c) in the case of an application made by virtue of subsection (1)(a)(iii) above, the disqualification subsists under or by virtue of any provision of the relevant external law or, as the case may be, is a disqualification for holding or obtaining a British Forces licence and relates to vehicles of the class, or of a class corresponding to the class, to which his application relates; and

(d) in the case of an application made by virtue of subsection (1)(a)(iv) above, the disqualification subsists under or by virtue of any provision of the law of the . . . country or territory under which the licence which he held was granted and relates to vehicles of the class, or of a class corresponding to the class, to which his application relates;

but a disqualification which does not prevent the person disqualified from obtaining a provisional licence or, as the case may be, a licence corresponding to a provisional licence is relevant to a full licence but not to a provisional licence.]

(2) The benefit of subsection (1) above does not extend—

(a) beyond the date when a licence is granted in pursuance of the application mentioned in subsection (1)(b) above or (as the case may be) in pursuance of section 99(7) [or (7A)] of this Act in consequence of the revocation or surrender so mentioned, or

(b) in a case where a licence is not in fact so granted, beyond the expiration of the period of one year or such shorter period as may be prescribed, beginning on the date of the application or (as the case may be) the revocation or surrender mentioned in subsection (1)(b) above [, or]

[(c) in a case where a licence is refused under section 92(3) of this Act [*q.v.*], beyond the day on which the applicant receives notice of the refusal.]

(3) The Secretary of State may by regulations provide that subsection (1) above shall also apply (where the requirements of that subsection are otherwise met) in the case of a person who has not previously held a licence to drive vehicles of the relevant class.

(4) Regulations made by virtue of subsection (3) above shall, if not previously revoked, expire at the end of the period of one year beginning with the day on which they came into operation.

(5) Regulations may provide that a person who becomes resident in Great Britain shall, during the prescribed period after he becomes so resident, be treated for the purposes of section 87 of this Act as the holder of a licence authorising him to drive motor vehicles of the prescribed classes if—

(a) he satisfies the prescribed conditions, and

(b) he is the holder of a permit of the prescribed description authorising him to drive vehicles under the law of a country outside the United Kingdom.

(6) Regulations made by virtue of subsection (5) above may provide for the application of any enactment relating to licences or licence holders, with or without modifications, in relation to any such permit and its holder respectively.

(7) Notwithstanding section 87 of this Act—

(a) a person who is not a holder of a licence may act as steersman of a motor vehicle, being a vehicle on which a speed limit of five miles per hour or less is imposed by or under section 86 of the Road Traffic Regulation Act 1984 [*q.v.*], under the orders of another person engaged in the driving of the vehicle who

[(i) is licensed in that behalf in accordance with the requirements of this Part and Part IV of this Act, or]

[(ii) is authorised by virtue of section 99A(1) of this Act to drive in Great Britain such a motor vehicle,]

and

(b) a person may cause or permit another person who is not the holder of a licence so to act.

[(8) In this Part of this Act—

"*British external licence*" means a licence granted in the Isle of Man or any of the Channel Islands under the relevant external law;

"*British Forces licence*" means a licence granted in the Federal Republic of Germany by the British authorities to members of the British Forces or of the civilian components of those Forces or their dependants; and

"*relevant external law*" means the law for the time being in force in the Isle of Man or any of the Channel Islands which corresponds to this Part of this Act.]

A25.185   *[Section 88 is printed as amended by the Road Traffic (Driver Licensing and Information Systems) Act 1989, s.3(2)–(5); the Road Traffic (New Drivers) Act 1995, s.10(4) and Sched. 2, paras 1 and 2; the Driving Licences (Community Driving Licence) Regulations 1996 (S.I. 1996 No. 1974), reg.2 and Sched. 1, para.1 (not reproduced in this work) (S.I. 1996 No. 1974 is stated to give effect to Directive 91/439/EEC (O.J. No. L237, August 24, 1991, p. 1) on driving licences); the Driving Licences (Community Driving Licence) Regulations 1998 (S.I. 1998 No. 1420), regs 2 and 3 (not reproduced in this work) (S.I. 1998 No. 1420 is stated to give effect to Directive 96/47/EC (O.J. No. L235, September 17, 1996, p. 1) and Directive 97/26/EC (O.J. No. L150, June 7, 1997, p. 41), both of which amended Directive 91/439/EEC.*

The Motor Vehicles (Driving Licences) Regulations 1999 (S.I. 1999 No. 2864) (q.v.) were made in part under section 88(5) and (6).

As to orders made under sections 88(8) and 89(2)(b), see the notes to section 89 below.

As to the term "Great Britain" in section 88(5), see the Driving Licences (Community Driving Licence) Regulations 1982 (S.I. 1982 No. 1555), reg.4(1) below.

A25.186   ***Community driving licence.*** *In relation to driving licences which came into force after May 31, 1990 (after December 31, 1990 for Northern Ireland driving licences) only, section 88 was amended by the Driving Licences (Community Driving Licence) Regulations 1990 (S.I. 1990 No. 144) on April 1, 1990 so that the words ", counterparts of licences" were inserted in section 88(6) after the word "licences".]*

Tests

89. Tests of competence to drive

A25.187   (1) A licence authorising the driving of motor vehicles of any class shall not be granted to any person unless he [meets the relevant residence requirement and satisfies the Secretary of State]—

> [(a) that at some time during the period of two years ending with the date the application is made but not earlier than the appointed day he has passed—
>
> > (i) the test of competence to drive prescribed by virtue of subsection (3) below, or
> > (ii) a Northern Ireland test of competence to drive which corresponds to such a test, or
> > (iii) a test of competence which under subsection (6) below is a sufficient test;
>
> or that, if it is available to him, he satisfies the alternative requirement of section 89A of this Act; or
>
> (b) that at some time not earlier than the appointed day he has held—
>
> > (i) a full licence authorising the driving of vehicles of that class, or
> > (ii) a full Northern Ireland licence authorising the driving of vehicles of that or a corresponding class;
>
> or that, if it is available to him, he satisfies the alternative requirement of section 89A of this Act [q.v.]; or
>
> (c) that at some time during the period of two years ending with the date the application is made he has passed a test of competence to drive vehicles of that

or a corresponding class . . . for the purpose of obtaining a British Forces licence; or

(d) that at some time not earlier than the appointed day he has held a full British external licence or a full British Forces licence to drive vehicles of that or a corresponding class or that, if it is available to him, he satisfies the alternative requirement of section 89A of this Act; or

(e) that at some time during the period of two years ending with the date the application is made he has passed a test of competence to drive vehicles of that or a corresponding class conducted under the law . . . of Gibraltar . . .; or]

[(ea) that either at the time of the application for the licence he holds a Community licence authorising the driving of vehicles of that or a corresponding class or at some time he has held such a Community licence; or]

[(f) that, at the time of the application for the licence, he holds an exchangeable licence authorising the driving of vehicles of that or a corresponding class.]

This subsection is subject to the provisions of this Part of this Act as to provisional licences and to the provisions of any regulations made by virtue of section 105(2)(f) of this Act.

[(1A) An applicant meets the relevant residence requirement referred to in subsection (1) above if on the date the application for the licence is made—

(a) in a case where he satisfies the Secretary of State in respect of paragraph (ea) of that subsection, he is normally resident in the United Kingdom or has been attending a course of study in the United Kingdom during the period of six months ending on that date;

(b) in a case where he satisfies the Secretary of State in respect of paragraph (f) of that subsection, he is normally resident in Great Britain but has not been so resident for more than the prescribed period; and

(c) in any other case, he is normally resident in Great Britain.]

[(2) For the purposes of subsection (1) above—

[(a) a licence which has been revoked under section 99(3) of this Act or under any corresponding provision of—

(i) the law of Northern Ireland,
(ii) the relevant external law, or
(iii) the law of an EEA State other than the United Kingdom,

as a licence granted in error shall be disregarded for the purposes of paragraph (b), (d) or (ea) (as the case may be) of that subsection;]

(b) *[repealed]*

(c) a British external licence to drive any class of goods vehicle or any class of passenger-carrying vehicle is to be disregarded for the purposes of paragraph (d) of that subsection unless the Secretary of State, by order made by statutory instrument, designates the relevant external law under which it is granted as one which makes satisfactory provision for the granting of such licences.]

[(2A) *[Approved training course for motor cyclists.]*]

(3)–(5A) *[Regulation-making powers.]*

(6) For the purposes of subsection [(1)(a)(iii) above or section 89A(2)(b)(iii) below], a test of competence shall be sufficient for the granting of a licence authorising the driving of—

(a) vehicles of any class, if at the time the test was passed it authorised the granting of a licence to drive vehicles of that class,

(b) vehicles of [all] classes which are designated by regulations as a group for the purposes of subsection (1)(a) above, if at the time the test was passed it authorised the granting of a licence to drive vehicles of any class included in the group, [and]

[(c) vehicles of all classes included in another such group, if a person passing the test is treated by virtue of regulations made for the purposes of this paragraph as competent also to drive vehicles of a class included in that other group.]

(7) If vehicles of any classes are designated by regulations as a group for the purposes of subsection (1)(b) above, a licence authorising the driving of vehicles of a class included in the group shall be deemed for the purposes of subsection [(1)(b)(i) above or section 89A(4)(a) below to authorise the driving of—

(a) vehicles of all classes included in the group [(except where regulations otherwise provide)], and

(b) vehicles of all classes included in another such group, if a person holding the licence is treated by virtue of regulations as competent also to drive vehicles of a class included in that other group.]

The reference in this subsection to a licence does not include a licence which has been revoked in pursuance of section 99(3) of this Act.

(8) For the purposes of this section and section 88(1) of this Act, an exchangeable licence issued in respect of a . . . country or territory shall not be treated as authorising a person to drive a vehicle of any [class] if—

(a) the licence is not for the time being valid for that purpose, or

(b) it was issued in respect of that [class] for a purpose corresponding to that mentioned in section 97(2) of this Act.

[(9) A test of competence falling within paragraphs (a)(ii), (c) or (e) of subsection (1) above shall be sufficient for the granting of a licence authorising the driving of—

(a) vehicles of all classes designated by regulations as a group for the purposes of subsection (1)(a) above, if [(except where regulations otherwise provide)] at the time the test was passed it authorised the granting of a licence to drive vehicles of any class included in the group, or of any class corresponding to a class included in the group, and

(b) vehicles of all classes included in another such group, if a person passing a test of competence authorising the granting of a licence to drive vehicles of a class included in the group mentioned in paragraph (a) above is treated by virtue of regulations as competent also to drive vehicles of a class included in that other group.]

[(10) A full Northern Ireland licence, a full British external licence, a full British Forces licence [, a Community licence] or an exchangeable licence shall be treated for the purposes of paragraphs (b)(ii), (d) [,(ea)] or (f) (as the case may be) of subsection (1) above as authorising the driving of—

(a) [(except where regulations otherwise provide)] vehicles of all classes designated by regulations as a group for the purposes of subsection (1)(b) above, if the licence authorises the driving of vehicles of any class included in the group, or any class corresponding to a class included in the group, and

(b) vehicles of all classes included in another such group, if by virtue of regulations a person holding a licence authorising him to drive vehicles of any class included in the group mentioned in paragraph (a) above is treated as competent also to drive vehicles of a class included in that other group.]

[(11) . . . in this section and section 89A "*the appointed day*" means the day appointed for the coming into force of section 1 of the Road Traffic (Driver Licensing and Information Systems) Act 1989 [*q.v.*].]

[Section 89 is printed as amended by the Road Traffic (Driver Licensing and Information Systems) Act **A25.188**
1989, ss.4(2) and (3) and 7, and Sched. 3, para.8(b)–(e); the Driving Licences (Community Driving Licence) Regulations 1996 (S.I. 1996 No. 1974), reg.2 and Sched. 1, para.2 (not reproduced in this work).

With effect from a date to be announced under the Transport Act 2000, s.275, the following words will be substituted at the beginning of section 89(6) for the word "for" by the Transport Act 2000, s.260 and Sched. 29, paras 1 and 2:

[Subject to regulations under section 99ZA of this Act, for]

Section 260 of the 2000 Act, together with Schedule 29, paragraphs 1 and 2 thereto, was brought into force on February 1, 2001 by the Transport Act 2000 (Commencement No. 3) Order 2001 (S.I. 2001 No. 57; not reproduced in this work), but S.I. 2001 No. 57 was itself amended by the Transport Act 2000 (Commencement No. 3) (Amendment) Order 2001 (S.I. 2001 No. 115; not reproduced in this work) so as to delete reference to (inter alia) section 260 and Schedule 29, paragraphs 1 and 2, from S.I. 2001 No. 57.

Also with effect from a date (or dates) to be announced, section 89(2A) and (5A) will be repealed by the Transport Act 2000, s.274 and Sched. 31, Pt V(1).

The Motor Vehicles (Driving Licences) Regulations 1999 (S.I. 1999 No. 2864) (q.v.) were made in part under section 89(1A), (2A), (3), (4), (5), (5A), (6), (7), (9) and (10); see, in particular, regulation 4.

The laws for the time being in force in (i) the Isle of Man and (ii) Jersey (which each corresponds to Part III of this Act) have been designated by the Driving Licences (Designation of Relevant External Law) Order 1996 (S.I. 1996 No. 3206; not reproduced in this work) as making satisfactory provision for the granting of licences to drive all classes of (a) goods vehicles and (b) passenger carrying vehicles.]

[89A. The alternative requirements to those in section 89

(1) The alternative requirements referred to in section 89(1) of this Act are the following.   **A25.189**

(2) The requirement which is alternative to that specified in section 89(1)(a) on an application by a person for a licence authorising the driving of motor vehicles of any class other than any class of goods vehicle or passenger-carrying vehicle prescribed for the purposes of subsection (3) below—

   (a) is available to that person if the application is made within the period of ten years beginning with the appointed day, and

   (b) is that at some time before the appointed day and during the period of ten years ending with the date the application is made he has passed—

      (i) the test of competence to drive prescribed by virtue of section 89(3) of this Act or a test of competence to drive which corresponds to such a test, or

      (ii) a Northern Ireland test of competence to drive which corresponds to any test falling within (i) above, or

      (iii) a test of competence which under section 89(6) of this Act is a sufficient test or a test of competence to drive which corresponds to such a test.

(3) The requirement which is alternative to that specified in section 89(1)(a) on an application by a person for a licence authorising the driving of any class of goods vehicle or passenger-carrying vehicle prescribed for the purposes of this subsection—

   (a) is available to that person if the application is made within the period of five years beginning with the appointed day, and

   (b) is that at some time before the appointed day and during the period of five years ending with the date the application is made he has passed—

    (i)   a test of competence to drive a heavy goods vehicle or public service vehicle of a class corresponding to the class of vehicle to which his application relates, or

    (ii)   a corresponding Northern Ireland test of competence to drive a heavy goods vehicle or public service vehicle of a class which corresponds to the class of goods vehicle or passenger-carrying vehicle to which his application relates.

(4) The requirement which is alternative to that specified in section 89(1)(b) on an application by a person for a licence authorising the driving of motor vehicles of any class other than any class of goods vehicle or passenger-carrying vehicle prescribed for the purposes of subsection (5) below is that at some time before the appointed day but not earlier than 1st January 1976 he has held—

    (a)   a full licence authorising the driving of vehicles of a class corresponding to the class of motor vehicle to which his application relates, or

    (b)   a full Northern Ireland licence authorising the driving of vehicles of a class corresponding to the class of motor vehicle to which his application relates.

(5) The requirement which is alternative to that specified in section 89(1)(b) on an application by a person for a licence authorising the driving of any class of goods vehicle or passenger-carrying vehicle prescribed for the purposes of this subsection is that at some time before the appointed day but not earlier than the beginning of the period of five years ending with the appointed day he has held—

    (a)   a full heavy goods vehicle or a public service vehicle driver's licence authorising the driving of vehicles of a class corresponding to the class of vehicle to which his application relates, or

    (b)   a full Northern Ireland licence to drive heavy goods vehicles of a class corresponding to the class of vehicle to which his application relates or a Northern Ireland licence to drive public service vehicles of a class corresponding to the class of vehicle to which his application relates.

(6) The requirement which is alternative to that specified in section 89(1)(d) on an application by a person for a licence authorising the driving of motor vehicles of any class—

    (a)   is available to that person if the application is made within the period of ten years beginning with the appointed day, and

    (b)   is that at some time before the appointed day and during the period of ten years ending with the date the application is made he has held a full British external licence or a full British Forces licence to drive vehicles of that or a corresponding class.

(7) In this section "*heavy goods vehicle*" and "*public service vehicle*" have the same meaning as they had for the purposes of Part IV of this Act or section 22 of the Public Passenger Vehicles Act 1981 before their repeal by section 1 of the Road Traffic (Driver Licensing and Information Systems) Act 1989.]

A25.190   *[Section 89A was inserted by the Road Traffic (Driver Licensing and Information Systems) Act 1989, s.4(4).*

The term "heavy goods vehicle" was defined for the purposes of Part IV of this Act before its repeal by section 1 of the Road Traffic (Driver Licensing and Information Systems) Act 1989 by section 120 as "(a) an articulated goods vehicle, or (b) a large goods vehicle, that is to say, a motor vehicle (not being an articulated goods vehicle) which is constructed or adapted to carry or to haul goods and the permissible maximum weight of which exceeds 7.5 tonnes".

The term "public service vehicle" was defined for the purposes of section 22 of the Public Passenger Vehicles Act 1981 by ibid., s.22(1) (as amended by the Transport Act 1985, s.1(3) and Sched. 1, para.5) as "a public service vehicle being used on a road for carrying passengers for hire or reward".

As to the prescription of classes of motor vehicle for the purposes of section 89A(5), see the Motor Vehicles (Driving Licences) Regulations 1999 (S.I. 1999 No. 2864), regs 49 and 52 below.]

90. Review of conduct of test by magistrates' court   *[Omitted.]*   A25.191

91. Repayment of test fees   *[Omitted.]*

Physical fitness

92. Requirements as to physical fitness of drivers

(1) An application for the grant of a licence must include a declaration by the applicant,   A25.192
in such form as the Secretary of State may require, stating whether he is suffering or has at
any time (or, if a period is prescribed for the purposes of this subsection, has during that
period) suffered from any relevant disability or any prospective disability.

(2) In this Part of this Act—

"disability" includes disease, [and the persistent misuse of drugs or alcohol, whether or
    not such misuse amounts to dependency]

"relevant disability" in relation to any person means—

(a) any prescribed disability, and

(b) any other disability likely to cause the driving of a vehicle by him in pursuance of
    a licence to be a source of danger to the public, and

"prospective disability" in relation to any person means any other disability which—

(a) at the time of the application for the grant of a licence or, as the case may be, the
    material time for the purposes of the provision in which the expression is used, is
    not of such a kind that it is a relevant disability, but

(b) by virtue of the intermittent or progressive nature of the disability or otherwise,
    may become a relevant disability in course of time.

(3) If it appears from the applicant's declaration, or if on inquiry the Secretary of State
is satisfied from other information, that the applicant is suffering from a relevant disability,
the Secretary of State must, subject to the following provisions of this section, refuse to
grant the licence.

(4) The Secretary of State must not by virtue of subsection (3) above refuse to grant a
licence—

(a) on account of any relevant disability which is prescribed for the purposes of this
    paragraph, if the applicant has at any time passed a relevant test and it does not
    appear to the Secretary of State that the disability has arisen or become more
    acute since that time or was, for whatever reason, not disclosed to the Secretary of
    State at that time,

(b) on account of any relevant disability which is prescribed for the purposes of this
    paragraph, if the applicant satisfies such conditions as may be prescribed with a
    view to authorising the grant of a licence to a person in whose case the disability is
    appropriately controlled,

(c) on account of any relevant disability which is prescribed for the purposes of this
    paragraph, if the application is for a provisional licence.

(5) Where as a result of a test of competence to drive [or of information obtained under
the relevant powers] the Secretary of State is satisfied that the person who took the test [or
in relation to whom the information was obtained] is suffering from a disability such that
there is likely to be a danger to the public—

   (a) if he drives any vehicle, . . .

   (b) if he drives a vehicle other than a vehicle of a particular [class], [or]

  [(c) if he drives a vehicle except in accordance with particular conditions,]

the Secretary of State must serve notice in writing to that effect on that person and must include in the notice a description of the disability.

  (6) Where a notice is served in pursuance of subsection (5)(a) above, then—

   (a) if the disability is not prescribed under subsection (2) above, it shall be deemed to be so prescribed in relation to the person [on whom the notice is served], and

   (b) if the disability is prescribed for the purposes of subsection (4)(c) above it shall be deemed not to be so prescribed in relation to him.

  [(7) Where a notice is served in pursuance of subsection (5)(b) above, the Secretary of State may—

   (a) if the person on whom the notice is served is an applicant for a licence, grant him a licence limited to vehicles of the particular class specified in the notice, or

   (b) if he held a licence which is revoked by the Secretary of State and he complies with subsection (7ZB) below, grant him a licence limited to vehicles of that class,

and, if the Secretary of State so directs in the notice, his entitlement to drive other classes of vehicle by virtue of section 98(2) of this Act shall be limited as specified in the notice.]

  [(7ZA) Where a notice is served in pursuance of subsection (5)(c) above, the Secretary of State may—

   (a) if the person on whom the notice is served is an applicant for a licence, grant him a licence authorising him to drive vehicles subject to the particular conditions specified in the notice, or

   (b) if he held a licence which is revoked by the Secretary of State and he complies with subsection (7ZB) below, grant him a licence authorising him to drive vehicles subject to those conditions,

and, if the Secretary of State so directs in the notice, any entitlement which the person has to drive vehicles by virtue of section 98(2) of this Act shall be subject to conditions as specified in the notice.]

  [(7ZB) A person complies with this subsection if—

   (a) he surrenders the existing licence and its counterpart, and

   (b) where the Secretary of State so requires, he provides his name, address, sex and date and place of birth and a photograph which is a current likeness of him.]

  [(7A) If he considers it appropriate to do so, the Secretary of State may, after serving a notice under any of the paragraphs of subsection (5) above, serve a further notice under that paragraph or a notice under another of those paragraphs; and on his serving the later notice the notice previously served shall cease to have effect and any licence previously granted in accordance with it shall be revoked by the later notice.]

  [(7B) In subsection (5) above the references to a test of competence to drive and to information obtained under the relevant powers are references respectively to a test of competence prescribed for the purposes of section 89 or so much of such a test as is required to be taken in pursuance of section 94(5)(c) of this Act and to information obtained in pursuance of section 94(5)(a) or (b) of this Act.]

[(7C) A person whose licence is revoked by virtue of subsection (7A) above must deliver the licence to the Secretary of State forthwith after the revocation and a person who, without reasonable excuse, fails to do so is guilty of an offence.]

[(7D) In subsection (7B) above the references to section 94 of this Act include references to that section as applied by section 99D of this Act.]

(8) In this section *"relevant test"*, in relation to an application for a licence, means any such test of competence as is mentioned in section 89 of this Act or a test as to fitness or ability in pursuance of section 100 of the Road Traffic Act 1960 as originally enacted, being a test authorising the grant of a licence in respect of vehicles of the classes to which the application relates.

(9) Without prejudice to subsection (8) above, for the purposes of subsection (4)(a) above—

[(a) an applicant shall be treated as having passed a relevant test if, and on the day on which, he passed a test of competence to drive which—

    (i) under a provision of the law of Northern Ireland or a relevant external law corresponding to subsections (3) and (4) or (6) of section 89 of this Act, either is prescribed in relation to vehicles of classes corresponding to the classes to which the application relates or is sufficient under that law for the granting of a licence authorising the driving of vehicles of those classes, or

    (ii) is sufficient for the granting of a British Forces licence authorising the driving of vehicles of those classes, and]

(b) in the case of an applicant who is treated as having passed a relevant test by virtue of paragraph (a) above, disclosure of a disability to [his licensing authority] shall be treated as disclosure to the Secretary of State.

[(10) A person who holds a licence authorising him to drive a motor vehicle of any class and who drives a motor vehicle of that class on a road is guilty of an offence if the declaration included in accordance with subsection (1) above in the application on which the licence was granted was one which he knew to be false.]

[Section 92 is printed as amended by the Road Traffic (Driver Licensing and Information Systems) Act 1989, ss.5(2)(a)–(c), (3)(a) and (b), (4) and (5)(a) and (b), and 16 and Sched. 6; the Road Traffic Act 1991, s.18(1); the Driving Licences (Community Driving Licence) Regulations 1996 (S.I. 1996 No. 1974), reg.2 and Sched. 1, para.3 (not reproduced in this work); the Driving Licences (Community Driving Licence) Regulations 1998 (S.I. 1998 No. 1420), regs 2 and 4 (not reproduced in this work).   **A25.193**

The Motor Vehicles (Driving Licences) Regulations 1999 (S.I. 1999 No. 2864) (q.v.) were made in part under section 92(2) and (4); see, in particular, regulations 71–73.

In relation to section 92(4)(a), see further the Road Traffic (Consequential Provisions) Act 1988, s.5 and Sched. 4, para.7(1) below.

As to the prescription of diabetes requiring insulin treatment for the purposes of section 92(4)(b), see the Motor Vehicles (Driving Licences) Regulations 1999 (S.I. 1999 No. 2864), reg.73(6) below.

Community driving licence. *In relation to driving licences which came into force after May 31, 1990 (after December 31, 1990 for Northern Ireland driving licences) only, section 92(7C) (as inserted by the Road Traffic (Driver Licensing and Information Systems) Act 1989, s.5(4)) was amended by the Driving Licences (Community Driving Licence) Regulations 1990 (S.I. 1990 No. 144) on April 1, 1990 so that the words "and its counterpart" were inserted after the words "the licence".]*   **A25.194**

93. Revocation of licence because of disability or prospective disability   **A25.195**
    [Omitted.]

94. Provision of information, etc., relating to disabilities

A25.196   (1) If at any time during the period for which his licence remains in force, a licence holder becomes aware—

(a) that he is suffering from a relevant or prospective disability which he has not previously disclosed to the Secretary of State, or

(b) that a relevant or prospective disability from which he has at any time suffered (and which has been previously so disclosed) has become more acute since the licence was granted,

the licence holder must forthwith notify the Secretary of State in writing of the nature and extent of his disability.

(2) The licence holder is not required to notify the Secretary of State under subsection (1) above if—

(a) the disability is one from which he has not previously suffered, and

(b) he has reasonable grounds for believing that the duration of the disability will not extend beyond the period of three months beginning with the date on which he first becomes aware that he suffers from it.

(3) A person who fails without reasonable excuse to notify the Secretary of State as required by subsection (1) above is guilty of an offence.

[(3A) A person who holds a licence authorising him to drive a motor vehicle of any class and who drives a motor vehicle of that class on a road is guilty of an offence if at any earlier time while the licence was in force he was required by subsection (1) above to notify the Secretary of State but has failed without reasonable excuse to do so.]

(4) If [the prescribed circumstances obtain in relation to a person who is an applicant for, or the holder of, a licence or if] the Secretary of State has reasonable grounds for believing that a person who is an applicant for, or the holder of, a licence may be suffering from a relevant or prospective disability, subsection (5) below applies for the purpose of enabling the Secretary of State to satisfy himself whether or not [that person may be suffering from that or any other relevant or prospective disability].

(5) The Secretary of State may by notice in writing served on the applicant or holder—

(a) require him to provide the Secretary of State, within such reasonable time as may be specified in the notice, with such an authorisation as is mentioned in subsection (6) below, or

(b) require him, as soon as practicable, to arrange to submit himself for examination—

(i) by such registered medical practitioner or practitioners as may be nominated by the Secretary of State, or

(ii) with respect to a disability of a prescribed description, by such officer of the Secretary of State as may be so nominated,

for the purpose of determining whether or not he suffers or has at any time suffered from a relevant or prospective disability, or

(c) except where the application is for, or the licence held is, a provisional licence, require him to submit himself for [such a test of competence to drive as the Secretary of State directs in the notice], being a test authorising the grant of a licence in respect of vehicles—

(i) of all or any of the classes to which the application relates, or

(ii) which he is authorised to drive (otherwise than by virtue of section 98(2) of this Act) by the licence which he holds,

as the case may be.

(6) The authorisation referred to in subsection (5)(a) above—

(a) shall be in such form and contain such particulars as may be specified in the notice by which it is required to be provided, and

(b) shall authorise any registered medical practitioner who may at any time have given medical advice or attention to the applicant or licence holder concerned to release to the Secretary of State any information which he may have, or which may be available to him, with respect to the question whether, and if so to what extent, the applicant or licence holder concerned may be suffering, or may at any time have suffered, from a relevant or prospective disability.

(7) If he considers it appropriate to do so in the case of any applicant or licence holder, the Secretary of State—

(a) may include in a single notice under subsection (5) above requirements under more than one paragraph of that subsection, and

(b) may at any time after the service of a notice under that subsection serve a further notice or notices under that subsection.

(8) If any person on whom a notice is served under subsection (5) above—

(a) fails without reasonable excuse to comply with a requirement contained in the notice, or

(b) fails any test of competence which he is required to take as mentioned in paragraph (c) of that subsection,

the Secretary of State may exercise his powers under sections 92 and 93 of this Act as if he were satisfied that the applicant or licence holder concerned is suffering from a relevant disability which is not prescribed for the purposes of any paragraph of section 92(4) of this Act or, if the Secretary of State so determines, as if he were satisfied that the applicant or licence holder concerned is suffering from a prospective disability.

(9) *[Secretary of State to defray expenses, etc., under subsection (5).]*

[Section 94 is printed as amended by the Road Traffic (Driver Licensing and Information Systems) Act   **A25.197**
1989, s.5(7) and (8); the Road Traffic Act 1991, s.18(2).
    The circumstances prescribed under section 94(4) for the purposes of section 94(5) are set out in regulations 74 and 75 of the Motor Vehicles (Driving Licences) Regulations 1999 (S.I. 1999 No. 2864) (q.v.).
    As to the application of section 94 to Community licence holders who are normally resident in Great Britain, see section 99D below.]

[94A. Driving after refusal or revocation of licence

(1) A person who drives a motor vehicle of any class on a road otherwise than in accor-   **A25.198**
dance with a licence authorising him to drive a motor vehicle of that class is guilty of an offence if—

[(a) at any earlier time the Secretary of State—

(i) has in accordance with section 92(3) of this Act refused to grant such a licence,
(ii) has under section 93(1) or (2) of this Act revoked such a licence, or
(iii) has served notice on that person in pursuance of section 99C(1) or (2) of this Act requiring him to deliver to the Secretary of State a Community licence authorising him to drive a motor vehicle of that or a corresponding class, and]

[(b) since that earlier time he has not been granted—

(i) a licence under this Part of this Act, or
(ii) a Community licence,

authorising him to drive a motor vehicle of that or a corresponding class.]

(2) Section 88 of this Act shall apply in relation to subsection (1) above as it applies in relation to section 87.]

A25.199 *[Section 94A was inserted by the Road Traffic Act 1991, s.18(3) and is printed as amended by the Driving Licences (Community Driving Licence) Regulations 1996 (S.I. 1996 No. 1974), reg.2 and Sched. 1, para.5 (not reproduced in this work).]*

95. Notification of refusal of insurance on grounds of health

A25.200 (1) If an authorised insurer refuses to issue to any person such a policy of insurance as complies with the requirements of Part VI of this Act on the ground that the state of health of that person is not satisfactory, or on grounds which include that ground, the insurer shall as soon as practicable notify the Secretary of State of that refusal and of the full name, address, sex and date of birth of that person as disclosed by him to the insurer.

(2) In subsection (1) above *"authorised insurer"* means a person or body of persons carrying on insurance business within Group 2 in Part II of Schedule 2 to the Insurance Companies Act 1982 and being a member of the Motor Insurers' Bureau (a company limited by guarantee and incorporated under the Companies Act 1929 on 14th June 1946).

96. Driving with uncorrected defective eyesight

A25.201 (1) If a person drives a motor vehicle on a road while his eyesight is such (whether through a defect which cannot be or one which is not for the time being sufficiently corrected) that he cannot comply with any requirement as to eyesight prescribed under this Part of this Act for the purposes of tests of competence to drive, he is guilty of an offence.

(2) A constable having reason to suspect that a person driving a motor vehicle may be guilty of an offence under subsection (1) above may require him to submit to a test for the purpose of ascertaining whether, using no other means of correction than he used at the time of driving, he can comply with the requirement concerned.

(3) If that person refuses to submit to the test he is guilty of an offence.

Granting of licences, their form and duration

97. Grant of licences

A25.202 (1) Subject to [the following provisions of this section] and section 92 of this Act [and, in the case of licences to drive large goods vehicles or passenger-carrying vehicles, to Part IV of this Act], the Secretary of State must . . . grant a licence to a person who—

(a) makes an application for it in such manner and containing such particulars as the Secretary of State may specify [and pays the fee (if any) which is prescribed],

(b) provides the Secretary of State with such evidence or further evidence in support of the application as the Secretary of State may require,

[(c) surrenders to the Secretary of State—

(i) any previous licence granted to him after 1st January 1976 and its counterpart,

(ii) any Community licence and its counterpart (if any) issued to him, and

(iii) any British external licence or British Forces licence or exchangeable licence held by him,

or provides the Secretary of State with an explanation for not surrendering them which the Secretary of State considers adequate,]

(d) is not [, in accordance with section 88(1B) of this Act, subject to a current disqualification which is relevant to the licence he applies for] and is not prevented from obtaining it by the provisions of section 89 of this Act [or section 4(1) of or paragraph 6(1) or 9(1) of Schedule 1 to the Road Traffic (New Drivers) Act 1995].

[(1A) Where any licence to be granted to an applicant would be in the form of a photo-card, the Secretary of State may under subsection (1)(*a*) and (*b*) above in particular require him to provide a photograph which is a current likeness of him.]

(2) If the application for the licence states that it is made for the purpose of enabling the applicant to drive a motor vehicle with a view to passing a test of competence to drive, any licence granted in pursuance of the application shall be a provisional licence for that purpose, and nothing in section 89 of this Act shall apply to such a licence.

(3) A provisional licence—

   (a) shall be granted subject to prescribed conditions,

   (b) shall, in any cases prescribed for the purposes of this paragraph, be restricted so as to authorise only the driving of vehicles of the classes so prescribed,

   (c) may, in the case of a person appearing to the Secretary of State to be suffering from a relevant disability or a prospective disability, be restricted so as to authorise only the driving of vehicles of a particular construction or design specified in the licence, . . .

   [(d) shall not authorise a person under the age of 21 years, before he has passed a test of competence to drive a motor bicycle,—

      (i) to drive a motor bicycle without a side-car unless it is a learner motor bicycle (as defined in subsection (5) below) or its first use (as defined in regulations) occurred before 1st January 1982 and the cylinder capacity of its engine does not exceed 125 cubic centimetres, or

      (ii) to drive a motor bicycle with a side-car unless its power to weight ratio is less than or equal to 0.16 kilowatts per kilogram,]

   [(e) except as provided under subsection (3B) below, shall not authorise a person, before he has passed a test of competence to drive, to drive on a road a motor [bicycle] [or moped] except where he has successfully completed an approved training course for motor cyclists or is undergoing training on such a course and is driving the motor [bicycle] [or moped] on the road as part of the training.]

[(3A) *[Regulation-making power.]*]

[(3B) *[Power to grant exemptions from section 97(3)(e) by regulation.]*]

(4) Regulations may authorise or require the Secretary of State to refuse a provisional licence authorising the driving of a motor [bicycle] [or moped] of a prescribed class if the applicant has held such a provisional licence and the licence applied for would come into force within the prescribed period—

   (a) beginning at the end of the period for which the previous licence authorised (or would, if not surrendered or revoked, have authorised) the driving of such a motor [bicycle] [or moped], or

   (b) beginning at such other time as may be prescribed.

(5) A learner motor [bicycle] is a motor [bicycle] which either is propelled by electric power or has the following characteristics—

   (a) the cylinder capacity of its engine does not exceed 125 cubic centimetres,

   [(b) the maximum net power output of its engine does not exceed eleven kilowatts.]

   (c) *[repealed.]*

[(6) In this section—

"maximum net power output", in relation to an engine, means the maximum net power output measured under full engine load, and

"power to weight ratio", in relation to a motor bicycle with a side-car, means the ratio of the maximum net power output of the engine of the motor bicycle to the weight of the combination with—

(a) a full supply of fuel in the tank,

(b) an adequate supply of other liquids needed for its propulsion, and

(c) no load other than its normal equipment, including loose tools.]

(7) *[Repealed.]*

A25.203   *[Section 97 is printed as amended by the Road Traffic (Driver Licensing and Information Systems) Act 1989, ss.6, 7 and 16, Sched. 3, para.9, and Sched. 6; the Road Traffic Act 1991, s.17(3); the Road Traffic (New Drivers) Act 1995, s.10(4) and Sched. 2, paras 1 and 2; the Driving Licences (Community Driving Licence) Regulations 1996 (S.I. 1996 No. 1974), reg.2 and Sched. 1, para.6 (not reproduced in this work); the Driving Licences (Community Driving Licence) Regulations 1998 (S.I. 1998 No. 1420), regs 2 and 6 (not reproduced in this work).*

With effect from a date to be announced under the Transport Act 2000, s.275, the following words will be substituted for the words "[the following provisions of this section]" at the beginning of section 97(1) by the Transport Act 2000, s.260 and Sched. 29, paras 1 and 3:

[subsection (2) below, section 92 of this Act and regulations under section 99ZA of this Act]

Section 260 of the 2000 Act, together with Schedule 29, paragraphs 1 and 3 thereto, was brought into force on February 1, 2001 by the Transport Act 2000 (Commencement No. 3) Order 2001 (S.I. 2001 No. 57; not reproduced in this work), but S.I. 2001 No. 57 itself was amended by the Transport Act 2000 (Commencement No. 3) (Amendment) Order 2001 (S.I. 2001 No. 115; not reproduced in this work) so as to delete reference to (inter alia) section 260 and Schedule 29, paragraphs 1 and 3, from S.I. 2001 No. 57.

Also with effect from a date (or dates) to be announced, section 97(3)(e), and the word "and" preceding it, section 97(3A) and (3B) will be repealed by the Transport Act 2000, s.274 and Sched. 31, Pt V(1).

As to the possible exemption for a holder of a full licence for a category A vehicle from the restriction imposed by section 97(3)(e) on driving a vehicle of another class included in category A, see the Motor Vehicle (Driving Licences) Regulations 1999 (S.I. 1999 No. 2864), reg.69(2B) and (2C) below.

The fixed penalty procedure applies to offences under section 97; see the Road Traffic Offenders Act 1988, Sched. 3.

Neither section 97(3) nor section 98(3) (in so far as they prevent such licence as is there mentioned from authorising any person to drive certain motor cycles) applies in the case of motor cycles in the service of a visiting force (as defined); see the Visiting Forces and International Headquarters (Application of Law) Order 1999 (S.I. 1999 No. 1736; not reproduced in this work), art.8(4).

The Motor Vehicles (Driving Licences) Regulations 1999 (S.I. 1999 No. 2864) (q.v.) were made in part under section 97(1), (1A), (3), (3A), (3B) and (4); see, in particular, regulation 3(5) and (6).

A25.204   ***Community driving licence.*** *In relation to driving licences which came into force after May 31, 1990 (after 31 December 1990 for Northern Ireland driving licences) only, section 97 was amended by the Driving Licences (Community Driving Licence) Regulations 1990 (S.I. 1990 No. 144) on April 1, 1990 so that the words "and its counterpart" were inserted in section 97(1)(c) after the words "1st June 1970" and also the word "them" was substituted in section 97(1)(c) for the word "it".]*

98. Form of licence

A25.205   [(1) A licence shall be in the form of a photocard of a description specified by the Secretary of State or such other form as he may specify and—

(a) the licence shall state whether, apart from subsection (2) below, it authorises its holder to drive motor vehicles of all classes or of certain classes only and, in the latter case, specify those classes,

(b) the licence shall specify (in such manner as the Secretary of State may determine) the restrictions on the driving of vehicles of any class in pursuance of the licence to which its holder is subject by virtue of section 101 of this Act and any conditions on the driving of vehicles of any class in pursuance of the licence to which its holder is subject by virtue of section 92(7ZA) of this Act, and

(c) in the case of a provisional licence, the licence or its counterpart shall specify (in such manner as the Secretary of State may determine) the conditions subject to which it is granted.]

[(1A) The Secretary of State may specify different descriptions of photocards, and different forms of licences not in the form of a photocard, for different cases and may determine the form of licence to be granted in any case.]

(2) Subject to subsections (3) [, (4) and (4A)] below, a licence which, apart from this subsection, authorises its holder to drive motor vehicles of certain classes only (not being—

[(a) a provisional licence, or]

[(b) any other prescribed description of licence)]

shall also authorise him to drive motor vehicles of all other classes subject to the same conditions as if he were authorised by a provisional licence to drive motor vehicles of those other classes.

(3) A licence shall not by virtue of subsection (2) above authorise a person to drive—

(a) a vehicle of a class for the driving of which he could not, by reason of the provisions of section 101 of this Act, lawfully hold a licence, or

(b) unless [he has either passed a test of competence to drive a motor bicycle or attained the age of 21 years, a motor bicycle] which, by virtue of section 97(3)(d) of this Act, a provisional licence would not authorise him to drive before he had passed that test [or attained that age (as the case may be)] [; or]

[(c) unless he has passed a test of competence to drive a motor bicycle [or moped] on a road in circumstances in which, by virtue of section 97(3)(e) of this Act, a provisional licence would not authorise him to drive it before he had passed that test.]

(4) In such cases [or as respects such classes of vehicles] as the Secretary of State may prescribe, the provisions of subsections (2) and (3) above shall not apply or shall apply subject to such limitations as he may prescribe.

[(4A) A licence shall not by virtue of subsection (2) above authorise a person on whom a notice under section 92(5)(b) of this Act [*q.v.*] has been served to drive motor vehicles otherwise than in accordance with the limits specified in the notice.]

(5) *[Repealed.]*

[Section 98 is printed as amended by the Road Traffic (Driver Licensing and Information Systems) Act **A25.206** *1989, ss.5(10)(a) and (b) and 7 and Sched. 3, para.11; the Road Traffic Act 1991, s.17(3); the Driving Licences (Community Driving Licence) Regulations 1996 (S.I. 1996 No. 1974), reg.2 and Sched. 1, para.7 (not reproduced in this work); the Driving Licences (Community Driving Licence) Regulations 1998 (S.I. 1998 No. 1420), regs 2 and 7 (not reproduced in this work).*

With effect from a date to be announced under the Transport Act 2000, s.275, the following words will be substituted for the word "below" in section 98(2) by the Transport Act 2000, s.260 and Sched. 29, paras 1 and 4:

[and to regulations under section 99ZA of this Act]

Section 260 of the 2000 Act, together with Schedule 29, paragraphs 1 and 4 thereto, was brought into force on February 1, 2001 by the Transport Act 2000 (Commencement No. 3) Order 2001 (S.I. 2001 No. 57; not reproduced in this work), but S.I. 2001 No. 57 itself was amended by the Transport Act 2000 (Commencement No. 3) (Amendment) Order 2001 (S.I. 2001 No. 115; not reproduced in this work) so as to delete reference to (inter alia) section 260 and Schedule 29, paragraphs 1 and 4, from S.I. 2001 No. 57.

Also with effect from a date (or dates) to be announced, section 97(3)(c), and the word "[or]" preceding it, will be repealed by the Transport Act 2000, s.274 and Sched. 31, Pt V(1).

As to the application of section 98(3) to visiting forces, etc., see the notes to section 97 above.

The Motor Vehicles (Driving Licences) Regulations 1999 (S.I. 1999 No. 2864) (q.v.) were made in part under section 98(2) and (4); see, in particular, regulations 19 and 69.

A25.207   ***Community driving licence.*** *In relation to driving licences which came into force after May 31, 1990 (after December 31, 1990 for Northern Ireland driving licences) only, section 98 was amended by the Driving Licences (Community Driving Licence) Regulations 1990 (S.I. 1990 No. 144) on April 1, 1990 so that:*

  (i)   *the word "and" was inserted at the end of section 98(1)(b), the word "and" at the end of section 98(1)(c) was deleted, and section 98(1)(d) was revoked;*

  (ii) *the words "person who holds a licence which" were substituted in section 98(2) for the words "licence which, apart from this subsection", and the word "may" was substituted in section 98(2) for the words "shall also authorise him to";*

  (iii) *the words "Subsection (2) above does not" were substituted in section 98(3) for the words "A licence shall not by virtue of subsection (2) above";*

  (iv) *the words "Subsection (2) above does not" were substituted in section 98(4A) (as inserted by the Road Traffic (Driver Licensing and Information Systems) Act 1989, s.5(10)(b)) for the words "A licence shall not by virtue of subsection (2) above"; and*

  (v)   *the amendment effected to section 98(1)(d) by section 7 of and Schedule 3, paragraph 11(a) to the Road Traffic (Driver Licensing and Information Systems) Act 1989 [inserting the words "specify those other classes" for the words "contain such statements as the Secretary of State considers appropriate for indicating the effect of that subsection"] will not take effect (in relation to such licences).]*

99. Duration of licences

A25.208   (1) [In so far as a licence authorises its holder to drive motor vehicles of classes other than any prescribed class of goods vehicle or any prescribed class of passenger-carrying vehicle, it] shall, unless previously revoked or surrendered, remain in force, subject to subsection (2) below—

  (a) except in a case falling within paragraph (b) or (c) of this subsection, for the period ending on the seventieth anniversary of the applicant's date of birth or for a period of three years, whichever is the longer,

  (b) except in a case falling within paragraph (c) of this subsection, if the Secretary of State so determines in the case of a licence to be granted to a person appearing to him to be suffering from a relevant or prospective disability, for such period of not more than three years and not less than one year as the Secretary of State may determine, and

  (c) in the case of a licence granted in exchange for a subsisting licence and in pursuance of an application requesting a licence for the period authorised by this paragraph, for a period equal to the remainder of that for which the subsisting licence was granted,

and any such period shall begin with the date on which the licence in question is expressed to come into force.

[(1A) In so far as a licence authorises its holder to drive any prescribed class of goods vehicle or passenger-carrying vehicle, it shall, unless previously revoked, suspended or surrendered, remain in force—

(a) except in a case falling within paragraph (c) or (d) of this subsection—

    (i) for the period ending on the forty-fifth anniversary of the applicant's date of birth or for a period of five years, whichever is the longer, or

    (ii) where the applicant's age at the date on which the licence is to come into force will exceed forty-five but not sixty-five years, for the period ending on the sixty-sixth anniversary of the applicant's date of birth or for a period of five years, whichever is the shorter,

(b) except in a case falling within paragraph (d) of this subsection, where the applicant's age at that date will exceed sixty-five years, for a period of one year,

(c) except in a case falling within paragraph (b) or (d) of this subsection, if the Secretary of State so determines in the case of a licence to be granted to a person appearing to him to be suffering from a relevant or prospective disability, for such period of not more than three years and not less than one year as the Secretary of State may determine, and

(d) in the case of a licence granted in exchange for a subsisting licence and in pursuance of an application requesting a licence for the period authorised by this paragraph, for a period equal to the remainder of that for which the subsisting licence was granted,

and any such period shall begin with the date on which the licence in question is expressed to come into force.]

(2) To the extent that a provisional licence authorises the driving of a motor [bicycle] [or moped] of a prescribed class it shall, unless previously surrendered or revoked, remain in force—

(a) for such period as may be prescribed, or

(b) if the licence is granted to the holder of a previous licence which was surrendered, revoked or treated as being revoked—

    (i) for the remainder of the period for which the previous licence would have authorised the driving of such a motor [bicycle] [or moped], or

    (ii) in such circumstances as may be prescribed, for a period equal to that remainder at the time of surrender or revocation.

[(2A) Where, in accordance with the preceding provisions of this section, a licence in the form of a photocard remains in force for a period of more than ten years, the holder of the licence must surrender it and its counterpart to the Secretary of State not later than the end of the period of ten years beginning with—

(a) the date shown on the licence as the date of issue, or

(b) if the licence was granted by way of renewal or replacement of a licence bearing the same photograph, the date shown on the earliest licence bearing that photograph as the date of issue of that licence.]

(3) Where it appears to the Secretary of State—

(a) that a licence granted by him to any person is required to be endorsed in pursuance of any enactment or was granted in error or with an error or omission in the particulars specified in the licence or required to be so endorsed on it, or

(b) that the particulars specified in a licence granted by him to any person do not comply with any requirement imposed since the licence was granted by any provision made by or having effect under any enactment, the Secretary of State may serve notice in writing on that person revoking the licence and requiring him to surrender the licence forthwith to the Secretary of State [and it shall be the duty of that person to comply with the requirement].

(4) Where the name or address of the licence holder as specified in a licence ceases to be correct, its holder must forthwith surrender the licence to the Secretary of State . . .

(5) A person who [without reasonable excuse] fails to comply with the duty under subsection [(2A),][(3) or] (4) above is guilty of an offence.

(6) Where a person who has a duty under this section to surrender his licence is not in possession of the licence in consequence of the fact that he has surrendered it to a constable or authorised person (within the meaning of Part III of the Road Traffic Offenders Act 1988) on receiving a fixed penalty notice given to him under section 54 of that Act, he does not fail to comply with the duty if he surrenders the licence to the Secretary of State immediately on its return.

[(7) On the surrender of a licence and its counterpart by a person in pursuance of subsection (2A), (3) and (4) above, the Secretary of State must (subject to the following provisions of this section) grant a new licence to that person and any licence granted under this subjection shall be granted free of charge.]

[(7A) Where the surrendered licence was revoked because it was granted in error or in consequence of an error or omission appearing to the Secretary of State to be attributable to the fault of the licence holder or in consequence of a current disqualification, subsection (7) shall not apply but the Secretary of State may, if the person is not currently disqualified, grant a new licence to that person on payment of that fee (if any) which is prescribed.]

[(7B) The Secretary of State may require a person to provide—

  (a) evidence of his name, address, sex and date and place of birth, and

  (b) a photograph which is a current likeness of him,

before granting a new licence to him under subsection (7) or (7A) above.]

[(8) A replacement licence granted pursuant to subsection (7) or (7A) above shall expire on the date on which the surrendered licence would have expired had it not been surrendered except that, where the period for which the surrendered licence was granted was based on an error with respect to the licence holder's date of birth such that (if that error had not been made) that licence would have been expressed to expire on a different date, the replacement licence shall expire on that different date.]

A25.209   *[Section 99 is printed as amended by the Road Traffic (Driver Licensing and Information Systems) Act 1989, ss.2(2) and 7 and Sched. 3, para.12; Driving Licences (Community Driving Licence) Regulations 1996 (S.I. 1996 No. 1974), reg.2 and Sched. 1, para.8 (not reproduced in this work); the Driving Licences (Community Driving Licence) Regulations 1998 (S.I. 1998 No. 1420), regs 2 and 8 (not reproduced in this work).*

The Motor Vehicles (Driving Licences) Regulations 1999 (S.I. 1999 No. 2864) (q.v.) were made in part under section 99(1) and (1A); see, in particular, regulations 15 and 49(2).

A25.210   **Community driving licence.** *In relation to driving licences which came into force after May 31, 1990 (after December 31, 1990 for Northern Ireland driving licences) only, section 99 was amended by the Driving Licences (Community Driving Licence) Regulations 1990 (S.I. 1990 No. 144) on April 1, 1990 so that:*

  (i)   *the following paragraphs were substituted for section 99(3)(a):*

    (a) that a licence granted by him to any person was granted in error or with an error or omission in the particulars specified in the licence, or (aa) that the counterpart of a licence granted by him to any person is required to be endorsed in pursuance of any enactment or was issued with an error or omission in the particulars specified in the counterpart or required to be so endorsed on it, or

(ii) *the words "or in its counterpart" were inserted in section 99(3)(b) after the word "person";*

(iii) *the words "and its counterpart" were inserted in the words following section 99(3)(b) after the second reference to the word "licence";*

(iv) *the words "and its counterpart" were inserted in section 99(4) after the words "surrender the licence";*

(v) *the words "and its counterpart" were inserted in section 99(6) after the first reference to the word "licence";*

(vi) *the word "them" was substituted in section 99(6) for the first reference to the words "the licence";*

(vii) *the word "them" was substituted in section 99(6) for the word "it";*

(viii) *the words "and its counterpart" were inserted in section 99(6) after the last reference to the word "licence";*

(ix) *the word "their" was substituted in section 99(6) for the word "its";*

(x) *the words "and its counterpart" were inserted in section 99(7) after the words "a licence"; and*

(xi) *the words "or the licence and its counterpart are" were substituted in section 99(7) for the words "or is".]*

[Driver training]

[99ZA. Compulsory driver training courses

Regulations may make provision about training in the driving of motor vehicles by means of courses provided in accordance with the regulations ("*driver training courses*").   **A25.211**

[With effect from a date to be announced under the Transport Act 2000, s.275, section 99ZA will be   **A25.212**
inserted by ibid., s.257.

Section 99ZA was brought into force on February 1, 2001 by the Transport Act 2000 (Commencement No. 3) Order 2001 (S.I. 2001 No. 57; not reproduced in this work), but S.I. 2001 No. 57 itself was amended by the Transport Act 2000 (Commencement No. 3) (Amendment) Order 2001 (S.I. 2001 No. 115; not reproduced in this work) so as to delete reference to (inter alia) section 257 from S.I. 2001 No. 57.

Sections 99ZB and 99ZC (noted below) also inserted by the 2000 Act, s.257, will be brought into force on a date to be announced; they specify certain matters which may be included in regulations made under section 99ZA.]

[99ZB. Requirements to complete training courses]   *[Omitted.]*   **A25.213**

[99ZC. Driver training courses: supplementary]   *[Omitted.]*

[Community licence holders]

[99A. Authorisation to drive in Great Britain

(1) A Community licence holder may drive, and a person may cause or permit a   **A25.214**
Community licence holder to drive, in Great Britain, a motor vehicle of any class which—

(a) he is authorised by his Community licence to drive, and

(b) he is not disqualified for holding or obtaining a licence under this Part of this Act to drive,

notwithstanding that he is not the holder of a licence under this Part of this Act.

(2) Subsections (3) and (4) below apply to a Community licence holder who is normally resident in Great Britain.

(3) In a case where the Community licence holder is authorised by his Community licence to drive motor vehicles of classes other than any prescribed class of goods vehicle or any prescribed class of passenger-carrying vehicle, he shall cease to be authorised by virtue of subsection (1) above to drive in Great Britain any such classes of motor vehicle from—

    (a) the date on which he attains the age of seventy years, or

    (b) the expiry of the period of three years beginning with the relevant date,

whichever is the later.

(4) In a case where the Community licence holder is authorised by his Community licence to drive any prescribed class of goods vehicle or any prescribed class of passenger-carrying vehicle, he shall cease to be authorised by virtue of subsection (1) above to drive in Great Britain any such class of vehicle from—

    [(a) except in a case falling within paragraph (b) or (c) of this subsection—

        (i) the date on which he attains the age of 45 years, or

        (ii) the expiry of the period of five years beginning with the relevant date, whichever is the later,]

    (b) where his age at the relevant date exceeds forty-five but not sixty-five years—

        (i) the date on which he attains the age of sixty-six years, or

        (ii) the expiry of the period of five years beginning with the relevant date,

whichever is the earlier, and

    (c) where his age at the relevant date exceeds sixty-five years, the expiry of the period of one year beginning with that date.

(5) A Community licence holder—

    (a) to whom a counterpart of his Community licence is issued under section 99B of this Act, and

    (b) who is authorised by virtue of subsection (1) above to drive in Great Britain motor vehicles of certain classes only,

may drive, in Great Britain, motor vehicles of all other classes subject to the same conditions as if he were authorised by a provisional licence to drive motor vehicles of those other classes.

(6) Subsections (3) and (4) of section 98 of this Act shall apply in relation to subsection (5) above as they apply in relation to subsection (2) of that section.

(7) For the purposes of this Part and Part IV of this Act a Community licence shall not be treated as authorising a person to drive a vehicle of any class if it is not for the time being valid for that purpose in the EEA State in respect of which it was issued.

(8) In this section *"relevant date"*, in relation to a Community licence holder who is normally resident in Great Britain, means—

    (a) in the case where he first became so resident on or before 1 January 1997, that date; and

    (b) in any other case, the date on which he first became so resident.]

A25.215   *[Section 99A (and the heading preceding it) was inserted by the Driving Licences (Community Driving Licence) Regulations 1996 (S.I. 1996 No. 1974), reg.2 and Sched. 1, para.9 (not reproduced in this work); the Driving Licences (Community Driving Licence) Regulations 1998 (S.I. 1998 No. 1420), regs 2 and 9 (not reproduced in this work).*

The Motor Vehicles (Driving Licences) Regulations 1999 (S.I. 1999 No. 2864) below were made in part under section 99A(3), (4) and (6). Attention is drawn in particular to regulation 4 of S.I. 1999 No. 2864 in connection with section 99A.]

[99B. Information about resident Community licence holders

(1) A Community licence holder who—

    (a) is normally resident in Great Britain, and

    (b) is authorised by his Community licence to drive medium-sized or large goods vehicles or passenger-carrying vehicles of any class,

shall, on or before the expiry of the period of twelve months beginning with the relevant date, deliver his Community licence to the Secretary of State and provide him with the information specified in, or required under, subsection (4) below.

(2) Subsection (1) above shall not apply to a Community licence holder from whom the Secretary of State has received a qualifying application (within the meaning of section 88(1A) of this Act) for the grant of a licence under this Part of this Act.

(3) The Secretary of State may issue to any Community licence holder who—

    (a) is normally resident in Great Britain, and

    (b) has delivered his Community licence to the Secretary of State, and provided him with the information specified in, or required under, subsection (4) below (whether or not in pursuance of this section),

a document (referred to in this Part of this Act in relation to a Community licence as a "*counterpart*") in such form and containing such information as the Secretary of State may determine but designed for the endorsement of particulars relating to the Community licence.

(4) The information referred to in subsections (1) and (3) above is—

    (a) the name and address in Great Britain of the Community licence holder;

    (b) his date of birth;

    (c) the classes of vehicle which he is authorised by his Community licence to drive;

    (d) the period of validity of the Community licence in the EEA State in respect of which it was issued;

    (e) whether the licence was granted in exchange for a licence issued by a state other than an EEA State; and

    (f) such other information as the Secretary of State may require for the purposes of the proper exercise of any of his functions under this Part or Part IV of this Act.

(5) The Secretary of State—

    (a) may endorse a Community licence delivered to him (whether or not in pursuance of this section) in such manner as he may determine with any part of the information specified in, or required under, subsection (4) above or with information providing a means of ascertaining that information or any part of it; and

    (b) must return the Community licence to the holder.

(6) Where it appears to the Secretary of State that a counterpart of a Community licence—

    (a) is required to be endorsed in pursuance of any enactment or was issued with an error or omission in the information contained in it or in the particulars required to be endorsed on it, or

    (b) does not comply with any requirement imposed since it was issued by any provision made by, or having effect under, any enactment, the Secretary of State may serve notice in writing on the Community licence holder requiring him to surrender the counterpart immediately to the Secretary of State and it shall be the duty of the Community licence holder to comply with any such requirement.

(7) Where the name or address of a Community licence holder as specified in the counterpart of his Community licence issued to him under this section ceases to be correct, the Community licence holder must surrender the counterpart and, in the case of a change of name, deliver his Community licence immediately to the Secretary of State and provide him with particulars of the alterations falling to be made in the name or address.

(8) On the surrender of a counterpart of a Community licence by any person in pursuance of subsection (6) or (7) above, the Secretary of State must issue to that person a new counterpart of the Community licence.

(9) On the delivery of a Community licence by any person in pursuance of subsection (7) above, the Secretary of State may endorse the Community licence with the correct name and must return the Community licence to that person.

(10) Where a Community licence holder has not complied with subsection (1) above, the Secretary of State may serve notice in writing on the holder requiring him to deliver his Community licence to the Secretary of State and to provide him with the information specified in, or required under, subsection (4) above within such period (not being less than 28 days from the date of service of the notice) as is specified in the notice.

(11) A person who drives a motor vehicle on a road is guilty of an offence if he fails without reasonable excuse—

    (a) to comply with a requirement contained in a notice served on him in pursuance of subsection (10) above, or

    (b) to comply with a requirement imposed under subsection (6) or (7) above.

(12) Where a Community licence holder who is required under subsection (6) or (7) above to surrender the counterpart of his Community licence or to deliver his Community licence is not in possession of it in consequence of the fact that he has surrendered it to a constable or authorised person (within the meaning of Part III of the Road Traffic Offenders Act 1988) on receiving a fixed penalty notice given to him under section 54 of that Act, he does not fail to comply with that requirement if he surrenders the counterpart or delivers the Community licence immediately on its return.

(13) In England and Wales, proceedings for an offence by virtue of subsection (11)(a) above shall not be instituted except by the Secretary of State or by a constable acting with the approval of the Secretary of State.

(14) In this section "*relevant date*" has the meaning given by section 99A(8) of this Act.]

A25.217   *[Section 99B was inserted by the Driving Licences (Community Driving Licence) Regulations 1996 (S.I. 1996 No. 1974), reg.2 and Sched. 1, para.10 (not reproduced in this work).]*

[99C. Revocation of authorisation conferred by Community licence because of disability or prospective disability

A25.218   (1) If the Secretary of State is at any time satisfied on inquiry—

    (a) that a Community licence holder who is normally resident in Great Britain at that time is suffering from a relevant disability, and

(b) that the Secretary of State would be required by virtue of section 92(3) of this Act to refuse an application made by him at that time for a licence authorising him to drive a vehicle of the class in respect of which his Community licence was issued or a class corresponding to that class,

the Secretary of State may serve notice in writing requiring the Community licence holder to deliver the Community licence and its counterpart (if any) immediately to the Secretary of State.

(2) If the Secretary of State is at any time satisfied on inquiry that a Community licence holder who is normally resident in Great Britain at that time is suffering from a prospective disability, the Secretary of State may—

(a) serve notice in writing requiring the Community licence holder to deliver the Community licence and its counterpart (if any) immediately to the Secretary of State, and

(b) on receipt of the Community licence and its counterpart (if any) grant to the Community licence holder, free of charge, a licence for a period determined by the Secretary of State under section 99(1)(b) of this Act.

(3) Where, in relation to a Community licence holder who is normally resident in Great Britain, the Secretary of State is at any time under a duty to serve notice on him in pursuance of section 92(5) of this Act, the Secretary of State may include in that notice a requirement that the Community licence holder deliver the Community licence and its counterpart (if any) immediately to the Secretary of State.

(4) A person who—

(a) is required under, or by virtue of, any of subsections (1) to (3) above to deliver his Community licence and its counterpart (if any) to the Secretary of State, but

(b) without reasonable excuse, fails to do so,

is guilty of an offence.

(5) Where a Community licence holder to whom a counterpart of his Community licence is issued under section 99B of this Act—

(a) is required under, or by virtue of, any of subsections (1) to (3) above to deliver his Community licence and its counterpart to the Secretary of State, and

(b) is not in possession of them in consequence of the fact that he has surrendered them to a constable or authorised person (within the meaning of Part III of the Road Traffic Offenders Act 1988) on receiving a fixed penalty notice given to him under section 54 of that Act,

he does not fail to comply with any such requirement if he delivers the Community licence and its counterpart to the Secretary of State immediately on their return.

(6) Where a Community licence holder is served with a notice in pursuance of any of subsections (1) to (3) above, he shall cease to be authorised by virtue of section 99A(1) of this Act to drive in Great Britain a motor vehicle of any class from such date as may be specified in the notice, not being earlier than the date of service of the notice.]

[Section 99C was inserted by the Driving Licences (Community Driving Licence) Regulations 1996 (S.I. 1996 No. 1974), reg.2 and Sched. 1, para.11 (not reproduced in this work).] **A25.219**

[99D. Information relating to disabilities, etc.

Section 94 of this Act shall apply to a Community licence holder who is normally resident in Great Britain as if— **A25.220**

(a) in subsection (1), for the words from the beginning to "aware" there were substituted "If a Community licence holder who is authorised by virtue of section 99A(1) of this Act to drive in Great Britain a motor vehicle of any class, is aware immediately before the relevant date (as defined by section 99A(8) of this Act), or becomes aware on or after that date",

(b) for subsection (3A) there were substituted—

"(3A) A person who is authorised by virtue of section 99A(1) of this Act to drive in Great Britain a motor vehicle of any class and who drives on a road a motor vehicle of that class is guilty of an offence if at any earlier time while he was so authorised he was required by subsection (1) above to notify the Secretary of State but has failed without reasonable excuse to do so.",

(c) in subsection (4), the words "an applicant for, or", in both places where they occur, were omitted,

(d) in subsection (5), the words "applicant or" and the words from the beginning of paragraph (c) to "provisional licence" were omitted,

(e) in subsection (6)(b), the words "applicant or", in both places where they occur, were omitted,

(f) in subsection (7), the words "applicant or" were omitted, and

(g) in subsection (8)—

    (i) for "93" there were substituted "99C", and

    (ii) the words "applicant or", in both places where they occur, were omitted.]

A25.221   *[Section 99D was inserted by the Driving Licences (Community Driving Licence) Regulations 1996 (S.I. 1996 No. 1974), reg.2 and Sched. 1, para.12 (not reproduced in this work).]*

A25.222   **[99E. Return of Community licences delivered to Secretary of State]**   *[Omitted.]*

Appeals

100. Appeals relating to licences

A25.223   (1) A person who is aggrieved by the Secretary of State's—

(a) refusal to grant or revocation of a licence in pursuance of section 92 or 93 of this Act, or

(b) determination under section 99(1)(b) of this Act to grant a licence for three years or less, or

(c) revocation of a licence in pursuance of section 99(3) of this Act,

or by a notice served on him in pursuance of section 92(5) [or 99C] of this Act may, after giving to the Secretary of State notice of his intention to do so, appeal to a magistrates' court acting for the petty sessions area in which he resides . . .

(2) On any such appeal the court . . . may make such order as it or he thinks fit and the order shall be binding on the Secretary of State.

(3) It is hereby declared that, without prejudice to section 90 of this Act, in any proceedings under this section the court . . . is not entitled to entertain any question as to whether the appellant passed a test of competence to drive if he was declared by the person who conducted it to have failed it.

A25.224   *[Section 100 is printed as amended by the Driving Licences (Community Driving Licence) Regulations 1996 (S.I. 1996 No. 1974), reg.2 and Sched. 1, para.14 (not reproduced in this work).*
Words relating exclusively and expressly to Scotland have been omitted from section 100.]

Disqualification (otherwise than on conviction)

101. Disqualification of persons under age

(1) A person is disqualified for holding or obtaining a licence to drive a motor vehicle of   A25.225
a class specified in the following Table if he is under the age specified in relation to it in the
second column of the Table.

[TABLE

Class of motor vehicle	Age (in years)
1. Invalid carriage	16
2. Moped	16
3. Motor bicycle	17
4. Agricultural or forestry tractor	17
5. Small vehicle	17
6. Medium-sized goods vehicle	18
7. Other motor vehicle	21]

(2) The Secretary of State may by regulations provide that subsection (1) above shall
have effect as if for the classes of vehicles and the ages specified in the Table in that subsection there were substituted different classes of vehicles and ages or different classes of
vehicles or different ages.

(3) Subject to subsection (4) below, the regulations may—

(a) apply to persons of a class specified in or under the regulations,

(b) apply in circumstances so specified,

(c) impose conditions or create exemptions or provide for the imposition of conditions
or the creation of exemptions,

(d) contain such transitional and supplemental provisions (including provisions
amending section 108, 120 or 183(5) of this Act) as the Secretary of State considers necessary or expedient.

(4) For the purpose of defining the class of persons to whom, the class of vehicles to
which, the circumstances in which or the conditions subject to which regulations made by
virtue of subsection (2) above are to apply where an approved training scheme for drivers is
in force, it is sufficient for the regulations to refer to a document which embodies the terms
(or any of the terms) of the scheme or to a document which is in force in pursuance of the
scheme.

(5) In subsection (4) above—

"*approved*" means approved for the time being by the Secretary of State for the purpose
of the regulations,

"*training scheme for drivers*" means a scheme for training persons to drive vehicles of a class
in relation to which the age which is in force under this section (but apart from any
such scheme) is 21 years,

but no approved training scheme for drivers shall be amended without the approval of the
Secretary of State.

[Section 101 is printed as amended by the Driving Licences (Community Driving Licence) Regulations   A25.226
1996 (S.I. 1996 No. 1974), reg.2 and Sched. 1, para.15 (not reproduced in this work).

The Motor Vehicles (Driving Licences) Regulations 1999 (S.I. 1999 No. 2864) (q.v.) were made in part under section 101(2) and (3); see, in particular, ibid., reg.9.

Section 101 (in so far as it prohibits persons aged under 21 years from holding or obtaining licences to drive motor vehicles or persons under 18 years from holding or obtaining licences to drive medium-sized goods vehicles, but subject to any regulations under section 101(2)) does not apply to vehicles in the service of a visiting force (as defined); see the Visiting Forces and International Headquarters (Application of Law) Order 1999 (S.I. 1999 No. 1736; not reproduced in this work), art.8(5).]

102. Disqualification to prevent duplication of licences

A25.227   A person is disqualified for obtaining a licence authorising him to drive a motor vehicle of any class so long as he is the holder of another licence authorising him to drive a motor vehicle of that class, whether the licence is suspended or not.

[Effects of disqualification]

[103. Obtaining licence, or driving, while disqualified

A25.228   (1) A person is guilty of an offence if, while disqualified for holding or obtaining a licence, he—

(a) obtains a licence, or

(b) drives a motor vehicle on a road.

(2) A licence obtained by a person who is disqualified is of no effect (or, where the disqualification relates only to vehicles of a particular class, is of no effect in relation to vehicles of that class).

(3) A constable in uniform may arrest without warrant any person driving a motor vehicle on a road whom he has reasonable cause to suspect of being disqualified.

(4) Subsections (1) and (3) above do not apply in relation to disqualification by virtue of section 101 of this Act.

(5) Subsections (1)(b) and (3) above do not apply in relation to disqualification by virtue of section 102 of this Act.

(6) In the application of subsections (1) and (3) above to a person whose disqualification is limited to the driving of motor vehicles of a particular class by virtue of—

(a) section 102 [117 or 117A] of this Act, or

(b) subsection (9) of section 36 of the Road Traffic Offenders Act 1988 (disqualification until test is passed),

the references to disqualification for holding or obtaining a licence and driving motor vehicles are references to disqualification for holding or obtaining a licence to drive and driving motor vehicles of that class.]

A25.229   *[Section 103 is printed as substituted by the Road Traffic Act 1991, s.19 (which also inserted the heading preceding section 103), and as subsequently amended by the Driving Licences (Community Driving Licence) Regulations 1996 (S.I. 1996 No. 1974), reg.2 and Sched. 1, para.16 (not reproduced in this work).]*

Miscellaneous

A25.230   **104. Conduct of proceedings in certain courts by or against the Secretary of State.**   *[Omitted.]*

105. Regulations under this Part and the Road Traffic Offenders Act 1988
[Omitted.]

106. Destination of fees for licences, etc.   *[Omitted.]*

107. Service of notices under sections 92, 93 and 99(3)   *[Omitted.]*

108. Interpretation

(1) In this Part of this Act—   **A25.231**

["*agricultural or forestry tractor*" means a motor vehicle which—

  (a) has two or more axles,

  (b) is constructed for use as a tractor for work off the road in connection with agriculture or forestry, and

  (c) is primarily used as such,]

"*articulated goods vehicle*" means a motor vehicle which is so constructed that a trailer designed to carry goods may by partial superimposition be attached to it in such manner as to cause a substantial part of the weight of the trailer to be borne by the motor vehicle, and "*articulated goods vehicle combination*" means an articulated goods vehicle with a trailer so attached,

["*British external licence*" and "*British Forces licence*" have the meanings given by section 88(8) [*q.v.*] of this Act,]

"*Community licence*" means a document issued in respect of [an EEA State] other than the United Kingdom by an authority of that or [another EEA State] (including the United Kingdom) authorising the holder to drive a motor vehicle, not being—

  (a) a document containing a statement to the effect that that or a previous document was issued in exchange for a document issued in respect of a State other than [an EEA State], or

  (b) a document in any of the forms for an international driving permit annexed to the Paris Convention on Motor Traffic of 1926 [*Cd 3510*], the Geneva Convention on Road Traffic of 1949 [*Cmd. 578*] or the Vienna Convention on Road Traffic of 1968 [*Cmnd. 4032*], [or]

  [(c) a document issued for a purpose corresponding to that mentioned in section 97(2) of this Act,]

["*counterpart*"—

  (a) in relation to a licence under this Part of this Act, means a document in such form as the Secretary of State may determine, issued with the licence, containing such information as he determines and designed for the endorsement of particulars relating to the licence, and

  (b) in relation to a Community licence, has the meaning given by section 99B of this Act,]

"*disability*" has the meaning given by section 92 of this Act,

"*disqualified*" means disqualified for holding or obtaining a licence [(or, in cases where the disqualification is limited, a licence to drive motor vehicles of the class to which the disqualification relates)], and "*disqualification*" is to be interpreted accordingly,

["*EEA Agreement*" means the Agreement on the European Economic Area signed at Oporto on 2nd May 1992 as adjusted by the Protocol signed at Brussels on 17th March 1993,]

["*EEA State*" means a State which is a Contracting Party to the EEA Agreement,]

["*exchangeable licence*" means a document authorising a person to drive a motor vehicle (not being a document mentioned in paragraph (b) of the definition of "Community licence")—

    (a) issued in respect of Gibraltar by an authority of Gibraltar,

    (b) issued in respect of a country or territory which is designed without restriction by an order under subsection (2)(a) below by an authority of that country or territory, or

    (c) issued in respect of a country or territory which is designated by a restricted order under subsection (2)(b) below by an authority of that country or territory, being a document which is a licence of a description specified in that order,

and a licence of a description so specified as to which provision is made as mentioned in subsection (2B) below is only an exchangeable licence to the extent that it authorises its holder to drive vehicles of a class specified in the order,]

["*full licence*" means a licence other than a provisional licence,]

["*large goods vehicle*" has the meaning given by section 121(1) of this Act,]

"*licence*" [(except where the context otherwise requires)] means a licence to drive a motor vehicle granted under this Part of this Act . . .,

"*maximum gross weight*", in relation to a motor vehicle or trailer, means the weight of the vehicle laden with the heaviest load which it is constructed or adapted to carry,

"*maximum train weight*", in relation to an articulated goods vehicle combination, means the weight of the combination laden with the heaviest load which it is constructed or adapted to carry,

["*medium-sized goods vehicle*" means a motor vehicle—

    (a) which is constructed or adapted to carry or to haul goods,

    (b) which is not adapted to carry more than nine persons inclusive of the driver, and

    (c) the permissible maximum weight of which exceeds 3.5 but not 7.5 tonnes,

and includes a combination of such a motor vehicle and a trailer where the relevant maximum weight of the trailer does not exceed 750 kilograms,]

["*moped*" means a motor vehicle which has fewer than four wheels and—

    (a) in the case of a vehicle the first use (as defined in regulations made for the purpose of section 97(3)(d) of this Act) of which occurred before 1st August 1977, has a cylinder capacity not exceeding 50 cubic centimetres and is equipped with pedals by means of which the vehicle is capable of being propelled, and

    (b) in any other case, has a maximum design speed not exceeding 50 kilometres per hour and, if propelled by an internal combustion engine, has a cylinder capacity not exceeding 50 cubic centimetres,]

["*motor bicycle*" means a motor vehicle which—

    (a) has two wheels, and

    (b) has a maximum design speed exceeding [45 kilometres per hour] and, if powered by an internal combustion engine, has a cylinder capacity exceeding 50 cubic centimetres,

and includes a combination of such a motor vehicle and a side-car,]

["*Northern Ireland driving licence*" or "*Northern Ireland licence*" means a licence to drive a motor vehicle granted under the law of Northern Ireland,]

["*passenger-carrying vehicle*" has the meaning given by section 121(1) of this Act,]

"*permissible maximum weight*", in relation to a goods vehicle (of whatever description), means—

    (a) in the case of a motor vehicle which neither is an articulated goods vehicle nor is drawing a trailer, the relevant maximum weight of the vehicle,

(b) in the case of an articulated goods vehicle—
 (i) when drawing only a semi-trailer, the relevant maximum train weight of the articulated goods vehicle combination,
 (ii) when drawing a trailer as well as a semi-trailer, the aggregate of the relevant maximum train weight of the articulated goods vehicle combination and the relevant maximum weight of the trailer,
 (iii) when drawing a trailer but not a semi-trailer, the aggregate of the relevant maximum weight of the articulated goods vehicle and the relevant maximum weight of the trailer,
 (iv) when drawing neither a semi-trailer nor a trailer, the relevant maximum weight of the vehicle,
(c) in the case of a motor vehicle (not being an articulated goods vehicle) which is drawing a trailer, the aggregate of the relevant maximum weight of the motor vehicle and the relevant maximum weight of the trailer,

"*prescribed*" means prescribed by regulations,

"*prospective disability*" has the meaning given by section 92 of this Act,

"*provisional licence*" means a licence granted by virtue of section 97(2) of this Act,

"*regulations*" means regulations made under section 105 of this Act,

"*relevant disability*" has the meaning given by section 92 of this Act,

["*relevant external law*" has the meaning given by section 88(8) [*q.v.*] of this Act,]

"*relevant maximum weight*", in relation to a motor vehicle or trailer, means—

(a) in the case of a vehicle to which regulations under section 49 of this Act apply which is required by regulations under section 41 of this Act to have a maximum gross weight for the vehicle marked on a plate issued by the Secretary of State under regulations under section 41, the maximum gross weight so marked on the vehicle,
(b) in the case of a vehicle which is required by regulations under section 41 of this Act to have a maximum gross weight for the vehicle marked on the vehicle and does not also have a maximum gross weight marked on it as mentioned in paragraph (a) above, the maximum gross weight marked on the vehicle,
(c) in the case of a vehicle on which a maximum gross weight is marked by the same means as would be required by regulations under section 41 of this Act if those regulations applied to the vehicle, the maximum gross weight so marked on the vehicle,
(d) in the case of a vehicle on which a maximum gross weight is not marked as mentioned in paragraph (a), (b) or (c) above, the notional maximum gross weight of the vehicle, that is to say, such weight as is produced by multiplying the unladen weight of the vehicle by the number prescribed by the Secretary of State for the class of vehicle into which that vehicle falls,

"*relevant maximum train weight*", in relation to an articulated goods vehicle combination, means—

(a) in the case of an articulated goods vehicle to which regulations under section 49 of this Act apply which is required by regulations under section 41 of this Act to have a maximum train weight for the combination marked on a plate issued by the Secretary of State under regulations under section 41, the maximum train weight so marked on the motor vehicle,
(b) in the case of an articulated goods vehicle which is required by regulations under section 41 of this Act to have a maximum train weight for the combination marked on the vehicle and does not also have a maximum train weight marked on it as mentioned in paragraph (a) above, the maximum train weight marked on the motor vehicle,

(c) in the case of an articulated goods vehicle on which a maximum train weight is marked by the same means as would be required by regulations under section 41 of this Act if those regulations applied to the vehicle, the maximum train weight so marked on the motor vehicle,

(d) in the case of an articulated goods vehicle on which a maximum train weight is not marked as mentioned in paragraph (a), (b) or (c) above, the notional maximum gross weight of the combination, that is to say, such weight as is produced by multiplying the sum of the unladen weights of the motor vehicle and the semi-trailer by the number prescribed by the Secretary of State for the class of articulated goods vehicle combination into which that combination falls,

"semi-trailer", in relation to an articulated goods vehicle, means a trailer attached to it in the manner described in the definition of articulated goods vehicle,

. . .

[*"small vehicle"* means a motor vehicle (other than an invalid carriage, moped or motor bicycle) which—

(a) is not constructed or adapted to carry more than nine persons inclusive of the driver, and

(b) has a maximum gross weight not exceeding 3.5 tonnes,

and includes a combination of such a motor vehicle and a trailer,]

. . .

"test of competence to drive" means such a test conducted under section 89 of this Act.

[*"approved training course for motor cyclists"* and, in relation to such a course, *"prescribed certificate of completion"* mean respectively any course of training approved under, and the certificate of completion prescribed in, regulations under section 97(3A) of this Act.]

(2), (2A), (2B), (3) *[Power to make orders designating countries, etc., for purposes of the definition of "exchangeable licences" in subsection (1).]*

A25.232   *[Section 108 is printed as amended by the Road Traffic (Driver Licensing and Information Systems) Act 1989, s.7 and Sched. 3, para.15(a)–(e) and (f); the Driving Licences (Community Driving Licence) Regulations 1996 (S.I. 1996 No. 1974), reg.2 and Sched. 1, para.19 (not reproduced in this work); the Deregulation (Exchangeable Driving Licences) Order 1998 (S.I. 1998 No. 1917), art.2 (not reproduced in this work); the Driving Licences (Community Driving Licence) Regulations 1998 (S.I. 1998 No. 1420), regs 2 and 11 (not reproduced in this work).*

With effect from a date (or dates) to be announced under the Transport Act 2000, s.275(1), the definitions of "approved training course for motor cyclists" and "prescribed certificate of completion" in section 108(1) will be repealed by the 2000 Act, s.724 and Sched. 31, Pt V(1).

The following orders have effect as if made under section 108(2): the Driving Licences (Exchangeable Licences) Order 1984 (S.I. 1984 No. 672), taking effect on June 1, 1984; the Driving Licences (Exchangeable Licences) Order 1985 (S.I. 1985 No. 65), taking effect on February 2, 1985; the Driving Licences (Exchangeable Licences) (No. 2) Order 1985 (S.I. 1985 No. 1461), taking effect on November 1, 1985; the Driving Licences (Exchangeable Licences) Order 1999 (S.I. 1999 No. 1641), taking effect on July 2, 1999, in respect of driving licences issued in the countries specified and granted to persons who had passed a driving test in vehicles with automatic transmission.

As a result of these orders the following countries have been designated for the purposes of section 108(2):

Australia	S.I. 1984 No. 672
Austria	S.I. 1985 No. 1461
Barbados	S.I. 1985 No. 65
British Virgin Islands	S.I. 1985 No. 65
Canada (Provinces and Territories of)	S.I. 1999 No. 1641
Cyprus	S.I. 1985 No. 65

Finland	S.I. 1985 No. 65
Hong Kong	S.I. 1984 No. 672
Japan	S.I. 1985 No. 1461
Kenya	S.I. 1984 No. 672
Malta	S.I. 1985 No. 65
New Zealand	S.I. 1984 No. 672
Norway	S.I. 1984 No. 672
Singapore	S.I. 1984 No. 672
South Africa	S.I. 1999 No. 1641
Sweden	S.I. 1984 No. 672
Switzerland	S.I. 1984 No. 672
Zimbabwe	S.I. 1985 No. 65.

On January 1, 1995, Austria, Finland and Sweden became members of the European Union (see the notice at O.J. No. LI, January 1, 1995, p. 221). As to driving licences in those countries, see further the Act of Accession (Austria, Finland and Sweden), Annex I, Part VI (a), paragraph 4, as substituted by Council Decision 95/1/EC, Euratom, ECSC (O.J. No. L1, January 1, 1995, p. 116).

The Motor Vehicles (Driving Licences) Regulations 1999 (S.I. 1999 No. 2864) below were made in part under section 108(1).

As to the European Economic Area, see the note to Regulation (EEC) 3820/85 below.]

109. Provisions as to Northern Ireland drivers' licences

(1) The holder of a [Northern Ireland driving licence] may drive, and a person may cause or permit the holder of such a licence to drive, in Great Britain, a motor vehicle of any class which he is authorised by that licence to drive, and which he is not disqualified from driving under this Part [or Part IV] of this Act, notwithstanding that he is not the holder of a licence under this Part of this Act.   **A25.233**

(2) Any driver holding a [Northern Ireland driving licence] shall be under the like obligation to produce such a licence as if it had been a licence granted under this Part of this Act, and the provisions—

(a) of this Act, and

(b) of the Road Traffic Offenders Act 1988, being the provisions connected with the licensing of drivers within the meaning of that Act,

as to the production of licences granted under this Part of this Act shall apply accordingly.

(3) The holder of any such licence who by an order of the court is disqualified for holding or obtaining a licence under this Part of this Act must produce the licence so held by him to the court within such time as the court may determine, and the court must, on production of the licence, forward it to the Secretary of State.

(4) If the holder fails to produce the licence within that time, he is guilty of an offence.

(5) If the holder of any such licence is convicted of an offence and the court orders particulars of the conviction to be endorsed in accordance with section 44 of the Road Traffic Offenders Act 1988, the court shall send those particulars to the Secretary of State.

[Section 109 is printed as amended by the Road Traffic (Driver Licensing and Information Systems) Act 1989, s.7 and Sched. 3, para.16.   **A25.234**

Community driving licence. *In relation to driving licences which came into force after May 31, 1990 (after December 31, 1990 for Northern Ireland driving licences) only, section 109 was amended by the Driving Licences (Community Driving Licence) Regulations 1990 (S.I. 1990 No. 144) on April 1, 1990 so that:*   **A25.235**

(i)   *the following words were substituted in section 109(2) for the words "as if it had been a licence granted under this Part of this Act":*

and its counterpart as if they had respectively been a licence granted under this Part of this Act and the counterpart to such a licence;

(ii) *the words "and counterparts of licences" were inserted in section 109(2) after the words "production of licences";*

(iii) *the words "and its counterpart" were inserted in section 109(3) after the word "him";*

(iv) *the words "and its counterpart" were inserted in section 109(3) after the last reference to the word "licence";*

(v)   *the word "them" was substituted in section 109(3) for the word "it";*
      and

(vi) *the words "and its counterpart" were inserted in section 109(4) after the word "licence".]*

PART IV

Licensing of Drivers of Large Goods Vehicles and Passenger-carrying Vehicles

110. Licensing of drivers of large goods vehicles and passenger-carrying vehicles

A25.236   (1) Licences under Part III of this Act to drive motor vehicles of classes which include large goods vehicles or passenger-carrying vehicles or large goods vehicles or passenger-carrying vehicles of any class shall be granted by the Secretary of State in accordance with this Part of this Act and shall, in so far as they authorise the driving of large goods vehicles or passenger-carrying vehicles, be otherwise subject to this Part of this Act in addition to Part III of this Act.

(2) In this Part of this Act—

["*Community licence*" has the same meaning as in Part III of this Act;]

["*LGV Community licence*" means a Community licence in so far as it authorises a person to drive large goods vehicles of any class;]

"*large goods vehicle driver's licence*" means a licence under Part III of this Act in so far as it authorises a person to drive large goods vehicles of any class; and

["*PCV Community licence*" means a Community licence in so far as it authorises a person to drive passenger-carrying vehicles of any class;]

"*passenger-carrying vehicle driver's licence*" means a licence under Part III of this Act in so far as it authorises a person to drive passenger-carrying vehicles of any class.

A25.237   *[Section 110 is printed as substituted by the Road Traffic (Driver Licensing and Information Systems) Act 1989, s.2 and Sched. 2; the Driving Licences (Community Driving Licence) Regulations 1996 (S.I. 1996 No. 1974), reg.2 and Sched. 1, para.20 (not reproduced in this work).]*

111. Functions of traffic commissioners

A25.238   (1) The traffic commissioner for any area constituted for the purposes of the Public Passenger Vehicles Act 1981 shall exercise the functions conferred by the following provisions of this Part of this Act relating to the conduct of

[(a) applicants for and holders of large goods vehicle and passenger-carrying vehicle drivers' licences, and]

[(b) holders of LGV Community licences and PCV Community licences.]

(2) Traffic commissioners shall, in the exercise of those functions, act in accordance with directions given by the Secretary of State; but such directions shall be general directions not relating to the exercise of functions in a particular case.

[Section 111 is printed as substituted by the Road Traffic (Driver Licensing and Information Systems) **A25.239**
Act 1989, s.2 and Sched. 2; the Driving Licences (Community Driving Licence) Regulations 1996 (S.I.
1996 No. 1974), reg.2 and Sched. 1, para.21 (not reproduced in this work).]

112. Grant of licences: fitness as regards conduct

The Secretary of State shall not grant to an applicant a large goods vehicle driver's   **A25.240**
licence or a passenger-carrying vehicle driver's licence unless he is satisfied, having regard
to his conduct, that he is a fit person to hold the licence applied for.

[Section 112 is printed as substituted by the Road Traffic (Driver Licensing and Information Systems) **A25.241**
Act 1989, s.2 and Sched. 2.]

113. Grant of licences: referral of matters of conduct to traffic commissioners

(1) Any question arising under section 112 of this Act relating to the conduct of an   **A25.242**
applicant for a licence may be referred by the Secretary of State to the traffic commissioner
for the area in which the applicant resides.

(2) On any reference under subsection (1) above, the traffic commissioner shall determine whether the applicant for the licence is or is not, having regard to his conduct, a fit
person to hold a licence to drive large goods vehicles or passenger-carrying vehicles, as the
case may be.

(3) A traffic commissioner to whom a reference has been made under this section may
require the applicant for the licence to furnish the commissioner with such information as he
may require and may, by notice to the applicant, require him to attend before the commissioner at the time and place specified by the commissioner to furnish the information and to
answer such questions (if any) relating to his application as the commissioner may put to him.

(4) If the applicant fails without reasonable excuse to furnish information to or attend
before or answer questions properly put by a commissioner when required to do so under
subsection (3) above, the commissioner may decline to proceed further with the application
and, if he does so, the commissioner shall notify the Secretary of State of that fact and the
Secretary of State shall refuse to grant the licence.

(5) The traffic commissioner to whom a reference has been made under this section
shall, unless he has declined to proceed further with the application, notify the Secretary of
State and the applicant of his determination in the matter and the decision of the commissioner shall be binding on the Secretary of State.

[Section 113 is printed as substituted by the Road Traffic (Driver Licensing and Information Systems) **A25.243**
Act 1989, s.2 and Sched. 2.]

114. Conditions of certain licences

(1) [The following licences, that is to say—   **A25.244**

   (a) a large goods vehicle or passenger-carrying vehicle driver's licence issued as a provisional licence,

   (b) a full large goods vehicle or passenger-carrying vehicle driver's licence granted to a
person under the age of 21, and

   (c) a LGV Community licence held by a person under the age of 21 who is normally
resident in Great Britain,]

shall be subject to the prescribed conditions, and if the holder of the licence fails, without
reasonable excuse, to comply with any of the conditions he is guilty of an offence.

(2) It is an offence for a person knowingly to cause or permit another person who is under the age of 21 to drive a large goods vehicle of any class or a passenger-carrying vehicle of any class in contravention of the prescribed conditions to which that other person's licence is subject.

A25.245   *[Section 114 is printed as substituted by the Road Traffic (Driver Licensing and Information Systems) Act 1989, s.2 and Sched. 2; the Driving Licences (Community Driving Licence) Regulations 1996 (S.I. 1996 No. 1974), reg.2 and Sched. 1, para.22 (not reproduced in this work).*

The Motor Vehicles (Driving Licences) Regulations 1999 (S.I. 1999 No. 2864) (q.v.) were made in part under section 114(1); see, in particular, ibid., reg.54.]

115. Revocation or suspension of licences

A25.246   (1) A large goods vehicle or passenger-carrying vehicle driver's licence—

(a) must be revoked if there come into existence, in relation to its holder, such circumstances relating to his conduct as may be prescribed;

(b) must be revoked or suspended if his conduct is such as to make him unfit to hold such a licence;

and where the licence is suspended under paragraph (b) above it shall during the time of suspension be of no effect.

(2) Where it appears that the conduct of the holder of a licence falls within both paragraph (a) and paragraph (b) of subsection (1) above, proceedings shall be taken or continued under paragraph (a) and not under paragraph (b) and accordingly the power to suspend the licence, rather than revoke it, shall not be available.

(3) Regulations made for the purposes of [this section [or any of sections 115A, 117 or 117A] of this Act]—

(a) may make different provision for large goods vehicles and for passenger-carrying vehicles and for different descriptions of persons; and

(b) shall provide for the determination of the cases in which,

[(i) under section 117 of this Act, a person whose licence has been revoked, or]
[(ii) under section 117A of this Act, a person on whom a notice is served in pursuance of section 115A(1)(a) of this Act,]

is to be disqualified indefinitely or for a period and, if for a period, for the determination of the period.

A25.247   *[Section 115 is printed as substituted by the Road Traffic (Driver Licensing and Information Systems) Act 1989, s.2 and Sched. 2, and as amended by the Road Traffic Act 1991, s.48 and Sched. 4, para.64; the Driving Licences (Community Driving Licence) Regulations 1996 (S.I. 1996 No. 1974), reg.2 and Sched. 1, para.23 (not reproduced in this work).*

The Motor Vehicles (Driving Licences) Regulations 1999 (S.I. 1999 No. 2864) (q.v.) were made in part under section 115(1) and (3).

The prescribed circumstances to which reference is made in 115(1)(a), are set out in S.I. 1999 No. 2864, reg.55(1) below; and see also ibid., reg.55(2) and (3).]

[115A. Community licence holders: cessation of authorisation, etc.

A25.248   (1) Where, in relation to a holder of a LGV Community licence or PCV Community licence who is normally resident in Great Britain—

(a) there exist immediately before the relevant date, or there come into existence on or after that date, such circumstances relating to his conduct as may be prescribed; or

(b) his conduct is such as to make him unfit to be authorised by virtue of section

99A(1) of this Act to drive in Great Britain a large goods vehicle or passenger-carrying vehicle (as the case may be),

the Secretary of State must serve notice on the holder requiring him to deliver the Community licence and its counterpart (if any) immediately to the Secretary of State and it shall be the duty of the holder to comply with that requirement.

(2) Where a notice is served in pursuance of subsection (1)(a) or (b) above on the holder of a LGV Community licence or a PCV Community licence, he shall cease to be authorised by virtue of section 99A(1) of this Act to drive in Great Britain a large goods vehicle or passenger-carrying vehicle (as the case may be) from such date as is specified in the notice, not being earlier than the date of service of the notice.

(3) Where it appears to the Secretary of State that the conduct of a Community licence holder falls within both paragraph (a) and paragraph (b) of subsection (1) above, the Secretary of State must serve notice on the holder in pursuance of the former paragraph only.

(4) Any Community licence holder who fails without reasonable excuse to comply with his duty under subsection (1) above is guilty of an offence.

(5) In this section *"relevant date"*, in relation to a Community licence holder who is normally resident in Great Britain, has the same meaning as in section 99A(8) of this Act.]

[Section 115A was inserted by the Driving Licences (Community Driving Licence) Regulations 1996   **A25.249**
(S.I. 1996 No. 1974), reg.2 and Sched. 1, para.24 (not reproduced in this work).

The prescribed circumstances to which reference is made in section 115(1)(a), are set out in the Motor Vehicles (Driving Licences) Regulations 1999 (S.I. 1999 No. 2864), reg.55(2) below; and see also ibid., reg.55(3) and (4).]

116. Revocation or suspension of licences: referral of matters of conduct to traffic commissioners

[(1) Any question arising—   **A25.250**

  (a) under section 116(1)(b) of this Act as to whether a person is or is not, by reason of his conduct, fit to hold a large goods vehicle or passenger-carrying vehicle driver's licence, as the case may be, or

  (b) under section 115A(1)(b) of this Act as to whether the holder of a LGV Community licence or PCV Community licence is or is not, by reason of his conduct, fit to be authorised by virtue of section 99A(1) of this Act to drive in Great Britain a large goods vehicle or passenger-carrying vehicle (as the case may be),

may be referred by the Secretary of State to the traffic commissioner for the area in which the holder of the licence resides.]

(2) Where, on any reference under [subsection (1)(a)] above, the traffic commissioner determines that the holder of the licence is not fit to hold a large goods vehicle or passenger-carrying vehicle driver's licence, as the case may be, he shall also determine whether the conduct of the holder of the licence is such as to require the revocation of his licence or only its suspension; and, if the former, whether the holder of the licence should be disqualified under section 117(2)(a) of this Act (and, if so, for what period) or under section 117(2)(b) of this Act.

[(2A) Where, on any reference under subsection (1)(b) above, the traffic commissioner determines that a Community licence holder is not fit to be authorised by virtue of section 99A(1) of this Act to drive in Great Britain a large goods vehicle or passenger-carrying vehicle (as the case may be), he shall also determine whether the Community licence holder—

  (a) should be disqualified under section 117A(2)(a) of this Act (and, if so, for what period) or under section 117A(2)(b) of this Act, or

(b) should be granted, free of charge, a large goods vehicle or passenger-carrying vehicle driver's licence (and, if so, from what date it shall take effect).]

(3) A traffic commissioner to whom a reference has been made under subsection (1) above may require the holder of the licence to furnish the commissioner with such information as he may require and may, by notice to the holder, require him to attend before the commissioner at the time and place specified by the commissioner to furnish the information and to answer such questions (if any) relating to the subject matter of the reference as the commissioner may put to him.

(4) If the holder of the licence fails without reasonable excuse to furnish information to or to attend before or answer questions properly put by a commissioner when required to do so under subsection (3) above, the commissioner may notify the failure to the Secretary of State and, if the commissioner does so,

[(a) in a case where the licence in question is a LGV Community licence or a PCV Community licence, the holder shall cease to be authorised by virtue of section 99A(1) of this Act to drive in Great Britain a large goods or passenger-carrying vehicle (as the case may be) from such date as is specified in a notice served on the holder by the Secretary of State; and]

[(b) in any other case, revoke the licence or suspend it for such period as he thinks fit.]

(5) Except where he has given such a notification as is mentioned in subsection (4) above, the traffic commissioner to whom a reference has been made under subsection (1) above shall notify his determination in the matter to the Secretary of State and the holder of the licence and the decision of the commissioner shall be binding on the Secretary of State.

(6) Where the Secretary of State, without making such a reference, determines to revoke or suspend a person's licence under section 115(1) of this Act he shall notify his determination in the matter to the holder of the licence and, where he suspends it, to the traffic commissioner for the area in which the holder of the licence resides.

A25.251   *[Section 116 is printed as substituted by the Road Traffic (Driver Licensing and Information Systems) Act 1989, s.2 and Sched. 2; the Driving Licences (Community Driving Licence) Regulations 1996 (S.I. 1996 No. 1974), reg.2 and Sched. 1, para.25 (not reproduced in this work).]*

117. Disqualification on revocation of licence

A25.252   (1) Where in pursuance of section 115(1)(a) of this Act the Secretary of State revokes a person's large goods vehicle or passenger-carrying vehicle driver's licence, the Secretary of State must, in accordance with the regulations made [in pursuance of section 115(3)], order that person to be disqualified indefinitely or for the period determined in accordance with the regulations.

(2) Where in pursuance of section 115(1)(b) of this Act the Secretary of State revokes a person's large goods vehicle or passenger-carrying vehicle driver's licence, the Secretary of State may—

(a) order the holder to be disqualified indefinitely or for such period as the Secretary of State thinks fit, or

(b) except where the licence is a provisional licence, if it appears to the Secretary of State that, owing to the conduct of the holder of the licence, it is expedient to require him to comply with the prescribed conditions applicable to provisional licences under Part III of this Act until he passes the prescribed test of competence to drive large goods vehicles or passenger-carrying vehicles of any class, order him to be disqualified for holding or obtaining a full licence until he passes such a test.

[(2A) *[Regulations applying subsections (1) and (2) where licence is treated as revoked under section 37(1) of the Road Traffic Offenders Act 1988.]*]

(3) If, while the holder of a large goods vehicle or passenger-carrying vehicle driver's licence is disqualified under subsection (1) above, the circumstances prescribed for the purposes of section 115(1)(a) of this Act cease to exist in his case, the Secretary of State must, on an application made to him for the purpose, remove the disqualification.

(4) Where the holder of a large goods vehicle or passenger-carrying vehicle driver's licence is disqualified under subsection (2)(a) above, the Secretary of State may, in such circumstances as may be prescribed, remove the disqualification.

(5) Where the holder of a full licence is disqualified under subsection (2)(b) above, the Secretary of State must not afterwards grant him a full licence to drive a large goods vehicle or passenger-carrying vehicle of any class unless satisfied that he has since the disqualification passed the prescribed test of competence to drive vehicles of that class, and until he passes that test any full licence obtained by him shall be of no effect.

(6) So long as the disqualification under subsection (1) or (2)(a) above of the holder of a large goods vehicle or passenger-carrying vehicle driver's licence continues in force, a large goods vehicle or passenger-carrying vehicle driver's licence must not be granted to him and any such licence obtained by him shall be of no effect.

(7) In this section "*disqualified*"—

(a) in a case of revocation on the ground of the conduct of the holder of the licence as a driver, means disqualified for holding or obtaining a licence under Part III of this Act to drive large goods vehicles of the prescribed classes and passenger-carrying vehicles of the prescribed classes; and

(b) in a case of revocation of a passenger-carrying vehicle driver's licence on the ground of the conduct of the holder otherwise than as a driver, means disqualified for holding or obtaining a licence under Part III of this Act to drive passenger-carrying vehicles of the prescribed classes.

[Section 117 is printed as substituted by the Road Traffic (Driver Licensing and Information Systems) Act 1989, s.2 and Sched. 2, and as amended by the Road Traffic Act 1991, s.48 and Sched. 4, para.65(1)–(3).   **A25.253**

The Motor Vehicles (Driving Licences) Regulations 1999 (S.I. 1999 No. 2864) (q.v.) were made in part under section 117(2A); see, in particular, regulation 57.]

[117A. Community licences: disqualification, etc.

(1) Where a notice is served on a Community licence holder in pursuance of section 115A(1)(a) of this Act, the Secretary of State must, in accordance with the regulations made in pursuance of section 115(3), order that person to be disqualified indefinitely or for the period determined in accordance with the regulations.   **A25.254**

(2) Where a notice is served on a Community licence holder in pursuance of section 115A(1)(b) of this Act, the Secretary of State may—

(a) order that person to be disqualified indefinitely or for such period as the Secretary of State thinks fit,

(b) if it appears to the Secretary of State that, owing to the conduct of the Community licence holder, it is expedient to require him to comply with the prescribed conditions applicable to provisional licences under Part III of this Act until he passes the prescribed test of competence to drive large goods vehicles or passenger-carrying vehicles of any class, order him to be disqualified for holding or obtaining a full licence until he passes such a test, or

(c) on receipt of the Community licence and its counterpart (if any), grant to the Community licence holder, free of charge, a large goods vehicle or passenger-carrying vehicle driver's licence which shall take effect from such date as the Secretary of State may determine.

[(3) Where, in pursuance of subsection (1) or (2) above, the Secretary of State orders a Community licence holder to be disqualified the Secretary of State must, on receipt of the Community licence and its counterpart (if any), grant to the Community licence holder, free of charge, a licence authorising the driving of the classes of vehicle which are unaffected by the disqualification.]

[(3A) The Secretary of State may require a person to provide—

(a) evidence of his name, address, sex and date and place of birth, and

(b) a photograph which is a current likeness of him,

before issuing a licence to him under subsection (3) above.]

(4) If, while the holder of a LGV Community licence or a PCV Community licence is disqualified under subsection (1) above, the circumstances prescribed for the purposes of section 115A(1)(a) of this Act cease to exist in his case, the Secretary of State must, on an application made to him for the purpose, remove the disqualification.

(5) Where the holder of a LGV Community licence or a PCV Community licence is disqualified under subsection (2)(a) above, the Secretary of State may, in such circumstances as may be prescribed, remove the disqualification.

(6) In this section "*disqualified*"—

(a) in a case where notice is served in pursuance of section 115A(1) of this Act on a Community licence holder on the ground of his conduct as a driver, means disqualified for holding or obtaining a licence under Part III of this Act to drive large goods vehicles of the prescribed classes and passenger-carrying vehicles of the prescribed classes; and

(b) in a case where notice is served in pursuance of section 115A(1) of this Act on a holder of a PCV Community licence on the ground of his conduct otherwise than as a driver, means disqualified for holding or obtaining a licence under Part III of this Act to drive passenger-carrying vehicles of the prescribed classes.]

A25.255   *[Section 117A was inserted by the Driving Licences (Community Driving Licence) Regulations 1996 (S.I. 1996 No. 1974), reg.2 and Sched. 1, para.26 (not reproduced in this work), and is printed as substituted by the Driving Licences (Community Driving Licence) Regulations 1998 (S.I. 1998 No. 1420), regs 2 and 12 (not reproduced in this work).]*

118. Revoked or suspended licences: surrender, return and endorsement

A25.256   (1) Where, in pursuance of section 115 of this Act, the Secretary of State revokes a licence, he must serve notice on the holder of the licence requiring him to deliver the licence forthwith to the Secretary of State, and it shall be the duty of the holder of the licence to comply with the requirement.

(2) Where, in pursuance of section 115 of this Act, the Secretary of State suspends a licence, then—

(a) where he does so without making any reference under section 116 of this Act to a traffic commissioner, the Secretary of State must serve notice on the holder of the licence requiring him to deliver the licence forthwith to the traffic commissioner for the area in which the holder of the licence resides;

(b) where he does so in pursuance of a determination of a traffic commissioner on such a reference, the traffic commissioner must, if the licence has not previously been delivered to him, serve notice on the holder of the licence requiring him to deliver the licence forthwith to the commissioner;

and it shall be the duty of the holder of the licence to comply with the requirement.

(3) Any holder of a licence who fails without reasonable excuse to comply with his duty under subsection (1) or (2) above is guilty of an offence.

(4) On the delivery of a licence by a person to the Secretary of State in pursuance of subsection (1) above, the Secretary of State must issue to him, on payment of such fee (if any) as may be prescribed, a licence authorising the driving of the classes of vehicles which are unaffected by the revocation.

[(4A) The Secretary of State may require a person to provide—

(a) evidence of his name, address, sex and date and place of birth, and

(b) a photograph which is a current likeness of him,

before issuing a licence to him under subsection (4) above.]

(5) On the delivery of a suspended licence to a traffic commissioner, the traffic commissioner must endorse the licence with particulars of the suspension and return it to the holder.

[Section 118 is printed as substituted by the Road Traffic (Driver Licensing and Information Systems) **A25.257**
Act 1989, s.2 and Sched. 2, and as subsequently amended by the Driving Licences (Community Driving Licence) Regulations 1998 (S.I. 1998 No. 1420), regs 2 and 12 (not reproduced in this work).
The Motor Vehicles (Driving Licences) Regulations 1999 (S.I. 1999 No. 2864) (q.v.) were made in part under section 118(4).

Community driving licence. *In relation to driving licences which came into force after May 31,* **A25.258**
1990 (after December 31, 1990 for Northern Ireland driving licences) only, section 118 (as prospectively inserted by the Road Traffic (Driver Licensing and Information Systems) Act 1989, s.2(1) and Sched. 2) was amended by the Driving Licences (Community Driving Licence) Regulations 1990 (S.I. 1990 No. 144) on April 1, 1990 so that:

(i) *the words "and its counterpart" were inserted in section 118(1) after the second reference to the words "the licence";*

(ii) *the words "and its counterpart" were inserted in section 118(2)(a) after the second reference to the words "the licence";*

(iii) *the words "licence and its counterpart have" were substituted in section 118(2)(b) for the words "licence has";*

(iv) *the word "them" was substituted in section 118(2)(b) for the third reference to the words "the licence";*

(v) *the words "and its counterpart" were inserted in section 118(4) after the first reference to the word "licence"; and*

(vi) *the following subsection was substituted for section 118(5):*

(5) On the delivery of a suspended licence and its counterpart to a traffic commissioner, the traffic commissioner must endorse the counterpart of the licence with particulars of the suspension and return the licence and its counterpart to the holder.]

119. Appeals to magistrates' court

(1) A person who, being the holder of, or an applicant for, a large goods vehicle or pas- **A25.259**
senger-carrying vehicle driver's licence [or the holder of a LGV Community licence or a PCV Community licence], is aggrieved by the Secretary of State's—

(a) refusal or failure to grant such a licence in pursuance of section 112 or 113(4) of this Act,

(b) suspension or revocation of such a licence in pursuance of section 115 or 116(4) of this Act, or

(c) ordering of disqualification under section 117(2) [or 117A(2)] of this Act,

[or by a notice served on him in pursuance of section 115A(1) or 116(4) of this Act] may, after giving to the Secretary of State and any traffic commissioner to whom the matter was referred notice of his intention to do so, appeal to a magistrates' court acting for the petty sessions area in which the holder of or applicant for the licence resides . . .

(2) On any appeal under [subsection (1) above (except paragraph (c) of that subsection)] the Secretary of State and, if the matter was referred to a traffic commissioner, the commissioner shall be respondent.

(3) On any appeal under subsection (1) above the court . . . may make such order as it thinks fit and the order shall be binding on the Secretary of State.

A25.260   *[Section 119 is printed as substituted by the Road Traffic (Driver Licensing and Information Systems) Act 1989, s.2 and Sched. 2; the Driving Licences (Community Driving Licence) Regulations 1996 (S.I. 1996 No. 1974), reg.2 and Sched. 1, para.27 (not reproduced in this work).*
Words in section 119 relating expressly and exclusively to Scotland have been omitted.]

120. Regulations

A25.261   (1) The Secretary of State may make regulations for any purpose for which regulations may be made under this Part of this Act and for prescribing anything which may be prescribed under this Part of this Act and generally for the purpose of carrying the provisions of this Part of this Act into effect.

(2) Regulations under this section may in particular require applicants for tests of competence under Part III of this Act to drive large goods vehicles or passenger-carrying vehicles or for large goods vehicle or passenger-carrying vehicle driver's licences (whether full or provisional) to have such qualifications, experience and knowledge as may be prescribed and, in particular, where they are to be authorised to drive large goods vehicles or passenger-carrying vehicles of any class at an age below the normal minimum age for driving vehicles of that class, to fulfil such requirements with respect to participation in an approved training scheme for drivers as may be prescribed.

(3) In subsection (2) above—

"*approved training scheme for drivers*" means a training scheme for drivers (as defined in section 101(5) of this Act [*q.v.*]) approved for the time being by the Secretary of State for the purposes of regulations under that section; and

"*normal minimum age for driving*", in relation to the driving of vehicles of any class, means the age which is in force under section 101 of this Act (but apart from any approved training scheme for drivers) in relation to that class of vehicle.

(4) Regulations under this section may make different provision as respects different classes of vehicles or as respects the same class of vehicles in different circumstances.

(5) Regulations under this section may provide that a person who contravenes or fails to comply with any specified provision of the regulations is guilty of an offence.

(6) The Secretary of State may by regulations provide that this Part of this Act shall not apply to large goods vehicles or passenger-carrying vehicles of such classes as may be prescribed either generally or in such circumstances as may be prescribed.

A25.262   *[Section 120 is printed as substituted by the Road Traffic (Driver Licensing and Information Systems) Act 1989, s.2 and Sched. 2.*

The Motor Vehicles (Driving Licences) Regulations 1999 (S.I. 1999 No. 2864) (q.v.) were made in part under section 120.]

121. Interpretation

(1) In this Part of this Act—   **A25.263**

["*conduct*" means—

    (a) in relation to an applicant for or the holder of a large goods vehicle driver's licence or the holder of a LGV Community licence, his conduct as a driver of a motor vehicle, and

    (b) in relation to an applicant for or the holder of a passenger-carrying vehicle driver's licence or the holder of a PCV Community licence, his conduct both as a driver of a motor vehicle and in any other respect relevant to his holding a passenger-carrying vehicle driver's licence or (as the case may be) his authorisation by virtue of section 99A(1) of this Act to drive in Great Britain a passenger-carrying vehicle of any class,

    including, in either case, such conduct in Northern Ireland;]

"*full licence*" means a large goods vehicle or passenger-carrying vehicle driver's licence other than a provisional licence;

["*large goods vehicle*" means a motor vehicle (not being a medium-sized goods vehicle within the meaning of Part III of this Act) which is constructed or adapted to carry or to haul goods and the permissible maximum weight of which exceeds 7.5 tonnes;]

"*passenger-carrying vehicle*" means—

    (a) a large passenger-carrying vehicle, that is to say, a vehicle used for carrying passengers which is constructed or adapted to carry more than 16 passengers, or

    (b) a small passenger-carrying vehicle, that is to say, a vehicle used for carrying passengers for hire or reward which is constructed or adapted to carry more than 8 but not more than 16 passengers;

    [and includes a combination of such a motor vehicle and a trailer]

"*notice*" means notice in writing and "*notify*" shall be construed accordingly;

"*prescribed*" means, unless the context requires otherwise, prescribed by regulations under section 120 of this Act;

"*provisional licence*" means a licence granted by virtue of section 97(2) of this Act [*q.v.*];

[and "*permissible maximum weight*" has the same meaning as in Part III of this Act.]

[Section 121 is printed as substituted by the Road Traffic (Driver Licensing and Information Systems)   **A25.264**
Act 1989, s.2 and Sched. 2 (as so substituted, although text is designated section 121(1), there are no other subsections); the Driving Licences (Community Driving Licence) Regulations 1996 (S.I. 1996 No. 1974), reg.2 and Sched. 1, para.28 (not reproduced in this work).

The Motor Vehicles (Driving Licences) Regulations 1999 (S.I. 1999 No. 2864) (q.v.) were made in part under section 121.

Community driving licence. *In relation to driving licences which came into force after May 31,*   **A25.265**
1990 (after December 31, 1990 for Northern Ireland driving licences) only, section 121 (as inserted by the Road Traffic (Driver Licensing and Information Systems) Act 1989, s.2(1) and Sched. 2) was amended by the Driving Licences (Community Driving Licence) Regulations 1990 (S.I. 1990 No. 144) on April 1, 1990 (and itself amended by the Driving Licences (Community Driving Licence) Regulations 1996 (S.I. 1996 No. 1974), reg.2 and Sched. 1, para.28) so that the following definition was inserted into section 121(1) at the appropriate place:

    "*counterpart*", in relation to a licence to drive under Part III of this Act [or a Community licence], has the same meaning as in that Part;]

122. Provisions as to Northern Ireland licences   *[Omitted.]*   **A25.266**

PART V

DRIVING INSTRUCTION

A25.267   *Note to Part V.* Part V of this Act (sections 123–142) does not apply to any person or vehicle in the service of a visiting force or headquarters (as defined); see the Visiting Forces and International Headquarters (Application of Law) Order 1999 (S.I. 1999 No. 1736; not reproduced in this work), art.8(1) and (2)(b).

Instructors to be registered or licensed

123. Driving instruction for payment to be given only by registered or licensed persons

A25.268   (1) No paid instruction in the driving of a motor car shall be given unless—

     (a) the name of the person giving the instruction is in the register of approved instructors established in pursuance of section 23 of the Road Traffic Act 1962 (in this Part of this Act referred to as "*the register*"), or

     (b) the person giving the instruction is the holder of a current licence granted under this Part of this Act authorising him to give such instruction.

(2) No paid instruction in the driving of a motor car shall be given unless there is fixed to and exhibited on that motor car in such manner as may be prescribed by regulations either—

     (a) a certificate in such form as may be so prescribed that the name of the person giving the instruction is in the register, or

     (b) a current licence granted under this Part of this Act authorising the person giving the instruction to give such instruction.

(3) For the purposes of subsections (1) and (2) above, instruction is paid instruction if payment of money or money's worth is, or is to be, made by or in respect of the person to whom the instruction is given for the giving of the instruction and for the purposes of this subsection instruction which is given—

     (a) free of charge to a person who is not the holder of a current licence to drive a motor vehicle granted under Part III of this Act (other than a provisional licence),

     (b) by, or in pursuance of arrangements made by, a person carrying on business in the supply of motor cars, and

     (c) in connection with the supply of a motor car in the course of that business,

shall be deemed to be given for payment of money by the person to whom the instruction is given.

(4) Where instruction is given in contravention of subsection (1) above—

     (a) the person by whom it is given, and

     (b) if that person is employed by another to give that instruction, that other, as well as that person,

is guilty of an offence.

(5) In proceedings against a person for an offence under subsection (4) above it shall be a defence for him to prove that he did not know, and had no reasonable cause to believe, that his name or, as the case may be, that of the person employed by him, was not in the register at the material time.

(6) If instruction is given in contravention of subsection (2) above, the person by whom it is given is guilty of an offence.

(7) Any reference in this Part of this Act to a current licence [or certificate] is a reference to a licence [or certificate] which has not expired and has not been cancelled, revoked or suspended.

[(8) In this Part of this Act—

"*paid instruction*", in relation to instruction in the driving of a motor car, shall be construed in accordance with subsection (3) above; and

"*provisional licence*" has the same meaning as in Part III of this Act.]

[*Section 123 is printed as amended by the Road Traffic (Driving Instruction by Disabled Persons) Act*   **A25.269**
1993, s.6 and Schedule, paras 1 and 2.
The register is now maintained under section 125 of this Act.
See further the Motor Cars (Driving Instruction) Regulations 1989 (S.I. 1989 No. 2057) (not reproduced in this work) which were made in part under this section.]

124. Exemption of police instructors from prohibition imposed by section 123

(1) Section 123(1) and (2) of this Act does not apply to the giving of instruction by a   **A25.270**
police instructor in pursuance of arrangements made by a chief officer of police or, under the authority of a chief officer of police, in pursuance of arrangements made by a local authority.

(2) In this section—

["*chief officer of police*" includes the Director General of the National Criminal Intelligence Service and the Director General of the National Crime Squad;]

["*police authority*" includes the Service Authority for the National Criminal Intelligence Service and the Service Authority for the National Crime Squad;]

["*police force*" includes the National Criminal Intelligence Service and the National Crime Squad;]

"*police instructor*" means a person who is—

(a) a member of a police force whose duties consist of or include, or have consisted of or included, the giving of instruction in the driving of motor cars to persons being members of a police force, or

(b) a civilian employed by a police authority for the purpose of giving such instruction to such persons, and

"*local authority*" means—

(a) in relation to England and Wales, the council of a county, metropolitan district, or London borough or the Common Council of the City of London,

(b) [*applies to Scotland.*]

(3) [*Repealed.*]

[*Section 124 is printed as amended by the Police Act 1997, s.134(1) and Sched. 9, para.58; the*   **A25.271**
Greater London Authority Act 1999, s.325 and Sched. 27, para.60 (see also ibid., s.423 and Sched. 34, Pt VII).]

Registration
                                                                                                    A25.272

125. The register of approved instructors   [*Omitted.*]

[125A. Registration of disabled persons   **A25.273**

(1) [*Right to apply as disabled instructor.*]

(2) *[Procedure for application.]*

(3) *[Need to notify relevant or prospective disability.]*

(4) *[Offence of failing to notify under subsection (3).]*

(5) *[Entry of disabled instructor on Register.]*

(6) *[Conditions for entry on Register.]*

(7) *[Regulations exempting from subsection (6).]*

(8) In this Part of this Act—

"*appropriate motor car*" means, subject to section 125B(2) of this Act, a motor car equipped with automatic transmission;

"*disability*" means a want of physical ability affecting the driving of motor cars; and

    (i) "*relevant disability*", in relation to a person, means any disability which is prescribed in regulations or any other disability likely to cause the driving of a motor car by him to be a source of danger to the public; and

    (ii) "*prospective disability*", in relation to a person, means any other disability which, at the material time, is not of such a kind that it is a relevant disability but, by virtue of the intermittent or progressive nature of the disability or otherwise, may become a relevant disability in course of time;

"*disabled person's limited driving licence*" means a licence of one of the following kinds, that is to say—

    (a) a licence to drive a motor car granted under Part III of this Act (not being a provisional licence) which is limited, by virtue of a notice served under section 92(5)(b) of this Act, to an appropriate motor car; . . .

    (b) a licence to drive a motor car granted under the law in force in Northern Ireland (not being a licence corresponding to a provisional licence) which is similarly limited by virtue of any corresponding provision of that law; [and]

    [(c) a Community licence authorising the driver of a motor car which is similarly limited by virtue of any corresponding provision of the law under which it was issued and a counterpart of that licence;]

"*emergency control assessment*" and "*emergency control certificate*" mean an assessment and a certificate under section 133A of this Act;

"*modifications*", in relation to a motor car, includes equipment; and

"*registered disabled instructor*" means a person whose name is in the register with an indication that he is disabled;

and any reference, in relation to a person, to the class of motor car covered by his disabled person's limited driving licence is a reference to the class of motor car specified in the notice served on him under section 92(5)(b) of this Act but disregarding any modifications specified in the notice.

A25.274   *[Section 125A was inserted by the Road Traffic (Driving Instruction by Disabled Persons) Act 1993, s.1 and is printed as subsequently amended by the Motor Cars (Driving Instruction) (Admission of Community Licence Holders) Regulations 1999 (S.I. 1999 No. 357; not reproduced in this work).]*

A25.275   **125B. Provisions supplementary to section 125A**   *[Omitted.]*

126. Duration of registration   *[Omitted.]*

127. Extension of duration of registration *[Omitted.]*

128. Removal of names from register *[Omitted.]*

Licences

129. Licences for giving instruction so as to obtain practical experience

[(1) A licence under this section is granted for the purpose of enabling a person to   A25.276
acquire practical experience in giving instruction in driving motor cars with a view to
undergoing [either—

(a) such part of the examination referred to in section 125(3)(a) of this Act, or

(b) such part of any examination prescribed for the purposes of section 125A(6)(a) of
this Act,]

as consists of a practical test of ability and fitness to instruct.]

(2) *[Application for licence.]*

(3) *[Refusal of licence.]*

(4) *[Notice of decision.]*

(5) *[Form of licence, and conditions.]*

(5A) *[Conditions on licence of disabled instructor.]*

(5B) *[Definition of "authorised motor car" in section 129(5A).]*

(6) *[Renewal of licence.]*

(7), (8) *[Notice of refusal of licence.]*

[Section 129 is printed as amended by the Road Traffic (Driving Instruction by Disabled Persons) Act   A25.277
1993, s.2(1).]

130. Revocation of licences *[Omitted.]*   A25.278

Appeals

131. Appeals against decisions of the Registrar *[Omitted.]*

Examinations and tests

132. Examinations and tests of ability to give driving instruction *[Omitted.]*

133. Review of examinations

(1) On the application of a person who has submitted himself for any part of an exam-   A25.279
ination of ability to give instruction in the driving of motor cars—

(a) the magistrates' court acting for the petty sessions area in which he resides, or

(b) *[applies to Scotland.],*

may determine whether that part of the examination was properly conducted in accordance with regulations.

(2) If it appears to the court . . . that that part of the examination was not so conducted,
the court . . . may order that any fee payable by the applicant in respect of that part shall
not be paid or, if it has been paid, shall be repaid.

(3) No appeal shall lie under section 131 of this Act in respect of any matter in respect of which an application may be made to a magistrates' court . . . under subsection (1) above.

A25.280   *[With effect from a date to be announced under the Transport Act 2000, s.275, the following amendments will be made to section 133 by the Transport Act 2000, s.260 and Sched. 29, paras 1 and 11:*

     (i)   *in section 133(1), the following words will be substituted for the words "submitted himself for any part of an examination of ability to give instruction in the driving of motor cars"—*

        [undergone relevant examination, or a part of such an examination]

     (ii)   *also in section 133(1), the following words will be substituted for the words "that part of the examination was properly conducted in accordance with regulations"—*

        [examination or part was properly conducted]

     (iii)   *in section 133(2), the following words will be substituted for the words "that part of the examination was not so"—*

        [the examination or part was not properly]

     (iv)   *also in section 133(2), the words "the examination or part" will be substituted for the words "that part", and*

     (v)   *the following text will be inserted after section 133(3)—*

        [(4) In this section *"a relevant examination"* means—

          (a)   an examination of ability to give instruction in the driving of motor cars,

          (b)   a test of continued ability and fitness to give instruction in the driving of motor cars (or appropriate motor cars), or

          (c)   an emergency control assessment.]

Section 260 of the 2000 Act, together with Schedule 29, paragraphs 1 and 11 thereto, was brought into force on February 1, 2001 by the Transport Act 2000 (Commencement No. 3) Order 2001 (S.I. 2001 No. 57; not reproduced in this volume), but S.I. 2001 No. 57 was itself amended by the Transport Act 2000 (Commencement No. 3) (Amendment) Order 2001 (S.I. 2001 No. 115; not reproduced in this work) so as to delete reference to (inter alia) section 260 and Schedule 29, paragraphs 1 and 11, from S.I. 2001 No. 57.

Words relating exclusively to Scotland have been omitted from section 133.

The regulations to which reference is made are the Motor Cars (Driving Instruction) Regulations 1989 (S.I. 1989 No. 2057) (not reproduced in this work) which were made in part under this section.]

[Disabled persons: emergency control certificates, etc.]

[133A. Assessment of disabled person's ability to control a motor car in an emergency

A25.281   (1) This section applies to any person who, by or under any provision of this Part of this Act,—

     (a)   is authorised to apply to undergo an emergency control assessment, or

     (b)   is required by the Registrar to submit himself for an emergency control assessment.

(2) An emergency control assessment is an assessment of whether the person being assessed would be able either—

     (a)   to take control of a motor car of a class covered by his disabled person's limited driving licence without any modifications, or

     (b)   to take control of a motor car of a class covered by his disabled person's limited driving licence only with appropriate modifications of such a motor car,

if an emergency arose while he was giving, in such a motor car, instruction in the driving of an appropriate motor car.

(3) Where a person is authorised to apply to undergo an emergency control assessment, for the application to be duly made, it must be made to the Secretary of State and must include—

(a) a declaration by the person making the application, in such form as the Secretary of State may require, stating every relevant disability or prospective disability from which the person is suffering or has at any time (or, if a period is prescribed by regulations, has during that period) suffered; and

(b) such other particulars as the Secretary of State may require.

(4) Where a person is required to submit himself for an emergency control assessment he must furnish to the Secretary of State such particulars as the Secretary of State may require.

[(4A) *[Regulation-making power.]*]

(5) An emergency control assessment—

(a) shall be conducted by a person appointed by the Secretary of State (in this section referred to as "*the assessor*"); and

(b) shall consist of such practical tests and other means of assessment as the Secretary of State may determine.

(6) On completing an emergency control assessment of a person, the assessor shall grant him an emergency control certificate if he is satisfied either—

(a) that, in the circumstances mentioned in subsection (2) above, that person would be able to take control of a motor car of a class covered by his disabled person's limited driving licence without any modifications, or

(b) that, in the circumstances mentioned in subsection (2) above, that person would be able to take control of a motor car of a class covered by his disabled person's limited driving licence only with appropriate modifications of such a motor car;

but if the assessor is not so satisfied, he shall refuse to grant a certificate to that person.

(7) An emergency control certificate granted to any person—

(a) shall specify the class of motor car covered by his disabled person's limited driving licence in relation to which the assessor is satisfied as mentioned in subsection (6)(a) or (b) above, specifying, in a case falling within paragraph (b), the modifications that are appropriate; and

(b) may include a recommendation that that person should undergo a further emergency control assessment after the end of such period as is specified in the certificate;

and shall otherwise be in such form as the Secretary of State may determine.

(8) Different modifications for different classes of motor car may be specified under subsection (7)(a) above.

(9) The assessor who has assessed any person under this section—

(a) if he grants an emergency control certificate, shall—

(i) give or send the certificate to that person, and
(ii) send a copy of the certificate to the Registrar; and

(b) if he refuses to grant such a certificate, shall—

(i) give notice in writing to that person of his decision and of the reasons for it, and
(ii) send a copy of the notice to the Registrar.]

[Section 133A was inserted by the Road Traffic (Driving Instruction by Disabled Persons) Act 1993,   **A25.282**
s.3; and it is printed as prospectively amended (with effect from a date to be announced under the Transport Act 2000, s.275) by the Transport Act 2000, s.260 and Sched. 29, paras 1 and 7 (which will insert section 133A(4A) (as noted above)).

Section 260 of the 2000 Act, together with Schedule 29, paragraphs 1 and 10 thereto, was brought into force on February 1, 2001 by the Transport Act 2000 (Commencement No. 3) Order 2001 (S.I. 2001 No. 57; not reproduced in this volume), but S.I. 2001 No. 57 was itself amended by the Transport Act 2000 (Commencement No. 3) (Amendment) Order 2001 (S.I. 2001 No. 115; not reproduced in this volume) so as to delete reference to (inter alia) section 260 and Schedule 29, paragraphs 1 and 10, from S.I. 2001 No. 57.]

A25.283   **133B. Further assessments**   *[Omitted.]*

[133C. Duty to disclose further disability

A25.284   (1) This section applies to—

(a) registered disabled instructors, and

(b) persons who hold licences under section 129 of this Act granted by virtue of sub-section (2)(b) of that section.

(2) If at any time a person to whom this section applies becomes aware—

(a) that he is suffering from a relevant or prospective disability which he has not previously disclosed to the Secretary of State under section 125A(3) or 133A(3) or (4) of this Act, or

(b) that a relevant or prospective disability from which he has at any time suffered (and which has been previously so disclosed) has become more acute since his current emergency control certificate was granted,

he must forthwith notify the Registrar in writing of the nature and extent of his disability.

(3) Subsection (2) above does not require a person to notify the Registrar if—

(a) the disability is one from which he has not previously suffered, and

(b) he has reasonable grounds for believing that the duration of the disability will not extend beyond the period of three months beginning with the date on which he first becomes aware that he suffers from it.

(4) A person who fails without reasonable excuse to notify the Registrar as required by subsection (2) above is guilty of an offence.]

A25.285   *[Section 133C was inserted by the Road Traffic (Driving Instruction by Disabled Persons) Act 1993, s.4.]*

[133D. Offences relating to giving by disabled person of paid driving instruction

A25.286   (1) This section applies to—

(a) registered disabled instructors, and

(b) persons who hold licences under section 129 of this Act granted by virtue of sub-section (2)(b) of that section.

(2) No person to whom this section applies shall give paid instruction in the driving of a motor car unless he is the holder of a current emergency control certificate.

(3) No person to whom this section applies shall give, in any unauthorised motor car, paid instruction in the driving of a motor car.

(4) Where instruction is given in contravention of this section—

(a) the person by whom it is given, and

(b) if that person is employed by another to give that instruction, that other, as well as that person,

is guilty of an offence.

(5) In subsection (3) above "*unauthorised motor car*", in relation to any person, means a motor car other than one which falls within the class of motor car specified in his current emergency control certificate and, where modifications are specified in that certificate, is modified in accordance with the specification.]

[*Section 133D was inserted by the Road Traffic (Driving Instruction by Disabled Persons) Act 1993, s.5.*]   **A25.287**

General and supplemental

134. Power to alter conditions for entry or retention in, and removal from, register and for grant or revocation of licences   *[Omitted.]*   **A25.288**

135. Power to prescribe form of certificate of registration, etc.

(1) Regulations may prescribe all or any of the following—   **A25.289**

   (a) a form of certificate for issue to persons whose names are in the register as evidence of their names being in the register,

   (b) a form of badge for use by such persons, and

   (c) an official title for such use.

(2) If a person whose name is not in the register—

   (a) takes or uses a title prescribed under this section, or

   (b) wears or displays a badge or certificate so prescribed, or

   (c) takes or uses any name, title, addition or description implying that his name is in the register,

he is guilty of an offence unless he proves that he did not know, and had no reasonable cause to believe, that his name was not in the register at the material time.

(3) If a person carrying on business in the provision of instruction in the driving of motor vehicles—

   (a) uses a title or description so prescribed in relation to any person employed by him whose name is not in the register, or

   (b) issues any advertisement or invitation calculated to mislead with respect to the extent to which persons whose names are in the register are employed by him,

he is guilty of an offence unless he proves that he did not know, and had no reasonable cause to believe, that the name or names in question were not in the register at the material time.

[*The Motor Cars (Driving Instruction) Regulations 1989 (S.I. 1989 No. 2057) (not reproduced in this work) were made in part under this section.*]   **A25.290**

136. Surrender of certificates and licences

Where—   **A25.291**

   (a) the name of a person to whom a certificate prescribed under section 135 of this Act has been issued is removed from the register in pursuance of this Part of this Act, or

   (b) a licence granted under this Part of this Act to a person expires or is revoked,

that person must, if so required by the Registrar by notice in writing, surrender the certificate or licence, as the case may be, to the Registrar within the period of fourteen days beginning with that on which the notice is given and, if he fails to do so, he is guilty of an offence.

137. Production of certificates and licences to constables and authorised persons

A25.292

(1) A person to whom a certificate prescribed under section 135 of this Act is issued, or to whom a licence under this Part of this Act is granted, must, on being so required by a constable or any person authorised in writing by the Secretary of State in that behalf, produce the certificate or licence for examination.

(2) Where—

(a) the name of a person is removed from the register, or

(b) a licence granted under this Part of this Act to a person expires or is revoked,

then, if that person fails to satisfy an obligation imposed on him by section 136 of this Act, a constable or a person authorised in writing by the Secretary of State in that behalf may require him to produce any such certificate issued to him or the licence, and upon its being produced may seize it and deliver it to the Registrar.

(3) A person who is required under subsection (1) or (2) above to produce a document and fails to do so is, subject to subsection (4) below, guilty of an offence.

(4) In proceedings against any person for an offence under subsection (3) above, it shall be a defence for him to show that—

(a) within seven days beginning with the day following that on which the production of the document was so required, it was produced—

   (i) where the requirement was made by a constable, at a police station specified at the time the production was required by the person required to produce the document,

   (ii) where the requirement was made by a person other than a constable, at a place specified at that time by that person, or

(b) the document was produced at that police station or, as the case may be, place as soon as was reasonably practicable, or

(c) it was not reasonably practicable for it to be produced at that police station or, as the case may be, place before the day on which the proceedings were commenced,

and for the purposes of this subsection the laying of the information . . . shall be treated as the commencement of the proceedings.

A25.293   *[Words relating exclusively and expressly to Scotland have been omitted from section 137.]*

138. Offences by corporations

A25.294

Where a body corporate is guilty of an offence under this Part of this Act and the offence is proved to have been committed with the consent or connivance of, or to be attributable to neglect on the part of, a director, manager, secretary or other similar officer of the body corporate, or a person who was purporting to act in any such capacity, he, as well as the body corporate, is guilty of that offence and liable to be proceeded against and punished accordingly.

A25.295   ### 139. Service of notices   *[Omitted.]*

140. Receipts   *[Omitted.]*

141. Regulations   *[Omitted.]*

[141A. Meaning of "motor car"

(1) Notwithstanding section 185(1) of this Act, in this Part of this Act "*motor car*" means   **A25.296**
a motor vehicle (other than an invalid carriage or motor cycle)—

    (a) which is not constructed or adapted to carry more than nine persons inclusive of
the driver, and

    (b) which has a maximum gross weight not exceeding 3.5 tonnes.

(2) In subsection (1) above "*maximum gross weight*" has the same meaning as in Part III of
this Act.]

[Section 141A was inserted by the Driving Licences (Community Driving Licence) Regulations 1996   **A25.297**
(S.I. 1996 No. 1974), reg.2 and Sched. 1, para.29 (not reproduced in this work).]

142. Index to Part V

The expressions listed in the left-hand column below are respectively defined or (as the   **A25.298**
case may be) fall to be construed in accordance with the provisions of this Part of this Act
listed in the right-hand column in relation to those expressions.

Expression	*Relevant provision*
[*Appropriate motor car*	Section 125A(8)]
["*Community licence*" and "*counterpart*" in relation thereto	Section 125(10)]
Current licence	Section 123(7)
[*Disability, prospective disability and relevant disability*	Section 125A(8)]
[*Disabled person's limited driving licence*	Section 125A(8)]
[*Emergency control assessment and emergency control certificate*	Section 125A(8)]
[*Paid instruction*	Section 123(8)]
[*Provisional licence*	Section 123(8)]
The register	Section 123
[*Registered disabled instructor*	Section 125A(8)]]
The Registrar	Section 125(2)
Regulations	Section 141

[Section 142 is printed as amended by the Road Traffic (Driving Instruction by Disabled Persons) Act   **A25.299**
1993, s.6 and Schedule, paras 1 and 8, and is printed as subsequently amended by the Motor Cars (Driving
Instruction) (Admission of Community Licence Holders) Regulations 1999 (S.I. 1999 No. 357; not
reproduced in this work).

Section 125(2) is not reproduced in this work; in that provision, "the registrar" is defined as the officer of
the Secretary of State by whom, on behalf of the Secretary of State, the register of approved instructors is
compiled and maintained. Section 125(10) (similarly, not reproduced in this work) was inserted by S.I.
1999 No. 357 and defines "Community licence" and "counterpart" as in Part III of this Act.]

PART VI

THIRD-PARTY LIABILITIES

Note to Part VI. Part VI of this Act (sections 143–162) does not apply to any person or   **A25.300**
vehicle in the service of a visiting force or headquarters (as defined); see the Visiting Forces
and International Headquarters (Application of Law) Order 1999 (S.I. 1999 No. 1736; not
reproduced in this work), art.8(1) and (2)(b).

143. Users of motor vehicles to be insured or secured against third-party risks

A25.301   (1) Subject to the provisions of this Part of this Act—

(a) a person must not use a motor vehicle on a road [or other public place] unless there is in force in relation to the use of the vehicle by that person such a policy of insurance or such a security in respect of third-party risks as complies with the requirements of this Part of this Act, and

(b) a person must not cause or permit any other person to use a motor vehicle on a road [or other public place] unless there is in force in relation to the use of the vehicle by that other person such a policy of insurance or such a security in respect of third-party risks as complies with the requirements of this Part of this Act.

(2) If a person acts in contravention of subsection (1) above he is guilty of an offence.

(3) A person charged with using a motor vehicle in contravention of this section shall not be convicted if he proves—

(a) that the vehicle did not belong to him and was not in his possession under a contract of hiring or of loan,

(b) that he was using the vehicle in the course of his employment, and

(c) that he neither knew nor had reason to believe that there was not in force in relation to the vehicle such a policy of insurance or security as is mentioned in subsection (1) above.

(4) This Part of this Act does not apply to invalid carriages.

A25.302   *[Section 143 is printed as amended by the Motor Vehicles (Compulsory Insurance) Regulations 2000 (S.I. 2000 No. 726; not reproduced in this work).*

In the explanatory note accompanying S.I. 2000 No. 726 it is stated that the regulations were made for the purpose of complying with Directive 72/166/EEC, O.J. No. L103, May 2, 1972, p. 2, as modified by Directive 84/5/EEC, O.J. No. L8, January 11, 1984, p. 17, and Directive 90/232/EEC, O.J. No. L129, May 19, 1990, p. 33, following the decision of the House of Lords in Cutter v. Eagle Star Insurance Co. Ltd; Clarke v. Kato [1998] 4 All E.R. 417.

Proceedings under section 143 are specified by the Prosecution of Offences Act 1985 (Specified Proceedings) Order 1999 (S.I. 1999 No. 904) below as being proceedings the conduct of which the Director of Public Prosecutions is not required to take over from the police under the Prosecution of Offences Act 1985, s.3(3)(a).]

144. Exceptions from requirement of third-party insurance or security

A25.303   (1) Section 143 of this Act does not apply to a vehicle owned by a person who has deposited and keeps deposited with the Accountant General of the Supreme Court the sum of [£500,000], at a time when the vehicle is being driven under the owner's control.

[(1A), (1B) *[Power to alter the sum in section 144(1) by order.]*]

(2) Section 143 does not apply—

(a) to a vehicle owned—

(i) by the council of a county or county district in England and Wales, [the Broads Authority,] the Common Council of the City of London, the council of a London borough, [a National Park authority], the Inner London Education Authority, [the London Fire and Emergency Planning Authority] or a joint authority (other than a police authority) established by Part IV of the Local Government Act 1985,

(ii) by a [council constituted under section 2 of the Local Government, etc. (Scotland) Act 1994] in Scotland, or

(iii) by a joint board or committee in England or Wales, or joint committee in Scotland, which is so constituted as to include among its members representatives of any such council,

at a time when the vehicle is being driven under the owner's control,

(b) to a vehicle owned by a police authority . . . , at a time when it is being driven under the owner's control, or to a vehicle at a time when it is being driven for police purposes by or under the direction of a constable, or by a person employed by a police authority, . . . or

[(ba) to a vehicle owned by the Service Authority for the National Criminal Intelligence Service or the Service Authority for the National Crime Squad, at a time when it is being driven under the owner's control, or to a vehicle at a time when it is being driven for the purposes of the body maintained by such an Authority by or under the direction of a constable, or by a person employed by such an Authority;]

(c) to a vehicle at a time when it is being driven on a journey to or from any place undertaken for salvage purposes pursuant to Part IX of the [Merchant Shipping Act 1995],

(d) to the use of a vehicle for the purpose of its being provided in pursuance of a direction under section 166(2)(b) of the Army Act 1955 or under the corresponding provision of the Air Force Act 1955,

[(da) to a vehicle owned by a health service body, as defined in section 60(7) of the National Health Service and Community Care Act 1990 [by a Primary Care Trust established under section 16A of the National Health Service Act 1977] [or by the Commission for Health Improvement], at a time when the vehicle is being driven under the owner's control,]

[(db) to an ambulance owned by a National Health Service trust established under Part I of the National Health Service and Community Care Act 1990 or the National Health Service (Scotland) Act 1978, at a time when a vehicle is being driven under the owner's control,]

(e) to a vehicle which is made available by the Secretary of State to any person, body or local authority in pursuance of section 23 or 26 of the National Health Service Act 1977 at a time when it is being used in accordance with the terms on which it is so made available,

(f) to a vehicle which is made available by the Secretary of State to any local authority, education authority or voluntary organisation in Scotland in pursuance of section 15 or 16 of the National Health Service (Scotland) Act 1978 at a time when it is being used in accordance with the terms on which it is so made available.

[Section 144 is printed as amended by the Norfolk and Suffolk Broads Act 1988 (c. iv); the Road Traffic   **A25.304**
(Consequential Provisions) Act 1988, s.4 and Sched. 3, para.36; the National Health Service and Community Care Act 1990, s.60(2) and Sched. 8; the Road Traffic Act 1991, s.20(1)–(3); the Local Government, etc. (Scotland) Act 1994, s.180(1) and Sched. 13, para.159(8); the Environment Act 1995, s.78 and Sched. 10, para.29; the Merchant Shipping Act 1995, ss.314(2), 316(2) and Sched. 13, para.85; the Police Act 1997, s.134(1) and Sched. 9, para.59; the Health Act 1999 (Supplementary and Consequential Provisions) Order 1999 (S.I. 1999 No. 2795; not reproduced in this work), art.4; the Greater London Authority Act 1999, ss.325, 328, 423 and Scheds 27 (para.61), 29 (para.54) (and see also the Greater London Authority Act 1999 (Commencement No. 5 and Appointment of Reconstitution Day) Order 2000, S.I. 2000 No. 1094; not reproduced in this work), and 34 (Pt VII); the Health Act 1999 (Supplementary, Consequential, etc., Provisions) Order 2000 (S.I. 2000 No. 90; not reproduced in this work), art.3(1) and Sched. 1, para.23.

As to the inclusion of the Local Government Residuary Body for England among the bodies specified in section 144(2), see the Local Government Residuary Body (England) Order 1995 (S.I. 1995 No. 401; not reproduced in this work).

The depositing of money for the purposes of section 144(1) with the Accountant General is governed by the Motor Vehicles (Third-Party Risks Deposits) Regulations 1992 (S.I. 1992 No. 1284) (not reproduced in this work).]

145. Requirements in respect of policies of insurance

A25.305   (1) In order to comply with the requirements of this Part of this Act, a policy of insurance must satisfy the following conditions.

(2) The policy must be issued by an authorised insurer.

(3) Subject to subsection (4) below, the policy—

(a) must insure such person, persons or classes of persons as may be specified in the policy in respect of any liability which may be incurred by him or them in respect of the death of or bodily injury to any person or damage to property caused by, or arising out of, the use of the vehicle on a road [or other public place] in Great Britain, and

[(aa) must, in the case of a vehicle normally based in the territory of another member State, insure him or them in respect of any civil liability which may be incurred by him or them as a result of an event related to the use of the vehicle in Great Britain if,—

(i) according to the law of that territory, he or they would be required to be insured in respect of a civil liability which would arise under that law as a result of that event if the place where the vehicle was used when the event occurred were in that territory, and

(ii) the cover required by that law would be higher than that required by paragraph (a) above, and]

(b) must [, in the case of a vehicle normally based in Great Britain,] insure him or them in respect of any liability which may be incurred by him or them in respect of the use of the vehicle and of any trailer, whether or not coupled, in the territory other than Great Britain and Gibraltar of each of the member States of the Communities according to

[(i) the law on compulsory insurance against civil liability in respect of the use of vehicles of the State in whose territory the event giving rise to the liability occurred; or

(ii) if it would give higher cover, the law which would be applicable under this Part of this Act if the place where the vehicle was used when that event occurred were in Great Britain; and]

(c) must also insure him or them in respect of any liability which may be incurred by him or them under the provisions of this Part of this Act relating to payment for emergency treatment.

(4) The policy shall not, by virtue of subsection (3)(a) above, be required—

(a) to cover liability in respect of the death, arising out of and in the course of his employment, of a person in the employment of a person insured by the policy or of bodily injury sustained by such a person arising out of and in the course of his employment, or

(b) to provide insurance of more than £250,000 in respect of all such liabilities as may be incurred in respect of damage to property caused by, or arising out of, any one accident involving the vehicle, or

(c)   to cover liability in respect of damage to the vehicle, or

(d)   to cover liability in respect of damage to goods carried for hire or reward in or on the vehicle or in or on any trailer (whether or not coupled) drawn by the vehicle, or

(e)   to cover any liability of a person in respect of damage to property in his custody or under his control, or

(f)   to cover any contractual liability.

[(4A)   In the case of a person—

(a)   carried in or upon a vehicle, or

(b)   entering or getting on to, or alighting from, a vehicle,

the provisions of paragraph (a) of subsection (4) above do not apply unless cover in respect of the liability referred to in that paragraph is in fact provided pursuant to a requirement of the Employers' Liability (Compulsory Insurance) Act 1969.]

(5)   In this Part of this Act "*authorised insurer*" means a person or body of persons carrying on insurance business within Group 2 in Part II of Schedule 2 to the Insurance Companies Act 1982 and being a member of the Motor Insurers' Bureau (a company limited by guarantee and incorporated under the Companies Act 1929 on 14th June 1946).

(6)   If any person or body of persons ceases to be a member of the Motor Insurers' Bureau, that person or body shall not by virtue of that cease to be treated as an authorised insurer for the purposes of this Part of this Act [or the Road Traffic (NHS Charges) Act 1999]—

(a)   in relation to any policy issued by the insurer before ceasing to be such a member, or

(b)   in relation to any obligation (whether arising before or after the insurer ceased to be such a member) which the insurer may be called upon to meet under or in consequence of any such policy or under section 157 of this Act [or section 1 of the Act of 1999] by virtue of making a payment in pursuance of such an obligation.

[Section 145 is printed as amended by the Motor Vehicles (Compulsory Insurance) Regulations   **A25.306**
1992 (S.I. 1992 No. 3036; not reproduced in this work); the Road Traffic (NHS Charges) Act 1999 (except in relation to military hospitals), s.18(1)(a) and (b); the Road Traffic (NHS Charges) Act 1999 (Commencement No. 1) Order 1999 (S.I. 1999 No. 1075; not reproduced in this work); the Motor Vehicles (Compulsory Insurance) Regulations 2000 (S.I. 2000 No. 726; not reproduced in this work).

As to the implementation of EC law by S.I. 2000 No. 726, see the notes to section 143 above.

As to section 145(2), see the Motor Vehicles (Compulsory Insurance) (No. 2) Regulations 1973 (S.I. 1973 No. 2143), reg.8, not reproduced in this work.]

146. Requirements in respect of securities   *[Omitted.]*   **A25.307**

147. Issue and surrender of certificates of insurance and of security

(1)   A policy of insurance shall be of no effect for the purposes of this Part of this Act   **A25.308**
unless and until there is delivered by the insurer to the person by whom the policy is effected a certificate (in this Part of this Act referred to as a "*certificate of insurance*") in the prescribed form and containing such particulars of any conditions subject to which the policy is issued and of any other matters as may be prescribed.

(2)   *[Certificate of security.]*

(3) Different forms and different particulars may be prescribed for the purposes of subsection (1) or (2) above in relation to different cases or circumstances.

(4) Where a certificate has been delivered under this section and the policy or security to which it relates is cancelled by mutual consent or by virtue of any provision in the policy or security, the person to whom the certificate was delivered must, within seven days from the taking effect of the cancellation—

    (a) surrender the certificate to the person by whom the policy was issued or the security was given, or

    (b) if the certificate has been lost or destroyed, make a statutory declaration to that effect.

(5) A person who fails to comply with subsection (4) above is guilty of an offence.

A25.309   *[As to section 147(1), see the Motor Vehicles (Compulsory Insurance) (No. 2) Regulations 1973 (S.I. 1973 No. 2143), reg.8, not reproduced in this work.*

As to the prescribed forms of certificates under section 147(3) and provisions relating to the forms and completion of certificates, see the Motor Vehicles (Third Party Risks) Regulations 1972 (S.I. 1972 No. 1217), Schedule below.]

148. Avoidance of certain exceptions to policies or securities

A25.310   (1) Where a certificate of insurance or certificate of security has been delivered under section 147 of this Act to the person by whom a policy has been effected or to whom a security has been given, so much of the policy or security as purports to restrict—

    (a) the insurance of the persons insured by the policy, or

    (b) the operation of the security,

(as the case may be) by reference to any of the matters mentioned in subsection (2) below shall, as respects such liabilities as are required to be covered by a policy under section 145 of this Act, be of no effect.

(2) Those matters are—

    (a) the age or physical or mental condition of persons driving the vehicle,

    (b) the condition of the vehicle,

    (c) the number of persons that the vehicle carries,

    (d) the weight or physical characteristics of the goods that the vehicle carries,

    (e) the time at which or the areas within which the vehicle is used,

    (f) the horsepower or cylinder capacity or value of the vehicle,

    (g) the carrying on the vehicle of any particular apparatus, or

    (h) the carrying on the vehicle of any particular means of identification other than any means of identification required to be carried by or under [the Vehicle Excise and Registration Act 1994].

(3) Nothing in subsection (1) above requires an insurer or the giver of a security to pay any sum in respect of the liability of any person otherwise than in or towards the discharge of that liability.

(4) Any sum paid by an insurer or the giver of a security in or towards the discharge of any liability of any person which is covered by the policy or security by virtue only of subsection (1) above is recoverable by the insurer or giver of the security from that person.

(5) A condition in a policy or security issued or given for the purposes of this Part of this Act providing—

(a) that no liability shall arise under the policy or security, or

(b) that any liability so arising shall cease,

in the event of some specified thing being done or omitted to be done after the happening of the event giving rise to a claim under the policy or security, shall be of no effect in connection with such liabilities as are required to be covered by a policy under section 145 of this Act.

(6) Nothing in subsection (5) above shall be taken to render void any provision in a policy or security requiring the person insured or secured to pay to the insurer or the giver of the security any sums which the latter may have become liable to pay under the policy or security and which have been applied to the satisfaction of the claims of third parties.

(7) Notwithstanding anything in any enactment, a person issuing a policy of insurance under section 145 of this Act shall be liable to indemnify the persons or classes of persons specified in the policy in respect of any liability which the policy purports to cover in the case of those persons or classes of persons.

[Section 148 is printed as amended by the Vehicle Excise and Registration Act 1994, s.63 and Sched. **A25.311**
3, para.24(1).]

149. Avoidance of certain agreements as to liability towards passengers

(1) This section applies where a person uses a motor vehicle in circumstances such that **A25.312**
under section 143 of this Act there is required to be in force in relation to his use of it such a policy of insurance or such a security in respect of third-party risks as complies with the requirements of this Part of this Act.

(2) If any other person is carried in or upon the vehicle while the user is so using it, any antecedent agreement or understanding between them (whether intended to be legally binding or not) shall be of no effect so far as it purports or might be held—

(a) to negative or restrict any such liability of the user in respect of persons carried in or upon the vehicle as is required by section 145 of this Act to be covered by a policy of insurance, or

(b) to impose any conditions with respect to the enforcement of any such liability of the user.

(3) The fact that a person so carried has willingly accepted as his the risk of negligence on the part of the user shall not be treated as negativing any such liability of the user.

(4) For the purposes of this section—

(a) references to a person being carried in or upon a vehicle include references to a person entering or getting on to, or alighting from, the vehicle, and

(b) the reference to an antecedent agreement is to one made at any time before the liability arose.

150. Insurance or security in respect of private use of vehicle to cover use under car-sharing arrangements

(1) To the extent that a policy or security issued or given for the purposes of this Part of **A25.313**
this Act—

(a) restricts the insurance of the persons insured by the policy or the operation of the security (as the case may be) to use of the vehicle for specified purposes (for example, social, domestic and pleasure purposes) of a non-commercial character, or

    (b) excludes from that insurance or the operation of the security (as the case may be)—

        (i) use of the vehicle for hire or reward, or

        (ii) business or commercial use of the vehicle, or

        (iii) use of the vehicle for specified purposes of a business or commercial character,

then, for the purposes of that policy or security so far as it relates to such liabilities as are required to be covered by a policy under section 145 of this Act, the use of a vehicle on a journey in the course of which one or more passengers are carried at separate fares shall, if the conditions specified in subsection (2) below are satisfied, be treated as falling within that restriction or as not falling within that exclusion (as the case may be).

    (2) The conditions referred to in subsection (1) above are—

    (a) the vehicle is not adapted to carry more than eight passengers and is not a motor cycle,

    (b) the fare or aggregate of the fares paid in respect of the journey does not exceed the amount of the running costs of the vehicle for the journey (which for the purposes of this paragraph shall be taken to include an appropriate amount in respect of depreciation and general wear), and

    (c) the arrangements for the payment of fares by the passenger or passengers carried at separate fares were made before the journey began.

    (3) Subsections (1) and (2) above apply however the restrictions or exclusions described in subsection (1) are framed or worded.

    (4) In subsections (1) and (2) above "*fare*" and "*separate fares*" have the same meaning as in section 1(4) of the Public Passenger Vehicles Act 1981 [*q.v.*].

A25.314   **151. Duty of insurers or persons giving security to satisfy judgment against persons insured or secured against third-party risks**   *[Omitted.]*

152. Exceptions to section 151   *[Omitted.]*

153. Bankruptcy, etc., of insured or secured persons not to affect claims by third parties   *[Omitted.]*

154. Duty to give information as to insurance or security where claim made

A25.315   (1) A person against whom a claim is made in respect of any such liability as is required to be covered by a policy of insurance under section 145 of this Act must, on demand by or on behalf of the person making the claim—

    (a) state whether or not, in respect of that liability—

        (i) he was insured by a policy having effect for the purposes of this Part of this Act or had in force a security having effect for those purposes, or

        (ii) he would have been so insured or would have had in force such a security if the insurer or, as the case may be, the giver of the security had not avoided or cancelled the policy or security, and

    (b) if he was or would have been so insured, or had or would have had in force such a security—

        (i) give such particulars with respect to that policy or security as were specified in any certificate of insurance or security delivered in respect of that policy or security, as the case may be, under section 147 of this Act, or

(ii) where no such certificate was delivered under that section, give the following particulars, that is to say, the registration mark or other identifying particulars of the vehicle concerned, the number or other identifying particulars of the insurance policy issued in respect of the vehicle, the name of the insurer and the period of the insurance cover.

(2) If without reasonable excuse, a person fails to comply with the provisions of subsection (1) above, or wilfully makes a false statement in reply to any such demand as is referred to in that subsection, he is guilty of an offence.

155. Deposits   *[Omitted.]*   **A25.316**

156. Power to require evidence of insurance or security on application for vehicle excise licence   *[Omitted.]*

Payments for treatment of traffic casualties

157. Payment for hospital treatment of traffic casualties

(1) Subject to subsection (2) below, where—   **A25.317**

(a) a payment, other than a payment under section 158 of this Act, is made (whether or not with an admission of liability) in respect of the death of, or bodily injury to, any person arising out of the use of a motor vehicle on a road or in a place to which the public have a right of access, and

(b) the payment is made—

   (i) by an authorised insurer, the payment being made under or in consequence of a policy issued under section 145 of this Act, or

   (ii) by the owner of a vehicle in relation to the use of which a security under this Part of this Act is in force, or

   (iii) by the owner of a vehicle who has made a deposit under this Part of this Act, and

(c) the person who has so died or been bodily injured has to the knowledge of the insurer or owner, as the case may be, received treatment at a hospital, whether as an in-patient or as an out-patient, in respect of the injury so arising,

the insurer or owner must pay the expenses reasonably incurred by the hospital in affording the treatment, after deducting from the expenses any moneys actually received in payment of a specific charge for the treatment, not being moneys received under any contributory scheme.

(2) The amount to be paid shall not exceed [£2,949.00] for each person treated as an in-patient or [£295.00] for each person treated as an out-patient.

(3) For the purposes of this section "*expenses reasonably incurred*" means—

(a) in relation to a person who receives treatment at a hospital as an in-patient, an amount for each day he is maintained in the hospital representing the average daily cost, for each in-patient, of the maintenance of the hospital and the staff of the hospital and the maintenance and treatment of the in-patients in the hospital, and

(b) in relation to a person who receives treatment at a hospital as an out-patient, reasonable expenses actually incurred.

[Section 157 is printed as amended by the Road Traffic Accidents (Payments for Treatment) Order 1995   **A25.318**
(S.I. 1995 No. 889) (not reproduced in this work) and the sums set out above in section 157(2) relate to treatment given after April 16, 1995 and examinations made after that date of persons who die or suffer bodily injury.]

158. Payment for emergency treatment of traffic casualties

A25.319   (1) Subsection (2) below applies where—

    (a) medical or surgical treatment or examination is immediately required as a result of bodily injury (including fatal injury) to a person caused by, or arising out of, the use of a motor vehicle on a road, and

    (b) the treatment or examination so required (in this Part of this Act referred to as "*emergency treatment*") is effected by a legally qualified medical practitioner.

(2) The person who was using the vehicle at the time of the event out of which the bodily injury arose must, on a claim being made in accordance with the provisions of section 159 of this Act, pay to the practitioner (or, where emergency treatment is effected by more than one practitioner, to the practitioner by whom it is first effected)—

    (a) a fee of [£21.40] in respect of each person in whose case the emergency treatment is effected by him, and

    (b) a sum, in respect of any distance in excess of two miles which he must cover in order—

        (i) to proceed from the place from which he is summoned to the place where the emergency treatment is carried out by him, and

        (ii) to return to the first mentioned place,

        equal to [41 pence] for every complete mile and additional part of a mile of that distance.

(3) Where emergency treatment is first effected in a hospital, the provisions of subsections (1) and (2) above with respect to payment of a fee shall, so far as applicable, but subject (as regards the recipient of a payment) to the provisions of section 159 of this Act, have effect with the substitution of references to the hospital for references to a legally qualified medical practitioner.

(4) Liability incurred under this section by the person using a vehicle shall, where the event out of which it arose was caused by the wrongful act of another person, be treated for the purposes of any claim to recover damage by reason of that wrongful act as damage sustained by the person using the vehicle.

A25.320   *[Section 158 is printed as amended by the Road Traffic Accidents (Payments for Treatment) Order 1995 (S.I. 1995 No. 889) (not reproduced in this work) and the sums set out above in section 158(2) relate to treatment given after April 16, 1995 and examinations made after that date of persons who die or suffer bodily injury.]*

159. Supplementary provisions as to payments for treatment

A25.321   (1) A payment falling to be made under section 157 or 158 of this Act in respect of treatment in a hospital must be made [to the hospital].

(2) A claim for a payment under section 158 of this Act may be made at the time when the emergency treatment is effected, by oral request to the person who was using the vehicle, and if not so made must be made by request in writing served on him within seven days from the day on which the emergency treatment was effected.

(3) Any such request in writing—

    (a) must be signed by the claimant or, in the case of a hospital, by an executive officer of [the hospital claiming the payment],

    (b) must state the name and address of the claimant, the circumstances in which the emergency treatment was effected, and that it was first effected by the claimant or, in the case of a hospital, in the hospital, and

(c) may be served by delivering it to the person who was using the vehicle or by sending it in a prepaid registered letter, or the recorded delivery service, addressed to him at his usual or last known address.

(4) A payment made under section 158 of this Act shall operate as a discharge, to the extent of the amount paid, of any liability of the person who was using the vehicle, or of any other person, to pay any sum in respect of the expenses or remuneration of the practitioner or hospital concerned of or for effecting the emergency treatment.

(5) A chief officer of police must, if so requested by a person who alleges that he is entitled to claim a payment under section 158 of this Act, provide that person with any information at the disposal of the chief officer—

(a) as to the identification marks of any motor vehicle which that person alleges to be a vehicle out of the use of which the bodily injury arose, and

(b) as to the identity and address of the person who was using the vehicle at the time of the event out of which it arose.

[Section 159 is printed as amended by the Health Authorities Act 1995, s.2(1) and (3) and Sched. 1,   **A25.322**
para.117; the Road Traffic (NHS Charges) Act 1999 (except in relation to military hospitals), s.18(2)(a) and (b); the Road Traffic (NHS Charges) Act 1999 (Commencement No. 1) Order 1999 (S.I. 1999 No. 1075; not reproduced in this work).

Effect has been given above to the presumed legislative intention underlying the amendment to section 159(3)(a). The text of the Road Traffic (NHS Charges) Act 1999, s.18(2), appears to refer to the text of section 159(3)(a) before it was amended by the Health Authorities Act 1995.

The functions of the Secretary of State exercisable under section 159 in relation to Wales have been transferred to the National Assembly for Wales by the National Assembly for Wales (Transfer of Functions) Order 1999 (S.I. 1999 No. 672; not reproduced in this work), art.2 and Sched. 1.]

General

160. Regulations   *[Omitted.]*   **A25.323**

161. Interpretation

(1) In this Part of this Act—   **A25.324**

[*"hospital"* means any institution which provides medical or surgical treatment for in-patients, other than—

(a) a health service hospital within the meaning of the National Health Service Act 1977 or the National Health Service (Scotland) Act 1978,

(b) one which is a military hospital for the purposes of section 15 of the Road Traffic (NHS Charges) Act 1999, or

(c) any institution carried on for profit,]

"policy of insurance" includes a covering note,

"salvage" means the preservation of a vessel which is wrecked, stranded or in distress, or the lives of persons belonging to, or the cargo or apparel of, such a vessel, and

"under the owner's control" means, in relation to a vehicle, that it is being driven by the owner or by a servant of the owner in the course of his employment or is otherwise subject to the control of the owner.

(2) In any provision of this Part of this Act relating to the surrender, or the loss or destruction, of a certificate of insurance or certificate of security, references to such a certificate—

(a) shall, in relation to policies or securities under which more than one certificate is issued, be construed as references to all certificates, and

(b) shall, where any copy has been issued of any certificate, be construed as including a reference to that copy.

(3) In this Part of this Act, any reference to an accident includes a reference to two or more causally related accidents.

A25.325 *[Section 161 is printed as amended by the Road Traffic (NHS Charges) Act 1999 (except in relation to military hospitals), s.18(3)(a); the Road Traffic (NHS Charges) Act 1999 (Commencement No. 1) Order 1999 (S.I. 1999 No. 1075; not reproduced in this work).*
The term "military hospital" is defined in the Road Traffic (NHS Charges) Act 1999, s.15(2) as:

a hospital (as defined by section 128 of the National Health Service Act 1977) maintained by a Minister of the Crown wholly or partly for purposes of any part of the armed forces of the Crown.]

162. Index to Part VI

A25.326 The expressions listed in the left-hand column below are respectively defined or (as the case may be) fall to be construed in accordance with the provisions of this Part of this Act listed in the right-hand column in relation to those expressions.

Expression	*Relevant provision*
Accident	Section 161(3)
Authorised insurer	Section 145(2)
Certificate of insurance	Sections 147(1) and 161(2)
Certificate of security	Sections 147(2) and 161(2)
Hospital	Section 161(1)
Policy of insurance	Section 161(1)
Prescribed	Section 160(1)
Regulations	Section 160(1)
Salvage	Section 161(1)
Under the owner's control	Section 161(1)

PART VII

MISCELLANEOUS AND GENERAL

Powers of constables and other authorised persons

163. Power of police to stop vehicles

A25.327 (1) A person driving a [mechanically propelled vehicle] on a road must stop the vehicle on being required to do so by a constable in uniform.

(2) A person riding a cycle on a road must stop the cycle on being required to do so by a constable in uniform.

(3) If a person fails to comply with this section he is guilty of an offence.

A25.328 *[Section 163 is printed as amended by the Road Traffic Act 1991, s.48 and Sched. 4, para.67.]*

164. Power of constables to require production of driving licence and in certain cases statement of date of birth

(1) Any of the following persons—   A25.329

    (a) a person driving a motor vehicle on a road,

    (b) a person whom a constable [or vehicle examiner] has reasonable cause to believe to have been the driver of a motor vehicle at a time when an accident occurred owing to its presence on a road,

    (c) a person whom a constable [or vehicle examiner] has reasonable cause to believe to have committed an offence in relation to the use of a motor vehicle on a road, or

    (d) a person—

        (i) who supervises the holder of a provisional licence while the holder is driving a motor vehicle on a road, or

        (ii) whom a constable [or vehicle examiner] has reasonable cause to believe was supervising the holder of a provisional licence while driving, at a time when an accident occurred owing to the presence of the vehicle on a road or at a time when an offence is suspected of having been committed by the holder of the provisional licence in relation to the use of the vehicle on a road,

must, on being so required by a constable [or vehicle examiner], produce his licence for examination, so as to enable the constable [or vehicle examiner] to ascertain the name and address of the holder of the licence, the date of issue, and the authority by which it was issued.

(2) [A person required by a constable under subsection (1) above to produce his licence] must in prescribed circumstances, on being so required by the constable, state his date of birth.

(3) If—

    [(a) the Secretary of State has—

        (i) revoked a licence under section [92,] 93 or 99 [*q.v.*] of this Act, or

        (ii) revoked or suspended a large goods vehicle driver's licence or a passenger-carrying vehicle driver's licence under section 115 [*q.v.*] of this Act, and] [or]

        [(iii) served notice requiring the delivery of a licence to him in pursuance of section 99C or 115A of this Act,]

    (b) the holder of the licence fails to deliver it to the Secretary of State [or the traffic commissioner, as the case may be] in pursuance of [section [92,] 93, 99 [99C, 115A or 118] (as the case may be)],

a constable [or vehicle examiner] may require him to produce it, and upon its being produced may seize it and deliver it to the Secretary of State.

(4) Where a constable has reasonable cause to believe that the holder of a licence, or any other person, has knowingly made a false statement for the purpose of obtaining the grant of the licence, the constable may require the holder of the licence to produce it to him.

[(4A) Where a constable to whom a provisional licence has been produced by a person driving a motor bicycle has reasonable cause to believe that the holder was not driving it as part of the training being provided on a training course for motor cyclists, the constable may require him to produce the prescribed certificate of completion of a training course for motor cyclists.]

(5) Where a person has been required under [section 26 or 27 of the Road Traffic Offenders Act 1988[, section 40B of the Child Support Act 1991] [, section 40 of the

Crime (Sentences) Act 1997, section 146 or 147 of the Powers of Criminal Courts (Sentencing) Act 2000] or section 223A or 436A of the Criminal Procedure (Scotland) Act 1975] to produce a licence to the court and fails to do so, a constable may require him to produce it and, upon its being produced, may seize it and deliver it to the court.

(6) If a person required under the preceding provisions of this section to produce a licence or state his date of birth [or to produce his certificate of completion of a training course for motor cyclists] . . . fails to do so he is, subject to subsections (7) [to (8A)] below, guilty of an offence.

(7) Subsection (6) above does not apply where a person required on any occasion under the preceding provisions of this section to produce a licence—

    (a) produces on that occasion a current receipt for the licence issued under section 56 of the Road Traffic Offenders Act 1988 [*q.v.*] and, if required to do so, produces the licence in person immediately on its return at a police station that was specified on that occasion, or

    (b) within seven days after that occasion produces such a receipt in person at a police station that was specified by him on that occasion and, if required to do so, produces the licence in person immediately on its return at that police station.

(8) In proceedings against any person for the offence of failing to produce a licence it shall be a defence for him to show that—

    (a) within seven days after the production of his licence was required he produced it in person at a police station that was specified by him at the time its production was required, or

    (b) he produced it in person there as soon as was reasonably practicable, or

    (c) it was not reasonably practicable for him to produce it there before the day on which the proceedings were commenced,

and for the purposes of this subsection the laying of the information . . . shall be treated as the commencement of the proceedings.

[(8A) Subsection (8) above shall apply in relation to a certificate of completion of a training course for motor cyclists as it applies in relation to a licence.]

(9) Where in accordance with this section a person has stated his date of birth to a constable, the Secretary of State may serve on that person a notice in writing requiring him to provide the Secretary of State—

    (a) with such evidence in that person's possession or obtainable by him as the Secretary of State may specify for the purpose of verifying that date, and

    (b) if his name differs from his name at the time of his birth, with a statement in writing specifying his name at that time,

and a person who knowingly fails to comply with a notice under this subsection is guilty of an offence.

(10) A notice authorised to be served on any person by subsection (9) above may be served on him by delivering it to him or by leaving it at his proper address or by sending it to him by post; and for the purposes of this subsection and section 7 of the Interpretation Act 1978 in its application to this subsection the proper address of any person shall be his latest address as known to the person giving the notice.

[(11) In this section—

"*licence*" means a licence under Part III of this Act or a Community licence,

"*vehicle examiner*" means an examiner appointed under section 66A of this Act;

and "*Community licence*", "*counterpart*", "*provisional licence*", "*training course for motor cyclists*" and, in relation to such a course, "*the prescribed certificate of completion*" have the same meanings as in Part III of this Act.]

[*Section 164 is printed as amended by the Road Traffic (Driver Licensing and Information Systems) Act* **A25.330**
1989, s.7 and Sched. 3, para.18(a)–(d); the Road Traffic Act 1991, ss.48, 83, Sched. 4, para.68(1)–(8) and Sched. 8; the Driving Licences (Community Driving Licence) Regulations 1996 (S.I. 1996 No. 1974), reg.2 and Sched. 1, para.30 (not reproduced in this work); the Driving Licences (Community Driving Licence) Regulations 1998 (S.I. 1998 No. 1420), regs 2 and 14 (not reproduced in this work); the Powers of Criminal Courts (Sentencing) Act 2000, s.165(1) and Sched. 9, para.117; the Child Support, Pensions and Social Security Act 2000, s.16(4).

With effect from a date to be announced under the Transport Act 2000, s.275, the following amendments will be made to section 164 by the Transport Act, s.260 and Sched. 29, paras 1 and 5:

(i) *the following text will be substituted for section 164(4A) (Transport Act 2000, Sched. 29, paras 1 and 5(1) and (2))—*

[(4A) If regulations make provision for the evidencing of the successful completion of driver training courses or a person's being within the exemption specified in subsection (2), or any exemption provided by virtue of subsection (3), of section 99ZA of this Act, a person driving on a road a motor vehicle which he—

(a) is not authorised so to drive without having successfully completed such a course, or

(b) would not be authorised so to drive apart from the exemption,

may be required by a constable to produce prescribed evidence of the successful completion by him of such a course or of his being within the exemption.]

(ii) *the following words will be substituted in section 164(6) for the words "his certificate of completion of a training course for motor cyclists" (Transport Act 2000, Sched. 29, paras 1 and 5(1) and (3))—*

[prescribed evidence of the successful completion by him of a driver training course or of his being within an exemption]

(iii) *the following words will be substituted in section 164(8A) for the words "a certificate of completion of a training course for motor cyclists" (Transport Act 2000, Sched. 29, paras 1 and 5(1) and (4))—*

[prescribed evidence of the successful completion of a driver training course or of being within an exemption]

and

(iv) *in section 164(11), the words ["counterpart" and "provisional licence"] will be substituted for the words from " 'counterpart,' to 'completion' " (Transport Act 2000, Sched. 29, paras 1 and 5(1) and (5)).*

Section 260 of the 2000 Act, together with Schedule 29, paragraphs 1 and 4 thereto, was brought into force on February 1, 2001 by the Transport Act 2000 (Commencement No. 3) Order 2001 (S.I. 2001 No. 57; not reproduced in this volume), but S.I. 2001 No. 57 was itself amended by the Transport Act 2000 (Commencement No. 3) (Amendment) Order 2001 (S.I. 2001 No. 115; not reproduced in this work) so as to delete reference to (inter alia) section 260 and Schedule 29, paragraphs 1 and 4, from S.I. 2001 No. 57.

Words in section 164(8) relating exclusively and expressly to Scotland have been omitted.

The circumstances in which a police constable may require a person to state his date of birth are prescribed in the Motor Vehicles (Driving Licences) Regulations 1999 (S.I. 1999 No. 2864), reg.83 (q.v.).

As to the application of section 164(1), (6) and (8) to domestic driving permits, Convention driving permits, British Forces (BFG) driving licences and to the holders of such licences and permits, see the Motor

Vehicles (Driving Licences) Regulations 1999 (S.I. 1999 No. 2864), reg.80, below; and see also the Motor Vehicles (International Circulation) Order 1975 (S.I. 1975 No. 1208), Sched. 3, para.5(1) and (2)(a), below.

Proceedings under section 164(6) and (9) are specified by the Prosecution of Offences Act 1985 (Specified Proceedings) Order 1999 (S.I. 1999 No. 904) below as being proceedings the conduct of which the Director of Public Prosecutions is not required to take over from the police under the Prosecution of Offences Act 1985, s.3(3)(a).

Reference is made in section 164(5) above (and also in section 27(3) of the Road Traffic Offenders Act 1998) to section 40B of the Child Support Act 1991. The latter section, together with section 39A of the 1991 Act, was inserted into the 1991 Act by the Child Support, Pensions and Social Security Act 2000, s.16(1) and (3). Sections 39A and 40B of the 1991 Act read as follows:

39A. Commitment to prison and disqualification from driving

(1) Where the Secretary of State has sought—

    (a) in England and Wales to levy an amount by distress under this Act; or

    (b) to recover an amount by virtue of section 36 or 38,

and that amount, or any portion of it, remains unpaid he may apply to the court under this section.

(2) An application under this section is for whichever the court considers appropriate in all the circumstances of—

    (a) the issue of a warrant committing the liable person to prison; or

    (b) an order for him to be disqualified from holding or obtaining a driving licence.

(3) On any such application the court shall (in the presence of the liable person) inquire as to—

    (a) whether he needs a driving licence to earn his living;

    (b) his means; and

    (c) whether there has been wilful refusal or culpable neglect on his part.

(4) The Secretary of State may make representations to the court as to whether he thinks it more appropriate to commit the liable person to prison or to disqualify him from holding or obtaining a driving licence; and the liable person may reply to those representations.

(5) In this section and section 40B, "*driving licence*" means a licence to drive a motor vehicle granted under Part III of the Road Traffic Act 1988.

(6) In this section "*the court*" means—

    (a) in England and Wales, a magistrates' court;

    (b) *[applies to Scotland]*

40B. Disqualification from driving: further provision

(1) If, but only if, the court is of the opinion that there has been wilful refusal or culpable neglect on the part of the liable person, it may—

    (a) order him to be disqualified, for such period specified in the order but not exceeding two years as it thinks fit, from holding or obtaining a driving licence (a "*disqualification order*"); or

    (b) make a disqualification order but suspend its operation until such time and on such conditions (if any) as it thinks just.

(2) The court may not take action under both sections 40 and this section.

(3) A disqualification order must state the amount in respect of which it is made, which to be the aggregate of—

(a) the amount mentioned in section 35(1), or so much of it as remains outstanding; and

(b) an amount (determined in accordance with regulations made by the Secretary of State) in respect of the costs of the application under section 39A.

(4) A court which makes a disqualification order shall require the person to whom it relates to produce any driving licence held by him, and its counterpart (within the meaning of section 108(1) of the Road Traffic Act 1988).

(5) On an application by the Secretary of State of the liable person, the court—

(a) may make an order substituting a shorter period of disqualification, or make an order revoking the disqualification order, if part of the amount referred to in subsection (3) (the "*amount due*") is paid to any person authorised to receive it; and

(b) must make an order revoking the disqualification order if all of the amount is so paid.

(6) The Secretary of State may make representations to the court as to the amount which should be paid before it would be appropriate to make an order revoking the disqualification order under subsection (5)(a), and the person liable may reply to those representations.

(7) The Secretary of State may make a further application under section 39A if the amount due has not been paid in full when the period of disqualification specified in the disqualification order expires.

(8) Where a court—

(a) makes a disqualification order;

(b) makes an order under subsection (5); or

(c) allows an appeal against a disqualification order,

it shall send notice of that fact to the Secretary of State; and the notice shall contain such particulars and be sent in such manner and to such address as the Secretary of State may determine.

(9) Where a court makes a disqualification order, it shall also send the driving licence and its counterpart, on their being produced to the court, to the Secretary of State at such address as he may determine.

(10) Section 80 of the Magistrates' Courts Act 1980 (application of money found on defaulter) shall apply in relation to a disqualification order under this section in relation to a liable person as it applies in relation to the enforcement of a sum mentioned in subsection (1) of that section.

(11) The Secretary of State may by regulations make provision in relation to disqualification orders corresponding to the provision he may make under section 40(11).

(12) *[Applies to Scotland]*

Community driving licence. *In relation to driving licences which came into force after May 31,*   **A25.331**
1990 (after December 31, 1990 for Northern Ireland driving licences) only, s.164 was amended by the Driving Licences (Community Driving Licence) Regulations 1990 (S.I. 1990 No. 144) on April 1, 1990 so that:

   (i)   *in the words following after section 164(1)(d), the words "and its counterpart" were inserted after the first reference to the word "licence" and also the words "they were" were substituted in section 164(1)(d) for the words "it was";*

   (ii)   *the words "and its counterpart" were inserted in section 164(3) after the words "fails to deliver it";*

   (iii)   *the words "produce the licence and its counterpart" were substituted in section 164(3) for the words "produce it";*

   (iv)   *the word "their" was substituted in section 164(3) for the word "its";*

   (v)   *the word "them" was substituted in section 164(3) for the word "it" in each of the last two places at which it occurs;*

   (vi)   *the words "and its counterpart" were inserted in section 164(4) after the word "it";*

   (vii)   *the words "and its counterpart" were inserted in section 164(5) after the words "a licence";*

   (viii)   *the word "them" was substituted for each reference in section 164(5) for the word "it";*

   (ix)   *the word "theirs" was substituted in section 164(5) for the word "its";*

   (x)   *the words "and its counterpart" were inserted in section 164(6) after the word "licence";*

   (xi)   *the words "and its counterpart" were inserted in the words immediately preceding section 164(7)(a) after the word "licence";*

   (xii)   *the words "and its counterpart" were inserted in section 164(7)(a) after the word "licence" (in two places), and the word "their" was substituted in section 164(7)(a) for the word "its";*

   (xiii)   *the words "and its counterpart" were inserted in section 164(7)(b) after the word "licence", and the word "their" was substituted in section 164(7)(b) for the word "its";*

   (xiv)   *the words "and its counterpart" were inserted in section 164(8) after the word "licence" (in two places);*

   (xv)   *the word "them" was substituted in section 164(8) for the word "it" in the 2nd, 3rd and 5th place at which it occurs;*

   (xvi)   *the word "their" was substituted in section 164(8) for the word "its"; and*

   (xvii)   *the word ", 'counterpart' " was inserted in section 164(11) after the word " 'licence' ".]*

165. Power of constables to obtain names and addresses of drivers and others, and to require production of evidence of insurance or security and test certificates

A25.332   (1) Any of the following persons—

   (a) a person driving a motor vehicle (other than an invalid carriage) on a road, or

   (b) a person whom a constable [or vehicle examiner] has reasonable cause to believe to have been the driver of a motor vehicle (other than an invalid carriage) at a time when an accident occurred owing to its presence on a road [or other public place], or

   (c) a person whom a constable [or vehicle examiner] has reasonable cause to believe to have committed an offence in relation to the use on a road of a motor vehicle (other than an invalid carriage),

must, on being so required by a constable [or vehicle examiner], give his name and address and the name and address of the owner of the vehicle and produce the following documents for examination.

   (2) Those documents are—

   (a) the relevant certificate of insurance or certificate of security (within the meaning of Part VI of this Act), or such other evidence that the vehicle is not or was not being driven in contravention of section 143 of this Act as may be prescribed by regulations made by the Secretary of State,

(b) in relation to a vehicle to which section 47 of this Act applies, a test certificate issued in respect of the vehicle as mentioned in subsection (1) of that section, and

(c) in relation to a goods vehicle the use of which on a road without a plating certificate or goods vehicle test certificate is an offence under section 53(1) or (2) of this Act, any such certificate issued in respect of that vehicle or any trailer drawn by it.

(3) Subject to subsection (4) below, a person who fails to comply with a requirement under subsection (1) above is guilty of an offence.

(4) A person shall not be convicted of an offence under [subsection (3)] above by reason only of failure to produce any certificate or other evidence . . . if in proceedings against him for the offence he shows that—

(a) within seven days after the date on which the production of the certificate or other evidence was required it was produced at a police station that was specified by him at the time when its production was required, or

(b) it was produced there as soon as was reasonably practicable, or

(c) it was not reasonably practicable for it to be produced there before the day on which the proceedings were commenced,

and for the purposes of this subsection the laying of the information . . . shall be treated as the commencement of the proceedings.

(5) A person—

(a) who supervises the holder of a provisional licence granted under Part III of this Act while the holder is driving on a road a motor vehicle (other than an invalid carriage), or

(b) whom a constable [or vehicle examiner] has reasonable cause to believe was supervising the holder of such a licence while driving, at a time when an accident occurred owing to the presence of the vehicle on a road or at a time when an offence is suspected of having been committed by the holder of the provisional licence in relation to the use of the vehicle on a road,

must, on being so required by a constable [or vehicle examiner], give his name and address and the name and address of the owner of the vehicle.

(6) A person who fails to comply with a requirement under subsection (5) above is guilty of an offence.

(7) In this section "*owner*", in relation to a vehicle which is the subject of a hiring agreement, includes each party to the agreement [and "*vehicle examiner*" means an examiner appointed under section 66A of this Act].

[Section 165 is printed as amended by the Road Traffic (Driver Licensing and Information Systems) Act 1989, s.7 and Sched. 3, para.19; the Road Traffic Act 1991, ss.48, 83, Sched. 4, para.69(1)–(4) and Sched. 8; the Motor Vehicles (Compulsory Insurance)Regulations 2000 (S.I. 2000 No. 726; not reproduced in this work; as to S.I. 2000 No. 726, see further the notes to section 143 of this Act). **A25.333**

Words in section 165(4) relating exclusively and expressly to Scotland have been omitted.

Proceedings under section 165(3) and (6) are specified by the Prosecution of Offences Act 1985 (Specified Proceedings) Order 1999 (S.I. 1999 No. 904) below as being proceedings the conduct of which the Director of Public Prosecutions is not required to take over from the police under the Prosecution of Offences Act 1985, s.3(3)(a).

Section 165 does not apply to any person or vehicle in the service of a visiting force or headquarters (as defined); see the Visiting Forces and International Headquarters (Application of Law) Order 1999 (S.I. 1999 No. 1736; not reproduced in this work), art.8(1) and (2)(b).

The requirements under this section to produce test certificates and to give names and addresses, are expressly applied to persons in connection with vehicles to which section 47 of this Act applies, notwithstanding that such persons (or the drivers) are or were at any material time persons in the service of a visiting force or headquarters; see S.I. 1999 No. 1736, art.8(6).

The requirement under section 165(1) to produce any certificate mentioned in section 165(2)(c) applies to any person in connection with a goods vehicle so mentioned, notwithstanding that such person (or the driver) is or was at any material time a person in the service of a visiting force or headquarters; see the Visiting Forces and International Headquarters (Application of Law) Order 1999 (S.I. 1999 No. 1736; not reproduced in this work), art.8(7).]

[166. Powers of certain officers as respects goods vehicles and passenger-carrying vehicles

A25.334   [A person authorised for the purpose by a traffic commissioner appointed under the Public Passenger Vehicles Act 1981,] may, on production if so required of his authority, exercise in the case of goods vehicles or passenger-carrying vehicles of any prescribed class all such powers as are, under section 164(1) or (3) or 165 of this Act [*q.v.*], exercisable by a constable.]

A25.335   *[Section 166 is printed as substituted by the Road Traffic (Driver Licensing and Information Systems) Act 1989, s.7 and Sched. 3, para.20, and as subsequently amended by the Road Traffic Act 1991, s.48 and Sched. 4, para.70.]*

167. Power of arrest in Scotland for reckless or careless driving or cycling

A25.336   *[Omitted.]*

Duty to give name and address

168. Failure to give, or giving false, name and address in case of reckless or careless or inconsiderate driving or cycling

A25.337   Any of the following persons—

       (a) the driver of a [mechanically propelled vehicle] who is alleged to have committed an offence under section 2 or 3 of this Act, or

       (b) the rider of a cycle who is alleged to have committed an offence under section 28 or 29 of this Act,

who refuses, on being so required by any person having reasonable ground for so requiring, to give his name or address, or gives a false name or address, is guilty of an offence.

[Section 168 is printed as amended by the Road Traffic Act 1991, s.48 and Sched. 4, para.71.

Proceedings under section 168 are specified by the Prosecution of Offences Act 1985 (Specified Proceedings) Order 1999 (S.I. 1999 No. 904) below as being proceedings the conduct of which the Director of Public Prosecutions is not required to take over from the police under the Prosecution of Offences Act 1985, s.3(3)(a).]

169. Pedestrian contravening constable's direction to stop to give name and address

A25.338   A constable may require a person committing an offence under section 37 of this Act to give his name and address, and if that person fails to do so he is guilty of an offence.

Duties in case of accident

170. Duty of driver to stop, report accident and give information or documents

A25.339   (1) This section applies in a case where, owing to the presence of a [mechanically propelled vehicle] on a road [or other public place], an accident occurs by which—

       (a) personal injury is caused to a person other than the driver of that [mechanically propelled vehicle], or

(b) damage is caused—

    (i) to a vehicle other than that [mechanically propelled vehicle] or a trailer drawn by that [mechanically propelled vehicle], or

    (ii) to an animal other than an animal in or on that [mechanically propelled vehicle] or a trailer drawn by that [mechanically propelled vehicle], or

    (iii) to any other property constructed on, fixed to, growing in or otherwise forming part of the land on which the road [or place] in question is situated or land adjacent to such land.

(2) The driver of the [mechanically propelled vehicle] must stop and, if required to do so by any person having reasonable grounds for so requiring, give his name and address and also the name and address of the owner and the identification marks of the vehicle.

(3) If for any reason the driver of the [mechanically propelled vehicle] does not give his name and address under subsection (2) above, he must report the accident.

(4) A person who fails to comply with subsection (2) or (3) above is guilty of an offence.

(5) If, in a case where this section applies by virtue of subsection (1)(a) above, the driver of [a motor vehicle] does not at the time of the accident produce such a certificate of insurance or security, or other evidence, as is mentioned in section 165(2)(a) of this Act—

(a) to a constable, or

(b) to some person who, having reasonable grounds for so doing, has required him to produce it,

the driver must report the accident and produce such a certificate or other evidence.
This subsection does not apply to the driver of an invalid carriage.

(6) To comply with a duty under this section to report an accident or to produce such a certificate of insurance or security, or other evidence, as is mentioned in section 165(2)(a) of this Act, the driver—

(a) must do so at a police station or to a constable, and

(b) must do so as soon as is reasonably practicable and, in any case, within twenty-four hours of the occurrence of the accident.

(7) A person who fails to comply with a duty under subsection (5) above is guilty of an offence, but he shall not be convicted by reason only of a failure to produce a certificate or other evidence if, within [seven] days after the occurrence of the accident, the certificate or other evidence is produced at a police station that was specified by him at the time when the accident was reported.

(8) In this section "*animal*" means horse, cattle, ass, mule, sheep, pig, goat or dog.

[Section 170 is printed as amended by the Road Traffic Act 1991, s.48 and Sched. 4,   **A25.340**
para.72(1)–(4); the Motor Vehicles (Compulsory Insurance) Regulations 2000 (S.I. 2000 No. 726;
not reproduced in this work; as to S.I. 2000 No. 726, see further the notes to section 143 of this Act).
    The provisions of section 170(5)–(7) do not apply to any person or vehicle in the service of a visiting
force or headquarters (as defined); see the Visiting Forces and International Headquarters (Application of
Law) Order 1999 (S.I. 1999 No. 1736; not reproduced in this work), art.8(1) and (2)(b).]

Other duties to give information or documents

171. Duty of owner of motor vehicle to give information for verifying compliance with requirement of compulsory insurance or security

(1) For the purpose of determining whether a motor vehicle was or was not being driven   **A25.341**
in contravention of section 143 of this Act on any occasion when the driver was required

under section 165(1) or 170 of this Act to produce such a certificate of insurance or security, or other evidence, as is mentioned in section 165(2)(a) of this Act, the owner of the vehicle must give such information as he may be required, by or on behalf of a chief officer of police, to give.

(2) A person who fails to comply with the requirement of subsection (1) above is guilty of an offence.

(3) In this section "*owner*", in relation to a vehicle which is the subject of a hiring agreement, includes each party to the agreement.

A25.342 *[Section 171 does not apply to any person or vehicle in the service of a visiting force or headquarters (as defined); see the Visiting Forces and International Headquarters (Application of Law) Order 1999 (S.I. 1999 No. 1736; not reproduced in this work), art.8(1) and (2)(b).]*

[172. Duty to give information as to identity of driver, etc., in certain circumstances

A25.343 (1) This section applies—

(a) to any offence under the preceding provisions of this Act except—

(i) an offence under Part V, or
(ii) an offence under section 13, 16, 51(2), 61(4), 67(9), 68(4), 96 or 120,

and to an offence under section 178 of this Act,

(b) to any offence under sections 25, 26 or 27 of the Road Traffic Offenders Act 1988,

(c) to any offence against any other enactment relating to the use of vehicles on roads, except an offence under paragraph 8 of Schedule 1 to the Road Traffic (Driver Licensing and Information Systems) Act 1989, and

(d) to manslaughter . . . by the driver of a motor vehicle.

(2) Where the driver of a vehicle is alleged to be guilty of an offence to which this section applies—

(a) the person keeping the vehicle shall give such information as to the identity of the driver as he may be required to give by or on behalf of a chief officer of police, and

(b) any other person shall if required as stated above give any information which it is in his power to give and may lead to identification of the driver.

(3) Subject to the following provisions, a person who fails to comply with a requirement under subsection (2) above shall be guilty of an offence.

(4) A person shall not be guilty of an offence by virtue of paragraph (a) of subsection (2) above if he shows that he did not know and could not with reasonable diligence have ascertained who the driver of the vehicle was.

(5) Where a body corporate is guilty of an offence under this section and the offence is proved to have been committed with the consent or connivance of, or to be attributable to neglect on the part of, a director, manager, secretary or other similar officer of the body corporate, or a person who was purporting to act in any such capacity, he, as well as the body corporate, is guilty of that offence and liable to be proceeded against and punished accordingly.

(6) Where the alleged offender is a body corporate . . . or the proceedings are brought against him by virtue of subsection (5) above or subsection (11) below, subsection (4) above shall not apply unless, in addition to the matters there mentioned, the alleged offender shows that no record was kept of the persons who drove the vehicle and that the failure to keep a record was reasonable.

(7) A requirement under subsection (2) may be made by written notice served by post; and where it is so made—

(a) it shall have effect as a requirement to give the information within the period of 28 days beginning with the day on which the notice is served, and

(b) the person on whom the notice is served shall not be guilty of an offence under this section if he shows either that he gave the information as soon as reasonably practicable after the end of that period or that it has not been reasonably practicable for him to give it.

(8) Where the person on whom a notice under subsection (7) above is to be served is a body corporate, the notice is duly served if it is served on the secretary or clerk of that body.

(9) For the purposes of section 7 of the Interpretation Act 1978 as it applies for the purposes of this section the proper address of any person in relation to the service on him of a notice under subsection (7) above is—

(a) in the case of the secretary or clerk of a body corporate, that of the registered or principal office of that body or (if the body corporate is the registered keeper of the vehicle concerned) the registered address, and

(b) in any other case, his last known address at the time of service.

(10) In this section—

"*registered address*", in relation to the registered keeper of a vehicle, means the address recorded in the record kept under [the Vehicle Excise and Registration Act 1994] with respect to that vehicle as being that person's address, and

"*registered keeper*", in relation to a vehicle, means the person in whose name the vehicle is registered under that Act;

and references to the driver of a vehicle include references to the rider of a cycle.

(11) *[Offences committed in Scotland.]]*

[Section 172 is printed as substituted by the Road Traffic Act 1991, s.21, and as subsequently amended   **A25.344**
by the Vehicle Excise and Registration Act 1994, s.63 and Sched. 3, para.24(1).
Words relating expressly and exclusively to Scotland have been omitted from section 172(1)(d) and (6).
Proceedings under section 172(3) are specified by the Prosecution of Offences Act 1985 (Specified Proceedings) Order 1999 (S.I. 1999 No. 904) below as being proceedings the conduct of which the Director of Public Prosecutions is not required to take over from the police under the Prosecution of Offences Act 1985, s.3(3)(a).]

Forgery, false statements, etc.

173. Forgery of documents, etc.

(1) A person who, with intent to deceive—   **A25.345**

(a) forges, alters or uses a document or other thing to which this section applies, or

(b) lends to, or allows to be used by, any other person a document or other thing to which this section applies, or

(c) makes or has in his possession any document or other thing so closely resembling a document or other thing to which this section applies as to be calculated to deceive,

is guilty of an offence.

(2) This section applies to the following documents and other things—

(a) any licence under any Part of this Act,

[(aa) any counterpart of a Community licence,]

(b) any test certificate, goods vehicle test certificate, plating certificate, certificate of conformity or Minister's approval certificate (within the meaning of Part II of this Act),

(c) any certificate required as a condition of any exception prescribed under section 14 of this Act,

[(cc) any seal required by regulations made under section 41 of this Act with respect to speed limiters,]

(d) [any plate containing particulars required to be marked on a vehicle by regulations under section 41 of this Act] or containing other particulars required to be marked on a goods vehicle by section 54 to 58 of this Act or regulations under those sections,

[(dd) any document evidencing the appointment of an examiner under section 66A of this Act,]

(e) any records required to be kept by virtue of section 74 of this Act,

(f) any document which, in pursuance of section 89(3) . . . of this Act, is issued as evidence of the result of a test of competence to drive,

[(ff) any certificate provided for by regulations under section 97(3A) of this Act relating to the completion of a training course for motor cyclists,]

(g) any [certificate under section 133A or any] badge or certificate prescribed by regulations made by virtue of section 135 of this Act,

(h) any certificate of insurance or certificate of security under Part VI of this Act,

(j) any document produced as evidence of insurance in pursuance of Regulation 6 of the Motor Vehicles (Compulsory Insurance) (No. 2) Regulations 1973 [*S.I. 1973 No. 2143; not reproduced in this work*],

(k) any document issued under regulations made by the Secretary of State in pursuance of his power under section 165(2)(a) of this Act to prescribe evidence which may be produced in lieu of a certificate of insurance or a certificate of security, . . .

(l) any international road haulage permit [, and].

[a certificate of the kind referred to in section 34B(1) of the Road Traffic Offenders Act 1988.]

(3) In the application of this section to England and Wales "*forges*" means makes a false document or other thing in order that it may be used as genuine.

A25.346 *[Section 173 is printed as amended by the Road Traffic (Driver Licensing and Information Systems) Act 1989, s.7 and Sched. 3, para.22; the Road Traffic Act 1991, ss.48, 83, Sched. 4, para.73(1)–(6), and Sched. 8; the Road Traffic (Driving Instruction by Disabled Persons) Act 1993, s.6 and Schedule, paras 1 and 9; the Driving Licences (Community Driving Licence) Regulations 1996 (S.I. 1996 No. 1974), reg.2 and Sched. 1, para.32 (not reproduced in this work).*

A further sub-paragraph (also designated "cc") is prospectively inserted into section 173(2) by the Transport Act 1982, s.23(3), as amended by the 1989 Act, s.4 and Sched. 2, para.12. It reads:

[(cc) any notice removing a prohibition under [section 69 or 70] of this Act;].

As to the application of section 173 to domestic driving permits, Convention driving permits, British Forces (BFG) driving licences and to the holders of such licences and permits, see the Motor Vehicles (Driving Licences) Regulations 1999 (S.I. 1999 No. 2864), reg.80 below; and see also the Motor Vehicles (International Circulation) Order 1975 (S.I. 1975 No. 1208), Sched. 3, para.5(1) and (2)(c) below.

A25.347 **Community driving licence.** *In relation to driving licences which came into force after May 31, 1990 (after December 31, 1990 for Northern Ireland driving licences) only, section 173 was amended by the Driving Licences (Community Driving Licence) Regulations 1990 (S.I. 1990 No. 144) (as themselves* *amended by the Driving Licences (Community Driving Licence) Regulations 1996 (S.I. 1996 No. 1974), reg.2 and Sched. 1, para.32 (not reproduced in this work)) on April 1, 1990 so that:*

   (*i*)   *the words "or, in the case of a licence to drive, any counterpart of such a licence", were inserted at the end of section 173(2)(a); and*

   (*ii*)   *the following subsection was inserted after section 173(3):*

   [(4) In this section *"counterpart"* and *"Community licence"* have the same meanings as in Part III of this Act.]*]*

174. False statements and withholding material information

(1) A person who knowingly makes a false statement for the purpose—   **A25.348**

   (a)   of obtaining the grant of a licence under any Part of this Act to himself or any other person, or

   (b)   of preventing the grant of any such licence, or

   (c)   of procuring the imposition of a condition or limitation in relation to any such licence, or

   (d)   of securing the entry or retention of the name of any person in the register of approved instructors maintained under Part V of this Act, or

   [(dd)   of obtaining the grant to any person of a certificate under section 133A of this Act, or]

   (e)   of obtaining the grant of an international road haulage permit to himself or any other person,

is guilty of an offence.

(2) A person who, in supplying information or producing documents for the purposes either of sections 53 to 60 and 63 of this Act or of regulations made under section 49 to 51, 61, 62 and 66(3) of this Act—

   (a)   makes a statement which he knows to be false in a material particular or recklessly makes a statement which is false in a material particular, or

   (b)   produces, provides, sends or otherwise makes use of a document which he knows to be false in a material particular or recklessly produces, provides, sends or otherwise makes use of a document which is false in a material particular,

is guilty of an offence.

(3) A person who—

   (a)   knowingly produces false evidence for the purposes of regulations under section 66(1) of this Act, or

   (b)   knowingly makes a false statement in a declaration required to be made by the regulations,

is guilty of an offence.

(4) A person who—

   (a)   wilfully makes a false entry in any record required to be made or kept by regulations under section 74 of this Act, or

   (b)   with intent to deceive, makes use of any such entry which he knows to be false,

is guilty of an offence.

(5) A person who makes a false statement or withholds any material information for the purpose of obtaining the issue—

(a) of a certificate of insurance or certificate of security under Part VI of this Act, or

(b) of any document issued under regulations made by the Secretary of State in pursuance of his power under section 165(2)(a) of this Act to prescribe evidence which may be produced in lieu of a certificate of insurance or a certificate of security,

is guilty of an offence.

A25.349   *[Section 174 is printed as amended by the Road Traffic (Driving Instruction by Disabled Persons) Act 1993, s.6 and Schedule, paras 1 and 10.*

As to the application of section 174 to Convention driving permits, see the Motor Vehicles (International Circulation) Order 1975 (S.I. 1975 No. 1208), art.1(9) below.]

175. Issue of false documents

A25.350   If a person issues—

(a) any such document as is referred to in section 174(5)(a) or (b) of this Act, or

(b) a test certificate or certificate of conformity (within the meaning of Part II of this Act),

and the document or certificate so issued is to his knowledge false in a material particular, he is guilty of an offence.

A25.351   *[With effect from a date to be announced under the Transport Act 1982, s.76(2), the following will be substituted for the text of section 175 by the 1982 Act, s.24 (as amended by the Road Traffic (Consequential Provisions) Act 1988, s.4 and Sched. 2, Pt I, para.13(a)):*

[[175.] Falsification of documents

(1) A person shall be guilty of an offence who issues—

(a) any such document as is referred to in paragraph (a) or (b) of [section 174(5)] of this Act;

(b) a test certificate, plating certificate, goods vehicle test certificate or certificate of conformity;

(c) a certificate of temporary exemption under regulations made under [section 48(4) or 53(5)(b)] of this Act; or

(d) a notice removing a prohibition under [section 69 or 70] of this Act;

if the document or certificate so issued is to his knowledge false in a material particular.

(2) A person who amends a certificate of conformity shall be guilty of an offence if the certificate as amended is to his knowledge false in a material particular.

(3) Expressions used in subsection (1)(b) and (2) above have the same meanings as they respectively have for the purposes of Part II of this Act.]*/

176. Power to seize articles in respect of which offences under sections 173 to 175 may have been committed

A25.352   (1) If a constable has reasonable cause to believe that a document produced to him—

(a) in pursuance of section 137 of this Act, or

(b) in pursuance of any of the preceding provisions of this Part of this Act,

is a document in relation to which an offence has been committed under section 173, 174 or 175 of this Act or under section 115 of the Road Traffic Regulation Act 1984 [*q.v.*], he may seize the document.

(2) When a document is seized under subsection (1) above, the person from whom it was taken shall, unless—

(a)　the document has been previously returned to him, or

(b)　he has been previously charged with an offence under any of those sections,

be summoned before a magistrates' court . . . to account for his possession of the document.

(3) The court . . . must make such order respecting the disposal of the document and award such costs as the justice of the case may require.

(4) If a constable, [an examiner appointed under section 66A] of this Act has reasonable cause to believe that a document or plate carried on a motor vehicle or by the driver of the vehicle is a document or plate to which this subsection applies, he may seize it.

For the purposes of this subsection the power to seize includes power to detach from a vehicle.

(5) Subsection (4) above applies to a document or plate in relation to which an offence has been committed under sections 173, 174 or 175 of this Act in so far as they apply—

(a)　to documents evidencing the appointment of examiners [under section 66A] of this Act, or

(b)　to goods vehicle test certificates, plating certificates, certificates of conformity or Minister's approval certificates (within the meaning of Part II of this Act), or

(c)　to plates containing plated particulars (within the meaning of that Part) or containing other particulars required to be marked on goods vehicles by sections 54 to 58 of this Act or regulations made under them, or

(d)　to records required to be kept by virtue of section 74 of this Act, or

(e)　to international road haulage permits.

(6) When a document or plate is seized under subsection (4) above, either the driver or owner of the vehicle shall, if the document or plate is still detained and neither of them has previously been charged with an offence in relation to the document or plate under section 173, 174 or 175 of this Act, be summoned before a magistrates' court . . . to account for his possession of, or the presence on the vehicle of, the document or plate.

(7) The court . . . must make such order respecting the disposal of the document or plate and award such costs as the justice of the case may require.

[Section 176 is printed as amended by the Road Traffic Act 1991, s.48 and Sched. 4, para.74(1)–(3).　　**A25.353**
With effect from a date to be announced under the Transport Act 1982, s.76(2), two amendments will be made in section 176 by the 1982 Act, s.24(2) (as amended by the Road Traffic (Consequential Provisions) Act 1988, s.4 and Sched. 2, para.13(b); see also the Road Traffic Act 1991, s.83 and Sched. 8). These amendments are:

(i)　the following words will be substituted in section 176(4) for the words from "a certifying officer" to "this Act";

[a certifying officer or a public service vehicle examiner appointed under the Public Passenger Vehicles Act 1981, an examiner appointed under [section 68] of this Act or an authorised inspector under section 8 of the Transport Act 1982]

and

(ii)　the following words will be added to section 176(5)(b) after the words "plating certificates":

[notices removing prohibitions under [section 69 or 70] of this Act].

Words relating exclusively and expressly to Scotland have been omitted from section 176(2), (3), (6) and (7).

A25.354   ***Community driving licence.*** *In relation to driving licences which came into force after May 31, 1990 (after December 31, 1990 for Northern Ireland driving licences) only, section 176 was amended by the Driving Licences (Community Driving Licence) Regulations 1990 (S.I. 1990 No. 144) (as themselves amended by the Driving Licences (Community Driving Licence) Regulations 1996 (S.I. 1996 No. 1974), reg.2 and Sched. 1, para.33 (not reproduced in this work)) on April 1, 1990 so that:*

(i)   *the following subsection was inserted after section 176(1):*

[(1A) Where a licence to drive or a counterpart of any such licence or of any Community licence may be seized by a constable under subsection (1) above, he may also seize the counterpart, the licence to drive or the Community licence (as the case may be) produced with it.]

(ii)   *the following subsection was inserted after section 176(3):*

[(3A) An order under subsection (3) above respecting the disposal of [any such licence or Community licence] to drive or a counterpart of a licence may include an order respecting the disposal of any document seized under subsection (1A) above.] *and*

(iii)   *the following subsection was inserted after section 176(7):*

[(8) In this section "*counterpart*" and "*Community licence*" have the same meanings as in Part III of this Act.]]

177. Impersonation of, or of person employed by, authorised examiner

A25.355   If a person, with intent to deceive, falsely represents himself to be, or to be employed by, a person authorised [in accordance with regulations made under section 41 of this Act with respect to the checking and sealing of speed limiters or a person authorised] by the Secretary of State for the purposes of section 45 of this Act, he is guilty of an offence.

A25.356   *[Section 177 is printed as amended by the Road Traffic Act 1991, s.48 and Sched. 4, para.75.*

With effect from a date to be announced under the Road Traffic (Vehicle Testing) Act 1999, s.9(2), the following text will be substituted by ibid., s.7(1) and Schedule, para.3(1), for the text of section 177:

[**177. Impersonation of authorised examiner, etc.**

A person is guilty of an offence if, with intent to deceive, he falsely represents himself—

(a)   to be, or to be employed by, a person authorised in accordance with regulations made under section 41 of this Act with respect to the checking and sealing of speed limiters, or

(b)   to be a person entitled under section 45 of this Act to carry out examinations of vehicles under that section.]]

Offences in Scotland

A25.357   **178. Taking motor vehicle without authority, etc.**   *[Omitted.]*

Inquiries

179. General power to hold inquiries   *[Omitted.]*

180. General provisions as to inquiries   *[Omitted.]*

181. General provisions as to accident inquiries   *[Omitted.]*

182. Special provisions as to accident inquiries in Greater London
[Omitted.]

Application to the Crown

183. Application to the Crown

(1) Subject to the provisions of this section—   **A25.358**

    (a) Part I of this Act,

    (b) Part II of this Act, except sections 68 to 74 and 77,

    (c) Part III of this Act, except section 103(3),

    (d) Part IV of this Act, and

    (e) in this Part, sections 163, 164, 168, 169, 170(1) to (4), 177, 178, 181 and 182,

apply to vehicles and persons in the public service of the Crown.

(2) Sections 49 to 63 and [sections 64A, 65 and 65A] of this Act apply—

    (a) to vehicles in the public service of the Crown only if they are registered or liable to be registered under [the Vehicle Excise and Registration Act 1994], and

    (b) to trailers in the public service of the Crown only while drawn by vehicles (whether or not in the public service of the Crown) which are required to be so registered.

(3) Where those sections so apply they do so subject to the following modifications—

    (a) examinations of such vehicles in pursuance of regulations under section 49 or 61(2)(a) of this Act may be made by or under the directions of examiners authorised by the Secretary of State for the purpose instead of by or under the directions of examiners appointed under section [66A of this Act], . . .

    (b) *[Repealed.]*

(4) Neither section 97(3) nor section 98(3) of this Act, in so far as they prevent such a licence as is there mentioned from authorising a person to drive certain [motor bicycles] [and mopeds], applies—

    (a) in the case of [motor bicycles] [and mopeds] owned by the Secretary of State for Defence and used for naval, military or air force purposes, or

    (b) in the case of [motor bicycles] [and mopeds] so used while being ridden by persons for the time being subject to the orders of a member of the armed forces of the Crown.

(5) Subject to regulations made under subsection (2) of section 101 of this Act, that section (in so far as it prohibits persons under 21 from holding or obtaining a licence to drive motor vehicles or persons under 18 from holding or obtaining a licence to drive medium-sized goods vehicles) does not apply—

    (a) in the case of motor vehicles owned by the Secretary of State for Defence and used for naval, military or air force purposes, or

    (b) in the case of vehicles so used while being driven by persons for the time being subject to the orders of a member of the armed forces of the Crown.

[(6) The functions under Part IV of this Act of traffic commissioners in relation to licences issued to persons subject to the Naval Discipline Act 1957, to military law or to air force law to drive large goods vehicles or passenger-carrying vehicles in the public service of the Crown shall be exercised by the prescribed authority.]

(7) Section 165 of this Act, in so far as it provides for the production of test certificates and the giving of names and addresses, applies to a person in connection with a vehicle to

which section 47 of this Act applies notwithstanding that he or the driver is or was at any material time in the public service of the Crown.

(8) Subsection (1) of section 165 of this Act, in so far as it provides for the production of any certificate mentioned in subsection (2)(c) of that section, applies to a person in connection with a goods vehicle so mentioned notwithstanding that he or the driver is or was at any material time in the public service of the Crown.

A25.359   *[Section 183 is printed as amended by the Road Traffic (Driver Licensing and Information Systems) Act 1989, s.7 and Sched. 3, para.23; the Road Traffic Act 1991, ss.48, 83, Sched. 4, para.77, and Sched. 8; the Motor Vehicles (EC Type Approval) Regulations 1992 (S.I. 1992 No. 3107); the Vehicle Excise and Registration Act 1994, s.63 and Sched. 3, para.24(1); the Driving Licences (Community Driving Licence) Regulations 1996 (S.I. 1996 No. 1974), reg.2 and Sched. 1, para.34 (not reproduced in this work); the Driving Licences (Community Driving Licence) Regulations 1998 (S.I. 1998 No. 1420), regs 2 and 15 (not reproduced in this work).*

With effect from a date to be announced under the Road Traffic (Consequential Provisions) Act 1988, s.8(3), ibid., s.4 and Sched. 2, Pt I, para.18, will effect the following amendments to section 183:

   (i)   in section 183(2), for "63" there will be substituted "63A";

   (ii) the following words will be inserted at the end of section 183(3)(a)—

     [or of authorised inspectors under section 8 of the Transport Act 1982]

     and

   (iii) section 183(3)(b) will be omitted.

The Motor Vehicles (Driving Licences) Regulations 1999 (S.I. 1999 No. 2864) (q.v.) were made in part under section 183(6).]

184. Application of sections 5 to 10 to persons subject to service discipline

A25.360   (1) Sections 5 to 10 of this Act, in their application to persons subject to service discipline, apply outside as well as within Great Britain and have effect as if—

   (a) references to proceedings for an offence under any enactment included references to proceedings for the corresponding service offence,

   (b) references to the court included a reference to any naval, military or air force authority before whom the proceedings take place,

   (c) references to a constable included references to a member of the provost staff,

   (d) references to a police station included references to a naval, military or air force unit or establishment,

   (e) references to a hospital included references to a naval, military or air force unit or establishment at which medical or surgical treatment is provided for persons subject to service discipline, and

   (f) in section 6(1) the reference to a traffic offence included a reference to the corresponding service offence.

(2) In relation to persons for the time being subject to service discipline, the power to arrest conferred on a constable by section 4(6) of this Act is also exercisable by a member of the provost staff and is so exercisable outside as well as within Great Britain.

(3) In this section—

"*corresponding service offence*", in relation to an offence under any enactment, means an offence under section 42 of the Naval Discipline Act 1957 or an offence against section 70 of the Army Act 1955 or section 70 of the Air Force Act 1955 committed by an act or omission which is punishable under that enactment or would be so punishable if committed in Great Britain, "*member of the provost staff*" means a provost officer or any person legally exercising authority under or on behalf of a provost officer,

"*persons subject to service discipline*" means persons subject to that Act of 1957, to military law or to air force law and other persons to whom section 42 of that Act of 1957 or section 70 of either of those Acts of 1955 for the time being applies,

"*provost officer*" means a person who is a provost officer within the meaning of that Act of 1957 or either of those Acts of 1955.

Interpretation

185. Meaning of "motor vehicle" and other expressions relating to vehicles

(1) In this Act—   A25.361

"*heavy locomotive*" means a mechanically propelled vehicle which is not constructed itself to carry a load other than any of the excepted articles and the weight of which unladen exceeds 11690 kilograms,

"*heavy motor car*" means a mechanically propelled vehicle, not being a motor car, which is constructed itself to carry a load or passengers and the weight of which unladen exceeds 2540 kilograms,

"*invalid carriage*" means a mechanically propelled vehicle the weight of which unladen does not exceed 254 kilograms and which is specially designed and constructed, and not merely adapted, for the use of a person suffering from some physical defect or disability and is used solely by such a person,

"*light locomotive*" means a mechanically propelled vehicle which is not constructed itself to carry a load other than any of the excepted articles and the weight of which unladen does not exceed 11690 kilograms but does exceed 7370 kilograms,

"*motor car*" means a mechanically propelled vehicle, not being a motor cycle or an invalid carriage, which is constructed itself to carry a load or passengers and the weight of which unladen—

(a) if it is constructed solely for the carriage of passengers and their effects, is adapted to carry not more than seven passengers exclusive of the driver and is fitted with tyres of such type as may be specified in regulations made by the Secretary of State, does not exceed 3050 kilograms,

(b) if it is constructed or adapted for use for the conveyance of goods or burden of any description, does not exceed 3050 kilograms, or 3500 kilograms if the vehicle carries a container or containers for holding for the purposes of its propulsion any fuel which is wholly gaseous at 17.5 degrees Celsius under a pressure of 1.013 bar or plant and materials for producing such fuel,

(c) does not exceed 2540 kilograms in a case not falling within sub-paragraph (a) or (b) above,

"*motor cycle*" means a mechanically propelled vehicle, not being an invalid carriage, with less than four wheels and the weight of which unladen does not exceed 410 kilograms,

"*motor tractor*" means a mechanically propelled vehicle which is not constructed itself to carry a load, other than the excepted articles, and the weight of which unladen does not exceed 7370 kilograms,

"*motor vehicle*" means, subject to section 20 of the Chronically Sick and Disabled Persons Act 1970 (which makes special provision about invalid carriages, within the meaning of that Act), a mechanically propelled vehicle intended or adapted for use on roads, and

"*trailer*" means a vehicle drawn by a motor vehicle.

(2) In subsection (1) *"excepted articles"* means any of the following: water, fuel, accumulators and other equipment used for the purpose of propulsion, loose tools and loose equipment.

186. Supplementary provisions about those expressions

A25.362

(1) For the purposes of section 185 of this Act, a side-car attached to a motor vehicle, if it complies with such conditions as may be specified in regulations made by the Secretary of State, is to be regarded as forming part of the vehicle to which it is attached and as not being a trailer.

(2) For the purposes of section 185 of this Act, in a case where a motor vehicle is so constructed that a trailer may by partial super-imposition be attached to the vehicle in such a manner as to cause a substantial part of the weight of the trailer to be borne by the vehicle, that vehicle is to be deemed to be a vehicle itself constructed to carry a load.

(3) For the purposes of section 185 of this Act, in the case of a motor vehicle fitted with a crane, dynamo, welding plant or other special appliance or apparatus which is a permanent or essentially permanent fixture, that appliance or apparatus is not to be deemed to constitute a load or goods or burden of any description, but is to be deemed to form part of the vehicle.

(4)–(6) *[Power to vary maximum and minimum weights under section 185 by regulations.]*

187. Articulated vehicles

A25.363

(1) Unless it falls within subsection (2) below, a vehicle so constructed that it can be divided into two parts both of which are vehicles and one of which is a motor vehicle shall (when not so divided) be treated for the purposes of the enactments mentioned in subsection (3) below as that motor vehicle with the other part attached as a trailer.

(2) A passenger vehicle so constructed that—

(a) it can be divided into two parts, both of which are vehicles and one of which is a motor vehicle, but cannot be so divided without the use of facilities normally available only at a workshop, and

(b) passengers carried by it when not so divided can at all times pass from either part to the other,

shall (when not so divided) be treated for the purposes of the enactments mentioned in subsection (3) below as a single motor vehicle.

(3) The enactments referred to in subsection (1) and (2) above are the Road Traffic Act 1960, Parts I and II of the Public Passenger Vehicles Act 1981, and the Traffic Acts.

(4) In this section *"passenger vehicle"* means a vehicle constructed or adapted for use solely or principally for the carriage of passengers.

188. Hover vehicles

A25.364

(1) For the purposes of the Road Traffic Acts, a hovercraft within the meaning of the Hovercraft Act 1968 (in this section referred to as a hover vehicle)—

(a) is a motor vehicle, whether or not it is intended or adapted for use on roads, but

(b) apart from that is to be treated, subject to subsection (2) below, as not being a vehicle of any of the classes defined in section 185 of this Act.

(2) *[Regulations as to application of provisions of this Act to hover vehicles.]*

189. Certain vehicles not to be treated as motor vehicles

(1) For the purposes of the Road Traffic Acts— A25.365

    (a) a mechanically propelled vehicle being an implement for cutting grass which is controlled by a pedestrian and is not capable of being used or adapted for any other purpose,

    (b) any other mechanically propelled vehicle controlled by a pedestrian which may be specified by regulations made by the Secretary of State for the purposes of this section and section 140 of the Road Traffic Regulation Act 1984 [*q.v.*], and

    (c) an electrically assisted pedal cycle of such a class as may be prescribed by regulations so made,

is to be treated as not being a motor vehicle.

(2) In subsection (1) above "*controlled by a pedestrian*" means that the vehicle either—

    (a) is constructed or adapted for use only under such control, or

    (b) is constructed or adapted for use either under such control or under the control of a person carried on it, but is not for the time being in use under, or proceeding under, the control of a person carried on it.

[*The Electrically Assisted Pedal Cycles Regulations 1983 (S.I. 1983 No. 1168) have effect as if made under section 189(1)(c); see further §1.32 in Vol. 1.*] A25.366

190. Method of calculating weight of motor vehicles and trailers

(1) This section applies for the purposes of the Traffic Acts and of any other enactments relating to the use of motor vehicles or trailers on roads. A25.367

(2) The weight unladen of a vehicle or trailer shall be taken to be the weight of the vehicle or trailer—

    (a) inclusive of the body and all parts (the heavier being taken where alternative bodies or parts are used) which are necessary to or ordinarily used with the vehicle or trailer when working on a road, but

    (b) exclusive of the weight of water, fuel or accumulators used for the purpose of the supply of power for the propulsion of the vehicle or, as the case may be, of any vehicle by which the trailer is drawn, and of loose tools and loose equipment.

[*Section 190 does not apply to tramcars: Tramcars and Trolley Vehicles (Modification of Enactments) Regulations 1992 (S.I. 1992 No. 1217), reg.7.*] A25.368

191. Interpretation of statutory references to carriages

A motor vehicle or trailer— A25.369

    (a) is to be deemed to be a carriage within the meaning of any Act of Parliament, whether a public general Act or a local Act, and of any rule, regulation or byelaw made under any Act of Parliament, and

    (b) if used as a carriage of any particular class shall for the purpose of any enactment relating to carriages of any particular class be deemed to be a carriage of that class.

[*Section 191 does not apply to tramcars: Tramcars and Trolley Vehicles (Modification of Enactments) Regulations 1992 (S.I. 1992 No. 1217), reg.7.*] A25.370

192. General interpretation of Act

(1) In this Act— A25.371

["*approved testing authority*" means a person authorised by the Secretary of State under section 8 of the Transport Act 1982 to carry on a vehicle testing business within the meaning of Part II of that Act,]

"*bridleway*" means a way over which the public have the following, but no other, rights of way: a right of way on foot and a right of way on horseback or leading a horse, with or without a right to drive animals of any description along the way,

"*carriage of goods*" includes the haulage of goods,

"*cycle*" means a bicycle, a tricycle, or a cycle having four or more wheels, not being in any case a motor vehicle,

"*driver*", where a separate person acts as a steersman of a motor vehicle, includes (except for the purposes of section 1 of this Act) that person as well as any other person engaged in the driving of the vehicle, and "*drive*" is to be interpreted accordingly,

"*footpath*", in relation to England and Wales, means a way over which the public have a right of way on foot only,

"*goods*" includes goods or burden of any description,

"*goods vehicle*" means a motor vehicle constructed or adapted for use for the carriage of goods, or a trailer so constructed or adapted,

["*highway authority*", in England and Wales, means—

    (a) in relation to a road for which he is the highway authority within the meaning of the Highways Act 1980, the Secretary of State, and

    (b) in relation to any other road, the council of the county, metropolitan district or London borough, or the Common Council of the City of London, as the case may be;]

"*international road haulage permit*" means a licence, permit, authorisation or other document issued in pursuance of a Community instrument relating to the carriage of goods by road between member States or an international agreement to which the United Kingdom is a party and which relates to the international carriage of goods by road,

"*owner*", in relation to a vehicle which is the subject of a hiring agreement or hire-purchase agreement, means the person in possession of the vehicle under that agreement,

. . .

"*prescribed*" means prescribed by regulations made by the Secretary of State,

"*road*",

    [(a)] in relation to England and Wales, means any highway and any other road to which the public has access, and includes bridges over which a road passes, [and]

    [(b) *[applies to Scotland]*.]

"*the Road Traffic Acts*" means the Road Traffic Offenders Act 1988 [*q.v.*], the Road Traffic (Consequential Provisions) Act 1988 [*q.v.*] (so far as it reproduces the effect of provisions repealed by that Act) and this Act,

"*statutory*", in relation to any prohibition, restriction, requirement or provision, means contained in, or having effect under, an enactment (including any enactment contained in this Act),

"*the Traffic Acts*" means the Road Traffic Acts and the Road Traffic Regulation Act 1984 [*q.v.*],

"*traffic sign*" has the meaning given by section 64(1) of the Road Traffic Regulation Act 1984 [*q.v.*],

"*tramcar*" includes any carriage used on any road by virtue of an order under the Light Railways Act 1896, and "*trolley vehicle*" means a mechanically propelled vehicle adapted for use on roads without rails [under] power transmitted to it from some external source [(whether or not there is in addition a source of power on board the vehicle)].

[(1A) In this Act—

(a) any reference to a county shall be construed in relation to Wales as including a reference to a county borough; and

(b) section 17(4) and (5) of the Local Government (Wales) Act 1994 (references to counties and districts to be construed generally in relation to Wales as references to counties and county boroughs) shall not apply.]

(2) [*Applies to Scotland.*]

(3) References in this Act to a class of vehicles are to be interpreted as references to a class defined or described by reference to any characteristics of the vehicles or to any other circumstances whatsoever [and accordingly as authorising the use of "category" to indicate a class of vehicles, however defined or described].

[Section 192 is printed as amended by the Road Traffic (Driver Licensing and Information Systems) Act **A25.372**
1989, s.7 and Sched. 3, para.24; the Road Traffic Act 1991, s.48 and Sched. 4, para.78(1)–(3); the New Roads and Street Works Act 1991, s.168(1) and Sched. 8, Pt IV, para.121(1) and (4); the Local Government (Wales) Act 1994, s.22(1) and Sched. 7, para.40(1); the Access to Justice Act 1999, s.106 and Sched. 15, Pt V(1).

In section 192(1), the definition of "approved testing authority" has been prospectively inserted by the Road Traffic (Consequential Provisions) Act 1988, s.4 and Sched. 2, Pt I, para.19. That definition will be brought into force on a date to be announced; see ibid., s.8(3). Until such date, the text of section 192(1) should be read as if that definition were omitted.

The Motor Vehicles (Driving Licences) Regulations 1999 (S.I. 1999 No. 2864) (q.v.) were made in part under section 192(1).]

[192A. Tramcars and other guided vehicles: drink and drugs

(1) Sections 4 to 11 of this Act shall not apply (to the extent that apart from this subsec-   **A25.373**
tion they would) to vehicles on any transport system to which Chapter I of Part II of the Transport and Works Act 1992 (offences involving drink or drugs on railways, tramways and certain other guided transport systems) applies.

(2) Subject to subsection (1) above, the Secretary of State may by regulations provide that sections 4 to 11 of this Act shall apply to vehicles on a system of guided transport specified in the regulations with such modifications as he considers necessary or expedient.

(3) Regulations under subsection (2) above may make different provision for different cases.

(4) In this section—

"*guided transport*" means transport by vehicles guided by means external to the vehicles (whether or not the vehicles are also capable of being operated in some other way), and

"*vehicle*" includes mobile traction unit.]

[Section 192A was inserted by the Transport and Works Act 1992, s.39.]   **A25.374**

193.   *[Repealed by the Road Traffic Act 1991, s.83 and Sched. 8.]*   **A25.375**

[193A. Tramcars and trolley vehicles

(1) The Secretary of State may by regulations provide that such of the provisions men-   **A25.376**
tioned in subsection (2) below as are specified in the regulations shall not apply, or shall apply with modifications—

(a) to all tramcars or to tramcars of any specified class, or

(b) to all trolley vehicles or to trolley vehicles of any specified class.

(2) The provisions referred to in subsection (1) above are the provisions of—

(a) sections 12, 40A to 42, 47, 48, 66, 68 to 73, 75 to 79, 83, 87 to 109, 143 to 165, 168, 170, 171, 178, 190 and 191 of this Act, and

(b) sections 1, 2, 7, 8, 22, 25 to 29, 31, 32, 34 to 48, [91A, 91B,] 96 and 97 of the Road Traffic Offenders Act 1988 (provisions requiring warning of prosecution, etc., and provisions connected with the licensing of drivers).

(3) Regulations under this section—

(a) may make different provision for different cases,

(b) may include such transitional provisions as appear to the Secretary of State to be necessary or expedient, and

(c) may make such amendments to any special Act as appear to the Secretary of State to be necessary or expedient in consequence of the regulations or in consequence of the application to any tramcars or trolley vehicles of any of the provisions mentioned in subsection (2) above.

(4) In this section "*special Act*" means a local Act of Parliament passed before the commencement of this section which authorises or regulates the use of tramcars or trolley vehicles.]

A25.377   *[Section 193A was inserted by the Road Traffic Act 1991, s.46(2); the Driving Licences (Community Driving Licence) Regulations 1996 (S.I. 1996 No. 1974), reg.2 and Sched. 1, para.35 (not reproduced in this work).]*

194. General index

A25.378   The expressions listed in the left-hand column below are respectively defined or (as the case may be) fall to be construed in accordance with the provisions of this Act listed in the right-hand column in relation to those expressions.

Expression	*Relevant provision*
Bridleway	Section 192
Carriage of goods	Section 192
Carriageway	Section 192
Cycle	Section 192
Drive	Section 192
Driver	Section 192
Footpath	Section 192
Footway	Section 192
Goods	Section 192
Goods vehicle	Section 192
Goods vehicle test certificate	Section 49(2)(b)
Heavy locomotive	Section 185
Heavy motor car	Section 185
Highway authority	Section 192
International road haulage permit	Section 192
Invalid carriage	Section 185
Light locomotive	Section 185
Local roads authority	Section 192
Motor car	Section 185
Motor cycle	Section 185

[continued on next page

Expression	Relevant provision
Motor tractor	Section 185
Motor vehicle	Sections 185, 186(1), 187, 188, 189
Owner	Section 192
Plating certificate	Section 49(2)(a)
Prescribed	Section 192
Public road	Section 192
Road	Section 192
Roads authority	Section 192
Road Traffic Acts	Section 192
Special road	Section 192 .
Statutory	Section 192
Test certificate	Section 45(2)
Traffic Acts	Section 192
Traffic sign	Section 192
Trailer	Section 185
Tramcar	Section 192
Trolley vehicle	Section 192
Trunk road	Section 192
Unladen weight	Section 190

*[With effect from a date to be announced under the Transport Act 2000, s.275, the following entries will   **A25.379**
be inserted into the appropriate place in section 194 by the Transport Act 2000, s.260 and Sched. 29, paras
1 and 6:*

[*Driver training course*   Section 99ZA]

*Section 260 of the 2000 Act, together with Schedule 29, paragraphs 1 and 6 thereto, was brought into
force on February 1, 2001 by the Transport Act 2000 (Commencement No. 3) Order 2001 (S.I. 2001
No. 57; not reproduced in this work), but S.I. 2001 No. 57 was itself amended by the Transport Act
2000 (Commencement No. 3) (Amendment) Order 2001 (S.I. 2001 No. 115; not reproduced in this
work) so as to delete reference to (inter alia) section 260 and Schedule 29, paras 1 and 6, from S.I. 2001
No. 57.]*

Supplementary

195. Provisions as to regulations   *[Omitted.]*   **A25.380**

196. Provision, etc., of weighbridges   *[Omitted.]*

197. Short title, commencement and extent

(1) This Act may be cited as the Road Traffic Act 1988.   **A25.381**

(2) This Act shall come into force, *subject to the transitory provisions in Schedule 5 to the Road
Traffic (Consequential Provisions) Act 1988,* at the end of the period of six months beginning
with the day on which it is passed.

(3) This Act, except section 80 and except as provided by section 184, does not extend
to Northern Ireland.

[The words printed in italics in section 197(2) have lapsed.]   **A25.382**

Sections 17 and 18   SCHEDULE 1

Supplementary Provisions in Connection with Proceedings for Offences
under Sections [15A,] 17 and 18(4)

A25.383   *Note.*   The heading to Schedule 1 is printed as amended by the Motor Vehicles (Safety
Equipment for Children) Act 1991, s.2(1).

Proceedings in England and Wales

A25.384   **1.**—(1) A person against whom proceedings are brought in England and Wales for an
offence under section [15A,] 17 or 18(4) of this Act is, upon information duly laid by him
and on giving the prosecution not less than three clear days' notice of his intention, entitled
to have any person to whose act or default he alleges that the contravention of that section
was due brought before the court in the proceedings.

(2) If, after the contravention has been proved, the original accused proves that the contravention was due to the act or default of that other person—

(a) that other person may be convicted of the offence, and

(b) if the original accused further proves that he has used all due diligence to secure
that section 17 or, as the case may be, 18(4) was complied with, he shall be acquitted of the offence.

(3) Where an accused seeks to avail himself of the provisions of sub-paragraphs (1) and
(2) above—

(a) the prosecution, as well as the person whom the accused charges with the offence,
has the right to cross-examine him, if he gives evidence, and any witness called by
him in support of his pleas, and to call rebutting evidence, and

(b) the court may make such order as it thinks fit for the payment of costs by any party
to the proceedings to any other party to the proceedings.

A25.385   *[Paragraph 1 of Schedule 1 is printed as amended by the Motor Vehicles (Safety Equipment for Children)
Act 1991, s.2(1).]*

A25.386   **2.**—(1) Where—

(a) it appears that an offence under section [15A,] 17 or 18(4) of this Act has been committed in respect of which proceedings might be taken in England and Wales
against some person (referred to below in this paragraph as "*the original offender*"), and

(b) a person proposing to take proceedings in respect of the offence is reasonably
satisfied—

(i)   that the offence of which complaint is made was due to an act or default of
some other person, being an act or default which took place in England and
Wales, and

(ii) that the original offender could establish a defence under paragraph 1 of this
Schedule,

the proceedings may be taken against that other person without proceedings first being
taken against the original offender.

(2) In any such proceedings the accused may be charged with, and on proof that the
contravention was due to his act or default be convicted of, the offence with which the original offender might have been charged.

A25.387   *[Paragraph 2 of Schedule 1 is printed as amended by the Motor Vehicles (Safety Equipment for Children)
Act 1991, s.2(1).]*

3.—(1) Where proceedings are brought in England and Wales against a person (referred to below in this paragraph as "*the accused*") in respect of a contravention of section 17 or 18(4) of this Act and it is proved—   **A25.388**

  (a) that the contravention was due to the act or default of some other person, being an act or default which took place in Scotland, and

  (b) that the accused used all due diligence to secure compliance with that section,

the accused shall, subject to the provisions of this paragraph, be acquitted of the offence.

  (2) The accused is not entitled to be acquitted under this paragraph unless within seven days from the date of the service of the summons on him—

  (a) he has given notice in writing to the prosecution of his intention to rely upon the provisions of this paragraph, specifying the name and address of the person to whose act or default he alleges that the contravention was due, and

  (b) he has sent a like notice to that person.

  (3) The person specified in a notice served under this paragraph is entitled to appear at the hearing and give evidence and the court may, if it thinks fit, adjourn the hearing to enable him to do so.

  (4) Where it is proved that the contravention of section 17 or 18(4) of this Act was due to the act or default of some person other than the accused, being an act or default which took place in Scotland, the court must (whether or not the accused is acquitted) cause notice of the proceedings to be sent to the Secretary of State.

[Paragraph 3 of Schedule 1 is printed as amended by the Motor Vehicles (Safety Equipment for Children)   **A25.389**
Act 1991, s.2(1).]

Proceedings in Scotland

4. *[Omitted.]*   **A25.390**

Proceedings in Great Britain

5.—[(1A) Subject to the provisions of this paragraph, in any proceedings (whether in   **A25.391**
England and Wales or Scotland) for an offence under section 15A of this Act it shall be a defence for the accused to prove—

  (a) if the offence is under subsection (3)(a) of that section—

    (i) that he purchased the equipment in question as being of a type which could be lawfully sold or offered for sale as conducive to the safety in the event of accident of prescribed classes of children in prescribed classes of motor vehicles and with a written warranty to that effect;

    (ii) that he had no reason to believe at the time of the commission of the alleged offence that it was not of such a type; and

    (iii) that it was then in the same state as when he purchased it;

  (b) if the offence is under subsection (3)(b) of that section, he provided information in relation to the equipment and it is alleged that it did not include appropriate information or included or consisted of inappropriate information—

    (i) that the information provided by him was information which had been provided to him with a written warranty to the effect that it was the information required to be provided by him under section 15A of this Act; and

    (ii) that he had no reason to believe at the time of the commission of the alleged offence that the information provided by him was not the information required to be provided under that section; or

(c) if the offence is under subsection (3)(b) of that section, he provided information in relation to the equipment and it is alleged that it was not provided in the manner required under that section—

   (i) that the information provided by him had been provided to him either with a written warranty to the effect that it was provided to him in the manner in which it was required to be provided by him under that section or with instructions as to the manner in which the information should be provided by him and with a written warranty to the effect that provision in that manner would comply with regulations under that section;

   (ii) that he had no reason to believe at the time of the commission of the alleged offence that he was not providing the information in the manner required under that section; and

   (iii) that the information was then in the same state as when it was provided to him or, as the case may be, that it was provided by him in accordance with the instructions given to him.]

(1) Subject to the provisions of this paragraph, in any proceedings (whether in England and Wales or Scotland) for an offence under section 17 or 18(4) of this Act it shall be a defence for the accused to prove—

(a) that he purchased the helmet or appliance in question as being of a type which—

   (i) in the case of section 17, could be lawfully sold or offered for sale under that section, and

   (ii) in the case of section 18(4), could be lawfully sold or offered for sale under section 18 as authorised for use in the manner in question,

and with a written warranty to that effect, and

(b) that he had no reason to believe at the time of the commission of the alleged offence that it was not of such a type, and

(c) that it was then in the same state as when he purchased it.

(2) A warranty is only a defence in any such proceedings if—

(a) the accused—

   (i) has, not later than three clear days before the date of the hearing, sent to the prosecutor a copy of the warranty with a notice stating that he intends to rely on it and specifying the name and address of the person from whom he received it, and

   (ii) has also sent a like notice of his intention to that person, and

(b) in the case of a warranty given by a person outside the United Kingdom, the accused proves that he had taken reasonable steps to ascertain, and did in fact believe in, the accuracy of the statement contained in the warranty.

(3) Where the accused is a servant of the person who purchased the [equipment, helmet or appliance in question under a warranty, or to whom the information in question was provided] under a warranty, he is entitled to rely on the provisions of this paragraph in the same way as his employer would have been entitled to do if he had been the accused.

(4) The person by whom the warranty is alleged to have been given is entitled to appear at the hearing and to give evidence and the court may, if it thinks fit, adjourn the hearing to enable him to do so.

A25.392   *[Paragraph 5 of Schedule 1 is printed as amended by the Motor Vehicles (Safety Equipment for Children) Act 1991, s.2(2) and (3).]*

A25.393   [**6.**—(1) An accused who in any proceedings for an offence under section 15A, 17 or 18(4) of this Act wilfully applies to equipment, information, a helmet or, as the case may be, an appliance a warranty not given in relation to it is guilty of an offence.

(2) A person who, in respect of equipment, a helmet or an appliance sold by him, or information provided by him, being equipment, a helmet, an appliance or information in respect of which a warranty might be pleaded under paragraph 5 of this Schedule, gives to the purchaser a false warranty in writing, is guilty of an offence, unless he proves that when he gave the warranty he had reason to believe that the statements of description contained in it were accurate.

(3) Where the accused in a prosecution for an offence under section 15A, 17 or 18(4) of this Act relies successfully on a warranty given to him or his employer, any proceedings under sub-paragraph (2) above in respect of the warranty may, at the option of the prosecutor, be taken before a court having jurisdiction in the place—

(a) where the equipment, helmet or appliance, or any of the equipment, helmets or appliances, to which the warranty relates was procured;

(b) where the information, or any of it, to which the warranty relates was provided; or

(c) where the warranty was given.]

[Paragraph 6 of Schedule 1 is printed as substituted by the Motor Vehicles (Safety Equipment for Children) Act 1991, s.2(4).]   **A25.394**

[**7.** In this Schedule, "*equipment*" means equipment to which section 15A of this Act applies and "*appliance*" means an appliance to which section 18 of this Act applies.]   **A25.395**

[Paragraph 7 of Schedule 1 is printed as substituted by the Motor Vehicles (Safety Equipment for Children) Act 1991, s.2(4).]   **A25.396**

SCHEDULE 2   Section 67

DEFERRED TESTS OF CONDITION OF VEHICLES

1. Where the driver is the owner of the vehicle, he may at the time of electing that the test shall be deferred—   **A25.397**

(a) specify a period of seven days within which the deferred test is to take place, being a period falling within the next thirty days, disregarding any day on which the vehicle is outside Great Britain, and

(b) require that the deferred test shall take place on premises then specified by him where the test can conveniently be carried out or that it shall take place in such area in England . . ., being a county district or Greater London [in such county or county borough in Wales], or such area in Scotland, being [the area of a council constituted under section 2 of the Local Government, etc. (Scotland) Act 1994], as he may specify at that time.

[Paragraph 1 of Schedule 2 is printed as amended by the Local Government (Wales) Act 1994, ss.22(1) and 66(8), Sched. 7, para.40(2), and Sched. 18; the Local Government, etc. (Scotland) Act 1994, s.180(1) and Sched. 13, para.159(9).]   **A25.398**

2. When the driver is not the owner of the vehicle he shall inform the examiner of the name and address of the owner of the vehicle and the owner shall be afforded an opportunity of specifying such a period, and such premises or area.   **A25.399**

3.—(1) Where under the preceding provisions of this Schedule a period has been specified within which the deferred test is to be carried out, the time for carrying it out shall be such time within that period as may be notified, being a time not earlier than two days after the giving of the notification.   **A25.400**

(2) Where no such period has been specified, the time for the carrying out of the deferred test shall be such time as may be notified, being a time not earlier than seven days after the giving of the notification.

(3) Where premises have been specified under the preceding provisions of this Schedule for the carrying out of the deferred test, and the test can conveniently be carried out on those premises, it must be carried out there.

(4) Where sub-paragraph (3) above does not apply, the place for carrying out the deferred test shall be such place as may be notified with the notification of the time for the carrying out of the test, and where an area has been so specified the place shall be a place in that area.

(5) Notwithstanding the preceding provisions of this paragraph, the time and place for the carrying out of the deferred test may be varied by agreement between an authorised examiner and the owner of the vehicle.

(6) In this paragraph—

"*notified*" means notified in writing to the owner of the vehicle on behalf of the Secretary of State, and

"*notification*" shall be construed accordingly,

and any notification under this paragraph may be given by post.

A25.401 **4.** The owner of the vehicle must produce it, or secure its production, at the time and place fixed for the carrying out of the deferred test.

A25.402 **5.**—(1) References in this Schedule to the owner of a vehicle are references to the owner of the vehicle at the time at which the election is made under section 67(6) of this Act that the test should be deferred.

(2) For the purposes of this Schedule—

(a) subject to sub-paragraph (b) below, if at the time at which that election is made the vehicle is in the possession of a person under a hire-purchase agreement or hiring agreement, that person shall be deemed to be the owner of the vehicle to the exclusion of any other person,

(b) if at that time the vehicle is being used under an international circulation permit, the person to whom the permit was issued shall be deemed to be the owner of the vehicle to the exclusion of any other person.

A25.403 Section 131   SCHEDULE 3

APPEALS UNDER SECTION 131 AGAINST DECISIONS OF THE REGISTRAR

[Prospectively repealed by the Transport Act 2000, s.274 and Sched. 31, Pt V(1).]

SCHEDULE 4

PROVISIONS NOT APPLICABLE TO TRAMCARS, ETC.

A25.404   *[Repealed by the Road Traffic Act 1991, s.83 and Sched. 8.]*

The Road Traffic Offenders Act 1988

(1988 c. 53)

An Act to consolidate certain enactments relating to the prosecution and punishment (including the punishment without conviction) of road traffic offences with amendments to give effect to recommendations of the Law Commission and the Scottish Law Commission.

A26.01

[15th November 1988]

ARRANGEMENT OF SECTIONS

PART I
TRIAL

Introductory

Trial

PART III

FIXED PENALTIES

Introductory

Giving notices to suspected offenders

Notices fixed to vehicles

The fixed penalty procedure

Conditional offer of fixed penalty

Proceedings in fixed penalty cases

PART I

TRIAL

Introductory

1. Requirement of warning, etc., of prosecutions for certain offences

A26.03   (1) Subject to section 2 of this Act, [a person shall not be convicted of an offence to which this section applies unless]—

(a) he was warned at the time the offence was committed that the question of prosecuting him for some one or other of the offences to which this section applies would be taken into consideration, or

(b) within fourteen days of the commission of the offence a summons . . . for the offence was served on him, or

(c) within fourteen days of the commission of the offence a notice of the intended prosecution specifying the nature of the alleged offence and the time and place where it is alleged to have been committed, was—

    (i) in the case of an offence under section 28 or 29 of the Road Traffic Act 1988 (cycling offences), served on him,

    (ii) in the case of any other offence, served on him or on the person, if any, registered as the keeper of the vehicle at the time of the commission of the offence.

[(1A) A notice required by this section to be served on any person may be served on that person—

(a) by delivering it to him;

(b) by addressing it to him and leaving it at his last known address; or

(c) by sending it by registered post, recorded delivery service or first class post addressed to him at his last known address.]

(2) A notice shall be deemed for the purposes of subsection (1)(c) above to have been served on a person if it was sent by registered post or recorded delivery service addressed to him at his last known address, notwithstanding that the notice was returned as undelivered or was for any other reason not received by him.

(3) The requirement of subsection (1) above shall in every case be deemed to have been complied with unless and until the contrary is proved.

(4) Schedule 1 to this Act shows the offences to which this section applies.

[Section 1 is printed as amended by the Road Traffic Act 1991, s.48 and Sched. 4, para.80; the   **A26.04**
Criminal Justice and Public Order Act 1994, s.168(1) and Sched. 9, para.6(3).
Words in section 1(1)(b) relating exclusively and expressly to Scotland have been omitted.
In note 16A to the code of practice for the detention, treatment and questioning of persons by police officers (Code C (1995) under the Police and Criminal Evidence Act 1984) it is stated that the service of a notice of intended prosecution under section 1 and section 2 of this Act does not amount to informing a person that he may be prosecuted for an offence and so does not preclude further questioning in relation to that offence; in this context, see also paragraph 16.5 of that code.]

2. Requirement of warning, etc.: supplementary

(1) The requirement of section 1(1) of this Act does not apply in relation to an offence   **A26.05**
if, at the time of the offence or immediately after it, an accident occurs owing to the presence on a road of the vehicle in respect of which the offence was committed.

(2) The requirement of section 1(1) of this Act does not apply in relation to an offence in respect of which—

(a) a fixed penalty notice (within the meaning of Part III of this Act) has been given or fixed under any provision of that Part, or

(b) a notice has been given under section 54(4) of this Act.

(3) Failure to comply with the requirement of section 1(1) of this Act is not a bar to the conviction of the accused in a case where the court is satisfied—

(a) that neither the name and address of the accused nor the name and address of the registered keeper, if any, could with reasonable diligence have been ascertained in time for a summons or, as the case may be, a complaint to be served or for a notice to be served or sent in compliance with the requirement, or

(b) that the accused by his own conduct contributed to the failure.

[(4) Failure to comply with the requirement of section 1(1) of this Act in relation to an offence is not a bar to the conviction of a person of that offence by virtue of the provisions of—

(a) section 24 of this Act, or

(b) any of the enactments mentioned in section 24(6);

but a person is not to be convicted of an offence by virtue of any of those provisions if section 1 applies to the offence with which he was charged and the requirement of section 1(1) was not satisfied in relation to the offence charged.]

A26.06   *[Section 2 is printed as amended by the Road Traffic Act 1991, s.4 and Sched. 4, para.81. See also the notes to section 1 of this Act.]*

3. Restriction on institution of proceedings for certain offences

A26.07   (1) *[Repealed.]*

(2) In England and Wales, proceedings for an offence under section 94(3) of the Road Traffic Act 1988 (notice about relevant or prospective disability) shall not be instituted except by the Secretary of State or by a constable acting with the approval of the Secretary of State.

[(2A) In subsection (2) above the reference to section 94(3) of the Road Traffic Act 1988 includes a reference to that section as applied by section 99D of that Act.]

A26.08   *[Section 3 is printed as amended by the Road Traffic (Driver Licensing and Information Systems) Act 1989, s.16 and Sched. 6; the Driving Licences (Community Driving Licence) Regulations 1996 (S.I. 1996 No. 1974), reg.3 and Sched. 2, para.1 (not reproduced in this work).]*

4. Offences for which local authorities in England and Wales may institute proceedings

A26.09   (1) The council of a county, metropolitan district or London borough or the Common Council of the City of London may institute proceedings for an offence under section [15A of the Road Traffic Act 1988 (safety equipment for children in motor vehicles) or under section 17 or 18 of that Act] (helmets and other head-worn appliances for motor cyclists).

(2) The council of a county, metropolitan district or London borough or the Common Council of the City of London may institute proceedings for an offence under section 27 of that Act (dogs on roads) relating to a road in their area.

(3) The council of a county, district or London borough or the Common Council of the City of London may institute proceedings for offences under section [35A(1), (2) or (5)] of the Road Traffic Regulation Act 1984 which are committed in connection with parking places provided by the council, or provided under any letting arrangements made by the council under section 33(4) of that Act.

(4) The council of a county, metropolitan district or London borough or the Common Council of the City of London may institute proceedings for an offence under section 47 or 52 of the Road Traffic Regulation Act 1984 in connection with a designated parking place controlled by the council.

(5) In England, the council of a county or metropolitan district and, in Wales, the council of a county [or county borough] may institute proceedings for an offence under section 53 of the Road Traffic Regulation Act 1984 in connection with a designated parking place in the council's area . . .

(6) In this section "*parking place*" means a place where vehicles, or vehicles of any class, may wait and "*designated parking place*" has the same meaning as in the Road Traffic Regulation Act 1984.

(7) This section extends to England and Wales only.

[(8) In relation to Wales, any reference in subsections (1) to (4) above to a county shall be read as including a reference to a county borough.]

[Section 4 is printed as amended by the Parking Act 1989, s.4 and Sched., para.10; the Motor Vehicles (Safety Equipment for Children) Act 1991, s.3(1); the Local Government (Wales) Act 1994, ss.22(1) and 66(8), Sched. 7, para.41, and Sched. 18.   **A26.10**
The term "designated parking place" is defined in the Road Traffic Regulation Act 1984, s.142(1) (q.v.).]

5. Exemption from Licensing Act offence

A person liable to be charged with an offence under [section 3A, 4], 5, 7 or 30 of the Road Traffic Act 1988 (drink and drugs) is not liable to be charged under section 12 of the Licensing Act 1872 with the offence of being drunk while in charge, on a highway or other public place, of a carriage.   **A26.11**

[Section 5 is printed as amended by the Road Traffic Act 1991, s.48 and Sched. 4, para.82.]   **A26.12**

6. Time within which summary proceedings for certain offences must be commenced

(1) Subject to subsection (2) below, summary proceedings for an offence to which this section applies may be brought within a period of six months from the date on which evidence sufficient in the opinion of the prosecutor to warrant the proceedings came to his knowledge.   **A26.13**

(2) No such proceedings shall be brought by virtue of this section more than three years after the commission of the offence.

(3) For the purposes of this section, a certificate signed by or on behalf of the prosecutor and stating the date on which evidence sufficient in his opinion to warrant the proceedings came to his knowledge shall be conclusive evidence of that fact.

(4) A certificate stating that matter and purporting to be so signed shall be deemed to be so signed unless the contrary is proved.

(5) *[Applies to Scotland.]*

(6) Schedule 1 to this Act shows the offences to which this section applies.

[The application of section 6 has been extended to offences under the Goods Vehicles (Licensing of Operators) Act 1995, ss. 9(3)(a) and (b), 38 and 39 by ibid., s.51 below; but Schedule 1 to this Act has not been amended to give effect to this amendment.]   **A26.14**

7. Duty of accused to provide licence

[(1)] A person who is prosecuted for an offence involving [obligatory or discretionary endorsement] and who is the holder of a licence must—   **A26.15**

(a) cause it to be delivered to the [proper officer] of the court not later than the day before the date appointed for the hearing, or

(b) post it, at such a time that in the ordinary course of post it would be delivered not later than that day, in a letter duly addressed to the clerk and either registered or sent by the recorded delivery service, or

(c) have it with him at the hearing.

[(2) In subsection (1) above *"proper officer"* means—

    (a) in relation to a magistrates' court in England and Wales, the justices' chief executive for the court, and

    (b) in relation to any other court, the clerk of the court.]

A26.16   *[Section 7 is printed as amended by the Road Traffic Act 1991, s.48 and Sched. 4, para.83; and (with effect from April 1, 2001) the Access to Justice Act 1999, s.90(1) and Sched. 13, paras 140 and 141 (see the Access to Justice Act 1999 (Commencement No. 7, Transitional Provisions and Savings) Order 2001 (S.I. 2001 No. 916; not reproduced in this work), arts 1(2) and 2(a)(ii)).*

     As to the application of section 7 to domestic driving permits, Convention driving permits and British Forces (BFG) driving licences and to the holders of such licences and permits, see the Motor Vehicles (Driving Licences) Regulations 1999 (S.I. 1999 No. 2864), reg.80, below. As to the application of section 7 to Community licences, see section 91A(1) below.

A26.17   ***Community driving licence.*** *In relation to driving licences which came into force after May 31, 1990 (after December 31, 1990 for Northern Ireland driving licences) only, section 7 was amended by the Driving Licences (Community Driving Licence) Regulations 1990 (S.I. 1990 No. 144) on April 1, 1990 so that the following words were inserted after section 7(c):*

     and the foregoing obligations imposed on him as respects the licence also apply as respects the counterpart to the licence.*]*

8. Duty to include date of birth and sex in written plea of guilty

A26.18   A person who—

    (a) gives a notification [to a justices' chief executive in pursuance of section 12(4)] of the Magistrates' Courts Act 1980 (written pleas of guilty), or

    (b) *[applies to Scotland.]*

in respect of an offence involving obligatory or discretionary disqualification or of such other offence as may be prescribed by regulations under section 105 of the Road Traffic Act 1988, must include in the notification or intimation a statement of the date of birth and sex of the accused.

A26.19   *[Section 8 is printed as amended by the Magistrates' Courts (Procedure) Act 1998, s.4(1)(a); and (with effect from April 1, 2001) the Access to Justice Act 1999, s.90(1) and Sched. 13, paras 140 and 142 (see the Access to Justice Act 1999 (Commencement No. 7, Transitional Provisions and Savings) Order 2001 (S.I. 2001 No. 916; not reproduced in this work), arts 1(2) and 2(a)(ii)).]*

Trial

9. Mode of trial

A26.20   An offence against a provision of the Traffic Acts specified in column 1 of Part I of Schedule 2 to this Act or regulations made under such a provision (the general nature of which offence is indicated in column 2) shall be punishable as shown against the offence in column 3 (that is, on summary conviction or on indictment or in either one way or the other).

A26.21   ### 10. Jurisdiction of district court in Scotland   *[Omitted.]*

11. Evidence by certificate as to driver, user or owner

A26.22   (1) In any proceedings in England and Wales for an offence to which this section applies, a certificate in the prescribed form, purporting to be signed by a constable and certifying that a person specified in the certificate stated to the constable—

(a) that a particular [mechanically propelled vehicle] was being driven or used by, or belonged to, that person on a particular occasion, or

(b) that a particular [mechanically propelled vehicle] on a particular occasion was used by, or belonged to, a firm and that he was, at the time of the statement, a partner in that firm, or

(c) that a particular [mechanically propelled vehicle] on a particular occasion was used by, or belonged to, a corporation and that he was, at the time of the statement, a director, officer or employee of that corporation,

shall be admissible as evidence for the purpose of determining by whom the vehicle was being driven or used, or to whom it belonged, as the case may be, on that occasion.

(2) Nothing in subsection (1) above makes a certificate admissible as evidence in proceedings for an offence except in a case where and to the like extent to which oral evidence to the like effect would have been admissible in those proceedings.

(3) Nothing in subsection (1) above makes a certificate admissible as evidence in proceedings for an offence—

(a) unless a copy of it has, not less than seven days before the hearing or trial, been served in the prescribed manner on the person charged with the offence, or

(b) if that person, not later than three days before the hearing or trial or within such further time as the court may in special circumstances allow, serves a notice in the prescribed form and manner on the prosecutor requiring attendance at the trial of the person who signed the certificate.

[(3A) Where the proceedings mentioned in subsection (1) above are proceedings before a magistrates' court inquiring into an offence as examining justices this section shall have effect with the omission of—

(a) subsection (2), and

(b) in subsection (3), paragraph (b) and the word "or" immediately preceding it.]

(4) In this section "*prescribed*" means prescribed by rules made by the Secretary of State by statutory instrument.

(5) Schedule 1 to this Act shows the offences to which this section applies.

[Section 11 is printed as amended by the Road Traffic Act 1991, s.48 and Sched. 4, para.84; the **A26.23**
Criminal Procedure and Investigations Act 1996, s.47 and Sched. 1, para.35.
    Section 11(3A) applies in relation to any alleged offence in relation to which Part I of the 1996 Act applies (see the Criminal Procedure and Investigations Act 1996 (Commencement) (Section 65 and Schedules 1 and 2) Order 1997 (S.I. 1997 No. 683); not reproduced in this work).
    The Evidence by Certificate Rules 1961 (S.I. 1962 No. 248; not reproduced in this work) have effect as if made under section 11; see further §3.53 in Vol. 1.]

12. Proof, in summary proceedings, of identity of driver of vehicle

(1) Where on the summary trial in England and Wales of an information for an offence **A26.24**
to which this subsection applies—

(a) it is proved to the satisfaction of the court, on oath or in manner prescribed by rules made under section 144 of the Magistrates' Courts Act 1980, that a requirement under section 172(2) of the Road Traffic Act 1988 [*q.v.*] to give information as to the identity of the driver of a particular vehicle on the particular occasion to which the information relates has been served on the accused by post, and

(b) a statement in writing is produced to the court purporting to be signed by the accused that the accused was the driver of that vehicle on that occasion, the court may accept that statement as evidence that the accused was the driver of that vehicle on that occasion.

(2) Schedule 1 to this Act shows the offences to which subsection (1) above applies.

(3) Where on the summary trial in England and Wales of an information for an offence to which section 112 of the Road Traffic Regulation Act 1984 [*q.v.*] applies—

(a) it is proved to the satisfaction of the court, on oath or in manner prescribed by rules made under section 144 of the Magistrates' Courts Act 1980, that a requirement under section 112(2) of the Road Traffic Regulation Act 1984 to give information as to the identity of the driver of a particular vehicle on the particular occasion to which the information relates has been served on the accused by post, and

(b) a statement in writing is produced to the court purporting to be signed by the accused that the accused was the driver of that vehicle on that occasion,

the court may accept that statement as evidence that the accused was the driver of that vehicle on that occasion.

(4) *[Applies to Scotland.]*

A26.25   *[Section 12 has been amended by the Road Traffic Act 1991, s.48 and Sched. 4, para.85 (which inserted section 12(4)).]*

13. Admissibility of records as evidence

A26.26   (1) This section applies to a statement contained in a document purporting to be—

(a) a part of the records maintained by the Secretary of State in connection with any functions exercisable by him by virtue of Part III of the Road Traffic Act 1988 or a part of any other records maintained by the Secretary of State with respect to vehicles [or of any records maintained with respect to vehicles by an approved testing authority in connection with the exercise by that authority of any functions conferred on such authorities, or on that authority as such an authority, by or under any enactment], or

(b) a copy of a document forming part of those records, or

(c) a note of any information contained in those records,

and to be authenticated by a person authorised in that behalf by the Secretary of State [or (as the case may be) the approved testing authority].

(2) A statement to which this section applies shall be admissible in any proceedings as evidence . . . of any fact stated in it to the same extent as oral evidence of that fact is admissible in those proceedings.

[(3) In the preceding subsections, except in Scotland—

"*copy*", in relation to a document, means anything onto which information recorded in the document has been copied, by whatever means and whether directly or indirectly;

"*document*" means anything in which information of any description is recorded; and

"*statement*" means any representation of fact, however made.]

[(3A) In any case where—

(a) a person is convicted by a magistrates' court of a summary offence under the Traffic Acts or the Road Traffic (Driver Licensing and Information Systems) Act 1989,

(b) a statement to which this section applies is produced to the court in the proceedings,

(c) the statement specifies an alleged previous conviction of the accused of an offence involving obligatory endorsment or an order made on the conviction, and

(d) the accused is not present in the person before the court when the statement is produced,

the court may take account of the previous conviction or order as if the accused had appeared and admitted it.

(3B) Section 104 of the Magistrates' Courts Act 1980 (under which the previous convictions may be adduced in the absence of the accused after giving him seven days' notice of them) does not limit the effect of subsection (3A) above.]

(4) In any case where—

(a) a statement to which this section applies is produced to a magistrates' court in any proceedings for an offence involving obligatory or discretionary disqualification [other than a summary offence under any of the enactments mentioned in subsection (3A) above],

(b) the statement specifies an alleged previous conviction of an accused person of any such offence or any order made on the conviction,

(c) it is proved to the satisfaction of the court, on oath or in such manner as may be prescribed by rules under section 144 of the Magistrates' Courts Act 1980, that not less than seven days before the statement is so produced a notice was served on the accused, in such form and manner as may be so prescribed, specifying the previous conviction or order and stating that it is proposed to bring it to the notice of the court in the event of or, as the case may be, in view of his conviction, and

(d) the accused is not present in person before the court when the statement is so produced,

the court may take account of the previous conviction or order as if the accused had appeared and admitted it.

(5) Nothing in the preceding provisions of this section enables evidence to be given in respect of any matter other than a matter of a description prescribed by regulations made by the Secretary of State.

(6) *[Regulation-making power.]*

[(7) Where the proceedings mentioned in subsection (2) above are proceedings before a magistrates' court inquiring into an offence as examining justices this section shall have effect as if—

(a) in subsection (2) the words "to the same extent as oral evidence of that fact is admissible in those proceedings" were omitted;

(b) in subsection (4) the word "and" were inserted at the end of paragraph (a);

(c) in subsection (4), paragraphs (c) and (d) and the words "as if the accused had appeared and admitted it" were omitted.]

[Section 13 is printed as prospectively amended by the Road Traffic (Consequential Provisions) Act **A26.27**
1988, s.4 and Sched. 2, Pt I, para.20; and as amended by the Civil Evidence Act 1995, s.15(1) and Sched. 1, para.15; the Criminal Procedure and Investigations Act 1996, s.47 and Sched. 1, para.36; the Magistrates' Court (Procedure) Act 1998, s.2(1) and (2).

Section 13(3A) (which applies to Scotland) was inserted by the Civil Evidence Act 1995, s.15(1) and Sched. 1, para.15. Two new subsections were later inserted by the Magistrates' Courts (Procedure) Act 1998, s.2(1); these were designated as section 13(3A) and (3B), with the consequence that there are two subsections designated as section 3(3A).

Section 13(7), which was inserted by the Criminal Procedure and Investigations Act 1996, s.47 and Sched. 1, para.36, applies in relation to any alleged offence in relation to which Part I of the 1996 Act applies (see the Criminal Procedure and Investigations Act 1996 (Commencement) (Section 65 and Schedules 1 and 2) Order 1997 (S.I. 1997 No. 683); not reproduced in this work).

Words in section 13(2) which relate exclusively and expressly to Scotland have been omitted.

With regard to the application of section 13 to records maintained for the purposes of the Motor Vehicles (International Circulation) Order 1975 (S.I. 1975 No. 1208), art.1, see ibid., art.1(10) below.]

14. Use of records kept by operators of goods vehicles

A26.28   In any proceedings [for an offence under section 40A of the Road Traffic Act 1988 or] for a contravention of or failure to comply with construction and use requirements (within the meaning of Part II of the Road Traffic Act 1988) or regulations under section 74 of that Act [*q.v.*], any record purporting to be made and authenticated in accordance with regulations under that section shall be evidence . . . of the matters stated in the record and of its due authentication.

A26.29   *[Section 14 is printed as amended by the Road Traffic Act 1991, s.48 and Sched. 4, para.86.*
Words in section 14 which relate exclusively and expressly to Scotland have been omitted.
As to the meaning of the term "construction and use requirements" in Part II of the Road Traffic Act 1988, see ibid., s.41(7) above.]

15. Use of specimens in proceedings for an offence under section 4 or 5 of the Road Traffic Act

A26.30   (1) This section and section 16 of this Act apply in respect of proceedings for an offence under [section 3A, 4 or 5 of the Road Traffic Act 1988 (driving offences connected with drink or drugs)] [*q.v.*]; and expressions used in this section and section 16 of this Act have the same meaning as in [sections 3A to 10] of that Act.

(2) Evidence of the proportion of alcohol or any drug in a specimen of breath, blood or urine provided by the accused shall, in all cases [(including cases where the specimen was not provided in connection with the alleged offence)], be taken into account and, subject to subsection (3) below, it shall be assumed that the proportion of alcohol in the accused's breath, blood or urine at the time of the alleged offence was not less than in the specimen.

[(3) That assumption shall not be made if the accused proves—

(a) that he consumed alcohol before he provided the specimen and—

(i) in relation to an offence under section 3A, after the time of the alleged offence, and

(ii) otherwise, after he had ceased to drive, attempt to drive or be in charge of a vehicle on a road or other public place, and

(b) that had he not done so the proportion of alcohol in his breath, blood or urine would not have exceeded the prescribed limit and, if it is alleged that he was unfit to drive through drink, would not have been such as to impair his ability to drive properly.]

(4) A specimen of blood shall be disregarded unless it was taken from the accused with his consent by a medical practitioner.

(5) Where, at the time a specimen of blood or urine was provided by the accused, he asked to be provided with such a specimen, evidence of the proportion of alcohol or any drug found in the specimen is not admissible on behalf of the prosecution unless—

(a) the specimen in which the alcohol or drug was found is one of two parts into which the specimen provided by the accused was divided at the time it was provided, and

(b) the other part was supplied to the accused.

[Section 15 is printed as amended by the Road Traffic Act 1991, s.48 and Sched. 4, para.87(1)–(4). **A26.31**
The code of practice for the identification of persons by police officers does not affect any procedure under section 15 or section 16 of this Act; see paragraph 1.15(i) of Code D (1995) under the Police and Criminal Evidence Act 1984.]

16. Documentary evidence as to specimens in such proceedings

(1) Evidence of the proportion of alcohol or a drug in a specimen of breath, blood or   **A26.32**
urine may, subject to subsections (3) and (4) below and to section 15(5) of this Act, be given by the production of a document or documents purporting to be whichever of the following is appropriate, that is to say—

(a) a statement automatically produced by the device by which the proportion of alcohol in a specimen of breath was measured and a certificate signed by a constable (which may but need not be contained in the same document as the statement) that the statement relates to a specimen provided by the accused at the date and time shown in the statement, and

(b) a certificate signed by an authorised analyst as to the proportion of alcohol or any drug found in a specimen of blood or urine identified in the certificate.

(2) Subject to subsections (3) and (4) below, evidence that a specimen of blood was taken from the accused with his consent by a medical practitioner may be given by the production of a document purporting to certify that fact and to be signed by a medical practitioner.

(3) Subject to subsection (4) below—

(a) a document purporting to be such a statement or such a certificate (or both such a statement and such a certificate) as is mentioned in subsection (1)(a) above is admissible in evidence on behalf of the prosecution in pursuance of this section only if a copy of it either has been handed to the accused when the document was produced or has been served on him not later than seven days before the hearing, and

(b) any other document is so admissible only if a copy of it has been served on the accused not later than seven days before the hearing.

(4) A document purporting to be a certificate (or so much of a document as purports to be a certificate) is not so admissible if the accused, not later than three days before the hearing or within such further time as the court may in special circumstances allow, has served notice on the prosecutor requiring the attendance at the hearing of the person by whom the document purports to be signed.

(5) *[Applies to Scotland.]*

(6) A copy of a certificate required by this section to be served on the accused or a notice required by this section to be served on the prosecutor may be served personally or sent by registered post or recorded delivery service.

[(6A) Where the proceedings mentioned in section 15(1) of this Act are proceedings before a magistrates' court inquiring into an offence as examining justices this section shall have effect with the omission of subsection (4).]

(7) In this section *"authorised analyst"* means—

(a) any person possessing the qualifications prescribed by regulations made under [section 27 of the Food Safety Act 1990] as qualifying persons for appointment as public analysts under those Acts, and

(b) any other person authorised by the Secretary of State to make analyses for the purposes of this section.

A26.33   *[Section 16 is printed as amended by the Food Safety Act 1990, s.59(1) and Sched. 3, para.38; the Criminal Procedure and Investigations Act 1996, s.47 and Sched. 1, para.37.*

Section 16(6A), which was inserted by the Criminal Procedure and Investigations Act 1996, s.47 and Sched. 1, para.37, applies in relation to any alleged offence in relation to which Part I of the 1996 Act applies (see the Criminal Procedure and Investigations Act 1996 (Commencement) (Section 65 and Schedules 1 and 2) Order 1997 (S.I. 1997 No. 683); not reproduced in this work).

See also the notes to section 15 of this Act.]

17. Provisions as to proceedings for certain offences in connection with the construction and use of vehicles and equipment

A26.34   (1) If in any proceedings for an offence under [section 40A, 41A, 41B or 42 of the Road Traffic Act 1988 (using vehicle in dangerous condition or contravention] of construction and use regulations) [*q.v.*]—

     (a) any question arises as to weight of any description specified in the plating certificate for a goods vehicle, and

     (b) a weight of that description is marked on the vehicle,

it shall be assumed, unless the contrary is proved, that the weight marked on the vehicle is the weight so specified.

     (2) If, in any proceedings for an offence—

     (a) under Part II of the Road Traffic Act 1988, except sections 47 and 75, or

     (b) under section 174(2) or (5) (false statement and deception) of that Act,

any question arises as to the date of manufacture of a vehicle, a date purporting to be such a date and marked on the vehicle in pursuance of regulations under that Part of that Act shall be evidence . . . that the vehicle was manufactured on the date so marked.

     (3) If in any proceedings for the offence of driving a . . . vehicle on a road, or causing or permitting a . . . vehicle to be so driven, in contravention of a prohibition under section 70(2) of the Road Traffic Act 1988 any question arises whether a weight of any description has been reduced to a limit imposed by construction and use requirements [, or so that it has ceased to be excessive,] the burden of proof shall lie on the accused.

     (4) *[Applies to Scotland.]*

A26.35   *[Section 17 is printed as amended by the Road Traffic Act 1991, ss.48, 83, Sched. 4, para.88(1)–(3), and Sched. 8.*

Words in section 17(2) relating exclusively and expressly to Scotland have been omitted.]

18. Evidence by certificate as to registration of driving instructors and licences to give instruction

A26.36   (1) A certificate signed by the Registrar and stating that, on any date—

     (a) a person's name was, or was not, in the register,

     (b) the entry of a person's name was made in the register or a person's name was removed from it,

     (c) a person was, or was not, the holder of a current licence under section 129 of the Road Traffic Act 1988 [*q.v.*], or

(d) a licence under that section granted to a person came into force or ceased to be in force,

shall be evidence of the facts stated in the certificate in pursuance of this section.

(2) A certificate so stating and purporting to be signed by the Registrar shall be deemed to be so signed unless the contrary is proved.

(3) In this section *"current licence"*, *"Registrar"* and *"register"* have the same meanings as in Part V of the Road Traffic Act 1988.

[For the definitions of "current licence", "Registrar", and "register", see section 142 of the Road Traffic   **A26.37**
Act 1988 above.]

19. Evidence of disqualification in Scotland   *[Omitted.]*   **A26.38**

[20. Speeding offences, etc.: admissibility of certain evidence   **A26.39**

(1) Evidence . . . of a fact relevant to proceedings for an offence to which this section applies may be given by the production of—

(a) a record produced by a prescribed device, and

(b) (in the same or another document) a certificate as to the circumstances in which the record was produced signed by a constable or by a person authorised by or on behalf of the chief officer of police for the police area in which the offence is alleged to have been committed;

but subject to the following provisions of this section.

(2) This section applies to—

(a) an offence under section 16 of the Road Traffic Regulation Act 1984 consisting in the contravention of a restriction on the speed of vehicles imposed under section 14 of that Act;

(b) an offence under subsection (4) of section 17 of that Act consisting in the contravention of a restriction on the speed of vehicles imposed under that section;

(c) an offence under section 88(7) of that Act (temporary minimum speed limits);

(d) an offence under section 89(1) of that Act (speeding offences generally);

(e) an offence under section 36(1) of the Road Traffic Act 1988 consisting in the failure to comply with an indication given by a light signal that vehicular traffic is not to proceed.

[(f) an offence under Part I or II of the Road Traffic Regulation Act 1984 of contravening or failing to comply with an order or regulations made under either of those Parts relating to the use of an area of road which is described as a bus lane or a route for use by buses only.]

(3) The Secretary of State may by order amend subsection (2) above by making additions to or deletions from the list of offences for the time being set out there; and an order under this subsection may make such transitional provision as appears to him to be necessary or expedient.

(4) A record produced or measurement made by a prescribed device shall not be admissible as evidence of a fact relevant to proceedings for an offence to which this section applies unless—

(a) the device is of a type approved by the Secretary of State, and

(b) any conditions subject to which the approval was given are satisfied.

(5) Any approval given by the Secretary of State for the purposes of this section may be given subject to conditions as to the purposes for which, and the manner and other circumstances in which, any device of the type concerned is to be used.

(6) In proceedings for an offence to which this section applies, evidence . . . —

(a) of a measurement made by a device, or of the circumstances in which it was made, or

(b) that a device was of a type approved for the purposes of this section, or that any conditions subject to which an approval was given were satisfied,

may be given by the production of a document which is signed as mentioned in subsection (1) above and which, as the case may be, gives particulars of the measurement or of the circumstances in which it was made, or states that the device was of such a type or that, to the best of the knowledge and belief of the person making the statement, all such conditions were satisfied.

(7) For the purposes of this section a document purporting to be a record of the kind mentioned in subsection (1) above, or to be a certificate or other document signed as mentioned in that subsection or in subsection (6) above, shall be deemed to be such a record, or to be so signed, unless the contrary is proved.

(8) Nothing in subsection (1) or (6) above makes a document admissible as evidence in proceedings for an offence unless a copy of it has, not less than seven days before the hearing or trial, been served on the person charged with the offence; and nothing in those subsections makes a document admissible as evidence of anything other than the matters shown on a record produced by a prescribed device if that person, not less than three days before the hearing or trial or within such further time as the court may in special circumstances allow, serves a notice on the prosecutor requiring attendance at the hearing or trial of the person who signed the document.

(8A) *[Applies to Scotland.]*

[(8A) Where the proceedings for an offence to which this section applies are proceedings before a magistrates' court inquiring into an offence as examining justices this section shall have effect as if in subsection (8) the words from "and nothing" to the end of the subsection were omitted.]

(9) In this section "*prescribed device*" means a device of a description specified in an order made by the Secretary of State.

(10) *[Orders under section 20(3) and (9) to be statutory instruments.]]*

A26.40 *[Section 20 is printed as substituted by the Road Traffic Act 1991, s.23, and as subsequently amended by the Criminal Justice (Scotland) Act 1995, s.117(1) and Sched. 6, para.172; the Criminal Procedure and Investigations Act 1996, s.47 and Sched. 1, para.38; the Road Traffic Offenders (Additional Offences and Prescribed Devices) Order 1997 (S.I. 1997 No. 384; not reproduced in this work).*

Subsection 20(8A) was inserted after section 20(8) (with effect from March 31, 1996) by the Criminal Justice (Scotland) Act 1995, s.117(1) and Sched. 6, para.172 (see the Criminal Justice (Scotland) Act 1995 (Commencement No. 2, Transitional Provisions and Savings) Order 1996 (S.I. 1996 No. 517; not reproduced in this work).

The text of section 20(8A) reproduced above (as so numbered) was inserted after section 20(8) by the Criminal Procedure and Investigations Act 1996, s.47 and Sched. 1, para.38, with effect from March 8, 1997 in relation to any alleged offence in relation to which Part I of the 1996 Act applies (see the Criminal Procedure and Investigations Act 1996 (Commencement) (Section 65 and Schedules 1 and 2) Order 1997 (S.I. 1997 No. 683); not reproduced in this work).

Words relating expressly and exclusively to Scotland in section 20(1) and (6) have been omitted.

The Road Traffic Offenders (Prescribed Devices) Order 1992 (S.I. 1992 No. 1209; not reproduced in this work) (prescribing devices designed or adapted for measuring by radar the speed of motor vehicles), the Road Traffic Offenders (Prescribed Devices) (No. 2) Order 1992 (S.I. 1992 No. 2843; not reproduced in this work) (prescribing devices designed or adapted for recording by photographic or other image recording means the position of motor vehicles in relation to light signals), the Road Traffic Offenders (Prescribed Devices) Order 1993 (S.I. 1993 No. 1698; not reproduced in this work) (prescribing (i) devices designed or adapted for recording a measurement of the speed of motor vehicles activated by means of sensors or cables on or near the surface of the highway; and (ii) devices designed or adapted for recording a measurement of the speed of motor vehicles activated by means of a light beam or beams), the Road Traffic Offenders (Additional Offences and Prescribed Devices) Order 1997 (S.I. 1997 No. 384; not reproduced in this work) (prescribing a camera designed or adapted to record the presence of a vehicle on an area of road which is a bus lane or a route for use by buses only), and the Road Traffic (Prescribed Devices) Order 1999 (S.I. 1999 No. 162; not reproduced in this work) (prescribing a device designed or adapted for recording a measurement of the speed of motor vehicles by (i) capturing by unattended cameras images of the motor vehicle at each of two predetermined points on the road; (ii) digitally recording each image and the time at which it is captured; and (iii) calculating the average speed of the motor vehicle over the distance between the two positions by reference to the times at which each image is captured) have been made under section 20.

The following radar speed measuring devices were approved by the Home Secretary under the former provision and have continuing effect as if given for the purposes of section 20(4): Road Traffic Act 1991 (Commencement No. 4 and Transitional Provisions) Order 1992 (S.I. 1992 No. 1286) (not reproduced in this work) (and see also the Radar Speed Measuring Devices Revocation of Approval dated July 31, 1997):

Device	Date of approval	Effective date for use
Gatso Mini Radar Mk 3	July 1, 1986	July 31, 1986
Gatso Mini Radar Mk 4	July 1, 1986	July 31, 1986
Kustom HR4	July 1, 1986	July 31, 1986
Kustom HR8	July 1, 1986	July 31, 1986
Kustom Falcon	December 22, 1986	January 1, 1986
Kustom Roadrunner	December 22, 1986	January 1, 1987
Muniquip K-GP	October 12, 1989	November 8, 1989

The following devices have been approved by the Home Secretary under the above provisions:

Radar	Date of approval	Extent of approval	Effective date for use
Gatsometer BV Type 24+AUS[1]	June 24, 1992	s.20(2)(a)–(d)	July 1, 1992
Serco Speed Enforcement System Type 1[2]	May 22, 1995	s.20(2)(a)–(b)	May 24, 1995
Kustom Cordless Falcon	September 15, 1997	s.20(2)(a)–(d)	October 31, 1997
Speedar SR1 speed measuring device	January 20, 1998	s.20(2)(a)–(d)	February 10, 1998

[1] the Radar Speed Measuring Device Conditional Approval 2000 dated November 8, 2000 (not reproduced in this work), limits the approval of the Gatsometer BV Type 24 + AUS to the detection of speeding offences of 30 mph or above

[2] approved when operating singly on a gantry and on range 1 or 2 settings with either Techspan Systems Controlled Motorway Indicator Type 450EE or Securité et Signalisation (SES) Controlled Motorway Indicator Type 450EE

Light signals	Date of approval	Extent of approval	Effective date for use
Gatsometer BV Type 36	December 17, 1992	s.20(e)	January 1, 1993
Traffiphot IIIG Red light Monitor	December 17, 1992	s.20(e)	January 1, 1993
Interface[3]	July 7, 1999	s.20(2)(e)	July 17, 1999

[3] for railway level crossing signals; when manufactured by Peek Traffic Ltd for use only with CE approved version of Traffiphot IIIG Red Light Monitor; when manufactured by B.I.C. Electronics Ltd for use only with CE approved version of Gatsometer BV Type 36

Road sensors	Date of approval	Extent of approval	Effective date for use
micro Mercury Speed Measuring System 90500	July 25, 1993	s.20(2)(a)–(d)	August 9, 1993
micro Mercury Vision System 92600	July 25, 1993	s.20(2)(a)–(d)	August 9, 1993
Speedmaster DS2	July 25, 1993	s.20(2)(a)–(d)	August 9, 1993
Autovision 2[4] Truvelo M4 Squared Speed	July 25, 1993	s.20(2)(a)–(d)	August 9, 1993
Measuring Device Speedman Enforcement System	July 25, 1993	s.20(2)(a)–(d)	August 9, 1993
Traffiphot "S" Speed Detection Device	February 27, 1994	s.20(2)(a)–(d)	March 11, 1994
Truvelo Combi S Speed Camera System[5]	May 29, 1997	s.20(2)(a)–(d)	June 23, 1997
Truvelo Combi S-mc Speed Camera System[6]	April 8, 1999	s.20(2)(a)–(d)	April 15, 1999
Speedmaster DS3	May 14, 1999	s.20(2)(a)–(d)	May 24, 1999
Autovision 3 (AV3)[7]	May 14, 1999	s.20(2)(a)–(d)	May 24, 1999
Leica XV2 Speed Laser	February 7, 2001	s.20(2)(a)–(d)	February 12, 2001

[4] subject to the condition that it is used in conjunction with the Speedmaster DS2

[5] comprising the M4 Squared MPC Speedmaster and the Robot DCE camera, subject to the condition tht a magenta filter is used when photographing the front of a vehicle

[6] comprising the M4 Squared MPC Speedmeter, the Robot DCE camera and a memory card facility, provided that a magenta filter is used when photographing the front of a vehicle

[7] when used with Speedmaster DS3

Light beams	Date of approval	Extent of approval	Effective date for use
LTI 20.20 TS/M Speed Measuring Device	October 16, 1993	s.20(2)(a)–(d)	November 1, 1993
Kustom Prolaser II Speed Measuring Device	August 26, 1995	s.20(2)(a)–(d)	September 18, 1995
LTI 20.20 TS/M "Speedscope" Speed Measuring Device	March 20, 1996	s.20(2)(a)–(d)	April 1, 1996
LASTEC Local Video System[8]	January 20, 1998	s.20(2)(a)–(d)	February 10, 1998
LaserCam Digital Camera System[8]	February 9, 1998	s.20(2)(a)–(d)	February 26, 1998
RIEGL LR90-235/P	September 28, 1998	s.20(2)(a)–(d)	October 16, 1998
Cleartone Stealth Speedlaser	April 25, 1999	s.20(2)(a)–(d)	May 5, 1999
Laser Data Interface (LDI)[9]	May 14, 1999	s.20(2)(a)–(d)	May 24, 1999
Autovision 3 (AV3)[10]	May 14, 1999	s.20(2)(a)–(d)	May 24, 1999
Unipar Urban Speed Ace	May 17, 1999	s.20(2)(a)–(d)	May 28, 1999
LTI 20.20 Ultralyte 100	July 7, 1999	s.20(2)(a)–(d)	July 15, 1999
Jenoptik LaserPatrol Speedlaser	October 6, 1999	s.20(2)(a)–(d)	October 15, 1999

[8] when used in conjunction with either the LTI 20.20 TS/M speed measuring device or with the LTI 20.20 TS/M "Speedscope" speed measuring device

[9] when used with both the Kustom ProLaser II speed measuring device and Autovision 3 (AV3)

[10] when used with both the Kustom ProLaser II speed measuring device and the Laser date Interface (LDI)

Distance over time speed measurement	Date of approval	Extent of approval	Effective date for use
Speed Violation Detection Deterrent (SVDD)	March 19, 1999	s.20(2)(a)–(d)	April 1, 1999

Bus lane enforcement camera	Date of approval	Extent of approval	Effective date for use
JAI BUS-ter 2001[11]	October 29, 1997	s.20(2)(f)	December 5, 1997
Peek Guardian Freelane	August 25, 1998	s.20(2)(f)	September 7, 1998
Peek Guardian Freelane MKII	September 22, 2000	s.20(2)(f)	October 3, 2000

[11] approved when operating with the TM1/B Transponder and Odometer and the London Transport Buses Locational Microwave Beacon]

A26.41   **21. Proceedings in which evidence of one witness sufficient in Scotland**
[Omitted.]

22. Notification of disability

A26.42   (1) If in any proceedings for an offence committed in respect of a motor vehicle it appears to the court that the accused may be suffering from any relevant disability or prospective disability (within the meaning of Part III of the Road Traffic Act 1988) the court must notify the Secretary of State.

(2) A notice sent by a court to the Secretary of State in pursuance of this section must be sent in such manner and to such address and contain such particulars as the Secretary of State may determine.

A26.43   *[As to the meaning of the terms "relevant disability" and "prospective disability" in Part III of the Road Traffic Act 1988, see ibid., s.92(2) above.]*

Verdict

A26.44   **23. Alternative verdicts in Scotland**   *[Omitted.]*

[24. Alternative verdicts: general

A26.45   (1) Where—

(a) a person charged with an offence under a provision of the Road Traffic Act 1988 specified in the first column of the Table below (where the general nature of the offences is also indicated) is found not guilty of that offence, but

(b) the allegations in the indictment or information . . . amount to or include an allegation of an offence under one or more of the provisions specified in the corresponding entry in the second column,

he may be convicted of that offence or of one or more of those offences.

Offence charged	Alternative
Section 1 (causing death by dangerous driving)	Section 2 (dangerous driving) Section 3 (careless, and inconsiderate, driving)

[continued on next page

Offence charged	Alternative
Section 2 (dangerous driving)	Section 3 (careless, and inconsiderate, driving)
Section 3A (causing death by careless driving when under influence of drink or drugs)	Section 3 (careless, and inconsiderate, driving) Section 4(1) (driving when unfit to drive through drink or drugs) Section 5(1)(a) (driving with excess alcohol in breath, blood or urine) Section 7(6) (failing to provide specimen)
Section 4(1) (driving or attempting to drive when unfit to drive through drink or drugs)	Section 4(2) (being in charge of a vehicle when unfit to drive through drink or drugs)
Section 5(1)(a) (driving or attempting to drive with excess alcohol in breath, blood or urine)	Section 5(1)(b) (being in charge of a vehicle with excess alcohol in breath, blood or urine)
Section 28 (dangerous cycling)	Section 29 (careless, and inconsiderate, cycling)

(2) Where the offence with which a person is charged is an offence under section 3A of the Road Traffic Act 1988, subsection (1) above shall not authorise his conviction of any offence of attempting to drive.

(3) Where a person is charged with having committed an offence under section 4(1) or 5(1)(a) of the Road Traffic Act 1988 by driving a vehicle, he may be convicted of having committed an offence under the provision in question by attempting to drive.

(4) Where by virtue of this section a person is convicted before the Crown Court of an offence triable only summarily, the court shall have the same powers and duties as a magistrates' court would have had on convicting him of that offence.

(5) *[Convictions and penalties in Scotland.]*

(6) This section has effect without prejudice to section 6(3) of the Criminal Law Act 1967 (alternative verdicts on trial on indictment), [sections 295, 138(4), 256 and 293 of and Schedule 3 to the Criminal Procedure (Scotland) Act 1995] and section 23 of this Act.]

[Section 24 is printed as substituted by the Road Traffic Act 1991, s.24; and as subsequently amended   **A26.46**
by the Criminal Procedure (Consequential Provisions) (Scotland) Act 1995, s.5 and Sched. 4, para.71(1) and (3).

Words relating expressly and exclusively to Scotland in section 24(1) have been omitted.]

After conviction

25. Information as to date of birth and sex

(1) If on convicting a person of an offence involving obligatory or discretionary   **A26.47**
disqualification or of such other offence as may be prescribed by regulations under section 105 of the Road Traffic Act 1988 the court does not know his date of birth, the court must order him to give that date to the court in writing.

(2) If a court convicting a person of such an offence in a case where—

(a) notification has been given [to a justices' chief executive in pursuance of section 12(4)] of the Magistrates' Courts Act 1980 (written pleas of guilty) . . . , and

(b) the notification or intimation did not include a statement of the person's sex,

does not know the person's sex, the court must order the person to give that information to the court in writing.

(3) A person who knowingly fails to comply with an order under subsection (1) or (2) above is guilty of an offence.

(4) Nothing in [section 7 of the Powers of Criminal Courts (Sentencing) Act 2000] (where magistrates' court commits a person to the Crown Court to be dealt with, certain powers and duties transferred to that court) applies to any duty imposed upon a magistrates' court by subsection (1) or (2) above.

(5) Where a person has given his date of birth in accordance with this section or section 8 of this Act, the Secretary of State may serve on that person a notice in writing requiring him to provide the Secretary of State—

(a) with such evidence in that person's possession or obtainable by him as the Secretary of State may specify for the purpose of verifying that date, and

(b) if his name differs from his name at the time of his birth, with a statement in writing specifying his name at that time.

(6) A person who knowingly fails to comply with a notice under subsection (5) above is guilty of an offence.

(7) A notice to be served on any person under subsection (5) above may be served on him by delivering it to him or by leaving it at his proper address or by sending it to him by post; and for the purposes of this subsection and section 7 of the Interpretation Act 1978 in its application to this subsection the proper address of any person shall be his latest address as known to the person serving the notice.

A26.48   *[Section 25 is printed as amended by the Magistrates' Courts (Procedure) Act 1998, s.4(1)(a); the Powers of Criminal Courts (Sentencing) Act 2000, s.165(1) and Sched. 9, para.118; and (with effect from April 1, 2001) the Access to Justice Act 1999, s.90(1) and Sched. 13, paras 140 and 142 (see the Access to Justice Act 1999 (Commencement No. 7, Transitional Provisions and Savings) Order 2001 (S.I. 2001 No. 916; not reproduced in this work), arts 1(2) and 2(a)(ii)).*

Words in section 25(2) relating exclusively and expressly to Scotland have been omitted.]

[26. Interim disqualification

A26.49   (1) Where a magistrates' court—

(a) commits an offender to the Crown Court under [section 6 of the Powers of Criminal Courts (Sentencing) Act 2000 or any enactment mentioned in subsection (4) of that section] applies, or

(b) remits an offender to another magistrates' court under [section 10 of that Act],

to be dealt with for an offence involving obligatory or discretionary disqualification, it may order him to be disqualified until he has been dealt with in respect of the offence.

(2) Where a court in England and Wales—

(a) defers passing sentence on an offender under [section 1 of that Act] in respect of an offence involving obligatory or discretionary disqualification, or

(b) adjourns after convicting an offender of such an offence but before dealing with him for the offence,

it may order the offender to be disqualified until he has been dealt with in respect of the offence.

(3) *[Applies to Scotland.]*

(4) Subject to subsection (5) below, an order under this section shall cease to have effect at the end of the period of six months beginning with the day on which it is made, if it has not ceased to have effect before that time.

(5) *[Applies to Scotland.]*

(6) Where a court orders a person to be disqualified under this section (*"the first order"*), no court shall make a further order under this section in respect of the same offence or any offence in respect of which an order could have been made under this section at the time the first order was made.

(7) Where a court makes an order under this section in respect of any person it must—

  (a) require him to produce to the court any licence held by him and its counterpart, and

  (b) retain the licence and counterpart until it deals with him or (as the case may be) cause them to be sent to the [proper officer] of the court which is to deal with him.

[(7A) In subsection (7) above *"proper officer"* means—

  (a) in relation to a magistrates' court in England and Wales, the justices' chief executive for the court, and

  (b) in relation to any other court, the clerk of the court.]

(8) If the holder of the licence has not caused it and its counterpart to be delivered, or has not posted them, in accordance with section 7 of this Act and does not produce the licence and counterpart as required under subsection (7) above, then he is guilty of an offence.

(9) Subsection (8) above does not apply to a person who—

  (a) satisfies the court that he has applied for a new licence and has not received it, or

  (b) surrenders to the court a current receipt for his licence and its counterpart issued under section 56 of this Act, and produces the licence and counterpart to the court immediately on their return.

(10) Where a court makes an order under this section in respect of any person, sections 44(1) [, 47(2) and 91A(5)] of this Act and section 109(3) of the Road Traffic Act 1988 (Northern Ireland drivers' licences) shall not apply in relation to the order, but—

  (a) the court must send notice of the order to the Secretary of State, and

  (b) if the court which deals with the offender determines not to order him to be disqualified under section 34 or 35 of this Act, it must send notice of the determination to the Secretary of State.

(11) A notice sent by a court to the Secretary of State in pursuance of subsection (10) above must be sent in such manner and to such address and contain such particulars as the Secretary of State may determine.

(12) Where on any occasion a court deals with an offender—

  (a) for an offence in respect of which an order was made under this section, or

  (b) for two or more offences in respect of any of which such an order was made,

any period of disqualification which is on that occasion imposed under section 34 or 35 of this Act shall be treated as reduced by any period during which he was disqualified by reason only of an order made under this section in respect of any of those offences.

(13) Any reference in this or any other Act (including any Act passed after this Act) to the length of a period of disqualification shall, unless the context otherwise requires, be construed as a reference to its length before any reduction under this section.

(14) In relation to licences which came into force before 1st June 1990, the references in this section to counterparts of licences shall be disregarded.]

A26.50 *[Section 26 is printed as substituted by the Road Traffic Act 1991, s.25, and as subsequently amended by the Driving Licences (Community Driving Licence) Regulations 1996 (S.I. 1996 No. 1974), reg.3 and Sched. 1, para.2 (not reproduced in this work); the Powers of Criminal Courts (Sentencing) Act 2000, s.165(1) and Sched. 9, para.119; and (with effect from April 1, 2001) the Access to Justice Act 1999, s.90(1) and Sched. 13, paras 140 and 143 (see the Access to Justice Act 1999 (Commencement No. 7, Transitional Provisions and Savings) Order 2001 (S.I. 2001 No. 916; not reproduced in this work), arts 1(2) and 2(a)(ii)).*

In amending section 26, the Access to Justice Act 1999 numbered the newly inserted subsection following section 26(7) as "(2)", but this has been emended editorially to "(7A)".

As to the application of section 26(7), (8) and (9)(b) to Community licences, see section 91A(1) below. As to references in section 26(9)(a) to a new licence, see further section 91A(2) below.

A26.51 **Community driving licence.** *In relation to driving licences which came into force after May 31, 1990 (after December 31, 1990 for Northern Ireland driving licences) only, section 26 was amended by the Driving Licences (Community Driving Licence) Regulations 1990 (S.I. 1990 No. 144) on April 1, 1990 so that:*

    (i) the words "and its counterpart" were inserted in section 26(2) after the words "held by him" and after the words (also in section 26(2)) "such licence"; and

    (ii) the words "and its counterpart" were inserted after the word "licence" in both section 26(4)(a) and (b), and the word "their" was substituted in section 26(4) for the word "its".]

PART II

SENTENCE

Introductory

27. Production of licence

A26.52 (1) Where a person who is the holder of a licence is convicted of an offence involving obligatory [or discretionary disqualification, and a court proposes to make an order disqualifying him or an order under section 44 of this Act, the court must, unless it has already received them,] require the licence to be produced to it.

(2) *[Repealed.]*

(3) If the holder of the licence has not caused it to be delivered, or posted it, in accordance with section 7 of this Act and does not produce it as required [under this section or [section 40 of the Crime (Sentences) Act 1997, section 146 or 147 of the Powers of Criminal Courts (Sentencing) Act 2000], or section 223A or 436A of the Criminal Procedure (Scotland) Act 1975][, or if the holder of the licence does not produce it and its counterpart as required by section 40B of the Child Support Act 1991, then,] unless he satisfies the court that he has applied for a new licence and has not received it—

    (a) he is guilty of an offence, and

    (b) the licence shall be suspended from the time when its production was required until it is produced to the court and shall, while suspended, be of no effect.

(4) Subsection (3) above does not apply where the holder of the licence—

    (a) has caused a current receipt for the licence issued under section 56 of this Act to be delivered to the [proper officer] of the court not later than the day before the date appointed for the hearing, or

(b) has posted such a receipt, at such time that in the ordinary course of post it would be delivered not later than that day, in a letter duly addressed to the [proper officer] and either registered or sent by the recorded delivery service, or

(c) surrenders such a receipt to the court at the hearing,

and produces the licence to the court immediately on its return.

[(5) In subsection (4) above "*proper officer*" means—

(a) in relation to a magistrates' court in England and Wales, the justices' chief executive for the court, and

(b) in relation to any other court, the clerk of the court.]

[*Section 27 is printed as amended by the Road Traffic Act 1991, s.48 and Sched. 4, para.91(1)–(4)*　**A26.53**
(see also section 83 and Schedule 8); the Powers of Criminal Courts (Sentencing) Act 2000, s.165(1) and Sched. 9, para.120; the Child Support, Pensions and Social Security Act 2000, s.16(5); and (with effect from April 1, 2001) the Access to Justice Act 1999, s.90(1) and Sched. 13, paras 140 and 144 (see the Access to Justice Act 1999 (Commencement No. 7, Transitional Provisions and Savings) Order 2001 (S.I. 2001 No. 916; not reproduced in this work), arts 1(2) and 2(a)(ii)).

As to the application of section 27(1) and (3) to domestic driving permits, Convention driving permits, British Forces (BFG) driving licences and to the holders of such licences and permits, see the Motor Vehicles (Driving Licences) Regulations 1999 (S.I. 1999 No. 2864), reg.80, below. As to the application of section 7 to Community licences, see section 91A(1) below.

As to the Child Support Act 1991, s.40B (to which reference is made in section 27(3) above), see the notes to section 164 of the Road Traffic Act 1988 above.

Community driving licence. *In relation to driving licences which came into force after May 31,*　**A26.54**
1990 (after December 31, 1990 for Northern Ireland driving licences) only, section 27 was amended by the Driving Licences (Community Driving Licence) Regulations 1990 (S.I. 1990 No. 144) on April 1, 1990 so that:

(i) *the words "and its counterpart" were inserted after the words "require the licence" in both section 27(1) and (2);*

(ii) *the words "and its counterpart" were inserted in section 27(3) after the first three references to the word "it", and the words "it and its counterpart are" were substituted (also in section 27(3)) for the words "it is";*

(iii) *the words "and its counterpart" were inserted in section 27(4)(a) after the word "licence"; and*

(iv) *in the concluding words of section 27(4), the words "and its counterpart" were inserted after the words "and produces the licence" and the word "their" was substituted for the word "its".]*

[28. Penalty points to be attributed to an offence

(1) Where a person is convicted of an offence involving obligatory endorsement, then,　**A26.55**
subject to the following provisions of this section, the number of penalty points to be attributed to the offence is—

(a) the number shown in relation to the offence in the last column of Part I or Part II of Schedule 2 to this Act, or

(b) where a range of numbers is shown, a number within that range.

(2) Where a person is convicted of an offence committed by aiding, abetting, counselling or procuring, or inciting to the commission of, an offence involving obligatory disqualification, then, subject to the following provisions of this section, the number of penalty points to be attributed to the offence is ten.

(3) Where both a range of numbers and a number followed by the words "(fixed penalty)" is shown in the last column of Part I of Schedule 2 to this Act in relation to an offence, that number is the number of penalty points to be attributed to the offence for the purposes of sections 57(5) and 77(5) of this Act; and, where only a range of numbers is shown there, the lowest number in the range is the number of penalty points to be attributed to the offence for those purposes.

(4) Where a person is convicted (whether on the same occasion or not) of two or more offences committed on the same occasion and involving obligatory endorsement, the total number of penalty points to be attributed to them is the number or highest number that would be attributed on a conviction of one of them (so that if the convictions are on different occasions the number of penalty points to be attributed to the offences on the later occasion or occasions shall be restricted accordingly).

(5) In a case where (apart from this subsection) subsection (4) above would apply to two or more offences, the court may if it thinks fit determine that that subsection shall not apply to the offences (or, where three or more offences are concerned, to any one or more of them).

(6) Where a court makes such a determination it shall state its reasons in open court and, if it is a magistrates' court . . . shall cause them to be entered in the register . . . of its proceedings.

(7)–(9) *[Alteration of numbers relating to offences in Schedule 2 by statutory instrument.]*]

A26.56   *[Section 28 is printed as substituted by the Road Traffic Act 1991, s.27.*
Words relating expressly and exclusively to Scotland in section 28(6) have been omitted.]

[29. Penalty points to be taken into account on conviction

A26.57   (1) Where a person is convicted of an offence involving obligatory endorsement, the penalty points to be taken into account on that occasion are (subject to subsection (2) below)—

    (a) any that are to be attributed to the offence or offences of which he is convicted, disregarding any offence in respect of which an order under section 34 of this Act is made, and

    (b) any that were on a previous occasion ordered to be endorsed on the counterpart of any licence held by him, unless the offender has since that occasion and before the conviction been disqualified under section 35 of this Act.

(2) If any of the offences was committed more than three years before another, the penalty points in respect of that offence shall not be added to those in respect of the other.

(3) In relation to licences which came into force before 1st June 1990, the reference in subsection (1) above to the counterpart of a licence shall be construed as a reference to the licence itself.]

A26.58   *[Section 29 is printed as substituted by the Road Traffic Act 1991, s.28.*
As to orders for endorsement made before 1 November 1982 (the date on which the Transport Act 1981, s.19, was brought into force by the Transport Act 1981 (Commencement No. 7) Order 1982 (S.I. 1982 No. 1451)), see the Road Traffic (Consequential Provisions) Act 1988, s.5 and Sched. 4, para.7(3) above.
As to the application of section 29(1) to Community licences, see section 91A(1) below.]

A26.59   ***Community driving licence.*** *In relation to driving licences which came into force after May 31, 1990 (after December 31, 1990 for Northern Ireland driving licences) only, section 29 was amended by the Driving Licences (Community Driving Licence) Regulations 1990 (S.I. 1990 No. 144) on April 1, 1990 so that the words "the counterpart of" were inserted after the words "endorsed on".]*

30. Penalty points: modification where fixed penalty also in question

(1) Sections 28 and 29 of this Act shall have effect subject to this section in any case **A26.60**
where—

- (a) a person is convicted of an offence involving [obligatory endorsement], and
- (b) the court is satisfied that his licence has been or is liable to be endorsed under section 57 or 77 of this Act in respect of an offence (referred to in this section as the "*connected offence*") committed on the same occasion as the offence of which he is convicted.

(2) . . . the number of penalty points to be attributed to the offence of which he is convicted is—

- (a) the number of penalty points to be attributed to that offence under section [28] of this Act apart from this section, less
- (b) the number of penalty points required to be endorsed on his licence under section 57 or 77 of this Act in respect of the connected offence [(except so far as they have already been deducted by virtue of this paragraph].

(3) *[Repealed.]*

[Section 30 is printed as amended by the Road Traffic Act 1991, s.48 and Sched. 4, para.92(1)–(4) **A26.61**
(see also section 83 and Schedule 8).

As to the application of section 30 to Community licences, see section 91A(1) below.

Community driving licence. *In relation to driving licences which came into force after May 31,* **A26.62**
1990 (after December 31, 1990 for Northern Ireland driving licences) only, section 30 was amended by the Driving Licences (Community Driving Licence) Regulations 1990 (S.I. 1990 No. 144) on April 1, 1990 so that:

- *(i) the words "the counterpart of" were inserted in section 30(1)(b) after the word "that"; and*
- *(ii) the words "the counterpart of" were inserted in section 30(2)(b) after the words "endorsed on".]*

31. Court may take particulars endorsed on licence into consideration

(1) Where a person is convicted of an offence involving [obligatory or discretionary **A26.63**
endorsement] and his licence is produced to the court—

- (a) any existing endorsement on his licence is prima facie evidence of the matters endorsed, and
- (b) the court may, in determining what order to make in pursuance of the conviction, take those matters into consideration.

(2) *[Applies to Scotland.]*

[Section 31 is printed as amended by the Road Traffic Act 1991, s.48 and Sched. 4, para.93. **A26.64**
As to the application of section 31 to Community licences, see section 91A(1) below.

Community driving licence. *In relation to driving licences which came into force after May 31,* **A26.65**
1990 (after December 31, 1990 for Northern Ireland driving licences) only, section 31 was amended by the Driving Licences (Community Driving Licence) Regulations 1990 (S.I. 1990 No. 144) on April 1, 1990 so that:

- *(i) the words "and its counterpart are" were substituted in section 31(1) for the second reference to the word "is"; and*
- *(ii) the words "the counterpart of" were inserted in section 31(1) after the word "on".]*

32. In Scotland, court may take extract from licensing records into account   **A26.66**
[Omitted.]

Fine and imprisonment

33. Fine and imprisonment

A26.67

(1) Where a person is convicted of an offence against a provision of the Traffic Acts specified in column 1 of Part I of Schedule 2 to this Act or regulations made under any such provision, the maximum punishment by way of fine or imprisonment which may be imposed on him is that shown in column 4 against the offence and (where appropriate) the circumstances or the mode of trial there specified.

(2) Any reference in column 4 of that Part to a period of years or months is to be construed as a reference to a term of imprisonment of that duration.

A26.68   **33A. Forfeiture of vehicles: Scotland**   *[Omitted.]*

Disqualification

34. Disqualification for certain offences

A26.69

(1) Where a person is convicted of an offence involving obligatory disqualification, the court must order him to be disqualified for such period not less than twelve months as the court thinks fit unless the court for special reasons thinks fit to order him to be disqualified for a shorter period or not to order him to be disqualified.

[(1A) Where a person is convicted of an offence under section 12A of the Theft Act 1968 (aggravated vehicle-taking), the fact that he did not drive the vehicle in question at any particular time or at all shall not be regarded as a special reason for the purposes of subsection (1) above.]

[(2) Where a person is convicted of an offence involving discretionary disqualification, and either—

(a) the penalty points to be taken into account on that occasion number fewer than twelve, or

(b) the offence is not one involving obligatory endorsement,

the court may order him to be disqualified for such period as the court thinks fit.]

(3) Where a person convicted of an offence under any of the following provisions of the Road Traffic Act 1988, that is—

(a) section 4(1) [*q.v.*] (driving or attempting to drive while unfit),

[(aa) section 3A (causing death by careless driving when under the influence of drink or drugs),]

(b) section 5(1)(a) [*q.v.*] (driving or attempting to drive with excess alcohol), and

(c) section 7(6) [*q.v.*] (failing to provide a specimen) where that is an offence involving obligatory disqualification,

has within the ten years immediately preceding the commission of the offence been convicted of any such offence, subsection (1) above shall apply in relation to him as if the reference to twelve months were a reference to three years.

[(4) Subject to subsection (3) above, subsection (1) above shall apply as if the reference to twelve months were a reference to two years—

(a) in relation to a person convicted of—

(i) manslaughter . . . or

(ii) an offence under section 1 of the Road Traffic Act 1988 (causing death by dangerous driving), or

(iii) an offence under section 3A of that Act (causing death by careless driving while under the influence of drink or drugs), and

(b) in relation to a person on whom more than one disqualification for a fixed period of 56 days or more has been imposed within the three years immediately preceding the commission of the offence.]

[(4A) For the purposes of subsection (4)(b) above there shall be disregarded any disqualification imposed under section 26 of this Act or [section 147 of the Powers of Criminal Courts (Sentencing) Act 2000] [*q.v.*] or section 223A or 436A of the Criminal Procedure (Scotland) Act 1975 (offences committed by using vehicles) and any disqualification imposed in respect of an offence of stealing a motor vehicle, an offence under section 12 or 25 of the Theft Act 1968, an offence under section 178 of the Road Traffic Act 1988, or an attempt to commit such an offence.]

(5) The preceding provisions of this section shall apply in relation to a conviction of an offence committed by aiding, abetting, counselling or procuring, or inciting to the commission of, an offence involving obligatory disqualification as if the offence were an offence involving discretionary disqualification.

(6) This section is subject to section 48 of this Act.

[Section 34 is printed as amended by the Road Traffic Act 1991, s.29(1)–(4); the Aggravated Vehicle-   **A26.70**
Taking Act 1992, s.3(2); the Powers of Criminal Courts (Sentencing) Act 2000, s.165(1) and Sched. 9,
para.121.

Words in section 34(4) relating expressly and exclusively to Scotland have been omitted.]

[34A. Reduced disqualification period for attendance on courses

(1) This section applies where—   **A26.71**

(a) a person is convicted of an offence under section 3A (causing death by careless driving when under influence of drink or drugs), 4 (driving or being in charge when under influence of drink or drugs), 5 (driving or being in charge with excess alcohol) or 7 (failing to provide a specimen) of the Road Traffic Act 1988, and

(b) the court makes an order under section 34 of this Act disqualifying him for a period of not less than twelve months.

(2) Where this section applies, the court may make an order that the period of disqualification imposed under section 34 shall be reduced if, by a date specified in the order under this section, the offender satisfactorily completes a course approved by the Secretary of State for the purposes of this section and specified in the order.

(3) The reduction made by an order under this section in a period of disqualification imposed under section 34 shall be a period specified in the order of not less than three months and not more than one quarter of the unreduced period (and accordingly where the period imposed under section 34 is twelve months, the reduced period shall be nine months).

(4) The court shall not make an order under this section unless—

(a) it is satisfied that a place on the course specified in the order will be available for the offender,

(b) the offender appears to the court to be of or over the age of 17,

(c) the court has explained the effect of the order to the offender in ordinary language, and has informed him of the amount of the fees for the course and of the requirement that he must pay them before beginning the course, and

(d) the offender has agreed that the order should be made.

(5) The date specified in an order under this section as the latest date for completion of a course must be at least two months before the last day of the period of disqualification as reduced by the order.

(6) An order under this section shall name the petty sessions area . . . in which the offender resides or will reside.]

A26.72   *[Section 34A was inserted by the Road Traffic Act 1991, s.30.*

Words in section 34A(6) relating expressly and exclusively to Scotland have been omitted.

The functions of the Secretary of State exercisable under section 34A in relation to Wales have been transferred to the National Assembly for Wales by the National Assembly for Wales (Transfer of Functions) Order 1999 (S.I. 1999 No. 672; not reproduced in this work), art.2 and Sched. 1.]

[34B. Certificates of completion of courses

A26.73   (1) An offender shall be regarded for the purposes of section 34A of this Act as having completed a course satisfactorily if (and only if) a certificate that he has done so is received by the [proper officer] of the supervising court before the end of the period of disqualification imposed under section 34.

(2) If the certificate referred to in subsection (1) above is received by the [proper officer] of the supervising court before the end of the period of disqualification imposed under section 34 but after the end of the period as it would have been reduced by the order, the order shall have effect as if the reduced period ended with the day on which the certificate is received by the [proper officer].

(3) The certificate referred to in subsection (1) above shall be a certificate in such form, containing such particulars, and given by such person, as may be prescribed by, or determined in accordance with, regulations made by the Secretary of State.

(4) A course organiser shall give the certificate mentioned in subsection (1) above to the offender not later than fourteen days after the date specified in the order as the latest date for completion of the course, unless the offender fails to make due payment of the fees for the course, fails to attend the course in accordance with the organiser's reasonable instructions, or fails to comply with any other reasonable requirements of the organiser.

(5) Where a course organiser decides not to give the certificate mentioned in subsection (1) above, he shall give written notice of his decision to the offender as soon as possible, and in any event not later than fourteen days after the date specified in the order as the latest date for completion of the course.

(6) An offender to whom a notice is given under subsection (5) above may, within such period as may be prescribed by rules of court, apply to the supervising court for a declaration that the course organiser's decision not to give a certificate was contrary to subsection (4) above; and if the court grants the application section 34A of this Act shall have effect as if the certificate had been duly received by the [proper officer] of the court.

(7) If fourteen days after the date specified in the order as the latest date for completion of the course the course organiser has given neither the certificate mentioned in subsection (1) above nor a notice under subsection (5) above, the offender may, within such period as may be prescribed by rules of court, apply to the supervising court for a declaration that the course organiser is in default; and if the court grants the application section 34A of this Act shall have effect as if the certificate had been duly received by the [proper officer] of the court.

(8) A notice under subsection (5) above shall specify the ground on which it is given, and the Secretary of State may by regulations make provision as to the form of notices under that subsection and as to the circumstances in which they are to be treated as given.

(9) Where the [proper officer of a court] receives a certificate of the kind referred to in subsection (1) above, or a court grants an application under subsection (6) or (7) above, the [officer or] court must send notice of that fact to the Secretary of State; and the notice must be sent in such manner and to such address, and must contain such particulars, as the Secretary of State may determine.]

[Section 34B was inserted by the Road Traffic Act 1991, s.30, and is printed as amended (with effect   **A26.74**
from April 1, 2001) by the Access to Justice Act 1999, s.90(1) and Sched. 13, paras 140 and 145 (see the Access to Justice Act 1999 (Commencement No. 7, Transitional Provisions and Savings) Order 2001 (S.I. 2001 No. 916; not reproduced in this work), arts 1(2) and 2(a)(ii)).

The functions of the Secretary of State exercisable under section 34B (except section 34B(9)) in relation to Wales have been transferred to the National Assembly for Wales by the National Assembly for Wales (Transfer of Functions) Order 1999 (S.I. 1999 No. 672; not reproduced in this work), art.2 and Sched. 1.

The Road Traffic (Courses for Drink-Drive Offenders) Regulations 1992 (S.I. 1992 No. 3013; not reproduced in this work) have been made under this section and section 34C.]

[34C. Provisions supplementary to sections 34A and 34B

(1) The Secretary of State may issue guidance to course organisers, or to any category   **A26.75**
of course organiser as to the conduct of courses approved for the purposes of section 34A of this Act; and—

  (a) course organisers shall have regard to any guidance given to them under this sub-section, and

  (b) in determining for the purposes of section 34B(6) whether any instructions or requirements of an organiser were reasonable, a court shall have regard to any guidance given to him under this subsection.

(2) In sections 34A and 34B and this section—

"course organiser", in relation to a course, means the person who, in accordance with regulations made by the Secretary of State, is responsible for giving the certificates mentioned in section 34B(1) in respect of the completion of the course;

[*"proper officer"* means—

  (a) in relation to a magistrates' court in England and Wales, the justices' chief executive for the court, and

  (b) *[applies to Scotland]*;]

"supervising court", in relation to an order under section 34A, means—

  (a) in England and Wales, a magistrates' court acting for the petty sessions area named in the order as the area where the offender resides or will reside;

  (b) *[applies to Scotland.]*

. . .

(3) *[Exercise of power to make regulations.]*]

[Section 34C was inserted by the Road Traffic Act 1991, s.30 and is printed as amended by the Access   **A26.76**
to Justice Act 1999, s.106 and Sched. 15, Pt V(1); and also (with effect from April 1, 2001) by the 1999 Act, ss.90(1) and 106, Scheds 13 (paras 140 and 146) and 15 (Pt V(7)) by the insertion of the definition of "proper officer" and the deletion of words at the end of section 34C(2) (see the Access to Justice Act 1999 (Commencement No. 7, Transitional Provisions and Savings) Order 2001 (S.I. 2001 No. 916; not reproduced in this work), arts 1(2) and 2(a)(ii) and (c)(ii)).

The functions of the Secretary of State exercisable under section 34C in relation to Wales have been transferred to the National Assembly for Wales by the National Assembly for Wales (Transfer of Functions) Order 1999 (S.I. 1999 No. 672; not reproduced in this work), art.2 and Sched. 1.

See further the note to section 34B above.]

35. Disqualification for repeated offences

A26.77   (1) Where—

  (a) a person is convicted of an offence [to which this subsection applies], and

  (b) the penalty points to be taken into account on that occasion number twelve or more,

the court must order him to be disqualified for not less than the minimum period unless the court is satisfied, having regard to all the circumstances, that there are grounds for mitigating the normal consequences of the conviction and thinks fit to order him to be disqualified for a shorter period or not to order him to be disqualified.

  [(1A) Subsection (1) above applies to—

  (a) an offence involving discretionary disqualification and obligatory endorsement, and

  (b) an offence involving obligatory disqualification in respect of which no order is made under section 34 of this Act.]

  (2) The minimum period referred to in subsection (1) above is—

  (a) six months if no previous disqualification imposed on the offender is to be taken into account, and

  (b) one year if one, and two years if more than one, such disqualification is to be taken into account;

and a previous disqualification imposed on an offender is to be taken into account if it [was for a fixed period of 56 days or more and was imposed] within the three years immediately preceding the commission of the latest offence in respect of which penalty points are taken into account under section 29 of this Act.

  (3) Where an offender is convicted on the same occasion of more than one offence [to which subsection (1) above applies]—

  (a) not more than one disqualification shall be imposed on him under subsection (1) above,

  (b) in determining the period of the disqualification the court must take into account all the offences, and

  (c) for the purposes of any appeal any disqualification imposed under subsection (1) above shall be treated as an order made on the conviction of each of the offences.

  (4) No account is to be taken under subsection (1) above of any of the following circumstances—

  (a) any circumstances that are alleged to make the offence or any of the offences not a serious one,

  (b) hardship, other than exceptional hardship, or

  (c) any circumstances which, within the three years immediately preceding the conviction, have been taken into account under that subsection in ordering the offender to be disqualified for a shorter period or not ordering him to be disqualified.

  (5) References in this section to disqualification do not include a disqualification imposed under section 26 of this Act or [section 147 of the Powers of Criminal Courts (Sentencing) Act 2000] [*q.v.*] [or section 223A or 436A of the Criminal Procedure (Scotland) Act 1975 (offences committed by using vehicles) or a disqualification imposed in respect of an offence of stealing a motor vehicle, an offence under section 12 or 25 of the Theft Act 1968, an offence under section 178 of the Road Traffic Act 1988, or an attempt to commit such an offence].

[(5A) The preceding provisions of this section shall apply in relation to a conviction of an offence committed by aiding, abetting, counselling, procuring, or inciting to the commission of, an offence involving obligatory disqualification as if the offence were an offence involving discretionary disqualification.]

(6) *[Applies to Scotland.]*

(7) This section is subject to section 48 of this Act.

[Section 35 is printed as amended by the Road Traffic Act 1991, s.48 and Sched. 4, para.95(1)–(7);   **A26.78** *the Powers of Criminal Courts (Sentencing) Act 2000, s.165(1) and Sched. 9, para.122.]*

[36. Disqualification until test is passed

(1) Where this subsection applies to a person the court must order him to be disqualified   **A26.79** until he passes the appropriate driving test.

(2) Subsection (1) above applies to a person who is disqualified under section 34 of this Act on conviction of—

   (a) manslaughter . . . by the driver of a motor vehicle, or

   (b) an offence under section 1 (causing death by dangerous driving) or section 2 (dangerous driving) of the Road Traffic Act 1988.

(3) Subsection (1) above also applies—

   (a) to a person who is disqualified under section 34 or 35 of this Act in such circumstances or for such period as the Secretary of State may by order prescribe, or

   (b) to such other persons convicted of such offences involving obligatory endorsement as may be so prescribed.

(4) Where a person to whom subsection (1) above does not apply is convicted of an offence involving obligatory endorsement, the court may order him to be disqualified until he passes the appropriate driving test (whether or not he has previously passed any test).

(5) In this section—

"appropriate driving test" means—

   (a) an extended driving test, where a person is convicted of an offence involving obligatory disqualification or is disqualified under section 35 of this Act,

   (b) a test of competence to drive, other than an extended driving test, in any other case,

"extended driving test" means a test of competence to drive prescribed for the purposes of this section, and

"test of competence to drive" means a test prescribed by virtue of section 89(3) of the Road Traffic Act 1988.

(6) In determining whether to make an order under subsection (4) above, the court shall have regard to the safety of road users.

(7) Where a person is disqualified until he passes the extended driving test—

   (a) any earlier order under this section shall cease to have effect, and

   (b) a court shall not make a further order under this section while he is so disqualified.

(8) Subject to subsection (9) below, a disqualification by virtue of an order under this section shall be deemed to have expired on production to the Secretary of State of evidence, in such form as may be prescribed by regulations under section 105 of the Road Traffic Act 1988, that the person disqualified has passed the test in question since the order was made.

(9) A disqualification shall be deemed to have expired only in relation to vehicles of such classes as may be prescribed in relation to the test passed by regulations under that section.

(10) Where there is issued to a person a licence on the counterpart of which are endorsed particulars of a disqualification under this section, there shall also be endorsed the particulars of any test of competence to drive that he has passed since the order of disqualification was made.

(11) For the purposes of an order under this section, a person shall be treated as having passed a test of competence to drive other than an extended driving test if he passes a corresponding test conducted—

(a) under the law of Northern Ireland, the Isle of Man, any of the Channel Islands, another [EEA State], Gibraltar or a designated country or territory . . ., or

(b) for the purposes of obtaining a British Forces licence (as defined by section 88(8) of [the Road Traffic Act 1988]);

and accordingly subsections (8) to (10) above shall apply in relation to such a test as they apply in relation to a test prescribed by virtue of section 89(3) of that Act.

[(11A) For the purposes of subsection (11) above *"designated country or territory"* means a country or territory designated by order under section 108(2) of the Road Traffic Act 1988 but a test conducted under the law of such a country or territory shall not be regarded as a corresponding test unless a person passing such a test would be entitled to an exchangeable licence as defined in section 108(1) of that Act.]

(12) This section is subject to section 48 of this Act.

(13) *[Orders under section 36(3) to be statutory instruments.]*

(14) The Secretary of State shall not make an order under subsection (3) above after the end of 2001 if he has not previously made such an order.]

A26.80 *[Section 36 is printed as substituted by the Road Traffic Act 1991, s.32, and as subsequently amended by the Driving Licences (Community Driving Licence) Regulations 1996 (S.I. 1996 No. 1974), reg.3 and Sched. 2, para.3 (not reproduced in this work); the Deregulation (Exchangeable Driving Licences) Order 1998 (S.I. 1998 No. 1917), art.3 (not reproduced in this work).*
Words in section 36(2)(a) relating expressly and exclusively to Scotland have been omitted.
As to the European Economic Area (EEA), see the note to Regulation (EEC) 3820/85 below.]

37. Effect of order of disqualification

A26.81 (1) Where the holder of a licence is disqualified by an order of a court, the licence shall be treated as being revoked with effect from the beginning of the period of disqualification.

[(1A) Where—

(a) the disqualification is for a fixed period shorter than 56 days in respect of an offence involving obligatory endorsement, or

(b) the order is made under section 26 of this Act,

subsection (1) above shall not prevent the licence from again having effect at the end of the period of disqualification.]

(2) Where the holder of the licence appeals against the order and the disqualification is suspended under section 39 of this Act, the period of disqualification shall be treated for the purpose of subsection (1) above as beginning on the day on which the disqualification ceases to be suspended.

(3) Notwithstanding anything in Part III of the Road Traffic Act 1988, a person disqualified by an order of a court under section [36] of this Act is (unless he is also disqualified otherwise than by virtue of such an order) entitled to obtain and to hold a provisional licence and to drive a motor vehicle in accordance with the conditions subject to which the provisional licence is granted.

[Section 37 is printed as amended by the Road Traffic Act 1991, ss.33, 48 and Sched. 4, para.96.   **A26.82**
The reference in section 37(3) to an order under section 36(1) includes a reference to an order made under earlier legislation; see the Road Traffic (Consequential Provisions) Act 1988, s.5 and Sched. 4, para.7(5) above.]

38. Appeal against disqualification

(1) A person disqualified by an order of a magistrates' court under section 34 or 35 of   **A26.83**
this Act may appeal against the order in the same manner as against a conviction.

(2) *[Applies to Scotland.]*

39. Suspension of disqualification pending appeal

(1) Any court in England and Wales (whether a magistrates' court or another) which   **A26.84**
makes an order disqualifying a person may, if it thinks fit, suspend the disqualification pending an appeal against the order.

(2) *[Applies to Scotland.]*

(3) Where a court exercises its power under subsection (1) or (2) above, it must send notice of the suspension to the Secretary of State.

(4) The notice must be sent in such manner and to such address and must contain such particulars as the Secretary of State may determine.

40. Power of appellate courts in England and Wales to suspend disqualification

(1) This section applies where a person has been convicted by or before a court in   **A26.85**
England and Wales of an offence involving obligatory or discretionary disqualification and has been ordered to be disqualified; and in the following provisions of this section—

   (a) any reference to a person ordered to be disqualified is to be construed as a reference to a person so convicted and so ordered to be disqualified, and

   (b) any reference to his sentence includes a reference to the order of disqualification and to any other order made on his conviction and, accordingly, any reference to an appeal against his sentence includes a reference to an appeal against any order forming part of his sentence.

(2) Where a person ordered to be disqualified—

   (a) appeals to the Crown Court, or

   (b) appeals or applies for leave to appeal to the Court of Appeal,

against his conviction or his sentence, the Crown Court or, as the case may require, the Court of Appeal may, if it thinks fit, suspend the disqualification.

(3) Where a person ordered to be disqualified has appealed or applied for leave to appeal to the House of Lords—

   (a) under section 1 of the Administration of Justice Act 1960 from any decision of a Divisional Court of the Queen's Bench Division which is material to his conviction or sentence, or

(b) under section 33 of the Criminal Appeal Act 1968 from any decision of the Court of Appeal which is material to his conviction or sentence,

the Divisional Court or, as the case may require, the Court of Appeal may, if it thinks fit, suspend the disqualification.

(4) Where a person ordered to be disqualified makes an application in respect of the decision of the court in question under section 111 of the Magistrates' Courts Act 1980 (statement of case by magistrates' court) or section 28 of the Supreme Court Act 1981 (statement of case by Crown Court) the High Court may, if it thinks fit, suspend the disqualification.

(5) Where a person ordered to be disqualified—

(a) applies to the High Court for an order of certiorari to remove into the High Court any proceedings of a magistrates' court or of the Crown Court, being proceedings in or in consequence of which he was convicted or his sentence was passed, or

(b) applies to the High Court for leave to make such an application,

the High Court may, if it thinks fit, suspend the disqualification.

(6) Any power of a court under the preceding provisions of this section to suspend the disqualification of any person is a power to do so on such terms as the court thinks fit.

(7) Where, by virtue of this section, a court suspends the disqualification of any person, it must send notice of the suspension to the Secretary of State.

(8) The notice must be sent in such manner and to such address and must contain such particulars as the Secretary of State may determine.

A26.86   **41. Power of High Court of Justiciary to suspend disqualification**
[Omitted.]

[41A. Suspension of disqualification pending determination of applications under section 34B

A26.87   (1) Where a person makes an application to a court under section 34B of this Act, the court may suspend the disqualification to which the application relates pending the determination of the application.

(2) Where a court exercises its power under subsection (1) above it must send notice of the suspension to the Secretary of State.

(3) The notice must be sent in such manner and to such address, and must contain such particulars, as the Secretary of State may determine.]

A26.88   *[Section 41A was inserted by the Road Traffic Act 1991, s.48 and Sched. 4, para.97.]*

42. Removal of disqualification

A26.89   (1) Subject to the provisions of this section, a person who by an order of a court is disqualified may apply to the court by which the order was made to remove the disqualification.

(2) On any such application the court may, as it thinks proper having regard to—

(a) the character of the person disqualified and his conduct subsequent to the order,

(b) the nature of the offence, and

(c) any other circumstances of the case,

either by order remove the disqualification as from such date as may be specified in the order or refuse the application.

(3) No application shall be made under subsection (1) above for the removal of a disqualification before the expiration of whichever is relevant of the following periods from the date of the order by which the disqualification was imposed, that is—

(a) two years, if the disqualification is for less than four years,

(b) one half of the period of disqualification, if it is for less than ten years but not less than four years,

(c) five years in any other case;

and in determining the expiration of the period after which under this subsection a person may apply for the removal of a disqualification, any time after the conviction during which the disqualification was suspended or he was not disqualified shall be disregarded.

(4) Where an application under subsection (1) above is refused, a further application under that subsection shall not be entertained if made within three months after the date of the refusal.

(5) If under this section a court orders a disqualification to be removed, the court—

(a) must cause particulars of the order to be endorsed on the licence, if any, previously held by the applicant, and

(b) may in any case order the applicant to pay the whole or any part of the costs of the application.

[(5A) Subsection (5)(a) above shall apply only where the disqualification was imposed in respect of an offence involving obligatory endorsement; and in any other case the court must send notice of the order made under this section to the Secretary of State.]

[(5B) A notice under subsection (5A) above must be sent in such manner and to such address, and must contain such particulars, as the Secretary of State may determine.]

(6) The preceding provisions of this section shall not apply where the disqualification was imposed by order under section 36(1) of this Act.

[Section 42 is printed as amended by the Road Traffic Act 1991, s.48 and Sched. 4, para.98.   **A26.90**
As to applications under section 42 where an order was made under section 93(5) of the Road Traffic Act 1972, see the Road Traffic (Consequential Provisions) Act 1988, s.5 and Sched. 4, para.7(6) above.
The reference in section 42(6) to an order under section 36(1) includes a reference to an order made under earlier legislation; see the Road Traffic (Consequential Provisions) Act 1988, s.5 and Sched. 4, para.7(5) above.
As to the application of section 42(5) to domestic driving permits, Convention driving permits, British Forces (BFG) driving licences and to the holders of such licences and permits, see the Motor Vehicles (Driving Licences) Regulations 1999 (S.I. 1999 No. 2864), reg.80. As to the application of section 7 to Community licences, see section 91A(1) below.

Community driving licence. *In relation to driving licences which came into force after May 31,*   **A26.91**
1990 (after December 31, 1990 for Northern Ireland driving licences) only, section 42 was amended by the Driving Licences (Community Driving Licence) Regulations 1990 (S.I. 1990 No. 144) on April 1, 1990 so that the words "the counterpart of" were inserted in section 42(5) after the words "endorsed on".]

43. Rule for determining end of period of disqualification

In determining the expiration of the period for which a person is disqualified by an order   **A26.92**
of a court made in consequence of a conviction, any time after the conviction during which the disqualification was suspended or he was not disqualified shall be disregarded.

Endorsement

44. Endorsement of licences

A26.93

(1) Where a person is convicted of an offence involving obligatory endorsement, the court must order there to be endorsed on any licence held by him particulars of the conviction and also—

    (a) if the court orders him to be disqualified, particulars of the disqualification, or

    (b) if the court does not order him to be disqualified—

        (i) particulars of the offence, including the date when it was committed, and

        (ii) the penalty points to be attributed to the offence.

(2) Where the court does not order the person convicted to be disqualified, it need not make an order under subsection (1) above if for special reasons it thinks fit not to do so.

(3) *[Applies to Scotland.]*

(4) This section is subject to section 48 of this Act.

A26.94   *[As to the application of section 44(1) to Community licences, see section 91A(1) below.*

A26.95   ***Community driving licence.*** *In relation to driving licences which came into force after May 31, 1990 (after December 31, 1990 for Northern Ireland driving licences) only, section 44 was amended by the Driving Licences (Community Driving Licence) Regulations 1990 (S.I. 1990 No. 144) on April 1, 1990 so that the words "the counterpart of " were inserted in section 44(1) after the words "endorsed on".]*

45. Effect of endorsement

A26.96

(1) An order that any particulars or penalty points are to be endorsed on any licence held by the person convicted shall, whether he is at the time the holder of a licence or not, operate as an order that any licence he may then hold or may subsequently obtain is to be so endorsed until he becomes entitled under subsection (4) below to have a licence issued to him free from the particulars or penalty points.

(2) On the issue of a new licence to a person, any particulars or penalty points ordered to be endorsed on any licence held by him shall be entered on the licence unless he has become entitled under subsection (4) below to have a licence issued to him free from those particulars or penalty points.

(3) *[Repealed.]*

(4) A person whose licence has been ordered to be endorsed is entitled to have [issued to him with effect from the end of the period for which the endorsement remains effective a new licence free from the endorsement if] he applies for a new licence in pursuance of section 97(1) of the Road Traffic Act 1988, surrenders any subsisting licence, pays the fee prescribed by regulations under Part III of that Act and satisfies the other requirements of section 97(1).

(5) An endorsement ordered on a person's conviction of an offence remains effective (subject to subsections (6) and (7) below)—

    (a) if an order is made for the disqualification of the offender, until four years have elapsed since the conviction, and

    (b) if no such order is made, until either—

        (i) four years have elapsed since the commission of the offence, or [(ii) an order is made for the disqualification of the offender under section 35 of this Act].

(6) Where the offence was one under section 1 or 2 of that Act (causing death by [dangerous] driving and [dangerous] driving), the endorsement remains in any case effective until four years have elapsed since the conviction.

(7) Where the offence was one—

[(a) under section 3A, 4(1) or 5(1)(a) of that Act (driving offences connected with drink or drugs), or]

(b) under section 7(6) of that Act (failing to provide specimen) involving obligatory disqualification,

the endorsement remains effective until eleven years have elapsed since the conviction.

[Section 45 is printed as amended by the Road Traffic (Driver Licensing and Information Systems) Act   **A26.97**
1989, ss.7 and 16 and Sched. 3, para.25(a) and (b); the Road Traffic Act 1991, s.48 and Sched. 4,
para.99(1)–(4). In section 45(4) the words printed within square brackets were substituted by section 7 of
and Schedule 3, paragraph 25(b) to, the 1989 Act for the words:

a new licence issued to him free from the endorsement if, after the end of the period for which the endorsement remains effective,

These words (i.e. those formerly in section 45(4)) have been restored in relation to the application of this
section to a Community driving licence; see the heading "Community driving licence" in the notes to this
section below.

Community driving licence. *In relation to driving licences which came into force after May 31,*   **A26.98**
1990 (after December 31, 1990 for Northern Ireland driving licences) only, section 45 was amended by the
Driving Licences (Community Driving Licence) Regulations 1990 (S.I. 1990 No. 144) on April 1, 1990
so that:

  (i) *the words "the counterpart of" were inserted in section 45(1) after the words "endorsed on";*

 (ii) *the words "the counterpart of" were inserted in section 45(1) after the words "operate as an order that";*

(iii) *the words "with its counterpart" were inserted in section 45(1) after the words "issued to him";*

 (iv) *the words "the counterpart of" were inserted in section 45(2) after the words "endorsed on";*

  (v) *the words "the counterpart of" were inserted in section 45(2) after the words "entered on";*

 (vi) *the words "with its counterpart" were inserted in section 45(2) after the words "issued to him";*

(vii) *the words "the counterpart of" were inserted in section 45(3) after the word "person";*

(viii) *the words "with its counterpart" were inserted in section 45(3) after the words "issued to him"; and*

 (ix) *the following words were substituted for the words from the beginning of section 45(4) to the word "effective':*

A person the counterpart of whose licence has been ordered to be endorsed is entitled to have issued to him with effect from the end of the period for which the endorsement remains effective a new licence with a counterpart free from the endorsement if

  (x) *the words "and its counterpart" were inserted in section 45(4) after the words "subsisting licence"; and*

 (xi) *the amendment effected to section 45 by section 7 of and Schedule 3, paragraph 25(b) to, the Road*
Traffic (Driver Licensing and Information Systems) Act 1989 [noted above] will not take effect
(in relation to such licences).]

46. Combination of disqualification and endorsement with probation orders and orders for discharge

A26.99   (1) Notwithstanding anything in [section 14(3) of the Powers of Criminal Courts (Sentencing) Act 2000] (conviction of offender . . . discharged to be disregarded for the purposes of enactments relating to disqualification), a court in England and Wales which on convicting a person of an offence involving obligatory or discretionary disqualification makes—

(a) a probation order, or

(b) an order discharging him absolutely or conditionally,

may on that occasion also exercise any power conferred, and must also discharge any duty imposed, on the court by sections 34, 35, 36 or 44 of this Act.

(2) A conviction—

(a) in respect of which a court in England and Wales has ordered a person to be disqualified, or

(b) of which particulars have been endorsed on any licence held by him,

is to be taken into account, notwithstanding anything in [section 14(1) of the Powers of Criminal Courts (Sentencing) Act 2000] (conviction of offender . . . discharged to be disregarded for the purpose of subsequent proceedings), in determining his liability to punishment or disqualification for any offence involving obligatory or discretionary disqualification committed subsequently.

(3) *[Applies to Scotland.]*

A26.100   *[Section 46 is printed as amended by the Criminal Justice Act 1991, s.100 and Sched. 11, para.38(1) and (2) (see also section 101(2) and Schedule 13); the Powers of Criminal Courts (Sentencing) Act 2000, s.165(1) and Sched. 9, para.123.*

As to the application of section 46(2) to Community licences, see section 91A(1) below.

A26.101   ***Community driving licence****. In relation to driving licences which came into force after May 31, 1990 (after December 31, 1990 for Northern Ireland driving licences) only, section 46 was amended by the Driving Licences (Community Driving Licence) Regulations 1990 (S.I. 1990 No. 144) on April 1, 1990 so that the words "the counterpart of" were inserted in section 46(2) after the words "endorsed on".]*

47. Supplementary provisions as to disqualifications and endorsements

A26.102   (1) In any case where a court exercises its power under section 34, 35 or 44 of this Act not to order any disqualification or endorsement or to order disqualification for a shorter period than would otherwise be required, it must state the grounds for doing so in open court and, if it is a magistrates' court . . . , must cause them to be entered in the register . . . of its proceedings.

(2) Where a court orders the endorsement of any licence held by a person it may [, and where a court orders the holder of a licence to be disqualified for a period of 56 days or more it must,] send the licence, on its being produced to the court, to the Secretary of State; and if the court orders the endorsement but does not send the licence to the Secretary of State it must send him notice of the endorsement.

[(2A) Subsection (2) above is subject to section 2(2) of and paragraph 7(2) of Schedule 1 to the Road Traffic (New Drivers) Act 1995 [*q.v.*] (obligation of court to send licence and its counterpart to the Secretary of State).]

(3) Where on an appeal against [an order for the endorsement of a licence or the disqualification of a person] the appeal is allowed, the court by which the appeal is allowed must send notice of that fact to the Secretary of State.

(4) A notice sent by a court to the Secretary of State in pursuance of this section must be sent in such manner and to such address and contain such particulars as the Secretary of State may determine, and a licence so sent in pursuance of this section must be sent to such address as the Secretary of State may determine.

[Section 47 is printed as amended by the Road Traffic Act 1991, s.48 and Sched. 4, para.100(1)–(3);   **A26.103**
the Road Traffic (New Drivers) Act 1995, s.10(4) and Sched. 2, paras 3 and 4.

As to the application of section 47 to domestic driving permits, Convention driving permits, British Forces (BFG) driving licences and to the holders of such licences and permits, see the Motor Vehicles (Driving Licences) Regulations 1999 (S.I. 1999 No. 2864), reg.80 below. As to the application of section 47(3) to Community licences, see section 91A(1) below.

Words relating exclusively and expressly to Scotland have been omitted from section 47(1).

Community driving licence. *In relation to driving licences which came into force after May 31,*   **A26.104**
1990 (after December 31, 1990 for Northern Ireland driving licences) only, s.47 was amended by the Driving Licences (Community Driving Licence) Regulations 1990 (S.I. 1990 No. 144) on April 1, 1990 so that:

   (i)   *the words "the counterpart of" were inserted in section 47(2) after the words "endorsement of";*

   (ii)   *the words "licence and its counterpart, on their" were substituted in section 47(2) for the words "licence, on its";*

   (iii)   *the words "and its counterpart" were inserted in section 47(2) after the words "send the licence"; and*

   (iv)   *the words "and the counterpart of a licence" were inserted in section 47(4) after the word "licence".]*

[48. Exemption from disqualification and endorsement for certain construction and use offences

(1) Where a person is convicted of an offence under section 40A of the Road Traffic Act   **A26.105**
1988 (using vehicle in dangerous condition, etc.) the court must not—

  (a) order him to be disqualified, or

  (b) order any particulars or penalty points to be endorsed on the counterpart of any licence held by him,

if he proves that he did not know, and had no reasonable cause to suspect, that the use of the vehicle involved a danger of injury to any person.

(2) Where a person is convicted of an offence under section 41A of the Road Traffic Act 1988 (breach of requirement as to brakes, steering-gear or tyres) the court must not—

  (a) order him to be disqualified, or

  (b) order any particulars or penalty points to be endorsed on the counterpart of any licence held by him,

if he proves that he did not know, and had no reasonable cause to suspect, that the facts of the case were such that the offence would be committed.

(3) In relation to licences which came into force before 1st June 1990, the references in subsections (1) and (2) above to the counterpart of a licence shall be construed as references to the licence itself.]

[Section 48 is printed as substituted by the Road Traffic Act 1991, s.48 and Sched. 4, para.101.   **A26.106**
As to the application of section 48(1) and (2) to Community licences, see section 91A(1) below.]

49. Offender escaping consequences of endorsable offence by deception

A26.107   (1) This section applies where in dealing with a person convicted of an offence involving obligatory endorsement a court was deceived regarding any circumstances that were or might have been taken into account in deciding whether or for how long to disqualify him.

(2) If—

(a) the deception constituted or was due to an offence committed by that person, and

(b) he is convicted of that offence,

the court by or before which he is convicted shall have the same powers and duties regarding an order for disqualification as had the court which dealt with him for the offence involving obligatory endorsement but must, in dealing with him, take into account any order made on his conviction of the offence involving obligatory endorsement.

A26.108   **50. Powers of district court in Scotland**   *[Omitted.]*

PART III

Fixed Penalties

A26.109   *Part III (sections 51–90).*   As to the application of the provisions of Part III, other than sections 75(12), 76(8) and 77(9), to Community licences where the licence holder has been issued with a counterpart, see section 91A(3) below.

Introductory

51. Fixed penalty offences

A26.110   (1) Any offence in respect of a vehicle under an enactment specified in column 1 of Schedule 3 to this Act is a fixed penalty offence for the purposes of this Part of this Act, but subject to subsection (2) below and to any limitation or exception shown against the enactment in column 2 (where the general nature of the offence is also indicated).

(2) An offence under an enactment so specified is not a fixed penalty offence for those purposes if it is committed by causing or permitting a vehicle to be used by another person in contravention of any provision made or restriction or prohibition imposed by or under any enactment.

(3) *[Power to vary fixed penalty offences by order.]*

A26.111   *[Proceedings under section 51(1) are specified by the Prosecution of Offences Act 1985 (Specified Proceedings) Order 1999 (S.I. 1999 No. 904) below as being proceedings the conduct of which the Director of Public Prosecutions is not required to take over from the police under the Prosecution of Offences Act 1985, s.3(3)(a).]*

52. Fixed penalty notices

A26.112   (1) In this Part of this Act "*fixed penalty notice*" means a notice offering the opportunity of the discharge of any liability to conviction of the offence to which the notice relates by payment of a fixed penalty in accordance with this Part of this Act.

(2) A fixed penalty notice must give such particulars of the circumstances alleged to constitute the offence to which it relates as are necessary for giving reasonable information about the alleged offence.

(3) A fixed penalty notice must state—

(a) the period during which, by virtue of section 78(1) of this Act, proceedings cannot be brought against any person for the offence to which the notice relates, being the period of twenty-one days following the date of the notice or such longer period (if any) as may be specified in the notice (referred to in this Part of this Act as the "*suspended enforcement period*"),

(b) the amount of the fixed penalty, and

(c) the [justices' chief executive] . . . to whom and the address at which the fixed penalty may be paid.

(4) *[Applies to Scotland.]*

[Section 52 is printed as amended (with effect from April 1, 2001) by the Access to Justice Act 1999, **A26.113**
s.90(1) and Sched. 13, paras 140 and 147 (see the Access to Justice Act 1999 (Commencement No. 7, Transitional Provisions and Savings) Order 2001 (S.I. 2001 No. 916; not reproduced in this work), arts 1(2) and 2(a)(ii)).

Words relating exclusively and expressly to Scotland have been omitted from section 52(3)(c).

When the fixed penalty provisions came into operation, a Home Office circular (circular 92/1985) recommended that 28 days (rather than the 21 days specified in section 52(3)(a)) should be allowed as the suspended enforcement period.]

[53. Amount of fixed penalty

(1) The fixed penalty for an offence is—   **A26.114**

(a) such amount as the Secretary of State may by order prescribe, or

(b) one half of the maximum amount of the fine to which a person committing that offence would be liable on summary conviction,

whichever is the less.

(2) Any order made under subsection (1)(a) may make different provision for different cases or classes of case or in respect of different areas.]

[Section 53 is printed as substituted by the Road Traffic Act 1991, s.48 and Sched. 4, para.102. **A26.115**
The Fixed Penalty Order 2000 (S.I. 2000 No. 2792) (q.v.) was made under this section.]

Giving notices to suspected offenders

54. Notices on-the-spot or at a police station

(1) This section applies where [in England and Wales] on any occasion a constable in   **A26.116**
uniform has reason to believe that a person he finds is committing or has on that occasion committed a fixed penalty offence.

(2) Subject to subsection (3) below, the constable may give him a fixed penalty notice in respect of the offence.

(3) Where the offence appears to the constable to involve obligatory endorsement, the constable may only give him a fixed penalty notice under subsection (2) above in respect of the offence if—

(a) he produces his licence for inspection by the constable,

(b) the constable is satisfied, on inspecting the licence, that he would not be liable to be disqualified under section 35 of this Act if he were convicted of that offence, and

(c) he surrenders his licence to the constable to be retained and dealt with in accordance with this Part of this Act.

(4) Where—

   (a) the offence appears to the constable to involve obligatory endorsement, and

   (b) the person concerned does not produce his licence for inspection by the constable,

the constable may give him a notice stating that if, within seven days after the notice is given, he produces the notice together with his licence in person to a constable or authorised person at the police station specified in the notice (being a police station chosen by the person concerned) and the requirements of subsection (5)(a) and (b) below are met he will then be given a fixed penalty notice in respect of the offence.

(5) If a person to whom a notice has been given under subsection (4) above produces the notice together with his licence in person to a constable or authorised person at the police station specified in the notice within seven days after the notice was so given to him and the following requirements are met, that is—

   (a) the constable or authorised person is satisfied, on inspecting the licence, that he would not be liable to be disqualified under section 35 of this Act if he were convicted of the offence, and

   (b) he surrenders his licence to the constable or authorised person to be retained and dealt with in accordance with this Part of this Act,

the constable or authorised person must give him a fixed penalty notice in respect of the offence to which the notice under subsection (4) above relates.

(6) A notice under subsection (4) above shall give such particulars of the circumstances alleged to constitute the offence to which it relates as are necessary for giving reasonable information about the alleged offence.

(7) A licence surrendered in accordance with this section must be sent to the fixed penalty clerk.

(8) *[Repealed.]*

(9) In this Part of this Act "*authorised person*", in relation to a fixed penalty notice given at a police station, means a person authorised for the purposes of this section by or on behalf of the chief officer of police for the area in which the police station is situated.

[(10) In determining for the purposes of subsections (3)(b) and (5)(a) above whether a person convicted of an offence would be liable to disqualification under section 35, it shall be assumed, in the case of an offence in relation to which a range of numbers is shown in the last column of Part I of Schedule 2 to this Act, that the number of penalty points to be attributed to the offence would be the lowest in the range.]

A26.117   *[Section 54 is printed as amended by the Road Traffic Act 1991, ss.48, 83, Sched. 4, para.103(1)–(3), and Sched. 8.*

A26.118   ***Community driving licence.*** *In relation to driving licences which came into force after May 31, 1990 (after December 31, 1990 for Northern Ireland driving licences) only, section 54 was amended by the Driving Licences (Community Driving Licence) Regulations 1990 (S.I. 1990 No. 144) on April 1, 1990 so that:*

   (i) *the words "and its counterpart" were inserted in section 54(3)(a) after the words "his licence";*

   (ii) *the words "and its counterpart" were inserted in section 54(3)(b) after the words "the licence";*

   (iii) *the words "and its counterpart" were inserted in section 54(3)(c) after the words "his licence";*

   (iv) *the words "and its counterpart" were inserted in section 54(4)(b) after the words "his licence";*

   (v) *the words "and its counterpart" were inserted in the words following section 54(4)(b) after the words "his licence";*

(vi)   the words "and its counterpart" were inserted in section 54(5) after the words "his licence";

(vii) the words "and its counterpart" were inserted in section 54(5)(a) after the word "licence";

(viii) the words "and its counterpart" were inserted in section 54(5)(b) after the words "his licence"; and

(ix)   the words "and a counterpart of a licence" were inserted in section 54(7) after the word "licence".]

55. Effect of fixed penalty notice given under section 54

(1) This section applies where a fixed penalty notice relating to an offence has been given to any person under section 54 of this Act, and references in this section to the recipient are to the person to whom the notice was given.

A26.119

(2) No proceedings shall be brought against the recipient for the offence to which the fixed penalty notice relates unless before the end of the suspended enforcement period he has given notice requesting a hearing in respect of that offence in the manner specified in the fixed penalty notice.

(3) Where—

(a) the recipient has not given notice requesting a hearing in respect of the offence to which the fixed penalty notice relates in the manner so specified, and

(b) the fixed penalty has not been paid in accordance with this Part of this Act before the end of the suspended enforcement period,

a sum equal to the fixed penalty plus one-half of the amount of that penalty may be registered under section 71 of this Act for enforcement against the recipient as a fine.

56. Licence receipts

(1) A constable or authorised person to whom a person surrenders his licence on receiving a fixed penalty notice given to him under section 54 of this Act must issue a receipt for the licence under this section.

A26.120

(2) The fixed penalty clerk may, on the application of a person who has surrendered his licence in those circumstances, issue a new receipt for the licence.

(3) A receipt issued under this section ceases to have effect—

(a) if issued by a constable or authorised person, on the expiration of the period of one month beginning with the date of issue or such longer period as may be prescribed, and

(b) if issued by the fixed penalty clerk, on such date as he may specify in the receipt,

or, if earlier, on the return of the licence to the licence holder.

[**Community driving licence**. In relation to driving licences which came into force after May 31, 1990 (after December 31, 1990 for Northern Ireland driving licences) only, section 56 was amended by the Driving Licences (Community Driving Licence) Regulations 1990 (S.I. 1990 No. 144) on April 1, 1990 so that:

A26.121

(i)   the words "and its counterpart" were inserted in section 56(1) after the words "his licence" and again (also in section 56(1)) after the words "the licence";

(ii) the words "and its counterpart" were inserted in section 56(2) after the words "his licence", and the word "them" was substituted (also in section 56(2)) for the words "the licence"; and

(iii) the words "and its counterpart" were inserted in section 56(3) after the word "licence".]

57. Endorsement of licences without hearings

A26.122   (1) Subject to subsection (2) below, where a person (referred to in this section as "the licence holder") has surrendered his licence to a constable or authorised person on the occasion when he was given a fixed penalty notice under section 54 of this Act, his licence may be endorsed in accordance with this section without any order of a court.

(2) A person's licence may not be endorsed under this section if at the end of the suspended enforcement period—

    (a) he has given notice, in the manner specified in the fixed penalty notice, requesting a hearing in respect of the offence to which the fixed penalty notice relates, and

    (b) the fixed penalty has not been paid in accordance with this Part of this Act.

(3) On the payment of the fixed penalty before the end of the suspended enforcement period, the fixed penalty clerk must endorse the relevant particulars on the licence and return it to the licence holder.

(4) Where any sum determined by reference to the fixed penalty is registered under section 71 of this Act for enforcement against the licence holder as a fine, the fixed penalty clerk must endorse the relevant particulars on the licence and return it to the licence holder—

    (a) if he is himself the clerk who registers that sum, on the registration of that sum, and

    (b) in any other case, on being notified of the registration by the clerk who registers that sum.

(5) References in this section to the relevant particulars are to—

    (a) particulars of the offence, including the date when it was committed, and

    (b) the number of penalty points to be attributed to the offence.

(6) On endorsing a person's licence under this section the fixed penalty clerk must send notice of the endorsement and of the particulars endorsed to the Secretary of State.

[(7) Subsections (3) and (4) above are subject to section 2(4)(a) of and paragraph 7(4)(a) of Schedule 1 to the Road Traffic (New Drivers) Act 1995 [*q.v.*]; and the fixed penalty clerk need not comply with subsection (6) above in a case where he sends a person's licence and its counterpart to the Secretary of State under section 2(4)(b) of or paragraph 7(4)(b) of Schedule 1 to that Act.]

A26.123   [*Section 57 is printed as amended by the Road Traffic (New Drivers) Act 1995, s.10(4) and Sched. 2, paras 3 and 5.*

A26.124   ***Community driving licence.*** *In relation to driving licences which came into force after May 31, 1990 (after December 31, 1990 for Northern Ireland driving licences) only, section 57 was amended by the Driving Licences (Community Driving Licence) Regulations 1990 (S.I. 1990 No. 144) on April 1, 1990 so that:*

    (i) *the words "and its counterpart" were inserted in section 57(1) after the second reference to the word "licence";*

    (ii) *the words "the counterpart of" were inserted in section 57(1) after the word "Act";*

    (iii) *the words "The counterpart of" were inserted at the beginning of section 57(2);*

    (iv) *the words "counterpart of the" were inserted in section 57(3) after the words "particulars on the", and the words "together with the licence" were inserted (also in section 57(3)) after the word "it";*

    (v) *the words "counterpart of the" were inserted in section 57(4) after the words "particulars on the", and the words "together with the licence" were inserted (also in section 57(4)) after the word "it"; and*

  (vi)   *the words "the counterpart of" were inserted in section 57(6) after the word "endorsing".]*

58. Effect of endorsement without hearing

(1) Where a person's licence is endorsed under section 57 of this Act he shall be treated for the purposes of sections 13(4), 28, 29 and 45 of this Act and of the Rehabilitation of Offenders Act 1974 as if—   **A26.125**

  (a)   he had been convicted of the offence,

  (b)   the endorsement had been made in pursuance of an order made on his conviction by a court under section 44 of this Act, and

  (c)   the particulars of the offence endorsed by virtue of section 57(5)(a) of this Act were particulars of his conviction of that offence.

(2) In relation to any endorsement of a person's licence under section 57 of this Act—

  (a)   the reference in section 45(4) of this Act to the order for endorsement, and

  (b)   the references in section 13(4) of this Act to any order made on a person's conviction,

are to be read as references to the endorsement itself.

*[**Community driving licence.** In relation to driving licences which came into force after May 31, 1990 (after December 31, 1990 for Northern Ireland driving licences) only, section 58 was amended by the Driving Licences (Community Driving Licence) Regulations 1990 (S.I. 1990 No. 144) on April 1, 1990 so that:*   **A26.126**

  (i)   *the words "the counterpart of" were inserted in section 58(1) after the word "Where"; and*

  (ii)   *the words "the counterpart of" were inserted in section 58(2) after the words "endorsement of".]*

59. Notification of court and date of trial in England and Wales

(1) On an occasion when a person is given a fixed penalty notice under section 54 of this Act in respect of an offence, he may be given written notification specifying the magistrates' court by which and the date on which the offence will be tried if he gives notice requesting a hearing in respect of the offence as permitted by the fixed penalty notice.   **A26.127**

(2) Subject to subsections (4) and (5) below, where—

  (a)   a person has been notified in accordance with this section of the court and date of trial of an offence in respect of which he has been given a fixed penalty notice, and

  (b)   he has given notice requesting a hearing in respect of the offence as permitted by the fixed penalty notice,

the provisions of the Magistrates' Courts Act 1980 shall apply as mentioned in subsection (3) below.

(3) Those provisions are to have effect for the purpose of any proceedings in respect of that offence as if—

  (a)   the allegation in the fixed penalty notice with respect to that offence were an information duly laid in accordance with section 1 of that Act, and

  (b)   the notification of the court and date of trial were a summons duly issued on that information by a justice of the peace for the area for which the magistrates' court notified as the court of trial acts, requiring the person notified to appear before that court to answer to that information and duly served on him on the date on which the notification was given.

(4) If, in a case within subsection (2) above, notice is served by or on behalf of the chief officer of police on the person who gave notice requesting a hearing stating that no proceedings are to be brought in respect of the offence concerned, that subsection does not apply and no such proceedings are to be brought against the person who gave notice requesting a hearing.

(5) Section 14 of that Act (proceedings invalid where accused did not know of them) is not applied by subsection (2) above in a case where a person has been notified in accordance with this section of the court and date of trial of an offence.

(6) *[Repealed.]*

A26.128   *[Section 59 will be brought into force on a date to be announced; see section 99(5) below. It is printed as amended by the Road Traffic Act 1991, s.83 and Sched. 8.]*

60. Court procedure in Scotland   *[Repealed by the Road Traffic Act 1991, s.83 and Sched. 8.]*

61. Fixed penalty notice mistakenly given: exclusion of fixed penalty procedures

A26.129   (1) This section applies where, on inspection of a licence sent to him under section 54(7) of this Act, it appears to the fixed penalty clerk that the person whose licence it is would be liable to be disqualified under section 35 of this Act if he were convicted of the offence in respect of which the fixed penalty notice was given.

(2) The fixed penalty clerk must not endorse the licence under section 57 of this Act but must instead send it to the chief officer of police.

(3) Nothing in this Part of this Act prevents proceedings being brought in respect of the offence in respect of which the fixed penalty notice was given where those proceedings are commenced before the end of the period of six months beginning with the date on which that notice was given.

(4) Where proceedings in respect of that offence are commenced before the end of that period, the case is from then on to be treated in all respects as if no fixed penalty notice had been given in respect of the offence.

(5) Accordingly, where proceedings in respect of that offence are so commenced, any action taken in pursuance of any provision of this Part of this Act by reference to that fixed penalty notice shall be void (including, but without prejudice to the generality of the preceding provision—

(a) the registration under section 71 of this Act of any sum, determined by reference to the fixed penalty for that offence, for enforcement against the person whose licence it is as a fine, and

(b) any proceedings for enforcing payment of any such sum within the meaning of sections 73 and 74 of this Act (defined in section 74(5)).

[(6) In determining for the purposes of subsection (1) above whether a person convicted of an offence would be liable to disqualification under section 35, it shall be assumed, in the case of an offence in relation to which a range of numbers is shown in the last column of Part I of Schedule 2 to this Act, that the number of penalty points to be attributed to the offence would be the lowest in the range.]

A26.130   *[Section 61 is printed as amended by the Road Traffic Act 1991, s.48 and Sched. 4, para.104.*

A26.131   ***Community driving licence.*** *In relation to driving licences which came into force after May 31, 1990 (after December 31, 1990 for Northern Ireland driving licences) only, section 61 was amended by the*

Driving Licences (Community Driving Licence) Regulations 1990 (S.I. 1990 No. 144) on April 1, 1990 so that:

    (i)   *the words "and its counterpart" were inserted in section 61(1) after the first reference to the word "licence";*

    (ii)   *the words "counterpart of the" were inserted in section 61(2) after the words "endorse the"; and*

    (iii)   *the words "together with the licence" were inserted in section 61(2) after the word "it".]*

Notices fixed to vehicles

62. Fixing notices to vehicles

(1) Where on any occasion a constable has reason to believe in the case of any station-   **A26.132**
ary vehicle that a fixed penalty offence is being or has on that occasion been committed in
respect of it, he may fix a fixed penalty notice in respect of the offence to the vehicle unless
the offence appears to him to involve obligatory endorsement.

(2) A person is guilty of an offence if he removes or interferes with any notice fixed to a
vehicle under this section, unless he does so by or under the authority of the driver or
person in charge of the vehicle or the person liable for the fixed penalty offence in question.

63. Service of notice to owner if penalty not paid

(1) This section applies where a fixed penalty notice relating to an offence has been fixed   **A26.133**
to a vehicle under section 62 of this Act.

(2) Subject to subsection (3) below, if at the end of the suspended enforcement period
the fixed penalty has not been paid in accordance with this Part of this Act, a notice under
this section may be served by or on behalf of the chief officer of police on any person who
appears to him (or to any person authorised to act on his behalf for the purposes of this
section) to be the owner of the vehicle.

Such a notice is referred to in this Part of this Act as a *"notice to owner"*.

(3) Subsection (2) above does not apply where before the end of the suspended enforcement period—

    (a)   any person has given notice requesting a hearing in respect of the offence in the
manner specified in the fixed penalty notice, and

    (b)   the notice so given contains a statement by that person to the effect that he was the
driver of the vehicle at the time when the offence is alleged to have been committed.

That time is referred to in this Part of this Act as the *"time of the alleged offence"*.

(4) A notice to owner—

    (a)   must give particulars of the alleged offence and of the fixed penalty concerned,

    (b)   must state the period allowed for response to the notice, and

    (c)   must indicate that, if the fixed penalty is not paid before the end of that period,
the person on whom the notice is served is asked to provide before the end of
that period to the chief officer of police by or on whose behalf the notice was
served a statutory statement of ownership (as defined in Part I of Schedule 4 to
this Act).

(5) For the purposes of this Part of this Act, the period allowed for response to a notice
to owner is the period of twenty-one days from the date on which the notice is served, or
such longer period (if any) as may be specified in the notice.

(6) A notice to owner relating to any offence must indicate that the person on whom it is served may, before the end of the period allowed for response to the notice, either—

    (a) give notice requesting a hearing in respect of the offence in the manner indicated by the notice, or

    (b) if—

        (i) he was not the driver of the vehicle at the time of the alleged offence, and

        (ii) a person purporting to be the driver wishes to give notice requesting a hearing in respect of the offence,

    provide, together with a statutory statement of ownership provided as requested in that notice, a statutory statement of facts (as defined by Part II of Schedule 4 to this Act) having the effect referred to in paragraph 3(2) of that Schedule (that is, as a notice requesting a hearing in respect of the offence given by the driver).

(7) In any case where a person on whom a notice to owner relating to any offence has been served provides a statutory statement of facts in pursuance of subsection (6)(b) above—

    (a) any notice requesting a hearing in respect of the offence that he purports to give on his own account shall be of no effect, and

    (b) no sum may be registered for enforcement against him as a fine in respect of the offence unless, within the period of two months immediately following the period allowed for response to the notice to owner, no summons . . . in respect of the offence in question is served on the person identified in the statement as the driver.

A26.134   *[Words relating exclusively and expressly to Scotland have been omitted from section 63(7).*

    Forms FP1 to FP6, Forms EC1 to EC6 and Form H for use in connection with sections 63 and 66 are prescribed by Schedule 1 to the Road Traffic (Owner Liability) Regulations 2000 (S.I. 2000 No. 2546; not reproduced in this work); forms to the like effect may be used.]

64. Enforcement or proceedings against owner

A26.135   (1) This section applies where—

    (a) a fixed penalty notice relating to an offence has been fixed to a vehicle under section 62 of this Act,

    (b) a notice to owner relating to the offence has been served on any person under section 63(2) of this Act before the end of the period of six months beginning with the day on which the fixed penalty notice was fixed to the vehicle, and

    (c) the fixed penalty has not been paid in accordance with this Part of this Act before the end of the period allowed for response to the notice to owner.

(2) Subject to subsection (4) below and to section 63(7)(b) of this Act, a sum equal to the fixed penalty plus one-half of the amount of that penalty may be registered under section 71 of this Act for enforcement against the person on whom the notice to owner was served as a fine.

(3) Subject to subsection (4) below and to section 65 of this Act, proceedings may be brought in respect of the offence against the person on whom the notice to owner was served.

(4) If the person on whom the notice to owner was served—

    (a) was not the owner of the vehicle at the time of the alleged offence, and

    (b) provides a statutory statement of ownership to that effect in response to the notice before the end of the period allowed for response to the notice, he shall not be liable in respect of the offence by virtue of this section nor shall any sum determined by reference to the fixed penalty for the offence be so registered by virtue of this section for enforcement against him as a fine.

(5) Subject to subsection (6) below—

(a) for the purposes of the institution of proceedings by virtue of subsection (3) above against any person on whom a notice to owner has been served, and

(b) in any proceedings brought by virtue of that subsection against any such person,

it shall be conclusively presumed (notwithstanding that that person may not be an individual) that he was the driver of the vehicle at the time of the alleged offence and, accordingly, that acts or omissions of the driver of the vehicle at that time were his acts or omissions.

(6) That presumption does not apply in any proceedings brought against any person by virtue of subsection (3) above if, in those proceedings, it is proved that at the time of the alleged offence the vehicle was in the possession of some other person without the consent of the accused.

(7) Where—

(a) by virtue of subsection (3) above proceedings may be brought in respect of an offence against a person on whom a notice to owner was served, and

(b) section 74(1) of this Act does not apply,

section 127(1) of the Magistrates' Courts Act 1980 (information must be laid within six months of time offence committed) . . . shall have effect as if for the reference to six months there were substituted a reference to twelve months.

[Words relating exclusively and expressly to Scotland in section 64(7) have been omitted.]   **A26.136**

65. Restrictions on proceedings against owner and others

(1) In any case where a notice to owner relating to an offence may be served under section   **A26.137**
63 of this Act, no proceedings shall be brought in respect of the offence against any person other than a person on whom such a notice has been served unless he is identified as the driver of the vehicle at the time of the alleged offence in a statutory statement of facts provided in pursuance of section 63(6)(b) of this Act by a person on whom such a notice has been served.

(2) Proceedings in respect of an offence to which a notice to owner relates shall not be brought against the person on whom the notice was served unless, before the end of the period allowed for response to the notice, he has given notice, in the manner indicated by the notice to owner, requesting a hearing in respect of the offence.

(3) Proceedings in respect of an offence to which a notice to owner relates may not be brought against any person identified as the driver of the vehicle in a statutory statement of facts provided in response to the notice if the fixed penalty is paid in accordance with this Part of this Act before the end of the period allowed for response to the notice.

(4) Once any sum determined by reference to the fixed penalty for an offence has been registered by virtue of section 64 of this Act under section 71 for enforcement as a fine against a person on whom a notice to owner relating to that offence has been served, no proceedings shall be brought against any other person in respect of that offence.

66. Hired vehicles

(1) This section applies where—   **A26.138**

(a) a notice to owner has been served on a vehicle-hire firm,

(b) at the time of the alleged offence the vehicle in respect of which the notice was served was let to another person by the vehicle-hire firm under a hiring agreement to which this section applies, and

(c) within the period allowed for response to the notice the firm provides the chief officer of police by or on whose behalf the notice was served with the documents mentioned in subsection (2) below.

(2) Those documents are a statement on an official form, signed by or on behalf of the firm, stating that at the time of the alleged offence the vehicle concerned was hired under a hiring agreement to which this section applies, together with—

(a) a copy of that hiring agreement, and

(b) a copy of a statement of liability signed by the hirer under that hiring agreement.

(3) In this section a *"statement of liability"* means a statement made by the hirer under a hiring agreement to which this section applies to the effect that the hirer acknowledges that he will be liable, as the owner of the vehicle, in respect of any fixed penalty offence which may be committed with respect to the vehicle during the currency of the hiring agreement and giving such information as may be prescribed.

(4) In any case where this section applies, sections 63, 64 and 65 of this Act shall have effect as if—

(a) any reference to the owner of the vehicle were a reference to the hirer under the hiring agreement, and

(b) any reference to a statutory statement of ownership were a reference to a statutory statement of hiring,

and accordingly references in this Part of this Act (with the exceptions mentioned below) to a notice to owner include references to a notice served under section 63 of this Act as it applies by virtue of this section.

This subsection does not apply to references to a notice to owner in this section or in section 81(2)(b) of or Part I of Schedule 4 to this Act.

(5) In any case where this section applies, a person authorised in that behalf by the chief officer of police to whom the documents mentioned in subsection (2) above are provided may, at any reasonable time within six months after service of the notice to owner (and on the production of his authority), require the firm to produce the originals of the hiring agreement and statement of liability in question.

(6) If a vehicle-hire firm fails to produce the original of a document when required to do so under subsection (5) above, this section shall thereupon cease to apply (and section 64 of this Act shall apply accordingly in any such case after that time as it applies in a case where the person on whom the notice to owner was served has failed to provide a statutory statement of ownership in response to the notice within the period allowed).

(7) This section applies to a hiring agreement under the terms of which the vehicle concerned is let to the hirer for a fixed period of less than six months (whether or not that period is capable of extension by agreement between the parties or otherwise); and any reference in this section to the currency of the hiring agreement includes a reference to any period during which, with the consent of the vehicle-hire firm, the hirer continues in possession of the vehicle as hirer, after the expiry of the fixed period specified in the agreement, but otherwise on the terms and conditions so specified.

(8) In this section—

"hiring agreement" refers only to an agreement which contains such particulars as may be prescribed and does not include a hire-purchase agreement within the meaning of the Consumer Credit Act 1974, and

"*vehicle-hire firm*" means any person engaged in hiring vehicles in the course of a business.

[The particulars to be contained in hiring agreements for the purposes of section 66(8) are prescribed in Schedule 2 to the Road Traffic (Owner Liability) Regulations 2000 (S.I. 2000 No. 2546; not reproduced in this work). As to forms for use in connection with section 66 and section 63, see the note to section 63 above.]   **A26.139**

67. False statements in response to notices to owner

A person who, in response to a notice to owner, provides a statement which is false in a material particular and does so recklessly or knowing it to be false in that particular is guilty of an offence.   **A26.140**

68. "Owner", "statutory statement" and "official form"

(1) For the purposes of this Part of this Act, the owner of a vehicle shall be taken to be the person by whom the vehicle is kept; and for the purposes of determining, in the course of any proceedings brought by virtue of section 64(3) of this Act, who was the owner of a vehicle at any time, it shall be presumed that the owner was the person who was the registered keeper of the vehicle at that time.   **A26.141**

(2) Notwithstanding the presumption in subsection (1) above, it is open to the defence in any proceedings to prove that the person who was the registered keeper of a vehicle at a particular time was not the person by whom the vehicle was kept at that time and to the prosecution to prove that the vehicle was kept by some other person at that time.

(3) References in this Part of this Act to statutory statements of any description are references to the statutory statement of that description defined in Schedule 4 to this Act; and that Schedule shall also have effect for the purpose of requiring certain information to be provided in official forms for the statutory statements so defined to assist persons in completing those forms and generally in determining what action to take in response to a notice to owner.

(4) In this Part of this Act "*official form*", in relation to a statutory statement mentioned in Schedule 4 to this Act or a statement under section 66(2) of this Act, means a document supplied by or on behalf of a chief officer of police for use in making that statement.

The fixed penalty procedure

69. Payment of penalty

(1) Payment of a fixed penalty under this Part of this Act must be made to such [justices' chief executive] . . . as may be specified in the fixed penalty notice relating to that penalty.   **A26.142**

(2) Without prejudice to payment by any other method, payment of a fixed penalty under this Part of this Act may be made by properly addressing, pre-paying and posting a letter containing the amount of the penalty (in cash or otherwise) and, unless the contrary is proved, shall be regarded as having been made at the time at which that letter would be delivered in the ordinary course of post.

(3) A letter is properly addressed for the purposes of subsection (2) above if it is addressed to the fixed penalty clerk at the address specified in the fixed penalty notice relating to the fixed penalty as the address at which the fixed penalty may be paid.

(4) References in this Part of this Act [(except in sections 75 to 77)], in relation to any fixed penalty or fixed penalty notice, to the fixed penalty clerk are references to the [justices' chief executive or] clerk specified in accordance with subsection (1) above in the

fixed penalty notice relating to that penalty or (as the case may be) in that fixed penalty notice.

A26.143   *[Section 69 is printed as amended by the Road Traffic Act 1991, s.48 and Sched. 4, para.105 and is printed as amended (with effect from April 1, 2001) by the Access to Justice Act 1999, s.90(1) and Sched. 13, paras 140 and 148 (see the Access to Justice Act 1999 (Commencement No. 7, Transitional Provisions and Savings) Order 2001 (S.I. 2001 No. 916; not reproduced in this work), arts 1(2) and 2(a)(ii)).*
Words relating exclusively and expressly to Scotland in section 69(1) have been omitted.]

70. Registration certificates

A26.144   (1) This section and section 71 of this Act apply where by virtue of section 55(3) or 64(2) of this Act a sum determined by reference to the fixed penalty for any offence may be registered under section 71 of this Act for enforcement against any person as a fine.

In this section and section 71 of this Act—

> (a) that sum is referred to as a "*sum payable in default*", and
>
> (b) the person against whom that sum may be so registered is referred to as the "*defaulter*".

(2) Subject to subsection (3) below, the chief officer of police may in respect of any sum payable in default issue a certificate (referred to in this section and section 71 as a "*registration certificate*") stating that the sum is registrable under section 71 for enforcement against the defaulter as a fine.

(3) *[Applies to Scotland.]*

(4) Where the chief officer of police or the fixed penalty clerk issues a registration certificate under this section, he must—

> (a) if the defaulter appears to him to reside in England and Wales, cause it to be sent to the [justices' chief executive] for the petty sessions area in which the defaulter appears to him to reside, and
>
> (b) *[applies to Scotland.]*

(5) A registration certificate issued under this section in respect of any sum payable in default must—

> (a) give particulars of the offence to which the fixed penalty notice relates,
>
> (b) indicate whether registration is authorised under section 55(3) or 64(2) of this Act, and
>
> (c) state the name and last known address of the defaulter and the amount of the sum payable in default.

A26.145   *[Section 70 is printed as amended (with effect from April 1, 2001) by the Access to Justice Act 1999, s.90(1) and Sched. 13, paras 140 and 149 (see the Access to Justice Act 1999 (Commencement No. 7, Transitional Provisions and Savings) Order 2001 (S.I. 2001 No. 916; not reproduced in this work), arts 1(2) and 2(a)(ii)).]*

71. Registration of sums payable in default

A26.146   [(1) Where, in England and Wales, a justices' chief executive receives a registration certificate issued under section 70 of this Act in respect of any sum payable in default—

> (a) if it appears to him that the defaulter resides in a petty sessions area for which he is the justices' chief executive, he must register that sum for enforcement as a fine in that area by entering it in the register of a magistrates' court acting for that area,
>
> (b) if it appears to him that the defaulter resides in any other petty sessions area in

England and Wales, he must send the certificate to the justices' chief executive for that area, or

(c) if it appears to him that the defaulter resides in Scotland, he must send the certificate to the clerk of the court of summary jurisdiction for the area in which the defaulter appears to him to reside.]

[(2) Where, in Scotland, the clerk of a court receives a registration certificate issued under section 70 of this Act in respect of any sum payable in default—

(a) if it appears to him that the defaulter resides in the area of the court, he must register that sum for enforcement as a fine by that court,

(b) if it appears to him that the defaulter resides in the area of any other court of summary jurisdiction in Scotland, he must send the certificate to the clerk of that court, or

(c) if it appears to him that the defaulter resides in England and Wales, he must send the certificate to the justices' chief executive for the petty sessions area in which the defaulter appears to him to reside.]

[(2A) Subsections (1) and (2) apply to executives and clerks who receive certificates pursuant to the provision they contain as they apply to the original recipients.]

(3) Where—

(a) the fixed penalty notice in question was given to the defaulter under section 54 of this Act in respect of an offence committed in Scotland, and

(b) the defaulter appears to the fixed penalty clerk to reside within the jurisdiction of the court of summary jurisdiction of which he is himself the clerk,

the fixed penalty clerk must register the sum payable in default for enforcement as a fine by that court.

(4), (5) *[Repealed by the Access to Justice Act 1999.]*

(6) On registering any sum under this section for enforcement as a fine, the [justices' chief executive] for a petty sessions area or, as the case may be, the clerk of a court of summary jurisdiction must give to the defaulter notice of registration—

(a) specifying the amount of that sum, and

(b) giving the information with respect to the offence and the authority for registration included in the registration certificate by virtue of section 70(5)(a) and (b) of this Act or (in a case within subsection (3) above) the corresponding information.

(7) On the registration of any sum in a magistrates' court or a court of summary jurisdiction by virtue of this section any enactment referring (in whatever terms) to a fine imposed or other sum adjudged to be paid on the conviction of such a court shall have effect in the case in question as if the sum so registered were a fine imposed by that court on the conviction of the defaulter on the date of the registration.

(8) Accordingly, in the application by virtue of this section of the provisions of the Magistrates' Courts Act 1980 relating to the satisfaction and enforcement of sums adjudged to be paid on the conviction of a magistrates' court, section 85 of that Act (power to remit a fine in whole or in part) is not excluded by subsection (2) of that section (references in that section to a fine not to include any other sum adjudged to be paid on a conviction) from applying to a sum registered in a magistrates' court by virtue of this section.

(9) For the purposes of this section, where the defaulter is a body corporate, the place where that body resides and the address of that body are either of the following—

(a) the registered or principal office of that body, and

(b) the address which, with respect to the vehicle concerned, is the address recorded in the record kept under [the Vehicle Excise and Registration Act 1994] as being that body's address.

A26.147 *[Section 71 is printed as amended by the Vehicle Excise and Registration Act 1994, s.63 and Sched. 3, para.25(1); and (with effect from April 1, 2001) by the Access to Justice Act 1999, ss.90(1) and 106, Scheds 13 (paras 140 and 150) and 15 (Pt V(7)) (see the Access to Justice Act 1999 (Commencement No. 7, Transitional Provisions and Savings) Order 2001 (S.I. 2001 No. 916; not reproduced in this work), arts 1(2) and 2(a)(ii) and (c)(ii)).]*

72. Notices on-the-spot or at a police station: when registration and endorsement invalid

A26.148

(1) This section applies where—

(a) a person who has received notice of the registration, by virtue of section 55(3) of this Act, of a sum under section 71 of this Act for enforcement against him as a fine makes a statutory declaration to the effect mentioned in subsection (2) below, and

(b) that declaration is, within twenty-one days of the date on which the person making it received notice of the registration, served on the [proper officer] of the relevant court.

(2) The statutory declaration must state—

(a) that the person making the declaration was not the person to whom the relevant fixed penalty notice was given, or

(b) that he gave notice requesting a hearing in respect of the alleged offence as permitted by the fixed penalty notice before the end of the suspended enforcement period.

(3) In any case within subsection (2)(a) above, the relevant fixed penalty notice, the registration and any proceedings taken before the declaration was served for enforcing payment of the sum registered shall be void.

(4) Where in any case within subsection (2)(a) above the person to whom the relevant fixed penalty notice was given surrendered a licence held by the person making the declaration, any endorsement of that licence made under section 57 of this Act in respect of the offence in respect of which that notice was given shall be void.

(5) In any case within subsection (2)(b) above—

(a) the registration, any proceedings taken before the declaration was served for enforcing payment of the sum registered, and any endorsement, in respect of the offence in respect of which the relevant fixed penalty notice was given, made under section 57 of this Act before the declaration was served, shall be void, and

(b) the case shall be treated after the declaration is served as if the person making the declaration had given notice requesting a hearing in respect of the alleged offence as stated in the declaration.

(6) The [proper officer] of the relevant court must—

(a) cancel an endorsement of a licence under section 57 of this Act that is void by virtue of this section on production of the licence to him for that purpose, and

(b) send notice of the cancellation to the Secretary of State.

(7) References in this section to the relevant fixed penalty notice are to the fixed penalty notice relating to the fixed penalty concerned.

A26.149 *[Section 72 is printed as amended (with effect from April 1, 2001) by the Access to Justice Act 1999, s.90(1) and Sched. 13, paras 140 and 151 (see the Access to Justice Act 1999 (Commencement No. 7,*

Transitional Provisions and Savings) Order 2001 (S.I. 2001 No. 916; not reproduced in this work), arts 1(2) and 2(a)(ii)).

Community driving licence. *In relation to driving licences which came into force after May 31,*   **A26.150**
1990 (after December 31, 1990 for Northern Ireland driving licences) only, section 72 was amended by the Driving Licences (Community Driving Licence) Regulations 1990 (S.I. 1990 No. 144) on April 1, 1990 so that:

(i)   *the words "and its counterpart" were inserted in section 72(4) after the words "a licence";*

(ii)   *the words "that counterpart" were substituted in section 72(4) for the words "that licence";*

(iii)   *the words "the counterpart of" were inserted in section 72(6)(a) after the words "endorsement of"; and*

(iv)   *the words "and its counterpart" were inserted in section 72(6)(a) after the words "the licence".]*

73. Notices fixed to vehicles: when registration invalid

(1) This section applies where—   **A26.151**

(a) a person who has received notice of the registration, by virtue of section 64(2) of this Act, of a sum under section 71 of this Act for enforcement against him as a fine makes a statutory declaration to the effect mentioned in subsection (2) below, and

(b) that declaration is, within twenty-one days of the date on which the person making it received notice of the registration, served on the [proper officer] of the relevant court.

(2) The statutory declaration must state either—

(a) that the person making the declaration did not know of the fixed penalty concerned or of any fixed penalty notice or notice to owner relating to that penalty until he received notice of the registration, or

(b) that he was not the owner of the vehicle at the time of the alleged offence of which particulars are given in the relevant notice to owner and that he has a reasonable excuse for failing to comply with that notice, or

(c) that he gave notice requesting a hearing in respect of that offence as permitted by the relevant notice to owner before the end of the period allowed for response to that notice.

(3) In any case within subsection (2)(a) or (b) above—

(a) the relevant notice to owner,

(b) the registration, and

(c) any proceedings taken before the declaration was served for enforcing payment of the sum registered,

shall be void but without prejudice, in a case within subsection (2)(a) above, to the service of a further notice to owner under section 63 of this Act on the person making the declaration.
This subsection applies whether or not the relevant notice to owner was duly served in accordance with that section on the person making the declaration.

(4) In any case within subsection (2)(c) above—

(a) no proceedings shall be taken, after the statutory declaration is served until the end of the period of twenty-one days following the date of that declaration, for enforcing payment of the sum registered, and

(b) where before the end of that period a notice is served by or on behalf of the chief officer of police on the person making the declaration asking him to provide a new statutory statement of ownership to that chief officer of police before the end of the period of twenty-one days from the date on which the notice is served, no such proceedings shall be taken until the end of the period allowed for response to that notice.

(5) Where in any case within subsection (2)(c) above—

(a) no notice is served by or on behalf of the chief officer of police in accordance with subsection (4) above, or

(b) such a notice is so served and the person making the declaration provides a new statutory statement of ownership in accordance with the notice,

then—

(i) the registration and any proceedings taken before the declaration was served for enforcing payment of the sum registered shall be void, and

(ii) the case shall be treated after the time mentioned in subsection (6) below as if the person making the declaration had given notice requesting a hearing in respect of the alleged offence as stated in the declaration.

(6) The time referred to in subsection (5) above is—

(a) in a case within paragraph (a) of that subsection, the end of the period of twenty-one days following the date of the statutory declaration,

(b) in a case within paragraph (b) of that subsection, the time when the statement is provided.

(7) In any case where notice is served by or on behalf of the chief officer of police in accordance with subsection (4) above, he must cause the [proper officer] of the relevant court to be notified of that fact immediately on service of the notice.

(8) References in this section to the relevant notice to owner are to the notice to owner relating to the fixed penalty concerned.

A26.152   *[Section 73 is printed as amended (with effect from April 1, 2001) by the Access to Justice Act 1999, s.90(1) and Sched. 13, paras 140 and 151 (see the Access to Justice Act 1999 (Commencement No. 7, Transitional Provisions and Savings) Order 2001 (S.I. 2001 No. 916; not reproduced in this work), arts 1(2) and 2(a)(ii)).]*

74. Provisions supplementary to sections 72 and 73

A26.153   (1) In any case within section 72(2)(b) or 73(2) of this Act—

(a) section 127(1) of the Magistrates' Courts Act 1980 (limitation of time), and

(b) *[applies to Scotland.]*

shall have effect as if for the reference to the time when the offence was committed or (as the case may be) the time when the contravention occurred there were substituted a reference to the date of the statutory declaration made for the purposes of section 72(1) or, as the case may be, 73(1).

(2) Where, on the application of a person who has received notice of the registration of a sum under section 71 of this Act for enforcement against him as a fine, it appears to the relevant court (which for this purpose may be composed of a single justice) that it was not reasonable to expect him to serve, within twenty-one days of the date on which he received the notice, a statutory declaration to the effect mentioned in section 72(2) or, as the case may be, 73(2) of this Act, the court may accept service of such a declaration by that person after that period has expired.

(3) A statutory declaration accepted under subsection (2) above shall be taken to have been served as required by section 72(1) or, as the case may be, section 73(1) of this Act.

(4) For the purposes of sections 72(1) and 73(1) of this Act, a statutory declaration shall be taken to be duly served on the [proper officer] of the relevant court if it is delivered to him, left at his office, or sent in a registered letter or by the recorded delivery service addressed to him at his office.

(5) In sections 72, 73 and this section—

(a) references to the relevant court are—

(i) in the case of a sum registered under section 71 of this Act for enforcement as a fine in a petty sessions area in England and Wales, references to any magistrates' court acting for that area, and

(ii) *[applies to Scotland.]*

[(b) references to the "*proper officer*" of the relevant court are—

(i) in the case of a magistrates' court, references to the justices' chief executive for the court, and

(ii) *[applies to Scotland]*, and]

(c) references to proceedings for enforcing payment of the sum registered are references to any process issued or other proceedings taken for or in connection with enforcing payment of that sum.

(6) For the purposes of sections 72, 73 and this section, a person shall be taken to receive notice of the registration of a sum under section 71 of this Act for enforcement against him as a fine when he receives notice either of the registration as such or of any proceedings for enforcing payment of the sum registered.

(7) Nothing in the provisions of sections 72 or 73 or this section is to be read as prejudicing any rights a person may have apart from those provisions by virtue of the invalidity of any action purportedly taken in pursuance of this Part of this Act which is not in fact authorised by this Part of this Act in the circumstances of the case; and, accordingly, references in those provisions to the registration of any sum or to any other action taken under or by virtue of any provision of this Part of this Act are not to be read as implying that the registration or action was validly made or taken in accordance with that provision.

[Section 74 is printed as amended (with effect from April 1, 2001) by the Access to Justice Act 1999, s.90(1) and Sched. 13, paras 140 and 152 (see the Access to Justice Act 1999 (Commencement No. 7, Transitional Provisions and Savings) Order 2001 (S.I. 2001 No. 916; not reproduced in this work), arts 1(2) and 2(a)(ii)).]   **A26.154**

[Conditional offer of fixed penalty]

[Note. The above heading was substituted by the Road Traffic Act 1991, s.34.]   **A26.155**

[75. Issue of conditional offer

(1) Where in England and Wales—   **A26.156**

(a) a constable has reason to believe that a fixed penalty offence has been committed, and

(b) no fixed penalty notice in respect of the offence has been given under section 54 of this Act or fixed to a vehicle under section 62 of this Act,

a notice under this section may be sent to the alleged offender by or on behalf of the chief officer of police.

(2)–(4) *[Apply to Scotland.]*

(5) A notice under this section is referred to in this section and sections 76 and 77 as a "*conditional offer*".

(6) Where a person issues a conditional offer, he must notify the [justices' chief executive] . . . specified in it of its issue and its terms; and [he] is referred to in this section and sections 76 and 77 as "*the fixed penalty clerk*".

(7) A conditional offer must—

   (a) give such particulars of the circumstances alleged to constitute the offence to which it relates as are necessary for giving reasonable information about the alleged offence,

   (b) state the amount of the fixed penalty for that offence, and

   (c) state that proceedings against the alleged offender cannot be commenced in respect of that offence until the end of the period of twenty-eight days following the date on which the conditional offer was issued or such longer period as may be specified in the conditional offer.

(8) A conditional offer must indicate that if the following conditions are fulfilled, that is—

   (a) within the period of twenty-eight days following the date on which the offer was issued, or such longer period as may be specified in the offer, the alleged offender—

      (i) makes payment of the fixed penalty to the fixed penalty clerk, and

      (ii) where the offence to which the offer relates is an offence involving obligatory endorsement, at the same time delivers his licence and its counterpart to that clerk, and

   (b) where his licence and its counterpart are so delivered, that clerk is satisfied on inspecting them that, if the alleged offender were convicted of the offence, he would not be liable to be disqualified under section 35 of this Act,

any liability to conviction of the offence shall be discharged.

(9) For the purposes of the condition set out in subsection (8)(b) above, it shall be assumed, in the case of an offence in relation to which a range of numbers is shown in the last column of Part I of Schedule 2 to this Act, that the number of penalty points to be attributed to the offence would be the lowest in the range.

(10) The Secretary of State may by order provide for offences to become or (as the case may be) to cease to be offences in respect of which a conditional offer may be sent under subsection (2)(b) above, and may make such modifications of the provisions of this Part of this Act as appear to him to be necessary for the purpose.

(11) *[Applies to Scotland.]*

(12) In relation to licences which came into force before 1st June 1990, the references in subsection (8) above to the counterpart of a licence shall be disregarded.]

A26.157   *[Section 75 is printed as substituted by the Road Traffic Act 1991, s.34; and is printed as amended (with effect from April 1, 2001) by the Access to Justice Act 1999, s.90(1) and Sched. 13, paras 140 and 153 (see the Access to Justice Act 1999 (Commencement No. 7, Transitional Provisions and Savings) Order 2001 (S.I. 2001 No. 916; not reproduced in this work), arts 1(2) and 2(a)(ii)).*

Words in section 75(6) relating expressly and exclusively to Scotland have been omitted.]

[76. Effect of offer and payment of penalty

A26.158   (1) This section applies where a conditional offer has been sent to a person under section 75 of this Act.

(2) No proceedings shall be brought against any person for the offence to which the conditional offer relates until—

(a) in England and Wales, the chief officer of police, or

(b) *[applies to Scotland.]*

receives notice in accordance with subsection (4) or (5) below.

(3) Where the alleged offender makes payment of the fixed penalty in accordance with the conditional offer, no proceedings shall be brought against him for the offence to which the offer relates.

(4) Where—

(a) the alleged offender tenders payment in accordance with the conditional offer and delivers his licence and its counterpart to the fixed penalty clerk, but

(b) it appears to the clerk, on inspecting the licence and counterpart, that the alleged offender would be liable to be disqualified under section 35 of this Act if he was convicted of the offence to which the conditional offer relates,

then subsection (3) above shall not apply and the clerk must return the licence and its counterpart to the alleged offender together with the payment and give notice that he has done so to the person referred to in subsection (2)(a) or (b) above.

(5) Where, on the expiry of the period of twenty-eight days following the date on which the conditional offer was made or such longer period as may be specified in the offer, the conditions specified in the offer in accordance with section 75(8)(a) of this Act have not been fulfilled, the fixed penalty clerk must notify the person referred to in subsection (2)(a) or (b) above.

(6) In determining for the purposes of subsection (4)(b) above whether a person convicted of an offence would be liable to disqualification under section 35, it shall be assumed, in the case of an offence in relation to which a range of numbers is shown in the last column of Part I of Schedule 2 to this Act, that the number of penalty points to be attributed to the offence would be the lowest in the range.

(7) In any proceedings a certificate that by a date specified in the certificate payment of a fixed penalty was or was not received by the fixed penalty clerk shall, if the certificate purports to be signed by that clerk, be evidence . . . of the facts stated.

(8) In relation to licences which came into force before 1st June 1990, the references in subsection (4) above to the counterpart of a licence shall be disregarded.

(9) *[Applies to Scotland.]*]

[Section 76 is printed as substituted by the Road Traffic Act 1991, s.34.
Words in section 76(7) relating expressly and exclusively to Scotland have been omitted.]

A26.159

[77. Endorsement where penalty paid

(1) Where—

A26.160

(a) in pursuance of a conditional offer a person (referred to in this section as the "*licence holder*") makes payment of the fixed penalty to the fixed penalty clerk and delivers his licence and its counterpart to the clerk, and

(b) the clerk is not required by subsection (4) of section 76 of this Act to return the licence and its counterpart to him and did not, before the payment was tendered, notify the person referred to in section 76(2)(a) or (b) of this Act under subsection (5) of that section,

the clerk must forthwith endorse the relevant particulars on the counterpart of the licence and return it to the licence holder together with the licence.

(2) *[Applies to Scotland.]*

(3) Subject to subsection (4) below, where a cheque tendered in payment is subsequently dishonoured—

(a) any endorsement made by a clerk under subsection (1) above remains effective, notwithstanding that the licence holder is still liable to prosecution in respect of the alleged offence to which the endorsement relates, and

(b) the clerk must, upon the expiry of the period specified in the conditional offer or, if the period has expired, forthwith notify the person referred to in section 76(2)(a) or (b) of this Act that no payment has been made.

(4) When proceedings are brought against a licence holder after a notice has been given in pursuance of subsection (3)(b) above, the court—

(a) must order the removal of the fixed penalty endorsement from the counterpart of the licence, and

(b) may, on finding the licence holder guilty, make any competent order of endorsement or disqualification and pass any competent sentence.

(5) The reference in subsection (1) above to the relevant particulars is to—

(a) particulars of the offence, including the date when it was committed, and

(b) the number of penalty points to be attributed to the offence.

(6) The fixed penalty clerk must send notice to the Secretary of State—

(a) of any endorsement under subsection (1) above and of the particulars endorsed,

(b) of any amendment under subsection (2) above, and

(c) of any order under subsection (4)(a) above.

(7) Where the counterpart of a person's licence is endorsed under this section he shall be treated for the purposes of sections 13(4), 28, 29 and 45 of this Act and of the Rehabilitation of Offenders Act 1974 as if—

(a) he had been convicted of the offence,

(b) the endorsement had been made in pursuance of an order made on his conviction by a court under section 44 of this Act, and

(c) the particulars of the offence endorsed by virtue of subsection (5)(a) above were particulars of his conviction of that offence.

(8) In relation to any endorsement of the counterpart of a person's licence under this section—

(a) the reference in section 45(4) of this Act to the order for endorsement, and

(b) the references in section 13(4) of this Act to any order made on a person's conviction,

are to be read as references to the endorsement itself.

(9) In relation to licences which came into force before 1st June 1990, the references in this section to the counterpart of a licence shall be disregarded or, as the case may require, construed as references to the licence itself.]

[(10) Subsection (1) above is subject to section 2(4)(a) of and paragraph 7(4)(a) of Schedule 1 to the Road Traffic (New Drivers) Act 1995 [*q.v.*] and the fixed penalty clerk need not send a notice falling within subsection (6)(a) above in a case where he sends a person's licence and its counterpart to the Secretary of State under section 2(4)(b) of or paragraph 7(4)(b) of Schedule 1 to that Act.]

A26.161   *[Section 77 is printed as substituted by the Road Traffic Act 1991, s.34, and as subsequently amended by the Road Traffic (New Drivers) Act 1995, s.10(4) and Sched. 2, paras 3 and 6.]*

Proceedings in fixed penalty cases

78. General restriction on proceedings

(1) Proceedings shall not be brought against any person for the offence to which a fixed   **A26.162**
penalty notice relates until the end of the suspended enforcement period.

(2) Proceedings shall not be brought against any person for the offence to which a fixed
penalty notice relates if the fixed penalty is paid in accordance with this Part of this Act
before the end of the suspended enforcement period.

79. Statements by constables

(1) In any proceedings a certificate that a copy of a statement by a constable with   **A26.163**
respect to the alleged offence (referred to in this section as a *"constable's witness statement"*)
was included in or given with a fixed penalty notice or a notice under section 54(3) of this
Act given to the accused on a date specified in the certificate shall, if the certificate
purports to be signed by the constable or authorised person who gave the accused the
notice, be evidence of service of a copy of that statement by delivery to the accused on
that date.

(2) In any proceedings a certificate that a copy of a constable's witness statement was
included in or served with a notice to owner served on the accused in the manner and on
a date specified in the certificate shall, if the certificate purports to be signed by any
person employed by the police authority for the police area in which the offence to which
the proceedings relate is alleged to have been committed, be evidence of service in the
manner and on the date so specified both of a copy of that statement and of the notice to
owner.

(3) Any address specified in any such certificate as is mentioned in subsection (2) above
as being the address at which service of the notice to owner was effected shall be taken for
the purposes of any proceedings in which the certificate is tendered in evidence to be the
accused's proper address, unless the contrary is proved.

(4) Where a copy of a constable's witness statement is included in or served with a notice
to owner served in any manner in which the notice is authorised to be served under this Part
of this Act, the statement shall be treated as duly served for the purposes of section 9 of the
Criminal Justice Act 1967 (proof by written statement) notwithstanding that the manner of
service is not authorised by subsection (8) of that section.

(5) In relation to any proceedings in which service of a constable's witness statement is
proved by certificate under this section—

 (a) that service shall be taken for the purposes of subsection (2)(c) of that section (copy
of statement to be tendered in evidence to be served before hearing on other
parties to the proceedings by or on behalf of the party proposing to tender it) to
have been effected by or on behalf of the prosecutor, and

 (b) subsection (2)(d) of that section (time for objection) shall have effect with the substitution, for the reference to seven days from the service of the copy of the statement, of a reference to seven days from the relevant date.

(6) In subsection (5)(b) above *"relevant date"* means—

 (a) where the accused gives notice requesting a hearing in respect of the offence in
accordance with any provision of this Part of this Act, the date on which he gives
that notice, and

 (b) where a notice in respect of the offence was given to the accused under section

54(4) of this Act but no fixed penalty notice is given in respect of it, the last day for production of the notice under section 54(5) at a police station in accordance with that section.

(7) This section does not extend to Scotland.

80. Certificates about payment

A26.164   In any proceedings a certificate—

(a) that payment of a fixed penalty was or was not received, by a date specified in the certificate, by the fixed penalty clerk, or

(b) that a letter containing an amount sent by post in payment of a fixed penalty was marked as posted on a date so specified,

shall, if the certificate purports to be signed by the fixed penalty clerk, be evidence . . . of the facts stated.

A26.165   *[Words relating exclusively and expressly to Scotland in section 80 have been omitted.]*

81. Documents signed by the accused

A26.166   (1) Where—

(a) any person is charged with a fixed penalty offence, and

(b) the prosecutor produces to the court a document to which this subsection applies purporting to have been signed by the accused,

the document shall be presumed, unless the contrary is proved, to have been signed by the accused and shall be evidence . . . in the proceedings of any facts stated in it tending to show that the accused was the owner, the hirer or the driver of the vehicle concerned at a particular time.

(2) Subsection (1) above applies to any document purporting to be—

(a) a notice requesting a hearing in respect of the offence charged given in accordance with a fixed penalty notice relating to that offence, or

(b) a statutory statement of any description defined in Schedule 4 to this Act or a copy of a statement of liability within the meaning of section 66 of this Act provided in response to a notice to owner.

A26.167   *[Words relating exclusively and expressly to Scotland in section 81(1) have been omitted.]*

Miscellaneous

82. Accounting for fixed penalties: England and Wales

A26.168   (1) In England and Wales, sums paid by way of fixed penalty for an offence shall be treated for the purposes of [section 60 of the Justices of the Peace Act 1997 (application of fines and fees)] as if they were fines imposed on summary conviction for that offence.

[(2) Where, in England and Wales, a [justices' chief executive] for a petty sessions area comprised in the area of one magistrates' courts committee ("*the first committee*") discharges functions in connection with a fixed penalty for an offence alleged to have been committed in a petty sessions area comprised in the area of another magistrates' courts committee ("*the second committee*")—

(a) the paying authority or authorities in relation to the second committee must make to the paying authority or authorities in relation to the first committee such payment in connection with the discharge of those functions as may be agreed between all the paying authorities concerned or, in default of such agreement, as may be determined by the Lord Chancellor, and

(b) any such payment between paying authorities shall be taken into account in determining for the purposes of [section 57 of the Justices of the Peace Act 1997] the net cost to the responsible authorities of the functions referred to in subsection (1) of that section.]

[(2A) In subsection (2) above "*paying authority*" and "*responsible authority*" have the same meaning as in section 55 of [the Justices of the Peace Act 1979][; except that, in relation to the Greater London Magistrates' Courts Authority, the Authority is the paying authority and responsible authority].]

(3) Subsection (2) above does not apply to functions discharged in connection with a fixed penalty on or after the registration of a sum determined by reference to the penalty under section 71 of this Act.

[Section 82 is printed as amended by the Police and Magistrates' Courts Act 1994, s.91(1) and Sched. 8, para.32; the Justices of the Peace Act 1997, s.73(3) and Sched. 5, para.25; and (with effect from April 1, 2001) the Access to Justice Act 1999, ss.83(3) and 90(1) and Scheds 12 (para.3) and 13 (paras 140 and 154) (see the Access to Justice Act 1999 (Commencement No. 7, Transitional Provisions and Savings) Order 2001 (S.I. 2001 No. 916; not reproduced in this work), arts 1(2) and 2(a)(ii)).]   **A26.169**

83. Powers of court where clerk deceived

(1) This section applies where—   **A26.170**

(a) in endorsing any person's licence under section 57 of this Act, the fixed penalty clerk is deceived as to whether endorsement under that section is excluded by section 61(2) of this Act by virtue of the fact that the licence holder would be liable to be disqualified under section 35 of this Act if he were convicted of the offence, or

(b) in endorsing any person's licence under section 77 of this Act the [justices' chief executive or] clerk of court specified in the conditional offer (within the meaning of that section) is deceived as to whether he is required by section 76(5) of this Act to return the licence without endorsing it by virtue of the fact that the licence holder would be liable to be disqualified under section 35 of this Act if he were convicted of the offence.

(2) If—

(a) the deception constituted or was due to an offence committed by the licence holder, and

(b) the licence holder is convicted of that offence,

the court by or before which he is convicted shall have the same powers and duties as it would have had if he had also been convicted by or before it of the offence of which particulars were endorsed under section 57 or, as the case may be, 77 of this Act.

[Section 83 is printed as amended (with effect from April 1, 2001) by the Access to Justice Act 1999, s.90(1) and Sched. 13, paras 140 and 155 (see the Access to Justice Act 1999 (Commencement No. 7, Transitional Provisions and Savings) Order 2001 (S.I. 2001 No. 916; not reproduced in this work), arts 1(2) and 2(a)(ii)).   **A26.171**

    Community driving licence. *In relation to driving licences which came into force after May 31, 1990 (after December 31, 1990 for Northern Ireland driving licences) only, section 83 was amended by the Driving Licences (Community Driving Licence) Regulations 1990 (S.I. 1990 No. 144) on April 1, 1990 so that:*   **A26.172**

    (i) the words "the counterpart of" were inserted in section 83(1)(a) after the word "endorsing";

    (ii) the words "the counterpart of" were inserted in section 83(1)(b) after the word "endorsing"; and

(iii)   *the words "and its counterpart without endorsing the counterpart" were substituted in section 83(1)(b) for the words "without endorsing it".]*

84. Regulations   *[Omitted.]*

85. Service of documents

A26.173   (1) Subject to any requirement of this Part of this Act with respect to the manner in which a person may be provided with any such document, he may be provided with the following documents by post (but without prejudice to any other method of providing him with them), that is to say—

    (a) any of the statutory statements mentioned in Schedule 4 to this Act, and

    (b) any of the documents mentioned in section 66(2) of this Act.

(2) Where a notice requesting a hearing in respect of an offence is permitted by a fixed penalty notice or notice to owner relating to that offence to be given by post, section 7 of the Interpretation Act 1978 (service of documents by post) shall apply as if that notice were permitted to be so given by this Act.

(3) A notice to owner may be served on any person—

    (a) by delivering it to him or leaving it at his proper address, or

    (b) by sending it to him by post,

and where the person on whom such a notice is to be served is a body corporate it is duly served if it is served on the secretary or clerk of that body.

(4) For the purposes of this Part of this Act and of section 7 of the Interpretation Act 1978 as it applies for the purposes of subsection (3) above the proper address of any person in relation to the service on him of a notice to owner is—

    (a) in the case of the secretary or clerk of a body corporate, that of the registered or principal office of that body or the registered address of the person who is or was the registered keeper of the vehicle concerned at the time of service, and

    (b) in any other case, his last known address at the time of service.

(5) In subsection (4) above, *"registered address"*, in relation to the registered keeper of a vehicle, means the address recorded in the record kept under [the Vehicle Excise and Registration Act 1994] with respect to that vehicle as being that person's address.

A26.174   *[Section 85 is printed as amended by the Vehicle Excise and Registration Act 1994, s.63 and Sched. 3, para.25(1).]*

86. Functions of traffic wardens

A26.175   (1) An order under section 95(5) of the Road Traffic Regulation Act 1984 may not authorise the employment of a traffic warden to discharge any function under this Part of this Act in respect of an offence if the offence appears to the traffic warden to be an offence involving obligatory endorsement [unless that offence was committed whilst the vehicle concerned was stationary].

(2) In so far as an order under that section authorises the employment of traffic wardens for the purposes of this Part of this Act, references in this Part of this Act to a constable or, as the case may be, to a constable in uniform include a traffic warden.

A26.176   *[Section 86 is printed as amended by the Road Traffic Act 1991, s.48 and Sched. 4, para.106.*
The Functions of Traffic Wardens Order 1970 (S.I. 1970 No. 1958) (q.v.) has effect as if made under the Road Traffic Regulation Act 1984, s.95(5).]

87. Guidance on application of Part III   *[Omitted.]*   A26.177

88. Procedure for regulations and orders   *[Omitted.]*

89. Interpretation

(1) In this Part of this Act—   A26.178

"*authorised person*" has the meaning given by section 54(9) of this Act,

. . .

"*chief officer of police*" (except in the definition of "*authorised person*") means, in relation to any fixed penalty notice [, notice to owner or conditional offer], the chief officer of police for the police area in which the fixed penalty offence in question is alleged to have been committed,

. . .

"*driver*" except in section 62 of this Act means, in relation to an alleged fixed penalty offence, the person by whom, assuming the offence to have been committed, it was committed,

. . . and

"*proceedings*", except in relation to proceedings for enforcing payment of a sum registered under section 71 of this Act, means criminal proceedings.

(2) In this Part of this Act—

  (a) references to a notice requesting a hearing in respect of an offence are references to a notice indicating that the person giving the notice wishes to contest liability for the offence or seeks a determination by a court with respect to the appropriate punishment for the offence,

  (b) references to an offence include an alleged offence, and

  (c) references to the person who is or was at any time the registered keeper of a vehicle are references to the person in whose name the vehicle is or was at that time registered under [the Vehicle Excise and Registration Act 1994].

[Section 89 is printed as amended by the Road Traffic Act 1991, s.48 and Sched. 4, para.107(1)–(3);   A26.179
the Vehicle Excise and Registration Act 1994, s.63 and Sched. 3, para.25(1); and the Access to Justice Act 1999, s.106 and Sched. 15, Pt V(1); and also (with effect from April 1, 2001) by the 1999 Act, s.105 and Sched. 15, Pt V(7) (see the Access to Justice Act 1999 (Commencement No. 7, Transitional Provisions and Savings) Order 2001 (S.I. 2001 No. 916; not reproduced in this work), arts 1(2) and 2(a)(ii)).

Two definitions ("chief constable" and "court of summary jurisdiction") which are applicable exclusively to Scotland have been omitted from section 89(1).]

90. Index to Part III

The expressions listed in the left-hand column below are respectively defined or (as the   A26.180
case may be) fall to be construed in accordance with the provisions of this Part of this Act listed in the right-hand column in relation to those expressions.

Expression	*Relevant provision*
Authorised person	Section 54(9)
Conditional offer	[Section 75(3)]
Fixed penalty	Section 53
Fixed penalty clerk	Section[s] 69(4) [and 75(4)]
Fixed penalty notice	Section 52

[continued on next page

Expression	Relevant provision
Fixed penalty offence	Section 51
Notice to owner	Sections 63(2) and 66(4)
Notice requesting a hearing in respect of an offence	Section 89(2)
Offence	Section 89(2)
Official form	Section 68(4)
Owner	Section 68(1)
Period allowed for response to a notice to owner	Section 63(5)
Proper address, in relation to the service of a notice to owner	Section 85(4)
Registered keeper	Section 89(2)
Statutory statement of facts	Part II of Schedule 4
Statutory statement of hiring	Part I of Schedule 4
Statutory statement of ownership	Part I of Schedule 4
Suspended enforcement period	Section 52(3)(a)
Time of the alleged offence	Section 63(3)

A26.181   *[Section 90 is printed as amended by the Road Traffic Act 1991, s.48 and Sched. 4, para.108(a) and (b).*

A "conditional offer" (which is defined in section 75(4)) is applicable only in Scotland.]

PART IV

Miscellaneous and General

91. Penalty for breach of regulations

A26.182   If a person acts in contravention of or fails to comply with—

(a) any regulations made by the Secretary of State under the Road Traffic Act 1988 other than regulations made under section 31, 45 or 132,

(b) any regulations made by the Secretary of State under the Road Traffic Regulation Act 1984, other than regulations made under section 28, Schedule 4, Part III of Schedule 9 or Schedule 12,

and the contravention of failure to comply is not made an offence under any other provision of the Traffic Acts, he shall for each offence be liable on summary conviction to a fine not exceeding level 3 on the standard scale.

[91A. Application to Community licence holders

A26.183   (1) The references in sections 7, 26(7) and (8) and (9)(b), 27, 29(1), 30, 31(1), 32, 42(5), 44(1), 46(2), 47(3) and 48(1) and (2) of this Act to a licence includes references to a Community licence; and accordingly the reference in section 27(3)(b) of this Act to the suspension of a licence is to be construed in relation to a Community licence as a reference to the Community licence holder ceasing to be authorised by virtue of section 99(a)(1) of the Road Traffic Act 1988 to drive in Great Britain a motor vehicle of any class.

(2) The references in sections 26(9)(a) and 27(3) of this Act to a new licence include references to a counterpart of a Community licence.

(3) In relation to a Community licence holder to whom a counterpart is issued under section 99B of the Road Traffic Act 1988, the references in Part III of this Act (except sections 75(12), 76(8) and 77(9) of this Act) to a licence include references to a Community licence.

(4) Where a court orders the endorsement of the counterpart of any Community licence held by a person, it must send notice of the endorsement to the Secretary of State.

(5) Where a court orders the holder of a Community licence to be disqualified, it must send the Community licence and its counterpart (if any), on their being produced to the court, to the Secretary of State.

(6) A notice sent by a court to the Secretary of State in pursuance of subsection (4) above must be sent in such manner and to such address and contain such particulars as the Secretary of State may determine, and a Community licence and its counterpart (if any) so sent in pursuance of subsection (5) above must be sent to such address as the Secretary of State may determine.

(7) Where a Community licence held by a person who is ordered by the court to be disqualified is sent to the Secretary of State in pursuance of subsection (5) above, the Secretary of State—

(a) must send to the licensing authority in the EEA State in respect of which the Community licence was issued the holder's name and address and particulars of the disqualification, and

(b) must (subject to subsection (8) below) return the Community licence to the holder—

(i) on the expiry of the period of disqualification, or

(ii) if earlier, on being satisfied that the holder has left Great Britain and is not normally resident there.

(8) Where—

(a) the Secretary of State would, apart from this subsection, be under a duty on the expiry of the period of disqualification to return a Community licence to a person in pursuance of subsection (7)(b)(i) above, but

(b) at that time, the person would not be authorised by virtue of section 99A(1) of the Road Traffic Act 1988 to drive in Great Britain a motor vehicle of any class,

the Secretary of State must send the Community licence to the licensing authority in the EEA State in respect of which it was issued and explain to them his reasons for so doing.

(9) A Community licence to be returned to any person under subsection (7) above may be returned to him by delivering it to him or by leaving it at his proper address or by sending it to him by post; and for the purposes of this subsection and section 7 of the Interpretation Act 1978 in its application to this subsection the proper address of any person shall be his latest address as known to the person returning the Community licence.

(10) In this section "*period of disqualification*" means, in relation to a Community licence holder, the period for which he is ordered by the court to be disqualified (otherwise than under section 36 of this Act).]

A26.184

[Section 91A was inserted by the Driving Licences (Community Driving Licence) Regulations 1996 (S.I. 1996 No. 1974), reg.3 and Sched. 2, para.4 (not reproduced in this work).

As to the European Economic Area (EEA), see the note to Regulation (EEC) 3820/85 below.]

[91B. Effect of endorsement on Community licence holders

A26.185   (1) An order that any particulars or penalty points are to be endorsed on the counterpart of any Community licence held by the person convicted shall operate as an order that—

(a) the counterpart of any Community licence which he may then hold, or

(b) the counterpart of any licence or Community licence which he may subsequently obtain,

is to be so endorsed until he becomes entitled under subsection (3) below to have a counterpart of his Community licence, or a licence and its counterpart, issued to him free from the particulars or penalty points.

(2) On the issue of a new counterpart of a Community licence or a new licence to a person, any particulars or penalty points ordered to be endorsed on the counterpart of any Community licence held by him shall be entered on the new counterpart or the counterpart of the new licence (as the case may be) unless he has become entitled under subsection (3) below to have a new counterpart of his Community licence or a new licence issued to him free from those particulars or penalty points.

(3) A person the counterpart of whose Community licence has been ordered to be endorsed is entitled to have issued to him with effect from the end of the period for which the endorsement remains effective (as determined in accordance with section 45(5) of this Act)—

(a) a new counterpart of any Community licence then held by him free from the endorsement if he makes an application to the Secretary of State for that purpose in such manner as the Secretary of State may determine, or

(b) a new licence with a counterpart free from the endorsement if he applies for a new licence in pursuance of section 97(1) of the Road Traffic Act 1988, surrenders any subsisting licence and its counterpart, pays the fee prescribed by regulations under Part III of that Act and satisfies the other requirements of section 97(1).]

A26.186   *[Section 91B was inserted by the Driving Licences (Community Driving Licence) Regulations 1996 (S.I. 1996 No. 1974), reg.3 and Sched. 2, para.5 (not reproduced in this work).]*

92. Application to Crown

A26.187   The following provisions of this Act apply to vehicles and persons in the public service of the Crown: sections 1, 2, 3, 15, 16 [, 20] and 49 and the provisions connected with the licensing of drivers.

A26.188   *[Section 92 is printed as amended by the Road Traffic Act 1991, s.48 and Sched. 4, para.109.]*

93. Application of sections 15 and 16 to persons subject to service discipline

A26.189   (1) Sections 15 and 16, in their application to persons subject to service discipline, apply outside as well as within Great Britain and have effect as if—

(a) references to proceedings for an offence under an enactment included references to proceedings for the corresponding service offence,

(b) references to the court included a reference to any naval, military, or air force authority before whom the proceedings take place,

(c) references to a constable included references to a member of the provost staff, and

(d) in section 15, subsection (4) were omitted.

(2) Expressions used in this section have the same meaning as in sections [3A] to 10 of the Road Traffic Act 1988 [*q.v.*].

[Section 93 is printed as amended by the Road Traffic Act 1991, s.48 and Sched. 4, para.110.]   **A26.190**

94. Proceedings in respect of offences in connection with Crown vehicles

(1) Where an offence under the Traffic Acts is alleged to have been committed in con-   **A26.191**
nection with a vehicle in the public service of the Crown, proceedings may be brought in
respect of the offence against a person nominated for the purpose on behalf of the
Crown.

(2) Subject to subsection (3) below, where any such offence is committed any person so
nominated shall also be guilty of the offence as well as any person actually responsible for
the offence (but without prejudice to proceedings against any person so responsible).

(3) Where any person is convicted of an offence by virtue of this section—

(a) no order is to be made on his conviction save an order imposing a fine,

(b) payment of any fine imposed on him in respect of that offence is not to be enforced
against him, and

(c) apart from the imposition of any such fine, the conviction is to be disregarded
for all purposes other than any appeal (whether by way of case stated or otherwise).

95. Destination of Scottish fines   *[Omitted.]*   **A26.192**

96. Meaning of "offence involving obligatory endorsement"

For the purposes of this Act, an offence involves obligatory endorsement if it is an   **A26.193**
offence under a provision of the Traffic Acts specified in column 1 of Part I of Schedule 2
to this Act or an offence specified in column 1 of Part II of that Schedule and either—

(a) the word "obligatory" (without qualification) appears in column 6 (in the case of
Part I) or column 3 (in the case of Part II) against the offence, or

(b) that word appears there qualified by conditions relating to the offence which are
satisfied.

97. Meaning of "offence involving obligatory disqualification" and "offence involving discretionary disqualification"

(1) For the purposes of this Act, an offence involves obligatory disqualification if it is an   **A26.194**
offence under a provision of the Traffic Acts specified in column 1 of Part I of Schedule 2
to this Act or an offence specified in column 1 of Part II of that Schedule and either—

(a) the word "obligatory" (without qualification) appears in column 5 (in the case of
Part I) or column 2 (in the case of Part II) against the offence, or

(b) that word appears there qualified by conditions or circumstances relating to the
offence which are satisfied or obtain.

(2) For the purposes of this Act, an offence involves discretionary disqualification if it is
an offence under a provision of the Traffic Acts specified in column 1 of Part I of Schedule
2 to this Act or an offence specified in column 1 of Part II of that Schedule and either—

(a) the word "discretionary" (without qualification) appears in column 5 (in the case of
Part I) or column 2 (in the case of Part II) against the offence, or

(b) that word appears there qualified by conditions or circumstances relating to the
offence which are satisfied or obtain.

98. General interpretation

A26.195   (1) In this Act—

"*disqualified*" means disqualified for holding or obtaining a licence and "*disqualification*" is to be construed accordingly,

"*drive*" has the same meaning as in the Road Traffic Act 1988,

"*licence*" means a licence to drive a motor vehicle granted under Part III of that Act . . .

"*provisional licence*" means a licence granted by virtue of section 97(2) of that Act [*q.v.*],

"*the provisions connected with the licensing of drivers*" means sections 7, 8, 22, 25 to 29, 31, 32, 34 to 48, [91A, 91B,] 96 and 97 of this Act,

"*road*"—

    (a) in relation to England and Wales, means any highway and any other road to which the public has access, and includes bridges over which a road passes, and

    (b) *[applies to Scotland.]*

"*the Road Traffic Acts*" means the Road Traffic Act 1988, the Road Traffic (Consequential Provisions) Act 1988 (so far as it reproduces the effect of provisions repealed by that Act) and this Act, and

"*the Traffic Acts*" means the Road Traffic Acts and the Road Traffic Regulation Act 1984.

[and "*Community licence*", "*counterpart*" and "*EEA State*" have the same meanings as in Part III of the Road Traffic Act 1988.]

(2) Sections 185 and 186 of the Road Traffic Act 1988 [*q.v.*] (meaning of "motor vehicle" and other expressions relating to vehicles) apply for the purposes of this Act as they apply for the purposes of that [Act].

(3) In the Schedules to this Act—

"*RTRA*" is used as an abbreviation for the Road Traffic Regulation Act 1984, and

"*RTA*" is used as an abbreviation for the Road Traffic Act 1988 [or, if followed by "1989", the Road Traffic (Driver Licensing and Information Systems) Act 1989].

(4) Subject to any express exception, references in this Act to any Part of this Act include a reference to any Schedule to this Act so far as relating to that Part.

A26.196   *[Section 98 is printed as amended by the Road Traffic (Driver Licensing and Information Systems) Act 1989, s.7 and Sched. 3, para.26; the Road Traffic Act 1991, s.48 and Sched. 4, para.111(2); the Driving Licences (Community Driving Licence) Regulations 1996 (S.I. 1996 No. 1974), reg.3 and Sched. 2, para.6 (not reproduced in this work).*

As to the European Economic Area (EEA), see the note to Regulation (EEC) 3820/85 below.

As to the meaning of the term "drive" in the Road Traffic Act 1988, see ibid., s.192 above. As to the meaning of "licence" in Part III of that Act, see ibid., s.108 above.]

99. Short title, commencement and extent

A26.197   (1) This Act may be cited as the Road Traffic Offenders Act 1988.

(2) This Act, except so far as it may be brought into force under subsection (3) or (5) below, shall come into force at the end of the period of six months beginning with the day on which it is passed.

(3), (4) *[Apply to Scotland.]*

(5) Section 59 of this Act shall come into force on such day or days as the Secretary of State may by order made by statutory instrument appoint.

(6) An order under subsection (3) or (5) above may contain such transitional provisions and savings (whether or not involving the modification of any provisions contained in an Act or in subordinate legislation (within the meaning of the Interpretation Act 1978)) as appear to the Secretary of State necessary or expedient in connection with the provisions brought (wholly or partly) into force by the order, and different days may be appointed for different purposes.

(7) This Act, except as provided by section 93, does not extend to Northern Ireland.

SCHEDULE 1   Sections 1, etc.

OFFENCES TO WHICH SECTIONS 1, 6, 11 AND 12(1) APPLY

1.—(1) Where section 1, 6, 11 or 12(1) of this Act is shown in column 3 of this Schedule   **A26.198**
against a provision of the Road Traffic Act 1988 specified in column 1, the section in question applies to an offence under that provision.

[**1A.** Section 1 also applies to—

(a) an offence under section 16 of the Road Traffic Regulation Act 1984 consisting in the contravention of a restriction on the speed of vehicles imposed under section 14 of that Act,

(b) an offence under subsection (4) of section 17 of that Act consisting in the contravention of a restriction on the speed of vehicles imposed under that section, and

(c) an offence under section 88(7) or 89(1) of that Act (speeding offences).]

(2) The general nature of the offence is indicated in column 2.

2. Section 6 also applies—   **A26.199**

(a) to an offence under section 67 of this Act, . . .

(b) *[applies to Scotland]* . . .

[(c) [to] an offence under section 1(5) of the Road Traffic (Driver Licensing and Information Systems) Act 1989] [and]

[(d) to an offence under paragraph 3(5) of Schedule 1 to the Road Traffic (New Drivers) Act 1995.]

3. Section 11 also applies to—

(a) any offence to which section 112 of the Road Traffic Regulation Act 1984 [*q.v.*] (information as to identity of driver or rider) applies except an offence under section 61(5) of that Act,

(b) any offence which is punishable under section 91 of this Act, . . .

[(bb) an offence under paragraph 3 of Schedule 1 to the Road Traffic (Driver Licensing and Information Systems) Act 1989, and]

(c) any offence against any other enactment relating to the use of vehicles on roads.

4. Section 12(1) also applies to—   **A26.200**

(a) any offence which is punishable under section 91 of this Act, . . .

[(aa) an offence under paragraph 3(1) of Schedule 1 to the Road Traffic (Driver Licensing and Information Systems) Act 1989, and]

(b) any offence against any other enactment relating to the use of vehicles on roads.

(1) *Provision creating offence*	(2) *General nature of offence*	(3) *Applicable provisions of this Act*
RTA section 1	Causing death by [dangerous] driving.	Section 11 of this Act.
RTA section 2	[Dangerous] driving.	Sections 1, 11 and 12(1) of this Act.
RTA section 3	Careless, and inconsiderate, driving.	Sections 1, 11 and 12(1) of this Act.
[RTA section 3A	Causing death by careless driving when under influence of drink or drugs.	Section 11 of this Act.]
RTA section 4	Driving or attempting to drive, or being in charge of a [mechanically propelled vehicle], when unfit to drive through drink or drugs.	Sections 11 and 12(1) of this Act.
RTA section 5	Driving or attempting to drive, or being in charge of a motor vehicle, with excess alcohol in breath, blood or urine.	Sections 11 and 12(1) of this Act.
RTA section 6	Failing to provide a specimen of breath for a breath test.	Sections 11 and 12(1) of this Act.
RTA section 7	Failing to provide specimen for analysis or laboratory test.	Sections 11 and 12(1) of this Act.
RTA section 12	Motor racing and speed trials.	Sections 11 and 12(1) of this Act.
RTA section 14	Driving or riding in a motor vehicle in contravention of regulations requiring wearing of seat belts.	Sections 11 and 12(1) of this Act.
RTA section 15	Driving motor vehicle with child not wearing seat belt.	Sections 11 and 12(1) of this Act.
RTA section 19	Prohibition of parking of heavy commercial vehicles on verges and footways.	Sections 11 and 12(1) of this Act.
RTA section 22	Leaving vehicles in dangerous positions.	Sections 1, 11 and 12(1) of this Act.
RTA section 23	Carrying passenger on motor-cycle contrary to section 23.	Sections 11 and 12(1) of this Act.
RTA section 24	Carrying passenger on bicycle contrary to section 24.	Sections 11 and 12(1) of this Act.
RTA section 25	Tampering with motor vehicles.	Section 11 of this Act.
RTA section 26(1)	Holding or getting onto vehicle in order to be carried.	Section 11 of this Act.
RTA section 26(2)	Holding onto vehicle in order to be towed.	Sections 11 and 12(1) of this Act.
RTA section 28	[Dangerous] cycling.	Sections 1, 11 and 12(1) of this Act.
RTA section 29	Careless, and inconsiderate, cycling.	Sections 1, 11 and 12(1) of this Act.
RTA section 30	Cycling when unfit through drink or drugs.	Sections 11 and 12(1) of this Act.

[continued on next page

(1) *Provision creating offence*	(2) *General nature of offence*	(3) *Applicable provisions of this Act*
RTA section 31	Unauthorised or irregular cycle racing, or trials of speed.	Sections 11 and 12(1) of this Act.
RTA section 33	Unauthorised motor vehicle trial on footpaths or bridleways.	Sections 11 and 12(1) of this Act.
RTA section 34	Driving motor vehicles elsewhere than on roads.	Sections 11 and 12(1) of this Act.
RTA section 35	Failing to comply with traffic directions.	Sections 1, 11 and 12(1) of this Act.
RTA section 36	Failing to comply with traffic signs.	Sections 1, 11 and 12(1) of this Act.
[RTA section 40A	Using vehicle in dangerous condition, etc.	Sections 11 and 12(1) of this Act.]
[RTA section 41A	Breach of requirement as to brakes, steering-gear or tyres.	Sections 11 and 12(1) of this Act.]
[RTA section 41B	Breach of requirement as to weight: goods and passenger vehicles.	Sections 11 and 12(1) of this Act.]
RTA section 42	[Breach of other construction and use requirements].	Sections 11 and 12(1) of this Act.
RTA section 47	Using, etc., vehicle without required test certificate being in force.	Sections 11 and 12(1) of this Act.
RTA section 53	Using, etc., goods vehicle without required plating certificate or goods vehicle test certificate being in force, or where Secretary of State is required by regulations under section 49 to be notified of an alteration to the vehicle or its equipment but has not been notified.	Sections 11 and 12(1) of this Act.
RTA section 63	Using, etc., vehicle without required certificate being in force showing that it, or a part fitted to it, complies with type approval requirements applicable to it, or using, etc., certain goods vehicles for drawing trailer when plating certificate does not specify maximum laden weight for vehicle and trailer, or using, etc., goods vehicle where Secretary of State has not been but is required to be notified under section 48 of alteration to it or its equipment.	Sections 11 and 12(1) of this Act.
RTA section 71	Driving, etc., . . . vehicle in contravention of prohibition on driving it as being unfit for service or overloaded, or refusing, neglecting or otherwise failing to comply with a direction to remove a . . . vehicle found overloaded.	Sections 11 and 12(1) of this Act.
RTA section 78	Failing to comply with requirement about weighing motor vehicle or obstructing authorised person.	Sections 11 and 12(1) of this Act.

[*continued on next page*

(1) *Provision creating offence*	(2) *General nature of offence*	(3) *Applicable provisions of this Act*
RTA section 87(1)	Driving [otherwise than in accordance with] a licence.	Sections 11 and 12(1) of this Act.
RTA section 87(2)	Causing or permitting a person to drive [otherwise than in accordance with] a licence.	Section 11 of this Act.
[RTA section 92(10)	Driving after making false declaration as to physical fitness.	Sections 6, 11 and 12(1) of this Act.]
RTA [section 94(3)] [and that subsection as applied by RTA section 99D]	Failure to notify the Secretary of State of onset of, or deterioration in, relevant or prospective disability.	Section 6 of this Act.
[RTA section 94(3A) [and that subsection as applied by RTA section 99D(b)]	Driving after such a failure.	Sections 6, 11 and 12(1) of this Act.]
[RTA section 94A	Driving after refusal of licence under section 92(3) [, revocation under section 93 or service of a notice under section 99C].	Sections 6, 11 and 12(1) of this Act.]
RTA section 99	Driving licence holder failing [to surrender licence and counterpart].	Section 6 of this Act.
[RTA section 99B(11)	Driving after failure to comply with a requirement under section 99B(6), (7) or (10).	Section 6 of this Act.]
RTA section 103(1)(a)	Obtaining driving licence while disqualified.	Section 6 of this Act.
RTA section 103(1)(b)	Driving while disqualified.	Sections 6, 11 and 12(1) of this Act.
[RTA section 114(1)	Failing to comply with conditions of LGV [, PCV licence or LGV Community licence].	Sections 11 and 12(1) of this Act.]
[RTA section 114(2)	Causing or permitting a person under 21 to drive LGV or PCV in contravention of conditions of that person's licence.	Section 11 of this Act.]
RTA section 143	Using motor vehicle, or causing or permitting it to be used, while uninsured or unsecured against third party risks.	Sections 6, 11 and 12(1) of this Act.
RTA section 163	Failing to stop vehicle when required by constable.	Sections 11 and 12(1) of this Act.
RTA section 164(6)	Failing to produce driving licence [, etc.] or to state date of birth.	Sections 11 and 12(1) of this Act.
RTA section 165(3)	Failing to give constable certain names and addresses or to produce certificate of insurance or certain test and other like certificates.	Sections 11 and 12(1) of this Act.
RTA section 165(6)	Supervisor of learner driver failing to give constable certain names and addresses.	Section 11 of this Act.

[continued on next page

(1) *Provision creating offence*	(2) *General nature of offence*	(3) *Applicable provisions of this Act*
RTA section 168	Refusing to give, or giving false, name and address in case of reckless, careless or inconsiderate driving or cycling.	Sections 11 and 12(1) of this Act.
RTA section 170	Failure by driver to stop, report accident or give information or documents.	Sections 11 and 12(1) of this Act.
RTA section 171	Failure by owner of motor vehicle to give police information for verifying compliance with requirement of compulsory insurance or security.	Sections 11 and 12(1) of this Act.
RTA section 174(1) or [(5)]	Making false statements in connection with licences under this Act and with registration as an approved driving instructor; or making false statement or withholding material information in order to obtain the issue of insurance certificates, etc.	Section 6 of this Act.
RTA section 175	Issuing false documents.	Section 6 of this Act.

[Schedule 1 is printed as corrected by a correction slip dated November 1990 and as amended by the Road **A26.202**
Traffic (Driver Licensing and Information Systems) Act 1989, ss.7, 16, Sched. 3, para.27(a)–(d), and Sched. 6; the Road Traffic Act 1991, ss.22, 83, Sched. 1, paras 1–17, and Sched. 8; the Road Traffic (New Drivers) Act 1995, s.10(4) and Sched. 2, paras 3 and 7; the Driving Licences (Community Driving Licence) Regulations 1996 (S.I. 1996 No. 1974), reg.3 and Sched. 2, para.7 (not reproduced in this work); the Driving Licences (Community Driving Licence) Regulations 1998 (S.I. 1998 No. 1420), regs 2 and 16(1) and (2) (not reproduced in this work).

Schedule 1 is also prospectively amended by the Transport Act 1982, s.24(3) (as itself amended by the Road Traffic (Consequential Provisions) Act 1988, s.4 and Sched. 2, Pt I, para.13(c)(iv)), which will add the words "falsely amending certificate of conformity" to column (2) of the entry relating to the Road Traffic Act 1988, s.175, with effect from a date to be announced; see the Transport Act 1982, s.76(2).

For the extension of offences to which section 6 applies, see the note to section 6 above.

Community driving licence. *In relation to driving licences which came into force after May 31,* **A26.203**
1990 (after December 31, 1990 for Northern Ireland driving licences) only, Schedule 1 was amended by the Driving Licences (Community Driving Licence) Regulations 1990 (S.I. 1990 No. 144) (as subsequently amended by the Driving Licences (Community Driving Licence) Regulations 1998 (S.I. 1998 No. 1420), reg.17 and Schedule (not reproduced in this work) on April 1, 1990 so that:

in the table, the words "and counterpart" were inserted after the word "licence" in column (2) of the entry relating to section 164(6) of the Road Traffic Act 1988 ("RTA").

SCHEDULE 2

PROSECUTION AND PUNISHMENT OF OFFENCES

PART I

OFFENCES UNDER THE TRAFFIC ACTS

Section 9, etc.

Offences under the Road Traffic Regulation Act 1984

(1) Provision creating offence	(2) General nature of offence	(3) Mode of prosecution	(4) Punishment	(5) Disqualification	(6) Endorsement	(7) Penalty points
RTRA section 5	Contravention of traffic regulation order.	Summarily.	Level 3 on the standard scale.			
RTRA section 8	Contravention of order regulating traffic in Greater London.	Summarily.	Level 3 on the standard scale.			
RTRA section 11	Contravention of experimental traffic order.	Summarily.	Level 3 on the standard scale.			
RTRA section 13	Contravention of experimental traffic scheme in Greater London.	Summarily.	Level 3 on the standard scale.			
RTRA section 16(1)	Contravention of temporary prohibition or restriction.	Summarily.	Level 3 on the standard scale.	[Discretionary if committed in respect of a speed restriction.	Obligatory if committed in respect of a speed restriction.	3–6 or 3 (fixed penalty)]

RTRA section 16C(1)	Contravention of prohibition or restriction relating to relevant event.	Summarily.	Level 3 on the standard scale.	—	—	—]
RTRA section 17(4)	Use of special road contrary to scheme or regulations.	Summarily.	Level 4 on the standard scale.	Discretionary if committed in respect of a motor vehicle otherwise than by unlawfully stopping or allowing the vehicle to remain at rest on a part of a special road on which vehicles are in certain circumstances permitted to remain at rest.	Obligatory if committed as mentioned in the entry in column 5.	[3–6 or 3 (fixed penalty) if committed in respect of a speed restriction, 3 in any other case].
RTRA section 18(3)	One-way traffic on trunk road.	Summarily.	Level 3 on the standard scale.			
RTRA section 20(5)	Contravention of prohibition or restriction for roads of certain classes.	Summarily.	Level 3 on the standard scale.			
RTRA section 25(5)	Contravention of pedestrian	Summarily.	Level 3 on the standard scale.	Discretionary if committed in	Obligatory if committed in	3

[continued on next page

Offences under the Road Traffic Regulation Act 1984—cont.

(1) Provision creating offence	(2) General nature of offence	(3) Mode of prosecution	(4) Punishment	(5) Disqualification	(6) Endorsement	(7) Penalty points
	crossing regulations.			respect of a motor vehicle.	respect of a motor vehicle.	
RTRA section 28(3)	Not stopping at school crossing.	Summarily.	Level 3 on the standard scale.	Discretionary if committed in respect of a motor vehicle.	Obligatory if committed in respect of a motor vehicle.	3
RTRA section 29(3)	Contravention of order relating to street playground.	Summarily.	Level 3 on the standard scale.	Discretionary if committed in respect of a motor vehicle.	Obligatory if committed in respect of a motor vehicle.	2
. . . RTRA section [35A(1)]	Contravention of order as to use of parking place.	Summarily.	(a) Level 3 on the standard scale in the case of an offence committed by a person in a street parking place reserved for disabled persons' vehicles or in an off-street parking place reserved for such			

[*continued on next page*

Provision creating offence	General nature of offence	Mode of prosecution	Punishment
RTRA section [35A(2)]	[Misuse of apparatus for collecting charges or of parking device or connected apparatus].	Summarily.	vehicles, where that person would not have been guilty of that offence if the motor vehicle in respect of which it was committed had been a disabled person's vehicle. (b) Level 2 on the standard scale in any other case. Level 3 on the standard scale.
RTRA section [35A(5)]	Plying for hire in parking place.	Summarily.	Level 2 on the standard scale.
RTRA section 43(5)	Unauthorised disclosure of information in respect of licensed parking place.	Summarily.	Level 3 on the standard scale.
RTRA section 43(10)	Failure to comply with term or	Summarily.	Level 3 on the standard scale.

Offences under the Road Traffic Regulation Act 1984—cont.

(1) Provision creating offence	(2) General nature of offence	(3) Mode of prosecution	(4) Punishment	(5) Disqualification	(6) Endorsement	(7) Penalty points
	conditions of licence to operate parking place.					
	Operation of public off-street parking place without licence.	Summarily.	Level 5 on the standard scale.			
RTRA section 47(1)	Contraventions relating to designated parking places.	Summarily.	(a) Level 3 on the standard scale in the case of an offence committed by a person in a street parking place reserved for disabled persons' vehicles where that person would not have been guilty of that offence if the motor vehicle in respect of which it was committed had been a disabled person's vehicle. (b) Level 2 in any			

RTRA section 47(3)	Tampering with parking meter.	Summarily.	other case. Level 3 on the standard scale.	
RTRA section 52(1)	Misuse of parking device.	Summarily.	Level 2 on the standard scale.	
RTRA section 53(5)	Contravention of certain provisions of designation orders.	Summarily.	Level 3 on the standard scale.	
RTRA section 53(6)	Other contraventions of designation orders.	Summarily.	Level 2 on the standard scale.	
RTRA section 61(5)	Unauthorised use of loading area.	Summarily.	Level 3 on the standard scale.	
RTRA section 88(7)	Contravention of minimum speed limit.	Summarily.	Level 3 on the standard scale.	
RTRA section 89(1)	Exceeding speed limit.	Summarily.	Level 3 on the standard scale.	Discretionary.
RTRA section 104(5)	Interference with notice as to immobilisation device.	Summarily.	Level 2 on the standard scale.	
RTRA section 104(6)	Interference with immobilisation device.	Summarily.	Level 3 on the standard scale.	
RTRA section 105(5)	Misuse of disabled person's badge (immobilisation devices).	Summarily.	Level 3 on the standard scale.	

Obligatory.　[3–6 or 3 (fixed penalty)].

[*continued on next page*

(1) Provision creating offence	(2) General nature of offence	(3) Mode of prosecution	(4) Punishment	(5) Disqualification	(6) Endorsement	(7) Penalty points
Offences under the Road Traffic Regulation Act 1984—cont.						
RTRA section 108(2) or that sub-section as modified by section 109(2), (3))	Non-compliance with notice (excess charge).	Summarily.	Level 3 on the standard scale.			
RTRA section 108(3) (or that subsection as modified by section 109(2) and (3))	False response to notice (excess charge).	Summarily.	Level 5 on the standard scale.			
RTRA section 112(4)	Failure to give information as to identity of driver.	Summarily.	Level 3 on the standard scale.			
RTRA section 115(1)	Mishandling or faking parking documents.	(a) Summarily. (b) On indictment.	(a) The statutory maximum. (b) 2 years.			
RTRA section 115(2)	False statement for procuring authorisation.	Summarily.	Level 4 on the standard scale.			
RTRA section 116(1)	Non-delivery of suspect document or article.	Summarily.	Level 3 on the standard scale.			

Provision	General nature of offence	Mode of prosecution	Punishment	Disqualification	Endorsement	Penalty points
RTRA section 117	Wrongful use of disabled person's badge.	Summarily.	Level 3 on the standard scale.			
RTRA section 129(3)	Failure to give evidence at inquiry.	Summarily.	Level 3 on the standard scale.			

Offences under the Road Traffic Act 1988

Provision	General nature of offence	Mode of prosecution	Punishment	Disqualification	Endorsement	Penalty points
RTA section 1	Causing death by [dangerous] driving.	On indictment.	[10 years].	Obligatory.	Obligatory.	[3–11]
RTA section 2	[Dangerous] driving.	(a) Summarily.	(a) 6 months or the statutory maximum or both.	[Obligatory.]	Obligatory.	[3–11]
		(b) On indictment.	(b) 2 years or a fine or both.			
RTA section 3	Careless, and inconsiderate, driving.	Summarily.	Level 4 on the standard scale.	Discretionary.	Obligatory.	3–9
[RTA section 3A	Causing death by careless driving when under influence of drink or drugs.	On indictment.	[10 years] or a fine or both.	Obligatory.	Obligatory.	[3–11]
RTA section 4(1)	Driving or attempting to drive when unfit to drive through drink or drugs.	Summarily.	6 months or level 5 on the standard scale or both.	Obligatory.	Obligatory.	[3–11]
RTA section 4(2)	Being in charge of a [mechanically	Summarily.	3 months or level 4 on the	Discretionary.	Obligatory.	10

[continued on next page

Offences under the Road Traffic Act 1988—cont.

(1) Provision creating offence	(2) General nature of offence	(3) Mode of prosecution	(4) Punishment	(5) Disqualification	(6) Endorsement	(7) Penalty points
	propelled vehicle] when unfit to drive through drink or drugs.		standard scale or both.			
RTA section 5(1)(a)	Driving or attempting to drive with excess alcohol in breath, blood or urine.	Summarily.	6 months or level 5 on the standard scale or both.	Obligatory.	Obligatory.	[3–11]
RTA section 5(1)(b)	Being in charge of a motor vehicle with excess alcohol in breath, blood or urine.	Summarily.	3 months or level 4 on the standard scale or both.	Discretionary.	Obligatory.	10
RTA section 6	Failing to provide a specimen of breath for a breath test.	Summarily.	Level 3 on the standard scale.	Discretionary.	Obligatory.	4
RTA section 7	Failing to provide specimen for analysis or laboratory test.	Summarily.	(a) Where the specimen was required to ascertain ability to drive or proportion of alcohol at the time offender was driving or	(a) Obligatory in case mentioned in column 4(a).	Obligatory.	(a) [3–11 in case mentioned in column 4(a).

Provision	General nature of offence	Mode of prosecution	Punishment	Disqualification	Endorsement	Penalty points
			attempting to drive, 6 months or level 5 on the standard scale or both. (b) In any other case, 3 months or level 4 on the standard scale or both.	(b) Discretionary in any other case.	Obligatory.	(b) 10 in any other case.
RTA section 12	Motor racing and speed trials on public ways.	Summarily.	Level 4 on the standard scale.	Obligatory.	Obligatory.	[3–11]
RTA section 13	Other unauthorised or irregular competitions or trials on public ways.	Summarily.	Level 3 on the standard scale.	Obligatory.		
RTA section 14	Driving or riding in a motor vehicle in contravention of regulations requiring wearing of seat belts.	Summarily.	Level 2 on the standard scale.			
RTA section 15(2)	Driving motor vehicle with child in front not wearing seat belt.	Summarily.	Level 2 on the standard scale.			
RTA section 15(4)	Driving motor vehicle with child in rear not wearing seat belt.	Summarily.	Level 1 on the standard scale.			

[continued on next page

Offences under the Road Traffic Act 1988—cont.

(1) Provision creating offence	(2) General nature of offence	(3) Mode of prosecution	(4) Punishment	(5) Disqualification	(6) Endorsement	(7) Penalty points
[RTA section 15A(3) or (4)	Selling, etc., in certain circumstances equipment as conducive to the safety of children in motor vehicles.	Summarily.	Level 3 on the standard scale.	—	—	—
RTA section 16	Driving or riding motor cycles in contravention of regulations requiring wearing of protective headgear.	Summarily.	Level 2 on the standard scale.			
RTA section 17	Selling, etc., helmet not of the prescribed type as helmet for affording protection for motor cyclists.	Summarily.	Level 3 on the standard scale.			
RTA section 18(3)	Contravention of regulations with respect to use of headworn appliances on motor cycles.	Summarily.	Level 2 on the standard scale.			

[continued on next page

RTA section 18(4)	Selling, etc., appliance not of prescribed type as approved for use on motor cycles.	Summarily.	Level 3 on the standard scale.			
RTA section 19	Prohibition of parking of heavy commercial vehicles on verges, etc.	Summarily.	Level 3 on the standard scale.			
RTA section 21	Driving or parking on cycle track.	Summarily.	Level 3 on the standard scale.			
RTA section 22	Leaving vehicles in dangerous positions.	Summarily.	Level 3 on the standard scale.	Discretionary if committed in respect of a motor vehicle.	Obligatory if committed in respect of a motor vehicle.	3
[RTA section 22A	Causing danger to road-users.	(a) Summarily. (b) On indictment.	(a) 6 months or the statutory maximum or both. (b) 7 years or a fine or both.	—	—	—]
RTA section 23	Carrying passenger on motor cycle contrary to section 23.	Summarily.	Level 3 on the standard scale.	Discretionary.	Obligatory.	[3]
RTA section 24	Carrying passenger on bicycle contrary to section 24.	Summarily.	Level 1 on the standard scale.			
RTA section 25	Tampering with	Summarily.	Level 3 on the			

Offences under the Road Traffic Act 1988—cont.

(1) Provision creating offence	(2) General nature of offence	(3) Mode of prosecution	(4) Punishment	(5) Disqualification	(6) Endorsement	(7) Penalty points
	motor vehicles.		standard scale.			
RTA section 26	Holding or getting on to vehicle, etc., in order to be towed or carried.	Summarily.	Level 1 on the standard scale.			
RTA section 27	Dogs on designated roads without being held on lead.	Summarily.	Level 1 on the standard scale.			
RTA section 28	[Dangerous] cycling.	Summarily.	[Level 4] on the standard scale.			
RTA section 29	Careless, and inconsiderate, cycling.	Summarily.	[Level 3] on the standard scale.			
RTA section 30	Cycling when unfit through drink or drugs.	Summarily.	Level 3 on the standard scale.			
RTA section 31	Unauthorised or irregular cycle racing or trials of speed on public ways.	Summarily.	Level 1 on the standard scale.			
RTA section 32	Contravening prohibition on persons under 14 driving electrically assisted	Summarily.	Level 2 on the standard scale.			

Provision	Offence	Mode of prosecution	Punishment	Disqualification	Endorsement	Penalty points
RTA section 33	pedal cycles. Unauthorised motor vehicle trial on footpaths or bridleways.	Summarily.	Level 3 on the standard scale.			
RTA section 34	Driving motor vehicles elsewhere than on roads.	Summarily.	Level 3 on the standard scale.			
RTA section 35	Failing to comply with traffic directions.	Summarily.	Level 3 on the standard scale.	Discretionary, if committed in respect of a motor vehicle by failure to comply with a direction of a constable or traffic warden.	Obligatory if committed as described in column 5.	3
RTA section 36	Failing to comply with traffic signs.	Summarily.	Level 3 on the standard scale.	Discretionary, if committed in respect of a motor vehicle by failure to comply with an indication given by a sign specified for the purposes of this paragraph in regulations under RTA section 36.	Obligatory if committed as described in column 5.	3
RTA section 37	Pedestrian failing to	Summarily.	Level 3 on the			

[continued on next page

Offences under the Road Traffic Act 1988—cont.

(1) Provision creating offence	(2) General nature of offence	(3) Mode of prosecution	(4) Punishment	(5) Disqualification	(6) Endorsement	(7) Penalty points
	stop when directed by constable regulating traffic.		standard scale.			
[RTA section 40A	Using vehicle in dangerous condition, etc.	Summarily.	(a) Level 5 on the standard scale if committed in respect of a goods vehicle or a vehicle adapted to carry more than eight passengers. (b) Level 4 on the standard scale in any other case.	Discretionary.	Obligatory.	3]
[RTA section 41A	Breach of requirement as to brakes, steering-gear or tyres.	Summarily.	(a) Level 5 on the standard scale if committed in respect of a goods vehicle or a vehicle adapted to carry more than eight	Discretionary.	Obligatory.	3]

[RTA section 41B	Breach of requirement as to weight: goods and passenger vehicles.	Summarily.	passengers. (b) Level 4 on the standard scale in any other case.
[RTA section 42	Breach of other construction and use requirements.	Summarily.	Level 5 on the standard scale.
RTA section 47	Using, etc., vehicle without required test certificate being in force.	Summarily.	(a) Level 4 on the standard scale if committed in respect of a goods vehicle or a vehicle adapted to carry more than eight passengers. (b) Level 3 on the standard scale in any other case. (a) Level 4 on the standard scale in the case of a vehicle adapted to carry more than eight passengers. (b) Level 3 on the

[continued on next page

Offences under the Road Traffic Act 1988—cont.

(1) Provision creating offence	(2) General nature of offence	(3) Mode of prosecution	(4) Punishment	(5) Disqualification	(6) Endorsement	(7) Penalty points
Regulations under RTA section 49 made by virtue of section 51(2)	Contravention of requirement of regulations (which is declared by regulations to be an offence) that driver of goods vehicle being tested be present throughout test or drive, etc., vehicle as and when directed.	Summarily.	standard scale in any other case. Level 3 on the standard scale.			
RTA section 53(1)	Using, etc., goods vehicle without required plating certificate being in force.	Summarily.	Level 3 on the standard scale.			
RTA section 53(2)	Using, etc., goods vehicle without required goods vehicle test certificate being	Summarily.	Level 4 on the standard scale.			

RTA section 53(3)	in force. Using, etc., goods vehicle where Secretary of State is required by regulations under section 49 to be notified of an alteration to the vehicle or its equipment but has not been notified.	Summarily.	Level 3 on the standard scale.
Regulations under RTA section 61 made by virtue of subsection (4)	Contravention of requirement of regulations (which is declared by regulations to be an offence) that driver of goods vehicle being tested after notifiable alteration be present throughout test and drive, etc., vehicle as and when directed.	Summarily.	Level 3 on the standard scale.
RTA section 63(1)	Using, etc., goods vehicle without required	Summarily.	Level 4 on the standard scale.

[continued on next page

Offences under the Road Traffic Act 1988—cont.

(1) Provision creating offence	(2) General nature of offence	(3) Mode of prosecution	(4) Punishment	(5) Disqualification	(6) Endorsement	(7) Penalty points
	certificate being in force showing that it complies with type approval requirements applicable to it.					
RTA section 63(2)	Using, etc., certain goods vehicles for drawing trailer when plating certificate does not specify maximum laden weight for vehicle and trailer.	Summarily.	Level 3 on the standard scale.			
RTA section 63(3)	Using, etc., goods vehicle where Secretary of State is required to be notified under section 59 of alteration to it or its equipment but has not been notified.	Summarily.	Level 3 on the standard scale.			
RTA section 64	Using goods vehicles with	Summarily.	Level 3 on the standard scale.			

[continued on next page

[RTA section 64A		unauthorised weights as well as authorised weights marked on it. Failure to hold EC certificate of conformity for unregistered light passenger vehicle [or motor cycle].
	Summarily.	Level 3 on the standard scale.
RTA section 65		Supplying vehicle or vehicle part without required certificate being in force showing that it complies with type approval requirements applicable to it.
	Summarily.	Level 5 on the standard scale.
[RTA section 65A		Light passenger vehicles [and motor cycles] not to be sold without EC certificate of conformity.
	Summarily.	Level 5 on the standard scale.
RTA section 67		Obstructing testing of vehicle by examiner on road
	Summarily.	Level 3 on the standard scale.

(1) Provision creating offence	(2) General nature of offence	(3) Mode of prosecution	(4) Punishment	(5) Disqualification	(6) Endorsement	(7) Penalty points
		Offences under the Road Traffic Act 1988—cont.				
	or failing to comply with requirements of RTA section 67 or Schedule 2.					
RTA section 68	Obstructing inspection, etc., of . . . vehicle by examiner or failing to comply with requirement to take . . . vehicle for inspection.	Summarily.	Level 3 on the standard scale.			
RTA section 71	Driving, etc., . . . vehicle in contravention of prohibition on driving it as being unfit for service, or refusing, neglecting or otherwise failing to comply with direction to remove a . . . vehicle found overloaded.	Summarily.	Level 5 on the standard scale.			

[*continued on next page*

RTA section 74	Contravention of regulations requiring goods vehicle operator to inspect, and keep records of inspection of, goods vehicles.	Summarily.	Level 3 on the standard scale.
RTA section 75	Selling, etc., unroadworthy vehicle or trailer or altering vehicle or trailer so as to make it unroadworthy.	Summarily.	Level 5 on the standard scale.
RTA section 76(1)	Fitting of defective or unsuitable vehicle parts.	Summarily.	Level 5 on the standard scale.
RTA section 76(3)	Supplying defective or unsuitable vehicle parts.	Summarily.	Level 4 on the standard scale.
RTA section 76(8)	Obstructing examiner testing vehicles to ascertain whether defective or unsuitable part has been fitted, etc.	Summarily.	Level 3 on the standard scale.
RTA section 77	Obstructing examiner testing condition of used	Summarily.	Level 3 on the standard scale.

Offences under the Road Traffic Act 1988—cont.

(1) Provision creating offence	(2) General nature of offence	(3) Mode of prosecution	(4) Punishment	(5) Disqualification	(6) Endorsement	(7) Penalty points
	vehicles at sale rooms, etc.					
RTA section 78	Failing to comply with requirement about weighing motor vehicle or obstructing authorised person.	Summarily.	Level 5 on the standard scale.			
RTA section 81	Selling, etc., pedal cycle in contravention of regulations as to brakes, bells, etc.	Summarily.	Level 3 on the standard scale.			
RTA section 83	Selling, etc., wrongly made tail lamps or reflectors.	Summarily.	Level 5 on the standard scale.			
[RTA section 87(1)	Driving otherwise than in accordance with a licence.	Summarily.	Level 3 on the standard scale.	Discretionary in a case where the offender's driving would not have been in accordance with any licence that could have been granted to him.	Obligatory in the case mentioned in column 5.	3–6]
RTA section 87(2)	Causing or permitting a	Summarily.	Level 3 on the standard scale.			

Provision	Offence	Mode of prosecution	Punishment	Disqualification	Endorsement	Penalty points
	...person to drive [otherwise than in accordance with] a licence.			—	—	—
[RTA section 92(7C)]	Failure to deliver licence revoked by virtue of section 92(7A) to Secretary of State.	Summarily.	Level 3 on the standard scale.			
[RTA section 92(10)]	Driving after making false declaration as to physical fitness.	Summarily.	Level 4 on the standard scale.	Discretionary.	Obligatory.	3–6
[RTA section 93(3)]	Failure to deliver revoked licence to Secretary of State.	Summarily.	Level 3 on the standard scale.	—	—	—
RTA [section 94(3)]	Failure to notify Secretary of State of onset of, or deterioration in, relevant or prospective disability [and that subsection as applied by RTA section 99D].	Summarily.	Level 3 on the standard scale.			
[RTA section 94(3A)]	Driving after such a failure [and that subsection as applied by RTA section 99D(b)].	Summarily.	Level 3 on the standard scale.	Discretionary.	Obligatory.	3–6

[continued on next page

Offences under the Road Traffic Act 1988—cont.

(1) Provision creating offence	(2) General nature of offence	(3) Mode of prosecution	(4) Punishment	(5) Disqualification	(6) Endorsement	(7) Penalty points
[RTA section 94A]	Driving after refusal of licence under section 92(3) [, revocation under section 93 or service of a notice under section 99C].	Summarily.	6 months or level 5 on the standard scale or both.	Discretionary.	Obligatory.	3–6
RTA section 96	Driving with uncorrected defective eyesight, or refusing to submit to test of eyesight.	Summarily.	Level 3 on the standard scale.	Discretionary.	Obligatory.	[3]
RTA section 99[(5)]	Driving licence holder failing [to surrender licence and counterpart].	Summarily.	Level 3 on the standard scale.	—	—	—
[RTA section 99B(11)]	Driving after failure to comply with a requirement under section 99B(6), (7) or (10).	Summarily.	Level 3 on the standard scale.	—	—	—
[RTA section 99C(4)	Failure to deliver Community licence to	Summarily.	Level 3 on the standard scale.	—	—	—

Provision	General nature of offence	Mode of prosecution	Punishment	Disqualification	Endorsement	Penalty points [6]
RTA section 103(1)(a)	Secretary of State when required by notice under section 99C. Obtaining driving licence while disqualified.	Summarily.	Level 3 on the standard scale.			
RTA section 103(1)(b)	Driving while disqualified.	(a) Summarily, in England and Wales. (b) Summarily, in Scotland. (c) On indictment, in Scotland.	(a) 6 months or level 5 on the standard scale or both. (b) 6 months or the statutory maximum or both. (c) 12 months or a fine or both.	Discretionary.	Obligatory.	[6]
RTA section 109	Failing to produce to court Northern Ireland driving licence.	Summarily.	Level 3 on the standard scale.		—	—
[RTA section 114	Failing to comply with conditions of LGV [, PCV licence or LGV Community licence], or causing or permitting person under 21 to drive LGV or PCV in	Summarily.	Level 3 on the standard scale.			

[continued on next page

Offences under the Road Traffic Act 1988—cont.

(1) Provision creating offence	(2) General nature of offence	(3) Mode of prosecution	(4) Punishment	(5) Disqualification	(6) Endorsement	(7) Penalty points
	contravention of such conditions.					
[RTA section 115A(4)]	Failure to deliver LGV or PCV Community licence when required by notice under section 115A.	Summarily.	Level 3 on the standard scale.	—	—	—
[RTA section 118]	Failing to surrender revoked or suspended LGV or PCV licence.	Summarily.	Level 3 on the standard scale.	—	—	—
Regulations made by virtue of RTA [section 120(5)]	Contravention of provisions of regulations (which is declared by regulations to be an offence) about [LGV or PCV] drivers' licences [or LGV or PCV Community licence].	Summarily.	Level 3 on the standard scale.			
RTA section 123(4)	Giving of paid driving	Summarily.	Level 4 on the standard scale.			

[*continued on next page*

RTA section 123(6)	instruction by unregistered and unlicensed persons or their employers. Giving paid instruction without there being exhibited on the motor car a certificate of registration or a licence under RTA Part V.	Summarily.	Level 3 on the standard scale.		
[RTA section 125A(4)	Failure, on application for registration as disabled driving instructor, to notify Registrar of onset of, or deterioration in, relevant or prospective disability.	Summarily.	Level 3 on the standard scale.		
[RTA section 133C(4)	Failure by registered or licensed disabled driving instructor to notify Registrar of onset of, or deterioration in, relevant or	Summarily.	Level 3 on the standard scale.		

Offences under the Road Traffic Act 1988—cont.

(1) Provision creating offence	(2) General nature of offence	(3) Mode of prosecution	(4) Punishment	(5) Disqualification	(6) Endorsement	(7) Penalty points
[RTA section 133D	prospective disability. Giving of paid driving instruction by disabled persons or their employers without emergency control certificate or in unauthorised motor car.	Summarily.	Level 3 on the standard scale.	—	—	—
RTA section 135	Unregistered instructor using title or displaying badge, etc., prescribed for registered instructor, or employer using such title, etc., in relation to his unregistered instructor or issuing misleading advertisement, etc.	Summarily.	Level 4 on the standard scale.			

Provision	General nature of offence	Mode of prosecution	Punishment	Disqualification	Endorsement	Penalty points
RTA section 136	Failure of instructor to surrender to Registrar certificate or licence.	Summarily.	Level 3 on the standard scale.			
RTA section 137	Failing to produce certificate of registration or licence as driving instructor.	Summarily.	Level 3 on the standard scale.			
RTA section 143	Using motor vehicle while uninsured or unsecured against third-party risks.	Summarily.	[Level 5] on the standard scale.	Discretionary.	Obligatory.	6–8
RTA section 147	Failing to surrender certificate of insurance or security to insurer on cancellation or to make statutory declaration of loss or destruction.	Summarily.	Level 3 on the standard scale.			
RTA section 154	Failing to give information, or wilfully making a false statement, as to insurance or security when claim made.	Summarily.	Level 4 on the standard scale.			
RTA section 163	Failing to stop motor vehicle or	Summarily.	Level 3 on the standard scale.			

[continued on next page

Offences under the Road Traffic Act 1988—cont.

(1) Provision creating offence	(2) General nature of offence	(3) Mode of prosecution	(4) Punishment	(5) Disqualification	(6) Endorsement	(7) Penalty points
	cycle when required by constable.					
RTA section 164	Failing to produce driving licence [, etc.] or to state date of birth, or failing to provide the Secretary of State with evidence of date of birth, etc.	Summarily.	Level 3 on the standard scale.			
RTA section 165	Failing to give . . . certain names and addresses or to produce certain documents.	Summarily.	Level 3 on the standard scale.			
RTA section 168	Refusing to give, or giving false, name and address in case of reckless, careless or inconsiderate driving or cycling.	Summarily.	Level 3 on the standard scale.			
RTA section 169	Pedestrian failing to give constable his	Summarily.	Level 1 on the standard scale.			

Provision creating offence	General nature of offence	Mode of prosecution	Punishment	Disqualification	Endorsement	Penalty points
	name and address after failing to stop when directed by constable controlling traffic.					
RTA section 170(4)	Failing to stop after accident and give particulars or report accident.	Summarily.	[Six months or level 5 on the standard scale or both].	Discretionary.	Obligatory.	[5–10]
RTA section 170(7)	Failure by driver, in case of accident involving injury to another, to produce evidence of insurance or security or to report accident.	Summarily.	Level 3 on the standard scale.			
RTA section 171	Failure by owner of motor vehicle to give police information for verifying compliance with requirement of compulsory insurance or security.	Summarily.	Level 4 on the standard scale.			
RTA section 172	Failure of person keeping vehicle and others to give police information as to identity of driver, etc., in the	Summarily.	Level 3 on the standard scale.	[Discretionary, if committed otherwise than by virtue of subsection (5) or (11).	Obligatory, if committed otherwise than by virtue of subsection	3]

[continued on next page

Offences under the Road Traffic Act 1988—cont.

(1) Provision creating offence	(2) General nature of offence	(3) Mode of prosecution	(4) Punishment	(5) Disqualification	(6) Endorsement	(7) Penalty points
RTA section 173	case of certain offences. Forgery, etc., of licences, [counterparts of licences,] test certificates, certificates of insurance and other documents and things.	(a) Summarily. (b) On indictment.	(a) The statutory maximum. (b) 2 years.		(5) or (11).	. . .]
RTA section 174	Making certain false statements, etc., and withholding certain material information.	Summarily.	Level 4 on the standard scale.			
RTA section 175 [[RTA section] [175(2)]]	Issuing false documents. Falsely amending certificate of conformity.	Summarily. Summarily.	Level 4 on the standard scale. [Level 4 on the standard scale.]			
RTA section 177	Impersonation of, or of person employed by, authorised examiner.	Summarily.	Level 3 on the standard scale.			

[*continued on next page*

				Discretionary.
RTA section 178	Taking, etc., in Scotland a motor vehicle without authority or, knowing that it has been so taken, driving it or allowing oneself to be carried in it without authority.	(a) Summarily. (b) On indictment.	(a) 3 months or the statutory maximum or both. (b) 12 months or a fine or both.	Discretionary.
RTA section 180	Failing to attend, give evidence or produce documents to, inquiry held by Secretary of State, etc.	Summarily.	Level 3 on the standard scale.	
RTA section 181	Obstructing inspection of vehicles after accident.	Summarily.	Level 3 on the standard scale.	
RTA Schedule 1 paragraph 6	Applying warranty to [equipment, protective helmet, appliance or information in defending proceedings under RTA section 15A,] 17 or 18(4) where no warranty given,	Summarily.	Level 3 on the standard scale.	

Offences under the Road Traffic Act 1984—cont.

Offences under this Act

(1) Provision creating offence	(2) General nature of offence	(3) Mode of prosecution	(4) Punishment	(5) Disqualification	(6) Endorsement	(7) Penalty points
	or applying false warranty.					
Section 25 of this Act	Failing to give information as to date of birth or sex to court or to provide Secretary of State with evidence of date of birth, etc.	Summarily.	Level 3 on the standard scale.			
Section 26 of this Act	Failing to produce driving licence to court making order for interim disqualification . . .	Summarily.	Level 3 on the standard scale.			
Section 27 of this Act	Failing to produce licence to court for endorsement on conviction of offence involving obligatory endorsement or on committal for sentence, etc., for offence involving	Summarily.	Level 3 on the standard scale.			

... obligatory or discretionary disqualification when no interim disqualification ordered					
Section 62 of this Act	Removing fixed penalty notice fixed to vehicle.	Summarily.	Level 2 on the standard scale.		
Section 67 of this Act	False statement in response to notice to owner.	Summarily.	Level 5 on the standard scale.		
[Offences under the Road Traffic (Driver Licensing and Information Systems) Act 1989]					
[RTA 1989, section 1(5)	Failure of holder of existing HGV or PSV driver's licence to surrender it upon revocation or surrender of his existing licence under Part III of RTA.	Summarily.	Level 3 on the standard scale.	—	—
[RTA 1989, Schedule 1, paragraph 3	Failing to comply with conditions of existing HGV driver's licence, or causing or permitting person under 21 to drive	Summarily.	Level 3 on the standard scale.	—	—

[continued on next page

[Offences under the Road Traffic (Driver Licensing and Information Systems) Act 1989]—cont.

(1) Provision creating offence	(2) General nature of offence	(3) Mode of prosecution	(4) Punishment	(5) Disqualification	(6) Endorsement	(7) Penalty points
	HGV in contravention of such conditions.					
[RTA 1989, Schedule 1, paragraph 8(2)	Contravention of provision of regulations (which is declared by regulations to be an offence) about existing HGV or PSV drivers' licences.	Summarily.	Level 3 on the standard scale.	—	—	—
[RTA 1989, Schedule 1, paragraph 10(4)	Taking PSV test before applying for licence or within prescribed period afterwards.	Summarily.	Level 3 on the standard scale.	—	—	—
[RTA 1989, Schedule 1, paragraph 10(5)	Taking PSV test after refusal of licence.	Summarily.	Level 3 on the standard scale.	—	—	—

[The entries in Part I of Schedule 2 are printed as amended by the Road Traffic (Driver Licensing and **A26.205**
Information Systems) Act 1989, ss.7, 16, Sched. 3, paras.28 and 29, and Sched. 6; the Parking Act 1989, s.4 and Schedule, para.11; the Motor Vehicles (Safety Equipment for Children) Act 1991, s.3(2) and (3); the New Roads and Street Works Act 1991, s.168(2) and Sched. 9; the Road Traffic Act 1991, ss.26, 83, Schedule 1, paras 1–31, and Sched. 8; the Motor Vehicles (EC Type Approval) Regulations 1992 (S.I. 1992 No. 3107); the Road Traffic (Driving Instruction by Disabled Persons) Act 1993, s.6 and Schedule, paras 1 and 11; the Criminal Justice Act 1993, s.67(1); the Road Traffic Regulation (Special Events) Act 1994, s.1(2); the Driving Licences (Community Driving Licence) Regulations 1996 (S.I. 1996 No. 1974), reg.3 and Sched. 2, para.8 (not reproduced in this work); the Driving Licences (Community Driving Licence) Regulations 1998 (S.I. 1998 No. 1420), regs 2 and 16(1) and (3) (not reproduced in this work); the Motor Cycles Etc. (EC Type Approval) Regulations 1999 (S.I. 1999 No. 2920).

The entries in Part I of Schedule 2 are further prospectively amended by the Transport Act 1982, s.24(3) (as itself amended by the Criminal Justice Act 1982, s.46(1) and (3)(c), and the Road Traffic (Consequential Provisions) Act 1988, s.4 and Sched. 2, Pt I, para.13(c)) [as to the entries relating to the Road Traffic Act 1988, s.175(1) and (2)]; when section 24(3) of the 1982 Act is brought into operation, the reference to section 175 of the Road Traffic Act 1988 will read "section 175(1)" and the entry relating to section 175(2) of that Act will become operative.

The traffic signs specified for the purposes of column 5 of the entry relating to section 36 of the Road Traffic Act 1988 are prescribed by regulation 10(2) of the Traffic Signs Regulations and General Directions 1994 (S.I. 1994 No. 1519) below.

Community driving licence. *In relation to driving licences which came into force after May 31,* **A26.206**
1990 (after December 31, 1990 for Northern Ireland driving licences) only, Schedule 2 was amended by the Driving Licences (Community Driving Licence) Regulations 1990 (S.I. 1990 No. 144) (as amended by the Driving Licences (Community Driving Licence) Regulations 1998 (S.I. 1998 No. 1420), reg.17 and Schedule (not reproduced in this work)) on April 1, 1990 so that:

(i) *in Part I of Schedule 2, the words "and counterpart" were inserted after the word "licence" in column (2) of the entry relating to section 109 of the Road Traffic Act 1988 ("RTA");*

(ii) *in Part I of Schedule 2, the words "and counterpart" were inserted after the word "licence" in column (2) of the entry relating to section 164 of the Road Traffic Act 1988 ("RTA");*

(iii) *in Part I of Schedule 2, the words "and counterpart" were inserted after the word "licence" in column (2) of the entry relating to section 26 of the Road Traffic Offenders Act 1988 ("this Act"); and*

(iv) *in Part I of Schedule 2, the words "and counterpart" were inserted after the word "licence" in column (2) of the entry relating to section 27 of the Road Traffic Offenders Act 1988 ("this Act");*

(v) *the words "and counterpart" were inserted in column (2) of the entry for section 92(7C) of the Road Traffic Act 1988 ("RTA") after the words "section 92(7A)";*

(vi) *the words "and counterpart" were inserted in column (2) of the entry for section 93(3) of the Road Traffic Act 1988 ("RTA") after the word "licence";*

(vii) *the words "and counterpart" were inserted in column (2) of the entry for section 118 of the Road Traffic Act 1988 ("RTA") after the word "licence".]*

PART II

OTHER OFFENCES

(1) Offence	(2) Disqualification	(3) Endorsement	(4) Penalty points
Manslaughter or, in Scotland, culpable homicide by the driver of a motor vehicle.	Obligatory.	Obligatory.	[3–11]
[An offence under section 12A of the Theft Act 1968 (aggravated vehicle-taking).	Obligatory.	Obligatory.	3–11]
Stealing or attempting to steal a motor vehicle.	Discretionary.	[—]	[—]
An offence or attempt to commit an offence in respect of a motor vehicle under section 12 of the Theft Act 1968 (taking conveyance without consent of owner, etc., or, knowing it has been so taken, driving it or allowing oneself to be carried in it).	Discretionary.	[—]	[—]
An offence under section 25 of the Theft Act 1968 (going equipped for stealing, etc.) committed with reference to the theft or taking of motor vehicles.	Discretionary.	[—]	[—]

[Part II of Schedule 2 is printed as amended by the Road Traffic Act 1991, ss.26, 83, Sched. 2, para.32(1)–(3), and Sched. 8; the Aggravated Vehicle-Taking Act 1992, s.3(1).]

SCHEDULE 3

FIXED PENALTY OFFENCES

(1) *Provision creating offence*	(2) *General nature of offence*
[Offences under the Parks Regulation (Amendment) Act 1926]	
[section 2(1)	Breach of parks regulations but only where the offence is committed in relation to regulation 4(27) (driving or riding a trade vehicle), 4(28) (exceeding speed limit) or 4(30) (unauthorised waiting by a vehicle or leaving a vehicle unattended) of the Royal and other Parks and Gardens Regulations 1977 [*S.I. 1977 No. 217; not reproduced in this work*].]
[Offences under the Highways Act 1835 and the Roads (Scotland) Act 1984]	
[Section 72 of the Highways Act 1835	Driving on the footway Cycling on the footway]
[Section 129(5) of the Roads (Scotland) Act 1984 . . .	Driving on the footway]
Offence under the Greater London Council (General Powers) Act 1974	
Section 15 of the Greater London Council (General Powers) Act 1974.	Parking vehicles on footways, verges, etc.
Offence under the Highways Act 1980	
Section 137 of the Highways Act 1980.	Obstructing a highway, but only where the offence is committed in respect of a vehicle.
Offences under the Road Traffic Regulation Act 1984	
RTRA section 5(1)	Using a vehicle in contravention of a traffic regulation order outside Greater London.
RTRA section 8(1)	Breach of traffic regulation order in Greater London.
RTRA section 11	Breach of experimental traffic order.
RTRA section 13	Breach of experimental traffic scheme regulations in Greater London.
RTRA section 16(1)	Using a vehicle in contravention of temporary prohibition or restriction of traffic in case of execution of works, etc.
RTRA section 17(4)	Wrongful use of special road.

[*continued on next page*

(1) *Provision creating offence*	(2) *General nature of offence*
Offences under the Road Traffic Regulation Act 1984—cont.	
RTRA section 18(3)	Using a vehicle in contravention of provision for one-way traffic on trunk road.
RTRA section 20(5)	Driving a vehicle in contravention of order prohibiting or restricting driving vehicles on certain classes of roads.
RTRA section 25(5)	Breach of pedestrian crossing regulations, except an offence in respect of a moving motor vehicle [other than a contravention of regulations 23, 24, 25 and 26 of the Zebra, Pelican and Puffin Pedestrian Crossings Regulations and General Directions 1997 [*q.v.*]].
. . .	
RTRA section [35A(1)]	Breach of an order regulating the use, etc., of a parking place provided by a local authority, but only where the offence is committed in relation to a parking place provided on a road.
RTRA section 47(1)	Breach of a provision of a parking place designation order and other offences committed in relation to a parking place designated by such an order, except any offence of failing to pay an excess charge within the meaning of section 46.
RTRA section 53(5)	Using vehicle in contravention of any provision of a parking place designation order having effect by virtue of section 53(1)(a) (inclusion of certain traffic regulation provisions).
RTRA section 53(6)	Breach of a provision of a parking place designation order having effect by virtue of section 53(1)(b) (use of any part of a road for parking without charge).
RTRA section 88(7)	Driving a motor vehicle in contravention of an order imposing a minimum speed limit under section 88(1)(b).
RTRA section 89(1)	Speeding offences under RTRA and other Acts.
Offences under the Road Traffic Act 1988	
RTA section 14	Breach of regulations requiring wearing of seat belts.
RTA section 15(2)	Breach of restriction on carrying children in the front of vehicles.
[RTA section 15(4)	Breach of restriction on carrying children in the rear of vehicles].

[*continued on next page*

(1) *Provision creating offence*	(2) *General nature of offence*
RTA section 16	Breach of regulations relating to protective headgear for motor cycle drivers and passengers.
RTA section 19	Parking a heavy commercial vehicle on verge or footway.
RTA section 22	Leaving vehicle in dangerous position.
RTA section 23	Unlawful carrying of passengers on motor cycles.
[RTA section 24	Carrying more than one person on a pedal cycle.]
RTA section 34	Driving motor vehicles elsewhere than on a road.
RTA section 35	Failure to comply with traffic directions.
RTA section 36	Failure to comply with traffic signs.
[RTA section 40A	Using vehicle in dangerous condition, etc.]
[RTA section 41A	Breach of requirement as to brakes, steering-gear or tyres.]
[RTA section 41B	Breach of requirement as to weight: goods and passenger vehicles.]
RTA section 42	[Breach of other construction and use requirements.]
RTA section 87(1)	Driving vehicle [otherwise than in accordance with] requisite licence.
. . .	
RTA section 163	Failure to stop vehicle on being so required by constable in uniform.

[Offences under the Vehicle Excise and Registration Act 1994 (c 22)]

[Section 33 of the Vehicle Excise and Registration Act 1994.	Using or keeping a vehicle on a public road without [vehicle licence, trade licence or nil licence] being exhibited in manner prescribed by regulations.]
[Section 42 of that Act.	Driving or keeping a vehicle without required registration mark.]
[Section 43 of that Act.	Driving or keeping a vehicle with registration mark obscured, etc.]
[Section 59 of that Act	Failure to fix prescribed registration mark to a vehicle in accordance with regulations made under section 23(4)(a) of that Act]

[The entries in Schedule 3 are printed as amended by the Crown Roads (Royal Parks) (Application of **A26.209**
Road Traffic Enactments) Order 1987 (S.I. 1987 No. 363; not reproduced in this work) as applied by the Road Traffic (Consequential Provisions) Act 1988, s.2(4) [q.v.]; the Parking Act 1989, s.4 and Schedule; the Fixed Penalties Offences Order 1990 (S.I. 1990 No. 335); the New Roads and Street Works Act 1991, s.168(2) and Sched. 9; the Road Traffic Act 1991, ss.48, 83, Sched. 4, para.112(1)–(4) and Sched. 8; the Fixed Penalty Offences Order 1992 (S.I. 1992 No. 345); the Vehicle Excise and Registration Act 1994, ss.63 and 65, Sched. 3, para.25(2) and Sched. 5; the Finance Act 1997, s.18 and Sched. 3, paras 1 and 8(1); the Fixed Penalty Offences Order 1999 (S.I. 1999 No. 1851).
As to fixed penalty parking offences, see the Fixed Penalty Order 2000 (S.I. 2000 No. 2792) below.]

SCHEDULE 4

STATUTORY STATEMENTS

PART I

STATUTORY STATEMENT OF OWNERSHIP OR HIRING

A26.210   **1.**—(1) For the purposes of Part III of this Act, a statutory statement of ownership is a statement on an official form signed by the person providing it and stating whether he was the owner of the vehicle at the time of the alleged offence and, if he was not the owner of the vehicle at that time, whether—

(a) he was never the owner, or

(b) he ceased to be the owner before, or became the owner after, that time,

and in a case within paragraph (b) above, stating, if the information is in his possession, the name and address of the person to whom, and the date on which, he disposed of the vehicle or (as the case may be) the name and address of the person from whom, and the date on which, he acquired it.

(2) An official form for a statutory statement of ownership shall—

(a) indicate that the person providing the statement in response to a notice to owner relating to an offence may give notice requesting a hearing in respect of the offence in the manner specified in the form, and

(b) direct the attention of any person proposing to complete the form to the information provided in accordance with paragraph 3(3) below in any official form for a statutory statement of facts.

A26.211   **2.**—(1) For the purposes of Part III of this Act, a statutory statement of hiring is a statement on an official form, signed by the person providing it, being a person by whom a statement of liability was signed, and stating—

(a) whether at the time of the alleged offence the vehicle was let to him under the hiring agreement to which the statement of liability refers, and

(b) if it was not, the date on which he returned the vehicle to the possession of the vehicle-hire firm concerned.

(2) An official form for a statutory statement of hiring shall—

(a) indicate that the person providing the statement in pursuance of a notice relating to an offence served under section 63 of this Act by virtue of section 66 of this Act may give notice requesting a hearing in respect of the offence in the manner specified in the form, and

(b) direct the attention of any person proposing to complete the form to the information provided in accordance with paragraph 3(3) below in any official form for a statutory statement of facts.

(3) In sub-paragraph (1) above "*statement of liability*", "*hiring agreement*" and "*vehicle-hire firm*" have the same meanings as in section 66 of this Act.

PART II

STATUTORY STATEMENT OF FACTS

A26.212   **3.**—(1) For the purposes of Part III of this Act, a statutory statement of facts is a statement on an official form, signed by the person providing it, which—

(a) states that the person providing it was not the driver of the vehicle at the time of the alleged offence, and

(b) states the name and address at the time when the statement is provided of the person who was the driver of the vehicle at the time of the alleged offence.

(2) A statutory statement of facts has effect as a notice given by the driver requesting a hearing in respect of the offence if it is signed by the person identified in the statement as the driver of the vehicle at the time of the alleged offence.

(3) An official form for a statutory statement of facts shall indicate—

(a) that if a person identified in the statement as the driver of the vehicle at the time of the alleged offence signs the statement he will be regarded as having given notice requesting a hearing in respect of the offence,

(b) that the person on whom the notice to owner relating to the offence is served may not give notice requesting a hearing in respect of the offence on his own account if he provides a statutory statement of facts signed by a person so identified, and

(c) that if the fixed penalty is not paid before the end of the period stated in the notice to owner as the period for response to the notice, a sum determined by reference to that fixed penalty may be registered without any court hearing for enforcement as a fine against the person on whom the notice to owner is served, unless he has given notice requesting a hearing in respect of the offence,

but that, in a case within paragraph (c) above, the sum in question may not be so registered if the person on whom the notice to owner is served provides a statutory statement of facts as mentioned in paragraph (b) above until two months have elapsed from the end of the period so stated without service of a summons or, in Scotland, complaint in respect of the offence on the person identified in that statement as the driver of the vehicle.

[Words relating expressly and exclusively to Scotland have been omitted from paragraph 3 of Schedule 4.]   **A26.213**

SCHEDULE 5   Section 75

SCOTLAND; ADDITIONAL OFFENCES OPEN TO CONDITIONAL OFFER   **A26.214**

[Omitted.]

The Road Traffic (Consequential Provisions) Act 1988

(1988 c. 54)

A27.01 An Act to make provision for repeals (including a repeal to give effect to a recommendation of the Law Commission and the Scottish Law Commission), consequential amendments, transitional and transitory matters and savings in connection with the consolidation of enactments in the Road Traffic Act 1988 and the Road Traffic Offenders Act 1988.

[15th November 1988]

ARRANGEMENT OF SECTIONS

1. Meaning of "the Road Traffic Acts", "the repealed enactments", etc.

A27.03 (1) In this Act—

"*the Road Traffic Acts*" means the Road Traffic Act 1988, the Road Traffic Offenders Act 1988 and, so far as it reproduces the effect of the repealed enactments, this Act, and

"*the repealed enactments*" means the enactments repealed or revoked by this Act.

(2) Expressions used in this Act and in the Road Traffic Act 1988 have the same meaning as in that Act.

2. Continuity, and construction of references to old and new law

A27.04 (1) The substitution of the Road Traffic Acts for the repealed enactments does not affect the continuity of the law.

(2) Anything done or having effect as if done under or for the purposes of a provision of the repealed enactments has effect, if it could have been done under or for the purposes of the corresponding provision of the Road Traffic Acts, as if done under or for the purposes of that corresponding provision.

(3) Any reference, whether express or implied, in the Road Traffic Acts or any other enactment, instrument or document to a provision of the Road Traffic Acts is to be read, in relation to the times, circumstances or purposes in relation to which the corresponding provision of the repealed enactments had effect and so far as the nature of the reference permits, as including a reference to that corresponding provision.

(4) Any reference, whether express or implied, in any enactment, instrument or document to a provision of the repealed enactments is to be read, in relation to the times, circumstances or purposes in relation to which the corresponding provision of the Road Traffic Acts has effect and so far as the nature of the reference permits, as including a reference to that corresponding provision.

[In the application of section 2 to section 34(3) of the Road Traffic Offenders Act 1988 (q.v.), see as to   **A27.05**
previous convictions section 5 of and Schedule 4, paragraph 7(4), to this Act below.]

3. Repeals   *[Omitted.]*   **A27.06**

4. Prospective and consequential amendments   *[Omitted.]*

5. Transitional provisions and savings

(1) Schedule 4 to this Act (which makes certain transitional provisions and contains   **A27.07**
savings in connection with the repeals made by this Act) shall have effect.

(2) Nothing in that Schedule affects the general operation of section 16 of the Interpretation Act 1978 (general savings implied on a repeal).

6.   *[Repealed by the Road Traffic Act 1991, s.83 and Sched. 8.]*   **A27.08**

7. Saving for law of nuisance

Nothing in the Road Traffic Acts authorises a person to use on a road a vehicle so con-   **A27.09**
structed or used as to cause a public or private nuisance . . . or affects the liability, whether under statute or common law, of the driver or owner so using such a vehicle.

[Words relating exclusively and expressly to Scotland have been omitted from section 7.]   **A27.10**

8. Short title, commencement and extent

(1) This Act may be cited as the Road Traffic (Consequential Provisions) Act 1988.

(2) This Act, except those provisions that may be brought into force in accordance with   **A27.11**
subsection (3) below, shall come into force at the end of the period of six months beginning with the day on which it is passed.

(3) [Paragraphs 15 to 20 of Schedule 2 to this Act]—

  (a) in Part I, paragraphs 1 and 15 to 20,

  (b) Part II (except paragraph 22 so far as relates to subsections (5) to (8) of the new section inserted by that paragraph, which therefore come into force in accordance with subsection (2) above), and

  (c) Parts III and IV,

shall come into force on such day as the Secretary of State may by order made by statutory instrument appoint, and different days may be so appointed for different provisions and for different purposes.

(4) An order under subsection (3) above bringing any provision of Part I of Schedule 2 to this Act (wholly or partly) into force may contain such transitional provisions and savings

(whether or not involving the modification of any provision contained in an Act or in subordinate legislation within the meaning of the Interpretation Act 1978) as appear to the Secretary of State necessary or expedient in connection with that provision.

(5) This Act does not extend to Northern Ireland except so far as it affects other enactments extending to Northern Ireland.

A27.12   *[Section 8 is printed as amended by the Road Traffic Act 1991, s.48 and Sched. 4, para.114.]*

*   *   *

Section 5   SCHEDULE 4

TRANSITIONAL PROVISIONS AND SAVINGS

General rules for old savings and transitional provisions

A27.13   **1.**—(1) The repeal by this Act of an enactment previously repealed subject to saving does not affect the continued operation of those savings.

(2) The repeal by this Act of a saving made on the previous repeal of an enactment does not affect the operation of the saving in so far as it is not specifically reproduced in the Road Traffic Acts but remains capable of having effect.

(3) Where the purpose of a repealed enactment was to secure that the substitution of the provisions of the Act containing that enactment for provisions repealed by that Act did not affect the continuity of the law, the repealed enactment, in so far as it is not specifically reproduced in the Road Traffic Acts, shall continue to have effect, in so far as it is capable of doing so, for the purposes of the Road Traffic Acts.

Old offences

A27.14   **2.** The Road Traffic Acts (including this Act so far as not included in that expression) do not affect the operation of the repealed enactments in relation to offences committed before the commencement of those Acts or to appeals against or suspension of disqualification by virtue of convictions for offences so committed or against orders made in consequence of such convictions.

Road Traffic Act 1974

A27.15   **3.**—(1) Any provision contained in an enactment passed or instrument made before 31 July 1974 which was not repealed by the Road Traffic Act 1974 and in which any expression was given the same meaning as in, or was otherwise to be construed by reference to, any provision of sections 68 to 82 of the Road Traffic Act 1972 which was repealed by that Act shall continue to be construed as if that provision had not been so repealed.

(2), (3) *[Power to make regulations implementing the Road Traffic Act 1974, s.9 (extension of construction and use regulations to lights).]*

Road Traffic (Drivers' Ages and Hours of Work) Act 1976

A27.16   **4.**—(1) Subject to sub-paragraph (2) below, a person who, immediately before 1st January 1976, fulfilled any of the conditions in paragraph 2(1) of Schedule 2 to the Road Traffic (Drivers' Ages and Hours of Work) Act 1976 shall not, by reason only of the provisions of section 101 of the Road Traffic Act 1988, be disqualified for holding or obtaining a licence authorising him to drive motor vehicles falling within the class described in paragraph 5 or 6 of the Table set out in section 101(1) of that Act.

(2) A person shall not be treated, by virtue of sub-paragraph (1) above, as entitled to the grant of a licence authorising him to drive a goods vehicle the permissible maximum weight of which exceeds 10 tonnes or a motor vehicle constructed solely for the carriage of passengers and their effects which is adapted to carry more than fifteen passengers inclusive of the driver.

Road Traffic Regulation Act 1984

5.—(1) Notwithstanding the repeal by this Act of the provisions of section 98 of and   **A27.17** Schedule 7 to the Road Traffic Regulation Act 1984 (prosecution of offences), those provisions shall, in relation to the interim period (within the meaning of Schedule 12 to that Act), continue to have effect in relation to offences under Schedule 12 to that Act.

(2) To the extent that section 135 of that Act (application to Isles of Scilly) applied to the repealed enactments, it shall continue to apply to the corresponding provisions of the Road Traffic Acts.

Payments for traffic casualties

6. *[Payments for accidents before April 1, 1987.]*   **A27.18**

Licences, disqualification and endorsement

7.—(1) For the purposes of section 92(4)(a) of the Road Traffic Act 1988, a person to whom   **A27.19** a licence was granted after the making of a declaration under paragraph (c) of the proviso to section 5(2) of the Road Traffic Act 1930 (which contained transitional provisions with respect to certain disabilities) shall be treated as having passed, at the time of the declaration, a relevant test in respect of vehicles of the classes to which the licence related.

(2) The references in sections 125(3)(d), 127(3)(d), 128(2)(b) and 130(2)(b) of the Road Traffic Act 1988 to section 34 or 36 of the Road Traffic Offenders Act 1988 and to Part III of the Road Traffic Act 1988 include a reference—

(a) to section 93 of the Road Traffic Act 1972 and to Part III of that Act, and

(b) to section 5 of the Road Traffic Act 1962 and Part II of the Road Traffic Act 1960, (but not to section 104 of the 1960 Act).

(3) For the purposes of section 29 of the Road Traffic Offenders Act 1988, an order for endorsement which was made before the commencement of section 19 of the Transport Act 1981 counts as an order made in pursuance of section 44 of the Road Traffic Offenders Act 1988 for the endorsement of three penalty points, unless a disqualification was imposed on the offender on that or any subsequent occasion.

(4) For the purposes of section 2 of this Act as it has effect for the purposes of section 34(3) of the Road Traffic Offenders Act 1988—

(a) a previous conviction of an offence under section 6(1) of the Road Traffic Act 1972, as it had effect immediately before the substitution of a new section 6(1) by the Transport Act 1981, shall be treated as a conviction of an offence under section 5(1)(a) of the Road Traffic Act 1988, and

(b) a previous conviction of an offence under section 9(3) of the 1972 Act, as it had effect immediately before the substitution of a new section 8(7) by the 1981 Act, shall be treated as a conviction of an offence under section 7(6) of the Road Traffic Act 1988.

(5) The references in sections 36(4), 37(3) and 42(6) of the Road Traffic Offenders Act 1988 to an order under subsection (1) of section 36 include a reference to an order under section 93(7) of the Road Traffic Act 1972, section 5(7) of the Road Traffic Act 1962 or section 104(3) of the Road Traffic Act 1960.

(6) Where, in pursuance of section 93(5) of the Road Traffic Act 1972, a period of disqualification was imposed on an offender in addition to any other period or periods then, for the purpose of determining whether an application may be made under section 42 of the Road Traffic Offenders Act 1988 for the removal of either or any of the disqualifications, the periods shall be treated as one continuous period of disqualification.

Hovercraft

A27.20   **8.** For the purposes of the Hovercraft Act 1968 (under which enactments and instruments relating, amongst other things, to motor vehicles may, if passed before the commencement of that Act, be applied to hovercraft) any enactment contained in the Road Traffic Acts, being an enactment derived from an enactment so passed, and any instrument made or having effect as if made under such an enactment, shall be treated as included among the enactments and instruments which can be so applied.

*   *   *

The London Regional Transport (No. 2) Act 1989

(1989 c. xi)

An Act to empower London Underground Limited to construct works and to acquire lands; to confer powers on London Regional Transport; and for other purposes. **A28.01**

[27th July 1989]

Whereas— **A28.02**

(1) By the London Regional Transport Act 1984 the London Transport Executive which were established by the Transport (London) Act 1969 were reconstituted on 29th June 1984 under the name of London Regional Transport (in this Act referred to as "*the Corporation*")
. . .

*   *   *

PART V

PROVISIONS FOR CORPORATION

20. Application of [section 172 of the Road Traffic Act 1988] to British Transport Police Force

(1) In this section— **A28.03**

"*the British Transport Police Force*" means the force established by the Scheme set out in the Schedule to the British Transport Police Force Scheme 1963 (Approval) Order 1964 [*S.I. 1964 No. 1456*];

"*level crossing*" has the same meaning as in section 1 of the Level Crossings Act 1983;

"*road*" has the same meaning as in [section 192 of the Road Traffic Act 1988]; and

"*subsidiary*" has the same meaning as in section 68 of the London Regional Transport Act 1984.

(2) In the application of [section 172 of the said Act of 1988] (which imposes a duty on the keeper of a vehicle to give information to a chief officer of police as to the identity of the driver, etc., in certain circumstances) to an offence alleged to be committed at a level crossing or on a road forming an access or approach to any garage, depot, railway or bus station, goods yard, workshop or other premises of the Corporation or any subsidiary of the Corporation, the expression "*chief officer of police*", where used in that section, shall include the chief constable of the British Transport Police Force.

[Section 20 is printed as amended by the Interpretation Act 1978, s.17(2)(a).] **A28.04**

*   *   *

The Road Traffic (Driver Licensing and Information Systems) Act 1989

(1989 c. 22)

A29.01   An Act to amend the law relating to driving licences and to regulate the operation of systems providing drivers of motor vehicles with guidance and information derived from automatically processed data or collecting, storing and processing the data.

[21st July 1989]

ARRANGEMENT OF SECTIONS

PART I

DRIVING LICENCES

*   *   *

SCHEDULES

PART I

DRIVING LICENCES

1. Abolition of special licences for driving HGVs and PSVs

A29.03   (1) On the appointed day Part IV of the Road Traffic Act 1988 and section 22 of the Public Passenger Vehicles Act 1981 (which require special driving licences to be held for driving heavy goods vehicles and public service vehicles) shall cease to have effect but the repeal of those provisions does not imply that it is lawful for a person to drive a heavy goods vehicle or a public service vehicle of any class on or after that day on the authority of an existing licence under Part III of the 1988 Act (ordinary licences) and, for the purposes of section 87 [*q.v.*] of that Act (offence of driving without Part III licence), his licence shall not be taken to authorise him to drive vehicles of those classes.

(2) Subsection (1) above shall not, however, invalidate existing licences for driving heavy goods vehicles or public service vehicles and the holder of such a licence may, during the currency of that licence and his existing licence under Part III of the 1988 Act, continue to

drive any heavy goods vehicle or public service vehicle which the first-mentioned licence authorises him to drive or a goods vehicle of any class or, as the case may be, a passenger-carrying vehicle of any class prescribed for the purposes of this subsection without obtaining a new licence under the said Part III.

(3) Any of the following proceedings pending at the appointed day, that is to say—

(a) any application questioning the conduct of a test of competence to drive under section 115 of the 1988 Act, and

(b) any reconsideration by, or appeal from, a licensing authority under section 116 of the 1988 Act or section 23 of the 1981 Act,

may be continued and, as the case may be, any order relative to the test (or fees) made or licence issued notwithstanding the repeals made by this Act and any order of eligibility to take a test so made shall be treated as relating to a corresponding test and any heavy goods vehicle or public service vehicle driver's licence so issued shall be treated as an existing licence.

(4) Where, during the currency of a person's existing licence for driving heavy goods vehicles or public service vehicles, his existing licence under Part III of the 1988 Act is revoked or surrendered, it shall be his duty to surrender his first-mentioned licence to the traffic commissioner for the traffic area in which he resides.

(5) A person who without reasonable excuse fails to comply with the duty under subsection (4) above is guilty of an offence.

(6) The provisions of Part I of Schedule 1 to this Act have effect for the purpose of re-enacting with modifications and assimilating the provisions of Part IV of the 1988 Act and the 1981 Act for the purposes of licences under those Acts continued in force by subsection (2) above and the transitory provisions of Part II of that Schedule shall also have effect.

(7) In this Part of this Act—

"*the appointed day*" means the day appointed for the coming into force of this section;

"*existing*", in relation to a licence, means in force immediately before the appointed day;

"*traffic area*" means a traffic area constituted for the purposes of the 1981 Act;

"*traffic commissioner*" means a traffic commissioner appointed for the purposes of the 1981 Act;

"*the 1981 Act*" means the Public Passenger Vehicles Act 1981;

"*the 1988 Act*" means the Road Traffic Act 1988;

and in subsection (2) above the reference to the vehicles which the holder of a heavy goods vehicle driver's licence is authorised to drive includes a reference to the vehicles which he is authorised to drive by virtue of regulations under paragraph 8(2)(a) of Schedule 1 to this Act and the reference to prescribed classes of goods vehicles or passenger-carrying vehicles is a reference to classes of goods vehicles or passenger-carrying vehicles (within the meaning of the 1988 Act) prescribed under that paragraph.

*   *   *

PART II

DRIVER INFORMATION SYSTEMS   **A29.04**

*   *   *

PART III

GENERAL

*   *   *

Section 1   SCHEDULE 1

EXISTING HGV AND PSV DRIVERS' LICENCES

PART I

EXISTING HGV AND PSV DRIVERS' LICENCES

Preliminary

A29.05   **1.** In this Part of this Schedule—

"*conduct*" means—

    (a)   in relation to the holder of an existing heavy goods vehicle licence, his conduct as a driver of a motor vehicle, and

    (b)   in relation to the holder of an existing public service vehicle licence, his conduct both as a driver of a motor vehicle and in any other respect relevant to his holding a public service vehicle licence,

including, in either case, such conduct in Northern Ireland;

"*existing licence*" means a licence to drive heavy goods vehicles or public service vehicles (as the case may be) continued in force by section 1(2) of this Act, and "*existing heavy goods vehicle licence*" and "*existing public service vehicle licence*" shall be construed accordingly;

"*full*", in relation to an existing heavy goods vehicle licence, indicates a licence other than a provisional licence;

"*heavy goods vehicle*" has the same meaning as it had for the purposes of Part IV of the 1988 Act before its repeal by section 1 of this Act and "*large goods vehicle*" has the same meaning;

"*notice*" means notice in writing and "*notify*" shall be construed accordingly;

"*passenger-carrying vehicle*" has the same meaning as it has in Part IV of the 1988 Act;

"*prescribed*", unless the context requires otherwise, means prescribed by regulations made under paragraph 8 below; and

"*public service vehicle*" has the same meaning as it had for the purposes of section 22 of the 1981 Act before its repeal by section 1 of this Act.

Functions of Secretary of State and Traffic Commissioners

A29.06   **2.**—(1) The functions conferred by the following provisions of this Part of this Schedule in relation to existing licences shall be functions of the Secretary of State except where, by any provision, the function is conferred on a traffic commissioner or any court.

(2) Traffic commissioners shall, in the exercise of those functions, act in accordance with directions given by the Secretary of State; but such directions shall be general directions not relating to the exercise of functions in a particular case.

Conditions of existing HGV licences

A29.07   **3.**—(1) An existing heavy goods vehicle licence issued as a provisional licence, or an existing full heavy goods vehicle licence held by a person under the age of 21, is subject to the prescribed conditions, and if the holder of the licence fails, without reasonable excuse, to comply with any of the conditions he is guilty of an offence.

(2) It is an offence for a person knowingly to cause or permit another person who is under the age of 21 to drive a heavy goods vehicle of any class in contravention of any prescribed conditions to which that other person's licence is subject.

Duration of existing licences

4.—(1) An existing heavy goods vehicle licence shall, unless previously revoked, suspended or surrendered, continue in force for 3 years from the date on which it is expressed to take effect.   **A29.08**

(2) Subject to sub-paragraph (3) below, a provisional heavy goods vehicle licence shall, unless previously revoked, suspended or surrendered, continue in force for 6 months from the date on which it is expressed to take effect.

(3) Sub-paragraph (2) above does not apply to a heavy goods vehicle licence treated as a provisional licence by virtue of regulations under paragraph 8 below.

(4) An existing public service vehicle licence shall, unless previously revoked, suspended or surrendered, continue in force for 5 years from the date on which it is expressed to take effect.

(5) If on the date on which an application is made under Part III of the 1988 Act for a licence to drive large goods vehicles or passenger-carrying vehicles, the applicant is the holder of an existing heavy goods vehicle licence or an existing public service vehicle licence, as the case may be, his existing licence shall not expire in accordance with the foregoing provisions before the application is disposed of.

Revocation or suspension of existing licences

5.—(1) An existing heavy goods vehicle licence or public service vehicle licence—   **A29.09**
  (a) must be revoked—
      (i) if its holder develops such physical disability as may be prescribed, or
      (ii) if there come into existence, in relation to its holder, such circumstances relating to his conduct as may be prescribed;
  (b) must be revoked or suspended if his conduct or physical disability is such as to make him unfit to hold such a licence;

and where the licence is suspended under paragraph (b) above it shall during the time of suspension be of no effect.

(2) Where it appears that the conduct or physical disability of the holder of an existing licence falls within both sub-paragraph (1)(a) above and sub-paragraph (1)(b) above, proceedings shall be taken or continued under sub-paragraph (1)(a) and not sub-paragraph (1)(b) and accordingly the power to suspend the licence, rather than revoke it, shall not be available.

(3) Regulations made for the purposes of sub-paragraph (1)(a) above—
  (a) may make different provision for heavy goods vehicles and for public service vehicles and for different descriptions of persons; and
  (b) shall provide for the determination of the cases in which, under paragraph 6 below, a person whose licence has been revoked is to be disqualified indefinitely or for a period and, if for a period, for the determination of the period.

(4) Any question arising under sub-paragraph (1)(b) above as to whether a person is or is not, by reason of his conduct, fit to hold a heavy goods vehicle licence or a public service

vehicle licence, as the case may be, may be referred by the Secretary of State to the traffic commissioner for the area in which the holder of the licence resides.

(5) Where, on any reference under sub-paragraph (4) above, the traffic commissioner determines that the holder of the licence is not fit to hold a heavy goods vehicle licence or a public service vehicle licence, as the case may be, he shall also determine whether the conduct of the holder of the licence is such as to require the revocation of his licence or only its suspension; and, if the former, whether the holder of the licence should be disqualified under paragraph 6(2)(a) below (and, if so, for what period) or under paragraph 6(2)(b) below.

(6) A traffic commissioner to whom a reference has been made under sub-paragraph (4) above may require the holder of the licence to furnish the commissioner with such information as he may require and may, by notice to the holder, require him to attend before the commissioner at the time and place specified by the commissioner to furnish the information and to answer such questions (if any) relating to the subject matter of the reference as the commissioner may put to him.

(7) If the holder of the licence fails without reasonable excuse to furnish information to or to attend before or answer questions properly put by a commissioner when required to do so under sub-paragraph (6) above, the commissioner may notify the failure to the Secretary of State and, if the commissioner does so, the Secretary of State may, as he thinks fit, revoke the licence or suspend it for such period as he thinks fit.

(8) Except where he has given such a notification as is mentioned in sub-paragraph (7) above, the traffic commissioner to whom a reference has been made under sub-paragraph (4) above shall notify the Secretary of State and the holder of the licence of his determination in the matter and the decision of the commissioner shall be binding on the Secretary of State.

(9) Where the Secretary of State, without making such a reference, determines to revoke or suspend a person's licence under sub-paragraph (1) above he shall notify his determination in the matter to the holder of the licence and, where he suspends it, to the traffic commissioner for the area in which the holder of the licence resides.

Disqualification on revocation of existing licences

A29.10   **6.**—(1) Where in pursuance of paragraph 5(1)(a) above the Secretary of State revokes a person's existing licence, the Secretary of State must, in accordance with the regulations made for the purposes of that paragraph, order that person to be disqualified indefinitely or for the period determined in accordance with the regulations.

(2) Where in pursuance of paragraph 5(1)(b) above the Secretary of State revokes an existing licence, he may—

   (a) order the holder to be disqualified indefinitely or for such period as the Secretary of State thinks fit, or

   (b) except where the licence is a provisional licence, if it appears to the Secretary of State that, owing to the conduct or physical disability of the holder of the licence, it is expedient to require him to comply with the prescribed conditions applicable to provisional licences under Part III of the 1988 Act until he passes the prescribed test of competence under that Part to drive large goods vehicles or passenger-carrying vehicles of any class, order him to be disqualified for holding or obtaining a full licence to drive until he passes such a test.

(3) If, while the holder of an existing licence is disqualified under sub-paragraph (1) above, the circumstances prescribed for the purposes of paragraph 5(1)(a)(ii) above cease to

exist in his case, the Secretary of State must, on an application made to him for the purpose, remove the disqualification.

(4) Where the holder of an existing licence is disqualified under sub-paragraph (2)(a) above, the Secretary of State may, in such circumstances as may be prescribed, remove the disqualification.

(5) Where the holder of an existing full licence is disqualified under sub-paragraph (2)(b) above, the Secretary of State must not afterwards grant him a full licence under Part III of the 1988 Act to drive large goods vehicles or passenger-carrying vehicles of any class unless satisfied that he has since the disqualification passed the prescribed test of competence under that Part to drive vehicles of that class, and until he passes that test any such full Part III licence obtained by him shall be of no effect.

(6) So long as the disqualification under sub-paragraph (1) or (2)(a) above of the holder of an existing licence continues in force, no licence under Part III of the 1988 Act to drive large goods vehicles or passenger-carrying vehicles (as the case may be) shall be granted to him and any such licence obtained by him shall be of no effect.

(7) In this paragraph "*disqualified*"—

(a) in a case of revocation on the ground of the conduct of the holder of the licence as a driver, means disqualified for holding or obtaining a licence under Part III of the 1988 Act to drive large goods vehicles of the prescribed classes and passenger-carrying vehicles of the prescribed classes; and

(b) in a case of revocation of a public service vehicle licence on the ground of the conduct of the holder otherwise than as a driver, means disqualified for holding or obtaining a licence under Part III of the 1988 Act to drive passenger-carrying vehicles of the prescribed classes.

Appeals relating to existing licences

7.—(1) The holder of an existing licence who is aggrieved by the Secretary of State's—   **A29.11**

(a) suspension or revocation of his licence under paragraph 5 above, or

(b) ordering of disqualification under paragraph 6 above,

may, after giving to the Secretary of State and any traffic commissioner to whom the matter was referred notice of his intention to do so, appeal to a magistrates' court acting for the petty sessions area in which the holder of the licence resides . . .

(2) On an appeal under sub-paragraph (1)(a) above the Secretary of State and, if the matter was referred to a traffic commissioner, the commissioner shall be respondent.

(3) On any appeal under sub-paragraph (1) above the court . . . may make such order as it thinks fit and the order shall be binding on the Secretary of State.

Regulations

8.—(1) The Secretary of State may make regulations for prescribing anything which may   **A29.12**
be prescribed under this Part of this Schedule and generally for the purpose of carrying its provisions into effect.

(2) Regulations under this paragraph may make different provision for different cases and circumstances and may in particular—

(a) provide that a full licence to drive heavy goods vehicles of a particular class shall also be treated for the purposes of this Part of this Schedule as a provisional licence to drive heavy goods vehicles of another prescribed class;

(b) make provision with respect to the custody and production of existing licences and requiring, and regulating the procedure on, the surrender or production to the Secretary of State, a traffic commissioner or any constable or officer of existing licences which have been revoked or suspended or have expired;

(c) provide for the issue by traffic commissioners of duplicate licences in place of existing licences lost or defaced on payment of the prescribed fee;

(d) provide that a person who contravenes or fails to comply with any specified provision is guilty of an offence; and

(e) provide that this Part of this Schedule shall not apply to prescribed classes of heavy goods vehicle or of public service vehicle either generally or in such circumstances as may be prescribed.

(3), (4) *[Exercise of regulation-making power.]*

Provisions as to existing Northern Ireland licences

A29.13   **9.**—(1) In this paragraph "*existing Northern Ireland licence*" means a licence specifically to drive heavy goods vehicles or public service vehicles granted under the law of Northern Ireland.

(2) The Secretary of State may exercise as respects Great Britain the like power of revoking or suspending any existing Northern Ireland licence and of making an order under paragraph 6(2) above as is conferred on him in relation to an existing heavy goods vehicle licence or public service vehicle licence by paragraphs 5(1)(b) and 6(2) above, and the provisions of paragraphs 5(1) and (4) to (9) and 6(2), (4), (5), (6), and (7) and the power to make regulations under paragraph 8(2)(b) shall have effect accordingly subject to the modification that references to the traffic commissioner for the area in which the holder of the licence resides shall be construed as references to the prescribed traffic commissioner.

(3) *[Revoked Northern Ireland licences.]*

(4) *[Appeals against revocation or suspension of Northern Ireland licences.]*

PART II

TRANSITORY PROVISIONS

A29.14   **10.** *[Repealed.]*

A29.15   **11.** Notwithstanding section 87 of the 1988 Act, a person who is the holder of a licence to drive motor vehicles granted under Part III of that Act and coming into force on or after 1 June 1990 and is also the holder of—

(a) a licence under Part IV of that Act to drive heavy goods vehicles of any class, or

(b) a licence under section 22 of the 1981 Act to drive public service vehicles of any class,

may drive, or be caused or permitted to drive, a heavy goods vehicle or (as the case may be) a public service vehicle of that class notwithstanding that his licence under Part III of the 1988 Act does not authorise him to drive such a vehicle.

A29.16   **12.** The power to make regulations under paragraph 8 above includes power to prescribe the classes of goods vehicle or passenger-carrying vehicle which, by virtue of section 1(2) of this Act, the holder of an existing licence is authorised to drive during the currency of his existing licence.

[Schedule 1 is printed as amended by section 16 of and Schedule 6 to this Act.

With effect from a date to be announced, paragraph 11 of Schedule 1 will be repealed by section 16 of and Schedule 6 to this Act.

Words in paragraph 7 relating expressly and exclusively to Scotland have been omitted.]

*   *   *

The Radioactive Material (Road Transport) Act 1991

(1991 c. 27)

A30.01 An Act to make new provision with respect to the transport of radioactive material by road; to repeal section 5(2) of the Radioactive Substances Act 1948; and for connected purposes.

[27th June 1991]

ARRANGEMENT OF SECTIONS

1. Preliminary

A30.03 (1) In this Act "*radioactive material*" means any material having a specific activity in excess of—

(a) 70 kilobecquerels per kilogram; or

(b) such lesser specific activity as may be specified in an order made by the Secretary of State;

and the power to make an order under this subsection shall be exercisable by statutory instrument which shall be subject to annulment in pursuance of a resolution of either House of Parliament.

(2) In this Act—

"*examiner*" means any examiner appointed under section 68(1) of the Road Traffic Act 1988;

"*inspector*" means any inspector appointed under subsection (3) below;

"*packaging*", in relation to radioactive material which has been consigned for transport, means an assembly of packaging components which encloses the material completely;

"*packaging components*" means components intended for use as part of the packaging of such material, and includes—

(a) receptacles, absorbent materials, spacing structures and radiation shielding; and

(b) devices for cooling, for absorbing mechanical shocks and for thermal insulation;

"*radioactive package*" means a package comprising radioactive material which has been consigned for transport and its packaging;

"*transport*" means transport by road.

(3) The Secretary of State may—

  (a) appoint as inspectors, to assist him in the execution of this Act and regulations made under it, such number of persons appearing to him to be qualified for the purpose as he may consider necessary; and

  (b) make to or in respect of any person so appointed such payments by way of remuneration, allowances or otherwise as he may with the approval of the Treasury determine.

[References to an examiner appointed under section 68(1) of the Road Traffic Act 1988 (see definition   **A30.04**
of "examiner" in section 1(2) above) are to be construed (as appropriate) as references to an examiner appointed under section 66A of the 1988 Act; see the Road Traffic Act 1991, s.9(2) below.]

2. Regulations

(1)–(3) *[Power to make regulations.]*   **A30.05**

(4) Any person who contravenes or fails to comply with any regulations under this section shall be guilty of an offence.

(5) *[Power to make regulations exercisable by statutory instrument.]*

(6) Subsection (2) of section 5 of the Radioactive Substances Act 1948 shall cease to have effect; and any regulations under that subsection which are in force at the commencement of this Act shall have effect as if made under this section.

[The Radioactive Material (Road Transport) (Great Britain) Regulations 1996 (S.I. 1996 No. 1350;   **A30.06**
not reproduced in this work) have been made under this section.]

3. Prohibitions and directions

(1) If it appears to an inspector or examiner, as respects any vehicle used to transport   **A30.07**
radioactive packages—

  (a) that the vehicle, or any radioactive package which is being transported by it, fails to comply with any regulations under section 2 above;

  (b) that the vehicle, or any radioactive package which is or was being transported by it, has been involved in an accident;

  (c) that any radioactive package which was being transported by the vehicle, or any radioactive material which was contained in such a package, has been lost or stolen,

he may prohibit the driving of the vehicle.

(2) If it appears to an inspector that any radioactive package or packaging component fails to comply with any regulations under section 2 above, he may prohibit the transport of that package or, as the case may require, the use of that component as part of the packaging of radioactive materials.

(3) A prohibition imposed under this section may apply either absolutely or for a specified purpose and either without any limitation of time or for a specified period.

(4) Where an inspector or examiner imposes a prohibition under subsection (1) above, he may also by a direction in writing require the person in charge of the vehicle to remove it (and, if it is a motor vehicle drawing a trailer, also to remove the trailer) to such place and

subject to such conditions as are specified in the direction; and the prohibition shall not apply to the removal of the vehicle or trailer in accordance with the direction.

(5) Where an inspector or examiner imposes a prohibition under this section, he shall forthwith give notice of the prohibition to the person in charge of the vehicle, package or packaging component, specifying the failure to comply or, as the case may be, the accident or other incident in consequence of which the prohibition is imposed and—

(a) stating whether the prohibition applies absolutely or for a specified purpose (and if the latter specifying the purpose); and

(b) stating whether the prohibition applies without limitation of time or for a specified period;

and any direction under subsection (4) above may be given either in such a notice or in a separate notice given to the person in charge of the vehicle.

(6) A prohibition under this section shall come into force as soon as notice of it has been given in accordance with subsection (5) above and shall continue in force—

(a) until it is removed under subsection (7) below; or

(b) in the case of a prohibition imposed only for a specified period, until either it is removed or that period expires, whichever first occurs.

(7) A prohibition under subsection (1) above may be removed by any inspector or examiner, and a prohibition under subsection (2) above may be removed by any inspector, if he is satisfied—

(a) in the case of a prohibition imposed in consequence of a failure to comply with any regulations under section 2 above, that appropriate action has been taken to remedy that failure;

(b) in the case of a prohibition imposed in consequence of an accident or other incident, either that no failure so to comply was occasioned by that accident or incident or that appropriate action has been taken to remedy any such failure which was so occasioned;

and on doing so, the inspector or examiner shall forthwith give notice of the removal of the prohibition to the person in charge of the vehicle, package or packaging component.

(8) Any person who contravenes a prohibition under this section, or fails to comply with a direction under subsection (4) above, shall be guilty of an offence.

4. Enforcement notices

A30.08   (1) If an inspector is of the opinion that any person is failing or is likely to fail to comply with any regulations under section 2 above which make provision for regulating the manufacture, or requiring the maintenance, of packaging components, he may serve a notice under this section on that person.

(2) A notice under this section shall—

(a) state that the inspector is of the said opinion;

(b) specify the matters constituting the failure to comply with the regulations in question or the matters making it likely that such a failure will occur, as the case may be;

(c) specify the steps that must be taken in order to remedy those matters and the period within which those steps must be taken.

(3) Any person who fails to comply with a notice under this section shall be guilty of an offence.

5. Powers of entry

(1) An inspector or examiner shall, on producing, if so required, some duly authenticated document showing his authority, have a right at all reasonable hours—

  (a) to enter any vehicle used to transport radioactive packages for the purpose of ascertaining—

    (i) whether the vehicle, or any radioactive package which is being transported by it, fails to comply with any regulations under section 2 above;

    (ii) whether the vehicle, or any radioactive package which is or was being transported by it, has been involved in an accident; and

    (iii) whether any radioactive package which was being transported by the vehicle, or any radioactive material which was contained in such a package, has been lost or stolen; and

  (b) in the case of an inspector, to enter any premises for the purpose of ascertaining whether there is on the premises any vehicle used for transporting radioactive packages, or any radioactive package or packaging component which fails to comply with regulations under section 2 above.

(2) If a justice of the peace, on sworn information in writing . . . is satisfied that there are reasonable grounds for entering any vehicle or premises for any such purpose as is mentioned in subsection (1) above and either—

  (a) that admission to the vehicle or premises has been refused, or a refusal is apprehended, and (in the case of premises) that notice of the intention to apply for the warrant has been given to the occupier; or

  (b) that an application for admission, or the giving of such a notice, would defeat the object of the entry, or that the case is one of urgency, or (in the case of premises) that they are unoccupied or the occupier temporarily absent,

he may by warrant signed by him authorise the inspector or examiner to enter and search the vehicle or premises, using reasonable force if need be.

(3) A warrant granted under this section shall continue in force until executed.

(4) An inspector or examiner who enters any vehicle or premises by virtue of this section, or of a warrant issued under it, may seize anything which he has reasonable grounds for believing is evidence in relation to an offence under section 2(4) above.

(5) Any person who intentionally obstructs any person exercising any power conferred by this section, or by a warrant issued under it, shall be guilty of an offence.

(6) If any person who enters any vehicle or premises by virtue of this section, or of a warrant issued under it, discloses any information thereby obtained with respect to any manufacturing process or trade secret, he shall, unless the disclosure was made in the performance of his duty, be guilty of an offence.

(7) *[Application to Scotland.]*

[In section 5(2), words relating expressly and exclusively to Scotland have been omitted.]

6. Offences and penalties

(1) Where an offence under this Act which has been committed by a body corporate is proved to have been committed with the consent or connivance of, or to be attributable to any neglect on the part of—

  (a) any director, manager, secretary or other similar officer of the body corporate; or

  (b) any person who was purporting to act in any such capacity, he as well as the body corporate shall be deemed to be guilty of that offence and shall be liable to be proceeded against and punished accordingly.

(2) Any person guilty of an offence under section 5(5) above shall be liable on summary conviction to a fine not exceeding level 3 on the standard scale.

(3) Any person guilty of any other offence under this Act shall be liable—

(a) on conviction on indictment, to a fine or to imprisonment for a term not exceeding two years or to both;

(b) on summary conviction, to a fine not exceeding the statutory maximum or to imprisonment for a term not exceeding two months or to both.

(4) The court by or before which any person is convicted of an offence under section 2(4) or 3(8) above in respect of any radioactive material may order the material to be destroyed or disposed of and any expenses reasonably incurred in connection with the destruction or disposal to be defrayed by that person.

A30.12 **7. Expenses**   *[Omitted.]*

8. Corresponding provision for Northern Ireland   *[Omitted.]*

9. Short title, repeals, commencement and extent   *[Omitted.]*

SCHEDULE

A30.13   Repeals

[Omitted.]

The Road Traffic Act 1991

(1991 c. 40)

An Act to amend the law about road traffic.

A31.01

[25th July 1991]

ARRANGEMENT OF SECTIONS

PART I

GENERAL

Section

A31.02

PART II

TRAFFIC IN LONDON

Section

Parking in London

Miscellaneous

PART III

SUPPLEMENTARY

Section

. . . .

86. Extent

SCHEDULES

PART I

GENERAL

*   *   *

9. Vehicle examiners

A31.03   (1) *[Repeals section 7 of the Public Passenger Vehicles Act 1981 and section 68(1) and (2) of the Road Traffic Act 1988 and inserts section 66A into the 1988 Act (q.v.).]*

(2) Any reference in any Act, or in any instrument made under any Act, to a certifying officer or public service vehicle examiner appointed under the Public Passenger Vehicles Act 1981 or to an examiner appointed under section 68(1) of the Road Traffic Act 1988 shall, so far as may be appropriate in consequence of the preceding provisions of this section, be construed as a reference to an examiner appointed under section 66A of the Road Traffic Act 1988.

*   *   *

31. Experimental period for section 30

A31.04   (1) Subject to the following provisions, no order shall be made under section 34A of the Road Traffic Offenders Act 1988 after the end of 1997 or such later time as may be specified in an order made by the Secretary of State.

(2) At any time before the restriction imposed by subsection (1) above has taken effect, the Secretary of State may by order provide that it shall not do so.

(3) In this section "*the experimental period*" means the period beginning when section 30 above comes into force and ending—

(a) when the restriction imposed by subsection (1) above takes effect, or

(b) if the Secretary of State makes an order under subsection (2) above, on a date specified in the order (being a date falling before the time when the restriction imposed by subsection (1) above would otherwise have taken effect).

(4) During the experimental period—

(a) no order shall be made under section 34A of the Road Traffic Offenders Act 1988 by virtue of a person's conviction under section 3A of the Road Traffic Act 1988, and

(b) no order shall be made under section 34A of the Road Traffic Offenders Act 1988 except by a magistrates' court acting for a petty sessions area . . . which is for the time being designated for the purposes of this section.

(5) In relation to orders made under section 34A during the experimental period, that section shall have effect with the omission of subsection (6) and section 34B shall have effect as if references to the supervising court were references to the court which made the order.

(6) The power to designate an area or district for the purposes of this section shall be exercisable by the Secretary of State by order, and includes power to revoke any designation previously made.

(7) An order under subsection (6) above shall specify the period for which an area or district is designated, and may—

(a) specify different periods for different areas or districts, and

(b) extend or abridge any period previously specified.

(8) The power to make an order under subsection (1) above shall not be exercisable after the end of 1997, and no more than one order may be made under that subsection.

(9) *[Orders to be made by statutory instrument.]*

[The words omitted from section 31(4)(b) relate exclusively to Scotland.   **A31.05**
*   The Courses for Drink-Drive Offenders (Experimental Period) (Termination of Restrictions) Order 1999 (S.I. 1999 No. 3130; not reproduced in this work) provided that the restriction imposed by section 31(1) would not take effect and, for the purposes of section 31(3), the experimental period ended on December 31, 1999.*
*   The functions of the Secretary of State exercisable under section 31(6) in relation to Wales have been transferred to the National Assembly for Wales by the National Assembly for Wales (Transfer of Functions) Order 1999 (S.I. 1999 No. 672; not reproduced in this work), art.2 and Sched. 1.]*

*   *   *

43. Permitted and special parking areas outside London

(1) Schedule 3 shall have effect for the purpose of making provision with respect to areas   **A31.06**
outside London corresponding to that made with respect to London, and areas within London, under sections 63 to 79 of this Act.

(2) In this section "*London*" has the same meaning as it has in Part II of this Act.

[The functions of the Secretary of State exercisable under section 43 and Schedule 3 in relation to Wales   **A31.07**
have been transferred to the National Assembly for Wales by the National Assembly for Wales (Transfer of Functions) Order 1999 (S.I. 1999 No. 672; not reproduced in this work), art.2 and Sched. 1.]

*   *   *

PART II

TRAFFIC IN LONDON

*   *   *

Parking in London

63. The Secretary of State's parking guidance   *[Repealed.]*   **A31.08**

64. Charges at designated parking places

[Amends section 46 of the Road Traffic Regulation Act 1984 (q.v.).]

65. Contravention of certain orders relating to parking places in London not to be criminal offence

[Amends sections 8, 11 and 47 of the Road Traffic Regulation Act 1984.]

66. Parking penalties in London

A31.09

(1) Where, in the case of a stationary vehicle in a designated parking place, a parking attendant has reason to believe that a penalty charge is payable with respect to the vehicle, he may—

(a) fix a penalty charge notice to the vehicle; or

(b) give such a notice to the person appearing to him to be in charge of the vehicle.

(2) For the purposes of this Part of this Act, a penalty charge is payable with respect to a vehicle, by the owner of the vehicle, if—

(a) the vehicle has been left—

    (i) otherwise than as authorised by or under any order relating to the designated parking place; or

    (ii) beyond the period of parking which has been paid for;

(b) no parking charge payable with respect to the vehicle has been paid; or

(c) there has, with respect to the vehicle, been a contravention of, or failure to comply with, any provision made by or under any order relating to the designated parking place.

(3) A penalty charge notice must state—

(a) the grounds on which the parking attendant believes that a penalty charge is payable with respect to the vehicle;

(b) the amount of the penalty charge which is payable;

(c) that the penalty charge must be paid before the end of the period of 28 days beginning with the date of the notice;

(d) that if the penalty charge is paid before the end of the period of 14 days beginning with the date of the notice, the amount of the penalty charge will be reduced by the specified proportion;

(e) that, if the penalty charge is not paid before the end of the 28 day period, a notice to owner may be served by the London authority on the person appearing to them to be the owner of the vehicle;

(f) the address to which payment of the penalty charge must be sent.

(4) In subsection (3)(d) above "*specified proportion*" means such proportion, applicable to all cases, as may be determined by the London authorities acting through the Joint Committee.

[(4A) If the amount to be paid after the penalty charge has been reduced by the specified proportion under subsection (3)(d) above is not a whole number of pounds an authority may reduce the amount further to the nearest pound.]

(5) A penalty charge notice fixed to a vehicle in accordance with this section shall not be removed or interfered with except by or under the authority of—

(a) the owner, or person in charge, of the vehicle; or

(b) the London authority for the place in which the vehicle in question was found.

(6) A person contravening subsection (5) above shall be guilty of an offence and liable on summary conviction to a fine not exceeding level 2 on the standard scale.

(7) Schedule 6 to this Act shall have effect with respect to penalty charges, notices to owners and other matters supplementing the provisions of this section.

[Section 66 is printed as amended by the London Local Authorities Act 1995 (c. x), s.8.

Section 66(4A) is stated only to apply to the boroughs of "participating councils", i.e. the Common Council of the City of London and the councils of London boroughs other than Tower Hamlets; see the London Local Authorities Act 1995 (c. x), ss.2 and 8.]

A31.10

67. Recovery of vehicles or of proceeds of disposal

[Amends section 101 of the Road Traffic Regulation Act 1984.]

A31.11

68. Charges for removal, storage and disposal of vehicles

[Amends section 102 of the Road Traffic Regulation Act 1984.]

69. Immobilisation of vehicles in parking places

(1) Where, in the case of a stationary vehicle in a designated parking place, a parking attendant has reason to believe that the vehicle has been permitted to remain at rest there in any of the circumstances specified in section 66(2)(a), (b) or (c) of this Act, he or another person acting under his direction may fix an immobilisation device to the vehicle.

A31.12

(2) On any occasion when an immobilisation device is fixed to a vehicle in accordance with this section, the person fixing the device shall also fix to the vehicle a notice—

(a) indicating that such a device has been fixed to the vehicle and warning that no attempt should be made to drive it or otherwise put it in motion until it has been released from that device;

(b) specifying the steps to be taken in order to secure its release; and

(c) giving such other information as may be prescribed.

(3) A vehicle to which an immobilisation device has been fixed in accordance with this section may only be released from that device by or under the direction of a person authorised by the relevant authority to give such a direction.

(4) Subject to subsection (3) above, a vehicle to which an immobilisation device has been fixed in accordance with this section shall be released from that device on payment in any manner specified in the notice fixed to the vehicle under subsection (2) above of—

(a) the penalty charge payable in respect of the parking; and

(b) such charge in respect of the release as may be required by the relevant authority.

(5) A notice fixed to a vehicle in accordance with this section shall not be removed or interfered with except by or under the authority of—

(a) the owner, or person in charge, of the vehicle; or

(b) the relevant authority.

(6) A person contravening subsection (5) above shall be guilty of an offence and liable on summary conviction to a fine not exceeding level 2 on the standard scale.

(7) Any person who, without being authorised to do so in accordance with this section, removes or attempts to remove an immobilisation device fixed to a vehicle in accordance with this section shall be guilty of an offence and shall be liable on summary conviction to a fine not exceeding level 3 on the standard scale.

(8) In this section "*relevant authority*" means the London authority for the place in which the vehicle in question was found.

70. Exemptions from section 69

A31.13   (1) Section 69(1) of this Act shall not apply in relation to a vehicle if—

    (a) a current disabled person's badge is displayed on the vehicle;

    (b) not more than 15 minutes have elapsed since the end of any period for which the appropriate charge was duly paid at the time of parking; or

    (c) not more than 15 minutes have elapsed since the end of any unexpired time (in respect of another vehicle) which is available at the relevant parking meter at the time of parking.

(2) In any case in which section 69(1) of this Act would apply to a vehicle but for subsection (1)(a) above and the vehicle was not, at the time at which it was parked, being used—

    (a) in accordance with regulations under section 21 of the Chronically Sick and Disabled Persons Act 1970; and

    (b) in circumstances falling within section 117(1)(b) of the Road Traffic Regulation Act 1984 (use where a disabled person's concession would be available),

the person in charge of the vehicle at that time shall be guilty of an offence and liable on summary conviction to a fine not exceeding level 3 on the standard scale.

(3) In this section "*disabled person's badge*" has the same meaning as in section 142(1) of the Road Traffic Regulation Act 1984, and "*parking meter*" has the same meaning as in section 46(2)(a) of that Act [*q.v.*].

A31.14   ### 71. Representations in relation to removal or immobilisation of vehicles
[Omitted.]

72. Appeals to parking adjudicator in relation to decisions under section 71
[Omitted.]

73. Appointment of parking adjudicators by joint committee of the London authorities   *[Omitted.]*

74. Fixing of certain parking and other charges for London   *[Omitted.]*

74A. Additional parking charges: reserve powers of Secretary of State   *[Omitted.]*

A31.15   ### 75. Immobilisation of vehicles in London by police

A31.16   *[Inserts section 106A into the Road Traffic Regulation Act 1984.]*

76. Special parking areas

A31.17   (1) Where a London authority applies to the Secretary of State for an order to be made under this section, the Secretary of State may make an order designating the whole, or any part, of that authority's area as a special parking area.

    [(1A) An application for an order under subsection (1) above may only be made—

    (a) by Transport for London, to the extent that the special parking area is to consist of GLA roads or trunk roads; or

(b) by a London local authority, to the extent that the special parking area is to consist of roads other than GLA roads and trunk roads.]

(2) *[Consultation before order made under section 76(1).]*

(3) While an order under this section is in force, the following provisions shall cease to apply in relation to the special parking area designated by the order—

    (a) section 8 of the Road Traffic Regulation Act 1984 (contravention of, or failure to comply with, an order under section 6 of that Act to be an offence), so far as it relates to the contravention of, or failure to comply with, any provision of such an order—

        (i) prohibiting or restricting the waiting of vehicles on any road; or

        (ii) relating to any of the matters mentioned in paragraph 7 or 8 of Schedule 1 to that Act (conditions for loading or unloading, or delivery or collecting);

    (b) section 11 of the Act of 1984 (contravention of, or failure to comply with, an experimental traffic order under section 9 of that Act to be an offence), so far as it relates to any contravention of, or failure to comply with, any provision of such an experimental traffic order—

        (i) prohibiting or restricting the waiting of vehicles on any road; or

        (ii) relating to any of the matters mentioned in paragraph 7 or 8 of Schedule 1 to that Act (conditions for loading or unloading, or delivery or collecting);

    [(c) section 16(1) of the Act of 1984 so far as it relates to the contravention of any provision of an order or notice under section 14 of that Act—

        (i) prohibiting or restricting the waiting of vehicles on any road; or

        (ii) relating to any of the matters mentioned in paragraph 7 or 8 of Schedule 1 to that Act;]

    [(ca) section 35A(1) (contravention of parking place orders) of the Act of 1984 so far as it applies in relation to stationary vehicles;]

    [(cb) section 61(5) (prohibition of vehicles in loading areas) of the Act of 1984 so far as it applies in relation to stationary vehicles;]

    (d) section 15 of the Greater London Council (General Powers) Act 1974 (parking of vehicles on verges, central reservations and footpaths etc., to be an offence);

    (e) section 19 of the Road Traffic Act 1988 (parking of heavy vehicles on verges, central reservations and footpaths, etc., to be an offence);

    (f) section 21 of the Act of 1988 (prohibition of driving or parking on cycle tracks), so far as it makes it an offence to park a motor vehicle wholly or partly on a cycle track.

(4) The Secretary of State may by order amend subsection (3) above by adding further provisions (but only in so far as they apply in relation to stationary vehicles).

(5) *[Consultation before making order under section 76(4).]*

[Section 76 is printed as amended by the Road Traffic Act 1991 (Amendment of Section 76(3)) Order 1995 (S.I. 1995 No. 1437; not reproduced in this work); the Greater London Authority Act 1999, s.285.   **A31.18**
The insertion of section 76(1A) is expressly stated not to affect the continuing validity of any order, or any application for an order, made before July 3, 2000 (when that provision took effect); see the Greater London Authority Act 1999, s.285(3).]

76A. Variation of special parking areas by Mayor of London   *[Omitted.]*   **A31.19**

77. Application of provisions in relation to special parking areas

(1) This section applies in relation to any vehicle which is stationary in a special   **A31.20** parking area (but which is not in a designated parking place) in circumstances in which an

offence would have been committed with respect to the vehicle but for section 76(3) above.

(2) A penalty charge shall be payable with respect to the vehicle by the owner of the vehicle.

(3) Section 66 of, and Schedule 6 to, this Act shall apply in relation to penalty charges payable by virtue of subsection (2) above, but subject to such modifications (if any) as the Secretary of State considers it appropriate to make in the order designating the special parking area in question.

(4) Where a parking attendant has reason to believe that a penalty charge is payable with respect to the vehicle by virtue of subsection (2) above, he or another person acting under his direction may fix an immobilisation device to the vehicle.

(5) Subsections (2) to (8) of section 69 of this Act shall apply in relation to a device fixed to a vehicle under subsection (4) above, but subject to such modifications (if any) as the Secretary of State considers it appropriate to make in the order designating the special parking area in question.

(6) An order under section 76 designating a special parking area may make such modifications of any provision of, or amended by, this Part of this Act as the Secretary of State considers appropriate in consequence of the provisions of section 76 or this section or of the order.

Miscellaneous

A31.21   **78. Enforcement**   *[Omitted.]*

79. Application to Crown and visiting forces

A31.22   (1) Nothing in Part II of this Act applies in relation to any vehicle which—

(a) at the relevant time is used or appropriated for use for naval, military or airforce purposes;

(b) belongs to any visiting forces (within the meaning of the Visiting Forces Act 1952); or

(c) at the relevant time is used or appropriated for use by any such forces.

(2) Sections 66 and 69 to 71 of this Act apply to—

(a) vehicles in the public service of the Crown which are required to be registered under [the Vehicle Excise and Registration Act 1994] (other than those which are exempted by subsection (1)(a) above); and

(b) persons in the public service of the Crown.

A31.23   *[Section 79 is printed as amended by the Vehicle Excise and Registration Act 1994, s.63 and Sched. 3, para.29.]*

A31.24   **80. Financial provisions**   *[Repealed.]*

81. Minor and consequential amendments   *[Omitted.]*

82. Interpretation of Part II—

A31.25   (1) In this Part of this Act—

"*Commissioner*" means the Commissioner of Police of the Metropolis or the Commissioner of Police for the City of London;

"designated parking place" means a parking place in London which is designated as a parking place under an order made under section 6, 9 or 45 of the Road Traffic Regulation Act 1984;

"the Director" means the Traffic Director for London appointed under section 52 of this Act;

[*"GLA road"* (subject to subsection (1C) below) has the same meaning as in the Highways Act 1980 (see sections 329(1) and 14D(1) of that Act);]

[*"GLA side road"* has the same meaning as in the Road Traffic Regulation Act 1984 (see sections 124A(9) and section 142(1) of that Act;]

"immobilisation device" has the same meaning as in section 104(9) of the Road Traffic Regulation Act 1984;

"the Joint Committee" has the meaning given by section 73(1) of this Act;

"local plan" has the meaning given in section 54(1) of this Act;

"local plan timetable" has the meaning given in section 54(7)(e) of this Act;

"London" means the area comprising the areas of the London boroughs, the City of London and the Temples;

"London authority" means—

(a) as respects parking, or any matter connected with or related to parking, on a GLA road (except in a designated parking place for which a London borough council or the Common Council of the City of London is the local authority by virtue of section 45(7) of the Road Traffic Regulation Act 1984 [as amended by the Greater London Authority Act 1999, s.281(4) and (5)]), Transport for London;

(b) as respects parking, or any matter connected or related to parking,

    (i) in a parking place such as is referred to in paragraph (a) above;

    (ii) on any road other than a GLA road or a trunk road,

any council of a London borough or the Common Council of the City of London;]

[*"London local authority"* means any council of a London borough or the Common Council of the City of London;]

[*"Minister of the Crown"* has the same meaning as in the Ministers of the Crown Act 1975;]

"Minister's trunk road local plan" has the meaning given in section 56(1);

"network plan" has the meaning given by section 53(1) of this Act;

"parking attendant" has the same meaning as in section 63A of the Road Traffic Regulation Act 1984 (which is inserted by section 44 of this Act);

"penalty charge" has the same meaning as in section 66 of this Act;

"prescribed" means prescribed by regulations made by the Secretary of State;

"priority route" means a road designated by a priority route order;

"priority route order" has the meaning given in section 50(1) of this Act;

"priority route network" has the meaning given in section 50(2) of this Act;

"road" has the same meaning as in the Road Traffic Regulation Act 1984;

[*"the Mayor's transport strategy"* means the transport strategy prepared and published by the Mayor of London under section 142 of the Greater London Authority Act 1999;]

"the Secretary of State's parking guidance" has the meaning given in section 63(1) of this Act;

"the Secretary of State's traffic management guidance" has the meaning given in section 51(1) of this Act;

"trunk road" has the same meaning as in section 10 of the Highways Act 1980;

"*trunk road local plan*" has the meaning given in section 55(3) of this Act;

"*vehicle hiring agreement*" and "*vehicle-hire firm*" have the same meanings as in section 66 of the Road Traffic Offenders Act 1988 (hired vehicles).

[(1A) Any functions conferred or imposed on the Greater London Authority by or under this Part of this Act shall be functions of the Authority which are exercisable by the Mayor acting on behalf of the Authority.]

[(1B) Subsection (1A) above does not apply in relation to any function expressly conferred or imposed on, or made exercisable by, the London Assembly.]

[(1C) In this Part of this Act, any reference to a GLA road includes a reference to a GLA side road.]

(2) For the purposes of this Part of this Act, the owner of a vehicle shall be taken to be the person by whom the vehicle is kept.

(3) In determining, for the purposes of this Part of the Act, who was the owner of a vehicle at any time, it shall be presumed that the owner was the person in whose name the vehicle was at that time registered under [the Vehicle Excise and Registration Act 1994].

(4) Section 28 of the Chronically Sick and Disabled Persons Act 1970 (power to define "*disability*" and other expressions) shall apply in relation to this Part of this Act as it applies to that Act.

(5) In determining, for the purposes of any provision of this Part of this Act, whether a penalty charge has been paid before the end of a particular period, it shall be taken to be paid when it is received by the London authority concerned.

(6), (7) *[Order and regulation-making power.]*

A31.26   *[Section 82 is printed as amended by the Vehicle Excise and Registration Act 1994, s.63 and Sched. 3, para.29; the Greater London Authoirty Act 1999, s.287; the Greater London Road Traffic (Various Provisions) Order 2001 (S.I. 2001 No. 1353; not reproduced in this work).]*

PART III

SUPPLEMENTARY

*   *   *

86. Extent

A31.27   Except in so far as it amends any enactment extending there, this Act does not extend to Northern Ireland.

*   *   *

Section 22   SCHEDULE 1

A31.28   AMENDMENT OF SCHEDULE 1 TO THE ROAD TRAFFIC OFFENDERS ACT 1988

[Omitted.]

Section 26   SCHEDULE 2

A31.29   AMENDMENT OF SCHEDULE 2 TO THE ROAD TRAFFIC OFFENDERS ACT 1988

[Omitted.]

SCHEDULE 3   Section 43

PERMITTED AND SPECIAL PARKING AREAS OUTSIDE LONDON

Permitted parking areas

1.—(1) *[Power of Secretary of State (following application from the appropriate local authority) to desig-*   **A31.30**
nate a permitted parking area by order.]

(2) *[Repealed.]*

(3) *[Need for Secretary of State to consult with police before making order.]*

(4) While an order under sub-paragraph (1) above is in force, the following provisions shall cease to apply in relation to the permitted parking area designated by the order—

    (a) section 35A(1) of the Road Traffic Regulation Act 1984 (offences), so far as it relates to the contravention of, or non-compliance with, any provision of an order made under section 35 of that Act (use of parking places) in relation to parking places provided under section 32(1)(b) of that Act (power of local authorities to provide free parking places on roads); . . .

    [(ab) section 35A(1) of the Act of 1984 (offences), so far as it relates to the contravention of, or non-compliance with any other provision of any order made under section 35 of that Act (use of parking places) applying in relation to a stationary vehicle.]

    (b) section 47(1) of the Act of 1984 (offences) in so far as it applies in relation to any designated parking place [; and]

    [(c) subsections (5) and (6) of section 53 of the Act of 1984 so far as those subsections apply in relation to stationary vehicles.]

(5) *[Power of Secretary of State to amend paragraph 1(4) above by order.]*

(6) *[Need for consultation before amending order under paragraph 1(5) above is made.]*

[Paragraph 1 of Schedule 3 is printed as amended by the Local Government (Wales) Act 1994, s.22(1)   **A31.31**
and Sched. 7, para.43 (see also ibid., s.66(8) and Sched. 18); the Road Traffic Act 1991 (Amendment of Schedule 3) (England and Wales) Order 1996 (S.I. 1996 No. 500; not reproduced in this work).

The functions of the Secretary of State exercisable under section 43 and Schedule 3 in relation to Wales have been transferred to the National Assembly for Wales by the National Assembly for Wales (Transfer of Functions) Order 1999 (S.I. 1999 No. 672; not reproduced in this work), art.2 and Sched. 1.]

Special parking areas

2.—(1) *[Power of Secretary of State (following an application from the appropriate local authority) to*   **A31.32**
designate a special parking area by order.]

(2) *[Repealed.]*

(3) *[Need for Secretary of State to consult with police before making order.]*

(4) While an order under sub-paragraph (1) above is in force, the following provisions shall cease to apply in relation to the special parking area designated by the order—

    (a) section 5 of the Road Traffic Regulation Act 1984 (contravention of a traffic regulation order under section 1 of that Act to be an offence), so far as it relates to the contravention of any provision of such an order prohibiting or restricting the waiting, or the loading and unloading, of vehicles;

    (b) section 11 of the Act of 1984 (contravention of, or failure to comply with, experimental traffic order under section 9 of that Act), so far as it relates to the contravention of, or failure to comply with, any provision of such an order prohibiting or restricting the waiting, or the loading and unloading, of vehicles;

[(ba) section 16(1) of the Act of 1984 (contravention of temporary orders under section 14 of that Act to be an offence) so far as it relates to the contravention of any provision of an order or notice under section 14 of that Act prohibiting or restricting the waiting, or the loading and unloading, of vehicles;]

[(bb) section 61(5) of the Act of 1984 (prohibition of vehicles in loading areas) so far as it applies in relation to stationary vehicles;]

(c) section 129(6) of the Roads (Scotland) Act 1984 (parking of a motor vehicle wholly or partly on a cycle track to be an offence);

(d) section 19 of the Road Traffic Act 1988 (parking of heavy vehicles on verges, central reservations and footpaths, etc., to be an offence);

(e) section 21 of the Act of 1988 (prohibition of driving or parking on cycle tracks), so far as it makes it an offence to park a motor vehicle wholly or partly on a cycle track.

(5) *[Power of Secretary of State to amend paragraph 2(4) above by order.]*

(6) *[Need for consultation before amending order under paragraph 2(5) above is made.]*

A31.33   *[Paragraph 2 of Schedule 3 is printed as amended by the Local Government (Wales) Act 1994, s.22(1) and Sched. 7, para.43 (see also ibid., s.66(8) and Sched. 18); the Road Traffic Act 1991 (Amendment of Schedule 3) (England and Wales) Order 1996 (S.I. 1996 No. 500; not reproduced in this work). See also the notes to Schedule 3, paragraph 1 above.]*

Control of parking in permitted and special parking areas

A31.34   **3.** *[Payment of penalty charges for contraventions of restrictions relating to permitted and special parking areas.]*

Orders under this Schedule

4. *[Orders under paragraphs 1 and 2 to be made by statutory instruments subject to annulment by either House of Parliament.]*

Section 48   SCHEDULE 4

A31.35   MINOR AND CONSEQUENTIAL AMENDMENTS

[Omitted.]

Section 52   SCHEDULE 5

A31.36   THE TRAFFIC DIRECTOR FOR LONDON

[Repealed.]

Section 66(7)   SCHEDULE 6

PARKING PENALTIES

A31.37   **1.** *[The notice to owner.]*

Representations against notice to owner

A31.38   **2.**—(1) Where it appears to the recipient that one or other of the grounds mentioned in sub-paragraph (4) below are satisfied, he may make representations to that effect to the London authority who served the notice on him.

(2) *[Form in which representations must be made.]*

(3) *[Right to disregard representations made after 28 days.]*

(4) The grounds are—

  (a) that the recipient—

    (i) never was the owner of the vehicle in question;

    (ii) had ceased to be its owner before the date on which the alleged contravention occurred; or

    (iii) became its owner after that date;

  (b) that the alleged contravention did not occur;

  (c) that the vehicle had been permitted to remain at rest in the parking place by a person who was in control of the vehicle without the consent of the owner;

  (d) that the relevant designation order is invalid;

  (e) that the recipient is a vehicle-hire firm and—

    (i) the vehicle in question was at the material time hired from that firm under a vehicle hiring agreement; and

    (ii) the person hiring it had signed a statement of liability acknowledging his liability in respect of any penalty charge notice fixed to the vehicle during the currency of the hiring agreement;

  (f) that the penalty charge exceeded the amount applicable in the circumstances of the case.

(5) *[Need to state name and address (if known) of transferee of vehicle if paragraph 2(4)(a)(ii) is relied on.]*

(6) *[Need to state name and address (if known) of transferee of vehicle if paragraph 2(4)(a)(iii) is relied on.]*

(7) *[Duty of authority receiving representations to consider them and to give notice of its decision.]*

3. *[Cancellation of notice to owner.]*   **A31.39**

4. *[Rejection of representations against notice to owner.]*

5. *[Adjudication by parking adjudicator.]*

6. *[Charge certificates.]*

7. *[Enforcement of charge certificate.]*

8. *[Invalid notices.]*

Offence of giving false information

9.—(1) A person who, in response to a notice to owner served under this Schedule, makes any representation under paragraph 2 or 5(2) above which is false in a material particular and does so recklessly or knowing it to be false in that particular is guilty of an offence.   **A31.40**

(2) Any person guilty of such an offence shall be liable on summary conviction to a fine not exceeding level 5 on the standard scale.

[The representations under paragraph 5(2) (to which reference is made in paragraph 9(1) above) are representations which the recipient of the notice to owner is entitled to make in respect of the notice and   **A31.41**

such additional representations made on an appeal to a parking adjudicator as may also fall within the terms of paragraph 2(4).]

10. *[Service by post.]*

Section 81	SCHEDULE 7

A31.42   MINOR AND CONSEQUENTIAL AMENDMENTS IN RELATION TO LONDON

[Omitted.]

Section 83	SCHEDULE 8

A31.43   REPEALS

[Omitted.]

The Aggravated Vehicle-Taking Act 1992

(1992 c. 11)

An Act to make provision with respect to persons who commit offences under section 12(1) of the Theft Act 1968 in relation to a mechanically propelled vehicle where additional circumstances are present relating to the driving of or damage to the vehicle. [6th March 1992]

A32.01

1. New offence of aggravated vehicle-taking

(1) *[Inserts section 12A into the Theft Act 1968, q.v.]*

A32.02

(2) The provisions of subsection (4) of section 12A of the Theft Act 1968 are without prejudice to the operation of—

  (a) [section 127 of the Powers of Criminal Courts (Sentencing) Act 2000] (under which a Crown Court has a general power to fine an offender convicted on indictment); and

  (b) section 17 of, and Schedule 1 to, the Magistrates' Courts Act 1980 (under which, with certain exceptions not material to section 12A, offences under the Theft Act 1968 are triable either way).

(3) Nothing in section 12A of the Theft Act 1968 applies to—

  (a) an offence under section 12(1) of that Act which was committed before this section comes into force; or

  (b) any driving, injury or damage which occurred before this section comes into force.

[Section 1 is printed as amended by the Powers of Criminal Courts (Sentencing) Act 2000, s.165(1) and Sched. 9, para.151.]

A32.03

2. Offence to be tried only summarily if value of damage is small

(1) In Schedule 2 to the Magistrates' Courts Act 1980 (offences for which the value involved is relevant to the mode of trial) after paragraph 2 there shall be inserted the following paragraph—

A32.04

"3. Offences under section 12A of the Theft Act 1968 (aggravated vehicle-taking) where no allegation is made under subsection 1(b) other than of damage, whether to the vehicle or other property or both.	The total value of the damage alleged to have been caused.	(1) In the case of damage to any property other than the vehicle involved in the offence, as for the corresponding entry in paragraph 1 above, substituting a reference to the time of the accident concerned for any reference to the material time.

[continued on next page

		(2) In the case of damage to the vehicle involved in the offence—
		(a) if immediately after the vehicle was recovered the damage was capable of repair—
		(i) what would probably then have been the market price for the repair of the damage, or
		(ii) what the vehicle would probably have cost to buy in the open market immediately before it was unlawfully taken, whichever is the less; or
		(b) if immediately after the vehicle was recovered the damage was beyond repair, what the vehicle would probably have cost to buy in the open market immediately before it was unlawfully taken."

(2) In the Magistrates' Courts Act 1980, at the end of section 22 (which introduces Schedule 2) there shall be added the following subsection—

"(12) Subsection (8) of section 12A of the Theft Act 1968 (which determines when a vehicle is recovered) shall apply for the purposes of paragraph 3 of Schedule 2 to this Act as it applies for the purposes of that section."

(3) In section 33 of the Magistrates' Courts Act 1980 (maximum penalties on summary conviction in pursuance of section 22)—

(a) in subsection (1), at the beginning of paragraph (a) there shall be inserted the words "subject to subsection (3) below"; and

(b) after subsection (2) there shall be inserted the following subsection—

"(3) Paragraph (a) of subsection (1) above does not apply to an offence under section 12A of the Theft Act 1968 (aggravated vehicle-taking)."

A32.05   **3. Obligatory disqualification**   *[Amends the Road Traffic Offenders Act 1988.]*

4. Short title, commencement and extent   *[Omitted.]*

The Transport and Works Act 1992

(1992 c. 42)

An Act to provide for the making of orders relating to, or to matters ancillary to, the construction or operation of railways, tramways, trolley vehicle systems, other guided transport systems and inland waterways . . . ; to make further provision in relation to railways, tramways, trolley vehicle systems and other guided transport systems; . . . and for connected purposes.

A33.01

[16th March 1992]

ARRANGEMENT OF SECTIONS

PART I

ORDERS AUTHORISING WORKS, ETC.

*   *   *

PART II

SAFETY OF RAILWAYS, ETC.

CHAPTER I   OFFENCES INVOLVING DRINK OR DRUGS

Preliminary

PART III

MISCELLANEOUS AND GENERAL

*　　　*　　　*

*　　　*　　　*

PART I

ORDERS AUTHORISING WORKS, ETC.

*　　　*　　　*

PART II

SAFETY OF RAILWAYS, ETC.

A33.03　*General note to Part II.*　All the functions of a Minister of the Crown under Part II of the Transport and Works Act 1992 exercisable in relation to Wales have been transferred to the National Assembly for Wales by the National Assembly for Wales (Transfer of Functions) Order 1999 (S.I. 1999 No. 672; not reproduced in this work), art.2 and Sched. 1.

CHAPTER I　　OFFENCES INVOLVING DRINK OR DRUGS

26. Transport systems to which Chapter I applies

A33.04　(1) This chapter applies to transport systems of any of the following kinds—

　(a) a railway;

　(b) a tramway;

　(c) a system which uses another mode of guided transport and is specified for the purposes of this Chapter by an order made by the Secretary of State.

(2) This chapter shall not apply to a transport system unless it is used, or is intended to be used, wholly or partly for the carriage of members of the public.

(3) *[Orders to be made by statutory instrument and subject to annulment by Parliament.]*

A33.05　*[Sections 4–11 of the Road Traffic Act 1988 do not apply to vehicles to which this chapter applies; see ibid., s.192A.*

Systems are specified for the purposes of Chapter I of Part II of this Act by the Transport (Guided Systems) Order 1992 (S.I. 1992 No. 2044) (not reproduced in this work).]

*　　　*　　　*

CHAPTER II   OTHER SAFETY PROVISIONS

*   *   *

Signs and barriers at private crossings

52. Placing of signs and barriers   *[Authorises operators of railways and tramways to* **A33.06**
*place crossing signs and barriers of a character prescribed by regulations or authorised by the Secretary of
State on or near private roads or paths which are near crossings.]*

53. Rights to enter land   *[Omitted.]* **A33.07**

54. Default powers of Secretary of State   *[Omitted.]*

55. Offence of failing to comply with sign

(1) A person who fails to comply with any requirement, restriction or prohibition con- **A33.08**
veyed by a crossing sign lawfully placed on or near a private road or path a place where
it crosses a railway or tramway shall be guilty of an offence.

(2) In any proceedings for an offence under this section, a crossing sign on or near a
private road or path near a place where it crosses a railway or tramway shall be taken to
have been lawfully placed there unless the contrary is proved.

(3) A person guilty of an offence under this section shall be liable on summary conviction to a fine not exceeding level 3 on the standard scale.

56. Interpretation of sections 52 to 55

(1) In sections 52 to 55 above (and this section)— **A33.09**

"*barrier*" includes gate;

"*cross*" means cross otherwise than by tunnel or bridge;

"*crossing sign*", in relation to a private road or path and any place where it crosses a
railway or tramway, means—

(a)   any object or device (whether fixed or portable), or

(b)   any line or mark on the road or path,

for conveying to users of the road or path warnings, information, requirements,
restrictions or prohibitions relating to the crossing;

"*fail*" includes refuse;

"*lawfully placed*" means placed in accordance with sections 52 to 54 above;

"*maintain*" includes repair and replace;

"*place*" includes erect and (in relation to a sign) display;

"*private road or path*" means any length of road or path to which the public does not have
access.

(2) *[Exercise of powers under sections 52–54.]*

CHAPTER III   SUPPLEMENTARY

57. Duty to consult   *[Omitted.]* **A33.10**

58. Prosecution

A33.11   No proceedings shall be instituted in England and Wales in respect of an offence under this Part [, other than an offence under section 41 or 43 above] except by or with the consent of the Secretary of State or the Director of Public Prosecutions.

A33.12   *[Section 58 is printed as amended by the Railways Act 1993, s.117(5)(b). Section 117 applies to railways, tramways, trolley vehicle systems and any transport system using any other mode of guided transport; ibid., s.117(6).*

Neither section 41 nor section 43 of the Railways Act 1993 is concerned with matters relating to road traffic.]

59. Offences by bodies corporate

A33.13   (1) Where an offence under this Part committed by a body corporate is committed with the consent or connivance of, or is attributable to any neglect on the part of, a director, manager, secretary or other similar officer of the body, or a person purporting to act in such a capacity, he as well as the body corporate shall be guilty of the offence.

(2) In subsection (1) above *"director"*, in relation to a body corporate whose affairs are managed by its members, means a member of the body corporate.

(3) *[Applies to Scotland.]*

PART III

MISCELLANEOUS AND GENERAL

*   *   *

67. Interpretation

A33.14   (1) In this Act, except where the context otherwise requires—

"carriageway" has the same meaning as in the Highways Act 1980 [*q.v.*] . . . ;

"guided transport" means transport by vehicles guided by means external to the vehicles (whether or not the vehicles are also capable of being operated in some other way);

"inland waterway" includes both natural and artificial waterways, and waterways within parts of the sea that are in Great Britain, but not any waterway managed or maintained by a person who is a harbour authority (within the meaning of the Harbours Act 1964) in relation to the waterway;

"operator", in relation to a transport system, means any person carrying on an undertaking which includes the system or any part of it or the provision of transport services on the system;

"railway" means a system of transport employing parallel rails which—

     (a) provide support and guidance for vehicles carried on flanged wheels, and

     (b) form a track which either is of a gauge of at least 350 millimetres or crosses a carriageway (whether or not on the same level),

but does not include a tramway;

"street" means—

     (a) in England and Wales, a street within the meaning of section 48 of the New Roads and Street Works Act 1991, together with land on the verge of a street or between two carriageways;

     (b) *[applies to Scotland.]*;

"*tramway*" means a system of transport used wholly or mainly for the carriage of passengers and employing parallel rails which—

   (a) provide support and guidance for vehicles carried on flanged wheels, and

   (b) are laid wholly or mainly along a street or in any other place to which the public has access (including a place to which the public has access only on making a payment);

"*trolley vehicle system*" means a system of transport by vehicles constructed or adapted for use on roads without rails under electric power transmitted to them by overhead wires (whether or not there is in addition a source of power on board the vehicles);

"*vehicle*" includes mobile traction unit.

(2) *[Relates to references to rights over land.]*

[Words relating expressly and exclusively to Scotland have been omitted from section 67.   **A33.15**
   For section 48 of the New Roads and Street Works Act 1991, see the notes to the Highways Act 1980, s.329.]

71. Extent

This Act shall not extend to Northern Ireland.   **A33.16**

*   *   *

The Vehicle Excise and Registration Act 1994

(1994 c. 22)

A34.01 An Act to consolidate the enactments relating to vehicle excise duty and the registration of vehicles.

[5th July 1994]

A34.02 *Visiting forces.* No excise duty is chargeable under the 1994 Act in respect of any vehicle in the service of a visiting force (as defined); see the Visiting Forces and International Headquarters (Application of Law) Order 1999 (S.I. 1999 No. 1736; not reproduced in this work), art.8(8).

ARRANGEMENT OF SECTIONS

PART I

VEHICLE EXCISE DUTY AND LICENCES

Main provisions

SCHEDULES

PART I

VEHICLE EXCISE DUTY AND LICENCES

Main provisions

1. Duty and licences

(1) A duty of excise ("*vehicle excise duty*") shall be charged in respect of every mechanically **A34.04** propelled vehicle which is used, or kept, on a public road in the United Kingdom and shall be paid on a licence to be taken out by the person keeping the vehicle.

(2) A licence taken out for a vehicle is in this Act referred to as a "*vehicle licence*".

2. Annual rates of duty

(1) Vehicle excise duty in respect of a vehicle of any description is chargeable by refer- **A34.05** ence to the annual rate currently applicable to it in accordance with the provisions of Schedule 1 which relate to vehicles of that description.

(2) But where vehicle excise duty is chargeable in respect of the keeping of a vehicle on a road (and not in respect of its use), the duty is chargeable in accordance with subsection (3) or (4).

(3) Where one or more vehicle licences have previously been issued for the use of the vehicle, duty in respect of the keeping of the vehicle on a road is chargeable by reference to

the annual rate currently applicable to a vehicle of the same description as that of the vehicle on the occasion of the issue of that licence (or the last of those licences).

(4) In any other case, duty in respect of such keeping is chargeable by reference to [the general rate currently specified in paragraph 1(2) of Schedule 1].

A34.06   *[Section 2 is printed as amended by the Finance Act 1996, s.18(3) and (5).]*

A34.07   **3. Duration of licences**   *[Omitted.]*

4. Amount of duty   *[Omitted.]*

5. Exempt vehicles

A34.08   (1) No vehicle excise duty shall be charged in respect of a vehicle if it is an exempt vehicle.

(2) Schedule 2 specifies descriptions of vehicles which are exempt vehicles.

A34.09   **6. Collection, etc., of duty**   *[Omitted.]*

Vehicle licences

7. Issue of vehicle licences

A34.10   (1) Every person applying for a vehicle licence shall—

    (a) make such a declaration, and

    (b) furnish such particulars,

(whether or not with respect to the vehicle for which the licence is to be taken out) as may be [specified] by the Secretary of State.

(2), (3) *[Content of declaration and particulars which may be prescribed.]*

[(3A) A person applying for a licence shall not be required to make a declaration specified for the purposes of subsection (1)(a) if he agrees to comply with such conditions as may be specified in relation to him by the Secretary of State.]

[(3B) The conditions which may be specified under subsection (3A) include—

    [(a)] a condition that particulars for the time being specified for the purposes of subsection (1)(b) are furnished by being transmitted to the Secretary of State by such electronic means as he may specify [; and]

    [(b) a condition requiring such payments as may be specified by the Secretary of State to be made to him in respect of—

        (i) steps taken by him for facilitating compliance by any person with any condition falling within paragraph (a); and

        (ii) in such circumstances as may be so specified, the processing of applications for vehicle licences where particulars are transmitted in accordance with that paragraph.]]

(4) A vehicle licence—

    (a) is issued for the vehicle specified in the application for the licence, and

    (b) does not entitle the person to whom it is issued to use or keep any other vehicle.

(5) The Secretary of State is not required to issue a vehicle licence for which an application is made unless he is satisfied—

(a) that the licence applied for is the appropriate licence for the vehicle specified in the application, and

(b) in the case of an application for a licence for a vehicle purporting to be the first application for a licence for the vehicle, that a licence has not previously been issued for the vehicle.

(6) *[Regulation-making power.]*

(7) Where, following an application made in accordance with regulations under paragraph 13 of Schedule 1, a licence is issued for a goods vehicle at the rate of duty applicable to a weight specified in the application which is lower than its actual weight, that lower weight is to be shown on the licence.

[(8) In this section "*special vehicle*" has the same meaning as in paragraph 4 of Schedule 1.]

[Section 7 is printed as amended by the Finance Act 1995, s.19 and Sched. 4, paras 1 and 30(1)(a)   **A34.11**
and (3); the Finance Act 1996, s.17(10), (14), and s.23 and Sched. 2, paras 1 and 2(1)–(3); the Finance (No. 2) Act 1997, s.14(1).]

8. Vehicles removed into UK   *[Omitted.]*   **A34.12**

9. Temporary vehicle licences

(1) Where an application is made for a vehicle licence for a vehicle for any period, the   **A34.13**
Secretary of State may, if he thinks fit, instead of issuing immediately a vehicle licence for that period—

(a) issue a vehicle licence (a "*temporary licence*") for fourteen days, or such other period as may be prescribed by regulations made by the Secretary of State, having effect from such day as may be so prescribed, and

(b) from time to time issue a further temporary licence for the vehicle.

(2) Nothing in this section affects the amount of any duty payable on a vehicle licence.

(3), (4) *[Payment of fee on application to an authorised body.]*

10. Transfer and surrender of vehicle licences

(1) Any vehicle licence may be transferred in the manner prescribed by regulations   **A34.14**
made by the Secretary of State.

(2) The holder of a vehicle licence may at any time surrender the licence to the Secretary of State.

(3) Where—

(a) a person surrenders under subsection (2) a temporary licence issued pursuant to an application for a vehicle licence, and

(b) a further vehicle licence issued pursuant to the application is either held by him at the time of the surrender of the temporary licence or received by him after that time,

the further licence ceases to be in force and the person shall immediately return it to the Secretary of State.

Trade licences

11. Issue of trade licences

(1) Where—   **A34.15**

(a) a motor trader or vehicle tester, or

(b) a person who satisfies the Secretary of State that he intends to commence business as a motor trader or vehicle tester,

applies to the Secretary of State (in the manner [specified] by the Secretary of State) to take out a licence under this section (a *"trade licence"*), the Secretary of State may, subject to the conditions [prescribed by regulations made by the Secretary of State], issue such a licence to him on payment of vehicle excise duty at the rate applicable to the licence.

[(1A) The power to prescribe conditions under subsection (1) includes, in particular, the power to prescribe conditions which are to be complied with after the licence is issued.]

(2) In the case of a motor trader who is a manufacturer of vehicles, a trade licence is a licence for—

(a) all vehicles which are from time to time temporarily in his possession in the course of his business as a motor trader,

(b) all vehicles kept and used by him solely for purposes of conducting research and development in the course of his business as such a manufacturer, and

(c) all vehicles which are from time to time submitted to him by other manufacturers for testing on roads in the course of that business.

(3) In the case of any other motor trader, a trade licence is a licence for all vehicles which are from time to time temporarily in his possession in the course of his business as a motor trader.

(4) In the case of a vehicle tester, a trade licence is a licence for all vehicles which are from time to time submitted to him for testing in the course of his business as a vehicle tester.

A34.16   *[Section 11 is printed as amended by the Finance Act 1995, s.19 and Sched. 4, paras 1 and 30(2) and (3); the Finance Act 1996, s.23 and Sched. 2, paras 1 and 3.]*

12. Use of vehicles by holders of trade licences

A34.17   (1) The holder of a trade licence is not entitled by virtue of the licence—

(a) to use more than one vehicle at any one time,

(b) to use a vehicle for any purpose other than a purpose prescribed by regulations made by the Secretary of State, or

(c) except in such circumstances as may be so prescribed, to keep any vehicle on a road if it is not being used on the road.

(2) The Secretary of State shall by regulations prescribe—

(a) the conditions subject to which trade licences are to be issued, and

(b) the purposes for which the holder of a trade licence may use a vehicle by virtue of the licence.

(3) The purposes which may be prescribed as those for which the holder of a trade licence may use a vehicle under the licence shall not include the conveyance of goods or burden of any description other than—

(a) a load which is carried solely for the purpose of testing or demonstrating the vehicle or any of its accessories or equipment and which is returned to the place of loading without having been removed from the vehicle except for that purpose or in the case of accident,

(b) in the case of a vehicle which is being delivered or collected, a load consisting of another vehicle used or to be used for travel from or to the place of delivery or collection,

(c) a load built in as part of the vehicle or permanently attached to it,

(d) a load consisting of parts, accessories or equipment designed to be fitted to the vehicle and of tools for fitting them to the vehicle, or

(e) a load consisting of a trailer other than a trailer which is for the time being a disabled vehicle.

(4) For the purposes of subsection (3), where a vehicle is so constructed that a trailer may by partial superimposition be attached to the vehicle in such a manner as to cause a substantial part of the weight of the trailer to be borne by the vehicle, the vehicle and the trailer are deemed to constitute a single vehicle.

(5) In subsection (3)(e) "*disabled vehicle*" includes a vehicle which has been abandoned or is scrap.

13. Trade licences: duration and amount of duty   *[Omitted.]*   **A34.18**

14. Trade licences: supplementary

(1) Nothing in sections 11 to 13 prevents a person entitled to take out a trade licence   **A34.19**
from holding two or more trade licences.

(2) The holder of a trade licence may at any time surrender the licence to the Secretary of State.

(3) *[Review of decision to refuse application for trade licence.]*

(4) *[Regulation-making power.]*

Additional duty, rebates, etc.

15. Vehicles becoming chargeable to duty at higher rate

(1) Where—   **A34.20**

(a) a vehicle licence has been taken out for a vehicle at any rate of vehicle excise duty, and

(b) at any time while the licence is in force the vehicle is used so as to subject it to a higher rate,

duty at the higher rate becomes chargeable in respect of the licence for the vehicle.

(2) For the purposes of subsection (1) a vehicle is used so as to subject it to a higher rate if it is used in an altered condition, in a manner or for a purpose which—

(a) brings it within, or

(b) if it was used solely in that condition, in that manner or for that purpose, would bring it within,

a description of vehicle to which a higher rate of duty is applicable.

[(2A) For the purpose of subsection (1) a vehicle is also used so as to subject it to a higher rate if—

(a) the rate of vehicle excise duty paid on a vehicle licence taken out for the vehicle was the rate applicable to a vehicle of the same description with respect to which the reduced pollution requirements are satisfied, and

(b) while the licence is in force, the vehicle is used at a time when those requirements are not satisfied with respect to it.]

(3) For the purposes of subsection (1) a vehicle in respect of which a lower rate of duty is chargeable by virtue of regulations under paragraph 13 of Schedule 1 is also used so as

to subject it to a higher rate if it is used in contravention of a condition imposed under or by virtue of sub-paragraph (2) of that paragraph.

(4) [Subject to section 7(5),] where duty at a higher rate becomes chargeable under sub-section (1) in respect of a vehicle licence, the licence may be exchanged for a new vehicle licence for the period—

(a) beginning with the date on which the higher rate of duty becomes chargeable, and

(b) ending with the period for which the original licence was issued.

(5) A new vehicle licence may be obtained under subsection (4) only on payment of the appropriate proportion of the difference between—

(a) the amount of duty payable on the original licence, and

(b) the amount of duty payable on a vehicle licence taken out for the period for which the original licence was issued but at the higher rate of duty.

(6) For the purposes of subsection (5) "*the appropriate proportion*" means the proportion which the number of months in the period—

(a) beginning with the date on which the higher rate of duty becomes chargeable, and

(b) ending with the period for which the original licence was issued,

bears to the number of months in the whole of the period for which the original licence was issued (any incomplete month being treated as a whole month).

(7) If the higher rate has been changed since the issue of the original licence, the amount under subsection (5)(b) is calculated as if that rate had been in force at all material times at the level at which it is in force when it becomes chargeable.

A34.21   *[Section 15 is printed as amended by the Finance Act 1995, s.19 and Sched. 4, paras 1, 16, 19 and 29; the Finance Act 1998, s.16 and Sched. 1, paras 1, 13 and 17.]*

16. Exceptions from charge at higher rate in case of tractive units

A34.22   (1) [Subject to subsection (9)] duty at a higher rate does not become chargeable under section 15—

(a) where subsection (2) applies in relation to a tractive unit, by reason of the tractive unit being used in accordance with subsection (3),

(b) where subsection (4) applies in relation to a tractive unit, by reason of the tractive unit being used in accordance with subsection (5), or

(c) where subsection (6) applies in relation to a tractive unit, by reason of the tractive unit being used in accordance with subsection (7).

(2) This subsection applies in relation to a tractive unit where—

(a) a vehicle licence for—

    (i) a tractive unit having two axles which is to be used only with semi-trailers with not fewer than two axles, or

    (ii) a tractive unit having two axles which is to be used only with semi-trailers with not fewer than three axles,

has been taken out for the tractive unit, and

(b) the rate of duty paid on taking out the licence is equal to or exceeds the rate of duty applicable to a tractive unit having two axles which—

(i) has [a revenue weight] equal to the maximum laden weight at which a tractive unit having two axles may lawfully be used in Great Britain with a semi-trailer with a single axle, and

(ii) is to be used with semi-trailers with any number of axles.

(3) The tractive unit is being used in accordance with this subsection where—

(a) it is used with a semi-trailer with a single axle, and

(b) when so used, the laden weight of the tractive unit and semi-trailer taken together does not exceed the maximum laden weight mentioned in subsection (2)(b)(i).

(4) This subsection applies in relation to a tractive unit where—

(a) a vehicle licence for a tractive unit having two axles which is to be used only with semi-trailers with not fewer than three axles has been taken out for the tractive unit, and

(b) the rate of duty paid on taking out the licence is equal to or exceeds the rate of duty applicable to a tractive unit having two axles which—

(i) has [a revenue weight] of 33,000 kilograms, and

(ii) is to be used with semi-trailers with not fewer than two axles.

(5) The tractive unit is being used in accordance with this subsection where—

(a) it is used with a semi-trailer with two axles, and

(b) when so used, the laden weight of the tractive unit and semi-trailer taken together does not exceed 33,000 kilograms.

(6) This subsection applies in relation to a tractive unit where—

(a) a vehicle licence for a tractive unit having three or more axles which is to be used only with semi-trailers with not fewer than two axles has been taken out for the tractive unit, and

(b) the rate of duty paid on taking out the licence is equal to or exceeds the rate of duty applicable to a tractive unit having three or more axles which—

(i) has [a revenue weight] equal to the maximum laden weight at which a tractive unit having three or more axles may lawfully be used in Great Britain with a semi-trailer with a single axle, and

(ii) is to be used with semi-trailers with any number of axles.

(7) The tractive unit is being used in accordance with this subsection where—

(a) it is used with a semi-trailer with a single axle, and

(b) when so used, the laden weight of the tractive unit and semi-trailer taken together does not exceed the maximum laden weight mentioned in subsection (6)(b)(i).

[(8) This subsection applies to a tractive unit (*"the relevant tractive unit"*) in relation to which subsection (2), (4) or (6) applies if—

(a) the rate of duty paid on taking out the licence for the relevant tractive unit is the rate applicable to a tractive unit of the appropriate description with respect to which the reduced pollution requirements are satisfied; and

(b) while the licence is in force, the relevant tractive unit is used at a time when the reduced pollution requirements are not satisfied with respect to it.]

[(9) Where subsection (8) applies, subsection (1) does not prevent duty becoming payable under section 15 at the rate applicable to a tractive unit of the appropriate description with respect to which the reduced pollution requirements are not satisfied.]

[(10) In this section "*the appropriate description*" means the description mentioned in paragraph (b) of whichever of subsections (2), (4) and (6) applies in relation to the relevant tractive unit.]

A34.23   *[Section 16 is printed as amended by the Finance Act 1995, s.19 and Sched. 4, paras 1, 16, 20 and 29; the Finance Act 1998, s.16 and Sched. 1, paras 1, 14 and 17.]*

17. Other exceptions from charge at higher rate

A34.24   (1) Where a vehicle licence has been taken out for a vehicle of any description, duty at a higher rate applicable to a vehicle of another description does not become chargeable under section 15 unless the vehicle as used while the licence is in force satisfies all the conditions which must be satisfied in order to bring the vehicle into the other description of vehicle for the purposes of vehicle excise duty.

(2) Where—

(a) duty has been paid in respect of a vehicle at a rate applicable under Part VIII of Schedule 1, and

(b) the vehicle is to a substantial extent being used for the conveyance of goods or burden belonging to a particular person (whether the person keeping the vehicle or not),

duty at a higher rate does not become chargeable under section 15 by reason only that the vehicle is used for the conveyance without charge in the course of their employment of employees of the person to whom the goods or burden belong.

(3)–(7) *[Repealed.]*

(8) This section does not have effect where section 15 applies by reason of the use of a vehicle in contravention of a condition imposed under or by virtue of paragraph 13(2) of Schedule 1.

A34.25   *[Section 17 is printed as amended by the Finance Act 1995, s.19 and Sched. 4, paras 1, 15 and 16 (see also ibid., s.162 and Sched. 29, Pt V(2)).]*

18. Vehicles for export becoming liable to VAT

A34.26   (1) Where, by virtue of sub-paragraph (2) of paragraph 23 of Schedule 2, a vehicle which is an exempt vehicle under sub-paragraph (1) of that paragraph is deemed never to have been an exempt vehicle under that sub-paragraph, vehicle excise duty is payable—

(a) by the person by whom the vehicle was acquired from its manufacturer, in relation to the whole period since the registration of the vehicle, or

(b) by any other person who is for the time being the keeper of the vehicle, in relation to the period since the vehicle was first kept by him,

unless, or except to the extent that, the Secretary of State waives payment of the duty.

(2) Subsection (1) is without prejudice to section 30; but duty with respect to a vehicle is not payable by a person under that subsection in relation to any part of a period if an amount with respect to it has been ordered to be paid by him under that section in relation to the part of the period.

A34.27   **19. Surrender of licences**   *[Omitted.]*

[19A. Payment for licences by cheque

(1) The Secretary of State may, if he thinks fit, issue a vehicle licence or a trade licence   **A34.28**
on receipt of a cheque for the amount of the duty payable on it.

(2) In a case where—

  (a) a vehicle licence or a trade licence is issued to a person on receipt of a cheque which is subsequently dishonoured, and

  (b) the Secretary of State sends a notice by post to the person informing him that the licence is void as from the time when it was granted,

the licence shall be void as from the time when it was granted.

(3) In a case where—

  (a) a vehicle licence or a trade licence is issued to a person on receipt of a cheque which is subsequently dishonoured,

  (b) the Secretary of State sends a notice by post to the person requiring him to secure that the duty payable on the licence is paid within such reasonable period as is specified in the notice,

  (c) the requirement in the notice is not complied with, and

  (d) the Secretary of State sends a further notice by post to the person informing him that the licence is void as from the time when it was granted,

the licence shall be void as from the time when it was granted.

(4) Section 102 of the Customs and Excise Management Act 1979 (payment for excise licences by cheque) shall not apply in relation to a vehicle licence or a trade licence.]

[Section 19A was inserted by the Finance Act 1995, s.19 and Sched. 4, paras 1 and 32(1).]   **A34.29**

[19B. Issue of licences before payment of duty

(1) The Secretary of State may, if he thinks fit, issue a vehicle licence or a trade licence   **A34.30**
to a person who has agreed with the Secretary of State to pay the duty payable on the licence in a manner provided for in the agreement.

(2) In a case where—

  (a) a vehicle licence or a trade licence is issued to a person in accordance with subsection (1),

  (b) the duty payable on the licence is not received by the Secretary of State in accordance with the agreement, and

  (c) the Secretary of State sends a notice by post to the person informing him that the licence is void as from the time when it was granted,

the licence shall be void as from the time when it was granted.

(3) In a case where—

  (a) paragraphs (a) and (b) of subsection (2) apply,

  (b) the Secretary of State sends a notice by post to the person requiring him to secure that the duty payable on the licence is paid within such reasonable period as is specified in the notice,

  (c) the requirement in the notice is not complied with, and

(d) the Secretary of State sends a further notice by post to the person informing him that the licence is void as from the time when it was granted,

the licence shall be void as from the time when it was granted.]

A34.31   *[Section 19B was inserted by the Finance Act 1997, s.19(1).]*

20. Combined road-rail transport of goods

A34.32   (1) This section applies where—

(a) goods are loaded on a relevant goods vehicle for transport between member States,

(b) the vehicle is transported by rail between the nearest suitable rail loading station to the point of loading and the nearest suitable rail unloading station to the point of unloading, and

(c) part of the rail transport of the vehicle takes place in the United Kingdom at a time when a vehicle licence for it is in force.

(2) Where this section applies, the holder of the licence is, on making a claim, entitled to receive from the Secretary of State (by way of rebate of the duty paid on the licence) an amount calculated by the method prescribed by regulations made by the Secretary of State.

[(3) In this section *"relevant goods vehicle"* means any vehicle the rate of duty applicable to which is provided for in Part VIII of Schedule 1 or which would be such a vehicle if Part VI of that Schedule did not apply to the vehicle.]

(4) *[Regulation-making power.]*

A34.33   *[Section 20 will come into force on a date to be appointed; see Schedule 4, paragraph 9 to this Act. Section 20 is printed as amended by the Finance Act 1995, s.19 and Sched. 4, paras 1, 16, 21 and 29.]*

PART II

REGISTRATION OF VEHICLES

Registration

A34.34   **21. Registration of vehicles**   *[Omitted.]*

                 22. Registration regulations   *[Omitted.]*

Registration marks

23. Registration marks

A34.35   (1) Where the Secretary of State registers a vehicle under section 21(1) he shall assign to the vehicle a mark (a *"registration mark"*) indicating the registered number of the vehicle.

(2) The Secretary of State may, in such circumstances as he may determine—

(a) assign a registration mark to a vehicle to which another registration mark has previously been assigned,

(b) assign to a vehicle (whether on its first registration or later) a registration mark previously assigned to another vehicle,

(c) (whether or not in connection with an assignment within paragraph (a) or (b)) withdraw any registration mark for the time being assigned to a vehicle, and

(d)   re-assign to a vehicle a registration mark previously assigned to it but subsequently withdrawn.

(3)–(5)   *[Regulation-making power.]*

[For the construction of the term "for the time being" in section 23(2), see Schedule 4, paragraph 11, to this Act.   **A34.36**

The Road Vehicles (Display of Registration Marks) Regulations 2001 (S.I. 2001 No. 561) below have been made (in part) under section 23.)]

24. Assignment of registration marks by motor dealers

(1)   The Secretary of State may by regulations make such provision as he considers appropriate with respect to the allocation of registration marks for vehicles to motor dealers who—   **A34.37**

(a)   apply for such allocations, and

(b)   appear to the Secretary of State suitable to receive them,

and with respect to the assigning of the marks to vehicles by motor dealers.

(2), (3)   *[Regulation-making power.]*

(4)–(6)   *[Review of refusal to allocate registration mark.]*

25. Charge on request for registration mark   *[Omitted.]*   **A34.38**

26. Retention of registration mark pending transfer

(1)   The Secretary of State may by regulations provide for a person in whose name a vehicle is registered under this Act to be granted a right, exercisable on a single occasion falling within a period prescribed by the regulations, to have the registration mark for the time being assigned to the vehicle assigned to some other vehicle which is registered under this Act—   **A34.39**

(a)   in that person's name, or

(b)   in the name of some other person nominated by him in accordance with the regulations.

(2)   Regulations under this section may, in particular, make provision—

(a)   for the manner in which an application for the grant of such a right (a "*right of retention*") is to be made to the Secretary of State,

(b)–(m)   *[Omitted.]*

(3)   *[Exemptions from fees or charges under section 26(2)(f) or (m).]*

(4)   *[Exemptions from fees under section 26(2)(f) or (l).]*

(5)   *[Regulations providing for no charge in connection with assignments.]*

(6)   *[Assignments of marks by Secretary of State.]*

27. Sale of rights to particular registration marks

(1)   This section applies to registration marks which either—   **A34.40**

(a)   have never been assigned to a vehicle, or

(b)   have been assigned to a vehicle but (as a result of having been subsequently withdrawn) are not for the time being so assigned,

and which are such as the Secretary of State may from time to time determine.

(2) The Secretary of State may by regulations make a scheme providing for registration marks to which this section applies to be assigned to vehicles registered under this Act in the names of, or of the nominees of, persons who have acquired rights under the scheme to have the marks so assigned.

(3) Regulations under this section may, in particular, make provision—

(a) for a person to acquire a right under the scheme to have a particular registration mark to which this section applies assigned to a vehicle registered under this Act in his name, or in the name of some other person nominated by him in accordance with the scheme, on payment of such sum as is payable in accordance with the scheme—

    (i) in respect of the acquisition of the right, and

    (ii) where no charge is to be made by virtue of paragraph in connection with an assignment pursuant to the right, in respect of such an assignment,

(b) with respect to—

    (i) the manner in which agreements for the sale of such a right (a "*relevant right*") may be effected,

    (ii) the terms which may be contained in, or incorporated into, such agreements, and

    (iii) rights and liabilities arising in connection with such agreements otherwise than under any such terms,

(c)–(n) *[Omitted.]*

(4), (5) *[Regulation-making powers.]*

(6) *[Exemption from fees in certain cases.]*

(7) *[Assignment of mark to be without prejudice to powers under section 23(2).]*

A34.41   *[The Sale of Registration Marks Regulations 1995 (S.I. 1995 No. 2880; not reproduced in this work) have been made in part under section 27.]*

Marking

28. Marking of engines and bodies

A34.42   (1) The Secretary of State may by regulations make such provision as he thinks appropriate with respect to the marking of the engines and bodies of vehicles.

(2) *[Regulation-making power.]*

PART III

OFFENCES

Offence of using or keeping unlicensed vehicle

29. Penalty for using or keeping unlicensed vehicle

A34.43   (1) If a person uses, or keeps, on a public road a vehicle (not being an exempt vehicle) which is unlicensed he is guilty of an offence.

(2) For the purposes of subsection (1) a vehicle is unlicensed if no vehicle licence or trade licence is in force for or in respect of the vehicle.

(3) [Subject to subsection (3A)] a person guilty of an offence under subsection (1) is liable on summary conviction to an excise penalty of—

(a) level 3 on the standard scale, or

(b) five times the amount of the vehicle excise duty chargeable in respect of the vehicle,

whichever is the greater.

[(3A) In the case of a person who—

(a) has provided the Secretary of State with a declaration or statement (in pursuance of regulations under section 22) that the vehicle will not during a period specified in the declaration or statement be used or kept on a public road, and

(b) commits an offence under subsection (1) within a period prescribed by regulations,

subsection (3) applies as if the reference in paragraph (a) to level 3 were a reference to level 4.]

(4) Where a vehicle for which a vehicle licence is in force is transferred by the holder of the licence to another person, the licence is to be treated for the purposes of subsection (2) as no longer in force unless it is delivered to the other person with the vehicle.

(5) Where—

(a) an application is made for a vehicle licence for any period, and

(b) a temporary licence is issued pursuant to the application,

subsection (4) does not apply to the licence applied for if, on a transfer of the vehicle during the currency of the temporary licence, the temporary licence is delivered with the vehicle to the transferee.

(6) The amount of the vehicle excise duty chargeable in respect of a vehicle is to be taken for the purposes of subsection (3)(b) to be an amount equal to the annual rate of duty applicable to the vehicle at the date on which the offence was committed.

(7) Where in the case of a vehicle kept (but not used) on a public road that annual rate differs from the annual rate by reference to which the vehicle was at that date chargeable under section 2(2) to (4), the amount of the vehicle excise duty chargeable in respect of the vehicle is to be taken for those purposes to be an amount equal to the latter rate.

(8) In the case of a conviction for a continuing offence, the offence is to be taken for the purposes of subsections (6) and (7) to have been committed on the date or latest date to which the conviction relates.

[Section 29 is printed as amended by the Finance Act 1996, s.23 and Sched. 2, paras 1 and 9(1), (2).   **A34.44**
    Proceedings under section 29(1) are specified by the Prosecution of Offences Act 1985 (Specified Proceedings) Order 1999 (S.I. 1999 No. 904) below as being proceedings the conduct of which the Director of Public Prosecutions is not required to take over from the police under the Prosecution of Offences Act 1985, s.3(3)(a).]

30. Additional liability for keeper of unlicensed vehicle

(1) Where the person convicted of an offence under section 29 is the person by whom   **A34.45**
the vehicle in respect of which the offence was committed was kept at the time at which it was committed, the court shall (in addition to any penalty which it may impose under that section) order him to pay the amount specified in subsection (2).

(2) The amount referred to in subsection (1) is an amount equal to one-twelfth of the annual rate of vehicle excise duty appropriate to the vehicle for each month, or part of a month, in the relevant period (within the meaning of section 31).

(3) In relation to any month or part of a month in the relevant period, the reference in subsection (2) to the annual rate of vehicle excise duty appropriate to the vehicle is a reference to the annual rate applicable to it at the beginning of that month or part.

(4) A vehicle is to be taken for the purposes of this section to have belonged throughout the relevant period to the description of vehicle to which it belonged for the purposes of vehicle excise duty at—

(a) the date on which the offence was committed, or

(b) if the prosecution so elect, the date when a vehicle licence for it was last issued,

except so far as it is proved to have fallen within some other description for the whole of any month or part of a month in that period.

(5) In the case of a conviction for a continuing offence, the offence is to be taken for the purposes of this section to have been committed on the date or latest date to which the conviction relates.

31. Relevant period for purposes of section 30

A34.46   (1) For the purposes of section 30 the relevant period is the period—

(a) ending with the date on which the offence was committed, and

(b) beginning as provided by subsections (2) to (4).

(2) Subject to subsection (4), if the person convicted has before the date of the offence notified the Secretary of State of his acquisition of the vehicle in accordance with regulations made by the Secretary of State, the relevant period begins with—

(a) the date on which the notification was received by the Secretary of State, or

(b) the expiry of the vehicle licence last in force for the vehicle,

whichever is the later.

(3) Subject to subsection (4), in any other case the relevant period begins with—

(a) the expiry of the vehicle licence last in force for the vehicle before the date on which the offence was committed, or

(b) if there has not at any time before that date been a vehicle licence in force for the vehicle, the date on which the vehicle was first kept by the person convicted.

(4) Where—

(a) the person convicted has been ordered to pay an amount under section 30 on the occasion of a previous conviction for an offence in respect of the same vehicle, and

(b) that offence was committed after the date specified in subsection (2) or (3) as the date with which the relevant period begins,

the relevant period instead begins with the month immediately following that in which the earlier offence was committed.

(5) Where the person convicted proves—

(a) that throughout any month or part of a month in the relevant period the vehicle was not kept by him, or

(b) that he has paid the duty due . . . in respect of the vehicle for any such month or part of a month,

any amount which the person is ordered to pay under section 30 is to be calculated as if that month or part of a month were not in the relevant period.

(6) Where a person has previously been ordered under section 36 to pay an amount for

a month or part of a month in the case of a vehicle, any amount which he is ordered to pay under section 30 in the case of the vehicle is to be calculated as if no part of that month were in the relevant period.

(7) In this section references to the expiry of a vehicle licence include a reference to—

(a) its surrender, and

(b) its being treated as no longer in force for the purposes of subsection (2) of section 29 by subsection (4) of that section.

(8) In the case of a conviction for a continuing offence, the offence is to be taken for the purposes of this section to have been committed on the date or latest date to which the conviction relates.

[Section 31 is printed as amended by the Finance Act 1995, s.19 and Sched. 4, paras 1 and 35(1) and (2) (see also ibid., s.162 and Sched. 29, Pt V(3)).]   **A34.47**

32. Sections 29 to 31: supplementary

(1) Where in the case of an offence under section 29 there is made against a person—   **A34.48**

(a) an order under [section 12 of the Powers of Criminal Courts (Sentencing) Act 2000] discharging him absolutely or conditionally,

(b) *[applies in Scotland]*, or

(c) *[applies in Northern Ireland]*,

he is to be treated for the purposes of sections 29 to 31 as having been convicted.

(2) Section 30 has effect subject to the provisions (applying with the necessary modifications) of any enactment relating to the imposition of fines by magistrates' courts and courts of summary jurisdiction, other than any conferring a discretion as to their amount.

(3) Where a sum is payable by virtue of an order under section 30—

(a) in England and Wales, the sum is to be treated as a fine, and the order as a conviction, for the purposes of Part III of the Magistrates' Courts Act 1980 (including any enactment having effect as if contained in that Part) and of any other enactment relating to the recovery or application of sums ordered to be paid by magistrates' courts,

(b) *[applies in Scotland]*, and

(c) *[applies in Northern Ireland]*.

[Section 32 is printed as amended by the Powers of Criminal Courts (Sentencing) Act 2000, s.165(1) and Sched. 9, para.158.]   **A34.49**

[32A. Immobilisation, removal and disposal of vehicles

Schedule 2A (which relates to the immobilisation of vehicles as regards which it appears that an offence under section 29(1) is being committed and to their removal and disposal) shall have effect.]   **A34.50**

[Section 32A was inserted by the Finance Act 1995, s.19 and Sched. 4, paras 1 and 36(1).]   **A34.51**

Other offences relating to licences

33. Not exhibiting licence

(1) A person is guilty of an offence if—   **A34.52**

(a) he uses, or keeps, on a public road a vehicle in respect of which vehicle excise duty is chargeable, and

(b) there is not fixed to and exhibited on the vehicle in the manner prescribed by regulations made by the Secretary of State a licence for, or in respect of, the vehicle which is for the time being in force.

[(1A) A person is guilty of an offence if—

(a) he uses, or keeps, on a public road an exempt vehicle,

(b) that vehicle is one in respect of which regulations under this Act require a nil licence to be in force, and

(c) there is not fixed to and exhibited on the vehicle in the manner prescribed by regulations made by the Secretary of State a nil licence for that vehicle which is for the time being in force.]

(2) A person guilty of an offence under subsection (1) [, or (1A)] is liable on summary conviction to a fine not exceeding level 1 on the standard scale.

[(3) Subsections (1) and (1A)—

(a) have effect subject to the provisions of regulations made by the Secretary of State, and

(b) are without prejudice to sections 29 and 43A.]

[(4) The Secretary of State may make regulations prohibiting a person from exhibiting on a vehicle [which is kept or used on a public road] anything—

(a) which is intended to be, or

(b) which could reasonably be,

mistaken for a licence which is for, or in respect of, the vehicle and which is for the time being in force.]

[(5) The reference to a licence in subsection (4) includes a reference to a nil licence.]

A34.53　　*[Section 33 is printed as amended by the Finance Act 1996, s.23 and Sched. 2, paras 1 and 10; the Finance Act 1997, s.18 and Sched. 3, paras 1, 4.*

For the application of the fixed penalty procedure to offences under section 33, see the Road Traffic Offenders Act 1988, Pt III and Sched. 3 above.]

34. Trade licences: penalties

A34.54　　(1) A person holding a trade licence or trade licences is guilty of an offence if he—

(a) uses at any one time on a public road a greater number of vehicles (not being vehicles for which vehicle licences are for the time being in force) than he is authorised to use by virtue of the trade licence or licences,

(b) uses a vehicle (not being a vehicle for which a vehicle licence is for the time being in force) on a public road for any purpose other than a purpose which has been prescribed under section 12(2)(b), or

(c) uses the trade licence, or any of the trade licences, for the purposes of keeping on a public road in any circumstances other than circumstances which have been prescribed under section 12(1)(c) a vehicle which is not being used on that road.

(2) A person guilty of an offence under subsection (1) is liable on summary conviction to an excise penalty of—

(a) level 3 on the standard scale, or

(b) five times the amount of the vehicle excise duty chargeable in respect of (in the case of an offence under subsection (1)(a)) the vehicles which he is not authorised to use or (in the case of an offence under subsection (1)(b) or (c)) the vehicle concerned,

whichever is the greater.

(3) The amount of the vehicle excise duty chargeable in respect of a vehicle is to be taken for the purposes of subsection (2) to be an amount equal to the annual rate of duty applicable to the vehicle at the date on which the offence was committed.

(4) Where in the case of a vehicle kept (but not used) on a public road that annual rate differs from the annual rate by reference to which the vehicle was at that date chargeable under section 2(2) to (4), the amount of the vehicle excise duty chargeable in respect of the vehicle is to be taken for those purposes to be an amount equal to the latter rate.

(5) In the case of a conviction for a continuing offence, the offence is to be taken for the purposes of subsections (3) and (4) to have been committed on the date or latest date to which the conviction relates.

35. Failure to return licence

(1) A person who knowingly fails to comply with section 10(3) is guilty of an offence.   A34.55

(2) A person guilty of an offence under subsection (1) is liable on summary conviction to a fine not exceeding level 3 on the standard scale.

[35A. Dishonoured cheques

(1) In a case where—   A34.56

    (a) a notice sent as mentioned in section 19A(2)(b) [or 19B(2)(c)] or a further notice sent as mentioned in section 19A(3)(d) [or 19B(3)(d)] [contains relevant information], and

    (b) the person fails to comply with the requirement [contained in the notice]

he shall be liable on summary conviction to a penalty of an amount found under subsection (2).

(2) The amount is whichever is the greater of—

    (a) level 3 on the standard scale;

    (b) an amount equal to five times the annual rate of duty that was payable on the grant of the licence or would have been so payable if it had been taken out for a period of twelve months.]

[(3) For the purposes of subsection (1)(a), *a relevant requirement* is—

    (a) a requirement to deliver up the licence within such reasonable period as is specified in the notice; or

    (b) a requirement to deliver up the licence within such reasonable period as is so specified and, on doing so, to pay the amount specified in subsection (4).]

[(4) The amount referred to in subsection (3)(b) is an amount equal to one-twelfth of the appropriate annual rate of vehicle excise duty for each month, or part of a month, in the relevant period.]

[(5) The reference in subsection (4) to the *appropriate annual rate of vehicle excise duty* is a reference to the annual rate which at the beginning of the relevant period—

    (a) in the case of a vehicle licence, was applicable to a vehicle of the description specified in the application, or

    (b) in the case of a trade licence, was applicable to a vehicle falling within [paragraph 1(2) of Schedule 1] (or to a vehicle falling within sub-paragraph (1)(c) of paragraph 2 of that Schedule if the licence was to be used only for vehicles to which that paragraph applies).]

[(6) For the purposes of subsection (4) *the relevant period* is the period—

(a)   beginning with the first day of the period for which the licence was applied for or, if later, the day on which the licence first was to have effect, and

(b)   ending with whichever is the earliest of the times specified in subsection (7).]

[(7) In a case where the requirement is a requirement to deliver up a vehicle licence, those times are—

(a)   the end of the month during which the licence was required to be delivered up,

(b)   the end of the month during which the licence was actually delivered up,

(c)   the date on which the licence was due to expire, and

(d)   the end of the month preceding that in which there first had effect a new vehicle licence for the vehicle in question;

and, in a case where the requirement is a requirement to deliver up a trade licence, those times are the times specified in paragraphs (a) to (c).]

A34.57   *[Section 35A was inserted by the Finance Act 1995, s.19 and Sched. 4, paras 1 and 32(2), and is printed as subsequently amended by the Finance Act 1997, s.19(2); the Finance Act 1998, s.19(1), (2) and (5); the Finance Act 1999, s.8(4) and (5).]*

36. Dishonoured cheques: additional liability

A34.58   (1) Where a person has been convicted of an offence under section [35A] in relation to a vehicle licence or a trade licence, the court shall (in addition to any penalty which it may impose under that section) order him to pay the amount specified in subsection (2).

(2) The amount referred to in subsection (1) is an amount equal to one-twelfth of the appropriate annual rate of vehicle excise duty for each month, or part of a month, in the relevant period.

(3) The reference in subsection (2) to the appropriate annual rate of vehicle excise duty is a reference to the annual rate which at the beginning of the relevant period—

(a)   in the case of a vehicle licence, was applicable to a vehicle of the description specified in the application, or

(b)   in the case of a trade licence, was applicable to a vehicle falling within [paragraph 1(2) of Schedule 1] (or to a vehicle falling within sub-paragraph (1)(c) of paragraph 2 of that Schedule if the licence was to be used only for vehicles to which that paragraph applies).

[(4) For the purposes of this section *the relevant period* is the period—

(a)   beginning with the first day of the period for which the licence was applied for or, if later, the day on which the licence was first to have effect, and

(b)   ending with whichever is the earliest of the times specified in subsection (4A).]

[(4A) In the case of a vehicle those times are—

(a)   the end of the month in which the order is made,

(b)   the date on which the licence was due to expire,

(c)   the end of the month during which the licence was delivered up, and

(d)   the end of the month preceding that in which there first had effect a new licence for the vehicle in question;

and, in the case of a trade licence, those times are the times specified in paragraphs (a) to (c).]

(5) Where a person has previously been ordered under section 30 to pay an amount for a month or part of a month in the case of a vehicle, any amount which he is ordered to pay under this section in the case of a vehicle licence for the vehicle is to be calculated as if no part of that month were in the relevant period.

[(6) Where—

(a) a person has been convicted of an offence under section 35 A in relation to a vehicle licence or a trade licence, and

(b) a requirement to pay an amount with respect to that licence has been imposed on that person by virtue of section 35A(3)(b),

the order to pay an amount under this section shall have effect instead of that requirement and the amount to be paid under the order shall be reduced by any amount actually paid in pursuance of the requirement.]

[Section 36 is printed as amended by the Finance Act 1995, s.19 and Sched. 4, paras 1, 6(2)(c), 16   **A34.59**
and 32(3); the Finance Act 1996, s.18(4)(c) and (5); the Finance Act 1998, s.19(3)–(5); the Finance
Act 1999, s.8(4) and (5).]

Offence of not paying duty chargeable at higher rate

37. **Penalty for not paying duty chargeable at higher rate**

(1) Where—   **A34.60**

(a) a vehicle licence has been taken out for a vehicle at any rate of vehicle excise duty,

(b) at any time while the licence is in force the vehicle is so used that duty at a higher rate becomes chargeable in respect of the licence for the vehicle under section 15, and

(c) duty at that higher rate was not paid before the vehicle was so used,
the person so using the vehicle is guilty of an offence.

(2) A person guilty of an offence under subsection (1) is liable on summary conviction . . . to an excise penalty of—

(a) level 3 on the standard scale . . ., or

(b) five times the difference between the duty actually paid on the licence and the amount of the duty at the higher rate,
whichever is the greater.

[Section 37 is printed as amended by the Finance Act 1995, s.19 and Sched. 4, paras 1 and 37(1) (see   **A34.61**
also ibid., s.162 and Sched. 29, Pt V(3)).]

38. **Additional liability for keeper of vehicle chargeable at higher rate**

(1) Where the person convicted of an offence under section 37 is the person by whom   **A34.62**
the vehicle in respect of which the offence was committed was kept at the time at which it was committed, the court shall (in addition to any penalty which it may impose under that section) order him to pay the amount specified in subsection (2).

(2) The amount referred to in subsection (1) is an amount equal to one-twelfth of the difference between—

(a) the rate of duty at which the licence in relation to which the offence was committed was taken out, and

(b) the relevant higher rate of duty (within the meaning of section 39) in relation to the vehicle,

for each month, or part of a month, in the relevant period (within the meaning of section 40).

(3) A vehicle is to be taken for the purposes of subsection (2) to have belonged throughout the relevant period to the description of vehicle to which it belonged for the purposes of vehicle excise duty at the date on which the offence was committed, except so far as it is proved to have fallen within some other description for the whole of any month or part of a month in that period.

(4) Where a person is convicted of more than one offence under section 37 in respect of the same vehicle (whether or not in the same proceedings), the court shall (in calculating the amount payable under this section in respect of any of the offences) reduce the amount in relation to any period by any amount ordered to be paid under this section in relation to the period in respect of any other such offence.

39. Relevant higher rate of duty for purposes of section 38

A34.63   (1) For the purposes of section 38 the relevant higher rate of duty in relation to a vehicle is the rate provided by this section.

(2) Where—

(a) at the time of the offence the vehicle had a [revenue weight] which exceeded that which it had when the licence in relation to which the offence was committed was taken out, and

(b) the licence was taken out at the rate applicable to the previous weight,

the relevant higher rate of duty is the rate which would have been applicable had the licence been taken out by reference to the higher weight.

(3) Where—

(a) the vehicle is a tractive unit,

(b) the licence in relation to which the offence was committed was taken out at a rate applicable to the use of the vehicle—

(i) only with semi-trailers having not fewer than two axles, or
(ii) only with semi-trailers having not fewer than three axles, and

(c) the offence consisted in using the vehicle with a semi-trailer with a smaller number of axles,

the relevant higher rate of duty is the rate which would have been applicable had the licence been taken out by reference to the use of the vehicle which constituted the offence.

(4) Where—

(a) the licence in relation to which the offence was committed was taken out at a rate applicable, by virtue of paragraph 13 of Schedule 1, to a weight lower than the [revenue weight] of the vehicle, and

(b) the offence consisted in using the vehicle in contravention of a condition imposed under or by virtue of sub-paragraph (2) of that paragraph,

the relevant higher rate of duty is the rate which would have been applicable had the licence been taken out by reference to the [revenue weight] of the vehicle.

(5) Where—

(a) the licence in relation to which the offence was committed was taken out at a rate lower than that applicable to it by reference to its [revenue weight], and

(b) none of subsections (2) to (4) apply,

the relevant higher rate of duty is the rate which would have been applicable had the licence been taken out by reference to the [revenue weight] of the vehicle.

(6) Where—

    (a) the licence in relation to which the offence was committed was taken out at a rate lower than that at which duty was chargeable in respect of the condition, manner or purpose of use of the vehicle which constituted the offence, and

    (b) none of subsections (2) to (5) apply,

the relevant higher rate of duty is the rate which would have been applicable had the licence been taken out by reference to the condition, manner or purpose of use of the vehicle which constituted the offence.

[Section 39 is printed as amended by the Finance Act 1995, s.19 and Sched. 4, paras 1, 16, 22 and 29.]   **A34.64**

40. Relevant period for purposes of section 38

(1) For the purposes of section 38 the relevant period is the period—   **A34.65**

    (a) ending with the date on which the offence was committed, and

    (b) beginning as provided by subsection (2) or (3).

(2) If the offence consists in the vehicle having a [revenue weight] which exceeds that which it had when the licence in relation to which the offence was committed was taken out, the relevant period begins with the date on which the vehicle [became a vehicle with a higher revenue weight].

(3) In any other case, the relevant period begins with the date on which the licence in relation to which the offence was committed first took effect.

(4) Where the person convicted proves—

    (a) that throughout any month or part of a month in the relevant period the vehicle was not kept by him, or

    (b) that he has paid the duty due (or an amount equal to the duty due) at the relevant higher rate in respect of the vehicle for any such month or part of a month,

any amount which the person is ordered to pay under section 38 is to be calculated as if that month or part of a month were not in the relevant period.

[Section 40 is printed as amended by the Finance Act 1995, s.19 and Sched. 4, paras 1, 16, 23 and 29.]   **A34.66**

41. Sections 37 to 40: supplementary

(1) Where in the case of an offence under section 37 there is made against a person—   **A34.67**

    (a) an order under [section 12 of the Powers of Criminal (Sentencing) Act 2000] discharging him absolutely or conditionally,

    (b) *[applies in Scotland]*, or

    (c) *[applies in Northern Ireland]*,

he is to be treated for the purposes of sections 38 to 40 as having been convicted.

(2) Section 38 has effect subject to the provisions (applying with the necessary modifications) of any enactment relating to the imposition of fines by magistrates' courts and courts of summary jurisdiction, other than any conferring a discretion as to their amount.

(3) Where a sum is payable by virtue of an order under section 38—

    (a) in England and Wales, the sum is to be treated as a fine, and the order as a conviction, for the purposes of Part III of the Magistrates' Courts Act 1980 (including any enactment having effect as if contained in that Part) and of any other enactment relating to the recovery or application of sums ordered to be paid by magistrates' courts,

(b) *[applies in Scotland]*, and

(c) *[applies in Northern Ireland]*.

A34.68   *[Section 41 is printed as amended by the Powers of Criminal Courts (Sentencing) Act 2000, s.165(1) and Sched. 9, para.159.]*

Offences relating to registration marks

42. Not fixing registration mark

A34.69   (1) If a registration mark is not fixed on a vehicle as required by virtue of section 23, the relevant person is guilty of an offence.

(2) A person guilty of an offence under subsection (1) is liable on summary conviction to a fine not exceeding level 3 on the standard scale.

(3) In subsection (1) "*the relevant person*" means the person driving the vehicle or, where it is not being driven, the person keeping it.

(4) It is a defence for a person charged with an offence under subsection (1) to prove that—

(a) he had no reasonable opportunity to register the vehicle under this Act, and

(b) the vehicle was being driven for the purpose of being so registered.

(5) It is a defence for a person charged with an offence under subsection (1) in relation to a vehicle—

(a) to which section 47 of the Road Traffic Act 1988 applies by virtue of subsection (2)(b) of that section, or

(b) *[applies in Northern Ireland]*,

(vehicles manufactured before the prescribed period and used before registration) to prove that he had no reasonable opportunity to register the vehicle under this Act and that the vehicle was being driven in accordance with subsection (6).

(6) A vehicle is being driven in accordance with this subsection if—

(a) it is being driven for the purposes of, or in connection with, its examination under section 45 of the Road Traffic Act 1988 in circumstances in which its use is exempted from subsection (1) of section 47 of that Act by regulations under sub-section (6) of that section, or

(b) *[applies in Northern Ireland]*.

A34.70   *[For the application of the fixed penalty procedure to offences under section 42, see the Road Traffic Offenders Act 1988, Pt III and Sched. 3 above.]*

43. Obscured registration mark

A34.71   (1) If a registration mark fixed on a vehicle as required by virtue of section 23 is in any way—

(a) obscured, or

(b) rendered, or allowed to become, not easily distinguishable,

the relevant person is guilty of an offence.

(2) A person guilty of an offence under subsection (1) is liable on summary conviction to a fine not exceeding level 3 on the standard scale.

(3) In subsection (1) "*the relevant person*" means the person driving the vehicle or, where it is not being driven, the person keeping it.

(4) It is a defence for a person charged with an offence under this section to prove that he took all steps which it was reasonably practicable to take to prevent the mark being obscured or rendered not easily distinguishable.

Other offences

[43A. Failure to have nil licence for exempt vehicle

(1) A person is guilty of an offence if—   **A34.72**

(a) he uses, or keeps, on a public road an exempt vehicle,

(b) that vehicle is one in respect of which regulations under this Act require a nil licence to be in force, and

(c) a nil licence is not for the time being in force in respect of the vehicle.

(2) A person guilty of an offence under subsection (1) is liable on summary conviction to a fine not exceeding level 2 on the standard scale.

(3) Subsection (1) has effect subject to the provisions of regulations made by the Secretary of State.

(4) The Secretary of State may, if he thinks fit, compound any proceedings for an offence under this section.]

[Section 43A was inserted by the Finance Act 1997, s.18 and Sched. 3, paras 1 and 5.]   **A34.73**

44. Forgery and fraud

(1) A person is guilty of an offence if he forges, fraudulently alters, fraudulently uses,   **A34.74**
fraudulently lends or fraudulently allows to be used by another person anything to which subsection (2) applies.

(2) This subsection applies to—

(a) a vehicle licence,

(b) a trade licence,

[(c) a nil licence,]

(d) a registration mark,

(e) a registration document, and

(f) a trade plate (including a replacement trade plate).

(3) A person guilty of an offence under this section is liable—

(a) on summary conviction, to a fine not exceeding the statutory maximum, and

(b) on conviction on indictment, to imprisonment for a term not exceeding two years or to a fine or . . . to both.

[Section 44 is printed as amended by the Finance Act 1997, s.18 and Sched. 3, paras 1, 6:   **A34.75**
The words omitted from section 44(3)(b) relate exclusively to Scotland.
For the application of the fixed penalty procedure to offences under section 44, see the Road Traffic Offenders Act 1988, Pt III and Sched. 3 above.]

45. False or misleading declarations and information

(1) A person who in connection with—   **A34.76**

(a) an application for a vehicle licence or a trade licence,

(b) a claim for a rebate under section 20, or

(c) an application for an allocation of registration marks,

makes a declaration which to his knowledge is either false or in any material respect misleading is guilty of an offence.

(2) A person who makes a declaration which—

(a) is required by regulations under this Act to be made in respect of a vehicle which is an exempt vehicle under paragraph 19 of Schedule 2, and

(b) to his knowledge is either false or in any material respect misleading,

is guilty of an offence.

[(2A) A person who makes a declaration or statement which—

(a) is required to be made in respect of a vehicle by regulations under section 22,and

(b) to his knowledge is either false or in any material respect misleading,

is guilty of an offence.]

(3) A person who—

(a) is required by [virtue of] this Act to furnish particulars relating to, or to the keeper of, a vehicle, and

(b) furnishes particulars which to his knowledge are either false or in any material respect misleading,

is guilty of an offence.

[(3A) A person who, in supplying information or producing documents for the purposes of any regulations made under section 61A [or 61B]—

(a) makes a statement which to his knowledge is false or in any material respect misleading or recklessly makes a statement which is false or in any material respect misleading, or

(b) produces or otherwise makes use of a document which to his knowledge is false or in any material respect misleading,

is guilty of an offence.]

[(3B) A person who—

(a) with intent to deceive, forges, alters or uses a certificate issued by virtue of section 61A [or 61B];

(b) knowing or believing that it will be used for deception lends such a certificate to another or allows another to alter or use it; or

(c) without reasonable excuse makes or has in his possession any document so closely resembling such a certificate as to be calculated to deceive,

is guilty of an offence.]

(4) A person guilty of an offence under this section is liable—

(a) on summary conviction, to a fine not exceeding the statutory maximum, and

(b) on conviction on indictment, to imprisonment for a term not exceeding two years or to a fine or . . . to both.

A34.77   *[Section 45 is printed as amended by the Finance Act 1995, s.19 and Sched. 4, paras 1, 16, 24 and 29; the Finance Act 1996, s.23 and Sched. 2, paras 1 and 11; the Finance Act 1998, s.16 and Sched.1, paras 1, 15 and 17(2).*

The words omitted from section 45(4)(b) relate exclusively to Scotland.
As to the reference in section 45(1)(b) to section 20, see Schedule 4, paragraph 9 below.
    Section 45 has been expressly applied by the Finance Act 2000, s.20(10) (not reproduced in this work) to declarations made under section 20 of the 2000 Act in connection with applications for refunds of vehicle excise duty.]

46. Duty to give information

(1) Where it is alleged that a vehicle has been used on a road in contravention of section   **A34.78**
29, 34 [, 37 or 43A]—

    (a) the person keeping the vehicle shall give such information as he may be required to give in accordance with subsection (7) as to the identity of the driver of the vehicle or any person who used the vehicle, and

    (b) any other person shall give such information as it is in his power to give and which may lead to the identification of the driver of the vehicle or any person who used the vehicle if he is required to do so in accordance with subsection (7).

(2) Where it is alleged that a vehicle has been kept on a road in contravention of section 29 [or 43A]—

    (a) the person keeping the vehicle shall give such information as he may be required to give in accordance with subsection (7) as to the identity of the person who kept the vehicle on the road, and

    (b) any other person shall give such information as it is in his power to give and which may lead to the identification of the person who kept the vehicle on the road if he is required to do so in accordance with subsection (7).

(3) Where it is alleged that a vehicle has at any time been used on a road in contravention of section 29 [or 43A], the person who is alleged to have so used the vehicle shall give such information as it is in his power to give as to the identity of the person who was keeping the vehicle at that time if he is required to do so in accordance with subsection (7).

(4) A person who fails to comply with subsection (1), (2) or (3) is guilty of an offence.

(5) A person guilty of an offence under subsection (4) is liable on summary conviction to a fine not exceeding level 3 on the standard scale.

(6) If a person is charged with an offence under subsection (4) consisting of failing to comply with subsection (1)(a) or (2)(a), it is a defence for him to show to the satisfaction of the court that he did not know, and could not with reasonable diligence have ascertained, the identity of the person or persons concerned.

(7) A person is required to give information in accordance with this subsection if he is required to give the information by or on behalf of—

    (a) a chief officer of police or, in Northern Ireland, the Chief Constable of the Royal Ulster Constabulary, or

    (b) the Secretary of State.

[Section 46 is printed as amended by the Finance Act 1997, s.18 and Sched. 3, paras 1, 7(1).   **A34.79**
    With effect from a date to be announced under the Police (Northern Ireland) Act 2000, s.79(1), the Royal Ulster Constabulary will be known as the Police Service of Northern Ireland (incorporating the Royal Ulster Constabulary) (ibid., s.1(1)). Subsequently, the reference in section 46(7)(a) above to the Chief Constable of the Royal Ulster Constabulary will be construed as a reference to the Chief Constable of the Police Service of Northern Ireland (2000 Act, s.78(2)(a)).]

[46A. Duty to give information: offences under regulations

A34.80   (1) Subsection (2) applies where it appears to the Secretary of State—

(a) that a person is a person by, through or to whom a vehicle has been sold or disposed of and that he has failed to comply with regulations made by virtue of section 22(1)(d) requiring him to furnish particulars prescribed by the regulations;

(b) that a person is a person by or through whom a vehicle has been sold or disposed of and that he has failed to comply with regulations made by virtue of section 22(1)(*dd*) requiring him to furnish a document prescribed by the regulations; or

(c) that a person is a person who is surrendering a vehicle licence, or who is not renewing a vehicle licence for a vehicle kept by him or who is keeping an unlicensed vehicle and that he has failed to comply with regulations made by virtue of section 22(1D) requiring him to furnish particulars or make a declaration prescribed by the regulations.

(2) The Secretary of State may serve a notice on the person in question requiring him to give the Secretary of State such information as it is in his power to give—

(a) as to the identity of any person who is keeping a specified vehicle or who has kept it at a specified time or during a specified period;

(b) as to the identity of any person by, through or to whom a specified vehicle has been sold or disposed of at a specified time or during a specified period; or

(c) which may lead to the identification of a person falling within paragraph (a) or (b).

(3) A person who fails to comply with a notice under subsection (2) is guilty of an offence.

(4) A person guilty of an offence under subsection (3) is liable on summary conviction to a fine not exceeding level 3 on the standard scale.

(5) In this section "*specified*" means specified in a notice under subsection (2).]

A34.81   *[Section 46A was inserted by the Finance Act 1996, s.23 and Sched. 2, paras 1 and 12.]*

PART IV

LEGAL PROCEEDINGS

Institution and conduct of proceedings

47. Proceedings in England and Wales or Northern Ireland

A34.82   (1) No proceedings for an offence under section 29, 34 [, 35A] or 37 shall be instituted in England and Wales or Northern Ireland except by the Secretary of State or a constable; and no such proceedings shall be instituted there by a constable except with the approval of the Secretary of State.

(2) Proceedings for an offence under—

(a) section 29, 34 [, 35A] or 37, or

(b) regulations under this Act,

may be commenced in England or Wales or Northern Ireland by the Secretary of State or a constable at any time within six months from the date on which evidence sufficient in his opinion to justify the proceedings came to his knowledge.

(3) No proceedings for any offence may be commenced by virtue of subsection (2) more than three years after the commission of the offence.

(4) A certificate—

(a) stating that the Secretary of State's approval is given for the institution by a constable of any proceedings specified in the certificate, and

(b) signed by or on behalf of the Secretary of State,

is conclusive evidence of that approval.

(5) A certificate—

(a) stating the date on which evidence such as is mentioned in subsection (2) came to the knowledge of the Secretary of State or a constable, and

(b) signed by or on behalf of the Secretary of State or constable, is conclusive evidence of that date.

(6) A certificate—

(a) including a statement such as is mentioned in paragraph (a) of subsection (4) or (5), and

(b) purporting to be signed as mentioned in paragraph (b) of the subsection concerned,

is to be deemed to be so signed unless the contrary is proved.

(7) The following provisions of the Customs and Excise Management Act 1979 do not apply to proceedings in England and Wales or Northern Ireland for any offence under this Act—

(a) section 145 (which would require such proceedings to be instituted by order of the Secretary of State and certain such proceedings to be commenced in the name of an officer of his), and

(b) section 146A (which would impose time-limits for bringing such proceedings).

[Section 47 is printed as amended by the Finance Act 1996, s.23 and Sched. 2, paras 1 and 14(1)(a).]   **A34.83**

48. Proceedings in Scotland   *[Omitted.]*   **A34.84**

49. Authorised persons

A person authorised by the Secretary of State for the purposes of this section may on behalf   **A34.85**
of the Secretary of State conduct and appear in any proceedings by or against the Secretary of State under this Act—

(a) in England and Wales, in a magistrates' court or before a district judge of a county court,

(b) *[applies in Scotland]*, and

(c) *[applies in Northern Ireland]*.

50. Time-limit for recovery of underpayments and overpayments   **A34.86**

No proceedings shall be brought—

(a) by the Secretary of State for the recovery of any underpayment of duty on a vehicle licence, or

(b) by any person for the recovery of any overpayment of duty on a vehicle licence taken out by him,

after the end of the period of twelve months beginning with the end of the period in respect of which the licence was taken out.

Evidence

51. Admissions

A34.87   (1) This section applies where in any proceedings in England and Wales or Northern Ireland for an offence under section 29 [, 34 or 43A]—

     (a) it is appropriately proved that there has been served on the accused by post a requirement under section 46(1) or (2) to give information as to the identity of—

         (i) the driver of, or a person who used, a particular vehicle, or

         (ii) the person who kept a particular vehicle on a road,

     on the particular occasion on which the offence is alleged to have been committed, and

     (b) a statement in writing is produced to the court purporting to be signed by the accused that he was—

         (i) the driver of, or a person who used, that vehicle, or

         (ii) the person who kept that vehicle on a road,

     on that occasion.

(2) Where this section applies, the court may accept the statement as evidence that the accused was—

     (a) the driver of, or a person who used, that vehicle, or

     (b) the person who kept that vehicle on a road,

on that occasion.

(3) In subsection (1) "*appropriately proved*" means proved to the satisfaction of the court—

     (a) on oath, or

     (b) in the manner prescribed—

         (i) in England and Wales, by rules under section 144 of the Magistrates' Courts Act 1980, or

         (ii) *[applies in Northern Ireland]*.

A34.88   *[Section 51 is printed as amended by the Finance Act 1997, s.18 and Sched. 3, paras 1, 7(2).]*

[51A. Admissions: offences under regulations

A34.89   (1) Subsection (2) applies in relation to any proceedings in England, Wales or Northern Ireland against a person for an offence on the grounds that—

     (a) a vehicle has been sold or disposed of by, through or to him and he has failed to furnish particulars prescribed by regulations made by virtue of section 22(1)(d);

     (b) a vehicle has been sold or disposed of by or through him and he has failed to furnish a document prescribed by regulations made by virtue of section 22(1)(dd); or

     (c) he has surrendered, or not renewed, a vehicle licence, or is keeping an unlicensed vehicle, and has failed to furnish any particulars or make a declaration prescribed by regulations made by virtue of section 22(1D).

(2) If—

     (a) it is appropriately proved that there has been served on the accused by post a requirement under section 46A to give information as to the identity of the person keeping the vehicle at a particular time, and

     (b) a statement in writing is produced to the court purporting to be signed by the accused that he was keeping the vehicle at that time, the court may accept the statement as evidence that the accused was keeping the vehicle at that time.

(3) In subsection (2) "*appropriately proved*" has the same meaning as in section 51.]

[*Section 51A was inserted by the Finance Act 1996, s.23 and Sched. 2, paras 1 and 13.*]　　**A34.90**

52. Records

(1) A statement to which this section applies is admissible in any proceedings as evidence　　**A34.91**
. . . of any fact stated in it with respect to matters prescribed by regulations made by the Secretary of State to the same extent as oral evidence of that fact is admissible in the proceedings.

(2) This section applies to a statement contained in a document purporting to be—

(a) a part of the records maintained by the Secretary of State in connection with any functions exercisable by him under or by virtue of this Act,

(b) a copy of a document forming part of those records, or

(c) a note of any information contained in those records,

and to be authenticated by a person authorised to do so by the Secretary of State.

[(3) In this section as it has effect in England and Wales . . . —

"*document*" means anything in which information of any description is recorded;

"*copy*", in relation to a document, means anything onto which information recorded in the document has been copied, by whatever means and whether directly or indirectly; and

"*statement*" means any representation of fact, however made.]

[(4) [*Applies to Scotland.*]]

[(5) [*Repealed.*]]

[(6) [*Applies to Scotland.*]]

[*Section 52 is printed as amended by the Civil Evidence Act 1995, s.15(1) and Sched. 1, para.19.*　　**A34.92**
Words in section section 52(3) relating exclusively to Northern Ireland have been omitted.]

53. Burden of proof

Where in any proceedings for an offence under section 29, 34, 37 or 45 any question arises　　**A34.93**
as to—

(a) the number of vehicles used,

(b) the character, weight or cylinder capacity of a vehicle,

(c) the seating capacity of a vehicle, or

(d) the purpose for which a vehicle has been used,

the burden of proof in respect of the matter lies on the accused.

54. Single witness sufficient in certain Scottish proceedings　　　*[Omitted.]*　　**A34.94**

55. Guilty plea by absent accused

(1) This section applies where, under section [12(5)] of the Magistrates' Courts Act　　**A34.95**
1980 . . ., a person is convicted in his absence of [an offence under section 29 or 35A] and it is appropriately proved that a relevant notice was served on the accused with the summons.

(2) In subsection (1) *"appropriately proved"* means—

    (a) in England and Wales, proved to the satisfaction of the court—

        (i) on oath, or

        (ii) in the manner prescribed by rules under section 144 of the Magistrates' Courts Act 1980, and

    (b) *[applies in Northern Ireland]*.

(3) In this section *"relevant notice"*, in relation to an accused, means a notice stating that, in the event of his being convicted of the offence, it will be alleged that an order requiring him to pay an amount specified in the notice falls to be made by the court—

    (a) in a case within subsection (1)(a), under section 30, or

    (b) in a case within subsection (1)(b), under section 36.

(4) Where this section applies, the court shall proceed under section 30, or section 36, as if the amount specified in the relevant notice were the amount calculated in accordance with that section.

(5) The court shall not so proceed if it is stated in the notification purporting to be given by or on behalf of the accused under—

    (a) section [12(4)] of the Magistrates' Courts Act 1980, or

    (b) *[applies in Northern Ireland]*,

that the amount specified in the relevant notice is inappropriate.

A34.96   *[Section 55 is printed as amended by the Finance Act 1996, s.23 and Sched. 2, paras 1 and 14(2); the Magistrates' Courts (Procedure) Act 1998, s.4.]*

Penalties, etc.

A34.97   **56. Application of penalties and fines**   *[Omitted.]*

PART V

SUPPLEMENTARY

Regulations and orders

A34.98   **57. Regulations**   *[Omitted.]*

58. Fees prescribed by regulations   *[Omitted.]*

59. Regulations: offences

A34.99   (1) A person who contravenes or fails to comply with any regulations under this Act (other than any regulations under section 24, 26, 27 or 28) is guilty of an offence.

(2) A person guilty of an offence under subsection (1) is liable on summary conviction to a fine not exceeding—

    (a) in the case of regulations prescribed by regulations made by the Secretary of State as regulations to which this paragraph applies, level 3 on the standard scale, and

    (b) in any other case, level 2 on the standard scale.

(3) The prescribing of regulations as regulations to which subsection (2)(a) applies does

not affect the punishment for a contravention of, or failure to comply with, the regulations before they were so prescribed.

(4) Regulations under section 24 or 28 may provide that a person who contravenes or fails to comply with any specified provision of the regulations is guilty of an offence.

(5) A person guilty of such an offence is liable on summary conviction to a fine not exceeding—

    (a) in the case of regulations under section 24, level 1 on the standard scale, and

    (b) in the case of regulations under section 28, level 3 on the standard scale.

[(6) The Secretary of State may, if he sees fit, compound any proceedings for an offence—

    (a) under subsection (1), or

    (b) under regulations under section 24 or 28.]

[Section 59 is printed as amended by the Finance Act 1996, s.23 and Sched. 2, paras 1 and 15.   **A34.100**
The Road Vehicles (Prescribed Regulations for the Purposes of Increased Penalties) Regulations 1987 (S.I. 1987 No. 2085; not reproduced in this work) have effect as if made under section 59(2)(a). References to S.I. 1987 No. 2085 are included (as appropriate) in the notes to the Road Vehicles (Registration and Licensing) Regulations 1971 (S.I. 1971 No. 450) below.
As to the person responsible for compliance with the Road Vehicles (Display of Registration Marks) Regulations 2001 (S.I. 2001 No. 561), see ibid., reg.19(1) below.
The Road Vehicles (Statutory Off-Road Notification) Regulations 1997 (S.I. 1997 No. 3025) are prescribed for the purposes of section 59(2)(a); see regulation 8 of S.I. 1997 No. 3025 below; as are the Road Vehicles (Display of Registration Marks) Regulations 2001 (S.I. 2001 No. 561), reg.11(1)–(3) below.]

60. Exercise of power to make orders   *[Omitted.]*   **A34.101**

Interpretation

[60A. Meaning of "revenue weight"

(1) Any reference in this Act to the revenue weight of a vehicle is a reference—   **A34.102**

    (a) where it has a confirmed maximum weight, to that weight; and

    (b) in any other case, to the weight determined in accordance with the following provisions of this section.

(2) For the purposes of this Act a vehicle which does not have a confirmed maximum weight shall have a revenue weight which, subject to the following provisions of this section, is equal to its design weight.

(3) Subject to subsection (4), the design weight of a vehicle is, for the purposes of this section—

    (a) in the case of a tractive unit, the weight which is required, by the design and any subsequent adaptations of that vehicle, not to be exceeded by an articulated vehicle which—

        (i) consists of the vehicle and any semi-trailer capable of being drawn by it, and

        (ii) is in normal use and travelling on a road laden;
    and

    (b) in the case of any other vehicle, the weight which the vehicle itself is designed or adapted not to exceed when in normal use and travelling on a road laden.

(4) Where, at any time, a vehicle—

    (a) does not have a confirmed maximum weight,

(b) has previously had such a weight, and

(c) has not acquired a different design weight by reason of any adaptation made since the most recent occasion on which it had a confirmed maximum weight,

the vehicle's design weight at that time shall be equal to its confirmed maximum weight on that occasion.

(5) An adaptation reducing the design weight of a vehicle shall be disregarded for the purposes of this section unless it is a permanent adaptation.

(6) For the purposes of this Act where—

(a) a vehicle which does not have a confirmed maximum weight is used on a public road in the United Kingdom, and

(b) at the time when it is so used—

(i) the weight of the vehicle, or

(ii) in the case of a tractive unit used as part of an articulated vehicle consisting of the vehicle and a semi-trailer, the weight of the articulated vehicle,

exceeds what, apart from this subsection, would be the vehicle's design weight,

it shall be conclusively presumed, as against the persons using the vehicle, that the vehicle has been temporarily adapted so as to have a design weight while being so used equal to the actual weight of the vehicle or articulated vehicle at that time.

(7) For the purposes of this Act limitations on the space available on a vehicle for carrying a load shall be disregarded in determining the weight which the vehicle is designed or adapted not to exceed when in normal use and travelling on a road laden.

(8) A vehicle which does not have a confirmed maximum weight shall not at any time be taken to have a revenue weight which is greater than the maximum laden weight at which that vehicle or, as the case may be, an articulated vehicle consisting of that vehicle and a semi-trailer may lawfully be used in Great Britain.

(9) A vehicle has a confirmed maximum weight at any time if at that time—

(a) it has a plated gross weight or a plated train weight; and

(b) that weight is the maximum laden weight at which that vehicle or, as the case may be, an articulated vehicle consisting of that vehicle and a semi-trailer may lawfully be used in Great Britain;

and the confirmed maximum weight of a vehicle with such a weight shall be taken to be the weight referred to in paragraph (a).

(10), (11) *[Apply to Northern Ireland.]*]

A34.103   *[Section 60A was inserted by the Finance Act 1995, s.19 and Sched. 4, paras 1, 16, 26 and 29.*

As to the modification of section 60A in its application to vehicles to which reference is made in the Goods Vehicles (Licensing of Operators) Act 1995, s.5(3), see the Goods Vehicles (Licensing of Operators) Regulations 1995 (S.I. 1995 No. 2869), reg.36 below.]

61. Vehicle weights

A34.104   (1) In this Act a reference to the plated gross weight of a goods vehicle or trailer is a reference—

(a) in the case of a trailer which may lawfully be used in Great Britain without a Ministry plate (within the meaning of regulations under section 41 or 49 of the Road Traffic Act 1988), to the maximum laden weight at which the trailer may lawfully be used in Great Britain, and

(b) otherwise, to the weight which is the maximum gross weight which may not be exceeded in Great Britain for the vehicle or trailer as indicated on the appropriate plate.

(2) In this Act a reference to the plated train weight of a vehicle is a reference to the weight which is the maximum gross weight which may not be exceeded in Great Britain for an articulated vehicle consisting of the vehicle and any semi-trailer which may be drawn by it as indicated on the appropriate plate.

(3) In subsections (1) and (2) "*appropriate plate*", in relation to a vehicle or trailer, means—

(a) where a Ministry plate (within the meaning of regulations under section 41 or 49 of the Road Traffic Act 1988) has been issued, or has effect as if issued, for the vehicle or trailer following the issue or amendment of a plating certificate (within the meaning of Part II of that Act), that plate, [and]

(b) where paragraph (a) does not apply but such a certificate is in force for the vehicle or trailer, that certificate, . . .

(c) *[repealed]*.

[(3A) Where it appears to the Secretary of State that there is a description of document which—

(a) falls to be treated for some or all of the purposes of the Road Traffic Act 1988 as if it were a plating certificate, or

(b) is issued under the law of any state in the European Economic Area for purposes which are or include purposes corresponding to those for which such a certificate is issued,

he may by regulations provide for references in this section to a plating certificate to have effect as if they included references to a document of that description.]

(4), (5) *[Repealed.]*

(6) In this Act "*weight unladen*"—

(a) in England and Wales and Scotland, has the same meaning as it has for the purposes of the Road Traffic Act 1988 by virtue of section 190 of that Act, and

(b) *[applies in Northern Ireland]*.

(7) *[Repealed.]*

(8) In this section "*trailer*" has the same meaning as in Part VIII of Schedule 1.

[Section 61 is printed as amended by the Finance Act 1995, s.19 and Sched. 4, paras 1, 16, 27 and   **A34.105**
29 (see also ibid., s.162 and Sched. 29, Pt V(2)).]

61A. Certificates, etc., as to vehicle weight   *[Power to make regulations for the issue*   **A34.106**
of certificates stating the design weight.]

[61B. Certificates as to reduced pollution

(1) *[Power to make regulations for applications, etc., for reduced pollution certificates for eligible vehicles.]*   **A34.107**

(2) For the purposes of this Act, the reduced pollution requirements are satisfied with respect to a vehicle at any time if, as a result of adaptations of the prescribed description having been made to the vehicle after the prescribed date, the prescribed requirements are satisfied at that time with respect to the rate and content of the vehicle's emissions.

(3) *[Additional regulation-making powers.]*

(4) In this section "*eligible vehicle*" means—

(a) a bus, as defined in paragraph 3(2) of Schedule 1;

(b) a vehicle to which paragraph 6 of Schedule 1 applies;

(c) a haulage vehicle, as defined in paragraph 7(2) of Schedule 1, other than a showman's vehicle; or

(d) a goods vehicle, other then one falling within paragraph 9(2) or 11(2) of Schedule 1.

(5) In this section *"prescribed"* means prescribed by regulations made by the Secretary of State.]

A34.108   *[Section 61B has been inserted by the Finance Act 1998, s.16 and Sched. 1, paras 1, 2 and 17(2).]*

62. Other definitions

A34.109   (1) In this Act, unless the context otherwise requires—

"axle", in relation to a vehicle, includes—

(a) two or more stub axles which are fitted on opposite sides of the longitudinal axis of the vehicle so as to form a pair in the case of two stub axles or pairs in the case of more than two stub axles,

(b) a single stub axle which is not one of a pair, and

(c) a retractable axle,

(*"stub axle"* meaning an axle on which only one wheel is mounted),

. . .

"business" includes the performance by a local or public authority of its functions,

"disabled person" means a person suffering from a physical or mental defect or disability,

"exempt vehicle" means a vehicle in respect of which vehicle excise duty is not chargeable,

. . .

"goods vehicle" means a vehicle constructed or adapted for use and used for the conveyance of goods or burden of any description, whether in the course of trade or not,

"motor dealer" means a person carrying on the business of selling or supplying vehicles,

"motor trader" means—

(a) a manufacturer or repairer of, or dealer in, vehicles, or

(b) any other description of person who carries on a business of such description as may be prescribed by regulations made by the Secretary of State,

and a person is treated as a dealer in vehicles if he carries on a business consisting wholly or mainly of collecting and delivering vehicles, and not including any other activities except activities as a manufacturer or repairer of, or dealer in, vehicles,

[*"nil licence"* means a document which is in the form of a vehicle licence and is issued by the Secretary of State in pursuance of regulations under this Act in respect of a vehicle which is an exempt vehicle,]

"public road"—

(a) in England and Wales and Northern Ireland, means a road which is repairable at the public expense, and

(b) *[applies in Scotland]*,

"registration mark" is to be construed in accordance with section 23(1),

"relevant right" is to be construed in accordance with section 27(3)(a) and (b),

"right of retention" is to be construed in accordance with section 26(1) and (2)(a),

"*rigid goods vehicle*" means a goods vehicle which is not a tractive unit,

. . .

"*showman's goods vehicle*" means a showman's vehicle which—

(a) is a goods vehicle, and

(b) is permanently fitted with a living van or some other special type of body or super-structure forming part of the equipment of the show of the person in whose name the vehicle is registered under this Act,

"*showman's vehicle*" means a vehicle—

(a) registered under this Act in the name of a person following the business of a travelling showman, and

(b) used solely by him for the purposes of his business and for no other purpose,

"*temporary licence*" is to be construed in accordance with section 9(1),

"*tractive unit*" means a goods vehicle to which a semi-trailer may be so attached that—

(a) part of the semi-trailer is superimposed on part of the goods vehicle, and

(b) when the semi-trailer is uniformly loaded, not less than twenty per cent. of the weight of its load is borne by the goods vehicle,

"*trade licence*" is to be construed in accordance with section 11,

"*vehicle*" means a mechanically propelled vehicle,

"*vehicle excise duty*" is to be construed in accordance with section 1(1),

"*vehicle licence*" is to be construed in accordance with section 1(2), and

"*vehicle tester*" means a person, other than a motor trader, who regularly in the course of his business engages in the testing on roads of vehicles belonging to other persons.

[(1A) For the purposes of this Act, a vehicle is not an electrically propelled vehicle unless the electrical motive power is derived from—

(a) a source external to the vehicle, or

(b) an electrical storage battery which is not connected to any source of power when the vehicle is in motion.]

(2) For the purposes of this Act and any other enactment relating to the keeping of vehicles on public roads, a person keeps a vehicle on a public road if he causes it to be on such a road for any period, however short, when it is not in use there.

[Section 62 is printed as amended by the Finance Act 1995, s.162 and Sched. 29, Pt V(2); the Finance Act 1996, s.15(3) and (4); the Finance Act 1997, s.18 and Sched. 3, paras 1 and 7(3).   **A34.110**

The following definition (although repealed by the Finance Act 1995) is expressly incorporated into the Goods Vehicles (Plating and Testing) Regulations 1988 (S.I. 1988 No. 1478), Sched. 2, para.7 below:

"*road construction vehicle*" means a vehicle—

(a) which is constructed or adapted for use for the conveyance of built-in road construction machinery, and

(b) which is not constructed or adapted for the conveyance of any other load except articles and material used for the purposes of such machinery.]

Other supplementary provisions

63. Consequential amendments   *[Omitted.]*   **A34.111**

64. Transitionals, etc.

A34.112   Schedule 4 has effect for—

    (a) making transitional provisions in consequence of this Act and savings in connection with the repeals and revocations made by this Act,

    (b) re-enacting provisions repealed by this Act when not in force, and

    (c) making transitory modifications of this Act.

A34.113   ### 65. Repeals and revocations   *[Omitted.]*

66. Commencement   *[Omitted.]*

67. Extent

A34.114   This Act extends to Northern Ireland.

A34.115   ### 68. Short title   *[Omitted.]*

SCHEDULES

Section 2   ## SCHEDULE 1

ANNUAL RATES OF DUTY

PART I

GENERAL

A34.116   [**1.**—(1) The annual rate of vehicle excise duty applicable to a vehicle in respect of which no other annual rate is specified by this Schedule is [the general rate].

(2) [Except in the case of a vehicle with a cylinder capacity not exceeding [1,200 cubic centimetres], the] general rate is £—.

[(2A) In the case of a vehicle having an engine capacity not exceeding [1,200 cubic centimetres], the general rate is £—.]

(3)–(5) *[Repealed.]*]

A34.117   *[Paragraph 1 of Schedule 1 is printed as amended by the Finance Act 1999, s.8(2), (3) and (5); the Finance Act 2000, s.20(1).*
The amounts of duty (and amendments to those amounts) are not reproduced.]

PART IA

A34.118   LIGHT PASSENGER VEHICLES: GRADUATED RATES OF DUTY

[Omitted.]

PART IB

[Omitted.]

PART II

MOTORCYCLES

2.—(1) The annual rate of vehicle excise duty applicable to a motorcycle which does   **A34.120**
not exceed 450 kilograms in weight unladen is—

[(a) if the cylinder capacity of the engine does not exceed 150 cubic centimetres [or the
     motorcycle is an electrically propelled vehicle], 10 per cent of the general rate
     specified in paragraph 1(2);

  (b) if the vehicle is a motorbicycle and the cylinder capacity of the engine exceeds 150
     cubic centimetres but does not exceed 250 cubic centimetres, 25 per cent of the
     general rate specified in paragraph 1(2);

  (c) in any other case, 40 per cent of the general rate specified in paragraph 1(2).]

[(1A), (1B) *[Rounding up or down of uneven amounts of duty.]*]

(2) Where a motorbicycle which was constructed before 1933 has an engine the cylinder
capacity of which exceeds 150 cubic centimetres, it is to be treated for the purposes of sub-
paragraph (1) as having an engine the cylinder capacity of which does not exceed 150 cubic
centimetres.

(3) In this paragraph—

"*motorcycle*" means a motorbicycle or a motortricycle,

"*motorbicycle*" includes a two-wheeled motor scooter, a bicycle with an attachment for pro-
     pelling it by mechanical power and a motorbicycle to which a side-car is attached, and

"*motortricycle*" includes a three-wheeled motor scooter and a tricycle with an attachment
     for propelling it by mechanical power.

(4) For the purposes of this paragraph the cylinder capacity of an engine shall be calculated in accordance with regulations made by the Secretary of State.

[Paragraph 2 of Schedule 1 is printed as amended by the Finance Act 1995, s.19 and Sched. 4, paras   **A34.121**
1, 7 and 16; the Finance Act 1996, ss.15(1) and (4) and 18(2) and (5) (see also ibid., s.205 and Sched.
41, Pt II(3)).
The amounts of duty are not reproduced.]

[PART III

BUSES]

[**3.**—(1) The annual rate of vehicle excise duty applicable to a bus [with respect to   **A34.122**
which the reduced pollution requirements are not satisfied] is—

  (a) if its seating capacity is nine to sixteen, the same as the basic goods vehicle rate;

  (b) if its seating capacity is seventeen to thirty-five, 133 per cent of the basic goods
     vehicle rate;

  (c) if its seating capacity is thirty-six to sixty, 200 per cent of the basic goods vehicle rate;

  (d) if its seating capacity is over sixty, 300 per cent of the basic goods vehicle rate.

[(1A) The annual rate of vehicle excise duty applicable to a bus with respect to which the reduced pollution requirements are satisfied is the general rate specified in paragraph 1(2).]

(2) In this paragraph "*bus*" means a vehicle which—

(a) is a public service vehicle (within the meaning given by section 1 of the Public Passenger Vehicles Act 1981), and

(b) is not an excepted vehicle [or a special concessionary vehicle].

(3) For the purposes of this paragraph an "*excepted vehicle*" is—

(a) a vehicle which has a seating capacity under nine,

(b) a vehicle which is a community bus,

(c) a vehicle used under a permit granted under section 19 of the Transport Act 1985 (educational and other bodies) and used in circumstances where the requirements mentioned in subsection (2) of that section are met, or

(d) a vehicle used under a permit granted under section 10B of the Transport Act (Northern Ireland) 1967 (educational and other bodies) and used in circumstances where the requirements mentioned in subsection (2) of that section are met.

(4) In sub-paragraph (3)(b) "*community bus*" means a vehicle—

(a) used on public roads solely in accordance with a community bus permit (within the meaning given by section 22 of the Transport Act 1985), and

(b) not used for providing a service under an agreement providing for service subsidies (within the meaning given by section 63(10)(b) of that Act).

(5) For the purposes of this paragraph the seating capacity of a vehicle shall be determined in accordance with regulations made by the Secretary of State.

(6) In sub-paragraph (1) references to the "*basic goods vehicle rate*" are to the rate applicable, by virtue of sub-paragraph (1) of paragraph 9, to a rigid goods vehicle [which—

(a) is not a vehicle with respect to which the reduced pollution requirements are satisfied; and

(b) falls] within column (3) of the table in that sub-paragraph and has a revenue weight exceeding 3,500 kilograms and not exceeding 7,500 kilograms.

(7), (8) [*Rounding up or down of uneven amounts of duty.*]]

A34.123   *[Paragraph 3 of Schedule 1 is printed as substituted by the Finance Act 1995, s.19 and Sched. 4, paras 1, 8 and 16, and is printed as subsequently amended by the Finance Act 1996, s.16(2) and (8); the Finance Act 1998, s.16 and Sched. 1, paras 1, 3 and 17.]*

[PART IV

SPECIAL VEHICLES]

A34.124   *[The heading to Part IV is printed as substituted by the Finance Act 1995, s.19 and Sched. 4, paras 1, 9(1) and (2) and 16.]*

A34.125   **4.**—(1) The annual rate of vehicle excise duty applicable to a [special vehicle is the same as the basic goods vehicle rate].

(2) In sub-paragraph (1) ["*special vehicle*" means a vehicle which has a revenue weight exceeding 3,500 kilograms [which is not a special concessionary vehicle and which is]]

(a), (b)   *[repealed]*,

[(bb)   a vehicle falling within sub-paragraph (2A) or (2B),]

(c)   a digging machine,

(d)   a mobile crane,

(e)   a works truck, or

[(ee)   a road roller.]

(f)   *[repealed.]*

[(2A)   A vehicle falls within this sub-paragraph if—

(a)   it is designed or adapted for use for the conveyance of goods or burden of any description; but

(b)   it is not so used or is not so used for hire or reward or for or in connection with a trade or business.]

[(2B)   A vehicle falls within this sub-paragraph if—

(a)   it is designed or adapted for use with a semi-trailer attached; but

(b)   it is not so used or, if it is so used, the semi-trailer is not used for the conveyance of goods or burden of any description.]

(3)   *[Repealed.]*

(4)   In sub-paragraph (2)(c) "*digging machine*" means a vehicle which is designed, constructed and used for the purpose of trench digging, or any kind of excavating or shovelling work, and which—

(a)   is used on public roads only for that purpose or for the purpose of proceeding to and from the place where it is to be or has been used for that purpose, and

(b)   when so proceeding does not carry any load except such as is necessary for its propulsion or equipment.

(5)   In sub-paragraph (2)(d) "*mobile crane*" means a vehicle which is designed and constructed as a mobile crane and which—

(a)   is used on public roads only as a crane in connection with work carried on on a site in the immediate vicinity or for the purpose of proceeding to and from a place where it is to be or has been used as a crane, and

(b)   when so proceeding does not carry any load except such as is necessary for its propulsion or equipment.

(6)   In sub-paragraph (2)(e) "*works truck*" means a goods vehicle which is—

(a)   designed for use in private premises, and

(b)   used on public roads only—

(i)   for carrying goods between private premises and a vehicle on a road in the immediate vicinity,

(ii)   in passing from one part of private premises to another or between private premises and other private premises in the immediate vicinity, or

(iii)   in connection with road works at or in the immediate vicinity of the site of the works.

[(7)   In sub-paragraph (1) reference to the "*basic goods vehicle rate*" is to the rate applicable, by virtue of sub-paragraph (1) of paragraph (9), to a rigid goods vehicle [which—

(a)   is not a vehicle with respect to which the reduced pollution requirements are satisfied; and

(b) falls] within column (3) of the table in that sub-paragraph and has a revenue weight exceeding 3,500 kilograms and not exceeding 7,500 kilograms.]

A34.126   *[Paragraph 4 of Schedule 1 is printed as amended by the Finance Act 1995, s.19 and Sched. 4, paras 1, 9(1) and (3), (6), and 16 (see also ibid., s.162 and Sched. 29, Pt V(2)); the Finance Act 1996, ss.16(3) and (8) and 17(1), (2), (3) and (11); the Finance Act 1998, s.16 and Sched. 1, paras 1, 4 and 17.*

The definition of "tractor" formerly contained in paragraph 4(3) (repealed by the Finance Act 1995) is expressly saved for the purposes of the Goods Vehicles (Licensing of Operators) Regulations 1995 (S.I. 1995 No. 2869) by ibid., Sched. 3, para.1 below; the former paragraph 4(3) is set out hereunder:

(3) In sub-paragraph (2)(a) *"tractor"* means—

    (a) an agricultural tractor, or

    (b) a tractor (other than an agricultural tractor) which is—
       (i) designed and constructed primarily for use otherwise than on roads, and
       (ii) incapable by reason of its construction of exceeding a speed of twenty-five miles per hour on the level under its own power.

The amount of duty is not reproduced.]

[PART IVA

SPECIAL CONCESSIONARY VEHICLES]

A34.127   *[The heading to Part IVA was inserted by the Finance Act 1995, s.19 and Sched. 4, paras 1, 10 and 16.]*

A34.128   **[4A.**—(1) The annual rate of vehicle excise duty applicable to a special concessionary vehicle is 25 per cent of the general rate specified in paragraph 1(2).

(2), (3) *[Rounding up or down of uneven amounts of duty.]]*

A34.129   *[Paragraph 4A of Schedule 1 was inserted by the Finance Act 1995, s.19 and Sched. 4, paras 1, 10 and 16.]*

A34.130   **[4B.**—(1) A vehicle is a special concessionary vehicle if it is—

    (a) an agricultural tractor, or

    (b) an off-road tractor.

(2) In sub-paragraph (1) *"agricultural tractor"* means a tractor used on public roads solely for purposes relating to agriculture, horticulture, forestry or activities falling within sub-paragraph (3).

(3) The activities falling within this sub-paragraph are—

    (a) cutting verges bordering public roads;

    (b) cutting hedges or trees bordering public roads or bordering verges which border public roads.

(4) In sub-paragraph (1) *"off-road tractor"* means a tractor which is not an agricultural tractor (within the meaning given by sub-paragraph (2)) and which is—

    (a) designed and constructed primarily for use otherwise than on roads, and

    (b) incapable by reason of its construction of exceeding a speed of twenty-five miles per hour on the level under its own power.]

A34.131   *[Paragraph 4B of Schedule 1 was inserted by the Finance Act 1995, s.19 and Sched. 4, paras 1, 10 and 16.]*

[**4C.**—(1) A vehicle is a special concessionary vehicle if it is a light agricultural vehicle.   **A34.132**

(2) In sub-paragraph (1) "*light agricultural vehicle*" means a vehicle which—

   (a) has a revenue weight not exceeding 1,000 kilograms,

   (b) is designed and constructed so as to seat only the driver,

   (c) is designed and constructed primarily for use otherwise than on roads, and

   (d) is used solely for purposes relating to agriculture, horticulture or forestry.]

[Paragraph 4C of Schedule 1 was inserted by the Finance Act 1995, s.19 and Sched. 4, paras 1, 10 and 16.]   **A34.133**

[**4D**. An agricultural engine is a special concessionary vehicle.]   **A34.134**

[Paragraph 4D of Schedule 1 was inserted by the Finance Act 1995, s.19 and Sched. 4, paras 1, 10 and 16.]   **A34.135**

[**4E.** A mowing machine is a special concessionary vehicle.]   **A34.136**

[Paragraph 4E of Schedule 1 was inserted by the Finance Act 1995, s.19 and Sched. 4, paras 1, 10 and 16.]   **A34.137**

[**4EE.** A steam powered vehicle is a special concessionary vehicle.]   **A34.138**

[Paragraph 4EE of Schedule 1 was inserted by the Finance Act 1996, s.16(1) and (8).]   **A34.139**

[**4F.**—(1) An electrically propelled vehicle [other than a motorcycle (within the meaning of Part II of this Schedule)] is a special concessionary vehicle.]   **A34.140**

(2) *[Repealed.]*

[Paragraph 4F of Schedule 1 was inserted by the Finance Act 1995, s.19 and Sched. 4, paras 1, 10 and 16, and is printed as subsequently amended by the Finance Act 1996, s.15(2) and (4) (see also ibid., s.205 and Sched. 41, Pt II(1)).]   **A34.141**

[**4G.** A vehicle is a special concessionary vehicle when it is—   **A34.142**

   (a) being used,

   (b) going to or from the place where it is to be or has been used, or

   (c) being kept for use,

for the purpose of clearing snow from public roads by means of a snow plough or similar device (whether or not forming part of the vehicle).]

[Paragraph 4G of Schedule 1 was inserted by the Finance Act 1995, s.19 and Sched. 4, paras 1, 10 and 16.]   **A34.143**

[**4H.** A vehicle is a special concessionary vehicle if it is constructed or adapted, and used, solely for the conveyance of machinery for spreading material on roads to deal with frost, ice or snow (with or without articles or material used for the purposes of the machinery).]   **A34.144**

[Paragraph 4H of Schedule 1 was inserted by the Finance Act 1995, s.19 and Sched. 4, paras 1, 10 and 16.]   **A34.145**

PART V

RECOVERY VEHICLES

A34.146   5.—(1) The annual rate of vehicle excise duty applicable to a recovery vehicle [is—

     (a) if it has a revenue weight exceeding 3,500 kilograms and not exceeding 12,000 kilograms, the same as the basic goods vehicle rate;

     (b) if it has a revenue weight exceeding 12,000 kilograms and not exceeding 25,000 kilograms, 300 per cent of the basic goods vehicle rate;

     (c) if it has a revenue weight exceeding 25,000 kilograms, 500 per cent of the basic goods vehicle rate.]

(2) In sub-paragraph (1) "*recovery vehicle*" means a vehicle which is constructed or permanently adapted primarily for any one or more of the purposes of lifting, towing and transporting a disabled vehicle.

(3) A vehicle is not a recovery vehicle if at any time it is used for a purpose other than—

     (a) the recovery of a disabled vehicle,

     (b) the removal of a disabled vehicle from the place where it became disabled to premises at which it is to be repaired or scrapped,

     (c) the removal of a disabled vehicle from premises to which it was taken for repair to other premises at which it is to be repaired or scrapped,

     (d) carrying fuel and other liquids required for its propulsion and tools and other articles required for the operation of, or in connection with, apparatus designed to lift, tow or transport a disabled vehicle, and

     (e) any purpose prescribed for the purposes of this sub-paragraph by regulations made by the Secretary of State.

(4) At any time when a vehicle is being used for either of the purposes specified in paragraphs (a) and (b) of sub-paragraph (3), use for—

     (a) the carriage of a person who, immediately before the vehicle became disabled, was the driver of or a passenger in the vehicle,

     (b) the carriage of any goods which, immediately before the vehicle became disabled, were being carried in the vehicle, or

     (c) any purpose prescribed for the purposes of this sub-paragraph by regulations made by the Secretary of State,

shall be disregarded in determining whether the vehicle is a recovery vehicle.

(5) A vehicle is not a recovery vehicle if at any time the number of vehicles which it is used to recover exceeds a number specified for the purposes of this sub-paragraph by an order made by the Secretary of State.

[(5A) A vehicle is not a recovery vehicle if it is a special concessionary vehicle.]

[(6) In sub-paragraph (1) references to the "*basic goods vehicle rate*" are to the rate applicable, by virtue of sub-paragraph (1) of paragraph (9), to a rigid goods vehicle [which—

     (a) is not a vehicle with respect to which the reduced pollution requirements are satisfied; and

     (b) falls] within column (3) of the table in that sub-paragraph and has a revenue weight exceeding 3,500 kilograms and not exceeding 7,500 kilograms.]

[(7), (8) *[Rounding up or down of uneven amounts of duty.]*]

[Paragraph 5 of Schedule 1 is printed as amended by the Finance Act 1995, s.19 and Sched. 4, paras   **A34.147**
*1, 11 and 16; the Finance Act 1996, s.16(4) and (8); the Finance Act 1998, s.16 and Sched. 1, paras
1, 5 and 17.*

The amount of duty is not reproduced.

*The Recovery Vehicles (Prescribed Purposes) Regulations 1989 (S.I. 1989 No. 1376) (q.v.) have effect
as if made under paragraph 5(3)(e) and (4)(c). The Recovery Vehicles (Number of Vehicles Recovered)
Order 1989 (S.I. 1989 No. 1226; not reproduced in this work), which has effect as if made under paragraph 5(5), prescribes two vehicles as the number prescribed for the purposes of paragraph 5(5).]*

PART VI

VEHICLES USED FOR EXCEPTIONAL LOADS

6.—(1) This paragraph applies to a vehicle which is—   **A34.148**

  (a) a heavy motor car used for the carriage of exceptional loads, or

  (b) a heavy locomotive, light locomotive or motor tractor used to draw trailers carry-
      ing exceptional loads,

[and which is not a special concessionary vehicle].

(2) The annual rate of vehicle excise duty applicable to a vehicle to which this paragraph
applies in respect of use for the carriage of exceptional loads, or to draw trailers carrying
exceptional loads, which is authorised by virtue of an order under—

  (a) section 44 of the Road Traffic Act 1988, or

  (b) *[applies in Northern Ireland]*,

is [the rate specified in sub-paragraph (2A)].

[(2A) The rate referred to in sub-paragraph (2) is—

  (a) in the case of a vehicle with respect to which the reduced pollution requirements
      are not satisfied, £—; and

  (b) in the case of a vehicle with respect to which those requirements are satisfied £—.]

(3) For the purposes of this paragraph an *exceptional load* is a load which—

  (a) by reason of its dimensions cannot be carried by a heavy motor car or trailer, or
      a combination of a heavy motor car and trailer, which complies in all respects
      with requirements of regulations under section 41 of the Road Traffic Act 1988
      . . ., or

  (b) by reason of its weight cannot be carried by a heavy motor car or trailer, or a com-
      bination of a heavy motor car and trailer, which has a total laden weight of not
      more than [41,000 kilograms] and which complies in all respects with such
      requirements.

[(3A) *[Repealed.]*]

(4) Expressions used in this paragraph and in the Road Traffic Act 1988 . . . have the
same meanings in this paragraph as in that Act . . .

[Paragraph 6 of Schedule 1 is printed as amended by the Finance Act 1995, s.19 and Sched. 14, paras   **A34.149**
*1, 12 and 16; the Finance Act 1996, s.16(5) and (8); the Finance Act 1998, s.16 and Sched. 1, paras
1, 6 and 17 (see also ibid., s.165 and Sched. 27, Pt I(3)); the Finance Act 1999, s.9 and Sched. 1, paras
1 and 2.*

The words omitted from paragraph 6(3) and (4) relate exclusively to Northern Ireland.

The amounts of duty (and amendments of those amounts) are not reproduced.]

PART VII

HAULAGE VEHICLES

A34.150

7.—(1) The annual rate of vehicle excise duty applicable to a haulage vehicle is—

[(a) if it is a showman's vehicle, the same as the basic goods vehicle rate;

(b) in any other case, [the rate specified in sub-paragraph (3A)].]

(2) In sub-paragraph (1) *"haulage vehicle"* means a vehicle (other than a vehicle to which Part IV, [IVA,] V or VI applies) which is constructed and used on public roads solely for haulage and not for the purpose of carrying or having superimposed on it any load except such as is necessary for its propulsion or equipment.

[(3) In sub-paragraph (1) references to the *"basic goods vehicle rate"* is to the rate applicable, by virtue of sub-paragraph (1) of paragraph (9), to a rigid goods vehicle [which—

(a) is not a vehicle with respect to which the reduced pollution requirements are satisfied; and

(b) falls] within column (3) of the table in that sub-paragraph and has a revenue weight exceeding 3,500 kilograms and not exceeding 7,500 kilograms.]

[(3A) The rate referred to in sub-paragraph (1)(b) is—

(a) in the case of a vehicle with respect to which the reduced pollution requirements are not satisfied, £—; and

(b) in the case of a vehicle with respect to which those requirements are satisfied, the general rate specified in paragraph 1(2).]

[(4)–(6) *[Repealed by the Finance Act 1998.]*]

A34.151

[Paragraph 7 of Schedule 1 is printed as amended by the Finance Act 1995, s.19 and Sched. 4, paras 1, 13 and 16; the Finance Act 1996, s.16(6) and (8); the Finance Act 1998, s.16 and Sched. 1, paras 1, 7 and 17. The amounts of duty are not reproduced.]

PART VIII

GOODS VEHICLES

Basic rate

A34.152

8.—*(1) The annual rate of vehicle excise duty applicable to a goods vehicle to which this paragraph applies is £—.*

(2) This paragraph applies to a goods vehicle—

(a) which has a plated gross weight or plated train weight . . . exceeding 3,500 kilograms but not exceeding 7,500 kilograms,

(b) which has a plated gross weight or plated train weight exceeding 7,500 kilograms but has such a weight only by virtue of section 61(3)(c) of this Act and is not a vehicle of a class prescribed by regulations made by the Secretary of State,

(c) which is a tower wagon with a plated gross weight . . . exceeding 7,500 kilograms, or

(d) which does not have a plated gross weight or plated train weight . . . but has a design weight exceeding 3,500 kilograms.

(3) In sub-paragraph (2)(c) "tower wagon" means a goods vehicle—

(a) into which there is built, as part of the vehicle, an expanding or extendible device designed for facilitating the erection, inspection, repair or maintenance of overhead structures or equipment, and

(b) which is not constructed or adapted for use, or used, for the conveyance of any load other than such a device or articles used in connection with it.

(4) This paragraph is subject to paragraph 12.

[**Repeal.** *Paragraph 8 of Schedule 1 has been repealed by the Finance Act 1995, s.19 and Sched. 4,*   **A34.153**
paras 1, 14(2) and 16 (see also ibid., s.162 and Sched. 29, Pt V(2)).
The text of paragraph 8 has been expressly saved for the purposes of the Goods Vehicles (Plating and Testing) Regulations 1988 (S.I. 1988 No. 1478), Sched. 2, para.6 below.
The words omitted from paragraph 8(2)(a), (c) and (d) relate exclusively to Northern Ireland.
The amount of duty is not reproduced.]

Rigid goods vehicles

9.—(1) [Subject to sub-paragraphs (2) and (3),] the annual rate of excise duty applic-   **A34.154**
able to a rigid goods vehicle which [is not a vehicle with respect to which the reduced pollution requirements are satisfied and which] has a [revenue weight exceeding 3,500
kilograms] shall be determined in accordance with the following table by reference to—

    (a) the [revenue weight] of the vehicle, and

    (b) the number of axles on the vehicle.

Table of Rates of Duty

[Omitted.]

[(2) The annual rate of vehicle excise duty applicable—

    (a) to any rigid goods vehicle which is a showman's goods vehicle with a revenue
weight exceeding 3,500 kilograms but not exceeding 44,000 kilograms, . . .

    (b) to any rigid goods vehicle which is an island goods vehicle with a revenue weight
exceeding 3,500 kilograms, [and]

    [(c) to any rigid goods vehicle which is used loaded only in connection with a person
learning to drive the vehicle or taking a driving test,]

shall be the basic goods vehicle rate.]

[(3) The annual rate of vehicle excise duty applicable to a rigid goods vehicle [which—

    (a) is not a vehicle with respect to which the reduced pollution requirements are
satisfied,

    (b) has a revenue weight exceeding 44,000 kilograms, and

    (c) is not an island goods vehicle,

shall be £—.]]

[(4) In sub-paragraph (2) the reference to the "*basic goods vehicle rate*" is to the rate applicable, by virtue of sub-paragraph (1) of paragraph (9), to a rigid goods vehicle [which—

    (a) is not a vehicle with respect to which the reduced pollution requirements are
satisfied; and

    (b) falls] within column (3) of the table in that sub-paragraph and has a revenue
weight exceeding 3,500 kilograms and not exceeding 7,500 kilograms.]

[(5) *[Repealed by the Finance Act 1998.]*]

[Paragraph 9 of Schedule 1 is printed as amended by the Finance Act 1995, s.19 and Sched. 4, paras   **A34.155**
*1, 14 and 16; the Finance Act 1996, s.17(1), (4) and (11) (see also ibid., s.205 and Sched. 41,
Pt II(2)); the Finance Act 1998, s.16 and Sched. 1, paras 1 and 8 (and see also ibid., s.165 and
Sched. 27, Pt I(3)).]*

A34.156   [**9A.**—(1) This paragraph applies to a rigid goods vehicle which—

     (a)   is a vehicle with respect to which the reduced pollution requirements are satisfied;

     (b)   is not a vehicle for which the annual rate of vehicle excise duty is determined under paragraph 9(2); and

     (c)   has a revenue weight exceeding 3,500 kilograms.

(2) Subject to sub-paragraph (3), the annual rate of vehicle excise duty applicable to a rigid goods vehicle to which this paragraph applies shall be determined in accordance with the table set out in paragraph 9B by reference to—

     (a)   the revenue weight of the vehicle, and

     (b)   the number of axles on the vehicle.

(3) The annual rate of vehicle excise duty applicable to a rigid goods vehicle to which this paragraph applies which has a revenue weight exceeding 44,000 kilograms shall be £—.]

A34.157   *[Paragraph 9A of Schedule 1 has been inserted by the Finance Act 1998, s.16 and Sched. 1, paras 1, 9 and 17.*

The amount of duty (and amendments to the amount) are not reproduced.]

A34.158   **9B.**   *[Rates of duty.]*

A34.159   **10.**—(1) The annual rate of vehicle excise duty applicable, in accordance with [paragraphs 9 and 9A], to a rigid goods vehicle which has a [revenue weight] exceeding 12,000 kilograms [, which does not fall within paragraph 9(2)(b) or (c)] and which is used for drawing a trailer which—

     (a)   has a [plated gross weight] exceeding 4,000 kilograms, and

     (b)   when so drawn, is used for the conveyance of goods or burden,

shall be increased by the amount of the supplement (the "*trailer supplement*") which is appropriate to the [plated gross weight] of the trailer being drawn.

(2) Where the plated gross weight . . . of the trailer—

     (a)   exceeds 4,000 kilograms, but

     (b)   does not exceed 12,000 kilograms,

the amount of the trailer supplement is [an amount equal to the amount of the general rate specified in paragraph 1(2)].

(3) Where the plated gross weight . . . of the trailer exceeds 12,000 kilograms, the amount of the trailer supplement is [an amount equal to 275 per cent of the amount of the general rate specified in paragraph 1(2)].

[(3A), (3B)   *[Rounding up or down of uneven amounts of trailer supplement.]*

(4) *[Repealed.]*

A34.160   *[Paragraph 10 of Schedule 1 is printed as amended by the Finance Act 1995, s.19 and Sched. 4, paras 1, 14(6)–(10) and 16 (see also ibid., s.162 and Sched. 29, Pt V(2)); the Finance Act 1996, s.17(1), (5) and (11); the Finance Act 1998, s.16 and Sched. 1, paras 1, 10 and 17.*

The amounts of trailer supplement are not reproduced.]

Tractive units

A34.161   **11.**—(1) [Subject to sub-paragraphs (2) and (3) [and paragraph 11C],] the annual rate of vehicle excise duty applicable to a tractive unit which [is not a vehicle with respect to which the reduced pollution requirements are satisfied and which] has a [revenue weight exceeding 3,500 kilograms] shall be determined in accordance with the following table by reference to—

(a) the [revenue weight] of the tractive unit,

(b) the number of axles on the tractive unit, and

(c) the types of semi-trailers, distinguished according to the number of their axles, which are to be drawn by it.

TABLE OF RATES OF DUTY

[Omitted.]

[(2) The annual rate of vehicle excise duty applicable—

(a) to any tractive unit which is a showman's goods vehicle with a revenue weight exceeding 3,500 kilograms but not exceeding 44,000 kilograms, . . .

(b) to any tractive unit which is an island goods vehicle with a revenue weight exceeding 3,500 kilograms, [and]

[(c) to any tractive unit to which a semi-trailer is attached which is used loaded only in connection with a person learning to drive the vehicle or taking a driving test,]

shall be the basic goods vehicle rate.]

[(3) The annual rate of vehicle excise duty applicable to a tractive unit [which—

(a) is not a vehicle with respect to which the reduced pollution requirements are satisfied,

(b) has a revenue weight exceeding 44,000 kilograms, and

(c) is not an island goods vehicle,

shall be £—.]]

[(4) In sub-paragraph (2) references to the "*basic goods vehicle rate*" is to the rate applicable, by virtue of sub-paragraph (1) of paragraph (9), to a rigid goods vehicle [which—

(a) is not a vehicle with respect to which the reduced pollution requirements are satisfied; and

(b) falls] within column (3) of the table in that sub-paragraph and has a revenue weight exceeding 3,500 kilograms and not exceeding 7,500 kilograms.]

[(5) *[Repealed by the Finance Act 1998.]*]

[Paragraph 11 of Schedule 1 is printed as amended by the Finance Act 1995, s.19 and Sched. 4, paras **A34.162** *1, 14(11) and (13) and 16; the Finance Act 1996, s.17(1), (6) and (11) (see also ibid., s.205 and Sched. 41, Pt II(2)); the Finance Act 1998, s.16 and Sched. 1, paras 1, 11 and 17 (see also ibid., s.165 and Sched. 27, Pt I(3)); the Finance Act 2000, s.24 and Sched. 5, paras 1 and 6(1)(a).*
The amount of duty (and amendments to the amount) are not reproduced.]

[**11A.**—(1) This paragraph applies to a tractive unit which—   **A34.163**

(a) is a vehicle with respect to which the reduced pollution requirements are satisfied;

(b) is not a vehicle for which the annual rate of vehicle excise duty is determined under paragraph 11(2); and

(c) has a revenue weight exceeding 3,500 kilograms.

(2) Subject to sub-paragraph (3) [and paragraph 11C], the annual rate of vehicle excise duty applicable to a tractive unit to which this paragraph applies shall be determined, in accordance with the table set out in paragraph 11B, by reference to—

(a) the revenue weight of the tractive unit,

(b) the number of axles on the tractive unit, and

(c) the types of semi-trailers, distinguished according to the number of their axles, which are to be drawn by it.

(3) The annual rate of vehicle excise duty applicable to a tractive unit to which this paragraph applies which has a revenue weight exceeding 44,000 kilograms shall be £—.]

A34.164   *[Paragraph 11A of Schedule 1 has been inserted by the Finance Act 1998, s.16 and Sched. 1, paras 1, 12 and 17, and is printed as amended by the Finance Act 2000, s.24 and Sched. 5, paras 1 and 6(1)(b). The amount of duty is not reproduced.]*

A34.165   **11B.**   *[Rates of duty.]*

              11C.   *[Rates of duty.]*

Farmers' goods vehicles and showmen's goods vehicles

A34.166   **12.** *[Repealed by the Finance Act 1995, s.19 and Sched. 4, paras 1, 14(14) and 16.]*

Vehicles with reduced plated weights

A34.167   **13.**—(1) The Secretary of State may by regulations provide that, on an application relating to a goods vehicle which is made in accordance with the regulations, the vehicle is treated for the purposes of this Part as if [its revenue weight were such lower weight as may be specified] in the application.

(2) The regulations may provide that the treatment of the vehicle as being of a lower weight is subject to—

(a) conditions prescribed by the regulations, or

(b) such further conditions as the Secretary of State may think fit to impose in any particular case.

A34.168   *[Paragraph 13 of Schedule 1 is printed as amended by the Finance Act 1995, s.19 and Sched. 4, paras 1, 14(15) and 16.]*

Vehicles for conveying machines

              14. A vehicle which—

A34.169   (a) is constructed or adapted for use and used for the conveyance of a machine or device and no other load except articles used in connection with the machine or device,

(b), (c) *[repealed]*,

is chargeable with vehicle excise duty at the rate which would be applicable to it if the machine or device were burden even if it is built in as part of the vehicle.

A34.170   *[Paragraph 14 of Schedule 1 is printed as amended by the Finance Act 1995, s.19 and Sched. 4, paras 1, 14(16) and 16 (see also ibid., s.162 and Sched. 29, Pt V(2)).]*

Goods vehicles used partly for private purposes

A34.171   **15.** *[Repealed by the Finance Act 1996, s.17(1) and (15).]*

Exceptions

A34.172   **16.**—(1) This Part does not apply to—

(a) a vehicle to which Part II, IV, [IVA,] V or VII applies, . . .

(b) *[repealed.]*

(2) This Part applies to a goods vehicle which is a vehicle to which paragraph 6 applies only if it is used on a public road and the use is not such as is mentioned in sub-paragraph (2) of that paragraph.

[Paragraph 16 of Schedule 1 is printed as amended by the Finance Act 1996, ss.16(7) and (8) and 17(1), (7) and (11) (see also ibid., s.205 and Sched. 41, Pt II(2)).]   **A34.173**

Meaning of "trailer"

17.—(1) In this Part *"trailer"* does not include—   **A34.174**

(a) an appliance constructed and used solely for the purpose of distributing on the road loose gritting material, [or]

(b) a snow plough,

(c)–(e) *[repealed].*

(2) *[Repealed.]*

[Paragraph 17 of Schedule 1 is printed as amended by the Finance Act 1995, s.19 and Sched. 4, paras 1, 14(17) and (18) and 16 (see also ibid., s.162 and Sched. 29, Pt V(2)).]   **A34.175**

[Meaning of "island goods vehicle"]

[18.—(1) In this Part *"island goods vehicle"* means any goods vehicle which—   **A34.176**

(a) is kept for use wholly or partly on the roads of one or more small islands; and

(b) is not kept or used on any mainland road, except in a manner authorised by sub-paragraph (2) or (3).

(2) The keeping or use of a goods vehicle on a mainland road is authorised by this sub-paragraph if—

(a) the road is one used for travel between a landing place and premises where vehicles disembarked at that place are loaded or unloaded, or both;

(b) the length of the journey, using that road, from that landing place to those premises is not more than five kilometres;

(c) the vehicle in question is one which was disembarked at that landing place after a journey by sea which began on a small island; and

(d) the loading or unloading of that vehicle is to take place, or has taken place, at those premises.

(3) The keeping or use of a goods vehicle on a mainland road is authorised by this sub-paragraph if—

(a) that vehicle has a revenue weight not exceeding 17,000 kilograms;

(b) that vehicle is normally kept at a base or centre on a small island; and

(c) the only journeys for which that vehicle is used are ones that begin or end at that base or centre.

(4) References in this paragraph to a *small island* are references to any such island falling within sub-paragraph (5) as may be designated as a small island by an order made by the Secretary of State.

(5) An island falls within this sub-paragraph if—

(a) it has an area of 23,000 hectares or less; and

(b) the absence of a bridge, causeway, tunnel, ford or other way makes it at all times impracticable for road vehicles to be driven under their own power from that island as far as the mainland.

(6) The reference in sub-paragraph (5) to *driving a road vehicle as far as the mainland* is a reference to driving it as far as any public road in the United Kingdom which is not on an island with an area of 230,000 hectares or less and is not a road connecting two such islands.

(7) In this paragraph—

"*island*" includes anything that is an island only when the tide reaches a certain height;

"*landing place*" means any place at which vehicles are disembarked after sea journeys;

"*mainland road*" means any public road in the United Kingdom, other than one which is on a small island or which connects two such islands; and

"*road vehicles*" means vehicles which are designed or adapted primarily for being driven on roads and which do not have any special features for facilitating their being driven elsewhere;

and references in this paragraph to the loading or unloading of a vehicle include references to the loading or unloading of its trailer or semi-trailer.]

A34.177   *[Paragraph 18 of Schedule 1 (and the italicised heading preceding paragraph 18) were inserted by the Finance Act 1995, s.19 and Sched. 4, paras 1, 14(19) and 16.*
The Vehicle Excise Duty (Designation of Small Islands) Order 1995 (S.I. 1995 No. 1397) below has been made under paragraph 18(4).]

[Other expressions]

A34.178   [**19.**—(1) In this Part "*driving test*" means any test of competence to drive mentioned in section 89(1) of the Road Traffic Act 1988.

(2) For the purposes of this Part a vehicle or a semi-trailer is used loaded if the vehicle or, as the case may be, the semi-trailer is used for the conveyance of goods or burden of any description.]

A34.179   *[Paragraph 19 of Schedule 1 (and the italicised heading preceding para.19) were inserted by the Finance Act 1996, s.17(1), (8) and (11).]*

Section 5   SCHEDULE 2

                          EXEMPT VEHICLES

                     Electrically propelled vehicles

A34.180   **1.** *[Repealed by the Finance Act 1995, s.19 and Sched. 4, paras 1, 2(a) and 5.]*

                          [Old vehicles]

A34.181   [**1A.**—(1) Subject to sub-paragraph (2), a vehicle is an exempt vehicle at any time if it was constructed [before 1st January 1973].

(2) A vehicle is not an exempt vehicle by virtue of sub-paragraph (1) if—

(a) an annual rate is specified in respect of it by any provision of Part III, V, VI, VII or VIII of Schedule 1; or

(b) it is a special vehicle, within the meaning of Part IV of Schedule 1, which—

(i) falls within sub-paragraph (3) or (4); and

(ii) is not a digging machine, mobile crane, works truck or road roller.

(3) A vehicle falls within this sub-paragraph if—

(a) it is designed or adapted for use for the conveyance of goods or burden of any description;

(b) it is put to a commercial use on a public road; and

(c) that use is not a use for the conveyance of goods or burden of any description.

(4) A vehicle falls within this sub-paragraph if—

(a) it is designed or adapted for use with a semi-trailer attached;

(b) it is put to a commercial use on a public road; and

(c) in a case where that use is a use with a semi-trailer attached, the semi-trailer is not used for the conveyance of goods or burden of any description.

(5) In sub-paragraph (2) "*digging machine*", "*mobile crane*" and "*works truck*" have the same meanings as in paragraph 4 of Schedule 1.

(6) In sub-paragraphs (3) and (4) "*commercial use*" means use for hire or reward or for or in connection with a trade or business.]

[Paragraph 1A of Schedule 2 and the heading preceding it were inserted by the Finance Act 1996, s.18(1) and (5), and paragraph 1A is printed as subsequently substituted by ibid., s.19(1) and (2); the Finance Act 1998, s.17.]   **A34.182**

Trams

2. A vehicle used on tram lines is an exempt vehicle.   **A34.183**

[Electrically assisted pedal cycles]

[2A.—(1) An electrically assisted pedal cycle is an exempt vehicle.   **A34.184**

(2) For the purposes of sub-paragraph (1) an electrically assisted pedal cycle is a vehicle of a class complying with such requirements as may be prescribed by regulations made by the Secretary of State for the purposes of this paragraph.]

[Paragraph 2A of Schedule 2 and the heading preceding it were inserted by the Finance Act 1996, s.15(5).]   **A34.185**

Vehicles not for carriage

3. A vehicle which is not constructed or adapted for use, or used, for the carriage of a driver or passenger is an exempt vehicle.   **A34.186**

[Police vehicles]

[3A. A vehicle is an exempt vehicle when it is being used for police purposes.]   **A34.187**

[Paragraph 3A of Schedule 2 and the heading preceding it were inserted by the Finance Act 1995, s.19 and Sched. 4, paras 1, 3 and 5.]   **A34.188**

Fire engines, etc.

4.—(1) A fire engine is an exempt vehicle.   **A34.189**

(2) In sub-paragraph (1) "*fire engine*" means a vehicle which—

(a) is constructed or adapted for use for the purpose of fire fighting or salvage (or both), and

(b) is used solely for the purposes of a fire brigade (whether or not one maintained under the Fire Services Act 1947 . . .

[The words omitted from paragraph 4(2)(b) relate exclusively to Northern Ireland.]   **A34.190**

A34.191   **5.** A vehicle which is kept by a fire authority is an exempt vehicle when it is being used or kept on a road for the purposes of the authority's fire brigade service.

Ambulances and health service vehicles

A34.192   **6.**—(1) An ambulance is an exempt vehicle.

(2) In sub-paragraph (1) *"ambulance"* means a vehicle which—

    (a) is constructed or adapted for, and used for no purpose other than, the carriage of sick, injured or disabled people to or from welfare centres or places where medical or dental treatment is given, and

    (b) is readily identifiable as a vehicle used for the carriage of such people by being marked "Ambulance" on both sides.

A34.193   **7.** A vehicle is an exempt vehicle when it is being used or kept on a road by—

    (a) a health service body (as defined in section 60(7) of the National Health Service and Community Care Act 1990) or a health and social services body (as defined in Article 7(6) of the Health and Personal Social Services (Northern Ireland) Order 1991) [*S.I. 1991 No. 194 (N.I. 1)*], or

    (b) a National Health Service trust established under Part I of the National Health Service and Community Care Act 1990 or the National Health Service (Scotland) Act 1978 or a Health and Social Services Trust established under the Health and Personal Social Services (Northern Ireland) Order 1991, [or]

    [(c) the Commission for Health Improvement], [or]

    [(d) a Primary Care Trust established under section 16A of the National Health Service Act 1977.]

A34.194   *[Paragraph 7 is printed as amended by the Health Act 1999 (Supplementary and Consequential Provisions) Order 1999 (S.I. 1999 No. 2795; not reproduced in this work), art.5; the Health Act 1999 (Supplementary, Consequential, etc., Provisions) Order 2000 (S.I. 2000 No. 90; not reproduced in this work), art.3(1) and Sched. 1, para.28).]*

A34.195   **8.** A vehicle which is made available by the Secretary of State—

    (a) to a person, body or local authority under section 23 or 26 of the National Health Service Act 1977, or

    (b) to a local authority, education authority or voluntary organisation in Scotland under section 15 or 16 of the National Health Service (Scotland) Act 1978,

and which is used in accordance with the terms on which it is so made available is an exempt vehicle.

A34.196   **9.**—(1) A veterinary ambulance is an exempt vehicle.

(2) In sub-paragraph (1) *"veterinary ambulance"* means a vehicle which—

    (a) is used for no purpose other than the carriage of sick or injured animals to or from places where veterinary treatment is given, and

    (b) is readily identifiable as a vehicle used for the carriage of such animals by being marked "Veterinary Ambulance" on both sides.

Mine rescue vehicles, etc.

A34.197   **10.** A vehicle used solely—

   (a) as a mine rescue vehicle, or

   (b) for the purpose of conveying or drawing emergency winding-gear at a mine,

is an exempt vehicle.

Lifeboat vehicles

11. A vehicle used or kept on a road for no purpose other than the haulage of a lifeboat and the conveyance of the necessary gear of the lifeboat which is being hauled is an exempt vehicle. **A34.198**

Road construction and maintenance vehicles

12–17. *[Repealed by the Finance Act 1995, s.19 and Sched. 4, paras 1, 2(b)–(g) and 5.]*

*[**Editorial note.** The following definition contained in paragraph 17(2) of Schedule 2 (repealed by the Finance Act 1995) has been expressly saved for the purposes of the Goods Vehicles (Licensing of Operators) Regulations 1995 (S.I. 1995 No. 2869) by ibid., reg.3(2) below and also for the Goods Vehicles (Plating and Testing) Regulations 1988 (S.I. 1988 No. 1478), Sched. 2 below:* **A34.199**

"*tower wagon*" means a goods vehicle—

   (a) into which there is built, as part of the vehicle, an expanding or extendible device designed for facilitating the erection, inspection, repair or maintenance of overhead structures or equipment, and

   (b) which is not constructed or adapted for use, or used, for the conveyance of any load other than—

      (i) such a device or articles used in connection with it, or

     (ii) articles used in connection with the installation or maintenance (by means of such a device) of materials or apparatus for lighting streets, roads or public places.*]*

Vehicles for disabled people

18. A vehicle (including a cycle with an attachment for propulsion by mechanical power) which— **A34.200**

   (a) is adapted, and used or kept on a road, for an invalid, and

   (b) does not exceed 508 kilograms in weight unladen,

is an exempt vehicle.

19.—(1) A vehicle is an exempt vehicle when it is being used, or kept for use, by or for the purposes of a disabled person who satisfies sub-paragraph (2) if— **A34.201**

   (a) the vehicle is registered under this Act in the name of the disabled person, and

   (b) no other vehicle registered in his name under this Act is an exempt vehicle under this paragraph or paragraph 7 of Schedule 4.

(2) A disabled person satisfies this sub-paragraph if—

   (a) he is in receipt of a disability living allowance by virtue of entitlement to the mobility component at the higher rate,

   (b) he is in receipt of a mobility supplement, or

   (c) he has obtained, or is eligible for, a grant under—

      (i) paragraph 2 of Schedule 2 to the National Health Service Act 1977,

     (ii) section 46(3) of the National Health Service (Scotland) Act 1978, or

    (iii) Article 30(3) of the Health and Personal Social Services (Northern Ireland) Order 1972 *[S.I. 1972 No. 1265 (N.I. 14)]*,

in relation to the vehicle.

[(2A) This paragraph shall have effect as if a person were in receipt of a disability living allowance by virtue of entitlement to the mobility component at the higher rate in any case where—

(a) he has ceased to be in receipt of it as a result of having ceased to satisfy a condition of receiving the allowance or of receiving the mobility component at that rate;

(b) that condition is either—

  (i) a condition relating to circumstances in which he is undergoing medical or other treatment as an in-patient in a hospital or similar institution; or

  (ii) a condition specified in regulations made by the Secretary of State;

  and

(c) he would continue to be entitled to receive the mobility component of the allowance at the higher rate but for his failure to satisfy that condition.]

(3) For the purposes of sub-paragraph (1) a vehicle is deemed to be registered under this Act in the name of a person in receipt of a disability living allowance by virtue of entitlement to the mobility component at the higher rate, or of a mobility supplement, if it is so registered in the name of—

(a) an appointee, or

(b) a person nominated for the purposes of this paragraph by the person or an appointee.

(4) In sub-paragraph (3) "*appointee*" means—

(a) a person appointed pursuant to regulations made under (or having effect as if made under) the Social Security Administration Act 1992 or the Social Security Administration (Northern Ireland) Act 1992 to exercise any of the rights and powers of a person in receipt of a disability living allowance, or

(b) a person to whom a mobility supplement is paid for application for the benefit of another person in receipt of the supplement.

(5) In this paragraph "*mobility supplement*" means a mobility supplement under—

(a) a scheme under the Personal Injuries (Emergency Provisions) Act 1939, or

(b) an Order in Council under section 12 of the Social Security (Miscellaneous Provisions) Act 1977,

or a payment appearing to the Secretary of State to be of a similar kind and specified for the purposes of this paragraph by an order made by him.

A34.202   *[Paragraph 19 of Schedule 2A is printed as amended by the Finance Act 1997, s.17.*
The Motor Vehicles (Exemption from Vehicles Excise Duty) Order 1985 (S.I. 1985 No. 722; not re-produced in this work) has effect as if made under paragraph 19.]

A34.203   **20.**—(1) A vehicle (other than an ambulance within the meaning of paragraph (6)) used for the carriage of disabled people by a body for the time being recognised by the Secretary of State for the purposes of this paragraph is an exempt vehicle.

(2) The Secretary of State shall recognise a body for the purposes of this paragraph if, on an application made to him in such manner as he may specify, it appears to him that the body is concerned with the care of disabled people.

(3) The issue by the Secretary of State of a nil licence in respect of a vehicle under this paragraph is to be treated as recognition by him for the purposes of this paragraph of the body by reference to whose use of the vehicle the document is issued.

(4) *[Repealed by the Finance Act 1997.]*

(5) The Secretary of State may withdraw recognition of a body for the purposes of this

paragraph if it appears to him that the body is no longer concerned with the care of disabled people.

[Paragraph 20 of Schedule 2 is printed as amended by the Finance Act 1997, s.18 and Sched. 3, paras   **A34.204**
1, 7(4) and 9 (see also ibid., s.113 and Sched. 18, Pt III).]

[Vehicles used between different parts of land]

[20A. A vehicle is an exempt vehicle if—   **A34.205**

(a) it is used only for purposes relating to agriculture, horticulture or forestry,

(b) it is used on public roads only in passing between different areas of land occupied by the same person, and

(c) the distance it travels on public roads in passing between any two such areas does not exceed 1.5 kilometres.]

[Paragraph 20A of Schedule 2 and the heading preceding it were inserted by the Finance Act 1995, s.19   **A34.206**
and Sched. 4, paras 1, 4 and 5.]

Vehicles used for short journeys between different parts of person's land

21. *[Repealed by the Finance Act 1995, s.19 and Sched. 4, paras 1, 2(b) and 5.]*   **A34.207**

Vehicle testing, etc.

22.—(1) A vehicle is an exempt vehicle when it is being used solely for the purpose of—   **A34.208**

(a) submitting it (by previous arrangement for a specified time on a specified date) for a compulsory test [, a vehicle weight test or a reduced pollution test], or

(b) bringing it away from [any such test].

[(1A) A vehicle is an exempt vehicle when it is being used solely for the purpose of—

(a) taking it (by previous arrangement for a specified time on a specified date) for a relevant re-examination, or

(b) bringing it away from such a re-examination.]

(2) A vehicle is an exempt vehicle when it is being used by an authorised person in the course of a compulsory test [, a vehicle weight test [, a reduced pollution test] or a relevant re-examination and is being so used] solely for the purpose of—

(a) taking it to, or bringing it away from, a place where a part of the test [or re-examination] is to be, or has been, carried out, or

(b) carrying out a part of the test [or re-examination].

[(2A) A vehicle is an exempt vehicle when it is being used by an authorised person solely for the purpose of warming up its engine in preparation for the carrying out of—

(a) a compulsory test [or a reduced pollution test] , or

(b) a relevant re-examination that is to be carried out for the purposes of an appeal relating to a determination made on a compulsory test [or a reduced pollution test].]

(3) Where the relevant certificate is refused on a compulsory test [, or a reduced pollution test] of a vehicle [or as a result of a relevant re-examination,] the vehicle is an exempt vehicle when it is being used solely for the purpose of—

(a) delivering it (by previous arrangement for a specified time on a specified date) at a place where relevant work is to be done on it, or

(b) bringing it away from a place where relevant work has been done on it.

(4) In this paragraph "*compulsory test*" means, as respects England and Wales and Scotland—

   (a) in the case of a vehicle for which by virtue of section 66(3) of the Road Traffic Act 1988 a vehicle licence cannot be granted unless certain requirements are satisfied, an examination such as is specified in sub-paragraph (5), and

   (b) otherwise, an examination under section 45 of the Road Traffic Act 1988 with a view to obtaining a test certificate without which a vehicle licence cannot be granted for the vehicle.

(5) The examinations referred to in sub-paragraph (4)(a) are—

   [(a) an examination under regulations under section 49(1)(b) or (c) of the Road Traffic Act 1988 (examination as to compliance with construction and use or safety requirements)],

   (b) an examination for the purposes of sections 54 to 58 of that Act (examination as to a . . . vehicle's compliance with type approval requirements), [and]

   (c) *[repealed]*

   (d) an examination under regulations under section 61(2)(a) of that Act (examinations in connection with alterations to . . . vehicles subject to type approval requirements).

(6) *[Applies to Northern Ireland.]*

[(6A) In this paragraph "*a vehicle weight test*" means any examination of a vehicle for which provision is made by regulations under—

   (a) section 61A of this Act,

   (b) section 49(1)(a) of the Road Traffic Act 1988 (tests for selecting plated weights and other plated particulars), or

   (c) Article 65(1)(a) of the Road Traffic (Northern Ireland) Order 1995 [*S.I. 1995 No. 2994 (NI 18)*].]

[(6AA) In this paragraph "*a reduced pollution test*" means any examination of a vehicle for which provision is made by regulations under sectio 61B of this Act.]

[(6B) In this paragraph "*a relevant re-examination*" means any examination or re-examination which is carried out in accordance with any provision or requirement made or imposed for the purposes of an appeal relating to a determination made on a compulsory test [, a vehicle weight test or a reduced pollution test].]

(7) In this paragraph "*authorised person*" means—

   (a) in the case of an examination within sub-paragraph (4)(b), a person who is, or is acting on behalf of, an examiner or inspector entitled to carry out such an examination or a person acting under the personal direction of such a person,

   (b) in the case of an examination within sub-paragraph (5), an examiner appointed under section 66A of the Road Traffic Act 1988, a person carrying out the examination under the direction of such an examiner or a person driving the vehicle in accordance with a requirement to do so under the regulations under which the examination is carried out, . . .

   (c) *[applies to Northern Ireland]* [and]

   [(d) in the case of a relevant re-examination—

        (i) the person to whom the appeal in question is made, or

        (ii) any person who, by virtue of an appointment made by that person, is authorised by or under any enactment to carry out that re-examination.]

(8) In this paragraph "*the relevant certificate*" means, as respects England and Wales and Scotland—

   (a) a test certificate (as defined in section 45(2) of the Road Traffic Act 1988), [or]

(b) a goods vehicle test certificate (as defined in section 49 of that Act), or

(c) a type approval certificate or Minister's approval certificate (as defined in sections 54 to 58 of that Act), [or]

[(d) a certificate issued by virtue of section 61B of this Act.]

(9) *[Applies to Northern Ireland.]*

(10) In this paragraph "*relevant work*" means—

(a) where the relevant certificate which is refused is a test certificate . . ., work done or to be done to remedy for a further compulsory test the defects on the ground of which the relevant certificate was refused, and

(b) in any other case, work done or to be done to remedy the defects on the ground of which the relevant certificate was refused (including work to alter the vehicle in some aspect of design, construction, equipment or marking on account of which the relevant certificate was refused).

[Paragraph 22 of Schedule 2 is printed as amended by the Finance Act 1996, ss.20 and 21(1), (5) and   **A34.209** *(6) (see also ibid., s.205 and Sched. 41, Pt II(4)); the Finance Act 1998, s.16 and Sched. 1, paras 1 and 16.*

Paragraph 22(7)(d) is expressed to take effect subject to section 21(3) of the Finance Act 1996, which substituted the text of paragraph 22(7)(c) (not reproduced in this work). As to the effective date of the repeal of the words in paragraph 22(10)(a) (which related to Northern Ireland), see the Finance Act 1996, s.21(6).]

Vehicles for export

23.—(1) A vehicle is an exempt vehicle if—   **A34.210**

(a) it has been supplied to the person keeping it by a taxable person within the meaning of section [3 of the Value Added Tax Act 1994], and

(b) the supply has been zero-rated under subsection [(8) of section 30] of that Act.

(2) If at any time the value added tax that would have been chargeable on the supply but for the zero-rating becomes payable under [subsection (10)] of that section (or would have become payable but for any authorisation or waiver under that subsection), the vehicle is deemed never to have been an exempt vehicle under sub-paragraph (1).

[Paragraph 23 is printed as amended by the Value Added Tax Act 1994, s.100(1) and Sched. 14,   **A34.211** *para.14.*

The term "taxable person" (in paragraph 23(1)(a) above) is defined in the Value Added Tax Act 1994, s.3, as a person who is (or who is required to be) registered under the 1994 Act. Exempt supplies for value added tax purposes are listed in Schedule 9 to the 1994 Act.]

Vehicles imported by members of foreign armed forces, etc.

24. The Secretary of State may by regulations provide that, in such cases, subject to   **A34.212** such conditions and for such period as may be prescribed by the regulations, a vehicle is an exempt vehicle if it has been imported by—

(a) a person for the time being appointed to serve with any body, contingent or detachment of the forces of any country prescribed by the regulations which is for the time being present in the United Kingdom on the invitation of Her Majesty's Government in the United Kingdom,

(b) a member of any country's military forces, except Her Majesty's United Kingdom forces, who is for the time being appointed to serve in the United Kingdom under the orders of any organisation so prescribed,

(c) a person for the time being recognised by the Secretary of State as a member of a civilian component of a force within sub-paragraph (a) or as a civilian member of an organisation within sub-paragraph (b), or

(d) any dependant of a description so prescribed of a person within sub-paragraph (a), (b) or (c).

A34.213   *[The Road Vehicles (Exemptions from Duty) Regulations 1986 (S.I. 1986 No. 1467) (q.v.) have effect as if made under paragraph 24.]*

[SCHEDULE 2A

IMMOBILISATION, REMOVAL AND DISPOSAL OF VEHICLES

Immobilisation

A34.214   1.—(1) The Secretary of State may make regulations under this Schedule with respect to any case where an authorised person has reason to believe that, on or after such date as may be prescribed, an offence under section 29(1) is being committed as regards a vehicle which is stationary on a public road.

(2) The regulations may provide that the authorised person or a person acting under his direction may—

(a) fix an immobilisation device to the vehicle while it remains in the place where it is stationary, or

(b) move it from that place to another place on the same or another public road and fix an immobilisation device to it in that other place.

(3) The regulations may provide that on any occasion when an immobilisation device is fixed to a vehicle in accordance with the regulations the person fixing the device shall also fix to the vehicle a notice—

(a) indicating that the device has been fixed to the vehicle and warning that no attempt should be made to drive it or otherwise put it in motion until it has been released from the device;

(b) specifying the steps to be taken to secure its release;

(c) giving such other information as may be prescribed.

(4) The regulations may provide that—

(a) a vehicle to which an immobilisation device has been fixed in accordance with the regulations may only be released from the device by or under the direction of an authorised person;

(b) subject to that, such a vehicle shall be released from the device if the first and second requirements specified below are met.

(5) The first requirement is that such charge in respect of the release as may be prescribed is paid in any manner specified in the immobilisation notice.

(6) The second requirement is that—

(a) a vehicle licence is produced in accordance with instructions specified in the immobilisation notice, and the licence is one which is in force for the vehicle concerned at the time the licence is produced, or

(b) where such a licence is not produced, such sum as may be prescribed is paid in any manner specified in the immobilisation notice.

(7) The regulations may provide that they shall not apply in relation to a vehicle if—

(a) a current disabled person's badge is displayed on the vehicle, or

(b) such other conditions as may be prescribed are fulfilled;

and *"disabled person's badge"* here means a badge issued, or having effect as if issued, under any regulations for the time being in force under section 21 of the Chronically Sick and Disabled Persons Act 1970 [*q.v.*] or any regulations for the time being in force under section 14 of the Chronically Sick and Disabled Persons (Northern Ireland) Act 1978 [*1978 c. 53*].

(8) The regulations may provide that an immobilisation notice shall not be removed or interfered with except by or on the authority of a person falling within a prescribed description.

[Schedule 2A was inserted by the Finance Act 1995, s.19 and Sched. 4, para.36(2).]   **A34.215**

Offences connected with immobilisation

2.—(1) The regulations may provide that a person contravening provision made under   **A34.216**
paragraph 1(8) is guilty of an offence and liable on summary conviction to a fine not exceeding level 2 on the standard scale.

(2) The regulations may provide that a person who, without being authorised to do so in accordance with provision made under paragraph 1, removes or attempts to remove an immobilisation device fixed to a vehicle in accordance with the regulations is guilty of an offence and liable on summary conviction to a fine not exceeding level 3 on the standard scale.

(3) The regulations may provide that where they would apply in relation to a vehicle but for provision made under paragraph 1(7)(a) and the vehicle was not, at the time it was stationary, being used—

(a) in accordance with regulations under section 21 of the Chronically Sick and Disabled Persons Act 1970 or regulations under section 14 of the Chronically Sick and Disabled Persons (Northern Ireland) Act 1978, and

(b) in circumstances falling within section 117(1)(b) of the Road Traffic Regulation Act 1984 [*q.v.*] or Article 174A(2)(b) of the Road Traffic (Northern Ireland) Order 1981 [*S.I. 1981 No. 154 (N.I. 1)*] (use where a disabled person's concession would be available),

the person in charge of the vehicle at that time is guilty of an offence and liable on summary conviction to a fine not exceeding level 3 on the standard scale.

(4) The regulations may provide that where—

(a) a person makes a declaration with a view to securing the release of a vehicle from an immobilisation device purported to have been fixed in accordance with the regulations,

(b) the declaration is that the vehicle is or was an exempt vehicle, and

(c) the declaration is to the person's knowledge either false or in any material respect misleading,

he is guilty of an offence.

(5) The regulations may provide that a person guilty of an offence by virtue of provision made under sub-paragraph (4) is liable—

(a) on summary conviction, to a fine not exceeding the statutory maximum, and

(b) on conviction on indictment, to imprisonment for a term not exceeding two years or to a fine or (except in Scotland) to both.

[Paragraph 2 of Schedule 2A; see the note to paragraph 1 above.]   **A34.217**

Removal and disposal of vehicles

A34.218   **3.**—[(1) The regulations may make provision with respect to any case where—

(a) an authorised person has reason to believe that an offence under section 29(1)—

    (i) is being committed as regards a vehicle which is stationary on a public road; or

    (ii) was being committed as regards a vehicle at a time when an immobilisation device which is fixed to the vehicle was fixed to it in accordance with the regulations;

and

(b) such conditions as may be prescribed are fulfilled.]

(2) The regulations may provide that [the authorised person, or a person acting under his direction], may remove the vehicle and deliver it into the custody of a person—

(a) who is identified in accordance with prescribed rules, and

(b) who agrees to accept delivery in accordance with arrangements agreed between that person and the Secretary of State;

and the arrangements may include provision as to the payment of a sum to the person into whose custody the vehicle is delivered.

(3) The regulations may provide that the person into whose custody the vehicle is delivered may dispose of it, and in particular provision may be made as to—

(a) the time at which the vehicle may be disposed of;

(b) the manner in which it may be disposed of.

(4) The regulations may make provision allowing a person to take possession of the vehicle if—

(a) he claims it before it is disposed of, and

(b) any prescribed conditions are fulfilled.

(5) The regulations may provide for a sum of an amount arrived at under prescribed rules to be paid to a person if—

(a) he claims after the vehicle's disposal to be or to have been its owner,

(b) the claim is made within a prescribed time of the disposal, and

(c) any other prescribed conditions are fulfilled.

(6) The regulations may provide that—

(a) the Secretary of State, or

(b) a person into whose custody the vehicle is delivered under the regulations,

may recover from the vehicle's owner (whether or not a claim is made under provision made under sub-paragraph (4) or (5)) such charges as may be prescribed in respect of all or any of the following, namely, its release, removal, custody and disposal; and "*owner*" here means the person who was the owner [when the vehicle was removed].

(7) The conditions prescribed under sub-paragraph (4) may include conditions as to—

(a) satisfying the person with custody that the claimant is the vehicle's owner;

(b) the payment of prescribed charges in respect of the vehicle's release, removal and custody;

(c) the production of a vehicle licence;

(d) payment of a prescribed sum where a vehicle licence is not produced.

(8) Without prejudice to anything in the preceding provisions of this paragraph, the regulations may include provision for purposes corresponding to those of sections 101 and 102 of the Road Traffic Regulation Act 1984 (disposal and charges) subject to such additions, omissions or other modifications as the Secretary of State thinks fit.

[Paragraph 3 of Schedule 2A was inserted (as were the other paragraphs in the Schedule) by the Finance Act 1995, s.19 and Sched. 4, para.36(2); the Finance Act 1997, s.20.]   **A34.219**

Offences as to securing possession of vehicles

4.—(1) The regulations may provide that where—   **A34.220**

(a) a person makes a declaration with a view to securing possession of a vehicle purported to have been delivered into the custody of a person in accordance with provision made under paragraph 3,

(b) the declaration is that the vehicle is or was an exempt vehicle, and

(c) the declaration is to the person's knowledge either false or in any material respect misleading,

he is guilty of an offence.

(2) The regulations may provide that a person guilty of such an offence is liable—

(a) on summary conviction, to a fine not exceeding the statutory maximum, and

(b) on conviction on indictment, to imprisonment for a term not exceeding two years or to a fine or (except in Scotland) to both.

[Paragraph 4 of Schedule 2A; see the note to paragraph 1 above.]   **A34.221**

Payment of sum where licence not produced

5.—(1) The regulations may make provision as regards a case where a person pays a   **A34.222**
prescribed sum in pursuance of provision made under—

(a) paragraph 1(6)(b), or

(b) paragraph 3(7)(d).

(2) The regulations may—

(a) provide for a voucher to be issued in respect of the sum;

(b) provide for setting the sum against the amount of any vehicle excise duty payable in respect of the vehicle concerned;

(c) provide for the refund of any sum;

(d) provide that where a voucher has been issued section 29(1) and any other prescribed provision of this Act shall not apply, as regards the vehicle concerned, in relation to events occurring in a prescribed period.

(3) The regulations may make provision—

(a) as to the information to be provided before a voucher is issued;

(b) as to the contents of vouchers;

(c) specifying conditions subject to which any provision under sub-paragraph (2)(b) to (d) is to have effect.

(4) The regulations may make provision as to any case where a voucher is issued on receipt of a cheque which is subsequently dishonoured, and in particular the regulations may—

(a) provide for a voucher to be void;

(b) provide that, where the sum concerned is set against the amount of any vehicle excise duty, the licence concerned shall be void;

(c) make provision under which a person is required to deliver up a void voucher or void licence.

A34.223 *[Paragraph 5 of Schedule 2A; see the note to paragraph 1 above.]*

Offences relating to vouchers

A34.224   **6.**—(1) The regulations may provide that—

   (a) a person is guilty of an offence if within such reasonable period as is found in accordance with prescribed rules he fails to deliver up a voucher that is void by virtue of provision made under paragraph 5(4);

   (b) a person guilty of such an offence shall be liable on summary conviction to a fine not exceeding level 3 on the standard scale.

(2) The regulations may provide that a person is guilty of an offence if within such reasonable period as is found in accordance with prescribed rules he fails to deliver up a licence that is void by virtue of provision made under paragraph 5(4), and that a person guilty of such an offence shall be liable on summary conviction to a penalty of whichever is the greater of—

   (a) level 3 on the standard scale;

   (b) an amount equal to five times the annual rate of duty that was payable on the grant of the licence or would have been so payable if it had been taken out for a period of twelve months.

(3) The regulations may provide that where a person is convicted of an offence under provision made by virtue of sub-paragraph (2) he must pay, in addition to any penalty, an amount found in accordance with prescribed rules.

(4) The regulations may provide that if—

   (a) a voucher is void by virtue of provision made under paragraph 5(4),

   (b) a person seeks to set the sum concerned against the amount of any vehicle excise duty, and

   (c) he knows the voucher is void,

he is guilty of an offence and liable on summary conviction to a fine not exceeding level 5 on the standard scale.

(5) The regulations may provide that a person who in connection with—

   (a) obtaining a voucher for which provision is made under paragraph 5, or

   (b) obtaining a refund of any sum in respect of which such a voucher is issued,

makes a declaration which to his knowledge is either false or in any material respect misleading is guilty of an offence.

(6) The regulations may provide that a person is guilty of an offence if he forges, fraudulently alters, fraudulently uses, fraudulently lends or fraudulently allows to be used by another person a voucher for which provision is made under paragraph 5.

(7) The regulations may provide that a person guilty of an offence under provision made under sub-paragraph (5) or (6) is liable—

   (a) on summary conviction, to a fine not exceeding the statutory maximum, and

   (b) on conviction on indictment, to imprisonment for a term not exceeding two years or to a fine or (except in Scotland) to both.

A34.225 *[Paragraph 6 of Schedule 2A; see the note to paragraph 1 above.]*

Vouchers: general

7. Without prejudice to anything in paragraphs 5(4) and 6 the regulations may include provision for purposes corresponding to those of sections 19A and 36 subject to such additions, omissions or other modifications as the Secretary of State thinks fit.   **A34.226**

[Paragraph 7 of Schedule 2A; see the note to paragraph 1 above.]   **A34.227**

Disputes

8. The regulations may make provision about the proceedings to be followed where a dispute occurs as a result of the regulations, and in particular provision may be made—   **A34.228**

    (a) for an application to be made to a magistrates' court . . .;

    (b) for a court to order a sum to be paid by the Secretary of State.

[Paragraph 8 of Schedule 2A; see the note to paragraph 1 above.   **A34.229**
The words omitted from paragraph 8(a) relate exclusively to Northern Ireland.]

Authorised persons

9. As regards anything falling to be done under the regulations (such as receiving payment of a charge or other sum or issuing a voucher) the regulations may provide that it may be done—   **A34.230**

    (a) by an authorised person, or

    (b) by an authorised person or a person acting under his direction.

[Paragraph 9 of Schedule 2A; see the note to paragraph 1 above.]   **A34.231**

Application of provisions

10.—(1) The regulations may provide that they shall only apply where the authorised person has reason to believe that the offence mentioned in paragraph 1(1) is being committed before such date as may be prescribed.   **A34.232**

(2) The regulations may provide that they shall only apply where the vehicle mentioned in paragraph 1(1) is in a prescribed area.

(3) Different dates may be prescribed under paragraph 1(1) or sub-paragraph (1) above in relation to different areas prescribed under sub-paragraph (2) above.

[Paragraph 10 of Schedule 2A; see the note to paragraph 1 above.]   **A34.233**

Interpretation

11.—(1) The regulations may make provision as to the meaning for the purposes of the regulations of *"owner"* as regards a vehicle.   **A34.234**

(2) In particular, the regulations may provide that for the purposes of the regulations—

    (a) the owner of a vehicle at a particular time shall be taken to be the person by whom it is then kept;

    (b) the person by whom a vehicle is kept at a particular time shall be taken to be the person in whose name it is then registered by virtue of this Act.

[Paragraph 11 of Schedule 2A; see the note to paragraph 1 above.]   **A34.235**

12.—(1) The regulations may make provision as to the meaning in the regulations of *"authorised person"*.   **A34.236**

(2) In particular, the regulations may provide that—

(a) references to an authorised person are to a person authorised by the Secretary of State for the purposes of the regulations;

(b) an authorised person may be a local authority or an employee of a local authority or a member of a police force or some other person;

(c) different persons may be authorised for the purposes of different provisions of the regulations.

A34.237   *[Paragraph 12 of Schedule 2A; see the note to paragraph 1 above.]*

13. In this Schedule—

(a) references to an immobilisation device are to a device or appliance which is an immobilisation device for the purposes of section 104 of the Road Traffic Regulation Act 1984 *[q.v.]* (immobilisation of vehicles illegally parked);

(b) references to an immobilisation notice are to a notice fixed to a vehicle in accordance with the regulations;

(c) *"prescribed"* means prescribed by regulations made under this Schedule.]

A34.238   *[Paragraph 13 of Schedule 2A; see the note to paragraph 1 above.*
The Vehicle Excise Duty (Immobilisation, Removal and Disposal of Vehicles) Regulations 1997 (S.I. 1997 No. 2439) below have been made in part under Schedule 2A.]

A34.239   Section 63   SCHEDULE 3

CONSEQUENTIAL AMENDMENTS

*   *   *

Section 64   SCHEDULE 4

TRANSITIONALS, ETC.

General transitionals and savings

A34.240   **1.** The substitution of this Act for the provisions repealed or revoked by this Act does not affect the continuity of the law.

2.—(1) Anything done, or having effect as done (including the making of subordinate legislation and the issuing of licences), under or for the purposes of any provision repealed or revoked by this Act has effect as if done under or for the purposes of any corresponding provision of this Act.

(2) Sub-paragraph (1) does not apply to the Vehicle Licences (Duration and Rate of Duty) Order 1980 *[S.I. 1980 No. 1183 (q.v.)]*.

A34.241   **3.** Any reference (express or implied) in this Act or any other enactment, or in any instrument or document, to a provision of this Act is (so far as the context permits) to be read as (according to the context) being or including in relation to times, circumstances and purposes before the commencement of this Act a reference to the corresponding provision repealed or revoked by this Act.

4. Any reference (express or implied) in any enactment, or in any instrument or document, to a provision repealed or revoked by this Act is (so far as the context permits) to be read as (according to the context) being or including in relation to times, circumstances and purposes after the commencement of this Act a reference to the corresponding provision of this Act.

5. Paragraphs 1 to 4 have effect in place of section 17(2) of the Interpretation Act 1978   **A34.242**
(but are without prejudice to any other provision of that Act).

Preservation of old transitionals and savings

6.—(1) The repeal by this Act of an enactment previously repealed subject to savings   **A34.243**
(whether or not in the repealing enactment) does not affect the continued operation of
those savings.

(2) The repeal by this Act of a saving made on the previous repeal of an enactment does
not affect the operation of the saving in so far as it remains capable of having effect.

(3) Where the purpose of an enactment repealed by this Act was to secure that the substitution of the provisions of the Act containing that enactment for provisions repealed by
that Act did not affect the continuity of the law, the enactment repealed by this Act continues to have effect in so far as it is capable of doing so.

Exemption for disabled passengers

7.—(1) Where—   **A34.244**
   (a) a vehicle is suitable for use by persons having a particular disability that so inca-
       pacitates them in the use of their limbs that they have to be driven and cared for
       by a full-time constant attendant,
   (b) the vehicle is registered under this Act in the name of a person who has such a dis-
       ability and is a person to whom this paragraph applies,
   (c) that person is sufficiently disabled to be eligible for an invalid tricycle under the
       National Health Service Act 1977, the National Health Service (Scotland) Act
       1978 or the Health and Personal Social Services (Northern Ireland) Order 1972
       [*S.I. 1972 No. 1265 (N.I. 14)*] but too disabled to drive it, and
   (d) no other vehicle registered in that person's name under this Act, or deemed to be
       so registered under sub-paragraph (3) of paragraph 19 of Schedule 2, is an exempt
       vehicle under that paragraph,

the vehicle is an exempt vehicle if used or kept for use by or for the purposes of that
person.

(2) This paragraph applies to a person if—
   (a) there remains valid a relevant certificate issued in respect of him before 13th
       October 1993 (the day on which the repeal of the provisions specified in section
       12(1) of the Finance (No. 2) Act 1992 came into force), or
   (b) an application for a relevant certificate in respect of him had been received by the
       Secretary of State or the Department of Health and Social Services for Northern
       Ireland before that date and a relevant certificate issued pursuant to that applic-
       ation remains valid.

(3) In this paragraph a *"relevant certificate"* means—
   (a) a certificate issued by the Secretary of State (or the Minister of Transport) con-
       taining a statement as described in Regulation 26(2)(b)(i) and (ii) of the Road
       Vehicles (Registration and Licensing) Regulations 1971 [*S.I. 1971 No. 450*] (as in
       force on 29th December 1972) or a statement to similar effect, or
   (b) a certificate issued by the Department of Health and Social Services for
       Northern Ireland (or the Ministry of Health and Social Services for Northern
       Ireland) containing a statement as described in Regulation 27(2)(b)(i) and (ii) of
       the Road Vehicles (Registration and Licensing) Regulations (Northern Ireland)

1973 [*S.R. & O. (N.I.) 1973 No. 490*] (as originally in force) or a statement to similar effect,

including (in either case) any renewal or continuation of such a certificate.

(4) For the purposes of sub-paragraph (2) a relevant certificate issued in respect of a person remains valid for as long as the matters stated in the certificate in relation to the person's disability remain unaltered.

(5) Where immediately before 13th October 1993 a person to whom this paragraph applies was under the age of five, the person ceases to be a person to whom this paragraph applies—

(a) if a relevant licence document is in force on the day on which he attains the age of five in respect of a vehicle used or kept for use for his purposes, when that licence document expires, and

(b) otherwise, on attaining the age of five.

(6) In sub-paragraph (5) "*relevant licence document*" means a document in the form of a licence issued under—

(a) Regulation 26(3A)(b) of the Road Vehicles (Registration and Licensing) Regulations 1971,

(b) Regulation 27(4)(b) of the Road Vehicles (Registration and Licensing) Regulations (Northern Ireland) 1973, or

(c) paragraph 4 or 6 of the Schedule to the Finance (No. 2) Act 1992 (Commencement No. 6 and Transitional Provisions and Savings) Order 1993 [*S.I. 1993 No. 2272 (q.v.)*],

or any re-enactment (with or without modifications) of any of those provisions.

(7) Regulations under section 22(2) of this Act which require a person to furnish information relating to a vehicle which is an exempt vehicle under this paragraph may require him to furnish (in addition) such evidence of the facts giving rise to the exemption as is prescribed by the regulations.

(8) In spite of the repeal by this Act of section 12(2) of the Finance (No. 2) Act 1992, paragraphs 4 to 8 of the Schedule to the Finance (No. 2) Act 1992 (Commencement No. 6 and Transitional Provisions and Savings) Order 1993 [*S.I. 1993 No. 2272 (q.v.)*] shall, until the coming into force of the first regulations made by virtue of sub-paragraph (7) (unless revoked and subject to any amendments), continue to have effect but subject to the modifications specified in sub-paragraph (9).

(9) The modifications referred to in sub-paragraph (8) are—

(a) the substitution of a reference to this paragraph for any reference to paragraph 2 of that Schedule,

(b) the addition of a reference to this Act after the first reference to the Vehicles (Excise) Act 1971 in paragraphs 4(4)(a) and 6(4)(a),

(c) the substitution of a reference to this Act for each other reference to the Vehicles (Excise) Act 1971, and

(d) the substitution of a reference to section 23 of this Act for any reference to section 19 of that Act and of a reference to subsection (3) of section 23 of this Act for any reference to subsection (2) of section 19 of that Act.

(10) Sections 44 and 45 of this Act have effect in relation to a vehicle which is an exempt vehicle under this paragraph as they have effect in relation to a vehicle which is an exempt vehicle under paragraph 19 of Schedule 2 to this Act.

(11) If and to the extent that, immediately before the coming into force of this Act, the Secretary of State had power to amend or revoke by order any provision of the Finance (No. 2) Act 1992 (Commencement No. 6 and Transitional Provisions and Savings) Order 1993, he has the same power in relation to so much of this paragraph as reproduces that provision.

[The reference in paragraph 7(3)(a) to the "Minister of Transport" is presumed to be of historical nature and is not directly affected by the Secretary of State for the Environment, Transport and the Regions Order 1997 (S.I. 1997 No. 2971).]   **A34.245**

Trade licences

8. *[Power to substitute by order different text for that of section 13.]*   **A34.246**

Combined road-rail transport of goods

9. Section 20 (and the references to it in sections 45(1)(b) and 57(5)) shall not come into force until such day as the Secretary of State may by order appoint.   **A34.247**

Regulations about registration and licensing

10. Regulation 12(1) of the Road Vehicles (Registration and Licensing) Regulations 1971 [*q.v.*] continues to have effect (until revoked) as if the amendments of section 23 of the Vehicles (Excise) Act 1971, as set out in paragraph 20 of Schedule 7 to that Act, which were made by paragraph 16(3) of Part III of Schedule 1 to the Finance Act 1987 had been in force when those Regulations were made.   **A34.248**

[The Finance Act 1987, Sched. 1, Pt III, para.16, has been repealed by section 65 of and Schedule 5, Part I, to this Act.]   **A34.249**

Assignment of registration marks

11. The inclusion in this Act of subsection (2), and the words "for the time being" in subsection (3), of section 23 (which reproduce the amendments of the Vehicles (Excise) Act 1971 made by section 10(2) and (3) of the Finance Act 1989) shall not be construed as affecting the operation of—   **A34.250**

(a) the Vehicles (Excise) Act 1971 or the Vehicles (Excise) Act (Northern Ireland) 1972, or

(b) any regulations made under either of those acts,

in relation to any time before 27th July 1989 (the day on which the Finance Act 1989 was passed).

SCHEDULE 5   Section 65 **A34.251**

REPEALS AND REVOCATIONS

*   *   *

The Road Traffic (New Drivers) Act 1995

(1995 c. 13)

A35.01 An Act to make provision about newly qualified drivers who commit certain offences, including provision with respect to tests of competence to drive.

[28th June 1995]

ARRANGEMENT OF SECTIONS

Introductory

Introductory

1. Probationary period for newly qualified drivers

(1) For the purposes of this Act, a person's probationary period is, subject to section **A35.03**
7, the period of two years beginning with the day on which he becomes a qualified
driver.

(2) For the purposes of this Act, a person becomes a qualified driver on the first occasion
on which he passes—

(a) any test of competence to drive mentioned in paragraph (a) or (c) of section 89(1)
of the Road Traffic Act 1988 [*q.v.*];

(b) any test of competence to drive conducted under the law of—

[(i) another EEA State,
(ii) the Isle of Man,
(iii) any of the Channel Islands, or
(iv) Gibraltar.]

(3) In subsection (2) "*EEA State*" means a State which is a contracting party to the EEA
Agreement but until the EEA Agreement comes into force in relation to Liechtenstein does
not include the State of Liechtenstein.

(4) In subsection (3) "*EEA Agreement*" means the Agreement on the European Economic
Area signed at Oporto on 2nd May 1992 as adjusted by the Protocol signed at Brussels on
17th March 1993.

[Section 1 is printed as amended by the Driving Licences (Community Driving Licence) Regulations **A35.04**
1996 (S.I. 1996 No. 1974), reg.5 and Sched. 4, para.5(1) and (2), read together with ibid., reg.1(2).
As to the EEA Agreement, the protocol of March 17, 1993 and the date on which the EEA Agreement
took effect in Liechtenstein, see the note to Regulation (EEC) 3820/85 below.]

2. Surrender of licences

(1) Subsection (2) applies where—   **A35.05**

(a) a person is the holder of a licence;

(b) he is convicted of an offence involving obligatory endorsement;

(c) the penalty points to be taken into account under section 29 of the Road Traffic
Offenders Act 1988 [*q.v.*] on that occasion number six or more;

(d) the court makes an order falling within section 44(1)(b) of that Act in respect of the
offence;

(e) the person's licence shows the date on which he became a qualified driver, or that
date has been shown by other evidence in the proceedings; and

(f) it appears to the court, in the light of the order and the date so shown, that the
offence was committed during the person's probationary period.

(2) Where this subsection applies, the court must send to the Secretary of State—

(a) a notice containing the particulars required to be endorsed on the counterpart of
the person's licence in accordance with the order referred to in subsection (1)(d);
and

(b) on their production to the court, the person's licence and its counterpart.

(3) Subsection (4) applies where—

(a) a person's licence and its counterpart have been sent to the fixed penalty clerk
under section 54(7) of the Road Traffic Offenders Act 1988 or delivered to the

fixed penalty clerk in response to a conditional offer issued under section 75 of that Act;

(b)   the offence to which the fixed penalty notice or the conditional offer relates is one involving obligatory endorsement;

(c)   the fixed penalty clerk endorses the number of penalty points to be attributed to the offence on the counterpart of the licence;

(d)   the penalty points to be taken into account by the fixed penalty clerk in respect of the offence number six or more;

(e)   the licence shows the date on which the person became a qualified driver; and

(f)   it appears to the fixed penalty clerk, in the light of the particulars of the offence endorsed on the counterpart of the licence and the date so shown, that the offence was committed during the person's probationary period.

(4) Where this subsection applies, the fixed penalty clerk—

(a)   may not return the licence and its counterpart under section 57(3) or (4) or 77(1) of the Road Traffic Offenders Act 1988; but

(b)   must send them to the Secretary of State.

(5) For the purposes of subsection (3)(d) the penalty points to be taken into account by the fixed penalty clerk in respect of the offence are the penalty points which would have been taken into account under section 29 of the Road Traffic Offenders Act 1988 if—

(a)   the person in question had been convicted of the offence; and

(b)   the number of penalty points to be attributed to the offence on that occasion had been determined in accordance with section 28(3) of that Act.

3. Revocation of licences

A35.06   (1) Where the Secretary of State receives—

(a)   a notice sent to him under section 2(2)(a) of particulars required to be endorsed on the counterpart of a person's licence, or

(b)   a person's licence and its counterpart sent to him in accordance with section 2(2)(b) or (4),

the Secretary of State must by notice served on that person revoke the licence.

(2) A revocation under subsection (1) shall have effect from a date specified in the notice of revocation which may not be earlier than the date of service of that notice.

4. Re-testing

A35.07   (1) Subject to subsection (5) and section 5, the Secretary of State may not under Part III of the Road Traffic Act 1988 grant a person whose licence has been revoked under section 3(1) a full licence to drive any class of vehicles in relation to which the revoked licence was issued as a full licence unless he satisfies the Secretary of State that within the relevant period he has passed a relevant driving test.

(2) In this section *"relevant driving test"* means, in relation to a person whose licence has been revoked, any test which—

(a)   falls within paragraph (a) or (b) of section 1(2); and

(b)   is a test of competence to drive any vehicle included in any class of vehicles in relation to which the revoked licence was issued as a full licence.

(3) If the Secretary of State grants a full licence to a person who is required to pass a relevant driving test in order to be granted that licence, the licence granted must (subject to

section 92 and Part IV of the Road Traffic Act 1988) be one authorising that person to drive all the classes of vehicles in relation to which the revoked licence was issued as a full licence.

(4) In subsection (1) "*the relevant period*" means the period beginning—

(a) after the date of the revocation of the licence; and

(b) not more than two years before the date on which the application for the full licence is made.

(5) Subsection (1) does not apply to a person whose licence has been revoked under section 3(1) if, before he passes a relevant driving test, an order is made in relation to him under section 36 of the Road Traffic Offenders Act 1988 (disqualification until test is passed).

5. Restoration of licence without re-testing in certain cases

(1) If the Secretary of State receives notice that a person whose licence has been revoked under section 3(1) is appealing against a conviction or endorsement which was the basis or formed part of the basis for the revocation, he must grant that person free of charge a full licence for a period prescribed by regulations.   **A35.08**

(2) Regulations under subsection (1) may in particular prescribe—

(a) a period expiring when the appeal is finally determined or abandoned; or

(b) a period expiring on the date on which the revoked licence would have expired if it had not been revoked.

(3) If the regulations prescribe a period other than that mentioned in subsection (2)(a), a licence granted under subsection (1) shall be treated as revoked if—

(a) following the appeal, the penalty points taken into account for the purposes of section 2 are not reduced to a number smaller than six; or

(b) the appeal is abandoned.

(4) If, in the case of a person whose licence has been revoked under section 3(1), the Secretary of State receives notice that a court—

(a) has quashed a conviction which was the basis or formed part of the basis for the revocation of the licence,

(b) has quashed an endorsement which was the basis or formed part of the basis for the revocation of the licence and has not on doing so ordered him to be disqualified, or

(c) has made an order which has the effect of reducing the penalty points taken into account for the purposes of section 2 to a number smaller than six,

then, subject to subsection (5), the Secretary of State must grant that person free of charge a full licence for a period expiring on the date on which the revoked licence would have expired if it had not been revoked.

(5) Subsection (4) does not require the Secretary of State to grant a licence to a person who has been granted a previous licence which has not been surrendered unless that person provides the Secretary of State with an explanation for not surrendering the previous licence that the Secretary of State considers adequate.

(6) If, in accordance with subsection (1) or (4), the Secretary of State grants a full licence to a person whose licence has been revoked under section 3(1), the licence granted must be one authorising that person to drive all the classes of vehicles in relation to which the revoked licence was issued as a full licence.

(7) Any licence granted in accordance with subsection (1) or (4) shall have effect for the

purposes of the Road Traffic Acts as if it were a licence granted under Part III of the Road Traffic Act 1988.

(8) Regulations may make provision for requiring such courts as may be prescribed to give notice to the Secretary of State—

(a) that a person whose licence has been or is due to be revoked under section 3(1) is appealing against a conviction or endorsement which is the basis or forms part of the basis for the revocation;

(b) that such an appeal has been abandoned.

(9) Regulations under this section may—

(a) include such incidental or supplementary provision as appears to the Secretary of State to be expedient;

(b) make different provision for different cases.

(10) Any regulations made under this section shall be made by the Secretary of State by statutory instrument which shall be subject to annulment in pursuance of a resolution of either House of Parliament.

A35.09   *[The New Drivers (Appeals Procedure) Regulations 1997 (S.I. 1997 No. 1098) below have been made in part under this section.]*

Miscellaneous and general

6. Newly qualified drivers holding test certificates

A35.10   Schedule 1 (which makes provision about newly qualified drivers who hold test certificates) shall have effect.

7. Early termination of probationary period

A35.11   For the purposes of this Act a person's probationary period comes to an end if—

(a) an order is made in relation to him under section 36 of the Road Traffic Offenders Act 1988 (order that a person be disqualified until he passes the appropriate driving test);

(b) after his licence is revoked under section 3(1), he is granted a full licence following the passing of a test which is a relevant driving test for the purposes of section 4; or

(c) after his test certificate is revoked under paragraph 5(1) of Schedule 1, or his licence and test certificate are revoked under paragraph 8(1) of that Schedule, he is granted a full licence following the passing of a test which is a relevant driving test for the purposes of paragraph 6 or 9 of that Schedule.

8. The Crown

A35.12   This Act applies to persons in the public service of the Crown.

9. Interpretation, etc.

A35.13   (1) Expressions used in this Act which are also used in Part III of the Road Traffic Act 1988 [*q.v.*] shall be construed in the same way as in that Act.

(2) Expressions used in this Act which are also used in the Road Traffic Offenders Act 1988 [*q.v.*] shall be construed in the same way as in that Act.

(3) In this Act "*notice*" means notice in writing.

(4) Section 107 of the Road Traffic Act 1988 (service of notices) applies to a notice

served under section 3 or paragraph 5 or 8 of Schedule 1 [as it applies to a notice served under Part III or IV of that Act].

(5) Any requirement under any provision of this Act that a licence and its counterpart, a test certificate or a notice must be sent to the Secretary of State is a requirement that the licence and its counterpart, the test certificate or the notice must be sent to the Secretary of State at such address as the Secretary of State may determine.

[Section 9 is printed as amended by the Driving Licences (Community Driving Licence) Regulations   **A35.14**
1996 (S.I. 1996 No. 1974), reg.5 and Sched. 4, para.5(1) and (3), read together with ibid., reg.1(2).]

10. Short title, commencement, extent, etc.

(1) This Act may be cited as the Road Traffic (New Drivers) Act 1995.   **A35.15**

(2) The provisions of this Act shall come into force on such day as the Secretary of State may by order made by statutory instrument appoint and different days may be so appointed for different provisions.

(3) Nothing in any provision of this Act applies to a person who becomes a qualified driver before the day on which the provision comes into force.

(4) The consequential amendments set out in Schedule 2 shall have effect.

(5) This Act does not extend to Northern Ireland.

[This Act was brought into force (in the main) on June 1, 1997 by the Road Traffic (New Drivers) Act   **A35.16**
1995 (Commencement) Order 1997 (S.I. 1997 No. 267; not reproduced in this work).]

SCHEDULES

SCHEDULE 1   Section 6
Newly Qualified Drivers Holding Test Certificates

PART I
General

Interpretation

1.—(1) In this Schedule "*test certificate*" means a certificate or other document which by   **A35.17**
virtue of regulations under section 89 of the Road Traffic Act 1988 is evidence that a person has not more than two years previously passed a test of competence to drive prescribed by virtue of such regulations.

(2) In this Schedule "*prescribed conditions*" means the prescribed conditions referred to in section 97(3) of the 1988 Act (subject to which provisional licences are granted).

Application of Schedule

2.—(1) Part II of this Schedule applies to any person to whom Part III or IV of this   **A35.18**
Schedule applies.

(2) Part III of this Schedule applies to a person who holds—

(a) a licence issued as a provisional licence; and

(b) a test certificate.

(3) Part IV of this Schedule applies to a person who falls within sub-paragraph (4) or (5).

(4) A person falls within this sub-paragraph if—

(a) he holds a licence issued as a full licence in relation to a class or certain classes of vehicles;

(b) he is treated under section 98(2) of the Road Traffic Act 1988 as authorised by a provisional licence to drive another class or other classes of vehicles; and

(c) he holds a test certificate which relates to that other class of vehicles or any of those other classes of vehicles.

(5) A person falls within this sub-paragraph if he holds—

(a) a licence issued as a full licence in relation to a class or certain classes of vehicles and has a provisional licence in relation to another class or other classes of vehicles; and

(b) a test certificate which relates to that other class of vehicles or any of those other classes of vehicles.

PART II

DUTY TO PROVIDE TEST CERTIFICATE

A35.19   **3.**—(1) Sub-paragraph (2) applies where—

(a) a person to whom this Part of this Schedule applies is prosecuted for an offence involving obligatory endorsement; and

(b) the time at which the offence for which he is prosecuted is alleged to have occurred is a time during his probationary period.

(2) Any obligations imposed on the person under section 7 of the Road Traffic Offenders Act 1988 as respects his licence and its counterpart shall also apply as respects his test certificate.

(3) If, in a case where sub-paragraph (2) applies—

(a) the person is convicted in the proceedings in question of an offence involving obligatory endorsement, and

(b) he has not previously caused his test certificate to be delivered or posted it to the [proper officer] of the court,

he must produce his test certificate to the court.

[(3A) In sub-paragraph (3) *"proper officer"* means—

(a) in relation to a magistrates' court in England and Wales, the justices' chief executive for the court, and

(b) in relation to any other court, the clerk of the court.]

(4) In a case where—

(a) the licence of a person to whom this Part of this Schedule applies has (with its counterpart) been sent to the fixed penalty clerk under section 54(7) of the Road Traffic Offenders Act 1988 or delivered to the fixed penalty clerk in response to a conditional offer issued under section 75 of that Act,

(b) the offence to which the fixed penalty notice or the conditional offer relates is one involving obligatory endorsement and occurring during his probationary period, and

(c) the person proposes to pay the fixed penalty to the fixed penalty clerk,

the person must ensure that when the fixed penalty is paid his test certificate is sent to the fixed penalty clerk to whom the payment is made.

(5) A person who without reasonable excuse fails to comply with sub-paragraph (3) or (4) is guilty of an offence and shall be liable on summary conviction to a fine not exceeding level 3 on the standard scale.

[Paragraph 3 of Schedule 1 is printed as amended (with effect from April 1, 2001) by the Access to Justice Act 1999, s.90(1) and Sched. 13, para.173 (see the Access to Justice Act 1999 (Commencement No. 7, Transitional Provisions and Savings) Order 2001 (S.I. 2001 No. 916; not reproduced in this work), arts 1(2) and 2(a)(ii)).]   **A35.20**

PART III

NEWLY QUALIFIED DRIVER WITH PROVISIONAL LICENCE AND TEST CERTIFICATE

Surrender of test certificate

4.—(1) Where the circumstances mentioned in section 2(1) exist with respect to a person to whom this Part of this Schedule applies, sub-paragraph (2) applies instead of section 2(2).   **A35.21**

(2) The court must send to the Secretary of State—

(a) a notice containing the particulars required to be endorsed on the counterpart of the person's licence in accordance with the order referred to in section 2(1)(d); and

(b) on its production to the court, the person's test certificate.

(3) Where—

(a) the circumstances mentioned in section 2(3)(a) to (d) and (f) exist with respect to a person to whom this Part of this Schedule applies,

(b) the fixed penalty clerk has received the person's test certificate in accordance with paragraph 3(4), and

(c) the test certificate shows the date on which the person became a qualified driver,

sub-paragraph (4) applies instead of section 2(4).

(4) The fixed penalty clerk must send to the Secretary of State—

(a) a notice containing the particulars endorsed on the counterpart of the person's licence; and

(b) the person's test certificate.

Revocation of test certificate

5.—(1) Where the Secretary of State—   **A35.22**

(a) has received a notice sent to him under paragraph 4 of particulars required to be endorsed or endorsed on the counterpart of a person's licence, and

(b) has received the person's test certificate sent to him under paragraph 4(2)(b) or (4)(b) or is satisfied that the person has been issued with a test certificate,

the Secretary of State must by notice served on that person revoke the test certificate.

(2) A revocation under sub-paragraph (1) shall have effect from a date specified in the notice of revocation which may not be earlier than the date of service of that notice.

(3) The effect of the revocation of a person's test certificate is that any prescribed conditions to which his provisional licence ceased to be subject when he became a qualified driver shall again apply.

Re-testing

6.—(1) Subject to Part V of this Schedule, the Secretary of State may not under Part III of the Road Traffic Act 1988 grant a person whose test certificate has been revoked   **A35.23**

under paragraph 5(1) a full licence to drive any class of vehicles that, immediately before his test certificate was revoked, he was permitted to drive without observing prescribed conditions, unless he satisfies the Secretary of State that within the relevant period he has passed a relevant driving test.

(2) In this paragraph "*relevant driving test*" means, in relation to a person whose test certificate has been revoked, any test which—

(a) falls within paragraph (a) or (b) of section 1(2); and

(b) is a test of competence to drive any vehicle included in any class of vehicles that, immediately before his test certificate was revoked, he was permitted to drive without observing prescribed conditions.

(3) If the Secretary of State grants a full licence to a person who is required to pass a relevant driving test in order to be granted that licence, the licence granted must (subject to section 92 and Part IV of the Road Traffic Act 1988) be one authorising that person to drive all the classes of vehicles that, immediately before his test certificate was revoked, he was permitted to drive without observing prescribed conditions.

(4) In sub-paragraph (1) "*the relevant period*" means the period beginning—

(a) after the date of the revocation of the test certificate; and

(b) not more than two years before the date on which the application for the full licence is made.

PART IV

NEWLY QUALIFIED DRIVER WITH FULL AND PROVISIONAL ENTITLEMENTS AND TEST CERTIFICATE

Surrender of licence and test certificate

A35.24   **7.**—(1) Where the circumstances mentioned in section 2(1) exist with respect to a person to whom this Part of this Schedule applies, sub-paragraph (2) applies instead of section 2(2).

(2) The court must send to the Secretary of State—

(a) a notice containing the particulars required to be endorsed on the counterpart of the person's licence in accordance with the order referred to in section 2(1)(d);

(b) on their production to the court, the person's licence and its counterpart; and

(c) on its production to the court, the person's test certificate.

(3) Where—

(a) the circumstances mentioned in section 2(3) exist with respect to a person to whom this Part of this Schedule applies, and

(b) the fixed penalty clerk has received the person's test certificate in accordance with paragraph 3(4),

sub-paragraph (4) applies instead of section 2(4).

(4) The fixed penalty clerk—

(a) may not return the person's licence and its counterpart under section 57(3) or (4) or 77(1) of the Road Traffic Offenders Act 1988; but

(b) must send them and the person's test certificate to the Secretary of State.

Revocation of licence and test certificate

A35.25   **8.**—(1) Where the Secretary of State—

(a) has received a notice sent to him under paragraph 7(2)(a) of particulars required to be endorsed on the counterpart of a person's licence or has received the licence and its counterpart under paragraph 7(2)(b) or (4)(b), and

(b) has received the person's test certificate sent to him under paragraph 7(2)(b) or (4)(b) or is satisfied that the person has been issued with a test certificate,

the Secretary of State must by notice served on that person revoke the licence and the test certificate.

(2) A revocation under sub-paragraph (1) shall have effect from a date specified in the notice of revocation which may not be earlier than the date of service of that notice.

Re-testing

9.—(1) Subject to Part V of this Schedule, the Secretary of State may not under Part **A35.26**
III of the Road Traffic Act 1988 grant a person whose licence and test certificate have been revoked under paragraph 8(1) a full licence to drive any class of vehicles mentioned in subparagraph (4), unless he satisfies the Secretary of State that within the relevant period he has passed a relevant driving test.

(2) In this paragraph "*relevant driving test*" means any test which—

(a) falls within paragraph (a) or (b) of section 1(2); and

(b) is a test of competence to drive any vehicle included in any class of vehicles mentioned in sub-paragraph (4).

(3) If the Secretary of State grants a full licence to a person who is required to pass a relevant driving test in order to be granted that licence, the licence granted must (subject to section 92 and Part IV of the Road Traffic Act 1988) be one authorising that person to drive all the classes of vehicles mentioned in sub-paragraph (4).

(4) The classes of vehicles are—

(a) any class of vehicles in relation to which the revoked licence was issued as a full licence; and

(b) any class of vehicles—

 (i) that he was treated under section 98(2) of the Road Traffic Act 1988 as authorised to drive under a provisional licence, or

 (ii) in relation to which the revoked licence was issued as a provisional licence,

and that, immediately before the test certificate was revoked, he was permitted to drive without observing prescribed conditions.

(5) In sub-paragraph (1) "*the relevant period*" means the period beginning—

(a) after the date of the revocation of the licence and the test certificate; and

(b) not more than two years before the date on which the application for the full licence is made.

PART V

SUPPLEMENTARY

Effect of disqualification until test is passed on re-testing rule

10. Where— **A35.27**

(a) a person's test certificate has been revoked under paragraph 5(1) or his licence and test certificate have been revoked under paragraph 8(1), but

(b) before he passes a relevant driving test, an order is made in relation to him under section 36 of the Road Traffic Offenders Act 1988 (disqualification until test is passed),

paragraph 6(1) or, as the case may be, paragraph 9(1) shall not apply to him.

Regulations

A35.28   **11.**—(1) The Secretary of State may by regulations make provision for cases where, after the Secretary of State has revoked a person's test certificate under paragraph 5(1), or a person's licence and test certificate under paragraph 8(1), he receives notice—

(a) that the person is appealing against a conviction or endorsement which was the basis or formed part of the basis for the revocation;

(b) that a court has quashed a conviction which was the basis or formed part of the basis for the revocation;

(c) that a court has quashed an endorsement which was the basis or formed part of the basis for the revocation and has not on doing so ordered that person to be disqualified;

(d) that a court has made an order which has the effect of reducing the penalty points taken into account for the purposes of section 2 to a number smaller than six.

(2) Regulations under sub-paragraph (1) may in particular make provision for—

(a) issuing licences for such period as may be prescribed;

(b) licences issued under the regulations to be treated as revoked in such circumstances as may be prescribed;

(c) re-issuing a test certificate which has been revoked under paragraph 5(1) or 8(1);

(d) suspending or terminating any prescribed conditions applied by virtue of paragraph 5(3);

(e) requiring such courts as may be prescribed to give notice to the Secretary of State of the matters mentioned in sub-paragraph (3).

(3) The matters referred to are—

(a) that a person whose certificate has been or is due to be revoked under paragraph 5(1) or whose licence and certificate have been or are due to be revoked under paragraph 8(1) is appealing against a conviction or endorsement which is the basis or forms part of the basis for the revocation;

(b) that such an appeal has been abandoned.

(4) Any regulations under this paragraph may—

(a) include such incidental or supplementary provision as appears to the Secretary of State to be expedient;

(b) make different provision for different cases.

(5) Any regulations under this paragraph shall be made by statutory instrument which shall be subject to annulment in pursuance of a resolution of either House of Parliament.

A35.29   *[The New Drivers (Appeals Procedure) Regulations 1997 (S.I. 1997 No. 1098) below have been made in part under this paragraph.]*

Section 10(4)   SCHEDULE 2

CONSEQUENTIAL AMENDMENTS

A35.30   *[Amends the Road Traffic Act 1988 (q.v.) and the Road Traffic Offenders Act 1988 (q.v.).]*

The Goods Vehicles (Licensing of Operators) Act 1995

(1995 c. 23)

An Act to consolidate Part V of the Transport Act 1968 and related provisions concerning the licensing of operators of certain goods vehicles.　**A36.01**

[19th July 1995]

Foreign goods vehicles. This Act is modified in its application to foreign goods vehicles; see further the Goods Vehicles (Licensing of Operators) (Temporary Use in Great Britain) Regulations 1996 (S.I. 1996 No. 2186) below.　**A36.02**

ARRANGEMENT OF SECTIONS

SCHEDULES

Functions of traffic commissioners

1. Functions of traffic commissioners   *[Omitted.]*   **A36.04**

Operators' licences

2. Obligation to hold operator's licence

(1) Subject to subsection (2) and section 4, no person shall use a goods vehicle on a road   **A36.05**
for the carriage of goods—

  (a) for hire or reward, or

  (b) for or in connection with any trade or business carried on by him,

except under a licence issued under this Act; and in this Act such a licence is referred to as
an "*operator's licence*".

(2) Subsection (1) does not apply to—

  (a) the use of a small goods vehicle within the meaning given in Schedule 1;

  (b) the use of a goods vehicle for international carriage by a haulier established in a
       member State other than the United Kingdom and not established in the United
       Kingdom;

  (c) the use of a goods vehicle for international carriage by a haulier established in
       Northern Ireland and not established in Great Britain; or

  (d) the use of a vehicle of any class specified in regulations.

(3) In subsection (2)(b) and (c) "*established*", "*haulier*" and "*international carriage*" have the
same meaning as in Community Council Regulation (EEC) No. 881/92 dated 26 March

1992 [*q.v.*] concerning access to the market in the carriage of goods by road within the Community to or from the territory of a member State or passing across the territory of one or more member States.

(4) It is hereby declared that, for the purposes of this Act, the performance by a local or public authority of their functions constitutes the carrying on of a business.

(5) A person who uses a vehicle in contravention of this section is guilty of an offence and liable on summary conviction to a fine not exceeding [level 5] on the standard scale.

A36.06   *[Section 2 is printed as amended by the Transport Act 2000, s.261(1) (with effect from February 1, 2001; see the Transport Act 2000 (Commencement No. 3) Order 2001 (S.I. 2001 No. 57; not reproduced in this work)) (the subsequent amendment of S.I. 2001 No. 57 by the Transport Act 2000 (Commencement No. 3) (Amendment) Order 2001 (S.I. 2001 No. 115; not reproduced in this volume) does not affect the amendment of section 2).*

Before February 1, 2001, section 2(5) provided for a level 4 fine and that level is the maximum applicable to any offence committed before February 1, 2001; see the Transport Act 2000, s.261(2).

As to the vehicles specified under section 2(2)(d), see Schedule 3, Part I, to the Goods Vehicles (Licensing of Operators) Regulations 1995 (S.I. 1995 No. 2869) below.]

[2A. Detention of vehicle used without operator's licence

A36.07   Schedule 1A (which relates to the detention, removal and disposal of goods vehicles in respect of which it appears that section 2 is contravened) shall have effect.]

A36.08   *[Section 2A was inserted by the Transport Act 2000, s.262(1) (with effect from February 1, 2001; see the Transport Act 2000 (Commencement No. 3) Order 2001 (S.I. 2001 No. 57; not reproduced in this work)) (the subsequent amendment of S.I. 2001 No. 57 by the Transport Act 2000 (Commencement No. 3) (Amendment) Order 2001 (S.I. 2001 No. 115; not reproduced in this volume) does not affect the insertion of section 2A).]*

3. "Standard" and "restricted" licences

A36.09   (1) An operator's licence may be either a standard licence or a restricted licence.

(2) A *standard licence* is an operator's licence under which a goods vehicle may be used on a road for the carriage of goods—

    (a) for hire or reward, or

    (b) for or in connection with any trade or business carried on by the holder of the licence.

(3) A *restricted licence* is an operator's licence under which a goods vehicle may be used on a road for the carriage of goods for or in connection with any trade or business carried on by the holder of the licence, other than that of carrying goods for hire or reward.

(4) Notwithstanding subsections (2) and (3), a company may use a goods vehicle on a road for the carriage of goods for hire or reward under a restricted licence instead of a standard licence if (but only if) the goods concerned are the property of a company which is—

    (a) a subsidiary of the first company,

    (b) a holding company for the first company, or

    (c) a subsidiary of a company which is a holding company both for that subsidiary and for the first company.

(5) A standard licence may authorise a goods vehicle to be used for the carriage of goods—

    (a) on both national and international transport operations; or

    (b) on national transport operations only.

(6) Except as provided in subsection (4) and subject to section 4, a person who uses a goods vehicle under a restricted licence for carrying goods for hire or reward is guilty of an offence and liable on summary conviction to a fine not exceeding £500.

(7) A person who uses a goods vehicle for carrying goods for hire or reward on international transport operations under a standard licence which covers the carriage of goods on national transport operations only is guilty of an offence and liable on summary conviction to a fine not exceeding £500.

4. Temporary exemptions

(1) A traffic commissioner may, for the purpose of—   **A36.10**

    (a) enabling an emergency to be dealt with, or

    (b) enabling some other special need to be met,

by notice in writing grant to any person falling within subsection (2) a temporary exemption from any requirement to hold a standard licence which would otherwise be imposed on him by sections 2 and 3 in respect of any vehicle specified in the notice or any vehicle of a class so specified.

(2) A person falls within this subsection if he is engaged exclusively in national transport operations which have only a minor impact on the transport market because of the nature of the goods carried or the short distances over which goods are carried.

(3) A temporary exemption granted under subsection (1) permits the person to whom it is granted to use the specified vehicle or (as the case may be) any vehicle of the specified class for the carriage of goods for hire or reward for the purposes of transport operations of his such as are referred to in subsection (2) (and, accordingly, sections 2(1) and 3(6) shall not to that extent apply to that person's use of goods vehicles).

(4) A temporary exemption has effect until consultations with the European Commission for the purposes of Article 2(2) of the 1974 Council Directive are completed.

Vehicles authorised to be used under a licence

5. Vehicles authorised to be used under operator's licence

(1) Subject to the following provisions of this section, the vehicles authorised to be used   **A36.11** under an operator's licence are—

    (a) any motor vehicle in the lawful possession of the licence-holder (whether that motor vehicle is specified in the licence or not); and

    (b) any trailer in the lawful possession of the licence-holder.

(2) An operator's licence may provide—

    (a) that no motor vehicle, or no trailer, whose relevant weight exceeds a weight specified in the licence is authorised to be used under it;

    (b) that no trailers are authorised to be used under the licence; or

    (c) that no motor vehicle that is not specified in the licence is authorised to be used under it.

(3) In subsection (2) "*relevant weight*", in relation to a motor vehicle or trailer of any prescribed class, means a weight of the description specified in relation to motor vehicles or trailers of that class by regulations.

(4) An operator's licence shall not authorise the use of any vehicle unless the place which is for the time being its operating centre—

(a) is in the area of the traffic commissioner by whom the licence was issued; or

(b) is outside that area but has not been the operating centre of that vehicle for a period of more than three months.

(5) For the purposes of subsection (4)(b), two or more successive periods which are not separated from each other by an interval of at least three months shall be treated as a single period having a duration equal to the total duration of those periods.

(6) A motor vehicle which is not specified in an operator's licence is not authorised to be used under that licence by virtue of subsection (1) after the period of one month beginning with—

(a) the day on which the vehicle was first in the lawful possession of the licence-holder, or

(b) (if later) the day on which the licence came into force,

unless, during that period, the licence-holder has given to the traffic commissioner by whom the licence was issued a notice in such form and containing such information about the vehicle as the commissioner may require, and has paid to him a prescribed fee.

(7) Where notice of a vehicle has been duly given and the prescribed fee has been duly paid under subsection (6), the traffic commissioner shall vary the licence by directing that the vehicle be specified in it.

(8) A motor vehicle specified in an operator's licence shall not, while it remains so specified, be capable of being effectively specified in any other operator's licence.

(9) Where it comes to the knowledge of the traffic commissioner by whom an operator's licence ("*the first licence*") was issued that a vehicle specified in that licence—

(a) has ceased to be used under the licence (otherwise than because of a fluctuation in business or because it is undergoing repair or maintenance), or

(b) is specified in another operator's licence,

he may vary the first licence by directing that the vehicle be removed from it.

A36.12   *[With effect from a date to be announced under the Transport Act 2000, s.275(1), the following text will be substituted by ibid., s.263 for section 5(6):*

[(6) A motor vehicle which is not specified in an operator's licence is not authorised to be used under that licence by virtue of subsection (1) unless the licence-holder—

(a) has given to the traffic commissioner by whom the licence was issued a notice in such form and containing such information about the vehicle as the commissioner may require, and

(b) has paid to him a prescribed fee.]

Section 5 is modified in its application to old-style licences by paragraph 5 of the Schedule to the Goods Vehicles (Licensing of Operators) Act 1995 (Commencement and Transitional Provisions) Order 1995 (S.I. 1995 No. 2181) below. As to firms, see the Goods Vehicles (Licensing of Operators) Regulations 1995 (S.I. 1995 No. 2869), reg.29(2) below. As to the vehicles to which reference is made in section 5(3), see S.I. 1995 No. 2869, reg.36 below.]

6. Maximum numbers of vehicles

A36.13   (1) An operator's licence—

(a) shall specify a maximum number for motor vehicles, and

(b) may specify a maximum number for motor vehicles whose relevant weight exceeds a weight specified in the licence.

(2) An operator's licence that does not contain a provision such as is mentioned in section 5(2)(b)—

(a) shall specify a maximum number for trailers, and

(b) may specify a maximum number for trailers whose relevant weight exceeds a weight specified in the licence.

(3) The number of motor vehicles which at any one time are being used under an operator's licence while not specified in that licence may not exceed the maximum number specified in the licence under subsection (1)(a) less however many motor vehicles are specified in the licence.

(4) Where, under subsection (1)(b), an operator's licence specifies a maximum number for motor vehicles whose relevant weight exceeds a specified weight—

(a) the number of such motor vehicles which at any one time are being used under the licence while not specified in it may not exceed that maximum number less however many motor vehicles whose relevant weight exceeds the specified weight are specified in the licence, and

(b) the number of such motor vehicles that are specified in the licence and are being used under it at any one time may not exceed that maximum number.

(5) The number of trailers being used under an operator's licence at any one time may not exceed the maximum number specified in the licence under subsection (2)(a).

(6) Where, under subsection (2)(b), an operator's licence specifies a maximum number for trailers whose relevant weight exceeds a specified weight, the number of such trailers being used under the licence at any one time may not exceed that maximum number.

(7) The definition of *"relevant weight"* in section 5(3) applies for the purposes of this section as it applies for the purposes of section 5(2).

(8) If subsection (3), (4)(a) or (b), (5) or (6) is contravened, the licence-holder is guilty of an offence and liable on summary conviction to a fine not exceeding level 4 on the standard scale.

[Section 6 does not apply to old-style licences; see paragraph 5(6) of the Schedule to the Goods Vehicles   **A36.14**
(Licensing of Operators) Act 1995 (Commencement and Transitional Provisions) Order 1995 (S.I. 1995 No. 2181) below.]

Operating centres

7. Operating centres to be specified in operators' licences

(1) A person may not use a place in the area of any traffic commissioner as an oper-   **A36.15**
ating centre for vehicles authorised to be used under any operator's licence issued to him by that commissioner unless that place is specified as an operating centre of his in that licence.

(2) Any person who contravenes subsection (1) is guilty of an offence and liable on summary conviction to a fine not exceeding level 4 on the standard scale.

(3) In this Act *"operating centre"*, in relation to any vehicle, means the base or centre at which the vehicle is normally kept, and references to an operating centre of the holder of an operator's licence are references to any place which is an operating centre for vehicles used under that licence.

8. Applications for operators' licences

A36.16   (1) An application for an operator's licence shall be made to the traffic commissioner for each area in which, if the licence is issued, the applicant will have an operating centre or operating centres.

(2) Accordingly, a person may hold separate operators' licences in respect of different areas; but he shall not at any time hold more than one such licence in respect of the same area.

(3) *[Statement by applicant for operator's licence.]*

(4) *[Provision of further information by applicant.]*

(5) *[Provision of particulars by applicant.]*

(6) *[Form of statement, information and particulars.]*

A36.17   *[As to firms, see the Goods Vehicles (Licensing of Operators) Regulations 1995 (S.I. 1995 No. 2869), reg.29(1) and (10) below.]*

9. Convictions, etc., subsequent to the making of an application

A36.18   (1) A person who has made an application for an operator's licence shall forthwith notify the traffic commissioner to whom it was made if, in the interval between the making of the application and the date on which it is disposed of, there occurs a notifiable conviction within the meaning given in paragraph 4 of Schedule 2.

(2) A person who—

  (a) has made an application for a standard licence, and

  (b) has included in that application particulars of a transport manager,

shall forthwith notify the traffic commissioner to whom the application was made if, in the interval between the making of the application and the date on which it is disposed of, there occurs any event affecting any information about the transport manager given to the commissioner under section 8.

(3) A person is guilty of an offence if he—

  (a) knowingly fails to comply with subsection (1), or

  (b) knowingly fails to comply with subsection (2) in a case where the event which occurs as mentioned in that subsection is the conviction of the transport manager of an offence such as is mentioned in paragraph 5 of Schedule 2;

and a person who is guilty of an offence under paragraph (a) or (b) is liable on summary conviction to a fine not exceeding level 4 on the standard scale.

(4) For the purposes of this section an application shall be taken to be disposed of—

  (a) in a case where the traffic commissioner is required, by virtue of regulations under section 57(2)(a), to cause a statement containing his decision on the application to be issued, on the date on which that statement is issued, and

  (b) in any other case, on the date on which the applicant receives notice from the traffic commissioner of his decision on the application.

A36.19   *[As to firms, see the Goods Vehicles (Licensing of Operators) Regulations 1995 (S.I. 1995 No. 2869), reg.29(10) below.]*

A36.20   **10. Publication by traffic commissioner of notice of application for licence**
[Omitted.]

11. Publication in locality affected of notice of application for licence
[Omitted.]

12. Objections to, and representations against, issue of operators' licences
[Omitted.]

Determination of applications

13. Determination of applications for operators' licences

(1) Subject to sections 11 and 45(2), on an application for a standard licence a traffic   **A36.21** commissioner shall consider—

(a) whether the requirements of subsections (3) and (5) are satisfied, and

(b) if he thinks fit, whether the requirements of subsection (6) are satisfied.

(2) Subject to sections 11 and 45(2), on an application for a restricted licence a traffic commissioner shall consider—

(a) whether the requirements of subsections (4) and (5) are satisfied, and

(b) if he thinks fit, whether the requirements of subsection (6) are satisfied.

(3) For the requirements of this subsection to be satisfied the traffic commissioner must be satisfied that the applicant fulfils the following requirements, namely—

(a) that he is of good repute,

(b) that he is of the appropriate financial standing, and

(c) that he is professionally competent;

and the traffic commissioner shall determine whether or not that is the case in accordance with Schedule 3.

(4) For the requirements of this subsection to be satisfied the applicant must not be unfit to hold an operator's licence by reason of—

(a) any activities or convictions of which particulars may be required to be given under section 8(4) by virtue of paragraph 1(e) or (f) of Schedule 2, or

(b) any conviction required to be notified in accordance with section 9(1).

(5) For the requirements of this subsection to be satisfied it must be possible (taking into account the traffic commissioner's powers under section 15(3) to issue a licence in terms that differ from those applied for) to issue a licence on the application in relation to which paragraphs (a) to (e) will apply—

(a) there are satisfactory arrangements for securing that—

    (i) Part VI of the Transport Act 1968 [*q.v.*] (drivers' hours), and

    (ii) the applicable Community rules, within the meaning of that Part,

  are complied with in the case of the vehicles used under the licence;

(b) there are satisfactory arrangements for securing that the vehicles used under the licence are not overloaded;

(c) there are satisfactory facilities and arrangements for maintaining the vehicles used under the licence in a fit and serviceable condition;

(d) at least one place in the traffic commissioner's area is specified in the licence as an operating centre of the licence-holder, and each place so specified is available and suitable for use as such an operating centre (disregarding any respect in which it may be unsuitable on environmental grounds);

(e) the capacity of the place so specified (if there is only one) or of both or all the places so specified taken together (if there are more than one) is sufficient to provide an operating centre for all the vehicles used under the licence.

(6) For the requirements of this subsection to be satisfied the provision of such facilities and arrangements as are mentioned in subsection (5)(c) must not be prejudiced by reason of the applicant's having insufficient financial resources for that purpose.

(7) In considering whether any of the requirements of subsections (3) to (6) are satisfied, the traffic commissioner shall have regard to any objection duly made under section 12(1)(a) in respect of the application.

(8) In considering whether the requirements of subsection (5) are satisfied, the traffic commissioner may take into account any undertakings given by the applicant (or procured by him to be given) for the purposes of the application, and may assume that those undertakings will be fulfilled.

(9) In considering whether subsection (5)(d) will apply in relation to a licence, the traffic commissioner may take into account any conditions that could be attached to the licence under section 21, and may assume that any conditions so attached will not be contravened.

(10) In considering whether subsection (5)(d) or (e) will apply in relation to a licence, the traffic commissioner may take into account (if that is the case) that any proposed operating centre of the applicant would be used—

(a) as an operating centre of the holders of other operators' licences as well as of the applicant; or

(b) by the applicant or by other persons for purposes other than keeping vehicles used under the licence.

(11) If the traffic commissioner determines that any of the requirements that he has taken into consideration in accordance with subsection (1) or (2) are not satisfied he shall refuse the application, but in any other case he shall, subject to sections 14 and 45(2), grant the application.

A36.22　　*[As to firms, see the Goods Vehicles (Licensing of Operators) Regulations 1995 (S.I. 1995 No. 2869), reg.29(3)–(5) below.]*

A36.23　　**14. Determination where objections, etc., are made on environmental grounds**　　*[Omitted.]*

15. Issue of operators' licences　　*[Omitted.]*

16. Duration of operators' licences

A36.24　　(1) The date on which an operator's licence is to come into force shall be specified in the licence.

(2) Subject to its revocation or other termination under any provision of this Act or any other statutory provision, an operator's licence (other than an interim licence issued under section 24) shall continue in force indefinitely.

(3) If the holder of an operator's licence requests the traffic commissioner by whom it was issued to terminate it at any time, the commissioner shall, subject to subsection (4), comply with the request.

(4) The traffic commissioner may refuse to comply with the request if he is considering giving a direction in respect of the licence under section 26 or 27.

(5) An operator's licence held by an individual terminates if he dies, if he becomes a patient within the meaning of Part VII of the Mental Health Act 1983, or . . .

[The words omitted from section 16(5) relate expressly and exclusively to Scotland.   **A36.25**
As to the application of section 16(2) to licences with expiry dates before the appointed day, see paragraph 2 of the Schedule to the Goods Vehicles (Licensing of Operators) Act 1995 (Commencement and Transitional Provisions) Order 1995 (S.I. 1995 No. 2181) below. As to prematurely terminated licences, see ibid., para.3 below. As to firms, see the Goods Vehicles (Licensing of Operators) Regulations 1995 (S.I. 1995 No. 2869), reg.29(11) below.]

Variation of licences

17. Variation of operators' licences   *[Omitted.]*   **A36.26**

18. Publication of notice of applications for variation in any locality affected
[Omitted.]

19. Objection to, and refusal of, applications to vary operators' licences on environmental grounds   *[Omitted.]*

20. Variation of licences: further provisions

(1) Where the holder of a restricted licence makes an application under section 17 to the   **A36.27**
traffic commissioner by whom the licence was issued to vary it by directing that it be converted into a standard licence—

   (a) section 9(2) and (3)(b) and (without prejudice to the generality of section 17(5)) section 13(1) shall apply in relation to that application as they apply in relation to an application for a standard licence; and

   (b) if the application is granted, section 22(2) shall apply to the giving of the direction to vary the restricted licence as it applies to the issuing of a standard licence.

(2) *[Application to vary standard licence so as to add international transport operations.]*

Conditions attached to licences

21. Conditions for securing road safety

(1) On issuing an operator's licence, or on varying such a licence under section 17,   **A36.28**
a traffic commissioner may attach to the licence such conditions as he thinks fit for preventing vehicles that are authorised to be used under it from causing danger to the public—

   (a) at any point where vehicles first join a public road on their way from an operating centre of the licence-holder (or last leave a public road on their way to such an operating centre); and

   (b) on any road (other than a public road) along which vehicles are driven between such a point and the operating centre.

(2) *[Variation or removal of conditions.]*

(3), (4) *[Representations as to conditions.]*

(5) In this section *"public road"* —

   (a) in relation to England and Wales, means a highway maintainable at the public expense for the purposes of the Highways Act 1980; and

   (b) *[applies to Scotland].*

(6) Any person who contravenes any condition attached under this section to a licence of which he is the holder is guilty of an offence and liable on summary conviction to a fine not exceeding level 4 on the standard scale.

22. Conditions as to matters required to be notified to traffic commissioner

A36.29   (1) On issuing an operator's licence, a traffic commissioner may attach to the licence such conditions as he thinks fit for requiring the holder to inform him—

     (a) of any change of a kind specified in the conditions in the organisation, management or ownership of the trade or business in the course of which vehicles are used under the licence or, if the licence is at any time suspended under section 26 or 28, were used under the licence immediately before its suspension;

     (b) where the licence-holder is a company, of any change, or of any change of a kind specified in the conditions, in the persons holding shares in the company; or

     (c) of any other event of a kind specified in the conditions which affects the licence-holder and which is relevant to the exercise of any powers of the traffic commissioner in relation to the licence.

(2) On issuing a standard licence, a traffic commissioner shall attach to it the following conditions, namely—

     (a) a condition requiring the licence-holder to inform the commissioner of any event which could affect the fulfilment by the licence-holder of any of the requirements of section 13(3), and to do so within 28 days of the event; and

     (b) a condition requiring the licence-holder to inform the commissioner of any event which could affect the fulfilment by a relevant transport manager of the requirements mentioned in section 13(3)(a) or (c), and to do so within 28 days of the event coming to the licence-holder's knowledge.

(3) In subsection (2)(b) the reference to a *"relevant transport manager"* is a reference to any transport manager employed by the licence-holder who is relied on by the licence-holder to fulfil the requirements of section 13(3)(c).

(4) In a case where the licence-holder is a company, no condition attached under subsection (2) shall be taken to require the company to inform the traffic commissioner of any change in the identity of the persons holding shares in the company unless the change is such as to cause a change in the control of the company.

(5) For the purposes of subsection (4), a change in the control of a company occurs when the beneficial ownership of more than half its equity share capital (as defined in section 744 of the Companies Act 1985) passes from one person to another person or from one group of persons to a wholly or substantially different group of persons.

(6) Any person who contravenes any condition attached under this section to a licence of which he is the holder is guilty of an offence and liable on summary conviction to a fine not exceeding level 4 on the standard scale.

A36.30   *[As to holding companies and their subsidiaries, see the Goods Vehicles (Licensing of Operators) Regulations 1995 (S.I. 1995 No. 2869), Sched. 2, para.2(i) below.]*

23. Conditions as to use of operating centres

A36.31   (1) On issuing an operator's licence, or on varying such a licence on an application of which notice has been published under section 17(3), a traffic commissioner may attach to the licence such conditions as he thinks fit for preventing or minimising any adverse effects on environmental conditions arising from the use of a place in his area as an operating centre of the licence-holder.

(2) The conditions which may be attached to a licence under this section shall be of such description as may be prescribed; and, without prejudice to the generality of the preceding provision, the descriptions which may be prescribed include conditions regulating—

  (a) the number, type and size of motor vehicles or trailers which may at any one time be at any operating centre of the licence-holder in the area of the traffic commissioner for any prescribed purpose;

  (b) the parking arrangements to be provided at or in the vicinity of any such centre; and

  (c) the hours at which operations of any prescribed description may be carried on at any such centre.

(3) *[Variation or removal of conditions.]*

(4), (5) *[Representations as to conditions.]*

(6) Any person who contravenes any condition attached under this section to a licence of which he is the holder is guilty of an offence and liable on summary conviction to a fine not exceeding level 4 on the standard scale.

Interim licences and interim variations

24. Interim operators' licences

(1) On an application for an operator's licence (a "*full*" licence), a traffic commissioner   **A36.32** may, if the applicant so requests, issue to him an interim licence.

(2) An *interim licence* is an operator's licence that (subject to its revocation or other termination under any provision of this Act or any other statutory provision) will continue in force until it terminates under subsection (4), (5) or (6).

(3) *[Terms in which interim licence issued.]*

(4)–(6) *[Termination of interim licence.]*

(7) *[Full licence taking effect on termination of interim licence.]*

(8) A request for the issuing of an interim licence—

  (a) shall not be treated as an application for an operator's licence for the purposes of section 10, 11, 12, 13, 14, 15(1) to (4), 36 or 37 or Schedule 4, but

  (b) shall be treated as such an application for the purposes of any other provision of this Act.

(9) *[Date on which an application is finally disposed of.]*

25. Interim variations   *[Omitted.]*   **A36.33**

Revocation, etc., of operators' licences

26. Revocation, suspension and curtailment of operators' licences
[Omitted.]

27. Revocation of standard licences   *[Omitted.]*

28. Disqualification

(1) Where, under section 26(1) or 27(1), a traffic commissioner directs that an operator's   **A36.34** licence be revoked, the commissioner may order the person who was the holder of the licence

to be disqualified (either indefinitely or for such period as the commissioner thinks fit) from holding or obtaining an operator's licence; and so long as the disqualification is in force—

    (a) any operator's licence held by him at the date of the making of the order (other than the licence revoked) shall be suspended, and

    (b) notwithstanding anything in section 13 or 24, no operator's licence may be issued to him.

(2) If a person applies for or obtains an operator's licence while he is disqualified under subsection (1)—

    (a) he is guilty of an offence and liable on summary conviction to a fine not exceeding level 4 on the standard scale, and

    (b) any operator's licence issued to him on the application, or (as the case may be) the operator's licence obtained by him, shall be void.

(3) An order under subsection (1) may be limited so as to apply only to the holding or obtaining of an operator's licence in respect of one or more specified traffic areas and, if the order is so limited—

    (a) paragraphs (a) and (b) of that subsection and subsection (2) shall apply only to any operator's licence to which the order applies, but

    (b) notwithstanding section 5(4)(b), no other operator's licence held by the person in question shall authorise the use by him of any vehicle at a time when its operating centre is in a traffic area in respect of which he is disqualified by virtue of the order.

(4) Where the traffic commissioner makes an order under subsection (1) in respect of any person, the commissioner may direct that if that person, at any time or during such period as the commissioner may specify—

    (a) is a director of, or holds a controlling interest in—

        (i) a company which holds a licence of the kind to which the order in question applies, or

        (ii) a company of which such a company is a subsidiary, or

    (b) operates any goods vehicles in partnership with a person who holds such a licence,

that licence of that company or, as the case may be, of that person, shall be liable to revocation, suspension or curtailment under section 26.

(5) The powers conferred by subsections (1) and (4) in relation to the person who was the holder of a licence shall be exercisable also—

    (a) where that person was a company, in relation to any director of that company, and

    (b) where that person operated vehicles under the licence in partnership with other persons, in relation to any of those other persons;

and any reference in this section or in section 26 or 29 to subsection (1) or (4) above includes a reference to that subsection as it applies by virtue of this subsection.

(6) *[Cancellation or variation of any order or direction.]*

(7) *[Effect of suspension of operator's licence.]*

(8) *[Criterion for holding controlling interest in company.]*

A36.35   *[As to firms, see the Goods Vehicles (Licensing of Operators) Regulations 1995 (S.I. 1995 No. 2869), reg.29(8) and (9) below. As to holding companies and their subsidiaries, see S.I. 1995 No. 2869, Sched. 2, para.2(n)–(p) below.]*

A36.36   **29. Revocation and disqualification, etc., supplementary provisions**   *[Omitted.]*

Review of operating centres

30. Periods of review for operating centres   *[Omitted.]*

31. Power to remove operating centres on review   *[Omitted.]*

32. Power to attach conditions on review   *[Omitted.]*

Transfer of operating centres

33. Transfer of operating centres   *[Omitted.]*

Environmental matters

34. Determinations as to environmental matters   *[Omitted.]*

Inquiries

35. Power of traffic commissioners to hold inquiries   *[Omitted.]*

Review of decisions and appeals

36. Review of decisions   *[Omitted.]*

37. Rights of appeal in connection with operators' licences   *[Omitted.]*

Forgery, false statements, etc.

38. Forgery of documents, etc.

(1) A person is guilty of an offence if, with intent to deceive, he—   A36.37

(a) forges, alters or uses a document or other thing to which this section applies;

(b) lends to, or allows to be used by, any other person a document or other thing to which this section applies; or

(c) makes or has in his possession any document or other thing so closely resembling a document or other thing to which this section applies as to be calculated to deceive.

(2) This section applies to the following documents and other things, namely—

(a) any operator's licence;

(b) any document, plate, mark or other thing by which, in pursuance of regulations, a vehicle is to be identified as being authorised to be used, or as being used, under an operator's licence;

(c) any document evidencing the authorisation of any person for the purposes of sections 40 and 41;

(d) any certificate of qualification under section 49; and

(e) any certificate or diploma such as is mentioned in paragraph 13(1) of Schedule 3.

(3) A person guilty of an offence under subsection (1) is liable—

(a) on summary conviction, to a fine not exceeding the statutory maximum;

(b) on conviction on indictment, to imprisonment for a term not exceeding two years or to a fine or to both.

(4) In the application of subsection (1) to England and Wales, "*forges*" means makes a false document or other thing in order that it may be used as genuine.

A36.38   *[With effect from a date to be announced, section 38(2)(c) will be amended by section 50 of and paragraph 5(1) of Schedule 5 to this Act.]*

39. False statements

A36.39   (1) A person is guilty of an offence if he knowingly makes a false statement for the purpose of—

    (a) obtaining the issue to himself or any other person of an operator's licence;

    (b) obtaining the variation of any such licence;

    (c) preventing the issue or variation of any such licence;

    (d) procuring the imposition of a condition or limitation in relation to any such licence; or

    (e) obtaining the issue to himself or any other person of a certificate of qualification under section 49 or a certificate or diploma such as is mentioned in paragraph 13(1) of Schedule 3.

(2) A person guilty of an offence under subsection (1) is liable on summary conviction to a fine not exceeding level 4 on the standard scale.

Enforcement, etc.

40. Inspection of maintenance facilities

A36.40   (1) An officer may, at any time which is reasonable having regard to the circumstances of the case, enter any premises of an applicant for an operator's licence or of the holder of such a licence and inspect any facilities on those premises for maintaining the vehicles used under the licence in a fit and serviceable condition.

(2) Any person who obstructs an officer in the exercise of his powers under subsection (1) is guilty of an offence and liable on summary conviction to a fine not exceeding level 3 on the standard scale.

41. Power to seize documents, etc.

A36.41   (1) If an officer has reason to believe that—

    (a) a document or article carried on or by the driver of a vehicle, or

    (b) a document produced to him in pursuance of this Act,

is a document or article in relation to which an offence has been committed under section 38 or 39, he may seize that document or article.

(2) Where—

    (a) a document or article is seized under subsection (1),

    (b) no person has, within six months of the date on which the document or article was seized, been charged since that date with an offence in relation to it under section 38 or 39, and

    (c) the document or article is still detained,

then any of the persons mentioned in subsection (3) may make an application to a magistrates' court . . .

(3) The persons who may make an application under subsection (2) are—

    (a) an officer;

    (b) the driver or owner of the vehicle;

    (c) the person from whom the document was seized.

(4) On an application under subsection (2), the magistrates' court . . . shall—

   (a) make such order respecting the disposal of the document or article, and

   (b) award such costs . . .,

as the justice of the case may require.

(5) *[Applies to Scotland.]*

[With effect from a date to be announced, section 41(1) and (2)(b) will be amended by section 50 of and   **A36.42**
paragraph 5(2) of Schedule 5 to this Act.
  The words omitted from section 41(2) and (4) relate exclusively to Scotland.]

42. Meaning of "officer" and powers of police constables

(1) In sections 40 and 41 *"officer"* means—   **A36.43**

   (a) an examiner appointed under section 66A of the Road Traffic Act 1988, or

   (b) any person authorised for the purposes of sections 40 and 41 by the traffic commissioner for any area.

(2) The powers conferred by sections 40 and 41 on an officer shall be exercisable also by a police constable.

[With effect from a date to be announced, section 42(1)(b) will be amended by section 50 of and para-   **A36.44**
graph 5(1) of Schedule 5 to this Act.]

43. Evidence by certificate

(1) In any proceedings for an offence under this Act a certificate such as is mentioned in   **A36.45**
subsection (2) shall be evidence . . . of the facts stated in it.

(2) The certificate referred to in subsection (1) is a certificate signed by or on behalf of a traffic commissioner which states—

   (a) that, on any date, a person was or was not the holder of an operator's licence issued by the commissioner;

   (b) that, by virtue of a direction given by the commissioner under regulations made under section 48(2)(b) or (3), a person is to be treated as having been the holder of an operator's licence on any date;

   (c) the date of the coming into force of any operator's licence issued by the commissioner;

   (d) the date on which any operator's licence issued by the commissioner ceased to be in force;

   (e) the terms and conditions of any operator's licence issued by the commissioner;

   (f) that a person is by virtue of an order of the commissioner disqualified from holding or obtaining an operator's licence, either indefinitely or for a specified period;

   (g) that a direction, having effect indefinitely or for a specified period, has been given by the commissioner under section 28(4) in relation to any person;

   (h) that an operator's licence was on any date or during any specified period suspended by virtue of a direction given by the commissioner under section 26(1); or

   (i) that, by virtue of a direction given by the commissioner under regulations made under section 48(2)(a), an operator's licence is to be treated as having been suspended on any date or during any specified period.

(3) Any such certificate which purports to be signed by or on behalf of a traffic commissioner shall be taken to be so signed unless the contrary is proved.

[The words omitted from section 43(1) relate exclusively to Scotland.]   **A36.46**

Miscellaneous

A36.47 **44. Assessors**   *[Omitted.]*

45. Fees   *[Omitted.]*

46. Holding companies and subsidiaries

A36.48   (1) The Secretary of State may by regulations make provision for the purpose of enabling any company or other body corporate which has one or more subsidiaries to hold an operator's licence under which the vehicles authorised to be used consist of or include vehicles belonging to or in the possession of any of its subsidiaries.

(2) Regulations under this section may—

(a) modify or supplement any of the provisions of this Act, other than the excepted provisions, so far as appears to the Secretary of State to be necessary or expedient for or in connection with the purpose mentioned in subsection (1), and

(b) may contain such other supplementary and incidental provisions as appear to the Secretary of State to be requisite.

(3) In this Act "*the excepted provisions*" means the following provisions (which are provisions that reproduce the effect of provisions of the Goods Vehicles (Operators' Licences, Qualifications and Fees) Regulations 1984 [*S.I. 1984 No. 176 (revoked)*]), namely—

(a) sections 3, 4, 9(2) and (3)(b), 13(3), 15(5) and (6), 20, 22(2) to (5), 27 and 49;

(b) in section 58, in subsection (1), the definitions of "*international transport operations*", "*national transport operations*", "*road transport undertaking*" and "*transport manager*", and subsection (4); and

(c) Schedule 3.

47. Partnerships

A36.49   Regulations may provide for this Act to apply in relation to partnerships with such modifications as may be specified in the regulations; but nothing in any such regulations may make modifications in any of the excepted provisions (within the meaning given in section 46(3)).

48. Operators' licences not to be transferable, etc.

A36.50   (1) Subject to any regulations under section 46, an operator's licence is neither transferable nor assignable.

(2) Regulations may make provision enabling a traffic commissioner, where the holder of an operator's licence issued by him has died or become a patient within the meaning of Part VII of the Mental Health Act 1983, to direct that the licence be treated—

(a) as not having terminated at the time when the licence-holder died or became a patient but as having been suspended (that is, as having remained in force but subject to the limitation that no vehicles were authorised to be used under it) from that time until the time when the direction comes into force; and

(b) as having effect from the time when the direction comes into force for a specified period and as being held during that period (for such purposes and to such extent as may be specified) not by the person to whom it was issued but by such other person carrying on that person's business, or part of that person's business, as may be specified.

(3) Regulations may make provision enabling a traffic commissioner in prescribed circumstances to direct that any operator's licence issued by him is to be treated (for such purposes, for such period and to such extent as may be specified) as held not by the person

to whom it was issued but by such other person carrying on that person's business, or part of that person's business, as may be specified.

(4) Regulations may make provision enabling a traffic commissioner to direct, for the purpose of giving effect to or supplementing a direction given by him by virtue of subsection (2) or (3), that this Act is to apply with specified modifications in relation to the person who is to be treated under the direction as the holder of an operator's licence; but nothing in any such regulations shall permit the commissioner to modify the operation of any of the excepted provisions (within the meaning given in section 46(3)).

(5) *[Applies to Scotland.]*

(6) In this section "*specified*", in relation to a direction, means specified—

  (a) in the regulations under which the direction was given; or

  (b) in the direction in accordance with those regulations.

49. Certificates of qualification

(1) On an application made to him by a person wishing to engage in a road transport undertaking in a member State other than the United Kingdom, the appropriate person shall issue to the applicant a certificate (a "*certificate of qualification*") as to such matters relating to—   **A36.51**

  (a) the applicant's repute,

  (b) his professional competence, or

  (c) (where relevant) his financial standing,

as the appropriate person is satisfied he may properly certify and as appear to him to be of assistance to the applicant in satisfying any requirements imposed by the law of the other member State as regards the repute, professional competence and financial standing of persons engaged in road transport undertakings in that member State.

(2) A certificate of qualification shall—

  (a) be in such form as the Secretary of State . . . may specify; and

  (b) have effect for the purposes of Article 3, 4 or (as the case may be) 5 of the 1977 Council Directive.

(3) *[Fee for certificate.]*

(4) *[Information relating to application.]*

(5) *[Meaning of "the appropriate person".]*

(6) *[Fees to be paid into Consolidated Fund.]*

[Section 49 is printed as amended by the Secretary of State for the Environment, Transport and the Regions Order 1997 (S.I. 1997 No. 2971).]   **A36.52**

Large goods vehicles

50. Large goods vehicles

(1) Schedule 5 (which requires certain documents to be carried by the drivers of large goods vehicles and makes other provision in connection with such vehicles) shall have effect.   **A36.53**

(2) This section and Schedule 5 shall come into force on such day as the Secretary of State may by order appoint; and different days may be appointed for different purposes and different provisions.

A36.54   *[No date has been appointed under section 50(2) for section 50 or Schedule 5 to come into force; these provisions were expressly excluded from the operation of the Goods Vehicles (Licensing of Operators) Act 1995 (Commencement and Transitional Provisions) Order 1995 (S.I. 1995 No. 2181) by ibid., art.2.]*

General provisions

51. Time for bringing proceedings

A36.55   Section 6 of the Road Traffic Offenders Act 1988 (time for bringing summary proceedings for certain offences) shall apply to an offence under section 9(3)(a) or (b), 38 or 39.

A36.56   ### 52. Destination of fines: Scotland   *[Omitted.]*

53. Method of calculating weight of motor vehicles

A36.57   For the purposes of this Act the weight unladen of a vehicle shall be taken to be the weight of the vehicle inclusive of the body and all parts (the heavier being taken where alternative bodies or parts are used) which are necessary to or ordinarily used with the vehicle when working on a road, but exclusive of the weight of water, fuel or accumulators used for the purpose of the supply of power for the propulsion of the vehicle, and of loose tools and loose equipment.

54. Saving for law of nuisance

A36.58   Nothing in this Act shall authorise a person to use on a road a vehicle so constructed or used as to cause a public or private nuisance . . . or affect the liability, whether under statute or common law, of the driver or owner so using such a vehicle.

A36.59   *[The words omitted from section 54 relate exclusively to Scotland.]*

55. Protection of public interests

A36.60   It is hereby declared that nothing in this Act is to be treated as conferring on the holder of an operator's licence any right to the continuance of any benefits arising from this Act or from any such licence or from any conditions attached to any such licence.

A36.61   ### 56. Secretary of State's power to hold inquiries   *[Omitted.]*

Regulations and orders

57. Regulations and orders

A36.62   (1) The Secretary of State may make regulations for any purpose for which regulations may be made under this Act, and for prescribing anything which may be prescribed under this Act, and generally for carrying this Act into effect.

(2) In particular, but without prejudice to the generality of subsection (1), the Secretary of State may make regulations with respect to the following matters—

    (a) the procedure on applications for, and the determination of questions in connection with, the issuing and variation of operators' licences and the procedure under, and the determination of questions for the purposes of, sections 26 to 32 and 36;

    (b) the issue of operators' licences and the issue on payment of the prescribed fee of copies of such licences in the case of licences lost or defaced;

    (c) the forms which operators' licences are to take in order to show a distinction—

    (i) between a standard licence and a restricted licence; and

    (ii) between a licence covering both international and national transport operations and a licence covering national transport operations only;

(d) the means by which vehicles may be identified, whether by plates, marks or otherwise, as being used or authorised to be used under an operator's licence;

(e) the custody, production, return and cancellation of operators' licences and of documents, plates and any other means of identification prescribed under paragraph (d);

(f) the payment of a prescribed fee in respect of any document, plate or other means of identification so prescribed that has been lost, defaced or broken;

(g) the notification to a traffic commissioner of vehicles which have ceased to be used under an operator's licence;

(h) the repayment (or partial repayment) in the prescribed circumstances of fees paid under this Act;

(i) the circumstances in which goods are to be treated for the purposes of this Act as carried for hire or reward and the circumstances in which goods are to be treated for those purposes as carried by any person for or in connection with a trade or business carried on by him.

(3) The power under subsection (2)(a) shall include power to require a person applying for an operator's licence to state in his application—

(a) whether his application is for a standard licence or a restricted licence, and

(b) (if his application is for a standard licence) whether his application is for a licence to cover both international and national transport operations or for one to cover national transport operations only.

(4) The power under subsection (2)(d) shall include power to require that any means of identification prescribed for a vehicle shall be carried notwithstanding that for the time being the vehicle is not being used for a purpose for which an operator's licence is required.

(5) The power under subsection (2)(d) shall also include power to make provision with respect to the means by which—

(a) any vehicle may be identified as being used under a standard licence or, as the case may be, a restricted licence; and

(b) any vehicle which is being used under a standard licence may be identified as being used under a licence that permits it to be used—

    (i) for both international and national transport operations, or

    (ii) for national transport operations only.

(6) The Secretary of State may make regulations for providing that any provision of this Act shall, in relation to vehicles brought temporarily into Great Britain, have effect subject to such modifications as may be prescribed.

(7) Any regulations under this Act may make—

(a) different provision for different cases or classes of case and different circumstances, and

(b) transitional provision,

and regulations made by virtue of subsection (2)(d) may make different provision for different traffic areas.

(8) A definition or description of a class of vehicles for the purposes of any regulation under this Act may be framed by reference to any characteristic of the vehicles or to any other circumstances whatever.

(9) Any person who contravenes a provision of regulations under this section, a contravention of which is declared by the regulations to be an offence, is guilty of an offence and liable on summary conviction to a fine not exceeding level 1 on the standard scale.

(10)–(12) *[Regulations under section 30(3) subject to approval by each House of Parliament; other regulations subject to annulment; consultation with representative organisations.]*

(13) Any power to make orders or regulations conferred on the Secretary of State by any provision of this Act shall be exercisable by statutory instrument.

A36.63   *[The Goods Vehicles (Licensing of Operators) Regulations 1995 (S.I. 1995 No. 2869) below, the Goods Vehicles (Licensing of Operators) (Fees) Regulations 1995 (S.I. 1995 No. 3000; not reproduced in this work), and the Goods Vehicles (Licensing of Operators) (Temporary Use in Great Britain) Regulations 1996 (S.I. 1996 No. 2186) below have been made (in part) under this section.]*

Interpretation

58. General interpretation

A36.64   (1) In this Act, unless the context otherwise requires—

"*area*", in relation to a traffic commissioner, means the traffic area for which he is the traffic commissioner;

"*articulated combination*" means a combination made up of—

    (a) a motor vehicle which is so constructed that a trailer may by partial superimposition be attached to the vehicle in such a manner as to cause a substantial part of the weight of the trailer to be borne by the vehicle, and

    (b) a trailer attached to it as described in paragraph (a);

"*carriage of goods*" includes haulage of goods;

"*contravention*", in relation to any condition or provision, includes a failure to comply with the condition or provision, and "*contravenes*" shall be construed accordingly;

"*the 1974 Council Directive*" means Community Council Directive No. 74/561/EEC dated 12 November 1974 [*O.J. No. L308, November 19, 1974, p. 18*] on admission to the occupation of road haulage operator in national and international transport operations, as amended by Community Council Directive No. 89/438/EEC dated 21 June 1989 [*O.J. No. L212, July 22, 1989, p. 101*];

"*the 1977 Council Directive*" means Community Council Directive No. 77/796/EEC dated 12 December 1977 [*O.J. No. L334, December 24, 1977, p. 37*] concerning the mutual recognition of diplomas, certificates and other evidence of formal qualifications for goods haulage operators and road passenger transport operators, including measures to encourage such operators effectively to exercise their right of freedom of establishment, as amended by Community Council Directive No. 89/438/EEC dated 21 June 1989;

"*driver*"—

    (a) where a separate person acts as steersman of a motor vehicle, includes that person as well as any other person engaged in the driving of the vehicle; and

    (b) in relation to a trailer, means the driver of the vehicle by which the trailer is drawn;

and "*drive*" shall be construed accordingly;

"*functions*" includes powers, duties and obligations;

"*goods*" includes goods or burden of any description;

"*goods vehicle*" means a motor vehicle constructed or adapted for use for the carriage of goods, or a trailer so constructed or adapted, but does not include a tramcar or trolley vehicle within the meaning of the Road Traffic Act 1988;

"holding company" and *"subsidiary"* have the meaning given by section 736 of the Companies Act 1985 [*not reproduced in this work*];

"international transport operations" and *"national transport operations"* have the same meaning as in the 1974 Council Directive;

"modification" includes addition, omission and alteration, and related expressions shall be construed accordingly;

"motor vehicle" and *"trailer"* have the same meaning as in section 253 of the Road Traffic Act 1960;

"operating centre" has the meaning given in section 7(3);

"operator's licence" has the meaning given in section 2(1);

"owner", in relation to any land in England and Wales, means a person, other than a mortgagee not in possession, who, whether in his own right or as trustee for any other person, is entitled to receive the rack rent of the land or, where the land is not let at a rack rent, would be so entitled if it were so let;

"plated weight", in relation to a vehicle, means a weight required to be marked on it by means of a plate in pursuance of regulations made by virtue of section 41 of the Road Traffic Act 1988 or required to be so marked by section 57 or 58 of that Act;

"prescribed" means prescribed by regulations;

"regulations" means regulations made by the Secretary of State under this Act;

"restricted licence" has the meaning given in section 3(3);

"road" —

    (a) in relation to England and Wales, means any highway and any other road to which the public has access, and includes bridges over which a road passes; and

    (b) [*applies to Scotland*];

"road transport undertaking" means an undertaking which involves the use of goods vehicles—

    (a) under an operator's licence, or

    (b) in accordance with the law of Northern Ireland or the law of any member State other than the United Kingdom;

"standard licence" has the meaning given in section 3(2);

"statutory provision" means a provision contained in an Act or in subordinate legislation within the meaning of the Interpretation Act 1978;

"traffic area" means a traffic area constituted for the purposes of the Public Passenger Vehicles Act 1981;

"transport manager", in relation to a business, means an individual who is in, or who is engaged to enter into, the employment of the holder of a standard licence and who, either alone or jointly with one or more other persons, has continuous and effective responsibility for the management of the transport operations of the business in so far as they relate to the carriage of goods;

"vehicle combination" means a combination of goods vehicles made up of one or more motor vehicles and one or more trailers all of which are linked together when travelling.

(2) For the purposes of this Act, the driver of a vehicle, if it belongs to him or is in his possession under an agreement for hire, hire-purchase or loan, and in any other case the person whose servant or agent the driver is, shall be deemed to be the person using the vehicle; and references to using a vehicle shall be construed accordingly.

(3) In this Act references to vehicles being authorised to be used under an operator's licence are to be read in accordance with section 5.

(4) For the purposes of this Act, a person who is an applicant for, or a holder of, a standard licence, or who is a transport manager, shall be regarded as being engaged in a road transport undertaking if—

    (a) in a case where that person is an individual, he is either—

        (i) the holder, or one of the joint holders, of an operator's licence, or

        (ii) in the employment of a person who carries on a road transport undertaking and that undertaking gives him responsibility for the operation of goods vehicles used under an operator's licence; or

    (b) in a case where that person is a company, either—

        (i) the company is the holder of an operator's licence, or

        (ii) the company is a subsidiary of the holder of an operator's licence and goods vehicles used under that licence belong to the company or are in its possession.

(5) Anything required or authorised by this Act to be done by or to a traffic commissioner by whom a licence was issued may be done by or to any person for the time being acting as traffic commissioner for the area for which the first-mentioned commissioner was acting at the time of the issuing of the licence.

A36.65   *[The term "motor vehicle" (to which reference is made in section 58(1)) is defined in the Road Traffic Act 1960, s.253(1), as "a mechnically propelled vehicle intended or adapted for use on roads"; and the same provision defines the term "trailer" as "a vehicle drawn by a motor vehicle".]*

Supplementary provisions

59. Transitional provisions, etc.

A36.66   (1) The transitional provisions and transitory modifications of this Act contained in Schedule 6 shall have effect.

(2) Without prejudice to the generality of paragraphs 2 to 4 of that Schedule, an existing licence shall continue in force as if it had been issued under this Act, and in this Act or any other enactment, instrument or document, any reference to, or including a reference to, an operator's licence issued under this Act shall, so far as the nature of the reference permits, be construed as including a reference to an existing licence.

(3) In subsection (2) *"existing licence"* means any operator's licence within the meaning of Part V of the Transport Act 1968 which was in force immediately before the commencement of this Act.

A36.67   *[This Act was, in the main, brought into force on January 1, 1996; see the Goods Vehicles (Licensing of Operators) Act 1995 (Commencement and Transitional Provisions) Order 1995 (S.I. 1995 No. 2181), art.2. By reference to the definitions of "appointed day" and "existing licence" in paragraph 1 of the Schedule to that order, it is clear that January 1, 1996 should be treated for the purposes of section 59(3) as the commencement date of this Act.]*

A36.68   **60. Consequential amendments and repeals**   *[Omitted.]*

61. Commencement

A36.69   (1) Subject to section 50(2) (which makes provision in relation to the commencement of section 50 and Schedule 5) this Act shall come into force on such day as the Secretary of State may by order appoint.

(2) An order under subsection (1) may contain such transitional provisions and savings as appear to the Secretary of State to be necessary or expedient in connection with the coming into force of any provision of this Act which reproduces the effect of any provision of the Deregulation and Contracting Out Act 1994 which was not brought into force before the appointed day.

(3) Where any provision of the Deregulation and Contracting Out Act 1994 was brought into force before the appointed day by an order containing transitional provisions or savings in connection with the coming into force of that provision, an order under subsection (1) may contain corresponding transitional provisions or savings in connection with the coming into force of any provision of this Act which reproduces the effect of that provision of that Act.

(4) In subsections (2) and (3) *"the appointed day"* means the day appointed under subsection (1).

[The Goods Vehicles (Licensing of Operators) (Commencement and Transitional Provisions) Order   **A36.70**
1995 (S.I. 1995 No. 2181) has been made under this section. It brought this Act (other than section 50
and Schedule 5) into force on January 1, 1996.]

62. Short title and extent

(1) This Act may be cited as the Goods Vehicles (Licensing of Operators) Act 1995.   **A36.71**

(2) The amendments specified in Schedule 7 and the repeals and revocations specified in Schedule 8 have the same extent as the enactments and instruments to which they relate.

(3) Subject to subsection (2), this Act does not extend to Northern Ireland.

SCHEDULES

SCHEDULE 1   Section 2

MEANING OF "SMALL GOODS VEHICLE"

1. For the purposes of section 2 a *small goods vehicle* is a goods vehicle falling within any   **A36.72**
of paragraphs 2 to 4.

2. A goods vehicle falls within this paragraph if it does not form part of a vehicle combination and—

(a) has a relevant plated weight not exceeding 3.5 tonnes, or

(b) if it does not have a relevant plated weight, has an unladen weight not exceeding 1525 kilograms.

3.—(1) A goods vehicle falls within this paragraph if it forms part of a vehicle combin-   **A36.73**
ation, other than an articulated combination, and the combination is such that—

(a) in a case where all the vehicles comprised in it, or all of those vehicles except any small trailer, have relevant plated weights, the aggregate of the relevant plated weights of those vehicles, exclusive of any such trailer, does not exceed 3.5 tonnes, or

(b) in any other case, the aggregate of the unladen weights of the vehicles comprised in the combination, exclusive of any small trailer, does not exceed 1525 kilograms.

(2) In this paragraph *"small trailer"* means a trailer having an unladen weight not exceeding 1020 kilograms.

4. A goods vehicle falls within this paragraph if it forms part of an articulated combination which is such that—

(a) in a case where the trailer comprised in the combination has a relevant plated weight, the aggregate of—

(i) the unladen weight of the motor vehicle comprised in the combination, and
(ii) the relevant plated weight of that trailer,

does not exceed 3.5 tonnes, or

(b) in any other case, the aggregate of the unladen weights of the motor vehicle and the trailer comprised in the combination does not exceed 1525 kilograms.

5. In any provision of paragraphs 2 to 4 *"relevant plated weight"* means a plated weight of the description specified in relation to that provision by regulations.

[SCHEDULE 1A

Detention of Vehicles used without Operator's Licence

A36.74   *Schedule 1A.*   Most of the paragraphs of this Schedule merely provide for the making of regulations for the purposes indicated in the italicised heading preceding the various paragraphs. As to the regulations, see further the note at the end of this Schedule.

Interpretation

A36.75   **1.**—(1) In this Schedule—

"authorised person" means—

(a) an examiner appointed by the Secretary of State under section 66A of the Road Traffic Act 1988 [*q.v.*], or

(b) a person acting under the direction of such an examiner;

"contents", in relation to a goods vehicle, means any goods carried by that vehicle;

"immobilisation device" means any device or appliance which is an immobilisation device for the purposes of section 104 of the Road Traffic Regulation Act 1984 [*q.v.*].

(2) Regulations may, for the purposes of regulations made by virtue of this Schedule, make provision as to the meaning of "owner" as regards a goods vehicle.

(3) Regulations made by virtue of sub-paragraph (2) may, in particular, provide that the owner of a motor vehicle at a particular time shall be taken to be—

(a) any person in whose name it is then registered by virtue of the Vehicle Excise and Registration Act 1994, or

(b) any person in whose operator's licence it is then specified.

Detention of property

A36.76   **2, 3.**   *[Omitted.]*

Immobilisation and removal

A36.77   **4–7.**   *[Omitted.]*

Return or disposal of vehicle

8–12.   *[Omitted.]*   **A36.78**

Return or disposal of contents of vehicle

13.   *[Omitted.]*   **A36.79**

Custody of property

14.   *[Omitted.]*   **A36.80**

Proceeds of sale

15.   *[Omitted.]*   **A36.81**

Disputes

16.   *[Omitted.]*   **A36.82**

Obstruction of authorised persons

17.   Regulations may provide that a person who intentionally obstructs an authorised   **A36.83**
person in the exercise of his powers under regulations made by virtue of paragraph 2 or 6
is guilty of an offence and liable on summary conviction to a fine not exceeding level 3 on
the standard scale.

Offences as to securing possession of property

18.—(1) Regulations may provide that where—   **A36.84**
   (a) a person makes a declaration with a view to securing the return of a goods vehicle
        under the regulations made by virtue of paragraph 10,
   (b) the declaration is that the vehicle was not being, or had not been, used in contra-
        vention of section 2, and
   (c) the declaration is to the person's knowledge either false or in any material respect
        misleading,

he is guilty of an offence.

   (2) Regulations may provide that a person guilty of such an offence is liable—
   (a) on summary conviction, to a fine not exceeding the statutory maximum, and
   (b) on conviction on indictment, to imprisonment for a term not exceeding two years
        or to a fine or to both.]

[Schedule 1A was inserted by the Transport Act 2000, s.262(2) (with effect from February 1, 2001;   **A36.85**
see the Transport Act 2000 (Commencement No. 3) Order 2001 (S.I. 2001 No. 57; not reproduced in this
work)) (the subsequent amendment of S.I. 2001 No. 57 by the Transport Act 2000 (Commencement No.
3) (Amendment) Order 2001 (S.I. 2001 No. 115; not reproduced in this volume) does not affect the inser-
tion of Schedule 1A).
As at April 1, 2001, no regulations had been made under this Schedule.]

INFORMATION ABOUT, AND CONVICTIONS OF, APPLICANTS FOR AND HOLDERS OF OPERATORS' LICENCES

Information to be given under section 8

A36.86   **1.** The information referred to in section 8(4) is the following—

(a) such particulars as the traffic commissioner may require with respect to the purposes for which the vehicles referred to in the statement under section 8(3) are proposed to be used;

(b) particulars of the arrangements for securing that—

(i) Part VI of the Transport Act 1968 (drivers' hours), and
(ii) the applicable Community rules, within the meaning of that Part,

will be complied with in the case of those vehicles;

(c) particulars of the arrangements for securing that those vehicles will not be overloaded;

(d) particulars of the facilities and arrangements for securing that those vehicles will be maintained in a fit and serviceable condition;

(e) particulars of any relevant activities carried on, at any time before the making of the application, by any relevant person;

(f) particulars of any notifiable convictions which have occurred during the five years preceding the making of the application;

(g) particulars of the financial resources which are or are likely to be available to the applicant;

(h) where the applicant is a company, the names of the directors and officers of—

(i) the company, and
(ii) any company of which that company is a subsidiary;

(i) where the vehicles referred to in the statement under section 8(3) are proposed to be operated by the applicant in partnership with other persons, the names of those other persons.

"Relevant person"

A36.87   **2.** In this Schedule *"relevant person"* means any of the following persons, namely—

(a) the applicant;

(b) any company of which the applicant is or has been a director;

(c) where the applicant is a company, any person who is a director of the company;

(d) where the applicant proposes to operate the vehicles referred to in the statement under section 8(3) in partnership with other persons, any of those other persons;

(e) any company of which any such person as is mentioned in sub-paragraph (c) or (d) is or has been a director; or

(f) where the applicant is a company, any company of which the applicant is a subsidiary.

"Relevant activities"

A36.88   **3.** In paragraph 1(e) *"relevant activities"* means any of the following—

(a) activities in carrying on any trade or business in the course of which vehicles of any description are operated;

(b) activities as a person employed for the purposes of any such trade or business; or

(c) activities as a director of a company carrying on any such trade or business.

"Notifiable convictions"

4. The following are *"notifiable convictions"*, namely—   **A36.89**

(a) any conviction of a relevant person of an offence such as is mentioned in paragraph 5, and

(b) any conviction of a servant or agent of a relevant person of an offence such as is mentioned in sub-paragraph (a), (b), (d), (f), (g), (i) or (j) of that paragraph.

Offences

5. The offences are—   **A36.90**

(a) an offence under section 53 of the Road Traffic Act 1988 (plating certificates and goods vehicle test certificates);

(b) an offence committed in relation to a goods vehicles consisting in the contravention of any provision (however expressed) contained in or having effect under any enactment (including any enactment passed after this Act) relating to—

    (i) the maintenance of vehicles in a fit and serviceable condition;

    (ii) limits of speed and weight laden and unladen, and the loading of goods vehicles; or

    (iii) the licensing of drivers;

(c) an offence under—

    (i) this Act;

    (ii) Part V of the Transport Act 1968 or section 233 or 235 of the Road Traffic Act 1960 so far as applicable (by virtue of Schedule 10 to the 1968 Act) to licences or means of identification under that Part;

    (iii) regulation 33(2) or (3) of the Goods Vehicles (Operators' Licences, Qualifications and Fees) Regulations 1984; or

    (iv) any regulation made under this Act or the Transport Act 1968 which is prescribed for the purposes of this paragraph;

(d) an offence under, or of conspiracy to contravene, Part VI of the Transport Act 1968 (drivers' hours) committed in relation to a goods vehicle;

(e) an offence under, or of conspiracy to contravene, section 13 of the Hydrocarbon Oil Duties Act 1979 (unlawful use of rebated fuel oil) committed in relation to a goods vehicle;

(f) an offence under section 173 or 174 of the Road Traffic Act 1988 (forgery, false statements and withholding of information) committed in relation to an international road haulage permit within the meaning of that Act;

(g) an offence under section 2 of the International Road Haulage Permits Act 1975 (removing, or causing or permitting the removal of, a goods vehicle or trailer from the United Kingdom in contravention of a prohibition imposed under that section);

(h) an offence under section 74 of the Road Traffic Act 1988 (operator's duty to inspect, and keep records of inspection of, goods vehicles);

(i) an offence under—

    (i) section 3 of the Control of Pollution Act 1974;

    (ii) section 2 of the Refuse Disposal (Amenity) Act 1978;

    (iii) section 1 of the Control of Pollution (Amendment) Act 1989; or

    (iv) section 33 of the Environmental Protection Act 1990;

    (j) an offence committed in relation to a goods vehicle consisting in the contravention of—

        (i) any provision (however expressed) prohibiting or restricting the waiting of vehicles which is contained in an order made under section 1, 6, 9 or 12 of the Road Traffic Regulation Act 1984, including any such order made by virtue of paragraph 3 of Schedule 9 to that Act (local authority powers to be exercisable also by Secretary of State); or

        (ii) any provision which is contained in a traffic regulation order, within the meaning of section 1 of that Act, by virtue of section 2(4) of that Act (lorry routes).

Repealed enactments

A36.91   **6.**—(1) In paragraph 5 any reference to an offence under a provision of the Road Traffic Act 1988 includes a reference to an offence under any corresponding provision of the Road Traffic Act 1972 repealed by the Road Traffic (Consequential Provisions) Act 1988.

    (2) In paragraph 5(j)—

    (a) the reference to a provision contained in an order made under section 1, 6, 9 or 12 of the Road Traffic Regulation Act 1984 includes a reference to a provision contained in an order made under any enactment repealed by the 1984 Act and re-enacted by any of those sections, including any such order made by virtue of section 84A(2) of the Road Traffic Regulation Act 1967; and

    (b) the reference to a provision contained in a traffic regulation order by virtue of section 2(4) of the 1984 Act includes a reference to a provision included in such an order by virtue of section 1(3AA) of the 1967 Act.

Sections 13 and 27   SCHEDULE 3

QUALIFICATIONS FOR STANDARD LICENCE

Good repute

A36.92   **1.**—(1) In determining whether an individual is of good repute, a traffic commissioner may have regard to any matter but shall, in particular, have regard to—

    (a) any relevant convictions of the individual or of his servants or agents; and

    (b) any other information in his possession which appears to him to relate to the individual's fitness to hold a licence.

    (2) In determining whether a company is of good repute, a traffic commissioner shall have regard to all the material evidence including, in particular—

    (a) any relevant convictions of the company or of any of its officers, servants or agents; and

    (b) any other information in his possession as to the previous conduct of—

        (i) any of the company's officers, servants or agents, or

        (ii) any of its directors, in whatever capacity,

    if that conduct appears to him to relate to the company's fitness to hold a licence.

    (3) For the purposes of this paragraph, the relevant convictions of any person are—

    (a) any conviction of that person of an offence such as is mentioned in paragraph 5 of Schedule 2;

    (b) any conviction of that person of an offence under the law of Northern Ireland or of the law of any country or territory outside the United Kingdom corresponding to an offence such as is mentioned in that paragraph;

(c) any conviction of that person of a serious offence within the meaning given in paragraph 3; and

(d) any conviction of that person of a road transport offence within the meaning given in paragraph 4.

[As to firms, see the Goods Vehicles (Licensing of Operators) Regulations 1995 (S.I. 1995 No. 2869),　　**A36.93**
reg.29(12)(a) below.]

[**2.** Without prejudice to the generality of a traffic commissioner's power under para-　　**A36.94**
graph 1 to determine that a person is not of good repute, a commissioner shall determine
that an individual is not of good repute if that individual has—

(a) more than one conviction of a serious offence; or

(b) been convicted of road transport offences.]

[Paragraph 2 of Schedule 3 is printed as substituted by the Goods Vehicle Operators (Qualifications)　　**A36.95**
Regulations 1999 (S.I. 1999 No. 2430), reg.2(1) below.]

3.—(1) A person has a conviction of a "*serious offence*" if—　　**A36.96**

(a) he has been convicted of any offence under the law of any part of the United Kingdom or under the law of a country or territory outside the United Kingdom, and

(b) on such conviction there was imposed on him for that offence a punishment falling within sub-paragraph (2).

(2) The punishments are—

(a) a sentence of imprisonment for a term exceeding three months;

(b) a fine exceeding level 4 on the standard scale;

(c) a community service order requiring him to perform work for more than 60 hours; and

(d) in the case of an offence committed under the law of a country or territory outside the United Kingdom, any punishment corresponding to those mentioned in paragraphs (a) to (c).

(3) In sub-paragraph (2)—

(a) the reference to a *sentence of imprisonment* includes a reference to any form of custodial sentence or order, other than one imposed under the enactments relating to mental health; and

(b) "*community service order*" means an order under [section 46 of the Powers of Criminal Courts (Sentencing) Act 2000] or under the Community Service by Offenders (Scotland) Act 1978.

[Paragraph 3 of Schedule 3 is printed as amended by the Powers of Criminal Courts (Sentencing) Act　　**A36.97**
2000, s.165(1) and Sched. 9, para.174.]

[**4.** "*Road transport offence*" means—　　**A36.98**

(a) an offence under the law of any part of the United Kingdom relating to road transport including, in particular—

　(i) an offence relating to drivers' hours of work or rest periods, the weights or dimensions of commercial vehicles, road or vehicle safety or the protection of the environment; and

　(ii) any other offence concerning professional liability; or

(b) any corresponding offence under the law of a country or territory outside the United Kingdom.]

A36.99 *[Paragraph 4 of Schedule 3 is printed as substituted by the Goods Vehicle Operators (Qualifications) Regulations 1999 (S.I. 1999 No. 2430), reg.2(2) below.]*

A36.100 **5.**—(1) Any reference in paragraphs 1 to 4 to an *offence under the law of any part of the United Kingdom* includes a reference to a civil offence (wherever committed) within the meaning of the Army Act 1955, the Air Force Act 1955 or (as the case may be) the Naval Discipline Act 1957.

(2) For the purposes of paragraphs 1 to 4—

(a) convictions which are spent for the purposes of the Rehabilitation of Offenders Act 1974 shall be disregarded; and

(b) a traffic commissioner may also disregard an offence if such time as he thinks appropriate has elapsed since the date of the conviction.

Appropriate financial standing

A36.101 **6.** *[Omitted.]*

Professional competence

7–12. *[Omitted.]*

A36.102 **13.**—(1) An individual shall be regarded as professionally competent if, and only if—

(a) he has demonstrated that he possesses the requisite skills by passing a written examination organised by an approved body and is the holder of a certificate to that effect issued by that body; or

(b) he is the holder of any other certificate of competence, diploma or other qualification recognised for the purposes of this sub-paragraph by the Secretary of State.

[(2) The written examination mentioned in sub-paragraph (1)(a) may be supplemented by an oral examination organised by the approved body in the form set out in Annex I to Council Directive No. 96/26/EC.]

[(2A) The certificate mentioned in sub-paragraph (1)(a) must take the form of the certificate set out in Annex IA to that Directive.]

(3) In sub-paragraph (1)—

"*approved body*" means—

(a) a body approved by the Secretary of State for the purposes of that sub-paragraph;

(b) a body approved by the Department of the Environment for Northern Ireland for the purposes of section 46A(5)(c) of the Transport Act (Northern Ireland) 1967 [*1967 c.37(N.I.)*]; or

(c) a body or authority designated for the purposes of Article 3.4 of [Council Directive No. 96/26/EC] by a member State other than the United Kingdom; and

[" *the requisite skills*" means knowledge corresponding to the level of training, for either national or international transport operations as the case may be, provided for in Annex I to that Directive in the subjects there listed.]

A36.103 *[Paragraph 13 of Schedule 3 is printed as amended by the Goods Vehicles Operators (Qualifications) Regulations 1999 (S.I. 1999 No. 2430), reg.4 below (subject to transitional provisions set out in S.I. 1999 No. 2430, reg.5(3)–(5)).*

The transitional provisions apply the text of paragraph 13 before its amendment by S.I. 1999 No. 2430 to (inter alia) certificates of professional competence issued before October 1, 1999. The unamended text read as follows:

13.—(1) An individual shall be regarded as professionally competent if, and only if—

(a) he has demonstrated that he possesses the requisite skills by passing a written examination organised by an approved body and is the holder of a certificate to that effect issued by that body; or

(b) he is the holder of any other certificate of competence, diploma or other qualification recognised for the purposes of this sub-paragraph by the Secretary of State.

(2) The written examination mentioned in sub-paragraph (1)(a) may take the form of a multiple-choice examination.

(3) In sub-paragraph (1)—

"*approved body*" means—

(a) a body approved by the Secretary of State for the purposes of that sub-paragraph;

(b) a body approved by the Department of the Environment for Northern Ireland for the purposes of section 46A(5)(c) of the Transport Act (Northern Ireland) 1967 [*1967 c.37(N.I.)*]; or

(c) a body or authority designated for the purposes of Article 3.4 of the 1974 Council Directive by a member State other than the United Kingdom; and

"*the requisite skills*" means skills in the subjects listed in Part A and, in the case of a licence to cover international operations, Part B, of the Annex to the 1974 Council Directive.]

14. In relation to a certificate of professional competence which was issued before 4   **A36.104**
February 1991, or which was issued on or after that date to a person who before that date passed the whole or any part of the examination leading to the issue of that certificate, paragraph 13 has effect with the following modifications—

(a) for sub-paragraph (1)(a) there shall be substituted—

"(a) he is the holder of a certificate issued by an approved body to the effect that he possesses the requisite skills; or";

(b) sub-paragraph (2) shall be omitted; and

(c) references in sub-paragraph (3) to the 1974 Council Directive shall be construed as references to that Directive as it had effect immediately before it was amended by Community Council Directive No. 89/438/EEC dated 21 June 1989.

[As to the revocation of paragraph 14 of Schedule 3 in accordance with transitional provisions relating to   **A36.105**
certificates of professional competence issued before February 4, 1991 or issued on or after that date to a person who had previously passed the examination leading to the issue of that certificate, see the Goods Vehicle Operators (Qualifications) Regulations 1999 (S.I. 1999 No. 2430), reg.5(4) and (5) below.]

Transport manager to be notified of proceedings

15.   *[Omitted.]*   **A36.106**

SCHEDULE 4

TRANSFER OF OPERATING CENTRES

[Omitted.]

LARGE GOODS VEHICLES

Meaning of "large goods vehicle"

A36.107   **1.**—(1) For the purposes of this Schedule, a large goods vehicle is a goods vehicle, other than a hauling vehicle, falling within any of sub-paragraphs (2) to (4).

(2) A goods vehicle falls within this sub-paragraph if—

(a) it has a relevant plated weight exceeding 16260 kilograms, or

(b) in the case of a vehicle which does not have a relevant plated weight, it has an unladen weight exceeding 5080 kilograms.

(3) A goods vehicle falls within this sub-paragraph if it forms part of a vehicle combination, other than an articulated combination, and the combination is such that—

(a) in a case where all the vehicles comprised in the combination, or all of those vehicles except any small trailer, have relevant plated weights, the aggregate of the relevant plated weights of the vehicles comprised in the combination, exclusive of any such trailer, exceeds 16260 kilograms, or

(b) in any other case, the aggregate of the unladen weights of the vehicles comprised in it, exclusive of any small trailer, exceeds 5080 kilograms;

and in this sub-paragraph *"small trailer"* means a trailer having an unladen weight not exceeding 1020 kilograms.

(4) A goods vehicle falls within this sub-paragraph if it forms part of an articulated combination which is such that—

(a) in a case where the trailer comprised in the combination has a relevant plated weight, the aggregate of—

(i) the unladen weight of the motor vehicle comprised in the combination, and
(ii) the relevant plated weight of that trailer,

exceeds 16260 kilograms, or

(b) in any other case, the aggregate of the unladen weights of the motor vehicle and the trailer comprised in the combination exceeds 5080 kilograms.

(5) In any provision of sub-paragraphs (2) to (4) *"relevant plated weight"* means a plated weight of the description specified in relation to that provision by regulations.

(6) In sub-paragraph (1) *"hauling vehicle"* means a motor tractor, a light locomotive, a heavy locomotive or the motor vehicle comprised in an articulated combination; and in this sub-paragraph *"motor tractor"*, *"light locomotive"* and *"heavy locomotive"* have the same meaning as in the Road Traffic Act 1960.

A36.108   *[The terms "motor tractor", "light locomotive" and "heavy locomotive" (to which reference is made in paragraph 1(6)) are defined in the Road Traffic Act 1960, s.253(6), (7) and (8), respectively (as amended by the Road Traffic Acts 1960 and 1972, Road Traffic Regulation Act 1984 and Transport Act 1968 (Metrication) Regulations 1981 (S.I. 1981 No. 1373)) in the following terms:*

(6) In this Act *"motor tractor"* means a mechanically propelled vehicle which is not constructed itself to carry a load, other than the following articles, that is to say, water, fuel, accumulators and other equipment used for the purpose of propulsion, loose tools and loose equipment, and the weight of which unladen does not exceed [7370 kilograms].

(7) In this Act *"light locomotive"* means a mechanically propelled vehicle which is not

constructed itself to carry a load, other than any of the articles aforesaid, and the weight of which unladen does not exceed [11690 kilograms] but does exceed [7370 kilograms].

(8) In this Act "*heavy locomotive*" means a mechnically propelled vehicle which is not constructed itself to carry a load, other than any of the articles aforesaid, and the weight of which unladen exceeds [11690 kilograms].*]*

Consignment notes

2.—(1) Subject to sub-paragraph (2), no goods shall be carried on a large goods vehicle   **A36.109** unless a document (a "*consignment note*") in the prescribed form and containing the prescribed particulars has been completed and signed in the prescribed manner and is carried by the driver of the vehicle.

(2) Sub-paragraph (1) shall not apply—

(a) to the carriage of goods on any journey or on a vehicle of any class exempted from that sub-paragraph by regulations; or

(b) to any carriage of goods which is lawful without the authority of an operator's licence.

(3) Subject to the provisions of regulations, a traffic commissioner may dispense with the observance, as respects the carriage of goods under an operator's licence issued by him, of any requirement of sub-paragraph (1), where he is satisfied that it is not reasonably practicable for that requirement to be observed.

(4) Such a dispensation may be granted—

(a) generally;

(b) as respects a particular vehicle; or

(c) as respects the use of vehicles for a particular purpose.

(5) The consignment note relating to the goods carried on a vehicle on any journey shall, at the conclusion of that journey, be preserved for the prescribed period by the person who used the vehicle for carrying the goods on that journey.

(6) Any person who—

(a) uses or drives a vehicle in contravention of sub-paragraph (1), or

(b) fails to comply with sub-paragraph (5),

is guilty of an offence and liable on summary conviction to a fine not exceeding level 4 on the standard scale.

Powers of entry and inspection

3.—(1) An officer may require any person to produce and permit him to inspect and   **A36.110** copy—

(a) any document which is required by or under paragraph 2 to be carried by that person as driver of a vehicle; or

(b) any document which that person is required by or under that paragraph to preserve;

and that document shall, if the officer so requires by notice in writing served on that person, be produced at the office of the traffic commissioner specified in the notice within such time (not being less than 10 days) from the service of the notice as may be so specified.

(2) An officer may at any time enter any large goods vehicle and inspect that vehicle and any goods carried on it.

(3) Where an officer has reason to believe—

(a) that a large goods vehicle is being kept on any premises, or

(b) that any such documents as are mentioned in sub-paragraph (1) are to be found on any premises,

he may, at any time which is reasonable having regard to the circumstances of the case, enter those premises and inspect any such vehicle, and inspect and copy any such document, which he finds there.

(4) For the purpose of exercising his powers under sub-paragraph (1)(a) or (2), an officer may detain the vehicle in question during such time as is required for the exercise of that power.

(5) The powers conferred by sub-paragraphs (1) to (4) are exercisable on production by the officer, if so required, of his authority.

(6) Any person who—

(a) fails to comply with any requirement under sub-paragraph (1), or

(b) obstructs any officer in the exercise of his powers under sub-paragraph (2), (3) or (4),

is guilty of an offence and liable on summary conviction to a fine not exceeding level 3 on the standard scale.

(7) In this paragraph "*officer*" has the meaning given in section 42(1) (as amended by paragraph 5 below).

(8) The powers conferred by this paragraph on an officer shall be exercisable also by a police constable who shall not, if wearing uniform, be required to produce any authority.

Falsification of consignment notes and records

A36.111   **4.**—(1) Any person who—

(a) makes, or causes to be made, any document required to be made under paragraph 2 which he knows to be false, or

(b) with intent to deceive, alters or causes to be altered any document required to be made under that paragraph,

is guilty of an offence.

(2) A person guilty of an offence under sub-paragraph (1) is liable—

(a) on summary conviction, to a fine not exceeding the statutory maximum;

(b) on conviction on indictment, to imprisonment for a term not exceeding two years or to a fine or to both.

Amendment of sections 38, 41 and 42 of this Act

A36.112   **5.**—(1) The following amendments shall take effect on the day appointed for the coming into force of paragraph 3, namely, in sections 38(2)(c) and 42(1)(b), after the words "sections 40 and 41" there shall be inserted the words "and paragraph 3 of Schedule 5".

(2) The following amendments shall take effect on the day appointed for the coming into force of paragraph 4, namely, in section 41(1) and (2)(b), after the words "section 38 or 39" there shall be inserted the words "or paragraph 4(1) of Schedule 5".

SCHEDULE 6   Section 59

Transitional Provisions, Transitory Modifications and Savings

General transitional provisions

1. The substitution of this Act for the provisions repealed and revoked by it shall not affect the continuity of the law.   **A36.113**

2. In so far as any thing done (including any subordinate legislation made or other instrument issued) under a provision repealed or revoked by this Act could have been done under the corresponding provision of this Act, it shall have effect as if done under that corresponding provision.

3. Any reference (express or implied) in this Act or any other enactment, instrument or document to—   **A36.114**

(a) any provision of this Act, or

(b) things done or falling to be done under or for the purposes of any provision of this Act,

shall, so far as the nature of the reference permits, be construed as including, in relation to the times, circumstances or purposes in relation to which the corresponding provision repealed or revoked by this Act had effect, a reference to that corresponding provision or (as the case may be) to things done or falling to be done under or for the purposes of that corresponding provision.

4. Any reference (express or implied) in any enactment, instrument or document to—

(a) a provision repealed or revoked by this Act, or

(b) things done or falling to be done under or for the purposes of such a provision,

shall, so far as the nature of the reference permits, be construed as including, in relation to the times, circumstances or purposes in relation to which the corresponding provision of this Act has effect, a reference to that corresponding provision or (as the case may be) to things done or falling to be done under or for the purposes of that corresponding provision.

5. Paragraphs 1 to 4 have effect, in relation to the substitution of this Act for the provisions repealed and revoked by it, in place of section 17(2) of the Interpretation Act 1978 (but without prejudice to any other provision of that Act).   **A36.115**

Meaning of "local authority" in relation to Scotland or Wales

6. *[Relates to section 12(2) (not reproduced in this work).]*

Meaning of "holding company" and "subsidiary"

7. For the purposes of this Act as it applies in relation to licences granted before 11 November 1990 (the date on which section 144(1) of the Companies Act 1989 came into force) the expressions "*holding company*" and "*subsidiary*" have the meaning given by section 736 of the Companies Act 1985 as originally enacted.   **A36.116**

SCHEDULE 7   Section 60(1)   **A36.117**

Consequential Amendments

[Omitted.]

SCHEDULE 8

REPEALS AND REVOCATIONS

[Omitted.]

The Crime (Sentences) Act 1997

(1997 c. 43)

An Act to make further provision with respect to the treatment of offenders and for connected purposes.   **A37.01**

[21st March 1997]

*   *   *

40. Fine defaulters

(1) This section applies in any case where a magistrates' court—   **A37.02**

    (a) has power under Part III of the 1980 Act to issue a warrant of commitment for default in paying a sum adjudged to be paid by a conviction of a magistrates' court (other than a sum ordered to be paid under section 71 of the Criminal Justice Act 1988 or section 2 of the Drug Trafficking Act 1994); or

    (b) would, but for [section 89 of the Powers of Criminal Courts (Sentencing) Act 2000] (restrictions on custodial sentences for persons under 21), have power to issue such a warrant for such default.

(2) Subject to subsection (3) below, the magistrates' court may, instead of issuing a warrant of commitment or, as the case may be, proceeding under section 81 of the 1980 Act (enforcement of fines imposed on young offenders), order the person in default to be disqualified, for such period not exceeding twelve months as it thinks fit, for holding or obtaining a driving licence.

(3) A magistrates' court shall not make an order under subsection (2) above unless the court has been notified by the Secretary of State that the power to make such orders is exercisable by the court and the notice has not been withdrawn.

(4) Where an order has been made under subsection (2) above for default in paying any sum—

    (a) on payment of the whole sum to any person authorised to receive it, the order shall cease to have effect;

    (b) on payment of a part of that sum to any such person, the number of weeks or months to which the order relates shall be reduced proportionately;

and the total number is so reduced if it is reduced by such number of complete weeks or months as bears to the total number the proportion most nearly approximating to, without exceeding, the proportion which the part paid bears to the whole sum.

(5) The Secretary of State may by order made by statutory instrument vary the period specified in subsection (2) above; but no such order shall be made unless a draft of the order has been laid before and approved by a resolution of each House of Parliament.

[(6) A court which makes an order under this section disqualifying a person from holding or obtaining a driving licence shall require him to produce any such licence held by him together with its counterpart.]

[(7) In this section—

"*driving licence*" means a licence to drive a motor vehicle granted under Part III of the Road Traffic Act 1988;

"*counterpart*", in relation to a driving licence, has the meaning given in relation to such a licence by section 108(1) of that Act.]

A37.03   *[Section 40 is printed as amended by the Powers of Criminal Courts (Sentencing) Act 2000, s.165(1) and Sched. 9, para.185.*

With effect from a date to be announced under the Criminal Justice and Court Services Act 2000, s.80, the number "18" will be substituted for the number "21" section 40(1)(b) by that Act, s.75 and Sched. 7, paras 135 and 140.]

The Private Hire Vehicles (London) Act 1998

(1998 c. 34)

An Act to provide for the licensing and regulation of private hire vehicles, and drivers and operators of such vehicles, within the metropolitan police district and the City of London; and for connected purposes. **A38.01**

[28th July 1998]

Commencement.   At the date at which this volume states the law (April 1, 2001) a number of the provisions of this Act (but not all) had been brought into force. A table listing the provisions in force on that date and the provisions in respect of which a prospective date for commencement had been announced is set out as a note to section 40 below. **A38.02**

ARRANGEMENT OF SECTIONS

Licences: general provisions

Further controls

Miscellaneous and supplementary

Introductory

1. Meaning of "private hire vehicle", "operator" and related expressions

A38.04   (1) In this Act—

(a) "*private hire vehicle*" means a vehicle constructed or adapted to seat fewer than nine passengers which is made available with a driver to the public for hire for the purpose of carrying passengers, other than a licensed taxi or a public service vehicle; and

(b) "*operator*" means a person who makes provision for the invitation or acceptance of, or who accepts, private hire bookings.

(2) Any reference in this Act to a vehicle being "*used as a private hire vehicle*" is a reference to a private hire vehicle which—

(a) is in use in connection with a hiring for the purpose of carrying one or more passengers; or

(b) is immediately available to an operator to carry out a private hire booking.

(3) Any reference in this Act to the operator of a vehicle which is being used as a private hire vehicle is a reference to the operator who accepted the booking for the hiring or to whom the vehicle is immediately available, as the case may be.

(4) In this Act "*private hire booking*" means a booking for the hire of a private hire vehicle for the purpose of carrying one or more passengers (including a booking to carry out as sub-contractor a private hire booking accepted by another operator).

(5) In this Act "*operating centre*" means premises at which private hire bookings are accepted by an operator.

Regulation of private hire vehicle operators in London

2. Requirement for London operator's licence

(1) No person shall in London make provision for the invitation or acceptance of, or accept, private hire bookings unless he is the holder of a private hire vehicle operator's licence for London (in this Act referred to as a "*London PHV operator's licence*"). **A38.05**

(2) A person who makes provision for the invitation or acceptance of private hire bookings, or who accepts such a booking, in contravention of this section is guilty of an offence and liable on summary conviction to a fine not exceeding level 4 on the standard scale.

3. London operator's licences

(1) Any person may apply to the [licensing authority] for a London PHV operator's licence. **A38.06**

(2) An application under this section shall state the address of any premises in London which the applicant proposes to use as an operating centre.

(3) The [licensing authority] shall grant a London PHV operator's licence to the applicant if [the authority] is satisfied that—

(a) the applicant is a fit and proper person to hold a London PHV operator's licence; and

(b) any further requirements that may be prescribed (which may include requirements relating to operating centres) are met.

(4) A London PHV operator's licence shall be granted subject to such conditions as may be prescribed and such other conditions as the [licensing authority] may think fit.

(5) A London PHV operator's licence shall be granted for five years or such shorter period as the [licensing authority] may consider appropriate in the circumstances of the case.

(6) A London PHV operator's licence shall—

(a) specify the address of any premises in London which the holder of the licence may use as an operating centre;

(b) be in such form and contain such particulars as the [licensing authority] may think fit.

(7) An applicant for a London PHV operator's licence may appeal to a magistrates' court against—

(a) a decision not to grant such a licence;

(b) a decision not to specify an address proposed in the application as an operating centre; or

(c) any condition (other than a prescribed condition) to which the licence is subject.

A38.07   *[Section 3 is printed as amended by the Greater London Authority Act 1999, s.254 and Sched. 21, paras 1–3.*

The Private Hire Vehicles (London) (Operators' Licences) Regulations 2000 (S.I. 2000 No. 3146) below have been made (in part) under section 3.]

4. Obligations of London operators

A38.08   (1) The holder of a London PHV operator's licence (in this Act referred to as a "*London PHV operator*") shall not in London accept a private hire booking other than at an operating centre specified in his licence.

(2) A London PHV operator shall secure that any vehicle which is provided by him for carrying out a private hire booking accepted by him in London is—

(a) a vehicle for which a London PHV licence is in force driven by a person holding a London PHV driver's licence; or

(b) a London cab driven by a person holding a London cab driver's licence.

(3) A London PHV operator shall—

(a) display a copy of his licence at each operating centre specified in the licence;

(b) keep at each specified operating centre a record in the prescribed form of the private hire bookings accepted by him there;

(c) before the commencement of each journey booked at a specified operating centre, enter in the record kept under paragraph (b) the prescribed particulars of the booking;

(d) keep at each specified operating centre such records as may be prescribed of particulars of the private hire vehicles and drivers which are available to him for carrying out bookings accepted by him at that centre;

(e) at the request of a constable or authorised officer, produce for inspection any record required by this section to be kept.

(4) If a London PHV operator ceases to use an operating centre specified in his licence he shall preserve any record he was required by this section to keep there for such period as may be prescribed.

(5) A London PHV operator who contravenes any provision of this section is guilty of an offence and liable on summary conviction to a fine not exceeding level 3 on the standard scale.

(6) It is a defence in proceedings for an offence under this section for an operator to show that he exercised all due diligence to avoid committing such an offence.

A38.09   *[The Private Hire Vehicles (London) (Operators' Licences) Regulations 2000 (S.I. 2000 No. 3146) below have been made (in part) under section 4.]*

5. Hirings accepted on behalf of another operator

A38.10   (1) A London PHV operator ("*the first operator*") who has in London accepted a private hire booking may not arrange for another operator to provide a vehicle to carry out that booking as a sub-contractor unless—

(a) the other operator is a London PHV operator and the sub-contracted booking is accepted at an operating centre in London;

(b) the other operator is licensed under section 55 of the Local Government (Miscellaneous Provisions) Act 1976 (in this Act referred to as "*the 1976 Act*") by the council of a district and the sub-contracted booking is accepted in that district; or

(c) the other operator accepts the sub-contracted booking in Scotland.

(2) A London PHV operator who contravenes subsection (1) is guilty of an offence and liable on summary conviction to a fine not exceeding level 3 on the standard scale.

(3) It is a defence in proceedings for an offence under this section for an operator to show that he exercised all due diligence to avoid committing such an offence.

(4) It is immaterial for the purposes of subsection (1) whether or not sub-contracting is permitted by the contract between the first operator and the person who made the booking.

(5) For the avoidance of doubt (and subject to any relevant contract terms), a contract of hire between a person who made a private hire booking at an operating centre in London and the London PHV operator who accepted the booking remains in force despite the making of arrangements by that operator for another contractor to provide a vehicle to carry out that booking as a sub-contractor.

Regulation of private hire vehicles in London

6. Requirements for private hire vehicle licence

(1) A vehicle shall not be used as a private hire vehicle on a road in London unless a private hire vehicle licence is in force for that vehicle.   **A38.11**

(2) The driver and operator of a vehicle used in contravention of this section are each guilty of an offence.

(3) The owner of a vehicle who permits it to be used in contravention of this section is guilty of an offence.

(4) It is a defence in proceedings for an offence under subsection (2) for the driver or operator to show that he exercised all due diligence to prevent the vehicle being used in contravention of this section.

(5) A person guilty of an offence under this section is liable on summary conviction to a fine not exceeding level 4 on the standard scale.

(6) In this section "*private hire vehicle licence*" means—

(a) except where paragraph (b) or (c) applies, a London PHV licence;

(b) if the vehicle is in use for the purposes of a hiring the booking for which was accepted outside London in a controlled district, a licence under section 48 of the 1976 Act issued by the council for that district; and

(c) if the vehicle is in use for the purposes of a hiring the booking for which was accepted in Scotland, a licence under section 10 of the Civic Government (Scotland) Act 1982 (in this Act referred to as "*the 1982 Act*"),

and for the purposes of paragraph (b) or (c) it is immaterial that the booking in question is a sub-contracted booking.

(7) This section does not apply to a vehicle used for the purposes of a hiring for a journey beginning outside London in an area of England and Wales which is not a controlled district.

7. London PHV licences

A38.12 (1) The owner of any vehicle constructed or adapted to seat fewer than nine passengers may apply to the [licensing authority] for a private hire vehicle licence for London (in this Act referred to as a "*London PHV licence*") for that vehicle.

(2) The [licensing authority] shall grant a London PHV licence for a vehicle if [the authority] is satisfied—

  (a) that the vehicle—

    (i) is suitable in type, size and design for use as a private hire vehicle;

    (ii) is safe, comfortable and in a suitable mechanical condition for that use; and

    (iii) is not of such design and appearance as would lead any person to believe that the vehicle is a London cab;

  (b) that there is in force in relation to the use of the vehicle a policy of insurance or such security as complies with the requirements of Part VI of the Road Traffic Act 1988; and

  (c) that any further requirements that may be prescribed are met.

(3) A London PHV licence may not be granted in respect of more than one vehicle.

(4) A London PHV licence shall be granted subject to such conditions as may be prescribed and such other conditions as the [licensing authority] may think fit.

(5) A London PHV licence shall be in such form and shall contain such particulars as the [licensing authority] may think fit.

(6) A London PHV licence shall be granted for one year or for such shorter period as the [licensing authority] may consider appropriate in the circumstances of the case.

(7) An applicant for a London PHV licence may appeal to a magistrates' court against a decision not to grant such a licence or against any condition (other than a prescribed condition) to which the licence is subject.

A38.13 *[Section 7 is printed as amended by the Greater London Authority Act 1999, s.254 and Sched. 21, paras 1, 2 and 4.]*

8. Obligations of owners of licensed vehicles

A38.14 (1) This section applies to the owner of any vehicle to which a London PHV licence relates.

(2) The owner shall present the vehicle for inspection and testing by or on behalf of the [licensing authority] within such period and at such place as [the authority] may by notice reasonably require.

The vehicle shall not be required to be presented under this subsection on more than three separate occasion during any one period of 12 months.

(3) The owner shall (without prejudice to section 170 of the Road Traffic Act 1988) report any accident to the vehicle materially affecting—

  (a) the safety, performance or appearance of the vehicle, or

  (b) the comfort or convenience of persons carried in the vehicle,

to the [licensing authority] as soon as reasonably practical and in any case within 72 hours of the accident occurring.

(4) If the ownership of the vehicle changes, the person who was previously the owner shall within 14 days of the change give notice to the Secretary of State of that fact and the name and address of the new owner.

(5) A person who, without reasonable excuse, contravenes any provision of this section is guilty of an offence and liable on summary conviction to a fine not exceeding level 3 on the standard scale.

[Section 8 is printed as amended by the Greater London Authority Act 1999, s.254 and Sched. 21, paras 1, 2 and 5.]   **A38.15**

9. Fitness of licensed vehicles

(1) A constable or authorised officer has power at all reasonable times to inspect and test, for the purpose of ascertaining its fitness, any vehicles to which a London PHV licence relates.   **A38.16**

(2) If a constable or authorised officer is not satisfied as to the fitness of such a vehicle he may by notice to the owner of the vehicle—

    (a) require the owner to make the vehicle available for further inspection and testing at such reasonable time and place as may be specified in the notice; and

    (b) if he thinks fit, suspend the London PHV licence relating to that vehicle until such time as a constable or authorised officer is satisfied as to the fitness of the vehicle.

(3) A notice under subsection (2)(b) shall state the grounds on which the licence is being suspended and the suspension shall take effect on the day on which it is served on the owner.

(4) A licence suspended under subsection (2)(b) shall remain suspended until such time as a constable or authorised officer by notice to the owner directs that the licence is again in force.

(5) If a licence remains suspended at the end of the period of two months beginning with the day on which a notice under subsection (2)(b) was served on the owner of the vehicle—

    (a) a constable or authorised officer may by notice to the owner direct that the licence is revoked; and

    (b) the revocation shall take effect at the end of the period of 21 days beginning with the day on which the owner is served with that notice.

(6) An owner may appeal against a notice under subsection (2)(b) or (5) to a magistrates' court.

10. Identification of licensed vehicles

(1) The [licensing authority] shall issue a disc or plate for each vehicle to which a London PHV licence relates which identifies that vehicle as a vehicle for which such a licence is in force.   **A38.17**

(2) No vehicle to which a London PHV licence relates shall be used as a private hire vehicle on a road in London unless the disc or plate issued under this section is exhibited on the vehicle in such manner as may be prescribed.

(3) The [licensing authority] may by notice exempt a vehicle from the requirement under subsection (2) when it is being used to provide a service specified in the notice if [the authority] considers it inappropriate (having regard to that service) to require the disc or plate in question to be exhibited.

(4) The driver and operator of a vehicle used in contravention of subsection (2) are each guilty of an offence.

(5) The owner of a vehicle who permits it to be used in contravention of subsection (2) is guilty of an offence.

(6) It is a defence in proceedings for an offence under subsection (4) for the driver or operator to show that he exercised all due diligence to prevent the vehicle being used in contravention of subsection (2).

(7) A person guilty of an offence under this section is liable on summary conviction to a fine not exceeding level 3 on the standard scale.

A38.18   *[Section 10 is printed as amended by the Greater London Authority Act 1999, s.254 and Sched. 21, paras 1, 2 and 6.]*

11. Prohibition of taximeters

A38.19   (1) No vehicle to which a London PHV licence relates shall be equipped with a taximeter.

(2) If such a vehicle is equipped with a taximeter, the owner of that vehicle is guilty of an offence and liable on summary conviction to a fine not exceeding level 3 on the standard scale.

(3) In this section *"taximeter"* means a device for calculating the fare to be charged in respect of any journey by reference to the distance travelled or time elapsed since the start of the journey (or a combination of both).

Regulation of drivers of private hire vehicles in London

12. Requirement for private hire vehicle driver's licence

A38.20   (1) No vehicle shall be used as a private hire vehicle on a road in London unless the driver holds a private hire vehicle driver's licence.

(2) The driver and operator of a vehicle used in contravention of this section are each guilty of an offence.

(3) The owner of a vehicle who permits it to be used in contravention of this section is guilty of an offence.

(4) It is a defence in proceedings against the operator of a vehicle for an offence under subsection (2) for the operator to show that he exercised all due diligence to prevent the vehicle being used in contravention of this section.

(5) A person guilty of an offence under this section is liable on summary conviction to a fine not exceeding level 4 on the standard scale.

(6) In this section *"private hire vehicle driver's licence"* means—

    (a) except where paragraph (b) or (c) applies, a London PHV driver's licence;

    (b) if the vehicle is in use for the purposes of a hiring the booking for which was accepted outside London in a controlled district in England and Wales, a licence under section 51 of the 1976 Act issued by the council for that district; and

    (c) if the vehicle is in use for a hiring the booking for which was accepted in Scotland, a licence under section 13 of the 1982 Act,

and for the purposes of paragraph (b) or (c) it is immaterial that the booking in question is a sub-contracted booking.

(7) This section does not apply to the use of a vehicle for the purposes of a hiring for a journey beginning ouside London in an area of England and Wales which is not a controlled district.

13. London PHV driver's licences

(1) Any person may apply to the [licensing authority] for private hire vehicle driver's **A38.21** licence for London (in this Act referred to as a "*London PHV driver's licence*").

(2) The [licensing authority] shall grant a London PHV driver's licence to an applicant if [the authority] is satisfied that—

- (a) the applicant has attained the age of 21, is (and has for at least three years been) authorised to drive a motor car and is a fit and proper person to hold a London PHV driver's licence; and
- (b) the requirement mentioned in subsection (3), and any further requirements prescribed by the [licensing authority], are met.

(3) The [licensing authority] shall require applicants to show to [the authority's] satisfaction (whether by taking a test or otherwise) that they possess a level—

- (a) of knowledge of London or parts of London; and
- (b) of general topographical skills,

which appears to [the authority] to be appropriate.

The [licensing authority] may impose different requirements in relation to different applicants.

(4) The [licensing authority] may send a copy of an application to the Commissioner of Police of the Metropolis or the Commissioner of Police for the City of London with a request for the Commissioner's observations; and the Commissioner shall respond to the request.

(5) A London PHV driver's licence—

- (a) may be granted subject to such conditions as the [licensing authority] may think fit;
- (b) shall be in such form and shall contain such particulars as the [licensing authority] may think fit; and
- (c) shall be granted for three years or for such shorter period as the [licensing authority] may consider appropriate in the circumstances of the particular case.

(6) An applicant may appeal to a magistrates' court against a decision not to grant a London PHV driver's licence or against any condition to which such a licence is subject.

(7) For the purposes of subsection (2), a person is authorised to drive a motor car if—

- (a) he holds a licence granted under Part III of the Road Traffic Act 1988 (other than a provisional licence) authorising him to drive a motor car; or
- (b) he is authorised by virtue of section 99A(1) or 109(1) of that Act (Community licences and Northern Ireland licences) to drive a motor car in Great Britain.

[Section 13 is printed as amended by the Greater London Authority Act 1999, s.254 and Sched. 21, **A38.22** *paras 1, 2 and 7.]*

14. Issue of driver's badges

(1) The [licensing authority] shall issue a badge to each person to whom [the authority] **A38.23** has granted a London PHV driver's licence.

(2) The [licensing authority] may prescribe the form of badges issued under this section.

(3) A person issued with such a badge shall, when he is the driver of a vehicle being used as a private hire vehicle, wear the badge in such position and manner as to be plainly and distinctly visible.

(4) The [licensing authority] may by notice exempt a person from the requirement under subsection (3), when he is the driver of a vehicle being used to provide a service specified in the notice if [the authority] considers it inappropriate (having regard to that service) to require the badge to be worn.

(5) Any person who without reasonable excuse contravenes subsection (3) is guilty of an offence and liable on summary conviction to a fine not exceeding level 3 in the standard scale.

A38.24   *[Section 14 is printed as amended by the Greater London Authority Act 1999, s.254 and Sched. 21, paras 1, 2 and 8.]*

Licences: general provisions

15. Applications for licences

A38.25   (1) An application for the grant of a licence under this Act shall be made in such form, and include such declarations and information, as the [licensing authority] may require.

(2) The [licensing authority] may require an applicant to furnish such further information as [the authority] may consider necessary for dealing with the application.

(3) The information which an applicant for a London PHV operator's licence may be required to furnish includes in particular information about—

    (a) any premises in London which he proposes to use as an operating centre;

    (b) any convictions recorded against him;

    (c) any business activities he has carried on before making the application;

    (d) if the applicant is or has been a director or secretary of a company, that company;

    (e) if the applicant is a company, information about the directors or secretary of that company;

    (f) if the applicant proposes to act as an operator in partnership with any other person, information about that person.

(4) An applicant for a London PHV driver's licence may be required by the [licensing authority]—

    (a) to produce a certificate signed by a registered medical practitioner to the effect that—

        (i) he is physically fit to be the driver of a private hire vehicle; and

        (ii) if any specific requirements of physical fitness have been prescribed for persons holding London PHV licences, that he meets those requirements; and

    (b) whether or not such a certificate has been produced, to submit to examination by a registered medical practitioner selected by the [licensing authority] as to his physical fitness to be the driver of such a vehicle.

(5) The provisions of this Act apply to the renewal of a licence as they apply to the grant of a licence.

A38.26   *[Section 15 is printed as amended by the Greater London Authority Act 1999, s.254 and Sched. 21, paras 1, 2 and 8.]*

16. Power to suspend or revoke licences

A38.27   (1) The [licensing authority] may suspend or revoke a licence under this Act for any reasonable cause including (without prejudice to the generality of this subsection) any ground mentioned below.

(2) A London PHV operator's licence may be suspended or revoked where—

  (a) the [licensing authority] is no longer satisfied that the licence holder is fit to hold such a licence; or

  (b) the licence holder has failed to comply with any condition of the licence or any other obligation imposed on him by or under this Act.

(3) A London PHV licence may be suspended or revoked where—

  (a) the [licensing authority] is no longer satisfied that the vehicle to which it relates is fit for use as a private hire vehicle; or

  (b) the owner has failed to comply with any condition of the licence or any other obligation imposed on him by or under this Act.

(4) A London PHV driver's licence may be suspended or revoked where—

  (a) the licence holder has, since the grant of the licence, been convicted of an offence involving dishonesty, indecency or violence;

  (b) the [licensing authority] is for any other reason no longer satisfied that the licence holder is fit to hold such a licence; or

  (c) the licence holder has failed to comply with any condition of the licence or any other obligation imposed on him by or under this Act.

[Section 16 is printed as amended by the Greater London Authority Act 1999, s.254 and Sched. 21, paras 1 and 2.]   **A38.28**

17. Suspension and revocation under section 16: procedure

(1) Where the [licensing authority] has decided to suspend or revoke a licence under   **A38.29** section 16—

  (a) [the authority] shall give notice of the decision and the grounds for the decision to the licence holder or, in the case of a London PHV licence, the owner of the vehicle to the which the licence relates; and

  (b) the suspension or revocation takes effect at the end of the period of 21 days beginning with the day on which that notice is served on the licence holder or the owner.

(2) If the [licensing authority] is of the opinion that the interests of public safety require the suspension or revocation of a licence to have immediate effect, and [the authority] includes a statement of that opinion and the reasons for it in the notice of suspension or revocation, the suspension or revocation takes effect when the notice is served on the licence holder or vehicle owner (as the case may be).

(3) A licence suspended under this section shall remain suspended until such time as the [licensing authority] by notice directs that the licence is again in force.

(4) The holder of a London PHV operator's or driver's licence, or the owner of a vehicle to which a PHV licence relates, may appeal to a magistrates' court against a decision under section 16 to suspend or revoke that licence.

[Section 17 is printed as amended by the Greater London Authority Act 1999, s.254 and Sched. 21, paras 1, 2 and 10.]   **A38.30**

18. Variation of operator's licence at the request of the operator

(1) The [licensing authority] may, on the application of a London PHV operator, vary   **A38.31** his licence by adding a reference to a new operating centre or removing an existing reference to an operating centre.

(2) An application for the variation of a licence under this section shall be made in such form, and include such declarations and information, as the [licensing authority] may require.

(3) The [licensing authority] may require an applicant to furnish such further information as he may consider necessary for dealing with the application.

(4) The [licensing authority] shall not add a reference to a new operating centre unless [the authority] is satisfied that the premises in question meet any requirements prescribed under section 3(3)(b).

(5) An applicant for the variation of a London PHV operator's licence under this section may appeal to a magistrates' court against a decision not to add a new operating centre to the licence.

A38.32   *[Section 18 is printed as amended by the Greater London Authority Act 1999, s.254 and Sched. 21, paras 1, 2 and 11.]*

19. [Variation of operator's licence by the licensing authority]

A38.33   (1) The [licensing authority] may—

      (a) suspend the operation of a London PHV operator's licence so far as relating to any operating centre specified in the licence; or

      (b) vary such a licence by removing a reference to an operating centre previously specified in the licence,

if [the authority] is no longer satisfied that the operating centre in question meets any requirements prescribed under section 3(3)(b) or for any other reasonable cause.

(2) Where the [licensing authority] has decided to suspend the operation of a licence as mentioned in subsection (1)(a) or vary a licence as mentioned in subsection (1)(b)—

      (a) [the authority] shall give notice of the decision and the grounds for it to the licence holder; and

      (b) the decision shall take effect at the end of the period of 21 days beginning with the day on which the licence holder is served with that notice.

(3) If the [licensing authority] is of the opinion that the interests of public safety require [the authority's] decision to have immediate effect, and [the authority] includes a statement of that opinion and the reasons for it in the notice, [the authority's] decision shall take effect when the notice is served on the licence holder.

(4) If a licence is suspended in relation to an operating centre, the premises in question shall not be regarded for the purposes of this Act as premises at which the licence holder is authorised to accept private hire bookings, until such time as the [licensing authority] by notice states that the licence is no longer suspended in relation to those premises.

(5) The holder of a London PHV operator's licence may appeal to a magistrates' court against a decision under subsection (1).

A38.34   *[Section 19 is printed as amended by the Greater London Authority Act 1999, s.254 and Sched. 21, paras 1, 2 and 12.]*

A38.35   **20. Fees for grant of licences, etc.**   *[Omitted.]*

21. Production of documents

A38.36   (1) The holder of a London PHV operator's licence or a London PHV driver's licence shall at the request of a constable or authorised officer produce his licence for inspection.

(2) The owner of a vehicle to which a London PHV licence relates shall at the request of a constable or authorised officer produce for inspection—

(a) the London PHV licence for that vehicle;

(b) the certificate of the policy of insurance or security required in respect of the vehicle by Part VI of the Road Traffic Act 1988.

(3) A document required to be produced under this section shall be produced either forthwith or—

(a) if the request is made by a constable, at any police station within London nominated by the licence holder or vehicle owner when the request is made, or

(b) if the request is made by an unauthorised officer, at such place as the officer may reasonably require,

before the end of the period of 6 days beginning with the day on which the request is made.

(4) A person who without reasonable excuse contravenes this section is guilty of an offence and liable on summary conviction to a fine not exceeding level 3 on the standard scale.

22. Return of licences, etc.

(1) The holder of a London PHV operator's licence shall return the licence to the [licensing authority] after the expiry or revocation of that licence, within the period of 7 days after the day on which the licence expires or the revocation takes effect.   **A38.37**

(2) The owner of a vehicle to which a London PHV licence relates shall return the licence and the plate or disc which was issued for the vehicle under section 10 to the [licensing authority] after the expiry or revocation of that licence within the period of 7 days after the day on which the licence expires or the revocation takes effect.

(3) The holder of a London PHV driver's licence shall return the licence and his driver's badge to the [licensing authority] after the expiry or revocation of that licence, within the period of 7 days after the day on which the licence expires or the revocation takes effect.

(4) On the suspension of a licence under this Act, the [licensing authority], a constable or an authorised officer may by notice direct the holder of the licence, or the owner of the vehicle, to return the licence to [the authority, constable or officer (as the case may be)] within the period of 7 days after the day on which the notice is served on that person.

A direction under this subsection may also direct—

(a) the return by the vehicle owner of the disc or plate which was issued for the vehicle under section 10 (in the case of a London PHV licence); or

(b) the return by the licence holder of the driver's badge (in the case of a London PHV driver's licence).

(5) A person who without reasonable excuse fails to comply with any requirement or direction under this section to return a licence, disc, plate or badge is guilty of an offence.

(6) A person guilty of an offence under this section is liable on summary conviction—

(a) to a fine not exceeding level 3 on the standard scale; and

(b) in the case of a continuing offence, to a fine not exceeding ten pounds for each day during which an offence continues after conviction.

(7) A constable or authorised officer is entitled to remove and retain the plate or disc from a vehicle to which an expired, suspended or revoked London PHV licence relates following—

(a) a failure to comply with subsection (2) or a direction under subsection (4);

(b) a suspension or revocation of the licence which has immediate effect by virtue of section 9(3) or 17(2).

A38.38   *[Section 22 is printed as amended by the Greater London Authority Act 1999, s.254 and Sched. 21, paras 1, 2 and 13.]*

A38.39   **23. Register of licences**   *[Omitted.]*

24. [Delegation of functions by the licensing authority]   *[Omitted.]*

25. Appeals

A38.40   (1) This section applies to any appeal which lies under this Act to a magistrates' court against a decision of the [licensing authority], a constable or an authorised officer in relation to, or to an application for, a licence under this Act.

(2) If the [licensing authority] has exercised the power to delegate functions under section 24, such an appeal shall be heard by the magistrates' court for the petty sessions area in which the person to whom the functions have been delegated has his office or principal office.

(3) Any such appeal shall be by way of complaint for an order and the Magistrates' Courts Act 1980 shall apply to the proceedings.

(4) The time within which a person may bring such an appeal is 21 days from the date on which notice of the decision appealed against is served on him.

(5) In the case of a decision where an appeal lies, the notice of the decision shall state the right of appeal to a magistrates' court and the time within which an appeal may be brought.

(6) An appeal against any decision of a magistrates' court in pursuance of an appeal to which this section applies shall lie to the Crown Court at the instance of any party to the proceedings in the magistrates' court.

(7) Where on appeal a court varies or reverses any decision of the [licensing authority], a constable or an authorised officer, the order of the court shall be given effect to by the [licensing authority] or, as the case may be, a constable or authorised officer.

A38.41   *[Section 25 is printed as amended by the Greater London Authority Act 1999, s.254 and Sched. 21, paras 1 and 2.]*

26. Effect of appeal on decision appealed against

A38.42   (1) If any decision of the [licensing authority] against which a right of appeal is conferred by this Act—

(a) involves the execution of any work or the taking of any action;

(b) makes it unlawful for any person to carry on a business which he was lawfully carrying on at the time of the decision,

the decision shall not take effect until the time for appealing has expired or (where an appeal is brought) until the appeal is disposed of or withdrawn.

(2) This section does not apply in relation to a decision to suspend, vary or revoke a licence if the notice of suspension, variation or revocation directs that, in the interests of public safety, the decision is to have immediate effect.

A38.43   *[Section 26 is printed as amended by the Greater London Authority Act 1999, s.254 and Sched. 21, paras 1 and 2.]*

27. Obstruction of authorised officers, etc.

(1) A person who wilfully obstructs a constable or authorised officer acting in pursuance   **A38.44**
of this Act is guilty of an offence and liable on summary conviction to a fine not exceeding
level 3 on the standard scale.

(2) A person who, without reasonable excuse—

   (a) fails to comply with any requirement properly made to such person by a constable
      or authorised officer acting in pursuance of this Act; or

   (b) fails to give a constable or authorised officer acting in pursuance of this Act any
      other assistance or information which he may reasonably require of such person
      for the purpose of performing his functions under this Act,

is guilty of an offence and liable on summary conviction to a fine not exceeding level 3 on
the standard scale.

(3) A person who makes any statement which he knows to be false in giving any information to an authorised officer or constable acting in pursuance of this Act is guilty of an offence
and liable on summary conviction to a fine not exceeding level 5 on the standard scale.

28. Penalty for false statements

A person who knowingly or recklessly makes a statement or furnishes information which   **A38.45**
is false or misleading in any material particular for the purpose of procuring the grant or
renewal of a licence under this Act, or the variation of an operator's licence under section
18, is guilty of an offence and liable on summary conviction to a fine not exceeding level 5
on the standard scale.

29. Saving for vehicle used for funerals and weddings

Nothing in this Act applies to any vehicle whose use as a private hire vehicle is limited to   **A38.46**
use in connection with funerals or weddings.

Further controls

30. Prohibition of certain signs, notices, etc.

(1) The [licensing authority] may make regulations prohibiting the display in London on   **A38.47**
or from vehicles (other than licensed taxis and public service vehicles) of any sign, notice or
other feature of a description specified in the regulations.

(2) [*Consultation before making regulations.*]

(3) Any person who—

   (a) drives a vehicle in respect of which a prohibition imposed by regulations under this
      section is contravened; or

   (b) causes or permits such a prohibition to be contravened in respect of any vehicle,

is guilty of an offence and liable on summary conviction to a fine not exceeding level 4 on
the standard scale.

[*Section 30 is printed as amended by the Greater London Authority Act 1999, s.254 and Sched. 21,*   **A38.48**
paras 1 and 2.]

31. Prohibition of certain advertisements

(1) This section applies to any advertisement—   **A38.49**

   (a) indicating that vehicles can be hired on application to a specified address in London;

(b) indicating that vehicles can be hired by telephone on a telephone number being the number of premises in London; or

(c) on or near any premises in London, indicating that vehicles can be hired at those premises.

(2) No such advertisement shall include—

(a) any of the following words, namely "taxi", "taxis", "cab" or "cabs", or

(b) any word so closely resembling any of those words as to be likely to be mistaken for it,

(whether alone or as part of another word), unless the vehicles offered for hire are London cabs.

(3) An advertisement which includes the word "minicab", "mini-cab" or "mini cab" (whether in the singular or plural) does not by reason only of that fact contravene this section.

(4) Any person who issues, or causes to be issued, an advertisement which contravenes this section is guilty of an offence and liable on summary conviction to a fine not exceeding level 4 on the standard scale.

(5) It is a defence for a person charged with an offence under this section to prove that—

(a) he is a person whose business it is to publish or arrange for the publication of advertisements;

(b) he received the advertisement in question for publication in the ordinary course of business; and

(c) he did not know and had no reason to suspect that its publication would amount to an offence under this section.

(6) In this section—

"*advertisement*" includes every form of advertising (whatever the medium) and references to the issue of an advertisement shall be construed accordingly;

"*telephone number*" includes any number used for the purposes of communicating with another by electronic means; and "*telephone*" shall be construed accordingly.

Miscellaneous and supplementary

A38.50   **32. Regulations**   *[Omitted.]*

33. Offences due to fault of other person

A38.51   (1) Where an offence by any person under this Act is due to the act or default of another person, then (whether proceedings are taken against the first mentioned person or not) that other person is guilty of the offence and is liable to be proceeded against and punished accordingly.

(2) Where an offence under this Act committed by a body corporate is proved to have been committed with the consent or connivance of, or attributable to any neglect on the part of, any director, manager, secretary or other similar officer of the body corporate (or any person purporting to act in that capacity), he as well as the body corporate is guilty of the offence is liable to be proceeded against and punished accordingly.

34. Service of notices

A38.52   (1) Any notice authorised or required under this Act to be given to any person may be served by post.

(2) For the purposes of section 7 of the Interpretation Act 1978 any such notice is properly addressed to a London PHV operator if it is addressed to him at any operating centre of his in London.

(3) Any notice authorised or required under this Act to be given to the owner of a vehicle shall be deemed to have been effectively given if it is given to the person who is for the time being notified to the [licensing authority] for the purposes of this Act as the owner of the vehicle (or, if more than one person is currently notified as the owner, if it is given to any of them).

[Section 34 is printed as amended by the Greater London Authority Act 1999, s.254 and Sched. 21,   **A38.53**
paras 1 and 2.]

35. References to the owner of a vehicle

(1) For the purposes of this Act the owner of a vehicle shall be taken to be the person by   **A38.54**
whom it is kept.

(2) In determining, in the course of any proceedings for an offence under this Act, who was the owner of a vehicle at any time it shall be presumed that the owner was the person who was the registered keeper of the vehicle at that time.

(3) Notwithstanding that presumption—

- (a) it is open to the defence to show that the person who was the registered keeper of a vehicle at any particular time was not the person by whom the vehicle was kept at the time; and

- (b) it is open to the prosecution to prove that the vehicle was kept at that time by some person other than the registered keeper.

(4) In this section *"registered keeper"*, in relation to a vehicle, means the person in whose name the vehicle was registered under the Vehicle Excise and Registration Act 1994.

36. Interpretation

In this Act, unless the context otherwise requires—   **A38.55**

"authorised officer" means an officer authorised in writing by the [licensing authority] for the purposes of this Act;

[*"controlled district"* means any area for which Part II of the 1976 Act is in force by virtue of—
- (a) a resolution passed by a district council under section 45 of that Act; or
- (b) section 255(4) of the Greater London Authority Act 1999;]

"driver's badge" means the badge issued to the holder's a London PHV driver's licence;

"hackney carriage" means a vehicle licensed under section 37 of the Town Police Clauses Act 1847 or any similar enactment;

"licensed taxi" means a hackney carriage, a London cab or a taxi licensed under Part II of the 1982 Act;

[*"the licensing authority"* means Transport for London;]

"London" means the area consisting of the metropolitan police district and the City of London (including the Temples);

"London cab" means a vehicle licensed under section 6 of the Metropolitan Public Carriage Act 1869;

"London PHV driver's licence" means a licence under section 13;

"London PHV licence" means a licence under section 7;

"*London PHV operator*" has the meaning given in section 4(1);

"*London PHV operator's licence*" means a licence under section 2;

"*notice*" means notice in writing;

"*operating centre*" has the meaning given in section 1(5);

"*operator*" has the meaning given in section 1(1);

"*prescribed*" means prescribed in regulations under section 32(1);

"*private hire vehicle*" has the meaning given in section 1(1);

"*public service vehicle*" has the same meaning as in the Public Passenger Vehicles Act 1981;

"*road*" means any length of highway or of any other road to which the public has access (including bridges over which a road passes);

"*the 1976 Act*" means the Local Government (Miscellaneous Provisions) Act 1976;

"*the 1982 Act*" means the Civic Government (Scotland) Act 1982; and

"*vehicle*" means a mechanically propelled vehicle (other than a tramcar) intended or adapted for use on roads.

A38.56   *[Section 35 is printed as amended by the Greater London Authority Act 1999, s.254 and Sched. 21, paras 1, 2 and 17; the Greater London Authority Act 1999 (Commencement No. 8 and Consequential Provisions) Order 2000 (S.I. No. 3145; not reproduced in this work).]*

A38.57   **37. Power to make transitional, etc., provisions**   *[Omitted.]*

38. Financial provisions   *[Omitted.]*

A38.58   *[Section 38 has been prospectively repealed by the Greater London Authority Act 1999, s.254 and Sched. 21, paras 1 and 19 (and see also ibid., s.423 and Sched. 34, Pt II). At the date at which this volume states the law (April 1, 2001) those provisions of the 1999 Act had not been brought into force.]*

39. Consequential amendments and repeals

A38.59   (1) Schedule 1 (minor and consequential amendments) shall have effect.

(2) The enactments mentioned in Schedule 2 are repealed to the extent specified.

40. Short title, commencement and extent

A38.60   (1) This Act may be cited as the Private Hire Vehicles (London) Act 1998.

(2) This Act (apart from this section) shall come into force on such date as the Secretary of State may by order made by statutory instrument appoint; but different dates may be appointed for different purposes.

An order under this subsection may contain any provision which could be made under section 37 in connection with any provision brought into force by the order.

(3) Any provision of this Act which amends or repeals any other Act has the same extent as the provision being amended or repealed.

(4) Subject to subsection (3), this Act extends only to England and Wales.

Private Hire Vehicles (London) Act 1998

Commencement Provisions

Provision	Commencement date	Authority	
Provision	*Commencement date*	*Authority*	**A38.61**
s.1	January 22, 2001	S.I. 2000 No. 3144	
s.2	October 22, 2001	S.I. 2000 No. 3144	
s.3	January 22, 2001	S.I. 2000 No. 3144	
s.4(1)	January 22, 2001	S.I. 2000 No. 3144	
s.4(3), (4)	January 22, 2001	S.I. 2000 No. 3144	
s.4(5), (6)	October 22, 2001	S.I. 2000 No. 3144	
s.5(1) to (4)	October 22, 2001	S.I. 2000 No. 3144	
s.5(5)	January 22, 2001	S.I. 2000 No. 3144	
s.15(1) to (3)	January 22, 2001	S.I. 2000 No. 3144	
s.15(5)	January 22, 2001	S.I. 2000 No. 3144	
s.16(1), (2)	January 22, 2001	S.I. 2000 No. 3144	
ss.17 to 20	January 22, 2001	S.I. 2000 No. 3144	
s.21(1)	January 22, 2001	S.I. 2000 No. 3144	
s.21(3)	January 22, 2001	S.I. 2000 No. 3144	
s.21(4)	October 22, 2001	S.I. 2000 No. 3144	
s.22(1)	January 22, 2001	S.I. 2000 No. 3144	
s.22(4)	January 22, 2001	S.I. 2000 No. 3144	
s.22(5), (6)	October 22, 2001	S.I. 2000 No. 3144	
ss.23 to 29	January 22, 2001	S.I. 2000 No. 3144	
s.32, 33	January 22, 2001	S.I. 2000 No. 3144	
s.34(1), (2)	January 22, 2001	S.I. 2000 No. 3144	
ss.36 to 38	January 22, 2001	S.I. 2000 No. 3144	
s.40	July 28, 1998	s.40(2)	

Commencement order. The following order had been made under section 40(2) of the 1998   **A38.62**
Act at the date at which this volume states the law:

The Private Hire Vehicles (London) Act 1998 (Commencement No. 1) Order 2000 (S.I.
2000 No. 3144) below

SCHEDULES

SCHEDULE 1

MINOR AND CONSEQUENTIAL AMENDMENTS

[Omitted.]   **A38.63**

SCHEDULE 2

REPEALS

[Omitted.]   **A38.64**

The Human Rights Act 1998

(1998 c. 42)

A39.01 An Act to give further effect to rights and freedoms guaranteed under the European Convention on Human Rights; to make provision with respect to holders of certain judicial offices who become judges of the European Court of Human Rights; and for connected purposes.

[9th November 1998]

ARRANGEMENT OF SECTIONS

Introduction

Introduction

1. The Convention rights

(1) In this Act "*the Convention rights*" means the rights and fundamental freedoms set out   **A39.03**
in—

   (a) Articles 2 to 12 and 14 of the Convention,

   (b) Articles 1 to 3 of the First Protocol, and

   (c) Articles 1 and 2 of the Sixth Protocol,

as read with Articles 16 to 18 of the Convention.

(2) Those Articles are to have effect for the purposes of this Act subject to any designated derogation or reservation (as to which see sections 14 and 15).

(3) The Articles are set out in Schedule 1.

(4) The Secretary of State may by order make such amendments to this Act as he considers appropriate to reflect the effect, in relation to the United Kingdom, of a protocol.

(5) In subsection (4) "*protocol*" means a protocol to the Convention—

   (a) which the United Kingdom has ratified; or

   (b) which the United Kingdom has signed with a view to ratification.

(6) No amendment may be made by an order under subsection (4) so as to come into force before the protocol concerned is in force in relation to the United Kingdom.

2. Interpretation of Convention rights

(1) A court or tribunal determining a question which has arisen in connection with a   **A39.04**
Convention right must take into account any—

   (a) judgment, decision, declaration or advisory opinion of the European Court of Human Rights,

   (b) opinion of the Commission given in a report adopted under Article 31 of the Convention,

   (c) decision of the Commission in connection with Article 26 or 27(2) of the Convention, or

(d) decision of the Committee of Ministers taken under Article 46 of the Convention, whenever made or given, so far as, in the opinion of the court or tribunal, it is relevant to the proceedings in which that question has arisen.

(2) Evidence of any judgment, decision, declaration or opinion of which account may have to be taken under this section is to be given in proceedings before any court or tribunal in such manner as may be provided by rules.

(3) In this section "*rules*" means rules of court or, in the case of proceedings before a tribunal, rules made for the purposes of this section—

(a) by the Lord Chancellor or the Secretary of State, in relation to any proceedings outside Scotland;

(b) *[relates to Scotland]*;

(c) *[relates to Northern Ireland]*.

Legislation

3. Interpretation of legislation

A39.05   (1) So far as it is possible to do so, primary legislation and subordinate legislation must be read and given effect in a way which is compatible with the Convention rights.

(2) This section—

(a) applies to primary legislation and subordinate legislation whenever enacted;

(b) does not affect the validity, continuing operation or enforcement of any incompatible primary legislation; and

(c) does not affect the validity, continuing operation or enforcement of any incompatible subordinate legislation if (disregarding any possibility of revocation) primary legislation prevents removal of the incompatibility.

4. Declaration of incompatibility

A39.06   (1) Subsection (2) applies in any proceedings in which a court determines whether a provision of primary legislation is compatible with a Convention right.

(2) If the court is satisfied that the provision is incompatible with a Convention right, it may make a declaration of that incompatibility.

(3) Subsection (4) applies in any proceedings in which a court determines whether a provision of subordinate legislation, made in the exercise of a power conferred by primary legislation, is compatible with a Convention right.

(4) If the court is satisfied—

(a) that the provision is incompatible with a Convention right, and

(b) that (disregarding any possibility of revocation) the primary legislation concerned prevents removal of the incompatibility,

it may make a declaration of that incompatibility.

(5) In this section "*court*" means—

(a) the House of Lords;

(b) the Judicial Committee of the Privy Council;

(c) the Courts-Martial Appeal Court;

(d) *[applies to Scotland]*;

(e) in England and Wales or Northern Ireland, the High Court or the Court of Appeal.

(6) A declaration under this section ("*a declaration of incompatibility*")—

(a) does not affect the validity, continuing operation or enforcement of the provision in respect of which it is given; and

(b) is not binding on the parties to the proceedings in which it is made.

5. Right of Crown to intervene

(1) Where a court is considering whether to make a declaration of incompatibility, the Crown is entitled to notice in accordance with rules of court. **A39.07**

(2) In any case to which subsection (1) applies—

(a) a Minister of the Crown (or a person nominated by him),

(b) a member of the Scottish Executive,

(c) a Northern Ireland Minister,

(d) a Northern Ireland department,

is entitled, on giving notice in accordance with rules of court, to be joined as a party to the proceedings.

(3) Notice under subsection (2) may be given at any time during the proceedings.

(4) A person who has been made a party to criminal proceedings (other than in Scotland) as the result of a notice under subsection (2) may, with leave, appeal to the House of Lords against any declaration of incompatibility made in the proceedings.

(5) In subsection (4)—

"*criminal proceedings*" includes all proceedings before the Courts-Martial Appeal Court; and

"*leave*" means leave granted by the court making the declaration of incompatibility or by the House of Lords.

Public authorities

6. Acts of public authorities

(1) It is unlawful for a public authority to act in a way which is incompatible with a Convention right. **A39.08**

(2) Subsection (1) does not apply to an act if—

(a) as the result of one or more provisions of primary legislation, the authority could not have acted differently; or

(b) in the case of one or more provisions of, or made under, primary legislation which cannot be read or given effect in a way which is compatible with the Convention rights, the authority was acting so as to give effect to or enforce those provisions.

(3) In this section "*public authority*" includes—

(a) a court or tribunal, and

(b) any person certain of whose functions are functions of a public nature,

but does not include either House of Parliament or a person exercising functions in connection with proceedings in Parliament.

(4) In subsection (3) "*Parliament*" does not include the House of Lords in its judicial capacity.

(5) In relation to a particular act, a person is not a public authority by virtue only of subsection (3)(b) if the nature of the act is private.

(6) *"An act"* includes a failure to act but does not include a failure to—

    (a) introduce in, or lay before, Parliament a proposal for legislation; or

    (b) make any primary legislation or remedial order.

7. Proceedings

A39.09   (1) A person who claims that a public authority has acted (or proposes to act) in a way which is made unlawful by section 6(1) may—

    (a) bring proceedings against the authority under this Act in the appropriate court or tribunal, or

    (b) rely on the Convention right or rights concerned in any legal proceedings,

but only if he is (or would be) a victim of the unlawful act.

(2) In subsection (1)(a) *"appropriate court or tribunal"* means such court or tribunal as may be determined in accordance with rules; and proceedings against an authority include a counterclaim or similar proceeding.

(3) If the proceedings are brought on an application for judicial review, the applicant is to be taken to have a sufficient interest in relation to the unlawful act only if he is, or would be, a victim of that act.

(4) *[Applies to Scotland.]*

(5) Proceedings under subsection (1)(a) must be brought before the end of—

    (a) the period of one year beginning with the date on which the act complained of took place; or

    (b) such longer period as the court or tribunal considers equitable having regard to all the circumstances,

but that is subject to any rule imposing a stricter time limit in relation to the procedure in question.

(6) In subsection (1)(b) *"legal proceedings"* includes—

    (a) proceedings brought by or at the instigation of a public authority; and

    (b) an appeal against the decision of a court or tribunal.

(7) For the purposes of this section, a person is a victim of an unlawful act only if he would be a victim for the purposes of Article 34 of the Convention if proceedings were brought in the European Court of Human Rights in respect of that act.

(8) Nothing in this Act creates a criminal offence.

(9) In this section *"rules"* means—

    (a) in relation to proceedings before a court or tribunal outside Scotland, rules made by the Lord Chancellor or the Secretary of State for the purposes of this section or rules of court,

    (b) *[applies to Scotland]*,

    (c) *[applies to Northern Ireland]*,

and includes provision made by order under section 1 of the Courts and Legal Services Act 1990.

(10) In making rules, regard must be had to section 9.

(11) The Minister who has power to make rules in relation to a particular tribunal may, to the extent he considers it necessary to ensure that the tribunal can provide an appropriate remedy in relation to an act (or proposed act) of a public authority which is (or would be) unlawful as a result of section 6(1), by order add to—

(a) the relief or remedies which the tribunal may grant; or

(b) the grounds on which it may grant any of them.

(12) An order made under subsection (11) may contain such incidental, supplemental, consequential or transitional provision as the Minister making it considers appropriate.

(13) *[Applies to Northern Ireland.]*

8. Judicial remedies

(1) In relation to any act (or proposed act) of a public authority which the court finds is (or would be) unlawful, it may grant such relief or remedy, or make such order, within its powers as it considers just and appropriate.   **A39.10**

(2) But damages may be awarded only by a court which has power to award damages, or to order the payment of compensation, in civil proceedings.

(3) No award of damages is to be made unless, taking account of all the circumstances of the case, including—

(a) any other relief or remedy granted, or order made, in relation to the act in question (by that or any other court), and

(b) the consequences of any decision (of that or any other court) in respect of that act,

the court is satisfied that the award is necessary to afford just satisfaction to the person in whose favour it is made.

(4) In determining—

(a) whether to award damages, or

(b) the amount of an award,

the court must take into account the principles applied by the European Court of Human Rights in relation to the award of compensation under Article 41 of the Convention.

(5) A public authority against which damages are awarded is to be treated—

(a) *[applies to Scotland]*,

(b) for the purposes of the Civil Liability (Contribution) Act 1978 as liable in respect of damage suffered by the person to whom the award is made.

(6) In this section—

"*court*" includes a tribunal;

"*damages*" means damages for an unlawful act of a public authority; and

"*unlawful*" means unlawful under section 6(1).

9. Judicial acts

(1) Proceedings under section 7(1)(a) in respect of a judicial act may be brought only—   **A39.11**

(a) by exercising a right of appeal;

(b) on an application . . . for judicial review; or

(c) in such other forum as may be prescribed by rules.

(2) That does not affect any rule of law which prevents a court from being the subject of judicial review.

(3) In proceedings under this Act in respect of a judicial act done in good faith, damages may not be awarded otherwise than to compensate a person to the extent required by Article 5(5) of the Convention.

(4) An award of damages permitted by subsection (3) is to be made against the Crown; but no award may be made unless the appropriate person, if not a party to the proceedings, is joined.

(5) In this section—

"*appropriate person*" means the Minister responsible for the court concerned, or a person or government department nominated by him;

"*court*" includes a tribunal;

"*judge*" includes a member of a tribunal, a justice of the peace and a clerk or other officer entitled to exercise the jurisdiction of a court;

"*judicial act*" means a judicial act of a court and includes an act done on the instructions, or on behalf, of a judge; and

"*rules*" has the same meaning as in section 7(9).

A39.12   *[The words omitted from section 9(1)(b) relate exclusively to Scotland.]*

10. Power to take remedial action

A39.13   (1) This section applies if—

  (a) a provision of legislation has been declared under section 4 to be incompatible with a Convention right and, if an appeal lies—

    (i) all persons who may appeal have stated in writing that they do not intend to do so;
    (ii) the time for bringing an appeal has expired and no appeal has been brought within that time; or
    (iii) an appeal brought within that time has been determined or abandoned; or

  (b) it appears to a Minister of the Crown or Her Majesty in Council that, having regard to a finding of the European Court of Human Rights made after the coming into force of this section in proceedings against the United Kingdom, a provision of legislation is incompatible with an obligation of the United Kingdom arising from the Convention.

(2) If a Minister of the Crown considers that there are compelling reasons for proceeding under this section, he may by order make such amendments to the legislation as he considers necessary to remove the incompatibility.

(3) If, in the case of subordinate legislation, a Minister of the Crown considers—

  (a) that it is necessary to amend the primary legislation under which the subordinate legislation in question was made, in order to enable the incompatibility to be removed, and

  (b) that there are compelling reasons for proceeding under this section,

he may by order make such amendements to the primary legislation as he considers necessary.

(4) This section also applies where the provision in question is in subordinate legislation and has been quashed, or declared invalid, by reason of incompability with a Convention right and the Minister proposes to proceed under paragraph 2(b) of Schedule 2.

(5) If the legislation is an Order in Council, the power conferred by subsection (2) or (3) is exercisable by Her Majesty in Council.

(6) In this section "*legislation*" does not include a Measure of the Church Assembly or of the General Synod of the Church of England.

(7) Schedule 2 makes further provision about remedial orders.

Other rights and proceedings

11. Safeguard for existing human rights

A person's reliance on a Convention right does not restrict—   **A39.14**

   (a) any other right or freedom conferred on him by or under any law having effect in any part of the United Kingdom; or

   (b) his right to make any claim or bring any proceedings which he could make or bring apart from sections 7 to 9.

12. Freedom of expression

(1) This section applies if a court is considering whether to grant any relief which, if   **A39.15**
granted, might affect the exercise of the Convention right to freedom of expression.

(2) If the person against whom the application for relief is made ("*the respondent*") is neither present nor represented, no such relief is to be granted unless the court is satisfied—

   (a) that the applicant has taken all practicable steps to notify the respondent; or

   (b) that there are compelling reasons why the respondent should not be notified.

(3) No such relief is to be granted so as to restrain publication before trial unless the court is satisfied that the applicant is likely to establish that publication should not be allowed.

(4) The court must have particular regard to the importance of the Convention right to freedom of expression and, where the proceedings relate to material which the respondent claims, or which appears to the court, to be journalistic, literary or artistic material (or to conduct connected with such material), to—

   (a) the extent to which—

      (i) the material has, or is about to, become available to the public; or
      (ii) it is, or would be, in the public interest for the material to be published;

   (b) any relevant privacy code.

(5) In this section—

"*court*" includes a tribunal; and
"*relief*" includes any remedy or order (other than in criminal proceedings).

13. Freedom of thought, conscience and religion

(1) If a court's determination of any question arising under this Act might affect the   **A39.16**
exercise by a religious organisation (itself or its members collectively) of the Convention right to freedom of thought, conscience and religion, it must have particular regard to the importance of that right.

(2) In this section "*court*" includes a tribunal.

Derogations and reservations

14. Derogations

(1) In this Act "*designated derogation*" means—   **A39.17**

   . . .

any derogation by the United Kingdom from an Article of the Convention, or of any protocol to the Convention, which is designated for the purposes of this Act in an order made by the Secretary of State.

(2) *[Repealed.]*

(3) If a designated derogation is amended or replaced it ceases to be a designated derogation.

(4) But subsection (3) does not prevent the Secretary of State from exercising his power under subsection (1) . . . to make a fresh designation order in respect of the Article concerned.

(5) The Secretary of State must by order make such amendments to Schedule 3 as he considers appropriate to reflect—

(a) any designation order; or

(b) the effect of subsection (3).

(6) A designation order may be made in anticipation of the making by the United Kingdom of a proposed derogation.

[Section 14 is printed as amended by the Human Rights Act (Amendment) Order 2001 (S.I. 2001 No. 1216), art.2.]

15. Reservations

(1) In this Act "*designated reservation*" means—

(a) the United Kingdom's reservation to Article 2 of the First Protocol to the Convention; and

(b) any other reservation by the United Kingdom to an Article of the Convention, or of any protocol to the Convention, which is designated for the purposes of this Act in an order made by the Secretary of State.

(2) The text of the reservation referred to in subsection (1)(a) is set out in Part II of Schedule 3.

(3) If a designated reservation is withdrawn wholly or in part it ceases to be a designated reservation.

(4) But subsection (3) does not prevent the Secretary of State from exercising his power under subsection (1)(b) to make a fresh designation order in respect of the Article concerned.

(5) The Secretary of State must by order make such amendments to this Act as he considers appropriate to reflect—

(a) any designation order; or

(b) the effect of subsection (3).

16. Period for which designated derogations have effect

(1) If it has not already been withdrawn by the United Kingdom, a designated derogation ceases to have effect for the purposes of this Act—

. . .

at the end of the period of five years beginning with the date on which the order designating it was made.

(2) At any time before the period—

(a) fixed by subsection (1) . . ., or

(b) extended by an order under this subsection,

comes to an end, the Secretary of State may by order extend it by a further period of five years.

(3) An order under section 14(1) . . . ceases to have effect at the end of the period for consideration, unless a resolution has been passed by each House approving the order.

(4) Subsection (3) does not affect—

(a) anything done in reliance on the order; or

(b) the power to make a fresh order under section 14(1) . . . .

(5) In subsection (3) "*period for consideration*" means the period of forty days beginning with the day on which the order was made.

(6) In calculating the period for consideration, no account is to be taken of any time during which—

(a) Parliament is dissolved or prorogued; or

(b) both Houses are adjourned for more than four days.

(7) If a designated derogation is withdrawn by the United Kingdom, the Secretary of State must by order make such amendments to this Act as he considers are required to reflect that withdrawal.

[Section 16 is printed as amended by the Human Rights Act (Amendment) Order 2001 (S.I. 2001 No. 1216), art.3.]

17. Periodic review of designated reservations

(1) The appropriate Minister must review the designated reservation referred to in section 15(1)(a)— **A39.20**

(a) before the end of the period of five years beginning with the date on which section 1(2) came into force; and

(b) if that designation is still in force, before the end of the period of five years beginning with the date on which the last report relating to it was laid under subsection (3).

(2) The appropriate Minister must review each of the other designated reservations (if any)—

(a) before the end of the period of five years beginning with the date on which the order designating the reservation first came into force; and

(b) if the designation is still in force, before the end of the period of five years beginning with the date on which the last report relating to it was laid under subsection (3).

(3) The Minister conducting a review under this section must prepare a report on the result of the review and lay a copy of it before each House of Parliament.

Judges of the European Court of Human Rights

18. *[Appointments to European Court of Human Rights.]* **A39.21**

Parliamentary procedure

19. Statements of compatibility

(1) A Minister of the Crown in charge of a Bill in either House of Parliament must, before Second Reading of the Bill— **A39.22**

(a) make a statement to the effect that in his view the provisions of the Bill are compatible with the Convention rights ("*a statement of compatibility*"); or

(b) make a statement to the effect that although he is unable to make a statement of compatibility the government nevertheless wishes the House to proceed with the Bill.

(2) The statement must be in writing and be published in such manner as the Minister making it considers appropriate.

Supplemental

20. Orders, etc., under this Act

A39.23 (1) Any power of a Minister of the Crown to make an order under this Act is exercisable by statutory instrument.

(2) The power of the Lord Chancellor or the Secretary of State to makes rules (other than rules of court) under section 2(3) or 7(9) is exercisable by statutory instrument.

(3) Any statutory instrument made under section 14, 15 or 16(7) must be laid before Parliament.

(4) No order may be made by the Lord Chancellor or the Secretary of State under section 1(4), 7(11) or 16(2) unless a draft of the order has been laid before, and approved by, each House of Parliament.

(5) Any statutory instrument made under section 18(7) or Schedule 4, or to which sub-section (2) applies, shall be subject to annulment in pursuance of a resolution of either House of Parliament.

(6) *[Applies to Northern Ireland.]*

(7) Any rules made under section 2(3)(c) or 7(9)(c) shall be subject to negative resolution; . . .

(8) *[Applies to Northern Ireland.]*

21. Interpretation, etc.

A39.24 (1) In this Act—

"*amend*" includes repeal and apply (with or without modifications);

"*the appropriate Minister*" means the Minister of the Crown having charge of the appropriate authorised government department (within the meaning of the Crown Proceedings Act 1947);

"*the Commission*" means the European Commission of Human Rights;

"*the Convention*" means the Convention for the Protection of Human Rights and Fundamental Freedoms, agreed by the Council of Europe at Rome on 4th November 1950 as it has effect for the time being in relation to the United Kingdom;

"*declaration of incompatibility*" means a declaration under section 4;

"*Minister of the Crown*" has the same meaning as in the Ministers of the Crown Act 1975;

"*Northern Ireland Minister*" includes the First Minister and the deputy First Minister in Northern Ireland;

"*primary legislation*" means any—

(a) public general Act;

(b) local and personal Act;

(c) private Act;

(d) Measure of the Church Assembly;

(e) Measure of the General Synod of the Church of England;

(f) Order in Council—

    (i) made in exercise of Her Majesty's Royal Prerogative;

    (ii) made under section 38(1)(a) of the Northern Ireland Constitution Act 1973 or the corresponding provision of the Northern Ireland Act 1998; or

    (iii) amending an Act of a kind mentioned in paragraph (a), (b) or (c);

and includes an order or other instrument made under primary legislation (otherwise than by the National Assembly for Wales, a member of the Scottish Executive, a Northern Ireland Minister or a Northern Ireland department) to the extent to which it operates to bring one or more provisions of that legislation into force or amends any primary legislation;

"*the First Protocol*" means the protocol to the Convention agreed at Paris on 20th March 1952;

"*the Sixth Protocol*" means the protocol to the Convention agreed at Strasbourg on 28th April 1983;

"*the Eleventh Protocol*" means the protocol to the Convention (restructuring the control machinery established by the Convention) agreed at Strasbourg on 11th May 1994;

"*remedial order*" means an order under section 10;

"*subordinate legislation*" means any—

(a) Order in Council other than one—

    (i) made in exercise of Her Majesty's Royal Prerogative;

    (ii) made under section 38(1)(a) of the Northern Ireland Constitution Act 1973 or the corresponding provision of the Northern Ireland Act 1998; or

    (iii) amending an Act of a kind mentioned in the definition of primary legislation;

(b) Act of the Scottish Parliament;

(c) Act of the Parliament of Northern Ireland;

(d) Measure of the Assembly established under section 1 of the Northern Ireland Assembly Act 1973;

(e) Act of the Northern Ireland Assembly;

(f) order, rules, regulations, scheme, warrant, byelaw or other instrument made under primary legislation (except to the extent to which it operates to bring one or more provisions of that legislation into force or amends any primary legislation);

(g) order, rules, regulations, scheme, warrant, byelaw or other instrument made under legislation mentioned in paragraph (b), (c), (d) or (e) or made under an Order in Council applying only to Northern Ireland;

(h) order, rules, regulations, scheme, warrant, byelaw or other instrument made by a member of the Scottish Executive, a Northern Ireland Minister or a Northern Ireland department in exercise of prerogative or other executive functions of Her Majesty which are exercisable by such a person on behalf of Her Majesty;

"*transferred matters*" has the same meaning as in the Northern Ireland Act 1998; and

"*tribunal*" means any tribunal in which legal proceedings may be brought.

(2) The references in paragraphs (b) and (c) of section 2(1) to Articles are to Articles of the Convention as they had effect immediately before the coming into force of the Eleventh Protocol.

(3) The reference in paragraph (d) of section 2(1) to Article 46 includes a reference to Articles 32 and 54 of the Convention as they had effect immediately before the coming into force of the Eleventh Protocol.

(4) The references in section 2(1) to a report or decision of the Commission or a decision of the Committee of Ministers include references to a report or decision made as provided by paragraphs 3, 4 and 6 of Article 5 of the Eleventh Protocol (transitional provisions).

(5) *[Abolishes death penalty under the Army Act 1955, the Air Force Act 1955 and the Naval Discipline Act 1957.]*

A39.25   **22. Short title, commencement, application and extent**

(1)–(3)   *[Omitted.]*

(4) Paragraph (b) of subsection (1) of section 7 applies to proceedings brought by or at the instigation of a public authority whenever the act in question took place; but otherwise that subsection does not apply to an act taking place before the coming into force of that section.

(5) This Act binds the Crown.

(6) This Act extends to Northern Ireland.

(7) *[Applies to section 21(5) of this Act; not reproduced in this work.]*

A39.26   *[All provisions of the Act (including section 7(1)) not previously in force were brought into force on October 2, 2000, see the Human Rights Act 1998 (Commencement No. 2) Order 2000 (S.I. 2000 No. 1851; not reproduced in this work).]*

Section 1(3)   SCHEDULE 1

A39.27   THE ARTICLES

PART I

THE CONVENTION

RIGHTS AND FREEDOMS

Article 2

Right to life

A39.28   1. Everyone's right to life shall be protected by law. No one shall be deprived of his life intentionally save in the execution of a sentence of a court following his conviction of a crime for which this penalty is provided by law.

2. Deprivation of life shall not be regarded as inflicted in contravention of this Article when it results from the use of force which is no more than absolutely necessary:

     (a) in defence of any person from unlawful violence;

     (b) in order to effect a lawful arrest or to prevent the escape of a person lawfully detained;

     (c) in action lawfully taken for the purpose of quelling a riot or insurrection.

Article 3

Prohibition of torture

No one shall be subjected to torture or to inhuman or degrading treatment or punishment.   **A39.29**

Article 4

Prohibition of slavery and forced labour

1. No one shall be held in slavery or servitude.   **A39.30**

2. No one shall be required to perform forced or compulsory labour.

3. For the purpose of this Article the term "*forced or compulsory labour*" shall not include:

   (a) any work required to be done in the ordinary course of detention imposed according to the provisions of Article 5 of this Convention or during conditional release from such detention;

   (b) any service of a military character or, in case of conscientious objectors in countries where they are recognised, service exacted instead of compulsory military service;

   (c) any service exacted in case of an emergency or calamity threatening the life or well-being of the community;

   (d) any work or service which forms part of normal civic obligations.

Article 5

Right to liberty and security

1. Everyone has the right to liberty and security of person. No-one shall be deprived of his liberty save in the following cases and in accordance with a procedure prescribed by law: **A39.31**

   (a) the lawful detention of a person after conviction by a competent court;

   (b) the lawful arrest or detention of a person for non-compliance with the lawful order of a court or in order to secure the fulfilment of any obligation prescribed by law;

   (c) the lawful arrest or detention of a person effected for the purpose of bringing him before the competent legal authority on reasonable suspicion of having committed an offence or when it is reasonably considered necessary to prevent his committing an offence or fleeing after having done so;

   (d) the detention of a minor by lawful order for the purpose of educational supervision or his lawful detention for the purpose of bringing him before the competent legal authority;

   (e) the lawful detention of persons for the prevention of the spreading of infectious diseases, of persons of unsound mind, alcoholics or drug addicts or vagrants;

   (f) the lawful arrest or detention of a person to prevent his effecting an unauthorised entry into the country or of a person against whom action is being taken with a view to deportation or extradition.

2. Everyone who is arrested shall be informed promptly, in a language which he understands, of the reasons for his arrest and of any charge against him.

3. Everyone arrested or detained in accordance with the provisions of paragraph 1(c) of this Article shall be brought promptly before a judge or other officer authorised by law to exercise judicial power and shall be entitled to trial within a reasonable time or to release pending trial. Release may be conditioned by guarantees to appear for trial.

4. Everyone who is deprived of his liberty by arrest or detention shall be entitled to take proceedings by which the lawfulness of his detention shall be decided speedily by a court and his release ordered if the detention is not lawful.

5. Everyone who has been the victim of arrest or detention in contravention of the provisions of this Article shall have an enforceable right to compensation.

Article 6

Right to a fair trial

A39.32   1. In the determination of his civil rights and obligations or of any criminal charge against him, everyone is entitled to a fair and public hearing within a reasonable time by an independent and impartial tribunal established by law. Judgment shall be pronounced publicly but the press and public may be excluded from all or part of the trial in the interest of morals, public order or national security in a democratic society, where the interests of juveniles or the protection of the private life of the parties so require, or to the extent strictly necessary in the opinion of the court in special circumstances where publicity would prejudice the interests of justice.

2. Everyone charged with a criminal offence shall be presumed innocent until proved guilty according to law.

3. Everyone charged with a criminal offence has the following minimum rights:
   (a) to be informed promptly, in a language which he understands and in detail, of the nature and cause of the accusation against him;
   (b) to have adequate time and facilities for the preparation of his defence;
   (c) to defend himself in person or through legal assistance of his own choosing or, if he has not sufficient means to pay for legal assistance, to be given it free when the interests of justice so require;
   (d) to examine or have examined witnesses against him and to obtain the attendance and examination of witnesses on his behalf under the same conditions as witnesses against him;
   (e) to have the free assistance of an interpreter if he cannot understand or speak the language used in court.

Article 7

No punishment without law

A39.33   1. No one shall be held guilty of any criminal offence on account of any act or omission which did not constitute a criminal offence under national or international law at the time when it was committed. Nor shall a heavier penalty be imposed than the one that was applicable at the time the criminal offence was committed.

2. This Article shall not prejudice the trial and punishment of any person for any act or omission which, at the time when it was committed, was criminal according to the general principles of law recognised by civilised nations.

Article 8

Right to respect for private and family life

A39.34   1. Everyone has the right to respect for his private and family life, his home and his correspondence.

2. There shall be no interference by a public authority with the exercise of this right except such as is in accordance with the law and is necessary in a democratic society in the interests of national security, public safety or the economic well-being of the country, for the prevention of disorder or crime, for the protection of health or morals, or for the protection of the rights and freedoms of others.

Article 9

Freedom of thought, conscience and religion

1. Everyone has the right to freedom of thought, conscience and religion; this right includes freedom to change his religion or belief and freedom, either alone or in community with others and in public or private, to manifest his religion or belief, in worship, teaching, practice and observance.   **A39.35**

2. Freedom to manifest one's religion or beliefs shall be subject only to such limitations as are prescribed by law and are necessary in a democratic society in the interests of public safety, for the protection of public order, health or morals, or for the protection of the rights and freedoms of others.

Article 10

Freedom of expression

1. Everyone has the right to freedom of expression. This right shall include freedom to hold opinions and to receive and impart information and ideas without interference by public authority and regardless of frontiers. This Article shall not prevent States from requiring the licensing of broadcasting, television or cinema enterprises.   **A39.36**

2. The exercise of these freedoms, since it carries with it duties and responsibilities, may be subject to such formalities, conditions, restrictions or penalties as are prescribed by law and are necessary in a democratic society, in the interests of national security, territorial integrity or public safety, for the prevention of disorder or crime, for the protection of health or morals, for the protection of the reputation or rights of others, for preventing the disclosure of information received in confidence, or for maintaining the authority and impartiality of the judiciary.

Article 11

Freedom of assembly and association

1. Everyone has the right to freedom of peaceful assembly and to freedom of association with others, including the right to form and to join trade unions for the protection of his interests.   **A39.37**

2. No restrictions shall be placed on the exercise of these rights other than such as are prescribed by law and are necessary in a democratic society in the interests of national security or public safety, for the prevention of disorder or crime, for the protection of health or morals or for the protection of the rights and freedoms of others. This Article shall not prevent the imposition of lawful restrictions on the exercise of these rights by members of the armed forces, of the police or of the administration of the State.

Article 12

Right to marry

Men and women of marriageable age have the right to marry and to found a family, according to the national laws governing the exercise of this right.   **A39.38**

Article 14

Prohibition of discrimination

A39.39 The enjoyment of the rights and freedoms set forth in this Convention shall be secured without discrimination on any ground such as sex, race, colour, language, religion, political or other opinion, national or social origin, association with a national minority, property, birth or other status.

Article 16

Restrictions on political activity of aliens

A39.40 Nothing in Articles 10, 11 and 14 shall be regarded as preventing the High Contracting Parties from imposing restrictions on the political activity of aliens.

Article 17

Prohibition of abuse of rights

A39.41 Nothing in this Convention may be interpreted as implying for any State, group or person any right to engage in any activity or perform any act aimed at the destruction of any of the rights and freedoms set forth herein or at their limitation to a greater extent than is provided for in the Convention.

Article 18

Limitation on use of restrictions on rights

A39.42 The restrictions permitted under this Convention to the said rights and freedoms shall not be applied for any purpose other than those for which they have been prescribed.

PART II

A39.43

THE FIRST PROTOCOL

Article 1

Protection of property

A39.44 Every natural or legal person is entitled to the peaceful enjoyment of his possessions. No one shall be deprived of his possessions except in the public interest and subject to the conditions provided for by law and by the general principles of international law.

The preceding provisions shall not, however, in any way impair the right of a State to enforce such laws as it deems necessary to control the use of property in accordance with the general interest or to secure the payment of taxes or other contributions or penalties.

Article 2

Right to education

A39.45 No person shall be denied the right to education. In the exercise of any functions which it assumes in relation to education and to teaching, the State shall respect the right of parents to ensure such education and teaching in conformity with their own religious and philosophical convictions.

Article 3

Right to free elections

The High Contracting Parties undertake to hold free elections at reasonable intervals by secret ballot, under conditions which will ensure the free expression of the opinion of the people in the choice of the legislature.   **A39.46**

PART III

THE SIXTH PROTOCOL   **A39.47**

Article 1

Abolition of the death penalty

The death penalty shall be abolished. No one shall be condemned to such penalty or executed.   **A39.48**

Article 2

Death penalty in time of war

A State may make provision in its law for the death penalty in respect of acts committed in time of war or of imminent threat of war; such penalty shall be applied only in the instances laid down in the law and in accordance with its provisions. The State shall communicate to the Secretary of the Council of Europe the relevant provisions of that law.   **A39.49**

SCHEDULE 2   Section 10(7)

REMEDIAL ORDERS

Orders

1.—(1) A remedial order may—   **A39.50**

  (a) contain such incidental, supplemental, consequential or transitional provision as the person making it considers appropriate;

  (b) be made so as to have effect from a date earlier than that on which it is made;

  (c) make provision for the delegation of specific functions;

  (d) make different provision for different cases.

(2) The power conferred by sub-paragraph (1)(a) includes—

  (a) power to amend primary legislation (including primary legislation other than that which contains the incompatible provision); and

  (b) power to amend or revoke subordinate legislation (including subordinate legislation other than that which contains the incompatible provision).

(3) A remedial order may be made so as to have the same extent as the legislation which it affects.

(4) No person is to be guilty of an offence solely as a result of the retrospective effect of a remedial order.

Procedure

A39.51   **2.** No remedial order may be made unless—

     (a) a draft of the order has been approved by a resolution of each House of Parliament made after the end of the period of 60 days beginning with the day on which the draft was laid; or

     (b) it is declared in the order that it appears to the person making it that, because of the urgency of the matter, it is necessary to make the order without a draft being so approved.

Orders laid in draft

A39.52   **3.**—(1) No draft may be laid under paragraph 2(a) unless—

     (a) the person proposing to make the order has laid before Parliament a document which contains a draft of the proposed order and the required information; and

     (b) the period of 60 days, beginning with the day on which the document required by this sub-paragraph was laid, has ended.

(2) If representations have been made during that period, the draft laid under paragraph 2(a) must be accompanied by a statement containing—

     (a) a summary of the representations; and

     (b) if, as a result of the representations, the proposed order has been changed, details of the changes.

Urgent cases

A39.53   **4.**—(1) If a remedial order ("*the original order*") is made without being approved in draft, the person making it must lay it before Parliament, accompanied by the required information, after it is made.

(2) If representations have been made during the period of 60 days beginning with the day on which the original order was made, the person making it must (after the end of that period) lay before Parliament a statement containing—

     (a) a summary of the representations; and

     (b) if, as a result of the representations, he considers it appropriate to make changes to the original order, details of the changes.

(3) If sub-paragraph (2)(b) applies, the person making the statement must—

     (a) make a further remedial order replacing the original order; and

     (b) lay the replacement order before Parliament.

(4) If, at the end of the period of 120 days beginning with the day on which the original order was made, a resolution has not been passed by each House approving the original or replacement order, the order ceases to have effect (but without that affecting anything previously done under either order or the power to make a fresh remedial order).

Definitions

A39.54   **5.** In this Schedule—

     "*representations*" means representations about a remedial order (or proposed remedial order) made to the person making (or proposing to make) it and includes any relevant Parliamentary report or resolution; and "*required information*" means—

(a) an explanation of the incompatibility which the order (or proposed order) seeks to remove, including particulars of the relevant declaration, finding or order; and

(b) a statement of the reasons for proceeding under section 10 and for making an order in those terms.

Calculating periods

6. In calculating any period for the purposes of this Schedule, no account is to be taken of any time during which—   **A39.55**

(a) Parliament is dissolved or prorogued; or

(b) both Houses are adjourned for more than four days.

[**7.** *[Applies to Scotland.]*]   **A39.56**

SCHEDULE 3   Sections 14(2), 15(2)   **A39.57**

DEROGATION AND RESERVATION

PART I

DEROGATION

[Repealed by the Human Rights Act (Amendment) Order 2001 (S.I. 2001 No. 1216), art.4]   **A39.58**

PART II

RESERVATION

At the time of signing the present (First) Protocol, I declare that, in view of certain provisions of the Education Acts in the United Kingdom, the principle affirmed in the second sentence of Article 2 is accepted by the United Kingdom only so far as it is compatible with the provision of efficient instruction and training, and the avoidance of unreasonable public expenditure.   **A39.59**

Dated 20 March 1952,

Made by the United Kingdom Permanent Representative to the Council of Europe.

SCHEDULE 4

JUDICIAL PENSIONS

[Omitted.]   **A39.60**

The Greater London Authority Act 1999

(1999 c. 29)

A40.01 An Act to establish and make provision about the Greater London Authority, the Mayor of London and the London Assembly; to make provision in relation to London borough councils and the Common Council of the City of London with respect to matters consequential on the establishment of the Greater London Authority; to make provision with respect to the functions of other local authorities and statutory bodies exercising functions in Greater London; to make provision about transport and road traffic in and around Greater London; to make provision about policing in Greater London and to make an adjustment of the metropolitan police district; and for connected purposes.

[11th November 1999]

ARRANGEMENT OF SECTIONS

* * *

PART IV

TRANSPORT

* * *

CHAPTER XI

HACKNEY CARRIAGES AND PRIVATE HIRE VEHICLES

* * *

CHAPTER XV

NEW CHARGES AND LEVIES

* * *

PART XII

SUPPLEMENTARY PROVISIONS

*   *   *

Miscellaneous and supplemental

*   *   *

SCHEDULES

*   *   *

PART IV

TRANSPORT

*   *   *

CHAPTER XI

HACKNEY CARRIAGES AND PRIVATE HIRE VEHICLES

253. **Hackney carriages**   *[Omitted.]*   **A40.03**

254. **The Private Hire Vehicles (London) Act 1998**

(1) Except as provided by the following provisions of this section, the functions of the **A40.04** Secretary of State under the Private Hire Vehicles (London) Act 1998 are transferred by this subsection to Transport for London.

(2) Subsection (1) above does not apply to any functions of the Secretary of State under section 37, 38 or 40 of that Act (transitional provisions, financial provisions and commencement etc).

(3) Schedule 21 to this Act (which makes amendments to the Private Hire Vehicles (London) Act 1998 in consequence of subsections (1) and (2) above) shall have effect.

(4) Any regulations made, licence issued, authorisation granted, or other thing done under the Private Hire Vehicles (London) Act 1998, other than section 37, 38 or 40, by or in relation to the Secretary of State before the coming into force of this section shall have effect as from the coming into force of this section as made, issued, granted or done by or in relation to Transport for London.

[Section 254 was brought into force on January 22, 2001 (in relation to Schedule 21, paragraphs **A40.05** *1–18, to this Act) by the Greater London Authority Act 1999 (Commencement No. 8 and Consequential Provisions) Order 2000 (S.I. 2000 No. 3145; not reproduced in this work). S.I. 2000 No. 3145 also brought paragraphs 1–18 of Schedule 21 into force on the same date.]*

255. Provisions consequent on alteration of metropolitan police district

A40.06   (1) Where, by virtue of the coming into force of section 323 below, the whole or any part of the area of a district council ceases to be within the metropolitan police district, the following provisions of this section shall have effect.

(2) The provisions of the Town Police Clauses Act 1847 with respect to hackney carriages, as incorporated in the Public Health Act 1875, shall apply throughout the council's area.

(3) The council's area shall constitute a single licensing area for the purposes of those provisions, without the passing of any resolution under Part II of Schedule 14 to the Local Government Act 1972 (extension resolutions).

(4) The provisions of Part II of the Local Government (Miscellaneous Provisions) Act 1976 (hackney carriages and private hire vehicles) shall also apply throughout the council's area, without the passing of any resolution under section 45 of that Act (application of Part II).

(5)–(7).   *[Omitted.]*

A40.07   *[Section 255 was brought into force on April 1, 2000 (in so far as not previously in force) by the Greater London Authority Act 1999 (Commencement No. 4 and Adaptation) Order 2000 (S.I. 2000 No. 801; not reproduced in this work).]*

*   *   *

CHAPTER XV

NEW CHARGES AND LEVIES

295. Road user charging

A40.08   (1) Each of the following bodies, namely—

(a) Transport for London,

(b) any London borough council, or

(c) the Common Council,

may establish and operate schemes for imposing charges in respect of the keeping or use of motor vehicles on roads in its area.

(2) Schedule 23 to this Act (which makes provision supplementing this section) shall have effect.

(3) For the purposes of this section and that Schedule *"motor vehicle"* has the meaning given in section 185(1) of the Road Traffic Act 1988, except that section 189 of that Act (exception for certain pedestrian controlled vehicles and electrically assisted pedal cycles) shall apply for those purposes as it applies for the purposes of the Road Traffic Acts.

A40.09   *[Section 295 was brought into force on May 8, 2000 (except in relation to Transport for London) and on July 3, 2000 (so far as not previously in force) by the Greater London Authority Act 1999 (Commencement No. 4 and Adaptation) Order 2000 (S.I. 2000 No. 801; not reproduced in this work).]*

*   *   *

PART XII

A40.10   SUPPLEMENTARY PROVISIONS

*   *   *

Miscellaneous and supplemental

*   *   *

425. Short title, commencement and extent

(1) This Act may be cited as the Greater London Authority Act 1999.   **A40.11**

(2) Apart from this section, section 420 above and any power of a Minister of the Crown to make regulations or an order (which accordingly come into force on the day on which this Act is passed) the provisions of this Act shall come into force on such day as the Secretary of State may by order appoint; and different days may be appointed for different purposes.

(3)–(6) *[Omitted.]*

(7) Subject to subsection (8) below, this Act does not extend to Northern Ireland.

(8) Any amendment or repeal made by this Act shall have the same extent as the enactment to which it relates.

*   *   *

SCHEDULE 23   Section 295

ROAD USER CHARGING

*   *   *

Offences

25.—(1) A person who, with intent to avoid payment of a charge imposed by a charging scheme or with intent to avoid being identified as having failed to pay such a charge,—   **A40.12**

(a) interferes with any equipment used for or in connection with charging under a charging scheme, [or]

(b) causes or permits the registration plate of a motor vehicle to be obscured . . .

is guilty of an offence.

[(1A) A person who makes or uses any false document with intent to avoid payment of, or being identified as having failed to pay, a charge imposed by a charging scheme or a penalty charge is guilty of an offence.]

(2) A person guilty of an offence under sub-paragraph (1) [or (1A)] above shall be liable on summary conviction to a fine not exceeding level 5 on the standard scale or to imprisonment for a term not exceeding six months or to both.

[(3) A person is guilty of an offence if he removes a penalty charge notice which has been fixed to a motor vehicle in accordance with regulations under paragraph 12 above unless—

(a) he is the registered keeper of the vehicle or a person using the vehicle with his authority; or

(b) he does so under the authority of the registered keeper or such a person or of the charging authority.]

[(4) A person guilty of an offence under sub-paragraph (3) above shall be liable on summary conviction to a fine not exceeding level 2 on the standard scale.]

A40.13   *[Schedule 23 was brought into force on May 8, 2000 (except in relation to Transport for London) (section 295 of this Act was formally brought into force for all other purposes on July 3, 2000) by the Greater London Authority Act 1999 (Commencement No. 4 and Adaptation) Order 2000 (S.I. 2000 No. 801; not reproduced in this work).*

Paragraph 25 of Schedule 23 is printed as amended (specifically, as respects England) by the Transport Act 2000, s.199 and Sched. 13, paras 1 and 10 (and see also ibid., s.274 and Sched. 31, Pt III) (with effect from February 1, 2001; see the Transport Act 2000 (Commencement No. 3) Order 2001 (S.I. 2001 No. 57; not reproduced in this work).]

*　　　*　　　*

The Powers of Criminal Courts (Sentencing) Act 2000

(2000 c. 6)

An Act to consolidate certain enactments relating to the powers of courts to deal with offenders and defaulters and to the treatment of such persons, with amendments to give effect to recommendations of the Law Commission and the Scottish Law Commission.   **A41.01**

[25th May 2000]

Table of Destinations

The table below indicates the provisions in the earlier legislation which correspond to those in the 2000 Act which fall within the scope of this work. In the table, a reference to a provision in the earlier legislation includes a reference to such provision as subsequently amended (and references to the amending legislation are excluded from the table).   **A41.02**

Children and Young Persons Act 1933	*Powers of Criminal Courts (Sentencing) Act 2000*
s.53(2), (3)	s.91(1)–(3)

Criminal Justice Act 1967	*Powers of Criminal Courts (Sentencing) Act 2000*
s.56(1)	s.6(1)–(3)
s.56(2)	s.6(4)
s.56(5)–(5C)	s.7
s.56(5D)	s.164(1)

Powers of Criminal Courts Act 1973	*Powers of Criminal Courts (Sentencing) Act 2000*
s.35(1)	s.130(1), (3)
s.35(1A)	s.130(4)
s.35(2)	s.130(5)
s.35(3)	s.130(6), (7)
s.35(3A), (3B)	s.130(8), (9)
s.35(3C), (3D)	s.130(10)
s.35(4), (4A)	s.130(11), (12)
s.36(1), (5)	s.132(1), (5)
s.37	s.133(1) to (4)
s.43(1)	s.143(1), (2), (4)
s.43(2)	ss.143(8), 147(6), 164(2)
s.43(1A)	s.143(5)
s.43(1B), (1C)	s.143(6), (7)
s.43(3)	s.143(3)
s.43(4)–(8)	s.144(1)–(5)
s.43A(1)–(3)	s.145(1)–(3)
s.44(1), (1A)	s.147(1), (2)
s.44(2)	s.147(3)
s.44(2A), (3)	s.147(4), (5)

Magistrates' Courts Act 1980	*Powers of Criminal Courts (Sentencing) Act 2000*
s.38A(1)–(5)	s.4(1)–(5)
s.38A(5A), (6)	s.4(6), (7)
s.40(1)	s.131(1), (2)
s.40(2)	s.163 (part)

Criminal Justice Act 1991	*Powers of Criminal Courts (Sentencing) Act 2000*
s.18(1)–(3)	s.128(1)–(3)
s.18(4)	s.128(5)
s.18(5)	ss.128(4), 138(3)
s.20(1), (1A)	s.126(1), (2)
s.20(1B)	s.136(1)
s.20(1C)	ss.126(3), 136(2)
s.20(2), (3)	s.126(4), (5)
s.20(4)	s.126(6)

Crime (Sentences) Act 1997	*Powers of Criminal Courts (Sentencing) Act 2000*
s.2(1)–(7)	s.109(1)–(7)
s.5(1), (2)	s.112(1), (2)
s.6(1), (3)	s.113(1), (3)
s.39(1)–(4)	s.146(1)–(4)
s.39(5)	Sched. 9, paras 117, 120
s.39(6)	s.146(5)

A41.03 *Commencement.* This Act took effect on August 25, 2000 (see section 168(1)).

ARRANGEMENT OF SECTIONS

PART I

POWERS EXERCISABLE BEFORE SENTENCE

*   *   *

Committal to Crown Court for sentence

Section

*   *   *

PART V

CUSTODIAL SENTENCES, ETC.

*   *   *

CHAPTER II

DETENTION AND CUSTODY OF YOUNG OFFENDERS

*   *   *

Detention at Her Majesty's pleasure or for specified period

*   *   *

CHAPTER III

REQUIRED CUSTODIAL SENTENCES FOR CERTAIN OFFENCES

PART VI

FINANCIAL PENALTIES AND ORDERS

Financial circumstances orders

Fines: general

Compensation orders

*   *   *

PART VII

FURTHER POWERS OF COURTS

Powers to deprive offender of property used, etc., for purposes of crime

* * *

PART VIII

MISCELLANEOUS AND SUPPLEMENTARY

* * *

Interpretation

SCHEDULES

* * *

* * *

PART I

POWERS EXERCISABLE BEFORE SENTENCE

*   *   *

Committal to Crown Court for sentence

3. Committal for sentence on summary trial of offence triable either way

(1) Subject to subsection (4) below, this section applies where on the summary trial of an offence triable either way a person aged 18 or over is convicted of the offence.   **A41.05**

(2) If the court is of the opinion—

  (a) that the offence or the combination of the offence and one or more offences associated with it was so serious that greater punishment should be inflicted for the offence than the court has power to impose, or

  (b) in the case of a violent or sexual offence, that a custodial sentence for a term longer than the court has power to impose is necessary to protect the public from serious harm from him,

the court may commit the offender in custody or on bail to the Crown Court for sentence in accordance with section 5(1) below.

(3) Where the court commits a person under subsection (2) above, section 6 below (which enables a magistrates' court, where it commits a person under this section in respect of an offence, also to commit him to the Crown Court to be dealt with in respect of certain other offences) shall apply accordingly.

(4) This section does not apply in relation to an offence as regards which this section is excluded by section 33 of the Magistrates' Courts Act 1980 (certain offences where value involved is small).

(5) The preceding provisions of this section shall apply in relation to a corporation as if—

  (a) the corporation were an individual aged 18 or over; and

  (b) in subsection (2) above, paragraph (b) and the words "in custody or on bail" were omitted.

4. Committal for sentence on indication of guilty plea to offence triable either way

(1) This section applies where—   **A41.06**

  (a) a person aged 18 or over appears or is brought before a magistrates' court ("*the court*") on an information charging him with an offence triable either way ("*the offence*");

  (b) he or his representative indicates that he would plead guilty if the offence were to proceed to trial; and

  (c) proceeding as if section 9(1) of the Magistrates' Courts Act 1980 were complied with and he pleaded guilty under it, the court convicts him of the offence.

(2) If the court has committed the offender to the Crown Court for trial for one or more related offences, that is to say, one or more offences which, in its opinion, are related to the offence, it may commit him in custody or on bail to the Crown Court to be dealt with in respect of the offence in accordance with section 5(1) below.

(3) If the power conferred by subsection (2) above is not exercisable but the court is still to inquire, as examining justices, into one or more related offences—

(a) it shall adjourn the proceedings relating to the offence until after the conclusion of its inquiries; and

(b) if it commits the offender to the Crown Court for trial for one or more related offences, it may then exercise that power.

(4) Where the court—

(a) under subsection (2) above commits the offender to the Crown Court to be dealt with in respect of the offence, and

(b) does note state that, in its opinion, it also has power so to commit him under section 3(2) above,

section 5(1) below shall not apply unless he is convicted before the Crown Court of one or more of the related offences.

(5) Where section 5(1) below does not apply, the Crown Court may deal with the offender in respect of the offence in any way in which the magistrates' court could deal with him if it had just convicted him of the offence.

(6) Where the court commits a person under subsection (2) above, section 6 below (which enables a magistrates' court, where it commits a person under this section in respect of an offence, also to commit him to the Crown Court to be dealt with in respect of certain other offences) shall apply accordingly.

(7) For the purposes of this section one offence is related to another if, were they both to be prosecuted on indictment, the charges for them could be joined in the same indictment.

A41.07   _[Section 9(1) of the Magistrates' Courts Act 1980 (to which reference is made in section 4(1)(c) above) requires a court, on a summary trial, to ask the accused whether he pleads guilty or not guilty.]_

5. Power of Crown Court on committal for sentence under sections 3 and 4

A41.08   (1) Where an offender is committed by a magistrates' court for sentence under section 3 or 4 above, the Crown Court shall inquire into the circumstances of the case and may deal with the offender in any way in which it could deal with him if he had just been convicted of the offence on indictment before the court.

(2) In relation to committals under section 4 above, subsection (1) above has effect subject to section 4(4) and (5) above.

6. Committal for sentence in certain cases where offender committed in respect of another offence

A41.09   (1) This section applies where a magistrates' court (_"the committing court"_) commits a person in custody or on bail to the Crown Court under any enactment mentioned in subsection (4) below to be sentenced or otherwise dealt with in respect of an offence (_"the relevant offence"_).

(2) Where this section applies and the relevant offence is an indictable offence, the committing court may also commit the offender, in custody or on bail as the case may require, to the Crown Court to be dealt with in respect of any other offence whatsoever in respect of which the committing court has power to deal with him (being an offence of which he has been convicted by that or any other court).

(3) Where this section applies and the relevant offence is a summary offence, the committing court may commit the offender, in custody or on bail as the case may require, to the Crown Court to be dealt with in respect of—

(a) any other offence of which the committing court has convicted him, being either—

(i) an offence punishable with imprisonment; or

(ii) an offence in respect of which the committing court has a power or duty to order him to be disqualified under section 34, 35 or 36 or the Road Traffic Offenders Act 1988 [*q.v.*] (disqualification for certain motoring offences); or

(b) any suspended sentence in respect of which the committing court has under section 120(1) below power to deal with him.

(4) The enactments referred to in subsection (1) above are—

(a) the Vagrancy Act 1824 (incorrigible rogues);

(b) sections 3 and 4 above (committal for sentence for offences triable either way);

(c) section 13(5) below (conditionally discharged person convicted of further offence);

(d) section 116(3)(b) below (offender convicted of offence committed during currency of original sentence); and

(e) section 120(2) below (offender convicted during operational period of suspended sentence).

7. Power of Crown Court on committal for sentence under section 6

(1) Where under section 6 above a magistrates' court commits a person to be dealt with by the Crown Court in respect of an offence, the Crown Court may after inquiring into the circumstances of the case deal with him in any way in which the magistrates' court could deal with him if it had just convicted him of the offence.   **A41.10**

(2) Subsection (1) above does not apply where under section 6 above a magistrates' court commits a person to be dealt with by the Crown Court in respect of a suspended sentence, but in such a case the powers under section 119 below (power of court to deal with suspended sentence) shall be exercisable by the Crown Court.

(3) Without prejudice to subsections (1) and (2) above, where under section 6 above or any enactment mentioned in subsection (4) of that section a magistrates' court commits a person to be dealt with by the Crown Court, any duty or power which, apart from this subsection, would fall to be discharged or exercised by the magistrates' court shall not be discharged or exercised by that court but shall instead be discharged or may instead be exercised by the Crown Court.

(4) Where under section 6 above a magistrates' court commits a person to be dealt with by the Crown Court in respect of an offence triable only on indictment in the case of an adult (being an offence which was tried summarily because of the offender's being under 18 years of age), the Crown Court's powers under subsection (1) above in respect of the offender after he attains the age of 18 shall be powers to do either or both of the following—

(a) to impose a fine not exceeding £5,000;

(b) to deal with the offender in respect of the offence in any way in which the magistrates' court could deal with him if it had just convicted him of an offence punishable with imprisonment for a term not exceeding six months.

*   *   *

PART V

CUSTODIAL SENTENCES, ETC.

*   *   *

CHAPTER II

DETENTION AND CUSTODY OF YOUNG OFFENDERS

*   *   *

Detention at Her Majesty's pleasure or for specified period

A41.11   **90. Offenders who commit murder when under 18: duty to detain at Her Majesty's pleasure**   *[Omitted.]*

91. Offenders under 18 convicted of certain serious offences: power to detain for specified period

A41.12   (1) Subsection (3) below applies where a person aged under 18 is convicted on indictment of—

    (a) an offence punishable in the case of a person aged 21 or over with imprisonment for 14 years or more, not being an offence the sentence for which is fixed by law; or

    (b) an offence under section 14 of the Sexual Offences Act 1956 (indecent assault on a woman); or

    (c) an offence under section 15 of that Act (indecent assault on a man) committed after 30th September 1997.

(2) Subsection (3) below also applies where a person aged at least 14 but under 18 is convicted of an offence under—

    (a) section 1 of the Road Traffic Act 1988 (causing death by dangerous driving); or

    (b) section 3A of that Act (causing death by careless driving while under influence of drink or drugs).

(3) If the court is of the opinion that none of the other methods in which the case may legally be dealt with is suitable, the court may sentence the offender to be detained for such period, not exceeding the maximum term of imprisonment with which the offence is punishable in the case of a person aged 21 or over, as may be specified in the sentence.

(4) Subsection (3) above is subject to (in particular) sections 79 and 80 above.

A41.13   *[With effect from a date to be announced under the Criminal Justice and Court Services Act 2000, s.80(2), the numeral "18" will be substituted in both section 91(1)(a) and in section 91(3) for the numeral "21" by the 2000 Act, s.74 and Sched. 7, paras 160 and 181.*

Sections 79 and 80 of this Act (to which reference is made in section 91(4) above) deal with general restrictions on imposing discretionary custodial sentences (section 79) and the length of custodial sentences: general provision (section 80).]

A41.14   **92. Detention under sections 90 and 91: place of detention, etc.**   *[Omitted.]*

*   *   *

CHAPTER III

REQUIRED CUSTODIAL SENTENCES FOR CERTAIN OFFENCES

109. Life sentence for second serious offence

(1) This section applies where—   A41.15

(a) a person is convicted of a serious offence committed after 30th September 1997; and

(b) at the time when that offence was committed, he was 18 or over and had been convicted in any part of the United Kingdom of another serious offence.

(2) The court shall impose a life sentence, that is to say—

(a) where the offender is 21 or over when convicted of the offence mentioned in subsection (1)(a) above, a sentence of imprisonment for life,

(b) where he is under 21 at that time, a sentence of custody for life under section 94 above,

unless the court is of the opinion that there are exceptional circumstances relating to either of the offences or to the offender which justify its not doing so.

(3) Where the court does not impose a life sentence, it shall state in open court that it is of that opinion and what the exceptional circumstances are.

(4) An offence the sentence for which is imposed under subsection (2) above shall not be regarded as an offence the sentence for which is fixed by law.

(5) An offence committed in England and Wales is a serious offence for the purposes of this section if it is any of the following, namely—

(a) an attempt to commit murder, a conspiracy to commit murder or an incitement to murder;

(b) an offence under section 4 of the Offences Against the Person Act 1861 (soliciting murder);

(c) manslaughter;

(d) an offence under section 18 of the Offences Against the Person Act 1861 (wounding, or causing grievous bodily harm, with intent);

(e) rape or an attempt to commit rape;

(f) an offence under section 5 of the Sexual Offences Act 1956 (intercourse with a girl under 13);

(g) an offence under section 16 (possession of a firearm with intent to injure), section 17 (use of a firearm to resist arrest) or section 18 (carrying a firearm with criminal intent) of the Firearms Act 1968; and

(h) robbery where, at some time during the commission of the offence, the offender had in his possession a firearm or imitation firearm within the meaning of that Act.

(6) An offence committed in Scotland is a serious offence for the purposes of this section if the conviction for it was obtained on indictment in the High Court of Justiciary and it is any of the following, namely—

(a) culpable homicide;

(b) attempted murder, incitement to commit murder or conspiracy to commit murder;

(c) rape or attempted rape;

(d) clandestine injury to women or an attempt to cause such injury;

(e) sodomy, or an attempt to commit sodomy, where the complainer, that is to say, the person against whom the offence was committed, did not consent;

   (f) assault where the assault—

     (i) is aggravated because it was carried out to the victim's severe injury or the danger of the victim's life; or

     (ii) was carried out with an intention to rape or to ravish the victim;

   (g) robbery where, at some time during the commission of the offence, the offender had in his possession a firearm or imitation firearm within the meaning of the Firearms Act 1968;

   (h) an offence under section 16 (possession of a firearm with intent to injure), section 17 (use of a firearm to resist arrest) or section 18 (carrying a firearm with criminal intent) of that Act;

   (i) lewd, libidinous or indecent behaviour or practices; and

   (j) an offence under section 5(1) of the Criminal Law (Consolidation) (Scotland) Act 1995 (unlawful intercourse with a girl under 13).

(7) An offence committed in Northern Ireland is a serious offence for the purposes of this section if it is any of the following, namely—

   (a) an offence falling within any of paragraphs (a) to (e) of subsection (5) above;

   (b) an offence under section 4 of the Criminal Law Amendment Act 1885 (intercourse with a girl under 14);

   (c) an offence under Article 17 (possession of a firearm with intent to injure), Article 18(1) (use of a firearm to resist arrest) or Article 19 (carrying a firearm with criminal intent) of the Firearms (Northern Ireland) Order 1981 *[S.I. 1981 No. 155]*; and

   (d) robbery where, at some time during the commission of the offence, the offender had in his possession a firearm or imitation firearm within the meaning of that Order.

A41.16   *[With effect from a date to be announced under the Criminal Justice and Court Services Act 2000, s.80(2), the words "a sentence of imprisonment for life" will be substituted for paragraphs (a) and (b) in section 109(2) by the 2000 Act, s.74 and Sched. 7, paras 160 and 189.]*

A41.17   **110. Minimum of seven years for third class A drug trafficking offence**
[Omitted.]

A41.18   **111. Minimum of three years for third domestic burglary**   *[Omitted.]*

112. Appeals where previous convictions set aside

A41.19   (1) This section applies where—

   (a) a sentence has been imposed on any person under subsection (2) of section 109, 110 or 111 above; and

   (b) any previous conviction of his without which that section would not have applied has been subsequently set aside on appeal.

(2) Notwithstanding anything in section 18 of the Criminal Appeal Act 1968, notice of appeal against the sentence may be given at any time within 28 days from the date on which the previous conviction was set aside.

113. Certificates of convictions for purposes of Chapter III

A41.20   (1) Where—

   (a) on any date after 30th September 1997 a person is convicted in England and Wales of a serious offence or a class A drug trafficking offence, or on any date after 30th November 1999 a person is convicted in England and Wales of a domestic burglary, and

  (b) the court by or before which he is so convicted states in open court that he has been convicted of such an offence on that date, and

  (c) that court, subsequently certifies that fact,

the certificate shall be evidence, for the purposes of the relevant section of this Chapter, that he was convicted of such an offence on that date.

(2) *[Applies to class A drug trafficking offences and domestic burglaries.]*

(3) In this section—

"*serious offence*", "*class A drug trafficking offence*" and "*domestic burglary*" have the same meanings as in sections 109, 110 and 111 respectively; and

"*the relevant section of this Chapter*", in relation to any such offence, shall be construed accordingly.

114. Offences under service law   *[Omitted.]*   **A41.21**

115. Determination of day when offence committed   *[Omitted.]*   **A41.22**

*   *   *

PART VI

FINANCIAL PENALTIES AND ORDERS

Financial circumstances orders

126. Powers to order statement as to offender's financial circumstances

(1) Where an individual has been convicted of an offence, the court may, before sentencing him, make a financial circumstances order with respect to him.   **A41.23**

(2) Where a magistrates' court has been notified in accordance with section 12(4) of the Magistrates' Courts Act 1980 that an individual desires to plead guilty without appearing before the court, the court may make a financial circumstances order with respect to him.

(3) In this section "*a financial circumstances order*" means, in relation to any individual, an order requiring him to give to the court, within such period as may be specified in the order, such a statement of his financial circumstances as the court may require.

(4) An individual who without reasonable excuse fails to comply with a financial circumstances order shall be liable on summary conviction to a fine not exceeding level 3 on the standard scale.

(5) If an individual, in furnishing any statement in pursuance of a financial circumstances order—

  (a) makes a statement which he knows to be false in a material particular,

  (b) recklessly furnishes a statement which is false in a material particular, or

  (c) knowingly fails to disclose any material fact,

he shall be liable on summary conviction to imprisonment for a term not exceeding three months or a fine not exceeding level 4 on the standard scale or both.

(6) Proceedings in respect of an offence under subsection (5) above may, notwithstanding anything in section 127(1) of the Magistrates' Courts Act 1980 (limitation of time), be commenced at any time within two years from the date of the commission of the offence

or within six months from its first discovery by the prosecutor, whichever period expires the earlier.

Fines: general

A41.24   **127. General power of Crown Court to fine offender convicted on indictment**   *[Omitted.]*

128. Fixing of fines

A41.25   (1) Before fixing the amount of any fine to be imposed on an offender who is an individual, a court shall inquire into his financial circumstances.

(2) The amount of any fine fixed by a court shall be such as, in the opinion of the court, reflects the seriousness of the offence.

(3) In fixing the amount of any fine to be imposed on an offender (whether an individual or other person), a court shall take into account the circumstances of the case including, among other things, the financial circumstances of the offender so far as they are known, or appear, to the court.

(4) Subsection (3) above applies whether taking into account the financial circumstances of the offender has the effect of increasing or reducing the amount of the fine.

(5) Where—

   (a) an offender has been convicted in his absence in pursuance of section 11 or 12 of the Magistrates' Courts Act 1980 (non-appearance of accused), or

   (b) an offender—

      (i) has failed to comply with an order under section 126(1) above, or

      (ii) has otherwise failed to co-operate with the court in its inquiry into his financial circumstances,

and the court considers that it has insufficient information to make a proper determination of the financial circumstances of the offender, it may make such determination as it thinks fit.

A41.26   **129. Remission of fines**   *[Omitted.]*

Compensation orders

130. Compensation orders against convicted persons

A41.27   (1) A court by or before which a person is convicted of an offence, instead of or in addition to dealing with him in any other way, may, on application or otherwise, make an order (in this Act referred to as a "*compensation order*") requiring him—

   (a) to pay compensation for any personal injury, loss or damage resulting from that offence or any other offence which is taken into consideration by the court in determining sentence; or

   (b) to make payments for funeral expenses or bereavement in respect of a death resulting from any such offence, other than a death due to an accident arising out of the presence of a motor vehicle on a road;

but this is subject to the following provisions of this section and to section 131 below.

(2) Where the person is convicted of an offence the sentence for which is fixed by law or falls to be imposed under section 109(2), 110(2) or 111(2) above, subsection (1) above shall have effect as if the words "instead of or" were omitted.

(3) A court shall give reasons, on passing sentence, if it does not make a compensation order in a case where this section empowers it to do so.

(4) Compensation under subsection (1) above shall be of such amount as the court considers appropriate, having regard to any evidence and to any representations that are made by or on behalf of the accused or the prosecutor.

(5) In the case of an offence under the Theft Act 1968, where the property in question is recovered, any damage to the property occurring while it was out of the owner's possession shall be treated for the purposes of subsection (1) above as having resulted from the offence, however and by whomever the damage was caused.

(6) A compensation order may only be made in respect of injury, loss or damage (other than loss suffered by a person's dependants in consequence of his death) which was due to an accident arising out of the presence of a motor vehicle on a road, if—

   (a) it is in respect of damage which is treated by subsection (5) above as resulting from an offence under the Theft Act 1968; or

   (b) it is in respect of injury, loss or damage as respects which—

      (i) the offender is uninsured in relation to the use of the vehicle; and

      (ii) compensation is not payable under any arrangements to which the Secretary of State is a party.

(7) Where a compensation order is made in respect of injury, loss or damage due to an accident arising out of the presence of a motor vehicle on a road, the amount to be paid may include an amount representing the whole or part of any loss of or reduction in preferential rates of insurance attributable to the accident.

(8) A vehicle the use of which is exempted from insurance by section 144 of the Road Traffic Act 1988 [*q.v.*] is not uninsured for the purposes of subsection (6) above.

(9) A compensation order in respect of funeral expenses may be made for the benefit of anyone who incurred the expenses.

(10) A compensation order in respect of bereavement may be made only for the benefit of a person for whose benefit a claim for damages for bereavement could be made under section 1A of the Fatal Accidents Act 1976; and the amount of compensation in respect of bereavement shall not exceed the amount for the time being specified in section 1A(3) of that Act.

(11) In determining whether to make a compensation order against any person, and in determining the amount to be paid by any person under such an order, the court shall have regard to his means so far as they appear or are known to the court.

(12) Where the court considers—

   (a) that it would be appropriate both to impose a fine and to make a compensation order, but

   (b) that the offender has insufficient means to pay both an appropriate fine and appropriate compensation,

the court shall give preference to compensation (though it may impose a fine as well).

[The text of the Fatal Accidents Act 1976, s.1A (so far as relevant to section 130(10) above), as **A41.28**
amended by the Damages for Bereavement (Variation of Sum) (England and Wales) Order 1990 (S.I. 1990 No. 2575; not reproduced in this work), reads as follows:

   (1) An action under this Act may consist of or include a claim for damages for bereavement.

(2) A claim for damages for bereavement shall only be for the benefit—

(a) of the wife or husband of the deceased; and

(b) where the deceased was a minor who was never married—

(i) of his parents, if he was legitimate; and
(ii) of his mother, if he was illegitimate.

(3) Subject to subsection (5) below, the sum to be awarded as damages under this section shall be [£7,500] . . .]

131. Limit on amount payable under compensation order of magistrates' court

A41.29   (1) The compensation to be paid under a compensation order made by a magistrates' court in respect of any offence of which the court has convicted the offender shall not exceed £5,000.

(2) The compensation or total compensation to be paid under a compensation order or compensation orders made by a magistrates' court in respect of any offence or offences taken into consideration in determining sentence shall not exceed the difference (if any) between—

(a) the amount or total amount which under subsection (1) above is the maximum for the offence or offences of which the offender has been convicted; and

(b) the amount or total amounts (if any) which are in fact ordered to be paid in respect of that offence or those offences.

132. Compensation orders: appeals, etc.

A41.30   (1) A person in whose favour a compensation order is made shall not be entitled to receive the amount due to him until (disregarding any power of a court to grant leave to appeal out of time) there is no further possibility of an appeal on which the order could be varied or set aside.

(2) *[Rule-making power.]*

(3) *[Powers of Court of Appeal.]*

(4) *[Power of House of Lords.]*

(5) Where a compensation order has been made against any person in respect of an offence taken into consideration in determining his sentence—

(a) the order shall cease to have effect if he successfully appeals against his conviction of the offence or, if more than one, all the offences, of which he was convicted in the proceedings in which the order was made;

(b) he may appeal against the order as if it were part of the sentence imposed in respect of the offence or, if more than one, any of the offences, of which he was so convicted.

133. Review of compensation orders

A41.31   (1) The magistrates' court for the time being having functions in relation to the enforcement of a compensation order (in this section referred to as "*the appropriate court*") may, on the application of the person against whom the compensation order was made, discharge the order or reduce the amount which remains to be paid; but this is subject to subsections (2) to (4) below.

(2) The appropriate court may exercise a power conferred by subsection (1) above only—

(a) at a time when (disregarding any power of a court to grant leave to appeal out of time) there is no further possibility of an appeal on which the compensation order could be varied or set aside; and

(b) at a time before the person against whom the compensation order was made has paid into court the whole of the compensation which the order requires him to pay.

(3) The appropriate court may exercise a power conferred by subsection (1) above only if it appears to the court—

(a) that the injury, loss or damage in respect of which the compensation order was made has been held in civil proceedings to be less than it was taken to be for the purposes of the order; or

(b) in the case of a compensation order in respect of the loss of any property, that the property has been recovered by the person in whose favour the order was made; or

(c) that the means of the person against whom the compensation order was made are insufficient to satisfy in full both the order and a confiscation order under Part VI of the Criminal Justice Act 1988 made against him in the same proceedings; or

(d) that the person against whom the compensation order was made has suffered a substantial reduction in his means which was unexpected at the time when the order was made, and that his means seem unlikely to increase for a considerable period.

(4) Where the compensation order was made by the Crown Court, the appropriate court shall not exercise any power conferred by subsection (1) above in a case where it is satisfied as mentioned in paragraph (c) or (d) of subsection (3) above unless it has first obtained the consent of the Crown Court.

(5) Where a compensation order has been made on appeal, for the purposes of subsection (4) above it shall be deemed—

(a) if it was made on an appeal brought from a magistrates' court, to have been made by that magistrates' court;

(b) if it was made on an appeal brought from the Crown Court or from the criminal division of the Court of Appeal, to have been made by the Crown Court.

134. Effect of compensation order on subsequent award of damages in civil   **A41.32**
proceedings   *[Omitted.]*

*   *   *

PART VII

FURTHER POWERS OF COURTS

Powers to deprive offender of property used, etc., for purposes of crime

143. Powers to deprive offender of property used, etc., for purposes of crime

(1) Where a person is convicted of an offence and the court by or before which he is con-   **A41.33**
victed is satisfied that any property which has been lawfully seized from him, or which was in his possession or under his control at the time when he was apprehended for the offence or when a summons in respect of it was issued—

(a) has been used for the purpose of committing, or facilitating the commission of, any offence, or

    (b) was intended by him to be used for that purpose,

the court may (subject to subsection (5) below) make an order under this section in respect of that property.

(2) Where a person is convicted of an offence and the offence, or an offence which the court has taken into consideration in determining his sentence, consists of unlawful possession of property which—

    (a) has been lawfully seized from him, or

    (b) was in his possession or under his control at the time when he was apprehended for the offence of which he has been convicted or when a summons in respect of that offence was issued,

the court may (subject to subsection (5) below) make an order under this section in respect of that property.

(3) An order under this section shall operate to deprive the offender of his rights, if any, in the property to which it relates, and the property shall (if not already in their possession) be taken into the possession of the police.

(4) Any power conferred on a court by subsection (1) or (2) above may be exercised—

    (a) whether or not the court also deals with the offender in any other way in respect of the offence of which he has been convicted; and

    (b) without regard to any restrictions on forfeiture in any enactment contained in an Act passed before 29th July 1988.

(5) In considering whether to make an order under this section in respect of any property, a court shall have regard—

    (a) to the value of the property; and

    (b) to the likely financial and other effects on the offender of the making of the order (taken together with any other order that the court contemplates making).

(6) Where a person commits an offence to which this subsection applies by—

    (a) driving, attempting to drive, or being in charge of a vehicle, or

    (b) failing to comply with a requirement made under section 7 of the Road Traffic Act 1988 (failure to provide specimen for analysis or laboratory test) in the course of an investigation into whether the offender had committed an offence while driving, attempting to drive or being in charge of a vehicle, or

    (c) failing, as the driver of a vehicle, to comply with subsection (2) or (3) of section 170 of the Road Traffic Act 1988 (duty to stop and give information or report accident),

the vehicle shall be regarded for the purposes of subsection (1) above (and section 144(1)(b) below) as used for the purpose of committing the offence (and for the purpose of committing any offence of aiding, abetting, counselling or procuring the commission of the offence).

(7) Subsection (6) above applies to—

    (a) an offence under the Road Traffic Act 1988 which is punishable with imprisonment;

    (b) an offence of manslaughter; and

    (c) an offence under section 35 of the Offences Against the Person Act 1861 (wanton and furious driving).

(8) Facilitating the commission of an offence shall be taken for the purposes of subsection (1) above to include the taking of any steps after it has been committed for the

purpose of disposing of any property to which it relates or of avoiding apprehension or detection.

144. Property which is in possession of police by virtue of section 143

(1) The Police (Property) Act 1897 shall apply, with the following modifications, to property which is in the possession of the police by virtue of section 143 above—   **A41.34**

- (a) no application shall be made under section 1(1) of that Act by any claimant of the property after the end of six months from the date on which the order in respect of the property was made under section 143 above; and
- (b) no such application shall succeed unless the claimant satisfies the court either—
  - (i) that he had not consented to the offender having possession of the property; or
  - (ii) where an order is made under subsection (1) of section 143 above, that he did not know, and had no reason to suspect, that the property was likely to be used for the purpose mentioned in that subsection.

(2) In relation to property which is in the possession of the police by virtue of section 143 above, the power to make regulations under section 2 of the Police (Property) Act 1897 (disposal of property in cases where the owner of the property has not been ascertained and no order of a competent court has been made with respect to it) shall, subject to subsection (3) below, include power to make regulations for disposal (including disposal by vesting in the relevant authority) in cases where no application by a claimant of the property has been made within the period specified in subsection (1)(a) above or no such application has succeeded.

(3) The regulations may not provide for the vesting in the relevant authority of property in relation to which an order has been made under section 145 below (court order as to application of proceeds of forfeited property).

(4) Nothing in subsection (2A)(a) or (3) of section 2 of the Police (Property) Act 1897 limits the power to make regulations under that section by virtue of subsection (2) above.

(5) In this section "*relevant authority*" has the meaning given by section 2(2B) of the Police (Property) Act 1897.

[The Police (Property) Act 1897, s.1(1) (to which reference is made in section 144(1)(a) above but which is not reproduced in this work), empowers a magistrates' court to make an order for the delivery of certain property in the hands of the police to the person appearing to the court to be the owner, or otherwise disposing of the property.]   **A41.35**

145. Application of proceeds of forfeited property

(1) Where a court makes an order under section 143 above in a case where—   **A41.36**

- (a) the offender has been convicted of an offence which has resulted in a person suffering personal injury, loss or damage, or
- (b) any such offence is taken into consideration by the court in determining sentence,

the court may also make an order that any proceeds which arise from the disposal of the property and which do not exceed a sum specified by the court shall be paid to that person.

(2) The court may make an order under this section only if it is satisfied that but for the inadequacy of the offender's means it would have made a compensation order under which the offender would have been required to pay compensation of an amount not less than the specified amount.

(3) An order under this section has no effect—

(a) before the end of the period specified in section 144(1)(a) above; or

(b) if a successful application under section 1(1) of the Police (Property) Act 1897 has been made.

A41.37   *[As to the Police (Property) Act 1897, s.1(1) (to which reference is made in section 145(3)(b) above), see the note to section 144 of this Act.]*

Driving disqualifications

146. Driving disqualification for any offence

A41.38   (1) The court by or before which a person is convicted of an offence committed after 31st December 1997 may, instead of or in addition to dealing with him in any other way, order him to be disqualified, for such period as it thinks fit, for holding or obtaining a driving licence.

(2) Where the person is convicted of an offence the sentence for which is fixed by law or falls to be imposed under section 109(2), 110(2) or 111(2) above, subsection (1) above shall have effect as if the words "instead of or" were omitted.

(3) A court shall not make an order under subsection (1) above unless the court has been notified by the Secretary of State that the power to make such orders is exercisable by the court and the notice has not been withdrawn.

(4) A court which makes an order under this section disqualifying a person for holding or obtaining a driving licence shall require him to produce—

(a) any such licence held by him together with its counterpart; or

(b) in the case where he holds a Community licence (within the meaning of Part III of the Road Traffic Act 1988), his Community licence and its counterpart (if any).

(5) In this section—

"*driving licence*" means a licence to drive a motor vehicle granted under Part III of the Road Traffic Act 1988;

"*counterpart*"—

(a) in relation to a driving licence, has the meaning given in relation to such a licence by section 108(1) of that Act; and

(b) in relation to a Community licence, has the meaning given by section 99B of that Act.

A41.39   *[Section 146 is derived from the Crime (Sentences) Act 1997, s.39(1)–(4) and (6); but modifications have been introduced into the text of what is now section 146(4) and (5) on the recommendation of the Law Commission.]*

147. Driving disqualification where vehicle used for purposes of crime

A41.40   (1) This section applies where a person—

(a) is convicted before the Crown Court of an offence punishable on indictment with imprisonment for a term of two years or more; or

(b) having been convicted by a magistrates' court of such an offence, is committed under section 3 above [*q.v.*] to the Crown Court for sentence.

(2) This section also applies where a person is convicted by or before any court of

common assault or of any other offence involving an assault (including an offence of aiding, abetting, counselling or procuring, or inciting to the commission of, an offence).

(3) If, in a case to which this section applies by virtue of subsection (1) above, the Crown Court is satisfied that a motor vehicle was used (by the person convicted or by anyone else) for the purpose of committing, or facilitating the commission of, the offence in question, the court may order the person convicted to be disqualified, for such period as the court thinks fit, for holding or obtaining a driving licence.

(4) If, in a case to which this section applies by virtue of subsection (2) above, the court is satisfied that the assault was committed by driving a motor vehicle, the court may order the person convicted to be disqualified, for such period as the court thinks fit, for holding or obtaining a driving licence.

(5) A court which makes an order under this section disqualifying a person for holding or obtaining a driving licence shall require him to produce—

(a) any such licence held by him together with its counterpart; or

(b) in the case where he holds a Community licence (within the meaning of Part III of the Road Traffic Act 1988), his Community licence and its counterpart (if any).

(6) Facilitating the commission of an offence shall be taken for the purposes of this section to include the taking of any steps after it has been committed for the purpose of disposing of any property to which it relates or of avoiding apprehension or detection.

(7) In this section *"driving licence"* and *"counterpart"* have the meanings given by section 146(5) above.

*   *   *

PART VIII

MISCELLANEOUS AND SUPPLEMENTARY

*   *   *

Interpretation

161. Meaning of "associated offence", "sexual offence", "violent offence"   **A41.41**
and "protecting the public from serious harm"   *[Omitted.]*

162. Meaning of "pre-sentence report"   *[Omitted.]*   **A41.42**

163. General definitions

In this Act, except where the contrary intention appears—   **A41.43**

"action plan order" means an order under section 69(1) above;

"the appropriate officer of the court" means, in relation to a magistrates' court, the clerk of the court;

"associated", in relation to offences, shall be construed in accordance with section 161(1) above;

"attendance centre" has the meaning given by section 62(2) above;

"attendance centre order" means an order under section 60(1) above (and, except where the contrary intention is shown by paragraph 8 of Schedule 3 or paragraph 4 of Schedule

7 or 8 to this Act, includes orders made under section 60(1) by virtue of paragraph 4(1)(c) or 5(1)(c) of Schedule 3 or paragraph 2(2)(a) of Schedule 7 or 8);

"*child*" means a person under the age of 14;

. . .

"*community order*" has the meaning given by section 33(1) above;

["*community punishment and rehabilitation order*" has the meaning given by section 45 of the Criminal Justice and Court Services Act 2000];

"*community [punishment] order*" [has the meaning given by section 44 of the Criminal Justice and Court Services Act 2000] (and, except where the contrary intention is shown by section 59 above or paragraph 7 of Schedule 3 to this Act or section 35 of the Crime (Sentences) Act 1997, includes orders made under section 46(1) by virtue of section 59 or paragraph 4(1)(b) or 5(1)(b) of Schedule 3 or the said section 35);

["*community rehabilitation order*" has the meaning given by section 43 of the Criminal Justice and Court Services Act 2000];

["*community rehabilitation period*" means the period for which a person subject to a community rehabilitation or community punishment and rehabilitation order is placed under supervision by the order];

"*community sentence*" has the meaning given by section 33(2) above;

"*compensation order*" has the meaning given by section 130(1) above;

"*court*" does not include a court-martial;

"*curfew order*" means an order under section 37(1) above (and except where the contrary intention is shown by section 59 above or paragraph 3 of Schedule 7 or 8 to this Act or section 35 of the Crime (Sentences) Act 1997, includes orders made under section 37(1) by virtue of section 59 or paragraph 2(2)(a) of Schedule 7 or 8 or the said section 35);

"*custodial sentence*" has the meaning given by section 76 above;

"*detention and training order*" has the meaning given by section 100(3) above;

"*drug treatment and testing order*" means an order under section 52(1) above;

"*falling to be imposed under section 109(2), 110(2) or 111(2)*" shall be construed in accordance with section 164(3) below;

"*guardian*" has the same meaning as in the Children and Young Persons Act 1933;

"*local authority accommodation*" means accommodation provided by or on behalf of a local authority, and "*accommodation provided by or on behalf of a local authority*" here has the same meaning as it has in the Children Act 1989 by virtue of section 105 of that Act;

["*local probation board*" means a local probation board established under section 4 of the Criminal Justice and Court Services Act 2000];

"*offence punishable with imprisonment*" shall be construed in accordance with section 164(2) below;

"*operational period*", in relation to a suspended sentence, has the meaning given by section 118(3) above;

"*order for conditional discharge*" has the meaning given by section 12(3) above;

"*period of conditional discharge*" has the meaning given by section 12(3) above;

"*pre-sentence report*" has the meaning given by section 162 above;

. . .

"*protecting the public from serious harm*" shall be construed in accordance with section 161(4) above;

"*referral order*" means an order under section 16(2) or (3) above;

"*the register*" means the register of proceedings before a magistrates' court required by rules under section 144 of the Magistrates' Courts Act 1980 to be kept by the clerk of the court;

"*reparation order*" means an order under section 73(1) above;

"*responsible officer*"—

(a) in relation to a curfew order, has the meaning given by section 37(12) above;

(b) in relation to a [community rehabilitation order], has the meaning given by section 41(6) above;

(c) in relation to a [community punishment order], has the meaning given by section 46(13) above;

(d) in relation to a [community and rehabilitation order], has (by virtue of section 51(4) above) the meaning given by section 41(13) or 46(13) above;

(e) in relation to a drug treatment and testing order, has the meaning given by section 54(3) above;

(f) in relation to an action plan order, has the meaning given by section 69(4) above; and

(g) in relation to a reparation order, has the meaning given by section 74(5) above;

except that in section 47 above references to "the responsible officer" shall be construed in accordance with that section;

"*review hearing*", in relation to a drug treatment and testing order, has the meaning given by section 54(6) above;

"*sentence of imprisonment*" does not include a committal—

(a) in default of payment of any sum of money;

(b) for want of sufficient distress to satisfy any sum of money; or

(c) for failure to do or abstain from doing anything required to be done or left undone;

and references to sentencing an offender to imprisonment shall be construed accordingly;

"*sexual offence*" has the meaning given by section 161(2) above;

"*supervision order*" means an order under section 63(1) above;

"*supervisor*", in relation to a supervision order, has the meaning given by section 63(3) above;

"*suspended sentence*" has the meaning given by section 118(3) above;

"*suspended sentence supervision order*" has the meaning given by section 122(1) above;

"*the testing requirement*", in relation to a drug treatment and testing order, has the meaning given by section 53(4) above;

"*the treatment provider*", in relation to such an order, has the meaning given by section 53(1) above;

"*the treatment requirement*", in relation to such an order, has the meaning given by section 53(1) above;

"*the treatment and testing period*", in relation to such an order, has the meaning given by section 52(1) above;

"*violent offence*" has the meaning given by section 161(3) above;

"*young person*" means a person aged at least 14 but under 18;

"*youth offending team*" means a team established under section 39 of the Crime and Disorder Act 1998;

A41.44

[Section 163 is printed as amended (as at April 1, 2001) by the Criminal Justice and Court Services Act 2000, ss.43(5), 44(5), 45(5), 74 and Sched. 7, paras 1–3, 160, 197(b) and (f) (and see also ibid., s.75 and Sched. 8) (as to the date on which these amendments took effect, see the Criminal Justice and Court Services Act 2000 (Commencement No. 4) Order 2001 (S.I. 2001 No. 919; not reproduced in this work), art.2(b) and (f)(i) and (iii)).

With effect from a date (or dates) to be announced under the Criminal Justice and Court Services Act 2000, s.80(2), the following amendments will be effected to section 163 by the 2000 Act, ss.70(4), 74 and 75 and Sched. 7 (paras 160 and 197) and Sched. 8:

(i) *the following definition of* "affected person" *will be inserted in the appropriate place (2000 Act, s.74 and Sched. 7, paras 160, 197(f))—*

["*affected person*"—
   (a) in relation to an exclusion order, has the meaning given by section 40A(13) above;
   (b) in relation to a community rehabilitation order, has the meaning given by section 41(12) above; and
   (c) in relation to a community punishment and rehabilitation order, has (by virtue of section 51(4) above), the meaning given by section 41(12) above]

(ii) *in the definition of* "attendance centre order" *the words* "4(1C)(c) or 5(1C)(c)" *will be substituted for the words* "4(1)(c) or 5(1)(c)" *(2000 Act, s.74 and Sched. 7, paras 160, 197(a)),*

(iii) *in the definition of* "community [punishment] order" *the words* "4(1C)(b) or 5(1C)(b)" *will be substituted for the words* "4(1)(b) or 5(1)(b)" *(2000 Act, s.74 and Sched. 7, paras 160, 197(c)),*

(iv) *in the definition of* "curfew order", *the following words will be inserted after the words* "section 59 above" *(2000 Act, s.74 and Sched. 7, paras 160, 197(d))—*

[or paragraph 6A of Schedule 3 to this Act]

(v) *also in the definition of* "curfew order", *the words* "or paragraph 4(1C)(a) of Schedule 3" *will be inserted after the words* "section 59" *(in the second place at which they appear) (2000 Act, s.74 and Sched. 7, paras 160, 197(d)),*

(vi) *at the end of the definition of* "custodial sentence", *the following words will be inserted (2000 Act, s.74 and Sched. 7, paras 160, 197(e))—*

[and, in relation to sentences passed before coming into force of section 61 of the Criminal Justice and Court Services Act 2000, includes a sentence of custody for life and a sentence of detention in a young offender institution]

(vii) *the following definitions (*"drug abstinence order" *and* "exclusion order"*) will be inserted at the appropriate places (2000 Act, s.74 and Sched. 7, paras 160, 197(f))—*

["*drug abstinence order*" means an order under section 58A(1) above];

["*exclusion order*" means an order under section 40A(1) above];

(viii) *in the definition of* "responsible officer", *the following text will be inserted after paragraph (a) (2000 Act, s.74 and Sched. 7, paras 160, 197(g)(i))—*

[(aa) in relation to an exclusion order, has the meaning given by section 40A(14) above]

(ix) *in the definition of* "responsible officer", *the following text will be inserted after paragraph (e) (2000 Act, s.74 and Sched. 7, paras 160, 197(g)(ii))—*

[(ee) in relation to a drug abstinence order, has the meaning given by section 58A(5) above];

and;

(x) *the following definitions (*"specified Class A drug" *and* "trigger offence"*) will be inserted at the appropriate places (2000 Act, s.70(4))—*

["*specified Class A Drug*" has the same meaning as in Part III of the Criminal Justice and Court Services Act 2000];

["*trigger offence*" has the same meaning as in Part III of the Criminal Justice and Court Services Act 2000].*]*

164. Further interpretive provisions

(1) For the purposes of any provision of this Act which requires the determination of the age of a person by the court or the Secretary of State, his age shall be deemed to be that which it appears to the court or (as the case may be) the Secretary of State to be after considering any available evidence.   **A41.45**

(2) Any reference in this Act to an offence punishable with imprisonment shall be constructed without regard to any prohibition or restriction imposed by or under this or any Act on the imprisonment of young offenders.

(3) For the purposes of this Act, a sentence falls to be imposed under section 109(2), 110(2) or 111(2) above if it is required by that provision and the court is not of the opinion there mentioned.

Final provisions

165. Consequential amendments, transitory modifications, transitional provisions and repeals   *[Omitted.]*   **A41.46**

166. Short title   *[Omitted.]*   **A41.47**

167. Extent

(1) Subject to subsections (2) to (4) below, this act extends to England and Wales only.   **A41.48**

(2) The following provisions also extend to Scotland, namely—

section 14;

sections 44, 49 and 51(6);

section 121(3);

section 159;

this section; and

Schedule 4.

(3) The following provisions also extend to Northern Ireland, namely—

sections 44, 49 and 51(6);

this section; and

Schedule 4.

(4) The extent of any amendment, repeal or revocation made by this Act is the same as that of the enactment amended, repealed or revoked.

(5) For the purposes of the Scotland Act 1998, any provision of this Act which extends to Scotland is to be taken to be a pre-commencement enactment within the meaning of that Act.

168. Commencement   *[Omitted.]*   **A41.49**

*   *   *

SCHEDULES

*   *   *

SCHEDULE 11

TRANSITIONAL PROVISIONS

PART I

GENERAL

Continuity of the law: general

A41.50   **1.**—(1) The substitution of this Act for the provisions repealed by it shall not affect the continuity of the law.

(2) Any thing done (including subordinate legislation made), or having effect as if done, under or for the purposes of any provision repealed by this Act shall, if it could have been done under or for the purposes of the corresponding provision of this Act and if in force or effective immediately before the commencement of that corresponding provision, have effect thereafter as if done under or for the purposes of that corresponding provision.

(3) Any reference (express or implied) in this Act or any other enactment, instrument or document to a provision of this Act shall (so far as the context permits) be construed as including, as respects times, circumstances or purposes in relation to which the corresponding provision repealed by this Act had effect, a reference to that corresponding provision.

(4) Any reference (express or implied) in any enactment instrument or document to a provision repealed by this Act shall (so far as the context permits) be construed, as respects times, circumstances and purposes in relation to which the corresponding provision of this Act has effect, as being or (according to the context) including a reference to the corresponding provision of this Act.

(5) Sub-paragraphs (1) to (4) above have effect instead of section 17(2) of the Interpretation Act 1978 (but are without prejudice to any other provision of that Act).

General saving for old transitional provisions and savings

A41.51   **2.**—(1) The repeal by this Act of a transitional provision or saving relating to the coming into force of a provision reproduced in this Act does not affect the operation of the transitional provision or saving, in so far as it is not specifically reproduced in this Act but remains capable of having effect in relation to the corresponding provision of this Act.

(2) The repeal by this Act of an enactment previously repealed subject to savings does not affect the continued operation of those savings.

(3) The repeal by this Act of a saving on the previous repeal of an enactment does not affect the operation of the saving in so far as it is not specifically reproduced in this Act but remains capable of having effect.

(4) Where the purpose of an enactment repealed by this Act was to secure that the substitution of the provisions of the Act containing that enactment for provisions repealed by

that Act did not affect the continuity of the law, the enactment repealed by this Act continues to have effect in so far as it is capable of doing so.

Use of existing forms, etc.

3. Any reference to an enactment repealed by this Act which is contained in a document made, served or issued after the commencement of that repeal shall be construed, except so far as a contrary intention appears, as a reference or (as the context may require) as including a reference to the corresponding provision of this Act.   **A41.52**

PART II

SPECIFIC PROVISIONS: REPLICATION OF OLD TRANSITIONAL PROVISIONS   **A41.53**

[Omitted.]

PART III

SPECIFIC PROVISIONS: MISCELLANEOUS TRANSITIONAL PROVISIONS

[Omitted.]

PART IV

INTERPRETATION

14. In this Schedule, where the context permits, "repeal" includes revoke.   **A41.54**

*   *   *

The Finance Act 2000

(2000 c. 17)

A42.01 An Act to grant certain duties, to alter other duties, and to amend the law relating to the National Debt and the Public Revenue, and to make further provisions in connection with Finance.

[28th July 2000]

*   *   *

23. Enforcement provisions for graduated rates

A42.02 Schedule 4 to this Act has effect with respect to vehicle licences for vehicles in respect of which vehicle excise duty is chargeable at different rates.

*   *   *

Section 23   SCHEDULE 4

VEHICLE EXCISE DUTY: ENFORCEMENT PROVISIONS FOR GRADUATED RATES

Introduction

A42.03 **1.**—(1) This Schedule applies to vehicles in respect of which different rates of vehicle excise duty are, under the provisions listed below, chargeable in respect of vehicles by reference to characteristics of the vehicle.

(2) The provisions referred to in sub-paragraph (1) are—

Part I of Schedule 1 to the Vehicle Excise and Registration Act 1994 (the general rate),

Part IA of that Schedule (graduated rates for light passenger vehicles first registered on or after 1st March 2001), or

Part II of that Schedule (motorcycles).

Particulars to be furnished on application for licence

A42.04 **2.** *[Regulation-making power.]*

Power to require evidence in support of application

A42.05 **3.** *[Regulation-making power.]*

Powers exercisable where licence issued on basis of incorrect application

A42.06 **4.** The powers conferred by paragraphs 5 to 11 below are exercisable in a case where—

(a) a vehicle licence is issued to a person on the basis of an application stating that the vehicle—

(i) is a vehicle to which this Schedule applies, or

(ii) is a vehicle to which this Schedule applies in respect of which a particular amount of vehicle excise duty falls to be paid, and

(b) the vehicle is not such a vehicle or, as the case may be, is one in respect of which duty falls to be paid at a higher rate.

Power to declare licence void

5. The Secretary of State may by notice sent by post to the person inform him that the licence is void as from the time when it was granted.   **A42.07**

If he does so, the licence shall be void as from the time when it was granted.

Power to require payment of balance of duty

6.—(1) The Secretary of State may by notice sent by post to the person require him to secure that the additional duty payable is paid within such reasonable period as is specified in the notice.   **A42.08**

(2) If that requirement is not complied with, the Secretary of State may by notice sent by post to the person inform him that the licence is void as from the time when it was granted.

If he does so, the licence shall be void as from the time when it was granted.

Power to require delivery up of licence

7. The Secretary of State may in a notice under paragraph 5 or 6(2) require the person to whom it is sent to deliver up the licence within such reasonable period as is specified in the notice.   **A42.09**

Power to require delivery up of licence and payment in respect of duty

8.—(1) The Secretary of State may in a notice under paragraph 5 or 6(2) require the person to whom it is sent—   **A42.10**

(a) to deliver up the licence within such reasonable period as is specified in the notice, and

(b) on doing so to pay an amount equal to the monthly duty shortfall for each month, or part of a month, in the relevant period.

(2) The "*monthly duty shortfall*" means one-twelfth of the difference between—

(a) the duty that would have been payable for a licence for a period of twelve months if the vehicle had been correctly described in the application, and

(b) that duty payable in respect of such a licence on the basis of the description in the application made.

For this purpose the amount of the duty payable shall be ascertained by reference to the rates in force at the beginning of the relevant period.

Failure to deliver up licence

9.—(1) A person who—   **A42.11**

(a) is required by notice under paragraph 7 or 8(1)(a) above to deliver up a licence, and

(b) fails to comply with the requirement contained in the notice,

commits an offence.

(2) A person committing such an offence is liable on summary conviction to a penalty not exceeding whichever is the greater of—

(a) level 3 on the standard scale, and

(b) five times the annual duty shortfall.

(3) The "*annual duty shortfall*" means the difference between—

(a) the duty that would have been payable for a licence for a period of twelve months if the vehicle had been correctly described in the application, and

(b) that duty payable in respect of a licence for period of twelve months in respect of the vehicle as described in the application.

For this purpose the amount of the duty payable shall be ascertained by reference to the rates in force at the beginning of the relevant period.

Failure to deliver up licence: additional liability

A42.12 **10.**—(1) Where a person has been convicted of an offence under paragraph 9, the court shall (in addition to any penalty which it may impose under that paragraph) order him to pay an amount equal to the monthly duty shortfall for each month, or part of a month, in the relevant period (or so much of the relevant period as falls before the making of the order).

(2) In sub-paragraph (1) the "*monthly duty shortfall*" has the meaning given by paragraph 8(2).

(3) Where—

(a) a person has been convicted of an offence under paragraph 9, and

(b) a requirement to pay an amount with respect to that licence has been imposed on that person by virtue of paragraph 8(1)(b),

the order to pay an amount under this paragraph has effect instead of that requirement and the amount to be paid under the order shall be reduced by any amount actually paid in pursuance of the requirement.

Meaning of the "relevant period"

A42.13 **11.** References in this Schedule to the "*relevant period*" are to the period—

(a) beginning with the first day of the period for which the licence was applied for or, if later, the day on which the licence first was to have effect, and

(b) ending with whichever is the earliest of the following times—

(i) the end of the month during which the licence was required to be delivered up;

(ii) the end of the month during which the licence was actually delivered up;

(iii) the date on which the licence was due to expire;

(iv) the end of the month preceding that in which there first had effect a new vehicle licence for the vehicle in question.

Construction and effect

A42.14 **12.**—(1) This Schedule and the Vehicle and Excise Registration Act 1994 shall be construed and have effect as if this Schedule were contained in that Act.

(2) References in any other enactment to that Act shall be construed and have effect accordingly as including references to this Schedule.

*   *   *

The Transport Act 2000

(2000 c. 38)

An Act to make provision for transport.

[30th November 2000]

*   *   *

PART III

ROAD USER CHARGING AND WORKPLACE PARKING LEVY

CHAPTER I

ROAD USER CHARGING

Charging schemes

163. Preliminary

(1) In this Part "*charging scheme*" means a scheme for imposing charges in respect of the   **A43.01** use or keeping of motor vehicles on roads.

(2) Charges imposed in respect of any motor vehicle by a charging scheme under this Part shall be paid—

  (a) by the registered keeper of the motor vehicle, or

  (b) in circumstances specified in regulations made by the appropriate national authority, by such person as is so specified.

(3) A charging scheme may be made—

  (a) by a non-metropolitan local traffic authority ("*a local charging scheme*"),

  (b) jointly by more than one non-metropolitan local traffic authority ("*a joint local charging scheme*"),

  (c) jointly by one or more non-metropolitan local traffic authorities and one or more London traffic authorities ("*a joint local-London charging scheme*"), or

  (d) by the Secretary of State or the National Assembly for Wales ("*a trunk road charging scheme*").

(4) In this Part references to a non-metropolitan local traffic authority are to a local traffic authority for an area outside Greater London.

(5) In this Part—

  (a) "*the charging authority*", in relation to a charging scheme under this Part made or proposed to be made by one authority, means the authority by which the charging scheme is or is proposed to be made, and

  (b) "*the charging authorities*", in relation to a charging scheme under this Part made or

2/745

proposed to be made jointly by more than one authority, means the authorities by which the charging scheme is or is proposed to be made.

(6) The power to make joint local-London charging schemes conferred by this Part does not limit any of the powers in Schedule 23 to the Greater London Authority Act 1999 (road user charging in Greater London).

A43.02   *[Sections 163–200 of this Act were brought into force (in England) on February 1, 2001; see the Transport Act 2000 (Commencement No. 3) Order 2001 (S. I. 2001 No. 57; not reproduced in this work).]*

* * *

Enforcement of charging schemes

A43.03   **173. Penalty charges**

(1) The appropriate national authority may by regulations make provision for or in connection with the imposition and payment of charges (*"charging scheme penalty charges"*) in respect of acts, omissions, events or circumstances relating to or connected with charging schemes under this Part.

(2) The regulations may include provision for or in connection with setting the rates of charging scheme penalty charges (which may include provision for discounts or surcharges).

(3) Charging scheme penalty charges in respect of any motor vehicle shall be paid—

    (a) by the registered keeper of the motor vehicle, or

    (b) in circumstances specified in regulations made by the appropriate national authority, by such person as is so specified.

(4) The Lord Chancellor may make regulations about the notification, adjudication and enforcement of charging scheme penalty charges.

(5) A person commits an offence if with intent to avoid payment of, or being identified as having failed to pay, a charge imposed by a charging scheme under this Part—

    (a) he interferes with any equipment used for or in connection with charging under the charging scheme, or

    (b) he causes or permits the registration plate of a motor vehicle to be obscured.

(6) A person commits an offence if he makes or uses any false document with intent to avoid payment of, or being identified as having failed to pay, charges imposed by a charging scheme under this Part or charging scheme penalty charges.

(7) A person commits an offence if he removes a notice of a charging scheme penalty charge which has been fixed to a motor vehicle in accordance with regulations under this section unless—

    (a) he is the registered keeper of the vehicle or a person using the vehicle with his authority, or

    (b) he does so under the authority of the registered keeper or such a person or of the charging authority or any of the charging authorities.

(8) A person guilty of an offence under subsection (5) or (6) is liable on summary conviction to—

    (a) a fine not exceeding level 5 on the standard scale, or

    (b) imprisonment for a term not exceeding six months,

or to both.

(9) A person guilty of an offence under subsection (7) is liable on summary conviction to a fine not exceeding level 2 on the standard scale.

[Section 173 was brought into force on February 1, 2001; see the note to section 163 above.]　　**A43.04**

174. Examination, entry, search and seizure

(1) The appropriate national authority may by regulations make provision enabling or requiring charging schemes under this Part to confer powers on persons specified in, or determined in accordance with, the regulations for or in connection with examining a motor vehicle for ascertaining—　　**A43.05**

   (a) whether any document required to be displayed while the motor vehicle is on a road in respect of which charges are imposed is so displayed,

   (b) whether any equipment required to be carried or fitted to the motor vehicle while the motor vehicle is on such a road is carried or fitted, is in proper working order or has been interfered with with intent to avoid payment of, or being identified as having failed to pay, a charge, or

   (c) whether any conditions relating to the use of any such equipment are satisfied.

(2) The appropriate national authority may by regulations make provision enabling or requiring charging schemes under this Part to confer power on any person authorised in writing by the charging authority, or any of the charging authorities, to enter a motor vehicle where he has reasonable grounds for suspecting that—

   (a) any equipment required to be carried in or fitted to it while it is on a road in respect of which charges are imposed has been interfered with with intent to avoid payment of, or being identified as having failed to pay, a charge imposed by the charging scheme, or

   (b) there is in the motor vehicle a false document which has been made or used with intent to avoid payment of, or being identified as having failed to pay, such a charge.

(3) A person commits an offence if he intentionally obstructs a person exercising any power conferred on him by a charging scheme under this Part by virtue of subsection (2).

(4) A person guilty of an offence under subsection (3) is liable on summary conviction to—

   (a) a fine not exceeding level 5 on the standard scale, or

   (b) imprisonment for a term not exceeding six months,

or to both

(5) The appropriate national authority may by regulations make provision enabling or requiring charging schemes under this Part to confer power on any person authorised in writing by the charging authority, or any of the charging authorities, to seize anything (if necessary by detaching it from a motor vehicle) and detain it as evidence of the commission of an offence under section 173(5) or (6).

(6) A charging scheme under this Part may not authorise an examination of, or entry into, a motor vehicle unless it is on a road.

[Section 174 was brought into force on February 1, 2001; see the note to section 163 above.]　　**A43.06**

175. Immobilisation, etc.

(1) The appropriate national authority may by regulations make a provision enabling or requiring charging schemes under this Part to make provision for or in connection with—　　**A43.07**

(a) the fitting of immobilisation devices to motor vehicles,

(b) the fixing of immobilisation notices to motor vehicles to which an immobilisation device has been fitted,

(c) the removal and storage of motor vehicles,

(d) the release of motor vehicles from immobilisation devices or from storage,

(e) the satisfaction of conditions before the release of a motor vehicle, and

(f) the sale or destruction of motor vehicles not released.

(2) A person commits an offence if he removes or interferes with an immobilisation notice fixed to a motor vehicle in accordance with provision included in a charging scheme under this Part by virtue of subsection (1) in contravention of such provision.

(3) A person commits an offence if he removes or attempts to remove an immobilisation device fitted to a motor vehicle in accordance with provision included in a charging scheme under this Part by virtue of subsection (1) in contravention of such provision.

(4) A person commits an offence if he intentionally obstructs a person exercising any power conferred on him by provision included in a charging scheme under this Part by virtue of subsection (1).

(5) A person guilty of an offence under subsection (2) is liable on summary conviction to a fine not exceeding level 2 on the standard scale.

(6) A person guilty of an offence under subsection (3) or (4) is liable on summary conviction to a fine not exceeding level 3 on the standard scale.

(7) In this section "*immobilisation device*" has the same meaning as in section 104 of the Road Traffic Regulation Act 1984 [*q.v.*]

(8) A charging scheme under this Part may not authorise or require the fitting of an immobilisation device to, or the removal of, a motor vehicle unless it is on a road.

A43.08   *[Section 175 was brought into force on February 1, 2001; see the note to section 163 above.]*

*   *   *

Section B

Statutory Instruments

Chronological List*

* An alphabetical list of statutory instruments is set out on p. 1007 below.

Statutory Instruments

Statutory Instruments

Alphabetical List

The Various Trunk Roads (Prohibition of Waiting) (Clearways) Order 1963

(S.I. 1963 No. 1172)

*   *   *

3. Interpretation

(1) In this Order the following expressions have the meanings hereby respectively assigned to them:—   **B1.01**

"*the [Act of 1984]*" means the [Road Traffic Regulation Act 1984];

"*main carriageway*", in relation to a trunk road, means any carriageway of that road used primarily by through traffic and excludes any lay-by;

"*lay-by*", in relation to a main carriageway of a trunk road, means any area intended for use for the waiting of vehicles, lying at a side of the road and bounded partly by a traffic sign consisting of a yellow dotted line on the road, or of a white dotted line and the words "lay-by" on the road, authorised by the [Secretary of State for the Environment, Transport and the Regions] under subsection (2) of [section 64 of the Road Traffic Regulation Act 1984], and partly by the outer edge of that carriageway on the same side of the road as that on which the sign is placed;

"*verge*" means any part of a road which is not a carriageway.

(2) The [Interpretation Act 1978] shall apply for the interpretation of this Order as it applies for the interpretation of an Act of Parliament and as if for the purposes of [section 17] of that Act this Order were an Act of Parliament and the Orders revoked by Article 2 were Acts of Parliament thereby repealed.   **B1.02**

[Article 3 is printed as amended by the Road Traffic Regulation Act 1967, Sched. 8, para.2; the Interpretation Act 1978, s.17(2); the Minister of Transport Order 1979 (S.I. 1979 No. 571); the Transfer of Functions (Transport) Order 1981 (S.I. 1981 No. 238); the Road Traffic Regulation Act 1984, s.144(1) and Sched. 10, para.2; the Secretary of State for the Environment, Transport and the Regions Order 1997 (S.I. 1997 No. 2971).]

4. Prohibition of waiting on main carriageways

Save as provided in Article 5 of this Order no person shall, except upon the direction or with the permission of a police constable in uniform, cause or permit any vehicle to wait on any of those main carriageways forming part of trunk roads which are specified in Schedule 1 to this Order.   **B1.03**

5. Exceptions to Article 4

Nothing in Article 4 of this Order shall apply—   **B1.04**

(a) so as to prevent a vehicle waiting on any main carriageway specified in Schedule 1 to this Order for so long as may be necessary to enable the vehicle, if it cannot be used for such purpose without waiting on that carriageway, to be used in connection with any building operation or demolition, the removal of any obstruction or potential obstruction to traffic, the maintenance, improvement or reconstruction of the road comprising that carriageway, or the erection, laying, placing, maintenance, testing, alteration, repair or removal of any structure, works, or apparatus in, on, under or over that road;

(b) to a vehicle being used for fire brigade, ambulance or police purposes;

(c) to a vehicle being used for the purposes of delivering or collecting postal packets as defined in section 87 of the Post Office Act 1953;

(d) so as to prevent a vehicle being used by or on behalf of a local authority from waiting on any main carriageway specified in Schedule 1 to this Order for so long as may be necessary to enable the vehicle, if it cannot be used for such a purpose without waiting on that carriageway to be used for the purpose of the collection of household refuse from, or the clearing of cesspools at, premises situated on or adjacent to the road comprising that carriageway;

(e) to a vehicle waiting on any main carriageway specified in Schedule 1 to this Order while any gate or other barrier at the entrance to premises to which the vehicle requires access or from which it has emerged is opened or closed, if it is not reasonably practicable for the vehicle to wait otherwise than on that carriageway while such gate or barrier is being opened or closed;

(f) to a vehicle waiting in any case where the person in control of the vehicle:—

    (i) is required by law to stop;

    (ii) is obliged to do so in order to avoid accident; or

    (iii) is prevented from proceeding by circumstances outside his control and it is not reasonably practicable for him to drive or move the vehicle to a place not on any main carriageway specified in Schedule 1 to this Order.

6. Restriction of waiting on verges, etc.

B1.05   No person shall cause or permit any vehicle to wait on any verge or lay-by immediately adjacent to a main carriageway specified in Schedule 1 to this Order for the purpose of selling goods from that vehicle unless the goods are immediately delivered at or taken into premises adjacent to the vehicle from which sale is effected.

*   *   *

The Drivers' Hours (Passenger Vehicles) (Exemptions) Regulations 1970

(S.I. 1970 No. 145)

[The text of these regulations is printed as amended by:

B2.01

the Drivers' Hours (Passenger Vehicles) (Exemptions) (Amendment) Regulations 1970 (S.I. 1970 No. 649) (May 12, 1970).

The amending regulations are referred to in the notes to the principal regulations by year and number. The date referred to above is the date on which the amending regulations came into force.]

1. Commencement and citation   *[Omitted.]*

B2.02

2. Interpretation

(1) In these Regulations, unless the context otherwise requires,—

B2.03

"*the Act*" means the Transport Act 1968,

"*emergency*" means an event which—

   (a) causes or is likely to cause such—

       (i) danger to the life or health of one or more individuals, or

      (ii) a serious interruption in the maintenance of public services for the supply of water, gas, electricity or drainage or of telecommunication or postal services, or

     (iii) a serious interruption in the use of roads, or

     (iv) a serious interruption in private transport or in public transport (not being an interruption caused by a trade dispute (within the meaning of the Trade Disputes Act 1906) involving persons who carry passengers for hire or reward), or

   (b) is likely to cause such serious damage to property,

as to necessitate the taking of immediate action to prevent the occurrence or continuance of such danger or interruption or the occurrence of such damage;

and any other expression which is also used in Part VI of the Act has the same meaning as in that Part of that Act.

(2) Any reference in these Regulations to an enactment or instrument shall be construed, unless the context otherwise requires, as a reference to that enactment or instrument as amended by any subsequent enactment or instrument.

(3) The [Interpretation Act 1978] shall apply for the interpretation of these Regulations as it applies for the interpretation of an Act of Parliament.

[The Trade Disputes Act 1906 was repealed by the Industrial Relations Act 1971, s.169 and Sched. 9. Cf. now the Trade Union and Labour Relations (Consolidation) Act 1992, s.244(1).]

B2.04

3. Exemptions from requirements as to drivers' hours

B2.05   (1) Any driver of a passenger vehicle who spends time on duty to deal with an emergency is, in accordance with paragraphs (2) and (3) of this Regulation, hereby exempted from the requirements of subsections (1) to (6) of section 96 of the Act in respect of the time so spent.

(2) Any time so spent by such a driver for the purposes of—

(a) subsection (1) of the said section 96 be deemed not to have been spent in driving vehicles to which Part VI of the Act applies, and

(b) subsections (1) to (6) of the said section 96 (including the expression "working day" used therein)—

(i) be deemed to have been spent by him off duty, and
(ii) if it would apart from the emergency have been spent in taking an interval for rest or an interval for rest and refreshment be deemed to have been so spent by him.

(3) The requirements of subsection (6) of the said section 96 shall, in relation to such a driver, be deemed to be satisfied in respect of a working week in which he spends time on such duty if he is off duty for a period of twenty-four hours in accordance with that subsection less a period equal to the total time which he spends on such duty in that week.

B2.06   **4.** Any driver of a passenger vehicle who spends time on duty during a working day to meet a special need, that is to say work done solely in connection with the collection and delivery of blood for the purposes of transfusion, is hereby exempted from the requirements of section 96(3) in relation to that day, subject to the conditions that—

(a) he is able to obtain rest and refreshment during that day for a period which is, or for periods which taken together are, not less than the time by which the working day exceeds ten hours,

(b) that day does not exceed fourteen hours, and

(c) he has not taken advantage of this exemption from the requirements of section 96(3) on more than one previous working day which forms part of the working week of which that day forms part.

B2.07   [**5.** Any driver of a passenger vehicle who spends time on duty during a working day to meet a special need, that is to say work done in connection with the carriage of persons suffering from physical or mental disability to or from any place at which social or recreational facilities for them are specially provided, is hereby exempted from the requirements of section 96(3) in relation to that day, subject to the conditions that—

(a) he is able to obtain rest and refreshment during that day for a period which is, or for periods which taken together are, not less than the time by which the working day exceeds ten hours,

(b) that day does not exceed fourteen hours, and

(c) he has not taken advantage of this exemption from the requirements of section 96(3) on more than one previous working day which forms part of the working week of which that day forms part.]

B2.08   [*Regulation 5 was added by S.I. 1970 No. 649.*]

The Drivers' Hours (Goods Vehicles) (Modifications) Order 1970

(S.I. 1970 No. 257)

[The text of this order is printed as amended by: **B3.01**

the Drivers' Hours (Passenger and Goods Vehicles) (Modifications) Order 1971 (S.I. 1971 No. 818) (May 29, 1971); and

the Drivers' Hours (Goods Vehicles) (Modifications) Order 1986 (S.I. 1986 No. 1459) (September 29, 1986).

The amending orders are referred to in the notes to the principal order by their years and numbers. The dates referred to above are the dates on which the orders came into force.]

1. Commencement and citation   *[Omitted.]*   **B3.02**

2. Interpretation

(1) In this Order, unless the context otherwise requires, "*the Act*" means the Transport   **B3.03**
Act 1968 and any other expression which is also used in Part VI of the Act has the same
meaning as in that Part of the Act.

(2) Any reference in this Order to a numbered section is a reference to the section
bearing that number in the Act except where otherwise expressly provided.

(3) Any reference in this Order to any enactment or instrument shall be construed,
unless the context otherwise requires, as a reference to that enactment or instrument as
amended by any subsequent enactment or instrument.

(4) The [Interpretation Act 1978] shall apply for the interpretation of this Order as it
applies for the interpretation of an Act of Parliament.

3.   *[Revoked by S.I. 1986 No. 1459.]*   **B3.04**

4. Exemptions for drivers engaged [in quarrying operations or] on building, construction and civil engineering work

There shall be added to the exemption provided for by section 96(9) (which provides   **B3.05**
that for the purposes of subsections (1) and (7) of section 96 no account is to be taken of
any time spent in driving a vehicle elsewhere than on a road if the vehicle is being so
driven in the course of operations of agriculture or forestry) the following exemption, that
is to say—

"For the purposes of subsections (1) and (7) of section 96 no account shall be taken
of any time spent in driving a goods vehicle elsewhere than on a road if the vehicle is
being so driven in the course of [operations of quarrying or of] carrying out any work
in the construction, reconstruction, alteration, extension or maintenance of, or of a
part of, a building, or of any other fixed works of construction or civil engineering
(including works for the construction, improvement or maintenance of a road) and, for

the purposes of this exemption, where the vehicle is being driven on, or on a part of, a road in the course of carrying out any work for the improvement or maintenance of, or of that part of, that road, it shall be treated as if it were being driven elsewhere than on a road."

B3.06   *[Article 4 is printed as amended by S.I. 1971 No. 818.]*

The Use of Invalid Carriages on Highways Regulations 1970

(S.I. 1970 No. 1391)

Editorial note. Although these regulations have been revoked by the Use of Invalid Carriages on Highways Regulations 1988 (S.I. 1988 No. 2268), they continue to apply to invalid carriages which were manufactured before January 30, 1989; see *ibid.*, reg.2(2) below. In consequence, the provisions of these regulations as to the use of invalid carriages have been retained in this edition; reference should be made to the thirteenth edition of this publication for the text of the regulations relating to the construction of such invalid carriages.

B4.01

1. Commencement, citation and interpretation

(1) *[Omitted.]*

B4.02

(2) The [Interpretation Act 1978] shall apply for the interpretation of these Regulations as it applies for the interpretation of an Act of Parliament.

[Regulation 1 is printed as amended by the Interpretation Act 1978, ss.17(2)(a) and 23(1).]

B4.03

2. Prescribed requirements and conditions for purposes of section 20(1) of the said Act of 1970

The requirements with which an invalid carriage (within the meaning of subsection (2) of the said section 20) must comply, and the conditions in accordance with which it must be used, in order that the modifications of the statutory provisions mentioned in subsection (1) of that section shall have effect in the case of the vehicle (being modifications of certain statutory provisions which relate to the use of vehicles on footways and roads) shall be—

B4.04

(a) that the vehicle is being used by a person for whose use it was constructed or adapted, being a person suffering from some physical defect or disability, or by some other person for the purposes only of taking the vehicle to or bringing it away from any place where work of maintenance or repair is to be or has been carried out to the vehicle; and

(b) the requirements (subject to the exceptions specified in relation thereto) as set out in Regulations 3 to 6 below.

[The reference to section 20 of the "said Act of 1970" and that to the "said section 20" are references to section 20 of the Chronically Sick and Disabled Persons Act 1970, to which reference is made in the recital of enabling powers.]

B4.05

3. Unladen weight   *[Omitted.]*

B4.06

4. Limit of speed   *[Omitted.]*

5. Brakes

B4.07   (1) *[Omitted.]*

(2) Every part of the braking system and of the means of operation thereof fitted to the vehicle shall be maintained in good and efficient working order and be properly adjusted.

(3) *[Omitted.]*

6. Lighting

B4.08   (1) Subject to paragraph (3) below, an invalid carriage when on the carriageway of any road shall during the hours of darkness carry—

(a) one lamp showing to the front a white light visible from a reasonable distance;

(b) one lamp showing to the rear a red light visible from a reasonable distance; and

(c) one unobscured and efficient red reflector facing to the rear.

(2) Every such lamp shall be kept properly trimmed, lighted, and in a clean and efficient condition, and every such lamp and reflector shall be attached to the vehicle in such position and manner, and shall comply with such conditions with respect thereto, as are specified in the Schedule to these Regulations.

(3) The foregoing provisions of this Regulation shall not apply in relation to a vehicle when it is on the carriageway of a road for the purpose only of crossing that carriageway in the quickest manner practicable in the circumstances.

(4) In this Regulation,—

(a) *"road"* means any highway and any other road to which the public has access not being (in either case) a footway within the meaning of section 20(2) of the said Act of 1970, and

(b) *"hours of darkness"* means the time between half-an-hour after sunset and half-an-hour before sunrise.

B4.09   *[As to the "said Act of 1970", see the note to regulation 2 above.]*

(See Regulation 6)   SCHEDULE

CONDITIONS AS TO LAMPS AND REFLECTORS

B4.10   **1.** The lamp showing a white light to the front shall be fixed on the centre line or offside of the vehicle.

2. The lamp showing a red light to the rear shall be so fixed that—

(a) its lateral position is on the centre line or offside of the vehicle,

(b) its longitudinal position is not more than 20 inches from the extreme rear of the vehicle,

(c) the maximum height from the ground of the highest part of the illuminated area of the lamp is 3 feet 6 inches, and

(d) the minimum height from the ground of the lowest part of the said area is 12 inches, and shall be marked—

(i) with the specification number of the British Standard for Cycle Rear Lamps, namely BS 3648, and

(ii) with the name, trade mark or other means of identification of the manufacturer of the lamp.

3. The reflector shall be so fixed that—

(a) its lateral position is on the centre line or offside of the vehicle,

(b) its longitudinal position is not more than 20 inches from the extreme rear of the vehicle,

(c) the maximum height from the ground of the highest part of the reflecting area of the reflector is 3 feet 6 inches, and

(d) the minimum height from the ground of the lowest part of the said area is 12 inches,

and shall be marked—

(i) with the specification number of the British Standard for Reflex Reflectors for Vehicles, namely, AU 40 followed by a marking "LI" or "LIA" and with the registered trade name or trade mark of the manufacturer of the reflector, or

(ii) with an approval mark (that is to say, a marking designated as an approval mark by the [Motor Vehicles (Designation of Approval Marks) Regulations 1979] [*S.I. 1979 No. 1088*]) incorporating the roman numeral I.

[The Schedule is printed as amended by the Interpretation Act 1978, ss.17(2)(a) and 23(1).]   **B4.11**

The Functions of Traffic Wardens Order 1970

(S.I. 1970 No. 1958)

*   *   *

B5.01 **2.** In this Order—

"[*the Act of 1988*]" and "[*the Act of 1984*]" mean respectively [the Road Traffic Act 1988] and [the Road Traffic Regulation Act 1984];

"*street parking place order*" means an order made under [the Act of 1984] relating to a street parking place;

"*traffic order*" means an order made under [section 1, 6, 9, 12 or 37 of or Schedule 9 to the Act of 1984].

B5.02 [*Article 2 is printed as amended by the Road Traffic Act 1972, s.205(2) and Sched. 10, para.3; the Road Traffic Regulation Act 1984, s.144(1) and Sched. 10, para.2.*]

B5.03 **3.**—(1) The functions set out in the Schedule to this Order are hereby prescribed as appropriate for discharge by traffic wardens.

(2) For the purposes of the discharge by traffic wardens of such functions, references to a constable or police constable in the following enactments shall include references to a traffic warden—

    (a) section 52 of the Metropolitan Police Act 1839 so far as it relates to the giving by the commissioner of directions to constables for preventing obstruction;

    (b) section 22 of the local Act of the second and third year of the reign of Queen Victoria, chapter 94, so far as it makes similar provision with respect to the City of London;

    (c) [sections 35 and 37 of the Act of 1988] (drivers and pedestrians to comply with traffic directions given by police constables);

    (d) [section 169 of the Act of 1988] (the power of constables to obtain the names and addresses of pedestrians failing to comply with traffic directions);

    (e) [section 11 of the Road Traffic Offenders Act 1988] (the giving of evidence of an admission by certificate).

    [(f) section 100(3) of the Road Traffic Regulation Act 1984 (the interim disposal of vehicles removed under section 99 of that Act);]

    [(g) sections 104 and 105 of the Road Traffic Regulation Act 1984 (the immobilisation of illegally parked vehicles).]

(3) For the purposes of the discharge by traffic wardens of the functions set out in the Schedule to this Order, references in section [165(1) of the Act of 1988] to a police constable shall, in so far as it applies to the furnishing of names and addresses, include references to a traffic warden if the traffic warden has reasonable cause to believe that there has been committed an offence—

    (a) in respect of a vehicle by its being left or parked on a road during the hours of darkness (as defined by the [Act of 1988]) without the lights or reflectors required by law;

(b) in respect of a vehicle by its obstructing a road, or waiting, or being left or parked, or being loaded or unloaded, in a road;

(c) in contravention of [section 35 of the Act of 1988];

(d) in contravention of a provision of [the Vehicle Excise and Registration Act 1994];

(e) created by [section 47 of the Act of 1984] (offences relating to parking places on highways where charges made).

[(4) References in section 164(1), (2) and (6) of the Road Traffic Act of 1988 to a constable or police constable shall include references to a traffic warden only where—

(a) the traffic warden has reasonable cause to believe that there has been committed an offence by causing a vehicle, or any part of it, to stop in contravention of regulations made under section 25 of the Road Traffic Regulation Act 1984 or an offence in contravention of section 22 of the Road Traffic Act 1988 (leaving vehicles in dangerous positions); or

(b) the traffic warden is employed to perform functions in connection with the custody of vehicles removed from a road or land in the open air in pursuance of regulations made under section 99 of the Road Traffic Regulation Act 1984 or from a parking place in pursuance of a street parking place order, and he has reasonable cause to believe that there has been committed an offence in respect of a vehicle by its obstructing a road, or waiting, or being left or parked, or being loaded or unloaded, in a road.]

[Article 3 is printed as amended by the Vehicles (Excise) Act 1971, s.39(4) and Sched. 7, Pt II,   **B5.04**
para.11; the Road Traffic Act 1972, s.205(2) and Sched. 10, para.3; the Road Traffic Regulation Act 1984, s.144(1) and Sched. 10, para.2; the Functions of Traffic Wardens (Amendment) Order 1993 (S.I. 1993 No. 1334); the Vehicle Excise and Registration Act 1994, s.64 and Sched. 4, para.4.

The definition of "hours of darkness" (to which reference is made in article 3(3)(a) above) had been included in earlier legislation and was re-enacted in the Road Traffic Act 1972, s.82. The definition was repealed, however, by the Road Traffic Act 1974. The term is now defined in the Road Vehicles Lighting Regulations 1989 (S.I. 1989 No. 1796), reg.3(2) (q.v.).]

SCHEDULE   Article 3
FUNCTIONS OF TRAFFIC WARDENS

1.—(1) Traffic wardens may be employed to enforce the law with respect to an   **B5.05**
offence—

(a) committed in respect of a vehicle by its being left or parked on a road during the hours of darkness (as defined by [the Act of 1988]) without the lights or reflectors required by law; or

(b) committed in respect of a vehicle by its obstructing a road, or waiting, or being left or parked, or being loaded or unloaded, in a road or other public place; or

(c) committed in contravention of a provision of [the Vehicle Excise and Registration Act 1994];

(d) created by [section 47 of the Act of 1984] (offences relating to parking places on highways where charges made).

[(e) committed by causing a vehicle, or any part of it, to stop in contravention of regulations made under section 25 of the Road Traffic Regulation Act 1984,]

[(2) For the purposes of the enforcement of the law with respect to such of the offences described in sub-paragraph (1) of this paragraph as are fixed penalty offences within the meaning of [section 51(1) of the Road Traffic Offenders Act 1988], . . . traffic wardens may exercise the functions conferred on constables by [Part III of the Road Traffic Offenders Act 1988].]

2.—(1) Traffic wardens may, under arrangements made with the Secretary of State or a local authority, be employed to act as parking attendants at street parking places provided or controlled by the Secretary of State or local authority.

(2) A traffic warden may exercise functions conferred on a traffic warden by a traffic order or a street parking place order.

B5.06   **3.** Without prejudice to the generality of paragraph 1 above, traffic wardens may be employed in connection with obtaining information under [section 172 of the Act of 1988] or [section 112 of the Act of 1984] (duty to give information as to identity of driver, etc., in certain cases).

4. Traffic wardens may be employed to perform functions in connection with the custody of vehicles removed from a road or land in the open air in pursuance of regulations under [section 99 of the Act of 1984] or from a parking place in pursuance of a street parking place order.

B5.07   **5.** Where a police authority provides school crossing patrols under [section 26 of the Act of 1984], whether as the appropriate authority or by agreement with the appropriate authority, traffic wardens appointed by that police authority may be employed to act as school crossing patrols.

6.—(1) Subject to the foregoing paragraphs, traffic wardens may be employed in the control and regulation of traffic (including foot passengers) or vehicles whether on a highway or not and to discharge any other functions normally undertaken by the police in connection with the control and regulation of traffic (including foot passengers) or vehicles.

(2) Nothing in this paragraph shall permit the functions described in sub-paragraph (1) to be exercised by a traffic warden who is in a moving vehicle.

B5.08   *[The Schedule is printed as amended by the Vehicles (Excise) Act 1971, s.39(4) and Sched. 7, Pt II, para.11; the Road Traffic Act 1972, s.205(2) and Sched. 10, para.3; the Road Traffic Regulation Act 1984, s.144(1) and Sched. 10, para.2; the Functions of Traffic Wardens (Amendment) Order 1986 (S.I. 1986 No. 1328); the Functions of Traffic Wardens (Amendment) Order 1993 (S.I. 1993 No. 1334); the Vehicle Excise and Registration Act 1994, s.64 and Sched. 4, para.4.*

As to the definition of "hours of darkness" (to which reference is made in paragraph 1(1)(a) above), see the note to article 3 of this order.]

The Vehicle and Driving Licences Records (Evidence) Regulations 1970

(S.I. 1970 No. 1997)

* * *

3. Matters prescribed for [section 13(5) of the Road Traffic Offenders Act 1988]

The following matters are prescribed for the purposes of [section 13(5) of the Road Traffic Offenders Act 1988]— **B6.01**

(1) in connection with the licensing of drivers under [Part III of the Road Traffic Act 1988]—

- (a) a document being, forming part of, or submitted in connection with, an application for a driving licence;
- (b) a driving licence;
- (c) a certificate of competence to drive;
- (d) the conviction of an offence specified in [Part I of Schedule 2 to the Road Traffic Offenders Act 1988 or the offence of manslaughter (or culpable homicide) specified in Part II of that Schedule] of any person or any order made by the Court as a result of any such conviction;

(2) in connection with the licensing and registration of mechanically propelled vehicles under the [Vehicle Excise and Registration Act 1994]—

- (a) a document being, forming part of, or submitted in connection with, an application for—
  - (i) a vehicle licence;
  - (ii) a trade licence;
  - (iii) a repayment of duty under [section 19 of the 1994 Act] or the recovery of underpayments or overpayments of duty under [section 50] of that Act;
- (b) a vehicle licence, trade licence, registration book or registration mark;
- (c) a document containing a declaration and particulars such as are prescribed under the [1994 Act] in relation to vehicles exempted from duty under that Act;
- (d) the conviction of an offence under the [1994 Act] of any person;

(3) in connection with the examination of a goods vehicle under regulations under [section 49 of the Road Traffic Act 1988]—

- (a) an application for an examination of a vehicle under the said regulations;
- (b) a notifiable alteration made to a vehicle and required by the said regulations to be notified to the [Secretary of State for the Environment, Transport and the Regions];
- (c) a plating certificate, goods vehicle test certificate, notification of the refusal of a goods vehicle test certificate, Ministry plate, Ministry test date disc or certificate of temporary exemption.

B6.02   *[Regulation 3 is printed as amended by the Vehicles (Excise) Act 1971, Sched. 7, para.11; the Road Traffic Act 1972, Sched. 10, para.3; the Minister of Transport Order 1979 (S.I. 1979 No. 571); the Transfer of Functions (Transport) Order 1981 (S.I. 1981 No. 238); the Vehicle Excise and Registration Act 1994, s.64 and Sched. 4, para.4; the Secretary of State for the Environment, Transport and the Regions Order 1997 (S.I. 1997 No. 2971).*

For the regulations under section 49 of the Road Traffic Act 1988, see the Goods Vehicles (Plating and Testing) Regulations 1988 (S.I. 1988 No. 1478) below.]

*   *   *

The Road Vehicles (Registration and Licensing) Regulations 1971

(S.I. 1971 No. 450)

[The text of these regulations is printed as amended by:

the Road Vehicles (Registration and Licensing) (Amendment) Regulations 1972 (S.I. 1972 No. 1865) (December 29, 1972);

the Road Vehicles (Registration and Licensing) (Amendment) (No. 2) Regulations 1975 (S.I. 1975 No. 1342) (September 1, 1975);

the Road Vehicles (Registration and Licensing) (Amendment) Regulations 1976 (S.I. 1976 No. 1680) (November 9, 1976);

the Road Vehicles (Registration and Licensing) (Amendment) Regulations 1983 (S.I. 1983 No. 1248) (September 14, 1983);

the Road Vehicles (Registration and Licensing) (Amendment) Regulations 1984 (S.I. 1984 No. 814) (August 1, 1984);

the Road Vehicles (Registration and Licensing) (Amendment) (No. 3) Regulations 1986 (S.I. 1986 No. 2101) (January 1, 1987);

the Road Vehicles (Registration and Licensing) (Amendment) Regulations 1987 (S.I. 1987 No. 2123) (January 1, 1988);

the Road Vehicles (Registration and Licensing) (Amendment) (No. 2) Regulations 1994 (S.I. 1994 No. 1911) (August 31, 1994);

the Road Vehicles (Registration and Licensing) (Amendment) (No. 3) Regulations 1994 (S.I. 1994 No. 3296) (January 30, 1995);

the Road Vehicles (Registration and Licensing) (Amendment) Regulations 1995 (S.I. 1995 No. 1470) (July 1, 1995); and

the Road Vehicles (Registration and Licensing) (Amendment) Regulations 1997 (S.I. 1997 No. 401) (March 24, 1997).

The amending regulations are referred to in the notes to the principal regulations by their years and numbers. The dates referred to above are the dates on which the amending regulations came into force.

The principal regulations have also been amended by the Road Vehicles (Registration and Licensing) (Amendment) Regulations 1973 (S.I. 1973 No. 870); the Road Vehicles (Registration and Licensing) (Amendment) Regulations 1975 (S.I. 1975 No. 1089); the Road Vehicles (Registration and Licensing) (Amendment) (No. 2) Regulations 1976 (S.I. 1976 No. 2089); the Road Vehicles (Registration and Licensing) (Amendment) Regulations 1977 (S.I. 1977 No. 230); the Road Vehicles (Registration and Licensing) (Amendment) Regulations 1978 (S.I. 1978 No. 1536); the Road Vehicles (Registration and Licensing) (Amendment) Regulations 1986 (S.I. 1986 No. 607); the Road Vehicles (Registration and Licensing) (Amendment) (No. 2) Regulations 1986 (S.I. 1986 No. 1177); the Road Vehicles (Registration and Licensing) (Amendment) Regulations 1993 (S.I. 1993 No. 1760); and the Road Vehicles (Registration and Licensing) (Amendment) Regulations 1994 (S.I. 1994 No. 1364); but these do not affect the text of any regulation set out in this work.]

*   *   *

ARRANGEMENT OF REGULATIONS

PART I

PRELIMINARY

PART II

LICENSING AND REGISTRATION

PART III

EXHIBITION OF LICENCES AND REGISTRATION MARKS

*   *   *

PART V

TRADE LICENCES

*   *   *

PART I

PRELIMINARY

1. Commencement and citation   *[Omitted.]*   **B7.03**

2. Revocation, savings and transitional provisions   *[Omitted.]*

3. Interpretation

(1) In these Regulations, unless the context otherwise requires, the following expressions   **B7.04** have the meanings hereby respectively assigned to them, that is to say—

["*the Act*" means the Vehicle Excise and Registration Act 1994];

"*agricultural machine*" has the same meaning as in [Schedule 1, paragraph 4(2),] to the Act [*q.v.*];

"*bicycle*" means a mechanically propelled bicycle (including a motor scooter, a bicycle with an attachment for propelling it by mechanical power and a mechanically propelled bicycle used for drawing a trailer or sidecar) not exceeding 8 hundredweight in weight unladen;

. . .

["*invalid carriage*"] means a mechanically propelled vehicle (including a cycle with an attachment for propelling it by mechanical power) which does not exceed [10] hundredweight in weight unladen and is adapted and used or kept on a road for an invalid or invalids;

"*owner*" in relation to a vehicle means the person by whom the vehicle is kept . . . and the expression "*ownership*" shall be construed accordingly;

"*pedestrian controlled vehicle*" means a mechanically propelled vehicle with three or more wheels which does not exceed 8 hundredweight in weight unladen and which is neither constructed nor adapted for use nor used for the carriage of a driver or passenger;

. . .

"*road*" has the same meaning as in [section 192 of the Road Traffic Act 1988];

"*trade licence*" has the meaning assigned to it by [section 11] of the Act;

"*trade plates*" has the meaning assigned thereto in Regulation 31 of these Regulations;

"*tricycle*" means a mechanically propelled tricycle (including a motor scooter and a tricycle with an attachment for propelling it by mechanical power) not exceeding 8 hundredweight in weight unladen and not being a pedestrian controlled vehicle;

["*valeting*" means the thorough cleaning of a vehicle before its registration by the Secretary of State under [section 21] of the Act or in order to prepare it for sale and includes removing wax and grease from the exterior, engine and interior, and "valeted" shall be construed accordingly;]

"*works truck*" means a mechanically propelled vehicle designed for use in private premises and used on a road only in delivering goods from or to such premises to or from a vehicle on a road in the immediate neighbourhood, or in passing from one part of any such premises to another or to other private premises in the immediate neighbourhood or in connection with road works while at or in the immediate neighbourhood of the site of such works.

[(1A) Any reference in these Regulations to a registration book shall be construed to include a reference to any registration document issued by the Secretary of State.]

(2) Any reference in these Regulations to any enactment shall be construed as a reference to that enactment as amended by or under any subsequent enactment.

(3) The [Interpretation Act 1978] shall apply for the interpretation of these Regulations as it applies for the interpretation of an Act of Parliament, and as if for the purposes of [section 17] of that Act these Regulations were an Act of Parliament and the Regulations revoked by Regulation 2 of these Regulations were Acts of Parliament thereby repealed.

B7.05   *[Regulation 3 is printed as amended by the Road Traffic Act 1972, Sched. 10, para.3; S.I. 1972 No. 1865; S.I. 1975 No. 1342; the Interpretation Act 1978, s.17(2)(a); S.I. 1986 No. 2101; S.I. 1994 No. 1911; the Vehicle Excise and Registration Act 1994, s.64 and Sched. 4, para.4; S.I. 1997 No. 401. Selected definitions only are reproduced in paragraph (1).*

The reference in the definition of "agricultural machine" to Schedule 1, paragraph 4(2), to the 1994 Act is an approximation to the provision in that Act most closely corresponding to the relevant provision in the Vehicles (Excise) Act 1971, Sched. 3, as enacted, that provision having subsequently been replaced.]

[3A. Exclusion for electrically assisted pedal cycles

B7.06   The provisions of Parts II and III of these Regulations do not apply to an electrically assisted pedal cycle for the time being prescribed for the purposes of [section 140 of the Road Traffic Regulation Act 1984] and [section 189 of the Road Traffic Act 1988].]

B7.07   *[Regulation 3A was inserted by S.I. 1983 No. 1248 and is printed as amended by the Road Traffic Regulation Act 1984, s.144(1) and Sched. 10, para.2; the Interpretation Act 1978, s.17(2)(a).]*

PART II

LICENSING AND REGISTRATION

*   *   *

12. Notification of change of ownership

B7.08   [(1) This regulation applies where the current vehicle registration book was issued in respect of the vehicle before 24th March 1997.]

[(1A)] On a change of ownership of a mechanically propelled vehicle the previous owner of the vehicle shall deliver the registration book issued in respect of the vehicle and may deliver any current licence issued in respect of the vehicle to the new owner and shall notify in writing forthwith the change of ownership to the [Secretary of State for the Environment, Transport and the Regions] stating the registration mark of the vehicle, its make and class and the name and address of the new owner.

(2) Upon acquiring the vehicle the new owner shall—

(a) if he intends to use or keep the vehicle upon public roads otherwise than under a trade licence, forthwith insert his name and address in the appropriate part of the registration book and deliver it to the [Secretary of State for the Environment, Transport and the Regions];

(b) if he does not intend to use or keep the vehicle upon public roads, forthwith notify the [Secretary of State for the Environment, Transport and the Regions] in writing that he is the owner of the vehicle, and he shall state in such notification the registration mark of the vehicle, its make and class, the name and address of the previous owner and the fact that he does not intend to use or keep the vehicle on public roads;

(c) if he intends to use the vehicle upon public roads solely under a trade licence, at the expiration of three months from the date when he became the owner of the vehicle or, if a further change of ownership occurs, on the date of that change, whichever is the sooner, notify the [Secretary of State for the Environment, Transport and the Regions] in writing of his name and address and those of the previous owner.

[Regulation 12 is printed as amended by the Minister of Transport Order 1979 (S.I. 1979 No. 571); **B7.09**
the Transfer of Functions (Transport) Order 1981 (S.I. 1981 No. 238); S.I. 1997 No. 401; the
Secretary of State for the Environment, Transport and the Regions Order 1997 (S.I. 1997 No. 2971).

The 1971 Regulations were made in part under the Vehicles (Excise) Act 1971, s.23, as substituted by
section 39 of and Schedule 7, Part I, paragraph 20, to that Act. Section 23 (as so substituted) was amended
by the Finance Act 1987. Under section 2(6) and (8) of, and Schedule 1, Part III, paragraph 16(4), to
the 1987 Act, regulation 12(1) was deemed as from May 15, 1987 to have effect as if the amendments
effected to section 23 of the 1971 Act by the 1987 Act, s.2(6) and (8) and Sched. 1, Pt III, para.16(3),
had been in force when regulation 12(1) was made. Regulation 12(1) continues to have effect as if the
amendments to section 23 of the Vehicles (Excise) Act 1971 (as set out in ibid., Sched. 7, Pt I, para.20)
effected by the Finance Act 1987 had been in force when the regulations were made; see the Vehicle Excise
and Registration Act 1994, s.64 and Sched. 4, para.10.

Contravention of either regulation 12(1A) or (2) is a summary offence for which the offender is liable to
a fine on level 3 of the standard scale under the Vehicle Excise and Registration Act 1994, s.59(2)(a), and
the Road Vehicles (Prescribed Regulations for the Purposes of Increased Penalties) Regulations 1987 (S.I.
1987 No. 2085; not reproduced in this work).]

12A. Notification of change of ownership: vehicle registration document issued on or after 24th March 1997

(1) This regulation applies where a vehicle registration document has been issued in **B7.10**
respect of the vehicle on or after 24th March 1997.

(2) On a change of ownership of a mechanically propelled vehicle, where the new
keeper is not a motor vehicle trader, the registered keeper—

  (a) shall forthwith send to the Secretary of State on that part of the registration document which relates to the change of keeper the following—

    (i) the name and address of the new keeper;

    (ii) the date on which the vehicle was transferred to the new keeper;

    (iii) a declaration signed by the registered keeper that the details given in
accordance with sub-paragraphs (i) and (ii) are correct to the best of his
knowledge; and

    (iv) a declaration signed by the new keeper that the details given in accordance
with sub-paragraphs (i) and (ii) are correct;

  (b) shall forthwith give to the new keeper that part of the registration document which
relates to the new keeper; and

  (c) may give to the new keeper any current licence issued in respect of the vehicle on
which vehicle excise duty has been paid.

(3) On a change of ownership of a mechanically propelled vehicle, where the new
keeper is a motor vehicle trader but the registered keeper is not such a trader, the registered
keeper—

  (a) shall forthwith send to the Secretary of State, on that part of the registration document which relates to the transfer to a motor vehicle trader, the following—

    (i) the name and address of the motor vehicle trader;

    (ii) the date on which the vehicle was transferred to the motor vehicle trader;

    (iii) a declaration signed by the registered keeper that he transferred the vehicle
to the motor vehicle trader on the date specified in accordance with sub-
paragraph (ii); and

    (iv) a declaration signed by the motor vehicle trader that the vehicle was transferred
to him and on the date specified in accordance with subparagraph (ii); and

  (b) shall forthwith give to the motor vehicle trader those parts of the registration document not required to be sent to the Secretary of State under sub-paragraph (a).

(4) Where a motor vehicle trader becomes the owner of a mechanically propelled vehicle, he shall—

(a) notify the Secretary of State of the transfer of the vehicle to him before he uses, or permits the use of, or keeps the vehicle on public roads otherwise than under a trade licence; or

(b) where he has not notified the Secretary of State in accordance with sub-paragraph (a), notify the Secretary of State of the transfer of the vehicle to him before the expiration of the period of three months beginning on the day after the date on which the vehicle was last owned by a person who was not a motor vehicle trader.

(5) Where a motor vehicle trader transfers a mechanically propelled vehicle to another person, he shall—

(a) where the transfer is to another motor vehicle trader, before the expiration of the period of three months beginning on the day after the date on which the vehicle was last owned by a person who was not a motor vehicle trader, give to the new keeper those parts of the registration document not required to be sent to the Secretary of State under paragraph 3(a); and

(b) in any other case, forthwith send to the Secretary of State on that part of the registration document which relates to the change of keeper the following:

(i) the name and address of the new keeper;
(ii) the date on which the vehicle was transferred to the new keeper;
(iii) a declaration signed by him that the details given in accordance with sub-paragraphs (i) and (ii) are correct to the best of his knowledge; and
(iv) a declaration signed by the new keeper that the details given in accordance with sub-paragraphs (i) and (ii) are correct.

(6) In this regulation *"motor vehicle trader"* means—

(a) any person who carries on business as a dealer in motor vehicles;
(b) any person who carries on business as an auctioneer of motor vehicles;
(c) any person who carries on business as a dismantler of motor vehicles; and
(d) in relation to a particular mechanically propelled vehicle—

(i) a finance company which has acquired that vehicle under an order for repossession; and
(ii) an insurance company which has acquired that vehicle on satisfaction of a total loss claim.]

B7.11 *[Regulation 12A was inserted by S.I. 1997 No. 401.*
Contravention of regulation 12A is an offence under the Vehicle Excise and Registration Act 1994, s.59.]

13. Notification of change of address of owner

B7.12 If the owner of a mechanically propelled vehicle changes his address he shall forthwith enter particulars of his new address in the space provided in the registration book issued in respect of the vehicle and send the book to the [Secretary of State for the Environment, Transport and the Regions].

B7.13 *[Regulation 13 is printed as amended by the Minister of Transport Order 1979 (S.I. 1979 No. 571) and the Transfer of Functions (Transport) Order 1981 (S.I. 1981 No. 238); the Secretary of State for the Environment, Transport and the Regions Order 1997 (S.I. 1997 No. 2971).*
Contravention of regulation 13 is a summary offence for which the offender is liable to a fine on level 3 of the standard scale under the Vehicle Excise and Registration Act 1994, s.59(2)(a), and the Road Vehicles

(Prescribed Regulations for the Purposes of Increased Penalties) Regulations 1987 (S.I. 1987 No. 2085; not reproduced in this work).]

*   *   *

PART III

EXHIBITION OF LICENCES AND REGISTRATION MARKS

16. Exhibition of licences

(1) Every licence issued under the Act and in force for a mechanically propelled   **B7.14**
vehicle . . . shall be fixed to and exhibited on the vehicle in accordance with the provisions of this Regulation at all times while the vehicle is being used or kept on a public road:

Provided that when such a licence is delivered up with an application for a new licence to [any post office authorised for the time being to issue vehicle licences in accordance with arrangements for that purpose made between the Post Office and the [Secretary of State for the Environment, Transport and the Regions]], no licence shall be required to be fixed to and exhibited on the vehicle until the new licence is obtained, when that licence shall be deemed to be the licence in force for the vehicle for the purposes of this Regulation.

(2) Each such licence shall be fixed to the vehicle in a holder sufficient to protect the licence from any effects of the weather to which it would otherwise be exposed.

(3) The licence shall be exhibited on the vehicle—

    (a) in the case of an invalid vehicle, tricycle or bicycle, other than a case specified in sub-paragraph (b) or (c) of this paragraph, on the near side of the vehicle in front of the driving seat so that all the particulars thereon are clearly visible by daylight from the near side of the road;

    (b) in the case of a bicycle drawing a side-car or to which a side-car is attached when the bicycle is being kept on a public road, on the near side of the handle-bars of the bicycle or on the near side of the side-car in front of the driving seat so that all the particulars thereon are clearly visible by daylight from the near side of the road;

    (c) in the case of any vehicle fitted with a glass windscreen in front of the driver extending across the vehicle to its near side, on or adjacent to the near side . . . of the windscreen, so that all particulars thereon are clearly visible by daylight from the near side of the road;

    (d) in the case of any other vehicle, if the vehicle is fitted with a driver's cab containing a near side window, on such window, or on the near side of the vehicle in front of the driver's seat or towards the front of the vehicle in the case of a pedestrian controlled vehicle and not less than 2 feet 6 inches and not more than 6 feet above the surface of the road, so that in each case all the particulars thereon are clearly visible by daylight from the near side of the road.

[Regulation 16 is printed as amended by S.I. 1972 No. 1865; S.I. 1976 No. 1680; the Minister of   **B7.15**
Transport Order 1979 (S.I. 1979 No. 571); the Transfer of Functions (Transport) Order 1981 (S.I. 1981 No. 238); S.I. 1995 No. 1470; the Secretary of State for the Environment, Transport and the Regions Order 1997 (S.I. 1997 No. 2971).]

*   *   *

[**19.**—(1) Save as provided in paragraph (2) below, no person shall use or cause or   **B7.16**
permit to be used on a road during the hours of darkness any motor vehicle unless every letter and number of the registration mark displayed on the back of—

(a) the motor vehicle if it is not drawing a trailer, or

(b) the trailer if the motor vehicle is drawing one trailer, or

(c) the rearmost trailer if the motor vehicle is drawing more than one trailer,

is illuminated so as to be easily legible in the absence of fog from every part of the relevant area, the diagonal of the square governing that area being—

(i) 15 metres in the case of a bicycle, an invalid vehicle and a pedestrian controlled vehicle, and

(ii) 18 metres in the case of any other vehicle.

(2) The provisions of paragraph (1) above do not apply in respect of—

(a) a works truck; or

(b) a vehicle which is not required to be fitted with a rear registration plate.]

B7.17   *[Regulation 19 is printed as substituted by S.I. 1984 No. 814.*

With effect from September 1, 2001, regulation 19 will be revoked by the Road Vehicles (Display of Registration Marks) Regulations 2001 (S.I. 2001 No. 561), reg.1(2) and Sched. 1 below.]

*   *   *

22. Trailers

B7.18   (1) Subject to paragraph (3) of this Regulation, where one or more trailers are attached to a mechanically propelled vehicle the owner of the vehicle shall ensure that there is displayed on the trailer or rearmost trailer (as the case may be) the registration mark of the mechanically propelled vehicle, and that such registration mark is fixed to and displayed on the trailer as if the trailer were a vehicle of the same class or description as the mechanically propelled vehicle.

(2) Where the registration mark of a mechanically propelled vehicle is fixed to and displayed on a trailer attached to it in accordance with the foregoing paragraph, the requirements of these Regulations as to the fixing to and display of a registration mark on the back of a mechanically propelled vehicle shall not apply to the vehicle drawing the trailer.

(3) Where the mechanically propelled vehicle is a restricted vehicle, the registration mark fixed to and displayed on the trailer in accordance with paragraph (1) of this Regulation may, instead of being that of the vehicle to which the trailer is attached, be that of any other restricted vehicle belonging to the owner of the vehicle to which the trailer is attached, and in such a case the duty in the said paragraph (1) as to fixing and display shall apply as if the other restricted vehicle were the vehicle to which the trailer was attached.

(4) In this Regulation "*restricted vehicle*" means a vehicle mentioned in [paragraph 21 of Schedule 2 to the Act or paragraph 4(2) of Schedule 1] thereto.

B7.19   *[Regulation 22 is printed as amended by the Vehicle Excise and Registration Act 1994, s.64 and Sched. 4, para.4.*

With effect from September 1, 2001, regulation 22 will be revoked by the Road Vehicles (Display of Registration Marks) Regulations 2001 (S.I. 2001 No. 561), reg.1(2) and Sched. 1 below.

In regulation 22(4), the reference to paragraph 4(2) of Schedule 1 to the 1994 Act is an approximation to the nearest provision of that Act corresponding to paragraph 2(1) of Schedule 2 to the Vehicles (Excise) Act 1971 as enacted (but replaced subsequently).]

*   *   *

PART V

TRADE LICENCES

*   *   *

[28A. Descriptions of businesses

[The following descriptions of business are prescribed for the purposes of sub-paragraph   **B7.20**
(b) of the definition of "motor trader" in section 16(8) of the Act:—

  (a)   the business of modifying vehicles, whether by the fitting of accessories or other-
        wise; and

  (b)   the business of valeting vehicles.]]

[Regulation 28A was inserted by S.I. 1986 No. 2101 and is printed as subsequently substituted by S.I.   **B7.21**
1994 No. 1911.]

*   *   *

30. Notification of change of address, etc.

If the holder of a trade licence changes the name of his business or his business address   **B7.22**
he shall notify this fact and the new name or address forthwith to the [Secretary of State for
the Environment, Transport and the Regions] and shall at the same time send to the
[Secretary of State for the Environment, Transport and the Regions] the licence for any
necessary amendment.

[Regulation 30 is printed as amended by the Minister of Transport Order 1979 (S.I. 1979 No. 571)   **B7.23**
and the Transfer of Functions (Transport) Order 1981 (S.I. 1981 No. 238); the Secretary of State for the
Environment, Transport and the Regions Order 1997 (S.I. 1997 No. 2971).

*   Contravention of regulation 30 is a summary offence for which the offender is liable to a fine on level 3 of*
the standard scale under the Vehicle Excise and Registration Act 1994, s.59(2)(a), and the Road Vehicles
(Prescribed Regulations for the Purposes of Increased Penalties) Regulations 1987 (S.I. 1987 No. 2085;
not reproduced in this work).]

31. Issue of trade plates and replacements therefor

(1) The [Secretary of State for the Environment, Transport and the Regions] shall issue   **B7.24**
to every holder of a trade licence in respect of that licence two plates (in these Regulations
referred to as "trade plates") appropriate to the class of vehicles on which they will be used
showing the general registration mark assigned to the holder of the licence, and one of the
plates so issued shall contain means whereby the licence may be fixed thereto:

    Provided that where the holder of a trade licence satisfies the [Secretary of State for the
Environment, Transport and the Regions] that the vehicles which he will use by virtue of
the licence include vehicles which would otherwise be liable to duty under Schedule 1 to the
Act and other vehicles he shall be entitled to be issued free of charge with [an additional
trade plate] in respect of the vehicles first mentioned in this proviso.

(2) Each trade plate shall remain the property of the [Secretary of State for the
Environment, Transport and the Regions] and shall be returned forthwith to the [Secretary
of State for the Environment, Transport and the Regions] if the person to whom it was
issued no longer holds a trade licence which is in force or if that person ceases to be a motor
trader or a vehicle tester.

(3) to (3C) *[Replacement of trade plates which have been lost, etc.]*

(4) In the case of the loss of any trade plate, if at any time after the issue of a replacement the original plate is found, the holder of the trade licence, if the plate is in his possession, shall forthwith return it to the [Secretary of State for the Environment, Transport

and the Regions], or if it is not in his possession but he becomes aware that it is found, shall take all reasonable steps to obtain possession of it and if successful shall forthwith return it to the [Secretary of State for the Environment, Transport and the Regions], so, however, that if possession is not obtained, such fact shall be notified to the [Secretary of State for the Environment, Transport and the Regions] by the holder of the licence.

B7.25   *[Regulation 31(1), (2) and (4) is printed as amended by the Minister of Transport Order 1979 (S.I. 1979 No. 571); the Transfer of Functions (Transport) Order 1981 (S.I. 1981 No. 238); S.I. 1994 No. 3296; the Secretary of State for the Environment, Transport and the Regions Order 1997 (S.I. 1997 No. 2971).*

Contravention of regulation 31(2) is a summary offence for which the offender is liable to a fine on level 3 of the standard scale under the Vehicle Excise and Registration Act 1994, s.59(2)(a), and the Road Vehicles (Prescribed Regulations for the Purposes of Increased Penalties) Regulations 1987 (S.I. 1987 No. 2085; not reproduced in this work).]

32. Alteration of trade plates and similar offences

B7.26   (1) No person shall alter, deface, mutilate or add anything to any trade plate or exhibit upon any mechanically propelled vehicle any trade plate which has been altered, defaced, mutilated or added to as aforesaid or upon which the figures or particulars have become illegible or the colour has become altered by fading or otherwise.

(2) No person shall exhibit on any mechanically propelled vehicle anything which could be mistaken for a trade plate.

33. Exhibition of trade plates and licences

B7.27   No person shall use a vehicle on a public road by virtue of a trade licence except in accordance with the following provisions, that is to say—

(a) there shall be fixed to and displayed on the vehicle the trade plates issued by the [Secretary of State for the Environment, Transport and the Regions] in such a manner that, if the trade plates contained a registration mark assigned to the vehicle, the provisions of Regulations 18 and 19 of these Regulations would be complied with, notwithstanding the vehicle may not have been first registered on or after 1st October 1938 or it is a works truck or an agricultural machine; and

(b) where in accordance with the provisions of the preceding paragraph a trade plate is required to be fixed to the front of a vehicle, the trade plate so fixed shall be that containing means for fixing the licence thereto, and the trade licence shall be fixed to the vehicle by means of that plate and exhibited on that plate so as to be at all times clearly visible by daylight.

B7.28   *[Regulation 33 is printed as amended by the Minister of Transport Order 1979 (S.I. 1979 No. 571) and the Transfer of Functions (Transport) Order 1981 (S.I. 1981 No. 238); the Secretary of State for the Environment, Transport and the Regions Order 1997 (S.I. 1997 No. 2971).*

Contravention of regulation 33 is a summary offence for which the offender is liable to a fine on level 3 of the standard scale under the Vehicle Excise and Registration Act 1994, s.59(2)(a), and the Road Vehicles (Prescribed Regulations for the Purposes of Increased Penalties) Regulations 1987 (S.I. 1987 No. 2085; not reproduced in this work).]

34. Restriction on use of trade plates and licences

B7.29   No person, not being the holder of a trade licence, shall use on a public road a vehicle on which there is displayed a trade plate or a trade licence, so, however, that nothing in this Regulation shall apply so as to prevent a person with the consent of the holder of the trade licence from driving a vehicle when the vehicle is being used on a public road by virtue of a trade licence [for a purpose prescribed in regulations 35 to 37 of these Regulations] and by the holder thereof.

[Regulation 34 is printed as amended by S.I. 1986 No. 2101.

Contravention of regulation 34 is a summary offence for which the offender is liable to a fine on level 3 of the standard scale under the Vehicle Excise and Registration Act 1994, s.59(2)(a), and the Road Vehicles (Prescribed Regulations for the Purposes of Increased Penalties) Regulations 1987 (S.I. 1987 No. 2085; not reproduced in this work).]

Purposes for which a vehicle may be used

35.—(1) In this Regulation, *"business purpose"*, in relation to a motor trader, means—

(a) a purpose connected with his business as a manufacturer or repairer of or dealer in mechanically propelled vehicles, . . .

(b) a purpose connected with his business as a manufacturer or repairer of or dealer in trailers carried on in conjunction with his business as a motor trader,

[(c) a purpose connected with his business of modifying vehicles (whether by the fitting of accessories or otherwise) or of valeting vehicles.]

(2) For the purposes of sub-paragraphs (a) to (k) of paragraph (4) of this Regulation, where a mechanically propelled vehicle is used on a public road by virtue of a trade licence and that vehicle is drawing a trailer, the vehicle and trailer shall be deemed to constitute a single vehicle.

(3) Save as provided in Regulation 36 of these Regulations, no person, being a motor trader and the holder of a trade licence, shall use any mechanically propelled vehicle on a public road by virtue of that licence unless it is a vehicle which is temporarily in his possession in the course of his business as a motor trader . . .

(4) Save as provided in the said Regulation 36 and without derogation from the provisions of the last preceding paragraph of this Regulation, no person, being a motor trader and the holder of a trade licence, shall use any mechanically propelled vehicle on a public road by virtue of that licence for a purpose other than a business purpose and other than one of the following purposes—

(a) for its test or trial or the test or trial of its accessories or equipment in the ordinary course of construction [modification] or repair or after completion in either such case;

(b) for proceeding to or from a public weighbridge for ascertaining its unladen weight or to or from any place for its registration or inspection by a person acting on behalf of the [Secretary of State for the Environment, Transport and the Regions];

(c) for its test or trial for the benefit of a prospective purchaser, for proceeding at the instance of a prospective purchaser to any place for the purpose of such test or trial, or for returning after such test or trial;

(d) for its test or trial for the benefit of a person interested in promoting publicity in regard to it, for proceeding at the instance of such a person to any place for the purpose of such test or trial, or for returning after such test or trial;

(e) for delivering it to the place where the purchaser intends to keep it;

(f) for demonstrating its operation or the operation of its accessories or equipment when being handed over to the purchaser;

(g) for delivering it from one part of his premises to another part of his premises, or for delivering it from his premises to the premises of, or between parts of premises of, another manufacturer or repairer of or dealer in mechanically propelled vehicles or removing it from the premises of another manufacturer or repairer of or dealer in mechanically propelled vehicles direct to his own business;

(h) for proceeding to or returning from a workshop in which a body or a special type of equipment or accessory is to be or has been fitted to it or in which it is to be or has been painted [valeted] or repaired;

(i) for proceeding from the premises of a manufacturer or repairer of or dealer in mechanically propelled vehicles to a place from which it is to be transported by train, ship or aircraft or for proceeding to the premises of such a manufacturer, repairer or dealer from a place to which it has been so transported;

(j) for proceeding to or returning from any garage, auction room or other place at which vehicles are usually stored or usually or periodically offered for sale and at which the vehicle is to be or has been stored or is to be or has been offered for sale as the case may be;

(k) for proceeding to or returning from a place where it is to be or has been tested, or for proceeding to a place where it is to be broken up or otherwise dismantled; or

(l) *[Revoked.]*

B7.32   *[Regulation 35 is printed as amended by the Minister of Transport Order 1979 (S.I. 1979 No. 571); the Transfer of Functions (Transport) Order 1981 (S.I. 1981 No. 238); S.I. 1986 No. 2101; S.I. 1987 No. 2123; S.I. 1994 No. 1911; the Secretary of State for the Environment, Transport and the Regions Order 1997 (S.I. 1997 No. 2971).]*

B7.33   **36.** No person, being a motor trader and who is a manufacturer of mechanically propelled vehicles and the holder of a trade licence, shall use any mechanically propelled vehicle, kept by him solely for the purposes of conducting research and development in the course of his business as such a manufacturer, on a public road by virtue of that licence except for such a purpose.

B7.34   **37.** No person, being a vehicle tester and the holder of a trade licence, shall use any mechanically propelled vehicle on a public road by virtue of that licence for any purpose other than testing it or any trailer drawn thereby or any of the accessories or equipment on such vehicle or trailer in the course of his business as a vehicle tester.

Conveyance of goods or burden

B7.35   **38.**—(1) No person, being a motor trader and the holder of a trade licence, shall use a mechanically propelled vehicle on a public road by virtue of that licence for the conveyance of goods or burden of any description other than—

(a) a load which is carried by a vehicle being used for a relevant purpose and is carried solely for the purpose of testing or demonstrating the vehicle or any of its accessories or equipment and which is returned to the place of loading without having been removed from the vehicle except for such last mentioned purpose or in the case of accident [or when the load consists of water, fertiliser or refuse]:
In this sub-paragraph *"relevant purpose"* means a purpose mentioned in Regulation 35(4)(a), (c), (d) and (f) of these Regulations; or

[(aa) in the case of a vehicle which is being delivered or collected and is being used for a relevant purpose, a load consisting of another vehicle used or to be used for travel from or to the place of delivery or collection:
In this sub-paragraph *"relevant purpose"* means a purpose mentioned in regulation 35(4)(e) to (j) of these Regulations;]

(b) *[revoked.]*

(c) any load built in as part of the vehicle or permanently attached thereto; or

(d) a load consisting of parts, accessories or equipment designed to be fitted to the vehicle and of tools for so fitting them, the vehicle being used for a relevant purpose;

In this sub-paragraph *"relevant purpose"* means a purpose mentioned in Regulation 35(4)(g), (h) or (i) of these Regulations; or

(e) a load consisting of a trailer, the vehicle carrying the trailer being used for a relevant purpose:

In this sub-paragraph *"relevant purpose"* means a purpose mentioned in Regulation 35(4)(e), (h) or (i) of these Regulations.

(2) No person, being a motor trader and who is a manufacturer of mechanically propelled vehicles and the holder of a trade licence, shall use any mechanically propelled vehicle, kept by him solely for the purpose of conducting research and development in the course of his business as such a manufacturer, on a public road by virtue of that licence for the conveyance of goods or burden of any description other than—

(a) a load which is carried solely for the purpose of testing the vehicle or any of its accessories or equipment and which is returned to the place of loading without having been removed from the vehicle except for such purpose or in the case of accident; or

(b) any load built in as part of the vehicle or permanently attached thereto,

and nothing in the last preceding paragraph of this Regulation shall be taken as applying to a mechanically propelled vehicle the use of which is restricted by this paragraph.

(3) For the purposes of this Regulation and the next succeeding Regulation, where a vehicle is so constructed that a trailer may by partial superimposition be attached to the vehicle in such a manner as to cause a substantial part of the weight of the trailer to be borne by the vehicle, the vehicle and the trailer shall be deemed to constitute a single vehicle.

[Regulation 38 is printed as amended by S.I. 1986 No. 2101; S.I. 1987 No. 2123; S.I. 1994 No. 1911.]   **B7.36**

39. No person, being a vehicle tester and the holder of a trade licence, shall use a mechanically propelled vehicle on a public road by virtue of that licence for the conveyance of goods or burden of any description other than—   **B7.37**

(a) a load which is carried solely for the purpose of testing or demonstrating the vehicle or any of its accessories or equipment and which is returned to the place of loading without having been removed from the vehicle except for such purpose or in the case of accident; or

(b) any load built in as part of the vehicle or permanently attached thereto.

40. Carriage of passengers

[No person, being the holder of a trade licence, shall use a mechanically propelled vehicle on a public road by virtue of that licence for carrying any person on the vehicle or on any trailer drawn by it except a person carried in connection with a purpose for which the holder of the trade licence may use the vehicle on the public road by virtue of that licence.]   **B7.38**

[Regulation 40 is printed as substituted by S.I. 1986 No. 2101.]   **B7.39**

*   *   *

The Drivers' Hours (Passenger and Goods Vehicles) (Modifications) Order 1971

(S.I. 1971 No. 818)

B8.01   *Editorial note.*   The text of section 96 of the Transport Act 1968 as modified by this order is set out as an appendix to this order.

PART I

GENERAL

*   *   *

B8.02   **2.**—(1)   In this Order, "*the Act*" means the Transport Act 1968 and any other expression which is also used in Part VI of the Act has the same meaning as in that Part.

(2)   The [Interpretation Act 1978] shall apply for the interpretation of this Order as it applies for the interpretation of an Act of Parliament, and as if for the purposes of [sections 16(1) and 17(2)(a)] of that Act this Order were an Act of Parliament and the Order revoked by Article 3 below were an Act of Parliament thereby repealed.

B8.03   *[Article 2 is printed as amended by the Interpretation Act 1978, s.17(2)(a).]*

PART II

DRIVERS OF PASSENGER VEHICLES

B8.04   **3.**   *[Revokes S.I. 1970 No. 356.]*

B8.05   **4.**—(1)   Where during any working day, or during each working day which falls wholly or partly within any working week, a driver spends all or the greater part of the time when he is driving vehicles to which Part VI of the Act applies in driving one or more passenger vehicles, then, as respects that driver and that working day or working week (as the case may be), the provisions of section 96 of the Act (permitted driving time and periods of duty of drivers of certain vehicles) and of section 103 thereof (interpretation of Part VI of the Act) mentioned in paragraphs (2) to (8) below shall have effect with the modifications or amendments respectively specified in those paragraphs.

(2)   Section 96(2) (interval for rest between periods of duty) shall have effect as if for the words from "if on any working day" onwards there were substituted the following words:—

"if on any working day a driver has been driving a vehicle or vehicles to which this Part of this Act applies—

(a)   for a period of five and a half hours and the end of that period does not mark the end of the working day; or

(b) for periods amounting in the aggregate to five and a half hours and there has not been between any of those periods an interval of not less than half an hour in which the driver was able to obtain rest and refreshment and the end of the last of those periods does not mark the end of the working day,

there shall, as respects the period mentioned in paragraph (a) above, at the end of that period or, in the case of the periods mentioned in paragraph (b) above, at the end of the last of those periods, be such an interval as aforesaid; but the requirements of the foregoing provisions of this subsection need not be satisfied in relation to a driver who, within any continuous period of eight and a half hours in the working day, drives for periods amounting in the aggregate to not more than seven and three-quarter hours, being periods of driving between which there is a period of, or there are periods amounting in the aggregate to, not less than forty-five minutes driving which the driver has not been driving, if—

    (i) the end of the last of those periods of driving marks the end of the working day, or

    (ii) at the end of the last of those periods, there is such an interval as is mentioned in paragraph (b) above.".

(3) Section 96(3) (the working day of a driver) shall have effect as if for paragraph (c) there were substituted the following paragraph:—

    "(c) if during that day all or the greater part of the time when he is driving vehicles to which this Part of this Act applies is spent in driving one or more passenger vehicles, shall not exceed sixteen hours.".

(4) Section 96(4) (interval for rest between working days) shall have effect as if for paragraphs (a) and (b) there were substituted the words "shall not be of less than ten hours except that on not more than three occasions in any working week the said interval may be of less than ten hours but not of less than eight and a half hours;".

(5) Section 96(5) and (8)(b) (maximum duty periods in a working week) shall not apply.

(6) Section 96(6) (off-duty periods in a working week) shall have effect as if for the words from "in the case of each working week of a driver" onwards there were substituted the following words:—

    "in the case of every two successive working weeks of a driver, a period of not less than twenty-four hours for which he is off duty, being a period either falling wholly in those weeks or beginning in the second of those weeks and ending in the first of the next two successive weeks; but where the requirements of the foregoing provisions of this subsection have been satisfied in the case of any two successive working weeks by reference to a period ending in the first of the next two successive weeks, no part of that period (except any part after the expiration of the first twenty-four hours of it) shall be taken into account for the purpose of satisfying those requirements in the case of the said next two successive weeks.".

(7) For section 96(7) there shall be substituted the following subsections:—

    "(7) If in the case of the working week of any driver the following requirements are satisfied, that is to say, that—

    (a) the driver does not drive any vehicle to which this Part of this Act applies for a period of, or for periods amounting in the aggregate to, more than four hours in more than two of the periods of twenty-four hours beginning at midnight which make up that working week (any such period of twenty-four hours in which the driver does drive for a period of, or for periods amounting in the aggregate to, more than four hours being in this subsection, and in sub-section (7B) below, referred to as '*a full time day*'); and

(b) the provisions of subsection (7B) of this section are complied with in relation to him as respects each full time day in that week,

then, subject to subsection (7A) of this section, the provisions of subsections (1) to (4) of this section shall not apply to that driver in that week, and where the said requirements are satisfied in the case of two successive working weeks of that driver the provisions of sub-section (6) of this section shall not apply to him as respects those working weeks.

(7A) Where in the case of the working week of a driver the requirements mentioned in subsection (7) above are satisfied but there is a working day of the driver which falls partly in that working week and partly in a working week in the case of which the said require-ments are not satisfied, then the provisions of subsections (1), (2) and (3) of this section shall nevertheless have effect in relation to the whole of that working day.

(7B) The following provisions shall apply as respects each full time day in a working week of a driver in the case of which the requirement mentioned in subsection (7)(a) above is satisfied, that is to say—

(a) each period of duty of that driver shall fall wholly within the full time day;

(b) there shall be an interval for rest of not less than ten hours immediately before his first period of duty and immediately after his last period of duty in the full time day or, if there is only one such period of duty therein, immediately before and after that period of duty;

(c) the driver shall not in the full time day drive a vehicle or vehicles to which this Part of this Act applies for periods amounting in the aggregate to more than ten hours;

(d) if in the full time day the driver has been driving a vehicle or vehicles to which this Part of this Act applies—

(i) for a period of five and a half hours and the end of that period of driving does not mark the end of his period of duty, or of the last of his periods of duty, in that day, or

(ii) for periods amounting in the aggregate to five and a half hours and there has not been between any of those periods of driving an interval of not less than half an hour in which the driver was able to obtain rest and refreshment and the end of the last of those periods of driving does not mark the end of his period of duty, or of the last of his periods of duty, in that day,

there shall be such an interval as aforesaid at the end of the period of driving men-tioned in sub-paragraph (i) above or of the last of the periods of driving mentioned in sub-paragraph (ii) above: provided however that the foregoing requirements of this paragraph need not be satisfied in relation to a driver who, within any contin-uous period of eight and a half hours falling wholly within the full time day, drives for periods amounting in the aggregate to not more than seven and three-quarter hours, being periods of driving between which there is a period of, or there are periods amounting in the aggregate to, not less than forty-five minutes during which the driver has not been driving, if the end of the last of those periods of driving marks the end of his period, or of the last of his periods, of duty in that day, or at the end of the last of those periods of driving there is such an interval as is mentioned in sub-paragraph (ii) above; and

(e) the period during which the driver is on duty in the full time day or, if there is more than one such period, the period between the beginning of his first period of duty in that day and the end of his last period of duty therein, shall not exceed 16 hours.

(8) The definition of '*working day*' in section 103 shall have effect for the purposes of sub-sections (1) to (4) and (6) to (8) of section 96 as if for the words from 'eleven hours' to the words 'nine and a half hours' there were substituted the words 'ten hours or (where permitted by virtue of section 96(4) of this Act) of not less than eight and a half hours'."

PART III

DRIVERS OF GOODS VEHICLES

5. *[Amends the Drivers' Hours (Goods Vehicles) (Modification) Order 1970 (S.I. 1970 No. 257)* **B8.06** *(q.v.).]*

APPENDIX (Transport Act 1968, s.96, as applied to drivers of passenger vehicles)

96. Permitted driving time and periods of duty

(1) Subject to the provisions of this section, a driver shall not on any working day drive **B8.07** a vehicle or vehicles to which this Part of this Act applies for periods amounting in the aggregate to more than ten hours.

(2) Subject to the provisions of this section, if on any working day a driver has been driving a vehicle or vehicles to which this Part of this Act applies—

  (a) for a period of five and a half hours and the end of that period does not mark the end of the working day; or

  (b) for periods amounting in the aggregate to five and a half hours and there has not been between any of those periods an interval of not less than half an hour in which the driver was able to obtain rest and refreshment and the end of the last of those periods does not mark the end of the working day,

there shall, as respects the period mentioned in paragraph (a) above, at the end of that period or, in the case of the periods mentioned in paragraph (b) above, at the end of the last of those periods, be such an interval as aforesaid; but the requirements of the foregoing provisions of this subsection need not be satisfied in relation to a driver who, within any continuous period of eight and a half hours in the working day, drives for periods amounting in the aggregate to not more than seven and three-quarter hours, being periods of driving between which there is a period of, or there are periods amounting in the aggregate to, not less than forty-five minutes during which the driver has not been driving, if—

  (i) the end of the last of those periods of driving marks the end of the working day, or

  (ii) at the end of the last of those periods there is such an interval as is mentioned in paragraph (b) above.

(3) Subject to the provisions of this section, the working day of a driver—

  (a) except where paragraph (b) or (c) of this subsection applies, shall not exceed eleven hours;

  (b) if during that day he is off duty for a period which is, or periods which taken together are, not less than the time by which his working day exceeds eleven hours, shall not exceed twelve and a half hours;

  (c) if during that day all or the greater part of the time when he is driving vehicles to which this Part of this Act applies is spent in driving one or more passenger vehicles, shall not exceed sixteen hours.

(4) Subject to the provisions of this section, there shall be, between any two successive working days of a driver, an interval for rest which shall not be of less than ten hours except that on not more than three occasions in any working week the said interval may be of less than ten hours but not of less than eight and a half hours, and for the purposes of this Part of this Act a period of time shall not be treated, in the case of an employee-driver, as not being an interval for rest by reason only that he may be called upon to report for duty if required.

(5) *[Inapplicable.]*

(6) Subject to the provisions of this section, there shall be, in the case of every two successive working weeks of a driver, a period of not less than twenty-four hours for which he is off duty, being a period either falling wholly in those weeks or beginning in the second of those weeks and ending in the first of the next two successive weeks; but where the requirements of the foregoing provisions of this subsection have been satisfied in the case of any two successive working weeks by reference to a period ending in the first of the next two successive weeks, no part of that period (except any part after the expiration of the first twenty-four hours of it) shall be taken into account for the purpose of satisfying those requirements in the case of the said next two successive weeks.

(7) If in the case of the working week of any driver the following requirements are satisfied, that is to say, that—

    (a) the driver does not drive any vehicle to which this Part of this Act applies for a period of, or for periods amounting in the aggregate to, more than four hours in more than two of the periods of twenty-four hours beginning at midnight which make up that working week (any such period of twenty-four hours in which the driver does drive for a period of, or for periods amounting in the aggregate to, more than four hours being in this subsection, and in subsection (7B) below, referred to as "*a full time day*"); and

    (b) the provisions of subsection (7B) of this section are complied with in relation to him as respects each full time day in that week,

then, subject to subsection (7A) of this section, the provisions of subsections (1) to (4) of this section shall not apply to that driver in that week, and where the said requirements are satisfied in the case of two successive working weeks of that driver the provisions of subsection (6) of this section shall not apply to him as respects those working weeks.

(7A) Where in the case of the working week of a driver the requirements mentioned in subsection (7) above are satisfied but there is a working day of the driver which falls partly in that working week and partly in a working week in the case of which the said requirements are not satisfied, then the provisions of subsections (1), (2) and (3) of this section shall nevertheless have effect in relation to the whole of that working day.

(7B) The following provisions shall apply as respects each full time day in a working week of a driver in the case of which the requirement mentioned in subsection (7)(a) above is satisfied, that is to say—

    (a) each period of duty of that driver shall fall wholly within the full time day;

    (b) there shall be an interval for rest of not less than ten hours immediately before his first period of duty and immediately after his last period of duty in the full time day or, if there is only one such period of duty therein, immediately before and after that period of duty;

    (c) the driver shall not in the full time day drive a vehicle or vehicles to which this Part of this Act applies for periods amounting in the aggregate to more than ten hours;

(d) if in the full time day the driver has been driving a vehicle or vehicles to which this Part of this Act applies—

  (i) for a period of five and a half hours and the end of that period of driving does not mark the end of his period of duty, or of the last of his periods of duty, in that day, or

  (ii) for periods amounting in the aggregate to five and a half hours and there has not been between any of those periods of driving an interval of not less than half an hour in which the driver was able to obtain rest and refreshment and the end of the last of those periods of driving does not mark the end of his period of duty, or of the last of his periods of duty, in that day,

there shall be such an interval as aforesaid at the end of the period of driving mentioned in sub-paragraph (i) above or of the last of the periods of driving mentioned in sub-paragraph (ii) above: provided however that the foregoing requirements of this paragraph need not be satisfied in relation to a driver who, within any continuous period of eight and a half hours falling wholly within the full time day, drives for periods amounting in the aggregate to not more than seven and three-quarter hours, being periods of driving between which there is a period of, or there are periods amounting in the aggregate to, not less than forty-five minutes during which the driver has not been driving, if the end of the last of those periods of driving marks the end of his period, or of the last of his periods, of duty in that day, or at the end of the last of those periods of driving there is such an interval as is mentioned in sub-paragraph (ii) above; and

(e) the period during which the driver is on duty in the full time day or, if there is more than one such period, the period between the beginning of his first period of duty in that day and the end of his last period of duty therein, shall not exceed sixteen hours.

(8) If on any working day a driver does not drive any vehicle to which this Part of this Act applies—

  (a) subsections (2) and (3) of this section shall not apply to that day, and

  (b) *[inapplicable.]*

(9) For the purposes of subsections (1) and (7) of this section no account shall be taken of any time spent driving a vehicle elsewhere than on a road if the vehicle is being so driven in the course of operations of agriculture or forestry.

(10) For the purposes of enabling drivers to deal with cases of emergency or otherwise to meet a special need, the [Secretary of State for the Environment, Transport and the Regions] may by regulations—

  (a) create exemptions from all or any of the requirements of subsections (1) to (6) of this section in such cases and subject to such conditions as may be specified in the regulations;

  (b) empower the traffic commissioner for any area, subject to the provisions of the regulations—

    (i) to dispense with the observance of all or any of those requirements (either generally or in such circumstances or to such extent as the commissioner thinks fit) in any particular case for which provision is not made under paragraph (a) of this subsection;

    (ii) to grant a certificate (which, for the purposes of any proceedings under this Part of this Act, shall be conclusive evidence of the facts therein stated) that any particular case falls or fell within any exemption created under the said paragraph (a) and regulations under this subsection may enable any dispensation under paragraph (b)(i) of this subsection to be granted retrospectively and provide for a document purporting to be a certificate granted by virtue of paragraph (b)(ii) of this subsection to be accepted in evidence without further proof.

(11) If any of the requirements of the domestic drivers' hours code is contravened in the case of any driver—

    (a) that driver; and

    (b) any other person (being that driver's employer or a person to whose orders that driver was subject) who caused or permitted the contravention,

shall be liable on summary conviction to a fine not exceeding level 4 on the standard scale; but a person shall not be liable to be convicted under this subsection if he proves to the court—

    (i) that the contravention was due to unavoidable delay in the completion of a journey arising out of circumstances which he could not reasonably have foreseen; or

    (ii) in the case of a person charged under paragraph (b) of this subsection, that the contravention was due to the fact that the driver had for any particular period or periods driven or been on duty otherwise than in the employment of that person or, as the case may be, otherwise than in the employment in which he is subject to the orders of that person, and that the person charged was not, and could not reasonably have become, aware of that fact.

(11A) Where, in the case of a driver of a motor vehicle, there is in Great Britain a contravention of any requirement of the applicable Community rules as to period of driving, or distance driven, or periods on or off duty, then the offender and any other person (being the offender's employer or a person to whose orders the offender was subject) who caused or permitted the contravention shall be liable on summary conviction to a fine not exceeding level 4 on the standard scale.

(11B) But a person shall not be liable to be convicted under subsection (11A) if—

    (a) he proves the matters specified in paragraph (i) of subsection (11); or

    (b) being charged as the offender's employer or a person to whose orders the offender was subject, he proves the matters specified in paragraph (ii) of that subsection.

(12) The [Secretary of State for the Environment, Transport and the Regions] may by order—

    (a) direct that subsection (1) of this section shall have effect with the substitution for the reference to ten hours of a reference to nine hours, either generally or with such exceptions as may be specified in the order;

    (b) direct that paragraph (a) of subsection (3) of this section shall have effect with the substitution for the reference to eleven hours of a reference to any shorter period, or remove, modify or add to the provisions of that subsection containing exceptions to the said paragraph (a);

    (c) remove, modify or add to any of the requirements of subsections (2), (4), (5) or (6) of this section or any of the exemptions provided for by subsections (7), (8) and (9) thereof;

and any order under this subsection may contain such transitional and supplementary provisions as the [Secretary of State for the Environment, Transport and the Regions] thinks necessary or expedient, including provisions amending any definition in section 103 of this Act which is relevant to any of the provisions affected by the order.

(13) In this Part of this Act "*the domestic drivers' hours code*" means the provisions of sub-sections (1) to (6) of this section as for the time being in force (and, in particular, as modified, added to or substituted by or under any instrument in force under section 95(1) of this Act or subsection (10) or (12) of this section).

[This version of the Transport Act 1968, s.96, is the text of section 96 as modified by the Drivers' Hours (Passenger and Goods Vehicles) (Modifications) Order 1971 (S.I. 1971 No. 818) above.

This version of section 96 is printed as further amended by the Secretary of State for the Environment Order 1970 (S.I. 1970 No. 1681); the European Communities Act 1972, s.4, and Sched. 4, para.9(2); the Road Traffic (Drivers' Ages and Hours of Work) Act 1976, s.2(1); the Secretary of State for Transport Order 1976 (S.I. 1976 No. 1775); the Transport Act 1978, s.10; the Minister of Transport Order 1979 (S.I. 1979 No. 571); the Transfer of Functions (Transport) Order 1981 (S.I. 1981 No. 238); the Criminal Justice Act 1982, ss.38 and 46(1); the Transport Act 1985, s.3 and Sched. 2, Pt II, para.1(2); the Community Drivers' Hours and Recording Equipment Regulations 1986 (S.I. 1986 No. 1457), reg.2; the Secretary of State for the Environment, Transport and the Regions Order 1997 (S.I. 1997 No. 2971).]

The Motor Vehicles (Third Party Risks) Regulations 1972

(S.I. 1972 No. 1217)

B9.01 *[The text of these regulations is printed as amended by:*

the Motor Vehicles (Third Party Risks) (Amendment) Regulations 1973 (S.I. 1973 No. 1821) (January 1, 1974);

the Motor Vehicles (Third Party Risks) (Amendment) Regulations 1974 (S.I. 1974 No. 792) (May 27, 1974);

the Motor Vehicles (Third Party Risks) (Amendment) (No. 2) Regulations 1974 (S.I. 1974 No. 2187) (January 31, 1975);

the Motor Vehicles (Third Party Risks) (Amendment) Regulations 1981 (S.I. 1981 No. 1567) (December 1, 1981);

the Motor Vehicles (Third Party Risks) (Amendment) Regulations 1992 (S.I. 1992 No. 1283) (July 1, 1992); and

the Motor Vehicles (Third Party Risks) (Amendment) Regulations 1997 (S.I. 1997 No. 97) (February 21, 1997).

The amending regulations are referred to in the notes to the principal regulations only by their years and numbers. The dates referred to above are the dates on which the amending regulations came into force.

The principal regulations have also been amended by the Motor Vehicles (Third Party Risks) (Amendment) Regulations 1999 (S.I. 1999 No. 2392), but these regulations do not affect the text of any provision which is printed in this work.]

B9.02   **1, 2. Commencement and citation**   *[Omitted.]*

3. Temporary use of existing forms   *[Omitted.]*

4. Interpretation

B9.03   (1) In these Regulations, unless the context otherwise requires, the following expressions have the meanings hereby respectively assigned to them:—

"*the Act*" means [the Road Traffic Act 1988];

"*company*" means an authorised insurer within the meaning of [Part VI] of the Act or a body of persons by whom a security may be given in pursuance of the said [Part VI];

"*motor vehicle*" has the meaning assigned to it by [sections 185, 186, 188 and 189 of the Act, but excludes any invalid carriage, tramcar or trolley vehicle to which [Part VI] of the Act does not apply;

"*policy*" means a policy of insurance in respect of third party risks arising out of the use of motor vehicles which complies with the requirements of [Part VI] of the Act and includes a covering note;

"*security*" means a security in respect of third party risks arising out of the use of motor vehicles which complies with the requirements of [Part VI] of the Act;

"*specified body*" means—

(a) any of the local authorities referred to in [paragraph (a) of section 144(2)] of the Act; or

(b) a Passenger Transport Executive established under an order made under section 9 of the Transport Act 1968, or a subsidiary of that Executive, being an Executive or subsidiary to whose vehicles [section 144(2)(a)] of the Act has been applied; or

(c) *[lapsed.]*

(2) Any reference in these Regulations to a certificate in Form A, B, C, D, E or F shall be construed as a reference to a certificate in the form so headed and set out in Part 1 of the Schedule to these Regulations which has been duly made and completed subject to and in accordance with the provisions set out in Part 2 of the said Schedule.

(3) Any reference in these Regulations to any enactment shall be construed as a reference to that enactment as amended by any subsequent enactment.

(4) The Interpretation Act [1978] shall apply for the interpretation of these Regulations as it applies for the interpretation of an Act of Parliament, and as if for the purposes of [sections 16(1) and 17(2)(a)] of that Act these Regulations were an Act of Parliament and the Regulations revoked by Regulation 2 of these Regulations were Acts of Parliament thereby repealed.

[Regulation 4 is printed as amended by the Interpretation Act 1978, s.17(2)(a).]

5. Issue of certificates of insurance or security

(1) A company shall issue to every holder of a security or of a policy other than a covering note issued by the company:— **B9.04**

  (a) in the case of a policy or security relating to one or more specified vehicles a certificate of insurance in Form A or a certificate of security in Form D in respect of each such vehicle;

  (b) in the case of a policy or security relating to vehicles other than specified vehicles such number of certificates in Form B or Form D as may be necessary for the purpose of complying with the requirements of [section 165(1) and (2)] of the Act and of these Regulations as to the production of evidence that a motor vehicle is not being driven in contravention of [section 143] of the Act:
    Provided that where a security is intended to cover the use of more than ten motor vehicles at one time the company by whom it was issued may issue one certificate only and the holder of the security may issue duplicate copies of such certificate duly authenticated by him.]

(2) Notwithstanding the foregoing provisions of this Regulation, where as respects third party risks a policy or security relating to a specified vehicle extends also to the driving by the holder of other motor vehicles, not being specified vehicles, the certificate may be in Form A or Form D, as the case may be, containing a statement in either case that the policy or security extends to such driving of other motor vehicles. Where such a certificate is issued by a company they may, and shall in accordance with a demand made to them by the holder, issue to him a further such certificate or a certificate in Form B.

(3) Every policy in the form of a covering note issued by a company shall have printed thereon or on the back thereof a certificate of insurance in Form C.

[Regulation 5 is printed as amended by the Interpretation Act 1978, s.17(2)(a) (cf. regulation 4(4) **B9.05** *above); S.I. 1997 No. 97.]*

6. Every certificate of insurance or certificate of security shall be issued not later than four days after the date on which the policy or security to which it relates is issued or renewed. **B9.06**

7. Production of evidence as alternatives to certificates

B9.07   The following evidence that a motor vehicle is not or was not being driven in contravention of [section 143] of the Act may be produced in pursuance of [section 165] of the Act as an alternative to the production of a certificate of insurance or a certificate of security:—

(1) a duplicate copy of a certificate of security issued in accordance with the proviso to sub-paragraph (b) of paragraph (1) of Regulation 5 of these Regulations;

(2) in the case of a motor vehicle of which the owner has for the time being deposited with the Accountant-General of the Supreme Court [the sum for the time being specified in section 144(1) of the Road Traffic Act 1988], a certificate in Form E signed by the owner of the motor vehicle or by some person authorised by him in that behalf that such sum is on deposit;

(3) in the case of a motor vehicle owned by a specified body, a police authority or the Receiver for the metropolitan police district, a certificate in Form F signed by some person authorised in that behalf by such specified body, police authority or Receiver as the case may be that the said motor vehicle is owned by the said specified body, police authority or Receiver.

[(4) in the case of a vehicle normally based [in the territory other than the United Kingdom and Gibraltar of a member state of the Communities or of [Austria, Czechoslovakia, Finland, the German Democratic Republic, Hungary, Norway, Sweden or Switzerland]] a document issued by the insurer of the vehicle which indicates the name of the insurer, the number or other identifying particulars of the insurance policy issued in respect of the vehicle and the period of the insurance cover. In this paragraph the territory of the state in which a vehicle is normally based is

(a) the territory of the state in which the vehicle is registered, or

(b) in cases where no registration is required for the type of vehicle, but the vehicle bears an insurance plate or distinguishing sign analogous to a registration plate, the territory of the state in which the insurance plate or the sign is issued, or

(c) in cases where neither registration plate nor insurance plate nor distinguishing sign is required for the type of vehicle, the territory of the state in which the keeper of the vehicle is permanently resident.]

B9.08   *[Regulation 7 is printed as amended by S.I. 1973 No. 1821; S.I. 1974 No. 792; S.I. 1974 No. 2187; the Interpretation Act 1978, s.17(2)(a) (cf. regulation 4(4) above); S.I. 1992 No. 1283.*
The German Democratic Republic has been incorporated into the Federal Republic of Germany and is (in effect) a member of the European Union. Austria, Finland and Sweden formally acceded to the European Union on January 1, 1995. Czechoslovakia has been divided into two separate republics.]

B9.09   **8.** Any certificate issued in accordance with paragraph (2) or (3) of the preceding Regulation shall be destroyed by the owner of the vehicle to which it relates before the motor vehicle is sold or otherwise disposed of.

*   *   *

12. Return of certificates to issuing company

B9.10   (1) The following provisions shall apply in relation to the transfer of a policy or security with the consent of the holder to any other person:—

(a) the holder shall, before the policy or security is transferred, return any relative certificates issued for the purposes of these Regulations to the company by whom they were issued; and

(b) the policy or security shall not be transferred to any other person unless and until the certificates have been so returned or the company are satisfied that the certificates have been lost or destroyed.

(2) In any case where with the consent of the person to whom it was issued a policy or security is suspended or ceases to be effective, otherwise than by effluxion of time, in circumstances in which the provisions of [section 147(4)] of the Act (relating to the surrender of certificates) do not apply, the holder of the policy or security shall within seven days from the date when it is suspended or ceases to be effective return any relative certificates issued for the purposes of these Regulations to the company by whom they were issued and the company shall not issue a new policy or security to the said holder in respect of the motor vehicle or vehicles to which the said first mentioned policy or security related unless and until the certificates have been returned to the company or the company are satisfied that they have been lost or destroyed.

(3) Where a policy or security is cancelled by mutual consent or by virtue of any provision in the policy or security, any statutory declaration that a certificate has been lost or destroyed made in pursuance of [section 147(4)] (which requires any such declaration to be made within a period of seven days from the taking effect of the cancellation) shall be delivered forthwith after it has been made to the company by whom the policy was issued or the security given.

(4) The provisions of the last preceding paragraph shall be without prejudice to the provisions of [paragraph (c) of subsection (1) of section 152] of the Act as to the effect for the purposes of that subsection of the making of a statutory declaration within the periods therein stated.

[Regulation 12 is printed as amended by the Interpretation Act 1978, s.17(2)(a) (cf. regulation 4(4)   **B9.11**
above).]

13. Issue of fresh certificates

Where any company by whom a certificate of insurance or a certificate of security has   **B9.12**
been issued are satisfied that the certificate has become defaced or has been lost or destroyed they shall, if they are requested to do so by the person to whom the certificate was issued, issue to him a fresh certificate. In the case of a defaced certificate the company shall not issue a fresh certificate unless the defaced certificate is returned to the company.

THE SCHEDULE

PART 1   **B9.13**

Forms of Certificates

FORM A

Certificate of Motor Insurance

Certificate No. ....   Policy No. ....(Optional)
1. Registration mark of vehicle.
2. Name of policy holder.
3. Effective date of the commencement of insurance for the purposes of the relevant law.
4. Date of expiry of insurance.

5. Persons or classes of persons entitled to drive.
6. Limitations as to use.

I/We hereby certify that the policy to which this certificate relates satisfies the requirements of the relevant law applicable in Great Britain.

....

Authorised Insurers

Note: For full details of the insurance cover
reference should be made to the policy.

Form B

Certificate of Motor Insurance

Certificate No. ....   Policy No. ....(Optional)

1. Description of vehicle.
2. Name of policy holder.
3. Effective date of the commencement of insurance for the purposes of the relevant law.
4. Date of expiry of insurance.
5. Persons or classes of persons entitled to drive.
6. Limitations as to use.

I/We hereby certify that the policy to which this certificate relates satisfies the requirements of the relevant law applicable in Great Britain.

....

Authorised Insurers

Note: For full details of the insurance cover
reference should be made to the policy.

Form C

Certificate of Motor Insurance

I/We hereby certify that this covering note satisfies the requirements of the relevant law applicable in Great Britain.

....

Authorised Insurers

Form D

Certificate No. ....   Policy No. ....(Optional)

1. Name of holder of security.
2. Effective date of the commencement of security for the purposes of the relevant law.
3. Date of expiry of security.
4. Conditions to which security is subject.

I/We hereby certify that the security to which this certificate relates satisfies the requirements of the relevant law applicable in Great Britain.

....
Persons giving security

Note: For full details of the cover
　　　reference should be made to the security.

FORM E

Certificate of Deposit

I/We hereby certify that I am/we are the owner(s) of the vehicle of which the registration mark is..........................and that in pursuance of the relevant law applicable in Great Britain I/we have on deposit with the Accountant-General of the Supreme Court [the sum for the time being specified in section 144(1) of the Road Traffic Act 1988]

Signed ....
on behalf of ....

FORM F

Certificate of Ownership

We hereby certify that the vehicle of which the registration mark is
..................................is owned by ....

Signed ....
on behalf of ....

[Part 1 of the Schedule is printed as amended by S.I. 1992 No. 1283.]

PART 2

Provisions relating to the forms and completion of certificates

[1. Every certificate shall be printed and completed in black [on a white background]. 　**B9.14**
This provision shall not prevent the reproduction of a seal or monogram or similar device referred to in paragraph 2 of this Part of this Schedule, or the presence of a background pattern (of whatever form and whether coloured or not) on the face of the form which does not materially affect the legibility of the certificate.]

[2. No certificate shall contain any advertising matter, either on the face or on the back thereof:

　Provided that the name and address of the company by whom the certificate is issued, or a reproduction of the seal of the company or any monogram or similar device of the company, or the name and address of an insurance broker, shall not be deemed to be advertising matter for the purposes of this paragraph if it is printed or stamped at the foot or on the back of such certificate, or if it forms, or forms part of, any such background pattern as is referred to in the foregoing paragraph.]

3. The whole of each form as set out in Part 1 of this Schedule shall in each case appear on the face of the form, the items being in the order so set out and the certification being set out at the end of the form.

4. The particulars to be inserted on the said forms shall so far as possible appear on the face of the form, but where in the case of any of the numbered headings in Forms A, B, or D, this cannot conveniently be done, any part of such particulars may be inserted on the back of the form, provided that their presence on the back is clearly indicated under the relevant heading.

5. The particulars to be inserted on any of the said forms shall not include particulars relating to any exceptions purporting to restrict the insurance under the relevant policy or the operation of the relevant security which are by [subsections (1) and (2) of section 148] of the Act rendered of no effect as respects the third party liabilities required by [sections 145 and 146] of the Act to be covered by a policy or security.

6. (1) In any case where it is intended that a certificate of insurance, certificate of security or a covering note shall be effective not only in Great Britain, but also in any of the following territories, that is to say, Northern Ireland, the Isle of Man, the Island of Guernsey, the Island of Jersey or the Island of Alderney, Forms A, B, C and D may be modified by the addition thereto, where necessary, of a reference to the relevant legal provisions of such of those territories as may be appropriate.

(2) A certificate of insurance or a certificate of security may contain either on the face or on the back of the certificate a statement as to whether or not the policy or security to which it relates satisfies the requirements of the relevant law in any of the territories referred to in this paragraph.

7. Every certificate of insurance or certificate of security shall be duly authenticated by or on behalf of the company by whom it is issued.

8. A certificate in Form F issued by a subsidiary of a Passenger Transport Executive or by a wholly-owned subsidiary of the [London Regional Transport] shall indicate under the signature that the issuing body is such a subsidiary of an Executive, which shall there be specified.

B9.15   *[Part 2 of the Schedule is printed as amended by the Interpretation Act 1978, s.17(2)(a) (cf. regulation 4(4) above); S.I. 1981 No. 1567; the London Regional Transport Act 1984, s.71(4); S.I. 1992 No. 1283.*

As to the dissolution of London Regional Transport and its replacement by Transport for London, see the Greater London Authority Act 1999, Pt IV, Chap. XVI (particularly ss.297 and 302).]

The Motor Vehicles (International Circulation) Order 1975

(S.I. 1975 No. 1208)

[The text of this order is printed as amended by: **B10.01**

the Motor Vehicles (International Circulation) (Amendment) Order 1985 (S.I. 1985 No. 459) (March 21, 1985);

the Motor Vehicles (International Circulation) (Amendment) Order 1989 (S.I. 1989 No. 993) (June 14, 1989 (arts 1–4), September 1, 1989 (art.5) and on a date to be announced under article 1 (art.6));

the Motor Vehicles (International Circulation) (Amendment) Order 1991 (S.I. 1991 No. 771) (April 3, 1991);

the Motor Vehicles (International Circulation) (Amendment) (No. 2) Order 1991 (S.I. 1991 No. 1727) (July 25, 1991);

the Motor Vehicles (International Circulation) (Amendment) Order 1996 (S.I. 1996 No. 1929) (August 6, 1996); and

the Driving Licences (Community Driving Licence) Regulations 1996 (S.I. 1996 No. 1974) (January 1, 1997).

The amending orders are referred to in the notes to the principal order only by their years and numbers. The dates referred to above are the dates on which the amendments took (or will take) effect. (S.I. 1996 No. 1974 came into force for certain purposes, not concerning the text of the principal order set out below on an earlier date.)

The Motor Vehicles (International Circulation) (Amendment) Order 1980 (S.I. 1980 No. 1095), below, also effects amendments to the principal order; but (apart from an amendment to Schedule 2 which is not reproduced) these are not yet in operation.]

1. Documents for drivers and vehicles going abroad

(1) The Secretary of State may issue for use outside the United Kingdom a driving   **B10.02**
permit in each or either of the forms A and B in Schedule 1 to this Order to a person who
has attained the age of eighteen years and satisfies the Secretary of State—

    (a) that he is competent to drive motor vehicles of the classes for which the permit is
    to be issued, and

    (b) that he is resident in the United Kingdom:

Provided that a permit in form A which is restricted to motor cycles or invalid carriages
may be issued to a person who is under eighteen years of age.

(2) The Secretary of State may issue for use outside the United Kingdom a document in
the form D in Schedule 1 to this Order for any motor vehicle registered under [the Vehicle
Excise and Registration Act 1994].

    (3), (4) *[Revoked.]*

(5) The Secretary of State may assign to a motor vehicle to which the Decision of 1957
of the Council of the Organisation for European Economic Co-operation applies, an

identification mark in the form of such a trade plate as may be required to be carried on such a vehicle under the provisions of section 1 of the Regulation attached to that Decision.

In this paragraph, "*the Decision of 1957 of the Council of the Organisation for European Economic Co-operation*" means the decision of the Council of the Organisation for European Economic Co-operation concerning the International Circulation of Hired Private Road Motor Vehicles adopted by that Council at its 369th Meeting, in June 1957.

(6) [The Secretary of State may charge a fee of £— for this issue of any such document as is mentioned in paragraph (1) or (2) of this article.]

(7) The Secretary of State may for the purpose of his functions under this Article carry out tests of the competency of applicants for driving permits and examination of vehicles.

(8) The Secretary of State may delegate any of his functions under this Article (including any power of charging fees and the carrying out of tests or examinations) to any body concerned with motor vehicles or to any Northern Ireland department.

[(9) Sections 173 and 174 of the Road Traffic Act 1988 (forgery of documents, etc., false statements and withholding material information) and Article 174 of the Road Traffic (Northern Ireland) Order 1981 [*S.I. 1981 No. 154*] (false statements in connection with forgery of, and fraudulent use of, documents, etc.) shall apply to a Convention driving permit as they apply to licences under that Act or under that Order.]

[(10) Section 13 of the Road Traffic Offenders Act 1988 and Article 190 of the said Order of 1981 (admissibility of records as evidence) shall apply to records maintained by the Secretary of State in connection with his functions under this Article, or by a body or Northern Ireland department to which in accordance with paragraph (8) of this Article he has delegated the function in connection with which the records are maintained, as that section or that Article apply to records maintained in connection with functions under that Act or under that Order, and the powers conferred by section 13(5) of the said Act of 1988 and Article 190(4) of the said Order of 1981 to prescribe a description of matter which may be admitted as evidence under that section or under that Article shall have effect in relation to the application of that section and that Article by this Article.]

B10.03   *[Article 1 is printed as amended by S.I. 1989 No. 993, art.4; the Vehicle Excise and Registration Act 1994, s.64 and Sched. 4, para.4; S.I. 1996 No. 1929.*
The amount of the fee referred in article 1(6) is not reproduced.]

[2. Visitors' driving permits

B10.04   (1) Subject to the provisions of this Article, it shall be lawful for a person resident outside the United Kingdom who is temporarily in Great Britain and holds—

(a) a Convention driving permit, or

(b) a domestic driving permit issued in a country outside the United Kingdom, or

(c) a British Forces (BFG) driving licence,

during a period of twelve months from the date of his last entry into the United Kingdom to drive, or except in the case of a holder of a British Forces (BFG) driving licence, for any person to cause or permit such a person to drive, in Great Britain a motor vehicle of any class [other than a large goods vehicle or a passenger-carrying vehicle] which he is authorised by that permit or that licence to drive, notwithstanding that he is not the holder of a driving licence under Part III of the Road Traffic Act 1988.

(2) Subject to the provisions of this Article, it shall be lawful for a person resident outside the United Kingdom who is temporarily in Great Britain and holds—

(a) a Convention driving permit, or

(b) a domestic driving permit issued in a country outside the United Kingdom, during a period of twelve months from the date of his last entry into the United Kingdom to drive, or for any person to cause or permit such a person to drive, in Great Britain—

    (i) in the case of any such person who is resident in [an EEA State], [the Isle of Man or Jersey] any [large goods vehicle or passenger-carrying vehicle]; and

    (ii) in the case of any other such person, a [large goods vehicle or passenger-carrying vehicle] brought temporarily into Great Britain,

which he is authorised by that permit to drive, notwithstanding that he is not the holder [of a large goods vehicle driver's licence or a passenger-carrying vehicle driver's licence]

(3) Subject to the provisions of this Article, it shall be lawful for a person resident outside the United Kingdom who is temporarily in Great Britain and holds a British Forces (BFG) public service vehicle driving licence during a period of twelve months from the date of his last entry into the United Kingdom to drive, or for any person to cause or permit such a person to drive, in Great Britain—

    (a) in the case of any such person who is resident in [an EEA State], [the Isle of Man or Jersey] any [passenger-carrying vehicle], and

    (b) in the case of any other such person, a [passenger-carrying vehicle] brought temporarily into Great Britain,

which he is authorised by that licence to drive, notwithstanding that he is not the holder of [a passenger-carrying vehicle driver's licence]

(4) Nothing in the preceding provisions of this Article shall authorise any person to drive, or any person to cause or permit any person to drive, a vehicle of any class at a time when he is disqualified by virtue of section 101 of the Road Traffic Act 1988 (persons under age) [*q.v.*], for holding or obtaining a driving licence authorising him to drive vehicles of that class, but in the case of any such person as is mentioned in paragraph (1), (2) or (3) of this Article, who is driving a vehicle which—

    (a) in the case of a person not resident in [an EEA State], [the Isle of Man or Jersey] is brought temporarily into Great Britain, and

    (b) is within the class specified in the first column of [paragraph (7)] of the Table in subsection (1) of that section, and

    (c) is either a vehicle registered in a Convention country or a goods vehicle in respect of which that person holds a certificate of competence which satisfies the international requirements,

the second column of that paragraph, in its application for the purposes of this paragraph, shall have effect as if for "21" there were substituted "18".

In this paragraph the following expressions have the meanings respectively assigned to them—

"*the international requirements*" means—

    (i) in relation to a person who is driving a goods vehicle on a journey to which Council Regulation (EEC) No. 3820/85 of 20th December 1985 [*q.v.*], on the harmonisation of certain social legislation relating to road transport applies, the requirements of Article 5(1)(b) (minimum ages for goods vehicle drivers) of that Regulation;

    (ii) in relation to a person who is driving a goods vehicle on a journey to which the European Agreement concerning the work of crews engaged in International Road Transport (AETR) signed at Geneva on 25th March 1971 [*q.v.*] applies, the requirements of Article 5(1)(b) (conditions to be fulfilled by drivers) of that Agreement;

"*Convention country*" means a country which is not [an EEA State] nor a party to the aforementioned European Agreement but is a party to the Convention on Road Traffic concluded at Geneva in the year 1949 [*Cmnd. 7991*], or the International Convention relative to Motor Traffic concluded at Paris in the year 1926 [*Cmnd. 3510*].

(5) This Article shall not authorise a person to drive a motor vehicle of any class if, in consequence of a conviction or of the order of a court, he is disqualified for holding or obtaining a driving licence under Part III of the Road Traffic Act 1988 [*q.v.*].

(6) The Secretary of State may by order contained in a statutory instrument withdraw the right conferred by paragraph (1)(b), (1)(c), (2)(b) or (3) of this Article, or any two or more of those rights either in the case of all domestic driving permits, British Forces (BFG) driving licences or British Forces (BFG) public service vehicle driving licences or in the case of such permits or licences of a description specified in the order or held by persons of a description so specified.

(7) In this Article—

"*Convention driving permit*" means a driving permit in the form A in Schedule 1 to this Order issued under the authority of a country outside the United Kingdom; whether or not that country is a party to the Convention on Road Traffic concluded at Geneva in the year 1949 [to a person who has given proof of his competence to drive], or a driving permit in the form B in the said Schedule issued under the authority of a country outside the United Kingdom which is a party to the International Convention relative to Motor Traffic concluded at Paris in the year 1926 but not to the Convention of 1949 [to a person who has given proof of his competence to drive];

"*domestic driving permit*" in relation to a country outside the United Kingdom means a document issued under the law of that country [to a person who has given proof of his competence to drive] and authorising the holder to drive motor vehicles, or a specified class of motor vehicles, in that country, and includes a driving permit issued [to such a person] by the armed forces of any country outside the United Kingdom for use in some other country outside the United Kingdom [but does not include a Community licence (within the meaning of Part III of the Road Traffic Act 1988)];

"*British Forces (BFG) driving licence*" means a driving licence issued in Germany to members of the British Forces or of the civilian component thereof or to the dependants of such members by the British authorities in that country in such a form and in accordance with such licensing system as may from time to time be approved by those authorities; and "*British Forces (BFG) public service vehicle driving licence*" means any such driving licence authorising the driving of public service vehicles of any class;

"*dependants*" in relation to such a member of the British Forces or the civilian component thereof, means any of the following persons, namely—

(a) the wife or husband of that member; and

(b) any other person wholly or mainly maintained by him or in his custody, charge or care; and

["*EEA Agreement*" means the Agreement on the European Economic Area signed at Oporto on 2nd May 1992 as adjusted by the Protocol signed at Brussels on 17th March 1993;]

["*EEA State*" means a State which is a Contracting Party to the EEA Agreement;]

"*public service vehicle*" has the same meaning as in the Public Passenger Vehicles Act 1981 [*q.v.*].

[and "*large goods vehicle*", "*passenger-carrying vehicle*", "*large goods vehicle driver's licence*" and "*passenger-carrying vehicle driver's licence*" have the same meaning as in Part IV of the Road Traffic Act 1988 [*q.v.*]]

(8) The provisions of this Article which authorise the holder of a permit or a licence to drive a vehicle during a specified period shall not be construed as authorising the driving of a vehicle at a time when the permit or the licence has ceased to be valid.]

[Article 2 is printed as substituted by S.I. 1989 No. 993, art.4, and as subsequently amended by S.I.   **B10.05**
1991 No. 771; S.I. 1996 Nos 1929 and 1974.

As from a date to be announced, article 2 will be amended by the Motor Vehicles (International Circulation) (Amendment) Order 1989 (S.I. 1989 No. 993), art.6 (q.v.).

As to the European Economic Area, see the note to Regulation (EEC) 3820/85 below.]

[3.—(1) It shall be lawful—   **B10.06**

  (a) for a member of a visiting force of a country to which Part I of the Visiting Forces Act 1952, for the time being applies who holds a driving permit issued under the law of any part of the sending country or issued by the service authorities of the visiting force, or

  (b) for a member of a civilian component of such a visiting force who holds such a driving permit, or

  (c) for a dependant of any such member of a visiting force or of a civilian component thereof who holds such a driving permit,

to drive, or for any person to cause or permit any such person to drive, in Great Britain, a motor vehicle of any class . . . which he is authorised by that permit to drive, notwithstanding that he is not the holder of a driving licence under Part III of the Road Traffic Act 1988 [*q.v.*].

(2) This Article shall not authorise a person to drive a motor vehicle of any class if, in consequence of a conviction or of the order of a court, he is disqualified for holding or obtaining a driving licence under Part III of the Road Traffic Act 1988.

(3) Nothing in this Article shall authorise any person to drive, or any person to cause or permit any other person to drive, a vehicle of any class at a time when he is disqualified by virtue of section 101 of the Road Traffic Act 1988 (persons under age) [*q.v.*], for holding or obtaining a driving licence authorising him to drive vehicles of that class.

(4) The interpretative provisions of the Visiting Forces Act 1952 shall apply for the interpretation of this Article and "*dependant*", in relation to a member of any such visiting force or a civilian component thereof, means any of the following persons namely—

  (a) the wife or husband of that member; and

  (b) any other person wholly or mainly maintained by him or in his custody, charge or care.]

[Article 3 is printed as substituted by S.I. 1989 No. 993, art.4, and as subsequently amended by S.I.   **B10.07**
1991 No. 771; S.I. 1996 No. 1929.

As to persons who are members of visiting forces, see Vol. 1, 2.36.]

4. Schedule 3 to this Order shall have effect as respects the driving permits referred to   **B10.08**
in Articles 2 and 3 of this Order.

5. Excise exemption and documents for vehicles brought temporarily into [United Kingdom]

(1) The next following paragraph shall apply to a vehicle brought temporarily into   **B10.09**
[United Kingdom] by a person resident outside the United Kingdom if the person bringing that vehicle into [United Kingdom]—

  (a) satisfies a registration authority that he is resident outside the United Kingdom and that the vehicle is only temporarily in [United Kingdom], and

(b) complies with any regulations made under paragraph (4) of this Article.

[(2) A vehicle to which this paragraph applies, and to which the temporary importation arrangements referred to in the Council Regulation on temporary importation from third countries do not apply and which would, but for this Order, be chargeable with excise duty under the Excise Act, shall be exempt from any duty of excise under that Act to the following extent,—

(a) in the case of a vehicle to which the Council Directive on the temporary importation of a private vehicle from another member State applies, the vehicle shall be exempt from excise duty if its importation is in accordance with the provisions of that Directive and it shall continue to be so exempt for as long as those provisions continue to be satisfied;

(b) in a case of a vehicle being used for, or in connection with,—

   (i) international carriage within the scope of the Council Regulation on common rules for the international carriage of passengers by coach and bus or the Council Regulation on access to the market in the carriage of goods within the Community, or

   (ii) a cabotage transport operation within the scope of the Council Regulation on passenger transport cabotage or the Council Regulation on goods transport cabotage, or

   (iii) a type of carriage which is exempt from any Community authorisation and from any carriage authorisation under the First Council Directive on the establishment of common rules for certain types of carriage of goods by road,

   the vehicle shall be exempt from excise duty if and so long as the vehicle is being so used in accordance with whichever of those instruments is applicable to the use of the vehicle.]

(3) A vehicle registered in the Isle of Man and brought temporarily into [United Kingdom] by a person resident outside the United Kingdom shall be exempt from any duty of excise under the Excise Act for a period not exceeding one year from the date of importation, if the person bringing that vehicle into [United Kingdom]—

(a) satisfies a registration authority that he is resident outside the United Kingdom and that the vehicle is only temporarily in [United Kingdom], and

(b) complies with any regulations made under paragraph (4) of this Article.

(4) The Secretary of State may by regulations provide—

(a) for the furnishing to a registration authority by a person who imports a vehicle to which either of the two last preceding paragraphs applies of such particulars as may be prescribed, and

[(b) for the recording by a registration authority of any particulars which the Secretary of State may by the regulations direct to be recorded, and for the manner of such recording, and for the making of any such particulars available for use by such persons as may be specified in the regulations on payment, in such cases as may be so specified, of such fee as may be prescribed, and]

(c) for the production to a registration authority of prescribed documents, and

(d) for the registration of vehicles which by virtue of this Article are exempt from excise duty and for the assignment of registration marks to, and for the issue of registration cards for, such vehicles.

(5) The following provisions of the Excise Act, that is to say:—

(a) [paragraphs (e), (f) and (h) of section 22(1) of] the Excise Act (which enable the Secretary of State to make regulations as respects registration books for vehicles in respect of which excise licences are issued), and

(b) [section 23(4) of the Excise Act] (which enables the Secretary of State to make regulations as to the display on a vehicle of the registration mark assigned to it), and

(c) [section 44 of the Excise Act] (which relates to forgery of licences, registration marks or registration documents),

shall apply in relation to a registration card issued, or a registration mark assigned, in pursuance of this Article as they apply in relation to a registration book or registration document issued, or a registration mark assigned, under the Excise Act.

(6) If regulations under this Article provide for the assignment of a registration mark on production of some document relating to a vehicle which is exempt from excise duty by virtue of this Article, then [paragraphs (e) and (f) of section 22(1) of the Excise Act] shall apply in relation to that document so as to authorise the Secretary of State to make regulations under that section requiring the production of that document for inspection by persons of classes prescribed by regulations made under that section.

(7) [Paragraphs (e) and (f) of section 22(1), section 23(4) and section 44] of the Excise Act shall, in [United Kingdom], apply in like manner in relation to a registration card issued, or a registration mark assigned, in pursuance of provisions corresponding to paragraph (4) of this Article in Northern Ireland.

(8) In relation to a motor vehicle brought temporarily into [United Kingdom] by a person resident outside the United Kingdom, references in [section 23] of the Excise Act and in [sections 22(1) and 23(4)] thereof to registration marks shall, where appropriate, include references to nationality signs.

(9) In this Article—

[*"The First Council Directive on the establishment of common rules for certain types of carriage of goods by road"* means the First Council Directive of 23rd July 1962 on the establishment of common rules for certain types of carriage of goods by road [*O.J. No. L70, August 6, 1962, p. 2005, as amended*];]

[*"the Council Directive on the temporary importation of a private vehicle from another member State"* means Council Directive (EEC) No. 83/182 of 28th March 1983 on tax exemptions within the community for certain means of transport temporarily imported into one Member State from another [*O.J. No. L105, April 23, 1983, p. 59*];]

[*"the Council Regulation on temporary importation from third countries"* means Council Regulation (EEC) No. 1855/89 of 14th June 1989 on the temporary importation of means of transport [*O.J. No. L186, June 30, 1989, p. 8*];]

[*"the Council Regulation on common rules for the international carriage of passengers by coach and bus"* means Council Regulation (EEC) No. 684/92 of 16th March 1992 on common rules for the international carriage of passengers by coach and bus [*q.v.*];]

[*"the Council Regulation on access to the market in the carriage of goods within the Community"* means Council Regulation (EEC) No. 881/92 of 26th March 1992 on access to the market in the carriage of goods by road within the Community to or from the territory of a Member State or passing across the territory of one or more Member States [*q.v.*];]

[*"the Council Regulation on passenger transport cabotage"* means Council Regulation (EEC) No. 2454/92 of 23rd July 1992 laying down conditions under which non-resident carriers may operate national road passenger transport services within a Member State [*q.v.*];]

[*"the Council Regulation on goods transport cabotage"* means Council Regulation (EEC) No. 3118/93 of 25th October 1993 laying down conditions under which non-resident carriers may operate national road haulage services within a Member State [*q.v.*] as it has effect in accordance with Council Regulation (EC) No. 3315/94 of 22nd December 1994;]

"*the Excise Act*" means [the Vehicle Excise and Registration Act 1994];

"*the date of importation*", in relation to a vehicle, means the date on which that vehicle was last brought into the United Kingdom;

["*registration authority*" means the Automobile Association, the Royal Automobile Club, the Royal Scottish Automobile Club, or the Secretary of State;]

and references to registration marks shall, where appropriate, include references to nationality signs.

B10.10   [(10) *[Applies to vehicles imported into Northern Ireland.]*]

B10.11   *[Article 5 is printed as amended by S.I. 1985 No. 459; S.I. 1991 No. 1727; S.I. 1996 No. 1929.]*

B10.12   **5A.** *[Revoked by S.I. 1996 No. 1929.]*

6.—(1) An application under Part V of the Transport Act 1968 for an operator's licence for a motor vehicle or trailer brought temporarily into Great Britain by a person resident outside the United Kingdom shall be made to the licensing authority for the purpose of the said Part V for the area where the vehicle is landed.

(2) Regulations made or having effect as if made, under sections 68–82 (provisions as to lighting of vehicles) of the Road Traffic Act 1972, may, either wholly or partially, and subject to any conditions, vary or grant exemptions from, the requirements of those sections in the case of motor vehicles or trailers brought temporarily into Great Britain by persons resident outside the United Kingdom or in the case of any class of such vehicles.

B10.13   *[Sections 68–80 and 81(1) of the Road Traffic Act 1972 were repealed by the Road Traffic Act 1974, s.24(3) and Sched. 7. Regulations relating to vehicle lighting are now principally made under section 41 of the Road Traffic Act 1988.]*

7. Interpretation, repeals, citation and commencement

B10.14   (1) In this Order—

"*the Secretary of State*" means [the Secretary of State for the Environment, Transport and the Regions];

"*prescribed*" means prescribed by regulations made by the Secretary of State.

(2) The Interpretation Act [1978] shall apply for the interpretation of this Order (except as provided by the next following paragraph of this Article) as it applies for the interpretation of an Act of Parliament and as if for the purposes of [sections 16(1) and 17(2)(a)] of that Act this Order (except as aforesaid) was an Act of Parliament and the Orders revoked by Article 8(1) of this Order were Acts of Parliament thereby repealed.

(3) *[Applies to Northern Ireland.]*

(4) Any reference in this Order to any enactment shall be taken as a reference to that enactment as amended by or under any other enactment; and any reference to an enactment which has effect subject to modifications specified in an enactment shall, when those modifications cease to have effect, then be construed as a reference to the first mentioned enactment as having effect without those modifications.

B10.15   *[Article 7 is printed as amended by the Secretary of State for Transport Order 1976 (S.I. 1976 No. 1775); the Interpretation Act 1978, s.17(2)(a); the Minister of Transport Order 1979 (S.I. 1979 No. 571); the Transfer of Functions (Transport) Order 1981 (S.I. 1981 No. 238); the Secretary of State for the Environment, Transport and the Regions Order 1997 (S.I. 1997 No. 2971).]*

*   *   *

SCHEDULE 1   Article 1

A

FORM OF INTERNATIONAL DRIVING PERMIT UNDER   **B10.16**
CONVENTION OF 1949

Page 1

** In a permit issued
by some other country
the name of that
country will appear
instead and pages 1
and 2 will be drawn
up in the language of
that country.*

United Kingdom of Great Britain and Northern Ireland*
International Motor Traffic

INTERNATIONAL DRIVING PERMIT
Convention on International Road Traffic of 1949.

Issued at ....

Date ....

Signature or seal of issuing authority.

Seal
or stamp
of
authority

Page 2

This permit is valid in the territory of all the Contracting States, with the exception of the territory of the Contracting State where issued, for the period of one year from the date of issue, for the driving of vehicles included in the category or categories mentioned on the last page of this permit.

List of Contracting States (optional)

It is understood that this permit shall in no way affect the obligation of the holder to conform strictly to the laws and regulations relating to residence or to the exercise of a profession which are in force in each country through which he travels.

Form of International Driving Permit under Convention of 1949

PART I Las

Particulars concerning the Driver:	Surname	1
	Other names*	2
	Place of birth**	3
	Date of birth***	4
	Permanent place of residence	5
Vehicles for which the permit is valid:		

Motor cycles, with or without a sidecar, invalid carriages and three-wheeled motor vehicles with an unladen weight not exceeding 400 kg (900 lbs.).	A
Motor vehicles used for the transport of passengers and comprising, in addition to the driver's seat, at most eight seats, or those used for the transport of goods and having a permissible maximum weight not exceeding 3,500 kg (7,700 lbs.). Vehicles in this category may be coupled with a light trailer.	B
Motor vehicles used for the transport of goods and of which the permissible maximum weight exceeds 3,500 kg (7,700 lbs.). Vehicles in this category may be coupled with a light trailer.	C
Motor vehicles used for the transport of passengers and comprising, in addition to the driver's seat, more than eight seats. Vehicles in this category may be coupled with a light trailer.	D
Motor vehicles of categories B, C or D, as authorised above, with other than a light trailer.	E

'Permissible maximum weight' of a vehicle means the weight of the vehicle and its maximum load when the vehicle is ready for the road.

'Maximum load' means the weight of the load declared permissible by the competent authority of the country of registration of the vehicle.

'Light trailers' shall be those of a permissible maximum weight not exceeding 750 kg (1,650 lbs.).

<div align="center">EXCLUSION</div> Holder of this permit is deprived of the right to drive in (country) .... by reason .... ⬭ Seal or stamp of authority .... Place .... Date .... Signature	Exclusions (countries I–VIII)
Should the above space be already filled, use any other space provided for 'Exclusion'.	

The entire last page (Parts I and II) shall be drawn up in French.

Additional pages shall repeat in other languages the text of Part I of the last page. They shall be drawn up in English, Russian, Chinese and Spanish, and other languages may be added.

Form of International Driving Permit under Convention of 1949

Page   PART II

1 ....
2 ....
3 ....
4 ....
5 ....

A   (Seal or stamp of authority)

B   (Seal or stamp of authority)

C   (Seal or stamp of authority)

D   (Seal or stamp of authority)

E   (Seal or stamp of authority)

Photograph

(Seal or stamp of authority)

....
Signature of holder****

EXCLUSIONS
(countries)

I ....   V ....

II ....   VI ....

III ....   VII ....

IV ....   VIII ....

* Father's or husband's name may be inserted.
** If known.
*** Or approximate age on date of issue.
**** Or thumb impression.

B

FORM OF INTERNATIONAL DRIVING PERMIT UNDER
CONVENTION OF 1926

Page 1

* In a permit issued by some other country the name of that country will appear instead and the permit will be drawn up in the language of that country.

United Kingdom of Great Britain and Northern Ireland*

International Motor Traffic

INTERNATIONAL DRIVING PERMIT

International Convention of April 24th, 1926

ISSUE OF PERMIT

Issued at ....

Date ....

Seal of authority

(Signature of issuing authority)

Page 2

** This should be a reference to the last page of the permit.

The present permit is valid in the territory of all the undermentioned contracting States for the period of one year from the date of issue for the driving of vehicles included in the category or categories mentioned on p. **

Here insert list of Contracting States

It is understood that this permit in no way diminishes the obligation of the holder to conform strictly to the laws and regulations relating to residence or to the exercise of a profession which are in force in each country through which he travels.

Page 3

PARTICULARS CONCERNING THE DRIVER

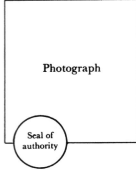

Photograph

Seal of authority

Surname .... (1)

Other names .... (2)

Place of birth .... (3)

Date of birth .... (4)

Home address .... (5)

Form of International Driving Permit under Convention of 1926
Page 4
(Name of country)
EXCLUSION

M. (surname and other names) ....
authorised as above by the authority of (country) ....
is deprived of the right to drive in (country) ....
by reason of ....
....
....

Seal of
authority

Place ....

Date ....

Signature ....

Page 5 and the following pages should repeat the particulars given on page 3 translated into as many languages as may be necessary to enable the International Permit to be used in all the Contracting States mentioned on page 2.

Here begin last page

A(1)	B(2)	C(3)
Seal of authority	Seal of authority	Seal of authority

(1) A.—Motor vehicles of which the laden weight does not exceed—
3,500 kilog.
(*In all languages.*)

(2) B.—Motor vehicles of which the laden weight exceeds—
3,500 kilog.
(*In all languages.*)

(3) C.—Motor cycles, with or without side-car.
(*In all languages.*)

(1) ....

(2) ....

(3) ....

(4) ....

(5) ....

D

B10.18   FORM OF INTERNATIONAL CERTIFICATE FOR MOTOR VEHICLES
UNDER CONVENTION OF 1926

Page 1

United Kingdom of Great Britain and Northern Ireland*

International Motor Traffic

INTERNATIONAL CERTIFICATE FOR MOTOR VEHICLES

International Convention of April 24th, 1926

———

ISSUE OF CERTIFICATE

Place ....

Date ....

(Seal
of
authority)   *Signature of issuing authority.*

* *In a permit issued by some other country the name of that country will appear instead and the permit will be drawn up in the language of that country.*

Page 2

This certificate is valid, in the territory of all the undermentioned contracting States, for the period of one year from the date of issue.

Here insert list of contracting States

Page 3

Owner	Surname	1
or	Other names	2
Holder	Home address	3
Class of vehicle		4
Name of maker of chassis		5
Type of chassis		6
Serial number of type or maker's number of chassis		7
Engine	Number of cylinders	8
	Engine number	9
	Stroke	10
	Bore	11
	Horse-power	12
Body	Shape ... ...:	13
	Colour	14
	Number of seats	15
Weight of car unladen (in kilos)		16
Weight of car fully laden (in kilos) if exceeding 3,500 kilos		17
Identification mark on the plates		18

Additional pages should repeat the particulars on page 3 translated into as many languages as may be necessary to enable the certificate to be used in all the contracting States mentioned on page 2 and these should be followed by pages for entrance and exit visas.

SCHEDULE 2

[Revoked by S.I. 1996 No. 1929.]

B10.19

SCHEDULE 3

Article 4

VISITORS' DRIVING PERMITS

1. In this Schedule *"driving permit"* means a driving permit which by virtue of this Order **B10.20** authorises a person to drive a motor vehicle without holding a driving licence under [Part III of the Road Traffic Act 1988]; [*"Convention driving permit"* has the meaning assigned it by article 2(7) of this Order]; and *"driving licence"* means a driving licence under the said [Part III].

2.—(1) A court by whom the holder of a driving permit is convicted shall— **B10.21**

(a) if in consequence of the conviction or of the order of the court he is disqualified for holding or obtaining a driving licence, or

(b) if the court orders particulars of the conviction to be endorsed on any driving licence held by him,

send particulars of the conviction to the Secretary of State.

(2) A court shall in no circumstances enter any particulars in a driving permit.

3.—(1) The holder of a driving permit disqualified in consequence of a conviction or of **B10.22** the order of a court for holding or obtaining a driving licence shall, if so required by the court, produce his driving permit within five days, or such longer time as the court may determine, and the court shall forward it to the Secretary of State.

[(2) The Secretary of State on receiving a permit forwarded under the foregoing sub-paragraph, shall—

(a) retain the permit until the disqualification ceases to have effect or until the holder leaves Great Britain, whichever is the earlier;

(b) send the holder's name and address, together with the particulars of the disqualification, to the authority by whom the permit was issued; and

(c) if the permit is a Convention driving permit, record the particulars of the disqualification on the permit.]

(3) A person failing to produce a driving permit in compliance with this paragraph shall be guilty of an offence which shall be treated for the purposes of [section 9 of the Road Traffic Offenders Act 1988] and of [Part I of Schedule 2 thereto as an offence against the provision specified in column 1 of that Part as section 27] and he shall be liable to be prosecuted and punished accordingly.

4.—(1) A court, on ordering the removal under [section 42(2) of the Road Traffic **B10.23** Offenders Act 1988] of a disqualification for holding or obtaining a driving licence, shall, if it appears that particulars of the disqualification have been forwarded to the Secretary of State under paragraph 2 of this Schedule, cause particulars of the order also to be forwarded to him . . .

[(2) The Secretary of State, on receiving particulars of a court order removing such a disqualification, shall—

(a) in the case of a permit on which particulars of a disqualification were recorded in accordance with paragraph 3(2)(c) of this Schedule, enter on the permit particulars of the order removing the disqualification;

(b) send the particulars of the order to the authority by whom the permit was issued; and

(c) return the permit to the holder.]

B10.24   **5.**—(1) In the following provisions of [the Road Traffic Act 1988], references to a driving licence shall include references to a driving permit.

(2) The said provisions are—

(a) [subsections (1) and (6) of section 164 (which authorises a police constable to require the production of a driving licence and in certain cases statement of date of birth by a person who is, or in certain circumstances has been, driving a vehicle),

(b) *[Lapsed.]*

(c) subsections (1) and (2) of section [173] (which relate to the use of a driving licence by a person other than the holder and to forgery of such a licence).

B10.25   *[Schedule 3 is printed as amended by the Interpretation Act 1978, s.17(2)(a) (cf. article 7(2) above); S.I. 1989 No. 993, art.2.]*

SCHEDULE 4

B10.26   REVOCATIONS

[Omitted.]

The 70 miles per hour, 60 miles per hour and 50 miles per hour (Temporary Speed Limit) Order 1977

[This order was varied by the 70 miles per hour, 60 miles per hour and 50 miles per hour (Temporary Speed Limit) (Variation) Order 1978 with effect from August 23, 1978. This order, which would otherwise have expired on November 30, 1978, was continued in force indefinitely by the 70 miles per hour (Temporary Speed Limit) (Continuation) Order 1978 (S.I. 1978 No. 1548).]

B11.01

*   *   *

2. Subject to Article 4 below, no person shall during the period of this Order drive a motor vehicle—   **B11.02**

(a) at a speed exceeding 50 miles per hour on the lengths of dual carriageway road specified in Part I of Schedule 1 to this Order,

(b) at a speed exceeding 60 miles per hour on the lengths of dual carriageway road specified in Schedule 2 to this Order, or

(c) at a speed exceeding 70 miles per hour on any other length of dual carriageway road.

3. Subject to Article 4 below, no person shall during the period of this Order drive a motor vehicle—   **B11.03**

(a) at a speed exceeding 50 miles per hour on the lengths of single carriageway road specified in Part II of Schedule 1 to this Order, or

(b) at a speed exceeding 60 miles per hour on any length of single carriageway road.

4. Nothing in this Order shall prohibit a person from driving a motor vehicle on a length of road at a speed exceeding that which would apply to that length under Article 2 or 3 above in a case where a higher speed limit is, after the coming into operation of this Order, prescribed in relation to that length by means of an Order under [section 84 of the Road Traffic Regulation Act 1984].   **B11.04**

[Article 4 is printed as amended by the Road Traffic Regulation Act 1984, s.144(1) and Sched. 10, para.2.]   **B11.05**

SCHEDULE 1

PART I

LENGTHS OF DUAL CARRIAGEWAY ROAD FOR WHICH A 50 MILES PER HOUR SPEED LIMIT IS
PRESCRIBED

Any dual carriageway sections of any of the lengths of road described in Part II of this Schedule.   **B11.06**

PART II

LENGTHS OF SINGLE CARRIAGEWAY ROAD FOR WHICH A 50 MILES PER HOUR SPEED LIMIT IS
PRESCRIBED

B11.07 *[In certain instances the lengths of road described below in this Part of this Schedule include short sections of dual carriageway road. These sections are covered by Part I of this Schedule.]*

A *Trunk Roads*

*   *   *

B *Other Roads*

*   *   *

SCHEDULE 2

B11.08   LENGTHS OF DUAL CARRIAGEWAY ROAD FOR WHICH A 60 MILES PER HOUR SPEED LIMIT
IS PRESCRIBED

A *Trunk Roads*

*   *   *

B *Other Roads*

*   *   *

The Motor Vehicles (Authorisation of Special Types) General Order 1979

(S.I. 1979 No. 1198)

[The text of this order is printed as amended by:

correction slip (October 1979);

the Motor Vehicles (Authorisation of Special Types) (Amendment) Order 1981 (S.I. 1981 No. 1664) (December 29, 1981);

the Motor Vehicles (Authorisation of Special Types) (Amendment) Order 1984 (S.I. 1984 No. 1810) (March 1, 1984);

the Motor Vehicles (Authorisation of Special Types) (Amendment) Order 1985 (S.I. 1985 No. 745) (May 31, 1985);

the Motor Vehicles (Authorisation of Special Types) (Amendment) Order 1986 (S.I. 1986 No. 313) (April 1, 1986);

the Motor Vehicles (Authorisation of Special Types) (Amendment) Order 1987 (S.I. 1987 No. 1327) (January 1, 1988);

the Motor Vehicles (Authorisation of Special Types) (Amendment) (No. 2) Order 1987 (S.I. 1987 No. 2161) (January 1, 1988);

the Motor Vehicles (Authorisation of Special Types) (Amendment) Order 1989 (S.I. 1989 No. 1662) (October 1, 1989);

the Motor Vehicles (Authorisation of Special Types) (Amendment) Order 1995 (S.I. 1995 No. 3052) (January 1, 1996);

the Motor Vehicles (Authorisation of Special Types) (Amendment) Order 1998 (S.I. 1998 No. 2249) (September 18, 1998); and

the Motor Vehicles (Authorisation of Special Types) (Amendment) (No. 2) Order 1998 (S.I. 1998 No. 2284) (December 1, 1998).

As to the application of S.I. 1987 Nos 1327 and 2161, reference should be made to the Motor Vehicles (Authorisation of Special Types) (Amendment) (No. 2) Order 1987 (S.I. 1987 No. 2161), art.6 below.

The amending orders are referred to in the notes to the principal order only by their years and numbers. The dates referred to above are the dates on which the amending orders came into force.]

Editorial note. This order sets out the authorisation to use vehicles in specified circumstances **B12.02** which do not comply with all the requirements of the Construction and Use Regulations. The order was made when the Motor Vehicles (Construction and Use) (Track Laying Vehicles) Regulations 1955 (S.I. 1955 No. 990) and the Motor Vehicles (Construction and Use) Regulations 1978 (S.I. 1978 No. 1017) were in force and the order refers expressly to provisions of both sets of regulations. The Road Vehicles (Construction and Use) Regulations 1986 (S.I. 1986 No. 1078), below, have consolidated both the 1955 and the 1978 Regulations and many amending regulations. The 1986 Regulations have a new presentation with more extensive use of tabulations, a more logical arrangement of material and simplified language. In consequence, it is not always possible to correlate references in this order precisely with provisions in the 1986 Regulations. Until the order is formally amended, therefore, care should be exercised in relating any provision of the order (other than articles 16, 17A and 18 (*q.v.*)) to any specific provision in the 1986 Regulations; whilst every care has been taken to indicate the latter provisions with such precision as is possible, in any case of doubt reference should be made to the original provisions referred to in the order.

ARRANGEMENT OF THE ORDER

PART I

PRELIMINARY

PART II

MISCELLANEOUS VEHICLES

PART III

ABNORMAL INDIVISIBLE LOADS, ENGINEERING PLANT AND OTHER VEHICLES CARRYING WIDE LOADS

PART I

PRELIMINARY

1. Commencement and citation   *[Omitted.]*   **B12.04**

2. Revocation   *[Omitted.]*

3. Interpretation

(1) In this Order, unless the context otherwise requires, the following expressions have **B12.05** the following meanings—

"abnormal indivisible load" means a load—

   (a) which cannot without undue expense or risk of damage be divided into two or more loads for the purpose of carriage on roads, and

   (b) which—

      (i) owing to its dimensions, cannot be carried by a heavy motor car or trailer or a combination of a heavy motor car and trailer complying in all respects with the requirements of the Construction and Use Regulations, or

      [(ii) owing to its weight, cannot be carried by a heavy motor car or trailer or a combination of a heavy motor car and trailer having a total laden weight of not more than—

         (a) prior to 1st October 1989, 32,520 kilograms, and
         (b) on or after 1st October 1989, 38,000 kilograms,

      and complying in all respects with the requirements of the Construction and Use Regulations;]

[*"agricultural motor vehicle"*, *"agricultural trailer"* and *"agricultural trailed appliance"* have the meanings respectively given to those expressions in [Regulation 3(2)] of the Construction and Use Regulations;]

"articulated vehicle", . . . *"locomotive"*, *"overall length"*, *"overall width"*, *"overhang"*, *"registered"*, *"straddle carrier"*, *"track laying"*, and *"wheeled"* have the same meanings respectively as in the Construction and Use Regulations;

"bank holiday" means a day which is a bank holiday under the Banking and Financial Dealings Act 1971;

"*chief officer of police*" and "*police area*", in relation to England and Wales, have respectively the same meanings as in the Police Act 1964 . . . ;

"*controlled by a pedestrian*" has the same meaning as in [section 189(2) of the Road Traffic Act 1988 [*q.v.*];]

"*Construction and Use Regulations*" means the [Road Vehicles (Construction and Use) Regulations 1986] [*S.I. 1986 No. 1078, q.v.*];

"*day*" means any day except a bank holiday, Christmas Day, Good Friday, Sunday or Saturday;

["*dual carriageway road*" has the same meaning as in Schedule 6 to the Road Traffic Regulation Act 1984 [*q.v.*];]

"*engineering plant*" means—

   (a) moveable plant or equipment which consists of a motor vehicle or trailer specially designed and constructed for the special purposes of engineering operations, and which cannot, owing to the requirements of those purposes, comply in all respects with the requirements of the Construction and Use Regulations . . . and which is not constructed primarily to carry a load other than excavated material raised from the ground by apparatus on the motor vehicle or trailer or materials which the vehicle or trailer is specially designed to treat while carried thereon, or

   (b) a mobile crane which does not comply in all respects with the requirements of the Construction and Use Regulations . . . ;

["*hours of darkness*" means the time between half an hour after sunset and half an hour before sunrise;]

"*lateral projection*", "*forward projection*" and "*rearward projection*" have the same meanings respectively as in [Regulation 81] of the Construction and Use Regulations and references in this Order to a special appliance or apparatus in relation to a vehicle, to a forward projection or a rearward projection in relation to a vehicle, to the distance between vehicles in relation to vehicles carrying a load, and to a combination of vehicles in relation to a motor vehicle which is drawing one or more trailers, shall be construed respectively in the same manner as is provided in the said [Regulation 81] for the purposes of [Regulation 82] of the said Regulations, and the provisions of sub-paragraphs [(b), (e), (h), (i) and (j)] of the said [Regulation 81] shall apply for the purposes of this Order as they apply for the purposes of the said [Regulations 81 and 82];

["*motorway*" has the same meaning as in regulation 3(1) of the Motorways Traffic (England and Wales) Regulations 1982 [*q.v.*], as regards England and Wales . . . ;]

"*the Minister*" means the Minister of Transport;

. . .

"*tractor*" means a motor tractor.

(2) Any reference in this Order to a numbered Article or Schedule is a reference to the Article or Schedule bearing that number in this Order except where otherwise expressly provided.

B12.06   *[Article 3 is printed as amended by the Interpretation Act 1978, ss.17(2)(a) and 23(1); S.I. 1984 No. 1810; S.I. 1987 Nos 1327 and 2161.*

For the Banking and Financial Dealings Act 1971, Sched. 1, see the note to the Road Vehicles (Construction and Use) Regulations 1986 (S.I. 1986 No. 1078), Sched. 12, para.1.

The terms "chief officer of police" and "police area" were defined in the Police Act 1964, s.62, as substituted by the Police and Magistrates' Courts Act 1994, s.44 and Sched. 5, para.15; section 62 has, however, been repealed by the Police Act 1996, s.104(2) and Sched. 9, Pt II. See now (by virtue of section 103(2) of and Schedule 8, paragraph 1(4), to the 1996 Act) section 1 of that Act (as amended by the Greater London Authority Act 1999, s.325 and Sched. 27, para.69 (and also ibid., s.423 and Sched. 34, Pt VII)) for the meaning of "police area" and section 101(1) for the meaning of "chief officer of police".

In the definitions of "chief officer of police" and "motorway" words relating expressly and exclusively to Scotland have been omitted.

References to the Minister of Transport refer to the Secretary of State for the Environment, Transport and the Regions; Transfer of Functions (Transport) Order 1981 (S.I. 1981 No. 238) and the Secretary of State for the Environment, Transport and the Regions Order 1997 (S.I. 1997 No. 2971).]

4. Speed limits

Nothing in this Order relating to the speed of vehicles shall be taken to authorise any speed which is in excess of any other speed limit imposed by or under any enactment.   **B12.07**

PART II

MISCELLANEOUS VEHICLES

5. Track laying vehicles (including those used for launching lifeboats)

The Minister authorises the use on roads of track laying motor vehicles and track laying trailers notwithstanding that such vehicles do not comply in all respects with the requirements of the Construction and Use Regulations . . . subject to the following conditions:—   **B12.08**

(1)(a) the vehicle shall be used only for the purpose of

    (i) demonstration, or

    (ii) enabling it to proceed to the nearest suitable railway station for conveyance to a port for shipment or to proceed to a port for shipment from a place in the immediate vicinity of that port where suitable railway facilities are not available,

(b) before the vehicle is so used the consent of every highway authority or every person responsible for the maintenance and repair of any road on which it is proposed that the vehicle shall be used shall in each case be obtained in writing, and

(c) the vehicle shall not be used for the carriage of goods or burden for hire or reward; or

[In condition (b) above, the expression *"person responsible for the maintenance and repair of any road"* includes any person who is so responsible to a highway authority pursuant to an agreement with that authority.]

(2) The vehicle shall be used only for drawing or in connection with the launching of lifeboats which are the property of the Royal National Lifeboat Institution.

[Article 5 is printed as amended by the Interpretation Act 1978, ss.17(2)(a) and 23(1); S.I. 1986 No. 313.]   **B12.09**

6. Naval, military, air force and aviation vehicles

The Minister authorises the use on roads of the vehicles specified in Column 1 of Schedule 1 notwithstanding that such vehicles do not comply in all respects with the requirements of the Regulations of the Construction and Use Regulations . . . specified opposite thereto in Column 2 of Schedule 1, subject to the vehicles being the property of, or for the time being under the control of, the persons respectively specified opposite thereto in Column 3 of Schedule 1.   **B12.10**

[Article 6 is printed as amended by the Interpretation Act 1978, ss.17(2)(a) and 23(1).]   **B12.11**

7. Grass cutting machines and hedge trimmers

The Minister authorises the use on roads of [motor vehicles] constructed or adapted for use as grass cutters or hedge trimmers (not, in either case, being vehicles controlled by a pedestrian) notwithstanding that such vehicles do not comply with [Regulations 8 or 82] of the Construction and Use Regulations subject to the following conditions:—   **B12.12**

(a) all other relevant requirements of the Construction and Use Regulations shall be complied with;

(b) the overall width of the vehicle [together with any equipment mounted on it], except when it is actually cutting grass or trimming hedges, shall not exceed [2.55] metres; and

(c) except where the vehicle is actually engaged in such operations, all cutting and trimming blades which form part of the machinery fitted to [or mounted on] the vehicle shall be effectively guarded so that no danger is caused or is likely to be caused to any person.

B12.13   *[Article 7 is printed as amended by the Interpretation Act 1972, ss.17(2)(a) and 23(1); S.I. 1984 No. 1810; S.I. 1995 No. 3052.]*

B12.14   **8.**   *[Revoked by S.I. 1984 No. 1810.]*

B12.15   **9.** The Minister authorises the use on roads of trailers constructed or adapted for use as grass cutters or hedge trimmers notwithstanding that such trailers do not comply in all respects with such of the requirements of the Construction and Use Regulations as apply to trailers, subject to the following conditions:—

(a) the requirements of [Regulation 27] of the Construction and Use Regulations, so far as they apply to trailers, shall be complied with;

(b) the unladen weight of the trailer shall not exceed—

   (i) 1020 kilograms if drawn by a locomotive, a motor tractor or a heavy motor car, or

   (ii) 815 kilograms in any other case;

(c) the overall width of the motor vehicle by which the trailer is drawn and, except when it is actually cutting grass or trimming hedges, the overall width of the trailer shall not exceed 2.6 metres;

(d) except when the trailer is actually engaged in such operations, where it is being drawn in such a manner that its longitudinal axis and that of the drawing vehicle are parallel but lie in different vertical planes, the width of road occupied by both vehicles shall not exceed 2.6 metres.

For the purposes of this paragraph, the said width shall be taken as a distance equivalent to the distance which, if both vehicles were treated as if they were one vehicle at a time when the one is drawing the other in the said manner, would fall to be measured as its overall width;

(e) except when the trailer is actually engaged in such operations, all cutting and trimming blades which form part of the machinery fitted to the trailer shall be effectively guarded so that no danger is caused or is likely to be caused to any person; and

(f) the trailer shall not be driven at a speed exceeding 20 miles per hour.

B12.16   *[Article 9 is printed as amended by the Interpretation Act 1978, ss.17(2)(a) and 23(1).]*

10. Pedestrian controlled road maintenance vehicles

B12.17   The Minister authorises the use on roads of motor vehicles constructed or adapted for the gritting of roads, the laying of road markings, the clearing of frost, snow or ice from roads or any other work of maintaining roads, being vehicles controlled by a pedestrian and not constructed or adapted for use or used for the carriage of a driver or passenger, notwithstanding that such vehicles do not comply in all respects with the requirements of [Regulations 16, 18, 23, and 61 of and Schedule 3 to] the Construction and Use Regulations subject to the following conditions:—

(a) all other relevant requirements of the Construction and Use Regulations shall be complied with;

(b) the weight of the vehicle, whether laden or unladen, shall not exceed 410 kilo-grams; and

(c) the vehicle shall be equipped with an efficient braking system capable of being set or with sufficient other means, not being a braking system, whereby it can be brought to a standstill and held stationary.

[Article 10 is printed as amended by the Interpretation Act 1978, ss.17(2)(a) and 23(1).]　　**B12.18**

11. Vehicles used for experiments or trials

The Minister authorises the use on roads of vehicles in or in connection with the conduct **B12.19** of experiments or trials under [section 283 of the Highways Act 1980] notwithstanding that such vehicles do not comply in all respects with the requirements of the Construction and Use Regulations . . .

[Article 11 is printed as amended by the Interpretation Act 1978, ss.17(2)(a) and 23(1).]　　**B12.20**

12. Straddle carriers

The Minister authorises the use on roads of straddle carriers notwithstanding that such **B12.21** vehicles do not comply in all respects with the requirements of [Regulations 8, 11, 18(2) and (3), 22, 45 and 66 of and Schedule 3 to] the Construction and Use Regulations, subject to the following conditions:—

(a) the vehicle shall not be used otherwise than for the purpose of demonstration or in the course of delivery on sale or when proceeding to or returning from a manu-facturer or repairer for the purpose of repair or overhaul and, when so used, shall carry no load other than its necessary gear or equipment:

Provided that a vehicle which does not comply with the said [Regulation 11] may, if it complies with the said [Regulations 8 and 22], be used whether laden or unladen in passing from one part of any private premises to any other part thereof or to other private premises in the immediate neighbourhood;

(b) the vehicle shall not travel at a speed exceeding 12 miles per hour;

(c) the overall width of the vehicle shall not exceed 2.9 metres;

(d) the vehicle shall not be used if the overall length of the vehicle or, where the vehicle is carrying a load, if the overall length of the vehicle together with the length of any forward projection and of any rearward projection of its load exceeds 9.2 metres except with the consent of the chief officer of police of every police area in which it is proposed that the vehicle will be used;

(e) save in so far as the chief officer of police of any police area in which it is proposed that the vehicle will be used dispenses, as respects the use of the vehicle in that area, with any of the requirements contained in this paragraph, the [user] of the vehicle shall, not less than two clear days before such use, apply to the chief officer of police of any such area for his consent to the use of the vehicle, and shall, when making the application, furnish to him particulars of the vehicle concerned, of its overall length, of the length of any forward projection or rearward projection of any load proposed to be carried, and of the roads on which it is proposed that the vehicle will be used; and

(f) all the relevant requirements of the Construction and Use Regulations other than those specified above shall be complied with.

[Article 12 is printed as amended by the Interpretation Act 1978, ss.17(2)(a) and 23(1); S.I. 1987 No. **B12.22** *1327.]*

[13. Agricultural motor vehicles, agricultural trailers and agricultural trailed appliances

B12.23   (1) Subject to the provisions of paragraph (2), the Secretary of State authorises the use on roads of—

     (a) an agricultural motor vehicle,

     (b) an agricultural trailer designed to perform functions, other than the carriage of goods, that necessitate an overall width of [2.55] metres being exceeded, or

     (c) an agricultural trailed appliance,

notwithstanding that the overall width of the vehicle exceeds [2.55] metres if the relevant conditions specified in Schedule 4 are complied with.

     (2) The authorisation specified in paragraph (1) applies only in so far as the width of a vehicle (including an agricultural implement which by virtue of Article 13B is treated as part of the vehicle) cannot, without undue expense or risk of damage, be reduced.]

B12.24   *[Article 13 (together with articles 13A–13C below) was substituted for the original text of article 13 by S.I. 1984 No. 1810. The text of article 13 is printed as subsequently amended by S.I. 1995 No. 3052.]*

[13A. Agricultural motor vehicle towing an off-set agricultural trailer or trailed appliance

B12.25   (1) The Secretary of State authorises the use on roads of an agricultural motor vehicle towing an agricultural trailer or agricultural trailed appliance in such a manner that the longitudinal axis of the motor vehicle and the longitudinal axis of the trailer are parallel but lie in different vertical planes and the width specified in paragraph (2) below exceeds [2.55] metres provided the relevant conditions specified in Schedule 4 are complied with.

     (2) The width referred to in paragraph (1) above is the distance equivalent to the distance which, if both the agricultural motor vehicle and the agricultural trailer or agricultural trailed appliance (when being drawn by the agricultural motor vehicle) are treated as one vehicle, would fall to be measured as its overall width.]

B12.26   *[Article 13A (together with article 13 above, and articles 13B and 13C below) was substituted for the original text of article 13 by S.I. 1984 No. 1810. The text of article 13A is printed as subsequently amended by S.I. 1995 No. 3052.]*

[13B. Provisions supplementary to Articles 13 and 13A

B12.27   For the purposes of Articles 13 and 13A and Schedule 4, an agricultural implement rigidly mounted on an agricultural motor vehicle, an agricultural trailer or an agricultural trailed appliance shall be treated as part of that vehicle, trailer or appliance whether or not—

     (a) the implement is permanently attached thereto, and

     (b) part of the weight of the implement is transmitted to the surface of the road, otherwise than by the wheels or tracks of the motor vehicle, trailer or appliance.]

B12.28   *[Article 13B (together with articles 13 and 13A above, and article 13C below) was substituted for the original text of article 13 by S.I. 1984 No. 1810.]*

[13C. Agricultural motor vehicles, agricultural trailers and agricultural trailed appliances with implements projecting rearwards or forwards

B12.29   (1) The Secretary of State authorises the use on roads of—

     (a) an agricultural motor vehicle,

   (b) an agricultural trailer, and

   (c) an agricultural trailed appliance,

with an agricultural implement rigidly mounted thereon whether or not—

     (i) the implement is permanently attached thereto, and

    (ii) part of the weight of the implement is transmitted to the surface of the road otherwise than by the wheels or tracks of the motor vehicle, trailer or appliance

provided that the requirements mentioned in paragraph (2) are complied with.

  (2) Those requirements are that:—

   (a) if any part of the implement projects rearwards of the rearmost part of the motor vehicle, trailer or appliance by more than a distance specified in an item in column 2 of Part I of Schedule 5 the conditions specified in that item in column 3 are complied with; and

   (b) if any part of the implement projects forwards of the foremost part of the motor vehicle, trailer or appliance by more than a distance specified in an item in column 2 of Part 1 of Schedule 5 the conditions specified in that item in column 3 are complied with.]

[Article 13C (together with articles 13, 13A and 13B above) was substituted for the original text of   **B12.30**
article 13 by S.I. 1984 No. 1810.]

14.   *[Revoked by S.I. 1984 No. 1810.]*   **B12.31**

15. Vehicles for moving excavated material

   The Minister authorises the use on roads of moveable plant or equipment (other than   **B12.32**
engineering plant) being a heavy motor car, trailer or articulated vehicle specially designed and constructed for use in private premises for the primary purpose of moving excavated material and fitted with a tipping body, moving platform or other similar device for discharging its load, and which cannot, owing to the requirements of that purpose, comply in all respects with the requirements of the Construction and Use Regulations, subject to the following conditions:—

   (a) the vehicle shall only be used in proceeding to and from private premises or between private premises and a port in either direction and shall carry no load other than its necessary gear or equipment;

   (b) a heavy motor car not forming part of an articulated vehicle shall not draw any trailer;

   (c) where a trailer is drawn by a motor vehicle the motor vehicle shall not draw any other trailer;

   (d) in a case where the overall width of the vehicle exceeds [5 metres] the conditions specified in Article 24 shall be complied with;

   (e) in the case of a heavy motor car not forming part of an articulated vehicle, and in the case of an articulated vehicle, the sum of the weights transmitted to the road surface by any two wheels in line transversely shall not exceed 22,860 kilograms and the sum of the weights so transmitted by all the wheels shall not exceed 50,800 kilograms;

   (f) in the case of a trailer, whether or not forming part of an articulated vehicle, the provisions of [Regulation 16(4), items 25 to 27 in the table, of and Schedule 3, paragraph 1, items 4(c), 11 and 14 in the table, to] the Construction and Use Regulations shall not apply if the trailer is equipped with an efficient brake or with suitable scotches or similar devices to hold it stationary when necessary;

(g) the overall length of a trailer shall not exceed 8.54 metres and the overall length of an articulated vehicle shall not exceed 13.4 metres;

(h) the vehicle shall not travel on any road, other than a [motorway], at a speed exceeding 12 miles per hour;

(i) every wheel of the vehicle shall be equipped with a pneumatic tyre;

(j) where the overall width of the vehicle exceeds 3.5 metres, at least one person, in addition to the person or persons employed as respects a motor vehicle in driving that vehicle, shall be employed in attending to that vehicle and any load carried thereby and any trailer drawn by that vehicle and any load carried on the trailer and to give warning to the driver of the said motor vehicle and to any other person of any danger likely to be caused to any such other person by reason of the presence of the vehicle or the vehicle and trailer on the road:

Provided that, where three or more vehicles authorised by this Article are travelling together in convoy, it shall be a sufficient compliance with this paragraph if only the foremost and rearmost vehicles in the convoy are attended in the manner prescribed in this paragraph;

(k) save in so far as the chief officer of police of any police area in which it is proposed that the vehicle will be used dispenses, as respects the use of the vehicle in that area, with any of the requirements contained in this paragraph as to length of notice or particulars to be given, the [user] of the vehicle, if its overall width exceeds 2.9 metres, before using it on a road, shall give at least two clear days' notice to the chief officer of police of any such area and such notice shall contain particulars of the vehicle concerned, of its overall width, and of the time, date and route of the proposed journey;

(l) subject to any variation in the time, date or route of the journey which may be directed by any such chief officer of police, the vehicle shall be used only in circumstances which accord with the particulars given in compliance with the foregoing paragraph as to the time, date and route of the journey and only if the overall width of the vehicle does not exceed the width of which particulars have been given as aforesaid;

in the case of the use of a vehicle in respect of which any of the requirements of the Construction and Use Regulations as to the weights of vehicles, whether laden or unladen, or the weights transmitted to the road surface by all or any of the wheels is not complied with, or, where a combination of vehicles is used, if any of the said requirements as to any or all of the vehicles in the combination is not complied with—

(i) save in so far as the highway authority for any road or the bridge authority for any bridge on which it is proposed that the vehicle or, as the case may be, the vehicles will be used dispenses, as respects the use of the vehicle or vehicles on that road or, as the case may be, on that bridge, with the requirements contained in this sub-paragraph as to length of notice or as to the form of notice or the particulars to be given, the [user] of the vehicle or, as the case may be, of the vehicles, before using the vehicle or vehicles on that road or that bridge, shall give to the highway authority for the road and the bridge authority for the bridge at least two clear days' notice in the form and containing the particulars specified in Part I of Schedule 2, and the provisions of Article 26(6) and (7) shall apply as respects any such notice, and

(ii) before using the vehicle or, as the case may be, the vehicles on any road or bridge the [user] of the vehicle or vehicles shall give to the highway authority for the road and to the bridge authority for the bridge an indemnity in the form specified in Part II of Schedule 2, and the provisions of Article 26(6) and (7) shall apply as respects any such indemnity,

and for the purposes of this sub-paragraph references to a combination of vehicles shall be construed in the same manner as is provided in [Regulation 81(g)] of the Construction and Use Regulations [and references to the highway authority for any road and to the bridge authority for any bridge shall be read as including references to any other person responsible for the maintenance and repair of the road or bridge in question pursuant to an agreement with the authority]; and

in a case specified in an item in column 2 of the Table below, all the Construction and Use Regulations shall apply with the exception of the Regulations which are specified opposite to that item in column 3 of that table and, in relation to items 2 and 3, save as provided in paragraph (f) above.

TABLE

1	2	3
Item	Case	Construction and Use Regulations not applicable
1	A heavy motor car not forming part of an articulated vehicle.	[Regulations 8, 16(4), 18(2) and (3), 22, 45, 63, 66, 75, 76, 78 to 80, and Schedule 3].
2	A trailer not forming part of an articulated vehicle.	[Regulations 8, 18(2) and (3), 22, 63 and 66].
3	An articulated vehicle.	[Regulations 7(1), 8, 16(4), 18(2) and (3), 22, 45, 63, 66, 75, 77 to 80, and Schedule 3].

[Article 15 is printed as amended by the Interpretation Act 1978, ss.17(2)(a) and 23(1); S.I. 1986 No. 313; S.I. 1987 No. 1327. See the editorial note on p. 1073.]   **B12.33**

16. Motor vehicles and trailers constructed for use outside the United Kingdom or which are new or improved types constructed for tests or trials or are equipped with new or improved equipment or types of equipment

(1) This Article applies to wheeled motor vehicles and trailers not falling within any   **B12.34** description of motor vehicle or trailer specified in Article 18 or 19 and references in this Article to motor vehicles and trailers shall be construed accordingly.

(1A) In this Article—

   "*the 1986 Regulations*" means the Road Vehicles (Construction and Use) Regulations 1986 [*S.I. 1986 No. 1078, q.v.*]; and

   "*the 1989 Regulations*" means the Road Vehicles Lighting Regulations 1989 [*S.I. 1989 No. 1796, q.v.*].

(2) The Minister authorises the use on roads—

   (A) of motor vehicles and trailers, or types of motor vehicles and trailers, constructed for use outside the United Kingdom and of new or improved types of motor vehicles and trailers constructed for tests or trials notwithstanding that such vehicles do not comply in all respects with the requirements of the 1986 Regulations and the 1989 Regulations, and

(B) of motor vehicles and trailers equipped with new or improved equipment or types of equipment notwithstanding that such vehicles do not comply in all respects with such of the requirements of the 1986 Regulations and the 1989 Regulations as cannot, by reason only of the said equipment, be complied with,

subject, in all cases, to the following conditions:—

(a) [subject to paragraph (3)] the vehicle shall not be used otherwise than—

(i) for or in connection with the testing or demonstration of the vehicle, or

(ii) in the course of delivery on sale, or

(iii) for proceeding to or returning from a manufacturer or repairer for the purpose of construction, repair or overhaul;

[(b) the relevant requirements, to the extent that they are applicable to the vehicle, shall be complied with or (as the case may be) shall not be contravened;]

(c) [subject to paragraph (7),] the vehicle shall not be used for the carriage of any load other than its necessary gear or equipment or such apparatus or ballast as may be necessary for the purpose of carrying out a test or trial of the vehicle;

(d) [subject to paragraph (8),] save in so far as the chief officer of police of any police area in which it is proposed that the vehicle will be used dispenses, as respects the use of the vehicle in that area, with any of the requirements contained in this sub-paragraph as to length of notice or particulars to be given, the [user] of the vehicle, if its overall width exceeds 2.9 metres or if its overall length exceeds that specified by any provision in [Regulation 7 of the 1986 Regulations] before using it on a road, shall give at least two clear days' notice to the chief officer of police of any such area and such notice shall contain particulars of the vehicle concerned, of its overall width and overall length, and of the width and length of any load proposed to be carried, and of the time, date and route of the proposed journey;

(e) [subject to paragraph (8),] subject to any variation in the time, date or route of the journey which may be directed by any such chief officer of police, the vehicle shall be used only in circumstances which accord with the particulars given in compliance with the foregoing sub-paragraph as to the time, date and route of the journey and only if the overall width and overall length of the vehicle and the width and length of any load carried thereon do not exceed the width and length of which particulars have been given as aforesaid;

(f) in the case of the use of a vehicle in respect of which any of the [1986 Regulations] as to the weights of vehicles, whether laden or unladen, or the weights transmitted to the road surface by all or any of the wheels is not complied with, or, where a combination of vehicles is used, if any of the said requirements as to any or all of the vehicles in the combination is not complied with—

(i) save in so far as the highway authority for any road or the bridge authority for any bridge on which it is proposed that the vehicle or, as the case may be, the vehicles will be used dispenses, as respects the use of the vehicle or vehicles on that road or, as the case may be, on that bridge, with the requirements contained in this sub-paragraph as to the length of notice or to the form of notice or the particulars to be given, the [user] of the vehicle or, as the case may be, of the vehicles, before using the vehicle or the vehicles on that road or that bridge shall give to the highway authority for the road and to the bridge authority for the bridge at least two clear days' notice in the form and containing the particulars specified in Part I of Schedule 2, and the provisions of Article 26(6) and (7) shall apply as respects any such notice, and

(ii) before using the vehicle or, as the case may be, the vehicles on any road or bridge the [user] of the vehicle or vehicles shall give to the highway authority for the road and to the bridge authority for the bridge an indemnity in the form specified in Part II of Schedule 2, and the provisions of Article 26(6) and (7) shall apply as respects any such indemnity,

and for the purposes of this sub-paragraph references to a combination of vehicles shall be construed in the same manner as is provided in [Regulation 81(g)] of the Construction and Use Regulations [and references to the highway authority for any road and to the bridge authority for any bridge shall be read as including references to any other person responsible for the maintenance and repair of the road or bridge in question pursuant to an agreement with the authority].

[(3) Paragraph (2)(a) shall not apply if the vehicle is being used in the following circumstances—

(a) a person ("*the approved person*") has been approved by the Secretary of State for the purposes of this article in respect of the vehicle;

(b) the vehicle is registered under the Vehicle Excise and Registration Act 1994 in the name of the approved person and no one else; and

(c) the requirement of paragraph (4) or (5) are met.]

[(4) The requirements of this paragraph are that the vehicle is being used by the approved person and he is using it for the sole purpose of making an evaluation of the vehicle.]

[(5) The requirements of this paragraph are that—

(a) the approved person has lent the vehicle to a person ("*the borrower*") for the borrower's own use on terms which include a requirement that the borrower must—

(i) supply to the approved person information or opinions derived from such use; and

(ii) return the vehicle to the approved person on demand;

(b) the vehicle is being used by the borrower in accordance with such terms; and

(c) the approved person requires the information or opinions for the purposes of evaluating the vehicle.]

[(6) For the purposes of paragraph (2) (b), the relevant requirements are the requirements of—

(a) the provisions of the 1986 Regulations (so far as they would otherwise apply to the vehicle) set out in the left hand column of Table I below as modified for the purposes of this Article in acccordance with the entries in the right hand column of that Table; and

(b) the provisions of the 1989 Regulations (so far as they would otherwise apply to the vehicle) set out in the left hand column of Table II below as modified for the purposes of this Article in accordance with the entries made in the right hand column of that Table.]

[(7) Paragraph (2)(c) shall not apply to the vehicle when it is being used in circumstances where all the provisions of the 1986 Regulations as to the weights of vehicles whether laden or unladen, or the weights transmitted to the road surface by all or any of the wheels are complied with.]

[(8) If a vehicle forms part of a combination of vehicles, paragraph (2)(d) and (e) shall have effect in relation to that vehicle as if—

(a) each reference to its overall length included a reference to the overall length of the combination of vehicles; and

(b) the reference to particulars of the vehicle were a reference to particulars of each vehicle in the combination.]

[(9) A reference to this Article to any enactment comprised in the 1986 Regulations or the 1989 Regulations is a reference to that enactment as from time to time amended or as from time to time re-enacted with or without modification.]

[(10) Nothing in this Article shall be construed as authorising a vehicle to be used when—

(a) the condition of the vehicle or its accessories or equipment;

(b) the purpose for which it is used;

(c) the number of passengers carried by it, or the manner in which they are carried; or

(d) the weight, position or distribution of its load, or the manner in which it is secured,

is such that the use of the vehicle involves a danger of injury to any person.]

[TABLE I

(see paragraph (6)(a))

Provision of the 1986 Regulations	*Subject matter*	*Modifications made to the 1986 Regulations for the purposes of this Article*
Regulation 10	Indication of overall travelling height	
Regulation 16	Braking systems	In regulation 16(1) for the words "to which regulation 15 does not apply" there shall be substituted the words "and has effect subject to the proviso in paragraph (f) of regulation 15".
Regulation 18(1)	Maintenance and efficiency of brakes	
Regulation 20	General requirements as to wheels and tracks	
Regulation 26	Mixing of tyres	
Regulation 27	Conditions and maintenance of tyres	
Regulation 29	Maintenance of steering gear	
Regulation 30	View to the front	
Regulation 34	Windscreen wipers and washers	
Regulation 37	Audible warning instruments	

[*continued on next page*

Provision of the 1986 Regulations	Subject matter	Modifications made to the 1986 Regulations for the purposes of this Article
Regulation 53	Mascots	
Regulation 54	Silencers—general	
Regulation 61	Emissions	
Regulation 62	Closets, etc.	
Regulations 81 and 82	Restrictions on the use of vehicles carrying wide or long loads or having fixed appliances or apparatus	In regulation 82(8)(c)(ii)(B)the reference to paragraph 1 of Schedule 12 to the 1986 Regulations shall be omitted.
Regulation 83	Number of trailers	
Regulation 84	Trailers drawn by motor cycles	
Regulation 86	Distance between motor vehicles and trailers	
Regulation 89	Leaving trailers at rest	
Regulation 90	Passengers in trailers	
Regulation 92	Attachment of side cars	
Regulation 97	Avoidance of excessive noise	
Regulation 98	Stopping of engine when stationary	
Regulation 99	Use of audible warning instruments	
Regulation 100	Maintenance and use of vehicles so as not to be a danger	
Regulation 101	Parking in darkness	
Regulation 102	Passengers on motor cycles	
Regulation 103	Obstruction	
Regulation 104	Driver's control	
Regulation 105	Opening doors	
Regulation 106	Reversing	
Regulation 107	Leaving motor vehicle unattended	

[*continued on next page*

Provision of the 1986 Regulations	Subject matter	Modifications made to the 1986 Regulations for the purposes of this Article
Regulation 108	Securing of suspended implements	
Regulation 109	Television sets]	

[TABLE II

(see paragraph (6)(b))

Provision of the 1989 Regulations	Subject matter	Modifications made to the 1989 Regulations for the purpose of this Article
Regulation 11	Colour of lights shown by lamps and reflectors	
Regulation 13	Lamps to show steady light	
Regulation 16	Restrictions on fitting blue warning beacons, special warning lamps and similar devices	
Regulation 17	Obligatory warning beacons	
Regulation 18	Obligatory lamps, reflectors, rear markings and devices	In regulation 18(1)(b) there shall be added at the end: "as if— (i) the requirements relating to the markings of lamps, retro-reflectors and rear markings were omitted; (ii) the requirements relating to angles of visibility were omitted; (iii) the requirements relating to the position of any lamp, retro-reflector or rear marking permitted any specified maximum measurement to be increased by 5 per cent and any specified minimum measurement to be decreased by 5 per cent; and (iv) the requirement relating to the fitting of a dim-dip device or running lamp in Table 1 of Schedule 1 were omitted."

[*continued on next page*

Provision of the 1989 Regulations	Subject matter	Modifications made to the 1989 Regulations for the purpose of this Article
Regulation 19	Restrictions on the obstruction of certain lamps and reflectors	
Regulation 21	Projecting trailers and vehicles carrying overhanging or projecting loads or equipment	
Regulation 22	Additional side marker lamps	In paragraph (1), after the words paragraph (2) there shall be inserted "and subject to paragraph (3)". In paragraph (3), there shall be added at the end: "as if— (i) the requirements relating to the markings of lamps, retro-reflectors and rear markings were omitted; (ii) the requirements relating to angles of visibility were omitted; and (iii) the requirements relating to the position of any lamp, retro-reflector or rear marking permitted any specified maximum measurement to be increased by 5 per cent and any specified minimum measurement to be decreased by 5 per cent."]

[Article 16 is printed as amended by the Interpretation Act 1978, ss.17(2)(a) and 23(1); S.I. 1981   **B12.35**
No. 1664; S.I. 1986 No. 313; S.I. 1987 No. 1327; S.I. 1998 No. 2249.]

17. Vehicles fitted with moveable platforms

(1) The Minister authorises the use on roads of a vehicle fitted with a moveable platform   **B12.36**
notwithstanding that the vehicle does not comply in all respects with the requirements of
[Regulations 7, 8, 11, 20, 23 or 82] of the Construction and Use Regulations subject to the
following conditions:—

  (a) all the relevant requirements of the Construction and Use Regulations other than
those specified above shall be complied with;

  (b) the vehicle shall not be used on a road unless its special equipment is fully retracted
except when the vehicle is at a place where it is being used to facilitate overhead
working;

  (c) any jacks with which the vehicle is fitted for stabilising it while the moveable platform is in use and which project from the sides of the vehicle shall be clearly visible to persons using the road within a reasonable distance of the vehicle; and

(d) the vehicle, except in respect of its special equipment when the vehicle is at a place where it is being used to facilitate overhead working, shall—

    (i) as respects its overall length, comply with [Regulation 7] of the said Regulations,

    (ii) as respects its overall width, comply with [Regulation 8] of the said Regulations,

    (iii) in the case of a vehicle other than a locomotive, as respects its overhang, comply with [Regulation 11] of the said Regulations.

(2) In this Article—

"*moveable platform*" means a platform which is attached to, and may be moved by means of, an extensible boom, and

"*special equipment*" means a moveable platform, the apparatus for moving the platform and any jacks fitted to the vehicle for stabilising it while the moveable platform is in use.

B12.37   *[Article 17 is printed as amended by the Interpretation Act 1978, ss.17(2)(a) and 23(1).]*

17A. Vehicles propelled by natural gas

B12.38   The Secretary of State authorises the use on roads of vehicles propelled by compressed natural gas notwithstanding that they do not comply with the requirements of regulations 40, 94(2) and (3) and 96 of, or of Schedule 4 or 5 to, the Road Vehicles (Construction and Use) Regulations 1986 [*S.I. 1986 No. 1078, q.v.*] subject to the following conditions—

(a) all other relevant requirements of the Road Vehicles (Construction and Use) Regulations 1986 shall be complied with;

(b) the compressed natural gas system shall comply with Schedule 5A; and

(c) Schedule 5B shall be complied with.]

B12.39   *[Article 17A was inserted by S.I. 1998 No. 2884.*
The heading to this article ("Vehicles propelled by natural gas") is not part of the official text, but was derived from the heading to the provision in S.I. 1998 No. 2884 which inserted it.]

PART III

ABNORMAL INDIVISIBLE LOADS, ENGINEERING PLANT AND OTHER VEHICLES CARRYING
WIDE LOADS

18. Vehicles for carrying or drawing abnormal indivisible loads

B12.40   (1) The Minister authorises the use on roads of heavy motor cars and trailers specially designed and constructed for the carriage of abnormal indivisible loads and of locomotives and tractors specially designed and constructed to draw trailers specially so designed and constructed notwithstanding that such vehicles do not comply in all respects with the requirements of the Construction and Use Regulations, subject—

(a) in a case where Article 22, 23, 25 or 26 applies to the conditions contained in such of those Articles as are applicable to that case;

(b) in a case where the overall width of the vehicle or of the vehicle together with the width of any lateral projection or projections of its load exceeds [5 metres], to the conditions contained in Article 24; and

(c) in all cases to the further conditions specified in paragraph (2) below.

[(1A) (a) In this article, "*the Construction and Use Regulations*" means the Road Vehicles (Construction and Use) Regulations 1986 [*S.I. 1986 No. 1078*].

(b) For the purposes of paragraph (2) below:

(i) "*Category 1*" shall consist of any vehicle or combination of vehicles where the total weight of the vehicle or vehicles carrying the load is not more than 46,000 kilograms;

"*Category 2*" shall consist of any motor vehicle or combination of vehicles where the total weight of the vehicle or vehicles carrying the load is not more than 80,000 kilograms;

"*Category 3*" shall consist of any motor vehicle or combination of vehicles where the total weight of the vehicle or vehicles carrying the load is not more than 150,000 kilograms;

(ii) a vehicle shall comply with the conditions of an appropriate category, and the category under the conditions of which a vehicle is being used shall be that indicated on the sign mentioned in paragraph (2)(t) below.]

(2) The conditions referred to in paragraph 1(c) above are as follows:—

(a) a heavy motor car or trailer which does not comply with Part II of the Construction and Use Regulations shall be used only, save as provided in paragraphs (i) and (m) of this Article, for or in connection with the carriage of an abnormal indivisible load;

(b) a locomotive or tractor which does not comply with Part II of the Construction and Use Regulations shall be used only for or in connection with the drawing of trailers the use of which on roads is authorised by this Article;

(c) the overall width of a heavy motor car [or a trailer] shall not exceed 2.9 metres unless it is used for or in connection with the carriage of a load which can only safely be carried on a heavy motor car which exceeds that overall width;

(d) the overall width of a locomotive or tractor shall not exceed 2.9 metres unless it is used for or in connection with the carriage of a load on a trailer which exceeds that overall width, being a load which can only be safely carried on such a trailer;

(e) [*revoked.*]

(f) notwithstanding anything in sub-paragraphs (c), (d) . . . above, the overall width of a heavy motor car, locomotive, tractor or trailer shall not exceed 6.1 metres;

(g) where, in relation to the load carried by a vehicle, there is a lateral projection on one or both sides of the vehicle the overall width of the vehicle together with the width of the projection, or, as the case may be, of both projections shall not exceed 6.1 metres;

(h) where a load is carried in such a manner that its weight rests—

(i) on one vehicle being a heavy motor car or a trailer, the overall length of the heavy motor car or, as the case may be, of the trailer together with the length of any forward and of any rearward projection of its load shall not exceed 27.4 metres; or

(ii) on more than one vehicle and the vehicles consist of—

(a) a motor vehicle drawing one trailer whether constituting an articulated vehicle or not, or

(b) any other combination of vehicles,

then, in the case at (a) above, the overall length of the trailer together with the length of any forward projection of the load extending beyond the foremost point of the trailer and of any rearward projection of the load shall not exceed 27.4 metres and, in the case at (b) above, the overall length of the vehicles together with the distance between vehicles and the length of any forward and of any rearward projection of the load shall not exceed 27.4 metres;

(i) the vehicle shall be so constructed that it is a wheeled vehicle;

(j) every wheel of the vehicle shall be equipped with a pneumatic tyre or a tyre of soft or elastic material;

[(k) The following restrictions on weight shall apply:

(i) for any vehicle or combination of vehicles carrying the load in Category 1:

    (a) regulations [75, 76 and 78] of the Construction and Use Regulations shall apply, and in respect of an articulated vehicle, regulation 77 shall apply save for a vehicle to which (b) below is applicable;

    [(aa) regulation 79 of the Construction and Use Regulations shall apply in the case of a vehicle with two or three closely spaced axles within the meaning of the Construction and Use Regulations;]

    (b) for an articulated vehicle with a total of 5 or more axles and with a relevant axle spacing specified in column 2 of the Table below, the total weight shall not exceed the weight specified for that item in column 3 of the Table.

TABLE

1	2	3
Item	Relevant axle spacing (in metres)	Weight (in kilograms)
1	at least 6.5	40,000
2	at least 7.0	42,000
3	at least 7.5	44,000
4	at least 8.0	46,000

    [(c) in the case of a semi-trailer within the meaning of the Construction and Use Regulations of which the outermost axles of a group of four axles are spaced at a distance apart of 3.25m or less and the smallest distance between any two adjoining axles in the group is at least 0.87m, the weight transmitted to the road surface by all the wheels of any one of those axles shall not exceed 6,000 kilograms;]

(ii) [save as provided in sub-paragraph (iia) below] for any vehicle or combination of vehicles carrying the load in Category 2:

    (a) the total weight shall be transmitted to the road through at least 5 axles;

    (b) the total weight imposed on the road by all the wheels of any one axle shall not exceed 12,500 kilograms, and by any one wheel, 6,250 kilograms;

    (c) if the distance between any two adjacent axles is at least 1.1 metres but less than 1.35 metres, the total weight imposed on the road by all the wheels of any one of those axles shall not exceed 12,000 kilograms, and by any one wheel, 6,000 kilograms;

(d) the distance between any two adjacent axles shall not be less than 1.1 metres;

(e) where the distance between the foremost and rearmost axles of the vehicle or vehicles carrying the load is at least as specified in an item in column 2 of the Table below, the total weight of the vehicle or combination of vehicles shall not exceed the weight given for that item in column 3 of the Table:

TABLE

1	*2*	*3*
Item	*Distance between foremost and rearmost axles (in metres)*	*Weight (in kilograms)*
1	5.07	38,000
2	5.33	40,000
3	6.0	45,000
4	6.67	50,000
5	7.33	55,000
6	8.0	60,000
7	8.67	65,000
8	9.33	70,000
9	10.0	75,000
10	10.67	80,000

(f) where the axles are in two or more groups (so that adjacent axles in each group are less than 2 metres apart and adjacent axles of different groups are more than 2 metres apart), then the total weight imposed on the road by all the wheels of any one group of axles shall not exceed 50,000 kilograms;

(iia) until 1st October 1989 an articulated vehicle in Category 2 need not meet the requirements of sub-paragraph (ii) above, but—

  (a) the total weight shall be transmitted to the road through at least 4 axles;

  (b) the total weight imposed on the road by all the wheels of any one axle shall not exceed 13,500 kilograms, and by any one wheel 6,750 kilograms;

  (c) if the total number of axles does not exceed 4, the total weight of the vehicle shall not exceed 46,000 kilograms;]

(iii) [save as provided in sub-paragraph (iiia) below] for any [vehicle] or combination of vehicles carrying the load in Category 3:

  (a) the total weight shall be transmitted to the road through at least 6 axles;

  (b) the total weight imposed on the road by all the wheels of any one axle shall not exceed 16,500 kilograms, and by any one wheel, 8,250 kilograms;

  (c) if the distance between any two adjacent axles is at least 1.1 metres but less than 1.35 metres, the total weight imposed on the road by all the wheels of any one of those axles shall not exceed 15,000 kilograms, and by any one wheel 7,500 kilograms;

  (d) the distance between any two adjacent axles shall not be less than 1.1 metres;

(e) where the distance between the foremost and rearmost axles of the vehicle or vehicles carrying the load is at least as specified in an item in column 2 of the Table below the total weight of the vehicle or combination of vehicles shall not exceed the weight given for that item in column 3 of the Table:

TABLE

1	2	3
Item	Distance between foremost and rearmost axles (in metres)	Weight (in kilograms)
1	5.77	80,000
2	6.23	85,000
3	6.68	90,000
4	7.14	95,000
5	7.59	100,000
6	8.05	105,000
7	8.50	110,000
8	8.95	115,000
9	9.41	120,000
10	9.86	125,000
11	10.32	130,000
12	10.77	135,000
13	11.23	140,000
14	11.68	145,000
15	12.14	150,000

(f) where the axles are in two or more groups (so that adjacent axles in each group are less than 1.5 metres apart and adjacent axles of different groups are more than 1.5 metres apart) then the total weight imposed on the road by all the wheels of any one group of axles shall not exceed 100,000 kilograms, or 90,000 kilograms for a group where the distance between any two adjacent axles of that group is less than 1.35 metres;

[(iiia) until 1st October 1989 a vehicle or combination of vehicles carrying the load in Category 3 need not meet the requirements of sub-paragraphs (c) to (f) of sub-paragraph (iii) above;]

(iv) for the purpose of this sub-paragraph (k):

"*axle*" shall mean any number of wheels in line transversely;

"*relevant axle spacing*" shall have the same meaning as in regulation 77(1) of the Construction and Use Regulations;

(v) regulation 3(7) and (8) of the Construction and Use Regulations shall apply to determine the number of wheels and axles for the purpose of this sub-paragraph and regulation 3(10) to determine the distance between axles.]

(l) the vehicle or combination of vehicles shall not carry more than one abnormal indivisible load at any one time:

Provided that—

(i) subject to compliance with all the requirements of the Construction and Use

Regulations with respect to the laden weights of vehicles and the weights transmitted to the road surface by all or any of the wheels, it shall be permissible for a vehicle or any vehicles comprised in a combination of vehicles to carry more than one abnormal indivisible load of the same character and, where any abnormal indivisible load is carried, to carry any articles of a similar character;

(ii) in the case of vehicles not falling within the foregoing proviso, it shall be permissible for a vehicle or any vehicles comprised in a combination of vehicles to carry more than one abnormal indivisible load each of the same character if—

[(a) the vehicle or combination of vehicles is in Category 1 or Category 2;]

(b) the overall length in relation to the vehicle or vehicles carrying the loads is such that the provisions of sub-paragraph (i) or (ii) of paragraph (h) above would be complied with were "18.3 metres" substituted for "27.4 metres" except that, where such compliance would be impossible by reason of the length of one of the loads if that were the only one carried, the aforesaid distance of 18.3 metres may be increased to such greater distance not exceeding 27.4 metres as may be necessary to permit the carriage of that load;

(c) the overall width of any vehicle together with the width of any lateral projection of its load does not exceed 2.9 metres or, where it would be impossible for the aforesaid distance to be complied with by reason of the width of one of the loads if that were the only one carried, such greater distance not exceeding 6.1 metres as may be necessary to permit the carriage of that load; and

(d) all the loads carried are loaded at the same place and conveyed to the same destination;

(m) where an abnormal indivisible load consists of engineering plant from which one or more constituent parts have been detached, such abnormal indivisible load and such constituent parts may be carried;

Provided that—

(i) no dimension of such constituent parts protrudes beyond any dimension of the vehicle or combination of vehicles on which such abnormal indivisible load and such constituent parts are being carried to an extent greater than such abnormal indivisible load would protrude if it were being carried without such constituent parts;

(ii) such abnormal indivisible load and such constituent parts are loaded at the same place and have the same destination; and

[(iii) the vehicle or combination of vehicles is in Category 1 or Category 2;]

[(n) in the case of a trailer whether manufactured before 1st January 1968 or on or after that date, [regulation 16] of the Construction and Use Regulations shall apply as it applies to trailers manufactured before 1st January 1968;]

(o) the conditions specified in Articles 21(1) and 27; and

(p) [for vehicles manufactured before 1st October 1989 and] in a case specified in column 2 of the Table below, all the Construction and Use Regulations shall apply with the exception of the Regulations which are specified opposite to that item in column 3 of that table, and, in relation to [item 3], save as provided in paragraph (n) above.

TABLE

1	2	3
Item	Case	Regulations that do not apply
1	A heavy motor car	8, 16 in so far as it relates to the requirement in item 18(c) of Schedule 3 to the Regulations, 15, 18 (except paragraph (1)), 22, 24, [25,] 45, 63, 75–80, 82 and 83(1).
2	A locomotive or tractor	8, 22, [25,] 45, 75(3), and 76.
3	A trailer	7, 8, 16 in so far as it relates to the requirements in [items 4, 11, 15 and 18] and 18 of Schedule 3 to the Regulations, 15, 18 (except paragraph (1)), 21, 22, 24, [25,] 63, 64, 75–80, 82 and 83(1)].

[(q) in relation to any vehicle or combination of vehicles in a Category specified in column 2 of the Table below and manufactured [on or after 1st October 1989] and any vehicle in Category 1 whenever manufactured, all the Construction and Use Regulations shall apply with the exception of the Regulations which are specified opposite to that item in column 3 of the Table:

TABLE

1	2	3
Item	Category	Regulations that do not apply
1	1	7, 8, 80 and 82.
2	2 and 3	7, 8, 15, 16, 18 (except paragraph (1)), [25,] 45, 64, 65, [75 in so far as it relates to items 1–4, 6–11, 15 and 16 of the Table, 76–80], 82 and 83(1).

[(r) a vehicle or combination of vehicles in Category 2 or Category 3, if manufactured on or after 1st October 1989, shall have a braking system complying with the construction, fitting and performance requirements set out in relation to category N3 motor vehicles and O4 trailers in Annexes I, II and VII to Council Directive 71/320/EEC [*O.J. No. L202, September 6, 1971, p. 37*], as amended by Council Directive 74/132/EEC [*O.J. No. L74, March 19, 1974, p. 7*], 75/524/EEC [*O.J. No. L236, September 8, 1975, p. 3*], 79/489/EEC [*O.J. No. L128, May 26, 1979, p. 12*], 85/647/EEC [*O.J. No. L380, December 31, 1985, p. 1*], and 88/194/EEC [*O.J. No. L92, April 9, 1988, p. 47*], ("*the amended Directive*") and, if appropriate, Annexes III, IV, V, VI and X to the amended Directive, modified as follows—

(i) for the purposes of each Type O test conducted in accordance with Annex II—

(a) a laden vehicle shall be a vehicle laden with the maximum technically permissible mass specified by the manufacturer for the vehicle speed specified for the test;

(b) for a trailer which is designed and constructed for use in a combination of vehicles in Category 3 and for which X (which is stated in the amended Directive as being a percentage of the force corresponding to the maximum mass borne by the wheels of the stationary vehicle) is specified in paragraph 2.2.1.2.1. of Annex II as having the values of 45 or 50, X shall have the value of 30;

(c) for a trailer mentioned in (b) above and for which the test speed is specified in paragraph 2.2.1.2.1. of Annex II as 60 km/h, the test speed shall be 48 km/h;

(d) for a drawing vehicle in category N3 which is designed and constructed for use with a semi-trailer within the meaning of the Construction and Use Regulations in a combination of vehicles in Category 3, if the performance of a service braking device is determined by measuring the stopping distance in relation to the initial speed, the stopping distance in paragraph 2.1.1.1.1. of Annex II shall be $0.15v + \dfrac{v^2}{77.5}$ or, if the performance of the device is determined by measuring the reaction time and the mean deceleration, the mean braking deceleration at normal engine speed in paragraph 2.1.1.1.1. of Annex II shall be at least 3m/section 2;

(e) for a drawing vehicle in category N3 mentioned in (d) above, if the performance of a secondary braking device is determined by measuring the stopping distance in relation to the initial speed, the stopping distance in paragraph 2.1.2.1. of Annex II shall be $0.15v + \dfrac{v^2}{37.5}$ or, if the performance of the device is determined by measuring the reaction time and the mean deceleration, the mean braking deceleration in paragraph 2.1.2.1. of Annex II shall be at least 1.45m/section 2;

(ii) the requirements of paragraphs 2.2.1.22 and 2.2.2.13 of Annex I and 1.1.4.2 and 1.4. of Annex II shall not apply;

(iii) in Annex I, in paragraph 2.2.1.23 the words "not mentioned in item 2.2.1.22 above" and in paragraph 2.2.2.14 the words "not mentioned in item 2.2.2.13 above" shall not apply;

(iv) for the purposes of Type I tests conducted in accordance with paragraph 1.3 of Annex II on a vehicle which is designed and constructed for use in a combination of vehicles in Category 3, a laden vehicle shall be a vehicle laden with the heaviest weight possible without the total weight imposed on the road by all the wheels of any one axle exceeding 12,500 kilograms; and

(v) if suitable and sufficient wheel chocks are provided in readily accessible positions and capable, when used in conjunction with any parking brakes fitted to the vehicle, of holding the vehicle stationary when loaded to its maximum mass on a gradient of 12%, the requirements of paragraph 2.1.3.2. of Annex II shall not apply;]

(s) (i) a vehicle in Category 2 or Category 3, if manufactured [on or after 1st October 1988], shall have a plate complying with the specification prescribed in the Road Vehicles (Marking of Special Weights) Regulations 1983 [*S.I. 1983 No. 910, as amended*] except that there need be no indication of any weight in respect of a speed not exceeding 12 miles per hour;

(ii) the plate fitted in accordance with paragraph (i) above shall be marked clearly with the words:

"SPECIAL TYPES USE";

(iii) if a vehicle is made up of several modules, each module may be fitted individually with a plate in accordance with paragraph (i) above, provided that the information required from the plate in relation to the vehicle as a whole can be readily determined from those individual plates;

(iv) a vehicle fitted with any plate in accordance with paragraph (i) above shall not be used at a weight in excess of any weight specified on that plate in relation to the speed at which the vehicle is travelling;

(v) a vehicle in Category 1 shall not be used at a weight in excess of any weight specified on a plate fitted in accordance with regulation 66 of the Construction and Use Regulations in relation to items 6, 7 and 8 in Part I or items 4, 5, and 6 in Part II of Schedule 8 to those Regulations;

(t) the vehicle or the drawing vehicle in a combination of vehicles shall be fitted with a sign indicating the relevant category and complying with the requirements specified in Schedule 6;

(u) notwithstanding sub-paragraph (p) above, regulation 7 of the Construction and Use Regulations shall not apply in the case of: .

(i) an articulated vehicle, or a motor vehicle and a trailer, where the semi-trailer is constructed such that the major part of the load platform does not extend over or between the wheels and is at a height that is below the height of the topmost point of the tyres of those wheels, measured on level ground and with any adjustable suspension at the normal travelling height, and where the height or stability of the load being carried necessitates the use of such a trailer,

(ii) a vehicle or combination of vehicles unable to comply with that regulation because of the requirements of sub-paragraphs (k)(ii)(e) or (k)(iii)(e) above;

(v) notwithstanding sub-paragraph (a) above, a vehicle consisting of two or more modules may, when being used in connection with the carriage of but not at the time carrying an abnormal indivisible load, be disassembled into two or more parts and arranged such that one part carries the others.]

B12.41　　*[Article 18 is printed as amended by S.I. 1985 No. 745; S.I. 1987 Nos 1327 and 2161; S.I. 1989 No. 1662.]*

19. Engineering plant

B12.42　　The Minister authorises the use on roads of engineering plant notwithstanding that such vehicles do not comply in all respects with the requirements of the Construction and Use Regulations . . . , subject to—

(1) the restriction specified in Article 21(2) [save as provided in paragraph (2A) below],

(2) in a case where Article 22, 23, 25 or 26 applies, the conditions specified in such of those Articles as are applicable [save as provided in paragraph (2A) below],

[(2A) in a case where a vehicle or combination of vehicles disregarding the date of its manufacture complies with the conditions specified in article 18(2)(k), (q), (r), (s) and (t), the conditions specified in Article 21(1) shall apply as if the use of the vehicle or combination of vehicles was authorised by Article 18.]

(3) in a case where the overall width of the vehicle, or of the vehicle together with the width of any lateral projection or projections of its load exceeds [5 metres], the conditions specified in Article 24, and

(4) in any case, the following conditions:—

[(a) engineering plant shall be used on a road only:

    (i) for testing or demonstration purposes or delivery on sale;

    (ii) for proceeding to or returning from a manufacturer or repairer for repair or maintenance;

    (iii) for proceeding to or from the site of engineering operations or when actually engaged in such operations;

(b) engineering plant may carry its own necessary gear and equipment but no other load except:

    (i) engineering plant other than a mobile crane when actually engaged on the construction, maintenance or repair of roads may carry materials which it is specifically designed to treat while being carried on the vehicle or materials which have been excavated and raised from the ground by apparatus on the motor vehicle or trailer, and

    (ii) a mobile crane when actually engaged in engineering operations may lift or transport a load;]

(c) engineering plant other than a mobile crane shall only draw a trailer which is engineering plant or a living van or office hut used in connection with the construction, maintenance and repair of roads;

(d) no mobile crane shall draw a trailer;

(e) the vehicle shall be so constructed that it is either a wheeled vehicle or a track laying vehicle;

(f) in the case of a wheeled motor vehicle [Regulations 4, 10, 18(2) and (3), 23, 27, 29 to 32, 34, 37, 39, 40, 48, 50, 52, 54 to 61, 65, 83, 86, 89, 94 to 101, 103 to 105 and 107] of the Construction and Use Regulations shall apply:

Provided that—

    (i) *[revoked]*

    (ii) in the case of a machine designed for use and used solely for the purpose of laying materials for the repair or construction of road surfaces, if the weight transmitted to the road surface by any two wheels in line transversely does not exceed 11,180 kilograms, the said [Regulation 23] shall not apply;

    (iii) in the case of a motor vehicle designed for use in work of construction or repair of road surfaces, the wheels of which are equipped with pneumatic tyres specially provided with smooth treads for such use and which is incapable by reason of its construction of exceeding a speed of 20 miles per hour on the level under its own power, [Regulation 27(1)(g)] of the said Regulations shall not apply;

(g) in the case of a wheeled trailer, [Regulations 4, 10, 18(2) and (3), 23, 27, 29, 34, 89, 95, 96, 100 and 103] of the Construction and Use Regulations shall apply:

Provided that in the case of a trailer designed for use in work of construction or repair of road surfaces and the wheels of which are equipped with pneumatic tyres specially provided with smooth treads for such use, [Regulation 27(1)(b)] of the said Regulations shall not apply;

(h) in the case of a track laying motor vehicle [Regulations 4, 18, 23, 27 to 31, 34, 37, 40, 54, 61, 86, 89, 91, 97 to 101, 103, 104, 106 and 107] of the Construction and Use Regulations shall apply:

Provided that—

    (i) in the case of a motor vehicle registered on or before 31st December 1951 [Regulations 31 and 34] of the said Regulations shall not apply, and

    (ii) in the case of a motor vehicle which is a road roller the said [Regulation 28] shall not apply;

(i) in the case of a track laying trailer [Regulations 4, 18, 23, 27 to 29, 34, 89, 100 and 103] of the Construction and Use Regulations shall apply:

Provided that in the case of a trailer which is a road roller the said [Regulation 28] shall not apply;

(j) all the wheels of a vehicle which are not equipped with pneumatic tyres or tyres of soft or elastic material shall be equipped with smooth tyres and have the edges rounded to a radius of not less than 12 millimetres and not more than 25 millimetres:

Provided that in the case of gritting machines designed for use and used for gritting frosted and icebound roads all or any of the tyres may be shod with diagonal cross bars of equal width of not less than 25 millimetres, extending the full breadth of the tyre and so arranged that the distance between adjacent cross bars is not greater than the width of the cross bars;

(k) in the case of any vehicle the weight transmitted to the road surface by any one wheel not equipped with pneumatic tyres where no other wheel is in the same line transversely or by all the wheels not equipped with pneumatic tyres in line transversely shall be such that the average weight per 25 millimetres width of tyre in contact with such surface does not exceed 765 kilograms;

(l) a motor vehicle shall be equipped with an efficient brake:
Provided that—

(i) in the case of a motor vehicle propelled by steam the engine shall be deemed to be an efficient brake if the engine is capable of being reversed, and

(ii) in the case of a motor vehicle registered on or after 1st January 1952 any brake required by this paragraph shall be capable of being set so as to hold the vehicle when stationary unless another brake fitted to the vehicle is capable of being so set;

(m) a trailer shall be equipped with an efficient brake or with suitable scotches or other similar devices to hold the vehicle stationary when necessary;

(n) no motor vehicle which exceeds 7.93 metres in overall length shall draw a trailer:
Provided that this paragraph shall not apply to a motor vehicle which is drawing a broken down vehicle in consequence of the breakdown;

(o) the sum of weights transmitted to the road surface by all the wheels and tracks of a vehicle shall not exceed 152,400 kilograms;

(p) the overall length of a vehicle shall not exceed 27.4 metres;

(q) the overall width of a vehicle shall not exceed 6.1 metres;

(r) as respects weight—

(i) the weight transmitted to the road surface by any one wheel of a vehicle, other than a heavy motor car registered on or before 31st December 1951 or a trailer manufactured before 1st January 1952, shall not exceed 11,430 kilograms, and for the purposes of this part of this sub-paragraph any two wheels shall be treated as one wheel if the distance between the centres of the areas of contact between such wheels and the road surface is less than 610 millimetres,

(ii) the weight transmitted to any strip of road surface upon which the wheels of a vehicle rest contained between any two parallel lines drawn on that surface at right angles to the longitudinal axis of the vehicle shall not exceed, if the parallel lines are not more than 610 millimetres apart, 45,720 kilograms and, thereafter, additional weight shall be permitted, for any distance apart of the parallel lines in excess of 610 millimetres but not exceeding a total distance apart of 2.13 metres, at a rate of 30,000 kilograms per metre and thereafter, additional weight shall be permitted, for any distance apart of the parallel lines in excess of 2.13 metres, at a rate of 10,000 kilograms per metre,

(iii) the total weight transmitted to the road surface by any wheels of a vehicle in line transversely not fitted with pneumatic tyres shall be such that the average weight per 25 millimetre width of tyre in contact with the road surface shall not exceed 765 kilograms, and

(iv) in the case of a track laying vehicle, in addition to the foregoing restrictions, the weight transmitted by each track thereof to any strip of road surface contained between any two parallel lines drawn on that surface at right angles to the longitudinal axis of the vehicle shall not exceed, if the parallel lines are not more than 610 millimetres apart, 11,430 kilograms, and, thereafter, additional weight shall be permitted, for any distance apart of the parallel lines in excess of 610 millimetres but not exceeding a total distance apart of 2.13 metres, at a rate of 7,500 kilograms per metre and, thereafter, additional weight shall be permitted, for any distance apart of the parallel lines in excess of 2.13 metres, at a rate of 2,500 kilograms per metre.

[Article 19 is printed as amended by the Interpretation Act 1978, ss.17(2)(a) and 23(1); S.I. 1981 No. 1664; S.I. 1987 No. 1327. See the editorial note on p. 1073.   **B12.43**

S.I. 1987 No. 1327 substituted the text of article 19(4)(a) and (b) above for the existing text of article 19(4)(a), i.e. without formally revoking existing article 19(4)(b) (which read "(b) a mobile crane shall not be used on a road to lift or transport goods or burden except when actually engaged in engineering operations;"). It would appear that the failure to revoke the existing regulation 19(4)(b) may have been an oversight; cf. the text of regulation 19(4)(a)(ii) above.]

*   *   *

20. Other vehicles carrying loads exceeding 4.3 metres in width

The Minister authorises the use on roads of motor vehicles and trailers carrying loads where the overall width of the vehicle on which the load is carried together with the width of any lateral projection or projections of the load exceeds 4.3 metres but does not exceed 6.1 metres, subject to the restrictions and conditions contained in [Articles 21(1)], 22, 24 and 25 and also to the condition that the vehicle complies in all respects with the requirements of the Construction and Use Regulations (other than [Regulation 82(1) and (2)]).   **B12.44**

[Article 20 is printed as amended by the Interpretation Act 1978, ss.17(2)(a) and 23(1); S.I. 1987 No. 1327.]   **B12.45**

21. Speed limits for vehicles authorised by Article 18, 19 or 20

[(1) A vehicle or combination of vehicles the use of which on roads is authorised by Article 18, if of Category 2 or Category 3 as defined in that article, or by Article 20, as indicated by an item in column 2 of the Table below, shall not travel at a speed exceeding that specified in column 3 for that item in relation to the type of road used: **B12.46**

TABLE

1	2	3		
Item	Authorisation	Speed (mph) Motorway	Dual Carriageway	Other road
1	Article 18 Category 2	40	35	30
2	Article 18 Category 3	30	25	20
3	Article 20	30	25	20]

(2) A vehicle the use of which on roads is authorised by Article 19 shall not travel on any road other than a [motorway] at a speed exceeding 12 miles per hour.

(3) *[Revoked.]*

B12.47   *[Article 21 is printed as amended by S.I. 1987 No. 1327.]*

22. Attendants

B12.48   (1) This Article applies in the case of a vehicle the use of which on roads is authorised by Article 20 and in a case where—

(a) the overall width of the vehicle the use of which on roads is authorised by Article 18 or 19 or of the vehicle together with the width of any lateral projection or projections of its load exceeds 3.5 metres, or

(b) the overall length of the vehicle the use of which on roads is authorised by Article 18 or 19 or of the vehicle together with the length of any forward projection and of any rearward projection of its load exceeds 18.3 metres, or

(c) as respects a motor vehicle (whether or not its use is authorised by Article 18 or 19) which is drawing a trailer or trailers the use of which is so authorised, a load is carried in such a manner that its weight rests on more than one of the vehicles being—

    (i) the motor vehicle and one trailer whether forming part of an articulated vehicle or not, or

    (ii) any other combination of vehicles,

and, in the case at (i) above, the overall length of the trailer together with the length of any forward projection of the load extending beyond the foremost point of the trailer and of any rearward projection of the load exceeds 18.3 metres and, in the case at (ii) above, the overall length of the vehicles together with the distance between vehicles and the length of any forward and of any rearward projection of the load exceeds 18.3 metres, or

(d) a motor vehicle (whether or not its use is authorised by Article 18 or 19) is drawing a trailer or trailers the use of which is so authorised and the overall length of the combination of vehicles together with the length of any forward projection of any load extending beyond the foremost point of the drawing vehicle comprised in the combination and the length of any rearward projection of any load extending beyond the rearmost point of the rearmost vehicle comprised therein exceeds 25.9 metres, or

(e) a vehicle the use of which is authorised by Article 18 or 19 is carrying a load having a forward projection exceeding 1.83 metres in length or a rearward projection exceeding 3.05 metres in length or is fitted with any special appliance or apparatus having such a projection.

(2) As respects a vehicle to which this Article applies at least one person, in addition to the person or persons employed in driving any motor vehicle to which this Article applies, shall be employed—

(a) to warn such driver or drivers, and any other person, of any danger likely to be caused to such other person by the presence of such vehicle, and any vehicle or vehicles being drawn by such vehicle on the road, and

(b) to attend to—

    (i) such vehicle and its load,

    (ii) any vehicle or vehicles drawn by such vehicle, and

    (iii) the load carried on any vehicle or vehicles so drawn.

(3) For the purposes of paragraph (2) above—

(a) in a case where a motor vehicle is drawing a trailer or trailers any person employed in pursuance of section 34 of the Road Traffic Act 1972 in attending that vehicle or any such trailer shall be treated as being an attendant required by that paragraph so long as he is also employed to discharge the duties mentioned in that paragraph,

(b) in a case where a motor vehicle is drawing a trailer or trailers and another motor vehicle is used for the purpose of assisting in their propulsion on the road, the person or persons employed in driving that other motor vehicle shall not be treated as a person or persons employed in attending to the first-mentioned vehicle or any vehicle or vehicles drawn thereby, and

(c) in a case where three or more vehicles to which that paragraph applies are travelling together in convoy, it shall be a sufficient compliance with the requirements of that paragraph if only the first and the last vehicles in the convoy are attended in the manner specified in that paragraph.

[Section 34 of the Road Traffic Act 1972 was repealed by the Road Traffic (Consequential Provisions)   **B12.49**
Act 1988, but (on the recommendation of the Law Commission; see Cm. 390) not re-enacted. It is assumed therefore that article 22(3)(a) above has now lapsed.]

23. Marking of projecting loads and fixed appliances or apparatus which project

(1) This Article applies in a case where a vehicle the use of which is authorised by Article   **B12.50**
18 or 19—

(a) carries a load which—

(i) has a forward or a rearward projection exceeding 1.83 metres in length, or
(ii) has a rearward projection exceeding 1.07 metres in length but not exceeding 1.83 metres in length, or

(b) is fitted with a special appliance or apparatus which—

(i) has a forward or a rearward projection exceeding 1.83 metres in length, or
(ii) has a rearward projection exceeding 1.07 metres in length but not exceeding 1.83 metres in length.

(2) Subject to the provisions of paragraphs (3), (4) and (5) of this Article—

(a) as respects a projection mentioned in sub-paragraph (a)(i) or in sub-paragraph (b)(i) of the foregoing paragraph the conditions specified in [paragraph 3 of Schedule 12] to the Construction and Use Regulations shall be complied with, and accordingly the provisions of the said [paragraph 3] shall apply in relation to that projection as they apply in relation to a relevant projection as mentioned in that paragraph, and

(b) as respects a projection mentioned in sub-paragraph (a)(ii) or in sub-paragraph (b)(ii) of the foregoing paragraph the conditions specified in [paragraph 4 of the said Schedule 12] shall be complied with, and accordingly the provisions of the said [paragraph 4] shall apply in relation to that projection as they apply in relation to a relevant projection as mentioned in that paragraph.

(3) Where, in any of the cases mentioned in paragraph (1) of this Article, a vehicle is carrying a load or is fitted with a special appliance or apparatus and the load or the appliance or apparatus has, in relation to the vehicle, a forward projection or a rearward projection, and another vehicle is attached to that end of the vehicle from which the load or, as the case may be, the appliance or apparatus projects and is attached to that vehicle in such a manner that—

(a) in the case where there is a forward projection, the foremost point of that other vehicle extends beyond the foremost part of the projection or, in the case where there is a rearward projection, the rearmost point of that other vehicle extends beyond the rearmost part of the projection, or

(b) in the case where there is a forward projection, the foremost part of the projection extends beyond the foremost point of that other vehicle or, in the case where there is a rearward projection the rearmost part of the projection extends beyond the rearmost point of that other vehicle, then—

   (i) in either of the cases mentioned in sub-paragraph (a) of this paragraph, the provisions of paragraph (2) of this Article shall not apply as respects any such projection, and

   (ii) in either of the cases mentioned in sub-paragraph (b) of this paragraph, the provisions of the said paragraph (2) shall apply as if each of the references in paragraph (1) of this Article to a rearward projection were treated as a reference to so much of a rearward projection as extends beyond the rearmost point of that other vehicle and as if the reference in the said paragraph (1) to a forward projection were treated as a reference to so much of a forward projection as extends beyond the foremost point of that other vehicle measured, in either case, when the longitudinal axis of each vehicle lies in the same vertical plane between vertical planes at right angles to the said longitudinal axis and passing, in the case of a rearward projection, through the rearmost point of the said other vehicle and that part of the projection furthest from that point or, in the case of a forward projection, through the foremost point of the said other vehicle and that part of the projection furthest from that point.

(4) This Article shall not apply to any motor vehicle or trailer being used—

   (a) for fire brigade, ambulance or police purposes or for defence purposes (including civil defence purposes), or

   (b) in connection with the removal of any obstruction to traffic

if, in any such case, compliance with any provision of this Article would hinder or be likely to hinder the use of the vehicle for the purpose for which it is being used on that occasion.

(5) Notwithstanding that paragraph (2)(a) provides for the conditions specified in [paragraph 3 of Schedule 12] to the Construction and Use Regulations to be complied with as respects a load which has a projection to which sub-paragraph (a)(i) of paragraph (1) of this Article applies, those conditions in relation to the exhibition of the end projection surface on that projection need not be complied with in the case of such a load which carries a rear marking in accordance with the [Road Vehicles Lighting Regulations 1989 [*S.I. 1989 No. 1796 (q.v.)*]].

B12.51   *[Article 23 is printed as amended by the Interpretation Act 1978, ss.17(2)(a) and 23(1).]*

24. Approval of the Minister as to the time, date and route of a journey by a vehicle or a vehicle and its load exceeding 4.3 metres in width

B12.52   [(1) This Article applies in the case of a vehicle the use of which on roads otherwise would be authorised by article 15, 18, 19 or 20 where the overall width of the vehicle or, if it is used for carrying a load, where the overall width of the vehicle together with the width of any lateral projection of its load, exceeds 5 metres.]

(2) Subject to the provisions of paragraph (3) of this Article, a vehicle mentioned in the foregoing paragraph shall be used only—

   (a) for the purpose of making such a journey between specified places as the Minister may have approved by notice in writing given to the owner of the vehicle and only at such times (if any), on such a date or dates (if any) and on such a route (if any) as the Minister may have specified in the said notice, or as the chief officer of police of any police area in which it is proposed that the vehicle shall be used may have specified, in relation to the use of the vehicle in that area, in a direction given to the [user] of the vehicle, and

(b) if the notice referred to in the foregoing sub-paragraph is carried on the vehicle at all times while it is being used for the purpose of making the journey for which the Minister's approval has been given.

(3) Where the effect of any such direction as is mentioned in sub-paragraph (a) of the foregoing paragraph is to vary, in relation to a time, a date or a route of the journey approved by the Minister under that sub-paragraph, the time, the date or dates or the route of the said journey, the vehicle shall not be used in accordance with that direction unless the Minister has given his further approval that the vehicle shall be so used.

[Article 24 is printed as amended by S.I. 1987 No. 1327.] B12.53

25. Notice to police

(1) This Article applies in a case where:— B12.54

(a) the overall width of a vehicle the use of which on roads is authorised by Article 18 or 19 or of the vehicle together with the width of any lateral projection or projections of its load exceeds 2.9 metres, or

(b) the overall length of a vehicle the use of which on roads is authorised by Article 18 or 19 or of the vehicle together with the length of any forward projection and of any rearward projection of its load exceeds 18.3 metres, or

(c) as respects a motor vehicle (whether or not its use is authorised by Article 18 or 19) which is drawing a trailer or trailers the use of which is so authorised, a load is carried in such a manner that its weight rests on more than one of the vehicles being—

   (i) the motor vehicle and one trailer whether constituting an articulated vehicle or not, or

   (ii) any other combination of vehicles,

and, in the case at (i) above, the overall length of the trailer together with the length of any forward projection of the load extending beyond the foremost point of the trailer and of any rearward projection of the load exceeds 18.3 metres and, in the case at (ii) above, the overall length of the vehicles together with the distance between vehicles and the length of any forward and of any rearward projection of the load exceeds 18.3 metres, or

(d) a motor vehicle (whether or not its use on roads is authorised by Article 18 or 19) is drawing a trailer or trailers the use of which is so authorised and the overall length of the combination of vehicles together with the length of any forward projection of any load extending beyond the foremost point of the drawing vehicle comprised in the combination and the length of any rearward projection of any load extending beyond the rearmost point of the rearmost vehicle comprised therein exceeds 25.9 metres, or

(e) a vehicle the use of which on roads is authorised by Article 18 or 19 is carrying a load having a forward projection or a rearward projection exceeding 3.05 metres in length or is fitted with any special appliance or apparatus having such a projection as aforesaid, or

(f) the total weight of a vehicle the use of which on roads is authorised by Article 18 or 19 or of such a vehicle and its load or, in a case where a motor vehicle (whether or not its use is so authorised), is drawing a trailer or trailers the use of which is so authorised, the total weight of the combination of vehicles or of the said combination and of any load carried by any vehicle or vehicles comprised therein exceeds [80,000 kilograms], or

(g) the use of a vehicle on roads is authorised by Article 20.

(2) Save in so far as the chief officer of police of any police area in which it is proposed that the vehicle or, as the case may be, the vehicles, will be used dispenses, as respects the use of the vehicle or vehicles in that area, with the requirements contained in this paragraph as to the length or the form of notice or the particulars to be given, the [user] of the vehicle, or, as the case may be, of the vehicles, before using the vehicle or vehicles on a road, shall give at least two clear days' notice to the chief officer of police of any such area and such notice shall, subject to any necessary modification, be in the form and contain the particulars specified in Part I of Schedule 2 [*not reproduced*].

(3) Subject to any variation in the time, date or route of the journey which may be directed by any such chief officer of police, and subject to any delay which may be occasioned by reason of a direction given by a police constable, in the interests of road safety or to avoid undue traffic congestion, to the driver of a vehicle to halt it in a place on or adjacent to the road on which the vehicle is travelling, the vehicle or vehicles shall be used only in circumstances which accord with the particulars given in compliance with paragraph (2) above as to the time, date and route of the journey and only if any dimension or measurement relating to the vehicle or the vehicles (including one relating to a combination of vehicles) or to a special appliance or apparatus or to a load to be carried, being a dimension or measurement of which particulars have been given as aforesaid, is not exceeded.

B12.55   *[Article 25 is printed as amended by S.I. 1987 No. 1327.]*

26. Notice and indemnity to highway and bridge authorities

B12.56   (1) This Article applies to—

(a) a vehicle the use of which on roads is authorised by Article 18 or 19, whether such vehicle is laden or unladen, or

(b) a combination of a motor vehicle (whether or not its use on roads is authorised under Article 18 or 19) and any trailer or trailers the use of which on roads is authorised under the said Articles, whether all or any part of such combination is laden or unladen,

and which, in either case, either—

(i) has a total weight exceeding [80,000 kilograms] or

(ii) does not comply in all respects with the requirements of the Construction and Use Regulations . . . with respect to

(a) the weights of vehicles, whether laden or unladen;

(b) the weights transmitted to the surface of the road by all or any of the wheels or tracks.

(2) In any case where this Article applies, the [user] of the vehicle or, as the case may be, of the combination of vehicles, shall give to the highway authority for any road and the bridge authority for any bridge on which it is proposed that the vehicle or, as the case may be, the combination of vehicles shall be used—

(a) at any time before such use an indemnity in the form specified in Part II of Schedule 2 [*not reproduced*]; and

(b) in any case to which sub-paragraph (i) of paragraph (1) above applies, at least [five clear days] (or such less period as the said highway authority or the said bridge authority, as the case may be, may agree) before such use, and in a case to which sub-paragraph (ii) of paragraph (1) above applies at least two clear days (or such less period as the said highway authority or the said bridge authority, as the case may be, may agree) before such a use, a notice in the form and containing the particulars specified in Part I of Schedule 2 [*not reproduced*].

[(2A) In any case where a London council or a metropolitan district council which is a highway authority or a bridge authority has—

(a) delegated all or any of its functions with respect to a road or bridge to another London council or (in the case of a metropolitan district council) another metropolitan district council; or

(b) entered into an agreement for the discharge of all or any of its functions with respect to a road or bridge by some other person,

the notice and indemnity which are required by the provisions of paragraph (2) above shall be treated as given in accordance with that paragraph if they are given to the other council or (as the case may be) to the other person.]

[(2B) In paragraph (2A) above "*London council*" means the council of a London borough or the Common Council of the City of London.]

(3) Where, in accordance with requirements specified in paragraph (2) above, notice is required to be given at least [five clear days] before a journey is proposed to be made by a combination of vehicles which include a trailer the use of which on roads is authorised by Article 18 and it is found impracticable to use any vehicle specified in the said notice (not being a vehicle the use of which on roads is authorised by Article 18 or 19) as a vehicle intended to draw the trailer, then any other vehicle of a similar type may be substituted therefor if at least two clear days' notice of the substitution is given to every authority to whom the notice was given, and thereupon the said notice shall have effect as if the substituted vehicle had always been specified therein as the vehicle intended to draw the trailer.

(4) If, by virtue of Article 18, a vehicle is to be used on roads to carry a vehicle specified in either item 1 or item 2 in column 1 of Schedule 1, being the property of, or for the time being under the control of, the persons respectively specified opposite thereto in column 3 of that Schedule, the requirement specified in paragraph (2) above that before such use an indemnity and at least [five clear days'] notice or at least two clear days' notice, as the case may be, shall be given to the authorities specified in that paragraph shall not apply provided that before the vehicle is used on a road—

(a) the notice and indemnity which are required by the provisions of paragraph (2) above are received by or posted to all the said authorities,

(b) the [user] of the carrying vehicle has consulted the Minister on the route proposed to be followed, and

(c) the proper naval, military or air force authority has certified in writing that the journey is urgent and in the national interest.

(5) The provisions of this Article shall not apply to the use on roads of any vehicle which is the property of, or for the time being under the control of, the Secretary of State for Defence.

(6) In the case of a trunk road—

(i) where by virtue of the provisions of [section 6 of the Highways Act 1980], the functions of the Minister with respect to maintenance are exercised in England by the council of a county [or of a metropolitan district] or of a London Borough [or by any other person acting pursuant to an agreement with the Minister] or the functions of the Secretary of State with respect to maintenance are exercised in Wales by the council of a county . . . , or

(ii) where by virtue of an agreement between, or having effect under paragraph 2 of

Schedule 6 to the Transport Act 1962 as if between, the Secretary of State or, as the case may be, the Minister, and either the British Railways Board, the London Transport Executive, the British Transport Docks Board, or the British Waterways Board, the maintenance or, as the case may be, the maintenance and repair of that part are carried out by such Executive or by any such Board,

the notice and indemnity required to be given to the Minister by paragraph (2) of this Article shall be treated as given in accordance with that paragraph only if addressed to, or included in any notice and indemnity given to, such council, Executive or Board [or person] as the case may be.

(7) Any notice and indemnity in respect of any part of a trunk road required by the foregoing paragraph to be addressed to, or included in any notice and indemnity given to, the British Railways Board shall be addressed to, or included in a notice and indemnity given to, the Board at the Headquarters of the Regional Railways Board responsible for the part of the railway system which is affected by any such agreement as is mentioned in that paragraph by virtue of the agreement applying to that part of the trunk road.

B12.57   *[Article 26 is printed as amended by the Interpretation Act 1978, ss.17(2)(a) and 23(1); S.I. 1986 No. 313; S.I. 1987 No. 1327.*

Words relating expressly and exclusively to Scotland have been omitted from paragraph (6)(i) above.

London Transport Executive became known as "London Regional Transport"; see the London Regional Transport Act 1984, s.1(2).

As to the dissolution of London Regional Transport and its replacement by Transport for London, see the Greater London Authority Act 1999, Pt IV, Chap. XVI (particularly ss.297 and 302).

As to the responsibility as highway authority for roads in London, see the 1999 Act, s.259.]

27. Restriction on the passage over bridges of vehicles carrying abnormal indivisible loads

B12.58   Where a motor vehicle the use of which on roads is authorised by Article 18 is so used or where a motor vehicle (whether or not its use is so authorised) is drawing a trailer or trailers the use of which is so authorised and an abnormal indivisible load is being carried by any such vehicle, the driver of the motor vehicle shall not cause or permit either that vehicle or, in the case of a combination of vehicles, any vehicle comprised in the combination—

(a) to enter on any bridge whilst there is on that bridge any other vehicle which is either carrying an abnormal indivisible load or is being used to draw a trailer carrying such a load the presence of which is known to or could reasonably be ascertained by him, or

(b) to remain stationary on any bridge except in circumstances beyond his control.

28. Breakdown on bridges of vehicles of excessive weight or carrying excessive loads

B12.59   (1) This Article applies where—

[(a) a vehicle (including an articulated vehicle) laden or unladen has a gross weight of more than:

(i) prior to [1st October 1989], 32,520 kilograms;

(ii) on or after [1st October 1989], 38,000 kilograms, and]

(b) the use on roads of a vehicle or of a trailer forming part of an articulated vehicle is authorised by Article 5(2), 6, 11, 15, 16, 18 or 19.

(2) Subject to the provisions of paragraph (3) below, where a vehicle or trailer is caused to stop for any reason while it is on a bridge, it shall, as soon as practicable, be moved clear of the bridge by appropriate action by the person in charge of the vehicle, without applying any concentrated load to the surface of that part of the road carried by the bridge.

(3) If the action described in paragraph (2) above is not practicable and it becomes necessary to apply any concentrated load to the said surface by means of jacks, rollers or other similar means, then the person in charge of the vehicle shall—

(a) before any such load is applied to that surface, seek the advice of the bridge authority for that bridge [or any other person responsible for the maintenance and repair of the bridge pursuant to an agreement with that authority] about the use of spreader plates to reduce the possibility of any damage caused by the application of such a load, and

(b) arrange that no such load shall be applied without using such spreader plates as the bridge authority [or such other person] may have advised.

[Article 28 is printed as amended by S.I. 1986 No. 313; S.I. 1987 Nos 1327 and 2161.]   **B12.60**

SCHEDULE 1

(see Article 6)

SERVICE AND AVIATION VEHICLES

B12.61

Column 1	*Column 2*	*Column 3*
1 Motor vehicles or trailers constructed either for actual combative purposes or for naval, military or air force training in connection therewith or for use with, or for the carriage or drawing of, instruments of war, including guns and machine guns.	Construction and Use Regulations—All . . .	The Secretary of State for Defence or the Secretary of State for [Trade and Industry], or any contractor making such vehicles for the said Secretaries of State, or any sub-contractor of such contractor.
2 Track laying motor vehicles or track laying trailers constructed either for actual combative purposes or for use with, or for the carriage or drawing of, instruments of of war, including guns and machine guns, ammunition, equipment or stores in connection therewith.	Construction and Use Regulations—All . . .	The Secretary of State for Defence or the Secretary of State for [Trade and Industry], or any contractor making such vehicles for the said Secretaries of State, or any sub-contractor of such contractor.
3 Motor vehicles or trailers constructed for the carriage of tanks.	Construction and Use Regulations—All . . .	The Secretary of State for Defence or the Secretary of State for [Trade and Industry], or any contractor making such vehicles for the said Secretaries of State, or any sub-contractor of such contractor.

[continued on next page

Column 1	Column 2	Column 3
4 Motor vehicles or trailers constructed for the carriage of searchlights or the necessary equipment therefor.	Construction and Use [Regulation 22].	The Secretary of State for Defence or the Secretary of State for [Trade and Industry], or any contractor making such vehicles for the said Secretaries of State, or any sub-contractor of such contractor.
5 Motor vehicles or trailers constructed for the carriage of aircraft or aircraft parts.	Construction and Use [Regulations 7, 8, 11, 81 and 82].	The Secretary of State for Defence or the Secretary of State for [Trade and Industry], or any contractor making such vehicles for the said Secretaries of State, or any sub-contractor of such contractor.
6 Motor tractors, heavy motor cars and trailers constructed for naval, military, air force or aviation purposes before 1st January 1949.	Construction and Use [Regulations 8, 11, 16, 18 and Schedule 3].	The Secretary of State for Defence or the Secretary of State for [Trade and Industry].
7 Heavy motor cars or trailers constructed for use and used only in connection with flying operations where the additional width is made necessary by the design of the equipment or its installation on the vehicle.	Construction and Use [Regulation 8].	The Secretary of State for Defence or the Secretary of State for [Trade and Industry], or any contractor making such vehicles for the said Secretaries of State, or any sub-contractor of such contractor.
8 Aircraft drawn by motor vehicles.	Construction and Use [Regulations 8, 16, 18 and 22 and Schedule 3].	The Secretary of State for Defence.
9 Motor vehicles or trailers used for the carriage of generating equipment, being equipment used for naval, military or air force purposes.	Construction and Use [Regulations 8, 75, 76 and 80].	The Minister of Transport.

B12.62   *[Schedule 1 is printed as amended by the Interpretation Act 1978, ss.17(2)(a) and 23(1); the Transfer of Functions (Trade and Industry) Order 1983 (S.I. 1983 No. 1127). See the editorial note on p. 1073.] As to references to the Minister of Transport, see the notes to article 3 above.]*

SCHEDULE 2

PART I

FORM OF NOTICE TO POLICE AND TO HIGHWAY AND BRIDGE AUTHORITIES   **B12.63**

[Omitted.]

PART II

FORM OF INDEMNITY

[Omitted.]

SCHEDULE 3

ORDERS REVOKED BY ARTICLE 2   **B12.64**

[Omitted.]

[SCHEDULE 4

(see Articles 13 and 13A)

CONDITIONS RELATING TO THE WIDTH OF AGRICULTURAL VEHICLES

1. If the overall width of the vehicle, or in the case of a combination of vehicles men-   **B12.65**
tioned in Article 13A(1), the overall width of the combination exceeds the width specified
in an item in column 2 of the Table below, the vehicle, or in the case of a combination of
vehicles, the drawing vehicle, shall not be driven at a speed exceeding that specified in
column 3 of that item.

1 *Item No.*	*2* *Overall width*	*3* *Maximum speed*
1 2	3.5 metres [2.55] metres	12 miles per hour 20 miles per hour

2. If—

  (a) the overall width of—   **B12.66**

      (i) an agricultural motor vehicle,

      (ii) an agricultural trailer,

      (iii) an agricultural trailed appliance, or

  (b) the width specified in Article 13A(2) of a combination of vehicles—

exceeds 3 metres and the whole or part of the journey to be made by the vehicle or combination will be on a road on which there is a speed limit of 40 miles per hour or less or will
cover a distance exceeding 5 miles, the operator of the vehicle shall—

      (a) before using the vehicle or combination on a road, give at least 24 hours
notice of the intended use to the chief officer of police for any police area in
which the operator proposes to use the vehicle or combination of vehicles and
the notice shall contain the following particulars:—

      (i) the time, date and route of the proposed journey,

      (ii) information about the vehicle or combination of vehicles including the overall width; and

  (b) use the vehicle or combination only in accordance with the particulars given in the notice mentioned above, subject to any variation in the time, date or route as may be directed by any chief officer of police as regards his police area,

so, however, that a chief officer of police may dispense, within his area, with the said requirements as to length of notice and information about the vehicle or combination.

B12.67   **3.** In a case where—

  (a) the width of an agricultural motor vehicle exceeds 3 metres, or

  (b) an agricultural motor vehicle is towing an agricultural trailer or agricultural trailed appliance in the manner described in Article 13A(1) and the width specified in Article 13A(2) exceeds 3 metres, or

  (c) an agricultural motor vehicle is towing an agricultural trailer or an agricultural trailed appliance in a manner not described in Article 13A(1) and the overall width of either the motor vehicle or the trailer or trailed appliance, or both, exceeds 3 metres,

the vehicle or the combination of vehicles shall not draw any trailer or, as the case may be, any other trailer, except

      (i) a two-wheeled trailer used solely for the carriage of equipment for use on the drawing vehicle,

      (ii) an agricultural trailed appliance, or

      (iii) an unladen trailer specially designed for use with the drawing vehicle when it is harvesting.

B12.68   **4.** If the overall width of an agricultural motor vehicle, an agricultural trailer on which an implement is mounted as mentioned in Article 13B, or an agricultural trailed appliance, or the width specified in Article 13A(2) of a combination of vehicles, exceeds 3.5 metres—

  (a) at least one person, other than the driver of the vehicle or, in the case of a combination of vehicles, the driver of the drawing vehicle, shall be employed to warn any other person (including the driver of the vehicle or the drawing vehicle) of any danger likely to be caused to that other person by the presence of the vehicle or the combination of vehicles on the road; and

  (b) the extremities of the vehicle or implement (including any blade or spike) shall be clearly visible at a reasonable distance to any person on the road (other than the driver of the vehicle or, in the case of a combination of vehicles, the driver of the drawing vehicle) and during the hours of darkness or in seriously reduced visibility this condition shall be satisfied by such means as may be required by the [Road Vehicles Lighting Regulations 1989 [*S.I. 1989 No. 1796, q.v.*]].

B12.69   **5.** The overall width of a vehicle, or the width specified in Article 13A(2) of a combination of vehicles, shall not exceed 4.3 metres.]

B12.70   *[Schedule 4 was inserted by S.I. 1984 No. 1810 and is printed as amended by the Interpretation Act 1978, ss.17(2)(a) and 23(1); S.I. 1995 No. 3052.]*

[SCHEDULE 5

(see Article 13C)

PART I

1 *Item No.*	2 *Distance of rearward or forward projection*	3 *Conditions to be complied with*	
1	1 metres	A	**B12.71**
2	2 metres	B	
3	4 metres	B	
		C	
4	6 metres	B	
		C	
		D	

PART II

1. In this Schedule:—   **B12.72**

"*Condition A*" is the condition that the end of each projection is clearly visible at a reasonable distance to any person using the road other than the driver of the vehicle, or in the case of a combination of vehicles, the driver of the drawing vehicle, and during the hours of darkness or in seriously reduced visibility this condition shall be satisfied by such means as may be required by the [Road Vehicles Lighting Regulations 1989].

"*Condition B*" is the condition that—

(a) the end of each projection is marked with a projection marker of a kind specified in relation to an end projection surface in [Part II of Schedule 12] to the Construction and Use Regulations and in respect of which the provisions specified, for the purposes of those Regulations, in [paragraph 3(b) of Part I] of that Schedule are complied with,

(b) each side of each projection is marked with a projection marker of a kind specified in relation to a side projection surface in [Part II] of that Schedule and in respect of which the provisions specified, for the purposes of the said Regulations, in [paragraph 3(c) of Part I] of that Schedule are complied with, and

(c) during the hours of darkness or in seriously reduced visibility the markers referred to in paragraphs (a) and (b) shall be illuminated in the manner described, in relation to the extremities of an appliance, in [paragraph 3(f) of Schedule 12] to the Construction and Use Regulations, and kept clean and unobstructed.

"*Condition C*" is the same condition as is specified, in relation to Articles 13 and 13A, in paragraph 2 of Schedule 4; and

"*Condition D*" is the same condition as is specified, in relation to Articles 13 and 13A, in paragraph 4(a) of Schedule 4.]

[Schedule 5 was inserted by S.I. 1984 No. 1810 and is printed as amended by the Interpretation Act 1978, ss.17(2)(a) and 23(1).   **B12.73**

There is no numbered paragraph in Part II of Schedule 5 following after paragraph 1.]

Article 17A   [SCHEDULE 5A

CONSTRUCTIONAL REQUIREMENTS FOR COMPRESSED NATURAL GAS
SYSTEMS FOR VEHICLE PROPULSION

1. Definitions

B12.74   In this Schedule—

"*articulating connector*" means a connector bridging the space between two separate and rigid vehicle structures;

"*bar*" means bar gauge;

"*compressed natural gas*" means natural gas stored at a pressure above 30 bar;

"*design pressure*" means the pressure which a part of a gas propulsion system has been designed to withstand;

"*gas container*" means a container fitted to a motor vehicle or a trailer and intended for the storage of natural gas for the purpose of the propulsion of the vehicle or of the drawing vehicle as the case may be;

"*g*" means gravity;

"*high pressure*" means designed to withstand a pressure exceeding 7 bar;

"*large bus*" means a vehicle constructed or adapted to carry more than 16 seated passengers in addition to the driver;

"*medium pressure*" means designed to withstand a pressure not exceeding 7 bar but exceeding 75 millibars;

"*millibars*" means millibars gauge;

"*mm*" means millimetres;

"*mm²*" means square millimetres;

"*N*" means newtons;

"*°C*" means degrees Celsius;

"*pipeline*" means any pipe or passage connecting any two parts of a gas propulsion system;

"*pressure relief device*" means a device to protect a gas container against over-pressure; and

"*regulator*" means a device which automatically reduces and controls the pressure of the gas flowing through it.

2. Gas containers

B12.75   (1) Any gas container shall—

(a) be suitable to be fitted to the vehicle to which it is fitted and be constructed from suitable materials;

(b) be capable of containing natural gas operating at a working pressure of 200 bar settled at 15°C with a maximum filling pressure of 260 bar;

(c) be free from any visible damage or defect and not have been the subject of any alteration or repair subsequent to its manufacture;

(d) be fitted with a manually operable isolation valve and a pressure relief device (but may in addition be fitted with an electrically operable isolation valve);

(e) be used for no more than 30 years from the date of manufacture, and

(f) be marked as follows in characters 6mm high (unless otherwise stated)—

(i) "CNG ONLY" in letters at least 25mm high;

(ii) the date of manufacture;

(iii) "DO NOT USE AFTER ......" in characters at least 25mm high, and specifying the month and year of expiry;

(iv) the design pressure at a temperature of 15°C;

(v) the date of the original pressure test, together with the identity of the testing station;

(vi) the date of any subsequent periodic pressure test carried out in accordance with paragraph 2 of Schedule 5B and the identity of the testing station, and

(vii) the design life of the gas container if less than 30 years.

(2) Any gas container shall be so mounted that—

(a) the effectiveness of any vehicle crumple zone is not impaired;

(b) it is securely attached to the vehicle by suitable mountings that will protect the gas container from displacement or damage due to vibration or other cause;

(c) the gas container and its mountings do not weaken the vehicle's structure or affect the vehicle's stability;

(d) it is placed in such a position that the risk of impact damage to the gas container and its isolation valve is, as far as practicable, reduced and it is placed or shielded so that the effects of any impact are, as far as practicable, reduced;

(e) it is placed in such a position or so shielded that the risk of damage from flying debris is minimised;

(f) it is placed in such a position or so insulated or shielded that the effects of any source of heat are minimised;

(g) it is suitably protected from external corrosion and abrasion; and

(h) subject to sub-paragraph (3), any leaking or vented gas will be directed safely to the atmosphere preventing as far as practicable the possibility of its entering the engine, or the passenger, driver or living compartment.

(3) Where a gas container is to be located in the driver, passenger or living compartment or in the vehicle boot, or in any space which is not so ventilated as to prevent the accumulation of gas, the valves, connections and pipework shall be enclosed in order to contain any gas leakage, either by—

(a) placing the gas container and its fittings within a durable enclosure which is sealed so that it is gas tight to the compartment, vehicle boot or space as the case may be and which is provided with permanent direct ventilation to the outside of the vehicle, or

(b) enclosing the neck and fittings of the gas container within a durable envelope which is gas tight to the compartment, vehicle boot or space as the case may be and which is provided with permanent direct ventilation to the outside of the vehicle.

(4) Any enclosure or envelope required for the purposes of sub-paragraph (3) shall not contain any source of ignition.

(5) Any ventilation opening required under sub-paragraph (3) shall—

(a) have a free area of not less than 600mm², and

(b) be terminated away from any openings into any vehicle compartment, away from any source of ignition and in a position where it is not liable to blockage.

(6) Any pressure relief device contained within any enclosure shall have a separate, dedicated vent line which may pass within the enclosure vent.

(7) In relation to every gas container, there shall be provided, either on the gas container itself or in documents which are readily available, information concerning—

(a) any particular installation requirements;

(b) details of any pressure relief devices fitted or required to be fitted to the gas container;

(c) recommended inspection intervals (which shall not be more than three years); and

(d) any recommended inspection procedure.

3. Gas container isolation

B12.76   (1) Any gas container shall be capable of being isolated from its supply pipework by means of an isolation valve connected directly to each gas container but not between the gas container and its pressure relief device.

(2) Any isolation valve shall be capable of shutting off all the gas flow from the gas container, except through the pressure relief device.

(3) Any isolation valve shall be marked clearly and permanently with the direction of operation.

(4) Any isolation valve shall be so protected as to ensure that its operation is unaffected by the collection of moisture or other foreign matter.

(5) Any gas container valve assembly shall be so placed as, so far as practicable, to be protected from damage.

(6) In this paragraph "*isolation valve*" means a manually operable isolation valve.

4. Pressure relief devices

B12.77   (1) Every gas container shall be provided with a suitable pressure relief device which complies with sub-paragraphs (3) to (7).

(2) Where a pressure regulator is fitted to a gas container, any pressure relief device attached to it shall comply with sub-paragraphs (3) to (7).

(3) Any pressure relief device shall be such that—

(a) there is an adequate discharge rate to ensure the safety of the system;

(b) any cooling effect of the gas during discharge will not affect the discharge rate;

(c) its relieving characteristics will not be impaired on exposure to fire;

(d) operation of the device will not inhibit the discharge rate from the device;

(e) its outlet size is not less than the size of inlet or outlet pipework of the gas container;

(f) it cannot be installed in the reverse flow direction;

(g) it is so protected as to ensure that its operation is unaffected by the collection of moisture or other foreign matter;

(h) if the device is adjustable, unauthorised interference with its settings is prevented; and

(i) it is marked clearly with the set pressure or temperature and with the flow direction.

(4) Any pressure relief device shall be placed so that—

(a) so far as practicable, the device and its outlets are protected from damage and blockage in the event of an accident;

(b) its discharge rate is not inhibited if an associated gas container is located within an enclosure; and

(c) it is away from any source of heat which could impair the designed operation of the device.

(5) The discharge from a pressure relief device shall terminate outside the vehicle and be directed or deflected away from any opening into the engine, driver, passenger or living compartment, vehicle boot, or any space which is not so ventilated as to prevent the accumulation of gas.

(6) The discharge from a pressure relief device shall not terminate near any source of heat or other potential source of ignition.

(7) A pressure relief device on any gas container or regulator located within the driver, passenger or living compartment, vehicle boot, or in any space which is not so ventilated as to prevent the accumulation of gas shall have its discharge vented separately and directly to the outside of the vehicle.

5. Pipelines

(1) Every pipeline shall be fixed in such a manner and position that—   **B12.78**

   (a) it will not be adversely affected by the heat of the exhaust system of any engine or by any other source of heat;

   (b) it is protected from vibration and strain in excess of that which it can reasonably be expected to withstand;

   (c) it is so placed or shielded as to minimise the risk from flying debris; and

   (d) in the case of a medium or high pressure pipeline it is so far as practicable accessible for inspection.

(2) Space as provided in sub-paragraph (4), every medium or high pressure pipeline shall—

   (a) a rigid line of seamless steel of high pressure hydraulic grade, suitable for service on road vehicles and designed for the full range of operating temperatures, pressures and loading which may occur, and

   (b) effectively protected against, or shielded from, or treated so as to be resistant to, external corrosion throughout its length unless it is made from material which is corrosion resistant under the conditions which it is likely to encounter in service.

(3) No unsupported length of any medium or high pressure pipeline shall exceed 600mm.

(4) Flexible hose may be used in a medium or high pressure pipeline if—

   (a) it is reinforced either by stainless steel wire braid or by textile braid, and

   (b) save in the case of a pipeline attached to a gas container for the purpose of filling that gas container, the flexibility which it provides is necessary for the construction or operation of the gas propulsion system of which it forms a part.

6. Unions and joints

(1) Every union and joint on a pipeline or gas container shall be so constructed and   **B12.79**
fitted that it will—

   (a) not be able to work loose or leak when in use, and

   (b) be readily accessible for inspection and maintenance;

(2) Every union on a medium or high pressure pipeline or on a gas container shall be made of suitable metal but such a union may contain non-metal washers and seals provided that such washers and seals are supported and constrained by metal components.

7. Filling connectors

B12.80   (1) Any filling connector for the refuelling of the vehicle shall be of a type which is used exclusively for natural gas filling and which is compatible with the filling nozzle without the use of an adapter fitting.

(2) Gas shall be prevented from flowing back from the gas container to the filling connector.

(3) Any filling connector shall be covered with a dust cap, which is secured permanently to the vehicle.

(4) Where a filling connector is placed on the outside of the vehicle, it shall be protected against unauthorised interference.

(5) The filling connector shall be located outside the driver or passenger compartment in a suitably protected, well ventilated and readily accessible position, away from any openings in the driver, passenger or living compartment.

8. Valves, safety devices and control equipment

B12.81   (1) Every gas propulsion system shall be so designed and constructed so that—

(a) the supply of gas to the engine is stopped by an automatic valve when—

(i) the engine is not running at all;
(ii) the engine is not running on the supply of gas, or
(iii) the engine ignition is oV;

(b) where the valve referred to in sub-paragraph (a) is not integral with the regulator, it shall be positioned upstream of the regulator so as to be able to isolate the gas container and filling point, and

(c) in the event of a rapid deceleration of the vehicle in an accident or similar occurrence, the supply of gas to the engine is automatically stopped at a point as close as is possible to the gas container and can only be restored manually.

(2) Where the engine or vehicle is constructed or adapted to run on one or more fuels as an alternative to gas or in addition to gas, the safety of the engine or the gas fuel system shall not be impaired by the presence of any other fuel system.

(3) In addition to the isolation valve required under paragraph 3 and the pressure relief device required under paragraph 4, every gas container shall, subject to sub-paragraph (4), be fitted with an automatically operated valve to prevent gas escaping from the gas container in the event of a fracture or failure of the pipeline or any component in the gas supply system.

(4) In the case of a group of gas containers inter-connected in such a manner that the pipework is protected in the event of an accident, the group of gas containers may be fitted with a single automatically operated valve or device to prevent gas escaping from the group of gas containers in the event of a fracture or failure of the pipeline or of any component in the gas supply system.

(5) Any electrically operated valve shall be constructed so as to open when electrical power is applied and close when electrical power is removed.

(6) Where a vehicle is equipped to operate on more than one fuel but not on a mixture of fuels, a fuel selection system shall be installed which—

(a) has a control switch which is readily accessible to the driver at all times and is clearly marked for the selection of each fuel or fuel mixture;

(b) has a change-over system, operated by the control switch mentioned in paragraph (a) to prevent the use of more than one fuel at a time, except for the fuel remaining in the common system during change-over; and

(c) does not impair the safety of the engine or the fuel system.

(7) All parts of every valve or cock which are in contact with gas shall be made of suitable metal, save that they may contain non-metal washers and seals if those washers and seals are supported and constrained by metal components.

9. Regulators

(1) Any regulator fitted shall be designed so that— **B12.82**

(a) it has a pre-set pressure and flow rating suitable for the part of the system to which it is attached;

(b) it incorporates a means of protecting the system downstream of the regulator from the upstream pressure in the event of failure of or leakage from the regulator;

(c) it is marked clearly and permanently with the fuel type, pressure and flow direction; and

(d) if the engine cooling system is utilised within the regulator, passage of gas into the engine cooling system is prevented.

(2) Any pressure relief device on a regulator shall comply with the requirement of paragraph 4(3) to (7).

(3) Any regulator shall be installed so that—

(a) it is in an accessible position for inspection and maintenance;

(b) it is in a position that is protected from heat sources;

(c) it is in a position where, as far as is practicable, any ventilation holes are prevented from being blocked, and

(d) it is securely attached to a secure mounting.

(4) Where a regulator is to be located in the driver, passenger or living compartment, or in the vehicle boot or in any other space which is not so ventilated as to prevent the accumulation of gas, it shall be enclosed in order to contain any gas leakage, either by—

(a) placing the gas container and its fillings within a durable enclosure which is—

(i) sealed so that it is gas tight to the compartment, vehicle boot or space as the case may be and which is,

(ii) provided with permanent direct ventilation to the outside of the vehicle, or

(b) enclosing the neck and fittings of the gas container within a durable envelope which is—

(i) gas tight to the compartment, vehicle boot or space as the case may be and which is,

(ii) provided with direct permanent ventilation to the outside of the vehicle.

(5) A regulator shall not be attached directly to the engine or to any part ancillary to the engine.

10. Special requirements for buses

In the case of a large bus there shall be fitted as near as practicable to the gas container **B12.83** a valve which stops the flow of gas into the gas supply pipeline in the event of—

(a) the angle of tilt of the vehicle exceeding that referred to in regulation 6 of the

Public Service Vehicles (Conditions of Fitness, Equipment, Use and Certification) Regulations 1981 [*S.I. 1981 No. 257, as amended, q.v.*], or

(b) the deceleration of the vehicle exceeding 5g.

11. Connections for articulated vehicles

B12.84   (1) Where a trailer is used for the carriage of any part of the gas supply system—

(a) an articulating connector complying with sub-paragraphs (2) to (8) shall be fitted between the part of the system on the vehicle and the part of the system on the trailer, and

(b) an articulating connector shall not be subjected to more than medium pressure.

(2) An articulating connector shall—

(a) be of a type suitable for natural gas systems;

(b) be designed to accept a compatible nozzle without the use of adapter fittings; and

(c) not be interchangeable with connections for other services.

(3) The gas supply pipework at the terminal on each station of the articulated unit shall be capable of withstanding a force at least 200N in any direction before deformation or failure occurs.

(4) Any articulating connector shall be designed so that separation can be achieved in a fail-safe manner, minimising the volume of gas released during the separation process and while the joint remains disconnected.

(5) Disconnection devices shall be designed to prevent unauthorised interference.

(6) Dust caps shall be fitted to exposed connections to keep out dirt and such dust caps shall be attached to the system.

(7) The articulating connector shall be properly supported and protected at all times.

(8) The articulating connector shall incorporate a breakaway coupling, which is designed to separate when a breakaway force of 200N or greater is applied in any direction and which has an automatic isolation system to minimise the release of gas in the event of the separation of the breakaway coupling.

12. Marking and labelling of the vehicle

B12.85   (1) Every vehicle is equipped to be fuelled by natural gas shall be fitted with a metal identification plate, located in a readily visible and accessible position, that is marked clearly and permanently to identify—

(a) that the vehicle has been constructed or adapted to run on natural gas, and

(b) the maximum system filling pressure.

This information is in addition to the information required by paragraph 2(1)(f) with respect to the gas container.

(2) The filling point for natural gas shall be identified adjacent to the point by the words "NATURAL GAS" or other suitable wording.

13. General requirements

B12.86   Every part of the gas system shall be—

(a) so far as practicable located and protected so as not to be exposed to accidental damage;

(b) soundly and properly constructed of materials which are compatible with one another and with the gas used or likely to be used and which are capable of withstanding the loads or stress likely to be met in operation, and

(c) so designed and constructed that the number of joints is kept to a minimum and that leakage of gas is unlikely to occur.]

[Schedule 5A was inserted by S.I. 1998 No. 2884.]   **B12.87**

[SCHEDULE 5B

GAS CONTAINER TESTING REQUIREMENTS

1. Before its first use on a vehicle, every gas container shall be pressure tested by an   **B12.88** accredited testing laboratory at a pressure of 1.5 times the working pressure of the gas container. The pressure test shall be carried out in accordance with the procedure set out in paragraph 4.7 of BS 5430: Part I: 1990 or, where an equivalent procedure has been specified by the manufacturer, in accordance with that procedure.

2. Without prejudice to the obligation imposed by regulation 100 of the Road Vehicles (Construction and Use) Regulations 1986, the owner of any vehicle, or, if it is in the possession of a different person, that person, shall ensure that any gas container used on that vehicle is subject to a periodic test by an accredited testing laboratory every three years, or with such greater frequency as the manufacturer specifies. The periodic test shall include—

(a) the pressure test specified in paragraph 1, and

(b) an internal and external visual inspection carried out in accordance with paragraphs 4.4.2 and 4.4.3 of BS 5430: Part I: 1990, or, where an equivalent procedure has been specified by the manufacturer, in accordance with that procedure.

3. (1) A gas container which has satisfied a test required under paragraph 1 or 2 shall be   **B12.89** permanently and legibly marked with—

(a) the month and year of the test, and

(b) the identity of the testing station.

(2) Where the gas container bears a previous test mark, the mark required under this paragraph shall be placed adjacent to that mark.

4. In this Schedule—

"an accredited testing laboratory" means a testing laboratory which has been accredited by the United Kingdom Accreditation Service or by an equivalent body in an EEA State under European Standard EN 45001: 1989 for general criteria for the operation of testing laboratories (British Standard BS 7501: 1989);

"BS 5430: Part I: 1990" means Part I of the British Standard for the periodic inspection, testing and maintenance of transportable gas containers (excluding dissolved acetylene gas containers), published in 1990 or any equivalent standard published by a recognised testing body in an EEA State in which case a reference to any provision of that British Standard is to be taken as a reference to the equivalent provision of any such equivalent standard;

"EEA State" means a State which is a contracting Party to the Agreement on the European Economic Area signed at Oporto on 2nd May 1992 as adjusted by the protocol signed at Brussels on 17th March 1993 [*Cm. 2073 and Cm. 2183*]; and

"gas container" has the meaning given in paragraph 1 of Schedule 5A.]

[Schedule 5B was inserted by S.I. 1998 No. 2884.   **B12.90**

As to the Agreement on the European Economic Area, see the editorial note to Regulation (EEC) 3820/85 below.]

[SCHEDULE 6

FORM OF IDENTIFICATION SIGN

(see Article 18(2)(t))

PART I

B12.91   **1.** The sign shall be mounted in a clearly visible position on the front of the vehicle, facing forwards, and as near to the vertical plane as practicable.

2. The sign shall be kept clean and unobscured at all times.

B12.92   **3.** The sign shall consist of white letters on a black background.

4. The sign shall take the form shown in Part II. Any variation in a dimension specified in Part II shall be treated as permitted for the purposes of this Order if the variation does not exceed 5 per cent of that dimension.

PART II

B12.93

400mm

250mm

105mm

70mm

Note: the category number 3 is shown as an example; the number could be 1, 2 or 3 depending upon the category of the vehicle or combination of vehicles.]

B12.94   *[Schedule 6 was inserted by S.I. 1987 No. 1327.]*

The Passenger and Goods Vehicles (Recording Equipment) Regulations 1979

(S.I. 1979 No. 1746)

[The text of these regulations is printed as amended by:

the Passenger and Goods Vehicles (Recording Equipment) (Amendment) Regulations 1984 (S.I. 1984 No. 144) (March 13, 1984);

the Community Drivers' Hours and Recording Equipment Regulations 1986 (S.I. 1986 No. 1457) (September 29, 1986);

the Passenger and Goods Vehicles (Recording Equipment) (Amendment) Regulations 1986 (S.I. 1986 No. 2076) (December 31, 1986);

the Passenger and Goods Vehicles (Recording Equipment) Regulations 1991 (S.I. 1991 No. 381) (April 1, 1991);

the Passenger and Goods Vehicles (Recording Equipment) Regulations 1994 (S.I. 1994 No. 1838), reg.3 (August 9, 1994); and

the Passenger and Goods Vehicles (Recording Equipment) Regulations 1996 (S.I. 1996 No. 941) (April 25, 1996).

The amending regulations are referred to in the notes to the principal regulations only by their years and numbers. The dates referred to above are the dates on which the amending regulations came into force.

The Passenger and Goods Vehicles (Recording Equipment) (Amendment) Regulations 1985 (S.I. 1985 No. 1801) were revoked by S.I. 1986 No. 2076.].

B13.01

1. Commencement, citation, revocation and interpretation

(1), (2) *[Omitted.]*

B13.02

(3) In these Regulations—

"*the Act of 1968*" means the Transport Act 1968;

["*the Community Recording Equipment Regulation*" means Council Regulation (EEC) No. 3821/85 on recording equipment in road transport [*q.v.*] as it has effect in accordance with—

(a) Commission Regulation (EEC) No. 3314/90;

(b) Commission Regulation (EEC) No. 3688/92; and

(c) Commission Regulation (EC) No. 2479/95;

and as read with the Community Drivers' Hours and Recording Equipment (Exemptions and Supplementary Provisions) Regulations 1986 [*S.I. 1986 No. 1456 (q.v.)*];]

[Regulation 1 is printed as amended by S.I. 1986 No. 1457; S.I. 1996 No. 941.]

B13.03

2. Installation and use of recording equipment

[Substitutes sections 97, 97A and 97B for section 97 of the Transport Act 1968 above.]

B13.04

3. Consequential adaptations of enactments

B13.05   *[Amends the Transport Act 1968, ss.98, 99 and 103 above, and the Road Traffic (Foreign Vehicles) Act 1972, Sched. 1.]*

[4. Installation or repair of recording equipment, checks and inspections

B13.06   (1) The Secretary of State shall be the competent authority in Great Britain—

(a) for the approval of fitters and workshops for the installation or repair of recording equipment in accordance with [Article 1] of the Community Recording Equipment Regulation; and

(b) for the nomination of bodies for the carrying out of checks and inspections of recording equipment in accordance with Chapter VI of Annex I to that Regulation.

(2) Any approval or nomination under this Regulation shall be in writing, shall specify its scope, shall provide for its withdrawal by the Secretary of State on notice given by him and, if the Secretary of State thinks fit, may contain conditions.

[(2A)(a) An approval or nomination shall be issued—

(i) in the case of an approval or nomination issued between 31st October and 31st December in any year, for a period ending on 31st January in the second year following the year of issue, and

(ii) in the case of any other approval or nomination, for a period ending on 31st January in the year following the year of issue.

(b) An approval or nomination issued and not withdrawn may, on application before the date of its expiry, be renewed for a further period ending on 31st January next following and thereafter for successive periods so ending.]

(3) Such conditions may in particular relate to—

(a) the fees to be charged for installing or repairing or, as the case may be, checking or inspecting recording equipment;

(b) the place where and equipment by means of which such activities are, or are to be, carried out;

(c) the procedure to be adopted in carrying out such activities;

(d) the records to be kept and the evidence to be furnished of the carrying out of such activities;

(e) the training of persons for carrying out such activities;

(f) the inspection by or on behalf of the Secretary of State of places where and equipment by means of which such activities are, or are to be, carried out; and

(g) the display, at the places where such activities are carried out, of signs indicating that such activities are carried out there by fitters or workshops approved or, as the case may be, bodies nominated, by the Secretary of State.

(4) The Secretary of State shall publish from time to time lists of—

(a) the fitters and workshops for the time being approved by him; and

(b) the bodies for the time being nominated by him;

and any list published under sub-paragraph (a) above shall specify the mark to be placed by each approved fitter or workshop on any seals which he or they affix to any recording equipment.

(5) In this Regulation *"recording equipment"* means equipment for recording information as to the use of a vehicle.]

[Regulation 4 was substituted by S.I. 1984 No. 144 (and a correction slip dated February 1984) and   **B13.07**
is printed as amended by S.I. 1986 No. 2076.]

5.   *[Revoked by S.I. 1986 No. 1457.]*   **B13.08**

The Motor Vehicles (International Circulation) (Amendment) Order 1980

(S.I. 1980 No. 1095)

B14.01 *Editorial note.* Articles 5, 6, 7, 8 and 10(2) to (4) of this order have been revoked by the Motor Vehicles (International Circulation) (Amendment) Order 1989 (S.I. 1989 No. 993) below. The revoked provisions had not been brought into force and have in effect been superseded by the amendments to the principal order effected by the 1989 Order.

1. Citation and commencement

B14.02 This Order may be cited as the Motor Vehicles (International Circulation) (Amendment) Order 1980 and shall come into operation—

(a) for all purposes of paragraph (1) of Article 10 on the first day of the month following that in which the Order is made, and

(b) for all other purposes, on the date on which the Convention on Road Traffic concluded at Vienna in 1968 [*Cmnd. 4032*] is first in force in respect of the United Kingdom, which date shall be notified in the London, Edinburgh and Belfast Gazettes.

B14.03 *[At April 1, 2001 no date is known to have been notified for the purpose of paragraph (b) above.]*

2. Interpretation

B14.04 In this Order "the principal Order" means the Motor Vehicles (International Circulation) Order 1975 [*S.I. 1975 No. 1208, q.v.*].

3. Documents for drivers going abroad

B14.05 For paragraph (1) of Article 1 of the principal Order there shall be substituted the following paragraphs:—

"(1) Subject to the following provisions of this Article, the Minister of Transport may issue to a person resident in the United Kingdom a driving permit in any of the forms A, B and C in Schedule 1 to this Order for use outside the United Kingdom.

(1A) A permit shall be issued to a person only for vehicles of a class or classes in respect of which that person either—

(a) holds a full licence, or has held and is entitled to obtain such a licence and is authorised to drive by virtue of [section 88(1) of the Road Traffic Act 1988] or any corresponding Northern Ireland provision (licence applied for or surrendered for correction of particulars, etc.); or

(b) holds a provisional licence, or has held and is entitled to obtain such a licence and is authorised to drive as mentioned in paragraph (a) above, and has passed the test of competence to drive or a test which is a sufficient test;

and in this paragraph '*full licence*' means a licence (granted under [Part III of the Road

Traffic Act 1988] or Part I of the Road Traffic Act (Northern Ireland) 1970) other than a provisional licence, and '*provisional licence*' and '*test of competence to drive*' have the same meaning as in the said [Part III] or the said Part I, and '*test of competence which is a sufficient test*' has the same meaning as in the said [Part III].

(1B) A permit in form A shall not be issued to any person who is under 18 years of age unless the permit is restricted to the driving of motor cycles or invalid carriages, or both.

(1C) A permit in form B shall not be issued to any person who is under 18 years of age.

(1D) A permit in form C shall be limited in its period of validity to three years, or, if shorter—

(a) the unexpired period of the permit holder's current United Kingdom driving licence; or

(b) where the permit holder is authorised to drive by virtue of [section 88(1) of the Road Traffic Act 1988] or any corresponding Northern Ireland provision (licence applied for or surrendered for correction of particulars, etc.) the remainder of the period for which he is so authorised together with the period of validity of any licence granted while he is so authorised.".

[Article 3 has not yet been brought into operation; see article 1(b) above.   **B14.06**
Article 3 is printed as amended by the Interpretation Act 1978, ss.17(2)(a) and 23(1).]

4. The following words shall be omitted from Article 1 of the principal Order:—   **B14.07**

(a) in paragraph (7) the words "tests of the competency of applicants for driving permits and", and

(b) in paragraph (8) the words "tests or".

[Article 4 has not yet been brought into operation; see article 1(b) above.]   **B14.08**

5. Visitors' driving permits   *[Revoked.]*   **B14.09**

6.   *[Revoked.]*

7.   *[Revoked.]*

8. Supplementary provisions   *[Revoked.]*

9. Schedules

In Schedule 1 to the principal Order after form B and before form D there shall be inserted as form C the form set out in the Schedule to this Order.   **B14.10**

[Article 9 has not yet been brought into operation; see article 1(b) above.]

10.–(1) *[Amended Schedule 2 (Fees) (now revoked) to principal order.]*   **B14.11**

(2)–(4) *[Revoked.]*

Article 9   SCHEDULE

C

B14.12   FORM OF INTERNATIONAL DRIVING PERMIT UNDER
CONVENTION OF 1968

Page No. 1 *(outside of front cover, coloured grey)*

** In a permit
issued by some
other country
the name of that
country and its
distinguishing
sign will appear
instead and
pages 1 and 2
will be drawn
up in the
language of that
country.*

United Kingdom of Great Britain and Northern Ireland   GB*

International Motor Traffic

INTERNATIONAL DRIVING PERMIT

No. ....

Convention on Road Traffic of 8 November, 1968

Valid until ....

Issued by ....

At ....

Date ....

Number of domestic
driving permit ....

```
   Seal
 or stamp
    of
the issuing        Signature of issuing authority or association.
 authority
    or
association
```

Page No. 2 *(inside front cover, coloured grey)*

This permit is not valid for the territory of the United Kingdom. It is valid for the territories of all the other Contracting Parties. The categories of vehicles for the driving of which it is valid are stated at the end of the booklet.

List of Contracting States (optional)

This permit shall in no way affect the obligation of the holder to conform to the laws and regulations relating to residence and to the exercise of a profession in each State through which he travels. In particular, it shall cease to be valid in a State if its holder establishes his normal residence there.

Form of International Driving Permit under Convention of 1968

Last left-hand page

PARTICULARS CONCERNING THE DRIVER Surname	1
Other names(^{1})	2
Place of birth(^{2})	3
Date of birth(^{3})	4
Home address	5

CATEGORIES OF VEHICLES FOR WHICH THE PERMIT IS VALID	
Motor cycles	A
Motor vehicles, other than those in category A, having a permissible maximum weight not exceeding 3,500kg. (7,700 lb.) and not more than eight seats in addition to the driver's seat	B
Motor vehicles used for the carriage of goods and whose permissible maximum weight exceeds 3,500kg. (7,700 lb.)	C
Motor vehicles used for the carriage of passengers and having more than eight seats in addition to the driver's seat	D
Combinations of vehicles of which the drawing vehicle is in a category or categories for which the driver is licensed (B and/or C and/or D), but which are not themselves in that category or categories	E

RESTRICTIVE CONDITIONS OF USE(^{4})

....

....

....

(^{1}) Father's or husband's name may be inserted here.

(^{2}) If the place of birth is unknown, leave blank.

(^{3}) If date of birth is unknown, state approximate age on date of issue of permit.

(^{4}) For example, "Must wear corrective lenses", "Valid only for driving vehicle No. ....", "Vehicle must be equipped to be driven by a one-legged person".

Form of International Driving Permit under Convention of 1968

Last right-hand page

1 ....

2 ....

3 ....

4 ....

5 ....

A (^{5})

B (^{5})

C (^{5})

D (^{5})

E (^{5})

Photograph

(^{5})

Signature of holder(^{6}) ....

DISQUALIFICATIONS:

The holder is deprived of the right to drive in the
territory of ....(^{7}) until ....
At .... on ....
on ....(^{8})

(^{8})

The holder is deprived of the right to drive in the
territory of ....(^{7}) until ....
At .... on ....
........................(^{8})   (^{8})

(^{5}) Seal or stamp of the authority or association issuing the permit. This seal or stamp shall be affixed against categories A, B, C, D and E only if the holder is licensed to drive vehicles in the category in question.

(^{6}) Or thumbprint.

(^{7}) Name of State.

(^{8}) Signature and seal or stamp of the authority which has invalidated the permit in its territory. If the spaces provided for disqualifications on this page have already been used, any further disqualifications should be entered overleaf.]

The Vehicle Licences (Duration and Rate of Duty) Order 1980

(S.I. 1980 No. 1183)

1. Citation and commencement   *[Omitted.]*   **B15.01**

2. Interpretation and application

(1) In this Order [*"the Act of 1994"* means the Vehicle Excise and Registration Act 1994].   **B15.02**

(2) *[Omitted.]*

[Article 2 is printed as amended by the Vehicle Excise and Registration Act 1994, s.64 and Sched. 4,   **B15.03**
para. 4.]

3. Commencement and duration of licences

Vehicle licences (other than licences for one calendar year) may be taken out—   **B15.04**

  (a) in the case of any vehicle licence, for any period of twelve months running from the beginning of the month in which the licence first has effect;

  (b) in the case of any vehicle the annual rate of duty applicable to which exceeds £18, for any period of six months running from the beginning of the month in which the licence first has effect;

  (c) in the case of a goods vehicle which is authorised to be used on roads by virtue of an order made under [section 44(1) of the Road Traffic Act 1988], and the unladen weight of which exceeds eleven tons, for any period of seven consecutive days.

[Article 3 is printed as amended by the Interpretation Act 1978, ss.17(2)(a) and 23(1).   **B15.05**
The Motor Vehicles (Authorisation of Special Types) General Order 1979 (S.I. 1979 No. 1198) (q.v.) has effect as if made under section 44(1) of the Road Traffic Act 1988.]

4. Rate of duty

The duty payable on a vehicle licence for a vehicle of any description shall—   **B15.06**

  (a) if the licence is taken out for a period of twelve months, be paid at the annual rate of duty applicable to vehicles of that description under [section 2 of the Act of 1994];

  (b) if the licence is taken out for a period of six months, be paid at a rate equal to one half of the said annual rate plus ten per cent, of that amount;

  (c) if the licence is taken out for a period of seven consecutive days, be paid at a rate equal to one fifty-second of the said annual rate plus ten per cent of that amount;

and in computing the rate of duty in accordance with paragraph (b) or paragraph (c) above, any fraction of 5p shall be treated as 5p if it exceeds 2.5p and shall otherwise be disregarded.

[Article 4 is printed as amended by the Vehicle Excise and Registration Act 1994, s.64 and Sched. 4,   **B15.07**
para. 4.]

5. Amendment of section 2 of the Act of 1971   *[Omitted.]*   **B15.08**

The Public Service Vehicles (Conditions of Fitness, Equipment, Use and Certification) Regulations 1981

(S.I. 1981 No. 257)

B16.01 *Editorial note.* As to the disapplication of the provisions of these regulations in respect of certain vehicles, see the Road Transport (International Passenger Services) Regulations 1984 (S.I. 1984 No. 748), reg.23 below.

None of the provisions of Parts II, III, IV or V of these regulations has effect in relation to a vehicle which is carrying out a cabotage transport operation in Great Britain in accordance with Council Regulation (EC) No. 12/98; see the Road Transport (Passenger Vehicles Cabotage) Regulations 1999 (S.I. 1999 No. 3413), regs 1(2) and 10(6) below.

B16.02 *[The text of these regulations is printed as amended by:*

the Public Service Vehicles (Conditions of Fitness, Equipment, Use and Certification) (Amendment) Regulations 1982 (S.I. 1982 No. 20) (February 22, 1982);

the Public Service Vehicles (Conditions of Fitness, Equipment, Use and Certification) (Amendment) (No. 2) Regulations 1982 (S.I. 1982 No. 1058) (September 2, 1982);

the Public Service Vehicles (Conditions of Fitness, Equipment, Use and Certification) (Amendment) (No. 3) Regulations 1982 (S.I. 1982 No. 1482) (November 22, 1982);

the Public Service Vehicles (Conditions of Fitness, Equipment, Use and Certification) (Amendment) (No. 2) Regulations 1986 (S.I. 1986 No. 1812) (November 26, 1986);

the Public Service Vehicles (Conditions of Fitness, Equipment, Use and Certification) (Amendment) (No. 2) Regulations 1989 (S.I. 1989 No. 2359, with correction slip dated January 1990) (January 11, 1990); and

the Public Service Vehicles (Conditions of Fitness, Equipment, Use and Certification) (Amendment) Regulations 1995 (S.I. 1995 No. 305) (March 14, 1995).

The amending regulations are referred to in the notes to the principal regulations only by their years and numbers. The dates referred to above are the dates on which the amending regulations came into force.

The principal regulations have also been amended by the Public Service Vehicles (Conditions of Fitness, Equipment, Use and Certification) (Amendment) Regulations 1984 (S.I. 1984 No. 1763), the Public Service Vehicles (Conditions of Fitness, Equipment, Use and Certification) (Amendment) Regulations 1986 (S.I. 1986 No. 370), the Public Service Vehicles (Conditions of Fitness, Equipment, Use and Certification) (Amendment) Regulations 1988 (S.I. 1988 No. 340), the Public Service Vehicles (Conditions of Fitness, Equipment, Use and Certification) (Amendment) Regulations 1989 (S.I. 1989 No. 322), the Public Service Vehicles (Conditions of Fitness, Equipment, Use and Certification) (Amendment) Regulations 1990 (S.I. 1990 No. 450), the Public Service Vehicles (Conditions of Fitness, Equipment, Use and Certification) (Amendment) Regulations 1991 (S.I. 1991 No. 456), the Public Service Vehicles (Conditions of Fitness, Equipment, Use and Certification) (Amendment) Regulations 1992 (S.I. 1992 No. 565), the Public Service Vehicles (Conditions of Fitness, Equipment, Use and Certification) (Amendment) Regulations 1993 (S.I. 1991 No. 3012), the Public Service Vehicles (Conditions of Fitness, Equipment, Use and Certification) (Amendment) Regulations 1997 (S.I. 1997 No. 84), the Public Service Vehicles (Conditions of Fitness, Equipment, Use and Certification) (Amendment) Regulations 1998 (S.I. 1998 No. 1670), and the Public Service Vehicles (Conditions of Fitness, Equipment, Use and Certification (Amendment) Regulations 2000 (S.I. 2000 No. 1431), but these do not affect the text of any provision printed in this work.]

ARRANGEMENT OF REGULATIONS

PART I

PRELIMINARY

Regulation

PART II

REGULATIONS RELATING TO THE CONDITIONS AS TO FITNESS OF PUBLIC SERVICE VEHICLES

Regulation

PART III

REGULATIONS RELATING TO THE EQUIPMENT OF PUBLIC SERVICE VEHICLES

Regulation

PART IV

REGULATIONS RELATING TO THE USE OF PUBLIC SERVICE VEHICLES

Regulation

*   *   *

SCHEDULES

Schedule

B16.04 **1. Commencement and citation** *[Omitted.]*

2. Revocation *[Omitted.]*

3. Interpretation

B16.05 (1) In these Regulations, unless the context otherwise requires, the following exceptions have the meanings hereby respectively assigned to them:—

"*the Act*" means the [Public Passenger Vehicles Act 1981];

"*articulated bus*" means a passenger vehicle so constructed that—

(a) it can be divided into two parts, both of which are vehicles and one of which is a motor vehicle, but cannot be so divided without the use of facilities normally available only at a workshop; and

(b) passengers carried by it when not so divided can at all times pass from either part to the other;

"*certificate of conformity*" means a certificate issued by the Minister in pursuance of [section 10(2)] of the Act;

"*certificate of initial fitness*" has the same meaning as in [section 6(1)] of the . . . Act . . .

"*the Commissioners*" means the traffic commissioners for any traffic area constituted for the purposes of [Part I] of the Act;

["*crew seat*" means a seat fitted to a vehicle and intended for use by crew (other than the driver), including any arm rests and foot rest with which the vehicle is fitted in relation to the seat, and which complies with the requirements specified in Regulation 28A;]

"*deck*" means a floor or platform upon which seats are provided for the accommodation of passengers;

"*double-decked vehicle*" means a vehicle having two decks one of which is wholly or partly above the other and each deck of which is provided with a gangway serving seats on that deck only;

"*ECE Regulation 36*" means Regulation No. 36 (uniform provisions concerning the construction of public service vehicles) which entered into force on 1st March 1976, annexed to the Agreement concerning the adoption of uniform conditions of approval and reciprocal recognition of approval for motor vehicle equipment and parts concluded at Geneva on 20th March 1958 [*Cmnd. 2535*] as amended [*Cmnd. 3562*], to which the United Kingdom is a party [*instrument of ratification deposited on January 15, 1961*];

"*emergency exit*" means an exit which is provided for use only in case of emergency;

"*entrance*" means any aperture or space provided to enable passengers to board the vehicle;

"*exit*" means any aperture or space provided to enable passengers to leave the vehicle;

"*gangway*" means the space provided for obtaining access from any entrance to the passengers' seats or from any such seat to an exit other than an emergency exit but does not include a staircase or any space in front of a seat or row of seats which is required only for the use of passengers occupying that seat or that row of seats;

"*half-decked vehicle*" means any vehicle not being a single-decked vehicle or a double-decked vehicle;

["*minibus*" means a motor vehicle which is constructed or adapted to carry more than 8 but not more than 16 seated passengers in addition to the driver;]

"*permanent top*" means any covering of a vehicle other than a hood made of canvas or other flexible material which is capable of being readily folded back so that no portion of such hood or any fixed structure of the roof remains vertically above any part of any seat of the vehicle, or, in the case of a double-decked vehicle, of any seat on the upper deck of the vehicle;

"*registered*" in relation to a vehicle, means registered under the Roads Act 1920 or, as the case may be, the Vehicles (Excise) Act 1949, the Vehicles (Excise) Act 1962 or the Vehicles (Excise) Act 1971 [or the Vehicle Excise and Registration Act 1994] and references to a vehicle being registered are references to the date on which it was first so registered;

"*safety glass*", "*safety glazing*" and "*specified safety glass*" have the same meanings as are respectively assigned to them in [Regulation 32(13)] of the Road Vehicles (Construction and Use) Regulations 1986] [*S.I. 1986 No. 1078, q.v.*];

"*single-decked vehicle*" means a vehicle on which no part of a deck or gangway is placed vertically above another deck or gangway;

"*type approval certificate*" means a certificate issued by the Minister in pursuance of [section 10(1)] of the Act;

"*vehicle*" means a public service vehicle within [section 1(1)] of the . . . Act . . . ; and

"*vehicle in the service of a visiting force or headquarters*" has the same meaning as in Article 8(6) of the Visiting Forces and International Headquarters (Application of Law) Order 1965 [*S.I. 1965 No. 1536*].

(2) For the purpose of these Regulations, the date when a motor vehicle is first used shall be taken to be such date as is the earlier of the undermentioned relevant dates applicable to that vehicle, that is to say—

    (a) in the case of a vehicle registered under the Roads Act 1920, the Vehicles (Excise) Act 1949, the Vehicles (Excise) Act 1962 or the Vehicles (Excise) Act 1971 [or the Vehicle Excise and Registration Act 1994] the relevant date is the date on which it was first so registered; and

    (b) in each of the following cases, that is to say—

        (i) in the case of a vehicle which is being or has been used under a trade licence within the meaning of section 16(1) of the Vehicles (Excise) Act 1971 (otherwise than for the purposes of demonstration or testing or of being delivered from premises of the manufacturer by whom it was made, or of a distributor of vehicles or dealer in vehicles to premises of a distributor of vehicles, dealer in vehicles or purchaser thereof, or to premises of a person obtaining possession thereof under a hiring agreement or hire purchase agreement);

        (ii) in the case of a vehicle belonging, or which has belonged, to the Crown which is or was used or appropriated for use for naval, military or air force purposes;

        (iii) in the case of a vehicle belonging, or which has belonged, to a visiting force or a headquarters within the meaning of Article 3 of the Visiting Forces and International Headquarters (Application of Law) Order 1965;

(iv) in the case of a vehicle which has been used on roads outside Great Britain and which has been imported into Great Britain; and

(v) in the case of a vehicle which has been used otherwise than on roads after being sold or supplied by retail and before being registered,

the relevant date is the date of manufacture of the vehicle.

In case (v) above "*sold or supplied by retail*" means sold or supplied otherwise than to a person acquiring the vehicle solely for the purpose of resale or re-supply for valuable consideration.

(3) Unless the context otherwise requires, any reference in these Regulations—

(a) to a numbered Regulation or Schedule is a reference to the Regulation or Schedule bearing that number in these Regulations, and

(b) to a numbered paragraph is to the paragraph bearing that number in the Regulation in which the reference occurs.

(4) The provisions of the Regulations in Part IV of these Regulations are in addition to, and not in derogation of, the provisions of any other Regulations made or having effect as if made under [section 41 of the Road Traffic Act 1988].

B16.06   *[Regulation 3 is printed as amended by the Interpretation Act 1978, ss.17(2)(a) and 23(1); S.I. 1982 No. 1058; S.I. 1986 No. 1812; the Vehicle Excise and Registration Act 1994, s.64 and Sched. 4, para.4.*

In relation to the definition of "the Commissioners", it should be noted that since the substitution of sections 4 and 5 of the Public Passenger Vehicles Act 1981 by the Transport Act 1985, s.3, there has been only one commissioner for each traffic area.

The Visiting Forces and International Headquarters (Application of Law) Order 1965 (to which reference is made in regulation 3(1) and (2)(b)(iii)) has been revoked and replaced by the Visiting Forces and International Headquarters (Application of Law) Order 1999 (S.I. 1999 No. 1736; not reproduced in this work). No textual amendment had been made to regulation 3 in consequence of that revocation; but by the Interpretation Act 1978, ss.17(2)(a) and 23(1) references to the earlier order may be treated as references to S.I. 1999 No. 1736.]

4. Exemptions—

B16.07   (1) Part IV of these Regulations does not apply to any vehicle in the public service of the Crown or in the service of a visiting force or headquarters.

(2) Parts III and IV of these Regulations do not apply to a motor vehicle belonging to a local education authority and which is from time to time used by that authority to provide free school transport whether the vehicle is being used wholly or partly to provide such transport or to provide a local bus service.

[(2A) Notwithstanding regulation 5, regulations 6 to 33, 35 to 44 and 45A shall not apply to a minibus which either complies with, or is required to comply with, or is exempted from the requirements specified in regulations 41 to 43 of the Road Vehicles (Construction and Use) Regulations 1986 for a minibus first used within the meaning of those Regulations on or after 1st April 1988.]

(3) Regulation 43 does not apply to a motor vehicle not belonging to a local education authority at any time when that vehicle is being used by that authority to provide free school transport, and to carry as the only fare-paying passengers pupils other than those for whom free school transport is provided.

(4) In this Regulation:—

(a) "*free school transport*" has the meaning given by section 46(3) of the Public Passenger Vehicles Act 1981 [*q.v.*] as regards England and Wales . . . ;

(b) *"pupil"* has the meaning given by [section 3(1) of the Education Act 1996 as regards England and Wales . . . ; and

(c) *[applies to Scotland.]*]

[Regulation 4 is printed as substituted by S.I. 1982 No. 20 and as amended by S.I. 1986 No. 1812;   **B16.08**
the Education Act 1996, s.582(3) and Sched. 39, para.1(4).
Words relating expressly and exclusively to Scotland have been omitted from subsection (4)(a) and (b).
The term "pupil" is defined in the Education Act 1996; section 3(1) of which provides that the term "pupil" means any person for whom education is being provided at a school, other than (a) a person who has attained the age of 19 for whom further education is being provided, or (b) a person for whom part-time education suitable to the requirements of persons of any age over compulsory school age is being provided.]

PART II

Regulations Relating to the Conditions as to Fitness of Public Service Vehicles

5. Conditions of fitness   *[Omitted.]*   **B16.09**

6. Stability

(1) The stability of a vehicle shall be such that—   **B16.10**

(a) in the case of a double-decked vehicle, the point at which overturning occurs would not be passed if, when the vehicle is complete, fully equipped for service and loaded with weights placed in the correct relative positions to represent the driver, a full complement of passengers on the upper deck only and a conductor (if carried), the surface on which the vehicle stands were tilted to either side to an angle of 28 degrees from the horizontal; and

(b) in the case of a single-decked vehicle and of a half-decked vehicle, the point at which overturning occurs would not be passed if, when the vehicle is complete, fully equipped for service and loaded with weights placed in the correct relative positions to represent [a full complement of passengers, a driver, any crew for whom a crew seat is provided, and any conductor intended to be carried on the vehicle otherwise than in a crew seat], the surface on which the vehicle stands were tilted to either side to an angle of 35 degrees from the horizontal.

(2) For the purpose of ascertaining whether the requirements of paragraph (1) have been complied with, the height of any stop used to prevent a wheel of the vehicle from slipping sideways shall not be greater than two-thirds of the distance between the surface upon which the vehicle stands before it is tilted and that part of the rim of that wheel which is nearest to that surface when the vehicle is loaded in accordance with the said requirements.

(3) For the purpose of this Regulation 63.5 kilograms shall be deemed to represent the weight of one person.

[Regulation 6 is printed as amended by S.I. 1982 No. 1058.]   **B16.11**

7.   *[Revoked by S.I. 1989 No. 2359.]*   **B16.12**

8.   *[Omitted.]*

9–12.   *[Revoked by S.I. 1989 No. 2359.]*

13–15.   *[Omitted.]*

16. Artificial lighting

B16.13 Subject to paragraph 4 of Schedule 2, adequate internal lighting shall be provided in every vehicle for the illumination—

(a) of each deck having a permanent top; and

(b) of any step or platform forming part of any entrance or exit other than an emergency exit;

and all lighting circuits shall be so arranged that an electrical failure of any lighting sub-circuit shall not be capable of extinguishing all the lights on any deck and at least one lamp shall be provided as near as practicable to the top of every staircase leading to an upper deck not having a permanent top.

B16.14 **17. Electrical equipment**   *[Omitted.]*

18. Body   *[Omitted.]*

19. Height of sides of body   *[Omitted.]*

20. Steps, platforms and stairs   *[Omitted.]*

21. Number, position and size of entrances and exits

B16.15 (1) For the purposes of this Regulation and Regulations 13, 22, 23, 24, 25 and 26—

(a) *"primary emergency exit"* means an emergency exit being an exit provided in a single-decked vehicle or in the lower deck of a double-decked vehicle which, subject to paragraph 8 of Schedule 2—

    (i) is situated so that passengers can step directly from the passage referred to in Regulation 26(1)(g) to the outside of the vehicle,

    (ii) has a clear height—

        (a) in the case of a vehicle which has a seating capacity not exceeding 14 passengers, of not less than 1.21 metres, and

        (b) in the case of any other vehicle, of not less than 1.37 metres,

    (iii) has a width of not less than 530 millimetres;

(b) *"secondary emergency exit"* means an emergency exit of which the dimensions are not less than 910 millimetres by 530 millimetres and which does not satisfy all the requirements of a primary emergency exit and which is not in the roof of a vehicle;

(c) neither of the foregoing definitions shall apply in relation to an emergency exit as required by paragraphs (7) and (8) but the exit so required shall be of dimensions not less than 1.52 metres by 455 millimetres;

(d) references to the seating capacity of a vehicle shall, in the case of a double-decked vehicle, be treated as references to the seating capacity of its lower deck;

(e) references to the distance between the centres or between the nearest points of the openings of two exits in a vehicle are references to the distance between lines drawn at right-angles to the longitudinal axis of the vehicle and passing respectively through the centres or, as the case may be, the nearest points of the openings of the exits at gangway level; and

(f) the references to the distance between the centre of an exit placed at the front end of a vehicle and the foremost part of the vehicle is a reference to the distance between lines drawn at right-angles to the longitudinal axis of the vehicle and passing through the centre of that exit and the said foremost part and the reference to the distance between the centre of an exit placed at the rear end of a vehicle and the rearmost part of the vehicle is a reference to the distance between lines drawn as aforesaid and passing through the centre of that exit and the said rearmost part.

(2) In this Regulation—

(a) *"pre-October 1981 vehicle"* means a vehicle manufactured before 1st October 1981 or first used before 1st April 1982; and

(b) *"post-October 1981 vehicle"* means a vehicle manufactured on or after 1st October 1981 and first used on or after 1st April 1982.

(3) Subject to paragraph 8 of Schedule 2, the following provisions of this Regulation shall apply with respect to the number and position of entrances and exits which shall be provided in a vehicle but a vehicle shall not be treated as failing to comply with any of those provisions by reason only that a number of exits is provided in a vehicle in excess of the number specified in relation to it by any provision of this Regulation.

(4) Subject to paragraphs (5) and (11), a vehicle which has a seating capacity for not more than 45 passengers shall be provided with two exits so placed as not to be on the same side of the vehicle, and

(a) in the case of a pre-October 1981 vehicle, one of which may be a primary emergency exit but neither of which shall be a secondary emergency exit;

(b) in the case of a post-October 1981 vehicle, one of which shall be a primary emergency exit and the other of which shall have dimensions which are not less than those specified in paragraph (1)(a) above in relation to a primary emergency exit;

Provided that this paragraph shall not apply in the case of a vehicle which has a seating capacity—

(i) exceeding 23 passengers and which is provided with an exit by virtue of its having a platform of a type described in [Regulation 20(1)(a)] which communicates with a deck (being in the case of a double-decked vehicle, the lower deck) by means of a doorless opening and has a doorless opening on the nearside of the vehicle contiguous with another such opening at the rear of the vehicle, these openings serving together as a means of entrance to or exit from the vehicle, and

(ii) not exceeding 12 passengers and of which the fuel tank is not placed behind the rear wheels if one exit of which, in the case of a post-October 1981 vehicle, the dimensions are not less than 1.21 metres in height by 530 millimetres in width is provided and is placed at the rear of the vehicle.

(5) Where the exits provided in accordance with paragraph (4) are so placed that the distance between their centres is—

(a) in the case of a vehicle first used before 1st January 1974 which has a seating capacity exceeding 30 passengers, less than 3.05 metres;

(b) in the case of a vehicle first used on or after 1st January 1974 which has a seating capacity exceeding 23 passengers, less than 3.05 metres;

(c) in the case of a vehicle first used on or after 1st January 1974 which has a seating capacity exceeding 14 but not exceeding 23 passengers, less than 2.44 metres,

a primary or secondary emergency exit shall be provided and placed so that there is a distance between the nearest points of the openings of that exit and one of the two exits mentioned in paragraph (4) of—

(i) in the cases mentioned in sub-paragraphs (a) and (b) above, not less than 3.05 metres, and

(ii) in the case mentioned in sub-paragraph (c) above, not less than 2.44 metres.

(6) Subject to paragraph (11), a vehicle which has a seating capacity exceeding 45 passengers shall be provided with three exits in respect of which the following provisions shall apply:—

(a) in the case of a pre-October 1981 vehicle one of the exits, but not more than one, may be a secondary emergency exit, and in the case of a post-October 1981 vehicle one of the exits shall be a primary emergency exit and any other exit (not being a secondary emergency exit) shall have dimensions not less than those specified in paragraph (1)(a) above in relation to primary emergency exits;

(b) two of the exits (neither being a secondary emergency exit) shall be so placed as not to be on the same side of the vehicle;

(c) where two exits are placed on the same side of the vehicle, the distance between their centres shall not be less than 3.05 metres; and

(d) one of the exits (not being a secondary emergency exit) shall be placed at the front end of the vehicle so that the distance between its centre and the foremost part of the vehicle is not more than 3.05 metres and another of the exits (not being a secondary emergency exit) shall be placed at the rear end of the vehicle so that the distance between its centre and the rearmost part of the vehicle is not more than 3.05 metres:

Provided that—

(i) in the case of a vehicle registered on or after 28th October 1964 and before 19th June 1968 the reference in sub-paragraph (c) above to 3.05 metres shall be replaced by a reference to 4.75 metres and sub-paragraph (d) shall not apply, and

(ii) in the case of any other vehicle first used before 1st January 1974 sub-paragraph (d) above shall apply with the omission of the words "(not being a secondary emergency exit)" in both places where they occur.

(7) In the case of a half-decked vehicle an emergency exit shall be provided in the roof of the vehicle so placed that the transverse centre line of that exit lies within 610 millimetres of the mid-point between the front edges of the foremost and of the rearmost passenger seats in the vehicle.

(8) Where, in the case of a double-decked vehicle which has a permanent top, access to the upper deck is obtained by means of an enclosed staircase, an emergency exit shall be provided on that deck and placed otherwise than on the nearside of the vehicle.

(9) Every entrance provided in a vehicle shall be placed on the nearside of the vehicle, but one or more entrances may be provided on the offside of the vehicle if—

(a) as respects any entrance so provided it is not also an exit provided in accordance with any of the foregoing provisions in this Regulation;

(b) every such entrance is fitted with a door which can be controlled only by the driver while sitting in his seat; and

(c) the device available to the driver for opening or closing that door is a separate and readily distinguishable device from that available to the driver for opening or closing any door fitted to the nearside of the vehicle:

[and one or more entrances may be provided on the rear face of the vehicle if each of those entrances is provided with a lifting platform or ramp for the benefit of disabled passengers;]

Provided that this paragraph shall not apply in the case of any such vehicle as is mentioned in the proviso to paragraph (4).

(10) A grab handle shall be fitted to every entrance and exit (other than an emergency exit) to assist passengers to board or alight from the vehicle.

(11) In the case of a vehicle—

(a) being a post-October 1981 vehicle,

(b) having a seating capacity for more than 16 passengers, and

(c) being a single-decked vehicle or a half-decked vehicle,

there shall be at least one emergency exit which complies with the requirements specified in paragraph (12) and which is either—

(i) in the front face of the vehicle, or

(ii) in the rear face of the vehicle, or

(iii) in the roof of the vehicle.

(12) The requirements referred to in paragraph (11) are, in respect of each exit therein referred to, as follows:—

(a) the dimensions of the aperture shall be such that it has a total area of not less than 4,000 square centimetres and shall include a rectangular area the dimensions of which are not less than 70 centimetres by 50 centimetres;

(b) the exit shall be so constructed that it can be opened by means available to persons inside the vehicle, and it may be so constructed that it can be opened also by persons outside the vehicle; and

(c) the exit shall be—

(i) ejectable, or

(ii) constructed of specified safety glass which can be readily broken by the application of reasonable force so as to afford a clear aperture having the dimensions referred to in sub-paragraph (a) above, and provided in a position adjacent to the exit with a suitable means, readily available to persons inside the vehicle, for breaking the glass, or

(iii) except where the exit is an exit in the roof, hinged.

[Regulation 21 is printed as amended by S.I. 1989 No. 2359.]

22. Width of entrances and exits　　*[Omitted.]*　　　　**B16.16**

23. Doors

(1) Subject to paragraph 9 of Schedule 2 and paragraph (4) the following conditions **B16.17** shall be complied with in the case of every vehicle:—

(a) means shall be provided for holding every entrance and exit door securely in the closed position and, where any such door is capable of remaining open when the vehicle is in motion or of being accidentally closed by the movement of the vehicle, means shall also be provided for holding that door securely in the open position;

(b) subject to paragraph (2), every entrance and exit door shall be provided with at least two devices (of which one may be a device provided for use in circumstances of normal operation only by a person authorised by the owner of the vehicle, and one, but not more than one, shall be provided on the outside of the vehicle) being in each case a device for operating the means for holding the door securely in the closed position, and every such device shall be so designed that a single movement of it will allow that door to be readily opened;

(c) the method of operation of any device mentioned in condition (b) above, the position of such a device where it is not placed on the door and the direction and points of application of any manual effort required to open any door, shall be clearly indicated; and there shall, in the case of a power-operated door, also be an indication that the said device may not be used by passengers except in an emergency;

(d) where any device mentioned in condition (b) above is not placed on the door, it shall be placed so as to be readily associated with that door and so that a person of normal height may conveniently operate the device without risk of being injured by movement of the door;

(e) in the case of every entrance and exit, any device mentioned in condition (b) above, other than such a device provided on the outside of an emergency exit on the upper deck of a double-decked vehicle or in the roof of a vehicle, shall be easily accessible to persons of normal height;

(f) the means and devices mentioned in conditions (a) and (b) above shall be so designed and fitted that they are unlikely to become dislodged or be operated accidentally but there shall be in the vehicle no means of a mechanical nature the operation of which would prevent the devices mentioned in the said condition (b) (devices for allowing entrance and exit doors to be opened in an emergency) when deliberately used, from allowing the entrance or exit doors for which they are provided to be readily opened;

(g) every door shall operate so as not to obstruct clear access to any entrance or exit from inside or outside the vehicle;

(h) being a vehicle having a power-operated door which, when open or being operated, projects laterally beyond the body of the vehicle at its widest point by more than 80 millimetres, shall be so constructed or adapted that it cannot move from rest under its own power when the door is open, and the door shall not be capable of being operated while the vehicle is in motion, except by the operation of such a device as is mentioned in condition (b) above;

(i) the storage and transmission system of the power for operating any power-operated door shall be such that operation of the doors does not adversely affect the efficient operation of the braking system of the vehicle and the apparatus shall be so designed and constructed that in the event of the system becoming inoperative the door shall be capable of being operated manually from inside and outside the vehicle; and

(j) the design of power-operated doors and their associated equipment at entrances and exits shall be such that, when opening or closing, the doors are unlikely to injure any passengers, and the vertical edges of any power-operated door which, when open or being operated, projects laterally beyond the body of the vehicle at its widest point by not more than 80 millimetres and which is installed in a vehicle not constructed or adapted as mentioned in condition (h) above shall be fitted with soft rubber.

[(1A) Schedule 3A shall have effect for the purpose of supplementing paragraph (1) in relation to power-operated doors fitted to certain vehicles.]

(2) A vehicle shall not be deemed to fail to comply with condition (b) or (f) of paragraph (1) by reason only of the fact that, for the purposes of securing the vehicle when unattended, any entrance or exit door has been fitted with a supplementary lock with or without an actuating mechanism if the lock is so designed and constructed that a single movement of any device mentioned in condition (b) above, being a device provided on the inside of the vehicle, will at all times allow that door to be readily opened.

(3) In determining for the purposes of conditions (h) and (j) of paragraph (1) whether, or the distance by which, a power-operated door, when open or being operated, projects laterally beyond the body of the vehicle at its widest point any moulding on the outside of the vehicle shall be disregarded.

(4) The references to exits in paragraph (1) do not include an emergency exit provided in accordance with the provisions of Regulation 21(11) unless such exit is a primary emergency exit or a secondary emergency exit.

B16.18   *[Regulation 23 is printed as amended by S.I. 1989 No. 2359.]*

24. Marking, positioning and operation of emergency exits

(1) Subject to the provisions of paragraph 10 of Schedule 2, every emergency exit, other **B16.19** than an emergency exit with which a vehicle is required to be fitted under Regulation 21(11) shall comply with the following conditions—

  (a) the emergency exit shall—

    (i) be clearly marked as such inside and outside the vehicle;

    (ii) be fitted with doors which open outwards or, in the case of a secondary emergency exit, be constructed of specified safety glass which can be readily broken by the application of reasonable force so as to afford a clear aperture of dimensions not less than those referred to in Regulation 21(1)(b);

    (iii) except in the case of an emergency exit provided in the roof of a vehicle, be readily accessible to passengers;

    (iv) in the case of a single-decked or half-decked vehicle or the lower deck of a double-decked vehicle, be so situated that passengers can step directly from the passage referred to in Regulation 26(1)(g) to the outside of the vehicle:

      Provided that this requirement shall not apply in the case of an emergency exit provided in the roof of the vehicle or in the case of a secondary emergency exit;

  (b) the means of operation of doors fitted to the emergency exit shall be clearly indicated;

  (c) the doors of the emergency exit shall not be fitted with any system of power operation; and

  (d) the means of operation of the doors of the emergency exit, other than those provided in the upper deck of a double-decked vehicle or in the roof of a vehicle, shall be readily accessible to persons of normal height standing at ground level outside the vehicle.

(2) Every emergency exit with which a vehicle is required to be fitted under Regulation 21(11) shall—

  (a) be clearly marked as an emergency exit—

    (i) on the inside of the vehicle, and

    (ii) in a case where the emergency exit can be opened from the outside, on the outside of the vehicle;

  (b) be accessible to persons inside the vehicle when the vehicle is tilted to either side through an angle of 99 degrees, measured from the normal vertical plane of the vehicle;

  (c) be clearly marked with its means of operation;

  (d) if hinged, open outwards; and

  (e) if ejectable, be fitted with a restraint which will prevent the part of the emergency exit which is ejected from becoming completely detached from the vehicle but which will not prevent egress from the vehicle by persons within it.

25. Access to exits   *[Omitted.]*   **B16.20**

26. Width of gangways

(1) [Subject to paragraphs (2) and (3) and to paragraph 11 of Schedule 2], the following **B16.21** conditions shall be complied with in the case of every vehicle:—

  (a) the width of every gangway shall be not less than—

    (i) 305 millimetres up to a height of 765 millimetres above the level of the deck of the vehicle,

(ii) 355 millimetres at heights exceeding 765 millimetres but not exceeding 1.22 metres above the level of the deck of the vehicle, and

(iii) 455 millimetres at heights exceeding 1.22 metres above the level of the deck of the vehicle;

(b) a vertical line projected upwards from the centre line of any gangway at deck level shall, to the height prescribed in Regulation 27 as the height of the gangway, be laterally not less than 150 millimetres from any part of the vehicle other than the roof above the gangway;

(c) being a vehicle which has a seating capacity exceeding 12 passengers, no part of any gangway which is within 910 millimetres of an entrance or exit (other than an emergency exit) to which it provides access shall be less than 530 millimetres in width; and

(d) being a double-decked vehicle which has a seating capacity exceeding 12 passengers, one gangway in the vehicle which serves as a joint means of access—

    (i) to both the upper and lower decks from any entrance, or

    (ii) to any exit from both the upper and lower decks,

shall where it lies between an entrance or exit (other than an emergency exit) and a staircase, be, at every level, not less than 910 millimetres in width;

(e) where a part of a gangway which adjoins an entrance or exit is divided by a handrail, the width of that part of the gangway at any point on each side of the handrail shall not be less than 455 millimetres;

(f) where two seats (being either two seats each for one passenger only or two portions of a continuous seat, each of such portions being for one passenger only measured in accordance with condition (b) of Regulation 28(1)) are placed parallel to the longitudinal axis of a vehicle and face each other and the space between those seats is not required for the purpose of obtaining access from an entrance to any other seat or from any other seat to an exit (not being an emergency exit), that space shall not for the purposes of this Regulation and Regulation 27 be treated as forming part of the gangway;

(g) between every exit, not being either—

    (i) an emergency exit provided in the roof of a vehicle, or

    (ii) an exit provided in accordance with the provisions of Regulation 21(11) unless it be a primary or secondary emergency exit,

and a gangway there shall be a passage—

    A. of dimensions not less than those prescribed for a gangway in condition (a) of paragraph (1);

    B. so designed that a vertical line projected upwards from the centre line of the passage at floor level to a height of 760 millimetres from the level of the deck is laterally not less than 150 millimetres from any part of the vehicle (excluding any cowling or cover which projects not more than 230 millimetres from the bulkhead of the vehicle into the passage at floor level and not more than 230 millimetres above the deck level and the provision of which is required by the projection of part of the chassis or mechanism of the vehicle into the body);

    C. which has a clear height at every point along the centre line of the passage of 1.52 metres from the deck level:

    Provided that—

        (i) for the purposes of sub-paragraphs A and B of this paragraph a seat placed below or in front of an emergency exit, being such an exit provided on the upper deck of a double-decked vehicle or in the roof of a vehicle or which is a secondary emergency exit within the meaning of Regulation 21 shall be deemed to form part of such a passage, and

(ii) sub-paragraph C of this paragraph shall not apply in the case of a passage leading to an emergency exit, being such an exit provided on the upper deck of a double-decked vehicle or in the roof of a vehicle or which is a secondary emergency exit within the meaning of Regulation 21, nor shall it apply in the case of a passage in a single-decked vehicle having a permanent top if the vehicle has a seating capacity not exceeding 14 passengers.

(2) Subject to paragraph 11 of Schedule 2, where any space in front of a seat in a vehicle adapted to carry more than 12 passengers is required for the accommodation of seated passengers, the space within 225 millimetres of the seat shall not be taken into account in measuring the width of a gangway;

Provided that the provisions of this paragraph shall not apply in relation to paragraph (1)(d) above where—

(i) the floor of the gangway is free of any obstruction; and
(ii) there are no other intrusions into the gangway space above the level of the deck of the vehicle.

[(3) The provisions of paragraph (1)(c) and (g) do not apply as regards a crew seat occupied by crew.]

[Regulation 26 is printed as amended by S.I. 1982 No. 1058.]   **B16.22**

27. Height of gangways   *[Omitted.]*   **B16.23**

28. Seats

(1) Subject to paragraph 13 of Schedule 2, [the following conditions shall, as regards   **B16.24**
every passenger seat, be complied with] in the case of every vehicle—

(a) the supports of all seats shall be securely fixed in position;

(b) a length of at least 400 millimetres measured horizontally along the front of each seat shall be allowed for the accommodation of a seated passenger:
Provided that in the case of a continuous seat fitted with arms for the purpose of separating the seating spaces, being arms so constructed that they can be folded back or otherwise put out of use, the seat shall be measured for the purposes of this paragraph as though it were not fitted with arms;

(c) every seat shall have a back rest so closed or otherwise constructed as to prevent, as far as practicable, the pockets of passengers from being picked;

(d) all passenger seats shall be so fitted—

(i) that the distance between any part of the back rest of any seat placed length-wise and the corresponding part of the back rest of the seat facing it shall be, in the case of a vehicle which has a seating capacity not exceeding 12 passengers, not less than 1.37 metres, and in any other case, not less than 1.60 metres, and

(ii) that there is a clear space of at least 610 millimetres in front of the back rest of any seat measured from the centre of each complete length of the seat allowed for the accommodation of a seated passenger in accordance with condition (b) above and a clear space of 200 millimetres in front of any part of that seat:
Provided that in the case of a seat for more than three passengers—

(a) in the case of a vehicle being used as a stage carriage, and
(b) in the case of any vehicle to which this regulation applies and which is first used on or after 1st April 1982

where access to that seat can be obtained only from one end of the seat, the said clear spaces shall respectively be at least 685 millimetres and 300 millimetres;

(e) there shall be a clear space of at least 480 millimetres between any part of the front edge of any transverse seat and any part of any other seat which faces it:

Provided that any support provided for a table shall be disregarded if there is a clear space of at least 225 millimetres between that support and the front edge of the nearest seat and the support is not in such a position as to cause discomfort to passengers occupying the seats;

(f) no seat shall be placed in such a position as to cause discomfort to passengers;

(g) there shall, as respects every seat, be a clear space measured vertically from the centre of each complete length of the seat allowed for the accommodation of a seated passenger in accordance with condition (b) above which shall be, in the case of a vehicle which has a seating capacity not exceeding 12 passengers, not less than 910 millimetres, and, in any other case, not less than 965 millimetres;

(h) where any seat is so placed that a passenger seated upon it is liable to be thrown through any entrance to or exit from the vehicle or down a stairway in the vehicle, an effective screen or guard shall be placed so as to afford adequate protection against that occurrence to a passenger occupying that seat; and

(i) the shortest distances between the edge of the well of any step in the vehicle and a vertical plane passing through the front edge of any seat shall be not less than 225 millimetres:

Provided that this condition shall not apply in the case of the well of a step provided as a means of obtaining access only to any forward-facing front passenger seat placed alongside the driver in a vehicle which has a seating capacity not exceeding 12 passengers.

(2) In this Regulation and in paragraph 13 of Schedule 2 the expression *"back rest"* includes any part of the vehicle which is available for seated passengers to lean against.

[(3) Paragraph (1)(b) above shall not apply to a wheelchair carried in a vehicle.]

[(4) Where a table is fitted to the rear of a seat and is so constructed that it can be folded back or otherwise put out of use, distances shall be measured for the purposes of paragraph (1)(d) with the table folded or put out of use.]

B16.25   *[Regulation 28 is printed as amended by S.I. 1982 No. 1058; S.I. 1989 No. 2359.*

The expression "stage carriage" was formerly defined in the Public Passenger Vehicles Act 1981, s.82(1), but the definition was revoked by the Transport Act 1985, s.139(3) and Sched. 9; for the meaning of that expression, see now Schedule 1, paragraph 16, to the 1985 Act above.]

[28A. Crew seats

B16.26   (1) Every crew seat shall be so constructed and located that when it is in use—

(a) the person by whom it is occupied—

(i) is adequately protected by means of arm rests from falling sideways either to the left or the right,

(ii) may conveniently place his feet either on a deck of the vehicle or on a foot rest, and

(iii) does not impede the driving of the vehicle either by obstructing the driver's field of vision or otherwise; and

(b) a space of at least 300 millimetres exists, along the whole width of the seat, between the foremost edge of the seat and any other part of the vehicle.

(2) Every crew seat shall be so constructed and located that when it is not in use—

(a) no part of it impedes the driving of the vehicle either by obstructing the driver's field of vision or otherwise; and

(b) every part of it which, when the seat is ready for or in use, protrudes into a gangway so that the provisions of Regulation 26(1)(c) and (g) are not complied with, is, as a result of automatic mechanism, retracted so that those provisions are complied with.

(3) The words "FOR CREW USE ONLY" shall be marked either on or near and in relation to every crew seat in letters not less than 10 millimetres tall and in a colour which contrasts with their background.

(4) The provisions of paragraph (1)(a) to (f) of Regulation 28 apply as respects a crew seat in the same manner as they apply as respects a seat to which that Regulation applies.]

[Regulation 28A was inserted by S.I. 1982 No. 1058.]   **B16.27**

29–34.   *[Omitted.]*   **B16.28**

PART III

REGULATIONS RELATING TO THE EQUIPMENT OF PUBLIC SERVICE VEHICLES

35. Fire extinguishing apparatus

[(1) There shall be carried by every vehicle suitable and efficient apparatus for extin-   **B16.29** guishing fire which is of one or more of the types specified in Schedule 4.]

(2) The apparatus referred to in paragraph (1) shall be—

(a) readily available for use,

(b) clearly marked with the appropriate British Standards Institution specification number, and

(c) maintained in good and efficient working order.

[(3) Paragraph (1) shall not apply to a vehicle if it carries apparatus for extinguishing fire which would meet the requirements of that paragraph were there substituted—

(a) for a reference in Schedule 4 to any British Standard, a reference to a corresponding standard;

(b) for the reference in Schedule 4 to a test fire rating of 8A or the reference in that Schedule to a test fire rating of 21B, a reference to an equivalent level of performance specified in the corresponding standard; and

(c) for the reference in paragraph (2)(b) to the appropriate British Standards Institution specification number, a reference to a marking indicating compliance with the corresponding standard.]

[(4) For the purposes of this regulation, *"corresponding standard"* in relation to a British Standard, means—

(a) a standard or code of practice of a national standards body or equivalent body of any EEA State;

(b) any international standard recognised for use as a standard by any EEA State; or

(c) a technical specification or code of practice which, whether mandatory or not, is recognised for use as a standard by a public authority of any EEA State,

where the standard code of practice, international standard or technical specification provides, in relation to fire extinguishers, a level of safety equivalent to that provided by the British Standard and contains a requirement as respects the markings of fire extinguishers equivalent to that provided by the British Standard.]

[(5) For the purposes of this regulation—

"*EEA State*" means a state which is a contracting party to the EEA Agreement but, until the EEA Agreement comes into force as regards Liechtenstein, does not include the State of Liechtenstein; and

"*EEA Agreement*" means the Agreement on the European Economic Area signed at Oporto on 2 May 1992 [*Cm. 2073*] as adjusted by the Protocol signed at Brussels on 17 March 1993 [*Cm. 2183*].]

B16.30   *[Regulation 35 is printed as amended by S.I. 1989 No. 2359; S.I. 1995 No. 305.]*
As to the European Economic Area, see the note to Regulation (EEC) 3820/85 below.]

36. First aid equipment

B16.31   (1) There shall be carried by every vehicle being used as an express carriage or as a contract carriage a receptacle which contains the items specified in Schedule 5.

(2) The receptacle referred to in paragraph (1) shall be—

(a) maintained in a good condition,

(b) suitable for the purpose of keeping the items referred to in the said paragraph in good condition,

(c) readily available for use, and

(d) prominently marked as a first aid receptacle.

(3) The items referred to in paragraph (1) shall be maintained in good condition and shall be of a good and reliable quality and of a suitable design.

B16.32   *[Section 82(1) of the Public Passenger Vehicles Act 1981 formerly included definitions of "contract carriage" and "express carriage". These definitions were repealed by the Transport Act 1985, s.139(3) and Sched. 8. For the meanings of these expressions, see now Schedule 1, paragraph 16, to the 1985 Act above.]*

PART IV

REGULATIONS RELATING TO THE USE OF PUBLIC SERVICE VEHICLES

37. Obstruction of entrances, exits and gangways

B16.33   No person shall, while passengers are being carried by a vehicle, cause or permit any unnecessary obstruction to any entrance or exit or gangway of the vehicle.

38. Obstruction of driver

B16.34   No person shall cause or permit any unnecessary obstruction of the driver of a vehicle.

39. Body maintenance

B16.35   No person shall use a vehicle while it is carrying passengers or cause or permit it to be so used unless the inside and the outside of the body of the vehicle and all windows and fittings and all passengers' seats are maintained in clean and good condition.

40. Lamps

B16.36   (1) No person shall use a vehicle during the hours of darkness while it is carrying passengers or cause or permit it to be so used unless every lamp provided in compliance with Regulation 16 for the internal illumination of the vehicle is at all times during such use kept lighted to such extent as is necessary to provide adequate illumination of every access from any seat in the vehicle to every exit in the vehicle and of every such marking as is required by Regulation 24 to be provided in relation to every emergency exit in the vehicle:

Provided that it shall not be necessary to keep lighted any lamp provided on the upper deck of a double-decked vehicle if a barrier is secured across the bottom of all staircases leading to that deck so as effectively to prevent passengers using any such staircase.

(2) In this Regulation, "*hours of darkness*" means the time between half-an-hour after sunset and half-an-hour before sunrise.

41. Use of device for operating power-operated doors

(1) Except as provided by paragraph (2), no person shall use or cause or permit to be used any device for operating the doors of a vehicle having power-operated doors, being a device such as is mentioned in condition (b) of Regulation 23(1) or, as the case may be, in paragraph 9(b)(ii) of Schedule 2. **B16.37**

(2) Paragraph (1) shall not apply—

(a) in an emergency, as to the use of a device by any person;

(b) otherwise than in an emergency, as to the use of a device by a person in accordance with an authorisation by the operator of the vehicle, save that no such use shall occur if—

    (i) the vehicle is in motion, and

    (ii) the doors, when fully opened, project more than 80 millimetres from the side of the vehicle.

42. Filling of petrol tank

While the engine of a vehicle is running no person shall cause or permit the filler cap fitted to the petrol tank of the vehicle to be removed or petrol to be put in its petrol tank. **B16.38**

43. Carriage of conductor

No person shall use or cause or permit to be used as a stage carriage any vehicle which has a seating capacity exceeding 20 passengers unless a person authorised to act as conductor of the vehicle is carried thereby: **B16.39**

Provided that this Regulation shall not apply—

    (i) in the case of a single-decked vehicle which has a seating capacity not exceeding 32 passengers and which is provided with only one emergency exit, if that exit and the entrance to the vehicle are both placed at the front of the vehicle and are readily visible to the driver from his seat and means are provided for the driver to be aware if any person outside the vehicle has been trapped by the closure of any door provided at that entrance, or

    (ii) in the case of any other vehicle, if a certifying officer has stated in writing that the construction and design of the vehicle is such that a conductor is not required for the purpose of the safety of the passengers.

44. Carriage of inflammable or dangerous substances

(1) No person shall use or cause or permit to be used any vehicle by which any highly inflammable or otherwise dangerous substance is carried unless that substance is carried in containers so designed and constructed, or unless the substance is so packed, that, notwithstanding an accident to the vehicle, it is unlikely that damage to the vehicle or injury to passengers carried by the vehicle will be caused by reason of the presence on it of that substance. **B16.40**

(2) The requirements of this Regulation are in addition to and not in derogation of the requirements of regulations made under the Petroleum (Consolidation) Act 1928 or under any other Act.

45. Markings

B16.41   No vehicle in respect of which, by virtue of [section 6(1)] of the . . . Act . . . , a certificate of initial fitness, or a certificate under [section 10] of the . . . Act . . . , or a certificate under [section 57 of the Road Traffic Act 1988] is required shall be used on a road unless the vehicle is marked with clearly legible characters—

    (i)   not less than 25 millimetres tall,

    (ii)   in a conspicuous position on the nearside of the vehicle,

    (iii)   in colours which contrast with their background, and

    (iv)   indicating the name of the owner (as defined in [section 82(1)] of the . . . Act . . . in relation to a vehicle to which that definition applies) of the vehicle and the owner's principal place of business.

B16.42   *[Regulation 45 is printed as amended by the Interpretation Act 1978, ss.17(2)(a) and 23(1).]*

[45A. Use of seats

B16.43   (1) No passenger shall be permitted to use a seat provided for a passenger unless it complies with the requirements specified in Regulation 28.

(2) No crew shall be permitted to use a crew seat unless it complies with the requirements specified in Regulation 28A.]

B16.44   *[Regulation 45A was inserted by S.I. 1982 No. 1058.]*

PART V

REGULATIONS RELATING TO CERTIFICATES OF INITIAL FITNESS, APPROVAL AS A TYPE
VEHICLE AND CONFORMITY TO AN APPROVED TYPE VEHICLE

B16.45   **46–57.**   *[Omitted.]*

SCHEDULES

SCHEDULE 1

B16.46   REGULATIONS REVOKED BY REGULATION 2

[Omitted.]

SCHEDULE 2

EXCEPTIONS FROM THE CONDITIONS PRESCRIBED IN PART II AS APPLICABLE TO VEHICLES
REGISTERED BEFORE CERTAIN DATES

*   *   *

B16.47   **4.** Regulation 16 (Artificial lighting) in so far as it consists of sub-paragraph (b), shall not apply in the case of a vehicle registered before 1st April 1959 and the requirements as to lighting circuits in that Regulation shall not apply in the case of a vehicle registered before 28th October 1964.

*   *   *

8. Regulation 21 (Number, position and size of entrances and exits) shall not apply—

(a) in so far as it consists of paragraphs (4) and (6) in the case of a vehicle registered before 1st April 1959 if it is provided with two exits so placed as not to be on the same side of the vehicle;

(b) in so far as it consists of paragraph (6) in the case of a vehicle registered on or after 1st April 1959 and before 28th October 1964 which has a seating capacity exceeding 45 passengers if—

    (i) the vehicle is provided with two exits (of which neither is a secondary emergency exit) and those exits are not on the same side of the vehicle, and

    (ii) in a case where those exits are so placed that the distance between their centres is less than 3.05 metres, a secondary emergency exit is provided in such a position that there is a distance of not less than 3.05 metres between the nearest points of the openings of that exit and of whichever of the exits mentioned in sub-paragraph (i) above is the nearer to that exit. For the purpose of this paragraph the reference to the distance between the centres and between the nearest points of the openings of the two exits there mentioned shall be construed in accordance with Regulation 21(1)(e);

(c) in so far as it consists of paragraph (9)—

    (i) in the case of a vehicle registered before 1st April 1959 (not being a single-decked vehicle having a permanent top) if it is provided with two exits so placed as not to be on the same sides of the vehicle; or

    (ii) in the case of a vehicle which—

        A. is provided with a platform such as is mentioned in proviso (i) to Regulation 21(4); or

        B. has a seating capacity not exceeding 14 passengers, if one means of exit and entrance is provided and is placed behind the rear wheels.

9. Regulation 23(1) (Doors) shall not apply—   **B16.48**

(a) in so far as it consists of sub-paragraph (j) in the case of a vehicle registered before 1st August 1968;

(b) save in so far as it consists of sub-paragraph (j) in the case of a vehicle registered before 19th June 1968 if—

    (i) every entrance door and every exit door can be readily opened from inside and outside the vehicle by one operation of the locking mechanism:

        Provided that a vehicle shall not be deemed to fail to comply with this sub-paragraph by reason only of the fact that, for the purpose of securing the vehicle when unattended, any entrance or exit door has been fitted with a supplementary lock with or without an actuating mechanism if the lock is so designed and constructed that the door can at all times be opened by a person inside the vehicle by one operation of the ordinary locking mechanism;

    (ii) except in the case of a vehicle registered before 1st April 1959, the device provided outside the vehicle for operating the locking mechanism of the door (not being a device provided in relation to an emergency exit on the upper deck of a double-decked vehicle or in the roof of a half-decked vehicle) is readily accessible to persons of normal height standing at ground level outside the vehicle;

    (iii) except in the case of a vehicle registered before 1st April 1959, means are provided for holding every entrance and exit door securely in the closed position;

    (iv) except in the case of a vehicle registered before 1st April 1959, all locks and fastenings fitted to entrance and exit doors are so designed and fitted that they are not likely to become dislodged or be operated accidentally, and, in the said excepted case, door handles or levers to door catches are so designed and fitted that they are not likely to become dislodged or be operated accidentally;

(v) where any entrances are provided with doors which are designed to remain open when the vehicle is in motion, suitable fastenings are provided to hold such doors securely in the opened position;

(vi) except in the case of a vehicle registered before 1st April 1959, every sliding door and every folding door fitted to an entrance or exit is provided with suitable fastenings to prevent it from being closed by any movement of the vehicle;

(vii) all doors can open so as not to obstruct clear access to any entrance or exit from inside or outside the vehicle; and

(viii) except in the case of a vehicle registered before 1st April 1959, the means by which a power-operated door may be opened are provided inside the vehicle on or adjacent to the door and their position is clearly indicated and there is also an indication that the said means may be used by passengers only in an emergency; and the storage and transmission system of the power for operating the door is such that operation of the doors does not adversely affect the efficient operation of the braking system of the vehicle and the apparatus is so designed and constructed that in the event of the system becoming inoperative the door can be operated manually from inside and outside the vehicle.

B16.49   **10.** Regulation 24(1)(b)(iv) (Marking, positioning and operation of emergency exits) shall not apply in the case of a vehicle registered before 1st April 1959, being a vehicle which is provided with a rear platform, if an emergency exit (of which the clear height at the centre line is not less than 1.52 metres and of which the width is not less than 455 millimetres) is provided from that platform to the rear of the vehicle and is enclosed by means of a door placed on the near-side of that platform.

11. The provisions of Regulation 26 (Width of gangways) specified in column 1 of the Table below shall not apply in the case of a vehicle specified, in relation to those provisions, in column 2 of that Table.

TABLE

1	2
Paragraph (1)(e)	A vehicle registered before 19th June 1968.
Paragraph (1) (d)	A double-decked vehicle registered before 19th June 1969 if no part of any gangway which serves as a joint means of access from any entrance to the upper and lower decks is less than 910 millimetres in width.
Paragraph (1) (a), (c) and (g) c.	A vehicle registered before 1st April 1959 if the width of every gangway is not less than 305 millimetres up to a height of 765 millimetres above the level of the deck and not less than 355 millimetres above that height.
Paragraph 1 (c)	A vehicle registered after 1st April 1959 and before 19th June 1968 if no part of any gangway which is within 915 millimetres of an exit (other than an emergency exit) to which it leads is less than 530 millimetres in width.

*　　*　　*

13. Regulation 28 (Seats) shall not apply—

  (a) in so far as it consists of paragraph (1)(d) in the case of a vehicle registered before   **B16.50**
1st April 1959 if all the passengers' seats in the vehicle are so fitted—

      (a) that no part of the back rest of any seat placed lengthwise is less than 1.37
metres from the corresponding part of the back rest of the seat facing it; and

      (b) there is in relation to every transverse seat in the vehicle a clear space of at
least 660 millimetres in front of the whole length of the top of the back rest
of that seat measured from the centre of each complete length of the seat
allowed for the accommodation of a seated passenger in accordance with
condition (b) of the said paragraph (1) but disregarding any handles or grips
which do not project more than 105 millimetres from the back rest;

  (b) in so far as it consists of paragraph (1)(f) and (g) in the case of a vehicle registered
before 1st April 1959 if no seat placed over the arch of a wheel of the vehicle is in
such a position as to cause discomfort to passengers;

  (c) in so far as it consists of paragraph (1)(h) in the case of a vehicle registered before
1st April 1959 if, as respects any transverse seat in the vehicle which is so placed
that a passenger seated upon it is liable to be thrown through any entrance to or
exit from the vehicle or down a stairway in the vehicle, an effective screen or guard
is placed so as to afford adequate protection against that occurrence to a passenger
occupying that seat.

SCHEDULE 3

Conditions Prescribed in Regulations in Part II, or Provisions Thereof,   **B16.51**
Applicable to Certain Vehicles Bearing a Designated Approval Mark

[Omitted.]

[SCHEDULE 3A (see regulation 23(1A))

1. Application

This Schedule applies to every vehicle registered on or after the 1st April 1980.   **B16.52**

2. Conditions

Save as provided below, the following conditions shall be complied with in relation to
every power-operated door which is—

  (a) fitted to a vehicle to which this Schedule applies, and

  (b) so situated in a vehicle that the whole of the door opening is more than 500
millimetres behind the transverse vertical plane that touches the back of the
driver's seat when the seat is in its rearmost position.

3.—(1) The first condition is that when the door is prevented from closing by the   **B16.53**
presence of a fixed vertical surface that is 60 millimetres high placed at right angles to the
direction of movement of the closing edge—

  (a) the force exerted on the surface does not exceed 150 newtons and

  (b) the door re-opens automatically and remains open until a closing control is operated manually.

(2) This condition shall not have to be met when a door is within 30 millimetres of its
fully closed position, but shall otherwise apply wherever the surface is placed within the

door opening (regardless of the stage of closure when the door first strikes the surface or of the part of the closing edge that strikes the surface).

4.—(1) The second condition is that whenever the door is closed on to the fingers or the palm of the hand—

(a) the door re-opens automatically and remains open until a closing control is operated manually, or

(b) the fingers or hand can be readily extracted from the door without injury.

(2) This condition shall not apply to a door fitted to a coach manufactured before the 1st of October 1992 or registered before the 1st of April 1993.

(3) In this paragraph *"coach"* has the same meaning as in the Road Vehicles (Construction and Use) Regulations 1986 [*S.I. 1986 No. 1078, as amended, q.v.*].

B16.54   **5.** The third condition is that a visual device, clearly visible to the driver at all times, is activated whenever the door is not fully closed.

6. Transitional and savings

B16.55   (1) This Schedule shall not have effect until 1st April 1993 in relation to a vehicle manufactured before the 14th May 1990 or first used before the 1st of October 1990.

(2) Nothing in this Schedule shall be construed as derogating from the requirements of regulation 23(1).]

B16.56   *[Schedule 3A was inserted by S.I. 1989 No. 2359.]*

[SCHEDULE 4 (see regulation 35)

FIRE EXTINGUISHING APPARATUS

B16.57   A fire extinguisher which complies in all respects with the specification for portable fire extinguishers issued by the British Standards Institution numbered BS 5423: 1977 or BS 5423: 1980 or BS 5423: 1987 and which—

(a) has a minimum test [fire] rating of 8A or 21B, and

(b) contains water or foam or contains and is marked to indicate that it contains, halon 1211 or halon 1301.]

B16.58   *[Schedule 4 is printed as substituted by S.I. 1989 No. 2359 and as subsequently amended by S.I. 1995 No. 305.]*

SCHEDULE 5 (see regulation 36)

FIRST AID EQUIPMENT

B16.59   (i)   Ten antiseptic wipes, foil packed.

(ii) One conforming disposable bandage (not less than 7.5 centimetres wide).

(iii) Two triangular bandages.

(iv) One packet of 24 assorted adhesive dressings.

(v)   Three large sterile unmedicated ambulance dressings (not less than 15.0 centimetres × 20.0 centimetres).

(vi)   Two sterile eye pads, with attachments.

(vii) Twelve assorted safety pins.

(viii) One pair of rustless blunt-ended scissors.

SCHEDULE 6

FORM OF CERTIFICATE OF INITIAL FITNESS   **B16.60**

[Omitted.]

SCHEDULE 7

FORM OF TYPE APPROVAL CERTIFICATE   **B16.61**

[Omitted.]

SCHEDULE 8

FORM OF DECLARATION OF CONFORMITY TO AN APPROVED TYPE VEHICLE   **B16.62**

[Omitted.]

SCHEDULE 9

FORM OF CERTIFICATE OF CONFORMITY   **B16.63**

[Omitted.]

The Motor Vehicles (Type Approval) (EEC Manufacturers) Regulations 1981

(S.I. 1981 No. 493)

1. Citation, commencement and interpretation

B17.01   (1) *[Omitted.]*

(2) In these Regulations expressions which are also used in [Part II of the Road Traffic Act 1988] have the same meanings as in that Part.

B17.02   *[Regulation 1 is printed as amended by the Interpretation Act 1978, ss.17(2)(a) and 23(1).]*

2. Application of provisions relating to type approval certificates and certificates of conformity

B17.03   (1) Subject to paragraph (2), the provisions—

(a) of sections 47 to 50 of the Road Traffic Act 1972 [and sections 54 to 62 of the Road Traffic Act 1988] (approval of design, construction, etc., of vehicles and vehicle parts); and

(b) of regulations made thereunder before the coming into operation of these Regulations,

so far as relating to type approval certificates and certificates of conformity, shall apply in relation to vehicles and vehicle parts manufactured in a member State of the Economic Community (other than the United Kingdom) or in Northern Ireland as they apply in relation to vehicles and vehicle parts manufactured in Great Britain.

(2) Nothing in the said provisions as applied by paragraph (1) shall require [the Secretary of State for the Environment, Transport and the Regions] to issue a type approval certificate before the expiration of the period of 12 months beginning with the day on which these Regulations came into operation.

(3) In consequence of paragraph (1) above any reference in the said provisions to a vehicle or vehicle part (including a reference which is to be construed as including such a reference) shall be construed as including a reference to a vehicle or vehicle part manufactured in a member State of the Economic Community (other than the United Kingdom) or in Northern Ireland.

B17.04   *[Regulation 2 is printed as amended by the Road Traffic (Consequential Provisions) Act 1988, s.2(4); the Secretary of State for the Environment, Transport and the Regions Order 1997 (S.I. 1997 No. 2971). These regulations came into operation on April 27, 1981; regulation 1(1).]*

The Motor Vehicles (Tests) Regulations 1981

(S.I. 1981 No. 1694)

[The text of these regulations is printed as amended by:　　　　　　　　　　**B18.01**

the Motor Vehicles (Tests) (Amendment) (No. 2) Regulations 1982 (S.I. 1982 No. 814) (July 15, 1982);

the Motor Vehicles (Tests) (Amendment) (No. 3) Regulations 1982 (S.I. 1982 No. 1477) (December 1, 1982);

the Motor Vehicles (Tests) (Amendment) (No. 2) Regulations 1983 (S.I. 1983 No. 1434) (November 1, 1983);

the Motor Vehicles (Tests) (Amendment) (No. 4) Regulations 1984 (S.I. 1984 No. 1126) (August 30, 1984);

the Motor Vehicles (Tests) (Amendment) Regulations 1985 (S.I. 1985 No. 45) (March 1, 1985);

the Motor Vehicles (Tests) (Amendment) (No. 3) Regulations 1988 (S.I. 1988 No. 1894) (November 29, 1988);

the Motor Vehicles (Tests) (Amendment) (No. 1) Regulations 1991 (S.I. 1991 No. 253) (March 18, April 1, 1991);

the Motor Vehicles (Tests) (Amendment) Regulations 1995 (S.I. 1995 No. 1457) (July 1, 1995);

the Motor Vehicles (Tests) (Amendment) Regulations 1998 (S.I. 1998 No. 1672) (August 1, 1998); and

the Motor Vehicles (Tests) (Amendment) Regulations 2000 (S.I. 2000 No. 1432) (June 26, 2000).

The amending regulations are referred to in the notes to the principal regulations only by their years and numbers. The dates referred to above are the dates on which the amending regulations came into force.

The principal regulations have also been amended by the Motor Vehicles (Tests) (Amendment) Regulations 1982 (S.I. 1982 No. 783), the Motor Vehicles (Tests) (Amendment) Regulations 1983 (S.I. 1983 No. 1147), the Motor Vehicles (Tests) (Amendment) Regulations 1984 (S.I. 1984 No. 401), the Motor Vehicles (Tests) (Amendment) (No. 2) Regulations 1984 (S.I. 1984 No. 727), the Motor Vehicles (Tests) (Amendment) (No. 3) Regulations 1984 (S.I. 1984 No. 815), the Motor Vehicles (Tests) (Amendment) (No. 2) Regulations 1985 (S.I. 1985 No. 834), the Motor Vehicles (Tests) (Amendment) (No. 3) Regulations 1985 (S.I. 1985 No. 1923), the Motor Vehicles (Tests) (Amendment) Regulations 1986 (S.I. 1986 No. 372), the Motor Vehicles (Tests) (Amendment) (No. 2) Regulations 1986 (S.I. 1986 No. 904), the Motor Vehicles (Tests) (Amendment) Regulations 1987 (S.I. 1987 No. 1144), the Motor Vehicles (Tests) (Amendment) Regulations 1988 (S.I. 1988 No. 339), the Motor Vehicles (Tests) (Amendment) (No. 2) Regulations 1988 (S.I. 1988 No. 989), the Motor Vehicles (Tests) (Amendment) Regulations 1989 (S.I. 1989 No. 321), the Motor Vehicles (Tests) (Amendment) (No. 2) Regulations 1989 (S.I. 1989 No. 920), the Motor Vehicles (Tests) (Amendment) (No. 3) Regulations 1989 (S.I. 1989 No. 1694) with corrigendum dated October 1989, the Motor Vehicles (Tests) (Amendment) Regulations 1990 (S.I. 1990 No. 449), the Motor Vehicles (Tests) (Amendment) (No. 2) Regulations 1990 (S.I. 1990 No. 628), the Motor Vehicles (Tests) (Amendment) (No. 3) Regulations 1990 (S.I. 1990 No. 1186), the Motor Vehicles (Tests) (Amendment) (No. 2) Regulations 1991 (S.I. 1991 No. 455), the Motor Vehicles (Tests) (Amendment) (No. 3) Regulations 1991 (S.I. 1991 No. 1525), the Motor Vehicles (Tests) (Amendment) (No. 4) Regulations 1991 (S.I. 1991 No. 2229), the Motor Vehicles (Tests) (Amendment) (No. 5) Regulations 1991 (S.I. 1991 No. 2791), the Motor Vehicles (Tests) (Amendment) Regulations 1992 (S.I. 1992 No. 566), the Motor Vehicles (Tests) (Amendment) (No. 2) Regulations 1992 (S.I. 1992 No.

1609), the Motor Vehicles (Tests) (Amendment) (No. 3) Regulations 1992 (S.I. 1992 No. 3160), the Motor Vehicles (Tests) (Amendment) Regulations 1993 (S.I. 1993 No. 3011), the Motor Vehicles (Tests) (Amendment) Regulations 1994 (S.I. 1994 No. 2136), the Motor Vehicles (Tests) (Amendment) (No. 2) Regulations 1995 (S.I. 1995 No. 2438), the Motor Vehicles (Tests) (Amendment) Regulations 1996 (S.I. 1996 No. 1751), the Motor Vehicles (Tests) (Amendment) Regulations 1997 (S.I. 1997 No. 81), the Motor Vehicles (Tests) (Amendment) (No. 2) Regulations 1997 (S.I. 1997 No. 1679), the Motor Vehicles (Tests) (Amendment) Regulations 1999 (S.I. 1999 No. 2199), the Motor Vehicles (Tests) (Amendment) (No. 2) Regulations 2000 (S.I. 2000 No. 2322), but these regulations do not affect the text of any provision which is printed in this work.]

* * *

3. Interpretation

B18.02   (1) In these Regulations, except where the context otherwise requires, the following expressions have the meanings hereby respectively assigned to them—

"[*the 1988 Act*]" means [the Road Traffic Act 1988];

. . .

["*the Construction and Use Regulations*" means the Road Vehicles (Construction and Use) Regulations 1986 [*S.I. 1986 No. 1078, q.v.*]];

. . .

["*agricultural motor vehicle*"], "*articulated bus*", "*articulated vehicle*", "*dual-purpose vehicle*", ["*exhaust system*",]["*minibus*",]["*Ministry plate*"], "*pedestrian controlled vehicle*", "*track laying*" and "*works truck*" have the meanings given by [Regulation 3(2)] of the Construction and Use Regulations;

. . .

["*child restraint*", "*disabled person's belt*", "*forward-facing seat*" and "*seat belt*" have the meanings given by regulation 47(8) of the Construction and Use Regulations;]

. . .

["*design gross weight*" means—

(a) in the case of a vehicle equipped with a Ministry plate, the weight shown thereon as the design weight, or, if no weight is so shown thereon, the weight shown thereon as the weight not to be exceeded in Great Britain;

(b) in the case of a vehicle which is not equipped with a Ministry plate, but which is equipped with a plate in accordance with regulation 66 of the Construction and Use Regulations, the maximum gross weight shown on the plate in respect of item 7 of Part I of Schedule 8 to those Regulations; and

(c) in any other case, the weight which the vehicle is designed or adapted not to exceed when in normal use and travelling on a road laden;]

. . .

"*goods vehicle*" means a motor vehicle constructed or adapted for use for the carriage of goods or burden of any description, including a living van but excluding—

[(i) a dual-purpose vehicle,
(ii) a motor caravan, and
(iii) a play bus].

. . .

"*living van*" means a vehicle, whether mechanically propelled or not, which is used as living accommodation by one or more persons, and which is also used for the carriage of goods or burden which are not needed by such one or more persons for the purpose of their residence in the vehicle;

. . .

"*motor bicycle*" means a two-wheeled motor cycle, whether having a side-car attached to it or not;

"*motor caravan*" means a motor vehicle (not being a living van) which is constructed or adapted for the carriage of passengers and their effects and which contains, as permanently installed equipment, the facilities which are reasonably necessary for enabling the vehicle to provide mobile living accommodation for its users;

. . .

["*play bus*" means a motor vehicle which was originally constructed to carry more than 12 passengers but which has been adapted primarily for the carriage of playthings for children (including articles required in connection with the use of those things);]

. . .

(2) Unless the context otherwise requires, any reference in these Regulations to—

  (a) a numbered section is a reference to the section bearing that number in [the 1988 Act];

  (b) a numbered Regulation or Schedule is a reference to the Regulation or Schedule bearing that number in these Regulations, and

  (c) a numbered paragraph is a reference to the paragraph bearing that number in the Regulation in which the reference appears.

(3) For the purposes of these Regulations the unladen weight of a vehicle shall be computed in accordance with Schedule 6 to the Vehicles (Excise) Act 1971.

(4), (5) *[Omitted.]*

[Regulation 3(1) as printed above contains only selected definitions.   **B18.03**
  Regulation 3 is printed as amended by the Interpretation Act 1978, ss.17(2)(a) and 23(1); S.I. 1982 No. 1477; S.I. 1983 No. 1434; S.I. 1985 No. 45; S.I. 1991 No. 253; S.I. 1998 No. 1672; S.I. 2000 No. 1432.
  Schedule 6 to the Vehicles (Excise) Act 1971 (see regulation 3(3)) was repealed by the Finance Act 1991.]

*   *   *

5. Classification of vehicles and application of regulations

(1) For the purposes of these Regulations motor vehicles to which they apply are   **B18.04**
classified as follows:
  Class I: Light motor bicycles
  [Class II: Motor bicycles]
  [Class III: Light motor vehicles other than motor bicycles]
  [Class IV: Motor cars and heavy motor cars not being vehicles with Classes III, IVA, V, VA, VI, VIA or VII]
  [Class IVA: Minibuses, other than vehicles to which paragraph (4) applies, not being vehicles within Classes III, V, VA, VI or VIA, in respect of which any forward-facing seat is fitted with a relevant seat belt]
  [Class V: Motor vehicles not being vehicles within Class VA which are—
    (a) Large passenger-carrying vehicles;
    (b) Public service vehicles—
      (i) of a type specified in paragraph (3), and
      (ii) constructed or adapted to carry more than 12 seated passengers, and
    (c) Play buses]

[Class VA: Motor vehicles, other than vehicles to which paragraph (4) applies, which are—
  (a) Large passenger-carrying vehicles;
  (b) Public service vehicles—
       (i) of a type specified in paragraph (3), and
       (ii) constructed or adapted to carry more than 12 seated passengers, and
  (c) Play buses]

   in respect of which any forward-facing seat is fitted with a relevant seat belt]

[Class VI: Public service vehicles, other than those of a type specified in paragraph (3), not being vehicles within Class VIA]
[Class VIA: Public service vehicles, not being vehicles to which paragraph (4) applies, other than those of a type specified in paragraph (3), in respect of which any forward-facing seat is fitted with a relevent seat-belt]
  Class VII: Goods vehicles of which the design gross weight is more than 3000 kilograms but does not exceed 3500 kilograms]

and (except where otherwise provided in these Regulations) any reference in these Regulations to a class of vehicles shall be construed accordingly.

(2) Save as provided in Regulation 6, these Regulations apply to every vehicle of a class specified in paragraph (1).

(3) The public service vehicles mentioned in paragraph (1) as included in [Class V or VA] are public service vehicles [which may lawfully be used on a road in the absence of a certificate of initial fitness by virtue of—]

  [(a) section 23(7) of the Transport Act 1985 (a bus being used to provide a community bus service)],

  (b) section 46 of the 1981 Act (a school bus belonging to a local education authority and being used to provide free school transport and carrying as fare-paying passengers persons other than those for whom the free school transport is provided, and a school bus being used, when it is not being used to provide free school transport, to provide a local bus service), [or]

  [(c) section 21(2) of the Transport Act 1985 (a small bus used under a permit granted under section 19 of that Act).]

[(4) This paragraph applies to vehicles, in respect of which—

  (a) a certificate of initial fitness has been issued on or after 1st August 1998; or

  (b) one or more forward-facing seats are fitted with a relevant seat belt, which, when so equipped, are of a type of vehicle in respect of which the Secretary of State is satisfied that the vehicle manufacturer holds—

       (i) an approval issued by or on behalf of the approval authority of an EEA State confirming compliance with the installation requirements of Community Directives 77/541 [*O.J. No. L220, August 29, 1977, p. 95*], 82/319 [*O.J. No. L139, May 19, 1982, p. 17*], 90/628 [*O.J. No. L341, December 6, 1990, p. 1*] or 96/36 [*O.J. No. L178, July 17, 1996, p. 15*]; and

       (ii) either—
            (A) an approval issued by or on behalf of the approval authority of an EEA State confirming compliance with the technical and installation requirements of Community Directives 76/115 [*O.J. No. L24, January 30, 1976, p. 6*], 81/575 [*O.J. No. L209, July 29, 1981, p. 30*], 82/318 [*O.J. No. L319, May 19, 1982, p. 9*], 90/629 [*O.J. No. L341, December 6, 1990, p. 14*] or 96/38[*O.J. No. L187, May 26, 1996, p. 95*]; or

(B) an approval issued by or on behalf of the competent authority of a contracting State confirming compliance with the technical and installation requirements of ECE Regulation 14, 14.01, 14.02 or 14.03.]

[(5) In this regulation—

"*approval authority*" has the same meaning as in Community Directive 70/156 [*O.J. L42, February 23, 1970, p. 1*];

"*certificate of initial fitness*" has the same meaning as in section 6 of the Public Passenger Vehicles Act 1981 [*q.v.*];

"*contracting State*" means a State which is a party to the International Agreement;

"*EEA State*" means a State which is a contracting party to the EEA Agreement;

"*EEA Agreement*" means the agreement on the European Economic Area signed at Oporto on 2nd May 1992 [*Cm. 2073*] as adjusted by the Protocol signed at Brussels on 17th March 1993 [*Cm. 2183*];

"*ECE Regulation*" and "*Community Directive*" have the meanings given by regulation 3(2) of the Construction and Use Regulations;

"*the International Agreement*" means the Agreement concerning the adoption of uniform conditions of approval for motor vehicle equipment and parts and reciprocal recognition thereof concluded at Geneva on 20th March 1958 [*Cmnd. 2535*] as amended [*Cmnd. 3562*] to which the United Kingdom is a party [*instrument of accession dated January 14, 1963 deposited with UN Secretary-General on January 15, 1963*]; and

"*relevant seat belt*" means a seat belt, not being a disabled person's belt or a child restraint, which—

(a) is fitted other than as required by regulation 47 of the Construction and Use Regulations; and

(b) on or after 1st August 1998 either—

    (i) has not undergone an examination and been found to comply with the prescribed statutory requirements referred to in item 28A in paragraph 3A of Schedule 2; or

    (ii) has undergone an examination and been found so to comply but is fitted in a vehicle in respect of which no test certificate has been issued to the effect that that is the case.]

[Regulation 5 is printed as amended by S.I. 1982 No. 814; S.I. 1982 No. 1477; S.I. 1984 No. **B18.05** *1126; S.I. 1988 No. 1894; S.I. 1991 No. 253; S.I. 1998 No. 1672.*

The classification of vehicles in regulation 5(1) is incorporated by reference into regulation 61(10AC), (10B) and (10BB) of the Road Vehicles (Construction and Use) Regulations 1986 (S.I. 1986 No. 1078) below.

As to the EEA agreement, see the note to Regulation (EEC) 3820/85 below.]

6. Exemptions

(1) Pursuant to [section 47(5)] the Secretary of State hereby prescribes the following **B18.06** vehicles as those to which [section 47] does not apply:

  (i) a heavy locomotive;

  (ii) a light locomotive;

  (iii) a motor tractor;

  (iv) a track laying vehicle;

  [(v) a goods vehicle, the design gross weight of which exceeds 3500 kilograms;]

  (vi) an articulated vehicle not being an articulated bus;

[(vii) a vehicle to which paragraph (1A) for the time being applies];

(viii) a works truck;

 (ix) a pedestrian controlled vehicle;

 (x) a vehicle (including a cycle with an attachment for propelling it by mechanical power) which is adapted, and used or kept on a road, for invalids, and which—

    (i) does not exceed 306 kilograms in weight unladen, or

    (ii) exceeds 306 kilograms but does not exceed 510 kilograms in weight unladen, and are supplied and maintained by or on behalf of the Department of Health and Social Security, the Scottish Office or the Welsh Office;

(xi) a vehicle temporarily in Great Britain displaying a registration mark mentioned in [Regulation 5 of the Motor Vehicles (International Circulation) Regulations 1985] [*S.I. 1985 No. 610; not reproduced in this work*], a period of twelve months not having elapsed since the vehicle was last brought into Great Britain;

(xii) a vehicle proceeding to a port for export;

(xiii) a vehicle in the service of a visiting force or of a headquarters (within the meaning given by Article 8(6) of the Visiting Forces and International Headquarters (Application of Law) Order 1965 [*S.I. 1965 No. 1536*]);

(xiv) a vehicle provided for police purposes and maintained in workshops approved by the Secretary of State as suitable for such maintenance, being a vehicle provided in England and Wales by a police authority or the Receiver for the Metropolitan Police District, or, in Scotland, by a police authority or a joint police committee;

(xv) a vehicle which has been imported into Great Britain and to which [section 47(2)(b)] applies, being a vehicle owned by or in the service of the naval, military or air forces of Her Majesty raised in the United Kingdom and used for naval, military or air force purposes;

(xvi) a vehicle in respect of which a test certificate issued in accordance with Article 34 of the Road Traffic (Northern Ireland) Order 1981 [*S.I. 1981 No. 154; not reproduced in this work*] is in force or which are licensed under the Vehicles (Excise) Act (Northern Ireland) 1972;

[(xvii) an electrically propelled goods vehicle the design gross weight of which does not exceed 3500 kilograms;] . . .

(xviii) subject to the provisions of paragraph (4), a hackney carriage or a cab in respect of which there is in force a licence under—

    (a) section 6 of the Metropolitan Public Carriage Act 1869, or

    (b) the Town Police Clauses Act 1847, . . . or any similar local statutory provision, to ply for hire;

(xix) subject to the provisions of paragraph (4), a private hire car in respect of which there is in force a licence granted by a local authority, or, in Scotland, by a local authority or a police authority;

[(xx) an agricultural motor vehicle].

[(xxi) a motor vehicle constructed and not merely adapted for the purpose of street cleansing or the collection or disposal of refuse or the collection or disposal of the contents of gullies and which is either—

    (a) a three wheeled vehicle, or

    (b) a vehicle which—

        (i) is incapable by reason of its construction of exceeding a speed of 20 miles per hour on the level under its own power, or

        (ii) has an inside track width of less than 810 millimetres;]

[(xxii) a goods vehicle, the design gross weight of which does not exceed 3500 kilograms and in respect of which a goods vehicle test certificate was issued between 1st February 1990 and 17th March 1991, while that certificate is valid; . . .]

[(xxiii) before 1st August 1991, a goods vehicle the design gross weight of which does not exceed 3500 kilograms and which is of a class specified in Schedule 2 to the Goods Vehicles (Plating and Testing) Regulations 1988 [*S.I. 1988 No. 1478, q.v.*].]

[(xxiv) a tramcar; and]

[(xxv) a trolley vehicle which is not an auxiliary trolley vehicle.]

    [(1A) This paragraph applies to a vehicle at a time when it is being used on a public road during any calendar week if—

(a) it is being used only in passing from land in the occupation of the person keeping the vehicle to other land in his occupation, and

(b) it has not been used on public roads for distances exceeding an aggregate of six miles in that calendar week,

and for the purposes of this paragraph *"public road"* has the meaning given in section 62(1) the Vehicle Excise and Registration Act 1994.]

    (2) Pursuant to [section 47(6)] the Secretary of State hereby exempts from [section 47(1)] the use of a vehicle—

(a)   (i) for the purpose of submitting it by previous arrangement for, or bringing it away from, an examination, or

    (ii) in the course of an examination, for the purpose of taking it to, or bringing it away from, any place where a part of the examination is to be or, as the case may be, has been, carried out, or of carrying out any part of the examination, the person so using it being either—

        (a) an examiner, or a Ministry Inspector or an inspector appointed by a designated council, or

        (b) a person acting under the personal direction of an examiner, a Ministry Inspector or a designated Council, or

   (iii) where a test certificate is refused on an examination—

        (a) for the purpose of delivering it by previous arrangement at, or bringing it away from, a place where work is to be or has been done on it to remedy for a further examination the defects on the ground of which the test certificate was refused; or

        (b) for the purpose of delivering it, by towing it, to a place where the vehicle is to be broken up;

(b) for any purpose for which the vehicle is authorised to be used on roads by an order under [section 44];

(c) where the vehicle has been imported into Great Britain, for the purpose of its being driven after arrival in Great Britain on the journey from the place where it has arrived in Great Britain to a place of residence of the owner or driver of the vehicle;

(d) for the purpose of removing it in pursuance of section 3 of the Refuse Disposal (Amenity) Act 1978 [*q.v.*], of moving or removing it in pursuance of regulations under [section 99 of the Road Traffic Regulation Act 1984], or of removing it from a parking place in pursuance of an order under [section 35(1) of the Road Traffic Regulation Act 1984], an order relating to a parking place designated under [section 45] thereof, or a provision of a designation order having effect by virtue of [section 53(3)] thereof;

(e) where the vehicle has been detained or seized by a police constable, for police purposes connected with such detention or seizure;

(f) where the vehicle has been removed, detained or seized or condemned as forfeited under any provision of the Customs and Excise Management Act 1979 for any purpose authorised by an officer of Customs and Excise;

(g) for the purpose of testing it by a motor trader as defined in [section 62(1) of the Vehicles Excise and Registration Act 1994], to whom a trade licence has been issued under that section, during the course of, or after completion of repairs carried out to that vehicle by that motor trader.

(3) Pursuant to [section 47(7)] the Secretary of State hereby exempts from [section 47(1)] the use of a vehicle on any island in any area mainly surrounded by water, being an island or area from which motor vehicles, unless constructed for special purposes, can at no time be conveniently driven to a road in any other part of Great Britain by reason of the absence of any bridge, tunnel, ford or other way suitable for the passage of such motor vehicle:

[Provided that—

(a) in relation to a vehicle in any of Classes I to [VIA],] this Regulation does not apply to any of the following islands, namely, the Isle of Wight, the islands of Arran, Bute, Great Cumbrae, Islay, Lewis, Mainland (Orkney), Mainland (Shetland), Mull, North Uist and Skye.

[and]

[(b) in relation to a vehicle in Class VII this Regulation does not apply in any of the following islands, namely, the Isle of Wight, the Islands of Lewis, Mainland (Orkney), Mainland (Shetland) and Skye.]

(4) The exemptions specified in paragraph (1)(xviii) and (xix) do not obtain unless the authority which issued the licence holds a certificate issued by the Secretary of State evidencing that he is satisfied that the issue of the licence is subject to the vehicle first passing an annual test relating to the prescribed statutory requirements; and, as from 1st January 1983,

(a) in the case of a vehicle of a kind mentioned in paragraph (1)(xviii) first used more than one year before the licence there mentioned was issued, or

(b) in the case of a vehicle of a kind mentioned in paragraph (1)(xix) first used more than three years before the licence there mentioned was issued

the authority which issued the licence also issued to the licensee a certificate recording that on the date on which the certificate was issued that authority was, as a result of a test, satisfied that the prescribed statutory requirements were satisfied.

(5) In this Regulation—

["*auxiliary trolley vehicle*" means a trolley vehicle which is adapted to operate under power provided from a source on board when it is not operating from power transmitted to it from some external source;]

"*private hire car*" means a motor vehicle which is not a vehicle licensed to ply for hire under the provisions of the Metropolitan Public Carriage Act 1869, Town Police Clauses Act 1847, . . . or any similar local statutory provision with respect to hackney carriages but which is kept for the purpose of being let out for hire with a driver for the carrying of passengers in such circumstances that it does not require to be licensed to ply for hire under the said provisions; and

"*test*" means an examination of a vehicle in relation to the prescribed statutory requirements conducted—

[(i) by a person appointed to act as an inspector under [section 45], or a person authorised as an examiner or acting on his behalf, or]

(ii) by a person on behalf of a police authority in England or Wales, or

(iii) [*applies to Scotland.*]

[Regulation 6 is printed as amended by the Interpretation Act 1978, ss.17(2)(a) and 23(1); S.I. 1983 No. 1434; the Road Traffic Regulation Act 1984, s.144(1) and Sched. 10, para.2; S.I. 1985 No. 45; S.I. 1991 No. 253; the Tramcars and Trolley Vehicles (Modification of Enactments) Regulations 1992 (S.I. 1992 No. 1217), reg.12(a) and (b); the Vehicle Excise and Registration Act 1994, s.64 and Sched. 4, para.4; S.I. 1995 No. 1457; S.I. 1998 No. 1672.

The Visiting Forces and International Headquarters (Application of Law) Order 1965 (to which reference is made in regulation 6(1)(xiii)) has been revoked and replaced by the Visiting Forces and International Headquarters (Application of Law) Order 1999 (S.I. 1999 No. 1736; not reproduced in this work). No textual amendment had been made to regulation 6 in consequence of that revocation; but by the Interpretation Act 1978, ss.17(2)(a) and 23(1) references to the earlier order may be treated as references to S.I. 1999 No. 1736.

The Vehicles (Excise) Act (Northern Ireland) 1972 (mentioned in regulation 6(1)(xvi) above) has been repealed by the Finance Act 1991.

Express references to Scottish legislation have been omitted from the text of regulation 6(1)(xviii)(b) and (5).]

*   *   *

The Motorways Traffic (England and Wales) Regulations 1982

(S.I. 1982 No. 1163)

B19.01   *Editorial note.*   Nothing contained in these regulations precludes any person, acting in accordance with Part IV (regulations 15 and 16) of the Traffic Signs (Temporary Obstructions) Regulations 1997 (S.I. 1997 No. 3053), from placing a flat traffic delineator, a keep right sign, a traffic cone, a traffic pyramid, a traffic triangle, or a warning lamp on a special road to which these regulations apply; nor, having so placed such item, from removing it; see S.I. 1997 No. 3053, reg.17 below.

B19.02   *[The text of these regulations is printed as amended by:*

the Motorways Traffic (England and Wales) (Amendment) Regulations 1983 (S.I. 1983 No. 374) (April 16, 1983);

the Motorways Traffic (England and Wales) (Amendment) Regulations 1984 (S.I. 1984 No. 1479) (October 17, 1984);

the Motorways Traffic (England and Wales) (Amendment) Regulations 1992 (S.I. 1992 No. 1364) (July 1, 1992);

the Motorways Traffic (England and Wales) (Amendment) Regulations 1995 (S.I. 1995 No. 158) (January 1, 1996); and

the Motorways Traffic (England and Wales) (Amendment) Regulations 1996 (S.I. 1996 No. 3053) (January 1, 1997).

The amending regulations are referred to in the notes to the principal regulations only by their years and numbers. The dates referred to above are the dates on which the amending regulations came into force.]

ARRANGEMENT OF REGULATIONS

B19.03   Regulation

1. Commencement and citation   *[Omitted.]*   **B19.04**

2. Revocation   *[Omitted.]*

3. Interpretation

(1) In these Regulations, the following expressions have the meanings hereby res-   **B19.05**
pectively assigned to them:—

  [(a) *"the 1984 Act"* means the Road Traffic Regulation Act 1984 [*q.v.*];]

  (b) [*"carriageway"* means that part of a motorway which—

     (i) is provided for the regular passage of vehicular motor traffic along the motor-
way; and

     (ii) where a hard shoulder is provided, has the approximate position of its left-
hand or near-side edge marked with a traffic sign of the type shown in
diagram 1012.1 in [Schedule 6 to the Traffic Signs Regulations and General
Directions 1994] [*S.I. 1994 No. 1519*]]:

  (c) *"central reservation"* means that part of a motorway which separates the carriageway
to be used by vehicles travelling in one direction from the carriageway to be used
by vehicles travelling in the opposite direction;

  (d) *"excluded traffic"* means traffic which is not traffic of Classes I or II;

  (e) *"hard shoulder"* means a part of the motorway which is adjacent to and situated on
the left hand or near side of the carriageway when facing in the direction in which
vehicles may be driven in accordance with Regulation 6, and which is designed to
take the weight of a vehicle;

  (f) *"motorway"* means any road or part of a road to which these Regulations apply by
virtue of Regulation 4;

  (g) *"verge"* means any part of a motorway which is not a carriageway, a hard shoulder,
or a central reservation.

(2) A vehicle shall be treated for the purposes of any provision of these Regulations as
being on any part of a motorway specified in that provision if any part of the vehicle
(whether it is at rest or not) is on the part of the motorway so specified.

(3) Any provision of these Regulations containing any prohibition or restriction relating
to the driving, moving or stopping of a vehicle, or to its remaining at rest, shall be construed
as a provision that no person shall use a motorway by driving, moving or stopping the
vehicle or by causing or permitting it to be driven or moved, or to stop or remain at rest, in
contravention of that prohibition or restriction.

(4) In these Regulations references to numbered classes of traffic are references to the
classes of traffic set out in Schedule 4 to the Highways Act 1980 [*q.v.*].

[Regulation 3 is printed as amended by the Road Traffic Regulation Act 1984, s.144(1) and Sched.   **B19.06**
10, para.2; S.I. 1984 No. 1479; S.I. 1992 No. 1364; the Interpretation Act 1978, ss.17(2)(a) and
23(1).]

[**4.** Subject to section 17(5) of the 1984 Act, these Regulations apply to every special road   **B19.07**
or part of a special road which can be used only by traffic of Class I or II.]

[Regulation 4 is printed as substituted by S.I. 1992 No. 1364.]   **B19.08**

5. Vehicles to be driven on the carriageway only

Subject to the following provisions of these Regulations, no vehicle shall be driven on any   **B19.09**
part of a motorway which is not a carriageway.

6. Direction of driving

B19.10 (1) Where there is a traffic sign indicating that there is no entry to a carriageway at a particular place, no vehicle shall be driven or moved onto that carriageway at that place.

(2) Where there is a traffic sign indicating that there is no left or right turn into a carriageway at a particular place, no vehicle shall be so driven or moved as to cause it to turn to the left or (as the case may be) to the right into that carriageway at that place.

(3) Every vehicle on a length of carriageway which is contiguous to a central reservation, shall be driven in such a direction that the central reservation is at all times on the right hand or off side of the vehicle.

(4) Where traffic signs are so placed that there is a length of carriageway (being a length which is not contiguous to a central reservation) which can be entered at one end only by vehicles driven in conformity with paragraph (1) of this Regulation, every vehicle on that length of carriageway shall be driven in such a direction only as to cause it to proceed away from that end of that length of carriageway towards the other end thereof.

(5) Without prejudice to the foregoing provisions of this Regulation, no vehicle which—

(a) is on a length of carriageway on which vehicles are required by any of the foregoing provisions of this Regulation to be driven in one direction only and is proceeding in or facing that direction, or

(b) is on any other length of carriageway and is proceeding in or facing one direction,

shall be driven or moved so as to cause it to turn and proceed in or face the opposite direction.

7. Restriction on stopping

B19.11 (1) Subject to the following provisions of this Regulation, no vehicle shall stop or remain at rest on a carriageway.

(2) Whether it is necessary for a vehicle which is being driven on a carriageway to be stopped while it is on a motorway—

(a) by reason of a breakdown or mechanical defect or lack of fuel, oil or water, required for the vehicle; or

(b) by reason of any accident, illness or other emergency; or

(c) to permit any person carried in or on the vehicle to recover or move any object which has fallen onto a motorway; or

(d) to permit any person carried in or on the vehicle to give help which is required by any other person in any of the circumstances specified in the foregoing provisions of this paragraph,

the vehicle shall, as soon and in so far as is reasonably practicable, be driven or moved off the carriageway on to, and may stop and remain at rest on, any hard shoulder which is contiguous to that carriageway.

(3)(a) A vehicle which is at rest on a hard shoulder shall so far as is reasonably practicable be allowed to remain at rest on that hard shoulder in such a position only that no part of it or of the load carried thereby shall obstruct or be a cause of danger to vehicles using the carriageway.

(b) A vehicle shall not remain at rest on a hard shoulder for longer than is necessary in the circumstances or for the purposes specified in paragraph 2 of this Regulation.

(4) Nothing in the foregoing provisions of this Regulation shall preclude a vehicle from

stopping or remaining at rest on a carriageway while it is prevented from proceeding along the carriageway by the presence of any other vehicle or any person or object.

8. Restriction on reversing

No vehicle on a motorway shall be driven or moved backwards except in so far as it is necessary to back the vehicle to enable it to proceed forwards or to be connected to any other vehicle.   **B19.12**

9. Restriction on the use of hard shoulders

No vehicle shall be driven or stop or remain at rest on any hard shoulder except in accordance with paragraphs (2) and (3) of Regulation 7.   **B19.13**

10. Vehicles not to use the central reservation or verge

No vehicle shall be driven or moved or stop or remain at rest on a central reservation or verge.   **B19.14**

11. Vehicles not to be driven by learner drivers

[(1) Subject to paragraph (3), a person shall not drive on a motorway a motor vehicle to which this regulation applies if he is authorised to drive that vehicle only by virtue of his being the holder of a provisional licence.   **B19.15**

(2) This regulation applies to—

    (a) a motor vehicle in category A or B or sub-category C1+E (8.25 tonnes), D1 (not for hire or reward), D1+E (not for hire or reward) or P, and

    (b) a motor vehicle in category B+E or sub-category C1 if the provisional licence authorising the driving of such a motor vehicle was in force at a time before 1st January 1997.

(3) Paragraph (1) shall not apply in relation to a vehicle if the holder of the provisional licence has passed a test of competence prescribed under section 89 of the Road Traffic Act 1988 [*q.v.*] for the grant of a licence to drive that vehicle.

(4) In this regulation—

    (a) the expression "*in force*" and expressions relating to vehicle categories shall be construed in accordance with regulations 3(2) and 4(2) respectively of the Motor Vehicles (Driving Licences) Regulations 1996 [*S.I. 1996 No. 2824, q.v.*];

    (b) "*provisional licence*", in relation to any vehicle, means a licence—

        (i) granted under section 97(2) of the Road Traffic Act 1988, or

        (ii) treated, by virtue of section 98 of that Act and regulations made thereunder, as authorising its holder to drive that vehicle as if he were authorised by a provisional licence to do so.]

[Regulation 11 is printed as substituted by S.I. 1996 No. 3053.   **B19.16**
The Motor Vehicles (Driving Licences) Regulations 1996 (to which reference is made in regulation 11(4)(a)) have been revoked and replaced with effect from November 12, 1999 by the Motor Vehicles (Driving Licences) Regulations 1999 (S.I. 1999 No. 2864) below. Attention is drawn in particular to regulations 3(2) and 4(2) of S.I. 1999 No. 2864.]

12. Restriction on use of right hand or off-side lane

[(1) This Regulation applies to—   **B19.17**

    [(a) a goods vehicle having a maximum laden weight exceeding 7.5 tonnes,]

    [(b) a passenger vehicle which is constructed or adapted to carry more than eight seated passengers in addition to the driver the maximum laden weight of which exceeds 7.5 tonnes;]

(c) a motor vehicle drawing a trailer; and

[(d) a vehicle which is a motor tractor, a light locomotive or a heavy locomotive.]

(2) Subject to the provisions of paragraph (3) below, no vehicle to which this Regulation applies shall be driven or moved or stop or remain at rest on the right hand or off-side lane of a length of carriageway which has three or more traffic lanes at any place where all the lanes are open for use by traffic proceeding in the same direction.

(3) The prohibition contained in paragraph (2) above shall not apply to a vehicle whilst it is being driven on any right hand or off-side lane such as is mentioned in that paragraph in so far as it is necessary for the vehicle to be driven to enable it to pass another vehicle which is carrying or drawing a load of exceptional width.

[(4) Nothing in this regulation shall have effect so as to require a vehicle to change lane during a period when it would not be reasonably practicable for it to do so without involving danger of injury to any person or inconvenience to other traffic.]

[(5) In this Regulation *"goods vehicle"*, *"passenger vehicle"* and *"maximum laden weight"* have the same meanings as in Schedule 6 to the 1984 Act.]

B19.18   *[Regulation 12 is printed as substituted by S.I. 1983 No. 374, and as subsequently amended by S.I. 1992 No. 1364; S.I. 1995 No. 158.]*

B19.19   **13. Restrictions affecting persons on foot on a motorway**   *[Revoked by S.I. 1992 No. 1364.]*

14. Restrictions affecting animals carried in vehicles

B19.20   The person in charge of any animal which is carried by a vehicle using a motorway shall, so far is practicable, secure that—

(a) the animal shall not be removed from or permitted to leave the vehicle while the vehicle is on a motorway, and

(b) if it escapes from, or it is necessary for it to be removed from, or permitted to leave, the vehicle—

(i) it shall not go or remain on any part of the motorway other than a hard shoulder, and

(ii) it shall whilst it is not on or in the vehicle be held on a lead or otherwise kept under proper control.

15. Use of motorway by excluded traffic

B19.21   (1) Excluded traffic is hereby authorised to use a motorway on the occasions or in the emergencies and to the extent specified in the following provisions of this paragraph, that is to say—

(a) traffic of Classes III or IV may use a motorway for the maintenance, repair, cleaning or clearance of any part of a motorway or for the erection, laying, placing, maintenance, testing, alteration, repair or removal of any structure, works or apparatus in, on, under or over any part of a motorway;

(b) pedestrians may use a motorway—

(i) when it is necessary for them to do so as a result of an accident or emergency or of a vehicle being at rest on a motorway in any of the circumstances specified in paragraph (2) of Regulation 7, or

(ii) in any of the circumstances specified in sub-paragraphs (b), (d), (e) or (f) of paragraph (1) of Regulation 16.

(2) The Secretary of State may authorise the use of a motorway by any excluded traffic on occasion or in emergency or for the purpose of enabling such traffic to cross a motorway or to secure access to premises abutting on or adjacent to a motorway.

(3) Where by reason of any emergency the use of any road (not being a motorway) by any excluded traffic is rendered impossible or unsuitable the Chief Officer of Police of the police area in which a motorway or any part of a motorway is situated, or any officer of or above the rank of superintendent authorised in that behalf by that Chief Officer, may—

(a) authorise any excluded traffic to use that motorway or that part of a motorway as an alternative road for the period during which the use of the other road by such traffic continues to be impossible or unsuitable, and

(b) relax any prohibition or restriction imposed by these Regulations in so far as he considers it necessary to do so in connection with the use of that motorway or that part of a motorway by excluded traffic in pursuance of any such authorisation as aforesaid.

16. Exceptions and relaxations

(1) Nothing in the foregoing provisions of these Regulations shall preclude any person **B19.22** from using a motorway otherwise than in accordance with the provisions in any of the following circumstances, that is to say—

(a) where he does so in accordance with any direction or permission given by a constable in uniform or with the indication given by a traffic sign;

(b) where, in accordance with any permission given by a constable, he does so for the purpose of investigating any accident which has occurred on or near a motorway;

(c) where it is necessary for him to do so to avoid or prevent an accident or to obtain or give help required as the result of an accident or emergency, and he does so in such manner as to cause as little danger or inconvenience as possible to other traffic on a motorway;

(d) where he does so in the exercise of his duty as a constable or as a member of a fire brigade or of an ambulance service;

(e) where it is necessary for him to do so to carry out in an efficient manner—

(i) the maintenance, repair, cleaning, clearance, alteration or improvement of any part of a motorway, or

(ii) the removal of any vehicle from any part of a motorway, or

(iii) the erection, laying, placing, maintenance, testing, alteration, repair or removal of any structure, works or apparatus in, on, under or over any part of a motorway; or

(f) where it is necessary for him to do so in connection with any inspection, survey, investigation or census which is carried out in accordance with any general or special authority granted by the Secretary of State.

(2) Without prejudice to the foregoing provisions of these Regulations, the Secretary of State may relax any prohibition or restriction imposed by these Regulations.

The Motor Vehicles (Type Approval for Goods Vehicles) (Great Britain) Regulations 1982

(S.I. 1982 No. 1271)

B20.01   *[The text of these regulations is printed as amended by:*

the Motor Vehicles (Type Approval for Goods Vehicles) (Great Britain) (Amendment) Regulations 1984 (S.I. 1984 No. 697) (June 20, 1984);

the Motor Vehicles (Type Approval for Goods Vehicles) (Great Britain) (Amendment) Regulations 1985 (S.I. 1985 No. 46) (March 1, 1985);

the Motor Vehicles (Type Approval for Goods Vehicles) (Great Britain) (Amendment) Regulations 1986 (S.I. 1986 No. 427) (April 4, 1986);

the Motor Vehicles (Type Approval for Goods Vehicles) (Great Britain) (Amendment) Regulations 1987 (S.I. 1987 No. 1508) (except as otherwise indicated, October 1, 1987);

the Motor Vehicles (Type Approval for Goods Vehicles) (Great Britain) (Amendment) Regulations 1988 (S.I. 1988 No. 1523) (October 1, 1988);

the Motor Vehicles (Type Approval for Goods Vehicles) (Great Britain) (Amendment) Regulations 1989 (S.I. 1989 No. 1579) (October 1, 1989);

the Motor Vehicles (Type Approval for Goods Vehicles) (Great Britain) (Amendment) Regulations 1991 (S.I. 1991 No. 1021) (May 20, 1991);

the Motor Vehicles (Type Approval for Goods Vehicles) (Great Britain) (Amendment) (No. 2) Regulations 1991 (S.I. 1991 No. 1970) (October 1, 1991);

the Motor Vehicles (Type Approval for Goods Vehicles) (Great Britain) (Amendment) Regulations 1992 (S.I. 1992 No. 25) (February 1, 1992); and

the Motor Vehicles (Type Approval for Goods Vehicles) (Great Britain) (Amendment) (No. 2) Regulations 1992 (S.I. 1992 No. 1342) (July 1, 1992);

the Motor Vehicles (Type Approval for Goods Vehicles) (Great Britain) (Amendment) (No. 3) Regulations 1992 (S.I. 1992 No. 3084) (January 1, 1993).

the Motor Vehicles (Type Approval for Goods Vehicles) (Great Britain) (Amendment) Regulations 1993 (S.I. 1993 No. 2200) (October 1, 1993);

the Motor Vehicles (Type Approval for Goods Vehicles) (Great Britain) (Amendment) Regulations 1995 (S.I. 1995 No. 1323) (June 12, 1995);

the Motor Vehicles (Type Approval for Goods Vehicles) (Amendment) Regulations 1996 [sic] (S.I. 1996 No. 2331) (October 1, 1996); and

the Motor Vehicles (Type Approval for Goods Vehicles) (Great Britain) (Amendment) (No. 2) Regulations 1996 (S.I. 1996 No. 3014) (July 1, 1997).

The amending regulations are referred to in the notes to the principal regulations only by their years and numbers. The dates referred to above are the dates on which the amending regulations came into force.

In addition to the above, the principal regulations have been amended by the Motor Vehicles (Type Approval for Goods Vehicles) (Great Britain) (Amendment) (No. 2) Regulations 1986 (S.I. 1986 No. 1089), the Motor Vehicles (Type Approval for Goods Vehicles) (Great Britain) (Amendment) Regulations 1994 (S.I. 1994 No. 2191), the Motor Vehicles (Type Approval for Goods Vehicles) (Great Britain) (Amendment) Regulations 1997 (S.I. 1997 No. 1365), the Motor Vehicles (Type Approval for Goods Vehicles) (Great Britain) (Amendment) (No. 2) Regulations 1997 (S.I. 1997 No. 2936), and the Motor

Vehicles (Type Approval for Goods Vehicles) (Great Britain) (Amendment) Regulations 1998 (S.I. 1998 No. 1006), but these regulations do not affect the text of any provision printed in this work.]

1. Commencement and citation   *[Omitted.]*   **B20.02**

2. Interpretation

(1) In these regulations—   **B20.03**

"the Construction and Use Regulations" means the [Road Vehicles (Construction and Use) Regulations 1986] [*S.I. 1986 No. 1078, q.v.*];

"the Great Britain Regulations" means the Motor Vehicles (Type Approval) (Great Britain) Regulations [1984] [*S.I. 1984 No. 981, q.v.*];

"the Plating and Testing Regulations" means the [Goods Vehicles (Plating and Testing) Regulations 1988] [*S.I. 1988 No. 1478, q.v.*];

"appropriate information document"—

    (i) in relation to a vehicle subject to type approval requirements, means a document in the form set out in Part I of Schedule 2, and

    (ii) in relation to a vehicle part subject to type approval requirements, means a document in the form set out in Part II of Schedule 2;

[*"axle weight"* has the same meaning given in the table in regulation 3(2) of the Construction and Use Regulations;]

"bi-purpose vehicle" means a vehicle constructed or adapted for the carriage of both goods and not more than 8 passengers, not being a vehicle to which the Great Britain Regulations apply nor a motor ambulance or a motor caravan;

"break-down vehicle" has the meaning given in [Regulation 3(1) of] the Plating and Testing Regulations;

"dual-purpose vehicle" has the meaning given in [the Table in regulation 3(2)] of the Construction and Use Regulations;

[*"emissions or noise item"* means an item in Part I of Schedule 1 in respect of which the subject matter specified in column (2) of that Part is "exhaust emissions" or "noise and silencers;"]

[*"Framework Directive vehicle"* means a vehicle to which these Regulations apply and is a "vehicle" within the meaning of Council Directive 70/156/EEC [*O.J. No. L42, February 23, 1970, p. 1*] as amended by Council Directive 87/403/EEC [*O.J. No. L220, August 8, 1987, p. 44*], Council Directive 92/53/EEC [*O.J. No. L225, August 10, 1992, p. 1*] and Commission Directive 93/81 [*O.J. No. L264, October 23, 1993, p. 49*];]

[*"hire agreement"* means an agreement for the bailment . . . of a vehicle which is not a hire-purchase agreement;]

[*"hire-purchase agreement"* has the same meaning as in the Consumer Credit Act 1974;]

[*"inter-urban motor coach"* means a vehicle designed and equipped for inter-urban transport having no spaces specifically intended for standing passengers, but able to carry for short distances passengers standing in the gangway;]

[*"long distance touring motor coach"* means a vehicle designed and equipped for long distance journeys, arranged to ensure the comfort of its seated passengers and which does not carry standing passengers;]

[*"maximum gross weight"* has the meaning given in the Table in regulation 3(2) of the Construction and Use Regulations;]

"*motor ambulance*" and "*motor caravan*" have the meanings given respectively in Regulation 2(1) of the Great Britain Regulations;

"*prescribed alteration*" means an alteration to a vehicle to which these Regulations apply which varies the number or nominal diameter of the tyres or the wheels and which is made before the vehicle is first used;

"*prescribed fee*", in relation to any matter provided for in these Regulations, means the fee prescribed for such matter in Regulations under section 50(1);

"*prescribed type approval requirements*", in relation to a vehicle or vehicle part subject to type approval requirements, means the type approval requirements prescribed therefor by [regulation 4];

"*public works vehicle*" has the meaning given in [the Table in regulation 3(2)] of the Construction and Use Regulations;

["*recovery vehicle*" has the meaning given in [paragraph 5(2) of Schedule 1 to the Vehicle Excise and Registration Act 1994] [*q.v.*];]

["*semi-trailer*" has the same meaning given in the table in regulation 3(2) of the Construction and Use Regulations;]

"*slow vehicle*" means a vehicle incapable by reason of its construction of a speed of more than 25 kilometres per hour on the level under its own power;

["*the type approval requirements*" means—

(a) the weights mentioned in Regulation 5; and

(b) the requirements with respect to the design, construction, equipment or marking requirements of vehicles or vehicle parts which—
  (i) relate to the items numbered in column (1) and listed in column (2) of Part I of Schedule 1; and
  (ii) are contained in instruments, other documents, or Parts of that Schedule, and consist of the requirements specified against each such item in column (3) of Part I of that Schedule (subject to such modifications and additions as are set out in Part I of that Schedule);]

"*vehicle subject to type approval requirements*" and "*vehicle part subject to type approval requirements*" have the meanings given in Regulation 4.

(2) *[Revoked.]*

(3) *[Omitted.]*

(4) For the purposes of these Regulations—

(a) a vehicle is to be regarded as being manufactured on or after a particular date if it is assembled to the stage where it includes all the parts of the vehicle which it needs to have to comply with any one or more of the prescribed type approval requirements; and

(b) the date on which a vehicle is to be regarded as being first used is the date on which it is first registered under [the Vehicle Excise and Registration Act 1994].

(5) *[Omitted.]*

B20.04   *[Regulation 2 is printed as amended by the Interpretation Act 1978, ss.17(2)(a) and 23(1); S.I. 1987 No. 1508; S.I. 1991 Nos 1021, 1970; S.I. 1992 No. 3084; the Vehicle Excise and Registration Act 1994, s.64 and Sched. 4, para.4; S.I. 1996 Nos 2331 and 3014.*

Words relating expressly and exclusively to Scotland have been omitted from the definition of "hire agreement" in regulation 2(1).

The definition of "hire-purchase agreement" in the Consumer Credit Act 1974 is reproduced in the notes to section 109 of the Road Traffic Regulation Act 1984 above.

Regulation 5 of these regulations is concerned with plated weights.]

2A. Interpretation of instruments in Schedule 1 *[Omitted.]*

3. Application of Regulations

(1) Subject to paragraph (2), these Regulations apply to—

 (a) every motor vehicle manufactured on or after 1st October 1982 and [not first used before] 1st April 1983 and which

  (i) has three or more wheels, and

  (ii) is either a goods vehicle, the [tractive] unit of an articulated vehicle or a bi-purpose vehicle; and

 (b) parts of any such vehicles.

(2) These Regulations do not apply to, or to the parts of, any of the following vehicles, that is to say—

 (a) a vehicle brought temporarily into Great Britain and which—

  (i) displays a registration mark mentioned in [Regulation 5 of the Motor Vehicles (International Circulation) Regulations 1985] [*S.I. 1985 No. 610*], and

  (ii) complies in every respect with the requirements relating to motor vehicles contained in:—

   (a) Article 21 and paragraph (1) of Article 22 of the Convention on Road Traffic concluded at Geneva on 19th September 1949 [*Cmnd. 7997*], and Part I, Part II (so far as it relates to direction indicators and stop lights) and Part III of Annex 6 to that Convention; or

   (b) paragraphs I, III and VIII of Article 3 of the International Convention relative to Motor Traffic concluded at Paris on 24th April 1926 [*T.S. No. 11 (1930)*];

 (b) a vehicle which is to be exported from Great Britain and which either—

  (i) has not been used on a road in Great Britain for any purpose except that of proceeding from the place where it was manufactured to the place from which it is to be taken out of Great Britain, or

  (ii) satisfies the criteria of—

   (A) being exempt from car tax by virtue of [section 7(1) of the Car Tax Act 1983],

   (B) being a vehicle in relation to which there has been a remission of car tax by virtue of [section 7(2) and (3) of that Act], or

   (C) being zero-rated under [Regulation 132 or 133 of the Value Added Tax Regulations 1995] [*S.I. 1995 No. 2158*];

 (c) a vehicle in the service of a visiting force or of a headquarters (as defined in Article 8(6) of the Visiting Forces and International Headquarters (Application of Law) Order 1965) [*S.I. 1965 No. 1536*];

 (d) a vehicle to which [sections 49 to 63 of the Road Traffic Act 1988] . . . have become applicable after a period of use on roads during which, by virtue of [section 183(2)] (which relates to vehicles in the public service of the Crown), those sections did not apply to that vehicle;

 [(e) a motor vehicle which is of a new or improved type, or is fitted with equipment of a new or improved type, and which has been constructed to that type or fitted with that equipment, for the purposes of tests or trials or for use as a prototype, and—

  (i) is not intended for general use on roads, and

  (ii) in the case of a vehicle first used on a road on or after 20th June 1984, remains in the ownership and the use of—

   (A) if the vehicle is of a new or improved type the manufacturer of the vehicle, or

(B) if the vehicle is fitted with equipment of a new or improved type the manufacturer of the equipment or the manufacturer of the vehicle on which that equipment is used;]

[(ee) a motor vehicle which is of a new or improved type provided that the conditions specified in paragraph (3) are satisfied;]

(f) a motor tractor, a light locomotive and a heavy locomotive;

(g) [an agricultural motor vehicle, engineering plant], a pedestrian-controlled vehicle, a straddle carrier, a works truck and a vehicle which is track-laying (all as defined in [the Table in regulation 3(2)] of the Construction and Use Regulations);

(h) a vehicle [the use of which on a road is authorised by] Article 15, 17 or 18 of the Motor Vehicles (Authorisation of Special Types) General Order 1979 [*S.I. 1979 No. 1198, q.v.*];

(i) a tower wagon as defined in [paragraph 8(3) of Schedule 1 to the Vehicle Excise and Registration Act 1994] [*q.v.*];

(j) a fire engine (including an air field crash tender);

(k) a road roller;

(l) a vehicle propelled by steam;

(m) a vehicle constructed for the purpose of preventing or reducing the effect of snow or ice on roads, either by spreading grit or other material, by scooping or sweeping, or by other means;

(n) a two-wheeled motor cycle, with or without a side-car;

(o) an electrically-propelled vehicle;

(p) a break-down vehicle;

(q), (r) *[revoked]*

(s) a motor ambulance; . . .

(t) a motor caravan;

[(u) a recovery vehicle first used before 1st January 1988.]

[(3) The conditions referred to in paragraph (2)(ee) are that—

(a) the manufacturer of the vehicle has made an application—

(i) in respect of a type vehicle in accordance with regulation 7 for a type approval certificate, or

(ii) in respect of another vehicle ("*the initial vehicle*") in accordance with regulation 8 for a Minister's approval certificate;

(b) an appointment has been made for a final examination of the type vehicle or the initial vehicle (as the case may be);

(c) the vehicle conforms with the type vehicle or the initial vehicle (as the case may be) in such of the relevant aspects of design, construction, equipment and marking as are mentioned in the information document accompanying the application pursuant to regulation 7 or 8;

(d) the vehicle complies with the relevant type approval requirements specified in Schedule 1;

(e) the Secretary of State has been notified of the vehicle identification number;

(f) the vehicle—

(i) was at the date of manufacture owned by the manufacturer of the vehicle and has remained in his ownership,

(ii) has not been offered for sale by him,

    (iii) has not been let or offered for letting under a hire agreement or a hire-purchase agreement, and

    (iv) has not been used on a road for any purpose other than for, or in connection with, publicity, demonstration or evaluation of vehicles of the new or improved type; and

  (g) the manufacturer of the vehicle intends that until pursuant to the application mentioned in sub-paragraph (a) there has been issued a type approval certificate or a Minister's approval certificate (as the case may be), the vehicle—

    (i) shall remain in his ownership,

    (ii) shall not be offered for sale by him,

    (iii) shall not be let or offered for letting under a hire agreement or a hire-purchase agreement, and

    (iv) shall not be used on a road for any purpose other than for, or in connection with, publicity, demonstration or evaluation of vehicles of the new or improved type.]

[Regulation 3 is printed as amended by the Interpretation Act 1978, ss.17(2)(a) and 23(1); S.I. 1984 **B20.07** *No. 697; S.I. 1985 No. 46; S.I. 1986 No. 427; S.I. 1987 No. 1508; S.I. 1991 No. 1021; S.I. 1992 No. 25; the Vehicle Excise and Registration Act 1994, s.64 and Sched. 4, para.4; S.I. 1996 No. 3014.*

For the provisions of the Car Tax Act 1983 and the Value Added Tax Regulations 1995 (to which reference is made in regulation 3(2)(b) above), see the notes to the Motor Vehicles (Type Approval) (Great Britain) Regulations 1984 (S.I. 1984 No. 981), reg.3 below.

The Visiting Forces and International Headquarters (Application of Law) Order 1965 (to which reference is made in regulation 3(2)(c)) has been revoked and replaced by the Visiting Forces and International Headquarters (Application of Law) Order 1999 (S.I. 1999 No. 1736; not reproduced in this work). No textual amendment had been made to regulation 3 in consequence of that revocation.]

[3A. Modifications in relation to which the Motor Vehicles (Approval) Regulations 1996 apply

(1) These Regulations shall have effect, in relation to vehicles to which Part III of the **B20.08** Approval Regulations apply, with the following modifications.

(2) Regulation 4 shall have effect subject to Regulation 5 of the Approval Regulations.

(3) Regulation 8 does not apply to an application for a Minister's approval certificate made on basis that the vehicle complies with the relevant requirements by virtue of the Approval Regulations.

(4) Regulations 5 and 13 do not apply in relation to any determination made for the purposes of such an application.

(5) Regulations 10, 11 and 12 do not apply to a vehicle in respect of which there is in force a Minister's approval certificate in the form prescribed by the Approval Regulations.

(6) Regulation 14 does not apply to any certificate issued on the basis that the vehicle complies with the relevant requirements by virtue of the Approval Regulations.

(7) Regulation 15 does not apply to any certificate in the form prescribed by the Approval Regulations.

(8) Regulations 18A and 19 do not apply to any vehicle to which Part III of the Approval Regulations (which contains provisions corresponding to Regulations 18A and 19) applies.

(9) In this Regulation—

"*the Approval Regulations*" means the Motor Vehicles (Approval) Regulations 1996 [*S.I. 1996 No. 3013*]; and "*the relevant requirements*", in relation to a vehicle, means the requirements prescribed under section 54 of the 1988 Act that are applicable to it.]

B20.09 *[Regulation 3A was inserted by S.I. 1996 No. 3014.*

The Motor Vehicles (Approval) Regulations 1996 (to which reference is made in regulation 3A) have been revoked and replaced by the Motor Vehicles (Approval) Regulations 2001 (S.I. 2001 No. 25) below. The Interpretation Act 1978, ss.17(2)(a) and 23, which enables references to the 1996 Regulations to be construed as references to the 2001 Regulations, is only applicable in the absence of a contrary intention (see 1978 Act, s.17(2)(a)); the fact that the scheme of the 2001 Regulations differs from that of the 1996 Regulations (e.g. there is no Part in the 2001 Regulations corresponding to Part III ("Goods Vehicles") of the 1996 Regulations and no regulation in the 2001 Regulations corresponding to regulation 5 (application of Part III) of the 1996 Regulations suggests that a "contrary intention" should be inferred. The text of the 1996 Regulations is reproduced in the nineteenth edition of this work.]

4. Application of type approval requirements

B20.10 (1) [Subject to paragraphs (2) to (6), regulation 3A] and to the exemptions specified in column (4) of [Part I of] Schedule 1, the type approval requirements are hereby prescribed as—

(a) a determination of the weights mentioned in Regulation 5 of every vehicle to which these Regulations apply; and

(b) the requirements which are applicable—

(i) from the date specified in column (5) of [Part I of] Schedule 1, and

(ii) in a case [where] a date is specified in column (6) of [Part I of] Schedule 1, until that date.

to every vehicle to which these Regulations apply and to the relevant parts of such vehicles.

(2) The requirements mentioned in paragraph (1) apply only in relation to a vehicle before it is first used on a road . . .

[(2A) [Subject to paragraph (4B),] in relation to a particular vehicle—

(a) a type approval requirement applicable to the vehicle at the date of manufacture shall continue to apply to it until it is first used; and

(b) a type approval requirement which is applicable to vehicles as from a date after that vehicle was manufactured shall not apply to the vehicle unless the subject matter of the requirement is the same as that of a requirement applicable to it on the date it was manufactured; . . .]

(3) [. . . If a vehicle or a vehicle part] is manufactured on or after a date, other than 1st October 1982, specified in an item in column (5) of [Part I of] Schedule 1, the type approval requirement specified in column (3) in that item shall not apply if the vehicle or, in the case of a vehicle part, the vehicle in which it is incorporated, is first used on a road within six months of that date.

(3A) [Revoked.]

(4) [Save as provided in paragraph (4A),] if a vehicle or a vehicle part is manufactured on or after a date specified in an item in column (6) of [Part I of] Schedule 1, the type approval requirement specified in column (3), in that item shall apply if the vehicle or, in the case of a vehicle part, the vehicle in which it is incorporated, is first used on a road within six months of that date.

[(4A) The provisions of paragraph (4) do not apply in respect of [any emissions or noise item] [2D, 2F, 2I, 4D(4) and 4E] in Part I of Schedule 1.]

[(4B) No emissions or noise item shall apply to a Framework Directive vehicle on or after the date specified in column (6) of the item.]

(5) Where in relation to an item listed in column (2) of [Part I of] Schedule 1 two or more instruments or other documents are specified in column (3) of [Part I of] Schedule 1 as alternatives (being instruments or documents containing substantially similar requirements) the requirements prescribed by paragraph (1) shall be the requirements contained in either or any of those instruments or documents, and subject to paragraphs (1), (2), (3), (6) and (7) where two or more items specified in column (1) of [Part I of] Schedule 1 have the same subject matter as that specified in column (2) of [Part I of] Schedule 1 the type approval requirements relate to either or, as the case may be, any of those items [; and for the purposes of this paragraph items 5A and 5B shall be regarded as items having the same subject matter].

(6) *[Revoked.]*

(7) A vehicle to which, or to a part of which, any such requirement as is mentioned in paragraph (1) is for the time being applicable is referred to in these Regulations as "*a vehicle subject to type approval requirements*" and a vehicle part to which any such requirement is so applicable is referred to in these Regulations as "*a vehicle part subject to type approval requirements*".

(8) Where a requirement is prescribed by these Regulations as a requirement applicable to a vehicle, or to a vehicle part, to which these Regulations apply that requirement shall, for the purposes of these Regulations, be regarded as being applicable to that vehicle or vehicle part by virtue of paragraphs (1) to (6) notwithstanding that the same requirement may have been, or may hereafter be, applied to that vehicle or vehicle part by or under any provision of the European Communities Act 1972 or by or under any other statutory provision.

[(8A) Where in relation to item 2 in [Part I of] Schedule 1, a date is specified in column (6) of that Schedule (being a date of cessation of application of type approval requirements), that date shall not apply to any vehicle for which, or for a model of which, there is a type approval certificate or (as the case may be) a Minister's approval certificate in force at the time but, in relation to such a vehicle, column (6) shall be read and shall have effect as if there appeared in that column a date one year later than the date specified therein.]

[(9) Where, in relation to item 4B(1), 4B(2), 4B(3), 4D(1), 4D(2) or 4D(3) in [Part I of] Schedule 1, a date is specified in column (6) of that Schedule (being a date of cessation of application of type approval requirements), that date shall not apply to any vehicle of a description set out in paragraph (10) but, in relation to any such vehicle, column (6) shall be read and shall have effect as if there was substituted in that column for the date specified therein the date mentioned in paragraph (10) in connection with a particular description of vehicle.]

[(10) The following descriptions of vehicles apply for the purposes of paragraph (9)—

   (a) vehicles having a maximum gross weight not exceeding 3.5 tonnes and propelled otherwise than by compression ignition engines and for which, or for a model of which, there is a type approval certificate or (as the case may be) a Minister's approval certificate in force on 1st October 1988 and, in relation to any such vehicle, the date substituted for the date specified in column (6) of [Part I of] Schedule 1 shall be 30th September 1989;

   (b) vehicles propelled by compression ignition engines, or propelled otherwise than by such engines if having a maximum gross weight exceeding 3.5 tonnes, and for which, or for a model of which, there is no type approval certificate or (as the case may be) Minister's approval certificate in force on 1st October 1989 and, in relation to any such vehicle, the date substituted for the date specified in column (6) of [Part I of] Schedule 1 shall be 30th September 1989; and

(c) vehicles propelled by compression ignition engines, or propelled otherwise than by such engines if having a maximum gross weight exceeding 3.5 tonnes, and for which, or for a model of which, there is a type approval certificate in force on 1st October 1989 and, in relation to any such vehicle, the date substituted for the date specified in column (6) of [Part I of] Schedule I shall be 30th September 1990.]

[(11) Where, in relation to item 4C(1), 4C(2) or 4C(3) in [Part I of] Schedule 1, a date is specified in column (6) of that Schedule, that date shall not apply to any vehicle for which, or for a model of which, there is a type approval certificate in force on 1st October 1989 but, in relation to any such vehicle, column (6) shall be read and shall have effect as if 30th September 1990 was substituted for the date specified therein.]

[(12) Where, in relation to item 6, 6A, 6B, 6C or 6D in [Part I of] Schedule 1, a date is specified in column (b) of that Schedule, that date shall not apply to any vehicle in categories M1, M2 or N1 but, in relation to any such vehicle, column (6) shall be read and shall have effect as if 30th September 1989 was substituted for the date specified therein.]

[(12A) In this regulation *"prescribed"* means prescribed under section 63(1) of the Road Traffic 1988.]

[(13) Schedule 1A shall have effect for the purpose of specifying, in relation to certain vehicles, dates which are to be read as if they appeared in column (5) of items 7 and 8 in [Part I of] Schedule 1.]

[(14) Schedules 1B and 1C (which treat certain emissions or noise items as if in certain circumstances specified dates were substituted for the entries in columns (5) and (6)) shall have effect.]

B20.11   *[Regulation 4 is printed as amended by S.I. 1984 No. 697; S.I. 1987 No. 1508; S.I. 1988 No. 1523; S.I. 1989 No. 1579; S.I. 1992 Nos 1342 and 3084; S.I. 1993 No. 2200; S.I. 1995 No. 1323; S.I. 1996 Nos 2331 and 3014.*

Paragraph (12A) of regulation 4 was inserted by S.I. 1996 No. 3014 as paragraph (13); but as a paragraph designated as paragraph (13) had been inserted at an earlier date by S.I. 1988 No. 1523, the paragraph inserted by S.I. 1996 No. 3014 has been designated paragraph (12A) by editorial emendation.]

*   *   *

The Driving Licences (Community Driving Licence) Regulations 1982

(S.I. 1982 No. 1555)

*   *   *

4. Temporary validity for Community licences

(1) In relation to a person who becomes normally resident in the United Kingdom and who holds a Community licence—

B21.01

- (a) [section 88(5) of the 1988 Act] (regulations may provide that holders of foreign permits who become resident in Great Britain may be treated temporarily as holding Part III licences); and
- (b) [regulation 80(1)–(3) of the Motor Vehicles (Driving Licences) Regulations 1999] [*S.I. 1999 No. 2864, q.v.*] (which makes such provision);

shall have effect as if the references to Great Britain were references to Great Britain, Northern Ireland or Gibraltar.

(2) In this Regulation "*Community licence*" has the same meaning as in [Part III of the Road Traffic Act 1988].

[Regulation 4 is printed as amended by the Interpretation Act 1978, ss.17(2)(a) and 23(1).]

B21.02

*   *   *

The Road Transport (International Passenger Services) Regulations 1984

(S.I. 1984 No. 748)

B22.01 *[The text of these regulations is printed as amended by:*

the Road Transport (International Passenger Services) (Amendment) Regulations 1987 (S.I. 1987 No. 1755) (November 1, 1987); and

the Road Transport (International Passenger Services) (Amendment) Regulations 1988 (S.I. 1988 No. 1809) (November 18, 1988).

The amending regulations are referred to in the notes to the principal regulations by their years and numbers. The dates referred to above are the dates on which the amending regulations came into force.

The principal regulations have been further amended by the Road Transport (International Passenger Services) (Amendment) Regulations 1990 (S.I. 1990 No. 1103); but the amending regulations do not affect the text of any provision which is printed in this work.]

ARRANGEMENT OF REGULATIONS

PART I

B22.02 GENERAL

Regulation

PART II

MODIFICATION OF THE ACT OF 1981 IN RELATION TO VEHICLES REGISTERED IN THE UNITED KINGDOM WHEN USED FOR THE INTERNATIONAL CARRIAGE OF PASSENGERS

Regulation

PART III

MODIFICATION OF THE ACT OF 1981 IN RELATION TO VEHICLES REGISTERED OUTSIDE THE UNITED KINGDOM

Regulation

PART IV

APPLICATIONS FOR ISSUE OF AUTHORISATIONS AND OTHER DOCUMENTS AND FEES IN RESPECT THEREOF

Regulation

PART V

PENALTIES, ENFORCEMENT, SUPPLEMENTARY AND CONSEQUENTIAL

Regulation

SCHEDULES

PART I

GENERAL

1. Citation, commencement and revocation   *[Omitted.]*   **B22.03**

2. Interpretation

(1) In these Regulations—   **B22.04**

(a) the references to the following provisions, that is to say—

      Council Regulation No. 117/66
      Council Regulation No. 516/72
      Council Regulation No. 517/72 and
      Commission Regulation No. 1016/68

are references, respectively, to the Community provisions more particularly described in Schedule 1 and references to "*the Council Regulations*" or "*the Commission Regulation*" shall be construed accordingly;

(b) "*ASOR*" means the Agreement on the International Carriage of Passengers by Road by means of Occasional Coach and Bus Services (ASOR) [*q.v.*], approved on behalf of the Economic Community pursuant to Council Decision (EEC) of 20th July 1982 concluding the Agreement [*O.J. No. L230, August 5, 1982, p. 38*], entering into force for the Economic Community on 1st December 1983, as read with Council Regulation (EEC) No. 56/83 on measures implementing the Agreement [*O.J. No. L10, January 13, 1983, p. 1*].

(c) "*ASOR State*" means—

    (i) a state, not being a member State, which is a Contracting Party to ASOR and to which the provisions of Sections II and III of ASOR apply in accordance with Article 18 thereof; or

    (ii) the Economic Community;

(d) "*ASOR regulated*" means, in relation to the carriage of passengers, the international carriage of passengers by road to which ASOR applies, namely in the circumstances specified in Article 1 thereof, that is to say, by means of occasional services (within the meaning of that Agreement) effected—

    (i) between the territories of two ASOR States, or starting and finishing in the territory of the same ASOR State; and

    (ii) should the need arise during such services, in transit through the territory of another ASOR State or through the territory of a state which is not an ASOR State; and

    (iii) using vehicles registered in the territory of an ASOR State which by virtue of their construction and their equipment, are suitable for carrying more than nine persons, including the driver, and are intended for that purpose

and references to the carriage of passengers which is ASOR regulated include unladen journeys of the vehicles concerned with such carriage;

(e) "*Community regulated*" means, in relation to the carriage of passengers, the international carriage of passengers by road to which Council Regulation No. 117/66 applies, namely in the circumstances mentioned in Article 4(1) thereof, that is to say—

    (i) where the place of departure is in the territory of a member State and the destination is in the territory of the same or another member State; and

    (ii) the vehicle is registered in a member State and in construction and equipment is suitable for carrying more than nine persons, including the driver, and is intended for that purpose,

and references to the carriage of passengers which is Community regulated include unladen journeys of the vehicles concerned with such carriage;

(f) "*ECMT State*" means a State which is a member of the European Conference of Ministers of Transport of the 17th November 1953 but not a member State or an ASOR State;

(g) "*the Secretary of State*" means [the Secretary of State for the Environment, Transport and the Regions];

(h) "*examiner*" has the same meaning as in section 7(1) of the Road Traffic (Foreign Vehicles) Act 1972 [*q.v.*];

(i) *"public service vehicle"* shall be construed in accordance with section 1 of the Act of 1981 [*q.v.*];

(j) *"the Act of 1981"* means the Public Passenger Vehicles Act 1981.

(2) Any reference in these Regulations to a numbered Regulation or Schedule is a reference to the Regulations or Schedule bearing that number in these Regulations.

[Regulation 2 is printed as amended by the Secretary of State for the Environment, Transport and the Regions Order 1997 (S.I. 1997 No. 2971).   **B22.05**

Council Regulations (EEC) 117/66, 516/72 and 517/72 (to which references are made in regulation 2(1)) have been repealed by Regulation (EEC) 684/92, art.21(1) (q.v.). References to the repealed Regulations should now be construed as references to Regulation (EEC) 684/92; see ibid., art.21(2). Commission Regulation (EEC) 1016/68 (to which reference is made in regulation 2(1)) has been repealed (subject to transitional provisions) by Regulation (EEC) 1839/92, arts 10, 11 (q.v.).]

3. Extent

These Regulations do not extend to Northern Ireland.   **B22.06**

PART II

MODIFICATIONS OF THE ACT OF 1981 IN RELATION TO VEHICLES REGISTERED IN THE UNITED KINGDOM WHEN USED FOR THE INTERNATIONAL CARRIAGE OF PASSENGERS

4. Community regulated regular, shuttle and works services by vehicles registered in the United Kingdom

(1) This Regulation applies to a vehicle registered in the United Kingdom which is being used for Community regulated carriage of passengers in so far as the vehicle—   **B22.07**

(a) is used to provide any service for the carriage of passengers such as is mentioned in Article 1, 2 or 6 of Council Regulation No. 117/66; and

(b) is so used in accordance with such of the requirements of the Council Regulations as apply in relation to the service in question.

(2) The provisions of the Act of 1981 shall have effect as if—

(a) *[lapsed.]*

(b) in relation to a vehicle to which this Regulation applies registered in Northern Ireland, sections 6, 12, 18, 22 . . . of the Act of 1981 were omitted.

[Regulation 4 is printed as it has effect after the repeal of section 30 of the Public Passenger Vehicles Act 1981.]   **B22.08**

5. Non-Community regulated regular and shuttle services by public service vehicles registered in the United Kingdom

(1) This Regulation applies to a public service vehicle registered in the United Kingdom which is being used for the international carriage of passengers by road which is not Community regulated but where the vehicle is being used to provide a service for the carriage of passengers of a description such as is mentioned in Article 1 or 2 of Council Regulation 117/66 (that is to say, a regular service, a special regular service or a shuttle service as defined in those Articles).   **B22.09**

(2) The provisions of the Act of 1981 [and Parts I and II of the Transport Act 1985] shall have effect as if—

(a) in relation to a vehicle to which this Regulation applies registered in Northern Ireland, sections 6, 12, 18 and 22 of the Act of 1981 were omitted; and

(b) in relation to a vehicle to which this Regulation applies registered in Great Britain or in Northern Ireland, for [section 6 of the Transport Act 1985 there shall be substituted the following section and section 35 of that Act shall be omitted]:—

"**[6.]**—(1) No person shall cause or permit a public service vehicle to be used on a road for the international carriage of passengers unless there is in force in relation to the use of the vehicle, and is carried on the vehicle, an international passenger transport authorisation.

(2) A certifying officer or a public service vehicle examiner may at any time, on production if so required of his authority, require the operator or the driver of any such vehicle as is referred to in subsection (1) above, to produce and to permit him to inspect and copy an international passenger transport authorisation relating to the use of the vehicle, and for that purpose may require the vehicle to be stopped and may detain the vehicle for such time as is requisite for the purpose of inspecting and copying the authorisation.

(3) A person who—

(a) without reasonable excuse contravenes subsection (1) of this section, or

(b) without reasonable excuse fails to comply with a requirement of a certifying officer or public service vehicle examiner, or wilfully obstructs such officer or examiner, in the exercise of his powers under subsection (2) of this section,

shall be guilty of an offence and shall be liable on summary conviction to a fine not exceeding level 3 on the standard scale (within the meaning of section 75 of the Criminal Justice Act 1982).

(4) In this section '*international passenger transport authorisation*' means a licence, permit, authorisation or other document issued by the Secretary of State in pursuance of an international agreement or arrangement to which the United Kingdom is for the time being a party."

B22.10   *[Regulation 5 is printed as amended by S.I. 1987 No. 1755.]*

6. Occasional services by vehicles registered in the United Kingdom (whether ASOR or Community regulated or not)

B22.11   (1) This Regulation applies to a vehicle registered in the United Kingdom which is being used for the international carriage of passengers by road—

(a) in so far as the vehicle is used to provide a service for the carriage of passengers which is Community regulated and is such as is mentioned—

(i) in paragraph 1(a) of Article 3 of Council Regulation No. 117/66 (that is to say, an occasional service described in that paragraph as a closed-door tour), or

(ii) in paragraph 1(b) of the said Article 3 (that is to say, an occasional service described in that paragraph where the passengers are carried on the outward journey and the return journey is made unladen), or

(iii) in paragraph 1(c) of the said Article 3 (that is to say, an occasional service, as mentioned in that paragraph, of any other description); or

(b) in so far as the vehicle is used to provide a service for the carriage of passengers which is ASOR regulated; or

(c) in so far as the vehicle is used as a public service vehicle for the carriage of passengers which is not ASOR regulated or Community regulated but is a service of a description such as is mentioned in any of the paragraphs of Article 3 of Council Regulation No. 117/66.

(2) The provisions of the Act of 1981 [and Parts I and II of the Transport Act 1985] shall have effect as if—

(a) in relation to a vehicle to which this Regulation applies registered in Northern Ireland, sections 6, 12, 18 and 22 of the Act of 1981 were omitted; and

(b) in relation to a vehicle to which this Regulation applies registered in Great Britain or in Northern Ireland, for [section 6 of the Transport Act 1985 there shall be substituted the following section and section 35 of that Act shall be omitted]:—

"[**6.**]—(1) No person shall cause or permit a vehicle to be used on a road for the international carriage of passengers unless—

(a) in relation to the use of the vehicle, in the case of such carriage which is ASOR regulated, the requirements of Articles 7, 8 and 9 of, and the Annex to, ASOR (which provide for the completion by the person by whom, or on whose behalf, a vehicle is used to provide an occasional service of a passenger waybill in respect of the service in question and for the carrying of the top copy of such waybill on the vehicle at all times while it is used on that service) are complied with and, in the case of any other such carriage, the requirements of Articles 2, 3 and 4 of, and of Annex 2 to, Commission Regulation No. 1016/68 (which provide as aforesaid) are complied with, or would be complied with if those provisions applied to the service; and

(b) the vehicle is used on the service in question in circumstances which accord in all respects with the particulars which have been specified in the said passenger waybill as applicable to that service.

(2) A certifying officer or a public service vehicle examiner may, at any time which is reasonable having regard to the circumstances of the case, enter any premises from which he has reason to believe that a vehicle is or is to be operated on a service for the international carriage of passengers and may, on production if so required of his authority, require the operator of the vehicle to produce and to permit him to inspect and copy a control document duly completed for the service, in the case of ASOR regulated carriage, in accordance with Articles 7, 8 and 9 of, and the Annex to, ASOR and, in the case of any other such carriage, in accordance with Articles 2, 3, and 4 of, and Annex 2 to, Commission Regulation No. 1016/68.

(3) A certifying officer or a public service vehicle examiner may, on production if so required of his authority—

(a) require the driver of a vehicle used for the international carriage of passengers to produce and to permit him to inspect and copy and to mark with an official stamp, in the case of a vehicle used for ASOR regulated carriage, the document required by Article 8(2) of ASOR and, in the case of any other such carriage, the document required by Article 3(2) of Commission Regulation No. 1016/68, to be kept on a vehicle to which that Article applies; and

(b) detain the vehicle for such time as is required for the purpose of inspecting, copying and marking the document.

(4) A person who—

(a) without reasonable excuse contravenes subsection (1) above, or

(b) without reasonable excuse fails to comply with a requirement of an officer or examiner, under subsection (2) or (3) above, or

(c) wilfully obstructs an officer or examiner in the exercise of his powers under either of those subsections,

shall be guilty of an offence and shall be liable on summary conviction to a fine not exceeding level 3 on the standard scale (within the meaning of section 75 of the Criminal Justice Act 1982).

(5) In this section—

'*ASOR*' means the Agreement on the International Carriage of Passengers by Road by means of Occasional Coach and Bus Services (ASOR) approved on behalf of the Economic Community pursuant to Council Decision (EEC) of 20th July 1982 concluding the Agreement entering into force for the Economic Community on 1st December 1983 [*q.v.*], as read with Council Regulation (EEC) No. 56/83 on measures implementing the Agreement;

'*ASOR State*' means—

    (a) a state, not being a member State, which is a Contracting Party to ASOR and to which the provisions of Section II and III of ASOR apply in accordance with Article 18 thereof; or

    (b) the Economic Community;

'*ASOR regulated*' means, in relation to the carriage of passengers, the international carriage of passengers by road to which ASOR applies namely in the circumstances specified in Article 1 thereof, that is to say, by means of occasional services (within the meaning of that Agreement) effected—

    (a) between the territories of two ASOR States, or starting and finishing in the territory of the same ASOR State; and

    (b) should the need arise during such services, in transit through the territory of another ASOR State or through the territory of a state which is not an ASOR State; and

    (c) using vehicles registered in the territory of an ASOR State which, by virtue of their construction and their equipment, are suitable for carrying more than nine persons, including the driver, and are intended for that purpose,

and references to the carriage of passengers which is ASOR regulated include unladen journeys of the vehicles concerned with such carriage;

'*Commission Regulation No. 1016/68*' means Regulation (EEC) No. 1016/68 of the Commission of 9th July 1968 prescribing the model control documents referred to in Articles 6 and 9 of Council Regulation No. 117/66/EEC as amended by and as read with Regulation (EEC) No. 2485/82 of the Commission of 13th September 1982; and

'*Council Regulation No. 117/66*' means Regulation No. 117/66/EEC of the Council of 28th July 1966 on the introduction of common rules for the international carriage of passengers by coach and bus [*q.v.*]."

B22.12   *[Regulation 6 is printed as amended by S.I. 1987 No. 1755.]*

PART III

MODIFICATIONS OF THE ACT OF 1981 IN RELATION TO VEHICLES REGISTERED OUTSIDE THE UNITED KINGDOM

7. Small vehicles registered outside the United Kingdom visiting Great Britain temporarily

B22.13   (1) This Regulation applies to a public service vehicle registered outside the United Kingdom which—

    (a) in construction and equipment is suitable for carrying not more than nine persons, including the driver, and is intended for that purpose;

    (b) is brought into Great Britain for the purpose of carrying passengers who are travelling to Great Britain from a place outside the United Kingdom, or who are travelling from the United Kingdom to any such place; and

(c) remains in Great Britain for a period not exceeding three months from the date of its entry therein.

(2) The provisions of the Act of 1981 shall, in relation to a vehicle to which this Regulation applies, have effect as if sections 6, 12, 18, 22 . . . of the Act of 1981 were omitted.

[Regulation 7 is printed as it has effect after the repeal of section 30 of the Public Passenger Vehicles Act 1981.]   **B22.14**

8. Community regulated regular, shuttle and works services by vehicles registered outside the United Kingdom

(1) This Regulation applies to a vehicle registered outside the United Kingdom which is being used for Community regulated carriage of passengers in so far as the vehicle—   **B22.15**

(a) is being used to provide any service for the carriage of passengers such as is mentioned in Article 1, 2 or 6 of Council Regulation 117/66; and

(b) is being so used in accordance with such of the requirements of the Council Regulations or, as the case may be, the Commission Regulation as apply to the service in question.

(2) The provisions of the Act of 1981 shall, in relation to a vehicle to which this Regulation applies, have effect as if sections 6, 12, 18, 22 . . . of the Act of 1981 were omitted.

[Regulation 8 is printed as it has effect after the repeal of section 30 of the Public Passenger Vehicles Act 1981.]   **B22.16**

9. Non-Community regulated regular and shuttle services by vehicles registered outside the United Kingdom

(1) This Regulation applies to a public service vehicle registered outside the United Kingdom which is being used for the international carriage of passengers which is not Community regulated in so far as the vehicle—   **B22.17**

(a) is being used to provide a service for the carriage of passengers of a description such as is mentioned in Article 1 or 2 of Council Regulation 117/66 (that is to say, a regular service, a special regular service or a shuttle service as defined in those Articles), and

(b) is so used by or on behalf of a person who is authorised, under the law of the country in which the vehicle is registered, to use the vehicle for the carriage of passengers on the journey in question or such parts thereof as are situated within that country.

(2) The provisions of the Act of 1981 shall in relation to a vehicle to which this Regulation applies, have effect as if sections 6, 18, 22 . . . of the Act of 1981 were omitted, and as if for section 12 of the Act of 1981 there were substituted the section set out in Schedule 2.

[Regulation 9 is printed as it has effect after the repeal of section 30 of the Public Passenger Vehicles Act 1981.]   **B22.18**

10. ASOR or Community regulated occasional services by vehicles registered outside the United Kingdom

(1) This Regulation applies to a vehicle registered outside the United Kingdom which is being used for ASOR or Community regulated carriage of passengers—   **B22.19**

(a) in so far as the vehicle is used to provide a service for the carriage of passengers such as is mentioned—

    (i) in paragraph 1(a) of Article 2 of ASOR or paragraph 1(a) of Article 3 of Council Regulation No. 117/66 (that is to say, an occasional service described in that paragraph as a closed-door tour), or

    (ii) in paragraph 1(b) of each of those Articles (that is to say an occasional service as described in that paragraph where passengers are carried on the outward journey and the return journey is made unladen), or

    (iii) in paragraph 1(c) of each of those Articles (that is to say, an occasional service as mentioned in that paragraph of any other description); and

(b) in so far as, in relation to the use of the vehicle—

    (i) in the case of a vehicle being used for ASOR regulated carriage, the requirements of Articles 7, 8 and 9 of, and Annex to, ASOR (which provides for the completion, by the person by whom or on whose behalf a vehicle is used to provide such an occasional service as aforesaid, of a passenger waybill in respect of the service in question and for the carrying of the top copy of such waybill on the vehicle at all times while it is used on that service) and in the case of a vehicle being used for Community regulated carriage, the requirements of Articles 2, 3 and 4 of, and Annex 2 to, Commission Regulation No. 1016/68 (which provides as aforesaid), have been complied with, and

    (ii) the vehicle is used on the service in question in circumstances which accord in all respects with particulars which, in pursuance of the said requirements, have been specified in the said passenger waybill as applicable to that service.

(2) In relation to a vehicle to which this Regulation applies, the provisions of the Act of 1981 shall have effect as if sections 6, 18, 22 . . . of the Act of 1981 were omitted and—

(a) in so far as the vehicle is used to provide a service for the carriage of passengers such as is mentioned—

    (i) in Article 2(1)(a) or (b) of ASOR or Article 3(1)(a) or (b) of Council Regulation No. 117/66, or

    (ii) in a case where the service is ASOR regulated and all the conditions mentioned in Article 5(2) of ASOR are fulfilled, in Article 2(1)(c) of ASOR, or

    (iii) in a case where the service is Community regulated and all the conditions mentioned in Article 5(2) of the said Council Regulation are fulfilled, in Article 2(1)(c) of that Regulation,

as if section 12 of the Act of 1981 were omitted; and

(b) in so far as the vehicle is used as a public service vehicle to provide a service for the carriage of passengers such as is mentioned in Article 2(1)(c) of ASOR or Article 2(1)(c) of the said Council Regulation and—

    (i) in a case where the service is ASOR regulated any of the conditions mentioned in Article 5(2) of ASOR are not fulfilled, or

    (ii) in a case where the service is Community regulated, any of the conditions mentioned in Article 5(2) of the said Council Regulation are not fulfilled,

as if for the said section 12 there were substituted the section set out in Schedule 2.

B22.20   *[Regulation 10 is printed as it has effect after the repeal of section 30 of the Public Passenger Vehicles Act 1981.]*

11. Certain occasional services by vehicles registered in ECMT States

B22.21   (1) This Regulation applies to a public service vehicle—

(a) which is registered in the territory of a State which is an ECMT State;

(b) which is brought into Great Britain for the purpose of carrying passengers who are making only a temporary stay therein or are in transit; and

(c) which remains in Great Britain for a period not exceeding three months from the date of its entry therein,

in so far as the vehicle—

(i) is used to provide a service for the carriage of passengers which is not ASOR or Community regulated but which is of a description such as is mentioned in Article 3(1)(a), (b) or (c) of Council Regulation No. 117/66, where the journey made by the vehicle in providing that service starts from a place situated in the territory of an ECMT State and ends at a place situated in the territory of such a State or in Great Britain, and

(ii) is so used by or on behalf of a person who is authorised, under the law in force in the State, in the territory of which it is registered to use the vehicle for the carriage of passengers on the journey in question or such part thereof as lies within the territory of that State.

(2) In relation to a vehicle to which this Regulation applies, the provisions of the Act of 1981 shall have effect as if sections 6, 18, 22 . . . of the Act of 1981 were omitted and as if—

(a) in so far as the vehicle is used to provide a service for the carriage of passengers such as is mentioned in paragraph 1(a) and 1(b) of Article 3 of Council Regulation No. 117/66, for section 12 of the Act of 1981 there were substituted the following sections [*sic*]:—

"**12.** No person shall cause or permit a public service vehicle to be used on a road for the international carriage of passengers unless there is in force in relation to the use of the vehicle, and is carried on the vehicle, a document which is issued by the competent authority of the country in which the vehicle is registered in the form set out in Schedule 3 to the Road Transport (International Passenger Service) Regulations 1984 and which is duly completed.";

and

(b) in so far as the vehicle is used for the carriage of passengers such as is mentioned in paragraph 1(c) of the said Article 3, for section 12 of the Act of 1981 there were substituted the section set out in Schedule 2.

[Regulation 11 is printed as it has effect after the repeal of section 30 of the Public Passenger Vehicles Act 1981.]   **B22.22**

12. Certain occasional services by vehicles not registered in a member State, an ASOR State or an ECMT State

(1) This Regulation applies to a public service vehicle—   **B22.23**

(a) which is registered in the territory of a State which is not a member State, an ASOR State or an ECMT State;

(b) which is brought into Great Britain for the purpose of carrying passengers who are making only a temporary stay therein or are in transit, being passengers who commenced their journey from the state in the territory of which the vehicle is registered or, as the case may be, from Northern Ireland; and

(c) which remains in Great Britain for a period not exceeding three months from the date of its entry therein,

in so far as the vehicle—

(i) is used to provide a service for the carriage of passengers which is not Community regulated but which is of a description such as is mentioned in Article 3(1)(a), (b) or (c) of Regulation No. 117/66, and

(iii) is so used by or on behalf of a person who is authorised, under the law in force in the state in the territory of which it is registered to use the vehicle for the carriage of passengers on the journey in question or such part thereof as lies within the territory of that state.

(2) The provisions of the Act of 1981 shall, in relation to a vehicle to which this Regulation applies, have effect as if sections 6, 18, 22 . . . of the Act of 1981 were omitted and as if for section 12 of the Act of 1981 there were substituted

[(a) in the case of a public service vehicle registered in the Union of Soviet Socialist Republics used to provide a service of a description such as is mentioned in Article 3(1)(a) or (b) of Regulation No. 117/66, the following section:—

"**12.** No person shall cause or permit a public service vehicle to be used on a road for the international carriage of passengers unless there is carried on the vehicle a list of the passengers carried by the vehicle;" and

(b) in any other case, the section set out in Schedule 2.]

B22.24   *[Regulation 12 is printed as it has effect after the repeal of section 30 of the Public Passenger Vehicles Act 1981; and as subsequently amended by S.I. 1988 No. 1809.]*

PART IV

Applications for Issue of Authorisations and other Documents and Fees in respect thereof

*   *   *

15. Applications for, and issue of, certificates and control documents for works and occasional services

B22.25   (1)–(3) *[Omitted.]*

(4) The top copy of every passenger waybill (being the document which, as mentioned in Article 7 of ASOR or Article 2 of the Commission Regulation is the document applicable in respect of the provision of a service for the carriage of passengers such as is mentioned in Article 2 of ASOR or Article 3 of Council Regulation No. 117/66), shall be retained, after the service in question has been provided, by the person by whom or on whose behalf it was provided and shall be sent to the Secretary of State so as to reach him not later than 31st March next following the end of the calendar year in which the service to which the waybill relates was provided.

(5) The duplicate of every such passenger waybill (being the duplicate which, by virtue of Article 7(1) of ASOR or Article 2(1) of Commission Regulation No. 1016/68 is required to be contained in a control document such as is mentioned in those Articles) shall not be detached from that document at any time during its period of validity.

PART V

Penalties, Enforcement, Supplementary and Consequential

16. Production, inspection and copying of documents in relation to ASOR or Community regulated services

B22.26   (1) Paragraph (2) below shall have effect in relation to a vehicle where it appears to an examiner that the vehicle—

(a) is being used for the provision of an ASOR regulated or Community regulated service; and

(b) is being used, or has been brought into Great Britain for the purpose of being used, in such circumstances as, by virtue of any of the provisions specified in paragraph (3) below, to require a document of a description referred to in that provision to be kept or carried on the vehicle.

(2) An examiner may, on production if so required of his authority—

(a) require the driver of a vehicle referred to in paragraph (1) above to produce the document and to permit him to inspect and copy it and (in the case of a document of a description referred to in any of the provisions specified in paragraph (3)(c) or (e) below) to mark it with an official stamp; and

(b) may detain the vehicle for such time as is required for the purpose of inspecting, copying and marking the document.

(3) The provisions referred to in paragraph (1) above as being specified in this paragraph are—

(a) Article 17 of Council Regulation No. 517/72 (which provides, inter alia, that the authorisation required by that Regulation for the use of a vehicle to provide a service for the carriage of passengers such as is mentioned in Article 1 thereof shall be carried on the vehicle);

(b) Articles 17 and 18 of Council Regulation No. 516/72 (which respectively provide, inter alia, that the authorisation required by that Regulation for the use of a vehicle to provide a service for the carriage of passengers such as is mentioned in Article 1 thereof shall be carried on the vehicle and that passengers using that service shall be provided with a ticket throughout the journey in question);

(c) Article 8(2) of ASOR and Article 3(2) of Commission Regulation No. 1016/68 (which provide that the top copy of the passenger waybill being the document which, by virtue of Article 7 of ASOR or Article 2 of Commission Regulation No. 1016/68, has been detached from the control document such as is mentioned in those Articles, and is the document applicable in respect of the provision of a service for the carriage of passengers such as is mentioned in Article 2 of ASOR or Article 3 of Council Regulation No. 117/66, shall be kept on the vehicle);

(d) Article 11(3) of ASOR and Article 5a(3) of Commission Regulation No. 1016/68 (which provide that the model document with stiff green covers referred to in Article 11 of ASOR must be carried on the vehicle); and

(e) Regulation 17.

[The text of regulation 16(3)(d) has been printed as it is believed that it was intended to read: the word **B22.27** *"of" has been substituted editorially for the word "or" immediately before the first reference to "ASOR", and the reference to "Commission Regulation No. 1016/68" has similarly been substituted for a reference to "Commission Regulation No. 1018/68" in the original text.]*

17. Carriage on the vehicle of certificate issued under Article 6 of Council Regulation No. 117/66

(1) In relation to a vehicle being used to provide a Community regulated service for the **B22.28** carriage of passengers such as is mentioned in Article 6 of Council Regulation No. 117/66 there shall be carried on the vehicle, at all times while it is being used, the certificate specified in Article 1 of Commission Regulation No. 1016/68, being the certificate which, by virtue of the said Article 6, is required to be in force in respect of the provision of that service.

(2) An examiner may, on production if so required of his authority—

(a) require the driver of a vehicle referred to in paragraph (1) above to produce the document and to permit him to inspect and copy it and to mark it with an official stamp; and

(b) may detain the vehicle for such time as is required for the purpose of inspecting, copying and marking the document.

18. Withdrawal of regular, special regular and shuttle service authorisations

B22.29

(1) If the Secretary of State is at any time satisfied that a holder of a regular, special regular or shuttle service authorisation issued by him—

(a) has failed to comply with the relevant Council Regulation, with the authorisation or any conditions specified therein; or

(b) has failed to operate, or is no longer operating, a service under the authorisation,

he may, by notice in writing to the holder, withdraw the authorisation.

(2) Where the Secretary of State decides to withdraw an authorisation in exercise of his powers under Council Regulation No. 516/72 or Council Regulation No. 517/72 he may do so by notice in writing to the holder of the authorisation.

(3) The withdrawal of an authorisation in accordance with this Regulation shall take effect on the date specified in the notice which shall be not earlier than 28 days after the date of the notice.

(4) Where an authorisation is withdrawn in accordance with this Regulation it shall be of no effect and the holder shall forthwith surrender the authorisation to the Secretary of State.

(5) At any time that is reasonable having regard to the circumstances of the case, an examiner may, on production if so required of his authority, enter any premises of the holder of an authorisation which has been withdrawn in accordance with this Regulation and may require the holder to produce the authorisation and, on its being produced, may seize it and deliver it to the Secretary of State.

(6) Where it appears to an examiner that a document produced to him in pursuance of Regulation 16 is an authorisation which has been withdrawn in accordance with this Regulation he may seize it and deliver it to the Secretary of State.

(7) In paragraph 1 of this Regulation "*relevant Council Regulation*" means in the case of a regular or special regular service authorisation Council Regulation No. 517/72 and in the case of a shuttle service authorisation Council Regulation No. 516/72.

19. Penalty for contravention of ASOR, the Council Regulations or the Commission Regulation

B22.30

(1) A person is guilty of an offence under this Regulation if without reasonable excuse, he uses a vehicle for Community regulated carriage of passengers by road or causes or permits such a vehicle to be used—

(a) to provide a service for the carriage of passengers such as is mentioned in Article 1 of Council Regulation No. 117/66 (that is to say, a regular service or a special regular service as defined in that Article), not being, in either such case, a service such as is mentioned in Article 6 of that Regulation, otherwise than under and in accordance with the terms of an authorisation issued under Article 2 of Council Regulation No. 517/72; or

(b) to provide a service for the carriage of passengers such as is mentioned in Article 2 of Council Regulation No. 117/66 (that is to say, a shuttle service as defined in that

Article), not being a service such as is mentioned in Article 6 of that Regulation, otherwise than under and in accordance with the terms of an authorisation issued under Article 2 of Council Regulation No. 516/72; or

(c) to provide a service for the carriage of passengers such as is mentioned in Article 6 of Council Regulation No. 117/66 (that is to say, a service provided by an undertaking for its own workers in relation to which the conditions mentioned in paragraph 1(a) and (b) of that Article are fulfilled) without there being in force in relation to the service a certificate issued under Article 1 of Commission Regulation No. 1016/68.

(2) A person shall be guilty of an offence under this Regulation if, without reasonable excuse, he uses a vehicle for ASOR regulated or Community regulated carriage by road, or causes or permits a vehicle to be so used, to provide a service for the carriage of passengers such as is mentioned in paragraph 1 of Article 2 of ASOR or Article 3 of Council Regulation No. 117/66 when there is not duly and correctly completed for the vehicle a passenger waybill, or when the top copy of the passenger waybill is not kept on the vehicle throughout the journey to which it refers, as required, in the case of a vehicle being used for ASOR regulated carriage, by Articles 7 and 8 of ASOR and, in the case of a vehicle being used for Community regulated carriage, by Articles 2 and 3 of Council Regulation No. 1016/68.

(3) A person guilty of an offence under this Regulation shall be liable on summary conviction to a fine not exceeding [level 3 on the standard scale].

[Regulation 19 is printed as amended by the Criminal Justice Act 1988, s.52.]   **B22.31**

20. Penalty relating to documents required in respect of ASOR and Community regulated services

A person who—   **B22.32**

(a) without reasonable excuse contravenes, or fails to comply with a requirement imposed by or under Regulation 15(4) or (5), 16(2)(a), 17(1) or (2), or 18(4) or (5), or by or under any provision of ASOR, the Council Regulations or the Commission Regulation referred to in any of those provisions; or

(b) wilfully obstructs an examiner in the exercise of his powers under Regulation 16(2), 17(1) or (2), or 18(5) or (6), or under any provision of ASOR, the Council Regulations or Commission Regulation referred to in any of those provisions

shall be liable on summary conviction to a fine not exceeding [level 3 on the standard scale].

[Regulation 20 is printed as amended by the Criminal Justice Act 1988, s.52.]   .   **B22.33**

21. Forgery and false statements, etc.

In sections 65(1)(a) (forgery) and 66(a) (false statements) of the Act of 1981 the references   **B22.34** to a licence under any Part of that Act shall include references to an authorisation, certificate or other document required by ASOR, any of the Council Regulations or the Commission Regulation, or by these Regulations, or by the Act of 1981 as modified by these Regulations, to be in force in relation to a vehicle, or to be kept or carried on a vehicle, used for the international carriage of passengers.

22. *[Amended the Road Traffic (Foreign Vehicles) Act 1972.]*   **B22.35**

23. Disapplication of requirements as to fitness, equipment type approval and certification of public service vehicles

None of the provisions of Parts II, III, IV and V of the Public Service Vehicles   **B22.36** (Conditions of Fitness, Equipment, Use and Certification) Regulations 1981 [*S.I. 1981 No.*

257, as amended (q.v.)] shall have effect in relation to a vehicle to which any provision of Part III of these Regulations applies or to a vehicle registered in Northern Ireland to which any provision of Part II of these Regulations applies.

SCHEDULE 1 (see regulation 2)

THE COUNCIL REGULATIONS AND THE COMMISSION REGULATION

B22.37   "*Council Regulation No. 117/66*" means Regulation No. 117/66/EEC of the Council of 28th July 1966 on the introduction of common rules for the international carriage of passengers by coach and bus [*O.J. No. L147, August 9, 1966, p. 2688*];

"*Council Regulation No. 516/72*" means Regulations (EEC) No. 516/72 of the Council of 28th February 1972 on the introduction of common rules for shuttle services by coach and bus between Member States [*O.J. No. L67, March 20, 1972, p. 13*];

"*Council Regulation No. 517/72*" means Regulation (EEC) No. 517/72 of the Council of 28th February 1972 on the introduction of common rules for regular and special regular services by coach and bus between Member States [*O.J. No. L67, March 20, 1972, p. 19*] as amended by Regulation (EEC) No. 1301/78 of the Council of 12th June 1978 [*O.J. No. L158, June 16, 1978, p. 1*];

"*Commission Regulation No. 1016/68*" means Regulation (EEC) No. 1016/68 of the Commission of 9th July 1968 prescribing the model control documents referred to in Articles 6 and 9 of Council Regulation No. 117/66 EEC [*O.J. No. L173, July 22, 1968, p. 8*] as amended by and as read with Regulation (EEC) No. 2485/82 of the Commission of 13th September 1982 [*O.J. No. L265, September 15, 1982, p. 5*].

B22.38   *[Council Regulations (EEC) 117/66, 516/72 and 517/72 (to which references are made in Schedule 1) have been repealed by Regulation (EEC) 684/92, art.21(1)(q.v.). References to the repealed Regulations should now be construed as references to Regulation (EEC) 684/92; see ibid., art.21(2). Commission Regulation (EEC) 1016/68 (to which reference is made in Schedule 1) has been repealed (subject to transitional provisions) by Regulation (EEC) 1839/92, arts 10, 11 (q.v.).]*

SCHEDULE 2 (see regulations 9, 10 and 11)

B22.39   "**12.**—(1) No person shall cause or permit a public service vehicle to be used on a road for the international carriage of passengers unless there is in force and is carried on the vehicle, an international passenger transport authorisation.

(2) An authorisation under this section may authorise the use of the vehicle or vehicles to which it relates on a specified occasion or during a specified period.

(3) In this section—

'*specified*' means specified in the authorisation; and

'*international passenger transport authorisation*' means a licence, permit, authorisation or other document issued by the Secretary of State in pursuance of an international agreement or arrangement to which the United Kingdom is for the time being a party."

B22.40   SCHEDULE 3 (see regulation 11(2))
                                     WAYBILL

[Omitted.]

The Motor Vehicles (Type Approval) (Great Britain) Regulations 1984

(S.I. 1984 No. 981)

[The text of these regulations is printed as amended by:

correction slip (August 1984);

the Motor Vehicles (Type Approval) (Great Britain) (Amendment) (No. 2) Regulations 1984 (S.I. 1984 No. 1761) (December 13, 1984);

the Motor Vehicles (Type Approval) (Great Britain) (Amendment) Regulations 1985 (S.I. 1985 No. 1651) (December 2, 1985);

the Motor Vehicles (Type Approval) (Great Britain) (Amendment) Regulations 1987 (S.I. 1987 No. 1509) (October 1, 1987);

the Motor Vehicles (Type Approval) (Great Britain) (Amendment) Regulations 1988 (S.I. 1988 No. 1522) (October 1, 1988);

the Motor Vehicles (Type Approval) (Great Britain) (Amendment) Regulations 1989 (S.I. 1989 No. 1580) (October 1, 1989);

the Motor Vehicles (Type Approval) (Great Britain) (Amendment) Regulations 1991 (S.I. 1991 No. 1022) (May 20, 1991);

the Motor Vehicles (Type Approval) (Great Britain) (Amendment) Regulations 1992 (S.I. 1992 No. 1341) (July 1, 1992);

the Motor Vehicles (Type Approval) (Great Britain) (Amendment) (No. 2) Regulations 1992 (S.I. 1992 No. 2161) (October 1, 1992);

the Motor Vehicles (Type Approval) (Great Britain) (Amendment) (No. 3) Regulations 1992 (S.I. 1992 No. 2908) (December 31, 1992);

the Motor Vehicles (Type Approval) (Great Britain) (Amendment) (No. 4) Regulations 1992 (S.I. 1992 No. 3173) (December 30, 1992);

the Motor Vehicles (Type Approval) (Great Britain) (Amendment) Regulations 1993 (S.I. 1993 No. 2201) (October 1, 1993);

the Motor Vehicles (Type Approval) (Great Britain) (Amendment) Regulations 1995 (S.I. 1995 No. 1322) (June 12, 1995);

the Motor Vehicles (Type Approval) (Great Britain) (Amendment) Regulations 1996 (S.I. 1996 No. 2330) (October 1, 1996); and

the Motor Vehicles (Type Approval) (Great Britain) (Amendment) (No. 2) Regulations 1996 (S.I. 1996 No. 3015) (July 1, 1997).

The amending regulations are referred to in the notes to the principal regulations only by their years and numbers. The dates referred to above are the dates on which the amending regulations came into force.

The principal regulations have also been amended by the Motor Vehicles (Type Approval) (Great Britain) (Amendment) Regulations 1984 (S.I. 1984 No. 1401), the Motor Vehicles (Type Approval) (Great Britain) (Amendment) Regulations 1986 (S.I. 1986 No. 739), the Motor Vehicles (Type Approval) (Great Britain) (Amendment) Regulations 1990 (S.I. 1990 No. 94), the Motor Vehicles (Type Approval) (Great Britain) (Amendment) (No. 2) Regulations 1990 (S.I. 1990 No. 1839), the Motor Vehicles (Type Approval) (Great Britain) (Amendment) (No. 2) Regulations 1991 (S.I. 1991 No. 1971), the Motor Vehicles (Type Approval) (Great Britain) (Amendment) Regulations 1994 (S.I. 1994 No. 2190), the Motor Vehicles (Type Approval) (Great Britain) (Amendment) Regulations 1997 (S.I. 1997 No. 1367), the Motor Vehicles (Type Approval) (Great Britain) (Amendment) (No. 2) Regulations 1997 (S.I. 1997 No. 1502), the Motor Vehicles (Type Approval) (Great Britain) (Amendment) (No. 3)

Regulations 1997 (S.I. 1997 No. 2933), and the Motor Vehicles (Type Approval) (Great Britain) (Amendment) Regulations 1998 (S.I. 1998 No. 1005), but these do not affect the text of any regulation printed in this work.]

B23.02   **1. Commencement and citation**   *[Omitted.]*

2. Interpretation

B23.03   (1) In these Regulations—

"*the Construction and Use Regulations*" means the [Road Vehicles (Construction and Use) Regulations 1986] [*S.I. 1986 No. 1078, q.v.*];

. . .

"*dual-purpose vehicle*" means a vehicle constructed or adapted for the carriage both of passengers and of goods or burden of any description, being a vehicle of which the unladen weight does not exceed 2040 kilograms, and which satisfies the following conditions as to construction, namely:—

(a) the vehicle must be permanently fitted with a rigid roof, with or without a sliding panel;

(b) the area of the vehicle to the rear of the driver's seat must—

(i) be permanently fitted with at least one row of transverse seats (fixed or folding) for two or more passengers and those seats must be properly sprung or cushioned and provided with upholstered back-rests, attached either to the seats or to a side or the floor of the vehicle; and

(ii) be lit on each side and at the rear by a window or windows of glass or other transparent material having an area or aggregate area of not less than 1850 square centimetres on each side and not less than 770 square centimetres at the rear; and

(c) the distance between the rearmost part of the steering wheel and the back-rests of the row of transverse seats satisfying the requirements specified in sub-paragraph (b)(i) above or, if there is more than one such row of seats, the distance between the rearmost part of the steering wheel and the back-rests of the rearmost such row must, when the seats are ready for use, be not less than one-third of the distance between the rearmost part of the steering wheel and the rearmost part of the floor of the vehicle;

["*emissions or noise item*" means an item in Part I of Schedule 1 in respect of which the subject matter specified in column (2) of that Part is "exhaust emissions" or "noise and silencers";]

["*Framework Directive vehicle*" means a vehicle to which these Regulations apply and which is a "vehicle" within the meaning of Council Directive 70/156/EEC [*O.J. No. L42, February 23, 1970, p. 1*] as amended by Council Directive 87/403/EEC [*O.J. No. L220, August 8, 1987, p. 44*], Council Directive 92/53/EEC [*O.J. No. L225, August 10, 1992, p. 1*] and Commission Directive 93/81 [*O.J. No. L264, October 23, 1993, p. 49*];]

. . .

["*hire agreement*" means an agreement for the bailment . . . of a vehicle which is not a hire-purchase agreement;]

["*hire-purchase agreement*" has the same meaning as in the Consumer Credit Act 1974;]

"*maximum gross weight*" means, in relation to a vehicle, the weight which it is designed or adapted not to exceed when in normal use and travelling on a road laden;

"*motor ambulance*" means a motor vehicle which is specially designed and constructed (and not merely adapted) for carrying, as equipment permanently fixed to the vehicle, equipment used for medical, dental or other health purposes and is used primarily for the carriage of persons suffering from illness, injury or disability;

"*motor caravan*" means a motor vehicle which is constructed or adapted for the carriage of passengers and their effects and which contains, as permanently installed equipment, the facilities which are reasonably necessary for enabling the vehicle to provide mobile living accommodation for its users;

. . .

"*the prescribed type approval requirements*", in relation to a vehicle or a vehicle part subject to type approval requirements, means the type approval requirements prescribed therefor by [regulation 4];

["*registered*" means registered under [the Vehicle Excise and Registration Act 1994];]

["*the type approval requirements*" means the requirements with respect to the design, construction, equipment or marking of vehicles or vehicle parts which—

  (a) relate to the items numbered in column (1) and listed in column (2) of Part I of Schedule 1; and

  (b) are contained in instruments, other documents, or Parts of that Schedule, and consist of the requirements, specified against each such item in column (3) of Part I of that Schedule (subject to such modifications and additions as are set out in Part I of that Schedule;]

. . .

(2) *[Revoked.]*

(3) For the purposes of these Regulations—

  (a) a motor vehicle is to be regarded as being manufactured on or after a particular date if it is first assembled on or after that date, even if it includes one or more parts which were manufactured before that date, and

  (b) the provisions of [regulation 3(3)] of the Construction and Use Regulations shall apply for determining when a motor vehicle is first used.

(4) Unless the context otherwise requires, any reference in these Regulations to—

  (a) a numbered Regulation or Schedule is a reference to the Regulation of or Schedule to these Regulations bearing that number, and

  (b) a numbered paragraph is a reference to the paragraph bearing that number in the Regulation in which that number appears, and

  (c) a numbered section is a reference to a section having that number in [the Road Traffic Act 1988].

[Regulation 2 is printed as amended by the Interpretation Act 1978, ss.17(2)(a) and 23; S.I. 1987 No. 1509; S.I. 1991 Nos 1022, 1971; S.I. 1992 Nos 2161, 2908, 3173; the Vehicle Excise and Registration Act 1994, s.64 and Sched. 4, para.4; S.I. 1996 Nos 2330 and 3015.   **B23.04**

In regulation 2(1), only selected definitions are included.

Words relating expressly and exclusively to Scotland have been omitted from the definition of "hire agreement" in regulation 2(1).

The definition of "hire-purchase agreement" in the Consumer Credit Act 1974 is reproduced in the notes to section 109 of the Road Traffic Regulation Act 1984 above.]

2A. Interpretation of instruments referred to in Schedule 1   *[Omitted.]*   **B23.05**

[[2B]. Interpretation of "low volume type approval vehicle"

(1) For the purposes of these Regulations a vehicle ("*the vehicle in question*") is a low volume   **B23.06**
type approval vehicle at a particular time if—

(a) since the 31st December immediately preceding that time [less] than 500 Minister's approval certificates have been issued with respect to vehicles of the relevant class; and

(b) no type approval certificate [is in force] with respect to a vehicle of the relevant class.

(2) Notwithstanding anything in paragraph (1) a vehicle shall be deemed to be a low volume type approval vehicle for the purposes of these Regulations if a Minister's approval certificate in the form set out in Part III Schedule 4 or a form to the like effect has been issued with respect to it.

(3) For the purposes of this Regulation, a vehicle is a vehicle of the relevant class if it is not the vehicle in question, but is a vehicle—

(a) of the same or a similar model; and

(b) manufactured by the same manufacturer;

as the vehicle in question.

(4) For the purposes of this regulation only, two or more vehicles manufactured by different bodies corporate shall be regarded as having been manufactured by the same manufacturer if at the date when the last of those vehicles was manufactured the bodies were interconnected within the meaning given by section 137(5) of the Fair Trading Act 1973.]

B23.07   *[Regulation 2B was inserted by S.I. 1992 No. 2908 and is printed as amended (before it took effect) by S.I. 1992 No. 3173 and as further amended by S.I. 1996 No. 3015.*

Section 137(5) of the Fair Trading Act 1973 (to which reference is made in regulation 2B(4)), as amended by the Restrictive Trade Practices Act 1976, s.44 and Sched. 6, and the Companies Consolidation (Consequential Provisions) Act 1985, s.30 and Sched. 2, provides:

. . . any two bodies corporate are to be treated as interconnected if one of them is a body corporate of which the other is a subsidiary (within the meaning of [section 736 of the Companies Act 1985]) or if both of them are subsidiaries (within the meaning of that section) of one and the same body corporate . . .]

3. Application

B23.08   (1) Subject to paragraph (2) these Regulations apply to—

(a) every motor vehicle manufactured on or after 1st October 1977 and [not first used before] 1st August 1978 which is constructed solely for the carriage of passengers and their effects or is a dual-purpose vehicle and in either case which—

(i) is adapted to carry not more than eight passengers exclusive of the driver and either has four or more wheels or, if having only three wheels, has a maximum gross weight of more than 1000 kilograms, or

(ii) has three wheels, a maximum gross weight not exceeding 1000 kilograms, and either a design speed exceeding [50 kilometres per hour] or an engine with a capacity exceeding 50 cubic centimetres, and is not a motor cycle with [or without] a side-car attached, and

(b) parts of any such motor vehicles.

(2) These Regulations do not apply to, or to parts of—

(a), (b) *[revoked]*

(c) a motor vehicle brought temporarily into Great Britain by a person resident abroad;

(d) a vehicle in the service of a visiting force or of a headquarters (as defined in Article 8(6) of the Visiting Forces and International Headquarters (Application of Law) Order 1965) [*S.I. 1965 No. 1536, not reproduced in this work*];

(e) *[revoked]*;

(f) a motor vehicle which is to be exported from Great Britain and which—

  (i) is exempt from car tax by virtue of [section 7(1) of the Car Tax Act 1983],

  (ii) is a vehicle in relation to which there has been a remission of car tax by virtue of [section 7(2) and (3) of that Act], or

  (iii) has been zero-rated under [Regulation 132 or 133 of the Value Added Tax Regulations 1995] [*S.I. 1995 No. 2518*];

(g) a motor vehicle which is of a new or improved type, or is fitted with equipment of a new or improved type, and which has been constructed to that type, or fitted with that equipment, for the purposes of tests or trials or for use as a prototype, and—

  (i) is not intended for general use on roads, and

  (ii) in the case of a vehicle first used on a road on or after 21st August 1984, remains in the ownership and the use of—

    (a) the manufacturer of the vehicle if the vehicle is of a new or improved type, or

    (b) the manufacturer of the equipment if the vehicle is fitted with equipment of a new or improved type or the manufacturer of the vehicle on which that equipment is used;

[(h) a motor vehicle which is of a new or improved type provided that the conditions specified in paragraph (3) are satisfied;]

 (i) a motor vehicle to which sections 45 to 51 and 61 have become applicable after a period of use on roads during which, by virtue of section 188(4) (which relates to vehicles in the public service of the Crown), those sections did not apply to that vehicle; or

 (j) [*revoked*]

[(k) a motor vehicle for which a first licence was granted under the Vehicles (Excise) Act (Northern Ireland) 1972 on or after 2nd December 1985 [and before 1st October 1991 (being the date on which that Act was repealed and the Vehicles (Excise) Act 1971 was extended to Northern Ireland by the Finance Act 1991)]; or]

[(l) a motor vehicle in respect of which there exists a certificate issued in accordance with the provisions of Article 31A of the Road Traffic (Northern Ireland) Order 1981 [*S.I. 1981 No. 154, not reproduced in this work*].]

[(3) The conditions referred to in paragraph (2)(h) are that—

 (a) the manufacturer of the vehicle has made an application—

  (i) in respect of a type vehicle in accordance with regulation 5 for a type approval certificate, or

  (ii) in respect of another vehicle ("*the initial vehicle*") in accordance with regulation 6 for a Minister's approval certificate;

 (b) an appointment has been made for a final examination of the type vehicle or the initial vehicle (as the case may be);

 (c) the vehicle conforms with the type vehicle or the initial vehicle (as the case may be) in such of the relevant aspects of design, construction, equipment and marking as are mentioned in the information document accompanying the application pursuant to regulation 5 or 6;

 (d) the vehicle complies with the relevant type approval requirements specified in Schedule 1;

 (e) the Secretary of State has been notified of the vehicle identification number;

 (f) the vehicle—

  (i) was at the date of manufacture owned by the manufacturer of the vehicle and has remained in his ownership,

  (ii) has not been offered for sale by him,

     (iii) has not been let or offered for letting under a hire agreement or a hire-purchase agreement, and

     (iv) has not been used on a road for any purpose other than for, or in connection with, publicity, demonstration or evaluation of vehicles of the new or improved type; and

  (g) the manufacturer of the vehicle intends that until pursuant to the application mentioned in sub-paragraph (a) there has been issued a type approval certificate or a Minister's approval certificate (as the case may be), the vehicle—

     (i) shall remain in his ownership,

     (ii) shall not be offered for sale by him,

     (iii) shall not be let or offered for letting under a hire agreement or a hire-purchase agreement, and

     (iv) shall not be used on a road for any purpose other than for, or in connection with, publicity, demonstration or evaluation of vehicles of the new or improved type.]

B23.09   *[Regulation 3 is printed as amended by the Interpretation Act 1978, ss.17(2)(a) and 23(1); S.I. 1984 No. 1761; S.I. 1985 No. 1651; S.I. 1987 No. 1509; S.I. 1991 No. 1022; the Vehicle Excise and Registration Act 1994, s.64 and Sched. 4, para.4; S.I. 1996 No. 3015.*

The Visiting Forces and International Headquarters (Application of Law) Order 1965 (to which reference is made in regulation 3(2)(d) has been revoked and replaced by the Visiting Forces and International Headquarters (Application of Law) Order 1999 (S.I. 1999 No. 1736; not reproduced in this work). No textual amendment had been made to regulation 3 in consequence of that revocation; but by the Interpretation Act 1978, ss.17(2)(a) and 23(1) references to the earlier order may be treated as references to S.I. 1999 No. 1736.

References to the Car Tax Act 1983 have been inserted in regulation 3(2)(f) to replace references to the Finance Act 1972, Sched. 7; however, as Schedule 7 to the 1972 Act had been repealed by the 1983 Act before these regulations were made, the Interpretation Act 1978 might not, strictly, be applicable.

Although car tax has been abolished, some of the provisions of the Car Tax Act 1983 remain in force. Section 7(1)–(3) read as follows:

  (1) Where the Commissioners are satisfied that a vehicle—

    (a) has been exported; or

    (b) is to be exported under arrangements approved by them,

they shall remit the tax on the vehicle or, if the tax has been paid, repay it (subject in the case of a vehicle registered before exportation, to such conditions as they think fit); but where such a vehicle is imported after having been exported the provisions of this Act shall apply in relation to it as they apply in relation to a vehicle made outside the United Kingdom and not previously imported.

  (2) Where it is shown to the satisfaction of the Commissioners that a person who acquires a chargeable vehicle is only temporarily in the United Kingdom or is about to become resident outside the United Kingdom the Commissioners may, subject to such conditions as they think necessary for the protection of the revenue, remit the tax on the vehicle or, if the tax has been paid and the vehicle is unused, repay the tax.

  (3) If—

    (a) tax has been remitted or repaid on a vehicle under subsection (2) above, and

    (b) the vehicle is found in the United Kingdom after the date by which the Commissioners directed, as a condition of the remission or repayment, that it should be exported, or any other condition imposed by the Commissioners under that subsection is not complied with, and

(c) the presence of the vehicle in the United Kingdom after that date or the non-observance of that condition has not been authorised for the purposes of this subsection by the Commissioners,

then the tax which would have been payable but for the remission or, as the case may be, an amount of tax equal to that repaid shall become payable forthwith by the person by whom the vehicle was acquired or by any other person in whose possession the vehicle is found in the United Kingdom, and shall be recoverable as a debt due to the Crown, unless, or except to the extent that, the Commissioners see fit to waive payment of the whole or part of it.

The Value Added Tax Regulations 1995 (S.I. 1995 No. 2518), regs 132 and 133 (to which reference is made in regulation 3(2)(f) above), which replace the Value Added Tax (General) Regulations 1985 (S.I. 1985 No. 886), regs 56 and 57, and the Value Added Tax (General) Regulations 1980 (S.I. 1980 No. 1536), regs 49 and 50, read as follows (as amended by the Value Added Tax (Amendment) Regulations 2000 (S.I. 2000 No. 258; not reproduced in this work), regs 1(3) and 6):

132. The Commissioners may, on application by an overseas visitor who intends to depart from the member States within 15 months and remain outside the member States for a period of at least 6 months, permit him within 12 months of his intended departure to purchase, from a registered person, a . . . motor vehicle without payment of VAT, for subsequent export, and its supply, subject to such conditions as they may impose, shall be zero-rated.

133. The Commissioners may, on application by any person who intends to depart from the member States within 9 months and remain outside the member States for a period of at least 6 months, permit him within 6 months of his intended departure to purchase, from a registered person, a new motor vehicle without payment of VAT, for subsequent export, and its supply, subject to such conditions as they may impose, shall be zero-rated.

The Vehicles (Excise) Act Northern Ireland 1972 (see regulation 3(2)(k) above) has been repealed by the Finance Act 1991.]

[3A. Modifications in relation to which the Motor Vehicles (Approval) Regulations 1996 apply

(1) These Regulations shall have effect, in relation to vehicles to which Part II of the Approval Regulations apply, with the following modifications.   **B23.10**

(2) Regulation 4 shall have effect subject to regulation 3 of the Approval Regulations.

(3) Regulation 6 does not apply to an application for a Minister's approval certificate made on the basis that the vehicle complies with the relevant requirements by virtue of the Approval Regulations.

(4) Regulation 8 does not apply in relation to any determination made for the purposes of such an application.

(5) Regulation 9 does not apply in relation to any certificate issued on the basis that the vehicle complies with the relevant requirements by virtue of the Approval Regulations.

(6) Regulation 10 does not apply in relation to any certificate in the form prescribed by the Approval Regulations.

(7) Regulations 13A and 14 do not apply to any vehicle to which Part II of the Approval Regulations apply (those Regulations containing provisions corresponding to regulations 13A and 14).

(8) In this regulation—

"*the Approval Regulations*" means the Motor Vehicles (Approval) Regulations 1996 [*S.I. 1996 No. 3013*]; and

"*the relevant requirements*" in relation to a vehicle, means the requirements prescribed under section 54 of the 1988 Act that are applicable to it.]

B23.11   *[Regulation 3A was inserted by S.I. 1996 No. 3015.*

The Motor Vehicles (Approval) Regulations 1996 (to which reference is made in regulation 3A) have been revoked and replaced by the Motor Vehicles (Approval) Regulations 2001 (S.I. 2001 No. 25) below. The Interpretation Act 1978, ss.17(2)(a) and 23, which enables references to the 1996 Regulations to be construed as references to the 2001 Regulations is only applicable in the absence of a contrary intention (see 1978 Act, s.17(2)(a)); the fact that the scheme of the 2001 Regulations differs from that of the 1996 Regulations (e.g. there is no Part in the 2001 Regulations corresponding to Part II ("Passenger Vehicles") of the 1996 Regulations and no regulation in the 2001 Regulations corresponding to regulation 3 (application of Part II) of the 1996 Regulations suggests that a "contrary intention" should be inferred. The text of the 1996 Regulations is reproduced in the nineteenth edition of this work.]

4. Type approval requirements—application

B23.12   (1) [Subject to paragraphs (1A) to (5), regulation 3A] and to the exemptions specified in column (4) of [Part I of] Schedule 1, the type approval requirements are hereby prescribed as requirements which are applicable—

(a) from the date specified in column (5) of [Part I of] Schedule 1, and

(b) in a case where a date is specified in column (6) of [Part I of] Schedule 1, until that date,

to vehicles to which these Regulations apply and to the relevant parts of such vehicles, before such vehicles are [registered].

[(1A) [Subject to paragraph (3B),] in relation to a particular vehicle—

(a) a type approval requirement applicable to the vehicle at the date of manufacture shall continue to apply to it until it is registered; and

(b) a type approval requirement which is applicable to vehicles as from a date after that vehicle was manufactured shall not apply to the vehicle unless the subject matter of the requirement is the same as that of a requirement applicable to it on the date it was manufactured;

. . .]

(2) [Save as provided in paragraph (2A) of this regulation, if a vehicle or vehicle part] is manufactured on or after a date (other than 1st August 1978) specified in an item in column (5) of [Part I of] Schedule 1, the type approval requirement specified in column (3) in that item shall not apply if the vehicle or, in the case of a vehicle part, the vehicle in which it is incorporated, is first used on a road within six months of that date.

[(2A) The provisions of paragraph (2) of this regulation do not apply in respect of item 14H in Part I of Schedule 1.]

(3) [Save as provided in paragraph (3A) of this regulation, if a vehicle or vehicle part] is manufactured on or after a date specified in an item in column (6) of [Part I of] Schedule 1, the type approval requirement specified in column (3) in that item shall apply if the vehicle or, in the case of a vehicle part, the vehicle in which it is incorporated, is first used on a road within six months of that date.

[(3A) The provisions of paragraph (3) of this regulation do not apply in respect of [any emissions or noise item].]

[(3B) No emissions or noise item shall apply to a Framework Directive vehicle on or after the date specified in column (6) of the item.]

(4) Where, in relation to an item listed in column (2) of [Part I of] Schedule 1, two or more instruments or other documents are specified in column (3) of [Part I of] Schedule 1 as alternatives, the requirements prescribed by paragraph (1) are the requirements contained in either or any of those instruments or documents, and subject to paragraphs (1), (2), (3), (5) and (6) where two or more items specified in column (1) of [Part I of] Schedule 1 have the same subject matter as is specified in column (2) of [Part I of] Schedule 1 the type approval requirements relate to either or, as the case may be, any of those items [; and for the purposes of this paragraph, items 2A and 2B shall be regarded as items having the same subject matter].

(5) *[Revoked.]*

(6) A vehicle to which, or to a part of which, any requirement mentioned in paragraph (1) is for the time being applicable by virtue of paragraphs (1) to (5) is referred to in these Regulations as "a vehicle subject to type approval requirements", and a vehicle part to which any such requirement is so applicable is referred to in these Regulations as "a vehicle part subject to type approval requirements".

[(7) Where a requirement is prescribed by these Regulations as a requirement applicable to a vehicle, or to a vehicle part, that requirement shall, for the purposes of these Regulations, be regarded as being applicable to that vehicle or vehicle part by virtue of paragraphs (1) to (5) notwithstanding that the same requirement may have been, or may hereafter be, applied to that vehicle or vehicle part by or under any provision of the European Communities Act 1972 or by or under any other statutory provision.]

[(8) Subject to paragraph (9), where in relation to item [4B,] 14B, 14C or 14D in [Part I of] Schedule 1, a date is specified in column (6) of that Schedule (being a date of cessation of application of type approval requirements), that date shall not apply to any vehicle for which, or for a model of which, there is a type approval certificate or (as the case may be) a Minister's approval certificate in force at the time but, in relation to any such vehicle, column (6) shall be read and shall have effect as if there appeared in that column a date one year later than the date specified therein.]

[(8A) Where, in relation to items 12A(1), 12A(2) and 12A(3) in [Part I of] Schedule 1, a date is specified in column (6) of that Schedule (being a date of cessation of application of type approval requirements), that date shall not apply to any vehicle for which, or for a model of which, there is a type approval certificate or (as the case may be) a Minister's approval certificate in force at that date.]

[(9) In relation to any vehicle—

    (a) which has 5 or more forward gears and a maximum power to maximum gross weight ratio of not less than 75 kilowatts per tonne; and

    (b) for which, or for a model of which, there is a type approval certificate or (as the case may be) a Minister's approval certificate in force on 30th September 1988,

notwithstanding the specification in item 14B or 14C in column (6) of [Part I of] Schedule 1 of any date, that column shall be read and have effect as if no date appeared therein.]

[(10) Schedule 1A shall have effect for the purpose of specifying, in relation to certain vehicles, dates which are to be read as if they appeared in column (5) of items 25 and 26 in [Part I of] Schedule 1.]

[(11) Schedules 1B and 1C (which treat certain emissions or noise items as if in certain circumstances specified dates were substituted for the entries in columns (5) and (6)) shall have effect].

[(12) In this regulation, *"prescribed"* means prescribed under sections 54 . . . of the Road Traffic Act 1988.]

B23.13   *[Regulation 4 is printed as amended by S.I. 1987 No. 1509; S.I. 1988 No. 1522; S.I. 1989 No. 1580; S.I. 1992 Nos 1341, 2161, 2908; S.I. 1993 No. 2201; S.I. 1995 No. 1322; S.I. 1996 Nos 2330 and 3015.]*

*   *   *

The Traffic Signs (Welsh and English Language Provisions) Regulations and General Directions 1985

(S.I. 1985 No. 713)

The Secretary of State for Wales, in exercise of the powers conferred by section 28(4) of the Road Traffic Regulation Act 1984 (hereinafter referred to as "the Act of 1984") and the Secretary of State for Wales, the Secretary of State for Transport and the Secretary of State for Scotland acting jointly in exercise of the powers conferred by sections 64(1) and 65(1) of the Act of 1984 and by the provision in column 5 of Part I of Schedule 4 to the Road Traffic Act 1972 which relates to section 22 of that Act as that provision is amended by paragraph 9 of Schedule 3 to the Secretary of State for Transport Order 1976 [*S.I. 1976 No. 1775; not reproduced in this work*] and in exercise of the powers conferred by section 2(2) and (3) of the Welsh Language Act 1967 and now vested in them and all other enabling powers, and after consultation with representative organisations in accordance with section 134(2) of the Act of 1984 and section 199(2) of the Road Traffic Act 1972 hereby make these Regulations and give these Directions.

B24.01

[*Although the Road Traffic Act 1972 has been repealed, the references to that Act in the recital of enabling powers have been retained for historical reasons. For sections 22 and 199(2) of the 1972 Act, see now sections 36 and 195(2), respectively, of the Road Traffic Act 1988; for Schedule 4, Part I, column 5, to the 1972 Act, see now Schedule 2, Part I, column 5, to the Road Traffic Offenders Act 1988.*]

B24.02

PART I

TRAFFIC SIGNS REGULATIONS

*   *   *

2. Interpretation

(1) In these Regulations the Main Regulations means the Traffic Signs Regulations 1981 [*S.I. 1981 No. 859*] as amended and a reference in Schedule 1 to these Regulations and Directions to "*Main Regulations*" or to "*Prif Reolau*" is similarly a reference to the Traffic Signs Regulations 1981 amended as aforesaid.

B24.03

(2) References in these Regulations to a numbered Regulation or numbered Schedule shall be construed, unless the context otherwise requires, as a reference to the Regulation bearing that number in these Regulations or to the Schedule bearing that number in these Regulations and Directions.

(3) References in these Regulations to a sign shown in a diagram in Schedule 1 shall include references to a variant of the sign which is specified in Schedule 1 as being a permitted variant.

(4) References in Schedule 1 to a sign without the prefix "W" before a diagram number are references to the sign bearing the same diagram number in Parts I and II of Schedule I to the Main Regulations and references in Schedule I to a sign with the prefix "W" before

a diagram number are references to the sign bearing the same diagram number which is prescribed for use in Wales by regulation 4(1).

(5) Nothing in these Regulations shall have effect so as to authorise any person not otherwise authorised to do so to place on or near a road any object or device for warning traffic of a temporary obstruction.

B24.04   *[The Traffic Signs Regulations 1981 (S.I. 1981 No. 859) have been revoked and replaced by the Traffic Signs Regulations 1994 (S.I. 1994 No. 1519), except for the purposes of these Regulations; see S.I. 1994 No. 1519, reg.2. The text of S.I. 1981 No. 859, so far as material is reproduced in the sixteenth edition of this work.]*

3. Authorisation by the Secretary of State

B24.05   Nothing in these Regulations shall be taken to limit the power of the Secretary of State under section 64 of the Act of 1984 to authorise the erection or retention of traffic signs of a character not prescribed by these Regulations.

4. Traffic Signs shown in Schedule 1

B24.06   (1) A sign shown in a diagram in Schedule 1 with the prefix "W" followed by a diagram number may be used in Wales in place of a sign bearing the same diagram number without the prefix "W" in Parts I or II of Schedule 1 to the Main Regulations.

(2) In the signs shown in the diagrams in Schedule 1, other than the signs shown in diagrams W605.1 and W629.1 and other than the signs therein which specifically prescribe the manner in which the two texts are to be displayed, either the Welsh or English text shall be placed above the other text.

B24.07   *[Diagram W605.1 is the sign exhibited by a school crossing patrol and diagram W629.1 is the sign prohibiting vehicles or combinations of vehicles exceeding the length indicated.]*

5. Application of the Main Regulations

B24.08   (1) Subject to the provisions of this Regulation, the provisions of the Main Regulations shall apply to a sign shown in a diagram in Schedule 1 with the prefix "W" followed by a diagram number as if it were a sign bearing the same diagram number without the prefix "W" in Schedule 1 to the Main Regulations.

Provided that—

(a) except as provided in paragraph (2) of this Regulation, references in subparagraphs (c), (d) and (e) of Regulation 12(1) of the Main Regulations to the signs specified in those subparagraphs showing distances in miles or in yards shall be construed as references to such signs in Schedule 1 showing distances in both the Welsh and English texts;

(b) references in subparagraph (g) of Regulation 12(1) of the Main Regulations to signs showing a period of time, day of the week, days of the month or months of the year shall be construed as references to such signs in Schedule 1 indicating these matters in both the Welsh and English texts;

(c) where, in accordance with the provisions of Regulation 12(1) of the Main Regulations, the indication given by a sign shown in a diagram in Schedule 1 is varied, the variation shall be made to both the Welsh and English texts of the sign; and

(d) Regulation 28(1) of the Main Regulations shall not apply to the sign shown in diagram 562 of Schedule 1 to the Main Regulations when used as directed in proviso (a) to Direction 3 in Part II of this Instrument in combination with any of the signs shown in diagrams W552, W554 and W554.1 in Schedule 1.

(2) A reference in Regulation 12(1)(c) of the Main Regulations to the sign shown in diagram 565.4 of Schedule 1 to the Main Regulations expressing distances in miles shall be construed as a reference to the sign showing distances by means of the letter "m" in diagram W564.4 in Schedule 1 and a similar reference in Regulation 12(1)(e) of the Main Regulations to the signs shown in diagrams 557.2 and 557.3 expressing distances in miles or yards shall be construed as references to the signs showing distances by means of the letters "m" or "yds" in diagrams W557.2 and W557.3 in Schedule 1.

(3) The provisions of Regulation 14 of and Schedule 7 to the Main Regulations shall apply as if in that Part of Schedule 7 specified in Column 1 of the following Table there were inserted the characters shown in that Part of Schedule 2 to these Regulations specified in Column 2 of the said Table opposite the Part in Column 1 to which it relates.

TABLE

Column 1 *Part of Schedule 7 to* *Main Regulations*	Column 2 *Part of Schedule 2 to these* *Regulations to be inserted*
Part　　I	Part A
Part　　II	Part B
Part　　IV	Part C
Part　　V	Part D
Part　　VI	Part E
Part　　VIII	Part F

[Diagrams 557.2 and 557.3 are plates for use in connection with diagram 557.1 (road hump ahead); **B24.09**
diagram 562 is a warning sign of other danger ahead; diagrams W552 (cattle grid), W554 (snow drifts)
and W554.1 (try your brakes) are plates for use in connection with diagram 562; and diagrams W557.2
and W557.3 are plates for use in connection with diagram 557.1]

6. Application of other enactments

A reference in any enactment to a traffic sign shown in a numbered diagram in the Main **B24.10**
Regulations shall be construed as including a reference to a sign bearing the same diagram number with the prefix "W" in Schedule 1.

SCHEDULE 1

[Warning and regulating signs; omitted.]　　　　　**B24.11**

SCHEDULE 2

[Proportion and form of letters, numerals and other characters; omitted.]　　　　**B24.12**

PART II

GENERAL DIRECTIONS

*　　　*　　　*

2. Interpretation

B24.13   (1) References in these Directions to "*Schedule 1*" shall be construed as references to Schedule 1 to these Regulations and Directions.

(2) In these Directions "*the Main Regulations*" means the Traffic Signs Regulations 1981 as amended; "*the Main Directions*" means the Traffic Signs General Directions 1981 [*S.I. 1981 No. 859*] as amended and a reference in Schedule 1 to these Regulations and Directions to "Main Directions" or to "Prif Gyfarwyddiadau" is similarly a reference to the Traffic Signs General Directions 1981 as amended.

(3) References in these Directions to a sign in a diagram in Schedule 1 shall include references to a variant of the sign which is specified in Schedule 1 as being a permitted variant.

(4) Nothing in these Directions shall have effect so as to authorise any person not otherwise authorised to do so to place on or near a road any object or device for warning traffic of a temporary obstruction.

B24.14   *[The Traffic Signs Directions 1981 (S.I. 1981 No. 859) have been revoked and replaced by the Traffic Signs Directions 1994 (S.I. 1994 No. 1519), except for the purposes of these Directions; see S.I. 1994 No. 1519, direction 2. The text of S.I. 1981 No. 859, so far as material, is reproduced in the sixteenth edition of this work.]*

3. Application of the Main Directions

B24.15   The Main Directions shall apply to a sign shown in a diagram in Schedule 1 with the prefix "W" followed by a diagram number as if it were a sign bearing the equivalent diagram number without the prefix "W" in Schedule 1 to the Main Regulations and the reference in Direction 12 of the Main Directions to signs which are specified beneath the diagrams showing the plates referred to in Direction 12 shall be construed as references to such signs beneath the corresponding diagrams in Schedule 1.
Provided that:—

   (a) notwithstanding anything to the contrary contained in Direction 11(3) of the Main Directions the plates shown in diagrams W552, W554 and W554.1 in Schedule 1 shall be used only in combination with the sign shown in diagram 562 of Schedule 1 to the Main Regulations; and

   (b) the references in Direction 17(ii) of the Main Directions to the sign shown in diagram 565.2 in Schedule 1 to the Main Regulations bearing words in the English language shall be construed as a reference to such sign in Schedule 1 in both the Welsh and English texts.

B24.16   *[Diagram 565.2 is a warning sign (slow—wet tar; and a number of specified variants). As to the other diagrams mentioned in direction 3, see the note to regulation 5.]*

The Removal and Disposal of Vehicles Regulations 1986

(S.I. 1986 No. 183)

[The text of the principal regulations is printed as amended by:

B25.01

the Removal and Disposal of Vehicles (Amendment) Regulations 1993 (S.I. 1993 No. 278) (June 1, 1993);

the Removal and Disposal of Vehicles (Amendment) (No. 2) Regulations 1993 (S.I. 1993 No. 1475) (July 5, 1993);

the Removal and Disposal of Vehicles (Amendment) (No. 3) Regulations 1993 (S.I. 1993 No. 1708) (July 12, 1993);

the Removal and Disposal of Vehicles (Amendment) Regulations 1994 (S.I. 1994 No. 1503) (July 4, 1994);

the Local Government Reorganisation (Wales) (Consequential Amendments No. 2) Order 1996 (S.I. 1996 No. 1008) (April 29, 1996); and

the Greater London Road Traffic (Various Provisions) Order 2001 (S.I. 2001 No. 1353) (April 4, 2001).

The amending regulations are referred to in the notes to the principal regulations only by their years and numbers. The dates referred to above are the dates on which the amending regulations came into force.

The principal regulations have also been amended by the Removal and Disposal of Vehicles (Amendment) Regulations 1998 (S.I. 1998 No. 2019), and the Removal and Disposal of Vehicles (Amendment) (Scotland) Regulations 1999 (S.I. 1999 No. 490), but the amending regulations do not affect any provision printed in this work.]

ARRANGEMENT OF REGULATIONS

PART I

GENERAL

PART II

REMOVAL OF VEHICLES

SCHEDULES

PART I

GENERAL

B25.03 **1. Commencement, citation and revocation**   *[Omitted.]*

2. Interpretation

B25.04 In these Regulations, unless the contrary intention appears, the following expressions have the meanings hereby assigned to them respectively, that is to say:—

"*the 1978 Act*" means the Refuse Disposal (Amenity) Act 1978;

"*the 1984 Act*" means the Road Traffic Regulation Act 1984;

"*motor vehicle*" has the meaning assigned to it in section 11(1) of the 1978 Act;

"*road*", in England and Wales, means any highway and any other road to which the public has access . . . ;

"*vehicle*", in relation to any matter prescribed by these Regulations for the purposes of any provision in sections 3 and 4 of the 1978 Act, means a motor vehicle, and in relation to any matter prescribed by these Regulations for the purposes of any provision in sections 99 and 101 of the 1984 Act has the meaning assigned to it in section 99(5) of that Act, and, in relation to any matter prescribed by these Regulations for the purposes of section 99 of the 1984 Act, any reference to a vehicle which has been permitted to remain at rest or which has broken down includes a reference to a vehicle which has been permitted to remain at rest or which has broken down before the coming into force of these Regulations.

B25.05 *[Words relating expressly and exclusively to Scotland have been omitted from the definition of "road" above.]*

PART II

REMOVAL OF VEHICLES

3. Power of constable to require removal of vehicles from roads

B25.06 (1) Except as provided by regulation 7 of these Regulations, this regulation applies to a vehicle which—

(a) has broken down, or been permitted to remain at rest, on a road in such a position or in such condition or in such circumstances as to cause obstruction to persons using the road or as to be likely to cause danger to such persons, or

(b) has been permitted to remain at rest or has broken down and remained at rest on a road in contravention of a prohibition or restriction contained in, or having effect under, any of the enactments mentioned in Schedule 1 to these Regulations.

(2) A constable may require the owner, driver or other person in control or in charge of any vehicle to which this regulation applies to move or cause to be moved the vehicle and any such requirement may include a requirement that the vehicle shall be moved from that road to a place which is not on that or any other road, or that the vehicle shall not be moved to any such road or to any such position on a road as may be specified.

(3) A person required to move or cause to be moved a vehicle under this regulation shall comply with such requirement as soon as practicable.

4. Power of constable to remove vehicles

Except as provided by regulation 7 of these Regulations, where a vehicle—   **B25.07**

(a) is a vehicle to which regulation 3 of these Regulations applies, or

(b) having broken down on a road or on any land in the open air, appears to a constable to have been abandoned without lawful authority, or

(c) has been permitted to remain at rest on a road or on any land in the open air in such a position or in such condition or in such circumstances as to appear to a constable to have been abandoned without lawful authority,

then, subject to the provisions of sections 99 and 100 of the 1984 Act, a constable may remove or arrange for the removal of the vehicle, and, in the case of a vehicle which is on a road, he may remove it or arrange for its removal from that road to a place which is not on that or any other road, or may move it or arrange for its removal to another position on that or another road.

[4A. Power of traffic warden to remove vehicles

(1) Except as provided by regulation 7 of these Regulations, a traffic warden may,   **B25.08** subject to sections 99 and 100 of the 1984 Act, remove or arrange for the removal of a vehicle to which regulation 3 of these Regulations applies to a place which is not on that or any other road, or may move it or arrange for its removal to another position on that or another road.

(2) This regulation applies only in respect of—

(a) a vehicle which is on a road in, and

(b) its removal in and to a place in,

England or Wales.]

[Regulation 4A was inserted by S.I. 1993 No. 278.]   **B25.09**

4B. Power of traffic wardens to remove vehicles   *[Applies to Scotland.]*   **B25.10**

5. Power of local authority to remove certain vehicles

(1) Except as provided by regulation 7 of these Regulations, where a vehicle (other than   **B25.11** a motor vehicle which a local authority have a duty to remove under section 3 of the 1978 Act)—

(a) having broken down on a road or on any land in the open air in the area of a local authority, appears to them to have been abandoned without lawful authority, or

(b) has been permitted to remain at rest on a road or on any land in the open air in the area of a local authority in such a position or in such condition or in such circumstances as to appear to them to have been abandoned without lawful authority,

the local authority may, subject to the provisions of sections 99 and 100 of the 1984 Act, remove or arrange for the removal of the vehicle to a place which is not on any road.

(2) In this regulation "*local authority*" means, in the case of a vehicle situate at a place—

(a) in England, the council of the district or of the London borough, or the Common Council of the City of London;

(b) *[applies to Scotland]*; or

(c) in Wales, the council of the [county or county borough],

within whose area is situate that place.

B25.12   *[Regulation 5 is printed as amended by S.I. 1996 No. 1008.*

The provisions of these regulations in their application to land within airports at Bristol, Coventry, Gloucester, Cheltenham, Liverpool, London Luton, Manchester and Southend have been modified by the Airports (Designation) (Removal and Disposal of Vehicles) Order 1990 (S.I. 1990 No. 54), as amended by the Airports (Designation) (Removal and Disposal of Vehicles) (Amendment) Order 1993 (S.I. 1993 No. 2117) (not reproduced in this work) so as to confer on the airport operators the functions exercisable under section 3 by local authorities. In relation to such airports, the regulations apply as if (inter alia) regulations 5 and 7 were omitted and as if regulation 10 were amended.]

[5A. Powers of parking attendants to remove vehicles

B25.13   (1) Except as provided by regulation 7 of these Regulations where, in the area of a particular local authority, a vehicle—

(a) has been permitted to remain at rest or has broken down and remained at rest on a road in Greater London in contravention of a prohibition or restriction contained in an order having effect under—

(i) section 6 of the 1984 Act so far as the order designates any parking place; or

(ii) section 9 of the 1984 Act so far as the order designates any parking place in an area in respect of which section 65 of the Road Traffic Act 1991 [*q.v.*] is in force;

(iii) section 46 of the 1984 Act so far as the order relates to a parking place in such an area;

(b) has been permitted to remain at rest or has broken down and remained at rest on a road outside Greater London in contravention of a prohibition or restriction contained in an order under section 46 of the 1984 Act in circumstances in which an offence would have been committed in respect of the vehicle but for paragraph 1(4)(b) of Schedule 3 to the Road Traffic Act 1991 (permitted parking areas); or

(c) has been permitted to remain at rest or has broken down and remained at rest on a road in contravention of a statutory prohibition or restriction in circumstances in which an offence would have been committed with respect to the vehicle but for section 76(3) of, or paragraph 1(4)(a) or 2(4) of Schedule 3 to, the Road Traffic Act 1991 (permitted parking areas or special parking areas),

a parking attendant acting on behalf of the local authority may, subject to the provisions of sections 99 and 100 of the 1984 Act, remove or arrange for the removal of the vehicle from the road to a place which is not on that or any other road, or may move it or arrange for its removal to another position on that or another road.

(2) Sub-paragraphs (ii) and (iii) of paragraph (1)(a) and paragraph (1)(b) above shall not apply in relation to a vehicle if—

(a) not more than 15 minutes have elapsed since the end of any period for which the appropriate charge was duly paid at the time of parking; or

(b) not more than 15 minutes have elapsed since the end of any unexpired time (in respect of another vehicle) which is available at the relevant parking meter at the time of parking.

(3) This regulation applies only in respect of—

(a) a vehicle which is on a road in, and

(b) its removal in and to a place in,

England or Wales.

[(4) In this regulation—

"*local authority*"—

(a) in relation to a vehicle which is on a road in Greater London, shall be construed in accordance with paragraphs (5) and (6) below; and,

(b) in relation to any other vehicle, has the same meaning as in section 100 of the 1984 Act;

"*London local authority*" means the council of a London borough or the Common Council of the City of London;

"*parking meter*" has the same meaning as in section 46(2)(a) of that Act.]

[(5) In relation to a vehicle which falls within paragraph (1)(a) above (vehicle parked in contravention of an order designating a parking place on a road in Greater London)—

(a) if the parking place is on a GLA road or GLA side road and the parking place was designated by Transport for London, "*local authority*" means Transport for London;

(b) in any other case, "*local authority*" means the London local authority in whose area the parking place is.]

[(6) In relation to a vehicle which has been permitted to remain at rest, or having broken down has been permitted to remain at rest, on a GLA road or GLA side road in contravention of a statutory prohibition or restriction in circumstances in which an offence would have been committed with respect to the vehicle but for section 76(3) of the Road Traffic Act 1991 (offence provisions not applying within a special parking area) "*local authority*" means Transport for London.]

[(7) For the purposes of this regulation the area of Transport for London shall be taken to be Greater London.]

[Regulation 5A was inserted by S.I. 1993 No. 1475 and is printed as subsequently substituted by S.I.   **B25.14**
1993 No. 1708, and as later amended by S.I. 2001 No. 1353.]

5B.   *[Applies only to Scotland.]*   **B25.15**

6. Method of removing vehicles

Any person removing or moving a vehicle under [regulation 4, 4A or 5 of these   **B25.16**
Regulations] may do so by towing or driving the vehicle or in such other manner as he may think necessary and may take such measures in relation to the vehicle as he may think necessary to enable him to remove or move it as aforesaid.

[Regulation 6 is printed as amended by S.I. 1993 No. 278. (Regulation 6 has been further amended by   **B25.17**
S.I. 1999 No. 490, but the amendment has not been noted as it applies only to Scotland.)]

7. Exception for Severn Bridge

B25.18 [Regulations 3, 4, 4A and 5] of these Regulations shall not apply in relation to any vehicle while on the central section of the specified carriageways (as defined in section 1 of the Severn Bridge Tolls Act 1965) of a road which crosses the Rivers Severn and Wye.

B25.19 *[Regulation 7 is printed as amended by S.I. 1993 No. 278.*
See also the note to regulation 5 above.]

B25.20 ### 8. Manner of giving notice to occupier of land before removing a vehicle therefrom *[Omitted.]*

9. Manner and period during which occupier of land may object
[Omitted.]

10. Period before which notice must be affixed to a vehicle in certain cases before removing it for destruction

B25.21 For the purposes of section 3(5) of the 1978 Act and section 99(4) of the 1984 Act, the period before the commencement of which a notice must be caused to be affixed to a vehicle by an authority who propose to remove it, before they remove it, being a vehicle which in the opinion of the authority is in such a condition that it ought to be destroyed, shall be seven days.

B25.22 *[See the note to regulation 5 above.]*

PART III

Disposal of Abandoned Vehicles

B25.23 **11–16.**   *[Omitted.]*

Regulation 3   SCHEDULE 1

Certain Enactments by or under which are Imposed Prohibitions or
Restrictions on the Waiting of Vehicles on Roads

. . .

B25.24 Section 52 of the Metropolitan Police Act 1839 and section 22 of the local Act of the second and third year of the reign of Queen Victoria, chapter 94 (relating to the prevention of obstruction in streets in London).

Section 21 of the Town Police Clauses Act 1847 (relating to the prevention of obstructions in streets in England and Wales elsewhere than in London).

Section 2 of the Parks Regulation (Amendment) Act 1926 (authorising the making of regulations as to Royal Parks).

[Section 36 of the Road Traffic Act 1988] (which makes it an offence to fail to conform to the indications given by certain traffic signs).

Section 1 of the 1984 Act (which authorises the making of orders regulating traffic on roads outside Greater London) . . .

Section 6 of the 1984 Act (authorising the making of orders regulating traffic on roads in Greater London).

Section 9 of the 1984 Act (authorising the making of experimental traffic orders).

Section 12 of the 1984 Act (relating to experimental traffic schemes in Greater London).

Section 14 of the 1984 Act (which provides for the restriction or prohibition of the use of roads in consequence of the execution of works).

[Section 16A of the Road Traffic Regulation Act 1984 (which provides for the restriction or prohibition of the use of roads in connection with the holding of certain special events).]

Section 17 of the 1984 Act (authorising the making of regulations with respect to the use of special roads).

Section 25 of the 1984 Act (authorising the making of regulations for crossings for foot passengers).

Sections 35 and 45 to 49 of the 1984 Act (relating to parking places for vehicles).

Section 57 of the 1984 Act (relating to the provision of parking places in England and Wales for bicycles and motor cycles).

Sections 66 and 67 of the 1984 Act (which empower the police to place traffic signs relating to local traffic regulations and temporary signs for dealing with traffic congestion and danger).

Any enactment in any local Act for the time being in force, and any byelaw having effect under any enactment for the time being in force, being an enactment or byelaw imposing or authorising the imposition of a prohibition or restriction similar to any prohibition or restriction which is or can be imposed by or under any of the above-mentioned enactments.

[Schedule 1 is printed as amended by the Interpretation Act 1978, ss.17(2)(a) and 23(1); S.I. 1994   **B25.25**
No. 1503.

References to Scottish legislation have been omitted from Schedule 1.]

SCHEDULE 2

FORM OF NOTICE TO OCCUPIER OF LAND BEFORE REMOVING ABANDONED VEHICLES   **B25.26**

[Omitted.]

The Removal and Disposal of Vehicles (Loading Areas) Regulations 1986

(S.I. 1986 No. 184)

PART I

GENERAL

B26.01   **1. Citation, commencement and revocation**   *[Omitted.]*

2. Interpretation

B26.02   In these Regulations—

"*the 1984 Act*" means the Road Traffic Regulation Act 1984;

"*loading area*" has the same meaning as in section 61 of the 1984 Act [*q.v.*];

"*vehicle*" has the same meaning as in section 99 of the 1984 Act [*q.v.*].

PART II

REMOVAL OF VEHICLES

3. Power to require the removal of vehicles from loading areas

B26.03   (1) This regulation applies to a vehicle which is in any part of a loading area while the parking of it in that part is prohibited by virtue of section 61 of the 1984 Act.

(2) Subject to paragraph (3) below, an officer of the local authority, duly authorised in writing by that authority, may require the owner, driver or other person in control or in charge of any vehicle to which this regulation applies to move it or cause it to be removed, and any such requirement may include a requirement that the vehicle shall be moved from the part of the loading area where it is to some other part of that loading area, or to a place on a highway, or to some other place which is not on a highway (being a place where the vehicle can be lawfully parked).

(3) When making any requirement under paragraph (2) above an officer of the local authority, if requested so to do by the owner, driver or other person in control or in charge of the vehicle, shall produce evidence of his authorisation.

(4) In this regulation and in regulation 4 below "*the local authority*" means—

  (a) in Greater London, the Council of the London borough or, as the case may be, the Common Council of the City,

  (b) elsewhere in England, . . . the council of the district in whose area is situated the part of the loading area where the vehicle in question is while parking is prohibited as mentioned in paragraph (1) above.

  [(c) in Wales, the council of the county or county borough.]

B26.04   *[Regulation 3 is printed as amended by the Local Government Reorganisation (Wales) (Consequential Amendments No. 2) Order 1996 (S.I. 1996 No. 1008; not reproduced in this work).]*

4. Power to remove vehicles

(1) Where, in the case of a vehicle to which regulation 3 above applies— **B26.05**

 (a) the owner, driver or other person in control or in charge of the vehicle refuses or fails to comply with a requirement, made under that regulation by a duly authorised officer of the local authority, to move it or cause it to be moved, or

 (b) no person who is in control or in charge of the vehicle and who is capable of moving it or causing it to be moved is present on or in the vicinity of the vehicle,

an officer of the local authority (who need not be the officer who has made any requirement as respects the vehicle under regulation 3 above) may move or arrange for the removal of the vehicle to another part of the loading area, or may remove it or arrange for its removal from the loading area to some other place which is not on a highway.

(2) Any person removing or moving a vehicle under this regulation may do so by towing or driving the vehicle or in such other manner as he may think necessary, and may take such measures in relation to the vehicle as he may think necessary to enable him to remove or move it as aforesaid.

PART III

DISPOSAL OF ABANDONED VEHICLES

5. Disposal of abandoned vehicles *[Omitted.]*   **B26.06**

The Road Vehicles (Construction and Use) Regulations 1986

(S.I. 1986 No. 1078)

B27.01   *Editorial note.*   These regulations revoked and replaced the Motor Vehicles (Construction and Use) (Track Laying Vehicles) Regulations 1955, as amended, and the Motor Vehicles (Construction and Use) Regulations 1978, as amended, on August 11, 1986. The 1986 Regulations are set out in a new presentation with more extensive use of tabulations, more logical arrangement of material and simplified language. Because of these changes, it is not possible to identify with precision the provisions in the 1986 Regulations which correspond to those in the revoked regulations. A table of comparison may be found at 3 W.R.T.L.B. 55; but where exact comparison is necessary, reference should be made to the actual provisions of the revoked regulations.

B27.02   *[The text of these regulations is printed as amended by:*

the Road Vehicles (Construction and Use) (Amendment) Regulations 1986 (S.I. 1986 No. 1597) (October 10, 1986);

the Road Vehicles (Construction and Use) (Amendment) Regulations 1987 (S.I. 1987 No. 676) (except as otherwise indicated, May 6, 1987);

the Road Vehicles (Construction and Use) (Amendment) (No. 2) Regulations 1987 (S.I. 1987 No. 1133) (July 31, 1987);

the Road Vehicles (Construction and Use) (Amendment) Regulations 1988 (S.I. 1988 No. 271) (March 18, 1988);

the Road Vehicles (Construction and Use) (Amendment) (No. 4) Regulations 1988 (S.I. 1988 No. 1178) (July 25, 1988);

the Road Vehicles (Construction and Use) (Amendment) (No. 5) Regulations 1988 (S.I. 1988 No. 1287) (January 1, 1989);

the Road Vehicles (Construction and Use) (Amendment) (No. 6) Regulations 1988 (S.I. 1988 No. 1524) (October 1, 1988);

the Road Vehicles (Construction and Use) (Amendment) (No. 7) Regulations 1988 (S.I. 1988 No. 1871) (January 1, 1989);

the Road Vehicles (Construction and Use) (Amendment) Regulations 1989 (S.I. 1989 No. 1478) (September 7, 1989);

the Road Vehicles (Construction and Use) (Amendment) (No. 2) Regulations 1989 (S.I. 1989 No. 1695) (October 30, 1989);

the Road Vehicles (Construction and Use) (Amendment) (No. 3) Regulations 1989 (S.I. 1989 No. 1865) (November 8, 1989);

the Road Vehicles (Construction and Use) (Amendment) (No. 4) Regulations 1989 (S.I. 1989 No. 2360) (January 11, 1990);

the Road Vehicles (Construction and Use) (Amendment) Regulations 1990 (S.I. 1990 No. 317) (March 19, 1990);

the Road Vehicles (Construction and Use) (Amendment) (No. 2) Regulations 1990 (S.I. 1990 No. 1131) (June 26, 1990);

the Road Vehicles (Construction and Use) (Amendment) (No. 3) Regulations 1990 (S.I. 1990 No. 1163) (June 29, 1990);

the Road Vehicles (Construction and Use) (Amendment) (No. 4) Regulations 1990 (S.I. 1990 No. 1981) (November 2, 1990);

the Road Vehicles (Construction and Use) (Amendment) (No. 5) Regulations 1990 (S.I. 1990 No. 2212) (December 10, 1990);

the Road Vehicles (Construction and Use) (Amendment) (No. 1) Regulations 1991 (S.I. 1991 No. 1526) (November 1, 1991);

the Road Vehicles (Construction and Use) (Amendment) (No. 2) Regulations 1991 (S.I. 1991 No. 1527) (August 1, 1991);

the Road Vehicles (Construction and Use) (Amendment) (No. 3) Regulations 1991 (S.I. 1991 No. 2003) (October 7, 1991);

the Road Vehicles (Construction and Use) (Amendment) (No. 4) Regulations 1991 (S.I. 1991 No. 2125) (October 17, 1991);

the Road Vehicles (Construction and Use) (Amendment) (No. 5) Regulations 1991 (S.I. 1991 No. 2710) (January 1, 1992);

the Road Vehicles (Construction and Use) (Amendment) Regulations 1992 (S.I. 1992 No. 352) (April 1, 1992);

the Road Vehicles (Construction and Use) (Amendment) (No. 2) Regulations 1992 (S.I. 1992 No. 422) (for the purposes of regulation 8, August 1, 1993; for all other purposes, August 1, 1992);

the Road Vehicles (Construction and Use) (Amendment) (No. 3) Regulations 1992 (S.I. 1992 No. 646) (April 1, 1992);

the Tramcars and Trolley Vehicles (Modification of Enactments) Regulations 1992 (S.I. 1992 No. 1217), reg.13 (July 1, 1992);

the Road Vehicles (Construction and Use) (Amendment) (No. 4) Regulations 1992 (S.I. 1992 No. 2016) (January 1, 1993);

the Road Vehicles (Construction and Use) (Amendment) (No. 5) Regulations 1992 (S.I. 1992 No. 2137) (December 31, 1992);

the Road Vehicles (Construction and Use) (Amendment) (No. 6) Regulations 1992 (S.I. 1992 No. 2909) (December 31, 1992);

the Road Vehicles (Construction and Use) (Amendment) (No. 7) Regulations 1992 (S.I. 1992 No. 3088) (January 1, 1993);

the Road Vehicles (Construction and Use) (Amendment) (No. 8) Regulations 1992 (S.I. 1992 No. 3285) (February 1, 1993);

the Road Vehicles (Construction and Use) (Amendment) (No. 1) Regulations 1993 (S.I. 1993 No. 1946) (September 1, 1993);

the Road Vehicles (Construction and Use) (Amendment) (No. 2) Regulations 1993 (S.I. 1993 No. 2199) (October 1, 1993);

the Road Vehicles (Construction and Use) (Amendment) (No. 3) Regulations 1993 (S.I. 1993 No. 3048) (January 1, 1994);

the Road Vehicles (Construction and Use) (Amendment) Regulations 1994 (S.I. 1994 No. 14) (July 1, 1994);

the Road Vehicles (Construction and Use) (Amendment) (No. 2) Regulations 1994 (S.I. 1994 No. 329) (March 24, 1994);

the Road Vehicles (Construction and Use) (Amendment) (No. 3) Regulations 1994 (S.I. 1994 No. 2192) (October 1, 1994);

the Road Vehicles (Construction and Use) (Amendment) (No. 4) Regulations 1994 (S.I. 1994 No. 3270) (February 1, 1995), with corrigendum dated May 1995;

the Road Vehicles (Construction and Use) (Amendment) Regulations 1995 (S.I. 1995 No. 551) (April 1, 1995);

the Road Vehicles (Construction and Use) (Amendment) (No. 2) Regulations 1995 (S.I. 1995 No. 737) (March 31, 1995);

the Road Vehicles (Construction and Use) (Amendment) (No. 3) Regulations 1995 (S.I. 1995 No. 1201) (June 1, 1995);

the Road Vehicles (Construction and Use) (Amendment) (No. 4) Regulations 1995 (S.I. 1995 No. 1458) (July 1, 1995);

the Road Vehicles (Construction and Use) (Amendment) (No. 5) Regulations 1995 (S.I. 1995 No. 2210) (September 25, 1995 and January 1, 1996);

the Road Vehicles (Construction and Use) (Amendment) (No. 6) Regulations 1995 (S.I. 1995 No. 3051) (January 1, 1996);

the Road Vehicles (Construction and Use) (Amendment) Regulations 1996 (S.I. 1996 No. 16) (February 1, 1996);

the Road Vehicles (Construction and Use) (Amendment) (No. 2) Regulations 1996 (S.I. 1996 No. 163) (March 6, 1996 and February 10, 1997);

the Gas Act 1995 (Consequential Modifications of Subordinate Legislation) Order 1996 (S.I. 1996 No. 252) (March 1, 1996);

the Road Vehicles (Construction and Use) (Amendment) (No. 3) Regulations 1996 (S.I. 1996 No. 2064) (September 1, 1996 and September 1, 1997);

the Road Vehicles (Construction and Use) (Amendment) (No. 4) Regulations 1996 (S.I. 1996 No. 2085) (September 2, 1996);

the Road Vehicles (Construction and Use) (Amendment) (No. 5) Regulations 1996 (S.I. 1996 No. 2329) (October 1, 1996);

the Road Vehicles (Construction and Use) (Amendment) (No. 6) Regulations 1996 (S.I. 1996 No. 3017) (July 1, 1997);

the Road Vehicles (Construction and Use) (Amendment) (No. 7) Regulations 1996 (S.I. 1996 No. 3033) (January 1, 1997);

the Road Vehicles (Construction and Use) (Amendment) (No. 8) Regulations 1996 (S.I. 1996 No. 3133) (January 3, 1997);

the Road Vehicles (Construction and Use) (Amendment) Regulations 1997 (S.I. 1997 No. 530) (October 1, 1997);

the Road Vehicles (Construction and Use) (Amendment) (No. 2) Regulations 1997 (S.I. 1997 No. 1096) (April 22, 1997);

the Road Vehicles (Construction and Use) (Amendment) (No. 4) Regulations 1997 (S.I. 1997 No. 1340) (July 1, 1997);

the Road Vehicles (Construction and Use) (Amendment) (No. 4) Regulations 1997 (S.I. 1997 No. 1458) (June 30, 1997);

the Road Vehicles (Construction and Use) (Amendment) (No. 5) Regulations 1997 (S.I. 1997 No. 1544) (August 1, 1997);

the Road Vehicles (Construction and Use) (Amendment) (No. 6) Regulations 1997 (S.I. 1997 No. 2935) (December 31, 1997);

the Road Vehicles (Construction and Use) (Amendment) Regulations 1998 (S.I. 1998 No. 1) (February 2, 1998);

the Road Vehicles (Construction and Use) (Amendment) (No. 2) Regulations 1998 (S.I. 1998 No. 1000) (April 30, 1998);

the Road Vehicles (Construction and Use) (Amendment) (No. 3) Regulations 1998 (S.I. 1998 No. 1188) (June 1, 1998);

the Road Vehicles (Construction and Use) (Amendment) (No. 4) Regulations 1998 (S.I. 1998 No. 1281) (August 1, 1998);

the Road Vehicles (Construction and Use) (Amendment) (No. 5) Regulations 1998 (S.I. 1998 No. 1563) (August 1, 1998);

the Road Vehicles (Construction and Use) (Amendment) (No. 6) Regulations 1998 (S.I. 1998 No. 2429) (November 1, 1998);

the Road Vehicles (Construction and Use) (Amendment) (No. 7) Regulations 1998 (S.I. 1998 No. 3112) (January 1, 1999);

the Road Vehicles (Construction and Use) (Amendment) Regulations 1999 (S.I. 1999 No. 1521) (August 1, 1999);

the Road Vehicles (Construction and Use) (Amendment No. 2) Regulations 1999 (S.I. 1999 No. 1959) (July 31, 1999);

the Road Vehicles (Construction and Use) (Amendment) Regulations 2000 (S.I. 2000 No. 1434) (August 1 and October 1, 2000);

the Road Vehicles (Construction and Use) (Amendment) (No. 2) Regulations 2000 (S.I. 2000 No. 1971) (August 30, 2000);

the Road Vehicles (Construction and Use) (Amendment) (No. 3) Regulations 2000 (S.I. 2000 No. 3197) (January 1, 2001);

the Road Vehicles (Construction and Use) (Amendment) Regulations 2001 (S.I. 2001 No. 306) (March 1, 2001); and

the Road Vehicles (Construction and Use) (Amendment) (No. 2) Regulations 2001 (S.I. 2001 No. 1043) (October 1, 1999);

The amending regulations are referred to in the notes to the principal regulations only by their years and numbers. The dates referred to above are the dates on which the amending regulations came into force.

The Road Vehicles (Construction and Use) (Amendment) (No. 2) Regulations 1988 (S.I. 1988 No. 1102) were revoked on July 12, 1988 (before they were due to take effect) by the Road Vehicles (Construction and Use) (Amendment) (No. 3) Regulations 1988 (S.I. 1988 No. 1177); regulation 3 of the latter regulations expressly stated that the principal regulations should have effect as if the Amendment No. 2 regulations had never been made.

The Amendment No. 2 regulations of 1988, have, in effect, been replaced by the Amendment No. 4 regulations of 1988 (see above), and hence neither the Amendment No. 2 regulations of 1988 nor the Amendment No. 3 regulations of 1988 are referred to in the notes to the principal regulations.

The Road Vehicles (Construction and Use) (Amendment No. 2) Regulations 1999 (S.I. 1999 No. 1959) amended the Road Vehicles (Construction and Use) (Amendment) Regulations 1999 (S.I. 1999 No. 1521) before the latter took effect.

The notes to the appropriate provisions of the regulations indicate where amendments effected by the Road Vehicles (Construction and Use) (Amendment) Regulations 2000 (S.I. 2000 No. 1434) took effect on October 1, 2000.

The Road Vehicles (Construction and Use) (Amendment) (No. 2) Regulations 2001 (S.I. 2001 No. 1043) will take effect from a date (October 1, 2001) after the date at which this volume states the law. The amendments effected by S.I. 2001 No. 1043 are accordingly noted in the notes to the appropriate provisions of the regulations and are not directly incorporated into the text.]

ARRANGEMENT OF REGULATIONS

PART I

PRELIMINARY

PART II

REGULATIONS GOVERNING THE CONSTRUCTION, EQUIPMENT AND MAINTENANCE OF
VEHICLES

A *Dimensions and manoeuvrability*

B *Brakes*

C *Wheels, Springs, Tyres and Tracks*

24. Tyres
25. Tyres for vehicles for which a plating certificate has been issued
26. Mixing of tyres
27. Condition and maintenance of tyres
28. Tracks

D *Steering*

29. Maintenance of steering gear

E *Vision*

30. View to the front
31, 32. Glass
33. Mirrors
34. Windscreen wipers and washers

F *Instruments and Equipment*

35. Speedometers
36. Maintenance of speedometers
36A, 36B. Speed limiters
36C. Speed limiters—authorised sealers
37. Audible warning instruments
38. Motor cycle sidestands

G *Fuel*

39A, 39B. Fuel tanks
40. Gas propulsion systems and gas-fired appliances

H *Minibuses*

41. Construction
42. Fire-extinguishing apparatus
43. First-aid equipment
44. Carriage of dangerous substances

I *Power-to-Weight Ratio*

. . . .

J *Protective Systems*

46. Seat belt anchorage points
47. Seat belts
48. Maintenance of seat belts and anchorage points
48A. Minibuses and coaches to be fitted with additional seat belts when used in certain
      circumstances
49. Rear under-run protection
50. Maintenance of rear under-run protective device
51. Sideguards
52. Maintenance of sideguards
53. Mascots

PART III

PLATES, MARKINGS, TESTING AND INSPECTION

PART IV

CONDITIONS RELATING TO USE

A *Laden Weight*

78. Maximum permitted wheel and axle weights
79. Maximum permitted weights for certain closely-spaced axles, etc.
79A. Saving for the Road Vehicles (Authorised Weight) Regulations 1998
80. Over-riding weight restrictions

B *Dimensions of Laden Vehicles*

81, 82. Restrictions on vehicles carrying wide or long loads or having fixed appliances or apparatus

C *Trailers and Sidecars*

83. Numbers of trailers
84. Trailers drawn by motor cycles
85. Trailers drawn by agricultural motor vehicles
86. Distance between motor vehicles and trailers
86A. Use of secondary couplings on trailers
86B. Use of mechanical coupling devices
87. Unbraked trailers
. . . .
89. Leaving trailers at rest
90. Passengers in trailers
. . . .
92. Attachment of sidecars
93. Use of sidecars

CA *Use of Motor Vehicles for the Carriage or Haulage of Dangerous Goods*

93A. Additional braking requirements for motor vehicles carrying or hauling dangerous goods

D *Use of Gas Propulsion Systems and Gas-fired Appliances*

94. Use of gas propulsion systems
95. Use of gas-fired appliances—general
96. Use of gas-fired appliances when vehicle is in motion

E *Control of Noise*

97. Avoidance of excessive noise
98. Stopping of engine when stationary
99. Use of audible warning instruments

F *Avoidance of Danger*

100. Maintenance and use of vehicle so as not to be a danger
100A. Speed of low platform trailers and restricted speed vehicles
101. Parking in darkness
102. Passengers on motor cycles
103. Obstruction
104. Driver's control
105. Opening of doors
106. Reversing
107. Leaving motor vehicles unattended
108. Securing of suspended implements
109. Television sets

SCHEDULES

PART I

PRELIMINARY

B27.04   **1. Commencement and citation**   *[Omitted.]*

2. Revocation   *[Omitted.]*

3. Interpretation

B27.05   (1) In these Regulations, unless the context otherwise requires—

(a) any reference to a numbered regulation or a numbered Schedule is a reference to the regulation or Schedule bearing that number in these Regulations,

(b) any reference to a numbered or lettered paragraph or sub-paragraph is a reference to the paragraph or sub-paragraph bearing that number or letter in the regulation or Schedule or (in the case of a sub-paragraph) paragraph in which the reference occurs, and

(c) any reference to a Table, or to a numbered Table, is a reference to the Table, or to the Table bearing that number, in the regulation or Schedule in which that reference occurs.

(2) In these Regulations, unless the context otherwise requires, the expressions specified in column 1 of the Table have the meaning, or are to be interpreted in accordance with the provisions, specified for them in column 2 of the Table.

TABLE

(regulation 3(2))

1	2
Expression	*Meaning*
The 1971 Act	The Vehicles (Excise) Act 1971.
The [1988 Act]	The [Road Traffic Act 1988].
The 1981 Act	The Public Passenger Vehicles Act 1981.
The 1984 Act	The Road Traffic Regulation Act 1984.
[The 1994 Act]	[The Vehicle Excise and Registration Act 1994].
The Approval Marks Regulations	The Motor Vehicles (Designation of Approval Marks) Regulations 1979 [*S.I. 1979 No. 1088, as amended*].
The Lighting Regulations	[The Road Vehicles Lighting Regulations 1989 [*S.I. 1989 No. 1796, q.v.*]].
The Plating and Test- ing Regulations	The [Goods Vehicles (Plating and Testing) Regulations 1988] [*S.I. 1988 No. 1478, q.v.*].
The Type Approval Regulations	The Motor Vehicles (Type Approval) Regulations 1980 [*S.I. 1980 No. 1182, as amended*].
The Type Approval Great Britain) Regulations	The Motor Vehicles (Type Approval) (Great Britain) Regulations 1984 [*S.I. 1984 No. 981, as amended, q.v.*].
The Type Approval for Goods Vehicles Regulations	The Motor Vehicles (Type Approval for Goods Vehicles) (Great Britain) Regulations 1982 [*S.I. 1982 No. 1271, as amended, q.v.*].
The Type Approval for Agricultural Vehicles Regulations	The Agricultural or Forestry Tractors and Tractor Compo- nents (Type Approval) Regulations 1988 [*S.I. 1988 No. 1567, as amended; not reproduced in this work*].
The Act of Accession	The Treaty concerning the Accession of the Kingdom of Denmark, Ireland, the Kingdom of Norway and the United Kingdom of Great Britain and Northern Ireland to the European Economic Community and the European Atomic Energy Community [*Cmnd. 5179–I*].
[agricultural or forestry tractor	an agricultural or forestry tractor within the meaning of Community Directive 82/890.]
agricultural motor vehicle	a motor vehicle which is constructed or adapted for use off roads for the purpose of agriculture, horticulture or forestry and which is primarily used for one or more of those purposes, not being a dual-purpose vehicle.
agricultural trailer	a trailer which is constructed or adapted for the purpose of agriculture, horticulture or forestry and which is only used

[continued on next page

1	*2*
Expression	*Meaning*
agricultural trailer—cont.	for one or more of those purposes, not being an agricultural trailed appliance.
agricultural trailed appliance	a trailer—
	(a) which is an implement constructed or adapted—
	(i) for use off roads for the purpose of agriculture, horticulture or forestry and which is only used for one or more of those purposes, and
	(ii) so that, save in the case of an appliance manufactured before 1st December 1985, or a towed roller, its maximum gross weight is not more than twice its unladen weight; but
	(b) which is not—
	(i) a vehicle which is used primarily as living accommodation by one or more persons, and which carries no goods or burden except those needed by such one or more persons for the purpose of their residence in the vehicle; or
	(ii) an agricultural, horticultural or forestry implement rigidly but not permanently mounted on any vehicle whether or not any of the weight of the implement is supported by one or more of its own wheels; so however that such an implement is an agricultural trailed appliance if
	—part of the weight of the implement is supported by one or more of its own wheels, and
	—the longitudinal axis of the greater part of the implement is capable of articulating in the horizontal plane in relation to the longitudinal axis of the rear portion of the vehicle which is mounted.
agricultural trailed appliance conveyor	an agricultural trailer which—
	(a) has an unladen weight which does not exceed 510kg;
	(b) is clearly and indelibly marked with its unladen weight;
	(c) has a pneumatic tyre fitted to each one of its wheels;
	(d) is designed and constructed for the purpose of conveying one agricultural trailed appliance or one agricultural, horticultural or forestry implement.
articulated bus	a bus so constructed that—
	(a) it can be divided into two parts, both of which are vehicles and one of which is a motor vehicle, but

[continued on next page

1	*2*
Expression	*Meaning*
articulated bus—cont.	cannot be so divided without the use of facilities normally available only at a workshop; and (b) passengers carried by it can at all times pass from either part to the other.
articulated vehicle	a heavy motor car or motor car, not being an articulated bus, with a trailer so attached that part of the trailer is superimposed on the drawing vehicle and, when the trailer is uniformly loaded, not less than 20% of the weight of its load is borne by the drawing vehicle.
axle	any reference to the number of axles of a vehicle is to be interpreted in accordance with paragraph (8).
axle weight	in relation to each axle of a vehicle, the sum of the weights transmitted to the road surface by all the wheels of that axle, having regard to the provisions of paragraph (8).
braking efficiency	the maximum braking force capable of being developed by the brakes of a vehicle, expressed as a percentage of the weight of the vehicle including any persons or load carried in the vehicle.
braking system	is to be interpreted in accordance with paragraph (6).
bus	a motor vehicle which is constructed or adapted to carry more than eight seated passengers in addition to the driver.
[car transporter	a trailer which is constructed and normally used for the purpose of carrying at least two other wheeled vehicles.]
cc	cubic centimetre(s).
close-coupled	in relation to wheels on the same side of a trailer, fitted so that at all times while the trailer is in motion they remain parallel to the longitudinal axis of the trailer, and that the distance between the centres of their respective areas of contact with the road surface does not exceed 1m.
closely spaced	[revoked.]
cm	centimetre(s).
cm^2	square centimetre(s).
[coach	a large bus with a maximum gross weight of more than 7.5 tonnes and with a maximum speed exceeding 60mph.]
Community Directive, followed by a number	the Directive adopted by the Council or the Commission of the European Communities of which identifying particulars are given in the item in column 3 of Table I in Schedule 2 in which that number appears in column 2; where such a

[*continued on next page*

1	*2*
Expression	*Meaning*
Community Directive—cont.	Directive amends a previous Directive mentioned in column 3(d) of the Table [the reference to the amending Directive includes a reference to] that previous Directive as so amended. Any reference to a Directive which has been amended by the Act of Accession is a reference to the Directive as so amended.
the Community Recording Equipment Regulation	[Council Regulation (EEC) 3821/85 of 20th December 1985 on recording equipment in road transport [*O.J. L370, December 31, 1985, p. 8 (q.v.)*], as read with the Community Drivers' Hours and Recording Equipment (Exemptions and Supplementary Provisions) Regulations 1986 [*S.I. 1986 No. 1456, as amended, q.v.*].]
[*combined transport operation*	shall be construed in accordance with paragraph 9 of Schedule 11A]
composite trailer	a combination of a converter dolly and a semi-trailer.
container	an article of equipment, not being a motor vehicle or trailer, having a volume of at least 8 cubic metres, constructed wholly or mostly of metal and intended for repeated use for the carriage of goods or burden.

converter dolly	[(a) a trailer which is—
	   (i) equipped with 2 or more wheels,
	   (ii) designed to be used in combination with a semi-trailer without any part of the weight of the semi-trailer being borne by the drawing vehicle, and
	   (iii) not itself a part either of the semi-trailer or the drawing vehicle when being so used; or
	(b) a trailer which is—
	   (i) equipped with 2 or more wheels;
	   (ii) designed to be used in combination with a semi-trailer with part of the weight of the semi-trailer being borne by the drawing vehicle;
	   (iii) not itself a part either of the semi-trailer or the drawing vehicle when being so used; and
	   (iv) used solely for the purposes of agriculture, horticulture or forestry, or for any two or for all of those purposes.]

Council Regulation (EEC), followed by a number	the Regulation adopted by the Council of the European Communities.
deck	a floor or platform on which seats are provided for the accommodation of passengers.

[continued on next page

1	*2*
Expression	*Meaning*
design weight	in relation to the gross weight, each axle weight or the train weight of a motor vehicle or trailer, the weight at or below which in the opinion of the Secretary of State or of a person authorised in that behalf by the Secretary of State the vehicle could safely be driven on roads.
double-decked vehicle	a vehicle having two decks one of which is wholly or partly above the other and each of which is provided with a gangway serving seats on that deck only.
dual-purpose vehicle	a vehicle constructed or adapted for the carriage both of passengers and of goods or burden of any description, being a vehicle of which the unladen weight does not exceed 2040kg, and which either—

(i) is so constructed or adapted that the driving power of the engine is, or by the appropriate use of the controls of the vehicle can be, transmitted to all the wheels of the vehicle; or

(ii) satisfies the following conditions as to construction, namely—

    (a) the vehicle must be permanently fitted with a rigid roof, with or without a sliding panel;

    (b) the area of the vehicle to the rear of the driver's seat must—

        (i) be permanently fitted with at least one row of transverse seats (fixed or folding) for two or more passengers and those seats must be properly sprung or cushioned and provided with upholstered back-rests, attached either to the seats or to a side or the floor of the vehicle; and

        (ii) be lit on each side and at the rear by a window or windows of glass or other transparent material having an area or aggregate area of not less that 1850 square centimetres on each side and not less than 770 square centimetres at the rear; and

    (c) the distance between the rearmost part of the steering wheel and the back-rests of the row of transverse seats satisfying the requirements specified in head (i) of sub-paragraph (b) (or, if there is more than one such row of seats, the distance between the rearmost part of the steering wheel and the back-rests of the rearmost such row) must, when the seats are ready for use, be not less than one-third of the distance between the rearmost part of the steering wheel and the rearmost part of the floor of the vehicle.

[continued on next page

1	*2*
Expression	*Meaning*
ECE Regulation, followed by a number	the Regulation, annexed to the Agreement concerning the adoption of uniform conditions of approval for Motor Vehicles Equipment and Parts and reciprocal recognition thereof concluded at Geneva on 20th March 1958 [*Cmnd. 2535*] as amended [*Cmnd. 3562*], to which the United Kingdom is party [*instrument of accession dated January 14, 1963 deposited with the Secretary-General of the United Nations on January 15, 1963*], of which identifying particulars are given in the item in column (3)(a), (b) and (c) of Table II in Schedule 2 in which that number appears in column (2); and where that number contains more than two digits, it refers to that Regulation with the amendments in force at the date specified in column (3)(d) in that item.
engine power in kilowatts (kW)	the maximum net power ascertained in accordance with Community Directive 80/1269.
engineering plant	(a) movable plant or equipment being a motor vehicle or trailer specially designed and constructed for the special purposes of engineering operations, and which cannot, owing to the requirements of those purposes, comply with all the requirements of these Regulations and which is not constructed primarily to carry a load other than a load being either excavated materials raised from the ground by apparatus on the motor vehicle or trailer or materials which the vehicle or trailer is specially designed to treat while carried thereon; or (b) a mobile crane which does not comply in all respects with the requirements of these Regulations.
[engineering equipment	engineering plant and any other plant or equipment designed and constructed for the purpose of engineering operations.]
exhaust system	a complete set of components through which the exhaust gases escape from the engine unit of a motor vehicle including those which are necessary to limit the noise caused by the escape of those gases.
first used	is to be interpreted in accordance with paragraph (3).
[Framework Directive	Council Directive 70/156/EEC [*O.J. L42, February 23, 1970, p. 1*] as amended by Council Directive 87/403/EEC [*O.J. L220, August 8, 1987, p. 44*], Council Directive 92/53/EEC [*O.J. L225, August 10, 1992, p. 1*] and Commission Directive 93/81 [*O.J. L264, October 23, 1993, p. 49*].]
gangway	the space provided for obtaining access from any entrance to the passengers' seats or from any such seat to an exit other than an emergency exit, but excluding a staircase and any space in front of a seat which is required only for the use of passengers occupying that seat or a seat in the same row of seats.

[continued on next page

1	2
Expression	*Meaning*
gas	any fuel which is wholly gaseous at 17.5°C under a pressure of 1.013 bar absolute.
gas-fired appliance	a device carried on a motor vehicle or trailer when in use on a road, which consumes gas and which is neither— (a) a device owned or operated by or with the authority of the British Gas Corporation for the purpose of detecting gas, nor (b) an engine for the propulsion of a motor vehicle, nor (c) a lamp which consumes acetylene gas.
goods vehicle	a motor vehicle or trailer constructed or adapted for use for the carriage or haulage of goods or burden of any description.
gritting trailer	a trailer which is used on a road for the purpose of spreading grit or other matter so as to avoid or reduce the effect of ice or snow on the road.
gross weight	(a) in relation to a motor vehicle, the sum of the weights transmitted to the road surface by all the wheels of the vehicle, (b) in relation to a trailer, the sum of the weights transmitted to the road surface by all the wheels of the trailer and of any weight of the trailer imposed on the drawing vehicle.
heavy motor car	a mechanically propelled vehicle, not being a locomotive, a motor tractor, or a motor car, which is constructed itself to carry a load or passengers and the weight of which unladen exceeds 2540kg.
indivisible load	a load which cannot without undue expense or risk of damage be divided into two or more loads for the purpose of conveyance on a road.
industrial tractor	a tractor, not being an agricultural motor vehicle, which— (a) has an unladen weight not exceeeding 7370kg, (b) is designed and used primarily for work off roads, or for work on roads in connection only with road construction or maintenance (including any such tractor when fitted with an implement or implements designed primarily for use in connection with such work, whether or not any such implement is of itself designed to carry a load), and (c) has a maximum speed not exceeding 20mph.
invalid carriage	a mechanically propelled vehicle the weight of which unladen does not exceed 254kg and which is specially designed and constructed, and not merely adapted, for the

[*continued on next page*

1	*2*
Expression	*Meaning*
invalid carriage—cont.	use of a person suffering from some physical defect or disability and is solely used by such a person.

kerbside weight	the weight of a vehicle when it carries—
	(a) in the case of a motor vehicle,
	    (i) no person; and
	    (ii) a full supply of fuel in its tank, an adequate supply of other liquids incidental to its propulsion and no load other than the loose tools and equipment with which it is normally equipped;
	(b) in the case of a trailer, no person and is otherwise unladen.

kg	kilogram(s).
km/h	kilometre(s) per hour.
kW	kilowatt(s).
[*large bus*	a vehicle constructed or adapted to carry more than 16 seated passengers in addition to the driver.]
[*light trailer*	a trailer with a maximum gross weight which does not exceed 3500kg.]
living van	a vehicle used primarily as living accommodation by one or more persons, and which is not also used for the carriage of goods or burden which are not needed by such one or more persons for the purpose of their residence in the vehicle.
locomotive	a mechanically propelled vehicle which is not constructed itself to carry a load other than the following articles, that is to say, water, fuel, accumulators and other equipment used for the purpose of propulsion, loose tools and loose equipment, and the weight of which unladen exceeds 7370kg.
longitudinal plane	a vertical plane parallel to the longitudinal axis of a vehicle.
[*low loader*	a semi-trailer which is constructed and normally used for the carriage of engineering equipment so constructed that the major part of the load platform does not extend over or between the wheels and the upper surface of which is below the height of the topmost point of the tyres of those wheels, measured on level ground and when— (a) any adjustable suspension is at the normal travelling height, (b) all pneumatic tyres are suitably inflated for use when the vehicle is fully laden, and (c) the semi-trailer is unladen, (see also the definition of stepframe low loader).]
[*low platform trailer*	a trailer fitted with tyres with a rim diameter size code less than 20 and displaying a rectangular plate which—

[continued on next page

1	*2*
Expression	*Meaning*
low platform trailer—cont.	(a) is at least 225mm wide and at least 175mm high; and (b) bears two black letters "L" on a white ground each at least 125mm high and 90mm wide with a stroke width of 12mm.]
m	metre(s).
m^2	square metre(s).
m^3	cubic metre(s).
[*maximum permitted axle weight*	in relation to an axle— (a) in the case of a vehicle which is equipped with a Ministry plate in accordance with regulation 70, the axle weight shown in column (2) of that plate (where the plate is in the form required by [Schedule 10 or 10B]) or in column (2) of that plate (where the plate is in the form required by [Schedule 10A or 10C]) in relation to that axle; (b) in the case of a vehicle which is not equipped with a Ministry plate but which is equipped with a plate in accordance with regulation 66, the maximum axle weight shown for that axle on the plate in respect of item 9 of Part I of Schedule 8 in the case of a motor vehicle and item 7 of Part II of Schedule 8 in the case of a trailer; and (c) in any other case, the weight which the axle is designed or adapted not to exceed when the vehicle is travelling on the road.]
maximum gross weight	(a) in the case of a vehicle equipped with a Ministry plate in accordance with regulation 70, the design gross weight shown in column (3) of that plate [(where the plate is in the form required by [Schedule 10 or 10B]) or in column (4) of that plate (where the plate is in the form required by [Schedule 10A or 10C])] or, if no such weight is shown, the gross weight shown in column (2) of that plate; (b) in the case of a vehicle not equipped with a Ministry plate, but which is equipped with a plate in accordance with regulation 66, the maximum gross weight shown on the plate in respect of item 7 of Part 1 of Schedule 8 in the case of a motor vehicle and item 6 of Part II of Schedule 8 in the case of a trailer; (c) in any other case, the weight which the vehicle is designed or adapted not to exceed when the vehicle is travelling on a road.

[*continued on next page*

1	*2*
Expression	*Meaning*
[*maximum total design axle weight* (an expression used only in relation to trailers)	(a) in the case of a trailer equipped with a Ministry plate in accordance with regulation 70, the sum of the relevant axle weights; (b) in the case of a trailer which is not equipped with a Ministry plate, but which is equipped with a plate in accordance with regulation 66, the sum of the maximum axle weights shown on the plate in respect of item 4 of Part II of Schedule 8; or (c) in the case of any other trailer, the sum of the axle weights which the trailer is designed or adapted not to exceed when the vehicle is travelling on a road; and for the purposes of sub-paragraph (a) the relevant axle weight, in respect to an axle, is the design axle weight shown in column (3) of the Ministry plate (where the plate is in the form required by [Schedule 10 or 10B]) or in column (4) of that plate (where the plate is in the form required by [Schedule 10A or 10C]) in relation to that axle or if no such weight is shown, the axle weight shown in column (2) of that plate in relation to that axle.]
maximum speed	the speed which a vehicle is incapable, by reason of its construction, of exceeding on the level under its own power when fully laden.
minibus	a motor vehicle which is constructed or adapted to carry more than 8 but not more than 16 seated passengers in addition to the driver.
Ministry plate	[is to be interpreted in accordance with regulation 70].
mm	millimetre(s).
motor ambulance	a motor vehicle which is specially designed and constructed (and not merely adapted) for carrying, as equipment permanently fixed to the vehicle, equipment used for medical, dental, or other health purposes and is used primarily for the carriage of persons suffering from illness, injury or disability.
motor car	a mechanically propelled vehicle, not being a motor tractor, a motor cycle or an invalid carriage, which is constructed itself to carry a load or passengers and the weight of which unladen— (a) if it is constructed solely for the carriage of passengers and their effects and is adapted to carry not more than seven passengers exclusive of the driver does not exceed 3050kg; (b) if it is constructed for use for the conveyance of goods or burden of any description, does not exceed 3050kg;

[*continued on next page*

1	*2*
Expression	*Meaning*
motor car—cont.	(c) does not exceed 2540kg in a case falling within neither of the foregoing paragraphs.
[*motor caravan*	a motor vehicle which is constructed or adapted for the carriage of passengers and their effects and which contains, as permanently installed equipment, the facilities which are reasonably necessary for enabling the vehicle to provide mobile living accommodation for its users.]
motor cycle	a mechanically propelled vehicle, not being an invalid carriage, having less than four wheels and the weight of which unladen does not exceed 410kg.
motor tractor	a mechanically propelled vehicle which is not constructed itself to carry a load, other than the following articles, that is to say, water, fuel, accumulators and other equipment used for the purpose of propulsion, loose tools and loose equipment, and the weight of which unladen does not exceed 7370kg.
motor vehicle	a mechanically propelled vehicle intended or adapted for use on roads.
mph	mile(s) per hour.
N/mm^2	newton(s) per square millimetre.
[*off-road vehicle*	an off-road vehicle as defined in Annex I to Council Directive 70/156/EEC of 6th February 1970 [*q.v.*] as read with Council Directive 87/403/EEC of 25th June 1987.]
overall height	the vertical distance between the ground and the point on the vehicle which is furthest from the ground, calculated when— (a) the tyres of the vehicle are suitably inflated for the use to which it is being put; (b) the vehicle is at its unladen weight; and (c) the surface of the ground under the vehicle is reasonably flat; but, in the case of a trolley bus, exclusive of the power collection equipment mounted on the roof of the vehicle.
overall length	in relation to a vehicle, the distance between transverse planes passing through the extreme forward and rearward projecting points of the vehicle inclusive of all parts of the vehicle, of any receptacle which is of a permanent character and accordingly strong enough for repeated use, and any fitting on, or attached to, the vehicle except— (i) for all purposes— (a) any driving mirror; (b) any expanding or extensible contrivance forming part of a turntable fire escape fixed to a vehicle;

[*continued on next page*

1	*2*
Expression	*Meaning*
overall length—cont.	(c) any snow-plough fixed in front of a vehicle;
	(d) any receptacle specially designed to hold and keep secure a seal issued for the purposes of customs clearance;
	(e) any tailboard which is let down while the vehicle is stationary in order to facilitate its unloading;
	(f) any tailboard which is let down in order to facilitate the carriage of, but which is not essential for the support of, loads which are in themselves so long as to extend at least as far as the tailboard when upright;
	(g) any fitting attached to a part of, or to a receptacle on, a vehicle which does not increase the carrying capacity of the part or receptacle but which enables it to be —transferred from a road vehicle to a railway vehicle or from a railway vehicle to a road vehicle, —secured to a railway vehicle by a locking device, and —carried on a railway vehicle by the use of stanchions:
	(h) any plate, whether rigid or movable, fitted to a trailer constructed for the purpose of carrying other vehicles and designed to bridge the gap between that trailer and a motor vehicle constructed for that purpose and to which the trailer is attached so that, while the trailer is attached to the motor vehicle, vehicles which are to be carried by the motor vehicle may be moved from the trailer to the motor vehicle before a journey begins, and vehicles which have been carried on the motor vehicle may be moved from it to the trailer after a journey ends;
	(i) any sheeting or other readily flexible means of covering or securing a load;
	(j) any receptacle with an external length, measured parallel to the longitudinal axis of the vehicle, not exceeding 2.5m;
	(k) any empty receptacle which itself forms a load;
	(l) any receptacle which contains an indivisible load of exceptional length;
	(m) any receptacle manufactured before 30th October 1985, not being a maritime container (namely a container designed primarily for

[*continued on next page*

1	*2*
Expression	*Meaning*

overall length—cont.	carriage on sea transport without an accompanying road vehicle); . . .
	 (n) any special appliance or apparatus as described in regulation 81(c) which does not itself increase the carrying capacity of the vehicle; [or]
	 [(o) any rearward projecting buffer made of rubber or other resilient material.]
	 (ii) for the purposes of [regulations 7, 13A, 13B and 13C]
	    (a) any part of a trailer (not being in the case of an agricultural trailed appliance a drawbar or other thing with which it is equipped for the purpose of being towed) designed primarily for use as a means of attaching it to another vehicle and any fitting designed for use in connection with any such part;
	    (b) the thickness of any front or rear wall on a semi-trailer and of any part forward of such front wall or rearward of such rear wall which does not increase the vehicle's load-carrying space.

overall width	the distance between longitudinal planes passing through extreme lateral projecting points of the vehicle inclusive of all parts of the vehicle, of any receptacle which is of permanent character and accordingly strong enough for repeated use, and any fitting on, or attached to, the vehicle except— (a) any driving mirror; (b) any snow-plough fixed in front of the vehicle; (c) so much of the distortion of any tyre as is caused by the weight of the vehicle; (d) any receptacle specially designed to hold and keep secure a seal issued for the purpose of customs clearance; (e) any lamp or reflector fitted to the vehicle in accordance with the Lighting Regulations; (f) any sideboard which is let down while the vehicle is stationary in order to facilitate its loading or unloading; (g) any fitting attached to part of, or to a receptacle on, a vehicle which does not increase the carrying capacity of the part or receptacle but which enables it to be —transferred from a road vehicle to a railway vehicle or from a railway vehicle to a road vehicle; —secured to a railway vehicle by a locking device; and —carried on a railway vehicle by the use of stanchions;

[continued on next page

1	*2*
Expression	*Meaning*
overall width—cont.	(h) any sheeting or other readily flexible means of covering or securing a load; (i) any receptacle with an external width, measured at right angles to the longitudinal axis of the vehicle, which does not exceed 2.5m; (j) any empty receptacle which itself forms a load; (k) any receptacle which contains an indivisible load of exceptional width; (l) any receptacle manufactured before 30th October 1985, not being a maritime container (namely a container designed primarily for carriage on sea transport without an accompanying road vehicle); . . . (m) any special appliance or apparatus as described in regulation 81(c) which does not itself increase the carrying capacity of the vehicle [; or] [(n) any apparatus fitted to a bus which enables it to be guided wholly or mainly by means of wheels bearing outwards against fixed apparatus, provided that no part of the apparatus projects more than 75mm beyond the side of the bus when the wheels of the bus are parallel to its longitudinal axis; and the reference in paragraph above to the side of a bus is a reference to the longitudinal plane passing through the extreme lateral projecting points of the vehicle inclusive of all parts of the vehicle, of any receptacle which is of permanent character and accordingly strong enough for repeated use, and any fitting on, or attached to, the vehicle except those items referred to in paragraphs (a) to (n).]
overhang	the distance measured horizontally and parallel to the longitudinal axis of a vehicle between two transverse planes passing through the following two points— (a) the rearmost point of the vehicle exclusive of— (i) any expanding or extensible contrivance forming part of a turntable fire escape fixed to a vehicle; (ii) in the case of a motor car constructed solely for the carriage of passengers and their effects and adapted to carry not more than eight passengers exclusive of the driver, any luggage carrier fitted to the vehicle; and (b) (i) in the case of a motor vehicle having not more than three axles of which only one is not a steering axle, the centre point of that axle;

[*continued on next page*

1	*2*
Expression	*Meaning*
overhang—cont.	(ii) in the case of a motor vehicle having three axles of which the front axle is the only steering axle and of a motor vehicle having four axles of which the two foremost are the only steering axles, a point 110mm behind the centre of a straight line joining the centre points of the two rearmost axles; and (iii) in any other case a point situated on the longitudinal axis of the vehicle and such that a line drawn from it at right angles to that axis will pass through the centre of the minimum turning circle of the vehicle.
passenger vehicle	a vehicle constructed solely for the carriage of passengers and their effects.
pedestrian-controlled vehicle	a motor vehicle which is controlled by a pedestrian and not constructed or adapted for use or used for the carriage of a driver or passenger.
pneumatic tyre	a tyre which— (a) is provided with, or together with the wheel upon which it is mounted forms, a continuous closed chamber inflated to a pressure substantially exceeding atmospheric pressure when the tyre is in the condition in which it is normally used, but is not subjected to any load; (b) is capable of being inflated and deflated without removal from the wheel or vehicle; and (c) is such that, when it is deflated and is subjected to a normal load, the sides of the tyre collapse.
public works vehicle	[a mechanically propelled vehicle which is used on a road by or on behalf of— (a) the Central Scotland Water Development Board; (b) a ferry undertaking; (c) a highway or roads authority; (d) a local authority; (e) a market undertaking; (f) the National Rivers Authority; (g) an operator of a telecommunications code system within the meaning of paragraph 1 (1) of Schedule 4 to the Telecommunications Act 1984; (h) a police authority; (i) the Post Office; (j) a public electricity supplier within the meaning of Part I of the Electricity Act 1989; (k) [a public gas transporter within the meaning of Part I of the Gas Act 1986];

[continued on next page

1	*2*
Expression	*Meaning*
public works vehicle—cont.	(l) a statutory undertaker within the meaning of section 329(1) of the Highways Act 1980 [*q.v.*]; (m) an undertaking for the supply of district heating; (n) a water authority within the meaning of the Water (Scotland) Act 1980; or (o) a water or sewerage undertaking within the meaning of the Water Act 1989; for the purpose of works which such a body has a duty or power to carry out, and which is used only for the carriage of— (i) the crew, and (ii) goods which are needed for works in respect of which the vehicle is used.]
recut pneumatic tyre	a pneumatic tyre in which all or part of its original tread pattern has been cut deeper or burnt deeper or a different tread pattern has been cut deeper or burnt deeper than the original tread pattern.
refuse vehicle	a vehicle designed for use and used solely in connection with street cleansing, the collection or disposal of refuse, or the collection or disposal of the contents of gullies or cesspools.
registered	registered under any of the following enactments— (a) the Roads Act 1920 (b) the Vehicles (Excise) Act 1949 (c) the Vehicles (Excise) Act 1962, or (d) the 1971 Act [or the 1994 Act] and, in relation to the date on which a vehicle was registered, the date on which it was first registered under any of those enactments.
relevant braking requirement	a requirement that the brakes of a motor vehicle (as assisted, where a trailer is being drawn, by the brakes on the trailer) comply— (i) in a case to which item 1 in Table 1 in regulation 18 applies, with the requirements specified in regulation 18(3) for vehicles falling in that item; (ii) in any other case, with the requirements specified in regulation 18(3) for vehicle classes (a) and (b) in item 2 of that Table (whatever the date of first use of the motor vehicle and the date of manufacture of any trailer drawn by it may be).
resilient tyre	a tyre, not being a pneumatic tyre, which is of soft or elastic material, having regard to paragraph (5).

[*continued on next page*

1	2
Expression	*Meaning*
[*restricted speed vehicle*	a vehicle displaying at its rear a "50" plate in accordance with the requirements of Schedule 13.]
[*retreaded tyre*	a tyre which has been reconditioned to extend its useful life by replacement of the tread rubber or by replacement of the tread rubber and renovation of the sidewall rubber.]
rigid vehicle	a motor vehicle which is not constructed or adapted to form part of an articulated vehicle or articulated bus.
[*rim diameter*	is to be interpreted in accordance with the British Standard BS AU 50: Part 2: Section 1: 1980 entitled "British Standard Automobile Series: Specification for Tyres and Wheels Part 2. Wheels and rims Section 1. Rim profiles and dimensions (including openings for valves)" which came into effect on 28th November 1980.]
[*rim diameter size code*	is to be interpreted in accordance with the British Standard referred to in the meaning given in this Table to "rim diameter".]
secondary braking system	a braking system of a vehicle applied by a secondary means of operation independent of the service braking system or by one of the sections comprised in a split braking system.
service braking system	the braking system of a vehicle which is designed and constructed to have the highest braking efficiency of any of the braking systems with which the vehicle is equipped.
semi-trailer	a trailer which is constructed or adapted to form part of an articulated vehicle [including (without prejudice to the generality of that) a vehicle which is not itself a motor vehicle but which has some or all of its wheels driven by the drawing vehicle].
silencer	a contrivance suitable and sufficient for reducing as far as may be reasonable the noise caused by the escape of exhaust gases from the engine of a motor vehicle.
single-decked vehicle	a vehicle upon which no part of a deck or gangway is vertically above another deck or gangway.
split braking system	in relation to a motor vehicle, a braking system so designed and constructed that— (a) it comprises two independent sections of mechanism capable of developing braking force such that, excluding the means of operation, a failure of any part (other than a fixed member or a brake shoe anchor pin) of one of the said sections will not cause a decrease in the braking force capable of being developed by the other section;

[*continued on next page*

1	*2*
Expression	*Meaning*
split braking system—cont.	(b) the said two sections are operated by a means of operation which is common to both sections; (c) the braking efficiency of either of the said two sections can be readily checked.
[*staircase*	a staircase by means of which passengers on a double-decked vehicle may pass to and from the upper deck of the vehicle.]
[*stepframe low loader*	a semi-trailer (not being a low loader) which is constructed and normally used for the carriage of engineering equipment and is so constructed that the upper surface of the major part of the load platform is at a height of less than 1m above the ground when measured on level ground and when— (a) any adjustable suspensions are at the normal travelling height, (b) all pneumatic tyres are suitably inflated for use when the vehicle is fully laden, and (c) the semi-trailer is unladen.]
stored energy	in relation to a braking system of a vehicle, energy (other than the muscular energy of the driver or the mechanical energy of a spring) stored in a reservoir for the purpose of applying the brakes under the control of the driver, either directly or as a supplement to his muscular energy.
straddle carrier	a motor vehicle constructed to straddle and lift its load for the purpose of transportation.
statutory power of removal	a power conferred by or under any enactment to remove or move a vehicle from any road or from any part of a road.
temporary use spare tyre	a pneumatic tyre which is designed for use on a motor vehicle only— (a) in the event of a failure of one of the tyres normally fitted to a wheel of the vehicle, and (b) at a speed lower than that for which such normally fitted tyres are designed.
three-wheeled motor cycle	a motor cycle having three wheels, not including a two-wheeled motor cycle with a sidecar attached.
towing implement	a device on wheels designed for the purpose of enabling a motor vehicle to draw another vehicle by the attachment of that device to that other vehicle in such a manner that part of that other vehicle is secured to and either rests on or is suspended from the device and some but not all of the wheels on which that other vehicle normally runs are raised off the ground.
track-laying	in relation to a vehicle, so designed and constructed that the weight thereof is transmitted to the road surface either by

[*continued on next page*

1	*2*
Expression	Meaning
track laying—cont.	means of continuous tracks or by a combination of wheels and continuous tracks in such circumstances that the weight transmitted to the road surface by the tracks is not less than half the weight of the vehicle.
trailer	means a vehicle drawn by a motor vehicle and is to be interpreted in accordance with paragraphs (9) and (11).
train weight	in relation to a motor vehicle which may draw a trailer, the maximum laden weight for the motor vehicle together with any trailer which may be drawn by it.
transverse plane	a vertical plane at right angles to the longitudinal axis of a vehicle.
trolley bus	a bus adapted for use on roads without rails and moved by power transmitted thereto from some external source.
unbraked trailer	any trailer other than one which, whether or not regulation 15 or 16 applies to it, is equipped with a braking system in accordance with one of those regulations.
unladen weight	the weight of a vehicle or trailer inclusive of the body and all parts (the heavier being taken where alternative bodies or parts are used) which are necessary to or ordinarily used with the vehicle or trailer when working on a road, but exclusive of the weight of water, fuel or accumulators used for the purpose of the supply of power for the propulsion of the vehicle or, as the case may be, of any vehicle by which the trailer is drawn, and of loose tools and loose equipment.
vehicle in the service of a visiting force or of a headquarters	a vehicle so described in Article 8(6) of the Visiting Forces and International Headquarters (Application of Law) Order 1965 [*S.I. 1965 No. 1536*].
wheel	a wheel the tyre or rim of which when the vehicle is in motion on a road is in contact with the ground; two wheels are to be regarded as one wheel in the circumstances specified in paragraph (7).
wheeled	in relation to a vehicle, so constructed that the whole weight of the vehicle is transmitted to the road surface by means of wheels.
wide tyre	a pneumatic tyre of which the area of contact with the road surface is not less than 300mm in width when measured at right angles to the longitudinal axis of the vehicle.
works trailer	a trailer designed for use in private premises and used on a road only in delivering goods from or to such premises to or from a vehicle on a road in the immediate neighbourhood, or in passing from one part of any such premises to another or to other private premises in the immediate neighbourhood or

[*continued on next page*

1	2
Expression	*Meaning*
works trailer—cont.	in connection with road works while at or in the immediate neighbourhood of the site of such works.
works truck	a motor vehicle (other than a straddle carrier) designed for use in private premises and used on a road only in delivering goods from or to such premises to or from a vehicle on a road in the immediate neighbourhood, or in passing from one part of any such premises to another or to other private premises in the immediate neighbourhood or in connection with road works while at or in the immediate neighbourhood of the site of such works.

[(2A) Without prejudice to section 17 of the Interpretation Act 1978 and subject to the context, a reference in these Regulations to any enactment comprised in subordinate legislation (within the meaning of that Act) is a reference to that enactment as from time to time amended or re-enacted with or without modification.]

(3) For the purpose of these Regulations, the date on which a motor vehicle is first used is—

(a) in the case of a vehicle not falling within sub-paragraph (b) and which is registered, the date on which it was registered;

(b) in each of the following cases—

(i) a vehicle which is being or has been used under a trade licence as defined in [section 11 of the 1994 Act] (otherwise than for the purposes of demonstration or testing or of being delivered from premises of the manufacturer by whom it was made or of a distributor of vehicles, or dealer in vehicles, to premises of a distributor of vehicles, dealer in vehicles or purchaser thereof or to premises of a person obtaining possession thereof under a hiring agreement or hire purchase agreement);

(ii) a vehicle belonging, or which has belonged, to the Crown and which is or was used or appropriated for use for naval, military or air force purposes;

(iii) a vehicle belonging, or which has belonged, to a visiting force or a headquarters or defence organisation to which in each case the Visiting Forces and International Headquarters (Application of Law) Order 1965 applies;

(iv) a vehicle which has been used on roads outside Great Britain before being imported into Great Britain; and

(v) a vehicle which has been used otherwise than on roads after being sold or supplied by retail and before being registered;

the date of manufacture of the vehicle.

In sub-paragraph (b)(v) of this paragraph "*sold or supplied by retail*" means sold or supplied otherwise than to a person acquiring it solely for the purpose of resale or re-supply for a valuable consideration.

(4) The date of manufacture of a vehicle to which the Type Approval for Goods Vehicles Regulations apply shall be the date of manufacture described in regulation 2(4)(a) of those Regulations.

(5) Save where otherwise provided in these Regulations a tyre shall not be deemed to be of soft or elastic material unless the said material is either—

(a) continuous round the circumference of the wheel; or

(b) fitted in sections so that so far as reasonably practicable no space is left between the ends thereof,

and is of such thickness and design as to minimise, so far as reasonably possible, vibration when the vehicle is in motion and so constructed as to be free from any defect which might in any way cause damage to the surface of a road.

(6) For the purpose of these Regulations a brake drum and a brake disc shall be deemed to form part of the wheel and not of the braking system.

(7) For the purpose of these Regulations other than regulations 26 and 27 any two wheels of a motor vehicle or trailer shall be regarded as one wheel if the distance between the centres of the areas of contact between such wheels and the road surface is less than 460mm.

(8) For the purpose of these Regulations other than regulations 26 and 27 in counting the number of axles of, and in determining the sum of the weights transmitted to the road surface by any one axle of, a vehicle, all the wheels of which the centres of the areas of contact with the road surface can be included between any two transverse planes less than [0.5] m apart shall be treated as constituting one axle.

[(8A) For the purposes of these Regulations, a reference to axles being closely-spaced is a reference to—

(a) two axles (not being part of a group of axles falling within sub-paragraph (b) or (c)) which are spaced at a distance apart of not more than 2.5m;

(b) three axles (not being part of a group of axles falling within sub-paragraph (c)) the outermost of which are spaced at a distance apart of not more than 3.25m; or

(c) four or more axles the outermost of which are spaced at a distance apart of not more than 4.6m;

the number of axles for the purposes of these paragraphs being determined in accordance with paragraph (8); and a reference to any particular number of closely-spaced axles shall be construed accordingly.]

(9) The provisions of these Regulations relating to trailers do not apply to any part of an articulated bus.

(10) For the purpose of [paragraph (8A) above,] of regulations 51, [76, 77 and 79] and [Schedules 11 and 11A] . . ., the distance between any two axles shall be obtained by measuring the shortest distance between the line joining the centres of the areas of contact with the road surface of the wheels of one axle and the line joining the centres of the areas of contact with the road surface of the wheels of the other axle.

(11) For the purpose of the following provisions only, a composite trailer shall be treated as one trailer (not being a semi-trailer or a converter dolly)—

(a) regulations 7, 76 and 83;

(b) paragraph (2) of, and items 3 and 10 in the Table in, regulation 75;

(c) item 2 in the Table in regulation 78.

[Regulation 3 is printed as amended by the Interpretation Act 1978, ss.17(2)(a) and 23(1); **B27.06** *S.I. 1987 Nos 676 and 1133; S.I. 1988 No. 1287; S.I. 1989 No. 1865; S.I. 1990 Nos*

317, 1131 and 1981; S.I. 1991 Nos 1526 and 2125; S.I. 1992 No. 2016; S.I. 1993 No. 2199; S.I. 1994 No. 329; the Vehicle Excise and Registration Act 1994, s.64 and Sched. 4, para.4; S.I. 1995 No. 3051; S.I. 1996 No. 252; S.I. 1996 No. 2329; S.I. 1998 Nos 118 and 3112.

The Visiting Forces and International Headquarters (Application of Law) Order 1965 (to which reference is made both in the table to regulation 3(2) and in regulation 3(3)(b)(iii)) has been revoked and replaced by the Visiting Forces and International Headquarters (Application of Law) Order 1999 (S.I. 1999 No. 1736; not reproduced in this work). No textual amendment had been made to regulation 3 in consequence of that revocation; but by the Interpretation Act 1978, ss.17(2)(a) and 23(1) references to the earlier order may be treated as references to S.I. 1999 No. 1736.

The vehicle categories formerly set out in Annex I of Directive 70/156/EEC are now set out in ibid., Annex II (as substituted by Directive 92/53/EEC); as to "off-road" vehicles, see paragraph 4 of Annex II below.]

[3A. Modification of Regulations in relation to vehicles for which a Minister's approval certificate has been issued under the Motor Vehicles (Approval) Regulations 1996

B27.07   Schedule 2A shall have effect for the purpose of modifying these Regulations in relation to vehicles in respect of which a Minister's approval certificate has been issued by virtue of the Motor Vehicles (Approval) Regulations 1996 [*S.I. 1996 No. 3013*].]

B27.08   *[Regulation 3A was inserted by S.I. 1996 No. 3017.*

The Motor Vehicles (Approval) Regulations 1996 (to which reference is made in regulation 3A) have been revoked and replaced by the Motor Vehicles (Approval) Regulations 2001 (S.I. 2001 No 25) below; see further the note to Schedule 2A, paragraph 2 below.]

4. Application and exemptions

B27.09   (1) Save where the context otherwise requires, these Regulations apply to both wheeled vehicles and track-laying vehicles.

(2) Where a provision is applied by these Regulations to a motor vehicle first used on or after a specified date it does not apply to that vehicle if it was manufactured at least six months before that date.

(3) Where an exemption from, or relaxation of, a provision is applied by these Regulations to a motor vehicle first used before a specified date it shall also apply to a motor vehicle first used on or after that date if it was manufactured at least six months before that date.

(4) The regulations specified in an item in column 3 of the Table do not apply in respect of a vehicle of a class specified in that item in column 2.

TABLE

(regulation 4(4))

1	2	3
Item	*Class of vehicle*	*Regulations which do not apply*
1	A vehicle proceeding to a port for export.	The regulations in Part II in so far as they relate to construction and equipment, except regulations 16 (in so far as it concerns parking brakes), 20, 30, 34, 37, [and 53]. Regulations 66 to 69 and 71.

[continued on next page

1	2	3
Item	Class of vehicle	Regulations which do not apply
2	A vehicle brought temporarily into Great Britain by a person resident abroad, provided that the vehicle complies in every respect with the requirements relating to motor vehicles or trailers contained in— (a) article 21 and paragraph (1) article 22 of the Convention on Road Traffic concluded at Geneva on 19th September 1949 [*Cmnd. 7997*] and [Part I,] Part II (so far as it relates to direction indicators and stop lights) and Part III of Annex 6 to that Convention; or (b) paragraphs I, III and VIII of article 3 of the International Convention relative to Motor Traffic concluded at Paris on 24th April 1926 [*Treaty Series No. 11 (1930)*].	The regulations in Part II in so far as they relate to construction and equipment except regulations 7, 8, . . ., 10, [10A,] 40, [and 53]. Regulations 66 to 69 and 71.
3	A vehicle manufactured in Great Britain which complies with the requirements referred to in item 2 above and contained in the Convention of 1949, or, as the case may be, 1926 referred to in that item as if the vehicle had been brought temporarily into Great Britain, and either— (a) is exempt from car tax by virtue of [section 7(1), (2) and (3) of the Car Tax Act 1983], or (b) has been zero rated under [regulation 132 or 133 of the Value Added Tax Regulations 1995]	The regulations in Part II in so far as they relate to construction and equipment, except regulations 7, 8, . . ., 10, [10A,] 40, [and 53]. Regulations 66 to 69 and 71.
4	A vehicle in the service of a visiting force or of a headquarters.	The regulations in Part II in so far as they relate to construction and equipment, except regulations . . ., 16 (in so far as it concerns parking brakes), 21, 53, . . . and 61. Regulations 66 to 69, [71 and 75 to 79 and 93A].

[*continued on next page*

1	*2*	*3*
Item	*Class of vehicle*	*Regulations which do not apply*
5	A vehicle which has been submitted for an examination under [section 45 or section 67A of the 1988 Act] while it is being used on a road in connection with the carrying out of that examination and is being so used by a person who is empowered under that section to carry out that examination, or by a person acting under the direction of a person so empowered.	The regulations in Part II . . . Regulations 75 to 79 and 100.
6	A motor car or a motor cycle in respect of which a certificate has been issued by the Officer in Charge of a National Collection of Road Transport, the Science Museum, London SW7, that it was designed before 1st January 1905 and constructed before 31st December 1905.	Regulation 16 (except in so far as it applies requirements 3 and 6 in Schedule 3), 21, 37(4), 63 and 99(4).
7	(a) A towing implement which is being drawn by a motor vehicle while it is not attached to any vehicle except the one drawing it if— (i) the towing implement is not being so drawn during the hours of darkness, and (ii) the vehicle by which it is being so drawn is not driven at a speed exceeding 20mph; or (b) a vehicle which is being drawn by a motor vehicle in the exercise of a statutory power of removal.	The regulations in Part II in so far as they relate to the construction and equipment of trailers, except regulation 20.
[8	Tramcars	The regulations in Parts II, III and IV].

(5) Any reference to a broken down vehicle shall include a reference to any towing implement which is being used for the drawing of any such vehicle.

(6) The Secretary of State is satisfied that it is requisite that the provisions of regulation 40(2) should apply, as from the date on which these Regulations come into operation, to track-laying vehicles registered before the expiration of one year from the making of these Regulations; and that, notwithstanding that those provisions will then apply to these vehicles, no undue hardship or inconvenience will be caused thereby.

[*Regulation 4 is printed as corrected by a corrigendum dated October 1986 and as amended by the* **B27.10** *Interpretation Act 1978, ss.17(2)(a) and 23(1); S.I. 1988 No. 271; S.I. 1992 No. 1217; S.I. 1994 No. 14; S.I. 1995 No. 1201; S.I. 1996 No. 3133; S.I. 1997 No. 530.*

For the provisions of the Car Tax Act 1983, s.7(1)–(3) (see item 3(a) in the table), and the Value Added Tax Regulations 1995 (S.I. 1995 No. 2518), regs 132 and 133 (see item 3(b) in the table), see the notes to the Motor Vehicles (Type Approval) (Great Britain) Regulations 1984 (S.I. 1984 No. 981), reg.3 above.]

5. Trade Descriptions Act 1968

Nothing in any provision of these Regulations whereby any vehicle or any of its parts or **B27.11** equipment is required to be marked with a specification number or the registered certification trade mark of the British Standards Institution or with an approval mark, or whereby such a marking is treated as evidence of compliance with a standard to which the marking relates, shall be taken to authorise any person to apply any such marking to the vehicle, part or equipment in contravention of the Trade Descriptions Act 1968.

6. Compliance with Community Directives and ECE Regulations

(1) For the purpose of any regulation which requires or permits a vehicle to comply with **B27.12** the requirements of a Community Directive or an ECE Regulation, a vehicle shall be deemed so to have complied at the date of its first use only if—

(a) one of the certificates referred to in paragraph (2) has been issued in relation to it; or

(b) the marking referred to in paragraph (3) has been applied; . . .

(c) it was, before it was used on a road, subject to a relevant type approval requirement as specified in paragraph (4) [or]

[(d) a sound-level measurement certificate issued by the Secretary of State under regulation 4 of the Motorcycles (Sound Level Measurement Certificates) Regulations 1980 [*S.I. 1989 No. 765, as amended; not reproduced in this work*].

(2) The certificates mentioned in paragraph (1) are—

(a) a type approval certificate issued by the Secretary of State under regulation 5 of the Type Approval Regulations or of the Type Approval for Agricultural Vehicles Regulations;

(b) a certificate of conformity issued by the manufacturer of the vehicle under regulation 6 of either of those Regulations; or

(c) a certificate issued under a provision of the law of any member state of the European Economic Community which corresponds to the said regulations 5 or 6,

being in each case a certificate issued by reason of the vehicle's conforming to the requirements of the Community Directive in question.

(3) The marking mentioned in paragraph (1) is a marking designated as an approval mark by regulation 4 of the Approval Marks Regulations, being in each case a mark shown in column 2 of an item in Schedule 2 to those Regulations which refers, in column 5, to the ECE Regulation in question, applied as indicated in column 4 in that item.

(4) A relevant type approval requirement is a requirement of the Type Approval (Great Britain) Regulations or that Type Approval for Goods Vehicles Regulations which appears—

(a) in column 4 of Table I in Schedule 2 in that item in which the Community Directive in question appears in column 3, or

(b) in column 4 of Table II in Schedule 2 in the item in which the ECE Regulation in question appears in column 3.

[*Regulation 6 is printed as amended by S.I. 1989 No. 1865.*]   **B27.13**

PART II

REGULATIONS GOVERNING THE CONSTRUCTION, EQUIPMENT AND MAINTENANCE OF
VEHICLES

A *Dimensions and Manoeuvrability*

[7. Length

B27.14   (1) Subject to paragraphs (2) to (6), the overall length of a vehicle or combination of vehicles of a class specified in an item in column 2 of the Table shall not exceed the maximum length specified in that item in column 3 of the Table, the overall length in the case of a combination of vehicles being calculated in accordance with regulation 81(g) and (h).

TABLE (regulation 7(1))

1	2	3
Item	Class of vehicle	Maximum length (metres)
	Vehicle combinations	
[1	A motor vehicle (other than a motor vehicle such as is mentioned in item 1A) drawing one trailer which is not a semi-trailer.	18.75]
[1A	Subject to paragraph (3C), a motor vehicle manufactured before 1st June 1998 and drawing one trailer, where the combination does not meet the requirements of paragraph (5A) and the trailer is not a semi-trailer.	18]
2	An articulated bus.	18
3	An articulated vehicle, the semi-trailer of which does not meet the requirements of paragraph (6) and is not a low loader.	15.5
3A	An articulated vehicle, the semi-trailer of which meets the requirements of paragraph (6) and is not a low loader.	16.5
3B	An articulated vehicle, the semi-trailer of which is a low loader.	18
	Motor vehicles	
4	A wheeled motor vehicle.	12
5	A track-laying motor vehicle.	9.2
	Trailers	
6	An agricultural trailed appliance manufactured on or after 1st December 1985.	15
7	A semi-trailer manufactured on or after 1st May 1983 which does not meet the requirements of paragraph (6) and is not a low loader.	12.2
7A	A composite trailer drawn by— (a) a goods vehicle being a motor vehicle having a maximum gross weight exceeding 3500kg; or (b) an agricultural motor vehicle.	14.04

[*continued on next page*

1	2	3
Item	*Class of vehicle*	*Maximum length (metres)*

8	A trailer (not being a semi-trailer or composite trailer) with at least 4 wheels which is—
	    (a) drawn by a goods vehicle being a motor vehicle having a maximum gross weight exceeding 3500kg;
	    or
	    (b) an agricultural trailer.
		12

9	Any other trailer not being an agricultural trailed appliance or a semi-trailer.	7

(2) In the case of a motor vehicle drawing one trailer where—

  (a) the motor vehicle is a showman's vehicle as defined in paragraph 7 of Schedule 3 to the 1971 Act; and

  (b) the trailer is used primarily as living accommodation by one or more persons and is not also used for the carriage of goods or burden which are not needed for the purpose of such residence in the vehicle,

item 1 in the Table applies with the substitution of 22m for 18m and item 1A in the Table does not apply.

(3) Items 1, 1A, 3, 3A and 3B of the Table do not apply to—

  (a) a vehicle combination which includes a trailer which is constructed and normally used for the conveyance of indivisible loads of exceptional length, or

  (b) a vehicle combination consisting of a broken down vehicle (including an articulated vehicle) being drawn by a motor vehicle in consequence of a breakdown, or

  (c) an articulated vehicle, the semi-trailer of which is a low loader manufactured before 1t April 1991.

(3A) Items 6, 7, 7A, 8 and 9 of the Table do not apply to—

  (a) a trailer which is constructed and normally used for the conveyance of indivisible loads of exceptional length,

  (b) a broken down vehicle (including an articulated vehicle) which is being drawn by a motor vehicle in consequence of a breakdown, or

  (c) a trailer being a drying or mixing plant designed for the production of asphalt or of bituminous or tar macadam and used mainly for the construction, repair or maintenance of roads, or a road planing machine so used.

(3B) Furthermore item 7 does not apply to—

  (a) a semi-trailer which is a car transporter,

  (b) a semi-trailer which is normally used on international journeys any part of which takes place outside the United Kingdom.

[(3C) Item 1A and the words "(other than a motor vehicle such as is mentioned in item 1A)" in item 1 of the Table shall cease to have effect after 31st December 2006.]

(4) Where a motor vehicle is drawing—

  (a) two trailers, then only one of those trailers may exceed an overall length of 7m;

  (b) three trailers, then none of those trailers shall exceed an overall length of 7m.

(5) Where a motor vehicle is drawing—

   (a) two or more trailers; or

   (b) one trailer constructed and normally used for the conveyance of indivisible loads of exceptional length—

then—

      (i) the overall length of that motor vehicle shall not exceed 9.2m; and

      (ii) the overall length of the combination of vehicles, calculated in accordance with regulation 81(g) and (h), shall not exceed 25.9m, unless the conditions specified in paragraphs 1 and 2 of Schedule 12 have been complied with.

[(5XA) A motor vehicle drawing a trailer which is not a semi-trailer shall (unless it is a vehicle such as is mentioned in item 1A of the Table in paragraph (1)) comply with the requirements of paragraph (5A).

The words in parenthesis in this paragraph shall cease to have effect after 31st December 2006.]

(5A) The requirements of this paragraph, in relation to a combination of vehicles, are that at least one of the vehicles in the combination is not a goods vehicle or, if both vehicles in the combination are goods vehicles that—

   (a) the maximum distance measured parallel to the longitudinal axis of the combination of vehicles from the foremost point of the loading area behind the driver's cab to the rear of the trailer, less the distance between the rear of the motor vehicle and the front of the trailer, does not exceed 15.65m; and

   (b) the maximum distance measured parallel to the longitudinal axis of the combination of vehicles from the foremost point of the loading area behind the driver's cab to the rear of the trailer does not exceed [16.4m];

but sub-paragraph (a) shall not apply if both vehicles in the combination are car transporters.

(6) The requirements of this paragraph, in relation to a semi-trailer, are that—

   (a) the longitudinal distance from the axis of the king-pin to the rear of the semi-trailer does not exceed—

      (i) 12.5m in the case of a car transporter, or

      (ii) 12m in any other case; and

   (b) no point in the semi-trailer forward of the transverse plane passing through the axis of the king-pin is more than—

      (i) 4.19m from the axis of the king-pin, in the case of a car transporter, or

      (ii) 2.04m from the axis of the king-pin, in any other case.

(6A) For the purposes of paragraph (5A)—

   (a) where the forward end of the loading area of a motor vehicle is bounded by a wall, the thickness of the wall shall be regarded as part of the loading area; and

   (b) any part of a vehicle designed primarily for use as a means of attaching another vehicle to it and any fitting designed for use in connection with any such part shall be disregarded in determining the distance between the rear of a motor vehicle and the front of a trailer being drawn by it.

(7) For the purpose of paragraph (6) the longitudinal distance from the axis of the king-pin to the rear of a semi-trailer is the distance between a transverse plane passing through the axis of the king-pin and the rear of the semi-trailer.

(7A) Where a semi-trailer has more than one king-pin or is constructed so that it can be used with a king-pin in different positions, references in this regulation to a distance from the king-pin shall be construed [(a) in relation to a vehicle which was manufactured after [1st January 1999], as a reference to the foremost king-pin or, as the case may be, the foremost king-pin position; and]

[(b) in relation to any other vehicle, as a reference to the rearmost king-pin or, as the case may be, the rearmost king-pin position.]

(7B) For the purposes of paragraphs (5A), (6) and (7)—

(a) a reference to the front of a vehicle is a reference to the transverse plane passing through the extreme forward projecting points of the vehicle; and

(b) a reference to the rear of a vehicle is a reference to the transverse plane passing through the extreme rearward projecting points of the vehicle,

inclusive (in each case) of all parts of the vehicle, of any receptacle which is of a permanent character and accordingly strong enough for repeated use, and any fitting on, or attached to, the vehicle but exclusive of—

(i) the things set out in sub-paragraph (i) of the definition of "overall length" in the Table in regulation 3(2), and

(ii) in the case of a semi-trailer, the things set out in sub-paragraph (ii)(a) of that definition.

(8) Where a broken down articulated vehicle is being towed by a motor vehicle in consequence of a breakdown—

(a) paragraph (5) shall have effect in relation to the combination of vehicles as if sub-paragraph (b) were omitted, and

(b) for the purposes of paragraph (4) and of paragraph (5) as so modified, the articulated vehicle shall be regarded as a single trailer.

(9) No person shall use or cause or permit to be used on a road, a trailer with an overall length exceeding 18.65m unless the requirements of paragraphs 1 and 2 of Schedule 12 are complied with.]

[Regulation 7 is printed as amended by S.I. 1990 Nos 317 and 1163; S.I. 1991 No. 2125; S.I.   **B27.15**
1998 Nos 1188 and 3112.

Following the 1991 amendments, the amended text of regulation 7 was reproduced in the Schedule to S.I. 1991 No. 2125 and that version is reproduced above with subsequent amendments.]

8. Width

(1) Save as provided in paragraph (2), overall width of a vehicle of a class specified in an   **B27.16** item in column 2 of the Table shall not exceed the maximum width specified in column 3 in that item.

TABLE

(regulation 8(1))

1	*2*	*3*
Item	*Class of vehicle*	*Maximum width (metres)*
1	A locomotive, other than an agricultural motor vehicle.	2.75
2	A refrigerated vehicle.	[2.60]

[continued on next page

1	*2*	*3*
Item	*Class of vehicle*	*Maximum width (metres)*
4	A trailer drawn by a motor vehicle having a maximum gross weight (determined as provided in Part I of Schedule 8 to these Regulations) exceeding 3500kg.	[2.55]
5	An agricultural trailer.	[2.55]
6	An agricultural trailed appliance.	[2.55]
7	Any other trailer drawn by a vehicle other than a motor cycle.	2.3
8	A trailer drawn by a motor cycle.	1.5

(2) Paragraph (1) does not apply to a broken down vehicle which is being drawn in consequence of the breakdown.

(3) No person shall use or cause or permit to be used on a road a wheeled agricultural motor vehicle drawing a wheeled vehicle trailer if, when the longitudinal axes of the vehicles are parallel but in different vertical planes, the overall width of the two vehicles, measured as if they were on one vehicle, exceeds [2.55] metres.

(4) In this regulation "*refrigerated vehicle*" means any vehicle which is specially designed for the carriage of goods at a low temperature and of which the thickness of each of the side walls, inclusive of insulation, is at least 45mm.

B27.17   *[Regulation 8 is printed as amended by S.I. 1988 No. 1871; S.I. 1995 No. 3051.]*

9. Height

B27.18   (1) The overall height of a bus shall not exceed 4.57m.

(2) *[Revoked.]*

[(2A) *[Revoked.]*

(3) *[Revoked.]*

B27.19   *[Regulation 9 is printed as amended by S.I. 1994 No. 329; S.I. 1995 No. 1201.]*

10. Indication of overall travelling height

B27.20   [(1) Subject to the provisions of this regulation, no person shall drive or cause or permit to be driven on a road a motor vehicle with an overall travelling height exceeding 3m unless a notice is displayed in the cab, in such a manner that it can easily be read by the driver, and the notice meets the requirements of paragraph (3).

(2) Subject to the provisions of this regulation, no person shall use or cause or permit to be used on a road a motor vehicle with an overall travelling height exceeding 3m if any letters or numbers are displayed in the cab, otherwise than in a notice which meets the requirements of paragraph (3)—

     (a) where they could be read by the driver; and

     (b) which could be understood as indicating a height associated with the vehicle or any trailer drawn by it.

(3) The requirements of this paragraph in respect of a notice are that—

  (a) the notice gives an indication of vehicle height expressed in feet and inches, or in both feet and inches and in metres;

  (b) the numbers giving the indication in feet and inches are at least 40mm tall;

  (c) the height expressed in feet and inches and (where applicable) the height expressed in metres are—

    (i) if the vehicle is a vehicle to which regulation 10A applies, not less than the predetermined height mentioned in regulation 10A(2)(a) or the overall travelling height (whichever is the greater), or

    (ii) if the vehicle is not a vehicle to which regulation 10A applies, not less than the overall travelling height;

  (d) if the vehicle is not a relevant vehicle, the height expressed in feet and inches does not exceed the overall travelling height by more than 150mm;

  (e) if the vehicle is a relevant vehicle, the height expressed in feet and inches does not exceed the overall travelling height by more than 1m;

  (f) if the height is expressed in both feet and inches and in metres, the height expressed in feet and inches and the height expressed in metres do not differ by more than 50mm; and

  (g) no other letters or numbers which could be understood as being an indication of any height associated with the vehicle or any trailer drawn by it are displayed in the notice.

(4) Paragraph (1) shall not apply if, having regard to the lengths of road which the driver might drive along in the course of fulfilling the purpose of the journey taking into account any possibility of unforeseen diversions and the driver having difficulty in finding his way, it is highly unlikely that the driver would during the course of the journey encounter any bridge or other overhead structure which does not exceed by at least 1m—

  (a) in the case of a vehicle to which regulation 10A applies, the maximum travelling height; or

  (b) in any other case, the overall travelling height.

(5) Paragraph (1) shall not apply to a vehicle on a particular journey and at a particular time if—

  (a) one or more documents are being carried in the vehicle which are within the easy reach of the driver and that or those documents describe a route or a choice of routes which the driver must take in order to fulfil the purpose of the journey without risk of the vehicle, its load or equipment or any trailer drawn by the vehicle, its load or equipment, colliding with any bridge or other overhead structure; and

  (b) the vehicle is on such a route which is so described or is off that route by reason of a diversion that could not reasonably have been foreseen at the beginning of the journey.

(6) Paragraph (1) shall not apply to a vehicle on a particular journey if—

  (a) one or more documents are being carried in the vehicle which are within the easy reach of the driver and that or those documents contain informations as to—

    (i) the height of bridges and other overhead structures under which the vehicle and any trailer drawn by it could pass, and

    (ii) the height of bridges and other overhead structures under which the vehicle and any trailer drawn by it could not pass,

without the vehicle, its load or equipment or any such trailer, its load or equipment, colliding with any bridge or other overhead structure; and

    (b) the information is such that, having regard in particular to the matters referred to in paragraph (7), it would enable any driver to fulfil the purpose of the journey without there being any risk of the vehicle, its load or equipment or any trailer, its load or equipment, colliding with any bridge or other overhead structure while on the journey.

  (7) The matters referred to in paragraph (6) are—

    (a) the roads which the driver might drive along in the course of fulfilling the purpose of the journey taking into account any possibility of unforeseen diversions and of the driver having difficulty in finding his way;

    (b) the height of bridges and other overhead structures that would be encountered were the vehicle to proceed along any of those roads; and

    (c) the setting of any device of a description specified in regulation 10A(2).

  (8) Paragraphs (1) and (2) shall not apply to motor vehicle if it has an overall travelling height of not more than 4m and—

    (a) it is a vehicle registered or put into circulation in an EEA State and is being used in international traffic; or

    (b) it is a motor vehicle drawing a trailer registered or put into circulation in an EEA State and that trailer is being used in international traffic.

  (9) For the purposes of this regulation—

    (a) *"EEA State"*, and *"high level equipment"* and *"maximum travelling height"* have the meanings given in regulation 10C;

    (b) *"overall travelling height"* in relation to a motor vehicle means—

        (i) if it is not drawing a trailer, the overall height for the time being of the vehicle, its equipment and load, or

       (ii) if it is drawing one or more trailers, the overall height for the time being of the combination of vehicles, their equipment and loads.

    (c) a motor vehicle is a *"relevant vehicle"* if at any particular time—

        (i) the vehicle or any trailer drawn by it is fitted with high level equipment with a maximum, height of more than 3m; and

       (ii) the overall travelling height is less than the maximum travelling height.

  (10) In paragraph (8), *"international traffic"* and *"registered or put into circulation"* have the same meanings as in article 3 of Community Directive 85/3 [*O.J. No. L2, January 3, 1985, p. 14*].]

B27.21   *[Regulation 10 was substituted (together with regulations 10A, 10B and 10C) by S.I. 1997 No. 530. As to the terms "international traffic" and "registered or put into circulation" (to which reference is made in regulation 10(10)), see now article 3(1) and (2) of Directive 96/53/EC below, which has repealed and replaced Directive 85/3/EEC.]*

[10A. Warning devices where certain high level equipment is fitted to a vehicle

B27.22   (1) Subject to the provisions of this regulation and regulations 10B and 10C, no person shall drive or cause or permit to be driven on a road a vehicle to which this regulation applies unless the vehicle is fitted with a warning device and the requirements specified in paragraph (2) are satisfied in respect of the device, the vehicle and any relevant trailer drawn by the vehicle.

  (2) The requirements are—

    (a) that the device, the vehicle and any relevant trailer drawn by it shall be constructed, maintained and adjusted, and the connections between the vehicle and those trailers are such, that the device would give a visible warning to the driver if, whilst the vehicle was being driven, the height of the highest point of any high level equipment fitted to the vehicle or any of those trailers were to exceed a predetermined height; and

(b) the predetermined height referred to in sub-paragraph (a) shall not exceed the overall travelling height by more than 1m.

(3) No person shall be taken to have failed to comply with paragraph (1) on the ground that a motor vehicle or a relevant trailer was not fitted with a warning device and the requirements in paragraph (2) were not being satisfied as mentioned in paragraph (1)—

(a) before 1st October 1998—

(i) if the motor vehicle was first used before 1st April 1998; or
(ii) the relevant trailer was manufactured before that date; or

(b) before 1st April 1998 in relation to any other motor vehicle or relevant trailer.

(4) Paragraph (1) shall not apply in relation to a particular journey if, having regard to the lengths of road which the driver might drive along in the course of fulfilling the purpose of the journey and taking into account any possibility of unforeseen diversions and the driver having difficulty in finding his way, it is highly unlikely that the driver would during the course of the journey be confronted with any bridge or other overhead structure which does not exceed the maximum travelling height by at least 1m.]

[10B. Vehicles to which regulation 10A applies

(1) Subject to the provisions of this regulation, regulation 10A applies to—   **B27.23**

(a) a motor vehicle first used on or after 1st April 1993, if the vehicle or any relevant trailer drawn by it, is fitted with high level equipment with a maximum height of more than 3m; and

(b) a motor vehicle first used before 1st April 1993, if any relevant trailer drawn by it is fitted with such equipment.

(2) Regulation 10A does not apply to a motor vehicle if it has an overall travelling height of not more than 4m and—

(a) it is a vehicle registered or put into circulation in an EEA State and is being used in international traffic; or

(b) it is a motor vehicle drawing a trailer registered or put into circulation in an EEA State and that trailer is being used in international traffic, and

in this paragraph, "*international traffic*" and "*registered or put into circulation*" have the same meanings as in article 3 of Community Directive 85/3.

(3) Regulation 10A does not apply to—

(a) an agricultural motor vehicle;

(b) an industrial tractor;

(c) a works truck;

(d) a motor vehicle owned by the Secretary of State for Defence and used for naval, military or air force purposes or a motor vehicle so used while being driven by a person for the time being subject to orders of a member of the armed forces of the Crown;

(e) a motor vehicle drawing a trailer owned by the Secretary of State for Defence and used for naval, military or air force purposes or a motor vehicle drawing such a trailer while being driven by a person for the time being subject to orders of a member of the armed forces of the Crown;

(f) a motor vehicle used by a fire brigade maintained under the Fire Services Act 1947;

(g) a motor vehicle that is constructed and normally used for the purpose of carrying at least two other vehicles;

(h) a motor vehicle drawing a car transporter; or

(i) a motor vehicle whose maximum travelling height does not exceed its overall travelling height.]

B27.24   *[Regulations 10A and 10B were inserted by S.I. 1997 No. 530.*
See note to regulation 10 with regard to the repeal of article 3 of Community Directive 85/3/EEC.]

B27.25   **[10C. Interpretation of regulations 10A and 10B**

(1) The following provisions of this regulation apply for the interpretation of this regulation and regulations 10A and 10B.

(2) Subject to paragraphs (4) and (5), a reference to high level equipment, in relation to a motor vehicle, is a reference to equipment which is so fitted to the vehicle that—

(a) the equipment can be raised by means of a power operated device, and

(b) the raising or lowering of the equipment is capable of altering the overall travelling height of the motor vehicle when the vehicle and every trailer drawn by it is unladen.

(3) Subject to paragraph (4) and (5), a reference to high level equipment, in relation to a trailer drawn by a motor vehicle, is a reference to equipment which is so fitted to the trailer that—

(a) the equipment can be raised by means of a power operated device, and

(b) the raising or lowering of the equipment is capable of altering the overall travelling height of the motor vehicle when the vehicle and every trailer drawn by it is unladen.

(4) A reference to high level equipment in relation to a tipper which is—

(a) a motor vehicle first used before 1st April 1998, or

(b) a trailer manufactured before that date,

shall be construed as not including the relevant part of the tipper.

(5) Where equipment fitted to a vehicle would otherwise be high level equipment, that equipment shall not be regarded as high level equipment if—

(a) the equipment is so designed and constructed that—

(i) it can be fixed in a stowed position by a locking device when travelling; and
(ii) it is not possible for a person in the cab to interfere with the locking device; and

(b) the equipment is fixed in that position by the locking device.

(6) The following expressions shall bear the following meanings—

(a) *"EEA State"* means a state which is a contracting party to the EEA Agreement; and

(b) *"EEA Agreement"* means the Agreement on the European Economic Area signed at Oporto on 2 May 1992 as adjusted by the Protocol signed at Brussels on 17 March 1993;

(c) *"maximum height"*, in relation to any high level equipment fitted to a vehicle, means the height of the highest point of that equipment above the ground when it is raised as far as possible by means of that device and the vehicle is unladen;

(d) *"maximum travelling height"*, in relation to a motor vehicle to which regulation 10A applies, means—

    (i) if the overall travelling height could be increased by raising any high level equipment fitted to the vehicle or to any relevant trailer drawn by [it] that is not for the time being at its maximum height, the greatest overall travelling height that could be achieved by raising such equipment (without making any other changes to the vehicle, its load or equipment or to any trailer drawn by it, its load or equipment); or

    (ii) in any other case, the overall travelling height;

(e) *"overall travelling height"* has the meaning given by regulation 10(9)(b);

(f) *"relevant part"*, in relation to a tipper, shall be construed in accordance with sub-paragraph (g);

(g) *"tipper"* means a vehicle that is so constructed that it can be unloaded by part of the vehicle (in this regulation referred to as the *"relevant part"*) being tipped sideways or rearwards, and

a reference to equipment fitted to a vehicle includes part of the vehicle.

(7) *"Relevant trailer"* means a trailer manufactured on or after 1st April 1993 not being—

(a) an agricultural trailer;

(b) an agricultural trailed appliance;

(c) a works trailer;

(d) a trailer used by a fire brigade maintained under the Fire Services Act 1947;

(e) a broken down vehicle (including an articulated vehicle) being drawn by a motor vehicle in consequence of a breakdown.

[Regulation 10C was inserted by S.I. 1997 No. 530 and is printed as subsequently amended by S.I.   **B27.26**
1998 No. 1188.

    As to the European Economic Area and the EEA agreement, see the note to Regulation (EEC) 3820/85 below.]

11. Overhang

(1) The overhang of a wheeled vehicle of a class specified in an item in column 2 of the   **B27.27**
Table [*see table on next page*] shall not, subject to any exemption specified in that item in column 4, exceed the distance specified in that item in column 3.

TABLE 1

(regulation 11(1))

1 Item	2 Class of vehicle	3 Maximum overhang	4 Exemptions
1	Motor tractor	1.83m.	(a) a track-laying vehicle (b) an agricultural motor vehicle

2	Heavy motor car and motor car	60% of the distance between the transverse plane which passes through the centre or centres of the foremost wheel or wheels and the transverse plane which passes through the foremost point from which the overhang is to be measured as provided in regulation 3(2).	(a) a bus
			(b) a refuse vehicle
			(c) a works truck
			(d) a track-laying vehicle
			(e) an agricultural motor vehicle
			(f) a motor car which is an ambulance
			(g) a vehicle designed to dispose of its load to the rear, if the overhang does not exceed 1.15m
			(h) a vehicle first used before 2nd January 1933
			(i) a vehicle first used before 1st January 1966 if—
			  (i) the distance between the centres of the rearmost and foremost axles does not exceed 2.29m, and
			  (ii) the distance specified in column 3 is not exceeded by more than 767mm
			(j) heating plant on a vehicle designed and mainly used to heat the surface of a road or other similar surface in the process of construction, repair or maintenance shall be disregarded

(2) In the case of an agricultural motor vehicle the distance measured horizontally and parallel to the longitudinal axis of the rear portion of the vehicle between the transverse planes passing through the rearmost point of the vehicle and through the centre of the rear or the rearmost axle should not exceed 3m.

[(3) A heavy motor car shall be taken to comply with the requirements of paragraph (1) if it meets the requirements of paragraph 7.6.2 of Annex I of Community Directive 97/27 [*O.J. No. L233, August 25, 1997, p. 1*].]

[Regulation 11 is printed as amended by S.I. 1998 No. 1188.]   **B27.28**

12. Minimum ground clearance

(1) Save as provided in paragraph (2), a wheeled trailer which is—   **B27.29**

   (a) a goods vehicle; and

   (b) manufactured on or after 1st April 1984,

shall have a minimum ground clearance of not less than 160mm if the trailer has an axle interspace of more than 6m but less than 11.5m, and a minimum ground clearance of not less than 190mm if the trailer has an axle interspace of 11.5m or more.

(2) Paragraph (1) shall not apply in the case of a trailer—

   (a) which is fitted with a suspension system which, by the operation of a control, the trailer may be lowered or raised, while that system is being operated to enable the trailer to pass under a bridge or other obstruction over a road provided that at such time the system is operated so that no part of the trailer (excluding any wheel) touches the ground or is likely to do so; or

   (b) while it is being loaded or unloaded.

(3) In this regulation—

"*axle interspace*" means—

   (a) in the case of a semi-trailer, the distance between the point of support of the semi-trailer at its forward end and, if it has only one axle, the centre of that axle or, if it has more than one axle, the point halfway between the centres of the foremost and rearmost of those axles; and

   (b) in the case of any other trailer, the distance between the centre of its front axle or, if it has more than one axle at the front, the point halfway between the centres of the foremost and rearmost of those axles, and the centre of its rear axle or, if it has more than one axle at the rear, the point halfway between the centre of the foremost and rearmost of those axles; and

"*ground clearance*" means the shortest distance between the ground and the lowest part of that portion of the trailer (excluding any part of a suspension, steering or braking system attached to any axle, any wheel and any air skirt) which lies within the area formed by the overall width of the trailer and the middle 70% of the axle interspace, such distance being ascertained when the trailer—

   (a) is fitted with suitable tyres which are inflated to a pressure recommended by the manufacturer, and

   (b) is reasonably horizontal and standing on ground which is reasonably flat.

13. [Turning circle — buses]

(1) This regulation applies to a bus first used on or after 1st April 1982.   **B27.30**

(2) Every vehicle to which this regulation applies shall be able to move on either lock so that [, both with and without all its wheels in contact with the ground,] no part of it projects outside the area contained between concentric circles with radii of [12.5m] and 5.3m.

[(2A) In relation to a vehicle manufactured before 1st June 1998 paragraph (2) shall have effect as if the words ", both with and without all its wheels in contact with the ground," were omitted.]

(3) When a vehicle to which this regulation applies moves forward from rest, on either lock, so that its outermost point describes a circle of [12.5m] radius, no part of the vehicle shall project beyond the longitudinal plane which, at the beginning of the manoeuvre, defines the overall width of the vehicle on the side opposite to the direction in which it is turning by more than—

    (a) 0.8m if it is a rigid vehicle; or

    (b) 1.2m if it is an articulated bus.

(4) For the purpose of paragraph (3) the two rigid portions of an articulated bus shall be in line at the beginning of the manoeuvre.

B27.31   *[Regulation 13 is printed as amended by S.I. 1998 No. 1188.]*

[13A. Turning circle—articulated vehicles other than those incorporating a car transporter

B27.32   [(1) Every vehicle to which this regulation applies shall be able to move on either lock so that, both with and without all its wheels in contact with the surface of the road and disregarding the things set out in paragraphs (a) to (m) in the definition of "overall width" and in paragraphs (i)(a) to (o) in the definition of "overall length" in the Table in regulation 3, no part of it projects outside the area contained between concentric circles with radii of 12.5m and 5.3m.

(2) This regulation applies to all articulated vehicles except the following:

    (a) an articulated vehicle, the semi-trailer of which—

        (i) was manufactured before 1st April 1990 and has an overall length that does not exceed the overall length it had on that date,

        (ii) is a car transporter,

        (iii) is a low loader,

        (iv) is a stepframe low loader, or

        (v) is constructed and normally used for the conveyance of indivisible loads of exceptional length;

    (b) an articulated vehicle having an overall length not exceeding 15.5m and of which the drawing vehicle was first used before 1st June 1998 or the trailer was first used before that date; or

    (c) an articulated vehicle when an axle of the trailer is raised to aid traction.

(3) In relation to a vehicle manufactured before 1st June 1998 paragraph (1) shall have effect as if the words "both with and without all its wheels in contact with the surface of the road and" were omitted.]

(4) An articulated vehicle shall be taken to comply with paragraph (1) if the semi-trailer comprised in it is, by virtue of paragraph 7.6.1.2 of Annex I of Community Directive 97/27/EC [*O.J. No. L233, August 25, 1997, p. 1*], deemed to comply with paragraph 7.6.1 of that Annex.]]

B27.33   *[Regulation 13A was inserted by S.I. 1990 No. 317 and was later amended by S.I. 1990 No. 1163; S.I. 1998 No. 1188.*
The text of regulation 13A as printed above was substituted by S.I. 2000 No. 3197.]

[13B. Turning circle—articulated vehicles incorporating a car transporter

(1) Subject to paragraphs (2) and (3) this regulation applies to an articulated vehicle **B27.34**
having an overall length exceeding 15.5m, the semi-trailer of which is a car transporter.

(2) This regulation does not apply to an articulated vehicle, the semi-trailer of which
satisfied the following conditions—

   (a) it was manufactured before the 1st April 1990, and

   (b) the distance from the front of the trailer to the rearmost axle is no greater than it
was on that date.

(3) This regulation does not apply to an articulated vehicle the semi-trailer of which is—

   (a) a low loader, or

   (b) a stepframe low loader.

(4) Every articulated vehicle to which this regulation applies shall be able to move on
either lock so that, [both with and without all its wheels in contact with the surface of the
road and] disregarding the things set out in [paragraphs (a) to (m) in the definition of
"overall width" and in paragraphs (i)(a) to (o) in the definition of "overall length"] in the
Table in regulation 3(2), no part of—

   (a) the motor vehicle drawing the car transporter, or

   (b) the car transporter to the rear of the transverse plane passing through the king pin,

projects outside the area between the concentric circles with radii of 12.5m and 5.3m.]

[(5) In relation to a vehicle manufactured before 1st June 1998 paragraph (4) shall have
effect as if the words "both with and without all its wheels in contact with the surface of the
road" were omitted.]

[(6) An articulated vehicle shall be taken to comply with paragraph (4) if the semi-trailer
comprised in it is, by virtue of paragraph 7.6.1.2 of Annex I of Community Directive
97/27/EC, deemed to comply with paragraph 7.6.1 of that Annex.]

[Regulation 13B was inserted by S.I. 1990 No. 317 and is printed as subsequently amended by S.I. **B27.35**
1998 No. 1188.]

[13C. Turning circle—heavy motor car

(1) This regulation applies to a vehicle which— **B27.36**

   (a) is a heavy motor car or a vehicle combination which consists of a heavy motor car
drawing one trailer which is not a semi-trailer;

   (b) was manufactured or, in the case of a vehicle combination, the part consisting of a
heavy motor car, was manufactured after 31st May 1998; and

   (c) is not a vehicle falling within any of the descriptions specified in paragraph (2).

(2) The descriptions of vehicle referred to in paragraph (1)(c) are—

   (a) a vehicle having 4 or more axles where the distance between the foremost and rearmost axles exceeds 6.4 metres;

   (b) a vehicle or a vehicle combination to which regulation 13, 13A or 13B applies;

   (c) a vehicle constructed and normally used for the carriage of indivisible loads of
abnormal length.

(3) Every vehicle to which this regulation applies shall be able to move on either lock so that,
both with and without all its wheels in contact with the surface of the road and disregarding
the things set out in paragraphs (a) to (m) in the definition of "overall width" and in paragraphs

(i)(a) to (o) in the definition of "overall length" in the Table in regulation 3(2), no part of it projects outside the area contained between concentric circles with radii of 12.5m and 5.3m.]

B27.37   *[Regulation 13C was inserted by S.I. 1998 No. 1188.]*

14. Connecting section and direction-holding of articulated buses

B27.38   (1) This regulation applies to every articulated bus first used on or after 1st April 1982.

(2) The connecting section of the two parts of every articulated bus to which this regulation applies shall be constructed so as to comply with the provisions relating to such a section specified in paragraph 5.9 in ECE Regulation 36 as regards vehicles within the scope of that Regulation.

(3) Every articulated bus to which this regulation applies shall be constructed so that when the vehicle is moving in a straight line the longitudinal median planes of its two parts coincide and form a continuous plane without any deflection.

B *Brakes*

15. Braking systems of certain vehicles first used on or after 1st April 1983

B27.39   [(1) Save as provided in paragraphs (2), (3) and (4), the braking system of every wheeled vehicle of a class specified in an item in column 2 of the Table which, in the case of a motor vehicle, is first used on or after 1st April 1983 or which, in the case of a trailer, is manufactured on or after 1st October 1982 shall comply with the construction, fitting and performance requirements specified in Annexes I, II and VII to Community Directive 79/489, and if relevant, Annexes III, IV, V, VI and VIII to that Directive in relation to the category of vehicles specified in that item in column 3.
  Provided that it shall be lawful for any vehicle of such a class which, in the case of a motor vehicle, was first used before 1st April 1983 or which, in the case of a trailer, was manufactured before 1st October 1982 to comply with the said requirements instead of complying with regulations 16 and 17.

(1A) Save as provided in paragraphs (2), (3), (3A) and (5), the braking system of every wheeled vehicle of a class specified in an item in column 2 of the Table which, in the case of a motor vehicle, is first used on or after the revelant date or which, in the case of a trailer, is manufactured on or after the relevant date shall comply with the construction, fitting and performance requirements specified in Annexes I, II and VII to Community Directive 85/647, and if relevant, Annexes III, IV, V, VI, VIII, X, XI and XII to that Directive in relation to the category of vehicles specified in that item in column 3.
  Provided that it shall be lawful for any vehicle of such a class which, in the case of a motor vehicle, was first used before the relevant date or which, in the case of a trailer, was manufactured before the relevant date to comply with the said requirements instead of complying with paragraph (1) or with regulations 16 and 17.

(1B) In paragraph (1A), the relevant date in relation to a vehicle of a class specified in item 1 or 2 of the Table is 1st April 1990, in relation to a vehicle specified in item 4 of that Table is 1st April 1992, in relation to a vehicle in items 7, 8, 9 or 10 of that Table is 1st October 1988 and in relation to a vehicle of any other class is 1st April 1989.

(1C) Save as provided in paragraphs (2), (3), (3A) and (5A), the braking system of every wheeled vehicle of a class specified in an item in column 2 of the Table which, in the case of a motor vehicle, is first used on or after 1st April 1992 or which, in the case of a trailer, is manufactured on or after 1st October 1991 shall comply with the construction, fitting and performance requirements specified in Annexes I, II and VII to Community Directive 88/194, and if relevant, Annexes III, IV, V, VI, VIII, X, XI and XII to that Directive in relation to the category of vehicles specified in that item in column 3.

Provided that it shall be lawful for any vehicle of such a class which, in the case of a motor vehicle, was first used before 1st April 1992 or which, in the case of a trailer, was manufactured before 1st October 1991 to comply with the said requirements instead of complying with paragraph (1) or (1A) or with regulations 16 and 17.

(1D) Save as provided in paragraphs (2), (3), (3A) and (5A), the braking system of every wheeled vehicle of a class specified in an item in column 2 of the Table which, in the case of a motor vehicle, is first used on or after 1st April 1995 or which, in the case of a trailer, is manufactured on or after that date shall comply with the construction, fitting and performance requirements specified in Annexes I, II, and VII to Community Directive 91/422, and if relevant, Annexes III, IV, V, VI, VIII, X, XI and XII to that Directive in relation to the category of vehicles specified in that item in column 3.

Provided that it shall be lawful for any vehicle of such a class which, in the case of a motor vehicle, was first used before 1st April 1995 or which, in the case of a trailer, was manufactured before that date to comply with the said requirements instead of complying with paragraph (1), (1A) or (1C) or with regulations 16 and 17.

(2) The requirements specified in paragraphs (1), (1A), (1C) and (1D) do not apply to—

   (a) an agricultural trailer or agricultural trailed appliance that is not, in either case, drawn at a speed exceeding 20mph;

   (b) a locomotive;

   (c) a motor tractor;

   (d) an agricultural motor vehicle unless it is first used after 1st June 1986 and is driven at more than 20mph;

   (e) a vehicle which has a maximum speed not exceeding 25 km/h;

   (f) a works trailer;

   (g) a works truck;

   (h) a public works vehicle;

   (i) a trailer designed and constructed, or adapted, to be drawn exclusively by a vehicle to which sub-paragraph (b), (c), (e), (g) or (h) of this paragraph applies;

   (j) a trailer falling within regulation 16(3)(b), (bb), (bc), (d), (e), (f) or (g);

 (ja) a trailer which is manufactured before 1st January 1997 and has a maximum total design axle weight that does not exceed 750kg; or]

   (k) a vehicle manufactured by Leyland Vehicles Limited and known as the Atlantean Bus, if first used before 1st October 1984.

(3) The requirements specified in paragraphs (1), (1A), (1C) and (1D) shall apply to the classes of vehicles specified in the Table so that—

   (a) in item 3, the testing requirement specified in paragraph 1.5.1 and 1.5.2 of Annex II to Community Directives 79/489, 85/647, 88/194 and 91/422 shall apply to every vehicle specified in that item other than—

      (i) a double-decked vehicle first used before 1st October 1983, or

     (ii) a vehicle of a type in respect of which a member state of the European Economic Community has issued a type approval certificate in accordance with Community Directive 79/489, 85/647, 88/194 or 91/422;

   (b) in items 2 and 3—

      (i) the requirements specified in paragraph 1.1.4.2 of Annex II to Community Directive 79/489, 85/647, 88/194 and 91/422 shall not apply in relation to any vehicle first used before 1st April 1996;

     (ii) those requirements shall not apply in relation to any relevant bus first used on or after that date;

(iii) sub-note (2) to paragraph 1.17.2 of Annex I to Community Directive 85/647, 88/194 and 91/422 shall not apply in relation to any vehicle,

and for the purposes of this sub-paragraph "*relevant bus*" means a bus that is not a coach;

(c) in items 1, 2, 3, 4, 5 and 6, in the case of vehicles constructed or adapted for use by physically handicapped drivers, the requirement in paragraph 2.1.2.1 of Annex I to Community Directive 79/489 that the driver must be able to achieve the braking action mentioned in that paragraph from his driving seat without removing his hands from the steering control shall be modified so as to require that the driver is able to achieve that action while continuing to steer the vehicle; and

(d) in items 1, 4, 5, 6, 7, 8, 9 and 10, the requirement specified in paragraph 1.1.4.2 of Annex II to Community Directive 79/489 shall not apply to a vehicle first used (in the case of a motor vehicle) or manufactured (in the case of a trailer) before the relevant date as defined in paragraph (1B) if either—

    (i) following a test in respect of which the fee numbered 26024/26250 to 26257, prescribed in Schedule 1 to the Motor Vehicles (Type Approval and Approval Marks) (Fees) Regulations 1990, or the corresponding fee prescribed under any corresponding previous enactment is payable, a document is issued by the Secretary of State indicating that, at the date of manufacture of the vehicle, the type to which it belonged complied with the requirements specified in Annex 13 to ECE Regulation 13.03, 13.04, 13.05 or 13.06; or

    (ii) as a result of a notifiable alteration to the vehicle within the meaning of regulation 3 of the Plating and Testing Regulations, a fitment has been approved as complying with the requirements mentioned in sub-paragraph (i).

(3A) The requirements specified in paragraphs (1A), (1C) and (1D) shall apply to a road tanker subject to the exclusion of paragraph 4.3 of Annex X to Community Directive 85/647.

(3B) No motor vehicle to which paragraph (1D) applies and which is first used on or after 1st April 1996 shall be fitted with an integrated retarder unless either—

(a) the motor vehicle is fitted with an anti-lock device which acts on the retarder and which complies with the requirements specified in Annex X to Community Directive 91/422; or

(b) the retarder is fitted with a cut-out device which allows the combined control to apply the service braking system alone and which can be operated by the driver from the driving seat;

and expressions (other than the word "*vehicle*") used in this paragraph which are also used in Annex I to Community Directive 85/647 shall, for the purposes of this paragraph, have the same meanings as in that Annex save that "*retarder*" shall not in any circumstances include a regenerative braking system.

(4) Instead of complying with paragraph (1) of this regulation, a vehicle to which this regulation applies may comply with ECE Regulation 13.03, 13.04, 13.05 or 13.06.

(5) Instead of complying with paragraph (1A) of this regulation, a vehicle to which this regulation applies may comply with ECE Regulation 13.05 or 13.06.

(5A) Instead of complying with paragraph (1C) or (1D) of this regulation, a vehicle to which this regulation applies may comply—

(a) in the case of a trailer manufactured before 1st April 1992, with ECE Regulation 13.05 or 13.06; or

(b) in the case of any vehicle not falling within sub-paragraph (a), with ECE Regulation 13.06.

(6) In paragraph (3A), the expression "*road tanker*" means any vehicle or trailer which carries liquid fuel in a tank forming part of the vehicle or trailer other than that containing the fuel which is used to propel the vehicle, and also includes any tank with a capacity exceeding 3m³ carried on a vehicle.

(7) In this regulation, and in relation to the application to any vehicle of any provision of Community Directive 85/647, 88/194 or 91/422, the definitions of "*semi-trailer*", "*full trailer*" and "*centre-axle trailer*" set out in that Directive shall apply and the meaning of "*semi-trailer*" in column 2 of the Table in regulation 3(2) shall not apply.

TABLE
(regulation 15(1))

1	2	3
Item	*Class of Vehicle*	*Vehicle category in the Community Directive*
1	Passenger vehicles and dual-purpose vehicles which have 3 or more wheels except— (a) dual-purpose vehicles constructed or adapted to carry not more than 2 passengers exclusive of the driver; (b) motor cycles with sidecar attached; (c) vehicles with three wheels, an unladen weight not exceeding 410kg, a maximum design speed not exceeding 50 km/h and an engine capacity not exceeding 50cc; (d) buses.	M1
2	Buses having a maximum gross weight which does not exceed 5000kg.	M2
3	Buses having a maximum gross weight which exceeds 5000kg.	M3
4	Dual-purpose vehicles not within item 1; and goods vehicles, having a maximum gross weight which does not exceed 3500kg, and not being motor cycles with a sidecar attached.	N1
	Goods vehicles with a maximum gross weight which—	
5	exceeds 3500kg but does not exceed 12,000kg;	N2
6	exceeds 12,000kg.	N3
	Trailers with a maximum total design axle weight which—	
7	does not exceed 750kg;	01
8	exceeds 750kg but does not exceed 3500kg;	02
9	exceeds 3500kg but does not exceed 10,000kg;	03
10	exceeds 10,000kg.	04]

[Regulation 15 is printed as amended by S.I. 1987 No. 676; S.I. 1990 No. 1981; S.I. 1992 No. 352; S.I. 1995 Nos 551 and 737; S.I. 1996 No. 3033. **B27.40**

The text reproduced above is based on a consolidated text (as subsequently amended) scheduled to S.I. 1995 No. 551 which incorporated the amendments effected by that instrument, by earlier instruments and by S.I. 1995 No. 737; it also incorporated a number of minor changes to spellings and punctuation.

S.I. 1996 No. 3033 (which substituted regulation 15(2)(j) and (ja) for regulation 15(2)(j)) disapplied the exemption from compliance in respect of trailers manufactured on or after January 1, 1997. S.I. 1996 No. 3033 expressly states (regulation 2(2)) that so far as any requirement is imposed by it such requirement is imposed in exercise of powers conferred by section 41 of the Road Traffic Act 1988 to the exclusion of powers under section 2(2) of the European Communities Act 1972.

The Motor Vehicles (Type Approval and Approval Marks) (Fees) Regulations 1990 (S.I. 1990 No. 461) to which reference is made in regulation 15(3)(d) have been revoked; see now the Motor Vehicles (Type Approval and Approval Marks) (Fees) Regulations 1999 (S.I. 1999 No. 2149); no formal amendment has, however, been made to regulation 15(3)(d) in consequence of the revocation of S.I. 1990 No. 461.

The following definitions (which are referred to in regulation 15(7)) are taken from Commission Directive 85/647/EEC:

"*Semi-trailer*" means a towed vehicle in which the axle(s) is (are) positioned behind the centre of gravity of the vehicle (when uniformly loaded) and which is equipped with a connecting device permitting horizontal and vertical forces to be transmitted to the drawing vehicle.

"*Full trailer*" means a towed vehicle having at least two axles, and equipped with a towing device which can move vertically (in relation to the trailer) and controls the direction of the front axle(s), but which transmits no significant static load to the drawing vehicle.

"*Centre-axle trailer*" means a towed vehicle equipped with a towing device which cannot move vertically (in relation to the trailer), and in which the axle(s) is (are) positioned close to the centre of gravity of the vehicle (when uniformly loaded) such that only a small static vertical load, not exceeding 10% of the maximum mass of the trailer or 1,000kg (whichever is the lesser) is transmitted to the drawing vehicle.

The maximum mass to be taken into consideration when classifying a centre-axle trailer shall be the mass transmitted to the ground by the axle(s) of the centre-axle trailer when coupled to the drawing vehicle and laden with a maximum load.]

16. Braking systems of vehicles to which regulation 15 does not apply

B27.41   (1) Save as provided in paragraphs (2) and (3), this regulation applies to every vehicle to which regulation 15 does not apply.

(2) Paragraph (4) of this regulation does not apply to a vehicle which complies with regulation 15 by virtue of the proviso to [regulation 15(1), (1A) [, (1C) or (1D)]], or which complies with Community Directive 79/489, 85/647 [, 88/194 or 91/422] or ECE Regulation 13.03, 13.04, 13.05 or 13.06].

(3) This regulation does not apply to the following vehicles, except in the case of a vehicle referred to in (a) in so far as the regulation concerns parking brakes (requirements 16 to 18 in Schedule 3)—

(a) a locomotive first used before 2nd January 1983, propelled by steam, and with an engine which is capable of being reversed;

[(b) a trailer which is designed for use and used for street cleansing and does not carry any load other than its necessary gear and equipment;]

[(ba) a trailer which has a maximum total design axle weight that does not exceed 750kg;]

[(bb) a trailer which—

(i) is an agricultural trailer manufactured before 1st July 1947;

(ii) is being drawn by a motor tractor or an agricultural motor vehicle at a speed not exceeding 10mph;

    (iii) has a laden weight not exceeding 4070kg; and

    (iv) is the only trailer being drawn;]

[(bc) a trailer which is being drawn by a motor cycle in accordance with regulation 84;]

  (c) an agricultural trailed appliance;

  (d) an agricultural trailed appliance conveyor;

  (e) a broken down vehicle;

  (f) before 1st October 1986—

    (i) a trailer with an unladen weight not exceeding 102kg which was manufactured before 1st October 1982; and

    (ii) a gritting trailer; or

  (g) on or after 1st October 1986, a gritting trailer with a maximum gross weight not exceeding 2000kg.

(4) Save as provided in paragraph (7), a vehicle of a class specified in an item in column 2 of the Table shall comply with the requirements shown in column 3 in that item, subject to any exemptions or modifications shown in column 4 in that item, references to numbers in column 3 being references to the requirements so numbered in Schedule 3.

    Provided that wheeled agricultural motor vehicles not driven at more than 20mph are excluded from all items other than items 21 to 23.

TABLE

(regulation 16(4))

1	2	3	4
Item	Class of vehicle	Requirement in Schedule 3	Exemptions or modifications
	Motor cars		
1	First used before 1st January 1915.	3, 6, 7, 13, 16	Requirements 13 and 16 do not apply to a motor car with less than 4 wheels.
2	First used on or after 1st January 1915 but before 1st April 1938.	1, 4, 6, 7, 9, 16	A works truck within items 1 to 11 is not subject to requirements 1, 2, 3 or 4 if it is equipped with one braking system with one means of operation.
3	First used on or after 1st April 1938 and being either a track-laying vehicle or a vehicle first used before 1st January 1968.	1, 4, 6, 7, 8, 9, 16	
4	Wheeled vehicles first used on or after 1st January 1968.	1, 4, 6, 7, 8, 9, [15,] 18	
	Heavy motor cars		
5	First used before 15th August 1928.	1, 6, 16	
6	First used on or after 15th August 1928 but before 1st April 1938.	1, 4, 6, 7, 8, 16	

[continued on next page

1	2	3	4
Item	Class of vehicle	Requirement in Schedule 3	Exemptions or modifications
	Heavy motor cars—cont.		
7	First used on or after 1st April 1938 and being either a track-laying vehicle or a vehicle first used before 1st January 1968.	1, 4, 6, 7, 8, 9, 16	
8	Wheeled vehicles first used on or after 1st January 1968.	1, 4, 6, 7, 8, 9, [15,] 18	
	Motor cycles		
9	First used before 1st January 1927.	3, and, in the case of three-wheeled vehicles, 16	
10	First used on or after 1st January 1927 but before 1st January 1968.	2, 7, and, in the case of three-wheeled vehicles, 16	
11	First used on or after 1st January 1968 and not being a motor cycle to which paragraph (5) applies.	2, 7, and, in the case of three-wheeled vehicles, 18	
	Locomotives		
12	Wheeled vehicles first used before 1st June 1955.	3, 6, 12, 16	
13	Wheeled vehicles first used on or after 1st June 1955 but before 1st January 1968.	3, 4, 6, 7, 8, 9, 18	
14	Wheeled vehicles first used on or after 1st January 1968.	3, 4, 6, 7, 8, 9, 18	
15	Track-laying vehicles.	3, 6, 16	
	Motor tractors		
16	Wheeled vehicles first used before 14th January 1931 and track-laying vehicles first used before 1st April 1938.	3, 4, 6, 7, 16	Industrial tractors within items 16 to 19 are subject to requirement 5 instead of requirement 4.
17	Wheeled vehicles first used on or after 14th January 1931 but before 1st April 1938.	3, 4, 6, 7, 9, 16	
18	Wheeled vehicles first used on or after 1st April 1938 but before 1st January 1968.	3, 4, 7, 8, 9, 16	
19	Wheeled vehicles first used on or after 1st January 1968.	3, 4, 6, 7, 8, 9, 18	
20	Track-laying vehicles first used on or after 1st April 1938.	3, 4, 6, 7, 8, 16	

[continued on next page

1	2	3	4
Item	*Class of vehicle*	*Requirement in Schedule 3*	*Exemptions or modifications*
	Wheeled agricultural motor vehicles not driven at more than 20mph		
21	First used before 1st January 1968.	3, 4, 6, 7, 8, 16	
22	First used on or after 1st January 1968 but before 9th February 1980.	3, 4, 6, 7, 8, 18	
23	First used on or after 9th February 1980.	3, 5, 6, 7, 8, 18	
	Invalid carriages		
24	Whenever first used.	3, 13	
	Trailers		
25	Manufactured before 1st April 1938.	3, 10, 14, 17	
26	Manufactured on or after 1st April 1938 and being either a track-laying vehicle, an agricultural trailer or a vehicle manufactured before 1st January 1968.	3, 8, 10, 14, 17	Agricultural trailers are not subject to requirement 8.
27	Wheeled vehicles manufactured on or after 1st January 1968, not being an agricultural trailer.	3, 4, 8, 11, 15, 18	Trailers equipped with brakes which come into operation on the overrun of the vehicle are not subject to requirement 15.

[(5) Subject to paragraphs (5B) and (6), the braking system of a motor cycle to which this regulation applies and which is—

(a) of a class specified in an item in column 2 of the Table below; and

(b) first used on or after 1st April 1987 and before 22nd May 1995;

shall comply with ECE Regulation 13.05, 78 or 78.01 [or Community Directive 93/143] in relation to the category of vehicles specified in that item in column 3.]

[(5A) Subject to paragraph (6), the braking system of a motor cycle to which this regulation applies and which is—

(a) of a class specified in an item in column 2 of the Table below [*on p. 1276*]; and

(b) first used on or after 22nd May 1995;

shall comply with ECE Regulation 78.01 [or Community Directive 93/143] in relation to the category of vehicles specified in that item in column 3.]

[[(5B)] In relation to a motor cycle with two wheels manufactured by Piaggio Veicoli Europei Societa per Azione and known as the Cosa 125, the Cosa 125E, the Cosa L125, the Cosa LX125, the Cosa 200, the Cosa 200E, the Cosa L200 or the Cosa LX200, paragraph (5) shall have effect as if ECE Regulation 13.05 were modified by—

[TABLE

(Regulation 16(5) and (5A))

1 Item	2 Class of vehicle	3 [Vehicle category in ECE Regulations or Community Directive 93/14 (as the case may be)]
1	Vehicles (without a sidecar attached) with two wheels, an engine capacity not exceeding 50cc and a maximum design speed not exceeding 50 km/h.	L1
2	Vehicles with three wheels (including two-wheeled vehicles with a sidecar attached) and with an engine capacity not exceeding 50cc and a maximum design speed not exceeding 50 km/h.	L2
3	Vehicles with two wheels (without a sidecar attached) and with— (a) an engine capacity exceeding 50cc, or (b) a maximum design speed exceeding 50 km/h.	L3
4	Vehicles with two wheels, a sidecar attached and— (a) an engine capacity exceeding 50cc, or (b) a maximum design speed exceeding 50 km/h.	L4]

(a) the omission of paragraph 4.4 (approval marks), and

(b) in paragraph 5.3.1.1, (independent braking devices and controls), the omission of the word "independent" in the first place where it appears,

but this paragraph shall not apply to a motor cycle first used on or after 1st July 1991.]

(6) Paragraph (5) does not apply to a works truck or to a vehicle constructed or assembled by a person not ordinarily engaged in the business of manufacturing vehicles of that description.

[(6A) Paragraph (5A) does not apply to—

(a) a vehicle with a maximum speed not exceeding 25 km/h; or

(b) a vehicle fitted for an invalid driver.]

(7) Instead of complying with the provisions of paragraph (4) of this Regulation an agricultural motor vehicle may comply with Community Directive 76/432 [or 96/63].

B27.42   *[Regulation 16 is printed as amended by S.I. 1987 No. 676; S.I. 1990 No. 1981; S.I. 1992 No. 352; S.I. 1995 No. 551; S.I. 1996 No. 3033; S.I. 1998 No. 2429.]*

17. Vacuum or pressure brake warning devices

B27.43   (1) Save as provided in paragraph (2), every motor vehicle which is equipped with a braking system which embodies a vacuum or pressure reservoir or reservoirs shall be equipped with a device so placed as to be readily visible to the driver of the vehicle and which is capable of indicating any impending failure of, or deficiency in, the vacuum or pressure system.

(2) The requirement specified in paragraph (1) does not apply in respect of—

(a) a vehicle to which [[paragraph (1), (1A) [, (1C) or (1D)]] of] regulation 15 applies, or which complies with the requirements of that regulation, of [Community Directive 79/489, 85/647 or [, 88/194 or 91/422]] or of ECE Regulation 13.03, 13.04 [, 13.05 or 13.06];

(b) an agricultural motor vehicle which complies with Community Directive 76/432 [or 96/63];

(c) a vehicle with an unladen weight not exceeding 3050kg propelled by an internal combustion engine, if the vacuum in the reservoir or reservoirs is derived directly from the inclusion system of the engine, and if, in the event of a failure of, or deficiency in, the vacuum system, the brakes of that braking system are sufficient under the most adverse conditions to bring the vehicle to rest within a reasonable distance; or

(d) a vehicle first used before 1st October 1937.

[Regulation 17 is printed as amended by S.I. 1987 No. 676; S.I. 1990 No. 1981; S.I. 1992 No. 352; S.I. 1995 No. 551; S.I. 1998 No. 2429.]   **B27.44**

[17A. Couplings on trailer pneumatic braking systems

(1) In this regulation—   **B27.45**

"*BS coupling*" means a coupling which—

     (a) is the type shown in figure 1, 4 or 5 of the British Standard specification; and

     (b) complies with the dimensions shown in that figure;

"*the British Standard specification*" means the British Standard specification for dimensions of "contact" type couplings for air pressure braking systems on trailers and semi-trailers and their towing vehicles, and the arrangements of these couplings on articulated and drawbar combinations, published by the British Standards Institution under reference number BS AU 138a: 1980;

"*coupling*", "*emergency line*", "*secondary line*" and "*service line*" have the same meanings as in the British Standard specification;

"*EEA Agreement*" means the Agreement on the European Economic Area signed at Oporto on the 2nd May 1992 as adjusted by the Protocol signed at Brussels on 17th March 1993; and

"*EEA State*" means a state which is a Contracting Party to the EEA Agreement.

(2) For the purposes of this regulation, a relevant coupling is a coupling that is physically capable of being connected to a BS coupling.

(3) Subject to paragraphs (6) and (7), no service line comprised in a pneumatic braking system fitted to a trailer shall be equipped with a relevant coupling unless that coupling—

     (a) is of the type shown in figure 2 of the British Standard specification;

     (b) complies with the dimensions shown in that figure; and

     (c) complies with paragraph 3.4.3 of that specification (except so far as it requires it to be of a type shown in that figure).

(4) Subject to paragraphs (6), (7) and (8) no emergency line comprised in a pneumatic braking system fitted to a trailer shall be equipped with a relevant coupling unless that coupling—

     (a) is of the type shown in figure 3 of the British Standard specification; and

     (b) complies with the dimensions shown in that figure.

(5) Subject to paragraphs (6), (7) and (8) no secondary line comprised in a pneumatic braking system fitted to a trailer shall be equipped with a relevant coupling unless that coupling—

(a) is of the type shown in figure 6 of the British Standard specification; and

(b) complies with the dimensions shown in that figure.

(6) For the purposes of paragraphs (3), (4) and (5), a reference to the dimensions shown in a figure in the British Standard specification does not include any dimension marked "M22×1.5".

(7) Paragraph (3) shall not apply to a relevant coupling which fulfils the requirements of—

(a) a standard or code of practice of a national standards body or equivalent body of any EEA State;

(b) any international standard recognised for use as a standard by any EEA State; or

(c) a technical specification or code of practice which, whether mandatory or not, is recognised for use as a standard by a public authority of any EEA State,

where the standard, code of practice, international standard or technical specification provides, in relation to couplings, a level of safety and compatibility with a BS coupling of the type shown in figure 1 of the British Standard specification equivalent to that provided by the British Standard specification as modified in accordance with paragraph (6).

(8) Paragraph (7) shall have effect—

(a) in relation to paragraph (4), as if for the words "paragraph (3)" there were substituted the words "paragraph (4)" and for the words "figure 1" there were substituted the words "figure 4"; and

(b) in relation to paragraph (5), as if for the words "paragraph (3)" there were substituted the words "paragraph (5)" and for the words "figure 1" there were substituted the words "figure 5".]

B27.46   *[Regulation 17A was inserted by S.I. 1996 No. 3033.*

S.I. 1996 No. 3033 expressly states (regulation 2(2)) that so far as any requirement is imposed by it such requirement is imposed in exercise of powers conferred by section 41 of the Road Traffic Act 1988 to the exclusion of the powers under section 2(2) of the European Communities Act 1972.

As to the European Economic Area and the EEA agreement, see the note to Regulation (EEC) 3820/85 below.]

18. Maintenance and efficiency of brakes

B27.47   (1) Every part of every braking system and of the means of operation thereof fitted to a vehicle shall be maintained in good and efficient working order and be properly adjusted.

[(1A) Without prejudice to paragraph (3), where a vehicle is fitted with an anti-lock braking system ("*the ABS*"), then while the condition specified in paragraph (1B) is fulfilled, any fault in the ABS shall be disregarded for the purposes of paragraph (1).]

[(1B) The condition is fulfilled while the vehicle is completing a journey at the beginning of which the ABS was operating correctly or is being driven to a place where the ABS is to undergo repairs.]

(2) Paragraph (3) applies to every wheeled motor vehicle except—

(a) an agricultural motor vehicle which is not driven at more than 20mph;

(b) a works truck; . . .

(c) a pedestrian-controlled vehicle [; and]

[(d) an industrial tractor.]

(3) Every vehicle to which this paragraph applies and which is of a class specified in an item in column 2 of Table I shall, subject to any exemption shown for that item in column 4, be so maintained that—

(a) its service braking system has a total braking efficiency not less than that shown in column (3)(a) for that item; and

(b) if the vehicle is a heavy motor car, a motor car first used on or after 1st January 1915 or a motor cycle first used on or after 1st January 1927, its secondary braking system has a total braking efficiency not less than that shown in column 3(b) for those items.

Provided that a reference in Table I to a trailer is a reference to a trailer required by regulation 15 or 16 to be equipped with brakes.

TABLE I

(regulation 18(3))

1	2	3		4
Item	Class of vehicle	Efficiencies %		Exemptions
		(a)	(b)	
1	A vehicle to which regulation 15 applies or which complies in all respects other than its braking efficiency with the requirements of that regulation or with [Community Directive 79/489, 85/647 [88/194 or 91/422]] or with ECE Regulation 13.03, 13.04 [, 13.05 or 13.06]—			A motor cycle.
	(a) when not drawing a trailer;	50	25	
	(b) when drawing a trailer	45	25	
2	A vehicle, not included in item 1 and not being a motor cycle, which is first used on or after 1st January 1968—			
	(a) when not drawing a trailer;	50	25	
	(b) when drawing a trailer manufactured on or after 1st January 1968;	50	25	
	(c) when drawing a trailer manufactured before 1st January 1968	40	15	
3	Goods vehicles [and buses (in each case)] first used on or after 15th August 1928 but before 1st January 1968 having an unladen weight exceeding 1525kg being—			
	(a) rigid vehicles with 2 axles not constructed to form part of an articulated vehicle—			
	(i) when not drawing a trailer	45	20	
	(ii) when drawing a trailer	40	15	
	(b) other vehicles, including vehicles constructed to form part of an articulated vehicle, whether or not drawing a trailer	40	15	

[continued on next page

1	*2*	*3*		*4*
Item	*Class of vehicle*	*Efficiencies* %		*Exemptions*
		(a)	(b)	
4	Vehicles not included in items 1 to 3—			(a) a bus;
	(a) having at least one means of operation applying to at least 4 wheels;	50	25	(b) an articulated vehicle;
	(b) having 3 wheels and at least one means of operation applying to all 3 wheels and not being a motor cycle with sidecar attached			(c) a vehicle constructed or adapted to form part of an articulated vehicle;
	(i) when not drawing a trailer	40	25	(d) a heavy motor car
	(ii) in the case of a motor cycle when drawing a trailer	40	25	which is a goods vehicle first used before 15th August 1928.
	(c) other			
	(i) when not drawing a trailer	30	25	
	(ii) in the case of a motor cycle when drawing a trailer.	30	25	

(4) A goods vehicle shall not be deemed to comply with the requirements of paragraph (3) unless it is capable of complying with those requirements both at the laden weight at which it is operating at any time and when its laden weight is equal to—

(a) if a plating certificate has been issued and is in force for the vehicle, the design gross weight shown in column (3) of that certificate or, if no such weight is so shown, the gross weight shown in column (2) of that certificate; and

(b) in any other case, the design gross weight of the vehicle.

Provided that in the case of a goods vehicle drawing a trailer, references in this paragraph to laden weight refer to the combined laden weight of the drawing vehicle and the trailer and references to gross weight and design gross weight are to be taken as references to train weight and design train weight respectively.

[(4A) A bus shall be deemed not to comply with the requirements of paragraph (3) unless it is capable of complying with those requirements both at its laden weight for the time being and at its relevant weight.]

[(4B) For the purposes of paragraph (4A), the relevant weight,—

(a) in relation to a bus first used on or after 1st April 1982, is its maximum gross weight; and

(b) in relation to a bus first used before that date, is the weight specified in paragraph (4C).]

[(4C) The weight referred to in paragraph (4B)(b) is—

$X + 63.5 (Y + Z)$ kg

where—

X is the unladen weight of that bus in kilograms;

Y is the number of passengers that the bus is constructed or adapted to carry seated in addition to the driver; and

Z is—

(a) in the case of a PSV which is not an articulated bus and has a standing capacity exceeding 8 persons, the standing capacity minus 8;

(b)　in the case of a PSV which is an articulated bus, the standing capacity; or

(c)　in any other case, nil.]

(5)　The brakes of every agricultural motor vehicle which is first used on or after 1st June 1986 and is not driven at more than 20mph, and of every agricultural trailer manufactured on or after 1st December 1985 shall be capable of achieving a braking efficiency of not less than 25% when the weight of the vehicle is equal to the total maximum axle weights which the vehicle is designed to have.

(6)　Every vehicle or combination of vehicles specified in an item in column 2 of Table II shall be so maintained that its brakes are capable, without the assistance of stored energy, of holding it stationary on a gradient of at least the percentage specified in column 3 in that item.

(7)　For the purpose of this regulation the date of manufacture of a trailer which is a composite trailer shall be deemed to be the same as the date of manufacture of the semi-trailer which forms part of the composite trailer.

TABLE II

(regulation 18(6))

1	2	3
Item	*Class of vehicle or combination*	*Percentage gradient*
1	A vehicle specified in item 1 of Table I—	
	(a)　when not drawing a trailer	16
	(b)　when drawing a trailer.	12
2	A vehicle to which requirement 18 in Schedule 3 applies by virtue of regulation 16.	16
3	A vehicle, not included in item 1, drawing a trailer manufactured on or after 1st January 1968 and required, by regulation 15 or 16, to be fitted with brakes.	16

(8)　A vehicle which is subject to, and which complies with the requirements in, item 1 and Tables I and II shall not be treated as failing, by reason of its braking efficiency, to comply with regulation 15 or with [Community Directive 79/489, 85/647 [, 88/194 or 91/422]] or ECE Regulation 13.03, 13.04 [, 13.05 or 13.06].

[(9)　In this regulation—

"*PSV*" means a public service vehicle within the meaning of section 1 of the Public Passenger Vehicles Act 1981 [*as amended by the Transport Act 1985, Sched. 8*];

"*standing capacity*", in relation to a PSV, means the number of persons that can be carried standing without an offence being committed under section 26 of the Public Passenger Vehicles Act 1981.]

[Regulation 18 is printed as amended by S.I. 1987 No. 676; S.I. 1990 No. 1981; S.I. 1992 No. 352; S.I. 1995 No. 551.]　　**B27.48**

19. Application of brakes of trailers

Where a trailer is drawn by a motor vehicle the driver (or in the case of a locomotive one of the persons employed in driving or tending the locomotive) shall be in a position readily　**B27.49** to operate any brakes required by these Regulations to be fitted to the trailer as well as the brakes of the motor vehicle unless a person other than the driver [(or in the case of a locomotive a person other than one of the persons employed in driving or tending the locomotive)] is in a position and competent efficiently to apply the brakes of the trailer.

Provided that this regulation shall not apply to a trailer which—

    (a) in compliance with these Regulations, is fitted with brakes which automatically come into operation on the overrun of the trailer; or

    (b) . . . is a broken down vehicle being drawn, whether or not in consequence of a breakdown, in such a manner that it cannot be steered by its own steering gear.

B27.50   *[Regulation 19 is printed as amended by S.I. 1990 No. 1981.]*

C *Wheels, Springs, Tyres and Tracks*

20. General requirements as to wheels and tracks

B27.51   Every motor cycle and invalid carriage shall be a wheeled vehicle, and every other motor vehicle and every trailer shall be either a wheeled vehicle or a track-laying vehicle.

B27.52   **21. Diameter of wheels**   *[Revoked by S.I. 1995 No. 1201.]*

B27.53   **22. Springs and resilient material**

(1) Save as provided in paragraphs (3) and (4), every motor vehicle and every trailer be equipped with suitable and sufficient springs between each wheel and the frame of the vehicle.

(2) Save as provided in paragraphs (3) and (4), in the case of a track-laying vehicle—

    (a) resilient material shall be interposed between the rims of the weight-carrying rollers and the road surface so that the weight of the vehicle, other than that borne by any wheel, is supported by the resilient material, and

    (b) where the vehicle is a heavy motor car, motor car, or trailer it shall have suitable springs between the frame of the vehicle and the weight-carrying rollers.

(3) This regulation does not apply to—

    (a) a wheeled vehicle with an unladen weight not exceeding 4070kg and which is—

        (i) a motor tractor any unsprung wheel of which is fitted with a pneumatic tyre;

        (ii) a motor tractor used in connection with railway shunting and which is used on a road only when passing from one railway track to another in connection with such use;

        (iii) a vehicle specially designed, and mainly used, for work on rough ground or unmade roads and every wheel of which is fitted with a pneumatic tyre and which is not driven at more than 20mph;

        (iv) a vehicle constructed or adapted for, and being used for, road sweeping and every wheel of which is fitted with either a pneumatic tyre or a resilient tyre and which is not driven at more than 20mph;

    (b) an agricultural motor vehicle which is not driven at more than 20mph;

    (c) an agricultural trailer, or an agricultural trailed appliance;

    (d) a trailer used solely for the haulage of felled trees;

    (e) a motor cycle;

    (f) a mobile crane;

    (g) a pedestrian-controlled vehicle all the wheels of which are equipped with pneumatic tyres;

(h) a road roller;

(i) a broken down vehicle; or

(j) a vehicle first used on or before 1st January 1932.

(4) Paragraphs (1) and (2)(b) do not apply to a works truck or a works trailer.

23. Wheel loads

(1) Subject to paragraph (2) this regulation applies to—   **B27.54**

(a) a semi-trailer with more than 2 wheels;

(b) a track-laying vehicle with more than 2 wheels; and

(c) any other vehicle with more than 4 wheels.

(2) This regulation does not apply to a road roller.

(3) Save as provided in paragraphs (4) and (5), every vehicle to which this regulation applies shall be fitted with a compensating arrangement which will ensure that under the most adverse conditions every wheel will remain in contact with the road and will not be subject to abnormal variations of load.

(4) Paragraph (3) does not apply in respect of a steerable wheel on which the load does not exceed—

(a) if it is a wheeled vehicle, [4250kg]; and

(b) if it is a track-laying vehicle, 2540kg.

(5) In the application of paragraph (3) to an agricultural motor vehicle, wheels which are in line transversely on one side of the longitudinal axis of the vehicle shall be regarded as one wheel.

[Regulation 23 is printed as amended by S.I. 1998 No. 3112.]   **B27.55**

24. Tyres

(1) Save as provided in paragraph (2), every wheel of a vehicle of a class specified in an   **B27.56**
item in column 2 of the Table shall be fitted with a tyre of a type specified in that item in column 3 which complies with any conditions specified in that item in column 4.

(2) The requirements referred to in paragraph (1) do not apply to a road-roller and are subject, in the case of any item in the Table, to the exemptions specified in that item in column 5.

TABLE

(regulation 24(1))

1	2	3	4	5
Item	Class of vehicle	Type of tyre	Conditions	Exemptions
1	Locomotives not falling into item 6	Pneumatic or resilient		
2	Motor tractors not falling in item 6	Pneumatic or resilient	No re-cut pneumatic tyre shall be fitted to any wheel of a	

[continued on next page

1	*2*	*3*	*4*	*5*
Item	*Class of vehicle*	*Type of tyre*	*Conditions*	*Exemptions*
2— cont.			vehicle with an unladen weight of less than 2540kg unless the diameter of the rim of the wheel is at least 405mm	
3	Heavy motor cars not falling in item 6	Pneumatic		The following, if every wheel not fitted with a pneumatic tyre is fitted with a resilient tyre— (a) a vehicle mainly used for work on rough ground; (b) a tower wagon; (c) a vehicle fitted with a turntable fire escape; (d) a refuse vehicle; (e) a works truck; (f) a vehicle first used before 3rd January 1933.
4	Motor cars not falling in item 6	Pneumatic	No re-cut tyre shall be fitted to any wheel of a vehicle unless it is— (a) an electrically propelled goods vehicle or, (b) a goods vehicle with an unladen weight of at least 2540 kg and the diameter of the rim of the wheel is at least 405mm	The following, if every wheel not fitted with a pneumatic tyre is fitted with a resilient tyre— (a) a vehicle mainly used for work on rough ground; (b) a refuse vehicle; (c) a works truck; (d) a vehicle with an unladen weight not exceeding— (i) 1270kg if electrically propelled; (ii) 1020kg in any other case; (e) a tower wagon; (f) a vehicle fitted with a turntable fire escape; (g) a vehicle first used before 3rd January 1933.

[continued on next page

1	2	3	4	5
Item	Class of vehicle	Type of tyre	Conditions	Exemptions
5	Motor cycles	Pneumatic	No re-cut tyre shall be fitted	The following, if every wheel not fitted with a pneumatic tyre is fitted with a resilient tyre— (a) a works truck; (b) a pedestrian-controlled vehicle
6	Agricultural motor vehicles which are not driven at more than 20mph	Pneumatic or resilient	The same as for item 2	The requirement in column 3 does not apply to a vehicle of which— (a) every steering wheel is fitted with a smooth-soled tyre which is not less than 60mm wide where it touches the road; and (b) in the case of a wheeled vehicle, every driving wheel is fitted with a smooth-soled tyre which— (i) is not less than 150mm wide if the unladen weight of the vehicle exceeds 3050kg, or 76mm wide in any other case, and either (ii) is shod with diagonal cross-bars not less than 76mm wide or more than 20mm thick extending the full breadth of the tyre and so arranged that the space between adjacent bars is not more than 76mm; or (iii) is shod with diagonal cross-bars of resilient material not less than 60mm wide extending the full breadth of the tyre and so arranged that the space between adjacent bars is not more than 76mm.

[*continued on next page*

1	*2*	*3*	*4*	*5*
Item	Class of vehicle	Type of tyre	Conditions	Exemptions
7	Trailers	Pneumatic	Except in the case of a trailer mentioned in paragraph (d) of column 5, no re-cut tyre shall be fitted to any wheel of a trailer drawn by a heavy motor car or a motor car if the trailer— (a) has an unladen weight not exceeding— (i) if it is a living van, 2040kg; or (ii) in any other case, 1020kg; or (b) is not constructed or adapted to carry any load, other than plant or other special appliance which is a permanent or essentially permanent fixture and has a gross weight not exceeding 2290kg	(a) an agricultural trailer manufactured before 1st December 1985; (b) an agricultural trailed appliance; (c) a trailer used to carry water for a road roller being used in connection with road works; (d) the following if every wheel which is not fitted with a pneumatic tyre is fitted with a resilient tyre— (i) a works trailer; (ii) a refuse vehicle; (iii) a trailer drawn by a heavy motor car every wheel of which is not required to be fitted with a pneumatic tyre; (iv) a broken down vehicle; or (v) a trailer drawn by a vehicle which is not a heavy motor car or a motor car.

(3) Save as provided in paragraph (4) a wheel of a vehicle may not be fitted with a temporary use spare tyre unless either—

(a) the vehicle is a passenger vehicle (not being a bus) first used before 1st April 1987; or

(b) the vehicle complies at the time of its first use with ECE Regulation 64 [or Community Directive 92/23].

(4) Paragraph (3) does not apply to a vehicle constructed or assembled by a person not ordinarily engaged in the trade or business of manufacturing vehicles of that description.

B27.57   *[Regulation 24 is printed as amended by S.I. 1992 No. 3088.]*

25. Tyre loads and speed ratings

B27.58   [(1) Save as provided in [paragraphs (3), (4), (7A) and (7B)] any tyre fitted to the axle of a vehicle—

(a) which is a class of vehicle specified in an item in column 2 of Table I; and

(b) in relation to which the date of first use is as specified in that item in column 3 of that Table;

shall comply with the requirements specified in that item in column 4 of that Table.

[TABLE I

(regulation 25(1))

1 Item	2 Class of vehicle	3 Date of first use	4 Requirements
1	Vehicles which are of one or more of the following descriptions, namely— (a) goods vehicles, (b) trailers, (c) buses, (d) vehicles of a class mentioned in column 2 in Table III	Before 1st April 1991	The requirements of paragraphs (5) and (6)
2	Vehicles which are of one or more of the following descriptions— (a) goods vehicles, (b) trailers, (c) buses, (d) vehicles of a class mentioned in column 2 in Table III, and do not fall within item 3 below	On or after 1st April 1991	The requirements of paragraphs (5), (6) and (7)
3	Vehicles of a class mentioned in paragraph (2)	On or after 1st April 1991	The requirements of paragraph (5)]

[(2) The classes of vehicle referred to in item 3 in column 2 of Table I are—

(a) engineering plant;

(b) track-laying vehicles;

(c) vehicles equipped with tyres of speed category Q;

(d) works trucks; and

(e) motor vehicles with a maximum speed not exceeding 30mph, not being vehicles of a class specified in—

    (i) items 2 and 3 of Table II; or

    (ii) paragraph (7A) or sub-paragraphs (a) to (d) of this paragraph;

or trailers while being drawn by such vehicles.]

(3) Paragraph (1) shall not apply to any tyre fitted to the axle of a vehicle if the vehicle is—

(a) broken down or proceeding to a place where it is to be broken up; and

(b) being drawn by a motor vehicle at a speed not exceeding 20mph.

(4) Where in relation to any vehicle first used on or after 1st April 1991 a tyre supplied by a manufacturer for the purposes of tests or trials of that tyre is fitted to an axle of that vehicle, [paragraph (7) shall not apply to that tyre while it is being used for those purposes.]

(5) The requirements of this paragraph are that the tyre, as respects strength, shall be designed and manufactured adequately to support the maximum permitted axle weight for the axle.

(6) The requirements of this paragraph are that the tyre shall be designed and [manufactured] adequately to support the maximum permitted axle weight for the axle when the vehicle is driven at the speed shown in column 3 in Table II in the item in which the vehicle is described in column 2 (the lowest relevant speed being applicable to a vehicle which is described in more than one item).

TABLE II

(regulation 25(6))

1	*2*	*3*	*4*	
Item	*Class of vehicle*	*Speed* (mph)	*Variation to the [load-capacity index] expressed as a percentage*	
			[Tyres marked in accordance with ECE Regulation 30, 30.01 or 30.02] [and relevant car tyres]	Tyres marked in accordance with ECE Regulation 54 [and relevant commercial vehicle tyres]
1	A vehicle of a class for which maximum speeds are prescribed by Schedule 6 to the 1984 Act [other than an agricultural motor vehicle]	The highest speed so prescribed	Single wheels: none Dual wheels: 95.5%	None
2	An electrically propelled vehicle used as a multi-stop local collection and delivery vehicle and having a maximum speed of not more than 25mph	[The maximum speed of the vehicle]	None	150%
3	An electrically propelled vehicle used as a multi-stop local collection and delivery vehicle and having a maximum speed of more than 25mph and not more than 40mph	[The maximum speed of the vehicle]	None	130%

[*continued on next page*

1	2	3	4	
Item	*Class of vehicle*	*Speed* (mph)	*Variation to the [load-capacity index] expressed as a percentage*	
			[Tyres marked in accordance with ECE Regulation 30, 30.01 or 30.02] [and relevant car tyres]	Tyres marked in accordance with ECE Regulation 54 [and relevant commercial vehicle tyres]
4	An electrically propelled vehicle used only within a radius of 25 miles from the permanent base at which it is normally kept and having a maximum speed of more than 40mph and not more than 50mph	[The maximum speed of the vehicle]	None	115%
5	A local service bus	50	None	110%
6	A restricted speed vehicle	50	None	The relevant % variation specified in Annex 8 to ECE Regulation 54 [or Appendix 8 to Annex II to Community Directive 92/23]
7	A low platform trailer [, an agricultural motor vehicle, an agricultural trailer, an agricultural trailed appliance or an agricultural trailed appliance conveyor]	40	None	The relevant % variation specified in Annex 8 to ECE Regulation 54 [or Appendix 8 to Annex II to Community Directive 92/23]
8	A municipal vehicle	40	None	115%
9	A multi-stop local collection and delivery vehicle if not falling within the class of vehicle described in items 2 or 3 above	40	None	115%
10	A light trailer or any trailer equipped with tyres of speed category F or G	60	Single wheels: 110%	The relevant variation specified in Annex 8 to ECE

[*continued on next page*

1	2	3	4	
Item	*Class of vehicle*	*Speed* (mph)	*Variation to the [load-capacity index] expressed as a percentage*	
			[Tyres marked in accordance with ECE Regulation 30, 30.01 or 30.02] [and relevant car tyres]	Tyres marked in accordance with ECE Regulation 54 [and relevant commercial vehicle tyres]
10—cont.				Regulation 54 [or Appendix 8 to Annex II to Community Directive 92/23]
11	A trailer not falling in items 6–10	60	Dual wheels: 105% Single wheels: none Dual wheels: 95.5%	None
12	A [motor] vehicle not fall-ing in items 1–11	70	Single wheels: none Dual wheels: 95.5%	None

(7) The requirement of this paragraph is that the tyre when first fitted to the vehicle [was marked with a designated approval mark or] complied with the requirements of [ECE Regulation 30, 30.01, 30.02] or 54, but this requirement shall not apply to a retreaded tyre.

[(7A) The requirements of paragraphs (6) and (7) shall not apply to [any tyre fitted to the axle of] a vehicle of a class specified in an item in column 2 of Table III while [the vehicle] is being driven or drawn at a speed not exceeding that specified in that item in column 3 of that Table.

TABLE III

(regulation 25(7A))

1	2	3
Item	*Class of vehicle*	*Speed (mph)*
1	Agricultural motor vehicles	20
2	Agricultural trailers	20
3	Agricultural trailed appliances	20
4	Agricultural trailed appliance conveyors	20
5	Works trailers	18]

[(7B) Paragraph (7C) applies where a tyre fitted to the axle of a vehicle—

(a) bears a speed category symbol and load-capacity index, being marks that were moulded on to or into the tyre at the time that it was manufactured;

(b) is designed and manufactured so as to be capable of operating safely at the speed and load indicated by those marks; and

(c) is designed so as to be capable of being fitted to the axle of a vehicle of a class specified in item 1, 2, 3 or 4 in column 2 of Table III above.]

[(7C) In the circumstances mentioned in paragraph (7B), paragraph (7) shall not apply to the tyre if—

(a) the vehicle is being driven or drawn at a speed that does not exceed the speed indicated by the speed category symbol or 50mph (whichever is the less), and

(b) the load on the tyre does not exceed the load indicated by the load-capacity index.]

(8) A vehicle of a class described in column 2 in Table II first used on or after 1st April 1991 shall not be used on a road—

(a) in the case where there is no entry in column 4 specifying a variation to the [load-capacity index] expressed as a percentage, if the load applied to any tyre fitted to the axle of the vehicle exceeds that indicated by the [load-capacity index]; or

(b) in the case where there is such an entry in column 4, if the load applied to any tyre fitted to the axle of the vehicle exceeds the variation to the [load-capacity index] expressed as a percentage.

(9) In this regulation—

"*designated approval mark*" means the marking designated as an approval mark by regulation 5 of the Approval Marks Regulations and shown at item 33 in Schedule 4 to those Regulations (that item being a marking relating to Community Directive 92/23);]

"*dual wheels*" means two or more wheels which are to be regarded as one wheel by virtue of paragraph 7 of regulation 3 in the circumstances specified in that paragraph;

"*load-capacity index*" has the same meaning as in [paragraph 2.28 of Annex II to Community Directive 92/23 or] paragraph 2.29 of ECE Regulation 30.02 or [paragraph 2.27] of ECE Regulation 54;

"*local service bus*" means a bus being used in the provision of a local service as defined in section 2 of the Transport Act 1985 [*q.v.*];

"*municipal vehicle*" means a motor vehicle or trailer limited at all times to use by a local authority, or a person acting in pursuance of a contract with a local authority, for road cleansing, road watering or the collection and disposal of refuse, night soil or the contents of cesspools, or the purposes of the enactments relating to weights and measures or the sale of food and drugs;

"*multi-stop local collection and delivery vehicle*" means a motor vehicle or trailer used for multi-stop collection and delivery services to be used only within a radius of 25 miles from the permanent base at which it is normally kept;

"*single wheels*" means wheels which are not dual wheels; and

"*speed category*" has the same meaning as in [paragraph 2.29 of Annex II to Community Directive 92/23 or] [paragraph 2.28] of ECE Regulation 54.

[(9A) For the purposes of this regulation, a tyre is a "*relevant car tyre*" if—

(a) it has been marked with a designated approval mark, and

(b) the first two digits of the approval number comprised in the mark are "02".]

[(9B) For the purposes of this regulation, a tyre is a *"relevant commercial vehicle tyre"* if—

(a) it has been marked with a designated approval mark, and

(b) the first two digits of the approval number comprised in the mark are "00".]

[(10) In this regulation any reference to the first use shall, in relation to a trailer, be construed as a reference to the date which is 6 months after the date of manufacture of the trailer.]

B27.59   *[Regulation 25 was substituted by S.I. 1990 No. 1981; and is printed as subsequently amended by S.I. 1991 No. 2710; S.I. 1992 No. 3088; S.I. 1995 No. 551.*

Paragraphs 2.28 and 2.29 of Annex II to Directive 92/23/EEC (to which reference is made in regulation 25(9)) and related paragraphs read as follows:

2.28.   "*load-capacity index*" means one or two numbers which indicate the load the tyre can carry in single or in single and dual formation at the speed corresponding to the associated speed category and when operated in conformity with the requirements governing utilization specified by the manufacturer. The list of these indices and their corresponding masses is given in Annex II, Appendix 2;

2.28.1.   on passenger car tyres there must be one load index only;

2.28.2.   on commercial vehicle tyres there may be one or two load indices, the first one for single formation and the second one, when present, for dual (twin) formation in which case the two indices are divided by a slash (/);

2.28.3.   a type of tyre may have either one or two sets of load capacity indices depending on whether or not the provisions of section 6.2.5 are applied;

2.29.   "*speed category*", expressed by the speed category symbol as shown in the table in 2.29.3;

2.29.1.   in the case of a passenger car tyre, the maximum speed which the tyre can sustain;

2.29.2.   in the case of a commercial vehicle tyre, the speed at which the tyre can carry the mass corresponding to the load capacity index;

2.29.3.   The speed categories are as shown in the table below:

Speed category symbol	*Corresponding speed* (km/h)
F	80
G	90
J	100
K	110
L	120
M	130
N	140
P	150
Q	160
R	170
S	180
T	190
U	200
H	210
V	240

2.29.4.   tyres suitable for maximum speeds higher than 240 km/h are identified by means of the letter code "Z" placed within the tyre size designation;

2.29.5   a type of tyre may have either one or two sets of speed category symbols depending on whether or not the provisions of section 6.2.5 are applied;/

26. Mixing of tyres

(1) Save as provided in paragraph (5) pneumatic tyres of different types of structure shall not be fitted to the same axle of a wheeled vehicle.   **B27.60**

(2) Save as provided in paragraphs (3) or (5), a wheeled motor vehicle having only two axles each of which is equipped with one or two single wheels shall not be fitted with—

(a) a diagonal-ply tyre or a bias-belted tyre on its rear axle if a radial-ply tyre is fitted on its front axle; or

(b) a diagonal-ply tyre on its rear axle if a bias-belted tyre is fitted on the front axle.

(3) Paragraph (2) does not apply to a vehicle to an axle of which there are fitted wide tyres not specially constructed for use on engineering plant or to a vehicle which has a maximum speed not exceeding 30mph.

(4) Save as provided in paragraph (5) pneumatic tyres fitted to—

(a) the steerable axles of a wheeled vehicle; [or]

(b) the driven axles of a wheeled vehicle, not being steerable axles,

shall all be of the same type of structure.

(5) Paragraphs (1), (2), and (4) do not prohibit the fitting of a temporary use spare tyre to a wheel of a passenger vehicle (not being a bus) unless it is driven at a speed exceeding 50mph.

(6) In this regulation—

"*axle*" includes—

(i) two or more stub axles which are fitted on opposite sides of the longitudinal axis of the vehicle so as to form—

(a) a pair in the case of two stub axles; and

(b) pairs in the case of more than two stub axles; and

(ii) a single stub axle which is not one of a pair;

"*a bias-belted tyre*" means a pneumatic tyre, the structure of which is such that the ply cords extend to the bead so as to be laid at alternate angles of substantially less than 90 degrees to the peripheral line of the tread, and are constrained by a circumferential belt comprising two or more layers of substantially inextensible cord material laid at alternate angles smaller than those of the ply cord structure;

"*a diagonal-ply tyre*" means a pneumatic tyre, the structure of which is such that the ply cords extend to the bead so as to be laid at alternate angles of substantially less than 90 degrees to the peripheral line of the tread, but not being a bias-belted tyre;

"*a driven axle*" means an axle through which power is transmitted from the engine of a vehicle to the wheels on that axle;

"*a radial-ply tyre*" means a pneumatic tyre, the structure of which is such that the ply cords extend to the bead so as to be laid at an angle of substantially 90 degrees to the peripheral line of the tread, the ply cord structure being stabilised by a substantially inextensible circumferential belt;

"*stub-axle*" means an axle on which only one wheel is mounted; and "*type of structure*", in relation to a tyre, means a type of structure of a tyre of a kind defined in the foregoing provisions of this paragraph.

B27.61   *[Regulation 26 is printed as amended by S.I. 1990 No. 1981.]*

27. Condition and maintenance of tyres

B27.62   (1) Save as provided in paragraphs (2), (3) and (4), a wheeled motor vehicle or trailer a wheel of which is fitted with a pneumatic tyre shall not be used on a road, if—

(a) the tyre is unsuitable having regard to the use to which the motor vehicle or trailer is being put or to the types of tyres fitted to its other wheels;

(b) the tyre is not so inflated as to make it fit for the use to which the motor vehicle or trailer is being put;

(c) the tyre has a cut in excess of 25mm or 10% of the section width of the tyre, whichever is the greater, measured in any direction on the outside of the tyre and deep enough to reach the ply or cord;

(d) the tyre has any lump, bulge or tear caused by separation or partial failure of its structure;

(e) the tyre has any of the ply or cord exposed;

(f) the base of any groove which showed in the original tread pattern of the tyre is not clearly visible;

(g) either—

(i) the grooves of the tread pattern of the tyre do not have a depth of at least 1mm throughout a continuous band measuring at least three-quarters of the breadth of the tread and round the entire outer circumference of the tyre; or

(ii) if the grooves of the original tread pattern of the tyre did not extend beyond three-quarters of the breadth of the tread, any groove which showed in the original tread pattern does not have a depth of at least 1mm; or

(h) the tyre is not maintained in such condition as to be fit for the use to which the vehicle or trailer is being put or has a defect which might in any way cause damage to the surface of the road or damage to persons on or in the vehicle or to other persons using the road.

(2) Paragraph (1) does not prohibit the use on a road of a motor vehicle or trailer by reason only of the fact that a wheel of the vehicle or trailer is fitted with a tyre which is deflated or not fully inflated and which has any of the defects described in sub-paragraph (c), (d) or (e) of paragraph (1), if the tyre and the wheel to which it is fitted are so constructed as to make the tyre in that condition fit for the use to which the motor vehicle or trailer is being put and the outer sides of the wall of the tyre are so marked as to enable the tyre to be identified as having been constructed to comply with the requirements of this paragraph.

(3) Paragraph (1)(a) does not prohibit the use on a road of a passenger vehicle (not being a bus) by reason only of the fact that a wheel of the vehicle is fitted with a temporary use spare tyre, unless the vehicle is driven at a speed exceeding 50mph.

(4) (a) Nothing in paragraph (1)(a) to (g) applies to—

(i) an agricultural motor vehicle that is not driven at more than 20mph;

(ii) an agricultural trailer;

(iii) an agricultural trailed appliance; or

(iv) a broken down vehicle or a vehicle proceeding to a place where it is to be broken up, being drawn, in either case, by a motor vehicle at a speed not exceeding 20mph.

(b) Nothing in paragraph (1)(f) and (g) applies to—

    (i) a three-wheeled motor cycle the unladen weight of which does not exceed 102kg and which has a maximum speed of 12mph; or

    (ii) a pedestrian-controlled works truck.

(c) Nothing in paragraph (1)(g) applies to a motor cycle with an engine capacity which does not exceed 50cc.

[(d) With effect from 1st January 1992, paragraph 1(f) and (g) shall not apply to the vehicles specified in sub-paragraph (e) of this paragraph but such vehicles shall comply with the requirements specified in sub-paragraph (f) of this paragraph.]

[(e) The vehicles mentioned in sub-paragraph (d) are—

    (i) passenger vehicles other than motor cycles constructed or adapted to carry no more than 8 seated passengers in addition to the driver;

    (ii) goods vehicles with a maximum gross weight which [does] not exceed 3500kg; and

    (iii) light trailers not falling within sub-paragraph (ii);

first used on or after 3rd January 1933.]

[(f) The requirements referred to in sub-paragraph (d) are that the grooves of the tread pattern of every tyre fitted to the wheels of a vehicle mentioned in sub-paragraph (e) shall be of a depth of at least 1.6mm throughout a continuous band [comprising] the central three-quarters of the breadth of tread and round the entire outer circumference of the tyre.]

(5) A recut pneumatic tyre shall not be fitted to any wheel of a motor vehicle or trailer if—

(a) its ply or cord has been cut or exposed by the recutting process; or

(b) it has been wholly or partially recut in a pattern other than the manufacturer's recut tread pattern.

(6) (a) In this regulation—

"*breadth of tread*" means the breadth of that part of the tyre which can contact the road under normal conditions of use measured at 90 degrees to the peripheral line of the tread;

"*original tread pattern*" means in the case of—

    a re-treaded tyre, the tread pattern of the tyre immediately after the tyre was re-treaded;

    a wholly recut tyre, the manufacturer's recut tread pattern;

    a partially recut tyre, on that part of the tyre which has been recut, the manufacturer's recut tread pattern, and on the other part, the tread pattern of the tyre when new; and

    any other tyre, the tread pattern of the tyre when the tyre was new;

"*tie-bar*" means any part of a tyre moulded in the tread pattern of the tyre for the purpose of bracing two or more features of such tread pattern;

"*tread pattern*" means the combination of plain surfaces and grooves extending across the breadth of the tread and round the entire outer circumference of the tyre but excludes any—

    (i) tie-bars or tread wear indicators;

    (ii) features which are designed to wear out substantially before the rest of the pattern under normal conditions of use; and

    (iii) other minor features; and

"*tread wear indicator*" means any bar, not being a tie-bar, projecting from the base of a groove of the tread pattern of a tyre and moulded between two or more features of the tread pattern of a tyre for the purpose of indicating the extent of the wear of such tread pattern.

(b) The references in [this regulation] to grooves are references—

if a tyre has been recut, to the grooves of the manufacturer's recut tread pattern; and

if a tyre has not been recut, to the grooves which showed when the tyre was new.

[(c) A reference in this regulation to first use shall, in relation to a trailer, be construed as a reference to the date which is 6 months after the date of manufacture of the trailer.]

B27.63   *[Regulation 27 is printed as amended by S.I. 1990 No. 1981; S.I. 1991 No. 2710.]*

28. Tracks

B27.64   (1) Every part of every track of a track-laying vehicle which comes into contact with the road shall be flat and have a width of not less than 12.5mm.

(2) The area of the track which is in contact with the road shall not at any time be less than 225cm^2 in respect of every 1000kg of the total weight which is transferred to the roads by the tracks.

(3) The tracks of a vehicle shall not have any defect which might damage the road or cause danger to any person on or in the vehicle or using the road, and shall be properly adjusted and maintained in good and efficient working order.

D *Steering*

29. Maintenance of steering gear

B27.65   All steering gear fitted to a motor vehicle shall at all times while the vehicle is used on a road be maintained in good and efficient working order and be properly adjusted.

E *Vision*

30. View to the front

B27.66   (1) Every motor vehicle shall be so designed and constructed that the driver thereof while controlling the vehicle can at all times have a full view of the road and traffic ahead of the motor vehicle.

(2) Instead of complying with the requirement of paragraph (1) a vehicle may comply with Community Directive 77/649, 81/643 [, 88/366, 90/630] or, in the case of an agricultural motor vehicle, 79/1073.

(3) All glass or other transparent material fitted to a motor vehicle shall be maintained in such condition that it does not obscure the vision of the driver while the vehicle is being driven on a road.

B27.67   *[Regulation 30 is printed as amended by S.I. 1991 No. 2003.]*

31. Glass

B27.68   (1) This regulation applies to a motor vehicle which is—

(a) a wheeled vehicle, not being a caravan, first used before 1st June 1978;

(b) a caravan first used before 1st September 1978; or

(c) a track-laying vehicle.

(2) The glass fitted to any window specified in an item in column 3 of the Table of a vehicle of a class specified in that item in column 2 shall be safety glass.

TABLE

(regulation 31(2))

1 Item	2 Class of vehicle	3 Windows
1	Wheeled vehicles first used on or after 1st January 1959, being passenger vehicles or dual-purpose vehicles.	Windscreens and all outside windows.
2	Wheeled vehicles first used on or after 1st January 1959, being goods vehicles (other than dual-purpose vehicles), locomotives or motor tractors.	Windscreens and all windows in front of and on either side of the driver's seat.
3	Wheeled vehicles not mentioned in item 1 or 2.	Windscreens and windows facing to the front on the outside, except glass fitted to the upper decks of a double-decked vehicle.
4	Track-laying vehicles.	Windscreens and windows facing to the front.

(3) For the purposes of this regulation any windscreen or window at the front of the vehicle the inner surface of which is at an angle exceeding 30 degrees to the longitudinal axis of the vehicle shall be deemed to face to the front.

[(4) In this regulation and in regulation 32—

"*caravan*" means a trailer which is constructed (and not merely adapted) for human habitation; and

["*designated approval mark*" means the marking designated as an approval mark by Regulation 5 of the Approval Marks Regulations and shown at item 31 or 32 in Schedule 4 to those Regulations (those items being markings relating to Community Directive 92/22); and]

"*safety glass*" means glass so constructed or treated if fractured it does not fly into fragments likely to cause severe cuts.]

[(5) Paragraph (2) does not apply to glass which is legibly and permanently marked with a designated approval mark.]

[Regulation 31 is printed as amended by S.I. 1987 No. 676; S.I. 1992 No. 3088.]   **B27.69**

32.—(1) This regulation applies to—   **B27.70**

(a) a caravan first used on or after 1st September 1978, and

(b) a wheeled motor vehicle and a wheeled trailer, not being a caravan, first used on or after 1st June 1978.

(2) Save as provided in paragraphs (3) to (9) the windows specified in column 2 of Table I in relation to a vehicle of a class specified in that column shall be constructed of the material specified in column 3 of the Table.

TABLE I

(regulation 32(2))

1	*2*	*3*
Item	*Window*	*Material*
1	Windscreens and other windows wholly or partly on either side of the driver's seat fitted to motor vehicles first used on or after 1st April 1985.	Specified safety glass (1980).
2	Windscreens and other windows wholly or partly on either side of the driver's seat fitted to a motor vehicle first used before 1st April 1985.	Specified safety glass, or specified safety glass (1980).
3	All other windows.	Specified safety glass, specified safety glass (1980), or safety glazing.

(3) The windscreens and all other windows of security vehicles or vehicles being used for police purposes shall not be subject to the requirements specified in paragraph (2), but shall be constructed of either safety glass or safety glazing.

(4) The windscreens of motor cycles not equipped with an enclosed compartment for the driver or for a passenger shall not be subject to the requirements specified in paragraph (2), but shall be constructed of safety glazing.

(5) Any windscreens or other windows which are wholly or partly in front of or on either side of the driver's seat, and which are temporarily fitted to motor vehicles to replace any windscreens or other windows which have broken, shall—

(a) be constructed of safety glazing; and

(b) be fitted only while the vehicles are being driven or towed either to premises where new windscreens or other windows are to be permanently fitted to replace the windscreens or other windows which have broken, or to complete the journey in the course of which the breakage occurred.

(6) Windows forming all or part of a screen or door in the interior of a bus first used on or after 1st April 1988, shall be constructed either of safety glazing or of specified safety glass (1980).

(7) Windows being—

(a) windows (other than windscreens) of motor vehicles being engineering plant, industrial tractors, agricultural motor vehicles (other than agricultural motor vehicles first used on or after 1st June 1986 and driven at more than 20mph) which are wholly or partly in front of or on either side of the driver's seat;

(b) windows of the upper deck of a double-decked bus; or

(c) windows in the roof of a vehicle,

shall be constructed of either specified safety glass, specified safety glass (1980) or safety glazing.

(8) In the case of motor vehicles and trailers which have not at any time been fitted with permanent windows and which are being driven or towed to a place where permanent windows are to be fitted, any temporary windscreens and any other temporary windows

shall be constructed of either specified safety glass, specified safety glass (1980) or safety glazing.

(9) No requirement in this regulation that a windscreen or other window shall be constructed of specified safety glass or of specified safety glass (1980) shall apply to a windscreen or other window which is—

(a) manufactured in France;

(b) marked with a marking consisting of the letters "TP GS" or "TP GSE"; and

(c) fitted to a vehicle first used before 1st October 1986.

(10) Save as provided in paragraph (11), the windscreens or other windows constructed in accordance with the foregoing provisions of this regulation of specified safety glass, specified safety glass (1980) or safety glazing and specified in column 3 of Table II in relation to a vehicle of a class specified in column 2 of that Table shall have a visual transmission for light of not less than the percentage specified in relation to those windows in column 4 when measured perpendicular to the surface in accordance with the procedure specified in a document specified in relation to those windows in column 5.

TABLE II

(regulation 32(10))

1	2	3	4	5
Item	Class of vehicle	Windows	Percentage	Documents specifying procedure
1	Motor vehicles first used before 1st April 1985	All windows	70	British Standard Specification No. 857 or No. 5282
2	Motor vehicles first used on or after 1st April 1985 and trailers	(a) Windscreens (b) All other windows	75 70	The documents mentioned in sub-paragraph (i), (ii) or (iii) of the definition in paragraph (13) of "specified safety glass (1980)".

(11) Paragraph (10) does not apply to—

(a) any part of any windscreen which is outside the vision reference zone;

(b) windows through which the driver when in the driver's seat is unable at any time to see any part of the road on which the vehicle is waiting or proceeding;

(c) windows in any motor ambulance which are not wholly or partly in front of or on either side of any part of the driver's seat; or

(d) windows in any bus, goods vehicle, locomotive, or motor tractor other than windows which—

    (i) are wholly or partly in front of or on either side of any part of the driver's seat;

    (ii) face the rear of the vehicle; or

(iii) form the whole or part of a door giving access to or from the exterior of the vehicle.

(12) For the purposes of this regulation any window at the rear of the vehicle is deemed to face the rear of the vehicle if the inner surface of such window is at an angle exceeding 30 degrees to the longitudinal axis of the vehicle.

[(12A) Paragraphs (2), (6), (7) and (8) do not apply to a window which is legibly and permanently marked with a designated approval mark.]

[(12B) Paragraph (10) does not apply to a window if—

(a) it is a window to which paragraph 12C applies and is legibly and permanently marked with a designated approval mark which does not comprise the Roman numeral "V" (other than as part of the combination "VI"); or

(b) it is not a window to which paragraph 12C applies and is legibly and permanently marked with a designated approval mark.]

[(12C) This paragraph applies to a side or rear window if—

(a) any part of it is on either side of or forward of the driver's seat; or

(b) any part of it is within the driver's indirect field of view obtained by means of the mirror or mirrors which are required to be fitted by regulation 33 when such mirrors are properly adjusted;

and for the purposes of this paragraph a mirror shall not be regarded as being required to be fitted by regulation 33 if, were it to be removed, the vehicle would nevertheless meet the requirements of regulation 33.]

(13) In this regulation, unless the context otherwise requires—

"British Standard Specification No. 857" means the British Standard Specification for Safety Glass for Land Transport published on 30th June 1967 under the number BS 857 as amended by Amendment Slip No. 1 published on 15th January 1973 under the number AMD 1088;

"British Standard Specification No. 5282" means the British Standard Specification for Road Vehicle Safety Glass published in December 1975 under the number BS 5282 as amended by Amendment Slip No. 1 published on 31st March 1976 under the number AMD 1927, and as amended by Amendment Slip No. 2 published on 31st January 1977 under the number AMD 2185;

"British Standard Specification BS AU 178" means the British Standard Specification for Road Vehicle Safety Glass published on 28th November 1980 under the number BS AU 178;

. . .

[*"designated approval mark"* means—

(a) in relation to a windscreen, the marking designated as an approval mark by regulation 5 of the Approval Marks Regulations and shown at item 31 in Schedule 4 to those Regulations, and

(b) in relation to a window other than a windscreen, the markings designated as approval marks by regulation 5 of those Regulations and shown at item 32 in Schedule 4 to those Regulations.]

"safety glazing" means material (other than glass) which is so constructed or treated that if fractured it does not fly into fragments likely to cause severe cuts;

"security vehicle" means a motor vehicle which is constructed (and not merely adapted) for the carriage of either—

(i) persons who are likely to require protection from any criminal offence involving violence; or

    (ii) dangerous substances, bullion, money, jewellery, documents or other goods or burden which, by reason of their nature or value, are likely to require protection from any criminal offence;

"*specified safety glass*" means glass complying with the requirements of either—

    (i) British Standard Specification No. 857 (including the requirements as to marking); or

    (ii) British Standard Specification No. 5282 (including the requirements as to marking);

"*specified safety glass (1980)*" means glass complying with the requirements of either—

    (i) the British Standard Specification for Safety Glass for Land Transport published on 30th June 1967 under the number BS 857 as amended by Amendment Slip No. 1 published on 15th January 1973 under the number AMD 1088, Amendment Slip No. 2 published on 30th September 1980 under the number AMD 3402, and Amendment Slip 4 published on 15th February 1981 under the number AMD 3548 (including the requirements as to marking); or

    (ii) British Standard Specification BS AU 178 (including the requirements as to marking); or

    (iii) ECE Regulation 43 (including the requirements as to marking);

"*vision reference zone*" means either—

    (i) the primary vision area as defined in British Standard Specification No. 857;

    (ii) Zone 1, as defined in British Standard Specification No. 5282;

    (iii) Zone B (as regards passenger vehicles other than buses) and Zone 1 (as regards all other vehicles) as defined in British Standard Specification BS AU 178 and in ECE Regulation 43; and

"*windscreen*" includes a windshield.

[Regulation 32 is printed as amended by S.I. 1987 No. 676; S.I. 1992 No. 3088.   **B27.71**

As to the application of the provisions of regulation 32 to vehicles in respect of which approval certificates have been issued under the "Approval Regulations", see Schedule 2A, paragraph 3, to these regulations.]

33. Mirrors

(1) Save as provided in paragraphs (5) and (6), a motor vehicle (not being a road roller)   **B27.72** which is of a class specified in an item in column 2 of the Table shall be fitted with such mirror or mirrors, if any, as are specified in that item in column 3; and any mirror which is fitted to such a vehicle shall, whether or not it is required to be fitted, comply with the requirements, if any, specified in that item in column 4.

(2) Save as provided in paragraph (5), each exterior mirror with which a vehicle is required to be fitted in accordance with item 2 or 6 of the Table shall, if the vehicle has a technically permissible maximum weight (as mentioned in Annex 1 to Community Directive 71/127) exceeding 3500kg, be a Class II mirror (as described in that Annex) and shall in any other case be a Class II or a Class III mirror (as described in that Annex).

(3) Save as provided in paragraph (5), in the case of a wheeled motor vehicle described in item 1, 2, 7 or 8 of the Table which is first used on or after 1st April 1969 the edges of any mirror fitted internally shall be surrounded by some material such as will render it unlikely that severe cuts would be caused if the mirror or that material were struck by any occupant of the vehicle.

(4) Save as provided in paragraph (5), in the case of a motor vehicle falling within paragraph (a) in column 4 of items 1 and 5, or within item 6, of the Table—

    (a) each mirror shall be fixed to the vehicle in such a way that it remains steady under normal driving conditions;

(b) each exterior mirror on a vehicle fitted with windows and a windscreen shall be visible to the driver, when in his driving position, through a side window or through the portion of the windscreen which is swept by the windscreen wiper;

(c) where the bottom edge of an exterior mirror is less than 2m above the road surface when the vehicle is laden, that mirror shall not project more than 20cm beyond the overall width of the vehicle or, in a case where the vehicle is drawing a trailer which has an overall width greater than that of the drawing vehicle, more than 20cm beyond the overall width of the trailer;

(d) each interior mirror shall be capable of being adjusted by the driver when in his driving position; and

(e) except in the case of a mirror which, if knocked out of its alignment, can be returned to its former position without needing to be adjusted, each exterior mirror on the driver's side of the vehicle shall be capable of being adjusted by the driver when in his driving position, but this requirement shall not prevent such a mirror from being locked into position from the outside of the vehicle.

TABLE

(regulation 33(1))

1	*2*	*3*	*4*
Item	*Class of vehicle*	*Mirrors to be fitted*	*Requirements to be complied with by any mirrors fitted*
1	A motor vehicle which is— (a) drawing a trailer, if a person is carried on the trailer so that he has an uninterrupted view to the rear and has an efficient means of communicating to the driver the effect of signals given by the drivers of other vehicles to the rear; (b) (i) a works truck; (ii) a track-laying agricultural motor vehicle; and (iii) a wheeled agricultural motor vehicle first used before 1st June 1978, if, in each case, the driver can easily obtain a view to the rear; (c) a pedestrian-controlled vehicle; (d) a chassis being driven from the place where it has been manufactured to the place where it is to receive a vehicle body; or (e) an agricultural motor vehicle which has an unladen weight exceeding 7370kg and which— (i) is a track-laying vehicle or (ii) is a wheeled vehicle first used before 1st June 1978	No requirement	(a) If the vehicle is a wheeled vehicle first used on or after 1st June 1978, item 2 of Annex I to Community Directive 71/127 or 79/795 or Annex II to Community Directive [86/562] [or 88/321 or paragraphs 4 to 8 of ECE Regulation 46.01] and paragraph (4) of this regulation. (b) In other cases, none, except as specified in paragraph (3).

[continued on next page

1	2	3	4
Item	*Class of vehicle*	*Mirrors to be fitted*	*Requirements to be complied with by any mirrors fitted*
2	A motor vehicle, not included in item 1, which is— (a) a wheeled locomotive or a wheeled motor tractor first used in either case on or after 1st June 1978; (b) an agricultural motor vehicle, not being a track-laying vehicle with an unladen weight not exceeding 7370kg (which falls in item 8) or a wheeled agricultural motor vehicle first used after 1st June 1986 which is driven at more than 20mph (which falls in item (6)); or (c) a works truck	At least one mirror fitted externally on the offside	None except as specified in paragraphs (2) and (3).
3	A wheeled motor vehicle not included in item 1 first used on or after 1st April 1983 which is— (a) a bus; or (b) a goods vehicle with a maximum gross weight exceeding 3500kg (not being an agricultural motor vehicle or one which is not driven at more than 20mph) other than a vehicle described in item 4	Mirrors complying with item 3 of Annex I to Community Directive 79/795 or with paragraph 2.1 of Annex III to Community Directive [86/562] [or 88/321 or paragraph 16.2.1 of ECE Regulation 46.01] or, except in the case of a goods vehicle first used on or after 1st April 1985, mirrors as required in the entry in this column in item 6	Item 2 of Annex I to Community Directive 71/127 or 79/795 or Annex II to Community Directive [86/562] [or 88/321 or paragraphs 4 to of ECE Regulation 46.01].
4	A goods vehicle not being an agricultural motor vehicle with a maximum gross weight exceeding 12,000kg which is first used on or after 1st October 1988	Mirrors complying with paragraph 2.1 of Annex III to Community Directive [86/562] [or 88/321 or paragraph 16.2.1 of ECE Regulation 46.01]	Annex II to Community Directive [86/562] [or 88/321 or paragraphs 4 to 8 of ECE Regulation 46.01].

[*continued on next page*

1	2	3	4
Item	*Class of vehicle*	*Mirrors to be fitted*	*Requirements to be complied with by any mirrors fitted*
5	A two-wheeled motor cycle with or without a sidecar attached	No requirement	(a) If the vehicle is first used on or after 1st October 1978, item 2 of Annex I to Community Directive 71/127, 79/795 or 80/780 or Annex II to Community Directive [86/562] [or 88/321 or paragraphs 4 to 8 of ECE Regulation 46.01] and paragraph (4) of this regulation. (b) In other cases, none.
6	A wheeled motor vehicle not in items 1 to 5, which is first used on or after 1st June 1978 (or, in the case of a Ford Transit motor car, 10th July 1978)	(i) At least one mirror fitted externally on the offside of the vehicle; and (ii) at least one mirror fitted internally, unless a mirror so fitted would give the driver no view to the rear of the vehicle; and (iii) at least one mirror fitted externally on the near-side of the vehicle unless a mirror which gives the driver an adequate view to the rear is fitted internally	Item 2 of Annex I to Community Directive 71/127 or 79/795 or Annex II to Community Directive [86/562] [or 88/321 or paragraphs 4 to 8 of ECE Regulation 46.01] and paragraphs (2) and (4) or this regulation.
7	A wheeled motor vehicle, not in items 1 to 5, first used before 1st June 1978 (or in the case of a Ford Transit motor car, 10th July 1978) and a track-laying motor vehicle which is not an agricultural motor vehicle first used on or after 1st January 1958, which in either case is— (a) a bus; (b) a dual-purpose vehicle; or (c) a goods vehicle	At least one mirror fitted externally on the offside of the vehicle and at least one mirror fitted either internally or externally on the near-side of the vehicle	None, except as specified in paragraph (3).
8	A motor vehicle, whether wheeled or track-laying, not in items 1 to 7	At least one mirror fitted either internally or externally	None, except as specified in paragraph (3).

[(5) Instead of complying with paragraphs (1) to (4) a vehicle may comply—

(a) if it is a goods vehicle with a maximum gross weight exceeding 3500kg first used on or after 1st April 1985 and before 1st August 1989, with Community Directive 79/795, 85/205 [, 86/562 or 88/321 or ECE Regulation 46.01];

(b) if it is a goods vehicle first used on or after 1st August 1989—

(i) in the case of a vehicle with a maximum gross weight exceeding 3500kg but not exceeding 12,000kg with Community Directive 79/795, 85/205 [, 86/562 or 88/321 or ECE Regulation 46.01]; and

(ii) in the case of a vehicle with a maximum gross weight exceeding 12,000kg with Community Directive 85/205 [, 86/562 or 88/321 or ECE Regulation 46.01];

(c) if it is an agricultural motor vehicle with Community Directive 71/127, 74/346, 79/795, 85/205 [, 86/562 or 88/321 or ECE Regulation 46.01];

(d) if it is a two-wheeled motor cycle with or without a side-car with Community Directive 71/127, 79/795, 80/780, 85/205 [, 86/562 or 88/321 or ECE Regulation 46.01]; and

(e) if it is any other vehicle with Community Directive 71/127, 79/795, 85/205 [, 86/562 or 88/321 or ECE Regulation 46.01].]

(6) Instead of complying with the provisions of column 4 in items 3, 5 or 6 of the Table a mirror may comply with the requirements as to construction and testing set out either in Annex I to Community Directive 71/127, excluding paragraphs 2.3.4 and 2.6, or in Annex I to Community Directive 79/795, excluding paragraphs 2.3.3 and 2.6.

(7) In this regulation "*mirror*" means a mirror to assist the driver of a vehicle to become aware of traffic—

(i) if it is an internal mirror, to the rear of the vehicle; and

(ii) if it is an external mirror fitted on one side of the vehicle, rearwards on that side of the vehicle.

In the case of an agricultural motor vehicle described in items 2 or 6 in the Table when drawing a trailer, the references to a vehicle in sub-paragraphs (i) and (ii) include references to the trailer so drawn.

[Regulation 33 has been printed as amended by S.I. 1988 No. 1178; S.I. 1992 No. 3088. **B27.73**
As to the application of the provisions of regulation 33 to vehicles in respect of which approval certificates have been issued under the "Approval Regulations", see Schedule 2A, paragraph 4, to these regulations.]

34. Windscreen wipers and washers

(1) Subject to paragraphs (4) and (5), every vehicle fitted with a windscreen shall, unless **B27.74** the driver can obtain an adequate view to the front of the vehicle without looking through the windscreen, be fitted with one or more efficient automatic windscreen wipers capable of clearing the windscreen so that the driver has an adequate view of the road in front of both sides of the vehicle and to the front of the vehicle.

(2) Save as provided in paragraphs (3), (4) and (5), every wheeled vehicle required by paragraph (1) to be fitted with a wiper or wipers shall also be fitted with a windscreen washer capable of cleaning, in conjunction with the windscreen wiper, the area of the windscreen swept by the wiper of mud or similar deposit.

(3) The requirement specified in paragraph (2) does not apply in respect of—

(a) an agricultural motor vehicle (other than a vehicle first used on or after 1st June 1986 which is driven at more than 20mph);

(b) a track-laying vehicle;

(c) a vehicle having a maximum speed not exceeding 20mph; or

(d) a vehicle being used to provide a local service, as defined in the Transport Act 1985.

(4) Instead of complying with paragraphs (1) and (2), a vehicle may comply with Community Directive 78/318.

(5) Instead of complying with paragraph (1) an agricultural motor vehicle may comply with Community Directive 79/1073.

(6) Every wiper and washer fitted in accordance with this regulation shall at all times while a vehicle is being used on a road be maintained in efficient working order and be properly adjusted.

F *Instruments and Equipment*

35. Speedometers

B27.75   (1) Save as provided in paragraphs (2) and (3), every motor vehicle shall be fitted with a speedometer which, if the vehicle is first used on or after 1st April 1984, shall be capable of indicating speed in both miles per hour and kilometers per hour, either simultaneously or, by the operation of a switch, separately.

(2) Paragraph (1) does not apply to—

(a) a vehicle having a maximum speed not exceeding 25mph;

(b) a vehicle which is at all times unlawful to drive at more than 25mph;

(c) an agricultural motor vehicle which is not driven at more than 20mph;

(d) a motor cycle first used before 1st April 1984 the engine of which has a cylinder capacity not exceeding 100cc;

(e) an invalid carriage first used before 1st April 1984;

(f) a works truck first used before 1st April 1984;

(g) a vehicle first used before 1st October 1937; or

(h) a vehicle equipped with recording equipment marked with a marking designated as an approval mark by regulation 5 of the Approval Marks Regulations and shown at item 3 in Schedule 4 to those Regulations (whether or not the vehicle is required to be equipped with that equipment) and which, as regards the visual indications given by that equipment of the speed of the vehicle, complies with the requirements relating to the said indications and installations specified in the Community Recording Equipment Regulation.

(3) Instead of complying with paragraph (1) a vehicle may comply with [Community Directive 97/39 [*O.J. No. L177, July 3, 1997, p. 1*]]or with ECE Regulation 39.

B27.76   *[Regulation 35 is printed as amended by S.I. 1998 No. 1188.*
As to the application of the provisions of regulation 35 to vehicles in respect of which approval certificates have been issued under the "Approval Regulations", see Schedule 2A, paragraph 5, to these regulations.]

36. Maintenance of speedometers

B27.77   (1) Every instrument for indicating speed fitted to a motor vehicle—

(a) in compliance with the requirements of regulation 35(1) or (3); or

(b) to which regulation 35(2)(h) relates and which is not, under the Community Recording Equipment Regulation, required to be equipped with the recording equipment mentioned in that paragraph,

shall be kept free from any obstruction which might prevent it being easily read and shall at all material times be maintained in good working order.

(2) In this regulation "*all material times*" means all times when the motor vehicle is in use on a road except when—

(a) the vehicle is being used on a journey during which, as a result of a defect, the instrument ceased to be in good working order; or

(b) as a result of a defect, the instrument has ceased to be in good working order and steps have been taken to have the vehicle equipped with all reasonable expedition, by means of repairs or replacement, with an instrument which is in good working order.

[36A. Speed limiters

[(1) Subject to paragraph (13), this regulation applies to every coach which—   **B27.78**

(a) was first used on or after 1st April 1974 and before 1st January 1988; and

(b) has, or if a speed limiter were not fitted to it would have, a maximum speed exceeding [112.65 km/h];

and a reference to this regulation to a paragraph (1) vehicle is a reference to a vehicle to which this regulation applies by virtue of this paragraph.

(2) Subject to paragraph (13), this regulation also applies to every bus which—

(a) is first used on or after 1st January 1988;

(b) has a maximum gross weight exceeding 7.5 tonnes; and

(c) has, or if a speed limiter were not fitted to it would have, a maximum speed exceeding [100 km/h];

and a reference in this regulation to a paragraph (2) vehicle is a reference to a vehicle to which this regulation applies by virtue of this paragraph.

(3) [*Revoked by S.I. 1997 No. 1340.*]

(4) Every vehicle to which this regulation applies shall be fitted with a speed limiter in respect of which such of the requirements of paragraphs (5) to (9) are met as apply to that speed limiter.

(5) Subject to paragraph (10), the requirements of this paragraph are that a speed limiter fitted to any vehicle must—

(a) be sealed by an authorised sealer in such a manner as to protect the limiter against any improper interference or adjustment and against any interruption of its power supply; and

(b) be maintained in good and efficient working order.

(6) The requirements of this paragraph are that a speed limiter fitted to a paragraph (1) vehicle must be calibrated to a set speed not exceeding [112.65 km/h].

[(7) The requirements of this paragraph are that a speed limiter fitted to a paragraph (2) vehicle must be calibrated to a set speed not exceeding 100 km/h.]

(8) Subject to paragraphs (11) and (12), the requirements of this paragraph are that a speed limiter fitted at any time to any paragraph (1) vehicle or a speed limiter fitted before 1st October 1994 to a paragraph (2) vehicle first used before that date must comply with—

(a) Part 1 of the British Standard; or

(b) the Annexes to Community Directive 92/24.

(9) The requirements of this paragraph are that a speed limiter (not being a speed limiter to which paragraph (8) applies) fitted to a paragraph (2) vehicle must comply with the Annexes to Community Directive 92/24.

[(9A) Until 1st July 1999, in relation to a vehicle used exclusively for transport operations in the United Kingdom and first used before 1st July 1998, paragraph (2)(c) and paragraph (7) shall have effect as if for "100 km/h" there were in each case substituted "105 km/h".]

(10) Paragraph (5)(a) shall have effect in relation to—

(a) a speed limiter fitted before 1st August 1992 to a vehicle first used before that date; or

(b) a speed limiter sealed outside the United Kingdom,

as if the words "by an authorised sealer" were omitted.

(11) Paragraph (8) does not apply to a speed limiter fitted before 1st October 1988.

(12) Paragraph (8) does not apply to a speed limiter fitted to a vehicle if the speed limiter complies with an equivalent standard.

(13) This regulation does not apply to a vehicle—

(a) being taken to a place where a speed limiter is to be installed, calibrated, repaired or replaced; or

(b) completing a journey in the course of which the speed limiter has accidentally ceased to function.

(14) In this regulation—

"authorised sealer" has the meaning given in Schedule 3B;

"equivalent standard" means—

(a) a standard or code of practice of a national standards body or equivalent body of any member State;

(b) any international standard recognised for use as a standard by any member State; or

(c) a technical specification or code of practice which, whether mandatory or not, is recognised for use as a standard by a public authority of any member State,

where the standard, code of practice, international standard or technical specification provides, in relation to speed limiters, a level of speed control equivalent to that provided by Part 1 of the British Standard.

"Part 1 of the British Standard" means the British Standard for Maximum Road Speed Limiters for Motor Vehicles which was published by the British Standards Institution under the number BS AU 217: Part 1: 1987 and which came into effect on 29th May 1987; as amended by Amendment Slip No. 1 under the number AMD 5969 which was published and came into effect on 30th June 1988;

"set speed", in relation to a calibrated speed limiter fitted to a vehicle, means the speed intended by the person who calibrated the speed limiter to be the mean speed of the vehicle when operating in a stabilised condition;

"speed limiter" means a device designed to limit the maximum speed of a motor vehicle by controlling the power output from the engine of the vehicle.

. . .]

B27.79   *[Regulation 36A was inserted by S.I. 1988 No. 271 and was later amended by S.I. 1988 No. 1524; S.I. 1992 No. 422 and substituted by S.I. 1993 No. 1946. The text of regulation 36A as printed above* *was substituted by S.I. 1993 No. 3048 and is printed as subsequently amended by the Vehicle Excise and Registration Act 1994, s.64 and Sched. 4, para.4; S.I. 1997 No. 1340.*

The explanatory note accompanying S.I. 1997 No. 1340 states that regulation 36A implements Directive 92/6/EEC and Directive 92/24/EEC.]

[**36B.**—(1) Subject to paragraphs (5) and (14), this regulation applies to every motor **B27.80** vehicle which—

(a) is a goods vehicle;

(b) has a maximum gross weight exceeding 7,500kg but not exceeding 12,000kg;

(c) is first used on or after 1st August 1992; and

(d) has, or if a speed limiter were not fitted to it would have, a relevant speed exceeding 60mph;

and a reference in this regulation to a paragraph (1) vehicle is a reference to a vehicle to which this regulation applies by virtue of this paragraph.

(2) Subject to paragraphs (5) and (14), this regulation also applies to every vehicle which—

(a) is a goods vehicle;

(b) has a maximum gross weight exceeding 12,000kg;

(c) is first used on or after 1st January 1988; and

(d) has, or if a speed limiter were not fitted to it would have, a relevant speed exceeding 56mph;

and a reference in this regulation to a paragraph (2) vehicle is a reference to a vehicle to which this regulation applies by virtue of this paragraph.

(3)–(5) *[Revoked.]*

(6) Every vehicle to which this regulation applies shall be fitted with a speed limiter in respect of which such of the requirements of paragraphs (7) to (11) are met as apply to that speed limiter.

(7) Subject to paragraph (12), the requirements of this paragraph are that a speed limiter fitted to any vehicle must—

(a) be sealed by an authorised sealer in such a manner as to protect the limiter against any improper interference or adjustment or against any interruption of its power supply; and

(b) be maintained in good and efficient working order.

(8) The requirements of this paragraph are that a speed limiter fitted to a paragraph (1) vehicle or a paragraph (3) vehicle must be calibrated to a set speed not exceeding 60mph.

[(9) Subject to paragraph (11A), the requirements of this paragraph are that a speed limiter fitted to a paragraph (2) vehicle must be set at a speed not exceeding 85 km/h and the stabilised speed of the vehicle must not exceed 90 km/h.]

(10) Subject to paragraph (13), the requirements of this paragraph are that a speed limiter fitted at any time to a paragraph (1) vehicle, a speed limiter fitted before 1st October 1994 to a paragraph (2) vehicle first used before that date or a speed limiter fitted at any time to a paragraph (3) vehicle must comply with—

(a) Part 1 of the British Standard; or

(b) the Annexes to Community Directive 92/24.

(11) The requirements of this paragraph are that a speed limiter (not being a speed limiter to which paragraph (10) applies) fitted to a paragraph (2) vehicle must comply with the Annexes to Community Directive 92/24.

[(11A) Where—

(a) a speed limiter fitted to a paragraph (2) vehicle is set at a particular speed above 85 km/h (approximately 52.8mph); and

(b) the processes used in the construction of the vehicle, the speed limiter and its other equipment were such as to ensure that, with the speed limiter set at that particular speed, the vehicle would have a stabilised speed of not more than 90 km/h (approximately 55.9mph),

the speed limiter of the vehicle shall, for the purposes of paragraph (9) and regulation 70A, be deemed to have been set at a speed of 85 km/h.]

(12) Paragraph (7)(a) shall have effect in relation to—

(a) a speed limiter fitted before 1st August 1992 to a vehicle first used before that date; or

(b) a speed limiter sealed outside the United Kingdom,

as if the words "by an authorised sealer" were omitted.

[(12A) Until 1st September 1997, paragraph (11A) shall have effect with the omission of the words "and regulation 70A".]

(13) Paragraph (10) does not apply to a speed limiter fitted to a vehicle if the speed limiter complies with an equivalent standard.

(14) This regulation does not apply to a vehicle—

(a) which is being taken to a place where a speed limiter is to be installed, calibrated, repaired or replaced;

(b) which is completing a journey in the course of which the speed limiter has accidentally ceased to function;

(c) is owned by the Secretary of State for Defence and used for naval, military or air force purposes;

(d) is used for naval, military or air force purposes while being driven by a person for the time being subject to the orders of a member of the armed forces of the Crown;

(e) while it is being used for fire brigade, ambulance or police purposes; or

[(f) at a time when it is being used on a public road during any calendar week if—

(i) it is being used only in passing from land in the occupation of the person keeping the vehicle to other land in his occupation, and

(ii) it has not been used on public roads for distances exceeding an aggregate of six miles in that calendar week,

and for the purposes of this paragraph "*public road*" has the meaning given in section 62(1) of the Vehicle Excise and Registration Act 1994 [*q.v.*].]

(15) In this regulation—

"*equivalent standard*", "*Part 1 of the British Standard*", . . . "*speed limiter*" and "*stabilised speed*" have the same meanings as in regulation 36A; . . .

"*relevant speed*" means a speed which a vehicle is incapable, by means of its construction, of exceeding on the level under its own power when unladen.

["*set speed*", in relation to a paragraph (1) vehicle, has the same meaning as in regulation 36A; and

subject to paragraph (11A), "*set*", in relation to a speed limiter fitted to a paragraph (2) vehicle, has the same meaning as in Community Directive 92/6 [*q.v.*]; and references to the speed at which a speed limiter is set shall be construed accordingly.]

(16) For the purposes of this regulation, a motor vehicle has a maximum gross trailer weight exceeding 5,000kg if—

(a) in the case of a vehicle equipped with a Ministry plate in accordance with regulation 70, the difference between its maximum gross weight and the relevant train weight exceeds 5,000kg;

(b) in the case of a vehicle not equipped with a Ministry plate, but which is equipped with a plate in accordance with regulation 66, the difference between its maximum gross weight and the weight shown on the plate in respect of item 8 of Part I of Schedule 8 exceeds 5,000kg; and

(c) in the case of any other vehicle, the vehicle is designed or adapted to be capable of drawing a trailer with a laden weight exceeding 5,000kg when travelling on a road;

and in sub-paragraph (a) "*the relevant train weight*" is the train weight shown in column (3) of the plate or, if no such weight is shown, the train weight shown in column (2) of the plate (where the plate is in the form required by [Schedule 10 or 10B]) or in column (4) of the plate (where the plate is in the form required by [Schedule 10A or 10C]).]

[Regulation 36B was inserted by S.I. 1991 No. 1527 and was later amended by S.I. 1992 No. 422   **B27.81**
and substituted by S.I. 1993 No. 1946.

The text of regulation 36B as printed above was substituted by S.I. 1993 No. 3048 and is printed as subsequently amended by S.I. 1994 No. 329; S.I. 1995 No. 1458; S.I. 1996 No. 2064.]

[36C. Speed limiters—authorised sealers

Schedule 3B (authorised sealers) shall have effect.]   **B27.82**

[Regulation 36C was inserted by S.I. 1992 No. 422.]   **B27.83**

37. Audible warning instruments

(1)(a) Subject to sub-paragraph (b), every motor vehicle which has a maximum speed of   **B27.84**
more than 20mph shall be fitted with a horn, not being a reversing alarm or a two-tone horn.

(b) Sub-paragraph (a) shall not apply to an agricultural motor vehicle, unless it is being driven at more than 20mph.

(2) Subject to paragraph (6), the sound emitted by any horn, other than a reversing alarm[, a boarding aid alarm] or a two-tone horn, fitted to a wheeled vehicle first used on or after 1st August 1973 shall be continuous and uniform and not strident.

(3) A reversing alarm [or a boarding aid alarm] fitted to a wheeled vehicle shall not be strident.

(4) Subject to paragraphs (5), (6) and (7) no motor vehicle shall be fitted with a bell, gong, siren or two-tone horn.

(5) The provisions of paragraph (4) shall not apply to motor vehicles—

(a) used for fire brigade, ambulance or police purposes;

(b) owned by a body formed primarily for the purposes of fire salvage and used for those or similar purposes;

(c) owned by the Forestry Commission or by local authorities and used from time to time for the purposes of fighting fires;

(d) owned by the Secretary of State for Defence and used for the purposes of the disposal of bombs or explosives;

(e) used for the purposes of the Blood Transfusion Service provided under the National Health Service Act 1977 or under the National Health Service (Scotland) Act 1947;

(f) used by her Majesty's Coastguard or the Coastguard Auxiliary Service to aid persons in danger or vessels in distress on or near the coast;

(g) owned by the National Coal Board and used for the purposes of rescue operations at mines;

(h) owned by the Secretary of State for Defence and used by the Royal Air Force Mountain Rescue Service for the purposes of rescue operations in connection with crashed aircraft or any other emergencies; or

(i) owned by the Royal National Lifeboat Institution and used for the purposes of launching lifeboats.

(6) The provisions of paragraphs (2) and (4) shall not apply so as to make it unlawful for a motor vehicle to be fitted with an instrument or apparatus (not being a two-tone horn) designed to emit a sound for the purpose of informing members of the public that goods are on the vehicle for sale.

(7) Subject to paragraph (8), the provisions of paragraph (4) shall not apply so as to make it unlawful for a vehicle to be fitted with a bell, gong or siren—

(a) if the purpose thereof is to prevent theft or attempted theft of the vehicle or its contents; or

(b) in the case of a bus, if the purpose thereof is to summon help for the driver, the conductor or an inspector.

(8) Every bell, gong or siren fitted to a vehicle by virtue of paragraph (7)(a), and every device fitted to a motor vehicle first used on or after 1st October 1982 so as to cause a horn to sound for the purpose mentioned in paragraph (7)(a), shall be fitted with a device designed to stop the bell, gong, siren or horn emitting noise for a continuous period of more than five minutes; and every such device shall at all times be maintained in good working order.

(9) Instead of complying with paragraphs (1), (2) and (4) to (8), a vehicle may comply with Community Directive 70/388 or ECE Regulation 28 or, if the vehicle is an agricultural motor vehicle, with Community Directive 74/151.

(10) In this regulation and in regulation 99—

(a) "*horn*" means an instrument, not being a bell, gong or siren, capable of giving audible and sufficient warning of the approach or position of the vehicle to which it is fitted;

(b) references to a bell, gong or siren include references to any instrument or apparatus capable of emitting a sound similar to that emitted by a bell, gong or siren;

(c) "*reversing alarm*" means a device fitted to a motor vehicle and designed to warn persons that the vehicle is reversing or is about to reverse; . . .

(d) "*two-tone horn*" means an instrument which, when operated, automatically produces a sound which alternates at regular intervals between two fixed notes[; and]

[(e) "*boarding aid alarm*" means an alarm for a power operated lift or ramp fitted to a bus to enable wheelchair users to board and alight and designed to warn persons that the lift or ramp is in operation.]

B27.85   *[Regulation 37 is printed as amended by S.I. 2000 No. 1971.]*

38. Motor cycle sidestands

B27.86   (1) No motor cycle first used on or after 1st April 1986 shall be fitted with any sidestand which is capable of—

(a) disturbing the stability of direction of the motor cycle when it is in motion under its own power; or

(b) closing automatically if the angle of the inclination of the motor cycle is inadvertently altered when it is stationary.

(2) In this regulation "*sidestand*" means a device fitted to a motor cycle which, when fully extended or pivoted to its open position, supports the vehicle from one side only and so that both the wheels of the motor cycle are on the ground.

G *Fuel*

39. Fuel tanks

[(1) This regulation applies to every fuel tank which is fitted to a wheeled vehicle for the purpose of supplying fuel to the propulsion unit or to an ancillary engine or to any other equipment forming part of the vehicle.]   **B27.87**

[(2) Subject to paragraphs (3) [,(3A)] and (4), every fuel tank to which this regulation applies—

(a) shall be constructed and maintained so that the leakage of any liquid from the tank is adequately prevented;

(b) shall be constructed and maintained so that the leakage of vapour from the tank is adequately prevented; and

(c) if it contains petroleum spirit (as defined in section 23 of the Petroleum (Consolidation) Act 1928) and is fitted to a vehicle first used on or after 1st July 1973, shall be—

(i) made only of metal; and

(ii) fixed in such a position and so maintained as to be reasonably secure from damage.]

[(3) Notwithstanding the requirement of paragraph (2)(b), the fuel tank may be fitted with a device which, by the intake of air or the emission of vapour, relieves changes of pressure in the tank.]

[(3A) Sub-paragraph (i) of paragraph 2(c) shall not have effect in relation to a two-wheeled motor cycle (with or without a side-car) first used on or after 1st February 1993.]

[(4)] Instead of complying with the requirements of paragraphs (2) and (3) as to construction, a vehicle may comply with the requirement of Community Directive 70/221 (in so far as they relate to fuel tanks) or ECE Regulation 34 or 34.01 or, if the vehicle is an agricultural motor vehicle, of Community Directive 74/151.

[Regulation 39 is printed as amended by S.I. 1990 No. 2212; S.I. 1992 No. 3285.   **B27.88**
As to the application of regulation 39(2)(c)(i) to vehicles in respect of which approval certificates have been issued under the "Approval Regulations", see Schedule 2A, paragraph 6, to these regulations.]

[**39A.** (1) Every vehicle to which this regulation applies shall be designed and constructed for running on unleaded petrol.   **B27.89**

(2) No person shall use or cause or permit to be used a vehicle to which this regulation applies on a road if it—

(a) has been deliberately altered or adjusted for running on leaded petrol, and

(b) as a direct result of such alteration or adjustment it is incapable of running on unleaded petrol.

(3) Subject to paragraph (4) this regulation applies to every motor vehicle which is—

(a) propelled by a spark ignition engine which is capable of running on petrol, and

(b) is first used on or after the 1st April 1991.

(4) Part I of Schedule 3A shall have effect for the purpose of excluding certain vehicles first used before specified dates from the application of this legislation.

(5) In this regulation "*petrol*", "*leaded petrol*" and "*unleaded petrol*" have the same meaning as in Community Directive 85/210.

(6) A vehicle shall be regarded for the purposes of this regulation as incapable of running on unleaded petrol at any particular time if and only if in its state of adjustment at that time prolonged continuous running on such petrol would damage the engine.]

B27.90   *[Regulation 39A was inserted by S.I. 1988 No. 1524.*

"Petrol" is defined by Council Directive 85/210/EEC, art.1, as "any volatile mineral oil intended for the operation of internal combustion spark-ignited engines used for the propulsion of vehicles". "Unleaded petrol" is defined by article 1 as "any petrol the contamination of which by lead compounds calculated in terms of lead, does not exceed 0.013 g Pb/1".]

B27.91   **[39B.** (1) Subject to paragraph (2), every fuel tank fitted to a vehicle to which regulation 39A applies shall be so constructed and fitted that it cannot readily be filled from a petrol pump delivery nozzle which has an external diameter of 23.6mm or greater without the aid of a device (such as a funnel) not fitted to the vehicle.

(2) Paragraph (1) does not apply to a vehicle in respect of which both of the following conditions are satisfied, that is to say—

(a) that at the time of its first use the vehicle is so designed and constructed that prolonged continuous running on leaded petrol would not cause any device designed to control the emission of carbon monoxide, hydrocarbons or nitrogen oxides to malfunction, and

(b) that it is conspicuously and legibly marked in a position immediately visible to a person filling the fuel tank with—

(i) the word "UNLEADED", or

(ii) the symbol shown in Part II of Schedule 3A.

(3) In this regulation "*fuel tank*", in relation to a vehicle, means a fuel tank used in connection with the propulsion of the vehicle.]

B27.92   *[Regulation 39B was inserted by S.I. 1988 No. 1524.]*

40. Gas propulsion systems and gas-fired appliances

B27.93   (1) A vehicle which is—

(a) a motor vehicle which first used gas as a fuel for its propulsion before 19th November 1982; or

(b) a trailer manufactured before 19th November 1982 to which there is fitted a gas container,

shall be so constructed that it complies either with the provisions of Schedule 4 or with the provisions of Schedule 5.

(2) A vehicle which is—

(a) a motor vehicle which first used gas as a fuel for its propulsion on or after 19th November 1982; or

(b) a motor vehicle first used on or after 1st May 1984 or a trailer manufactured on or after 19th November 1982 which is in either case equipped with a gas container or a gas-fired appliance,

shall comply with the provisions of Schedule 5.

(3) The requirements of this regulation are in addition to, and not in derogation from, the requirements of any regulations made under powers conferred by the Petroleum (Consolidation) Act 1928, the Health and Safety at Work, etc., Act 1974, the Control of Pollution Act 1974 or any other Act or of any codes of practice issued under the Health and Safety at Work etc., Act 1974.

(4) In this regulation "*gas container*" has the meaning given in Schedule 4 where compliance with the provisions of that Schedule is concerned and otherwise has the meaning given in Schedule 5.

H *Minibuses*

41. Minibuses

The requirements specified in Schedule 6 shall apply to every minibus first used on or after 1st April 1988 except a vehicle—

  (a) manufactured by Land Rover UK Limited and known as the Land Rover; or

  (b) constructed or adapted for the secure transport of prisoners.

B27.94

42. Fire-extinguishing apparatus

(1) No person shall use, or cause or permit to be used, on a road a minibus first used on or after 1st April 1988 unless it carries suitable and efficient apparatus for extinguishing fire which is of a type specified in Part I of Schedule 7.

B27.95

(2) The apparatus referred to in paragraph (1) above shall be—

  (a) readily available for use;

  (b) clearly marked with the appropriate British Standards Institution specification number; and

  (c) maintained in good and efficient working order.

(3) This regulation does not apply to a vehicle manufactured by Land Rover UK Limited and known as the Land Rover.

43. First-aid equipment

(1) No person shall use, or cause or permit to be used, on a road a minibus first used on or after 1st April 1988 unless it carries a receptacle which contains the items specified in Part II of Schedule 7.

B27.96

(2) The receptacle referred to in paragraph (1) above shall be—

  (a) maintained in a good condition;

  (b) suitable for the purpose of keeping the items referred to in the said paragraph in good condition;

  (c) readily available for use; and

  (d) prominently marked as first aid receptacle.

(3) The items referred to in paragraph (1) above shall be maintained in good condition and shall be of a good and reliable quality and of a suitable design.

(4) This regulation does not apply to a vehicle manufactured by Land Rover UK Limited and known as the Land Rover.

44. Carriage of dangerous substances

B27.97   (1) Save as provided in paragraph (2), no person shall use or cause or permit to be used on a road a minibus by which any highly inflammable or otherwise dangerous substance is carried unless that substance is carried in containers so designed and constructed, and unless the substance is so packed, that, notwithstanding an accident to the vehicle, it is unlikely that damage to the vehicle or injury to passengers in the vehicle will be caused by the substance.

(2) Paragraph (1) shall not apply in relation to the electrolyte of a battery installed in an electric wheelchair provided that the wheelchair is securely fixed to the vehicle.

(3) This regulation does not apply to a vehicle manufactured by Land Rover UK Limited and known as Land Rover.

I *Power-to-Weight Ratio*

B27.98   **45. Power-to-weight ratio**   *[Revoked by S.I. 1995 No. 1201.]*

J *Protective Systems*

[46. Seat belt anchorage points

B27.99   (1) Save as provided by paragraph (2), this regulation applies to—

(a) every wheeled motor car first used on or after 1st January 1965;

(b) every three-wheeled motor cycle the unladen weight of which exceeds 255kg and which was first used on or after 1st September 1970; and

(c) every heavy motor car first used on or after 1st October 1988.

(2) This regulation does not apply to—

(a) a goods vehicle (other than a dual-purpose vehicle) which was first used—

(i) before 1st April 1967; or

(ii) on or after 1st April 1980 and before 1st October 1988 and has a maximum gross weight exceeding 3500kg; or

(iii) before 1st April 1980 or, if the vehicle is of a model manufactured before 1st October 1979, was first used before 1st April 1982 and in either case, has an unladen weight exceeding 1525kg;

(b) a bus, being—

(i) a minibus—

(a) if first used before 1st October 1988, constructed or adapted to carry more than twelve passengers; or

(b) if first used on or after 1st October 1988, having a maximum gross weight exceeding 3500kg; or

(ii) a large bus (other than a coach first used on or after 1st October 1988);

(c) an agricultural motor vehicle;

(d) a motor tractor;

(e) a works truck;

(f) an electrically-propelled goods vehicle first used before 1st October 1988;

(g) a pedestrian-controlled vehicle;

(h) a vehicle which has been used on roads outside Great Britain and has been imported into Great Britain, whilst it is being driven from the place where it has arrived in Great Britain to a place of residence of the owner or driver of the vehicle, or from any such place to a place where, by previous arrangement, it will be provided with such anchorage points as are required by this regulation and such seat belts as are required by regulation 47;

(i) a vehicle having a maximum speed not exceeding 16mph;

(j) a motor cycle equipped with a driver's seat of a type requiring the driver to sit astride it, and which is constructed or assembled by a person not ordinarily engaged in the trade or business of manufacturing vehicles of that description; or

(k) a locomotive.

(3) A vehicle which was first used before 1st April 1982 shall be equipped with anchorage points which are designed to hold securely in position on the vehicle seat belts for the driver's seat and specified passenger's seat (if any).

(4) Save as provided in paragraph (4A) or (4B) a vehicle which is first used on or after 1st April 1982 shall be equipped with anchorage points which—

(a) are designed to hold securely in position on the vehicle seat belts for—

    (i) in the case of a minibus, motor ambulance or a motor caravan—

        (A) if first used before 1st October 1988, the driver's seat and the specified passenger's seat (if any); or

        (B) if first used on or after 1st October 1988, the driver's seat and any forward-facing front seat; and

    (ii) in the case of any other passenger or dual-purpose vehicle, every forward-facing seat constructed or adapted to accommodate one adult;

    (iii) in every other case, every forward-facing front seat and every non-protected seat, and

(b) comply with the technical and installation requirements of Community Directive 76/115 or 81/575 or 82/318 [or 90/629] [or 96/38] or ECE Regulation 14 [or 14.01 or 14.02] [or 14.03] whether or not those instruments apply to the vehicle, so, however, that the requirements in those instruments which relate to testing shall not apply.

(4A) The requirements specified in paragraph (4) shall not apply to—

(a) a goods vehicle first used on or after 1st October 1988 and having a maximum gross weight exceeding 3500kg, but any such vehicle shall be equipped with two belt anchorages designed to hold securely in position on the vehicle lap belts for the driver's seat and each forward-facing front seat; or

(b) a coach equipped with anchorage points which are designed to hold securely in position on the vehicle seat belts for all exposed forward-facing seats and which—

    (i) comply with the requirements in paragraph (4)(b); or

    (ii) in any case where the anchorage points form part of a seat, do not when a forward horizontal force is applied to them become detached from the seat of which they form part before that seat becomes detached from the vehicle.

(4B) Instead of complying with the requirements in paragraph (4), a vehicle may comply [with—

(a) Community Directive 76/115 or 81/575 or 82/318 [or 90/629] [or 96/38]; or

(b) ECE Regulation 14 or 14.01 or 14.02 [or 14.03].]

(5) Save as provided in paragraph (5A), a vehicle of a type mentioned in paragraphs (4), (4A) and (4B) which is fitted with anchorage points other than those required by those paragraphs shall comply with the requirements in paragraph (4)(b), or in the case of a coach the requirements in paragraph (4A)(b)(ii), in respect of any additional anchorage points as well as in respect of the anchorage points required by paragraph (4), (4A) or (4B) to be provided.

(5A) The requirements in paragraph (5) shall not apply in respect of any additional anchorage points first fitted before 1st April 1986 in the case of a vehicle of a type mentioned in paragraph (4)(a)(i)(a), or before 1st October 1988 in the case of a vehicle of any other type.

(6) In this regulation—

    (a) the expressions *"exposed forward-facing seat"*, *"forward-facing seat"*, *"forward-facing front seat"*, *"lap belt"*, *"seat-belt"* and *"specified passenger's seat"* have the same meaning as in regulation 47(8); . . .

    [(b) a seat is a *"non-protected seat"* if it is not a front seat and the screen zones within the protected area have a combined surface area of less than 800cm^2; and]

    [(c) *"screen zone"* and *"protected area"* in relation to a seat, shall be construed in accordance with paragraph 4.3.3 of Annex 1 to Community Directive 81/575.]

B27.100   *[Regulation 46 was substantially amended by S.I. 1987 No. 1133. The text of regulation 46, as so amended, was set out in the Schedule to S.I. 1987 No. 1133 and the above text is the text so printed as subsequently amended by S.I. 1989 No. 1478; S.I. 1991 No. 2003; S.I. 1994 No. 3270; S.I. 1998 No. 2429.*

    With effect from October 1, 2001 (a date after the date on which this volume states the law), the following text will be substituted by S.I. 2001 No. 1043 for the above text of regulation 46:

[46. Seat belt anchorage points

(1) This regulation applies to a motor vehicle which is not an excepted vehicle and is—

    (a) a bus first used on or after 1st April 1982;

    (b) a wheeled motor car first used on or after 1st January 1965;

    (c) a three-wheeled motor cycle which has an unladen weight exceeding 255 kg and which was first used on or after 1st September 1970; or

    (d) a heavy motor car first used on or after 1st October 1988.

(2) Each of the following is an excepted vehicle—

    (a) a goods vehicle (other than a dual-purpose vehicle)—

        (i) first used before 1st April 1967;

        (ii) first used on or after 1st April 1980 and before 1st October 1988 and having a maximum gross weight exceeding 3500 kg; or

        (iii) first used before 1st April 1980 or, if the vehicle is of a model manufactured before 1st October 1979, first used before 1st April 1982 and, in either case, having an unladen weight exceeding 1525 kg;

    (b) an agricultural motor vehicle;

    (c) a motor tractor;

    (d) a works truck;

    (e) an electrically propelled goods vehicle first used before 1st October 1988;

    (f) a pedestrian-controlled vehicle;

    (g) a vehicle which has been used on roads outside Great Britain, whilst it is being driven from the place at which it arrived in Great Britain to a place of residence of the owner or driver of the vehicle, or from any such place to a place where, by previous arrangement, it will be provided with such anchorage points as are required by this regulation and with such seat belts as are required by regulation 47;

    (h) a vehicle having a maximum speed not exceeding 16 mph;

(i) a motor cycle equipped with a driver's seat of a type requiring the driver to sit astride it, and which is constructed or assembled by a person not ordinarily engaged in the trade or business of manufacturing vehicles of that description;

(j) a locomotive.

(3) A vehicle which falls within a description specified in column (2) of an item in the Table below shall be equipped with anchorage points for seat belts for the use of persons sitting in the seats specified in column (3) of that item and those anchorage points ("*mandatory anchorage points*") shall comply with the requirements specified in column (4).

TABLE

(1) *Item*	(2) *Description of vehicle*	(3) *Seats for which mandatory anchorage points are to be provided*	(4) *Technical and installation requirements*
1.	Any vehicle first used before 1st April 1982	The driver's seat and specified passenger seat (if any)	Anchorage points must be designed to hold seat belts securely in position on the vehicle
2.	Minibus constructed or adapted to carry not more than 12 seated passengers in addition to the driver, motor ambulance or motor caravan which, in any such case, was first used on or after 1st April 1982 but before 1st October 1988	The driver's seat and specified passenger seat (if any)	The technical and installation (but not the testing) requirements of Community Directive 76/115, 81/575, 82/318, 90/629 or 96/38 or ECE Regulation 14, 14.01, 14.02. 14.03, 14.04 or 14.05 whether or not those instruments apply to the vehicle
3.	Minibus (not being a vehicle falling within item 7 or 8) having a gross weight not exceeding 3500 kg, motor ambulance or motor caravan which, in any such case, was first used on or after 1st October 1988	The driver's seat and each forward-facing front seat	The requirements specified in column (4) of item 2
4.	Goods vehicle first used on or after 1st October 1988 but before 1st October 2001 and having a maximum gross weight exceeding 3500 kg	The driver's seat and each forward-facing front seat	2 or 3 anchorage points designed to hold seat belts securely in position

[*continued on next page*

(1) Item	(2) Description of vehicle	(3) Seats for which mandatory anchorage points are to be provided	(4) Technical and installation requirements
5.	Goods vehicle first used on or after 1st October 2001 and having a maximum gross weight exceeding 3500 kg	All forward-facing front seats	The technical and installation requirements of Community Directive 96/38 or ECE Regulation 14.04 or 14.05
6.	Coach first used on or after 1st October 1988 but before 1st October 2001	All exposed forward-facing seats	The requirements specified in column (4) of item 2 or, if the anchorage points were fitted before 1st October 2001 and form part of a seat, a requirement that they do not, when a forward horizontal force is applied ot them, become detached from the seat before the seat becomes detached from the vehicle
7.	Bus (other than an urban bus) having a gross vehicle weight exceeding 3500 kg and first used on or after 1st October 2001	Anochorage points for every forward-facing and every rearward-facing seat	The requirements specified in column (4) of item 5
8.	Bus (other than an urban bus) having a gross vehicle weight not exceeding 3500 kg and first used on or after 1st October 2001	Every forward-facing and every rearward-facing seat	The requirements specified in column (4) of item 5
9.	Passenger or dual-purpose vehicle (other than a bus) first used on or after 1st April 1982 and not falling within any of items 2 to 8	Every forward-facing seat constructed or adapted to accommodate no more than one adult	The requirements specified in column (4) of item 2
10.	Vehicle (other than a bus) first used on or after 1st April 1982 and not falling within any of items 2 to 9	Every forward-facing front seat and every non-protected seat	The requirements specified in column (4) of item 2

(4) Any anchorage fitted after 1st October 2001 to a bus not falling within item 7 or 8 of the Table in paragraph (3) must comply with the technical and installation (but not the testing) requirements of Community Directive 76/115, 81/575, 82/318, 90/629 or 96/38 or ECE Regulation 14, 14.01, 14.02, 14.03, 14.04 or 14.05 whether or not those instruments apply to the vehicle.

(5) Subject to paragraph (6), where a vehicle to which this regulation applies and which falls within a class specified in an item of the Table in paragraph (3) is fitted with non-mandatory anchorage points, those anchorage points shall comply with the requirements applicable to the mandatory anchorage points specified for that item.

(6) Paragraph (5) does not apply to non-mandatory anchorage points fitted to—

(a) a minibus before 1st April 1986; or

(b) any other vehicle before 1st October 1988.

(7) For the purposes of this regulation—

(a) the expressions "*exposed forward-facing seat*", "*forward-facing front seat*", "*lap belt*", "*seat belt*" and "*specified passenger's seat*" have the same meaning as in regultaion 47(8);

(b) "*mandatory anchorage points*" has the meaning given in paragraph (3) and "*non-mandatory anchorage points*" means anchorage points which are not mandatory anchorage points;

(c) a seat is a "*non-protected seat*" if it is not a front seat and the screen zones within the protected area have a combined surface area of less than 800 cm^2;

(d) "*screen zone*" and "*protected area*" in relation to a seat shall be construed in accordance with paragraph 4.3.3 of Annex I to Community Directive 81/575; and

(e) "*urban bus*" means a bus designed for urban use with standing passengers and includes a vehicle which is—

    (i) a Class I vehicle as defined by paragraph 2.1.2.1.3.1.1 of Annex I of Community Directive 97/27/EC [*O.J. No. L233, August 25, 1997, p. 1*];

    (ii) a Class II vehicle as defined by paragraph 2.1.2.1.3.1.2 of that Annex; or

    (iii) a Class A vehicle as defined by paragraph 2.1.2.1.3.2.1 of that Annex.

(8) A vehicle which is not required by this regulation to comply with the technical and installation requirements of Community Directive 76/115, 81/575, 82/318, 90/629 or 96/38 or ECE Regulation 14, 14.01, 14.02, 14.03, 14.04 or 14.05 shall nevertheless be taken to comply with the provisions of this regulation if it does comply with those requirements.]

The explanatory notes accompanying S.I. 2001 No. 1043 state that that instrument gives effect to Directive 96/36/EC, Directive 96/38/EC and Directive 2000/3/EC.

As to the application of the provisions of regulation 46 to vehicles in respect of which approval certificates have been issued under the "Approval Regulations", see Schedule 2A, paragraph 7, to these regulations.]

[47. Seat belts

(1) This regulation applies to every vehicle to which regulation 46 applies.   **B27.101**

(2) Save as provided in paragraph (4) a vehicle to which—

(a) this regulation applies which was first used before 1st April 1981 shall be provided with—

    (i) a body-restraining belt, designed for use by an adult, for the driver's seat; and

    (ii) a body-restraining belt for the specified passenger's seat (if any);

(b) this regulation applies which is first used on or after 1st April 1981 shall be provided with three-point belts for the driver's seat and for the specified passenger's seat (if any);

(c) regulation 46(4)(a)(ii) or (iii) applies which is first used on or after 1st April 1987 shall be fitted with seat belts additional to those required by sub-paragraph (b) as follows—

    (i) for any forward-facing front seat alongside the driver's seat, not being a specified passenger's seat, a seat belt which is a three-point belt, or a lap belt installed in accordance with paragraph 3.1.2.1 of Annex 1 to Community Directive 77/541 or a disabled person's belt;

    (ii) in the case of a passenger or dual-purpose vehicle having not more than two forward-facing seats behind the driver's seat with either—

        (A) an inertia reel belt for at least one of those seats, or

        (B) a three-point belt, a lap belt, a disabled person's belt or a child restraint for each of those seats;

    (iii) in the case of a passenger or dual-purpose vehicle having more than two forward-facing seats behind the driver's seat, with either—

        (A) an inertia reel belt for one of those seats being an outboard seat and a three-point belt, a lap belt, a disabled person's belt or a child restraint for at least one other of those seats;

        (B) a three-point belt for one of those seats and either a child restraint or a disabled person's belt for at least one other of those seats; or

        (C) a three-point belt, a lap belt, a disabled person's belt or a child restraint for each of those seats;

(d) regulation 46(4)(a)(i)(B) applies shall be fitted with seat belts as follows—

    (i) for the driver's seat and the specified passenger's seat (if any) a three-point belt; and

    (ii) for any forward-facing front seat which is not a specified passenger's seat, a three-point belt or a lap belt installed in accordance with the provisions of sub-paragraph (c)(i);

(e) regulation 46(4A)(b) applies shall be equipped with seat belts which shall be three-point belts, lap belts or disabled person's belts.

Where a lap belt is fitted to a forward-facing front seat of a minibus, a motor ambulance or a motor caravan, or to an exposed forward-facing seat [(other than the driver's seat or any crew seat) of a coach either—

    (i) there shall be provided padding to a depth of not less than 50mm, on that part of the surface or edge of any bar, or the top or edge of any screen or partition, which would be likely to be struck by the head of a passenger wearing the lap belt in the event of an accident; or

    (ii) the technical and installation requirements of Annex 4 to ECE Regulation 21 shall be met, in respect of any such bar, screen or partition,

but nothing in sub-paragraph (i) above shall require padding to be provided on any surface more than 1m from the centre of the line of intersection of the seat cushion and the back rest or more than 150mm on either side of the longitudinal vertical plane which passes through the centre of that line, nor shall it require padding to be provided on any instrument panel of a minibus.]

(3) Every seat belt for an adult, other than a disabled person's belt, provided for a vehicle in accordance with paragraph (2)(b), (c), (d) or (e) shall, except as provided in paragraph (6), comply with the installation requirements specified in paragraph 3.2.2 to 3.3.4 of Annex I to Community Directive 77/541 [or 82/319 or 90/628] [or 96/36] whether or not [those Directives apply] to the vehicle.

(4) The requirements specified in paragraph (2) do not apply—

(a) to a vehicle while it is being used under a trade licence within the meaning of section 16 of the 1971 Act;

(b) to a vehicle, not being a vehicle to which the Type Approval (Great Britain) Regulations apply, while it is being driven from premises of the manufacturer by whom it was made, or of a distributor of vehicles or dealer in vehicles—

    (i) to premises of a distributor of or dealer in vehicles or of the purchaser of the vehicle, or

    (ii) to premises of a person obtaining possession of the vehicle under a hiring agreement or hire-purchase agreement;

(c) in relation to any seat for which there is provided—

    (i) a seat belt which bears a mark including the specification number of the British Standard for Passive Belt Systems, namely BSAU 183:1983 and including the registered certification trade mark of the British Standards Institution; . . .

    (ii) a seat belt designed for use by an adult which is a harness belt comprising a lap belt and shoulder straps which bears a British Standard mark or a mark including the specification number for the British Standard for Seat Belt Assemblies for Motor Vehicles, namely BS 3254:1960 or [BS 3254: Part 1: 1988] and including the registered certification trade mark of the British Standards Institution, or [the marking designated as an approval mark by regulations 4 of the Approval Marks Regulations and shown at item 16 or 16A in Schedule 2 to those Regulations];

    [(iii) a seat belt which satisfies the requirements of a standard corresponding to the British Standard referred to in sub-paragraph (i); or]

    [(iv) a seat belt designated for use by an adult which is a harness belt comprising a lap belt and shoulder straps and which satisfies the requirements of a standard corresponding to any of the British Standards referred to in sub-paragraph (ii).]

(d) in relation to the driver's seat or the specified passenger's seat (if any) of a vehicle which has been specially designed and constructed, or specially adapted, for the use of a person suffering from some physical defect or disability, in a case where a disabled person's belt for an adult person is provided for use for that seat;

(e) to a vehicle to which regulation 46(4A)(a) applies.

(5) Every seat belt provided in pursuance of paragraph (2) shall be properly secured to the anchorage points provided for it in accordance with regulation 46; or, in the case of a child restraint, to anchorages specially provided for it or, in the case of a disabled person's belt, secured to the vehicle or to the seat which is being occupied by the person wearing the belt.

(6) Paragraph (3), in so far as it relates to the second paragraph of paragraph 3.3.2 of the Annex there mentioned (which concerns the locking or releasing of a seat belt by a single movement) does not apply in respect of a seat belt fitted for—

(a) a seat which is treated as a specified passenger's seat by virtue of the provisions of sub-paragraph (ii) in the definition of "specified passenger's seat" in paragraph (8); or

(b) any forward-facing seat for a passenger alongside the driver's seat of a goods vehicle which has an unladen weight of more than 915kg and has more than one such seat, any such seats for passengers being joined together in a single structure; or

(c) any seat (other than the driver's seat) fitted to a coach.

(7) Every seat belt, other than a disabled person's belt or a seat belt of a kind mentioned in paragraph [4(c)] above, provided for any person in a vehicle to which this regulation applies shall be legibly and permanently marked—

(a) . . . with a British Standard mark or a designated approval mark; . . .

Provided this paragraph shall not operate so as to invalidate the exception permitted in paragraph (6).

[(7A) Paragraph (7) does not apply to—

(a) a seat belt for an adult . . . that satisfies the requirements of a standard corresponding to either of the British Standards referred to in sub-paragraph (i)(a) of the definition of "British Standard mark" in paragraph (8); or

(b) a child restraint that satisfies the requirements of a standard corresponding to any of the British Standards referred to in sub-paragraph (i)(b) of that definition.]

[(7B) For the purposes of this regulation a reference to a standard corresponding to a specified British Standard is a reference to—

(a) a standard or code of practice of a national standards body or equivalent body of any EEA State;

(b) any international standard recognised for use as a standard by any EEA State; or

(c) a technical specification recognised for use as a standard by a public authority of any EEA State,

where the standard, code of practice, international standard or technical specification provides in relation to seat belts, a level of safety equivalent to that provided by the British Standard and contains a requirement as respects the marking of seat belts equivalent to that provided by the British Standard.]

[(7C) For the purposes of paragraph (7B)—

(a) *"EEA State"* means a State which is a contracting Party to the EEA Agreement but, until the EEA Agreement comes into force in relation to Liechtenstein, does not include the state of Liechtenstein; and

(b) *"EEA Agreement"* [*Cm. 2073*] means the Agreement on the European Economic Area signed at Oporto on 2nd May 1992 as adjusted by the Protocol signed at Brussels on 17th March 1993 [*Cm. 2183*].]

(8) In this regulation—

"body-restraining belt" means a seat belt designed to provide restraint for both the upper and lower parts of the trunk of the wearer in the event of an accident to the vehicle;

"British Standard mark" means a mark consisting of—

(i) the specification number of one of the following British Standards for Seat Belt Assemblies for Motor Vehicles, namely—
(a) if it is a seat belt for an adult, BS 3254:1960 [BS 3254: Part 1: 1988]; or
(b) if it is a child restraint, BS 3254:1960, or BS 3254:1960 as amended by Amendment No. 16 published on 31st July 1986 under the number AMD 5210, [BS 3254: Part 2: 1988] [or BS 3254: Part 2: 1991], BS AU 185, BS AU 186 or 186a, BS AU 202 [, BS AU 202a or BS AU 202b]; and, in either case,

(ii) the registered certification trade mark of the British Standards Institution;

"child restraint" means a seat belt for the use of a young person which is designed either to be fitted directly to a suitable anchorage or to be used in conjunction with a seat belt for an adult and held in place by the restraining action of that belt;
Provided that for the purposes of paragraph (2)(c)(ii)(B) and (2)(c)(iii) it means only such seat belts fitted directly to a suitable anchorage and excludes belts marked with the specification numbers BS AU 185 and BS AU 186 or 186a;

"crew seat" has the same meaning as in regulation 3(1) of the Public Service Vehicles (Conditions of Fitness, Equipment, Use and Certification) Regulations 1981 [*q.v.*];

"designated approval mark" means

(a) if it is a seat belt other than a child restraint, the marking designated as an approval mark by regulation 4 of the Approval Marks Regulations and shown at [items 16 and 16A] of Schedule 2 to those Regulations or the marking designated as an approval mark by regulation 5 of those Regulations and shown at item 23 [, 23A and 23B] in Schedule 4 to those Regulations and

(b) if it is a child restraint, [any] of the markings designated as approval marks by regulation 4 of those Regulations and shown at [items 44, 44A, [, 44B and 44C]] in Schedule 2 to those Regulations;

"disabled person's belt" means a seat belt which has been specially designed or adapted for use by an adult or young person suffering from some physical defect or disability and which is intended for use solely by such a person;

"exposed forward-facing seat" means—

(i) a forward-facing front seat (including any crew seat) and the driver's seat; and

(ii) any other forward-facing seat which is not immediately behind and on the same horizonal plane as a forward-facing high-backed seat;

"forward-facing seat" means a seat which is attached to a vehicle so that it faces towards the front of the vehicle in such a manner that a line passing through the centre of both the front and the back of the seat is at an angle of 30° or less to the longitudinal axis of the vehicle;

"forward-facing front seat" means—

(i) any forward-facing seat alongside the driver's seat; or

(ii) if the vehicle normally has no seat which is a forward-facing front seat under sub-paragraph (i) of this definition, each forward-facing seat for a passenger which is foremost in the vehicle;

"forward-facing high-backed seat" means a forward-facing seat which is also a high-backed seat;

"high-backed seat" means a seat the highest part of which is at least 1 metre above the deck of the vehicle;

"inertia reel belt" means a three-point belt of either of the types required for a front out-board seating position by paragraph 3.1.1 of Annex 1 to Community Directive 77/541;

"lap belt" means a seat belt which passes across the front of the wearer's pelvic region and which is designed for use by an adult;

"seat" includes any part designed for the accommodation of one adult of a continuous seat designed for the accommodation of more than one adult;

"seat belt" means a belt intended to be worn by a person in a vehicle and designed to prevent or lessen injury to its wearer in the event of an accident to the vehicle and includes, in the case of a child restraint, any special chair to which the belt is attached;

"specified passenger's seat" means—

(i) in the case of a vehicle which has one forward-facing front seat alongside the driver's seat, that seat, and in the case of a vehicle which has more than one such seat, the one furthest from the driver's seat; or

(ii) if the vehicle normally has no seat which is the specified passenger's seat under sub-paragraph (i) of this definition the forward-facing front seat for a passenger which is the foremost in the vehicle and furthest from the driver's seat, unless there is a fixed partition separating that seat from the space in front of it along-side the driver's seat; and "*three-point belt*" means a seat belt which—

   (i)   restrains the upper and lower parts of the torso;

   (ii)   includes a lap belt;

   (iii)   is anchored at not less than three points; and

   (iv)   is designed for use by an adult.]

B27.102   *[Regulation 47 was substantially amended by S.I. 1987 No. 1133. The text of regulation 47, as so amended, was set out in the Schedule to S.I. 1987 No. 1133 and the above text is the text so printed as subsequently amended by S.I. 1989 No. 1478; S.I. 1991 No. 2003; S.I. 1994 No. 3270; S.I. 1996 No. 163; S.I. 1998 No. 2429.*

With effect from October 1, 2001 (a date after the date at which this volume states the law), the following amendments will be effected to regulation 47 by S.I. 2001 No. 1043:

   (i)   *in regulation 47(2)(c), the following words will be substituted for the words "regulation 46(4)(a)(ii) or (iii)"—*

[item 9 or 10 of the Table in regulation 46(3)]

   (ii)   *in regulation 47(2)(d), the following words will be substituted for the words "regulation 46(4)(a)(i)(B)"—*

[item 3 of the Table in regulation 46(3)]

   (iii)   *in regulation 47(2)(e), the following words will be substituted for the words "regulation 46(4A)(b)"—*

[item 6 of the Table in regulation 46(3)]

   (iv)   *a semi-colon will be inserted at the end of regulation 47(2)(e),*

   (v)   *the following text (regulation 47(2)(f) to (j)) will be inserted after regulation 47(2)(e)—*

   [(f)   item 5 of the Table in regulation 46(3) applies shall be fitted—

      (i)   as respects the driver's seat with a three-point belt or a lap belt; and

      (ii)   as respects every other forward-facing front seat with a three-point belt, a lap belt installed in accordance with paragraph 3.1.2.1 of Annex I to Community Directive 77/541 or a disabled person's belt;]

   [(g)   item 7 of the Table in regulation 46(3) applies shall be fitted, as respects every forward-facing seat, with—

      (i)   an inertia reel belt;

      (ii)   a retractable lap belt installed in compliance with paragraph 3.1.10 of Annex I to Community Directive 96/36 or 2000/3;

      (iii)   a disabled person's belt; or

      (iv)   a child restraint;]

   [(h)   item 7 of the Table in regulation 46(3) applies shall be fitted, as respects every rearward-facing seat, with—

      (i)   an inertia reel belt;

      (ii)   a retractable lap belt;

      (iii)   a disabled person's belt; or

      (iv)   a child restraint;]

   [(i)   item 8 of the Table in regulation 46(3), as respects every forward-facing seat, with—

      (i)   an inertia reel belt;

      (ii)   a disabled person's belt; or

      (iii)   a child restraint;]

   [(j)   item 8 of the Table in regulation 46(3), as respects every rearward-facing seat, with—

       (i) an inertia reel belt;
      (ii) a retractable lap belt;
     (iii) a disabled person's belt; or
     (iv) a child restraint;]

(vi) in regulation 46(3), the following words will be substituted for the words "paragraph (2)(b), (c), (d) or (e)"—

[any of paragraphs (2)(b) to (j)]

(vii) also in regulation 47(3), the following words will be substituted for the words "[or 82/319" to "96/36]"—

[, 82/319, 90/628, 96/36 or 2000/3]

(viii) in regulation 47(4)(a), the following words will be substituted for the words "section 16 of the 1971 Act"—

[section 11 of the Vehicle Excise and Registration Act 1994 [*q.v.*]]

(ix) in regulation 47(4)(e), the following words will be substituted for the words "regulation 46(4A)(a)"—

[item 4 of the Table in regulation 46(3)]

(x) the following text (regulation 47(4A)) will be inserted after regulation 47(4)—

[(4A) Vehicles constructed or adapted for the secure transport of prisoners shall not be required to comply with the requirements of paragraph (2) in relation to seats for persons other than the driver and any front seat passenger provided that those seats shall have seat belt anchorage points provided for them in accordance with regulation 46.]

(xi) in regulation 47(5), the following words will be inserted after the words "disabled person's belt"—

[first fitted before 1st October 2001]

(xii) a semi-colon followed by the word "or" will be inserted at the end of regulation 47(7)(a),

(xiii) the following text (regulation 47(7)(b)) will be inserted after regulation 47(7)(a)—

[(b) with an EC Component Type-Approval Mark complying with Annex III to Community Directive 2000/3]

and

(xiv) in regulation 47(8), the following definition ("retractable lap belt") will be inserted after the definition of "lap belt"—

["*retractable lap belt*" means a lap belt with either an automatically locking retractor (as defined in paragraph 1.8.3 of Annex I to Community Directive 77/541) or an emergency locking retractor (as defined in paragraph 1.8.4 of Annex I to Community Directive 77/541).]

As to the European Economic Area and the EEA agreement, see the editorial note to Regulation (EEC) 3820/85 below.

As to the application of the provisions of regulation 47 (so far as it relates to seat belts for adults) to vehicles in respect of which approval certificates have been issued under the "Approval Regulations", see Schedule 2A, paragraph 8, to these regulations.]

48. Maintenance of seat belts and anchorage points

(1) This regulation applies to every seat belt with which a motor vehicle is required to be   **B27.103** provided in accordance with regulation 47 and to the anchorages, fastenings, adjusting device and retracting mechanism (if any) of every such seat belt [and also to every anchorage with which a goods vehicle is required to be provided in accordance with regulation 46(4A)(a)].

(2) For the purposes of this regulation the anchorages and anchorage points of a seat

belt shall, in the case of a seat which incorporates integral seat belt anchorages, include the system by which the seat assembly itself is secured to the vehicle structure.

(3) The anchorage points provided for seat belts shall be used only as anchorages for the seat belts for which they are intended to be used or capable of being used.

(4) Save as provided in paragraph (5) below—

(a) all load-bearing members of the vehicle structure or panelling within 30cm of each anchorage point shall be maintained in a sound condition and free from serious corrosion, distortion or fracture;

(b) the adjusting device and (if fitted) the retracting mechanism of the seat belt shall be so maintained that the belt may be readily adjusted to the body of the wearer, either automatically or manually, according to the design of the device and (if fitted) the retracting mechanism;

(c) the seat belt and its anchorages, fastenings and adjusting device shall be maintained free from any obvious defect which would be likely to affect adversely the performance by the seat belt of the function of restraining the body of the wearer in the event of an accident to the vehicle;

(d) the buckle or other fastening of the seat belt shall—

(i) be so maintained that the belt can be readily fastened or unfastened;
(ii) be kept free from any temporary or permanent obstruction; and
(iii) except in the case of a disabled person's seat belt, be readily accessible to a person sitting in the seat for which the seat belt is provided;

(e) the webbing or other material which forms the seat belt shall be maintained free from cuts or other visible faults (as, for example, extensive fraying) which would be likely to affect adversely the performance of the belt when under stress;

(f) the ends of every seat belt, other than a disabled person's seat belt, shall be securely fastened to the anchorage points provided for them; and

(g) the ends of every disabled person's seat belt shall, when the seat belt is being used for the purpose for which it was designed and constructed, be securely fastened either to some part of the structure of the vehicle or to the seat which is being occupied by the person wearing the belt so that the body of the person wearing the belt would be restrained in the event of an accident to the vehicle.

(5) No requirement specified in paragraph (4) above applies if the vehicle is being used—

(a) on a journey after the start of which the requirement ceased to be complied with; or

(b) after the requirement ceased to be complied with and steps have been taken for such compliance to be restored with all reasonable expedition.

(6) Expressions which are used in this regulation and are defined in regulation 47 have the same meaning in this regulation as they have in regulation 47.

B27.104   *[Regulation 48 is printed as amended by S.I. 1987 No. 1133.*

With effect from October 1, 2001 (a date after the date at which this volume states the law), the following amendment will be effected to regulation 48(1) by S.I. 2001 No. 1043: the words "regulation 46(3) and item 4 in the Table in that regulation" will be substituted for the words "regulation 46(4A)(a)".]

[48A. Minibuses and coaches to be fitted with additional seat belts when used in certain circumstances

B27.105   (1) No person shall use or cause or permit to be used on a road a coach or minibus wholly or mainly for the purpose of carrying a group of 3 or more children in the following circumstances unless the appropriate number of forward-facing passenger seats fitted to the vehicle meet the requirements of this regulation.

(2) The circumstances are that—

(a) the group of children are on an organised trip; and

(b) the journey is being made for the purposes of the trip.

(3) In paragraph (1), the reference to the appropriate number is a reference to the number of children being carried in the vehicle (excluding disabled children in wheelchairs).

(4) Without prejudice to the generality of paragraph (2)(a), a group of children shall, for the purposes of this regulation, be regarded as being on an organised trip if they are being carried to or from their school or from one part of their school premises to another.

(5) Without prejudice to the meaning of paragraph (2)(b), paragraph (1) shall not apply to a vehicle if it is being used in the provision of a bus service of a description specified in paragraph 2 of the Schedule to the Fuel Duty Grant (Eligible Bus Services) Regulations 1985 [*S.I. 1985 No. 1886; not reproduced in this work*] or if it is otherwise being used wholly or mainly for the purpose of providing a transport service for the general public.

(6) For a forward-facing passenger seat to meet the requirements of this regulation a seat belt must be provided for it, and—

(a) if paragraph (3) of regulation 47 does not (in whole or part) apply to the seat belt and the seat belt was first fitted to the vehicle after 10th February 1997, the seat belt must comply with that paragraph to the extent (if any) that it would have to so comply were—

(i) that regulation to apply to all motor vehicles, and

(ii) there substituted for the words "provided" to "or (e)", in that paragraph, the words "provided for any person in a vehicle to which this regulation applies";

(b) if paragraph (5) of regulation 47 does not apply to the seat belt and the seat belt is a seat belt for an adult (not being a disabled person's belt) that was first fitted to the vehicle after 10th February 1997, the seat belt must comply with the requirements specified in paragraph (7) below;

(c) if paragraph (5) of regulation 47 does not apply to the seat belt and the seat belt is a child restraint that was first fitted to the vehicle after 10th February 1997, the seat belt must be properly secured to anchorages provided for it;

(d) if paragraph (5) of regulation 47 does not apply to the seat belt and the seat belt is a disabled person's belt that was first fitted to the vehicle after 10th February 1997, the seat belt must be properly secured to the vehicle or to the seat;

(e) if regulation 47 does not apply to the vehicle and the seat belt was first fitted to the vehicle after 10th February 1997, the seat belt must comply with paragraph (7) of that regulation to the extent (if any) that it would have to so comply were that regulation to apply to all motor vehicles; and

(f) if regulation 48 does not apply to the seat belt and the seat belt was first fitted to the vehicle after 10th February 1997, the requirements of paragraph (4) of that regulation must be met in relation to the anchorages, fastenings, adjusting device and retracting mechanism (if any) of the seat belt to the extent (if any) that those requirements would have to be met were that paragraph to apply to all anchorages, fastenings, adjusting devices and retracting mechanisms of seat belts fitted to motor vehicles, and paragraph (2) of regulation 48 shall apply for the purposes of sub-paragraph (f) above as it applies for the purposes of that regulation.

(7) The requirements referred to in paragraph (6)(b) are that the seat belt must be properly secured to the anchorage points provided for it and, in a case where any of those anchorage points is first fitted to the vehicle after 10th February 1997 the anchorage points to which it is secured must comply—

(a) if the vehicle is a coach, with the requirements specified in regulation 46(4)(b) or (4A)(b)(ii); or

(b) in any other case, with the requirements specified in regulation 46(4)(b).

(8) Until 10th February 1998, this regulation shall not apply to a coach first used before 1st October 1988.

(9) In this regulation—

"*school*" has the meaning given by [section 4(1) of the Education Act 1996];

"*forward-facing passenger seat*" means a forward-facing seat which is not the driver's seat; and

"*child restraint*", "*disabled person's belt*", "*forward-facing seat*", "*seat*", and "*seat belt*" have the meanings given in regulation 47.

(10) For the purpose of this regulation, a child is a person who is aged 3 years or more but is under the age of 16 years.]

B27.106   *[Regulation 48A was inserted by S.I. 1996 No. 163 and is printed as subsequently amended by the Education Act 1996, s.582(3) and Sched. 39, para.1(4).*

S.I. 1996 No. 163 is expressly stated (in relation to this provision) to have been made in exercise of powers under section 41 of the Road Traffic Act 1988 to the exclusion of powers under section 2(2) of the European Communities Act 1972.

With effect from October 1, 2001 (a date after the date at which this volume states the law), the following text (regulation 48A(3A)) will be inserted by S.I. 2001 No. 1043 after regulation 48A(3):

[(3A) For the purposes of this regulation a rearward-facing seat shall be treated as a forward-facing seat which meets the requirements of this regulation if the coach or minibus concerned was first used on or after 1st October 2001, and the rearward-facing seat complies with the requirements of regulations 46 and 47.]

Section 4(1) of the Education Act 1996 (as substituted by the Education Act 1997, s.51) defines a "school" (see regulation 48A(9) above) as an educational establishment which is outside the further education sector and the higher education sector and is an institution for providing—(a) primary education, (b) secondary education, or (c) both primary and secondary education, whether or not the institution also provides part-time education suitable to the requirements of junior pupils or further education.]

49. Rear under-run protection

B27.107   (1) Save as provided in paragraph (2), this regulation applies to a wheeled goods vehicle being either—

(a) a motor vehicle with a maximum gross weight which exceeds 3500kg and which was first used on or after 1st April 1984; or

(b) a trailer manufactured on or after 1st May 1983 with an unladen weight which exceeds 1020kg.

(2) This regulation does not apply to—

(a) a motor vehicle which has a maximum speed not exceeding 15mph;

(b) a motor car or a heavy motor car constructed or adapted to form part of an articulated vehicle;

  (c) an agricultural trailer;

  (d) engineering plant;

  (e) a fire engine;

  (f) an agricultural motor vehicle;

  (g) a vehicle fitted at the rear with apparatus specially designed for spreading material on a road;

  (h) a vehicle so constructed that it can be unloaded by part of the vehicle being tipped rearwards;

  (i) a vehicle owned by the Secretary of State for Defence and used for naval, military or air force purposes;

  (j) a vehicle to which no bodywork has been fitted and which is being driven or towed—

      (i) for the purpose of a quality or safety check by its manufacturer or a dealer in, or distributor of, such vehicles; or

     (ii) to a place where, by previous arrangement, bodywork is to be fitted or work preparatory to the fitting of bodywork is to be carried out; or

    (iii) by previous arrangement to premises of a dealer in, or distributor of, such vehicles;

  (k) a vehicle which is being driven or towed to a place where by previous arrangement a device is to be fitted so that it complies with this regulation;

  (l) a vehicle specially designed and constructed, and not merely adapted, to carry other vehicles loaded onto it from the rear;

  (m) a trailer specially designed and constructed, and not merely adapted, to carry round timber, beams or girders, being items of exceptional length;

  (n) a vehicle fitted with a tail lift so constructed that the lift platform forms part of the floor of the vehicle and this part has a length of at least 1m measured parallel to the longitudinal axis of the vehicle;

  (o) a trailer having a base or centre in a country outside Great Britain from which it normally starts its journeys, provided that a period of not more than 12 months has elapsed since the vehicle was last brought into Great Britain;

  (p) a vehicle specially designed, and not merely adapted, for the carriage and mixing of liquid concrete;

  (q) a vehicle designed and used solely for the delivery of coal by means of a special conveyor which is carried on the vehicle and when in use is fitted to the rear of the vehicle so as to render its being equipped with a rear under-run protective device impracticable; or

  (r) an agricultural trailed appliance.

(3) Subject to the provisions of paragraphs (4), (5) and (6), every vehicle to which this regulation applies shall be equipped with a rear under-run protective device.

(4) A vehicle to which this regulation applies and which is fitted with a tail lift, bodywork or other part which renders its being equipped with a rear under-run protective device impracticable shall instead be equipped with one or more devices which do not protrude beyond the overall width of the vehicle (excluding any part of the device or the devices) and which comply with the following requirements—

  (a) where more than one device is fitted, not more than 50cm shall lie between one device and the device next to it;

  (b) not more than 30cm shall lie between the outermost end of a device nearest to the outermost part of the vehicle to which it is fitted and a longitudinal plane passing through the outer end of the rear axle of the vehicle on the same side of the vehicle or, in a case where the vehicle is fitted with more than one rear axle, through the outer end of the widest rear axle on the same side of the vehicle, and paragraph II.5.4.2 in the Annex to Community Directive 79/490 shall not have effect in a case where this requirement is met; and

(c) the device or, where more than one device is fitted, all the devices together, shall have the characteristics specified in paragraphs II.5.4.5.1 to II.5.4.5.5.2 in the Annex to the said Directive save—

   (i) as provided in sub-paragraphs (a) and (b) above;
   (ii) that for the reference in paragraph II.5.4.5.1 in that Annex to 30cm there is substituted a reference to 35cm; and
   (iii) that the distance of 40cm specified in paragraph II.5.4.5 in that Annex may be measured exclusive of the said tail-lift, bodywork or other part.

(5) The provisions of paragraph (3) shall have effect so that in the case of—

(a) a vehicle which is fitted with a demountable body, the characteristics specified in paragraph II.5.4.2 in the Annex to the said Directive have effect as if the reference to 10cm were a reference to 30cm and as if in paragraph II.5.4.5.1 the reference to 30cm were a reference to 35cm; and

(b) a trailer with a single axle to two close-coupled axles, the height of 55cm referred to in paragraph II.5.4.5.1 in that Annex is measured when the coupling of the trailer to the vehicle by which it is drawn is at the height recommended by the manufacturer of the trailer.

(6) Instead of complying with paragraphs (3) to (5) a vehicle may comply with [Community Directive 97/19 [*O.J. No. L125, May 16, 1997, p. 1*]].

(7) In this regulation—

"*rear under-run protective device*" means a device within the description given in paragraph II.5.4 in the Annex to Community Directive 79/490.

B27.108   *[Regulation 49 is printed as amended by S.I. 1998 No. 1188.*
Item II.5.4 of the Annex to Directive 79/490/EEC (see regulation 49(7)) reads as follows:

II.5.4   A device for protection against underrunning from the rear, hereinafter referred to as "*device*", generally consists of a cross-member and linking components connected to the chassis side-members or to whatever replaces them.

It must have the following characteristics:

II.5.4.1.   The device must be fitted as close to the rear of the vehicle as possible. When the vehicle is unladen [*as defined in Directive 70/156/EEC, Annex I, item 2.6: "Weight of the vehicle with bodywork in running order, or weight of the chassis with cab if the manufacturer does not fit the bodywork (including coolant, oils, fuel, tools, spare wheel and driver"; Annex I has since been superseded (see Directive 92/53/EEC)*], the lower edge of the device must at no point be more than 55cm above the ground;

II.5.4.2.   The width of the device must at no point exceed the width of the rear axle measured at the outermost points of the wheels, excluding the bulging of the tyres close to the ground, nor must it be more than 10cm shorter on either side. Where there is more than one rear axle, the width to be considered is that of the widest rear axle;

II.5.4.3.   The section height of the cross-member must be not less than 10cm. The lateral extremities of the cross-member must not bend to the rear or have a sharp outer edge; this condition is fulfilled when the lateral extremities of the cross-member are rounded on the outside and have a radius of curvature of not less than 2.5mm;

II.5.4.4.   The device may be so designed that its position at the rear of the vehicle can be varied. In this event, there must be a guaranteed method of securing it in the service position so that any unintentional change of position is precluded. It must be possible for the operator to vary the position of the device by applying a force not exceeding 40 daN;

II.5.4.5.   The device must offer adequate resistance to forces applied parallel to the longitudinal axis of the vehicle, and be connected, when in the service position, with the chassis side-members or whatever replaces them.

This requirement will be satisfied if it is shown that both during and after the application the horizontal distance between the rear of the device and the rear extremity of the vehicle does not exceed 40cms at any of the points P1, P2 and P3. In measuring this distance, any part of the vehicle which is more than 3m above the ground when the vehicle is unladen must be excluded;

II.5.4.5.1.   Points P1 are located 30cm from the longitudinal planes tangential to the outer edges of the wheels on the rear axle; points P2, which are located on the line joining points P1, are symmetrical to the median longitudinal plane of the vehicle at a distance from each other of 70 to 100cm inclusive, the exact position being specified by the manufacturer. The height above the ground of points P1 and P2 must be defined by the vehicle manufacturer within the lines that bound the device horizontally. The height must not, however, exceed 60cm when the vehicle is unladen. P3 is the centre-point of the straight line joining points P2;

II.5.4.5.2   A horizontal force equal to 12.5% of the maximum technically permissible weight of the vehicle but not exceeding 2.5×10^4 N must be applied successively to both points P1 and to point P3;

II.5.4.5.3.   A horizontal force equal to 50% of the maximum technically permissible weight of the vehicle but not exceeding 10×10^4 N must be applied successively to both points P2;

II.5.4.5.4.   The forces specified in items II.5.4.5.2 and II.5.4.5.3. above must be applied separately. The order in which the forces are applied may be specified by the manufacturer;

II.5.4.5.5.   Whenever a practical test is performed to verify compliance with the above mentioned requirements, the following conditions must be fulfilled;

II.5.4.5.5.1.   The device must be connected to the chassis side-members of the vehicle or to whatever replaces them;

II.5.4.5.5.2.   The specified forces must be applied by rams which are suitably articulated (e.g. by means of universal joints) and must be parallel to the median longitudinal plane of the vehicle via a surface not more than 25cm in height (the exact height must be indicated by the manufacturer) and 20cm wide, with a radius of curvature of 5 ± 1mm at the vertical edges; the centre of the surface is placed successively at points P1, P2 and P3.]

50. Maintenance of rear under-run protective device

B27.109   Every device fitted to a vehicle in compliance with the requirements of regulation 49 shall at all times when the vehicle is on a road be maintained free from any obvious defect which would be likely to affect adversely the performance of the device in the function of giving resistance in the event of an impact from the rear.

51. Sideguards

B27.110   (1) Save as provided in paragraph (2), this regulation applies to a wheeled goods vehicle being—

(a) a motor vehicle first used on or after 1st April 1984 with a maximum gross weight which exceeds 3500kg; or

(b) a trailer manufactured on or after 1st May 1983 with an unladen weight which exceeds 1020kg; or

(c) a semi-trailer manufactured before 1st May 1983 which has a relevant plate showing a gross weight exceeding 26,000kg and which forms part of an articulated vehicle with a relevant train weight exceeding 32,520kg.

(2) This regulation does not apply to—

(a) a motor vehicle which has a maximum speed not exceeding 15mph;

(b) an agricultural trailer;

(c) engineering plant;

(d) a fire engine;

(e) an agricultural motor vehicle;

(f) a vehicle so constructed that it can be unloaded by part of the vehicle being tipped sideways or rearwards;

(g) a vehicle owned by the Secretary of State for Defence and used for naval, military or air force purposes;

(h) a vehicle to which no bodywork has been fitted and which is being driven or towed—

(i) for the purpose of a quality or safety check by its manufacturer or a dealer in, or distributor of, such vehicles;

(ii) to a place where, by previous arrangement, bodywork is to be fitted or work preparatory to the fitting of bodywork is to be carried out; or

(iii) by previous arrangement to premises of a dealer in, or distributor of, such vehicles;

(i) a vehicle which is being driven or towed to a place where by previous arrangement a sideguard is to be fitted so that it complies with this regulation;

(j) a refuse vehicle;

(k) a trailer specially designed and constructed, and not merely adapted, to carry round timber, beams or girders, being items of exceptional length;

(l) a motor car or a heavy motor car constructed or adapted to form part of an articulated vehicle;

(m) a vehicle specially designed and constructed, and not merely adapted, to carry other vehicles loaded onto it from the front or the rear;

(n) a trailer with a load platform—

(i) no part of any edge of which is more than 60mm inboard from the tangential plane; and

(ii) the upper surface of which is not more than 750mm from the ground throughout that part of its length under which a sideguard would have to be fitted in accordance with paragraph (5)(d) to (g) if this exemption did not apply to it;

(o) a trailer having a base or centre in a country outside Great Britain from which it normally starts its journeys, provided that a period of not more than 12 months has elapsed since the vehicle was last brought into Great Britain; or

(p) an agricultural trailed appliance.

[(2A) This regulation also applies to a wheeled goods vehicle, whether of a description falling within paragraph (2) or not, which is a semi-trailer some or all of the wheels of which are driven by the drawing vehicle.]

(3) Every vehicle to which this regulation applies shall be securely fitted with a sideguard to give protection on any side of the vehicle where—

(a) if it is a semi-trailer, the distance between the transverse planes passing through the centre of its foremost axle and through the centre of its king pin or, in the case of a vehicle having more than one king pin, the rearmost one, exceeds 4.5m; or

(b) if it is any other vehicle, the distance between the centres of any two consecutive axles exceeds 3m.

(4) Save as provided in paragraphs (6) and (7), a sideguard with which a vehicle is by this regulation required to be fitted shall comply with all the specifications listed in paragraph (5).

(5) Those specifications are—

(a) the outermost surface of every sideguard shall be smooth, essentially rigid and either flat or horizontally corrugated, save that—

(i) any part of the surface may overlap another provided that the overlapping edges face rearwards or downwards;

(ii) a gap not exceeding 25mm measured longitudinally may exist between any two adjacent parts of the surface provided that the foremost edge of the rearward part does not protrude outboard of the rearmost edge of the forward part; and

(iii) domed heads of bolts or rivets may protrude beyond the surface to a distance not exceeding 10mm;

(b) no part of the lowest edge of a sideguard shall be more than 550mm above the ground when the vehicle to which it is fitted is on level ground and, in the case of a semi-trailer, when its load platform is horizontal;

(c) in a case specified in an item in column 2 of the Table the highest edge of a sideguard shall be as specified in that item in column 3;

(d) the distance between the rearmost edge of a sideguard and the transverse plane passing through the foremost part of the tyre fitted to the wheel of the vehicle nearest to it shall not exceed 300mm;

(e) the distance between the foremost edge of a sideguard fitted to a semi-trailer and a transverse plane passing through the centre of the vehicle's king pin or, if the vehicle has more than one king pin, the rearmost one, shall not exceed 3m;

(f) the foremost edge of a sideguard fitted to a semi-trailer with landing legs shall, as well as complying with sub-paragraph (e), not be more than 250mm to the rear of a transverse plane passing through the centre of the leg nearest to that edge;

(g) the distance between the foremost edge of a sideguard fitted to a vehicle other than a semi-trailer and a transverse plane passing through the rearmost part of the tyre fitted to the wheel of the vehicle nearest to it shall not exceed 300mm if the vehicle is a motor vehicle and 500mm if the vehicle is a trailer;

(h) the external edges of a sideguard shall be rounded at a radius of at least 2.5mm;

(i) no sideguard shall be more than 30mm inboard from the tangential plane;

(j) no sideguard shall project beyond the longitudinal plane from which, in the absence of a sideguard, the vehicle's overall width would fall to be measured;

(k) every sideguard shall cover an area extending to at least 100mm upwards from its lowest edge, 100mm downwards from its highest edge, and 100mm rearwards and inwards from its foremost edge, and no sideguard shall have a vertical gap measuring more than 300mm nor any vertical surface measuring less than 100mm; and

(l) except in the case of a vehicle described in paragraph (1)(c) every sideguard shall be capable of withstanding a force of 2 kilonewtons applied perpendicularly to any part of its surface by the centre of a ram face of which is circular and not more than 220mm in diameter, and during such application—

    (i) no part of the sideguard shall be deflected by more than 150mm, and

    (ii) no part of the sideguard which is less than 250mm from its rearmost part shall be deflected by more than 30mm.

TABLE

(regulation 51(5))

1	2	3
Item	Case	Requirement about highest edge of sideguard
1	Where the floor of the vehicle to which the side-guard is fitted— (i) extends laterally outside the tangential plane; (ii) is not more than 1.85m from the ground; (iii) extends laterally over the whole of the length of the sideguard with which the vehicle is required by this regulation to be fitted; and (iv) is wholly covered at its edge by a side-rave the lower edge of which is not more than 150 mm below the underside of the floor.	Note more than 350mm below the lower edge of the side-rave.
2	Where the floor of the vehicle to which the sideguard is fitted— (i) extends laterally outside the tangential plane; and (ii) does not comply with all of the provisions specified in sub-paragraphs (ii), (iii) and (iv) in item 1 above, and any part of the structure of the vehicle is cut within 1.85m of the ground by the tangential plane.	Not more than 350mm below the structure of the vehicle where it is cut by the tangential plane.
3	Where— (i) no part of the structure of the vehicle is cut within 1.85m of the ground by the tangential plane; and	Not less than the height of the upper surface of the load carrying structure of the vehicle.

[*continued on next page*

1	2	3
Item	*Case*	*Requirement about highest edge of sideguard*
3—*cont.*	(ii) the upper surface of the load carrying structure of the vehicle is less than 1.5m from the ground.	
4	A vehicle specially designed, and not merely adapted, for the carriage and mixing of liquid concrete.	Not less than 1m from the ground.
5	Any other case.	Not less than 1.5m from the ground.

(6) The provisions of paragraph (4) apply—

(a) in the case of an extendible trailer when it is, by virtue of the extending mechanism, extended to a length greater than its minimum, so as not to require, in respect of any additional distance solely attributed to the extension, compliance with the specifications mentioned in paragraph (5)(d) to (g);

(b) in the case of a vehicle designed and constructed, and not merely adapted, to be fitted with a demountable body or to carry a container, when it is not fitted with a demountable body or carrying such a container as if it were fitted with such a body or carrying such a container; and

(c) only so far as it is practicable in the case of—

(i) a vehicle designed solely for the carriage of a fluid substance in a closed tank which is permanently fitted to the vehicle and provided with valves and hose or pipe connections for loading or unloading; and

(ii) a vehicle which requires additional stability during loading or unloading or while being used for operations for which it is designed or adapted and is fitted on one or both sides with an extendible device to provide such stability.

(7) In the case of a motor vehicle to which this regulation applies and which is of a type which was required to be approved by the Type Approval for Goods Vehicles Regulations before 1st October 1983—

(a) if the bodywork of the vehicle covers the whole of the area specified as regards a sideguard in paragraph (5)(b), (c), (d) and (g) above the other provisions of that paragraph do not apply to that vehicle; and

(b) if the bodywork of the vehicle covers only part of that area the part of that area which is not so covered shall be fitted with a sideguard which complies with the provisions of paragraph (5) above save that there shall not be a gap between—

(i) the rearmost edge of the sideguard or the rearmost part of the bodywork (whichever is furthest to the rear) and the transverse plane mentioned in paragraph (5)(d) of more than 300mm;

(ii) the foremost edge of the sideguard or the foremost part of the bodywork (whichever is furthest to the front) and the transverse plane mentioned in paragraph (5)(g) of more than 300mm; or

(iii) any vertical or sloping edge of any part of the bodywork in question and the edge of the sideguard immediately forwards or rearwards thereof of more than 25mm measured horizontally.

(8) In this regulation—

"*relevant plate*" means a Ministry plate, where fitted, and in other cases a plate fitted in accordance with regulation 66;

"*relevant train weight*" means the train weight shown in column 2 of the Ministry plate, where fitted, and in other cases the maximum train weight shown at item 8 of the plate fitted in accordance with regulation 66; and

"*tangential plane*", in regulation to a sideguard, means the vertical plane tangential to the external face of the outermost part of the tyre (excluding any distortion caused by the weight of the vehicle) fitted to the outermost wheel at the rear and on the same side of the vehicle.

[(9) Instead of complying with the foregoing provisions of this regulation a vehicle may comply with Community Directive 89/297.]

B27.111   *[Regulation 51 is printed as amended by S.I. 1987 No. 676; S.I. 1989 No. 1695.]*

52. Maintenance of sideguards

B27.112   Every sideguard fitted to a vehicle in compliance with the requirements of regulation 51 shall at all times when the vehicle is on a road be maintained free from any obvious defect which would be likely to affect adversely its effectiveness.

53. Mascots

B27.113   (1) Subject to paragraph (2), no mascot, emblem or other ornamental object shall be carried by a motor vehicle first used on or after 1st October 1937 in any position where it is likely to strike any person with whom the vehicle may collide unless the mascot is not liable to cause injury to such person by reason of any projection thereon.

(2) Instead of complying with the requirements of paragraph (1) a vehicle may comply with Community Directive 74/483 or 79/488 or ECE Regulation 26.01.

[53A. Strength of superstructure

B27.114   (1) This regulation applies to every coach which is—

(a) a single decked vehicle;

(b) equipped with a compartment below the deck for the luggage of passengers; and

(c) first used on or after [1st April 1993].

(2) Every vehicle to which this regulation applies shall comply with the requirements of ECE Regulation 66.]

B27.115   *[Regulation 53A was inserted by S.I. 1987 No. 1133 and is printed as subsequently amended by S.I. 1989 No. 2360.]*

[53B. Additional exits from double-decked coaches

B27.116   (1) This regulation applies to every coach which is—

(a) a double-decked vehicle; and

(b) first used on or after 1st April 1990.

(2) Subject to the following provisions of this regulation, every vehicle to which this regulation applies shall be equipped with two staircases, one of which shall be located in one half of the vehicle and the other in the other half of the vehicle.

(3) Instead of being equipped with two staircases in accordance with paragraph (2), a vehicle to which this regulation applies may be equipped in accordance with the following provisions of this regulation with a hammer or other similar device with which in case of emergency any side window of the vehicle may be broken.

(4) Where a vehicle is equipped with—

    (a) a staircase located in one half of the vehicle; and

    (b) an emergency exit complying with regulation 21(8) of the Public Service Vehicles (Conditions of Fitness, Equipment, Use and Certification) Regulations 1981 [*S.I. 1981 No. 257 (q.v.)*] located in the same half of the upper deck of the vehicle;

the hammer or the similar device shall be located in the other half of that deck.

(5) Any hammer or other similar device with which a vehicle is equipped pursuant to this regulation shall be located in a conspicuous and readily accessible position in the upper deck of the vehicle.

(6) There shall be displayed, in a conspicuous position in close proximity to the hammer or other similar device, a notice which shall contain in clear and indelible lettering—

    (a) in letters not less than 25mm high, the heading "IN EMERGENCY"; and

    (b) in letters not less than 10mm high, instructions that in case of emergency the hammer or device is to be used first to break any side window by striking the glass near the edge of the window and then to clear any remaining glass from the window aperture.

(7) For the purposes of this regulation a staircase, emergency exit, hammer or other similar device (as the case may be) shall be considered to be located in the other half of the vehicle if the shortest distance between any part of that staircase, exit, hammer or device (as the case may be) and any part of any other staircase, emergency exit, hammer or device is not less than one half of the overall length of the vehicle.]

[Regulation 53B was inserted by S.I. 1987 No. 1133.]   **B27.117**

K Control of Emissions

54. [Silencers—general]

(1) Every vehicle propelled by an internal combustion engine shall be fitted with an   **B27.118**
exhaust system including a silencer and the exhaust gases from the engine shall not escape into the atmosphere without first passing through the silencer.

(2) Every exhaust system and silencer shall be maintained in good and efficient working order and [shall not after the date of manufacture be altered] so as to increase the noise made by the escape of exhaust gases.

(3) Instead of complying with paragraph (1) a vehicle may comply with Community Directive 77/212, 81/334, 84/372 [, 84/424 or 92/97 or ECE Regulation 51.02] or, in the case of a motor cycle other than a moped, 78/1015, 87/56 or 89/235.

(4) In this regulation "*moped*" has the meaning given to it in paragraph (5) [*sic*] of Schedule 9.

[Regulation 54 is printed as amended by S.I. 1994 No. 14; S.I. 1996 No. 2329.]   **B27.119**

55. [Noise limits—certain vehicles with 3 or more wheels—general]

(1) Save as provided in [paragraphs (1A) and (2)] and regulation 59, this regulation   **B27.120**
applies to every wheeled motor vehicle having at least three wheels and first used on or after 1st October 1983 which is—

(a) a vehicle, not falling within sub-paragraph (b) or (c), with or without bodywork;

(b) a vehicle not falling within sub-paragraph (c) which is—

   (i) engineering plant;

   (ii) a locomotive other than an agricultural motor vehicle;

   (iii) a motor tractor other than an industrial tractor or an agricultural motor vehicle;

   (iv) a public works vehicle;

   (v) a works truck; or

   (vi) a refuse vehicle; or

(c) a vehicle which—

   (i) has a compression ignition engine;

   (ii) is so constructed or adapted that the driving power of the engine is, or by appropriate use of the controls can be, transmitted to all wheels of the vehicle; and

   (iii) falls within category I.1.1, I.1.2, or I.1.3 specified in Article 1 of Community Directive 77/212.

[(1A) This regulation does not apply to a vehicle to which an item in the Table in regulation 55A applies.]

(2) This regulation does not apply to—

(a) a motor cycle with a sidecar attached;

(b) an agricultural motor vehicle which is first used before 1st June 1986 or which is not driven at more than 20mph;

(c) an industrial tractor;

(d) a road roller;

(e) a vehicle specially constructed, and not merely adapted, for the purposes of fighting fires or salvage from fires at or in the vicinity of airports, and having an engine power exceeding 220kW;

(f) a vehicle which runs on rails; or

(g) a vehicle manufactured by Leyland Vehicles Ltd. and known as the Atlantean Bus, if first used before 1st October 1984.

(3) Save as provided in paragraphs (4) and (5), every vehicle to which this regulation applies shall be so constructed that it complies with the requirements set out in item 1, 2, 3 or 4 of the Table [*see table on pp. 1342, 1343*]; a vehicle complies with those requirements if—

(a) its sound level does not exceed the relevant limit specified in column 2(a), (b) or (c), as the case may be, in the relevant item when measured under the conditions specified in column 3 in that item and by the method specified in column 4 in that item using the apparatus prescribed in paragraph (6); and

(b) in the case of a vehicle referred to in paragraph 1(a) (other than one having less than four wheels or a maximum speed not exceeding 25 km/h) or 1(c), the device designed to reduce the exhaust noise meets the requirements specified in column 5 in that item.

(4) Save as provided in paragraph (5), paragraph (3) applies to every vehicle to which this regulation applies and which is first used on or after 1st April 1990, unless it is equipped with 5 or more forward gears and has a maximum power to maximum gross weight ratio not less than 75kW per 1000kg, and is of a type in respect of which a type approval certificate has been issued under the Type Approval (Great Britain) Regulations as if, for the reference to items 1, 2, 3 or 4 of the Table there were substituted a reference to item 4 of the Table.

(5) Paragraph (4) does not apply to a vehicle in category 5.2.2.1.3 as defined in Annex I to Directive 84/424 and equipped with a compression ignition engine, a vehicle in category 5.2.2.1.4 as defined in that Annex, or a vehicle referred to in paragraph 1(b) unless it is first used on or after 1st April 1991.

(6) The apparatus prescribed for the purposes of paragraph 3(a) and [regulation 56(2)(a) and Schedule 7A] is a sound level meter of the type described in Publication No. 179 of the International Electrotechnical Commission, in either its first or second edition, a sound level meter complying with the specification for Type 0 or Type 1 in Publication No. 651 (1979) "Sound Level Meters" of the International Electrotechnical Commission, or a sound level meter complying with the specifications of the British Standard Number BS 5969: 1981 which came into effect on 29th May 1981.

[(6A) A vehicle shall be deemed to satisfy the requirements of this regulation if it is so constructed that it complies with the requirements specified in column 4 of item 2 in the Table in regulation 55A as they apply to a vehicle first used on or after the date specified in column 3 of that item.]

(7) Instead of complying with the preceding provisions of this regulation a vehicle may comply at the time of its first use with Community Directive 77/212, 81/334, 84/372 [, 84/424, 92/97 or 96/20 or ECE Regulation 51.02].

[Regulation 55 is printed as amended by S.I. 1989 No. 1865; S.I. 1994 No. 14; S.I. 1996 No. 2329.]   **B27.121**

B27.122

[TABLE
(regulation 55(3))]

1	2 Limits of sound level			3	4	5
Item	*(a)* Vehicle referred to in paragraph (1)(a)	*(b)* Vehicle referred to in paragraph (1)(c)	*(c)* Vehicle referred to in paragraph (1)(c)	*Conditions of measurement*	*Method of measurement*	*Requirements for exhaust device*
1	Limits specified in paragraph I.1 of the Annex to Community Directive 77/212.	89dB(a)	82dB(a)	Conditions specified in paragraph I.3 of the Annex to Community Directive 77/212.	Method specified in paragraph I.4.1 of the Annex to Community Directive 77/212.	Requirements specified in heading II of the Annex to Community Directive 77/212 (except paragraphs II.2 and II.5).
2	Limits specified in paragraph 5.2.2.1 of Annex I to Community Directive 81/334.	89dB(a)	82dB(a)	Conditions specified in paragraph 5.2.2.3 of Annex I to Community Directive 81/334.	Method specified in paragraph 5.2.2.4 of Annex I to Community Directive 81/334. Interpretation of results as specified in paragraph 5.2.2.5 of that Annex.	Requirements specified in section 3 and paragraphs 5.1 and 5.3.1 of Annex I to Community Directive 81/334.
3	Limits specified in paragraph 5.2.2.1 of Annex I to Community Directive 84/372.	89dB(a)	82dB(a)	Conditions specified in paragraph 5.2.2.3 of Annex I to Community Directive 84/372.	Method specified in paragraph 5.2.2.4 of Annex I to Community Directive 84/372, except that vehicles with 5 or more	Requirements specified in section 3 and paragraphs 5.1 and 5.3.1 of Annex I to Community Directive 84/372.

4	Limits specified in paragraph 5.2.2.1 of Annex I of Community Directive 84/424.	Vehicles with engine power— —less than 75kW —84dB(a) —not less than 75kW —86dB(a)	Limits specified in paragraph 5.2.2.1 of Annex I to Community Directive 84/424.	Conditions specified in paragraph 5.2.2.3 of Annex I to Community Directive 84/424.	Method specified in paragraph 5.2.2.4 of Annex I to Community Directive 84/424, except that vehicles with 5 or more forward gears and a maximum power to maximum gross weight ratio not less than 75kW per 1000 kg may be tested in 3rd gear only. Interpretation of results as specified in paragraph 5.2.2.5 of that Annex.	Requirements specified in section 3 and paragraphs 5.1 and 5.3.1 of Annex I to Community Directive 84/424.
					forward gears and a with 5 or more forward gears and a maximum power to maximum gross weight ratio not less than 75kW per 1000 kg may be tested in 3rd gear only. Interpretation of results as specified in paragraph 5.2.2.5 of that Annex.	

[55A. Noise limits—certain vehicles first used on or after 1st October 1996 —general

B27.123   (1) A motor vehicle to which an item in the Table below applies shall be so constructed that it meets the requirements specified in column 4 of that item; and an item in that Table applies to a vehicle if it is of the description specified in column 2 of that item.

This paragraph has effect subject to the following provisions of this regulation, regulation 59 and Schedule 7XA.

THE TABLE

(1) Item	(2) *Vehicles to which the item applies*	(3) *Earliest date of first use (see column 2)*	(4) *The requirements*	(5) *Modification of Community Directives in relation to special vehicles (see paragraph (4)(c))*
1	1. All motor vehicles with less than 4 wheels and first used on or after the date specified in column 3 of this item. 2. All special vehicles first used on or after the date specified in column 3 of this item. 3. All motor vehicles first first used on or after the date specified in column 3 of this item with a maximum speed not exceeding 25 km/h.	1st October 1996	The requirement of— (a) regulation 55 as they would apply to the vehicle but for paragraph (1A) of that regulation; or (b) paragraphs 3 and 5.2 of Annex I to Community Directive 92/97 or 96/20.	For paragraph 5.2.2.1 of Annex I, substitute— "The sound level measured in accordance with 5.2.2.2 to 5.2.2.5 of this Annex shall not exceed— (a) in the case of vehicles with engine power of less than 75kW, 84 dB(a) (b) in the case of vehicles with engine power not less than 75 kW, 86 dB(a)."
2	All motor vehicles first used on or after the date specified in column 3 of this item, not being a vehicle to which item 1 applies.	1st October 1996	The requirements of paragraphs 3 and 5 of Annex I to Community Directive 92/97 or 96/20	

(2) Paragraph (1) does not apply to—

(a) a vehicle with fewer than 3 wheels; or

(b) a vehicle of a description mentioned in regulation 55(2).

(3) In this regulation, "*special vehicle*" means a vehicle which is—

(a) engineering plant;

(b) a locomotive other than an agricultural motor vehicle;

(c) a motor tractor other than an industrial tractor or an agricultural motor vehicle;

(d) a public works vehicle; or

(e) a works truck.

(4) For the purposes of this regulation—

(a) subject to paragraphs (b), (c), (d) and (e), the Community Directives referred to in this regulation shall have effect in relation to a vehicle that is not a "vehicle" within the meaning of the Framework Directive but is of a class of a description specified in column 2 of an item in the Table in regulation 15 (whether or not regulation 15 applies to the vehicle) as it has effect in relation to a vehicle of the category specified in column 3 of that item;

(b) subject to paragraphs (c), (d) and (e), a vehicle that does not fall within sub-paragraph (a) and is not a "vehicle" within the meaning of the Framework Directive shall be regarded as meeting the requirements of paragraph 5 of a Community Directive mentioned in the Table if it meets—

  (i) the requirements of that paragraph as it applies to a vehicle in category M_1 or N_1 within the meaning of the Community Directive, or

  (ii) the requirements of that paragraph as it applies to a vehicle that is not in either of those categories;

(c) subject to sub-paragraphs (d) and (e), in relation to a special vehicle the Community Directives mentioned in column 4 of an item in the Table shall have effect with the modifications (if any) specified in column 5 of the item;

(d) a requirement in paragraph 5.2.2.1 of Annex I to Community Directive 92/97 for a sound level not to exceed a specified limit in specified circumstances shall be read as a requirement for the sound level not to exceed that limit by more than the amount mentioned in paragraph 4.1 of Annex V to the Community Directive in those circumstances;

(e) a requirement in paragraph 5.2.2.1 of Annex I to Community Directive 96/20 for a sound level not to exceed a specified limit in specified circumstances shall be read as a requirement for the sound level not to exceed that limit by more than the amount mentioned in paragraph 4.1 of Annex III to the Directive in those circumstances.

(5) Instead of complying with paragraph (1) a vehicle may comply at the time of its first use—

(a) in the case of a vehicle to which item 1 of the Table applies, with Community Directive 77/212, 81/334, 84/424, 92/97 or 96/20 or ECE Regulation 51.02; or

(b) in the case of a vehicle to which item 2 of the Table applies, with Community Directive 92/97 or 96/20 or ECE Regulation 51.02.]

[Regulation 55A was inserted by S.I. 1996 No. 2329.   **B27.124**
* The Framework Directive (i.e. Directive 70/156/EEC, as amended) defines a vehicle in article 2 (as substituted by Directive 92/53/EEC) as:*

any motor vehicle intended for use on the road, being complete or incomplete, having at least four wheels and a maximum design speed exceeding 25 km/h, and its trailers, with the exception of vehicles which run on rails and of agricultural and forestry tractors and all mobile machinery.*]*

56. Noise limits—agricultural motor vehicles and industrial tractors

(1) Save as provided in regulation 59, this regulation applies to every wheeled vehicle   **B27.125**
first used on or after 1st April 1983 being an agricultural motor vehicle or an industrial tractor, other than—

(a) an agricultural motor vehicle which is first used on or after 1st June 1986 and which is driven at more than 20mph; or

(b) a road roller.

(2) Every vehicle to which this regulation applies should be so constructed—

(a) that its sound level does not exceed—

(i) if it is a vehicle with engine power of less than 65kW, 89 dB(a);

(ii) if it is a vehicle with engine power of 65kW or more, and first used before 1st October 1991, 92 dB(a); or

(iii) if it is a vehicle with engine power of 65kW or more, and first used on or after 1st October 1991, 89 dB(a),

when measured under the conditions specified in paragraph I.3 of Annex VI of Community Directive 74/151 by the method specified in paragraph I.4.1 of that Annex using the apparatus prescribed in regulation 55(6); and

(b) that the device designed to reduce the exhaust noise meets the requirements specified in paragraph II.1 of the Annex and, if fibrous absorbent material is used, the requirements specified in paragraphs II.4.1 to II.4.3 of that Annex.

[57. Noise limits—construction requirements relating to motor cycles

B27.126 (1) Subject to regulation 59, this regulation applies to every motor vehicle first used on or after 1st April 1983 which is—

(a) a moped; or

(b) a two-wheeled motor cycle, whether or not with sidecar attached, which is not a moped.

(2) A vehicle to which this regulation applies shall be so constructed that it meets,—

(a) if it is first used before 1st April 1991, the requirements of item 1 or 2 of the Table in Part I of Schedule 7A;

(b) if it is used on or after that date, the requirements of item 2 of that Table.

(3) Instead of complying with paragraph (2), a vehicle first used before 1st April 1991 may comply at the time of its first use with Community Directive 78/1015, 87/56 or 89/235.

(4) Instead of complying with paragraph (2), a vehicle first used on or after 1st April 1991 may comply at the time of its first use with Community Directive 87/56 or 89/235.

(5) In this regulation "*moped*" has the meaning given to it in paragraph 5 of Schedule 9.]

B27.127 *[Regulation 57 was originally amended by S.I. 1989 No. 1865. The text of regulation 57 printed above was substituted by S.I. 1994 No. 14.]*

[57A. Exhaust systems—motor cycles

B27.128 (1) Any original silencer forming part of the exhaust system of a vehicle to which regulation 57 applies, being a vehicle first used before 1st February 1996, shall—

(a) be so constructed that the vehicle meets the requirements specified in paragraph 3 (other than sub-paragraphs 3.2 and 3.3) of Annex I to Community Directive 78/1015 and be marked in accordance with sub-paragraph 3.3 of that Annex; or

(b) be so constructed that the vehicle meets the requirements specified in paragraph 3 (other than sub-paragraphs 3.2 and 3.3) of Annex I to Community Directive 89/235 and be marked in accordance with sub-paragraph 3.3 of that Annex.

(2) Any original silencer forming part of the exhaust system of a vehicle to which

regulation 57 applies, being a vehicle first used on or after 1st February 1996, shall be so constructed that the vehicle meets the requirements specified in paragraph 3 (other than sub-paragraphs 3.2 and 3.3) of Annex I to CommunityDirective 89/235 and be marked in accordance with sub-paragraph 3.3 of that Annex.

(3) A vehicle fitted with an original silencer may,—

(a) if the vehicle is first used before 1st February 1996, instead of complying with paragraph (1), comply at the time of first use with Community Directive 78/1015, 87/56 or 89/235; or

(b) if the vehicle is first used on or after that date, instead of complying with paragraph (2), comply at the time of first use with Community Directive 89/235.

(4) Where any replacement silencer forms part of the exhaust system of a vehicle to which regulation 57 applies, being a vehicle first used on or after 1st January 1985, the first requirement or the second requirement as set out below must be met in respect of the silencer.

(5) In order for the first requirement to be met in respect of a silencer forming part of the exhaust system of a vehicle (in this paragraph referred to as "*the vehicle in question*"),—

(a) if the vehicle in question is first used before 1st April 1991, the silencer must be so constructed that, were it to be fitted to an unused vehicle of the same model as the vehicle in question, the unused vehicle would meet—

(i) the requirements of item 1 or 3 of the Table in Part I of Schedule 7A; and

(ii) the requirements specified in paragraph 3 (other than sub-paragraphs 3.2 and 3.3) of Annex I to Community Directive 78/1015 or 89/235,

and the silencer must be marked in accordance with sub-paragraph 3.3 of Annex I to Community Directive 78/1015 or 89/235;

(b) if the vehicle in question is first used on or after the 1st April 1991 but before 1st February 1996, the silencer must be so constructed that, were it to be fitted to an unused vehicle of the same model as the vehicle in question, the unused vehicle would meet—

(i) the requirements of item 3 of the Table in Part I of Schedule 7A; and

(ii) the requirements specified in paragraph 3 (other than sub-paragraphs 3.2 and 3.3) of Annex I to Community Directive 78/1015 or 89/235,

and the silencer must be marked in accordance with sub-paragraph 3.3 of Annex I to Community Directive 78/1015 or 89/235;

(c) if the vehicle in question is first used on or after 1st February 1996, the silencer must be so constructed that, were it to be fitted to an unused vehicle of the same model as the vehicle in question, the unused vehicle would meet—

(i) the requirements of item 3 of the Table in Part I of Schedule 7A; and

(ii) the requirements specified in paragraph 3 (other than sub-paragraphs 3.2 and 3.3) of Annex I to Community Directive 89/235,

and the silencer must be marked in accordance with sub-paragraph 3.3 of Annex I to that Directive.

(6) In order for the second requirement to be met in respect of a silencer forming part of the exhaust system of a vehicle (in Part II of Schedule 7A referred to as "*the vehicle in question*"),—

(a) if the vehicle is first used before 1st April 1991, the silencer must meet the requirements of paragraph 2, 3 or 4 of Part II of Schedule 7A; or

(b) if the vehicle is first used on or after that date, the silencer must meet the requirements of paragraph 4 of Part II of Schedule 7A.

(7) Any requirements specified in paragraph (5) or in Part II of Schedule 7A relating to the silencer were it to be fitted to an unused vehicle of the same model as the vehicle in question (as defined in that paragraph or in paragraph (6) for the purposes of that Part, as the case may be) shall be deemed to be met if they are met by the silencer as fitted to the vehicle in question at the time that it is first fitted.

(8) For the purposes of this regulation, Community Directive 89/235 shall have effect as if—

    (a) in Annex I, for sub-paragraph 3.4.1, there were substituted—

        "3.4.1. After removal of the fibrous material, the vehicle must meet the relevant requirements"; and

        for sub-paragraph 3.4.3 there were substituted—

        "3.4.3. After the exhaust system has been put into a normal state for road use by one of the following conditioning methods, the vehicle must meet the relevant requirements:";

    (b) references in Annex I as so modified to a vehicle meeting the relevant requirements were,—

        (i) in relation to an original silencer, references to a vehicle meeting the requirements of item 2 of the Table in Part I of Schedule 7A; and

        (ii) in relation to a replacement silencer, references to a vehicle meeting the requirements of item 3 of that Table;

    (c) in Annex II there were omitted sub-paragraphs 3.1.2, 3.4 and 3.5 and in sub-paragraph 3.2—

        (i) the words "and the name referred to in 3.1.2", and

        (ii) the words after "legible".

[(8A) For the purposes of paragraphs (1)(b) and (2) in their application to vehicles with a design speed not exceeding 50 km/h, Community Directive 89/235/EEC shall have effect as if it were not only modified in accordance with paragraph (8) but were further modified by the omission of—

    (a) sub-paragraph 3.1.3 of Annex II; and

    (b) in sub-paragraph 3.2 of that Annex, the words "and 3.1.3".]

(9) In relation to a replacement silencer which is—

    (a) fitted to a vehicle before 1st February 1997; and

    (b) clearly and indelibly marked with the name or trade mark of the manufacturer of the silencer and with that manufacturer's part number relating to it,

paragraphs (5) and (6) of this regulation and Parts II and III of Schedule 7A shall have effect as if they contained no reference to a silencer being marked.

(10) For the purposes of this regulation, a silencer forming part of the exhaust system of a vehicle shall not be regarded as being marked in accordance with sub-paragraph 3.3 of Annex I to Community Directive 78/1015 or 89/235, paragraph (9) of this regulation or any paragraph of Part II of Schedule 7A if the marking is so obscured by any part of the vehicle that it cannot easily be read.

(11) Until 1st February 1996, for the purposes of paragraph (6), a vehicle first used on or after 1st April 1991 shall be treated as a vehicle first used before 1st April 1991.

(12) Part III of Schedule 7A shall have effect for the purpose of exempting certain silencers from the provisions of paragraph (4).

(13) No person shall use a motor cycle on a road or cause or permit such a vehicle to be

so used if any part of the exhaust system has been indelibly marked by the manufacturer of that part with the words "NOT FOR ROAD USE" or words to that effect.

(14) In this regulation—

"*original silencer*", in relation to a vehicle, means a silencer which was fitted to the vehicle when it was manufactured;

"*replacement silencer*", in relation to a vehicle, means a silencer fitted to the vehicle, not being an original silencer; and

"*trade mark*" has the same meaning as in the Trade Marks Act 1938.]

[*Regulation 57A was inserted by S.I. 1994 No. 14 and is printed as subsequently amended by S.I. 1996 No. 16.*   **B27.129**

    The Trade Marks Act 1938 (see regulation 57A(14)) has been repealed by the Trade Marks Act 1994; the term "trade mark" is defined in section 1(1) of the 1994 Act.]

[57B. Noise limits—maintenance requirements relating to motor cycles

(1) No person shall use or cause or permit to be used on a road a motor cycle to which regulation 57 applies if the three conditions specified below are all fulfilled.   **B27.130**

(2) The first condition is fulfilled if the vehicle does not meet the noise limit requirements.

(3) The second condition is fulfilled if—

    (a) any part of the vehicle is not in good and efficient working order, or

    (b) the vehicle has been altered.

(4) The third condition is fulfilled if the noise made by the vehicle would have been materially less (so far as applicable)—

    (a) were all parts of the vehicle in good and efficient working order, or

    (b) had the vehicle not been altered.

(5) For the purposes of this regulation, a vehicle meets the noise limit requirements if,—

    (a) in the case of a vehicle first used before 1st April 1991 and not fitted with a replacement silencer, it meets the requirements of item 1 or 2 of the Table in Part I of Schedule 7A;

    (b) in the case of a vehicle first used before 1st April 1991 and fitted with a replacement silencer, it meets the requirements of item 1 or 3 of that Table;

    (c) in the case of a vehicle first used on or after 1st April 1991 and not fitted with a replacement silencer, it meets the requirements of item 2 of that Table;

    (d) in the case of a vehicle first used on or after 1st April 1991 and fitted with a replacement silencer, it meets the requirements of item 3 of that Table.

(6) In this regulation, "*replacement silencer*" has the same meaning as in regulation 57A.]

[*Regulation 57B was inserted by S.I. 1994 No. 14.*]   **B27.131**

58. Noise limits—vehicles not subject to regulations 55 to 57, first used on or after 1st April 1970   [*Revoked by S.I. 1995 No. 1201.*]   **B27.132**

59. [Exceptions to regulations 55 to 57B]

Regulations 55, [55A,] 56, [57, [57A and 57B]] do not apply to a motor vehicle which is—   **B27.133**

    (a) proceeding to a place where, by previous arrangement—

(i) noise emitted by it is about to be measured for the purpose of ascertaining whether or not the vehicle complies with such of those provisions as apply to it; or

(ii) the vehicle is about to be mechanically adjusted, modified or equipped for the purpose of securing that it so complies; or

(b) returning from such a place immediately after the noise has been so measured.

B27.134   *[Regulation 59 is printed as amended by S.I. 1989 No. 1865; S.I. 1994 No. 14; S.I. 1995 No. 1201; S.I. 1996 No. 2329.]*

60. Radio interference suppression

B27.135   [(1) Subject to paragraphs (1B), (1D), (1E) and (2)—

(a) every vehicle to which this sub-paragraph applies shall be so constructed that it complies with the requirements of paragraph 6 of Annex I to Community Directive 72/245 or paragraph 6 (as read with paragraph 8) of Annex I to Community Directive 95/54 (whether or not those Community Directives apply to the vehicle); and

(b) every agricultural and forestry tractor which is propelled by a spark ignition engine and is first used on or after 1st April 1974 shall be so constructed that it meets the requirements of paragraph 6 of Community Directive 72/245, 75/322 or 95/54.]

[(1A) Paragraph (1)(a) applies to every wheeled vehicle which is propelled by a spark ignition engine and—

(a) is first used on or after 1st April 1974 and before 1st January 1996; or

(b) is first used on or after 1st January 1996 and is a "vehicle" within the meaning of the Framework Directive.]

[(1B) For the purposes of paragraph (1)—

(a) a requirement in paragraph 6.2.2 of Community Directive 72/245 or 75/322 for any description of radiation level not to exceed a specified limit when measured in specified circumstances shall be read as a requirement for that description of radiation level not to exceed that limit by more than the amount mentioned in paragraph 9.2 of those Community Directives when measured in those circumstances; and

(b) a requirement in paragraph 6.2.2 or 6.3.2 of Community Directive 95/54 for any description of radiation level not to exceed a specified limit when measured in specified circumstances shall be read as a requirement for that description of radiation level not to exceed that limit by more than the amount mentioned in paragraph 7.3.1 of the Community Directive when measured in those circumstances.]

[(1C) Subject to paragraph (1F), on and after 1st October 2002 no person shall use or cause or permit to be used on a road a vehicle—

(a) in respect of which an EC certificate of conformity has been issued; and

(b) which is fitted with any electrical/electronic sub-assembly that was not fitted to the vehicle when the certificate was issued,

unless the electrical/electronic sub-assembly is marked in accordance with the requirements of Community Directive 95/54/EC.]

[(1D) Instead of complying with paragraph (1)(a) a vehicle may comply at the time of first use with Community Directive 72/245 or 95/54 or ECE Regulation 10 or 10.01.]

[(1E) Instead of complying with paragraph (1)(b) a vehicle may comply at the time of first use with Community Directive 75/322.]

[(1F) Paragraph (1C) shall not apply to a vehicle of a type described in article 2(6) of Community Directive 95/54/EC; and for the purposes of this paragraph "type" has the same meaning as in article 2(6) of that Directive.]

(2) This regulation does not apply to a vehicle constructed or assembled by a person not ordinarily engaged in the trade or business of manufacturing vehicles of that description, but nothing in this paragraph affects the application to such vehicles of the Wireless Telegraphy (Control of Interference from Ignition Apparatus) Regulations 1973 [*S.I. 1973 No. 1217; not reproduced in this work*].

[(3) In this regulation "*electrical/electronic sub-assembly*" has the same meaning as in Community Directive 95/54.]

[Regulation 60 is printed as amended by S.I. 1996 No. 2329.   **B27.136**
The term "electrical/electronic sub-assembly" (see regulation 60(3)) is defined by Directive 95/54/EC, Annex I, para.2.1.10 as follows:

"*Electrical/electronic sub-assembly*" (ESA) means an electrical and/or electronic device or set(s) of devices intended to be part of a vehicle, together with any associated electrical connections and wiring, which performs one or more specialized functions. An ESA may be approved at the request of a manufacturer as either a "component" or a "separate technical unit (STU)" (see Directive 70/156/EEC, Article 2).]

61. Emission of smoke, vapour, gases, oily substances, etc.

(1) Subject to [paragraph (3B)], every vehicle shall be constructed [and maintained] so   **B27.137**
as not to emit any avoidable smoke or avoidable visible vapour.

(2) Every motor vehicle using solid fuel shall be fitted with—

   (a) a tray or shield to prevent ashes and cinders from falling onto the road; and

   (b) an efficient appliance to prevent any emission of sparks or grit.

[(2A) Paragraphs (3), (3A), (3C), (4A), (5)(b), (5)(c), (6), (7), (8), (9), (10) and (11) shall not apply to motor vehicles first used on or after 1st January 2001.]

(3) Subject to paragraph (3B)], and to the exemptions specified in an item in column 4 of [Table I] [*see table on pp. 1356, 1357*], every wheeled vehicle of a class specified in that item in column 2 shall be constructed so as to comply with the requirements specified in that item in column 3.

[(3A) A motor vehicle to which an item in Table II [*see pp. 1358 et seq.*] applies shall be so constructed as to comply with the requirements relating to conformity of production models set out in the provisions specified in that item in column 4 of that Table.]

[(3B) Instead of complying with paragraph (1) a vehicle may comply with a relevant instrument.]

[(3C) Instead of complying with such provisions of items 1, 2 and 3 in Table I as apply to it, a vehicle may at the time of its first use comply with a relevant instrument.]

(4) [For the purposes of paragraphs (3B) and (3C), a reference to a vehicle complying with a relevant instrument is a reference to a vehicle complying]—

   (a) if it is propelled by a compression ignition engine, with Community Directive 72/306 (or, in the case of an agricultural vehicle [first used before 1st January 2001], 77/537) or ECE Regulation 24.01, 24.02 or 24.03; or

   [(b) if it is propelled by a spark ignition engine, with an instrument mentioned in column (4)(a) of Table II.]

[(4A) In relation to a vehicle which—

(a) has an engine the cylinder capacity of which is less than 700cc and has a rated power speed of more than 3,000 revolutions per minute;

(b) is first used before 1st October 1998,

Community Directive 91/542 shall have effect for the purposes of this regulation as if for the figure "0.15" in the Table in paragraph 6.2.1 and 8.3.1.1 there were substituted "0.25".

For the purposes of this paragraph, *"rated power speed"* has the same meaning as in Community Directive 96/1.]

(5) No person shall use, or cause or permit to be used, on a road any motor vehicle—

(a) from which any smoke, visible vapour, grit, sparks, ashes, cinders or oily substance is emitted if that emission causes, or is likely to cause, damage to any property or injury or danger to any person who is, or who may reasonably be expected to be, on the road;

(b) which is subject to the requirement in item 2 of [Table I] [*see pp. 1356, 1357*] (whether or not it is deemed to comply with that requirement by virtue of paragraph (4)), if the fuel injection equipment, the engine speed governor or any other parts of the engine by which it is propelled have been altered or adjusted so as to increase the emission of smoke; or

(c) which is subject to the requirement in item 1 of [Table I] [*see p. 1356*] if the device mentioned in column 2 in that item is used while the vehicle is in motion.

(6) No person shall use, or cause or permit to be used, on a road a motor vehicle to which item 3 of [Table I] applies unless it is so maintained that the means specified in column 3 of that item are in good working order.

[(7) Subject to paragraphs . . . (8), (9) and (10), no person shall use, or cause or permit to be used, on a road a motor vehicle to which an item in Table II [*see pp. 1358–1364*] applies if, in relation to the emission of the substances specified in column (6) of the item, the vehicle does not comply with the requirements relating to conformity of production models specified in column (4) unless the following conditions are satisfied in respect to it—

(a) the failure to meet those requirements in relation to the emission of those substances does not result from an alteration to the propulsion unit or exhaust system of the vehicle,

(b) [neither would those requirements] be met in relation to the emission of those substances nor would such emissions be materially reduced if maintenance work of a kind which would fall within the scope of a normal periodic service of the vehicle were to be carried out on the vehicle, and

(c) the failure to meet those requirements in relation to such emissions does not result from any device designed to control the emission of carbon monoxide, hydrocarbons, oxides of nitrogen, or particulates fitted to the vehicle being other than in good and efficient working order.]

(7A)–(7H) *[Revoked.]*

[(8) Paragraph (7) shall not apply to a vehicle first used before 26th June 1990.]

[(9) Where—

(a) a vehicle is fitted with a device of the kind referred to in sub-paragraph (c) of paragraph (7),

(b) the vehicle does not comply with the requirements specified in that paragraph in respect to it, and

(c) the conditions specified in sub-paragraphs (a) and (b) of that paragraph are satisfied in respect to the vehicle,

nothing in paragraph (7) shall prevent the vehicle being driven to a place where the device is to be repaired or replaced.]

[(10) Where a vehicle is constructed or assembled by a person not ordinarily engaged in the business of manufacturing motor vehicles of that description [and is first used before [July 1st, 1998]], the date on which it is first used shall, for the purposes of paragraphs (3A), (7), (8) and (9), be regarded as being the 1st January immediately preceding the date of manufacture of the engine by which it is propelled.

However, the date on which a vehicle is first used shall not, by virtue of the foregoing provisions of this paragraph, be regarded in any circumstances as being later than the date on which it would otherwise have been regarded as being first used had those provisions been omitted.]

[(10A) Without prejudice to paragraphs (1) and (7) and subject to the following provisions of this regulation, no person shall use, or cause or permit to be used on a road, a vehicle first used on or after 1st August 1975 and propelled by a four-stroke spark ignition engine, if the vehicle is in such a condition and running on such fuel that—

(a) when the engine is idling the carbon monoxide content of the exhaust emissions from the engine exceeds—

  (i) in the case of a vehicle first used before 1st August 1986, 4.5%; or
  (ii) in the case of a vehicle first used on or after 1st August 1986, 3.5%;

  of the total exhaust emissions from the engine by volume; and

(b) when the engine is running without load at a rotational speed of 2,000 revolutions per minute, the hydrocarbon content of those emissions exceeds 0.12% of the total exhaust emissions from the engine by volume.]

[(10AA) Without prejudice to paragraphs (1) and (7) and subject to the following provisions of this regulation, no person shall use, or cause or permit to be used on a road, a vehicle to which this paragraph applies and which is propelled by a spark ignition engine, if the vehicle is in such a condition and running on such fuel that Part I of Schedule 7B applies to the vehicle.]

[(10AB) [Subject to paragraph (10B)], paragraph (10AA) applies to—

(a) a passenger car which—

  (i) is first used on or after 1st August 1992 and before [1st August 1995], and
  (ii) is of a description mentioned in the Annex to the emissions publication;

(b) a vehicle which—

  (i) is not a passenger car,
  (ii) is first used on or after 1st August 1994 . . . and
  (iii) is of a description mentioned in the Annex to the emissions publication; [or]

(c) a passenger car which is first used on or after [1st August 1995]; . . .

and in this paragraph, "*emissions publication*" has the meaning given in Part I of Schedule 7B.]

[(10AC)   [*Revoked by S.I. 1998 No. 1563.*]]

[(10AD) Paragraph (10A) does not apply to—

(a) a vehicle to which paragraph (10AA) applies; or

(b) a vehicle if, at the date that the engine was manufactured, that engine was incapable of meeting the requirements specified in that paragraph.]

[(10AE) Paragraph (10AA) does not apply to a vehicle if, at the date that the engine was manufactured, that engine was incapable of meeting the requirements specified in that paragraph.]

[(10B) [Paragraphs (10A) and (10AA) do not] apply to—

    (a) *[revoked]*

    (b) a vehicle being driven to a place where it is to undergo repairs;

    (c) a vehicle which was constructed or assembled by a person not ordinarily engaged in the business of manufacturing motor vehicles of that description [and is first used before [1st July 1998]];

    (d) an exempt vehicle within the meaning given by paragraph (12)(a) . . .;

    (e) a goods vehicle with a maximum gross weight exceeding 3,500kg;

    (f) engineering plant, an industrial tractor, or a works truck; . . .

    (g) *[revoked.]*

    [(h) a vehicle first used before 1st August 1987 if the engine is a rotary piston engine; and for the purposes of this paragraph *"the engine"*, in relation to a vehicle, means the engine by which it is propelled.]

[(10BA) Without prejudice to paragraphs (1) and (7), no person shall use, or cause or permit to be used on a road, a vehicle propelled by a compression ignition engine, if the vehicle is in such a condition and running on such fuel that Part II of Schedule 7B applies to the vehicle.]

[(10BB) Paragraph (10BA) shall not apply to—

    (a) a vehicle if, at the date that the engine was manufactured, that engine was incapable of meeting the requirements specified in that paragraph;

    (b) a vehicle being driven to a place where it is to undergo repairs;

    (c) an exempt vehicle within the meaning given by paragraph (12)(a);

    (d) engineering plant, an industrial tractor or a works truck; and

    (e) a vehicle in Class III, IV, V or VII within the meaning of the Motor Vehicles (Tests) Regulations 1981 and first used before 1st August 1979.]

[(10BC)   *[Revoked by S.I. 1998 No. 1563.]*]

[(10C) For the purposes of this regulation—

    (a) any rotary piston engine shall be deemed to be a four-stroke engine; and

    (b) *"rotary piston engine"* means an engine in which the torque is provided by means of one or more rotary pistons and not by any reciprocating piston.]

[(11) Subject to Schedule 7XA] in this regulation, a reference to a vehicle to which an item in Table II [*see pp. 1358 et seq.*] applies is a reference to a vehicle which—

    (a) is of a class specified in that item in column (2) of that Table,

    (b) is first used on or after the date specified in that item in column (3) of that Table, and

    (c) is not exempted by the entry in that item in column (5) of that Table,]

[and for the purposes of determining whether a vehicle is a vehicle to which [any item numbered 8 or more] in that Table applies, regulation 4(2) shall be disregarded.]

[(11A) In this regulation, "*passenger car*" means a motor vehicle which—

(a) is constructed or adapted for use for the carriage of passengers and is not a goods vehicle;

(b) has no more than five seats in addition to the driver's seat; and

(c) has a maximum gross weight not exceeding 2,500kg.]

[(12) In Table II [and paragraphs (10B) and (10BB)]—

(a) "*exempt vehicle*" means—

    (i) a vehicle with less than 4 wheels,
    (ii) a vehicle with a maximum gross weight of less than 400kg,
    (iii) a vehicle with a maximum speed of less than 25 km/h, or
    (iv) an agricultural motor vehicle;

(b) "*direct injection*" means a fuel injection system in which the injector communicates with an open combustion chamber or the main part of a divided combustion chamber;

(c) "*indirect injection*" means a fuel injection system in which the injector communicates with the subsidiary part of a divided combustion chamber;

(d) a reference in column (5) to a vehicle complying with an item is a reference to a vehicle that complies with the provisions specified in that item in column (4) whether the vehicle is or is not within the class of vehicles to which that item applies and any instrument mentioned in that item shall for the purposes of the reference have effect as if it applied to the vehicle in question (whether it would otherwise have done so or not).]

[Regulation 61 is printed as amended by S.I. 1988 No. 1524; S.I. 1990 No. 1131; S.I. 1991 No. **B27.138**
1526; S.I. 1992 Nos 2016, 2137, 2909, 3285; S.I. 1993 No. 2199; S.I. 1994 No. 2192; S.I. 1995 No. 2210; S.I. 1996 Nos 2085, 2329 and 3017; S.I. 1997 Nos 1458, 1544 and 2935; S.I. 1998 Nos 1000 and 1563; S.I. 2000 No. 3197.

As to the modification of the provisions of regulation 61 in relation to vehicles in respect of which approval certificates containing the letter "A" have been issued under the "Approval Regulations", see Schedule 2A, paragraph 9, to these regulations.

As to the issue of fixed penalty notices for contraventions of regulation 61, see the Road Traffic (Vehicles Emissions) (Fixed Penalty) Regulations 1997 (S.I. 1997 No. 3058) below.]

[TABLE I]

(regulation 61(3))

1	2	3	4
Item	Class of vehicle	Requirements	Exemptions

1	Vehicles propelled by a compression ignition engine and equipped with a device designed to facilitate starting the engine by causing it to be supplied with excess fuel.	Provision shall be made to ensure the device cannot readily be operated by a person inside the vehicle.	(a) a works truck;
			(b) a vehicle on which the device is so designed and maintained that—
			  (i) its use after the engine has started cannot cause the engine to be supplied with excess fuel, or
			  (ii) it does not cause any increase in the smoke or visible vapour emitted from the vehicle.

2	Vehicles first used on or after 1st April 1973 and propelled by a compression ignition engine.	The engine of the vehicle shall be of a type for which there has been issued by a person authorised by the Secretary of State a type test certificate in accordance with the British Standard Specification for the Performance of Diesel Engines for Road Vehicles published on 19th May 1971 under number BS AU 141a: 1971. In the case of an agricultural motor vehicle (other than one which is first used after 1st June 1986 and is driven at more than 20mph), an industrial tractor, a works truck or engineering plant, for the purposes of that Specification as to the exhaust gas opacity, measurements shall be made with the engine running at 80% of its full load over the speed range from maximum speed down to the speed	(a) a vehicle manufactured before 1st April 1973 and propelled by an engine known as the Perkins 6.354 engine; (b) a vehicle propelled by an engine having not more than 2 cylinders and being an agricultural motor vehicle (other than one which is first used on or after 1st June 1986 and which is driven at more than 20 mph), an industrial tractor, a works truck or engineering plant.

		at which maximum torque occurs as declared by the manufacturer of the vehicle for those purposes.	
3	Vehicles first used on or after 1st January 1972 and propelled by a spark ignition engine other than a 2-stroke engine.	The engine shall be equipped with means sufficient to ensure that, while the engine is running, any vapours or gases in the engine crank case, or in any other part of the engine to which vapours or gases may pass from that case, are prevented, so far as is reasonably practicable, from escaping into the atmosphere otherwise than through the combustion chamber of the engine.	(a) a two-wheeled motor cycle with or without a sidecar attached; (b) . . . [(c) a vehicle to which any item in Table II applies.]
4	. . .	. . .	. . .

[Table I is printed as amended by S.I. 1990 No. 1131; S.I. 1993 No. 2199.]

TABLE II
(regulation 61(3A), (3C), (7), (11) and (12))

(1) Item	(2) Class of Vehicle	(3) Date of First Use	(4) Design, construction and equipment requirements		(5) Vehicles exempted from requirements	(6) Emitted substances
			(a) Instrument	(b) Place in instrument where requirements are stated		
1	Vehicles propelled by a spark ignition engine.	1st October 1982	Community Directive 78/665 or ECE Regulation 15.03	Annex I, paragraphs 3 and 5. Paragraphs 5, 8 and 11.	(a) A vehicle whose maximum gross weight exceeds 3,500kg; (b) A vehicle which complies with the requirements of item 2, 4, 5, 8, 11, 12 or 13; (c) A vehicle whose maximum speed is less than 50 km/h; (d) An exempt vehicle.	Carbon monoxide, hydrocarbons and oxides of nitrogen.
2	All vehicles.	1st April 1991	Community Directive 83/351 or ECE Regulation 15.04	Annex I, paragraphs 5, 7 and 8. Paragraphs 5, 8 and 12.	(a) A vehicle propelled by a compression ignition engine and whose maximum gross weight exceeds 3,500kg; (b) A vehicle which complies with the requirements of item 4, 5, 8, 11, 12 or 13; (c) A vehicle within the meaning given by Article 1 of Community Directive 88/77 which complies with the requirements of item 6, 9, or 10;	Carbon monoxide, hydrocarbons and oxides of nitrogen.

					(d) An industrial tractor, works truck, or engineering plant; (e) A vehicle whose maximum speed is less than 50 km/h (f) An exempt vehicle.	
3	Industrial tractors, works trucks and engineering plant propelled in each case by a compression ignition engine.	1st April 1993	ECE Regulation 49	Paragraphs 5 and 7.	A vehicle which complies with the requirements of item 6, 9, 10, 11, 12 or 13.	Carbon monoxide, hydrocarbons and oxides of nitrogen.
4	Passenger vehicles which— (a) are constructed or adapted to carry not more than 5 passengers excluding the driver, and (b) have a maximum gross weight of not more than 2,500kg, not being off-road vehicles.	1st April 1991	Community Directive 88/76 or Community Directive 89/458 or ECE Regulation 83	Annex I, paragraphs 5, 7 and 8. Annex I, paragraphs 5, 7 and 8. Paragraphs 5, 8 and 13.	(a) A vehicle which complies with the requirements of item 2, 8, 11, 12 or 13; (b) A vehicle whose maximum speed is less than 50 km/h; (c) An exempt vehicle.	Carbon monoxide, hydrocarbons and oxides of nitrogen.
5	Vehicles which are not of a description specified in this column in item 4 but which— (a) are propelled by a spark ignition engine and have a maximum gross weight of not more than 2,000kg, or	1st April 1992	Community Directive 88/76 or ECE Regulation 8.3	Annex I, paragraphs 5, 7 and 8. Paragraphs 5, 8 and 13.	(a) A vehicle within the meaning given by Article 1 of Community Directive 88/77 and which complies with the requirements of item 6, 9, 10, 11, 12 or 13; (b) An industrial tractor, works truck or engineering plant; (c) A vehicle whose maximum speed is less than 50 km/h;	Carbon monoxide, hydrocarbons and oxides of nitrogen.

[continued on next page

(1) Item	(2) Class of Vehicle	(3) Date of First Use	(4) Design, construction and equipment requirements		(5) Vehicles exempted from requirements	(6) Emitted substances
			(a) Instrument	(b) Place in instrument where requirements are stated		
5—cont.	(b) are propelled by a compression ignition engine and have a maximum gross weight of more than 3,500kg.	1st April 1991			(d) A vehicle which complies with the requirements of item 8; (e) An exempt vehicle.	
6	All vehicles propelled by compression ignition engines.	1st April 1991	Community Directive 88/77 or ECE Regulation 49.01	Annex I, paragraphs 6, 7 and 8. Paragraphs 5, 6 and 7.	(a) A vehicle whose maximum gross weight is less than 3,500kg and which complies with the requirements of item 2; (b) A vehicle which complies with the requirements of item 4, 5, 8, 9, 10, 11, 12 or 13; (c) A fire appliance which is first used before 1st October 1992; (d) An industrial tractor, works truck or engineering plant; (e) An exempt vehicle.	Carbon monoxide, hydrocarbons and oxides of nitrogen.
7	Passenger vehicles which— (a) are constructed or adapted to carry not	1st April 1991	Community Directive 88/436	Annex I, paragraphs 5, 7 and 8 as far as they relate to particulate emissions.	(a) A vehicle which complies with the requirements of item 8, 11, 12 or 13; (b) A vehicle whose maximum speed is less than 50 km/h;	Particulates.

	more than 5 passengers excluding the driver; (b) have a maximum gross weight of not more than 2,500kg, and (c) are propelled by a compression ignition engine of the indirect injection type.				(c) An off-road vehicle; (d) An exempt vehicle.	Carbon monoxide, hydrocarbons, oxides of nitrogen and particulates.
8	All vehicles	31st December 1992	Community Directive 91/441 or ECE Regulation 83.01	Annex I, paragraphs 5, 7 and 8. Paragraphs 5, 8 and 13.	(a) A vehicle within the meaning given by Article 1 of Community Directive 88/77 and which— (i) complies with the requirements of item 6 and is first used before 1st October 1993, or (ii) complies with the requirements of item 9, 10, 11, 12 or 13; (b) An industrial tractor, works truck or engineering plant; (c) A vehicle whose maximum speed is less than 50 km/h; (d) An exempt vehicle.	
9	All vehicles propelled by a compression ignition engine.	1st October 1993	Community Directive 91/542	Annex I, paragraphs 6, 7 and 8 (excluding line B in the Tables in	(a) A vehicle which complies with the requirements of item 8, 10, 11, 12 or 13;	Carbon monoxide, hydrocarbons, oxides of

[continued on next page]

(1) Item	(2) Class of Vehicle	(3) Date of First Use	(4) Design, construction and equipment requirements		(5) Vehicles exempted from requirements	(6) Emitted substances
			(a) Instrument	(b) Place in instrument where requirements are stated		
9— cont.			or ECE Regulation 49.02	sub-paragraphs 6.2.1 and 8.3.1.1). Paragraphs 5, 6 and 7 (excluding line B in the Tables in sub-paragraphs 5.2.1 and 7.4.2.1).	(b) An industrial tractor, works truck or engineering plant; (c) An exempt vehicle.	nitrogen and particulates.
10	All vehicles propelled by a compression ignition engine.	1st October 1996	Community Directive 91/542 or ECE Regulation 49.02	Annex I, paragraphs 6, 7 and 8 (excluding line A in the Tables in sub-paragraphs 6.2.1 and 8.3.1.1). Paragraphs 5, 6 and 7 (excluding line A in the Tables in sub-paragraphs 5.2.1 and 7.4.2.1).	(a) A vehicle which complies with the requirements of item 8, 11, 12 or 13; (b) An industrial tractor, works truck or engineering plant; (c) An exempt vehicle.	Carbon monoxide, hydrocarbons, oxides of nitrogen and particulates.
11	All vehicles.	1st October 1994	Community Directive 93/59	Annex I, paragraphs 5, 7 and 8.	(a) A vehicle within the meaning given by Article 1 of Community Directive 88/77 and which complies with the requirements of items 9, 10, 12 or 13 [or ECE Regulation 83.02];	Carbon monoxide, hydrocarbons, oxides of nitrogen and particulates.

12	All vehicles.	1st January 1997	Community Directive 94/12	Annex I, paragraphs 5, 7 and 8.	(a) A vehicle within the meaning given by Article 1 of Community Directive 88/77 and which complies with the requirements of items 9, 10, 11 or 13 [or ECE Regulation 83.03]; (b) An industrial tractor, works truck or engineering plant; (c) Vehicles whose maximum speed is less than 50 km/h; (d) An exempt vehicle.	Carbon monoxide, hydrocarbons, oxides of nitrogen and particulates.
13	All vehicles.	1st October 1997	Community Directive 96/69	Annex I, paragraphs 5, 7 and 8.	(a) A vehicle within the meaning given by Article 1 of Community Directive 88/77 and which complies with the requirements of items 9, 10, or 12 [or ECE Regulation 83.04]; (b) A vehicle as defined in column 2 of item 14; (c) An industrial tractor, works truck or engineering plant;	Carbon monoxide, hydrocarbons, oxides of nitrogen and particulates.

[continued on next page]

(1) Item	(2) Class of Vehicle	(3) Date of First Use	(4) Design, construction and equipment requirements		(5) Vehicles exempted from requirements	(6) Emitted substances
			(a) Instrument	(b) Place in instrument where requirements are stated		
13—cont.					(d) Vehicles whose maximum speed is less than 50 km/h; (e) An exempt vehicle.	
14	Vehicles falling within (a) Class II or III, as specified in the Annex to Community Directive 96/69 [q.v.], of category N₁, or (b) Category M and specified in footnote (²) of that Annex. Note: references to categories M and N₁ are to those categories as specified in Annex II of the Framework Directive [q.v.].	1st October 1998	Community Directive 96/69	Annex 1, paragraphs 5, 7 and 8.		Carbon monoxide, hydrocarbons, oxides of nitrogen and particulates.

[Table II was inserted by S.I. 1990 No. 1131 and is printed as substituted by S.I. 1997 No. 1544; and subsequently amended by S.I. 2000 No. 3197. S.I. 2000 No. 3197 purported to add the words "or ECE Regulation 83.04" to the entry in column (4)(a) in item 14 above, but there is no such entry.]

[61A. Emission of smoke, vapour, gases, oily substances, etc.—further requirements for certain motor vehicles first used on or after 1st January 2001

(1) This regulation shall apply to motor vehicles first used on or after 1st January 2001. **B27.141**

(2) Subject to paragraphs (5) to (7) and Schedule 7XA, a motor vehicle in any category shall comply with such design, construction and equipment requirements and such limit values as may be specified for a motor vehicle of that category and weight by any Community Directive specified in item 1 or 2 of the Table and from such date as is specified by that Community Directive.

(3) Subject to paragraphs (4) to (7) and Schedule 7XA, no person shall use, or cause or permit to be used, on a road a motor vehicle if the motor vehicle does not comply with such limit values as may apply to it by virtue of any Community Directive specified in item 1 or 2 of the Table, and from such date as is specified by that Community Directive, unless the following conditions are satisfied with respect to it—

(a) the failure to meet the limit values does not result from an alteration to the propulsion unit or exhaust system of the motor vehicle;

(b) neither would those limit values be met nor the emissions of gaseous and particulate pollutants and smoke and evaporative emissions be materially reduced if maintenance work of any kind which would fall within the scope of a normal periodic service of the vehicle were carried out on the motor vehicle; and

(c) the failure to meet those limit values does not result from any device designed to control the emission of gaseous and particulate pollutants and smoke and evaporative emissions which is fitted to the motor vehicle being other than in good and efficient working order.

(4) Subject to paragraphs (5) to (7) and Schedule 7XA, where—

(a) a motor vehicle is fitted with a device of the kind referred to in sub-paragraph (c) of [this paragraph];

(b) the motor vehicle does not comply with the limit values applying to it which are referred to in that paragraph; and

(c) the conditions specified in sub-paragraphs (a) and (b) of paragraph (3) are satisfied in respect of the motor vehicle

nothing in this paragraph shall prevent the motor vehicle being driven to a place where the device is to be repaired or replaced.

(5) Subject to paragraph (6), if the Secretary of State has exempted any motor vehicle produced in a small series from one or more of the provisions of the Community Directive specified in item 1 of the Table in accordance with the procedure in Article 8(2)(a) of the Framework Directive then paragraphs (2) to (4) shall not apply to that motor vehicle insofar as it has been so exempted.

(6) If any motor vehicle has been exempted from one or more of the provisions of a Community Directive specified in item 1 of the Table in accordance with paragraph (5), then in the Table as it applies to that motor vehicle there shall be deemed to be substituted, for the reference to Community Directive 96/69/EC or ECE Regulation 83.04, Community Directive 98/69/EC and 1999/102/EC—

(a) in the case of passenger cars as defined in regulations 61(11A), a reference to Community Directive 94/12/EC or ECE Regulation 83.03; and

(b) in the case of other motor vehicles of category M, a reference to Community Directive 93/59/EEC or ECE Regulation 83.02

and in any such case paragraphs (2) to (4) shall apply to the motor vehicle as if they referred to the substituted Community Directives or ECE Regulations.

(7) If any motor vehicle has been exempted from one or more of the provisions of a Community Directive specified in item 1 or 2 of the Table in accordance with Schedule 7XA, then in the Table as it applies to that motor vehicle there shall be deemed to be substituted—

(a) for the reference to Community Directive 98/69/EC and 1999/102/EC, a reference to Community Directive 96/69/EC or ECE Regulation 83.04; and

(b) for the reference to Community Directive 1999/96/EC, a reference to Community Directive 91/542/EEC or ECE Regulation 49.02

and in any such case paragraphs (2) to (4) shall apply to the motor vehicle as if they referred to the substituted Community Directives or ECE Regulations.

(8) In this regulation—

(a) *"category"* means a category for the purpose of Annex II of the Framework Directive;

(b) *"date as is specified"* means the date specified by the relevant Community Directive as that from which Member States are required to prohibit the registration or the entry into service of motor vehicles which do not comply with the limit values specified by the relevant Community Directive or, in the case of emission control and monitoring systems and devices, the date specified by the relevant Community Directive for the fitting of such equipment;

(c) *"limit values"* means the permitted amounts of gaseous and particulate pollutants and smoke and evaporative emissions;

(d) *"small series"* means the motor vehicles within a family of types as defined in Annex XII of the Framework Directive which are registered or enter into service in a period of twelve months beginning on 1st January in any year where the total number of motor vehicles does not exceed the small series limits specified in that Annex.

TABLE

(Regulation 61A)

Item	Community Directive of ECE Regulation	Amending Community Directive or ECE Regulation
1.	70/220/EEC	96/69/EC or ECE Regulation 83.04 98/69/EC 1999/102/EC
2.	88/77/EEC or ECE Regulation 49.01	91/542/EEC or ECE Regulation 49.02 1999/96/EC]

B27.142   *[Regulation 61A was inserted by S.I. 2000 No. 3197; and is printed as amended by S.I. 2001 No. 306.]*

62. Closets, etc.

(1) No wheeled vehicle first used after 15th January 1931 shall be equipped with any closet or urinal which can discharge directly on to a road.   **B27.143**

(2) Every tank into which a closet or urinal with which a vehicle is equipped empties, and every closet or urinal which does not empty into a tank, shall contain chemicals which are non-inflammable and non-irritant and provide an efficient germicide.

63. Wings

(1) Save as provided in paragraph (4), this regulation applies to—   **B27.144**
  (a) invalid carriages;
  (b) heavy motor cars, motor cars and motor cycles, not being agricultural motor vehicles or pedestrian-controlled vehicles;
  (c) agricultural motor vehicles driven at more than 20mph; and
  (d) trailers.

(2) Subject to paragraphs (3) and (5), every vehicle to which this regulation applies shall be equipped with wings or other similar fittings to catch, so far as practicable, mud or water thrown up by the rotation of its wheels or tracks.

(3) The requirements specified in paragraph (2) apply, in the case of a trailer with more than two wheels, only in respect of the rearmost two wheels.

(4) Those requirements do not apply in respect of—
  (a) a works truck;
  (b) a living van;
  (c) a water cart;
  (d) an agricultural trailer drawn by a motor vehicle which is not driven at a speed in excess of 20mph;
  (e) an agricultural trailed appliance;
  (f) an agricultural trailed appliance conveyor;
  (g) a broken down vehicle;
  (h) a heavy motor car, motor car or trailer in an unfinished condition which is proceeding to a workshop for completion;
  (i) a trailer used for or in connection with the carriage of round timber and the rear wheels of any heavy motor car or motor car drawing a semi-trailer so used; or
  (j) a trailer drawn by a motor vehicle the maximum speed of which is restricted to 20mph or less under Schedule 6 to the 1984 Act.

(5) Instead of complying with paragraph (2) a vehicle may comply with Community Directive 78/549.

64. Spray suppression devices

(1) Save as provided in paragraph (2), this regulation applies to every wheeled goods vehicle which is—   **B27.145**
  (a) a motor vehicle first used on or after 1st April 1986 having a maximum gross weight exceeding 12,000kg;
  (b) a trailer manufactured on or after 1st May 1985 having a maximum gross weight exceeding 3500kg; or

(c) a trailer, whenever manufactured, having a maximum gross weight exceeding 16,000kg and 2 or more axles.

(2) This regulation does not apply to—

(a) a motor vehicle so constructed that the driving power of its engine is, or can by use of its controls be, transmitted to all the wheels on at least one front axle and on at least one rear axle;

(b) a motor vehicle of which no part which lies within the specified area is less than 400mm vertically above the ground when the vehicle is standing on reasonably flat ground;

(c) a works truck;

(d) a works trailer;

(e) a broken down vehicle;

(f) a motor vehicle which has a maximum speed not exceeding 30mph;

(g) a vehicle of a kind specified in sub-paragraphs (b), (c), (d), (e), (f), (g), (h), (j), (o) or (p) or regulation 51(2);

(h) a vehicle specially designed, and not merely adapted, for the carriage and mixing of liquid concrete; or

(i) a vehicle which is being driven or towed to a place where by previous arrangement a device is to be fitted so that it complies with the requirements specified in paragraph (3).

[(2A) This regulation shall not apply to a vehicle fitted with a spray-suppression system in accordance with the requirements of Annex III of Community Directive 91/226 if the spray-suppression devices with which the vehicle is equipped are legibly and permanently marked with a designated approval mark.]

(3) A vehicle to which this regulation applies and which is of a class specified in an item in column 2 of the Table shall not be used on a road on or after the date specified in column 3 in that item, unless it is fitted in relation to the wheels on each of its axles, with such containment devices as satisfy the technical requirements and other provisions about containment devices specified in the British Standard Specification, provided that in the case of a containment device fitted before 1st January 1985 the said requirements shall be deemed to be complied with if that containment device substantially conforms to those requirements.

TABLE

(regulation 64(3))

1	2	3
Item	Class of vehicle	Date
1	A trailer manufactured before 1st January 1975	1st October 1987
2	A trailer manufactured on or after 1st January 1975 but before 1st May 1985	1st October 1986
3	A trailer manufactured on or after 1st May 1985	1st May 1985
4	A motor vehicle	1st April 1986

(4) In this regulation—

["*the British Standard Specification*" means—

(a) in relation to a containment device fitted before 1st May 1987, Part 1a of the amended Specification and Part 2 of the original Specification; and

(b) in relation to a containment device fitted on or after 1st May 1987, Part 1a and Part 2a of the amended Specification;]

["*designated approval mark*" means the marking designated as an approval mark by regulation 5 of the Approval Marks Regulations [*i.e. as amended by S.I. 1992 No. 634*] and shown at item 30 in Schedule 4 to those Regulations;]

["*the original Specification*" means the British Standard Specification for Spray Reducing Devices for Heavy Goods Vehicles published under the reference BS AU 200: Part 1: 1984 and BS AU 200: Part 2: 1984;]

["*the amended Specification*" means the original Specification as amended and published under the reference BS AU 200: Part 1a: 1986 and BS AU 200: Part 2a: 1986;]

["*containment device*" means any device so described in the original Specification or the amended Specification;]

"*the specified area*" means the area formed by the overall length of the vehicle and the middle 80% of the shortest distance between the inner edges of any two wheels on opposite sides of the vehicle (such distance being ascertained when the vehicle is fitted with suitable tyres inflated to a pressure recommended by the manufacturer, but excluding any bulging of the tyres near the ground).

(5) Nothing in this regulation derogates from any requirement in regulation 63.

[Regulation 64 is printed as amended by S.I. 1986 No. 1597; S.I. 1992 No. 646.]   **B27.146**

65. Maintenance of spray suppression devices

Every part of every containment device with which a vehicle is required to be fitted by the provisions of regulation 64 shall at all times when the vehicle is on a road be maintained free from any obvious defect which would be likely to affect adversely the effectiveness of the device.   **B27.147**

PART III

PLATES, MARKINGS, TESTING AND INSPECTION

66. Plates for goods vehicles and buses

(1) This regulation applies to—   **B27.148**

(a) a wheeled heavy motor car or motor car first used on or after 1st January 1968 not being—

   (i) a dual-purpose vehicle;
   (ii) an agricultural motor vehicle;
   (iii) a works truck;
   (iv) a pedestrian-controlled vehicle; . . .
   (v) save as provided in sub-paragraph (b) below, a passenger vehicle; [or]
   [(vi) a vehicle which is exempt from section 63(1) of the Road Traffic Act 1988 by virtue of regulation 14(6) of the Motor Vehicles (Approval) Regulations 1996.]

(b) a bus (whether or not it is an articulated bus) first used on or after 1st April 1982;

(c) a wheeled locomotive or motor tractor first used on or after 1st April 1973 not being—

    (i) an agricultural motor vehicle;

    (ii) an industrial tractor;

    (iii) a works truck;

    (iv) engineering plant; or

    (v) a pedestrian-controlled vehicle;

(d) a wheeled trailer manufactured on or after 1st January 1968 which exceeds 1020kg in weight unladen not being—

    (i) a trailer not constructed or adapted to carry any load, other than plant or special appliances or apparatus which is a permanent or essentially permanent fixture, and not exceeding 2290kg in total weight;

    (ii) a living van not exceeding 2040kg in weight unladen and fitted with pneumatic tyres;

    (iii) a works trailer;

    (iv) a trailer mentioned in regulation 16(3)(b) to (g); or

    (v) a trailer which was manufactured and used outside Great Britain before it was first used in Great Britain; and

(e) a converter dolly manufactured on or after 1st January 1979.

(2) Every vehicle to which this regulation applies shall be equipped with a plate securely attached to the vehicle in a conspicuous and readily accessible position which either—

(a) contains the particulars required, in the case of a motor vehicle by Part I of Schedule 8 or, in the case of a trailer, by Part II of that Schedule and complies with the provisions of Part III of that Schedule; or

(b) complies with the requirements specified in the Annex to Community Directive 78/507 or, in the case of a vehicle first used before 1st October 1982, in the Annex to Community Directive 76/114, such requirements being in any case modified as provided in paragraph (3).

(3) Instead of the particulars required by items 2.1.4 to 2.1.7 of that Annex, the plate required by paragraph (2)(b) shall show, for a vehicle of a class specified in column 2 of the Table against an item of that Annex so specified in column 1, the following particulars—

(a) the maximum permitted weight for that class, if any, shown in column 3 of the Table;

(b) where the maximum weight shown in column 4 of the Table exceeds the maximum permitted weight, the maximum weight in a column on the plate to the right of the maximum permitted weight; and

(c) if no weight is shown in column 3 of the Table, the maximum weight shown in column 4 of the Table, in the right hand column of the plate.

TABLE

(regulation 66(3))

1	2	3	4
Item in Annex to Directive	*Class of vehicle*	*Maximum permitted weight*	*Maximum weight*
2.1.4 (Laden weight of vehicle)	(i) Motor vehicles	The maximum gross weight in Great Britain referred to in item 10 in Part I of Schedule 8.	The maximum gross weight referred to in item 7 in Part I of Schedule 8.
	(ii) Trailers, other than semi-trailers	The maximum gross weight in Great Britain referred to in item 8 in Part II of Schedule 8.	The maximum gross weight referred to in item 6 in Part II of Schedule 8.
	(iii) Semi-trailers		The maximum gross weight referred to in item 6 in Part II of Schedule 8.
2.1.5 (Train weight of motor vehicle)	Motor vehicles constructed to draw a trailer	The lower of— (a) the maximum train weight referred to in item 8 in Part I of Schedule 8; and (b) the maximum laden weight specified, in the case of vehicles constructed to form part of an articulated vehicle, in regulation 77, and, in other cases, in regulation 76.	The maximum train weight referred to in item 8 in Part I of Schedule 8.
2.1.6 weight of vehicle)	(i) Motor vehicles	The maximum weight in Great Britain for each axle referred to in item 9 in Part I of Schedule 8.	The maximum weight for each axle referred to in item 6 in Part I of Schedule 8.
	(ii) Trailers	The maximum weight in Great Britain for each axle referred to in item 7 in Part II of Schedule 8.	The maximum weight for each axle referred to in item 4 in Part II of Schedule 8.
2.1.7 (Load imposed by semi-trailer)	Semi-trailers		The maximum load imposed on the drawing vehicle referred to in item 5 in Part II of Schedule 8.

(4) Part III of Schedule 8 applies for determining the relevant weights to be shown on a plate in accordance with this regulation.

[(5) Where, in accordance with the provisions of this regulation and of Schedule 8, a motor vehicle first used, or a trailer manufactured, after 31st December 1998, is required to be equipped with a plate showing the maximum gross weight in Great Britain or the maximum weight in Great Britain for each axle of the vehicle, the plate may instead show particulars of the maximum authorised weight for the vehicle of, as the case may be, the maximum authorised weight for each axle of the vehicle.]

[(6) In paragraph (5) the references to the *maximum authorised weight* for a vehicle and *maximum authorised* [*weight*] for each axle of a vehicle mean those weights determined in accordance with the Motor [*sic*] Vehicles (Authorised Weight) Regulations 1998 [*S.I. 1998 No. 3111 below*].]

[(7) The plate for a vehicle which falls within paragraph (1)(a) and which is a motor vehicle first used after 31st December 1998 need not include the particulars referred to in paragraph 9 or 10 of Part I of Schedule 8.]

B27.149   *[Regulation 66 is printed as amended by S.I. 1996 No. 3017; S.I. 1998 No. 3112.*
The Motor Vehicles (Approval) Regulations 1996 (to which reference is made in regulation 66(1)(a)(vi)) have been revoked and replaced by the Motor Vehicles (Approval) Regulations 2001 (S.I. 2001 No. 25) below; see further the note to Schedule 2A, paragraph 2 below.
The word "weight" (in the second place where it occurs in regulation 66(6)) has been added editorially.]

67. Vehicle identification numbers

B27.150   (1) This regulation applies to a wheeled vehicle which is first used on or after 1st April 1980 and to which the Type Approval (Great Britain) Regulations apply.

(2) A vehicle to which this regulation applies shall be equipped with a plate which is in a conspicuous and readily accessible position, is affixed to a vehicle part which is not normally subject to replacement and shows clearly and indelibly—

  (a) the vehicle identification number in accordance with the requirements specified—
    (i) in the case of a vehicle first used before 1st April 1987, in paragraphs 3.1.1 and 3.1.2 of the Annex to Community Directive 76/114/EEC; or
    (ii) in any case, in sections 3 and 4 of the Annex to Community Directive 78/507/EEC;
  (b) the name of the manufacturer; and
  (c) the approval reference number of either—
    (i) the type approval certificate which relates to the vehicle model or the model variant of the vehicle model, as the case may be, issued in accordance with the provisions of regulation 9(1) of, and Part I of Schedule 3 to, the Type Approval (Great Britain) Regulations; or
    (ii) the Minister's approval certificate which relates to the vehicle, issued in accordance with the provisions of regulation 9(2) of, and Part 1A of Schedule 4 to, the said Regulations.

Provided that the information required under sub-paragraph (c) above may be shown clearly and indelibly on an additional plate which is fitted in a conspicuous and readily accessible position and which is affixed to a vehicle part which is not normally subject to replacement.

(3) The vehicle identification number of every vehicle to which this regulation applies shall be marked on the chassis, frame or other similar structure, on the offside of the vehicle, in a clearly visible and accessible position, and by a method such as hammering or stamping, in such a way that it cannot be obliterated or deteriorate.

[As to the application of the provisions of regulation 67 to vehicles in respect of which approval certificates have been issued under the "Approval Regulations", see Schedule 2A, paragraph 10, to these regulations.]   **B27.151**

68. Plates—agricultural trailed appliances

(1) Save as provided in paragraph (3) below, every wheeled agricultural trailed appliance manufactured on or after 1st December 1985 shall be equipped with a plate affixed to the vehicle in a conspicuous and readily accessible position and which is clearly and indelibly marked with the particulars specified in paragraph (2) below.   **B27.152**

(2) Those particulars are—

  (a) the name of the manufacturer of the appliance;

  (b) the year in which the appliance was manufactured;

  (c) the maximum gross weight;

  (d) the unladen weight; and

  (e) the maximum load which would be imposed by the appliance on the drawing vehicle.

(3) In the case of a towed roller consisting of several separate rollers used in combination, a single plate shall satisfy the requirements specified in paragraph (2) above.

69. Plates—motor cycles

(1) This regulation applies to every motor cycle first used on or after 1st August 1977 which is not—   **B27.153**

  (a) propelled by an internal combustion engine with a cylinder capacity exceeding 150cc if the vehicle was first used before 1st January 1982 or 125cc if it was first used on or after 1st January 1982;

  (b) a mowing machine; or

  (c) a pedestrian-controlled vehicle.

(2) Every vehicle to which this regulation applies shall be equipped with a plate which is securely affixed to the vehicle in a conspicuous and readily accessible position and which complies with the requirements of Schedule 9.

70. Ministry plates

(1) Every goods vehicle to which the Plating and Testing Regulations apply and in respect of which a plating certificate has been issued shall, from the date specified in paragraph (2), be equipped with a Ministry plate securely affixed, so as to be legible at all times, in a conspicuous and readily accessible position, and in the cab of the vehicle if it has one.   **B27.154**

(2) That date is in the case of—

  (a) a vehicle to which the Type Approval for Goods Vehicles Regulations apply, the date of the fourteenth day after the plate was issued; or

  (b) any other vehicle, the date by which it is required, by the said Regulations, to be submitted for examination for plating.

[(3) In these Regulations "*Ministry plate*" means a plate which—

  (a) is issued by the Secretary of State following the issue or amendment of a plating certificate; and

  (b) subject to paragraph (4), contains the particulars required by Schedule 10, 10A, 10B or 10C.]

[(4) Instead of particulars of the gross weight, train weight and axle weights of the vehicle to which it relates, a Ministry plate may contain particulars of the maximum authorised weight for the vehicle, maximum authorised weight for a combination of which the vehicle forms part and maximum authorised axle weights for the vehicle, determined in accordance with the Road Vehicles (Authorised Weight) Regulations 1998 [*S.I. 1998 No. 3111, above*] and the form of the plate shall be amended accordingly.]

B27.155   *[Regulation 70 is printed as amended by S.I. 1998 No. 3112.]*

[70A. Speed limiters—plates

B27.156   [(1) This regulation applies to every vehicle to which regulation 36A or 36B applies and which is fitted with a speed limiter.

(2) Every vehicle to which this regulation applies shall be equipped with a plate which meets the requirements specified in paragraph (3).

(3) [Subject to regulation 36B(11A)] the requirements are that the plate is in a conspicuous position in the driving compartment of the vehicle and is clearly and indelibly marked with the speed at which the speed limiter has been set.]

B27.157   *[Regulation 70A was inserted by S.I. 1988 No. 271 and was later amended by S.I. 1988 No. 1524; S.I. 1992 No. 422; and substituted by S.I. 1993 No. 1946.*
The text of regulation 70A as printed above was substituted by S.I. 1993 No. 3048 and is printed as subsequently amended by S.I. 1996 No. 2064.]

[70B. Plate relating to dimensions

B27.158   (1) This regulation applies to a vehicle which is not a goods vehicle fitted in accordance with regulation 70 with a Ministry plate containing the particulars required by Schedule 10A or 10C and which is either—

     (a) a bus or a heavy motor car and which is manufactured after 31st May 1998; or

     (b) a trailer used in combination with a vehicle falling within paragraph (a) and manufactured after 31st May 1998.

(2) A vehicle to which this regulation applies shall not be used unless—

     (a) the vehicle is equipped with a plate securely attached to the vehicle in a conspicuous and readily accessible position and containing the particulars as to the dimensions of the vehicle specified in Annex III of Community Directive 96/53/EC [*q.v.*]; or

     (b) those particulars are included in the particulars shown on the plate with which the vehicle is equipped in accordance with regulation 66.]

B27.159   *[Regulation 70B was inserted by S.I. 1998 No. 1188.]*

71. Marking of weights on certain vehicles

B27.160   (1) This regulation applies to a vehicle (other than an agricultural motor vehicle which is either a track-laying vehicle not exceeding 3050kg in unladen weight or a wheeled vehicle) which is—

     (a) a locomotive;

     (b) a motor tractor;

     (c) [a bus] which is registered under [the 1994 Act] (or any enactment repealed thereby) . . . ; or

     (d) an unbraked wheeled trailer, other than one mentioned in [regulation 16(3)(b), (bb), (c), (d), (e), (f), or (g)].

(2) There shall be plainly marked in a conspicuous place on the outside of a vehicle to which this regulation applies, on its near side—

    (a) if it is a vehicle falling in paragraph (1)(a), (b) or (c), its unladen weight; and

    (b) if it is a vehicle falling in paragraph (1)(d), its maximum gross weight.

[Regulation 71 is printed as amended by S.I. 1990 No. 1981; S.I. 1994 No. 329; the Vehicle Excise   **B27.161**
and Registration Act 1994, s.64 and Sched. 4, para.4; S.I. 1996 No. 3033.]

[71A. Marking of date of manufacture of trailers

(1) This regulation applies to a trailer that—   **B27.162**

    (a) is not a motor vehicle;

    (b) is manufactured on or after 1st January 1997; and

    (c) has a maximum total design axle weight not exceeding 750kg.

(2) The year of manufacture of every trailer to which this regulation applies shall be marked on the chassis, frame or other similar structure on the nearside of the vehicle, in a clearly visible and accessible position, and by a method such as hammering or stamping, in such a way that it cannot be obliterated or deteriorate.]

[Regulation 71A was inserted by S.I. 1996 No. 3033.   **B27.163**
S.I. 1996 No. 3033 expressly states (regulation 2(2)) that so far as any requirement is imposed by it such requirement is imposed in exercise of powers conferred by section 41 of the Road Traffic Act 1988 to the exclusion of the powers under section 2(2) of the European Communities Act 1972.]

72. Additional markings

(1) This regulation applies to every goods vehicle to which the Plating and Testing   **B27.164**
Regulations apply and for which a plating certificate has been issued.

(2) Without prejudice to the provisions of regulation 70, any weight which by virtue of regulation 80 may not be exceeded in the case of a goods vehicle to which this regulation applies may be marked on either side, or on both sides, of the vehicle.

(3) Where at any time by virtue of any provision contained in regulation 75 a goods vehicle to which this regulation applies may not be used in excess of a weight which is less than the gross weight which may not be exceeded by that vehicle by virtue of regulation 80, the first mentioned weight may be marked on either side, or on both sides, of the vehicle.

(4) Where at any time by virtue of any provision contained in regulation 76 and 77 a goods vehicle to which this regulation applies is drawing, or being drawn by, another vehicle and those vehicles may not be used together in excess of a laden weight applicable to those vehicles by virtue of any such provision, that weight may be marked on either side, or on both sides, of that goods vehicle.

73. Test date discs

(1) Every Ministry test date disc which is issued, following the issue of a goods vehicle   **B27.165**
test certificate, in respect of a trailer to which the Plating and Testing Regulations apply and for which a plating certificate has been issued shall be carried on the trailer in a legible condition and in a conspicuous and readily accessible position in which it is clearly visible by daylight from the near side of the road, from the date of its issue until but not beyond the date of expiry of that test certificate or the date of issue of a further test certificate for that trailer, whichever date is the earlier.

(2) In this regulation "*Ministry test date disc*" means a plate issued by the Secretary of State for a goods vehicle, being a trailer, following the issue of a goods vehicle test certificate for

that trailer under the Plating and Testing Regulations and containing the following particulars—

    (a) the identification mark allotted to that trailer and shown in that certificate;

    (b) the date until which that certificate is valid; and

    (c) the number of the vehicle testing station shown in that certificate.

74. Testing and inspection

B27.166   (1) Subject to the conditions specified in paragraph (2), the following persons are hereby empowered to test and inspect the brakes, silencers, steering gear and tyres of any vehicle, on any premises where that vehicle is located—

    (a) a police constable in uniform;

    (b) a person appointed by the Commissioner of Police of the Metropolis to inspect public carriages for the purposes of the Metropolitan Public Carriage Act 1869;

    (c) a person appointed by the police authority for a police area to act for the purposes of [section 67 of the 1988 Act];

    (d) a goods vehicle examiner as defined in [section 68 of the 1988 Act];

    (e) a certifying officer as defined in section 7(1) of the 1981 Act; and

    (f) a public service vehicle examiner appointed as mentioned in section 7(2) of the 1981 Act.

    (2) Those conditions are—

    (a) any person empowered as there mentioned shall produce his authorisation if required to do so;

    (b) no such person shall enter any premises unless the consent of the owner of those premises has first been obtained;

    (c) no such person shall test or inspect any vehicle on any premises unless—

        (i) the owner of the vehicle consents thereto;

        (ii) notice has been given to that owner personally or left at his address not less than 48 hours before the time of the proposed test or inspection, or has been sent to him at least 72 hours before that time by the recorded delivery service to his address last known to the person giving the notice; or

        (iii) the test or inspection is made within 48 hours of an accident to which [section 170 of the 1988 Act] applies and in which the vehicle was involved.

    (3) For the purposes of this regulation, the owner of the vehicle shall be deemed to be in the case of a vehicle—

    (a) which is for the time being registered under [the 1994 Act], and is not being used under a trade licence under that Act the person appearing as the owner of the vehicle in the register kept by the Secretary of State under that Act;

    (b) used under a trade licence, the holder of the licence; or

    (c) exempt from excise duty by virtue of the Motor Vehicles (International Circulation) Order 1975 [*S.I. 1975 No. 1208 (q.v.)*], the person resident outside the United Kingdom who has brought the vehicle into Great Britain;

and in cases (a) and (b) the address of the owner as shown on the said register or, as the case may be, on the licence may be treated as his address.

B27.167   *[Regulation 74 is printed as amended by the Interpretation Act 1978, ss.17(2)(a) and 23(1); the Vehicle Excise and Registration Act 1994, s.64 and Sched. 4, para.4.]*

PART IV

CONDITIONS RELATING TO USE

A *Laden Weight*

75. Maximum permitted laden weight of a vehicle

(1) Save as provided in paragraph (2), the laden weight of the vehicle of a class specified **B27.168**
in an item in column 2 of the Table shall not exceed the maximum permitted laden weight
specified in that item in column 3.

(2) The maximum permitted laden weight of a vehicle first used before 1st June 1973
which falls in item 1 or 2 shall not be less than would be the case if the vehicle fell in item 9.

TABLE

(regulation 75(1))

1	2	3
Item	*Class of vehicle*	*Maximum permitted laden weight (kg)*
1	A wheeled heavy motor car or motor car which is not described in items [1A, 2], 4 or 5 and which complies with the relevant braking requirement [(see regulation 78(3) to (6) in relation to buses)]	[The weight determined in accordance with Part I of Schedule 11]
[1A	A wheeled heavy motor car or motor car which is not described in item 2, 4 or 5, which complies with the relevant braking requirement—and in which— (a) every driving axle not being a steering axle is fitted with twin tyres; and (b) either every driving axle is fitted with road friendly suspension or no axle has an axle weight exceeding 9,500 kg	The weight determined in accordance with Part IA of Schedule 11]
2	A wheeled heavy motor car or motor car (not being an agricultural motor vehicle) which forms part of an articulated vehicle and which complies with the relevant braking requirement	The weight specified in column (5) in Part II of Schedule 11 in the item which is appropriate having regard to columns (2), (3) and (4) in that Part
3	A wheeled trailer, including a composite trailer, but not including a semi-trailer, which is drawn by a motor tractor, heavy	As for item 1

[continued on next page

1	*2*	*3*
Item	*Class of vehicle*	*Maximum permitted laden weight (kg)*
3—*cont.*	motor car or motor car which complies with the relevant braking requirement, other than a trailer described in items 6, 7, 8 or 11	
[4	An articulated bus (see regulation 78(3) to (5))	27,000]
5	A wheeled agricultural motor vehicle	As for item 1, but subject to a maximum of 24,390
6	A balanced agricultural trailer, as defined in paragraph (4), which is not described in items 8, 11 or 16	As for item 1, but subject to a maximum of 18,290
7	An unbalanced agricultural trailer, as defined in paragraph (4), which is not described in items 8, 11 or 16	18,290 inclusive of the weight imposed by the trailer on the drawing vehicle
8	A wheeled trailer manufactured on or after 27th February 1977 and fitted with brakes which automatically come into operation on the over-run of the trailer (whether or not it is fitted with any other brake), except an agricultural trailer which is being drawn by an agricultural motor vehicle, which complies with the requirements specified in items 3, 14 and 17 of Schedule 3 and of which the brakes can be applied either by the driver of the drawing vehicle or by some other person on that vehicle or on the trailer	3,500
9	A wheeled heavy motor car or motor car not described in items 1, 2, 4 or 5—	
	(a) with not more than 4 wheels	14,230
	(b) with more than 4 but not more than 6 wheels	20,330
	(c) with more than 6 wheels	24,390
10	A wheeled trailer not described in items 3, 6, 7, 8 or 11 having less than 6 wheels, and not forming part of an articulated vehicle; and an agricultural trailed appliance	14,230

[*continued on next page*

1	2	3
Item	*Class of vehicle*	*Maximum permitted laden weight (kg)*
11	A trailer manufactured before 27th February 1977 and having no brakes other than— (i) a parking brake and (ii) brakes which come into operation on the over-run of the trailer	3,560
12	A wheeled locomotive, not described in item 5, which is equipped with suitable and sufficient springs between each wheel and the vehicle's frame and with a pneumatic tyre or a tyre of soft or elastic material fitted to each wheel— (a) if having less than 6 wheels (b) if having 6 wheels (c) if having more than 6 wheels	 22,360 26,420 30,490
13	A track-laying locomotive with resilient material interposed between the rims of the weight-carrying rollers and the road so that the weight of the vehicle (other than that borne by any wheels and the portion of the track in contact with the road) is supported by the resilient material	22,360
14	A locomotive not described in items 5, 12 or 13	20,830
15	A track-laying heavy motor car or motor car	22,360
16	A track-laying trailer	13,210

(3) The maximum total weight of all trailers, whether laden or unladen, drawn at any one time by a locomotive shall not exceed [44,000kg].

[(3A) Nothing in item 1 or 1A of the Table shall prevent a vehicle being used on a road if—

(a) a plating certificate in respect of the vehicle was in force immediately before the 1st January 1993; and

(b) the laden weight of the vehicle does not exceed the weight shown in that certificate as being the weight not to be exceeded in Great Britain.]

(4) [In this Part of these Regulations and in Schedule 11—]

["*air spring*" means a spring operated by means of air or other compressible fluid under pressure;]

["*air suspension*" means a suspension system in which at least 75 per cent of the spring effect is caused by an air spring;]

"*balanced agricultural trailer*" means an agricultural trailer the whole of the weight of which is borne by its own wheels; and

"*unbalanced agricultural trailer*" means an agricultural trailer of which some, but not more than 35 per cent, of the weight is borne by the drawing vehicle and the rest of the weight is borne by its own wheels.

[(5) For the purposes of this Part of these Regulations and Schedule 11, an axle shall be regarded as fitted with a road friendly suspension if its suspension is—

(a) an air suspension, or

(b) a suspension, not being an air suspension, which is regarded as being equivalent to an air suspension for the purposes of Community Directive 92/7.]

[(6) For the purposes of this Part of these Regulations and Schedule 11, an axle shall be regarded as fitted with twin tyres if it would be regarded as fitted with twin tyres for the purposes of Community Directive 92/7.]

B27.169   *[Regulation 75 is printed as amended by S.I. 1992 No. 2016; S.I. 1998 No. 3112.]*

76. Maximum permitted laden weight of a vehicle and trailer, other than an articulated vehicle

B27.170   (1) The total laden weight of a motor vehicle and the trailer or trailers (other than semi-trailers) drawn by it shall not, in a case specified in an item in column 2 of the Table, exceed the maximum permitted train weight specified in that item in column 3.

[(1A) This regulation is subject to Schedule 11A (exemptions relating to combined transport operations).]

[(2) In this regulation, the expressions "*road friendly suspension*", "*twin tyres*" and "*unbalanced agricultural trailer*" shall be construed in accordance with regulation 75(4), (5) and (6).]

TABLE

(regulation 76(1))

1	*2*	*3*
Item	*Vehicle combination*	*Maximum permitted laden weight (kg)*
[1	A wheeled trailer which is drawn by a wheeled motor tractor, heavy motor car (not being in any case an agricultural motor vehicle), where— (a) the combination has a total of 4 axles and is being used for international transport; and (b) the drawing vehicle is a vehicle which was first used on or after 1st April 1973 and complies with the relevant braking requirement	35,000]

[continued on next page

1	*2*	*3*
Item	*Class of vehicle*	*Maximum permitted laden weight (kg)*
[1A	A wheeled trailer which is drawn by a wheeled motor tractor, heavy motor car or motor car (not being in any case an agricultural motor vehicle), where the combination has a total of 4 axles and the following conditions are satisfied in relation to the drawing vehicle, namely— (a) it was first used on or after 1st April 1973; (b) it complies with the relevant braking requirement; (c) every driving axle not being a steering axle is fitted with twin tyres; and (d) every driving axle is fitted with road friendly suspension	35,000]
[1AA	A wheeled trailer which is drawn by a wheeled motor tractor, heavy motor car or motor car (not being in any case an agricultural motor vehicle), where the combination has a total of 5 or more axles and the following conditions are satisfied in relation to the drawing vehicle, namely— (a) it was first used on or after 1st April 1973; (b) it complies with the relevant braking requirement; (c) every driving axle not being a steering axle is fitted with twin tyres; and (d) either every driving axle is fitted with road friendly suspension or no axle has an axle weight exceeding 8,500kg	38,000]
[1B	A wheeled trailer, not being part of a combination described in items 1, 1A or 1AA which is drawn by a wheeled motor tractor heavy motor car or motor car (not being in any case an agricultural motor vehicle), where—	

[continued on next page

1	2	3
Item	*Class of vehicle*	*Maximum permitted laden weight (kg)*
[1B— *cont.*	(a) the trailer is fitted with power-assisted brakes which can be operated by the driver of the drawing vehicle and are not rendered ineffective by the non-rotation of its engine; and (b) the drawing vehicle is equipped with a warning device so placed as to be readily visible to the driver of the vehicle and which is capable of indicating any impending failure of, or deficiency in, the vacuum or pressure system	32,520]
1C	A wheeled trailer which is of a description specified in item 8 in the Table of regulation 75 drawn by a wheeled motor tractor, heavy motor car or motor car (not being in any case an agricultural motor vehicle), the drawing vehicle being a vehicle which— (a) was first used on or after 1st April 1973; and (b) complies with the relevant braking requirement	29,500
2	A wheeled agricultural motor vehicle drawing a wheeled unbalanced agricultural trailer, if the distance between the rearmost axle of the trailer and the rearmost axle of the drawing vehicle does not exceed 2.9m	20,000
3	A wheeled trailer or trailers drawn by a wheeled motor tractor, heavy motor car, motor car or agricultural motor vehicle, not being a combination of vehicles mentioned in items 1 [, 1A, [1AA,] 1B, 1C] or 2	24,390
4	A track-laying trailer drawn by a motor tractor, heavy motor car or motor car, whether wheeled or track-laying and a wheeled trailer, drawn by a track-laying vehicle being a motor tractor, heavy motor car or motor car	22,360

B27.171   *[Regulation 76 is printed as amended by S.I. 1992 No. 2016; S.I. 1994 No. 329.]*

77. Maximum permitted laden weight of an articulated vehicle

(1) Except as provided in paragraph (2), the laden weight of an articulated vehicle of a   **B27.172**
class specified in an item in column 2 of the Table shall not exceed the weight specified in
column 3 in that item.

TABLE
(regulation 77(1))

1	*2*	*3*
Item	Class of vehicle	Maximum permitted laden weight (kg)
1	An articulated vehicle which complies with the relevant braking requirement	Whichever is the lower of— (a) the weight specified in column (3) of Part III of Schedule 11 in the item in which the spacing between the rearmost axles of the motor vehicle and the semi-trailer is specified in column (2), . . . ; and (b) if the vehicle is of a description specified in an item in column (2) of Part IV of Schedule 11, the weight specified in column (3) of that item
2	An articulated vehicle which does not comply with the relevant braking requirement if the trailer has— (a) less than 4 wheels (b) 4 wheels or more	 20,330 24,390

(2) This regulation does not apply to an agricultural motor vehicle, an agricultural
trailer or an agricultural trailed appliance.

[(2A) This regulation is subject to Schedule 11A (exemptions relating to combined transport operations).]

[(3) In Part IV of Schedule 11, "*road friendly suspension*" and "*twin tyres*" shall be construed
in accordance with regulation 75(5) and (6).]

[Regulation 77 is printed as amended by S.I. 1992 No. 2016; S.I. 1994 No. 329.]   **B27.173**

78. Maximum permitted wheel and axle weights

(1) The weight transmitted to the road by one or more wheels of a vehicle as mentioned   **B27.174**
in an item in column 2 of the Table shall not exceed the maximum permitted weight
specified in that item in column 3.

(2) The Parts of the Table have the following application—

    (a) Part I applies to wheeled heavy motor cars, motor cars and trailers which comply
       with the relevant braking requirement and to wheeled agricultural motor vehicles,

agricultural trailers and agricultural trailed appliances; items 1(b) and 2 also apply to buses;

(b) Part II applies to wheeled heavy motor cars, motor cars and trailers which do not fall in Part I;

(c) Part III applies to wheeled locomotives; and

(d) Part IV applies to track-laying vehicles.

TABLE

(regulation 78(1))

PART I

(wheeled heavy motor cars, motor cars and trailers which comply with the relevant braking requirement and wheeled agricultural motor vehicles, agricultural trailers and agricultural trailed appliances; and, in respect of items 1(b) and 2, buses)

1	*2*	*3*
Item	*Wheel criteria*	*Maximum permitted weight (kg)*
1	Two wheels in line transversely each of which is fitted with a wide tyre or with two pneumatic tyres having the centres of their areas of contact with the road not less than 300mm apart, measured at right angles to the longitudinal axis of the vehicle—	
	(a) if the wheels are on the sole driving axle of a motor vehicle [not being a bus],	10,500
	(b) if the vehicle is a bus which has 2 axles and of which the weight transmitted to the road surface by its wheels is calculated in accordance with regulation 78(5),	10,500
	(c) in any other case	10,170
2	Two wheels in line transversely otherwise than as mentioned in item 1	9,200
3	More than two wheels in line transversely—	
	(a) in the case of a vehicle manufactured before 1st May 1983 [where] the wheels are on one axle of a group of . . . closely spaced axles . . .,	10,170
	(b) in the case of a vehicle manufactured on or after 1st May 1983,	10,170
	(c) in any other case	11,180

[*continued on next page*

1	2	3
Item	Wheel criteria	Maximum permitted weight (kg)
4	One wheel not transversely in line with any other wheel—	
	(a) if the wheel is fitted as described in item 1,	5,090
	(b) in any other case	4,600

Part II

(wheeled heavy motor cars, motor cars and trailers not falling in Part I)

1	2	3
Item	Wheel criteria	Maximum permitted weight (kg)
5	More than two wheels transmitting weight to a strip of the road surface on which the vehicle rests contained between two parallel lines at right angles to the longitudinal axis of the vehicle—	
	(a) less than 1.02m apart,	11,180
	(b) 1.02m or more apart but less than 1.22m apart,	16,260
	(c) 1.22m or more apart but less than 2.13m apart	18,300
6	Two wheels in line transversely	9,200
7	One wheel, where no other wheel is in the same line transversely	4,600

Part III

(wheeled locomotives)

1	2	3
Item	Wheel criteria	Maximum permitted weight (kg)
8	Two wheels in line transversely (except in the case of a road roller, or a vehicle with not more than four wheels first used before 1st June 1955)	11,180
9	Any two wheels in the case of a wheeled locomotive having not more than four wheels first used before 1st June 1955 (not being a road roller or an agricultural motor vehicle which is not driven at more than 20mph)	Three quarters of the total weight of the locomotive

PART IV

(track-laying vehicles)

1	2	3
Item	Wheel criteria	Maximum permitted weight (kg)
10	The weight of a heavy motor car, motor car or trailer transmitted to any strip of the road surface on which the vehicle rests contained between two parallel lines 0.6m apart at right angles to the longitudinal axis of the vehicle	10,170
11	Two wheels in line— (a) heavy motor cars or motor cars with 2 wheels, (b) heavy motor cars or motor cars with more than 2 wheels	8,130 7,630
12	One wheel, where no other wheel is in the same line transversely, on a heavy motor car or a motor car	4,070

(3) In the case of an articulated bus, or, subject to paragraph (4), of a bus first used before 1st April 1988, the laden weight, for the purposes of . . . regulation 75, and the weight transmitted to the road surface by wheels of the vehicle, for the purposes of items 1 and 2 of the Table in this regulation, shall be calculated with reference to the vehicle when it is complete and fully equipped for service with—

(a) a full supply of water, oil and fuel; and

(b) weights of 63.5kg for each person (including crew)—

(i) for whom a seat is provided in the position in which he may be seated; and

(ii) who may by or under any enactment be carried standing, the total of such weights being reasonably distributed in the space in which such persons may be carried, save that in the case of a bus (not being an articulated bus) only the number of such persons exceeding 8 shall be taken into account.

(4) The weights for the purposes referred to in paragraph (3) may, in the case of a bus to which that paragraph applies, be calculated in accordance with paragraph (5) instead of paragraph (3).

(5) In the case of a bus first used on or after 1st April 1988, the weights for the purposes referred to in paragraph (3) shall be calculated with reference to the vehicle when it is complete and fully equipped for service with—

(a) a full supply of water, oil and fuel;

(b) a weight of 65kg for each person (including crew)—

(i) for whom a seat is provided, in the position in which he may be seated; and

(ii) who may by or under any enactment be carried standing, the total of such weights being reasonably distributed in the space in which such persons may be so carried, save that in the case of a bus (not being an articulated bus) only the number of such persons exceeding 4 shall be taken into account;

(c) all luggage space within the vehicle but not with the passenger compartment loaded at the rate of 100kg per m³ or 10kg per person mentioned in sub-paragraph (b) above, whichever is the less; and

(d) any area of the roof of the vehicle constructed or adapted for the storage of luggage loaded with a uniformly distributed load at the rate of 75kg per m².

[(6) Regulation 75 shall not apply to a two axle bus if—

(a) its laden weight as calculated in accordance with paragraph (5) does not exceed 17,000kg; and

(b) the distance between the two axles is at least 3.0m.]

[Regulation 78 is printed as amended by S.I. 1987 No. 676; S.I. 1992 No. 2016.]   **B27.175**

79. Maximum permitted weights for certain closely spaced axles, etc.

(1) This regulation applies to—   **B27.176**

(a) a wheeled motor vehicle which complies with the relevant braking requirement;

(b) a wheeled trailer which is drawn by such a motor vehicle; and

(c) an agricultural motor vehicle, an agricultural trailer and an agricultural trailed appliance.

[(2) Save as provided in paragraph (5), where a vehicle to which this regulation applies is of a description specified in an item in column 2 of Part V of Schedule 11 and has two closely-spaced axles, the total weight transmitted to the road surface by all the wheels of those axles shall not exceed the maximum permitted weight specified in column 3 of that item.]

[(3) Save as provided in paragraph (5), where a vehicle to which this regulation applies is of a description specified in an item in column 2 of Part VI of Schedule 11 and has three closely-spaced axles, the total weight transmitted to the road surface by all the wheels of those axles shall not exceed the weight specified in column 3.]

[(4) Save as provided by paragraph (5), where a vehicle is fitted with four or more closely-spaced axles, the weight transmitted to the road surface by all the wheels of those axles shall not exceed 24,000kg.]

(5) Nothing in paragraphs (2), (3) or (4) of this regulation shall apply so as to prevent a vehicle first used before 1st June 1973 from being used on a road at a weight as respects those axles at which it could be used if it fell within item 5 in the Table in regulation 78 [and nothing in those paragraphs shall prevent a vehicle being used on a road if—

(a) a plating certificate in respect of the vehicle was in force immediately before the 1st January 1993; and

(b) no axle has an axle weight exceeding the weight shown in that certificate as being the weight not to be exceeded in Great Britain for that axle.]

[(6) In Parts V and VI of Schedule 11, *"air suspension"*, *"road friendly suspension"* and *"twin tyres"* shall be construed in accordance with regulation 75(4), (5) and (6).]

[(7) Paragraph (6) applies to a semi-trailer if—

(a) it has a total of three axles;

(b) the outermost axles are spaced at a distance apart of at least 0.7m but not more than 3.25m, such distances being obtained as provided in regulation 3(10);

(c) each axle is fitted with suspension devices in which air springs are used to support a substantial part of the weight borne on that axle; and

(d) the devices are so interconnected and maintained that under any relevant condition of load the weight transmitted to the road surface by all the wheels of any one axle does not exceed the total weight transmitted to the road surface by all the wheels of any other axle by more than 500kg.]

[(8) For the purposes of paragraphs (6) and (7), in relation to a semi-trailer any two adjoining axles of which are spaced at such a distance apart as is specified in an item in column 2 of Part VI of Schedule 11—

(a) *"air spring"* means a spring operated by means of air or other compressible fluid under pressure;

(b) *"relevant condition of load"* means a condition of load which causes the weight transmitted to the road surface by all the wheels of any one axle to exceed the weight shown in column 3 of that item;

(c) *"relevant weight"* means the weight shown in column 4 of that item.]

B27.177   *[Regulation 79 is printed as amended by S.I. 1988 No. 1287; S.I. 1992 No. 2016.]*

[79A. Saving for the Road Vehicles (Authorised Weight) Regulations 1998

B27.178   Nothing in regulations 75 to 79 shall be taken to prohibit the use of a vehicle in circumstances where the maximum authorised weight for the vehicle, for any vehicle combination of which the vehicle forms part and for any axle of the vehicle, as determined in accordance with the Road Vehicles (Authorised Weight) Regulations 1998 [*S.I. 1998 No. 3111 below*], is not exceeded.]

B27.179   *[Regulation 79A was inserted by S.I. 1998 No. 3112.]*

80. Over-riding weight restrictions

B27.180   (1) Subject to [paragraphs (2), (2A), (2B), (2C) and (4)], no person shall use, or cause or permit to be used, on a road a vehicle—

(a) fitted with a plate in accordance with regulation 66, but for which no plating certificate has been issued, if any of the weights shown on the plate is exceeded;

(b) for which a plating certificate has been issued, if any of the weights shown in column (2) of the plating certificate is exceeded; or

(c) required by regulation 68 to be fitted with a plate, if the maximum gross weight referred to in paragraph (2)(c) of that regulation is exceeded.

(2) Where any two or more axles are fitted with a compensating arrangement in accordance with regulation 23 the sum of the weights shown for them in the plating certificate shall not be exceeded. In a case where a plating certificate has not been issued the sum of the weights referred to shall be that shown for the said axles in the plate fitted in accordance with regulation 66.

[(2A) Paragraph (1) shall not apply to a vehicle for which a plating certificate has been issued in the form set out in Schedule 10A or 10C where—

(a) the vehicle is being used for international transport; and

(b) none of the weights shown in column (3) of the plating certificate is exceeded.]

[(2B) Where both a train weight and a maximum train weight are shown in column (2) of a plating certificate issued for a motor vehicle, paragraph (1)(b) in so far as it relates to train weights shall not apply to the motor vehicle if—

(a) the motor vehicle is a wheeled heavy motor car drawing a wheeled trailer and the requirements set out in Part II of Schedule 11A are for the time being fulfilled; or

(b) the motor vehicle is comprised in an articulated vehicle and the requirements set out in Part III of Schedule 11A are for the time being fulfilled,

and the train weight of the motor vehicle does not exceed the maximum train weight shown in column (2) of the certificate.]

(3) Nothing in regulations 75 to 79 [or in the Road Vehicles (Authorised Weight) Regulations 1998 [*S.I. 1998 No. 3111 below*]] shall permit any such weight as is mentioned in the preceding provisions of this regulation to be exceeded and nothing in this regulation shall permit any weight prescribed by regulations 75 to 79 [or in the Road Vehicles (Authorised Weight) Regulations 1998] in relation to the vehicle in question to be exceeded.

[(4) Paragraph (1) shall not apply where a vehicle is used on a road before 1st January 2000 if—

(a) the vehicle is fitted with a plate in accordance with regulation 66(1)(b) and the maximum gross weight and the maximum weight for any axle of the vehicle are not exceeded; or

(b) there is in force a plating certificate for the vehicle that was issued before 1st January 1999 and the design weight of the vehicle is not exceeded; and

(c) in either case the maximum authorised weight for the vehicle, maximum authorised weight for a combination of which the vehicle forms part and maximum authorised weight for any axle of the vehicle, determined in accordance with the Road Vehicles (Authorised Weight) Regulations 1998, are not exceeded.]

[Regulation 80 is printed as amended by S.I. 1994 No. 329; S.I. 1997 No. 1096; S.I. 1998 No. 3112.   **B27.181**
The reference to paragraph (2C) in regulation 80(1) seems to have been made in error. There is no provision designated as regulation 80(2C); a reference to paragraph (2C) was inserted by S.I. 1994 No. 329 and deleted by S.I. 1997 No. 1096; but a further amendment to regulation 80(1) (effected by S.I. 1998 No. 3112) seems to have been made on the basis that the reference to paragraph (2C) was extant, and renewed it.
Other than as stated, compliance with the Road Vehicles (Authorised Weight) Regulations 1998 (S.I. 1998 No. 3111 below) provides no defence to a contravention of this regulation; see S.I. 1998 No. 3111, reg.5(1) below. But as to the application of regulation 80 after January 1, 2002 to vehicles fitted with one or more retractable (or loadable) axles, see S.I. 1998 No. 3111, reg.5(2).]

B *Dimensions of Laden Vehicles*

81. Restrictions on use of vehicles carrying wide or long loads or having fixed appliances or apparatus

For the purpose of this regulation, regulation 82 and Schedule 12—   **B27.182**

(a) "*lateral projection*", in relation to a load carried by a vehicle, means that part of the load which extends beyond a side of the vehicle;

(b) the width of any lateral projection shall be measured between longitudinal planes passing through the extreme projecting point of the vehicle on that side on which the projection lies and the part of the projection furthest from that point;

(c) references to a special appliance or apparatus, in relation to a vehicle, are references to any crane or other special appliance or apparatus fitted to the vehicle which is a permanent or essentially permanent fixture;

(d) "*forward projection*" and "*rearward projection*"—

(i) in relation to a load carried in such a manner that its weight [is borne by] only one vehicle, mean respectively that part of the load which extends beyond the foremost point of the vehicle and that part which extends beyond the rearmost point of the vehicle;

    (ii) in relation to a load carried in such a manner that part of its weight [is borne by] more than one vehicle, mean respectively that part of the load which extends beyond the foremost point of the foremost vehicle by which the load is carried except where the context otherwise requires and that part of the load which extends beyond the rearmost point of the rearmost vehicle by which the load is carried; and

    (iii) in relation to any special appliance or apparatus, mean respectively that part of the appliance or apparatus which, if it were deemed to be a load carried by the vehicle, would be a part of a load extending beyond the foremost point of the vehicle and that part which would be a part of a load extending beyond the rearmost point of the vehicle,

and references in regulation 82 and Schedule 12 to a forward projection or to a rearward projection in relation to a vehicle shall be construed accordingly;

(e) the length of any forward projection or of any rearward projection shall be measured between transverse planes passing—

    (i) in the case of a forward projection, through the foremost point of the vehicle and that part of the projection furthest from that point; and

    (ii) in the case of a rearward projection, through the rearmost point of the vehicle and that part of the projection furthest from that point.

In this and the foregoing sub-paragraph "*vehicle*" does not include any special appliance or apparatus or any part thereof which is a forward projection or a rearward projection;

(f) references to the distance between vehicles, in relation to vehicles carrying a load, are references to the distance between the nearest points of any two adjacent vehicles by which the load is carried, measured when the longitudinal axis of each vehicle lies in the same vertical plane.

    For the purposes of this sub-paragraph, in determining the nearest point of two vehicles any part of either vehicle designed primarily for use as a means of attaching the one vehicle to the other and any fitting designed for use in connection with any such part shall be disregarded;

(g) references to a combination of vehicles, in relation to a motor vehicle which is drawing one or more trailers, are references to the motor vehicle and the trailer or trailers drawn thereby, including any other motor vehicle which is used for the purpose of assisting in the propulsion of the trailer or the trailers on the road;

(h) the overall length of a combination of vehicles shall be taken as the distance between the foremost point of the drawing vehicle comprised in the combination and the rearmost point of the rearmost vehicle comprised therein, measured when the longitudinal axis of each vehicle comprised in the combination lies in the same vertical plane;

(i) the extreme projecting point of a vehicle is the point from which the overall width of the vehicle is calculated in accordance with the definition of overall width contained in regulation 3(2);

(j) without prejudice to sub-paragraph (e) the foremost or, as the case may be, the rearmost point of a vehicle is the foremost or rearmost point from which the overall length of the vehicle is calculated in accordance with the definition of overall length contained in regulation 3(2); and

(k) an agricultural, horticultural or forestry implement rigidly but not permanently mounted on an agricultural motor vehicle, agricultural trailer or agricultural trailed appliance, whether or not part of its weight is supported by one or more of its own wheels, shall not be treated as a load, or special appliance, on that vehicle.

82.—(1) No load shall be carried on a vehicle so that the overall width of the   B27.184
vehicle together with the width of any lateral projections or projection of its load exceeds
4.3m.

(2) Subject to the following provisions of this regulation, no load shall be carried on a
vehicle so that—

    (a) the load has a lateral projection or projections on either side exceeding 305mm; or

    (b) the overall width of the vehicle and of any lateral projection or projections of its
        load exceeds 2.9m.

Provided that this paragraph does not apply to the carriage of—

    (i) loose agricultural produce not baled or crated; or

    (ii) an indivisible load if—

        (A) it is not reasonably practicable to comply with this paragraph and the
            conditions specified in [paragraphs 1 and 5] of Schedule 12 are com-
            plied with; and

        (B) where the overall width of the vehicle together with the width of any
            lateral projection or projections of its loads exceeds 3.5m, the conditions
            specified in paragraph 2 of Schedule 12 are complied with.

(3) Where a load is carried so that its weight rests on a vehicle or vehicles, the length
specified in paragraph (5) shall not exceed 27.4m.

[(4) A load shall not be carried so that its weight is borne by a vehicle or vehicles if
either—

    (a) the length specified in paragraph (5) exceeds 18.65m; or

    (b) the load is borne by a trailer or trailers and the length specified in paragraph (6)
        exceeds 25.9m,

unless the conditions specified in paragraphs 1 and 2 of Part I of Schedule 12 are complied
with.]

(5) The length referred to in paragraphs (3) and (4)(a) is—

    (a) where the [weight of the load is borne by] a single vehicle, the overall length of the
        vehicle together with the length of any forward and rearward projection of the
        load;

    (b) where the [weight of the load is borne by] a motor vehicle and one trailer, whether
        or not forming an articulated vehicle, the overall length of the trailer together with
        the length of any projection of the load in front of the foremost point of the trailer
        and of any rearward projection of the load; and

    (c) in any other case, the overall length of all the vehicles [which bear the weight of
        the load], together with the length of any distance between them and of any
        forward or rearward projection of the load.

(6) The length referred to in paragraph (4)(b) is the overall length of the combination of
vehicles, together with the length of any forward or rearward projection of the load.

(7) Subject to the following provisions of this regulation no person shall use, or cause or
permit to be used, on a road a vehicle, not being a straddle carrier, carrying a load or fitted
with a special appliance or apparatus if the load, appliance or apparatus has a forward projection of a length specified in an item in column 2 of the Table, or rearward projection of
a length specified in an item in column 3, unless the conditions specified in that item in
column 4 are complied with.

TABLE

(regulation 82(7))

1	2	3	4	
Item	*Length of forward projection*	*Length of rearward projection*	*Conditions to be complied with*	
			(a) if the load consists of a racing boat propelled solely by oars	(b) in any other case
1	Exceeding 1m but not exceeding 2m	—	Para 4 of Schedule 12	—
2	Exceeding 2m but not exceeding 3.05m	—	Para 4 of Schedule 12	Paras 2 and 3 of Schedule 12
3	Exceeding 3.05m	—	Paras 1 and 4 of Schedule 12	Paras 1, 2 and 3 of Schedule 12
4	—	Exceeding 1m but not exceeding 2m	Para 4 of Schedule 12	Para 4 of Schedule 12
5	—	Exceeding 2m but not exceeding 3.05m	Para 4 of Schedule 12	Para 3 of Schedule 12
6	—	Exceeding 3.05m	Paras 1 and 4 of Schedule 12	Paras 1, 2 and 3 of Schedule 12

(8) Subject to the following provisions of this regulation, no person shall use, or cause or permit to be used, on a road a straddle carrier carrying a load if—

(a) the load has a rearward projection exceeding 1m unless the conditions specified in paragraph 4 of Schedule 12 are met;

(b) the load has a forward projection exceeding 2m or a rearward projection exceeding 3m; or

(c) the overall length of the vehicle together with the length of any forward projection and of any rearward projection of its load exceeds 12.2m;

Provided that—

(i) sub-paragraph (a) does not apply to a vehicle being used in passing from one part of private premises to another part thereof or to other private premises in the immediate neighbourhood;

(ii) sub-paragraphs (b) and (c) do not apply to a vehicle being used as in proviso (i) above if—

(A) the vehicle is not being driven at a speed exceeding 12mph; and

(B) where the overall length of the vehicle together with the length of any forward projection and of any rearward projection of its load exceeds 12.2m, the conditions specified in paragraphs 1 and 2 of Schedule 12 are complied with.

(9) Where another vehicle is attached to that end of a vehicle from which a projection extends, then for the purposes of any requirement in this regulation to comply with paragraph 3 or 4 of Schedule 12, that projection shall be treated as a forward or rearward projection only if, and to the extent that it extends beyond the foremost point or, as the case may be, the rearmost point, of that other vehicle, measured when the longitudinal axis of each vehicle lies in the same vertical plane.

(10) In the case of a vehicle being used—

(a) for fire brigade, ambulance or police purposes or for defence purposes (including civil defence purposes); or

(b) in connection with the removal of any obstruction to traffic,

if compliance with any provision of this regulation would hinder or be likely to hinder the use of the vehicle for the purpose for which it is being used, that provision does not apply to that vehicle while it is being so used.

(11) No person shall use, or cause or permit to be used, on a road an agricultural, horticultural or forestry implement rigidly, but not permanently, mounted on a wheeled agricultural motor vehicle, agricultural trailer, or agricultural trailed appliance, whether or not part of its weight is supported by one or more of its own wheels if—

(a) the overall width of the vehicle together with the lateral projection of the implement exceeds [2.55]m; or

(b) the implement projects more than 1m forwards or rearwards of the vehicle,

so however, that this restriction shall not apply in a case where—

(i) part of the weight of the implement is supported by one or more of its own wheels; and

(ii) the longitudinal axis of the greater part of the implement is capable of articulating in the horizontal plane in relation to the longitudinal axis of the rear portion of the vehicle.

[Regulation 82 is printed as amended by S.I. 1991 No. 2125; S.I. 1995 No. 3051.]   **B27.185**

C *Trailers and Sidecars*

83. Number of trailers   **B27.186**

(1) No person shall use, or cause or permit to be used, on a road a wheeled vehicle of a class specified in an item in column 2 of the Table drawing a trailer, subject to any exceptions which may be specified in that item in column 3.

TABLE

(regulation 83(1))

1	*2*	*3*
Item	*Class of vehicles*	*Exceptions*
1	A straddle carrier	—
2	An invalid carriage	—
3	An articulated bus	—

[continued on next page

1	*2*	*3*
Item	*Class of vehicles*	*Exceptions*
4	A bus not being an articulated bus or a mini-bus	(a) 1 broken down bus where no person other than the driver is carried in either vehicle or [(b) 1 trailer]
5	A locomotive	3 trailers
6	A motor tractor	[1 trailer] 2 trailers if neither is laden
7	A heavy motor car or a motor car not described in items 1, 3 or 4	2 trailers if one of them is a towing implement and part of the other is secured to and either rests on or is suspended from that implement 1 trailer in any other case
8	An agricultural motor vehicle	(a) in respect of trailers other than agricultural trailers and agricultural trailed appliances, such trailers as are permitted under items 5, 6 or 7 above, as the case may be; or (b) in respect of agricultural trailers and agricultural trailed appliances— (i) 2 unladen agricultural trailers, or (ii) 1 agricultural trailer and 1 agricultural trailed appliance, or (iii) 2 agricultural trailed appliances

(2) For the purposes of items 5, 6 and 7 of the Table—

   (a) an unladen articulated vehicle, when being drawn by another motor vehicle because it has broken down, shall be treated as a single trailer; and

   (b) a towed roller used for the purposes of agriculture, horticulture or forestry and consisting of several separate rollers shall be treated as one agricultural trailed appliance.

(3) No track-laying motor vehicle which exceeds 8m in overall length shall draw a trailer other than a broken down vehicle which is being drawn in consequence of the breakdown.

[(4) For the purpose of this regulation, the word "*trailer*" does not include a vehicle which is drawn by a steam powered vehicle and which is used solely for carrying water for the purpose of the drawing vehicle.]

B27.187   *[Regulation 83 is printed as amended by S.I. 1987 No. 676; S.I. 1989 No. 2360.]*

84. Trailers drawn by motor cycles

B27.188   (1) Save as provided in paragraph (2), no person shall use, or cause or permit to be used, on a road a motor cycle—

(a) drawing behind it more than one trailer;

(b) drawing behind it any trailer carrying a passenger;

(c) drawing behind it a trailer with an unladen weight exceeding 254kg;

(d) with not more than 2 wheels, without a sidecar, and with an engine capacity which does not exceed 125cc, drawing behind it any trailer; or

(e) with not more than 2 wheels, without a sidecar and with an engine capacity exceeding 125cc, drawing behind it any trailer unless—

    (i) the trailer has an overall width not exceeding 1m;

    (ii) the distance between the rear axle of the motor cycle and the rearmost part of the trailer does not exceed 2.5m;

    (iii) the motor cycle is clearly and indelibly marked in a conspicuous and readily accessible position with its kerbside weight;

    (iv) the trailer is clearly and indelibly marked in a conspicuous and readily accessible position with its unladen weight; and

    (v) the laden weight of the trailer does not exceed 150kg or two-thirds of the kerbside weight of the motor cycle, whichever is the less.

(2) The provisions of paragraph (1)(b), (d) and (e) do not apply if the trailer is a broken down motor cycle and one passenger is riding it.

85. Trailers drawn by agricultural motor vehicles

(1) No person shall use, or cause or permit to be used, on a road a wheeled agricultural motor vehicle drawing one or more wheeled trailers if the weight of the drawing vehicle is less than a quarter of the weight of the trailer or trailers, unless the brakes fitted to each trailer in compliance with regulation 15 or 16 are operated directly by the service braking systems fitted to the motor vehicle. **B27.189**

(2) No person shall use, or cause or permit to be used, on a road any motor vehicle drawing an agricultural trailer of which—

(a) more than 35 per cent of the weight is borne by the drawing vehicle; or

(b) the gross weight exceeds 14,230kg, unless it is fitted with brakes as mentioned in paragraph (1).

(3) No person shall use, or cause or permit to be used, on a road an agricultural trailer manufactured on or after 1st December 1985 which is drawn by a motor vehicle first used on or after 1st June 1986 unless the brakes fitted to the trailer—

(a) in accordance with regulation 15 can be applied progressively by the driver of the drawing vehicle, from his normal driving position and while keeping proper control of that vehicle, using a means of operation mounted on the drawing vehicle; or

(b) automatically come into operation on the over-run of the trailer.

86. Distance between motor vehicles and trailers

(1) Where a trailer is attached to the vehicle immediately in front of it solely by means of a rope or chain, the distance between the trailer and that vehicle shall not in any case exceed 4.5m; and shall not exceed 1.5m unless the rope or chain is made clearly visible to any other person using the road within a reasonable distance from either side. **B27.190**

(2) For the purpose of determining the said distance any part of either vehicle designed primarily for use as a means of attaching the one vehicle to the other and any fitting designed for use in connection with any such part shall be disregarded.

[86A. Use of secondary coupling on trailers

B27.191   (1) No person shall use or cause or permit to be used on a road a motor vehicle drawing one trailer if the trailer—

     (a) is a trailer to which regulation 15 applies; and

     (b) is not fitted with a device which is designed to stop the trailer automatically in the event of the separation of the main coupling while the trailer is in motion,

unless the requirements of paragraph (2) are met in relation to the motor vehicle and trailer.

(2) The requirements of this paragraph, in relation to a motor vehicle drawing a trailer, are that a secondary coupling is attached to the motor vehicle and trailer in such a way that, in the event of the separation of the main coupling while the trailer is in motion,—

     (a) the drawbar of the trailer would be prevented from touching the ground; and

     (b) there would be some residual steering of the trailer.

(3) No person shall use or cause or permit to be used on a road a motor vehicle drawing one trailer if—

     (a) the trailer is a trailer to which regulation 15 applies;

     (b) the trailer is fitted with a device which is designed to stop the trailer automatically in the event of the separation of the main coupling while the trailer is in motion;

     (c) the operation of the device in those circumstances depends upon a secondary coupling linking the device to the motor vehicle; and

     (d) the trailer is not also fitted with a device which is designed to stop the trailer automatically in those circumstances in the absence of such a secondary coupling,

unless the requirements of paragraph (4) are met in relation to the motor vehicle and trailer.

(4) The requirements of this paragraph, in relation to a motor vehicle drawing a trailer, are that the secondary coupling is attached to the motor vehicle and trailer in such a way that, in the event of the separation of the main coupling while the trailer is in motion, the device of the kind referred to in paragraph (3)(b) and (c) fitted to the trailer would stop the trailer.

(5) This regulation is without prejudice to any other provision in these Regulations.]

B27.192   *[Regulation 86A was inserted by S.I. 1995 No. 1201.]*

[86B. Use of mechanical coupling devices

B27.193   (1) This regulation applies to every light passenger vehicle first used on or after 1st August 1998 in respect of which an EC certificate of conformity has effect.

(2) No person shall use or cause or permit to be used on a road any vehicle to which this regulation applies unless any mechanical coupling device which is attached to it complies with the relevant technical and installation requirements of Annexes I, V, VI and VII of Community Directive 94/20 [*O.J. No. L195, July 29, 1994, p. 1*] and is marked in accordance with sub-paragraphs 3.3.4 to 3.3.5 of Annex I to that Directive.

(3) For the purposes of this regulation, in a case where a vehicle is drawing a trailer a mechanical coupling device shall not be regarded as being attached to that vehicle if it forms part of the trailer.

(4) In this regulation *"mechanical coupling device"* shall be construed in accordance with paragraph 2.1 of Annex I to Community Directive 94/20.]

[Regulation 86B was inserted by S.I. 1998 No. 1281.]   **B27.194**

87. Unbraked trailers

(1) Save as provided in paragraph (2), no person shall use, or cause or permit to be used, on a road an unbraked wheeled trailer if—   **B27.195**

(a) its laden weight exceeds its maximum gross weight; or

(b) it is drawn by a vehicle of which the kerbside weight is less than twice the sum of the unladen weight of the trailer and the weight of any load which the trailer is carrying.

(2) This regulation does not apply to—

(a) an agricultural trailer; or

(b) a trailer mentioned in [paragraph (b), (bb), (bc), (c), (d), (e), (f) or (g) of regulation 16(3)].

[Regulation 87 is printed as amended by S.I. 1987 No. 676; S.I. 1996 No. 3033.]   **B27.196**

88. Use of bridging plates between motor vehicle and trailer   *[Revoked by*   **B27.197**
S.I. 1998 No. 2429.]

89. Leaving trailers at rest

No person in charge of a motor vehicle, or trailer drawn thereby, shall cause or permit such trailer to stand on a road when detached from the drawing vehicle unless one at least of the wheels of the trailer is (or, in the case of a track-laying trailer, its tracks are) prevented from revolving by the setting of [a parking brake] or the use of a chain, chock or other efficient device.   **B27.198**

[Regulation 89 is printed as amended by S.I. 1996 No. 3033.]   **B27.199**

90. Passengers in trailers

(1) Save as provided in paragraph (2), no person shall use, or cause or permit to be used, on a road any trailer for the carriage of passengers for hire or reward.   **B27.200**

(2) The provisions of paragraph (1) do not apply in respect of a wheeled trailer which is, or is carrying, a broken down motor vehicle if—

(a) the trailer is drawn at a speed not exceeding 30mph; and

(b) where the trailer is, or is carrying, a broken down bus, it is attached to the drawing vehicle by a rigid draw bar.

(3) Save as provided in paragraph (4), no person shall use, or cause or permit to be used, on a road a wheeled trailer in which any person is carried and which is a living van having either—

(a) less than 4 wheels; or

(b) 4 wheels consisting of two close-coupled wheels on each side.

(4) The provisions of paragraph (3) do not apply in respect of a trailer which is being tested by—

(a) its manufacturer;

(b) a person by whom it has been, or is being, repaired; or

(c) a distributor of, or dealer in, trailers.

B27.201   **91. Attendance on trailers and certain other vehicles**   *[Revoked by the Road Traffic (Consequential Provisions) Act 1988.]*

92. Attachment of sidecars

B27.202   Every sidecar fitted to a motor cycle shall be so attached that the wheel thereof is not wholly outside the space between transverse planes passing through the extreme projecting points at the front and at the rear of the motor cycle.

93. Use of sidecars

B27.203   No person shall use or cause or permit to be used on a road any two-wheeled motor cycle registered on or after 1st August 1981, not being a motor cycle brought temporarily into Great Britain by a person resident abroad, if there is a sidecar attached to the right (or off) side of the motor cycle.

[CA *Use of Motor Vehicles for the Carriage or Haulage of Dangerous Goods*]

[93A. Additional braking requirements for motor vehicles carrying or hauling dangerous goods

B27.204   (1) Subject to paragraph (5), no person shall use or cause or permit to be used a motor vehicle for the carriage or haulage of dangerous goods on a road if it is a vehicle within the meaning of the Framework Directive and—

    (a) its maximum gross weight exceeds 16,000kg; or

    (b) it is drawing a trailer which has a maximum total design axle weight exceeding 10,000kg,

unless the vehicle meets the requirements of paragraph (2).

(2) Subject to paragraph (6), in order for a motor vehicle to meet the requirements of this paragraph—

    (a) it must not be drawing more than one trailer;

    (b) without prejudice to regulation 15, it must be fitted with an anti-lock braking system that meets the requirements of paragraph (1) of marginal 220 521 of Appendix B.2 to Annex B to the ADR;

    (c) it must be fitted with an endurance braking system (which may consist of one device or a combination of several devices) that meets the requirements of sub-paragraphs (a) to (d) of paragraph (2) of marginal 220 522 of Appendix B.2 to Annex B to the ADR;

    (d) if it is not drawing a trailer, it must meet the requirements of the 4th, 5th, 6th and 7th sub-paragraphs of paragraph (2) of marginal 10 221 of Annex B to the ADR;

    (e) without prejudice to regulation 15, if it is drawing a trailer with a maximum total design axle weight exceeding 10,000kg—

        (i) the trailer must be fitted with an anti-lock braking system that meets the requirements of paragraph (2) of marginal 220 521 of Appendix B.2 to Annex B to the ADR, and

        (ii) the electrical connections between the motor vehicle and the trailer must meet the requirements of paragraph (3) of marginal 220 521 of Appendix B.2 to Annex B to the ADR;

    (f) if it is drawing a trailer, the combination of vehicles must meet the requirements of the 4th, 5th, 6th and 7th sub-paragraphs of paragraph (2) of marginal 10 221 of Annex B to the ADR;

(g) if it is drawing a trailer fitted with an endurance braking system, the trailer must meet the requirements of paragraph (3) of marginal 220 522 of Appendix B.2 to Annex B to the ADR; and

(h) if it is drawing a trailer, the requirements of either paragraph (3) or (4) must be met.

(3) The requirements of this paragraph are that the motor vehicle meets the requirements of paragraph (2)(e) of marginal 220 522 of Appendix B.2 to Annex B to the ADR.

(4) The requirements of this paragraph are that the motor vehicle—

(a) does not contravene the restriction mentioned in sub-paragraph (f) of paragraph (2) of marginal 220 522 of Appendix B.2 to Annex B to the ADR; and

(b) meets the requirements of the second sentence of that sub-paragraph in relation to the trailer.

(5) Paragraph (1) does not apply to a motor vehicle manufactured before 1st January 1997.

(6) Sub-paragraph (e) of paragraph (2) does not apply to a trailer manufactured before 1st January 1997.

(7) For the purposes of this regulation, Annex B to the ADR (including the Appendices to that Annex) shall have effect as if—

(a) references to ECE Regulation 13 (however expressed) were references to ECE Regulation 13.06 or 13.07;

(b) references to Directive 71/320/EEC [*O.J. No. L202, September 6, 1971, p. 37*] were references to Community Directive 91/422 [*O.J. No. L233, September 22, 1991, p. 21*];

(c) references to the corresponding EEC Directive, an relation to Annex 5 to ECE Regulation 13, were references to paragraph 1.5 of Annex II to Community Directive 91/422.

(8) Subject to paragraph (9), a reference in this regulation to dangerous goods is a reference to a load comprising explosives of such type and in such quantity that it could not be carried by road in a single transport unit of Type I and II without there being a contravention of the restrictions set out in marginal 11 401 of Annex B to the ADR as read with marginal 11 402 of that Annex.

(9) For the purposes of paragraph (8)—

(a) marginal 11 402 of Annex B to the ADR shall have effect with the omission of the words "in conformity with the prohibitions of mixed loading contained in 11 403"; and

(b) "*transport unit of Type I or II*" means a transport unit of Type I or a transport unit of Type II as defined in marginal 11 204 of that Annex.

(10) In this regulation, "*ADR*" means the 1995 edition of the "European Agreement concerning the International Carriage of Dangerous Goods by Road (ADR)" produced by the Department of Transport and published by Her Majesty's Stationery Office (ISBN 0-11-551265-9).]

[Regulation 93A was inserted by S.I. 1996 No. 3133.   **B27.205**
The 1995 edition of the ADR (see regulation 93A(10)) has been superseded. See now the consolidated text (July 1, 2001) published by the United Nations (ISBN 92 113 9069 9) and available from the Stationery Office. It is understood that the Department of Transport, Local Government and the Regions will not produce further editions of the ADR.]

94. Use of gas propulsion systems

B27.206   (1) No person shall use, or cause or permit to be used, on a road a vehicle with a gas propulsion system unless the whole of such system is in a safe condition.

(2) No person shall use, or cause or permit to be used, in any gas supply system for the propulsion of a vehicle when the vehicle is on a road any fuel except liquefied petroleum gas.

(3) No person shall use, or cause or permit to be used, on a road a vehicle which is propelled by gas unless the gas container in which such fuel is stored is on the motor vehicle, and not on any trailer, and in the case of an articulated vehicle on the portion of the vehicle to which the engine is fitted.

(4) In this regulation and in regulation 95 *"liquefied petroleum gas"* means—

  (a) butane gas in any phase which meets the requirements contained in the specification of commercial butane and propane issued by the British Standards Institution under the number BS4250:1975 published on 29th August 1975; or

  (b) propane gas in any phase which meets the requirements contained in the said specification; or

  (c) any mixture of such butane gas and such propane gas.

95. Use of gas-fired appliances—general

B27.207   (1) No person shall use, or cause or permit to be used, in or on a vehicle on a road any gas-fired appliance unless the whole of such appliance and the gas system attached thereto is in an efficient and safe condition.

(2) No person shall use, or cause or permit to be used, in any gas-fired appliance in or on a vehicle on a road any fuel except liquefied petroleum gas as defined in regulation 94(4).

(3) No person shall use, or cause or permit to be used, in or on a vehicle on a road any gas-fired appliance unless the vehicle is so ventilated that—

  (a) an ample supply of air is available for the operation of the appliance;

  (b) the use of the appliance does not adversely affect the health or comfort of any person using the vehicle; and

  (c) any unburnt gas is safely disposed of to the outside of the vehicle.

(4) No person shall use, or cause or permit to be used, on a road a vehicle in or on which there is—

  (a) one gas-fired appliance unless the gas supply for such appliance is shut off at the point where it leaves the container or containers at all times when the appliance is not in use;

  (b) more than one gas-fired appliance each of which has the same supply of gas unless the gas supply for such appliances is shut off at the point where it leaves the container or containers at all times when none of such appliances is in use; or

  (c) more than one gas-fired appliance each of which does not have the same supply of gas unless each gas supply for such appliances is shut off at the point where it leaves the container or containers at all times when none of such appliances which it supplies is in use.

96. Use of gas-fired appliances when a vehicle is in motion

(1) Subject to paragraph (2), this regulation applies to every motor vehicle and trailer.   **B27.208**

(2) Paragraphs (3) and (4) do not apply to a vehicle constructed or adapted for the conveyance of goods under controlled temperatures.

(3) No person shall use, or cause or permit to be used, in any vehicle to which this paragraph applies, while the vehicle is in motion on a road, any gas-fired appliance except—

(a) a gas-fired appliance which is fitted to engineering plant while the plant is being used for the purposes of the engineering operations for which it was designed;

(b) a gas-fired appliance which is permanently attached to a bus, provided that any appliance for heating or cooling the interior of the bus for the comfort of the driver and any passengers does not expose a naked flame on the outside of the appliance; or

(c) in any other vehicle, a refrigerating appliance or an appliance which does not expose a naked flame on the outside of the appliance and which is permanently attached to the vehicle and designed for the purpose of heating any part of the interior of the vehicle for the comfort of the driver and any passengers.

(4) No person shall use, or cause or permit to be used, in any vehicle to which this paragraph applies, while the vehicle is in motion on a road, any gas-fired appliance to which—

(a) sub-paragraph (3)(a) refers, unless the appliance complies with the requirements specified in paragraphs 12 and 13 of Schedule 5 and the gas system to which it is attached complies with the requirements specified in paragraphs 2 to 9 and 15 of Schedule 5; or

(b) sub-paragraph (3)(b) refers, unless the appliance complies with the requirements specified in paragraphs 12, 13 and 14 of Schedule 5 and the gas system to which it is attached complies with the requirements specified in paragraphs 2 to 9, 11 and 15 of Schedule 5; or

(c) sub-paragraph (3)(c) refers, unless the appliance complies—

(i) if it is fitted to a motor vehicle, with the requirements specified in paragraphs 12, 13 and 14 of Schedule 5; and

(ii) in any other case, with the requirements specified in paragraphs 12 and 13 of Schedule 5;

and the gas system to which the appliance is attached complies with the requirements specified in paragraphs 2 to 9 and 15 of Schedule 5.

(5) No person shall use, or cause or permit to be used, in a vehicle to which this regulation applies which is in motion on a road any gas-fired appliance unless it is fitted with a valve which stops the supply of gas to the appliance if the appliance fails to perform its function and causes gas to be emitted.

E *Control of Noise*

97. Avoidance of excessive noise

No motor vehicle shall be used on a road in such manner as to cause any excessive   **B27.209**
noise which could have been avoided by the exercise of reasonable care on the part of the driver.

98. Stopping of engine when stationary

B27.210   (1) Save as provided in paragraph (2), the driver of a vehicle shall, when the vehicle is stationary, stop the action of any machinery attached to or forming part of the vehicle so far as may be necessary for the prevention of noise [or of exhaust emissions].

(2) The provisions of paragraph (1) do not apply—

(a) when the vehicle is stationary owing to the necessities of traffic;

(b) so as to prevent the examination or working of the machinery where the examination is necessitated by any failure or derangement of the machinery or where the machinery is required to be worked for a purpose other than driving the vehicle; or

(c) in respect of a vehicle propelled by gas produced in plant carried on the vehicle, to such plant.

B27.211   *[Regulation 98 is printed as amended by S.I. 1998 No. 1.*

As to the issue of fixed penalty notices for contraventions of this regulation, see the Road Traffic (Vehicle Emissions) (Fixed Penalty) Regulations 1997 (S.I. 1997 No. 3058) below.]

99. Use of audible warning instruments

B27.212   (1) Subject to the following paragraphs, no person shall sound, or cause or permit to be sounded, any horn, gong, bell or siren fitted to or carried on a vehicle which is—

(a) stationary on a road, at any time, other than at times of danger due to another moving vehicle on or near the road; or

(b) in motion on a restricted road, between 23.30 hours and 07.00 hours in the following morning.

(2) The provisions of paragraph (1)(a) do not apply in respect of the sounding of a reversing alarm when the vehicle to which it is fitted is about to move backwards and its engine is running [or in respect of the sounding of a boarding aid alarm.]

(3) No person shall sound, or cause or permit to be sounded, on a road any reversing alarm [or any boarding aid alarm] fitted to a vehicle—

(a) unless the vehicle is a goods vehicle which has a maximum gross weight not less than 2000kg, a bus, engineering plant, [a refuse vehicle,] or a works truck; or

(b) if the sound of the alarm is likely to be confused with a sound emitted in the operation of a pedestrian crossing established, or having effect as if established, under Part III of the 1984 Act.

(4) Subject to the provisions of the following paragraphs, no person shall sound, or cause or permit to be sounded a gong, bell, siren or two-tone horn, fitted to or otherwise carried on a vehicle (whether it is stationary or not).

(5) Nothing in paragraph (1) or (4) shall prevent the sounding of—

(a) an instrument or apparatus fitted to, or otherwise carried on, a vehicle at a time when the vehicle is being used for one of the purposes specified in regulation 37(5) and it is necessary or desirable to do so either to indicate to other road users the urgency of the purposes for which the vehicle is being used, or to warn other road users of the presence of the vehicle on the road; or

(b) a horn (not being a two-tone horn), bell, gong or siren—

(i) to raise alarm as to the theft or attempted theft of the vehicle or its contents, or

(ii) in the case of a bus, to summon help for the driver, the conductor or an inspector.

(6) Subject to the provisions of section 62 of the Control of Pollution Act 1974 and notwithstanding the provisions of paragraphs (1) and (4) above, a person may, between 12.00 hours and 19.00 hours, sound or cause or permit to be sounded an instrument or apparatus, other than a two-tone horn, fitted to or otherwise carried on a vehicle, being an instrument or apparatus designed to emit a sound for the purpose of informing members of the public that the vehicle is conveying goods for sale, if when the apparatus or instrument is sounded, it is sounded only for that purpose.

(7) For the purposes of this regulation the expressions which are referred to in regulation 37(10) have the meanings there given to them and the expression *"restricted road"* in paragraph (1) means a road which is a restricted road for the purpose of section 81 of the 1984 Act [*q.v.*].

[Regulation 99 is printed as amended by S.I. 1987 No. 676; S.I. 2000 No. 1971.   **B27.213**
The Control of Pollution Act 1974, s.62, regulates the use of loudspeakers in streets.]

F *Avoidance of Danger*

100. Maintenance and use of vehicle so as not to be a danger, etc.

(1) A motor vehicle, every trailer drawn thereby and all parts and accessories of such   **B27.214**
vehicle and trailer shall at all times be in such condition, and the number of passengers carried by such vehicle or trailer, the manner in which any passengers are carried in or on such vehicle or trailer, and the weight, distribution, packing and adjustment of the load of such vehicle or trailer shall at all times be such, that no danger is caused or is likely to be caused to any person in or on the vehicle or trailer or on a road.
Provided that the provisions of this regulation with regard to the number of passengers carried shall not apply to a vehicle to which the Public Service Vehicles (Carrying Capacity) Regulations 1984 [*S.I. 1984 No. 1406; not reproduced in this work*] apply.

(2) The load carried by a motor vehicle or trailer shall at all times be so secured, if necessary by physical restraint other than its own weight, and be in such a position, that neither danger nor nuisance is likely to be caused to any person or property by reason of the load or any part thereof falling or being blown from the vehicle or by reason of any other movement of the load or any part thereof in relation to the vehicle.

(3) No motor vehicle or trailer shall be used for any purpose for which it is so unsuitable as to cause or be likely to cause danger or nuisance to any person in or on the vehicle or trailer or on a road.

[100A. Speed of low platform trailers and restricted speed vehicles

(1) No person shall use, or cause or permit to be used, on a road a vehicle displaying the   **B27.215**
rectangular plate described in the definition of "low platform trailer" in the Table in regulation 3(2) or anything resembling such a plate at a speed exceeding 40mph.

(2) No person shall use, or cause or permit to be used on a road a vehicle displaying the rectangular plate described in Schedule 13 (Plate for restricted speed vehicle) or anything resembling such a plate at a speed exceeding 50mph.]

[Regulation 100A was inserted by S.I. 1990 No. 1981.]   **B27.216**

101. Parking in darkness

(1) Save as provided in paragraph (2) no person shall, except with the permission of a   **B27.217**
police officer in a uniform, cause or permit any motor vehicle to stand on a road at any time

between . . . sunset and . . . sunrise unless the near side of the vehicle is as close as may be to the edge of the carriageway.

(2) The provisions of paragraph (1) do not apply in respect of any motor vehicle—

   (a) being used for fire brigade, ambulance or police purposes or for defence purposes (including civil defence purposes) if compliance with those provisions would hinder or be likely to hinder the use of the vehicle for the purpose for which it is being used on that occasion;

   (b) being used in connection with—

      (i) any building operation or demolition;

      (ii) the repair of any other vehicle;

      (iii) the removal of any obstruction to traffic;

      (iv) the maintenance, repair or reconstruction of any road; or

      (v) the laying, erection, alteration or repair in or near to any road of any sewer, main pipe or apparatus for the supply of gas, water or electricity, of any telecommunication apparatus as defined in Schedule 2 to the Telecommunication Act 1984 or of the apparatus of any electric transport undertaking;

if, in any such case, compliance with those provisions would hinder or be likely to hinder the use of the vehicle for the purpose for which it is being used on that occasion;

   (c) on any road in which vehicles are allowed to proceed in one direction only;

   (d) standing on a part of a road set aside for the parking of vehicles or as a stand for hackney carriages or as a stand for buses or as a place at which such vehicles may stop for a longer time than is necessary for the taking up and setting down of passengers where compliance with those provisions would conflict with the provisions of any order, regulations or byelaws governing the use of such part of a road for that purpose; or

   (e) waiting to set down or pick up passengers in accordance with regulations made or directions given by a chief officer of police in regard to such setting down or picking up.

B27.218   *[Regulation 101 is printed as amended by S.I. 1991 No. 2125.]*

102. Passengers on motor cycles

B27.219   If any person in addition to the driver is carried astride a two-wheeled motor cycle on a road (whether a sidecar is attached to it or not) suitable supports or rests for the feet shall be available on the motor cycle for that person.

103. Obstruction

B27.220   No person in charge of a motor vehicle or trailer shall cause or permit the vehicle to stand on a road so as to cause any unnecessary obstruction of the road.

B27.221   *[Offences under regulation 103 have been designated as fixed penalty parking offences by the Schedule to the Fixed Penalty Order 2000 (S.I. 2000 No. 2792) below.]*

104. Driver's control

B27.222   No person shall drive or cause or permit any other person to drive, a motor vehicle on a road if he is in such a position that he cannot have proper control of the vehicle or have a full view of the road and traffic ahead.

105. Opening of doors

No person shall open, or cause or permit to be opened, any door of a vehicle on a road so as to injure or endanger any person.   **B27.223**

106. Reversing

No person shall drive, or cause or permit to be driven, a motor vehicle backwards on a road further than may be requisite for the safety or reasonable convenience of the occupants of the vehicle or other traffic, unless it is a road roller or is engaged in the construction, maintenance or repair of the road.   **B27.224**

107. Leaving motor vehicle unattended

(1) Save as provided in paragraph (2), no person shall leave or cause or permit to be left, on a road a motor vehicle which is not attended by a person licensed to drive it unless the engine is stopped and any parking brake with which the vehicle is required to be equipped is effectively set.   **B27.225**

(2) The requirement specified in paragraph (1) as to the stopping of the engine shall not apply in respect of a vehicle—

    (a) being used for ambulance, fire brigade or police purposes; or

    (b) in such a position and condition as not to be likely to endanger any person or property and engaged in an operation which requires its engine to be used to—

        (i) drive machinery forming part of, or mounted on, the vehicle and used for purposes other than driving the vehicle; or

        (ii) maintain the electrical power of the batteries of the vehicle at a level required for driving that machinery or apparatus.

(3) In this regulation "*parking brake*" means a brake fitted to a vehicle in accordance with requirement 16 or 18 in Schedule 3.

108. Securing of suspended implements

Where a vehicle is fitted with any apparatus or appliance designed for lifting and part of the apparatus or appliance consists of a suspended implement, the implement shall at all times while the vehicle is in motion on a road and when the implement is not attached to any load supported by the appliance or apparatus be so secured either to the appliance or apparatus or to some part of the vehicle that no danger is caused or is likely to be caused to any person on the vehicle or on the road.   **B27.226**

109. Television sets

(1) No person shall drive, or cause or permit to be driven, a motor vehicle on a road, if the driver is in such a position as to be able to see, whether directly or by reflection, a television receiving apparatus or other cinematographic apparatus used to display anything other than information—   **B27.227**

    (a) about the state of the vehicle or its equipment;

    (b) about the location of the vehicle and the road on which it is located;

    (c) to assist the driver to see the road adjacent to the vehicle; or

    (d) to assist the driver to reach his destination.

(2) In this regulation "*television receiving apparatus*" means any cathode ray tube carried on a vehicle and on which there can be displayed an image derived from a television broadcast, a recording or a camera or computer.

B27.228

SCHEDULE 1

REGULATIONS REVOKED BY REGULATION 2

[Omitted.]

COMMUNITY DIRECTIVES AND ECE REGULATIONS

TABLE I

Community Directives

| 1 | 2 | 3 | | | 4 | |
| Item | Reference No | Community Directives | | | Item No. in Schedule 1 to— | |
		(a) Date	(b) Official Journal Reference	(c) Subject matter	(d) Previous Directives included	(a) The Type Approval (Great Britain) Regulations	(b) The Type Approval for Goods Vehicles Regulations
1	70/157	6.2.70	L42, 23.2.70, p. 16	The permissible sound level and the exhaust system of motor vehicles			
2	70/220	20.3.70	L76, 6.4.70, p. 1	Measures to be taken against air pollution by gases from spark ignition engines of motor vehicles			
3	70/221	20.3.70	L76, 6.4.70, p. 23	Liquid fuel tanks and rear protective devices for motor vehicles and their trailers			
4	70/388	27.7.70	L176, 10.8.70, p. 12	Audible warning devices for motor vehicles		10	
5	71/127	1.3.71	L68, 22.3.71, p. 1	The rear-view mirrors of motor vehicles			
6	71/320	[26.7.71]	L202, 6.9.71, p. 37	The braking devices of certain categories of motor vehicles and their trailers			

[continued on next page

1 Item	*2* Reference No	*3* Community Directives				*4* Item No. in Schedule 1 to—	
		(a) Date	*(b)* Official Journal Reference	*(c)* Subject matter	*(d)* Previous Directives included	*(a)* The Type Approval (Great Britain) Regulations	*(b)* The Type Approval for Goods Vehicles Regulations
7	72/245	20.6.72	L152, 6.7.72, p. 15	The suppression of radio interference produced by spark ignition engines fitted to motor vehicles		2A	5A
8	72/306	2.8.72	L190, 20.8.72, p. 1	The emission of pollutants from diesel engines for use in vehicles		5	3
9	73/350	7.11.73	L321, 22.11.73, p. 33	The permissible sound level and the exhaust system of motor vehicles	70/157		4A
10	74/132	11.2.74	L74, 19.3.74, p. 7	The braking devices of certain categories of motor vehicles and their trailers	71/320		
11	74/151	4.3.74	L84, 28.3.74, p. 25	Parts and characteristics of agricultural motor vehicles (see Note 1)			
12	74/290	28.5.74	L159, 15.6.74, p. 61	Measures to be taken against air pollution by gases from spark ignition engines for motor vehicles	70/220		
13	74/346	25.6.74	L191, 15.7.74, p. 1	Rear-view mirrors for agricultural motor vehicles (see Note 1);			

14	74/347	25.6.74	L191, 15.7.74, p. 1	Field of vision and windscreen wipers for agricultural motor vehicles (see Note 1)		19	
15	74/483	17.9.74	L266, 2.10.74, p. 4	External projections of motor vehicles			
16	75/322	20.5.75	L147, 9.6.75, p. 28	Suppression of radio interference from spark ignition engines of agricultural motor vehicles (see Note 1)		20	
17	75/443	26.6.75	L196, 26.7.75, p. 1	Reverse and speedometer equipment of motor vehicles			
18	75/524	25.7.75	L236, 8.9.75, p. 3	The braking devices of certain categories of motor vehicles and their trailers	71/320 as amended by 74/132	13A	
19	76/114	18.12.75	L24, 30.1.76, p. 1	Statutory plates and inscriptions for motor vehicles and trailers			
20	76/115	18.12.75	L24, 30.1.76, p. 6	Anchorages for motor vehicle seat belts		12A	
21	76/432	6.4.76	L122, 8.5.76, p. 1	Braking devices of agricultural vehicles (see Note 1)			
22	77/102	30.11.76	L32, 3.2.77, p. 32	Measures to be taken against air pollution by gases from spark ignition engines of motor vehicles	70/220 as amended by 74/290		
23	77/212	8.3.77	L66, 12.3.77, p. 33	The permissible sound level and the exhaust system of motor vehicles	70/157 as amended by 73/350	14B	4B, 4C, 4D

[continued on next page

1 Item	*2* Reference No	*3* Community Directives				*4* Item No. in Schedule 1 to—	
		(a) Date	*(b)* Official Journal Reference	*(c)* Subject matter	*(d)* Previous Directives included	*(a)* The Type Approval (Great Britain) Regulations	*(b)* The Type Approval for Goods Vehicles Regulations
24	77/537	28.6.77	L220, 29.8.77, p. 38	Emission of pollution from diesel engines for agricultural motor vehicles (see Note 1)			
25	77/541	28.6.77	L220, 29.8.77, p. 95	Seat belts and restraint systems for motor vehicles		12A	
26	77/649	27.9.77	L267, 19.10.77, p. 1	Field of vision of motor vehicle drivers			
27	78/318	21.12.77	L81, 28.3.78, p. 49	Wiper and washer systems of motor vehicles		22	
28	78/507	19.5.78	L155, 13.6.78, p. 31	Statutory plates and inscriptions for motor vehicles and trailers	76/114		
29	78/549	12.6.78	L168, 26.6.78, p. 45	Wheel guards of motor vehicles			
30	78/665	14.7.78	L223, 14.8.78, p. 48	Measures to be taken against air pollution by gases from spark ignition engines of motor vehicles	70/220 amended by 74/290 and 77/102	4B, 4C	2
31	78/1015	23.11.78	L349, 13.12.78, p. 21	The permissible sound level and exhaust system of motor cycles			

32	79/488	18.4.79	L128, 26.5.79, p. 1	External projections of motor vehicles	74/483	19A	
33	79/489	18.4.79	L128, 26.5.79, p. 12	The braking devices of certain categories of motor vehicles and their trailers	71/320 as amended by 74/132 and 75/524	13B	6, 6C
34	79/490	18.4.79	L128, 26.5.79, p. 22	Liquid fuel tanks and rear under-run protection	70/221		
35	79/795	20.7.79	L239, 22.9.79, p. 1	The rear-view mirrors of motor vehicles	71/127	10A	
36	79/1073	22.11.79	L331, 27.12.79, p. 20	Field of vision and windscreen wipers for agricultural motor vehicles	74/347		
37	80/780	22.7.80	L229, 30.8.80, p. 49	Rear-view mirrors for motor cycles			
38	80/1269	16.12.80	L375, 31.12.80, p. 46	The engine power of motor vehicles			
39	81/334	13.4.81	L131, 18.5.81, p. 6	The permissible sound level and exhaust system of motor vehicles	70/157 as amended by 73/350 and 77/212	14C	4B, 4C, 4D
40	81/575	29.7.81	L209, 29.7.81, p. 30	Anchorages for motor vehicle seat belts	76/115	12A	
41	81/576	29.7.81	L209, 29.7.81, p. 32	Seat belts and restraint systems for motor vehicles	77/541	12A	
42	81/643	29.7.81	L231, 15.8.81, p. 41	Field of vision of motor vehicle drivers	77/649		

[continued on next page

| | | Community Directives | | | | Item No. in Schedule 1 to— | |
| 1 | 2 | 3 | | | | 4 | |
Item	Reference No	(a) Date	(b) Official Journal Reference	(c) Subject matter	(d) Previous Directives included	(a) The Type Approval (Great Britain) Regulations	(b) The Type Approval for Goods Vehicles Regulations
43	82/318	2.4.82	L139, 19.5.82, p. 9	Anchorages for motor vehicle seat belts	76/115 as amended by 81/575	12A	
44	82/319	2.4.82	L139, 19.5.82, p. 17	Seat belts and restraint systems for motor vehicles	77/541 as amended by 81/576	12A	
45	82/890	17.12.82	L378, 31.12.82, p. 45	Agricultural motor vehicles			
46	83/351	16.6.83	L197, 20.7.82, p. 1	Air pollution by gases from positive ignition engines of motor vehicles	70/220 as amended by 74/290, 77/102 and 78/665	4C	
47	84/372	3.7.84	L196, 26.7.84, p. 47	The permissible sound level and exhaust system of motor vehicles	70/157 as amended by 73/350, 77/212 and 81/334		
48	84/424	3.9.84	L238, 6.9.84, p. 31	The permissible sound level and exhaust system of motor vehicles	70/157 as amended by 73/350,		

[48A]	85/3	19.12.84	L2, 3.1.85, p. 14	The weights, dimensions and other technical characteristics of certain road vehicles	77/212, 81/334 and 84/372	10B	]
49	85/205	18.2.85	L90, 29.3.85, p. 1	Mirrors	71/127 as amended by 79/795		
[49A]	85/210	20.3.85	L96, 3.4.85, p. 25	The lead content of petrol]			
[50]	85/647	23.12.85	L380, 31.12.85, p. 1	The braking devices of certain motor vehicles and their trailers	71/320 as amended by 74/132, 75/524 and 79/489]		
[50A]	86/360	24.7.86	L217, 5.8.86, p. 19	The weights, dimensions and other technical characteristics of certain road vehicles	85/3		
[51]	86/562	6.11.86	L327, 27.11.86, p. 49	Mirrors	71/127 as amended by 79/795 and 85/205]		]
[51A]	87/56	18.12.86	L24, 27.1.87, p. 42	The permissible sound level and exhaust system of motor cycles	78/1015		
[52]	88/76	3.12.87	L36, 9.2.88, p. 1	Measures to be taken against air pollution by gases from the engines of motor vehicles	70/220 as amended by 74/290	4D	] 2B]

[continued on next page

| *1* | *2* | *3* Community Directives | | | | *4* Item No. in Schedule 1 to— | |
Item	Reference No	*(a)* Date	*(b)* Official Journal Reference	*(c)* Subject matter	*(d)* Previous Directives included	*(a)* The Type Approval (Great Britain) Regulations	*(b)* The Type Approval for Goods Vehicles Regulations
52—cont.					77/102, 78/665, and 83/351		]
[53	89/297	13.4.89	L124, 5.5.89, p. 1	Lateral protection (side guards) of certain motor vehicles and their trailers			
[54	88/77	3.12.87	L36, 9.2.88, p. 33	Measures to be taken against the emission of gaseous pollutants from diesel engines for use in vehicles		4E	2D]
[54A	88/194	24.3.88	L92, 9.4.88, p. 47	The braking devices of certain categories of motor vehicles and their trailers	71/320 as amended by 74/132, 75/524, 79/489 and 85/647		
[55	88/195	24.3.88	L92, 9.4.88, p. 50	Engine power of motor vehicles	80/1269		]
[55A	88/218	11.4.88	L98, 15.4.88, p. 48	The weights, dimensions and other technical characteristics of certain road vehicles	85/3 as amended by 86/360		]

[55B]	88/321	16.5.88	L147, 14.6.88, p. 77	Mirrors	71/127 as amended by 79/795, 85/205 and 86/562	10C	]
[55C]	88/366	17.5.88	L181, 12.7.88, p. 40	Field of vision of motor vehicle drivers	77/649 as amended by 81/643		]
[56]	88/436	16.6.88	L124, 6.8.88, p. 1	Measures to be taken against air pollution by gases from engines of motor vehicles (restriction of particulate pollution emissions from diesel engines)	70/220 as amended by 74/290, 77/102, 78/665, 83/351 and 88/76	4D	2C]
[56A]	89/235	13.3.89	L98, 11.4.89, p.1	The permissible sound level and exhaust systems of motor cycles	78/1015 amended by 87/56	—	—]
[[56 AA]	89/338	27.4.89	L142, 25.5.89, p. 3	The weights, dimensions and other technical characteristics of certain road vehicles	85/3 as amended by 86/360 and 88/218		
[57]	89/458	18.7.89	L226, 3.8.89, p. 1	Measures to be taken against air pollution by emissions from motor vehicles	70/220 as amended by 74/290, 77/102, 78/665, 83/351,		]

[continued on next page

1	2	3 Community Directives				4 Item No. in Schedule 1 to—	
Item	Reference No	(a) Date	(b) Official Journal Reference	(c) Subject matter	(d) Previous Directives included	(a) The Type Approval (Great Britain) Regulations	(b) The Type Approval for Goods Vehicles Regulations
57—cont.							
[57A	89/460	18.7.89	L.226, 3.8.89, p. 5	The weights, dimensions and other technical characteristics of certain road vehicles	88/76 and 88/436; 85/3 as amended by 86/360, 88/218 and 89/338		]
[57B	89/461	18.7.89	L.226, 3.8.89, p. 7	The weights, dimensions and other technical characteristics of certain road vehicles	85/3 as amended by 86/360, 88/218, 89/338 and 89/460		]
[58	90/628	30.10.90	L.341, 6.12.90, p. 1	Safety belts and restraint systems of motor vehicles	77/541 as amended by 81/576 and 82/319	12A	]
[59	90/269	30.10.90	L.341, 6.12.90, p. 14	Anchorages for motor vehicle safety belts	76/115 as amended by 81/575 and 82/318	12A	]

[60	90/630	30.10.90	L341, 6.12.90, p. 20	Field of vision of motor vehicle drivers	77/649 as amended by 81/643 and 88/366		]
[60A	91/60	4.2.91	L37, 9.2.91, p. 37	The weights, dimensions and other technical characteristics of certain vehicles	85/3 as amended by 86/360, 88/218, 89/338, 89/460 and 89/641		
[61	91/226	27.3.91	L103, 23.4.91, p. 5	Spray-suppression systems of certain categories of motor vehicles and their trailers			]
[61A	91/422	15.7.91	L233, 22.8.91, p. 21	The braking devices of certain categories of motor vehicles and their trailers	71/320 as amended by 74/132, 75/524, 79/489, 85/647 and 88/194		]
[62	92/7	10.2.91	L57, 2.3.92, p. 29	The weights, dimensions and other technical characteristics of certain road vehicles	85/3 as amended by 86/360, 88/218, 89/338, 89/460 and 89/641		]
[63	91/441	26.6.91	L242, 30.8.91, p. 1	Measures to be taken against air pollution by emissions from motor vehicles	70/220 as amended by 74/290	4G	]2F]

[continued on next page

1	2	3 Community Directives				4 Item No. in Schedule 1 to—	
Item	*Reference No*	*(a) Date*	*(b) Official Journal Reference*	*(c) Subject matter*	*(d) Previous Directives included*	*(a) The Type Approval (Great Britain) Regulations*	*(b) The Type Approval for Goods Vehicles Regulations*
63— cont.					77/102, 78/665, 83/351, 88/76, 88/436 and 89/458		
[64	91/542	1.10.91	L295, 25.10.91, p. 1	Measures to be taken against the emission of gaseous pollutants from diesel engines for use in vehicles	88/77	4H	2G]
[64A	92/6	10.2.92	L57, 2.4.92, p. 27	The installation and use of speed limitation devices			]
[65	92/22	31.3.92	L129, 14.5.92, p. 11	Safety glazing and glazing materials on motor vehicles and their trailers			]
[66	92/23	31.3.92	L129, 14.5.92, p. 95	Tyres of motor vehicles and their trailers and their fittings			]
[67	92/24	31.3.92	L 129, 14.5.92, p. 154	Speed limitation devices or similar speed limitation on-board certain categories of motor vehicles	—	—	]

Item	Directive	Date	Official Journal reference	Subject	Amends		
[67A	93/14	5.4.93	L121, 15.5.93, p. 1	The braking of two or three-wheel motor vehicles		4K	]
[68	93/59	28.6.93	—	Measures to be taken against air pollution by emissions from motor vehicles	70/220 as amended by 74/290, 77/102, 78/665, 83/351, 88/76, 88/436, 89/458 and 91/441		2I]
[69	94/12	23.3.94	L100, 19.4.94, p. 42	Measures to be taken against air pollution by emissions from motor vehicles	70/220 as amended by 74/290, 77/102, 78/665,	4L	2J]
[69A	94/20	30.5.94	L195, 29.7.94, p. 1	Mechanical coupling devices of motor vehicles and their trailers	83/351, 88/76, 88/436, 89/458, 91/441 and 93/59		]
[70	92/97	10.11.92	L371, 19.12.92, p. 1	Permissible sound level and the exhaust system of motor vehicles	70/157 as amended by 73/350, 77/212, 81/334, 84/372	14G	4F]

[continued on next page]

1	2	3 Community Directives				4 Item No. in Schedule 1 to—	
Item	Reference No	(a) Date	(b) Official Journal Reference	(c) Subject matter	(d) Previous Directives included	(a) The Type Approval (Great Britain) Regulations	(b) The Type Approval for Goods Vehicles Regulations
70—cont.					and 84/424		
[71]	95/54	31.10.95	L266, 8.11.95, p. 1	The suppression of radio interference of motor vehicles	72/245	2B	5B]
[72]	96/1	22.1.96	L40, 17.2.96, p. 1	Measures to be taken against the emission of gaseous pollutants from diesel engines for use in vehicles	88/77 as amended by 91/542	4N	2L]
[73]	96/20	27.3.96	L92, 13.4.96, p. 23	Permissible sound level and the exhaust system of motor vehicles	70/157 as amended by 73/350, 77/212, 81/334, 84/372 84/424 and 92/97	14I	4G]
[73A]	96/36	17.6.96	L178, 17.6.96, p. 15	Safety belts and restraint systems of motor vehicles	77/541 as amended by 81/576, 82/319 and 90/628		]

[continued on next page

[73B	96/38	17.6.96	L187, 26.7.96, p. 95	Anchorage for motor vehicle safety belts	76/115 as amended by 81/575, 82/318 and 90/629
[74	96/53	25.7.96	L234, 17.9.96, p. 59	Maximum dimensions in national and international traffic and maximum weights in international traffic	
[74A	96/63	30.9.96	L253, 5.10.96, p. 13	Braking devices of wheeled agricultural or forestry tractors	76/432
[74B	96/69	08.10.96	L282, 1.11.96, p. 64	Measures to be taken against air pollution by emissions from motor vehicles	70/220 as amended by 74/290, 77/102, 78/665, 83/351, 88/76, 88/436, 89/491, 91/441, 93/59, 94/12, and 96/44
[75	97/19	18.4.97	L125, 16.5.97, p. 1	Liquid fuel tanks and rear under-run protection of motor vehicles and their trailers	70/221 as amended by 79/490 and 81/333
[76	97/27	22.7.97	L233, 25.8.97, p. 1	Masses and dimensions of certain categories of vehicle and their trailers	

| Item | Reference No | Community Directives | | | | Item No. in Schedule 1 to— | |
1	2	(a) Date	(b) Official Journal Reference	(c) Subject matter	(d) Previous Directives included	(a) The Type Approval (Great Britain) Regulations	(b) The Type Approval for Goods Vehicles Regulations
[77	97/39	27.4.97	L177, 5.7.97, p. 15	Reverse and speedometer equipment of motor vehicles	75/443		]
[78	98/69	13.10.98	L350, 28.12.98, p. 1	Measures to be taken against air pollution by emissions from motor vehicles	70/220 as amended by 74/290, 77/102, 78/665, 83/351, 88/76, 88/436, 89/491, 91/441, 93/59, 94/12, 96/44 and 96/69		
[79	1999/96	13.12.99	L44, 16.2.2000, p. 1	Measures to be taken against the emission of gaseous and particulate pollutants from compression ignition engines for use in vehicles and the emission of gaseous pollutants from	88/77 as amended by 91/542 and 96/1		]

[80]	1999/102	15.12.99	L334, 28.12.99, p. 43	positive ignition engines fuelled with natural gas or liquefied petroleum gas for use in vehicles Measures to be taken against air pollution by emissions from motor vehicles	70/220 as amended by 74/290, 77/102, 78/665, 83/351, 88/76, 88/436, 89/491, 91/441, 93/59, 94/12, 96/44, 96/69 and 98/69]

NOTE 1. This item is to be interpreted as including reference to the amendments made by Community Directive 82/890 (item 45).

[Table I in Schedule 2 is printed as amended by S.I. 1987 No. 676; S.I. 1988 Nos 1178 and 1524; S.I. 1989 Nos 1695 and 1865; S.I. 1990 Nos 1131, 1981; S.I. 1991 No. 2003; S.I. 1992 Nos 646, 2016, 2137 and 3088; S.I. 1993 No. 1946 and 2199; S.I. 1994 No. 14; S.I. 1995 Nos 551 and 2210; S.I. 1996 Nos 2064, 2329 and 3033; S.I. 1998 Nos 1188, 1281 and 2429; S.I. 2000 No. 3197.

With effect from October 1, 2001, the term "90/269" in column 2 of item 59 in table I will be replaced by the term "90/629" by S.I. 2001 No. 1043 (although it is stated in the explanatory note to S.I. 2001 No. 1043 that this is a correction, seemingly it does not take effect until the same date as the other provisions of S.I. 2001 No. 1043).]

TABLE II

ECE REGULATIONS

Item	Reference No.	ECE Regulations				Item No. in Schedule 1 to—	
		(a) Number	(b) Date	(c) Subject matter	(d) Date of amendment	(a) The Type Approval (Great Britain) Regulations	(b) The Type Approval for Goods Vehicles Regulations
1	10	10	17.12.68	Radio interference suppression	—	2A	5A
2	10.01	10	17.12.68	Radio interference suppression	19.3.78	2A	5A
3	13.03	13	29.5.69	Brakes	4.1.79	13C, 13D	6A, 6B, 6D
4	13.04	13	29.5.69	Brakes	11.8.81	13C, 13D	6A, 6B, 6D
[4A]	13.05	13	29.5.69	Brakes	26.11.84		—
[4B]	13.06	13	29.5.69	Brakes	22.11.90		—
[4C]	13.07	13	29.5.69	Brakes	18.9.94		—
[5A]	14	14	30.1.70	Anchorages for seat belts	—	12A	—
6	14.01	14	30.1.70	Anchorages for seat belts	28.4.76	12A	—
[6A]	14.02	14	30.1.70	Anchorages for seat belts	22.11.84	12A	—
[6C]	14.03	—	30.1.70	Anchorages for seat belts	29.1.92		—
7	15.03	15	11.3.70	Emission of gaseous pollutants	6.3.78	4B	2A
8	15.04	15	11.3.70	Emission of gaseous pollutants	20.10.81	4C	2A
9	16.03	16	14.8.70	Seat belts and restraint systems	9.12.79	12A	—
10	24.01	24	23.8.71	Emission of pollutants by a diesel engine	11.9.73	5A	3A
11	24.02	24	23.8.71	Emission of pollutants by a diesel engine	11.2.80	5A	3A
12	24.03	24	23.8.71	Emission of pollutants by a diesel engine	20.4.86		—
13	26.01	26	28.4.72	External projections	11.9.73	19A	—
[13A]	30	30	1.4.75	Pneumatic tyres for motor vehicles and their trailers	—	17, 17A	—
[13B]	30	30.01	1.4.75	Pneumatic tyres for motor vehicles and their trailers	25.9.77	17, 17A	—

[13C]	30.02	1.4.75	Pneumatic tyres for motor vehicles and their trailers	5.10.87	17, 17A	]
14	34	25.7.75	Prevention of fire risks	—	—	—
15	34.01	25.7.75	Prevention of fire risks	18.1.79	—	—
16	36	21.11.75	Construction of public service vehicles	—	—	—
17	39	11.7.78	Speedometers	—	20B	—
18	43	15.9.80	Safety glass and glazing materials	—	15B	—
19	43.01	15.9.80	Safety glass and glazing materials	12.11.82	15B	—
20	44	1.2.81	Child restraints	—	—	—
21	44.01	1.2.81	Child restraints	1.2.84	—	]
[21A]	46.01	21.10.84	Mirrors	30.5.88	—	]
[21AA]	49.01	14.5.90	Emissions of gaseous pollutants	—	—	]
[21AB]	49.02	15.4.82	Emissions of gaseous pollutants	—	—	]
[21B]	49	15.4.82	Emissions of gaseous pollutants	30.12.92	—	]
[21BA]	51.02	18.4.95	Noise emissions from motor vehicles having at least 4 wheels	—	14E	4D(4) or 4E]
[21C]	54	1.3.83	Pneumatic tyres for commercial vehicles and their trailers	—	17A	—
22	64	1.8.85	Vehicles with temporary-use spare wheels/tyres	—	—	—
[23]	78	15.10.88	Brakes	—	—	—
[24]	78.01	15.10.88	Brakes	22.11.90	—	—
25	83	5.11.89	Emissions of gaseous pollutants	—	4F	2H]
26	83.01	5.11.89	Emissions of gaseous pollutants	30.12.92	4K	2F]

[Table II in Schedule 2 is printed as amended by S.I. 1989 No. 1478; S.I. 1990 Nos 1131 and 1981; S.I. 1991 No. 2710; S.I. 1992 Nos 352, 2016, 2137 and 3088; S.I. 1993 No. 2199; S.I. 1994 No. 3270; S.I. 1996 Nos 2329 and 3133.

Item 21AA in table II was positioned after what is now item 21B before that item (formerly 21A) was re-numbered by S.I. 1992 No. 3088.

With effect from October 1, 2001, the following items will be inserted by S.I. 2001 No. 1043 after item 6A:

6B	14.03	30.1.70	Anchorages for seat belts	29.1.92	—	]
6C	14.04	30.1.70	Anchorages for seat belts	18.1.98	—	]
6D	14.05	30.1.70	Anchorages for seat belts	4.2.99	—	]

Regulation 3A   SCHEDULE 2A

VEHICLES FOR WHICH A MINISTER'S APPROVAL CERTIFICATE HAS BEEN ISSUED UNDER THE
MOTOR VEHICLES (APPROVAL) REGULATIONS 1996

PART I

INTERPRETATION

1. General interpretation

B27.231 (1) In this Schedule—

"*the Approval Regulations*" means the Motor Vehicles (Approval) Regulations 1996;

"*approval certificate*" means a Minister's approval certificate in the form prescribed by the Approval Regulations;

"*approval date*", in relation to a vehicle in respect of which an approval certificate has been issued, is the date that the certificate was issued;

"*goods vehicle approval certificate*" means an approval certificate which appears to have been issued on the basis that the vehicle to which Part III of the Approval Regulations applies;

"*passenger vehicle approval certificate*" means an approval certificate which appears to have been issued on the basis that the vehicle is a vehicle to which Part II of the Approval Regulations applies.

B27.232 *[Schedule 2A (paragraphs 1–9 and 10) was inserted by S.I. 1996 No. 3017. As to the "Approval Regulations", see the note to paragraph 2 of this Schedule.]*

2. Interpretation of references to a vehicle complying with the approval requirements and to a vehicle exempt from the approval requirements

B27.233 (1) Subject to paragraph 3, references in this Schedule to a vehicle complying with or being exempt from the approval requirements shall be construed in accordance with the following provisions of this paragraph.

(2) Subject to sub-paragraphs (4) and (5), a vehicle in respect of which a goods vehicle approval certificate has been issued shall be regarded as complying with or exempt from the approval requirements in relation to a specified subject matter if and only if it for the time being satisfies at least one of the conditions in regulation 6(5) of the Approval Regulations in relation to that subject matter.

(3) Subject to sub-paragraphs (4) and (5), a vehicle in respect of which a passenger vehicle approval certificate has been issued shall be regarded as complying with or exempt from the approval requirements in relation to a specified subject matter if and only if it for the time being satisfies at least one of the conditions in regulation 4(5) of the Approval Regulations in relation to that subject matter.

(4) A vehicle in respect of which an approval certificate has been issued shall be regarded as neither complying with nor being exempt from the approval requirements in relation to any subject matter if—

   (a) the certificate is a goods vehicle approval certificate and the vehicle is not for the time being a vehicle to which Part III of the Approval Regulations applies; or

   (b) the certificate is a passenger vehicle approval certificate and the vehicle is not for the time being a vehicle to which Part II of the Approval Regulations applies.

(5) For the purposes of this paragraph, the Approval Regulations shall have effect with the omission of regulations 4(8) and 6(7).

[Schedule 2A (paragraphs 1–9 and 10) was inserted by S.I. 1996 No. 3017.
The "Approval Regulations" (i.e. the Motor Vehicles (Approval) Regulations 1996, to which reference is made in paragraph 2 of Schedule 2A) have been revoked and replaced by the Motor Vehicles (Approval) Regulations 2001 (S.I. 2001 No. 25) below. The Interpretation Act 1978, ss.17(2)(a) and 23, which enables references to the 1996 Regulations to be construed as references to the 2001 Regulations is only applicable in the absence of a contrary intention (see 1978 Act, s.17(2)(a)); the fact that the scheme of the 2001 Regulations differs from that of the 1996 Regulations (e.g. there are no Parts in the 2001 Regulations corresponding to Part II ("Passenger Vehicles") and Part III ("Goods Vehicles") of the 1996 Regulations suggests that a "contrary intention" should be inferred. The text of the 1996 Regulations is reproduced in the nineteenth edition of this work.]

B27.234

PART II

MODIFICATION OF THE REGULATIONS

3. Part exemption from regulation 32 (glazing)

Regulation 32(2), (7) and (10) shall not apply to a vehicle in respect of which a passenger vehicle approval certificate has been issued, if it complies with or is exempt from the approval requirements relating to glazing.

B27.235

[Schedule 2A (paragraphs 1–9 and 10) was inserted by S.I. 1996 No. 3017.
References in these paragraphs to approval certificates are to approval certificates issued under the "Approval Regulations". As to the "Approval Regulations", see the note to paragraph 2 of this Schedule.]

B27.236

4. Exemption from regulation 33 (mirrors)

Regulation 33 shall not apply to a vehicle in respect of which a passenger vehicle approval certificate has been issued, if it complies with or is exempt from the approval requirements relating to rear view mirrors.

B27.237

[Schedule 2A (paragraphs 1–9 and 10) was inserted by S.I. 1996 No. 3017.
References in these paragraphs to approval certificates are to approval certificates issued under the "Approval Regulations". As to the "Approval Regulations", see the note to paragraph 2 of this Schedule.]

B27.238

5. Exemption from regulation 35 (speedometers)

Regulation 35 shall not apply to a vehicle in respect of which a passenger approval certificate has been issued, if it complies with or is exempt from the approval requirements relating to speedometers.

B27.239

[Schedule 2A (paragraphs 1–9 and 10) was inserted by S.I. 1996 No. 3017.
References in these paragraphs to approval certificates are to approval certificates issued under the "Approval Regulations". As to the "Approval Regulations", see the note to paragraph 2 of this Schedule.]

B27.240

6. Exemption from regulation 39(2)(c)(i) (fuel tanks to be made of metal)

Regulation 39(2)(c)(i) shall not apply to a vehicle in respect of which either a passenger vehicle approval certificate or a goods vehicle approval certificate has been issued, if it complies with the approval requirements relating to general vehicle construction.

B27.241

[Schedule 2A (paragraphs 1–9 and 10) was inserted by S.I. 1996 No. 3017.
References in these paragraphs to approval certificates are to approval certificates issued under the "Approval Regulations". As to the "Approval Regulations", see the note to paragraph 2 of this Schedule.]

B27.242

7. Exemption from regulation 46 (seat belt anchorages)

Regulation 46 shall not apply to a vehicle in respect of which a passenger vehicle approval certificate has been issued, if it complies with or is exempt from the approval requirements relating to anchorage points.

B27.243

B27.244   *[Schedule 2A (paragraphs 1–9 and 10) was inserted by S.I. 1996 No. 3017.*
References in these paragraphs to approval certificates are to approval certificates issued under the "Approval Regulations". As to the "Approval Regulations", see the note to paragraph 2 of this Schedule.]

8. Part exemption from regulation 47 (seat belts)

B27.245   Regulation 47, so far as it relates to seat belts for adults, shall not apply to a vehicle in respect of which a passenger vehicle approval certificate has been issued, if it complies with or is exempt from the approval requirements relating to seat belts (including the requirements relating to the installation of seat belts).

B27.246   *[Schedule 2A (paragraphs 1–9 and 10) was inserted by S.I. 1996 No. 3017.*
References in these paragraphs to approval certificates are to approval certificates issued under the "Approval Regulations". As to the "Approval Regulations", see the note to paragraph 2 of this Schedule.]

9. Modifications to regulation 61 (emissions)

B27.247   (1) Regulation 61 shall have effect with the following modifications in relation to a vehicle in respect of which there has been issued an approval certificate containing the letter "A" pursuant to regulation 12(2)(c) of the Approval Regulations.

(2) For the purposes of paragraphs (3A), (7), (8) and (9), the date of first use of the vehicle shall be regarded as being 1st January immediately preceding the date of manufacture of the engine by which it is propelled.
However, the date on which the vehicle is first used shall not, by virtue of this paragraph, be regarded in any circumstances as being later than the date on which it would otherwise have been regarded as being first used had this paragraph been omitted.

(3) Paragraphs 10(A) and 10(AA) shall not apply to the vehicle if it complies with or is exempt from the approval requirements relating to exhaust emissions.

B27.248   *[Schedule 2A (paragraphs 1–9 and 10) was inserted by S.I. 1996 No. 3017.*
References in these paragraphs to approval certificates are to approval certificates issued under the "Approval Regulations". As to the "Approval Regulations", see the note to paragraph 2 of this Schedule.]

B27.249   **[9A.** Paragraphs (10A), (10AA) and (10BA) of regulation 61 shall not apply to a vehicle in respect of which either a passenger vehicle approval certificate or a goods vehicle approval certificate has been issued, if it complies with, or is exempt from, the approval requirements relating to exhaust or smoke emissions.]

B27.250   *[Paragraph 9A was inserted into Schedule 2A by S.I. 2000 No. 3917.*
References in paragraph 9A to approval certificates are to approval certificates issued under the "Approval Regulations". As to the "Approval Regulations", see the note to paragraph 2 of this Schedule.]

[9B. Modifications to regulation 61A (emissions)

B27.251   (1) Regulation 61A shall not apply to a vehicle in respect of which either a passenger vehicle approval certificate or a goods vehicle approval certificate has been issued, if it complies with or is exempt from the approval requirements relating to exhaust or smoke emissions.

(2) Regulation 61A shall have effect with the following modifications in relation to a vehicle in respect of which there has been issued an approval certificate containing the letter "A" pursuant to regulation 12(2)(c) of the Approval Regulations.

(3) For the purposes of paragraphs (2) and (3) of regulation 61A, the date as is specified (as defined in regulation 61A) shall be regarded as being the 1st January immediately preceeding the date of manufacture of the engine by which the vehicle is propelled; provided that the date as is specified shall not in any circumstances be regarded as being later than the date on which the motor vehicle would otherwise have been regarded as being first used.]

[Paragraph 9B was inserted into Schedule 2A by S.I. 2000 No. 3917.   **B27.252**

References in paragraph 9B to approval certificates are to approval certificates issued under the "Approval Regulations". As to the "Approval Regulations", see the note to paragraph 2 of this Schedule.

Vehicles in respect of which approval certificates have been issued under regulation 12(2)(c) of the Approval Regulations which were in force when regulation 9B was enacted (i.e. the Motor Vehicles (Approval) Regulations 1996 (S.I. 1996 No. 3013)), are, by reference to ibid., Sched. 1, para.3, vehicles constructed for the personal use of the constructor, etc. As to the revocation of S.I. 1996 No. 3013, see the note to paragraph 2 of this Schedule.]

10. Modification to regulation 67 (vehicle identification numbers)

Regulation 67 shall not apply to a vehicle in respect of which an approval certificate has   **B27.253**
been issued if—

   (a) the vehicle is equipped with a plate which is in a conspicuous and readily accessible position, is affixed to a vehicle part which is not normally subject to replacement and shows clearly and indelibly the identification number shown on the certificate and the name of the manufacturer; and

   (b) that number is marked on the chassis, frame or other similar structure, on the offside of the vehicle, in a clearly visible and accessible position, and by a method such as hammering or stamping, in such a way that it cannot be obliterated or deteriorate.

[Schedule 2A (paragraphs 1–9 and 10) was inserted by S.I. 1996 No. 3017.   **B27.254**

References in these paragraphs to approval certificates are to approval certificates issued under the "Approval Regulations". As to the "Approval Regulations", see the note to paragraph 2 of this Schedule.]

SCHEDULE 3 (see regulation 16)

BRAKING REQUIREMENTS

1. The braking requirements referred to in regulation 16(4) are set out in the Table and   **B27.255**
are to be interpreted in accordance with paragraphs 2 to 5 of this Schedule.

TABLE

(Schedule 3)

Number	Requirement
1	The vehicle shall be equipped with— (a) one efficient braking system having two means of operation; (b) one efficient split braking system having one means of operation; or (c) two efficient braking systems each having a separate means of operation, and in the case of a vehicle first used on or after 1st January 1968, no account shall be taken of a multi-pull means of operation unless, at first application, it operates a hydraulic, electric or pneumatic device which causes the application of brakes with total braking efficiency not less than 25%.
2	The vehicle shall be equipped with— (a) one efficient braking system having two means of operation; or (b) two efficient braking systems each having a separate means of operation.

[continued on next page

Number	*Requirement*
3	The vehicle shall be equipped with an efficient braking system.
4	The braking system shall be so designed that in the event of failure of any part (other than a fixed member or a brake shoe anchor pin) through or by means of which the force necessary to apply the brakes is transmitted, there shall still be available for application by the driver brakes sufficient under the most adverse conditions to bring the vehicle to rest within a reasonable distance. The brakes so available shall be applied to— (a) in the case of a track-laying vehicle, one track on each side of the vehicle; (b) in the case of a wheeled motor vehicle, one wheel if the vehicle has 3 wheels and otherwise to at least half the wheels; and (c) in the case of a wheeled trailer, at least one wheel if it has only 2 wheels and otherwise at least 2 wheels. This requirement applies to the braking systems of both a trailer and the vehicle by which it is being drawn except that if the drawing vehicle complies with regulation 15 [Community Directive 79/489, 85/647 [, 88/194 or 91/422]] or ECE Regulation 13.03, 13.04 [, 13.05 or 13.06], the requirement applies only to the braking system of the drawing vehicle. It does not apply to vehicles having split braking systems (which are subject to regulation 18(3)(b)) or to road rollers. (The expressions *"part"* and *"half the wheels"* are to be interpreted in accordance with paragraphs (3) and (4) respectively.)
5	The braking system shall be so designed and constructed that, in the event of the failure of any part thereof, there shall still be available for application by the driver a brake sufficient under the most adverse conditions to bring the vehicle to rest within a reasonable distance.
6	The braking system of a vehicle, when drawing a trailer which complies with regulation 15 [Community Directive 79/489, 85/647 or 88/194] or ECE Regulation 13.03, 13.04 [, 13.05 or 13.06], shall be so constructed that, in the event of a failure of any part (other than a fixed member or brake shoe anchor pin) of the service braking system of the drawing vehicle (excluding the means of operation of a split braking system) the driver can still apply brakes to at least one wheel of the trailer, if it has only 2 wheels, and otherwise to at least 2 wheels, by using the secondary braking system of the drawing vehicle. (The expression *"part"* is to be interpreted in accordance with paragraph 3.)
7	The application of any means of operation of a braking system shall not affect or operate the pedal or hand lever of any other means of operation.
8	The braking system shall not be rendered ineffective by the non-rotation of the engine of the vehicle or, in the case of a trailer, the engine of the drawing vehicle (steam-propelled vehicles, other than locomotives and buses, are excluded from this requirement).
9	At least one means of operation shall be capable of causing brakes to be applied directly, and not through the transmission gear, to at least half the wheels of the vehicle. This requirement does not apply to a works truck with an unladen weight not exceeding 7370kg, or to an industrial tractor; and it does not apply to a vehicle with more than 4 wheels if—

[*continued on next page*]

Number	Requirement
	(a) the drive is transmitted to all wheels other than the steering wheels without the interposition of a differential driving gear or similar mechanism between the axles carrying the driving wheels; and (b) the brakes applied by one means of operation apply directly to 2 driving wheels on opposite sides of the vehicle; and (c) the brakes applied by another means of operation act directly on all the other driving wheels. (The expression "*half the wheels*" is to be interpreted in accordance with paragraph (4).)
10	The brakes of a trailer shall come into operation automatically on its overrun or, in the case of a track-laying trailer drawn by a vehicle having steerable wheels at the front or a wheeled trailer, the driver of, or some other person on, the drawing vehicle or on the trailer shall be able to apply the brakes on the trailer.
11	The brakes of a trailer shall come into operation automatically on its overrun or the driver of the drawing vehicle shall be able to apply brakes to all the wheels of the trailer, using the means of operation which applies the service brakes of the drawing vehicle.
12	The brakes of the vehicle shall apply to all wheels other than the steering wheels.
13	The brakes of the vehicle shall apply to at least 2 wheels.
14	The brakes of the vehicle shall apply in the case of a wheeled vehicle to at least 2 wheels if the vehicle has no more than 4 wheels and to at least half the wheels if the vehicle has more than 4 wheels; and in the case of a track-laying vehicle to all the tracks.
15	The brakes shall apply to all the wheels.
16	The parking brake shall be so designed and constructed that— (a) in the case of a wheeled heavy motor car or motor car, its means of operation is independent of the means of operation of any split braking system with which the vehicle is fitted; (b) in the case of a motor vehicle other than a motor cycle or an invalid carriage, either— (i) it is capable of being applied by direct mechanical action without the intervention of any hydraulic, electric or pneumatic device; or (ii) the vehicle complies with requirement 15; and (c) it can at all times when the vehicle is not being driven or is left unattended be set so as— (i) in the case of a track-laying vehicle, to lock the tracks; and (ii) in the case of a wheeled vehicle, to prevent the rotation of at least one wheel in the case of a three wheeled vehicle and at least two wheels in the case of a vehicle with more than three wheels.
17	The parking brake shall be capable of being set so as effectively to prevent two at least of the wheels from revolving when the trailer is not being drawn.

[*continued on next page*

Number	*Requirement*
18	The parking brake shall be so designed and constructed that— (a) in the case of a motor vehicle, its means of operation (whether multi-pull or not) is independent of the means of operation of any braking system required by regulation 18 to have a total braking efficiency of not less than 50%; and (b) in the case of a trailer, its brakes can be applied and released by a person standing on the ground by a means of operation fitted to the trailer; and (c) in either case, its braking force, when the vehicle is not being driven or is left unattended (and in the case of a trailer, whether the braking force is applied by the driver using the service brakes of the drawing vehicle or by a person standing on the ground in the manner indicated in sub-paragraph (b)) can at all times be maintained in operation by direct mechanical action without the intervention of any hydraulic, electric or pneumatic device and, when so maintained, can hold the vehicle stationary on a gradient of at least 16% without the assistance of stored energy.

B27.256   *[Paragraph 1 of Schedule 3 is printed as amended by S.I. 1987 No. 676; S.I. 1990 No. 1981; S.I. 1992 No. 352; S.I. 1995 No. 551.]*

B27.257   **2.** For the purposes of requirement 3 in the Table, in the case of a motor car or heavy motor car propelled by steam and not used as a bus, the engine shall be deemed to be an efficient braking system with one means of operation if the engine is capable of being reversed and, in the case of a vehicle first used on or after 1st January 1927, is incapable of being disconnected from any of the driving wheels of the vehicle except by the sustained effort of the driver.

B27.258   **3.** For the purpose of requirements 4 and 6 in the Table, in the case of a wheeled motor car and of a vehicle first used on or after 1st October 1938 which is a locomotive, a motor tractor, a heavy motor car or a track-laying motor car, every moving shaft which is connected to or supports any part of a braking system shall be deemed to be part of the system.

B27.259   **4.** For the purpose of [requirements 4, 9 and 14] in the Table, in determining whether brakes apply to at least half the wheels of a vehicle, not more than one front wheel shall be treated as a wheel to which brakes apply unless the vehicle is—

    (a) a locomotive or motor tractor with more than 4 wheels;

    (b) a heavy motor car or motor car first used before 1st October 1938;

    (c) a motor car with an unladen weight not exceeding 1020kg;

    (d) a motor car which is a passenger vehicle but is not a bus;

    (e) a works truck;

    (f) a heavy motor car or motor car with more than 3 wheels which is equipped in respect of all its wheels with brakes which are operated by one means of operation; or

    (g) a track-laying vehicle.

B27.260   *[Paragraph 4 of Schedule 3 is printed as amended by S.I. 1987 No. 676.]*

B27.261   **5.** In this Schedule a "*multi-pull means of operation*" means a device forming part of a braking system which causes the muscular energy of the driver to apply the brakes of that system progressively as a result of successive applications of that device by the driver.

[SCHEDULE 3A (see regulations 39A and 39B)

EXCLUSION OF CERTAIN VEHICLES FROM THE APPLICATION OF REGULATION 39A

PART I

1.—(1) In this Part—   B27.262

"*EEC type approval certificate*" means a certificate issued by a member state of the European Economic Community in accordance with Community Directive 70/220 as originally made or with any amendments which have from time to time been made before 5th September 1988;

"*engine capacity*" means in the case of a reciprocating engine, the nominal swept volume and, in the case of a rotary engine, double the nominal swept volume;

. . .

"*relevant authority*" means—

(a) in relation to an EEC type approval certificate issued by the United Kingdom, the Secretary of State, and

(b) in relation to an EEC type approval certificate issued by any other member state of the European Economic Community, the authority having power under the law of that state to issue that certificate.

(2) The reference in this Schedule to a M1 category vehicle is reference to a vehicle described as M1 in Council Directive 70/156/EEC [*q.v.*] of 6th February 1970 as amended at 5th September 1988.

[2] A vehicle of a description specified in column 2 of the Table below is excluded from the application of regulation 39A if it is first used before the date specified in column 3 and the conditions specified in paragraph 3 are satisfied in respect to it on that date.

[3] The conditions referred to in paragraph 2 are—

(a) that the vehicle is a model in relation to which there is in force an EEC type approval certificate issued before 1st October 1989;

(b) that the manufacturer of the vehicle has supplied to the relevant authority which issued the EEC type approval certificate, a certificate stating that adapting vehicles of that model to the fuel requirements specified in the Annexes to Community Directive 88/76 would entail a change in material specification of the inlet or exhaust valve seats or a reduction in the compression ratio or an increase in the engine capacity to compensate for loss of power; and

(c) that the relevant authority has accepted the certificate referred to in sub-paragraph (b).

TABLE

Item	Description of vehicle	Date before which vehicle must be first used
(1)	(2)	(3)
1.	Vehicles with an engine capacity of less than 1400cc.	1.4.92
2.	Vehicles with an engine capacity of not less than 1400cc and not more than 2000cc.	1.4.94

[*continued on next page*

Item (1)	Description of vehicle (2)	Date before which vehicle must be first used (3)
3.	M1 category vehicles with an engine capacity of more than 2000cc and which— (a) are constructed or adapted to carry not more than 5 passengers excluding the driver, or (b) have a maximum gross weight of not more than 2500kg not being in either case, an off-road vehicle.	1.4.93

PART II

B27.263

SYMBOL INDICATING THAT VEHICLE CAN RUN ON UNLEADED PETROL

[Omitted.]]

B27.264   *[Schedule 3A was inserted by S.I. 1988 No. 1524 and is printed as subsequently amended by S.I. 1990 No. 1131.*

The date September 5, 1988 (to which reference is made in paragraph 1(2) of Schedule 3A) is the date on which S.I. 1988 No. 1524 (which added Schedule 3A) was made; it seems to have no significance vis-à-vis Council Directive 70/156/EEC.]

[SCHEDULE 3B (see regulation 36C)

AUTHORISED SEALERS

PART I

GENERAL

B27.265   **1.** The Secretary of State may authorise—

(a) an individual proposing to seal speed limiters other than on behalf of another person;

(b) a firm; or

(c) a corporation;

to seal speed limiters for the purposes of regulation 36A or 36B and a person or body so authorised is referred to in this Schedule as an *"authorised sealer"*.

2. An authorised sealer shall comply with the conditions set out in Part II of this Schedule and with such other conditions as may from time to time be imposed by the Secretary of State.

B27.266   **3.** *[Entitlement to charge for sealing a speed limiter.]*

4. *[Withdrawal of authorisation granted under paragraph 1.]*

5. *[Events terminating an authorisation granted under paragraph 1.]*

PART II

THE CONDITIONS

6. An authorised sealer shall not—   **B27.267**

(a) seal a speed limiter fitted to a vehicle to which regulation 36A applies unless he is satisfied that the speed limiter fulfils the requirements of paragraph (3)(a), (b) and (d) of that regulation, or

(b) seal a speed limiter fitted to a vehicle to which regulation 36B applies unless he is satisfied that the speed limiter fulfils the requirements of paragraph (3)(a), (b) and (d) of that regulation.

7. When sealing a speed limiter fitted to a vehicle to which regulation 36A applies, an authorised sealer shall do so in such a manner that the speed limiter fulfils the requirements of paragraph (3)(c) of that regulation.

8. When sealing a speed limiter fitted to a vehicle to which regulation 36B applies, an   **B27.268** authorised sealer shall do so in such a manner that the speed limiter fulfils the requirements of paragraph (3)(c) of that regulation.

9. When an authorised sealer has sealed a speed limiter fitted to a vehicle to which section 36A applies he shall supply the owner with a plate which fulfils the requirements of regulation 70A.

10. When an authorised sealer has sealed a speed limiter fitted to a vehicle to which   **B27.269** section 36B applies he shall supply the owner with a plate which fulfils the requirements of regulation 70B.]

[Schedule 3B was inserted by S.I. 1992 No. 422.]   **B27.270**

SCHEDULE 4 (see regulation 40)

GAS CONTAINERS

PART I

Definitions relating to gas containers

1. In this Schedule, unless the context otherwise requires, the following expressions have   **B27.271** the meanings hereby assigned to them respectively, that is to say—

"*gas container*" means a container fitted to a motor vehicle or a trailer and intended for the storage of gaseous fuel for the purpose of the propulsion of the vehicle or the drawing vehicle as the case may be;

"*gas cylinder*" means a container fitted to a motor vehicle or a trailer and intended for the storage of compressed gas for the purpose of the propulsion of the vehicle or the drawing vehicle as the case may be;

"*compressed gas*" means gaseous fuel under a pressure exceeding 1.0325 bar above atmospheric pressure;

"*pipeline*" means all pipes connecting a gas container or containers—

(a) to the engine or the mixing device for the supply of a mixture of gas and air to the engine; and

(b) to the filling point on the vehicle;

"*pressure pipeline*" means any part of a pipeline intended for the conveyance of compressed gas; and

"*reducing valve*" means an apparatus which automatically reduces the pressure of the gas passing through it.

Gas containers

B27.272   **2.** Every gas container shall—

(a) be securely attached to the vehicle in such manner as not to be liable to displacement or damage due to vibration or other cause; and

(b) be so placed or insulated as not to be adversely affected by the heat from the exhaust system.

Pipelines

B27.273   **3.**—(1) Every pipeline shall be supported in such manner as to be protected from excessive vibration and strain.

(2) No part of a pipeline shall be in such a position that it may be subjected to undue heat from the exhaust system.

(3) Every pressure pipeline shall be made of steel solid drawn.

(4) The maximum unsupported length of a pressure pipeline shall not exceed 920mm.

Unions

B27.274   **4.**—(1) Every union shall be so constructed and fitted that it will—

(a) not be liable to work loose or develop leakage when in use; and

(b) be readily accessible for inspection and adjustment.

(2) No union on a pressure pipeline or on a gas cylinder shall contain a joint other than a metal to metal joint.

Reducing valves

B27.275   **5.** Every reducing valve shall be—

(a) so fitted as to be readily accessible; and

(b) so constructed that there can be no escape of gas when the engine is not running.

Valves and cocks

B27.276   **6.**—(1) Every valve or cock intended to be subjected to a pressure exceeding 6.8948 bar shall be of forged steel or of brass or bronze complying with the specification contained in Part II of this Schedule.

(2) A valve or cock shall be fitted to the pipeline to enable the supply of gas from the container or containers to the mixing device to be shut off.

(3)(a) In the case of a pressure pipeline the valve or cock shall be placed between the reducing valve and the container and shall be readily visible and accessible from the outside of the vehicle and a notice indicating its position and method of operation shall be affixed in a conspicuous position on the outside of the vehicle carrying the gas container or containers.

(b) In other cases, if the valve or cock is not so visible and accessible as aforesaid, a notice indicating its position shall be affixed in a conspicuous position on the outside of the vehicle carrying the container or containers.

Pressure gauges

7. Every pressure gauge connected to a pressure pipeline shall be so constructed as not to be liable to deterioration under the action of the particular gases employed and shall be so constructed and fitted that—   **B27.277**

    (a) in the event of failure of such pressure gauge no gas can escape into any part of the vehicle;

    (b) it is not possible owing to leakage of gas into the casing of the pressure gauge for pressure to increase therein to such extent as to be liable to cause a breakage of the glass thereof; and

    (c) in the event of failure of such pressure gauge the supply of gas thereto may be readily cut off.

Charging connections

8.—(1) Every connection for charging a gas container shall be outside the vehicle and in the case of a public service vehicle no such connection shall be within 610mm of any entrance or exit.   **B27.278**

(2) An efficient shut-off valve shall be fitted as near as practicable to the filling point.

Provided that in cases where compressed gas is not used a cock or an efficient non-return valve may be fitted in lieu thereof.

(3) Where compressed gas is used an additional emergency shut-off valve shall be fitted adjacent to the valve referred to in sub-paragraph (2) of this paragraph.

(4) A cap shall be fitted to the gas filling point on the vehicle and where compressed gas is used this cap shall be made of steel with a metal to metal joint.

Trailers

9.—(1) Where a trailer is used for the carriage of a gas cylinder, a reducing valve shall be fitted on the trailer.   **B27.279**

(2) No pipe used for conveying gas from a trailer to the engine of a vehicle shall contain compressed gas.

Construction, etc., of system

10. Every part of a gas container propulsion system shall be—   **B27.280**

    (a) so placed or protected as not to be exposed to accidental damage and shall be soundly and properly constructed of suitable and well-finished materials capable of withstanding the loads and stresses likely to be met with in operation and shall be maintained in an efficient, safe and clean condition; and

    (b) so designed and constructed that leakage of gas is not likely to occur under normal working conditions, whether or not the engine is running.

PART II

SPECIFICATION FOR BRASS OR BRONZE VALVES

Manufacture of valves

1. The stamping or pressing from which each valve is manufactured shall be made from bars produced by (a) extrusion, (b) rolling, (c) forging, (d) extrusion and drawing, or (e) rolling and drawing.   **B27.281**

Heat treatment

B27.282   **2.** Each stamping or pressing shall be heat treated so as to produce an equiaxed microstructure in the material.

Freedom from defects

B27.283   **3.** All stampings or pressings and the bars from which they are made shall be free from cracks, laminations, hard spots, segregated materials and variations in composition.

Tensile test

B27.284   **4.** Tensile tests shall be made on samples of stampings or pressings taken at random from any consignment. The result of the tensile test shall conform to the following conditions—

Yield Stress.—Not less than 231.6 N/mm^2.
Ultimate Tensile Stress.—Not less than 463.3 N/mm^2.
Elongation on 50mm gauge length.—Not less than 25%.

Note.—When the gauge length is less than 50mm the required elongation shall be proportionately reduced.

The fractured test piece shall be free from piping and other defects (see paragraph 3 of this Part of this Schedule).

SCHEDULE 5 (see regulations 40 and 96)

GAS SYSTEMS

Definitions

B27.285   **1.** In this Schedule—

"*check valve*" means a device which permits the flow of gas in one direction and prevents the flow of gas in the opposite direction;

"*design pressure*" means the pressure which a part of a gas system has been designed and constructed safely to withstand;

"*double-check valve*" means a device which consists of two check valves in series and which permits the flow of gas in one direction and prevents the flow of gas in the opposite direction;

"*excess flow valve*" means a device which automatically and instantaneously reduces to a minimum the flow of gas through the valve when the flow rate exceeds a set value;

"*fixed gas container*" means a gas container which is attached to a vehicle permanently and in such a manner that the container can be filled without being moved;

"*gas container*" means any container, not being a container for the carriage of gas as goods, which is fitted to or carried on a motor vehicle or trailer and is intended for the storage of gas for either—

(a) the propulsion of the motor vehicle, or

(b) the operation of a gas-fired appliance;

"*high pressure*" means a pressure exceeding 1.0325 bar absolute;

"*high pressure pipeline*" means a pipeline intended to contain gas at high pressure;

"*pipeline*" means any pipe or passage connecting any two parts of a gas propulsion system of a vehicle or of a gas-fired appliance supply system on a vehicle or any two points on the same part of any such system;

"*portable gas container*" means a gas container which may be attached to a vehicle but which can readily be removed;

"*pressure relief valve*" means a device which opens automatically when the pressure in the part of the gas system to which it is fitted exceeds a set value, reaches its maximum flow capacity when the set value is exceeded by 10% and closes automatically when the pressure falls below a set value; and

"*reducing valve*" means a device which automatically reduces the pressure of the gas passing through it, and includes regulator devices.

Gas containers

2.—(1) Every gas container shall—   **B27.286**

(a) be capable of withstanding the pressure of the gas which may be stored in the container at the highest temperature which the gas is likely to reach,

(b) if fitted inside the vehicle be so arranged as to prevent so far as is practicable the possibility of gas entering the engine, passenger or living compartments due to leaks or venting from the container or valves connections and gauges immediately adjacent to it, and the space containing those components shall be so ventilated and drained as to prevent the accumulation of gas,

(c) be securely attached to the vehicle in such a manner as not to be liable to displacement or damage due to vibration or other cause, and

(d) be so placed and so insulated or shielded as not to suffer any adverse effect from the heat of the exhaust system of any engine or any other source of heat.

(2) Every portable gas container shall be either—

(a) hermetically sealed, or

(b) fitted with a valve or cock to enable the flow of gas from the container to be stopped.

(3) Every fixed gas container shall—

(a) be fitted with—

(i) at least one pressure relief valve, and

(ii) at least one manually operated valve which may be extended by an internal dip tube inside the gas container so as to indicate when the container has been filled to the level corresponding to the filling ratio specified in the British Standards Institution Specification for Filling Ratios and Developed Pressure for Liquefiable and Permanent Gases (as defined, respectively, in paragraphs 3.2 and 3.5 of the said Specification) published in May 1976 under the number BS 5355, and

(b) be conspicuously and permanently marked with its design pressure.

(4) If any fixed gas container is required to be fitted in a particular attitude or location, or if any device referred to in sub-paragraph (3) above requires the container to be fitted in such a manner, then it shall be conspicuously and permanently marked to indicate that requirement.

(5) If the operation of any pressure relief valve or other device referred to in sub-paragraph (3) above may cause gas to be released from the gas container an outlet shall be provided to lead such gas to the outside of the vehicle so as not to suffer any adverse effect from the heat of the exhaust system of any engine or any other source of heat, and that outlet from the pressure relief valve shall not be fitted with any other valve or cock.

Filling systems for fixed gas containers

3.—(1) Every connection for filling a fixed gas container shall be on the outside of the   **B27.287**
vehicle.

(2) There shall be fitted to every fixed gas container either—

   (a) a manually operated shut-off valve and an excess flow valve, or

   (b) a manually operated shut-off valve and a single check valve, or

   (c) a double-check valve,

and all parts of these valves in contact with gas shall be made entirely of suitable metal except that they may contain non-metal washers and seals provided that such washers and seals are supported and constrained by metal components.

(3) In every case where a pipe is attached to a gas container for the purpose of filling the gas container there shall be fitted to the end of the pipe furthest from the gas container a check valve or a double-check valve.

(4) There shall be fitted over every gas filling point on a vehicle a cap which shall—

   (a) prevent any leakage of gas from the gas filling point,

   (b) be secured to the vehicle by a chain or some other suitable means,

   (c) be made of suitable material; and

   (d) be fastened to the gas filling point by either a screw thread or other suitable means.

Pipelines

B27.288   **4.**—(1) Every pipeline shall be fixed in such a manner and position that—

   (a) it will not be adversely affected by the heat of the exhaust system of any engine or any other source of heat,

   (b) it is protected from vibration and strain in excess of that which it can reasonably be expected to withstand, and

   (c) in the case of a high pressure pipeline it is so far as is practicable accessible for inspection.

(2) Save as provided in sub-paragraph (4) below, every high pressure pipeline shall be—

   (a) a rigid line of steel, copper or copper alloy of high pressure hydraulic grade, suitable for service on road vehicles and designed for a minimum service pressure rating of not less than 75 bar absolute, and

   (b) effectively protected against, or shielded from, or treated so as to be resistant to, external corrosion throughout its length unless it is made from material which is corrosion resistant under the conditions which it is likely to encounter in service.

(3) No unsupported length of any high pressure pipeline shall exceed 600mm.

(4) Flexible hose may be used in a high pressure pipeline if—

   (a) it is reinforced either by stainless steel wire braid or by textile braid,

   (b) its length does not exceed 500mm, and

   (c) save in the case of a pipeline attached to a gas container for the purpose of filling that container the flexibility which it provides is necessary for the construction or operation of the gas system of which it forms a part.

(5) If a high pressure pipeline or part of such a pipeline is so constructed or located that it may, in the course of its normal use (excluding the supply of fuel from a gas container), contain liquid which is prevented from flowing, a relief valve shall be incorporated in that pipeline.

Unions and joints

B27.289   **5.**—(1) Every union and joint on a pipeline or gas container shall be so constructed and fitted that it will—

(a) not be liable to work loose or leak when in use, and

(b) be readily accessible for inspection and maintenance.

(2) Every union on a high pressure pipeline or on a gas container shall be made of suitable metal but such a union may contain non-metal washers and seals provided that such washers and seals are supported and constrained by metal components.

Reducing valves

6. Every reducing valve shall be made of suitable materials and be so fitted as to be readily accessible for inspection and maintenance.   **B27.290**

Pressure relief valves

7.—(1) Every pressure relief valve which is fitted to any part of a gas system (including a gas container) shall—   **B27.291**

(a) be made entirely of suitable metal and so constructed and fitted as to ensure that the cooling effect of the gas during discharge shall not prevent its effective operation,

(b) be capable, under the most extreme temperatures likely to be met (including exposure to fire), of a discharge rate which prevents the pressure of the contents of the gas system from exceeding its design pressure,

(c) have a maximum discharge pressure not greater than the design pressure of the gas container,

(d) be so designed and constructed as to prevent unauthorised interference with the relief pressure setting during service, and

(e) have outlets which are—

    (i) so sited that so far as is reasonably practicable in the event of an accident the valve and its outlets are protected from damage and the free discharge from such outlets is not impaired, and

    (ii) so designed and constructed as to prevent the collection of moisture and other foreign matter which could adversely affect their performance.

(2) The pressure at which a pressure relief valve is designed to start lifting shall be clearly and permanently marked on every such valve.

(3) Every pressure relief valve which is fitted to a gas container shall communicate with the vapour space in the gas container and not with any liquefied gas.

Valves and cocks

8.—(1) A valve or cock shall be fitted to every supply pipeline as near as practicable to every fixed gas container and such valve or cock shall by manual operation enable the supply of gas from the gas container to the gas system to be stopped, and save as provided in sub-paragraph (2) below, shall—   **B27.292**

(a) if fitted on the outside of the vehicle, be readily visible and accessible from the outside of the vehicle, or

(b) if fitted inside the vehicle be readily accessible for operation and be so arranged as to prevent so far as is practicable the possibility of gas entering the engine, passenger or living compartments due to leaks, and the space containing the valve or cock shall be so ventilated and drained as to prevent the accumulation of gas in that space.

(2) Where a fixed gas container supplies no gas system other than a gas propulsion system and the gas container is so located that it is not practicable to make the valve or cock referred to in sub-paragraph (1) above readily accessible there shall be fitted an electrically-operated valve which shall either be incorporated in the valve or cock referred to in sub-paragraph (1) above or be fitted immediately downstream from it and shall—

(a) be constructed so as to open when the electric power is applied and to close when the electric power is cut off,

(b) be so fitted as to shut off the supply of gas from the gas container to the gas system when the engine is not running, and

(c) if fitted inside the vehicle be so arranged as to prevent as far as is practicable the possibility of gas entering the engine, passenger or living compartments due to leaks, and the space containing the valve shall be so ventilated and drained as to prevent the accumulation of gas in that space.

(3) A notice clearly indicating the position, purpose and method of operating every valve or cock referred to in sub-paragraphs (1) and (2) above shall be fixed—

(a) in all cases, in a conspicuous position on the outside of the vehicle, and

(b) if every case where the valve or cock is located inside the vehicle in a conspicuous position adjacent to the gas container.

(4) In the case of a high pressure pipeline for the conveyance of gas from the gas container an excess flow valve shall be fitted as near as practicable to the gas container and such valve shall operate in the event of a fracture of the pipeline or other similar failure.

(5) All parts of every valve or cock referred to in this paragraph which are in contact with gas shall be made of suitable metal, save that they may contain non-metal washers and seals provided that such washers and seals are supported and constrained by metal components.

Gauges

B27.293   **9.** Every gauge connected to a gas container or to a pipeline shall be so constructed as to be unlikely to deteriorate under the action of the gas used or to be used and shall be so constructed and fitted that—

(a) no gas can escape into any part of the vehicle as a result of any failure of the gauge, and

(b) in the event of any failure of the gauge the supply of gas to the gauge can be readily stopped.

Provided that the requirement specified in sub-paragraph (b) above shall not apply in respect of a gauge as an integral part of a gas container.

Propulsion systems

B27.294   **10.**—(1) Every gas propulsion system shall be so designed and constructed that—

(a) the supply of gas to the engine is automatically stopped by the operation of a valve when the engine is not running at all or is not running on the supply of gas, and,

(b) where a reducing valve is relied on to comply with sub-paragraph (a) above, the supply of gas to the engine is automatically stopped by the operation of an additional valve when the engine is switched off.

(2) Where the engine of a vehicle is constructed or adapted to run on one or more fuels as alternatives to gas, the safety and efficiency of the engine and any fuel system shall not be impaired by the presence of any other fuel system.

Special requirements for buses

B27.295   **11.** In the case of a bus there shall be fitted as near as practicable to the gas container a valve which shall stop the flow of gas into the gas supply pipeline in the event of—

(a) the angle of tilt of the vehicle exceeding that referred to in regulation 6 of the Public Services Vehicles (Conditions of Fitness, Equipment, Use and Certification) Regulations 1981 [*S.I. 1981 No. 257, q.v.*], and

(b) the deceleration of the vehicle exceeding 5 g.

Gas-fired appliances

12. Every part of a gas-fired appliance shall be—   **B27.296**

(a) so designed and constructed that leakage of gas is unlikely to occur, and

(b) constructed of materials which are compatible both with each other and with the gas used.

13. Every gas-fired appliance shall be—   **B27.297**

(a) so located as to be easily inspected and maintained,

(b) so located and either insulated or shielded that its use shall not cause or be likely to cause danger due to the presence of any flammable material,

(c) so constructed and located as not to impose undue stress on any pipe or fitting, and

(d) so fastened or located as not to work loose or move in relation to the vehicle.

14. With the exception of catalytic heating appliances, every appliance of the kind   **B27.298**
described in regulation 96(3)(b) or (c) which is fitted to a motor vehicle shall be fitted with a
flue which shall be—

(a) connected to an outlet which is on the outside of the vehicle,

(b) constructed and located so as to prevent any expelled matter from entering the vehicle, and

(c) located so that it will not cause any adverse effect to, or suffer any adverse effect from, the exhaust outlet of any engine or any other source of heat.

General requirements

15. Every part of a gas propulsion system or a gas-fired appliance system, excluding the   **B27.299**
appliance itself, shall be—

(a) so far as is practicable so located or protected as not to be exposed to accidental damage,

(b) soundly and properly constructed of materials which are compatible with one another and with the gas used or to be used and which are capable of withstanding the loads and stresses likely to be met in operation, and

(c) so designed and constructed that leakage of gas is unlikely to occur.

SCHEDULE 6 (see regulation 41)

CONSTRUCTION OF MINIBUSES

The requirements referred to in regulation 41 are as follows—   **B27.300**

Exhaust pipes

1. The outlet of every exhaust pipe fitted to a minibus shall be either at the rear or on   **B27.301**
the off side of the vehicle.

Doors—number and position

2.—(1) Every minibus shall be fitted with at least—   **B27.302**

(a) one service door on the near side of the vehicle; and

(b) one emergency door either at the rear or on the off side of the vehicle so, however, that any emergency door fitted on the off side of the vehicle shall be in addition to the driver's door and there shall be no requirement for an emergency door on a minibus if it has a service door at the rear in addition to the service door on the near side.

(2) No minibus shall be fitted with any door on its off side other than a driver's door and an emergency door.

Emergency doors

B27.303   **3.** Every emergency door fitted to a minibus, whether or not required pursuant to these Regulations, shall—

    (a) be clearly marked, in letters not less than 25mm high, on both the inside and the outside, "EMERGENCY DOOR" or "FOR EMERGENCY USE ONLY", and the means of its operation shall be clearly indicated on or near the door;

    (b) if hinged, open outwards;

    (c) be capable of being operated manually; and

    (d) when fully opened, give an aperture in the body of the vehicle not less than 1210mm high nor less than 530mm wide.

Power-operated doors

B27.304   **4.**—(1) Every power-operated door fitted to a minibus shall—

    (a) incorporate transparent panels so as to enable a person immediately inside the door to see any person immediately outside the door;

    (b) be capable of being operated by a mechanism controlled by the driver of the vehicle when in the driving seat;

    (c) be capable, in the event of an emergency or a failure of the supply of power for the operation of the door, of being opened from both inside and outside the vehicle by controls which—

        (i) over-ride all other controls;

        (ii) are placed on, or adjacent to, the door, and

        (iii) are accompanied by markings which clearly indicate their position and method of operation and state that they may not be used by passengers except in an emergency;

    (d) have a soft edge so that a trapped finger is unlikely to be injured; and

    (e) be controlled by a mechanism by virtue of which if the door, when closing, meets a resistance exceeding 150 Newtons, either

    —the door will cease to close and begin to open, or

    —the closing force will cease and the door will become capable of being opened manually.

(2) No minibus shall be equipped with a system for the storage or transmission of energy in respect of the opening or closing of any door which, either in normal operation or if the system fails, is capable of adversely affecting the operation of the vehicle's braking system.

Locks, handles and hinges of doors

B27.305   **5.** No minibus shall be fitted with—

    (a) a door which can be locked from the outside unless, when so locked, it is capable of being opened from inside the vehicle when stationary;

    (b) a handle or other device for opening any door, other than the driver's door, from inside the vehicle unless the handle or other device is designed so as to prevent, so far as is reasonably practicable, the accidental opening of the door, and is fitted with a guard or transparent cover or so designed that it must be raised to open the door;

(c) a door which is not capable of being opened, when not locked, from inside and outside the vehicle by a single movement of the handle or other device for opening the door;

(d) a door in respect of which there is not a device capable of holding the door closed so as to prevent any passenger falling through the doorway;

(e) a side door which opens outwards and is hinged at the edge nearest the rear of the vehicle except in the case of a door having more than one rigid panel;

(f) a door, other than a power-operated door, in respect of which there is not either—

　(i) a slam lock of the two-stage type; or

　(ii) a device by means of which the driver, when occupying the driver's seat, is informed if the door is not securely closed, such device being operated by movement of the handle or other device for opening the door or, in the case of a handle or other device with a spring-return mechanism, by movement of the door as well as of the handle or other device.

Provided that the provisions of sub-paragraphs (a), (c), (d) and (f) of this paragraph shall not apply in respect of a near side rear door forming part of a pair of doors fitted at the rear of a vehicle if that door is capable of being held securely closed by the other door of that pair.

View of doors

6.—(1) Save as provided in sub-paragraph (2), every minibus shall be fitted with mirrors or other means so that the driver, when occupying the driver's seat, can see clearly the area immediately inside and outside every service door of the vehicle.   **B27.306**

(2) The provisions of sub-paragraph (1) shall be deemed to be satisfied in respect of a rear service door if a person 1.3 metres tall standing 1 metre behind the vehicle is visible to the driver when occupying the driver's seat.

Access to doors

7.—(1) Save as provided in sub-paragraph (2), there shall be unobstructed access from every passenger seat in a minibus to at least two doors one of which must be on the nearside of the vehicle and one of which must be either at the rear or on the offside of the vehicle.   **B27.307**

(2) Access to one only of the doors referred to in sub-paragraph (1) may be obstructed by either or both of—

(a) a seat which when tilted or folded does not obstruct access to that door, and

(b) a lifting platform or ramp which—

　(i) does not obstruct the handle or other device on the inside for opening the door with which the platform or ramp is associated, and

　(ii) when the door is open, can be pushed or pulled out of the way from the inside so as to leave the doorway clear for use in an emergency.

Grab handles and hand rails

8. Every minibus shall be fitted as respects every side service door with a grab handle or a hand rail to assist passengers to get on or off the vehicle.   **B27.308**

Seats

9.—(1) No seat shall be fitted to any door of a minibus.   **B27.309**

(2) Every seat and every wheelchair anchorage fitted to a minibus shall be fixed to the vehicle.

(3) No seat, other than a wheelchair, fitted to a minibus shall be less than 400mm wide, and in ascertaining the width of a seat no account shall be taken of any arm-rests, whether or not they are folded back or otherwise put out of use.

(4) No minibus shall be fitted with an anchorage for a wheelchair in such a manner that a wheelchair secured to the anchorage would face either side of the vehicle.

(5) No minibus shall be fitted with a seat—

(a) facing either side of the vehicle and immediately forward of a rear door unless the seat is fitted with an arm-rest or similar device to guard against a passenger on that seat falling through the doorway; or

(b) so placed that a passenger on it would, without protection, be liable to be thrown through any doorway which is provided with a power-operated door or down any steps, unless the vehicle is fitted with a screen or guard which affords adequate protection against that occurrence.

Electrical equipment and wiring

B27.310   **10.**—(1) Save as provided in sub-paragraph (2) no minibus shall be fitted with any—

(a) electrical circuit which is liable to carry a current exceeding that for which it was designed;

(b) cable for the conduct of electricity unless it is suitably insulated and protected from damage;

(c) electrical circuit, other than a charging circuit, which includes any equipment other than—

(i) a starter motor,
(ii) a glow plug,
(iii) an ignition circuit, and
(iv) a device to stop the vehicle's engine,

unless it includes a fuse or circuit breaker so, however, that one fuse or circuit breaker may serve more than one circuit; or

(d) electrical circuit with a voltage exceeding 100 volts unless there is connected in each pole of the main supply of electricity which is not connected to earth a manually operated switch which is—

(i) capable of disconnecting the circuit, or, if there is more than one, every circuit, from the main supply,
(ii) not capable of disconnecting any circuit supplying any lamp with which the vehicle is required to be fitted, and
(iii) located inside the vehicle in a position readily accessible to the driver.

(2) The provisions of sub-paragraph (1) do not apply in respect of a high tension ignition circuit or a circuit within a unit of equipment.

Fuel tanks

B27.311   **11.** No minibus shall be fitted with a fuel tank or any apparatus for the supply of fuel which is in the compartments or other spaces provided for the accommodation of the driver or passengers.

Lighting of steps

B27.312   **12.** Every minibus shall be provided with lamps to illuminate every step at a passenger exit or in a gangway.

General construction and maintenance

13. Every minibus, including all bodywork and fittings, shall be soundly and properly constructed of suitable materials and maintained in good and serviceable condition, and shall be of such design as to be capable of withstanding the loads and stresses likely to be met in the normal operation of the vehicle.   **B27.313**

Definitions

14. In this Schedule—   **B27.314**

"*driver's door*" means a door fitted to a minibus for use by the driver;

"*emergency door*" means a door fitted to a minibus for use by passengers in an emergency; and

"*service door*" means a door fitted to a minibus for use by passengers in normal circumstances.

SCHEDULE 7

FIRE-EXTINGUISHING APPARATUS AND FIRST-AID EQUIPMENT FOR MINIBUSES

[PART I

(see regulation 42)

FIRE EXTINGUISHING APPARATUS

A fire extinguisher which complies in all respects with the specification for portable fire extinguishers issued by the British Standards Institution numbered BS 5423:1977 or BS 5423:1980 or BS 5423:1987 and which—   **B27.315**

(a) has a minimum test fire rating of 8A or 21B, and

(b) contains water or foam or contains, and is marked to indicate that it contains halon 1211 or halon 1301.]

[Part I of Schedule 7 was substituted by S.I. 1989 No. 2360.]   **B27.316**

PART II

(see regulation 43)

FIRST AID EQUIPMENT

(i) Ten antiseptic wipes, foil packed;   **B27.317**
(ii) One conforming disposable bandage (not less than 7.5cm wide);
(iii) Two triangular bandages;
(iv) One packet of 24 assorted adhesive dressings;
(v) Three large sterile unmedicated ambulance dressings (not less than 15.0cm × 20.0cm);
(vi) Two sterile eye pads, with attachments;
(vii) Twelve assorted safety pins; and
(viii) One pair of rustless blunt-ended scissors.

Regulations 55A(1) and 61(11)   [SCHEDULE 7XA

END OF SERIES EXEMPTIONS

PART I

MODIFICATION OF [REGULATIONS 55A, 61 AND 61A] IN RELATION TO END OF SERIES
VEHICLES

B27.318   *Note.* The heading to Part I is printed as amended by S.I. 2000 No. 3197.

B27.319   **1. Modification of [regulations 55A, 61 and 61A]**

(1) An item numbered 2 or higher in the Table in regulation 55A shall not apply to—

(a) a type approval end of series vehicle;

(b) a non-type approval end of series vehicle; or

(c) a late entry into service vehicle,

if it is first used before the first anniversary of the date specified in column 3 of the item.

(2) An item numbered 8, 9 or 11 in Table II of regulation 61 shall not apply to a type approval end of series vehicle if it is first used before the first anniversary of the date specified in column 3 of the item.

(3) An item numbered 9 or 11 in Table II of regulation 61 shall not apply to a non-type approval end of series vehicle if it is first used before the first anniversary of the date specified in column 3 of the item.

(4) An item numbered 10 or higher (other than 11) in Table II of regulation 61 shall not apply to—

(a) a type approval end of series vehicle;

(b) a non-type approval end of series vehicle; or

(c) a late entry into service vehicle,

if it is first used before the first anniversary of the date specified in column 3 of the item.

[(4A) Paragraphs (2) to (4) of regulation 61A and an item numbered 1 or 2 in the Table in that regulation shall not apply to—

(a) a type approval end of series vehicle;

(b) a non-type approval end of series vehicle; or

(c) a late entry into service vehicle;

if it is used before the first anniversary of the date as is specified (as defined in regulation 61A) by the relevant Community Directive in item 1 or 2 in the Table in regulation 61A.]

(5) Parts II, III and IV of this Schedule shall have effect for the purpose of interpreting the expressions "*type approval end of series vehicle*", "*non-type approval end of series vehicle*" and "*late entry into service vehicle*" respectively for the purposes of this paragraph.

B27.320   *[Schedule 7XA (paragraphs 1–13) was inserted by S.I. 1996 No. 2329. Paragraph 1 is printed as subsequently amended by S.I. 2000 No. 3197.]*

PART II

MEANING OF "TYPE APPROVAL END OF SERIES VEHICLE" IN PART I

2. Meaning of "type approval end of series vehicle" for the purposes of paragraph 1

(1) For the purposes of paragraph 1, a vehicle is a type approval end of series vehicle, in relation to item 8, 9 or 11 in Table II in regulation 61, if it meets the requirements of sub-paragraph (3) in relation to the item.

B27.321

(2) For the purposes of paragraph 1, a vehicle is a type approval end of series vehicle, in relation to an item numbered 2 or higher in the Table in regulation 55A or an item numbered 10 or higher (other than item 11) in Table II in regulation 61 [or an item numbered 1 or 2 in the Table in regulation 61A] if—

   (a) by virtue of Schedule 1C to the Type Approval for Goods Vehicles Regulations, or

   (b) by virtue of Schedule 1C to the Type Approval (Great Britain) Regulations,

(both of which Schedules in certain circumstances defer the date on which certain requirements relating to exhaust emissions, noise and silencers cease to apply) the type approval requirements that applied to the vehicle on the date specified in column 3 of the item [or, in relation to item 1 or 2 of the Table in regulation 61A, on the date as is specified (as defined in regulation 61A) by the relevant Community Directive] are the same as the type approval requirements that applied to the vehicle immediately before the date so specified in that column of that item [or in relation to item 1 or 2 of regulation 61A, the date as is specified by the relevant Community Directive].

(3) A vehicle meets the requirements of this sub-paragraph, in relation to the item, if—

   (a) it was manufactured during the relevant period;

   (b) one of the following conditions is satisfied—

      (i) a certificate of conformity was issued in respect of the vehicle before the date specified in column 3 of the item by virtue of a TAC issued before the date specified in column 4 of the Table in paragraph 6 in relation to the item, or

      (ii) a sub-MAC was issued in respect of the vehicle before the date specified in column 3 of the item by virtue of a MAC issued before the date specified in column 4 of that Table;

   (c) it was in the territory of a relevant state at some time before the date specified in column 3 of the item; and

   (d) the number of relevant vehicles which were—

      (i) manufactured before that vehicle was manufactured, and

      (ii) still in existence on the date specified in column 3 of that item, was less than the specified number of 50 (whichever is the greater).

(4) For the purposes of sub-paragraph (3)—

   (a) "*MAC*" means a Minister's approval certificate issued under section 58(1) of the Road Traffic Act 1988;

   (b) "*sub-MAC*" means a Minister's approval certificate issued under section 58(4) of the Road Traffic Act 1988; and

   (c) "*TAC*" means a type approval certificate.

[Schedule 7XA (paragraphs 1–13) was inserted by S.I. 1996 No. 2329. Paragraph 2 is printed as subsequently amended by S.I. 2000 No. 3197.]

B27.322

3. Meaning of "relevant vehicle" for the purposes of this Part

B27.323   (1) For the purposes of paragraph 2(3)(d), in relation to a particular vehicle to which Type Approval for Goods Vehicles Regulations apply (in this paragraph referred to as "*the vehicle in question*") and a particular item, a "*relevant vehicle*" is a vehicle (other than the vehicle in question) which—

(a) is a vehicle to which those Regulations apply;

(b) meets the requirements specified in paragraphs (a) to (c) of paragraph 2(3);

(c) was manufactured by the manufacturer of the vehicle in question; and

(d) had not been registered under the Vehicles (Excise) Act 1971 or the Vehicle Excise and Registration Act 1994 before the date specified in column 3 of the item.

(2) For the purposes of paragraph 2(3)(d) in relation to a particular vehicle to which the Type Approval (Great Britain) Regulations apply (in this paragraph referred to as "*the vehicle in question*") and a particular item, a "*relevant vehicle*" is a vehicle (other than the vehicle in question) which—

(a) is a vehicle to which these Regulations apply;

(b) meets the requirements specified in paragraphs (a) to (c) of paragraph 2(3);

(c) was manufactured by the manufacturer of the vehicle in question; and

(d) had not been registered under the Vehicle Excise and Registration Act 1994 before the date specified in column 3 of the item.

B27.324   *[Schedule 7XA (paragraphs 1–13) was inserted by S.I. 1996 No. 2329.]*

4. Meaning of "specified number" for the purposes of this Part

B27.325   (1) For the purposes of paragraph 2(3)(d), in relation to a particular vehicle to which the Type Approval (Great Britain) Regulations apply (in this paragraph referred to as "*the vehicle in question*") and a particular item, "*the specified number*" is 10% of the total number of vehicles to which those Regulations apply that were both—

(a) manufactured by the manufacturer of the vehicle in question; and

(b) registered under the Vehicles Excise Act 1971 or the Vehicle Excise and Registration Act 1994 during the one-year period ending immediately before the date specified in column 3 of the item.

(2) For the purposes of paragraph 2(3)(d), in relation to a particular vehicle to which the Type Approval for Goods Vehicles Regulations apply (in this paragraph referred to as "*the vehicle in question*") and a particular item, "*the specified number*" is 10% of the total number of vehicles to which those Regulations apply that were both—

(a) manufactured by the manufacturer of the vehicle in question, and

(b) registered under the Vehicles Excise Act 1971 or the Vehicle Excise and Registration Act 1994 during the one-year period ending immediately before the date specified in column 3 of the item.

B27.326   *[Schedule 7XA (paragraphs 1–13) was inserted by S.I. 1996 No. 2329.]*

5. Circumstances in which a vehicle is to be regarded as having been in the territory of a relevant state for the purposes of this Part

B27.327   (1) For the purposes of paragraph 2(3)(c)—

(a) at any material time before the 5th November 1993, "*relevant state*" means a member State;

(b) in relation to any time on or after 5th November 1993 but before 1st May 1995, "*relevant state*" means an EEA State other than Liechtenstein; and

(c) in relation to any time on or after 1st May 1995, "*relevant state*" means any EEA State.

(2) For the purposes of this paragraph—

"*EEA agreement*" means the Agreement on the European Economic Area signed at Oporto on the 2nd May 1992 as adjusted by the protocol signed at Brussels on the 17th March 1993; and

"*EEA State*" means a State which is a contracting party to the EEA agreement.

[Schedule 7XA (paragraphs 1–13) was inserted by S.I. 1996 No. 2329.   **B27.328**
As to the European Economic Area and the EEA agreement (see paragraph 5(2) above), see the note to Regulation (EEC) 3820/85 below.]

6. Meaning of "relevant period" for the purposes of this Part

For the purposes of this Part, "*the relevant period*" in relation to an item numbered 8, 9 or   **B27.329**
11 in Table II in regulation 61 is the period—

   (a) beginning on the date specified in column 2 of the Table below against that item; and

   (b) ending immediately before the date specified in column 3 of the Table below against that item.

THE TABLE

1	2	3	4	5
Item in Table II in regulation 61	Date on which the relevant period begins	Date immediately before which the relevant period ends	Date before which type approval, etc. needs to be granted	Date in column 3 of Table II in regulation 61
8	1st August 1990	1st September 1992	1st July 1992	31st December 1992
9	1st April 1991	1st October 1993	1st October 1993	1st October 1993
11	1st August 1992	1st August 1994	1st October 1993	1st October 1994

[Schedule 7XA (paragraphs 1–13) was inserted by S.I. 1996 No. 2329.]   **B27.330**

PART III

MEANING OF "NON-TYPE APPROVAL END OF SERIES VEHICLE" IN PART I

7. Meaning of "non-type approval end of series vehicle" in paragraph 1

(1) For the purposes of paragraph 1 a vehicle is a non-type approval end of series   **B27.331**
vehicle in relation to an item if it meets the requirements of sub-paragraph (2) in relation to the item.

(2) A vehicle meets the requirements of this sub-paragraph in relation to an item if—

   (a) it is a vehicle to which neither the Type Approval (Great Britain) Regulations nor the Type Approval for Goods Vehicles Regulations apply;

   (b) it was manufactured during the relevant period;

   (c) no EC certificate of conformity has been issued in respect of the vehicle;

   (d) it was in the territory of a relevant state at some time before the end of the relevant period; and

(e) the number of relevant vehicles which were both—

    (i) manufactured before that vehicle was manufactured, and

    (ii) still in existence on the date specified in column 3 in the item [or in relation to item 1 or 2 of the Table in regulation 61A, on the date as is specified (as defined in regulation 61A) by the relevant Community Directive], is less than the specified number, of 50, whichever is the greater.

B27.332   *[Schedule 7XA (paragraphs 1–13) was inserted by S.I. 1996 No. 2329. Paragraph 7 is printed as subsequently amended by S.I. 2000 No. 3197.]*

8. Meaning of "relevant vehicle" for the purposes of this Part

B27.333   For the purposes of paragraph 7(2)(e), in relation to a particular vehicle (in this paragraph referred to as "*the vehicle in question*") and a particular item, a "*relevant vehicle*" is a vehicle (other than the vehicle in question) which—

(a) meets the requirements specified in paragraphs (a) to (d) of paragraph 7(2);

(b) is a "vehicle" within the meaning of either Community Directive 70/220 [*O.J. No. L76, April 6, 1972, p. 1*] (as amended by Community Directive 83/351 [*O.J. No. L197, July 20, 1983, p. 1*] or Community Directive 88/77 [*O.J. No. L36, February 9, 1988, p. 33*];

(c) was manufactured by the manufacturer of the vehicle in question;

(d) had not been registered under the Vehicles (Excise) Act 1971 or the Vehicle Excise and Registration Act 1994 during the relevant period.

B27.334   *[Schedule 7XA (paragraphs 1–13) was inserted by S.I. 1996 No. 2329.*
The term "vehicle" is defined in article 1 of Directive 70/220/EEC (as substituted by Directive 83/351/EEC) (see paragraphs 8(b) and 9(2)(b)) as—

any vehicle with a positive-ignition engine or with a compression-ignition engine, intended for use on the road, with or without bodywork, having at least four wheels, a permissible maximum mass of at least 400kg and a maximum design speed equal to or exceeding 50 km/h, with the exception of agricultural tractors and machinery and public works vehicles.

The term is defined in Directive 88/77/EEC, art.1, as—

any vehicle propelled by a diesel engine, intended for use on the road, with or without bodywork, having at least four wheels and a maximum design speed exceeding 25 km/h, with the exception of vehicles of category M_1 as defined in section 0.4 of Annex I to Directive 70/156/EEC, having a total mass not exceeding 3.5 tonnes, and vehicles which run on rails, agricultural tractors and machines and public works vehicles.

The categories of motor vehicles are now set out in Annex II to Directive 70/156/EEC (q.v.). Article 1 of Directive 70/220/EEC has been substituted by Directive 98/77/EC (O.J. No. L286, October 23, 1998, p. 34) and now defines a "vehicle" as "any vehicle as defined in Annex II, Section A, to Directive 70/156/EEC".]

9. Meaning of "specified number" for the purposes of this Part

B27.335   (1) For the purposes of paragraph 7(2)(e), in relation to a particular vehicle (in this paragraph referred to as "*the vehicle in question*") and a particular item, "*the specified number*" is 10% of the total number of vehicles that—

(a) are vehicles to which neither the Type Approval (Great Britain) Regulations nor the Type Approval for Goods Vehicles Regulations apply; and

(b) meet the requirements of sub-paragraph (2).

(2) A vehicle meets the requirements of this paragraph if it—

(a) is a *"vehicle"* within the meaning of either Community Directive 83/351 or Community Directive 88/77;

(b) was manufactured by the manufacturer of the vehicle in question; and

(c) was registered under the Vehicles (Excise) Act 1971 or the Vehicle Excise and Registration Act 1994 during the one-year period ending immediately before the date specified in column 3 of that item [or, in relation to item 1 or 2 of the Table in regulation 61A, before the date as is specified (as defined in regulation 61A) by the relevant Community Directive].

[Schedule 7XA (paragraphs 1–13) was inserted by S.I. 1996 No. 2329. Paragraph 9 is printed as **B27.336**
subsequently amended by S.I. 2000 No. 3197.
As to the meaning of "vehicle" (see paragraph 9(2)(a) above), see the note to paragraph 8 above.]

10. Circumstances in which a vehicle is to be regarded as having been in the territory of a relevant state for the purposes of this Part

Paragraph 5 in Part II of this Schedule shall have effect for the purposes of paragraph   **B27.337**
7(2)(d) as it has effect for the purposes of paragraph 2(3)(c).

[Schedule 7XA (paragraphs 1–13) was inserted by S.I. 1996 No. 2329.]   **B27.338**

11. Meaning of "relevant period" for the purposes of this Part

For the purposes of paragraphs [*sic*] 7(2)(d), *"the relevant period"*—   **B27.339**

(a) in relation to an item numbered 9 or 11 in Table II in regulation 61 is the period—

  (i) beginning on the date specified in column 2 of the Table below against the item, and

  (ii) ending immediately before the date specified in column 3 of the Table below against the item; and

(b) in relation to any item in the Table in regulation 55A or any item numbered 10 or higher (other than 11) in the said Table II is the two-year period ending immediately before the date specified in column 3 of that item [; and]

[(c) in relation to an item numbered 1 or 2 in the Table in regulation 61A is the two year period ending immediately before the date as is specified (as defined in regulation 61A) by the relevant Community Directive in the Table].

THE TABLE

1	2	3	4
Item in Table II in regulation 61	Date on which relevant period begins	Date immediately before which the relevant period ends	Date in column 3 of Table II in regulation 61
9	1st April 1991	1st October 1993	1st October 1993
11	1st August 1992	1st August 1994	1st October 1994

[Schedule 7XA (paragraphs 1–13) was inserted by S.I. 1996 No. 2329. Paragraph 11 is printed as   **B27.340**
subsequently amended by S.I. 2000 No. 3197.]

PART IV

MEANING OF "LATE ENTRY INTO SERVICE VEHICLE" IN PART I

12. Meaning of "late entry into service vehicle" in paragraph 1

B27.341 For the purposes of paragraph 1, a vehicle is a late entry into service vehicle, in relation to an item, if—

(a) no EC certificate of conformity has been issued in respect of the vehicle;

(b) it was in the territory of a relevant state at some time before the date specified in column 3 of the item [or, in relation to item 1 or 2 of the Table in regulation 61A, before the date as is specified (as defined in regulation 61A) by the relevant Community Directive];

(c) it was manufactured at least two years before that date.

B27.342 *[Schedule 7XA (paragraphs 1–13) was inserted by S.I. 1996 No. 2329. Paragraph 12 is printed as subsequently amended by S.I. 2000 No. 3197.]*

13. Circumstances in which a vehicle is to be regarded as having been in the territory of a relevant state for the purposes of this Part

B27.343 Paragraph 5 in Part II of this Schedule shall have effect for the purposes of paragraph 12(b) as it has effect for the purposes of paragraph 2(3)(c).]

B27.344 *[Schedule 7XA (paragraphs 1–13) was inserted by S.I. 1996 No. 2329.]*

Regulations 57, 57A and 57B   [SCHEDULE 7A

MOTOR CYCLE NOISE AND MOTOR CYCLE SILENCERS

PART I

B27.345 **1.**—(1) For the purposes of these Regulations a vehicle meets the requirements of an item in the Table below if its sound level does not exceed by more than 1 dB(a) the relevant limit specified in column 2 in that item when measured under the conditions specified in column 3 in that item by the method specified in column 4 in that item using the apparatus prescribed in regulation 55(6).

(2) In this Part of this Schedule, "*moped*" has the same meaning as in regulation 57.

TABLE

1	2		3	4
	Limits of sound level			
Item	*Mopeds*	*Vehicles other than mopeds*	*Conditions of measurement*	*Methods of measurement*
1	73 dB(a)	Limit determined in accordance with paragraph 2.1.1 of Annex I to Community	Conditions specified in paragraph 2.1.3 of Annex I to Community	Methods specified in paragraph 2.1.4 of Annex I to Community Directive 78/1015

[continued on next page

1	2		3	4
	Limits of sound level			
Item	*Mopeds*	*Vehicles other than mopeds*	*Conditions of measurement*	*Methods of measurement*
1— *cont.*		Directive 78/1015 by reference to the cubic capacity of the vehicle	Directive 78/1015	
2	73 dB(a)	First stage limit determined in accordance with paragraph 2.1.1 of Annex I to Community Directive 87/56 by reference to the cubic capacity of the vehicle	Conditions specified in paragraph 2.1.3 of Annex I to Community Directive 87/56	Methods specified in paragraph 2.1.4 of Annex I to Community Directive 87/56
3	74 dB(a)	The limit specified in item 2 plus 1 dB(a)	As in item 2	As in item 2

PART II

2. The requirements of this paragraph are that the silencer— **B27.346**

  (a) is so constructed that—

    (i) it meets the requirements of paragraphs 3 and 4 of British Standard BS AU 193:1983;

    (ii) were it to be fitted to an unused vehicle of the same model as the vehicle in question, the unused vehicle would meet the requirements of paragraph 5.2 of that Standard; and

  (b) is clearly and indelibly marked "BS AU 193/T2".

3. The requirements of this paragraph are that the silencer— **B27.347**

  (a) is so constructed that—

    (i) it meets the requirements of paragraphs 3 and 4 of British Standard BS AU 193a:1990;

    (ii) were it to be fitted to an unused vehicle of the same model as the vehicle in question, the unused vehicle would meet the requirements of paragraph 5.2 of that Standard; and

  (b) is clearly and indelibly marked "BS AU 193a:1990/T2".

4. The requirements of this paragraph are that the silencer— **B27.348**

  (a) is so constructed that—

    (i) it meets the requirements of paragraphs 3 and 4 of British Standard BS AU 193a:1990;

  (ii) were it to be fitted to an unused vehicle of the same model as the vehicle in question, the unused vehicle would meet the requirements of paragraph 5.3 of that Standard; and

 (b) is clearly and indelibly marked "BS AU 193a:1990/T3".

B27.349 **5.** In this Part of this Schedule—

 (a) "*British Standard BS AU 193:1983*" means the British Standard Specification for replacement motor cycle and moped exhaust systems published by the British Standards Institution under reference number BS AU 193:1983;

 (b) "*British Standard BS AU 193a:1990*" means the British Standard Specification for replacement motor cycle and moped exhaust systems published by the British Standards Institution under reference number BS AU 193a:1990.

PART III

B27.350 **6.** Paragraph (4) of regulation 57A shall not apply to a replacement silencer if the second requirement referred to in that regulation would be met were there substituted in Part II of this Schedule,—

 (a) for the references to provisions in either of the British Standard Specifications, references to equivalent provisions in a corresponding standard; and

 (b) for the references to a mark, references to a mark made pursuant to that corresponding standard indicating that the silencer complies with those equivalent provisions.

B27.351 **7.** In this Part of this Schedule, "*corresponding standard*", in relation to a British Standard Specification, means—

 (a) a standard or code of practice of a national standards body or equivalent body of any member State;

 (b) any international standard recognised for use as a standard by any member State; or

 (c) a technical specification or code of practice which, whether mandatory or not, is recognised for use as a standard by a public authority of any member State,

where the standard, code of practice, international standard or technical specification provides, in relation to motor cycles, a level of noise limitation and safety equivalent to that provided by the British Standard Specification and contains a requirement as respects the marking of silencers equivalent to that provided by that instrument.

B27.352 **8.** A reference in this part of this Schedule to a British Standard Specification is a reference to British Standard BS AU 193:1983 or British Standard BS AU 193a:1990; and "*either of the British Standard Specifications*" shall be construed accordingly.

B27.353 **9.** In this Part of this Schedule, "*British Standard BS AU 193:1983*" and "*British Standard BS AU 193a:1990*" have the same meanings as in Part II of this Schedule.]

B27.354 *[Schedule 7A was inserted by S.I. 1994 No. 14.]*

[SCHEDULE 7B   Regulation 61(10AA),
(10AB) and (10BA)

EMISSIONS FROM CERTAIN MOTOR VEHICLES

PART I

VEHICLES PROPELLED BY SPARK IGNITION ENGINES

1. This Part of this Schedule applies to a vehicle if, when the engine is running without load at a normal idling speed, the carbon monoxide content of the exhaust emissions from the engine exceeds the relevant percentage of the total exhaust emissions from the engine by volume.   **B27.355**

[Schedule 7B (paragraphs 1–9) was inserted by S.I. 1995 No. 2210.]   **B27.356**

2. This Part of this Schedule also applies to a vehicle if, when the engine is running without load at a fast idling speed,—   **B27.357**

(a) the carbon monoxide content of the exhaust emissions from the engine exceeds 0.3% of the total exhaust emissions from the engine by volume;

(b) the hydrocarbon content of those emissions exceeds 0.02% of the total exhaust emissions from the engine by volume; or

(c) the lambda value is not within the relevant limits.

[Schedule 7B (paragraphs 1–9) was inserted by S.I. 1995 No. 2210.]   **B27.358**

3. For the purposes of this Part of this Schedule the relevant percentage, in respect of a vehicle, is—   **B27.359**

(a) if the vehicle is of a description specified in the Annex to the emissions publication, the percentage shown against that description of vehicle in column 2(a) of that Annex; or

(b) if the vehicle is not of such a description, 0.5%.

[Schedule 7B (paragraphs 1–9) was inserted by S.I. 1995 No. 2210.]   **B27.360**

4. For the purposes of this Part of this Schedule, in the case of a vehicle of a description specified in the Annex to the emissions publication, the engine shall be regarded as running at a normal idling speed if and only if the engine is running at a rotational speed between the minimum and maximum limits shown against that description of vehicle in columns 2(b) and (c) respectively of that Annex.   **B27.361**

[Schedule 7B (paragraphs 1–9) was inserted by S.I. 1995 No. 2210.]   **B27.362**

5. For the purposes of this Part of this Schedule an engine shall be regarded as running at a fast idling speed if—   **B27.363**

(a) the vehicle is of a description specified in the Annex to the emissions publication and the engine is running at a rotational speed between the minimum and maximum limits shown against that description of vehicle in columns 3(e) and (f) respectively of that Annex; or

(b) the vehicle is not of such a description and the engine is running at a rotational speed between 2,500 and 3,000 revolutions per minute.

[Schedule 7B (paragraphs 1–9) was inserted by S.I. 1995 No. 2210.]   **B27.364**

6. For the purposes of this Part of this Schedule, the lambda value, in respect of a vehicle, shall be regarded as being within relevant limits, if and only if—   **B27.365**

    (a) the vehicle is of a description specified in the Annex to the emissions publication and the lambda value is between the minimum and maximum limits shown against that description of vehicle in columns 3(c) and (d) respectively of that Annex; or

    (b) the vehicle is not of such a description and the lambda value is between 0.97 and 1.03.

B27.366   *[Schedule 7B (paragraphs 1–9) was inserted by S.I. 1995 No. 2210.]*

B27.367   **7.** In this Part of this Schedule—

    (a) a reference to the lambda value, in relation to a vehicle at any particular time, is a reference to the ratio by mass of air to petrol vapour in the mixture entering the combustion chambers divided by 14.7; and

    [(b) *"the emissions publication"* is the publication entitled "In-Service Exhaust Emissions Standards for Road Vehicles—Sixth Edition" (ISBN 0-9526457-5-0) published by the Department of the Environment, Transport and the Regions.]

B27.368   *[Schedule 7B (paragraphs 1–9) was inserted by S.I. 1995 No. 2210. Paragraph 7 is printed as subsequently amended by S.I. 1996 No. 2085; S.I. 1997 No. 1544; S.I. 1998 No. 1563, S.I. 1999 Nos 1521 and 1959; S.I. 2000 No. 1434.]*

PART II

VEHICLES PROPELLED BY COMPRESSION IGNITION ENGINES

B27.369   **8.** This Part of this Schedule applies to a vehicle if [when tested in accordance with point 8.2.2 of Annex II of Council Directive 96/96/EC [*O.J. No. L46, February 17, 1997, p. 1*] as replaced by Article 1 of Commission Directive 1999/52/EC [*O.J. No. L142, June 5, 1999, p. 26*]], the coefficient of absorption of the exhaust emissions from the engine of the vehicle immediately after leaving the exhaust system exceeds—

    (a) if the engine of the vehicle is turbo-charged, 3.0 per metre, or

    (b) in any other case, 2.5 per metre.

B27.370   *[Schedule 7B (paragraphs 1–9) was inserted by S.I. 1995 No. 2210. Paragraph 8 is printed as subsequently amended by S.I. 2000 No. 1434.]*

B27.371   **9.** In this Part of this Schedule—

    (a) *"coefficient of absorption"* shall be construed in accordance with paragraph 3.5 of Annex VII to Community Directive 72/306 . . .

    (b) *[revoked by S.I. 2000 No. 1434.]*

B27.372   *[Schedule 7B (paragraphs 1–9) was inserted by S.I. 1995 No. 2210. Paragraph 9 is printed as subsequently amended by S.I. 2000 No. 1434.*

Paragraph 3.5 of Annex VII to Directive 72/306/EEC (to which reference is made at paragraph 9(a) above) provides:

3.5.   **Measuring scales**

3.5.1.   The light-absorption coefficient k shall be calculated by the formula $\Phi = \Phi_o \cdot e^{-kL}$, where L is the effective length of the light path through the gas to be measured, Φ_o the incident flux and Φ the emergent flux. When the effective length L of a type of opacimeter cannot be assessed directly from its geometry, the effective length L shall be determined

—either by the method described in item 4 of this Annex; or

—through correlation with another type of opacimeter for which the effective length is known.

3.5.2. The relationship between the 0–100 linear scale and the light absorption coefficient k is given by the formula

$$k=-\frac{1}{L}\log_c\left(1-\frac{N}{100}\right)$$

where N is a reading on the linear scale and k the corresponding value of the absorption coefficient.

3.5.3. The indicating dial of the opacimeter shall enable an absorption coefficient of $1{\cdot}7\mathrm{m}^{-1}$ to be read with an accuracy of $0{\cdot}025\mathrm{m}^{-1}.]$

SCHEDULE 8 (see regulation 66)

PLATES FOR CERTAIN VEHICLES

PART I

Particulars to be shown on plate for motor vehicles (including motor vehicles forming   **B27.373**
part of articulated vehicles)

1. Manufacturer's name.

2. Vehicle type.

3. Engine type and power (a).

4. Chassis or serial number.

5. Number of axles.

6. Maximum axle weight for each axle (b).

7. Maximum gross weight (c).

8. Maximum train weight (d).

9. Maximum weight in Great Britain for each axle (b), (e).

10. Maximum gross weight in Great Britain (c), (e).

(a) The power need not be shown in the case of a motor vehicle manufactured before 1st October 1972 (hereinafter in this Schedule referred to as "*an excepted vehicle*") and shall not be shown in the case of any motor vehicle which is propelled otherwise than by a compression ignition engine.

(b) This weight as respects each axle is the sum of the weights to be transmitted to the road surface by all the wheels of that axle.

(c) This weight is the sum of the weights to be transmitted to the road surface by all the wheels of the motor vehicle (including any load imposed by a trailer, whether forming part of an articulated vehicle or not, on the motor vehicle).

(d) This weight is the sum of the weights to be transmitted to the road surface by all the wheels of the motor vehicle and of any trailer drawn, but this item need not be completed where the motor vehicle is not constructed to draw a trailer.

(b), (c), (d) References to the weights to be transmitted to the road surface by all or any of the wheels of the vehicle or any trailer drawn are references to the weights so to be transmitted both of the vehicle or trailer and of any load or persons carried by it.

(e) This item need not be completed in the case of an excepted vehicle or in the case of a vehicle which is a locomotive or motor tractor.

PART II

B27.374   Particulars to be shown on plate for trailers (including trailers forming part of articulated vehicles)

1. Manufacturer's name.
2. Chassis or serial number.
3. Number of axles.
4. Maximum weight for each axle (a).
5. Maximum load imposed on drawing vehicle (b).
6. Maximum gross weight (c).
7. Maximum weight in Great Britain for each axle (a), (e).
8. Maximum gross weight in Great Britain (c), (f).
9. Year of manufacture (d).

   (a) This weight as respects each axle is the sum of the weights to be transmitted to the road surface by all the wheels of that axle.

   (b) Only for trailers forming part of articulated vehicles or where some of the weight of the trailer or its load is to be imposed on the drawing vehicle. This item need not be completed in the case of a converter dolly [manufactured before 1st February 1992].

   (c) This weight is the sum of the weights to be transmitted to the road surface by all the wheels of the trailer, including any weight of the trailer to be imposed on the drawing vehicle.

   (a), (b), (c) References to the weights to be transmitted to the road surface by all or any of the wheels of the trailer are references to the weight so to be transmitted both of the trailer and of any load or persons carried by it and references to the weights to be imposed on the drawing vehicle are references to the weights so to be imposed both of the trailer and of any load or persons carried by it except where only the load of the trailer is imposed on the drawing vehicle.

   (d) This item need not be completed in the case of a trailer manufactured before 1st April 1970.

   (e) This item need not be completed in the case of a trailer manufactured before 1st October 1972.

   (f) This item need not be completed in the case of a trailer manufactured before 1st October 1972 or which forms part of an articulated vehicle.

B27.375   *[Part II of Schedule 8 is printed as amended by S.I. 1991 No. 1526.]*

PART III

B27.376   **1.** The power of an engine, which is to be shown only in the case of a compression ignition engine on the plate in respect of item 3 in Part I of this Schedule, shall be the amount in kilowatts equivalent to the installed power output shown in a type test certificate issued—

   (a) by a person authorised by the Secretary of State for the type of engine to which the engine conforms; and

   (b) in accordance with either—

      (i) the provisions relating to the installed brake power output specified in the British Standard Specification for the Performance of Diesel Engines for Road Vehicles published on 19th May 1971 under the number BS AU 141a:1971;

(ii) the provisions relating to the net power specified in Community Directive 80/1269 but after allowance has been made for the power absorbed by such equipment, at its minimum power setting, driven by the engine of the vehicle as is fitted for the operation of the vehicle (other than its propulsion) such power being measured at the speed corresponding to the engine speed at which maximum engine power is developed; or

(iii) the provisions of Annex 10 of ECE Regulations 24.02 as further amended with effect from 15th February 1984 [or Annex 10 of ECE Regulation 24.03 or Community Directive 88/195] relating to the method of measuring internal combustion engine net power, but after allowance has been made for the power absorbed by any disconnectable or progressive cooling fan, at its maximum setting, and by any other such equipment, at its minimum power setting, driven by the engine of the vehicle as is fitted for the operation of the vehicle (other than its propulsion), such power being measured at the speed corresponding to the engine speed at which maximum engine power is developed.

[Paragraph 1 of Part III of Schedule 8 is printed as amended by S.I. 1990 No. 1131.]   **B27.377**

2.—(1) [Subject to paragraph 3A,] the weights to be shown on the plate in relation to   **B27.378**
items 6, 7 and 8 in Part I and in relation to items 4, 5 and 6 in Part II shall be the weight limits at or below which the vehicle is considered fit for use, having regard to its design, construction and equipment and the stresses to which it is likely to be subject in use, by the Secretary of State if the vehicle is one to which the Type Approval for Goods Vehicles Regulations [or the Motor Vehicles (Approval) Regulations 2001] *[S.I. 2001 No. 25 below]* apply, and by the manufacturer if the vehicle is one to which those Regulations do not apply.

Provided that, where alterations are made to a vehicle which may render the vehicle fit for use at weights which exceed those referred to above in this paragraph and shown on the plate—

(a) there may be shown on the plate, in place of any of those weights, such new weights as the manufacturer of the vehicle or any person carrying on business as a manufacturer of motor vehicles or trailers (or a person duly authorised on behalf of that manufacturer or any such person) or a person authorised by the Secretary of State considers to represent the weight limits at or below which the vehicle will then be fit for use, having regard to its design, construction and equipment and to those alterations and to the stresses to which it is likely to be subject in use; and

(b) the name of the person who has determined the new weights shall be shown on the plate as having made that determination and, where he is a person authorised by the Secretary of State, his appointment shall be so shown.

(2) In relation to a vehicle manufactured on or after 1st October 1972, in the foregoing paragraph—

(a) the references to equipment shall not be treated as including a reference to the type of tyres with which the vehicle is equipped; and

(b) for the words "weight limits at or below" in both places where they occur there shall be substituted the words "maximum weights at".

[Paragraph 2 of Part III of Schedule 8 is printed as amended by S.I. 2001 No. 306.]   **B27.379**

3. [Subject to paragraph 3A,] the weights to be shown on the plate in respect of—   **B27.380**

(a) item 9 in Part I of this Schedule shall be the weights shown at item 6 in that Part and in respect of item 7 in Part II of this Schedule shall be the weights shown at item 4 in that Part, in each case reduced so far as necessary to indicate the maximum weight applicable to each axle of the vehicle, if the vehicle is not to be used in contravention of regulations 23, 75, 78 or 79, and if the tyres with which the vehicle is equipped are not, as respects strength, to be inadequate to support the weights to be so shown at item 9 and item 7;

(b) item 10 in the said Part I shall be the weight shown at item 7 in that Part and in respect of item 8 in the said Part II shall be the weight shown at item 6 in that Part, in each case reduced so far as necessary to indicate the maximum permissible weight applicable if the vehicle is not to be used in contravention of regulation 75 if the tyres with which the vehicle is equipped are not, as respects strength, to be inadequate to support the weights to be so shown at item 10 and item 8.

B27.381   *[Paragraph 3 of Part III of Schedule 8 is printed as amended by S.I. 2001 No. 306.]*

B27.382   [**3A.** In the case of a vehicle—

(a) which complies with the requirements specified in regulation 4(2) of the Motor Vehicles (Approval) Regulations 2001;

(b) in respect of which a Minister's approval certificate has been issued under section 58 of the 1988 Act for the purposes of the type approval requirements prescribed by those Regulations; and

(c) in respect of which a Minister's approval certificate has not subsequently been issued under that section for the purposes of the type approval requirements prescribed by the Type Approval for Goods Vehicles Regulations,

the weight shown on the plate in relation to items 7 and 10 in Part I of this Schedule shall be 3,500 kg.]

B27.383   *[Paragraph 3A of Part III of Schedule 8 was inserted by S.I. 2001 No. 306.]*

B27.384   **4.**—(1) Subject to sub-paragraph (2) of this paragraph weights on plates first affixed to a vehicle on or after 1st October 1972 shall be shown in kilograms and weights on plates first so affixed before that date shall be shown in tons and decimals thereof.

(2) Where a new weight is first shown on a plate by virtue of the proviso to paragraph 2(1) the weight shall be shown as if it was on a plate first affixed to a vehicle on the date it was first shown.

5. All letters and figures shown on the plate shall be not less than 6mm in height.

B27.385   **6.** In this Schedule references to the manufacturer of a motor vehicle or trailer are in relation to—

(a) a vehicle constructed with a chassis which has not previously formed part of another vehicle, references to the person by whom that chassis was made;

(b) any other vehicle, references to the person by whom that vehicle was constructed.

SCHEDULE 9 (see regulation 69)

PLATES FOR MOTOR CYCLES

B27.386   **1.** The plate required by regulation 69 shall be firmly attached to a part of the motor cycle which is not normally subject to replacement during the life of the motor cycle.

2. The plate shall be in the form shown in the diagram in this paragraph, shall have dimensions not less than those shown in that diagram and shall show the information provided for in that diagram and detailed in the Notes below.

Diagram of Plate

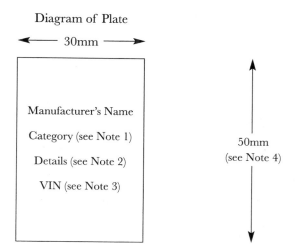

Notes:

1. The categories are "standard motor cycle" and "moped".

2. The details are—

(a) for standard motor cycles—

(i) the engine capacity,
(ii) the maximum engine power, and
(iii) the power to weight ratio,

provided that the details under (ii) and (iii) need not be shown for a vehicle first used before 1st January 1982;

(b) for mopeds—

(i) the engine capacity,
(ii) the kerbside weight, and
(iii) the maximum speed.

3. The vehicle identification number (VIN) shall be marked in the form used by the manufacturer to identify any one individual vehicle.

4. In the case of a plate fitted to a vehicle first used before 1st January 1982 or to a moped this dimension shall be 40mm.

3. The information on the plate shall be shown in characters not less than 4mm in height and in the positions on the plate indicated in the diagram above.   **B27.387**

4. No information, other than that provided for in the diagram above, shall be marked within the rectangle which is shown in that diagram.

5. In this Schedule and, in respect of the definition of "moped", in regulations 54 and 57—   **B27.388**

"*maximum engine power*" means the maximum net power the motor cycle engine will develop, in kilowatts, when measured in accordance with the test conditions specified in the International Standard number ISO 4106 developed by the technical committee of the International Organisation for Standardisation, and approved by member bodies, including the United Kingdom, and published under the reference ISO 1978 4106–09–01;

"*moped*" means a motor cycle which—

(a) has a kerbside weight not exceeding 250kg, and

(b) if propelled by an internal combustion engine, has an engine with a cylinder capacity which does not exceed 50cc, and

(c) is designed to have a maximum speed not exceeding 30mph when driven under the conditions set out in paragraph 6;

"*power to weight ratio*" means the ratio of the maximum engine power to the kerbside weight of the vehicle measured, as regards the maximum engine power, in kilowatts and, as regards the kerbside weight, in 1000kg;

"*standard motor cycle*" means a motor cycle which is not a moped.

B27.389   **6.** A motor cycle shall be regarded as complying with paragraph (c) of the definition of "moped" in paragraph 5 if it cannot exceed 35mph when tested under the following conditions—

(a) the surface on which it is tested shall be dry asphalt or concrete;

(b) the rider shall be a person not exceeding 75kg in weight;

(c) no passenger or load shall be carried;

(d) the test route shall be so located that acceleration to, and deceleration from, maximum speed can take place elsewhere than on the test route itself;

(e) the test route shall not have a gradient exceeding 5%;

(f) when being driven along the test route, the motor cycle shall be driven in such manner and in such gear as to achieve the maximum speed of which it is capable; and

(g) if the motor cycle is fitted with a device which can, without the use of specialist tools or equipment, be readily modified or removed so as to increase its maximum speed, the test shall be carried out with the device in the modified condition or, as the case may be, without the device.

SCHEDULE 10 (see regulation 70)

MINISTRY PLATE

PLATE	DEPARTMENT OF TRANSPORT			Serial No.
	[Road Traffic Act 1988, Sections 41 and 54] Examination of Goods Vehicles			DTp REF. No.
REGISTRATION/IDENTIFICATION MARK	YEAR OF ORIGINAL REGISTRATION	YEAR OF MANUFACTURE	FUNCTION	MAKE AND MODEL
CHASSIS/SERIAL No.		UNLADEN WEIGHT		
(1) DESCRIPTION OF WEIGHTS APPLICABLE TO VEHICLE	(2) WEIGHTS NOT TO BE EXCEEDED IN GREAT BRITAIN		(3) DESIGN WEIGHTS (if higher than shown in col (2))	
	KILOGRAMS		KILOGRAMS	DATE OF ISSUE
AXLE WEIGHT (Axles numbered from front to rear)	AXLE 1			
	AXLE 2			
	AXLE 3			
	AXLE 4			
GROSS WEIGHT (see warning opposite)				
TRAIN WEIGHT (see warning opposite)				

WARNING
1. A reduced gross weight may apply in certain cases to a vehicle towing or being towed by another.
2. A reduced train weight may apply depending on the type of trailer drawn.
3. All weights shown are subject to fitting of correct tyres.

NOTES: 1. A Ministry plate may contain the words "MINISTRY OF TRANSPORT" or "DEPARTMENT OF TRANSPORT", and may contain the words "Road Safety Act 1967, Sections 8 and 9" or the words "Road Traffic Act 1972, Sections 40 and 45" [or the words "Road Traffic Act 1988, Sections 41 and 49"]. (In a case where the Type Approval for Goods Vehicles Regulations do not apply.) It may also contain additional columns in Columns (2) and (3) showing the weights in tons.

2. Entries in respect of train weight are required in the case of—(a) a motor vehicle constructed or adapted to draw a trailer and is first used on or after 1st April 1983.

3. A Ministry plate shows the unladen weight and function of the vehicle in a case where the Type Approval for Goods Vehicles Regulations apply.

4. A Ministry plate may have separate spaces for the "make" and "model" of the vehicle.

5. A Ministry plate may have no "Reference Number" or may refer to the "Department of the Environment Reference No".

[SCHEDULE 10A (see regulation 70)]

MINISTRY PLATE

DEPARTMENT OF TRANSPORT
[Road Traffic Act 1988, Sections 41, 49 and 54]
Examination of Goods Vehicles

PLATE VTG 6A			SERIAL NUMBER		DTp REF No
REGISTRATION/ IDENTIFICATION MARK	YEAR OF ORIGINAL REG	YEAR OF MANUFACTURE	FUNCTION	UNLADEN WEIGHT	
MANUFACTURER/MODEL					
TYPE APPROVAL/ VARIANT No					
VEHICLE IDENTIFICATION No					
(1) DESCRIPTION OF WEIGHTS APPLICABLE TO VEHICLE	(2) WEIGHT NOT TO BE EXCEEDED IN Gt. BRITAIN	(3) EEC MAXIMUM PERMITTED WEIGHTS (See Note 4)	(4) DESIGN WEIGHTS (if higher than shown in column 2)		
GROSS WEIGHT (See warning below)					
TRAIN WEIGHT (See warning below)					
MAXIMUM TRAIN WEIGHT (See Note 3)					
AXLE WEIGHTS (Axles numbered from front to rear) Axle 1					
Axle 2					
Axle 3					
Axle 4					
MAXIMUM KINGPIN LOAD (Semi-trailers only)					

5. VEHICLE DIMENSIONS

	MAXIMUM	MINIMUM
LENGTH (L)		
WIDTH (W)		
a. (See Note 1) COUPLING CENTRE TO VEHICLE FOREMOST PART		
b. (See Note 2) COUPLING CENTRE TO VEHICLE REARMOST PART		

DATE OF ISSUE

N.B. ALL WEIGHTS IN KILOGRAMS/ALL DIMENSIONS IN MILLIMETRES.

WARNING

a. A reduced gross weight may apply in certain cases to a vehicle towing or being towed by another.
b. A reduced train weight may apply depending on the type of trailer drawn.
c. All weights shown are subject to the fitting of correct tyres.

NOTES

1. This dimension only applies to drawing vehicles of trailers and semi-trailers.
2. This dimension only applies to trailers and semi-trailers.
3. This weight only applies to a 3 axle tractor with a 2 or 3 axle semi-trailer carrying a 40 foot ISO container as a combined transport operation.
4. Where there is no weight shown in the EEC maximum permitted weights column this is because there is no EEC standard relating to that weight.

NOTES

1. Entries in respect of train weight are required in the case of—(a) a motor vehicle constructed or adapted to form an articulated vehicle; and (b) a rigid vehicle which is constructed or adapted to draw a trailer and is first used on or after 1st April 1983.
2. A Ministry plate shows the unladen weight and function of the vehicle in a case where the Type Approval for Goods Vehicles Regulations apply.
3. A Ministry plate may have no "Reference Number".]

[Schedule 10A was inserted by S.I. 1987 No. 676 and is printed as amended by the Interpretation Act 1978, ss. 17(2)(a) and 23(1).]

B27.392   [SCHEDULE 10B (see regulation 3(2))

Department of Transport *ROAD TRAFFIC ACT 1988 SECTIONS 41, 49, 57 & 59* *EXAMINATION OF GOODS VEHICLES*				Serial No.	**V**
Plate VTG 6T Rev. 92				DTp Ref. No.	
Reg./Ident. Mark	Vehicle Identification No.			Type Approval No./Variant	
Manufacturer/ Model					Speed Limiter Exempt
Function *(See note 3 below)*		Year of Original Registration			Year of Manufacture

(1) Description of Weights applicable to vehicle	(2) Weights not to be exceeded in GL Britain		(3) Design Weights *(If higher than shown in column 2)*	
Gross Weight *(See notes 1 & 4 below)*				
Train Weight *(See note 2 below)*				
Max. Train Weight *(See note 5 below)*				Date of Issue
Axle Weights *(Axles numbered from front to rear) (See note 1 overleaf)* — Axle 1				👑 **DEPARTMENT OF**
Axle 2				
Axle 3				**TRANSPORT GREAT BRITAIN**
Axle 4				

NOTES
1. A reduced gross weight and/or axle weight may apply in certain cases to a vehicle towing or being towed by another.
2. The MAXIMUM permissible train weight can vary depending on the type of suspension and trailer drawn.
3. If the last letter in the function box is "R" road friendly suspension is fitted.
4. All weights shown are subject to the fitting of correct tyres.
5. This weight applies to combined transport operations.

Tyre use conditions applicable to vehicle

N. B. All weights in Kilograms

Note: A weight is not required in the box for Maximum Train Weight unless the vehicle is capable of being lawfully used on a road in Great Britain, having regard to Schedule 11A, at a greater train weight than the train weight at which it could lawfully be used ignoring that Schedule.]

B27.393   *[Schedule 10B was inserted by S.I. 1994 No. 329.]*

[SCHEDULE 10C (see regulation 3(2))　　　　　**B27.394**

Department of Transport *ROAD TRAFFIC ACT 1988 SECTIONS 41, 49, 57 & 59* *EXAMINATION OF GOODS VEHICLES* This is issued as proof of compliance with the Weights and Dimensions Directive 86/3/EEC	Serial No.	**B**
	DTp Ref. No.	

Plate VTG 6A

Reg./Ident. Mark		Vehicle Identification No.		Type Approval No./Variant	
Manufacturer/ 　　　Model				Speed Limiter Exempt	
Function *(See note 3 below)*		Year of Original Registration		Year of Manufacture	

(1) Description of Weights applicable to vehicle	(2) Weights not to be exceeded in Gt. Britain	(3) EEC Maximum permitted weights *(See note 8 below)*	(4) Design Weights *(If higher than shown in column 2)*	Length		Width	
Gross Weight *(See notes 1 & 4 below)*				a　Coupling centre to vehicle foremost part *(See note 6 below)*	Max	Min	
Train Weight *(See note 2 below)*				b　Coupling centre to vehicle rearmost part *(See note 7 below)*	Max	Min	
Max. Train Weight *(See note 5 below)*				Date of Issue			
Axle Weights *(Axles numbered from front to rear) (See note 1 overleaf)*	Axle 1			👑 DEPARTMENT OF TRANSPORT GREAT BRITAIN			
	Axle 2						
	Axle 3						
	Axle 4			Tyre use conditions applicable to vehicle			
Maximum Kingpin Load *(Semi-Trailers only)*				NOTES *(cont'd)*			

NOTES
1. A reduced gross weight and/or axle weight may apply in certain cases to a vehicle towing or being towed by another.
2. The MAXIMUM permissible train weight can vary depending on the type of suspension and trailer drawn.
3. If the last letter in the function box is "R" road friendly suspension is fitted.
4. All weights shown are subject to the fitting of correct tyres.
5. This weight applies to combined transport operations.

NOTES *(cont'd)*
6. This dimension only applies to drawing vehicles of trailers and semi-trailers.
7. This dimension only applies to trailers and semi-trailers.
8. Where there is no weight shown in the EEC maximum permitted weights column this is because there is no EEC standard relating to that weight.

N. B. All weights in Kilograms

Note: A weight is not required in the box for Maximum Train Weight unless the vehicle is capable of being lawfully used on a road in Great Britain, having regard to Schedule 11A, at a greater train weight than the train weight at which it could lawfully be used ignoring that Schedule.]

[Schedule 10C was inserted by S.I. 1994 No. 329.]　　　　　**B27.395**

SCHEDULE 11 (see regulations 75, 77 and 79)

Maximum Permitted Weights, etc.

[PART I (see regulation 75)

MAXIMUM PERMITTED LADEN WEIGHTS OF (1) TRAILERS AND (2) HEAVY MOTOR CARS AND
MOTOR CARS NOT FITTED WITH ROAD FRIENDLY SUSPENSION; IN EACH CASE NOT FORMING
PART OF AN ARTICULATED VEHICLE

B27.396   1. The maximum permitted laden weight of a two or three axle vehicle to which this
Part applies of a description specified in column 2 of Table I below shall, for the purposes
of regulation 75, be the weight specified in column 3 of that item.

2. In the case of a vehicle to which this Part applies and which is not of a description
specified in an item in column 2 of Table I below, the maximum permitted laden weight
shall, for the purposes of regulation 75, be the weight specified in column 4 of Table II
below in the item which is appropriate having regard to columns 2 and 3 of that Table.

Table I

MAXIMUM PERMITTED LADEN WEIGHTS OF CERTAIN TWO AND THREE AXLE VEHICLES

(1) Item	(2) Description of Vehicle	(3) Maximum permitted laden weight (kg)
1	A two axle trailer in which— (a) the two axles are closely spaced, and (b) the distance between the foremost axle of the trailer and the rearmost axle of the drawing vehicle is at least 4.2m	18,000
2	A three axle trailer in which— (a) the three axles are closely spaced, and (b) the distance between the foremost axle of the trailer and the rearmost axle of the drawing vehicle is at least 4.2m	24,000
3	A two axle motor vehicle which is a goods vehicle in which the distance between the foremost and rearmost axles is at least 3.0m	17,000
4	A two axle trailer in which the distance between the foremost axle and the rearmost axle is at least 3.0m	18,000

Table II

MAXIMUM PERMITTED LADEN WEIGHTS OF VEHICLES NOT FALLING WITHIN TABLE I

(1) Item	(2) No. of axles	(3) Distance between foremost and rearmost axles (metres)	(4) Maximum permitted laden weight (kg)
1	2	Less than 2.65	14,230
2	2	At least 2.65	16,260
3	3 or more	Less than 3.0	16,260
4	3 or more	At least 3.0 but less than 3.2	18,290

[*continued on next page*

(1) Item	(2) No. of axles	(3) Distance between foremost and rearmost axles (metres)	(4) Maximum permitted laden weight (kg)
5	3 or more	At least 3.2 but less than 3.9	20,330
6	3 or more	At least 3.9 but less than 4.9	22,360
7	3	At least 4.9	25,000
8	4 or more	At least 4.9 but less than 5.6	25,000
9	4 or more	At least 5.6 but less than 5.9	26,420
10	4 or more	At least 5.9 but less than 6.3	28,450
11	4 or more	At least 6.3	30,000]

[Part I of Schedule 11 is printed as substituted by S.I. 1992 No. 2016.]   **B27.397**

[PART IA (see regulation 75)

MAXIMUM PERMITTED GROSS WEIGHTS FOR HEAVY CARS AND MOTOR CARS IF THE DRIVING
AXLES ARE FITTED WITH ROAD FRIENDLY SUSPENSION, ETC., AND IN EACH CASE NOT
FORMING PART OF AN ARTICULATED VEHICLE

1. Subject to paragraph 2, the maximum permitted gross weight of a vehicle to which   **B27.398**
this Part applies shall, for the purposes of regulation 75, be the weight shown in column 4
of the Table below in the item which is appropriate, having regard to columns 2 and 3 in
that Table.

2. In the case of a vehicle to which this Part applies being a two axle goods vehicle which
has a distance between its axles of at least 3.0m, the maximum permitted laden weight for
the purposes of regulation 75 shall be 17,000kg.

Table

MAXIMUM PERMITTED LADEN WEIGHT

(1) Item	(2) No. of axles	(3) Distance between foremost and rearmost axles (metres)	(4) Maximum permitted laden weight (kg)
1	2	Less than 2.65	14,230
2	2	At least 2.65	16,260
3	3 or more	Less than 3.0	16,260
4	3 or more	At least 3.0 but less than 3.2	18,290
5	3 or more	At least 3.2 but less than 3.9	20,330
6	3 or more	At least 3.9 but less than 4.9	22,360
7	3 or more	At least 4.9 but less than 5.2	25,000
8	3	At least 5.2	26,000
9	4 or more	At least 5.2 but less than 6.4	The distance in metres between the foremost and rearmost axles multiplied by 5,000, rounded up to the next 10kg
10	4 or more	At least 6.4	32,000]

[Part IA of Schedule 11 was inserted by S.I. 1992 No. 2016.]   **B27.399**

PART II (see regulation 75)

MAXIMUM PERMITTED LADEN WEIGHTS FOR HEAVY MOTOR CARS AND MOTOR CARS
FORMING PART OF ARTICULATED VEHICLES

B27.400

1	2	3	4	5
Item	No. of axles	Distance between foremost and rearmost axles (metres)	Weight not exceeded by any axle not being the foremost or rearmost (kg)	Maximum permitted laden weight (kg)
1	2	At least 2.0	—	14,230
2	2	At least 2.4	—	16,260
3	2	At least 2.7	—	17,000
4	3 or more	At least 3.0	8,390	20,330
5	3 or more	At least 3.8	8,640	22,360
6	3 or more	At least 4.0	10,500	22,500
7	3 or more	At least 4.3	9,150	24,390
8	3 or more	At least 4.9	10,500	24,390

B27.401   *[Part II of Schedule 11 is printed as amended by S.I. 1987 No. 676.]*

PART III (see regulation 77)

MAXIMUM PERMITTED LADEN WEIGHT OF ARTICULATED VEHICLES

B27.402

1	2		3
Item	Relevant axle spacing (metres)		Maximum weight (kg)
	(a) Where motor vehicle has 2 axles	(b) Where motor vehicle has more than 2 axles	
1	At least 2.0	At least 2.0	20,330
2	At least 2.2	At least 2.2	22,360
3	At least 2.6	At least 2.6	23,370
4	At least 2.9	At least 2.9	24,390
5	At least 3.2	At least 3.2	25,410
6	At least 3.5	At least 3.5	26,420
7	At least 3.8	At least 3.8	27,440
8	At least 4.1	At least 4.1	28,450
9	At least 4.4	At least 4.4	29,470
10	At least 4.7	At least 4.7	30,490
11	At least 5.0	At least 5.0	31,500
12	At least 5.3	At least 5.3	32,520
13	At least 5.5	At least 5.4	33,000
14	At least 5.8	At least 5.6	34,000
15	At least 6.2	At least 5.8	35,000
16	At least 6.5	At least 6.0	36,000
17	At least 6.7	At least 6.2	37,000
18	At least 6.9	At least 6.3	38,000

B27.403   *[Part III of Schedule 11 is printed as amended by S.I. 1994 No. 329.]*

[PART IV (see regulation 77)

MAXIMUM PERMITTED LADEN WEIGHT OF ARTICULATED VEHICLES

(1) Item	(2) Type of articulated vehicle	(3) Maximum permitted weight (kg)	
1	Motor vehicle first used on or after 1st April 1973 and semi-trailer having a total of 5 or more axles	38,000	**B27.404**
2	Motor vehicle with 2 axles first used on or after 1st April 1973 and semi-trailer with 2 axles while being used for international transport	35,000	
3	Motor vehicle with 2 axles first used on or after 1st April 1973 in which— (a) every driving axle not being a steering axle is fitted with twin tyres; and (b) every driving axle is fitted with road friendly suspension; and a semi-trailer with 2 axles	35,000	
4	[Motor vehicle and semi-trailer having a total of 4 or more axles and not described in item 1, 2 or 3]	32,520	
5	Motor vehicle with 2 axles first used on or after 1st April 1973 in which— (a) every driving axle not being a steering axle is fitted with twin tyres; and (b) every driving axle is fitted with road friendly suspension; and a semi-trailer with 1 axle	26,000	
6	Motor vehicle with 2 axles and a semi-trailer with 1 axle being a combination not described in item 5	25,000]	

[*Part IV of Schedule 11 is printed as substituted by S.I. 1992 No. 2016 and as subsequently amended by S.I. 1994 No. 329.*]   **B27.405**

[PART V (regulation 79(2))

VEHICLES WITH TWO CLOSELY-SPACED AXLES

(1) Item	(2) Description of vehicle	(3) Maximum permitted weight of the two closely-spaced axles (kg)	
1	A motor vehicle or trailer in which (in either case) the distance between the two closely-spaced axles is less than 1.3 metres	16,000	**B27.406**
2	A vehicle being— (a) a motor vehicle in which the distance between the two closely-spaced axles is at least 1.3m, or (b) a trailer in which that distance is at least 1.3m and less than 1.5m, not being a vehicle described in item 3 or 4	18,000	

[*continued on next page*

(1) Item	(2) Description of vehicle	(3) Maximum permitted weight of the two closely-spaced axles (kg)

3	A motor vehicle in which the distance between the two closely-spaced axles is at least 1.3m and—
	  (a) every driving axle not being a steering axle is fitted with twin tyres; and
	  (b) either every driving axle is fitted with road friendly suspension or neither of the two closely-spaced axles has an axle weight exceeding 9,500kg
		19,000

4	A trailer in which—
	  (a) the two closely-spaced axles are driven from the motor vehicle drawing the trailer and are fitted with twin tyres; and
	  (b) either those axles are fitted with road friendly suspension or neither of them has an axle weight exceeding 9,500kg
		19,000

5	A trailer in which the distance between the two closely-spaced axles is at least 1.5m and less than 1.8m	19,320
6	A trailer in which the distance between the two closely-spaced axles is at least 1.8m	20,000]

B27.407   *[Part V of Schedule 11 is printed as substituted by S.I. 1992 No. 2016.]*

[PART VI (regulation 79(3))

VEHICLES WITH THREE CLOSELY-SPACED AXLES

B27.408

(1) Item	(2) Description of vehicle	(3) Maximum permitted weight of the three closely-spaced axles (kg)
1	A vehicle in which the smallest distance between any two of the three closely-spaced axles is less than 1.3m	21,000
2	A vehicle in which the smallest distance between any two of the three closely-spaced axles is at least 1.3m and at least one of those axles does not have air suspension	22,500
3	A vehicle in which the smallest distance between any two of the three closely-spaced axles is at least 1.3m and all three axles are fitted with air suspension	24,000

B27.409   *[Part VI of Schedule 11 is printed as substituted by S.I. 1992 No. 2016.]*

PART VII

B27.410   *[Revoked by S.I. 1992 No. 2016.]*

[SCHEDULE 11A (see regulations 76(1A), 77(2A) and [80(2B)])

EXEMPTIONS RELATING TO COMBINED TRANSPORT OPERATIONS

Note.   Schedule 11A was inserted by S.I. 1994 No. 329 and the heading to the Schedule is **B27.411** printed as amended by S.I. 1997 No. 1096.

PART I

GENERAL

1. Regulation 76 does not apply to a wheeled heavy motor car drawing one wheeled **B27.412** trailer if the requirements set out in Part II of this Schedule are for the time being fulfilled.

[Schedule 11A (paragraphs 1, 2, 3–8, and 9) was inserted by S.I. 1994 No. 329.]   **B27.413**

2. Regulation 77 does not apply to an articulated vehicle if the requirements set out in **B27.414** Part III of this Schedule are for the time being fulfilled.

[Schedule 11A (paragraphs 1, 2, 3–8, and 9) was inserted by S.I. 1994 No. 329.]   **B27.415**

[**2A.** Regulation 75, 76, 77 and 78 do not apply to an articulated vehicle if the require- **B27.416** ments set out in Part IIIA of this Schedule are for the time being fulfilled.]

[Paragraph 2A of Schedule 11A was inserted by S.I. 1998 No. 3112.]

PART II

DRAWBAR COMBINATIONS

3.—(1) The drawing vehicle and trailer must each be carrying a relevant receptacle as **B27.417** part of a combined transport operation, each such receptacle being on a journey—

   (a) to a railhead from which the relevant receptacle is, as part of the operation, to be transported in a relevant manner by railway pursuant to a relevant contract made before the journey began; or

   (b) from a railhead to which the relevant receptacle has, as part of the operation, been transported in a relevant manner by railway.

(2) There must be carried in the cab of the drawing vehicle a document or documents—

   (a) if the vehicle is on a journey to a railhead, specifying the railhead, the date the relevant contract was made and the parties thereto;

   (b) if the vehicle is on a journey from a railhead, specifying the railhead and the date and time at which the receptacles were collected from that railhead.

[Schedule 11A (paragraphs 1, 2, 3–8, and 9) was inserted by S.I. 1994 No. 329.]   **B27.418**

4. The following conditions must be satisfied in relation to the drawing vehicle, namely— **B27.419**

   (a) it complies with the relevant braking requirement;

   (b) every driving axle not being a steering axle is fitted with twin tyres; and

   (c) either every driving axle is fitted with road friendly suspension or no axle has an axle weight exceeding 8,500kg.

[Schedule 11A (paragraphs 1, 2, 3–8, and 9) was inserted by S.I. 1994 No. 329.]   **B27.420**

B27.421   **5.**—(1) The motor vehicle and trailer must have a total of at least 6 axles.

(2) The total laden weight of the motor vehicle and trailer must not exceed 44,000kg.

B27.422   *[Schedule 11A (paragraphs 1, 2, 3–8, and 9) was inserted by S.I. 1994 No. 329.]*

PART III

ARTICULATED VEHICLES

B27.423   **6.**—(1) The motor vehicle comprised in the articulated vehicle must be being used for the conveyance of a loading unit as part of a combined transport operation, the loading unit being on a journey—

    (a) to a railhead from which the loading unit is, as part of the operation, to be transported in a relevant manner by railway pursuant to a relevant contract made before the journey began; or

    (b) from a railhead to which the loading unit has, as part of the operation, been transported in a relevant manner by railway.

(2) If the loading unit is a bi-modal vehicle, the semi-trailer comprised in the articulated vehicle must be the bi-modal vehicle in its semi-trailer mode.

(3) If the loading unit is a relevant receptacle, the relevant receptacle must be being carried on the semi-trailer comprised in the articulated vehicle.

(4) There must be carried in the cab of the motor vehicle a document or documents—

    (a) if the vehicle is on a journey to a railhead, specifying the railhead, the date the contract was made and the parties thereto;

    (b) if the vehicle is on a journey from a railhead, specifying the railhead and the date and time at which the loading unit was collected from that railhead.

B27.424   **7.** The following conditions must be satisfied in relation to the motor vehicle, namely—

    (a) it complies with the relevant braking requirements;

    (b) it has at least three axles;

    (c) every driving axle not being a steering axle is fitted with twin tyres; and

    (d) either every driving axle is fitted with road friendly suspension or no axle has an axle weight exceeding 8,500kg.

B27.425   *[Schedule 11A (paragraphs 1, 2, 3–8, and 9) was inserted by S.I. 1994 No. 329.]*

B27.426   [**8.**—(1) The articulated vehicle must have a total of at least 6 axles.

(2) The laden weight of the articulated vehicle must not exceed the weight determined in accordance with sub-paragraph (3).

(3) The weight for the purposes of sub-paragraph (2) is the number of kilograms equal to the product of the distance measured in metres between the king-pin and the centre of the rearmost axle of the semi-trailer by 5500 and rounded up to the nearest 10kg, if that number is less than 44000kg.]

B27.427   *[Schedule 11A (paragraphs 1, 2, 3–8, and 9) was inserted by S.I. 1994 No. 329. Paragraph 8 is printed as substituted by S.I. 1998 No. 3112.]*

[PART IIIA

ARTICULATED VEHICLES (ALTERNATIVE REQUIREMENTS)]

[8A.—(1) The requirements of paragraph 6 are fulfilled.   **B27.428**

(2) The vehicle is one which falls within the first indent of paragraph 1 of Article 3 of Community Directive 96/53 [*q.v.*] (vehicles used in international traffic or put into circulation in any other Member State) and complies with the limit values specified in paragraph 2.2.2 of Annex I and the other relevant requirements of that Directive.]

[Paragraph 8A of Schedule 11A, and the Part IIIA heading immediately preceding it, was inserted by   **B27.429**
S.I. 1998 No. 3112.]

PART IV

INTERPRETATION

9.—(1) In this Schedule—   **B27.430**

"*bi-modal vehicle*" means a semi-trailer which can be adapted for use as a railway vehicle;

"*journey*", except in sub-paragraph (3), means a journey by road;

"*loading unit*" means a bi-modal vehicle [, road-rail semi-trailer] or a relevant receptacle;

"*railhead*" means a facility for the transhipment of—

    (a) bi-modal vehicles from the ground onto the track of a railway, or

    (b) relevant receptacles from road vehicles onto railway vehicles situated on the track of a railway, [or]

    [(c) road-rail semi-trailers from the ground onto railway vehicles on the track of a railway,]

or vice versa;

"*relevant contract*" means a contract for the transport of a loading unit by railway;

"*relevant receptacle*" means a receptacle (not being a vehicle) having a length of at least 6.1m designed and constructed for repeated use for the carriage of goods on, and for transfer between, road vehicles and railway vehicles;

["*road-rail semi-trailer*" means a semi-trailer constructed or adapted so as to be capable of being both used as a semi-trailer on roads and carried on a railway vehicle;]

"*road friendly suspension*" and "*twin tyres*" have the meanings given by regulation 75; and

"*network*", "*network licence*", "*railway vehicle*", "*track*" and "*train*" have the meanings given by section 83 of the Railways Act 1993.

(2) The definition of "*railway*" in section 67(1) of the Transport and Works Act 1992 shall have effect for the purposes of this Schedule as it has effect for the purposes of that Act, and cognate expressions shall be construed accordingly.

(3) In these Regulations, a reference to a combined transport operation is a reference to the transport of a loading unit on a journey where—

    (a) part of the journey is by railway on a network operated by the British Railways Board or under a network licence;

    (b) part of the journey is by road; and

    (c) no goods are added to or removed from the loading unit between the time when the journey begins and the time when it ends.

(4) Subject to sub-paragraph (5), for the purposes of this Schedule—

    (a) a bi-modal vehicle shall be regarded as being transported by railway in a relevant manner if and only if the vehicle in its railway vehicle mode is travelling by railway as part of a train; . . .

(b) a relevant receptacle shall be regarded as being transported by railway in a relevant manner if and only if it is being carried on a railway vehicle which forms part of a train [; and]

[(c) a road-rail semi-trailer shall be regarded as being transported by railway in a relevant manner if and only if it is being carried on a railway vehicle which forms part of a train.]

(5) A relevant receptacle shall be regarded, for the purposes of this Schedule, as not being transported by railway in a relevant manner at any time when—

(a) the relevant receptacle is in or on a motor vehicle or trailer; and

(b) the motor vehicle or trailer is being carried on a railway vehicle.]

[(6) A road-rail semi-trailer shall be regarded, for the purposes of this Schedule, as not being transported by railway in a relevant manner at any time when it is being carried on a railway vehicle as part of an articulated vehicle.]

B27.431   *[Schedule 11A (paragraphs 1, 2, 3–8, and 9) was inserted by S.I. 1994 No. 329. Paragraph 9 is printed as amended by S.I. 1997 No. 1096.*

The Railways Act 1993, s.83(1), defines "network", "network licence", "railway vehicle", "track" and "train" in the following terms:

"*network*" means—

(a) any railway line, or combination of two or more railway lines, and

(b) any installations associated with any of the track comprised in that line or those lines,

together constituting a system of track and other installations which is used for and in connection with the support, guidance and operation of trains;

"*network licence*" means a licence authorising a person—

(a) to be the operator of a network;

(b) to be the operator of a train being used on a network for any purpose comprised in the operation of that network; and

(c) to be the operator of a train being used on a network for a purpose preparatory or incidental to, or consequential on, using a train as mentioned in paragraph (b) above;

"*railway vehicle*" includes anything which, whether or not it is constructed or adapted to carry any person or load, is constructed or adapted to run on flanged wheels over or along track;

"*track*" means any land or other property comprising the permanent way of any railway, taken together with the ballast, sleepers and metals laid thereon, whether or not the land or other property is also used for other purposes; and any reference to track includes a reference to—

(a) any level crossings, bridges, viaducts, tunnels, culverts, retaining walls, or other structures used or to be used for the support of, or otherwise in connection with, track; and

(b) any walls, fences or other structures bounding the railway or bounding any adjacent or adjoining property;

"*train*" means—

(a) two or more items of rolling stock coupled together, at least one of which is a locomotive; or

(b) a locomotive not coupled to any other rolling stock;

The Transport and Works Act 1992, s.67(1), defines "railway" in the following terms:

"*railway*" means a system of transport employing parallel rails which—

    (a) provide support and guidance for vehicles carried on flanged wheels, and

    (b) form a track which either is of a gauge of at least 350 millimetres or crosses a carriageway (whether or not on the same level),

but does not include a tramway;]

SCHEDULE 12 (see regulations 81 and 82)

CONDITIONS TO BE COMPLIED WITH IN RELATION TO THE USE OF VEHICLES CARRYING WIDE OR LONG LOADS OR VEHICLES CARRYING LOADS OR HAVING FIXED APPLIANCES OR APPARATUS WHICH PROJECT

PART I

Advance notice to police

1. (a) Before using on a road a vehicle or vehicles to which this paragraph applies, the   **B27.432** owner shall give notice of the intended use to the Chief Officer of Police for any area in which he proposes to use the vehicle or vehicles. The notice shall be given so that it is received by the date after which there are at least two working days before the date on which the use of the vehicle or vehicles is to begin, and shall include the following details—

    (i) time, date and route of the proposed journey, and

  [(ia) in a case to which regulation 7(9) applies, the overall length of the trailer,]

   (ii) in a case to which regulation 82(2) applies, the overall length and width of the vehicle by which the load is carried and the width of the lateral projection or projections of its load,

  (iii) in a case to which regulation 82(4)(a) applies, the overall length and width of each vehicle by which the load is carried, the length of any forward or rearward projection and, where the load rests on more than one vehicle, the distance between the vehicles,

  (iv) in a case to which regulation 82(4)(b) applies, the overall length of the combination of vehicles and the length of any forward or rearward projection of the load, and

  (v) in a case to which regulation 82(7) and (8) applies, the overall length of the vehicle and the length of any forward or rearward projection of the load or special appliance or apparatus.

The Chief Officer of Police for any police area may, at his discretion, accept a shorter period of notice or fewer details.

(b) The vehicle or vehicles shall be used only in accordance with the details at (a) subject to any variation in the time, date or route which may be directed by—

    (i) any such Chief Officer of Police to the owner of the vehicle or vehicles, or

   (ii) a police constable to the driver in the interests of road safety or in order to avoid undue traffic congestion by halting the vehicle or vehicles in a place on or adjacent to the road on which the vehicle or vehicles are travelling.

(c) In this paragraph—

    (i) "*Chief Officer of Police*" has, in relation to England and Wales, the same meaning as in the Police Act 1964 . . . ,

   (ii) "*working day*" means a day which is not a Sunday, a bank holiday, Christmas Day or Good Friday, and

  (iii) "*bank holiday*" means a day which is a bank holiday by or under the Banking and Financial Dealings Act 1971, either generally or in the locality in which the road is situated.

B27.433 *[Paragraph 1 of Part I of Schedule 12 is printed as amended by S.I. 1991 No. 2125.*

Words relating expressly and exclusively to Scotland have been omitted from paragraph 1(c) above.

The term "chief officer of police" was defined in the Police Act 1964, s.62, as substituted by the Police and Magistrates' Courts Act 1994, s.44 and Sched. 5, para.15; section 62 has, however, been repealed by the Police Act 1996, s.104(2) and Sched. 9, Pt II. Reference should now be made (by virtue of section 103(2) of and Schedule 8, paragraph 1(4), to the 1996 Act) to section 1 of that Act (as amended by the Greater London Authority Act 1999, s.325 and Sched. 27, para.69 (and see also ibid., s.423 and Sched. 34, Pt VII)) for the meaning of "police area" and to section 101(1) for the meaning of "chief officer of police".

The following are stated by the Banking and Financial Dealings Act 1971, Sched. 1, para.1, to be bank holidays in England and Wales:

Easter Monday.
The last Monday in May.
The last Monday in August.
26th December, if it be not a Sunday.
27th December in a year in which 25th or 26th December is a Sunday.

Days may be substituted for or added to the above list by royal proclamation. In recent years January 1 (or 2), and the first Monday in May have been so added.]

Attendants

B27.434 **2.** At least one person in addition to the person or persons employed in driving a motor vehicle to which this paragraph applies shall be employed—

  (a) in attending to that vehicle and its load and any other vehicle or vehicles drawn by that vehicle and the load or loads carried on the vehicle or vehicles so drawn, and

  (b) to give warning to the driver of the said motor vehicle and to any person of any danger likely to be caused to any such person by reason of the presence of the said vehicle or vehicles on the road.

Provided that, where three or more vehicles as respects which the conditions in this paragraph are applicable are travelling together in convoy, it shall be a sufficient compliance with this paragraph if only the foremost and rearmost vehicles in the convoy are attended in the manner prescribed in this paragraph.

For the purpose of this paragraph when a motor vehicle is drawing a trailer or trailers—

  (i) any person employed in pursuance of section 34 of the 1972 Act in attending that vehicle or any such trailer shall be treated as being an attendant required by this paragraph so long as he is also employed to discharge the duties mentioned in this paragraph; and

  (ii) when another motor vehicle is used for the purpose of assisting in their propulsion on the road, the person or persons employed in driving that other motor vehicle shall not be treated as a person or persons employed in attending to the first-mentioned vehicle or any vehicle or vehicles drawn thereby.

B27.435 *[Section 34 of the Road Traffic Act 1972 (to which reference is made in paragraph 2 of Schedule 12 above) was repealed by the Road Traffic (Consequential Provisions) Act 1988 but not re-enacted. It seems therefore that paragraph 2(i) above has lapsed.]*

Marking of longer projections

B27.436 **3.** (a) Every forward and rearward projection to which this paragraph applies shall be fitted with—

    (i) an end marker, except in the case of a rearward projection which is fitted with a rear marking in accordance with the Lighting Regulations, and

    (ii) where required by sub-paragraphs (c) and (d) of this paragraph, two or more side markers;

which shall be of the size, shape and colour described in Part II of this Schedule;

(b) the end marker shall be so fitted that—

    (i) it is as near as is practicable in a transverse plane,

    (ii) it is not more than 0.5m from the extreme end of the projection,

    (iii) the vertical distance between the lowest point of the marker and the road surface is not more than 2.5m,

    (iv) it, and any means by which it is fitted to the projection, impedes the view of the driver as little as possible, and

    (v) it is clearly visible within a reasonable distance to a person using the road at the end of the vehicle from which the projection extends;

(c) where the forward projection exceeds 2m or the rearward projection exceeds 3m, one side marker shall be fitted on the right hand side and one on the left hand side of the projection so that—

    (i) each marker is as near as is practicable in a longitudinal plane,

    (ii) no part extends beyond the end of the projection,

    (iii) the vertical distance between the lowest part of each marker and the surface of the road is not more than 2.5m,

    (iv) the horizontal distance between each marker and the end marker or as the case may be, the rear marking carried in accordance with the Lighting Regulations does not exceed 1m, and

    (v) each marker is clearly visible within a reasonable distance to a person using the road on that side of the projection;

(d) where—

    (i) a forward projection exceeds 4.5m, or

    (ii) a rearward projection exceeds 5m,

extra side markers shall be fitted on either side of the projection so that the horizontal distance between the extreme projecting point of the vehicle from which the projection extends and the nearest point on any side marker from that point, and between the nearest points of any adjacent side markers on the same side does not exceed—

2.5m in the case of a forward projection, or

3.5m in the case of a rearward projection.

For the purposes of this sub-paragraph the expression "*the vehicle*" shall not include any special appliance or apparatus or any part thereof which is a forward projection or a rearward projection within the meaning of regulation 81;

(e) the extra side markers required by this sub-paragraph shall also meet the requirements of (i), (iii) and (v) of sub-paragraph (c);

(f) every marker fitted in accordance with this paragraph shall be kept clean and unobscured and [between sunset and sunrise] be illuminated by a lamp which renders it readily visible from a reasonable distance and which is so shielded that its light, except as reflected from the marker, is not visible to other persons using the road.

[Paragraph 3 of Part I of Schedule 12 is printed as amended by S.I. 1991 No. 2125.]   **B27.437**

Marking of shorter projections

4. A projection to which this paragraph applies shall be rendered clearly visible to other persons using the road within a reasonable distance, in the case of a forward projection,   **B27.438**

from the front thereof or, in the case of a rearward projection, from the rear thereof and, in either case, from either side thereof.

[*Marking of wide loads*

B27.439 **5.** (a) Subject to sub-paragraph (d), every load carried on a vehicle in circumstances where this paragraph applies shall be fitted on each side and in the prescribed manner, with—

    (i) a prescribed marker in such a position that it is visible from the front of the vehicle, and

    (ii) a prescribed marker in such a position that it is visible from the rear of the vehicle.

  (b) For the purposes of sub-paragraph (a)—

    (i) a marker on a side of the load is fitted in the prescribed manner if at least part of it is within 50mm of a longitudinal plane passing through the point on that side of the load which is furthest from the axis of the vehicle; and

    (ii) a prescribed marker is a marker of the size, shape and colour described in Part II of this Schedule.

  (c) Every marker fitted pursuant to this paragraph shall be kept clean and between sunset and sunrise be illuminated by a lamp which renders it readily visible from a reasonable distance and which is so shielded that its light, except as reflected from the marker, is not visible to other persons using the road.

  (d) If the load does not extend beyond the longitudinal plane passing through the extreme projecting point on one side of the vehicle, it shall not be necessary for a marker to be fitted to the load on that side.]

B27.440 *[Paragraph 5 of Part I of Schedule 12 was inserted by S.I. 1991 No. 2125.]*

PART II

PROJECTION MARKERS

B27.441 [(see paragraphs 3(a) and 5(b) of this Schedule)]

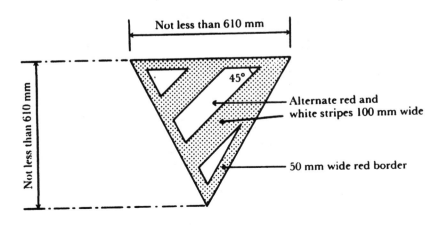

DIAGRAM OF SIDE MARKER SURFACE

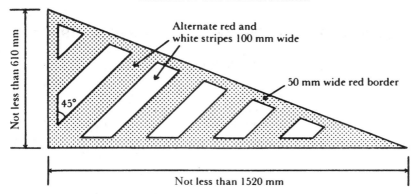

[Part II of Schedule 12 is printed as amended by S.I. 1991 No. 2125.]   **B27.442**

[SCHEDULE 13 (see regulation 3(2))

PLATE FOR RESTRICTED SPEED VEHICLE

1.—[(1)] A vehicle displays a plate in accordance with the requirements of this   **B27.443**
Schedule if a plate in respect of which the following conditions are satisfied is displayed on
the vehicle in a prominent position.

(2) The conditions are—

(a) the plate must be in the form shown in the diagram below;

(b) the plate must be at least 150mm wide and at least 120mm high;

(c) the figures "5" and "0" must be at least 100mm high and 50mm wide with a stroke
width of at least 12mm, the figures being black on a white background; and

(d) the border must be black and between 3mm and 5mm wide.

[Schedule 13 was inserted by S.I. 1990 No. 1981.
    The reference "(1)" at the beginning of the text of paragraph 1 of this Schedule has been added editor-   **B27.444**
ially. There are no numbered paragraphs after paragraph 1.]

The Fixed Penalty (Procedure) Regulations 1986

(S.I. 1986 No. 1330)

B28.01 *[The text of these regulations is printed as amended by:*

the Fixed Penalty (Procedure) (Amendment) Regulations 2001 (S.I. 2001 No. 926) (April 1, 2001).

The amending regulations are referred to in the notes to the principal regulations only by their year and number. The date referred to above is the date on which the amending regulations came into force.]

B28.02 **1.**—(1) *[Omitted.]*

(2) In these Regulations any reference to a section is a reference to a section of [the Road Traffic Offenders Act 1988].

(3) These Regulations do not extend to Scotland.

B28.03 *[Regulation 1 is printed as amended by the Interpretation Act 1978, ss.17(2)(a) and 23(1).]*

B28.04 **2.**—(1) Subject to paragraph (2) below, in the documents described in column 1 of the Schedule to these Regulations and referred to in the provisions of the Act specified in column 2 of the Schedule there shall be provided the information or, as the case may be, further information prescribed in column 3 of the Schedule.

(2) The information prescribed in the Schedule in relation to a fixed penalty notice need not be provided if the offender's driving licence would not be subject to endorsement on conviction of the offence in respect of which the notice was given.

B28.05 **3.**—(1) A copy of any fixed penalty notice given or affixed under [section 54 or section 62] shall be forwarded by or on behalf of the constable or traffic warden giving or affixing the notice to the fixed penalty clerk unless the fixed penalty clerk has notified the chief officer of police that he does not wish to receive a copy of any such notice.

(2) Where a fixed penalty notice has been given to a person under [section 54] and that person has surrendered his driving licence in accordance with that section the driving licence shall be forwarded by or on behalf of the constable to the fixed penalty clerk.

B28.06 *[Regulation 3 is printed as amended by the Interpretation Act 1978, ss.17(2)(a) and 23(1).]*

B28.07 **4.**—(1) Where a constable has issued a fixed penalty notice to a person under [section 54(5)], he shall send a notice indicating that fact to the chief officer of police together with that person's driving licence.

(2) Subject to paragraph (3) below, on receipt of the documents referred to in paragraph (1) above the chief officer of police shall send the driving licence and a copy of the notice issued under [section 54(4)] to the fixed penalty clerk and notify him that a fixed penalty notice has been issued under [section 54(5)].

(3) The chief officer of police shall not send a copy of the notice issued under [section 54(4)] to the fixed penalty clerk under paragraph (2) above if the fixed penalty clerk has

notified the chief officer of police that he does not wish to receive a copy of any such notice.

[Regulation 4 is printed as amended by the Interpretation Act 1978, ss.17(2)(a) and 23(1).]   **B28.08**

5.—(1) On receipt of the remittance in respect of a fixed penalty the fixed penalty clerk   **B28.09**
shall notify the chief officer of police that the remittance has been received.

(2) If payment of the fixed penalty is made by a person otherwise than as required by the fixed penalty notice the fixed penalty clerk shall return the remittance to that person.

(3) Where a remittance in respect of a fixed penalty is sent by a person to a [justices' chief executive]who is not the fixed penalty clerk specified in the fixed penalty notice, the [justices' chief executive] shall return the remittance to that person.

[Regulation 5 is printed as amended by S.I. 2001 No. 926.]   **B28.10**

6. Where—   **B28.11**
  (a) the suspended enforcement period has expired; and
  (b) the fixed penalty has not been paid; and
  (c) either the person to whom the fixed penalty notice was given has requested a hearing under [section 55(2)] or [63(3)] or no registration certificate has been issued under [section 70(2)],

the chief officer of police shall notify the fixed penalty clerk accordingly and the fixed penalty clerk shall, where an endorsable offence is involved, return the driving licence to the person to whom the fixed penalty notice was given.

[Regulation 6 is printed as amended by the Interpretation Act 1978, ss.17(2)(a) and 23(1).]   **B28.12**

7. Where—   **B28.13**
  (a) the suspended enforcement period has expired; and
  (b) the fixed penalty has not been paid; and
  (c) a registration certificate has been issued under [section 70(2)],

the chief officer of police shall notify the fixed penalty clerk accordingly.

[Regulation 7 is printed as amended by the Interpretation Act 1978, ss.17(2)(a) and 23(1).]   **B28.14**

8. Where in a case involving an endorsable offence any sum determined by reference to   **B28.15**
the fixed penalty is registered under [section 71] for enforcement against the licence holder as a fine the [justices' chief executive for] the court where the sum is registered shall notify the fixed penalty clerk to whom the driving licence was sent that the sum has been registered.

[Regulation 8 is printed as amended by the Interpretation Act 1978, ss.17(2)(a) and 23(1); S.I. 2001   **B28.16**
No. 926.]

9. Where a fixed penalty notice is issued under [section 54(2)] or [(5)] the fixed penalty   **B28.17**
clerk shall not accept payment of the fixed penalty after the expiry of the suspended enforcement period.

[Regulation 9 is printed as amended by the Interpretation Act 1978, ss.17(2)(a) and 23(1).]   **B28.18**

10. Where a fixed penalty is paid within the suspended enforcement period the fixed   **B28.19**
penalty clerk shall send a receipt for the payment, if requested, to the payer.

B28.20   **11.** For the purposes of [section 56(3)(a)] (which provides that a licence receipt issued by a constable is to cease to have effect on the expiration of the period of one month beginning with the date of issue) there shall be prescribed a longer period of two months beginning with the same date.

B28.21   *[Regulation 11 is printed as amended by the Interpretation Act 1978, ss.17(2)(a) and 23(1).]*

Regulation 2   SCHEDULE

INFORMATION OR FURTHER INFORMATION TO BE PROVIDED IN CERTAIN DOCUMENTS
MENTIONED IN [PART III OF THE ROAD TRAFFIC OFFENDERS ACT 1988]

B28.22

Document	Provision of Act	Information or further information to be provided
1. Fixed penalty notice	[Section 52(1)]	(i) The name of the police force of which the constable giving the notice is a member. (ii) The serial number of the fixed penalty notice. (iii) Whether the notice relates to an endorsable offence. (iv) The name, date of birth and address of the person to whom the notice is given. (v) The date, time and place of the alleged offence. (vi) The details of the vehicle including the registration number. (vii) The documents, if any, to be produced at a police station and the period within which they must be produced. (viii) An explanation of the action to be taken by the driver where (a) he has not or (b) he has surrendered the licence. (ix) The fact that the person to whom the notice is given may opt for trial. (x) The method of paying the fixed penalty. (xi) The name, rank and number of the constable issuing the fixed penalty notice. (xii) Guidance to the driver as to the legal consequences of a fixed penalty notice.
2. Receipt for driving licence	[Section 56(1)]	(i) Whether the driving licence is full or provisional. (ii) The driver number as shown on the licence. (iii) The groups of vehicles which the driver is entitled to drive. (iv) The expiry date of the licence. (v) The duration of the validity of the licence receipt. (vi) The method of obtaining a new receipt on the expiry of an old receipt. (vii) The name, rank and number of the constable issuing the fixed penalty notice.

[continued on next page

Document	Provision of Act	Information or further information to be provided
3. Receipt for driving licence	[Section 56(2)]	(i) The date of issue of receipt. (ii) The code of the magistrates' court issuing receipt. (iii) The name, address and date of birth of driver. (iv) Whether the driving licence is full or provisional. (v) The driver number as shown on the licence. (vi) The groups of vehicles which the driver is entitled to drive. (vii) The expiry date of the licence. (viii) The duration of the validity of the licence receipt.
4. Registration certificate	[Section 70]	(i) The serial number and date, time and place of issue of the notice to owner, notice to hirer or fixed penalty notice (as case may be). (ii) The vehicle registration number. (iii) The driver number. (iv) The amount of the appropriate fixed penalty. (v) The sum to be registered in default of payment of the fixed penalty.
5. Notice requesting new statutory statement	[Section 73(4)]	(i) The particulars of the statutory declaration. (ii) The details of the alleged fixed penalty offence. (iii) A request to furnish a statutory statement of ownership. (iv) The period allowed for a response to the notice. (v) The consequences of providing, or, as the case may be, not providing the statutory statement of ownership.
6. Statement of liability	[Section 66(2)]	(i) The name, date of birth and address of hirer. (ii) The duration of the hiring agreement.

[The Schedule is printed as amended by the Interpretation Act 1978, ss.17(2)(a) and 23(1).]   **B28.23**

The Community Drivers' Hours and Recording Equipment (Exemptions and Supplementary Provisions) Regulations 1986

(S.I. 1986 No. 1456)

B29.01   *[The text of these regulations is printed as amended by:*

> *the Community Drivers' Hours and Recording Equipment (Exemptions and Supplementary Provisions) (Amendment) Regulations 1986 (S.I. 1986 No. 1669) (October 26, 1986);*
>
> *the Community Drivers' Hours and Recording Equipment (Exemptions and Supplementary Provisions) (Amendment) Regulations 1987 (S.I. 1987 No. 805) (June 1, 1987);*
>
> *the Community Drivers' Hours and Recording Equipment (Exemptions and Supplementary Provisions) (Amendment) Regulations 1988 (S.I. 1988 No. 760) (May 20, 1988); and*
>
> *the Community Drivers' Hours and Recording Equipment (Amendment) Regulations 1998 (S.I. 1998 No. 2006) (August 24, 1998).*

The amending regulations are referred to in the notes to the principal regulations by their years and numbers. The dates referred to above are the dates on which the amending regulations came into force.]

1. Citation, commencement, interpretation and revocation

B29.02   (1) *[Omitted.]*

(2) In these Regulations—

"*the Community Drivers' Hours Regulation*" means Council Regulation (EEC) No. 3820/85 of 20th December 1985 on the harmonisation of certain social legislation relating to road transport [*q.v.*];

"*the Community Recording Equipment Regulation*" means Council Regulation (EEC) No. 3821/85 of 20th December 1985 on recording equipment in road transport [*q.v.*];

"*permissible maximum weight*" has the same meaning as in [section 108 of the Road Traffic Act 1988].

(3) Subject to paragraph (2) above, any expression used in these Regulations which is used in the Community Drivers' Hours Regulation has the same meaning as in that Regulation.

(4) *[Revocations.]*

B29.03   *[Regulation 1 is printed as amended by the Interpretation Act 1978, ss.17(2)(a) and 23(1).]*

2. Exemption from the Community Drivers' Hours Regulation

B29.04   [(1) Pursuant to Article 13(1) of the Community Drivers' Hours Regulation, exemption is granted from all the provisions of that Regulation, except Article 5 (minimum ages for drivers) in respect of any vehicle falling within a description specified in Part I of the Schedule to these Regulations.

(2) Pursuant to Article 13(2) of the Community Drivers' Hours Regulation, exemption is granted from all the provisions of that Regulation, except Article 5, in respect of any vehicle falling within a description specified in Part II of the Schedule to these Regulations.]

[Regulation 2 is printed as substituted by S.I. 1987 No. 805.]   **B29.05**

3. Supplementary provisions relating to the Community Drivers' Hours Regulation

(1) Pursuant to Article 6(1) of the Community Drivers' Hours Regulation, the applic-   **B29.06** ation of the fourth sub-paragraph of that Article shall be extended to national passenger services other than regular passenger services.

(2) Pursuant to Article 7(3) of the Community Drivers' Hours Regulation, if—

(a) the driver of a vehicle which is engaged in the national carriage of passengers on a regular service observes in a relevant area, immediately after any period of driving not exceeding four hours, a break of at least 30 minutes; and

(b) it was not possible for him to observe, at any time during that period of driving, a break of at least 15 minutes,

that period of driving shall be disregarded for the purposes of Article 7(1) of that Regulation.

(3) In paragraph (2) above "*relevant area*", in relation to the driver of a vehicle which is engaged in the national carriage of passengers on a regular service, means any of the following areas, namely—

(a) the London Borough of Camden;

(b) the Royal Borough of Kensington and Chelsea;

(c) the London Borough of Islington;

(d) the City of Westminster,

[(e) in the City of Birmingham, an area comprising Digbeth Coach Station, Rea Street, Bradford Street, Barford Street, Cheapside and Birchall Street;]

[(f) in the City of Bristol, an area comprising Marlborough Street Coach Station, Marlborough Street, Maudlin Street, Lower Maudlin Street, Earl Street and Whitson Street;]

[(g) in the City of Leeds, an area comprising Wellington Street Coach Station, Wellington Street, York Place, Queen Street, Little Queen Street and King Street;]

[(h) in the City of Leicester, an area comprising St Margaret's Bus Station, Abbey Street, Gravel Street, Church Gate, Mansfield Street, Sandacre Street, New Road, Burleys Way and St Margaret's Way;]

[(i) in the City of Nottingham, an area comprising Victoria Bus Station, Glasshouse Street, Huntingdon Street, York Street, Cairns Street, Woodborough Road, Mansfield Road, Milton Street, Lower Parliament Street and Union Road; and]

[(j) in the City of Oxford, an area comprising Oxpens Coach Park, Oxpens Road, Thames Street and Holybush Hill,]

in which passengers are taken up or set down in the course of the service.

[Regulation 3 is printed as amended by S.I. 1986 No. 1669.]   **B29.07**

4. Exemption from the Community Recording Equipment Regulation

[(1) Pursuant to Article 3(2) of the Community Recording Equipment Regulation,   **B29.08** exemption is granted from the provisions of that Regulation in respect of any vehicle falling within a description specified in Part I of the Schedule to these Regulations.

(2) Pursuant to Article 3(3) of the Community Recording Equipment Regulation, exemption is granted from the provisions of that Regulation in respect of:

(a) any vehicle falling within a description specified in Part II of the Schedule to these Regulations; and

(b) any vehicle which is being used for collecting sea coal.]

B29.09   *[Regulation 4 is printed as substituted by S.I. 1987 No. 805.]*

5. Application of the Community Recording Equipment Regulation

B29.10   (1) Pursuant to Article 3(4) of the Community Recording Equipment Regulation, that Regulation shall apply (notwithstanding the exception in Article 3(1)) to vehicles used for the carriage of postal articles on national transport operations except—

(a) vehicles which have a permissible maximum weight which does not exceed 3.5 tonnes; and

(b) vehicles which are being used by the Post Office in connection with the carriage of letters.

(2) In paragraph (1) above "*letter*" has the same meaning as in the Post Office Inland Post Scheme 1979.

(3) This Regulation shall not have effect—

(a) before 1st April 1988 in relation to vehicles which have a permissible maximum weight of 7.5 tonnes or more; or

(b) before 1st January 1990 in relation to vehicles which have a permissible maximum weight which exceeds 3.5 tonnes but which is less than 7.5 tonnes.

SCHEDULE

EXEMPTED VEHICLES

[PART I

VEHICLES EXEMPTED BY REGULATIONS 2(1) AND 4(1)]

B29.11   *[The text of the original Schedule was designated as Part I (and Part II of the Schedule was added) by S.I. 1987 No. 805, which also substituted the heading to what is now Part I.]*

B29.12   **1.** Any vehicle used for the carriage of passengers which is by virtue of its construction and equipment suitable for carrying not more than 17 persons including the driver and is intended for that purpose.

B29.13   **2.**—(1) Any vehicle which, on or after 1st January 1990, is being used by a public authority to provide public services otherwise than in competition with professional road hauliers.

(2) A vehicle does not fall within the description specified in this paragraph unless the vehicle—

[(a) is being used by a health service body—

(i) to provide ambulance services in pursuance of its duty under the National Health Service Act 1977, the National Health Service and Community Care Act 1990 or the National Health Service (Scotland) Act 1978; or

(ii) to carry staff, patients, medical supplies or equipment in pursuance of its general duties under that Act;]

(b) is being used by a local authority for the purposes of the Local Authority Social Services Act 1970 or the Social Work (Scotland) Act 1968 to provide, in the exercise of social services functions—

    (i) services for old persons; or

    (ii) services for persons to whom section 29 of the National Assistance Act 1948 (welfare arrangements for physically and mentally handicapped persons) applies;

(c) is being used by Her Majesty's Coastguard, a general lighthouse authority or a local lighthouse authority;

(d) is being used by a harbour authority within the limits of a harbour for the improvement, maintenance or management of which the authority is responsible;

(e) is being used by an airports authority within the perimeter of an airport owned or managed by the authority;

(f) is being used by the British Railways Board, London Regional Transport, any wholly owned subsidiary of London Regional Transport, a Passenger Transport Executive or a local authority for the purpose of maintaining railways; or

(g) is being used by the British Waterways Board for the purpose of maintaining navigable waterways.

(3) In this paragraph—

"airport" means an aerodrome within the meaning given by section 105(1) of the Civil Aviation Act 1982;

"airports authority" means the British Airports Authority or a local authority which owns or manages an airport;

"general lighthouse authority" and *"local lighthouse authority"* have the meanings given by section 634 of the Merchant Shipping Act 1894;

"harbour" and *"harbour authority"* have the meanings given by section 57(1) of the Harbours Act 1964;

[*"health service body"*—

    (a) in relation to England and Wales, means a Health Authority, a Special Health Authority or an NHS trust (each within the meaning of the National Health Service Act 1977);

    (b) in relation to Scotland, means the Agency, a Health Board, a Special Health Board or an NHS trust (each within the meaning of the National Health Service (Scotland) Act 1978).]

"local authority", unless the contrary intention appears, means—

    (a) in relation to England and Wales, a county or district council, a London borough council or the Common Council of the City of London; and

    (b) *[applies to Scotland.]*

"social services functions"—

    (a) in relation to England and Wales, has the meaning given by section 3(1) of the Local Authority Social Services Act 1970; and

    (b) *[applies to Scotland.]*

"wholly owned subsidiary", in relation to London Regional Transport, has the meaning given by section 68 of the London Regional Transport Act 1984.

[Paragraph 2 in the Schedule is printed as amended by S.I. 1998 No. 2006.   **B29.14**

The term "aerodrome" (see paragraph 2(3) above) is defined by the Civil Aviation Act 1982, s.105(1), as follows:

> *"aerodrome"* means any area of land or water designated, equipped, set apart or commonly used for affording facilities for the landing and departure of aircraft and includes any area or space, whether on the ground, on the roof of a building or elsewhere, which is designed, equipped, or set apart for affording facilities for the landing and departure of aircraft capable of descending or climbing vertically;

The Merchant Shipping Act 1894, s.634 (repealed by the Merchant Shipping Act 1995) designated "any person or body of persons having by law or usage authority over local lighthouses, buoys or beacons" as "local lighthouse authorities"; it also designated Trinity House, the Commissioners of Northern Lighthouses and the Commissioners of Irish Lights as "general lighthouse authorities". The 1995 Act, s.195(2), designates each harbour authority (as respects its area), and any other existing local lighthouse authority (as respects its area) as local lighthouse authorities. By ibid., s.195(1), the same authorities as were designated under the 1894 Act are designated as general lighthouse authorities.

The Local Authority Social Services Act 1970, s.3(1) (as substituted by the Local Government, Planning and Land Act 1980, s.183(1)), designates as "social services functions" those local authority functions matters relating to which stand referred to the authority's social services committee by virtue of section 2 of that Act (i.e. functions conferred by enactments listed in Schedule 1 to the 1970 Act or designated by the Secretary of State).

As to the dissolution of London Regional Transport and its replacement by Transport for London, see the Greater London Authority Act 1999, Pt IV, Chap. XVI (particularly ss.297 and 303).]

B29.15   **3.**—(1) Any vehicle which is being used by an agricultural, horticultural, forestry or fishery undertaking to carry goods within a 50 kilometre radius of the place where the vehicle is normally based, including local administrative areas the centres of which are situated within that radius.

(2) A vehicle which is being used by a fishery undertaking does not fall within the description specified in this paragraph unless the vehicle is being used—

    (a) to carry live fish; or

    (b) to carry a catch of fish from the place of landing to a place where it is to be processed.

4. Any vehicle which is being used to carry animal waste or carcases which are not intended for human consumption.

B29.16   **5.** Any vehicle which is being used to carry live animals between a farm and a local market or from a market to a local slaughterhouse.

6. Any vehicle which is being used—

    (a) as a shop at a local market;

    (b) for door-to-door selling;

    (c) for mobile banking, exchange or saving transactions;

    (d) for worship;

    (e) for the lending of books, records or cassettes; or

    (f) for cultural events or exhibitions,

and is specially fitted for that use.

B29.17   **7.**—(1) Any vehicle used for the carriage of goods which has a permissible maximum weight not exceeding 7.5 tonnes and is carrying material or equipment for the driver's use in the course of his work within a 50 kilometre radius of the place where the vehicle is normally based.

(2) A vehicle does not fall within the description specified in this paragraph if driving the vehicle constitutes the driver's main activity.

8. Any vehicle which operates exclusively on an island which does not exceed 2300 square kilometres in area and is not linked to the rest of Great Britain by a bridge, ford or tunnel open for use by motor vehicles.

9. Any vehicle used for the carriage of goods which has a permissible maximum weight not exceeding 7.5 tonnes and is propelled by means of gas produced on the vehicle or by means of electricity.   **B29.18**

10.—(1) Any vehicle which is being used for driving instruction with a view to obtaining a driving licence.

(2) A vehicle does not fall within the description specified in this paragraph if the vehicle or any trailer or semi-trailer drawn by it is being used for the carriage of goods—

    (a) for hire or reward; or

    (b) for or in connection with any trade or business.

11. Any tractor which, on or after 1st January 1990, is used exclusively for agricultural and forestry work.   **B29.19**

[PART II

VEHICLES EXEMPTED BY REGULATIONS 2(2) AND 4(2)

12. Any vehicle which is being used by the Royal National Lifeboat Institution for the purpose of hauling lifeboats.   **B29.20**

13. Any vehicle which was manufactured before 1st January 1947.

14. Any vehicle which is propelled by steam.]

[**15.**—(1) Any vehicle which is by virtue of its construction and equipment suitable for carrying passengers and which on the occasion on which it is being driven—   **B29.21**

    (a) is a vintage vehicle;

    (b) is not carrying more than 9 persons including the driver;

    (c) is not used for carrying passengers with a view to profit; and

    (d) is being driven—

        (i) in a vintage vehicle rally or to or from such a rally, or

        (ii) to or from a museum, or other place where the vehicle is to be or has been displayed to members of the public, or

        (iii) to or from a place where the vehicle is to be or has been repaired, maintained or tested.

(2) For the purposes of this paragraph:—

    (a) a vehicle is a vintage vehicle on any occasion on which it is being driven if it was manufactured more than 25 years before that occasion; and

(b) *"vintage vehicle rally"* means an event in which a collection of historic vehicles are driven on a road open to the public along a predetermined route.]

B29.22   *[Part II of this Schedule was added by S.I. 1987 No. 805 (which at the same time designated the original text of the Schedule as Part I) and is printed as subsequently amended by S.I. 1988 No. 760.]*

The Drivers' Hours (Harmonisation with Community Rules) Regulations 1986

(S.I. 1986 No. 1458)

1. Citation, commencement, interpretation and revocation

B30.01

(1) *[Omitted.]*

(2) In these Regulations "*the 1968 Act*" means the Transport Act 1968.

(3) *[Revocation.]*

2. Domestic drivers' hours code, etc.

(1) Subject to the provisions of this Regulation, the domestic drivers' hours code shall **B30.02** not apply in relation to any Community driving or work of a driver of a vehicle to which Part VI of the 1968 Act applies.

(2) Paragraphs (3) and (4) below apply where during any working day a driver of a vehicle to which Part VI of the 1968 Act applies spends time both on Community driving or work and on domestic driving or work.

(3) Any time spent on Community driving or work shall be regarded for the purpose of—

(a) applying the limits in the domestic drivers' hours code on periods of driving or length of working day; or

(b) calculating periods of driving for the purposes of section 96(7) of the 1968 Act,

as time spent on domestic driving, or as the case may be, domestic work.

(4) Without prejudice to paragraph (3) above, any time spent on Community driving or work shall not be regarded for the purposes of any of the provisions of the domestic drivers' hours code as constituting or forming part of an interval for rest or an interval for rest and refreshment.

(5) In this Regulation "*the domestic drivers' hours code*" has the meaning given by section 96(13) of the 1968 Act [*q.v.*].

(6) In this Regulation—

(a) any reference to Community driving or work is a reference to driving or, as the case may be, work to which the applicable Community Rules apply; and

(b) any reference to domestic driving or work is a reference to driving or, as the case may be, work to which Part VI of the 1968 Act applies and those Rules do not apply.

3. Meaning of "working week"

[Amends section 103(1) and (5) of the 1968 Act, q.v.]

B30.03

The Drivers' Hours (Goods Vehicles) (Modifications) Order 1986

(S.I. 1986 No. 1459)

B31.01 *Editorial note.* The text of section 96 of the Transport Act 1968 as modified by this order is set out as an appendix to this order.

1. Citation, commencement, interpretation and revocation

B31.02 (1) *[Omitted.]*

(2) In this Order "*the 1968 Act*" means the Transport Act 1968.

(3) *[Revokes S.I. 1970 No. 257, art.3, and S.I. 1971 No. 818, art.5(a).]*

2. Goods vehicles generally

B31.03 Where during any working day a driver spends all or the greater part of the time when he is driving vehicles to which Part VI of the 1968 Act applies in driving goods vehicles, that Part of that Act shall have effect, as respects that driver and that working day, as if—

(a) subsections (2), (3)(b), (4) to (6) and (8)(b) of section 96 were omitted;

(b) for the words "subsections (1), (2) and (3)" in subsection (7) of that section there were substituted the words "subsections (1) and (3)(a)";

(c) for the words "subsections (2) and (3)" in subsection (8)(a) of that section there were substituted the words "subsection (3)(a)"; and

(d) for the definition of "working day" in section 103(1) there were substituted the following definition—

"*working day*', in relation to any driver, means—

(a) any working period (that is to say, any period during which he is on duty) which does not fall to be aggregated with the whole or part of any other such period or periods by virtue of paragraph (b) of this definition; and

(b) where a working period is followed by one or more other such periods beginning within the 24 hours next after the beginning of that working period, the aggregate of that working period and so much of the other such period or periods as fall within those 24 hours;".

3. Light goods vehicles

B31.04 (1) Where during any working week a driver spends all of the time when he is driving vehicles to which Part VI of the 1968 Act applies in driving light goods vehicles and, in so far as he drives such a vehicle during that week otherwise than for social, domestic or pleasure purposes, he does so—

(a) solely in connection with the carrying on by him or by his employer of the profession of medical practitioner, nurse, midwife, dentist or veterinary surgeon;

    (b) wholly or mainly in connection with the carrying out of any service of inspection, cleaning, maintenance, repair, installation or fitting;

    (c) solely while he is acting as a commercial traveller and is carrying in the vehicle (apart from the effects of any person carried in it) no goods other than goods carried for the purpose of soliciting orders;

    (d) solely while he is acting in the course of his employment by the Automobile Association, the Royal Automobile Club or Royal Scottish Automobile Club; or

    (e) solely in connection with the carrying on by him or by his employer of the business of cinematography or of radio or television broadcasting,

that Part of that Act shall have effect, as respects that driver and any working day falling wholly within that working week, not only with the modifications made by article 2 above but also as if subsections (3)(a) and (8)(a) of section 96 were omitted.

  (2) In this article *"light goods vehicle"* means a vehicle which—

    (a) is a goods vehicle which has a permissible maximum weight within the meaning of [section 108 of the Road Traffic Act 1988] not exceeding 3.5 tonnes; or

    (b) is a dual purpose vehicle within the meaning of [Regulation 3(2) of the Road Vehicles (Construction and Use) Regulations 1986] [*S.I. 1986 No. 1078, q.v.*],

and (in either case) is a vehicle to which Part VI of the 1968 Act applies.

[Article 3 is printed as amended by the Interpretation Act 1978, ss.17(2)(a) and 23.]   **B31.05**

    APPENDIX (Transport Act 1986, s.96, as applied to drivers of goods vehicles)

96. Permitted driving time and periods of duty

  (1) Subject to the provisions of this section, a driver shall not on any working day drive   **B31.06** a vehicle or vehicles to which this Part of this Act applies amounting in the aggregate to more than ten hours.

  (2) *[Inapplicable.]*

  (3) Subject to the provisions of this section, the working day of a driver—

    (a) except where paragraph (b) or (c) of this subsection applies, shall not exceed eleven hours;

    (b) *[inapplicable.]*

  (4)–(6) *[Inapplicable.]*

  (7) If in the case of the working week of any driver the following requirement is satisfied, that is to say, that, in each of the periods of twenty-four hours beginning at midnight which make up that week, the driver does not drive a vehicle to which this Part of this Act applies for a period of, or periods amounting in the aggregate to, more than four hours, the foregoing provisions of this section shall not apply to him in that week, except that the provisions of subsections (1) and (3)(a) shall nevertheless have effect in relation to the whole of any working day falling partly in that week and partly in a working week in the case of which that requirement is not satisfied.

  (8) If on any working day a driver does not drive any vehicle to which this Part of this Act applies—

    (a) subsection (3)(a) of this section shall not apply to that day, and

    (b) *[inapplicable.]*

(9) For the purposes of subsections (1) and (7) of this section no account shall be taken of any time spent driving a vehicle elsewhere than on a road if the vehicle is being so driven in the course of operations of agriculture or forestry.

(10) For the purpose of enabling drivers to deal with cases of emergency or otherwise to meet a special need, the [Secretary of State for the Environment, Transport and the Regions] may by regulations—

    (a) create examinations from all or any of the requirements of subsections (1) to (6) of this section in such cases and subject to such conditions as may be specified in the regulations;

    (b) empower the traffic commissioner for any area, subject to the provisions of the regulations—

        (i) to dispense with the observance of all or any of those requirements (either generally or in such circumstances or to such extent as the commissioner thinks fit) in any particular case for which provision is not made under paragraph (a) of this subsection;

        (ii) to grant a certificate (which, for the purposes of any proceedings under this Part of this Act, shall be conclusive evidence of the facts therein stated) that any particular case falls or fell within any exemption created under the said paragraph (a)

and regulations under this subsection may enable any dispensation under paragraph (b)(i) of this subsection to be granted retrospectively and provide for a document purporting to be a certificate granted by virtue of paragraph (b)(ii) of this subsection to be accepted in evidence without further proof.

(11) If any of the requirements of the domestic drivers' hours code is contravened in the case of any driver—

    (a) that driver; and

    (b) any other person (being that driver's employer or a person to whose orders that driver was subject) who caused or permitted the contravention,

shall be liable on summary conviction to a fine not exceeding level 4 on the standard scale; but a person shall not be liable to be convicted under this subsection if he proves to the court—

        (i) that the contravention was due to unavoidable delay in the completion of a journey arising out of circumstances which he could not reasonably have foreseen; or

        (ii) in the case of a person charged under paragraph (b) of this subsection, that the contravention was due to the fact that the driver had for any particular period or periods driven or been on duty otherwise than in the employment of that person or, as the case may be, otherwise than in the employment in which he is subject to the orders of that person, and that the person charged was not, and could not reasonably have become, aware of that fact.

(11A) Where, in the case of a driver of a motor vehicle, there is in Great Britain a contravention of any requirement of the applicable Community rules as to period of driving, or distance driven, or periods on or off duty, then the offender and any other person (being the offender's employer or a person to whose orders the offender was subject) who caused or permitted the contravention shall be liable on summary conviction to a fine not exceeding level 4 on the standard scale.

(11B) But a person shall not be liable to be convicted under subsection (11A) if—

    (a) he proves the matters specified in paragraph (i) of subsection (11); or

(b) being charged as the offender's employer or a person to whose orders the offender was subject, he proves the matters specified in paragraph (ii) of that subsection.

(12) The [Secretary of State for the Environment, Transport and the Regions] may by order—

    (a) direct that subsection (1) of this section shall have effect with the substitution for the reference to ten hours of a reference to nine hours, either generally or with such exceptions as may be specified in the order;

    (b) direct that paragraph (a) of subsection (3) of this section shall have effect with the substitution for the reference to eleven hours of a reference to any shorter period, or remove, modify or add to the provisions of that subsection containing exceptions to the said paragraph (a);

    (c) remove, modify or add to any of the requirements of subsections (2), (4), (5) or (6) of this section or any of the exemptions provided for by subsections (7), (8) and (9) thereof;

and any order under this subsection may contain such transitional and supplementary provisions as the [Secretary of State for the Environment, Transport and the Regions] thinks necessary or expedient, including provisions amending any definition in section 103 of this Act which is relevant to any of the provisions affected by the order.

(13) In this Part of this Act *"the domestic drivers' hours code"* means the provisions of subsections (1) to (6) of this section as for the time being in force (and, in particular, as modified, added to or substituted by or under any instrument in force under section 95(1) of this Act or subsection (10) or (12) of this section).

[This version of the Transport Act 1968, s.96, is the text of section 96 as modified by the Drivers' Hours (Goods Vehicles) (Modifications) Order 1986 (S.I. 1986 No. 1459), art.2 (goods vehicles generally); in relation to light goods vehicles, subsections (3)(a) and (8)(a) are also inapplicable (see S.I. 1986 No. 1459, art.3).

* This version of section 96 is printed as further amended by the Secretary of State for the Environment Order 1970 (S.I. 1970 No. 1681); the European Communities Act 1972, s.4, and Sched. 4, para.9(2); the Road Traffic (Drivers' Ages and Hours of Work) Act 1976, s.2(1); the Secretary of State for Transport Order 1976 (S.I. 1976 No. 1775); the Transport Act 1978, s.10; the Minister of Transport Order 1979 (S.I. 1979 No. 571); the Transfer of Functions (Transport) Order 1981 (S.I. 1981 No. 238); the Criminal Justice Act 1982, ss.38 and 46(1); the Transport Act 1985, s.3 and Sched. 2, Pt II, para.1(2); the Community Drivers' Hours and Recording Equipment Regulations 1986 (S.I. 1986 No. 1457), reg.2; the Secretary of State for the Environment, Transport and the Regions Order 1997 (S.I. 1997 No. 2971).]*

B31.07

The Road Vehicles (Exemptions from Duty) Regulations 1986

(S.I. 1986 No. 1467)

*   *   *

B32.01 2.—(1) In these Regulations—

["*the 1994 Act*" means the Vehicle Excise and Registration Act 1994];

"*dependant*" means any of the following members of an entitled person's household, namely, his spouse, or any other person wholly or mainly maintained by him or in his custody, charge or care;

"*entitled person*" means a person falling within paragraph (a) or (b) of regulation 3;

"*member of a visiting force*" means a person for the time being appointed to serve with any body, contingent or detachment of the forces of any country specified in Part I of the Schedule to these Regulations, which is for the time being present in the United Kingdom on the invitation of Her Majesty's Government, and shall include a person for the time being recognised by the Secretary of State as a member of a civilian component of such force;

"*member of a headquarters or organisation*" means a member of any country's military forces, except a member of Her Majesty's United Kingdom forces, who is for the time being appointed to serve in the United Kingdom under the orders of any headquarters or organisation specified in Part II of the Schedule to these Regulations, and shall include a person for the time being recognised by the Secretary of State as a civilian member of such headquarters or organisation.

(2) Any reference in these Regulations to a numbered regulation is a reference to the regulation having that number in these Regulations, except where otherwise expressly provided.

B32.02 *[Regulation 2 is printed as amended by the Vehicle Excise and Registration Act 1994, s.64 and Sched. 4, para.4.]*

3. Exemption from duty

B32.03 Subject to regulations 4 and 5, a mechanically propelled vehicle shall not be chargeable with any duty under [the 1994 Act] if it has been imported into any part of the United Kingdom other than Northern Ireland by or on behalf of—

(a) a member of a visiting force;

(b) a member of a headquarters or organisation; or

(c) a dependant of a person falling within paragraph (a) or (b) of this regulation,

and if there is produced in relation to the vehicle evidence that the person importing it has not been required to pay any duty or tax chargeable in respect of its import.

B32.04 *[Regulation 3 is printed as amended by the Vehicle Excise and Registration Act 1994, s.64 and Sched. 4, para.4.]*

4. Period of exemption

An exemption from duty pursuant to regulation 3 shall subsist only for a period of 12 months commencing on the date on which the first vehicle licence is issued under [the 1994 Act] for the vehicle in respect of which the exemption is claimed.   **B32.05**

[Regulation 4 is printed as amended by the Vehicle Excise and Registration Act 1994, s.64 and Sched. 4, para.4.]   **B32.06**

5. Conditions to be observed during period of exemption

During the period prescribed by regulation 4, the owner of or, as the case may be, the person keeping the vehicle in respect of which the exemption is claimed shall comply with the provisions of Part II and Part III of the Road Vehicles (Registration and Licensing) Regulations 1971 [*S.I. 1971 No. 450, as amended (q.v.)]* (being provisions as to the licensing and registration of mechanically propelled vehicles, and as to the exhibition of licences and the form and display of registration marks).   **B32.07**

[So far as Part III of the Road Vehicles (Registration and Licensing) Regulations 1971 (S.I. 1971 No. 450) above is concerned with the exhibition of registration marks, it will be superseded on September 1, 2001 by the Road Vehicles (Display of Registration Marks) Regulations 2001 (S.I. 2001 No. 561) below.]   **B32.08**

6. Cessation of exemption

An exemption from duty pursuant to regulation 3 shall cease to apply if, at any time during the period prescribed by regulation 4, the person who imported the vehicle in respect of which the exemption is claimed becomes liable to pay any duty or tax chargeable in respect of the import of that vehicle.   **B32.09**

SCHEDULE   Regulation 2(1)

PART I

LIST OF COUNTRIES

Antigua and Barbuda	Grenada	**B32.10**
Australia	Guyana	
Bahamas	Iceland	
Bangladesh	India	
Barbados	Italy	
Belgium	Jamaica	
Belize	Jordan	
Botswana	Kenya	
Burma	Kiribati	
Canada	Lesotho	
Cyprus	Luxembourg	
Denmark	Malawi	
Dominica	Malaysia	
Fiji	Malta	
France	Mauritius	
Gambia	Nauru	
Germany, Federal Republic of	Netherlands	
Ghana	New Zealand	
Greece	Nigeria	

Norway
Pakistan
Papua New Guinea
Portugal
Saint Lucia
Saint Vincent and the Grenadines
Seychelles
Sierra Leone
Singapore
Solomon Islands
South Africa
Spain
Sri Lanka

Swaziland
Tanzania
Tonga
Trinidad and Tobago
Turkey
Tuvalu
Uganda
United States of America
Vanuatu
Western Samoa
Zambia
Zimbabwe

PART II

LIST OF HEADQUARTERS AND ORGANISATIONS

B32.11 The Supreme Headquarters Allied Powers Europe (SHAPE)
The Headquarters of the Supreme Allied Commander, Europe (SACEUR)
The Headquarters of the Supreme Allied Commander Atlantic (SACLANT)
The Headquarters of the Allied Commander in Chief Channel (CINCHAN)
The Channel Committee (CHANCOMTEE)
The Headquarters of the Commander of the Allied Maritime Air Force, Channel (COMMAIRCHAN)
The Headquarters of the Commander in Chief of the Eastern Atlantic Area (CINCEASTLANT)
The Headquarters of the Commander in Chief United Kingdom Air (CINCUKAIR)
The Headquarters of the Commander of the Maritime Air Eastern Atlantic Area (COMMAIREASTLANT)
The Headquarters of the Commander Submarines, East Atlantic (COMSUBEASTLANT)

The Drivers' Hours (Goods Vehicles) (Exemptions) Regulations 1986

(S.I. 1986 No. 1492)

1. Citation, commencement and revocation   *[Omitted.]*   **B33.01**

2. Exemptions from requirements as to drivers' hours

(1) A driver who during any working day spends all or the greater part of the time when   **B33.02**
he is driving vehicles to which Part VI of the Transport Act 1968 applies in driving goods
vehicles and who spends time on duty during that working day to deal with any of the cases
of emergency specified in paragraph (2) below is exempted from the requirements of
section 96(1) and (3)(a) of that Act in respect of that working day subject to the condition
that he does not spend time on such duty (otherwise than to deal with the emergency) for a
period of or periods amounting in the aggregate to more than 11 hours.

(2) The cases of emergency referred to in paragraph (1) above are—

  (a) events which cause or are likely to cause such—

      (i) danger to life or health of one or more individuals or animals, or

      (ii) a serious interruption in the maintenance of public services for the supply of
water, gas, electricity or drainage or of telecommunication or postal services,
or

      (iii) a serious interruption in the use of roads, railways, ports or airports,

    as to necessitate the taking of immediate action to prevent the occurrence or con-
tinuance of such danger or interruption and

  (b) events which are likely to cause such serious damage to property as to necessitate
the taking of immediate action to prevent the occurrence of such damage.

The Drivers' Hours (Goods Vehicles) (Keeping of Records) Regulations 1987

(S.I. 1987 No. 1421)

ARRANGEMENT OF REGULATIONS

B34.03   **1. Commencement and citation**   *[Omitted.]*

2. Revocation   *[Omitted.]*

3. Interpretation

B34.04   In these Regulations, unless the context otherwise requires—

"*the Act*" means the Transport Act 1968;

"*driver's record book*" means a book which complies with regulation 5, and any reference in relation to a driver's record book to a front sheet, instructions to drivers for completion of sheets, and weekly record sheets is a reference to those components of a driver's record book referred to in regulation 5;

"*operator's licence*" has the same meaning as in section 60(1) of the Act [*q.v.*]; and "*passenger vehicles*" and "*goods vehicles*" have the same meaning as in section 95(2) of the Act [*q.v.*].

4. Application of Regulations

Subject to the provisions of regulations 12 and 13 these Regulations apply to drivers of goods vehicles and to employers of employee-drivers of such vehicles but they do not so apply in relation to a journey made or work done by a driver in a case where the journey or, as the case may be, the work is a journey or work to which the applicable Community rules apply.   **B34.05**

5. Form of driver's record book

A driver's record book shall contain—   **B34.06**

(a) a front sheet;

(b) instructions to drivers for completion of sheets;

(c) notes for guidance on use of the book; and

(d) weekly record sheets divided up into boxes for entry of information relating to each day of the week and a duplicate of each weekly record sheet together with one sheet of carbon paper or other means whereby an entry on a weekly record sheet may be simultaneously reproduced on the duplicate of that sheet

each of which shall conform to the model in the Schedule to these Regulations and shall have the standard A6 format (105×148mm) or a larger format.

6. Issue of driver's record books

(1) Where an employee-driver is required by these Regulations to enter information in a driver's record book the employer shall issue to him and from time to time as may be necessary while the employee-driver remains in the employment of that employer supply him with a new driver's record book.   **B34.07**

(2) If on the date of the coming into operation of these Regulations or at any time thereafter an employee-driver has more than one employer in relation to whom he is an employee-driver of a vehicle, the employer who is to issue a new driver's record book to him shall be the employer for whom the employee-driver first acts in the course of his employment on or after the said date or time.

(3) Where during the currency of a driver's record book an employee-driver ceases to be employed by an employer who has issued that book to him he shall return that book, (including all unused weekly record sheets), to that employer and, if he is at that time employed by some other person or persons in relation to whom he is an employee-driver of a vehicle, that other person, or if there is more than one such other person, that one of them for whom he first acts in the course of his employment after ceasing to be so employed as aforesaid, shall issue a new driver's record book to him in accordance with the provisions of paragraph (1) above.

7. Entries in driver's record books

(1) An employer of an employee-driver or an owner-driver shall enter or secure that there is entered on the front sheet the information specified in items 4 and 6 of that sheet.   **B34.08**

(2) The entries referred to in paragraph (1) shall be made—

(a) in the case of an employer, before the driver's record book is issued to the driver pursuant to regulation 6, and

(b) in the case of an owner-driver before the book is used.

(3) (a) For the purpose of entering the information specified in item 4, the address shall, in the case of an owner-driver, be the address of the driver's place of business.

(b) For the purpose of entering the information specified in item 6 the Operator's Licence No. shall be the serial number of the operator's licence granted under Part V of the Act by virtue of which each goods vehicle used by the driver during the currency of the record book is an authorised vehicle for the purposes of the said Part V.

(4) A driver shall enter, and where he is an employee-driver, his employer shall cause him to enter, in accordance with the instructions to drivers for the completion of sheets—

(a) on the front sheet the information specified in relation to the front sheet in those instructions; and

(b) in the appropriate boxes in the weekly record sheet the information specified in relation to weekly record sheets in those instructions.

(5) A driver when making an entry in a weekly record sheet (including signing such a sheet) shall ensure, by the use of the carbon paper or otherwise, that the entry is simultaneously reproduced on the duplicate of that sheet.

8. Manner of keeping driver's record books—supplementary

B34.09   (1) Where a weekly record sheet has been completed by an employee-driver he shall deliver the driver's record book (including the duplicate of the weekly record sheet which has been completed) to the employer who issued or should have issued the record book to him within a period of seven days from the date when the weekly record sheet was completed or earlier if so required by the employer.

(2) An employer to whom a driver's record book has been delivered pursuant to paragraph 1 above shall—

(a) examine the weekly record sheeet which has been completed and sign it and its duplicate;

(b) detach the duplicate sheet; and

(c) return the book to the driver before he is next on duty.

(3) When all the weekly record sheets in a driver's record book have been used, the driver shall retain the book for a period of fourteen days from the date on which the book was last returned to him pursuant to paragraph (2)(c) above and shall then return the book to the employer as soon as is reasonably practicable.

(4) When a weekly record sheet has been completed by an owner-driver he shall, within a period of seven days from the date of its being completed, detach the duplicate sheet and deliver it to the address which is required to be entered in item 4 on the front sheet.

(5) An employee-driver or an owner-driver shall not be treated as having failed to comply with any of the requirements of paragraphs (1) and (4) above with respect to the period within which the duplicate of a weekly record sheet shall be delivered if he can show that it was not reasonably practicable to comply with that requirement and that the duplicate of the weekly record sheet was delivered as soon as it was reasonably practicable to do so.

(6) A driver who is in possession of a driver's record book in which he has made any entry pursuant to regulation 7 shall not, until all the weekly record sheets in that book have been completed, make any entry in any other record book.

(7) An employee-driver shall not make any entry in a driver's record book pursuant to regulation 7 if the book was not supplied to him by his employer unless a driver's record book so supplied was not available to him.

(8) No person shall erase or obliterate any entry once made in a driver's record book, and if a correction is required it shall be made by striking the original entry through in such a way that it may still be read and by writing the appropriate correction near to the entry so struck through, and any person making such a correction shall initial it.

9. Production of driver's record book by employee-drivers

(1) Where an employee-driver has or has had during any period more than one employer in relation to whom he is an employee-driver each employer, who is not the employer who is required by these Regulations to issue a driver's record book to that employee-driver, shall require that driver to produce his current driver's record book and shall enter on the front sheet the information contained in item 5.   **B34.10**

(2) An employee-driver shall produce his current driver's record book for inspection by the employer who issued it to him, or by any other person in relation to whom he is at any time during the period of the currency of that book an employee-driver, whenever required to do so by that employer or that other person.

10. Driver's record books to be carried by drivers

A driver shall have his current driver's record book (including all unused record sheets) in his possession at all times when he is on duty.   **B34.11**

11. Preservation of driver's record books

(1) An owner-driver shall preserve his driver's record book intact when it has been completed or he has ceased to use it, and the employer of an employee-driver to whom any driver's record book relating to that employee-driver has been returned shall preserve that book intact, for the period specified in paragraph (3) below.   **B34.12**

(2) An employer of an employee-driver or an owner-driver who has detached duplicates of weekly sheets pursuant to regulation 8(2)(b) or as the case may be regulation 8(4) shall preserve those sheets for the period specified in paragraph (3) below.

(3) The period for which driver's record books and duplicates of weekly record sheets must be preserved as required by this regulation shall be one year reckoned, in the case of an owner-driver, from the day on which that book was completed or ceased to be used by him, or in the case of an employee-driver, from the day on which that book was returned to his employer pursuant to regulation 8(3).

12. Exemptions

(1) Where a driver does not during any working day drive any goods vehicle other than a vehicle the use of which is exempted from any requirement to have an operator's licence or, in the case of a vehicle in the public service of the Crown, would be so exempted by virtue of section 60(2) of the Act, were it not such a vehicle, that driver and, if he is an employee-driver, his employer, shall be exempted for that period from the specified requirements.   **B34.13**

(2) (a) Where in any working day a driver does not drive a goods vehicle for more than four hours and does not drive any such vehicle outside a radius of 50 kilometres from the operating centre of the vehicle, then he and, if he is an employee-driver, his employer shall be exempted for that period from the specified requirements.

(b) For the purposes of computing the period of four hours mentioned in sub-paragraph (a) above no account shall be taken of any time spent in driving a vehicle elsewhere than on a road if the vehicle is being so driven in the course of operations of agriculture, forestry or quarrying or in the course of carrying out work in the construction, reconstruction, alteration or extension or maintenance of, or of a part of, a building, or of any other fixed works of construction of [*sic*] civil engineering (including works for the construction, improvement or maintenance of a road) and, for the purposes of this sub-paragraph, where the vehicle is being driven on, or on a part of, a road in the course of carrying out of any work for the improvement or maintenance of, or that part of, that road, it shall be treated as being driven elsewhere than on a road.

(3) Where during any working day a driver does not spend all or the greater part of the time when he is driving vehicles to which Part VI of the Act applies in driving goods vehicles, then he and, if he is an employee-driver, his employer shall be exempted for that working day from the specified requirements.

(4) Where a vehicle is used in such circumstances that by virtue of regulation 5 of the Community Drivers' Hours and Recording Equipment (Exemptions and Supplementary Provisions) Regulations 1986 [*S.I. 1986 No. 1456, q.v.*] Council Regulation (EEC) No. 3821/85 of 20th December 1985 on recording equipment in road transport [*q.v.*] applies to the vehicle, the driver of the vehicle and, if he is an employee-driver, his employer shall be exempted from the specified requirements in relation to the use of the vehicle in those circumstances.

(5) (a) In this regulation "*the specified requirements*" means the provisions of regulations 7 and 10.

(b) In paragraph (2)(a) above "*operating centre*" has the same meaning as in section 92 of the Act [*as amended*] [*q.v.*].

13. Drivers of goods vehicles and passenger vehicles

(1) Subject to the provisions of regulation 12(3), regulations 7 and 10 apply to a driver who in any working week drives goods and passenger vehicles as they apply to a driver who only drives a goods vehicle and the information to be entered in the driver's record book pursuant to regulation 7 shall be information in relation to his employment in connection with both goods and passenger vehicles.

(2) If a driver of both goods vehicles and passenger vehicles has a different employer in relation to his employment in connection with goods vehicles from his employer in relation to his employment in connection with passenger vehicles his employer for the purpose of regulation 6 shall be his employer in relation to his employment in connection with goods vehicles notwithstanding the provisions of regulation 6(2).

[The Schedule is set out on the following four pages.]

SCHEDULE

MODEL FOR DRIVER'S RECORD BOOK

(a) *Front sheet*   **B34.15**

RECORD BOOK FOR DRIVERS IN ROAD TRANSPORT

1. Date book first used...

2. Date book last used...

3. Surname, first name(s), and address of holder of book...
....
....

4. Name, address, telephone number and stamp (if any) of employer/undertaking........
....
....

5. Name, address, telephone number and stamp (if any) of any other employer(s).........
....
....

6. Operator's Licence No. (Nos)...

(b) *Instructions to drivers for completion of sheets*   **B34.16**

INSTRUCTIONS TO DRIVERS FOR COMPLETION OF SHEETS

FRONT SHEET

1. Enter your surname, first name(s) and address (item 3). Owner-drivers need not make any entry in item 3 unless their personal address is different from the address of their place of business.

2. Enter the date on which you first use the book (item 1).

3. Immediately after you have completed all the weekly sheets enter in item 2 the date on which you last made an entry in a weekly sheet. If you cease to be employed by the employer who issued you with a record book enter the last date on which you were employed in item 2.

WEEKLY RECORD SHEET

4. Use a new sheet each week. A week runs from midnight on Sunday/Monday to midnight the next Sunday/Monday.

5. Complete boxes 1 and 2 at the beginning of each week in which you work as a driver.

6. Each day on which you do not work as a driver complete boxes 3–9 in accordance with the instructions below.

7. Enter in box 3 for the day in question the registration number of any vehicle used during that day.

8. Complete boxes 4 and 5 at the beginning of each day on which you do work as a driver.

9. Complete boxes 6, 7, 8 and 9 at the end of the day's work.

B34.17   (c) *Notes for guidance on the use of book*

NOTES FOR GUIDANCE ON THE USE OF RECORD BOOKS

FOR EMPLOYERS

1. After completing items 4 and 6 on the front sheet, issue a record book to the drivers employed by you.

2. Give the holder the necessary instructions for correct use of the book.

3. When the record book is handed in to you by the drivers employed by you within seven days of the end of each week of driving, examine and sign the weekly record sheet (including the duplicate sheet) for the week to which it relates. Tear out and keep the duplicate sheets, leaving the top sheets in the book and return the book to the driver before he is next on duty.

4. When the used books have been handed back to you by the drivers employed by you preserve them together with the duplicate sheets for not less than one year.

FOR EMPLOYEE-DRIVERS

5. Ensure that items 1 and 3 on the front sheet are completed before you use the book.

6. This record book is personal. Carry it with you when on duty and produce it to any authorised inspecting officer on request. Hand it over to your employer when you leave the undertaking.

7. Produce this record book to your employer within 7 days of the end of each week of driving, so that he can check and countersign your entries. Keep the top sheets in the book.

8. When the book is completed, complete item 2 on the front sheet and keep the book for 2 weeks so that it can be produced at any time to an authorised inspecting officer and then hand it to your employer.

FOR OWNER-DRIVERS

9. Ensure that items 1, 3 (if applicable), 4 and 6 on the front sheet are completed before you use the record book. Enter your business address in item 4.

10. This record book is personal. Carry it with you when on duty and produce it to any authorised inspecting officer on request.

11. Tear out and keep the duplicate of each weekly record sheet at the end of the week to which it relates.

12. When the book is completed, complete item 2 on the front sheet. Preserve the used books and the duplicate sheets for not less than a year.

GENERAL

13. All entries must be made in ink or with a ball-point pen.

14. If you have to correct an entry, strike the incorrect entry through, write the correct entry near it and initial the correction.

(These notes are for guidance only and reference should be made to Part VI of the Transport Act 1968 and the Drivers' Hours (Keeping of Records) Regulations 1987 for particulars of the statutory provisions.)

[The weekly sheet is set out on the next page.]

(d) *Weekly record sheets*

WEEKLY SHEET

1. DRIVER'S NAME

2. PERIOD COVERED BY SHEET
WEEK COMMENCING (DATE) ....
TO WEEK ENDING (DATE) ....

DAY ON WHICH DUTY COMMENCED	REGISTRATION NO. OF VEHICLE(S) 3	PLACE WHERE VEHICLE(S) BASED 4	TIME OF GOING ON DUTY 5	TIME OF GOING OFF DUTY 6	TIME SPENT DRIVING 7	TIME SPENT ON DUTY 8	SIGNATURE OF DRIVER 9
MONDAY							
TUESDAY							
WEDNESDAY							
THURSDAY							
FRIDAY							
SATURDAY							
SUNDAY							

10. CERTIFICATION BY EMPLOYER

I HAVE EXAMINED THE ENTRIES IN THIS SHEET
SIGNATURE ....
POSITION HELD ....

The Motor Vehicles (Authorisation of Special Types) (Amendment) (No. 2) Order 1987

(S.I. 1987 No. 2161)

1. *[Citation.]*   **B35.01**

2–5. *[Amend the Motor Vehicles (Authorisation of Special Types) General Order 1979 (referred to as the "Principal Order").]*

6.—(1) This article applies to an order made before 1st January 1988 under section 42   **B35.02**
of the Road Traffic Act 1972 otherwise than by statutory instrument.

(2) Nothing in the Motor Vehicles (Authorisation of Special Types) (Amendment) Order 1987 [*S.I. 1987 No. 1327; not reproduced in this work*] or this order shall affect the Principal Order as applied by an order such as is mentioned in paragraph (1) above.

The Goods Vehicles (Plating and Testing) Regulations 1988

(S.I. 1988 No. 1478)

B36.01 *[The text of these regulations is printed as amended by:*

the Goods Vehicles (Plating and Testing) (Amendment) Regulations 1990 (S.I. 1990 No. 448) (April 2, 1990);

the Goods Vehicles (Plating and Testing) (Amendment) (No. 1) Regulations 1991 (S.I. 1991 No. 252) (March 18, 1991);

the Goods Vehicles (Plating and Testing) (Amendment) Regulations 1993 (S.I. 1993 No. 2048) (October 1, 1993);

the Goods Vehicles (Plating and Testing) (Amendment) (No. 2) Regulations 1993 (S.I. 1993 No. 3013) (January 2, 1994);

the Goods Vehicles (Plating and Testing) (Amendment) Regulations 1994 (S.I. 1994 No. 328) (March 24, 1994);

the Goods Vehicles (Plating and Testing) (Amendment) Regulations 1995 (S.I. 1995 No. 1456) (July 1, 1995);

the Goods Vehicles (Plating and Testing) (Amendment) Regulations 1997 (S.I. 1997 No. 82) (March 3, 1997);

the Goods Vehicles (Plating and Testing) (Amendment) (No. 2) Regulations 1997 (S.I. 1997 No. 263) (March 5, 1997);

the Goods Vehicles (Plating and Testing) (Amendment) Regulations 2000 (S.I. 2000 No. 1433) (June 26, 2000); and

the Goods Vehicles (Plating and Testing) (Amendment) Regulations 2001 (S.I. 2001 No. 307) (March 1, 2001).

The amending regulations are referred to in the notes to the principal regulations only by their years and numbers. The dates referred to above are the dates on which the amending regulations came into force.

The principal regulations have also been amended by the Goods Vehicles (Plating and Testing) (Amendment) Regulations 1989 (S.I. 1989 No. 320), the Goods Vehicles (Plating and Testing) (Amendment) (No. 2) Regulations 1989 (S.I. 1989 No. 1693), the Goods Vehicles (Plating and Testing) (Amendment) (No. 2) Regulations 1991 (S.I. 1991 No. 454), the Goods Vehicles (Plating and Testing) (Amendment) Regulations 1992 (S.I. 1992 No. 564), the Goods Vehicles (Plating and Testing) (Amendment) (No. 2) Regulations 1992 (S.I. 1992 No. 2447), the Goods Vehicles (Plating and Testing) (Amendment) Regulations 1998 (S.I. 1998 No. 1671), and the Goods Vehicles (Plating and Testing) (Amendment) (No. 2) Regulations 1998 (S.I. 1998 No. 3113), but these do not affect the text of any provision which is printed in this publication.]

PART I

GENERAL

B36.02 **1. Commencement and citation**   *[Omitted.]*

2. Revocation   *[Omitted.]*

3. Interpretation

(1) In these Regulations, except where the context otherwise requires, the following **B36.03**
expressions have the meanings hereby respectively assigned to them:—

["*the 1994 Act*" means the Vehicle Excise and Registration Act 1994;]

["*the 1988 Act*" means the Road Traffic Act 1988] [*q.v.*];

"*the Construction and Use Regulations*" means the Road Vehicles (Construction and Use)
Regulations 1986 [*S.I. 1986 No. 1078, as amended (q.v.)*];

"*the National Type Approval for Goods Vehicles Regulations*" means the Motor Vehicles (Type
Approval for Goods Vehicles) (Great Britain) Regulations 1982 [*S.I. 1982 No. 1271, as
amended (q.v.)*];

"*agricultural motor vehicle*", "*agricultural trailer*", "*agricultural trailed appliance*", "*agricultural
trailed appliance conveyor*", "*articulated vehicle*", "*converter dolly*", "*dual-purpose vehicle*", "*engineering plant*", [*exhaust system,*] "*Ministry plate*", "*registered*", "*semi-trailer*", "*straddle carrier*",
"*track-laying*", "*works trailer*", and "*works truck*" have the same meanings respectively as
in the Construction and Use Regulations;

"*appeal officer*" means the person appointed by the Secretary of State for the purposes of
appeals to the Secretary of State;

["*appropriate day*", means—

(a) in relation to a vehicle which is a motor vehicle, the last day of the calendar month
in which falls the first anniversary of the date on which it was registered; and

(b) in relation to a vehicle which is a trailer, the last day of the calendar month in which
falls the first anniversary of the date on which it was first sold or supplied by retail;]

. . .

"*auxiliary station*" means a vehicle testing station which is regularly not open for the carrying out of re-tests on certain normal working days;

"*break-down vehicle*" means a motor vehicle—

(a) on which is permanently mounted apparatus designed for raising one disabled
vehicle partly from the ground and for drawing that vehicle when so raised; and

(b) which is not equipped to carry any load other than articles required for the operation of, or in connection with, that apparatus or for repairing disabled vehicles;

["*design gross weight*" means—

(a) in the case of a vehicle equipped with a Ministry plate, the weight shown thereon
as the design weight or, if no weight is so shown thereon, the weight shown
thereon as the weight not to be exceeded in Great Britain;

(b) in the case of a vehicle which is not equipped with a Ministry plate, but which is
equipped with a plate in accordance with regulation 66 of the Construction and
Use Regulations, the maximum gross weight shown on the plate in respect of
item 7 of Part I of Schedule 8 to those Regulations; and

(c) in any other case, the weight which the vehicle is designed or adapted not to
exceed when in normal use and travelling on a road laden;]

"*examination*" means any operation being—

(a) a first examination;

(b) a re-test;

(c) a periodical test;

(d) a re-examination under regulation 33; or

[(e) an examination or re-examination for the purposes of an appeal against a determination made under these Regulations;]

["*first examination*" means an examination or, as the case may be, examinations for which a vehicle is submitted under regulation 9;]

"*Goods Vehicle Centre*" means the Goods Vehicle Centre at Welcombe House, 91–92 The Strand, Swansea, SA1 2DH;

"*living van*" means a vehicle whether mechanically propelled or not which is used as living accommodation by one or more persons, and which is also used for the carriage of goods or burden which are not needed by such one or more persons for the purpose of their residence in the vehicle;

"*Ministry test date disc*" means a plate issued by the Secretary of State for a goods vehicle being a trailer, following the issue of a goods vehicle test certificate for that trailer under these Regulations and containing—

(a) the identification mark allotted to that trailer and shown in that certificate;

(b) the date until which that certificate is valid; and

(c) the number of the vehicle testing station shown in the said certificate;

"*notifiable alteration*", in relation to a vehicle, means—

(a) an alteration made in the structure or fixed equipment of the vehicle which varies the carrying capacity or towing capacity of the vehicle;

(b) an alteration, affecting any part of a braking system or the steering system with which the vehicle is equipped or of the means of operation of either of those systems; or

(c) any other alteration made in the structure or fixed equipment of the vehicle which renders or is likely to render the vehicle unsafe to travel on roads at any weight equal to any plated weight shown in the plating certificate for that vehicle;

["*out of hours*" means at any time either—

(a) on any day which is a Saturday, Sunday, Good Friday, Christmas Day or a Bank holiday (as defined in the Banking and Financial Dealings Act 1971); or

(b) on any other day, other than between—
   (i) 8.00 am and 5.00 pm on a Monday to Thursday inclusive, or
   (ii) 8.00 am and 4.30 pm on a Friday;]

"*periodical test*", in relation to a vehicle, means a goods vehicle test carried out under Part IV of these Regulations on a vehicle in respect of which a goods vehicle test certificate has been issued on a first examination of it or as a result of a re-test following that examination or as a result of an appeal under any provision in these Regulations;

"*plated particulars*" means those particulars which are required to be shown in a Ministry plate under Schedule [10B] to the Construction and Use Regulations;

"*plated weights*" means such of the plated particulars related to gross weight, axle weight for each axle and train weight as are required to be shown in column (2) on the Ministry plate;

"*play bus*" means a motor vehicle which was originally constructed to carry more than 12 passengers but which has been adapted primarily for the carriage of play things for children (including articles required in connection with the use of those things);

["*the prescribed construction and use requirements*", in relation to a vehicle, mean those of the requirements specified in Part I of Schedule 3 which apply to the vehicle and the requirements of Part II of that Schedule;]

"*re-test*", in relation to a vehicle, means an examination which is

(a) an examination for plating and a goods vehicle test carried out on a vehicle under Part III of these Regulations subsequent to a first examination of that vehicle as a result of which a notice of refusal was issued; or

(b) a goods vehicle test carried out on a vehicle under Part IV of these Regulations subsequent to a periodical test of that vehicle as a result of which a notice of refusal was issued;

"*Secretary of State*" means the [Secretary of State for the Environment, Transport and the Regions];

"*sender*" means a person who informs the Secretary of State of a notifiable alteration under regulation 30;

"*sold or supplied by retail*", in relation to a trailer, means sold or supplied otherwise than to a person acquiring solely for the purpose of resale or of resupply for a valuable consideration;

. . .

["*vehicle testing station*" means a station provided by the Secretary of State under section 52(2) of the 1988 Act or such other place as he may consider appropriate for the purposes of carrying out an examination.]

(2) Any reference in these Regulations to—

(a) an examination for plating includes, in relation to a vehicle to which regulation 18 applies, an examination provided for in that regulation; and

(b) a vehicle of a make, model and type shall, in relation to a trailer, include a reference to a vehicle of a make and bearing a serial number.

(3) For the purpose of these Regulations, in counting the number of axles of a vehicle, where the centres of the areas of contact between all the wheels and the road surface can be included between any two vertical planes at right angles to the longitudinal axis of the vehicle less than [0.5] metres apart, those wheels shall be treated as constituting one axle.

(4) For the purpose of these Regulations, in determining when a trailer is first sold or supplied by retail the date of such first sale or supply by retail shall in the case of a trailer which is constructed with a chassis be taken to be the date on which that chassis (with or without a body mounted on it) is first sold or supplied by retail and in the case of any other trailer be taken to be the date the trailer is first sold or supplied by retail.

[(4A) Without prejudice to section 17 of the Interpretation Act 1978 and subject to the context, a reference in these Regulations to any enactment comprised in subordinate legislation (within the meaning of that Act) is a reference to that enactment as from time to time amended or as from time to time re-enacted with or without modification.]

(5) Unless the context otherwise requires, any reference in these Regulations to—

(a) a numbered regulation or Schedule is a reference to the regulation or Schedule bearing that number in these Regulations;

(b) a numbered paragraph is a reference to the paragraph bearing that number in the regulation or Schedule in which the reference appears;

(c) a vehicle is a reference to a vehicle to which these Regulations apply.

[Regulation 3 is printed as amended by S.I. 1990 No. 448; S.I. 1991 No. 252; S.I. 1993 Nos 2048 and 3013; S.I. 1994 No. 328; the Vehicle Excise and Registration Act 1994, s.64 and Sched. 4, para.4; S.I. 1997 Nos 82 and 263; the Secretary of State for the Environment, Transport and the Regions Order 1997 (S.I. 1997 No. 2971); S.I. 2000 No. 1433. **B36.04**

As to the Banking and Financial Dealings Act 1971, see the note to the Road Vehicles (Construction and Use) Regulations 1986 (S.I. 1986 No. 1078), Sched. 12, para.1 above.]

4. Application

B36.05   (1) Subject to paragraph (2), these Regulations apply to goods vehicles being—

    (a) heavy motor cars and motor cars constructed or adapted for the purpose of forming part of an articulated vehicle;

    (b) other heavy motor cars;

    [(c) other motor cars, the design gross weight of which exceeds 3500 kilograms;]

    (d) semi-trailers;

    (e) converter dollies of any unladen weight manufactured on or after 1st January 1979; or

    (f) trailers, not being converter dollies or semi-trailers, the unladen weight of which exceeds 1020 kilograms.

   (2) Nothing in these Regulations applies to goods vehicles of any of the classes of vehicle specified in Schedule 2.

B36.06   *[Regulation 4 is printed as amended by S.I. 1991 No. 252.]*

B36.07   **5. Prescribed requirements for tests**   *[Omitted.]*

       6. Supervision of tests   *[Omitted.]*

       7. Authority to drive and duties of driver

B36.08   (1) The person who drove the vehicle to an examination shall, except so far as he is permitted to be absent by the person who is carrying out the examination, be present throughout the whole of the examination, and shall drive the vehicle and operate its controls when and in such a manner as he may be directed by the person who is carrying out the examination to do so.

   (2) The person who is carrying out an examination is authorised to drive the vehicle on a road or elsewhere.

   (3) A contravention of this regulation is hereby declared to be an offence.

            *   *   *

PART V

REGULATIONS GOVERNING NOTIFIABLE ALTERATIONS, AMENDMENTS OF PLATING CERTIFICATES AND RE-EXAMINATION IN CONNECTION THEREWITH

30. Secretary of State to be informed of notifiable alterations

B36.09   In the event of a notifiable alteration being made to a vehicle in respect of which a plating certificate has been issued, and before the vehicle to which the alteration has been made is used on roads, particulars of that alteration on a form approved by the Secretary of State shall be sent to him at the Goods Vehicle Centre, and any such form may contain a request by the sender for an amendment to be made as respects a plated weight shown on the plating certificate for the vehicle.

B36.10   *[As to the consequences of failure to notify the Secretary of State, see the Road Traffic Act 1988, s.53(3) above.]*

            *   *   *

PART VI

Miscellaneous Matters

*   *   *

39. General provisions as to fees

(1) In this Regulation *"exceptional circumstances"* means an accident, a fire, an epidemic, severe weather, a failure in the supply of essential services or other unexpected happening (excluding a breakdown or mechanical defect in a vehicle or non-delivery of spare parts therefor).

B36.11

(2), (3) *[Omitted.]*

[The definition of "exceptional circumstances" in regulation 39(1) is applied by regulation 46.]

B36.12

*   *   *

PART VIII

Exemptions

44. [Exemptions from section 53(1) and (2) of the 1988 Act]

(1) The provisions of [section 53(1) and (2) of the 1988 Act] do not apply to the use of a vehicle for any of the following purposes—

B36.13

(a) the purpose of submitting it by previous arrangement for, or of bringing it away from, or being used in the course of or in connection with any examination;

(b) where a goods vehicle test certificate is refused on an examination—

   (i) the purpose of delivering it by previous arrangement at, or bringing it away from, a place where work is to be or has been done on it to remedy the defects on the grounds of which the certificate was refused; or

   (ii) the purpose of delivering it, by towing it, to a place where it is to be broken up;

(c) when unladen, the purpose of being driven or drawn by a vehicle driven under a trade licence issued under [section 11 of the 1994 Act];

(d) the purpose of being driven or drawn where it has been imported into Great Britain after arrival in Great Britain on the journey from the place where it has arrived in Great Britain to a place where it is to be kept by the person importing the vehicle or by any other person on whose behalf the vehicle has been imported, and in this sub-paragraph the reference to a vehicle being imported into Great Britain is a reference, in the case of a vehicle which has been so imported more than once, to the first such importation, and in determining for the purposes of this sub-paragraph when a vehicle was first so imported any such importation as is referred to in paragraph 24 of Schedule 2 shall be disregarded;

(e) any purpose for which it is authorised to be used on roads by an order under [section 44 of the 1988 Act];

(f) any purpose connected with its seizure or detention [by a constable];

(g) any purpose connected with its removal, detention, seizure, condemnation or forfeiture under any provision in the Customs and Excise Management Act 1979; and

(h) the purpose of removing it under section 3 of the Refuse Disposal (Amenity) Act 1978 [*q.v.*], or under section 99 of the Road Traffic Regulation Act 1984 or of removing it from a parking place in pursuance of an order under section 35(1) of the Road Traffic Regulation Act 1984, an order relating to a parking place designated under section 45 thereof, or a provision of a designation order having effect by virtue of section 53(3) thereof.

(2) The provisions of [section 53(1) and (2) of the 1988 Act] shall not apply to the use of a vehicle in so far as such use occurs in any place (excluding the Isle of Wight, the islands of Lewis, Mainland (Orkney), Mainland (Shetland) and Skye) being an island or to any area mainly surrounded by water, being an island or area from which motor vehicles not constructed for special purposes can at no time be conveniently driven to a road in any other part of Great Britain by reason of the absence of any bridge, tunnel, ford or other way suitable for the passage of such motor vehicles.

B36.14   *[Regulation 44 is printed as amended by S.I. 1990 No. 448; the Vehicle Excise and Registration Act 1994, s.64 and Sched. 4, para.4.]*

45. [Exemption from section 63(2) of the 1988 Act]

B36.15   Motor vehicles other than those manufactured on or after 1st October 1982 and first used on or after 1st April 1983, not constructed or adapted to form part of an articulated vehicle, are hereby exempted from the provisions of [section 63(2) of the 1988 Act].

[Regulation 45 is printed as amended by S.I. 1990 No. 448.]

46. Certificates of temporary exemption

B36.16   (1) [The Secretary of State] may issue in respect of a vehicle a certificate of temporary exemption, by virtue of which that vehicle shall not, during the period specified in paragraph (2)(d), be subject to the provisions of [section 53(1) or (2) of the 1988 Act], where—

    (a) he is satisfied that by reason of exceptional circumstances, as defined in regulation 39(1) affecting either a vehicle testing station or the vehicle, an examination cannot be completed by a date fixed under these Regulations for carrying out the examination; and

    (b) the use of the vehicle on or after that date would be unlawful by virtue of the said provisions.

(2) Every certificate of temporary exemption shall be on a form approved by the Secretary of State and shall be signed by a person duly authorised on his behalf and shall contain—

    (a) in the case of a certificate issued for a motor vehicle, the registration mark (if any) exhibited on the vehicle or, if no such mark is so exhibited, the chassis or serial number marked on the vehicle or, if no such number is so marked, the identification mark which shall have been allotted to the vehicle by the Secretary of State in the notice of appointment relating to the first examination of the vehicle;

    (b) in the case of a certificate issued for a trailer, the identification mark which shall have been allotted to the trailer by the Secretary of State in the notice of appointment (if any) relating to the first examination of the trailer or shall have otherwise been allotted to the trailer by the Secretary of State under these Regulations;

    (c) the date on which the certificate is issued; and

    (d) the period during which the vehicle is exempted from the provisions of [section 53(1) or (2) of the 1988 Act] so, however, that no such period shall exceed three months in duration.

B36.17   *[Regulation 46 is printed as amended by S.I. 1990 No. 448; S.I. 1997 No. 82.]*

*   *   *

SCHEDULE 2   Regulation 4

Classes of Vehicle to which these Regulations do not Apply

1. Dual-purpose vehicles not constructed or adapted to form part of an articulated vehicle.   **B36.18**

2. Mobile cranes as defined in [paragraph 4(5) of Schedule 1 to the 1994 Act].

3. Break-down vehicles.   **B36.19**

4. Engineering plant and plant, not being engineering plant, which is movable plant or equipment being a motor vehicle or trailer (not constructed primarily to carry a load) especially designed and constructed for the special purposes of engineering operations.

5. Trailers being drying or mixing plant designed for the production of asphalt or of bituminous or tar macadam.   **B36.20**

[**6.** Tower wagons as defined in—

  (a) paragraph 8 of Schedule 1 to the Vehicle Excise and Registration Act 1994 as originally enacted; or

  (b) paragraph 17 of Schedule 2 to that Act as originally enacted.]

7. Road construction vehicles as defined in [section 61 of the Vehicle Excise and Registration Act 1994 as originally enacted [*q.v.*]] and road rollers.   **B36.21**

8. Vehicles designed for fire fighting or fire salvage purposes.

9. Works trucks, straddle carriers used solely as works trucks, and works trailers.   **B36.22**

10. Electrically-propelled motor vehicles.

11. Vehicles used solely for one or both of the following purposes—   **B36.23**

  (a) clearing frost, ice or snow from roads by means of a snow plough or similar contrivance, whether forming part of the vehicle or not, and

  (b) spreading material on roads to deal with frost, ice or snow.

12. Motor vehicles used for no other purpose than the haulage of lifeboats and the conveyance of the necessary gear of the lifeboats which are being hauled.

[**13.** Living vans the design gross weight of which does not exceed 3500 kilograms.]   **B36.24**

14. Vehicles constructed or adapted for, and used primarily for the purpose of, carrying equipment permanently fixed to the vehicle which equipment is used for medical, dental, veterinary, health, educational, display, clerical or experimental laboratory purposes, such use—

  (a) not directly involving the sale, hire or loan of goods from the vehicle; and

  (b) not directly or indirectly involving drain cleaning or sewage or refuse collection.

15. Trailers which have no other brakes than a parking brake and brakes which automatically come into operation on the over-run of the trailer.   **B36.25**

[**16.** A motor vehicle at a time when it is being used on a public road during any calendar week if—

   (a) it is being used only in passing from land in the occupation of the person keeping the vehicle to other land in his occupation, and

   (b) it has not been used on public roads for distances exceeding an aggregate of six miles in that calendar week,

and to a trailer drawn by a motor vehicle that is being used on a public road in such circumstances.

For the purposes of this paragraph "*public road*" has the meaning given in section 62(1) of the Vehicle Excise and Registration Act 1994.]

B36.26   **17.** Agricultural motor vehicles and agricultural trailed appliances.

18. Agricultural trailers and agricultural trailed appliance conveyors drawn on roads only by an agricultural motor vehicle.

B36.27   [**18A.** Converter dollies used solely for the purposes of agriculture, horticulture and forestry, or for any one or two of those purposes.]

19. Public service vehicles (as defined in section 1 of the Public Passenger Vehicles Act 1981 [*q.v.*]).

B36.28   **20.** Licensed taxis (as defined in section 13(3) of the Transport Act 1985 [*q.v.*]).

21. Vehicles used solely for the purposes of funerals.

B36.29   **22.** Goods vehicles to which any of the prescribed construction and use requirements do not apply by virtue of either of the following items in the Table in regulation 4(4) of the Construction and Use Regulations [*q.v.*] namely—

   (a) item 1 (which relates to vehicles proceeding to a port for export);

   (b) item 4 (which relates to vehicles in the service of a visiting force or of a headquarters).

B36.30   **23.** Vehicles equipped with a new or improved equipment or types of equipment and used, solely by a manufacturer of vehicles or their equipment or by an importer of vehicles, for or in connection with the test or trial of any such equipment.

24. Motor vehicles brought into Great Britain and displaying a registration mark mentioned in regulation 5 of the Motor Vehicles (International Circulation) Regulations 1971 [*S.I. 1971 No. 937*], a period of twelve months not having elapsed since the vehicle in question was last brought into Great Britain.

B36.31   **25.** Motor vehicles for the time being licensed under the Vehicles (Excise) Act (Northern Ireland) 1972.

26. Vehicles having a base or centre in any of the following islands, namely, Arran, Bute, Great Cumbrae, Islay, Mull, Tiree or North Uist from which the use of the vehicle on a journey is normally commenced.

B36.32   **27.** Trailers brought into Great Britain and having a base or centre in a country outside Great Britain from which the use of the vehicle on a journey is normally commenced, a period of twelve months not having elapsed since the vehicle in question was last brought into Great Britain.

28. Track-laying vehicles.

29. Steam propelled vehicles.

30. Motor vehicles first used before 1st January 1960, used unladen and not drawing a laden trailer, and trailers manufactured before 1st January 1960 and used unladen.

For the purposes of this paragraph any determination as to when a motor vehicle is first used shall be made as provided in regulation 3(3) of the Construction and Use Regulations [*q.v.*].

31. Motor vehicles constructed, and not merely adapted, for the purpose of street cleansing, or the collection or disposal of refuse or the collection or disposal of the contents of gullies and which are either—

   (a) three-wheeled vehicles, or

   (b) vehicles which—

      (i) are incapable by reason of their construction of exceeding a speed of 20 miles per hour on the level under their own power, or

      (ii) have an inside track width of less than 810 millimetres.

32. Vehicles designed and used for the purpose of servicing or controlling or loading or unloading aircraft while so used—

   (a) on an aerodrome as defined in section 105(1) of the Civil Aviation Act 1982;

   (b) on roads outside such an aerodrome if, except when proceeding directly from one part of such an aerodrome to another part thereof, the vehicles are unladen and are not drawing a laden trailer.

33. Vehicles designed for use, and used on an aerodrome mentioned in paragraph 32, solely for the purpose of road cleansing, the collection or disposal of refuse or the collection or disposal of the contents of gullies or cesspools.

34. Vehicles provided for police purposes and maintained in workshops approved by the Secretary of State as suitable for such maintenance, being vehicles provided in England and Wales by a police authority or the Receiver for the metropolitan police district, or, in Scotland, by a police authority or a joint police committee.

35. Heavy motor cars or motor cars constructed or adapted for the purpose of forming part of an articulated vehicle and which are used for drawing only a trailer falling within a class of vehicle specified in paragraph 13, 14 or 15 of this Schedule or a trailer being used for or in connection with any purpose for which it is authorised to be used on roads by an order under [section 44(1) of the 1988 Act] being an order authorising that trailer or any class or description of trailers comprising that trailer to be used on roads.

36. Play buses.

[**37.** A vehicle—

   (a) which complies with the requirements specified in regulation 4(2) of the Motor Vehicles (Approval) Regulations 2001 [*S.I. 2001 No. 25, q.v.*];

   (b) in respect of which a Minister's approval certificate has been issued under section 58 of the 1988 Act for the purposes of the type approval requirements prescribed by those Regulations; and

   (c) in respect of which a Minister's approval certificate has not subsequently been

issued under that section for the purposes of the type approval requirements prescribed by the National Type Approval for Goods Vehicles Regulations [*as defined in
regulation 3 above*].]

B36.38   [*Schedule 2 is printed as amended by S.I. 1990 No. 448; S.I. 1991 No. 252; S.I. 1995 No. 1456;
S.I. 2001 No. 307.*

*The reference in paragraph 7 above to section 61 of the Vehicle Excise and Registration Act 1994 would
appear to be intended to be a reference to section 62(1) of that Act.*

*For the definition of the term "aerodrome" in the Civil Aviation Act 1982, s.105(1) (cf. paragraph 32
above), see the notes to the Community Drivers' Hours and Recording Equipment (Exemptions and
Supplementary Provisions) Regulations 1986 (S.I. 1986 No. 1456), Schedule, para.2 above.*]

*   *   *

The Use of Invalid Carriages on Highways Regulations 1988

(S.I. 1988 No. 2268)

1. Citation and commencement   *[Omitted.]*   **B37.01**

2. Revocation and saving

(1) Subject to paragraph (2), the Use of Invalid Carriages on Highways Regulations   **B37.02**
1970 [*S.I. 1970 No. 1391, q.v.*] ("*the 1970 Regulations*") are hereby revoked.

(2) Nothing in these Regulations shall apply to invalid carriages manufactured before
30th January 1989, and the 1970 Regulations shall continue to apply to such invalid
carriages as if these Regulations had not been made.

3. Interpretation

In these Regulations—   **B37.03**

the "*1970 Act*" means the Chronically Sick and Disabled Persons Act 1970;

the "*1986 Regulations*" means the Road Vehicles (Construction and Use) Regulations
1986 [*S.I. 1986 No. 1078 (q.v.)*];

a "*Class 1 invalid carriage*" means an invalid carriage which is not mechanically propelled;

a "*Class 2 invalid carriage*" means a mechanically propelled invalid carriage which is so
constructed or adapted as to be incapable of exceeding a speed of 4 miles per hour
on the level under its own power;

a "*Class 3 invalid carriage*" means a mechanically propelled invalid carriage which is so
constructed or adapted as to be capable of exceeding a speed of 4 miles per hour
but incapable of exceeding a speed of 8 miles per hour on the level under its own
power;

"*horn*" has the meaning given by regulation 37(10)(a) of the 1986 Regulations;

"*reversing alarm*" has the meaning given by regulation 37(10)(c) of the 1986
Regulations;

"*road*" has the meaning given by section 142(1) of the Road Traffic Regulation Act
1984 [*q.v.*];

"*two-tone horn*" has the meaning given by regulation 37(10)(d) of the 1986
Regulations.

4. Prescribed conditions for purposes of section 20(1) of the 1970 Act

The conditions in accordance with which an invalid carriage must be used, in order that   **B37.04**
the modifications of the statutory provisions mentioned in subsection (1) of section 20 of
the 1970 Act [*q.v.*] shall have effect in the case of the invalid carriage (being modifications
of certain statutory provisions which relate to the use of vehicles on footways and roads)
shall be—

   (a) in the case of Class 1, Class 2 and Class 3 invalid carriages that the invalid carriage must be used—

      (i) by a person falling within a class of persons for whose use it was constructed or adapted, being a person suffering from some physical defect or physical disability;

      (ii) by some other person for the purposes only of taking the invalid carriage to or bringing it away from any place where work of maintenance or repair is to be or has been carried out to the invalid carriage;

      (iii) by a manufacturer for the purposes only of testing or demonstrating the invalid carriage;

      (iv) by a person offering to sell the invalid carriage for the purpose only of demonstrating it; or

      (v) by a person giving practical training in the use of the invalid carriage for that purpose only;

   (b) in the case of Class 1, Class 2 and Class 3 invalid carriages, that any horn fitted to it must not be sounded in the circumstances set out in regulation 5;

   (c) in the case of Class 3 invalid carriages only—

      (i) that the invalid carriage must not be used by a person who is aged under 14 years;

      (ii) that, when being used on a footway, the invalid carriage must not be driven at a speed greater than 4 miles per hour;

      (iii) that the invalid carriage must not be used on a footway unless the device fitted in accordance with regulation 10(1)(a) is operating; and

      (iv) that the invalid carriage must not be used at any time unless the speed indicator fitted to it in accordance with regulation 10(1)(b) is operating.

B37.05   **5.** The circumstances referred to in regulation 4(b) are that the invalid carriage is either—

   (a) stationary on a road, at any time, other than at times of danger due to another moving vehicle on or near the road; or

   (b) in motion on a road which is a restricted road for the purposes of section 81 of the Road Traffic Regulation Act 1984 between 23.30 hours and 07.00 hours in the following morning.

6. Prescribed requirements for purposes of section 20(1) of the 1970 Act

B37.06   The requirements with which an invalid carriage must comply in order that the modifications of the statutory provisions mentioned in subsection (1) of section 20 of the 1970 Act [*q.v.*] shall have effect in the case of the invalid carriage (being modifications of certain statutory provisions which related to the use of vehicles on footways and roads) shall be—

   (a) that it shall be a Class 1, Class 2 or Class 3 invalid carriage; and

   (b) the requirements specified in regulations 7 to 14.

7. Unladen weight

B37.07   (1) The unladen weight of a Class 1 or Class 2 invalid carriage shall not exceed 113.4 kilograms.

(2) The unladen weight of a Class 3 invalid carriage shall not exceed 150 kilograms.

(3) In this regulation "*unladen weight*" means the weight of the invalid carriage inclusive of the weight of water, fuel or accumulators used for the purpose of the supply of power for its propulsion and of loose tools, but exclusive of the weight of any other load or of a person carried by the invalid carriage.

8. Means of stopping

(1) A Class 2 or Class 3 invalid carriage shall be so constructed and maintained that it meets the requirements set out in paragraphs (2) to (4).   **B37.08**

(2) The invalid carriage shall be capable of being brought to rest in all conditions of use with reasonable directional stability and within a reasonable distance.

(3) When the invalid carriage is not being propelled or is left unattended it shall be capable of being held stationary indefinitely in all conditions of use on a gradient of at least 1 in 5.

(4) The requirements of paragraphs (2) and (3) shall not be regarded as met unless the necessary braking effect can be achieved by the appropriate use—

  (a) of the invalid carriage's propulsion unit transmission gear or of both the propulsion unit and transmission gear;

  (b) of a separate system fitted to the vehicle (which may be a system which operates upon the propulsion unit or transmission gear); or

  (c) of a combination of the means of achieving a braking effect referred to in sub-paragraphs (a) and (b);

and in the case of paragraph (3) without depending upon any hydraulic or pneumatic device or on the flow of electrical current.

9. Lighting

A Class 2 or Class 3 invalid carriage when on the carriageway of any road shall comply with the requirements specified in [the Road Vehicles Lighting Regulations 1989 [*S.I. 1989 No. 1796 (q.v.)*]] as if it was a motor vehicle within the meaning of [the Road Traffic Act 1988] and as if any reference to an invalid carriage in those Regulations included an invalid carriage within the meaning of the 1970 Act.   **B37.09**

[Regulation 9 is printed as amended by the Interpretation Act 1978, ss.17(2)(a) and 23(1).]   **B37.10**

10. Speed device and speed indicator

(1) A Class 3 invalid carriage shall be fitted with—   **B37.11**

  (a) a device which is capable of limiting the maximum speed of the invalid carriage to 4 miles per hour on the level under its own power and which can be put into operation by the user; and

  (b) a speed indicator.

(2) A speed indicator fitted in accordance with this regulation shall be kept free from any obstruction which might prevent it being easily seen by the user of the invalid carriage and shall be maintained in efficient working order.

(3) In this regulation, "*speed indicator*" means a device fitted to an invalid carriage for the purpose of indicating to the user of the invalid carriage whether the device referred to in paragraph (1)(a) is in operation.

11. Width

The overall width of a Class 3 invalid carriage shall not exceed 0.85 metres.   **B37.12**

12. Audible warning instrument

(1) A Class 3 invalid carriage shall be fitted with a horn, not being a reversing alarm or a two-tone horn.   **B37.13**

(2) The sound emitted by any horn fitted to an invalid carriage shall be continuous and uniform and not strident.

13. Vision

B37.14   (1) A Class 2 or Class 3 invalid carriage shall be so constructed that the user of the invalid carriage can at all times have a full view of the road and traffic ahead when controlling the invalid carriage.

(2) Any windscreen or window fitted to a Class 2 or Class 3 invalid carriage shall be made of safety glass or safety glazing and shall be maintained in such condition that it does not obscure the vision of the user of the invalid carriage while the invalid carriage is being driven.

(3) In this regulation—

"*safety glass*" means glass so manufactured or treated that if fractured it does not fly into fragments likely to cause severe cuts; and

"*safety glazing*" means material other than glass so manufactured or treated that if fractured it does not fly into fragments likely to cause severe cuts.

14. Rear view mirrors

B37.15   (1) A Class 3 invalid carriage shall be fitted either internally or externally with a rear view mirror.

(2) Any rear view mirror fitted to an invalid carriage shall be so constructed or treated that if fractured it does not fly into fragments likely to cause severe cuts.

(3) In this regulation "*rear view mirror*" means a mirror to assist the user of the invalid carriage to become aware of traffic to the rear of the invalid carriage.

The Motor Vehicles (International Circulation) (Amendment) Order 1989

(S.I. 1989 No. 993)

1. Citation and commencement

This Order may be cited as the Motor Vehicles (International Circulation) (Amendment) Order 1989 and shall come into force for all purposes except the purposes of articles 5 and 6 on the day after the day on which it is made, for all purposes of article 5 on 1 September 1989 and for all purposes of article 6 on the date on which the Convention on Road Traffic concluded at Vienna in 1968 [*Cmnd. 4032*] is first in force in respect of the United Kingdom, which date shall be notified in the London, Edinburgh and Belfast Gazettes.

B38.01

[This order was made on June 13, 1989.]

2. Interpretation, revocation and variation

(1) In this Order "*the principal Order*" means the Motor Vehicles (International Circulation) Order 1975 [*S.I. 1975 No. 1208, q.v.*] as amended by the Motor Vehicles (International Circulation) (Amendment) Order 1980 [*S.I. 1980 No. 1095, q.v.*] and the Motor Vehicles (International Circulation) (Amendment) Order 1985 [*S.I. 1985 No. 459*].

B38.02

(2) Articles 5, 6, 7 and 8 and paragraphs (2), (3) and (4) of article 10 of the Motor Vehicles (International Circulation) (Amendment) Order 1980 and articles 3 and 4 of the Motor Vehicles (International Circulation) (Amendment) Order 1985 are hereby revoked.

(3) *[Amends Schedule 3 to the principal order.]*

3. Documents for drivers of vehicles going abroad   *[Amends article 1 of the principal order.]*

B38.03

4. Visitors' driving permits   *[Substitutes articles 2 and 3 of the principal order.]*

5. Fees for documents   *[Amends Schedule 2 to the principal order; not reproduced.]*

6. Vienna Convention on Road Traffic 1968

(1) In paragraph (4) of article 2 of the principal Order, as substituted by article 4 of this Order, in the definition of "Convention country" after the words "but is a party to" there shall be inserted the words "the Convention on Road Traffic concluded at Vienna in the year 1968 [*Cmnd. 4032*]".

B38.04

(2) In paragraph (7) of article 2 of the principal Order, as so substituted, for the definition of "Convention driving permit" there shall be substituted the following definition:

"'*Convention driving permit*' means either—

  (i) a driving permit in the form A in Schedule 1 to this Order issued under the authority of a country outside the United Kingdom, whether or not that country is a party to the Convention on Road Traffic concluded at Geneva in the year 1949 but not so issued as aforesaid after the expiry of a period of five years from the date of the entry into force of the Convention on Road Traffic concluded at Vienna in the year 1968 in accordance with Article 47(1) thereof, if that country is a party to that Convention, or

(ii) a driving permit in the form B in that Schedule issued under the authority of a country outside the United Kingdom which is a party to the International Convention relative to Motor Traffic concluded at Paris in the year 1926, but not to the Convention of 1949 nor to the Convention of 1968, or

(iii) a driving permit in the form C in that Schedule issued under the authority of a country outside the United Kingdom which is a party to the Convention of 1968;".

(3) At the end of paragraph (8) of article 2 of the principal Order as so substituted, there shall be added the following words "and, without prejudice to the provisions of paragraph (4) above, a Convention driving permit in the form C in Schedule 1 to this Order shall, if the validity of the permit is by special endorsement thereon made conditional upon the holder wearing certain devices or upon the vehicle being equipped in a certain manner to take account of his disability, not be valid at a time when any such condition is not satisfied".

The Recovery Vehicles (Prescribed Purposes) Regulations 1989

(S.I. 1989 No. 1376)

1. *[Citation and commencement.]*   **B39.01**

2. *[Revocation.]*

3. The purposes specified in Schedule 1 to these Regulations are hereby prescribed for   **B39.02**
the purposes of [paragraph 5(3) of Schedule 1 to the Vehicle Excise and Registration Act
1994] [*q.v.*].

[Regulation 3 is printed as amended by the Vehicle Excise and Registration Act 1994, s.64 and Sched.   **B39.03**
4, para.4.]

4. The purposes specified in Schedule 2 to these Regulations are hereby prescribed for   **B39.04**
the purposes of [paragraph 5(4) of Schedule 1 to the Vehicle Excise and Registration Act
1994] [*q.v.*].

[Regulation 4 is printed as amended by the Vehicle Excise and Registration Act 1994, s.64 and Sched.   **B39.05**
4, para.4.]

5. In paragraph 2 of Schedule 1 the following expressions have the following   **B39.06**
meanings—

"*local authority*" means—

    (a) in relation to England, a district council, a London borough council or the
        Common Council of the City of London;

    (b) *[applies to Scotland]*;

    (c) in relation to Wales, a district council;

"*road*" has the meaning given—

    (a) in relation to England and Wales by the Road Traffic Act 1988 [*q.v.*]; and

    (b) *[applies to Scotland.]*

SCHEDULE 1   Regulation 3

PURPOSES PRESCRIBED FOR THE PURPOSES OF [PARAGRAPH 5(3) OF SCHEDULE 1 TO THE
VEHICLE EXCISE AND REGISTRATION ACT 1994]

[The heading is printed as amended by the Vehicle Excise and Registration Act 1994, s.64 and Sched. 4,   **B39.07**
para.4.]

1. Carrying any person who, immediately before a vehicle became disabled, was the   **B39.08**
driver of or a passenger in that vehicle, together with his personal effects, from the premises
at which that vehicle is to be repaired or scrapped to his original intended destination.

2. At the request of—

    (a) a constable, or

(b) a local authority,

empowered by or under statute to remove a vehicle from a road, removing such a vehicle to a place nominated by the constable or the local authority.

B39.09   *[Paragraph 2 of Schedule 1 is printed as corrected by a correction slip dated September 1989.]*

B39.10   **3.** Proceeding to a place at which the vehicle will be available for use for either of the purposes specified in [paragraph 5(3)(a) and (b) of Schedule 1 to the Vehicle Excise and Registration Act 1994] [*q.v.*] and remaining temporarily at such a place so as to be available for such use.

B39.11   *[Paragraph 3 of Schedule 1 is printed as amended by the Vehicle Excise and Registration Act 1994, s.64 and Sched. 4, para.4.]*

B39.12   **4.** Proceeding from—

(a) a place where the vehicle has remained temporarily so as to be available for such use;

(b) a place where the vehicle has recovered a disabled vehicle; or

(c) any premises mentioned in [paragraph 5(3)(b) or (c) of Schedule 1 to the Vehicle Excise and Registration Act 1994] to which the vehicle has removed a disabled vehicle.

B39.13   *[Paragraph 4 of Schedule 1 is printed as amended by the Vehicle Excise and Registration Act 1994, s.64 and Sched. 4, para.4.]*

Regulation 4   SCHEDULE 2

Purposes Prescribed for the Purposes of [Paragraph 5(4) of Schedule 1 to the Vehicle Excise and Registration Act 1994]

B39.14   *[The heading is printed as amended by the Vehicle Excise and Registration Act 1994, s.64 and Sched. 4, para.4.]*

B39.15   **1.** Repairing a disabled vehicle at the place where it became disabled or to which it has been moved in the interests of safety after becoming disabled.

2. Drawing or carrying one trailer if the trailer was immediately before a vehicle became disabled, being drawn or carried by the disabled vehicle.

The Road Vehicles Lighting Regulations 1989

(S.I. 1989 No. 1796)

Editorial note. The explanatory note accompanying the 1989 Regulations draws attention specifically to the drafting of certain of the provisions in the regulations relating to contraventions. These, unlike the corresponding provisions in the earlier regulations, are drafted so that contraventions are offences under section 42(1)(b) of the Road Traffic Act 1988 (*q.v.*), rather than under section 42(1)(a).

The explanatory notes also included the following explanation of European approval marks:

7. The following explanation of European approval marks is added for convenience—

EXPLANATION OF EUROPEAN APPROVAL MARKS
EXAMPLES OF MARKINGS

HCR

021507

UN: ECE Dipped and
Main-Beam Halogen Headlamp

III

011471

E.C. Class III Triangular Shaped
Rectro Reflector

Notes—

1. An E within a circle indicates a device which has been approved to a UN: ECE Regulation. (United Nations: Economic Commission for Europe, based in Geneva.)

2. An e within a rectangle indicates a device which has been approved to an EEC Directive. (European Economic Community, based in Brussels.)

3. The number within the circle or rectangle beside the E or e is the distinguishing number of the country that issued the approval. 11 stands for the United Kingdom.

4. An arrow below the circle or rectangle means, in the case of a headlamp, that it dips to the left. A double-headed arrow means that the headlamp bulb holder can be adjusted so as to dip either to the left or to the right.

5. In the case of a motor vehicle registered for use in the United Kingdom which is fitted with European-approved headlamps, an arrow (single or double headed) is required to be present below the approval mark on the lenses of the headlamps.

6. An arrow below the circle or rectangle means, in the case of any other type of lamp, that the lamp is "handed" and must be fitted to the side of the vehicle to which the arrow points except in the case of a direction indicator of category 3, 4 or 5, in which case the lamp is fitted on the side of the vehicle and the arrow points towards the front of the vehicle.

7. The symbols above the circle or rectangle identify the function, category or class of device as follows—

A	Front position lamp (or end-outline marker lamp)
C	Dipped-beam headlamp
R	Main-beam headlamp
S	Sealed-beam headlamp
H	Halogen headlamp
B	Front fog lamp (white or yellow)
1	Category 1 front direction indicator (suitable for fitting at least 40mm from a headlamp or front fog lamp)
1a	Category 1a front direction indicator (suitable for fitting at least 20mm from a headlamp or front fog lamp)
1b	Category 1b front direction indicator (suitable for fitting less than 20mm from a headlamp or front fog lamp)
2a	Category 2a rear direction indicator (with single level of intensity)
2b	Category 2b rear director indicator (with dual level of intensity)
3	Category 3 front-side direction indicator
4	Category 4 front-side direction indicator
5	Category 5 side-repeater direction indicator
11	Category 11 front ⎫ direction indicators
12	Category 12 rear ⎬ for motor
13	Category 13 side repeater ⎭ cycles only
SM	Side marker lamp
R	Rear position lamp
B or F	Rear fog lamp (red)
S1	Stop lamp with single level of intensity
S2	Stop lamp with two levels of intensity
AR	Reversing lamp
I	Class I retro reflector
IA	Class IA retro reflector
III	Class III retro reflector (triangular—for trailers only)
IIIA	Class IIIA retro reflector (triangular—for trailers only)
No symbol	No A, R, S1 or S2 is required on a position lamp or a stop lamp approved for use only on motor cycles
	Common combinations of symbols—
R–S1	Rear position lamp which is also a stop lamp
HCR	Halogen headlamp emitting both main and dipped-beam

Other combinations of symbols are possible.

B40.02

[The text of these regulations has been amended by:

the Tramcars and Trolley Vehicles (Modification of Enactments) Regulations 1992 (S.I. 1992 No. 1217), reg.14 (July 1, 1992);

the Road Vehicles Lighting (Amendment) Regulations 1994 (S.I. 1994 No. 2280) (October 1, 1994 and April 1, 1995);

the Road Vehicles Lighting (Amendment) Regulations 1996 (S.I. 1996 No. 3016) (July 1, 1997); and

the Road Vehicles Lighting (Amendment) Regulations 2001 (S.I. 2001 No. 560) (March 21, 2001).

The amending regulations are referred to in the notes to the principal regulations by their years and numbers only. The dates referred to above are the dates on which the amending regulations came into force.]

ARRANGEMENTS OF REGULATIONS

PART I

PRELIMINARY

Regulation

PART II

REGULATIONS GOVERNING THE FITTING OF LAMPS, REFLECTORS, REAR MARKINGS AND DEVICES

Regulation

21. Projecting trailers and vehicles carrying overhanging or projecting loads or equipment
22. Additional side marker lamps

PART III

REGULATIONS GOVERNING THE MAINTENANCE AND USE OF LAMPS, REFLECTORS, REAR MARKINGS AND DEVICES

Regulation

23. Maintenance of lamps, reflectors, rear markings and devices
24. Requirements about the use of front and rear position lamps, rear registration plate lamps, side marker lamps and end-outline marker lamps
25. Requirements about the use of headlamps and front fog lamps
26. Requirements about the use of warning beacons
27. Restrictions on the use of lamps other than those to which regulation 24 refers

PART IV

TESTING AND INSPECTION OF LIGHTING EQUIPMENT AND REFLECTORS

Regulation

28. Testing and inspection of lighting equipment and reflectors

SCHEDULES

Schedule

1. Obligatory lamps, reflectors, rear markings and devices
2. Front position lamps
3. Dim-dip devices and running lamps
4. Dipped-beam headlamps
5. Main-beam headlamps
6. Front fog lamps
7. Direction indicators
8. Hazard warning signal devices
9. Side marker lamps
10. Rear position lamps
11. Rear fog lamps
12. Stop lamps
13. End-outline marker lamps
14. Reversing lamps
15. Rear registration plate lamps
16. Warning beacons
17. Side retro reflectors
18. Rear retro reflectors
19. Rear markings
20. Pedal retro reflectors
21. Front retro reflectors
22. Diagram showing where unlit parking is not permitted near a junction
23. Example of marking showing the vertical downwards inclination of the dipped-beam headlamps

PART I

PRELIMINARY

1. Commencement, citation and revocations   *[Omitted.]*   **B40.04**

2. Statement under section 43(3) of the Road Traffic Act 1988   *[Omitted.]*   **B40.05**

3. Interpretation

(1) Unless the context otherwise requires, any reference in these Regulations—   **B40.06**

    (a) to a numbered regulation or Schedule is a reference to the regulation or Schedule bearing that number in these Regulations,

    (b) to a numbered paragraph is to the paragraph bearing that number in the regulation or Schedule in which the reference occurs, and

    (c) to a numbered or lettered sub-paragraph is to the sub-paragraph bearing that number in the paragraph in which the reference occurs.

(2) In these Regulations, unless the context otherwise requires, any expressions for which there is an entry in column 1 of the Table has the meaning given against it in column 2 or is to be construed in accordance with directions given against it in that column.

TABLE

1 *Expression*	2 *Meaning*
"The Act"	The Road Traffic Act 1988 [*q.v.*].
"The Construction and Use Regulations"	The Road Vehicles (Construction and Use) Regulations 1986 [*S.I. 1986 No. 1078 (q.v.)*].
"The Designation of Approval Marks Regulations"	The Motor Vehicles (Designation of Approval Marks) Regulations 1979 [*S.I. 1979 No. 1088, as amended; not reproduced in this work*].
"Agricultural vehicle"	A vehicle constructed or adapted for agriculture, grass cutting, forestry, land levelling, dredging or similar operations and primarily used for one or more of these purposes, and includes any trailer drawn by an agricultural vehicle.
"Angles of visibility"	A requirement for a lamp or reflector fitted to a vehicle to have specified horizontal and vertical angles of visibility is a requirement that at least 50 per cent of the apparent surface must be visible from any point within those angles when every door, tailgate, boot lid, engine cover, cab or other movable part of the vehicle is in the closed position.
"Apparent surface"	For any given direction of observation, is the orthogonal projection of a light-emitting surface in a plane perpendicular to the direction of observation and touching that surface.
"Articulated bus"	Has the same meaning as in the Construction and Use Regulations.

[continued on next page

1 *Expression*	2 *Meaning*
"Articulated vehicle"	Has the same meaning as in the Construction and Use Regulations.
"Breakdown vehicle"	A vehicle used to attend an accident or breakdown or to draw a broken down vehicle.
"Bus"	Has the same meaning as in the Construction and Use Regulations.
"Caravan"	A trailer which is constructed (and not merely adapted) for human habitation.
"cc"	Cubic centimetre or centimetres (as the case may be).
"Circuit-closed tell-tale"	A light showing that a device has been switched on.
"cm"	Centimetre or centimetres (as the case may be).
"cm²"	Square centimetre or centimetres (as the case may be).
"Combat vehicle"	A vehicle of a type described at item 1, 2 or 3 in column 1 of Schedule 1 to the Motor Vehicles (Authorisation of Special Types) General Order 1979 [*S.I. 1979 No. 1198 (q.v.)*].
[*"Community Directive 76/756/EEC, as last amended by Directive 89/278/EEC"*]	Council Directive 76/756/EEC of 27.7.76 (O.J. L262, 27.9.76, p. 1) as amended by Commission Directive 80/233/EEC of 21.11.79 (O.J. L51, 25.2.80, p. 8), Commission Directive 82/244/EEC of 17.3.82 (O.J. L109, 22.4.82, p. 31), Council Directive 83/276/EEC of 26.5.83 (O.J. L151, 9.6.83, p. 47), Commission Directive 84/8/EEC of 14.12.83 (O.J. L9, 12.1.84, p. 24) and Commission Directive 89/278/EEC of 23.3.89 (O.J. L109, 20.4.89, p. 38).
[*"Community Directive 76/756/ EEC, as last amended by Directive 91/663/EEC"*]	Council Directive 76/756/EEC as last amended by Directive 89/278/EEC and further amended by Commission Directive 91/663/EEC (O.J. L366, 31.12.91, p. 17).]
"Daytime hours"	The time between half an hour before sunrise and half an hour after sunset.
"Dim-dip device"	A device which is capable of causing a dipped-beam headlamp to operate at reduced intensity.
"Dipped beam"	A beam of light emitted by a lamp which illuminates the road ahead of the vehicle without causing undue dazzle or discomfort to oncoming drivers or other road users.
"Direction indicator"	A lamp on a vehicle used to indicate to other road users that the driver intends to change direction to the right or to the left.
"Dual-purpose vehicle"	Has the same meaning as in the Construction and Use Regulations.
"Emergency vehicle"	A motor vehicle of any of the following descriptions—

[continued on next page

1 *Expression*	2 *Meaning*

"Emergency vehicle"—cont.	(a) a vehicle used for fire brigade, ambulance or police purposes;
	(b) an ambulance, being a vehicle (other than an invalid carriage) which is constructed or adapted for the purposes of conveying sick, injured or disabled persons and which is used for such purposes;
	(c) a vehicle owned by a body formed primarily for the purposes of fire salvage and used for those or similar purposes;
	(d) a vehicle owned by the Forestry Commission or by a local authority and used from time to time for the purposes of fighting fires;
	(e) a vehicle owned by the Secretary of State for Defence and used—
	   (i) for the purposes of the disposal of bombs or explosives,
	   (ii) by the Naval Emergency Monitoring Organisation for the purposes of a nuclear accident or an incident involving radioactivity,
	   (iii) by the Royal Air Force Mountain Rescue Service for the purposes of rescue operations or any other emergencies, or
	   (iv) by the Royal Air Force Armament Support Unit;
	(f) a vehicle primarily used for the purposes of the Blood Transfusion Service provided under the National Health Service Act 1977 or under the National Health Service (Scotland) Act 1978;
	(g) a vehicle used by Her Majesty's Coastguard or Coastguard Auxiliary Service for the purposes of giving aid to persons in danger or vessels in distress on or near the coast;
	(h) a vehicle owned by the British Coal Corporation and used for the purposes of rescue operations at mines;
	(i) a vehicle owned by the Royal National Lifeboat Institution and used for the purposes of launching lifeboats; and
	(j) a vehicle primarily used for the purposes of conveying any human tissue for transplanting or similar purposes.

"End-outline marker lamp"	A lamp fitted near the outer edge of a vehicle in addition to the front and rear position lamps to indicate the presence of a wide vehicle.

[*continued on next page*

1 *Expression*	2 *Meaning*
"Engineering plant"	Has the same meaning as in the Construction and Use Regulations.
"Extreme outer edge"	In relation to a side of a vehicle, the vertical plane parallel with the longitudinal axis of the vehicle, and coinciding with its lateral outer edge, disregarding the projection of— (a) so much of the distortion of any tyre as is caused by the weight of the vehicle, (b) any connections for tyre pressure gauges, (c) any anti-skid devices which may be mounted on the wheels, (d) rear-view mirrors, (e) lamps and reflectors, (f) customs seals affixed to the vehicle, and devices for securing and protecting such seals, and (g) special equipment.
"Front fog lamp"	A lamp used to improve the illumination of the road in front of a motor vehicle in conditions of seriously reduced visibility.
"Front position lamp"	A lamp used to indicate the presence and width of a vehicle when viewed from the front.
"First used"	References to the date of first use of a vehicle shall be construed in accordance with regulation 3(3) of the Construction and Use Regulations.
"Hazard warning signal device"	A device which is capable of causing all the direction indicators with which a vehicle, or a combination of vehicles, is fitted to operate simultaneously.
"Headlamp"	A lamp used to illuminate the road in front of a vehicle and which is not a front fog lamp.
"Headlamp levelling device"	Either— (a) an automatic headlamp levelling device by means of which the downward inclination of any dipped-beam headlamp is automatically maintained regardless of the load on the vehicle, or (b) a manual headlamp levelling device by means of which the downward inclination of any dipped-beam headlamp may be adjusted by a manual control operable from the driving seat of the vehicle.
"Home forces"	The naval, military or air forces of Her Majesty raised in the United Kingdom.
"Home forces' vehicle"	A vehicle owned by, or in the service of, the home forces and used for naval, military or air force purposes.

[continued on next page

1 *Expression*	2 *Meaning*
"Horse-drawn"	In relation to a vehicle, means that the vehicle is drawn by a horse or other animal.
"Hours of darkness"	The time between half an hour after sunset and half an hour before sunrise.
"Illuminated area"	The expression, in relation to a headlamp, front fog lamp and reversing lamp, in each case fitted with a reflector, means the orthogonal projection of the full aperture of the reflector on a plane (touching the surface of the lamp) at right angles to the longitudinal axis of the vehicle to which the lamp is fitted. If the light-emitting surface extends over only part of the full aperture of the reflector, then the projection of only that part shall be taken into account. In the case of a dipped-beam headlamp, the illuminated area is limited by the apparent trace of the cut-off on the lens. The expression, in relation to any other lamp, means the part of the orthogonal projection of the light-emitting surface on a plane (touching the surface of the lamp) at right angles to the longitudinal axis of the vehicle to which it is fitted, the boundary of which is such that if the straight edge of an opaque screen touches it at any point 98 per cent of the total intensity of the light is shown in the direction parallel to the longitudinal axis of the vehicle. Accordingly, for the purposes of determining the lower, upper and lateral edges of the lamp, only a screen placed with its straight edge horizontally or vertically needs to be considered.
"Industrial tractor"	Has the same meaning as in the Construction and Use Regulations.
"Installation and performance requirements"	In relation to any lamp, reflector, rear marking or device, the requirements specified in the Schedules to these Regulations relating to that lamp, reflector, rear marking or device.
"Invalid carriage"	A mechanically propelled vehicle constructed or adapted for the carriage of one person, being a person suffering from some physical defect or disability.
"Kerbside weight"	Has the same meaning as in the Construction and Use Regulations.
"kg"	Kilogram or kilograms (as the case may be).
"Light-emitting surface"	In relation to a lamp, that part of the exterior surface of the lens through which light is emitted when the lamp is lit, and in relation to a retro reflector that part of the exterior surface of the retro reflector from which light can be reflected.

[continued on next page

1 *Expression*	2 *Meaning*
"*m*"	Metre or metres (as the case may be).
"*Main beam*"	A beam of light emitted by a headlamp which illuminates the road over a long distance ahead of the vehicle.
"*Matched pair*"	In relation to lamps, a pair of lamps in respect of which— (a) both lamps emit light of substantially the same colour and intensity, and (b) both lamps are of the same size and of such a shape that they are symmetrical to one another.
"*Maximum distance from the side of the vehicle*"	The expression means— (a) in relation to a lamp fitted to a vehicle, the shortest distance from the boundary of the illuminated area to an extreme outer edge of the vehicle, and (b) in relation to a retro reflector fitted to a vehicle, the shortest distance from the boundary of the reflecting area to an extreme outer edge of the vehicle.
"*Maximum gross weight*"	Has the same meaning as in the Construction and Use Regulations.
"*Maximum height above the ground*"	The height above which no part of the illuminated area in the case of a lamp, or the reflecting area in the case of a retro reflector, extends when the vehicle is at its kerbside weight and when each tyre with which the vehicle is fitted is inflated to the pressure recommended by the manufacturer of the vehicle.
"*Maximum speed*"	Has the same meaning as in the Construction and Use Regulations.
"*Minimum height above the ground*"	The height below which no part of the illuminated area in the case of a lamp, or the reflecting area in the case of a retro reflector, extends when the vehicle is at its kerbside weight and when each tyre with which the vehicle is fitted is inflated to the pressure recommended by the manufacturer of the vehicle.
"*mm*"	Millimetre or millimetres (as the case may be).
"*Motor bicycle combination*"	A combination of a solo motor bicycle and a sidecar.
"*Motor tractor*"	Has the same meaning as in the Construction and Use Regulations.
"*Motorway*"	Has the same meaning as in Schedule 6 of the Road Traffic Regulation Act 1984 [*q.v.*].
"*Movable platform*"	A platform which is attached to, and may be moved by means of, an extendible boom.
"*mph*"	Mile per hour or miles per hour (as the case may be).

[*continued on next page*

1 *Expression*	2 *Meaning*
"*Obligatory*"	In relation to a lamp, reflector, rear marking or device, means a lamp, reflector, rear marking or device with which a vehicle, its load or equipment is required by these Regulations to be fitted.
"*Operational tell-tale*"	A warning device readily visible or audible to the driver and showing whether a device that has been switched on is operating correctly or not.
"*Optional*"	In relation to a lamp, reflector, rear marking or device, means a lamp, reflector, rear marking or device with which a vehicle, its load or equipment is not required by these Regulations to be fitted.
"*Overall length*"	Has the same meaning as in the Construction and Use Regulations.
"*Overall width*"	Has the same meaning as in the Construction and Use Regulations.
"*Pair*"	In relation to lamps, reflectors or rear markings means a pair of lamps, reflectors or rear markings, including a matched pair, one on each side of the vehicle, in respect of which the following conditions are met— (a) each lamp, reflector or rear marking is at the same height above the ground, and (b) each lamp, reflector or rear marking is at the same distance from the extreme outer edge of the vehicle. In the case of an asymmetric vehicle, those conditions shall be deemed to be met if they are as near as practicable to being met.
"*Passenger vehicle*"	Has the same meaning as in the Construction and Use Regulations.
"*Pedal cycle*"	A vehicle which is not constructed or adapted to be propelled by mechanical power and which is equipped with pedals, including an electrically assisted pedal cycle prescribed for the purposes of section 189 of the Act and section 140 of the Road Traffic Regulation Act 1984.
"*Pedal retro reflector*"	A retro reflector attached to or incorporated in the pedals of a pedal cycle or motor bicycle.
"*Pedestrian-controlled vehicle*"	Has the same meaning as in the Construction and Use Regulations.
["*Prescribed sign*"	A sign which is of a type shown in Schedule 21A and complies with the requirements of that Schedule.]
"*Rear fog lamp*"	A lamp used to render a vehicle more readily visible from the rear in conditions of seriously reduced visibility.

[*continued on next page*

1 *Expression*	2 *Meaning*
"Rear position lamp"	A lamp used to indicate the presence and width of a vehicle when viewed from the rear.
"Rear retro reflector"	A retro reflector used to indicate the presence and width of a vehicle when viewed from the rear.
"Rear registration plate lamp"	A lamp used to illuminate the rear registration plate.
"Reflecting area"	In relation to a retro reflector fitted to a vehicle, the area of the orthogonal projection on a vertical plane (touching the surface of the reflector)— (a) at right angles to the longitudinal axis of the vehicle of that part of the reflector designed to reflect light in the case of a front or a rear retro reflector, and (b) parallel to the longitudinal axis of the vehicle of that part of the reflector designed to reflect light in the case of a side retro reflector.
"Reversing lamp"	A lamp used to illuminate the road to the rear of a vehicle for the purpose of reversing and to warn other road users that the vehicle is reversing or about to reverse.
"Road clearance vehicle"	A mechanically propelled vehicle used for dealing with frost, ice or snow on roads.
"Running lamp"	A lamp (not being a front position lamp, an end-outline marker lamp, headlamp or front fog lamp) used to make the presence of a moving motor vehicle readily visible from the front.
"Separation distance"	In relation to two lamps or two retro reflectors the expression means, except where otherwise specified, the shortest distance between the orthogonal projections in a plane perpendicular to the longitudinal axis of the vehicle of the illuminated areas of the two lamps or the reflecting areas of the two reflectors.
"Service braking system"	Has the same meaning as in the Construction and Use Regulations.
"Side marker lamp"	A lamp fitted to the side of a vehicle or its load and used to render the vehicle more visible to other road users.
"Side retro reflector"	A reflector fitted to the side of a vehicle or its load and used to render the vehicle more visible from the side.
"Solo motor bicycle"	A motor bicycle without a sidecar.
"Special equipment"	A movable platform fitted to a vehicle, the apparatus for moving the platform and any jacks fitted to the vehicle for stabilising it while the movable platform is in use.

[continued on next page

1 *Expression*	2 *Meaning*
"Special warning lamp"	A lamp, fitted to the front or rear of a vehicle, capable of emitting a blue flashing light and not any other kind of light.
"Stop lamp"	A lamp used to indicate to road users that the brakes of a vehicle or combination of vehicles are being applied.
"Traffic sign"	Has the same meaning given by section 64(1) of [the Road Traffic Regulation Act 1984].
"Trailer"	A vehicle constructed or adapted to be drawn by another vehicle.
"Unrestricted dual-carriageway road"	A dual-carriageway within the meaning given by paragraph 2 of Schedule 6 to the Road Traffic Regulation Act 1984 on which a motor vehicle may lawfully be driven at a speed exceeding 50mph.
"Unladen weight"	Has the same meaning as in the Construction and Use Regulations.
"Vehicle in the service of a visiting force or of a headquarters"	Has the same meaning as in the Construction and Use Regulations.
"Visiting vehicle"	Has the meaning given by regulation 3(1) of the [Motor Vehicles (International Circulation) Regulations 1985 [*S.I. 1985 No. 610; not reproduced in this work*]].
"Warning beacon"	A lamp that is capable of emitting a flashing or rotating beam of light throughout 360° in the horizontal plane.
"Wheel"	Has the same meaning as in the Construction and Use Regulations (see also paragraph (7)).
"Wheeled"	Has the same meaning as in the Construction and Use Regulations.
"Work lamp"	A lamp used to illuminate a working area or the scene of an accident, breakdown or roadworks in the vicinity of the vehicle to which it is fitted.
"Works trailer"	Has the same meaning as in the Construction and Use Regulations.
"Works truck"	Has the same meaning as in the Construction and Use Regulations.

(3) Material designed primarily to reflect light is, when reflecting light, to be treated for the purposes of these Regulations as showing a light, and material capable of reflecting an image is not, when reflecting the image of a light, to be so treated.

(4) In these Regulations a reference to one lamp, except in the case of a dipped-beam headlamp, a main-beam headlamp and a front fog lamp, includes any combination of two or more lamps, whether identical or not, having the same function and emitting light of the same colour, if it comprises devices the aggregate illuminated area of which occupies 60 per cent or more of the area of the smallest rectangle circumscribing those illuminated areas.

(5) In these Regulations a reference to two lamps includes—

    (a) a single illuminated area which—

        (i) is placed symmetrically in relation to the longitudinal axis of the vehicle,

        (ii) extends on both sides to within 400mm of the extreme outer edge of the vehicle,

        (iii) is not less than 800mm long, and

        (iv) is illuminated by not less than two sources of light, and

    (b) any number of illuminated areas which—

        (i) are juxtaposed,

        (ii) if on the same transverse plane have illuminated areas which occupy not less than 60 per cent of the area of the smallest rectangle circumscribing their illuminated areas,

        (iii) are placed symmetrically in relation to the median longitudinal plane of the vehicle,

        (iv) extend on both sides to within 400mm of the extreme outer edge of the vehicle,

        (v) do not have a total length of less than 800mm, and

        (vi) are illuminated by not less than two sources of light.

(6) Where a part fitted to a vehicle is required by these Regulations to be marked with a British Standard mark, the requirements shall not be regarded as met unless, in addition to being marked as required, the part complied with the relevant British Standard at the time when the part was first fitted to the vehicle.

(7) A reference in these Regulations to the number of wheels of a vehicle shall be construed in accordance with regulation 3 of the Construction and Use Regulations.

(8) A reference in a Schedule to there being no requirement in relation to a lamp, reflector, rear marking or device is without prejudice to any other provision in these Regulations affecting same.

B40.07　　*[Regulation 3 is printed as amended by S.I. 1994 No. 2280.*

In regulation 3(2), table, reference is made in the definition of "visiting vehicle" to the Motor Vehicles (International Circulation) Regulations 1985 (S.I. 1985 No. 610). By regulation 3 of the 1985 Regulations, the term is defined as "a vehicle brought temporarily into Great Britain by a person resident outside the United Kingdom". See further regulation 5(b) of these regulations.]

[3A. Equivalent standards

B40.08　　(1) Nothing in these Regulations shall render unlawful any act or omission which would have been lawful were—

    (a) there to be substituted for any reference to a British Standard in these Regulations a reference to a corresponding standard, and

    (b) regulation 3(6) to apply in relation to that corresponding standard and the markings relating to that corresponding standard as it applies to a British Standard.

(2) For the purposes of this regulations, "*corresponding standard*", in relation to a relevant British Standard Specification, means—

    (a) a standard or code of practice of a national standards body or equivalent body of any State within the European Economic Area;

    (b) any international standard recognised for use as a standard by any State within the European Economic Area;

    (c) a technical specification or code of practice which, whether mandatory or not, is recognised for use as a standard by a public authority of any State within the European Economic Area, where the standard, code of practice, international standard or technical specification provides, in relation to lamps, retro reflectors and rear markings, a level of safety equivalent to that provided by that British Standard Specification and contains a requirement as respects the marking of such parts equivalent to that provided by that instrument.]

[Regulation 3A was inserted by S.I. 1994 No. 2280.   **B40.09**
As to the European Economic Area, see the note to Regulation (EEC) 3820/85 below.]

4. Exemptions—General

(1) Where a provision is applied by these Regulations to a motor vehicle first used on or   **B40.10**
after a specified date it does not apply to any vehicle manufactured at least six months before that date.

(2) Where an exemption from, or a relaxation of, a provision is applied by these Regulations to a motor vehicle first used before a specified date it shall also apply to a motor vehicle first used on or after that date if it was manufactured at least six months before that date.

(3) Nothing in these Regulations shall require any lamp or reflector to be fitted between sunrise and sunset to—

  (a) a vehicle not fitted with any front or rear position lamp,

  (b) an incomplete vehicle proceeding to a works for completion,

  (c) a pedal cycle,

  (d) a pedestrian-controlled vehicle,

  (e) a horse-drawn vehicle,

  (f) a vehicle drawn or propelled by hand, or

  (g) a combat vehicle.

(4) Without prejudice to regulation 16, for the purposes of these Regulations a lamp shall not be treated as being a lamp if it is—

  (a) so painted over or masked that it is not capable of being immediately used or readily put to use; or

  (b) an electric lamp which is not provided with any system of wiring by means of which that lamp is, or can readily be, connected with a source of electricity.

5. Exemptions—Temporarily imported vehicles and vehicles proceeding to a port for export

Part II of these Regulations does not apply to—   **B40.11**

  (a) any vehicle having a base or centre in a country outside Great Britain from which it normally starts its journeys, provided that a period of not more than 12 months has elapsed since the vehicle was last brought into Great Britain;

  (b) a visiting vehicle;

  (c) any combination of two or more vehicles, one of which is drawing the other or others, if the combination includes any vehicle of the type mentioned in sub-paragraph (a) or (b); or

  (d) a vehicle proceeding to a port for export,

if in each case the vehicle or combination of vehicles complies in every respect with the requirements about lighting equipment and reflectors relating thereto contained in the Convention on Road Traffic concluded at Geneva on 19th September 1949 [*Cmnd. 7997*] or the International Convention relating to Motor Traffic concluded at Paris on 24th April 1926 [*T.S. No. 11 (1930)*].

6. Exemptions—Vehicles towing or being towed

B40.12   (1) No motor vehicle first used before 1st April 1986 and no pedal cycle or trailer manufactured before 1st October 1985 is required by regulation 18 to be fitted with any rear position lamp, stop lamp, rear direction indicator, rear fog lamp or rear reflector whilst a trailer fitted with any such lamp or reflector is attached to its rear.

(2) No trailer manufactured before 1st October 1985 is required by regulation 18 to be fitted with any front position lamp whilst being drawn by a passenger vehicle.

(3) No trailer is required by regulation 18 to be fitted with any stop lamp whilst being drawn by a vehicle which is not required by regulation 18 to be fitted with any such lamp.

(4) Paragraph (3) shall apply respectively to rear fog lamps and direction indicators as it applies to stop lamps.

(5) No trailer manufactured before 1st October 1990 is required by regulation 18 to be fitted with any stop lamp or direction indicator whilst being drawn by a motor vehicle fitted with one or two stop lamps and two or more direction indicators if the dimensions of the trailer are such that when the longitudinal axes of the drawing vehicle and the trailer lie in the same vertical plane such stop lamps and at least one direction indicator on each side of the vehicle are visible to an observer in that vertical plane from a point 6m behind the rear of the trailer whether it is loaded or not.

(6) No rear marking is required to be fitted to any vehicle by regulation 18 if another vehicle in a combination of which it forms part would obscure any such marking.

(7) Where a broken-down vehicle is being drawn by another vehicle—
- (a) regulations 18 and 23 shall not apply to the broken-down vehicle between sunrise and sunset, and
- (b) between sunset and sunrise those regulations shall apply to the broken-down vehicle only in respect of rear position lamps and reflectors.

(8) The references in paragraphs (3) and (4) to a vehicle which is required to be fitted with a lamp shall be construed as if paragraph (1) did not have effect.

7. Exemptions—Military vehicles

B40.13   (1) Regulation 18 does not apply to a home forces' vehicle or to a vehicle in the service of a visiting force or of a headquarters whilst being used—
- (a) in connection with training which is certified in writing for the purposes of this regulation by a person duly authorised in that behalf to be training on a special occasion and of which not less than 48 hours' notice has been given by that person to the chief officer of police of every police area in which the place selected for the training is wholly or partly situate; or
- (b) on manoeuvres within such limits and during such period as may from time to time be specified by Order in Council under the Manoeuvres Act 1958.

(2) Where not less than 6 nor more than 12 vehicles being home forces' vehicles or vehicles of a visiting force or of a headquarters are proceeding together in a convoy on tactical or driving exercises which are authorised in writing by a person duly authorised in that behalf, and of which not less than 48 hours' notice in writing has been given by that person to the chief officer of police of every police area through which it is intended that the convoy shall pass and the interval between any two vehicles in such convoy does not exceed 20m—
- (a) front position lamps shall be required only on the vehicle leading the convoy; and
- (b) rear position lamps shall be required only on the rearmost vehicle provided that every other vehicle in the convoy carries a bright light under the vehicle illuminating either a part of the vehicle or anything attached to the vehicle or the road

surface beneath the vehicle, in such a manner that the presence of the vehicle can be detected from the rear.

(3) No lamp is required to be fitted to any home forces' vehicle or any vehicle in the service of a visiting force or of a headquarters if the vehicle is constructed or adapted for combat and is such that compliance with these provisions is impracticable and it is fitted with two red rear position lamps and two red rear retro reflectors when on a road between sunset and sunrise. Such lamps and reflectors need not meet any of the requirements specified in Schedules 10 and 18.

(4) Part II of these Regulations does not apply to a vehicle in the service of a visiting force or of a headquarters if the vehicle complies in every respect with the requirements as to lighting equipment and reflectors relating thereto contained in a Convention referred to in regulation 5.

8. Exemptions—Invalid carriages

An invalid carriage having a maximum speed not exceeding 4mph is required by these Regulations to be fitted with lamps and reflectors only when it is used on the carriageway of a road between sunset and sunrise otherwise than for the sole purpose of crossing it.   **B40.14**

9. Exemptions—Vehicles drawn or propelled by hand

A vehicle drawn or propelled by hand which has an overall width, including any load, not exceeding 800mm is required by these Regulations to be fitted with lamps and reflectors only when it is used on the carriageway of a road between sunset and sunrise other than—   **B40.15**

    (a) close to the near side or left-hand edge of the carriageway, or

    (b) to cross the carriageway.

[9A. Exemptions—Tramcars

Parts II to IV of these Regulations do not apply to tramcars.]   **B40.16**

[Regulation 9A was inserted by S.I. 1992 No. 1217.]   **B40.17**

[9B. Modifications in relation to vehicles approved under the Motor Vehicles (Approval) Regulations 1996

(1) In this regulation—   **B40.18**

"*the Approval Regulations*" means the Motor Vehicles (Approval) Regulations 1996 [*S.I. 1996 No. 3013*];

"*coefficient of luminous intensity*" has the same meaning as in ECE Regulation 3.01;

"*ECE Regulation 3.01*" means Regulation 3 (with the amendments in force on 20th March 1982), annexed to the Agreement concerning the adoption of uniform conditions of approval for Motor Vehicles Equipment and Parts and reciprocal recognition therefor concluded at Geneva on the 20th March 1958 [*Cmnd. 2535*] to which the United Kingdom is a party;

"*passenger vehicle approval certificate*" means a Minister's approval certificate in the form prescribed by the Approval Regulations which appears to have been issued on the basis that the vehicle is a vehicle to which Part II of those Regulations applies;

"*relevant vehicle*" means a vehicle—

    (a) in respect of which a passenger vehicle approval certificate containing the letter "P" has been issued pursuant to regulation 12(2)(b) of the Approval Regulations; or

    (b) which is a "transitional provision vehicle" as defined by Schedule 6 to the Approval Regulations in respect of which a passenger vehicle approval certificate containing the letter "A" has been issued pursuant to regulation 12(2)(c) of the Approval Regulations;

"*standard mark*" means a mark which when applied to a lamp, reflector or device indicates compliance with the requirements of a particular instrument; and a reference to the instrument to which a standard mark relates shall be construed accordingly.

(2) The requirements of the Schedules to these Regulations, so far as they require any lamp, reflector or device to bear a particular standard mark (or one of two or more standard marks), shall not apply to a lamp, reflector or device if it is fitted to a relevant vehicle and—

(a) in the case of a lamp or device, it meets the requirements as to intensity; and

(b) in the case of a reflector, it meets the requirements as to coefficient of luminous intensity,

of the instrument to which the standard mark (or as the case may be one of those standard marks) relates.

(3) The requirements of these Regulations so far as they require headlamps (including a filament lamp fitted to a headlamp) fitted to a vehicle to bear a particular standard mark (or one of two or more standard marks) shall not apply to the headlamps fitted to a relevant vehicle if they emit sufficient light to illuminate the road in front of the vehicle on both main beam and dipped beam.

(4) Table 1 of Schedule 1 shall apply to a vehicle in respect of which a passenger vehicle approval certificate has been issued as if the entry that relates to dim-dip devices and running lamps were omitted.

(5) Paragraph (5)(markings) of Part I of Schedule 7 shall apply to a vehicle in respect of which a passenger approval certificate has been issued as if the vehicle were of a description falling within sub-paragraph (b) of that paragraph.]

B40.19   *[Regulation 9B was inserted by S.I. 1996 No. 3016.*
The Motor Vehicles (Approval) Regulations 1996 (to which reference is made in regulation 9B(1)) have been revoked and replaced by the Motor Vehicles (Approval) Regulations 2001 (S.I. 2001 No. 25) below. The Interpretation Act 1978, ss.17(2)(a) and 23, which enables references to the 1996 Regulations to be construed as references to the 2001 Regulations is only applicable in the absence of a contrary intention (see 1978 Act, s.17(2)(a)); the fact that the scheme of the 2001 Regulations differs from that of the 1996 Regulations (e.g. there is no Part in the 2001 Regulations corresponding to Part II ("Passenger Vehicles")) of the 1996 Regulations suggests that a "contrary intention" should be inferred. The text of the 1996 Regulations is reproduced in the nineteenth edition of this work.]

10. Provision as respects Trade Descriptions Act 1968

B40.20   Where by any provision in these Regulations any vehicle or any of its parts or equipment is required to be marked with a specification number or a registered certification trade mark of the British Standards Institution or with any approval mark, nothing in that provision shall be taken to authorise any person to apply any such number or mark to the vehicle, part or equipment in contravention of the Trade Descriptions Act 1968.

PART II

REGULATIONS GOVERNING THE FITTING OF LAMPS, REFLECTORS, REAR MARKINGS AND DEVICES

11. Colour of light shown by lamps and reflectors

B40.21   (1) No vehicle shall be fitted with a lamp [or retro reflective material] which is capable of showing a red light to the front, except—

(a) a red and white chequered domed lamp, or a red and white segmented mast-mounted warning beacon, fitted to a fire service control vehicle and intended for use at the scene of an emergency;

(b) a side marker lamp or a side retro reflector;

(c) retro reflective material or a retro reflector designed primarily to reflect light to one or both sides of the vehicle and attached to or incorporated in any wheel or tyre of—

   (i) a pedal cycle and any sidecar attached to it;

   (ii) a solo motor bicycle or a motor bicycle combination; or

   (iii) an invalid carriage; or

(d) a traffic sign.

(2) No vehicle shall be fitted with a lamp [or retro reflective material] which is capable of showing any light to the rear, other than a red light, except—

(a) amber light from a direction indicator or side marker lamp;

(b) white light from a reversing lamp;

(c) white light from a work lamp;

(d) light to illuminate the interior of a vehicle;

(e) light from an illuminated rear registration plate;

(f) light for the purposes of illuminating a taxi meter;

(g) in the case of a bus, light for the purposes of illuminating a route indicator;

(h) blue light and white light from a chequered domed lamp fitted to a police control vehicle and intended for use at the scene of an emergency;

(i) white light from a red and white chequered domed lamp, or a red and white segmented mast-mounted warning beacon, fitted to a fire service control vehicle and intended for use at the scene of an emergency;

(j) green light and white light from a chequered domed lamp fitted to an ambulance control vehicle and intended for use at the scene of an emergency;

(k) blue light from a warning beacon or rear special warning lamp fitted to an emergency vehicle, or from any device fitted to a vehicle used for police purposes;

(l) amber light from a warning beacon fitted to—

   (i) a road clearance vehicle;

   (ii) a vehicle constructed or adapted for the purpose of collecting refuse;

   (iii) a breakdown vehicle;

   (iv) a vehicle having a maximum speed not exceeding 25mph or any trailer drawn by such a vehicle;

   (v) a vehicle having an overall width (including any load) exceeding 2.9m;

   (vi) a vehicle used for the purposes of testing, maintaining, improving, cleansing or watering roads or for any purpose incidental to any such use;

   (vii) a vehicle used for the purpose of inspecting, cleansing, maintaining, adjusting, renewing or installing any apparatus which is in, on, under or over a road, or for any purpose incidental to any such use;

   (viii) a vehicle used for or in connection with any purpose for which it is authorised to be used on roads by an order under section 44 of the Act;

   (ix) a vehicle used for escort purposes when travelling at a speed not exceeding 25mph;

   (x) a vehicle used by the Commissioners of Customs and Excise for the purpose of testing fuels;

   (xi) a vehicle used for the purpose of surveying;

   (xii) a vehicle used for the removal or immobilisation of vehicles in exercise of a statutory power or duty;

(m) green light from a warning beacon fitted to a vehicle used by a medical practitioner registered by the General Medical Council (whether with full, provisional or limited registration);

(n) yellow light from a warning beacon fitted to a vehicle for use at airports;

(o) light of any colour from a traffic sign which is attached to a vehicle;

(p) reflected light from amber pedal retro reflectors;

(q) reflected light of any colour from retro reflective material or a retro reflector designed primarily to reflect light to one or both sides of the vehicle and attached to or incorporated in any wheel or tyre of—

    (i) a pedal cycle and any sidecar attached to it;

    (ii) a solo motor bicycle or motor bicycle combination; or

    (iii) an invalid carriage;

(r) reflected light from amber retro reflective material on a road clearance vehicle;

(s) reflected light from yellow retro reflective registration plates;

[(sa) reflected blue, yellow and white light from a retro reflective plate displaying a distinguishing sign in accordance with Council Regulation (EC) No. 2411/98 [*Council Regulation of November 3, 1998 on the recognition in intra-Community traffic of the distinguishing sign of the Member State in which motor vehicles and their trailers are registered; O.J. No. L299, November 10, 1998, p. 1*]];

(t) reflected light from yellow retro reflective material incorporated in a [prescribed rear marking fitted in the appropriate manner to]—

    (i) a motor vehicle having a maximum gross weight exceeding 7500kg;

    (ii) a motor vehicle first used before 1st August 1982 having an unladen weight exceeding 3000kg;

    (iii) a trailer having a maximum gross weight exceeding 3500kg;

    (iv) a trailer manufactured before 1st August 1982 having an unladen weight exceeding 1000kg;

    (v) a trailer which forms part of a combination of vehicles one of which is of a type mentioned in a previous item of this sub-paragraph;

    (vi) a load carried by any vehicle; . . .

(u) reflected light from orange retro reflective material incorporated in a sign fitted to the rear of a vehicle carrying a dangerous substance within the meaning of the Dangerous Substances (Conveyance by Road in Road Tankers and Tank Containers) Regulations 1981 [*S.I. 1981 No. 1059*] or the Road Traffic (Carriage of Dangerous Substances in Packages, etc.) Regulations 1986 [*S.I. 1986 No. 1951*].

[(v) reflected light from yellow retro reflective material incorporated in a prescribed sign and fitted to the rear of a bus; or]

[(w) reflected light from yellow retro reflective material incorporated in a sign fitted to the rear of a bus in accordance with paragraph (4).]

[(3) For the purposes of paragraph (2)(t), a rear marking fitted to a vehicle is a prescribed rear marking fitted in the appropriate manner if the rear marking—

(a) is a rear marking of a description specified in the entry applicable to that vehicle in the right hand column of paragraph 1 of Part I of Schedule 19, and

(b) complies with paragraphs 2 to 7 of that Part of that Schedule.]

[(4) For the purposes of paragraph (2)(w), a sign ("*the secondary sign*") is fitted to the rear of a bus in accordance with this paragraph if—

(a) a prescribed sign is also fitted to the rear of a bus;

(b) the total area of the retro reflective material incorporated in the secondary sign is no greater than the area of the prescribed sign; and

(c) the secondary sign satisfies the requirements specified—

    (i) in the case of a bus which is owned or hired by a local education authority or any person managing an education establishment attended by children under the age of 16 years, in paragraphs (5) or (6); or

    (ii) in any other case, in paragraph (6).]

[(5) The requirements referred to in paragraph (4)(c)(i) are that the secondary sign contains no words or other markings apart from words or markings identifying the local education authority or the educational establishment (as the case may be).]

[(6) The requirements referred to in paragraph (4)(c)(ii) are that the secondary sign contains no words or other markings apart from words or other markings which—

(a) indicate that children are on board the bus when it is in motion or likely to be on board the bus or in its vicinity when it is stationary, and

(b) are calculated to reduce the risk of road accidents involving such children.]

[Regulation 11 is printed as amended by S.I. 1994 No. 2280; S.I. 2001 No. 560.   **B40.22**
S.I. 1981 No. 1059 (to which reference is made in regulation 11(2)(u)) has been revoked by the Road Traffic (Carriage of Dangerous Substances in Road Tankers and Tank Containers) Regulations 1992 (S.I. 1992 No. 743) and S.I. 1986 No. 1951 (to which reference is also made) has been revoked by the Road Traffic (Carriage of Dangerous Substances in Packages, etc.) Regulations 1992 (S.I. 1992 No. 743); see now the Carriage of Dangerous Goods by Road Regulations 1996 (S.I. 1996 No. 2095; not reproduced in this work).]

12. Movement of lamps and reflectors

(1) Save as provided in paragraph (2), no person shall use, or cause or permit to be used, **B40.23** on a road any vehicle to which, or to any load or equipment of which, there is fitted a lamp, reflector or marking which is capable of being moved by swivelling, deflecting or otherwise while the vehicle is in motion.

(2) Paragraph (1) does not apply in respect of—

(a) a headlamp which can be dipped only by the movement of the headlamp or its reflector;

(b) a headlamp which is capable of adjustment so as to compensate for the effect of the load carried by the vehicle;

(c) a lamp or reflector which can be deflected to the side by the movement of, although not necessarily through the same angle as, the front wheel or wheels of the vehicle when turned for the purpose of steering the vehicle;

(d) a headlamp or front fog lamp which can be wholly or partially retracted or concealed;

(e) a direction indicator fitted to a motor vehicle first used before 1st April 1986;

(f) a work lamp;

(g) a warning beacon;

(h) an amber pedal retro reflector; or

(i) retro reflective material or a retro reflector of any colour which is fitted so as to reflect light primarily to one or both sides of the vehicle and is attached to or incorporated in any wheel or tyre of—

    (i) a pedal cycle and any sidecar attached to it;

    (ii) a solo motor bicycle or motor bicycle combination; or

    (iii) an invalid carriage.

13. Lamps to show a steady light

(1) Save as provided in paragraph (2), no vehicle shall be fitted with a lamp which auto- **B40.24** matically emits a flashing light.

(2) Paragraph (1) does not apply in respect of—

    (a) a direction indicator;

    (b) a headlamp fitted to an emergency vehicle;

    (c) a warning beacon or special warning lamp;

    (d) a lamp or illuminated sign fitted to a vehicle used for police purposes;

    (e) a green warning lamp used as an anti-lock brake indicator; or

    (f) lamps forming part of a traffic sign.

14. Filament lamps

B40.25   (1) Where a motor vehicle first used on or after 1st April 1986 or any trailer manufactured on or after 1st October 1985 is equipped with any lamp of a type that is required by any Schedule to these Regulations to be marked with an approval mark, no filament lamp other than a filament lamp referred to in the Designation of Approval Marks Regulations in—

    (a) regulation 4 and Schedule 2, items 2 or 2A, 8, 20, 37 or 37A; or

    (b) regulation 5 and Schedule 4, item 18,

shall be fitted to any such lamp.

    (2) *[Revoked.]*

B40.26   *[Regulation 14 is printed as amended by S.I. 1994 No. 2280.]*

15. General requirements for electrical connections

B40.27   (1) Every motor vehicle first used on or after 1st April 1991 shall be so constructed that every position lamp, side marker lamp, end-outline marker lamp and rear registration plate lamp with which the vehicle is fitted is capable of being switched on and off by the operation of one switch and, save as provided in paragraph (2), not otherwise.

    (2) Sub-paragraph (a) of paragraph (1) shall not prevent one or more position lamps from being capable of being switched on and off independently of any other lamp referred to in that sub-paragraph.

16. Restrictions on fitting blue warning beacons, special warning lamps and similar devices

B40.28   No vehicle, other than an emergency vehicle, shall be fitted with—

    (a) a blue warning beacon or special warning lamp, or

    (b) a device which resembles a blue warning beacon or a special warning lamp, whether the same is in working order or not.

17. Obligatory warning beacons

B40.29   (1) Subject to paragraph (2), no person shall use, or cause or permit to be used, on an unrestricted dual-carriageway road any motor vehicle with four or more wheels having a maximum speed not exceeding 25mph unless it or any trailer drawn by it is fitted with at least one warning beacon which—

    (a) complies with Schedule 16, and

    (b) is showing an amber light.

    (2) Paragraph (1) shall not apply in relation to—

    (a) any motor vehicle first used before 1st January 1947; and

    (b) any motor vehicle, or any trailer being drawn by it, to which paragraph (1) would otherwise apply, when that vehicle or trailer is on any carriageway of an unrestricted dual-carriageway road for the purpose only of crossing that carriageway in the quickest manner practicable in the circumstances.

[17A. Signs on buses carrying children

(1) Subject to paragraph (2), no person shall use or cause or permit to be used on a road a bus when it is carrying a child to or from his school unless—

   (a) a prescribed sign is fitted to the front of the bus and is plainly visible to road users ahead of the bus, and

   (b) a prescribed sign is fitted to the rear of the bus and is plainly visible to road users behind the bus.

B40.30

(2) Paragraph (1) does not apply where a bus is on a bus service of a description specified in paragraph 2 of the Schedule to the Fuel Duty Grant (Eligible Bus Services) Regulations 1985 [*S.I. 1985 No. 1886; not reproduced in this work*].

(3) For the purposes of this regulation—

   (a) a reference to a bus carrying a child to or from his school is a reference to a bus carrying a child—

      (i) to, or to a place within the vicinity of, his school on a day during term time before he has attended the school on that day; or

      (ii) from, or from a place within the vicinity of, his school on a day during term time after he has finished attending the school on that day;

   (b) "*school*" has the meaning given by [section 4(1) of the Education Act 1996]; and

   (c) a reference to a child is a reference to a child under the age of 16 years.]

B40.31

[Regulation 17A was inserted by S.I. 1994 No. 2280, and is printed as subsequently amended by the Education Act 1996, s.582(3) and Sched. 39, para.1(4).

For the definition of "school" in section 4(1) of the Education Act 1996, see the notes to the Road Vehicles (Construction and Use) Regulations 1986 (S.I. 1986 No. 1078), reg.48A above.]

18. Obligatory lamps, reflectors, rear markings and devices

(1) Save as provided in the foregoing provisions of these Regulations and in paragraph (2), every vehicle of a class specified in a Table in Schedule 1 shall be fitted with lamps, reflectors, rear markings and devices which—

   (a) are of a type specified in column 1 of that Table, and

   (b) comply with the relevant installation, alignment and performance requirements set out in the Schedule or Part of a Schedule shown against that type in column 2 of that Table.

B40.32

(2) The requirements specified in paragraph (1) do not apply in respect of a lamp, reflector, rear marking or device of a type specified in column 1 of a Table in the case of a vehicle shown against it in column 3 of that Table.

(3) The requirements specified in paragraph (1) apply without prejudice to any additional requirements specified in regulations 20 and 21.

(4) The Schedules referred to in the Tables in Schedule 1 are Schedules 2 to 21.

19. Restrictions on the obscuration of certain obligatory lamps and reflectors

Every vehicle shall be so constructed that at least part of the apparent surface of any—

   (a) front and rear position lamp,

   (b) front and rear direction indicator, and

   (c) rear retro reflector,

B40.33

which is required by these Regulations to be fitted to a vehicle is visible when the vehicle is viewed from any point directly in front of or behind the lamp or reflector, as appropriate, when every door, tailgate, boot lid, engine cover, cab or other movable part of the vehicle is in a fixed open position.

20. Optional lamps, reflectors, rear markings and devices

B40.34   Every optional lamp, reflector, rear marking or device fitted to a vehicle, being of a type specified in an item in column 2 of the Table below, shall comply with the provisions shown in column 3 of that Table.

TABLE

(1) Item No	(2) Type of lamp, reflector, rear marking or device	(3) Provisions with which compliance is required	
1	Front position lamp	Schedule 2, Part II	
2	Dim-dip device and running lamp	Schedule 3, Part II	
3	Dipped-beam headlamp	Schedule 4, Part II	
4	Main-beam headlamp	Schedule 5, Part II	
5	Front fog lamp	Schedule 6	
7	Direction indicator	Schedule 7, Part II	and Parts I of
8	Hazard warning signal device	Schedule 8	Schedules 2 to 5, 7, 9 to 13
9	Side marker lamp	Schedule 9, Part II	and 17 to 21 to
10	Rear position lamp	Schedule 10, Part II	the extent
11	Rear fog lamp	Schedule 11, Part II	specified in
12	Stop lamp	Schedule 12, Part II	Parts II of
13	End-outline marker lamp	Schedule 13, Part II	those Schedules.
14	Reversing lamp	Schedule 14	
15	Warning beacon	Schedule 16	
16	Side retro reflector	Schedule 17, Part II	
17	Rear retro reflector	Schedule 18, Part II	
18	Rear marking	Schedule 19, Part II	
19	Pedal retro reflector	Schedule 20, Part II	
20	Front retro reflector	Schedule 21, Part II	

21. Projecting trailers and vehicles carrying overhanging or projecting loads or equipment

B40.35   (1) No person shall use, or cause or permit to be used, on a road in the circumstances mentioned in paragraph (2)—

   (a) any trailer which forms part of a combination of vehicles which projects laterally beyond any preceding vehicle in the combination; or

   (b) any vehicle [or] combination of vehicles which carries a load or equipment

in either case under the conditions specified in an item in column 2 of the Table below, unless the vehicle or combination of vehicles complies with the requirements specified in that item in column 3 of that Table.

TABLE

(1) Item No	(2) Conditions	(3) Requirements
1	A trailer which is not fitted with front position lamps and which projects laterally on any side so that the distance from the outermost part of the projection to the outermost part of the illuminated area of the obligatory front position lamp on that side fitted to any preceding vehicle in the combination exceeds 400mm.	A lamp showing white light to the front shall be fitted to the trailer so that the outermost part of the illuminated area is not more than 400mm from the outermost projection of the trailer. The installation and performance requirements relating to front position lamps do not apply to any such lamp.
2	A trailer which is not fitted with front position lamps and which carries a load or equipment which projects laterally on any side of the trailer so that the distance from the outermost projection of the load or equipment to the outermost part of the illuminated area of the obligatory front position lamp on that side fitted to any preceding vehicle in the combination exceeds 400mm.	A lamp showing white light to the front shall be fitted to the trailer or the load or equipment so that the outermost part of the illuminated area is not more than 400mm from the outermost projection of the load or equipment. The installation and performance requirements relating to front position lamps do not apply to any such lamp.
3	A vehicle which carries a load or equipment which projects laterally on any side of the vehicle so that the distance from the outermost part of the load or equipment to the outermost part of the illuminated area of the obligatory front or rear position lamp on that side exceeds 400mm.	Either— (a) the obligatory front or rear position lamp shall be transferred from the vehicle to the load or equipment to which must also be attached a white front or a red rear reflecting device; or (b) an additional front or rear position lamp and a white front or a red rear reflecting device shall be fitted to the vehicle, load or equipment. All the installation, performance and maintenance requirements relating to front or rear position lamps shall in either case be complied with except that for the purpose of determining the lateral position of such lamps and reflecting devices any reference to the vehicle shall be taken to include the load or equipment except special equipment on a vehicle fitted with a movable platform or the jib of any crane.

[*continued on next page*

(1) *Item No*	(2) *Conditions*	(3) *Requirements*
4	A vehicle which carries a load or equipment which projects beyond the rear of the vehicle or, in the case of a combination of vehicles, beyond the rear of the rearmost vehicle in the combination, more than— (a) 2m in the case of an agricultural vehicle or a vehicle carrying a fire escape; or (b) 1m in the case of any other vehicle.	An additional rear lamp capable of showing red light to the rear and a red reflecting device, both of which are visible from a reasonable distance, shall be fitted to the vehicle or the load in such a position that the distance between the lamp and the reflecting device, and the rearmost projection of the load or equipment does not exceed 2m in the case mentioned in sub-paragraph (a) in column 2 of this item or 1m in any other case. The installation and performance requirements relating to rear position [lamps and rear retro reflectors do not apply to any such additional lamp and reflecting device].
5	A vehicle which carries a load or equipment which projects beyond the front of the vehicle more than— (a) 2m in the case of an agricultural vehicle or a vehicle carrying a fire fire escape; or (b) 1m in the case of any other vehicle.	An additional front lamp capable of showing white light to the front and a white reflecting device, both visible from a reasonable distance shall be fitted to the vehicle or the load in such a position that the distance between the lamp and the the reflecting device, and the foremost projection of the load or equipment, does not exceed 2m in the case mentioned in sub-paragraph (a) in column 2 of this item or 1m in any other case. The installation and performance requirements relating to front position lamps and front retro reflectors do not apply to any such additional lamp and reflecting device.
6	A vehicle which carries a load or equipment which obscures any obligatory lamp, reflector or rear marking.	Either— (a) the obligatory lamp, reflector or rear marking shall be transferred to a position on the vehicle, load or equipment where it is not obscured; or (b) an additional lamp, reflector or rear marking shall be fitted to the vehicle, load or equipment. All the installation, performance and maintenance requirements relating to obligatory lamps, reflectors or rear markings shall in either case be complied with.

(2) The circumstances referred to in paragraph (1) are—

(a) as regards item 6 in the Table, in so far as it relates to obligatory stop lamps and direction indicators, all circumstances; and

(b) as regards items 1 to 5 in the Table and item 6 in the Table, except in so far as it relates to obligatory stop lamps and direction indicators, the time between sunset and sunrise or, except in so far as it relates to obligatory reflectors, when visibility is seriously reduced between sunrise and sunset.

[Regulation 21 is printed as amended by S.I. 1994 No. 2280.]   **B40.36**

22. Additional side marker lamps

(1) Save as provided in paragraph (2), no person shall use, or cause or permit to be used,   **B40.37** on a road between sunset and sunrise, or in seriously reduced visibility between sunrise and sunset, any vehicle or combination of vehicles of a type specified in an item in column 2 of the Table below unless each side of the vehicle or combination of vehicles is fitted with the side marker lamps specified in that item in column 3 and those lamps are kept lit.

TABLE

(1) *Item No*	(2) *Vehicle or combination of vehicles*	(3) *Side marker lamps*
1	Any vehicle or combination of vehicles the overall length of which (including any load) exceeds 18.3m.	There shall be fitted— (a) one lamp no part of the light-emitting surface of which is more than 9.15m from the foremost part of the vehicle or vehicles (in either case inclusive of any load); (b) one lamp no part of the light-emitting surface of which is more than 3.05m from the rearmost part of the vehicle or vehicles (in either case inclusive of any load); and (c) such other lamps as are required to ensure that not more than 3.05m separates any part of the light-emitting surface of one lamp and any part of the light-emitting surface of the next lamp.
2	A combination of vehicles the overall length of which (including any load) exceeds 12.2m but does not exceed 18.3m and carrying a load supported by any two of the vehicles but not including a load carried by an articulated vehicle.	There shall be fitted— (a) one lamp no part of the light-emitting surface of which is forward of, or more than 1530mm rearward of, the rearmost part of the drawing vehicle; and (b) if the supported load extends more than 9.15m rearward of

[continued on next page

(1) *Item No*	(2) *Vehicle or combination of vehicles*	(3) *Side marker lamps*
2—*cont.*		the rearmost part of the drawing vehicle, one lamp no part of the light-emitting surface of which is forward of, or more than 1530mm rearward of, the centre of the length of the load.

(2) The requirements specified in paragraph (1) do not apply to—

   (a) a combination of vehicles where any vehicle being drawn in that combination has broken down; or

   (b) a vehicle (not being a combination of vehicles) having an appliance or apparatus or carrying a load of a kind specified in the Table to regulation 82(7) or in regulation 82(8) of the Construction and Use Regulations [*q.v.*], if the conditions specified in paragraphs 3 and 4 (which provide for the special marking of projections from vehicles) of Schedule 12 to those Regulations are complied with in relation to the special appliance or apparatus or load as if the said conditions had been expressed in the said regulation 82 to apply in the case of every special appliance or apparatus or load of a kind specified in that regulation.

(3) Every side marker lamp fitted in accordance with this regulation shall comply with Part I of Schedule 9.

PART III

REGULATIONS GOVERNING THE MAINTENANCE AND USE OF LAMPS, REFLECTORS, REAR MARKINGS AND DEVICES

23. Maintenance of lamps, reflectors, rear markings and devices

B40.38   (1) No person shall use, or cause or permit to be used, on a road a vehicle unless every lamp, reflector, rear marking and device to which this paragraph applies is in good working order and, in the case of a lamp, clean.

(2) Save as provided in paragraph (3), paragraph (1) applies to—

   (a) every—

      (i) front position lamp,

      (ii) rear position lamp,

      (iii) headlamp,

      (iv) rear registration plate lamp,

      (v) side marker lamp,

      (vi) end-outline marker lamp,

      (vii) rear fog lamp,

      (viii) retro reflector, and

      (ix) rear marking of a type specified in Part I of . . . Schedule 19,

with which the vehicle is required by these Regulations to be fitted; and

   (b) every—

      (i) stop lamp,

      (ii) direction indicator,

      (iii) running lamp,

(iv) dim-dip device,

(v) headlamp levelling device, and

(vi) hazard warning signal device,

with which it is fitted.

(3) Paragraph (2) does not apply to—

(a) a rear fog lamp on a vehicle which is part of a combination of vehicles any part of which is not required by these Regulations to be fitted with a rear fog lamp;

(b) a rear fog lamp on a motor vehicle drawing a trailer;

(c) a defective lamp, reflector, dim-dip device or headlamp levelling device on a vehicle in use on a road between sunrise and sunset, if any such lamp, reflector or device became defective during the journey which is in progress or if arrangements have been made to remedy the defect with all reasonable expedition; or

(d) a lamp, reflector, dim-dip device, headlamp levelling device or rear marking on a combat vehicle in use on a road between sunrise and sunset.

[Regulation 23 is printed as amended by S.I. 1994 No. 2280.]   **B40.39**

24. Requirements about the use of front and rear position lamps, rear registration plate lamps, side marker lamps and end-outline marker lamps

(1) Save as provided in paragraphs (5) and (9), no person shall—   **B40.40**

(a) use, or cause or permit to be used, on a road any vehicle which is in motion—

(i) between sunset and sunrise, or

(ii) in seriously reduced visibility between sunrise and sunset; or

(b) allow to remain at rest, or cause or permit to be allowed to remain at rest, on a road any vehicle between sunset and sunrise

unless every front position lamp, rear position lamp, rear registration plate lamp, side marker lamp and end-outline marker lamp with which the vehicle is required by these Regulations to be fitted is kept lit and unobscured.

(2) Save as provided in paragraphs (5) and (9), where a solo motor bicycle is not fitted with a front position lamp, no person shall use it, or cause or permit it to be used, on a road (other than when it is parked) between sunset and sunrise or in seriously reduced visibility between sunrise and sunset, unless a headlamp is kept lit and unobscured.

(3) Save as provided in paragraphs (5) and (9), no person shall allow to remain parked, or cause or permit to be allowed to remain parked between sunset and sunrise—

(a) a motor bicycle combination which is required to be fitted only with a front position lamp on the sidecar; or

(b) a trailer to the front of which no other vehicle is attached and which is not required to be fitted with front position lamps,

unless a pair of front position lamps is fitted and kept lit and unobscured.

(4) Save as provided in paragraphs (5) and (9), no person shall allow to remain parked, or cause or permit to be allowed to remain parked between sunset and sunrise a solo motor bicycle which is not required to be fitted with a front position lamp, unless a front position lamp is fitted and kept lit and unobscured.

(5) Paragraphs (1), (2), (3) and (4) shall not apply in respect of a vehicle of a class specified in paragraph (7) which is parked on a road on which a speed limit of 30mph or less is in force and the vehicle is parked—

(a) in a parking place for which provision is made under section 6, or which is authorised under section 32 or designated under section 45 of the Road Traffic Regulation Act 1984, or which is set apart as a parking place under some other enactment or instrument and the vehicle is parked in a manner which does not contravene the provision of any enactment or instrument relating to the parking place; or

(b) in a lay-by—

    (i) the limits of which are indicated by a traffic sign consisting of the road marking shown in diagram 1010 in [Schedule 6 of the Traffic Signs Regulations and General Directions 1994] [*S.I. 1994 No. 1519, q.v.*]; or

    (ii) the surface of which is of a colour or texture which is different from that of the part of the carriageway of the road used primarily by through traffic; or

    (iii) the limits of which are indicated by a continuous strip of surface of a different colour or texture from that of the surface of the remainder of the carriageway of the road; or

(c) elsewhere than in such a parking place or lay-by if—

    (i) the vehicle is parked in one of the circumstances described in paragraph (8); and

    (ii) no part of the vehicle is less than 10m from the junction of any part of the carriageway of any road with the carriageway of the road on which it is parked whether that junction is on the same side of the road as that on which the vehicle is parked or not.

(6) Sub-paragraph (5)(c)(ii) shall be construed in accordance with the diagram in Schedule 22.

(7) The classes of vehicle referred to in paragraph (5) are—

(a) a motor vehicle being a goods vehicle the unladen weight of which does not exceed 1525kg;

(b) a passenger vehicle other than a bus;

(c) an invalid carriage; and

(d) a motor cycle or a pedal cycle in either case with or without a sidecar;

not being—

    (i) a vehicle to which a trailer is attached;

    (ii) a vehicle which is required to be fitted with lamps by regulation 21; or

    (iii) a vehicle carrying a load, if the load is required to be fitted with lamps by regulation 21.

(8) The circumstances referred to in paragraph (5)(c) are that—

(a) the vehicle is parked on a road on which the driving of vehicles otherwise than in one direction is prohibited at all times and its left or near side is as close as may be and parallel to the left-hand edge of the carriageway or its right or off side is as close as may be and parallel to the right-hand edge of the carriageway; or

(b) the vehicle is parked on a road on which such a prohibition does not exist and its left or near side is as close as may be and parallel to the edge of the carriageway.

(9) Paragraphs (1), (2), (3) and (4) do not apply in respect of—

(a) a solo motor bicycle or a pedal cycle being pushed along the left-hand edge of a carriageway;

(b) a pedal cycle waiting to proceed provided it is kept to the left-hand or near side edge of a carriageway; or

(c) a vehicle which is parked in an area on part of a highway on which roadworks are being carried out and which is bounded by amber lamps and other traffic signs so as to prevent the presence of the vehicle, its load or equipment being a danger to persons using the road.

[Regulation 24 is printed as amended by the Interpretation Act 1978, ss.17(2)(a) and 23(1).]   **B40.41**

25. Requirements about the use of headlamps and front fog lamps

(1) Save as provided in paragraph (2), no person shall use, or cause or permit to be used,   **B40.42**
on a road a vehicle which is fitted with obligatory dipped-beam headlamps unless every such lamp is kept lit—

(a) during the hours of darkness, except on a road which is a restricted road for the purposes of section 81 of the Road Traffic Regulation Act 1984 [*q.v.*] by virtue of a system of street lighting when it is lit; and

(b) in seriously reduced visibility.

(2) The provisions of paragraph (1) do not apply—

(a) in the case of a motor vehicle fitted with one obligatory dipped-beam headlamp or a solo motor bicycle or motor bicycle combination fitted with a pair of obligatory dipped-beam headlamps, if a main-beam headlamp or a front fog lamp is kept lit;

(b) in the case of a motor vehicle, other than a solo motor bicycle or motor bicycle combination, fitted with a pair of obligatory dipped-beam headlamps, if—

(i) a pair of main-beam headlamps is kept lit; or
(ii) in seriously reduced visibility, a pair of front fog lamps which is so fitted that the outermost part of the illuminated area of each lamp in the pair is not more than 400mm from the outer edge of the vehicle is kept lit;

(c) to a vehicle being drawn by another vehicle;

(d) to a vehicle while being used to propel a snow plough; or

(e) to a vehicle which is parked.

(3) For the purposes of this regulation a headlamp shall not be regarded as lit if its intensity is reduced by a dim-dip device.

26. Requirements about the use of warning beacons

No person shall use, or cause or permit to be used, on an unrestricted dual-carriageway   **B40.43**
road a vehicle which is required to be fitted with at least one warning beacon by regulation 17 unless every such beacon is kept lit.

27. Restrictions on the use of lamps other than those to which regulation 24 refers

No person shall use, or cause or permit to be used, on a road any vehicle on which any   **B40.44**
lamp, hazard warning signal device or warning beacon of a type specified in an item in column 2 of the Table below is used in a manner specified in that item in column 3.

TABLE

(1) Item No	(2) Type of lamp, hazard warning signal device or warning beacon	(3) Manner of use prohibited
1	Headlamp	(a) Used so as to cause undue dazzle or discomfort to other persons using the road. (b) Used so as to be lit when a vehicle is parked.
2	Front fog lamp	(a) Used so as to cause undue dazzle or discomfort to other persons using the road. (b) Used so as to be lit at any time other than in conditions of seriously reduced visibility. (c) Used so as to be lit when a vehicle is parked.
3	Rear fog lamp	(a) Used so as to cause undue dazzle or discomfort to the driver of a following vehicle. (b) Used so as to be lit at any time other than in conditions of seriously reduced visibility. (c) Save in the case of an emergency vehicle, used so as to be lit when a vehicle is parked.
4	Reversing lamp	Used so as to be lit except for the purpose of reversing the vehicle.
5	Hazard warning signal device	Used other than— (i) to warn persons using the road of a temporary obstruction when the vehicle is at rest; or (ii) on a motorway or unrestricted dual-carriageway, to warn following drivers of a need to slow down due to a temporary obstruction ahead; or (iii) in the case of a bus, to summon assistance for the driver or any person acting as a conductor or inspector on the vehicle. [or] [(iv) in the case of a bus to which prescribed signs are fitted as described in sub-paragraphs (a) and (b) of regulation 17A(1), when the vehicle is stationary and children under the age of 16 years

[*continued on next page*

(1) *Item No*	(2) *Type of lamp, hazard warning signal device or warning beacon*	(3) *Manner of use prohibited*
5— *cont.*		are entering or leaving, or are about to enter or leave, or have just left the vehicle.]
6	Warning beacon emitting blue light and special warning lamp	Used so as to be lit except— (i) at the scene of an emergency; or (ii) when it is necessary or desirable either to indicate to persons using the road the urgency of the purpose for which the vehicle is being used, or to warn persons of the presence of the vehicle or a hazard on the road.
7	Warning beacon emitting amber light	Used so as to be lit except— (i) at the scene of an emergency; (ii) when it is necessary or desirable to warn persons of the presence of the vehicle; and (iii) in the case of a breakdown vehicle, while it is being used in connection with, and in the immediate vicinity of, an accident or breakdown, or while it is being used to draw a broken-down vehicle.
8	Warning beacon emitting green light	Used so as to be lit except whilst occupied by a medical practitioner registered by the General Medical Council (whether with full, provisional or limited registration) and used for the purposes of an emergency.
9	Warning beacon emitting yellow light	Used so as to be lit on a road.
10	Work lamp	(a) Used so as to cause undue dazzle or discomfort to the driver of any vehicle. (b) Used so as to be lit except for the purpose of illuminating a working area, accident, breakdown or works in the vicinity of the vehicle.
11	Any other lamp	Used so as to cause undue dazzle or discomfort to other persons using the road.

[Regulation 27 is printed as amended by S.I. 1994 No. 2280.]

PART IV

TESTING AND INSPECTION OF LIGHTING EQUIPMENT AND REFLECTORS

28. Testing and inspection of lighting equipment and reflectors

B40.46   The provisions of regulation 74 of the Construction and Use Regulations [*q.v.*] apply in respect of lighting equipment and reflectors with which a vehicle is required by these Regulations to be fitted in the same way as they apply in respect of brakes, silencers, steering gear and tyres.

SCHEDULE 1

OBLIGATORY LAMPS, REFLECTORS, REAR MARKINGS AND DEVICES

TABLE I

B40.47   Motor vehicle having three or more wheels not being a vehicle to which any other Table in this Schedule applies

(1) *Type of lamp, reflector, rear marking or device*	(2) *Schedule in which relevant installation and performance requirements are specified*	(3) *Exceptions*
Front position lamp	Schedule 2: Part I	None.

Dim-dip device or running lamp	Schedule 3:
	Part I
		A vehicle having a maximum speed not exceeding 40mph;
		
		A vehicle first used before 1st April 1987;
		
		A home forces' vehicle;
		
		A vehicle in respect of which the following conditions are satisfied—
		  (a) there is fitted to the vehicle all the lighting and light-signalling devices listed in items 1.5.7 to 1.5.20 of Annex I of [Community Directive 76/756/EEC as last amended by Directive 89/278/EEC or Community Directive 76/756/EEC as last amended by Directive 91/663/EEC] which are required to be fitted under that Annex; and
		  (b) all those devices are so installed that they comply with the requirements set out in items 3 and 4 of that Annex including, in particular, item 4.2.6 (Alignment of dipped-beam headlamps).

[*continued on next page*

(1) *Type of lamp, reflector, rear marking or device*	(2) *Schedule in which relevant installation and performance requirements are specified*	(3) *Exceptions*
Dipped-beam headlamp	Schedule 4: Part I	A vehicle having a maximum speed not exceeding 15mph;
		A vehicle first used before 1st April 1986 being an agricultural vehicle or a works truck;
		A vehicle first used before 1st January 1931.
Main-beam headlamp	Schedule 5: Part I	A vehicle having a maximum speed not exceeding 25mph;
		A vehicle first used before 1st April 1986 being an agricultural vehicle or a works truck;
		A vehicle first used before 1st January 1931.
Direction indicator	Schedule 7: Part I	An invalid carriage having a maximum speed not exceeding 4mph and any other vehicle having a maximum speed not exceeding 15mph;
		An agricultural vehicle having an unladen weight not exceeding 255kg;
		A vehicle first used before 1st April 1986 being an agricultural vehicle, an industrial tractor or a works truck;
		A vehicle first used before 1st January 1936.
Hazard warning signal device	Schedule 8: Part I	A vehicle not required to be fitted with direction indicators;
		A vehicle first used before 1st April 1986.
Side marker lamp	Schedule 9: Part I	A vehicle having a maximum speed not exceeding 25mph;
		A passenger vehicle;
		An incomplete vehicle proceeding to a works for completion or to a place where it is to be stored or displayed for sale;
		A vehicle the overall length of which does not exceed 6m;
		A vehicle first used before 1st April 1991;
		[A vehicle first used before 1st April 1996 in respect of which the following conditions are satisfied]—

[*continued on next page*

(1) Type of lamp, reflector, rear marking or device	(2) Schedule in which relevant installation and performance requirements are specified	(3) Exceptions
Side marker lamp—*cont.*		(a) there is fitted to the vehicle all the lighting and light-signalling devices listed in items 1.5.7 to 1.5.20 of Annex I of [Community Directive 76/756/ EEC as last amended by Directive 89/278/EEC or Community Directive 76/756/ EEC as last amended by Directive 91/663/EEC] which are required to be fitted under that Annex; and (b) all those devices are so installed that they comply with the requirements set out in items 3 and 4 of that Annex including, in particular, item 4.2.6 (Alignment of dipped-beam headlamps).
Rear position lamp	Schedule 10: Part I	None.
Rear fog lamp	Schedule 11: Part I	A vehicle having a maximum speed not exceeding 25mph; A vehicle first used before 1st April 1986 being an agricultural vehicle or a works truck; A vehicle first used before 1st April 1980; A vehicle having an overall width which does not exceed 1300mm.
Stop lamp	Schedule 12: Part I	A vehicle having a maximum speed not exceeding 25mph; A vehicle first used before 1st April 1986 being an agricultural vehicle or a works truck; A vehicle first used before 1st January 1936.
End-outline marker lamp	Schedule 13: Part I	A vehicle having a maximum speed not exceeding 25mph; A motor vehicle having an overall width not exceeding 2100mm; An incomplete vehicle proceeding to a works for completion or to a place where it is to be stored or displayed for sale;

[*continued on next page*

(1) *Type of lamp, reflector, rear marking or device*	(2) *Schedule in which relevant installation and performance requirements are specified*	(3) *Exceptions*
End-outline marker-lamp —*cont.*		A motor vehicle first used before 1st April 1991.
Rear registration plate lamp	Schedule 15	A vehicle not required to be fitted with a rear registration plate; A works truck.
Side retro reflector	Schedule 17: Part I	A vehicle having a maximum speed not exceeding 25mph; A goods vehicle— 　(a)　first used on or after 1st April 1986, the overall length of which does not exceed 6m; or 　(b)　first used before 1st April 1986, the overall length of which does not exceed 8m; A passenger vehicle; An incomplete vehicle proceeding to a works for completion or to a place where it is to be stored or displayed for sale; A vehicle primarily constructed for moving excavated material and being used by virtue of an Order under section 44 of the Act; A mobile crane or engineering plant.
Rear retro reflector	Schedule 18: Part I	None.
Rear marking	Schedule 19: Part I	A vehicle having a maximum speed not exceeding 25mph; A vehicle first used before 1st August 1982, the unladen weight of which does not exceed 3050kg; A vehicle the maximum gross weight of which does not exceed 7500kg; A passenger vehicle not being an articulated bus; A tractive unit for an articulated vehicle; An incomplete vehicle proceeding to a works for completion or to a place where it is to be stored or displayed for sale; A vehicle first used before 1st April 1986 being an agricultural vehicle, a works truck or engineering plant;

[*continued on next page*

(1) *Type of lamp, reflector, rear marking or device*	(2) *Schedule in which relevant installation and performance requirements are specified*	(3) *Exceptions*
Rear marking —cont.		A vehicle first used before 1st January 1940; A home forces' vehicle; A vehicle constructed or adapted for— (a) fire fighting or fire salvage; (b) servicing or controlling aircraft; (c) heating and dispensing tar or other material for the construction or maintenance of roads; or (d) transporting two or more vehicles or vehicle bodies or two or more boats.

TABLE II

B40.48 Solo motor bicycle and motor bicycle combination

(1) *Type of lamp or reflector*	(2) *Schedule in which relevant installation and performance requirements are specified*	(3) *Exceptions*
Front position lamp	Schedule 2: Part I	A solo motor bicycle fitted with a headlamp.
Dipped-beam headlamp	Schedule 4: Part I	A vehicle first used before 1st January 1931.
Main-beam headlamp	Schedule 5: Part I	A vehicle having a maximum speed not exceeding 25mph; A vehicle first used before 1st January 1972 and having an engine with a capacity of less than 50cc; A vehicle first used before 1st January 1931.
Direction indicator	Schedule 7: Part I	A vehicle having a maximum speed not exceeding 25mph; A vehicle first used before 1st April 1986; A vehicle which is constructed or adapted primarily for use off roads

[*continued on next page*

(1) *Type of lamp or reflector*	(2) *Schedule in which relevant installation and performance requirements are specified*	(3) *Exceptions*
Direction indicator—*cont.*		(whether by reason of its tyres, suspension, ground clearance or otherwise) and which can carry only one person or which, in the case of a motor bicycle combination, can carry only the rider and one passenger in the sidecar.
Rear position lamp	Schedule 10: Part I	None.
Stop lamp	Schedule 12: Part I	A vehicle having a maximum speed not exceeding 25mph; A vehicle first used before 1st April 1986 and having an engine with a capacity of less than 50cc; A vehicle first used before 1st January 1936.
Rear registration plate lamp	Schedule 15	A vehicle not required to be fitted with a rear registration plate.
Rear retro reflector	Schedule 18: Part I	None.

TABLE III

Pedal cycle

(1) *Type of lamp or reflector*	(2) *Schedule in which relevant installation and performance requirements are specified*	(3) *Exceptions*
Front position lamp	Schedule 2: Part I	None.
Rear position lamp	Schedule 10: Part I	None.
Rear retro reflector	Schedule 18: Part I	None.
Pedal retro reflector	Schedule 20: Part I	A pedal cycle manufactured before 1st October 1985.

TABLE IV

B40.50 Pedestrian-controlled vehicle, horse-drawn vehicle and track-laying vehicle

(1) Type of lamp or reflector	(2) Schedule in which relevant installation and performance requirements are specified	(3) Exceptions
Front position lamp	Schedule 2: Part I	None.
Rear position lamp	Schedule 10: Part I	None.
Rear retro reflector	Schedule 18: Part I	None.

TABLE V

B40.51 Vehicle drawn or propelled by hand

(1) Type of lamp or reflector	(2) Schedule in which relevant installation and performance requirements are specified	(3) Exceptions
Front position lamp	Schedule 2: Part I	None.
Rear position lamp	Schedule 10: Part I	A vehicle fitted with a rear retro reflector.
Rear retro reflector	Schedule 18: Part I	A vehicle fitted with a rear position lamp.

TABLE VI

B40.52 Trailer drawn by a motor vehicle

(1) Type of lamp, reflector or rear marking	(2) Schedule in which relevant installation and performance requirements are specified	(3) Exceptions
Front position lamp	Schedule 2: Part I	A trailer with an overall width not exceeding 1600mm; A trailer manufactured before 1st October 1985 the overall length of which, excluding any drawbar and any

[*continued on next page*

(1) *Type of lamp, reflector or rear marking*	(2) *Schedule in which relevant installation and performance requirements are specified*	(3) *Exceptions*
Front position lamp—*cont.*		fitting for its attachment, does not exceed 2300mm; A trailer constructed or adapted for the carriage and launching of a boat.
Direction indicator	Schedule 7: Part I	A trailer manufactured before 1st September 1965; An agricultural vehicle or a works trailer in either case manufactured before 1st October 1990.

Side marker lamp	Schedule 9:
	Part I
		A trailer the overall length of which, excluding any drawbar and any fitting for its attachment, does not exceed—
		   (a) 6m,
		   (b) 9.15m in the case of a trailer manufactured before 1st October 1990;
		An incomplete trailer proceeding to a works for completion or to a place where it is to be stored or displayed for sale;
		
		An agricultural vehicle or a works trailer;
		
		A caravan;
		
		A trailer constructed or adapted for the carriage and launching of a boat;
		
		[A trailer manufactured before 1st October 1995 in respect of which the following conditions are satisfied]—
		   (a) there is fitted to the trailer all the lighting and light-signalling devices listed in items 1.5.7 to 1.5.20 of Annex I of [Community Directive 76/756/EEC as last amended by Directive 89/278/EEC or Community Directive 76/756/EEC as last amended by Directive 91/663/EEC] which are required to be fitted under that Annex; and
		   (b) all those devices are so installed and maintained that they comply with the requirements

[continued on next page

(1) *Type of lamp, reflector or rear marking*	(2) *Schedule in which relevant installation and performance requirements are specified*	(3) *Exceptions*
Side marker lamp—*cont.*		set out in items 3 and 4 of that Annex.
Rear position lamp	Schedule 10: Part I	None.
Rear fog lamp	Schedule 11: Part I	A trailer manufactured before 1st April 1980;
		A trailer the overall width of which does not exceed 1300mm;
		An agricultural vehicle or a works trailer.
Stop lamp	Schedule 12: Part I	An agricultural vehicle or a works trailer.
End-outline marker lamp	Schedule 13: Part I	A trailer having an overall width not exceeding 2100mm;
		An incomplete trailer proceeding to a works for completion or to a place where it is to be stored or displayed for sale;
		An agricultural vehicle or a works trailer;
		A trailer manufactured before 1st October 1990.
Rear registration plate lamp	Schedule 15	A trailer not required to be fitted with a rear registration plate.
Side retro reflector	Schedule 17: Part I	A trailer the overall length of which, excluding any drawbar, does not exceed 5m;
		An incomplete trailer proceeding to a works for completion or to a place where it is to be stored or displayed for sale;
		Engineering plant;
		A trailer primarily constructed for moving excavated material and which is being used by virtue of an Order under section 44 of the Act.
Front retro reflector	Schedule 21: Part I	A trailer manufactured before 1st October 1990;
		An agricultural vehicle or a works trailer.
Rear retro reflector	Schedule 18: Part I	None.

[*continued on next page*

(1) Type of lamp, reflector or rear marking	(2) Schedule in which relevant installation and performance requirements are specified	(3) Exceptions
Rear marking	Schedule 19: Part I	A trailer manufactured before 1st August 1982 the unladen weight of which does not exceed 1020kg; A trailer the maximum gross weight of which does not exceed 3500kg; An incomplete trailer proceeding to a works for completion or to a place where it is to be stored or displayed for sale; An agricultural vehicle, a works trailer or engineering plant; A trailer drawn by a bus; A home forces' vehicle; A trailer constructed or adapted for— (a) fire fighting or fire salvage; (b) servicing or controlling aircraft; (c) heating and dispensing tar or other material for the construction or maintenance of roads; (d) carrying asphalt or macadam, in each case being mixing or drying plant; or (e) transporting two or more vehicles or vehicle bodies or two or more boats.

TABLE VII

Trailer drawn by a pedal cycle   **B40.53**

(1) Type of lamp, reflector or rear marking	(2) Schedule in which relevant installation and performance requirements are specified	(3) Exceptions
Rear position lamp	Schedule 10: Part I	None.
Rear retro reflector	Schedule 18: Part I	None.

[Tables I and VI in Schedule 1 are printed as amended by S.I. 1994 No. 2280.]   **B40.54**

(Regulations 18 and 20)   SCHEDULE 2

PART I

REQUIREMENTS RELATING TO OBLIGATORY FRONT POSITION LAMPS AND TO OPTIONAL
FRONT POSITION LAMPS TO THE EXTENT SPECIFIED IN PART II

B40.55   **1.**   Number—

(a) Any vehicle not covered by sub-paragraph (b), (c), (d), (e) or (f):	Two
(b) A pedal cycle with less than four wheels and without a sidecar:	One
(c) A solo motor bicycle:	One
(d) A motor bicycle combination with a headlamp on the motor bicycle:	One, on the sidecar
(e) An invalid carriage:	One
(f) A vehicle drawn or propelled by hand:	One

B40.56   **2.**   Position—

(a) Longitudinal:	No requirement
(b) Lateral—	
(i) Where two front position lamps are required to be fitted—	
(A) Maximum distance from the side of the vehicle—	
(1) A motor vehicle first used on or after 1st April 1986:	400mm
(2) A trailer manufactured on or after 1st October 1985:	150mm
(3) Any other vehicle manufactured on or after 1st October 1985:	400mm
(4) A motor vehicle first used before 1st April 1986 and any other vehicle manufactured before 1st October 1985:	510mm
(B) Minimum separation distance between front position lamps:	No requirement
(ii) Where one front position lamp is required to be fitted—	
(A) A sidecar forming part of a motor bicycle combination:	On the centre-line of the sidecar or on the side of the sidecar furthest from the motor bicycle
(B) Any other vehicle:	On the centre-line or offside of the vehicle
(c) Vertical—	
(i) Maximum height above the ground—	
(A) Any vehicle not covered by sub-paragraph (b), (c) or (d):	1500mm or, if the structure of the vehicle makes this impracticable, 2100mm
(B) A motor vehicle first used before 1st April 1986 and a trailer manufactured before 1st October 1985:	2300mm

(C) A motor vehicle, first used on or after 1st April 1986, having a maximum speed not exceeding 25mph: 2100mm

(D) A [bus] and a road clearance vehicle   No requirement

(ii) Minimum height above the ground   No requirement

3. Angles of visibility—   **B40.57**

(a) A motor vehicle (not being a motor bicycle combination or an agricultural vehicle) first used on or after 1st April 1986 and a trailer manufactured on or after 1st October 1985—

(i) Horizontal—

(A) Where one lamp is required to be fitted: 80° to the left and to the right

(B) Where two lamps are required to be fitted: 80° outwards and 45° inwards (5° inwards in the case of a trailer)

(ii) Vertical—

(A) Any case not covered by sub-paragraph (B):   15° above and below the horizontal

(B) Where the highest part of the illuminated area of the lamp is less than 750 mm above the ground: 15° above and 5° below the horizontal

(b) Any other vehicle: Visible to the front

4. Alignment: To the front

5. Markings [(see also regulation 3(6))]—   **B40.58**

(a) A motor vehicle (other than a solo motor bicycle or a motor bicycle combination) first used on or after 1st January 1972 and a trailer manufactured on or after 1st October 1985:   An approval mark

(b) A solo motor bicycle and a motor bicycle combination in either case first used on or after 1st April 1986:   An approval mark

(c) Any other vehicle manufactured or first used on or after 1st October 1990 [and before the 1st October 1995]:   An approval mark or a British Standard mark

[(ca) Any other vehicle manufactured on or after 1st October 1995:   An approval mark or the British Standard mark which is specified in sub-paragraph (b) of the definition of "British Standard mark" below.]

(d) Any other vehicle: No requirement

6. Size of illuminated area: No requirement

7. Colour: White or, if incorporated in a headlamp which is capable of emitting only a yellow light, yellow   **B40.59**

8.   Wattage: No requirement

B40.60   **9.**   Intensity—
(a) A front position lamp bearing any of the   No requirement
markings mentioned in paragraph 5:
(b) Any other front position lamp: Visible from a reasonable
distance

10.   Electrical connections: No individual requirement

B40.61   **11.**   Tell-tale: No requirement

12.   Other requirements—
(a) Except in the case of a vehicle covered by sub-paragraph (b), where two front
position lamps are required to be fitted they shall form a pair.
(b) In the case of a trailer manufactured before 1st October 1985 and a motor
bicycle combination, where two front position lamps are required to be fitted
they shall be fitted on each side of the longitudinal axis of the vehicle.

B40.62   **13.**   Definitions—
In this Schedule—
"*approval mark*" means—
(a) in relation to a solo motor bicycle or a motor bicycle combination, a marking
designated as an approval mark by regulation 4 of the Designation of Approval
Marks Regulations and shown at item 50A of Schedule 2 to those Regulations,
and
(b) in relation to any other . . . vehicle . . . , either—
    (i) a marking designated as an approval mark by regulation 5 of the
Designation of Approval Marks Regulations and shown at item 5 of
Schedule 4 to those Regulations, or
    (ii) a marking designated as an approval mark by regulation 4 of the
Designation of Approval Marks Regulations and shown at item 7 of
Schedule 2 to those Regulations;
["*British Standard mark*" means—
(a) the mark indicated in the specification for photometric and physical requirements for lighting equipment published by the British Standards Institution
under the references BS 6102: Part 3: 1986 namely "6102/3"; or
(b) the mark indicated in the specification for photometric and physical requirements for lighting equipment published by the British Standards Institution
under the references BS 6102: Part 3: 1986 as amended by AMD 5821 published on the 29th April 1988, namely "6102/3".]

B40.63   *[Part I of Schedule 2 is printed as amended by S.I. 1994 No. 2280.]*

PART II

REQUIREMENTS RELATING TO OPTIONAL FRONT POSITION LAMPS

B40.64   **1.** In the case of a solo motor bicycle first used on or after 1st April 1991 which is not
fitted with any obligatory front position lamp, not more than two may be fitted which must
comply with the requirement specified in paragraph 7 of Part I. Where two are fitted these
shall be situated as close together as possible.

2. In the case of a solo motor bicycle first used on or after 1st April 1991 which is fitted with one obligatory front position lamp, not more than one additional lamp may be fitted which must comply with the requirement specified in paragraph 7 of Part I and shall be situated as close as possible to the obligatory front position lamp.

3. In the case of any other vehicle the only requirement prescribed by these Regulations in respect of any which are fitted is that in paragraph 7 of Part I. **B40.65**

SCHEDULE 3 (Regulations 18 and 20)

PART I

REQUIREMENTS RELATING TO OBLIGATORY DIM-DIP DEVICES AND RUNNING LAMPS

1. A dim-dip device fitted to satisfy regulation 18 shall cause light to be emitted from the dipped-beam filament of each obligatory dipped-beam headlamp, each such light having, so far as is practicable, an intensity of between 10 and 20 per cent of the intensity of the normal dipped beam. **B40.66**

2. Running lamps fitted to satisfy regulation 18 shall be in the form of a matched pair of front lamps, each of which—
  (a) is fitted in a position in which an obligatory front position lamp may lawfully be fitted, and
  (b) is capable of emitting white light to the front having an intensity of not less than 200 candelas, measured from directly in front of the centre of the lamp in a direction parallel to the longitudinal axis of the vehicle, and of not more than 800 candelas in any direction.

[**3.** The electrical connections to the obligatory dim-dip device shall be such that the light output specified in paragraph 1 above is automatically emitted whenever the following four conditions are satisfied, namely— **B40.67**
  (a) the engine is running, or the key or devices which control the starting or stopping of the engine are in the normal position for when the vehicle is being driven
  (b) the obligatory main beam and dipped beam headlamps are switched off;
  (c) any front fog lamp fitted to the vehicle is switched off; and
  (d) the obligatory front position lamps are switched on.]

[**4.** The electrical connections to the obligatory running lamps shall be such that the light output specified in paragraph 2 above is automatically emitted, whenever the conditions set out in sub-paragraphs (a), (b) and (c) of paragraph 3 are satisfied.]

[Part I of Schedule 3 is printed as amended by S.I. 1994 No. 2280.] **B40.68**

PART II

REQUIREMENTS RELATING TO OPTIONAL DIM-DIP DEVICES AND RUNNING LAMPS

There is no requirement relating to an optional dim-dip device or an optional running lamp. **B40.69**

(Regulations 18 and 20) SCHEDULE 4

PART I

REQUIREMENTS RELATING TO OBLIGATORY DIPPED-BEAM HEADLAMPS AND TO OPTIONAL
DIPPED-BEAM HEADLAMPS TO THE EXTENT SPECIFIED IN PART II

B40.70 **1.** Number—

(a)	Any vehicle not covered by sub-paragraph (b), (c), (d) or (e):	Two
(b)	A solo motor bicycle and a motor bicycle combination:	One
(c)	A motor vehicle with three wheels, other than a motor bicycle combination, first used before 1st January 1972:	One
(d)	A motor vehicle with three wheels, other than a motor bicycle combination, first used on or after 1st January 1972 and which has an unladen weight of not more than 400kg and an overall width of not more than 1300mm:	One
(e)	A bus first used before 1st October 1969:	One

B40.71 **2.** Position—

(a)	Longitudinal:	No requirement
(b)	Lateral—	
	(i) Where two dipped-beam headlamps are required to be fitted—	
	(A) Maximum distance from the side of the vehicle—	
	(1) Any vehicle not covered by sub-paragraph (2) or (3):	400mm
	(2) A vehicle first used before 1st January 1972:	No requirement
	(3) An agricultural vehicle, engineering plant and an industrial tractor:	No requirement
	(B) Minimum separation distance between a pair of dipped-beam headlamps:	No requirement
	(ii) Where one dipped-beam headlamp is required to be fitted—	
	(A) Any vehicle not covered by sub-paragraph (B):	(i) On the centre-line of the motor vehicle (disregarding any sidecar forming part of a motor bicycle combination), or (ii) At any distance from the side of the motor vehicle (disregarding any sidecar forming part of a motor bicycle combination) provided that a duplicate lamp is fitted on

the other side so that together they form a matched pair. In such a case, both lamps shall be regarded as obligatory lamps.

(B) A bus first used before 1st October 1969:

No requirement

(c) Vertical—
  (i) Maximum height above the ground—
    (A) Any vehicle not covered by sub-paragraph (b):

1200mm

    (B) A vehicle first used before 1st January 1952, an agricultural vehicle, a road clearance vehicle, an aerodrome fire tender, an aerodrome runway sweeper, an industrial tractor, engineering plant and a home forces' vehicle:

No requirement

  (ii) Minimum height above the ground—
    (A) Any vehicle not covered by sub-paragraph (b):

500mm

    (B) A vehicle first used before 1st January 1956:

No requirement

3. Angles of visibility: No requirement   **B40.72**

4. Alignment—
When a vehicle is at its kerbside weight and has a weight of 75kg on the driver's seat, and any manual headlamp levelling device control is set to the stop position, the alignment of every dipped-beam headlamp shall, as near as practicable, be as follows:
  (a) In the case of a vehicle having a maximum speed exceeding 25mph—
    (i) If the dipped-beam headlamp bears an approval mark its aim shall be set so that the horizontal part of the cut-off of the beam pattern is inclined downwards as indicated by the vehicle manufacturer in a marking on the vehicle, as mentioned in sub-paragraph 12(b) or, where no such marking is provided—
      (A) 1.3 per cent if the height of the centre of the headlamp is not more than 850mm above the ground, or
      (B) 2 per cent if the height of the centre of the headlamp is more than 850mm above the ground;
    (ii) If the dipped-beam headlamp does not bear an approval mark and the headlamp can also be used as a main-beam headlamp its aim shall be set so that the centre of the main-beam pattern is horizontal or inclined slightly below the horizontal;
    (iii) If the dipped-beam headlamp does not bear an approval mark and the headlamp cannot also be used as a main-beam headlamp its aim shall be set so as not to cause undue dazzle or discomfort to other persons using the road;
  (b) In the case of a vehicle having a maximum speed not exceeding 25mph—
    (i) If the dipped-beam headlamp bears an approval mark or not and the headlamp can also be used as a main-beam headlamp its aim shall be set so

that the centre of the main-beam pattern is horizontal or inclined slightly below the horizontal;

(ii) If the dipped-beam headlamp bears an approval mark or not and the headlamp cannot also be used as a main-beam headlamp its aim shall be set so as not to cause undue dazzle or discomfort to other persons using the road.

B40.73 5. Markings—

(a) Any vehicle not covered by sub-paragraph (b), (c) or (d):   An approval mark or a British Standard mark

(b) A motor vehicle first used before 1st April 1986:   No requirement

(c) A three-wheeled motor vehicle, not being a motor bicycle combination, first used on or after 1st April 1986 and having a maximum speed not exceeding 50mph: No requirement

(d) A solo motor bicycle and a motor bicycle combination: No requirement

B40.74 6. Size of illuminated area: No requirement

7. Colour: White or yellow

8. Wattage—

(a) A motor vehicle with four or more wheels first used on or after 1st April 1986:   No requirement

(b) A three-wheeled motor vehicle, not being a motor bicycle combination, first used on or after 1st April 1986—

    (i) having a maximum speed not exceeding 50mph: 15 watts minimum

    (ii) having a maximum speed exceeding 50 mph: No requirement

(c) A motor vehicle with four or more wheels first used before 1st April 1986:   30 watts minimum

(d) A three-wheeled motor vehicle, not being a motor bicycle combination, first used before 1st April 1986:   24 watts minimum

(e) A solo motor bicycle and a motor bicycle combination—

    (i) having an engine not exceeding 250cc and a maximum speed not exceeding 25mph: 10 watts minimum

    (ii) having an engine not exceeding 250cc and a maximum speed exceeding 25mph: 15 watts minimum

    (iii) having an engine exceeding 250cc: 24 watts minimum

9. Intensity: No requirement

B40.75 10. Electrical connections—
Where a matched pair of dipped-beam headlamps is fitted they shall be capable of being switched on and off simultaneously and not otherwise.

11. Tell-tale: No requirement

12. Other requirements—

    (a) Every dipped-beam headlamp shall be so constructed that the direction of the beam of light emitted therefrom can be adjusted whilst the vehicle is stationary.

    (b) Every vehicle which—

        (i) is fitted with dipped-beam headlamps bearing an approval mark,

        (ii) has a maximum speed exceeding 25mph, and

        (iii) is first used on or after 1st April 1991

    shall be marked with a clearly legible and indelible marking, as illustrated in Schedule 23, close to either the headlamps or the manufacturer's plate showing the setting recommended by the manufacturer for the downward inclination of the horizontal part of the cut-off of the beam pattern of the dipped-beam headlamps when the vehicle is at its kerbside weight and has a weight of 75kg on the driver's seat. That setting shall be a single figure—

        (A) between 1 and 1.5 per cent if the height of the centre of the headlamp is not more than 850mm above the ground, and

        (B) between 1 and 2 per cent if the height of the centre of the headlamp is more than 850mm above the ground.

    (c) Every dipped-beam headlamp fitted to a vehicle first used on or after 1st April 1986 in accordance with this part of this Schedule shall be designed for a vehicle which is intended to be driven on the left-hand side of the road.

    (d) Where two dipped-beam headlamps are required to be fitted they shall form a matched pair.

13. Definitions—

In this Schedule—

"*approval mark*" means either—

    (a) a marking designated as an approval mark by regulation 5 of the Designation of Approval Marks Regulations and shown at item 12 or 13 or 14 or 16 or, in the case of a vehicle having a maximum 25mph, 27 or 28 of Schedule 4 to those Regulations, or

    (b) a marking designated as an approval mark by regulation 4 of the Designation of Approval Marks Regulations and shown at item 1A or 1B or 1C or 1E or 5A or 5B or 5C or 5E or 8C or 8D or 8E or 8F or 8G or 8H or 8K or 8L or 20C or 20D or 20E or 20F or 20G or 20H or 20K or 20L or 31A or 31C or, in the case of a vehicle having a maximum speed not exceeding 25mph, 1H or 1I or 5H or 5I or Schedule 2 to those Regulations; and

"*British Standard mark*" means the specification for sealed beam headlamps published by the British Standards Institution under the reference BS AU 40: Part 4A: 1966 as amended by Amendment AMD 2188 published in December 1976, namely "B.S. AU40".

PART II

REQUIREMENTS RELATING TO OPTIONAL DIPPED-BEAM HEADLAMPS

1. In the case of a vehicle with three or more wheels having a maximum speed exceeding 25mph first used on or after 1st April 1991, two and not more than two may be fitted and the only requirements prescribed by these Regulations in respect of any which are fitted are—

    (a) those specified in paragraphs 2(c), 4, 7, 10 and 12 (a) of Part I,

    (b) that they are designed for a vehicle which is intended to be driven on the right-hand side of the road,

(c) that they form a matched pair, and

(d) that their electrical connections are such that not more than one pair of dipped-beam headlamps is capable of being illuminated at a time.

2. In the case of any other vehicle, any number may be fitted and the only requirements prescribed by these Regulations in respect of any which are fitted are those specified in paragraphs 2(c), 4, 7 and 12(a) of Part I.

(Regulations 18 and 20)   SCHEDULE 5

PART I

REQUIREMENTS RELATING TO OBLIGATORY MAIN-BEAM HEADLAMPS AND TO OPTIONAL
MAIN-BEAM HEADLAMPS TO THE EXTENT SPECIFIED IN PART II

B40.79 **1.** Number—

(a)	Any vehicle not covered by sub-paragraph (b), (c) or (d):	Two
(b)	A solo motor bicycle and motor bicycle combination:	One
(c)	A motor vehicle with three wheels, other than a motor bicycle combination, first used before 1st January 1972:	One
(d)	A motor vehicle with three wheels, other than a motor bicycle combination, first used on or after 1st January 1972 and which has an unladen weight of not more than 400kg and an overall width of not more than 1300mm:	One

B40.80 **2.** Position—

(a) Longitudinal: No requirement

(b) Lateral—

(i) Where two dipped-beam headlamps are required to be fitted—

(A) Maximum distance from the side of the vehicle: The outer edges of the illuminated areas must in no case be closer to the side of the vehicle than the outer edges of the illuminated areas of the obligatory dipped-beam headlamps.

(B) Maximum separation distance between a pair of main-beam headlamps: No requirement

(ii) Where one main-beam headlamp is required to be fitted: (i) On the centre-line of the motor vehicle (disregarding any sidecar forming part of a motor bicycle combination), or
(ii) At any distance from

the side of the vehicle (disregarding any sidecar, forming part of a motor bicycle combination) provided that a duplicate lamp is fitted on the other side so that together they form a matched pair. In such a case, both lamps shall be treated as obligatory lamps.

    (c) Vertical: No requirement

3. Angles of visibility: No requirement   **B40.81**

4. Alignment: To the front

5. Markings—   **B40.82**
    (a) Any vehicle not covered by sub-paragraph (b), (c), or (d):   An approval mark or a British Standard mark
    (b) A motor vehicle first used before 1st April 1986:   No requirement
    (c) A three-wheeled motor vehicle, not being a motor bicycle combination, first used on or after 1st April 1986 and having a maximum speed not exceeding 50mph: No requirement
    (d) A solo motor bicycle and a motor bicycle combination: No requirement

6. Size of illuminated area: No requirement

7. Colour: White or yellow   **B40.83**

8. Wattage—
    (a) A motor vehicle, other than a solo motor bicycle or motor bicycle combination, first used on or after 1st April 1986:   No requirement
    (b) A motor vehicle, other than a solo motor bicycle or a motor bicycle combination, first used before 1st April 1986:   30 watts minimum
    (c) A solo motor bicycle and a motor bicycle combination—
        (i) having an engine not exceeding 250cc: 15 watts minimum
        (ii) having an engine exceeding 250cc: 30 watts minimum

9. Intensity: No requirement   **B40.84**

10. Electrical connections—
    (a) Every main-beam headlamp shall be so constructed that the light emitted therefrom—
        (i) can be deflected at the will of the driver to become a dipped beam, or
        (ii) can be extinguished by the operation of a device which at the same time either—

(A) causes the lamp to emit a dipped beam, or

(B) causes another lamp to emit a dipped beam.

(b) Where a matched pair of main-beam headlamps is fitted they shall be capable of being switched on and off simultaneously and not otherwise.

B40.85 **11.** Tell-tale—

(a) Any vehicle not covered by sub-paragraph (b):   A circuit-closed tell-tale shall be fitted

(b) A motor vehicle first used before 1st April 1986:   No requirement

12. Other requirements—

(a) Every main-beam headlamp shall be so constructed that the direction of the beam of light emitted therefrom can be adjusted whilst the vehicle is stationary.

(b) Except in the case of a bus first used before 1st October 1969, where two main-beam headlamps are required to be fitted they shall form a matched pair.

B40.86 **13.** Definitions—

In this Schedule—

"*approval mark*" means—

(a) a marking designated as an approval mark by regulation 5 of the Designation of Approval Marks Regulations and shown at item 12 or 13 or 17 of Schedule 4 to those Regulations; or

(b) a marking designated as an approval mark by regulation 4 of the Designation of Approval Marks Regulations and shown at item 1A or 1B or 1F or 5A or 5B or 5F or 8C or 8D or 8E or 8F or 8M or 8N or 20C or 20D or 20E or 20F or 20M or 20N or 31A or 31D of Schedule 2 to those Regulations; and

"*British Standard mark*" means the specification for sealed beam headlamps published by the British Standards Institution under the reference BS AU 40: Part 4a: 1966 as amended by Amendment AMD 2188 published in December 1976, namely "B.S. AU40".

PART II

REQUIREMENTS RELATING TO OPTIONAL MAIN-BEAM HEADLAMPS

B40.87 Any number may be fitted and the only requirements prescribed by these Regulations in respect of any which are fitted are those specified in paragraphs 7, 10 and 12(a) of Part I and, in the case of a motor vehicle first used on or after 1st April 1991, paragraph 5 of Part I.

(Regulation 20)   SCHEDULE 6

REQUIREMENTS RELATING TO OPTIONAL FOG LAMPS

B40.88 **1.** Number—

(a) Any vehicle not covered by sub-paragraph (b):   No requirement

(b) A motor vehicle, other than a motor bicycle or motor bicycle combination, first used on or after 1st April 1991:   Not more than two

2. Position—

(a) Longitudinal: No requirement

(b) Lateral—
    (i) Where a pair of front fog lamps is used in conditions of seriously reduced visibility in place of the obligatory dipped beam headlamps—

Maximum distance from side of vehicle:	400mm
(ii) in all other cases:	No requirement

(c) Vertical—
    (i) Maximum height above the ground—

(A) Any vehicle not covered by sub-paragraph (B):	1200mm
(B) An agricultural vehicle, a road clearance vehicle, an aerodrome fire tender, an aerodrome runway sweeper, an industrial tractor, engineering plant and a home forces' vehicle:	No requirement
(ii) Minimum height above the ground:	No requirement

3. Angles of visibility:	No requirement	**B40.89**
4. Alignment:	To the front and so aimed that the upper edge of the beam is, as near as practicable, 3 per cent below the horizontal when the vehicle is at its kerbside weight and has a weight of 75kg on the driver's seat	
5. Markings—		**B40.90**
(a) A vehicle first used on or after 1st April 1986:	An approval mark	
(b) A vehicle first used before 1st April 1986:	No requirement	
6. Size of illuminated area:	No requirement	
7. Colour:	White or yellow	
8. Wattage:	No requirement	
9. Intensity:	No requirement	
10. Electrical connections:	No individual requirement	**B40.91**
11. Tell-tale:	No requirement	

12. Other requirements—
Every front fog lamp shall be so constructed that the direction of the beam of light emitted therefrom can be adjusted whilst the vehicle is stationary.

13. Definitions—
In this Schedule "*approval mark*" means either—
  (a) a marking designated as an approval mark by regulation 5 of the Designation of

Approval Marks Regulations and shown at item 19 of Schedule 4 to those Regulations; or

(b) a marking designated as an approval mark by regulation 4 of the Designation of Approval Marks Regulations and shown at item 19 or 19A of Schedule 2 to those Regulations.

(Regulations 18 and 20) SCHEDULE 7

PART I

REQUIREMENTS RELATING TO OBLIGATORY DIRECTION INDICATORS AND TO OPTIONAL DIRECTION INDICATORS TO THE EXTENT SPECIFIED IN PART II

B40.92 1. Number (on each side of a vehicle)—

(a) A motor vehicle with three or more wheels, not being a motor bicycle combination, first used on or after 1st April 1986:

One front indicator (Category 1, 1a or 1b), one rear indicator (Category 2, 2a or 2b) and one side repeater indicator (Category 5) or, in the case of a motor vehicle having a maximum speed not exceeding 25mph, one front indicator (Category 1, 1a or 1b) and one rear indicator (Category 2, 2a or 2b).

(b) A trailer manufactured on or after 1st October 1985 drawn by a motor vehicle:

One rear indicator (Category 2, 2a or 2b) or, in the case of a trailer towed by a solo motor bicycle or a motor bicycle combination, one rear indicator (Category 12).

(c) A solo motor bicycle and a motor bicycle combination, in each case first used on or after 1st April 1986:

One front indicator (Category 1, 1a, 1b or 11) and one rear indicator (Category 2, 2a, 2b or 12).

(d) A motor vehicle first used on or after [1st April 1936] and before 1st April 1986, a trailer manufactured on or after [1st April 1936] and before 1st October 1985, a pedal cycle with or without a sidecar or a trailer, a horse-drawn vehicle and a vehicle drawn or propelled by hand:

Any arrangement of indicators so as to satisfy the requirements for angles of visibility in paragraph 3.

(e) A motor vehicle first used before 1st April 1936 and any trailer manufactured before that date:

Any arrangement of indicators so as to make the intention of the driver clear to other road users.

B40.93 2. Position—

(a) Longitudinal—

(i) A side repeater indicator which is required

Within 2600mm of the

to be fitted in accordance with paragraph 1(a):	front of the vehicle
(ii) Any other indicator:	No requirement

(b) Lateral—

  (i) Maximum distance from the side of the vehicle—

(A) Any vehicle not covered by sub-paragraph (b):	400mm
(B) A motor vehicle first used before 1st April 1986, a trailer manufactured before 1st October 1985, a solo motor bicycle, a pedal cycle, a horse-drawn vehicle and a vehicle drawn or propelled by hand:	No requirement

  (ii) Minimum separation distance between indicators on opposite sides of a vehicle—

(A) A motor vehicle (other than a solo motor bicycle or a motor bicycle combination or an invalid carriage having a maximum speed not exceeding 8mph) first used on or after 1st April 1986, a trailer manufactured on or after 1st October 1985, a horse-drawn vehicle, a pedestrian-controlled vehicle and a vehicle drawn or propelled by hand:	500mm or, if the overall width of the vehicle is less than 1400mm, 400mm
(B) A solo motor bicycle having an engine exceeding 50cc and first used on or after 1st April 1986—	
(1) Front indicators:	300mm
(2) Rear indicators:	240mm
(C) A solo motor bicycle having an engine not exceeding 50cc and first used on or after 1st April 1986 and a pedal cycle—	
(1) Front indicators:	240mm
(2) Rear indicators:	180mm
(D) A motor bicycle combination first used on or after 1st April 1986:	400mm
(E) An invalid carriage having a maximum speed not exceeding 8mph—	
(1) Front indicators:	240mm
(2) Rear indicators:	300mm
(F) A motor vehicle first used before 1st April 1986 and a trailer manufactured before 1st October 1985:	No requirement

  (iii) Minimum separation distance between a front indicator and any dipped-beam headlamp or front fog lamp—

(A) Fitted to a motor vehicle, other than a solo motor bicycle or a motor bicycle combination, first used on or after [1st April 1995]:	(a) in the case of a Category 1 indicator, 40mm; (b) in the case of a Category 1a indicator, 20mm;

                                                       (c) in the case of a Category 1b indicator, no requirement

          (B) Fitted to a solo motor bicycle or a motor bicycle combination in either case first used on or after 1st April 1986:   100mm

          (C) Fitted to any other vehicle: No requirement

     (c) Vertical—

          (i) Maximum height above the ground—

               (A) Any vehicle not covered by sub-paragraph (b) or (c):   1500mm or, if the structure of the vehicle makes this impracticable, 2300mm

               (B) A motor vehicle first used before 1st April 1986 and a trailer manufactured before 1st October 1985:   No requirement

               (C) A motor vehicle having a maximum speed not exceeding 25mph: No requirement

          (ii) Minimum height above the ground: 350mm

B40.94   **3.**   Angles of visibility—

     (a) A motor vehicle first used on or after 1st April 1986 and a trailer manufactured on or after 1st October 1985—

          (i) Horizontal (see diagrams in Part III of this Schedule)—

               (A) A front or rear indicator fitted to a motor vehicle, other than a solo motor bicycle or a motor bicycle combination, having a maximum speed exceeding 25mph and every rear indicator fitted to a trailer: 80° outwards and 45° inwards

               (B) A front or rear indicator fitted to a solo motor bicycle or a motor bicycle combination: 80° outwards and 20° inwards

               (C) A front or rear indicator fitted to a motor vehicle, other than a solo motor bicycle or a motor bicycle combination, having a maximum speed not exceeding 25mph: 80° outwards and 3° inwards

               (D) A side repeater indicator fitted to a motor vehicle or a trailer: Between rearward angles of 5° outboard and 60° outboard or, in the case of a motor vehicle having a maximum speed not exceeding 25mph where it is impracticable to comply with the 5° angle, this may be replaced by 10°.

          (ii) Vertical—

               (A) Except as provided by sub-paragraph (B) or (C):   15° above and below the horizontal

(B) Where the highest part of the illuminated area of the lamp is less than 1900mm above the ground and the vehicle is a motor vehicle having a maximum speed not exceeding 25mph:

15° above and 10° below the horizontal

(C) Where the highest part of the illuminated area of the lamp is less than 750mm above the ground:

15° above and 5° below the horizontal

(b) A motor vehicle first used before 1st April 1986, a trailer manufactured before 1st October 1985, a pedal cycle, a horse-drawn vehicle and a vehicle drawn or propelled by hand:

Such that at least one (but not necessarily the same) indicator on each side is plainly visible to the rear in the case of a trailer and both to the front and rear in the case of any other vehicle.

4. Alignment—   **B40.95**
   (a) A front indicator:
   (b) A rear indicator:
   (c) A side repeater indicator (Category 5):

To the front
To the rear
As shown in the first sketch in Part III of this Schedule

5. Markings—
   (a) A motor vehicle, other than a solo motor bicycle or a motor bicycle combination, first used on or after 1st April 1986 and a trailer, other than a trailer drawn by a solo motor bicycle or a motor bicycle combination, manufactured on or after 1st October 1985:

An approval mark and, above such mark, the following numbers—
(a) in the case of a front indicator, "1", "1a", or "1b",
(b) in the case of a rear indicator, "2", "2a" or "2b";
(c) in the case of a side repeater indicator, "5".

   (b) A solo motor bicycle and a motor bicycle combination in either case first used on or after 1st April 1986, a trailer, manufactured on or after 1st October 1985, drawn by such a solo motor bicycle or a motor bicycle combination, a pedal cycle, a horse-drawn vehicle and a vehicle drawn or propelled by hand:

An approval mark and, above such mark, the following numbers—
(a) in the case of a front indicator, "1", "1a", "1b" or "11";
(b) in the case of a rear indicator, "2", "2a", "2b" or "12";
(c) in the case of a side repeater indicator, "5".

   (c) A motor vehicle first used before 1st April 1986 and a trailer manufactured before 1st October 1985:

No requirement

6. Size of illuminated area: No requirement   **B40.96**

7. Colour—
   (a) Any vehicle not covered by sub-paragraph (b):   Amber
   (b) An indicator fitted to a motor vehicle first used
       before 1st September 1965 and any trailer drawn
       thereby—
       (i) if it shows only the front: White or amber
       (ii) if it shows only the rear: Red or amber
       (iii) if it shows both to the front and to the   Amber
             rear.

B40.97   8. Wattage—
   (a) Any front or rear indicator which emits a   15 to 36 watts
       flashing light and does not bear an approval
       mark:
   (b) Any other indicator: No requirement

   9. Intensity—
   (a) An indicator bearing an approval mark: No requirement
   (b) An indicator not bearing an approval mark: Such that the light is
                                                               plainly visible from a
                                                               reasonable distance

B40.98   10. Electrical conditions—
   (a) All indicators on one side of a vehicle together with all indicators on that side of
       any trailer drawn by the vehicle, while so drawn, shall be operated by one
       switch.
   (b) All indicators on one side of a vehicle or combination of vehicles showing a
       flashing light shall flash in phase, except that in the case of a solo motor bicycle,
       a motor bicycle combination and a pedal cycle, the front and rear direction
       indicators on one side of the vehicle may flash alternately.

   11. Tell-tale—
   (a) One or more indicators on each side of a vehicle to which indicators are fitted
       shall be so designed and fitted that the driver when in his seat can readily be
       aware when it is in operation; or
   (b) The vehicle shall be equipped with an operational tell-tale for front and rear
       indicators (including any rear indicator on the rearmost of any trailers drawn by
       the vehicle).

B40.99   12. Other requirements—
   (a) Every indicator (other than a semaphore arm, that is an indicator in the form of
       an illuminated sign which when in operation temporarily alters the outline of
       the vehicle to the extent of at least 150mm measured horizontally and is visible
       from both the front and rear of the vehicle) shall when in operation show a light
       which flashes constantly at the rate of not less than 60 nor more than 120 flashes
       per minute. However, in the event of a failure, other than a short-circuit of an
       indicator, any other indicator on the same side of the vehicle or combination of
       vehicles may continue to flash, but the rate may be less than 60 or more than
       120 flashes per minute. Every indicator shall when in operation perform
       efficiently regardless of the speed of the vehicle.
   (b) Where two front or rear direction indicators are fitted to a motor vehicle first
       used on or after 1st April 1986, and two rear direction indicators are fitted to a

trailer manufactured on or after 1st October 1985, in each case they shall be fitted so as to form a pair.

(c) [*Revoked.*]

13. Definitions— B40.100

In this Schedule "*approval mark*" means either—

(a) a marking designated as an approval mark by regulation 5 of the Designation of Approval Marks Regulations and shown at item 9 of Schedule 4 to those Regulations; or

(b) a marking designated as an approval mark by regulation 4 of the Designation of Approval Marks Regulations and shown at item 6 or, in the case of a solo motor bicycle or a motor bicycle combination, a pedal cycle, a horse-drawn vehicle or a vehicle drawn or propelled by hand, at item 50 of Schedule 2 to those Regulations.

[*Part I of Schedule 7 is printed as amended by S.I. 1994 No. 2280.*] B40.101

PART II

REQUIREMENTS RELATING TO OPTIONAL DIRECTION INDICATORS

1. No vehicle shall be fitted with a total of more than one front indicator nor more than two rear indicators, on each side. B40.102

2. Any number of side indicators may be fitted to the side (excluding the front and rear) of a vehicle.

3. The only other requirements prescribed by these Regulations in respect of any which are fitted are those specified in paragraphs 5, 7, 8, 9, 10, 11, 12(a) and 12(b) of Part I.

PART III

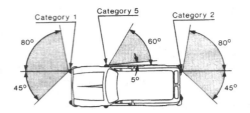

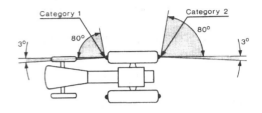

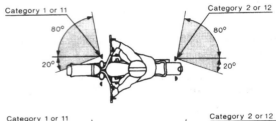

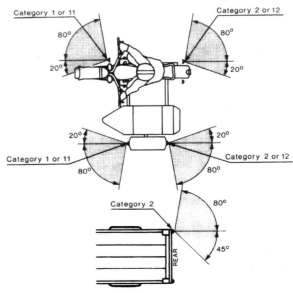

SCHEDULE 8   (Regulations 18 and 20)

REQUIREMENTS RELATING TO OBLIGATORY AND OPTIONAL HAZARD WARNING SIGNAL
DEVICES

Every hazard warning signal device shall—   **B40.104**

    (a) be operated by one switch;

    (b) cause all the direction indicators with which a vehicle or a combination of vehicles is equipped to flash in phase;

    (c) be provided with a circuit-closed tell-tale in the form of a flashing light which may operate in conjunction with any direction indicator tell-tale; and

    (d) be able to function even if the device which controls the starting and stopping of the engine is in a position which makes it impossible to start the engine.

SCHEDULE 9   (Regulations 18, 20 and 22)

PART I

REQUIREMENTS RELATING TO OBLIGATORY SIDE MARKER LAMPS AND TO OPTIONAL SIDE
MARKER LAMPS TO THE EXTENT SPECIFIED IN PART II

1. Number—   **B40.105**

    (a) A vehicle not covered by sub-paragraph (b) which is—

        (i) a motor vehicle first used on or after 1st April 1991 or a trailer manufactured on or after 1st October 1990:   On each side: two and as many more as are sufficient to satisfy the requirements of paragraph 2(a)

        (ii) a trailer manufactured before 1st October 1990:   One on each side

    (b) Long vehicles and vehicle combinations to which regulation 22 applies: The numbers required by regulation 22

2. Position—   **B40.106**

    (a) Longitudinal—

        (i) A vehicle of a type mentioned in sub-paragraph 1(a)(i)—

            (A) Maximum distance from the front of the vehicle, including any drawbar, in respect of the foremost side marker lamp on each side: 4m

            (B) Maximum distance from the rear of the vehicle in respect of the rearmost side marker lamp on each side: 1m

            (C) Maximum separation distance between the light-emitting surfaces of adjacent side marker lamps on the same side of the vehicle: 3m or, if this is not practicable, 4m

        (ii) A vehicle of a type mentioned in sub-paragraph 1(a)(ii):   Such that no part of the light-emitting surface is forward of, or more than

1530mm to the rear of, the centre point of the overall length of the trailer

(b) Lateral: No requirement
(c) Vertical—
    (i) Maximum height above the ground: 2300mm
    (ii) Minimum height above the ground: No requirement

B40.107   **3.**   Angles of visibility—
    (a) Horizontal: 45° to the left and to the right when viewed in a direction at right angles to the longitudinal axis of the vehicle

    (b) Vertical: No requirement

4.   Alignment: To the side

5.   Markings: No requirement

B40.108   **6.**   Size of illuminated area: No requirement

7.   Colour: Amber
or, if within 1m of the rear of the vehicle it may be red or, if the vehicle is a trailer manufactured before 1st October 1990, it may be white when viewed from the front and red when viewed from the rear

8.   Wattage: No requirement

9.   Intensity: Visible from a reasonable distance

B40.109   **10.**   Electrical connections: No individual requirement

11.   Tell-tale: No requirement

PART II

REQUIREMENTS RELATING TO OPTIONAL SIDE MARKER LAMPS

B40.110   Any number may be fitted and the only requirement prescribed by these Regulations in respect of any which are fitted is that specified in paragraph 7 of Part I.

SCHEDULE 10   (Regulations 18 and 20)

PART I

REQUIREMENTS RELATING TO OBLIGATORY REAR POSITION LAMPS AND TO OPTIONAL REAR
POSITION LAMPS TO THE EXTENT SPECIFIED IN PART II

1. Number—   **B40.111**
   (a) Any vehicle not covered by sub-paragraph (b),   Two
      (c), (d), (e), (f), (g) or (h):
   (b) A bus first used before 1st April 1955:   One
   (c) A solo motor bicycle: One
   (d) A pedal cycle with less than four wheels and   One
      without a sidecar:
   (e) A trailer drawn by a pedal cycle and a trailer, the   One
      overall width of which does not exceed 800mm,
      drawn by a solo motor bicycle or by a motor
      bicycle combination:
   (f) An invalid carriage having a maximum speed   One
      not exceeding 4mph:
   (g) A vehicle drawn or propelled by hand: One
   (h) A motor vehicle having three or more wheels and   Four
      a maximum speed not exceeding 25mph and a
      trailer drawn by any such vehicle if, in either
      case, the structure of the vehicle makes it
      impracticable to meet all of the relevant require-
      ments of paragraphs 2 and 3 below with two
      lamps:

2. Position—   **B40.112**
   (a) Longitudinal: At or near the rear
   (b) Lateral—
      (i) Where two lamps are required to be fitted—
         (A) Maximum distance from the side of
            the vehicle—
            (1) Any vehicle not covered by sub-   400mm
               paragraph (2):
            (2) A motor vehicle first used before   800mm
               1st April 1986 and any other
               vehicle manufactured before 1st
               October 1985:
         (B) Minimum separation distance
            between a pair of rear position
            lamps—
            (1) Any vehicle not covered by sub-   500mm. If the overall
               paragraph (2):   width of the vehicle is less
                                       than 1400mm, 400mm or
                                       if less than 800mm,
                                     300mm
            (2) A motor vehicle first used before   No requirement
               1st April 1986 and any other
                vehicle manufactured before 1st
                October 1985:

(ii) Where one lamp is required to be fitted:

On the centre-line or off side of the vehicle

(iii) Where four lamps are required to be fitted—
  (A) Maximum distance from the side of the vehicle—
    (1) One pair of lamps:

Such that they satisfy the relevant requirements in sub-paragraph 2(b)(i)(A)

    (2) The other pair of lamps:

No requirement

  (B) Minimum separation distance between rear position lamps—
    (1) One pair of lamps:

Such that they satisfy the relevant requirements in sub-paragraph 2(b)(i)(B)

    (2) The other pair of lamps:

No requirement

(c) Vertical—
  (i) Maximum height above the ground where one or two rear position lamps are required to be fitted—
    (A) Any vehicle not covered by sub-paragraph (B) or (C):

1500mm or, if the structure of the vehicle makes this impracticable, 2100mm

    (B) A bus first used before 1st April 1986:

No requirement

    (C) A motor vehicle first used before 1st April 1986 not being a bus, a trailer manufactured before 1st October 1985, an agricultural vehicle, a horse-drawn vehicle, an industrial tractor and engineering plant:

2100mm

  (ii) Maximum height above the ground where four rear position lamps are required to be fitted—
    (A) One pair of lamps:

Such that they satisfy the relevant requirements in paragraph 2(c)(i)

    (B) The other pair of lamps:

No requirement

  (iii) Minimum height above the ground—
    (A) A vehicle not covered by sub-paragraph (B):

350mm

    (B) A motor vehicle first used before 1st April 1986 and any other vehicle manufactured before 1st October 1985:

No requirement

3. Angles of visibility—
  (a) A motor vehicle, other than a motor bicycle combination, first used on or after 1st April 1986 and a trailer manufactured on or after 1st October 1985—
    (i) Horizontal—
      (A) Where two lamps are required to be fitted:

45° inwards and 80° outwards

(B) Where one lamp is required to be fitted:	80° to the left and to the right
(C) Where four lamps are required to be fitted—	
(1) The outer pair of lamps:	0° inwards and 80° outwards
(2) The inner pair of lamps:	45° inwards and 80° outwards
(ii) Vertical—	
(A) Where one or two rear position lamps are required to be fitted—	
(1) Any vehicle not covered by sub-paragraph (2) or (3):	15° above and below the horizontal
(2) Where the highest part of the illuminated area of the lamp is less than 1500mm above the ground:	15° above and 10° below the horizontal
(3) Where the highest part of the illuminated area of the lamp is less than 750mm above the ground:	15° above and 5° below the horizontal
(B) Where four rear position lamps are required to be fitted—	
(1) One pair of lamps:	Such that they satisfy the relevant requirements in paragraph 3(a)(ii)(A)
(2) The other pair of lamps:	Visible to the rear
(b) A motor vehicle, other than a motor bicycle combination, first used before 1st April 1986 and any other vehicle manufactured before 1st October 1985:	Visible to the rear
(c) A vehicle drawn or propelled by hand, a pedal cycle, a horse-drawn vehicle and a motor bicycle combination:	Visible to the rear

4. Alignment:	To the rear

5. Markings [(see also regulation 3(6))]—	**B40.114**
(a) A motor vehicle or a trailer not covered by sub-[paragraph (b), (c), (d) or (e)]:	An approval mark
(b) A motor vehicle first used before 1st January 1974 and a trailer, other than a trailer drawn by a pedal cycle, manufactured before that date:	No requirement
(c) A solo motor bicycle and a motor bicycle combination, in each case first used before 1st April 1986, and a trailer manufactured before 1st October 1985 and drawn by a solo motor bicycle or a motor bicycle combination:	No requirement
(d) A pedal cycle, a trailer drawn by a pedal cycle, an invalid carriage having a maximum speed not exceeding 4mph, a horse-drawn vehicle and a vehicle drawn or propelled by hand [in each case manufactured before 1st October 1995]:	An approval mark or a British Standard mark

[(e) A pedal cycle, a trailer drawn by a pedal cycle, an invalid carriage having a maximum speed not exceeding 4mph, a horse-drawn vehicle and a vehicle drawn or propelled by hand in each case manufactured on or after 1st October 1995.	An approval mark or the British Standard mark which is specified in sub-paragraph (c) of the definition of "British Standard mark".]

6. Size of illuminated area: No requirement

B40.115   **7.** Colour: Red

8. Wattage: No requirement

9. Intensity—
   (a) A rear position lamp bearing any of the markings mentioned in paragraph 4:   No requirement
   (b) Any other rear position lamp: Visible from a reasonable distance

10. Electrical connections: No individual requirement

11. Tell-tale: No requirement

B40.116   **12.** Other requirements—
   (a) Except in the case of a motor vehicle first used before 1st April 1986, any other vehicle manufactured before 1st October 1985 and a motor bicycle combination, where two rear position lamps are required to be fitted they shall form a matched pair and where four rear position lamps are required to be fitted they shall form two matched pairs.
   (b) *[Revoked.]*

13. Definitions—
In this Schedule—
"approval mark" means—
   (a) in relation to a solo motor bicycle, a motor bicycle combination and a trailer drawn by a solo motor bicycle or a motor bicycle combination, a marking designated as an approval mark by regulation 4 of the Designation of Approval Marks Regulations and shown at item 50A of Schedule 2 to those Regulations, and
   (b) in relation to any other motor vehicle or any other trailer, either—
     (i) a marking designated as an approval mark by regulation 5 of the Designation of Approval Marks Regulations and shown at item 6 or, if combined with a stop lamp, at item 8 of Schedule 4 to those Regulations, or
     (ii) a marking designated as an approval mark by regulation 4 of the Designation of Approval Marks Regulations and shown at item 7A or, if combined with a stop lamp, at item 7C of Schedule 2 to those Regulations; and
"British Standard mark" means—
   (a) the mark indicated in the specification for cycle rear lamps and published by the British Standards Institution under the reference 3648:1963 as amended by Amendment PD 6137 published in May 1967 and by AMD 4753 published in July 1985, or
   (b) the mark indicated in the specification for photometric and physical require-

ments for lighting equipment published by the British Standards Institution under the reference BS 6102: Part 3: 1986, namely "BS 6102/3". [or]

[(c) the mark indicated in the specification for photometric and physical requirements for lighting equipment published by the British Standards Institution under the reference BS 6102: Part 3: 1986 as amended by AMD 5821 published on the 29th April 1988, namely "6102/3".]

[Part I of Schedule 10 is printed as amended by S.I. 1994 No. 2280.]   **B40.117**

PART II

REQUIREMENTS RELATING TO OPTIONAL REAR POSITION LAMPS

Any number may be fitted and the only requirement prescribed by these Regulations in respect of any which are fitted is that specified in paragraph 7 of Part I.   **B40.118**

SCHEDULE 11   (Regulations 18 and 20)

PART I

REQUIREMENTS RELATING TO OBLIGATORY REAR FOG LAMPS AND TO OPTIONAL REAR FOG LAMPS TO THE EXTENT SPECIFIED IN PART II

1. Number: One   **B40.119**

2. Position—
    (a) Longitudinal: At or near the rear of the vehicle

    (b) Lateral—
        (i) Where one rear fog lamp is fitted: On the centre-line or off side of the vehicle (disregarding any sidecar forming part of a motor bicycle combination)

        (ii) Where two lamps are fitted: No requirement
    (c) Vertical—
        (i) Maximum height above the ground—
            (A) Any vehicle not covered by sub-paragraph (B):   1000mm
            (B) An agricultural vehicle, engineering plant and a motor tractor: 2100mm
        (ii) Minimum height above the ground: 250mm
    (d) Minimum separation distance between a rear fog lamp and a stop lamp—
        (i) In the case of a rear fog lamp which does not share a common lamp body with a stop lamp: A distance of 100mm between the light-emitting surfaces of the lamps when viewed in a direction parallel to the longitudinal axis of the vehicle

        (ii) In the case of a rear fog lamp which shares a common lamp body with a stop lamp: 100mm

B40.120	**3.**	Angles of visibility—	
		(a) Horizontal:	25° inwards and out-wards. However, where two rear fog lamps are fitted it shall suffice if throughout the sector so defined at least one lamp (but not necessarily the same lamp) is visible
		(b) Vertical:	5° above and below the horizontal
	4.	Alignment:	To the rear
B40.121	**5.**	Markings:	An approval mark
	6.	Size of illuminated area:	No requirement
	7.	Colour:	Red
	8.	Wattage:	No requirement
	9.	Intensity:	No requirement
	10.	Electrical connections:	No rear fog lamp shall be fitted to any vehicle so that it can be illuminated by the application of any braking system on the vehicle
B40.122	**11.**	Tell-tale:	A circuit-closed tell-tale shall be fitted

12. Other requirements—
Where two rear fog lamps are fitted to a motor vehicle first used on or after 1st April 1986 or to a trailer manufactured on or after 1st October 1985 they shall form a matched pair.

13. Definitions—
In this Schedule "*approval mark*" means either—
(a) a marking designated as an approval mark by regulation 5 of the Designation of Approval Marks Regulations and shown at item 20 of Schedule 4 to those Regulations; or
(b) a marking designated as an approval mark by regulation 4 of the Designation of Approval Marks Regulations and shown at item 38 of Schedule 2 to those Regulations.

PART II

REQUIREMENTS RELATING TO OPTIONAL REAR FOG LAMPS

B40.123　**1.** In the case of a motor vehicle first used before 1st April 1980 and any other vehicle manufactured before 1st October 1979, any number may be fitted and the only requirements prescribed by these Regulations in respect of any which are fitted are those specified in paragraphs 2(d), 7 and 10 of Part I.

2. In the case of a motor vehicle first used on or after 1st April 1980 and any other vehicle manufactured on or after 1st October 1979, not more than two may be fitted and the requirements prescribed by these Regulations in respect of any which are fitted are all those specified in this Schedule.

SCHEDULE 12　　　　(Regulations 18 and 20)

PART I

REQUIREMENTS RELATING TO OBLIGATORY STOP LAMPS AND TO OPTIONAL STOP LAMPS TO
THE EXTENT SPECIFIED IN PART II

1. Number—　　　　　　　　　　　　　　　　　　　　　　　　　　　　**B40.124**

   (a) Any vehicle not covered by sub-paragraph (b) or (c):　　Two

   (b) A solo motor bicycle, a motor bicycle combination, an invalid carriage and a trailer drawn by a solo motor bicycle or a motor bicycle combination:　　One

   (c) Any other motor vehicle first used before 1st January 1971 and any other trailer manufactured before that date:　　One

2. Position—　　　　　　　　　　　　　　　　　　　　　　　　　　　**B40.125**

   (a) Longitudinal:　　No requirement

   (b) Lateral—

     (i) Maximum distance from the side of the vehicle—

       (A) Where two stop lamps are fitted:　　One each side of the longitudinal axis of the vehicle

       (B) Where only one stop lamp is fitted:　　On the centre-line or off side of the vehicle (disregarding any sidecar forming part of a motor bicycle combination)

     (ii) Minimum separation distance between two obligatory stop lamps:　　400mm

   (c) Vertical—

     (i) Maximum height above ground—

       (A) Any vehicle not covered by sub-paragraph (B):　　1500mm or, if the structure of the vehicle makes this impracticable, 2100mm

       (B) A motor vehicle first used before 1st January 1971, a trailer manufactured before that date and a motor vehicle having a maximum speed not exceeding 25mph:　　No requirement

(ii)	Minimum height above the ground—	
	(A) Any vehicle not covered by sub-paragraph (B):	350mm
	(B) A motor vehicle first used before 1st January 1971 and a trailer manufactured before that date:	No requirement

B40.126 **3.** Angles of visibility—
    (a) A motor vehicle first used on or after 1st January 1971 and a trailer manufactured on or after that date—

(i) Horizontal:	45° to the left and to the right
(ii) Vertical—	
(A) Except in a case specified in sub-paragraph (B) or (C):	15° above and below the horizontal
(B) Where the highest part of the illuminated area of the lamp is less than 1500 mm above the ground:	15° above and 10° below the horizontal
(C) Where the highest part of the illuminated area of the lamp is less than 750 mm above the ground:	15° above and 5° below the horizontal
(b) A motor vehicle first used before 1st January 1971 and a trailer manufactured before that date:	Visible to the rear

    4. Alignment: To the rear

B40.127 **5.** Markings—

(a) Any vehicle not covered by sub-paragraph (b) or (c):	An approval mark
(b) A motor vehicle first used before 1st February 1974 and a trailer manufactured before that date:	No requirement
(c) A solo motor bicycle and a motor bicycle combination, in each case first used before 1st April 1986, and a trailer manufactured before 1st October 1985 drawn by a solo motor bicycle or a motor bicycle combination:	No requirement

    6. Size of illuminated area: No requirement

    7. Colour: Red

    8. Wattage—

(a) A stop lamp fitted to a motor vehicle first used before 1st January 1971 or a trailer manufactured before that date and a stop lamp bearing an approval mark:	No requirement
(b) Any other stop lamp:	15 to 36 watts

B40.128 **9.** Intensity: No requirement

    10. Electrical connections—
      (a) Every stop lamp fitted to—

    (i) a solo motor bicycle or a motor bicycle combination first used on or after 1st April 1986 shall be operated by the application of every service brake control provided for the use of the rider;

    (ii) any other motor vehicle, shall be operated by the application of the service braking system.

(b) Every stop lamp fitted to a trailer drawn by a motor vehicle shall be operated by the application of the service braking system of that motor vehicle.

11. Tell-tale: No requirement

12. Other requirements—

Where two stop lamps are required to be fitted, they shall form a pair.

13. Definitions—   **B40.129**

In this Schedule "*approval mark*" means—

(a) in relation to a solo motor bicycle, a motor bicycle combination or a trailer drawn by a solo motor bicycle or a motor bicycle combination, a marking designated as an approval mark by regulation 4 of the Designation of Approval Marks Regulations and shown at item 50A of Schedule 2 to those Regulations; and

(b) in relation to any other vehicle, either—

    (i) a marking designated as an approval mark by regulation 5 of the Designation of Approval Marks Regulations and shown at item 7 or, if combined with a rear position lamp, at item 8 of Schedule 4 to those Regulations; or

    (ii) a marking designated as an approval mark by regulation 4 of the Designation of Approval Marks Regulations and shown at item 7B or, if combined with a rear position lamp, at item 7C of Schedule 2 to those Regulations.

PART II

REQUIREMENTS RELATING TO OPTIONAL STOP LAMPS

Any number may be fitted, and the requirements prescribed by these Regulations in respect of any which are fitted are all those specified in Part I except—   **B40.130**

(a) those specified in paragraphs 1, 2 and 3; and

(b) in the case of a stop lamp fitted to a pedal cycle, those specified in paragraphs 5 and 8; and

(c) in the case of a stop lamp fitted to a motor vehicle not being a motor bicycle, first used on or after 1st April 1991 either centrally or in such a manner as to project light through the rear window the intensity of the light emitted to the rear of the vehicle shall be not less than 20 candelas and not more than 60 candelas when measured from directly behind the centre of the lamp in a direction parallel to the longitudinal axis of the vehicle.

SCHEDULE 13   (Regulations 18 and 20)

PART I

REQUIREMENTS RELATING TO OBLIGATORY END-OUTLINE MARKER LAMPS AND TO OPTIONAL END-OUTLINE MARKER LAMPS TO THE EXTENT SPECIFIED IN PART II

1. Number: Two visible from the front   **B40.131**
and two visible from the rear

2. Position—

    (a) Longitudinal: No requirement

    (b) Lateral—

        (i) Maximum distance from the side of the vehicle: 400mm

        (ii) Minimum separation distance between a pair of end-outline marker lamps: No requirement

    (c) Vertical—

        (i) At the front of a motor vehicle   The horizontal plane tangential to the upper edge of the illuminated area of the lamp shall not be lower than the horizontal plane tangential to the upper edge of the transparent zone of the windscreen

        (ii) At the front of a trailer and at the rear of any vehicle: At the maximum height compatible with:

        (a) the requirements relating to the lateral position and to being a pair, and

        (b) the use for which the vehicle is constructed

3. Angles of visibility—

    (a) Horizontal: 0° inwards and 80° outwards

    (b) Vertical: 5° above and 20° below the horizontal

4. Alignment: Such that white light is shown towards the front and red light is shown towards the rear

5. Markings: An approval mark

6. Size of illuminated area: No requirement

7. Colour: White towards the front and red towards the rear

8. Wattage: No requirement

9. Intensity: No requirement

10. Electrical connections: No individual requirement

11. Tell-tale: No requirement

12. Other requirements—

The two lamps which emit white light towards the front, and the two lamps which emit red light towards the rear, shall in each case form a matched pair. The white front lamp and red rear lamp on one side of a vehicle may be combined into a single lamp with a single light source.

13. Definitions—

In this Schedule, "*approval mark*" means the approval mark for a front or rear position lamp, as the case may be.

PART II

REQUIREMENTS RELATING TO OPTIONAL END-OUTLINE MARKER LAMPS

Any number may be fitted, and the only requirement prescribed by these Regulations in respect of any which are fitted is that specified in paragraph 7 of Part I.   **B40.134**

SCHEDULE 14   (Regulation 20)

REQUIREMENTS RELATING TO OPTIONAL REVERSING LAMPS

1. Number:	Not more than two	**B40.135**
2. Position:	No requirement	
3. Angles of visibility:	No requirement	
4. Alignment:	To the rear	
5. Markings—		
(a) A motor vehicle first used on or after 1st April 1986 and a trailer manufactured on or after 1st October 1985:	An approval mark	
(b) A motor vehicle first used before 1st April 1986 and a trailer manufactured before 1st October 1985:	No requirement	
6. Size of illuminated area:	No requirement	**B40.136**
7. Colour:	White	
8. Wattage—		
(a) A reversing lamp bearing an approval mark:	No requirement	
(b) A reversing lamp not bearing an approval mark:	The total wattage of any one reversing lamp shall not exceed 24 watts	
9. Intensity:	No requirement	
10. Electrical connections:	No requirement	

11.	Tell-tale—	
	(a) A motor vehicle first used on or after 1st July 1954, provided that the electrical connections are such that the reversing lamp or lamps cannot be illuminated other than automatically by the selection of the reverse gear of the vehicle:	No requirement
	(b) Any other motor vehicle first used on or after 1st July 1954:	A circuit-closed tell-tale shall be fitted
	(c) A motor vehicle first used before 1st July 1954:	No requirement
	(d) Any vehicle which is not a motor vehicle:	No requirement

B40.137 **12.** Definitions—

In this Schedule *"approval mark"* means either—

    (a) a marking designated as an approval mark by regulation 5 of the Designation of Approval Marks Regulations and shown at item 21 of Schedule 4 to those Regulations; or

    (b) a marking designated as an approval mark by regulation 4 of the Designation of Approval Marks Regulations and shown at item 23 or 23A of Schedule 2 to those Regulations.

(Regulation 18)   SCHEDULE 15

REQUIREMENTS RELATING TO OBLIGATORY REAR REGISTRATION PLATE LAMPS

B40.138	**1.**	Number:	
	2.	Position:	Such that the lamp or lamps are capable of adequately illuminating the rear registration plate
	3.	Angles of visibility:	
	4.	Alignment:	
	5.	Markings—	
		(a) A motor vehicle first used on or after 1st April 1986 and a trailer manufactured on or after 1st October 1985:	An approval mark
		(b) A motor vehicle first used before 1st April 1986 and a trailer manufactured before 1st October 1985:	No requirement
B40.139	**6.**	Size of illuminated area:	No requirement
	7.	Colour:	White
	8.	Wattage:	No requirement
	9.	Intensity:	No requirement
	10.	Electrical connections:	No individual requirement
	11.	Tell-tale:	No requirement

12. Definitions—

In this Schedule "*approval mark*" means—

(a) in relation to a solo motor bicycle, a motor bicycle combination and a trailer drawn by a solo motor bicycle or a motor bicycle combination, a marking designated as an approval mark by regulation 4 of the Designation of Approval Marks Regulations and shown at item 50A of Schedule 2 to those Regulations; and

(b) in relation to any other motor vehicle and any other trailer, either—

(i) a marking designated as an approval mark by regulation 5 of the Designation of Approval Marks Regulations and shown at item 10 of Schedule 4 to those Regulations; or

(ii) a marking designated as an approval mark by regulation 4 of the Designation of Approval Marks Regulations and shown at item 4 of Schedule 2 to those Regulations.

SCHEDULE 16   (Regulations 17 and 20)

REQUIREMENT RELATING TO OBLIGATORY AND OPTIONAL WARNING BEACONS

1. Number: Sufficient to satisfy the   **B40.141**
                                       requirements of para-
                                       graph 3

2. Position—

Every warning beacon shall be so mounted on the vehicle that the centre of the lamp is at a height not less than 1200mm above the ground.

3. Angles of visibility—

The light shown from at least one beacon (but not necessarily the same beacon) shall be visible from any point at a reasonable distance from the vehicle or any trailer being drawn by it.

4. Markings: No requirement

5. Size of illuminated area: No requirement

6. Colour: Blue, amber, green or   **B40.142**
                                       yellow in accordance with
                                       Regulation 11

7. Wattage: No requirement

8. Intensity: No requirement

9. Electrical connections: No requirement

10. Tell-tale: No requirement

11. Other requirements—

The light shown by any one warning beacon shall be displayed not less than 60 nor more than 240 equal times per minute and the intervals between each display of light shall be constant.

(Regulations 18 and 20)   SCHEDULE 17

PART I

REQUIREMENTS RELATING TO OBLIGATORY SIDE RETRO REFLECTORS AND OPTIONAL SIDE
RETRO REFLECTORS TO THE EXTENT SPECIFIED IN PART II

B40.143   **1.**   Number—

(a) A motor vehicle first used on or after 1st April 1986 and a trailer manufactured on or after 1st October 1985:   On each side: two and as many more as are sufficient to satisfy the requirements of paragraph 2(a)

(b) A motor vehicle first used before 1st April 1986 and a trailer manufactured before 1st October 1985:   On each side: Two

B40.144   **2.**   Position—

(a) Longitudinal—

(i) A motor vehicle first used on or after 1st April 1986 and a trailer manufactured on or after 1st October 1985—

(A) Maximum distance from the front of the vehicle, including any drawbar, in respect of the foremost reflector on each side: 4m

(B) Maximum distance from the rear of the vehicle in respect of the rearmost reflector on each side: 1m

(C) Maximum separation distance between the reflecting areas of adjacent reflectors on the same side of the vehicle: 3m or, if this is not practicable, 4m

(ii) A motor vehicle first used before 1st April 1986 and a trailer manufactured before 1st October 1985—

(A) Maximum distance from the rear of the vehicle in respect of the rearmost reflector on each side: 1m

(B) The other reflector on each side of the vehicle: Towards the centre of the vehicle

(b) Lateral: No requirement

(c) Vertical—

(i) Maximum height above the ground: 1500mm

(ii) Minimum height above the ground: 350mm

B40.145   **3.**   Angles of visibility—

(a) A motor vehicle first used on or after 1st April 1986 and a trailer manufactured on or after 1st October 1985—

(i) Horizontal: 45° to the left and to the right when viewed in a direction at right angles to

	the longitudinal axis of the vehicle
(ii) Vertical—	
(A) Except in a case specified in sub-paragraph (b):	15° above and below the horizontal
(B) Where the highest part of the reflecting area is less than 750mm above the ground:	15° above and 5° below the horizontal
(b) A motor vehicle first used before 1st April 1986 and a trailer manufactured before 1st October 1985:	Plainly visible to the side

4.   Alignment: To the side

5.   Markings: An approval mark

6.   Size of reflecting area: No requirement

7.   Colour—   **B40.146**
    (a) Any vehicle not covered by sub-paragraph (b):   Amber or if within 1m of the rear of the vehicle it may be red

    (b) A solo motor bicycle, a motor bicycle combination, a pedal cycle with or without a sidecar or an invalid carriage: No requirement

8.   Other requirements: No side retro reflector shall be triangular

9.   Definitions—
    (a) In this Schedule "*approval mark*" means either—
        (i) a marking designated as an approval mark by regulation 4 of the Designation of Approval Marks Regulations and shown at item 3 or 3B of Schedule 2 to those Regulations and which includes the marking I or IA; or
        (ii) a marking designated as an approval mark by regulation 5 of the Designation of Approval Marks Regulations and shown at item 4 of Schedule 4 to those Regulations and which includes the marking I; and
    (b) In this Schedule references to "*maximum distance from the front of the vehicle*" and "*maximum distance from the rear of the vehicle*" are references to the maximum distance from that end of the vehicle (as determined by reference to the overall length of the vehicle exclusive of any special equipment) beyond which no part of the reflecting area of the side retro reflector extends.

PART II

REQUIREMENTS RELATING TO OPTIONAL SIDE RETRO REFLECTORS

Any number may be fitted, and the only requirements prescribed by these Regulations in respect of any which are fitted are those specified in paragraphs 7 and 8 of Part I.   **B40.147**

PART I

REQUIREMENTS RELATING TO OBLIGATORY REAR RETRO REFLECTORS AND OPTIONAL REAR
RETRO REFLECTORS TO THE EXTENT SPECIFIED IN PART II

B40.148   **1.**   Number—

(a)	Any vehicle not covered by sub-paragraph (b) or (c):	Two
(b)	A solo motor bicycle, a pedal cycle with less than four wheels and with or without a sidecar, a trailer drawn by a pedal cycle, a trailer the overall width of which does not exceed 800mm drawn by a solo motor bicycle or a motor bicycle combination, an invalid carriage having a maximum speed not exceeding 4mph and a vehicle drawn or propelled by hand:	One
(c)	A motor vehicle having three or more wheels and a maximum speed not exceeding 25mph and a trailer drawn by any such vehicle if, in either case, the structure of the vehicle makes it impracticable to meet all of the requirements of paragraphs 2 and 3 below with two reflectors:	Four

B40.149   **2.**   Position—

(a)	Longitudinal:	At or near the rear
(b)	Lateral—	
	(i) Where two rear reflectors are required to be fitted—	
	(A) Maximum distance from the side of the vehicle—	
	(1) Any vehicle not covered by sub-paragraph (2), (3) or (4):	400mm
	(2) A bus first used before 1st October 1954 and a horse-drawn vehicle manufactured before 1st October 1985:	No requirement
	(3) A vehicle constructed or adapted for the carriage of round timber:	765mm
	(4) Any other motor vehicle first used before 1st April 1986 and any other vehicle manufactured before 1st October 1985:	610mm
	(B) Minimum separation distance between a pair of rear reflectors—	
	(1) Any vehicle not covered by sub-paragraph (2):	600mm. If the overall width of the vehicle is less than 1300mm, 400mm or if less than 800mm, 300mm
	(2) A motor vehicle first used before 1st April 1986 and any other	No requirement

vehicle manufactured before 1st
October 1985:

(ii) Where one rear reflector is required to be
fitted:

On the centre-line or off
side of the vehicle

(iii) Where four rear reflectors are required to
be fitted—

(A) Maximum distance from the side of
the vehicle—

(1) One pair of reflectors:

Such that they satisfy
the relevant require-
ments in sub-paragraph
2(b)(i)(A)

(2) The other pair of reflectors:

No requirement

(B) Minimum separation distance
between rear reflectors—

(1) One pair of reflectors:

Such that they satisfy the
relevant requirements in
sub-paragraph 2(b)(i)(B)

(2) The other pair of reflectors:

No requirement

(c) Vertical—

(i) Maximum height above the ground where
one or two rear reflectors are required to be
fitted—

(A) Any vehicle not covered by sub-paragraph (b):

900mm or, if the struc-
ture of the vehicle makes
this impracticable,
1200mm

(B) A motor vehicle first used before 1st
April 1986 and any other vehicle
manufactured before 1st October
1985:

1525mm

(ii) Maximum height above the ground where
four rear reflectors are required to be
fitted—

(A) One pair of reflectors:

Such that they satisfy the
relevant requirements in
paragraph 2(c)(i)

(B) The other pair of reflectors:

2100mm

(iii) Minimum height above the ground—

(A) Any vehicle not covered by sub-paragraph (b):

350mm

(B) A motor vehicle first used before 1st
April 1986 and any other vehicle
manufactured before 1st October
1985:

No requirement

3.   Angles of visibility—   **B40.150**

(a) A motor vehicle (not being a motor bicycle
combination) first used on or after 1st April
1986 and a trailer manufactured on or after
1st October 1985—

(i) Where one or two rear reflectors are
required to be fitted—

(A) Horizontal—	
(1) Where two rear reflectors are required to be fitted:	30° inwards and outwards
(2) Where one rear reflector is required to be fitted:	30° to the left and to the right
(B) Vertical—	
(1) Except in a case specified in sub-paragraph (2):	15° above and below the horizontal
(2) Where the highest part of the reflecting area is less than 750 mm above the ground:	15° above and 5° below the horizontal
(ii) Where four rear reflectors are required to be fitted—	
(A) One pair of reflectors:	Such that they satisfy the relevant requirements in paragraph 3(a)(i)
(B) The other pair of reflectors:	Plainly visible to the rear
(b) A motor vehicle (not being a motor bicycle combination) first used before 1st April 1986 and a trailer manufactured before 1st October 1985:	Plainly visible to the rear
(c) A motor bicycle combination, a pedal cycle, a sidecar attached to a pedal cycle, a horse-drawn vehicle and a vehicle drawn or propelled by hand:	Plainly visible to the rear

B40.151

4. Alignment:	To the rear
5. Markings—	
(a) A motor vehicle first used—	
(i) On or after 1st April 1991:	An approval mark incorporating "I" or "IA"
(ii) On or after 1st July 1970 and before 1st April 1991:	(A) An approval mark incorporating "I" or "IA", or
	(B) A British Standard mark which is specified in sub-paragraph (i) of the definition of "British Standard mark" below followed by "LI" or "LIA"; or
	(C) In the case of a vehicle manufactured in Italy, an Italian approved marking
(iii) Before 1st July 1970:	No requirement
(b) A trailer (other than a broken-down motor vehicle) manufactured—	
(i) On or after 1st October 1989:	An approval mark incorporating "III" or "IIIA"
(ii) On or after 1st July 1970 and before 1st October 1989:	(A) An approval mark incorporating "III" or "IIIA"; or

(B) A British Standard mark which is specified in sub-paragraph (i) of the definition of "British Standard mark" below followed by "LIII" or "LIIIA", or

(C) In the case of a trailer manufactured in Italy, an Italian approved marking

(iii) Before 1st July 1970:

No requirement

(c) A pedal cycle, an invalid carriage having a maximum speed not exceeding 4mph, a horse-drawn vehicle and a vehicle drawn or propelled by hand, in each case manufactured—

    (i) On or after 1st October 1989:

(A) An approval mark incorporating "I" or "IA"; or

(B) A British Standard mark which is specified in sub-paragraph (ii) of the definition of "British Standard mark" below

    (ii) On or after 1st July 1970 and before 1st October 1989:

(A) Any of the markings mentioned in sub-paragraph (c)(i) above; or

(B) A British Standard mark which is specified in sub-paragraph (i) of the definition of "British Standard mark" below followed by "LI" or "LIA"

    (iii) Before 1st July 1970:

No requirement

6. Size of reflecting area: No requirement   **B40.152**

7. Colour: Red

8. Other requirements—
    (a) Except in the case of a motor vehicle first used before 1st April 1986, any other vehicle manufactured before 1st October 1985 and a motor bicycle combination, where two rear reflectors are required to be fitted they shall form a pair. Where four rear reflectors are required to be fitted they shall form two pairs.
    (b) No vehicle, other than a trailer or a broken-down motor vehicle being towed, may be fitted with triangular-shaped rear reflectors.
    (c) *[Revoked.]*

9. Definitions—   **B40.153**
In this Schedule—
    (a) *"approval mark"* means either—
        (i) a marking designated as an approval mark by regulation 4 of the

Designation of Approval Marks Regulations and shown at item 3 or 3A or 3B of Schedule 2 to those Regulations; or

(ii) a marking designated as an approval mark by regulation 5 of the Designation of Approval Marks Regulations and shown at item 4 of Schedule 4 to those Regulations;

(b) *"British Standard mark"* means either—

  (i) the mark indicated in the specification for retro reflectors for vehicles, including cycles, published by the British Standards Institution under the reference B.S. AU40: Part 2: 1965, namely "AU 40"; or

  (ii) the mark indicated in the specification for photometric and physical requirements of reflective devices published by the British Standards Institution under the reference BS6102: Part 2: 1982, namely "BS 6102/2"; and

(c) *"Italian approved marking"* means—

a mark approved by the Italian Ministry of Transport, namely, one including two separate groups of symbols consisting of "IGM" or "DGM" and "C.1." or "C.2.".

B40.154   *[Part I of Schedule 18 is printed as amended by S.I. 1994 No. 2280.]*

PART II

REQUIREMENTS RELATING TO OPTIONAL REAR RETRO REFLECTORS

B40.155   Any number may be fitted and the only requirements prescribed by these Regulations in respect of any which are fitted are those specified in paragraphs 7 and 8(b) of Part I.

(Regulations 18 and 20)   **SCHEDULE 19**

PART I

REQUIREMENTS RELATING TO OBLIGATORY REAR MARKINGS AND OPTIONAL REAR MARKINGS TO THE EXTENT SPECIFIED IN PART II

GENERAL REQUIREMENTS

B40.156   **1.**   Description

(a) A motor vehicle first used on or after 1 April 1996, the overall length of which—

  (i) does not exceed 13m: A rear marking of a type shown in diagram 1, 2, 3 or 4 of this Schedule

  (ii) exceeds 13m: A rear marking of a type shown in diagram 5, 6, 7 or 8 in Part IV of this Schedule

(b) A motor vehicle first used before 1 April 1996, the overall length of which—

  (i) does not exceed 13m: A rear marking of a type shown in diagram 1, 2 or 3 in Part III of this Schedule or a rear marking of a type shown

(ii) exceeds 13m:

in diagram 1, 2, 3 or 4 of Part IV of this Schedule A rear marking of a type shown in diagram 4 or 5 in Part III of this Schedule or a rear marking of a type shown in diagram 5, 6, 7 or 8 in Part IV of this Schedule

(c) A trailer manufactured on or after 1 October 1995 if it forms part of a combination of vehicles the overall length of which—

    (i) does not exceed 11m:

A rear marking of a type shown in diagram 1, 2, 3 or 4 in Part IV of this Schedule

    (ii) exceeds 11m but does not exceed 13m:

A rear marking of a type shown in Part IV of this Schedule

    (iii) exceeds 13m:

A rear marking of a type shown in diagram 5, 6, 7 or 8 in Part IV of this Schedule

(d) A trailer manufactured before 1 October 1995 if it forms part of a combination of vehicles the overall length of which—

    (i) does not exceed 11m:

A rear marking of a type shown in diagram 1, 2 or 3 in Part III of this Schedule or a rear marking of a type shown in diagram 1, 2, 3 or 4 in Part IV of this Schedule

    (ii) exceeds 11m but does not exceed 13m:

A rear marking of a type shown in Part III or Part IV of this Schedule

    (iii) exceeds 13m:

A rear marking of a type shown in diagram 4 or 5 in Part III of this Schedule or a rear marking of a type shown in diagram 5, 6, 7 or 8 in Part IV of this Schedule

2. Position—

  (a) Longitudinal:

At or near the rear of the vehicle

B40.157

  (b) Lateral—

    (i) A rear marking of a type shown in diagram 2, 3 or 5 in Part III of this Schedule and a rear marking of a type shown in diagram 2, 3, 4, 6, 7 or 8 in Part IV of this Schedule:

Each part shall be fitted as near as practicable to the outermost edge of the vehicle on the side thereof on which it is fitted so that

(ii) A rear marking of a type shown in diagram 1 or 4 in Part III of this Schedule and a rear marking of a type shown in diagram 1 or 5 in Part IV of this Schedule:

no part of the marking projects beyond the outermost part of the vehicle on either side

The marking shall be fitted so that the vertical centre-line of the marking lies on the vertical plane through the longitudinal axis of the vehicle and no part of the marking projects beyond the outermost part of the vehicle on either side

(c) Vertical:

The lower edge of every rear marking shall be at a height of not more than 1700mm nor less than 400mm above the ground whether the vehicle is laden or unladen

B40.158 3. Visibility:

Plainly visible to the rear

4. Alignment:

The lower edge of every rear marking shall be fitted horizontally. Every part of a rear marking shall lie within 20° of a transverse vertical plane at right angles to the longitudinal axis of the vehicle and shall face to the rear

B40.159 5. Markings—
(a) A motor vehicle or trailer not covered by subparagraph (b):

In respect of any rear marking of a type shown in Part III of this Schedule a British Standard mark or in respect of any rear marking of a type shown in Part IV of this Schedule an approval mark

(b) A motor vehicle first used on or after 1 April 1996 and a trailer manufactured on or after 1 October 1995:

An approval mark

B40.160 6. Colour:

Red fluorescent material in the stippled areas shown in any of the

diagrams in Part III or IV
of this Schedule and
yellow retro reflective
material in any of the
areas so shown, being
areas not stippled and not
constituting a letter. All
letters shall be coloured
black

7. Other requirements—   **B40.161**

A rear marking of a type shown in a diagram in Part III of this Schedule shall comply
with the requirements of that Part.

The two parts of every rear marking of a type shown in diagrams 2, 3 or 5 in Part III
and diagrams 2, 3, 6 and 7 in Part IV of this Schedule shall form a pair and the four
parts of every rear marking of a type shown in diagrams 4 and 8 in Part IV of this
Schedule shall form two pairs.

8. Definitions—

In this Schedule—

(a) "*approval mark*" means a marking designated as an approval mark by regulation
3 of the Designation of Approval Marks Regulations and shown at item 70 of
Schedule 2 to those Regulations; and

(b) "*British Standard mark*" means the specification for rear markings for vehicles published by the British Standards Institution under the reference BS AU 152:
1970, namely "BS AU 152".

PART II

REQUIREMENTS RELATING TO OPTIONAL REAR MARKINGS

Subject to regulation 11(2), any number of rear markings shown in Parts III and IV may be   **B40.162**
fitted to the rear of a vehicle.

PART III

REAR MARKINGS PRESCRIBED FOR MOTOR VEHICLES FIRST USED BEFORE 1 APRIL 1996 AND
TRAILERS MANUFACTURED BEFORE 1 OCTOBER 1995

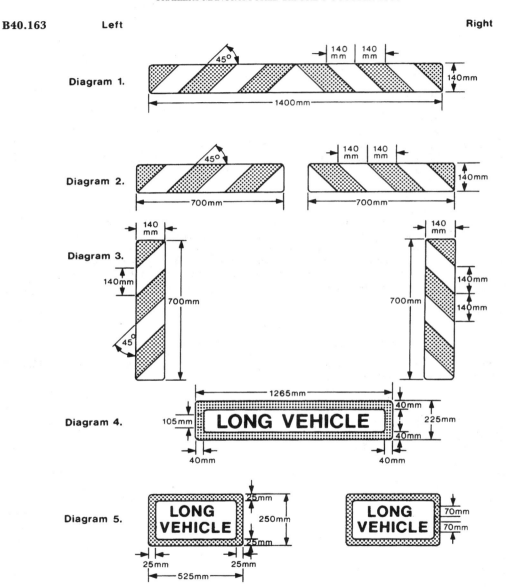

ADDITIONAL PROVISIONS RELATING TO THE ABOVE DIAGRAMS

1. A rear marking of a type shown in one of the above diagrams shall have the dimensions shown in relation to that diagram.   **B40.164**

2. Any variation in a dimension (other than as to the height of a letter) specified in any of the diagrams shall be treated as permitted for the purposes of this Schedule if the variation—
- (a) in the case of a dimension so specified as 250mm or as over 250mm does not exceed 2.5 per cent of that dimension;
- (b) in the case of a dimension so specified as 40mm or as over 40mm but as under 250mm does not exceed 5 per cent of that dimension; or
- (c) in the case of a dimension so specified as under 40mm does not exceed 10 per cent of that dimension.

3. Any variation in a dimension as to the height of a letter specified in any of those diagrams shall be treated as permitted for the purposes of this Schedule if the variation—   **B40.165**
- (a) in the case of a dimension so specified as 105mm does not exceed 2.5 per cent of that dimension; or
- (b) in the case of a dimension so specified as 70mm does not exceed 5 per cent of that dimension.

4. Any variation in a dimension as to the angle of hatching specified in any of those diagrams shall be treated as permitted for the purposes of this Schedule if the variation does not exceed 5 degrees.

5. A rear marking of a type shown in diagram 1 or 4 above shall be constructed in the form of a single plate, and every rear marking shown in diagrams 2, 3 or 5 above shall be constructed in the form of two plates of equal size and shape.   **B40.166**

6. The height of each half of the marking shown in diagram 3 above may be reduced to a minimum of 140mm provided the width is increased so that each half of the marking has a minimum area of $980cm^2$.

7. All letters incorporated in any rear marking of a type shown in diagrams 4 or 5 above shall have the proportions and form of letters as shown in Part II of Schedule 13 to the Traffic Signs Regulations 1994 [*S.I. 1994 No. 1519, q.v.*].

PART IV

REAR MARKINGS PRESCRIBED FOR MOTOR VEHICLES WHENEVER FIRST USED AND TRAILERS
WHENEVER MANUFACTURED

B40.167   **Left**   **Right**

Diagram 1.

Diagram 2.

Diagram 3.

Diagram 4.

Left   Right

Diagram 5.

Diagram 6.

Diagram 7.

Diagram 8.

,,

[Schedule 19 is printed as substituted by S.I. 1994 No. 2280.]   **B40.168**

(Regulations 18 and 20)   SCHEDULE 20

PART I

REQUIREMENTS RELATING TO OBLIGATORY PEDAL RETRO REFLECTORS AND OPTIONAL
PEDAL RETRO REFLECTORS TO THE EXTENT SPECIFIED IN PART II

B40.169	**1.** Number:	Two reflectors on each pedal
	2. Position—	
	(a) Longitudinal:	On the leading edge and the trailing edge of each pedal
	(b) Lateral:	No requirement
	(c) Vertical:	No requirement
B40.170	**3.** Angles of visibility:	Such that the reflector on the leading edge of each pedal is plainly visible to the front and the reflector on the trailing edge of each pedal is plainly visible to the rear
	4. Markings:	A British Standard mark
	5. Size of reflecting area:	No requirement
B40.171	**6.** Colour:	Amber

7. Definitions—
In this Schedule "*British Standard mark*" means the specification for photometric and physical requirements of reflective devices published by the British Standards Institution under the reference BS 6102: Part 2: 1982, namely "BS 6102/2".

PART II

REQUIREMENTS RELATING TO OPTIONAL PEDAL RETRO REFLECTORS

B40.172   Any number may be fitted and the only requirement prescribed by these Regulations in respect of any which are fitted is that specified in paragraph 6 of Part I.

(Regulations 18 and 20)   SCHEDULE 21

PART I

REQUIREMENTS RELATING TO OBLIGATORY FRONT RETRO REFLECTORS AND TO OPTIONAL FRONT RETRO REFLECTORS TO THE EXTENT SPECIFIED IN PART II

B40.173	**1.** Number:	Two

2. Position—
   (a) Longitudinal: No requirement
   (b) Lateral—
       (i) Maximum distance from the side of the   150mm
           trailer:
       (ii) Minimum separation distance between a   600mm or, if the overall
            pair of front reflectors: width of the trailer is less
                                                          than 1400mm, 400mm
   (c) Vertical—
       (i) Maximum height above the ground: 900mm or, if the structure
                                                          of the trailer makes this
                                                          impracticable, 1500mm
       (ii) Minimum height above the ground: 350mm

3. Angles of visibility—   **B40.174**
   (a) Horizontal: 30° outwards and 5°
                                                          inwards
   (b) Vertical—
       (i) Any case not covered by sub-paragraph   15° above and below the
           (ii):   horizontal
       (ii) Where the highest point of the reflecting   15° above and 5° below
            area is less than 750mm above the ground: the horizontal

4. Alignment: To the front

5. Markings: An approval mark

6. Size of reflecting area: No requirement

7. Colour: White   **B40.175**

8. Other requirements—
   (a) Where two front reflectors are required to be fitted they shall form a pair.
   (b) Triangular shaped retro reflectors shall not be fitted to the front of any trailer.

9. Definitions—
   In this Schedule—
   "*approval mark*" means either—
   (a) a marking designated as an approval mark by regulation 4 of the Designation of
       Approval Marks Regulations and shown at item 3 or 3A or 3B of Schedule 2 to
       those Regulations; or
   (b) a marking designated as an approval mark by regulation 5 of the Designation of
       Approval Marks Regulations and shown at item 4 of Schedule 4 to those
       Regulations.

PART II

REQUIREMENTS RELATING TO OPTIONAL FRONT RETRO REFLECTORS

Any number may be fitted and the only requirements prescribed by these Regulations in   **B40.176**
respect of any which are fitted are those specified in paragraph 8(b) of Part I and that the
colour shall not be red.

B40.177   (Regulation 3(2))   [SCHEDULE 21A

Colour

Shaded areas—yellow retro reflective material
Border and silhouette—black

Dimensions

A $\begin{cases} \text{Front—not less than 250mm.} \\ \text{Rear—not less than 400mm.} \end{cases}$ B $\begin{cases} \text{Front—not more than 20mm.} \\ \text{Rear—not more than 30mm.} \end{cases}$]

B40.178   *[Schedule 21A was inserted by S.I. 1994 No. 2280.]*

SCHEDULE 22   (Regulation 24(3))

DIAGRAM SHOWING WHERE UNLIT PARKING IS NOT PERMITTED NEAR A JUNCTION

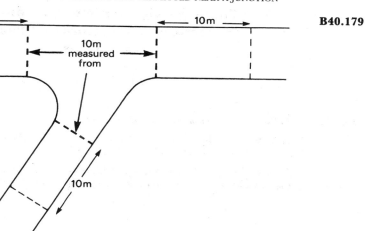

B40.179

SCHEDULE 23   (Schedule 4, Part I, Paragraphs 4 and 12)

EXAMPLE OF MARKING SHOWING THE VERTICAL DOWNWARDS INCLINATION OF THE DIPPED-BEAM HEADLAMPS WHEN THE VEHICLE IS AT ITS KERBSIDE WEIGHT AND HAS A WEIGHT OF 75KG ON THE DRIVER'S SEAT

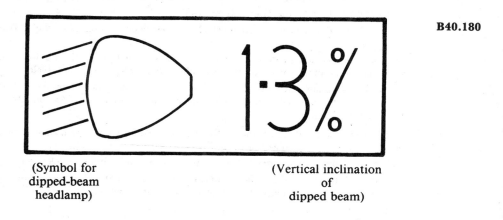

B40.180

(Symbol for dipped-beam headlamp)

(Vertical inclination of dipped beam)

The Public Service Vehicles (Conduct of Drivers, Inspectors, Conductors and Passengers) Regulations 1990

(S.I. 1990 No. 1020)

B41.01   *[The text of these regulations is printed as amended by:*

the Public Service Vehicles (Conduct of Drivers, Inspectors, Conductors and Passengers) (Amendment) Regulations 1995 (S.I. 1995 No. 186) (March 1, 1995).

The amending regulations are referred to in the notes to the principal regulations only by their year and number. The date referred to above is the date on which the amending regulations came into force.]

PART I

B41.02   **1. Citation and commencement**   *[Omitted.]*

2. Revocation   *[Omitted.]*

PART II

3. Interpretation

B41.03   (1) In this Part of the Regulations unless the context otherwise requires—

"*the 1981 Act*" means the Public Passenger Vehicles Act 1981;

"*the 1985 Act*" means the Transport Act 1985;

"*licence*" means a licence to drive a vehicle granted under section 22 of the 1981 Act [*q.v.*];

"*ticket*" means a document which, in accordance with the terms and conditions under which it has been issued, constitutes a valid authority to travel on a vehicle;

"*vehicle*" means any vehicle used as a public service vehicle as defined in the 1981 Act but excluding any vehicle used under a permit granted by virtue of section 19 of the 1985 Act [*q.v.*].

(2) For the purposes of this Part of the Regulations, a sum payable by a passenger on the vehicle shall not be regarded as a fare unless—

(a)   it is computed in accordance with a fare table available on the vehicle; and

(b)   the fare table contains sufficient information to enable the passenger to ascertain the fare for his journey or the manner in which it is computed.

(3) In this Part of the Regulations, in relation to a vehicle—

"*conductor*" means a person, not being the driver, who is authorised by the operator to act as a conductor on the vehicle, but does not include an inspector; and

"*driver*" means a person who is the holder of a licence and who is for the time being responsible for driving the vehicle.

(4) In this Part of the Regulations, any reference to a numbered regulation is a reference to the regulation bearing that number in this Part of the Regulations.

(5) In this Part of the Regulations, any reference to a numbered or lettered paragraph or sub-paragraph is a reference to the paragraph or sub-paragraph bearing that number or letter in the regulation or (in the case of a sub-paragraph) paragraph in which the reference appears.

4. The conduct of drivers, inspectors and conductors

(1) A driver shall not, when a vehicle is in motion, hold a microphone or any attachment   **B41.04**
thereto unless it is necessary for him, either in an emergency or on grounds of safety, to speak into the microphone.

(2) Subject to paragraph (3), a driver shall not, when a vehicle is in motion, speak to any person either directly or by means of a microphone.

(3) Nothing in paragraph (2) shall prevent—

(a) the driver of a vehicle from—

   (i) speaking in circumstances when he is obliged to do so by reason of an emergency or on grounds of safety; or

   (ii) speaking to a relevant person in relation to the operation of the vehicle provided that he can do so without being distracted from his driving of the vehicle; and

(b) the driver of a vehicle which is being used to provide a relevant service from making short statements from time to time limited to indicating the location of the vehicle or operational matters provided that he can do so without being distracted from his driving of the vehicle.

(4) In this regulation—

(a) "*relevant person*" is a person fulfilling one of the following descriptions—

   (i) an employee of the operator;

   (ii) when the operator is a firm, a partner of the firm;

   (iii) if the operator is an individual, that individual; or

   (iv) if the operator is a company, a director; and

(b) "*relevant service*" is a service for the carriage of passengers for hire or reward at separate fares which is neither—

   (i) an excursion or tour within the meaning of section 137(1) of the 1985 Act [*q.v.*]; nor

   (ii) a service the primary purpose of which is sightseeing, not falling within sub-paragraph (i).

5.   *[Omitted.]*   **B41.05**

6. The conduct of passengers

(1) No passenger on a vehicle shall—   **B41.06**

(a) where the vehicle has a door which passengers are by a notice informed is for a particular purpose, use that door for any other purpose, unless otherwise directed or authorised by a driver, inspector or conductor;

(b) put at risk or unreasonably impede or cause discomfort to any person travelling on or entering or leaving the vehicle, or a driver, inspector, conductor or employee of the operator when doing his work on the vehicle;

(c) throw or trail any article from the vehicle;

    (d) smoke or carry lighted tobacco or light a match or a cigarette lighter in or on any part of the vehicle where passengers are by a notice informed that smoking is prohibited, unless the vehicle has been hired as a whole and both the operator and the hirer have given their permission to the contrary;

    (e) except with the permission of the operator, distribute any paper or other article for the purpose of giving or seeking information about or comment upon any matter;

    (f) except with the permission of the operator, sell or offer for sale any article;

  [(g) speak to the driver whilst the vehicle is in motion except—

       (i) in an emergency;
      (ii) for reasons of safety; or
     (iii) to give directions as to the stopping of the vehicle;]

    (h) without reasonable cause distract the driver's attention, obstruct his vision or give any signal which might reasonably be interpreted by the driver as a signal—

       (i) to stop the vehicle in an emergency; or
      (ii) to start the vehicle;

    (j) travel on any part of the vehicle which is not provided for the carriage of passengers;

    (k) remain on the vehicle, when directed to leave by the driver, inspector or conductor on the following grounds—

       (i) that his remaining would result in the number of passengers exceeding the maximum seating capacity or the maximum standing capacity marked on the vehicle in accordance with the Public Service Vehicles (Carrying Capacity) Regulations 1984 [*S.I. 1984 No. 1406; not reproduced in this work*];
      (ii) that he has been causing a nuisance, or
     (iii) that his condition is such as would be likely to cause offence to a reasonable passenger or that the condition of his clothing is such that his remaining would be reasonably expected to soil the fittings of the vehicle or the clothing of other passengers;

    (l) play or operate any musical instrument or sound reproducing equipment to the annoyance of any person on the vehicle or in a manner which is likely to cause annoyance to any person on the vehicle; or

  (m) intentionally interfere with any equipment with which the vehicle is fitted.

(2) Subject to paragraph (3), a passenger on a vehicle who has with him any article or substance mentioned in paragraph (4) or any animal—

    (a) if directed by the driver, inspector or conductor to put it in a particular place on the vehicle, shall put it where directed; and

    (b) if requested to move it from the vehicle by the driver, inspector or conductor, shall remove it.

(3) Paragraph (2)(b) shall not apply to the bearer of a card issued by the Guide Dogs for the Blind Association who has with him a guide dog unless—

    (a) the vehicle is—

       (i) a double-decked vehicle; or
      (ii) a single-decked vehicle of which the overall length is 8.5 metres or more; and there are already two or more dogs on board; or

    (b) the vehicle is a single-decked vehicle of which the overall length is less than 8.5 metres and there is already one dog or more than one dog on board.

(4) The article or substance referred to in paragraph (2) is—

    (a) any bulky or cumbersome article;

(b) any article or substance which causes or is likely to cause annoyance to any person on the vehicle; or

(c) any article or substance which would be reasonably expected to constitute—

    (i) a risk of injury to any person on the vehicle; or

    (ii) a risk of damage to the property of any person on the vehicle or to the vehicle.

(5) In this regulation, *"double-decked vehicle"*, *"single-decked vehicle"* and *"overall length"* have the meanings given by the Road Vehicles (Construction and Use) Regulations 1986 [*S.I. 1986 No. 1078, q.v.*].

[Regulation 6 is printed as amended by S.I. 1995 No. 186.]   **B41.07**

7.—(1) No passenger on a vehicle being used for the carriage of passengers at separate   **B41.08** fares shall use any ticket which has—

(a) been altered or defaced;

(b) been issued for use by another person on terms that it is not transferable; or

(c) expired.

(2) Save as provided in paragraph (3), every passenger on a vehicle being used for the carriage of passengers at separate fares shall—

(a) declare, if so requested by the driver, inspector or conductor, the journey which he intends to take, is taking or has taken in the vehicle;

(b) where the vehicle is being operated by the driver without a conductor—

    (i) save as provided in (ii) below, immediately on boarding the vehicle, pay the fare for the journey he intends to take to the driver or, where appropriate, by inserting in any fare-collection equipment provided on the vehicle the money or token required to pay that fare; or

    (ii) if otherwise directed by the driver, an inspector or a notice displayed on the vehicle, shall pay the fare for his journey in accordance with the direction;

(c) where the vehicle is being operated by the driver with a conductor, pay the fare for the journey which he intends to take, is taking, or has taken in the vehicle to the conductor immediately on being requested to do so by the conductor or an inspector;

(d) accept and retain for the rest of his journey any ticket which is provided on payment of a fare in accordance with sub-paragraph (b) or (c);

(e) produce during his journey any ticket which has been issued to him either under sub-paragraph (d) or before he started his journey for inspection by the driver, inspector or conductor on being requested to do so by the driver, inspector or conductor; and

(f) as soon as he has completed the journey for which he has a ticket, either—

    (i) leave the vehicle; or

    (ii) pay the fare for any further journey which he intends to take on the vehicle.

(3) Paragraph (2)(b) and (c) do not apply to a passenger who has with him a ticket which was issued to him before his journey in respect of that journey, provided he complies with all such directions in relation to the ticket as may be–

(a) printed on the ticket;

(b) displayed on the vehicle; or

(c) given by the driver, inspector or conductor.

(4) Any passenger who—

(a) fails to comply with paragraph (2)(b) or (c); or

(b) does not have with him a ticket which was issued to him before his journey in respect of that journey;

shall pay the fare for his journey to the driver, inspector or conductor on request and in any case before he leaves the vehicle unless otherwise agreed by the driver, inspector or conductor.

(5) Any passenger on a vehicle being used for the carriage of passengers at separate fares who has with him a ticket which he is not entitled to retain for any reason including—

(a) the alteration or defacement of the ticket;

(b) the fact that the ticket, having been issued for use by another person, was not transferable to him;

(c) the expiry of the ticket; or

(d) a mistake in consequence of which the ticket was issued;

shall surrender the ticket to a driver, inspector or conductor on being required to do so.

B41.09   8.—(1) Any passenger on a vehicle who is reasonably suspected by the driver, inspector or conductor of the vehicle of contravening any provision of these Regulations shall give his name and address to the driver, inspector or conductor on demand.

(2) Any passenger on a vehicle who contravenes any provision of these Regulations may be removed from the vehicle by the driver, inspector or conductor of the vehicle or on the request of the driver, inspector or conductor by a police constable.

B41.10   **9.** *[Applies to Scotland.]*

PART III

B41.11   **10. Amendment of Regulations**   *[Omitted.]*

SCHEDULE

B41.12   (Regulations revoked by regulation 2)

[Omitted.]

The Tramcars and Trolley Vehicles (Modification of Enactments) Regulations 1992

(S.I. 1992 No. 1217)

PART I

PRELIMINARY

1. Citation and commencement   *[Omitted.]*   **B42.01**

2. Interpretation

(1) In these Regulations—   **B42.02**

"*the 1984 Act*" means the Road Traffic Regulation Act 1984 [*q.v.*];

"*the 1988 Act*" means the Road Traffic Act 1988 [*q.v.*];

"*duobus*" means a trolley vehicle which—

(a) is adapted to operate under power provided from a source on board when it is not operating from power transmitted to it from some external source;

(b) has a maximum speed when it is operating solely under power provided from a source on board which is at least—

   (i) 75% of its maximum speed when it is operating solely under power transmitted to it from an external source, or

   (ii) 30 miles per hour,

   whichever is the less; and

(c) is designed to have a range of at least 10 miles when operating solely under power provided from a source on board;

"*maximum speed*", in relation to a trolley vehicle and a source of power, means the speed which the trolley vehicle is incapable, by reason of its construction, of exceeding on the level under that source of power when unladen.

(2) A reference in these Regulations to an order or regulations made under an enactment shall be read as including a reference to an order or regulations having effect as if made under that enactment.

PART II

MODIFICATIONS TO THE 1984 ACT

3. Modifications relating to tramcars

(1) Subject to Part IV of these Regulations, the following sections of the 1984 Act—   **B42.03**

(a) section 1 (traffic regulation orders),

(b) section 6 (orders similar to traffic orders in London),

(c) section 9 (experimental orders), and

(d) section 18 (one-way traffic on trunk roads),

shall have effect in relation to tramcars so that such vehicles are exempt from any order under any of those sections.

B42.04   **4.**—(1) Save as provided below, section 14 (temporary prohibition or restriction of traffic on roads) shall have effect in relation to tramcars so that such vehicles are exempt from any order or notice under that section.

(2) Nothing in paragraph (1) above shall affect the operation of any provision in an order or notice under that section restricting the speed of vehicles.

5. Modifications relating to trolley vehicles

B42.05   (1) Subject to Part IV of these Regulations and save as provided below, the following sections of the 1984 Act—

(a)   section 1 (traffic regulation orders),

(b)   section 6 (orders similar to traffic orders in London),

(c)   section 9 (experimental orders), and

(d)   section 18 (one-way traffic on trunk roads),

shall have effect in relation to trolley vehicles so that such vehicles are exempt from any order under any of those sections.

(2) Nothing in paragraph (1) above shall affect the operation of any provision in an order under section 1 of the 1984 Act prohibiting or restricting the waiting of vehicles or the loading or unloading of vehicles.

(3) Nothing in paragraph (1) above shall affect the operation of an order under section 6 of the 1984 Act in so far as it is made in respect of the matters referred to in paragraph 15 of Schedule 1 to that Act.

(4) Nothing in paragraph (1) above shall affect the operation of any provision in an order under section 9 of the 1984 Act prohibiting or restricting the waiting of vehicles or the loading or unloading of vehicles.

(5) Nothing in paragraph (1) above shall affect the operation of an order under section 9 of the 1984 Act as respects traffic on roads in Greater London in so far as it is made in respect of the matters referred to in paragraph 15 of Schedule 1 to that Act or imposes a speed limit.

B42.06   **6.**—(1) Save as provided below, section 14 (temporary prohibition or restriction of traffic on roads) shall have effect in relation to trolley vehicles so that such vehicles are exempt from any order or notice under that section.

(2) Nothing in paragraph (1) above shall affect the operation of any provision in an order or notice under that section—

(a)   prohibiting or restricting the waiting of vehicles or the loading and unloading of vehicles;

(b)   restricting the speed of vehicles;

(c)   prohibiting or restricting overtaking; or

(d)   prohibiting or restricting the use of a road or part of the width of a road by vehicular traffic or by any class of vehicular traffic.

PART III

MODIFICATIONS TO THE 1988 ACT

7. Modifications relating to tramcars

The following provisions of the 1988 Act shall not apply to tramcars—   **B42.07**

section 40A (using vehicle in dangerous condition, etc.);
section 68 (inspection of public passenger vehicles and goods vehicles);
sections 69 to 73 (prohibition of unfit vehicles);
section 75 (vehicles not to be sold in unroadworthy condition or as altered so as to be unroadworthy);
section 76 (fitting and supply of defective or unsuitable vehicle parts);
section 77 (testing condition of used vehicles at sale rooms, etc.);
sections 78 and 79 (weighing of motor vehicles);
section 83 (offences to do with reflectors and tail lamps);
section 190 (method of calculating weight of motor vehicles and trailers); and
section 191 (interpretation of statutory references to carriages).

8.   *[Amends section 87 of the Road Traffic Act 1988 (q.v.) as it applies to tramcars.]*

9. Modifications relating to trolley vehicles

Subject to Part IV of these Regulations, the following provisions of the 1988 Act shall not apply to trolley vehicles—   **B42.08**

section 40A (using a vehicle in a dangerous condition);

section 77 (testing condition of used vehicle in sale rooms, etc.); and

sections 78 and 79 (weighing of motor vehicles).

10. Subject to Part IV of these Regulations, section 68 of the 1988 Act (inspection of public passenger vehicles and goods vehicles) shall apply to trolley vehicles as if subsection (4) were omitted.   **B42.09**

PART IV

DUOBUSES

11. Nothing in Parts II or III of these Regulations affects the operation of the 1984 Act or the 1988 Act in relation to duobuses.   **B42.10**

PART V

AMENDMENTS TO SUBORDINATE LEGISLATION

12–14.   *[Omitted.]*   **B42.11**

PART VI

TRANSITIONAL

15. An order made under—   **B42.12**

(a) section 1, 14, 18 or 84 of the 1984 Act; or

(b) as respects any road outside Greater London under section 9 of that Act, before the coming into force of these Regulations shall not apply to tramcars or trolley vehicles (other than duobuses).

B42.13 *[The regulations came into force on July 1, 1992; regulation 1.]*

B42.14 **16.** An order made under—

(a) section 1, 14, 18 or 84 of the 1984 Act; or

(b) as respects any road outside Greater London under section 9 of that Act,

before the coming into force of these Regulations shall have effect thereafter, in relation to duobuses, as if the provisions of section 141 of that Act (as originally enacted) and the corresponding provisions of earlier enactments had never been passed.

B42.15 *[See the note to regulation 15 above.]*

17. Any regulations made under section 41 of the 1988 Act before the coming into force of these Regulations shall have effect thereafter in relation to trolley vehicles as if section 193 of and Schedule 4 to that Act (as originally enacted) and the corresponding provisions of earlier enactments had never been passed.

B42.16 *[See the note to regulation 15 above.]*

The Road Vehicles (Prohibition) Regulations 1992

(S.I. 1992 No. 1285)

[These regulations have been amended by the Road Vehicles (Prohibition) (Amendment) Regulations 1997 (S.I. 1997 No. 83), but these regulations do not affect any of the provisions reproduced in this work.].   **B43.01**

1. Preliminary   *[Citation and commencement.]*   **B43.02**

2. Interpretation

(1) In these Regulations—   **B43.03**

"the 1981 Regulations" means the Motor Vehicles (Tests) Regulations 1981 *[S.I. 1981 No. 1694 (q.v.)]* as from time to time amended;

"the 1988 Regulations" means the Goods Vehicles (Plating and Testing) Regulations 1988 *[S.I. 1988 No. 1478 (q.v.)]* as from time to time amended;

"the 1988 Act" means the Road Traffic Act 1988 *[q.v.]*;

"authorised constable" means a constable authorised to act for the purpose of section 72 of the 1988 Act by or on behalf of a chief officer of police;

"vehicle examiner" has the meaning given by section 66A of the 1988 Act;

"prohibition" means a prohibition under section 69 of the 1988 Act; and

"relevant test certificate", in relation to a prohibition, means a test certificate issued in respect of the vehicle after the prohibition had been imposed.

(2) A reference to an inspection by a vehicle examiner shall be read as including a reference to an inspection under the direction of a vehicle examiner.

3. Exemptions from section 71(1) of the 1988 Act

(1) The driving of a vehicle on a road—   **B43.04**

(a) solely for the purpose of submitting it by previous arrangement for a specified time on a specified date for an inspection by a vehicle examiner or authorised constable with a view to the removal of the prohibition;

(b) solely for the purpose of submitting it by previous arrangement for a specified time on a specified date for an inspection by a vehicle examiner with a view to the removal of the prohibition and the issue of either a test certificate or a goods vehicle test certificate;

(c) in the course of an inspection with a view to the removal of a prohibition; or

(d) within 3 miles from where it is being, or has been, repaired solely for the purpose of its test or trial with a view to the removal of a prohibition,

is exempted from section 71(1)(a) and (b) of the 1988 Act.

(2) Where a prohibition has been imposed with a direction under section 69A(3) of the 1988 Act, the driving of the vehicle on a road solely for the purpose of submitting it by

previous arrangement at a specified time for an examination under section 45(3) of the 1988 Act with a view to obtaining a test certificate or bringing it away from such an examination is exempted from section 71(1)(a) and (b) of that Act.

(3) Where—

(a) a prohibition has been imposed with a direction under section 69A(3) of the 1988 Act, and

(b) a relevant test certificate has been issued,

the driving of the vehicle on a road to a police station with a view to the prohibition being removed under regulation 4(3) of these Regulations is exempted from section 71(1)(a) and (b) of that Act.

4. Removal of prohibitions imposed with a direction under section 69A(3) of the 1988 Act

B43.05   (1) This regulation applies where a prohibition has been imposed with a direction under section 69A(3) of the 1988 Act.

(2) Where a vehicle examiner has issued a relevant test certificate, the prohibition may be removed by—

(a) the vehicle examiner who issued the certificate, or

(b) a person who has been authorised for the purpose by or on behalf of the Secretary of State and to whom the certificate has been produced.

(3) The prohibition may also be removed by a person who has been authorised for the purpose by or on behalf of a chief officer of police and to whom a relevant test certificate has been produced at a police station.

5. Removal of prohibitions imposed with a direction under section 69A(4)

B43.06   (1) This regulation applies where a prohibition has been imposed under section 69A(4) of the 1988 Act.

(2) The requirements relating to the inspection of the vehicle which have to be complied with before the prohibition can be removed are that the vehicle must have been inspected by a vehicle examiner or an authorised constable.

B43.07   ### 6. Appeals to the Secretary of State relating to prohibitions   *[Omitted.]*

7. Fees relating to inspection of goods vehicles   *[Omitted.]*

8. Fees relating to the inspection of vehicles other than goods vehicles
[Omitted.]

9. Revocations   *[Omitted.]*

The Goods Vehicles (Community Authorisations) Regulations 1992

(S.I. 1992 No. 3077)

Editorial note. The Goods Vehicles (Community Authorisations) Regulations 1992 were **B44.01** made under the European Communities Act 1972, s.2(2), and are expressly stated (in the explanatory note) to give effect to Council Regulation (EEC) 881/92 below.

ARRANGEMENT OF REGULATIONS

1. Commencement and citation   *[Omitted.]*   **B44.03**

2. Purpose and interpretation   **B44.04**

(1) These Regulations implement the Council Regulation.

(2) In these Regulations—

"*actual holder*", in relation to a person established as a haulier in Great Britain, has the meaning which it bears in regulation 32A(1) of the 1984 Regulations [*q.v.*];

"*Community authorisation*" means a Community authorisation issued under the Council Regulation;

"*competent authority*" has the meaning given by regulation 4 of these Regulations;

"*the Council Regulation*" means Council Regulation (EEC) No. 881/92 of 26th March 1992 [*q.v.*] on access to the market in the carriage of goods by road within the Community to or from the territory of a member State or passing across the territory of one or more member States;

"*the First Council Directive*" means the First Council Directive of 23 July 1962 on the establishment of common rules for certain types of carriage of goods by road [*O.J. No. L70, August 6, 1962, p. 2005/62, as amended; not reproduced in this work*];

"*operating centre*" has the meaning which it bears in section 92(1) of the Transport Act 1968 [*q.v.*];

"*operator's licence*" means an operator's licence within the meaning of section 60(1) of the Transport Act 1968 [*q.v.*] or section 14 of the Transport Act (Northern Ireland) 1967;

"*standard operator's licence*" means an operator's licence which is a standard licence within the meaning of regulation 3(2) of the 1984 Regulations [*q.v.*];

"*the 1984 Regulations*" means the Goods Vehicles (Operators' Licences, Qualifications and Fees) Regulations 1984 [*S.I. 1984 No. 176, as amended (q.v.)*]; and

"*traffic area*" means a traffic area constituted for the purposes of the Public Passenger Vehicles Act 1981 [*as amended by the Traffic Areas (Reorganisation) (No. 2) Order 1983 (S.I. 1983 No. 1714; not reproduced in this work) and the Traffic Areas (Reorganisation) Order 1991 (S.I. 1991 No. 288; not reproduced in this work)*],

and, subject thereto, expressions used which are also used in the Council Regulation have the meaning which they bear in that Regulation.

B44.05 *[The Goods Vehicles (Operators' Licences, Qualifications and Fees) Regulations 1984 (S.I. 1984 No. 176) have been revoked by the Goods Vehicles (Licensing of Operators) Regulations 1995 (S.I. 1995 No. 2869) below.]*

3. Use of goods vehicle without Community authorisation

B44.06 A person who uses a vehicle in the United Kingdom in contravention of Article 3.1 of the Council Regulation shall be guilty of an offence and liable on summary conviction to a fine not exceeding level 4 on the standard scale.

4. Competent authorities

B44.07 The competent authority for the purposes of the Council Regulation and of these Regulations shall be—

(a) in relation to a haulier with an operating centre in a traffic area in Great Britain, the traffic commissioner for that area, and

(b) in relation to a haulier established in Northern Ireland, the Department of the Environment for Northern Ireland.

B44.08 ### 5. Entitlement to the issue of Community authorisation   *[Omitted.]*

6. Rights of appeal   *[Omitted.]*

7. Effect of failure to comply with conditions governing use of Community authorisation

B44.09 A person who uses a vehicle in the United Kingdom under a Community authorisation and, without reasonable excuse, fails to comply with any of the conditions governing the use of that authorisation under the Council Regulation shall be guilty of an offence and liable on summary conviction to a fine not exceeding level 4 on the standard scale.

8. Authorised inspecting officers

B44.10 Authorised inspecting officers for the purposes of the Council Regulation shall be police constables and—

(a) in Great Britain, examiners appointed under section 56(1) of the Road Traffic Act 1972 or section 66A(1) of the Road Traffic Act 1988 [*q.v.*], and

(b) *[applies to Northern Ireland]*.

9. Return of documents

(1) The holder of a Community authorisation which is withdrawn by the competent authority in accordance with Article 8.2 of the Council Regulation shall within 7 days of such withdrawal return to the competent authority which issued it the original authorisation and all certified true copies of it.   **B44.11**

(2) The holder of a Community authorisation shall return to the competent authority which issued it such certified true copies of the authorisation as the authority may require pursuant to any reduction in the number of vehicles at the disposal of the holder or any decision of the authority under Article 8.3 of the Council Regulation to suspend certified true copies of that authorisation.

(3) A person who, without reasonable excuse, fails to comply with any provision of paragraphs (1) or (2) above shall be guilty of an offence and liable on summary conviction to a fine not exceeding level 4 on the standard scale.

10. Supply of information

(1) The holder of a Community authorisation shall furnish such information as the competent authority which issued it may reasonably require from time to time to enable the authority to decide whether the holder is entitled to retain that authorisation.   **B44.12**

(2) A person who, without reasonable excuse, fails to supply any information required under paragraph (1) above shall be guilty of an offence and liable on summary conviction to a fine not exceeding level 4 on the standard scale.

11. Death, bankruptcy, etc., of holder of Community authorisation

Where a person is treated as the holder of an operator's licence by virtue of a direction under Regulation 32A of the 1984 Regulations or by virtue of regulations made under section 33(2) of the Transport Act (Northern Ireland) 1967, such person shall also be treated as the holder of any Community authorisation held by the actual holder of that operator's licence, for the same period as is specified in that direction or under such regulations.   **B44.13**

[The 1984 Regulations have been revoked; see the note to regulation 2 above.   **B44.14**
As to the continuance of an operator's licence by the direction of a traffic commissioner following the death, bankruptcy, etc., of the holder, see the Goods Vehicles (Licensing of Operators) Regulations 1995 (S.I. 1995 No. 2869), reg.31 below.]

12. Bodies corporate

(1) Where an offence under these Regulations has been committed by a body corporate and it is proved to have been committed with the consent or connivance of, or to be attributable to any neglect on the part of, any director, manager, secretary or other similar officer of the body corporate or any person who was purporting to act in any such capacity, he as well as the body corporate shall be guilty of the offence and shall be liable to be proceeded against and punished accordingly.   **B44.15**

(2) Where the affairs of a body corporate are managed by its members, paragraph (1) above shall apply in relation to the acts and defaults of a member in connection with his functions of management as if he were a director of the body corporate.

(3) Where an offence under these Regulations has been committed by a Scottish partnership and it is proved to have been committed with the consent or connivance of, or to be attributable to any neglect on the part of, a partner, he as well as the partnership shall be guilty of the offence and shall be liable to be proceeded against and punished accordingly.

B44.16   **13.** *[Revoked by the Goods Vehicles (International Road Haulage Permits) (Revocation) Regulations 1995 (S.I. 1995 No. 1290).]*

14. *[Revoked by the Goods Vehicles (Licensing of Operators) Act 1995, s.60(2) and Sched. 8, Pt II.]*

15. *[Revoked by the Goods Vehicles (Licensing of Operators) (Temporary Use in Great Britain) Regulations 1996 (S.I. 1996 No. 2186).]*

The Motor Vehicles (Wearing of Seat Belts by Children in Front Seats) Regulations 1993

(S.I. 1993 No. 31)

Editorial note. The Motor Vehicles (Wearing of Seat Belts by Children in Front Seats) Regulations 1993 are expressly stated (in the explanatory note) to implement partially Council Directive 91/671/EEC (O.J. No. L373, December 31, 1991, p. 26). The explanatory note adds that the Directive applies only to vehicles of less than 3.5 tonnes which have four or more wheels and a design speed of more than 25 km/h; and it continues to the effect that the Directive does not apply to passenger vehicles with more than eight passenger seats if they are designed to carry standing passengers. (Article 1(1) of the Directive provides: "This Directive shall apply to all motor vehicles in categories M^1, M^2 (except for rear seats and vehicles of a maximum permissible weight exceeding 3.5 tonnes and those which include places specially designed for standing passengers) and N^1 (except for rear seats), as defined in Annex I to Directive 70/156/EEC, intended for use on the road, having at least four wheels and a maximum speed exceeding 25 km/h". However, vehicle categories are now set out in Annex II to Directive 70/156/EEC, as substituted by Directive 92/53/EEC (*q.v.*).)

B45.01

ARRANGEMENT OF REGULATIONS

1. Citation, commencement and revocations   *[Omitted.]*   **B45.03**

2. General interpretation

(1) In these Regulations—   **B45.04**

"*the Act*" means the Road Traffic Act 1988;

"*Construction and Use Regulations*" means the Road Vehicles (Construction and Use) Regulations 1986 [*S.I. 1986 No. 1078, as amended (q.v.)*];

"*front seat*", in relation to a vehicle, means a seat which is wholly or partially in the front of the vehicle and "*rear seat*", in relation to a vehicle, means any seat which is not a front seat (see also regulation 4);

"*maximum laden weight*" has the meaning given by Part IV of Schedule 6 to the Road Traffic Regulation Act 1984 [*q.v.*];

"*medical certificate*" has the meaning given by Schedule 1 to these Regulations;

"*restraint system*" means a system combining a seat fixed to the structure of the vehicle by appropriate means and a seat belt for which at least one anchorage point is located on the seat structure;

"*seat belt*", except in this Regulation, includes a child restraint and references to wearing a seat belt shall be construed accordingly;

"*disabled person's belt*", "*lap belt*", "*seat*", and "*three point belt*" have the meanings given by regulation 47(8) of the Construction and Use Regulations [*q.v.*].

(2) Without prejudice to section 17 of the Interpretation Act 1978, a reference to a provision of the Construction and Use Regulations is a reference to that provision as from time to time amended or as from time to time re-enacted with or without modification.

(3) In these Regulations—

"*child*" means a person under the age of 14 years;

"*large child*" means a child who is not a small child; and

"*small child*" means a child who is—

    (a) aged under 12 years; and

    (b) under 150 centimetres in height.

(4) In these Regulations, "*adult belt*" means a seat belt in respect of which one or more of the following requirements is satisfied, namely that—

    (a) It is a three-point belt which has been marked in accordance with regulation 47(7) of the Construction and Use Regulations;

    (b) it is a lap belt which has been so marked;

    (c) it is a seat belt that falls within regulation 47(4)(c)(i) or (ii) of those Regulations;

    (d) it is a seat belt fitted in a relevant vehicle ("*the vehicle in question*") and comprised in a restraint system—

        (i) of a type which has been approved by an authority of another member State for use by all persons who are either aged 13 years or more or of 150 centimetres or more in height, and

        (ii) in respect of which, by virtue of such approval, the requirements of the law of another member State corresponding to these Regulations would be met were it to be worn by persons who are either aged 13 years or more or of 150 centimetres or more in height when travelling in the vehicle in question in that State.

(5) In these Regulations, "*child restraint*" means a seat belt or other device in respect of which the following requirements are satisfied, namely that—

    (a) it is a seat belt or any other description of restraining device for the use of a child which is—

        (i) designed either to be fitted directly to a suitable anchorage or to be used in conjunction with an adult belt and held in place by the restraining action of the belt, and

        (ii) marked in accordance with regulation 47(7) of the Construction and Use Regulations; or

(b) it is a seat belt consisting of or comprised in a restraint system fitted in a relevant vehicle ("*the vehicle in question*"), being a restraint system—

(i) of a type which has been approved by an authority of another member State for use by a child, and

(ii) in respect of which, by virtue of such approval, the requirements of the law of that State corresponding to these Regulations would be met were it to be worn by a child when travelling in the vehicle in question in that State.

(6) Subject to paragraph (7), for the purposes of these Regulations, a seat shall be regarded as provided with an adult belt if an adult belt is fixed in such a position that it can be worn by an occupier of that seat.

(7) A seat shall not be regarded as provided with an adult belt if the belt—

(a) has an inertia reel mechanism which is locked as a result of the vehicle being, or having been, on a steep incline, or

(b) does not comply with the requirements of regulation 48 of the Construction and Use Regulations.

(8) For the purposes of these Regulations, a seat shall be regarded as provided with a child restraint if a child restraint is—

(a) fixed in such a position that it can be worn by an occupier of that seat, or

(b) elsewhere in or on the vehicle but—

(i) could readily be fixed in such a position without the aid of tools, and

(ii) is not being worn by a child for whom it is appropriate and who is occupying another seat.

(9) For the purposes of these Regulations, a seat belt is appropriate—

(a) in relation to a child aged under 3 years, if it is a child restraint of a description prescribed for a child of his height and weight by regulation 5;

(b) in relation to a child aged 3 years or more, if it is a child restraint of a description prescribed for a child of his height and weight by regulation 5 or is an adult belt; or

(c) in relation to a person aged 14 years or more, if it is an adult belt.

(10) Unless the context otherwise requires, in these Regulations—

(a) any reference to a numbered regulation is a reference to the regulation bearing that number in these Regulations; and

(b) a numbered paragraph is a reference to the paragraph bearing that number in the regulation or Schedule in which the reference appears.

3. Interpretation of references to relevant vehicles

(1) In these Regulations, "*relevant vehicle*" means—   **B45.05**

(a) a passenger car,

(b) a light goods vehicle, or

(c) a small bus.

(2) For the purposes of this regulation—

"*light goods vehicle*" means a goods vehicle which—

(a) has four or more wheels,

(b) has a maximum design speed exceeding 25 kilometres per hour,

(c) has a maximum laden weight not exceeding 3.5 tonnes;

"*passenger car*" has the same meaning as in section 15 of the Act;

"*small bus*" means a motor vehicle which—

(a) is constructed or adapted for use for the carriage of passengers and is not a goods vehicle,

(b) has more than 8 seats in addition to the driver's seat,

(c) has four or more wheels,

(d) has a maximum design speed exceeding 25 kilometres per hour,

(e) has a maximum laden weight not exceeding 3.5 tonnes, and

(f) is not constructed or adapted for the carriage of standing passengers.

4. Interpretation of reference to the front of a vehicle

B45.06   (1) This regulation has effect for the purpose of defining in relation to a vehicle what part of the vehicle is to be regarded as the front of the vehicle for the purposes of section 15(1) of the Act and these Regulations.

(2) Subject to paragraph (3), every part of the vehicle forward of the transverse vertical plane passing through the rearmost part of the driver's seat shall be regarded as the front of the vehicle; and accordingly no part of the vehicle to the rear of that plane shall be regarded as being in the front of the vehicle.

(3) Where a vehicle has a deck which is above the level of the driver's head when he is in the normal driving position, no part of the vehicle above that level shall be regarded as being in the front of the vehicle.

5. Description of seat belts to be worn by children

B45.07   (1) For a child of any particular height and weight travelling in a particular vehicle, the description of seat belt prescribed for the purpose of section 15(1) of the Act to be worn by him is—

(a) if he is a small child and the vehicle is a relevant vehicle, a child restraint of a description specified in sub-paragraph (a) or (b) of paragraph (2);

(b) if he is a small child and the vehicle is not a relevant vehicle, a child restraint of a description specified in sub-paragraph (a) of paragraph (2);

(c) if he is a large child, a child restraint of a description specified in sub-paragraph (a) of paragraph (2) or an adult belt.

(2) The descriptions of seat belt referred to in paragraph (1) are—

(a) a child restraint with the marking required under regulation 47(7) of the Construction and Use Regulations if the marketing indicates that it is suitable for his weight and either indicates that it is suitable for his height or contains no indication as respects height;

(b) a child restraint which would meet the requirements of the law of another member State corresponding to these Regulations were it to be worn by that child when travelling in that vehicle in that State.

6. Vehicles to which section 15(1) of the Act does not apply

B45.08   Two-wheeled motor cycles with or without sidecars are exempt from the prohibition in section 15(1) of the Act.

7. Exemptions

B45.09   (1) The prohibition in section 15(1) of the Act shall not apply in relation to—

(a) a small child aged 3 years or more if a seat belt of a description prescribed by regulation 5 for a small child of his height and weight is not available for him in the front or rear of the vehicle and he is wearing an adult belt;

(b) a child for whom there is a medical certificate;

(c) a child aged under 1 year in a carry cot provided that the carry cot is restrained by straps;

(d) a disabled child who is wearing a disabled person's belt; or

(e) a child riding in a motor car first used before 1st January 1965 if—

    (i) the vehicle has no rear seat, and

    (ii) apart from the driver's seat no seat in the vehicle is provided with a seat belt which is appropriate for that child,

and for the purposes of this paragraph, the date on which a vehicle is first used shall be determined in accordance with regulation 3(3) of the Construction and Use Regulations.

(2) The prohibition in section 15(1) of the Act shall not apply in relation to a child riding in a vehicle which—

(a) is being used to provide a local service within the meaning of the Transport Act 1985 [*q.v.*]; and

(b) is neither a motor car nor a passenger car.

(3) The prohibition in section 15(1) of the Act shall not apply in relation to a large child if no appropriate seat belt is available for him in the front of the vehicle.

(4) For the purpose of this regulation, a reference to a seat belt being available shall be construed in accordance with Schedule 2.

SCHEDULE 1   Regulation 2(1)

MEANING OF "MEDICAL CERTIFICATE"

PART I

1. Subject to paragraph 2, in these Regulations, "*medical certificate*", in relation to a person **B45.10** driving or riding in a vehicle, means—

(a) a valid certificate signed by a medical practitioner to the effect that it is inadvisable on medical grounds for him to wear a seat belt, or

(b) a valid certificate to such effect issued by the authority having power to issue such a certificate under the law of another member State corresponding to these Regulations.

2. A certificate shall not be regarded as a medical certificate in relation to a person driving or riding in a vehicle for the purposes of these Regulations unless—

(a) it specifies its period of validity and bears the symbol shown in Part II of this Schedule; or

(b) the person is aged under 14 years and the vehicle is not a relevant vehicle.

3. Paragraph 2 does not apply in relation to a certificate issued before 1st January 1995. **B45.11**

PART II
(see paragraph 2(a) in Part I of this Schedule)

Regulation 7(4)   SCHEDULE 2

INTERPRETATION OF REFERENCE TO AVAILABILITY OF SEAT BELTS

B45.12   **1.** For the purposes of these Regulations, in relation to a child riding in a vehicle,—

    (a) if any front seat in the vehicle (other than the driver's seat) is provided with an adult belt, that belt shall be regarded as being available for him in the front of the vehicle unless the requirements of paragraph 2 are satisfied in relation to that person, that seat and that belt; and

    (b) if any rear seat in the vehicle is provided with an adult belt, that belt shall be regarded as being available for him in the rear of the vehicle unless the requirements of paragraph 2 are satisfied in relation to that person, the seat and that belt.

B45.13   **2.** The requirements of this paragraph are satisfied in relation to a particular child (*"the child in question"*) and a particular seat (*"the relevant seat"*) provided with a particular seat belt (*"the relevant belt"*) if—

    (a) another person is wearing the relevant belt;

    (b) another child is occupying the relevant seat and wearing a child restraint which is an appropriate child restraint for that child;

    (c) another person, being a person holding a medical certificate, is occupying the relevant seat;

    (d) a disabled person (not being the child in question) is occupying the relevant seat and wearing a disabled person's belt;

    (e) by reason of his disability, it would not be practicable for the child in question to wear the relevant belt;

    (f) the child in question is prevented from occupying the relevant seat by the presence of a carry cot which is restrained by straps and in which there is a child aged under 1 year;

    (g) the child in question is prevented from occupying the relevant seat by the presence of a child restraint which could not readily be removed without the aid of tools; or

    (h) the relevant seat is specially designed so that—

        (i) its configuration can be adjusted in order to increase the space in the vehicle available for goods or personal effects, and

        (ii) when it is so adjusted the seat cannot be used as such,

    and the configuration is adjusted in the manner described in sub-paragraph (i) above and it would not be reasonably practicable for the goods and personal effects being carried in the vehicle to be so carried were the configuration not so adjusted.

3. Paragraphs 2(b) and (d) shall not apply unless the presence of the other person renders it impracticable for the child in question to wear the relevant belt.   **B45.14**

4. Paragraph 2(f) shall not apply if it would be reasonably practicable for the carry cot to be carried in any other part of the vehicle where it could be restrained by straps so as to render it practicable for the child in question to wear the relevant belt.

5. Paragraph 2(g) shall not apply if the child restraint is appropriate for the child in question.

The Motor Vehicles (Wearing of Seat Belts) Regulations 1993

(S.I. 1993 No. 176)

B46.01   *Editorial note.*   The Motor Vehicles (Wearing of Seat Belts) Regulations 1993 are expressly stated (in the explanatory note) to implement partially Council Directive 91/671/EEC (O.J. No. L373, December 31, 1991, p. 26). As to the vehicles to which the Directive applies, see the editorial note to the Motor Vehicles (Wearing of Seat Belts by Children in Front Seats) Regulations 1993 (S.I. 1993 No. 31) above.

ARRANGEMENT OF REGULATIONS

PART I

INTRODUCTION

PART II

ADULTS IN THE FRONT OR REAR OF A VEHICLE

PART III

CHILDREN IN THE REAR OF A VEHICLE

SCHEDULES

PART I

INTRODUCTION

1. **Citation, commencement and revocations**　　*[Omitted.]*　　**B46.03**

2. **General interpretation**

(1) In these Regulations—　　　　　　　　　　　　　　　　**B46.04**

"*the Act*" means the Road Traffic Act 1988;

"*the Construction and Use Regulations*" means the Road Vehicles (Construction and Use) Regulations 1986 [*S.I. 1986 No. 1078, as amended (q.v.)*];

"*licensed hire car*" has the meaning given by sections 13(3) of the Transport Act 1985 [*q.v.*];

"*licensed taxi*" has the meaning given by section 13(3) of the Transport Act 1985;

"*maximum laden weight*" has the meaning given by Part IV of Schedule 6 to the Road Traffic Regulation Act 1984 [*q.v.*];

"*medical certificate*" has the meaning given in Schedule 1 to these Regulations;

"*passenger car*" has the same meaning as in section 15 of the Act;

"*private hire vehicle*" means a motor vehicle which has no more than 8 seats in addition to the driver's seat, other than a licensed taxi or a public service vehicle (within the meaning of the Public Passenger Vehicles Act 1981 [*q.v.*]), which is provided for hire with the services of a driver for the purpose of carrying passengers and which displays a sign pursuant to either section 21 of the Vehicles (Excise) Act 1971 or section 48(2) of the Local Government (Miscellaneous Provisions) Act 1976 or any similar enactment;

"*rear seat*" in relation to a vehicle means a seat not being the driver's seat, a seat alongside the driver's seat or a specified passenger seat;

"*restraint system*" means a system combining a seat fixed to the structure of the vehicle by appropriate means and a seat belt for which at least one anchorage point is located on the seat structure;

"*seat belt*" except in this regulation, includes a child restraint and references to wearing a seat belt shall be construed accordingly;

"*trade licence*" has the meaning given by [section 11(1) of the Vehicle Excise and Registration Act 1994] [*q.v.*];

"*disabled person's belt*", "*lap belt*", "*seat*", "*specified passenger seat*" and "*three point belt*" have the meanings given by regulation 47(8) of the Construction and Use Regulations.

(2) Without prejudice to section 17 of the Interpretation Act 1978, a reference to a provision in any subordinate legislation (within the meaning of that Act) is a reference to that provision as from time to time amended or as from time to time re-enacted with or without modification.

(3) In these Regulations—

"*child*" means a person under the age of 14 years;

"*large child*" means a child who is not a small child; and

"*small child*" means a child who is—

　(a)　aged under 12 years, and

　(b)　under 150 centimetres in height.

(4) In these Regulations, "*adult belt*" means a seat belt in respect of which one or more of the following requirements is satisfied, namely that—

    (a) it is a three-point belt which has been marked in accordance with regulation 47(7) of the Construction and Use Regulations,

    (b) it is a lap belt which has been so marked,

    (c) it is a seat belt that falls within regulation 47(4)(c)(i) or (ii) of those Regulations;

    (d) it is a seat belt fitted in a relevant vehicle ("*the vehicle in question*") and comprised in a restraint system—

       (i) of a type which has been approved by an authority of another member State for use by all persons who are either aged 13 years or more or of 150 centimetres or more in height, and

       (ii) in respect of which, by virtue of such approval, the requirements of the law of another member State corresponds to these Regulations would be met were it to be worn by persons who are either aged 13 years or more or of 150 centimetres or more in height when travelling in the vehicle in question in that State.

(5) In these Regulations, "*child restraint*" means a seat belt or other device in respect of which the following requirements are satisfied, namely that—

    (a) it is a seat belt or any other description of restraining device for the use of a child which is—

       (i) designed either to be fitted directly to a suitable anchorage or to be used in conjunction with an adult seat belt and held in place by the restraining action of that belt, and

       (ii) marked in accordance with regulation 47(7) of the Construction of Use Regulations; or

    (b) it is a seat belt consisting of or comprised in a restraint system fitted in a relevant vehicle ("*the vehicle in question*"), being a restraint system—

       (i) of a type which has been approved by an authority of another member State for use by a child, and

       (ii) in respect of which, by virtue of such approval, the requirements of the law of that State corresponding to these Regulations would be met were it to be worn by a child when travelling in the vehicle in question in that State.

(6) Subject to paragraph (7), for the purposes of these Regulations, a seat shall be regarded as provided with an adult seat belt if it is fixed in such a position that it can be worn by an occupier of that seat.

(7) A seat shall not be regarded as provided with an adult belt if the seat belt—

    (a) has an inertia reel mechanism which is locked as a result of the vehicle being, or having been, on a steep incline, or

    (b) does not comply with the requirements of regulation 48 of the Construction and Use Regulations.

(8) For the purposes of these Regulations, a seat belt is appropriate—

    (a) in relation to a child aged under 3 years, if it is of a description prescribed for a child of his height and weight by regulation 8;

    (b) in relation to a child aged 3 years or more, if it is a child restraint of a description prescribed for a child of his height and weight by regulation 8 or is an adult belt; or

    (c) in relation to a person aged 14 years or more, if it is an adult belt.

(9) For the purposes of these Regulations, any reference to a seat belt being available shall be construed in accordance with Schedule 2 to these Regulations.

(10) Unless the context otherwise requires, in these Regulations—

    (a) any reference to a numbered regulation is a reference to the regulation bearing that number in these Regulations; and

    (b) a numbered paragraph is a reference to the paragraph bearing that number in the regulation or Schedule in which the reference appears.

[Regulation 2 is printed as amended by the Vehicle Excise and Registration Act 1994, s.64 and Sched.   **B46.05**
4, para.4.
Section 21 of the Vehicles (Excise) Act 1971 was repealed by the Finance Act 1994, s.258 and Sched.
26.]

3. Interpretation of reference to relevant vehicles

(1) In these Regulations, *"relevant vehicle"* means—   **B46.06**

    (a) a passenger car,

    (b) a light goods vehicle, or

    (c) a small bus.

(2) For the purposes of this regulation—

"light goods vehicle" means a goods vehicle which—

    (a) has four or more wheels,

    (b) has a maximum design speed exceeding 25 kilometres per hour,

    (c) has a maximum laden weight not exceeding 3.5 tonnes; and

"small bus" means a motor vehicle which—

    (a) is constructed or adapted for use for the carriage of passengers and is not a goods vehicle,

    (b) has more than 8 seats in addition to the driver's seat,

    (c) has four or more wheels,

    (d) has a maximum design speed exceeding 25 kilometres per hour;

    (e) has a maximum laden weight not exceeding 3.5 tonnes, and

    (f) is not constructed or adapted for the carriage of standing passengers.

PART II
ADULTS IN THE FRONT OR REAR OF A VEHICLE

4. General

This Part of these Regulations shall have effect for the purpose of section 14 of the Act.   **B46.07**

5. Requirement for adults to wear adult belts

(1) Subject to the following provisions of these Regulations, every person—   **B46.08**

    (a) driving a motor vehicle (other than a two-wheeled motor cycle with or without a sidecar);

    (b) riding in a front seat of a motor vehicle (other than a two-wheeled motor cycle with or without a sidecar); or

(c) riding in a rear seat of a motor car or a passenger car which is not a motor car;

shall wear an adult belt.

(2) Paragraph (1) does not apply to a person under the age of 14 years.

6. Exemptions

B46.09   (1) The requirements of regulation 5 do not apply to—

(a) a person holding a medical certificate;

(b) a person using a vehicle constructed or adapted for the delivery of goods or mail to consumers or addressees, as the case may be, while engaged in making local rounds of deliveries or collections;

(c) a person driving a vehicle while performing a manoeuvre which includes reversing;

(d) a qualified driver (within the meaning given by regulation 9 of the Motor Vehicles (Driving Licences) Regulations 1987) who is supervising the holder of a provisional licence (within the meaning of Part III of the Act) while that holder is performing a manoeuvre which includes reversing;

(e) a person by whom, as provided in the Motor Vehicles (Driving Licences) Regulations 1987, a test of competence to drive is being conducted and his wearing a seat belt would endanger himself or any other person;

(f) a person driving or riding in a vehicle while it is being used for fire brigade or police purposes or for carrying a person in lawful custody (a person who is being so carried being included in this exemption);

(g) the driver of—

(i) a licensed taxi while it is being used for seeking hire, or answering a call for hire, or carrying a passenger for hire, or

(ii) a private hire vehicle while it is being used to carry a passenger for hire;

(h) a person riding in a vehicle, being used under a trade licence, for the purpose of investigating or remedying a mechanical fault in the vehicle;

(j) a disabled person who is wearing a disabled person's belt; or

(k) a person riding in a vehicle while it is taking part in a procession organised by or on behalf of the Crown.

(2) Without prejudice to paragraph (1)(k), the requirements of regulation 5 do not apply to a person riding in a vehicle which is taking part in a procession held to mark or commemorate an event if either—

(a) the procession is one commonly or customarily held in the police area or areas in which it is being held, or

(b) notice in respect of the procession was given in accordance with section 11 of the Public Order Act 1986.

(3) The requirements of regulation 5 do not apply to—

(a) a person driving a vehicle if the driver's seat is not provided with an adult belt;

(b) a person riding in the front of a vehicle if no adult belt is available for him in the front of the vehicle;

(c) a person riding in the rear of a vehicle if no adult belt is available for him in the rear of the vehicle.

B46.10   *[The Motor Vehicles (Driving Licences) Regulations 1987 have been revoked and are now replaced by the Motor Vehicles (Driving Licences) Regulations 1999 (S.I. 1999 No. 2864). For the meaning of "qualified driver" in the 1999 Regulations, see ibid., reg.17 below.]*

PART III

CHILDREN IN THE REAR OF A VEHICLE

7. General

This Part of these Regulations has effect for the purposes of section 15(3) and (3A) of the Act.   **B46.11**

8. Description of seat belts to be worn by children

(1) For a child of any particular height and weight travelling in a particular vehicle, the description of seat belt prescribed for the purpose of section 15(3) of the Act to be worn by him is—   **B46.12**

(a) if he is a small child and the vehicle is a relevant vehicle, a child restraint of a description specified in sub-paragraph (a) or (b) of paragraph (2);

(b) if he is a small child and the vehicle is not a relevant vehicle, a child restraint of a description specified in sub-paragraph (a) of paragraph (2);

(c) if he is a large child, a child restraint of a description specified in sub-paragraph (a) of paragraph (2) or an adult belt.

(2) The descriptions of seat belt referred to in paragraph (1) are—

(a) a child restraint with the marking required under regulation 47(7) of the Construction and Use Regulations if the marking indicates that it is suitable for his weight and either indicates that it is suitable for his height or contains no indication as respects height;

(b) a child restraint which would meet the requirements of the law of another member State corresponding to these Regulations were it to be worn by that child when travelling in that vehicle in that State.

9. Vehicles to which section 15(3) and (3A) of the Act do not apply

The following classes of vehicles are exempt from the prohibition in section 15(3) and (3A) of the Act, that is to say—   **B46.13**

(a) vehicles which are neither motor cars nor passenger cars;

(b) licensed taxis and licensed hire cars in which (in each case) the rear seats are separated from the driver by a fixed partition.

10. Exemptions

(1) The prohibitions in section 15(3) and (3A) of the Act do not apply in relation to—   **B46.14**

(a) a small child aged 3 years or more if a seat belt of a description prescribed by regulation 8 for a small child of his height and weight is not available in the front or rear of the vehicle and he is wearing an adult belt;

(b) a child for whom there is a medical certificate;

(c) a child aged under 1 year in a carry cot provided that the carry cot is restrained by straps; or

(d) a disabled child who is wearing a disabled person's belt.

(2) The prohibition in section 15(3) of the Act does not apply in relation to a small child in a passenger car if no appropriate seat belt is available for him in the front or in the rear of the vehicle.

(3) The prohibition in section 15(3) of the Act does not apply in relation to a small child

in a vehicle other than a passenger car if no appropriate seat belt is available for him in the rear of the vehicle.

(4) The prohibition in section 15(3) of the Act does not apply in relation to a large child in any vehicle if no appropriate seat belt is available for him in the rear of the vehicle.

(5) The prohibition in section 15(3A) of the Act does not apply in relation to a child if no appropriate seat belt is available for him in the front of the vehicle.

Regulation 2(1)

SCHEDULE 1

MEANING OF "MEDICAL CERTIFICATE"

PART I

B46.15 **1.** Subject to paragraph 2, in these Regulations, "*medical certificate*", in relation to a person driving or riding in a vehicle, means—

(a) a valid certificate signed by a medical practitioner to the effect that it is inadvisable on medical grounds for him to wear a seat belt, or

(b) a valid certificate to such effect issued by the authority having power to issue such a certificate under the law of another member State corresponding to these Regulations.

2. A certificate shall not be regarded as a medical certificate in relation to a person driving or riding in a vehicle for the purposes of these Regulations unless—

(a) it specifies its period of validity and bears the symbol shown in Part II of this Schedule; or

(b) the person is aged under 14 years and the vehicle is not a relevant vehicle.

B46.16 **3.** Paragraph 2 does not apply in relation to a certificate issued before 1st January 1995.

PART II

(see paragraph 2(a) in Part I of this Schedule)

Regulation 2(9)

SCHEDULE 2

INTERPRETATION OF REFERENCES TO AVAILABILITY OF SEAT BELTS

B46.17 **1.** For the purpose of these Regulations, in relation to a person aged 14 years or more riding in a vehicle—

(a) if any front seat in a vehicle (other than the driver's seat) is provided with an adult belt, that belt shall be regarded as being available for him in the front of the vehicle unless the requirements of paragraph 3 are satisfied in relation to that person, that seat and that belt; and

(b) if any rear seat in the vehicle is provided with an adult belt, that belt shall be regarded as being available for him in the rear of the vehicle unless the requirements of paragraph 3 are satisfied in relation to that person, that seat and that belt.

2. For the purpose of these Regulations, in relation to a child riding in a vehicle—

(a) if any front seat in the vehicle (other than the driver's seat) is provided with an appropriate seat belt, that belt shall be regarded as an appropriate seat belt available for him in the front of the vehicle unless the requirements of paragraph 3 are satisfied in relation to that child, that seat and that belt; and

(b) if any rear seat in a vehicle is provided with an appropriate seat belt, that belt shall be regarded as an appropriate seat belt available for him in the rear of the vehicle unless the requirements of paragraph 3 are satisfied in relation to that child, that seat and that belt.

3. The requirements of this paragraph are satisfied in relation to a particular person **B46.18** (*"the person in question"*) and a particular seat (*"the relevant seat"*) provided with a particular seat belt (*"the relevant belt"*) if—

(a) another person is wearing the relevant belt;

(b) a child is occupying the relevant seat and wearing a child restraint which is an appropriate child restraint for that child;

(c) another person, being a person holding a medical certificate, is occupying the relevant seat;

(d) a disabled person (not being the person in question) is occupying the relevant seat and wearing a disabled person's belt;

(e) by reason of his disability, it would not be practicable for the person in question to wear the relevant belt;

(f) the person in question is prevented from occupying the relevant seat by the presence of a carry cot which is restrained by straps and in which there is a child aged under 1 year;

(g) the person in question is prevented from occupying the relevant seat by the presence of a child restraint which could not readily be removed without the aid of tools; or

(h) the relevant seat is specially designed so that—

(i) its configuration can be adjusted in order to increase the space in the vehicle available for goods or personal effects, and

(ii) when it is so adjusted the seat cannot be used as such,
and the configuration is adjusted in the manner described in sub-paragraph (i) and it would not be reasonably practicable for the goods and personal effects being carried in the vehicle to be so carried were the configuration not so adjusted.

4. Paragraph 3 shall have effect in relation to regulation 10(5) as if sub-paragraphs (a) to (d) of that paragraph were omitted.

5. Paragraph (3b) and (d) shall not apply unless the presence of the other person renders **B46.19** it impracticable for the person in question to wear the relevant belt.

6. Paragraph 3(f) shall not apply if it would be reasonably practicable for the carry cot to be carried in any other part of the vehicle where it could be restrained by straps so as to render it practicable for the person in question to wear the relevant belt.

7. Paragraph 3(g) shall not apply if—

    (a) the person in question is a child; and

    (b) the child restraint is appropriate for him.

8. A child restraint shall be regarded as provided for a seat for the purposes of this Schedule if—

    (a) it is fixed in such a position that it can be worn by an occupier of that seat, or

    (b) it is elsewhere in or on the vehicle but—

        (i) it could readily be fixed in such a position without the aid of tools, and

        (ii) it is not being worn by a child for whom it is appropriate and who is occupying another seat.

Regulation 1(2)

SCHEDULE 3

REVOCATIONS

[Omitted.]

The Finance (No. 2) Act 1992 (Commencement No. 6 and Transitional Provisions and Savings) Order 1993

(S.I. 1993 No. 2272)

Editorial note. As to the saving of paragraphs 4 to 8 of the Schedule to this order following the repeal of section 12(2) of the Finance (No. 2) Act 1992, see the Vehicle Excise and Registration Act 1994, Sched. 4, para.7(8) and (9) above.

B47.01

1, 2. *[Omitted.]*

B47.02

3. Transitional provisions and savings

The transitional provisions and savings set out in the Schedule to this Order shall have effect.

B47.03

SCHEDULE

TRANSITIONAL PROVISIONS AND SAVINGS

Article 3

1.—(1) In this Schedule—

B47.04

"*appropriate authority*" means the Secretary of State for Social Security, the Secretary of State for Scotland or the Department of Health and Social Services for Northern Ireland;

"*licence*" means a licence under the Act for a mechanically propelled vehicle;

"*qualified disabled person*" has the meaning given in paragraph 2(2) below;

"*relevant certificate*" has the meaning given in paragraph 2(3) below;

"*the Act*" means the Vehicles (Excise) Act 1971 [*q.v.*];

"*the appointed day*" means 13th October 1993;

"*the 1971 Regulations*" means the Road Vehicles (Registration and Licensing) Regulations 1971 [*S.I. 1971 No. 450, as amended (q.v.)*]; and

"*the 1973 Regulations*" means the Road Vehicles (Registration and Licensing) Regulations (Northern Ireland) 1973 [*S.R. & O. (N.I.) 1973 No. 490 (not reproduced in this work)*].

(2) In this Schedule any reference to the Secretary of State for Social Security shall include a reference to his statutory predecessor.

(3) In this Schedule any reference to the Department of Health and Social Services for Northern Ireland shall include a reference to its statutory predecessor.

(4) Without prejudice to section 17 of the Interpretation Act 1978, a reference in this Schedule to a provision of either the 1971 Regulations or the 1973 Regulations is, unless otherwise stated, a reference to that provision as from time to time amended or as from time to time re-enacted with or without modification.

2, 3. *[Lapsed.]*

[The provisions of paragraphs 2 and 3 of the Schedule have been re-enacted in the Vehicle Excise and Registration Act 1994, Sched. 4, para.7(1)–(5) above.]

B47.05

B47.06   **4.**—(1) This paragraph applies only to Great Britain.

(2) The owner of a mechanically propelled vehicle which is exempt from duty by virtue of [paragraph 7 of Schedule 4 to the Vehicle Excise and Registration Act 1994] shall annually—

> (a) make the prescribed declaration and furnish the prescribed particulars as if, subject to sub-paragraph (3) below, he desired to take out a licence for the vehicle; and

> (b) include with the prescribed declaration and particulars, the relevant certificate issued in respect of him.

(3) Such declaration, particulars and certificate shall be forwarded to the Secretary of State.

(4) Upon receipt of such declaration, particulars and certificate, the Secretary of State shall—

> (a) if the vehicle has not previously been registered under the Act [or the 1994 Act], register the vehicle, assign to the vehicle a registration mark and issue to the owner a registration book with the appropriate particulars of the vehicle in respect of which it is issued entered therein, and any registration mark so assigned shall be deemed to be assigned under [section 23 of the 1994 Act] for the purposes of [sub-section (3) of section 23 of the 1994 Act] and the 1971 Regulations; and

> (b) issue to the owner of the vehicle a document in respect thereof in the form of a licence valid for a period of twelve months running from the beginning of the month in which the document first has effect with the word "NIL" marked in the space provided for indicating the amount of duty payable.

(5) If at any time duty becomes chargeable under the Act in respect of a mechanically propelled vehicle to which this paragraph applies the owner of the vehicle shall forthwith return to the Secretary of State any document issued by him for exhibition on the vehicle which indicates that no duty was payable in respect of it.

(6) The provisions of regulation 7 (which relates to the alteration of licences and similar offences) and regulation 16 (which relates to the exhibition of licences) of the 1971 Regulations shall apply in relation to a vehicle to which this paragraph applies as if each reference therein to a licence issued under [the 1994 Act] included a reference to any such document issued in respect of the vehicle as is mentioned in sub-paragraph (5) above.

(7) In this paragraph, the expressions "*prescribed*" and "*owner*" have the meanings given in Part I of the 1971 Regulations.

B47.07   *[Paragraph 4 of the Schedule is printed as amended by the Vehicle Excise and Registration Act 1994, s.64 and Sched. 4, para.7(9).]*

B47.08   **5.** The provisions of Parts II and III of the 1971 Regulations as to registration and matters incidental thereto shall extend to the vehicles to which paragraph 4 above applies subject to the modifications specified in that paragraph.

    6, 7. *[Apply to Northern Ireland.]*

B47.09   **8.**—(1) Paragraphs 4 to 7 above shall have effect as if they were contained in regulations made under the Act.

(2) Without prejudice to the generality of sub-paragraph (1), any vehicle registered under either paragraph 4(4)(a) or paragraph 6(4)(a) shall be deemed to be registered under [the 1994 Act].

B47.10   *[Paragraph 8 of the Schedule is printed as amended by the Vehicle Excise and Registration Act 1994, s.64 and Sched. 4, para.7(9).]*

The Traffic Signs Regulations and General Directions 1994

(S.I. 1994 No. 1519)

Editorial note. All the functions of a Minister of the Crown under the Traffic Signs and General Directions 1994 which are exercisable in relation to Scotland have been transferred to the Scottish Ministers by the Scotland Act 1998 (Transfer of Functions to the Scottish Ministers etc.) Order 1999 (S.I. 1999 No. 1750; not reproduced in this work), art.2 and Sched. 1.

B48.01

[The text of the regulations and general directions has been amended by:

the Traffic Signs General (Amendment) Directions 1995 (S.I. 1995 No. 2769) (November 10, 1995);

the Traffic Signs (Amendment) Regulations and General Directions 1995 (S.I. 1995 No. 3107) (January 5, 1996); and

the Road Traffic Signs General (Amendment) Directions 1999 (S.I. 1999 No. 1723) (June 16, 1999).

The amending regulations are referred to in the notes to the principal regulations and general directions only by their years and numbers. The dates referred to above are the dates on which the amending regulations came into force.]

B48.02

ARRANGEMENT OF INSTRUMENT

PART I

THE TRAFFIC SIGNS REGULATIONS 1994

SECTION 1

Preliminary

B48.03

SECTION 2

General provisions

SCHEDULES

Schedule

. . . .

17. Illumination of signs
18. Interpretation of "unladen vehicle"

PART II

THE TRAFFIC SIGNS GENERAL DIRECTIONS 1994

*   *   *

PART I

THE TRAFFIC SIGNS REGULATIONS 1994

SECTION 1

Preliminary

1. Citation and commencement

B48.04   This Part of this Instrument—

     (a) may be cited—

         (i) as the Traffic Signs Regulations 1994, and

         (ii) together with Part II below, as the Traffic Signs Regulations and General Directions 1994; and

     (b) shall come into force on 12th August 1994.

2. Revocations

B48.05   The Instruments specified in Appendix 2 to this Instrument, so far as they consist of or comprise regulations, are hereby revoked except that for the purposes of the Traffic Signs (Welsh and English Language Provisions) Regulations 1985 [*S.I. 1985 No. 713, q.v.*] the revocations of the Regulations marked with an asterisk in Appendix 2 shall have no effect.

B48.06   *[The "asterisked" instruments listed in Appendix 2 are the Traffic Signs Regulations and General Directions 1981 (S.I. 1981 No. 859), the Traffic Signs (Amendment) Regulations 1982 (S.I. 1982 No. 1879), the Traffic Signs General (Amendment) Directions 1982 (S.I. 1982 No. 1880), the Traffic Signs General (Amendment) Directions 1983 (S.I. 1983 No. 1086), the Traffic Signs (Amendment) Regulations 1983 (S.I. 1983 No. 1088) and the Traffic Signs (Amendment) Regulations and General Directions 1984 (S.I. 1984 No. 966).]*

3. Savings

B48.07   (1) Subject to paragraph (2), any traffic sign which immediately before the coming into force of these Regulations is placed on or near any road shall be treated as prescribed by these Regulations, notwithstanding any provisions of these Regulations to the contrary, provided that—

     (a) it is a sign prescribed, or to be treated as if prescribed, by the 1981 Regulations; and

     (b) it continues to comply with those Regulations,

as if those Regulations had not been revoked.

     (2) Paragraph (1) shall cease to have effect—

     (a) on 1st January 1996 in relation to any road markings shown in diagrams RM 2 to RM 29 in the Second Schedule to the Traffic Signs Regulations 1957 [*S.I. 1957 No. 13, as amended*], in relation to the sign shown in diagram 623 in Schedule 1 and any road markings shown in diagrams 1005 to 1008, 1013, 1015, 1016, 1027, 1028, 1030, 1031 and 1034 to 1039 in Schedule 2 to the Traffic Signs Regulations 1964 [*S.I. 1964 No. 1857, as amended*]; and

     (b) on 1st January 1999 in relation to any sign shown in any of the diagrams 508, 509, 537.1, 537.2, 537.3, 537.4, 542.1, 542.2, 554 (when varied to "Ice" or "Snowdrifts"), 556.3, 556.4, 577, 603, 605.1 and 622.1A (when varied to indicate a 16.5 tonne maximum gross weight prohibition) in Schedule 1 and diagrams 1016.1, 1018, 1020 and 1021 in Schedule 2 to the 1981 Regulations; and

     (c) on 1st January 2005 in relation to any sign shown in any of the diagrams 403 to 405, 412A to 418, 422 to 433, 435 to 459, 468 to 472, and 474 to 495 in the First Schedule to the Traffic Signs Regulations 1957, in diagrams 742, 746, 837, and

838 in Schedule 1 to the Traffic Signs Regulations 1964, and in diagrams 626.1, 627, 628.1, 641, 642.1, 653, 734.7, 739.3, 742.1, 742.2, 742.3, 742.4, 742.5, 742.6, 747, 748, 749, 750, 751, 752, 752.1, 753, 753.1, 758, 759, 837.1, 838.1 and 905 in Schedule 1 to the 1981 Regulations; and

(d) on 1st January 2015 in relation to any sign shown in diagrams 728.1, 728.2, 729, 729.1, 729.2, 729.3, 730, 730.1, 732, 732.1, 732.2, 733, 733.1, 734.1, 734.2, 734.3, 734.4, 734.5, 734.6, 734.8, 734.9, 734.10, 736, 736.1, 737.1, 760 and 761 in Schedule 1 to the 1981 Regulations.

(3) A sign which is of the size, colour and type shown in diagram 701, 702, 702.1, 703, 703.1, 703.2, 703.3, 704, 705, 706, 707, 708, 709, 710, 710.1, 711.1, 712, 712.1, 713, 714, 715, 716, 717, 718, 718.1, 718.2, 718.3, 719, 719.1, 719.2, 719.3A, 719.4, 720, 721.1, 722, 723, 724, 724.1, 724.2, 725, 726, 727, 727.2, 728, 728.1, 728.2, 728.3, 729, 729.1, 729.2, 729.3, 730, 730.1, 732, 732.1, 732.2, 732.4, 732.5, 733, 733.1, 734.1, 734.2, 734.3, 734.4, 734.5, 734.6, 734.7, 734.8, 734.9, 734.10, 735.1, 735.2, 736, 736.1, 737.1, 739, 739.1, 739.2, 739.3, 739.4, 739.5, 741, 741.1 or 905 in Schedule 1 to the 1981 Regulations may be erected on or near a road after the coming into force of these Regulations, notwithstanding that it is not of the size, colour and type shown in any diagram in these Regulations, provided that the design or manufacture of the sign had begun before the coming into force of these Regulations.

4. Interpretation—general

In these Regulations unless the context otherwise requires—

"*the 1984 Act*" means the Road Traffic Regulation Act 1984 [*q.v.*];

"*the 1988 Act*" means the Road Traffic Act 1988 [*q.v.*];

"*the 1981 Regulations*" means the Traffic Signs Regulations and General Directions 1981;

"*articulated vehicle*" means a motor vehicle with a trailer so attached to it as to be partially superimposed upon it;

"*automatic half-barrier level crossing*" means a level crossing where barriers are installed to descend automatically across part of the road when a railway vehicle or tramcar approaches and the operation of the barriers is monitored remotely from the crossing;

"*automatic barrier crossing (L)*" means a level crossing where barriers are installed to descend automatically across part of the road when a railway vehicle or tramcar approaches and the driver of the railway vehicle or tramcar is required to monitor the operation of the barriers when the railway vehicle or tramcar is at or near the crossing;

"*automatic open crossing (L)*" means a level crossing without automatic barriers where light signals are so installed as to be operated automatically by a railway vehicle or tramcar approaching the crossing and the driver of the railway vehicle or tramcar is required to monitor the operation of the light signals when the railway vehicle or tramcar is at or near the crossing;

"*automatic open crossing (R)*" means a level crossing without automatic barriers where light signals are so installed as to be operated automatically by a railway vehicle or tramcar approaching the crossing and the operation of the light signals is monitored remotely from the crossing;

"*automatic level crossing*" means an automatic half-barrier level crossing, an automatic barrier crossing (L), an automatic open crossing (L) or an automatic open crossing (R);

"*central reservation*" means—

(a) any land between the carriageways of a road comprising two carriageways; or

(b) any permanent work (other than a traffic island) in the carriageway of a road,

which separates the carriageway or, as the case may be, the part of the carriageway which is to be used by traffic moving in one direction from the carriageway or part of the carriageway which is to be used (whether at all times or at particular times only) by traffic moving in the other direction;

"*contra-flow*" means a part of a carriageway of a road where—

    (a) traffic is authorised to proceed in the opposite direction to the usual direction of traffic on that part; or

    (b) a specified class of traffic is authorised to proceed in the opposite direction to other traffic on that carriageway;

"*cycle lane*" means a part of the carriageway of a road which—

    (a) starts with the marking shown in diagram 1009; and

    (b) is separated from the rest of the carriageway—

        (i) if it may not be used by vehicles other than pedal cycles, by the marking shown in diagram 1049; or

        (ii) if it may be used by vehicles other than pedal cycles, by the marking shown in diagram 1004 or 1004.1;

"*dual carriageway road*" means a road which comprises a central reservation;

"*enactment*" includes any Act or subordinate legislation as defined in section 21(1) of the Interpretation Act 1978;

"*excursion or tour*" has the meaning given in section 137(1) of the Transport Act 1985 [*q.v.*];

"*goods vehicle*" means a motor vehicle or trailer constructed or adapted for use for the carriage or haulage of goods or burden of any description;

"*hours of darkness*" means the time between half an hour after sunset and half an hour before sunrise;

"*level crossing*" means a place where a road is crossed by a railway or a tramway on a reserved track on the level;

"*local bus*" means a public service vehicle used for the provision of a local service not being an excursion or tour;

"*local service*" has the meaning given in section 2 of the Transport Act 1985 [*q.v.*];

"*major road*" means the road at a road junction into which there emerges vehicular traffic from a minor road;

"*manually operated*" means a change from one sign to another or one signal aspect to another set in process by an operator;

"*maximum gross weight*" means—

    (a) in the case of a motor vehicle not drawing a trailer or in the case of a trailer, its maximum laden weight;

    (b) in the case of an articulated vehicle, its maximum laden weight (if it has one) and otherwise the aggregate maximum laden weight of all the individual vehicles forming part of that articulated vehicle; and

    (c) in the case of a motor vehicle (other than an articulated vehicle) drawing one or more trailers, the aggregate maximum laden weight of the motor vehicle and the trailer or trailers drawn by it,

and the foregoing references to the maximum laden weight of a vehicle (including a vehicle which is a trailer) are references—

        (i) in the case of a vehicle as respects which a gross weight not to be exceeded in Great Britain is specified in construction and use requirements (as defined by section [41(7)] of the 1988 Act), to the weight so specified, or

        (ii) in the case of a vehicle as respects which no such weight is so specified, to the weight which the vehicle is designed or adapted not to exceed when in normal use and travelling on a road laden.

"*minor road*" means a road on which, at its junction with another road, there is placed the sign shown in diagram 601.1 or 602 or the road marking shown in diagram 1003;

"*mobile road works*" means works on a road carried out by or from a vehicle or vehicles which move slowly along the road or which stop briefly from time to time along that road;

"*motorway*" means a special road—

(a) which in England or Wales (save as otherwise provided by or under regulations made under, or having effect as if made under, section 17 of the 1984 Act) can only be used by traffic of Class I or II as specified in Schedule 4 to the Highways Act 1980 [*q.v.*]; or

(b) [*applies to Scotland*];

"*non-primary route*" means a route, not being a primary route or a motorway or part of a primary route or of a motorway;

"*passenger vehicle*" means a vehicle constructed or adapted for the carriage of passengers and their effects;

"*pedal cycle*" means a unicycle, bicycle, tricycle, or cycle having four or more wheels, not being in any case mechanically propelled unless it is an electrically assisted pedal cycle of such class as is to be treated as not being a motor vehicle for the purposes of the 1984 Act;

"*pedestrian zone*" means an area—

(a) which has been laid out to improve amenity for pedestrians; and

(b) to which the entry of vehicles is prohibited or restricted;

"*Pelican crossing*" means a pedestrian crossing which conforms to The "Pelican" Pedestrian Crossings Regulations and General Directions 1987 [*S.I. 1987 No. 16*];

"*plate*" means a sign which by virtue of general directions given in exercise of the power conferred by section 65 of the 1984 Act must always be placed in combination or in conjunction with another sign and which is supplementary to that other sign;

"*police vehicle*" means a vehicle being used for police purposes or operating under the instructions of a chief officer of police;

"*primary route*" means a route, not being a route comprising any part of a motorway, in respect of which the Secretary of State—

(a) in the case of a trunk road is of the opinion, and

(b) in any other case after consultation with the traffic authority for the road comprised in the route is of the opinion,

that it provides the most satisfactory route for through traffic between places of traffic importance;

"*principal road*" means a road for the time being classified as a principal road—

(a) by virtue of section 12 of the Highways Act 1980 (whether as falling within subsection (1) or classified under subsection (3)), or

(b) [*applies to roads in Scotland*];

"*public service vehicle*" has the meaning given in section 1 of the Public Passenger Vehicles Act 1981 [*q.v.*];

"*retroreflecting material*" means material which reflects a ray of light back towards the source of that light;

"*road maintenance vehicle*" means a vehicle which—

(a) in England and Wales is specially designed or adapted for use on a road by or on behalf of a highway authority for the purposes of the Highways Act 1980 for the purposes of road maintenance; or

(b) [*applies to Scotland*];

"*road marking*" means a traffic sign consisting of a line or mark or legend on a road;

"*route*" includes any road comprised in a route;

"*scheduled express service*" means a service provided by a public service vehicle—

(a) used to carry passengers for hire or reward at separate fares otherwise than in the provision of a local service; and

(b) which is operated in accordance with a timetable;

"*school bus*" means a vehicle constructed or adapted to carry 12 or more passengers and being used to carry persons to or from a school as defined in [section 4(1) of the Education Act 1996] . . .;

"*sign*" means a traffic sign;

"*stud*" means a prefabricated device fixed or embedded as a mark in the carriageway of a road;

"*taxi*" means—

(a) in England and Wales, a vehicle licensed under—

(i) section 37 of the Town Police Clauses Act 1847 [*as amended by the Transport Act 1985, s.16(a) and Sched. 8*]; or

(ii) section 6 of the Metropolitan Public Carriage Act 1869 [*as amended by the Statute Law (Repeals) Act 1976, and by the Transport Act 1981, ss.35(1) and 40(1) and Sched. 12, Pt III*];

or under any similar enactment; and

(b) *[applies to Scotland]*;

"*taxi rank*" means an area of carriageway reserved for use by taxis waiting to pick up passengers;

"*temporary statutory provision*" means—

(a) a provision having effect under section 9 (experimental traffic orders), section 12 (experimental traffic schemes in Greater London) or section 14 (temporary restriction of traffic on roads) of the 1984 Act or under a provision referred to in section 66 (traffic signs for giving effect to local traffic regulations) of that Act;

(b) a prohibition, restriction or requirement indicated by a traffic sign placed pursuant to section 67 (emergencies and temporary obstructions) of the 1984 Act; or

(c) *[applies to Scotland]*;

"*terminal sign*" means a sign placed in accordance with direction 8 or 9 of the Traffic Signs General Directions 1994 [*Part II of this Instrument below*];

["*tourist attraction*" means a permanently established destination or facility which—

(a) attracts or is used by visitors to an area;

(b) is open to the public without prior booking during normal opening hours;

(c) *[applies to Scotland]*; and

(d) if located in Wales is recognised by the Wales Tourist Board.]

"*Tourist Information Centre*" means a staffed information service centre recognised and supported by the English, Scottish or Wales Tourist Board;

"*Tourist Information Point*" means a display of tourist information approved by a regional, area or local tourist board;

"*traffic lane*" means, in relation to a road, a part of the carriageway having, as a boundary which separates it from another such part, a road marking of the type shown in diagram 1004.1, 1004.1, 1005, 1005.1, 1008, 1008.1, 1010, 1013.1, 1013.3, 1040, 1040.2 or 1049;

"*tramcar*" has the meaning given in section 141A(4) of the 1984 Act [*q.v.*];

"*trolley vehicle*" has the meaning given in section 141A(4) of the 1984 Act;

"*trunk road*" as respects England and Wales has the meaning given in section 329(1) of the Highways Act 1980 . . .;

"*unladen vehicle*" has the meaning given in Schedule 18;

"*variable message sign*" has the meaning given in regulation 46(1);

"*with-flow lane*" means a traffic lane reserved for a specified class of traffic proceeding in the same direction as general traffic in an adjoining traffic lane; and

"*works bus*" means a vehicle constructed or adapted to carry 12 or more passengers (excluding the driver) which has been provided by an employer for the purpose of carrying persons employed by him or on his behalf to or from their place of employment and is being used for that purpose.

[Regulation 4 is printed as amended by S.I. 1995 No. 3107; the Education Act 1996, s.582(3) and   **B48.09**
Sched. 39, para.1(4).

  The words omitted from the definitions of "school bus" and "trunk road" apply to Scotland.

  In the definition of "maximum gross weight", the reference to section 41(7) of the 1988 Act has been inserted editorially in place of a reference to section 41(8).

  As to "Pelican" crossings, see now the Zebra, Pelican and Puffin Pedestrian Crossings Regulations and General Directions 1997 (S.I. 1997 No. 2400) below.

5. Interpretation of "speed limit"

(1) In these Regulations "*speed limit*" means—   **B48.10**

    (a) a maximum or minimum limit of speed on the driving of vehicles on a road—

        (i) imposed by an order under section 14 of the 1984 Act (temporary prohibition or restriction of traffic on roads);

        (ii) imposed by regulations under section 17 of the 1984 Act (traffic regulation on special roads);

        (iii) arising by virtue of the road being restricted for the purposes of section 81 of the 1984 Act (general speed limit for restricted roads);

        (iv) imposed by an order under section 84 of the 1984 Act (speed limits on roads other than restricted roads);

        (v) imposed by an order under section 88 of the 1984 Act (temporary speed limits); or

        (vi) imposed by or under a local Act; or

    (b) a maximum limit of speed on the driving of vehicles on a road advised by a traffic authority,

and "*maximum speed limit*" and "*minimum speed limit*" should be construed accordingly.

(2) In these Regulations "*national speed limit*" means any prohibition imposed on a road by the 70 miles per hour, 60 miles per hour and 50 miles per hour (Temporary Speed Limit) Order 1977 [*q.v.*] or by regulation 3 of the Motorways (Speed Limit) Regulations 1974 [*S.I. 1974 No. 502; not reproduced in this work*].

6. References in the Regulations

In these Regulations, unless it is expressly provided otherwise or the context otherwise   **B48.11**
requires—

    (a) a reference to a numbered regulation is a reference to the regulation so numbered in these Regulations;

    (b) a reference to a numbered paragraph is a reference to the paragraph so numbered in the regulation in which the reference occurs;

    (c) a reference to a sub-paragraph followed by a number or letter is a reference to the sub-paragraph bearing that number or letter in the paragraph in which the reference occurs;

(d) a reference to a numbered diagram is a reference to the diagram so numbered in a Schedule to these Regulations;

(e) a reference to a sign or road marking shown in a diagram in a Schedule to these Regulations means a sign or road marking of the size, colour and type shown in that diagram and prescribed by these Regulations and includes a reference to that sign or road marking as varied in accordance with these Regulations;

(f) a reference to the information, warning, requirement, restriction, prohibition or speed limit conveyed by a sign shown in a diagram includes a reference to that information, warning, requirement, restriction, prohibition or speed limit, however expressed, as varied to accord with any variation of the diagram made in accordance with these Regulations; and

(g) in any provision which includes a table, references to a table or to a numbered table are to the table or as the case may be to the table so numbered in that provision.

7. Interpretation of Schedules 1 to 12

B48.12   (1) In any untitled table under or beside any diagram (in this paragraph referred to as "*the diagram*") in Schedules 1 to 12—

(a) in item 1 any regulations which are specified are regulations in these Regulations in which a specific reference is made to the diagram;

(b) in item 2 any directions which are specified are directions in the Traffic Signs General Directions 1994 in which a specific reference is made to the diagram;

(c) in item 3 any diagrams which are specified are diagrams in the Schedules to these Regulations which show signs which may or must be placed in conjunction or in combination with the sign shown in the diagram;

(d) in item 4 any item which is specified is an item in Schedule 16 which specifies permitted variants to the diagram; and

(e) in item 5 any item which is specified is an item in Schedule 17 which specifies the illumination requirements for the sign shown in the diagram.

(2) The table entitled "Table of combinations" under or beside any diagram in Part III of Schedule 12 indicates the manner in which the sign shown in that diagram may be varied in accordance with paragraphs (6) to (8) of regulation 17.

(3) Dimensions indicated on any diagram shown in Schedules 1 to 12 are expressed in millimetres unless otherwise specified.

SECTION 2

General provisions

8. Authorisations by the Secretary of State

B48.13   Nothing in these Regulations shall be taken to limit the powers of the Secretary of State under section 64 of the 1984 Act to authorise the erection or retention of traffic signs of a character not prescribed by these Regulations.

9. Temporary obstructions

B48.14   Nothing in these Regulations shall have effect so as to authorise any persons not otherwise authorised to do so to place on or near a road any object or device for warning traffic of a temporary obstruction.

10. Application of section 36 of the Road Traffic Act 1988 to signs and disqualification for offences

(1) Section 36 of the 1988 Act shall apply to— **B48.15**

(a) the signs shown in any of the diagrams 601.1, 602, 606, 610, 611.1, 614, 616, 626.2, 629.2, 629.2A, 784, 953, 953.1 and 7023 and to the sign shown in diagram 602 when placed in combination with that shown in diagram 778 or 778.1;

(b) the red light signal when displayed by the light signals prescribed by regulation 30 or by regulation 32;

(c) the road markings shown in diagram 1013.1 or 1013.3 insofar as those markings convey the requirements specified in regulation 26;

(d) the road marking shown in diagram 1003 insofar as that marking conveys the requirements specified in regulation 25;

(e) the road markings shown in diagrams 1043, 1044 and 1045;

(f) the light signals prescribed by regulation 30(2) as varied in accordance with regulation 31 when they are displaying the green arrow signals shown in diagrams 3000.4, 3000.6, 3002, 3003, 3004, 3005, 3006, 3007, 3008, 3009.1, 3011.1 and 3011.2 insofar as they convey the restrictions specified in paragraphs (1)(f) and (1)(g) of regulation 33; and

(g) the light signal shown in diagram 3013.1.

(2) The signs hereby specified for the purposes of column 5 of the entry in Schedule 2 to the Road Traffic Offenders Act 1988 [*q.v.*] relating to offences under section 36 of the 1988 Act are—

(a) the signs shown in diagrams 601.1 and 616;

(b) the signs shown in diagrams 629.2 and 629.2A;

(c) the sign shown in diagram 784;

(d) the red light signal when displayed by the light signals prescribed by regulation 30 or by regulation 32;

(e) the road markings shown in diagram 1013.1 or 1013.3 insofar as those markings convey the requirements specified in regulation 26(2); and

(f) the light signals prescribed by regulation 30(2) when they are displaying the green arrow signals shown in diagrams 3000.4, 3000.6, 3002, 3003, 3004, 3005, 3006, 3007, 3008, 3009.1, 3011.1 and 3011.2 insofar as they convey the restrictions specified in paragraphs (1)(f) and (1)(g) of regulation 33.

11. Signs, markings and signals to be of the sizes, colours and types shown in the diagrams

(1) Subject to the provisions of these Regulations, a sign for conveying information or a **B48.16**
warning, requirement, restriction, prohibition or speed limit of the description specified under a diagram in Schedules 1 to 7, Part II of Schedule 10 and Schedule 12 to traffic on roads shall be of the size, colour and type shown in the diagram.

(2) The signs shown in diagrams 515.1, 515.1A, 515.2, 1012.2, 1012.3, 1049.1 and 7102 shall be of the size, colour and type shown in the two parts of those diagrams.

(3) In Schedule 6, a road marking shown in a diagram as a horizontal line shall be laid transversely, and a marking shown as a vertical line shall be laid longitudinally, to the flow of traffic, except so far as the nature of the diagram or the caption to the diagram indicates that it may or should be laid in another direction.

(4) The road marking shown in diagram 1055 shall be white, silver or light grey in colour.

12. Variations of dimensions

B48.17

(1) Where any diagram in Schedules 1 to 12 specifies a dimension for an element of a sign together with a dimension for that element in brackets, the dimensions so specified shall, subject to paragraph (2), be alternatives.

(2) Subject to paragraphs (3) and (4), where alternative dimensions are specified for more than one element of a sign, the dimensions chosen for each element must correspond with one another so that the shape and proportions of the sign are as shown in the diagram.

(3) Paragraph (2) does not apply to the road marking shown in diagram 1009 and the respective lengths of the lines comprised in that sign and of the gaps between them may be either—

    (a) 600 and 300 millimetres, in which case the width of the lines may be 100, 150 or 200 millimetres; or

    (b) 300 and 150 millimetres, in which case the width of the lines shall be 100 millimetres.

(4) Paragraph (2) does not apply to the road markings shown in diagrams 1013.3, 1035, 1036.1, 1036.2, 1037.1, 1040, 1040.2, 1040.4 and 1041.

(5) Where any diagram in Schedules 1 to 12 specifies a maximum and a minimum dimension for an element of a sign, the dimension chosen for that element shall, subject to the footnote to Table 1, be not more than the maximum and not less than the minimum.

(6) Where maximum and minimum dimensions are specified for more than one element of a sign, the dimensions chosen for each element must correspond with one another so that the shape and proportions of the sign are as shown in the diagram.

(7) Where a sign shown in diagram 606, 607, 609, 610, 611.1, 612, 613, 614, 616, 636, 638, 642, 643, 644 or 645 is placed temporarily on a road by a constable or a person acting under the instructions (whether general or specific) of the chief officer of police for the purposes of indicating a temporary statutory provision, any dimension in the diagram for the diameter of a roundel, or for the sign may be reduced so long as any dimension shown in the diagram for the diameter of a roundel or for the measurement horizontally of the sign is at least 200 millimetres, and the height of any lettering is at least 20 millimetres.

(8) Any sign shown in diagrams 960, 960.1, 7201, 7202, 7203, 7203.1, 7204, 7205, 7206, 7207, 7210, 7211, 7212, 7213, 7214, 7215, 7216, 7217, 7218, 7220, 7221, 7230, 7231, 7232, 7233, 7234, 7235, 7236, 7237, 7238, 7239, 7240, 7250, 7251, 7252, 7253, 7254, 7255, 7256 or in a diagram in Schedule 7 (other than diagrams 2032, 2130, 2208, 2708, 2711, 2712, 2713, 2714, 2715, 2922, 2923 and 2932) shall be of such dimensions as, having regard to the character of the road and the speed of the vehicular traffic generally using it, are necessary to accommodate any place name, route symbol or number, arrow, indication of distance, symbol or any other indication which, in accordance with these Regulations, may be shown on the sign and which it is appropriate to show for the purpose for which that sign is placed on the road.

(9) Any sign shown in a diagram in Part III of Schedule 12 shall be of such dimensions as, having regard to the character of the road and the speed of traffic generally using it, are necessary to accommodate the route symbols or arrows appropriate to the number of traffic lanes and the nature of the road works in relation to which the sign is placed.

(10) Any dimension (not being an angle or specified as a maximum or minimum) specified in these Regulations shall be treated as permitted by these Regulations if it is varied in accordance with the following Tables, subject, in the case of Tables 1 and 2, to the Notes to those Tables.

TABLE 1
DIAGRAMS IN SCHEDULES 1 TO 5, 7, 10 AND 12—HEIGHT OF LETTERS OR NUMBERS

(1) Item	(2) Dimensions shown in diagrams	(3) Permitted variations
1.	100 millimetres or more	Up to 5% of the dimension
2.	Less than 100 millimetres	Up to 7.5% of the dimension

B48.18

NOTE: Where the height of letters or numbers is expressed as a range within maximum and minimum dimensions the permitted variations indicated in this Table shall apply to those dimensions shown as the maximum and minimum.

TABLE 2
DIAGRAMS IN SCHEDULE 6—ALL DIMENSIONS

(1) Item	(2) Dimensions shown in diagrams	(3) Permitted variations
1.	3 metres or more	(i) Up to 15% of the dimension where the varied dimension is greater than the specified dimension; or (ii) Up to 10% of the dimension where the varied dimension is less than the specified dimension.
2.	300 millimetres or more, but less than 3 metres	(i) Up to 20% of the dimension where the varied dimension is greater than the specified dimension; or (ii) Up to 10% of the dimension where the varied dimension is less than the specified dimension.
3.	10 millimetres or more, but less than 300 millimetres	(i) Up to 30% of the dimension where the varied dimension is greater than the specified dimension; or (ii) Up to 10% of the dimension where the varied dimension is less than the specified dimension.
4.	Less than 10 millimetres	(i) Up to 2 millimetres more than the dimension where the varied dimension is greater than the specified dimension; or (ii) Up to 1 millimetre less than the dimension where the varied dimension is less than the specified dimension.

B48.19

NOTE: Where a dimension denoting the length or width of a road marking is varied in accordance with this Table, and there is a space between two parts of the marking, the dimensions of that space may be varied as required to accommodate the variation of the length or width of the marking, provided that the character of the marking is maintained.

TABLE 3

ALL DIMENSIONS OTHER THAN THOSE IN TABLES 1 AND 2

B48.20

(1) *Item*	(2) *Dimensions shown in diagrams*	(3) *Permitted variations*
1.	300 millimetres or more	Up to 5% of the dimension
2.	50 millimetres or more, but less than 300 millimetres	Up to 7.5% of the dimension
3.	Less than 50 millimetres	Up to 10% of the dimension

(11) Any variation of any angle specified in any diagram in Schedule 1, 6 or 8, except diagrams 1043 and 1044, shall be treated as permitted by these Regulations if the variation does not exceed 5 degrees.

(12) Where—

    (a) overall dimensions are given for a sign shown in any diagram in the Schedules to these Regulations; and

    (b) the legend on that sign is varied in accordance with regulation 17 and with item 4 of the table appearing under or beside that diagram,

the overall dimensions or the number of lines filled by the legend, or both, may be varied so far as necessary to give effect to the variation of the legend.

13. Proportions and form of letters, numerals, symbols and other characters

B48.21   (1) Subject to paragraphs (2), (3) and (5)—

    (a) all letters, numerals and other characters incorporated in the signs or parts of the signs shown in the diagrams in Schedules 1 to 5, 7, 10 and 12 which have a red, blue, brown, black or green background (other than those incorporated in the bottom panel of diagram 674, diagrams 973, 973.1, 2401, 2402, 2403, 2607, 2610, 2610.1, 2610.2, the top panels of diagrams 2919 and 2920, the petrol price display in diagram 2919, and diagrams 5001.1, 5001.2, 5003, 5003.1, 5005 and 5005.1, the top and bottom panels of diagram 7008 and the words "National Trust for Scotland" used in conjunction with the symbol shown in diagram T303 in Part IV of Schedule 14) and the signs shown in diagrams 2714 and 2715 shall have the proportions and form shown in Part I of Schedule 13; and

    (b) all letters, numerals and other characters incorporated in the signs or the parts of signs shown in the diagrams in Schedules 1 to 5, 7, 10 and 12 which have a white, yellow or orange background (other than those incorporated in the bottom panel of diagram 674, diagrams 973, 973.1, 2401, 2402, 2403, 2610, 2610.1, 2610.2, 2714, 2715, the top panels of diagrams 2919 and 2920, and the top and bottom panels of diagram 7008) shall have the proportions and form shown in Part II of Schedule 13.

(2) Letters and numerals used for the purpose of indicating a route number on any sign shown in a diagram in Part X of Schedule 7 (other than those incorporated in

diagram 2913 and 2914) shall have the proportions and form shown in Part III of Schedule 13, except where a route number is indicated in brackets on a sign shown in diagram 2904, 2904.1, 2906, 2908 or 2909 in which case those letters and numerals shall have the proportions and form shown in either Part I or Part III of Schedule 13 as appropriate.

(3) Letters and numerals used for the purpose of indicating a route number on any sign shown in a diagram in Part III of Schedule 12 when used on a motorway shall have the proportions and form shown in Part IV of Schedule 13.

(4) Subject to and within the limits of any dimension specified as a maximum or minimum in diagrams 973, 973.1, 2401, 2402, 2403, 2607, 2610, 2610.1, 2610.2, the top panels of diagrams 2919 and 2920, the petrol price display in diagram 2919, and the top and bottom panels of diagram 7008 any letters or numerals or other characters incorporated in those diagrams may have proportions and form other than the proportions and form shown in Schedule 13.

(5) All letters, numerals, symbols and other characters incorporated in variable message signs shall have the general proportions and form shown in Part V of Schedule 13 where the construction or method of operation of the sign does not permit the use of letters, numerals and other characters of the proportions and form shown in Part I, II, III or IV of Schedule 13 or of symbols shown in diagrams in Schedules 1 to 5, 10 or 12.

(6) All letters, numerals and other characters incorporated in the road markings shown in the diagrams in Schedule 6 shall have the proportions and form shown in Part VI of Schedule 13.

(7) Symbols incorporated in signs for the purpose of indicating diversion routes to be followed in an emergency shall have the proportions and form shown in Part VII of Schedule 13.

(8) Symbols incorporated in signs for the purpose of indicating the type of a tourist attraction shall have the proportions and form shown in Schedule 14.

14. Signs attached to vehicles

(1) A sign attached to a vehicle of the description and in the position on that vehicle specified in an item in column (2) of the Table, when the vehicle is on a road which is subject to a maximum speed limit specified in column (3) of that item, shall be of the size, colour and type shown in one of the diagrams specified in column (4) of that item.   **B48.22**

TABLE

(1) *Item*	(2) *Description of vehicle, and position*	(3) *Maximum speed limit*	(4) *Diagram numbers*
1.	Road maintenance vehicle, on the front	30mph or under	610, 7001 and 7001.1
2.	Road maintenance vehicle, on the rear	30mph or under	610, 7001, 7001.1, 7401, 7401.1, 7402, 7403 and 7404

[*continued on next page*

(1) *Item*	(2) *Description of vehicle, and position*	(3) *Maximum speed limit*	(4) *Diagram numbers*
3.	Road maintenance vehicle, on the rear	More than 30 mph	7401, 7401.1, 7402, 7403 and 7404
4.	Police vehicle, on the front or the rear	70mph or under	829.1, 829.2, 829.3 and 829.4

(2) The operating requirements for the lamps that form part of the signs shown in diagrams 7401, 7402 and 7403 are that—

(a) the lamps shall be illuminated only when the signs are being used in accordance with the Table; and

(b) each lamp shall show an intermittent amber light at a rate of flashing of not less than 60 nor more than 90 flashes per minute, and in such a manner that the lights of one horizontal pair are always shown when the lights of the other horizontal pair are not shown.

SECTION 3

Warning, regulatory and informatory traffic signs

15. Sign shown in diagram 610 and its significance

B48.23   (1) Except as provided in paragraphs (2) and (3), the requirement conveyed by the sign shown in diagram 610 shall be that vehicular traffic passing the sign must keep to the left of the sign where the arrow is pointed downwards to the left, or to the right of the sign where the arrow is pointed downwards to the right.

(2) On an occasion where a vehicle is being used for fire brigade, ambulance or police purposes and the observance of the requirement specified in paragraph (1) would be likely to hinder the use of that vehicle for one of those purposes then, instead of that requirement, the requirement conveyed by the sign in question shall be that the vehicle shall not proceed beyond that sign in such a manner or at such a time as to be likely to endanger any person.

(3) The requirement specified in paragraph (1) does not apply to a tramcar or trolley vehicle.

16. Signs shown in diagrams 601.1, 602, 778, 778.1 and 784 and their significance

B48.24   (1) The requirements conveyed to vehicular traffic on roads by a sign shown in the diagram specified in column (2) of an item in the Table are specified in column (3) of that item.

TABLE

(1) Item	(2) Diagram number	(3) Requirements
1.	601.1	(a) Every vehicle shall stop before crossing the transverse line shown in diagram 1002.1 or, if that line is not clearly visible, before entering the major road in respect of which the sign shown in diagram 601.1 has been provided; and
		(b) no vehicle shall cross the transverse line shown in diagram 1002.1 or, if that line is not clearly visible, enter the major road in respect of which the sign shown in diagram 601.1 has been provided, so as to be likely to endanger the driver of or any passenger in any other vehicle or to cause that driver to change the speed or course of his vehicle in order to avoid an accident.
2.	602	No vehicle shall cross the transverse line shown in diagram 1003 nearer to the major road at the side of which that line is placed, or if that line is not clearly visible, enter that major road, so as to be likely to endanger the driver of or any passenger in any other vehicle or to cause that driver to change the speed or course of his vehicle in order to avoid an accident.
3.	602 when placed in combination with 778 or 778.1	No vehicle shall cross the transverse line shown in diagram 1003 nearer to the level crossing at the side of which that line is placed, or if that line is not clearly visible, enter that level crossing, so as to be likely to endanger the driver of or any passenger in any railway vehicle or tramcar or to cause that driver to change the speed of his vehicle in order to avoid an accident.
4.	784	No abnormal transport unit shall proceed onto or over an automatic half-barrier level crossing or an automatic open crossing (R) unless—
		(a) the driver of the unit has used a telephone provided at or near the crossing for the purpose of obtaining from a person, authorised in that behalf by the railway or tramway authority, permission for the unit to proceed;

[continued on next page

(1) *Item*	(2) *Diagram number*	(3) *Requirements*
4.— *cont.*		(b) that permission has been obtained before the unit proceeds; and (c) the unit proceeds in accordance with any terms attached to that permission. Provided that sub-paragraphs (b) and (c) above shall not apply if— (i) on the use by the driver of the telephone placed at or near the crossing he receives an indication for not less than two minutes that the telephone at the other end of the telephone line is being called, but no duly authorised person answers it, or he receives no indication at all due to a fault or malfunction of the telephone; and (ii) the driver then drives the unit on to the crossing with the reasonable expectation of crossing it within times specified in a railway or tramway notice at that telephone as being times between which railway vehicles or tramcars do not normally travel over that crossing.

(2) In this regulation—

"*abnormal transport unit*" means—

    (a) a motor vehicle or a vehicle combination—

        (i) the overall length of which, inclusive of the load (if any) on the vehicle or the combination, exceeds 55 feet; or

        (ii) the overall width of which, inclusive of the load (if any) on the vehicle or the combination, exceeds 9 feet 6 inches; or

        (iii) the maximum gross weight of which exceeds 38 tonnes; or

    (b) a motor vehicle, or a vehicle combination, which in either case is incapable of proceeding, or is unlikely to proceed, over an automatic railway level crossing at a speed exceeding 5 miles per hour;

"*driver*", in relation to an abnormal transport unit, means where that unit is a single motor vehicle the driver of that vehicle and, where that unit is a vehicle combination, the driver of the only or the foremost motor vehicle forming part of that combination; and

"*vehicle combination*" means a combination of vehicles made up of one or more motor vehicles and one or more trailers all of which are linked together when travelling.

17. Permitted variants

B48.25   (1) Where the circumstances in which a sign shown in a diagram in a Schedule (other than Schedule 6) to these Regulations is to be placed so require or where appropriate in those circumstances, the form of the sign shall or may be varied—

(a) in the manner (if any) allowed or required in item 4 of the untitled table below or beside the diagram; or

(b) in the manner allowed or required in column (3) of an item in Schedule 16, if the diagram is one whose number is given in column (2) of that item.

(2) A symbol in the form of a prescribed sign to which direction 7 of the Traffic Signs General Directions 1994 applies shall not be incorporated in a sign in accordance with item 31 of Schedule 16, except in circumstances where it could be placed as a sign in accordance with that direction.

(3) A symbol incorporated as mentioned in paragraph (2) shall or may be varied in the same manner as the sign which the symbol represents or from which it is derived.

(4) In each of the signs shown in diagrams 780, 780.1 and 780.2 the safe height shown on the sign shall be varied where necessary so that it is between 1 and 2 feet (450 to 600 millimetres) less than the height of the lowest part of the overhead wire, of which the sign gives warning, over the highest part of the surface of the carriageway beneath that wire.

(5) Where a sign shown in a diagram in Schedule 7 indicates a road or a route, and that road or route is temporarily closed, there may be affixed to the sign or to that part of the sign where that road or route is indicated, in order to cancel temporarily the indication, a board coloured red and displaying in white lettering the words "Road temporarily closed" or "Route temporarily closed".

(6) In this paragraph and paragraphs (7) and (8)—

(a) "*combination sign*" means a sign shown in diagram 7201, 7210, 7211, 7212, 7213, 7214, 7215, 7216, 7217, 7218, 7220, 7221, 7230, 7231, 7232, 7233, 7234, 7235, 7236, 7237, 7238, 7239 or 7240;

(b) "*panel*" means a sign shown in diagram 7260, 7261, 7262, 7263, 7264, 7270, 7271, 7272, 7273, 7274 or 7275 when used as part of a combination sign and references to a panel whose number is shown in a Table of combinations are to a sign shown in a diagram having a number so shown;

(c) "*permitted combination*" means one of the combinations specified in paragraph (8);

(d) "*the table*" in relation to a combination sign means the Table of combinations appearing below or beside the diagram in which that sign is shown;

(e) "*top panel*" means a panel shown at the top of a combination sign and "*bottom panel*" means a panel shown at the bottom of such a sign.

(7) If and only if the top and bottom panels of the sign as varied together constitute a permitted combination, a combination sign may be varied in the following ways—

(a) by substituting for the top panel or, where a top panel is not shown, by adding as a top panel, a panel whose number is shown in item (1) of the table;

(b) by substituting for the bottom panel or, where a bottom panel is not shown, by adding as a bottom panel, a panel whose number is shown in item (2) of the table;

(c) if the word "none" appears in item (1) of the table, by omitting the top panel;

(d) if the word "none" appears in item (2) of the table, by omitting the bottom panel.

(8) Each of the following is a permitted combination—

(a) a top panel whose number appears in item (1) of a column in the table and a bottom panel whose number appears in item (2) of the same column;

(b) a top panel whose number appears in item (1) of a column in the table and, if the word "none" appears in item (2) of the same column, no bottom panel;

(c) a bottom panel whose number appears in item (2) of a column in the table and, if the word "none" appears in item (1) of the same column, no top panel;

(d) if the word "none" appears in both items of the same column of the table, no top panel and no bottom panel.

(9) Where the form of a sign is varied in accordance with these Regulations, the information, warning, requirement, restriction, prohibition or speed limit conveyed to traffic by the sign is varied to accord with the form of the sign as varied.

18. Illumination of signs

B48.26 (1) Subject to paragraph (2), every sign shown in a diagram whose number is indicated in column (2) of an item in Schedule 17 shall be illuminated in the manner and at the times described in column (3) of that item.

(2) Where a sign shown in a diagram whose number is indicated in column (2) of an item in Schedule 17 is placed for the purpose of conveying to vehicular traffic a warning, information, prohibition, restriction or requirement which applies only at certain times, the sign shall be illuminated in accordance with that Schedule only during those times.

(3) Where a sign shown in a diagram whose number is indicated in column (2) of an item in Schedule 17 is illuminated by means of external lighting, then that means of lighting shall be fitted to—

(a) the sign; or

(b) the structure on which the sign is mounted or which is otherwise specially provided,

except that if a sign is mounted on a bridge, tunnel or similar structure over a road the means of lighting may alternatively be mounted separately in a manner such as to illuminate the face of the sign effectively.

B48.27 **19.**—(1) Nothing in this regulation shall apply to the signs shown in diagrams 560, 561, 776, 781, 5001.1, 5001.2, 5003, 5003.1, 5005 and 5005.1.

(2) Subject to the provisions of regulation 18 and paragraph (1), any sign shown in a diagram in Schedules 1 to 5, 7, 10 and 12—

(a) when placed as part of a road works scheme must, and

(b) in other situations may,

be illuminated by the use of retroreflecting material in accordance with the following provisions of this regulation.

(3) Subject to paragraph (4), where retroreflecting material is used on any part of a sign shown in a diagram, all other parts of that sign shall also be illuminated by means of retroreflecting material.

(4) No retroreflecting material shall be applied to—

(a) any part of a sign coloured black;

(b) that part of the sign shown in diagram 605.2 which is coloured fluorescent yellow, unless the retroreflecting material is applied to that part in horizontal strips with a gap between each strip, or unless the retroreflecting material is itself also fluorescent;

(c) that part of a sign shown in diagram 2714 or 2715 which is coloured orange,

and in this paragraph the word "*part*", in relation to a sign, means any part of that sign which is uniformly coloured and bounded by parts of a different colour.

20. Illumination of plates

(1) Where a plate is placed in combination with a sign shown in a diagram in Schedules 1 to 5 or 12, and that sign is illuminated in accordance with regulation 18, the plate shall, subject to paragraph (2), be illuminated by the same means as the sign.

B48.28

(2) Paragraph (1) shall not apply where the means of lighting provided for the illumination of the sign adequately illuminates the plate.

21. Illumination of signs shown in diagrams 560 and 561

(1) The signs shown in diagrams 560 and 561 shall not be illuminated by the fitting of a means of internal or external lighting.

B48.29

(2) A sign shown in a diagram whose number appears in column (2) of an item in the Table and having the dimension specified in column (3) of that item shall be illuminated by either of the methods prescribed in paragraph (3) which are shown in column (4) of the item, and by no other method.

(3) The prescribed methods of illumination are—

TABLE

(1) Item	(2) Diagram number	(3) Dimension	(4) Method of illumination
1.	560	150 millimetres diameter	Paragraph 3(a) or (b)
2.	560	75 millimetres or more but less than 150 millimetres diameter	Paragraph 3(c) or (d)
3.	561	180 square centimetres area	Paragraph 3(b) or (e)

(a) the use of 14 circular reflectors of the corner cube type, each reflector having a diameter of 22 millimetres;

(b) the use of retroreflecting material extending over the whole surface of the sign;

(c) the use of a single circular reflector of the corner cube type extending over the whole surface of the sign;

(d) the use of reflectors consisting of bi-convex lenses extending over the whole surface of the sign; and

(e) the use of a single rectangular reflector of the corner cube type extending over the whole surface of the sign.

22. Buses and coaches

(1) In the signs shown in the permitted variants of diagrams 618.1, 618.2, 618.3, 618.3A, 620 and 820, in diagrams 877, 954, 954.1, 954.2, 954.3, 970, 973, 973.1, 974, 975, 1025, 1025.1, 1025.2 and 1025.3 and in the permitted variant of diagram 1028.2 the expressions "*bus*", "*buses*" and "*buses and coaches*" have the meanings given in paragraphs (2) and (3).

B48.30

(2) "*Buses*" in the signs referred to in paragraph (1) means—

(a) before 1st January 1997—

(i) public service vehicles used for the provision of local services or scheduled express services;

    (ii) school buses; or

    (iii) works buses; and

  (b) after 31st December 1996—

    (i) motor vehicles constructed or adapted to carry more than 8 passengers (exclusive of the driver); and

    (ii) local buses not so constructed or adapted;

and "*bus*" shall be construed accordingly.

(3) The expression "*buses and coaches*" referred to in paragraph (1) means until 31st December 1996 vehicles constructed or adapted to carry 12 or more passengers (exclusive of the driver).

23. Bus lanes

B48.31   (1) In the sign shown in diagram 962, 962.2, 963, 963.2, 964, 1048 or 1048.1 the expression "*bus lane*" has the meaning given in paragraphs (2) and (3).

(2) Before 1st January 1997 "*bus lane*" in the signs referred to in paragraph (1) means a traffic lane reserved for—

  (a) public service vehicles used in the provision of local services or scheduled express services;

  (b) school buses;

  (c) works buses; and

  (d) pedal cycles and taxis where indicated on the sign shown in diagram 958 or 959 and pedal cycles where indicated on the sign shown in diagram 960, 962.2, 963.2 or 1048.1.

(3) After 31st December 1996 "*bus lane*" in the signs referred to in paragraph (1) means a traffic lane reserved for—

  (a) motor vehicles constructed or adapted to carry more than 8 passengers (exclusive of the driver);

  (b) local buses not so constructed or adapted; and

  (c) pedal cycles and taxis where indicated on the sign shown in diagram 958 or 959 and pedal cycles where indicated on the sign shown in diagram 960, 962.2, 963.2 or 1048.1.

24. Bus symbols

B48.32   (1) Before 1st January 1997 the symbol representing a bus ("*the bus symbol*") in the sign or the permitted variant of the sign shown in a diagram whose number is indicated in column (2) of an item in the Table refers to the vehicles indicated in column (3) of that item.

TABLE

(1) *Item*	(2) *Diagram number*	(3) *Vehicles*
1.	952	All motor vehicles constructed or adapted to carry more than 12 passengers (exclusive of the driver), except— (a) public service vehicles used

[continued on next page

(1) Item	(2) Diagram number	(3) Vehicles
1.— cont.		in the provision of local services; (b) scheduled express services; (c) school buses; or (d) works buses.
2.	953, the permitted variant of 953.1 with the bus symbol, the permitted variants of 958 and 959 without the legend "local", 960, 962, 962.2, 963, 963.2 and 970	(a) Public service vehicles used in the provision of local services; (b) scheduled express services; (c) school buses; or (d) works buses.
3.	(a) The permitted variants of 640.2A, 665 and 666 with the bus symbol; (b) 969 and 2106; (c) the permitted variants of 958 and 959 with the legend "& coaches" placed on the symbol; and (d) the permitted variants of diagrams 832.3, 832.4, 832.5, 832.6 and 832.7	All motor vehicles constructed or adapted to carry 12 or more passengers (exclusive of the driver).
4.	972	Public service vehicles used in the provision of excursions or tours.

(2) After 31st December 1996 the bus symbol when incorporated into any sign refers to—

(a) motor vehicles constructed or adapted to carry more than 8 passengers (exclusive of the driver); or

(b) local buses not so constructed or adapted.

(3) In the signs shown in diagrams 953, the permitted variant of 953.1, 958, 959 and 960 the word "local" on the bus symbol indicates that the road or the traffic lane on or near which the sign has been placed shall be used only by local buses.

SECTION 4

Road markings

25. Road marking shown in diagram 1003 and its significance

(1) The requirements conveyed to vehicular traffic on roads by the road marking shown in diagram 1003 shall be as follows.   **B48.33**

(2) Except as provided by paragraphs (3) and (4), the requirement conveyed by the transverse lines shown in diagram 1003, whether or not they are placed in conjunction with the sign shown in diagram 602 or 1023, shall be that no vehicle shall proceed past such one of those lines as is nearer the major road into that road in a manner or at a time likely to endanger the driver of or any passenger in a vehicle on the major road or to cause the driver of such a vehicle to change its speed or course in order to avoid an accident.

(3) Wherever the transverse lines are placed in conjunction with the sign shown in diagram 602, and that sign is at the same time placed in combination with the sign shown in diagram 778 or 778.1 at a level crossing, then the requirement shall be that no vehicle shall proceed past such one of those lines as is nearer the level crossing in a manner or at a time likely to endanger the driver of or any passenger in a railway vehicle or tramcar, or to cause that driver to change the speed of his vehicle in order to avoid an accident.

(4) Wherever the transverse lines are placed in advance of a point in the road where the width of the carriageway narrows significantly, then the requirement shall be that no vehicle shall proceed past such one of these lines as is nearer to the point of narrowing in a manner or at a time likely to endanger the driver of or any passenger in a vehicle that is proceeding in the opposite direction to the first-mentioned vehicle, or to necessitate the driver of such a vehicle to change its speed or course in order to avoid an accident.

26. Road markings shown in diagrams 1013.1 and 1013.3 and their significance

B48.34   (1) A road marking for conveying the requirements specified in paragraph (2) and the warning specified in paragraph (5) shall be of the size, colour and type shown in diagram 1013.1 or 1013.3.

(2) The requirements conveyed by the road marking mentioned in paragraph (1) shall be that—

    (a) subject to paragraph (3), no vehicle shall stop on any length of road along which the marking has been placed at any point between the ends of the marking; and

    (b) subject to paragraph (4), every vehicle proceeding on any length of road along which the marking has been so placed that, as viewed in the direction of travel of the vehicle, a continuous line is on the left of a broken line or of another continuous line, shall be so driven as to keep the first-mentioned continuous line on the right hand or off side of the vehicle.

(3) Nothing in paragraph (2)(a) shall apply—

    (a) so as to prevent a vehicle stopping on any length of road so long as may be necessary for any of the following purposes—

        (i) to enable a person to board or alight from the vehicle,

        (ii) to enable goods to be loaded on to or to be unloaded from the vehicle,

        (iii) to enable the vehicle to be used in connection with—

            (A) any building operation or demolition;

            (B) the removal of any obstruction to traffic;

            (C) the maintenance, improvement or reconstruction of that length of road; or

            (D) the laying, erection, alteration or repair in or near that length of road of any sewer or of any main, pipe or apparatus for the supply of gas, water or electricity, or of any telecommunications apparatus as defined in paragraph 1(1) of Schedule 2 to the Telecommunications Act 1984,

        if the vehicle cannot be used for such a purpose without stopping on the length of road;

    (b) so as to prevent a vehicle stopping in a lay-by;

    (c) to a vehicle for the time being used for fire brigade, ambulance or police purposes;

    (d) to a pedal bicycle not having a sidecar attached thereto, whether additional means of propulsion by mechanical power are attached to the bicycle or not;

(e) to a vehicle stopping in any case where the person in control of the vehicle is required by law to stop, or is obliged to do so in order to avoid an accident, or is prevented from proceeding by circumstances outside his control;

(f) to anything done with the permission or at the direction of a constable in uniform or in accordance with the direction of a traffic warden; or

(g) to a vehicle on a road with more than one traffic lane in each direction.

(4) Nothing in paragraph (2)(b) shall be taken to prohibit a vehicle from being driven across, or so as to straddle, the continuous line referred to in that paragraph, if it is safe to do so and if necessary to do so—

(a) to enable the vehicle to enter, from the side of the road on which it is proceeding, land or premises adjacent to the length of road on which the line is placed, or another road joining that road;

(b) in order to pass a stationary vehicle;

(c) owing to circumstances outside the control of the driver;

(d) in order to avoid an accident;

(e) in order to pass a road maintenance vehicle which is in use, is moving at a speed not exceeding 10 miles per hour, and is displaying to the rear the sign shown in diagram 610 or 7403;

(f) in order to pass a pedal cycle moving at a speed not exceeding 10 miles per hour;

(g) in order to pass a horse that is being ridden or led at a speed not exceeding 10 miles per hour; or

(h) for the purposes of complying with any direction of a constable in uniform or a traffic warden.

(5) The warning conveyed by the road marking mentioned in paragraph (1) shall be that no vehicle while travelling next to a broken line placed on the left of a continuous line, as viewed in the direction of travel of the vehicle, should cross or straddle the first-mentioned line unless it is seen by the driver of the vehicle to be safe to do so.

[The term "telecommunications apparatus" is defined in the Telecommunications Act 1984, Sched. 2, **B48.35**
para.1(1), as including:

any apparatus falling within the definition in section 4(3) of this Act and any apparatus not so falling which is designed or adapted for use in connection with the running of a telecommunication system and, in particular—(a) any line, that is to say, any wire, cable, tube, pipe or other similar thing (including its casing or coating) which is so designed or adapted; and (b) any structure, pole or other thing in, on, by or from which any telecommunication apparatus is or may be installed, supported, carried or suspended; and references to the installation of telecommunication apparatus shall be construed accordingly.

Section 4(3) of that Act defines the term "telecommunication apparatus" (except where the extended definition in Schedule 2 applies) as:

apparatus constructed or adapted for use—(a) in transmitting or receiving anything falling within paragraphs (a) to (d) of subsection (1) above [(a) speech, music and other sounds; (b) visual images; (c) signals for the impartation . . . of any matter otherwise than in the form of sounds or visual images; or (d) signals serving for the actuation or control of machinery or apparatus.] which is to be or has been conveyed by means of a telecommunication system; or (b) in conveying, for the purposes of such a system, anything falling within those paragraphs.]

27. Permitted variants

B48.36
(1) Where the circumstances in which a road marking shown in a diagram in Schedule 6 is to be placed so require or where appropriate in those circumstances, the form of the marking shall or may be varied as follows—

(a) in the manner (if any) allowed or required in item 4 of the untitled table below or beside the diagram; or

(b) in the manner allowed or required in column (3) of an item in Schedule 16, if the diagram is one whose number is given in column (2) of that item.

(2) In the road marking shown in diagram 1035, route numbers, place names and the direction in which any arrow-head points shall be varied to accord with the circumstances but the words "turn left", "ahead" or "turn right" shall not be included in the marking.

(3) Where the form of a road marking is varied in accordance with this regulation, the information, warning, requirement, restriction, prohibition or speed limit conveyed by the marking is varied to accord with the form of marking as varied.

28. Illumination of road markings

B48.37
(1) Subject to paragraph (2) a road marking shown in diagram 1001, 1002.1, 1003, 1003.1, 1003.3, 1003.4, 1004, 1004.1, 1005, 1005.1, 1008, 1008.1, 1009, 1010, 1012.1, 1012.2, 1012.3, 1013.1, 1013.3, 1014, 1022, 1023, 1024, 1024.1, 1036.1, 1036.2, 1037.1, 1039, 1040, 1040.2, 1040.3, 1040.4, 1040.5, 1041, 1042, 1046, 1049, 1060, 1060.1, 1061 or 1061.1 shall be illuminated with retroreflecting material.

(2) Paragraph (1) shall not apply to a road marking shown in diagram 1003, 1023 or 1049 when varied for use on a cycle track as defined in the Highways Act 1980 or the Roads (Scotland) Act 1984.

(3) Subject to paragraph (4), studs incorporating reflectors or retroreflecting material and so spaced as to form a single line of studs not less than 3 nor more than 4.5 metres apart shall be fitted—

(a) between the two lines constituting the marking shown in diagram 1013.1 unless that marking—

(i) is placed on an automatic level crossing;

(ii) is placed on a length of the road situated within 90 metres of the transverse stop line shown in diagram 1001 provided in association with any such crossing; or

(iii) is so placed that the continuous lines shown in version B of diagram 1013.1 are more than 175 millimetres apart and are separated by an area of cross-hatching so shown;

(b) between the two continuous parallel lines forming part of the marking shown in diagram 1013.3.

(4) Where the marking shown in diagram 1013.1 is placed in any of the cases referred to in paragraphs (i), (ii) and (iii) of paragraph (3)(a) then the studs mentioned in paragraph (3) shall be fitted either in opposite pairs within the width of each of the two lines or in a single line between them.

(5) Subject to the foregoing provisions of this regulation, and to paragraph (6), any road marking may be illuminated with retroreflecting material, and studs incorporating reflectors or retroreflecting material may be used with a road marking shown in diagram 1004, 1004.1, 1005, 1005.1, 1008, 1008.1, 1009, 1010, 1012.1, 1012.2, 1012.3, 1025.2, 1025.3, 1035, 1040, 1040.2, 1040.3, 1040.4, 1040.5, 1041 or 1042 in such a manner that

any such stud shall not be fitted to any part of the marking coloured white or yellow but shall be applied to the surface of the carriageway in the gaps between parts of the marking.

(6) In the case of a road marking shown in diagram 1012.1, 1012.2, 1012.3 or 1042 the studs shall, if fitted, be applied to the surface of the carriageway at the side of and adjacent to the line shown in the diagram.

(7) Reflectors or retroreflecting material incorporated in studs shall be white except that in the case of studs used with a road marking shown in diagram 1009, 1010, 1012.1, 1012.2, 1012.3, 1025.2, 1025.3, 1040.3, 1041 or 1042 the reflectors or retroreflecting material shall reflect—

(a) red light where the near side edge of a carriageway is indicated to drivers of approaching vehicles, or when placed in conjunction with the markings shown in diagrams 1041 and 1042 to indicate the off side edge of a carriageway;

(b) amber light to indicate the off side edge of a carriageway which is contiguous to a central reservation or to traffic cones or cylinders at road works or the road marking shown in diagram 1040.3, or which carries traffic in one direction only; and

(c) green light when placed in conjunction with a road marking shown in diagram 1009, 1010, 1025.2 or 1025.3 where the edge of any part of the carriageway available for through traffic at a road junction, a lay-by or a parking place is so indicated to drivers of approaching vehicles.

(8) The colour of the parts of the stud other than the reflectors or retroreflecting material shall either be the same as the reflectors or retroreflecting material, or be white, or be a natural metallic finish or other neutral colour, or shall be fluorescent green/yellow in the case of studs placed temporarily at road works.

29. Height of road markings and size of studs

(1) The size and shape of a stud incorporating reflectors or retroreflecting material shall be such that the part which is visible above the surface of the road can be contained within—   **B48.38**

(a) an overall length in the direction of travel of traffic of not less than 35 millimetres and not exceeding 250 millimetres; and

(b) an overall width of not less than 84 millimetres and not exceeding 230 millimetres.

(2) No road marking or stud shall project above the surface of the adjacent carriageway more than 6 millimetres at any point except—

(a) a depressible stud, which shall not project above that surface more than 25 millimetres at its highest point, whether depressed or not;

(b) a non-depressible stud, which shall not project above that surface more than 20 millimetres at its highest point;

(c) the road marking shown in diagram 1003.4, which shall not project above that surface more than 125 millimetres at its highest point or 6 millimetres at its perimeter;

(d) the road marking shown in diagram 1012.2, the raised ribs on which shall project above the surface of the remainder of the marking by 11 millimetres; or

(e) the road marking shown in diagram 1012.3, the raised ribs on which shall project above the surface of the remainder of the marking by 8 millimetres; and

(f) the road marking shown in diagram 1049.1, the height of which above the surface of the adjacent carriageway shall be within the range of dimensions indicated on the second part of that diagram illustrating the cross-section of the marking.

(3) In this regulation, the expression *"depressible stud"* means a stud so fitted that the height by which it, or part of it, projects above the surface of the adjacent carriageway is apt to be reduced when pressure is applied to the stud from above; and *"non-depressible stud"* and *"depressed"* shall be construed accordingly.

SECTION 5

Light signals and warning lights

30. Use of different types of light signals

B48.39　　　(1) Light signals used for the control of vehicular traffic shall be of the size, colour and type prescribed in paragraph (2), (3), (5), (7) or (9).

(2) Subject to regulation 31, light signals used to control vehicular traffic at road junctions, at places where the headroom or the width of the road is permanently restricted, or at places where pedestrians cross the road (other than Pelican crossings) shall be of the size, colour and type shown in diagram 3000, 3000.3, 3000.4, 3000.5 or 3000.6 and be illuminated in the sequence prescribed in paragraph (4).

(3) Light signals used to control vehicular traffic consisting solely of pedal cycles shall be of the size, colour and type shown in diagram 3000.2 and be illuminated in the sequence prescribed in paragraph (4).

(4) The sequence of illumination of the lights shown by the signals prescribed in paragraphs (2) and (3) shall be as follows—

(a) red,

(b) red and amber together,

(c) green,

(d) amber,

provided that where the light signals are varied as prescribed in regulation 31, the green arrow shown in diagram 3000.4 or 3000.6 and shown as a permitted variant of diagram 3000.3 or 3000.5 or one of the green arrows shown as a permitted variant of diagram 3000.3, 3000.4 or 3000.6 may be illuminated while any of the lights referred to in sub-paragraphs (a), (b), (c) and (d) are illuminated.

(5) Light signals used to control vehicular traffic entering or proceeding along a motorway or dual carriageway road shall be—

(a) of the size, colour and type shown in diagram 6031.1 or 6032.1; and

(b) operated as prescribed in paragraph (6).

(6) The operating requirements for the light signals prescribed in paragraph (5) are that—

(a) each lamp shall show an intermittent red light at a rate of flashing of not less than 60 nor more than 90 flashes per minute, and in such a manner that the lights of one vertical pair are always shown when the lights of the other vertical pair are not shown; and

(b) the red cross or the white symbol shown in diagram 6031.1 or 6032.1 shall be illuminated by a steady light when the red lights are flashing.

(7) Light signals used to control road traffic at level crossings, swinging or lifting bridges,

tunnels, airfields or in the vicinity of premises used regularly by fire, police or ambulance service vehicles shall be—

    (a) of the size, colour and type shown in diagram 3014; and

    (b) illuminated in the sequence prescribed in paragraph (8).

(8) The sequence for the illumination of the light signals prescribed in paragraph (7) shall be as follows—

    (a) a single steady amber light,

    (b) two intermittent red lights, each of which will be shown at a rate of flashing of not less than 60 nor more than 90 flashes per minute, and in such a manner that one light is always shown when the other light is not shown.

(9) Light signals used to control tramcars shall—

    (a) be of the size, colour and type shown in diagram 3013; and

    (b) display the aspects shown in diagrams 3013.1, 3013.2, 3013.3, 3013.4 and 3013.5 in the sequence prescribed in paragraph (10).

(10) The sequence for the illumination of the light signals prescribed in paragraph (9) shall be as follows—

    (a) the horizontal line shown in diagram 3013.1,

    (b) the vertical line shown in diagram 3013.2 or either of the diagonal lines shown in diagram 3013.3 or 3013.4,

    (c) the central circle shown in diagram 3013.5.

(11) When the light signals prescribed in paragraph (9) ("*tram signals*") are affixed to the light signals mentioned in paragraph (2) ("*standard signals*") in the manner shown in diagram 3000.3, 3000.4, 3000.5 or 3000.6 their aspect may be such that they convey to the driver of a tramcar a significance (within the meaning of regulation 33) which is different from that conveyed at the same time to the drivers of other vehicular traffic by the aspect of the standard signals to which the tram signals are affixed.

31. Permitted variants of green arrow light signals

(1) A lens or lenses of the size and colour shown in either diagram 3001 or 3001.1 **B48.40** which, when illuminated, shows a green arrow—

    (a) may be substituted for the lens showing the green light in the light signals referred to in regulation 30(2) using any of the methods shown in diagram 3003, 3005, 3006, 3011.1 or 3011.2; or

    (b) may be affixed to the light signals referred to in regulation 30(2) or to those signals as altered in accordance with sub-paragraph (a) using any of the methods shown in diagram 3000.4, 3000.6, 3002, 3004, 3005, 3006, 3007, 3008, 3009.1, 3011.1 or 3011.2.

(2) The direction of the arrow prescribed as the permitted variant of diagram 3000.3 and shown in diagram 3000.4 may be varied so that the head of the arrow points to any position on the 90° arc shown in diagram 3002 or 3004.

(3) The direction of the arrow prescribed as the permitted variant of diagrams 3000 and 3000.5 and shown in diagram 3000.6 may be varied so that the head of the arrow points to any position on the 180° arc shown in diagram 3003 or 3009.1.

(4) The direction of any arrow prescribed as a permitted variant of diagrams 3000.3 and 3000.4 where the arrow is substituted for the green light may be varied so that the head of the arrow points to any position on the 90° arcs shown in diagram 3005 or 3006,

provided that there is a difference of not less than 45° between the directions in which paired arrows point.

(5) The direction of either of the green arrows included in diagram 3000.4, where the sign shown in that diagram has been varied by the substitution of a green arrow for the tram signal aspect, may be varied so that the head of the arrow points to any position on the 45° arcs shown in diagram 3007 or 3008 provided that there is a difference of not less than 45° between the directions in which paired arrows point.

(6) The direction of either of the green arrows included in diagram 3000.6, where the sign shown in that diagram has been varied by the substitution of a green arrow for the tram signal aspect, may be varied so that—

(a) when the arrows are illuminated and extinguished simultaneously, the head of the upper arrow may point in any direction on the 135° arc and the head of the lower arrow may point in any direction on either of the two 45° arcs shown in diagram 3011.1, provided that there is a difference of not less than 45° between the directions in which the two arrows point; and

(b) when the arrows are illuminated and extinguished independently, the head of either of the arrows may point in any direction on the two 180° arcs shown in diagram 3011.2, provided that there is a difference of not less than 45° between the directions in which the two arrows point.

32. Portable light signals

B48.41 Portable light signals—

(a) shall be of the size, colour and type shown in diagram 3000.1; and

(b) shall be illuminated in the sequence prescribed by regulation 30(4).

33. Significance of light signals

B48.42 (1) The significance of the light signals prescribed in paragraphs (2) and (3) of regulation 30 and in regulation 32 shall be as follows—

(a) except as provided in sub-paragraphs (b), (f) and (g) the red signal shall convey the prohibition that vehicular traffic other than tramcars shall not proceed beyond the stop line;

(b) when a vehicle is being used for fire brigade, ambulance or police purposes and the observance of the prohibition conveyed by the red signal in accordance with sub-paragraph (a) would be likely to hinder the use of that vehicle for the purpose for which it is being used, then sub-paragraph (a) shall not apply to the vehicle, and the red signal shall convey the prohibition that that vehicle shall not proceed beyond the stop line in a manner or at a time likely to endanger any person or to cause the driver of any vehicle proceeding in accordance with the indications of light signals operating in association with the signals displaying the red signal to change its speed or course in order to avoid an accident;

(c) except as provided in sub-paragraph (f), the red-with-amber signal shall denote an impending change to green or a green arrow in the indication given by the signals but shall convey the same prohibition as the red signal;

(d) the green signal shall indicate that vehicular traffic other than tramcars may proceed beyond the stop line and proceed straight on or to the left or to the right;

(e) the amber signal shall, when shown alone, convey the same prohibition as the red signal, except that, as respects any vehicle other than a tramcar which is so close to the stop line that it cannot safely be stopped without proceeding beyond the stop line, it shall convey the same indication as the green signal or green arrow signal which was shown immediately before it;

(f) save as provided in sub-paragraph (g), the green arrow signal shall indicate that vehicular traffic other than tramcars may, notwithstanding any other indication given by the signals, proceed beyond the stop line only in the direction indicated by the arrow for the purpose of proceeding in that direction through the junction controlled by those signals; and

(g) where more than one green arrow is affixed to light signals in accordance with regulation 31(1)(b), vehicular traffic other than tramcars may, notwithstanding any other indication given by the signals, proceed beyond the stop line only in the direction indicated by any one of the green arrows for the purpose of proceeding in that direction through the junction controlled by those signals.

(2) Vehicular traffic proceeding beyond a stop line in accordance with paragraph (1) shall proceed with due regard to the safety of other road users and subject to any direction given by a constable in uniform or a traffic warden or to any other applicable prohibition or restriction.

(3) The significance of the light signals prescribed in regulation 30(5) shall be as follows—

(a) when placed beside the carriageway of a road, they shall convey the prohibition that vehicular traffic (other than vehicles being used in the circumstances described in paragraph (1)(b)) shall not proceed beyond the signals; and

(b) when displayed on a gantry over the carriageway, they shall convey the prohibition that vehicular traffic (other than vehicles being used in the circumstances described in paragraph (1)(b)) proceeding in the traffic lane immediately below the signals shall not proceed beyond them in that lane,

and for the purposes of this paragraph light signals which are mounted on a post situated beside the carriageway but which are projected over it or part of it shall be treated as light signals placed beside the carriageway of that road.

(4) The significance of the light signals prescribed in regulation 30(7) shall be as follows—

(a) the amber signal shall convey the prohibition that traffic shall not proceed beyond the stop line on the carriageway, except for a vehicle which is so close to the stop line that it cannot safely be stopped without proceeding beyond the stop line; and

(b) the intermittent red signals shall convey the prohibition that traffic shall not proceed beyond the stop line.

(5) The significance of the light signals prescribed in regulation 30(9) shall be as follows—

(a) the aspect shown in diagram 3013.1 shall convey the prohibition that a tramcar shall not proceed beyond the stop line;

(b) the aspect shown in diagram 3013.2 shall indicate that a tramcar may proceed beyond the stop line and proceed straight ahead;

(c) the aspect shown in diagram 3013.3 shall indicate that a tramcar may proceed beyond the stop line and proceed to the left;

(d) the aspect shown in diagram 3013.4 shall indicate that a tramcar may proceed beyond the stop line and proceed to the right; and

(e) the aspect shown in diagram 3013.5 shall convey the prohibition that a tramcar shall not proceed beyond the stop line except that, as respects a tramcar which is so close to the stop line that it cannot safely be stopped without proceeding beyond the stop line, it shall convey the same indication as the aspect which was shown immediately before it.

(6) In this regulation—

(a) *"primary signals"* means light signals erected on or near the carriageway of a road and sited near either one or both ends of the stop line, or if there is no stop line, sited at either or both edges of the carriageway or part of the carriageway which is in use by traffic approaching and controlled by the signals;

(b) *"secondary signals"* means light signals erected on or near the carriageway facing traffic approaching from the direction of the primary signals but sited beyond those signals as viewed from the direction of travel of such traffic;

(c) *"stop line"* in relation to light signals means the road marking shown in diagram 1001 placed on a carriageway in conjunction with those light signals being either primary signals alone, or secondary signals alone or both primary and secondary signals and, where no stop line is provided or the stop line is not visible, references in the preceding paragraphs of this regulation to the stop line are—

(i) in a case where the sign shown in diagram 7011 is placed in conjunction with the light signals, to be treated as references to that sign; and

(ii) in any other case, to be treated as references to the post or other structure on which the primary signals are mounted; and

(d) any reference to light signals, to the signals or to a signal of a particular colour is, where secondary signals have been placed, a reference to the light signals displayed by both the primary and secondary signals or, as the case may be, by the primary signals operating without the secondary signals or by the secondary signals operating without the primary signals.

34. Light signals for lane control of vehicular traffic

(1) A light signal placed above the carriageway and facing the direction of oncoming vehicular traffic used for the control of that traffic proceeding along the traffic lane over which those signals have been placed shall be of the size, colour and type shown in diagram 5001.1, 5001.2, 5003, 5003.1, 5005 or 5005.1.

(2) The height of the centre of each light signal from the surface of the carriageway in the immediate vicinity shall be not less than 5.5 metres nor more than 9 metres.

(3) The signals prescribed by this regulation shall be so designed that—

(a) the red cross shown in diagram 5003 or 5003.1 (*"the red cross"*) can be internally illuminated in such a manner as to show a steady red light;

(b) the green arrow shown in diagram 5001.1 or 5001.2 (*"the downward green arrow"*) can be internally illuminated in such a manner as to show a steady green light;

(c) the white arrow shown in diagram 5005 or 5005.1 (*"the diagonal white arrow"*) can be internally illuminated in such a manner as to show a steady white light; and

(d) whenever one of the signals referred to in sub-paragraphs (a) to (c) is illuminated neither of the other signals referred to in those sub-paragraphs shall be illuminated when placed over the same traffic lane.

(4) The significance of the light signals prescribed in this regulation shall be as follows—

(a) the red cross shall convey to vehicular traffic proceeding in the traffic lane above which it is displayed the prohibition that such traffic shall not proceed beyond the red cross in the traffic lane until that prohibition is cancelled by a display over that traffic lane of the downward green arrow or diagonal white arrow or by a display over that traffic lane or beside the carriageway of the traffic sign shown in diagram 5015 or 6001;

(b) the downward green arrow shall convey to vehicular traffic proceeding in the traffic lane above which it is displayed the information that such traffic may proceed or continue to do so in the lane beneath the arrow; and

(c) the diagonal white arrow shall convey to vehicular traffic proceeding in the traffic lane above which it is displayed the warning that such traffic should move into the adjacent traffic lane in the direction indicated by the arrow as soon as traffic conditions permit.

35. Warning signal for motorways and dual carriageway roads

(1) A traffic sign for conveying the warning specified in paragraph (2) to vehicular traffic on a motorway or a dual carriageway road shall be a light signal of the size, colour and type shown in diagram 6023. **B48.44**

(2) The warning conveyed by the light signal shall be that—

(a) there is a hazard ahead on the motorway or dual carriageway road; and

(b) drivers should drive at a speed which does not exceed 30 miles per hour until they are certain that the hazard has been passed or removed.

(3) When the light signal prescribed by this regulation is operated, each lamp shall show an intermittent amber light at a rate of flashing of not less than 60 nor more than 90 flashes per minute and in such a manner that one light is always shown when the other light is not shown.

36. Matrix signs for motorways and dual carriageway roads

(1) In this regulation "*matrix sign*" means a sign shown in a diagram in Part I of Schedule 11 for conveying to traffic on motorways and dual carriageway roads information or a warning, requirement, restriction, prohibition or speed limit— **B48.45**

(a) relating to or arising out of temporary hazardous conditions on or near the motorway or dual carriageway road; and

(b) specified under a diagram contained in Part I of that Schedule.

(2) A matrix sign shall be a light signal and shall be of the size, colour and type prescribed by this regulation and shown in a diagram in Part I of Schedule 11.

(3) Where a matrix sign is placed beside the carriageway of a road the warning, requirement, restriction, prohibition or speed limit conveyed by the sign shall apply to all vehicular traffic facing that sign and proceeding along the carriageway beside which the sign is placed.

(4) For the purposes of this regulation a sign which is mounted on a post situated beside the carriageway but is projected over it or part of it shall be treated as a sign placed beside the carriageway of that road.

(5) Where a matrix sign mounted on a gantry or other structure is so placed that a traffic lane of the carriageway passes directly beneath it, the warning, requirement, restriction, prohibition or speed limit conveyed by the sign shall apply only to vehicular traffic facing that sign and proceeding along the traffic lane passing directly beneath it.

(6) The legend or symbol in a matrix sign shall be displayed by means of white or off-white light and except in the case of the sign shown in diagram 6012 shall be accompanied by the four lamps prescribed in paragraph (7).

(7) The four lamps mentioned in paragraph (6)—

(a) shall be of the size, colour and type shown in diagram 6022 when placed beside the carriageway or in diagram 6021 when mounted on a gantry or other structure over the carriageway; and

(b) when a matrix sign other than the one shown in diagram 6012 is displayed, each lamp shall show an intermittent amber light at a rate of flashing of not less than 60 nor more than 90 flashes per minute and in such a manner that one horizontal pair of lights is always shown when the lights of the other horizontal pair of lights is not shown.

37. Light signals for pedestrians

B48.46   (1) Light signals for conveying to pedestrians the information mentioned in paragraph (3) shall be of the size, colour and type shown in diagram 4002.

(2) The signals shall be so designed that—

(a) the red figure shown in diagram 4002 ("*the red signal*") can be internally illuminated by a steady light;

(b) the green figure shown in diagram 4002 ("*the green signal*") can be internally illuminated by a steady light;

(c) when one signal is illuminated the other signal is not illuminated; and

(d) the green signal is and remains illuminated only for so long as there is conveyed to vehicular traffic a requirement, prohibition or restriction against entering that part of the carriageway across which the light signals for pedestrians are facing, being a requirement, prohibition or restriction indicated by—

(i) the light signals prescribed in paragraphs (2), (3) or (9) of regulation 30;

(ii) the light signals prescribed in regulation 30(2) varied in accordance with regulation 31 as respects the direction of the green arrow; or

(iii) a traffic sign shown in diagram 606, 612, 613 or 616.

(3) The period during which, in the interests of safety, pedestrians—

(a) should not cross the carriageway shall be shown by the red signal during such time as it is illuminated; and

(b) may cross the carriageway shall be shown by the green signal during such time as it is illuminated by the steady light.

(4) Any audible signal emitted by any device for emitting audible signals provided in conjunction with the green signal, and any tactile signal made by any device for making tactile signals similarly provided, shall convey to pedestrians the information mentioned in paragraph (3)(b).

(5) A sign of the size, colour and type shown in diagram 4003 shall during such time as the word "WAIT" is illuminated indicate to pedestrians the warning mentioned in sub-paragraph (a) of paragraph (3).

B48.47   **38.**—(1) Light signals conveying to pedestrians at level crossings the prohibition mentioned in paragraph (2) shall be of the size, colour and type shown in diagram 4006 and so designed that—

(a) the red figure shown in diagram 4006 is internally illuminated by an intermittent red light which is shown at a rate of flashing of not less than 60 nor more than 90 flashes per minute; and

(b) the red figure is illuminated only when the intermittent red lights prescribed in regulation 30(8)(b) are illuminated.

(2) The red figure when illuminated in the manner described in paragraph (1) shall convey the prohibition that pedestrians shall not proceed beyond the transverse road marking shown in diagram 1003.2 on the footway or diagram 1001 on the carriageway.

39. School crossing patrol signs and warning lights

(1) A sign which is exhibited by a school crossing patrol for the purpose of stopping any vehicle in accordance with section 28 of the 1984 Act shall be of the size, colour and type shown in diagram 605.2.

B48.48

(2) A sign for conveying a warning to vehicular traffic, which is approaching a place in a road where children on their way to or from school or on their way from one part of a school to another cross or seek to cross that road ("*a crossing place*"), that the crossing place lies ahead and is being patrolled by a school crossing patrol or is otherwise in use by such children—

   (a) shall be a light signal of the size, colour and type shown in diagram 4004, each lamp of which when operated shall show an intermittent amber light at a rate of flashing of not less than 60 nor more than 90 flashes per minute and in such a manner that one light is always shown when the other light is not shown; and

   (b) may be erected on or near part of the road in advance of a crossing place in relation to oncoming traffic.

40. Cattle crossing signs and warning lights

(1) A sign of the size, colour and type shown in diagram 4005 may be erected on or near a road in advance of a place in that road where cattle under the supervision of a herdsman on their way from one part of a farm to another cross the road ("*a cattle crossing*") to convey to oncoming traffic the warning specified in paragraph (2).

B48.49

(2) The warning conveyed by the sign shall be that—

   (a) a cattle crossing lies ahead and may be in use; and

   (b) traffic should be prepared to stop.

(3) When the sign is operated, each lamp shall show an intermittent amber light at a rate of flashing of not less than 60 nor more than 90 flashes per minute and in such a manner that one light is always shown when the other light is not shown.

SECTION 6

Miscellaneous traffic signs

41. Certain temporary signs

(1) A temporary sign shall be of such size, colour and type as is specified in this regulation.

B48.50

(2) The shape of a temporary sign shall be—

   (a) rectangular;

   (b) rectangular but with the corners rounded; or

   (c) pointed at one end but otherwise rectangular in accordance with (a) or (b).

(3) A temporary sign may incorporate—

   (a) wording;

   (b) numerals;

   (c) arrows or chevrons;

(d) any appropriate symbol taken from any diagram in any Schedule; and

(e) the arms, badge or other device of a traffic authority, police authority or an organisation representative of road users,

and shall be of a size appropriate to the circumstances in which it is placed.

(4) Every letter and numeral incorporated in a temporary sign other than any letter incorporated in the sign in accordance with paragraph (3)(e) shall be not less than 40 nor more than 350 millimetres in height, and every arrow so incorporated shall be not less than 250 nor more than 1000 millimetres in length.

(5) Every letter, numeral, arrow, chevron or symbol, other than a sign shown in a diagram in Schedules 1 to 5 when used as a symbol, incorporated in a temporary sign shall be—

(a) black on a background of white or of yellow;

(b) white on a blue background;

(c) blue on a white background;

(d) if the sign conveys information or warnings of the kind mentioned in sub-paragraphs (c) or (d) of paragraph (7), white on a red background, except where it is placed on a motorway when it shall be black on a yellow background; or

(e) if the sign is a variable message sign, yellow on a black background or black on a yellow background, except when the sign is not in use when it shall display a plain black or grey face.

(6) No temporary sign shall convey to traffic any information, warning, requirement, restriction or prohibition of a description which can be conveyed either by a sign shown in a diagram in Schedules 1 to 12 or by a sign so shown placed in combination or in conjunction with another sign so shown in such a diagram.

(7) In this regulation "*temporary sign*" means a sign placed temporarily on or near a road for conveying to traffic—

(a) information as respects deviations or alternative traffic routes;

(b) information as respects the route which may conveniently be followed on the occasion of a sports meeting, exhibition or other public gathering which in each case it is anticipated will attract a considerable volume of traffic;

(c) information as to the date from which works are to be executed on or near a road;

(d) information or warnings as to the avoidance of any temporary hazards occasioned by works being executed on or near a road, by adverse weather conditions or other natural causes, by the failure of street lighting or by malfunction of or damage to any apparatus, equipment or facility used in connection with the road or anything situated on, near or under it or by damage to the road itself; or

(e) requests for information by the police in connection with a road traffic accident.

B48.51   *[Nothing in the Traffic Signs (Temporary Obstructions) Regulations 1997 (S.I. 1997 No. 3053) below affects regulation 41; see S.I. 1997 No. 3053, reg.17.]*

42. Flashing beacons

B48.52   (1) A beacon—

(a) showing an intermittent amber light and placed in combination with a temporary sign within the meaning of regulation 41 or the sign shown in diagram 562, 610, 7001, 7009, 7010, 7012, 7013, 7019, 7020, 7021 or 7022, and in compliance with the requirements in paragraph (2); or

(b) showing an intermittent blue light and placed by a constable or a person acting under instructions (whether general or specific) of the chief officer of police in combination with a sign shown in diagram 606, 609, 610, 616, 633, 829.1, 829.2, 829.3, 829.4 or 7105, and in compliance with (c) and (d) of the requirements in paragraph (2),

shall convey the warning that drivers of vehicles should take special care.

(2) The requirements mentioned in paragraph (1) are—

(a) the peak intensity of light emitted by the lens or lenses of each such beacon shall be—

  (i) if the period between individual flashes does not exceed of a second, not less than 100 candela on the principal axis of the relevant lens;

  (ii) if the period between individual flashes exceeds of a second, not less than 2000 candela on the principal axis; or

  (iii) if the period between the cessation of a double flash and the start of the succeeding double flash exceeds of a second, not less than 1000 candela on the principal axis;

(b) each lens shall be of such shape and size that the perimeter of its area projected horizontally onto a vertical plane shall be capable of lying wholly inside a square having sides of 200 millimetres in length and wholly outside a square having sides of 100 millimetres in length;

(c) the height of the centre of the lenses from the surface of the carriageway in the immediate vicinity shall be not less than 800 nor more than 1500 millimetres; and

(d) the rate of flashing shall be not less than 40 nor more than 150 individual or double flashes per minute.

43. Road danger lamps

(1) A lamp showing a steady or intermittent amber light which— **B48.53**

(a) conforms to British Standard Specification BS3143: Part 1: 1985 amended by Amendment No. 1 dated February 1985; or BS3143: Part 2: 1990; or an equivalent specification of a European Economic Area State; and

(b) is illuminated separately and by a single source of light,

shall indicate to traffic the limits of a temporary obstruction of the road and in this regulation is called a "*road danger lamp*".

(2) The height of the centre of each lens of a road danger lamp from the surface of the road in the immediate vicinity of the lamp shall not exceed 1500 millimetres where the speed limit on the road is 40 miles per hour or less, or 1200 millimetres where the speed limit on the road is more than 40 miles per hour.

(3) Where a road danger lamp which shows an intermittent light is placed—

(a) within 50 metres of a street lamp lit by electricity on a road subject to a speed limit of 40 miles per hour or less, the lamp shall operate in such a way that the rate of flashing shall be not less than 40 nor more than 150 flashes per minute; and

(b) on roads other than those mentioned in sub-paragraph (a), the rate of flashing shall be not less than 900 flashes per minute.

44. Cones, delineators and cylinders

(1) The sign shown in diagram 7101 shall, subject to paragraph (2), consist of a conically **B48.54**
shaped device made of rubber or flexible plastic material of which—

(a) the base is coloured red, black, grey or brown;

(b) the base is a polygon having not more than eight sides, which would be contained wholly within a circle with a diameter of three quarters of the height of the device; and

(c) the part of the device coloured white is illuminated with white retroreflecting material,

and information about the manufacture of the sign required in order to comply with British Standard Specification BS 873: Part 8: 1985 or an equivalent specification of a European Economic Area State, occupying an area not exceeding 30 square centimetres, may be indicated on the part of the sign coloured white in characters not exceeding 5 millimetres in height, at least 90% of the remaining area of white colour shall be illuminated with white retroreflecting material, and the part of the device coloured red may be illuminated with red retroreflecting material.

(2) A rotating device which is red and not illuminated by means of retroreflecting material and which displays one or more of the signs shown in diagram 560 or 561, which shall be coloured amber, intermittently while rotating and constantly while static, may be mounted on top of the sign shown in diagram 7101.

(3) The sign shown in diagram 7102 shall consist of a device made of rubber or flexible plastic material of which—

(a) the base is coloured red, black, grey or brown, except that a white line 100 millimetres wide at an angle of not more than 60° to the road surface and illuminated with retroreflecting material may be marked on one side of the base at right angles to the face of the device;

(b) the base has a maximum width (measured parallel to the face of the device) of three quarters of the height of the device, a minimum length of three quarters of the height of the device and is no more than 70 millimetres high at the outermost edge; and

(c) the part of the device coloured white is illuminated with white retroreflecting material,

and information about the manufacture of the sign required in order to comply with British Standard Specification BS 873: Part 8: 1985 or an equivalent specification of a European Economic Area State, occupying an area not exceeding 30 square centimetres, may be indicated on the part of the sign coloured white in characters not exceeding 5 millimetres in height and, if only one side of the device is illuminated in accordance with this paragraph, the reverse side shall be coloured red or grey in material which is not retroreflecting, and the part of the device coloured red may be illuminated with red retroreflecting material.

(4) The sign shown in diagram 7103 shall consist of a cylindrically shaped device made of rubber or flexible plastic material and—

(a) the part of the device coloured white shall be illuminated with white retroreflecting material; and

(b) information about the manufacture of the sign required in order to comply with British Standard Specification BS 873: Part 8: 1985 or an equivalent specification of a European Economic Area State, occupying an area not exceeding 30 square centimetres, may be indicated on the part of the sign coloured white in characters not exceeding 5 millimetres in height, and at least 90% of the remaining area of white colour shall be illuminated with white retroreflecting material; and

(c) the part of the device coloured red may be illuminated with red retroreflecting material.

45. Refuge indicator lamps

A lamp in the form of an illuminated spherical globe for conveying the warning that drivers of vehicles are approaching a street refuge may be placed subject to the following conditions— **B48.55**

(a) the globe shall be white;

(b) the globe shall have a diameter of not less than 290 nor more than 310 millimetres; and

(c) the height of the centre of the globe above the surface of the carriageway in the immediate vicinity shall be not less than 3800 millimetres nor more than 5000 millimetres.

46. Variable message signs

(1) A device may display at different times— **B48.56**

(a) a sign shown in a diagram in Schedules 1 to 5, 7, 11 or 12;

(b) a legend of a type shown in Schedule 15 in accordance with the provisions of that Schedule; or

(c) a blank grey or a blank black face,

and in these Regulations such a device is referred to as a "*variable message sign*".

(2) A variable message sign shall be of a size appropriate to display the messages referred to in sub-paragraphs (a) and (b) of paragraph (1), having regard to the normal speed of traffic on the road on or near which the sign is situated.

(3) If the construction or method of operation of a variable message sign prevents the sign from being displayed in the colours shown for it in the appropriate diagram in Schedules 1 to 5, 7, Part I of Schedule 11 or Schedule 12, a black legend or symbol on a white or yellow background may be displayed as a white, off-white or yellow legend or symbol on a dark background, provided that any red triangle or red circle forming part of the sign is retained.

(4) When a variable message sign displays the sign shown in diagram 670, any sign shown in a diagram in Part I of Schedule 11 other than diagram 6012, or a legend of the type shown in Schedule 15, it may also display four lamps of the size, colour and type specified in regulation 36(7), save that the rate of flashing shall be not less than 60 nor more than 150 flashes per minute and the distance between the lamps shall be varied to accord with the overall size of the variable message sign.

(5) The display of a blank black or grey face on a variable message sign accompanied by four flashing lamps of the kind mentioned in paragraph (4) shall indicate to drivers that they should take special care.

(6) A variable message sign which displays alternately the signs shown in diagrams 7023 and 7024 shall be manually operated.

SCHEDULE 1   Regulation 11(1) and (5)

WARNING SIGNS

(OTHER THAN THOSE FOR RAILWAY AND TRAMWAY LEVEL CROSSINGS, BUS AND PEDAL CYCLE FACILITIES, AND ROAD WORKS)

Editorial note. The diagrams representing the actual traffic signs are not reproduced in this work, but the signs in Schedule 1 are described below by means of (in the main) the legends accompanying the signs. The dimensions of the components of the various signs **B48.57** are specified in marks accompanying the diagrams (not reproduced) and variations of wording (where permissible) are referred to in notes accompanying the diagrams (not reproduced), often by means of a cross reference to Schedule 16. The accompanying notes also cross refer to Schedule 17 for information regarding the illumination requirements for the signs. The diagrams are reproduced in numerical sequence but there are gaps in the numbering.

501	junction ahead controlled by a diagram 601.1 or diagram 602 sign (inverted red triangle)
502	distance to a junction ahead controlled by diagram 601.1 sign ("STOP 100yds")
503	distance to a junction ahead controlled by a diagram 602 sign ("GIVE WAY 50yds")
504.1	crossroads ahead (black symbol within red triangle)
505.1	T-junction ahead (black symbol within red triangle)
506.1	side road ahead (black symbol within red triangle)
507.1	staggered junction ahead (black symbol within red triangle)
510	roundabout ahead (black symbol within red triangle)
511	reduction in speed necessary for a change of road layout ahead ("REDUCE SPEED NOW" in white letters on red background edged in white)
512	bend ahead (black symbol within red triangle)
512.1	junction on bend ahead (black symbol within red triangle)
512.2	alternative to diagram 512.1
513	double bend ahead, first to the left (black symbol within red triangle)
513.1	adverse camber on a bend ("Adverse camber" in black letters on white background)
513.2	advisory speed limit at a bend or other hazard ("Max speed 30" in black letters on white background)
515	sharp deviation of route (white chevrons on black background)
515.1	alternative to diagram 515
515.1A	sharp deviation of route at roundabout (white chevrons on black background)
515.2	sharp deviation of route at roundabout (black chevrons set between white paving blocks)
516	road narrows on both sides ahead (black symbol within red triangle)
517	road narrows on right ahead (black symbol within red triangle)
518	convergence of traffic to a single file in each direction ("Single file traffic" in black letters on white background)
519	road only wide enough for one line of vehicles ("Single track road" in black letters on white background)
520	dual carriageway ahead (black symbol within red triangle)
521	two-way traffic (black symbol within red triangle)
522	two-way traffic on route crossing ahead (black symbol within red triangle)
523.1	steep hill downwards ahead (black symbol within red triangle)
524.1	steep hill upwards ahead (black symbol within red triangle)
525	drivers should engage low gear for steep hill ("Low gear now" in black letters on white background)
526	drivers should keep in low gear for steep hill or tight bend ("Keep in low gear" in black letters on white background)
527	drivers should keep in low gear for distance indicated ("Low gear for 1 miles" in black letters on white background)

528	hump bridge ahead (black symbol within red triangle)
528.1	end of bridge parapet, abutment wall, tunnel mouth or other obstruction adjacent to carriageway (vertical rectangles with diagonal yellow and black stripes)
529	opening or swing bridge ahead (black symbol within red triangle)
529.1	tunnel ahead (black symbol within red triangle)
530	maximum headroom available at hazard (alternatives in feet+inches and in metres) (black symbol within red triangle)
530.1	reduced headroom over part of road due to overhanging building ahead ("Overhanging building" in black letters on white background)
530.2	reduced headroom at hazard (alternative types) (horizontal rectangles with diagonal yellow and black stripes, one version culminating in inverted black triangle in middle)
531.1	maximum headroom available at arch bridge ahead (alternatives in feet+inches and in metres) (black symbol within red triangle)
531.2	high vehicles to use the middle of road at arch bridge ahead ("ARCH BRIDGE High vehicles use middle of road" in black letters on white background)
532.2	maximum headroom available in the centre of a road at an arch bridge (arc with alternative black and yellow stripes surmounted by sign or signs as in diagram 531.1)
532.3	maximum headroom available at the side of and in the centre of a road at an arch bridge (sign or signs as in diagram 531.1 at side of bridge and sign or signs as in diagram 531.1 in centre of bridge)
543	traffic signs ahead (coloured lights symbol within red triangle)
543.1	traffic signals ahead which only operate at certain times ("Part time signals" in black letters on white background)
544	pedestrian crossing ahead (black symbol within red triangle)
544.1	pedestrians in road ahead (black symbol within red triangle)
544.2	elderly or disabled pedestrians likely to cross road ahead (black symbol within red triangle)
545	children going to or from school or playground ahead (black symbol within red triangle)
546	school ahead ("School" in black letters on white background)
547.1	school crossing patrol ahead ("Patrol" in black letters on white background)
547.2	children's playground ahead ("Playground" in black letters on white background)
547.3	no footway for distance indicated ("No footway for 400 yards" in black letters on white background)
547.4	elderly pedestrians likely to cross road ahead ("Elderly people" in black letters on white background)
547.5	zebra pedestrian crossing on road hump ahead ("Humped Zebra Crossing" in black letters on white background)
547.6	pelican pedestrian crossing on road hump ahead ("Humped Pelican Crossing" in black letters on white background)
547.7	disabled children likely to cross road ahead ("Disabled children" in black letters on white background)
548	cattle likely to be in road ahead (black symbol within red triangle)
548.1	supervised cattle crossing ahead ("When lights show 200yds" in black letters on white background)
549	sheep likely to be in road ahead (black symbol within red triangle)
550	wild horses or ponies likely to be in road ahead (black symbol within

red triangle)

550.1	accompanied horses or ponies likely to be in road ahead (black symbol within red triangle)
551	wild animals likely to be in road ahead (black symbol within red triangle)
551.1	migratory toad crossing ahead (black symbol within red triangle)
551.2	wild fowl likely to be in road ahead (black symbol within red triangle)
552	cattle grid ahead ("Cattle grid" in black letters within red triangle)
553	by-pass of cattle grid ("Horse drawn vehicles and animals" and directional arrow in black letters on white background)
553.1	agricultural vehicles likely to be in road ahead (black symbol within red triangle)
553.2	agricultural vehicles likely to be in road ahead ("Farm traffic" in black letters on white background)
554	worded warning sign ("ford" in black letters within red triangle)
554.1	risk of brake failure after crossing a ford or before descending a steep gradient ("Try your brakes" in black letters within red triangle)
554.2	risk of ice or packed snow ahead (black symbol within red triangle)
554.3	ice ahead ("Ice" in black letters on white background)
555	quayside or river bank ahead (black symbol within red triangle)
556	uneven road ahead (black symbol within red triangle)
556.1	soft verges ahead (black symbol within red triangle)
566.2	soft verges for distance indicated ("Soft verges for 2 miles" in black letters on white background)
557	slippery road ahead (black symbol within red triangle)
557.1	road hump or series of road humps ahead (black symbol within red triangle)
557.2	road humps ahead for the distance indicated ("Humps for mile" in black letters on white background)
557.3	road humps ahead in the direction and for the distance indicated ("Humps for 300 yards" and directional arrow in black letters on white background)
557.4	road hump in the distance indicated ("Hump 20 yards" in black letters on white background)
558	low flying aircraft or sudden aircraft noise likely ahead (black symbol within red triangle)
558.1	low flying helicopters or sudden helicopter noise likely ahead (black symbol within red triangle)
558.2	gliders likely ahead ("Gliders" in black letters on white background)
559	risk of falling or fallen rocks likely (black symbol within red triangle)
560	edge of carriageway or obstruction near that edge (solid red circle)
561	alternative to diagram 560 (solid red rectangle (upright))
562	other danger ahead (black symbol within red triangle)
563	nature of other danger ahead ("Accident" in black letters on white background)
563.1	warning of light signals as shown in diagram 3014 ahead ("FIRE STATION STOP when lights show" in black letters on white background together with two red and one yellow lights on black background)
570	distance over which hazard or prohibition extends ("For 2 miles" in black letters on white background)
572	distance ahead to hazard ("400yds" in black letters on white background)
573	distance and direction to hazard ("250yds" and directional arrow in black letters on white background)

574	area infected by animal diseases ("ANIMAL DISEASE RABIES INFECTED AREA AHEAD" in white letters on red background)
575	large vehicles likely to be in middle of road because of narrowness of carriageway ("Oncoming vehicles in middle of road" in black letters on white background)
581	side winds likely ahead (black symbol within red triangle)
582	slow moving military vehicles likely to be crossing or in road ahead (black symbol within red triangle)
583	slow moving vehicles likely on incline ahead (black symbol within red triangle)
583.1	distance over which slow moving vehicles likely to be encountered ahead ("Slow lorries for 2 miles" in black letters on white background)

SCHEDULE 2   Regulation 11(1)

REGULATORY SIGNS

(OTHER THAN THOSE FOR RAILWAY AND TRAMWAY LEVEL CROSSINGS, BUS AND PEDAL CYCLE FACILITIES, AND ROAD WORKS)

Editorial note. The diagrams representing the actual traffic signs are not reproduced in   **B48.58**
this work, but the signs in Schedule 2 are described below by means of (in the main) the legends accompanying the signs. The dimensions of the components of the various signs are specified in marks accompanying the diagrams (not reproduced) and variations of wording (where permissible) are referred to in notes accompanying the diagrams (not reproduced), often by means of a cross reference to Schedule 16. The accompanying notes also cross refer to Schedule 17 for information regarding the illumination requirements for the signs. The diagrams are reproduced in numerical sequence but there are gaps in the numbering.

601.1	vehicular traffic must comply with the requirements prescribed in reg.16 ("STOP" in white letters on a red hexagonal background edged with white)
602	vehicular traffic must comply with the requirements prescribed in reg.16 ("GIVE WAY" in black letters within an inverted red triangle)
605.2	vehicular traffic must comply with the requirements of section 28 of the 1984 Act when the sign is exhibited by a school crossing patrol ("STOP" in black letters above a black symbol on a yellow background surrounded by a red circle)
606	vehicular traffic must proceed in direction indicated by arrow (horizontal arrow in white on blue background within circle edged in white)
607	one way traffic ("One way" in black letters on white background)
608	dual carriageway ("Dual carriageway" in black letters on white background
609	vehicular traffic must turn ahead in direction indicated by arrow (arrow in white on blue background within circle edged in white)
610	vehicular traffic must comply with requirements of reg.15 (angled arrow in white on blue background within circle edged in white)
611	vehicular traffic may reach the same destination by proceeding either side of sign (two white arrows within blue circle)
611.1	vehicular traffic entering junction must give priority to vehicles from the right at transverse road marking (diagram 1003.3) associated with sign

(or, if line not visible, at road junction) and proceed past marking in diagram 1003.4 in direction indicated by arrows (three white arrows within blue circle)

612   no right turn for vehicular traffic (black arrow on white background pointing to right crossed through in red without red circle)

613   no left turn for vehicles (black arrow on white background pointing to left crossed through in red within red circle)

614   no U-turns for vehicles (black symbol on white background crossed through in red within red circle)

615   priority must be given to vehicles from opposite direction (small red arrow and larger black arrow pointing in opposite directions on white background within red circle)

615   same as diagram 615 ("Give way to oncoming vehicles" in black letters on white background)

616   no entry for vehicular traffic (horizontal white bar on red background within circle edged in white)

617   all vehicles prohibited except non-mechanically propelled vehicles pushed by pedestrians (red circle with white centre)

618   all vehicles prohibited from "play street" during times indicated except for access ("Play Street [*time*] to sunset except for access" in black letters on white background)

618.1   all vehicles prohibited during the times indicated, except for access/specified vehicles ("No vehicles [*time*] except for . . ." in black letters on white background)

618.2   entry to pedestrian zone restricted except for loading/specified vehicles (alternative types) ("PEDESTRIAN ZONE [red circle with white centre (with or without symbol)] except for [symbol] [times to be specified]")

618.3   entry to and waiting in pedestrian zone restricted, except for loading/specified vehicles (alternative types) ("PEDESTRIAN ZONE [red circle (with or without symbol)] except for . . . [diagram 636] At any time")

618.3A   entry to and waiting in pedestrian zone restricted, except for loading/access/specified vehicles ("PEDESTRIAN ZONE [red circle with white centre] except for . . [symbol may be included] [diagram 636] At any time")

618.4   end of restrictions associated with pedestrian zone ([symbol] "Pedestrian Zone ENDS" in black letters on white background)

619   motor vehicles prohibited (black symbols (motorcyle and motor car) within red circle)

619.1   motor vehicles except motorcycles without sidecars prohibited (black symbol (motor car) within red circle)

619.2   motorcycles prohibited (black symbol (motorcycle) within red circle)

620   vehicles requiring access to premises or land adjacent to the road exempt from prohibition conveyed by associated sign ("Except for access" in black letters on white background)

620.1   goods vehicles requiring to enter road for loading or unloading of goods exempt from prohibition conveyed by associated sign ("Except for loading by" [symbol] in black letters on white background)

622.1A   goods vehicles exceeding maximum gross weight indicated on the goods vehicle symbol prohibited (black symbol [goods vehicle indicating weight] on white background within red circle)

622.2   end of prohibition of goods vehicles exceeding maximum gross weight indicated by diagram 622.1A (grey symbol on white background crossed

	through within grey circle)
622.4	articulated vehicles prohibited ("No articulated vehicles" in black letters on white background within red circle)
622.5	horse drawn vehicles prohibited (black symbol on white background within red circle)
622.6	ridden or accompanied horses prohibited (black symbol on white background within red circle)
625.1	pedestrians prohibited (black symbol on white background within red circle)
626.2	vehicles exceeding maximum gross weight indicated prohibited from crossing bridge or other structure ("WEAK BRIDGE" in black letters on white background above indication of "m g w" in black letters on white background within red circle on grey background)
627.1	exemption for unladen vehicles from prohibition conveyed by diagram 626.2 ("Except for empty vehicles" in black letters on white background set below diagram 626.2)
629	vehicles exceeding width indicated prohibited (permitted width in black characters on white background preceded and followed by black arrowheads pointing inwards within red circle)
629.1	vehicles or combinations of vehicles exceeding length indicated prohibited (black symbol above permitted length and two arrows pointing outwards on white background within red circle)
629.2	vehicles exceeding height indicated prohibited (permitted height in black characters on white background above and below black arrowheads pointing inwards within red circle)
629.2A	as diagram 629.2, but height indicated in metric and imperial units.
632	no overtaking (black and red symbols (cars) on white background within red circle)
633	vehicular traffic must not proceed beyond the sign where displayed temporarily by uniformed police officer or traffic warden ("STOP [symbol] POLICE")
636	temporary prohibition of waiting except for loading and unloading (blue circle crossed with diagonal bar in red within red circle, on yellow background)
636.1	temporary prohibition of loading and unloading ("No loading" in black letters on yellow background)
637	continuous prohibition on waiting except for loading and unloading (alternative types) (rectangular panel displaying diagram 636 and "At any time" in black letters on yellow background)
637.2	prohibition on waiting (and loading and unloading) in pedestrian zone (alternative types) ("Pedestrian Zone" [diagram 636] "At any time" in black letters on yellow background (to which may be added "No loading" [days] and [times] in black letters on white background)
637.3	continuous prohibition on waiting except for loading and unloading for at least 4 consecutive months (rectangular panel displaying diagram 636 and "At any time [dates]" in black letters on yellow background)
638	continuous prohibition on loading and unloading ("No loading at any time" in black letters on white background)
638.1	loading and unloading prohibited during the periods and in the direction indicated ("No loading [days] [times]" together with directional arrow in black letters on white background)
639	waiting prohibited except for loading and unloading during the period

and in the direction indicated (diagram 636   [*times*] together with directional arrow in black characters on yellow background)

639.1A   waiting prohibited during period indicated on upper portion except in accordance with conditions shown on lower portion (rectangular panel with diagram 636, [*dates*] and [*times*] in black letters on yellow background in upper portion; letter "P" in white on blue patch in lower portion with "Except [*times*]   *xx* mins   No return within *xx* mins" in black letters on white background)

640   waiting prohibited during period and in direction indicated on upper portion and loading and unloading prohibited during period and in direction indicated on lower portion (rectangular panel with [*dates*] and [*times*] in black letters on yellow background and diagram 636 in upper portion; with "No loading   [*days*]   [*times*]" and directional arrow in black letters on white background in lower portion)

640.1   waiting, loading and unloading prohibited at parking place where parking temporarily suspended (indication on parking meter cover) (diagram 636 and "No loading" in black letters on yellow background)

640.2A   waiting by goods vehicles over maximum gross weight shown prohibited during the periods and in the direction indicated (yellow rectangular panel with black symbol displaying permitted weight, diagram 636, [*days*] and [*times*], in black letters and directional arrow)

640.3   entrance to designated off-highway loading area in which waiting restrictions apply ("Loading area   diagram 636   Except by permitted vehicles   [*days*]   [*times*]" in black letters on yellow background)

640.4   waiting prohibited in designated off-highway loading area during period indicated except by permitted vehicles (diagram 636   "Except by permitted vehicles   [*days*]   [*times*]" in black letters on yellow background)

640.5   end of designated off-highway loading area in which waiting restrictions apply (rectangular panel, in left-hand portion diagram 636 displayed in grey and white crossed through; in right-hand portion "End of loading area" in black letters on yellow background)

642   no stopping on main carriageway (blue circle surrounded in red and crossed through diagonally in red)

642.2   no stopping at school entrance during periods indicated (diagram 642 "No stopping   [*days*]   [*times*]   on school entrance markings" in black letters on yellow background)

642.3   no stopping in lay-by except in emergency (diagram 642   "No stopping except in emergency")

643   restriction or prohibition conveyed by associated sign applies in both directions (black arrows on white background pointing left and right)

644   restriction or prohibition conveyed by associated sign applies in direction indicated (black arrow on white background pointing to left or right)

645   end of restriction or prohibition conveyed by associated sign or, when used with diagram 7001 (road works or temporary obstruction of carriageway ahead), end of all restrictions or prohibitions associated with road works ("End" in black letters on white background)

646   no stopping during periods indicated except for so long as may be necessary for the purpose of picking up or setting down passengers (rectangular panel; in upper portion, diagram 642   "URBAN CLEARWAY [*days*]' in black letters on yellow background; in left-hand side of lower portion, "am   [*times*]" in black letters on white background; in right-

hand side of lower portion "pm   [*times*]" in white letters on black background)

647   end of restriction on stopping (rectangular panel; in upper portion diagram 642   "URBAN CLEARWAY" in black letters on yellow background; in lower portion, "End" in black letters on white background)

650.1   prohibition on stopping by vehicles other than taxis during period indicated (diagram 642   "No stopping   [*times*]   except taxis" in black letters on yellow background)

650.1   prohibition on waiting by vehicles other than taxis during period indicated (diagram 642   "No waiting   [*times*]   except taxis" in black letters on yellow background)

651   use of verge maintained in mown or ornamental condition by specified traffic prohibited ("No motor vehicles, cycles, animals, pedestrians on mown verge" in black letters on white background below three red circles enclosing black symbols on white backgrounds)

660   parking place reserved for permit holders ("P" in white on blue patch and "Permit holders only" in black letters on white background)

660.3   parking place reserved for holders of residents' permits ("P" in white on blue patch, "Resident permit holders only" in black letters on white background, and "A", "B" and "C" in white on black patches)

660.4   part of carriageway reserved for loading and unloading (white symbol on blue patch and "Loading only" in black letters on white background)

660.5   parking place reserved for voucher parking during period indicated ("P" in white and white coat of arms on blue patches, [*days*], [*times*], and "Voucher parking only   *x* hour limit" in black letters on white background)

661   parking place reserved for diabled badge holders ("P" in white on blue patch, disabled symbol in black on orange patch, and "Disabled badge holders only" in black letters on white background)

661.1   restrictions on length of waiting time and return period ("P" in white on blue patch; actual restrictions indicated in black letters on white background)

661.2   "pay and display" ticket-regulated parking place ("P" in white on blue patch, "pay at meter", two arrows and "Display ticket" in black letters on white background)

661.3   location of "pay and display" ticket machine

661.4   drivers must obtain and display parking tickets (alternative types) ("P" in white on blue patch and "Have you paid and displayed?" in black letters on white background)

662   period during which waiting is limited and display of disc is required at parking place in a disc zone ("Disc Zone", "P" in white on blue patch, [*days*], [*times*], and "*xx* mins   No return within *x* hours" in black letters on white background)

663   entrance to controlled parking zone ("Meter ZONE",   diagram 636, [*days*], and [*times*] in black letters on white background)

663.1   entrance to voucher parking zone (coat of arms in white on blue patch, "Voucher parking ZONE'   diagram 636   [*days*], [*times*] and "*x* hour limit" in black letters on white background)

664   end of controlled or voucher parking zone (diagram 636 reproduced in grey on white and crossed through above wording "Zone ENDS" in black letters on white background)

665   entrance to controlled parking zone applying to goods vehicles over maximum gross weight shown (diagram 636, black lorry symbol

displaying permitted weight, "ZONE" and [*days*] and [*times*] in black letters on white background)

666   end of controlled parking zone applying to goods vehicles over a maximum weight shown (diagram 636 reproduced in grey on white and crossed through above goods vehicle symbol, and wording "Zone ENDS" in black letters on white background)

667   vehicles may be parked partially on verge or footway

667.1   vehicles may be parked partially on verge or footway during period indicated

667.2   end of area where vehicles may be parked partially on verge or footway

668   vehicles may be parked wholly on verge or footway

668.1   vehicles may be parked wholly on verge or footway during period indicated

668.2   end of area where vehicles may be parked wholly on verge or footway

669   nature of and distance to prohibition, restriction or requirement ahead ("Entry to . . . Street mile ahead" in white letters on blue background)

669.1   same as diagram 669 ("Low bridge . . . miles ahead" in white letters on blue background above diagram 629.2A)

670   maximum speed limit (black numerals on white background within red circle)

671   national speed limits apply (black diagonal bar across white circle)

672   minimum speed limit (white numerals within blue circle edged in white)

673   end of minimum speed limit (diagram 673 crossed through in red)

674   entrance to 20mph speed limit zone ("20" displayed within diagram 670 above "ZONE" [town name may be added])

675   end of 20mph speed limit zone ("30" displayed within diagram 670 above "20" in grey within grey circle and crossed through, and "Zone ENDS" in black on white background)

Regulation 11(1)   SCHEDULE 3

SIGNS FOR RAILWAY AND TRAMWAY LEVEL CROSSINGS

B48.59   *Editorial note.* The diagrams representing the actual traffic signs are not reproduced in this work, but the signs in Schedule 3 are described below by means of (in the main) the legends accompanying the signs. The dimensions of the components of the various signs are specified in marks accompanying the diagrams (not reproduced) and variations of wording (where permissible) are referred to in notes accompanying the diagrams (not reproduced), often by means of a cross reference to Schedule 16. The accompanying notes also cross refer to Schedule 17 for information regarding the illumination requirements for the signs. The diagrams are reproduced in numerical sequence but there are gaps in the numbering.

770   level crossing with gate or barrier ahead (black symbol (gate) within red triangle)

771   railway level crossing without gate or barrier ahead (black symbol (engine) within red triangle)

772   tramcars crossing ahead (black symbol (tram) within red triangle)

773   light signals in diagram 3014 ahead (two red and one yellow lights on black background above "STOP when lights show" in black letters on white background)

774   location of railway or tramcar level crossing without gate or barrier (two white bars edged in red with arrow heads at their ends set diagonally to each other)

775   vehicular traffic must not stop within area of railway or tramway level crossing ("KEEP CROSSING CLEAR" in black letters on white background with black surround)

776   another train or tramcar may be about to pass over crossing ("ANOTHER TRAIN COMING" within circle in black letters on red background)

777   level crossing ahead is crossed by more than one railway or tramway track, and more than one train or tramcar may pass over it in quick succssion ("ANOTHER TRAIN COMING if lights continue to show" in black letters on white background with black surround)

778   open level crossing without light signals (black symbol on white background with black surround)

778.1   open tramway level crossing without light signals (black symbol on white background with black surround)

779   electrified overhead cable ahead (black symbol within red triangle)

780   safe height beneath electrified overhead cable ahead

780.1   safe height beneath electrified overhead cable in direction and at distance indicated

780.2   safe height beneath electrified overhead cable ahead provided with a load gauge

781   load gauge giving audible warning to drivers where vehicle exceeds safe height under electrified overhead cables

782   risk of grounding at railway or tramway level crossing or hump backed bridge

783   drivers of large or slow vehicles must phone and get permission before using an automatic railway or tramway level crossing ("DRIVERS OF LONG LOW VEHICLES phone before crossing" in white letters on blue background edged in white)

784   drivers of large or slow vehicles must stop and telephone before using an automatic railway or tramway level crossing ("Drivers of LARGE or SLOW VEHICLES must phone and get permission to cross" in white letters on blue background edged in white)

785   details of telephone number for contacting railway or tramway operator

786   place where large or slow vehicles should wait near an automatic railway or tramway level crossing while the driver obtains permission to cross

787   site of emergency telephone or telephone at or near railway or tramway level crossing

788   direction to emergency telephone, etc.

789   countdown markers to concealed railway or tramway level crossing

789.1, 2   as diagram 789

790   new method of controlling traffic at railway or tramway level crossing ahead

Regulation 11(1)   SCHEDULE 4

OTHER INFORMATORY SIGNS

B48.60   *Editorial note.*   The diagrams representing the actual traffic signs are not reproduced in this work, but the signs in Schedule 4 are described below by means of (in the main) the legends accompanying the signs. The dimensions of the components of the various signs are specified in marks accompanying the diagrams (not reproduced) and variations of wording (where permissible) are referred to in notes accompanying the diagrams (not reproduced), often by means of a cross reference to Schedule 16. The accompanying notes also cross refer to Schedule 17 for information regarding the illumination requirements for the signs. The diagrams are reproduced in numerical sequence but there are gaps in the numbering.

801	parking place ("P" in white on blue background edged in white)
804.1	parking place for goods vehicles (black symbol (lorry) on white background with black surround)
804.2	parking place for motor cars (black symbol (car) on white background with black surround)
804.3	parking place for motorised caravans or caravans drawn by motor vehicles (black symbol (car end and caravan) on white background with black surround)
810	one way traffic in direction indicated (sign for pedestrians)
811	traffic has priority over traffic from the opposite direction (large white arrow and smaller red arrow in opposite directions on blue background edged in white)
811.1	explanatory plate for diagram 811 ("Priority over oncoming vehicles" in black letters on white background with black surround)
814.1–3	signs for pedestrians relating to subway/overbridge
816	no through road for vehicular traffic (letter "T" on which horizontal is red edged in white and is broader than the vertical which is coloured white, all on a blue background edged in white)
816.1	alternative to diagram 816 with street nameplate to one side of sign
817	no through road for vehicular traffic in direction indicated from junction ahead (main road shown as white on blue background with side road from junction terminating with red bar (edged with white) at right angle to side road, all edged in white)
817.2	escape lane ahead for vehicles unable to stop on steep hill
818	section of dual carriageway begins directly ahead
818.1	distance to section of dual carriageway ahead
818.1A	distance over which a short length of dual carriageway road beginning directly ahead extends
820	road unsuitable for type of vehicle indicated
821	road ahead only wide enough for one line of vehicles, but has passing places at intervals
822	passing place on narrow road
823–825	distance in hundreds of yards to a roundabout or next point at which driver may leave motorway or other route
826	depth of water at a ford
826.1	alternative to diagram 826 using metric and imperial units
827.1	hospital ahead without accident and emergency facilities
827.2	hospital ahead with accident and emergency facilities
829.1	potential danger temporarily ahead and consequent need to proceed

	with caution ("POLICE SLOW" in white letters on blue background edged in white)
829.2	accident ahead and consequent need to proceed with caution ("POLICE ACCIDENT" in white letters on blue background edged in white)
829.3	traffic should use hard shoulder in emergency ("POLICE USE HARD SHOULDER" in white letters on blue background edged in white)
829.4	end of temporary permission for traffic to use hard shoulder ("POLICE REJOIN MAIN CARRIAGEWAY" in white letters on blue background edged in white)
830	vehicles will be required to stop at traffic survey ahead ("STOP AT CENSUS POINT" in white letters on blue background edged in white)
830.1	vehicles may be directed to stop at traffic survey ahead ("CENSUS STOP if directed" in white letters on blue background edged in white)
830.2	goods vehicles may be directed to stop ahead by uniformed police officer for purposes of section 67, section 68 or section 78 of Road Traffic Act 1988 ("GOODS VEHICLES STOP if directed" in white letters on blue background edged in white)
830.3	vehicles should stay in lane for purposes of traffic survey or weight check ahead ("STAY IN LANE" in white letters on blue background edged in white)
831	vehicles should reduce speed on approaching traffic survey ahead ("SLOW CENSUS POINT" in white letters on blue background edged in white)
831.1	vehicle excise licence check point ahead ("Department of Transport VEHICLE EXCISE LICENCE CHECK" in white letters on blue background edged in white)
832	location of traffic survey ("CENSUS POINT" in white letters on blue background edged in white)
832.1	vehicle check point ahead ("Department of Transport CHECK POINT AHEAD" in white letters on blue background)
832.2	vehicle condition check point ahead ("Department of Transport VEHICLE CONDITION INSPECTION" in white letters on blue background)
832.3	goods vehicles may be directed to leave motorway at junction ahead (rectangular panel displaying black symbol and "Leave m'way if directed" in black letters on yellow background)
832.4	goods vehicles may be directed to enter a check point ahead (square panel displaying black symbol and "Enter Check Point if directed" in black letters on yellow background)
832.5	goods vehicles should keep to left lane on approach to check point ahead (square panel displaying black symbol and "Keep to left lane" in black letters on yellow background)
832.6	goods vehicles should get into left lane and other vehicles should use right-hand lane of a 2-lane carriageway on approach to goods vehicle check point ahead ([top panel] "GET IN LANE"; [second panel divided vertically into two by broken line] black symbol above arrow pointing upwards on left and "Other Vehicles" above arrow pointing upwards on right; [bottom panel] "Goods vehicle Check Point [*distance*]" in black letters on yellow background)
832.7	goods vehicles should get into left lane of a 3-lane carriageway on approach to goods vehicle check point ahead ([top panel] "GET IN LANE"; [second panel divided vertically into three by broken lines] "Any Vehicle" above arrow pointing upwards on left and black symbol crossed through

in red above arrow pointing upwards in each of other two panels; [bottom panel] "Goods vehicle Check Point [*distance*]" in black letters on yellow background)

832.8 goods vehicles should leave main carriageway of road on approach to goods vehicle check point (rectangular panel displaying arrow pointing diagonally and "All goods vehicles" in black letters on yellow background)

832.9 direction to commerical vehicle check point (rectangular panel with arrowhead displaying arrowhead and "Check point" in black letters on yellow background)

832.10 end of goods vehicle check point area (rectangular panel with "Goods vehicle restrictions END" in black letters on yellow background)

833 entrance to private access road or property ("IN")

834 exit from private access road or property ("OUT")

835 exit from private access road or property to public road not allowed ("NO EXIT" in white letters on blue background edged in white)

836 entry to private access road or property from public road not allowed ("NO ENTRY" in white letters on blue background edged in white)

857 information about tourist attractions, etc.

857.1 information relating to taxi rank for number of taxis specified

864 approved vehicle testing station

865 motor cycle testing station

868 additional traffic lane joining from left ahead

868.1 additional traffic lanes joining from right ahead

872 number of traffic lanes reduced ahead

873 additional traffic lane joining from left ahead; traffic on main carriageway has priority over joining traffic from right-hand lane of slip road

874 additional traffic lanes joining from right ahead; traffic in right-hand lane joins main carriageway; traffic on main carriageway has priority over joining traffic

875 additional traffic lanes joining from right ahead; traffic in right-hand lane of slip road has priority over traffic in left-hand lane

876 distance to change in number of lanes indicated by diagrams 868 to 875

877 junction ahead where left-hand lane is dedicated to traffic turning left and must not be used by other traffic, except buses, and where right-hand lane is available both for traffic proceeding ahead and turning right

Regulation 11(1)   SCHEDULE 5

SIGNS FOR BUS, TRAM AND PEDAL CYCLE FACILITIES

B48.61   *Editorial note.*   The diagrams representing the actual traffic signs are not reproduced in this work, but the signs in Schedule 5 are described below by means of (in the main) the legends accompanying the signs. The dimensions of the components of the various signs are specified in marks accompanying the diagrams (not reproduced) and variations of wording (where permissible) are referred to in notes accompanying the diagrams (not reproduced), often by means of a cross reference to Schedule 16. The accompanying notes also cross refer to Schedule 17 for information regarding the illumination requirements for the signs. The diagrams are reproduced in numerical sequence but there are gaps in the numbering.

950	cycle route ahead (black symbol within red triangle)
950.1	training or testing of child cyclists ahead
951	riding of pedal cycles prohibited (black symbol within red circle)
952	buses prohibited (black symbol within red circle)
953	route for buses and pedal cycles only (white symbols on blue background within circle edged in white)
953.1	route for use by tramcars only (white symbol on blue background within circle edged in white)
953.3	explanatory plate for diagrams 953, 953.1 ("Only")
954	buses excluded from restriction or prohibition conveyed by associated sign ("Except buses")
954.1	same as diagram 954 applying to buses and coaches ("Except buses and coaches")
954.2	same as diagram 954 applying to local buses ("Except local buses")
954.3	same as diagram 954 applying to buses and pedal cycles ("Except buses and cycles")
954.4	same as diagram 954 applying to pedal cycles ("Except cycles")
955	route for use by pedal cycles only (white symbol on blue background within circle edged in white)
956	route for use by pedal cycles and pedestrians only (white symbols on blue background within circle edged in white)
957	route comprising two ways, separated, by marking in diagram 1049 or 1049.1 or by physical means, for use by pedal cycles only and by pedestrians only (white symbols separated by vertical white line on blue background within circle edged in white)
958	with-flow bus lane ahead
958.1	with-flow cycle lane ahead
959	with-flow bus lane which pedal cycles may also use (note: any vehicle may enter the bus lane to stop, load or unload where this is not prohibited)
959.1	with-flow cycle lane
960	contra-flow bus lane (note: any vehicle may enter the bus lane to stop, load or unload where this is not prohibited)
960.1	contra-flow cycle lane
961	times of operation of bus lane or cycle lane
962	bus lane on road junction ahead
962.1	cycle lane on road at junction ahead or cycle track crossing road
962.2	contra-flow bus lane which pedal cycles may also use on road at junction ahead
963	bus lane with traffic proceeding from right
963.1	cycle lane with traffic proceeding from right
963.2	contra-flow bus lane which pedal cycles may also use with traffic proceeding from right
963.3	tramway with traffic proceeding in both directions
964	end of bus lane
965	end of cycle lane, track or route
966	pedal cyclists to dismount at end of, or at break in, cycle lane, track or route
967	route recommended for pedal cycles
968, 968.1	parking place for pedal cycles
969	parking place for buses
970	stopping place for buses
971	stopping place for tramcars

972	stopping point for buses carrying tourists to allow passengers to take photographs
973	stopping place for London buses
973.1	"request" stopping place for London buses
974	stopping by vehicles other than buses prohibited during periods indicated (rectangular panel displaying 642 and "No stopping [*times*] except buses" on yellow background)
975	place where buses may stand and stopping of other vehicles is prohibited during periods indicated (square panel displaying diagram 642 and "BUS STAND No stopping [*times*] except buses" in black letters on yellow background)

Regulation 11   SCHEDULE 6

ROAD MARKINGS

B48.62   *Editorial note.*   The diagrams representing the actual traffic signs are not reproduced in this work, but the signs in Schedule 6 are described below by means of (in the main) the legends accompanying the signs. The dimensions of the components of the various signs are specified in marks accompanying the diagrams (not reproduced) and variations of wording (where permissible) are referred to in notes accompanying the diagrams (not reproduced), often by means of a cross reference to Schedule 16. The accompanying notes also cross refer to Schedule 17 for information regarding the illumination requirements for the signs. The diagrams are reproduced in numerical sequence but there are gaps in the numbering.

N.B.   all diagrams included in Schedule 6 are marked on the surface of the roadway, usually in white.

1001	vehicular traffic must not proceed beyond the line when required to stop by light signals or by a police constable in uniform or a traffic warden (solid white line)
1002.1	vehicular traffic must not proceed beyond the line when required to stop by the sign shown in diagram 601.1 (solid white line)
1003	vehicular traffic must give way in accordance with regulation 25 (broken double white lines)
1003.1	vehicular traffic approaching roundabout should give way at or immediately beyond the line to vehicles circulating on carriageway of roundabout (broken single white line)
1003.2	pedestrians approaching level crossing should wait behind the line when barriers are closed or when light signals (diagram 3014) are showing or if these are neither barriers nor light signals until it is safe to proceed (broken single white line)
1003.3	vehicular traffic approaching roundabout with small central island or approaching junction marked by sign at diagram 611.1 should give way at or immediately beyond line to traffic circulating on carriageway of roundabout (broken white line)
1003.4	direction of traffic flow at junction marked by sign at diagram 611.1 (three arrows circling small white circle on roadway)
1004	vehicular traffic on roads with speed limit of 40mph or less should not straddle or cross line unless safe to do so; when line used in conjunction with diagram 967, motor vehicles should not enter cycle lane unless lane is clear of pedal cycles (broken white line)

1004.1	as diagram 1004 on roads with speed limit of more than 40mph (broken white line (increased lengths of lines and intervals))
1005	division of carriageway into lanes where vehicles normally proceed in same direction on roads with speed limit of 40mph or less (except where diagram 1004 is used) (broken white line (long intervals between short lines))
1005.1	as diagram 1005 on roads with speed limit of more than 40mph (except when diagram 1004.1 is used) (broken white line (increased lengths of lines and intervals))
1008	division between opposing flows of traffic on carriageway with speed limit of 40mph or less (except when diagram 1004 is used) (broken white line))
1008.1	division between opposing flows of traffic on carriageway with speed limit of more than 40mph (except when diagram 1004.1 is used) (broken white line))
1009	edge of carriageway at road injunction, exit from private drive on to public road, or (laid diagonally) start of cycle lane (broken white line)
1010	edge of carriageway at road junction, exit from private drive on to public road or lay-by; (laid diagonally) start of traffic lane, the boundary of which is indicated by diagram 1049; most suitable path for high vehicles through arch bridge (used in conjunction with diagram 1014 or 1024.1); (laid alongside tram rails) edge of carriageway used by tramcars; or division between main carriageway and traffic lane leaving main carriageway at a junction ahead (broken white line)
1012.1	edge of carriageway available for through traffic other than at road junction, exit from a private drive on to public road or a lay-by (unbroken white line)
1012.2	alternative to diagram 1012.1 incorporating audible and tactile warning (in form of raised rib) for use on motorways
1012.3	as diagram 1012.2, but for use on all-purpose roads with hard strips
1013.1	alternative methods of showing warning prescribed in regulation 26 (double white lines)
1013.3	as diagram 1013.1; adjacent part of carriageway which vehicular traffic should not enter unless it is seen by driver to be safe to do so
1014	direction in which vehicular traffic should pass (used in conjunction with diagram 1013.1, 1013.3, 1040, 1040.3, 1040.4 or 1049 ahead); obstruction on carriageway ahead; (used with diagram 1010) most suitable path for high vehicles through arch bridge (arrow)
1017	waiting of vehicles on side of a length of road prohibited for less than that specified in caption to diagram 1018.1 (single yellow line)
1018.1	waiting of vehicles on side of a length of road prohibited at any time during period of at least four consecutive months (double yellow lines)
1019	loading or unloading of vehicles on side of a length of road prohibited for a time less than that specified in caption to diagram 1020.1 (short yellow line at right angle to edge of carriageway)
1020.1	loading or unloading of vehicles on side of a length of road prohibited at any time during period of at least four consecutive months (two short yellow lines at right angle to edge of carriageway)
1022	approach to road junction at or near which is placed the sign in diagram 601.1 and the road marking in diagram 1002.1 ("STOP")

1023	approach to road junction at or near marking in diagram 1003 or diagrams 602 and 1003 (inverted triangle)
1024	vehicular traffic should proceed with caution because of potential danger ahead ("SLOW")
1024.1	path to be taken by high vehicles through arch bridge or route to avoid low bridge ("HIGH VEHS")
1025	stopping place for buses on part of carriageway also used by through traffic ("BUS STOP" in yellow inside yellow box with broken lines)
1025.1	as diagram 1025 where other vehicles prohibited from stopping at certain times ("BUS STOP" in yellow inside box with broken lines and single yellow line at edge of carriageway)
1025.2	stopping place for buses in lay-by ("BUS STOP" in yellow; area of lay-by marked off by broken line in yellow)
1025.3	as diagram 1025.2 where other vehicles prohibited from stopping at certain times ("BUS STOP" in yellow; area of stop marked off from carriageway by broken line in yellow and edge of carriageway and edges of bus stop marked with single (solid) yellow line)
1026	part of carriageway to be kept clear of stationary vehicles ("KEEP CLEAR" preceded and followed by line at right angle to edge of carriageway)
1026.1	part of carriageway outside entrance to off-street premises, or where kerb is dropped to provide convenient crossing place for pedestrians, to be kept clear of stationary vehicles (single line with short "bar" at each end)
1027	part of carriageway outside school entrance to be kept clear of stationary vehicles ("SCHOOL—KEEP—CLEAR" in yellow preceded and followed by wavy lines in yellow)
1028.2	alternative types of taxi rank either at edge or in centre of carriageway ("TAXIS" in yellow; area boxed off with broken yellow lines)
1028.3	alternative types of parking bays reserved for disabled badge holders either at edge or in centre of carriageway ("DISABLED"; area boxed off with broken lines)
1028.4	alternative types of parking bays reserved for doctor permit holders either at edge or in centre of carriageway ("DOCTOR"; area boxed off with broken lines)
1029	direction in which pedestrians should look for approaching traffic
1032	designated parking place (longitudinal markings)
1033	echelon parking spaces subject to such conditions (if any) as may be in force
1035	appropriate traffic lanes for different destinations
1036.1	vehicular traffic must turn left (alternative diagrams)
1036.2	vehicular traffic must only proceed ahead (alternative diagrams)
1037.1	vehicular traffic must turn right (alternative diagrams)
1038	appropriate traffic lanes for different manoeuvres
1039	place where traffic streams divide or bifurcate
1040	part of carriageway which vehicles should not enter unless it is seen by driver to be safe to do so (two broken lines converging on a point with diagonals between them)
1040.2	length or road which drivers should not overtake by passing through marking unless it is seen by driver to be safe to do so (two parallel lines with diagonals between them)

1040.3	reduction in number of lanes on motorway/all-purpose dual carriageway
1040.4	part of carriageway adjacent to edge which vehicles should not enter unless seen by driver to be safe to do so (broken line at angle from edge of carriageway with diagonals between it and edge of carriageway)
1040.5	end of hard shoulder
1041	part of carriageway where vehicles pass in same direction on both sides of marking, and should not enter the area covered by the marking unless it is seen by driver to be clear to do so (two broken lines converging on a point with chevrons between them)
1042	part of verge or hard shoulder or motorway between main motorway carriageway and carriageway of slip road, or at bifurcation or convergence of motorways which vehicles must not enter except in an emergency (two solid lines converging on a point with thick chevrons between them)
1043, 1044	area of carriageway at a junction (other than a roundabout) which vehicles must not enter in a manner which then causes any part of the vehicle to remain stationary within area due to the presence of stationary vehicles, except that vehicles waiting to complete a right turn may remain stationary within the area for so long as prevented from completing that turn by reason either of on-coming vehicles or of the presence of other stationary vehicles waiting in or near that area to complete a right turn; when diagrams are used in conjunction with diagrams 615 and 811 on an area of carriageway which at any point is less than 4.5m in width, vehicles must not enter the marked area in a manner which then causes any part of the vehicle to remain stationary within that area due to the presence of on-coming vehicles or other stationary vehicles (alternative types) (rhombus with several diagonals in each direction in yellow)
1045	area of carriageway at a level crossing which vehicles must not enter in a manner which then causes any part of the vehicle to remain at rest within the marked area due to the presence of stationary vehicles (yellow rectangle covering both carriageways with patterned cross hatching)
1046	no entry for vehiclar traffic (alternative type) ("NO ENTRY")
1048	with-flow lane reserved for buses and other vehicles as indicated in diagram 959 or a contra-flow lane reserved for buses ("BUS LANE")
1048.1	contra-flow reserved for buses and pedal cycles ("BUS AND [cycle symbol] LANE")
1049	boundary of bus or cycle lane; where varied to 150mm wide and used in conjunction with diagram 957, the division of route into part reserved for pedal cycles and part for pedestrians (unbroken white line)
1049.1	division of route into part reserved for pedal cycles and part for pedestrians (raised white marking)
1050	direction of possible traffic movements at end of bus lane
1055	pedestrian crossing at which traffic subject to control by police in uniform or traffic warden, or the most suitable crossing for pedestrians near traffic signals or pedestrian crossing signals (square marks)
1057	cycle lane, track or route
1058	end of cycle lane, track or route

1059	directions in which pedal cycles should travel on cycle lane, track or route
1060	road hump with round top extending across whole width of carriage-way
1060.1	road hump with round top and tapered ends
1061	road hump with flat top extending across whole width of carriageway
1061.1	road hump with flat top and tapered ends
1063	limits of measured lengths of road for assessing speed of vehicular traffic by police

Regulation 11(1)

SCHEDULE 7

B48.63 *Editorial note.* The diagrams representing the traffic signs in Schedule 7 being essentially for information are not listed.

PART I

PRIMARY ROUTE DIRECTIONAL SIGNS

Diagrams 2001 to 2034 [*not reproduced*]

PART II

NON-PRIMARY ROUTE DIRECTIONAL SIGNS

Diagrams 2101 to 2138 [*not reproduced*]

PART III

TOURIST ATTRACTION SIGNS

Diagrams 2201 to 2216 [*not reproduced*]

PART IV

[SIGNS FOR SERVICES AND TOURIST FACILITIES]

Diagrams 2301 to 2329 [*not reproduced*]

PART V

BOUNDARY SIGNS

Diagrams 2401 to 2403 [*not reproduced*]

PART VI

DIRECTIONAL SIGNS TO PARKING PLACES

Diagrams 2501 to 2509 [*not reproduced*]

PART VII

DIRECTIONAL SIGNS FOR CYCLISTS AND PEDESTRIANS

Diagrams 2601 to 2610.2 [*not reproduced*]

PART VIII

TEMPORARY AND EMERGENCY DIRECTIONAL SIGNS

Diagrams 2701 to 2716 [*not reproduced*]

PART IX

OTHER NON-MOTORWAY DIRECTIONAL SIGNS

Diagrams 2801 to 2807 [*not reproduced*]

PART X

MOTORWAY SIGNS

Diagrams 2901 to 2932 [*not reproduced*]

[Schedule 7 has been amended by S.I. 1995 No. 3107.]   **B48.64**

SCHEDULE 8   Regulations 30, 31, 32

LIGHT SIGNALS FOR THE CONTROL OF VEHICULAR TRAFFIC

Editorial note. The diagrams representing the actual traffic signs are not reproduced in this   **B48.65**
work, but the signs in Schedule 8 are described below by means of (in the main) the legends
accompanying the signs. The dimensions of the components of the various signs are
specified in marks accompanying the diagrams (not reproduced) and variations of wording
(where permissible) are referred to in notes accompanying the diagrams (not reproduced),
often by means of a cross reference to Schedule 16. The accompanying notes also cross
refer to Schedule 17 for information regarding the illumination requirements for the signs.
The diagrams are reproduced in numerical sequence but there are gaps in the numbering.

3000	lights signals for the control of vehicular traffic at road junctions, where the headroom or width of road is permanently reduced, or where pedestrians cross the road (other than "Pelican" crossings) (red, yellow and green traffic signals)
3000.1	portable light signals (red, yellow and green traffic signals)
3000.2	light signals solely for pedal cycles (red, yellow and green traffic signals, the latter two displaying only a symbol of a cycle)
3000.3	as diagram 3000, but with additional signal as in diagram 3001, 3001.1, or 3013
3000.4	as diagram 3000, but with two additional signals as in diagram 3001, 3001.1, and 3013

3000.5	alternative arrangement of signals in diagram 3000.3
3000.6	alternative arrangement of signals in diagram 3000.4
3001	green arrow for inclusion within light signals (reg.31)
3001.1	same as diagram 3001
3002	light signals shown in diagram 3000.3 with green arrow as in diagram 3001 or 3001.1 substituted for tram signal shown in diagram 3013
3003	lights signals shown at diagram 3000 with a green arrow as in diagram 3001 or 3001.1 substituted for green signal
3004	same as diagram 3002
3005	light signals as in diagram 3000.3, with green arrows as in diagram 3001 or 3001.1 substituted for green aspect and tram signal shown in diagram 3013
3006	as diagram 3005
3007	light signals in diagram 3000.4 with green arrow as in diagram 3001 or 3001.1 substituted for tram signal shown in diagram 3013.
3008	same as diagram 3007
3009.1	light signals in diagram 3000 with green arrow as in diagram 3001 or 3001.1 added below green signal
3011.1	lights signals shown at diagram 3000 with a green arrow as in diagram 3001 or 3001.1 substituted for green signal, and a second arrow added below that (arrows illuminated and extinguished simultaneously)
3011.2	as diagram 3011.1 (arrows illuminated and extinguished separately)
3013	light signal for control of tramcars
3013.1	as diagram 3013, conveying prohibition prescribed by regulation 33(5)(a)
3013.2	as diagram 3013, conveying prohibition prescribed by regulation 33(5)(b)
3013.3	as diagram 3013, conveying prohibition prescribed by regulation 33(5)(c)
3013.4	as diagram 3013, conveying prohibition prescribed by regulation 33(5)(d)
3013.5	as diagram 3013, conveying prohibition prescribed by regulation 33(5)(e)
3014	light signals for control of traffic at level crossings, swing or lifting bridges, tunnels, airfields or in vicinity of premises used regularly by fire, police or ambulance service vehicles (two red and one orange light signals on black background mounted on red and white chequered surround)

Regulations 37–40   SCHEDULE 9

LIGHT SIGNALS FOR PEDESTRIANS AND ANIMAL CROSSINGS

B48.66   *Editorial note.* The diagrams representing the actual traffic signs are not reproduced in this work, but the signs in Schedule 9 are described below by means of (in the main) the legends accompanying the signs. The dimensions of the components of the various signs are specified in marks accompanying the diagrams (not reproduced) and variations of wording (where permissible) are referred to in notes accompanying the diagrams (not reproduced), often by means of a cross reference to Schedule 16. The accompanying notes also cross refer to Schedule 17 for information regarding the illumination requirements for the signs.

4002	light signals for pedestrians
4003	instructions to pedestrians above push button control for calling up pedestrian phases at light signals
4004	children likely to be crossing road on their way to or from school ahead (alternative types) (two amber light signals on black background)

| 4005 | cattle crossing ahead |
| 4006 | light signal at level crossings for pedestrians |

SCHEDULE 10

Regulation 34

Editorial note. The diagrams representing the traffic signs in Schedule 10 being in the main for information are not listed.

B48.67

PART I

LANE CONTROL SIGNALS

Diagrams 5001.1 to 5005.1 [*not reproduced*]

PART II

LANE CONTROL SIGNS

Diagrams 5010 to 5015 [*not reproduced*]

SCHEDULE 11

Regulation 36

PART I

MATRIX SIGNS
(FOR MOTORWAYS AND DUAL CARRIAGEWAYS)

Editorial note. The diagrams representing the actual traffic signs are not reproduced in this work, but the signs in Schedule 11 are described below by means of (in the main) the legends accompanying the signs. The dimensions of the components of the various signs are specified in marks accompanying the diagrams (not reproduced) and variations of wording (where permissible) are referred to in notes accompanying the diagrams (not reproduced), often by means of a cross reference to Schedule 16. The accompanying notes also cross refer to Schedule 17 for information regarding the illumination requirements for the signs. The diagrams are reproduced in numerical sequence but there are gaps in the numbering.

B48.68

6001	temporary maximum speed advised
6002	vehicular traffic must move to next lane on the right
6003	vehicular traffic must leave at next junction
6006	closure of one lane of a three-lane carriageway ahead
6006.1	closure of two lanes of a three-lane carriageway ahead
6006.2	closure of all lanes of a three-lane carriageway ahead
6008	closure of right-hand lane of a two-lane carriageway ahead
6008.1	closure of both lanes of a two-lane carriageway ahead
6009	closure of one lane or a four-lane carriageway ahead
6009.1	closure of two lanes of a four-lane carriageway ahead
6009.2	closure of three lanes of a four-lane carriageway ahead
6009.3	closure of all lanes of a four-lane carriageway ahead
6011	risk of fog ahead

6012   end of temporary restrictions indicated by previous signs

6021   gantry mounted signal with flashing amber lamps displaying signs at diagram 6001, 6002, 6003 or 6011

6022   post mounted signal with flashing amber lamps displaying signs at diagram 6001, 6003, 6006, 6006.1, 6008, 6009, 6009.1, 6009.2 or 6011

PART II

LIGHT SIGNALS
(FOR MOTORWAYS AND DUAL CARRIAGEWAYS)

6023   light signal conveying the warning under regulation 35

6031.1   light signals (motorways and dual carriageways) for conveying requirements of regulation 33(3)(b)

6032.1   light signals for conveying requirements of regulation 33(3)(a)

Regulation 11(1)   **SCHEDULE 12**

B48.69   *Editorial note.* The diagrams representing the traffic signs in Schedule 12 being mainly for information, only selected signs are listed below. The dimensions of the components of the various signs are specified in marks accompanying the diagrams (not reproduced) and variations of wording (where permissible) are referred to in notes accompanying the diagrams (not reproduced), often by means of a cross reference to Schedule 16. The accompanying notes also cross refer to Schedule 17 for information regarding the illumination requirements for the signs. The diagrams are reproduced in numerical sequence but there are gaps in the numbering.

PART I

MISCELLANEOUS WARNING, INFORMATORY AND REGULATORY SIGNS FOR ROAD WORKS

. . . .

7011   point beyond which vehicular traffic must not proceed when required to stop by regulation 33 in accordance with indication given by portable light signals in diagram 3000.1 and when road marking diagram 1001 is not placed on carriageway (rectangular panel with "WHEN RED LIGHT SHOWS WAIT HERE" in white letters on red background edged in white)

. . . .

7023   vehicular traffic must not proceed into length of road where one-way working is temporarily necessary (manually operated sign) (octagonal panel with "STOP" in white letters on red background edged in white)

7024   vehicular traffic may proceed into length of road where one-way working is temporarily necessary (manually operated sign) (octagonal panel with "GO" in white letters on green background edged in white)

Regulation 11(1)   **PART II**

ROAD WORKS DELINEATORS AND BARRIERS

7101   edge of route for vehicular traffic through or past temporary obstruction (traffic cone)

7101   edge of route for vehicular traffic through or past temporary obstruction
              on motorway or dual carriageway road (flat traffic delineator)
7103   line of division of traffic flows on one carriageway, or edge of route for
              vehicular traffic through or past temporary obstruction, or boundary
              between two carriageways of a dual carriageway which may not be
              crossed except for fire brigade, ambulance or police purposes (traffic
              cylinder)
              . . . .
7105   barrier to mark length of road closed to traffic or to guide traffic past
              obstruction (barrier in alternate red and white stripes)

PART III   Regulation 11(1)

SIGNS FOR LANE CLOSURES AND CONTRA-FLOW WORKING AT ROAD WORKS

Diagrams 7201 to 7290 [*not reproduced*]

PART IV   Regulation 11(1)

SIGNS FOR ROAD WORKS ENTRANCES AND EXITS

Diagrams 7301 to 7307 [*not reproduced*]

PART V   Regulation 11(1)

SIGNS MOUNTED ON ROAD WORKS VEHICLES

              . . . .
7402   lanes closed to traffic ahead by vehicles carrying out mobile road works
7403   other traffic to keep to right of vehicles carrying out mobile road works
              . . . .

SCHEDULE 13

PART I   Regulation 13(1)   **B48.70**

PROPORTIONS AND FORM OF LETTERS, NUMERALS AND OTHER CHARACTERS
(FOR USE ON A SIGN OR PARTS OF A SIGN WITH A RED, BLUE, BROWN, BLACK OR GREEN
BACKGROUND AND ON THE SIGNS SHOWN IN DIAGRAMS 2714 AND 2715)

[*not reproduced*]

PART II   Regulation 13(1)

PROPORTIONS AND FORM OF LETTERS, NUMERALS AND OTHER CHARACTERS
(FOR USE ON A SIGN OR PARTS OF A SIGN WITH A WHITE, YELLOW OR ORANGE BACKGROUND
OTHER THAN THE SIGNS SHOWN IN DIAGRAMS 2714 AND 2715)

[*not reproduced*]

Regulation 13(3)

PART III

PROPORTIONS AND FORM OF LETTERS, NUMERALS AND OTHER CHARACTERS
(FOR ROUTE NUMBERS ON PERMANENT MOTORWAY SIGNS WITH BLUE BACKGROUNDS)

[*not reproduced*]

Regulation 13(3)

PART IV

PROPORTIONS AND FORM OF LETTERS, NUMERALS AND OTHER CHARACTERS
(FOR ROUTE NUMBERS ON TEMPORARY MOTORWAY SIGNS WITH YELLOW BACKGROUNDS)

[*not reproduced*]

Regulation 13(5)

PART V

PROPORTIONS AND FORM OF LETTERS, NUMERALS AND OTHER CHARACTERS FOR USE ON
VARIABLE MESSAGE SIGNS
(WHERE THE CHARACTERS SHOWN IN PARTS I, II, III AND IV CANNOT BE USED BECAUSE OF
THE METHOD OF CONSTRUCTION OR OPERATION OF THE SIGN)

[*not reproduced*]

Regulation 13(6)

PART VI

PROPORTIONS AND FORM OF LETTERS, NUMERALS AND OTHER CHARACTERS FOR USE IN
THE ROAD MARKINGS SHOWN IN SCHEDULE 6

(a) with a height of 1.6 metres [*not reproduced*]

(b) with a height of 2.8 metres [*not reproduced*]

(c) for use in the road markings shown in diagrams 1027.1, 1028.2, 1028.3, 1028.4, 1029
and 1033 [*not reproduced*]

Regulation 13(5)

PART V

PROPORTIONS AND FORM OF LETTERS, NUMERALS AND OTHER CHARACTERS
(SYMBOLS FOR USE ON DIRECTIONAL SIGNS TO INDICATE DIVERSION ROUTES)

[*not reproduced*]

SCHEDULE 14

B48.71   Regulation 13(8)

PART I

PROPORTIONS AND FORM OF SYMBOLS INDICATING THE TYPE OF TOURIST ATTRACTION IN
ENGLAND, SCOTLAND AND WALES

Diagrams T1 to T9 [*not reproduced*]

PART II   Regulation 13(8)

PROPORTIONS AND FORM OF SYMBOLS INDICATING THE TYPE OF TOURIST ATTRACTION IN ENGLAND AND WALES

Diagrams T101 to T133 [*not reproduced*]

PART III   Regulation 13(8)

PROPORTIONS AND FORM OF SYMBOLS INDICATING THE TYPE OF TOURIST ATTRACTION IN ENGLAND ONLY

Diagrams T201 to T203 [*not reproduced*]

PART IV   Regulation 13(8)

PROPORTIONS AND FORM OF SYMBOLS INDICATING THE TYPE OF TOURIST ATTRACTION IN SCOTLAND ONLY

Diagrams T301 to T303 [*not reproduced*]

PART V   Regulation 13(8)

PROPORTIONS AND FORM OF SYMBOLS INDICATING THE TYPE OF TOURIST ATTRACTION IN WALES ONLY

Diagrams T401 and T402 [*not reproduced*]

SCHEDULE 15   Regulation 46

LEGENDS FOR USE ON VARIABLE MESSAGE SIGNS

PART I   **B48.72**

SIGNS AUTOMATICALLY ACTIVATED BY VEHICULAR TRAFFIC

Paragraph 1 [*not reproduced*]

PART II

LEGENDS GIVING WARNING OF ADVERSE WEATHER OR OTHER TEMPORARY HAZARDS

Paragraph 2 [*not reproduced*]

PART III

INFORMATION ON DIVERSION ROUTES

Paragraph 3 [*not reproduced*]

PART IV

OTHER LEGENDS

Paragraph 4 [*not reproduced*]

Regulation 17

SCHEDULE 16

PERMITTED VARIANTS

B48.73

Items 1 to 42 [*not reproduced*]

Regulation 18, 19

SCHEDULE 17

ILLUMINATION OF SIGNS

B48.74

(1) Item	(2) Diagram numbers	(3) Method of Illumination
1.	501, 504.1, 505.1, 506.1, 507.1, 510, 512, 512.1, 512.2, 513, 516, 517, 520, 521, 522, 523.1, 524.1, 528, 529, 529.1, 530, 531.1, 532.2 (in respect of the triangle symbols), 532.3 (in respect of the triangle symbols), 543 (other than when used with 547.6), 544 (other than when used with 547.5), 544.1, 544.2, 545, 555, 601.1, 602, 606 (other than when used as described in item 6 or item 7), 609, 610 (other than when used as described in item 7), 611 (other than when used as described in item 7), 611.1, 612 (other than when used as described in item 6), 613 (other than when used as described in item 6), 614 (other than when used as described in item 6), 615, 616 (other than when used as described in item 7), 617 (other than when used with 618), 618.2, 618.3, 618.3A, 618.4, 619, 619.1, 619.2, 622.1A, 622.2, 622.4, 626.2, 629, 629.1, 629.2, 629.2A, 632, 642 (if the diameter is more than 450mm), 652, 669, 669.1, 770, 771, 772, 779, 782, 784, 790, 818, 818.1, 818.1A, 868, 868.1, 872, 873, 874, 875, 950 (other than when used with	(1) Where the sign is erected on a road within 50 metres of any lamp lit by electricity which forms part of a system of street-lighting furnished by means of at least three such lamps placed not more than 183 metres apart, that sign shall be illuminated by a means of internal or external lighting either for so long as that system is illuminated, or throughout the hours of darkness, unless it is erected temporarily for any of the following reasons— (a) for the purpose of a temporary statutory provision; (b) by reason of some emergency; or (c) if that road is a road subject to a speed limit of 30mph or under, by reason of the execution of works, or of any obstruction on the road. (2) Where any such sign is erected in such a manner that it is not required to be illuminated throughout the hours of darkness by a means of internal or external lighting, it shall be illuminated by the use of retroreflecting material in accordance with the provisions of regulation 19.

[*continued on next page*

(1) Item	(2) Diagram numbers	(3) Method of Illumination
1.— cont.	950.1), 952, 953, 953.1, 2901, 2902, 2902.1, 2903, 2904, 2904.1, 2905, 2906, 2908, 2909, 2910, 2910.1, 2911, 2912, 2915, 2917, 2918, 2919, 2920, 2921, 2929, 2930, 2931, 5010, 5011, 7001, 7002, 7004, 7005, 7006, 7009, 7010, 7011, 7012, 7013, 7201, 7202, 7203, 7203.1, 7204, 7205, 7206, 7207, 7210, 7211, 7212, 7213, 7214, 7215, 7216, 7217, 7218, 7220, 7221, 7230, 7231, 7232, 7233, 7234, 7235, 7236, 7237, 7238, 7239, 7240, 7250, 7251, 7252, 7253, 7254, 7255, 7260, 7261, 7262, 7263, 7264, 7265, 7266, 7270, 7271, 7272, 7273, 7274, 7275, 7290	
2.	2711	The sign shall be internally illuminated.
3.	955 (other than when used as described in item 7), 956, 957	(1) Where the sign is a terminal sign and is erected on a road within 50 metres of any lamp lit by electricity which forms part of a system of street-lighting furnished by means of at least three such lamps placed not more than 183 metres apart, that sign shall be illuminated by a means of internal or external lighting either for so long as that system is illuminated, or throughout the hours of darkness. (2) Where the sign is erected in such a manner that it is not required to be illuminated throughout the hours of darkness by a means of internal or external lighting, it shall be illuminated by the use of retroreflecting material in accordance with the provisions of regulation 19.
4.	515, 515.1, 515.1A, 528.1, 548, 549, 550, 550.1, 551, 551.1, 551.2, 552, 553.1, 554, 554.1, 554.2, 556, 556.1, 557, 558, 558.1, 559, 562,	The sign may be illuminated by a means of internal or external lighting but if not so illuminated throughout the hours of darkness,

[*continued on next page*

(1) Item	(2) Diagram numbers	(3) Method of Illumination
4.—cont.	574, 581, 582, 583, 633, 642 (if the diameter is 450mm or less), 646, 647, 663, 663.1, 664, 665, 666, 774, 775, 777, 783, 785, 786, 787, 788, 789, 789.1, 789.2, 801, 811, 816, 817, 820, 821, 822, 823, 824, 825, 827.1, 827.2, 829.1, 829.2, 829.3, 829.4, 830, 830.1, 830.2, 830.3, 831, 831.1, 832, 832.1, 832.2, 832.3, 832.4, 832.5, 832.6, 832.7, 832.8, 832.9, 832.10, 877, 950 (when used with 950.1), 951, 958, 958.1, 959, 959.1, 960, 960.1, 962, 962.1, 962.2, 964, 969, 2001, 2002, 2003, 2004, 2005, 2006, 2007, 2008, 2009, 2010, 2011, 2012, 2013, 2014, 2015, 2016, 2017, 2018, 2019, 2020, 2021, 2022, 2023, 2024, 2025, 2026, 2027, 2028, 2029, 2030, 2030.1, 2031, 2032, 2033, 2034, 2101, 2101.1, 2101.2, 2102, 2103, 2104, 2105, 2106, 2107, 2108, 2109, 2110, 2111, 2112, 2113, 2113.1, 2114, 2115, 2115.1, 2116, 2117, 2118, 2119, 2120, 2121, 2122, 2123, 2124, 2125, 2126, 2127, 2128, 2129, 2130, 2131, 2132, 2133, 2134, 2135, 2136, 2137, 2138, 2301, 2302, 2303, 2304, 2305, 2306, 2307, 2308, 2309, 2310, 2311, 2312, 2312.1, 2313, 2314, 2315, 2315.1, 2501, 2502, 2503, 2504, 2505, 2506, 2507, 2508, 2509, 2702, 2703, 2704, 2705, 2706, 2707, 2708, 2709, 2710, 2713.1, 2716, 2803, 2804, 2805, 2806, 2913, 2914, 2916, 2922, 2923, 2924, 2925, 2926, 2927, 2928, 2932, 5012, 5013, 5014, 5015, 7003, 7014, 7015, 7019, 7020, 7104, 7105, 7301, 7302, 7303, 7304, 7305, 7306, 7307	it shall be illuminated by the use of retroreflecting material in accordance with the provisions of regulation 19.
5.	543 (when used with 547.6), 544 (when used with 547.5), 557.1, 7023, 7024, 7401, 7402, 7403	The sign shall be illuminated by a means of internal or external lighting throughout the hours of darkness.

[*continued on next page*

(1) *Item*	(2) *Diagram numbers*	(3) *Method of Illumination*
6.	606, 612, 613, 614	Where the sign is fixed to light signals prescribed by regulation 30, or by regulation 30 as varied by regulation 31, it shall be illuminated by a means of internal lighting at all times except when the light signals to which it is fixed are being maintained or repaired.
7.	606, 610, 611, 616, 955	Where the sign is mounted in a bollard fitted with a means of lighting it internally, the sign shall be illuminated throughout the hours of darkness by that means of internal lighting.
8.	502, 503, 511, 513.1, 513.2, 518, 519, 525, 526, 527, 530.1, 531.2, 543.1, 546, 547.1, 547.2, 547.3, 547.4, 547.5, 547.6, 547.7, 548.1, 553, 553.2, 554.3, 556.2, 557.2, 557.3, 557.4, 558.2, 563, 563.1, 570, 572, 573, 575, 583.1, 607, 608, 615.1, 618, 618.1, 620, 620.1, 627.1, 643, 644, 645, 773, 778, 778.1, 780, 780.1, 780.2, 804.1, 804.2, 804.3, 811.1, 817.2, 876, 950.1, 953.2, 954, 954.1, 954.2, 954.3, 954.4, 961, 7001.1, 7001.2, 7021, 7022, 7208, 7209, 7256, 7401.1	See regulation 20.
9.	530.2, 532.2 and 532.3 in respect of parts of the signs other than the triangle symbols, 617 when used 618, 622.5, 622.6, 625.1, 636, 636.1, 637, 637.1, 637.2, 637.3, 638, 638.1, 639, 639.1A, 640, 640.1, 640.2A, 640.3, 640.4, 640.5, 642.2, 642.3, 650.1, 650.2, 651, 660, 660.3, 660.4, 660.5, 661, 661.1, 661.2, 661.3, 661.4, 662, 667, 667.1, 667.2, 668, 668.1, 668.2, 810, 814.1, 814.2, 814.3, 814.4, 816.1, 826, 826.1, 833, 834, 835, 836, 857, 857.1, 864, 865, 963, 963.1, 963.2, 963.3, 965, 966, 967, 968, 968.1, 970, 971, 972, 973, 973.1, 974, 975, 2201, 2202,	The sign or plate may be left unlit, or be illuminated either by means of internal or external with lighting or by the use of retroreflecting material.

[continued on next page

(1) *Item*	(2) *Diagram numbers*	(3) *Method of Illumination*
9.— *cont.*	2203, 2204, 2205, 2206, 2207, 2208, 2209, 2210, 2211, 2212, 2213, 2214, 2215, 2216, 2316, 2317, 2318, 2319, 2320, 2321, 2322, 2323, [2324, 2325, 2326, 2327, 2328, 2329,] 2401, 2402, 2403, 2601, 2602, 2603, 2604, 2605, 2606, 2607, 2608, 2609, 2610, 2610.1, 2610.2, 2701, 2712, 2713, 2801, 2802, 2807, 7007, 7008, 7016, 7017, 7018, 7404	
10.	670, 671, 672, 673 (if the diameter is 600mm, 900mm or 1500mm)	(1) Where the sign is a terminal sign and is erected on a trunk or principal road within 50 metres of a street lamp lit by electricity, it shall throughout the hours of darkness— (a) be continuously illuminated by means of internal or external lighting and may also be illuminated by the use of retroreflecting material; or (b) while the street lamp is lit, be continuously illuminated by means of external lighting and shall also be illuminated by the use of retroreflecting material. (2) If any sign is required to be illuminated in the manner and at the times described in paragraph (1) above— (a) every sign shown in the same diagram as the first-mentioned sign which is erected at or near the same point on the road or the same junction for the same purpose as the first-mentioned sign shall be continuously illuminated throughout the same period by the same means of lighting as the first-mentioned sign; and (b) if any of the signs is illuminated by the use of retroflecting material, every other such sign shall be similarly illuminated.

[continued on next page

(1) Item	(2) *Diagram numbers*	(3) *Method of Illumination*
11.	670, 671, 672, 673, 674, 675	If the sign is not required by item 10 to be illuminated by lighting throughout the hours of darkness or throughout such hours while a street lamp is lit, it may be illuminated— (a) throughout the hours of darkness by means of internal or external lighting; or (b) throughout any period during the hours of darkness by the use of retroreflecting material; and if so illuminated paragraph (2) of item 10 shall apply as if the sign were a sign required by paragraph (1) of item 10 to be illuminated by lighting throughout the hours of darkness or throughout such hours while a street lamp is lit.
12.	1001, 1002.1, 1003, 1003.1, 1003.2, 1003.3, 1003.4, 1004, 1004.1, 1005, 1005.1, 1008, 1008.1, 1009, 1010, 1012.1, 1012.2, 1012.3, 1013.1, 1013.3, 1014, 1017, 1018.1, 1019, 1020.1, 1022, 1023, 1024, 1024.1, 1025, 1025.1, 1025.2, 1025.3, 1026, 1026.1, 1027.1, 1028.2, 1028.3, 1028.4, 1029, 1032, 1033, 1035, 1036.1, 1036.2, 1037.1, 1038, 1039, 1040, 1040.2, 1040.3, 1040.4, 1040.5, 1041, 1042, 1043, 1044, 1045, 1046, 1048, 1048.1, 1049, 1049.1, 1050, 1055, 1057, 1058, 1059, 1060, 1060.1, 1061, 1061.1, 1063	See regulation 28.
13.	560, 561	See regulation 21.
14.	776	The sign shall be illuminated by an intermittent red light flashing at a rate of not less than 54 nor more than 90 flashes per minute.
15.	515.2, 532.2, 605.2, 2714, 2715, 3014 (in respect of the backing board)	The parts of the sign coloured other than black or orange shall be illuminated by the use of

[continued on next page

(1) Item	(2) Diagram numbers	(3) Method of Illumination
15.— cont.		retroreflecting material in accordance with the provisions of regulation 19. Any parts of the sign coloured orange may be so illuminated. The part of the sign in diagram 605.2 coloured yellow shall be fluorescent, except as provided in regulation 19(4).
16.	7101, 7102, 7103	See regulation 44.

B48.75   *[Schedule 17 is printed as amended by S.I. 1995 No. 3107.]*

Regulation 4   SCHEDULE 18

INTERPRETATION OF "UNLADEN VEHICLE"

B48.76   **1.** In these Regulations "*unladen vehicle*" means, subject to paragraph 3 of this Schedule—

(a) a motor vehicle not drawing a trailer or otherwise forming part of a combination of vehicles; or

(b) a combination of vehicles comprising one motor vehicle drawing one or more trailers,

in relation to which the conditions specified in paragraph 2 below are satisfied.

2. The conditions mentioned in paragraph 1 above are—

(a) that the motor vehicle is a motor car, a heavy motor car, or a motor tractor;

(b) that no goods or burden are being carried in the motor vehicle or if the motor vehicle is drawing one or more trailers, in that combination of vehicles; and

(c) that not more than 2 persons (excluding the driver) are being carried in the motor vehicle or, if the motor vehicle is drawing one or more trailers, in that combination of vehicles.

B48.77   **3.** For the purposes of this Schedule—

(a) in the case of a motor vehicle so constructed that it is fitted with a crane, dynamo, plant or other special appliance or apparatus which is a permanent or essentially permanent fixture, the appliance or apparatus is not to be deemed to constitute goods or burden of any description; and

(b) water, fuel or accumulators used for the purpose of the supply of power for the propulsion of a vehicle or, as the case may be, of any vehicle by which a trailer is drawn, and loose tools and loose equipment are not to be deemed to constitute goods or burden of any description.

PART II

THE TRAFFIC SIGNS GENERAL DIRECTIONS 1994

1. Citation and commencement

This Part of this Instrument—   **B48.78**

(a) may be cited—

    (i) as the Traffic Signs General Directions 1994, and

    (ii) together with Part I above, as the Traffic Signs Regulations and General Directions 1994; and

(b) shall come into force on 12th August 1994.

2. Revocations

The Instruments specified in Appendix 2 to this Instrument, so far as they consist of   **B48.79**
or comprise directions, are hereby revoked except that for the purposes of the Traffic
Signs (Welsh and English Language Provisions) Regulations and General Directions
1985 the revocations of the Directions marked with an asterisk in Appendix 2 shall have
no effect.

[See the note to regulation 2 of this Instrument.]   **B48.80**

3. Interpretation

(1) In these Directions—   **B48.81**

"*the 1971 Regulations*" means the "Zebra" Pedestrian Crossing Regulations 1971 [*S.I. 1971 No. 1524*];

"*controlled parking zone*" has the meaning given in direction 23;

"*former Directions*" means the Directions revoked by these Directions;

"*the Regulations*" means the Traffic Signs Regulations 1994 [*q.v.*],

and the expressions listed in paragraph (2) have the same meaning as in the Regulations.

(2) Those expressions are—

"the 1981 Regulations";
"the 1984 Act";
"automatic level crossing";
"central reservation";
"cycle lane";
"dual carriageway road";
"hours of darkness";
"level crossing";
"manually operated";
"maximum gross weight";
"motorway";

. . .

"non-primary route";
"pedal cycle";
"pedestrian zone";
"plate";
"primary route";
"principal road";
"road marking";

"route";
"sign";
. . .
"stud";
"temporary statutory provision";
"traffic lane"; and
"variable message sign".

B48.82   [(3) Regulation 5 (interpretation of "speed limit") shall apply for the interpretation of these Directions as it applies for the interpretation of the Regulations.]

[Direction 3 is printed as amended by S.I. 1995 No. 2769.
The "Zebra" Pedestrian Crossings Regulations 1971 have been revoked and replaced by the Zebra, Pelican and Puffin Pedestrian Crossings Regulations and General Directions 1997 (S.I. 1997 No. 2400) below.]

4. References in the Directions

B48.83   In these Directions, unless it is expressly provided otherwise or the context otherwise requires,—

     (a) a reference to a numbered direction is a reference to the direction so numbered in these Directions;

     (b) a reference to a numbered paragraph is a reference to the paragraph so numbered in the direction in which the reference occurs;

     (c) a reference to a sub-paragraph followed by a number or letter is a reference to the sub-paragraph bearing that number or letter in the direction in which the reference occurs;

     (d) a reference to a numbered diagram is a reference to the diagram so numbered in a Schedule to the Regulations;

     (e) a reference to a sign shown in a diagram in a Schedule to the Regulations includes a reference to that sign as varied in accordance with the Regulations;

     (f) a reference to a numbered regulation or Schedule is a reference to the regulation of, or to the Schedule to, the Regulations so numbered; and

     (g) in any direction which includes a table, references to a table are to the table in that direction.

5. Saving

B48.84   Any sign, which immediately before the coming into force of these Directions was placed on or near any road in conformity with the former Directions, so long as it continues to conform with those Directions as though they had not been revoked, shall be treated as if placed in conformity with these Directions, notwithstanding any provision of these Directions to the contrary.

6. Signs to be placed only at sites approved by the Secretary of State

B48.85   A sign shown in diagram 601.1, or in diagram 1040 or 1040.2 (when either is varied to include a continuous white line bounding the hatched marking), shall not be placed for the first time at any site except with the approval of the Secretary of State.

7. Signs to be placed only to indicate the effect of a statutory prohibition

B48.86   (1) Except as provided by paragraph (3), the signs to which this paragraph applies may be placed on or near a road only to indicate the effect of an Act, order, regulation, byelaw or notice ("*the effect of a statutory provision*") which prohibits or restricts the use of the road by traffic.

(2) Paragraph (1) applies to—

(a) the signs shown in diagrams 606, 607, 609, 612, 613, 614, 616, 617, 618, 618.1, 618.2, 618.3, 618.3A, 618.4, 619, 619.1, 619.2, 620, 620.1, 622.1A, 622.2, 622.4, 622.5, 622.6, 625.1, 626.2, 627.1, 629, 629.1, 629.2, 629.2A, 632, 636, 636.1, 637, 637.1, 637.2, 637.3, 638, 638.1, 639, 639.1A, 640, 640.2A, 640.3, 640.4, 640.5, 642, 642.2, 642.3, 643, 644, 646, 647, 650.1, 650.2, 651, 652, 660, 660.3, 660.4, 660.5, 661, 661.1, 661.2, 661.3, 661.4, 662, 663, 663.1, 664, 665, 666, 667, 667.1, 667.2, 668, 668.1, 668.2, 669, 669.1, 670, 671, 672, 673, 674, 675, 804.1, 804.2, 804.3, 810, 951, 952, 953, 953.1, 953.2, 954, 954.1, 954.2, 954.3, 954.4, 955, 956, 957, 958, 958.1, 959, 959.1, 960, 960.1, 961, 962, 962.1, 962.2, 963, 963.1, 963.2, 963.3, 964, 969, 974, 975, 1017, 1018.1, 1019, 1020.1, 1025.1, 1025.3, 1028.2, 1028.3, 1028.4, 1032, 1033, 1036.1, 1036.2, 1037.1, 1046, 1048, 1048.1, 1049, 1049.1, 1050, 2003, 2007, 2009, 2010, 2107, 2108, 2123, 2124, 5001.1, 5001.2, 5003, 5003.1, 5005, 5005.1, 7201, 7203.1, 7204, 7207, 7210, 7211, 7212, 7213, 7214, 7215, 7216, 7217, 7218, 7220, 7230, 7231, 7232, 7233, 7234, 7260, 7261, 7262, 7263, 7282, 7283 and 7284; and

(b) any sign which, by virtue of regulation 17 and item 31 of Schedule 16, incorporates as a symbol a sign shown in a diagram specified in sub-paragraph (a).

(3) The sign shown in a diagram whose number is specified in an item in column (2) of the Table may be placed at the place or in the circumstances specified in column (3) of that item notwithstanding that it does not in those circumstances indicate the effect of a statutory provision.

TABLE

(1) Item	(2) Diagram	(3) Circumstances
1.	606	On the central island of a roundabout or in combination with a plate of the type shown in diagram 608.
2.	609	On a road approaching its junction with a dual carriageway road or in combination with a plate of the type shown in diagram 608.
3.	616, 1046	At a site which has been approved by the Secretary of State.
4.	629.2, 629.2A	On— (a) a road which passes under or through a bridge, tunnel or other structure which limits the height of vehicles using that road; or (b) any such bridge, tunnel or other structure.

[*continued on next page*

(1) Item	(2) Diagram	(3) Circumstances
5.	2003, 2007, 2009, 2107, 2108	When including a symbol represented in— (a) any diagram in Schedule 1; or (b) diagram 629.2 or 629.2A in the circumstances specified in item 4 above.
6.	669, 669.1	When placed to indicate that the prohibition indicated by the sign shown in diagram 629.2 or 629.2A is ahead, provided that that sign has been placed in the circumstances specified in item 4 above.

(4) The sign shown in diagram 626.2 may be placed only to indicate the effect of a statutory provision which restricts the use of a road carried by a bridge or other structure—

(a) in the case of vehicles required to be marked with their maximum gross weight, to any vehicle with a maximum gross weight not exceeding that indicated on the sign; or

(b) in the case of vehicles not required to be marked with their maximum gross weight but required to be marked with their unladen weight, to any vehicle with an unladen weight not exceeding the maximum gross weight indicated on the sign.

8. The placing of certain signs to indicate the beginning of a restriction, requirement, prohibition or speed limit

B48.87   (1) This direction applies to a sign which is shown in diagram 616, 617, 618, 618.1, 618.2, 618.3, 618.3A, 619, 619.1, 619.2, 620, 620.1, 622.1A, 622.4, 622.5, 622.6, 625.1, 626.2, 627.1, 629, 629.1, 629.2, 629.2A, 632, 642, 646, 663, 663.1, 665, 667, 667.1, 668, 668.1, 670, 672, 674, 951, 952, 953, 953.1, 955, 956 or 957 and which is placed to indicate the point at which a restriction, requirement, prohibition or speed limit applying to traffic on a road [(in this direction and in direction 8A called "*the relevant road*")] begins.

(2) Subject to paragraphs (3) and (4) [and to direction 8A], a sign to which this direction applies shall be placed on the relevant road at or as near as practicable to the point referred to in paragraph (1)—

(a) where the road has only one carriageway, on each side of the carriageway of the road; or

(b) where the road has more than one carriageway, on each side of each carriageway in relation to which the restriction, requirement, prohibition or speed limit begins.

(3) Where the relevant road has one carriageway, signs to which this direction applies need only be placed on one side of the relevant road to indicate the point at which a restriction, requirement, prohibition (but not a speed limit) begins—

(a) where the restriction, requirement or prohibition applies only to traffic on one side of the relevant road; or

(b) at a junction where—

(i) traffic proceeding on another road on which it is permitted to proceed only in one direction turns into the relevant road; or

(ii) the relevant road is less than 5 metres wide.

(4) Where a length of road which passes under or through a bridge, tunnel or other structure is subject to a prohibition on vehicles exceeding a particular height, the sign shown in diagram 629.2 or 629.2A may be placed on the bridge, tunnel or other structure to indicate the prohibition in addition to or instead of the signs placed as required by paragraph (2).

[Direction 8 is printed as amended by S.I. 1995 No. 2769.]   **B48.88**

[8A. Beginning of a speed limit—further provisions

(1) Direction 8(2) does not apply where a speed limit in force on the relevant road   **B48.89**
begins—

   (a) at a point where the relevant road begins, being a point where it has no junction with another road; or

   (b) at a point where the relevant road has a junction with another road and the same speed limit is in force on both roads.

(2) This paragraph applies where the relevant road has a junction (*"the junction"*) with the side of another road (*"the other road"*) and a maximum speed limit is in force on the other road which is different from the speed limit in force on the relevant road.

(3) Where paragraph (2) applies, it is sufficient compliance with regulation 8(2), for the purpose of indicating the beginning of the speed limit on the relevant road to traffic entering it from the other road, if a sign shown in diagram 670, 674 or 675 is erected not more than 20 metres from the junction, on the left hand or near side of the carriageway of the relevant road as viewed in the direction of travel of such traffic or, where the relevant road is a dual carriageway road, on the left hand or near side of the carriageway by which traffic may pass into the relevant road from the other road.

(4) Where paragraph (2) applies, for the purpose of indicating the speed limit in force on the other road to traffic entering that road from the relevant road, signs shown in diagram 670, 674 or 675 shall (subject to paragraph (5)) be erected not further than 20 metres from the junction and so as to be visible to such traffic, on each side of the carriageway of the relevant road or, where the relevant road is a dual carriageway road, on each side of the carriageway by which traffic may pass from the relevant road into the other road.

(5) Paragraph (4) does not apply if—

   (a) the maximum speed limit in force on the other road is greater than that in force on the relevant road; and

   (b) signs indicating that maximum speed limit have been placed on the other road in accordance with direction 10 on each side of, and not more than 100 metres from, the junction.]

[Direction 8A was inserted by S.I. 1995 No. 2769.]   **B48.90**

9. The placing of certain signs to indicate the end of a restriction, requirement, prohibition or speed limit

(1) When a sign shown in diagram 618.4, 622.2, 645, 647, 664, 666, 667.2, 668.2, 673,   **B48.91**
675 or 964 is placed to indicate the point at which traffic on a road ceases to be subject to a restriction, requirement, prohibition or speed limit, the sign shall be placed on the road as near as practicable to that point.

(2) Where a length of road ceases to be subject to a speed limit and becomes subject to

a national speed limit, the sign shown in diagram 671 shall be placed at or as near as practicable to the point where the speed limit ends and a national speed limit begins, except in a case where a restriction of speed has been imposed under section 14 of the 1984 Act by reason of works which are being or are proposed to be executed on or near the road in which case—

(a) the sign shown—

(i) in diagram 7006; or

(ii) in diagram 7001 when placed in combination with the plate shown in diagram 645;

shall be placed as indicated above in this paragraph; and

(b) the sign shown in diagram 671 may also be so placed.

(3) When a sign shown in diagram 671, 673 or 675 is placed to indicate the point at which traffic on a road ceases to be subject to a speed limit—

(a) where the road has only one carriageway, one such sign shall be placed on each side of the carriageway of the road; or

(b) where the road has more than one carriageway, one such sign shall be placed on each side of each carriageway on which the speed limit ends.

[(4) Where a road (*"the relevant road"*) has a junction with the side of another road (*"the other road"*) and—

(a) a maximum speed limit is in force on the other road; and

(b) a national speed limit is in force on the relevant road,

then, for the purpose of indicating the national speed limit to traffic entering the relevant road from the other road, a sign shown in diagram 671 or 675 shall be placed on the relevant road in accordance with paragraph (5).]

[(5) The sign shall be placed not more than 20 metres from the junction with the other road on the left hand or near side of the relevant road as viewed in the direction of travel of a vehicle entering the relevant road from the other road or, if the relevant road is a dual carriageway road, on the left hand or near side of the carriageway by which a vehicle may pass into the relevant road from the other road.]

[(6) Where a road (*"the relevant road"*) has a junction with the side of another road (*"the other road"*) and—

(a) a national speed limit is in force on the other road; and

(b) a maximum speed limit is in force on the relevant road,

then, for the purpose of indicating the national speed limit to traffic entering the other road from the relevant road, traffic signs shown in diagram 671 or 675 shall be placed in accordance with paragraph (7) on the relevant road not further than 20 metres from the junction.]

[(7) If the relevant road has one carriageway, one such sign shall be placed on each side of that carriageway and, if the relevant road is a dual carriageway road, one such sign shall be placed on each side of the carriageway by which traffic may pass from the relevant road into the other road.]

B48.92   *[Direction 9 is printed as amended by S.I. 1995 No. 2769.]*

10. Repeater signs

B48.93   (1) Paragraph (2) applies to the signs shown in diagrams 614, 632, 636, 636.1, 637, 637.1, 637.2, 637.3, 638, 638.1 when the arrow is omitted, 639 when the arrow is omitted,

640 when the arrow is omitted, 642, 646, 670, 672, 956, 957, 959, 959.1, 960, 960.1 and 961.

(2) Signs to which this paragraph applies shall be placed at regular intervals along a road which is subject to a restriction, requirement, prohibition or speed limit which can be indicated by the signs, except that the sign shown in diagram 670 shall not be placed along a road which is—

(a) in England and Wales a restricted road as defined by section 82 of the 1984 Act and in Scotland a road as respects which there is in force an order prohibiting the driving of motor vehicles at a speed exceeding 30 miles per hour and on which there is provided a system of carriageway lighting furnished by means of lamps placed not more than 185 metres apart; or

(b) a motorway on which a national speed limit is in force.

(3) The sign shown in diagram 671 shall be placed at regular intervals along the length of a road (other than a motorway) on which—

(a) there is a system of street or carriageway lighting furnished by lamps lit by electricity placed not more than 183 metres apart in England and Wales or not more than 185 metres apart in Scotland; and

(b) a national speed limit is in force.

11. Signs to be placed only on specified types of road

(1) The signs shown in diagrams 2001, 2002, 2003, 2004, 2005, 2006, 2007, 2008, 2009, 2010, 2011, 2012, 2013, 2014, 2015, 2016, 2017, 2018, 2019, 2020, 2021, 2022, 2023, 2024, 2025, 2030, 2030.1, 2032, 2033, 2034, 2313, 2314, 2315 and 2315.1 may be placed only on or near a primary route. **B48.94**

(2) The signs shown in diagrams 2026, 2027, 2028 and 2029 may be placed only on a primary route, or on a non-primary route at a junction with a primary route.

12.—(1) The signs shown in diagrams 2101, 2101.1, 2101.2, 2102, 2103, 2104, 2105, 2106, 2107, 2108, 2109, 2110, 2111, 2112, 2113, 2113.1, 2114, 2115, 2115.1, 2116, 2117, 2118, 2119, 2120, 2121, 2122, 2123, 2124, 2128, 2130, 2131, 2133, 2135, 2138, 2310, 2311, 2312 and 2312.1 may be placed only on or near a non-primary route. **B48.95**

(2) The signs shown in diagrams 2125, 2126, 2127, 2132, 2134, 2136, 2137, 2322, 2323 and 2807 may be placed only on or near a non-primary route, or on a primary route at a junction with a non-primary route.

(3) The signs shown in diagrams 1012.3, 2031, 2129, 2201, 2202, 2203, 2204, 2205, 2206, 2207, 2208, 2209, 2210, 2211, 2212, 2213, 2214, 2215, 2216, 2301, 2302, 2303, 2304, 2305, 2306, 2307, 2308, 2309, 2316, 2317, 2318, 2319, 2320, 2321, [2324, 2325, 2326, 2327, 2328, 2329] 2401, 2402, 2403, 2501, 2502, 2503, 2504, 2505, 2506, 2507, 2508, 2509, 2601, 2602, 2603, 2604, 2605, 2606, 2607, 2608, 2609, 2610, 2610.1, 2610.2, 2701, 2702, 2703, 2704, 2705, 2706, 2707, 2708, 2709, 2710, 2712, 2713.1, 2801, 2802, 2803, 2804, 2805, 2806 and 7240 may not be placed on a motorway.

[Direction 12 is printed as amended by S.I. 1995 No. 3107.] **B48.96**

13.—(1) The signs shown in diagrams 832.3, 1012.2, 1042, 2901, 2903, 2904, 2904.1, 2905, 2906, 2908, 2909, 2910, 2910.1, 2911, 2912, 2913, 2914, 2915, 2916, 2917, 2918, 2919, 2920, 2922, 2923, 2924, 2925, 2926, 2927, 2928, 2929, 2930, 2931, 2932, 7002, 7212, 7220, 7230 and 7233 may be placed only on or near a motorway. **B48.97**

(2) The signs shown in diagrams 2902 and 2902.1 may be placed only on a motorway or on another road at a junction with a motorway.

B48.98   14.—(1) The signs shown in diagrams 823, 824, 825, 868, 868.1, 872, 873, 874, 875 and 876 may be placed only on or near—

(a) a motorway when the colour of the background of the sign is blue;

(b) a primary route when the colour of the background of the sign is green; or

(c) a non-primary route when the colour of the background of the sign is white.

(2) The sign shown in diagram 877 may be placed only on or near—

(a) a primary route when the colour of the background of the sign is green; or

(b) a non-primary route when the colour of the background of the sign is white.

[14A. Speed limits of 20 miles per hour

B48.99   (1) The sign shown in diagram 674 may only be placed on a road if no point on any road (not being a cul-de-sac less than 80 metres long), to which the speed limit indicated by the sign applies, is situated more than 100 metres from a traffic calming feature.

(2) In paragraph (1) "*traffic calming feature*" means—

(a) a road hump constructed pursuant to section 90A of the Highways Act 1980 ("*the 1980 Act*") . . . and in accordance with the Highways (Road Humps) Regulations 1999 [*S.I. 1999 No. 1025; not reproduced in this work*] . . .;

(b) traffic calming works constructed in accordance with section 90G of the 1980 Act . . . and in accordance with the Highways (Traffic Calming) Regulations 1999 [*S.I. 1999 No. 1026; not reproduced in this work*] . . .;

(c) a refuge for pedestrians which was constructed pursuant to section 68 of the 1980 Act . . . after 15th June 1999 and is so constructed as to encourage a reduction in the speed of traffic using the carriageway;

(d) a variation of the relative widths of the carriageway or of any footway pursuant to section 75 of the 1980 Act . . . which—

(i) was carried out after 15th June 1999 for the purpose of encouraging a reduction in the speed of traffic using the carriageway; and

(ii) had the effect of reducing the width of the carriageway; or

(e) a horizontal bend in the carriageway through which all vehicular traffic has to change direction by no less than 70 degress within a distance of 32 metres as measured at the inner kerb radius.

(3) For the purposes of paragraph (1) the distance of 100 metres shall be measured along roads to which the speed limit indicated by the sign shown in diagram 674 applies.]

B48.100   *[Direction 14A has been inserted by S.I. 1999 No. 1723.*
The words omitted from direction 14A(2) relate exclusively to Scotland.]

15. Signs to be placed only in conjunction with specified road markings (except signs for prohibitions and restrictions on waiting, etc.)

B48.101   (1) Save as provided in paragraph (2), a sign shown in a diagram whose number appears and is placed in the circumstances (if any) or is in the form (if any) specified in an item in column (2) in the Table may be placed on a road only in conjunction with a road marking shown in a diagram whose number appears and is in the form (if any) specified in column (3) of that item.

TABLE

(1) Item	(2) Sign diagram number	(3) Road marking diagram number
1.	557.1	1060, 1060.1, 1061 or 1061.1
2.	601.1	1002.1 and 1022
3.	602	1003 and 1023
4.	611.1 if placed in conjunction with diagram 602	1003, 1003.4 and 1023
5.	611.1	1003.3 and 1003.4
6.	957	1057
7.	959	1048 and 1049
8.	959.1	1049 varied to a width of 150 millimetres and 1057
9.	960	1048 and 1049
10.	960 varied to include pedal cycle symbol	1048.1 and 1049
11.	960.1	1049 varied to a width of 150 millimetres and 1057

(2) The provisions of paragraph (1) requiring the placing of a sign shown in diagram 601.1, 602 or 611.1 in conjunction with a road marking shall not apply during the execution of works on a road near the sign—

(a) if those works necessitate the temporary removal of the marking; or

(b) if the sign is erected only temporarily in connection with the execution of works on a road.

16. Road markings to be placed only in conjunction with other road markings or specified signs (except road markings for prohibitions and restrictions on waiting, etc.)

(1) A road marking shown in a diagram whose number appears and is placed in the circumstances (if any) specified in an item in column (2) of the Table may be placed on the carriageway of a road only in conjunction with a road marking or sign shown in a diagram whose number appears and is in the form (if any) specified in column (3) of that item.   **B48.102**

TABLE

(1) Item	(2) Road marking diagram number	(3) Road marking or sign diagram number
1.	1001 unless placed at a site where traffic is from time to time controlled by a constable	3000, 3000.1, 3000.2, 3000.3, 3000.4, 3000.5, 3000.6 or 3014
2.	1002.1 and 1022	601.1

[*continued on next page*

(1) Item	(2) _Road marking diagram number_	(3) _Road marking or sign diagram number_
3.	1003.3	611.1 and 1003.4
4.	1003.4	611.1
5.	1022	601.1 and 1002.1
6.	1023	1003
7.	1024.1	1010 and 1014
8.	1048	1049 and either 959 or 960
9.	1048.1	1049 and 960 varied to include the pedal cycle symbol
10.	1049	957 and 1057, or 1048 and either 959 or 960, or 1048.1 and 960 varied to include the pedal cycle symbol, or 1057 and either 959.1 or 960.1
11.	1049.1	957 and 1057
12.	1050	964 and 1049
13.	1057	955, 956, 957, 959.1, 960.1 or 967
14.	1058	1057
15.	1059	1057
16.	1060, 1060.1, 1061, 1061.1 unless placed in a zone indicated by the sign shown in diagram 674	557.1

(2) A road marking shown in diagram 1003, 1023 or 1049 when varied in size to conform with any of the smaller dimensions prescribed for it may be placed on the carriageway only in conjunction with the marking shown in diagram 1057 and with one or more of the signs shown in diagrams 955, 957, 959.1, 960.1 and 967.

(3) The road marking shown in diagram 1009 when varied in size to conform with the smallest dimensions prescribed for it may be placed on the carriageway only to mark the junction of a cycle track and another road and in conjunction with the road markings shown in diagrams 1003 and 1023 and having the smaller dimensions prescribed for them.

17. The placing of the signs shown in diagrams 615 and 811

B48.103 The signs shown in diagrams 615 and 811 may be placed on a road only in conjunction with one another.

18. Signs to be placed only in combination with specified plates or other signs

B48.104 (1) A sign shown in a diagram whose number appears and is placed in the circumstances (if any) specified in an item in column (2) of the Table may be placed on a road only in combination with a plate shown in the diagram whose number appears in column (3) of that item.

TABLE

(1) Item	(2) Sign diagram number	(3) Plate diagram number
1.	501 when placed in advance of the sign shown in diagram 601.1	502
2.	501 when placed in advance of the sign shown in diagram 602	503
3.	544.2	547.4
4.	553.1	553.2
5.	554.2	554.3
6.	556.1	556.2
7.	557.1	557.2, 557.3 or 557.4
8.	562	563, 563.1 or 7022
9.	583	583.1
10.	615	615.1
11.	617	618 or 618.1
12.	779	780, 780.1 or 780.2
13.	811	811.1
14.	953	953.2
15.	953.1	953.2

(2) The sign shown in diagram 545 may be placed on a road only in combination with a plate shown in diagram 546, 547.1, 547.2, 547.3 or 547.7 or the sign shown in diagram 4004.

(3) A sign shown in diagram 515.1A or 515.2 may be placed on a road only in combination with the sign shown in diagram 606.

19. Plates to be placed only in combination with specified signs

(1) A plate shown in a diagram whose number appears and is in the form (if any) specified in an item in column (2) of the Table may be placed on a road only in combination with a sign shown in a diagram whose number appears and is placed in the circumstances (if any) specified in column (3) of that item.   **B48.105**

TABLE

(1) Item	(2) Plate diagram number	(3) Sign diagram number
1.	502	501
2.	503	501

[continued on next page

(1) Item	(2) Plate diagram number	(3) Sign diagram number
3.	511	504.1, 505.1, 506.1, 507.1, 510, 512, 512.1, 512.2, 513, 516, 517, 520, 523.1, 524.1, 528 or 556
4.	511 when varied to "HEAVY PLANT CROSSING"	504.1, 505.1, 506.1, 507.1, 512.1 or 512.2
5.	513.1	512, 512.1, 512.2 or 513
6.	513.2	512, 512.1, 512.2, 513 or 7009
7.	518	516, 517 or 520
8.	519	516 or 517
9.	525	523.1 or 524.1
10.	526	512, 512.1, 512.2, 513, 523.1, 524.1 or 554.1
11.	527	523.1 or 524.1
12.	530.1	530
13.	530.2	530, 629.2 or 629.2A
14.	531.2	531.1
15.	543.1	543, 3000, 3000.3, 3000.4, 3000.5 or 3000.6
16.	546	545
17.	547.1	545
18.	547.2	545
19.	547.3	544.1 or 545
20.	547.4	544.2
21.	547.5	544
22.	547.6	543
23.	547.7	545
24.	548.1	548 when placed in advance of the sign shown in diagram 4005
25.	553	552
26.	553.2	553.1
27.	554.3	554.2, 622.1A, 622.4, 629, 629.1 or 632
28.	556.2	556.1
29.	557.2	557.1
30.	557.3	557.1

[*continued on next page*

(1) Item	(2) Plate diagram number	(3) Sign diagram number
31.	557.4	557.1
32.	558.2	558
33.	563	562
34.	563.1	562
35.	570	513, 516 when placed in combination with 518 or 519, 517 when placed in combination with 518 or 519, 521, 523.1, 524.1, 548, 549, 550, 550.1, 551, 551.1, 551.2, 553.1, 554.2, 556, 556.1, 557, 558, 558.1, 559, 581, 582, 614, 615, 632, 642, 811, 7001 or 7009
36.	572	504.1, 505.1, 506.1, 507.1, 516, 517, 520, 521, 522, 523.1, 524.1, 528, 529, 529.1, 530, 531.1, 543, 544, 544.1, 544.2, 545, 552, 554, 555, 562, 770, 771, 772, 782, 950, 7001 or 7009
37.	573	516, 517, 523.1, 524.1, 528, 529, 529.1, 530, 531.1, 543, 544, 544.1, 544.2, 545, 552, 554, 555, 562, 770, 771, 772, 782, 950, 7001 or 7009
38.	575	516, 517, 528 or 529.1
39.	583.1	583
40.	607	606 or 609
41.	608	501, 601.1, 602, 606, 609 or 610
42.	615.1	615
43.	618	617
44.	618.1	617
45.	620	619, 619.1, 619.2, 622.1A, 622.5, 622.6, 629, 629.1 or 952
46.	620.1	619 or 619.1
47.	627.1	626.2
48.	643	636 or 642
49.	644	636 or 642
50.	645	614, 615, 632, 642, 811 or 7001
51.	773	529, 529.1, 558, 770, 771 or 772

[*continued on next page*

(1) Item	(2) Plate diagram number	(3) Sign diagram number
52.	778	602
53.	778.1	602
54.	780	779
55.	780.1	779
56.	780.2	779
57.	804.1	801
58.	804.2	801
59.	804.3	801
60.	811.1	811
61.	817.2	523.1 and either 523 or 526, or 554.1 and 526
62.	876	868, 868.1, 872, 873, 874 or 875
63.	950.1	950
64.	953.2	953 or 953.1
65.	954	606, 609, 612, 613, 616, 629 or 629.1
66.	954.1	606, 609, 612, 613, 616, 629 or 629.1
67.	954.2	606, 609, 612, 613, 616, 629, 629.1 or 952
68.	954.3	606, 609, 612 or 613
69.	954.4	606, 609, 612, 613 or 816
70.	961	958, 958.1, 959 or 959.1
71.	7001.1	7001
72.	7001.2	7001
73.	7021	7001
74.	7022	562
75.	7208	7202, 7206 or 7207
76.	7209	7203, 7203.1, 7204 or 7205
77.	7256	7250, 7251, 7252, 7253, 7254 or 7255
78.	7401.1	7401

(2) A plate shown in diagram 954.3 or 954.4 shall not be placed in combination with the sign shown in diagram 616.

20. Placing of road markings and signs to indicate prohibitions and restrictions on waiting, loading and unloading and parking

(1) Subject to paragraphs (2) and (3)—   **B48.106**

(a) the road marking shown in diagram 1018.1 may be placed on a side of a road only for the purpose of indicating a statutory prohibition or restriction on the waiting of vehicles which applies on that side of the road at all times of day on every day of the year or on every day in a period of at least four consecutive months;

(b) the road marking shown in diagram 1017 may be placed on a side of a road only for the purpose of indicating a statutory prohibition or restriction on the waiting of vehicles which is not a restriction of the kind mentioned in sub-paragraph (a).

(2) In this direction, references to a statutory prohibition or restriction on the waiting of a vehicle do not include references to any such prohibition or restriction imposed—

(a) on waiting for the purpose of loading or unloading goods from a vehicle or picking up or setting down passengers from a vehicle;

(b) expressly to limit the duration of waiting of vehicles within a particular period; or

(c) on the waiting of goods vehicles (as defined by section 192(1) of the Road Traffic Act 1988) but of no other class of vehicle.

(3) A road marking shown in diagram 1017 or 1018.1 shall not be placed on a road on which a marking shown in diagram 1025.1 or 1025.3 is placed, or on which the marking shown in diagram 1027.1 is placed in conjunction with the sign shown in diagram 642.2 unless the restrictions indicated by the marking shown in diagram 1017 or 1018.1 apply on that road at times other than those indicated on the sign shown in diagram 642.2.

21.—(1) The road marking shown in diagram 1020.1 may be placed on a side of the   **B48.107** carriageway of a road only for the purpose of indicating a statutory prohibition or restriction on the waiting of vehicles for the purpose of their being loaded or unloaded which applies on that side of the road at all times of the day on every day of the year or on every day in a period of at least four consecutive months.

(2) The road marking shown in diagram 1019 may be placed on a side of the carriageway of a road only for the purpose of indicating a statutory prohibition or restriction on the waiting of vehicles for the purpose of their being loaded or unloaded (but not for indicating a statutory prohibition or restriction which expressly limits the duration of waiting by vehicles within a particular period for that purpose) which is not a restriction of the kind mentioned in paragraph (1).

22.—(1) Except where it is placed to indicate the effect of a temporary statutory pro-   **B48.108** vision, a sign shown in a diagram whose number appears in column (2) of an item in the Table shall not be placed except—

(a) on or near the side of a road, and

(b) in conjunction with, and on the same side of the road as, a road marking which is shown in a diagram and is in the form (if any) indicated in column (3) of that item.

TABLE

(1) Item	(2) Sign diagram number	(3) Road marking diagram number
1.	637	1018.1
2.	637.3	1018.1
3.	638	1020.1
4.	638.1	1019
5.	639	1017
6.	639.1A	1017 and 1028.4 (when no legend appears) or 1033
7.	640	1017 and 1019
8.	642.2	1027.1
9.	642.3	1018.1 and 1020.1
10.	650.1	1028.2 when indicating "TAXIS"
11.	650.2	1028.2 when indicating "TAXIS"
12.	660	1028.3 when varied to indicate "LARGE OR SLOW VEHICLES ONLY", 1028.4 when indicating "DOCTOR" or when no legend appears, or 1033
13.	660.3	1028.4 when indicating "DOCTOR" or when no legend appears, or 1033
14.	660.4	1028.3 when varied to indicate "LOADING ONLY", or 1033
15.	660.5	1028.4 when no legend appears, 1032 or 1033
16.	661	1028.3 or 1033 when either road marking is indicating "DISABLED" or when no legend appears
17.	661.1	1028.4 when no legend appears, 1032 or 1033
18.	661.2	1028.4 when no legend appears, 1032 or 1033
19.	662	1028.4 when no legend appears, 1032 or 1033
20.	974	1025.1 or 1025.3
21.	975	1025.1 or 1025.3 when either marking is varied to "BUS STAND"

(2) Subject to paragraph (3) the sign shown in diagram 637.2 may be placed only on a road within a pedestrian zone where a sign shown in diagram 618.2, 618.3 or 618.3A is placed at each entrance into the zone for vehicular traffic.

(3) The sign shown in diagram 637.2 shall not be used on a road within the pedestrian zone to which the sign relates except in conjunction with—

    (a) the road marking shown in diagram 1017 or 1018.1 unless—

        (i) the road does not comprise a carriageway and footway which are separately defined;

        (ii) the entry of vehicular traffic into the pedestrian zone is restricted at the same times as those at which the waiting of vehicles is prohibited as indicated on the upper panel of the sign in diagram 637.2; and

        (iii) the prohibition on the waiting of vehicles applies uniformly throughout every road in the zone, and

    (b) where there is a prohibition on the loading and unloading of vehicles, the road marking shown in diagram 1019 or 1020.1 unless—

        (i) the road does not comprise a carriageway and footway which are separately defined;

        (ii) the entry of vehicular traffic into the pedestrian zone is restricted at the same times as those at which the loading and unloading of vehicles is prohibited as indicated on the lower panel of the sign in diagram 637.2; and

        (iii) the prohibition on the loading and unloading of vehicles applies uniformly throughout every road in the zone.

23.—(1) Subject to paragraph (2) a road marking shown in a diagram whose number appears and is in the form (if any) specified in an item in column (2) of the Table may be placed on the carriageway only in conjunction with, and on the same side of the road as, a sign shown in a diagram whose number appears and is in the form specified (if any) in column (3) of that item.

B48.109

TABLE

(1) Item	(2) Road marking diagram number	(3) Sign diagram number
1.	1017	637.2, 639, 639.1A or 640
2.	1018.1	637, 637.2, 637.3 or 642.3
3.	1019	637.2, 638.1 or 640
4.	1020.1	637.2, 638 or 642.3
5.	1025.1	974 or 975
6.	1025.3	974 or 975
7.	1028.2 when indicating "TAXIS"	650.1 or 650.2
8.	1028.2 when varied to "BUSES" or "COACHES"	969
9.	1028.3 when indicating "DISABLED" or when no legend appears	661

[continued on next page

(1) *Item*	(2) *Road marking diagram number*	(3) *Sign diagram number*
10.	1028.3 when varied to "LARGE OR SLOW VEHICLES ONLY"	660 varied to "Large or slow vehicles only"
11.	1028.3 when varied to "LOADING ONLY"	660.4
12.	1028.4 when indicating "DOCTOR"	660 varied to "Doctor permit holders only"
13.	1028.4 when no legend appears	639.1A, 660, 660.3, 660.5, 661.1, 661.2, 661.3, 662 or 801
14.	1033 when indicating "DISABLED"	661

(2) Paragraph (1) shall not apply to a road marking placed on a road within a controlled parking zone, except where the road marking is placed to indicate restrictions different from the restrictions indicated on a sign shown in diagram 663 or 663.1 placed at the entrances for vehicular traffic into the zone.

(3) In this direction and direction 24, "*controlled parking zone*" means either—

    (a) an area—

        (i) in which, except where parking places have been provided, every road has been marked with one or more of the road markings shown in diagrams 1017, 1018.1, 1019 and 1020.1; and

        (ii) into which each entrance for vehicular traffic has been indicated by a sign shown in diagram 663 or 663.1; or

    (b) an area—

        (i) in which at least one of the signs shown in diagram 640.2A has been placed on each side of every road; and

        (ii) into which each entrance for vehicular traffic has been indicated by a sign shown in diagram 665.

B48.110   **24.** A sign shown in diagram 663, 663.1, 664, 665 or 666 may be placed only at the boundary of a controlled parking zone.

25. Signs to be placed only at specified sites or for specified purposes

B48.111   The sign shown in diagram 545, when placed in combination with the plate shown in diagram 547.1, or with a plate shown in either diagram 546 or 547.1 together with the sign shown in diagram 4004, may be placed only near a school crossing place as defined by regulation 39(2).

B48.112   **26.** The sign shown in diagram 551.1 may be placed on or near a road only—

    (a) at a site which is approved as a migratory toad crossing by or on behalf of the Secretary of State; and

    (b) during February, March, April and May in each year.

B48.113   **27.** The sign shown in diagram 574 may be placed only in or near an infected place or area for the purposes of the Animal Health Act 1981 and shall be removed as soon as it ceases to be in or near such a place or area.

28. A sign shown in diagram 830, 830.1, 831 or 832, except when varied to contain the words "WEIGHT CHECK", and the sign shown in diagram 830.3 except when placed in connection with a weight check, may be placed only in connection with a traffic census the taking of which on a road has been approved— **B48.114**

(a) by the traffic authority for that road;

(b) by the chief officer of police of the police area in which the road is situated; and

(c) by or on behalf of the Secretary of State.

29. A sign shown in diagram 833, 834, 835 or 836 may be placed only to regulate the movement of vehicular traffic into and out of premises with more than one access to a road. **B48.115**

30. The sign shown in diagram 957 may be placed on a road only when the road has been divided into a part reserved for the use of pedal cycles only and a part reserved for use by pedestrians only by either or both of the following means— **B48.116**

(a) the road marking shown in diagram 1049 (when that marking is varied to be 150 millimetres wide) or 1049.1;

(b) the presence on the road of works such as distinctive colouring of the surface of each part, a kerb or other device.

31. Restrictions on the placing of temporary signs

The signs shown in any diagram in Schedule 12 other than diagrams 7014 and 7103 may be placed only in connection with the execution of works on or near a road or a temporary obstruction thereon, and any such sign so placed and any other sign shown in a diagram in Schedules 1 to 11 so placed shall not be retained on or near the road after the completion of the works or the removal of the obstruction, as the case may be, unless— **B48.117**

(a) it is a sign of the type shown in diagram 7009, in which case that sign may be retained on or near a road after the completion of the works for so long as the traffic authority for the road thinks fit; or

(b) it is a sign of the type shown in diagram 7012 bearing the words "NO GIVE WAY MARKINGS" or "NO STOP MARKINGS", in which case that sign shall be removed as soon as the road markings have been replaced and in any event not later than 28 days after the completion of the works.

32. A sign shown in diagram 790 or 7014 may be placed on or near a road only in connection with works involving an alteration in the layout of the carriageway or involving the removal of or a change in the road markings or other traffic signs placed on or near a road or, in the case of the sign shown in diagram 790, at an automatic railway level crossing, and may be retained for not more than 3 months after completion of those works. **B48.118**

33.—(1) No sign of the kind referred to in regulation 41 may be retained at any place for more than six months (or such longer period as the Secretary of State may approve) after the placing of the sign there or in any event after the sign has ceased to be needed at that place. **B48.119**

(2) The sign shown in diagram 2701 may be retained on or near a road for not more than six months after completion of the housing development to which it refers.

34.—(1) A sign shown in diagram 7023 or 7024 may be placed on or near a road only where one-way working is necessary owing to a temporary closure to vehicular traffic of a part of the width of the carriageway of the road. **B48.120**

(2) A sign shown in diagram 829.1, 829.2, 829.3, 829.4 or 1063 may be placed on or near a road only by a constable in uniform or a person acting under the instructions or authority of the chief officer of police.

(3) A sign shown in diagram 554 (when varied to "Flood" or "No smoking"), 554.2 (when placed in conjunction with the plate shown in diagram 554.3), or 562 (when placed in combination with the plate shown in diagram 563 varied to "Accident", "Census", "Dust cloud", "Fallen tree", "Overhead cable repairs" or "Smoke") may be retained only on or near a road for so long as the hazard indicated by the sign continues to exist or is expected to recur in the near future.

(4) The sign shown in diagram 950 may be placed in combination with the plate shown in diagram 950.1 only while the training or testing of child cyclists is in progress.

35. Placing of signs varied to show metric units

B48.121
(1) Where the indication given by a sign shown in diagram 629, 629.1, 780, 780.1 or 780.2 is varied in accordance with regulation 17 and item 2 of Schedule 16, that sign may be placed only in combination with another sign of the same type whose indication has not been so varied.

(2) Paragraph (1) shall apply when a sign shown in diagram 629 or 629.1 is incorporated as a symbol into another sign.

36. Mounting and backing of signs

B48.122
(1) Where a sign shown in a diagram (other than the diagrams referred to in paragraphs (2) to (4) of direction 38 or 39) in Schedules 1 to 5, 7, Part II of Schedule 10, Schedule 12 or a sign prescribed in regulation 41 is mounted on a post specially provided for the purpose ("*the post*"), that part of the post which extends above ground level shall be coloured grey or black, except that—

(a) where the post is made of aluminium, concrete, galvanised metal or wood, the post may retain its natural colour; and

(b) where the post is not likely to be readily visible to pedestrians if wholly coloured grey or black, a yellow or white band not less than 140 nor more than 160 millimetres deep may be provided on the post, the lower edge of the band being not less than 1500 nor more than 1700 millimetres above ground level.

(2) Where a beacon or lamp of a kind prescribed by regulation 42 or 43 is mounted on a structure specially provided for the purpose, the structure shall be coloured grey, red, white or yellow, or in alternate bands of red and white or of black and white.

(3) The post provided for the mounting of the sign shown in diagram 605.2 shall be coloured in alternate black and yellow bands each 300 millimetres deep with a black band uppermost below the bottom of the sign face, and the yellow bands may be illuminated by means of retroreflecting material.

(4) A post or other support provided for the mounting of a sign shown in diagram 651, 970, 971, 972, 973, 973.1, 2610, 2610.1, 2610.2, 7104 or 7105 may be of any colour.

B48.123
37.—(1) The back of any sign shown in a diagram in Schedules 1 to 5, 7, Part II of Schedule 10 or in Schedule 12, or prescribed in regulation 41, other than a sign shown in diagram 651, 970, 971, 972, 973, 973.1, 2610, 2610.1, 2610.2, 7101, 7102, 7103, 7104 or 7105, and the back of any backing board or other fitting provided for the assembly of such a sign including any container enclosing apparatus for the illumination of that sign, shall be coloured—

(a) black if the sign is mounted on the same post as that on which light signals prescribed in regulation 30(2) (or those signals as varied by regulation 31) or light signals prescribed in regulation 30(3) and regulation 32 are mounted; or

(b) grey, black or in a non-reflective metallic finish in any other case, except that—

  (i) information about sites for placing and the ownership of the sign may be indicated on the back of the sign in characters not exceeding 15 millimetres in height; and

  (ii) information about the manufacture of the sign required in order to comply with British Standard Specification BS 873 or an equivalent specification of a European Economic Area State, occupying an area not exceeding 30 square centimetres, may be indicated on the back of the sign in characters not exceeding 5 millimetres in height.

(2) The back of a sign shown in diagram 7104 or 7105 shall be coloured grey, red, white, black or yellow, except that—

(a) information about sites for placing and the ownership of the sign may be indicated on the back of the sign in characters not exceeding 15 millimetres in height; and

(b) information about the manufacture of the sign required in order to comply with British Standard Specification BS 873 or an equivalent specification of a European Economic Area State, occupying an area not exceeding 30 square centimetres, may be indicated on the back of the sign in characters not exceeding 5 millimetres in height.

(3) The back of a sign shown in diagram 651, 970, 971, 972, 973, 973.1, 2610, 2610.1 or 2610.2 may be of any colour.

(4) The front of any backing board for a sign mounted otherwise than as described in paragraph (1)(a) shall be coloured either grey or yellow.

(5) Any sign shown in a diagram in Schedules 1 to 5, 7, Part II of Schedule 10, or Schedule 12 which has a red or black border may have a white edge added not less than 10 nor more than 20 millimetres wide, outside that border.

(6) In this direction "*backing board*" in relation to a sign includes any background against which the sign is displayed.

38. Mounting of the sign shown in diagram 781

The sign shown in diagram 781 shall be mounted on two posts and so much of each post as extends above ground level shall be coloured black and white in alternate horizontal bands, each band being not less than 250 nor more than 335 millimetres deep. **B48.124**

39. Mounting of the signs shown in diagrams 560 and 561

(1) A sign shown in diagram 560 or 561 shall be so placed that the top of the sign is not less than 550 nor more than 1000 millimetres above the surface of the adjacent carriageway. **B48.125**

(2) Where a sign shown in diagram 560 or 561 is mounted on a post specially provided for the purpose that part of the post which extends above ground level shall be coloured black and white in alternate horizontal bands, each band being not less than 225 nor more than 350 millimetres deep.

(3) The signs shown in diagrams 560 and 561 shall be so erected as to display—

(a) the colour red on the left hand edge of the carriageway as viewed by the drivers of approaching vehicles; and

(b) the colour white on the right hand edge of the carriageway when so viewed, unless the edge is the edge of the carriageway of a dual carriageway road when the colour amber shall be displayed.

40. Mounting of refuge indicator lamps

B48.126   (1) Save as provided in paragraph (2), where the lamp prescribed in regulation 45 is mounted on a post specially provided for the purpose—

     (a) if the post is placed on a street refuge or central reservation of a zebra crossing and yellow globes are attached to or mounted on the post—

        (i) the part of the post between ground level and the point where the yellow globes are mounted or attached shall be coloured black and white in alternate horizontal bands, the lowest band visible to approaching traffic being coloured black and not less than 275 millimetres nor more than 1 metre deep, and each other band being not less than 275 nor more than 335 millimetres deep; and

        (ii) beyond the point referred to in sub-paragraph (a)(i) any remaining part of the post shall be coloured in accordance with sub-paragraph (b); and

     (b) if the post—

        (i) is a post placed as mentioned in sub-paragraph (a) but yellow globes are not attached to or mounted on it; or

        (ii) is placed elsewhere than on a zebra crossing,

the post shall be coloured grey or black but with two white bands (each band being not less than 275 nor more than 335 millimetres deep) so arranged that—

        (i) at least 275 nor more than 335 millimetres extend between the nearest edges of the two bands; and

        (ii) the upper edge of the uppermost band is not less than 275 nor more than 335 millimetres below the lowest part of the lamp,

and the white bands may be internally illuminated.

(2) Where a post of the kind mentioned in paragraph (1) consists of aluminium, concrete or galvanised metal it may remain in its natural colour.

(3) In this paragraph "*zebra crossing*" has the same meaning as in the 1971 Regulations and "*yellow globes*" means globes in relation to which Part II of Schedule 2 to the 1971 Regulations is complied with.

41. Mounting and backing of light signals, matrix signs and warning lights

B48.127   (1) Light signals such as are prescribed in regulations 30, 31, 32, 34, 35, 37 and 38, the matrix signals prescribed in regulation 36 and the warning lights prescribed in regulations 39(2) and 40 may be placed on or near a road only if they are so placed that they face the stream of traffic to which they are intended to convey the warnings, information, requirements, restrictions or prohibitions prescribed by the Regulations.

(2) The containers enclosing the lamps of each of the types of light signals, matrix signs or warning lights mentioned in paragraph (1) shall be coloured black except that, if those containers enclose lamps of the light signals prescribed in paragraph (5) or (7) of regulation 30, or in regulation 34 or 35, the matrix signs prescribed in regulation 36 or the warning lights prescribed in regulation 39(2) and 40, they may be coloured grey instead of black.

(3) Any of the kinds of light signals mentioned in paragraph (1) other than the signals prescribed in regulation 30(7) may be mounted on a backing board, which shall be

coloured black and may have a white border not less than 45 nor more than 55 milli-metres wide.

(4) In the case of the light signals prescribed in regulation 30(7) the back of the backing board shown in diagram 3014 may be coloured black or grey.

(5) In the case of the matrix signs prescribed in regulation 36, an identification number may be shown on the front of the backing board below the signal in the manner shown in diagram 6022.

(6) Without prejudice to paragraph (7), where light signals prescribed in any of the regulations specified in paragraph (1) or shown in a diagram in Part I of Schedule 10 or in Schedule 11 are mounted on a post specially provided for the purpose, that part of the post which extends above ground level shall be coloured grey or black and may have one yellow or white band not less than 140 nor more than 160 millimetres deep, the lower edge of the band being not less than 1500 nor more than 1700 millimetres above ground level.

(7) The light signals, matrix signs or warning lights prescribed in regulation 32, instead of being mounted on a post coloured in accordance with paragraph (6), may be mounted on a post coloured yellow (but having no yellow or white band as specified in paragraph (6)) or on a tripod coloured yellow.

42. Placing of road marking shown in diagram 1001 in conjunction with light signals

(1) The light signals prescribed in paragraph (2), (3) or (7) of regulation 30 may be placed only in conjunction with the road marking shown in diagram 1001, except that this paragraph shall not apply while works which necessitate the temporary removal of that road marking are being executed on a road near the light signals.   **B48.128**

(2) Where both primary and secondary signals within the meaning of regulation 33(6) have been erected, the references in paragraph (1) to light signals shall be construed as references to—

(a) both the primary and the secondary signals;

(b) the primary signals operating alone; or

(c) the secondary signals operating alone,

as the case may be.

43. Placing of road marking shown in diagram 1014 in conjunction with the road marking shown in diagram 1013.1 or 1013.3

(1) At least one road marking of the type shown in diagram 1014 shall be placed in conjunction with a road marking of the type shown in diagram 1013.1 or 1013.3 on the length of carriageway which extends backwards from the commencement of any continuous line marked on the carriageway as a part of the road marking shown in diagram 1013.1 or 1013.3, such commencement being viewed in the direction of travel of a vehicle driven so as to have and keep that continuous line on the right hand or off side thereof in accordance with regulation 26(2)(b).   **B48.129**

(2) If more than one road marking of the type shown in diagram 1014 is placed on a length of carriageway, then the road markings shall be so spaced apart that one follows in line behind the other.

44. Placing of light signals prescribed in regulation 30(5) and in regulation 35 and signs and light signals shown in Schedule 11

The light signals prescribed in regulation 30(5) and regulation 35 and the signs and light signals shown in any diagram in Schedule 11 may be displayed only on or near—   **B48.130**

(a) a motorway; or

(b) a dual carriageway road.

B48.131   **45.** The light signals prescribed in regulation 30(5) shall not be displayed over or in relation to a traffic lane at the same time as any sign shown in diagram 6001, 6002, 6003, 6006, 6006.1, 6008, 6009, 6009.1, 6009.2, 6011 or 6012 is also being displayed over or in relation to that same traffic lane and at the same place on that lane.

B48.132   **46.** A sign shown in diagram 6021 or 6031.1 may be displayed only over a traffic lane and a sign shown in diagram 6006, 6006.1, 6006.2, 6008, 6008.1, 6009, 6009.1, 6009.2, 6009.3, 6022 or 6032.1 may be displayed only at the side of the carriageway to which the indications given by the sign relate, or projecting over part of that carriageway, so as to communicate information to drivers in all traffic lanes.

47. Placing of light signals prescribed in regulation 32

B48.133   Portable light signals may be placed for the control of vehicular traffic only at a site approved by the traffic authority except—

(a) where the signals are being operated and maintained by and are under the regular supervision of a constable during the progress of a temporary scheme of traffic control;

(b) on a length of road along which

(i) there is no junction carrying vehicular traffic to or from it; and

(ii) the width of the carriageway is temporarily restricted so as to carry only one line of traffic;

(c) at a level crossing when work in relation to that crossing is being carried out; or

(d) on a road adjacent to the temporary site of road, building or engineering works used for the movement of vehicles, materials, plant or equipment within the site of the works.

48. Placing of various light signals

B48.134   (1) The light signals shown in diagram 4004 may be placed only in conjunction with the sign shown in diagram 545 when placed in conjunction with the plate shown in diagram 546 or 547.1.

(2) The light signals shown in diagram 4005 may be placed on or near a road only when the sign shown in diagram 548 in conjunction with the plate shown in diagram 548.1 is placed in advance of those signals.

(3) The light signals shown in diagram 4006 may be placed only in conjunction with the light signals shown in diagram 3014.

(4) The sign shown in diagram 4003 may be placed only in conjunction with the light signals shown in diagram 4002 for the purpose of conveying to pedestrians the indications specified in diagram 4003.

(5) The light signals shown in diagram 4002 may be placed only in conjunction with the light signals prescribed in paragraphs (2) or (3) of regulation 30.

(6) The light signal shown in diagram 776 may be placed only at or near a level crossing and the legend shall be displayed to road traffic in black letters on a red background which is internally illuminated by means of electricity only when a railway vehicle or tramcar has just passed over the level crossing and another is approaching.

49. Approval of signs and signals

(1) Save as provided in this direction, the light signals prescribed in regulations 30, **B48.135**
31, 32, 34, 35, 37 and 38, the matrix signs prescribed in regulation 36, the warning lights
prescribed in regulations 39(2) and 40, the audible and tactile signals prescribed in regulation 37, a sign shown in diagram 618.3A, 776 or 2509, any light signals or signs shown in
a diagram in Schedule 11, variable message signs and any other signs not continuously in
use over a period of 24 hours and which are capable of being brought into and taken out
of use by the operation of any electrical or other apparatus may be placed on or near a
road only if at the time that they are first placed—

(a) the signal, sign or any apparatus (including the content of all instructions stored in, or
executable by it) used in connection with the signal or sign is approved in writing in
accordance with the relevant requirements laid down by the Secretary of State; and

(b) in the case of signals prescribed in regulation 30(7) or regulation 38 the signals are
to be erected at or near a level crossing, and the site for, and the number and dis-
position of, those signals has first been approved in writing by or on behalf of the
Secretary of State.

(2) Paragraph (1)(b) shall not apply to signals displayed to indicate the effect of Orders
made by the Secretary of State under—

(a) section 66 of the British Transport Commission Act 1957;

(b) section 124 of the Transport Act 1968; or

(c) section 1 of the Level Crossings Act 1983.

(3) If, after a signal or sign has been placed in accordance with an approval under paragraph (1), the signal, sign or any apparatus used in connection with the signal or sign is
altered, the signal or sign shall not be further used unless that alteration is approved in
writing by or on behalf of the Secretary of State.

(4) Paragraphs (1) and (3) shall not apply to variable message signs which are only manually operated without any assistance by electrical or mechanical means.

(5) When any signal or sign has been placed in accordance with an approval under paragraph (1), the signal, the sign or any apparatus used in connection with the signal or sign,
including any alterations approved in accordance with paragraph (3), shall be regarded as
continuing to be approved until notice is given in writing by the Secretary of State—

(a) to the traffic authority; and

(b) either—

(i) to the supplier of the equipment; or

(ii) where an alteration has been approved in accordance with paragraph (3), to
the person who carried out the alteration,

of a date after which the signal, sign or apparatus is no longer to be so regarded.

(6) Where notice is given under paragraph (5) that a signal, sign or any apparatus used in
connection with the signal or sign shall no longer be regarded as being approved that signal,
sign or apparatus shall be removed from the road on or before the date given in the notice.

[The functions of the Secretary of State exercisable under direction 49 in relation to Wales have been **B48.136**
transferred to the National Assembly for Wales by the National Assembly for Wales (Transfer of Functions)
Order 1999 (S.I. 1999 No. 672; not reproduced in this work), art.2 and Sched 1.]

50. Approval of studs

(1) Studs incorporating reflectors, retroreflecting material or a steady or intermittent **B48.137**
light source may be placed on a road only if such studs are approved in writing in accordance with requirements laid down by the Secretary of State.

(2) When any stud has been placed in accordance with an approval under paragraph (1), the stud shall be regarded as continuing to be approved until notice is given in writing by the Secretary of State to the supplier and to the traffic authority of a date after which the stud is no longer to be so regarded.

(3) Where notice is given under paragraph (2) that a stud is no longer to be regarded as being approved that stud shall be removed from the road on or before the date given in the notice.

51. Special directions by the Secretary of State

B48.138   Nothing in these Directions shall be taken to limit the power of the Secretary of State acting as the appropriate Minister by any special direction to dispense with, add to or modify any of the requirements of these Directions in their application to any particular case.

The Vehicle Excise Duty (Designation of Small Islands) Order 1995

(S.I. 1995 No. 1397)

1.   *[Omitted.]*

2. The islands listed in the Schedule to this Order are hereby designated as small islands   **B49.01**
for the purposes of paragraph 18 (meaning of island goods vehicle) of Schedule 1 to the
Vehicle Excise and Registration Act 1994.

THE SCHEDULE

DESIGNATED SMALL ISLANDS

Inner Hebrides
Canna
Coll
Colonsay
Eigg
Gigha
Iona
Islay
Jura
Kerrera
Lismore
Luing
Muck
Mull
Pabay
Raasay
Rum
Scarba
Shuna
Tiree
Ulva

Orkney Islands
Copinsay
Eday
Egilsay
Fara
Faray
Flotta
Graemsay

Hoy
North Ronaldsay
Papa Stronsay
Papa Westray
Pentland Skerries
Rousay
Sanday
South Walls
Stroma
Stronsay
Westray
Wyre

Outer Hebrides
Barra
Benbecula
Berneray
Eriskay
North Uist
Scalpay
South Uist
Vatersay

Scilly Isles
Bryher
St Agnes
St Martin's
St Mary's
Tresco

Shetland Islands   **B49.02**
Bressay
Fair Isle
Fetlar
Foula
Out Skerries
Papa Stour
Unst
Uyea
Whalsay
Yell

Other Islands
Arran
Bardsey Island
Brownsea Island
Bute
Caldey Island
Isle of Ewe
Flat Holm
Great Cumbrae
Inch Marnock
Little Cumbrae
Lundy
Isle of May
Rathlin
St Kilda
Sanda
Scalpay
Skokholm

The Goods Vehicles (Licensing of Operators) Act 1995 (Commencement and Transitional Provisions) Order 1995

(S.I. 1995 No. 2181)

B50.01   *Editorial note.*   This order has no effect in relation to foreign goods vehicles; see the Goods Vehicles (Licensing of Operators) (Temporary Use in Great Britain) Regulations 1996 (S.I. 1996 No. 2186), reg.31(3) below.

B50.02   **1.** This Order may be cited as the Goods Vehicles (Licensing of Operators) Act 1995 (Commencement and Transitional Provisions) Order 1995.

B50.03   **2.** The Goods Vehicles (Licensing of Operators) Act 1995, except section 50 and Schedule 5, shall come into force on the 1st January 1996.

B50.04   **3.** The Schedule to this Order (transitional provisions) shall have effect.

Article 3   THE SCHEDULE

TRANSITIONAL PROVISIONS

1. Interpretation

B50.05   In this Schedule—

"*the 1968 Act*" means the Transport Act 1968;

"*the 1995 Act*" means the Goods Vehicles (Licensing of Operators) Act 1995;

"*the appointed day*" means 1st January 1996;

"*existing licence*" means an operator's licence within the meaning of Part V of the 1968 Act which was in force immediately before the appointed day; and

"*old-style licence*" means an existing licence in respect of which no direction has been given under paragraph 10 below.

2. Licences with expiry dates before the appointed day

B50.06   (1) This paragraph applies to an existing licence if—

(a)   on the date that the licence was due to expire proceedings were pending before the traffic commissioner on an application by the holder of the licence for the grant to him of a new licence in substitution therefor; and

(b)   the licence was in force immediately before the appointed day by virtue of that application and section 67(4) of the 1968 Act.

(2) An existing licence to which this paragraph applies shall, unless previously revoked

or otherwise terminated under any provision of the 1995 Act or any other statutory provision, terminate upon the requirements of sub-paragraph (3) below being met.

(3) The requirements of this sub-paragraph are that—

(a) the application, and

(b) any appeal under (or having effect as an appeal under) section 37 of the 1995 Act arising out of that application,

are disposed of.

(4) Section 16(2) of the 1995 Act shall have effect subject to this paragraph.

3. Prematurely terminated licences

(1) This paragraph applies to an existing licence if—   **B50.07**

(a) a traffic commissioner has, before the appointed day, given a direction under section 69 of the 1968 Act that an existing licence be terminated on a date earlier than that on which it would otherwise expire under section 67 of that Act; and

(b) the date specified in the direction as the date on which the licence is to terminate is on or after the appointed day.

(2) Subject to sub-paragraph (3), an existing licence to which this paragraph applies shall, unless previously revoked or otherwise terminated under any provision of the 1995 Act or any other statutory provision, terminate on the date specified in the direction as the date on which the licence is to terminate.

(3) If, on the date on which an existing licence is due to expire by virtue of sub-paragraph (2) above, proceedings are pending before the traffic commissioner on an application by the holder of that licence for the grant to him of a new licence in substitution therefor, the existing licence shall, subject to its revocation or other termination under any provision of the 1995 Act or any other statutory provision, continue in force until—

(a) the application, and

(b) any appeal under section 37 of the 1995 Act arising out of the application,

are disposed of.

(4) Section 16(2) of the 1995 Act shall have effect subject to this paragraph.

4. Statements of intent

Where—   **B50.08**

(a) the holder of an old-style licence had made or procured to be made—

(i) for the purposes of his application for the licence, or

(ii) for the purposes of an application for the variation of the licence, a statement of intent in writing; and

(b) the application was determined before the appointed day,

the statement shall, for the purposes of the 1995 Act, have effect on and after the appointed day as if it were an undertaking recorded in the licence.

5. Authorised vehicles

(1) Section 5 of the 1995 Act (which replaces section 61 of the 1968 Act) shall have   **B50.09**
effect in relation to an old-style licence as if for subsection (1) there were substituted—

"(1) Subject to subsection (2) of this section, the vehicles authorised to be used under an operator's licence shall be—

(a) such motor vehicles, being vehicles in the lawful possession of the holder of the licence as are specified in the licence;

(b) trailers from time to time in the lawful possession of the holder of the licence, not exceeding at any time such maximum number as is specified in the licence;

(c) unless the licence does not permit the addition of vehicles under this paragraph and subject to subsection (6) of this section, motor vehicles not exceeding such maximum number as is specified in the licence, being vehicles in the lawful possession of the holder of the licence.

For the purposes of paragraphs (b) and (c) of this subsection different types of trailers or different types of motor vehicles, as the case may be, may be distinguished in a licence and a maximum number may be specified in the licence for trailers or vehicles of each type.".

(2) Section 5(2) and (3) of the 1995 Act shall not have effect in relation to an old-style licence.

(3) Subject to sub-paragraph (4) below, section 5(6) of the 1995 Act shall have effect in relation to an old-style licence as if for the words "subsection (1)" there were substituted the words "subsection (1)(c)".

(4) In section 5(6) of the 1995 Act, the words "and has paid him a prescribed fee" shall not have effect in relation to a notice given to the traffic commissioner under section 61(3) of the 1968 Act before the appointed day.

(5) In section 5(7) of the 1995 Act, the words "and the prescribed fee has been duly paid under subsection (6)" shall not have effect in relation to a notice to the traffic commissioner under section 61(3) of the 1968 Act before the appointed day.

(6) Section 6 of the 1995 Act shall not have effect in relation to an old-style licence.

B50.10   **6. Variation of old-style licences**   *[Application of section 17 of the 1995 Act (not reproduced in this work) to old-style licences.]*

7. Publication of notices of applications for licences made before the appointed day   *[Application of section 11 of the 1995 Act (not reproduced in this work) to applications for licences before the appointed day.]*

B50.11   **8. Publication of notices of applications for the variation of licences made before the appointed day**   *[Application of section 18 of the 1995 Act (not reproduced in this work) to applications made before the appointed day.]*

9. Publication of notices of applications for the variation of old-style licences made on or after the appointed day   *[Application of section 18 of the 1995 Act (not reproduced in this work) to applications in respect of old-style licences on or after the appointed day.]*

10. Conversion of old-style licences

B50.12   (1) The traffic commissioner by whom an old-style licence was issued may at any time after the appointed day vary the licence by directing—

(a) that any maximum number specified in the licence under (or having effect as specified in the licence under) section 5(1)(b) or (c) of the 1995 Act (as substituted by paragraph 5 above) shall cease to have effect;

(b) that a provision such as is mentioned in section 5(2) of the 1995 Act be included in the licence;

(c) that a maximum number of motor vehicles be specified in the licence in accordance with section 6(1)(a) of the 1995 Act;

(d) that a maximum number of trailers be specified in the licence in accordance with section 6(2)(a) of the 1995 Act;

(e) that a provision such as is mentioned in section 6(1)(b) or (2)(b) of the 1995 Act be included in the licence;

(f) that any statement having effect as an undertaking by virtue of paragraph 4 above immediately before the direction or a statement to the like effect be recorded in the licence as an undertaking; or

(g) that an alteration of any other description be made which appears to the traffic commissioner to be consequential to the coming into force of the 1995 Act;

or any two or more of those things; and paragraph 5 of this Schedule shall be disregarded for the purposes of paragraphs (b) to (e) above.

(2) The powers under sub-paragraph (1) above shall be exercised in such a way as appears to the traffic commissioner—

(a) to put the licence into a form that would have been appropriate had the 1995 Act been in force at the time it was granted; and

(b) to leave the holder of the licence in the same position as he was immediately before the licence is varied or as near to that position as is practicable using those powers while meeting the requirements of paragraph (a) above.

(3) If it appears to a traffic commissioner that an old-style licence is in a form that would have been appropriate had the 1995 Act been in force at the time it was granted, he may at any time after the appointed day give a direction that no variation is to be made to the licence under this paragraph.

(4) A traffic commissioner shall not exercise his powers under this paragraph without first giving the holder of the licence an opportunity to make representations to the commissioner with respect to the proposed variation.

11. Revocation, etc., of old-style licences *[Application of section 26 of the 1995 Act (not reproduced in this work) to old-style licences.]* **B50.13**

12. Periods of review of operating centres

(1) *[Application of section 30(2) of the 1995 Act (not reproduced in this work) to existing licences.]*

(2) *[Disapplication of sections 30–32 of the 1995 Act (not reproduced in this work) to licences to which paragraph 2 or paragraph 3 of this Schedule applies.]*

13. Removal of operating centres on review *[Application of section 31 of the 1995 Act (not reproduced in this work) to certain representations to the traffic commissioners before the appointed day.]* **B50.14**

14. Fees *[Omitted.]*

The Deregulation and Contracting Out Act 1994 (Commencement No. 4 and Transitional Provisions) Order 1995

(S.I. 1995 No. 2835)

B51.01 **1.** *[Citation.]*

2. *[Commencement of Deregulation and Contracting Out Act 1994.]*

B51.02 **3.** The Schedule to this Order (transitional provisions) shall have effect.

Article 3   THE SCHEDULE

TRANSITIONAL PROVISIONS

1. Interpretation

B51.03 In this Schedule—

"*the 1981 Act*" means the Public Passenger Vehicles Act 1981 [*q.v.*];

"*the 1994 Act*" means the Deregulation and Contracting Out Act 1994;

"*the appointed day*" means 1st January 1996;

"*existing licence*" means a PSV operator's licence which was in force immediately before the appointed day;

"*PSV operator's licence*" has the same meaning as in the 1981 Act;

"*old-style licence*" means an existing licence in respect of which no direction has been given under paragraph 6 below.

2. Licences with expiry dates prior to the appointed day

B51.04 (1) This paragraph applies to an existing licence if—

    (a) on the date that the licence was due to expire, proceedings were pending before the traffic commissioner on an application by the holder of the licence for the grant to him of a new licence in substitution for it; and

    (b) the licence was in force immediately before the appointed day by virtue of that application and section 15(3) or (4) or 50(2) of the 1981 Act.

(2) Subject to paragraph (4) below, an existing licence to which this paragraph applies shall, unless previously revoked or otherwise terminated under any provision of the 1981 Act or any other statutory provision, terminate upon the requirements of sub-paragraph (3) below being met.

(3) The requirements of this sub-paragraph are that—

    (a) the application, and

    (b) any appeal under section 50 of the 1981 Act arising out of the application,

are disposed of.

(4) Section 15(4) of the 1981 Act as it was in force immediately before the appointed day shall, notwithstanding anything in the 1994 Act, continue to have effect in relation to an existing licence to which this paragraph applies.

(5) Section 15(2) of the 1981 Act shall, on and after the appointed day, have effect subject to this paragraph.

3. Prematurely terminated licences

(1) This paragraph applies to an existing licence if—   **B51.05**

    (a) a traffic commissioner has before the appointed day curtailed the period of validity of the licence under section 17(2) of the 1981 Act; and

    (b) the expiry date of the licence is the appointed day or any day thereafter.

(2) Subject to sub-paragraphs (3) and (4) below, an existing licence to which this paragraph applies shall, unless previously revoked or otherwise terminated under any provision of the 1981 Act or any other statutory provision, terminate on the expiry date.

(3) If, immediately before an existing licence is due to expire by virtue of sub-paragraph (2) above, proceedings are pending before the traffic commissioner on an application by the holder of that licence for the grant to him of a new licence in substitution for it, the existing licence shall, subject to its revocation or other termination under any provision of the 1981 Act or any other statutory provision, continue in force until—

    (a) the application, and

    (b) any appeal under section 50 of the 1981 Act arising out of the application,

are disposed of.

(4) Section 15(4) of the 1981 Act as it was in force immediately before the appointed day shall, notwithstanding anything in the 1994 Act, continue to have effect in relation to an existing licence to which this paragraph applies.

(5) For the purposes of this paragraph, the expiry date of a licence that has, before the appointed day, been curtailed under subsection (2) of section 17 of the 1981 Act is the date on which it would have expired by virtue of the curtailment had the 1994 Act not been passed and no application were made for a licence in substitution for it.

(6) Section 15(2) of the 1981 Act shall, on and after the appointed day, have effect subject to this paragraph.

4. Statements of intent

(1) Where—   **B51.06**

    (a) the holder of an old-style licence had made or procured to be made—

        (i) for the purposes of his application for the licence, or

        (ii) for the purposes of an application for the variation of the licence, a statement of intent in writing; and

    (b) the application was determined before the appointed day,

the statement shall for the purposes of the 1981 Act, on and after the appointed day, have effect as if it were an undertaking recorded in the licence.

5. Variation of an old-style licence *[Application of section 16(6) of the 1981 Act (not* **B51.07** *reproduced in this work) to old-style licences.]*

6. Conversion of old-style licences

(1) The traffic commissioner by whom an old-style licence was issued may at any time   **B51.08** after the appointed day vary the licence by directing—

(a) that any statement of intent having effect as an undertaking by virtue of paragraph 4 above immediately before the variation, or a statement that appears to the traffic commissioner to be to the like effect, be recorded as an undertaking in the licence; or

(b) that an alteration of any other description be made which appears to the traffic commissioner to be consequential to the coming into force of the 1994 Act;

or both of those things.

(2) The powers under paragraph (1) above shall be exercised in such a way as appears to the traffic commissioner—

(a) to put the licence into a form that would have been appropriate had the 1994 Act been in force at the time it was granted; and

(b) to leave the holder of the licence in the same position as he was immediately before the licence is varied or as near to that position as is practicable using those powers while meeting the requirements of paragraph (a) above.

(3) A traffic commissioner shall not exercise his powers under this paragraph without first giving the holder of the licence an opportunity to make representations to the commissioner with respect to the proposed variation.

B51.09 **7. Fees** *[Omitted.]*

The Goods Vehicles (Licensing of Operators) Regulations 1995

(S.I. 1995 No. 2869)

Editorial note. These regulations are modified in relation to their application to foreign goods vehicles by the Goods Vehicles (Licensing of Operators) (Temporary Use in Great Britain) Regulations 1996 (S.I. 1996 No. 2186) below.

B52.01

ARRANGEMENT OF REGULATIONS

PART I

GENERAL

B52.02

*   *   *

PART VII

OTHER MATTERS

SCHEDULES

PART I

GENERAL

1. Commencement and citation   *[Omitted.]*

B52.03

2. Revocation   *[Omitted.]*

3. Interpretation

B52.04   (1) In these Regulations, unless the context otherwise requires, any reference to—

(a) a numbered section is a reference to the section bearing that number in the Goods Vehicles (Licensing of Operators) Act 1995 [*q.v.*];

(b) a numbered regulation or Schedule is a reference to the regulation or, as the case may be, the Schedule bearing that number in these Regulations; and

(c) a numbered paragraph is a reference to the paragraph bearing that number in the regulation in which the reference appears.

(2) In these Regulations, unless the context otherwise requires—

"*the 1995 Act*" means the Goods Vehicles (Licensing of Operators) Act 1995;

"*application for a licence*" means an application for an operator's licence for which publication is required by section 10(1);

"*application for the variation of a licence*" means an application for the variation of an operator's licence for which publication is required by section 17(3) and "*application*" when used otherwise than as part of those expressions means—

(a) an application for a licence, or

(b) an application for the variation of a licence;

"*Applications and Decisions*" means a statement issued by a traffic commissioner under regulation 21;

"*company*" shall be construed as provided in section 735 of the Companies Act 1985;

"*disc*" means a disc issued in accordance with regulation 23(1) and (2) or 27(2);

"*dual purpose vehicle*" has the meaning given in column 2 of the Table in regulation 3(2) of the Road Vehicles (Construction and Use) Regulations 1986 [*S.I. 1986 No. 1078, as amended (q.v.)*];

"*farm*" includes a market garden;

"*firm*" has the same meaning as in section 4 of the Partnership Act 1890 [*not reproduced in this work*];

"*goods vehicle*" has the same meaning as in section 58(1) but excludes a small goods vehicle as described in Schedule 1 to the 1995 Act;

"*keeper*", in relation to a goods vehicle, is the person in whose name the vehicle is registered under the Vehicle Excise and Registration Act 1994 [*q.v.*];

"*licence*" means an operator's licence (whether standard or restricted) as defined in section 2(1) and, where the context so requires, includes the documentation which evidences the grant of an application;

"*licence-holder*", and "*holder*" in relation to a licence, mean the person to whom the licence was issued;

"*motor vehicle*" means a mechanically propelled vehicle intended or adapted for use on roads;

"*maintenance*" in relation to a goods vehicle includes inspection, repair and fuelling;

"*officer*" has the meaning given in section 42;

"*recovery vehicle*" has the same meaning as in Part V of Schedule 1 to the Vehicle Excise and Registration Act 1994;

"*relevant conviction*" means any conviction mentioned in paragraph 5 of Schedule 2 to the 1995 Act or any conviction of contravening any provision of the law of

Northern Ireland or of a country or territory outside the United Kingdom corresponding to any such conviction, not being in either case a spent conviction within the meaning of section 1(1) of the Rehabilitation of Offenders Act 1974 [*not reproduced in this work*];

"*showman's goods vehicle*" has the same meaning as in section 62 of the Vehicle Excise and Registration Act 1994;

"*tower wagon*" has the same meaning as in paragraph 17(2) of Schedule 2 to the Vehicle Excise and Registration Act 1994 (as originally enacted);

"*trade licence*" is a licence granted under section 11 of the Vehicle Excise and Registration Act 1994;

"*visiting force*", "*headquarters*" and "*vehicle in the service of a visiting force or a headquarters*" have the same meanings as in the Visiting Forces and International Headquarters (Application of Law) Order 1965 [*S.I. 1965 No. 1536.*]

[*The Visiting Forces and International Headquarters (Application of Law) Order 1965 (to which reference is made in regulation 3(2)) has been revoked and replaced by the Visiting Forces and International Headquarters (Application of Law) Order 1999 (S.I. 1999 No. 1736; not reproduced in this work). No textual amendment has been made to regulation 3 in consequence of that revocation; but by the Interpretation Act 1978, ss.17(2)(a) and 23(1) references to the earlier order may be treated as references to S.I. 1999 No. 1736.*] **B52.05**

PART II

APPLICATIONS

4–9.   *[Omitted.]*   **B52.06**

PART III

OBJECTIONS AND REPRESENTATIONS

10–13.   *[Omitted.]*   **B52.07**

PART IV

OPERATING CENTRES

14–19.   *[Omitted.]*   **B52.08**

PART V

INQUIRIES

20.   *[Omitted.]*   **B52.09**

PART VI

APPLICATIONS AND DECISIONS

21, 22.   *[Omitted.]*   **B52.10**

PART VII

OTHER MATTERS

23. Identification of motor vehicles

B52.11   (1) The traffic commissioner shall, when any motor vehicle to be used under a licence is specified in the licence, issue to the licence-holder a disc in respect of the vehicle.

(2) The disc shall clearly indicate (by colour or other means)—

(a) whether a vehicle is being used under a standard licence or under a restricted licence; and

(b) in the case of a vehicle being used under a standard licence, whether the vehicle covers both international and national transport operations or national transport operations only.

(3) The licence-holder shall, during such time as any motor vehicle is specified in the licence and whether or not for the time being the vehicle is being used for the purpose for which a licence is required, cause a disc appropriate to the vehicle to be fixed to, and exhibited in a legible condition on, that vehicle in a waterproof container—

(a) in the case of a vehicle fitted with a front windscreen, on the near side and near the lower edge of the windscreen with the obverse side facing forwards;

(b) in the case of a vehicle not fitted with a front windscreen, in a conspicuous position on the front or near side of the vehicle.

(4) At no time shall any person except the traffic commissioner, or a person authorised to do so on his behalf, write on or make any other alteration to a disc.

B52.12   *[A contravention of regulation 23(3) or regulation 23(4) is an offence under section 57(9) of the 1995 Act; see regulation 32 below.]*

B52.13   **24. Temporary addition of a motor vehicle**   *[Omitted.]*

25. Notification of change of address

B52.14   If during the currency of a licence the address for correspondence as notified in the licence-holder's application or as subsequently notified under this regulation ceases to be an effective address for correspondence the licence-holder shall within 28 days from the date of such event notify the traffic commissioner by whom the licence was granted of an effective address for correspondence.

B52.15   *[A contravention of regulation 25 is an offence under section 57(9) of the 1995 Act; see regulation 32 below.]*

26. Production of licence for examination

B52.16   (1) The licence-holder shall produce the licence for inspection by an officer or a police constable on being required by such a person to do so, and the licence-holder may do so at any operating centre covered by the licence or at his head or principal place of business within the traffic area in which any such operating centre lies or, if the requirement is made by a police constable, at a police station chosen by the licence-holder.

(2) The licence-holder shall comply with any requirement mentioned in paragraph (1) within 14 days of the day on which the requirement is made.

B52.17   *[A contravention of regulation 26 is an offence under section 57(9) of the 1995 Act; see regulation 32 below.*

...ing companies and their subsidiaries, see Schedule 2, paragraph 3(b), to these regulations ...w.]

27. Issue of copies of licences and discs

(1) If a licence or disc has been lost, destroyed or defaced, the person to whom it was   **B52.18**
issued shall forthwith notify in writing the traffic commissioner by whom the licence or disc
was issued.

(2) If—

   (a) the traffic commissioner is satisfied that a licence or disc has been lost, destroyed or
        defaced; and

   (b) in the case of a licence or disc which has been defaced, it is surrendered to the
        traffic commissioner,

the traffic commissioner shall issue a copy (so marked) which shall have effect as the original licence or disc.

(3) Where a licence or disc has been lost and after a copy has been issued the lost licence
or disc is found by or comes into the possession of the licence-holder he shall forthwith
return the original licence or disc to the traffic commissioner.

[A contravention of regulation 27(1) or regulation 27(3) is an offence under section 57(9) of the 1995   **B52.19**
Act; see regulation 32 below.]

28. Return of licences and discs

(1) If the licence-holder ceases to use under the licence any motor vehicle specified in   **B52.20**
the licence he shall within 21 days beginning with the date of ceasing to use the vehicle or
vehicles notify the traffic commissioner by whom the licence was issued and return to that
traffic commissioner the licence for variation and the disc relating to the vehicle.

(2) If a licence is varied under section 17, 31, 32 or 36 its holder shall, when required by
the traffic commissioner so to do, return to the traffic commissioner—

   (a) the licence; and

   (b) if the number of motor vehicles specified in the licence has been reduced, the disc
        relating to any vehicle no longer specified in the licence.

(3) If a licence is revoked, surrendered, suspended, curtailed or terminated for any other
reason, or if a traffic commissioner has given a direction in respect of a licence under
section 26(2), the licence-holder shall on or before the date specified in a notice to that
effect, send or deliver to the office of the traffic area of the traffic commissioner by whom
the licence was issued—

   (a) the licence; and

   (b) the disc relating to any motor vehicle which the traffic commissioner may specify,

   for cancellation, retention during the time of suspension, or alteration as the case may be.

(4) The notice referred to in paragraph (3) shall be delivered personally to the licence-
holder or sent to him by recorded delivery service at the address shown in his application or
last notified in accordance with regulation 25.

(5) In the event of the traffic commissioner deciding to make a variation under paragraph 9 of the Schedule to the Goods Vehicles (Licensing of Operators) Act 1995
(Commencement and Transitional Provisions) Order 1995 [*S.I. 1995 No. 2181; paragraph 9
of the Schedule is not reproduced in this work*] the licence-holder shall return the licence to the
traffic commissioner for him to amend the licence so that it conforms to the variation before
returning it to the holder.

[A contravention of regulation 28(1), regulation 28(2), regulation 28(3) or regulation 28(5) is an offence under section 57(9) of the 1995 Act; see regulation 32 below and the note thereto.]

29. Partnerships

B52.22   (1) The provision in section 8(2) that a person shall not at the same time hold more than one operator's licence in respect of the same area shall apply so that a firm shall be treated as a person separate from any partner of that firm or an individual in any other partnership.

(2) For the purposes of authorising goods vehicles to be used under section 5(1) when the licence-holder is a firm, any vehicle in the lawful possession of any partner of a firm shall be regarded as in the lawful possession of the firm.

(3) The provisions of section 13(3) shall apply in any case where an applicant for a standard licence is a firm so that the traffic commissioner is required to satisfy himself that—

    (a) every one of the partners of that firm is of good repute;

    (b) the firm satisfies the requirement of appropriate financial standing; and

    (c) either—

        (i) if one of the firm's partners manage the road transport business carried on by the firm, he, or if more than one each of whom, is professionally competent, or

        (ii) the firm employs a transport manager or transport managers who, or if more than one each of whom, is of good repute and professionally competent.

(4) The provisions of section 13(4) shall apply in any case where an applicant for a restricted licence is a firm so that the traffic commissioner is required to satisfy himself that every one of the partners of that firm is not unfit to hold an operator's licence by reason of any activities or convictions covered by section 34(a) or (b).

(5) The provisions of section 13(6) shall apply in any case where an applicant is a firm and in such case the financial resources referred to in that subsection shall be those of the firm.

(6) *[Application of section 26 to firms.]*

(7) *[Application of section 27(1) to firms.]*

(8) The provisions of section 28 shall apply to the revocation of an operator's licence held by a firm and in such a case the powers conferred by subsections (1) and (4) shall be exercisable in respect of each and every partner of that firm.

(9) Except in a case falling within paragraph (9) [*sic*] any requirement, obligation or prohibition (however expressed) placed on a person making an application or on the licence-holder by, or in pursuance of, a provision in the 1995 Act or these Regulations, shall apply where the licence-holder is a firm and the duty to meet the requirement or obligation or to comply with the prohibition shall apply to the partners of that firm severally as well as jointly.

(10) Where an application is made by, or the licence-holder is a firm a requirement or obligation placed on the applicant or licence-holder by virtue of sections 8(4), 9(1) or 17(2) of the 1995 Act to inform the traffic commissioner of a notifiable conviction within the meaning given in paragraph 4 of Schedule 2 to the 1995 Act shall apply in relation to the notifiable conviction of each partner of that firm, and the duty to meet the requirement shall apply to the person convicted.

(11) The provisions in section 16(5) as to the events on which an operator's licence held by an individual terminates apply in a case where such a licence is held by a firm, if—

(a) the partnership is dissolved; or

(b) one or more of the persons dies or becomes a patient within the meaning of Part VII of the Mental Health Act 1983, or . . .

(12) In Schedule 3 to the 1995 Act—

(a) the provisions in paragraph 1 as regards determining whether an individual is of good repute apply, in a case of a firm in respect of each of the partners of that firm as they apply to an individual;

(b) *[applies to paragraph 6 (not reproduced in this work)]*;

(c) *[applies to paragraph 8(2) (not reproduced in this work)]*; and

(d) *[applies to paragraphs 10 and 11 (not reproduced in this work)]*.

[The reference in regulation 29(9) to "paragraph (9)" is a drafting or typographical error and a refer-   **B52.23**
ence to "paragraph (10)" might have been intended.

The words omitted from regulation 29(11)(b) refer expressly and exclusively to Scotland.]

30. Holding companies and subsidiaries

(1) A holding company may apply to the traffic commissioner for any traffic area—   **B52.24**

(a) if it does not already hold a licence in respect of that area, for the issue of a licence; or

(b) if it already holds a licence in respect of that area, for a variation of its licence by a direction under section 17(1)(a),

which would have the effect, if the application were granted, of including in the licence to be issued to, or already held by, the holding company, goods vehicles in the lawful possession of a subsidiary of that company specified in the application.

(2) An application by a holding company under paragraph (1) shall, unless

(a) the subsidiary is not the licence-holder; or

(b) the licence or variation applied for by the holding company will not take effect until any licence held by the subsidiary has been surrendered or has otherwise terminated,

be accompanied by an application by the subsidiary for the variation of the licence held by the subsidiary by a direction under section 17(1)(b) for the removal therefrom of all or some of the goods vehicles authorised to be used thereunder, being the vehicles to which the application of the holding company relates.

(3) Where a holding company, on an application under paragraph (1), signifies to the traffic commissioner its desire that the provisions of this regulation should have effect as respects a subsidiary of that company, then, in relation to the application and to any licence granted to the holding company, or held by the holding company and varied, on that application, and to the use of any goods vehicles authorised to be used under any such licence, the 1995 Act and these Regulations shall have effect subject to the modifications specified in Schedule 2.

(4) The provisions of this regulation shall cease to have effect as respects a holding company and its subsidiary—

(a) if the holding company gives notice to the traffic commissioner who issued or varied its licence that it desires that this regulation should, as from any date, cease to apply to the holding company and that subsidiary, as from that date; or

(b) as from the date on which that subsidiary ceases to be a subsidiary of that holding company.

(5) *[Publication of notice of application under regulation 30(4)(a).]*

(6) Where the provisions of this regulation cease to have effect as respects a holding company and its subsidiary by virtue of paragraph (4)(b) the company which was the holding company shall within 21 days of the event which caused the subsidiary to cease to be a subsidiary of that company—

   (a) notify the traffic commissioner by whom the licence was issued, and

   (b) supply all material details of the event, and

   (c) return to the traffic commissioner the licence and the discs relating to the motor vehicles authorised to be used thereunder,

and in so far as the holding company fails to satisfy those requirements the company which was the subsidiary company shall, on being so directed by the traffic commissioner, within 7 days of that direction supply the details, or return the licence and the discs, as the case may require.

(7) In a case where the applicant for, or the holder of, a standard licence is a holding company and the goods vehicles used, or to be used, under the licence belong to, or are in the possession of, a subsidiary of that holding company, the provisions of these Regulations apply as if—

   (a) the road transport undertaking and any operating centre of the subsidiary were the road transport undertaking and an operating centre of the holding company;

   (b) for purposes of, or relating to, the reputation and financial standing of the holding company, the activities, relevant convictions and financial resources of the subsidiary were activities, convictions and resources of the holding company; and

   (c) in relation to a transport manager, his employment by the subsidiary were employment by the holding company.

B52.25   *[A contravention of regulation 30(6) is an offence under section 57(9) of the 1995 Act; see regulation 32 below.]*

31. Continuance of licence on death, bankruptcy, etc.

B52.26   (1) In this regulation, *"actual holder"* in relation to a licence means the person to whom the licence was issued.

(2) This regulation applies in the event—

   (a) of the death of the actual holder of a licence;

   (b) of the actual holder of a licence becoming a patient under Part VII of the Mental Health Act 1983, or . . .;

   (c) of the bankruptcy of the actual holder of a licence;

   (d) in the case of a company, of the actual holder of a licence going into liquidation or an administration order being made in relation to the actual holder; or

   (e) of the appointment of a receiver or manager of the trade or business of the actual holder of a licence.

(3) After the happening of either of the events mentioned in paragraphs (2)(a) or (b) the traffic commissioner may direct that the licence shall not be treated as terminated when the actual holder died or became a patient but suspended until the date when a direction under paragraph (4) comes into force.

(4) After the happening of any of the events mentioned in paragraph (2) the traffic commissioner may direct that a person carrying on the trade or business of the actual holder of the licence is to be treated for the purposes of the 1995 Act as if he were the holder thereof for such purpose and to such extent as is specified in the direction for a period not exceeding—

(a) if it appears to the traffic commissioner that there are special circumstances, 18 months;

(b) in any other case, 12 months,

from the date of the coming into force of that direction.

(5) The powers under paragraph (4) shall be exercisable in relation to a standard licence whether or not the person carrying on the trade or business of the actual holder of the licence satisfies the requirement of professional competence.

(6) Where a person is treated as if he were the licence-holder by virtue of a direction under this regulation—

(a) any goods vehicle which had been in the lawful possession of the actual holder of the licence shall for the purposes of the 1995 Act be treated as if it was in the lawful possession of that person; and

(b) if the licence is a standard licence, nothing in section 27 shall oblige the traffic commissioner to revoke the licence by reason only of that person not satisfying the requirement of professional competence.

[The words omitted from regulation 31(2)(b) relate expressly and exclusively to Scotland.]   **B52.27**

32. Offences

Any contravention of, or failure to comply with, a provision in regulations 23(3), 23(4), 25, 26, 27(1), 27(3), 28(1), 28(2), 28(3), 28(4) [*sic*] or 30(6), is hereby declared to be an offence and for the purposes of section 57(9) any provision mentioned above shall be regarded as made under the 1995 Act.   **B52.28**

[The reference in regulation 32 to regulation "28(4)" would appear to be a drafting or typographical error; it is probable that a reference to regulation 28(5) was intended.]   **B52.29**

33. Classes of vehicle for which a licence is not required

(1) The classes of vehicle specified under section 2(2)(d) as those to which section 2(1) does not apply are the classes mentioned in Part I of Schedule 3.   **B52.30**

(2) The relevant plated weight of a goods vehicle, for the purposes of Schedule 1 to the 1995 Act (meaning of "*small goods vehicle*") is the gross weight not to be exceeded in Great Britain of the vehicle as shown on a Ministry plate as defined in column 2 of the Table in regulation 3(2) of the Road Vehicles (Construction and Use) Regulations 1986 or, if no such plate has been issued in respect of that vehicle, the maximum gross weight of the vehicle as shown on a plate affixed to the vehicle by virtue of regulation 66 of those Regulations.

34. Period for service of notice of review on ground of procedural irregularity   [*Omitted.*]   **B52.31**

35. Manner of service of notice of review on ground of procedural irregularity   [*Omitted.*]

36. Meaning of "relevant weight"

(1) A motor vehicle or trailer of any prescribed class referred to in section 5(3) means any vehicle described in section 2(1) as needing an operator's licence, and the relevant weight of such a vehicle is its revenue weight.   **B52.32**

(2) For purposes of this regulation "*revenue weight*" shall have the meaning given in section 60A of the Vehicle Excise and Registration Act 1994 [*q.v.*].

(3) In its application to this regulation, section 60A of that Act shall have effect as if—

(a) subsection (6) of that section were omitted; and

(b) no provision had been made under section 61A(2) of that Act.

SCHEDULE 1

B52.33   NOTICE OF APPLICATION FOR A LICENCE OR A VARIATION OF A LICENCE

[Omitted.]

Regulation 30(3)   SCHEDULE 2

MODIFICATIONS IN RELATION TO HOLDING COMPANIES AND SUBSIDIARIES

B52.34   **1.** The 1995 Act and these Regulations have effect as if any reference (except in this Schedule) to a provision which is modified by this Schedule were a reference to that provision as so modified.

B52.35   **2.** The 1995 Act has effect as if—

(a) goods vehicles in the lawful possession of the subsidiary were in the lawful possession of the holding company;

(b) where a goods vehicle is used in circumstances in which, but for the provisions of regulation 30, the subsidiary would be deemed to be the user, the holding company were the user;

(c) a trade or business carried on by the subsidiary were carried on by the holding company;

(d) the subsidiary were an applicant for the grant or variation of the licence;

(e) any operating centre of the subsidiary were an operating centre of the holding company;

(f) any person who is a director of the subsidiary were a director of the holding company;

(g) any person who is an employee of the subsidiary were an employee of the holding company;

(h) *[modification of section 10(1) (not reproduced in this work)]*;

(i) in section 22(1) the reference in paragraph (b) to persons holding shares in the company included a reference to persons holding shares in the subsidiary, and the reference in paragraph (c) to the licence-holder included a reference to the subsidiary;

(j) *[modification of section 17(3) (not reproduced in this work)]*;

(k)–(m) *[modification of section 26(1) and section 26(5) (not reproduced in this work)]*;

(n) in section 28(1) the reference to the licence-holder included a reference to the subsidiary;

(o) in section 28(4)(a) after sub-paragraph (ii) there were inserted the following sub-paragraph—

"(iii) a company which is a subsidiary of such a company; or";

(p) in section 28(5) there were substituted for paragraph (a) "where that person is a company or other body corporate which is the licence-holder in respect of a subsidiary of that company or other body corporate in pursuance of Regulations made under section 46 of this Act, in relation to any director of that company or other body corporate or of that subsidiary.".

3. These Regulations shall have effect as if—   **B52.36**

(a) *[modifies regulation 8 (not reproduced in this work)]*;

(b) in regulation 26 the reference to the licence-holder included a reference to the subsidiary.

SCHEDULE 3   Regulation 33

CLASSES OF VEHICLES FOR WHICH A LICENCE IS NOT REQUIRED

PART I

1. Any tractor as defined in paragraph 4(3) of Part IV of Schedule 1 to the Vehicle Excise and Registration Act 1994 (as originally enacted) while being used for one or more of the purposes specified in Part II of this Schedule.   **B52.37**

2. A dual-purpose vehicle and any trailer drawn by it.

3. A vehicle used on a road only in passing from private premises to other private premises in the immediate neighbourhood belonging (except in the case of a vehicle so used only in connection with excavation or demolition) to the same person, provided that the distance travelled on a road by any such vehicle does not exceed in the aggregate 9.654 kilometres, (6 miles), in any one week.   **B52.38**

4. A motor vehicle constructed or adapted primarily for the carriage of passengers and their effects, and any trailer drawn by it, while being so used.

5. A vehicle which is being used for funerals.   **B52.39**

6. A vehicle which is being used for police, fire brigade or ambulance purposes.

7. A vehicle which is being used for fire-fighting or rescue operations at mines.   **B52.40**

8. A vehicle on which no permanent body has been constructed, which is being used only for carrying burden which either is carried solely for the purpose of test or trial, or consists of articles and equipment which will form part of the completed vehicle when the body is constructed.

9. A vehicle which is being used under a trade licence.   **B52.41**

10. A vehicle in the service of a visiting force or of a headquarters.

11. A vehicle used by or under the control of Her Majesty's United Kingdom forces.   **B52.42**

12. A trailer not constructed primarily for the carriage of goods but which is being used incidentally for that purpose in connection with the construction, maintenance or repair of roads.

B52.43   **13.** A road roller and any trailer drawn by it.

14. A vehicle while being used under the direction of HM Coastguard or of the Royal National Lifeboat Institution for the carriage of life-boats, life-saving appliances or crew.

B52.44   **15.** A vehicle fitted with a machine, appliance, apparatus or other contrivance which is a permanent or essentially permanent fixture, provided that the only goods carried on the vehicle are—

(a) required for use in connection with the machine, appliance, apparatus or contrivance or the running of the vehicle;

(b) to be mixed by the machine, appliance, apparatus or contrivance with other goods not carried on the vehicle on a road in order to thrash, grade, clean or chemically treat grain;

(c) to be mixed by the machine, appliance, apparatus or contrivance with other goods not carried on the vehicle in order to make fodder for animals; or

(d) mud or other matter swept up from the surface of a road by the use of the machine, appliance, apparatus or other contrivance.

B52.45   **16.** A vehicle while being used by a local authority for the purposes of the enactments relating to weights and measures or the sale of food and drugs.

17. A vehicle while being used by a local authority in the discharge of any function conferred on or exercisable by that authority under Regulations made under the Civil Defence Act 1948.

18. A steam-propelled vehicle.

B52.46   **19.** A tower wagon or trailer drawn thereby, provided that the only goods carried on the trailer are goods required for use in connection with the work on which the tower wagon is ordinarily used as such.

20. A vehicle while being used for the carriage of goods within an aerodrome within the meaning of section 105(1) of the Civil Aviation Act 1982.

B52.47   **21.** An electrically propelled vehicle.

22. A showman's goods vehicle and any trailer drawn thereby.

B52.48   **23.** A vehicle permitted to carry out cabotage in the United Kingdom under Community Council Regulation (EEC) No. 3118/93 dated 25 October 1993 [*q.v.*] laying down conditions under which non-resident carriers may operate national road haulage services within a Member State.

24. A goods vehicle first used before 1 January 1977 which has an unladen weight not exceeding 1525 kilograms and for which the maximum gross weight, as shown on a plate affixed to the vehicle by virtue of regulation 66 of the Motor Vehicles (Construction and Use) Regulations 1986 or any provision which that regulation replaced, exceeds 3500 kilograms but does not exceed 3556.21 kilograms (3½ tons).

B52.49   **25.** A vehicle while being used by a highway authority for the purposes of section 196 of the Road Traffic Act 1988.

26. A vehicle being held ready for use in an emergency by an undertaking for the supply of water, electricity, gas or telephone services.

27. A recovery vehicle.   **B52.50**

28. A vehicle which is being used for snow clearing, or for the distribution of grit, salt or other materials on frosted, icebound or snow-covered roads or for going to or from the place where it is to be used for the said purposes or for any other purpose directly connected with those purposes.

29. A vehicle proceeding to or from a station provided by the Secretary of State under   **B52.51**
section 45 of the Road Traffic Act 1988 for the purposes of an examination of that vehicle under that section provided that—

   (a) the only load being carried is a load required for the purposes of the examination; and

   (b) it is being carried at the request of the Secretary of State.

[The definition of "aerodrome" in the Civil Aviation Act 1982, s.105(1) (to which reference is made in   **B52.52**
paragraph 20 above) is reproduced in the notes to the Community Drivers' Hours and Recording Equipment
(Exemptions and Supplementary Provisions) Regulations 1986 (S.I. 1986 No. 1456), Schedule, Pt I,
para.2 above.]

PART II

PURPOSES REFERRED TO IN PARAGRAPH 1 OF PART I OF THIS SCHEDULE

1. Hauling—   **B52.53**
   (a) threshing appliances;
   (b) farming implements;
   (c) a living van for the accommodation of persons employed to drive the tractor; or
   (d) supplies of water or fuel required for the tractor.

2. Hauling articles for a farm required by the keeper, being either the occupier of the farm or a contractor employed to do agricultural work on the farm by the occupier of the farm.

3. Hauling articles for a forestry estate required by the keeper where the keeper is the   **B52.54**
occupier of that estate or employed to do forestry work on the estate by the occupier or a contractor employed to do forestry work on the estate by the occupier.

4. Hauling within 24.135 kilometres, (15 miles), of a farm or a forestry estate occupied by the keeper, agricultural or woodland produce of that farm or estate.

5. Hauling within 24.135 kilometres, (15 miles), of a farm or a forestry estate occupied   **B52.55**
by the keeper, material to be spread on roads to deal with frost, ice or snow.

6. Hauling a snow plough or a similar contrivance for the purpose of clearing snow; and

7. Hauling—   **B52.56**
   (a) soil for landscaping or similar works; or
   (b) a mowing machine,
where the keeper is a local authority.

SCHEDULE 4

B52.57

INQUIRIES

[Omitted.]

SCHEDULE 5

B52.58

LIST OF REGULATIONS REVOKED

[Omitted.]

The Public Service Vehicles (Operators' Licences) Regulations 1995

(S.I. 1995 No. 2908)

ARRANGEMENT OF REGULATIONS

1. Citation and commencement   *[Omitted.]*

B53.02

2. Revocation   *[Omitted.]*

3. Interpretation

(1) In these Regulations, unless the context otherwise requires—

B53.03

"*the 1981 Act*" means the Public Passenger Vehicles Act 1981 [*q.v.*];

"*the 1985 Act*" means the Transport Act 1985;

"*designated sporting event*" has the same meaning as in the Sporting Events (Control of
Alcohol) Act 1985;

"*disc*" means an operator's disc issued under section 18 [*q.v.*];

"*fax*" means the making of a facsimile copy of a document by the transmission of
electronic signals;

"*holder*" in relation to a licence means the person to whom that licence was granted;

"*licence*" means a PSV operator's licence and "*special licence*" has the same meaning as in section 12(2) of the 1985 Act [*q.v.*];

"*local authority*" has the meaning given by section 14A(4);

"*Notices and Proceedings*" has the same meaning as in regulation 3 of the Public Service Vehicles (Traffic Commissioners: Publications and Inquiries) Regulations 1986 [*S.I. 1986 No. 1629*; *not reproduced in this work*];

"*traffic regulation conditions*" has the meaning given by section 7(1) of the 1985 Act; and

"*vehicle examiner*" means an examiner appointed under section 66A of the Road Traffic Act 1988 [*q.v.*].

(2) Unless the context otherwise requires, any reference in these Regulations to:

(a) a numbered section is a reference to the section bearing that number in the 1981 Act;

(b) a numbered regulation is a reference to the regulation bearing that number in these Regulations;

(c) a numbered paragraph is a reference to the paragraph bearing that number in the regulation in which the reference appears.

B53.04   **4. Inspection of applications**   *[Omitted.]*

5. Objections to applications for licences   *[Omitted.]*

6. Determination of applications   *[Omitted.]*

7. Description of conditions attached to licences   *[Omitted.]*

8, 9. Requirements of notice and consideration of representations
[Omitted.]

10. Forms of and particulars to be contained on discs

B53.05   (1) There shall be specified on every disc the date on which it comes into force and the date on which it expires.

(2) The disc shall clearly indicate (by colour or other means)—

(a) whether a vehicle is being used under a standard licence or under a restricted licence; and

(b) in the case of a vehicle being used under a standard licence, whether the licence covers both international and national transport operations or national transport operations only.

11. The coming into force and expiry of discs

B53.06   (1) A disc shall not come into force more than a month after it is issued.

(2) A disc shall expire—

(a) if paragraph (3) applies to the disc, at the end of the 1 year period of the relevant licence in which the disc comes into force;

(b) in any other case, at the end of the 5 year period of the relevant licence in which the disc comes into force.

(3) This paragraph applies—

(a) to a disc which comes into force during the first 5 year period of the relevant licence if and only if a notice of election is in force immediately before the licence is granted; and

(b) to a disc which comes into force during any other 5 year period of the relevant licence if and only if a notice of election is in force immediately before the beginning of the period.

(4) For the purposes of this regulation a notice of election, in relation to a licence, is a notice in which the holder states (or stated when he was applying for the licence) that he wishes to pay the fee for the issue of any disc connected with the licence on an annual basis.

(5) A notice of election shall come into force on the day on which the holder serves it on the traffic commissioner and shall remain in force until revoked in accordance with paragraph (6).

(6) The holder of a licence may not earlier than 42 days before the end of a 5 year period of the relevant licence serve a notice on the traffic commissioner revoking a notice of election.

(7) Paragraph (3) of regulation 5 shall apply to the service of a notice under this regulation as it applies to service of a notice under that paragraph.

(8) For the purposes of this regulation, "*relevant licence*", in relation to a disc, means the licence in respect of which the disc is issued.

(9) For the purposes of this regulation, the 1 year periods of a licence, are—

(a) the period of 1 year beginning with the first day of the month in which the relevant licence comes into force; and

(b) each consecutive period of 1 year.

(10) For the purposes of this regulation, the 5 year periods of a licence, are—

(a) the period of 5 years beginning with the first day of the month in which the relevant licence comes into force; and

(b) each consecutive period of 5 years.

(11) Notwithstanding anything in the foregoing provisions of this regulation, paragraph (2)(a) shall not apply to a disc unless at the time the disc is issued a provision in regulations under the 1981 Act is in force which prescribes different fees for the issue of a disc according to whether paragraph (3) does or does not apply.

12. Manner in which discs are to be fixed and exhibited

The prescribed manner in which a disc is to be fixed and exhibited for the purposes of   **B53.07**
section 18 is by so fixing it to the vehicle that it—

(a) is adjacent to the licence issued under the Vehicle Excise and Registration Act 1994 [*q.v.*];

(b) does not interfere unduly with the driver's view; and

(c) can easily be read in daylight from the outside of the vehicle.

13. Issue of a duplicate licence or disc and prohibition on unauthorised alteration of a disc

(1) If a licence or disc has been lost or destroyed, the holder shall forthwith notify the   **B53.08**
traffic commissioner who granted the licence or disc so that he may provide a duplicate, marked as such.

(2) If a licence or disc has been notified as lost or destroyed in accordance with paragraph

(1) and is subsequently recovered by the holder, then the holder shall use the duplicate licence or disc and return the original to the traffic commissioner.

(3) At no time shall any person except the traffic commissioner, or a person authorised to do so on his behalf, write on or otherwise alter a disc, but in the event that a disc becomes illegible by ordinary wear and tear the holder shall forthwith return the illegible disc so that the traffic commissioner may provide a duplicate, marked as such.

14. Compulsory return of licences and discs

B53.09   (1) In the event of the suspension, surrender or other termination—

    (a) at any time of a continuous licence; or

    (b) prior to the date of expiry specified in a term licence,

the holder shall return that licence to the traffic commissioner by whom it was granted for retention during the time of the suspension, or for cancellation, as the case may be, and shall at the same time return to that commissioner any discs which have been issued in relation to the licence.

(2) On the removal of a suspension referred to in paragraph (1) the commissioner shall return the licence together with any discs which were issued in relation to the licence.

(3) In the event of the traffic commissioner deciding—

    (a) to attach an additional condition or any traffic regulation conditions to a licence;

    (b) to alter or remove a condition or any traffic regulation conditions attached to a licence; or

    (c) to vary or remove any undertaking in a licence,

the holder shall return that licence to the traffic commissioner for him to make the appropriate addition, alteration, variation or removal before returning it to the holder.

(4) In the event of the traffic commissioner deciding to vary one or more conditions attached to a licence under section 16(1), so reducing the maximum number of vehicles which may be used under the licence below the number of discs which have been issued to the holder, the holder shall return to that commissioner such number of discs as will leave the holder with only the same number of discs as is equal to the reduced maximum number of vehicles.

(5) In the event of a disc ceasing to have effect prior to the date of expiry, the holder shall return the disc to the traffic commissioner who issued it.

(6) For the purposes of this regulation, a requirement to return a licence or disc to a traffic commissioner is a requirement for it to be—

    (a) delivered to the office of his traffic area; or

    (b) sent to the traffic commissioner at the office of his traffic area by recorded delivery service,

within the period of 14 days beginning with the date on which the holder receives the notice from the traffic commissioner requiring it to be returned.

(7) For the purposes of this regulation, if a licence or disc is sent by recorded delivery service in accordance with paragraph (6), it shall be regarded as having been returned at the date that it is delivered at the appropriate office in the traffic area.

(8) In this regulation—

"*term licence*" means a licence which by virtue of the Deregulation and Contracting Out (Commencement) (No. 4) Order 1995 [*S.I. 1995 No. 2835, q.v.*], has an expiry date; and

"*continuous licence*" means a licence that is not a term licence.

15. Voluntary return of discs   *[Omitted.]*   **B53.10**

16. Production of licences and discs for examination

(1) Unless its loss or destruction has been previously notified to the traffic comm-   **B53.11**
issioner in accordance with regulation 13(1) or (2), a licence or a disc shall be produced by
the holder for examination if he is so required by any police constable, vehicle examiner
or by any person authorised by the traffic commissioner for any traffic area to examine
the licence or disc, and any such requirement shall be complied with in not more than 14
days.

(2) Any such requirement as is mentioned in paragraph (1) may be complied with by the
holder producing the licence or disc within the traffic area of the traffic commissioner by
whom the licence was granted at the operating centre or principal place of business of the
holder.

17. Notification of decisions   *[Omitted.]*   **B53.12**

18. Review of decisions   *[Omitted.]*

19. Notices generally   *[Omitted.]*

20. Notification of change of address

If during the currency of a licence the address for correspondence as notified in the   **B53.13**
licence holder's application or as subsequently notified under this regulation ceases to be an
effective address for correspondence the holder shall within 28 days from the date of such
event notify the traffic commissioner by whom the licence was granted of an effective
address for correspondence.

21. Relevant convictions

The convictions specified in the Schedule hereto are hereby prescribed as relevant   **B53.14**
convictions for the purposes of the 1981 Act.

22. Operators under hiring arrangements

The person who is to be regarded as the operator of a vehicle which is made available   **B53.15**
by one holder of a licence to another under a hiring arrangement is the holder from whom
the vehicle is hired in a case where—

   (a) the holder to whom the vehicle is hired is not, under the hiring arrangement,
      entitled to keep the vehicle in his possession for a total period of more than 14
      days;

   (b) not less than 14 days have elapsed between the finish of any previous period
      (of whatever duration) in which the hirer to whom the vehicle is hired was entitled
      to the use of the vehicle under a hiring arrangement with the holder from whom
      the vehicle is hired and the start of the period mentioned in sub-paragraph (a)
      above;

   (c) at all times when the vehicle is being used for carrying passengers for hire or
      reward during the period mentioned in sub-paragraph (a) above there is affixed to
      the vehicle a disc which has been issued to the holder from whom the vehicle is
      hired;

   (d) the vehicle, if made available to the holder of a restricted licence, is not adapted to
      carry more than sixteen passengers; and

(e) the vehicle is not a licensed taxi made available to or by the holder of a special licence.

23. Termination of licences held by companies

B53.16   In a case where a licence is held by a company the events relating to the holder on the occurrence of which the licence is to terminate are as follows—

(a) the making of a winding-up order; and

(b) the passing of a resolution for voluntary winding-up.

24. Computation of time

B53.17   Any day which is a bank holiday under the Banking and Financial Dealings Act 1971 shall be excluded from the computation of any period of a specified number of days prescribed in these Regulations.

B53.18   *[As to bank holidays under the Banking and Financial Dealings Act 1971, see the note to the Road Vehicles (Construction and Use) Regulations 1986 (S.I. 1986 No. 1078), Sched. 12, para.1 above.]*

25. Post Office

B53.19   Section 16(1A) (limit on number of vehicles to be used under a restricted licence) shall not apply in respect of a licence held at any time by the Post Office.

26. Savings

B53.20   Notwithstanding the revocation of the Public Service Vehicles (Operators' Licences) Regulations 1986 by these Regulations, regulation 12(3) of those Regulations (which require a licence to be returned if its period of validity is curtailed) shall continue to have effect in relation to a licence if its period of validity is curtailed before 1st January 1996.

Regulation 21   SCHEDULE

RELEVANT CONVICTIONS PRESCRIBED BY REGULATION 21

B53.21   **1.** A conviction of any of the offences specified in paragraph 2 below—

(a) of the holder of a licence, or the applicant for a licence;

(b) where the holder of a licence, or the applicant for a licence, is a partnership, of a partner in that partnership;

(c) of any transport manager whom the holder of a licence employs or proposes to employ, and of any transport manager whom an applicant for a licence employs or proposes to employ; and

(d) of any person appointed or otherwise engaged as an officer, employee or agent of the holder of, or of an applicant for, a licence in relation to any business which such holder or applicant carries on, or proposes to carry on.

B53.22   **2.** The offences referred to in paragraph 1 above are offences in relation to a public service vehicle or the operation thereof—

(a) under or by virtue of the 1981 Act;

(b) under sections 5(1), 8(1), 11, 13, 16(1), 17(4) and 18(3) of the Road Traffic Regulation Act 1984 [*q.v.*];

(c) under section 1(2) of the Sporting Events (Control of Alcohol, etc.) Act 1985;

(d) under or by virtue of Parts I and II and section 101 of the 1985 Act;

(e) under or by virtue of Parts I, II, III, IV and VI and sections 164(6) and (9), 165(3) and (6), 168, 170(7), 171(2), 172(3) and (4), 173(1), 174(1) and (2) and (5) in Part VII of the Road Traffic Act 1988;

(f) under section 91 of the Road Traffic Offenders Act 1988;

(g) relating to—

    (i) the speed at which vehicles may be driven,

    (ii) drivers' hours or the keeping of drivers' records under or by virtue of Part VI of the Transport Act 1968 [*q.v.*],

    (iii) new bus grants under section 32 of, and Schedule 8 to, the Transport Act 1968, grants towards bus fuel duty under section 92 of the Finance Act 1965,

    (iv) a duty of excise imposed by or under the Vehicles (Excise) Act 1971 or the Vehicle Excise and Registration Act 1994, and

(h) under section 92 of the Licensing (Scotland) Act 1976 and section 70 of the Criminal Justice (Scotland) Act 1980;

or other offences under the law in force in any part of Great Britain which are serious offences as defined in paragraph 1(4) of Schedule 3 [*q.v.*] or road transport offences as defined in paragraph 1(5) of that Schedule.

[The Sporting Events (Control of Alcohol, etc.) Act 1985, s.1(2) (to which reference is made in paragraph 2(c)) prohibits specified persons from knowingly causing or permitting intoxicating liquor to be carried on a vehicle to which section 1 applies, e.g. a public service vehicle used to carry passengers to or from a designated sporting event.]   **B53.23**

The Deregulation (Parking Equipment) Order 1996

(S.I. 1996 No. 1553)

B54.01 **1. Citation, commencement and interpretation**

(1) *[Citation.]*

(2) *[Commencement.]*

(3) In this Order, *"the 1984 Act"* means the Road Traffic Regulation Act 1984.

2. Removal of requirement for parking equipment to be approved by the Secretary of State

B54.02 (1) Subject to article 3 below—

(a) the provisions of the 1984 Act mentioned in the first column of the Schedule to this Order *[not reproduced in this work]* are hereby repealed to the extent specified in the second column of that Part, and

(b) paragraphs 3(b), 4(c)(ii), 5 and 7 of the Schedule to the Parking Act 1989 (which are spent in consequence of the repeals mentioned in sub-paragraph (a) above) are hereby repealed.

(2) In Schedule 10 to the 1984 Act, in paragraph 13, for the words "subsections (1) to (4)" there shall be substituted the words "subsections (1) to (3)".

3. Supplementary provisions

B54.03 (1) Nothing in article 2 above shall affect the validity of any order having effect by virtue of the 1984 Act and made before this Order comes into force, but—

(a) any provision in such an order having effect by virtue of section 4(3), 7(3) or 35(1)(iii) or (3) of the 1984 Act shall apply to any apparatus or device which has not been approved by the Secretary of State to the extent (if any) that the provision would, apart from this paragraph, have applied to it had it been approved by him, and

(b) any provision in such an order having effect by virtue of section 35(3A), 46(2)(a), (b) or (c) or 51 of the 1984 Act shall apply to any apparatus or device which is of a type and design that has not been approved by the Secretary of State to the extent (if any) that the provision would, apart from this paragraph, have applied to it had apparatus or devices of that type and design been approved by him.

(2) Without prejudice to section 16 of the Interpretation Act 1978, the repeals made by this Order of sections 35A(4), 47(5), 52(2) and 115(2A) of the 1984 Act (presumptions relating to the approval of the Secretary of State) and to section 130(2)(a) of that Act (application to the Crown) shall not have effect in relation to proceedings for an offence committed before this Order comes into force.

THE SCHEDULE

Repeals

B54.04 *[The effect of the repeals listed in this Schedule, so far as material to this work, has been noted against the appropriate provisions of the Road Traffic Regulation Act 1984.]*

The Private Crossings (Signs and Barriers) Regulations 1996

(S.I. 1996 No. 1786)

ARRANGEMENT OF REGULATIONS

B55.01

PART VI

PART I

Preliminary

B55.02   **1. Citation and commencement**   *[Omitted.]*

2. Interpretation

B55.03   (1) In these Regulations, where the context so admits, the following expressions have the meanings hereby respectively assigned to them—

   "*crossing*" means a level crossing;

   "*crossing operator*" means an operator of a railway or tramway that is crossed in any place by a relevant road or a private path;

   "*relevant road*" means a private road that crosses, or a private road and a private path that cross, a railway or tramway;

   "*retroreflecting material*" means material which reflects a ray of light back towards the source of that light;

   "*sign*" includes a road marking and a light signal;

   "*the 1992 Act*" means the Transport and Works Act 1992 [*q.v.*];

   "*the 1994 Regulations*" means the Traffic Signs Regulations and General Directions 1994 [*S.I. 1994 No. 1519 (q.v.)*].

   (2) Except where otherwise provided, any reference in these Regulations to a numbered regulation or Schedule shall be construed as a reference to the regulation or Schedule bearing that number in these Regulations and any reference in these Regulations to a numbered diagram shall be construed as a reference to the diagram bearing that number in Schedule 1 to these Regulations.

PART II

General Provisions

3. Signs to be of the size, colour and type shown in diagrams

B55.04   Subject to the provisions of these Regulations, for the purposes of section 52 of the 1992 Act, a crossing operator may cause or permit the placement on or near the relevant road or private path of a sign of a size, colour and type described and shown—

(a) in a diagram in Schedule 1; or

(b) in a diagram in Schedule 3 to the 1994 Regulations; or

(c) in one of the diagrams numbered 601.1, 602, 953.1 and 953.2, 963.3, 966, 971, 1001, 1002.1, 1003, 1003.2, 1004, 1004.1, 1005, 1005.1, 1008, 1008.1, 1010, 1012.1, 1013.1, 1014, 1022, 1023, 1026, 1045, 3000.3, 3000.4, 3000.5, 3000.6, 3013, 3013.1, 3013.2, 3013.3, 3013.4, 3013.5 and 3014 in Schedules 2, 5, 6 and 8 to the 1994 Regulations.

PART III

Signs shown in Schedule 1

4. Colours of backs of signs

The back of any sign shown in a diagram in Schedule 1 and any post or other structure   **B55.05**
specially provided for mounting the sign shall be coloured black or grey.

5. Dimensions

(1) Any variation in a dimension specified in Schedule 1 shall be treated as permitted by   **B55.06**
these Regulations if the variation is not more than 5% more or less than the dimension
specified.

(2) In the diagrams in Schedule 1 the dimensions given are expressed in millimetres.

6. Permitted variants

(1) Where the circumstances so require the indication given by a sign shown in a   **B55.07**
diagram in Schedule 1 may be varied in the respect (if any) shown below the diagram relating to that sign.

(2) Where a sign in a diagram in Schedule 1 contains an indication as to the penalty
relating to a failure to obey the requirements on that sign, the indication of the penalty may
be varied when necessary to accord with changes in the legislation governing the nature
and level of penalty.

7. Illumination of signs

(1) Subject to paragraphs (2) and (3) of this regulation all parts other than the back of   **B55.08**
every sign shown in a diagram in Schedule 1 shall be illuminated by means of
retroreflecting material.

(2) No retroreflecting material shall be applied to—

(a) any part of a sign coloured black; or

(b) the red and green lights in the signs shown in diagrams 107 and 108 and prescribed in regulation 8.

(3) Retroreflecting material need not be applied to a sign at a crossing which is not used
by motor vehicles.

8. Miniature stop lights

(1) The signs shown in diagrams 107 and 108 shall contain red and green lamps which   **B55.09**
are internally illuminated by a steady light in such a manner that—

    (a) when one light is illuminated the other is not illuminated;

    (b) the green lamp is and remains illuminated for so long as no railway or tramway vehicle is approaching the vicinity of the crossing from either direction; and

    (c) the red lamp is and remains illuminated for so long as the green lamp is not illuminated.

(2) The lenses of the lamps shall be—

    (a) circular and not less than 60 millimetres in diameter; or

    (b) rectangular with each side measuring not less than 60 millimetres;

and the distance between the edges of the lenses of the green lamp and the red lamp shall be not less than 40 millimetres.

(3) The information, warnings, requirements and prohibitions conveyed by the lamps described in paragraphs (1) and (2) shall be as follows—

    (a) the red lamp when illuminated shall convey the warning that a railway or tramway vehicle is approaching the vicinity of the crossing and the prohibition that persons must not proceed across the crossing;

    (b) the green lamp when illuminated shall convey the information that no railway or tramway vehicle is approaching the vicinity of the crossing and persons may proceed across the crossing;

    (c) if neither the red nor green lamp is illuminated persons should either telephone the crossing operator or proceed across the crossing with caution after having ascertained that no railway or tramway vehicle is approaching the vicinity of the crossing in accordance with the instructions shown on the sign.

PART IV

SIGNS SHOWN IN THE 1994 REGULATIONS

9. Proportions and significance, etc., of signs

B55.10   The provisions made by the 1994 Regulations in relation to the proportions, illumination and significance of, and requirements conveyed by, a sign shall have effect where the sign is placed under the authority of these Regulations, as if the relevant road or private path on or near to which it is placed were a road within the meaning of the Road Traffic Regulation Act 1984 [*q.v.*].

PART V

BARRIERS

10. Barriers to be of the character described in Schedule 2 or Schedule 3

B55.11   For the purposes of section 52 of the 1992 Act, where a railway or tramway is crossed in any place by a relevant road, the operator of that railway or tramway may cause or permit a barrier to be placed on or near the relevant road near the crossing if it is, in the case of a gate, of the character described in Schedule 2, or, in the case of any other form of barrier, of the character described in Schedule 3.

PART VI

SIGNS RELATING TO TELEPHONES

11. Placement of signs relating to telephones

The authority which these Regulations give for the placement of signs relating to tel-   **B55.12**
ephones at a crossing shall only apply where telephones are, or are to be, provided on both
sides of the crossing and connected direct to the crossing operator.

SCHEDULE 1   Regulation 3

CROSSING SIGNS

Editorial note. The diagrams representing the actual traffic signs are not reproduced in this   **B55.13**
work, but the signs in Schedule 1 are described below by means of (in the main) the legends
accompanying the signs. The dimensions of the components of the various signs are
specified in marks accompanying the diagrams (not reproduced) and variations of wording
(where permissible) are referred to in notes accompanying the diagrams (not reproduced).

101   warning signs for non-vehicular crossing ("Stop   Look   Listen   Beware of
       trains") (black lettering on white background with red border) (permitted
       variant: "tram" for "trains")

102   instructions for use at vehicular crossing without telephone (top panel: "Stop
       Look   Listen   Notify crossing operator before crossing with a vehicle which
       is unusually long, wide, low, heavy or slow moving"; lower panel includes
       advice on crossing and maximum penalty for offence) (top panel, white let-
       tering on red background; lower panel, black lettering on white background)
       (permitted variant: telephone number of crossing operator may be added)

103   instructions for use at vehicular crossing with telephone (top panel: "Stop
       Always telephone before crossing with vehicles or animals to find out if there
       is time to cross.   Tell the crossing operator if the vehicle is large or slow
       moving"; lower panel includes advice on crossing and maximum penalty for
       offence) (top panel, white lettering on red background; lower panel, black let-
       tering on white background)

104   operating instructions for barrier ("Hold down to lower   Maximum penalty
       for not closing barriers £1000   Pump to raise both barriers   In the event of
       failure phone crossing operator") (black lettering and border on white back-
       ground)

105   indication of penalty for failure to shut gate at vehicular crossing (black let-
       tering and border on white background)

106   target for crossing gate (circle on red background)

107   sign for use with miniature stop lights at crossing with telephone ("Red [cir-
       cular lamp on black square] STOP   Green [circular lamp on black square]
       Clear   IF NO LIGHT—PHONE CROSSING OPERATOR") (black lettering and
       border on white background) (permitted variant: lenses of lamps may be rec-
       tangular instead of circular)

108   sign for use with miniature stop lights at crossing without telephone ("Red
       [circular lamp on black square] STOP   Green [circular lamp on black
       square] Clear   IF NO LIGHT—PROCEED WITH CAUTION") (black lettering and
       border on white background) (permitted variant: lenses of lamps may be rec-
       tangular instead of circular)

109   instructions for use at crossing with miniature stop lights and user-operated
       gates (black lettering and border on white background)

110 instructions for use at crossing with miniature stop lights and user-operated barriers (black lettering and border on white background)

111 reminder to close gates at crossing with user-operated gates (black lettering and border on white background)

112 reminder to lower barriers at crossing with user-operated barriers (black lettering and border on white background)

113 special sign for use at vehicular crossing where railway or tramway is equipped with overhead electric wire and road approaches are on a gradient (black lettering, symbols and border with white background) (permitted variant: telephone number of operator may be added)

114 instructions to non-vehicular traffic at crossing with miniature stop lights (black lettering and border on white background)

115 instructions to shut and fasten gate at crossing with gates (black lettering and border on white background)

116 danger sign for use at crossing where railway or tramway is equipped with overhead electric wires (word "DANGER" and flash symbol in red; other lettering in black; white background with no border)

117 danger sign for use at crossing where track has electric live rail or rails (word "DANGER" and flash symbol in red; other lettering in black; white background with no border)

118 supplementary sign for use with diagram 103 or diagram 107 where crossing used for animal traffic (black lettering on white background with red border)

119 instructions to horse riders to dismount at crossing where railway or tramway is equipped with overhead electric wires

Regulation 10 **SCHEDULE 2**

B55.14

GATES

[Omitted.]

Regulation 10 **SCHEDULE 3**

B55.15

BARRIERS OTHER THAN GATES

[Omitted.]

The Goods Vehicles (Licensing of Operators) (Temporary Use in Great Britain) Regulations 1996

(S.I. 1996 No. 2186)

ARRANGEMENT OF REGULATIONS

Regulation

SCHEDULES

Schedule

B56.02   **1. Citation and commencement**   *[Omitted.]*

2. Revocation   *[Omitted.]*

3. Interpretation

B56.03   (1) In these Regulations—

"*the Act*" means the Goods Vehicles (Licensing of Operators) Act 1995 [*q.v.*];

"*Community cabotage authorisation*" means an authorisation granted pursuant to Council Regulation (EEC) No. 3118/93 of 25th October 1993 laying down conditions under which non-resident carriers may operate national road haulage services within a Member State, as amended by Council Regulation (EC) No. 3315/94 [*q.v.*], and Commission Regulation (EC) No. 792/94 [*q.v.*];

"*Council Regulation No. 881/92*" means Council Regulation (EEC) No. 881/92 of 26th March 1992 on access to the market in the carriage of goods by road within the Community to or from the territory of a Member State or passing across the territory of one or more Member States [*q.v.*];

"*foreign goods vehicle*" means a goods vehicle—

(a) which is operated by a person who is not established in the United Kingdom and has been brought temporarily into Great Britain;

(b) which is not being used for international carriage by a haulier who is established in a Member State other than the United Kingdom;

(c) which is engaged in carrying goods by road on a journey some part of which has taken place, or will take place, outside the United Kingdom; and

(d) which, except in the case of use under a Community cabotage authorisation, is not used at any time during the said journey for the carriage of goods loaded at one place in the United Kingdom and delivered at another place in the United Kingdom;

"*international carriage*" has the meaning which it bears in Council Regulation No. 881/92;

"*loading*" includes attaching to a drawing vehicle a trailer which has been loaded with goods before it is so attached, and "*loaded*" shall be construed accordingly;

"*Northern Ireland goods vehicle*" means a goods vehicle of which the operating centre is in Northern Ireland and—

(a) which has been brought temporarily into Great Britain;

(b) which is not being used for international carriage by a haulier who is established in Northern Ireland and is not established in Great Britain;

(c) which is engaged in carrying goods by road on a journey some part of which has taken place, or will take place, outside Great Britain; and

(d) which—
  (i) in the case of a motor vehicle, is registered in Northern Ireland or Great Britain; or
  (ii) in the case of a trailer, is drawn in Great Britain only by a motor vehicle which is a Northern Ireland goods vehicle; and

"*relief vehicle*" means a vehicle used for transporting goods which is sent to replace a vehicle which has broken down, and which continues the haul under cover of the licence, permit, or other document issued for the vehicle which has broken down.

(2) For the purposes of these Regulations—

(a) the permissible laden weight and the permissible pay load of a vehicle shall be determined by reference to the law of the country where the vehicle is registered or, in the case of a trailer which is not registered, by reference to the law of the country where the drawing vehicle is registered; and

(b) a combination of a motor vehicle drawing a trailer shall be treated, for the purpose of determining the permissible laden weight or the permissible pay load, as the case may be, as a single vehicle.

(3) In these Regulations, unless the context otherwise requires, a reference to a numbered regulation or Schedule is a reference to the regulation or Schedule bearing that number in these Regulations.

4. Exemptions for foreign vehicles used for certain purposes

Notwithstanding anything in regulations 8 to 30, section 2(1) of the Act (Users of certain goods vehicles to hold operators' licences) shall not apply to the use in Great Britain of a foreign goods vehicle for the carriage of any goods specified in paragraph 1, 2, 4, 5, 6, 7 or 8 of Schedule 2.   **B56.04**

5. Exemptions for Northern Ireland or foreign goods vehicles used for the carriage of goods between Member States of the European Community

Notwithstanding anything in regulations 8 to 30, section 2(1) of the Act shall not apply to the use in Great Britain of a Northern Ireland or foreign goods vehicle for the carriage of goods between Member States of the European Community—   **B56.05**

(a) where the vehicle is—
  (i) loaded or unloaded at a place not more than 25 kilometres from the coast of Great Britain and unloaded or loaded (as the case may be) at a place not more than 25 kilometres from the coast of another Member State, and the distance between the place where the goods are loaded on to the vehicle and the place where they are off-loaded from the vehicle, when measured in a straight line (but disregarding so much of that distance as lies over the sea in a case where the vehicle is carried on sea transport specially constructed and equipped for the carriage of commercial vehicles and operated as a regular service) does not exceed 100 kilometres; or
  (ii) a motor vehicle, or trailer drawn by a foreign goods vehicle, having a permissible laden weight not exceeding 6 metric tons or a permissible pay load not exceeding 3.5 metric tons; or
  (iii) a relief vehicle; or

(b) where the goods so carried are those specified in paragraphs 9, 16, 17, 18, 20, 21, 26 or 28 of Schedule 2; or

(c) where the vehicle is being used on a journey for combined transport as defined in Article 1 of Council Directive (EEC) No. 92/106 on the establishment of common rules for certain types of combined transport of goods between Member States [*O.J.*

No. L368, December 17, 1992, p. 38], and there is carried on the vehicle, or, in the case of a trailer, on the vehicle drawing it, a document which satisfies the requirements of Article 3 of that Directive, or a document issued by the competent authority of the Member State where the vehicle, or, in the case of a trailer, the vehicle drawing it, is registered certifying that the vehicle is being used on such a journey; or

(d) where the goods are being carried for or in connection with any trade or business carried on by the undertaking carrying them and each of the following conditions are fulfilled:—

    (i) the goods are the property of the undertaking carrying them or have been sold, bought, let out on hire or hired, produced, extracted, processed or repaired by that undertaking;

    (ii) the purpose of the journey is to carry the goods to or from the undertaking carrying them or to move them either inside that undertaking, or outside for that undertaking's own requirements;

    (iii) the vehicle used for such carriage is being driven by an employee of the undertaking;

    (iv) except in the case of a replacement vehicle during a short breakdown of the vehicle normally used, the vehicle used for carrying the goods is owned by the undertaking carrying them or has been bought by it on deferred terms or hired in accordance with the conditions on the use of vehicles hired without drivers for the carriage of goods by road contained in Council Directive (EEC) No. 84/647 [*O.J. No. L335, December 22, 1984, p. 72*].

B56.06   *[The term "combined transport" is defined for the purposes of Directive 92/106/EEC, by ibid., art.1, as—*

the transport of goods between Member States where the lorry, trailer, semi-trailer, with or without tractor unit, swap body or container of 20 feet or more uses the road on the initial or final leg of the journey and, on the other leg, rail or inland waterway or maritime services where this section exceeds 100 km as the crow flies and make the initial or final road transport leg of the journey;

—between the point where the goods are loaded and the nearest suitable rail loading station for the initial leg, and between the nearest suitable rail unloading station and the point where the goods are unloaded for the final leg, or;

—within a radius not exceeding 150 km as the crow flies from the inland waterway port or seaport of loading or unloading.*]*

6. Exemption for Northern Ireland or foreign goods vehicles with international licences

B56.07   Notwithstanding anything in regulations 8 to 30, section 2(1) of the Act shall not apply to the use in Great Britain of a Northern Ireland or foreign goods vehicle for the carriage of goods for hire or reward if the vehicle is being used by virtue of a licence issued pursuant to the scheme adopted by Resolution of the Council of Ministers of Transport on 14th June 1973 [*CM(73)5 Final, ECMT 20th Annual Report and Resolutions of the Council of Ministers (1973), pp. 64, 65, ISBN 92–821*] and the licence is carried on the vehicle or, if the vehicle is a trailer, on the motor vehicle by which it is drawn.

7. Exemption for foreign goods vehicles with Community cabotage authorisations and for Northern Ireland goods vehicles carrying goods in Great Britain or between Northern Ireland and Great Britain

B56.08   (1) Notwithstanding anything in regulations 8 to 30, section 2(1) of the Act shall not apply to the use in Great Britain of a foreign goods vehicle permitted to carry out cabotage in the United Kingdom under Council Regulation (EEC) No. 3118/93 laying down conditions under which non-resident carriers may operate national road haulage services within a member State [*q.v.*].

(2) Section 2(1) of the Act shall not apply to the use in Great Britain of a Northern Ireland goods vehicle for the carriage of goods between places of loading or unloading in Great Britain or between one such place in Northern Ireland and another such place in Great Britain.

8. Exemption for Albanian goods vehicles

(1) In this regulation "*Albanian goods vehicle*" means a foreign goods vehicle which is owned or operated by a person who is authorised under the law of the Republic of Albania to engage in the international carriage of goods by road for hire or reward or on his own account and which, in the case of a motor vehicle, is registered in the Republic of Albania. **B56.09**

(2) Section 2(1) of the Act shall not apply to the use in Great Britain of an Albanian goods vehicle for the carriage of any goods.

9. Exemptions and modifications for Austrian goods vehicles

(1) In this regulation "*Austrian goods vehicle*" means a foreign goods vehicle— **B56.10**
  (a) which, in the case of a motor vehicle, is owned by or operated by or on behalf of a person—
    (i) who is authorised under Austrian law to use that vehicle for the carriage of goods in the Republic of Austria; or
    (ii) who, if Austrian law permits him so to use that vehicle without being so authorised, uses that vehicle primarily or substantially for that purpose in that country; and
  (b) which, in the case of a trailer, is drawn in Great Britain only by a motor vehicle which is an Austrian goods vehicle.

(2) Section 2(1) of the Act shall not apply to the use in Great Britain of an Austrian goods vehicle for the carriage of any goods specified in paragraph 1, 2, 4, 5, 6, 7, 8, 9, 10, 15, 17, 18, 19, 20, 21, 24, 26 or 27 of Schedule 2.

(3) Section 2(1) of the Act shall not apply to the use in Great Britain of an Austrian goods vehicle which is a vehicle specified in Schedule 3.

(4) In relation to an Austrian goods vehicle used for the carriage of any goods, for or in connection with any trade or business carried on by the user of the vehicle, in a case to which neither of the preceding exemptions applies, section 2(1) of the Act shall have effect as set out in Schedule 4.

(5) In relation to an Austrian goods vehicle used for the carriage of goods in a case to which neither of the preceding exemptions nor the preceding modification apply, section 2(1) of the Act shall have effect as set out in Schedule 5.

10. Exemption for Bulgarian goods vehicles

(1) In this regulation "*Bulgarian goods vehicle*" means a foreign goods vehicle— **B56.11**
  (a) which, in the case of a motor vehicle, is registered in the Republic of Bulgaria; and
  (b) which, in the case of a trailer, is drawn in Great Britain only by a motor vehicle which is a Bulgarian goods vehicle.

(2) Section 2(1) of the Act shall not apply to the use in Great Britain of a Bulgarian goods vehicle for the carriage of any goods.

11. Exemption for Channel Islands goods vehicles

B56.12

(1) In this regulation "*Channel Islands goods vehicle*" means a foreign goods vehicle—

(a) which, in the case of a motor vehicle, is registered in the Channel Islands; and

(b) which, in the case of a trailer, is drawn in Great Britain only by a motor vehicle which is a Channel Islands goods vehicle.

(2) Section 2(1) of the Act shall not apply to the use in Great Britain of a Channel Islands goods vehicle for the carriage of any goods.

12. Exemptions and modifications for Cypriot goods vehicles

B56.13

(1) In this regulation "*Cypriot goods vehicle*" means a foreign goods vehicle which is owned by, or operated by or on behalf of, a person who is authorised under the law of the Republic of Cyprus to use the vehicle in that country for the international carriage of goods, and which, in the case of a motor vehicle, is registered in the Republic of Cyprus.

(2) Section 2(1) of the Act shall not apply to the use in Great Britain of a Cypriot goods vehicle for the carriage of any goods specified in paragraph 1, 2, 3, 5, 9, 10, 16, 22, 23 or 24 of Schedule 2.

(3) Section 2(1) of the Act shall not apply to the use in Great Britain of a Cypriot goods vehicle specified in Schedule 3.

(4) Section 2(1) of the Act shall not apply to the use in Great Britain of a Cypriot goods vehicle which is a vehicle used for the recovery of a damaged vehicle.

(5) In relation to a Cypriot goods vehicle used for the carriage of goods, for or in connection with any trade or business carried on by the user of the vehicle, in a case to which none of the preceding exemptions apply, section 2(1) of the Act shall have effect as if for the words from "(a) hire or reward" to the end of that subsection there were substituted the words "for or in connection with any trade or business carried on by him unless there is carried on the vehicle or, if that vehicle is a trailer, on the motor vehicle by which it is drawn a document containing the following particulars:—

(a) the place at which and the date on which the document was made out;

(b) the name and address of the carrier and a description of the nature of his business;

(c) if the goods carried, or to be carried, or any of them, are to be collected from or delivered to, any person other than the carrier, the name and address of that person and a description of the nature of his business;

(d) the place or places at which the vehicle is to be loaded or unloaded;

(e) the nature and gross weight, or other indication of quantity, of the goods;

(f) the carrying capacity of the vehicle by weight;

(g) the index mark and registration number of the vehicle, or if the vehicle does not carry an index mark or any registration number, the chassis number of the vehicle;

(h) the place of entry of the vehicle into, or of exit from, the United Kingdom;

(i) the signature of the carrier or his authorised agent.".

(6) In relation to a Cypriot goods vehicle used for the carriage of goods in a case to which none of the preceding exemptions nor the preceding modification apply, section 2(1) of the Act shall have effect as set out in Schedule 5.

13. Exemption for Czech goods vehicles

(1) In this regulation "*Czech goods vehicle*" means a foreign goods vehicle—   **B56.14**

   (a) which, in the case of a motor vehicle, is registered in the Czech Republic; and

   (b) which, in the case of a trailer, is drawn in Great Britain only by a motor vehicle which is a Czech goods vehicle.

(2) Section 2(1) of the Act shall not apply to the use in Great Britain of a Czech goods vehicle for the carriage of any goods.

14. Exemption for Faroese goods vehicles

(1) In this regulation "*Faroese goods vehicle*" means a foreign goods vehicle—   **B56.15**

   (a) which, in the case of a motor vehicle, is registered in the Faroe Islands; and

   (b) which, in the case of a trailer, is drawn in Great Britain only by a motor vehicle which is a Faroese goods vehicle.

(2) Section 2(1) of the Act shall not apply to the use in Great Britain of a Faroese goods vehicle for the carriage of any goods.

15. Exemptions and modifications for Estonian goods vehicles

(1) In this regulation—   **B56.16**

"*Estonian goods vehicle*" means a foreign goods vehicle—

   (a) which, in the case of a motor vehicle, is registered in the Republic of Estonia; and

   (b) which, in the case of a trailer, is owned by or operated by or on behalf of a person who under Estonian law is authorised to use that vehicle for the carriage of goods in the Republic of Estonia.

"*relevant date*" means the date on which the Agreement between the Government of the United Kingdom of Great Britain and Northern Ireland and the Republic of Estonia on international road transport signed on 16th August 1995 [*Cm. 3105, 17 W.R.T.L.B. [149]*] comes into force.

(2) On and after the relevant date, section 2(1) of the Act shall not apply to the use in Great Britain of an Estonian goods vehicle for the carriage of any goods specified in paragraphs 4, 5, 9, 18, 20, 21, 22, 23 or 24 of Schedule 2 and in such a case these provisions shall have effect as if the words "or broken-down" were added after "damaged" in paragraph 5.

(3) Section 2(1) of the Act shall not apply to the use in Great Britain of an Estonian goods vehicle specified in paragraph 1 of Schedule 3.

(4) In relation to an Estonian goods vehicle being used for the carriage of goods in a case to which the preceding exemptions do not apply, section 2(1) of the Act shall have effect as set out in Schedule 5.

16. Exemption for Hungarian goods vehicles

(1) In this regulation "*Hungarian goods vehicle*" means a foreign goods vehicle—   **B56.17**

   (a) which, in the case of a motor vehicle, is registered in the Republic of Hungary; and

   (b) which, in the case of a trailer, is drawn in Great Britain only by a motor vehicle which is a Hungarian goods vehicle.

(2) Section 2(1) of the Act shall not apply to the use in Great Britain of a Hungarian goods vehicle for the carriage of any goods.

17. Exemption for Jordanian goods vehicles

B56.18 (1) In this regulation "*Jordanian goods vehicle*" means a foreign goods vehicle which is owned or operated by a person who is authorised under the law of the Hashemite Kingdom of Jordan to engage in the international carriage of goods by road for hire or reward or on his own account and which, in the case of a motor vehicle, is registered in the Hashemite Kingdom of Jordan.

(2) Section 2(1) of the Act shall not apply to the use in Great Britain of a Jordanian goods vehicle for the carriage of any goods.

18. Exemption for Latvian goods vehicles

B56.19 (1) In this regulation—

"*Latvian goods vehicle*" means a foreign goods vehicle which is owned or operated by a person who is authorised under the law of the Republic of Latvia to engage in the international carriage of goods by road for hire or reward or on his own account and which, in the case of a motor vehicle, is registered in the Republic of Latvia; and

"*relevant date*" means the date on which the Agreement between the Government of the United Kingdom of Great Britain and Northern Ireland and the Government of the Republic of Latvia on international road transport signed on 6th December 1993 [*Cm. 2526*] comes into force.

(2) On and after the relevant date, section 2(1) of the Act shall not apply to the use in Great Britain of a Latvian goods vehicle for the carriage of any goods.

19. Exemption for Lithuanian goods vehicles

B56.20 (1) In this regulation—

"*Lithuanian goods vehicle*" means a foreign goods vehicle which is owned or operated by a person who is authorised under the law of the Republic of Lithuania to engage in the international carriage of goods by road for hire or reward or on his own account and which, in the case of a motor vehicle, is registered in the Republic of Lithuania; and

"*relevant date*" means the date on which the Agreement between the Government of the United Kingdom of Great Britain and Northern Ireland and the Government of the Republic of Lithuania on international road transport signed on 2nd November 1994 [*Cm. 2999, 17 W.R.T.L.B. [99]*] comes into force.

(2) On and after the relevant date, section 2(1) of the Act shall not apply to the use in Great Britain of a Lithuanian goods vehicle for the carriage of any goods.

20. Exemption for Manx goods vehicles

B56.21 (1) In this regulation "*Manx goods vehicle*" means a foreign goods vehicle—

    (a) which, in the case of a motor vehicle, is registered in the Isle of Man; and

    (b) which, in the case of a trailer, is drawn in Great Britain only by a motor vehicle which is a Manx goods vehicle.

(2) Section 2(1) of the Act shall not apply to the use in Great Britain of a Manx goods vehicle for the carriage of any goods.

21. Exemption and modification for Moroccan goods vehicles

B56.22 (1) In this regulation—

"*Moroccan goods vehicle*" means a foreign goods vehicle which is owned or operated by a person who is authorised under the law of the Kingdom of Morocco to engage in the international carriage of goods by road for hire or reward or on his own account and which, in the case of a motor vehicle, is registered in the Kingdom of Morocco; and

"relevant date" means the date on which the Agreement between the Government of the United Kingdom of Great Britain and Northern Ireland and the Government of the Kingdom of Morocco on international road transport signed on 15th April 1994 [*Cm. 2703, replaced by Cm. 3480; see 17 W.R.T.L.B. [307]*] comes into force.

(2) On and after the relevant date, section 2(1) of the Act shall not apply to the use in Great Britain of a Moroccan goods vehicle for the carriage of any goods specified in paragraph 2, 9, or 31 of Schedule 2.

(3) In relation to a Moroccan goods vehicle used for the carriage of goods in a case to which the preceding exemption applies, section 2(1) of the Act shall have effect as set out in Schedule 5.

[The agreement with Morocco entered into force on April 12, 2000 (see 19 W.R.T.L.B. [183]) and is supplemented by an administrative memorandum (see ibid.).]   **B56.23**

22. Exemption and modification for Northern Ireland goods vehicles

(1) Section 2(1) of the Act shall not apply to the use of a Northern Ireland goods vehicle for the carriage of goods for hire or reward where there is in force in relation to the use of that vehicle in Northern Ireland or, in the case of a trailer, the vehicle by which it is drawn, a licence under section 17 of the Transport Act (Northern Ireland) 1967 [*c. 37(N.I.)*].   **B56.24**

(2) In relation to a Northern Ireland goods vehicle used for the carriage of goods otherwise than for hire or reward, section 2(1) of the Act shall have effect as set out in Schedule 4.

23. Exemption for Polish goods vehicles

(1) In this regulation *"Polish goods vehicle"* means a foreign goods vehicle—   **B56.25**
  (a) which, in the case of a motor vehicle, is registered in the Republic of Poland; and
  (b) which, in the case of a trailer, is drawn in Great Britain only by a motor vehicle which is a Polish goods vehicle.

(2) Section 2(1) of the Act shall not apply to the use in Great Britain of a Polish goods vehicle for the carriage of any goods.

24. Exemption for Romanian goods vehicles

(1) In this regulation *"Romanian goods vehicle"* means a foreign goods vehicle—   **B56.26**
  (a) which, in the case of a motor vehicle, is registered in Romania; and
  (b) which, in the case of a trailer, is drawn in Great Britain only by a motor vehicle which is a Romanian goods vehicle.

(2) Section 2(1) of the Act shall not apply to the use in Great Britain of a Romanian goods vehicle for the carriage of any goods.

25. Exemption for Slovak goods vehicles

(1) In this regulation *"Slovak goods vehicle"* means a foreign goods vehicle—   **B56.27**
  (a) which, in the case of a motor vehicle, is registered in the Slovak Republic; and
  (b) which, in the case of a trailer, is drawn in Great Britain only by a motor vehicle which is a Slovak goods vehicle.

(2) Section 2(1) of the Act shall not apply to the use in Great Britain of a Slovak goods vehicle for the carriage of any goods.

26. Exemptions and modification for the Republics of the former Soviet Union goods vehicles

B56.28

(1) In this regulation *"Republic of the former Soviet Union goods vehicle"* means a foreign goods vehicle which is not provided for elsewhere in these Regulations—

(a) which is owned by, or operated on behalf of, a person who is authorised under the law of a Republic of the former Union of Soviet Socialist Republics to use the vehicle in that country for the international carriage of goods; and

(b) which, in the case of a motor vehicle, is registered in a Republic of the former Union of Soviet Socialist Republics; and

(c) which, in the case of a trailer, is drawn in Great Britain only by a motor vehicle which is a Republic of the former Soviet Union goods vehicle.

(2) Subject to paragraphs (6) and (7) below, section 2(1) of the Act shall not apply to the use of a Republic of the former Soviet Union goods vehicle for the carriage of any goods specified in paragraph 4, 5 or 8 of Schedule 2.

(3) Subject to paragraphs (6) and (7) below, section 2(1) of the Act shall not apply to the use of a Republic of the former Soviet Union goods vehicle for the carriage of any goods specified in paragraph 21, 22 or 23 of Schedule 2 if the goods are to be, or are being, returned to the country of origin of the vehicle or are to be, or are being, taken to another country.

(4) Subject to paragraphs (6) and (7) below, section 2(1) of the Act shall not apply to the use of a Republic of the former Soviet Union goods vehicle which is a vehicle specified in paragraph 2 or 3 of Schedule 3.

(5) Subject to paragraphs (6) and (7) below, in relation to a Republic of the former Soviet Union goods vehicle being used for the carriage of goods in a case to which none of the preceding exemptions apply, section 2(1) shall have effect as set out in Schedule 5.

(6) The foregoing exemptions and modification shall not apply unless there is carried on the vehicle or, if the vehicle is a trailer, on the motor vehicle by which it is drawn—

(a) in the case of the carriage of goods under a contract to which the Convention on the Contract for the International Carriage of Goods by Road (as given the force of law in the United Kingdom by section 1 of the Carriage of Goods by Road Act 1965 [*not reproduced in this work*]) applies, a consignment note made out in accordance with that Convention and containing the particulars specified therein, or

(b) in the case of the carriage of goods otherwise than under such a contract, a document or documents containing the following particulars:

   (i) the date of the document and the place at which it is made out;

   (ii) the name and address of the sender of the goods, if any;

   (iii) the name and address of the carrier;

   (iv) the date and place of taking over of the goods, if any, and the place designated for delivery, if any;

   (v) the name and address of the consignee, if any;

   (vi) the description in common use of the nature of the goods and the method of packing, and, in the case of dangerous goods, their generally recognised description;

   (vii) the number of packages and their special marks and numbers;

   (viii) the gross weight of the goods and their quantity otherwise expressed;

(ix) charges relating to the carriage (carriage charges, supplementary charges, Customs duties and other charges incurred during the journey); and

(x) the requisite instructions for Customs and other formalities.

(7) The foregoing exemptions and modification shall not apply to the use of a Republic of the former Soviet Union goods vehicle for the carriage of goods between a place in Great Britain and a place in a country other than Great Britain or a Republic of the former Soviet Union, or vice versa, unless there is carried on the vehicle, or if the vehicle is a trailer, on the motor vehicle by which it is drawn, a permit for the use of the vehicle for that purpose issued with the authority of the Secretary of State.

27. Exemption for Swiss goods vehicles

(1) In this regulation "*Swiss goods vehicle*" means a foreign goods vehicle—   B56.29

(a) which, in the case of a motor vehicle, is registered in the Swiss Confederation; and

(b) which, in the case of a trailer, is drawn in Great Britain only by a motor vehicle which is a Swiss goods vehicle.

(2) Section 2(1) of the Act shall not apply to the use in Great Britain of a Swiss goods vehicle for the carriage of any goods.

28. Exemptions and modification for Tunisian goods vehicles

(1) In this regulation "*Tunisian goods vehicle*" means a foreign goods vehicle which—   B56.30

(a) in the case of a motor vehicle, is registered in the Republic of Tunisia; and

(b) in the case of a trailer, is operated by a person who is authorised under Tunisian law to use that vehicle for the international carriage of goods for hire or reward or on his own account.

(2) Section 2(1) of the Act shall not apply to the use in Great Britain of a Tunisian goods vehicle for the carriage of any goods specified in paragraph 1, 2, 3, 4, 5, 6, 7, 8, 9, 10, 13, 18, 19, 21, 24 or 30 of Schedule 2.

(3) Section 2(1) of the Act shall not apply to the use in Great Britain of a Tunisian goods vehicle which is a vehicle specified in Schedule 3.

(4) In relation to a Tunisian goods vehicle being used for the carriage of goods in a case to which none of the preceding exemptions apply, section 2(1) of the Act shall have effect as set out in Schedule 5.

29. Exemption and modification for Turkish goods vehicles

(1) In this regulation "*Turkish goods vehicle*" means a foreign goods vehicle—   B56.31

(a) which, in the case of a motor vehicle, is registered in the Republic of Turkey; and

(b) which, in the case of a trailer, is owned by or operated by or on behalf of a person who is authorised under Turkish law to use that vehicle for the carriage of goods in the Turkish Republic.

(2) Section 2(1) of the Act shall not apply to the use in Great Britain of a Turkish goods vehicle for the carriage of any goods specified in paragraph 1, 2, 3, 4, 5, 6, 7, 8, 9, 17, 21, 26, 27 or 30 of Schedule 2.

(3) In relation to a Turkish goods vehicle being used for the carriage of goods in a case to which the preceding exemption does not apply, section 2(1) of the Act shall have effect as set out in Schedule 5.

30. Exemptions and modification for Ukrainian goods vehicles

B56.32

(1) In this regulation—

"*Ukrainian goods vehicle*" means a foreign goods vehicle—

   (a) which, in the case of a motor vehicle, is registered in the Ukraine; and

   (b) which, in the case of a trailer, is owned by or operated by or on behalf of a person who under Ukrainian law is authorised to use that vehicle for the carriage of goods in the Ukraine.

"*relevant date*" means the date on which the Agreement between the Government of the United Kingdom of Great Britain and Northern Ireland and the Government of the Ukraine on international road transport signed on 13th December 1995 [*Cm. 3158, 17 W.R.T.L.B. [149]*] comes into force.

(2) On and after the relevant date, section 2(1) of the Act shall not apply to the use in Great Britain of a Ukrainian goods vehicle for the carriage of any goods specified in paragraphs 4, 5, 9, 18 and 20 to 24 of Schedule 2 and in such a case these provisions shall have effect as if the words "or broken-down" were added after "damaged" in paragraph 5.

(3) Section 2(1) of the Act shall not apply to the use in Great Britain of a Ukrainian goods vehicle—

   (a) specified in paragraph 1 of Schedule 3, or

   (b) where the goods are being carried for or in connection with any trade or business carried on by the undertaking carrying them and each of the following conditions are fulfilled—

      (i) the goods are the property of the undertaking carrying them or have been sold, bought, let out on hire or hired, produced, extracted, processed or repaired by that undertaking;

      (ii) the purpose of the journey is to carry the goods to or from the undertaking carrying them or to move them either inside that undertaking or outside for that undertaking's own requirements;

      (iii) the vehicle used for such carriage is being driven by an employee of the undertaking;

      (iv) except in the case of a replacement vehicle during a short breakdown of the vehicle normally used, the vehicle used for carrying the goods is owned by the undertaking carrying them or has been bought by it on deferred terms or hired in accordance with the conditions on the use of vehicles hired without drivers for the carriage of goods by road contained in Council Directive (EEC) No. 84/647;

      (v) the carriage in Great Britain is part of a journey between Great Britain and the Ukraine.

(4) In relation to a Ukrainian goods vehicle being used for the carriage of goods in a case to which the preceding exemptions do not apply, section 2(1) of the Act shall have effect as set out in Schedule 5.

B56.33

[The agreement with the Ukraine entered into force on June 10, 2000 and has been re-issued as Cm. 4879.]

31. Simplified procedure for the grant, etc., of operators' licences

B56.34

(1) The Act shall have effect subject to the modifications set out in Part I of Schedule 6 in relation to any foreign goods vehicles [to which Regulations 4 to 30 do not apply].

(2) The Goods Vehicles (Licensing of Operators) Regulations 1995 [*S.I. 1995 No. 2869 above*] shall have effect subject to the amendments set out in Part II of the said Schedule in relation to foreign goods vehicles [to which Regulations 4 to 30 do not apply].

(3) The Goods Vehicles (Licensing of Operators) Act 1995 (Commencement and Transitional Provisions) Order 1995 [*S.I. 1995 No. 2181 (q.v.)*] and the Goods Vehicles (Licensing of Operators) (Fees) Regulations 1995 [*S.I. 1995 No. 3000; not reproduced in this work*] shall not have effect in relation to any foreign goods vehicles.

[The square brackets which appear in regulation 31(1) and (2) are part of the official text and do not relate to editorial emendations. The words enclosed within those brackets did not appear in the corresponding provisions of the revoked regulations.]　　**B56.35**

SCHEDULE 1　　　　　　　　　　Regulation 2　**B56.36**

REVOCATIONS

[Omitted.]

SCHEDULE 2　　　Regulations 4, 5, 9(2), 12(2),
　　　　　　　　　　15(2) and (3), 21(2), 26(2),
　　　　　　　　　　26(3), 28(2), 29(2) and 30(2)

EXEMPTION FROM SECTION 2(1) OF THE ACT FOR CERTAIN GOODS
CARRIED BY CERTAIN GOODS VEHICLES

1. Luggage being carried to or from an airport.　　**B56.37**

2. Goods being carried to or from an airport in a case where an air service has been diverted.

3. Luggage being carried in trailers drawn by passenger vehicles.　　**B56.38**

4. Postal packets (as defined by section 87 of the Post Office Act 1953 [*not reproduced in this work*]).

5. Damaged vehicles.　　**B56.39**

6. Animal corpses (other than those intended for human consumption) for the purpose of disposal.

7. Bees or fish stock.　　**B56.40**

8. The body of a deceased person.

9. Goods for medical or surgical care in emergency relief and in particular for relief in natural disasters.　　**B56.41**

10. Goods carried in connection with household removals by undertakings using specialised personnel and equipment for that purpose.

11. Household effects.　　**B56.42**

12. Live animals, other than animals intended for slaughter.

B56.43　**13.** Spare parts for ocean-going ships.

14. Spare parts and provisions for ships.

B56.44　**15.** Spare parts and provisions for ocean-going ships where such ships have been re-routed.

16. Spare parts and provisions for ocean-going ships and aircraft.

B56.45　**17.** Goods which by reason of their value are carried in vehicles constructed or adapted for the carriage of goods requiring special security precautions and which are accompanied by guards.

18. Works of art.

B56.46　**19.** Antiques.

20. Goods carried exclusively for publicity or educational purposes.

B56.47　**21.** Properties, equipment or animals being carried to or from theatrical, musical, cinematographic or circus performances or sporting events, exhibitions or fairs, or to or from the making of radio or television broadcasts or films.

22. Goods, properties or animals being carried to or from theatrical, musical, film or circus programmes, or sporting events.

B56.48　**23.** Goods or properties intended for the making of radio or television broadcasts or films.

24. Goods carried for fairs and exhibitions.

B56.49　**25.** Goods carried for international fairs and exhibitions.

26. Refuse.

B56.50　**27.** Garbage.

28. Sewage.

B56.51　**29.** Perishable foodstuffs in a state of refrigeration.

30. Broken down vehicles.

Regulations 9(3), 12(3), 15(3), 26(4), 28(3) and 30(3)　　SCHEDULE 3

EXEMPTIONS FROM SECTION 2(1) OF THE ACT FOR CERTAIN FOREIGN GOODS
VEHICLES

B56.52　**1.** A vehicle having a permissible laden weight not exceeding 6 metric tons or a permissible pay load not exceeding 3.5 metric tons.

2. A goods vehicle used for the carriage of an abnormal indivisible load or other wide load provided that the requirements of the Motor Vehicles (Authorisation of Special Types) General Order 1979 [*S.I. 1979 No. 1198 above*] are complied with.

3. A relief vehicle.

SCHEDULE 4   Regulations 9(4) and 22(2)

MODIFICATION TO SECTION 2(1) OF THE ACT IN RELATION TO CERTAIN FOREIGN GOODS VEHICLES AND NORTHERN IRELAND VEHICLES

"**2.**—(1) Subject to subsection (2) of this section and to the other provisions of this   **B56.53** Part of this Act, no person shall use a goods vehicle on a road for the carriage of goods for or in connection with any trade or business carried on by him unless there is carried on the vehicle, or, if that vehicle is a trailer, on the motor vehicle by which it is drawn, a document containing particulars of the user of the goods vehicle, his trade or business, the goods being carried, their loading and unloading points, the vehicle, and the route."

SCHEDULE 5   Regulations 9(5), 12(6), 15(4), 21(3), 26(5), 28(5), 29(3) and 30(4)

MODIFICATION TO SECTION 2(1) OF THE ACT IN RELATION TO CERTAIN FOREIGN GOODS VEHICLES

"**2.**—(1) Subject to subsection (2) of this section and to the other provisions of this Part   **B56.54** of this Act, no person shall use a goods vehicle on a road for the carriage of goods—

(a)   for hire or reward, or

(b)   for or in connection with any trade or business carried on by him,

except under a permit carried on the vehicle or, if the vehicle is a trailer, on the motor vehicle by which it is drawn, issued with the authority of the Secretary of State, and authorising the vehicle to be used for the carriage of goods on the journey on which the goods are being carried."

SCHEDULE 6   Regulation 31

PART I

MODIFICATIONS TO THE GOODS VEHICLES (LICENSING OF OPERATORS) ACT 1995 IN RELATION TO FOREIGN GOODS VEHICLES

The Act shall have effect—   **B56.55**

(a)   as if for section 5(1) there were substituted the following—

"(1) The vehicles authorised to be used under an operator's licence are—
(a) any motor vehicle in the lawful possession of the licence-holder that is specified in the licence;
(b) any trailer in the lawful possession of the licence-holder, and for the purposes of this section different types of trailers may be distinguished in a licence and a maximum number may be specified in the licence for trailers of each type.";

(b) as if sections 5(4) to (7), 6(1)(a), (3) and (4), and 7 were omitted;

(c) as if for section 8(1), there were substituted the following—

"(1) A person applying for an operator's licence with a view to enabling goods vehicles brought temporarily into Great Britain to be used shall apply to such traffic commissioner as the Secretary of State may from time to time direct and shall not at any time hold more than one such licence";

(d) as if sections 8(2), (3)(b) and (5) were omitted;

(e) as if for section 8(4), there were substituted the following—

"(4) A person applying for an operator's licence shall also give to the traffic commissioner details of—

(a) the notifiable convictions within the meaning given in paragraph 4 of Schedule 2, and

(b) a prohibition under section 69 or 70 of the Road Traffic Act 1988 of the driving of a vehicle of which he was the owner when the prohibition was imposed.";

(f) as if in section 9(1), there was inserted at the end of the subsection ", or a prohibition under section 69 or 70 of the Road Traffic Act 1988 of the driving of a vehicle which he owned", and section 9(2) was omitted;

(g) as if sections 10, 11, 12, 13(2) to (11), 14 and 15 were omitted;

(h) as if for section 13(1) there were substituted the following—

"(1) On an application for an operator's licence the traffic commissioner shall consider whether the applicant satisfies the requirement that he is a fit and proper person to hold an operator's licence having regard in particular to his previous known conduct in respect of the use and operation of motor vehicles in the United Kingdom.";

(i) as if in section 16(1) there were substituted the following—

"(1) The operator's licence shall specify in the licence—

(a) the date on which it is to come into force, and

(b) the date when it will terminate, which date shall not be less than three months after the coming into force of the licence.";

(j) as if section 16(2) and (4) and the words "subject to subsection (4)" in section 16(3) were omitted;

(k) as if in section 17(1) there were substituted the following—

"(1) On the application of the holder of an operator's licence, the traffic commissioner by whom the licence was issued may vary the licence by directing that any vehicle may cease to be specified in the licence and at the same time direct that another [similar] vehicle shall be specified in the licence as a substitute.";

(l) as if sections 17(3) to (5), and 18 to 21 were omitted;

as if in section 22(1) there were substituted the following—

"(1) On issuing an operator's licence, a traffic commissioner may attach to the licence such conditions as he thinks fit for requiring the holder to inform him of any event of a kind specified in the conditions which affect the licence-holder and which is relevant to the exercise of any powers of the traffic commissioner in relation to the licence.";

as if section 22(2) to (6), and 23 to 25 were omitted;

(o) as if in section 26(1) there were substituted the following—

"(1) Subject to the provisions of section 29, the traffic commissioner by whom an operator's licence was issued may direct that it be revoked, suspended or curtailed on the grounds—

(a) that during the five years ending with the date on which the direction is given there has been either a conviction of the licence-holder of a notifiable conviction within the meaning of paragraph 4 of Schedule 2, or a prohibition under section 69 or 70 of the Road Traffic Act 1988 of the driving of a vehicle of which the licence-holder was the owner when the prohibition was imposed, or

(b) that since the licence was issued or varied he has learned that a statement of fact was false or statement of expectation has not been fulfilled.";

(p) as if sections 26(2) to (10) and (11)(c) and (d), and 27 were omitted;

(q) as if in section 28(1) there were substituted the following—

"(1) Where, under section 26(1) a traffic commissioner directs that an operator's licence be revoked, the commissioner may order the person who was the holder of the licence to be disqualified (either indefinitely or for such period as the commissioner thinks fit) from holding or obtaining an operator's licence in Great Britain.";

(r) as if section 28(3) were omitted;

(s) as if sections 30 to 34 and sections 40, 44 and 49 were omitted.

[In paragraph (k) of Part I of Schedule 6, the square brackets used in the substituted text of section 17(1) are part of the official text and do not represent editorial emendations.]   **B56.56**

PART II

MODIFICATIONS TO THE GOODS VEHICLES (LICENSING OF OPERATORS) REGULATIONS 1995
IN RELATION TO FOREIGN GOODS VEHICLES

The Goods Vehicles (Licensing of Operators) Regulations 1995 [*S.I. 1995 No. 2869 (above)*]   **B56.57**
shall have effect:—

(a) as if regulations 4(c), 7, 9(1) and (3), 10 to 19, 21(1)(a)(i) and (iii), 21(1)(d), 22(1)(b) and (c), 22(2)(b), 22(3), 28(2) and (5), 29(1), (3) to (5), (7), and (12), 31 and 36 were omitted;

(b) as if in regulation 8(1) for the words "grant of that application would lead to a contravention of section 8(2)" there were substituted "applicant already holds an operator's licence in Great Britain";

(c) as if in regulation 21(1)(b) the words "or section 27" were omitted;

(d) as if in regulation 23(2) there were substituted the following—

"The disc shall clearly indicate (by colour or other means) that the vehicle is a foreign goods vehicle.";

(e) as if in regulation 26(1), for the words "and the licence-holder may do so" to the end there were substituted "at a place specified by the person requiring its production";

(f) as if in regulation 33(2) for the words "on a plate affixed to the vehicle by virtue of regulation 66 of those Regulations" there were substituted "in accordance with the legal requirements of the State of establishment of the operator of the foreign goods vehicle".

The New Drivers (Appeals Procedure) Regulations 1997

(S.I. 1997 No. 1098)

1. Citation, commencement and interpretation

B57.01   (1)   *[Omitted.]*

(2) In these Regulations—

"*the Act*" means the Road Traffic (New Drivers) Act 1995;

"*appellate court*" means—

    (a) in England and Wales, the Crown Court, the High Court or the Court of Appeal, as the case may be;

    (b) *[applies to Scotland.]*

"*relevant appeal*" means an appeal against—

    (a) a conviction, or

    (b) an order of a court in England and Wales for the endorsement of a licence or . . .;

which is, or forms part of, the basis for the revocation of the licence or a test certificate.

B57.02   *[The words omitted from the definition of "relevant appeal" relate exclusively to Scotland.]*

2. Licences granted pending appeal

B57.03   (1) There is prescribed for the purposes of section 5(1) of the Act (duration of licences granted without retesting pending appeal) a period expiring on the date on which the revoked licence would have expired if it had not been revoked.

(2) Where the Secretary of State has—

    (a) revoked a person's test certificate under paragraph 5(1) of Schedule 1 to the Act or, as the case may be, revoked a person's licence and test certificate under paragraph 8(1) of that Schedule, and

    (b) received notice that the person is making a relevant appeal, he must, if that person surrenders to him any previous licence granted to him or provides an explanation for not surrendering it that the Secretary of State considers adequate, grant to that person a full licence in accordance with paragraph (3) below.

(3) A licence granted under paragraph (2) above shall—

    (a) have effect for the purposes of the Road Traffic Acts as if it were a licence granted under Part III of the Road Traffic Act 1988,

    (b) subject to section 92 and Part IV of that Act, authorise the driving of all classes of vehicle which, immediately before his test certificate was revoked, the person was permitted to drive without observing the prescribed conditions, and

    (c) subject to paragraph (4) below, be for a period expiring on the date on which a licence granted under Part III of that Act would have expired.

(4) A licence granted under paragraph (2) shall be treated as revoked if—

(a) following the appeal, the penalty points taken into account for the purposes of section 2(1) of the Act are not reduced to a number smaller than six, or

(b) the appeal is abandoned.

3. Notices of appeal

(1) Subject to paragraphs (2) and (3) below, notice of a relevant appeal shall be given to the Secretary of State—   **B57.04**

(a) in England and Wales, by the magistrates' court or Crown Court in which the case is heard;

(b) *[applies to Scotland.]*

(2) Notice of a relevant appeal from a magistrates' court or Crown Court by case stated shall be given to the Secretary of State by the High Court.

(3) Notice of a further appeal from a decision of an appellate court shall be given to the Secretary of State by the appellate court from which the appeal is made.

(4) A notice pursuant to this regulation shall be given—

(a) in the case of an appeal by case stated, as soon as reasonably practicable after the day on which the case is lodged in the High Court;

(b) in the case of any other appeal—

(i) where leave to appeal or for abridgement of time is necessary, as soon as reasonably practicable after the court has granted such leave or abridgement, or

(ii) in any other case, as soon as reasonably practicable after notice of appeal is duly given by the appellant.

4. Notice of abandonment of appeal

Notice of the abandonment of any relevant appeal shall be given to the Secretary of State—   **B57.05**

(a) in England and Wales, by the appellate court to which the appeal is made, or

(b) *[applies to Scotland]*,

as soon as reasonably practicable after the day on which notice of the abandonment of the appeal is duly given.

The Zebra, Pelican and Puffin Pedestrian Crossings Regulations and General Directions 1997

(S.I. 1997 No. 2400)

B58.01   *Editorial note.*   All the functions of a Minister of the Crown under the Zebra, Pelican and Puffin Pedestrian Crossings and General Directions 1997 which are exercisable in relation to Scotland have been transferred to the Scottish Ministers by the Scotland Act 1998 (Transfer of Functions to the Scottish Ministers etc.) Order 1999 (S.I. 1999 No. 1750; not reproduced in this work), art.2 and Sched. 1.

B58.02   *[The regulations and directions have been amended by:*

the Pelican and Puffin Pedestrian Crossings General (Amendment) Directions 1998 (S.I. 1998 No. 901) (April 1, 1998).

The amending directions are referred to in the notes to the regulations and directions only by their year and number. The date referred to above is the date on which the amending directions came into force.]

ARRANGEMENT OF INSTRUMENT

PART I
The Zebra, Pelican and Puffin Pedestrian Crossings Regulations 1997

SECTION I
Preliminary

SECTION II
Form of crossings

*   *   *

PART I

THE ZEBRA, PELICAN AND PUFFIN PEDESTRIAN CROSSINGS REGULATIONS 1997

SECTION I

Preliminary

B58.04 **1. Citation and commencement**   *[Omitted.]*

2. Revocation

B58.05 (1) The "Zebra" Pedestrian Crossings Regulations 1971 [*S.I. 1971 No. 1524*], the "Zebra" Pedestrian Crossings (Amendment) Regulations 1990 [*S.I. 1990 No. 1828*] and, so far as they consist of or comprise regulations, the "Pelican" Pedestrian Crossings Regulations and General Directions 1987 [*S.I. 1987 No. 16*] are hereby revoked.

(2) Any crossing which, immediately before the coming into force of these Regulations, was constituted a Pelican or a Zebra crossing in accordance with the regulations revoked by paragraph (1) which were applicable to it ("*the applicable regulations*") shall, notwithstanding the revocation of the applicable regulations, be treated as constituted in accordance with these Regulations for so long as the traffic signs situated at or near it and the manner in which its presence and limits are indicated comply with the applicable regulations.

(3) Paragraph (2) shall cease to have effect on 15th December 2002.

B58.06 *[The text of the "Zebra" Pedestrian Crossings Regulations 1971 (S.I. 1971 No. 1524) and that of the "Pelican" Pedestrian Crossings Regulations and General Directions 1987 (S.I. 1987 No. 16) may be found in the eighteenth edition of this work.]*

3. Interpretation

B58.07 (1) In these Regulations unless the context otherwise requires—

"*the 1984 Act*" means the Road Traffic Regulation Act 1984;

"*the 1994 Regulations*" means the Traffic Signs Regulations 1994 [*Part I of S.I. 1994 No. 1519, q.v.*];

"*carriageway*" means—

(a) in relation to a crossing on a highway in England or Wales . . ., a way constituting or comprised in the highway or road being a way over which the public has a right of way for the passage of vehicles; and

(b) in relation to a crossing on any other road in England or Wales to which the public has access, that part of the road to which vehicles have access,

but does not include in either case any central reservation (whether within the limits of the crossing or not);

"*central reservation*" means—

(a) in relation to a road comprising a single carriageway, any provision (including a refuge for pedestrians) which separates one part of the carriageway from another part;

(b) in relation to a road which comprises two or more carriageways any land or permanent work which separates those carriageways from one another;

"*controlled area*" means a Pelican controlled area, a Puffin controlled area or a Zebra controlled area;

"*crossing*" means a crossing for pedestrians established—

(a) in the case of a trunk road, by the Secretary of State pursuant to section 24 of the 1984 Act; and

(b) in the case of any other road, by a local traffic authority pursuant to section 23 of that Act;

"*driver*" in relation to a vehicle which is a motor cycle or pedal cycle means the person riding the vehicle who is in control of it;

"*give-way line*" means a road marking placed adjacent to a Zebra crossing in accordance with regulation 6(1) and Schedule 1;

"*indicator for pedestrians*" means the traffic sign of that description prescribed for the purposes of a Pelican crossing by regulation 5(2)(a) and paragraphs 2(c) and 5 of Part I and Part II of Schedule 2;

"*layout or character*" in relation to a road means the layout or character of the road itself and does not include the layout or character of any land or premises adjacent to the road;

"*mm*" means millimetres;

"*one-way street*" means a road on which the driving of vehicles otherwise than in one particular direction is prohibited;

"*pedestrian demand unit*" means the traffic sign of that description prescribed for the purposes of a Puffin crossing by regulation 5(3)(a) and paragraphs 1(b) and 3 of Part I and Part II of Schedule 3;

"*pedestrian light signals*" means the traffic sign of that description prescribed for the purposes of a Pelican crossing by regulation 5(2)(a) and paragraphs 2(b) and 4 of Part I of Schedule 2;

"*Pelican controlled area*" means an area of carriageway in the vicinity of a Pelican crossing the limits of which are indicated in accordance with regulation 6(2) and Schedule 4;

"*Pelican crossing*" means a crossing—

(a) at which there are traffic signs of the size, colour and type prescribed by regulation 5(2)(a) and Schedule 2;

(b) the limits of which are indicated in accordance with regulation 5(2)(b) and Schedule 4;

"*primary signal*" means vehicular light signals so placed as to face vehicular traffic approaching a Pelican or a Puffin crossing and placed beyond the stop line and in front of the line of studs nearest the stop line indicating the limits of the crossing in accordance with regulation 6(3) and Schedule 4;

"*Puffin controlled area*" means an area of the carriageway in the vicinity of a Puffin crossing the limits of which are indicated in accordance with regulation 6(2) and Schedule 4;

"*Puffin crossing*" means a crossing—

(a) at which there are traffic signs of the size, colour and type prescribed by regulation 5(3)(a) and Schedule 3;

(b) the limits of which are indicated in accordance with regulation 5(3)(b) and Schedule 4;

"*refuge for pedestrians*" means a part of a road to which vehicles do not have access and on which pedestrians may wait after crossing one part of the carriageway and before crossing the other;

"*retroreflecting material*" means material which reflects a ray of light back towards the source of that light;

"*road marking*" means a traffic sign consisting of a line or mark or legend on a road and includes a stud;

"*secondary signal*" means vehicular light signals so placed as to face vehicular traffic approaching a Pelican or Puffin crossing but sited beyond the furthest limit of the crossing as viewed from the direction of travel of the traffic;

"*stop line*" means, in relation to a vehicle approaching a Pelican or Puffin crossing, the transverse continuous white line (indicated in accordance with regulation 6(3) and Schedule 4 and parallel to the limits of the crossing) which is on the same side of the crossing as the vehicle;

"*stud*" means a mark or device on the carrriageway, whether or not projecting above the surface of the carriageway;

"*system of staggered crossings*" means two or more Pelican crossings or two or more Puffin crossings provided on a road on which there is a central reservation and where—

(a) there is one crossing on each side of the central reservation; and

(b) taken together the two crossings do not lie along a straight line;

"*two-way street*" means a road which is not a one-way street;

"*vehicular light signals*" means, in relation to a Pelican or Puffin crossing, the traffic sign of that description prescribed (in the case of a Pelican crossing) by regulation 5(2)(a) and paragraphs 2(a) and 3 of Part I of Schedule 2 or (in the case of a Puffin crossing) by regulation 5(3)(a) and paragraphs 1(a) and 2 of Part I of Schedule 3;

"*Zebra controlled area*" means an area of carriageway in the vicinity of a Zebra crossing the limits of which are indicated in accordance with regulation 6(1) and Part II of Schedule 1; and

"*Zebra crossing*" means a crossing—

(a) at which there are traffic signs of the size, colour and type prescribed by regulation 5(1)(a) and Part I of Schedule 1; and

(b) the limits of which are indicated in accordance with regulation 5(1)(b) and Part II of Schedule 1.

(2) In these Regulations, unless it is expressly provided otherwise or the context otherwise requires—

(a) a reference to a numbered regulation or Schedule is a reference to the regulation or, as the case may be, the Schedule so numbered in these Regulations;

(b) a reference in a regulation or Schedule to a numbered paragraph is a reference to the paragraph so numbered in the regulation or, as the case may be, in the Schedule in which the reference occurs; and

(c) a reference to a sub-paragraph followed by a number or letter is a reference to the sub-paragraph bearing that number or letter in the paragraph in which the reference occurs.

B58.08   *[The words omitted from the definition of "carriageway" relate exclusively to Scotland.]*

4. Application of Regulations

B58.09   These Regulations apply to a crossing which is a Zebra, Pelican or Puffin crossing.

SECTION II

Form of crossings

5. Traffic signs and road markings for indicating crossings

(1) A Zebra crossing shall be indicated by—   **B58.10**

  (a) the placing at or near the crossing of traffic signs of the size, colour and type specified in Part I of Schedule 1;

  (b) the placing on the carriageway to indicate the limits of the crossing of road markings of the size, colour and type specified in Part II of Schedule 1.

(2) A Pelican crossing shall be indicated by—

  (a) the placing at or near the crossing of traffic signs of the size, colour and type specified in Schedule 2;

  (b) the placing on the carriageway to indicate the limits of the crossing of road markings of the size, colour and type specified in Schedule 4.

(3) A Puffin crossing shall be indicated by—

  (a) the placing at or near the crossing of traffic signs of the size, colour and type specified in Schedule 3;

  (b) the placing on the carriageway to indicate the limits of the crossing of road markings of the size, colour and type specified in Schedule 4.

6. Give-way and stop lines and controlled areas

(1) On each side of a Zebra crossing, there shall be laid out a Zebra controlled area   **B58.11**
(including a give-way line) indicated by road markings of the size, colour and type, and generally in the manner, specified in Part II of Schedule 1.

(2) On each side of a Pelican or Puffin crossing, there shall be laid out a Pelican controlled area or a Puffin controlled area indicated by road markings of the size, colour and type, and generally in the manner, specified in Schedule 4.

(3) A stop line or stop lines of the size, colour and type specified in Schedule 4 shall be placed next to a Pelican or Puffin crossing in the manner specified in that Schedule.

7. Dimensions

(1) Dimensions indicated on any diagram shown in the Schedules to these Regulations   **B58.12**
are expressed in millimetres.

(2) A dimension (other than one specified as a maximum or minimum dimension) specified in a diagram in Schedule 2 or 3 may be varied if, in the case of a dimension of the length specified in column (2) of an item in the table below, the variation does not exceed the extent specified in column (3) of the item.

TABLE

(1) Item	(2) Length of dimension	(3) Extent of variation
(1)	less than 10mm	1mm
(2)	10mm or more but less than 50mm	10% of the dimension
(3)	50mm or more but less than 300mm	7.5% of the dimension
(4)	300mm or more	5% of the dimension

(3) A dimension (other than one specified as a maximum or minimum dimension) specified in any diagram in Schedule 1 or in Schedule 4 may be varied if, in the case of a dimension of the length specified in column (2) of an item in the table below, the variation does not exceed the extent specified in column (3) of the item.

TABLE

(1) Item	(2) Length of dimension	(3) Extent of variation
(1)	300mm or more	(i) 20% of the dimension where the varied dimension is greater than the specified dimension; or (ii) 10% of the dimension where the varied dimension is less than the specified dimension
(2)	less than 300mm	(i) 30% of the dimension where the varied dimension is greater than the specified dimension; or (ii) 10% of the dimension where the varied dimension is less than the specified dimension.

(4) Where maximum and minimum dimensions are specified for any element of a traffic sign or road marking, the dimension chosen for that element must not be less than the minimum and must not exceed the maximum.

(5) Where any diagram in a Schedule to these Regulations specifies a dimension for an element of a traffic sign or road marking together with a dimension for that element in brackets, the dimensions so specified shall be alternatives.

(6) A dimension specified in the 1994 Regulations in relation to a traffic sign prescribed by those Regulations and referred to in these Regulations may be varied to the extent permitted by the 1994 Regulations.

8. Additional equipment

B58.13   A traffic authority may provide at, or fix to any traffic sign or post placed for the purposes of, a crossing in accordance with these Regulations any object, device, apparatus or equipment—

(a) in connection with the proper operation of the crossing; or

(b) which they consider appropriate for giving information or assistance to disabled persons wishing to use the crossing.

9. Additional traffic signs

B58.14   In addition to the traffic signs prescribed in regulation 5 a traffic sign shown in diagram 610, 611, 612, 613 or 616 in Schedule 2 or diagram 810 in Schedule 4, or a road marking shown in diagram 1029 or the white triangular markings included in the road marking shown in diagram 1061 of Schedule 6, to the 1994 Regulations may, if the traffic authority think fit, be placed at or near a crossing.

10. Non-compliance with requirements of this Section

B58.15   (1) Where, as respects a crossing or controlled area, the requirements of this Section of these Regulations as to the placing of traffic signs and road markings to indicate the crossing or controlled area have not been complied with in every respect, the crossing or, as the case may be, the controlled area shall nevertheless be treated as complying with these Regulations if the non-compliance—

   (a)   is not such as materially to affect the general appearance of the crossing or the controlled area;

   (b)   does not, in the case of a Pelican or Puffin crossing, affect the proper operation of the vehicular and pedestrian signals at the crossing; and

   (c)   does not relate to the size of the controlled area.

(2)   Nothing in any other provision of these Regulations shall be taken to restrict the generality of paragraph (1).

SECTION III

Significance of traffic signs at crossings

11. Scope of Section III

The provisions of this Section of these Regulations (except regulation 16) are made under section 64(1) of the Road Traffic Regulation Act 1984 for the purpose of prescribing the warnings, information, requirements, restrictions and prohibitions which are to be conveyed to traffic by traffic signs and road markings of the size, colour and type prescribed by Section II.   **B58.16**

12. Significance of vehicular light signals at Pelican crossings

(1)   The significance of the vehicular light signals prescribed by regulation 5(2)(a) and paragraph 3 of Schedule 2 for the purpose of indicating a Pelican crossing shall be as follows—   **B58.17**

   (a)   the green signal shall indicate that vehicular traffic may proceed beyond the stop line and across the crossing;

   (b)   the green arrow signal shall indicate that vehicular traffic may proceed beyond the stop line and through the crossing only for the purpose of proceeding in the direction indicated by the arrow;

   (c)   except as provided by sub-paragraph (e) the steady amber signal shall convey the same prohibition as the red signal except that, as respects a vehicle which is so close to the stop line that it cannot safely be stopped without proceeding beyond the stop line, it shall convey the same indication as the green signal or, if the amber signal was immediately preceded by a green arrow signal, as that green arrow signal;

   (d)   except as provided in sub-paragraph (e), the red signal shall convey the prohibition that vehicular traffic shall not proceed beyond the stop line;

   (e)   when a vehicle is being used for fire brigade, ambulance, national blood service or police purposes and the observance of the prohibition conveyed by the steady amber or the red signal in accordance with sub-paragraph (c) or (d) would be likely to hinder the use of that vehicle for the purpose for which it is being used, then those sub-paragraphs shall not apply to the vehicle, and the steady amber and the red signal shall each convey the information that the vehicle may proceed beyond the stop line if the driver—

      (i)   accords precedence to any pedestrian who is on that part of the carriageway which lies within the limits of the crossing or on a central reservation which lies between two crossings which do not form part of a system of staggered crossings; and

(ii) does not proceed in a manner or at a time likely to endanger any person or any vehicle approaching or waiting at the crossing, or to the driver of any such vehicle to change its speed or course in order to avoid an accident; and

(f) the flashing amber signal shall convey the information that traffic may proceed across the crossing but that every pedestrian who is on the carriageway or a central reservation within the limits of the crossing (but not if he is on a central reservation which lies between two crossings forming part of a system of staggered crossings) before any part of a vehicle has entered those limits, has the right of precedence within those limits over that vehicle, and the requirement that the driver of a vehicle shall accord such precedence to any such pedestrian.

(2) Vehicular traffic proceeding beyond a stop line in accordance with paragraph (1) shall proceed with due regard to the safety of other road users and subject to any direction given by a constable in uniform or a traffic warden or to any other applicable prohibition or restriction.

(3) In this regulation, references to the "*stop line*" in relation to a Pelican crossing where the stop line is not visible are to be treated as references to the post or other structure on which the primary signal is mounted.

13. Significance of vehicular light signals at Puffin crossings

B58.18   (1) The significance of the vehicular light signals at a Puffin crossing prescribed by regulation 5(3)(a) and paragraph 2 of Schedule 3 shall be as follows—

(a) the green signal shall indicate that vehicular traffic may proceed beyond the stop line and across the crossing;

(b) the green arrow signal shall indicate that vehicular traffic may proceed beyond the stop line and through the crossing only for the purpose of proceeding in the direction indicated by the arrow;

(c) except as provided by sub-paragraph (f), the amber signal shall, when shown alone, convey the same prohibition as the red signal, except that, as respects any vehicle which is so close to the stop line that it cannot safely be stopped without proceeding beyond the stop line, it shall convey the same indication as the green signal or, if the amber signal was immediately preceded by a green arrow signal, as that green arrow signal;

(d) except as provided in sub-paragraph (f), the red signal shall convey the prohibition that vehicular traffic shall not proceed beyond the stop line;

(e) except as provided by sub-paragraph (f), the red-with-amber signal shall denote an impending change to green in the indication given by the signals but shall convey the same prohibition as the red signal;

(f) when a vehicle is being used for fire brigade, ambulance, national blood service or police purposes and the observance of the prohibition conveyed by the amber, red or red-with-amber signal in accordance with sub-paragraph (c), (d) or (e) would be likely to hinder the use of that vehicle for the purpose for which it is being used, then those sub-paragraphs shall not apply to the vehicle, and the red signal, red-with-amber and amber signals shall each convey the information that the vehicle may proceed beyond the stop line if the driver—

(i) accords precedence to any pedestrian who is on that part of the carriageway which lies within the limits of the crossing or on a central reservation which lies between two crossings which do not form part of a system of staggered crossings; and

(ii) does not proceed in a manner or at a time likely to endanger any person or any vehicle approaching or waiting at the crossing, or to cause the driver of any such vehicle to change its speed or course in order to avoid an accident.

(2) Vehicular traffic proceeding beyond a stop line in accordance with paragraph (1) shall proceed with due regard to the safety of other road users and subject to any direction given by a constable in uniform or a traffic warden or to any other applicable prohibition or restriction.

(3) In this regulation, references to the "*stop line*" in relation to a Puffin crossing where the stop line is not visible are to be treated as references to the post or other structure on which the primary signal is mounted.

14. Significance of give-way lines at Zebra crossings

A give-way line included in the markings placed pursuant to regulation 5(1)(b) and Part II of Schedule 1 shall convey to vehicular traffic proceeding towards a Zebra crossing the position at or before which a vehicle should be stopped for the purpose of complying with regulation 25 (precedence of pedestrians over vehicles at Zebra crossings).   **B58.19**

15. Significance of pedestrian light signals and figures on pedestrian demand units

(1) The significance of the red and steady green pedestrian light signals whilst they are illuminated at a Pelican crossing and of the red and green figures on a pedestrian demand unit whilst they are illuminated at a Puffin crossing shall be as follows—   **B58.20**

  (a) the red pedestrian light signal and the red figure shall both convey to a pedestrian the warning that, in the interests of safety, he should not cross the carriageway; and

  (b) the steady green pedestrian light signal and the steady green figure shall both indicate to a pedestrian that he may cross the carriageway and that drivers may not cause vehicles to enter the crossing.

(2) The flashing green pedestrian light signal at a Pelican crossing shall convey—

  (a) to a pedestrian who is already on the crossing when the flashing green signal is first shown the information that he may continue to use the crossing and that, if he is on the carriageway or a central reservation within the limits of that crossing (but not if he is on a central reservation which lies between two crossings which form part of a system of staggered crossings) before any part of a vehicle has entered those limits, he has precedence over that vehicle within those limits; and

  (b) to a pedestrian who is not already on the crossing when the flashing green light is first shown the warning that he should not, in the interests of safety, start to cross the carriageway.

(3) Any audible signal emitted by any device for emitting audible signals provided in conjunction with the steady green pedestrian light signal or the green figure, and any tactile signal given by any device for making tactile signals similarly provided, shall convey to a pedestrian the same indication as the steady green pedestrian light signal or as the green figure as the case may be.

16. Significance of additional traffic signs

A traffic sign placed in accordance with regulation 9 shall convey the information, prohibition or requirement specified in relation to it by the 1994 Regulations.   **B58.21**

SECTION IV

Movement of traffic at crossings

17. Scope of Section IV

B58.22   This Section of these Regulations is made under section 25 of the 1984 Act with respect to the movement of traffic at and in the vicinity of crossings.

18. Prohibition against the stopping of vehicles on crossings

B58.23   The driver of a vehicle shall not cause the vehicle or any part of it to stop within the limits of a crossing unless he is prevented from proceeding by circumstances beyond his control or it is necessary for him to stop to avoid injury or damage to persons or property.

19. Pedestrians not to delay on crossings

B58.24   No pedestrian shall remain on the carriageway within the limits of a crossing longer than is necessary for that pedestrian to pass over the crossing with reasonable despatch.

20. Prohibition against the stopping of vehicles in controlled areas

B58.25   (1) For the purposes of this regulation and regulations 21 and 22 the word *"vehicle"* shall not include a pedal bicycle not having a sidecar attached to it, whether or not additional means of propulsion by mechanical power are attached to the bicycle.

(2) Except as provided in regulations 21 and 22 the driver of a vehicle shall not cause it or any part of it to stop in a controlled area.

21. Exceptions to regulation 20

B58.26   Regulation 20 does not prohibit the driver of a vehicle from stopping it in a controlled area—

(a) if the driver has stopped it for the purpose of complying with regulation 25 or 26;

(b) if the driver is prevented from proceeding by circumstances beyond his control or it is necessary for him to stop to avoid injury or damage to persons or property; or

(c) when the vehicle is being used for police, fire brigade or ambulance purposes.

22. Further exceptions to regulation 20

B58.27   (1) Regulation 20 does not prohibit the driver of a vehicle from stopping it in a controlled area—

(a) for so long as may be necessary to enable the vehicle to be used for the purposes of—

(i) any building operation, demolition or excavation;

(ii) the removal of any obstruction to traffic;

(iii) the maintenance, improvement or reconstruction of a road; or

(iv) the laying, erection, alteration, repair or cleaning in or near the crossing of any sewer or of any main, pipe or apparatus for the supply of gas, water or electricity, or of any telecommunications apparatus kept installed for the purposes of a telecommunications code system or of any other telecommunications apparatus lawfully kept installed in any position,

but only if the vehicle cannot be used for one of those purposes without stopping in the controlled area; or

(b) if the vehicle is a public service vehicle being used—

(i) in the provision of a local service; or

(ii) to carry passengers for hire or reward at separate fares,

and the vehicle, having proceeded past the crossing to which the controlled area relates, is waiting in that area in order to take up or set down passengers; or

(c) if he stops the vehicle for the purposes of making a left or right turn.

(2) In paragraph (1) "*local service*" has the meaning given in section 2 of the Transport Act 1985 [*q.v.*] but does not include an excursion or tour as defined by section 137(1) of that Act.

23. Prohibition against vehicles proceeding across Pelican or Puffin crossings

When vehicular light signals at a Pelican or Puffin crossing are displaying the red light signal the driver of a vehicle shall not cause it to contravene the prohibition given by that signal by virtue of regulation 12 or 13.

B58.28

24. Prohibition against vehicles overtaking at crossings

(1) Whilst any motor vehicle (in this regulation called "*the approaching vehicle*") or any part of it is within the limits of a controlled area and is proceeding towards the crossing, the driver of the vehicle shall not cause it or any part of it—

B58.29

(a) to pass ahead of the foremost part of any other motor vehicle proceeding in the same direction; or

(b) to pass ahead of the foremost part of a vehicle which is stationary for the purpose of complying with regulation 23, 25 or 26.

(2) In paragraph (1)—

(a) the reference to a motor vehicle in sub-paragraph (a) is, in a case where more than one motor vehicle is proceeding in the same direction as the approaching vehicle in a controlled area, a reference to the motor vehicle nearest to the crossing; and

(b) the reference to a stationary vehicle is, in a case where more than one vehicle is stationary in a controlled area for the purpose of complying with regulation 23, 25 or 26, a reference to the stationary vehicle nearest the crossing.

[For the application of the fixed penalty procedure to overtaking a moving or stationary vehicle on a zebra, pelican or puffin crossing contrary to regulation 24, see the Road Traffic Offences Act 1988, Pt III and Sched. 3 above.]

B58.30

25. Precedence of pedestrians over vehicles at Zebra crossings

(1) Every pedestrian, if he is on the carriageway within the limits of a Zebra crossing, which is not for the time being controlled by a constable in uniform or traffic warden, before any part of a vehicle has entered those limits, shall have precedence within those limits over that vehicle and the driver of the vehicle shall accord such precedence to any such pedestrian.

B58.31

(2) Where there is a refuge for pedestrians or central reservation on a Zebra crossing, the parts of the crossing situated on each side of the refuge for pedestrians or central reservation shall, for the purposes of this regulation, be treated as separate crossings.

26. Precedence of pedestrians over vehicles at Pelican crossings

When the vehicular light signals at a Pelican crossing are showing the flashing amber signal, every pedestrian, if he is on the carriageway or a central reservation within the limits

B58.32

of the crossing (but not if he is on a central reservation which forms part of a system of staggered crossings) before any part of a vehicle has entered those limits, shall have precedence within those limits over that vehicle and the driver of the vehicle shall accord such precedence to any such pedestrian.

Regulations 5(1) and 6(1)   SCHEDULE 1

Traffic Signs and Road Markings to Indicate Zebra Crossings and Zebra
Controlled Areas

PART I

TRAFFIC SIGNS

B58.33   **1.**—(1) Subject to the following provisions of this Part of this Schedule the traffic signs which are to be placed at or near a Zebra crossing for the purpose of indicating it shall consist of globes each of which is—

(a) coloured yellow or fluorescent yellow;

(b) not less than 275 nor more than 335mm in diameter;

(c) illuminated by a flashing light or, where the Secretary of State so authorises in writing in relation to a particular crossing a constant steady light; and

(d) mounted on a post or bracket so that the lowest part of a globe is not less than 2.1 metres nor more than 3.1 metres above the surface of the ground immediately beneath it.

(2) One globe shall be placed at each end of the crossing and, if there is a refuge for pedestrians or central reservation on the crossing, one or more globes may, if the traffic authority thinks fit, be placed on the refuge or central reservation.

B58.34   **2.** Where a globe is mounted on or attached to a post, whether or not specially provided for the purpose—

(a) the post shall be coloured in alternate black and white bands, the lowest band being coloured black;

(b) the bands shall be not less than 275mm nor more than 335mm wide except that the lowest band may be up to 1 metre wide; and

(c) the post may be internally illuminated.

B58.35   **3.** A globe or the post on which it is mounted may be fitted with all or any of the following—

(a) a backing board or other device designed to improve the conspicuousness of the globe;

(b) a shield or other device designed to prevent or reduce light shining into adjacent premises;

(c) a light to illuminate the crossing.

B58.36   **4.** A crossing shall not be taken to have ceased to be indicated in accordance with this Part of this Schedule by reason only of—

(a) the imperfection, disfigurement or discolouration of any globe or post, or

(b) the failure of illumination of any of the globes.

5. Nothing in this Part of this Schedule shall be taken to restrict regulation 8 or 9.

PART II

ROAD MARKINGS

6. Road markings

Subject to the following provisions of this Part of this Schedule— **B58.37**

(a) within the limits of a Zebra crossing the carriageway shall be marked with a series of alternate black and white stripes;

(b) the Zebra controlled areas shall be marked with give-way lines, a line of studs and zig-zag lines,

of the size and type, and generally in the manner, shown in the diagram at the end of this Part of this Schedule.

7. Number of studs and stripes

The number of studs and stripes may be varied. **B58.38**

8. Limits of the crossing

(1) If it provides a reasonable contrast with the white stripes, the colour of the surface of **B58.39** the carriageway may be used to indicate the stripes shown coloured black in the diagram.

(2) The white stripes may be illuminated by retroreflecting material.

(3) Subject to paragraph (4) each black and each white stripe shall be of the same size and not less than 500mm nor more than 715mm wide as measured across the carriageway.

(4) The first stripe at each end may be up to 1300mm wide and, if the traffic authority consider it appropriate in relation to a particular crossing having regard to the layout of the carriageway or other special circumstances, the other stripes may be not less than 380mm nor more than 840mm wide as measured across the carriageway.

9. Studs

(1) The studs may be omitted altogether. **B58.40**

(2) If studs are provided—

  (a) they shall be coloured white, silver or light grey;

  (b) they shall be either—

     (i) circular in shape with a diameter of not less than 95mm nor more than 110mm; or

     (ii) square in shape with each side not less than 95mm nor more than 110mm long;

  (c) they may be illuminated by retroreflecting material;

  (d) if they consist of a device fixed to the carriageway, they shall—

     (i) not be fitted with reflecting lenses;

     (ii) be so fixed that they do not project more than 20mm above the adjacent surface of the carriageway at their highest points nor more than 6mm at their edges;

  (e) the distance from the centre of any stud to the centre of the next stud in the same line shall not be less than 250mm nor more than 715mm and the distance between the edge of the carriageway at each end of a line of studs and the centre of the nearest stud shall be not more than 1.3 metres; and

(f) the two lines of studs need not be at right angles to the edge of the carriageway, but shall form straight lines and, so far as is reasonably practicable, shall be parallel to each other.

10. Zig-zag lines

B58.41

(1) The pattern of the central zig-zag lines may be reversed or, on a road having a carriageway not more than 6 metres wide, those lines may be omitted altogether so long as they are replaced by the road marking shown in diagram 1004 in Schedule 6 to the 1994 Regulations.

(2) Subject to sub-paragraph (4) the number of marks in a zig-zag line shall not be less than 8 nor more than 18 and a zig-zag line need not contain the same number of marks as any other zig-zag line.

(3) Each mark in a zig-zag line shall be coloured white and may be illuminated by retro-reflecting material.

(4) Where the traffic authority is satisfied that, by reason of the layout or character of any roads in the vicinity of a Zebra crossing, it would be impracticable to lay out a Zebra controlled area in accordance with this Schedule—

(a) the number of marks in any zig-zag line in that area may be reduced to not less than 2; and

(b) the length of any of the marks may be varied to not less than 1 metre.

11. Give-way line

B58.42

(1) The give-way line shall be coloured white and may be illuminated by retroreflecting material.

(2) The angle of the give-way line in relation to, and its distance from, the edge of the crossing may be varied, if the traffic authority is satisfied that the variation is necessary having regard to the angle of the crossing in relation to the edge of the carriageway.

(3) The maximum distance of 3 metres between the give-way line and the limits of the crossing shown in the diagram in this Part of this Schedule may, if the traffic authority think fit having regard to the layout or character of the road in the vicinity of the crossing, be increased to not more than 10 metres.

12. Discolouration or partial displacement of markings

B58.43

A Zebra crossing or a Zebra controlled area shall not be deemed to have ceased to be indicated in accordance with this Schedule by reason only of the discolouration or partial displacement of any of the road markings prescribed by this Schedule, so long as the general appearance of the pattern of the lines is not impaired.

[the diagram is set out on the facing page

DIAGRAM

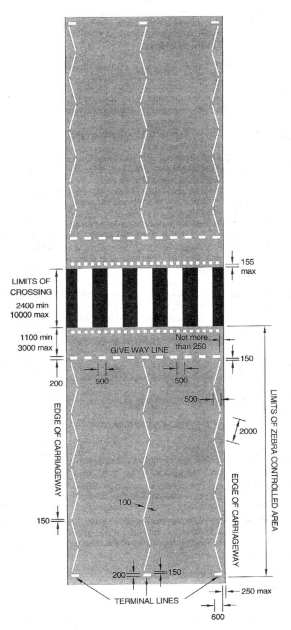

Regulation 5(2)(a)   SCHEDULE 2

TRAFFIC SIGNS TO INDICATE PELICAN CROSSINGS

PART I

TRAFFIC SIGNS TO BE PLACED AT OR NEAR PELICAN CROSSINGS

1. Interpretation

B58.44   In this Schedule "*push button*" has the meaning given by paragraph 5(c).

2. Traffic signs

B58.45   The traffic signs which are to be placed at or near a Pelican crossing shall consist of a combination of—

(a) vehicular light signals;

(b) pedestrian light signals; and

(c) indicators for pedestrians,

of the size, colour and type specified in the following provisions of this Part of this Schedule, together with any additional traffic signs placed in accordance with regulation 9.

3. Vehicular light signals

B58.46   (1) The vehicular light signals shall be of the size, colour and type of the signals shown in diagram 3000 in Schedule 8 to the 1994 Regulations, except that a green arrow may be substituted for the green aspect in the manner shown in diagram 3003 in that Schedule or in accordance with any variant permitted by those Regulations in respect of that diagram.

(2) The lamp showing an amber light shall be capable of showing a light which is either steady or which flashes at a rate of not less than 70 nor more than 90 flashes per minute.

(3) The vehicular light signals shall be illuminated in the following sequence—

(a) steady green,

(b) steady amber,

(c) steady red,

(d) flashing amber.

4. Pedestrian light signals

B58.47   (1) The pedestrian light signals shall be of the size, colour and type of the signals shown in diagram 4002 in Schedule 9 to the 1994 Regulations.

(2) The signals shall be so designed that—

(a) they operate in the following sequence—

(i) steady red,

(ii) steady green,

(iii) flashing green;

(b) the red figure can be internally illuminated by a steady light;

(c) the green figure can be internally illuminated by a steady light or a light which flashes at a rate of not less than 70 nor more than 90 flashes per minute; and

(d) when one signal is illuminated the other is not.

(3) The signals may incorporate a device for emitting audible signals whilst the green figure is illuminated by a steady light.

5. Indicators for pedestrians

The indicators for pedestrians—   **B58.48**

(a) shall be of the size, colour and type shown in the diagram in Part II of this Schedule;

(b) shall be so constructed that the word "WAIT" as shown on the diagram can be illuminated;

(c) shall incorporate a push button or other switching device (referred to in this Schedule as a *"push button"*) which can be used by pedestrians with the effect described in paragraphs 6 and 7;

(d) shall be so constructed that the instruction for pedestrians shown in the diagram can be internally illuminated; and

(e) may be so constructed that a device giving audible or tactile signals is provided for use when the green figure shown in the diagram is illuminated by a steady light.

6. Co-ordination of light signals and indicators for pedestrians

(1) The vehicular light signals, pedestrian light signals and the indicators for pedestrians   **B58.49**
shall be so constructed that—

(a) before the signals and indicators are operated by the pressing of a push button (or by remote control in accordance with paragraph 7)—

  (i) the vehicular light signals show a green or red light,

  (ii) the pedestrian light signals show a red light,

  (iii) the word "WAIT" on the indicators for pedestrians is not illuminated,

  (iv) any device for giving tactile signals is inactive; and

  (v) any device for giving audible signals is silent;

(b) when a push button is pressed or the signals and indicators are operated by remote control—

  (i) the signals and indicators show lights in the sequences specified in descending order in—
    (a) column (1) in the case of vehicular light signals;
    (b) in column (2) in the case of pedestrian light signals; and
    (c) in column (3) in the case of indicators for pedestrians,
    of either Part III or Part IV of this Schedule;

  (ii) when the pedestrian light signals are showing a steady green light, the word "WAIT" in the indicators for pedestrians is not illuminated;

  (iii) when the pedestrian light signals are showing a flashing green light, the word "WAIT" in the indicators for pedestrians is illuminated immediately and the signals and indicators are caused to show lights in the sequence specified in paragraph (i) above at the end of the next vehicle period; and

  (iv) when the pedestrian light signals are showing a red light, the word "WAIT" in the indicators for pedestrians is illuminated immediately and the vehicular light signals and indicators for pedestrians are caused to show lights in the sequence specified in paragraph (i);

(c) the periods during which lights are shown by the signals and indicators, begin and end in relation to each other as shown in either Part III or Part IV of this Schedule as if each horizontal line in those Parts represented one moment of time, subsequent moments occurring in descending order, but the distances between the horizontal lines do not represent the lengths of the periods during which lights shown by the signals and indicator are, or are not, lit.

(2) Where a device for emitting audible signals is provided pursuant to paragraph 4(3) or (5)(e), it shall be so constructed that the device operates only when the pedestrian light signals are showing a steady green light and at the same time the vehicular light signals are showing a red light.

(3) Where a device for giving tactile signals is provided pursuant to paragraph 5(e), it shall be so constructed that, when it is operating, a regular movement perceptible to touch by pedestrians is made only when the pedestrian light signals are showing a steady green light and at the same time the vehicular light signals are showing a red light.

(4) In this paragraph "*vehicle period*" means such period as may be fixed from time to time in relation to a Pelican crossing, being a period which begins when the vehicular light signals cease to show a flashing amber light and during which those signals show a green light.

7. Operation by remote control

B58.50   The vehicular light signals, pedestrian light signals, indicators for pedestrians and any device for giving tactile signals or emitting audible signals, when they are placed at or near a Pelican crossing may also be so constructed that they can be operated by remote control.

PART II

INDICATOR FOR PEDESTRIANS

[Diagram omitted.]

PART III

SEQUENCE OF OPERATION OF VEHICULAR AND PEDESTRIAN LIGHT SIGNALS AND INDICATOR FOR PEDESTRIANS (BUT NOT THE AUDIBLE OR TACTILE SIGNALS)

Sequence of vehicular traffic light signals (1)	Sequence of pedestrian signals	
	Pedestrian light signals (2)	*Indicator for pedestrians* (3)
Green light	Red light	The word "WAIT" is illuminated
Amber light		
Red light		
	Green light	The word "WAIT" is not illuminated
Flashing amber light	Flashing green light	The word "WAIT" is illuminated
	Red light	
Green light		

PART IV

ALTERNATIVE SEQUENCE OF OPERATION OF VEHICULAR AND PEDESTRIAN LIGHT SIGNALS
AND INDICATOR FOR PEDESTRIANS (BUT NOT THE AUDIBLE OR TACTILE SIGNALS)

Sequence of vehicular traffic light signals (1)	Sequence of pedestrian signals	
	Pedestrian light signals (2)	Indicator for pedestrians (3)
Green light	Red light	The word "WAIT" is illuminated
Amber light		
Red light		
	Green light	The word "WAIT" is not illuminated
Flashing amber light	Flashing green light	The word "WAIT" is illuminated
	Red light	
Green light		

SCHEDULE 3   Regulation 5(3)(a)

TRAFFIC SIGNS TO INDICATE PUFFIN CROSSINGS

PART I

TRAFFIC SIGNS TO INDICATE PUFFIN CROSSINGS

1. Traffic signs at or near a Puffin crossing

The traffic signs which are to be placed at or near a Puffin crossing by virtue of regul-   **B58.51**
ation 5(3)(a) shall consist of a combination of—

    (a) vehicular light signals: and

    (b) pedestrian demand units,

of the size, colour and type specified in the following provisions of this Schedule, together
with any additional traffic signs placed in accordance with regulation 9.

2. Vehicular light signals

(1) The vehicular light signals shall be of the size, colour and type shown in diagram   **B58.52**
3000 in Schedule 8 to the 1994 Regulations, except that a green arrow may be substituted
for the green aspect in the manner shown in diagram 3003 in that Schedule or in
accordance with any variant permitted by those Regulations in respect of that diagram.

(2) The vehicular lights shall be illuminated in the following sequence—

    (a) red,

    (b) red and amber together,

    (c) green,

    (d) amber.

3. Pedestrian demand unit

B58.53 (1) A pedestrian demand unit shall be placed at each end of a crossing.

(2) Each such unit shall consist of a device the principal features of which are a signal display of the size, colour and type shown in the diagram in Part II of this Schedule and which—

(a) complies with the requirements of sub-paragraph (3); and

(b) includes a push button or other switching device which in some way indicates to pedestrians that it has been operated.

(3) The requirements referred to in sub-paragraph (2)(a) are—

(a) the signal display must comprise a red figure and a green figure, both of which can be internally illuminated;

(b) while one figure is illuminated the other figure must not be capable of being illuminated; and

(c) the green figure must be capable of being illuminated only whilst there is conveyed to vehicular traffic, by means of the red vehicular light signal prescribed by paragraph 2, a prohibition against entering the limits of the Puffin crossing at or near which the unit is displayed and at no other time.

(4) The pedestrian demand unit may incorporate a device for emitting tactile or audible signals whilst the green figure is illuminated.

(5) Units consisting of only the red and green figures or the push button and legend comprised in a pedestrian demand unit may be provided at a crossing in addition to pedestrian demand units.

PART II

PEDESTRIAN DEMAND UNIT

[Diagram omitted.]

Regulation 5(2)(b) and   SCHEDULE 4
(3)(b) and 6(2) and (3)

PART I

ROAD MARKINGS TO INDICATE PELICAN AND PUFFIN CROSSINGS, PELICAN AND PUFFIN
CONTROLLED AREAS AND STOP LINES

1. Interpretation of Schedule

B58.54 In this Schedule except where otherwise stated,—

(a) a reference to a "*crossing*" is to a Pelican crossing or a Puffin crossing;

(b) a reference to a "*controlled area*" is to a Pelican controlled area or a Puffin controlled area;

(c) a reference to a numbered diagram is a reference to the diagram in Part II of this Schedule so numbered.

2. Indication of limits of crossings and of controlled areas and stop lines

B58.55 (1) Subject to the provisions of this Schedule, the limits of a crossing on a two-way street and of its controlled areas and stop lines shall be indicated by road markings consisting of lines and studs on the carriageway of the size and type shown—

(a) in diagram 1 where there is no central reservation;

(b) in diagram 2 where there is a central reservation, but the crossing does not form part of a system of staggered crossings; and

(c) in diagram 3 where the crossing forms part of a system of staggered crossings.

(2) Subject to the provisions of this Schedule, the limits of a crossing on a one-way street and of its controlled areas and stop lines shall be indicated by road markings consisting of lines and studs placed on the carriageway of the size and type shown—

(a) in diagram 4 where there is no central reservation;

(b) in diagram 5 where there is a central reservation but the crossing does not form part of a system of staggered crossings; and

(c) in diagram 6 where the crossing forms part of a system of staggered crossings.

(3) The two lines of studs indicating the limits of a crossing need not be at right angles to the edge of the carriageway, but shall form straight lines and shall, as near as is reasonably practicable, be parallel to each other.

3. Controlled areas and stop lines on a two-way street

(1) Where a crossing is on a two-way street the road markings to indicate each controlled area and stop line shall consist of—   **B58.56**

(a) a stop line parallel to the nearer row of studs indicating the limits of the crossing and extending, in the manner indicated in the appropriate diagram, across the part of the carriageway used by vehicles approaching the crossing from the side on which the stop line is placed; and

(b) two or more longitudinal zig-zag lines or, in the case of a road having more than one carriageway, two or more such lines on each carriageway, each zig-zag line containing not less than 8 nor more than 18 marks and extending away from the crossing.

(2) Subject to paragraph (3), where a central reservation is provided, the road marking shown in diagram 1040 in Schedule 6 to the 1994 Regulations may be placed between the zig-zag lines on the approaches to the central reservation.

(3) Where a central reservation is provided connecting crossings which form part of a system of staggered crossings, the road marking shown in diagram 1040.2 in Schedule 6 to the 1994 Regulations shall be placed in the manner indicated in diagram 3.

(4) The distance between the studs and the terminal marks on the exit sides shall be not less than 1700mm nor more than 3000mm.

4. Controlled areas and stop line on a one-way street

(1) Where a crossing is on a one-way street the road markings to indicate a controlled area and stop line shall consist of—   **B58.57**

(a) a stop line parallel to the nearer row of studs indicating the limits of the crossing and extending—

(i) in the case of a crossing of the type shown in diagram 4 or 5, from one edge of the carriageway to the other; and

(ii) in the case of a crossing of the type shown in diagram 6, from the edge of the carriageway to the central reservation; and

(b) two or more zig-zag lines, each containing not less than 8 nor more than 18 marks and extending away from the crossing.

(2) Subject to paragraph (3), where a central reservation is provided, the road marking shown in diagram 1041 in Schedule 6 to the 1994 Regulations may be placed between the zig-zag lines on the approaches to the central reservation.

(3) Where a central reservation is provided connecting crossings which form part of a system of staggered crossings, the road marking mentioned in paragraph (2) shall be placed in the manner indicated in diagram 6.

5. Variations in relation to a controlled area or stop line

B58.58　(1) Where the traffic authority is satisfied that, by reason of the layout or character of the roads in the vicinity of a crossing, it is impracticable to indicate a controlled area in accordance with the requirements of the preceding provisions of this Schedule, the following variations shall be permitted—

 (a)　the number of marks in each zig-zag line may be reduced to not less than 2;

 (b)　the marks comprised in a zig-zag line may be varied to a length of not less than 1 metre, in which case—

  (i)　each mark in each zig-zag line must be of the same or substantially the same length as the other marks in the same line;

  (ii)　and the number of marks in each line must be not more than 8 nor less than 2.

(2) The angle of a stop line in relation to the nearer line of studs indicating the limits of a crossing may be varied, if the traffic authority is satisfied that the variation is necessary having regard to the angle of the crossing in relation to the edge of the carriageway.

(3) The maximum distance of 3 metres between a stop line and the nearer line of studs indicating the limits of the crossing shown in the diagrams in this Schedule may be increased to such greater distance, not exceeding 10 metres, as the traffic authority may decide.

(4) Each zig-zag line in a controlled area need not contain the same number of marks as the others and the pattern of the central lines may be reversed or, if the carriageway is not more than 6 metres wide, may be omitted altogether if replaced by the road marking shown in diagram 1004 in Schedule 6 to the 1994 Regulations.

6. Colour and illumination of road markings

B58.59　Subject to paragraph 7, the road markings shown in the diagrams in this Schedule shall be coloured white and may be illuminated by retroreflecting material.

7. Form and colour of studs

B58.60　(1) The studs shown in the diagrams in this Schedule shall be—

 (a)　coloured white, silver or light grey and shall not be fitted with reflective lenses; and

 (b)　either circular in shape with a diameter of not less than 95mm nor more than 110mm or square in shape with the length of each side being not less than 95mm nor more than 110mm.

(2) Any stud which is fixed or embedded in the carriageway shall not project more than 20mm above the carriageway at its highest point nor more than 6mm at its edges.

8. Supplementary

B58.61　The requirements of this Schedule shall be regarded as having been complied with in the case of any crossing or controlled area, if most of the road markings comply with those requirements, even though some of the studs or lines do not so comply by reason of discolouration, temporary removal or a displacement or for some other reason, so long as the general appearance of the road markings as a whole is not thereby materially impaired.

PART II

DIAGRAM 1

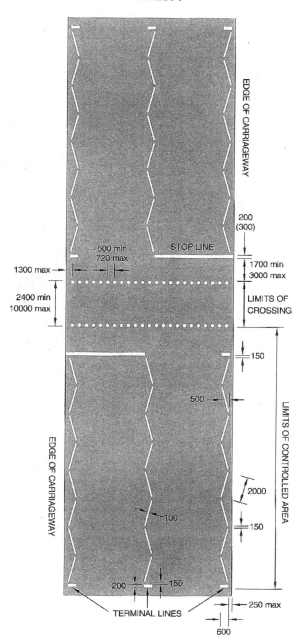

DIAGRAM 2

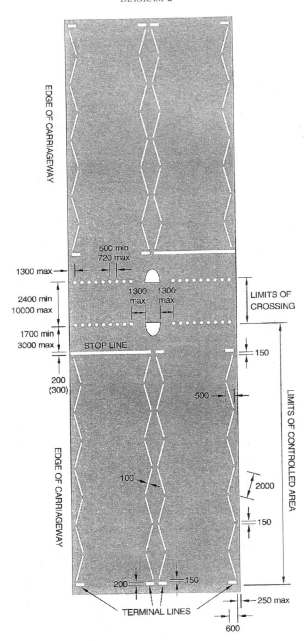

DIAGRAM 3

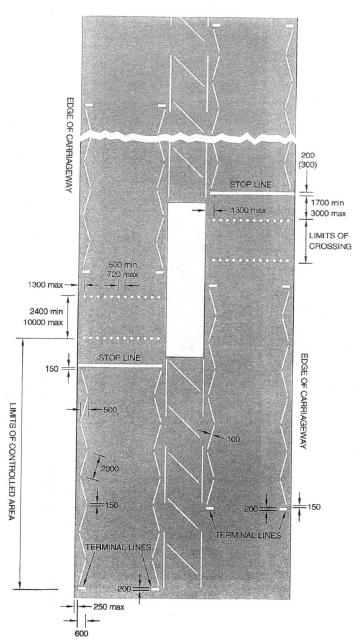

DIAGRAM 4

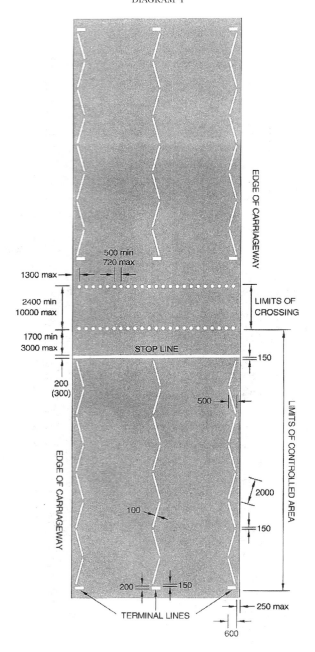

DIAGRAM 5

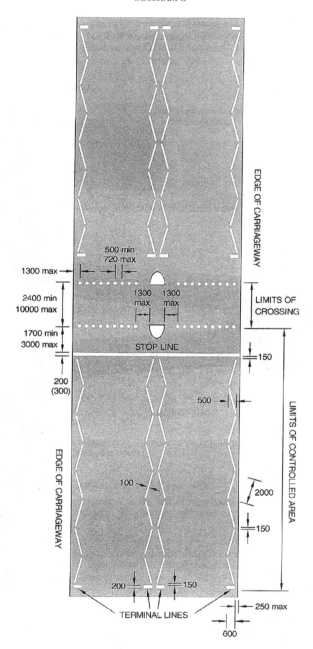

DIAGRAM 6

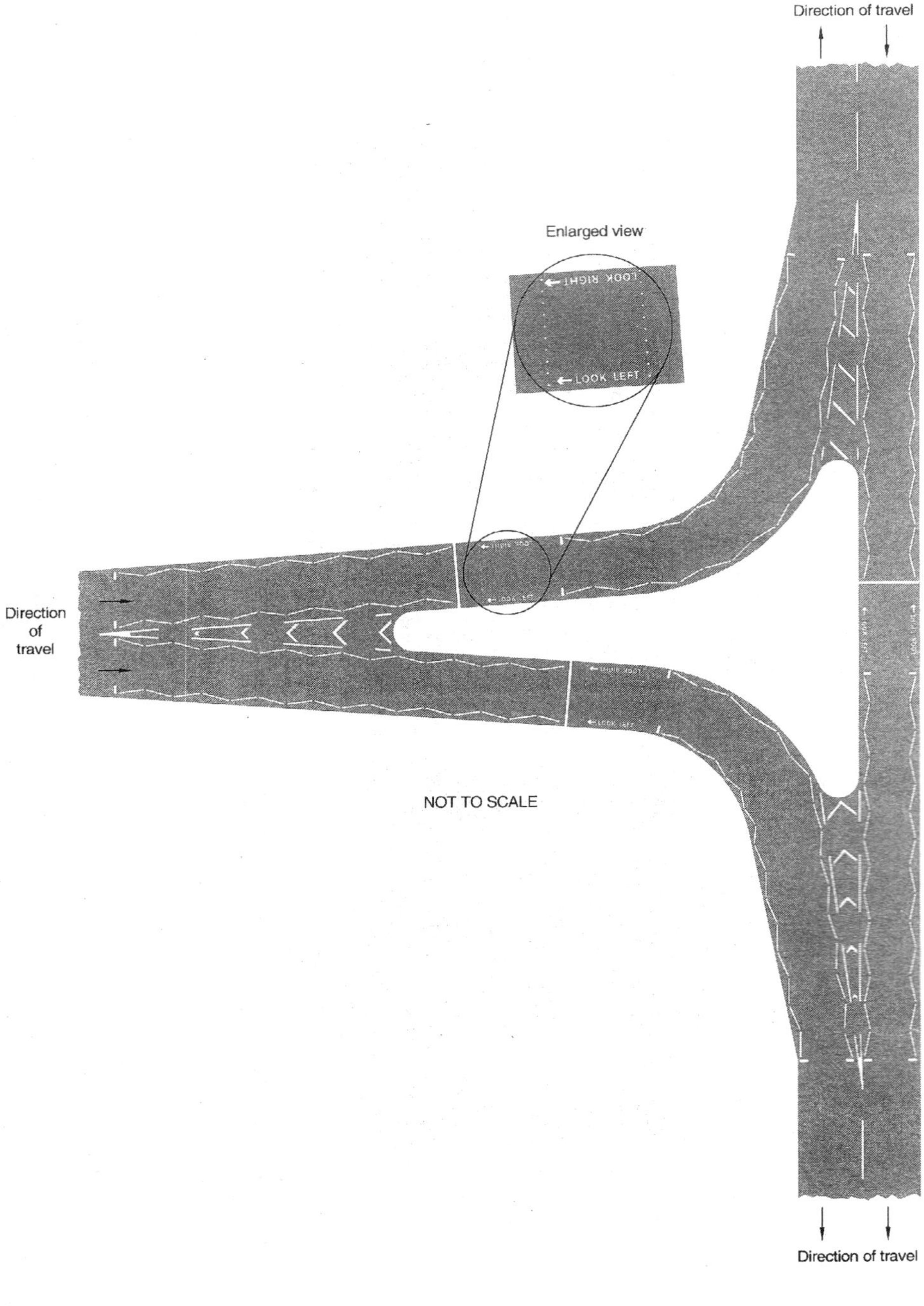

Direction of travel

Enlarged view

LOOK RIGHT

LOOK LEFT

Direction of travel

Direction
of
travel

NOT TO SCALE

Direction of travel

PART II

THE PELICAN AND PUFFIN PEDESTRIAN CROSSINGS GENERAL DIRECTIONS 1997

1. Citation and commencement   *[Omitted.]*   **B58.62**

2. Revocation

So far as they consist of or comprise general directions, the "Pelican" Pedestrian   **B58.63**
Crossings Regulations and General Directions 1987 are hereby revoked.

[See the note to regulation 2 of this instrument.]   **B58.64**

3. Interpretation

(1) In these Directions—   **B58.65**

    (a) *"the Regulations"* means the Zebra, Pelican and Puffin Pedestrian Crossings Regulations 1997 [*i.e. Part I of this Instrument*], and

    (b) the expressions listed in paragraph (2) have the same meanings as in the Regulations.

(2) Those expressions are—

"the 1994 Regulations";
"carriageway";
"central reservation";
"indicator for pedestrians";
"one-way street";
"pedestrian light signals";
"pedestrian demand unit";
"Pelican crossing";
"primary signal";
"Puffin crossing";
"secondary signal";
"system of staggered crossings";
"two-way street"; and
"vehicular light signals".

(3) In these Directions a reference to a numbered paragraph is to the paragraph so numbered in the direction in which the reference occurs.

4. Vehicular light signals at Pelican and Puffin crossings

(1) In this direction references to the left or right hand side of a crossing are to the left or   **B58.66**
right hand side as viewed from the direction of travel of vehicular traffic approaching the
crossing.

(2) Subject to paragraph (4) the vehicular light signals to be provided facing each direction of approaching traffic at a Pelican or Puffin crossing which is on a two-way street and is of a type specified in column (1) of the table below shall be as specified in relation to that type of crossing in column (2).

TABLE

(1) *Type of crossing on a two-way street*	(2) *Vehicular light signals facing each direction of traffic*
Crossing not forming part of a system of staggered crossings and not having a refuge for pedestrians or central reservation within the limits of the crossing	One primary signal on the left hand side of the crossing and one secondary signal on the right hand side of the crossing
Crossing not forming part of a system of staggered crossings and having a refuge for pedestrians or central reservation within the limits of the crossing	One primary signal on the left hand side of the crossing and one secondary signal on the right hand side or on the refuge for pedestrians or central reservation
Crossing forming part of a system of staggered crossings	One primary signal on the left hand side of the crossing and one other signal, which may be either a primary signal or a secondary signal, on the right hand side of the crossing

(3) Subject to paragraph (4) the vehicular light signals to be provided facing the direction of approaching traffic at a Pelican or Puffin crossing which is on a one-way street and is of a type specified in column (1) of the table below shall be as specified in relation to that type of crossing in column (2).

TABLE

(1) *Type of crossing on a one-way street*	(2) *Vehicular light signals to be provided*
Crossing not forming part of a system of staggered crossings and not having a refuge for pedestrians or central reservation within the limits of the crossing	One primary signal on the left hand side of the crossing and one other signal, which may be either a primary or a secondary signal, on the right hand side of the crossing
Crossing not forming part of a system of staggered crossings and having a refuge for pedestrians or central reservation within the limits of the crossing	One primary signal on each side of the crossing and one other signal which may be either a primary signal (in which case it must be on the refuge for pedestrians or the central reservation) or a secondary signal
Crossing forming part of a system of staggered crossings	One primary signal on the left hand side of the crossing and a signal, which may be either a primary or a secondary signal, on the right hand side of the crossing

(4) In addition to the signals required to be placed by paragraph (2) or (3) the traffic authority may place such other primary or secondary signals at a Pelican or Puffin crossing as it thinks fit.

5. Pedestrian light signals and indicators for pedestrians at Pelican crossings

B58.67   (1) At least one pedestrian light signal and at least one indicator for pedestrians shall be placed at each end of a Pelican crossing.

(2) Each pedestrian light signal shall be so placed as to be clearly visible to any person on the other side of the carriageway who wishes to use the crossing.

(3) Where there is a central reservation in a Pelican crossing, at least one indicator for pedestrians shall be placed on the central reservation.

(4) Each indicator for pedestrians shall be so placed that the push button on it may be reached by any person wishing to press it.

6. Pedestrian demand units at Puffin crossings

(1) At least one pedestrian demand unit shall be placed at each end of a Puffin crossing.   **B58.68**

(2) Each pedestrian demand unit shall be so placed that the push button on it may be reached by any person wishing to press it.

7. Additional traffic signs

A traffic sign of the size, colour and type shown in diagram 610 or 611 in Schedule 2   **B58.69** to the 1994 Regulations may only be placed on a refuge for pedestrians or a central reservation within the limits of a Pelican or Puffin crossing or on a central reservation which lies between two Pelican or Puffin crossings which form part of a system of staggered crossings.

8. Colouring of containers and posts

(1) The containers of vehicular light signals at a Pelican or Puffin crossing—   **B58.70**
   (a) shall be coloured black; and
   (b) may be mounted on a backing board,

and, if so mounted the backing board shall be coloured black and may have a white border not less than 45mm nor more than 55mm wide which may be made of reflective material.

(2) The containers of pedestrian light signals at a Pelican crossing shall be coloured black.

(3) Where, at a Pelican or Puffin crossing, vehicular light signals, pedestrian light signals, an indicator for pedestrians or a pedestrian demand unit is mounted on a post specially provided for the purpose, the part of the post extending above ground level shall be of a single colour, which may be grey, [black,] brown, dark green or dark blue but may have marked on it one yellow or white band not less than 140mm nor more than 160mm deep, the lower edge of the band being not less than 1.5 metres nor more than 1.7 metres above the level of the immediately adjacent ground.

(4) Any box attached to a post or other structure on which vehicular light signals, pedestrian light signals, an indicator for pedestrians or a pedestrian demand unit are mounted and housing apparatus designed to control, or to monitor, the operation of the signals or unit shall be coloured grey, black, brown, dark green or dark blue.

[Direction 8 is printed as amended by S.I. 1998 No. 901.]   **B58.71**

9. Approval of equipment

(1) In this direction *"equipment"* means all equipment (including the content of all   **B58.72** instructions stored in, or executable by it) capable of giving visible, audible or tactile signals used in connection with vehicular light signals, pedestrian light signals, indicators for pedestrians or pedestrian demand units to secure that those signals, indicators or units comply with the relevant provisions of the Regulations.

(2) All equipment placed on a road for the purposes of a Pelican or Puffin crossing shall be of a type approved in writing by the Secretary of State.

(3) If, after equipment has been placed in accordance with an approval under paragraph (2), the signals, indicator or unit used in connection with it is altered, the signal, indicator or unit shall not be further used unless that alteration is approved in writing by the Secretary of State.

(4) When any equipment which has been placed at a Pelican or Puffin crossing is of a type approved under paragraph (2), the equipment shall, subject to paragraph (3), be regarded as continuing to be approved until notice is given in writing by the Secretary of State—

    (a) to the traffic authority; and

    (b) either—

        (i) to the supplier of the equipment; or

        (ii) where an alteration has been approved in accordance with paragraph (3), to the person who carried out the alteration,

of a date which the equipment is no longer to be so regarded.

(5) Where notice is given under paragraph (4) that equipment is no longer to be regarded as being approved, the equipment and, unless the Secretary of State approves any alternative equipment for the same purpose, any signal, indicator or unit in connection with it shall be removed from the road on or before the date given in the notice.

10. Special directions by the Secretary of State

B58.73 Nothing in these Directions shall be taken to limit the power of the Secretary of State by any special direction to dispense with, add to or modify any of the requirements of these Directions in their application to any particular case.

APPENDIX

B58.74 EXERCISE OF POWERS

[Omitted.]

The Vehicle Excise Duty (Immobilisation, Removal and Disposal of Vehicles) Regulations 1997

(S.I. 1997 No. 2439)

[The text of the regulations is printed as amended by:

    the Vehicle Excise Duty (Immobilisation, Removal and Disposal of Vehicles) (Amendment) Regulations 1997 (S.I. 1997 No. 3063) (February 2, 1998); and

    the Vehicle Excise Duty (Immobilisation, Removal and Disposal of Vehicles (Amendment) Regulations 1998 (S.I. 1998 No. 1217) (June 15, 1998).

    The amending regulations are referred to in the notes to the principal regulations only by their years and numbers. The dates referred to above are the dates on which the amending regulations came into force.

    The principal regulations have also been amended by the Vehicle Excise Duty (Immobilisation, Removal and Disposal of Vehicles) (Amendment) Regulations 1999 (S.I. 1999 No. 35); the Vehicle Excise Duty (Immobilisation, Removal and Disposal of Vehicles) (Amendment) Regulations 2001 (S.I. 2001 No. 936), but these do not affect the text of any provision printed in this work.]

B59.01

ARRANGEMENT OF REGULATIONS

PART I

PRELIMINARY

B59.02

PART II

IMMOBILISATION OF VEHICLES

PART III

REMOVAL AND DISPOSAL OF VEHICLES

PART IV

VOUCHERS

PART V

DISPUTES

*   *   *

PART I

PRELIMINARY

B59.03 **1. Citation, commencement and revocation**   *[Omitted.]*

2. Interpretation

B59.04   (1) In these Regulations—

"*the 1994 Act*" means the Vehicle Excise and Registration Act 1994;

"*authorised person*" has the meaning given by regulation 3;

"*custodian*" in relation to a vehicle has the meaning given by regulation 9(3);

"*disabled person's badge*" has the meaning given by paragraph 1(7) of Schedule 2A to the 1994 Act;

"*G.B. records*" means the records kept under the 1994 Act by the Driver and Vehicle Licensing Agency on behalf of the Secretary of State and "*G.B. registration mark*" means a registration mark assigned to a vehicle registered in those records;

["*local authority*" means—

    (a) in relation to England, a county council, a district council, a London borough council or the Common Council of the City of London;

    (b) in relation to Wales, a county council or county borough council;

    (c) *[applies to Northern Ireland]*;]

    [(d) *[applies to Scotland]*.]

"*N.I. records*" means the records kept under the 1994 Act by Driver and Vehicle Licensing Northern Ireland on behalf of the Secretary of State and "*N.I. registration mark*" means a registration mark assigned to a vehicle registered in those records;

["*public service vehicle*"—

(a) in relation to [Great Britain] has the meaning given by section 1 of the Public Passenger Vehicles Act [*q.v.*]; and

(b) *[applies to Northern Ireland]*;]

"*release*" in relation to a vehicle means release from an immobilisation device;

"*surety payment*" means a sum payable by virtue of regulation 6(3)(b) or regulation 12(2)(c)(ii) where a vehicle licence is not produced; and

"*voucher*" means a voucher issued under regulation 15(2).

(2) References to the prescribed charge for any matter are to the charge specified in relation to that matter in Schedule 1 to these Regulations.

(3) References to the "*owner*" of a vehicle at a particular time are to the person by whom it was then kept and the person in whose name the vehicle is registered at a particular time shall be taken, unless the contrary is shown, to be the person by whom the vehicle was kept at that time.

(4) Except where it is expressly provided otherwise, references in these Regulations to a numbered regulation are to the regulation in these Regulations so numbered and references to a numbered paragraph are to the paragraph so numbered in the regulation in which the reference occurs.

[Regulation 2 is printed as amended by S.I. 1997 No. 3063; S.I. 1998 No. 1217.]   **B59.05**

3. Authorised persons

(1) In these Regulations a reference to an authorised person is to a person authorised by   **B59.06** the Secretary of State for the purposes of these Regulations.

(2) An authorised person may be a local authority, an employee of a local authority, a member of a police force or any other person.

(3) Different persons may be authorised for different purposes, but a person who is an authorised person for the purposes of regulation 17 shall not act as an authorised person for any other purpose.

4. Disapplication of the Regulations

(1) These Regulations shall not apply in relation to a vehicle [which is on a public road]   **B59.07** in any of the circumstances specified in paragraph (2).

(2) The circumstances are that—

(a) a current disabled person's badge is displayed on the vehicle;

(b) the vehicle is an exempt vehicle and a current nil licence is displayed on it;

(c) a badge issued pursuant to the British Medical Association car badge scheme is displayed on the vehicle;

(d) the vehicle appears to an authorised person to have been abandoned;

(e) the vehicle is a public service vehicle being used for the carriage of passengers;

(f) the vehicle is being used for the purpose of the removal of any obstruction to traffic, the maintenance, improvement or reconstruction of a public road, or the laying, erection, alteration, repair or cleaning in or near a road of any traffic sign or sewer or of any main, pipe or apparatus for the supply of gas, water or electricity, or of any telegraph or telephone wires, cables, posts or supports;

(g) the vehicle is being used by the Post Office in connection with the delivery or collection of postal packets and each side of the vehicle is clearly marked with the words "Post Office" or "Royal Mail"; or

(h) the vehicle is stationary at a time when, having been immobilised or removed under these Regulations, less than 24 hours have elapsed since it was released or, as the case may be, removed.

(3) In this regulation *"nil licence"* means a document which—

(a) was issued by the Secretary of State in accordance with regulations under the 1994 Act;

(b) is in the form of a vehicle licence; and

(c) has "NIL" marked in the space provided for indicating the amount of vehicle excise duty payable.

B59.08 *[Regulation 4 is printed as amended by S.I. 1997 No. 3063.]*

PART II

IMMOBILISATION OF VEHICLES

5. Power to immobilise vehicles

B59.09 (1) This regulation applies where an authorised person has reason to believe that an offence under section 29(1) of the 1994 Act is being committed as regards a vehicle which is stationary on a public road . . .

(2) Where this regulation applies, without prejudice to the institution of proceedings for any offence under the 1994 Act, the authorised person or a person acting under his direction may—

(a) fix an immobilisation device to the vehicle while it remains in the place where it is stationary, or

(b) move it from that place to another place on the same or another public road and fix an immobilisation device to it in that other place.

(3) Where an immobilisation device is fixed to a vehicle in accordance with this regulation, the person fixing the device shall also fix to the vehicle an immobilisation notice which—

(a) indicates that the device has been fixed to the vehicle and warns that no attempt should be made to drive it or otherwise put it in motion until it has been released from the device;

(b) states the reason why the device has been fixed;

(c) specifies the steps to be taken to secure its release including the charges payable under these Regulations and the person to whom and the means by which those charges may be paid.

B59.10 *[Regulation 5 is printed as amended by S.I. 1997 No. 3063; S.I. 1998 No. 1217.]*

6. Release of immobilised vehicles

B59.11 (1) A vehicle to which an immobilisation device has been fixed in accordance with regulation 5—

(a) may be released only by or under the direction of an authorised person; and

(b) subject to sub-paragraph (a) above, shall be released—

(i) where there is produced to an authorised person a vehicle licence for the vehicle which was in force when the vehicle was immobilised; or

(ii) where an authorised person is satisfied that the vehicle was immobilised in any of the circumstances specified in regulation 4(2) or that the vehicle was at the time it was immobilised an exempt vehicle; or

(iii) if the first and second requirements specified in paragraphs (2) and (3) are met.

(2) The first requirement is that the prescribed charge for the release of the vehicle from the immobilisation device is paid in any manner specified in the immobilisation notice.

(3) The second requirement is that—

(a) a vehicle licence is produced in accordance with instructions specified in the immobilisation notice and the licence is one which is in force for the vehicle concerned at the time the licence is produced; or

(b) where such a licence is not produced, the prescribed charge for a surety payment is paid in any manner specified in the immobilisation notice.

7. Removal of or interference with immobilisation notice or device

(1) An immobilisation notice shall not be removed or interfered with except by or under the authority of an authorised person. **B59.12**

(2) A person contravening paragraph (1) shall be guilty of an offence and liable on summary conviction to a fine not exceeding level 2 on the standard scale.

(3) Any person who, without being authorised to do so in accordance with regulation 6, removes or attempts to remove an immobilisation device fixed to a vehicle in accordance with these Regulations is guilty of an offence and shall be liable on summary conviction to a fine not exceeding level 3 on the standard scale.

8. Other offences connected with immobilisation

(1) Where these Regulations would apply in relation to a vehicle but for the provisions of regulation 4(1) and (2)(a) and the vehicle was not, at the time it was stationary, being used— **B59.13**

(a) in accordance with regulations under section 21 of the Chronically Sick and Disabled Persons Act 1970 [*q.v.*] or with regulations under section 14 of the Chronically Sick and Disabled Persons (Northern Ireland) Act 1978, and

(b) in circumstances falling within section 117(1)(b) of the Road Traffic Regulation Act 1984 [*q.v.*] or Article 174A(2)(b) of the Road Traffic (Northern Ireland) Order 1981 [*S.I. 1981 No. 154*] (use where a disabled person's concession would be available),

the person in charge of the vehicle at that time is guilty of an offence and liable on summary conviction to a fine not exceeding level 3 on the standard scale.

(2) Where—

(a) a person makes a declaration with a view to securing the release of a vehicle from an immobilisation device purported to have been fixed in accordance with these Regulations,

(b) the declaration is that the vehicle is or was an exempt vehicle, and

(c) the declaration is to the person's knowledge either false or in any material respect misleading,

that person is guilty of an offence.

(3) A person guilty of an offence by virtue of paragraph (2) is liable—

(a) on summary conviction, to a fine not exceeding the statutory maximum, and

(b) on conviction on indictment, to imprisonment for a term not exceeding two years or to a fine or to both.

PART III

REMOVAL AND DISPOSAL OF VEHICLES

9. Removal of vehicles

B59.14　(1) This regulation applies where an authorised person has reason to believe that an offence under section 29(1) of the 1994 Act—

　　(a) is being committed as regards a vehicle which is stationary on a public road . . .; or

　　(b) was being committed as regards a vehicle at a time when an immobilisation device which is fixed to the vehicle was fixed to it in accordance with these Regulations and the conditions prescribed in paragraph (2) are fulfilled.

　(2) The conditions are—

　　(a) 24 hours have elapsed since the device was fixed to the vehicle, and

　　(b) the vehicle has not been released in accordance with these Regulations.

　(3) In a case where this regulation applies, the authorised person or a person acting under his direction, may remove the vehicle and deliver it to a person authorised by the Secretary of State to keep vehicles so removed in his custody (in these Regulations called a "*custodian*").

B59.15　*[Regulation 9 is printed as amended by S.I. 1997 No. 3063; S.I. 1998 No. 1217.]*

B59.16　**10. Disposal of removed vehicles**　*[Omitted.]*

11. Recovery of prescribed charges

B59.17　(1) Where a vehicle has been removed and delivered into the custody of a custodian in accordance with regulation 9(3), the Secretary of State or the custodian may (whether or not any claim is made under regulation 12 or 14) recover from the person who was the owner of the vehicle when the vehicle was removed the prescribed charges for—

　　(a) its removal and storage; and

　　(b) if the vehicle has been disposed of, its disposal.

　(2) Where, by virtue of paragraph (1)(a), any sum is recoverable in respect of a vehicle by a custodian, he shall be entitled to retain custody of it until that sum is paid.

12. Taking possession of a vehicle

B59.18　(1) A person ("*the claimant*") may take possession of a vehicle which has been removed and delivered to a custodian and has not been disposed of under regulation 10, if the conditions specified in paragraph (2) are satisfied.

　(2) The conditions are—

　　(a) the claimant satisfies the custodian that he is the owner of the vehicle or that he is authorised by the owner to take possession of the vehicle;

　　(b) except where the claimant produces a vehicle licence in respect of the vehicle which was in force when the vehicle was immobilised or, where it was not immobilised, it was removed, or the custodian is satisfied that these Regulations did not apply to the vehicle at the time it was immobilised or removed, the claimant pays to the custodian—

　　　(i) the prescribed charge in respect of the removal of the vehicle; and

　　　(ii) the prescribed charge for the storage of the vehicle during the period whilst it was in the custody of the custodian; and

    (c) the claimant either—

        (i) produces to the custodian a vehicle licence in respect of the vehicle which is in force at the time the vehicle is claimed; or

        (ii) pays to the custodian the prescribed charge for the surety payment.

    (3) On giving the claimant possession of a vehicle pursuant to this regulation, the custodian shall give the claimant a statement of the right of the owner or person in charge of the vehicle at the time it was immobilised or, where it was not immobilised, it was removed to appeal pursuant to regulation 17(2), of the steps to be taken in order to appeal and of the address to which representations to an authorised person made as mentioned in that regulation should be sent.

13. Offences as to securing possession of vehicles

    (1) Where—   **B59.19**

    (a) a person makes a declaration with a view to securing possession of a vehicle purported to have been delivered into the custody of a custodian in accordance with regulation 9(3);

    (b) the declaration is that the vehicle is or was an exempt vehicle, and

    (c) the declaration is to the person's knowledge either false or in any material respect misleading,

that person is guilty of an offence.

    (2) A person guilty of an offence under paragraph (1) is liable—

    (a) on summary conviction, to a fine not exceeding the statutory maximum, and

    (b) on conviction on indictment, to imprisonment for a term not exceeding two years or to a fine or to both.

14. Claim by owner of a vehicle after its disposal   *[Omitted.]*   **B59.20**

PART IV

Payment of Sum where Licence is not Produced

15. Issue of vouchers

    (1) This regulation applies where a surety payment has been made in respect of a vehicle under either—   **B59.21**

    (a) regulation 6(3)(b); or

    (b) regulation 12(2)(c)(ii).

    (2) Where this regulation applies a voucher shall be issued in respect of the surety payment to the person making the payment by an authorised person, in a case falling within paragraph (1)(a), or by the custodian, in a case falling within paragraph (1)(b).

    (3) Where a voucher is so issued section 29(1) of the 1994 Act shall not apply as regards the vehicle concerned if it is used or kept on a public road without a vehicle licence being in force for it at any time during the period of 24 hours beginning with the time when the voucher was issued.

    (4) Neither an authorised person nor a custodian shall issue a voucher unless they have been furnished with information as to the identity of the owner of the vehicle.

(5) A voucher shall contain the following information—

(a) the registration mark of the vehicle concerned;

(b) the date and time of day when the vehicle was released from the immobilisation device; or, as the case may be, possession of it was taken;

(c) the name and address of the owner or assumed owner;

(d) the amount paid and the means by which it was paid;

(e) the name and address of the person procuring the release of the vehicle or, as the case may be, taking possession of it;

(f) particulars as to how a refund may be obtained in accordance with paragraph (6).

(6) The owner of a vehicle as respects which a voucher has been issued under this regulation shall be entitled to a refund of the amount of the surety payment represented by the voucher if—

(a) within the period of 15 days beginning with the date on which the voucher was issued, the voucher is surrendered to a person authorised to issue vouchers or a custodian; and

(b) a valid vehicle licence for the vehicle whose registration mark is given in the voucher is produced at the same time.

(7) Where a voucher is issued on receipt of a cheque which is subsequently dishonoured—

(a) the voucher shall be void;

(b) the person to whom the voucher is issued shall be required to deliver it up; and

(c) no refund shall be payable under paragraph (6).

16. Offences relating to vouchers

B59.22   (1) Where a person who, in connection with—

(a) obtaining a voucher under regulation 15, or

(b) obtaining a refund of any sum in respect of which a voucher was issued,

makes a declaration which to his knowledge is either false or in any material respect misleading, he is guilty of an offence.

(2) A person is guilty of an offence if he forges, fraudulently alters, fraudulently uses or fraudulently lends a voucher or fraudulently allows a voucher to be used by another person.

(3) A person guilty of an offence under paragraph (1) or (2) is liable—

(a) on summary conviction, to a fine not exceeding the statutory maximum, and

(b) on conviction on indictment, to imprisonment for a term not exceeding two years or to a fine or to both.

PART V

DISPUTES

17. Disputes

B59.23   (1) This regulation applies to a dispute which has arisen because—

(a) a person ("*the claimant*"), in order to secure the release or to obtain possession of a vehicle, has paid a charge in accordance with regulation 6 or 12 and alleges that the charge ("*the disputed charge*") should be refunded to him on the ground that, at the time the vehicle was immobilised or, where it was not immobilised, it was removed,—

(i) a vehicle licence was in force for the vehicle; or

(ii) any of the circumstances specified in regulation 4(2) applied to the vehicle; and

(b) the person to whom the disputed charge was paid refuses to refund the charge.

(2) The claimant under a dispute to which this regulation applies may appeal against the refusal of a refund by sending, to the authorised person whose name is given for this purpose in the statement under regulation 12(3) at the address so given, written representations stating the grounds on which a refund is claimed.

(3) The authorised person to whom the appeal is made may disregard any representations which are received by him after the end of the period of 28 days beginning with the date on which the vehicle was released or, as the case may be, on which possession was taken of it.

(4) The authorised person shall consider any representations duly made and any evidence provided in support of them and notify the claimant whether or not he accepts that either of the grounds mentioned in paragraph (1)(a) have been established and—

(a) if the authorised person notifies the claimant that one of those grounds has been established, the Secretary of State shall refund the disputed charge;

(b) if the authorised person rejects the appeal he shall so inform the claimant and at the same time notify him of his right to make a further appeal under paragraph (5).

[(5) A claimant who has made an appeal to an authorised person under paragraph (2) may make a further appeal to the appropriate court in accordance with paragraph (6)—

(a) if his appeal under paragraph (2) has been rejected under paragraph (4) and the further appeal is made within 28 days of his being served with notification to that effect under paragraph (4)(b); or

(b) if the authorised person has not notified him of the outcome of his appeal in accordance with paragraph (4) and 56 days have elapsed since he appealed,

and, if the court finds that either of the gounds mentioned in paragraph (1)(a) have been established, it shall order the Secretary of State to refund the disputed charge.]

[(6) A further appeal in accordance with paragraph (5) lies—

(a) in relation to a vehicle that was stationary on a public road in England or Wales, to a magistrates' court by way of complaint;

(b) *[applies to Scotland]*;

(c) *[applies to Northern Ireland]*.]

[Regulation 17 is printed as amended by S.I. 1998 No. 1217.]   **B59.24**

SCHEDULE 1

THE PRESCRIBED CHARGES   **B59.25**

[Omitted.]

SCHEDULE 2

STEPS TO BE TAKEN TO ASCERTAIN OWNERSHIP OF A REMOVED VEHICLE   **B59.26**

[Omitted.]

The Road Vehicles (Statutory Off-Road Notification) Regulations 1997

(S.I. 1997 No. 3025)

B60.01 *Editorial note.* These regulations were made under the Vehicle Excise and Registration Act 1994, s.22(1D), (1E), 1G) and (2), and s.57(1)–(3). As to offences under section 22(1D), see further section 46A of that Act above.

B60.02 *[The text of these regulations is printed as amended by:*

the Road Vehicles (Statutory Off-Road Notification) (Amendment) Regulations 1999 (S.I. 1999 No. 713) (April 1, 1999).

The amending regulations are referred to in the notes to the principal regulations only by their year and number. The date referred to above is the date on which the amending regulations came into force.]

ARRANGEMENT OF REGULATIONS

B60.03 Regulation

B60.04 **1. Citation and commencement**   *[Omitted.]*

2. Interpretation

B60.05 (1) In these Regulations—

"*the 1994 Act*" means the Vehicle Excise and Registration Act 1994 [*q.v.*];

"*keeper*" in relation to a vehicle means the person by whom the vehicle is kept;

"*the required declaration*" means a declaration in writing made to the Secretary of State by a person surrendering a vehicle licence or the keeper of a vehicle to the effect that (except for use under a trade licence) he does not for the time being intend to use or keep the vehicle on a public road and will not do so without first taking out a vehicle licence (or if appropriate a nil licence) for the vehicle;

"*the required particulars*" in relation to a vehicle are particulars furnished in writing to the Secretary of State of—

   (a) the registration mark of the vehicle;

   (b) the make and model of the vehicle; and

   (c) the address of the premises at which the vehicle is to be kept; and *"vehicle"* means a mechanically propelled vehicle which is—

  (a) registered in the records kept under the 1994 Act by the Driver and Vehicle Licensing Agency on behalf of the Secretary of State; and

  (b) kept in Great Britain,

and a reference to a vehicle which is *"unlicensed"* is to a vehicle for which no vehicle licence is for the time being in force.

(2) For the purposes of these Regulations a person is a *"motor vehicle trader"* in relation to a vehicle if he falls within a description mentioned in column (2) of an item in the table below and the vehicle falls within the description mentioned in column (3) of that item—

TABLE

(1) Item	(2) Descriptions of person	(3) Descriptions of vehicle
1.	The holder of a trade licence	A vehicle temporarily in his possession in the course of the business by virtue of which he is a person eligible to hold such a licence
2.	An auctioneer of mechanically propelled vehicles	A vehicle temporarily in his possession in the course of his business as such an auctioneer
3.	A motor dealer	A vehicle temporarily in his possession in the course of his business as a motor dealer
4.	A person who carries on business as a dismantler of vehicles	A vehicle temporarily in his possession in the course of that business
5.	An authorised insurer	A vehicle temporarily in his possession in consequence of settling a claim under a policy of insurance relating to the vehicle
6.	The holder of a licence under Part III of the Consumer Credit Act 1974 [*not reproduced in this work*]	A vehicle temporarily in his possession under an order for the repossession of the vehicle made in pursuance of a personal credit agreement relating to the vehicle

(3) In paragraph (2) above *"authorised insurer"* has the meaning given in section 145(5) of the Road Traffic Act 1988 [*q.v.*] and "personal credit agreement" has the meaning given in section 8(1) of the Consumer Credit Act 1974.

  [*The term "personal credit agreement" is defined by the Consumer Credit Act 1974, s.8(1), as "an agreement between an individual ('the debtor') and any other person ('the creditor') by which the creditor provides the debtor with credit of any amount".*]   **B60.06**

3. Application

  These Regulations have effect for the purpose of prescribing the particulars to be furnished and the declarations to be made, and the times at which and the manner in which they are to be furnished or made, by a person—   **B60.07**

(a) who surrenders a vehicle licence for a vehicle;

(b) who does not renew such a licence; or

(c) who keeps an unlicensed vehicle.

4. Exemptions

B60.08   These Regulations shall not apply in relation to a vehicle—

(a) which is an exempt vehicle falling within a description specified in paragraph 2, 2A, 3, 23 or 24 of Schedule 2 to the 1994 Act; or

(b) in relation to which the following conditions are satisfied—

(i) neither a vehicle licence nor a nil licence was in force for the vehicle on 31st January 1998;

(ii) such a licence has not been taken out for the vehicle for a period starting after that date; and

(iii) the vehicle has not been used or kept on a public road on or after that date.

5. Surrender of vehicle licence

B60.09   (1) When after 31st January 1998 the holder of a vehicle licence surrenders it under section 10(2) of the 1994 Act, he shall make the required declaration and furnish the required particulars in relation to the vehicle for which the licence was taken out.

(2) Paragraph (1) does not apply where the vehicle to which the licence relates is no longer kept by the holder of the licence or the holder is a motor vehicle trader in relation to that vehicle.

6. [Expiry of vehicle licence or nil licence]

B60.10   Where, on or after 31st January 1998, a vehicle licence [or a nil licence] ceases to be in force for a vehicle by reason of the expiration of the period for which the licence was granted and [a vehicle licence or a nil licence] for the vehicle is not taken out so as to run from the expiration of that period, the keeper of the vehicle shall make the required declaration and furnish the required particulars in relation to the vehicle—

(a) if he is a motor trader, not later than the end of the period of three months starting with the day following the expiration of that period; or

(b) in any other case, not later than that day.

B60.11   *[Regulation 6 is printed as amended by S.I. 1999 No. 713.]*

7. Person keeping an unlicensed vehicle

B60.12   (1) Subject to paragraph (2) where at any time after 31st January 1999—

(a) a person keeps an unlicensed vehicle; and

(b) a period of 12 months has elapsed throughout which the vehicle has been kept in Great Britain unlicensed and within which a nil licence has not been in force, the required declaration has not been made and the required particulars have not been furnished in relation to the vehicle,

then, unless a vehicle licence (or if appropriate a nil licence) for the vehicle has been taken out so as to run from the end of that period of 12 months, the keeper of the vehicle shall, not later than the day following the end of that period, make the required declaration and furnish the required particulars in relation to the vehicle.

(2) For the purposes of paragraph (1)(b) above, where a vehicle licence has been surr-

endered under section 10(2) of the 1994 Act, the vehicle to which it relates shall be taken to be unlicensed from the first day of the month in which the licence was surrendered.

(3) On a change of keeper of an unlicensed vehicle, unless a vehicle licence (or if appropriate a nil licence) for the vehicle is taken out, the new keeper shall make the required declaration and furnish the required particulars in relation to the vehicle—

    (a) if he is a motor vehicle trader, not later than the end of the period of three months beginning with the day following the day on which the change of keeper occurs; or

    (b) in any other case, not later than the day following the day on which the change of keeper occurs.

[8. Offences against these Regulations

These Regulations are hereby prescribed as regulations to which section 59(2)(a) of the 1994 Act applies.]   **B60.13**

[Regulation 8 was inserted by S.I. 1999 No. 713.]   **B60.14**

The Traffic Signs (Temporary Obstructions) Regulations 1997

(S.I. 1997 No. 3053)

ARRANGEMENT OF REGULATIONS

PART I

PRELIMINARY

PART II

SIGNIFICANCE OF TRAFFIC SIGNS

PART III

SIZE, COLOUR AND TYPE OF TRAFFIC SIGNS

PART IV

PLACING OF TRAFFIC SIGNS

PART V

SAVINGS

Regulation
17. Saving for the 1994 Regulations
18. The Motorways Traffic (England and Wales) Regulations 1982 and the Motorways Traffic (Scotland) Regulations 1995

SCHEDULES TO REGULATIONS

Schedule
1. The road vehicle sign
2. The traffic pyramid
3. The traffic triangle

PART I

PRELIMINARY

1, 2.   *[Omitted.]*   **B61.02**

3. Interpretation

(1) In these Regulations—   **B61.03**

"*the 1994 Regulations*" means the Traffic Signs Regulations 1994 [*Part I of S.I. 1994 No. 1519, q.v.*];

"*EEA State*" means a State which is a contracting Party to the Agreement on the European Economic Area signed at Oporto on 2nd May 1992 [*Cm. 2073*] as adjusted by the protocol signed at Brussels on 17th March 1993 [*Cm. 2183*];

"*flat traffic delineator*" means a traffic sign which is of the size, colour and type prescribed by regulation 9;

"*keep right sign*" means a traffic sign which is of the size, colour and type prescribed by regulation 8;

"*reflectorised*" means illuminated with retroreflecting material, that is to say material which reflects a ray of light back towards the source of that light;

"*road vehicle sign*" means a traffic sign which is of the size, colour and type prescribed by regulation 10;

"*traffic cone*" means a traffic sign which is of the size, colour and type prescribed by regulation 11;

"*traffic pyramid*" means a traffic sign which is of the size, colour and type prescribed by regulation 12;

"*traffic triangle*" means a traffic sign which is of the size, colour and type prescribed by regulation 13; and

"*warning lamp*" means a traffic sign which is of the size, colour and type prescribed by regulation 14.

(2) Unless otherwise specified, a reference in these Regulations to a numbered regulation or to a numbered Schedule is a reference to the regulation of or, as the case may be, the Schedule to these Regulations so numbered.

(3) The dimensions given in the diagrams in the Schedules to these Regulations are all in millimetres.

B61.04 *[As to the European Economic Area agreement, see the editorial note to Regulation (EEC) 3820/85 below.]*

PART II

SIGNIFICANCE OF TRAFFIC SIGNS

4. Keep right sign

B61.05 (1) In addition to the requirement conveyed by the sign shown in diagram 610 of the 1994 Regulations in accordance with those Regulations, a keep right sign shall convey to vehicular traffic a warning of a temporary obstruction.

(2) Section 36 of the Road Traffic Act 1998 [*q.v.*] shall apply to the keep right sign.

5. Flat traffic delineator and traffic cone

B61.06 In addition to indicating the edge of a route for vehicular traffic through or past a temporary obstruction, in accordance with the 1994 Regulations, a traffic cone and a flat traffic delineator shall each convey to such traffic on a road a warning of an obstruction in the road.

6. Road vehicle sign

B61.07 A road vehicle sign shall convey to vehicular traffic using a road a warning of a temporary obstruction in the road caused by a stationary vehicle.

7. Traffic pyramid, traffic triangle and warning lamp

B61.08 A traffic pyramid, a traffic triangle and a warning lamp shall each convey to vehicular traffic using a road a warning of a temporary obstruction in the road, other than an obstruction caused by the carrying out of works.

PART III

SIZE, COLOUR AND TYPE OF TRAFFIC SIGNS

8. Keep right sign

B61.09 A keep right sign shall consist of a device which is—

(a) of the colour and type of the traffic sign shown in diagram 610 of Schedule 2 to the 1994 Regulations varied so that the arrow points downwards to the right;

(b) of the size shown in that diagram except that its minimum diameter shall be 900 millimetres instead of 270 millimetres; and

(c) illuminated in accordance with the provisions of paragraph (2) in column (3) of item 1 of Schedule 17 to the 1994 Regulations.

9. Flat traffic delineator

B61.10 A flat traffic delineator shall consist of a device which is of the type specified in, and complies with the provisions of, regulation 44(3) of the 1994 Regulations and is of the colour and type of the traffic sign shown in the two parts of diagram 7102 in Schedule 12 to those Regulations, except that—

(a) its minimum height may be 450 millimetres instead of 750 millimetres; and

(b) it shall not have the optional white strip on its base referred to in regulation 44(3)(a) and shown in the second part of diagram 7102.

10. Road vehicle sign

A road vehicle sign shall consist of a device which is of the size, colour and type specified in the diagram in Schedule 1.   **B61.11**

11. Traffic cone

A traffic cone shall consist of a device which—

(a) complies with the requirements of regulation 44(1) of the 1994 Regulations; and   **B61.12**

(b) is of the size, colour and type of the traffic sign shown in diagram 7101 in Schedule 12 to the 1994 Regulations.

12. Traffic pyramid

A traffic pyramid shall consist of a device which is—   **B61.13**

(a) pyramidically shaped with at least 3 visible faces, each of which is of the size and colour specified in one of the diagrams in Schedule 2;

(b) made of rubber or flexible plastic material; and

(c) so constructed that it can stand upright firmly on the surface of a road.

13. Traffic triangle

A traffic triangle shall consist of a device which is—   **B61.14**

(a) of the size, colour and type specified in either of the diagrams in Schedule 3; and

(b) legibly and permanently marked—

(i) in the case of a triangle of the size, colour and type specified in the first diagram in Schedule 3, with the specification number of the British Standard for an Advance Warning Triangle to indicate a temporary obstruction, namely BS:AU47:1965 as amended by amendment No. 1 of 6th May 1966, or the specification number of an equivalent standard which has been approved by a recognised standardising body in an EEA State; or

(ii) in the case of a triangle of the size, colour and type specified in the second diagram in Schedule 3, with the marking designated as an approval mark by regulation 4 of the Motor Vehicles (Designation of Approval Marks) Regulations 1979 [*S.I. 1979 No. 1088; not reproduced in this work*] and shown in item 27 of Schedule 2 to those Regulations.

14. Warning lamp

A warning lamp shall consist of a device which—   **B61.15**

(a) shows an intermittent amber light having a flashing rate of not less than 55 nor more than 150 flashes per minute; and

(b) is illuminated by either—

(i) a single source of light; or

(ii) two or more sources of light mounted adjacent to each other and flashing in such a manner that all the sources of light are illuminated and extinguished simultaneously.

PART IV

PLACING OF TRAFFIC SIGNS

15. Authorisation to place traffic signs

B61.16

(1) Subject to paragraph (4) of this regulation, a person who is in charge of or accompanies an emergency or a breakdown vehicle which is temporarily obstructing a road is hereby authorised to place a keep right sign for the purpose of warning vehicular traffic of the obstruction created by the vehicle and to indicate the way past the vehicle.

(2) Subject to paragraph (4) of this regulation, any person not otherwise authorised to do so is hereby authorised to place a road vehicle sign on a vehicle or a flat traffic delineator, traffic cone, traffic pyramid, traffic triangle or warning lamp on any road for the purpose of warning traffic of a temporary obstruction in the road, other than one caused by the carrying out of works.

(3) In paragraph (1) above, the expressions "*emergency vehicle*" and "*breakdown vehicle*" have the meanings given in regulation 3(2) of the Road Vehicles Lighting Regulations 1989 [*S.I. 1989 No. 1796, q.v.*].

(4) The authorisations given by paragraphs (1) and (2) of this regulation are subject to the conditions specified in regulation 16.

16. Conditions of authorisation

B61.17

(1) In this regulation—

    (a) "*placed*" in relation to a traffic sign means placed in pursuance of an authorisation given by regulation 15;

    (b) references to "*the obstruction*" are to the temporary obstruction in relation to which a traffic sign is placed; and

    (c) references to "*the road*" are to the road on which the obstruction is situated.

(2) A traffic sign which has been placed shall be removed as soon as the obstruction has been removed.

(3) A flat traffic delineator, keep right sign, traffic cone, traffic pyramid or traffic triangle shall be placed in an upright position.

(4) A flat traffic delineator, keep right sign, traffic cone or traffic pyramid shall be placed so as to guide traffic past the obstruction.

(5) A traffic sign referred to in column (2) of an item in the table below may be placed only if the conditions specified in column (3) of the item are complied with.

TABLE

(1) *Item*	*(2)* *Traffic sign*	*(3)* *Conditions*
1.	Flat traffic delineator	1. At least three other flat traffic delineators must also be placed in relation to the obstruction. 2. Each flat traffic delineator must be so placed as to face traffic approaching the obstruction from the side of the obstruction on which it is placed.

[*continued on next page*

(1) Item	(2) Traffic sign	(3) Conditions
2.	Road vehicle sign	1. It must be placed to face traffic approaching the stationary vehicle from the front, rear or side of the vehicle on which it is placed. 2. It must be securely fixed to the stationary vehicle. 3. It must not obscure any registration plate, lamps or reflectors of the stationary vehicle.
3.	Traffic cone	At least three other traffic cones must also be placed in relation to the obstruction.
4.	Traffic pyramid	At least three other traffic pyramids must also be placed in relation to the obstruction.
5.	Traffic triangle	1. A traffic triangle must be placed at least 45 metres away from the obstruction. 2. A traffic triangle must be so placed as to face traffic approaching the obstruction from the side of the obstruction on which it is placed.
6.	Warning lamp	1. A warning lamp may be used only in conjunction with another traffic sign lawfully placed in accordance with these Regulations being— (a) a flat traffic delineator; (b) a keep right sign; (c) a road vehicle sign; (d) a traffic cone; (e) a traffic pyramid; or (f) a traffic triangle and shall be so placed as not to obscure that other traffic sign from the view of approaching traffic. 2. Not more than one warning lamp shall be placed in conjunction with each such other traffic sign.

PART V

SAVINGS

17. Saving for the 1994 Regulations

Nothing in these Regulations shall affect regulation 41 (temporary traffic signs) of the 1994 Regulations.   **B61.18**

18. The Motorways Traffic (England and Wales) Regulations 1982 and the Motorways Traffic (Scotland) Regulations 1995

Nothing in the Motorways Traffic (England and Wales) Regulations 1982 [*S.I. 1982 No. 1163, as amended, q.v.*] or the Motorways Traffic (Scotland) Regulations 1995 [*S.I. 1995 No. 2507, as amended; not reproduced in this work*] shall preclude any person, acting in accordance with an authorisation conferred by Part IV of these Regulations, from placing a flat traffic delineator, keep right sign, traffic cone, traffic pyramid, traffic triangle or warning lamp on, or having placed it there removing it from, a special road to which either of those Regulations apply.   **B61.19**

Regulation 10

SCHEDULE 1

THE ROAD VEHICLE SIGN

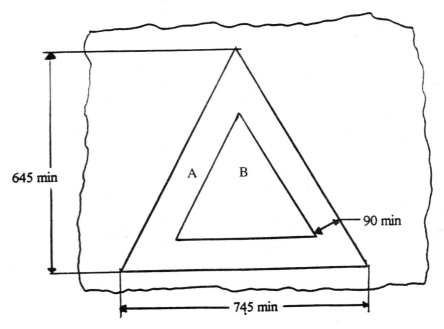

1. A road vehicle sign shall be a flexible sheet on which appears a triangle.

2. The triangle shall be equilateral. The area marked A in the diagram shall be coloured red, and shall be reflectorised to Class 1 of British Standard BS 873 Part 6 or an equivalent standard which has been approved by a recognised standardising body in an EEA State.

B61.21 3. The area marked B in the diagram may be coloured white, in which case it shall be reflectorised to Class 1 of British Standard BS 873 Part 6 or an equivalent standard which has been approved by a recognised standardising body in an EEA State. If the area marked B is not coloured white it shall be of the same colour as the background specified in note 4 below.

4. The background shall be coloured yellow which shall be fluorescent and may also be reflectorised.

B61.22 5. The total area of the sheet, including the red triangle, shall be not less than 0.8 square metres.

SCHEDULE 2   Regulation 12   **B61.23**

THE TRAFFIC PYRAMID—FIRST DIAGRAM

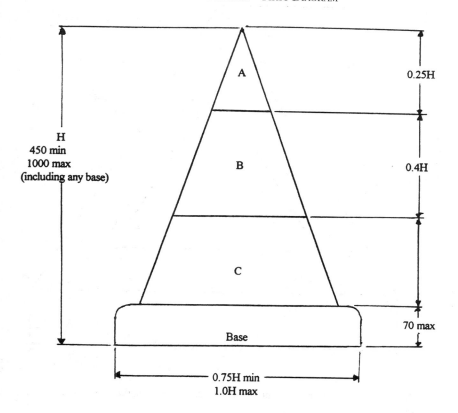

1. The areas marked A B and C in the diagram indicate areas of the surface on each face of the pyramid as follows:

A—Surface coloured red which may be reflectorised.

B—White surface which must be reflectorised.

C—Surface coloured red which may be reflectorised. Up to 50% of this surface may be obscured by constructional components.

2. The pyramid shall not be directly illuminated either internally or externally.   **B61.24**

3. The base may be of any colour or it may be omitted.

B61.25   THE TRAFFIC PYRAMID—SECOND DIAGRAM

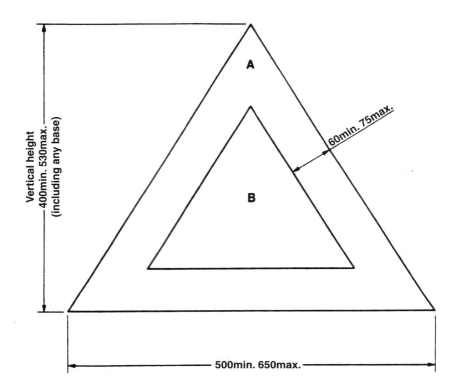

1. The areas marked A and B in the diagram indicate areas of the surface on each face of the pyramid as follows:

A—Suface coloured red which may be reflectorised.

B—White surface which must be reflectorised.

B61.26   2. Each outer edge of the triangular face shall be the same length.

3. The pyamid shall not be directly illuminated either internally or externally.

SCHEDULE 3   Regulation 13   **B61.27**

THE TRAFFIC TRIANGLE—FIRST DIAGRAM

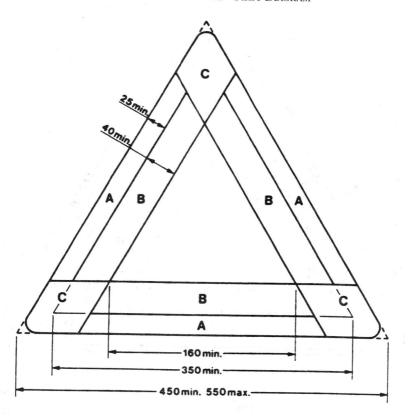

1. The areas marked A B and C in the diagram indicate areas of the surface on the face of the triangle as follows:

A—Red reflectorised surface. Not more than a total of 15 square centimetres may be obscured by constructional components.

B—Red fluorescent surface.

C—May have either red reflectorised surface or a combination of both red reflectorised and red fluorescent surface. Not more than 10 square centimetres in each corner may be obscured by constructional components.

2. The corners shall be radiused.   **B61.28**

3. All sides shall be the same length.

4. The reflectorised areas of the surface may be internally illuminated provided that such illumination is steady, presents a uniform appearance throughout that area and does not impair the retroreflecting properties of that area of the surface. The triangle shall not be directly illuminated externally.

B61.29   THE TRAFFIC TRIANGLE—SECOND DIAGRAM

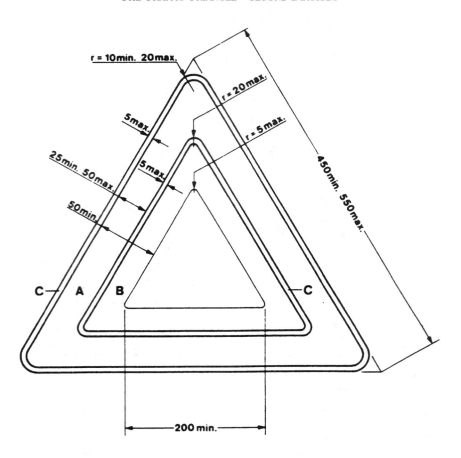

1. The areas marked A B and C in the diagram indicate areas of the surface on the face of the triangle as follows:

A—Red reflectorised surface.

B—Red fluorescent surface (having an area of not less than 315 square centimetres).

B61.30   C—Red edging which may be omitted.

2. The corners shall be radiused.

3. All sides shall be the same length.

4. The reflectorised areas of the surface may be internally illuminated provided that such illumination is steady, presents a uniform appearance throughout that area and does not impair the retroreflecting properties of that area of the surface. The triangle shall not be directly illuminated externally.

The Road Traffic (Vehicle Emissions) (Fixed Penalty) Regulations 1997

(S.I. 1997 No. 3058)

Editorial note. These regulations were made under the Environment Act 1995, s.87. The Arrangement of regulations set out below has been compiled editorially and is not part of the official text.

B62.01

ARRANGEMENT OF REGULATIONS

B62.02

1. Citation and commencement   *[Omitted.]*

B62.03

2. Interpretation

(1) In these Regulations—

B62.04

(a) "*an authorised person*" means a person authorised to issue fixed penalty notices in accordance with regulation 4;

(b) "*fixed penalty*" means, subject to regulation 9, a penalty—

    (i) of £60 in the case of a fixed penalty offence relating to regulation 61 of the 1986 Regulations, or

    (ii) of £20 in the case of a fixed penalty offence relating to regulation 98 of the 1986 Regulations;

(c) "*fixed penalty notice*" means a notice offering a person an opportunity to discharge any liability to conviction for a fixed penalty offence by payment of a penalty of the amount prescribed in sub-paragraph (b);

(d) "*fixed penalty offence*" means an offence under section 42 of the Road Traffic Act 1988 [*q.v.*] consisting of—

    (i) a contravention of, or failure to comply with, regulation 61 of the 1986 Regulations;

    (ii) a contravention of, or failure to comply with, regulation 98 of the 1986 Regulations;

    (iii) using on a road a motor vehicle which does not comply with a requirement of regulation 61 of the 1986 Regulations or causing or permitting a motor vehicle to be so used; or

    (iv) using on a road a motor vehicle which does not comply with a requirement of regulation 98 of the 1986 Regulations or causing or permitting a motor vehicle to be so used;

(e) *"the 1986 Regulations"* means the Road Vehicles (Construction and Use) Regulations 1986 [*S.I. 1986 No. 1078, as amended (q.v.)*];

(f) *"a participating authority"* means—

    (i) Birmingham City Council;

    (ii) Bristol City Council;

    (iii) Canterbury City Council;

    (iv) Glasgow City Council;

    (v) Middlesbrough Borough Council;

    (vi) the Council of the City and County of Swansea; and

    (vii) Westminster City Council;

(g) *"the period for paying"* in relation to any fixed penalty notice, means the period of 28 days beginning with the day on which the notice was issued.

(2) Unless the context otherwise requires any reference in these Regulations to a numbered regulation is to the regulation in these Regulations bearing that number and any reference in a regulation to a numbered paragraph is to the paragraph of that regulation bearing that number.

3. Powers of participating authorities

B62.05   (1) A participating authority may within its area—

(a) take such steps as are required, including the carrying out of tests on the emissions from vehicles, to enforce the provisions of regulation 61 of the 1986 Regulations, and

(b) take such steps as are required to enforce the provisions of regulation 98 of the 1986 Regulations,

and each of the offences referred to in the definition of "fixed penalty offence" in regulation 2(1)(d) is hereby prescribed as an offence for the purposes of section 87(2)(o) of the Environment Act 1995.

(2) In connection with the discharge of an authority's functions under paragraph (1) an authorised person of that authority may require the driver of any vehicle to disclose to him—

(a) his name and address; and

(b) his date of birth.

(3) Any person who fails to comply with a requirement under paragraph (2) shall be guilty of an offence and be liable on summary conviction to a fine not exceeding level 5 on the standard scale.

4. Persons to issue fixed penalty notices

B62.06   (1) A participating authority may authorise any officer of the authority, or any other person, who has successfully completed a course of training on checking emissions approved by the Secretary of State, to issue fixed penalty notices in accordance with these

Regulations in respect of fixed penalty offences relating to regulation 61 of the 1986 Regulations.

(2) A participating authority may authorise any officer of the authority or any other person to issue fixed penalty notices in accordance with these Regulations in respect of fixed penalty offences relating to regulation 98 of the 1986 Regulations.

5. Issue of fixed penalty notices

(1) Where—   **B62.07**

   (a) a test has been carried out on the emissions from a vehicle, and

   (b) in consequence of that test an authorised person considers that a fixed penalty offence relating to regulation 61 of the 1986 Regulations has been committed by the person using that vehicle,

he may issue a fixed penalty notice to that person.

(2) Where an authorised person considers that a fixed penalty offence relating to regulation 98 of the 1986 Regulations has been committed by the driver of a vehicle, he may issue a fixed penalty notice to that person.

(3) A fixed penalty notice in accordance with paragraph (1) or (2) shall be issued as soon as is reasonably practicable and, in any case, not later than 24 hours after the commission of the offence in connection with which it is issued.

(4) A fixed penalty notice issued in accordance with paragraph (1) or (2) shall give such reasonable particulars of the circumstances alleged to constitute the fixed penalty offence to which the notice relates as are necessary for giving reasonable information of the offence and shall state—

   (a) the name and address of the person to whom the notice is issued;

   (b) the registered number of the vehicle concerned;

   (c) the date of the offence;

   (d) the monetary amount of the fixed penalty which may be paid;

   (e) the person to whom, and the address at which, the fixed penalty may be paid and any correspondence relating to the fixed penalty notice may be sent;

   (f) the person to whom and the address at which any request for a hearing may be sent;

   (g) the method or methods by which payment of the fixed penalty may be made;

   (h) the period for paying the fixed penalty, and

   (i) the consequences of the fixed penalty not being paid before the expiration of the period.

(5) A fixed penalty notice may be issued under this regulation either by giving it to the person to whom it is issued or by properly addressing, pre-paying and posting a letter containing the notice to that person and shall, for the purposes of these Regulations, be taken to have been issued at the time when it is so given or a letter containing it is so posted.

6. Proceedings or conviction

(1) Where a fixed penalty notice has been issued to a person in accordance with reg-   **B62.08**
ulation 5, no proceedings shall be instituted against that person for the offence in connection with which the notice was issued before the expiration of the period for paying the penalty, unless he has given a notice requesting a hearing in accordance with regulation 7.

(2) A person shall not be convicted for an offence in connection with which a fixed penalty notice has been issued if the fixed penalty is paid before the expiration of the period for paying it.

7. Request for a hearing

B62.09   (1) A person to whom a fixed penalty notice has been issued may give notice requesting a hearing in respect of the offence to which the fixed penalty notice relates.

(2) A notice requesting a hearing under paragraph (1) shall be in writing and shall be given to the person specified for this purpose in the fixed penalty notice at the address so specified not later than the end of the period of 28 days beginning with the day after the day on which the fixed penalty notice was issued.

(3) Where a hearing has been requested in accordance with paragraphs (1) and (2), the fixed penalty shall not be payable.

8. Prosecution in respect of an offence

B62.10   (1) Where a person to whom a fixed penalty notice has been issued in respect of an offence committed in England or Wales gives a notice requesting a hearing in respect of the offence in accordance with regulation 7, the fixed penalty notice may be treated as an information for the purposes of a prosecution for the offence in connection with which it was issued.

(2) *[Applies to Scotland.]*

9. Increase in fixed penalty

B62.11   Where the person liable to pay the fixed penalty fails to pay it before the expiration of the period for paying it without having given notice requesting a hearing under regulation 7, the amount of the fixed penalty shall be increased—

    (a) to £90, in the case of an offence relating to regulation 61 of the 1986 Regulations, and

    (b) to £40, in the case of an offence relating to regulation 98 of the 1986 Regulations.

10. Recovery of unpaid fixed penalties

B62.12   (1) Any fixed penalty payable under a fixed penalty notice issued in England or Wales which is unpaid after the end of the period for paying it shall, if a county court so orders, be recoverable by execution issued from the county court or otherwise as if it were payable under an order of that court.

(2) *[Applies to Scotland.]*

11. Enforcement by execution

B62.13   (1) Subject to paragraphs (2) and (3), an unpaid fixed penalty, which is recoverable in accordance with regulation 10 as if it were payable under a county court order, shall be treated for purposes of enforcement by execution as if it were a Part II debt specified in article 2(1)(a) of the Enforcement of Road Traffic Debts Order 1993 *[S.I. 1993 No. 2073, not reproduced in this work]* ("the 1993 Order").

(2) Article 3(1) of the 1993 Order (no warrant of execution to be issued until the time for serving a statutory declaration has expired) shall not apply to a warrant of execution to enforce payment of an unpaid fixed penalty.

(3) For the purposes of the enforcement of payment of an unpaid fixed penalty, any reference in the 1993 Order to "*the authority*" shall be a reference to a participating authority.

12. Withdrawal of a fixed penalty notice

(1) A fixed penalty notice may be withdrawn in any case in which an authorised person **B62.14** determines that it ought not to have been issued or ought not to have been issued to the person named as the person to whom it was issued.

(2) Where a fixed penalty notice has been withdrawn in accordance with paragraph (1)—

(a) any amount paid by way of fixed penalty in pursuance of that notice shall be repaid to the person who paid it, and

(b) no proceedings shall be continued or instituted against that person for the offence in connection with which the withdrawn notice was issued.

The Motor Cycles (Protective Helmets) Regulations 1998

(S.I. 1998 No. 1807)

B63.01   *[The text of these regulations is printed as amended by:*

the Motor Cycles (Protective Helmets) (Amendment) Regulations 2000 (S.I. 2000 No. 1488) (June 30, 2000).

The amending regulations are referred to in the notes to the principal regulations only by their year and number. The date referred to above is the date on which the amending regulations came into force.]

B63.02   **1. Citation and commencement**   *[Omitted.]*

2. Revocation   *[Omitted.]*

3. Interpretation

B63.03   In these Regulations—

(a) "*EEA State*" means a state which is a contracting party to the Agreement on the European Economic Area signed at Oporto on 2nd May 1992 as adjusted by the Protocol signed at Brussels on 17th March 1993 [*Cm. 2073 and Cm. 2183*];

[(aa) "*ECE Regulation 22*" means Regulation No. 22 set out in Addendum 21 to the UN ECE Agreement;

[(aaa) "*ECE Regulation 22.05*" means ECE Regulation 22 as amended by the 05 series of amendments and all previous amendments in force on 30th June 2000;]

[(aaaa) "*the UN ECE Agreement*" means the Agreement of the United Nations Economic Commission for Europe concluded at Geneva on 20th March 1958 as amended [*Cmnd. 2535 and Cmnd. 3562*] concerning the adoption of uniform technical prescriptions for wheeled vehicles, equipment and parts which can be fitted to and/or used on wheeled vehicles and the condition for the reciprocal recognition of approvals granted on the basis of these prescriptions, to which the United Kingdom is a part by virtue of an instrument of accession dated 14th January 1963 deposited with the Secretary General of the United Nations on 15th January 1963;]

(b) a reference to a numbered regulation is a reference to the regulation so numbered in these Regulations; and

(c) a reference to a numbered paragraph is a reference to the paragraph so numbered in the regulation in which the reference occurs.

B63.04   *[Regulation 3 is printed as amended by S.I. 2000 No. 1488.*
As to the European Economic Area, see further the note to Regulation (EEC) 3820/85 below.]

4. Protective headgear

(1) Save as provided in paragraph (2), every person driving or riding (otherwise than in   **B63.05**
a side-car) on a motor bicycle when on a road shall wear protective headgear.

(2) Nothing in paragraph (1) shall apply to any person driving or riding on a motor
bicycle if—

(a) it is a mowing machine; or

(b) it is for the time being propelled by a person on foot.

(3) In this regulation—

"motor bicycle" means a two-wheeled motor cycle, whether or not having a side-car
attached, and for the purposes of this definition where the distance measured between
the centre of the area of contact with the road surface of any two wheels of a motor
cycle is less than 460 millimetres, those wheels shall be counted as one wheel;

"protective headgear" means a helmet which—

(a) either—

(i) bears a marking applied by its manufacturer indicating compliance with the
specifications contained in one of the British Standards (whether or not as
modified by any amendment) mentioned in Schedule 2 to these Regulations;
or

(ii) is of a type manufactured for use by persons on motor cycles which by virtue
of its shape, material and construction could reasonably be expected to afford
to the wearer a degree of protection from accidental injury similar to or
greater than that provided by a helmet of a type prescribed by regulation 5.

(b) if worn with a chin cup attached to or held in position by a strap, is provided with
an additional strap (to be fastened under the wearer's jaw) for securing the helmet
to the head; and

(c) is securely fastened to the head by means of straps provided for that purpose; and
"strap" includes any fastening device.

5. Prescribed types of recommended helmet

(1) The types of helmet hereby prescribed as types of helmet recommended as affording   **B63.06**
protection to persons on or in motorcycles from injury in the event of an accident are
helmets which as regards their shape, construction and other qualities conform—

(a) with British Standard 6658: 1985 as amended by Amendment Slip number 1 published on 28th February 1986 and are marked with the number of that standard,
. . .

(b) with any other standard accepted by an EEA State which offers in use equivalent
levels of safety, suitability and fitness for purpose and are marked with a mark to
indicate that standard,

[and in each case] are marked with an approved certification mark of an approved
body (whether or not they are required to be so marked by the standard in point)[, or]

[(c) with ECE Regulation 22.05 including the approval, marking and conformity of
production requirements of that Regulation].

(2) For the purposes of this regulation—

(a) an approved certification mark is—

(i) the certification mark of the British Standards Institution; or

(ii) a certification mark which indicates that a conformity assessment equivalent to that of the British Standards Institution has been undertaken, and

(b) an approved body is—

(i) the British Standards Institution; or

(ii) any body approved by an EEA State to undertake conformity assessments equivalent to those undertaken by the British Standards Institution.

B63.07   *[Regulation 5 is printed as amended by S.I. 2000 No. 1488.]*

6. Saving for the Trade Descriptions Act 1968 and the Consumer Protection Act 1987

B63.08   Nothing in regulation 5(1) shall be taken to authorise any person to apply any number or mark referred to therein in contravention of the Trade Descriptions Act 1968 or the Consumer Protection Act 1987.

Regulation 2   SCHEDULE 1

B63.09   REVOCATIONS

[Omitted.]

SCHEDULE 2

BRITISH STANDARDS

B63.10   **1.** British Standard 2001: 1956 as amended by the following Amendment Slips—

Number	*Date of Publication*
1	11th January 1957
2	23rd November 1959
3	27th February 1962
4	11th June 1964
5	13th March 1968
6	18th February 1972

2. British Standard 1869: 1960 as amended by the following Amendment Slips—

Number	*Date of Publication*
1	29th May 1963
4	3rd December 1965
5	13th March 1968
6	10th August 1971
7	3rd January 1972
8	15th May 1973
9	1st February 1974
10	2nd September 1974
11	1st March 1975

B63.11   **3.** British Standard 2495: 1960 as amended by the following Amendment Slips—

Number	*Date of Publication*
1	29th May 1963
2	22nd February 1965
3	7th December 1965

Number	Date of Publication
4	22nd July 1966
5	10 August 1971
6	3rd January 1972
7	1st February 1974
8	1st March 1975

4. British Standard 2001: 1972 as amended by the following Amendment Slips—

Number	Date of Publication
1	12th December 1972
2	26th January 1973
3	1st February 1974
4	2nd September 1974
5	1st March 1975

5. British Standard 5361: 1976   **B63.12**

6. British Standard 2495: 1977

7. British Standard 5361: 1976 as amended by the following Amendment Slips—   **B63.13**

Number	Date of Publication
1	30th September 1977
2	31st August 1978
3	31st August 1979
4	29th February 1980

8. British Standard 2495: 1977 as amended by the following Amendment Slips—

Number	Date of Publication
1	30th September 1977
2	31st August 1978
3	31st August 1979
4	29th February 1980

9. British Standard 5361: 1976 as amended by the following Amendment Slips—   **B63.14**

Number	Date of Publication
1	30th September 1977
2	31st August 1978
3	31st August 1979
4	29th February 1980
5	27th February 1981

10. British Standard 2495: 1977 as amended by the following Amendment Slips—

Number	Date of Publication
1	30th September 1977
2	31st August 1978
3	31st August 1979
4	29th February 1980
5	27th February 1981

11. British Standard 6658: 1985 as amended by the following Amendment Slips—   **B63.15**

Number	Date of Publication
1	28th February 1986

The Motor Vehicles (EC Type Approval) Regulations 1998

(S.I. 1998 No. 2051)

B64.01   *Editorial note.*   The explanatory note accompanying these regulations states that the regulations implement Directive 70/156/EEC, Directive 87/403/EEC and Directive 98/14/EC relating to the establishment of national systems for granting EC type approval for light passenger vehicles and motor vehicle parts. Regulations 12 and 13 below give effect to the "end of series" derogations permitted by Directive 70/156/EEC, art.8(2)(b).

B64.02   *[The text of these regulations is printed as amended by:*

> *the Motor Vehicles (EC Type Approval) (Amendment) Regulations 1999 (S.I. 1999 No. 778) (April 14, 1999);*

> *the Motor Vehicles (EC Type Approval) (Amendment No. 2) Regulations 1999 (S.I. 1999 No. 2324) (September 16, 1999);*

> *the Motor Vehicles (EC Type Approval) (Amendment) Regulations 2000 (S.I. 2000 No. 869) (April 20, 2000); and*

> *the Motor Vehicles (EC Type Approval) (Amendment) (No. 2) Regulations 2000 (S.I. 2000 No. 2730) (November 7, 2000).*

> *The amending regulations are referred to in the notes to the principal regulations only by their years and numbers. The dates referred to above are the dates on which the amending regulations came into force.]*

ARRANGEMENT OF REGULATIONS

PART I

PRELIMINARY

PART II

EC TYPE APPROVAL GRANTED BY THE SECRETARY OF STATE

. . . .

PART III

LICENSING AND REGISTRATION

PART IV

MISCELLANEOUS

SCHEDULES

PART I

PRELIMINARY

1. Citation, commencement and extent *[Omitted.]* B64.04

2. Revocation *[Omitted.]* B64.05

3. Interpretation

(1) In these Regulations—

"*the 1981 Order*" means the Road Traffic (Northern Ireland) Order 1981 [*S.I. 1981 No. 154 (N.I. 1)*]; B64.06

"*the 1988 Act*" means the Road Traffic Act 1988 [*q.v.*];

"*the 1980 Regulations*" means the Motor Vehicles (Type Approval) Regulations 1980 [*S.I. 1980 No. 1182, as amended, not reproduced in this work*];

"*the 1984 Regulations*" means the Motor Vehicles (Type Approval) (Great Britain) Regulations 1984 [*S.I. 1984 No. 981, as amended, q.v.*];

"*the 1985 Regulations*" means the Motor Vehicles (Type Approval) Regulations (Northern Ireland) 1985 [*S.R. 1985 No. 294, as amended*];

"*the 1987 Regulations*" means the Motor Vehicles (Type Approval) (EEC) Regulations (Northern Ireland) 1987 [*S.R. 1987 No. 306; revoked by S.R. 1994 No. 240*];

"*the 1994 Act*" means the Vehicle Excise and Registration Act 1994 [*q.v.*];

"*the Framework Directive*" means Council Directive 70/156/EEC [*O.J. No. L42, February 23, 1970, p. 1*] as amended by Council Directives 87/403/EEC [*O.J. No. L220, August 8, 1987, p. 44*], and 92/53/EEC [*O.J. No. L225, August 10, 1992, p. 1*] and Commission Directives 93/81/EEC [*O.J. No. L264, October 23, 1993, p. 49*] and 98/14/EC [*O.J. No. L91, March 25, 1998, p. 1*];

"*EC certificate of conformity*" means any certificate of conformity issued by a manufacturer—

(a) under regulation 5 of these Regulations, or

(b) under any provision of the law of a Member State other than the United Kingdom giving effect to Article 6 of the Framework Directive;

"*EC type approval*" means—

(a) vehicle type approval for a light passenger vehicle granted pursuant to the Framework Directive (an "*EC vehicle type approval*"), or

(b) system, component or separate technical unit type approval granted pursuant to a separate Directive (an "*EC system, component or separate technical unit type approval*"),

and references to an application for EC type approval and other cognate expressions shall be construed accordingly;

"*EC type approval certificate*" means a type approval certificate issued—

(a) by the Secretary of State under regulation 4(5) of these Regulations, or

(b) under any provision of the law of a Member State other than the United Kingdom giving effect to Article 4 of the Framework Directive;

"*light passenger vehicle*" has the meaning given in section 85 of the 1988 Act; and

"*separate Directive*" means a Directive specified in the second column of an item in Schedule 1 to these Regulations as read with Directives (if any) specified in the third column of that item.

(2) Other expressions used in these Regulations which are also used in the Framework Directive shall have the same meaning as in the Framework Directive and cognate expressions shall be construed accordingly.

(3) Unless the context otherwise requires, any reference in these Regulations to—

(a) a numbered regulation is a reference to the regulation bearing that number in these Regulations,

(b) a numbered paragraph is a reference to the paragraph bearing that number in the regulation in which the reference appears, and

(c) a numbered Schedule is a reference to the Schedule so numbered in these Regulations.

PART II

EC TYPE APPROVAL GRANTED BY THE SECRETARY OF STATE

B64.07   **4. Applications for grant or amendment of EC type approval**   *[Omitted.]*

5. EC certificates of conformity and approval marks   *[Omitted.]*

6. Tests and associated checks   *[Omitted.]*

7. Duty to co-operate with the Secretary of State   *[Omitted.]*

8. Information concerning restrictions on the use of components and separate technical units   *[Omitted.]*

9. Withdrawal or suspension of EC type approval   *[Omitted.]*

PART III

LICENSING AND REGISTRATION

10. Powers of the Secretary of State in a case where a vehicle is a serious   **B64.08**
risk to road safety   *[Omitted.]*

11. Conditions for grant of first licence or registration

(1) Subject to paragraphs (4) to (10), where application is made for a first licence under   **B64.09**
the 1994 Act for a light passenger vehicle the licence shall not be granted unless one of the
conditions in paragraph (3) is satisfied.

(2) Subject to paragraphs (4) to (10), the Secretary of State shall not register a light passenger vehicle under section 21 of the 1994 Act as applied by regulations under section
22(2) of that Act to vehicles in respect of which duty is not chargeable under that Act,
unless one of the conditions in paragraph (3) is satisfied.

(3) The conditions referred to in paragraphs (1) and (2) are that—

   (a) it is shown that an EC certificate of conformity has effect with respect to the vehicle,

   (b) a Minister's approval certificate issued under section 58(1) of the 1988 Act has
     effect with respect to the vehicle,

   (c) a Minister's approval certificate issued under section 58(4) of the 1988 Act has
     effect with respect to the vehicle and is—

      (i) in a form prescribed by regulation 9(4) of the 1984 Regulations,
      (ii) endorsed in accordance with regulation 9(6) of the 1984 Regulations, or
     (iii) in a form prescribed by regulation 9(4) of the 1985 Regulations,

   (d) the vehicle falls within—

      (i) regulation 3(2)(g) of the 1984 Regulations, or
      (ii) regulation 3(2)(g) of the 1985 Regulations, or

   (e) section 63, 65 and 65A of the 1988 Act or Articles 31E and 31G of the 1981
     Order have become applicable to the vehicle after a period of use on roads during
     which, by virtue of section 183(2) of the 1988 Act or Article 214 of the 1981 Order
     (which relates to vehicles in service of the Crown), those sections or Articles did not
     apply to it.

(4) Paragraphs (1) and (2) shall not apply for a vehicle which—

   (a) conforms with a type vehicle in respect of which a national type approval
     certificate was issued before 1st January 1996,

   (b) conforms with a vehicle in respect of which a Minister's approval certificate was
     issued under section 58(1) of the 1988 Act before 1st January 1996, or

   (c) belongs to the same type as a vehicle registered under section 21 of the 1994 Act
     before 1st January 1996.

(5) This paragraph applies to a vehicle belonging to a type of vehicle in respect of which
a national type approval certificate has been issued before 1st January 1998 as an incomplete vehicle.

(6) Paragraphs (1) and (2) shall not apply at any time before 1st January 2000—

   (a) for a vehicle to which paragraph (5) applies and which—

      (i) conforms with a type vehicle in respect of which a national type approval
        certificate was issued before the 1st January 1998,

      (ii) conforms with a vehicle in respect of which a Minister's approval certificate
        was issued under section 58(1) of the 1988 Act before 1st January 1998, or

(iii) belongs to the same type as a vehicle registered under section 21 of the 1994 Act before 1st January 1998.

(7) Paragraphs (1) and (2) shall not apply to a special purpose vehicle unless a manufacturer of such vehicle—

(a) makes a request for the grant or amendment of EC type approval to the Secretary of State, and

(b) submits an application for EC type approval to the Secretary of State in accordance with regulation 4.

(8) For the purposes of paragraphs (4)(a) and (6)(a)(i), a vehicle in respect of which a national certificate of conformity has effect shall be taken to conform with the relevant type vehicle; and for the purposes of paragraphs (4)(a) and (6)(a)(ii) a vehicle in respect of which a Minister's approval certificate issued under section 58(4) of the 1988 Act has effect shall be taken to conform with the relevant vehicle in respect of which such a certificate was issued under section 58(1) of that Act.

(9) For the purposes of paragraphs (4) and (6), a vehicle belongs to a particular type only if it would be treated for the purposes of the Framework Directive as belonging to that type.

(10) Paragraphs (1) and (2) shall not apply in relation to—

(a) the licensing or registration by a public or local authority of any vehicle intended by that authority to be used by them for the purposes of civil defence (within the meaning of the Civil Defence Act 1948 [*not reproduced in this work*]), or

(b) the licensing or registration by a police autority of any vehicles intended to be used for police purposes.

(11) Where the Secretary of State, by virtue of this regulation, refuses to grant a first licence for a vehicle, he shall give notice of his decision to the applicant.

(12) Where the Secretary of State, by virtue of this regulation, refuses to register a vehicle in respect of which duty is not chargeable under the 1994 Act, he shall give notice of his decision to the person who appears to him to be the keeper of the vehicle.

(13) In this regulation—

(a) references to a Minister's approval certificate issued under section 58(1) of the 1988 Act includes references to a Department's approval certificate issued under Article 31A(4) of the 1981 Order, and

(b) the reference to a Minister's approval certificate issued under section 58(4) of that Act includes a reference to a Department's approval certificate issued under Article 31A(5) of that Order.

(14) In this regulation—

"*conform*" means conform (within the meaning of section 55(3) of the 1988 Act or Article 31A(7) of the 1981 Order) with the relevant aspects of design, construction, equipment and marking (as defined in section 54(6) of that Act or Article 31A(7) of that Order),

"*national certificate of conformity*" means a certificate of conformity issued under section 57(1) of the 1988 Act or Article 31A(3) of the 1981 Order, and

"*national type approval certificate*" means a type approval certificate issued under section 55(2) of the 1988 Act or Article 31A(2) of the 1981 Order.

B64.10   *[Regulation 11 is expressly incorporated into the Road Traffic Act 1988, ss.64A(2)(a) and 65A(3)(a). There is no paragraph (b) to follow regulation 11(6)(a).]*

12. End of series vehicles for EC type approval

(1) This regulation applies to an EC type approval if— **B64.11**

 (a) it has been granted by the Secretary of State or under any provision of the law of a Member State other than the United Kingdom giving effect to Article 4 of the Framework Directive, and

 (b) the Secretary of State is satisfied that it is going to cease to have effect in consequence of the provisions of the Framework Directive or a separate Directive.

(2) Subject to paragraph (3), the Secretary of State may, at the request of the holder of an EC type approval to which this regulation applies, direct that every relevant EC certificate of conformity shall continue to have effect for the purposes of—

 (a) Part II of the 1988 Act,

 (b) Part IV of the 1981 Order, and

 (c) this Part of these Regulations,

for the period of 12 months for complete vehicles as from the date on which the EC type approval lost its validity and for the period of 18 months for completed vehicles as from the date on which the EC type approval lost its validity.

(3) A direction under paragraph (2)—

 (a) may be given only at a time when the EC type approval has effect,

 (b) shall cease to have effect if—

  (i) the EC type approval is withdrawn under regulation 9(2), or

  (ii) the EC type approval is withdrawn under any provision of the law of a Member State other than the United Kingdom giving effect to Article 4 of the Framework Directive, or

  (iii) ceases to have effect for a reason other than that referred to in sub-paragraph (1)(b), and

 (c) shall have effect subject to regulations 9(6) and (9) and 11.

(4) For the purposes of paragraph (2), an EC certificate of conformity is a relevant EC certificate of conformity for an EC type approval (as from the time that the EC type approval ceases to have effect) if the vehicle to which it relates is an end of series vehicle.

(5) If, following a request by a holder of an EC type approval, the Secretary of State refuses to exercise his powers under paragraph (2), he shall give notice of his decision to the holder.

(6) In this regulation *"end of series vehicle"* has the meaning given in Part I of Schedule 2.

13. End of series vehicles for national type approval

(1) This regulation applies to a national type approval if— **B64.12**

 (a) it has been granted by the Secretary of State under any provision of the 1984 Regulations or by the Department of the Environment for Northern Ireland under any provision of the 1985 Regulations, and

 (b) the Secretary of State is satisfied that it is going to cease to have effect in consequence of the provisions of regulation 11 of these Regulations.

(2) The Secretary of State may, at the request of the holder of a national type approval to which this regulation applies, direct that every relevant certificate of conformity shall continue to have effect for the purposes of—

 (a) Part II of the 1988 Act,

 (b) Part IV of the 1981 Order, and

 (c) this Part of these Regulations,

for the period of 12 months for complete vehicles as from the date on which the national type approval lost its validity and for the period of 18 months for completed vehicles as from the date on which the national type approval lost its validity.

(3) Such a direction—

(a) may be given only at a time when the national type approval has effect; and

(b) shall cease to have effect if—

    (i) the national type approval is cancelled or suspended under regulation 8(1) of the 1984 Regulations or regulation 8(1) of the 1985 Regulations, or

    (ii) the national type approval otherwise ceases to have effect for a reason other than that referred to in sub-paragraph (1)(b).

(4) For the purposes of paragraph (2), a certificate of conformity is a relevant certificate of conformity issued in accordance with the requirements of regulation 9(3) of the 1984 Regulations or regulation 9(3) of the 1985 Regulations (as from the time that the national type approval ceases to have effect) if the vehicle to which it relates is an end of series vehicle.

(5) If, following a request by a holder of national type approval, the Secretary of State refuses to exercise his powers under paragraph (2), he shall give notice of his decision to the holder.

(6) In this regulation "*end of series vehicle*" has the meaning given in Part II of Schedule 2.

PART IV

MISCELLANEOUS

14. Forgery, false statements, etc.

(1) A person who, with intent to deceive—

(a) forges, alters or uses a document to which this paragraph applies. or

(b) lends to, or allows to be used by, any other person a document to which this paragraph applies, or

(c) makes or has in his possession any document so closely resembling a document to which this paragraph applies as to be calculated to deceive, shall be guilty of an offence.

(2) A person guilty of an offence under paragraph (1) shall be liable—

(a) on summary conviction, to a fine not exceeding the statutory maximum, or

(b) on conviction on indictment, to imprisonment for a term not exceeding 2 years, or to a fine, or to both.

(3) Paragraph (1) applies to an EC type approval certificate and to an EC certificate of conformity.

(4) A person who, in supplying information or producing documents for the purposes of these Regulations—

(a) makes a statement which he knows to be false in a material particular or recklessly makes a statement which is false in material particular, or

(b) produces, provides, sends or otherwise makes use of a document which he knows to be false in a material particular or recklessly produces, provides, sends or otherwise makes use of a document which is false in a material particular, shall be liable on summary conviction to a fine not exceeding level 4 on the standard scale.

15. Duty to give reasons, etc. *[Omitted.]*   **B64.14**

16. Review of decisions *[Omitted.]*

17. Service of notices *[Omitted.]*

18. Provision of testing stations *[Omitted.]*

19. Transitional

(1) An application for an EC type approval made under the 1980 Regulations or the   **B64.15**
1987 Regulations or the Motor Vehicles (EC Type Approval) Regulations 1992 before the
coming into force of these Regulations shall have effect as if it had been made under these
Regulations.

(2) Nothing in these Regulations shall affect the validity of anything done under the
1980 Regulations or the 1987 Regulations or the Motor Vehicles (EC Type Approval)
Regulations 1992 before the coming into force on these Regulations.

(3) This regulation does not apply to an application relating to the provisions set out in
Part II of Schedule 2 to the 1980 Regulations or Part II of Schedule 3 to the 1987
Regulations.

[These regulations came into force on September 23, 1998 in accordance with regulation 1(1).]   **B64.16**

Regulation 3(1)

SCHEDULE 1

SEPARATE DIRECTIVES

Item No	Principal Directives	Amending Directives	Official Journal References	Subject matter
1	70/157/EEC	73/350/EEC* 77/212/EEC 81/334/EEC* 84/372/EEC* 89/424/EEC 89/491/EEC* 92/97/EEC 96/20/EC* [1999/101/EC*]	L42, 23.2.70, p. 16 L321, 22.11.73, p. 33 L66, 12.3.77, p. 33 L131, 18.5.81, p. 6 L196, 26.7.84, p. 47 L238, 6.9.84, p. 31 L238, 15.8.89, p. 43 L371, 19.12.92, p. 1 L92, 13.4.96, p. 23 L334, 28.12.99, p. 41]	Sound levels
2	70/220/EEC	74/290/EEC 77/102/EEC* 78/665/EEC* 83/351/EEC 88/76/EEC 88/436/EEC 89/458/EEC 89/491/EEC* 91/441/EEC 93/59/EEC 94/12/EC† 96/44/EC* 96/69/EC† [98/69/EC†] [98/77/EC*] [1999/102/EC*]	L176, 6.4.70, p. 1 L159, 15.6.74, p. 61 L32, 3.2.77, p. 32 L223, 14.8.78, p. 48 L197, 20.7.83, p. 1 L36, 9.2.88, p. 1 L214, 6.8.88, p. 1 L226, 3.8.89, p. 43 L238, 15.8.89, p. 43 L242, 30.8.91, p. 1 L186, 28.7.93, p. 21 L100, 19.4.94, p. 42 L210, 20.8.96, p. 25 L282, 1.11.96, p. 64 L350, 28.12.98, p. 1] L286, 23.10.98, p. 34] L334, 28.12.99, p. 43]	Emissions

3	70/221/EEC	74/490/EEC*, 81/433/EEC*, 97/19/EC*, [2000/8/EC†]	L76, 6.4.70, p. 23; L128, 26.5.79, p. 22; L131, 18.5.91, p. 4; L125, 16.5.97, p. 1; L106, 3.5.2000, p. 7	Fuel tanks/rear protective devices
4	70/222/EEC		L76, 6.4.70, p. 25	Rear registration plate space
5	70/311/EEC	92/62/EC*, [1999/7/EC*]	L133, 18.6.70, p. 10; L199, 18.7.92, p. 33; L40, 13.2.99, p. 36]	Steering equipment
6	70/387/EEC	[98/90/EC*]	L176, 10.8.70, p. 5; L337, 12.12.98, p. 29]	Doors, latches and hinges
7	70/388/EEC		L176, 10.8.70, p. 12	Audible warning
8	71/127/EEC	79/795/EEC*, 85/205/EEC*, 86/562/EEC*, 88/321/EEC*	L68, 22.3.71, p. 1; L239, 22.9.79, p. 1; L90, 29.3.85, p. 1; L327, 2.11.867, p. 49; L147, 14.6.88, p. 77	Rear visibility
9	71/320/EEC	74/132/EEC*, 75/524/EEC, 79/489/EEC*, 85/647/EEC*, 88/194/EEC*, 91/422/EEC*, 98/12/EC*	L202, 6.9.71, p. 37; L74, 19.3.74, p. 7; L236, 8.9.75, p. 3; L128, 26.5.79, p. 12; L380, 31.12.85, p. 1; L92, 9.4.88, p. 47; L233, 22.9.91, p. 21; L81, 18.3.98, p. 1	Braking
10	72/245/EEC	89/491/EEC*, 95/54/EC*	L152, 6.7.72, p. 15; L238, 15.8.89, p. 43; L266, 8.11.95, p. 1	Suppression (radio)

Note: for footnotes, see end of table

[continued on next page]

Item No	Principal Directives	Amending Directives	Official Journal References	Subject matter
11	72/306/EEC	89/491/EEC* 97/20/EC*	L190, 20.8.72, p. 1 L238, 15.8.89, p. 43 L125, 16.5.97, p. 21	Diesel smoke
12	74/60/EC	78/632/EEC [2000/4/EC†]	L38, 11.2.74, p. 2 L206, 29.7.78, p. 26 L87, 8.4.2000, p. 22]	Interior fittings
13	74/61/EEC	95/56/EC*	L38, 11.2.74, p. 22 L286, 29.11.85, p. 1	Anti-theft and immobiliser
14	74/297/EEC	91/662/EEC*	L165, 20.6.74, p. 16 L366, 31.12.91, p. 1	Protective steering
15	74/408/EEC	81/577/EEC 96/37/EC*	L221, 12.8.74, p. 1 L209, 29.7.81, p. 34 L187, 25.7.96, p. 28	Seat strength
16	74/483/EEC	79/488/EEC*	L266, 2.10.74, p. 4 L128, 26.5.79, p. 1	Exterior projections
17	75/443/EEC	97/39/EC*	L196, 26.7.75, p. 1 L177, 5.7.97, p. 15	Speedometer and reverse gear
18	76/114/EEC	78/507/EEC*	L24, 30.1.76, p. 1 L155, 13.6.78, p. 31	Plates (statutory)
19	76/115/EEC	81/575/EEC* 82/318/EEC 90/629/EEC* 96/38/EC*	L24, 30.1.76, p. 6 L209, 29.7.81, p. 30 L139, 19.5.82, p. 9 L341, 6.12.90, p. 14 L187, 26.7.96, p. 95	Seat belt anchorages
20	76/756/EEC	80/233/EEC* 82/244/EEC* 83/276/EEC	L262, 27.9.76, p. 1 L51, 25.2.80, p. 8 L109, 22.4.82, p. 31 L151, 9.6.83, p. 47	Installation of lighting and light signalling devices

	Community Directive	Amending Directive(s)	Official Journal reference	Subject matter
21	76/757/EEC	84/8/EEC 89/278/EEC* 91/663/EEC* 97/28/EC*	L9, 12.1.84, p. 24 L109, 20.4.89, p. 38 L366, 31.12.91, p. 17 L171, 30.6.97, p. 1 L262, 27.9.76, p. 32	Reflex reflectors
22	76/758/EEC	97/29/EC*	L171, 30.6.97, p. 11 L262, 27.9.76, p. 54 L265, 12.9.89, p. 1	End-outline, front-position (side), rear-position (side), stop, side marker, daytime running lamps
23	76/759/EEC	89/277/EEC* [1999/15/EC*]	L171, 30.6.97, p. 25 L262, 27.9.96, p. 71 L109, 20.4.89, p. 25 L97, 12.4.99, p. 14]	Direction indicators
24	76/760/EEC	97/31/EC*	L262, 27.9.76, p. 85 L171, 30.6.97, p. 49	Rear registration plate lamps
25	76/761/EEC	89/517/EEC* [1999/17/EC*]	L262, 27.6.76, p. 96 L265, 12.9.89, p. 15 L97, 12.4.99, p. 45]	Headlamps (including bulbs)
26	76/762/EEC	[1999/18/EC*]	L262, 27.9.76, p. 122 L97, 12.4.99, p. 82]	Fog lamps (front)
27	77/389/EEC	96/64/EC*	L154, 13.6.77, p. 41 L258, 11.10.96, p. 26	Towing hooks
28	77/538/EEC	89/518/EEC* [1999/14/EC*]	L220, 29.6.77, p. 60 L265, 12.9.89, p. 24 L97, 12.4.99, p. 1]	Rear fog lamps
29	77/539/EEC	97/32/EC*	L200, 29.8.77, p. 72 L171, 30.6.97, p. 63	Reversing lamps
30	77/540/EEC	[1999/16/EC*]	L220, 29.8.77, p. 83 L97, 12.4.99, p. 33]	Parking lamps

[continued on next page

Note: for footnotes, see end of table

Item No	Principal Directives	Amending Directives	Official Journal References	Subject matter
31	77/541/EEC	81/576/EEC* 82/319/EEC* 90/628/EEC* 96/36/EC* [2000/3/EC*	L220, 29.8.77, p. 95 L209, 29.7.81, p. 32 L139, 19.5.82, p. 17 L341, 6.12.90, p. 1 L178, 17.7.96, p. 15 L53, 25.2.2000, p. 1]	Seat belts
32	77/649/EEC	81/643/EEC* 88/366/EEC* 90/630/EEC*	L267, 19.10.77, p. 1 L231, 15.8.81, p. 41 L181, 12.7.88, p. 40 L341, 6.12.90, p. 20	Forward vision
33	78/316/EEC	93/91/EC* 94/53/EC*	L81, 28.3.78, p. 3 L284, 19.11.93, p. 25 L299, 22.11.94, p. 26	Identification of controls
34	78/317/EEC		L81, 28.3.78, p. 27	Defrost/demist
35	78/318/EEC	94/68/EC*	L81, 28.3.78, p. 49 L354, 31.12.94, p. 1	Wash/wipe
36	74/548/EEC		L168, 26.6.78, p. 40	Heating systems
37	78/549/EEC	94/78/EC*	L168, 26.6.78, p. 45 L354, 31.12.94, p. 10	Wheel guards
38	78/932/EEC		L325, 20.11.78, p. 1	Head restraints
39	80/1268/EEC	89/491/EEC* 93/116/EC* [1999/100/EC*	L375, 31.12.80, p. 36 L238, 15.8.89, p. 43 L329, 30.12.93, p. 39 L334, 28.12.99, p. 36]	CO_2 emissions/fuel consumption
40	80/1269/EEC	88/195/EEC 89/491/EEC* 97/91/EC*	L375, 20.11.78, p. 46 L92, 9.4.88, p. 50 L238, 15.8.89, p. 43 L195, 16.5.97, p. 21	Engine power

41	88/77/EEC	[1999/99/EC*]	L334, 28.12.99, p. 32]	Diesel emissions
		91/542/EEC	L36, 9.2.88, p. 33	
			L295, 25.10.91, p. 1	
		[1999/96/EC†]	L44, 16.12.2000, p. 1]	
42	89/297/EEC		L124, 5.5.89, p. 1	Lateral protection
43	91/226/EEC		L103, 24.4.91, p. 5	Spray-suppression systems
44	92/21/EEC	95/48/EC*	L129, 14.5.92, p. 1	Masses and dimensions (cars)
			L233, 30.9.95, p. 73	
45	92/22/EEC		L129, 14.5.92, p. 11	Safety glass
46	92/23/EEC		L129, 14.5.92, p. 95	Tyres
47	92/24/EEC		L129, 14.5.92, p. 154	Speed limiters
48	97/27/EC†		L233, 25.8.97, p. 1	Masses and dimensions (other than vehicles referred to in item 44)
49	92/114/EEC		L409, 31.12.92, p. 17	External projections forward of the cabs
50	94/20/EC†		L195, 29.7.94, p. 1	Couplings
51	95/28/EC†		L281, 23.11.95, p. 1	Flammability
53	96/79/EC†	[1999/98/EC*]	L18, 21.1.97, p. 7	Frontal impact
			L9, 13.1.2000, p. 14]	
54	96/27/EC†		L169, 8.7.96, p. 1	Side impact
[55	98/91/EC†		L11, 16.01.1999, p. 25	Transport of dangerous goods]
[56	2000/40/EC†		L203, 10.08.2000, p. 9	Front protective devices]

Note: The Directives marked with a * are Commission Directives, while those with a † are Directives of the European Parliament and the Council. The other Directives are Council Directives.

[*Schedule 1 is printed as amended by S.I. 1999 Nos 778 and 2324; S.I. 2000 Nos 869 and 2730.*]

PART I

MEANING OF END OF SERIES VEHICLE FOR THE PURPOSES OF REGULATION 12

B64.18   **1.**—(1) For the purposes of regulation 12, a vehicle is an *end of series vehicle* for an EC type approval to which regulation 12 applies, if—

    (a) an EC certificate of conformity has been issued in respect of the vehicle under the EC type approval (whether before or after the giving of the direction by the Secretary of State),

    (b) the vehicle was in the territory of an EEA State at a time when the EC type approval had effect,

    (c) it was manufactured with the intention that it should be supplied by retail for use in the United Kingdom,

    (d) it was not registered under the 1994 Act on the date on which the relevant EC type approval ceased to have effect, and

    (e) it is a vehicle forming part of the allocation of vehicles to a relevant person under sub-paragraphs (2) and (3) of this Part of this Schedule.

(2) The Secretary of State shall make an allocation in accordance with sub-paragraph (3) to each relevant person who makes a request to him under regulation 12 not later than one month before the relevant EC type approval ceases to have effect.

(3) The Secretary of State shall allocate to each relevant person in respect of each vehicle model manufactured in conformity with the relevant EC type approval—

    (a) the number of vehicles of that model in respect of which the request is made, or

    (b) the number of vehicles of that model for which an EC certificate of conformity was issued on or after the date of manufacture and which remained valid for at least 3 months after its date of issue but subsequently lost its validity because of the provisions of the Framework Directive or a Separate Directive,

whichever is the less.

    2.—(1) In this Part of this Schedule—

B64.19   (a) *"EEA Agreement"* means the Agreement on the European Economic Area signed at Oporto on 2nd May 1992 as adjusted by the Protocol signed at Brussels on 17th March 1993 [*Cm. 2073 and Cm. 2183*],

    (b) *"EEA State"* means a State which is a contracting party to the EEA Agreement,

    (c) *"relevant person"* means a person who has made a request to the Secretary of State under regulation 12, and

    (d) *"the relevant EC type approval"* means the EC type approval in respect of which the request has been made to the Secretary of State under regulation 12.

(2) For the purposes of this Schedule, a vehicle shall be regarded as manufactured when its final assembly is completed.

B64.20   *[As to the EEA agreement, see the note to Regulation (EEC) 3820/85 below.]*

PART II

MEANING OF END OF SERIES VEHICLE FOR THE PURPOSES OF REGULATION 13

3.—(1) For the purposes of regulation 13, a vehicle is an *end of series vehicle*, for a national **B64.21**
type approval to which regulation 13 applies, if—

(a) a certificate of conformity has been issued in respect of the vehicle under the relevant national type approval (whether before or after the giving of the direction),

(b) it was manufactured with the intention that it should be supplied by retail for use in the United Kingdom,

(c) it was not registered under the 1994 Act on the date on which the relevant national type approval ceases to have effect, and

(d) it is a vehicle forming part of the allocation of vehicles to a relevant person under sub-paragraphs (2) and (3).

(2) The Secretary of State shall make an allocation in accordance with sub-paragraph (3) to each relevant person who makes a request to him under regulation 13 not later than one month before the relevant national type approval ceases to have effect.

(3) The Secretary of State shall allocate to each relevant person in respect of each vehicle model manufactured in conformity with the relevant national type approval—

(a) the number of vehicles of that model in respect of which the request is made, or

(b) the number of vehicles of that model for which a certificate of conformity was issued on or after the date of manufacture and which remained valid for at least 3 months after its date of issue but subsequently lost its validity because of the provisions of the Directive or one or more of the separate Directives,

whichever is the less.

4.—(1) In this Part of this Schedule—   **B64.22**

(a) a "*relevant person*" means a person who has made a request to the Secretary of State under regulation 13, and

(b) "*the relevant national type approval*" means the national type approval in respect of which a request has been made to the Secretary of State under regulation 13.

(2) For the purposes of this Part of this Schedule, a vehicle shall be regarded as manufactured when its final assembly is completed.

SCHEDULE 3   Regulation 2

REVOCATIONS   **B64.23**

[Omitted.]

The Road Vehicles (Authorised Weight) Regulations 1998

(S.I. 1998 No. 3111)

B65.01   *[The text of these regulations is printed as amended by:*

> *the Road Vehicles (Authorised Weight) (Amendment) Regulations 2000 (S.I. 2000 No. 3224) (January 1, 2001; February 1, 2001; and January 1, 2002); and*

> *the Road Vehicles (Authorised Weight) (Amendment) Regulations 2001 (S.I. 2001 No. 1125) (April 17, 2001).*

> *The amending regulations are referred to in the notes to the principal regulations only by their years and numbers. The dates referred to above are the dates on which the amending regulations came into force (the dates on which the amendments effected by S.I. 2000 No. 3224 took effect, or will take effect, are noted against the amended provisions, as appropriate).*

> *S.I. 2001 No. 1125 also amended S.I. 2000 No. 3224; as to this amendment, see the notes to regulation 2 of the principal regulations below.]*

B65.02   *Editorial note.*   The Arrangement of regulations set out below has been added editorially and does not form part of the text of the regulations.

ARRANGEMENT OF REGULATIONS

B65.03   Regulation

> . . . .
> 2. Interpretation
> 3. Application of Regulations
> 4. Maximum authorised weights
> 5. Saving for regulation 80 of the 1986 Regulations (over-riding weight restrictions)

SCHEDULES

Schedule
> 1. Maximum authorised weights for vehicles
> 2. Maximum authorised weights for vehicle combinations
> 3. Maximum authorised axle weights

B65.04   **1. Citation and commencement**   *[Omitted.]*

2. Interpretation

B65.05   (1) In these Regulations

"*the 1986 Regulations*" means the Road Vehicles (Construction and Use) Regulations 1986 [*S.I. 1986 No. 1078, as amended (q.v.)*];

"*articulated bus or coach*" means a single vehicle which is a bus or coach consisting of 2 or more rigid sections which—

    (a) articulate relative to one another;

    (b) are intercommunicating so that passengers can move freely between them; and

    (c) are permanently connected so that they can only be separated by an operation using facilities normally found only in a workshop;

"*articulated vehicle*" means a tractor unit to which a semi-trailer is attached;

"*axle weight*" means the sum of the weights transmitted to the road surface by all the wheels of an axle, and for the purpose of calculating axle weight the 2 axles comprised in a tandem axle and all the axles comprised in a triaxle shall be treated as one axle;

"*axle-lift device*" means a device permanently fitted to the vehicle for the purpose of reducing or increasing the load on the axles, according to the loading conditions of the vehicle either—

    (a) by means of raising the wheels clear off the ground or by lowering them to the ground, or

    (b) without raising the wheels off the ground,

in order to reduce wear on the tyres when the vehicle is not fully laden and, or alternatively, to make it easier for the vehicle to move off on slippery ground by increasing the load on the driving axle;

"*centre-axle trailer*" means a trailer having only a single axle or group of axles which is positioned at or close to the centre of gravity so that, when the trailer is uniformly loaded, the static vertical load transmitted to the towing vehicle does not exceed 10 per cent of the maximum authorised weight for the axle or group of axles or 1000kg, whichever is the less;

"*kg*" means kilograms;

"*low pollution engine*" means an engine which—

    (a) is fuelled solely by gas; or

    (b) is fuelled predominantly by gas and has a minimum gas tank capacity of 400 litres; or

    (c) being a diesel engine, complies with at least the requirements for the emission of gaseous and particulate pollutants specified in paragraphs 6.2.1 of Annex I to Directive 88/77/EEC [*O.J. No. L36, February 9, 1988, p. 33*] as amended by Directive 91/542/EEC [*O.J. No. L295, October 25, 1991, p. 1*], the maximum masses of which as shown on line B in the table to that paragraph are—

Mass of carbon monoxide (CO) g/kWh	*Mass of hydrocarbons (HC) g/kWh*	*Mass of nitrogen oxides (Nox) g/kWh*	*Mass of particulates (PT) g/kWh*
4.0	1.1	7.0	0.15

"*loadable axle*" means an axle the load on which can be varied without the axle being raised by the use of an axle-lift device;

"*m*" means metres;

"*maximum authorised weight*" in relation to a vehicle, vehicle combination or axle means the maximum authorised weight for the vehicle, vehicle combination or axle determined in accordance with these Regulations;

"*retractable axle*" means an axle which is raised or lowered by an axle-lift device, either by raising the wheels of the vehicle clear off the ground or by lowering them to the ground.

"*rigid motor vehicle*" means a motor vehicle which is not a tractor unit or an articulated bus;

"*road friendly suspension*" means a suspension system whereby at least 75 per cent of the spring effect is produced by air or other compressible fluid under pressure or suspension recognised as being equivalent within the Community as defined in Annex II of Council Directive 96/53/EC [*O.J. No. L235, September 17, 1996, p. 59*];

"*semi-trailer*" means a trailer which is constructed or adapted to be drawn by a tractor unit and includes a vehicle which is not itself a motor vehicle but has some or all of its wheels driven by the drawing vehicle;

"*steering axle*" means an axle that can be positively steered by the action of the driver;

"*tandem axle*" means a group of 2 axles not more than 2.5m apart so linked together that the load applied to one axle is applied to the other; references to "*driving tandem axle*" include a tandem axle where either or both the axles comprising the tandem axle are driven and references to a "*non-driving tandem axle*" are to a tandem axle where neither of the axles comprising it is driven;

"*tractor unit*" means a motor vehicle by which a trailer partially superimposed on it may be drawn so that, when the trailer is fully loaded, not less than 20 per cent of its load is borne by the drawing vehicle;

"*triaxle*" means—

    (a) a group of 3 axles in which no axle is more than 3.25m apart from any other axle; or

    (b) a group of more than 3 axles in which no axle is more than 4.6m from any other axle,

and in either case so linked together that the load applied to one axle is transferred to both or all the others; and

"*vehicle combination*" means an articulated vehicle or a rigid motor vehicle drawing a trailer.

(2) For the purposes of these Regulations the distance between any 2 axles of a vehicle or vehicle combination shall be taken to be the shortest distance between the line joining the centres of the areas of contact with the road surface of the wheels of one axle and the line joining the centres of the areas of contact with the road surface of the wheels of the other axle.

(3) In these Regulations, except where otherwise specified,—

    (a) a reference to a numbered regulation is a reference to the regulation in these Regulations so numbered;

    (b) a reference to a numbered paragraph is a reference to the paragraph so numbered in the regulation or the Schedule in which the reference occurs;

    (c) a reference to a numbered sub-paragraph is a reference to the sub-paragraph so numbered in the paragraph in which the reference occurs; and

    (d) a reference to a numbered Schedule is a reference to the Schedule to these Regulations so numbered.

B65.06   *[Regulation 2 is printed as amended by S.I. 2000 No. 3224 (on January 1, 2001).*

The amendment effected by S.I. 2000 No. 3224 was set out in regulation 3(1) of that instrument. Ibid., reg.3(2), provided as follows:

The expressions listed below shall be construed in accordance with the provisions indicated—

first used	regulation 3(3) of the 1986 Regulations *[S.I. 1986 No. 1078]*
complies with	regulation 6 of the 1986 Regulations
diesel engine	paragraph 2.2 Directive 88/77/EEC as amended by Directive 91/542/EEC, Annex 1
gas	regulation 3(2) of the 1986 Regulations
trailer	regulation 3(2) of the 1986 Regulations
wheel	regulation 3(2) of the 1986 Regulations

The effect of ibid., reg.3(2) (which also took effect on January 1, 2001) is not clear; in particular, it is not clear whether the expressions referred to were intended to be introduced as textual amendments into regulation 2 of the principal regulations. However, S.I. 2000 No. 3224, reg.3(2), has been prospectively revoked by S.I. 2001 No. 1125 with effect from April 17, 2001. Nevertheless, if S.I. 2000 No. 3224, reg.3(2), is properly to be regarded as textually amending regulation 2 of the principal regulations it would seem that the textual amendment would survive the revocation of S.I. 2000 No. 3224, reg.3(2) (see the Interpretation Act 1978, ss.16(1)(b) and 23(1)). S.I. 2001 No. 1125 will insert the following definitions (at the appropriate places) into regulation 2 of the principal regulations (and such definitions seem to be intended to supersede the substance of S.I. 2000 No. 3224, reg.3(2)) with effect from April 17, 2001:

"complies with" shall, in relation to the requirements of a Community Directive, be construed in accordance with regulation 6 of the 1986 Regulations *[S.I. 1986 No. 1078, as amended]*;

"diesel engine" shall be construed in accordance with paragraph 2.2 of Directive 88/77/EEC as amended by Directive 91/542/EEC, Annex 1;

"Directive 88/77/EEC" means Council Directive 88/77 of 3 December 1987 on the approximation of the laws of the member states relating to the measures to be taken against the emission of gaseous and particulate pollutants from diesel engines for use in vehicles;

"Directive 91/542/EEC" means Council Directive 91/542 of 1 October 1991 amending Directive 88/77/EEC;

"first used" shall be construed in accordance with regulation 3(3) of the 1986 Regulations;

"gas" has the meaning given in regulation 3(2) of the 1986 Regulations;

"trailer" and *"semi-trailer"* have the meanings given in regulation 3(2) of the 1986 Regulations; and

"wheel" has the meaning given in regulation 3(2) of the 1986 Regulations; and

The following amendment will also take effect on April 17, 2001 in the table in the definition of "low pollution engine" in accordance with S.I. 2001 No. 1125:

the term "(NOx)" will be substituted in the heading to the third column for "(Nox)".*]*

3. Application of Regulations

These Regulations apply to all wheeled motor vehicles and trailers which fall within category M_2, M_3, N_2, N_3, O_3 or O_4 of the vehicle categories defined in Annex II of Directive 70/156/EEC as substituted by Directive 92/53/EC *[below]* except where vehicle combinations which for the time being fulfil the requirements of Part II, III or IIIA of Schedule 11A to the 1986 Regulations (exemptions relating to combined transport operations).   **B65.07**

4. Maximum authorised weights

B65.08   (1) Subject to paragraph (2) and regulation 5, no vehicle to which these Regulations apply and which is of a description specified in a Schedule to these Regulations shall be used on a road if—

(a) the weight of the vehicle exceeds the maximum authorised weight for the vehicle determined in accordance with Schedule 1;

(b) where the vehicle is used as part of a vehicle combination, the weight of the combination exceeds the maximum authorised weight for the combination determined in accordance with Schedule 2; or

(c) the axle weight of any axle of the vehicle exceeds the maximum authorised axle weight for that axle determined in accordance with Schedule 3.

(2) A vehicle to which any of the provisions of regulations 75 to 79 of the 1986 Regulations apply, so long as it is so used that those provisions are complied with, shall be taken to comply with these Regulations.

B65.09   *[With effect from January 1, 2002, the following amendments will be made to regulation 4 by S.I. 2000 No. 3224:*

(i) the following words will be inserted at the end of regulation 4(1)(c) (after the words "Schedule 3)—

[or if any of the other requirements of that Schedule are not complied with.]

and

(ii) the following words will be inserted at the end of regulation 4(2)—

[except, in the case of a vehicle fitted with one or more retractable loadable axles, for the provisions of paragraphs 3 or 4 of Schedule 3.] *]*

5. Saving for regulation 80 of the 1986 Regulations (over-riding weight restrictions)

B65.10   Nothing in these Regulations shall prejudice or affect regulation 80 of the 1986 Regulations and a person using or permitting a vehicle to be used contrary to the provisions of that regulation commits an offence even if the weights authorised by these Regulations are not exceeded.

B65.11   *[With effect from January 1, 2002, the following amendments will be made to regulation 5 by S.I. 2000 No. 3224:*

(i) the words "Compliance with" will be substituted in the heading to regulation 5 for the words "Saving for",

(ii) the existing text of regulation 5 will be re-numbered as regulation 5(1),

(iii) the following words will be inserted at the beginning of regulation 5(1) (as re-numbered)—

[Subject to paragraph (2),]

and

(iv) the following text will be added after regulation 5(1) (as re-numbered)—

[(2) Regulation 80 of the 1986 Regulations [*S.I. 1986 No. 1078, as amended by S.I. 1994 No. 329; S.I. 1997 No. 1096; and S.I. 1998 No. 3112*] shall not be contravened when a vehicle to which paragraph 3 of Schedule 3 applies is operated in accordance with sub-paragraph (3) of that paragraph.] *]*

SCHEDULE 1 Regulation 4(1)(a)

MAXIMUM AUTHORISED WEIGHTS FOR VEHICLES

1. Weight not to be exceeded in any circumstances

(1) Subject to paragraph 2, the maximum authorised weight for a vehicle of a descrip- **B65.12**
tion specified in column (2) of an item in Table 1 below and having the number of axles
specified in column (3) shall be the weight specified in column (4) of the item.

TABLE 1

(1) Item	(2) Description of vehicle	(3) Number of axles	(4) Maximum authorised weight (kg)
1.	Rigid motor vehicle	2	18000
2.	Tractor unit	2	18000
3.	Trailer which is not a semi-trailer or a centre-axle trailer	2	18000
4.	Trailer which is not a semi-trailer or centre-axle trailer	3 or more	2400
5.	Rigid motor vehicle which satisfies at least one of the conditions specified in sub-paragraph (2)	3	26000
6.	Rigid motor vehicle not falling within item 5	3	2500
7.	Tractor unit which satisfies at least one of the conditions specified in sub-paragraph (2)	3 or more	26000
8.	Tractor unit not falling within item 7	3 or more	25000
9.	Articulated bus	Any number	28000
10.	Rigid motor vehicle which satisfies at least one of the conditions specified in sub-paragraph (2)	4 or more	32000
11.	Rigid motor vehicle not falling within item 10	4 or more	30000

(2) The conditions referred to in items 5, 7 and 10 of Table 1 are that—

(a) the driving axle if it is not a steering axle is fitted with twin tyres and road friendly suspension; or

(b) each driving axle is fitted with twin tyres and the maximum weight for each axle does not exceed 9500kg.

2. Weight by reference to axle spacing

For a vehicle of a description specified in column (2) of an item in Table 2 below and **B65.13**
having the number of axles specified in column (3) of that item, the authorised weight in
kilograms shall be the number equal to the product of the distance measured in metres
between the foremost and rearmost axles of the vehicle multiplied by the factor specified in
column (4) and rounded up to the nearest 10kg, if that number is less than the maximum
authorised weight determined in accordance with paragraph 1.

TABLE 2

(1) Item	(2) _Description of vehicle_	(3) _Number of axles_	(4) _Factor to determine maximum authorised weight_
1.	Rigid motor vehicle	2	6000
2.	Tractor unit	2	6000
3.	Trailer which is not a semi-trailer or centre-axle trailer	2	6000
4.	Rigid motor vehicle	3	5500
5.	Tractor unit	3 or more	6000
6.	Trailer which is not a semi-trailer or centre-axle trailer	3 or more	5000
7.	Rigid motor vehicle	4 or more	5000
8.	Articulated bus	Any number	5000

Regulation 4(1)(b) SCHEDULE 2

MAXIMUM AUTHORISED WEIGHTS FOR VEHICLE COMBINATIONS

1. Weight not to be exceeded in any circumstances

B.65.14 (1) Subject to paragraph 2, the maximum authorised weight for a vehicle combination of a description of vehicle specified in column (2) of an item in Table 3 below and having the number of axles specified in column (3) shall be the weight specified in column (4) of the item.

TABLE 3

(1) Item	(2) _Description of combination_	(3) _Number of axles_	(4) _Maximum authorised weight (kg)_
1.	Articulated vehicle	3	26000
2.	Rigid motor vehicle towing a trailer satisfying the condition specified in sub-paragraph (2)	3	26000
3.	Rigid motor vehicle not falling within item 2 drawing a trailer	3	22000
4.	Articulated vehicle satisfying the conditions specified in sub-paragraph (3)	4	38000
5.	Articulated vehicle not falling within item 4	4	36000
6.	Rigid motor vehicle towing a trailer satisfying the condition specified in sub-paragraph (2)	4	36000
7.	Rigid motor vehicle not falling witin item 6 drawing a trailer	4	30000
8.	Articulated vehicle	5 or more	40000

[_continued on next page_

(1) *Item*	(2) *Description of combination*	(3) *Number of axles*	(4) *Maximum authorised weight (kg)*
9.	Rigid motor vehicle towing a trailer satisfying the condition specified in sub-paragraph (2)	5 or more	40000
10.	Rigid motor vehicle not falling within item 9 drawing a trailer	5 or more	34000
11.	Articulated vehicle satisfying the conditions specified in sub-paragraph (4)	6 or more	41000
12.	Rigid motor vehicle towing a trailer satisfying each of the conditions specified in sub-paragraphs (2) and (4)	6 or more	41000
[13.	Articulated vehicles satisfying each of the conditions specified in sub-paragraphs (4) and (5)	6 or more	44000]
[14.	Rigid motor vehicles towing a trailer satisfying each of the conditions specified in sub-paragraphs (2), (4) and (5)	6 or more	44000]

(2) The condition referred to in items 2, 6, 9 and 12 of Table 3 is that the distance between the rear axle of the motor vehicle and the front axle of the trailer is not less than 3m.

(3) The conditions referred to in item 4 of Table 3 are that—

(a) the combination consists of a 2-axle tractor unit and a 2-axle semi-trailer;

(b) the weight of the tractor unit comprised in the combination does not exceed 18000kg;

(c) the sum of the axle weights of the semi-trailer does not exceed 20000kg; and

(d) the driving axle is fitted with twin tyres and road friendly suspension.

(4) The conditions referred to in items 11 and 12 of Table 3 are that—

(a) the axle weight of each driving axle does not exceed 10500kg; and

(b) either—

(i) each driving axle is fitted with twin tyres and road friendly suspension; or

(ii) each driving axle which is not a steering axle is fitted with twin tyres and the axle weight of each such axle does not exceed 8500kg;

(c) each axle of the trailer is fitted with road friendly suspension; and

(d) each vehicle comprised in the combination has at least 3 axles.

[(5) The condition referred to in items 13 and 14 of Table 3 is that the vehicle is fitted with a low pollution engine.]

[*Paragraph 1 of Schedule 2 is printed as amended (on February 1, 2001) by S.I. 2000 No. 3224.*   **B65.15**
(It has been assumed that the addition of sub-paragraph (5) to paragraph 1 was intended by S.I. 2000 No. 3224, although the text of ibid., reg.6(b) is ambiguous. The matter has been clarified, however, by S.I. 2001 No. 1125 which revoked the original amendment and inserted a like-worded provision as sub-paragraph (5) of paragraph 1; but the latter instrument only takes effect on April 17, 2001.)
With effect from April 17, 2001, the following amendments will be made to paragraph 1 of Schedule 2 by S.I. 2001 No. 1125:

(i) the words ", 12 and 14" will be substituted in paragraph 1(2) for the words "and 12", and

(ii) the words ", 12, 13 and 14" will be substituted in paragraph 1(4) for the words "and 12".

2. Weight by reference to axle spacing

B65.16   For a vehicle combination of a description specified in column (2) in Table 4 below and having the number of axles specified in column (3), the maximum authorised weight in kilograms shall be the product of the distance measured in metres between the king-pin and the centre of the rearmost axle of the semi-trailer multiplied by the factor specified in column (4) and rounded up to the nearest 10kg, if that weight is less than the authorised weight determined in accordance with paragraph 1.

TABLE 4

(1) Item	(2) Description of vehicle combination	(3) Number of axles	(4) Factor to determine maximum authorised weight
1.	Articulated vehicle	3 or more	5500

Regulation 4(1)(c)   SCHEDULE 3

MAXIMUM AUTHORISED AXLE WEIGHTS

1. Weight not to be exceeded in any circumstances

B65.17   (1) Subject to paragraph 2, the maximum authorised weight for an axle of a description specified in column (2) of an item in Table 5 below shall be the weight specified in column (3) of the item.

TABLE 5

(1) Item	(2) Description of axle	(3) Maximum authorised weight (kg)
1.	Single driving axle	11500
2.	Single non-driving axle	10000
3.	Driving tandem axle which meets either of the conditions specified in sub-paragraph (2)	19000
4.	Driving tandem axle not falling within item 3	18000
5.	Non-driving tandem axle	20000
6.	Triaxle	24000

(2) The conditions referred to in item 3 of Table 5 are that—

(a) the driving axle is fitted with twin tyres and road friendly suspension; or

(b) each driving axle is fitted with twin tyres and no axle has an axle weight exceeding 9500kg.

2. Weight by reference to axle spacing

B65.18   For an axle of a description specified in column (2) of an item in Table 6 below, if the dimension specified in column (3) is of the length specified in column (4), the maximum authorised weight shall be the weight specified in column (5) of the item, if that weight is less than the maximum authorised weight determined in accordance with paragraph 1.

TABLE 6

(1) Item	(2) Description of axle	(3) Specified dimension	(4) Length m	(5) Maximum authorised weight (kg)
1.	Driving tandem axle	Distance between the 2 axles comprised in the tandem axle	Less than 1	11500
2.	Driving tandem axle	Distance between the 2 axles comprised in the tandem axle	Not less than 1 but less than 1.3	16000
3.	Non-driving tandem axle	Distance between the 2 axles comprised in the tandem axle	Less than 1	11000
4.	Non-driving tandem axle	Distance between the 2 axles comprised in the tandem axle	Not less than 1 but less than 1.3	16000
5.	Non-driving tandem axle	Distance between the 2 axles comprised in the tandem axle	Not less than 1.3 but less than 1.8	18000
6.	Triaxle	Distance between any one axle comprised in the triaxle and the nearer of the other 2 axles	1.3 or less	21000

[With effect from January 1, 2002, the following amendment will be made to paragraph 1(1) of   **B65.19** *Schedule 3 by S.I. 2000 No. 3224:*

the words "paragraphs 2 to 4" will be substituted for the words "paragraph 2".

With effect from the same date, the following paragraphs will be added to Schedule 3 by S.I. 2000 No. 3224:

[3. Requirements relating to retractable and loadable axles

(1) This paragraph applies to a vehicle which—

(a) is fitted with one or more retractable axles or with one or more loadable axles; and

(b) is first used on or after 1 January 2002.

(2) Subject to sub-paragraph (3), under all driving conditions other than those described in sub-paragraph (3), the maximum authorised weight on any axle shall be the weight specified in column (3) of Table 5 or in column (5) of Table 6 (as may be appropriate) and the retractable axle or the loadable axle shall lower to the ground automatically if—

(a) the front axle on the vehicle is laden to that maximum authorised weight, or

(b) in the case of a vehicle having a group of axles, the nearest axle or axles is or are laden to that maximum authorised weight;

and in paragraph (a) above "*axle*" is a reference to an axle described in column (2) of items 1 or 2 of Table 5 in Schedule 3 and in paragraph (b) above "*group of axles*" is a reference to an axle described in column (2) of items 3 to 6 of that Table.

(3) The driving conditions referred to in sub-paragraph (2) exist where a vehicle is on a slippery surface and, accordingly in order to help vehicles or vehicle combinations to move off on slippery ground, and to increase the traction of their tyres on slippery surfaces, the axle-lift device may also actuate the retractable axle or the loadable axle of the vehicle or semi-trailer to increase the weight on the driving axle of the vehicle, subject as follows:—

   (a) the weight corresponding to the load on each axle of the vehicle may exceed the relevant maximum authorised weight by up to 30 per cent, so long as it does not exceed the value stated by the manufacturer for this special purpose;

   (b) the weight corresponding to the remaining load on the front axle shall remain above zero;

   (c) the retractable axle or the loadable axle shall be actuated only by a special control device; and

   (d) after the vehicle has moved off and reached a speed of 30 kms per hour, the axle shall automatically lower again to the ground or be reloaded.]

[**4.** Every retractable axle or loadable axle fitted to a vehicle to which these Regulations apply, and any system for its operation, shall be designed and installed in such a manner as to protect it against improper use or tampering.]]

The Motor Cycles (Eye Protectors) Regulations 1999
(S.I. 1999 No. 535)

[The text of these regulations is printed as amended by:

    the Motor Cycles (Eye Protectors) (Amendment) Regulations 2000 (S.I. 2000 No. 1489) (June 30, 2000).   **B66.01**

    The amending regulations are referred to in the notes to the principal regulations only by their year and number. The date referred to above is the date on which the amending regulations came into force.]

1. Citation and commencement   *[Omitted.]*   **B66.02**

2. Interpretation   **B66.03**

In these Regulations—

[(aa)   "*ECE Regulation 22*" means Regulation No. 22 set out in Addendum 21 to the UN ECE Agreement;]

[(aaa)   "*ECE Regulation 22.05*" means ECE Regulation 22 as amended by the 05 series of amendments and all previous amendments in force on 30th June 2000;]

[(aaaa)   "*the UN ECE Agreement*" means the Agreement of the United Nations Economic Commission for Europe concluded at Geneva on 20th March 1958 at amended *[Cmnd. 2535 and Cmnd. 3562]* concerning the adoption of uniform technical pre-scriptions for wheeled vehicles, equipment and parts which can be fitted to and/or used on wheeled vehicles and the conditions for the reciprocal recognition of approvals granted on the basis of these prescriptions, to which the United Kingdom is a party by virtue of an instrument of accession dated 14th January 1963 deposited with the Secretary General of the United Nations on 15th January 1963;]

(a)   "*EEA State*" means a State which is a contracting party to the Agreement on the European Economic Area signed at Oporto on 2nd May 1992 as adjusted by the Protocol signed at Brussels on 17th March 1993 *[Cm. 2073 and Cm. 2183]*;

(b)   "*eye protector*" means an appliance designed or adapted for use with any headgear or by being attached to or placed upon the head by a person driving or riding on a motor bicycle and intended for the protection of the eyes;

(c)   "*motor bicycle*" means a two-wheeled motor cycle, whether or not having a side-car attached, and for the purposes of this definition, where the distance measured between the centre of the area of contact with the road surface of any two wheels of a motor cycle is less than 460 millimetres, those wheels shall be counted as one wheel.

[Regulation 2 is printed as amended by S.I. 2000 No. 1489.   **B66.04**
As to the EEA states, see the note "European Economic Area" to Regulation (EEC) 3820/85 below.]

3. Revocation   *[Omitted.]*   **B66.05**

4. Prescribed types of authorised eye protector

(1)   Subject to paragraph (3), the types of eye protector hereby prescribed as authorised for use by persons driving or riding (otherwise than in a side-car) on a motor bicycle are—   **B66.06**

(a) those which conform—

    (i) to the requirements relating to Grade X in British Standard BS 4110:1979 and are marked with that Grade and the number of that standard,

    (ii) to the requirements relating to Grades XA, YA or ZA in British Standards BS 4110:1979 as amended by Amendment No. 1 (AMD 3368), Amendment No. 2 (AMD 4060) and Amendment No. 3 (AMD 4630) and are marked with the number of that standard and the Grade to which they conform, or

    (iii) to any other standard accepted by an EEA State, which offers in use levels of safety, suitability and fitness for purpose equivalent to those offered by the standards referred to in paragraph (i) or (ii) above, and are marked with a mark to indicate that standard,

and in each case are marked with an approved certification mark of an approved body (whether or not they are required to be so marked by the standard in point);

[(aa) those which conform with ECE Regulation 22.05 including the approval, marking and conformity of production requirements of that Regulation;]

(b) those which comply with the requirements of Council Directive 89/686/EEC [*O.J. No. L399 December 30, 1989, p. 18*] of the 21st December 1989 on the approximation of the laws of the Member States relating to personal protective equipment as amended by Council Directives 93/68/EEC [*O.J. No. L220 August 30, 1993, p. 1*] of 22nd July 1993, 93/95/EEC [*O.J. No. L276 November 9, 1993, p. 11*] of 29th October 1993 and 96/58/EEC [*O.J. No. L236 September 18, 1996, p. 44*] of 3rd September 1996; or

(c) those which were first used before 1st April 1989 and fulfil all of the following requirements—

    (i) they are fitted with lenses that are designed to correct a defect in sight,

    (ii) they transmit 50 per cent or more of the light, and

    (iii) they do not fly into fragments if fractured.

(2) For the purposes of this regulation:

(a) an approved certification mark is—

    (i) the certification mark of the British Standards Institution; or

    (ii) a certification mark which indicates that a conformity assessment equivalent to that of the British Standards Institution has been undertaken, and

(b) an approved body is—

    (i) the British Standards Institution; or

    (ii) any body approved by an EEA State to undertake conformity assessments equivalent to those undertaken by the British Standards Institution.

(3) The types of eye protector prescribed by paragraph (1) are not prescribed as authorised for use by persons to whom paragraph (4) applies.

(4) This paragraph applies to any person driving or riding on a motor bicycle if—

(a) it is a mowing machine;

(b) it is for the time being propelled by a person on foot;

(c) it is a vehicle brought temporarily into Great Britain by a person resident outside the United Kingdom which has not remained in the United Kingdom for a period of more than one year from the date it was last brought into the United Kingdom; or

(d) that person is in the armed forces of the Crown, is on duty and is wearing an eye protector supplied to him as part of his service equipment.

[Regulation 4 is printed as amended by S.I. 2000 No. 1489.]

SCHEDULE

Regulation 3   **B66.08**

[Revocations.]

The Prosecution of Offences Act 1985 (Specified Proceedings) Order 1999

(SI 1999 No. 904)

B67.01   **1, 2.**   *[Omitted.]*

B67.02   **3.**—(1) Subject to paragraphs (2) and (3) below, proceedings for the offences mentioned in the Schedule to this Order are hereby specified for the purposes of section 3 of the Prosecution of Offences Act 1985 (which, amongst other things, places a duty on the Director of Public Prosecutions to take over the conduct of all criminal proceedings, other than specified proceedings, instituted on behalf of a police force).

(2) Where a summons has been issued in respect of an offence mentioned in the Schedule to this Order, proceedings for that offence cease to be specified when the summons is served on the accused unless the documents described in section 12(3)(b) of the Magistrates' Courts Act 1980 (pleading guilty by post etc.) are served upon the accused with the summons.

(3) Proceedings for an offence cease to be specified if at any time a magistrates' court begins to receive evidence in those proceedings; and for the purpose of this paragraph nothing read out before the court under section 12(7) of the Magistrates' Courts Act 1980 shall be regarded as evidence.

Article 3   SCHEDULE

OFFENCES PROCEEDINGS FOR WHICH ARE SPECIFIED BY ARTICLE 3(1)

B67.03   **1.** Fixed penalty offences within the meaning of section 51(1) of the Road Traffic Offenders Act 1988.

B67.04   **2.** The offences under section 29(1) of the Vehicle Excise and Registration Act 1994.

B67.05   **3.** The offences under sections 17(2), 18(3), 24(3), 26(1) and (2), 29, 31(1), 42(b), 47(1), 87(2), 143, 164(6) and (9), 165(3) and (6), 168 and 172(3) of the Road Traffic Act 1988.

B67.06   **4.** All offences under the Road Traffic Regulation Act 1984 other than those under sections 35A(2), 43(5) and (12), 47(3), 52(1), 108(3), 115(1) and (2), 116(1) and 129(3) or those mentioned in paragraph 1 above.

B67.07   **5.** The offences arising by contravention of Regulations 3(9)(a) (involving a pedal cycle) and 3(9)(b) and 4(27), (28) and (30) of the Royal and Other Open Spaces Regulations 1997 [*S.I. 1997 No. 1639; not reproduced in this work*].

The Public Service Vehicles (Community Licences) Regulations 1999

(S.I. 1999 No. 1322)

Editorial note. The Arrangement of regulations set out below has been added editorially and does not form part of the text of the regulations.

B68.01

1. Citation, commencement and extent

(1)   *[Omitted.]*

B68.03

(2) These Regulations shall not extend to Northern Ireland.

2. Purpose and interpretation

(1) These Regulations implement Article 3A of the Council Regulation.

B68.04

(2) In these Regulations—

"*the 1981 Act*" means the Public Passenger Vehicles Act 1981 [*q.v.*];

"*the Council Regulation*" means Council Regulation (EEC) No. 684/92 of 16 March 1992 on common rules for the international carriage of passengers by coach and bus, as amended by Council Regulation (EC) No. 11/98 of 11 December 1997 [*q.v.*];

"*international operations*", "*national operations*", "*operating centre*", "*PSV operator's licence*", "*restricted licence*", "*standard licence*" and "*traffic commissioner*" have the meaning given to them by section 82(1) of the 1981 Act [*q.v.*];

"*operator*" has the meaning given by section 81 of the 1981 Act;

"*public service vehicle*" has the meaning given by section 1 of the 1981 Act [*q.v.*];

"*traffic area*" means a traffic area constituted for the purposes of the 1981 Act;

"*Transport Tribunal*" means the Transport Tribunal constituted as provided in Schedule 4 to the Transport Act 1985;

and subject thereto, expressions used which are also used in the Council Regulation have the meaning which they bear in that Regulation.

3. Use of public service vehicles without Community licence

B68.05   A person who uses a vehicle in Great Britain in contravention of Article 3A(1) of the Council Regulation shall be guilty of an offence and liable on summary conviction to a fine not exceeding level 4 on the standard scale.

4. Competent authorities

B68.06   The competent authority for the purposes of Article 3A of the Council Regulation and of these Regulations shall be, in relation to the operator of a public service vehicle who has an operating centre in a traffic area in Great Britain, the traffic commissioner for that area.

5. Entitlement to the issue of a Community licence

B68.07   A person shall be entitled to be issued by the competent authority with a Community licence under Article 3A(2) of the Council Regulation if he holds a standard licence which authorises use on both national and international operations, or a restricted licence.

6. Rights of appeal

B68.08   A person who—

(a) is aggrieved by the refusal of the competent authority to issue a Community licence to him, or

(b) being the holder of a Community licence, is aggrieved by the decision of the competent authority who issued it to withdraw it,

may appeal to the Transport Tribunal.

7. Effect of failure to comply with conditions governing use of Community licences

B68.09   A person who uses a public service vehicle in Great Britain under a Community licence and, without reasonable excuse, fails to comply with any of the conditions governing the use of that licence under the Council Regulation, shall be guilty of an offence and liable on summary conviction to a fine not exceeding level 4 on the standard scale.

8. Authorised inspecting officers

B68.10   Authorised inspecting officers for the purposes of the Council Regulation shall be examiners appointed under section 66A(1) of the Road Traffic Act 1988 [*q.v.*] and police constables.

9. Return of documents

B68.11   (1) Where a Community licence is withdrawn by the competent authority in accordance with condition 5 of the model Community licence set out in the Annex to the Council Regulation, the holder of that licence shall within 7 days of such withdrawal return to the competent authority which issued it the original licence and all certified true copies of it.

(2) The holder of a Community licence shall return to the competent authority which issued it such certified true copies of the licence as the authority may require pursuant to—

(a) any decision of the authority to reduce the maximum number of vehicles (being vehicles having their operating centre in the area of that authority) which the holder is authorised, under section 16(1) of the 1981 Act, to use under the PSV operator's licence held by him, or

(b) any decision of the authority under the condition 5 referred to in paragraph (1) to suspend or withdraw certified true copies of the Community licence.

(3) A person who, without reasonable excuse, fails to comply with any provision of paragraph (1) or (2) shall be guilty of an offence and liable on summary conviction to a fine not exceeding level 4 on the standard scale.

10. Supply of information

(1) The holder of a Community licence shall furnish such information as the competent authority which issued it may reasonably require from time to time to enable the authority to decide whether the holder is entitled to retain that licence. **B68.12**

(2) A person who, without reasonable excuse, fails to supply any information required under paragraph (1) shall be guilty of an offence and liable on summary conviction to a fine not exceeding level 4 on the standard scale.

11. Death, bankruptcy, etc., of holder of Community licence

Where a person is authorised to carry on the business of the holder of a PSV operator's licence by virtue of an authorisation under section 57(4)(b) of the 1981 Act, such person shall be treated as the holder of any Community licence held by the holder of the PSV operator's licence, for the same period as is specified in that authorisation. **B68.13**

12. Bodies corporate

(1) Where an offence under these Regulations has been committed by a body corporate and it is proved to have been committed with the consent or connivance of, or to be attributable to any neglect on the part of, any director, manager, secretary or other similar officer of the body corporate or any person who was purporting to act in any such capacity, he as well as the body corporate shall be guilty of the offence and shall be liable to be proceeded against and punished accordingly. **B68.14**

(2) Where the affairs of a body corporate are managed by its members, paragraph (1) shall apply in relation to the acts and defaults of a member in connection with his functions of management as if he were a director of the body corporate.

(3) Where an offence under these Regulations has been committed by a Scottish partnership and it is proved to have been committed with the consent or connivance of, or to be attributable to any neglect on the part of, a partner, he as well as the partnership shall be guilty of the offence and shall be liable to be proceeded against and punished accordingly.

13. Modification of the Road Traffic (Foreign Vehicles) Act 1972 *[Amends the 1972 Act, q.v.]* **B68.15**

The Goods Vehicle Operators (Qualifications) Regulations 1999

(SI 1999 No. 2430)

B69.01 **1. Citation, commencement, interpretation and extent**   *[Omitted.]*

B69.02 **2. Good repute**   *[Amends Good Vehicles (Licensing of Operators) Act 1995, Sched. 3, para.2, q.v.]*

B69.03 **3. Financial standing**   *[Omitted.]*

B69.04 **4. Professional competence**   *[Amends Goods Vehicles (Licensing of Operators) Act 1995, Sched. 3, para.13, q.v.]*

B69.05 **5. Transitional provisions and savings**

(1), (2) *[Transitional provisions relating to matters of financial standing.]*

(3) The amendments made by Regulation 4 above shall not apply in relation to a certificate of professional competence—

(a) which was issued before 1st October 1999; or

(b) which was issued on or after that date to a person who before that date passed the whole or any part of the examination leading to the issue of that certificate.

(4) In relation to a certificate of professional competence which was issued before 4th February 1991, or which was issued on or after that date to a person who before that date passed the whole or any part of the examination leading to the issue of that certificate, Schedule 3 to the Act shall have effect as if for paragraph 13 there was substituted the following paragraph—

"13.—(1) An individual shall be regarded as professionally competent if, and only if—

(a) he is the holder of a certificate issued by an approved body to the effect that he possesses the requisite skills; or

(b) he is the holder of any other certificate of competence, diploma or other qualification recognised for the purposes of this sub-paragrah by the Secretary of State.

(2) In sub-paragraph (1)—

'approved body' means—

(a) a body approved by the Secretary of State for the purposes of that sub-paragraph;

(b) a body approved by the Department of the Environment for Northern Ireland for the purposes of section 46A(5)(c) of the Transport Act (Northern Ireland) 1967; or

(c) a body or authority designated by a member state other than the United Kingdom for the purposes of Article 3.4 of Council Directive No. 74/561/EEC as it had effect immediately before it was amended by Council

Directive No. 89/438/EEC; and

'*the requisite skills*' means skills in the subjects listed in Part A and, in the case of a licence to cover international operations, Part B, of the Annex to Council Directive No. 74/561/EEC as it had effect immediately before it was amended by Council Directive No. 89/438/EEC."

(5) Paragraph 14 of Schedule 3 to the Act [*q.v.*] (which is superseded by paragraph (4) above) shall be omitted.

The Motor Vehicles (Driving Licences) Regulations 1999

(S.I. 1999 No. 2864)

B70.01   *[The text of these regulations is printed as amended by:*

> *the Motor Vehicles (Driving Licences) (Amendment) Regulations 2000 (S.I. 2000 No. 2766) (November 1, 2000);*
>
> *the Motor Vehicles (Driving Licences) (Amendment) (No. 2) Regulations 2000 (S.I. 2000 No. 3157) (January 1, 2001);*
>
> *the Motor Vehicles (Driving Licences) (Amendment) Regulations 2001 (S.I. 2001 No. 53) (February 1, 2001);*
>
> *the Motor Vehicles (Driving Licences) (Amendment) (No. 2) Regulations 2001 (S.I. 2001 No. 236) (February 1, 2001); and*
>
> *the Motor Vehicles (Driving Licences) (Amendment) (No. 3) Regulations 2001 (S.I. 2001 No. 937) (April 5, 2001).*

The amending regulations are referred to in the notes to the principal regulations only by their years and numbers. The dates referred to above are the dates on which the amending regulations came into force.

The Motor Vehicles (Driving Licences) (Amendment) (No. 2) Regulations 2001 (S.I. 2001 No. 236) amended the Motor Vehicles (Driving Licences) (Amendment) Regulations 2001 (S.I. 2001 No. 53) on the day on which the earlier regulations came into force.]

B70.02   ARRANGEMENT OF REGULATIONS

PART I

PRELIMINARY

Regulation

PART II

LICENCES

Categories of entitlement

Regulation

PART III

TESTS OF COMPETENCE TO DRIVE

Preliminary

PART VI

DISABILITIES

PART VII

SUPPLEMENTARY

Transitional provisions

Miscellaneous

SCHEDULES

PART I

PRELIMINARY

1. Citation and commencement   *[Omitted.]*   B70.03

2. Revocation and saving

(1) The regulations specified in Schedule 1 [*not reproduced*] are hereby revoked.   B70.04

(2) Subject to otherwise herein provided, and without prejudice to the operation of sections 16 and 17 of the Interpretation Act 1978, the revocation of those regulations

shall not affect the validity of any application or appointment made, notice or approval given, licence, certificate or other document granted or issued or other thing done thereunder and any reference in such application, appointment, notice, approval, licence, certificate or other document or thing to a provision of any regulation hereby revoked, whether specifically or by means of a general description, shall, unless the context otherwise requires, be construed as a reference to the corresponding provision of these Regulations.

3. Interpretation

B70.05   (1) In these Regulations, unless the context otherwise requires, the following expressions have the following meanings—

"*1981 Act*" means the Public Passenger Vehicles Act 1981 [*q.v.*];

"*1985 Act*" means the Transport Act 1985 [*q.v.*];

"*ambulance*" means a motor vehicle which—

    (a) is constructed or adapted for, and used for no other purpose than, the carriage of sick, injured or disabled people to or from welfare centres or places where medical or dental treatment is given, and

    (b) is readily identifiable as such a vehicle by being marked "Ambulance" on both sides;

"*appropriate driving test*" and "*extended driving test*" have the same meanings respectively as in section 36 of the Offenders Act [*q.v.*];

["*certified direct access instructor*" has the meaning given by regulation 64(2);]

"*Construction and Use Regulators*" means the Road Vehicles (Construction and Use) Regulations 1986 [*S.I. 1986 No. 1078, q.v.*];

"*controlled by a pedestrian*" in relation to a vehicle means that the vehicle either—

    (a) is constructed or adapted for use under such control; or

    (b) is constructed or adapted for use either under such control or under the control of a person carried on it but is not for the time being in use under, or proceeding under, the control of a person carried on it;

["*disability assessment test*" means a test of competence to drive for which a person is required, by notice under section 94(5)(c) of the Traffic Act, to submit himself; and "*disability assessment licence*" means a provisional licence granted to enable him to drive a motor vehicle for the purposes of preparing for, and taking, such a test];

"*dual purpose vehicle*" means a motor vehicle which is constructed or adapted both to carry or haul goods and to carry more than eight persons in addition to the driver;

"*exempted goods vehicle*" and "*exempted military vehicle*" have the meanings respectively given in regulation 51;

"*extended driving test*" means a test of a kind prescribed by regulation 41;

"*full*", in relation to a licence of any nature, means a licence granted otherwise than as a provisional licence;

"*Group 1 licence*" and "*Group 2 licence*" have the meanings respectively given in regulation 70;

"*incomplete large vehicle*" means—

    (a) an incomplete motor vehicle, typically consisting of a chassis and a complete or incomplete cab, which is capable of becoming, on the completion of its construction, a medium-sized or large goods vehicle or a passenger-carrying vehicle, or

(b) a vehicle which would be an articulated goods vehicle but for the absence of a fifth-wheel coupling,

and which is not drawing a trailer;

"*large motor bicycle*" means—

(a) in the case of a motor bicycle without a side-car, a bicycle the engine of which has a maximum net power output exceeding 25 kilowatts or which has a power to weight ratio exceeding 0.16 kilowatts per kilogram, or

(b) in the case of a motor bicycle and side-car combination, a combination having a power to weight ratio exceeding 0.16 kilowatts per kilogram;

"*LGV trainee driver's licence*" has the meaning given in regulation 54;

"*maximum authorised mass*"—

(a) in relation to a goods vehicle, has the same meaning as "permissible maximum weight" in section 108(1) of the Traffic Act [*q.v.*];

(b) in relation to an incomplete large vehicle, means its working weight, and

(c) in relation to any other motor vehicle or trailer, has the same meaning as "maximum gross weight" in regulation 3(2) of the Construction and Use Regulations [*q.v.*];

"*maximum speed*" means the speed which the vehicle is incapable, by reason of its construction, of exceeding on the level under its own power when fully laden;

"*maximum net power output*" has the same meaning as in section 97 of the Traffic Act [*q.v.*];

"*mobile project vehicle*" means a vehicle which has a maximum authorised mass exceeding 3.5 tonnes, is constructed or adapted to carry not more than eight persons in addition to the driver and carries principally goods or burden consisting of—

(a) play or educational equipment and articles required in connection with the use of such equipment, or

(b) articles required for the purposes of display or of an exhibition,

and the primary purpose of which is use as a recreational, educational or instructional facility when stationary;

"*Northern Ireland test*" means a test of competence to drive conducted under the law of Northern Ireland;

"*Offenders Act*" means the Road Traffic Offenders Act 1988 [*q.v.*];

"*passenger-carrying vehicle recovery vehicle*" means a vehicle (other than an articulated goods vehicle combination as defined in section 108(1) of the Traffic Act) which—

(a) has an unladen weight not exceeding 10.2 tonnes,

(b) is being operated by the holder of a PSV operator's licence, and

(c) is being used for the purpose of—

(i) proceeding to, or returning from, a place where assistance is to be, or has been, given to a damaged or disabled passenger-carrying vehicle; or

(ii) giving assistance to or moving a disabled passenger-carrying vehicle or moving a damaged vehicle;

"*penalty points*" means penalty points attributed to an offence under section 28 of the Offenders Act [*q.v.*];

"*power to weight ratio*", in relation to a motor bicycle, means the ratio of the maximum net power output of the engine of the vehicle to its weight (including the weight of any side-car) with—

(a) a full supply of fuel in the tank,

(b) an adequate supply of other liquids needed for its propulsion, and

(c) no load other than its normal equipment, including loose tools;

"*practical test*" means a practical test of driving skills and behaviour or, where a test is by virtue of these Regulations required to be conducted in two parts, the part of it which consists of that test and includes such a test conducted as part of an extended driving test;

"*propelled by electrical power*", in relation to a motor vehicle, means deriving motive power solely from an electrical storage battery carried on the vehicle and having no connection to any other source of power when the vehicle is in motion;

"*PSV operator's licence*" has the meaning given by section 82(1) of the 1981 Act [*q.v.*];

"*standard access period*" has the meaning given by regulation 22;

"*standard motor bicycle*" means a motor bicycle which is not a large motor bicycle;

"*test*" means any test of competence to drive conducted pursuant to section 89 of the Traffic Act including an extended driving test;

"*test pass certificate*" means a certificate in the form specified in regulation 48(1)(a);

"*theory test*" means, where a test is by virtue of these Regulations to be conducted in two parts, the part that consists of the theoretical test and includes such a test conducted as part of an extended driving test;

"*theory test pass certificate*" means a certificate in the form specified in regulation 47(2)(a);

"*Traffic Act*" means the Road Traffic Act 1988 [*q.v.*];

"*traffic commissioner*" means, in relation to an applicant for or the holder of a licence, the traffic commissioner in whose area the applicant or holder resides;

"*unitary test*" means a test which, by virtue of these Regulations, is to consist of a single test of both practical driving skills and behaviour and knowledge of the Highway Code and other matters and includes such a test conducted as an extended driving test;

"*unladen weight*" has the same meaning as in regulation 3(2) of the Construction and Use Regulations [*q.v.*] and, in the case of a road roller, includes the weight of any object for the time being attached to the vehicle, being an object specially designed to be so attached for the purpose of temporarily increasing the vehicle's weight;

"*vehicle with automatic transmission*" means a class of vehicle in which either—

(a) the driver is not provided with any means whereby he may vary the gear ratio between the engine and the road wheels independently of the accelerator and the brakes, or

(b) he is provided with such means but they do not include a clutch pedal or lever which he may operate manually,

(and accordingly a vehicle with manual transmission is any other class of vehicle);

"*working weight*" means the weight of a vehicle in working condition on a road but exclusive of the weight of any liquid coolant and fuel used for its propulsion.

(2) In these Regulations, unless the context otherwise requires—

(a) a reference to a licence being in force is a reference to it being in force in accordance with section 99 of the Traffic Act, save that for the purpose of these Regulations a licence shall remain in force notwithstanding that it is—

(i) surrendered to the Secretary of State or is revoked otherwise than by notice under section 93(1) or (2) of the Traffic Act (revocation because of disability or prospective diability), or

(ii) treated as revoked by virtue of sections 37(1) of the Offenders Act, and

(b) a reference to the expiry of a licence is a reference to the time at which it ceases to be so in force (and "*expired*" shall be construed accordingly).

(3) Except where otherwise expressly provided, any reference in these Regulations to a numbered regulation or Schedule is a reference to the regulation or Schedule bearing that number in these Regulations, and any reference to a numbered paragraph (otherwise than as part of a reference to a numbered regulation) is a reference to the paragraph bearing that number in the regulation or Schedule in which the reference occurs.

(4) Where a statement or certificate (but not a distinguishing mark specified in regulation 16) is required under these Regulations to be in a form prescribed herein, the reference is to a certificate or statement in that form (or as nearly in that form as circumstances permit), adapted to the circumstances of the case and duly completed and signed where required.

(5) For the purposes of section 97(3)(d) of the Traffic Act and these Regulations the date of first use of a motor bicycle means—

(a) except in a case to which paragraph (b) applies, the date on which it was first registered under the Roads Act 1920, the Vehicles (Excise) Act 1949, the Vehicles (Excise) Act 1962 or the Vehicles (Excise) Act 1971;

(b) in the case of a motor bicycle which was used in any of the following circumstances before the date on which it was first registered, namely:—

(i) where the bicycle was used under a trade licence as defined in section 16 of the Vehicles (Excise) Act 1971, otherwise than for the purposes of demonstration or testing or of being delivered from premises of the manufacturer by whom it was made, or of a distributor of vehicles or dealer in vehicles to premises of a distributor of vehicles, dealer in vehicles or purchaser thereof, or to premises of a person obtaining possession thereof under a hiring agreement or hire purchase agreement,

(ii) where the bicycle belonged to the Crown and is or was used or appropriated for use for naval, military or air force purposes,

(iii) where the bicycle belonged to a visiting force or a headquarters or defence organisation to which the Visiting Forces and International Headquarters (Application of Law) Order 1965 [*S.I. 1965 No. 1536*] applied,

(iv) where the bicycle had been used on roads outside Great Britain and was imported into Great Britain, or

(v) where the bicycle had been used otherwise than on roads after being sold or supplied by retail and before being registered,

the date of manufacture of the bicycle.

(6) In paragraph (5)(b)(v) "*sold or supplied by retail*" means sold or supplied otherwise than to a person acquiring solely for the purpose of re-sale or re-supply for a valuable consideration.

[Regulation 3 is printed as amended by S.I. 2000 No. 3157; S.I. 2001 No. 53. **B70.06**
The Visiting Forces and International Headquarters (Application of Law) Order 1965 (to which reference is made in regulation 3(5)(b)(iii)) has been revoked and replaced by the Visiting Forces and International Headquarters (Application of Law) Order 1999 (S.I. 1999 No. 1736; not reproduced in this work). No textual amendment has been made to regulation 3 in consequence of that revocation; but by the Interpretation Act 1978, ss.17(2)(a) and 23(1) references to the earlier order may be treated as references to S.I. 1999 No. 1736.]

PART II

LICENCES

Categories of entitlement

4. Classification of vehicles

B70.07   (1) Subject to regulations 5 and 78, the Secretary of State shall grant licences authorising the driving of motor vehicles in accordance with the categories and sub-categories specified in column (1) and defined in column (2) of Schedule 2 and those categories and sub-categories are designated as groups for the purposes of section 89(1)(b) of the Traffic Act.

(2) In these Regulations, expressions relating to vehicle categories have the following meanings—

(a) any reference to a category or sub-category identified by letter, number or word or by any combination of letters, numbers and words is a reference to the category or sub-category defined in column (2) of Schedule 2 opposite that letter or combination in column (1) of the Schedule,

(b) "*sub-category*" means, in relation to category A, B, C, C+E, D or D+E, a class of vehicles comprising part of the category and identified as a sub-category thereof in column (2) of Schedule 2, and

(c) unless the context otherwise requires, a reference to a category includes a reference to sub-categories of that category.

5. Classes for which licences may be granted

B70.08   (1) A licence authorising the driving of motor vehicles of a class included in a category or sub-category shown in Part 1 of Schedule 2 may be granted to a person who is entitled thereto by virtue of—

(a) holding or having held a full licence, a full Northern Ireland licence, full British external licence, full British Forces licence, exchangeable licence or Community licence authorising the driving of vehicles of that class, or

(b) having passed a test for a licence authorising the driving of motor vehicles of that class or a Northern Ireland or Gibraltar test corresponding to such a test.

(2) A licence authorising the driving of motor vehicles of a class included in any category or sub-category shown in Part 2 of Schedule 2 may not be granted to a person unless, at a time before 1st January 1997—

(a) in the case of a person applying for a full licence—

(i) he held a full licence authorising the driving of motor vehicles of that class or a class which by virtue of these Regulations corresponds to a class included in that category or sub-category, or

(ii) he passed a test which at the time it was passed authorised the driving of motor vehicles of such a class or a Northern Ireland test corresponding to such a test;

(b) in the case of a person applying for a provisional licence, he held a provisional licence authorising the driving of vehicles of that class or a class which by virtue of these Regulations corresponds to a class included in that category or sub-category.

(3) A licence authorising the driving of motor vehicles included in sub-category B1 (invalid carriages), which are specified in Part 3 of Schedule 2, may not be granted to a person unless, at a time before 12th November 1999—

(a) in the case of a person applying for a full licence, he held a full licence authorising the driving of motor vehicles included in sub-category B1 (invalid carriages) or a class of motor vehicles which by virtue of these Regulations corresponds to vehicles included in that sub-category, or

(b) in the case of a person applying for a provisional licence, he held a provisional licence authorising the driving of motor vehicles included in sub-category B1 (invalid carriages) or a class of motor vehicles which by virtue of these Regulations corresponds to vehicles included in that sub-category.

6. Competence to drive classes of vehicle: general

(1) Where a person holds, or has held, a relevant full licence authorising him to drive vehicles included in any category or, as the case may be, sub-category he is deemed competent to drive—   **B70.09**

    (a) vehicles of all classes included in that category or sub-category unless by that licence he is or was authorised to drive—

        (i) only motor vehicles of a specified class within that category or sub-category, in which case he shall be deemed competent to drive only vehicles of that class, or

        (ii) only motor vehicles adapted on account of a disability, in which case he shall be deemed competent to drive only such classes of vehicle included in that category or sub-category as are so adapted (and for the purposes of this paragraph, a motor bicycle with a side-car may be treated in an appropriate case as a motor vehicle adapted on account of a disability),

and

    (b) all classes of vehicle included in any other category or sub-category which is specified in column (3) of Schedule 2 as an additional category or sub-category in relation to that category or sub-category unless by that licence he is or was authorised to drive—

        (i) only motor vehicles having automatic transmission, in which case he shall, subject to paragraph (2), be deemed competent to drive only such classes of motor vehicle included in the additional category or sub-category as have automatic transmission, or

        (ii) only motor vehicles adapated on account of a disability, in which case he shall be deemed competent to drive only such classes of vehicle included in the additional category or sub-category as are so adapted.

(2) Where the additional category is F, K or P, paragraph (1)(b)(i) shall not apply.

(3) In this regulation and regulations 7 and 8, "*relevant full licence*" means a full licence granted under Part III of the Traffic Act, a full Northern Ireland licence or a Community licence.

7. Competence to drive classes of vehicle: special cases

(1) A person who has held, for a period of at least two years, a relevant full licence authorising the driving of vehicles included in category C, other than vehicles included in sub-category C1, may also drive a motor vehicle of a class included in category D which is—   **B70.10**

    (a) damaged or defective and being driven to a place of repair or being road tested following repair, and

    (b) is not used for the carriage of any person who is not connected with its repair or road testing, unless by that licence he is authorised to drive only vehicles having automatic transmission, in which case he shall be deemed competent to drive only such of the vehicles mentioned in sub-paragraphs (a) and (b) as have automatic transmission.

(2) A person who holds a relevant full licence authorising the driving of vehicles included in category D, other than vehicles included in sub-category D1 or D1 (not for hire or reward), may drive a passenger-carrying vehicle recovery vehicle unless by that licence he is authorised to drive only vehicles having automatic transmission, in which case he shall be deemed competent to drive only passenger-carrying vehicle recovery vehicles having automatic transmission.

(3) A person may drive an incomplete large vehicle—

(a) having a working weight exceeding 3.5 tonnes but not exceeding 7.5 tonnes if he holds a relevant full licence authorising the driving of vehicles in sub-category C1, or

(b) having a working weight exceeding 7.5 tonnes if he holds a relevant full licence authorising the driving of vehicles in category C, other than vehicles in sub-category C1,

unless by that licence he is authorised to drive only motor vehicles having automatic transmission, in which case he shall be deemed competent to drive only incomplete large vehicles of the appropriate weight specified in paragraph (a) or (b) which have automatic transmission.

(4) A person who holds a relevant full licence authorising the driving of vehicles included in category B, other than vehicles in sub-categories B1 and B1 (invalid carriages), may drive—

(a) an exempted goods vehicle other than—

(i) a passenger-carrying vehicle recovery vehicle, or
(ii) a mobile project vehicle,

(b) an exempted military vehicle, and

(c) a passenger-carrying vehicle in respect of which the conditions specified in regulation 50(2) or (3) are satisfied,

unless by that licence he is authorised to drive only motor vehicles having automatic transmission, in which case he shall be deemed competent to drive only such of the vehicles mentioned in sub-paragraphs (a), (b) and (c) as have automatic transmission.

(5) A person who—

(a) holds a relevant full licence authorising the driving of vehicles of a class included in category B, other than vehicles in sub-categories B1 or B1 (invalid carriages),

(b) has held that licence for an aggregate period of not less than 2 years, and

(c) is aged 21 or over,

may drive a mobile project vehicle on behalf of a non-commercial body—

(i) to or from the place where the equipment it carries is to be, or has been, used, or the display or exhibition is to be, or has been, mounted, or

(ii) to or from the place where a mechanical defect in the vehicle is to be, or has been, remedied, or

(iii) in such circumstances that by virtue of paragraph 22 of Schedule 2 to the Vehicle Excise and Registration Act 1994 [*q.v.*] the vehicle is not chargeable with duty in respect of its use on public roads,

unless by that licence he is authorised to drive only vehicles having automatic transmission, in which case he shall be deemed competent to drive only mobile project vehicles having automatic transmission.

(6) A person who—

(a) holds a relevant full licence authorising the driving of vehicles of a class included in category B, other than vehicles in sub-categories B1 or B1 (invalid carriages),

(b) has held that licence for an aggregate period of not less than 2 years,

(c) is aged 21 or over,

(d) if he is aged 70 or over, is not suffering from a relevant disability in respect of which the Secretary of State would be bound to refuse to grant him a Group 2 licence, and

(e) receives no consideration for so doing, other than out-of-pocket expenses,

may drive, on behalf of a non-commercial body for social purposes but not for hire or reward, a vehicle of a class included in sub-category D1 which has no trailer attached and has a maximum authorised mass—

(i) not exceeding 3.5 tonnes, excluding any part of that weight which is attributable to specialised equipment intended for the carriage of disabled passengers, and

(ii) not exceeding 4.25 tonnes otherwise,

unless such a person is by that licence authorised to drive only vehicles having automatic transmission, in which case he shall be deemed competent to drive only such vehicles in sub-category D1 as conform to the above specification and have automatic transmission.

(7) A person who holds a relevant full licence authorising the driving of vehicles of a class included in category B, other than vehicles in sub-categories B1 or B1 (invalid carriages), may drive a vehicle of a class included in category B+E where—

(a) the trailer consists of a vehicle which is damaged or defective and is likely to represent a road safety hazard or obstruction to other road users,

(b) the vehicle is driven only so far as is reasonably necessary in the circumstances to remove the hazard or obstruction, and

(c) he receives no consideration for driving the vehicle,

unless by that licence he is authorised to drive only motor vehicles having automatic transmission, in which case he shall be deemed competent to drive, in the circumstances mentioned above, only vehicles included in category B+E having automatic transmission.

8. Competence to drive classes of vehicle: dual purpose vehicles

(1) Subject to paragraph (2), a person who is a member of the armed forces of the   **B70.11**
Crown may drive a dual purpose vehicle when it is being used to carry passengers for naval, military or air force purposes—

(a) where the vehicle has a maximum authorised mass not exceeding 3.5 tonnes, if he holds a relevant full licence authorising the driving of vehicles included in category B other than vehicles in sub-categories B1 or B1 (invalid carriages),

(b) where the vehicle has a maximum authorised mass exceeding 3.5 tonnes but not exceeding 7.5 tonnes, if he holds a relevant full licence authorising the driving of vehicles included in sub-category C1,

(c) in any other case, if he holds a relevant full licence authorising the driving of vehicles included in category C other than vehicles in sub-category C1.

(2) Where the person is authorised by his licence to drive only motor vehicles included in the relevant category or sub-category having automatic transmission, he may drive only dual purpose vehicles having automatic transmission.

9. Minimum ages for holding or obtaining licences

B70.12 (1) Subsection (1) of section 101 of the Traffic Act shall have effect as if for the classes of vehicle and the ages specified in the Table in that subsection there were substituted classes of vehicle and ages in accordance with the following provisions of this regulation.

(2) In item 3 (motor bicycles), the age of 21 is substituted for the age of 17 in a case where the motor bicycle is a large motor bicycle except in the following cases, namely—

(a) a case where a person has passed a test on or after 1st January 1997 for a licence authorising the driving of a motor vehicle of a class included in category A, other than sub-category A1, and the standard access period has elapsed,

(b) a case where the large motor bicycle—

(i) is owned or operated by the Secretary of State for Defence, or

(ii) is being driven by a person for the time being subject to the orders of a member of the armed forces of the Crown

and is being used for naval, military or air force purposes, and

(c) a case where a person holds a licence authorising the driving of a large motor bicycle by virtue of having passed a test before 1st January 1997.

(3) An item 4 (agricultural and forestry tractors), in the case of an agricultural or forestry tractor which—

(a) is so constructed that the whole of its weight is transmitted to the road surface by means of wheels,

(b) has an overall width not exceeding 2.45 metres, and

(c) is driven either—

(i) without a trailer attached to it, or

(ii) with a trailer which has an overall width not exceeding 2.45 metres and is either a two-wheeled or close-coupled four-wheeled trailer,

the age of 16 is substituted for the age of 17 in the case of a person who has passed a test prescribed in respect of category F, or is proceeding to, taking or returning from, such a test.

(4) In item 5 (small vehicles), the age of 16 is substituted for the age of 17 in the case of a small vehicle driven without a trailer attached where the driver of the vehicle is a person in respect of whom an award of the higher rate component of the disability living allowance made in pursuance of section 73 of the Social Security Contributions and Benefits Act 1992 (whether before or after his 16th birthday) is still in force.

(5) In item 6 (medium-sized goods vehicles), the age of 21 is substituted for the age of 18 in the case of a vehicle drawing a trailer where the maximum authorised mass of the combination exceeds 7.5 tonnes.

(6) In item 7 (other vehicles, including large goods and passenger-carrying vehicles), the age of 18 is substituted for the age of 21 in the case of a person driving a vehicle of a class included in sub-category D1 which is an ambulance and which is owned or operated by—

(a) a health service body (as defined in section 60(7) of the National Health Service and Community Care Act 1990), or

(b) a National Health Service Trust established under Part I of that Act or under the National Health Service (Scotland) Act 1978.

(7) In item 7, the age of 18 is substituted for the age of 21 in the case of a motor vehicle and trailer combination which is in sub-category C1 + E and the maximum authorised mass of the combination does not exceed 7.5 tonnes.

(8) In item 7, the age of 18 is substituted for the age of 21 in the case of a person who is registered as an employee of a registered employer in accordance with the Training Scheme, where he is driving a vehicle which is—

(a) of a class to which his training agreement applies, and

(b) owned or operated by his employer or by a registered LGV driver training establishment.

(9) In item 7, the age of 18 is substituted for the age of 21 in relation to a passenger-carrying vehicle—

(a) in the case of a person who holds a provisional licence, and

(b) in the case of a person who holds a full passenger-carrying vehicle driver's licence, where he is driving a vehicle which is operated under a PSV operator's licence, a permit granted under section 19 of the 1985 Act or a community bus permit granted under section 22 of that Act and he is either—

(i) not engaged in the carriage of passengers, or
(ii) engaged in the carriage of passengers on a regular service over a route which does not exceed 50 kilometres, or
(iii) is driving a vehicle of a class included in sub-category D1.

(10) In items 6 and 7, the age of 17 is substituted for the ages of 18 and 21 respectively in the case of—

(a) motor vehicles owned or operated by the Secretary of State for Defence, or

(b) motor vehicles driven by persons for the time being subject to the orders of a member of the armed forces of the Crown,

when they are being used for naval, military or air force purposes.

(11) In item 7, in the case of an incomplete large vehicle—

(a) which has a working weight not exceeding 3.5 tonnes, the age of 17 is substituted for the age of 21;

(b) which has a working weight exceeding 3.5 tonnes but not exceeding 7.5 tonnes, the age of 18 is substituted for the age of 21.

(12) In item 7, the age of 17 is substituted for the age of 21 in the case of a road roller which—

(a) is propelled otherwise than by steam,

(b) has no wheel fitted with pneumatic, soft or elastic tyres,

(c) has an unladen weight not exceeding 11.69 tonnes, and

(d) is not constructed or adapted for the conveyance of a load other than the following things, namely water, fuel or accumulators used for the purpose of the supply of power to or propulsion of the vehicle, loose tools and objects specially designed to be attached to the vehicle for the purpose of temporarily increasing its weight.

(13) In this regulation—

(a) for the purposes of paragraph (3)—

(i) any implement fitted to a tractor shall be deemed to form part of the tractor notwithstanding that it is not a permanent or essentially permanent fixture,

     (ii) *"closed-coupled"*, in relation to wheels on the same side of a trailer, means fitted so that at all times while the trailer is in motion the wheels remain parallel to the longitudinal axis of the trailer and that the distance between the centres of their respective areas of contact with the road surface does not exceed 840 millimetres, and

     (iii) *"overall width"*, in relation to a vehicle, means the width of the vehicle measured between vertical planes parallel to the longitudinal axis of the vehicle and passing through the extreme projecting points thereof exclusive of any driving mirror and so much of the distortion of any tyre as is caused by the weight of the vehicle;

   (b) for the purposes of paragraph (8), *"registered"*, *"training agreement"* and *"the Training Scheme"* have the meanings respectively given in regulation 54;

   (c) in paragraph (9), expressions used which are also used in Council Regulation 3820/85/EEC [*q.v.*] have the same meanings as in that Regulation.

Applications for licences

    10–12.   *[Omitted.]*

     13. *[Revoked by S.I. 2001 No. 53.]*

     14. *[Omitted.]*

Provisional licences

15. Duration of provisional licences authorising the driving of motor bicycles

    (1) Subject to paragraph (2), there is prescribed for the purposes of section 99(2) of the Traffic Act—

   (a) a motor bicycle of any class, and

   [(b) the same period as is provided by section 99(1) of the Traffic Act in relation to a licence to which section 99(1) applies.]

   (2) There are prescribed for the purposes of section 99(2)(b)(ii) of that Act the circumstances that—

   (a) the previous licence was surrendered or revoked, otherwise than under subsection (3) or (4) of section 99 of the Traffic Act, or treated as being revoked under section 37(1) of the Offenders Act,

   (b) if it has not been so surrendered or revoked, a period of at least one month, commencing on the date of surrender or revocation, would have elapsed before the previous licence would have expired, and

   (c) the licence when granted would come into force within the period of one year beginning on the date of surrender or revocation of the previous licence.

    [Regulation 15 is printed as amended by S.I. 2001 No. 53.]

16. Conditions attached to provisional licences

    (1) A provisional licence of any class is granted subject to the conditions prescribed in relation to a licence of that class in the following paragraphs.

   (2) Subject to the following paragraphs, the holder of a provisional licence shall not drive a vehicle of a class which he is authorised to drive by virtue of that licence—

(a) otherwise than under the supervision of a qualified driver who is present with him in or on the vehicle,

(b) unless a distinguishing mark in the form set out in Part 1 of Schedule 4 is displayed on the vehicle in such manner as to be clearly visible to other persons using the road from within a reasonable distance from the front and and from the back of the vehicle, or

(c) while it is being used to draw a trailer.

(3) The condition specified in paragraph (2)(a) shall not apply when the holder of the provisional licence—

(a) is driving a motor vehicle of a class included in sub-category B1 or B1 (invalid carriages) or in category F, G, H or K which is constructed to carry only one person and not adapted to carry more than one person;

(b) is riding a moped or a motor bicycle with or without a side-car; or

(c) is driving a motor vehicle, other than a vehicle of a class included in category C, C+E, D or D+E, on a road in an exempted island.

(4) The condition specified in paragraph (2)(b) shall not apply—

(a) when the holder of the provisional licence is driving a motor vehicle on a road in Wales, and

(b) a distinguishing mark in the form set out in Part 2 of Schedule 4 is displayed on the motor vehicle in the manner described in paragraph (2)(b).

(5) The condition specified in paragraph (2)(c) shall not apply to the holder of a provisional licence authorising the driving of a vehicle of a class included in category B+E, C+E, D+E or F, in relation to motor vehicles of that class.

(6) The holder of a provisional licence authorising the driving of—

(a) a moped, or

(b) a motor bicycle with or without a side-car,

shall not drive such a vehicle while carrying on it another person.

(7) The holder of a provisional licence authorising the driving of a motor bicycle other than a learner motor bicycle shall not drive such a vehicle otherwise than under the supervision of a certified direct access instructor . . . who is—

(a) present with him on the road while riding another motor bicycle,

(b) able to communicate with him by means of a radio which is not hand-held while in operation,

(c) supervising only that person or only that person and another person who holds such a provisional licence, and

(d) carrying a valid certificate issued in respect of him by the Secretary of State under regulation 65(4),

while he and the instructor are wearing apparel which is fluorescent or (during hours of darkness) is either fluorescent or luminous.

[(7A) The holder of a provisional licence authorising the driving of a moped or a learner motor bicycle shall not drive such a vehicle on a road when undergoing relevant training, unless the instructor giving the training is at all times—

(a) present with him on the road while riding another moped or learner motor bicycle or any motor bicycle, and

(b) supervising only him or him and not more than 3 other persons each of whom holds such a provisional licence.]

[(7B) In paragraph (7A)—

(a) "*relevant training*" means training (otherwise than as part of an approved training course for motor cyclists) in how to drive a moped or learner motor cycle given by a professional instructor; and

(b) "*professional instructor*" means an instructor paid money or money's worth for giving such training.]

(8) The holder of a passenger-carrying vehicle driver's provisional licence shall not drive a vehicle which he is authorised to drive by that licence while carrying any passenger in the vehicle other than—

(a) the person specified in paragraph (2)(a), or

(b) a person who holds a passenger-carrying vehicle driver's licence and either is giving or receiving instruction in the driving of passenger-carrying vehicles, or has given or received or is to give or receive, such instruction.

(9) The conditions specified in paragraphs (2)(a), (7) and (8) shall not apply when the holder of the provisional licence is undergoing a test.

(10) The conditions specified in paragraphs (2), (6), (7) and (8) shall not apply in relation to the driving of motor vehicles of a class in respect of which the provisional licence holder has been furnished with a valid test pass certificate stating that he has passed a test for the grant of a licence authorising him to drive vehicles of that class.

(11) The condition specified in paragraph (7)(b) shall not apply in the case of a provisional licence holder who is unable, by reason of impaired hearing, to receive directions from the supervising instructor by radio where the licence holder and the instructor are employing a satisfactory means of communication which they have agreed before the start of the journey.

[(11A) The holder of a disability assessment licence shall not drive a vehicle of a class which he is authorised to drive by virtue of the licence otherwise than during a period which—

(a) commences with the beginning of such period prior to the taking of the disability assessment test required by a relevant notice as is specified in writing by the Secretary of State when serving that notice; and

(b) ends with the completion of the test;

and, for these purposes, a "relevant notice" is a notice under section 94(5)(c) of the Traffic Act requiring the person to submit to a disability assessment test.]

(12) In the case of an LGV trainee driver's licence issued as a provisional licence, this regulation shall apply as modified by regulation 54.

(13) In this regulation—

(a) "*exempted island*" means any island outside the mainland of Great Britain from which motor vehicles, unless constructed or adapted specially for that purpose, cannot at any time be conveniently driven to a road in any other part of Great Britain by reason of the absence of any bridge, tunnel, ford or other way suitable for the passage of such motor vehicles but excluding any of the following islands, namely, the Isle of Wight, St. Mary's (Isles of Scilly), the islands of Arran, Barra, Bute, Great Cumbrae, Islay, the island which comprises Lewis and Harris, Mainland Orkney, Mainland Shetland, Mull, the island which comprises North Uist, Benbecula and South Uist and Tiree;

(b) "*provisional licence*", in relation to a class of vehicles, includes a full licence which is treated, by virtue of section 98 of the Traffic Act, as authorising its holder to drive vehicles of that class as if he held a provisional licence therefor;

(c) *"qualified driver"* shall be interpreted in accordance with regulation 17.

[Regulation 16 is printed as amended by S.I. 2000 No. 3157; S.I. 2001 No. 53.]   **B70.17**

17. Meaning of "qualified driver"

(1) Subject to paragraph (2), a person is a qualified driver for the purposes of regulation 16 if he—   **B70.18**

(a) is 21 years of age or over,

(b) holds a relevant licence,

(c) has the relevant driving experience, and

(d) in the case of a disabled driver, he is supervising a provisional licence holder who is driving a vehicle of a class included in category B and would in an emergency be able to take control of the steering and braking functions of the vehicle in which he is a passenger.

(2) In the case of a person who is a member of the armed forces of the Crown acting in the course of his duties for naval, military or air force purposes sub-paragraphs (a) and (c) of paragraph (1) shall not apply.

(3) For the purposes of this regulation—

(a) *"disabled driver"* means a person who holds a relevant licence which is limited by virtue of a declaration made with his application for the licence or a notice served under section 92(5)(b) of the Traffic Act to vehicles of a particular class;

(b) *"full licence"* includes a full Northern Ireland licence and a Community licence;

(c) *"relevant licence"* means—

(i) in the case of a disabled driver, a full licence authorising the driving of a class of vehicles in category B other than vehicles in sub-category B1 or B1 (invalid carriages), and

(ii) in any other case, a full licence authorising the driving of vehicles of the same class as the vehicle being driven by the provisional licence holder;

(d) a person has relevant driving experience if he satisfies either of the following requirements—

(i) he has held the relevant licence for a continuous period of not less than 3 years or for periods amounting in aggregate to not less than 3 years, or

(ii) he is supervising a provisional licence holder driving a vehicle in category C, D, C+E or D+E, held the relevant licence on 6th April 1998, has held it continuously since that date and has held a full licence authorising the driving of vehicles in category B for a continuous period of not less than 3 years or for periods amounting in aggregate to not less than 3 years; and

(e) for the purposes of sub-paragraph (d)(ii) a person shall be regarded as holding a relevant licence during any period in which he holds a provisional licence and a valid test pass certificate entitling him to a full licence authorising the driving of vehicles of the same class as the vehicle being driven by the provisional licence holder.

18. Conditions attached to provisional licences: holders of driving permits other than licences granted under Part III of the Traffic Act

A holder of a provisional licence authorising the driving of vehicles of any class who also holds a permit by virtue of which he is at any time—   **B70.19**

(a) treated, by virtue of regulation 80, as the holder, for the purposes of section 87 of the Traffic Act, of a licence authorising the driving of vehicles of that class, or

(b) entitled, pursuant to article 2(1) of the Motor Vehicles (International Circulation) Order 1975 [*S.I. 1975 No. 1208, q.v.*], to drive motor vehicles of that class,

need not comply with regulation 16 at that time.

19. Full licences not carrying provisional entitlement

B70.20   (1) The application of sections 98(2) and 99A(5) of the Traffic Act is limited or excluded in accordance with the following paragraphs.

(2) Subject to paragraphs (3), (4), (5), (6), (11) and (12), the holder of a full licence which authorises the driving of motor vehicles of a class included in a category or sub-category specified in column (1) of the table at the end of this regulation may drive motor vehicles—

(a) of other classes included in that category or sub-category, and

(b) of a class included in each category or sub-category specified, in relation to that category or sub-category, in column (2) of the table,

as if he were authorised by a provisional licence to do so.

(3) Section 98(2) shall not apply to a full licence if it authorises the driving only of motor vehicles adapted on account of a disability, whether pursuant to an application in that behalf made by the holder of the licence or pursuant to a notice served under section 92(5)(b) of the Traffic Act.

(4) In the case of a full licence which authorises the driving of a class of standard motor bicycles, other than bicycles included in sub-category A1, section 98(2) shall not apply so as to authorise the driving of a large motor bicycle by a person under the age of 21 before the expiration of the standard access period.

(5) In the case of a full licence which authorises the driving of motor bicycles of a class included in sub-category A1 section 98(2) shall not apply so as to authorise the driving of a large motor bicycle by a person under the age of 21.

(6) In the case of a full licence which authorises the driving of a class of vehicles included in category C or C+E, paragraph (2) applies subject to the provisions of regulation 54.

(7) Subject to paragraphs (8), (9), (10), (11) and (12), the holder of a Community licence to whom section 99A(5) of the Traffic Act applies and who is authorised to drive in Great Britain motor vehicles of a class included in a category or sub-category specified in column (1) of the Table at the end of this regulation may drive motor vehicles—

(a) of other classes included in that category or sub-category, and

(b) of a class included in each category or sub-category specified, in relation to that category or sub-category, in column (2) of the Table,

as if he were authorised by a provisional licence to do so.

(8) Section 99A(5) shall not apply to a Community licence if it authorises the driving only of motor vehicles adapted on account of a disability.

(9) In the case of a Community licence which authorises the driving of a class of standard motor bicycle other than bicycles included in sub-category A1, section 99A(5) shall not apply so as to authorise the driving of a large motor bicycle by a person under the age of 21 before the expiration of the period of two years commencing on the date when that person passed a test for a licence authorising the driving of that class of standard motor

bicycle (and in calculating the expiration of that period, any period during which that person has been disqualified for holding or obtaining a licence shall be disregarded).

(10) In the case of a Community licence which authorises the driving only of motor bicycles of a class included in sub-category A1 section 98(2) shall not apply so as to authorise the driving of a large motor bicycle by a person under the age of 21.

(11) Except to the extent provided in paragraph (12), section 98(2) shall not apply to a full licence, and section 99A(5) shall not apply to a Community licence, in so far as it authorises its holder to drive motor vehicles of any class included in category B+E, C+E, D+E, or K or in sub-category B1 (invalid carriages), C1 or D1 (not for hire or reward).

(12) A person—

(a) who holds a full licence authorising the driving only of those classes of vehicle included in a category or sub-category specified in paragraph (11) which have automatic transmission (and are not otherwise adapted on account of a disability), or

(b) who holds a Community licence, to whom section 99A(5) of the Traffic Act applies and who is authorised to drive in Great Britain only those classes of vehicle included in a category or sub-category specified in paragraph (11) which have automatic transmission (and are not otherwise adapted on account of a disability),

may drive motor vehicles of all other classes included in that category or sub-category which have manual transmission as if he were authorised by a provisional licence to do so.

TABLE

(1) *Full licence held*	(2) *Provisional entitlement included*
A1	A, B, F and K
A	B and F
B1	A, B and F
B	A, B+E, G and H
C	C1+E, C+E
D1	D1+E
D	D1+E, D+E
F	B and P
G	H
H	G
P	A, B, F and K

Miscellaneous

20. Signatures on licences

In order that a licence may show the usual form of signature of its holder—　　B70.21

(a) where the Secretary of State so requires, a person applying for a licence shall provide the Secretary of State with a specimen of his signature which can be electronically recorded and reproduced on the licence;

(b) where no such requirement is made, a person to whom a licence is granted shall forthwith sign it in ink in the space provided.

21. Lost or defaced licences　　*[Omitted.]*　　　B70.22

PART III

TESTS OF COMPETENCE TO DRIVE

Preliminary

22. Interpretation of Part III

B70.23   In this Part of these Regulations—

"*applicant in person*" means a person making an application for an appointment for a test or a part of a test with a view to taking the test or that part thereof himself;

"*appointed person*" means a person appointed by the Secretary of State to conduct theory tests under paragraph (1)(a)(ii) or (2)(a) of regulation 23;

"*DSA examiner*" means a person appointed by the Secretary of State to conduct practical or unitary tests under paragraph (1)(a) or (2)(a) of regulation 24;

"*large vehicle instructor*" means a person operating an establishment for providing instruction in the driving of vehicles included in category B+E, C, C+E, D or D+E, including an establishment which provides tuition to prepare persons for the theory test;

"*motor bicycle instructor*" means a person operating an establishment for providing instruction in the driving of vehicles included in categories A or P, including an establishment which provides tuition to prepare persons for the theory test;

"*standard access period*" means the period of two years commencing on the date when a person passes a test for a licence authorising the driving of standard motor bicycles of any class, other than a class included in the sub-category A1, but disregarding—

(a) any period during which the person is disqualified under section 34 or 35 of the Offenders Act [*q.v.*],

(b) in a case where the person has been disqualified under section 36 of the Offenders Act [*q.v.*], the period beginning on the date of the court order under subsection (1) of that section and ending on the date when the disqualification is deemed by virtue of that section to have expired in relation to standard motor bicycles of that class,

(c) in a case where the Secretary of State has revoked the person's licence or test pass certificate under section 3(2) of, or Schedule 1 to, the Road Traffic (New Drivers) Act 1995 [*q.v.*], the period beginning on the date of the notice of revocation under that Act and ending on the date when the person passes the relevant driving test within the meaning of that Act, and

(d) any period during which the licence has ceased to be in force;

"*working day*" means a day other than a Saturday, Sunday, bank holiday, Christmas Day or Good Friday (and "*bank holiday*" means a day to be observed as such under section 1 of and Schedule 1 to the Bank [*sic*] and Financial Dealings Act 1971).

B70.24   *[For the Banking and Financial Dealings Act 1971, Sched. 1, see the note to the Road Vehicles (Construction and Use) Regulations 1986 (S.I. 1986 No. 1078), Sched. 12, para.1 above.]*

Appointment of persons to conduct tests

B70.25   **23–25.**   *[Omitted.]*

Applications for tests

B70.26   **26–36.**   *[Omitted.]*

Requirements at tests

37–39.   *[Omitted.]*

Nature and conduct of tests

40–42.   *[Omitted.]*

Entitlements upon passing test

43. Entitlement upon passing a test other than an appropriate driving test

(1) Where a person passes a test other than an appropriate driving test prescribed in respect of any category for a licence which (by virtue of regulation 37) authorises the driving of motor vehicles included in that category or in a sub-category thereof, or has passed a Northern Ireland test of competence corresponding to that test, the Secretary of State shall grant to him a licence in accordance with [the following provisions of this regulation].

(2) Subject to [regulations 44 and 44A], the licence shall authorise the driving of all classes of motor vehicle included in that category or sub-category unless—

  (a) the test or, as the case may be, the practical test is passed on a motor vehicle with automatic transmission, in which case it shall authorise the driving only of such classes of vehicle included in that category or sub-category as have automatic transmission;

  (b) the test or, as the case may be, the practical test, is passed on a motor vehicle which is adapted on account of a disability of the person taking the test, in which case it shall authorise the driving only of such classes of vehicle included in that category or sub-category as are so adapted (and for the purposes of this paragraph, a motor bicycle with a side-car may be treated in an appropriate case as a motor vehicle adapted on account of a disability).

(3) [Subject to paragraphs (5) and (6), the licence shall] in addition authorise the driving of all classes of motor vehicle included in a category or sub-category which is specified in column (3) of Schedule 2 as an additional category or sub-category in relation to a category or sub-category specified in column (1) of that Schedule unless—

  (a) the test or, as the case may be, the practical test is passed on a motor vehicle with automatic transmission, in which case it shall (subject to paragraph (4)) authorise the driving only of such classes of vehicle included in the additional category or sub-category as have automatic transmission;

  (b) the test or, as the case may be, the practical test is passed on a motor vehicle which is adapted on account of a disability of the person taking the test in which case it shall authorise the driving only of such classes of vehicle included in the additional category or sub-category as are so adapted.

(4) Where the additional category is F, K or P, paragraph (3)(a) shall not apply.

[(5) Where a person has passed a test (or Northern Ireland test of competence corresponding to such a test) for a licence authorising the driving of vehicles included in category B, the effect of paragraph (3) in relation to the driving of vehicles in category P shall be as follows—

  (a) the licence granted by the Secretary of State shall authorise the driving of vehicles within class P if and only if—

  (i) the test was passed before 1st February 2001;

(ii) the person concerned held at the date on which he passed the test the prescribed certificate of successful completion by him of an approved training
course for motor cyclists and that certificate was at that time valid in accordance with regulation 68(2); or

(iii) the person concerned holds the prescribed certificate of successful completion by him of an approved training course for motor cyclists and that certificate was furnished to him after the date on which he passed the test, and

(b) where a certificate referred to in sub-paragraph (a)(ii) or (iii) shows that the person
concerned has successfully completed an approved training course for riders of
three-wheeled mopeds, the only vehicles in category P authorised by the licence
to be driven shall be three-wheeled mopeds.

[(6) In relation to the first item of Schedule 2 (category A), the effect of paragraph (3)
shall be that a licence authorising the driving of vehicles in category A shall in addition
authorise the driving of vehicles in category B1, if and only if, the test, or as the case may
be the practical test, is passed before 1st February 2001.]

B70.30   *[Regulation 43 is printed as amended by S.I. 2001 Nos 53 and 236.]*

44. Entitlement upon passing a test other than an appropriate driving test: category A

B70.31   (1) This regulation applies where a person has passed a test (or a Northern Ireland test
of competence corresponding to such a test) for a licence authorising the driving of motor
bicycles of any class other than a class included in sub-category A1.

(2) Where this regulation applies the Secretary of State shall grant to the person who
passed the test—

(a) in a case where he has passed the practical test (or the Northern Ireland test of
competence corresponding to the practical test) on a motor bicycle without a side-
car, the engine of which has a maximum net power output of not less than 35 kilowatts, a licence authorising him to drive all classes of motor vehicle included in
category A;

(b) subject to paragraph (3), in a case where the practical test (or the Northern Ireland
test of competence corresponding to the practical test) was passed on any other
motor bicycle without a side-car, a licence authorising him to drive standard motor
bicycles;

(c) in a case where he has passed the practical test (or the Northern Ireland test of competence corresponding to the practical test) on a motor bicycle and side-car combination and the engine of the bicycle has a maximum net power output of not less
than 35 kilowatts, a licence authorising him to drive all classes of motor bicycle and
side-car combinations included in category A;

(d) subject to paragraph (4), in a case where the practical test (or the Northern Ireland
test of competence corresponding to the practical test) was passed on a motor
bicycle and a side-car combination the power to weight ratio of which does not
exceed 0.16 kw/kg. but which does not fall within paragraph (c), a licence authorising him to drive standard motor bicycles and side-car combinations.

(3) A licence granted to a person by virtue of paragraph (2)(b) shall authorise him to
drive all classes of motor vehicle included in category A upon the expiration of the standard access period.

(4) A licence granted to a person by virtue of paragraph (2)(d) shall authorise him to
drive all classes of motor bicycle and side-car combinations included in category A upon
the expiration of the standard access period.

[**44A. Entitlement upon passing a test other than an appropriate driving test:**   **B70.32**
category P

(1) This regulation applies where a person has passed a test (or Northern Ireland test of competence corresponding to such a test) for a licence authorising the driving of vehicles included in category P.

(2) Where this regulation applies the Secretary of State shall grant to the person who passed the test—

(a) in a case where the test was passed on a three-wheeled moped, a licence authorising the driving of all vehicles having three wheels included in category P;

(b) in any other case, a licence authorising the driving of all vehicles included in category P.]

[Regulation 44A was inserted by S.I. 2001 No. 53.]   **B70.33**

45. Upgrading of entitlements by virtue of passing second test

(1) A person who has passed tests for a licence authorising the driving of motor vehicles   **B70.34**
included in—

(a) category D or sub-category D1 as specified in column (1) of Table A in Schedule 9, and

(b) category C+E or sub-category C1+E as respectively specified at the top of columns (2) and (3) of Table A,

is deemed, subject to the following paragraphs of this regulation, competent to drive (in addition to the classes of motor vehicle in respect of which the tests were passed) vehicles included in the category or sub-category shown in column (2) or (3) of Table A in relation to the relevant test pass in column (1).

(2) Where, in a case to which paragraph (1) applies, each practical test is passed on a vehicle having automatic transmission the person pasing the tests is deemed competent to drive only such classes of vehicle in the upgrade category as have automatic transmission.

(3) A person who has passed a test for a licence authorising the driving of—

(a) motor vehicles included in a category or sub-category specified in column (A) of Table B in Schedule 9 which have automatic transmission, and

(b) motor vehicles included in a category or sub-category specified at the head of one of the columns in that table numbered (1) to (8) which have manual transmission,

is, subject to the following paragraphs of this regulation, deemed competent to drive in addition to the classes of vehicle in respect of which the tests were passed all vehicles included in the category or sub-category shown in the relevant numbered column of Table B in relation to the relevant test pass mentioned in column (A).

(4) Where a person has passed tests for a licence authorising the driving of—

(a) motor vehicles in category D not more than 5.5 metres in length having automatic transmission, and

(b) motor vehicles in category C, other than vehicles in sub-category C1, having manual transmission,

he is deemed competent to drive vehicles in category D not more than 5.5 metres in length which have manual transmission.

(5) In the case of a person who holds a licence which, by virtue of regulation 76 (notwithstanding that he may not have passed a test authorising the driving of such vehicles), authorises the driving of a class of vehicles in category D when used under a section

19 permit or (if not so used) are driven otherwise than for hire or reward, Tables A and B shall be read as if—

    (a) for "D" there were substituted "vehicles in category D, driven otherwise than for hire or reward", and

    (b) for "D+E" there were substituted "vehicles in category D+E driven otherwise than for hire or reward".

(6) In the case of a person who has passed a test for a licence authorising the driving only of those classes of vehicle in category C+E which are drawbar trailer combinations, paragraphs (1), (2) and (3) and Tables A and B in Schedule 9 shall apply as if he had passed a test for a licence authorising only the driving of the corresponding classes of vehicle in category C.

(7) Where, in Table B, the upgrade category is qualified by the expression "(a)", the person is deemed competent to drive only such classes of vehicle therein as have automatic transmission.

(8) Where a person has passed a test prescribed in respect of category B+E which authorises the driving only of classes of vehicle having automatic transmission and a test prescribed in respect of any class of vehicle in category C or D which authorises the driving of vehicles with manual transmission, he is deemed competent to drive vehicles in category B+E with manual transmission.

(9) Where a person, who is the holder of a licence which authorises the driving of motor vehicles included in categories B and B+E and sub-categories C1, C1+E (8.25 tonnes), D1 (not for hire or reward) and D1+E (not for hire or reward) which have automatic transmission, passes a test prescribed in respect of category B, B+E, C or D which authorises the driving of vehicles with manual transmission, he is deemed competent to drive vehicles in category B+E and in sub-categories C1, C1+E (8.25 tonnes), D1 (not for hire or reward) and D1+E (not for hire or reward) which have manual transmission.

(10) Where a person has passed tests for a licence authorising the driving of—

    (a) motor vehicles included in category B, other than vehicles included in sub-categories B1 and B1 (invalid carriages), having automatic transmission, and

    (b) motor vehicles included in category B+E, C or D having manual transmission,

he is deemed competent to drive vehicles in category B which have manual transmission.

(11) In this regulation—

    (a) "*upgrade category*" means the additional category or sub-category which the person passing the tests (or holding the licence and passing the test) is deemed competent to drive by virtue of the relevant provision of this regulation, and

    (b) a reference to a test or a practical test includes, as the case may be, a reference to a Northern Ireland test of competence or a Northern Ireland practical test corresponding thereto.

46. Entitlement upon passing an appropriate driving test

B70.35   (1) Where a person—

    (a) is disqualified by order of a court under section 36 of the Offenders Act until he passes the appropriate driving test, and

    (b) passes the appropriate driving test for a licence authorising the driving of a class of motor vehicles included in any category or sub-category,

the disqualification shall, subject to paragraph (8), be deemed to have expired in relation to that class and such other classes of motor vehicle as are specified in paragraphs (2), (3), (4), (5) and (6).

(2) Subject to paragraph (4), the disqualification shall be deemed to have expired in relation to all classes of vehicle included in the category or sub-category referred to in paragraph (1)(b) unless—

(a) the test or, as the case may be, the practical test is passed on a motor vehicle with automatic transmission, in which case the disqualification shall be deemed to have expired only in relation to such classes of vehicle included in that category or sub-category as have automatic transmission;

(b) the test or, as the case may be, the practical test is passed on a motor vehicle which is adapted on account of a disability of the person taking the test, in which case the disqualification shall be deemed to have expired only in relation to such classes of motor vehicle included in that category or sub-category as are so adapted (and for the purposes of this paragraph, a motor bicycle with a side-car may be treated in an appropriate case as a motor vehicle adapted on account of a disability).

(3) The disqualification shall be deemed to have expired in relation to all classes of vehicle included in any other category which is specified in column (3) of Schedule 2 as being an additional category or sub-category in relation to that category or sub-category unless—

(a) subject to paragraph (5), the test or, as the case may be, the practical test is passed on a vehicle with automatic transmission, in which case the disqualification shall be deemed to have expired only in relation to such classes of motor vehicle included in the additional category or sub-category as have automatic transmission;

(b) the test or, as the case may be, the practical test, is passed on a vehicle which is adapted on account of a disability of the person taking the test, in which case the disqualification shall be deemed to have expired only in relation to such classes of motor vehicle included in the additional category or sub-category as are so adapted.

(4) Where, at the date on which a person is disqualified—

(a) he holds a licence which was granted pursuant to regulation 44(2)(b) or (d), and

(b) the standard access period has not expired,

the disqualification shall not, by virtue of paragraph (2) or (7), be deemed to have expired—

(i) in a case to which regulation 44(2)(b) applies, in relation to large motor bicycles, or

(ii) in a case to which regulation 44(2)(d) applies, in relation to large motor bicycle and side-car combinations,

until the standard access period has expired.

(5) Paragraph (3)(a) shall not apply where the additional category is F, G, H, K, L or P.

(6) Where a person who is disqualified passes the practical test on a vehicle of a class included in category A, other than sub-category A1, the disqualification shall be deemed to have expired additionally in relation to all classes of vehicle included in—

(a) categories B, B+E, C, C+E, D and D+E, unless that test is passed on a vehicle with automatic transmission, in which case the disqualification shall be deemed to have expired only in relation to such classes of motor vehicle included in those categories as have automatic transmission;

(b) categories F, G, H and L.

(7) Where the person who is disqualified passes the practical test on a vehicle of a class included in category B, other than a vehicle included in sub-category B1, the disqualification shall be deemed to have expired additionally in relation to all classes of vehicle included in—

(a) categories A, B+E, C, C+E, D and D+E, unless that test is passed on a vehicle with automatic transmission, in which case the disqualification shall be deemed to have expired only in relation to such classes of motor vehicle included in those categories as have automatic transmission;

(b) categories G, H and L.

(8) Where a person is, pursuant to regulation 56, disqualified by the Secretary of State until he passes a driving test prescribed in respect of a class of large goods or passenger-carrying vehicle, the disqualification shall not be deemed to have expired in relation to any class of large goods or passenger-carrying vehicle until he passes that test.

Test results

47. Evidence of result of theory test

B70.36

(1) For the purpose of ascertaining whether a candidate has demonstrated a knowledge and sound understanding of the specified matters in accordance with these Regulations the person conducting a theory test shall arrange for the test to be marked—

(a) in the case of a test conducted before 4th January 2000 in respect of which no request has been made for the theory test pass certificate or failure statement to be furnished on the day of the test, as soon as practicable after completion of the test, and

(b) in any other case, on the day of the test.

(2) A person conducting the theory test shall, upon completion of the marking of the test, furnish—

(a) a person who passes the test with a theory test pass certificate in the form set out in Part 1 of Schedule 10;

(b) a person who fails to pass the test with a failure statement in the form set out in Part 2 of Schedule 10.

(3)–(8) *[Omitted.]*

48. Evidence of the result of practical or unitary test

B70.37

(1) A person conducting a practical or unitary test shall upon completion of the test furnish—

(a) a person who passes the test with a test pass certificate in the form set out in Part 1 of Schedule 11;

(b) a person who fails to pass the test with a statement in the form set out in Part 2 of Schedule 11.

(2), (3) *[Omitted.]*

PART IV

GOODS AND PASSENGER-CARRYING VEHICLES

General

49. Part III of the Traffic Act: prescribed classes of goods and passenger-carrying vehicle

B70.38

(1) All classes of motor vehicle included in categories C, C+E, D and D+E, except vehicles of classes included in sub-categories C1, C1+E (8.25 tonnes) D1 (not for hire or

reward) and D1+E (not for hire or reward), are prescribed for the purposes of section 89A(3) of the Traffic Act.

(2) Subject to paragraph (3), all classes of motor vehicle included in categories C, C+E, D and D+E, except vehicles of classes included in sub-categories C1+E (8.25 tonnes), D1 (not for hire or reward) and D1+E (not for hire or reward), are prescribed for the purposes of section 99(1) and (1A) of the Traffic Act.

(3) In the case of a licence in force at a time before 1st January 1997, paragraph (2) above shall apply as if "C1," was inserted after "sub-categories".

(4) All classes of motor vehicle included in categories C, C+E, D and D+E, except vehicles of classes included in sub-categories C1+E (8.25 tonnes), D1 (not for hire or reward) and D1+E (not for hire or reward), are prescribed for the purposes of section 99A(3) and (4) of the Traffic Act.

50. Part IV of the Traffic Act: prescribed classes of large goods and passenger-carrying vehicle

(1) Part IV of the Traffic Act and regulations 54 to 57 shall not apply to a large goods **B70.39** vehicle—

   (a) of a class included in category F, G or H or sub-category C1+E (8.25 tonnes), or

   (b) which is an exempted goods vehicle or an exempted military vehicle.

(2) Part IV of the Traffic Act and regulations 54 to 57 shall not apply to a passenger-carrying vehicle manufactured more than 30 years before the date when it is driven and not used for hire or reward or for the carriage of more than eight passengers;

(3) Part IV of the Traffic Act and regulations 54 to 57 shall not apply to a passenger-carrying vehicle when it is being driven by a constable for the purpose of removing or avoiding obstruction to other road users or other members of the public, for the purpose of protecting life or property (including the passenger-carrying vehicle and its passengers) or for other similar purposes.

(4) All classes of large goods and passenger-carrying vehicle to which Part IV of the Traffic Act applies are prescribed for the purposes of section 117(7) and 117A(6) of the Traffic Act.

51. Exempted goods vehicles and military vehicles

(1) For the purposes of this Part of these Regulations, an exempted goods vehicle is a **B70.40** vehicle falling within any of the following classes—

   (a) a goods vehicle propelled by steam;

   (b) any road construction vehicle used or kept on the road soley for the conveyance of built-in road construction machinery (with or without articles or materials used for the purpose of that machinery);

   (c) any engineering plant other than a mobile crane;

   (d) a works truck;

   (e) an industrial tractor;

   (f) an agricultural motor vehicle which is not an agricultural or forestry tractor;

   (g) a digging machine;

   (h) a goods vehicle which, in so far as it is used on a road—

      (i) is used only in passing from land in the occupation of a person keeping the vehicle to other land in the occupation of that person, and

      (ii) is not used on roads for distances exceeding an aggregate of 9.7 kilometres in any calendar week;

(j) a goods vehicle, other than an agricultural motor vehicle, which—

      (i) is used only for purposes relating to agriculture, horticulture or forestry,

      (ii) is used on roads only in passing between different areas of land occupied by the same person, and

      (iii) in passing between any two such areas does not travel a distance exceeding 1.5 kilometres on roads;

(k) a goods vehicle used for no other purpose than the haulage of lifeboats and the conveyance of the necessary gear of the lifeboats which are being hauled;

(l) a goods vehicle manufactured before 1st January 1960, used unladen and not drawing a laden trailer;

(m) an articulated goods vehicle the unladen weight of which does not exceed 3.05 tonnes;

(n) a goods vehicle in the service of a visiting force or headquarters as defined in the Visiting Forces and International Headquarters (Application of Law) Order 1965;

(o) a goods vehicle driven by a constable for the purpose of removing or avoiding obstruction to other road users or other members of the public, for the purpose of protecting life or property (including the vehicle and its load) or for other similar purposes;

(p) a goods vehicle fitted with apparatus designed for raising a disabled vehicle partly from the ground and for drawing a disabled vehicle when so raised (whether by partial superimposition or otherwise) being a vehicle which—

      (i) is used solely for dealing with disabled vehicles;

      (ii) is not used for the conveyance of any goods other than a disabled vehicle when so raised and water, fuel, accumulators and articles required for the operation of, or in connection with, such apparatus or otherwise for dealing with disabled vehicles; and

      (iii) has an unladen weight not exceeding 3.05 tonnes;

(q) a passenger-carrying vehicle recovery vehicle; and

(r) a mobile project vehicle.

(2) For the purposes of this Part of these Regulations, an exempted military vehicle is a large goods or passenger-carrying vehicle falling within any of the following classes—

(a) a vehicle designed for fire fighting or fire salvage purposes which is the property of, or for the time being under the control of, the Secretary of State for Defence, when being driven by a member of the armed forces of the Crown;

(b) a vehicle being driven by a member of the armed forces of the Crown in the course of urgent work of national importance in accordance with an order of the Defence Council in pursuance of the Defence (Armed Forces) Regulations 1939 which were continued permanently in force, in the form set out in Part C of Schedule 2 to the Emergency Laws (Repeal) Act, 1959, by section 2 of the Emergency Powers Act 1964; or

(c) an armoured vehicle other than a track-laying vehicle which is the property of, or for the time being under the control of, the Secretary of State for Defence.

(3) In this Regulation—

"*digging machine*" has the same meaning as in paragraph 4(4) of Schedule 1 to the Vehicle Excise and Registration Act 1994 [*q.v.*];

"*agricultural motor vehicle*", "*engineering plant*", "*industrial tractor*" and "*works truck*" have the same meaning as in regulation 3(2) of the Construction and Use Regulations [*q.v.*];

"*public road*" has the same meaning as in section 62(1) of the Vehicle Excise and Registration Act 1994 [*q.v.*];

"*road construction machinery*" means a machine or device suitable for use for the construction and repair of roads and used for no purpose other than the construction and repair of roads; and

"*road construction vehicle*" means a vehicle which—

   (a) is constructed or adapted for use for the conveyance of road construction machinery which is built in as part of, or permanently attached to, that vehicle, and

   (b) is not constructed or adapted for the conveyance of any other load except articles and materials used for the purposes of such machinery.

[*The Visiting Forces and International Headquarters (Application of Law) Order 1965 (to which reference is made in regulation 51(1)(n)) has been revoked and replaced by the Visiting Forces and International Headquarters (Application of Law) Order 1999 (S.I. 1999 No. 1736; not reproduced in this work). No textual amendment has been made to regulation 3 in consequence of that revocation; but by the Interpretation Act 1978, ss.17(2)(a) and 23(1) references to the earlier order may be treated as references to S.I. 1999 No. 1736.*]   **B70.41**

52. Correspondences

(1) For the purposes of section 89A(5) of the Traffic Act, a heavy goods vehicle or public service vehicle of a class specified in column (1) of the table at the end of this regulation corresponds to a class of large goods vehicle or passenger-carrying vehicle, as the case may be, specified in column (2) of that table in relation to the class of vehicle in column (1).   **B70.42**

(2) For the purposes of paragraph (1), where a heavy goods vehicle driver's licence held before 1st April 1991 was restricted to vehicles having a permissible maximum weight not exceeding 10 tonnes by virtue of—

   (a) paragraph 3(3) and (5) of Schedule 2 to the Road Traffic (Drivers' Ages and Hours of Work) Act 1976; or

   (b) paragraph (1) or (2) of regulation 31 of the Heavy Goods Vehicles (Drivers' Licences) Regulations 1977 [*S.I. 1977 No. 1309*];

before those enactments ceased to have effect, such restriction shall be disregarded.

TABLE

(1) *Class of heavy goods or public service vehicle*	(2) *Corresponding class of large goods or passenger-carrying vehicle*
Heavy goods vehicles 1 1A 2 2A	*Large goods vehicles* Categories C and C+E Categories C and C+E (limited, in each case, to vehicles with automatic transmission) Category C and vehicles in category C+E which are drawbar trailer combinations Category C and vehicles in category C+E which are drawbar trailer combinations (limited, in each case, to vehicles with automatic transmission)

[*continued on next page*

(1) *Class of heavy goods or public service vehicle*	(2) *Corresponding class of large goods or passenger-carrying vehicle*
3	Category C and vehicles in category C+E which are drawbar trailer combinations
3A	Category C and vehicles in category C+E which are drawbar trailer combinations (limited, in each case, to vehicles with automatic transmission)
Public service vehicles	*Passenger-carrying vehicles*
1	Categories D and D+E
1A	Categories D and D+E (limited, in each case, to vehicles with automatic transmission)
2	Categories D and D+E
2A	Categories D and D+E (limited, in each case, to vehicles with automatic transmission)
3	Category D
3A	Category D (limited to vehicles with automatic transmission)
4	Sub-category D1 and vehicles in category D not more than 5.5 metres in length
4A	Sub-category D1 and vehicles in category D not more than 5.5 metres in length (limited, in each case, to vehicles with automatic transmission)

53. Part IV of the Traffic Act: dual purpose vehicles

B70.43   (1) Except in the case of a vehicle mentioned in paragraph (2), Part IV of the Traffic Act and regulations 54 to 57 shall apply to dual purpose vehicles to the extent that they apply to passenger-carrying vehicles.

(2) Part IV of the Traffic Act and regulations 54 to 57 shall apply to any dual purpose vehicle which is—

    (a) driven by a member of the armed forces of the Crown, and

    (b) used to carry passengers for naval, military or air force purposes,

to the extent that they apply to large goods vehicles.

Persons under the age of 21

54. Large goods vehicles drivers' licences issued to persons under the age of 21: trainee drivers

B70.44   (1) A large goods vehicle driver's licence granted to a person under the age of 21 is subject to the conditions prescribed, for the purposes of section 114(1) of the Traffic Act, in the following paragraphs.

(2) In the case of an LGV trainee driver's licence, whether issued as a provisional or a full licence or treated as a provisional licence by virtue of section 98 of the Traffic Act and regulation 19, the holder shall not drive a large goods vehicle of any class which the licence authorises him to drive unless—

    (a) he is a registered employee of a registered employer, and

    (b) the vehicle is a large goods vehicle of a class to which his training agreement applies and is owned or operated by that registered employer or by a registered LGV driver training establishment.

(3) In the case of a licence held by a person who is a member of the armed forces of the Crown, the holder shall not drive a large goods vehicle of any class unless it is owned or operated by the Secretary of State for Defence and is being used for naval, military or air force purposes.

(4) In the case of an LGV trainee driver's full licence, the holder shall not drive a large goods vehicle of any class if the vehicle is being used to draw a trailer except under the supervision of a person who is present with him in the vehicle and who holds a full large goods vehicle driver's licence authorising the driving of a vehicle of that class which is not an LGV trainee driver's licence.

(5) In the case of an LGV trainee driver's full licence authorising the driving of a class of vehicles included in category C, the holder shall not drive large goods vehicles of a class included in category C+E, other than vehicles included in sub-category C1+E the maximum authorised mass of which does not exceed 7.5 tonnes, as if he were authorised by a provisional licence to do so before the expiration of a period of two years commencing on the date on which he passed the test for that full licence.

(6) In this regulation—

"*LGV trainee driver's licence*" means a large goods vehicle driver's licence which—

    (a) authorises its holder to drive vehicles of a class included in category C or C+E,

    (b) is held by a person, other than a member of the armed forces of the Crown, who was under the age of 21 on the date of the application, and

    (c) is in force for a period during the whole or part of which that person is under the age of 21;

"*registered*", in relation to an employee, employer or training establishment, means registered for the time being by the Training Committee in accordance with the Training Scheme;

"*training agreement*", in relation to an individual who is undergoing, or is to undergo, driver training under the Training Scheme, means the agreement between that individual and a registered employer;

"*the Training Committee*" means the National Joint Training Committee for Young LGV Drivers in the Road Goods Transport Industry which is referred to in the Training Scheme;

"*the Training Scheme*" means the Young Large Goods Vehicle (LGV) Drivers Training Scheme which has been established by the Road Haulage and Distribution Training Council and approved by the Secretary of State for the purpose of regulations under section 101(2) of the Traffic Act on 30th September 1996 for training young drivers of large goods vehicles.

Drivers' conduct

55. Large goods vehicle drivers' licences and LGV Community licences: obligatory revocation or withdrawal and disqualification

(1) The prescribed circumstances for the purposes of section 115(1)(a) of the Traffic Act are that, in the case of the holder of a large goods vehicle driver's licence who is under the age of 21, he has been convicted (or is, by virtue of section 58 of the Offenders Act, to be treated as if he had been convicted) of an offence as a result of which the number of penalty points to be taken into account under section 29 of the Offenders Act [*q.v.*] exceeds three.   **B70.45**

(2) The prescribed circumstances for the purposes of section 115A(1)(a) of the Traffic Act are that, in the case of the holder of an LGV Community licence who is under the age of 21, he has been convicted (or is, by virtue of section 58 of the Offenders Act, to be treated as if he had been convicted) of an offence as a result of which the number of penalty points to be taken into account under section 29 of the Offenders Act exceeds three.

(3) Where—

    (a) a large goods vehicle drivers' licence is revoked under section 115(1)(a) of the Traffic Act, or

    (b) the Secretary of State serves a notice on a person in pursuance of section 115A(1)(a) of that Act,

the cases in which the person whose licence has been revoked or, as the case may be, on whom the notice has been served must be disqualified indefinitely or for a fixed period shall be determined by the Secretary of State.

(4) Where the Secretary of State makes a determination under paragraph (3) that a person is to be disqualified for a fixed period he shall be disqualified until he reaches 21 years of age or for such longer period as the Secretary of State shall determine.

56. Holders of licences who are disqualified by order of a court

B70.46   (1) This regulation applies where a person's large goods vehicle or passenger-carrying vehicle driver's licence is treated is revoked by virtue of section 37(1) of the Offenders Act (effect of disqualification by court order) and where it applies subsections (1) and (2) of section 117 of the Traffic Act are modified in accordance with paragraphs (2) to (6).

(2) Where the licence which is treated as revoked is a large goods vehicle driver's licence held by a person under the age of 21—

    (a) the Secretary of State must order that person to be disqualified either indefinitely or for a fixed period, and

    (b) where the Secretary of State determines that he shall be disqualified for a fixed period, he must be disqualified until he reaches the age of 21 or for such longer period as the Secretary of State determines.

(3) Where the licence which is treated as revoked is a large goods vehicle driver's licence held by any other person or is a passenger-carrying vehicle driver's licence—

    (a) the Secretary of State may order that person to be disqualified either indefinitely or for such fixed period as he thinks fit, or

    (b) except where the licence is a provisional licence, if it appears to the Secretary of State that, owing to that person's conduct, it is expedient to require him to comply with the prescribed conditions applicable to provisional licences until he passes a test, the Secretary of State may order him to be disqualified for holding or obtaining a full licence until he passes a test.

(4) Where the Secretary of State orders him to be disqualified until he passes a test, that test shall be a test prescribed by these Regulations for a licence authorising the driving of any class of vehicle in category C (other than sub-category C1), C+E, D or D+E which, prior to his disqualification by order of the court, he was authorised to drive by the revoked licence.

(5) Any question as to whether a person—

    (a) shall be disqualified indefinitely or for a fixed period or until he passes a test, or

    (b) if he is to be disqualified for a fixed period, what that period should be, or

(c) if he is to be disqualified until he passes a test, which test he should be required to pass,

may be referred by the Secretary of State to the traffic commissioner.

(6) Where the Secretary of State determines that a person shall be disqualified for a fixed period, that period shall commence on the expiration of the period of disqualification ordered by the court.

(7) Where this regulation applies, subsections (3) to (6) of section 116 of the Traffic Act shall apply, but as if—

(a) subsection (4)(a) were omitted,

(b) for the words "in any other case, revoke the licence or suspend it" in subsection (4)(b) there were substituted "suspend the licence", and

(c) the references to sections 115(1) and 116(1) of that Act were references to this regulation.

57. Removal of disqualification

(1) Subject to paragraphs (2) and (3), the Secretary of State may remove a disqualification for a period of more than two years imposed under section 117(2)(a) of the Traffic Act, after consultation with the traffic commissioner in a case which was referred to him, if an application for the removal of the disqualification is made after the expiration of whichever is relevant of the following periods commencing on the date of the disqualification—   **B70.47**

(a) two years, if the disqualification is for less than four years;

(b) one half of the period of the disqualification, if it is for less than ten years, but not less than four years;

(c) five years in any other case.

(2) An application may not be made if the applicant has during the relevant period been convicted (or treated as convicted) of an offence by virtue of which he has incurred—

(a) penalty points, or

(b) an endorsement of a Northern Ireland driving licence held by him, or of its counterpart, with particulars of a conviction pursuant to provisions for the time being in force in Northern Ireland that correspond to sections 44 and 45 of the Offenders Act.

(3) Where an application under paragraph (1) for the removal of a disqualification is refused, a further such application shall not be entertained if made within three months after the date of refusal.

PART V

APPROVED TRAINING COURSES FOR RIDERS OF MOTOR BICYCLES AND MOPEDS

Approved training courses

58. Provision of approved training courses

(1) For the purposes of section 97(3)(e) of the Traffic Act an approved training course is a course for riders of motor bicycles or mopeds both complying with and conducted in accordance with this Part of these Regulations and approved by the Secretary of State.   **B70.48**

(2)–(5)   *[Omitted.]*

59. Nature and conduct of training courses   *[Omitted.]*   **B70.49**

Instructors

B70.50   **60. Certified instructors**   *[Omitted.]*

B70.51   **61. Persons authorised as assistant instructors**   *[Omitted.]*

B70.52   **62. Withdrawal of approval to provide training courses or to act as instructor**
[Omitted.]

B70.53   **63. Cessation of conduct of training**   *[Omitted.]*

B70.54   **64. Approved training courses conducted on large motor bicycles**

(1) An approved training course for a person holding a provisional licence authorising the driving of large motor bicycles and undertaken by him on a motor bicycle other than a learner motor bicycle must be conducted by a certified direct access instructor.

(2) *"Certified direct access instructor"* means a person authorised (or deemed to have been authorised) in accordance with regulation 65.

B70.55   **65. Certified direct access instructors**

(1) An approved training body may, subject to the following provisions of this regulation, authorise instructors to conduct on his behalf the instruction of persons who hold provisional licences authorising the riding of large motor bicycles in the riding of motor bicycles other than learner motor bicycles.

(2) A person may not be authorised under paragraph (1) unless he—

   (a) holds a full licence to drive motor bicycles,

   (b) either—

      (i) was authorised on 30th January 1998 to conduct instruction by an approved training body in accordance with [the Motor Vehicles (Driving Licences) Regulations 1996 [*S.I. 1996 No. 2824*]] and has held that licence for a period of, or periods amounting in aggregate to, not less than 2 years, or

      (ii) if he was not so authorised, is at least 21 years of age and has held that licence for a period of, or periods amounting in aggregate to, not less than 3 years.

   (c) is a certified instructor, and

   (d) has successfully completed the Secretary of State's assessment course for certified direct access instructors.

(3)–(9)   *[Omitted.]*

B70.56   *[Regulation 65 is printed as amended by S.I. 2000 No. 2766.]*

Miscellaneous

B70.57   **66. Eligibility to undertake approved training course**   *[Omitted.]*

B70.58   **67. Ratio of trainees to instructors**   *[Omitted.]*

B70.59   **68. Evidence of successful completion of course**

(1) The certified instructor or the certified direct access instructor who conducted element (E) of the prescribed training course shall furnish a person who successfully com-

pletes an approved training course with a certificate in the form set out in Part 3 of Schedule 13 and signed by that instructor.

(2)–(4) *[Omitted.]*

69. Exemptions from Part V

(1) Subject to paragraph (2), section 98(3)(c) of the Traffic Act shall not apply to a person who is a provisional entitlement holder by virtue of having passed a test for the time being prescribed in respect of category P on or after 1st December 1990 and such a person shall be exempt from the requirement imposed by section 89(2A) of that Act.

(2) Paragraph (1) shall cease to apply to a person if he is disqualified by order of a court under section 36 of the Offenders Act.

[(2A) Subject to paragraph (2C), section 89(2A) of the Traffic Act shall not apply to a person who is for the time being a holder of a full licence for a class of vehicle included in category A in respect of a test of competence to drive a vehicle of any other class included in that category.]

[(2B) Subject to paragraph (2C), a person who is for the time being the holder of a full licence for a class of vehicle included in category A shall be exempt from the restriction imposed by section 97(3)(e) on his driving a vehicle of another class included in that category.]

[(2C) The exemptions conferred by paragraphs (2A) and (2B) shall not apply in relation to the holder of a full licence authorising him only to drive a vehicle included in category A having automatic transmission in respect of—

(a) a test of competence to drive a vehicle having manual transmission; or

(b) his driving a vehicle having manual transmission.]

(3) A provisional licence or provisional entitlement holder who is resident on an exempted island shall be exempt from the requirement imposed by section 89(2A) of the Traffic Act in respect of a test of competence to drive a motor bicycle of any class taken, or to be taken, on an island, whether or not that island is an exempted island.

(4) A provisional licence holder who is resident on an exempted island shall be exempt from the restriction imposed by section 97(3)(e) of the Traffic Act if he satisfies either of the conditions set out in paragraph (6).

(5) Section 98(3)(c) of the Traffic Act shall not apply to a provisional entitlement holder who is resident on an exempted island if he satisfies either of the conditions set in paragraph (6).

(6) The conditions referred to in paragraphs (4) and (5) are that he is—

(a) driving on an exempted island, whether or not he is also resident on that island; or

(b) driving on an island which is not an exempted island for the purpose of—
   (i)   undertaking, or travelling to or from, an approved training course,
   (ii) undergoing, or travelling to or from a place where he is to take or where he has taken, a test of competence prescribed in respect of category A or P.

(7) In this regulation—

"exempted island" means any island in Great Britain other than—

(a) the Isle of Wight, the island which comprises Lewis and Harris, the island which comprises North Uist, Benbecula and South Uist, Mainland Orkney and Mainland Shetland, and

(b) any other island from which motor vehicles vehicles not constructed or adapted for special purposes can at some time be conveniently driven to a road in any other part of Great Britain because of the presence of a bridge, tunnel, ford or other way suitable for the passage of such motor vehicles;

"*provisional licence holder*" means a person who holds a provisional licence which, subject to section 97(3) of the Traffic Act, authorises the driving of motor bicycles of any class; and

"*provisional entitlement holder*" means a person who holds a full licence which is treated, by virtue of section 98 of the Traffic Act and regulation 19, as authorising him to drive motor bicycles of any class as if he held a provisional licence therefor.

B70.61   *[Regulation 69 is printed as amended by S.I. 2001 No. 53.]*

PART VI

DISABILITIES

70. Licence groups

B70.62   (1) In this Part of these Regulations—

"*Group 1 licence*" means a licence in so far as it authorises its holder to drive classes of motor vehicle included in—

(a) categories A, B, B+E, F, G, H, K, L and P,

(b) the former category N,

"*Group 2 licence*" means, subject to paragraphs (2) and (3), a licence in so far as it authorises its holder to drive classes of motor vehicle included in any other category, and

"*licence*" includes, unless the context otherwise requires, a Northern Ireland licence and a Community licence.

(2) In so far as a licence authorises its holder to drive vehicles of a class included in sub-categories C1, C1+E (8.25 tonnes), D1 (not for hire or reward) and D1+E (not for hire or reward) it is a Group 1 licence while it remains in force if—

(a) it was in force at a time before 1st January 1997, or

(b) it is granted upon the expiry of a licence which was in force at a time before 1st Janaury 1997 and comes into force not later than 31st December 1997.

(3) Subject to paragraph (6)(d) of regulation 7, a licence shall be a Group 1 licence in so far as it authorises, by virtue of paragraphs (4), (5) and (6) of that regulation, the driving of a class of motor vehicles which is not included in a category or sub-category specified in relation to a Group 1 licence in paragraph (1) or (2) above.

71. Disabilities prescribed in respect of Group 1 and 2 licences

B70.63   (1) The following disabilities are prescribed for the purposes of section 92(2) of the Traffic Act as relevant disabilities in relation to an applicant for, or a person who holds, a Group 1 or Group 2 licence—

(a) epilepsy;

(b) severe mental disorder;

(c) liability to sudden attacks of disabling giddiness or fainting which are caused by any disorder or defect of the heart as a result of which the applicant for the licence or, as the case may be, the holder of the licence has a device implanted in his body, being a device which, by operating on the heart so as to regulate its action, is designed to correct the disorder or defect;

(d) liability to sudden attacks of disabling giddiness or fainting, other than attacks falling within paragraph (1)(c); and

(e) persistent misuse of drugs or alcohol, whether or not such misuse amounts to dependency.

(2) The disability prescribed in paragraph (1)(c) is prescribed for the purpose of section 92(4)(b) of the Traffic Act in relation to an applicant for a Group 1 or Group 2 licence if the applicant suffering from that disability satisfies the Secretary of State that—

(a) the driving of a vehicle by him in pursuance of the licence is not likely to be a source of danger to the public; and

(b) he has made adequate arrangements to receive regular medical supervision by a cardiologist (being a supervision to be continued throughout the period of the licence) and is conforming to those arrangements.

(3) The following disabilities are prescribed for the purposes of paragraphs (a) and (c) of section 92(4) of the Traffic Act namely, any disability consisting solely of any one or more of—

(a) the absence of one or more limbs,

(b) the deformity of one or more limbs, or

(c) the lost of use of one or more limbs, which is not progressive in nature.

(4) In this regulation—

(a) in paragraph (1)(b), the expression "*severe mental disorder*" includes mental illness, arrested or incomplete development of the mind, psychopathic disorder and severe impairment of intelligence or social functioning;

(b) in paragraph (2)(b), the expression "*cardiologist*" means a registered medical practitioner who specialises in disorders or defects of the heart and who, in that connection, holds a hospital appointment;

(c) in paragraph (3), references to a limb include references to a part of a limb, and the reference to loss of use, in relation to a limb, includes a reference to a deficiency of limb movement or power.

72. Disabilities prescribed in respect of Group 1 licences

(1) There is prescribed for the purposes of section 92(2) of the Traffic Act as a relevant **B70.64** disability in relation to an applicant for, or a person who holds, a Group 1 licence, the inability to read in good light (with the aid of corrective lenses if necessary) a registration mark fixed to a motor vehicle and containing letters and figures 79.4 millimetres high at a distance of—

(a) 12.3 metres, in the case of an applicant for a licence authorising only the driving of motor vehicles of a class included in category K, or

(b) 20.5 metres, in any other case.

(2) Epilepsy is prescribed for the purposes of section 92(4)(b) of the Traffic Act in relation to an applicant for a Group 1 licence who either—

(a) has been free from any epileptic attack during the period of one year immediately preceding the date when the licence is granted; or

(b) (if not so free from attack) has had an epileptic attack whilst asleep more than three years before the date when the licence is granted and has had attacks only whilst asleep between the date of that attack and the date when the licence is granted, where the Secretary of State is satisfied that the driving of a vehicle by him in accordance with the licence is not likely to be a source of danger to the public.

(3) The disability described in paragraph (1) is prescribed for the purposes of section 94(5)(b) of the Traffic Act in relation to an applicant for, or a person who holds, a Group 1 licence.

73. Disabilities prescribed in respect of Group 2 licences

B70.65   (1) There is prescribed for the purpose of section 92(2) of the Traffic Act as a relevant disability in relation to an applicant for, or a person who holds, a Group 2 licence, the inability to read in good light (with the aid of corrective lenses if necessary) a registration mark fixed to a motor vehicle and containing letters and figures 79.4 millimetres high at a distance of 20.5 metres.

(2) There is also prescribed for the purposes of section 92(2) of the Traffic Act as a relevant disability in relation to a person other than an excepted licence holder who is an applicant for or who holds a Group 2 licence, such abnormality of sight in one or both eyes that he cannot meet the relevant standard of visual acuity.

(3) The relevant standard of visual acuity for the purposes of paragraph (2) means—

    (a) in the case of a person who—

        (i) was the holder of a valid Group 2 licence or obsolete vocational licence upon each relevant date specified in column (1) of Table 1 at the end of this regulation, and

        (ii) if he is an applicant for a Group 2 licence, satisfies the Secretary of State that he has had adequate recent driving experience and has not during the period of 10 years immediately before the date of the application been involved in any road accident in which his defective eyesight was a contributory factor,

    the standard prescribed in relation to him in column (2) of Table 1;

    (b) in the case of a person who—

        (i) does not fall within sub-paragraph (a), and

        (ii) was or is the holder of a valid Group 2 licence upon the relevant date specified in column (1) of Table 2 at the end of this regulation,

    the standard prescribed in relation to him in column (2) of Table 2;

    (c) in the case of any other person, a standard of visual acuity (with the aid of corrective lenses if necessary) of at least 6/9 in the better and eye and at least 6/12 in the worse eye and, if corrective lenses are necessary, an uncorrected acuity of at least 3/60 in both eyes.

(4) There is prescribed for the purposes of section 92(2) of the traffic Act in relation to a person—

    (a) to whom paragraph (3)(c) applies, and

    (b) who is able to meet the relevant standard of visual acuity prescribed in that sub-paragraph only with the aid of corrective lenses,

poor toleration of the correction made by the lenses.

(5) There is prescribed for the purposes of section 92(2) as a relevant disability in relation to a person who is an applicant for or who holds a Group 2 licence, sight in only one eye unless—

    (a) he held an obsolete vocational licence on 1st April 1991, the traffic commissioner who granted the last such licence knew of the disability before 1st January 1991, and—

    (i) in a case of a person who also held such a licence on 1st Janaury 1983, the visual acuity in his sighted eye is no worse than 6/12, or

    (ii) in any other case, the visual acuity in his sighted eye is no worse than 6/9, and

if he is an applicant for a Group 2 licence, he satisfies the Secretary of State that he has had adequate recent driving experience and has not during the period of 10 years immediately before the date of the application been involved in any road accident in which his defective eyesight was a contributory factor; or

  (b) the person is an excepted licence holder.

(6) Diabetes requiring insulin treatment is prescribed for the purposes of section 92(2) in relation to an applicant for or a person who holds a Group 2 licence unless the person suffering from the disability held an obsolete vocational licence on 1st April 1991 and the traffic commissioner who granted the last obsolete vocational licence knew of the disability before 1st January 1991.

(7) Liability to seizures arising from a cause other than epilepsy is prescribed for the purposes of section 92(2) in relation to an applicant for or a person who holds a Group 2 licence.

(8) Epilepsy is prescribed for the purposes of section 92(4)(b) of the Traffic Act in the case of an applicant for a Group 2 licence suffering from epilepsy who satisfies the Secretary of State that—

  (a) during the period of 10 years immediately preceding the date when the licence is granted—

    (i) he has been free from any epileptic attack, and

    (ii) he has not required any medication to treat epilepsy, and

  (b) that the driving of a vehicle by him in accordance with the licence is not likely to be a source of danger to the public.

[(9) Diabetes requiring insulin treatment is prescribed for the purposes of section 92(4)(b) in the case of a person who—

  (a) is an applicant for a licence authorising the driving of vehicles in sub-category C1, C1+E or C1+E (8.25 tonnes), and

  (c) satisfies the Secretary of State that he has for at least 4 weeks been undergoing treatment with insulin,

provided that he satisfies the conditions mentioned in paragraph (10).]

(10) The conditions referred to in paragraph (9) are that—

  (a) *[revoked by S.I. 2001 No. 937.]*

  (b) he has not, during the period of 12 months ending on the date of the application, required the assistance of another person to treat an episode of hypoglycaemia suffered whilst he was driving,

  (c) he makes an arrangement to undergo at intervals of not more than 12 months an examination by a hospital consultant specialising in the treatment of diabetes and so far as is reasonably practicable conforms to that arrangement,

  (d) his application is supported by a report from such a consultant sufficient to satisfy the Secretary of State that he has a history of responsible diabetic control with a minimal risk of incapacity due to hypoglycaemia . . .

[(dd) he provides a declaration signed by him that he will—

    (i) so far as reasonably practicable comply with such directions regarding his treatment for diabetes as may for the time being be given to him by the doctor supervising that treatment;

    (ii) immediately report to the Secretary of State in writing any significant change in his condition; and

    (iii) provide such evidence as the Secretary of State may request that he continues to carry out the monitoring referred to in sub-paragraph (e) below,]

(e) he regularly monitors his condition and, in particular, undertakes blood glucose monitoring at least twice daily and at times relevant to—

    (i) if he has held a licence authorising the driving of vehicles in sub-category C1, C1 + E or C1 + E (8.25 tonnes) for at least 12 months since starting his insulin treatment, the driving of such vehicles, and

    (ii) in any other case, the driving of motor vehicles generally,]

(f) the Secretary of State is satisfied that the driving of such a vehicle in pursuance of the licence is not likely to be a source of danger to the public.

(11) In this regulation—

(a) references to measurements of visual acuity are references to visual acuity measured on the Snellen Scale;

(b) *"excepted licence holder"* means a person who—

    (i) was the holder of a licence authorising the driving of vehicles included in sub-categories C1 and C1 + E (8.25 tonnes) which was in force at a time before 1st January 1997, and

    (ii) is an applicant for, or the holder of, a Group 2 licence solely by reason that the licence applied for or held authorises (or would, if granted, authorise) the driving of vehicles included in those sub-categories.

(c) *"obsolete vocational licence"* means a licence to drive heavy goods vehicles granted under Part IV of the Traffic Act as originally enacted or a licence to drive public service vehicles granted under section 22 of the 1981 Act which was in force a time before 1 April 1991.

TABLE 1

(1) *Person holding Group 2 licence or obsolete vocational licence on:*	(2) *Standard of visual acuity applicable:*
1. 1 January 1983 and 1 April 1991	Acuity (with the aid of corrective lenses if necessary) of at least 6/12 in the better eye or at least 6/36 in the worse eye or uncorrected acuity of at least 3/60 in at least one eye
2. 1 March 1992, but not on 1 January 1983	Acuity (with the aid of corrective lenses if necessary) of at least 6/9 in the better eye or at least 6/12 in the worse eye, or uncorrected acuity of at least 3/60 in at least one eye.

TABLE 2

(1) *Person holding Group 2 licence on:*	(2) *Standard of visual acuity applicable:*
1. 31 December 1996, but not on 1 March 1992.	Acuity (with the aid of corrective lenses if necessary) of at least 6/9 in the better eye and at least 6/12 in the worse eye and, if corrected lenses are needed to meet that standard, uncorrected acuity of at least 3/60 in at least one eye.
2. On or after 1 January 1997 but not on 31 December 1996.	Acuity (with the aid of corrective lenses if necessary) of at least 6/9 in the better eye and at least 6/12 in the worse eye and, if corrected lenses are needed to meet that standard, uncorrected acuity of at least 3/60 in both eyes.

[Regulation 73 is printed as amended by S.I. 2001 No. 937 (on April 5, 2001, a date after the date at **B70.66**
which this volume states the law; for the text of regulation 73 immediately before that date, see the Second
Supplement to the nineteenth edition).]

74. Disabilities requiring medical investigation: high risk offenders

(1) Subject to paragraph (2), the circumstances prescribed for the purposes of subsection　**B70.67**
(5) of section 94 of the Traffic Act, under subsection (4) of that section, are that the person
who is an applicant for, or holder of, a licence—

(a) has been disqualified by an order of a court by reason that the proportion of
alcohol in his body equalled or exceeded—

(i) 87.5 microgrammes per 100 millilitres of breath, or
(ii) 200 milligrammes per 100 millilitres of blood, or
(iii) 267.5 milligrammes per 100 millilitres of urine;

(b) has been disqualified by order of a court by reason that he has failed, without
reasonable excuse, to provide a specimen when required to do so pursuant to
section 7 of the Traffic Act; or

(c) has been disqualified by order of a court on two or more occasions within any
period of 10 years by reason that—

(i) the proportion of alcohol in his breath, blood or urine exceeded the limit prescribed by virtue of section 5 of the Traffic Act, or
(ii) he was unfit to drive through drink contrary to section 4 of that Act.

(2) For the purposes of paragraph (1)(a) and (b) a court order shall not be taken into
account unless it was made on or after 1st June 1990 and paragraph (1)(c) shall not apply to
a person unless the last such order was made on or after 1st June 1990.

75. Examination by an officer of the Secretary of State

(1) There are prescribed for the purposes of section 94(5)(b)(ii) (examination of a licence　**B70.68**
applicant or holder by an officer of the Secretary of State) the following disabilities—

(a) impairment of visual acuity or of the central or peripheral visual field;

(b) a disability consisting of any one or more of the following—

(i) the absence of one or more limbs,
(ii) the deformity of one or more limbs,

  (iii) the loss of use of one or more limbs whether or not progressive in nature, and

  (iv) impairment of co-ordination of movement of the limbs or of co-ordination between a limb and the eye;

 (c) impairment of cognitive functions or behaviour;

(2) In paragraph (1)(b), a reference to a limb includes a reference to part of a limb, and the reference to loss of use in relation to a limb includes a reference to impairments of limb movement, power or sensation.

PART VII

SUPPLEMENTARY

Transitional provisions

76. Effect of change in classification of vehicles for licensing purposes

B70.69 (1) In a licence (whether full or provisional) granted before 1st January 1997, a reference to motor vehicles in an old category shall be construed as a reference to motor vehicles in the new category corrresponding thereto and a reference to motor vehicles of a class included in an old category shall be construed as a reference to vehicles of the corresponding class included in the new category.

(2) Where a licence granted before 1st January 1997 authorises only the driving of a class of motor vehicles included in an old category having automatic transmission, it shall authorise the driving of the corresponding class of vehicles in the new category having automatic transmission.

(3) For the purposes of paragraphs (1) and (2), a reference in a licence to motor vehicles in an old category (or a class included in that category) includes a reference in a licence granted before 1st June 1990 to a group or class of motor vehicles which is, by virtue of any enactment, to be construed as a reference to vehicles in the old category (or a class included in that category).

(4) In this regulation—

"*old category*" and "*class included in an old category*" mean respectively a category and a class of vehicles specified in column (1) of the table at the end of this regulation,

"*new category*" and "*class included in a new category*", in relation to an old category, mean respectively the category (or, as the case may be, the sub-category) and the class of vehicles specified in column (2) of the table as corresponding to the relevant old category or class included therein, and

"*section 19 permit*" means a permit granted under section 19 of the 1985 Act.

TABLE

(1) *Old category or class*	(2) *Corresponding new category or class*
A	A
B1	B1
B1, limited to invalid carriages	B1 (invalid carriages)
B	B
B plus E	B + E

[continued on next page

(1) *Old category or class*	(2) *Corresponding new category or class*
C1	C1
C1 plus E	C1 + E (8.25 tonnes)
C	C
C plus E	C + E
C plus E, limited to drawbar trailer combinations only	Vehicles in category C + E which are drawbar trailer combinations
D1	D1 (not for hire or reward)
D1 plus E	D1 + E (not for hire or reward)
D, limited to 16 seats	D1
D, limited to vehicles not more than 5.5 metres in length	D1 and vehicles in category D not more than 5.5 metres in length
D, limited to vehicles not driven for hire or reward	Vehicles in category D which are either driven while being used in accordance with a section 19 permit or, if not being so used, driven otherwise than for hire or reward
D	D
D plus E	D + E
F	F
G	G
H	H
K	K
L	L
P	P

77. Saving in respect of entitlement to Group M

(1) Where a person was authorised by virtue of regulations revoked by these Regulations **B70.70** (whether or not he is also the holder of a licence granted before 1st October 1982) to drive, or to apply for the grant of a licence authorising the driving of, vehicles of a class included in the former group M (trolley vehicles used for the carriage of passengers with more than 16 seats in addition to the driver's seat), he shall continue to be so authorised and any licence granted to such a person shall be construed as authorising the driving of vehicles of that class.

(2) A person who is authorised to drive vehicles of a class included in the former group M shall, to the extent that he is so authorised, be deemed to be the holder of a Group 1 licence.

78. Saving in respect of entitlement to former category N

(1) Where on 31st December 1996 a person was, by virtue of regulations then in force, **B70.71** the holder of, or entitled to apply for the grant of, a licence authorising the driving of vehicles included in—

(a) the former category N (vehicles exempt from vehicle excise duty under section 7(1) of the Vehicles (Excise) Act 1971) alone, or

(b) category F or A and the former category N,

the Secretary of State may, notwithstanding anything otherwise contained in these Regulations, grant to such a person a licence authorising the driving of vehicles in the former category N (with or without vehicles in either or both of the other categories as the case may be) and a person holding such a licence shall be authorised to drive such vehicles.

(2) Where on 31st December 1996 a person was the holder of, or entitled to apply for the grant of, a licence authorising the driving of vehicles included in category B and the former category N, he shall continue to be authorised to drive vehicles in that former category and any licence granted to such a person authorising the driving of vehicles included in category B shall be construed as authorising also the driving of vehicles in that former category.

79. Saving in respect of entitlement to drive mobile project vehicles

B70.72   In relation to a person who was at a time before 1st January 1997 the holder of a licence authorising the driving of vehicles of a class included in category B (except a licence authorising only the driving of vehicles included in sub-category B1 or B1 (invalid carriages)), regulation 7(5) shall apply as if paragraphs (b) and (c) and the words "on behalf of a non-commercial body" were omitted.

Miscellaneous

80. Persons who become resident in Great Britain

B70.73   (1) A person who becomes resident in Great Britain who is—

  (a) the holder of a relevant permit, and

  (b) not disqualified for holding or obtaining a licence in Great Britain

shall, during the period of one year after he becomes so resident, be treated for the purposes of section 87 of the Traffic Act as the holder of a licence authorising him to drive all classes of small vehicle, motor bicycle or moped which he is authorised to drive by that permit.

(2) A person who becomes resident in Great Britain who is—

  (a) the holder of a British external licence granted in the Isle of Man or Jersey authorising the driving of large goods vehicles of any class, and

  (b) not disqualified for holding or obtaining a licence in Great Britain

shall, during the period of one year after he becomes so resident, be treated for the purposes of section 87 of the Traffic Act as the holder of a licence authorising him to drive large goods vehicles of all classes which he is authorised to drive by that licence.

(3) A person who becomes resident in Great Britain who is—

  (a) the holder of a British external licence granted in the Isle of Man or Jersey authorising the driving of passenger-carrying vehicles of any class, and

  (b) not disqualified for holding or obtaining a licence in Great Britain

shall, during the period of one year after he becomes so resident, be treated for the purposes of section 87 of the Traffic Act as the holder of a licence authorising him to drive passenger-carrying vehicles of all classes which he is authorised to drive by that licence.

(4) The enactments mentioned in paragraph (5) shall apply in relation to—

  (a) holders of relevant permits and holders of British external licences of the classes mentioned in paragraphs (2) and (3), or

  (b) (as the case may be) those licences and permits,

with the modifications contained in paragraph (5).

(5) The modifications referred to in paragraph (4) are that—

  (a) section 7 of the Offenders Act shall apply as if—

(i) the references to a licence were references to a relevant permit or a British external licence, and

(ii) the words after paragraph (c) thereof were omitted;

(b) section 27(1) and (3) of the Offenders Act shall apply as if—

(i) the references to a licence were references to a relevant permit or a British external licence,

(ii) the references to the counterpart of a licence were omitted, and

(iii) in subsection (3) the words ", unless he satisfies the Court that he has applied for a new licence and has not received it" were omitted;

(c) section 42(5) of the Offenders Act shall apply as if for the words "endorsed on the counterpart of the licence" onwards there were substituted the words "notified to the Secretary of State";

(d) section 47 of the Offenders Act shall apply as if for subsection (2) there were substituted—

"(2) Where a court orders the holder of a relevant permit or a British external licence to be disqualified it must send the permit or the licence, on its being produced to the court, to the Secretary of State who shall keep it until the disqualification has expired or been removed or the person entitled to it leaves Great Britain and in any case has made a demand in writing for its return to him.

'*Relevant permit*' has the meaning given by regulation 80 of the Motor Vehicles (Driving Licences) Regulations 1999.";

(e) section 164(1), (6) and (8) of the Traffic Act shall apply as if the references therein to a licence were references to a relevant permit or a British external licence and the references to a counterpart of a licence were omitted; and

(f) section 173 of the Traffic Act(e) shall apply as if after paragraph (aa) there were added—

"(ab) a relevant permit (within the meaning of regulation 80 of the Motor Vehicles (Driving Licences) Regulations 1999,

(ac) a British external licence,".

(6) In this regulation "*relevant permit*" means—

(i) a "domestic driving permit",

(ii) a "Convention driving permit", or

(iii) a "British Forces (BFG) driving licence",

within the meaning of article 2(7) of the Motor Vehicles (International Circulation) Order 1975 which is—

(a) for the time being valid for the purposes for which it was issued, and

(b) is not a domestic driving permit or a British Forces (BFG) driving licence in respect of which any order made, or having effect as if made, by the Secretary of State is for the time being in force under article 2(6) of that Order.

81. Service personnel

The traffic commissioner for the South Eastern and Metropolitan Traffic Areas is hereby prescribed for the purposes of section 183(6) of the Traffic Act (discharge of Part IV functions in relation to HM Forces). **B70.74**

82. Northern Ireland licences

(1) The traffic commissioner for the North Western Traffic Area is hereby prescribed for the purposes of section 122(2) of the Traffic Act. **B70.75**

(2) For the purposes of section 122(4) of the Traffic Act, the magistrates' court or sheriff to whom an appeal shall lie by the holder of a Northern Ireland licence, being a person who is not resident in Great Britain and who is aggrieved by the suspension or revocation of the licence or by the ordering of disqualification for holding or obtaining a licence, shall be—

(a) such a magistrates' court or sheriff as he may nominate at the time he makes the appeal; or

(b) in the absence of a nomination of a particular court under sub-paragraph (a), the magistrates' court in whose area the office of the traffic commissioner for the North Western Traffic Area is situated.

83. Statement of date of birth

B70.76 (1) The circumstances in which a person specified in section 164(2) of the Traffic Act shall, on being required by a police constable, state his date of birth are—

(a) where that person fails to produce forthwith for examination his licence on being required to do so by a police constable under that section; or

(b) where, on being so required, that person produces a licence—

(i) which the police constable in question has reason to suspect was not granted to that person, was granted to that person in error or contains an alteration in the particulars entered on the licence (other than as described in paragraph (ii)) made with intent to deceive; or

(ii) in which the driver number has been altered, removed or defaced;

(c) where that person is a person specified in subsection (1)(d) of that section and the police constable has reason to suspect that he is under 21 years of age.

(2) In paragraph (1), "*driver number*" means the number described as the driver number in the licence.

Regulation 2 SCHEDULE 1

B70.77 *[Regulations revoked]*

Regulations 4 to 6 and 43 SCHEDULE 2

CATEGORIES AND SUB-CATEGORIES OF VEHICLE FOR LICENSING PURPOSES

PART 1

B70.78

(1) *Category or sub-category*	(2) *Classes of vehicle included*	(3) *Additional categories and sub-categories*
A	Motor bicycles.	B1, K and P
A1	A sub-category of category A comprising learner motor bicycles.	P
B	Motor vehicles, other than vehicles included in category A, F, K or P, having a maximum	F, K and P

[continued on next page]

(1) *Category or*	(2) *Classes of vehicle included sub-category*	(3) *Additional categories and sub-categories*
B—*cont.*	authorised mass not exceeding 3.5 tonnes and not more than eight seats in addition to the driver's seat, including: (i) a combination of any such vehicle and a trailer where the trailer has a maximum authorised mass not exceeding 750 kilograms, and (ii) a combination of any such vehicle and a trailer where the maximum authorised mass of the combination does not exceed 3.5 tonnes and the maximum authorised mass of the trailer does not exceed the unladen weight of the tractor vehicle.	
B1	A sub-category of category B comprising motor vehicles having three or four wheels and an unladen weight not exceeding 550 kilograms.	K and P
B + E	Combinations of a motor vehicle and trailer where the tractor vehicle is in category B but the combination does not fall within that category.	None
C	Motor vehicles having a maximum authorised mass exceeding 3.5 tonnes, other than vehicles falling within category D, F, G or H, including any such vehicle drawing a trailer having a maximum authorised mass not exceeding 750 kilograms.	None
C1	A sub-category of category C comprising motor vehicles having a maximum authorised mass exceeding 3.5 tonnes but not exceeding 7.5 tonnes, including any such vehicle drawing a trailer having a maximum authorised mass not exceeding 750 kilograms.	None
D	Motor vehicles constructed or adapted for the carriage of passengers having more than eight seats in addition to the driver's seat, including any such vehicle drawing a trailer having a maximum authorised mass not exceeding 750 kilograms.	None
D1	A sub-category of category D comprising motor vehicles having more than eight but not more than 16 seats in addition to the driver's seat and including any such vehicle drawing a trailer with a maximum authorised mass not exceeding 750 kilograms.	None
C + E	Combinations of a motor vehicle and trailer where the tractor vehicle is in category C but	B + E

[*continued on next page*

(1) *Category or*	(2) *Classes of vehicle included sub-category*	(3) *Additional categories and sub-categories*
C + E—*cont.*	the combination does not fall within that category.	
C1 + E	A sub-category of category C + E comprising combinations of a motor vehicle and trailer where: (a) the tractor vehicle is in sub-category C1, (b) the maximum authorised mass of the trailer exceeds 750 kilograms but not the unladen weight of the tractor vehicle, and (c) the maximum authorised mass of the combination does not exceed 12 tonnes.	B + E
D + E	Combinations of a motor vehicle and trailer where the tractor vehicle is in category D but the combination does not fall within that category	B + E
D1 + E	A sub-category of category D + E comprising combinations of a motor vehicle and trailer where: (a) the tractor vehicle is in sub-category D1, (b) the maximum authorised mass of the trailer exceeds 750 kilograms but not the unladen weight of the tractor vehicle, (c) the maximum authorised mass of the combination does not exceed 12 tonnes, and (d) the trailer is not used for the carriage of passengers.	B + E
F	Agricultural or forestry tractors, including any such vehicle drawing a trailer but excluding any motor vehicle included in category H.	K
G	Road rollers.	None
H	Track-laying vehicles steered by their tracks.	None
K	Mowing machines which do not fall within category A and vehicles controlled by a pedestrian.	None
P	Mopeds.	None

PART 2

(1) *Sub-category*	(2) *Classes of vehicle included*	(3) *Additional categories and sub-categories*	**B70.79**
C1 + E (8.25 tonnes)	A sub-category of category C + E comprising combinations of a motor vehicle and trailer in sub-category C1 + E, the maximum authorised mass of which does not exceed 8.25 tonnes.	None	
D1 (not for hire or reward)	A sub-category of category D comprising motor vehicles in sub-category D1 driven otherwise than for hire or reward.	None	
D1 + E (not for hire or reward)	A sub-category of category D + E comprising motor vehicles in sub-category D1 + E driven otherwise than for hire or reward.	None	
L	Motor vehicles propelled by electrical power.	None	

PART 3

(1) *Sub-category*	(2) *Classes of vehicle included*	(3) *Additional categories and sub-sub-categories*	**B70.80**
B1 (invalid carriages)	A sub-category of category B conmprising motor vehicles which are invalid carriages.	None	

[*The categories of driving licences issued by EC Member States have been harmonised by Directive* **B70.81**
91/439/EEC of July 29, 1991 (O.J. No. L237, August 24, 1991, p. 1), as amended. The Directive requires the mutual recognition of driving licences issued in the various Member States, including those issued before the implementation of the Directive. Tables of equivalences between the categories of driving licences issued before the implementation of the Directive and the harmonised categories of driving licences have been published as an Annex to Decision 2000/275/EC (O.J. No. L91, April 12, 2000, pp. 1–50). When an existing driving licence is exchanged for a Community model driving licence, the entitlement to drive under the latter will be determined by reference to the published equivalences.]

SCHEDULE 3   Regulation 14

LICENCE FEES

PART 1

[*Omitted.*]   **B70.82**

PART 2

INTERPRETATION

B70.83   In Part 1 of this Schedule—

"*first licence*" means a licence (other than a licence falling within paragraph 3 of the Table in Part 1) granted to a person—

(a) who has not held a licence before, or

(b) whose last licence was a full licence which expired before 31st December 1978, or

(c) whose last licence was a provisional licence which was granted before 1st October 1982;

"*short Group 2 licence*" means a Group 2 licence which, when granted upon the expiry of a period of disqualification, must (by virtue of the expiry date of the licence which was revoked upon disqualification) expire not later than three months after the date it is granted.

Regulation 16   SCHEDULE 4

Distinguishing Marks to be Displayed on a Motor Vehicle being Driven under a Provisional Licence

PART 1

B70.84   Diagram of distinguishing mark to be displayed on a motor vehicle in England, Wales or Scotland.

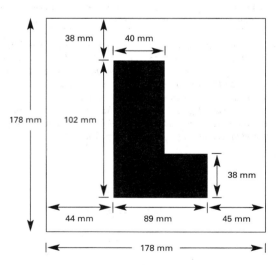

Red letter on white ground.

The corners of the ground can be rounded off.

PART 2

Diagram of optional distinguishing mark to be displayed on a motor vehicle in Wales if a   **B70.85**
mark in the form set out in Part 1 is not displayed.

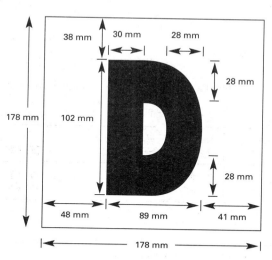

Red letter on white ground
The corners of the ground can be rounded off.

SCHEDULE 5   Regulation 35

FEES FOR PRACTICAL AND UNITARY TESTS   **B70.86**

[Omitted.]

SCHEDULE 6   Regulation 38

EVIDENCE OF IDENTITY OF TEST CANDIDATES   **B70.87**

[Omitted.]

SCHEDULE 7   Regulation 40

SPECIFIED MATTERS FOR THEORY TEST   **B70.88**

[Omitted.]

Regulation 40   SCHEDULE 8

B70.89   SPECIFIED REQUIREMENTS FOR PRACTICAL OR UNITARY TEST

[Omitted.]

Regulation 45   SCHEDULE 9

B70.90   UPGRADED ENTITLEMENTS ON PASSING SECOND TEST

TABLE A

(1) *Test prescribed in respect of:—*	*Prescribed test also passed for:—* (2) *Category C+E*	(3) *Sub-category C1+E*
D	D+E	D1+E
D1	D1+E	D1+E

TABLE B

B70.91

(A) *Automatic test pass:—*	*Manual test pass in category (or sub-category):—*							
	(1) *C1*	(2) *C*	(3) *C1+E*	(4) *C+E*	(5) *D1*	(6) *D*	(7) *D1+E*	(8) *D+E*
C1	—	—	C1	C1 & C1+E	C1	C1	C1	C1
C	—	—	—	C	C1	C	C1	C
C1+E	—	C1+E	—	—	D1+E (a)	C1+E	C1+E	C1+E
C+E	—	—	—	—	D1+E (a)	D+E (a)	—	C+E
D1	D1	D1	D1 & D1+E	D1 & D1+E	—	—	—	D1&D1+E
D	—	D	—	D1 & D+E	—	—	—	D
D1+E	—	D1+E	D1+E	D1+E	—	D1+E	—	—
D+E	—	—	—	D+E	—	—	—	—

Regulation 47   SCHEDULE 10

B70.92   FORMS OF CERTIFICATE AND STATEMENT OF THEORY TEST RESULT

[Omitted.]

Regulation 48   SCHEDULE 11

B70.93   FORMS OF CERTIFICATE AND STATEMENT OF PRACTICAL OR UNITARY TEST RESULT

[Omitted.]

SCHEDULE 12   Regulation 59

Elements of an Approved Training Course   **B70.94**

[Omitted.]

SCHEDULE 13   Regulations 60, 65 and 68

Approved Motor Bicycle Training Courses: Forms of Certificate   **B70.95**

[Omitted.]

The Motor Cycles Etc. (EC Type Approval) Regulations 1999

(S.I. 1999 No. 2920)

B71.01 *Editorial note.* These regulations implement Directive 92/61/EEC (the "Framework Directive") and other Directives listed in Schedule 1.

The Arrangement of regulations set out below has been added editorially and does not form part of the text of the regulations.

B71.02 *[The text of these regulations is printed as amended by:*

the Motor Cycles Etc. (EC Type Approval) (Amendment) Regulations 2001 (S.I. 2001 No. 368) (March 15, 2001).

The amending regulations are referred to in the notes to the principal regulations only by their year and number. The date referred to above is the date on which the amending regulations came into force.]

ARRANGEMENT OF REGULATIONS

PART I

PRELIMINARY

PART II

EC TYPE APPROVAL GRANTED BY THE SECRETARY OF STATE

PART III

Licensing of Vehicles

PART IV

Offences

PART V

Miscellaneous

* * *

SCHEDULES

PART I

Preliminary

1. Commencement, citation and extent

(1)   *[Omitted.]*   **B71.04**

(2) These Regulations extend to Northern Ireland.

2. Revocation   *[Omitted.]*   **B71.05**

3. Interpretation

(1) In these Regulations—   **B71.06**

"*the 1981 Order*" means the Road Traffic (Northern Ireland) Order 1981 [*S.I. 1981 No. 154 (NI 1) as amended; not reproduced in this work*];

"*the 1988 Act*" means the Road Traffic Act 1988 [*q.v.*];

"*the 1994 Act*" means the Vehicle Excise and Registration Act 1994 [*q.v.*];

"*the 1995 Order*" means the Road Traffic (Northern Ireland) Order 1995 [*S.I. 1995 No. 197 (NI 3)*];

"*the Framework Directive*" means Council Directive 92/61/EEC of 30th June 1992 relating to the type approval of two or three-wheel motor vehicles [*O.J. No. L225, August 10, 1992, p. 72*];

"*cm³*" means cubic centimetres;

"*EC certificate of conformity*" means any certificate of conformity issued by the holder of an EC type approval certificate—

    (a) under regulation 8, or

    (b) under any provision of the law of an EEA State other than the United Kingdom giving effect to Article 7 of the Framework Directive;

"*EC component type approval*" means type approval of a separate technical unit or component granted pursuant to the Framework Directive and a separate Directive;

"*EC type approval*" means EC vehicle type approval or EC component type approval;

"*EC type approval certificate*" means a type approval certificate issued—

    (a) under regulation 7, or

    (b) under any provision of the law of an EEA State other than the United Kingdom giving effect to Article 5 of the Framework Directive;

"*EC vehicle type approval*" means type approval of a vehicle granted pursuant to the Framework Directive;

"*EEA Agreement*" means the Agreement on the European Economic Area signed at Oporto on 2nd May 1992 as adjusted by the Protocol signed at Brussels on 17th March 1993 [*Cm. 2073 and Cm. 2183*];

"*EEA State*" means a State which is a contracting Party to the EEA Agreement;

"*kg*" means kilogram(s);

"*km/h*" means kilometre(s) per hour;

"*kW*" means kilowatt(s);

"*mm*" means millimetre(s);

"*moped*" means a two or three wheel vehicle fitted with an engine having a cylinder capacity not exceeding 50 cm³ if of the internal combustion type and a maximum design speed of not more than 45 km/h;

"*motor cycle*" means a two-wheel vehicle with or without a sidecar, fitted with an engine having cylinder capacity of more than 50 cm³ if of the internal combustion type and/or having a maximum design speed of more than 45 km/h;

"*motor tricycle*" means a vehicle with three symmetrically arranged wheels fitted with an engine having a cyclinder capacity of more than 50 cm³ if of the internal combustion type and/or a maximum design speed of more than 45 km/h;

"*quadricycle*" means a motor vehicle with four wheels having the following characteristics—

    (a) a light quadricycle whose unladen mass is less than 350 kg, not including the mass of batteries in the case of an electric vehicle, whose maximum design speed is not more than 45 km/h and whose engine cylinder capacity does not exceed 50 cm³ for spark-ignition engines (or whose maximum net power is no more than 4kW for other types of engines); or

    (b) a quadricycle other than one falling within sub-paragraph (a), whose unladen mass is not more than 400 kg (550 kg for a vehicle intended for carrying goods), not including the mass of batteries in the case of an electric vehicle, whose maximum net engine power does not exceed 15 kW;

"*separate Directive*" means a Directive specified in Schedule 1.

(2) For the purposes of determining the number of wheels which a vehicle has, two wheels shall be considered as one wheel where—

  (a) they are mounted on the same axle, and

  (b) the distance between the centres of their areas of contact with the ground is less than 460 mm.

(3) Other expressions used in these Regulations which are also used in the Framework Directive shall have the same meaning as in that Directive and cognate expressions shall be construed accordingly.

[As to the EEA agreement, see further the note to Regulation (EEC) 3820/85 below.] **B71.07**

4. Vehicles to which these Regulations apply

(1) These Regulations apply to the following vehicles, if they are intended to travel on the road— **B71.08**

  (a) mopeds;

  (b) motor cycles;

  (c) motor tricycles; and

  (d) quadricycles.

This is subject to paragraph (2).

(2) These Regulations do not apply to—

  (a) vehicles with a maximum design speed not exceeding 6 km/h;

  (b) vehicles intended for pedestrian control;

  (c) vehicles intended for use by the physically handicapped;

  (d) vehicles intended for use in competitions, on roads or whatever the terrain;

  (e) tractors and machines, used for agricultural or similar purposes;

  (f) vehicles designed primarily for off-road leisure use having wheels arranged symmetrically with one wheel at the front of the vehicle and two at the rear.

PART II

EC TYPE APPROVAL GRANTED BY THE SECRETARY OF STATE

5. Applications for grant or amendment of EC type approval *[Omitted.]* **B71.09**

6. Grant or refusal of applications

(1) The Secretary of State may refuse to grant EC vehicle type approval if he is not satisfied that the applicant has made adequate arrangements for complying with regulation 9. **B71.10**

(2) The Secretary of State may refuse to grant EC component type approval if he is not satisfied that the applicant has made adequate arrangements for complying with regulations 9, 11 and 12.

(3) The Secretary of State may grant EC component type approval of a separate technical unit or component subject to such restrictions on its use or conditions as to fitting it as are described in Article 7(3) of the Framework Directive.

(4) Without prejudice to paragraphs (1) to (3) the Secretary of State shall make any decision under this regulation in accordance with—

    (a) the Framework Directive,

    (b) any relevant separate Directives, and

    (c) in particular, the requirement of the Framework Directive that a member State granting EC type approval must ensure that adequate arrangements have been made to ensure that production vehicles, components and separate technical units (as the case may be) conform to the EC approved type.

(5) Where the Secretary of State decides to refuse an application made under regulation 5, he shall give notice of the refusal to the applicant.

(6) Where the Secretary of State decides to impose restrictions on EC component type approval under paragraph (3), he shall, unless the applicant has consented to the restrictions or conditions, give notice of his decision to the applicant.

7. Issue of certificate

B71.11   (1) Where the Secretary of State decides to grant or amend an EC type approval he shall issue an EC type approval certificate or (as the case may be) an amended EC type approval certificate.

(2) An EC type approval certificate shall be in the form required by the Framework Directive or the relevant separate Directive (as the case may be).

8. EC certificates of conformity and approval marks

B71.12   (1) The holder of an EC vehicle type approval granted by the Secretary of State shall comply with the requirements of the first sentence of Article 7(1) of the Framework Directive (holders of EC vehicle type approval to issue certificates of conformity).

(2) The holder of an EC component type approval granted by the Secretary of State shall comply with Articles 7(2) and (4) and 8 of the Framework Directive (holders of EC component type approval to issue certificates of conformity and affix markings) so far as those provisions are applicable.

9. Conformity of production

B71.13   The holder of an EC type approval granted by the Secretary of State shall comply with paragraphs 1.1 to 1.1.6 of Annex VI to the Framework Directive (provisions relating to checking the conformity of production).

10. Duty to co-operate with the Secretary of State

B71.14   (1) The holder of an EC type approval granted by the Secretary of State shall permit the Secretary of State to carry out his obligations in relation to the approval under—

    (a) Article 4(3) and (5) of the Framework Directive (duty to ensure that provisions relating to checking the conformity of production continue to be observed), or

    (b) any similar provision under a separate Directive.

(2) The holder of an EC type approval granted by the Secretary of State shall co-operate with any person acting on behalf of the Secretary of State in connection with the obligations mentioned in paragraph (1).

11. Information concerning restrictions on use of components and separate technical units

B71.15   Where the Secretary of State has granted EC component type approval subject to restrictions as permitted by regulation 6(3), the holder of the type approval shall comply with the requirements of Article 7(5) of the Framework Directive (duty to supply detailed information on restrictions and to give fitting instructions).

12. Information concerning separate technical units of non-original equipment

Where the Secretary of State has granted EC component type approval for a separate technical unit of non-original equipment in connection with one or more types of vehicle, the holder of the type approval shall comply with the requirements of Article 7(6) of the Framework Directive (duty to supply information identifying those vehicles).

B71.16

13. Withdrawal of EC type approval   *[Omitted.]*

B71.17

14. Suspension of EC type approval   *[Omitted.]*

B71.18

15. Powers of the Secretary of State in cases of serious risk to road safety
[Omitted.]

B71.19

PART III

LICENSING OF VEHICLES

16. Grant of first licence or nil licence

(1) Where a person applies on or after 30th November 1999 for a licence or nil licence under the 1994 Act for a vehicle to which these Regulations apply, and no licence or nil licence has previously been granted under that Act for that vehicle, the Secretary of State shall not grant the licence or nil licence unless—

B71.20

(a) it is shown that an EC certificate of conformity has effect with respect to the vehicle, or

(b) it is shown that a Minister's approval certificate issued under section 58(1) or (4) of the 1988 Act has effect with respect to the vehicle, or

(c) it is shown that a Department's approval certificate issued under Article 31A(4) or (5) of the 1981 Order has effect with respect to the vehicle, or

(d) the application is made before 17th June 2003 and the vehicle belongs to the same type as a vehicle used before 17th June 1999.

(2) Where, by virtue of this regulation, the Secretary of State refuses to grant a licence or nil licence for a vehicle, he shall give notice of his decision to the applicant.

(3) For the purposes of paragraph (1), a vehicle belongs to a particular type only if it would be treated for the purposes of the Framework Directive as belonging to that type.

(4) This regulation is subject to regulations 17 and 18.

17. Vehicles used for the purposes of the Crown, the police and civil defence

Regulation 16 shall not apply in relation to—

B71.21

(a) an application by a public or local authority in respect of a vehicle intended by that authority to be used by them for the purposes of civil defence (within the meaning of the Civil Defence Act 1948), or

(b) an application by a public or local authority in respect of a vehicle intended to be used for police purposes, or

(c) an application in respect of a vehicle to which sections 63, 65 and 65A of the 1988 Act or Articles 31E and 31G of the 1981 Order have become applicable after a period of use on roads during which, by virtue of section 183(2) of the 1988 Act or Article 214 of the 1981 Order (which relate to vehicles in the service of the Crown) those sections or Articles did not apply to it.

18. Prototypes

B71.22   Regulation 16 shall not apply in relation to a vehicle of a new or improved construction, or a vehicle fitted with new or improved equipment, which—

(a) has been so constructed, or fitted with such equipment, for the purposes of tests or trials or for use as a prototype, and

(b) is not intended for general use on roads, and

(c) remains in the ownership and use of the manufacturer of the vehicle or (as the case may be) the manufacturer of the equipment.

PART IV

OFFENCES

19. Amendments of Acts and Orders

B71.23   The amendments set out in Schedule 2 shall have effect.

20. Forgery and deception

B71.24   (1) A person who, with intent to deceive—

(a) forges, alters or uses an EC type approval certificate or an EC certificate of conformity, or

(b) lends an EC type approval certificate or an EC certificate of conformity to another person, or

(c) allows an EC type approval certificate or an EC certificate of conformity to be used by another person, or

(d) makes any document so closely resembling an EC type approval certificate or an EC certificate of conformity as to be calculated to deceive, or

(e) has in his possession any document so closely resembling an EC type approval certificate or an EC certificate of conformity as to be calculated to deceive,

shall be guilty of an offence.

(2) A person who commits an offence under paragraph (1) shall be liable—

(a) on summary conviction, to a fine not exceeding the statutory maximum, or

(b) on conviction on indictment, to imprisonment for a term not exceeding 2 years, or to a fine or both.

21. False statements and documents

B71.25   A person who, in supplying information or producing documents for the purposes of these Regulations—

(a) makes a statement which he knows to be false in a material particular, or

(b) recklessly makes a statement which is false in a material particular, or

(c) produces, provides, sends or otherwise makes use of a document which he knows to be false, in a material particular, or

(d) recklessly produces, provides, sends or otherwise makes use of a document which is false in a material particular,

shall be liable on summary conviction to a fine not exceeding level 4 on the standard scale.

PART V

MISCELLANEOUS

SCHEDULE 1   Regulation 3(1)

SEPARATE DIRECTIVES   **B71.31**

Item	Principal Directives	Amending Directives	Official Journal Reference	Subject Matter and (where applicable) the Chapter of the Annex
1	93/14/EEC		L121, 15.5.93, p. 1	Braking of two or three-wheel motor vehicles
2	93/29/EEC		L188, 29.7.93, p. 1	Identification of controls, tell-tales and indicators for two or three-wheel motor vehicles
3	93/30/EEC		L188, 29.7.93, p. 11	Audible warning devices for two or three-wheel motor vehicles
4	93/31/EEC		L188, 29.7.93, p. 19	Stands for two-wheel motor vehicles
5	93/32/EEC		L188, 29.7.93, p. 28	Passenger hand holds for two-wheel motor vehicles
6	93/33/EEC	1999/24/EC*	L104, 21.4.1999, p. 16 L188, 29.7.93, p. 32	Protective devices intended to prevent the unauthorised use of two or three-wheel motor vehicles

[continued on next page

Item	Principal Directives	Amending Directives	Official Journal Reference	Subject Matter and (where applicable) the Chapter of the Annex
7	93/34/EEC	1999/23/EC*	L104, 21.4.1999, p. 13 L188, 29.7.93, p. 38	Statutory markings for two or three-wheel motor vehicles
8	93/92/EEC	1999/25/EC*	L104, 21.4.1999, p. 19 L311, 14.12.93, p. 1	Installation of lighting and light-signalling devices on two or three-wheel motor vehicles
9	93/93/EEC		L311, 14.12.93, p. 76	Masses and dimensions of two or three-wheel motor vehicles
10	93/94/EEC		L311, 14.12.93, p. 83	Space for mounting the rear registration plate of two or three-wheel motor vehicles
11	95/1/EC†	1999/26/EC*	L118, 6.5.1999, p. 32 L52, 8.3.95, p. 1	Maximum design speed, maximum torque and maximum engine power of two or three-wheel motor vehicles
12	97/24/EC†		L226, 18.8.97, p. 1	Certain components and characteristics of two or three-wheel motor vehicles Chapter 1 Tyres Chapter 2 Lighting and light-signalling devices Chapter 3 External projections Chapter 4 Rear view mirrors Chapter 5 Measures to counter pollution Chapter 6 Fuel tanks Chapter 7 Measures to counter tampering Chapter 8 Electromagnetic compability Chapter 9 Permissible sound level and exhaust systems

[*continued on next page*

Item	Principal Directives	Amending Directives	Official Journal Reference	Subject Matter and (where applicable) the Chapter of the Annex
12— cont.				Chapter 10 Coupling devices and attachments
				Chapter 11 Safety belt anchorages and safety belts
				Chapter 12 Glazing, windscreen wipers and washers and de-icing and de-misting devices
[13		2000/7/EC†	L106, 3.5.2000, p. 1	Speedometers for two or three-wheeled motor vehicles]

Note: the Directives marked with a * are Commission Directives, while those marked with a † are Directives of the European Parliament and the Council. The other Directives are Council Directives.

[Schedule 1 is printed as amended by S.I. 2001 No. 368.]   **B71.32**

SCHEDULE 2   Regulation 19

AMENDMENTS OF ACTS AND ORDERS

[Amends, inter alia, the Road Traffic Act 1988, q.v., and the Road Traffic Offenders Act 1988, q.v.]   **B71.33**

The Road Transport (Passenger Vehicles Cabotage) Regulations 1999

(S.I. 1999 No. 3413)

B72.01   *Editorial note.*   The Arrangement of regulations set out below has been added editorially and does not form part of the text of the regulations.

B72.02   *[The text of these regulations is printed as amended by:*

the Road Transport (Passenger Vehicles Cabotage) (Amendment) Regulations 2000 (S.I. 2000 No. 3114) (December 28, 2000).

The amending regulations are referred to in the notes to the principal regulations only by their year and number. The date referred to above is the date on which the amending regulations came into force.]

ARRANGEMENT OF REGULATIONS

B72.03   Regulation

1.   Commencement, citation and interpretation

B72.04   (1)   *[Omitted.]*

(2)   In these Regulations—

"*the Council Regulation*" means Council Regulation (EC) No. 12/98 [*q.v.*] of 11 December 1997 laying down the conditions under which non-resident carriers may operate national road passenger transport services within a member State;

"*the 1981 Act*" means the Public Passenger Vehicles Act 1981 [*q.v.*];

"*Community carrier*" means a road passenger transport carrier established in a member state of the European Community other than the United Kingdom;

"*road*" has the meaning given in section 192(1) of the Road Traffic Act 1988 [*q.v.*];

"*traffic commissioner*" has the meaning given in section 4 of the 1981 Act;

"*UK cabotage operations*" means cabotage transport operations in Great Britain or between Great Britain and Northern Ireland.

2. Extent

These Regulations apply in Great Britain.　　　　**B72.05**

3. Cabotage without a Community licence

(1) A person commits an offence if he uses a vehicle on a road, or causes or permits a　　**B72.06**
vehicle to be so used, for the purpose of UK cabotage operations which are carried out by
a Community carrier without a valid Community licence.

(2) A person who is guilty of an offence under paragraph (1) above shall be liable on
summary conviction to a fine not exceeding level 4 on the standard scale.

4. Use of a vehicle in Great Britain without a control document

(1) A person commits an offence if he uses a vehicle on a road, or causes or permits a　　**B72.07**
vehicle to be so used, for the purposes of UK cabotage operations which—

(a) take the form of occasional services in Great Britain or between Great Britain and
Northern Ireland, and

(b) are carried out in contravention of Article 6(1) of the Council Regulation.

(2) A person who is guilty of an offence under paragraph (1) above shall be liable on
summary conviction to a fine not exceeding level 4 on the standard scale.

5. Competent authorities in Great Britain

(1) For the purposes of Article 11(4) of the Council Regulation the competent authority of　　**B72.08**
the member State of establishment shall be the traffic commissioner for the area in which the
carrier has his operating centre (*"the appropriate traffic commissioner"*).

[(2) For the purposes of Articles 7, 9 and 11(2) and (3) of the Council Regulation the
competent authority shall be the Secretary of State.]

[Regulation 5 is printed as amended by S.I. 2000 No. 3114.]　　　　**B72.09**

6. Appeals

(1) A carrier who is aggrieved by an administrative penalty imposed on him by the　　**B72.10**
Secretary of State under Article 11(2) of the Council Regulation may request the Secretary
of State to review that decision.

(2) A carrier who is aggrieved by an administrative penalty imposed on him by the appropriate traffic commissioner under Article 11(4) of the Council Regulation may appeal to
the Transport Tribunal.

7. Production of documents

(1) The driver of a vehicle which is required, under Article 5 of the Council Regulation,　　**B72.11**
to have on board a Community licence commits an offence if he fails, without reasonable
cause, to produce the licence when requested to do so by an authorised inspecting officer.

(2) References in paragraph (1) above to a Community licence include references to a
certified true copy of a licence.

(3) The driver of a vehicle which is required, under Article 6(1) of the Council
Regulation, to have on board a control document commits an offence if he fails, without
reasonable cause, to produce the control document when requested to do so by an authorised inspecting officer.

(4) A person who is guilty of an offence under paragraph (1) or (3) above is liable on summary conviction to a fine not exceeding level 3 on the standard scale.

8. Authorised inspecting officers

B72.12 Authorised inspecting officers for the purposes of the Council Regulation shall in Great Britain be constables in uniform, and examiners appointed under section 66A of the Road Traffic Act 1988.

9. Bodies corporate

B72.13 (1) Where an offence under these Regulations has been committed by a body corporate and it is proved to have been committed with the consent or connivance of, or to be attributable to any neglect on the part of, any director, manager, secretary or other similar officer of the body corporate or any person who was purporting to act in any such capacity, he as well as the body corporate shall be guilty of the offence and shall be liable to be proceeded against and punished accordingly.

(2) Where the affairs of a body corporate are managed by its members, paragraph (1) above shall apply in relation to the acts and defaults of a member in connection with his functions of management as if he were a director of the body corporate.

(3) Where an offence under these Regulations has been committed by a Scottish partnership and is proved to have been committed with the consent or connivance of, or to be attributable to any neglect on the part of a partner, he as well as the partnership shall be guilty of the offence and shall be liable to be proceeded against and punished accordingly.

10. Modification of certain enactments and of the Public Service Vehicles (Conditions of Fitness, Equipment, Use and Certification) Regulations 1981

B72.14 (1)–(5) *[Amend, inter alia, the Road Traffic (Foreign Vehicles) Act 1972, q.v., and the Public Passenger Vehicles Act 1981, q.v.]*

(6) None of the provisions of Parts II, III, IV and V of the Public Service Vehicles (Conditions of Fitness, Equipment, Use and Certification) Regulations 1981 [*S.I. 1981 No. 257, as amended, q.v.*] shall have effect in relation to a vehicle which is carrying out a cabotage transport operation in Great Britain in accordance with the Council Regulation.

The Disabled Persons (Badges for Motor Vehicles) (England) Regulations 2000

(S.I. 2000 No. 682)

Editorial note. These regulations provide for a Community-model parking card for disabled persons in conformity with Council Recommendation 98/37/EC of June 4, 1998 (O.J. No. L167, June 12, 1998, p. 25).

B73.01

[The text of the regulations is printed as amended by:

B73.02

the Disabled Persons (Badges for Motor Vehicles) (England) (Amendment) Regulations 2000 (S.I. 2000 No. 1507) July 1, 2000).

The amending regulations are referred to in notes to the principal regulations only by their year and number. The date referred to above is the date on which the amending regulations came into force.]

ARRANGEMENT OF REGULATIONS

PART I

PRELIMINARY

PART II

ISSUE, DURATION AND REVOCATION OF BADGES

PART III

FORM AND DISPLAY OF BADGES

*　　　*　　　*

PART I

PRELIMINARY

1. Citation, commencement and extent

B73.04

(1)   *[Omitted.]*

(2) These Regulations extend to England.

2. Interpretation

B73.05

(1) In these Regulations—

"*the 1970 Act*" means the Chronically Sick and Disabled Persons Act 1970 [*q.v.*];

"*the 1982 Regulations*" has the meaning given by regulation 3(1);

"*the 1984 Act*" means the Road Traffic Regulation Act 1984 [*q.v.*];

"*disabled person*" means a person more than 2 years old and falling within at least one of the prescribed descriptions in regulation 4;

"*disabled person's badge*" means, [subject to paragraph (1A), a badge in the form prescribed by regulation 11 issued by a local authority for display on a motor vehicle driven by a disabled person, or used for the carriage of a disabled person, and includes a replacement badge issued in accordance with regulation 7;

"*disabled person's concession*" has the meaning given by section 117(3) of the 1984 Act;

"*holder*", in relation to a disabled person's badge, means the individual or institution to whom a disabled person's badge was issued;

"*institution*" means an institution concerned with the care of disabled persons to which a disabled person's badge may be issued in accordance with section 21(4) of the 1970 Act;

"*individual's badge*" means a disabled person's badge issued to an individual disabled person;

"*institutional badge*" means a disabled person's badge issued to an institution;

"*issuing authority*", in relation to a disabled person's badge, means the local authority which issued the badge; and

"*local authority*" means a county council, district council, the Council of the Isles of Scilly, a London borough council or the Common Council of the City of London.

[(1A) For the purposes of regulations 12 to 16, the definition of "*disabled person's badge*" in paragraph (1) shall include a badge issued under regulations having effect in Scotland or Wales under section 21 of the Chronically Sick and Disabled Persons Act 1970.]

(2) In these Regulations a reference to an order made under any provision of the 1984 Act is to an order made, or having effect as if made, under that provision including an order varying or revoking an order made or having effect as if made under that Act.

(3) In these Regulations "*relevant conviction*" means—

(a) any conviction of—

    (i) the holder of a disabled person's badge; or

    (ii) any other person using such a badge with the holder's consent,

for an offence specified in paragraph (4); or

(b) any conviction of a person other than the holder of a disabled person's badge of an offence under section 117(1) of the 1984 Act where the badge was displayed on the vehicle with the consent of the holder at any time during which the offence was being committed.

(4) The offences mentioned in paragraph (3)(a) are—

(a) any offence under section 5, 8, 11 or 16(1) of the 1984 Act so far as it relates to any contravention of or failure to comply with any provision of an order made under section 1, 6, 9 or 14 of that Act—

  (i) prohibiting or restricting the waiting of vehicles on any road; or
  (ii) relating to any of the matters mentioned in paragraph 7 or 8 of Schedule 1 to that Act; or

(b) any offence under section 35A(1) and (2), 47(1), 53(5), 53(6) or 117(1) of that Act.

(5) Any notice given under these Regulations shall be in writing.

[Regulation 2 is printed as amended by S.I. 2000 No. 1507.]   **B73.06**

3. Amendment of 1982 Regulations and transitional provisions

[Revoked; see now the Disabled Persons (Badges for Motor Vehicles) (Wales) Regulations (S.I. 2000   **B73.07**
No. 1786), reg.3(2) and (3) below.]

PART II

ISSUE, DURATION AND REVOCATION OF BADGES

4. Descriptions of disabled persons

(1) The prescribed descriptions of disabled person to whom a local authority may issue   **B73.08**
a disabled person's badge are a person who is more than 2 years old who falls within one or
more of the descriptions specified in paragraph (2).

(2) The descriptions are a person who—

(a) receives the higher rate of the mobility component of the disability living allowance in accordance with section 73 of the Social Security and Benefits Act [1992];

(b) uses a motor vehicle supplied by the Department of Social Security or the Scottish Executive or is in receipt of a grant pursuant to section 5(2)(a) of the National Health Service Act 1977 or section 46 of the National Health Service (Scotland) Act 1978;

(c) is registered as blind under section 29(4)(g) of the National Assistance Act 1948 or, in Scotland, is a blind person within the meaning of section 64(1) of that Act;

(d) receives a mobility supplement under article 26A of the Naval, Military and Air Forces etc. (Disablement and Death) Service Pensions Order 1983 [*S.I. 1983 No. 883, as amended*] including such a supplement by virtue of any scheme or order under article 25A of the Personal Injuries (Civilians) Scheme 1983 [*S.I. 1983 No. 686, as amended*];

(e) drives a motor vehicle regularly, has a severe disability in both upper limbs and is unable to turn by hand the steering wheel of a motor vehicle even if that wheel is fitted with a turning knob; or

(f) has a permanent and substantial disability which causes inability to walk or very considerable difficulty in walking.

[Regulation 4 is printed as amended by S.I. 2000 No. 1507.]   **B73.09**

5. Institutional badges

An institutional badge may be issued to an institution for a motor vehicle when the   **B73.10**
vehicle is to be used to carry disabled persons as specified in regulation 4(2).

B73.11   **6. Fee for issue and period of issue of a badge**   *[Omitted.]*

B73.12   **7. Replacement badges**   *[Omitted.]*

B73.13   **8. Grounds for refusal to issue a badge**   *[Omitted.]*

B73.14   **9. Return of badge to issuing authority**   *[Omitted.]*

B73.15   **10. Appeals**   *[Omitted.]*

PART III

FORM AND DISPLAY OF BADGES

11. Form of badge

B73.16   A disabled person's badge is in the prescribed form if—

    (a) the front and reverse of the badge are in the form shown in—

        (i) Part I of the Schedule to these Regulations in the case of an individual's badge; or

        (ii) Part II of the Schedule in the case of an institutional badge, and

    (b) the badge complies with the specifications in Part III of the Schedule.

B73.17   *[The text of the Schedule is not reproduced.]*

12. Manner in which a badge is to be displayed

B73.18   For the purposes of section 21(4A) of the 1970 Act a disabled person's badge is displayed on a vehicle in the prescribed manner if—

    (a) the badge is exhibited on the dashboard or fascia of the vehicle, or

    (b) where the vehicle is not fitted with a dashboard or fascia, the badge is exhibited in a conspicuous position on the vehicle,

so that the front of the badge is clearly legible from the outside of the vehicle.

13. Display of an individual's badge when a vehicle is being driven

B73.19   (1) This regulation prescribes for the purposes of section 21(4A) of the 1970 Act the circumstances in which an individual's badge may be displayed while a vehicle is being driven.

(2) An individual's badge may be displayed on a vehicle while the holder is either driving or being carried in it.

(3) An individual's badge may also be displayed on a vehicle if—

    (a) the vehicle is being used for the collection of the holder and no other purpose;

    (b) a disabled person's concession (other than a concession relating to parking) would be available to a vehicle lawfully displaying a disabled person's badge; and

    (c) it would not be practicable for the vehicle to be lawfully driven to, or to stop at, the place at which the holder is to be collected if the concession did not apply to the vehicle.

(4) An individual's badge may be displayed on a vehicle if—

(a) the vehicle, after being driven by or carrying the holder, is leaving the place where he got out;

(b) a disabled person's concession (other than a concession relating to parking) is available to a vehicle lawfully displaying a disabled person's badge; and

(c) it would not have been practicable for the vehicle to have left that place if the concession did not apply to the vehicle.

14. Display of an individual's badge when a vehicle is parked

(1) This regulation prescribes for the purposes of section 21(4A) of the 1970 Act the circumstances in which an individual's badge may be displayed while a vehicle is parked.   **B73.20**

(2) An individual's badge may be displayed on a vehicle while it is parked if it—

(a) has been driven by the holder, or has been used to carry the holder, to the place where it is parked; or

(b) is to be driven by the holder, or is to be used to carry the holder, from that place.

15. Display of institutional badge when a vehicle is being driven

(1) This regulation prescribes for the purposes of section 21(4A) of the 1970 Act the circumstances in which an institutional badge may be displayed while a vehicle is being driven.   **B73.21**

(2) An institutional badge may be displayed on a vehicle while it is being driven by or on behalf of the holder and is carrying a disabled person.

(3) An institutional badge may also be displayed on a vehicle while it is being driven by or on behalf of the holder and—

(a) the vehicle is being used for the collection of a disabled person and for no other purpose;

(b) a disabled person's concession (other than a concession relating to parking) is available to a vehicle lawfully displaying a disabled person's badge; and

(c) it would not have been practicable for the vehicle to be lawfully driven to or to stop at the place at which the disabled person is to be collected if that concession did not apply to the vehicle.

(4) An institutional badge may also be displayed on a vehicle while it is being driven by or on behalf of the holder and—

(a) the vehicle, after carrying a disabled person, is leaving the place where he got off;

(b) a disabled person's concession (other than a concession relating to parking) is available to a vehicle lawfully displaying a disabled person's badge; and

(c) it would not have been practicable for the vehicle to have left that place if the concession had not applied to the vehicle.

16. Display of an institutional badge when a vehicle is parked

(1) This regulation prescribes for the purposes of section 21(4A) of the 1970 Act the circumstances in which an institutional badge may be displayed while a vehicle is parked.   **B73.22**

(2) An institutional badge may be displayed on a vehicle while it is parked if it has been, or is to be, used by or on behalf of the holder for carrying a disabled person to or from the place where it is parked.

B73.23   (Regulation 11)   THE SCHEDULE

PART I

FORM OF INDIVIDUAL'S BADGE

[Omitted.]

PART II

FORM OF INSTITUTIONAL BADGE

[Omitted.]

PART III

SPECIFICATIONS FOR BADGE

[Omitted.]

The Local Authorities' Traffic Orders (Exemptions for Disabled Persons) (England) Regulations 2000

(S.I. 2000 No. 683)

Editorial note. The Arrangement of regulations set out below has been added editorially **B74.01**
and does not form part of the text of the regulations.

ARRANGEMENT OF REGULATIONS

1. Citation and commencement   *[Omitted.]*   **B74.03**

2. Amendment of the Local Authorities' Traffic Orders (Exemptions for   **B74.04** Disabled Persons) (England and Wales) Regulations 1986   *[Revoked.]*

3. Interpretation

(1) In these Regulations—   **B74.05**

"*the 1984 Act*" means the Road Traffic Regulation Act 1984;

"*the Badges Regulations*" means the Disabled Persons (Badges for Motor Vehicles) (England) Regulations 2000 [*S.I. 2000 No. 682, q.v.*];

"*bus lane*" has the meaning given by regulation 23(3) of the Traffic Signs Regulations 1994 [*S.I. 1994 No. 1519, q.v.*];

"*cycle lane*" has the meaning given by regulation 4 of the Traffic Signs Regulations 1994;

"*disabled person's badge*" means a badge which was—

(a) issued, or has effect as if issued, to a disabled person or an institution under the Badges Regulations or under regulations having effect in Scotland or Wales under section 21 of the Chronically Sick and Disabled Persons Act 1970 [*q.v.*]; and

(b) has not ceased to be in force;

"*hours of operation*" in relation to a bus lane or a cycle lane means the periods during which the restrictions, by virtue of which it is a bus lane or cycle lane, apply;

"*local authority*" means a county council, district council, the Council of the Isles of Scilly, a London borough council or the Common Council of the City of London;

"*parking disc*" has the meaning given by regulation 8(5); and

"*road*" in relation to Greater London includes a street as defined by section 6(6) of the 1984 Act [*q.v.*].

(2) In these Regulations—

(a) a reference to an order which includes a provision of a specified kind includes a reference to an order which applies a provision of that kind in an existing order; and

(b) a reference to an order made under any provision of the 1984 Act includes a reference to an order having effect as if made under that Act and to an order varying or revoking an order made or having effect as if made under that Act.

4. Meaning of "relevant position"

B74.06 (1) A vehicle displays a disabled person's badge in the relevant position if it is displayed in the manner prescribed by regulation 12 of the Badges Regulations.

(2) A vehicle displays a parking disc in the relevant position if—

(a) the disc is exhibited on the dashboard or fascia of the vehicle; or

(b) where the vehicle does not have a dashboard or fascia, the disc is exhibited in a conspicuous position on the vehicle,

so that, when marked to show the quarter-hour period during which a period of waiting began, that period is clearly legible from the outside of the vehicle.

5. Application

B74.07 (1) These Regulations apply to—

(a) any order made in relation to a road by a county or district council in England or by the Council of the Isles of Scilly under section 1, 9, 35, 45 or 46 of the 1984 Act;

(b) any order made in relation to a road by a London borough council or the Common Council of the City of London under section 6, 9, 45 and 46 of the 1984 Act except so far as the order applies to an excepted area or any part of one.

(2) Each of the following is an expected area—

(a) the City of London;

(b) the City of Westminster;

(c) the Royal Borough of Kensington and Chelsea;

(d) that part of the London borough of Camden, bounded by and including the borough boundary, Euston Road, Upper Woburn Place, Tavistock Square, Woburn Place, Russell Square, Southampton Road, Theobalds Road and Clerkenwell Road.

6. Exemption in favour of vehicles displaying disabled person's badges

B74.08 (1) The following provisions of these Regulations have effect for requiring local authorities to include, in orders to which these Regulations apply, exemptions in favour of a vehicle displaying a disabled person's badge.

(2) Any exemption from a provision which these Regulations require to be included in an order may be limited to vehicles of the same class as those to which the provision applies.

7. Exemption from prohibitions on waiting beyond a specified time

B74.09 (1) This regulation applies to an order made under section 1, 6, 9, 35, 45 or 46 of the 1984 Act if—

    (a) the order includes a provision prohibiting the waiting of vehicles or vehicles of any class in a road either—

        (i) beyond a specified period; or

        (ii) where less than a specified period has elapsed since a previous period of waiting by the same vehicle in that road, and

    (b) the prohibition does not apply to all vehicles except disabled persons' vehicles.

(2) An order to which this regulation applies shall include an exemption from the prohibition in favour of any vehicle displaying a disabled person's badge in the relevant position.

8. Exemptions from prohibitions on waiting at all times or during specified periods

(1) This regulation applies to an order made under section 1, 6, 9, 35, 45 or 46 of the 1984 Act which includes a provision which—   **B74.10**

    (a) prohibits (except for the purposes of loading or unloading) the waiting of vehicles, or any class of vehicles, in a road at all times of day or during one or more specified periods of the day;

    (b) does not apply to a bus lane or cycle lane during its hours of operation; and

    (c) is not a provision of the kind referred to in regulation 7(1).

(2) An order to which this regulation applies shall include an exemption from the prohibition in accordance with whichever of paragraphs (3) and (4) is appropriate in favour of any vehicle displaying a disabled person's badge in the relevant position.

(3) Where the period of the prohibition does not exceed 3 hours the exemption shall be for the whole of that period.

(4) Where the period of the prohibition exceeds 3 hours the exemption shall be for a period of 3 hours subject to the conditions that—

    (a) the period of exempted waiting does not begin less than one hour after a previous period of exempted waiting by the same vehicle in the same road on the same day;

    (b) a parking disc is displayed in the relevant position on the vehicle marked to show the quarter-hour period during which the period of exempted waiting began.

(5) In this regulation "*parking disc*" means a device which—

    (a) is 125 millimetres square and coloured blue, if issued on or after 1st April 2000 or orange, if issued before that date;

    (b) has been issued by a local authority and has not ceased to be valid; and

    (c) is capable of showing the quarter-hour period during which a period of waiting has begun.

9. Exemptions from other provisions of orders under section 45 or 46 of the Road Traffic Regulation Act 1984

(1) This regulation applies to an order made under section 45 or 46 of the 1984 Act which prescribes—   **B74.11**

    (a) a charge to be paid for a vehicle or vehicle of any class left in a parking place designated by the order;

    (b) a maximum period during which a vehicle may wait in a parking place; or

    (c) a period which must elapse before a vehicle taken away from a parking place may be left there again.

(2) An order to which this regulation applies shall include an exemption, from each of the matters so prescribed, in favour of a vehicle displaying a disabled person's badge in the relevant position.

The Local Authorities' Traffic Orders (Exemptions for Disabled Persons) (Wales) Regulations 2000

(S.I. 2000 No. 1785)

Editorial note. The official text of these regulations is produced in two languages, but only the English language text is reproduced below. In regulation 3 (interpretation), the Welsh language equivalents of the terms defined (in English) are reproduced (as in the official English language text) in parenthesis immediately following the defined terms.

The Arrangement of regulations set out below has been added editorially and does not form part of the text of the regulations.

B75.01

ARRANGEMENT OF REGULATIONS

B75.02

3. Interpretation

(1) In these Regulations —

B75.03

"*the 1984 Act*" ("*Deddf 1984*") means the Road Traffic Regulation Act 1984;

"the Badges Regulations" ("*y Rheoliadau Bathodynnau*") means the Disabled Persons (Badges for Motor Vehicles) (Wales) Regulations 2000 [*S.I. 2000 No. 1786 below*];

"*bus lane*" ("*lôn bysiau*") has the meaning given by regulation 23(3) of the Traffic Signs Regulations 1994 [*S.I. 1994 No. 1519 above*];

"*cycle lane*" ("*lôn beiciau*") has the meaning given by regulation 4 of the Traffic Signs Regulations 1994;

"*disabled person's badge*" ("*bathodyn person anabl*") means a badge which was—

(a) issued, or has effect as if issued, to a disabled person or an institution under the Badges Regulations or under regulations having effect in Scotland or England under section 21 of the Chronically Sick and Disabled Persons Act 1970; and

(b) has not ceased to be in force;

"*hours of operation*" ("*oriau gweithredu*") in relation to a bus lane or a cycle lane means the periods during which the restrictions, by virtue of which it is a bus lane or cycle lane, apply;

2/1993

"*local authority*" ("*awdurdod ileol*") means a county council, or county borough council; and "*parking disc*" ("*disg barcio*") has the meaning given by regulation 8(5).

(2) In these Regulations —

    (a) a reference to an order which includes a provision of a specified kind includes a reference to an order which applies a provision of that kind in an existing order; and

    (b) a reference to an order made under any provision of the 1984 Act includes a reference to an order having effect as if made under that Act and to an order varying or revoking an order made or having effect as if made under that Act.

4. Meaning of "relevant position"

B75.04   (1) A vehicle displays a disabled person's badge in the relevant position if it is displayed in the manner prescribed by regulation 12 of the Badges Regulations.

(2) A vehicle displays a parking disc in the relevant position —

    (a) if the disc is exhibited on the dashboard or fascia of the vehicle; or

    (b) if where the vehicle does not have a dashboard or fascia, the disc is exhibited in a conspicuous position on the vehicle,

so that when marked to show the quarter-hour period during which a period of waiting began, that period is clearly legible from the outside of the vehicle.

5. Application

B75.05   These Regulations apply to any order made in relation to a road by a county or county borough council in Wales under section 1, 9, 35, 45 or 46 of the 1984 Act.

6. Exemption in favour of vehicles displaying disabled person's badges

B75.06   (1) The following provisions of these Regulations have effect for requiring local authorities to include, in orders to which these Regulations apply, exemptions in favour of a vehicle displaying a disabled person's badge.

(2) Any exemption from a provision (which these Regulations require to be included) in an order may be limited to vehicles of the same class as those to which the provision applies.

7. Exemption from prohibitions on waiting beyond a specified time

B75.07   (1) This regulation applies to an order made under section 1, 9, 35, 45 or 46 of the 1984 Act —

    (a) if the order includes a provision prohibiting the waiting of vehicles or vehicles of any class in a road either —

        (i) beyond a specified period; or

        (ii) where less than a specified period has elapsed since a previous period of waiting by the same vehicle in that road, and

    (b) if the prohibition does not apply to all vehicles except disabled persons' vehicles.

(2) An order to which this regulation applies shall include an exemption from the prohibition in favour of any vehicle displaying a disabled person's badge in the relevant position.

8. Exemptions from prohibitions on waiting at all times or during specified periods

B75.08   (1) This regulation applies to an order made under section 1, 9, 35, 45 or 46 of the 1984 Act which includes a provision which —

(a) prohibits (except for the purposes of loading or unloading) the waiting of vehicles, or any class of vehicles, in a road at all times of day or during one or more specified periods of the day;

(b) does not apply to a bus lane or cycle lane during its hours of operation; and

(c) is not a provision of the kind referred to in regulation 7(1).

(2) An order to which this regulation applies shall include an exemption from the prohibition in accordance with whichever of paragraphs (3) and (4) is appropriate in favour of any vehicle displaying a disabled person's badge in the relevant position.

(3) Where the period of the prohibition does not exceed three hours the exemption shall be for the whole of that period.

(4) Where the period of the prohibition exceeds three hours the exemption shall be for a period of three hours, subject to the following conditions:—

(a) the period of exempted waiting does not begin less than one hour after a previous period of exempted waiting by the same vehicle in the same road on the same day;

(b) a parking disc is displayed in the relevant position on the vehicle marked to show the quarter-hour period during which the period of exempted waiting began.

(5) In this regulation "*parking disc*" means a device which—

(a) is 125 millimetres square and coloured blue, if issued on or after the day these Regulations come into force or orange, if issued before that date;

(b) has been issued by a local authority and has not ceased to be valid; and

(c) is capable of showing the quarter-hour period during which a period of waiting has begun.

9. Exemptions from other provisions of orders under section 45 or 46 of the Road Traffic Regulation Act 1984

(1) This regulation applies to an order made under section 45 or 46 of the 1984 Act which prescribes—   **B75.09**

(a) a charge to be paid for a vehicle or vehicle of any class left in a parking place designated by the order;

(b) a maximum period during which a vehicle may wait in a parking place; or

(c) a period which must elapse before a vehicle taken away from a parking place may be left there again.

(2) An order to which this regulation applies shall include an exemption from each of the matters so prescribed in favour of a vehicle displaying a disabled person's badge in the relevant position.

The Disabled Persons (Badges for Motor Vehicles) (Wales) Regulations 2000

(S.I. 2000 No. 1786)

B76.01   *Editorial note.*   The official text of these regulations is produced in two languages, but only the English language text is reproduced below. In regulation 2 (interpretation), the Welsh language equivalents of the terms defined (in English) are reproduced (as in the official English language text) in parenthesis immediately following the defined terms.

ARRANGEMENT OF REGULATIONS

PART I

PRELIMINARY

PART II

ISSUE, DURATION AND REVOCATION OF BADGES

PART III

FORM AND DISPLAY OF BADGES

*   *   *

PART I

PRELIMINARY

1. Citation, commencement and extent

(1) *[Omitted.]*   **B76.03**

(2) These Regulations apply to Wales.

2. Interpretation

(1) In these Regulations—   **B76.04**

"*the 1970 Act*" ("*Deddf 1970*") means the Chronically Sick and Disabled Persons Act 1970 [*q.v.*];

"*the 1982 Regulations*" ("*Rheoliadau 1982*") has the meaning given by regulation 3(1) below;

"*the 1983 Act*" ("*Deddf 1984*") means the Road Traffic Regulation Act 1984 [*q.v.*];

"*disabled person*" ("*person anabl*") means a person more than two years old and who corresponds to at least one of the prescribed descriptions in regulation 4(2);

"*disabled person's badge*" ("*bathodyn person anabl*") means, subject to paragraph (6) below, a badge in the form prescribed by regulation 11 and issued by a local authority for display on a motor vehicle driven by a disabled person, or to carry a disabled person and includes a replacement badge for one that was lost etc. issued in accordance with regulation 7;

"*disabled person's concession*" ("*consesiwn person anabl*") has the meaning given by section 117(3) of the 1984 Act;

"*holder*" ("*deiliad*") in relation to a disabled person's badge, means the individual or institution to whom a disabled person's badge was issued;

"*individual's badge*" ("*bathodyn unigolyn*") means a disabled person's badge issued to an individual disabled person;

"*institution*" ("*sefydliad*") means an institution concerned with the care of disabled persons to which a disabled person's badge may be issued in accordance with section 21(4) of the 1970 Act,

"*institutional badge*" ("*bathodyn sefydliad*") means a disabled person's badge issued to an institution;

"*issuing authority*" ("*awdurdod rhoi*"), in relation to a disabled person's badge, means the local authority which issued the badge; and

"*local authority*" ("*awdurdod ileol*") means a county council or county borough council.

(2) In these Regulations a reference to an order made under any provision of the 1984 Act is to an order made, or having effect as if made, under that provision, including an order varying or revoking an order made or having effect as if made under that Act.

(3) In these Regulations "*relevant conviction*" ("*collfarn berthnasol*") means

(a) any conviction of—

(i) the holder of a disabled person's badge; or

(ii) any other person using such a badge with the holder's consent,

for an offence specified in paragraph (4); or

(b) any conviction of a person other than the holder of a disabled person's badge of an offence under section 117(1) of the 1984 Act where the badge was displayed on the vehicle with the consent of the holder at any time during which the offence was being committed.

(4) The offences mentioned in paragraph (3)(a) above are—

(a) any offence under sections 5, 8, 11 or 16(1) of the 1984 Act so far as it relates to any contravention of or failure to comply with any provision of an order made under sections 1, 6, 9 or 14 of that Act—

(i) prohibiting or restricting the waiting of vehicles on any road or part of a road; or

(ii) relating to any of the matters mentioned in paragraphs 7 or 8 of Schedule 1 to that Act; or

(b) any offence under sections 35A(1) and (2), 47(1), 53(5), 53(6) or 117(1) of that Act.

(5) Any notice given under these Regulations shall be in writing.

(6) For the purposes of regulations 12 to 16 the definition of *"disabled person's badge"* in paragraph (1) above shall include a badge issued under regulations having effect in England or Scotland under section 21 of the Chronically Sick and Disabled Persons Act 1970.

3. Revocation of 1982 Regulations and transitional provisions

B76.05   (1) The Disabled Persons (Badges for Motor Vehicles) Regulations 1982 [S.I. 1982 No. 1740, as amended] (in these Regulations called *"the 1982 Regulations"*), are revoked.

(2) Without prejudice to section 17 of the Interpretation Act 1978

(a) any application made to a local authority or other thing done under the 1982 Regulations before the coming into force of these Regulations by or in relation to a local authority in Wales shall have effect as if made or done, and may be continued under the corresponding provision of these Regulations;

(b) any badge issued by a local authority in Wales under the 1982 Regulations shall have effect as if issued under these Regulations and shall remain in force until

(i) the happening of an event specified in regulation 9(1) or the giving of a notice in accordance with regulation 9(2); or

(ii) the issue of a replacement in accordance with regulation 7.

(3) Any order made under the 1984 Act which refers to a disabled person's badge shall, in relation to times falling after the coming into force of these Regulations, have effect as if the reference included a reference to a badge issued, or having effect as if issued, in accordance with these Regulations.

PART II

Issue, Duration and Revocation of Badges

4. Descriptions of disabled persons

B76.06   (1) The prescribed descriptions of a disabled person to whom a local authority may issue a disabled person's badge are a person who is more than two years old who fits one or more of the descriptions specified in paragraph (2).

(2) The descriptions are a person who—

(a) receives a higher rate of the mobility component of the disability living allowance in accordance with section 73 of the Social Security Contributions and Benefits Act 1992;

(b) uses a motor vehicle supplied by the Department of Social Security or the Scottish Executive or is in receipt of a grant pursuant to section 5(2)(a) of the National

Health Service Act 1977 or section 46 of the National Health Service (Scotland) Act 1978;

(c) is registered as blind under section 29(4)(g) of the National Assistance Act 1948 or, in Scotland, is a blind person within the meaning of section 64(1) of that Act;

(d) receives a mobility supplement under article 26A of the Naval, Military and Air Forces etc. (Disablement and Death) Service Pensions Order 1983 including such a supplement by virtue of any scheme or order under article 25A of the Personal Injuries (Civilians) Scheme 1983;

(e) drives motor vehicles regularly, has a severe disability in both upper limbs and is unable to turn by hand the steering wheel of a motor vehicle even if that wheel is fitted with a turning knob; or

(f) has a permanent and substantial disability which causes inability to walk or very considerable difficulty in walking.

5. Institutional badges

An institutional badge may be issued by an authority to an institution for a motor vehicle when the vehicle is to be used to carry disabled persons as specified in regulation 4(2).   **B76.07**

6. Fee for issue and period of issue of a badge   *[Omitted.]*   **B76.08**

7. Replacement of badges that have been lost, etc.   *[Omitted.]*

8. Grounds for refusal to issue a badge   *[Omitted.]*   **B76.09**

9. Return of badge to issuing authority   *[Omitted.]*

10. Appeals   *[Omitted.]*   **B76.10**

PART III

FORM AND DISPLAY OF BADGES

11. Form of badge

A disabled person's badge is in the prescribed form if—   **B76.11**

(a) the front and reverse of the badge are in the form shown—
    (i) in Part I of the Schedule to these Regulations in the case of an individual's badge; or
    (ii) in Part II of the Schedule in the case of an institutional badge; and

(b) the badge complies with the specifications in Part III of the Schedule.

12. Manner in which a badge is to be displayed

For the purposes of section 21(4A) of the 1970 Act a disabled person's badge is displayed on a vehicle in the prescribed manner if—   **B76.12**

(a) the badge is exhibited on the dashboard or fascia of the vehicle, or

(b) where the vehicle is not fitted with a dashboard or fascia, the badge is exhibited in a conspicuous position on the vehicle, so that the front of the badge is clearly legible from the outside of the vehicle.

13. Display of an individual's badge when a vehicle is being driven

B76.13   (1) This regulation prescribes for the purposes of section 21(4A) of the 1970 Act the circumstances in which an individual's badge may be displayed while a vehicle is being driven.

(2) An individual's badge may be displayed on a vehicle while the holder is either driving or being carried in it.

(3) An individual's badge may also be displayed on a vehicle—

(a) if the vehicle is being used for the collection of the holder and no other purpose;

(b) if a disabled person's concession (other than a concession relating to parking) is available to a vehicle lawfully displaying a disabled person's badge; and

(c) if it would not be practicable for the vehicle to be lawfully driven to, or to stop at, the place at which the holder is to be collected if the concession did not apply to the vehicle.

(4) An individual's badge may be displayed on a vehicle—

(a) if the vehicle, after being driven by or carrying the holder, is leaving the place where the holder got out;

(b) if the disabled person's concession (other than a concession relating to parking) is available to a vehicle lawfully displaying a disabled person's badge; and

(c) if it would not be practicable for the vehicle to be driven from that place if the concession did not apply to the vehicle.

14. Display of an individual's badge when a vehicle is parked

B76.14   (1) This regulation prescribes for the purposes of section 21(4A) of the 1970 Act the circumstances in which an individual's badge may be displayed while a vehicle is parked.

(2) An individual's badge may be displayed on a vehicle while it is parked if it—

(a) has been driven by the holder, or has been used to carry the holder, to the place where it is parked; or

(b) is to be driven by the holder, or is to be used to carry the holder, from that place.

15. Display of institutional badge when a vehicle is being driven

B76.15   (1) This regulation prescribes for the purposes of section 21(4A) of the 1970 Act the circumstances in which an institutional badge may be displayed while a vehicle is being driven.

(2) An institutional badge may be displayed on a vehicle while it is being driven by or on behalf of the holder and is carrying a disabled person.

(3) An institutional badge may also be displayed on a vehicle while it is being driven by or on behalf of the holder and—

(a) the vehicle is being used for the collection of a disabled person and for no other purpose;

(b) a disabled person's concession (other than a concession relating to parking) is available to a vehicle lawfully displaying a disabled person's badge; and

(c) it would not have been practicable for the vehicle to be lawfully driven to or to stop at the place at which the disabled person is to be collected if that concession did not apply to the vehicle.

(4) An institutional badge may also be displayed on a vehicle while it is being driven by or on behalf of the holder and—

(a) the vehicle, after carrying a disabled person, is leaving the place where the disabled person got off;

(b) a disabled person's concession (other than a concession relating to parking) is available to a vehicle lawfully displaying a disabled person's badge; and

(c) it would not have been practicable for the vehicle to have left that place if the concession had not applied to the vehicle.

16. Display of an institutional badge when a vehicle is parked

(1) This regulation prescribes for the purposes of section 21(4A) of the 1970 Act the circumstances in which an institutional badge may be displayed while a vehicle is parked.   **B76.16**

(2) An institutional badge may be displayed on a vehicle while it is parked if it has been, or is to be, used by or on behalf of the holder for carrying a disabled person to or from the place where it is parked.

SCHEDULE

[Omitted]

The Fixed Penalty Order 2000

(S.I. 2000 No. 2792)

B77.01   **1. Citation and commencement**   *[Omitted]*

2. Fixed penalties

B77.02   The fixed penalty for an offence shown in column (1) of the Schedule to this Order shall be the amount shown in relation to that offence in column (2) of the Schedule.

B77.03   **3. Revocations**   *[Omitted]*

SCHEDULE

FIXED PENALTIES

B77.04

(1) *Offence*	(2) *Fixed penalty*
A fixed penalty offence involving obligatory endorsement	£60.00
A fixed penalty parking offence committed in Greater London on a red route	£60.00
Any other fixed penalty parking offence committed in Greater London	£40.00
Any other fixed penalty offence	£30.00

In this Schedule—

"*fixed penalty parking offence*" means—

(i) an offence under the Road Traffic Regulation Act 1984 [*q.v.*] which is a fixed penalty offence, which does not involve obligatory endorsement and which is committed in respect of a stationary vehicle;

(ii) an offence under section 15(1) of the Greater London Council (General Powers) Act 1974 [*c.xxiv; not reproduced in this work*];

(iii) an offence under section 137(1) of the Highways Act 1980 [*q.v.*];

(iv) an offence under section 19 of the Road Traffic Act 1988 [*q.v.*];

(v) an offence under section 42 of the Road Traffic Act 1988 consisting in the causing of an unnecessary obstruction of a road in breach of regulation 103 of the Road Vehicles (Construction and Use) Regulations 1986 [*S.I. 1986 No. 1078 above*]; or

(vi) an offence under the Parks Regulation Acts 1872 and 1926 [not reproduced in this work] consisting in the failure to comply with, or acting in contravention of, regulation 4(30) of the Royal Parks and Other Open Spaces Regulations 1997 [*not reproduced in this work*];

"*red route*" means a length of road affected by either or both of the following traffic signs, namely—

(i) a traffic sign lawfully placed on the road, being a traffic sign which bears the words "Red Route", with or without any other word or any sign or other indication; or

(ii) a traffic sign consisting of a red line or mark is lawfully placed on the road;

"*traffic sign*" means a traffic sign for the purposes of section 64(1) of the Road Traffic Regulation Act 1984 which conveys any restriction of prohibition under an order made under that Act.

The Private Hire Vehicles (London) Act 1998 (Commencement No. 1) Order 2000

(S.I. 2000 No. 3144)

B78.01   **1.**—(1) This Order may be cited as the Private Hire Vehicles (London) Act 1998 (Commencement No. 1) Order 2000.

(2) In this Order "*the Act*" means the Private Hire Vehicles (London) Act 1998.

B78.02   **2.** The following provisions of the Act shall come into force on 22nd January 2001—

Sections 1, 3, 4(1), (3) and (4), 5(5), 15(1) to (3) and (5), 16(1) and (2), 17 to 20, 21(1) and (3), 22(1) and (4), 23 to 29, 32, 33, 34(1) and (2) and 36 to 38.

B78.03   **3.** The following provisions of the Act shall come into force on 22nd October 2001—

Sections 2, 4(5) and (6), 5(1) to (4), 21(4) and 22(5) and (6).

The Private Hire Vehicles (London) (Operators' Licences) Regulations 2000

(S.I. 2000 No. 3146)

ARRANGEMENT OF REGULATIONS

PART I

GENERAL

B79.01

*   *   *

PART III

LICENCES

PART IV

RECORDS

PART V

OTHER MATTERS

PART I

GENERAL

B79.02   **1. Citation and commencement**   *[Omitted.]*

2. Interpretation

B79.03   In these Regulations, unless the context otherwise requires—

"*the 1998 Act*" means the Private Hire Vehicles (London) Act 1998 [*q.v.*];

"*application*" means an application for the grant or variation of a licence;

"*business name*" means a name which if used by a person for the purpose of carrying on business would make him subject to the Business Names Act 1985;

"*CB apparatus*" means wireless telegraphy apparatus known as "Citizens' Band" which is designed or adapted, or has facilities permitting its adaptation, for the purpose of transmitting spoken messages on the frequency band 26.1 MHz to 28 MHz;

"*certificate of insurance*" and "*certificate of security*" shall be construed in accordance with section 147 of the Road Traffic Act 1988 [*q.v.*];

"*Community licence*" and "*Northern Ireland licence*" have the same meanings as in section 108(1) of the Road Traffic Act 1988 [*q.v.*];

"*driving licence*" means a licence to drive a motor car granted under Part III of the Road Traffic Act 1988 [*q.v.*] (other than a provisional licence), or a licence authorising the driving of a motor car by virtue of section 99A(1) or 109(1) of that Act (Community licences and Northern Ireland licences);

"*firm*" has the same meaning as in section 4 of the Partnership Act 1890;

"*licence*" means a London PHV operator's licence;

"*licensing authority*" means the person appointed under section 24(1) of the 1998 Act for the purpose of exercising the functions of the Secretary of State under that Act or, where no such appointment has been made, the Secretary of State(e);

"*MOT test certificate*" means, in relation to a vehicle to which section 47 of the Road Traffic Act 1998 [*q.v.*] applies, a test certificate issued in respect of the vehicle as mentioned in subsection (1) of that section;

"*national insurance number*" has the same meaning as in regulation 1(2) of the Social Security (Contributions) Regulations 1979 [*S.I. 1979 No. 591*];

"*officer*", in relation to a body corporate, shall be construed in accordance with section 744 of the Companies Act 1985;

"*operator*" means a London PHV operator and in relation to a licence means the operator to whom the licence was granted;

"*registered keeper*" means, in relation to a vehicle, the person in whose name the vehicle is registered under the Vehicle Excise and Registration Act 1994 [*q.v.*];

"*registration mark*" means, in relation to a vehicle, the mark assigned to the vehicle in accordance with section 23 of the Vehicle Excise and Registration Act 1994 [*q.v.*];

"*variation*" means a variation of a licence at the operator's request under section 18 of the 1998 Act [*q.v.*]; and

"*wireless telegraphy apparatus*" shall be construed in accordance with section 19(1) of the Wireless Telegraphy Act 1949.

PART II
APPLICATIONS

3. Manner of making applications   *[Omitted.]*   **B79.04**

4. Fees   *[Omitted.]*

5. Determination of applications   *[Omitted.]*   **B79.05**

PART III
LICENCES

6. Grant and variation   *[Omitted.]*   **B79.06**

7. Fees   *[Omitted.]*

8. Refund of fees   *[Omitted.]*   **B79.07**

9. Conditions

(1) Every licence shall be granted subject to the conditions set out in the following provisions of this regulation.   **B79.08**

(2) In respect of any operating centre specified in the licence which is accessible to members of the public, the operator shall maintain in force a policy of insurance against public liability risks which provides a minimum indemnity of £5,000,000 in respect of any one event.

(3) The operator shall, if required to do so by a person making a private hire booking—

(a) agree the fare for the journey booked, or

(b) provide an estimate of that fare.

(4) If, during the currency of the licence—

(a) any conviction is recorded—

    (i) where the operator is an individual, against him,

    (ii) where the operator is a firm, against any partner of that firm, or

    (iii) where the operator is another type of body or group of persons, against that body or group or any officer of that body or group;

(b) any information provided in the application for the grant of the licence, or for any variation thereof, changes; or

(c) any driver ceases to be available to the operator for carrying out bookings, by virtue of that driver's unsatisfactory conduct in connection with the driving of a private hire vehicle,

the operator shall, within 14 days of the date of such event, give the licensing authority notice containing details of the conviction or change, as the case may be, or, in the case falling within sub-paragraph (c), the name of the driver and the circumstances of the case.

(5) No CB apparatus shall be used in connection with a private hire booking at any operating centre specified in the licence or in any private hire vehicle available for carrying out bookings accepted at any such operating centre.

(6) The operator shall preserve records in accordance with regulation 16(1)(a) and (b).

(7) The operator shall establish and maintain a procedure for dealing with—

(a) complaints, and

(b) lost property,

arising in connection with any private hire booking accepted by him and shall keep and preserve records in accordance with regulations 14, 15 and 16(1)(c).

(8) Where an operator provides a London cab for the purpose of carrying out a private hire booking, any fare payable in respect of the booking shall be calculated as if the vehicle was a private hire vehicle unless the fare shown on the taximeter is less.

(9) In the case of a licence granted following an election made under regulation 7(2) or (5), the operator must, during the currency of the licence, continue to meet the requirement that no more than two private hire vehicles are available to him for carrying out bookings accepted by him at all the operating centres specified in his licence.

PART IV

RECORDS

10. Form of record of private hire bookings

B79.09   The record which an operator is required to keep by virtue of section 4(3)(b) of the 1998 Act at each operating centre specified in his licence of the private hire bookings accepted by him there shall be kept—

(a) in writing, or

(b) in such other form that the information contained in it can easily be reduced to writing.

11. Particulars of private hire bookings

B79.10   Before the commencement of each journey booked at an operating centre specified in his licence an operator shall enter the following particulars of the booking in the record referred to in regulation 10—

(a) the date on which the booking is made and, if different, the date of the proposed journey,

(b) the name of the person for whom the booking is made or other identification of him, or, if more than one person, the name or other identification of one of them;

(c) the agreed time and place of collection, or, if more than one, the agreed time and place of the first;

(d) the main destination specified at the time of the booking;

(e) any fare or estimated fare quoted;

(f) the name of the driver carrying out the booking or other identification of him;

(g) if applicable, the name of the other operator to whom the booking has been sub-contracted, and

(h) the registered number of the vehicle to be used or such other means of identifying it as may be adopted.

12. Particulars of private hire vehicles

B79.11   (1) For the purposes of section 4(3)(d) of the 1998 Act, an operator shall keep at each operating centre specified in his licence a record, containing the particulars set out in paragraph (2), of each private hire vehicle which is available to him for carrying out bookings accepted by him at that centre.

(2) In relation to each vehicle the particulars referred to in paragraph (1) are—

(a) the make, model and colour;

(b) the registration mark;

(c) the name and address of the registered keeper;

(d) in the case of a vehicle to which section 47 of the Road Traffic Act 1988 applies, a copy of the current MOT test certificate;

(e) a copy of the current certificate of insurance or certificate of security;

(f) the date on which the vehicle became available to the operator; and

(g) the date on which the vehicle ceased to be so available.

13. Particulars of drivers

(1) For the purposes of section 4(3)(d) of the 1998 Act, an operator shall keep at each operating centre specified in his licence a record, containing the particulars set out in paragraph (2), of each driver who is available to him for carrying out bookings accepted by him at that centre.   **B79.12**

(2) In relation to each driver the particulars referred to in paragraph (1) are—

(a) his surname, forenames, address and date of birth;

(b) his national insurance number;

(c) a photocopy of his driving licence;

(d) a photograph of him;

(e) the date on which he became available to the operator, and

(f) the date on which he ceased to be so available.

14. Record of complaints

(1) An operator shall keep at each operating centre specified in his licence a record containing—   **B79.13**

(a) the particulars set out in paragraph (2) of any complaint made in respect of a private hire booking accepted by him at that centre; and

(b) the particulars set out in paragraph (2)(d), (e), and (f) of any other complaint made in respect of his undertakings as an operator at that centre.

(2) In relation to each complaint the particulars referred to in paragraph (1) are—

(a) the date of the related booking;

(b) the name of the driver who carried out the booking;

(c) the registration mark of the vehicle used;

(d) the name of the complainant and any address, telephone number or other contact details provided by him;

(e) the nature of the complaint, and

(f) details of any investigation carried out and subsequent action taken as a result.

15. Record of lost property

(1) An operator shall keep at each operating centre specified in his licence a record, containing the particulars set out in paragraph (2), of any lost property found—   **B79.14**

(a) at that centre, or

(b) in any private hire vehicle used to carry out a booking accepted by him there.

(2) In relation to each item of lost property the particulars referred to in paragraph (1) are—

(a) the date on which it was found;

(b) the place where it was found and if it was found in a vehicle, the registration mark of that vehicle;

(c) a description of the item;

(d) evidence to show that, where practical, an attempt was made to return the item to the owner and whether or not this was successful, and

(e) in the case of any unclaimed item which has been disposed of, how it was disposed of.

(3) An operator shall keep at each operating centre specified in his licence a record, containing the particulars set out in paragraph (4), of any property reported to him at that centre as having been lost.

(4) In relation to each item of property reported as having been lost the particulars referred to in paragraph (3) are—

(a) the date of the report;

(b) the date on which it is alleged to have been lost;

(c) the place where it is alleged to have been lost;

(d) a description of the item, and

(e) evidence to show that, where practical, an attempt was made to find the item.

16. Preservation of records

B79.15   (1) Subject to paragraph (3), an operator shall preserve the particulars of—

(a) each private hire booking recorded in accordance with regulation 11 for six months from the date on which the booking was accepted;

(b) each private hire vehicle and driver recorded in accordance with regulations 12 and 13 for twelve months from the date on which the vehicle or, as the case may be, the driver ceased to be available for carrying out bookings;

(c) each complaint and item of lost property recorded in accordance with regulations 14 and 15 for six months from the date on which they were entered in the respective record.

(2) Where an operator tape-records a private hire booking he shall preserve the tape-recording of that conversation for a period of six months.

(3) For the purpose of section 4(4) of the 1998 Act, if an operator ceases to use an operating centre specified in his licence, he shall, in relation to that operating centre, preserve—

(a) the record referred to in regulation 10 for six months; and

(b) the records kept in accordance with regulations 12 and 13 for twelve months, from the date of the last entry.

PART V

OTHER MATTERS

B79.16   **17. Register of licences**   *[Omitted.]*

18. Issue of replacement licences *[Omitted.]* **B79.17**

19. Continuance of licence on death, bankruptcy, etc.

(1) This regulation applies in relation to a licence granted in the sole name of an indi- **B79.18**
vidual in the event of—

(a) the death of that individual;

(b) the bankruptcy of that individual; or

(c) that individual becoming a patient under Part VII of the Mental Health Act 1983.

(2) After the happening of the event mentioned in paragraph (1)(a) the licensing authority may direct that the licence shall not be treated as terminated when the individual died
but suspended until the date when a direction under paragraph (3) comes into force.

(3) After the happening of any of the events mentioned in paragraph (1) the licensing
authority may direct that a person carrying on the business of the operator is to be treated
for the purposes of the 1998 Act as if he were the operator for such purpose and to such
extent as is specified in the direction for a period not exceeding—

(a) six months from the date of the coming into force of that direction; or

(b) if less, the remainder of the period of the licence.

20. Transitional provisions

(1) Subject to paragraph (2), where an application is received by the licensing authority **B79.19**
before 22nd August 2001 but no determination under regulation 5 has been made in relation to that application before 22nd October 2001, the licensing authority shall—

(a) issue the applicant with a temporary permit, in the terms applied for, to make provision for the invitation or acceptance of, or accept, private hire bookings, or

(b) make a temporary variation of the applicant's licence in the terms applied for,
which shall have effect from the latter date as if it were a licence granted or, as the
case may be, variation made under the 1998 Act.

(2) Any temporary permit issued or variation made under paragraph (1) shall, unless the
permit or, as the case may be, the licence to which the variation applies, has already been
suspended or revoked under the 1998 Act, cease to have effect for the purposes of that
Act—

(a) on the grant or variation of a licence pursuant to the outstanding application; or

(b) where no such licence is granted or varied, on the expiry of the period of 28 days
commencing on the date specified in paragraph (3).

(3) The date referred to in paragraph (2)(b) is—

(a) the date of service of the notice given in accordance with regulation 5 of a decision in relation to the outstanding application; or

(b) where an appeal is brought against that decision, the date of disposal or withdrawal of that appeal.

The Motor Vehicles (Approval) Regulations 2001

(S.I. 2001 No. 25)

ARRANGEMENT OF REGULATIONS

PART I

GENERAL

PART II

APPROVAL REQUIREMENTS FOR RELEVANT VEHICLES

PART III

MISCELLANEOUS

SCHEDULES

PART I

GENERAL

1. Citation and commencement   *[Omitted.]*   **B80.02**

2. Revocation   *[Omitted.]*   **B80.03**

3. Interpretation

(1) In these Regulations, unless the context otherwise requires—   **B80.04**

"*the 1970 Directive*" means Council Directive 70/156/EEC of 6th February 1970 on the approximation of the laws of the member states relating to the type-approval of motor vehicles and their trailers [*O.J. No. 142, February 23, 1970, p.1*] as last amended by Directive 98/14/EC of 25th March 1998 [*O.J. No. L91, March 25, 1998, p.1*];

"*the 1982 Regulations*" means the Motor Vehicles (Type Approval for Goods Vehicles) (Great Britain) Regulations 1982 [*S.I. 1982 No. 1271, q.v.*];

"*the 1984 Regulations*" means the Motor Vehicles (Type Approval) (Great Britain) Regulations 1984 [*S.I. 1984 No. 981, q.v.*];

"*the 1988 Act*" means the Road Traffic Act 1988 [*q.v.*];

"*ambulance*", "*armoured vehicle*", "*hearse*" and "*motor caravan*" have the meanings given by paragraph 1 of Schedule 2;

"*approval requirements*", in relation to a vehicle, means the requirements prescribed by section 54 of the 1988 Act as they apply to that vehicle and which are set out in regulation 5(1);

"*axle weight*", "*gross weight*", "*kerbside weight*", "*maximum gross weight*" and "*maximum permitted axle weight*" have the meanings given in regulation 3(2) of the Construction and Use Regulations;

"*the Construction and Use Regulations*" means the Road Vehicles (Construction and Use) Regulations 1986 [*S.I. 1986 No. 1078, q.v.*];

"*design gross weight*" means the weight which the vehicle is designed or adapted not to exceed when in normal use and travelling on a road laden;

"*EEA State*" means a State which is a contracting party to the Agreement on the European Economic Area signed at Oporto on 2nd May 1992 as adjusted by the Protocol signed at Brussels on 17th March 1993 [*Cm. 2972 and Cm. 2183*];

"*family of types*" has the meaning as in Annex XII of the 1970 Directive;

"*goods vehicle*" means a vehicle of a kind specified in regulation 4(1)(b);

"*kg*" means kilograms;

"*kph*" means kilometres per hour;

"*the Lighting Regulations*" means the Road Vehicles Lighting Regulations 1989 [*S.I. 1989 No. 1796, q.v.*];

"*mm*" means millimetres;

"*mph*" means miles per hour;

"*registered*" means registered under the Vehicle Excise and Regulation Act 1994 [*q.v.*];

"*relevant vehicle*" has the meaning given in regulation 4(3);

"*Schedule 2 vehicle*" has the meaning given in Schedule 2;

"*subject matter*" means a subject matter in relation to which approval requirements are specified in Schedule 3 or 4 and "*applicable subject matter*" in relation to a vehicle means a subject matter as respects which approval requirements are applicable to the vehicle in accordance with these Regulations;

"*wheel*" has the meaning given in regulation 3(2) of the Construction and Use Regulations.

(2) References to vehicles of categories M1, M2, M3, N1, N2 and N3 are to vehicles of those categories as defined in Annex II.A of the 1970 Directive.

(3) A reference in any provision of these Regulations to a prescribed fee is a reference to the fee (if any) for the time being prescribed for the purposes of that provision in regulations made under section 61 of the 1988 Act.

(4) Paragraphs (7) and (8) of regulation 3 of the Construction and Use Regulations (determination of the numbers of wheels and axles of a vehicle) shall apply for the purposes of these Regulations other than item 16 of Schedule 3 as they apply for the purposes of the Construction and Use Regulations other than regulations 26 and 27.

(5) For the purposes of these Regulations, a vehicle is to be regarded as being manufactured on or after a particular date if it is first assembled on or after the date, even if it includes one or more parts which were manufactured before that date.

(6) Schedule 6 of these Regulations—

(a) defines expressions relating to Community instruments and ECE Regulations (including references to complying with provisions of such instruments); and

(b) sets out details of Community instruments and ECE Regulations referred to in these Regulations.

B80.05   *[As to the EEA states, see further the note to Regulation (EEC) 3820/85 below.]*

PART II

APPROVAL REQUIREMENTS FOR RELEVANT VEHICLES

4. Application of Regulations

B80.06   (1) These Regulations apply to every motor vehicle—

(a) to which the 1984 Regulations apply; or

(b) to which the 1982 Regulations apply and which either has a design gross weight not exceeding 3,500 kg or complies with the requirements specified in paragraph (2).

(2) The requirements referred to in paragraph (1)(b) are that the vehicle in question—

(a) has a design gross weight exceeding 3,500 kg but not exceeding 5,500 kg;

(b) has a kerbside weight not exceeding 3,425 kg; and

(c) belongs to the same family of types as at least one vehicle to which these Regulations apply by virtue of paragraph (1) and which has been granted a Minister's approval certificate on the basis that it complies with the approval requirements by virtue of these Regulations or the Motor Vehicle (Approval) Regulations 1996 [*S.I. 1996 No. 3013; revoked by these regulations*].

(3) In these Regulations, "*relevant vehicle*" means a vehicle to which these Regulations apply.

5. Approval requirements for relevant vehicles

B80.07   (1) Subject to the following provisions of this regulation, the following are prescribed under section 54 of the 1988 Act as requirements as to the design, construction, equipment and marking of relevant vehicles—

(a) in the case of any relevant vehicle, compliance with the requirements set out in column 3 of the Table in Schedule 3; and

(b) in the case of any relevant vehicle which is not a Schedule 2 vehicle, and in relation to each item in the Table in Schedule 4 for which is specified in column 3(a) of that Table a date which is, or falls before, the date of manufacture of the vehicle, compliance with the requirements of the Community instruments set out in column 3(b) of that Table in relation to that item, or with any equivalent requirement of the ECE Regulations set out in column 3(c) of that Table.

(2) Subject to paragraph (3), the requirements of paragraph (1)(b) shall not apply to a relevant vehicle until 1st August 2001.

(3) Where, in the case of any relevant vehicle which is of category M1 and to which the requirements of paragraph (1)(b) would not otherwise apply, a person making an application in accordance with regulation 6 requests the Secretary of State in writing at the time of making the application that the provisions of paragraph (1)(b) be applied for the purposes of the application, those provisions shall so apply.

(4) The items in Schedule 3 numbered 1, 3, 6, 7, 8, 9, 10, 11, 14, 15, 16 and 19 and the items in Schedule 4 numbered 3, 8, 10, 11, 26, 27 and 28 shall not apply to goods vehicles.

(5) The requirements set out or referred to in column 3 of the Tables in Schedules 3 and 4 have effect subject to the exceptions and modifications set out in column 5 of those Tables.

(6) An entry in column 4 of an item in the Table in Schedules 3 and 4 shall have effect for the purposes of interpreting or otherwise supplementing the entries in that item and, for convenience, expressions that are defined in that column are printed in bold type.

(7) Where a provision of any Community instrument or ECE Regulation is applied by Schedule 4, that provision as so applied shall (except in so far as the contrary intention appears) have effect in relation to—

(a) a vehicle to which the 1984 Regulations apply as it has effect in relation to a vehicle of category M1; and

(b) a vehicle to which the 1982 Regulations apply as it has effect in relation to a vehicle of category N1.

(8) A relevant vehicle shall be regarded as complying with all the requirements prescribed under section 54 of the 1988 Act if at least one of the following three conditions are satisfied in relation to each applicable subject matter mentioned in Schedule 3 or 4—

(a) that the vehicle complies with the requirements set out in paragraph (1);

(b) that requirements applicable to the vehicle are prescribed by regulation 4 of the 1984 Regulations or by regulation 4 of the 1982 Regulations in relation to the subject matter and the vehicle complies with those requirements;

(c) that there is produced to the Secretary of State evidence that satisfies him that the vehicle has been found by a competent authority in another EEA State to comply with requirements applicable to the vehicle equivalent to those prescribed in relation to the subject matter.

(9) For the purposes of paragraph (8)(b), the requirement prescribed by regulation 4 of the 1984 Regulation in relation to the subject mentioned in item 6 of column 2 of the Table in Schedule 3 to these Regulations (lamps, reflectors and devices) shall be regarded as the requirements prescribed in relation to—

(a) installation of lighting and signalling equipment;

(b) direction indicators;

    (c) headlamps and filament lamps;

    (d) side, rear and stop lamps;

    (e) rear reflectors; and

    (f) rear fog lamps.

(10) For the purposes of paragraph (8), regulation 4(1A) of the 1984 Regulations shall have effect as if—

    (a) for sub-paragraph (a), there were substituted—

        "(a) an entry in column (6) of Part I of Schedule 1 shall not apply to the vehicle if the vehicle was manufactured before the date specified or having effect as if specified in that entry;"; and

    (b) the words after sub-paragraph (b) were omitted.

(11) For the purposes of paragraph (8), regulation 4(2A) of the 1982 Regulations shall have effect as if—

    (a) for sub-paragraph (a), there were substituted—

        "(a) an entry in column (6) of Part I of Schedule 1 shall not apply to the vehicle if the vehicle was manufactured before the date specified or having effect as if specified in that entry;"; and

    (b) the words after sub-paragraph (b) were omitted.

(12) If a relevant vehicle complies with all the requirements prescribed by—

    (a) regulation 4 of the 1984 Regulations (disregarding paragraph (9)); or

    (b) regulation 4 of the 1982 Regulations (disregarding paragraph (10)),

that are applicable to it, the requirements prescribed by this regulation shall not apply to it.

PART III

MISCELLANEOUS

B80.08   **6. Application for Minister's approval certificate**   *[Omitted.]*

        7. Assignment of vehicle identification numbers   *[Omitted.]*

B80.09   **8. Criteria for determining design weights**   *[Omitted.]*

        9. Appeals   *[Omitted.]*

B80.10   **10. Refusal of application or appeal without an examination or a complete examination**   *[Omitted.]*

        11. Form of certificate   *[Omitted.]*

B80.11   **12. Replacement certificates**   *[Omitted.]*

        13. Notices   *[Omitted.]*

B80.12   **14. Obligatory certificates**

(1) Subject to paragraph (2) below, this regulation applies to all relevant vehicles.

(2) This regulation does not apply—

(a) to any ambulance or a motor caravan;

(b) to any registered vehicle;

(c) to a vehicle more than 10 years after the time when it was manufactured; or

(d) to a vehicle that meets the requirements specified in paragraph (3).

(3) The requirements referred to in paragraph (2)(d) are that—

(a) the person by whom the vehicle is kept ("*the keeper*") is a member of a visiting force or of a member of the civilian component of a visiting force;

(b) the vehicle has been imported into the United Kingdom for the personal use of the keeper or of his dependants;

(c) there is not in force with respect to the vehicle—

  (i) a Minister's approval certificate issued in pursuance of these Regulations;
  (ii) a certificate of conformity;
  (iii) a Minister's approval certificate in a form prescribed by regulation 14 of the 1982 Regulations or regulation 9 of the 1984 Regulations, or
  (iv) an EC certificate of conformity; and

(d) not more than one other vehicle which meets the requirements of sub-paragraphs (a), (b) and (c) is kept in the United Kingdom by the keeper.

(4) In paragraph (3) the expressions "*member of a visiting force*" and "*member of a civilian component of a visiting force*" shall bear the same meanings as in Part I of the Visiting Forces Act 1952 [*not reproduced in this work*].

(5) The day appointed for the purposes of section 63(1) of the 1988 Act in relation to every vehicle—

(a) to which this regulation applies; but

(b) which is not of a class for which a day had previously been appointed for those purposes,

is 1st February 2001.

(6) Without prejudice to any other Regulations having effect by virtue of section 63(1) of the 1988 Act, all vehicles to which this regulation applies are vehicles of a prescribed class for the purposes of that section.

(7) The type approval requirements prescribed for the purposes of section 63(1) of the 1988 Act, in relation to every vehicle to which this regulation applies, are the approval requirements.

(8) Section 63(1) of the 1988 Act shall not apply to the use of a relevant vehicle—

(a) for the purpose of submitting it (by previous arrangement for a specified time on a specified date) before it is registered for an examination pursuant to an application under these Regulations;

(b) for the purpose of bringing it away, before it is registered, from such an examination;

(c) by an authorised person for the purpose of—

  (i) taking it to, or bringing it away from, a place where a part of such an examination is to be, or has been, carried out, or
  (ii) carrying out a part of such an examination, or
  (iii) warming up its engine in preparation for such an examination, before it is registered;

(d) where an application under regulation 6 is refused following such an examination, for the purpose of—

(i) delivering it (by previous arrangement for a specified time on a specified date) at a place where relevant work is to be done on it, or

(ii) bringing it away from a place where relevant work has been done on it, before it is registered.

(9) In this regulation—

"*authorised person*" means an examiner appointed under 66A of the 1988 Act or a person carrying out such an examination under the direction of such an examiner;

"*relevant work*" means work done or to be done to remedy the defects on the grounds of which the application was refused (including work to alter the vehicle in some aspect of design, construction, equipment or marking on account of which the certificate was refused).

B80.13   **15. Licences not to be issued for vehicles unless appropriate certificates are in force**   *[Omitted.]*

SCHEDULES

SCHEDULE 1

B80.14   *[Revocations]*

Regulation 3(1)   SCHEDULE 2

SCHEDULE 2 VEHICLES

B80.15   **1. Meaning of "Schedule 2 vehicle"**

A Schedule 2 vehicle is a relevant vehicle which is—

(a) a left hand drive vehicle;

(b) a personally imported vehicle;

(c) an amateur built vehicle;

(d) a vehicle manufactured in very low volume;

(e) a vehicle manufactured using parts of a registered vehicle;

(f) a disabled person's vehicle;

(g) a rebuilt vehicle;

(h) a motor caravan as defined in Annex II.A of the 1970 Directive;

(i) an ambulance as defined in Annex II.A of the 1970 Directive;

(j) a hearse as defined in Annex II.A of the 1970 Directive; or

(k) an armoured vehicle as defined in Annex II.A of the 1970 Directive.

2. Personally imported vehicles

B80.16   (1) A vehicle is a personally imported vehicle if—

(a) it has been imported by a person entering the United Kingdom;

(b) that person had, at the time the vehicle was imported, been normally resident in a country other than the United Kingdom for a continuous period of at least 12 months;

(c) that person intends to become normally resident in the United Kingdom;

(d) the vehicle has been in the possession of that person and used by him in the country where he has been normally resident for a period of at least 6 months before its importation; and

(e) the vehicle is intended for his personal or household use in the United Kingdom.

(2) For the purposes of this paragraph a person shall be treated as being normally resident in the country where he usually lives—

(a) for a period of, or periods together amounting to, at least 185 days in a period of 12 months;

(b) because of his occupational ties; and

(c) because of his personal ties.

(3) In the case of a person with no occupational ties, sub-paragraph (2) shall apply with the omission of paragraph (b), provided that his personal ties show close links with that country.

(4) Where a person has his occupational ties in one country and his personal ties in another country, he will be treated, for the purposes of this paragraph, as being normally resident in that latter country provided that either—

(a) his stay in the former country is in order to carry out a task of a definite duration, or

(b) he returns regularly to the country where he has his personal ties.

(5) Notwithstanding paragraph (4), a United Kingdom citizen whose personal ties are in the United Kingdom but whose occupational ties are in a country other than the United Kingdom shall be treated for the purpose of this paragraph as normally resident in the country of his occupational ties, provided that he has lived there for a period of, or periods together amounting to, at least 185 days in a period of 12 months.

3. Amateur built vehicles

(1) A vehicle is an amateur built vehicle if— **B80.17**

(a) the vehicle was constructed or assembled for the personal use of a relevant individual; and

(b) the construction or assembly or a substantial part of the construction or assembly was carried out by—

(i) the individual referred to in paragraph (a),

(ii) one or more relevant individuals acting on his behalf and under his direction, or

(iii) the individual referred to in paragraph (a) and one or more relevant individuals acting on his behalf and under his direction.

(2) For the purposes of this paragraph, a reference to a relevant individual, in relation to a motor vehicle, is a reference to an individual who did not, at any time during the period when the construction or assembly of the vehicle was being carried out, carry on a business in the course of which motor vehicles are normally constructed or assembled.

4. Vehicles manufactured in very low volume

(1) A vehicle is a vehicle manufactured in very low volume if the condition specified in either paragraph (2) or paragraph (3) is complied with. **B80.18**

(2) The condition specified in this paragraph is that the total number of vehicles of the family of types to which the vehicle in question belongs which are manufactured in the

world for any period of 12 months falling within the period of 36 months immediately preceding the month in which the vehicle was manufactured does not exceed 200.

(3) The condition specified in this paragraph is that the number of vehicles of the type variant to which the vehicle in question belongs which are manufactured in the world for any period of 12 months falling within the period of 36 months immediately preceding the month in which the vehicle was manufactured does not exceed 20.

(4) For the purposes of sub-paragraph (3), a type variant consists exclusively of vehicles which do not differ in at least the following essential respects—

    (a) the manufacturer;

    (b) essential aspects of construction and design, that is to say in:

        (i) obvious and fundamental differences in the chassis, floor pan or other parts of the vehicle's structure, or

        (ii) the power plant (whether internal combustion, electric or hybrid);

    (c) body style (by way of example, saloon, hatchback, coupe, cabriolet or estate);

    (d) the following further characteristics of the power plant:

        (i) its working principle (whether positive ignition or compression ignition, and whether four stroke or two stroke),

        (ii) the number and arrangement of its cylinders,

        (iii) differences in maximum power of more than 30% (the highest is more than 1.3 times the lowest), or

        (iv) engine capacity differences of more than 20% (the highest is more than 1.2 times the lowest);

    (e) number, position or interconnection of the powered axles; or

    (f) number or position of the steered axles.

5. Vehicles manufactured using parts of a registered vehicle

B80.19   A vehicle is a vehicle manufactured using parts of a registered vehicle if—

    (a) it is constructed or assembled by a person carrying on a business in the course of which motor vehicles are normally constructed or assembled;

    (b) it is equipped with an engine which has previously been used as the engine of another vehicle which had been registered under the Vehicle Excise and Registration Act 1994 or any earlier Act relating to the registration of mechanically propelled vehicles; and

    (c) it is equipped with one or more of the following components taken from the same vehicle as the engine—

        (i) chassis;

        (ii) body;

        (iii) suspension;

        (iv) an axle;

        (v) transmission; or

        (vi) steering assembly.

6. Disabled person's vehicle

B80.20   (1) A vehicle is a disabled person's vehicle if it is adapted or specially constructed so as to enable a person who has a disability to travel in the vehicle, whether as the driver or a passenger, in safety and reasonable comfort.

(2) In sub-paragraph (1), "*disability*" has the meaning given by section 1 of the Disability Discrimination Act 1995 [*not reproduced in this work*].

7. Rebuilt vehicles

A vehicle is a rebuilt vehicle if it—　　　　　　　　　　　　**B80.21**

(a) is a vehicle to which the Secretary of State is required by regulation 7 to assign a vehicle identification number;

(b) does not fall within either of the classes defined by paragraphs 3 or 5; and

(c) has been rebuilt using a replacement chassis, or an integral chassis body, which is of the same design and construction as that of the original vehicle and which—

(i) was supplied for the purpose without having been previously used, or

(ii) previously formed part of a registered vehicle.

SCHEDULE 3

[Approval requirements for relevant vehicles.]　　　　**B80.22**

SCHEDULE 4

[Approval requirements for relevant vehicles except Schedule 2 vehicles.]　　　　**B80.23**

SCHEDULE 5

[Form of approval certificate.]　　　　**B80.24**

SCHEDULE 6　　　　Regulation 3(6)

COMMUNITY INSTRUMENTS AND ECE REGULATIONS

PART I

1. References to Community Instruments

(1) The Directives referred to in these Regulations are set out in Part II of this Schedule;　　**B80.25** those marked with an asterisk are Commission Directives, those marked with a cross are Directives of the European Parliament and the Council and the other Directives are Council Directives.

(2) A reference in these Regulations to a Directive shown in column 2 of Part II of this Schedule as last amended by a Directive shown in column 3 against that Directive shall be read as follows.

(3) The reference shall be read as a reference to the Directive shown in column 2 as amended by the Directives shown in column 3 against that Directive down as far as (and including) the Directive referred to as the last amending Directive.

2.—(1) For the purposes of these Regulations, where a vehicle does not comply with an　　**B80.26** item in Schedule 3 or 4 of these Regulations, it shall nevertheless be regarded as complying with that item if—

(a) that item contains a reference to a Directive (*"the base Directive"*) not followed by the words *"as last amended by"*; and

(b) the vehicle would comply with that item were there substituted for that reference, a reference to the base Directive as last amended by a Directive shown against the base Directive in column 3 of Part II of this Schedule.

(2) For the purposes of these Regulations, where a vehicle does not comply with an item in Schedule 3 or 4 of these Regulations, it shall nevertheless be regarded as complying with that item if—

(a) that item contains a reference to a Directive ("*the base Directive*") as last amended by another Directive ("*the amending Directive*"); and

(b) the vehicle would comply with that item were there substituted for that reference, a reference to the base Directive as last amended by a Directive shown—

(i) against the base Directive, and

(ii) below the amending Directive in column 3 of Part II of this Schedule.

3. References to ECE Regulations

B80.27   (1) A reference in these Regulations to an ECE Regulation followed by a number which is not itself followed by a full-stop and 2 digits (for example "ECE Regulation 30") shall be read as a reference to the ECE Regulation of that number which came into force on the date shown against that number in column (4) of Part III of this Schedule.

(2) A reference in these Regulations to an ECE Regulation followed by a number which is itself followed by a full-stop and 2 digits (for example "ECE Regulation 30.01") shall be read as a reference to the ECE Regulation of that number with the amendments in force on the dates shown against the number in column (4) of Part III of this Schedule.

B80.28   **4.**—(1) For the purposes of these Regulations, where a vehicle does not comply with an item in Schedule 3 or 4 of these Regulations, it shall nevertheless be regarded as complying with that item if—

(a) that item contains a reference to an ECE Regulation ("*the base Regulation*") that is not followed by a full-stop and 2 digits; and

(b) the vehicle would comply with that item were there substituted for that reference, a reference to an entry in column (3) of Part III of this Schedule shown against that Regulation.

(2) For the purposes of these Regulations, where a vehicle does not comply with an item in Schedule 3 or 4 of these Regulations, it shall nevertheless be regarded as complying with that item if—

(a) that item contains a reference to an ECE Regulation ("*the base Regulation*") that is followed by a full-stop and 2 digits; and

(b) the vehicle would comply with that item were there substituted for that reference, a reference to an entry in column 3 of Part III of this Schedule shown—

(i) against that Regulation, and

(ii) below the entry in that column for that ECE Regulation and those 2 digits.

B80.29   **5.** In these Regulations, "*ECE Regulation*" means a Regulation annexed to the Agreement concerning the adoption of uniform conditions of approval for motor vehicle equipment and parts and reciprocal recognition thereof concluded at Geneva on 20th March 1958 [*Cmnd. 2535*] as amended [*Cmnd. 3562*] to which the United Kingdom is a party [*instrument of accession deposited on January 15, 1963*].

PART II

REFERENCES TO COMMUNITY DIRECTIVES

References in Schedule 3   **B80.30**

(1) Subject matter of Directive	(2) Principal Directive	(3) Amending Directive	(4) Official Journal reference
Radio interference suppression	72/245/EEC		L152, 6.7.72, p. 15
		89/491/EEC*	L238, 15.8.89, p. 43
		95/54/EC	L226, 8.11.95, p. 1
Protective steering	74/297/EEC		L165, 20.6.74, p. 16
		91/662/EEC*	L366, 31.12.91, p. 1
Diesel smoke	72/306/EEC		L190, 20.8.72, p. 1
		97/20/EC*	L125, 16.5.97, p. 21
Roadworthiness	77/143/EEC		L47, 18.2.77, p. 47
		88/449/EEC	L222, 12.8.88, p. 10
		91/225/EEC	L103, 24.4.91, p. 3
		91/328/EEC	L178, 6.7.91, p. 29
		92/55/EEC	L225, 10.8.92, p. 68
Rear view mirrors	71/127/EEC		L68, 22.3.71, p. 1
		79/795/EEC*	L239, 22.9.79, p. 1
		85/205/EEC*	L90, 29.3.85, p. 1
		86/562/EEC*	L327, 02.11.86, p. 49
		88/321/EEC*	L147, 14.6.88, p. 77
Seat belt anchorages	76/115/EEC		L24, 30.1.76, p. 6
		81/575/EEC	L209, 29.7.81, p. 30
		82/318/EEC*	L139, 19.5.82, p. 9
		90/629/EEC*	L341, 6.12.90, p. 14
		96/38/EC*	L187, 26.7.96, p. 95
Seat belts	77/541/EEC		L220, 29.8.77, p. 95
		81/576/EEC	L209, 29.7.81, p. 32
		82/319/EEC*	L139, 19.5.82, p. 17
		90/628/EEC*	L341, 6.12.90, p. 1
		96/36/EC*	L178, 17.7.96, p. 15
Braking	71/320/EEC*		L202, 6.9.71, p. 37
		74/132/EEC*	L74, 19.3.74, p. 7
		75/524/EEC*	L236, 8.9.75, p. 3
		79/489/EEC*	L128, 26.5.79, p. 12
		85/647/EEC*	L38, 31.12.85, p. 1
		88/194/EEC*	L92, 9.4.88, p. 47
		91/422/EEC*	L233, 22.9.91, p. 21
		98/12/EC*	L81, 18.3.98, p. 1
Braking of 2/3 wheeled vehicles	93/14/EEC		L121, 15.5.93, p. 1
Seat strength	74/408/EEC		L221, 12.8.74, p. 1
		81/577/EEC	L209, 29.7.81, p. 34
		96/37/EC*	L187, 25.7.96, p. 28
Tyres	92/23/EEC		L129, 14.5.92, p. 95
Interior fittings	74/60/EEC		L38, 11.2.74, p. 2
		78/632/EEC*	L206, 29.7.68, p. 26

[continued on next page

(1) *Subject matter of Directive*	(2) *Principal Directive*	(3) *Amending Directive*	(4) *Official Journal reference*
Forward vision	77/649/EEC		L267, 19.10.77, p. 1
		81/643/EEC*	L231, 15.8.81, p. 41
		88/366/EEC*	L181, 12.7.88, p. 40
		90/630/EEC*	L341, 6.12.90, p. 20
External projections	74/483/EEC		L266, 2.10.74, p. 4
		79/488/EEC*	L128, 26.5.79, p. 1
Masses and dimensions	9/21/EEC		L129, 14.5.92, p. 1
		95/48/EEC*	L233, 30.9.95, p. 73

B80.31   References in Schedule 4

(1) *Subject matter of Directive*	(2) *Principal Directive*	(3) *Amending Directive*	(4) *Official Journal reference*
Protective steering	74/297/EEC		L165, 20.6.74, p. 16
		91/662/EEC*	L366, 31.12.91, p. 1
Exhaust emissions	70/220/EEC		L76, 6.4.70, p. 1
		91/441/EEC	L242, 30.8.91, p. 1
		93/59/EEC	L186, 28.7.93, p. 21
		94/12/EC[+]	L100, 19.4.94, p. 42
		96/69/EC[+]	L282, 1.11.96, p. 64
		98/77/EC[+]	L286, 23.10.98, p. 34
		98/69/EC[+]	L350, 28.12.98, p. 1
Anti-theft devices	74/61/EEC		L38, 11.2.70, p. 22
		95/56/EC*	L286, 29.11.95, p. 1
Seat belt anchorages	76/115/EEC		L24, 30.1.76, p. 1
		82/318/EEC*	L139, 19.5.82, p. 9
		90/629/EEC*	L341, 6.12.90, p. 14
		96/38/EC*	L187, 26.7.96, p. 95
Seat belts	77/541/EEC		L220, 29.8.77, p. 45
		90/628/EEC	L341, 6.12.90, p. 1
		96/36/EC*	L178, 17.7.90, p. 15
Braking	71/320/EEC		L202, 6.9.71, p. 37
		91/422/EEC*	L238, 27.8.91, p. 25
		98/12/EC*	L81, 18.3.98, p. 1
Noise and silencers	70/157/EEC		L42, 23.2.70, p. 16
		84/424/EEC	L238, 6.9.84, p. 31
		92/97/EEC	L371, 19.12.92, p. 1
Carbon dioxide emissions and fuel consumption	80/1268/EEC		L375, 31.12.80, p. 46
		93/116/EC*	L329, 30.12.93, p. 39
Frontal impact	96/79/EC[+]		L18, 21.1.97, p. 7
Side impact	96/27/EC[+]		L169, 8.7.96, p. 1

PART III

REFERENCES TO ECE REGULATIONS

References in Schedule 3

(1) Subject matter of Regulation	(2) ECE Regulation	(3) Amending Series	(4) Date
Radio interference suppression	10		17 Dec 1968
		10.01	23 June 1978
		10.02	3 Sept 1997
Rear reflectors	3		1 Nov 1963
		3.01	18 Aug 1982
		3.02	11 July 1985
Rear view mirrors	46		29 Sept 1975
		46.01	5 Oct 1987
Tyres	30		1 April 1975
		30.01	10 Oct 1977
		30.02	21 April 1981

References in Schedule 4

(1) Subject matter of Regulation	(2) ECE Regulation	(3) Amending Series	(4) Date
Protective steering	12		1 June 1969
		12.01	8 Oct 1980
		12.02	14 Nov 1982
		12.03	24 Aug 1993
Exhaust emissions	83		5 Nov 1989
		83.01	30 Dec 1992
		83.02	7 Dec 1996
		83.04	13 Nov 1999
Anti-theft devices	18		1 March 1971
		18.02	3 Sept 1997
Alarm systems	97		1 Jan 1996
		97.01	13 Jan 2000
Seat belt anchorages	14		1 April 1970
		14.02	22 Nov 1984
		14.03	29 Jan 1992
		14.04	18 Jan 1998
		14.05	4 Feb 1999
Seat belts	16		1 Dec 1970
		16.04	22 Dec 1985
Braking	13		1 June 1970
		13.06	22 Nov 1990
		13.07	18 Sep 1994
		13.08	26 March 1995
		13.09	28 Aug 1996
		13H	11 May 1998

[*continued on next page*

(1) Subject matter of Regulation	(2) ECE Regulation	(3) Amending Series	(4) Date
Noise and silencers	51		15 July 1982
		51.01	27 April 1988
		51.02	18 April 1995
Carbon dioxide emissions from fuel consumption	101		1 Jan 1997
Frontal impact	94		1 Oct 1995
		94.01	2 Aug 1998
Side impact	95		6 July 1995
		95.01	12 Aug 1998

The Road Vehicles (Display of Registration Marks) Regulations 2001

(S.I. 2001 No. 561)

[The text of these regulations is printed as amended by:

B81.01

the Road Vehicles (Display of Registration Marks) (Amendment) Regulations 2001 (S.I. 2001 No. 1079) (September 1, 2001).

The amending regulations are referred to in the notes to the principal regulations only by their year and number. The date referred to above is the date on which the amending regulations came into force. (The amending regulations are stated to come into force, for the purposes of their own commencement provisions and for regulation 17 of the principal regulations (to which they do not refer), on March 21, 2001.)

ARRANGEMENT OF REGULATIONS

PART I

PRELIMINARY

PART II

REGISTRATION PLATES

PART III

REGISTRATION MARKS

PART IV

MISCELLANEOUS

SCHEDULES

PART I

PRELIMINARY

1. Citation, commencement and revocation

B81.03 (1) These Regulations may be cited as the Road Vehicles (Display of Registration Marks) Regulations 2001 and shall come into force—

(a) for the purposes of this paragraph and regulation 17, on 21st March 2001, and

(b) for all other purposes, on 1st September 2001.

(2) The regulations specified in Schedule 1 are hereby revoked.

2. Interpretation: general

B81.04 (1) In these Regulations the following expressions shall have the following meanings—

"*the Act*" means the Vehicle Excise and Registration Act 1994 [*q.v.*];

"*agricultural machine*" means a vehicle which is—

(a) an agricultural tractor, as defined in paragraph 4B(2) of Schedule 1 to the Act [*q.v.*], or

(b) an off-road tractor, as defined in paragraph 4B(4) of that Schedule, or

(c) a light agricultural vehicle, as defined in paragraph 4C(2) of that Schedule, or

(d) an agricultural engine, or

(e) a mowing machine,

"*the Council Regulation*" means Council Regulation (EC) No. 2411/98 [*O.J. No. L299, November 10, 1998, p. 1*] on the recognition in intra-community traffic of the distinguishing signs of member states in which motor vehicles are registered;

"*dual purpose plate*" means a plate or other device which displays both the registration mark of the vehicle and the international distinguishing sign of the United Kingdom in accordance with the Council Regulation;

"*EEA State*" means a state which is a contracting party to the Agreement on the European Economic Area signed at Oporto on 2nd May 1992 as adjusted by the Protocol signed at Brussels on 17th March 1993;

"*motor cycle*" means a vehicle having 2 wheels and includes a vehicle of that description in combination with a sidecar;

"*motor tricycle*" means a vehicle having 3 wheels symmetrically arranged;

"*quadricycle*" means a vehicle having four wheels, a maximum net engine power not exceeding 15 kilowatts and an unladen mass (excluding the mass of batteries in the case of an electrically-powered vehicle) not exceeding—

    (a) 550 kilograms in the case of a goods vehicle, and

    (b) 400 kilograms in any other case;

"*registration plate*" means a plate or other device displaying the registration mark of the vehicle and in the case of a dual purpose plate means such part of the plate as is not intended for the display the international distinguishing sign of the United Kingdom in accordance with the Council Regulation;

"*prescribed font*" means the style shown in Schedule 4 for a character of the height specified in that Schedule;

"*relevant date*" means—

    (a) in Great Britain, 1st October 1938, and

    (b) in Northern Ireland, 1st January 1948;

"*works truck*" means a vehicle which is—

    (a) designed for use in private premises, and

    (b) used on public roads only—

        (i) for carrying goods between private premises and a vehicle on a road in the immediate vicinity, or

        (ii) in passing from one part of private premises to another or between private premises and other private premises in the immediate vicinity, or

        (iii) in connection with road works at or in the immediate vicinity of the site of the works

(2) Unless the context otherwise requires, a reference in these Regulations to—

    (a) a registration plate fixed or to be fixed to a vehicle, or

    (b) a registration mark displayed or to be displayed on a plate,

is to be construed, where the vehicle is towing a trailer, so as to include a reference to the registration plate which is required under these Regulations to be fixed to the trailer or a reference to the mark displayed on the plate fixed to that trailer.

[As to the EEA states, see further the note to Regulation (EEC) 3820/85 below.]　　　　**B81.05**

3. Exempt vehicles

Nothing in these Regulations applies to—　　　　**B81.06**

    (a) an invalid vehicle, that is a vehicle the unladen weight of which does not exceed 254 kilograms and which is specially designed and constructed, and not merely adapted, for the use of a person suffering from a physical disability and solely used by that person; or

(b) a pedestrian-controlled vehicle, that is a vehicle the unladen weight of which does not exceed 450 kilograms which is neither constructed nor adapted for the carriage of a driver or passenger.

PART II

REGISTRATION PLATES

4. Interpretation of Part II

B81.07   In this Part the following expressions shall have the following meanings—

"*diagonal length*", in relation to a relevant area, means the length of a line drawn diagonally across the square enclosing the area (so that the extent of the relevant area is thereby delimited);

"*relevant area*", in relation to a registration plate, means the area contained in a square described on the ground—

(a) in front of the vehicle in the case of a plate fixed on the front of the vehicle, and

(b) behind the vehicle in the case of a plate fixed on the rear of the vehicle,

where one corner of the square is immediately below the middle of the plate and the diagonal of the square from that corner is parallel to the longitudinal axis of the vehicle;

"*relevant type-approval directive*" means—

(a) in the case of a motor cycle, motor tricycle or quadricycle—

(i) Council Directive 93/94/EEC [*O.J. No. L311, December 14, 1993, p. 83*] (as amended by Commission Directive 99/26/EC [*O.J. No. L118, May 6, 1999, p. 32*] as regards the space to be provided for fixing of the rear registration plate, and

(ii) Council Directive 93/92/EEC [*O.J. No. L311, December 14, 1993, p. 1*] as regards the rear registration plate lamp;

(b) in the case of any other vehicle or a trailer—

(i) Council Directive 70/222/EEC [*O.J. No. L75, April 6, 1970, p. 25*] as regards the space to be provided for fixing of the rear registration plate, and

(ii) Council Directive 76/760/EEC [*O.J. No. L262, September 27, 1976, p. 85*] (as amended by Commission Directive 97/31/EC [*O.J. No. L171, June 30, 1997, p. 49*] as regards the rear registration plate lamp.

5. Fixing of rear registration plates: vehicles registered on or after the relevant date

B81.08   (1) This regulation applies to vehicles, other than works trucks, road rollers and agricultural machines, first registered on or after the relevant date.

(2) A registration plate must be fixed on the rear of—

(a) the vehicle, or

(b) where the vehicle is towing a trailer, the trailer, or

(c) where the vehicle is towing more than one trailer, the rearmost trailer.

(3) Where a vehicle (or, in a case where the plate is required to be fixed on a trailer, that trailer) has been constructed so as to satisfy the requirements of the relevant type-approval directive, whether or not it is required by law to satisfy them, the plate may be fixed in the space provided in accordance with those requirements but if it is not so fixed it must be fixed in the manner required by paragraph (5).

(4) Except as provided in paragraph (3) the plate must be fixed in the manner required by paragraph (5).

(5) This paragraph requires the plate to be fixed—

(a) vertically or, where that is not reasonably practicable, in a position as close to the vertical as is reasonably practicable, and

(b) in such a position that in normal daylight the characters of the registration mark are easily distinguishable from every part of a relevant area having the diagonal length specified in paragraph (6).

(6) The diagonal length of the relevant area is—

(a) in the case of a mark having characters the width of which is at least 57 milli-metres, 22 metres,

(b) in the case of a mark having characters the width of which is 50 millimetres, 21.5 metres,

(c) in the case of a mark having characters the width of which is 44 millimetres, 18 metres.

6. Fixing of front registration plates: vehicles registered on or after the relevant date

(1) This regulation applies to vehicles, other than works trucks, road rollers and agricul-tural machines, first registered on or after the relevant date.   **B81.09**

(2) Except as provided in paragraph (5), a registration plate must be fixed on the front of the vehicle in the manner required by paragraph (3).

(3) This paragraph requires the plate to be fixed—

(a) vertically or, where that is not reasonably practicable, in a position as close to the vertical as is reasonably practicable,

(b) in such a position that in normal daylight the characters of the registration mark are easily distinguishable from every part of a relevant area having the diagonal length specified in paragraph (4).

(4) The diagonal length of the relevant area is—

(a) in the case of a mark having characters the width of which is at least 57 milli-metres, 22 metres,

(b) in the case of a mark having characters the width of which is 50 millimetres, 21.5 metres,

(c) in the case of a mark having characters the width of which is 44 millimetres, 18 metres.

(5) In the case of a motor cycle or a motor tricycle which does not have a body of a type which is characteristic of the body of a four-wheeled vehicle—

(a) a registration plate must not be fixed on the front of a vehicle if it was first reg-istered on or after 1st September 2001,

(b) a plate need not be fixed on the front of the vehicle if it was first registered before 1st September 2001.

7. Fixing of registration plates: vehicles registered before the relevant date

(1) This regulation applies to vehicles, other than works trucks, road rollers and agricul-tural machines, first registered before the relevant date.   **B81.10**

(2) Except as provided in paragraph (4), a registration plate must be fixed in the manner required by paragraph (3) on—

(a) the front of the vehicle, and

(b) the rear of—

(i) the vehicle or,

(ii) where the vehicle is towing a trailer, the trailer or,

(iii) where the vehicle is towing more than one trailer, the rearmost trailer.

(3) This paragraph requires each plate to be fixed—

(a) in a vertical position or, where that is not possible, in a position as close to the vertical as is reasonably practicable, and

(b) in such a position that in normal daylight the characters of the registration mark are easily distinguishable, in the case of a plate fixed on the front of the vehicle, from in front of the vehicle and, in the case of a plate fixed on the rear of the vehicle or trailer, from behind the vehicle or trailer.

(4) In the case of a motor cycle and a motor tricycle which does not have a body of a type which is characteristic of the body of a four-wheeled vehicle, a registration plate need not be fixed on the front of the vehicle.

8. Fixing of registration plates: works trucks, road rollers and agricultural machines

B81.11   (1) This regulation applies to works trucks, road rollers and agricultural machines.

(2) A registration plate must be fixed on the vehicle in a vertical position or, where that is not possible, in a position as close to the vertical as is reasonably practicable—

(a) on both sides of the vehicles, so that the characters of the mark are easily distinguishable from both sides of the vehicle, or

(b) on the rear of the vehicle, so that the characters of the mark are easily distinguishable from behind the vehicle, or

(c) where the vehicle is towing a trailer or trailers and the plate is not fixed on the sides of the vehicle, on the trailer or the rearmost trailer (as the case may be) so that the characters of the mark are easily distinguishable from behind the trailer.

(3) Where the towing vehicle is an agricultural machine, a plate fixed on the trailer may, instead of displaying the registration mark of the towing vehicle, display the mark of any other agricultural machine kept by the keeper of the towing vehicle.

9. Lighting of rear registration plates

B81.12   (1) This regulation applies to vehicles other than—

(a) works trucks,

(b) road rollers,

(c) agricultural machines, and

(d) vehicles first registered before the relevant date.

(2) Where the vehicle is being used on a road between sunset and sunrise the registration plate fixed on the rear of—

(a) the vehicle, or

(b) where the vehicle is towing a trailer, the trailer or,

(c) where the vehicle is towing more than one trailer, the rearmost trailer, must be lit in accordance with this regulation.

(3) Where a vehicle (or, in a case where the plate is required to be fixed on a trailer, that trailer) has been constructed so as to satisfy the requirements of the relevant type-approval directive, whether or not it is required by law to satisfy them, that plate may be lit by a lamp which complies with those requirements but if it is not so lit it must be lit in the manner required by paragraph (5).

(4) Except as provided in paragraph (3) that plate must be lit in the manner required by paragraph (5).

(5) This paragraph requires the plate to be lit so that it is easily distinguishable from every part of a relevant area having a diagonal length

(a) in the case of a plate displaying a mark having characters with a width of 44 millimetres, of 15 metres, and

(b) in any other case, of 18 metres.

10. Specifications for registration plates

(1) A registration mark must be displayed on a registration plate conforming to the requirements prescribed by this regulation.   **B81.13**

(2) In the case of a vehicle first registered on or after 1st September 2001 the registration plate must conform to the requirements set out in Part 1 of Schedule 2.

(3) Subject to paragraph (4), in the case of a vehicle first registered on or after 1st January 1973 but before 1st September 2001 the registration plate must conform either to the requirements set out in Part 2 of Schedule 2 or to the requirements set out in Part 1 of that Schedule.

(4) Where on or after 1st September 2001 a new registration plate is fixed to a vehicle to which paragraph (3) applies to replace a plate previously fixed thereto, the plate must conform to the requirements set out in Part 1 of Schedule 2.

(5) In the case of a vehicle first registered before 1st January 1973, the registration plate must conform either to one of the requirements set out in Part 3 of Schedule 2 or to the requirements set out in Part 2 of that Schedule or to the requirements set out in Part 1 of that Schedule.

(6) The corners of a registration plate may be rounded off provided that the requirements of regulation 14(9) (margins around registration marks) are not thereby infringed.

11. Further requirements for registration plates

(1) No reflex-reflecting material may be applied to any part of a registration plate and the plate must not be treated in such a way that the characters of the registration mark become, or are caused to act as, retroreflective characters.   **B81.14**

(2) A registration plate must not be treated in any other way which renders the characters of the registration mark less easily distinguishable to the eye or which would prevent or impair the making of a true photographic image of the plate through the medium of camera and film or any other device.

(3) A registration plate must not be fixed to a vehicle—

(a) by means of a screw, bolt or other fixing device of any type or colour,

(b) by the placing of a screw, bolt or other fixing device in any position, or

(c) in any other manner,

which has the effect of changing the appearance or legibility of any of the characters of the registration mark, which renders the characters of the registration mark less easily distinguishable to the eye or which prevents or impairs the making of a true photographic image of the plate through the medium of camera and film or any other device.

(4) Section 59(2)(a) of the Act (regulations the contravention of which attracts a level 3 fine) applies to paragraphs (1), (2) and (3) of this regulation.

PART III

REGISTRATION MARKS

12. Interpretation of Part III

B81.15
(1) In this Part and in Schedule 3, the following expressions shall have the following meanings—

(a) "*diagram*" means a diagram shown in Part 2 of Schedule 3 and a reference to a numbered diagram is a reference to the diagram identified by that number in that part of that Schedule,

(b) "*Table A*" means the table in Part 1 of Schedule 3,

(c) "*Table B*" means the table in Part 3 of Schedule 3,

(d) a reference to "*relevant character height*" is a reference to the height of the characters in the registration mark shown at the head of column (2), (3) or (4) of Table B as the case may be.

(2) Any provision as to measurement contained in this Part or in Schedule 3 shall be taken to be complied with—

(a) in the case of a provision prescribing character height, if the height of the character is not more than 1 millimetre more or less than the measurement prescribed herein, and

(b) in the case of a provision prescribing any other dimension, if the dimension of the character or the space in question is not more than 0.5 millimetres more or less than the measurement prescribed herein.

(3) For the purpose of any provision contained in this Part or in Schedule 3 as to the spacing between characters or between groups of characters or as to the width of a margin the measurement shall be made—

(a) in the case of a horizontal spacing requirement, between vertical lines passing through the extreme edges of each character or group of characters or between a vertical line passing through the extreme edge of a character and the lateral edge of the plate (as the case may be), and

(b) in the case of a vertical spacing requirement, between horizontal lines passing through the extreme edges of each group of characters or between a horizontal line passing through the extreme edge of a group of characters and the top or bottom edge of the plate (as the case may be).

13. Layout of marks

B81.16
(1) Subject to paragraphs (2) and (3), a registration mark of a description specified in column (1) of Table A must be laid out on the registration plate in conformity with one of the diagrams specified in relation to that description in column (2) of Table A.

(2) A mark displayed on a motor cycle may not be laid out in conformity with diagram 1a, 2a, 3a, 4a, 5a, 6a, 7a, 8a or 9a.

(3) A mark may not be laid out in conformity with diagram 2c, 3c, 4b or 7b if it is displayed on—

   (a) a registration plate fixed to a vehicle first registered on or after 1st September 2001, or

   (b) a new registration plate fixed to a vehicle on or after 1st September 2001 to replace a plate previously fixed thereto (except where the vehicle was first registered before 1st January 1973).

14. Size and spacing of characters

(1) Except in the cases mentioned in paragraphs (2) and (3), each character in a registration mark must be 79 millimetres high.   **B81.17**

(2) In the case of a registration mark displayed on a vehicle first registered before 1st September 2001, a character in a registration mark may be 89 millimetres high unless—

   (a) the vehicle was first registered on or after 1st January 1973 and the mark is displayed on a new registration plate fixed to the vehicle to replace a plate previously fixed thereto, or

   (b) the vehicle is a motor cycle, motor tricycle, quadricycle, agricultural machine, works truck or road roller.

(3) In the case of a registration mark fixed on a motor cycle, motor tricycle, quadricycle, agricultural machine, works truck or road roller, each character of the mark may be 64 millimetres high.

(4) The width of each character of a mark other than the letter "I" and the figure "1" must be—

   (a) in the case of a mark displayed—

      (i) on a registration plate fixed to a vehicle first registered on or after 1st September 2001, or

      (ii) on a new registration plate fixed to a vehicle on or after 1st September 2001 to replace a plate previously fixed thereto (except where the vehicle was first registered before 1st January 1973),

that shown in line 1 of Table B in relation to the relevant character height,

   (b) in any other case, that shown in line 2 of Table B in relation to the relevant character height.

(5) The width of every part of the stroke forming a character in a mark must be that shown in line 3 of Table B in relation to the relevant character height.

(6) Except in a case to which paragraph (11) applies, the spacing between any two characters within a group must be that shown in line 4 of Table B in relation to the relevant character height.

(7) The horizontal spacing between groups of characters in a mark must be that shown in line 5 of Table B in relation to the relevant character height.

(8) The vertical spacing between groups of characters must be shown in line 6 of Table B in relation to the relevant character height.

(9) The width of a margin between the mark and the top, bottom and lateral edges of the registration plate must be not less than that shown in line 7 of Table B in relation to the relevant character height.

(10) Paragraph (11) applies where—

(a) one or both of the characters is "I" or "1",

(b) those characters are either 79 millimetres or 89 millimetres high,

(c) the mark is displayed on a vehicle first registered before 1st September 2001,

(d) the registration plate displaying the mark was fixed to the vehicle before 1st September 2001 or, if that is not the case, the vehicle was first registered before 1st January 1973 and,

(e) the plate is made of cast or pressed metal with raised characters.

(11) Where this paragraph applies the spacing between—

[(a)] two characters one of which is "I" or "1" must be within the limits shown in line 8 of Table 8 in relation to the relevant character height, and

[(b)] two characters both of which are "I" or "1" must be within the limits shown in line 9 of Table B in relation to the relevant character height,

but where one or more characters in a group is "I" or "1" all the characters within that group must be evenly spaced.

B81.18   [*Regulation 14 is printed as amended by S.I. 2001 No. 1079.*]

15. Style of characters

B81.19   (1) In the case of a registration mark displayed—

(a) on a registration plate fixed to a vehicle first registered on or after 1st September 2001, or

(b) on a new registration plate fixed to a vehicle on or after 1st September 2001 to replace a plate previously fixed thereto (except where the vehicle was first registered before 1st January 1973),

each of the characters of the mark must be in the prescribed font.

(2) Except in a case to which paragraph (1) applies, each of the characters of the registration mark must either be in the prescribed font or in a style which is substantially similar to the prescribed font so that the character is easily distinguishable and in particular, but without prejudice to the generality of those requirements, characters must not be formed in any way described in paragraph (4) or in a manner which is similar to any of those ways.

(3) For the purposes of paragraph (2), a character shall not be treated as being in a style which is not substantially similar to the prescribed font merely by virtue of the fact that it has, or does not have, serifs.

(4) The ways of forming characters referred to in paragraph (2) are their formation—

(a) in italic script,

(b) using a font, other than italic script, in which the characters are not vertical,

(c) using a font in which the curvature or alignment of the lines of the stroke is substantially different from the prescribed font,

(d) using multiple strokes,

(e) using a broken stroke,

(f) in such a way as to make a character or more than one character appear like a different character or characters.

PART IV

MISCELLANEOUS

16. International distinguishing signs and other material

(1) No material other than a registration mark may be displayed on a registration plate except material complying with the requirements of any of the relevant standards mentioned in Schedule 2.   **B81.20**

(2) Where a mark is displayed on a dual purpose plate—

(a) no material other than the international distinguishing sign of the United Kingdom displayed in accordance with the Council [Regulation] may be placed in the space provided on the plate for that purpose;

(b) no part of the international distinguishing sign must encroach beyond the extreme left of the registration mark (that is to say the outside edge of the margin prescribed by these Regulations).

(3) Unless it forms part of a dual purpose plate a registration plate may not be combined with a plate or device of any kind containing material which would not be permitted to be displayed on a dual purpose plate.

[Regulation 16 is printed as amended by S.I. 2001 No. 1079.]   **B81.21**

17. Optional early use of new-specification plates and prescribed font

(1) This regulation applies in a case where, on or after 21st March and before 1st September 2001 a registration mark on a vehicle—   **B81.22**

(a) is displayed on a registration plate which conforms to the specification set out in Part 1 of Schedule 2 and is otherwise fixed on the vehicle and lit in accordance with the requirements of Part II of these Regulations,

(b) conforms to the requirements of regulations 13 and 14 as to layout and spacing of characters in so far as they apply to vehicles first registered on or after 1st September 2001, and

(c) is comprised of characters each of which is in the prescribed font.

(2) Where this regulation applies—

(a) regulations 17 to 22 of the Road Vehicles (Registration and Licensing) Regulations 1971 [*S.I. 1971 No. 450, as amended*] or, as the case may be,

(b) regulations 18 to 23 of the Road Vehicles (Registration and Licensing) Regulations (Northern Ireland) 1973 [*S.R.&O. (N.I.) 1973 No. 490, as amended*],

(which provide for the format and means of display of registration plates and marks) shall cease to apply in respect of that vehicle and any trailer being towed by it and the provisions of these Regulations shall apply instead.

18. Saving for vehicles constructed before 1st January 1973

For the purposes of these Regulations a vehicle which was first registered on or after 1st January 1973 shall be treated as if it was first registered before that date if—   **B81.23**

(a) it is an exempt vehicle for the purposes of paragraph 1A(1) of Schedule 2 to the Act, or

(b) not being such a vehicle, it was constructed before 1st January 1973.

19. Offences under section 59 of the Act

B81.24   (1) For the purposes of section 59(1) of the Act (regulations: offences), the person responsible for complying with these Regulations is the person driving the vehicle or, where it is not being driven, the person keeping it.

(2) Paragraph (1) does not apply to a regulation the breach of which would constitute an offence under section 42(1) of the Act (not fixing a registration mark as required by virtue of section 23).

SCHEDULE 1

REGULATIONS REVOKED

B81.25

Title of Regulations	Number	Extent of revocation
The Road Vehicles (Registration and Licensing) Regulations 1971	1971/450	Regulations 17 to 22 and Schedules 2 and 3.
The Road Vehicles (Registration and Licensing) (Amendment) Regulations 1972	1972/1865	Regulation 6.
The Road Vehicles (Registration and Licensing) Regulations (Northern Ireland) 1973	S.R. & O. (N.I.) 1973 No. 490	Regulations 18 to 23 and Schedule 2 and 3.
The Road Vehicles (Registration and Licensing) (Amendment) Regulations 1975	1975/1089	The whole instrument.
The Road Vehicles (Registration and Licensing) (Amendment) (No. 2) Regulations (Northern Ireland) 1976	1976/2180	Regulations 2(6), (8) and (9).
The Road Vehicles (Registration and Licensing) (Amendment) Regulations 1984	1984/814	The whole instrument.

SCHEDULE 2

REQUIREMENTS FOR REGISTRATION PLATES

PART I

VEHICLES REGISTERED AND NEW REGISTRATION PLATES FITTED ON OR AFTER 1ST SEPTEMBER 2001 (MANDATORY SPECIFICATION)

B81.26   **1.** The plate must be made of retroreflecting material which, as regards its construction, colour and other qualities, complies with the requirements of—

(a) the British Standard specification for retroreflecting number plates published on 15 January 1998 under number BS AU 145d [*ISBN 0 580 28985 0*], or

(b) any other relevant standard or specification recognised for use in an EEA State and which, when in use, offers a performance equivalent to that offered by a plate complying with the British Standard specification,

and which, in either case, is marked with the number (or such other information as is necessary to permit identification) of that standard or specification.

2. Where the registration mark is displayed on the front of the vehicle, it must have black characters on a white background.   **B81.27**

3. Where the registration mark is displayed on the back of the vehicle, it must have black characters on a yellow background.   **B81.28**

PART 2

VEHICLES REGISTERED ON OR AFTER 1ST JANUARY 1973 AND BEFORE 1ST SEPTEMBER 2001 (OPTIONAL SPECIFICATION)

1. The plate must be made of reflex-reflecting material which, as regards its construction, colour and other qualities, complies with the requirements of—   **B81.29**

   (a) the British Standard Specification for reflex-reflecting number plates, published on 11 September 1972 under the number BS AU 145a [*ISBN 0 580 07327 0*], or

   (b) any other relevant standard or specification recognised for use in an EEA State and which, when in use, offers a performance equivalent to that offered by a plate complying with the British Standard specification,

and which, in either case, is marked with the number (or such other information as is necessary to permit identification) of that standard or specification.

2. Where the registration mark is displayed on the front of the vehicle, it must have black characters on a white background.   **B81.30**

3. Where the registration mark is displayed on the back of the vehicle, it must have black characters on a yellow background.   **B81.31**

PART 3

VEHICLES REGISTERED BEFORE 1ST JANUARY 1973 (OPTIONAL SPECIFICATIONS)

A. Requirements where the vehicle carries a registration plate which is constructed so that the mark may be illuminated from behind by virtue of the translucency of its characters

1. The registration mark must be formed of white translucent characters on a black background on the surface of that plate.   **B81.32**

2. When the registration mark is illuminated during the hours of darkness, the characters on that plate must appear white against a black background.

B. Requirements where the vehicle carries a registration plate which is not so constructed

Either of the following is permitted—

1. A plate made of reflex-reflecting material complying with the requirements of the British Standard Specification for reflex-reflecting number plates published on 31 October 1967 under the number BS AU 145 [*revised in 1972 to BS AU 145a*] and which displays black characters on a white background where it is fixed on the front of the vehicle and black characters on a yellow background where it fixed on the rear of the vehicle.   **B81.33**

2. A plate displaying white, silver or light grey letters and numbers on a black surface having every character indelibly inscribed on the surface or so attached to the surface that it cannot readily be detached from it, which may either—

   (a) be made of cast or pressed metal with raised characters, or

(b) consist of a plate to which separate characters are attached, or

(c) consist of a plastic plate having either reverse engraved characters or characters of a foil type, or

(d) consist of an unbroken rectangular area on the surface of the vehicle which is either flat or, if there is no flat area where the mark is required to be displayed, an area which is almost flat.

Regulations 12, 13 and 14 — SCHEDULE 3

LAYOUT OF REGISTRATION MARKS

PART 1

TABLE A

PERMITTED LAYOUTS FOR REGISTRATION MARKS

B81.34

(1) *Description of mark*	(2) *Permitted layouts*
1. A group consisting of two letters and two numbers followed by a group of 3 letters (for example DE51 ABC).	Diagrams 1a and 1b.
2. A group consisting of a single letter and not more than 3 numbers followed by a group of 3 letters (for example A123 ABC).	Diagrams 2a, 2b and 2c.
3. A group of 3 letters followed by a group consisting of not more than 3 numbers and a single letter (for example ABC 123A).	Diagrams 3a, 3b and 3c.
4. A group of 4 numbers followed by a single letter or a group of 2 letters (for example 1234 AB, 1234 A).	Diagrams 4a and 4b.
5. A group of not more than 3 numbers followed by a group of not more than 3 letters (for example 123 ABC, 123 AB, 12 A).	Diagrams 5a and 5b.
6. A group of not more than 3 letters followed by a group of not more than 3 numbers (for example ABC 123, AB 123, A 12).	Diagrams 6a and 6b.
7. A single letter or group of 2 letters followed by a group of 4 numbers (for example AB 1234, A 1234).	Diagrams 7a and 7b.
8. A group of 3 letters followed by a group of 4 numbers (for example ABZ 1234, being a form of mark issued only in Northern Ireland).	Diagrams 8a and 8b.
9. A group of 4 numbers followed by a group of 3 letters (for example 1234 ABZ, being a form of mark issued only in Northern Ireland).	Diagrams 9a and 9b.

PART 2

DIAGRAMS SHOWING PERMITTED LAYOUTS   **B81.35**

Diagram 1a

Diagram 1b

Diagram 2a

Diagram 2b

Diagram 2c

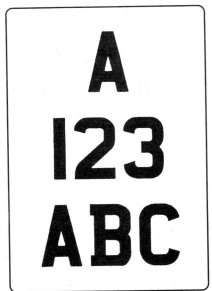

Diagram 3a

Diagram 3b

Diagram 3c

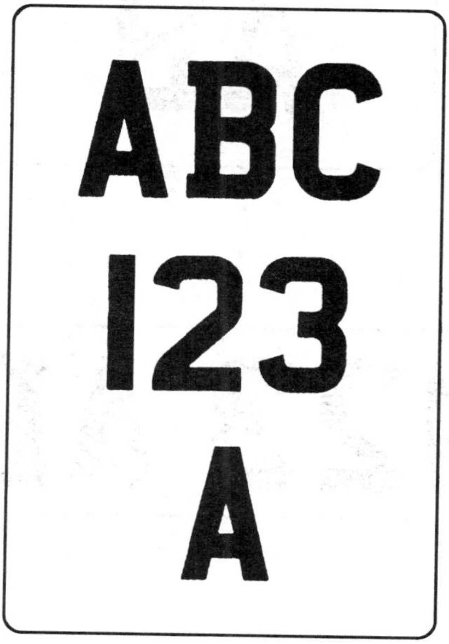

Diagram 4a

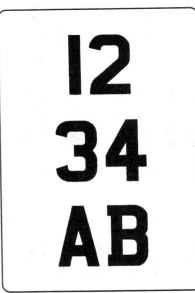

Diagram 4b

Diagram 5a

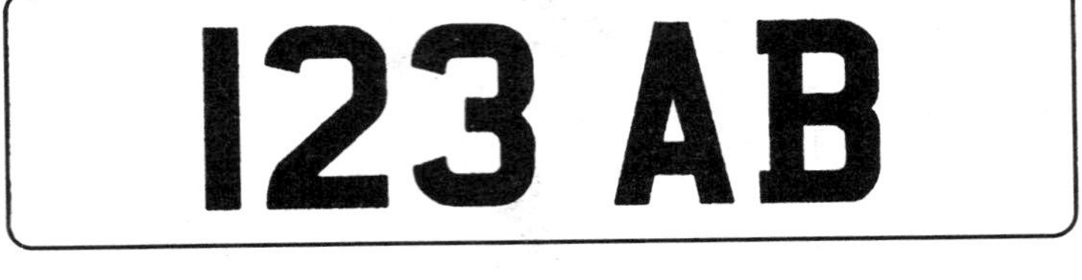

Diagram 5b

Diagram 6a

AB 123

Diagram 6b

AB
123

Diagram 7a

AB 1234

Diagram 7b

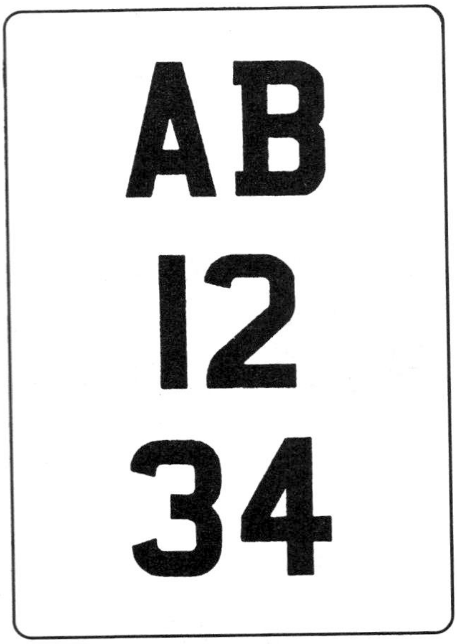

AB 12 34

Diagram 8a

ABZ 1234

Diagram 8b

ABZ
1234

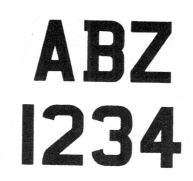

Diagram 9a

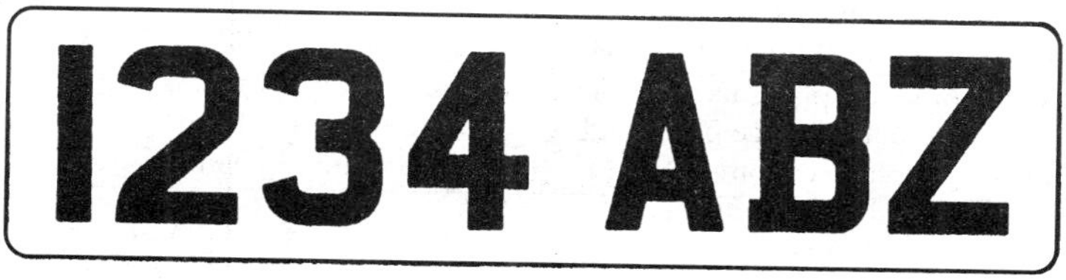
1234 ABZ

Diagram 9b

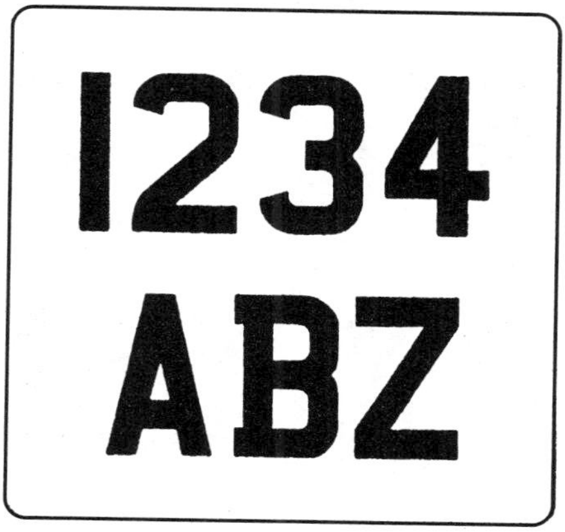
1234
ABZ

PART 3

Table B

STROKE AND CHARACTER WIDTH, SPACING AND MARGINS

B81.36

(1) *Relevant dimension*	*Relevant character height:*		
	(2) 89 mm.	(3) 79 mm.	(4) 64 mm.
1. Character width (all new registration plates from 1.9.01 except replacement of "classic" plates)	—	50 mm.	44 mm.
2. Character width (other registration plates)	64 mm.	57 mm.	44 mm.
3. Stroke width	16 mm.	14 mm.	10 mm.
4. Space between two characters within group: general rule	13 mm.	11 mm.	10 mm.
5. Horizontal space between groups	38 mm.	33 mm.	30 mm.
6. Vertical space between groups	19 mm.	19 mm.	13 mm.
7. Minimum margin	13 mm.	11 mm.	11 mm.
8. Pressed/embossed plates fixed before 1.9.01 and "classic" plates: space permitted between "I" or "1" and another character	13 to 37 mm.	11 to 33 mm.	—
9. Pressed/embossed plates fixed before 1.9.01 and "classic" plates: space permitted between characters if both "I" or "1"	13 to 60 mm.	11 to 54 mm.	—

SCHEDULE 4

PRESCRIBED FONT

PART 1

FONT DESCRIBED FOR CHARACTERS 79 MILLIMETRES IN HEIGHT   **B81.37**

123456789
ABCDEFGHJ
KLMNOPQRS
TUVYZWX

PART 2

FONT PRESCRIBED FOR CHARACTERS 64 MILLIMETRES IN HEIGHT

123456789
ABCDEFGH
JKLMNOPQ
RSTUVWXYZ

Section C

European Union Legislation

European Union Legislation

Citation of provisions of the EC Treaty. Following the renumbering of the provisions of the EC Treaty and the EU Treaty by article 12 of and the Annex to the Treaty of Amsterdam (O.J. No. C340, November 10, 1997, pp. 78 and 86–91) references in the notes in this volume to articles in the EC Treaty as so renumbered are (in accordance with the practice of the European Court of Justice) in the form "article 71 EC", whereas any reference to an article as numbered before the Treaty of Amsterdam took effect is in the form "article 75 of the EC Treaty" or "EC Treaty, art. 75". No editorial change in the style of citation has been incorporated into the texts of legislation. The Treaty of Amsterdam entered into force in accordance with *ibid.*, art.14(2), on May 1, 1999 (see the information at O. J. No. C120, May 1, 1999, p. 24).

The texts in this section are reproduced from the *Official Journal of the European Communities* published by the Office for Official Publications of the European Communities.

Council Directive 70/156/EEC
of February 6, 1970

on the approximation of the laws of the Member States relating to the type approval of motor vehicles and their trailers

Editorial note. The only part of this Directive which is reproduced below is Annex II which sets out the international classification of motor vehicles (formerly set out in a note to Annex I (model information document)) which is incorporated by reference into other texts, *e.g.* regulation 3(2) of the Road Vehicles (Construction and Use) Regulations 1986 (S.I. 1986 No. 1078) (*q.v.*).

C1.01

*   *   *

[ANNEX II

DEFINITION OF VEHICLE CATEGORIES AND VEHICLE TYPES

A. Vehicle categories are defined according to the following international classification: C1.02

1.   Category M: Motor Vehicles with at least four wheels used for the carriage of passengers.

      Category M_1:   Vehicles used for the carriage of passengers and comprising no more than eight seats in addition to the driver's seat.

      Category M_2:   Vehicles used for the carriage of passengers, comprising more than eight seats in addition to the driver's seat, and having a maximum mass not exceeding 5 tonnes.

      Category M_3:   Vehicles used for the carriage of passengers, comprising more than eight seats in addition to the driver's seat, and having a maximum mass exceeding 5 tonnes.

2.   Category N: Motor vehicles with at least four wheels used for the carriage of goods.

      Category N_1:   Vehicles used for the carriage of goods and having a maximum mass not exceeding 3.5 tonnes.

      Category N_2:   Vehicles used for the carriage of goods and having a maximum mass exceeding 3.5 tonnes but not exceeding 12 tonnes.

      Category N_3:   Vehicles used for the carriage of goods and having a maximum mass exceeding 12 tonnes.

In the case of a towing vehicle designed to be coupled to a semi-trailer or centre-axle trailer, the mass to be considered for classifying the vehicle is the mass of the tractor vehicle in running order, increased by the mass corresponding to the maximum static vertical load transferred to the tractor vehicle by the semi-trailer or centre-axle trailer and, where applicable, by the maximum mass of the tractor vehicle's own load.

3.   Category O: Trailers (including semi-trailers).   C1.03

      Category O_1:   Trailers with a maximum mass not exceeding 0.75 tonnes.

      Category O_2:   Trailers with a maximum mass exceeding 0.75 tonnes but not exceeding 3.5 tonnes.

      Category O_3:   Trailers with a maximum mass exceeding 3.5 tonnes but not exceeding 10 tonnes.

      Category O_4:   Trailers with a maximum mass exceeding 10 tonnes.

In the case of a semi-trailer or centre-axle trailer, the maximum mass to be considered for classifying the trailer corresponds to the static vertical load transmitted to the ground by the axle or axles of the semi-trailer or centre-axle trailer when coupled to the towing vehicle and carrying its maximum load.

4.   Vehicles in categories M and N, above, considered to be off-road vehicles under the load and checking conditions set out in item 4.4. and pursuant to the definitions and sketches of item 4.5.

C1.04

4.1.   Vehicles in category N_1 with a maximum mass not exceeding two tonnes and motor vehicles in category M_1 are considered to be off-road vehicles if they have:
— at least one front axle and at least one rear axle designed to be driven simultaneously including vehicles where the drive to one axle can be disengaged,
— at least one differential locking mechanism or at least one mechanism having a similar effect and if they can climb a 30% gradient calculated for a solo vehicle.

In addition, they must satisfy at least five of the following six requirements:
— the approach angle must be at least 25 degrees,
— the departure angle must be at least 20 degrees,
— the ramp angle must be at least 20 degrees
— the ground clearance under the front axle must be at least 180mm,
— the ground clearance under the rear axle must be at least 180mm,
— the ground clearance between the axles must be at least 200mm.

4.2.   Vehicles in category N_1 with a maximum mass exceeding two tonnes or in category N_2, M_2 or M_3 with a maximum mass not exceeding 12 tonnes are considered to be off-road vehicles either if all their wheels are designed to be driven simultaneously, including vehicles where the drive to one axle can be disengaged, or if the following three requirements are satisfied:
— at least one front axle and at least one rear axle are designed to be driven simultaneously, including vehicles where the drive to one axle can be disengaged,
— there is at least one differential locking mechanism or at least one mechanism having a similar effect,
— they can climb a 25% gradient calculated for a solo vehicle.

C1.05

4.3.   Vehicles in category M_3 with a maximum mass exceeding 12 tonnes or in category N_3 are to be considered to be off-road vehicles either if the wheels are designed to be driven simultaneously, including vehicles where the drive to one axle can be disengaged, or if the following requirements are satisfied:
— at least half the wheels are driven,
—there is at least one differential locking mechanism or at least one mechanism having a similar effect,
— they can climb a 25% gradient calculated for a solo vehicle,
— at least four of the following six requirements are satisfied:
— the approach angle must be at least 25 degrees,
— the departure angle must be at least 25 degrees,
— the ramp angle must be at least 25 degrees,
— the ground clearance under the front axle must be at least 250mm,
— the ground clearance between the axles must be at least 300mm,
— the ground clearance under the rear axle must be least 250mm.

4.4.   Load and checking conditions.

4.4.1 Vehicles in category N_1 with a maximum mass not exceeding two tonnes and   **C1.06**
vehicles in category M_1 must be in running order, namely with coolant fluid,
lubricants, fuel, tools, spare-wheel and a driver considered to weigh a standard
75 kilograms.

4.4.2. Motor vehicles other than those referred to in 4.4.1. must be loaded to the technically permissible maximum mass stated by the manufacturer.

4.4.3. The ability to climb the required gradients (25% and 30%) is verified by simple
calculation. In exceptional cases, however, the technical services may ask for a
vehicle of the type concerned to be submitted to it for an actual test.

4.4.4. When measuring approach and departure angles and ramp angles, no account is   **C1.07**
taken of underrun protective devices.

4.5. Definitions and sketches of approach and departure angles, ramp angle and
ground clearance.

4.5.1. *"Approach angle"* means the maximum angle between the ground plane and
planes tangential to the tyres of the front wheels, under a static load, such that
no point of the vehicle ahead of the front axle is situated below these planes and
no rigid part of the vehicle, with the exception of any steps, is situated below
these planes.

4.5.2. *"Departure angle"* means the maximum angle between the ground plane and   **C1.08**
planes tangential to the tyres of the rear wheels, under a static load, such that no
point of the vehicle behind the rearmost axle is situated below these planes and
no rigid part of the vehicle is situated below these planes.

4.5.3. *"Ramp angle"* means the minimum angle between two planes, perpendicular to
the median longitudinal plane of the vehicle, tangential to the tyres of the
front wheels and to the tyres of the rear wheels respectively, under a static load,
the intersection of which touches the rigid underside of the vehicle apart from
the wheels. This angle defines the steepest ramp over which the vehicle can
pass.

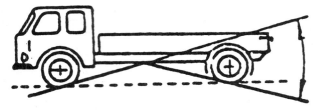

4.5.4. *"Ground clearance between the axles"* means the shortest distance between the ground plane and the lowest fixed point of the vehicle.
Multi-axled bogies are considered to be a single axle.

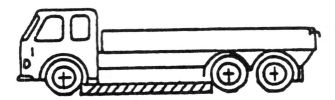

4.5.5. *"Ground clearance beneath one axle"* means the distance beneath the highest point of the arc of a circle passing through the centre of the tyre footprint of the wheels on one axle (the inner wheels in the case of twin tyres) and touching the lowest fixed point of the vehicle between the wheels.
No rigid part of the vehicle may project into the shaded area of the diagram. Where appropriate, the ground clearance of several axles is indicated in accordance with their arrangement, for example 280/250/250.

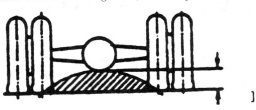

B. DEFINITION OF VEHICLE TYPE

1.   For the purposes of category M_1:
A *"type"* shall consist of vehicles which do not differ in at least the following essential respects:
— the manufacturer,
— the manufacturer's type designation,
— essential aspects of construction and design:
    — chassis/floor pan (obvious and fundamental differences),
    — power plant (internal combustion/electric/hybrid).
"Variant" of a type means vehicles within a type which do not differ in at least the following essential respects:
— body style (e.g. saloon, hatchback, coupe, cabriolet, wagon, etc.),
— power plant:

— working principle (as in item 3.2.1.1 of Annex III),
— number and arrangement of cylinders,
— power differences of more than 30% (the highest is more than 1.3 times the lowest),
— capacity differences of more than 20% (the highest is more than 1.2 times the lowest),
— powered axles (number, position, interconnection),
— steered axles (number and position).

"*Version*" of a variant means vehicles which consist of permitted combinations of items shown in the information package in accordance with Annex III and Annex VIII.

Full identification of the vehicle just from the designations of type, variant and version must be consistent with a single accurate definition of all the technical characteristics required for the vehicle to be put into service, and particularly the parameter(s) necessary for determining the taxes applicable to the vehicle. These parameters will be established in the relevant Annexes which cover the information to be provided for type-approval purposes.]

[Annex II is printed as substituted by Directive 92/53/EEC.]   **C1.11**

*   *   *

Regulation (EEC) 3820/85
of December 20, 1985

on the harmonisation of certain social legislation
relating to road transport

C2.01   *European Economic Area.* The Agreement on the European Economic Area was signed at Oporto on May 2, 1992 and entered into force on January 1, 1994. The agreement was originally signed by the EFTA countries (Austria, Finland, Iceland, Liechtenstein, Norway, Sweden and Switzerland) and the EC Member States at that date (Belgium, Denmark, France, Germany, Greece, Ireland, Italy, Luxembourg, the Netherlands, Portugal, Spain and the United Kingdom) (O.J. No. L1, January 3, 1994, p. 3). However, the agreement was not ratified by Switzerland and in consequence a protocol adjusting the original agreement was signed by the remaining states (*op. cit.*, p. 572). Following Switzerland's withdrawal from the original agreement, the position of Liechtenstein was for a time uncertain. Subsequently (on January 1, 1995), Austria, Finland and Sweden became members of the European Union. For practical purposes, it seems that the European Economic Area in effect now means the territory of the European Union (within which area Community law applies) plus Iceland, Norway and (from May 1, 1995; see Decision 1/95 of the EEA Council, O.J. No. L86, April 20, 1995, p. 58) Liechtenstein. The agreement expressly adapts a number of provisions of Community law but does so expressly "for the purposes of the agreement". The agreement has itself been amended on a number of occasions since it came into operation. In view of the limited application of adaptations effected by the agreement, they are not expressly incorporated into this work.

    For the purposes of the agreement, Regulation (EEC) 3820/85 has been adapted by Annex XIII, Chapter II, paragraph 20, as amended.

THE COUNCIL OF THE EUROPEAN COMMUNITIES,

C2.02   Having regard to the Treaty establishing the European Economic Community, and in particular [Article 71] thereof;

Having regard to the Council Decision of 13 May 1965 on the harmonisation of certain provisions affecting competition in transport by rail, road and inland waterway [*O.J. No. 88, May 24, 1965, p. 1500/65*], and in particular Section III thereof,

Having regard to the proposal from the Commission [*O.J. No. C100, April 12, 1984, p. 3, O.J. No. C223, September 3, 1985, p. 5*],

Having regard to the opinion of the European Parliament [*O.J. No. C122, May 20, 1985, p. 168*],

Having regard to the opinion of the Economic and Social Committee [*O.J. No. C104, April 25, 1985, p. 4, O.J. No. C303, November 25, 1985, p. 29*],

Whereas in the field of road transport, Community social legislation is set out in Regulation (EEC) No. 543/69 [*O.J. No. L77, March 29, 1969, p. 49*] as last amended by Regulation (EEC) No. 2829/77 [*O.J. No. L334, December 24, 1977, p. 1*]; whereas that legislation aims at the harmonisation of conditions of competition between methods of inland transport, especially with regard to the road sector and the improvement of working conditions and road safety; whereas progress made in these fields must be safeguarded and extended; whereas, however, it is necessary to make the provisions of the said Regulation more flexible without undermining their objectives;

Whereas, taking into account the amendments set out hereinafter, in order to clarify matters, all the relevant provisions should be brought together in a single text, and in consequence thereof, Regulation (EEC) No. 543/69 should be repealed; whereas, however, the exemptions set out in Article 4 for certain vehicles and the provisions of Article 15 for certain passenger transport operations should be maintained in force for a certain time;

Whereas the provisions of this Regulation dealing with working conditions cannot be allowed to prejudice the right of the two sides of industry to lay down, by collective bargaining or otherwise, provisions more favourable to workers; whereas, in order not only to promote social progress but also to improve road safety, each Member State must retain the right to adopt certain appropriate measures;

Whereas in view of the fall in the number of drivers' mates and conductors it is no longer necessary to regulate the rest periods of crew members other than the driver;

Whereas the replacement of the flexible week by a fixed week would make it easier for drivers to organize their work and improve checking;

Whereas a system should be defined to apply to international road transport operations to or from a third country or between two countries in transit through the territory of a Member State; whereas the provisions of the European Agreement concerning the Work of Crews of Vehicles engaged in International Road Transport (AETR) [*q.v.*] of 1 July 1970 should apply to those transport operations; whereas in the case of vehicles registered in a State which is not a Contracting Party to AETR, those provisions will only apply to that part of the journey effected within the Community;

Whereas, since the subject matter of the AETR Agreement falls within the scope of this Regulation, the power to negotiate and conclude the Agreement lies with the Community; whereas, however, the particular circumstances in which the AETR negotiations took place warrant, by way of exception, a procedure whereby the Member States of the Community individually deposit the instruments of ratification or accession in a concerted action but nonetheless act in the interest and on behalf of the Community;

Whereas, in order to ensure the supremacy of Community law in intra-Community transport, Member States should enter a reservation when depositing their instruments of ratification or accession whereby international transport operations between Member States are not to be regarded as international transport operations within the meaning of the Agreement;

Whereas the possibilities provided for in the Agreement itself for bilateral agreements between Contracting Parties derogating from the said Agreement as regards frontier zone and transit transport operations are a matter which in principle fall within the competence of the Community;

Whereas, if an amendment to the internal Community rules in the field in question necessitates a corresponding agreement to the Agreement, the Member States will act jointly to obtain such an amendment to the Agreement in accordance with the procedure laid down therein;

Whereas certain transport operations may be exempted from the application of this Regulation;

Whereas it is desirable to amplify and clarify certain definitions and to bring up to date certain provisions, in particular concerning the exceptions for certain categories of vehicles;

Whereas it is desirable to lay down provisions concerning the minimum ages for drivers engaged in the carriage of goods or of passengers—bearing in mind here certain vocational training requirements—and concerning also the minimum age for drivers' mates and conductors; whereas for the purposes of vocational training, Member States must be able to reduce the approved minimum age for drivers' mates to 16 years;

Whereas, with regard to driving periods, it is desirable to set limits on continuous driving time and on daily driving time, but without prejudice to any national rules whereby drivers are prohibited from driving for longer than they can with complete safety;

Whereas a longer driving day, together with a shorter driving time over a two-week period is likely to facilitate the management of transport undertakings and to contribute to social progress;

Whereas the provisions on breaks in driving should be adjusted because of the longer daily driving time;

Whereas, with regard to rest periods, it is desirable to lay down the minimum duration of and other conditions governing the daily and weekly rest periods of crew members;

Whereas trips would be made easier if the driver were able to split up his daily rest period, in particular to avoid his having to take a meal and lodging in the same place;

Whereas it is beneficial to social progress and to road safety to lengthen weekly rest periods, while enabling these periods to be shortened, provided that the driver can compensate for parts of his rest period which have not been taken in a place of his choosing within a given time;

Whereas many road transport operations within the Community involve transport by ferry-boat or by rail for part of the journey; whereas provisions regarding daily rest periods and breaks which are appropriate to such operations should therefore be provided for in the rules;

Whereas, in the interests of road safety, the payment of bonuses for distance travelled and/or tonnage carried which might endanger road safety must be prohibited;

Whereas it is desirable to provide that exceptions may be made from this Regulation for certain national transport operations with special characteristics; whereas in the event of exceptions Member States should ensure that the standard of social protection and road safety is not jeopardised;

Whereas it is justified, given the specific nature of passenger transport, to redefine the category of vehicles that the Member States may exempt from application of the Regulation in the field of national transport;

Whereas the Member States should be entitled, with the Commission's authorisation, to grant exceptions from the provisions of the Regulation in exceptional circumstances; whereas in urgent cases, it should be possible to grant these exceptions for a limited time without prior authorisation from the Commission;

Whereas in the case of drivers of vehicles used for regular passenger services, a copy of the timetable and an extract from the undertaking's duty roster may replace the recording equipment; whereas it would be useful for the application of this Regulation and the prevention of abuse, to have delivered to drivers who so request extracts from their duty rosters;

Whereas it is desirable, in the interest of effective control, that regular international passenger services, with the exception of certain border services should no longer be exempt from the obligation to install and use recording equipment;

Whereas it is desirable to emphasise the importance of and the need for compliance with this Regulation by employers and drivers;

Whereas the Commission should monitor the way the situation with Member States develops and submit to the Council and to the European Parliament a report on the application of the rules every two years;

Whereas, in order that this Regulation may be applied and that compliance therewith may be checked, it is appropriate for Member States to give each other assistance.

[The preamble is printed as amended by the Treaty of Amsterdam, art.12(1) and (3).]   **C2.03**

HAS ADOPTED THIS REGULATION:

SECTION I

DEFINITIONS

Article 1

In this Regulation: **C2.04**

1. *"carriage by road"* means any journey made on roads open to the public of a vehicle, whether laden or not, used for the carriage of passengers or goods;

2. *"vehicles"* means motor vehicles, tractors, trailers and semi-trailers, defined as follows:

   (a) *"motor vehicle"*: any mechanically self-propelled vehicle circulating on the road, other than a vehicle running on rails, and normally used for carrying passengers or goods;

   (b) *"tractor"*: any mechanically self-propelled vehicle circulating on the road, other than a vehicle running on rails, and specially designed to pull, push or move trailers, semi-trailers, implements or machines;

   (c) *"trailer"*: any vehicle designed to be coupled to a motor vehicle or a tractor;

   (d) *"semi-trailer"*: a trailer without a front axle coupled in such a way that a substantial part of its weight and of the weight of its load is borne by the tractor or motor vehicle;

3. *"driver"* means any person who drives the vehicle even for a short period, or who is carried in the vehicle in order to be available for driving if necessary;

4. *"week"* means the period between 00.00 hours on Monday and 24.00 hours on Sunday;

5. *"rest"* means any uninterrupted period of at least one hour during which the driver may freely dispose of his time;

6. *"permissible maximum weight"* means the maximum authorised operating weight of the vehicle fully laden;

7. *"regular passenger services"* means national and international services as defined in Article 1 of Council Regulation No. 117/66/EEC of 28 July 1966 on the introduction of common rules for the international carriage of passengers by coach and bus [*q.v.*].

[As to Regulation (EEC) 117/66, art.1, see Regulation (EEC) 684/92, arts 2 and 21(2) below.]   **C2.05**

SECTION II

SCOPE

Article 2

1. This Regulation applies to carriage by road, as defined in Article 1(1), within the Community.   **C2.06**

2. The European Agreement concerning the Work of Crews of Vehicles engaged in International Road Transport (AETR) [*q.v.*] shall apply instead of the present rules to international road transport operations;

— to and/or from third countries which are Contracting Parties to the Agreement, or in transit through such countries, for the whole of the journey where such operations are carried out by vehicles registered in a Member State or in one of the said third countries;

— to and/or from a third country which is not a Contracting Party to the Agreement in the case of any journey made within the Community where such operations are carried out by vehicles registered in one of those countries.

Article 3

C2.07   The Community shall enter into any negotiations with third countries which may prove necessary for the purpose of implementing this Regulation.

Article 4

C2.08   This Regulation shall not apply to carriage by:

1. vehicles used for the carriage of goods where the maximum permissible weight of the vehicle, including any trailer or semi-trailer, does not exceed 3.5 tonnes;

2. vehicles used for the carriage of passengers which, by virtue of their construction and equipment, are suitable for carrying not more than nine persons, including the driver, and are intended for that purpose;

3. vehicles used for the carriage of passengers on regular services where the route covered by the service in question does not exceed 50 kilometres;

4. vehicles with a maximum authorised speed not exceeding 30 kilometres per hour;

5. vehicles used by or under the control of the armed services, civil defence, fire services, and forces responsible for maintaining public order;

6. vehicles used in connection with the sewerage, flood protection, water, gas and electricity services, highway maintenance and control, refuse collection and disposal, telegraph and telephone services, carriage of postal articles, radio and television broadcasting and the detection of radio or television transmitters or receivers;

7. vehicles used in emergencies or rescue operations;

8. specialised vehicle used for medical purposes;

9. vehicles transporting circus and fun-fair equipment;

10. specialised breakdown vehicles;

11. vehicles undergoing road tests for technical development, repair or maintenance purposes, and new or rebuilt vehicles which have not yet been put into service;

12. vehicles used for non-commercial carriage of goods for personal use;

13. vehicles used for milk collection from farms and the return to farms of milk containers or milk products for animal feed.

SECTION III

CREW

Article 5

C2.09   1. The minimum ages for drivers engaged in the carriage of goods shall be as follows:

(a) for vehicles, including, where appropriate, trailers or semi-trailers, having a permissible maximum weight of not more than 7.5 tonnes, 18 years;

(b) for other vehicles:
  — 21 years, or
  — 18 years provided that the person concerned holds a certificate of profes-
    sional competence recognised by one of the Member States confirming that
    he has completed a training course for drivers of vehicles intended for the
    carriage of goods by road, in conformity with Community rules on the
    minimum level of training for road transport drivers.

2. Any driver engaged in the carriage of passengers shall have reached the age of 21 years.
Any driver engaged in the carriage of passengers on journeys beyond a 50 kilometre
radius from the place where the vehicle is normally based must also fulfil one of the following conditions:

(a) he must have worked for at least one year in the carriage of goods as a driver of
     vehicles with a permissible maximum weight exceeding 3.5 tonnes;

(b) he must have worked for at least one year as a driver of vehicles used to provide
     passenger services on journeys within a 50 kilometre radius from the place where
     the vehicle is normally based, or other types of passenger services not subject to
     this Regulation, provided the competent authority considers that he has by so
     doing acquired the necessary experience;

(c) he must hold a certificate of professional competence recognised by one of the
     Member States confirming that he has completed a training course for drivers
     of vehicles intended for the carriage of passengers by road, in conformity
     with Community rules on the minimum level of training for road transport
     drivers.

3. The minimum age for drivers' mates and conductors shall be 18 years.

4. A driver engaged in the carriage of passengers shall not be subject to the conditions
laid down in paragraph 2, second paragraph, (a), (b) and (c) if he has carried on that
occupation for at least one year prior to 1 October 1970.

5. In the case of internal transport operations carried out within a 50 kilometre radius
of the place where the vehicle is based, including local administrative areas the centres of
which are situated within that radius, Member States may reduce the minimum age for
drivers' mates to 16 years, on condition that this is for purposes of vocational training and
subject to the limits imposed by their national law in employment matters.

SECTION IV

DRIVING PERIODS

Article 6

1. The driving period between any two daily rest periods or between a daily rest period   **C2.10**
and a weekly rest period, hereinafter called "*daily driving period*", shall not exceed nine hours.
It may be extended twice in any one week to 10 hours.
   A driver must, after no more than six daily driving periods, take a weekly rest period as
defined in Article 8(3).
   The weekly rest period may be postponed until the end of the sixth day if the total
driving time over the six days does not exceed the maximum corresponding to six daily
driving periods.
   In the case of the international carriage of passengers, other than on regular services, the
terms "six" and "sixth" in the second and third subparagraphs shall be replaced by
"twelve" and "twelfth" respectively.

Member States may extend the application of the previous subparagraph to national passenger services within their territory, other than regular services.

2. The total period of driving in any one fortnight shall not exceed 90 hours.

C2.11 *[For the extension of the application of article 6(1) to national passenger services, see the Community Drivers' Hours and Recording Equipment (Exemptions and Supplementary Provisions) Regulations 1986 (S.I. 1986 No. 1456), reg.3(1) above.]*

SECTION V

Breaks and Rest Periods

Article 7

C2.12 1. After four-and-a-half hours' driving, the driver shall observe a break of at least 45 minutes, unless he begins a rest period.

2. This break may be replaced by breaks of at least 15 minutes each distributed over the driving period or immediately after this period in such a way as to comply with the provisions of paragraph 1.

3. By way of exception from paragraph 1, in the case of national carriage of passengers on regular services Member States may fix the minimum break at not less than 30 minutes after a driving period not exceeding four hours. Such exceptions may be granted only in cases where breaks in driving over 30 minutes could hamper the flow of urban traffic and where it is not possible for drivers to take a 15-minute break within four-and-a-half hours of driving prior to a 30-minute break.

4. During these breaks, the driver may not carry out any other work. For the purposes of this Article, the waiting time and time not devoted to driving spent in a vehicle in motion, a ferry, or a train shall not be regarded as "other work".

5. The breaks observed under this Article may not be regarded as daily rest periods.

C2.13 *[For exceptions under national legislation in accordance with article 7(3), see the Community Drivers' Hours and Recording Equipment (Exemptions and Supplementary Provisions) Regulations 1986 (S.I. 1986 No. 1456), reg.3(2) above.]*

Article 8

C2.14 1. In each period of 24 hours, the driver shall have a daily rest period of at least 11 consecutive hours, which may be reduced to a minimum of nine consecutive hours not more than three times in any one week, on condition that an equivalent period of rest be granted as compensation before the end of the following week.

On days when the rest is not reduced in accordance with the first subparagraph, it may be taken in two or three separate periods during the 24-hour period, one of which must be of at least eight consecutive hours. In this case the minimum length of the rest shall be increased to 12 hours.

2. During each period of 30 hours when a vehicle is manned by at least two drivers, each driver shall have a rest period of not less than eight consecutive hours.

3. In the course of each week, one of the rest periods referred to in paragraphs 1 and 2 shall be extended, by way of weekly rest, to a total of 45 consecutive hours. This rest period may be reduced to a minimum of 36 consecutive hours if taken at the place where the vehicle is normally based or where the driver is based, or to a minimum of 24 consecutive hours if taken elsewhere. Each reduction shall be compensated by an equivalent rest taken *en bloc* before the end of the third week following the week in question.

4. A weekly rest period which begins in one week and continues into the following week may be attached to either of these weeks.

5. In the case of the carriage of passengers to which Article 6(1), fourth or fifth sub-paragraph applies, the weekly rest period may be postponed until the week following that in respect of which the rest is due and added on to that second week's weekly rest.

6. Any rest taken as compensation for the reduction of the daily and/or weekly rest periods must be attached to another rest of at least eight hours and shall be granted, at the request of the person concerned, at the vehicle's parking place or driver's base.

7. The daily rest period may be taken in a vehicle, as long as it is fitted with a bunk and is stationary.

Article 9

Notwithstanding Article 8(1) where a driver engaged in the carriage of goods or pass-   **C2.15**
engers accompanies a vehicle which is transported by ferryboat or train, the daily rest period may be interrupted not more than once, provided the following conditions are fulfilled:
— that part of the daily rest period spent on land must be able to be taken before or after the portion of the daily rest period taken on board the ferry-boat or train,
— the period between the two portions of the daily rest period must be as short as possible and may on no account exceed one hour before embarkation or after disembarkation, customs formalities being included in the embarkation or disembarkation operations,
— during both portions of the rest period the driver must be able to have access to a bunk or couchette.

The daily rest period, interrupted in this way, shall be increased by two hours.

SECTION VI

PROHIBITION OF CERTAIN TYPES OF PAYMENT

Article 10

Payments to wage-earning drivers, even in the form of bonuses or wage supplements,   **C2.16**
related to distances travelled and/or the amount of goods carried shall be prohibited, unless these payments are of such a kind as not to endanger road safety.

SECTION VII

EXCEPTIONS

Article 11

Each Member may apply higher minima or lower maxima than those laid down in   **C2.17**
Articles 5 to 8 inclusive. Nevertheless, the provisions of this Regulation shall remain applic-able to drivers engaged in international transport operations on vehicles registered in another Member State.

Article 12

Provided that road safety is not thereby jeopardised and to enable him to reach a suitable   **C2.18**
stopping place, the driver may depart from the provisions of this Regulation to the extent

necessary to ensure the safety of persons, of the vehicle or of its load. The driver shall indicate the nature of and reason for his departure from those provisions on the record sheet of the recording equipment or in his duty roster.

Article 13

C2.19   1. Each Member State may grant exceptions on its own territories or, with the agreement of the States concerned, on the territory of another Member State from any provision of this Regulation applicable to carriage by means of a vehicle belonging to one or more of the following categories:

    (a) vehicles used for carrying passengers, which by virtue of their construction and equipment are suitable for carrying not more than 17 persons, including the driver, and are intended for that purpose;

    (b) vehicles used by public authorities to provide public services which are not in competition with professional road hauliers;

    (c) vehicles used by agricultural, horticultural, forestry or fishery undertakings for carrying goods within a 50 kilometre radius of the place where the vehicle is normally based, including local administrative areas the centres of which are situated within that radius;

    (d) vehicles used for carrying animal waste or carcases which are not intended for human consumption;

    (e) vehicles used for carrying live animals from farms to the local markets and vice versa or from markets to the local slaughterhouses;

    (f) vehicles used as shops at local markets or for door-to-door selling, or used for mobile banking, exchange or saving transactions, for worship, for the lending of books, records or cassettes, for cultural events or exhibitions, and specially fitted for such uses;

    (g) vehicles carrying material or equipment for the driver's use in the course of his work within a 50 kilometre radius of the place where the vehicle is normally based, provided that driving the vehicle does not constitute the driver's main activity and that the exception does not seriously prejudice the objectives of the Regulation. The Member States may make such exceptions subject to individual authorisation;

    (h) vehicles operating exclusively on islands not exceeding 2,300 square kilometres in areas which are not linked to the rest of the national territory by a bridge, ford or tunnel open for use by motor vehicles;

    (i) vehicles used for the carriage of goods and propelled by means of gas produced on the vehicle or of electricity or equipped with a governor in so far as such vehicles are regarded, under the legislation of the Member State of registration, as equivalent to vehicles propelled by a petrol or diesel engine, the maximum weight of which, including the weight of trailers or semi-trailers, does not exceed 3.5 tonnes;

    (j) vehicles used for driving instruction with a view to obtaining a driving licence;

    (k) tractors used exclusively for agricultural and forestry work.

Member States shall inform the Commission of the exceptions granted under this paragraph.

2. Member States may, after authorisation by the Commission, grant exceptions from the application of the provisions of this Regulation to transport operations carried out in exceptional circumstances, if such exceptions do not seriously jeopardise the objectives of the Regulation.

In urgent cases they may grant a temporary exception for a period not exceeding 30 days, which shall be notified immediately to the Commission.

The Commission shall notify the other Member States of any exception pursuant to this Regulation.

[For exemptions under national legislation in accordance with article 13(1), see the Community Drivers'   **C2.20**
Hours and Recording Equipment (Exemptions and Supplementary Provisions) Regulations 1986 (S.I.
1986 No. 1456), reg.2 and Schedule above.

The United Kingdom has been authorised to exempt from the application of this Regulation "vehicles
which travel exclusively within the boundaries of airports, which must be used in connection with the
operation of airports and which are not authorised or technically approved for travel on the public highway
outside" airports; see Commission Decision 94/451/EC (O.J. No. L187, July 22, 1994, p. 9; not repro-
duced in this work), art.1(1).

Exemptions under national legislation in accordance with article 13(2) are likely (in the main) to be of
short duration, and will normally be noted in Wilkinson's Road Traffic Law Bulletin.]

SECTION VIII

CONTROL PROCEDURES AND PENALTIES

Article 14

1. In the case of   **C2.21**
   — regular national passenger services, and
   — regular international passenger services whose route terminals are located
     within a distance of 50 kilometres as the crow flies from a frontier between
     two Member States and whose route length does not exceed 100 kilometres;

which are subject to this Regulation, a service timetable and a duty roster shall be drawn up by the undertaking.

2. The duty roster shall show, in respect of each driver, the name, place where based and the schedule laid down in advance for various periods of driving, other work and availability.

3. The duty roster shall include all the particulars specified in paragraph 2 for a minimum period covering both the current week and the weeks immediately preceding and following that week.

4. The duty roster shall be signed by the head of the undertaking or by a person authorised to represent him.

5. Each driver assigned to a service referred to in paragraph 1 shall carry an extract from the duty roster and a copy of the service timetable.

6. The duty roster shall be kept by the undertaking for one year after expiry of the period covered. The undertaking shall give an extract from the roster to the drivers concerned who request it.

7. This Article shall not apply to the drivers of vehicles fitted with recording equipment used in accordance with the provisions of Council Regulation (EEC) No. 3821/85 of 20 December 1985 on recording equipment in road transport [*q.v.*].

Article 15

1. The transport undertaking shall organise drivers' work in such a way that drivers are   **C2.22**
able to comply with the relevant provisions of this Regulation and of Regulation (EEC) No. 3821/85.

2. The undertaking shall make periodic checks to ensure that the provisions of these two Regulations have been complied with. If breaches are found to have occurred, the undertaking shall take appropriate steps to prevent their repetition.

Article 16

C2.23   1. The Commission shall produce a report every two years on the implementation of this Regulation by Member States and developments in the fields in question. The Commission shall forward the report to the Council and the European Parliament within 13 months of expiry of the two-year period covered by the report.

2. To enable the Commission to draw up the report referred to in paragraph 1, Member States shall communicate the necessary information to the Commission every two years, using a standard form. This information must reach the Commission not later than 30 September following the date on which the two-year period covered by the report expires.

3. The Commission shall draw up the standard form after consulting the Member States.

C2.24   *[The information required to be supplied under article 16(2) must be provided in accordance with the model form annexed to Commission Decision 93/173/EEC, O.J. No. L72, March 25, 1993, p. 33; not reproduced in this work.]*

Article 17

C2.25   1. Member States shall, in due time and after consulting the Commission, adopt such laws, regulations or administrative provisions as may be necessary for the implementation of this Regulation.
Such measures shall cover, *inter alia*, the organisation of, procedure for and means of control and the penalties to be imposed in case of breach.

2. Member States shall assist each other in applying this Regulation and in checking compliance therewith.

3. Within the framework of this mutual assistance the competent authorities of the Member States shall regularly send one another all available information concerning:
— breaches of this Regulation committed by non-residents and any penalties imposed for such breaches;
— penalties imposed by a Member State on its residents for such breaches committed in other Member States.

SECTION IX

FINAL PROVISIONS

Article 18

C2.26   1. Regulation (EEC) No. 543/69 is hereby repealed . . .

2. References to the Regulation repealed under paragraph 1 shall be construed as references to this Regulation.

C2.27   *[The words omitted from article 18 relate to transitional provisions which expired on December 31, 1989.]*

C2.28   **Article 19**   *[Commencement.]*

This Regulation shall be binding in its entirety and directly applicable in all Member States.

Regulation (EEC) 3821/85
of December 20, 1985

on recording equipment in road transport

European Economic Area. As to the Agreement on the European Economic Area generally, see the note to Regulation (EEC) 3820/85, above.

For the purposes of that agreement, Regulation (EEC) 3821/85 has been adapted by *ibid.*, Annex XIII, Chapter II, para.21, as amended.

[The text of this regulation is printed as amended by:

Commission Regulation (EEC) 3314/90 (O.J. No. L318, November 17, 1990, p. 20) (November 20, 1990);

Council Regulation (EEC) 3572/90, art.3 (O.J. No. L353, December 17, 1990, p. 12) (December 17, 1990);

Commission Regulation (EEC) 3688/92 (O.J. No. L374, December 22, 1992, p. 12) (December 25, 1992);

Act of Accession of Austria, Finland and Sweden to the European Union (O.J. No. C241, August 29, 1994, p. 21), as amended by Council Decision 95/1/EC (O.J. No. L1, January 1, 1995, p. 1);

Commission Regulation (EC) 2479/95 (O.J. No. L256, October 26, 1995, p. 8) (January 1, 1996);

Commission Regulation (EC) 1056/97 (O.J. No. L154, June 12, 1997, p. 21) (January 1, 1996); and

Council Regulation (EC) 2135/98 (O.J. No. L274, October 9, 1998, p. 1) (October 10, 1998).

The amending Regulations are referred to in the notes to the principal Regulation only by their reference numbers. The dates referred to above in relation to Regulations are the dates on which the amending Regulations came into force. The Act of Accession (Austria, Finland, Sweden) as amended by Council Decision 95/1/EC came into force on January 1, 1995 (see the notice at O.J. No. L1, January 1, 1995, p. 221); any reference to the "Act of Accession (Austria, Finland, Sweden)" is a reference to that Act as amended by that Decision.]

THE COUNCIL OF THE EUROPEAN COMMUNITIES,

Having regard to the Treaty establishing the European Economic Community, and in particular [Article 71] thereof,

Having regard to the proposal from the Commission [*O.J. No. C100, April 12, 1984, p. 3, O.J. No. C223, September 3, 1985, p. 5*],

Having regard to the opinion of the European Parliament [*O.J. No. C122, May 20, 1985, p. 168*],

Having regard to the opinion of the Economic and Social Committee [*O.J. No. C104, April 25, 1985, p. 4, O.J. No. C303, November 25, 1985, p. 29*],

Whereas Regulation (EEC) No. 1463/70 [*O.J. No. L164, July 27, 1970, p. 1*] as last amended by Regulation (EEC) No. 2828/77 [*O.J. No. L334, December 24, 1977, p. 11*] introduced recording equipment in road transport;

Whereas, taking into account the amendments set out hereinafter, in order to clarify matters, all the relevant provisions should be brought together in a single text, and in consequence thereof, Regulation (EEC) No. 1463/70 of the Council should be repealed; whereas, however, the exemptions set out in Article 3(1) for certain passenger services should be maintained in force for a certain time;

C3.01

C3.02

Whereas the use of recording equipment that may indicate the periods of time referred to in Regulation (EEC) No. 3820/85 on the harmonisation of certain social legislation relating to road transport [*q.v.*] is intended to ensure effective checking on that social legislation;

Whereas the obligation to use such recording equipment can be imposed only for vehicles registered in Member States; whereas furthermore certain of such vehicles may, without giving rise to difficulty, be excluded from the scope of this Regulation;

Whereas the Member States should be entitled with the Commission's authorisation, to grant certain vehicles exemptions from the provisions of the Regulation in exceptional circumstances; whereas, in urgent cases, it should be possible to grant these exemptions for a limited time without prior authorisation from the Commission;

Whereas, in order to ensure effective checking, the equipment must be reliable in operation, easy to use and designed in such a way as to minimise any possibility of fraudulent use; whereas to this end recording equipment should in particular be capable of providing, on separate sheets for each driver and in a sufficiently precise and easily readable form, recorded details of the various periods of time;

Whereas automatic recording of other details of a vehicle's journey, such as speed and distance covered, will contribute significantly to road safety and will encourage sensible driving of the vehicle; whereas, consequently, it appears appropriate to provide for the equipment also to record those details;

Whereas it is necessary to set Community construction and installation standards for recording equipment and to provide for an EEC approval procedure, in order to avoid throughout the territory of the Member States any impediment to the registration of vehicles fitted with such recording equipment, to their entry into service or use, or to such equipment being used;

Whereas, in the event of differences of opinion between Member States concerning cases of EEC type approval, the Commission should be empowered to take a decision on a dispute within six months if the States concerned have been unable to reach a settlement;

Whereas it would be helpful in implementing this Regulation and preventing abuses to issue drivers who so request with a copy of their record sheets;

Whereas, in order to achieve the aims hereinbefore mentioned of keeping a check on work and rest periods, it is necessary that employers and drivers be responsible for seeing that the equipment functions correctly and that they perform with due care the operations described;

Whereas the provisions governing the number of records sheets that a driver must keep with him must be amended following the replacement of the flexible week by a fixed week;

Whereas technical progress necessitates rapid adaptation of the technical specifications set out in the Annexes to this Regulation; whereas, in order to facilitate the implementation of the measures necessary for this purpose, provision should be made for a procedure establishing close co-operation between the Member States and the Commission within an Advisory Committee;

Whereas Member States should exchange the available information on breaches established;

Whereas, in order to ensure that recording equipment functions reliably and correctly, it is advisable to lay down uniform requirements for the periodic checks and inspections to which the equipment is to be subject after installation,

C3.03   *[The preamble is printed as amended by the Treaty of Amsterdam, art.12(1) and (3).]*

HAS ADOPTED THIS REGULATION:

CHAPTER I

PRINCIPLES AND SCOPE

Article 1

Recording equipment within the meaning of this Regulation shall, as regards con-   **C3.04**
struction, installation, use and testing, comply with the requirements of this Regulation [and
of Annexes I or IB and II thereto], which shall form an integral part of this Regulation.

[Article 1 is printed as amended by Regulation (EC) 2135/98.]   **C3.05**

Article 2

For the purposes of this Regulation the definitions set out in Article 1 of Regulation   **C3.06**
(EEC) No. 3820/85 *[q.v.]* shall apply.

Article 3

1. Recording equipment shall be installed and used in vehicles registered in a Member   **C3.07**
State which are used for the carriage of passengers or goods by road, except the vehicles
referred to in Articles 4 and 14(1) of Regulation (EEC) No. 3820/85.

2. Member States may exempt vehicles mentioned in Article 13(1) of Regulation (EEC)
No. 3820/85 from application of this Regulation. Member States shall inform the
Commission of any exemption granted under this paragraph.

3. Member States may, after authorisation by the Commission, exempt from application
of this Regulation vehicles used for the transport operations referred to in Article 13(2) of
Regulation (EEC) No. 3820/85. In urgent cases they may grant a temporary exemption for
a period not exceeding 30 days, which shall be notified immediately to the Commission.
The Commission shall notify the other Member States of any exemption granted pursuant
to this paragraph.

4. In the case of national transport operations, Member States may require the installation and use of recording equipment in accordance with this Regulation in any of the vehicles for which its installation and use are not required by paragraph 1.

[For exemptions under national legislation in accordance with article 3(2), see the Community Drivers'   **C3.08**
Hours and Recording Equipment (Exemptions and Supplementary Provisions) Regulations 1986 (S.I.
1986 No. 1456), reg.4 and Schedule above.

For the extension under national legislation in accordance with article 3(4) of the application of
Regulation (EEC) 3821/85 to vehicles used for the carriage of postal articles on national transport oper-
ations, see S.I. 1986 No. 1456, reg.5 above.

The United Kingdom has been authorised to exempt from the application of this Regulation "transport
vehicles" which are "vehicles which travel exclusively within the boundaries of airports, which must be used
in connection with the operation of airports and which are not authorised or technically approved for travel
on the public highway outside" airports, provided that "the objectives of Regulation (EEC) 3820/85 are
not called into question"; see Commission Decision 94/451/EC (O.J. No. L187, July 22, 1994, p. 9;
not reproduced in this work), art.1(2).]

CHAPTER II

TYPE APPROVAL

Article 4

[For the purposes of this Chapter, the words *"recording equipment"* shall mean "recording   **C3.09**
equipment or its components".]

Applications for EEC approval of a type of recording equipment or of a model record sheet [or memory card] shall be submitted, accompanied by the appropriate specifications, by the manufacturer or his agent to a Member State. No application in respect of any one type of recording equipment or of any one model record sheet [or memory card] may be submitted to more than one Member State.

C3.10   *[Article 4 is printed as amended by Regulation (EC) 2135/98.]*

Article 5

C3.11   [A Member State shall grant EC component type-approval to any type of recording equipment, to any model record sheet or memory card which conforms to the requirements laid down in Annex I or IB to this Regulation, provided the Member State is in a position to check that production models conform to the approved type.]

[The system's security must comply with the technical requirements laid down in Annex IB. The Commission, acting in accordance with the procedure laid down in Article 18, shall ensure that the said Annex stipulates that recording equipment may not be granted EC component type-approval until the whole system (the recording equipment itself, driver card and electrical gearbox connections) has demonstrated its capacity to resist attempts to tamper with or alter the data on its driving times. The tests necessary to establish this shall be carried out by experts with up to date tampering techniques.]

Any modifications or additions to an approved model must receive additional EEC type approval from the Member State which granted the original EEC type approval.

[Article 5 is printed as amended by Regulation (EC) 2135/98.]

Article 6

C3.12   Member States shall issue to the applicant an EEC approval mark, which shall conform to the model shown in Annex II, for each type of recording equipment or model record sheet [or memory card] which they approve pursuant to Article 5.

C3.13   *[Article 6 is printed as amended by Regulation (EC) 2135/98.]*

Article 7

C3.14   The competent authorities of the Member State to which the application for type approval has been submitted shall, in respect of each type of recording equipment or model record sheet [or memory card] which they approve or refuse to approve, either send within one month to the authorities of the other Member States a copy of the approval certificate accompanied by copies of the relevant specifications, or, if such is the case, notify those authorities that approval has been refused; in cases of refusal they shall communicate the reasons for their decision.

C3.15   *[Article 7 is printed as amended by Regulation (EC) 2135/98.]*

Article 8

C3.16   1. If a Member State which has granted EEC type approval as provided for in Article 5 finds that certain recording equipment or record sheets [or memory card] bearing the EEC type approval mark which it has issued do not conform to the prototype which it has approved, it shall take the necessary measures to ensure that production models conform to the approved prototype. The measures taken may, if necessary, extend to withdrawal of EEC type approval.

2. A Member State which has granted EEC type approval shall withdraw such approval if the recording equipment or record sheet [or memory card] which has been approved is not in conformity with this Regulation to its Annexes or displays in use any general defect which makes it unsuitable for the purpose for which it is intended.

3. If a Member State which has granted EEC type approval is notified by another Member State of one of the cases referred to in paragraphs 1 and 2, it shall also, after consulting the latter Member State, take the steps laid down in those paragraphs, subject to paragraph 5.

4. A Member State which ascertains that one of the cases referred to in paragraph 2 has arisen may forbid until further notice the placing on the market and putting into service of the recording equipment or record sheets [or memory card]. The same applies in the cases mentioned in paragraph 1 with respect to recording equipment or record sheets [or memory card] which have been exempted from EEC initial verification, if the manufacturer, after due warning, does not bring the equipment into line with the approved model or with the requirements of this Regulation.

In any event, the competent authorities of the Member States shall notify one another and the Commission, within one month, of any withdrawal of EEC type approval or of any other measures taken pursuant to paragraphs 1, 2 and 3 shall specify the reasons for such action.

5. If a Member State which has granted an EEC type approval disputes the existence of any of the cases specified in paragraphs 1 or 2 notified to it, the Member States concerned shall endeavour to settle the dispute and the Commission shall be kept informed.

If talks between the Member States have not resulted in agreement within four months of the date of the notification referred to in paragraph 3 above, the Commission, after consulting experts from all Member States and having considered all the relevant factors, *e.g.* economic and technical factors, shall within six months adopt a decision which shall be communicated to the Member States concerned and at the same time to the other Member States. The Commission shall lay down in each instance the time limit for implementation of its decision.

[Article 8 is printed as amended by Regulation (EC) 2135/98.]   **C3.17**

Article 9

1. An applicant for EEC type approval of a model record sheet shall state on his application the type or types of recording equipment on which the sheet in question is designed to be used and shall provide suitable equipment of such type or types for the purpose of testing the sheet.   **C3.18**

2. The competent authorities of each Member State shall indicate on the approval certificate for the model record sheet the type or types of recording equipment on which that model sheet may be used.

Article 10

No Member State may refuse to register any vehicle fitted with recording equipment, or prohibit the entry into service or use of such vehicle for any reason connected with the fact that the vehicle is fitted with such equipment, if the equipment bears the EEC approval mark referred to in Article 6 and the installation plaque referred to in Article 12.   **C3.19**

Article 11

All decisions pursuant to this Regulation refusing or withdrawing approval of a type of recording equipment or model record sheet [or memory card] shall specify in detail the reasons on which they are based. A decision shall be communicated to the party concerned, who shall at the same time be informed of the remedies available to him under the laws of the Member States and of the time-limits for the exercise of such remedies.   **C3.20**

[Article 11 is printed as amended by Regulation (EC) 2135/98.]   **C3.21**

CHAPTER III

INSTALLATION AND INSPECTION

Article 12

C3.22   1. Recording equipment may be installed or repaired only by fitters or workshops approved by the competent authorities of Member States for that purpose after the latter, should they so desire, have heard the views of the manufacturers concerned.

[The period of administrative validity of approved workshop and fitter cards shall not exceed one year.]

[If a card issued to an approved workshop or fitter is to be extended, is damaged, malfunctions, is lost or stolen, the authority shall supply a replacement card within five working days of receiving a detailed request to that effect.]

[Where a new card is issued to replace an old one, the new card shall bear the same "workshop" information number, but the index shall be increased by one. The authority issuing the card shall maintain a register of lost, stolen or defective cards.]

[Member States shall take any measure necessary to prevent the cards distributed to approved fitters and workshops being falsified.]

[2. The approved fitter or workshop shall place a special mark on the seals which it affixes and, in addition, shall enter for recording equipment in conformity with Annex IB, the electronic security data for carrying out, in particular, the authentification checks. The competent authorities of each Member State shall maintain a register of the marks and electronic security data used and of approved workshop and fitter cards issued.]

[3. The component authorities of the Member States shall forward to the Commission the lists of approved fitters and workshops and the cards issued to them and shall forward to it copies of the marks and of the necessary information relating to the electronic security data used.]

4. For the purpose of certifying that installation of recording equipment took place in accordance with the requirements of this Regulation an installation plaque affixed as provided in [Annexes I and IB] shall be used.

[5. Any seal may be removed by the fitters or workshops approved by competent authorities under paragraph 1 of this Article, or in the circumstances described in Annex I, Chapter V, paragraph 4 [or in Annex IB, section VI(c)] to this Regulation.]

C3.23   *[Article 12 is printed as amended by Regulation (EEC) 3688/92; Regulation (EC) 2135/98.]*

CHAPTER IV

USE OF EQUIPMENT

[Article 13

C3.24   The employer and drivers shall ensure the correct functioning and proper use of, on the one hand, the recording equipment and, on the other, the driver card where a driver is required to drive a vehicle fitted with recording equipment in conformity with Annex IB.]

C3.25   *[Article 13 is printed as substituted by Regulation (EC) 2135/98.]*

Article 14

C3.26   [1. The employer shall issue a sufficient number of record sheets to drivers of vehicles fitted with recording equipment in conformity with Annex I, bearing in mind the fact that these sheets are personal in character, the length of the period of service and the possible obligation to replace sheets which are damaged, or have been taken by an authorised inspecting officer. The employer shall issue to drivers only sheets of an approved model suitable for use in equipment installed in the vehicle.]

[Where the vehicle is fitted with recording equipment in conformity with Annex IB, the employer and the driver shall ensure that, taking into account the length of the period of service, the printing on request referred to in Annex IB can be carried out correctly in the event of an inspection.]

2. The undertaking shall keep the record sheets in good order for at least a year after their use and shall give copies to the drivers concerned who request them. The sheets shall be produced or handed over at the request of any authorised inspecting officer.

[3. The driver card as defined in Annex IB shall be issued, at the request of the driver, by the competent authority of the Member State where the driver has his normal residence.]

[A Member State may require any driver subject to the provisions of Regulation (EEC) No. 3820/85 and normally resident on its territory to hold a driver card.]

[(a) For the purposes of this Regulation *"normal residence"* means the place where a person usually lives, that is for at least 185 days in each calendar year, because of personal and occupational ties, or, in the case of a person with no occupational ties, because of personal ties which show close links between that person and the place where he is living.

However, the normal residence of a person whose occupational ties are in a different place from his personal ties and who consequently lives in turn in different places situated in two or more Member States shall be regarded as being the place of his personal ties, provided that such person returns there regularly. This last condition need not be met where the person is living in a Member State in order to carry out a fixed-term assignment.]

[(b) Drivers shall give proof of their place of normal residence by any appropriate means, such as their identity card or any other valid document.]

[(c) Where the competent authorities of the Member State issuing the driver card have doubts as to the validity of a statement as to normal residence made in accordance with point (b), or for the purposes of certain specific controls, they may request any additional information or evidence.]

[(d) The competent authorities of the issuing Member State shall, as far as this can be done, ensure that the applicant does not already hold a valid driver card.]

[4. (a) The competent authority of the Member State shall personalise the driver card in accordance with the provisions of Annex IB.

For administrative purposes, the driver card may not be valid for more than five years.

The driver may hold one valid driver card only. The driver authorised to use only his own personalised driver card. The driver shall not use a driver card which is defective or which has expired.

When a new driver card is issued replacing the old, the new card shall bear the same driver card issue number but the index shall be increased by one. The issuing authority shall keep records of issued, stolen, lost or defective driver cards for a period at least equivalent to their period of administrative validity.

If the driver card is damaged, malfunctions or is lost or stolen, the authority shall supply a replacement card within five working days of receiving a detailed request to that effect.

In the event of a request for the renewal of a card whose expiry date is approaching, the authority shall supply a new card before the expiry date provided that the request was sent to it within the time limits laid down in the second sub-paragraph of Article 15(1).]

[(b) Driver cards shall be issued only to applicants who are subject to the provisions of Regulation (EEC) No. 3820/85.]

[(c) The driver card shall be personal. It may not, during its official period of validity, be withdrawn or suspended for whatever reason unless the competent authority of a Member State finds that the card has been falsified, or the driver is using a card of which he is not the holder, or that the card card held has been obtained on the basis of false declarations and/or forged documents. If such suspension or withdrawal measures are taken by a Member State other than the Member State of issue, the former shall return the card to the authorities of the Member State which issued it and shall indicate the reasons for returning it.]

[(d) Driver cards issued by Member States shall be mutually recognised.

Where the holder of a valid driver card issued by a Member State has established his normal place of residence in another Member State, he may ask for his card to be exchanged for an equivalent driver card; it shall be the responsibility of the Member State which carries out the exchange to verify if necessary whether the card produced is actually still valid.

Member States carrying out an exchange shall return the old card to the authorities of the Member State of issue and indicate the reasons for so doing.]

[(e) Where a Member State replaces or exchanges a driver card, the replacement or exchange, and any subsequent replacement or renewal, shall be registered in that Member State.]

[(f) Member States shall take all the necessary measures to prevent any possibility of driver cards being falsified.]

[5. Member States shall ensure that data needed to monitor compliance with Regulation (EEC) No. 3820/85 and Council Directive 92/6/EEC of 10 February 1992 on the installation and use of speed limitation devices for certain categories of motor vehicles in the Community [*q.v.*] which are recorded and stored by recording equipment in conformity with Annex IB to this Regulation can be made available for at least 365 days after the date of their recording and that they can be made available under conditions that guarantee the security and accuracy of the data.]

[Member States shall take any measures necessary to ensure that the resale or decommissioning of recording equipment cannot detract, in particular, from the satisfactory application of this paragraph.]

C3.27   *[Article 14 is printed as amended by Regulation (EC) 2135/98.]*

Article 15

C3.28   1. Drivers shall not use dirty or damaged record sheets [or driver card]. The sheets shall be adequately protected on this account.

[Where a driver wishes to renew his driver card, he shall apply to the competent authorities of the Member State in which he has his normal residence not later than 15 working days before the expiry date of the card.]

In case of damage to a sheet bearing recordings, drivers shall attach the damaged sheet to the spare sheet used to replace it.

[If the driver card is damaged, malfunctions or is lost or stolen, the driver shall apply within seven calendar days for its replacement to the competent authorities of the Member State in which he has his normal residence.]

2. Drivers shall use the records sheets [or driver card] every day on which they are driving, starting from the moment they take over the vehicle. The record sheet [or driver

card] shall not be withdrawn before the end of the daily working period unless its withdrawal is otherwise authorised. No record sheet [or driver card] be used to cover a period longer than that for which it is intended.

When, as a result of being away from the vehicle, a driver is unable to use the equipment fitted to the vehicle, the periods of time indicated in paragraph 3, second indent (b), (c) and (d) below shall be entered on the sheet, either manually, by automatic recording or other means, legibly and without dirtying the sheet.

Drivers shall amend the record sheets as necessary should there be more than one driver on board the vehicle, so that the information referred to in Chapter II(1) to (3) of Annex I is recorded on the record sheet of the driver who is actually driving.

3. Drivers shall:

— ensure that the time recorded on the sheet agrees with the official time in the country of registration of the vehicle,

— operate the switch mechanisms enabling the following periods of time to be recorded separately and distinctly:

(a) under the sign ⊗ : driving time;

(b) under the sign ⚒ : all other periods of work;

(c) under the sign ▨ : other periods of availability, namely:

— waiting time, i.e. the period during which drivers need to remain at their posts only for the purpose of answering any calls to start or resume driving or to carry out other work,

— time spent beside the driver while the vehicle is in motion,

— time spent on a bunk while the vehicle is in motion;

(d) under the sign ⊨ : breaks in work and daily rest periods.

4. Each Member State may permit all the periods referred to in paragraph 3, second indent (b) and (c) to be recorded under the sign ▨ on the record sheets used on vehicles registered in its territory.

5. Each crew member shall enter the following information on his record sheet:

(a) on beginning to use the sheet—his surname and first name;

(b) the date and place where use of the sheet begins and the date and place where such use ends;

(c) the registration number of each vehicle to which he is assigned, both at the start of the first journey recorded on the sheet and then, in the event of a change of vehicle, during the use of the sheet;

(d) the odometer reading:

— at the start of the first journey recorded on the sheet;

— at the end of the last journey recorded on the sheet;

— in the event of a change of vehicle during a working day (reading on the vehicle to which he was assigned and reading on the vehicle to which he is to be assigned);

(e) the time of any change of vehicle.

[5A. The driver shall enter in the recording equipment in conformity with Annex IB the symbols of the countries in which he begins and ends his daily work period. However, a

Member State may require drivers of vehicles engaged in transport operations inside its territory to add more detailed geographic specifications to the country symbol provided that the Member State has notified them to the Commission before 1 April 1998 and that they do not number more than 20.]

[The above data entries shall be activated by the driver, and may be entirely manual or automatic if the recording equipment is linked to a satellite tracking system.]

6. The [recording equipment defined in Annex I] shall be so designed that it is possible for an authorised inspecting officer, if necessary after opening the equipment, to read the recordings relating to the nine hours preceding the time of the check without permanently deforming, damaging or soiling the sheet.

The equipment shall, furthermore, be so designed that it is possible, without opening the case, to verify that recordings are being made.

[7. Where the driver drives a vehicle fitted with recording equipment in conformity with Annex I, he must be able to produce, whenever an inspecting officer so requests:

— the record sheets for the current week and, in any event, the sheet for the last day on which he drove during the previous week,

— the driver card if he holds one, and

— print-outs from the recording equipment defined in Annex IB relating to the periods of time indicated in paragraph 3, second indent, (a), (b), (c) and (d) if he drove a vehicle fitted with such recording equipment during the period referred to in the first indent of this paragraph.]

[Where the driver drives a vehicle fitted with recording equipment in conformity with Annex IB, he must be able to produce, whenever an inspecting officer so requests:

— the driver card of which he is the holder,

— the record sheeds corresponding to the same period as the one referred to in the first indent of the previous sub-paragraph during which he drove a vehicle fitted with recording equipment in conformity with Annex I.]

[An authorised inspecting officer may check compliance with Regulation (EEC) No. 3820/85 by analysis of the record sheets, of the displayed or printed data which have been recorded by the recording equipment or by the driver card or, failing this, by analysis of any other supporting document that justifies non-compliance with a provision, such as those laid down in Article 16(2) and (3).]

[8. It shall be forbidden to falsify, suppress or destroy data recorded on the record sheet, stored in the recording equipment or on the driver card, or print-outs from the recording equipment as defined in Annex IB. The same applies to any manipulation of the recording equipment, record sheet or driver card which may result in data and/or printed information being falsified, suppressed or destroyed. No device which could be used to this effect shall be present on the vehicle.]

C3.29   *[Article 15 is printed as amended by Regulation (EC) 2135/98.]*

Article 16

C3.30   1. In the event of breakdown or faulty operation of the equipment, the employer shall have it repaired by an approved fitter or workshop, as soon as circumstances permit.

If the vehicle is unable to return to the premises within a period of one week calculated from the date of the breakdown or of the discovery of defective operation, the repair shall be carried out en route.

Measures taken by Member States pursuant to Article 19 may give the competent authorities power to prohibit the use of the vehicle in cases where breakdown or faulty operation has not been put right as provided in the foregoing subparagraphs.

[2. While the recording equipment is unserviceable or malfunctioning, drivers shall mark on the record sheet or sheets, or on a temporary sheet to be attached to the record sheet or to the driver card, on which he shall enter data enabling him to be identified (driver's card number and/or name and/or driving licence number), including his signature, all information for the various periods of time which are no longer recorded or printed out correctly by the recording equipment.]

[If a driver card is damaged, malfunctions or is lost or stolen, the driver shall, at the end of his journey, print out the information relating to the periods of time recorded by the recording equipment and mark on that document the details that enable him to be identified (the driver card number and/or name and/or driving licence number), including his signature.]

[3. If a driver card is damaged or if it malfunctions, the driver shall return it to the competent authority of the Member State in which he has his normal residence. Theft of the driver card shall be the subject of a formal declaration to the competent authorities of the State where the theft occurred.]

[Loss of the driver card must be reported in a formal declaration to the competent authorities of the State that issued it and to the competent authorities of the Member State of normal residence where they are different.]

[The driver may continue to drive without a driver card for a maximum period of 15 calendar days or for a longer period if this is necessary for the vehicle to return to its premises, provided he can prove the impossibility of producing or using the card during this period.]

[Where the authorities of the Member State in which the driver has his normal residence are different from those which issued his card and where the latter are requested to renew, replace or exchange the driver card, they shall inform the authorities which issued the old card of the precise reasons for its renewal, replacement or exchange.]

[Article 16 is printed as amended by Regulation (EC) 2135/98.]   **C3.31**

CHAPTER V

FINAL PROVISIONS

[Article 17

1. The amendments necessary to adapt the Annexes to technical progress shall be adopted in accordance with the procedure laid down in Article 18.   **C3.32**

2. The technical specifications relating to the following sections of Annex IB shall be adopted as soon as possible and if possible before 1 July 1998 by the same procedure:

(a) Chapter II
   — (d) 17:
      displaying and printing of faults in the recording equipment,
   — (d) 18:
      displaying and printing of faults in the driver card,
   — (d) 21:
      displaying and printing of summary reports;

(b) Chapter III
   — (a) 6.3:
      standards for the protection of vehicle electronics against electrical interference and magnetic fields,
   — (a) 6.5:
      protection (security) of the total system,

— (c) 1:

warning signals indicating the internal malfunctioning of the recording equipment

— (c) 5:

format of the warnings,

— (f):

maximum tolerances;

(c) Chapter IV, A:

— 4:

standards,

— 5:

security, including data protection,

— 6:

temperature range,

— 8:

electrical characteristics,

— 9:

logical structure of the driver card,

— 10:

functions and commands,

— 11:

elementary files;

and Chapter IV, B;

(d) Chapter V:

printer and standard print-outs.]

C3.33   *[Article 17 is printed as substituted by Regulation (EC) 2135/98.]*

[Article 18

C3.34   1. Where reference is made to the procedure laid down in this Article, the Commission shall be assisted by a committee composed of the representatives of the Member States and chaired by the representative of the Commission.

2. The representative of the Commission shall submit to the committee a draft of the measures to be taken. The committee shall deliver its opinion on the draft within a time limit which the chairman may lay down according to the urgency of the matter. The opinion shall be delivered by the majority laid down in [Article 205(2)] of the Treaty in the case of decisions which the Council is required to adopt on a proposal from the Commission. The votes of the representatives of the Member States within the committee shall be weighted in the manner set out in that Article. The chairman shall not vote.

3. (a) The Commission shall adopt the measures envisaged if they are in accordance with the opinion of the committee.

(b) If the measures envisaged are not in accordance with the opinion of the committee, or if no opinion is delivered, the Commission shall, without delay, submit to the Council a proposal relating to the measures to be taken. The Council shall act by a qualified majority.

If, on the expiry of a period of three months from the date of referral to the Council, the Council has not acted, the proposed measures shall be adopted by the Commission.]

C3.35   *[Article 18 is printed as substituted by Regulation (EC) 2135/98 and as subsequently amended by the Treaty of Amsterdam, art.12(1) and (3).]*

Article 19

1. Member States shall, in good time and after consulting the Commission, adopt such   **C3.36**
laws, regulations or administrative provisions as may be necessary for the implementation
of this Regulation.

Such measures shall cover, inter alia, the re-organisation of, procedure for, and means of
carrying out, checks on compliance and the penalties to be imposed in case of breach.

2. Member States shall assist each other in applying this Regulation and in checking
compliance therewith.

3. Within the framework of this mutual assistance the competent authorities of the
Member States shall regularly send one another all available information concerning:
  — breaches of this Regulation committed by non-residents and any penalties
    imposed for such breaches,
  — penalties imposed by a Member State on its residents for such breaches com-
    mitted in other Member States.

Article 20   *[Repeal of Regulation (EEC) 1463/70.]*   **C3.37**

[Article 20A   *[Lapsed.]]*   **C3.38**

Article 21   *[Commencement.]*   **C3.39**

This Regulation shall be binding in its entirety and directly applicable in all Member States.

ANNEX I

REQUIREMENTS FOR CONSTRUCTION, TESTING, INSTALLATION AND INSPECTION

I DEFINITIONS

In this Annex: **C3.40**
  (a) Recording equipment means:
       equipment intended for installation in road vehicles to show and record automat-
       ically or semi-automatically details of the movement of those vehicles and of
       certain working periods of their drivers;
  (b) Record sheet means:
       a sheet designed to accept and retain recorded data, to be placed in the recording
       equipment and on which the marking devices of the latter inscribe a continuous
       record of the information to be recorded;
  (c) The constant of the recording equipment means:
       the numerical characteristics giving the value of the input signal required to show
       and record a distance travelled of one kilometre; this constant must be expressed
       either in revolutions per kilometre ($k = \ldots$ rev/km), or in impulses per kilometre
       ($k = \ldots$ imp/km);
  (d) Characteristic coefficient of the vehicle means:
       the numerical characteristic giving the value of the output signal emitted by the
       part of the vehicle linking it with the recording equipment (gearbox output shaft or
       axle) while the vehicle travels a distance of one measured kilometre under normal
       test conditions (see Chapter VI, point 4 of this Annex). The characteristic
       coefficient is expressed either in revolutions per kilometre ($w = \ldots$ rev/km) or in
       impulses per kilometre ($w = \ldots$ imp/km);

(e) Effective circumference of wheel tyres means:
the average of the distances travelled by the several wheels moving the vehicle (driving wheels) in the course of one complete rotation. The measurement of these distances must be made under normal test conditions (see Chapter VI, point 4 of this Annex) and is expressed in the form: 1 = . . . mm.

    II   GENERAL CHARACTERISTICS AND FUNCTIONS OF RECORDING EQUIPMENT

C3.41   The equipment must be able to record the following:

1. distance travelled by the vehicle;

2. speed of the vehicle;

3. driving time;

4. other periods of work or of availability;

5. breaks from work and daily rest periods;

6. opening of the case containing the record sheet;

[7. for electronic recording equipment which is equipment operating by signals transmitted electrically from the distance and speed sensor, any interruption exceeding 100 milliseconds in the power supply of the recording equipment (except lighting), in the power supply of the distance and speed sensor and any interruption in the signal lead to the distance and speed sensor.]

For vehicles used by two drivers the equipment must be capable of recording simultaneously but distinctly and on two separate sheets details of the periods listed under 3, 4 and 5.

C3.42   *[Chapter II of Annex I is printed as amended by Regulation (EEC) 3314/90 which inserted item 7 into Chapter II. Transitional provisions relating to this amendment are set out in Regulation (EEC) 3314/90, art. 3 (q.v.).]*

    III   CONSTRUCTION REQUIREMENTS FOR RECORDING EQUIPMENT

(a) General points

C3.43   1. *Recording equipment shall include the following:*

    1.1. Visual instruments showing:
      — distance travelled (distance recorder),
      — speed (speedometer),
      — time (clock).

    1.2. Recording instruments comprising:
      — a recorder of the distance travelled,
      — a speed recorder,
      — one or more time recorders satisfying the requirements laid down in Chapter III (c) 4.

    [1.3. A means of marking showing on the record sheet individually:
      — each opening of the case containing that sheet,
      — for electronic recording equipment, as defined in point 7 of Chapter II, any interruption exceeding 100 milliseconds in the power supply of the recording equipment (except lighting), not later than at switching-on the power supply again,
      — for electronic recording equipment, as defined in point 7 of Chapter II, any interruption exceeding 100 milliseconds in the power supply of the distance

and speed sensor and any interruption in the signal lead to the distance and speed sensor.]

2. Any inclusion in the equipment of devices additional to those listed above must not interfere with the proper operation of the mandatory devices or with the reading of them. The equipment must be submitted for approval complete with any such additional devices.

3. *Materials*

3.1. All the constituent parts of the recording equipment must be made of materials with sufficient stability and mechanical strength and stable electrical and magnetic characteristics.

3.2. Any modification in a constituent part of the equipment or in the nature of the materials used for its manufacture must, before being applied in manufacture, be submitted for approval to the authority which granted type-approval for the equipment.

4. *Measurement of distance travelled*

The distances travelled may be measured and recorded either:
— so as to include both forward and reverse movement; or
— so as to include only forward movement.

Any recording of reversing movements must on no account affect the clarity and accuracy of the other recordings.

5. *Measurement of speed*

5.1. The range of speed measurement shall be as stated in the type approval certificate.

5.2. The natural frequency and the damping of the measuring device must be such that the instruments showing and recording the speed can, within the range of measurement, follow acceleration changes of up to 2m/section 2, within the limits of accepted tolerances.

6. *Measurement of time (clock)*

6.1. The control of the mechanism for resetting the clock must be located inside a case containing the record sheet; each opening of that case must be automatically recorded on the record sheet.

6.2. If the forward movement mechanism of the record sheet is controlled by the clock, the period during which the latter will run correctly after being fully wound must be greater by at least 10% than the recording period corresponding to the maximum sheet-load of the equipment.

7. *Lighting and protection*

7.1. The visual instruments of the equipment must be provided with adequate non-dazzling lighting.

7.2. For normal conditions of use, all the internal parts of the equipment must be protected against damp and dust. In addition they must be made proof against tampering by means of casings capable of being sealed.

(b) Visual instruments

1. *Distance travelled indicator (distance recorder)* **C3.44**

1.1. The value of the smallest grading on the instrument showing distance travelled must be 0.1 kilometres. Figures showing hectometres must be clearly distinguishable from those showing whole kilometres.

1.2. The figures on the distance recorder must be clearly legible and must have an apparent height of at least 4mm.

1.3. The distance recorder must be capable of reading up to at least 99,999.9 kilometres.

2. *Speed indicators (speedometer)*

2.1. Within the range of measurement, the speed scale must be uniformly graduated by 1, 2, 5 or 10 kilometres per hour. The value of a speed graduation (space between two successive marks) must not exceed 10% of the maximum speed shown on the scale.

2.2. The range indicated beyond that measured need not be marked by figures.

2.3. The length of each space on the scale representing a speed difference of 10 kilometres per hour must not be less than 10 millimetres.

2.4. On an indicator with a needle, the distance between the needle and the instrument face must not exceed three millimetres.

3. *Time indicator (clock)*

The time indicator must be visible from outside the equipment and give a clear, plain and unambiguous reading.

(c) Recording instruments

C3.45   1. *General points*

1.1. All equipment, whatever the form of the record sheet (strip or disc) must be provided with a mark enabling the record sheet to be inserted correctly, in such a way as to ensure that the time shown by the clock and the time-marking on the sheet correspond.

1.2. The mechanism moving the record sheet must be such as to ensure that the latter moves without play and can be freely inserted and removed.

1.3. For record sheets in disc form, the forward movement device must be controlled by the clock mechanism. In this case, the rotating movement of the sheet must be continuous and uniform, with a minimum speed of seven millimetres per hour measured at the inner border of the ring marking the edge of the speed recording area.

In equipment of the strip type, where the forward movement device of the sheets is controlled by the clock mechanism the speed of rectilinear forward movement must be at least 10 millimetres per hour.

1.4. Recording of the distance travelled, of the speed of the vehicle and of any opening of the case containing the record sheet or sheets must be automatic.

2. *Recording distance travelled*

2.1. Every kilometre of distance travelled must be represented on the record by a variation of at least one millimetre on the corresponding coordinate.

2.2. Even at speeds reaching the upper limit of the range of measurement, the record of distances must still be clearly legible.

3. *Recording speed*

3.1. Whatever the form of the record sheet, the speed recording stylus must normally move in a straight line and at right angles to the direction of travel of the record sheet.

However, the movement of the stylus may be curvilinear, provided the following conditions are satisfied:

— the trace drawn by the stylus must be perpendicular to the average circumference (in the case of sheets in disc form) or to the axis (in the case of sheets in strip form) of the area reserved for speed recording,

— the ratio between the radius of curvature of the trace drawn by the stylus and the width of the area reserved for speed recording must be not less than 2.4 to 1 whatever the form of the record sheet,

— the markings on the time-scale must cross the recording area in a curve of the same radius as the trace drawn by the stylus. The spaces between the markings on the time-scale must represent a period not exceeding one hour.

3.2. Each variation in speed of 10 kilometres per hour must be represented on the record by a variation of at least 1.5 millimetres on the corresponding coordinate.

4. *Recording time*

4.1. Recording equipment must be so constructed that the period of driving time is always recorded automatically and that it is possible, through the operation where necessary of a switch device to record separately the other periods of time as indicated in Article 15(3), second indent (b), (c) and (d) of the Regulation.

4.2. It must be possible, from the characteristics of the traces, their relative positions and if necessary the signs laid down in Article 15 of the Regulation to distinguish clearly between the various periods of time.

The various periods of time should be differentiated from one another on the record by differences in the thickness of the relevant traces, or by any other system of at least equal effectiveness from the point of view of legibility and ease of interpretation of the record.

4.3. In the case of vehicles with a crew consisting of more than one driver, the recordings provided for in point 4.1 must be made on two separate sheets, each sheet being allocated to one driver. In this case, the forward movement of the separate sheets must be effected either by a single mechanism or by separate synchronised mechanisms.

(d) Closing device

1. The case containing the record sheet or sheets and the control of the mechanism for resetting the clock must be provided with a lock.   **C3.46**

2. Each opening of the case containing the record sheet or sheets and the control of the mechanism for resetting the clock must be automatically recorded on the sheet or sheets.

(e) Markings

1. The following markings must appear on the instrument face of the equipment: **C3.47**

— close to the figure shown by the distance recorder, the unit of measurement of distance, indicated by the abbreviation "km",

— near the speed scale, the marking "km/h",

— the measurement range of the speedometer in the form "Vmin . . . km/h, Vmax . . . km/h". This marking is not necessary if it is shown on the descriptive plaque of the equipment.

However, these requirements shall not apply to recording equipment approved before 10 August 1970.

2. The descriptive plaque must be built into the equipment and must show the following markings, which must be visible on the equipment when installed:

— name and address of the manufacturer of the equipment,

— manufacturer's number and year of construction,

— approval mark for the equipment type,
— the constant of the equipment in the form "k=. . . rev/km" or "k=. . . imp/km",
— optionally, the range of speed measurement, in the form indicated in point 1,
— should the sensitivity of the instrument to the angle of inclination be capable of affecting the readings given by the equipment beyond the permitted tolerances, the permissible angle expressed as:

where a is the angle measured from the horizontal position of the front face (fitted the right way up) of the equipment for which the instrument is calibrated, while b and c represent respectively the maximum permissible upward and downward deviations from the angle of calibration a.

(f) Maximum tolerances (visual and recording instruments)

C3.48   1. On the test bench before installation:

     (a) distance travelled:
       1% more or less than the real distance, where that distance is at least one kilometre;

     (b) speed:
       3 km/h more or less than the real speed;

     (c) time:
       ± two minutes per day with a maximum of 10 minutes per seven days in cases where the running period of the clock after rewinding is not less than that period.

   2. On installation:

     (a) distance travelled:
       2% more or less than the real distance, where that distance is at least one kilometre;

     (b) speed;
       4 km/h more or less than the real speed;

     (c) time:
       ± two minutes per day, or
       ± 10 minutes per seven days.

   3. In use:

     (a) distance travelled:
       4% more or less than the real distance, where that distance is at least one kilometre;

     (b) speed:
       6 km/h more or less than the real speed;

     (c) time:
       ± two minutes per day, or
       ± 10 minutes per seven days.

   4. The maximum tolerances set out in points 1, 2 and 3 are valid for temperatures between 0° and 40°C, temperatures being taken in close proximity to the equipment.

5. Measurement of the maximum tolerances set out in points 2 and 3 shall take place under the conditions laid down in Chapter VI.

[Chapter III of Annex I is printed as amended by Regulation (EEC) 3314/90.

Before the amendments effected by Regulation (EEC) 3314/90 took effect, paragraph 1.3 under the heading "(a) General Points" and paragraph 4.1 under the heading "(c) Recording instruments" read as follows:

1.3. A marking device showing on the record sheet each opening of the case containing that sheet.

4.1. Recording equipment must be so constructed that it is possible, through the operation where necessary of a switch device, to record automatically and separately four periods of time as indicated in Article 15 of the Regulation.

Transitional provisions relating to these provisions are set out in Regulation (EEC) 3314/90, art.3 (q.v.).]

IV   RECORD SHEETS

(a) General points

1. The record sheets must be such that they do not impede the normal functioning of the instrument and that the records which they contain are indelible and easily legible and identifiable.

The record sheets must retain their dimensions and any records made on them under normal conditions of humidity and temperature.

In addition it must be possible to write on the sheets, without damaging them and without affecting the legibility of the recordings, the information referred to in Article 15(5) of the Regulation.

Under normal conditions of storage, the recordings must remain clearly legible for at least one year.

2. The minimum recording capacity of the sheets, whatever their form, must be 24 hours.

If several discs are linked together to increase the continuous recording capacity which can be achieved without intervention by staff, the links between the various discs must be made in such a way that there are no breaks in or overlapping of recordings at the point of transfer from one disc to another.

(b) Recording areas and their graduation

1. The record sheets shall include the following recording areas:

— an area exclusively reserved for data relating to speed,
— an area exclusively reserved for data relating to distance travelled,
— one or more areas for data relating to driving time, to other periods of work and availability to breaks from work and to rest periods for drivers.

2. The area for recording speed must be scaled off in divisions of 20 kilometres per hour or less. The speed corresponding to each marking on the scale must be shown in figures against that marking. The symbol "km/h" must be shown at least once within the area. The last marking on the scale must coincide with the upper limit of the range of measurement.

3. The area for recording distance travelled must be set out in such a way that the number of kilometres travelled may be read without difficulty.

4. The area or areas reserved for recording the periods referred to in point 1 must be so marked that it is possible to distinguish clearly between the various periods of time.

(c) Information to be printed on the record sheets

C3.52   Each sheet must bear, in printed form, the following information:

— name and address or trade name of the manufacturer,

— approval mark for the model of the sheet,

— approval mark for the type or types of equipment in which the sheet may be used,

— upper limit of the speed measurement range, printed in kilometres per hour.

By way of minimal additional requirements, each sheet must bear, in printed form a time-scale graduated in such a way that the time may be read directly at intervals of fifteen minutes while each five minute interval may be determined without difficulty.

(d) Free space for handwritten insertions

C3.53   A free space must be provided on the sheets such that drivers may as a minimum write in the following details:

— surname and first name of the driver,

— date and place where use of the sheet begins and date and place where such use ends,

— the registration number or numbers of the vehicle or vehicles to which the driver is assigned during the use of the sheet,

— odometer readings from the vehicle or vehicles to which the driver is assigned during the use of the sheet,

— the time at which any change of vehicle takes place.

V   INSTALLATION OF RECORDING EQUIPMENT

C3.54   1. Recording equipment must be positioned in the vehicle in such a way that the driver has a clear view from his seat of speedometer, distance recorder and clock while at the same time all parts of those instruments, including driving parts, are protected against damage.

2. It must be possible to adapt the constant of the recording equipment to the characteristic coefficient of the vehicle by means of a suitable device, to be known as an adaptor.

Vehicles with two or more rear axle ratios must be fitted with a switch device whereby these various ratios may be automatically brought into line with the ratio for which the equipment has been adapted to the vehicle.

3. After the equipment has been checked on installation, an installation plaque shall be affixed to the vehicle beside the equipment or in the equipment itself and in such a way as to be clearly visible. After every inspection by an approved fitter or workshop requiring a change in the setting of the installation itself, a new plaque must be affixed in place of the previous one.

The plaque must show at least the following details:

— name, address or trade name of the approved fitter or workshop,

— characteristic coefficient of the vehicle, in the form "w = . . . rev/km" or "w = . . . imp/km",

— effective circumference of the wheel tyres in the form "1 = . . . mm",

— the dates on which the characteristic coefficient of the vehicle was determined and the effective measured circumference of the wheel tyres.

4. *Sealing*

The following parts must be sealed:

(a) the installation plaque, unless it is attached in such a way that it cannot be removed without the markings thereon being destroyed;

(b) the two ends of the link between the recording equipment proper and the vehicle;

(c) the adaptor itself and the point of its insertion into the circuit;

(d) the switch mechanism for vehicles with two or more axle ratios;

(e) the links joining the adaptor and the switch mechanism to the rest of the equipment;

(f) the casings required under Chapter III (a) 7.2.

[(g) any cover giving access to the means of adapting the constant of the recording equipment to the characteristic coefficient of the vehicle.]

In particular cases, further seals may be required on approval of the equipment type and a note of the positioning of these seals must be made on the approval certificate.

[The seals mentioned in (b), (c) and (e) are authorised to be removed:

— in case of emergency,

— to install, to adjust or to repair a speed limitation device or any other device contributing to road safety,

provided that the recording equipment continues to function reliably and correctly and is resealed by an approved fitter or workshop immediately after fitting the speed limitation device or any other device contributing to road safety or within seven days in other cases]; for each occasion that these seals are broken a written statement giving the reasons for such action must be prepared and made available to the competent authority.

[5. The cables connecting the recording equipment to the transmitter must be protected by a continuous plastic-coated rust-protected steel sheath with crimped ends except where an equivalent protection against manipulation is guaranteed by other means (for example by electronic monitoring such as signal encryption) capable of detecting the presence of any device, which is unnecessary for the correct operation of the recording equipment and whose purpose is to prevent the accurate operation of the recording equipment by short circuiting or interruption or by modification of the electronic data from the speed and distance sensor. A joint, comprised of sealed connections, is deemed to be continuous within the meaning of this Regulation.

The aforementioned electronic monitoring may be replaced by an electronic control which ensures that the recording equipment is able to record any movement of the vehicle, independent from the signal of the speed and distance sensor.]

[For the purpose of the application of the present point, M 1 and N 1 vehicles are those defined in Part A of Annex II to Council Directive 70/156/EEC [*q.v.*]. For those vehicles that are equipped with tachographs in compliance with the Regulation and are not designed to install an armoured cable between the distance and speed sensors and the recording equipment, then an adaptor shall be fitted as close as possible to the distance and speed sensors.]

[The armoured cable shall be fitted from the adaptor to the recording equipment.]

[Chapter V of Annex I is printed as amended by Regulation (EEC) 3688/92; Regulation (EC)   **C3.55** *2479/95; Regulation (EC) 1056/97.]*

VI   CHECKS AND INSPECTIONS

The Member States shall nominate the bodies which shall carry out the checks and in-   **C3.56** spections.

1. *Certification of new or repaired instruments*

Every individual device, whether new or repaired, shall be certified in respect of its correct operation and the accuracy of its readiness and recordings, within the limits laid down in Chapter III (f) 1, by means of sealing in accordance with Chapter V (4)(f).

For this purpose the Member States may stipulate an initial verification, consisting of a check on and confirmation of the conformity of a new or repaired device with the type-approved model and/or with the requirements of the Regulation and its Annexes, or may delegate the power to certify to the manufacturers or to their authorised agents.

2. *Installation*

When being fitted to a vehicle, the equipment and the whole installation must comply with the provisions relating to maximum tolerances laid down in Chapter III (f) 2.

The inspection tests shall be carried out by the approved fitter or workshop on his or its responsibility.

3. *Periodic inspections*

    (a) Periodic inspections of the equipment fitted to vehicles shall take place at least every two years and may be carried out in conjunction with roadworthiness tests of vehicles.

        These inspections shall include the following checks:

        — that the equipment is working correctly,

        — that the equipment carries the type approval mark,

        — that the installation plaque is affixed,

        — that the seals on the equipment and on the other parts of the installation are intact,

        — the actual circumference of the tyres.

    (b) An inspection to ensure compliance with the provision of Chapter III (f) 3 on the maximum tolerances in use shall be carried out at least once every six years, although each Member State may stipulate a shorter interval or such inspection in respect of vehicles registered in its territory. Such inspections must include replacement of the installation plaque.

4. *Measurement of errors*

The measurement of errors on installation and during use shall be carried out under the following conditions, which are to be regarded as constituting standard test conditions:

        — vehicle unladen, in normal running, order

        — tyre pressures in accordance with the manufacturer's instructions,

        — tyre wear within the limits allowed by law,

        — movement of the vehicle: the vehicle must proceed, driven by its own engine, in a straight line and on a level surface, at a speed of 50 ± 5 km/h; provided that it is of comparable accuracy, the test may also be carried out on an appropriate test bench.

[ANNEX IB

REQUIREMENTS FOR CONSTRUCTION, TESTING, INSTALLATION, AND INSPECTION

I   DEFINITIONS

In this Annex:

(a) *"recording equipment"* means:

C3.57   the total equipment intended for installation in road vehicles to show, record and store automatically or semi-automatically details of the movement of such vehicles and of certain work periods of their drivers. This equipment includes cables, sensors, an electronic driver information device, one (two) card reader(s) for the insertion of one or two driver memory card(s), an integrated or separate printer, display instruments, facilities for downloading the data memory, facilities to display or print information on demand and facilities for the input of the places where the daily work period begins and ends;

(b) *"data memory"* **means:**

an electronic storage system built into the reording equipment, capable of storing at least 365 calendar days from the recording equipment. The memory should be protected in such a way as to prevent unauthorised access to and manipulation of the data and detect any such attempt;

(c) *"driver card (with memory)"* **means:**

a removable information transfer and storage device allocated by the authorities of the Member States to each individual driver for the purposes of identification of the driver and storage of essential data. The format and technical specifications of the driver card (with memory) shall meet the requirements laid down in Chapter IV of this Annex;

(d) *"the constant of the recording equipment"* **means:**

the numerical characteristic giving the value of the input signal required to show and record a distance travelled of one kilometre; this constant must be expressed either in revolutions per kilometre ($k = \ldots$ rev/km) or in impulses per kilometre ($k = \ldots$ imp/km);

(e) *"characteristic coefficient of the vehicle"* **means:**

the numerical characteristic giving the value of the output signal emitted by the part of the vehicle linking it with the recording equipment (gearbox output shaft or axle) while the vehicle travels a distance of one kilometre under normal test conditions (see Chapter VII(e)). The characteristic coefficient is expressed either in revolutions per kilometre ($w = \ldots$ rev/km) or in impulses per kilometre ($w = \ldots$ imp/km);

(f) *"effective circumference of the wheel tyres"* **means:**

the average of the distances travelled by each of the wheels moving the vehicle (driving wheels) in the course of one complete rotation. The measurement of these distances must be made under normal test conditions (see Chapter VII(e)) and is expressed in the form "$l = \ldots$ mm"; where the appropriate measurement of these distances may be based on a theoretical calculation which takes into account the distribution of the maximum authorised weight on the axles;

(g) *"test station card"* **means:**

a removable data transfer and storage device for use in the card reader of the recording equipment, issued by the authorities of the Member State to their authorised bodies. The test station card identifies the body and allows for testing, calibration and programming of the recording equipment;

(h) *"control card"* **means:**

a removable data transfer and storage device for use in the card reader of the recording equipment, issued by the authorities of the Member States to competent authorities to get access to the data stored in the data memory or in the driver cards for reading, printing and/or downloading;

(i) *"company data card"* **means:**

a removable data transfer and storage device issued by the Member State's authorities to the owner of vehicles fitted with recording equipment.

The company data card allows for displaying, downloading and printing of the data stored in the (item of) recording equipment fitted in the company's vehicle(s);

(j) *"calendar day"* **means:**

a day ranging from 00.00 hours to 24.00 hours. All calendar days relate to UTC time (universal time co-ordinated);

(k) **_"downloading"_** **means:**

copy of a part or of a complete set of data stored in the data memory of the vehicle or in the memory of the driver card.

Downloading may not alter or delete any stored data.

Downloaded data are protected in such a way as to make attempts to data manipulation detectable; origin of dowloaded data must be authenticatable.

Downloaded data are kept in a format that can be used by any authorised person;

(l) **_"vehicle identification"_** **means:**

number(s) identifying the vehicle on the basis of its VIN and/or its VRN.

II   GENERAL CHARACTERISTICS AND FUNCTIONS OF RECORDING EQUIPMENT

C3.58   The equipment must be able to record, store, display and print the following:

(a) Recording and storing in the data memory

1.   distance travelled by the vehicle with an accuracy of 1km;

2.   speed of the vehicle;

2.1.   momentary speed of the vehicle at a frequency of 1 s for the last 24 hours of use of the vehicle;

2.2.   exceeding the authorised speed of the vehicle, defined as any period of more than 1 minute during which the vehicle speed exceeds 90 km/h for N_3 vehicles or 105 km/h for M_3 vehicles (with time, date, maximum speed of the overspeeding, average speed during the period concerned);

3.   periods of driving time (times and dates), with an accuracy of 1 minute;

4.   other periods of work or of availability (times and dates) with an accuracy of 1 minute;

5.   breaks from work and daily rest periods (times and dates) with an accuracy of 1 minute;

6.   for electronic recording equipment which is equipment operated by signals transmitted electrically from the distance and speed sensor, any interruption exceeding 100 milliseconds in the power supply of the recording equipment (except lighting), in the power supply of the distance and speed sensor and any interruption in the signal lead to the distance and speed sensor, with date, time, duration and driver card issue number;

7.   the driver card issue number with times and dates of insertion and removal;

8.   for each driver card that is inserted for the first time after it was used in another item of recording equipment
   — current driving time since the last break or rest period,
   — driving time for the day after the last rest period of at least eight hours,
   — driving times for the day between two rest periods of at least eight hours for the preceding 27 calendar days with date, time and duration,
   — total of the driving times for the current week and the preceding week and the total of the driving times of the two completed preceding weeks,
   — rest periods of at least eight hours' duration for the day and the preceding 27 calendar days in each case with date, time and duration,
   — the VRN of the vehicles driven;

9.   date, time and duration of driving without an inserted or a functioning driver card;

10. data recorded on the places at which the daily work period began and ended;

11. automatically identifiable system faults of the recording equipment with date, time and driver card issue number;

12. faults in the driver card with date and time and driver card issue number;

13. workshop card number of the authorised fitter or workshop with date of at least the last installation inspection and/or periodic inspection of the recording equipment in accordance with Chapter VII(c) and (d);

14. control card number with date of control card insertion and type of control (display, printing, downloading). In case of downloading, period downloaded should be recorded;

15. time adjustment with date, time and card issue number;

16. driving status (single/crew driving — driver/co-driver);

(b) Storing on the driver card

1. the essential data for the periods listed under point (a)(3), (4) and (5) for a period of at least the last 28 calendar days combined with the "VRN" identification of the vehicle driven and the data under point (a)(10), (14) and (16);   **C3.59**

2. the events and faults according to point (a)(6), (11) and (15) with the "VRN" identification of the vehicle driven;

2.1. date and time of insertion and removal of the driver card and distance travelled during the corresponding period;

2.2. date and time of insertion and removal of the co-driver card with issue number;

3. data must be recorded and stored on the driver card in such a way as to rule out any possibility of falsification;

(c) Recording and storing in the case of two drivers

for vehicles used by two drivers the driving time listed under point (a)(3) must be recorded and stored on the driver card of the driver who is driving the vehicle. The equipment must record and store in the data memory and on the two other cards simultaneously but distinctly details of the information listed under point (a)(4) and (5);   **C3.60**

(d) Displaying or printing on request for an authorised user

1. driver card issue number, expiry date of the card;   **C3.61**

2. the surname and first name of the driver who is the cardholder;

3. current driving time since the last break or rest period;

4. driving time for the day after the last rest period of at least eight hours;

5. driving times for the day between two rest periods of at least eight hours for the preceding 27 calendar days on which the driver has driven, with date, time and duration;

6. total of the driving times for the current week and the preceding week and total times for the two completed preceding weeks;

7. the other periods of work and availability;

8. rest periods of at least eight hours' duration for the day and the preceding 27 days in each case with date, time and duration;

9. "VRN" identification of vehicles driven for at least the last 28 calendar days with the distance travelled per vehicle and day, time of first insertion and last removal of the driver card and the time of change of vehicle;

10. time adjustment with date, time and card issue number;

11. interruption of power supply to the recording equipment with date, time, duration and driver card issue number (as defined in point (a)(6));

12. sensor interruption with date, time, duration and driver card issue nuber (as defined in point (a)(6));

13. the "VIN" and/or "VRN" identification of the vehicle driven;

14. driving without driver card as defined in point (a)(9) for the last 28 calendar days;

15. details of the information stored concerning the driver (as defined in point (c));

16. recorded data on the places where the daily work period began and ended;

17. the automatically identifiable system faults of the recording equipment with date, time and driver card issue number;

18. the faults in the driver card with date and time and driver card issue number;

19. control card number with date of control card insertion and type of control (display, printing, downloading). In the case of downloading, period downloaded should be recorded;

20. exceeding the authorised speed as defined in point (a)(2.2), with date, time and driver card issue number for the current week and in any case including the last day of the previous week;

21. summary reports whereby compliance with Regulations (EEC) No. 3820/85 and (EEC) No. 3821/85 and Directive 88/599/EEC can be checked.

III CONSTRUCTION AND FUNCTIONAL REQUIREMENTS FOR RECORDING EQUIPMENT

(a) General points

C3.62

1.1. Any inclusion in or connection to the recording equipment of any device, or devices, approved or otherwise, must not interfere with, or be capable of interfering with, the proper operation of the recording equipment. The recording equipment must be submitted for approval complete with any such included devices.

1.2. The recording equipment must be capable of operating correctly in all the climatic conditions normally encountered in Community territory.

2. *Materials*

2.1. All the constituent parts of the recording equipment must be made of sufficient stability and mechanical strength and with stable electrical and magnetic characteristics.

2.2. Any modification in a constituent part of the equipment or in the nature of the materials used for its manufacture must, before being used, be submitted for approval to the authority which granted type-approval for the recording equipment.

3. *Measurement of distance travelled*

The distance travelled may be measured and recorded either:
— so as to include both forward and reverse movements, or
— so as to include only forward movement.

Any recordings of reversing movements must on no account affect the clarity and accuracy of the other recordings.

4. *Measurement of speed*

4.1 The range of speed measurement must be as stated in the type-approval certificate.

4.2 The natural frequency and the damping of the measuring device must be such that the instruments showing and recording the speed can, within the range of measurements, follow acceleration changes of up to 2 m/s^2, within the limits of accepted tolerances.

5. *Measurement of time (clock)*

Time is digital. Update is performed (if necessary) at the authorised workshop. The internal clock time is UTC. The driver can change the offset of the time displayed on the display screen.

5.1. The measurement of time is effected automatically in the recording equipment.

5.2. The clock time in the memory can be reset only when an authorised workshop card is inserted.

6. *Lighting and protection*

6.1. The visual instruments of the equipment must be provided with adequate non-dazzling lighting.

6.2. For normal conditions of use, all the internal parts of the equipment must be protected against damp and dust. In addition, they must be made tamper-proof by means of casings capable of being sealed.

6.3. Protection against electrical interference and magnetic fields must be provided complying with standards for electronics in vehicles.

6.4. The cables connecting the recording equipment to the transmitter must be protected by electronic monitoring, such as signal encryption, capable of detecting the presence within that part of the system of any device, not otherwise necessary for the correct operation of the recording equipment, which is capable of preventing the accurate operation of the recording equipment by any short circuit, interruption or modification of the electronic data from the speed and distance sensor, or by the duplication of any other approved devices, when that device is connected and put into operation.

6.5. The total system, including the connections to the speed and distance sensor must be tamper-proof.

6.6. The recording equipment must self-detect faults.

(b) Visual instruments

Indications must be visible from outside the recording equipment and give a clear, plain and unambiguous reading including where there are two drivers.   **C3.63**

The display instrument must enable the information referred to in Chapter II(d) to be displayed on request. The request can take place selectively or sequentially.

(c) Warning signals

1. A warning to the driver of at least 30 seconds if the vehicle is driven: **C3.64**
    — without the driver card in place,
    — with a malfunctioning card,

— with the driver card in the wrong slot,
— when the recording equipment has detected one or more cases of internal malfunctioning, in particular those referred to in Chapter II(d)(17) and (18),
— above the speed limit as defined in Chapter II(a)(2.2).

2. A warning to the driver before exceeding four and a half hours driving time per
period of driving time and nine hours daily driving time, 15 minutes before and at
the time of exceeding the limit.

3. A warning to the driver, 15 minutes before and at the time of failing to observe the
required eight hours daily rest period within the last 24 hours.

4. Additional warnings may be installed at the request of the vehicle owner.

5. *Format of the warnings*

Warnings may be either auditory or visual, or a combination of both and must be
clearly recognisable by the user.

(d) Memory

C3.65

1. The periods of time referred to in Chapter II(a)(3), (4) and (5) must be stored whenever there is any change of activity or status.

2. The period of driving time must always be stored automatically when the vehicle is
in motion.

3. The other periods of time as indicated in Article 15(3), second indent (b), (c) and (d)
of the Regulation must always be stored separately through the operation where
necessary of an activity selection device.

(e) Markings

C3.66

1. The following details must appear on the instrument face of the recording equipment:
— near the figure indicating the distance, the unit of measurement of distance,
indicated by the abbreviation "km",
— near the figure showing the speed, the entry "km/h".

2. The descriptive plaque must be visible on the recording equipment and must show
the following details:
— name and address of the manufacturer of the equipment,
— manufacturer's number and year of manufacture of the equipment,
— approval mark for the recording equipment type,
— the constant of the recording equipment in the form "k = . . . rev/km" or
"k = . . . imp/km",
— optionally, the range of speed measurements, in the form indicated in 1.

This information may also be shown on demand by the recording equipment.

(f) Maximum tolerances (display and recording instruments)

C3.67

1. The maximum tolerances relate to distance travelled, speed and time and are
measured on the dynamometer before installation and, under the circumstances
referred to in Chapter VII, on installation, during periodic inspection and in
use.

2. The maximum tolerances set out in 1 are valid for extreme temperatures
corresponding to climatic conditions normally encountered in Community territory.

IV CARDS WITH MEMORY

A.   DRIVER CARD (WITH MEMORY)

1. Insertion/removal

The recording equipment must be so designed that the driver card (with memory) is locked   **C3.68**
in position on its proper insertion into the card reader and that the relevant driver card data
are automatically stored in the data memory of the recording equipment. The release of
the driver card may function only when the vehicle is stationary and after the relevant data
have been stored on the driver card.

2. Memory capacity of the driver card

The capacity of the driver card must be sufficient to store at least 28 calendar days of data   **C3.69**
referred to in Chapter II(c) for the actual driver. Should the data card be full the new data
will replace the oldest data.

3. Visible data

Page 1 will contain: **C3.70**

  (a) the word "Driver card" printed in large type in the official language or languages
      of the Member State issuing the card;

      "Driver card" in the other official languages of the Community, printed to form
      the background of the licence:

      es: TARJETA DEL CONDUCTOR
      dk: FØRERKORT
      de: FAHRERKARTE
      el: KAPTA OΔHΓOY
      en: DRIVER CARD
      fr: CARTE DE CONDUCTEUR
      ga: CÁRTA TIOMÁNAÍ
      it: CARTA DEL CONDUCENTE
      nl: BESTUURDERSKAART
      pt: CARTÃO DE CONDUTOR
      fi: KULJETTAJAKORTTI
      sv: FÖRARKORT;

  (b) the name of the Member States issuing the card (optional);

  (c) the distinguishing sign of the Member States issuing the card, printed in negative
      in a blue rectangle and encircled by 12 yellow stars; the distinguishing signs are as
      follows:

      B   Belgium
      DK   Denmark
      D   Germany
      GR   Greece
      E   Spain
      F   France
      IRL Ireland
      I   Italy
      L   Luxembourg
      NL   The Netherlands
      A   Austria
      P   Portugal
      FIN Finland

S   Sweden
UK The United Kingdom

(d) information specific to the card issued, numbered as follows:

1. surname of the holder;
2. first name(s) of the holder;
3. date and place of birth;
4. (a) date of issue of the card;
   (b) date of expiry of the card;
   (c) the name of the issuing authority (may be printed on page 2);
   (d) a different number from the one under heading 5, for administrative purposes (optional);
5. (a) driving licence number including number of replacement issue;
   (b) driver card issue number including the index number of replacement issue;
6. photograph of the holder;
7. signature of the holder;
8. normal place residence, or postal address of the holder (optional).

The data referred to in 1, 2, 3, 4(b) and 5(a) and (b) will also be stored in the driver card memory.

Page 2 will contain:

(a) an explanation of the numbered items which appear on pages 1 and 2 of the card;
(b) with the specific written agreement of the holder, information which is not related to the administration of the driver card may also be added, such addition will not alter in any way the use of the model as a driver card.

COMMUNITY MODEL DRIVER CARD

Page 2

DRIVER CARD   MEMBER STATE
1.
2.
3.
4a.   4c.
4b.   (4d.)
5a.
5b.
7.

(8.)

1.   Surname   2. Name   3. Date and place of birth
4a. Card issuing date
4b. Administrative expiry date of card
4c. Issuing authority
(4d.) No for national administrative purposes
5a. Driving licence number   5b. Driver card number
6.   Photograph
7.   Signature   (8.) Address

Please return to:

NAME OF AUTHORITY AND ADDRESS

SPECIMEN COMMUNITY MODEL DRIVER CARD: BELGIAN CARD
(For information)

BESTUURDERSKAART   KONINKRIJK BELGIË
1. Ruyter
2. Georges
3. 01.04.73   Milano
4a. 01.07.98   4c. B-9000 Gent
4b. 30.06.03
5a. DA 003 360
5b. 11 ABC 334455
7.

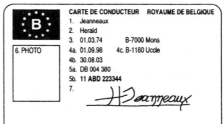

CARTE DE CONDUCTEUR   ROYAUME DE BELGIQUE
1. Jeanneaux
2. Herald
3. 01.03.74   B-7000 Mons
4a. 01.09.98   4c. B-1180 Uccle
4b. 30.08.03
5a. DB 004 380
5b. 11 ABD 223344
7.

4. Standards

The driver card and recording equipment must conform to the following standards: **C3.71**
— ISO 7810,
— ISO 7816-1,
— ISO 7816-2,
— ISO 7816-3,
— draft ISO 7816-4,
— draft ISO 10373,
— the detailed functional specifications defined within systems of identification cards intended for use in surface transport.

5. Security, including data protection

The various components of the driver card are intended to exclude any falsification or tampering and to detect any attempt of that kind.   **C3.72**

6. Temperature range

C3.73 The driver card must be capable of operating correctly in all the climatic conditions normally encountered in Community territory.

7. Lifetime

C3.74 The card must be capable of operating correctly for a five-year period if used within the environmental and electrical specifications.

8. Electrical characteristics

C3.75 The electrical characteristics of the card must correspond to the specifications applicable to electronics in vehicles.

9. Logical structure of the driver card

C3.76 The logical structure of the card must be defined in such a way as to guarantee its proper operation and its compatibility with any recording equipment complying with this Annex.

10. Functions and commands

C3.77 The card's functions and commands must cover all the functions referred to in Chapter I(c) and Chapter II(b).

11. Elementary files

C3.78 The specifications of elementary files must be within the framework of the standards referred to in 4.

12. Special provisions

C3.79 After consulting the Commission, Member States may add colours or markings, such as national symbols and security features, without prejudice to the other provisions of this Annex.

B.   TEST STATION CARD (WITH MEMORY), CONTROL CARD (WITH MEMORY) AND COMPANY DATA CARD (WITH MEMORY)

C3.80 The specifications of the test station, control and company data cards (with memory) must be such that they operate correctly when used as provided for in Chapter I(g), (h) and (i) and are compatible with any recording equipment complying with this Annex. The structure of the cards must be so designed as to give access only to the authorised user and only for the exercise of the functions which each card is intended to fulfil.

V   PRINTER AND STANDARD PRINTOUTS

C3.81 1. Printers must be so designed as to produce the print-outs referred to in Chapter II(d) with a degree of definition likely to avoid any ambiguity when they are read. Print-outs must remain clearly legible and identifiable under normal conditions of storage for at least one year.

They must retain their dimensions and recordings under normal conditions of humidity and temperature.

It must also be possible to add handwritten notes, such as the driver's signature, to these documents.

2. The minimum capacity of print-outs, whatever their form, must be sufficient to allow the printing of the information referred to in Chapter II(d).

If several print-outs have to be linked together to increase printing capacity, the links between the various documents must be made in such a way that there are no breaks in the data at the points linked which could jeopardise interpretation of the data.

VI INSTALLATION OF RECORDING EQUIPMENT

(a) Installation

1. The recording equipment must be protected against accidental damage.   **C3.82**

2. It must be possible for authorised agents to adapt the constant of the recording equipment to the characteristic coefficient of the vehicle by means of a suitable device, to be known as an adaptor.

Vehicles with two or more axle ratios must be fitted with a switch device whereby these various ratios will automatically be brought into line with the ratio for which the equipment has been adapted to the vehicle by the adaptor.

(b) Installation plaque

After the equipment has been checked on installation, an installation plaque which is   **C3.83**
clearly visible must be affixed on, in or beside the equipment. After every inspection by an approved fitter or workshop requiring a change in the calibration of the installation, a new plaque must be affixed in place of the previous one.

The plaque must bear at least the following details:
— name, address or trade name of the approved fitter or workshop,
— characteristic coefficient of the vehicle, in the form "w = . . . rev/km" or "w = . . . imp/km",
— effective circumference of the wheel tyres in the form "l = . . . mm",
— the date on which the characteristic coefficient of the vehicle was determined and the effective circumference of the wheel tyres measured,
— the last eight digits of the chassis number of the vehicle.

(c) Sealing

1. The following parts must be sealed: **C3.84**
    (a) any connection which, if disconnected, would cause undetectable alterations to be made or data to be lost;
    (b) any cover giving access to the circuits or mechanisms, any alteration of which would affect the proper operation of the recording equipment or which would allow unauthorised alteration of the equipment's characteristics;
    (c) the installation plaque, unless it is attached in such a way that it cannot be removed without the markings thereon being destroyed.

2. In all cases, the location of the seals must be mentioned on the type-approval certificate and their effectiveness tested as part of the type-approval procedures.

3. The seals mentioned in 1(b) may be removed:
    — in case of emergency,
    — to install, to adjust or to repair a speed limitation device or any other device contributing to road safety, provided that the recording equipment continues to function reliably and correctly and is resealed by an approved fitter or workshop (in accordance with Chapter VII) immediately after fitting the speed limitation

device or any other device contributing to road safety or within seven days in other cases.

On each occasion that these seals are broken a written statement giving the reasons for such action must be prepared and made available to the competent authority.

VII CHECKS AND INSPECTIONS

(a) Approval of test stations (fitters and workshops)

C3.85 The Member States will nominate the bodies to carry out the checks and inspections.

(b) Certification of new or repaired instruments

C3.86 Every individual device, whether new or repaired, must be certified in respect of its proper operation and the accuracy of its readings and recordings, within the limits laid down in Chapter III(f)(1) by means of sealing in accordance with Chapter VI(c)(1) or equivalent digital information in the data memory of the recording equipment.

(c) Installation inspection and programming

C3.87 1. When being fitted to a vehicle, the recording equipment and the whole installation must comply with the provisions relating to maximum tolerances laid down in Chapter III(f)(2).

2. The following programming of the recording equipment must be carried out:
   — the date of the installation test,
   — the universal time co-ordinated (UTC),
   — the "VIN" and "VRN" vehicle identification,
   — the number of the workshop card of the approved fitter or approved workshop.

(d) Periodic inspections

C3.88 1. Periodic inspections of the equipment fitted to vehicles must take place after any repair of the equipment or after any alteration of the characteristic coefficient of the vehicle or of the effective circumference of the tyres or at least once within two years of the last inspection; they may be carried out in conjunction with roadworthiness tests on vehicles.

These inspections must include the following checks:
   — that the recording equipment is working properly, including the downloading of data to and from the workshop card,
   — that compliance with the provisions of Chapter III(f)(2) on the maximum tolerances on installation is ensured,
   — that the recording equipment carries the type-approval mark,
   — that the installation plaque is affixed,
   — that the seals on the equipment and on the other parts of the installation are intact,
   — the actual circumference of the tyres.

2. The following programming of the recording equipment must be carried out:
   — the date of the periodic inspection,
   — the universal time co-ordinated (UTC),
   — the "VIN" and "VRN" vehicle identification
   — the number of the card of the approved workshop.

3. Such inspections must include replacement of the installation plaque or equivalent digital information in the data memory of the recording equipment.

(e) Measurement of errors

The measurement of errors on installation and during use must be carried out under the following conditions, which are to be regarded as constituting standard test conditions: **C3.89**
— vehicle unladen, in normal running order,
— tyre pressures in accordance with the manufacturer's instructions,
— tyre wear within the limits allowed by national law,
— vehicle movement: the vehicle must advance under its own engine power in a straight line on level ground and at a speed of 50 ± 5 km/h. The measuring distance must be at least 1000m,
— provided that it is of comparable accuracy, an appropriate dynamometer may also be used for the test.]

[Annex IB ws inserted by Regulation (EC) 2135/98.]   **C3.90**

ANNEX II

APPROVAL MARK AND CERTIFICATE

I   APPROVAL MARK   **C3.91**

1. The approval mark shall be made up of:

     — a rectangle, within which shall be placed the letter "e" followed by a distinguishing number or letter for the country which has issued the approval in accordance with the following conventional signs:

[Austria	12,]
Belgium	6,
Denmark	18,
[Finland	17,]
Germany	1,
Greece	GR,
Spain	9,
France	2,
Ireland	IRL,
Italy	3,
Luxembourg	13,
Netherlands	4,
Portugal	21,
[Sweden	5,]
United Kingdom	11,
and	

     — an approval number corresponding to the number of the approval certificate drawn up for prototype of the recording equipment or the record sheet, placed at any point within the immediate proximity of this rectangle.

[Paragraph 1 of Annex II is printed as amended by the Act of Accession (Austria, Finland, Sweden), Annex I.]   **C3.92**

2. The approval mark shall be shown on the descriptive plaque of each set of equipment and on each record sheet. It must be indelible and must always remain clearly legible.   **C3.93**

3. The dimensions of the approval mark drawn below are expressed in millimetres, these dimensions being minima. The ratios between the dimensions must be maintained.

C3.94

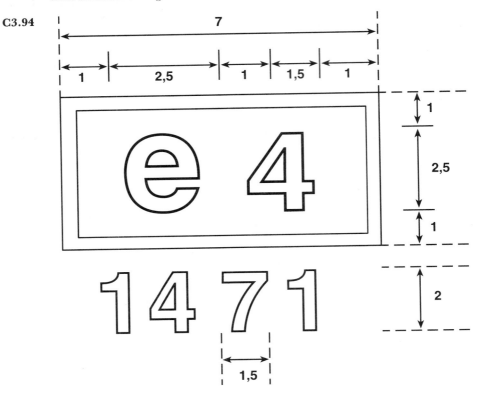

C3.95   *[The characters "e 4" and "1471" are stated to be for guidance only.]*

II APPROVAL CERTIFICATE

A State having granted approval shall issue the applicant with an approval certificate, the **C3.96** model for which is given below. When informing other Member States of approvals issued or, if the occasion should arise, withdrawn, a Member State shall use copies of that certificate.

APPROVAL CERTIFICATE

Name of competent administration ....

Notification concerning [*the items which are not applicable should be deleted*]:

— approval of a type of recording equipment

— withdrawal of approval of a type of recording equipment

— approval of a model record sheet

— withdrawal of approval of a record sheet

....

Approval No ....

1. Trade mark or name ....

2. Name of type or model..

3. Name of manufacturer ....

4. Address of manufacturer ....

....

5. Submitted for approval on ....

6. Tested at ....

7. Date and number of test report ....

8. Date of approval ....

9. Date of withdrawal of approval ....

10. Type or types of recording equipment in which sheet is designed to be used

....

11. Place ....

12. Date ....

13. Descriptive documents annexed ....

---

14. Remarks ....

....

(Signature)

Regulation (EEC) 3314/90
of November 16, 1990

adapting to technical progress Council Regulation (EEC) 3821/85 on recording equipment in road transport

C4.01   THE COMMISSION OF THE EUROPEAN COMMUNITIES

Having regard to the Treaty establishing the European Economic Community,

Having regard to Council Regulation (EEC) No. 3821/85 of 20 December 1985 on recording equipment in road transport [*q.v.*], and in particular Articles 17 and 18 thereof,

Whereas it is necessary to eliminate the possibilities of fraud in the use of electronic recording equipment in road transport in particular those caused by the interruption of the power supply or of the distance and speed sensor;

Whereas in the light of experience and in view of the current state of the art it is possible to indicate such interruptions clearly on the record sheets in order to facilitate application of the Regulation and to discourage this kind of fraudulent use;

Whereas it is appropriate to implement this new technology in the Community construction and installation standards for electronic recording equipment;

Whereas in order to ensure effective checking and correct registration of driving time in particular, driving time should be recorded automatically and the other periods, when the driver is not driving the vehicle, should be recorded according to the sign indicated on the switch mechanism;

Whereas current recording equipment already provides for this automatic recording of driving time and therefore in the light of experience and current state of the art the construction standards for the recording equipment should be adapted accordingly;

Whereas the measures provided for in this Regulation are in accordance with the opinion of the Committee for Adaptation of Regulation (EEC) No. 3821/85 to Technical Progress,

HAS ADOPTED THIS REGULATION:

C4.02   **Article 1**   *[Amends Regulation (EEC) 3821/85, Annex I (q.v.).]*

Article 2

C4.03   As from 1 July 1991 Member States shall no longer grant EEC approval to any type of recording equipment which does not comply with the provisions of Regulation (EEC) No. 3821/85, as amended by this Regulation.

Article 3

C4.04   As from 1 January 1996 the recording equipment of any new vehicle brought into service for the first time shall comply with Regulation (EEC) No. 3821/85, as amended by this Regulation.

Article 4

This Regulation shall enter into force on the third day following its publication in the *Official Journal of the European Communities.*   **C4.05**

[Regulation (EEC) 3314/90 was published on November 17, 1990.]   **C4.06**

This Regulation shall be binding in its entirety and directly applicable in all Member States.   **C4.07**

Directive 91/439/EEC
of July 29, 1991

on driving licences

C5.01 *Editorial note.* Only selected provisions of this Directive (which have been incorporated into the provisions of the Convention on driving disqualifications below) are reproduced. The full text of the Directive (as originally adopted) is reproduced at O.J. No. L237, August 24, 1991, pp. 1–24).

* * *

Article 3

C5.02 1, 2. *[Omitted.]*

3. . . .
— *"Motor vehicle"* means any power-driven vehicle, other than a motorcycle, which is normally used for carrying persons or goods by road or for drawing, on the road, vehicles used for the carriage of persons or goods. This term shall include trolleybuses, i.e. vehicles connected to an electric conductor and not rail-borne. It shall not include agricultural or forestry tractors;

. . .

* * *

Article 9

C5.03 For the purpose of this Directive, *"normal"* residence means the place where a person usually lives, that is for at least 185 days in each calendar year, because of personal and occupational ties, or, in the case of a person with no occupational ties, because of personal ties which show close links between that person and the place where he is living.

However, the normal residence of a person whose occupational ties are in a different place from his personal ties and who consequently lives in turn in different places situated in two or more Member States shall be regarded as being the place of his personal ties, provided that such person returns there regularly. This last condition need not be met where the person is living in a Member State in order to carry out a task of a definite duration. Attendance at a university or school shall not imply transfer of normal residence.

* * *

Directive 92/6/EEC
of February 10, 1992

on the installation and use of speed limitation devices for certain categories of motor vehicles in the Community

Editorial note. This Directive (and also Directive 92/94/EEC (O.J. No. L129, May 14, 1992, p. 92) relating to EC type approval for speed limitation devices) is implemented by regulation 36B of the Road Vehicles (Construction and Use) Regulations 1986 (S.I. 1986 No. 1078), *q.v.* For the purposes of regulation 36B, the term "*set*" in relation to a speed limiter has the meaning attributed to it in this Directive and the references in regulation 36B to the speed at which a speed limiter is set are construed accordingly (regulation 36B(15)).

C6.01

THE COUNCIL OF THE EUROPEAN COMMUNITIES,

Having regard to the Treaty establishing the European Economic Community, and in particular [Article 71] thereof,

C6.02

Having regard to the proposal from the Commission,

Having regard to the opinion of the European Parliament,

Having regard to the opinion of the Economic and Social Committee,

Whereas one of the objectives of a common transport policy is to lay down common rules applicable to international transport within the Community and to facilitate the circulation of vehicles;

Whereas the growth of road traffic and the resulting increase in danger and nuisance present all Member States with road safety and environmental problems of a serious nature;

Whereas the available engine power for heavy goods vehicles and buses needed for climbing slopes enables them to be driven on level roads at excessive speeds that are not compatible with the specifications of other components of those vehicles such as brakes and tyres; whereas, for that reason and for reasons of environmental protection in certain Member States, speed limitation devices were made compulsory for certain categories of motor vehicles;

Whereas the beneficial effects of speed limitation devices with regard to protection of the environment and energy consumption, the wear and tear of the motor and tyres and road safety will be increased if such devices are in general use;

Whereas the use of speed limitation devices serves no purpose unless the appliances are of a degree of technical perfection such as will provide an adequate guarantee that no fraud is possible;

Whereas, as a first step, requirements should be introduced in the case only of the heaviest categories of motor vehicles which are most involved in international transport and thereafter, depending on technical possibilities and experiences in Member States, could be extended to lighter categories of motor vehicles;

Whereas, in certain Member States, vehicles intended exclusively for the carriage of dangerous goods must be equipped with speed limitation devices set at maximum speeds lower than those provided for by this Directive; whereas, in this specific case, the Member States in question should be allowed to maintain such regulations for vehicles registered within their territory because they enhance road safety and civil protection of the public, in accordance with the objectives of this Directive;

Whereas the installation of speed limitation devices on category M3 and N3 vehicles covered by this Directive, registered before it is brought into effect and intended exclusively for national transport operations could entail excessive costs in certain Member States; whereas it should therefore be made possible for those Member States to postpone the application of Articles 2 and 3 of this Directive to the vehicles concerned;

Whereas this Directive does not affect Member States' prerogatives as regards speed restriction provisions for traffic,

C6.03   *[The preamble is printed as amended by the Treaty of Amsterdam, art.12(1) and)3.]*

HAS ADOPTED THIS DIRECTIVE:

Article 1

C6.04   For the purpose of this Directive, "*motor vehicle*" means any power-driven vehicle falling within one of the categories listed below, intended for use on the road and having at least four wheels and a maximum design speed exceeding 25 km/h:

     —category M3 vehicles having a maximum weight exceeding 120 metric tonnes,
     —category N3 vehicles,

categories M3 and N3 being understood to be those defined in Annex I to Directive 70/156/EEC.

C6.05   *[The classification of motor vehicles is now contained in Annex II of Directive 70/156/EEC above.]*

Article 2

C6.06   Member States shall take the necessary steps to ensure that motor vehicles of the category M3 referred to in Article 1 shall be used on the road only if speed limitation devices are installed for which the maximum speed is set at 100 km/h.

Article 3

C6.07   1. Member States shall take the necessary measures to ensure that motor vehicles of category N3 shall be used on the road only if equipped with a device set in such a way that their speed cannot exceed 90 km/h; bearing in mind the technical tolerance which is allowed, at the present state of technology, between the regulating value and the actual speed of traffic, the maximum speed on this device shall be set at [85 km/h].

     2. Member States shall be authorized to set the maximum speed of the device at less than 85 km/h in vehicles used exclusively for the carriage of dangerous goods and registered in their territory.

C6.08   *[Article 3 is printed as corrected by a corrigendum of O.J. No. L244, September 30, 1993, p. 34.]*

Article 4

C6.09   1. Articles 2 and 3 shall be applicable to vehicles registered as from 1 January 1994.

     2. Articles 2 and 3 shall also be applicable, at the latest from 1 January 1995, to vehicles registered between 1 January 1988 and 1 January 1994.

However, where these vehicles are used exclusively for national transport operations, Articles 2 and 3 may be applied at the latest from 1 January 1996.

Article 5

1. Until Community provisions on these matters are applied, the speed limitation **C6.10**
devices referred to in Articles 2 and 3 must satisfy the technical requirements laid down by
the competent national authorities.

2. Speed limitation devices shall be installed by workshops or bodies approved by the
Member States.

Article 6

The requirements of Articles 2 and 3 do not apply to motor vehicles used by armed **C6.11**
forces, civil defence, fire and other emergency services and forces responsible for maintaining public order.

The same shall apply for motor vehicles which:
—by their construction, cannot drive faster than the limits provided for in Articles 2 and 3,
—are used for scientific tests on roads,
—are used only for public services in urban areas.

Article 7

1. Member States shall bring into force the laws, regulations and administrative prov- **C6.12**
isions necessary to comply with this Directive before 1 October 1993. They shall immediately inform the Commission thereof.

When these provisions are adopted by Member States, they shall contain a reference to
this Directive or shall be accompanied by such reference at the time of their official publication. The procedure for making such reference shall be adopted by Member States.

2 Member States shall communicate to the Commission the text of the provisions of
national law which they adopt in the field covered by this Directive.

Article 8

This Directive is addressed to the Member States. **C6.13**

Regulation (EEC) 684/92

of March 16, 1992

on common rules for the international carriage of passengers by coach and bus

C7.01   *European Economic Area.*   As to the Agreement on the European Economic Area generally, see the note to Regulation (EEC) 3820/85 above.

For the purposes of that agreement, Regulation (EEC) 684/92 has been adapted by *ibid.*, Annex XIII, Chapter II, para.32, as substituted by Decision 7/94 of the EEA Joint Committee, Annex 11, Chapter II, para.11 (O.J. No. L160, June 28, 1994, p. 84).

Regulation (EC) 11/98 (which amends Regulation (EEC) 684/92) has also been adapted for the purposes of the Agreement on the European Economic Area by Annex XIII, Chapter II, para.32 of the agreement, as amended by Decision 121/98 of the EEA Joint Committee (O.J. No. L297, November 18, 1999, p. 50).

C7.02   *[The text of this Regulation is printed as amended by:*

Regulation (EC) 11/98 (O.J. No. L4, January 8, 1998, p. 1) (December 11, 1998 and June 11, 1999).

The amending Regulation is referred to in the notes to the principal Regulation only by its reference number. The dates referred to above are the dates from which the amending Regulation took effect. The amendments effected by Regulation (EC) 11/98 took effect on December 11, 1998 unless otherwise indicated in the notes.]

THE COUNCIL OF THE EUROPEAN COMMUNITIES,

C7.03   Having regard to the Treaty establishing the European Economic Community, and in particular [Article 71] thereof,

Having regard to the proposal from the Commission,

Having regard to the opinion of the European Parliament,

Having regard to the opinion of the Economic and Social Committee,

Whereas, in accordance with [Article 71(1) (a)] of the Treaty, the establishment of a common transport policy entails, *inter alia*, laying down common rules applicable to the international carriage of passengers by road;

Whereas such rules were laid down in Council Regulations No. 117/66/EEC [*O.J. No. L147, August 9, 1966, p. 2688/66*], (EEC) No. 516/72 [*O.J. No. L67, March 20, 1972, p. 13, as amended*] and (EEC) No. 517/72 [*O.J. No. L67, March 20, 1972, p. 19, as amended*] and whereas this Regulation does not call in question the liberalisation achieved by those Regulations;

Whereas freedom to provide services constitutes a basic principle of the common transport policy and requires that carriers from all Member States be guaranteed access to international transport markets without discrimination on grounds of nationality or place of establishment;

Whereas there should be provision for flexible arrangements subject to certain conditions for shuttle services with accommodation, special regular services and certain occasional services, in order to satisfy market demand;

Whereas, while maintaining authorisation arrangements for regular services and shuttle services without accommodation, certain rules should be amended, particularly as regards authorisation procedures;

Whereas observance of the Treaty rules on competition must be guaranteed;

Whereas administrative formalities should be reduced as far as possible without the abandonment of the controls and penalties that guarantee the correct application of this Regulation;

Whereas it is for the Member States to adopt the measures necessary for the implementation of this Regulation;

Whereas the application of this Regulation should be monitored by means of a report to be submitted by the Commission and any future action in this area should be considered in the light of that report,

[The preamble is printed as amended by the Treaty of Amsterdam, art.12(1) and (3).]   **C7.04**

HAS ADOPTED THIS REGULATION:

SECTION I

GENERAL PROVISIONS

Article 1—Scope

1. This Regulation shall apply to the international carriage of passengers by coach and   **C7.05**
bus within the territory of the Community by carriers for hire or reward or own-account carriers established in a Member State in accordance with its law, using vehicles which are registered in that Member State and are suitable, by virtue of their construction and equipment, for carrying more than nine persons, including the driver, and are so intended, and to the movement of such vehicles empty in connection with such carriage.

Change of vehicle or interruption of carriage to enable part of a journey to be made by another means of transport shall not affect the application of this Regulation.

2. In the event of carriage from a Member State to a third country and vice versa, this Regulation shall apply to the part of the journey on the territory of the Member State of picking up or setting down, after conclusion of the necessary agreement between the Community and the third country concerned.

3. Pending the conclusion of agreements between the Community and the third countries concerned, this Regulation shall not affect provisions relating to the carriage referred to in paragraph 2 contained in bilateral agreements concluded by Member States with those third countries. However, Member States shall endeavour to adapt those agreements to ensure compliance with the principle of non-discrimination between Community carriers.

Article 2—Definitions

For the purposes of this Regulation, the following definitions shall apply: **C7.06**

1. *Regular services*

1.1. Regular services are services which provide for the carriage of passengers at specified intervals along specified routes, passengers being taken up and set down at predetermined stopping points. Regular services shall be open to all, subject, where appropriate, to compulsory reservation. [The regular nature of the service shall not be affected by any adjustment to the service operating conditions.]

1.2. Services, by whomsoever organised, which provide for the carriage of specified categories of passengers to the exclusion of other passengers, insofar as such services are operated under the conditions specified in 1.1, shall be deemed to be regular services. Such services are hereinafter called "special regular services".

Special regular services shall include:

(a) the carriage of workers between home and work,

(b) carriage to and from the educational institution for school pupils and students,

(c) the carriage of soldiers and their families between their state of origin and the area of their barracks,

(d) . . .

The fact that a special service may be varied according to the needs of users shall not affect its classification as a regular service.

1.3. The organisation of parallel temporary services, serving the same public as existing regular services, . . ., the non-serving of certain stops and the serving of additional stops on existing regular services shall be governed by the same rules as existing regular services.

2. *Shuttle services*

2.1. Shuttle services are services whereby, by means of repeated outward and return journeys, groups of passengers assembled in advance are carried from a single area of departure to a single area of destination. These groups, made up of passengers who have completed the outward journey, are carried back to the place of departure in the course of a subsequent journey. "*Area of departure*" and "*area of destination*" mean respectively the place where the journey begins and the place where the journey ends, together with, in each case, localities within a radius of 50km.

Outside the areas of departure and destination, groups may be picked up and set down respectively at up to three different places.

The areas of departure and destination and the additional picking-up and setting-down points may be within the territory of one or more Member States.

2.2. . . .

2.3. For the purposes of point 2, a group assembled in advance is a group for which a body or person responsible in accordance with the rules of the State of establishment has taken charge of conclusion of the contract or collective payment of the services or has received all reservations and payments before departure.

3. *Occasional services*

[3.1. Occasional services are services which do not meet the definition of regular services, including special regular services and which are characterised above all by the fact that they carry groups of passengers assembled on the initiative of the customer or the carrier himself.

The organisation of parallel or temporary services comparable to existing regular services and serving the same public as the latter shall be subject to authorisation in accordance with the procedure laid down in Section II.]

3.2. . . .

3.3. The services referred to in point 3 shall not cease to be occasional services solely because they are provided at certain intervals.

3.4. Occasional services may be provided by a group of carriers acting on behalf of the same contractor, and travellers may catch a connection en route, with a different carrier of the same group, in the territory of one of the Member States.

The names of such carriers and the connection points en route shall be communicated to the competent authorities of the Member States concerned, in accordance with the procedures to be determined by the Commission . . .

[4. *Own-account transport operations*

Own-account transport operations are those carried out for non-commercial and non-profit-making purposes by a natural or legal person, provided that:

— the transport activity is only an ancillary activity for that natural or legal person,

— the vehicles used are the property of that natural or legal person or have been obtained on deferred terms by them or have been the subject of a long-term leasing contract and are driven by a member of the staff of the natural or legal person or by the natural person himself.]

[*Article 2 is printed as amended by Regulation (EC) 11/98.*]   **C7.07**

Article 3—Freedom to provide services

1. Any carrier for hire or reward referred to in Article 1 shall be permitted to carry out   **C7.08**
the transport services defined in Article 2 without discrimination as to nationality or place of establishment if he:

— is authorised in the State of establishment to undertake carriage by means of regular services including special regular services or occasional services by coach and bus;

— satisfies the conditions laid down in accordance with Community rules on admission to the occupation of road passenger transport operator in national and international transport operations;

— meets legal requirements on road safety as far as the standards for drivers and vehicles are concerned.

2. Any own-account carrier referred to in Article 1 shall be permitted to carry out the transport services defined in Article 13 without discrimination as to nationality or place of establishment if he:

— is authorised in the State of establishment to undertake carriage by coach and bus in accordance with the market-access conditions laid down by national legislation;

— meets legal requirements on road safety as far as the standards for drivers and vehicles are concerned.

[*Article 2 is printed as amended by Regulation (EC) 11/98.*]   **C7.09**

[Article 3A—Community licence

1. In order to carry out international passenger transport operations by coach and bus,   **C7.10**
any carrier meeting the criteria laid down in Article 3(1) must hold a Community licence issued by the competent authorities of the Member State of establishment in accordance with the model set out in the Annex.

2. The competent authorities of the Member State of establishment shall issue the holder with the original of the Community licence, which shall be kept by the carrier, and the number of certified true copies corresponding to the number of vehicles used for the international carriage of passengers at the disposal of the holder of the Community licence, either in full ownership, or in another form, notably by virtue of an instalment-purchase contract, a hire contract or a leasing contract.

3. The Community licence shall be established in the name of the carrier and shall be non-transferable. A certified true copy of the Community licence shall be carried on the vehicle and shall be presented at the request of any authorised inspecting officer.

4. The Community licence shall be issued for a period of five years which shall be renewable.

5. The Community licence shall replace the document issued by the competent authorities of the Member State of establishment certifying that the carrier has access to the market for the international carriage of passengers by road.

6. When an application for a licence is submitted, and at least every five years thereafter, the competent authorities of the Member State of establishment shall verify whether the carrier meets or continues to meet the conditions laid down in Article 3(1).

7. Where the conditions referred to in Article 3(1) are not met, the competent authorities of the Member State of establishment shall refuse to issue or renew a Community licence by means of a reasoned decision.

8. Member States shall guarantee the right of the applicant for, or holder of, a Community licence to appeal against a decision by the competent authorities of the Member State of establishment to refuse or withdraw this licence.

9. Member States shall inform the Commission no later than 31 January of every year of the number of carriers holding a Community licence as at 31 December of the previous year and of the number of certified true copies corresponding to the number of vehicles in circulation on that date.

10. Member States may decide that the Community licence shall also be valid for national transport operations.]

C7.11 *[Article 3A was inserted by Regulation (EC) 11/98 with effect from June 11, 1999.*
Article 3A has been implemented in Great Britain by the Public Service Vehicles (Community Licences) Regulations 1999 (S.I. 1999 No. 1322, q.v.)]

[**Article 4—Access to the market**

C7.12 1. Occasional services as defined in Article 2(3.1) shall not require authorisation.

2. Special regular services defined in Article 2(1.2) shall not require authorisation if they are covered by a contract concluded between the organiser and the carrier.

3. Empty journeys by vehicles in connection with the transport operations referred to in paragraphs 1 and 2 shall likewise not require authorisation.

4. Regular services as defined in the first sub-paragraph of Article 2(1.1) and special regular services not covered by a contract between the organiser and the carrier shall require authorisation in accordance with Articles 5 to 10.

5. Arrangements for own-account transport operations are set out in Article 13.]

C7.13 *[Article 4 is printed as substituted by Regulation (EC) 11/98.]*

SECTION II

[REGULAR SERVICES SUBJECT TO AUTHORISATION]

C7.14 *Note.* The heading to Section II is printed as substituted by Regulation (EC) 11/98.

Article 5—Nature of authorisation

C7.15 1. Authorisations shall be issued in the name of the transport undertaking; they may not be transferred by the latter to third parties. However, the carrier who has received the authorisation may, with the consent of the authority referred to in Article 6(1), operate the service through a sub-contractor. In this case, the name of the latter undertaking and its role as sub-contractor shall be indicated in the authorisation. The sub-contractor must fulfil the conditions laid down in Article 3(1).

[In the case of undertakings associated for the purpose of operating a regular service, the authorisation shall be issued in the names of all the undertakings.] It shall be given to the undertaking that manages the operation and copies shall be given to the others. The authorisation shall state the names of all the operators.

[2. The period of validity of an authorisation shall not exceed five years.] It may be set at less either at the request of the applicant or by mutual consent of the competent authorities of the Member States on whose territory passengers are picked up or set down.

3. Authorisations shall specify the following:

(a) the type of service;

(b) the route of the service, giving in particular the place of departure and the place of destination;

(c) the period of validity of the authorisation;

[(d) the stops and the timetable.]

4. Authorisations shall conform to a model drawn up by the Commission [in accordance with the procedure laid down in Article 16A].

[5. Authorisations shall entitle their holder(s) to operate regular services in the territories of all Member States over which the routes of the services pass.]

[6. The operator of a regular service may use additional vehicles to deal with temporary and exceptional situations.

In this case, the carrier must ensure that the following documents are carried on the vehicle:

— a copy of the authorisation of the regular service,

— a copy of the contract between the operator of the regular service and the undertaking providing the additional vehicles or an equivalent document,

— a certified true copy of the Community licence issued to the operator of the regular service.]

[Article 5 is printed as amended by Regulation (EC) 11/98.]　　　　**C7.16**

Article 6—Submission of applications for authorisation

[1. Applications for authorisation of regular services shall be submitted to the competent authorities of the Member State in whose territory the place of departure is situated, hereinafter referred to as the "*authorising authority*". The *place of departure* shall mean "one of the termini of the service".]　　　**C7.17**

2. Applications shall conform to a model drawn up by the Commission in accordance with the procedure laid down in Article [16A].

[3. Persons applying for authorisation shall provide any further information which they consider relevant or which is requested by the authorising authority, in particular a driving schedule making it possible to monitor compliance with Community legislation on driving and rest periods and a copy of the Community licence for international carriage of passengers by road for hire or reward provided for in Article 3A.]

[Article 6 is printed as amended by Regulation (EC) 11/98.]　　　　**C7.18**

[Article 7—Authorising procedure

C7.19   1. Authorisations shall be issued in agreement with the authorities of all the Member States in whose territories passengers are picked up or set down. The authorising authority shall forward to such authorities—as well as to the competent authorities of Member States whose territories are crossed without passengers being picked up or set down—a copy of the application, together with copies of any other relevant documentation, and its assessment.

2. The competent authorities of the Member States whose agreement has been requested shall notify the authorising authority of their decision on the application within two months. The time limit shall be calculated from the date of receipt of the request for an opinion which is shown in the acknowledgement of receipt. If within this period the authorising authority has received no reply, the authorities consulted shall be deemed to have given their agreement and the authorising authority shall grant the authorisation.

The authorities of the Member States whose territories are crossed without passengers being picked up or set down may notify the authorising authority of their comments within the time limits laid down in the first sub-paragraph.

3. Subject to paragraphs 7 and 8, the authorising authority shall take a decision on the application within four months of the date of submission of the application by the carrier.

4. Authorisation shall be granted unless:

(a) the applicant is unable to provide the service which is the subject of the application with equipment directly available to him;

(b) in the past the applicant has not complied with national or international legislation on road transport, and in particular the conditions and requirements relating to authorisations for international road passenger services, or has committed serious breaches of legislation in regard to road safety, in particular with regard to the rules applicable to vehicles and driving and rest periods for drivers;

(c) in the case of an application for renewal of authorisation, the conditions of authorisation have not been complied with;

(d) it is shown that the service in question would directly compromise the existence of regular services already authorised, except in cases in which the regular services in question are carried out by a single carrier or group of carriers only;

(e) it appears that the operation of services covered by the application is aimed only at the most lucrative of the services existing on the links concerned;

(f) a Member State decides on the basis of a detailed analysis that the said service would seriously affect the viability of a comparable rail service on the direct sections concerned. Any decision pursuant to this provision, together with the reasons therefor, shall be notified to the carriers affected.

As from 1 January 2000, in the event that an existing international bus service is seriously affecting the viability of a comparable rail service on the direct sections concerned, a Member State may, with the agreement of the Commission, suspend or withdraw the authorisation to run the international bus service after having given six months' notice to the carrier.

The fact that a carrier offers lower prices than are offered by other road carriers or the fact that the link in question is already operated by other road carriers may not in itself constitute justification for rejecting the application.

5. The authorising authority and the competent authorities of all the Member States involved in the procedure to reach the agreement provided for in paragraph 1 may refuse applications only on the basis of reasons compatible with this Regulation.

6. If the procedure for reaching the agreement referred to in paragraph 1 does not

enable the authorising authority to decide on an application, the matter may be referred to the Commisison within the time limit of five months calculated from the date of submission of the application by the carrier.

7. After consulting the Member States concerned, the Commision shall within ten weeks take a decision which shall take effect within thirty days of the notification of the Member States concerned.

8. The Commission decision shall continue to apply until such time as agreement is reached between the Member States concerned.

9. Having completed the procedure laid down in this article, the authorising authority shall inform all the authorities referred to in paragraph 1 of its decision, sending them a copy of any authorisation; the competent authorities of the transit Member States may indicate that they do not wish to be so informed.]

[Article 7 is printed as substituted by Regulation (EC) 11/98.]   **C7.20**

Article 8—Grant and renewal of authorisations

1. Once the procedures referred to in Article 7 have been completed, the authorising   **C7.21**
authority shall grant the authorisation or shall formally refuse the application.

2. Decisions refusing an application must state the reasons on which they are based. Member States shall ensure that transport undertakings are given the opportunity to make representations in the event of their application being refused.

3. Article 7 shall apply, *mutatis mutandis*, to applications for the renewal of authorisations or for alteration of the conditions under which the services subject to authorisation must be carried out.

In the event of a minor alteration to the operating conditions, in particular adjustment [of intervals] of fares and timetables, the authorising authority need only supply the other Member States concerned with the information in question.

The Member States concerned may also agree that the authorising authority alone shall decide on alterations to the conditions under which a service is operated.

[Article 8 is printed as amended by Regulation (EC) 11/98.]   **C7.22**

Article 9—Lapse of an authorisation

1. Without prejudice to Article 14 of Regulation (EEC) No. 1191/69 [*Regulation (EEC)*   **C7.23**
1191/69 on action by member states concerning the obligations inherent in the concept of public service in transport by rail, road and inland waterway (O.J. No. L156, June 28, 1969, p. 1), as amended], an authorisation for a regular service shall lapse at the end of its period of validity or three months after the authorising authority has received from its holder notice of his intention to withdraw the service. Such notice must contain a proper statement of reasons.

2. Where demand for a service has ceased to exist, the period mentioned in paragraph 1 shall be reduced to one month.

3. The authorising authority shall inform the competent authorities of the other Member States concerned that the authorisation has lapsed.

4. . . .

5. The holder of the authorisation shall notify users of the service concerned of its withdrawal one month beforehand by means of appropriate publicity.

[Article 9 is printed as amended by Regulation (EC) 11/98.]   **C7.24**

Article 10—Obligations of carriers

C7.25 1. Save in the event of force majeure, the operator of a regular service shall, until the authorisation expires, take all measures to guarantee a transport service that fulfils the standards of continuity, regularity and capacity and complies with the other conditions laid down by the competent authority in accordance with Article 5(3).

2. The carrier shall display the route of the service, the bus stops, the timetable, the fares and the conditions of carriage—insofar as these are not laid down by law—in such a way as to ensure that such information is readily available to all users.

3. Without prejudice to Regulation (EEC) No. 1191/69, it shall be possible for the Member States concerned, by common agreement and in agreement with the holder of the authorisation, to make changes to the operating conditions governing a regular service.

SECTION III

[Occasional Services and other Services Exempt from Authorisation]

C7.26 *Note.*   The heading to Section III is printed as amended by Regulation (EC) 11/98.

[Article 11—Journey form

C7.27 1. The services referred to in Article 4(1) shall be carried out under cover of a journey form.

2. A carrier operating occasional services shall fill out a journey form before each journey.

3. The journey form shall contain at least the following information:

(a) the type of service;

(b) the main itinerary;

(c) the carrier(s) involved.

4. The books of journey forms shall be supplied by the competent authorities of the Member State where the transport undertaking is established or by bodies appointed by those authorities.

5. The Commission shall, in accordance with the procedure provided for in Article 16A, lay down the model for the journey form and the way in which it is to be used.]

C7.28 *[Article 11 is printed as substituted by Regulation (EC) 11/98.]*

Article 12—Local excursions

C7.29 Within the framework [of] . . . an international occasional service, a carrier may carry out occasional services (local excursions) in a Member State other than that in which it is established.

Such services shall be intended for non-resident passengers previously carried by the same carrier on one of the international services mentioned in the first sub-paragraph and must be carried out with the same vehicle or another vehicle from the same carrier or group of carriers.

C7.30 *[Article 12 is printed as amended by Regulation (EC) 11/98. (Although the word "of" in the first line of text has been formally repealed, it has been reinstated editorially; cf. article 1(13) of Regulation (EC) 11/98.)]*

SECTION IV

OWN-ACCOUNT TRANSPORT OPERATIONS

Article 13

1. Own-account road transport operations defined in point 4 of Article 2 shall be exempt from any system of authorisation but shall be subject to a system of certificates.   **C7.31**

2. . . .

3. The certificates provided for in paragraph 1 shall be issued by the competent authority of the Member State in which the vehicle is registered and shall be valid for the entire journey including transit.

They must conform to a model determined by the Commission [in accordance with the procedure laid down in Article 16A].

[Article 13 is printed as amended by Regulation (EC) 11/98.]   **C7.32**

SECTION V

CONTROLS AND PENALTIES

Article 14—Transport tickets

1. Passengers using a regular service, excluding special regular services, shall throughout their journey possess transport tickets, either individual or collective, which indicate: **C7.33**

— the points of departure and destination and, where appropriate, the return journey;

— the period of validity of the ticket;

— the price of transport].

2. The transport ticket provided for in paragraph 1 shall be presented at the request of any authorised inspecting officer.

[Article 14 is printed as amended by Regulation (EC) 11/98.]   **C7.34**

Article 15—Inspections on the road and in undertakings

1. The authorisation or control document shall be carried on the vehicle and shall be presented at the request of any authorised inspecting officer.   **C7.35**

In the case of the services covered by Article 4(2), the contract or a certified true copy of it shall serve as a control document.

2. Carriers operating coaches and buses in international passenger transport shall allow all inspections intended to ensure that operations are being conducted correctly, in particular as regards driving and rest periods. In the context of implementation of this Regulation, authorised inspecting officers shall be empowered to:

(a) check the books and other documentation relating to the operation of the transport undertaking;

(b) make copies of, or take extracts from, the books and documentation on the premises;

(c) have access to all the transport undertaking's premises, sites and vehicles;

(d) require the production of any information contained in books, documentation or data bases.

[Article 16—Penalties and mutual assistance

C7.36   1. The competent authorities of the Member State where the carrier is established shall withdraw the Community licence provided for in Article 3A where the holder:

— no longer meets the conditions laid down in Article 3(1),

— has supplied inaccurate information concerning the data which were required for the issue of the Community licence.

2. The authorising authority shall withdraw an authorisation if the holder no longer fulfils the conditions on the basis of which the authorisation was issued under this Regulation, in particular where the Member State in which the carrier is established so requests. The authority shall immediately inform the competent authorities of the Member State concerned.

3. In the case of a serious breach of repeated minor breaches of road safety regulations, in particular with regard to the rules applicable to vehicles, driving and rest periods for drivers and the provision without authorisation of parallel or temporary services, as referred to in Article 2(1.3), the competent authorities of the Member State of establishment of the carrier who committed the breach may *inter alia* withdraw the Community licence or make temporary and/or partial withdrawals of the certified true copies of the Community licence.

These penalties shall be determined in accordance with the seriousness of the breach committed by the holder of the Community licence and with the total number of certified true copies that he possesses in respect of his international trade.

4. The competent authorities of the Member States shall prohibit a carrier from operating on their territory an international passenger service under this Regulation if he repeatedly commits serious breaches of the regulations governing road safety, in particular with regard to the rules applicable to vehicles and driving and rest periods for drivers. They shall immediately inform the competent authorities of the Member State concerned.

5. Member States shall on request provide each other with any relevant information in their possession concerning:

— breaches of this Regulation and of any other Community rules applicable to the international carriage of passengers by coach and bus committed in their territory by a carrier from another Member State, and the penalties imposed,

— the penalties imposed on their own carriers in respect of breaches committed in the territory of another Member State.]

C7.37   *[Article 16 is printed as substituted by Regulation (EC) 11/98.]*

[Article 16A

C7.38   Where the procedure referred to in this Article is to be followed the Commission shall be assisted by the advisory committee set up by Council Regulation (EC) No. 12/98 of 11 December 1997, laying down the conditions under which non-resident carriers may operate national road passenger transport services within a Member State [*q.v.*] and chaired by the representative of the Commission.

The representative of the Commission shall submit to the committee a draft of the measures to be taken. The committee shall deliver its opinion on the draft, within a time limit which the chairman may lay down according to the urgency of the matter, if necessary by taking a vote.

The opinion shall be recorded in the minutes; in addition, each Member State shall have the right to ask to have its position recorded in the minutes.

The Commission shall take the utmost account of the opinion delivered by the committee. It shall inform the committee of the manner in which its opinion has been taken into account.]

[Article 16A was inserted by Regulation (EC) 11/98.]

C7.39

SECTION VI

TRANSITIONAL AND FINAL PROVISIONS

Article 17—Transitional provision

Authorisations for services existing on the date of entry into force of this Regulation shall continue to be valid until they expire insofar as the services in question remain subject to authorisation.

C7.40

Article 18—Agreements between Member States

1. Member States may conclude bilateral and multilateral agreements on the further liberalisation of the services covered by this Regulation, in particular as regards the authorisation system and the simplification or abolition of control documents.

C7.41

2. Member States shall inform the Commission of any agreements concluded under paragraph 1.

Article 19—Implementation

Member States shall, before 1 June 1992 and after consulting the Commission, adopt the measures necessary for the implementation of this Regulation and notify such measures to the Commission.

C7.42

[Member States shall adopt measures relating in particular to the means of carrying out checks and the system of penalties applicable to infringements of the provisions of this Regulation, and take all the measures necessary to ensure that those penalties are applied. The penalties thus provided for shall be effective, proportionate and dissuasive. Member States shall notify the relevant measures to the Commission within 12 months of the date on which this Regulation comes into force and shall notify any subsequent changes as soon as possible. They shall ensure that all such measures are applied without discrimination as to the nationality or place of establishment of the carrier.]

[Article 19 is printed as amended by Regulation (EC) 11/98.]

C7.43

Article 20—Commission report and proposal *[Omitted.]*

C7.44

Article 21—Repeals

1. Regulations No. 117/66/EEC, (EEC) No. 516/72 and (EEC) No. 517/72 are hereby repealed.

C7.45

2. References to the Regulations repealed shall be taken as references to this Regulation.

Article 22—Entry into force and application

C7.46   This Regulation shall enter into force on the third day following that of its publication in the *Official Journal of the European Communities*.

It shall apply from 1 June 1992.

C7.47   *[This Regulation was published at O.J. No. L74, March 20, 1992, p. 1.]*

This Regulation shall be binding in its entirety and directly applicable in all Member States.

[ANNEX

EUROPEAN COMMUNITY   **C7.48**

(a)

(Heavy-duty, blue—dimension DIN A4)

(First page of the licence)

(Text in the official language(s) or one of the official languages of the
Member State issuing the licence)

Distinctive symbol of the Member State (¹) issuing the licence	Designation of the competent authority or body

LICENCE NO. . . .

**for the international carriage of passengers by coach and bus
for hire or reward**

The holder of this licence (²) ....
....
....
....

is authorised to carry out international carriage of passengers by road for hire or reward in
the territory of the Community pursuant to the conditions laid down by Council
Regulation (EEC) No. 684/92 of 16 March 1992, as amended by Regulation (EC) No.
11/98 and in accordance with the general provisions of this licence.

Comments: ....
....
....
....
....

This licence is valid from.. to ....
Issued in ...., on ....
.... (³)

(¹) **(B)** Belgium, **(DK)** Denmark, **(D)** Germany, **(GR)** Greece, **(E)** Spain, **(F)** France, **(IRL)**
Ireland, **(I)** Italy, **(L)** Luxembourg, **(NL)** Netherlands, **(A)** Austria, **(P)** Portugal, **(FIN)**
Finland, **(S)** Sweden, **(UK)** United Kingdom.
(²) Full name or business name of the carrier.
(³) Signature and stamp of the competent authority or body issuing the licence.

General provisions

C7.49

1. This licence is issued pursuant to Council Regulation (EEC) No. 648/92 of 16 March 1992 on common rules for the international carriage of passengers by coach and bus, as amended by Regulation (EC) No. 11/98.

2. This licence is issued by the competent authorities of the Member State of establishment of the carrier for hire or reward who:

   — is authorised in the Member State of establishment to undertake carriage by means of regular services, including special regular services or occasional services by coach and bus,

   — satisfies the conditions laid down in accordance with Community rules on admission to the occupation of road passenger transport operator in national and international transport operations,

   — meets legal requirements on road safety as far as the standards for drivers and vehicles are concerned.

3. This licence permits the international carriage of passengers by coach and bus for hire or reward on all transport links for journeys carried out in the territory of the Community:

   — where the place of departure and place of destination are situated in two different Member States, with or without transit through one or more Member States or third countries,

   — from a Member State to a third country and vice versa, with or without transit through one or more Member States or third countries,

   — between third countries crossing the territory of one or more Member States in transit,

   and empty journeys in connection with transport operations under the conditions laid down by Regulation (EEC) No. 648/92.

   In the case of a transport operation from a Member State to a third country and vice versa, Regulation (EEC) No. 684/92, is applicable, for the journey made in the territory of the Member State of picking up or setting down, once the necessary agreement between the Community and the third country in question has been concluded.

4. This licence is personal and non-transferable.

5. This licence may be withdrawn by the competent authority of the Member State of issue in particular where the carrier:

   — no longer meets the conditions laid down in Article 3(1) of Regulation (EEC) No. 648/92,

   — has supplied inaccurate information regarding the data required for the issue or renewal of the licence,

   — has committed a serious breach or repeated minor breaches of road safety regulations, in particular with regard to the rules applicable to vehicles, driving and rest periods for drivers and the provision, without authorisation, of parallel or temporary services as referred to in Article 2(1.3) of Regulation (EEC) No. 684/92. The competent authorities of the Member State of establishment of the carrier who committed the breach may, *inter alia*, withdraw the Community licence or make temporary and/or partial withdrawals of the certified true copies of the Community licence.

These penalties are determined in accordance with the seriousness of the breach committed by the holder of the Community licence and with the total number of certified true copies that he possesses in respect of his international trade.

6. The original of the licence must be kept by the carrier. A certified true copy of the licence must be carried on the vehicle carrying out an international transport operation.

7. This licence must be presented at the request of any inspecting officer.

8. The holder must, on the territory of each Member State, comply with the laws, regulations and administrative measures in force in that State, particularly with regard to transport and traffic.

9. "*Regular services*" means services which provide for the carriage of passengers at specified intervals along specified routes, passengers being taken up and set down at predetermined stopping points. Regular services shall be open to all, subject, where appropriate, to compulsory reservation.

The regular nature of the service shall not be affected by any adjustment to the service operating conditions.

Regular services require authorisation.

"*Special regular services*" means regular services which provide for the carriage of specified categories of passengers, to the exclusion of other passengers, at specified intervals along specified routes, passengers being taken up and set down at predetermined stopping points.

Special regular services shall include:

(a) the carriage of workers between home and work;
(b) carriage to and from the educational institution for school pupils and students;
(c) the carriage of soldiers and their families between their homes and the area of their barracks.

The fact that a special service may be varied according to the needs of users shall not affect its classification as a regular service.

Special regular services do not require authorisation if they are covered by a contract between the organiser and the carrier.

The organisation of parallel or temporary services, serving the same public as existing regular services, requires authorisation.

"*Occasional services*" means services which do not fall within the definition of regular services, including special regular services, and whose main characteristic is that they carry groups constituted on the initiative of a customer or of the carrier himself. The organisation of parallel or temporary services comparable to existing regular services and serving the same public as the latter shall be subject to authorisation in accordance with the procedure laid down in Section II of Regulation (EEC) No. 684/92. These services shall not cease to be occasional services solely because they are provided at certain intervals.

Occasional services do not require authorisation.]

[The Annex is printed as substituted by Regulation (EC) 11/98.]

Regulation (EEC) 881/92
of March 26, 1992

on access to the market in the carriage of goods by road within the Community to or from the territory of a Member State or passing across the territory of one or more Member States

C8.01 *Editorial note.* The provisions implementing this Regulation are set out in the Goods Vehicles (Community Authorisations) Regulations 1992 (S.I. 1992 No. 3077) above.

C8.02 *European Economic Area.* As to the Agreement on the European Economic Area generally, see the note to Regulation (EEC) 3820/85 above.

For the purposes of that agreement, Regulation (EEC) 881/92 has been adapted by *ibid.*, Annex XIII, Chapter II, para.26a, as inserted by Decision 7/94 of the EEA Joint Committee, Annex 11, Chapter II, para.10 (O.J. No. L160, June 28, 1994, p. 80). As to the adaptation of documents, see Appendix 1 to Annex 11 of Decision 7/94 of the EEA Joint Committee (*op. cit.*, p. 90).

C8.03 *[The text of this Regulation is printed as amended by:*

Act of Accession of Austria, Finland and Sweden to the European Union (O.J. No. C241, August 29, 1994, p. 21), as amended by Council Decision 95/1/EC (O.J. No. L1, 1 January 1995, p. 1).

The Act of Accession (Austria, Finland, Sweden) as amended by Council Decision 95/1/EC came into force on January 1, 1995 (see the notice at O.J. No. L1, January 1, 1995, p. 221); any reference to the "Act of Accession (Austria, Finland, Sweden)" is a reference to that Act as amended by that Decision.]

THE COUNCIL OF THE EUROPEAN COMMUNITIES,

C8.04 Having regard to the Treaty establishing the European Economic Community, and in particular [Article 71] thereof,

Having regard to the proposal from the Commission,

Having regard to the opinion of the European Parliament,

Having regard to the opinion of the Economic and Social Committee,

Whereas the establishment of a common transport policy involves, inter alia, laying down common rules applicable to access to the market in the international carriage of goods by road within the territory of the Community; whereas those rules must be laid down in such a way as to contribute to the attainment of the internal transport market;

Whereas these uniform arrangements for market access also involve introducing the freedom to provide services by eliminating all restrictions imposed on the provider of services because of his nationality or the fact that he is established in a Member State other than that in which the service is to be provided;

Whereas, as regards carriage from a Member State to a non-member country and vice versa, implementation of the freedom to provide services for the journey within the territory of the Member State of loading or unloading should be deferred until appropriate agreements with the non-member countries concerned have been concluded or amended, in order to guarantee compliance with the principle of non-discrimination and equality of conditions of competition between Community carriers;

Whereas, following the judgment of the Court of Justice of 22 May 1985 in Case 13/83 [*European Parliament v. EC Council [1985] E.C.R. 1513*] and the conclusions adopted on 28 and 29 June 1985 by the European Council on the Commission communication on the completion of the internal market, on 21 June 1988 the Council adopted Regulation (EEC) No. 1841/88 [*O.J. No. L163, June 30, 1988, p. 1*] amending Regulation (EEC) No. 3164/76 on access to the market in the international carriage of goods by road [*O.J. No. L357, December 29, 1976, p. 1, as amended*];

Whereas under Article 4a of Regulation (EEC) No. 3164/76 inserted by Regulation (EEC) No. 1841/88 from January 1, 1993, Community quotas, bilateral quotas between Member States and quotas for transit traffic to and from non-member countries will be abolished for the types of carriage referred to in that Article, and arrangements for access to a market without quantitative restrictions based on qualitative criteria which hauliers must meet will be introduced;

Whereas these qualitative criteria are laid down principally in Council Directive 74/561/EEC of 12 November 1974 on admission to the occupation of road haulage operator in national and international transport operations, as last amended by Council Directive 89/483/EEC of 21 June 1989 [*O.J. No. L308, November 19, 1974, p. 1, as amended*];

Whereas pursuant to Article 4b of Regulation (EEC) No. 3164/76, as inserted by Regulation (EEC) No. 1841/88, the Council must adopt the measures necessary for the implementation of the aforementioned Article 4a;

Whereas with regard to the rules for applying the access arrangements the international carriage of goods by road must be made conditional on the possession of a quota-free Community transport authorisation;

Whereas at present, under the First Council Directive of 23 July 1962 on the establishment of common rules for certain types of carriage of goods by road between Member States [*O.J. No. L70, August 6, 1962, p. 2005/62, as amended*], a certain number of types of carriage are exempt from any quota and carriage authorisation system; whereas, within the framework of the new organisation of the market introduced by this Regulation, a system of exemption from Community authorisation and from any other carriage authorisation must be maintained for some of those types of transport, because of their special nature;

Whereas the conditions governing the issue and withdrawal of authorisations and the types of carriage to which they apply, their periods of validity and the detailed rules for their use must be determined,

[The preamble is printed as amended by the Treaty of Amsterdam, art.12(1) and (3).]   **C8.05**

HAS ADOPTED THIS REGULATION:

Article 1

1. This Regulation shall apply to the international carriage of goods by road for hire or reward for journeys carried out within the territory of the Community.   **C8.06**

2. In the event of carriage from a Member State to a non-member country and vice versa, this Regulation shall apply to that part of any journey carried out within the territory of the Member State of loading or unloading, after conclusion of the necessary agreement between the Community and the non-member country concerned.

3. Pending the conclusion of agreements between the Community and the non-member countries concerned, this Regulation shall not affect:

— provisions relating to the carriage referred to in paragraph 2 included in bilateral agreements concluded by Member States with those non-member countries. However, Member States shall endeavour to adapt those agreements to ensure compliance with the principle of non-discrimination between Community hauliers,

— provisions relating to the carriage referred to in paragraph 2 included in bilateral agreements concluded between Member States which either under bilateral authorisations or under liberalisation arrangements, allow loading and unloading in a Member State by hauliers not established in that State.

Article 2

C8.07   For the purposes of this Regulation:

— "*vehicle*" shall mean a motor vehicle registered in a Member State or a coupled combination of vehicles the motor vehicle of which at least is registered in a Member State and which are used exclusively for the carriage of goods,

— "*international carriage*" shall mean:

— a journey undertaken by a vehicle the point of departure and the point of arrival of which are in two different Member States, with or without transit through one or more Member States or non-member countries;

— a journey undertaken by a vehicle from a Member State to a non-member country or vice versa, with or without transit through one or more Member States or non-member countries;

— a journey undertaken by a vehicle between non-member countries, with transit through the territory of one or more Member States;

— an unladen journey in conjunction with such carriage.

Article 3

C8.08   1. International carriage shall be carried out subject to Community authorisation.

2. Community authorisation shall be issued by a Member State, in accordance with Articles 5 and 7, to any haulier carrying goods by road for hire or reward who:

— is established in a Member State, hereinafter referred to as the "*Member State of establishment*", in accordance with the legislation of that Member State,

— is entitled in that Member State, in accordance with the legislation of the Community and of that State concerning admission to the occupation of road haulage operator, to carry out the international carriage of goods by road.

Article 4

C8.09   The Community authorisation referred to in Article 3 shall replace the document issued by the competent authorities of the Member State of establishment, where such a document exists, certifying that the haulier has been granted access to the market in the international carriage of goods by road.

For carriage falling within the scope of this Regulation it shall also replace both the Community authorisations and the bilateral authorisations exchanged between Member States which are necessary until this Regulation comes into force.

Article 5

C8.10   1. The Community authorisation referred to in Article 3 shall be issued by the competent authorities of the Member State of establishment.

2. The Member State shall issue the holder with the original of the Community authorisation, which shall be kept by the haulage undertaking, and the number of certified true copies corresponding to the number of vehicles at the disposal of the holder of the Community authorisation, whether wholly owned or, for example, under hire purchase, hire or leasing contracts.

3. The Community authorisation shall correspond to the model set out in Annex I, which also lays down the conditions governing its use.

4. The Community authorisation shall be made out in the haulier's name, he may not transfer it to any third party. A certified true copy shall be kept in the vehicle and must be produced whenever required by an authorised inspecting officer.

Article 6

The Community authorisation shall be issued for a renewable period of five years.   **C8.11**

Article 7

Whenever an application for a Community authorisation is lodged, not more than five years after issue and subsequently at least every five years, the competent authorities of the Member State of establishment shall verify whether the haulier satisfies or still satisfies the conditions laid down in Article 3(2).   **C8.12**

Article 8

1. If the conditions laid down in Article 3(2) are not satisfied, the competent authorities of the Member State of establishment shall reject an application for the issue or renewal of a Community authorisation, by means of a reasoned decision.   **C8.13**

2. The competent authorities shall withdraw a Community authorisation where the holder:

— no longer satisfies the conditions laid down in Article 3(2),

— has supplied incorrect information in relation to the data required for the issue of a Community authorisation.

3. In the event of serious infringements or repeated minor infringements of carriage regulations, the competent authorities of the Member State of establishment of the haulier who has committed such infringements may *inter alia* temporarily or partially suspend the certified true copies of the Community authorisation.

These sanctions shall be determined having regard to the seriousness of the infringement committed by the holder of the Community authorisation and having regard to the total number of certified copies that he holds in respect of international traffic.

Article 9

The Member States shall guarantee that the applicant or the holder of a Community authorisation is able to appeal against any decision by the competent authorities of the Member State of establishment to refuse or withdraw an authorisation.   **C8.14**

Article 10

By 31 January each year Member States shall inform the Commission of the number of hauliers possessing Community authorisations on 31 December of the previous year and of the number of certified true copies corresponding to the vehicles in circulation at that date.   **C8.15**

Article 11

1. The Member States shall give each other mutual assistance in ensuring the application and monitoring of this Regulation.   **C8.16**

2. Where the competent authorities of a Member State are aware of an infringement of this Regulation attributable to a haulier from another Member State, the Member State within the territory [in which the infringement is ascertained] shall inform the competent authorities of the Member State in which the haulier is established and may ask the competent authorities of the Member State of establishment to impose sanctions in accordance with this Regulation.

3. In the event of a serious infringement or repeated minor infringements of carriage regulations, the competent authorities of the Member State in which the haulier is established shall examine the ways in which the sanctions provided for in Article 8(3) are applied and shall communicate their decision to the competent authorities of the Member State [in which the infringements were ascertained].

C8.17   *[Article 11 is printed as corrected by a corrigendum at O.J. No. L213, July 29, 1992, p. 36.]*

C8.18   **Article 12**   *[Repeal of Regulation (EEC) 3164/76, Directive 75/130/EEC, art.4, Directive 65/269/EEC, Decision 80/48/EEC.]*

Article 13

C8.19   The First Council Directive of 23 July 1962 is hereby amended as follows:

1. The title shall be replaced by: "First Council Directive of 23 July 1962 on the establishment of common rules for certain types of carriage of goods by road";

2. Article 1 shall be replaced by:

"Article 1

1. Under the conditions laid down in paragraph 2, Member States shall liberalise the types of international carriage of goods by road for hire or reward and on own account listed in the Annex where such carriage is performed to or from or in transit through their territory.

2. The types of carriage and unladen journeys made in conjunction with the carriage listed in the Annex shall be exempted from Community authorisation and from any carriage authorisation";

3. Annex II shall be deleted and the text of Annex I shall be replaced by that appearing in Annex II to this Regulation.

Article 14

C8.20   The Member States shall communicate to the Commission the measures they take to implement this Regulation.

Article 15

C8.21   This Regulation shall enter into force on the day following its publication in the Official Journal of the European Communities.

It shall apply from 1 January 1993.

C8.22   *[This Regulation was published at O.J. No. L95, April 9, 1992, p. 1.]*

This Regulation shall be binding in its entirety and directly applicable in all Member States.

ANNEX I

"ANNEX

EUROPEAN ECONOMIC COMMUNITY   .**C8.23**
(a)

(Blue card—DIN A4)

(First page of the authorisation)

(Text in (one of) the official language(s) of the Member State issuing the authorisation)

State issuing the authorisation Distinguishing sign (^{1})	Name of the competent authority or body

AUTHORISATION No. .....

for the international carriage of goods by road for hire or reward

This authorisation entitles (^{2}) ....
....
....
....

to engage in the international carriage of goods by road for hire or reward by any route, for journeys or parts of journeys effected for hire or reward within the territory of the Community, as laid down in Council Regulation (EEC) No. 881/92 of 26 March 1992 and subject to the general provisions of this authorisation.

Particular remarks: ....
....
....
....
....

This authorisation shall be valid from .... to ....

Issued in ...., on ....
....(^{3})

Notes   [*these notes are part of the official text*]

(^{1}) The distinguishing signs are [(a) Austria as from 1 January 1997,] (B) Belgium, (DK) Denmark, (D) Germany, (GR) Greece, (ES) Spain, (F) France, [(FIN) Finalnd,] (IRL) Ireland, (I) Italy, (L) Luxembourg, (NL) Netherlands, (P) Portugal, [(S) Sweden,] (UK) United Kingdom.

(^{2}) Name or business name and full address of the haulier.

(^{3}) Signature and stamp of the issuing competent authority or body.

(b)

(Second page of the authorisation)

(Text in (one of) the official language(s) of the Member State issuing the authorisation)

GENERAL PROVISIONS

C8.24   This authorisation is issued under Council Regulation (EEC) No. 881/92 of 26 March 1992, on access to the market in the carriage of goods by road within the Community to or from the territory of a Member State or passing across the territory of one or more Member States (¹).

It entitles the holder to engage in the international carriage of goods by road for hire or reward by any route for journeys or parts of journeys effected within the territory of the Community and, where appropriate, subject to the conditions laid down herein:

— where the point of departure and the point of arrival are situated in two different Member States, with or without transit through one or more Member States or non-member countries,

— from a Member State to a non-member country or vice versa, with or without transit through one or more Member States or non-member countries,

— between non-member countries with transit through the territory of one or more Member States,

and unladen journeys in connection with such carriage

In the case of carriage from a Member State to a non-member country or vice versa, this authorisation is valid for that part of the journey effected on the territory of the Member State of loading or unloading upon conclusion of the necessary agreement between the Community and the non-member country in question in accordance with Regulation (EEC) No. 881/92.

The authorisation is personal to the holder and is not transferable.

It may be withdrawn by the competent authority of the Member State which issued it, notably where the haulier has:

— not complied with all the conditions for using the authorisation,

— supplied incorrect information with regard to the data needed for the issue or extension of the authorisation.

The original of the authorisation must be kept by the haulage undertaking.

A certified copy of the authorisation must be kept in the vehicle (²). In the case of a coupled combination of vehicles it must accompany the motor vehicle. It covers the coupled combination of vehicles even if the trailer or semi-trailer is not registered or authorised to use the roads in the name of the authorisation holder or if it is registered or authorised to use the roads in another Member State.

The authorisation must be produced whenever required by an authorised inspecting officer.

Within the territory of each Member State the holder must comply with the laws, regulations and administrative provisions in force in that State, in particular with regard to transport and traffic.

Notes [*these notes form part of the official text*]

(^{1}) See O.J. L95, 9 April 1992, p. 1.
(^{2}) "*Vehicle*" means a motor vehicle registered in a Member State or a coupled combination of vehicles, the motor vehicle of which at least is registered in a Member State, used exclusively for the carriage of goods."

[*Annex I is printed as amended by the Act of Accession (Austria, Finland, Sweden), Annex I.*]   **C8.25**

ANNEX II

"*ANNEX*

Types of carriage to be exempted from any Community authorisation and from any carriage authorisation

1. Carriage of mail as a public service.   **C8.26**

2. Carriage of vehicles which have suffered damage or breakdown.

3. Carriage of goods in motor vehicles the permissible laden weight of which, including that of trailers, does not exceed six tonnes or the permissible payload of which, including that of trailers, does not exceed 3.5 tonnes.

4. Carriage of goods in motor vehicles provided the following conditions are fulfilled:

  (a) the goods carried must be the property of the undertaking or must have been sold, bought, let out on hire or hired, produced, extracted, processed or repaired by the undertaking;

  (b) the purpose of the journey must be to carry the goods to or from the undertaking or to move them, either inside the undertaking or outside for its own requirements;

  (c) motor vehicles used for such carriage must be driven by employees of the undertaking;

  (d) the vehicles carrying the goods must be owned by the undertaking or have been bought by it on deferred terms or hired provided that in the latter case they meet the conditions of Council Directive 84/647/EEC of 19 December 1984 on the use of vehicles hired without drivers for the carriage of goods by road [*O.J. No. L335, December 22, 1984, p. 72*].

  This provision shall not apply to the use of a replacement vehicle during a short breakdown of the vehicle normally used;

  (e) carriage must be no more than ancillary to the overall activities of the undertaking.

5. Carriage of medicinal products, appliances, equipment and other articles required for medical care in emergency relief, in particular for natural disasters."

Editorial note. This Annex is substituted for Annex I in First Council Directive of July 23,   **C8.27**
1962 (O.J. No. L70, August 6, 1962, p. 2005/62).

Regulation (EEC) 3688/92
of December 21, 1992

adapting to technical progress Council Regulation (EEC) 3821/85 on recording equipment in road transport

C9.01   THE COMMISSION OF THE EUROPEAN COMMUNITIES,

Having regard to the Treaty establishing the European Economic Community,

Having regard to Council Regulation (EEC) No. 3821/85 of 20 December 1985 on recording equipment in road transport [*q.v.*], as last amended by Regulation (EEC) No. 3572/90 [*q.v.*], and in particular Articles 17 and 18 thereof,

Whereas it is necessary to eliminate the possibilities of fraud in the use of the electronic recording equipment in road transport;

Whereas in the light of experience and in view of the current state of the art it is possible to protect the connecting cables of the appliance to the impulse transmitter in order to make them inviolable;

Whereas, having regard to the lifetime of the existing recording equipment, there is a need to implement this new technology in the Community construction and installation standards for electronic recording equipment;

Whereas it is necessary to break the seal of the recording equipment to install a speed limitation device on the vehicle; whereas such an action is permitted by the Regulation only in an emergency case; whereas it is advisable consequently to amend the Regulation accordingly;

Whereas the measures provided for in this Regulation are in accordance with the opinion of the Committee for Adaptation of Regulation (EEC) No. 3821/85 to Technical Progress,

HAS ADOPTED THIS REGULATION

C9.02   **Article 1**   *[Amends Regulation (EEC) 3821/85, art.12 and Annex I (q.v.).]*

Article 2

C9.03   As from 1 January 1994, Member States shall no longer grant EEC approval to any type of recording equipment which does not comply with the provisions of Regulation (EEC) No. 3821/85, as amended by this Regulation.

Article 3

C9.04   As from 1 January 1996, the recording equipment of any new vehicle brought into service for the first time shall comply with Regulation (EEC) No. 3821/85, as amended by this Regulation.

Article 4

This Regulation shall enter into force on the third day following its publication in the   **C9.05**
Official Journal of the European Communities.

[Regulation (EEC) 3688/92 was published in O.J. No. L374, December 22, 1992, p. 12.]   **C9.06**

This Regulation shall be binding in its entirety and directly applicable in all Member States.

Regulation (EEC) 3118/93
of October 25, 1993

laying down the conditions under which non-resident carriers may operate national road haulage services within a Member State

C10.01 *European Economic Area.* As to the Agreement on the European Economic Area generally, see the note to Regulation (EEC) 3820/85 above.

For the purposes of that agreement, Regulation (EEC) 3118/93 has been adapted by *ibid.*, Annex XIII, Chapter II, para.26*c*, as inserted by Decision 7/94 of the EEA Joint Committee, Annex 11, Chapter II, para.10 (O.J. No. L160, June 28, 1994, p. 82) and as subsequently amended.

As to the adaptation of documents, see Appendix 2 to Annex 11 to Decision 7/94 (*op. cit.*, p. 93). As to the mutual recognition of cabotage authorisations, see the communication at O.J. No. C178, June 30, 1994, p. 25.

C10.02 *[The text of this Regulation is printed as amended by:*

Council Regulation (EC) 3315/94 (O.J. No. L350, December 31, 1994, p. 9) (January 1, 1995).

The amending Regulation is referred to in the notes to the principal Regulation only by its reference number. The date referred to above is the date on which the amending Regulation came into force.]

THE COUNCIL OF THE EUROPEAN COMMUNITIES,

C10.03 Having regard to the Treaty establishing the European Economic Community, and in particular [Article 71] thereof,

Having regard to the proposal from the Commission,

Having regard to the opinion of the European Parliament,

Having regard to the opinion of the Economic and Social Committee,

Whereas, pursuant to [Article 71(1)(b)] of the Treaty, the establishment of a common transport policy entails, *inter alia*, laying down the conditions under which non-resident carriers may operate transport services within a Member State;

Whereas this provision implies the removal of all restrictions against the person providing the services in question on the grounds of his nationality or the fact that he is established in a different Member State from the one in which the service is to be provided;

Whereas, in order for this provision to be implemented smoothly and flexibly, provision should be made for a transitional cabotage system prior to the implementation of the definitive system;

Whereas only carriers who are holders of Community authorisations provided for in Council Regulation (EEC) No. 881/92 of 26 March 1992 on access to the market in the carriage of goods by road within the Community to or from the territory of a Member State or passing through the territory of one or more Member States [*q.v.*] or carriers authorised to operate certain categories of international haulage services may be permitted to carry out cabotage;

Whereas such a transitional system should entail the introduction of a progressive quota of Community cabotage authorisations;

Whereas the conditions for the issue and use of the said cabotage authorisations should be determined;

Whereas the provisions of the host Member State applicable to cabotage operations should be fixed;

Whereas provisions should be adopted so that action can be taken in the event of serious disturbance of the transport markets affected; whereas for that purpose it is necessary to introduce a suitable decision-making procedure and for the required statistical data to be collected;

Whereas it is desirable that Member States should grant each other mutual assistance with a view to the sound application on the system introduced; particularly in respect of penalties applicable in the event of infringements; whereas penalties should be non-discriminatory and in proportion to the seriousness of the infringements; whereas there is a need to provide for the possibility of lodging an appeal;

Whereas the Commission should periodically submit a report on the application of this Regulation;

Whereas in order to meet the obligations devolving upon the Council, it is necessary to fix the date of entry into force of a definitive system enabling cabotage operations to be effected without quantitative restrictions,

[The preamble is printed as amended by the Treaty of Amsterdam, art.12(1) and (3).]   **C10.04**

HAS ADOPTED THIS REGULATION:

Article 1

1. Any road haulage carrier for hire or reward who is a holder of the Community auth-   **C10.05**
orisation provided for in Regulation (EEC) No. 881/92 shall be entitled, under the conditions laid down in this Regulation, to operate on a temporary basis national road haulage services for hire and reward in another Member State, hereinafter referred to respectively as "*cabotage*" and as the "*host Member State*", without having a registered office or other establishment therein.

2. In addition, any carrier entitled in the Member State of establishment, in accordance with that Member State's legislation, to carry out the road haulage operations for hire or reward mentioned in points 1, 2 and 3 of the Annex to the First Directive [*First Council Directive of July 23, 1962 on the establishment of certain common rules for international transport (carriage of goods by road; O.J. No. 70, August 6, 1962, p. 2005/62), as last amended by Regulation (EEC) 881/92, art.13 above*] shall be permitted, under the conditions set out in this Regulation, to carry out, as the case may be, cabotage operations of the same kind or cabotage operations with vehicles in the same category.

3. Permission to carry out cabotage operations, within the framework of the types of carriage referred to in point 5 of the Annex to the First Directive, shall be unrestricted.

4. Any undertaking entitled in the Member State of establishment, in accordance with that Member State's legislation, to carry out road haulage operations for own account shall be permitted to carry out cabotage operations on own account as defined in point 4 of the Annex to the First Directive.

The Commission shall adopt the detailed rules for implementing this paragraph.

Article 2

1. With a view to the progressive introduction of the definitive system defined in Article   **C10.06**
12, cabotage operations shall be carried out from 1 January 1994 to 30 June 1998 within the framework of Community cabotage quotas, without prejudice to Article 1(3).

Cabotage authorisations shall correspond to the model in Annex I.

· [A Community cabotage quota shall consist of cabotage authorisations, each valid for two months; in accordance with the following table:]

Year	Number of authorisations
[1994	30000
1995	46296
1996	60191
1997	83206
1 January to 30 June 1998	54091]

2. At the request of a Member State, to be submitted before 1 November of each year, one cabotage authorisation may be converted into two short-duration authorisations, each valid for one month.

The short-duration cabotage authorisations shall correspond to the model in Annex II.

3. The quota shall be allocated amongst the Member States as follows:

	1995	1996	1997	1 January to 30 June 1998
[Belgium	3647	4742	6223	4045
Denmark	3538	4600	6037	3925
Germany	5980	7774	10203	6632
Greece	1612	2096	2751	1789
Spain	3781	4916	6452	4194
France	4944	6428	8436	5484
Ireland	1645	2139	2808	1826
Italy	4950	6435	8445	5490
Luxembourg	1699	2209	2899	1885
Netherlands	5150	6695	8786	5711
Austria	0	0	4208	2736
Portugal	2145	2789	3661	2380
Finland	1774	2307	3029	1969
Sweden	2328	3027	3973	2583
United Kingdom	3103	4034	5295	3442]

C10.07   *[Article 2 is printed as amended by Regulation (EC) 3315/94.]*

Article 3

C10.08   1. The cabotage authorisations referred to in Article 2 shall allow the recipient to carry out the cabotage operations.

2. Cabotage authorisations shall be distributed by the Commission to the Member States of establishment and issued to carriers applying for them by the competent authority or body of the Member State of establishment.

They shall bear the distinctive sign of the Member State of establishment.

3. A cabotage authorisation shall be made out in the name of the carrier. That carrier may not transfer it to a third party. Each cabotage authorisation may be used by only one vehicle at a time.

"*Vehicle*" means a motor vehicle registered in the Member State of establishment or a coupled combination of vehicles of which at least the motor vehicle is registered in the Member State of establishment and which are used exclusively for the carriage of goods.

The non-resident carrier shall have the vehicle at his disposal either under full ownership or an another basis, *inter alia*, a hire-purchase, hire or leasing contract.

In the case of hiring, the vehicle shall be hired by the carrier in the Member State of establishment to carry out cabotage operations. However, the non-resident carrier may, in order to complete a cabotage operation interrupted because of a breakdown or an accident, hire a vehicle in the host Member State under the same conditions as resident carriers.

The cabotage authorisation and the hiring contract, if any, shall accompany the motor vehicle.

4. The cabotage authorisation must be produced whenever requested by inspecting officers.

5. The date from which a cabotage authorisation is valid must be entered on the authorisation before it is used by the competent authority or body of the Member State of establishment.

Article 4

Transport operations effected under a cabotage authorisation shall be entered in a book of record sheets and the sheets shall be returned with the authorisation to the competent authority or body of the Member State of establishment which issued the authorisation within eight days of the expiry of the validity of the authorisation.   **C10.09**

The book of record sheets shall correspond to the model in Annex III.

Article 5

1. At the end of each quarter and within three months, which may be reduced by the Commission to one month in the case referred to in Article 7, the competent authority or body of each Member State shall communicate to the Commission the data concerning the cabotage operations carried out during that quarter by resident carriers, such data being expressed in tonnes carried and in tonnes/kilometres.   **C10.10**

The communication shall be effected by means of a table, the model for which is set out in Annex IV [*not reproduced in this work*].

2. The Commission shall send to the Member States as soon as possible summary statements drawn up on the basis of the data submitted under paragraph 1.

Article 6

1. The performance of cabotage transport operations shall be subject, save as otherwise provided in Community Regulations, to the laws, regulations and administrative provisions in force in the host Member State in the following areas: **C10.11**

(a) rates and conditions governing the transport contract;

(b) weights and dimensions of road vehicles; such weights and dimensions may, where appropriate, exceed those applicable in the carrier's Member State of establishment, but they may under no circumstances exceed the technical standards certified by the proof of compliance referred to in Article 1(1) of Council Directive 86/364/EEC [*O.J. No. L221, August 7, 1986, p. 7*];

(c) requirements relating to the carriage of certain categories of goods, in particular dangerous goods, perishable foodstuffs, live animals;

(d) driving and rest time;

(e) value added tax (VAT) on transport services. In this area Article 21(1)(a) of Directive 77/388/EEC [*Council Directive 77/388/EEC of May 17, 1977 on the harmonisation for the laws of the Member States relating to turn-over taxes—common system of value added tax: uniform basis of assessment (O.J. No. L145, June 13, 1977, p. 1), as amended*] shall apply to the services referred to in Article 1 of this Regulation.

2. The technical standards of construction and equipment which vehicles used to carry out cabotage operations must meet shall be those laid down for vehicles put into circulation in international transport.

3. The provisions referred to in paragraph 1 shall be applied to non-resident transport operators on the same conditions as those which that Member State imposes on its own nationals, so as to prevent any open or hidden discrimination on grounds of nationality or place of establishment.

4. If it is established that, in the light of experience, the list of areas covered by the host Member State's laws, regulations and administrative provisions referred to in paragraph 1 needs to be adapted, the Council shall amend that list, acting by a qualified majority on a proposal from the Commission.

Article 7

C10.12

1. In the event of serious disturbance of the national transport market in a given geographical area due to or aggravated by cabotage, any Member State may refer the matter to the Commission with a view to the adoption of safeguard measures and shall provide the Commission with the necessary information and notify it of the measures it intends to take as regards resident carriers.

2. or the purposes of paragraph 1:
— "*serious disturbance of the national transport market in a given geographical area*" means the existence on the market of problems specific to it, such that there is a serious and potentially enduring excess of supply over demand implying a threat to the financial stability and survival of a significant number of road haulage undertakings,
— "*geographical area*" means an area covering all or part of the territory of a Member State or extending to all or part of the territory of other Member States.

3. The Commission shall examine the situation, on the basis in particular of the latest quarterly data referred to in Article 5 and, after consulting the Advisory Committee set up by Article 5 of Regulation (EEC) No. 3916/90 [*O.J. No. L375, December 31, 1990, p. 10*] shall decide within one month of receipt of the relevant Member State's request whether or not safeguard measures are necessary and shall adopt them if they are necessary.

Such measures may involve the temporary exclusion of the area concerned from the scope of this Regulation.

The measures introduced in accordance with this Article shall remain in force for a period not exceeding six months, renewable once within the same limits of validity.

The Commission shall without delay notify the Member States and the Council of any decision taken pursuant to this paragraph.

4. If the Commission decides to take safeguard measures concerning one or more Member States, the competent authorities of the Member States involved shall be required to take measures of equivalent scope in respect of resident carriers and shall inform the Commission thereof.

These measures shall be applied at the latest as from the same date as the safeguard measures decided on by the Commission.

5. Any Member State may submit a Commission decision as referred to in paragraph 3 to the Community within 30 days of its notification.

The Council, acting by a qualified majority within 30 days of referral by a Member State or, if there are referrals by several Member States, of the first referral, may take a different decision.

The limits of validity laid down in the third sub-paragraph of paragraph 3 shall apply to the Council's decision.

The competent authorities of the Member States concerned shall be required to take measures of equivalent scope in respect of resident carriers and shall inform the Commission thereof.

If the Council takes no decision within the period referred to in the second sub-paragraph, the Commission decision shall become final.

6. Where the Commission considers that the measures referred to in paragraph 3 need to be prolonged, it shall submit a proposal to the Council, which shall take a decision by qualified majority.

Article 8

1. Member States shall assist one another in applying this Regulation.   **C10.13**

2. Without prejudice to any criminal proceedings the competent authorities of the host Member State shall be empowered to impose penalties on a non-resident carrier who has committed infringements of this Regulation or of Community or national transport legislation in their territory during a cabotage operation. They shall impose such penalties on a non-discriminatory basis and in accordance with paragraph 3.

3. The penalties referred to in paragraph 2 may, *inter alia*, consist of a warning, or, in the event of serious or repeated infringements, a temporary ban on cabotage transport within the territory of the host Member State where the infringement was committed.

Where a falsified cabotage authorisation is produced, the false document shall be confiscated immediately and forwarded as soon as possible to the competent authority of the carrier's Member State of establishment.

4. The competent authority of the host Member State shall inform that of the Member State of establishment of the infringements recorded and any penalties imposed on the carrier and may, in the event of serious or repeated infringements, at the same time transmit a request that a penalty be imposed.

In the event of serious or repeated infringements, the competent authority of the Member State of establishment shall decide whether an appropriate penalty should be imposed on the carrier concerned; the authority shall take into account any penalty imposed in the host Member State and ensure that the penalties imposed on the carrier concerned are, as a whole, proportional to the infringement or infringements which gave rise to such penalties.

The penalty imposed by the competent authority of the Member State of establishment, after consulting the competent authorities of the host Member State, may extend to withdrawal of authorisation to pursue the activity of road haulage operator.

The competent authority of the Member State of establishment may also, pursuant to its national law, arraign the carrier concerned before a competent national court or tribunal.

It shall inform the competent authority of the host Member State of the decisions taken pursuant to the preceding paragraphs.

Article 9

C10.14   Member States shall ensure that any applicant for, or holder of, an authorisation may appeal against a decision refusing or withdrawing that authorisation and against any other administrative penalty taken against him by the competent authority of the Member State of establishment or of the host Member State.

Article 10

C10.15   Member States shall adopt in good time and communicate to the Commission the laws, regulations and administrative provisions relating to the implementation of this Regulation.

Article 11

C10.16   Every two years and, for the first time by 30 June 1996, the Commission shall submit a report to the Community on the application of this Regulation.

Article 12

C10.17   1. This Regulation shall enter into force on 1 January 1994.

2. The Community authorisation and quota system for cabotage operations provided for in Article 2 shall cease to apply on 1 July 1998.

3. From that date any non-resident carrier meeting the conditions laid down in Article 1 shall be entitled to operate, on a temporary basis and without quantitative restrictions, national road haulage services in another Member State, without having a registered office or other establishment in that State.

The Commission shall submit to the Council, where appropriate, taking account of experience acquired, of developments in the transport market and of progress made towards harmonisation in the transport sector, a proposal on the detailed rules accompanying the definitive system as regards an appropriate system for observing the market in cabotage operations and the adjustment of the safeguard measures provided for in Article 7.

This Regulation shall be binding in its entirety and directly applicable in all Member States.

ANNEX I

(a)

(Thick green paper—format DIN A4)   **C10.18**

(First page of cabotage authorisation)

(Deadlines of periods of validity)

[(Text to be worded in the official language(s) or one of the official languages of the
Member State issuing the authorisation)]

COMMISSION OF THE EUROPEAN COMMUNITIES	(Impressed stamp of the Commission of the European Communities)	State issuing the authorisation/ international distinguishing sign (^{1})	Competent authority or agency

[CABOTAGE AUTHORISATION No. . . .

**for the national carriage of goods by road in a Member State of the
European Community performed by a non-resident carrier (cabotage)**

This authorisation entitles ....
....
....
....
....
.... (^{2})

to carry goods by means of a motor vehicle or a coupled combination of vehicles, within a
Member State of the European Community other than that in which the holder of this
authorisation is established, and to move such vehicle or combination unladen over any
part of the territory of the aforesaid Community, as laid down in Regulation (EEC) No.
3118/93 and subject to the general provisions of this authorisation.]

This authorisation is valid for a period of two months

from ....   to ....

issued at ....   date ....

(^{3})

_____

[(^{1}) Distinguishing signs of the country:
    Belgium (B), Denmark (DK), Germany (D), Greece (GR), Spain (E), France (F),
    Ireland (IRL), Italy (I), Luxembourg (L), Netherlands (NL), Austria (a), Portugal
    (P), Finland (FIN), Sweden (S), United Kingdom (GB) (as from 1 January 1996: UK).]
(^{2}) Name, or registered business name, and full address of carrier.
(^{3}) Signature and stamp of the competent authority or agency issuing the authorisation.

(b)

(Second page of cabotage authorisation)

[(Text to be worded in the official language(s) or one of the official languages of the Member State issuing the authorisation)]

General provisions

This authorisation permits the national carriage of goods by road in any Member State other than that in which the holder of the authorisation is established (cabotage).

It is personal to the holder and non-transferable.

It may be withdrawn by the competent authority of the Member State which issued it or, where the authorisation is a forgery, by the Member State in which the cabotage transport operations are carried out.

It may be used for only one vehicle at a time. Vehicle means a motor vehicle registered in the Member State of establishment or a coupled combination of vehicles of which at least the motor vehicle is registered in the Member State of establishment and which are used exclusively for the carriage of goods.

In the case of a coupled combination of vehicles, it shall accompany the motor vehicle.

It must be carried in the vehicle and must be accompanied by a book of record sheets for all national cabotage operations effected under it.

The cabotage authorisation and the book of record sheets must be filled in before the cabotage operations begin.

The authorisation and the book of record sheets for national cabotage operations must be produced together whenever required by an authorised inspecting officer.

Save as otherwise provided in Community regulations, the performance of cabotage transport operations shall be subject to the laws, regulations and administrative provisions in force in the host Member State in the following areas:

   (a) rates and conditions governing the transport contract;
   (b) weights and dimensions of road vehicles; such weights and dimensions may, where appropriate, exceed those applicable in the carrier's Member State of establishment but they may under no circumstances exceed the technical standards set out in the certificate of conformity;
   (c) requirements relating to the carriage of certain categories of goods, in particular dangerous goods, perishable foodstuffs, live animals;
   (d) driving and rest time;
   (e) VAT on transport services.

The technical standards of construction and equipment which vehicles used to carry out cabotage operations must meet those laid down for vehicles put into circulation in international transport.

This authorisation must be returned to the competent issuing authority or agency within eight days following its date of expiry.

C10.20   *[Annex I is printed as amended by Regulation (EC) 3315/94.]*

ANNEX II

(a)

(Thick pink paper—format DIN A4)

(First page of short-term cabotage authorisation)

(Deadlines of periods of validity)

[(Text to be worded in the official language(s) or one of the official languages of the
Member State issuing the authorisation)]

COMMISSION OF THE EUROPEAN COMMUNITIES	(Impressed stamp of the Commission of the European Communities)	State issuing the authorisation/ international distinguishing sign (¹)	Competent authority or agency

[**CABOTAGE AUTHORISATION No. . . . .**

**for the national carriage of goods by road in a Member State of the
European Community performed by a non-resident carrier (cabotage)**

This authorisation entitles ....

....

....

....

....

.... (²)

to carry goods by means of a motor vehicle or a coupled combination of vehicles, within a
Member State of the European Community other than that in which the holder of this
authorisation is established, and to move such vehicle or combination unladen over any
part of the territory of the aforesaid Community, as laid down in Regulation (EEC) No.
3118/93 and subject to the general provisions of this authorisation.]

This authorisation is valid for a period of one month

from ....   to ....

issued at ....   date ....

(³)

[(¹) Distinguishing signs of the country:
    Belgium (B), Denmark (DK), Germany (D), Greece (GR), Spain (E), France (F), Ireland
    (IRL), Italy (I), Luxembourg (L), Netherlands (NL), Austria (a), Portugal (P), Finland
    (FIN), Sweden (S), United Kingdom (GB) (as from 1 January 1996: UK).]
(²) Name, or registered business name, and full address of carrier.
(³) Signature and stamp of the competent authority or agency issuing the authorisation.

C10.22   (b)

(Second page of cabotage authorisation)

[(Text to be worded in the official language(s) or one of the official languages of the Member State issuing the authorisation)]

General provisions

This authorisation permits the national carriage of goods by road in any Member State other than that in which the holder of the authorisation is established (cabotage).

It is personal to the holder and non-transferable.

It may be withdrawn by the competent authority of the Member State which issued it or, where the authorisation is a forgery, by the Member State in which the cabotage transport operations are carried out.

It may be used for only one vehicle at a time. Vehicle means a motor vehicle registered in the Member State of establishment or a coupled combination of vehicles of which at least the motor vehicle is registered in the Member State of establishment and which are used exclusively for the carriage of goods.

In the case of a coupled combination of vehicles, it shall accompany the motor vehicle.

It must be carried in the vehicle and must be accompanied by a book of record sheets for all national cabotage operations effected under it.

The cabotage authorisation and the book of record sheets must be filled in before the cabotage operations begin.

The authorisation and the book of record sheets for national cabotage operations must be produced together whenever required by an authorised inspecting officer.

Save as otherwise provided in Community regulations, the performance of cabotage transport operations shall be subject to the laws, regulations and administrative provisions in force in the host Member State in the following areas:

    (a) rates and conditions governing the transport contract;

    (b) weights and dimensions of road vehicles; such weights and dimensions may, where appropriate, exceed those applicable in the carrier's Member State of establishment but they may under no circumstances exceed the technical standards set out in the certificate of conformity;

    (c) requirements relating to the carriage of certain categories of goods, in particular dangerous goods, perishable foodstuffs, live animals;

    (d) driving and rest time;

    (e) VAT on transport services.

The technical standards of construction and equipment which vehicles used to carry out and cabotage operations must meet shall be those laid down for vehicles put into circulation in international transport.

This authorisation must be returned to the competent issuing authority or agency within eight days following its date of expiry.

C10.23   *[Annex II is printed as amended by Regulation (EC) 3315/94.]*

ANNEX III

(a)   **C10.24**

(Format DIN A4)

(Front cover of book of record sheets)

[(Text to be worded in the official language(s) or one of the official languages of the
Member State issuing the book)]

State issuing the book of record sheets   Competent authority or agency

International distinguishing sign of
Member State (^{1})
                                                         Book No. . . .

BOOK OF RECORD SHEETS FOR NATIONAL CABOTAGE TRANSPORT
OPERATIONS CARRIED OUT UNDER CABOTAGE AUTHORISATION
No . . .

This book is valid until ....(^{2}).

Issued at .... date ....

(^{3})

_____

[(^{1}) Distinguishing signs of the country:
    Belgium (B), Denmark (DK), Germany (D), Greece (GR), Spain (E), France (F), Ireland
    (IRL), Italy (I), Luxembourg (L), Netherlands (NL), Austria (a), Portugal (P), Finland
    (FIN), Sweden (S), United Kingdom (GB) (as from 1 January 1996: UK)].
(^{2}) The period of validity may not exceed that of the cabotage authorisation.
(^{3}) Stamp of the competent authority or agency issuing the book.

(b)

(Inside front cover of book of record sheets)

1. [(Text to be worded in the official language(s) or one of the official languages of the Member State issuing the book)]

2. (Text in the official language or languages of issuing Member State)

General provisions

1. This book of record sheets contains 25 detachable sheets, numbered 1 to 25, on which details must be given, at the time of loading, of all goods transported under the cabotage authorisation to which they relate. Each book is numbered and that number is marked on every page of the book.

2. The carrier is responsible for the proper completion of the records of national cabotage operations.

3. The book must accompany the cabotage authorisation to which it relates and be kept on board the vehicle travelling laden or unladen under the said authorisation. It must be produced whenever required by an authorised inspecting officer.

4. Record sheets must be used in numerical order and the successive loading operations must be entered in chronological order.

5. Each item in the record sheet must be completed accurately and legibly by printing in indelible ink.

6. Not later than eight days after the end of the month to which the sheet relates, each completed record sheet must be returned to the competent authority or agency of the Member State which issued this book. Where an operation spans two census periods, the date of loading determines the period which the record must cover (e.g. an operation beginning towards the end of January and ending in the early part of February should be included in the January return).

(c)

(Front of the page inserted before the 25 detachable sheets)

(Text in the official language or languages of the issuing Member State)

Explanatory notes

The information to be given on the following sheets relates to all goods transported under the cabotage authorisation to which this record book relates.

A separate line on this sheet must be completed for each consignment of goods loaded.

Column 2:	give, where appropriate, the information requested by the issuing Member State;
Column 3:	give the day (01, 02 . . . 31) of the month indicated at the top of the sheet during which the vehicle departed under load;
Column 4 and 5:	specify the place and, if necessary to make this clear, the department, province, "Land", etc.;
Column 6:	use the following distinguishing signs:

> [— Belgium: B
> — Denmark: DK
> — Germany: D
> — Greece: GR
> — Spain: E
> — France: F
> — Ireland: IRL
> — Italy: I
> — Luxembourg: L
> — Netherlands: NL
> — Portugal: P
> — Finland: FIN
> — Sweden: S
> — United Kingdom: GB (as from 1 January 1996: UK)
> and from 1 January 1997:
> — Austria: A]

Column 7:	state the distance travelled between the place of loading and the place of unloading;
Column 8:	give the weight in tonnes to one decimal point (e.g. 10.0 t) of the consignment of goods in the same way as for the customs declaration; do not include the weight of containers or pallets;
Column 9:	in addition, describe as accurately as possible the goods in the consignment;
Column 10:	for official use only.

C10.27

Name and address of carrier

(d)

Month/Year

../....

Authorisation number:

Book number:

Record sheet number:

GOODS CARRIED

Order number		Date of departure	Place of loading	Place of unloading	Country	Distance (km)	Tonnage (. . .)	Descriptions of goods	Code
1	2	3	4	5	6	7	8	9	10
1									
2									
3									
4									
5									
6									
7									
8									
9									

[Annex III is printed as amended by Regulation (EC) 3315/94.]

ANNEX IV

[Omitted; see article 5.]

Regulation (EC) 792/94
of April 8, 1994

laying down detailed rules for the application of Council Regulation (EEC) 3118/93 to road haulage operators on own account

C11.01   *European Economic Area.*   As to the Agreement on the European Economic Area generally, see the note to Regulation (EEC) 3820/85 above.

For the purposes of that agreement, Regulation (EC) 792/94 has been adapted by *ibid.*, Annex XIII, Chapter II, para.26D, as inserted by Decision 20/94 of the EEA Joint Committee, art.1 (O.J. No. L325, December 17, 1994, p. 72).

THE COMMISSION OF THE EUROPEAN COMMUNITIES,

C11.02   Having regard to the Treaty establishing the European Community,

Having regard to Council Regulation (EEC) No. 3118/93 of 25 October 1993 laying down the conditions under which non-resident carriers may operate national road haulage services within a Member State [*q.v.*], and in particular Article 1(4) thereof,

Whereas cabotage authorisations should be issued both to undertakings entitled to carry out road haulage operations on own account and to undertakings performing road haulage operations for hire or reward;

Whereas the host Member State should consider the cabotage authorisation as sufficient evidence that an undertaking is entitled to carry out road haulage operations on own account in accordance with point 4 of the Annex to the First Council Directive of 23 July 1962 on the establishment of common rules for certain types of carriage of goods by road [*O.J. No. L70, August 6, 1962, p. 2005/62*], as last amended by Regulation (EEC) No. 881/92 [*q.v., Annex II of which substitutes the text of the Annex to the 1962 Directive*];

Whereas all conditions for the issue and use of cabotage authorisations as laid down by Regulation (EEC) No. 3118/93 shall apply to road haulage cabotage operations on own account;

Whereas this Regulation should apply as from 1 January 1994 in order to cover own-account cabotage operations already carried out under Regulation (EEC) No. 3118/93,

HAS ADOPTED THIS REGULATION:

Article 1

C11.03   Undertakings entitled in the Member State of establishment, in accordance with that Member State's legislation, to carry out road haulage operations on own account, shall be entitled to receive the cabotage authorisations referred to in Article 2 of Regulation (EEC) No. 3118/93, under the same conditions as undertakings performing road haulage operations for hire or reward.

Article 2

C11.04   The authorities of the host Member State shall consider the cabotage authorisations as sufficient evidence that the undertaking is entitled to carry out road haulage operations on own account, as defined in point 4 of the Annex to the First Directive.

Article 3

This Regulation shall enter into force on the day of its publication in the *Official Journal*   **C11.05**
of the European Communities.

It shall apply with effect from 1 January 1994.

The Regulation shall be binding in its entirety and directly applicable in all Member States.

Council Directive 96/53/EC
of July 25, 1996

laying down for certain road vehicles circulating within the Community the maximum authorised dimensions in national and international traffic and the maximum authorised weights in international traffic

C12.01   *Editorial note.*   The provisions of Directive 96/53/EC are incorporated into various provisions of English law, *e.g.* the Road Vehicles (Construction and Use) Regulations 1986 (S.I. 1986 No. 1078), reg.70B and Sched. 11A, para.8A.

THE COUNCIL OF THE EUROPEAN UNION,

C12.02   Having regard to the Treaty establishing the European Community, and in particular [Article 71] thereof,

Having regard to the proposal from the Commission,

Having regard to the opinion of the Economic and Social Committee,

Acting in accordance with the procedure laid down in [Article 252] of the Treaty,

(1) Whereas Council Directive 85/3/EEC of 19 December 1984 on the weights, dimensions and certain other technical characteristics of certain road vehicles [*O.J. No. L2, January 3, 1985, p. 14, as last amended by Directive 92/7/EEC, O.J. No. L57, March 2, 1992, p. 29*] established, in the framework of the common transport policy, common standards permitting improved use of road vehicles in traffic between Member States;

(2) Whereas Directive 85/3/EEC has been significantly amended on many occasions; whereas on the occasion of its further amendment it should for reasons of clarity and rationality be recast in a single text together with Council Directive 86/364/EEC of 24 July 1986 [*O.J. No. L221, August 7, 1986, p. 48*] relating to proof of compliance of vehicles with Directive 85/3/EEC;

(3) Whereas differences between standards in force in the Member States with regard to the weights and dimensions of commercial road vehicles could have an adverse effect on the conditions of competition and constitute an obstacle to traffic between Member States;

(4) Whereas, under the principle of subsidiarity, action should be taken at Community level in order to remove this obstacle;

(5) Whereas the above-mentioned standards reflect a balance between the rational and economical use of commercial road vehicles and the requirements of infrastructure maintenance, road safety and the protection of the environment and the fabric of life;

(6) Whereas common standards on the dimensions of vehicles intended for the carriage of goods should remain stable in the long term;

(7) Whereas additional technical requirements related to the weights and dimensions of vehicles may apply to commercial vehicles registered or put into circulation in a Member State; whereas these requirements must not constitute an obstacle to the circulation of commercial vehicles between Member States;

(8) Whereas the definition of "thick-walled refrigerated vehicle" in Article 2 of Directive 85/3/EEC, as amended by Directive 89/388/EEC [*O.J. No. L142, May 25, 1989, p. 3*], should be broadened in order to permit Member States to allow refrigerated vehicles no longer meeting the insulation requirements defined in that Article to circulate in their territory;

(9) Whereas its is necessary to clarify the concept of "indivisible load" in order to ensure uniform application of this Directive in respect of permits for vehicles or vehicle combinations carrying such loads;

(10) Whereas the tonne is universally used and understood as the unit of measurement for vehicle weight and is, therefore, applied in this Directive whilst recognising that the formal unit of weight is the newton;

(11) Whereas, in implementation of the internal market, the scope of this Directive should be extended to national transport insofar as it concerns characteristics that significantly affect the conditions of competition in the transport sector and in particular the values relating to the maximum authorised length and width of vehicles and vehicle combinations intended for the carriage of goods;

(12) Whereas, for the other vehicle characteristics, Member States are authorised to apply in their territory different values from those laid down in this Directive only to vehicles used in national traffic;

(13) Whereas road trains using extensible coupling systems in practice attain a maximum length of 18,75m when fully extended; whereas the same maximum length should be authorised for road trains using fixed coupling systems;

(14) Whereas they maximum authorised width of 2,50m for vehicles intended for the carriage of goods can leave insufficient internal space for the efficient loading of pallets, which has given rise to the application of different tolerances beyond that level in the legislation of the Member States concerning domestic traffic; whereas a general adaptation to the current situation is therefore necessary in order to provide for clarity in technical requirements, bearing in mind the road safety aspects of these characteristics;

(15) Whereas if the maximum width of vehicles intended for the carriage of goods is increased to 2,55m, that standard should also be applied to buses; whereas, in respect of buses, it is however necessary to provide for a transitional period to allow the manufacturers concerned to adapt industrial plant;

(16) Whereas, to prevent excessive road damage and to ensure manoeuvrability, when authorising and using vehicles preference should be given to pneumatic or equivalent suspension rather than mechanical suspension; whereas certain maximum axle loads should not be exceeded, and the vehicle must be capable of turning though 360° within certain limit values for the path followed;

(17) Whereas Member States should be permitted, in national goods transport, to allow vehicles or vehicle combinations with dimensions deviating from those laid down in this Directive to circulate in their territory if the transport operations carried out by such vehicles are defined by this Directive as not significantly affecting international competition in the transport sector, *i.e.* operations carried out by specialised vehicles and operations carried out according to a modular concept;

(18) Whereas, in the case of modular concept operations, there should be provision for a transitional period to enable a Member State to adapt its road infrastructure;

(19) Whereas vehicles or vehicle combinations constructed applying new technologies or new concepts, according to standards which deviate from those laid down by this Directive, should be allowed to carry out local transport operations for a trial period to enable profit to be drawn from technical progress;

(20) Whereas vehicles which entered into service before the date of implementation of this Directive and which do not comply with the dimension characteristics laid down in this Directive, owing to previously differing national provisions or methods of measurement, should be allowed for a transitional period to continue to provide transport services within the Member State in which the vehicle is registered or put into circulation;

(21) Whereas progress has been made towards adopting Type-Approval Directives for vehicle combinations with five or six axles; whereas, the requirements regarding conformity with characteristics other than weights and dimensions as laid down in Annex II of Directive 85/3/EEC should therefore be deleted;

(22) Whereas such a modification is also necessary in order to avoid rules conflicting with international conventions on road traffic and circulation;

(23) Whereas in order to facilitate the monitoring of compliance with this Directive, it is necessary to ensure that vehicles carry proof of such compliance;

(24) Whereas this Directive does not affect the obligations of the Member States concerning the deadlines for transposition into national law and for application of the Directives which this Directive replaces,

C12.03   *[The preamble is printed as amended by the Treaty of Amsterdam, art.12(1) and (3).]*

HAS ADOPTED THIS DIRECTIVE:

Article 1

C12.04   1. This Directive applies to:

(a) the dimensions of motor vehicles in categories M2, M3 and N2 and N3 and their trailers in categories 03 and 04, as defined in Annex II to Council Directive 70/156/EEC of 6 February 1970 on the approximation of the laws of the Member States relating to the type approval of motor vehicles and their trailers [*q.v.*];

(b) the weights and certain other characteristics of the vehicles defined in (a) and specified in Annex I (2) to this Directive.

2. All the values of weights indicated in Annex I are valid as circulation standards and thus refer to loading conditions, not production standards, which will be defined in a later Directive.

Article 2

C12.05   For the purposes of this Directive:

"*motor vehicle*" shall mean any power-driven vehicle which travels on the road by its own means,

"*trailer*" shall mean any vehicle intended to be coupled to a motor vehicle excluding semi-trailers, and constructed and equipped for the carriage of goods,

"*semi-trailer*" shall mean any vehicle intended to be coupled to a motor vehicle in such a way that part of it rests on the motor vehicle with a substantial part of its weight and of the weight of its load being borne by the motor vehicle, and constructed and equipped for the carriage of goods,

"*vehicle combination*" shall mean either:

— a road train consisting of a motor vehicle coupled to a trailer; or

— an articulated vehicle consisting of a motor vehicle coupled to a semi-trailer,

"*conditioned vehicle*" shall mean any vehicle whose fixed or movable superstructures are specially equipped for the carriage of goods at controlled temperatures and whose side walls, inclusive of insulation, are each at least 45mm thick, "*bus*" shall mean a vehicle with more than nine seats including the driver's seat, constructed and equipped to carry passengers and their luggage. It may have one or two decks and may also draw a luggage trailer,

"*articulated bus*" shall mean a bus consisting or two rigid sections connected to each other by an articulated section. On this type of vehicle the passenger compartments in each of the two rigid sections shall be intercommunicating. The articulated section shall permit the free movement of travellers between the rigid sections. Connection and disconnection of the two sections shall be possible only in a workshop,

"*maximum authorised dimensions*" shall mean the maximum dimensions for use of a vehicle, as laid down in Annex I to this Directive,

"*maximum authorised weight*" shall mean the maximum weight for use of a laden vehicle in international traffic,

"*maximum authorised axle weight*" shall mean the maximum weight for use in international traffic of a laden axle or group of axles,

"*indivisible load*" shall mean a load that cannot, for the purposes of carriage by road, be divided into two or more loads without undue expense or risk of damage and which owing to its dimensions or mass cannot be carried by a motor vehicle complying with this Directive in all respects,

"*tonne*" shall mean the weight executed by the mass of a tonne and shall correspond to 9,8 kilonewtons (kN),

All maximum authorised dimensions specified in Annex I shall be measured in accordance with Annex I to Directive 70/156/EEC, with no positive tolerances.

Article 3

1. A Member State may not reject or prohibit the use in its territory: **C12.06**

— in international traffic, of vehicles registered or put into circulation in any other Member State for reasons relating to their weights and dimensions,

— in national traffic, of goods vehicles registered or put into circulation in any other Member State for reasons relating to their dimensions,

provided that such vehicles comply with the limit values specified in Annex I.

This provision shall apply notwithstanding the fact that:

(a) the said vehicles are not in conformity with the requirements of that Member State with regard to certain weight and dimension characteristics not covered by Annex I;

(b) the competent authority of the Member State in which the vehicles are registered or put into circulation has authorised limits not referred to in Article 4(1) exceeding those laid down in Annex I.

2. However, paragraph 1(a) shall not affect the right of Member States, with due regard to Community law, to require vehicles registered or put into circulation in their own territory to be in conformity with their national requirements on weight and dimension characteristics not covered by Annex I.

3. Member States may require conditioned vehicles to carry an ATP certificate or ATP certification plate provided for in the Agreement of 1 September 1970 on the international carriage of perishable foodstuffs and on the special equipment to be used for such carriage.

Article 4

1. Member States shall not allow the normal circulation of vehicles or vehicle combinations for the national transport of goods in their own territory which are not in   **C12.07**

conformity with the characteristics set out in points 1.1, 1.2, 1.4 to 1.8, 4.2 and 4.4 of Annex I.

2. Member States may nonetheless allow circulation in their territory of vehicles or vehicle combinations for the national transport of goods freight which are not in conformity with the characteristics set out in 1.3, 2, 3, 4.1 and 4.3 of Annex I.

3. Vehicles or vehicle combinations which exceed the maximum dimensions may only be allowed to circulate on the basis of special permits issued without discrimination by the competent authorities, or on the basis of similar non-discriminatory arrangements agreed on a case-by-case basis with those authorities, where these vehicles or vehicle combinations carry or are intended to carry indivisible loads.

4. Member States may allow vehicles or vehicle combinations used for goods transport which carry out certain national transport operations that do not significantly affect international competition in the transport sector to circulate in their territory with dimensions deviating from those laid down in points 1.1, 1.2, 1.4 to 1.8, 4.2 and 4.4 of Annex I.

Transport operations shall be considered not significantly to affect international competition in the transport sector if one of the conditions under (a) and (b) is fulfilled:

(a) the transport operations are carried out in a Member State's territory by specialised vehicles or specialised vehicle combinations in circumstances in which they are not normally carried out by vehicles from other Member States, *e.g.* operations linked to logging and the forestry industry;

(b) the Member State which permits transport operations to be carried out in its territory by vehicles or vehicle combinations with dimensions deviating from those laid down in Annex I also permits motor vehicles, trailers and semi-trailers which comply with the dimensions laid down in Annex I to be used in such combinations as to achieve at least the loading length authorised in that Member State, so that every operator may benefit from equal conditions of competition (modular concept).

The Member State concerned which has to adapt its road infrastructure in order to be able to fulfil the condition under (b) may nevertheless prohibit, until 31 December 2003 at the latest, the circulation in its territory, in national goods transport operations, of vehicles or vehicle combinations which exceed current national standards on dimensions, provided that national legislation continues to apply to all Community carriers in a non-discriminatory manner.

The Member States shall inform the Commission of the measures taken pursuant to this paragraph.

5. Member States may allow vehicles or vehicle combinations incorporating new technologies or new concepts which cannot comply with one or more requirements of this Directive to carry out certain local transport operations for a trial period. Member States shall inform the Commission thereof.

6. Member States may allow vehicles or vehicle combinations used for goods transport and registered or put into circulation before the implementation of this Directive to circulate in their territory until 31 December 2006 with dimensions exceeding those laid down in points 1.1, 1.2, 1.4 to 1.8, 4.2 and 4.4 of Annex I by virtue of differing national provisions or methods of measurement.

Article 5

Without prejudice to Article 4(6):

(a) articulated vehicles put into circulation before 1 January 1991 which do not comply with the specifications contained in points 1.6 and 4.4 of Annex I shall be deemed to comply with such specifications for the purposes of Article 3 if they do not exceed a total length of 15,50m;

(b) road trains, the motor vehicle of which was put into circulation before 31 December 1991 and which do not comply with the specifications contained in points 1.7 and 1.8 of Annex I, shall until 31 December 1998 be deemed to comply with such specifications for the purposes of Article 3 if they do not exceed a total length of 18,00m.

Article 6

1. Member States shall take the necessary measures to ensure that Article 1 vehicles referred to in Article 1 and complying with this Directive carry one of the proofs referred to in (a), (b) and (c):   **C12.09**

(a) a combination of the following two plates:

— the "manufacturer's plate" established and attached in accordance with Directive 76/114/EEC [*O.J. No. L24, January 30, 1976, p. 1, as amended by Directive 78/507/EEC, O.J. No. L155, June 13, 1978, p. 31*],

— the plate relating to dimensions, in accordance with Annex III, established and attached in accordance with Directive 76/114/EEC;

(b) a single plate established and attached in accordance with Directive 76/114/EEC and containing the information on the two plates referred to in (a);

(c) a single document issued by the competent authorities of the Member State in which the vehicle is registered or put into circulation. Such document shall bear the same headings and information as the plates referred to in (a). It shall be kept in a place easily accessible to inspection and shall be adequately protected.

2. If the characteristics of the vehicle no longer correspond to those indicated on the proof of compliance, the Member State in which the vehicle is registered shall take the necessary steps to ensure that the proof of compliance is altered.

3. The plates and documents referred to in paragraph 1 shall be recognised by the Member States as the proof of vehicle compliance provided for in this Directive.

4. Vehicles carrying proof of compliance may be subject:

— as regards common standards on weights, to random checks,

— as regards common standards on dimensions, only to checks where there is a suspicion of non-compliance with this Directive.

5. The middle column of the proof of compliance relating to weights shall contain, where appropriate, the Community weight standards applicable to the vehicle in question. As regards vehicles referred to in point 2.2.2(c) of Annex I, the entry "44 tonnes" shall be included in brackets under the maximum authorised weight of the vehicle combination.

6. Each Member State may decide, in respect of any vehicle registered or put into circulation in its territory, that the maximum weights authorised by its national legislation shall be indicated in the proof of compliance in the left-hand column and the technically permissible weights in the right-hand column.

Article 7

This Directive shall not preclude the application of road traffic provisions in force in each Member State which permit the weight and/or dimensions of vehicles on certain roads or civil engineering structures to be limited, irrespective of the State of registration of such vehicles.   **C12.10**

Article 8

C12.11   Article 3 shall not apply in Ireland and the United Kingdom until 31 December 1998:

(a) as regards the standards referred to in points 2.2, 2.3.1, 2.3.3, 2.4 and 3.3.2 of Annex I:

— with the exception of the articulated vehicles referred to in point 2.2.2 where:
  (i)   the total laden weight does not exceed 38 tonnes;
  (ii) the weight on any tri-axle at the spacing specified in point 3.3.2 does not exceed 22,5 tonnes,

— with the exception of the vehicles referred to in points 2.2.3, 2.2.4, 2.3 and 2.4, where the total laden weight does not exceed:
  (i)   35 tonnes for the vehicles referred to in points 2.2.3 and 2.2.4;
  (ii)   17 tonnes for the vehicles referred to in point 2.3.1;
  (iii) 30 tonnes for the vehicles referred to in point 2.3.3, subject to compliance with the conditions specified in that point and in point 4.3;
  (iv)   27 tonnes for the vehicles referred to in point 2.4,

(b) as regards the standard referred to in point 3.4 of Annex I, with the exception of the vehicles referred to in point 2.2, 2.3 and 2.4, where the weight per driving axle does not exceed 10,5 tonnes.

Article 9

C12.12   As regards the standard referred to in point 1.2(a) of Annex I, a Member State may reject or prohibit the use in its territory, until 31 December 1999, of buses with a width exceeding 2,5m.

Member States shall inform the Commission of the measures taken pursuant to this Article. The Commission shall inform the other Member States thereof.

Article 10

C12.13   The Directive listed in Annex IV, Part A, shall be repealed with effect from the date in Article 11, without prejudice to the obligations of the Member States concerning the deadlines for transposition set out in Annex IV, Part B.

References to the repealed Directives shall be construed as references to this Directive and shall be read in accordance with the correlation table set out in Annex V.

Article 11

C12.14   1. Member States shall bring into force the laws, regulations and administrative provisions necessary to comply with this Directive by 17 September 1997. They shall forthwith inform the Commission thereof.

When Member States adopt these measures, they shall contain a reference to this Directive or shall be accompanied by such reference on the occasion of their official publication. The methods of making such reference shall be laid down by Member States.

2. Member States shall communicate to the Commission the text of the main provisions of domestic law which they adopt in the field covered by this Directive.

Article 12

C12.15   This Directive shall enter into force on the day of its publication in the *Official Journal of the European Communities*.

C12.16   *[This Directive was published at O.J. No. L235, September 17, 1996, pp. 59–75.]*

Article 13

This Directive is addressed to the Member States.

ANNEX I

MAXIMUM WEIGHTS AND DIMENSIONS AND RELATED CHARACTERISTICS OF
VEHICLES

1.   **Maximum authorised dimensions**
for the vehicles referred to in
Article 1(1)(a)

1.1	*Maximum length:*	
	— motor vehicle	12,00m
	— trailer	12,00m
	— articulated vehicle	16,50m
	— road train	18,75m
	— articulated bus	18,00m
1.2	*Maximum width:*	
	(a) all vehicles	2,55m
	(b) superstructures of conditioned vehicles	2,60m
1.3	*Maximum height (any vehicle)*	4,00m

1.4   Removable superstructures and standardised freight items such as containers are included in the dimensions specified in points 1.1, 1.2, 1.3, 1.6, 1.7, 1.8 and 4.4

1.5   Any motor vehicle or vehicle combination which is in motion must be able to turn within a swept circle having an outer radius of 12,50m and an inner radius of 5,30m

1.6   Maximum distance between the axis of the fifth-wheel king-pin and the rear of a semi-trailer   12,00m

1.7   Maximum distance measured parallel to the longitudinal axis of the road train from the foremost external point of the loading area behind the cabin to the rearmost external point of the trailer of the combination, minus the distance between the rear of the drawing vehicle and the front of the trailer   15,65m

1.8	Maximum distance measured parallel to the longitudinal axis of the road train from the foremost external point of the loading area behind the cabin to the rearmost external point of the trailer of the combination	16,40m

2.   **Maximum authorised vehicle weight (in tonnes)**

2.1	*Vehicles forming part of a vehicle combination*	
2.1.1	Two-axle trailer	18 tonnes
2.1.2	Three-axle trailer	24 tonnes
2.2	*Vehicle combinations*	
2.2.1	Road trains with five or six axles	
	(a) two-axle motor vehicle with three-axle trailer	40 tonnes
	(b) three-axle motor vehicle with two or three-axle trailer	40 tonnes
2.2.2	Articulated vehicles with five or six axles	
	(a) two-axle motor vehicle with three-axle semi-trailer	40 tonnes
	(b) three-axle motor vehicle with two or three-axle semi-trailer	40 tonnes
	(c) three-axle motor vehicle with two or three-axle semi-trailer carrying a 40-foot ISO container as a combined transport operation	44 tonnes
2.2.3	Road trains with four axles consisting of a two-axle motor vehicle and a two-axle trailer	36 tonnes
2.2.4	Articulated vehicles with four axles consisting of a two-axle motor vehicle and a two-axle semi-trailer, if the distance between the axles of the semi-trailer:	
2.2.4.1	is 1,3m or greater but not more than 1,8m	36 tonnes
2.2.4.2	is greater than 1,8m	36 tonnes +2 tonnes margin when the maximum authorised weight (MAW) of the motor vehicle (18 tonnes) and the MAW of the tandem axle of the semi-trailer (20 tonnes) are respected and the driving axle is fitted with twin tyres and air suspension or suspension recognised as being equivalent within the Community as defined in Annex II

2.3	*Motor vehicles*	
2.3.1	Two-axle motor vehicles	18 tonnes
2.3.2	Three-axle motor vehicles	— 25 tonnes — 26 tonnes where the driving axle is fitted with twin tyres and air suspension or suspension recognised as being equivalent within the Community as defined in Annex II, or where each driving axle is fitted with twin tyres and the maximum weight of each axle does not exceed 9,5 tonnes
2.3.3	Four-axle motor vehicles with two steering axles	— 32 tonnes where the driving axle is fitted with twin tyres and air suspension or suspension recognised as being equivalent within the Community as defined in Annex II, or where each driving axle is fitted with twin tyres and the maximum weight of each axle does not exceed 9,5 tonnes
2.4	*Three-axle articulated buses*	28 tonnes

3. Maximum authorised axle weight of the vehicles referred to in Article 1(1)(b) (in tonnes)

3.1	*Single axles* Single non-driving axle	10 tonnes
3.2	*Tandem axles of trailers and semi-trailers* The sum of the axle weights per tandem axle must not exceed, if the distance (d) between the axles is:	
3.2.1	less than 1m (d < 1,0)	11 tonnes
3.2.2	between 1,0m and less than 1,3m (1,0 ≤ d < 1,3	16 tonnes
3.2.3	between 1,3m and less than 1,8m (1,3 ≤ d < 1,8)	18 tonnes
3.2.4	1,8m or more (1,8 ≤ d)	20 tonnes
3.3	*Tri-axles of trailers and semi-trailers* The sum of the axle weights per tri-axle must not exceed, if the distance (d) between the axles is:	
3.3.1	1,3m or less (d ≤ 1,3)	21 tonnes
3.3.2	over 1,3m and up to 1,4m (1,3 < d ≤ 1,4)	24 tonnes

3.4	*Driving axle*	
3.4.1	Driving axle of the vehicles referred to in 2.2.1 and 2.2.2	11,5 tonnes
3.4.2	Driving axle of the vehicles referred to in points 2.2.3, 2.2.4, 2.3 and 2.4	11,5 tonnes
3.5	*Tandem axles of motor vehicles* The sum of the axle weights per tandem axle must not exceed, if the distance (d) between the axles is:	
3.5.1	less than 1m (d < 1,0)	11,5 tonnes
3.5.2	1,0m or greater but less than 1,3m (1,0 ≤ d < 1,3)	16 tonnes
3.5.3	1,3m or greater but less than 1,8m (1,3 ≤ d < 1,8)	— 18 tonnes — 19 tonnes where the driving axle is fitted with twin tyres and air suspension or suspension recognised as being equivalent within the Community as defined in Annex II, or where each driving axle is fitted with twin tyres and where the maximum weight for each axle does not exceed 9,5 tonnes

C12.21 **4. Related characteristics of the vehicles referred to in Article 1(1)(b)**

4.1 *All vehicles*
The weight borne by the driving axle or driving axles of a vehicle or vehicle combination must not be less than 25% of the total laden weight of the vehicle or vehicle combination, when used in international traffic

4.2 *Road trains*
The distance between the rear axle of a motor vehicle and the front axle of a trailer must not be less than 3,00m.

4.3 *Maximum authorised weight depending on the wheelbase*
The maximum authorised weight in tonnes of a four-axle motor vehicle may not exceed five times the distance in metres between the axles and the foremost and rearmost axles of the vehicle

4.4 *Semi-trailers*
The distance measured horizontally between the axis of the fifth-wheel king-pin and any point at the front of the semi-trailer must not exceed 2,04m

ANNEX II

CONDITIONS RELATING TO EQUIVALENCE BETWEEN CERTAIN NON-AIR SUSPENSION SYSTEMS AND AIR SUSPENSION FOR VEHICLE DRIVING AXLE(S)

1. DEFINITION OF AIR SUSPENSION

    A suspension system is considered to be air suspended if at least 75% of the spring   **C12.22**
    effect is caused by the air-spring.

2. EQUIVALENCE TO AIR SUSPENSION

    A suspension recognised as being equivalent to air suspension must conform to the   **C12.23**
    following:

2.1. during free transient low frequency oscillation of the sprung mass above the driving axle or bogie, the measured frequency and damping with the suspension carrying its maximum load must fall within the limits defined in points 2.2 to 2.5;

2.2. each axle must be fitted with hydraulic dampers. On tandem axle bogies, the dampers must be positioned to minimise the oscillation of the bogies;

2.3. the mean damping ratio D must be more than 20% of critical damping for the suspension in its normal conditions with hydraulic dampers in place and operating;

2.4. the damping ratio D of the suspension with all hydraulic dampers removed or anticipated must be not more than 50% of D;

2.5. the frequency of the sprung mass above the driving axle or bogie in a free transient vertical oscillation must not be higher than 2,0 Hz;

2.6. the frequency and damping of the suspension are given in paragraph 3. The test procedures for measuring the frequency and damping are laid down in paragraph 4.

3. DEFINITION OF FREQUENCY AND DAMPING

    In this definition a sprung mass M (kg) above a driving axle or bogie is considered. The   **C12.24**
    axle or bogie has a total vertical stiffness between the road surface and the sprung mass of K Newtons/metre (N/m) and a total damping coefficient of C Newtons per metre per second (N.s/m). The vertical displacement of the sprung mass is Z. The equation of motion for free oscillation of the spring mass is:

$$M \frac{d^2 Z}{dt^2} + C \frac{dZ}{dt} + kZ = 0$$

    The frequency of oscillation of the sprung mass F (rad/sec) is:

$$F = \sqrt{\frac{K}{M} - \frac{C^2}{4M^2}}$$

    The damping is critical when $C = C_o$,

    where

$$C_o = 2\sqrt{KM}$$

    The damping ratio as a fraction of critical damping is C/C_o.

    During free transient oscillation of the sprung mass the vertical motion of the mass will follow a damped sinusoidal path (Figure 2). The frequency can be estimated by measuring the time for as many cycles of oscillation as can be observed. The damping can be estimated by measuring the heights of successive peaks of the oscillation in the same direction. If the peak amplitudes of the first and second cycles of the oscillation are A_1 and A_2, then the damping ratio D is:

$$D = \frac{C}{C_o} = \frac{1}{2\pi} \ln \frac{A_1}{A_2}$$

"In" being the natural logarithm of the amplitude ratio.

4.   TEST PROCEDURE

C12.25   To establish by test the damping ratio D, the damping ratio with hydraulic dampers removed, and the frequency F of the suspension, the loaded vehicle should either:

(a) be driven at low speed (5 km/hr ± 1 km/hr) over an 80mm step with the profile shown in Figure 1. The transient oscillation to be analysed for frequency and damping occurs after the wheels on the driving axle have left the step;

     or

(b) be pulled down by its chassis so that the driving axle load is 1,5 times its maximum static value. The vehicle held down is suddenly released and subsequent oscillation analysed;

     or

(c) be pulled up by its chassis so that the sprung mass is lifted by 80mm above the driving axle. The vehicle held up is suddenly dropped and the subsequent oscillation analysed;

     or

(d) be subjected to other procedures insofar as it has been proved by the manufacturer, to the satisfaction of the technical department, that they are equivalent.

The vehicle should be instrumented with a vertical displacement transducer between driving axle and chassis, directly above the driving axle. From the trace, the time interval between the first and second compression peaks can be measured to find the frequency F and the amplitude ratio to obtain the damping. For twin-drive bogies, vertical displacement transducers should be fitted between each driving axle and the chassis directly above it.

Figure 1

Step for suspension tests

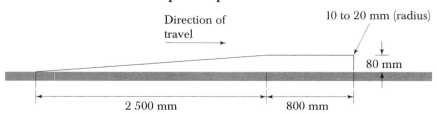

Figure 2

A damped transient response

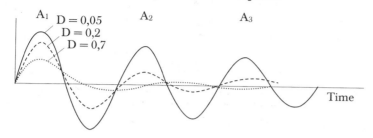

ANNEX III

PLATE RELATING TO DIMENSIONS REFERRED TO IN ARTICLE 6(1)(a)

I. The plate relating to dimensions, as far as possible affixed next to the plate referred to   **C12.26**
    in Directive 76/114/EEC, must contain the following data:

1. name of the manufacturer ([1]);

2. vehicle identification number ([1]);

3. length of the motor vehicle, trailer or semi-trailer (L);

4. width of the motor vehicle, trailer or semi-trailer (W);

5. data for the measurement of the length of vehicle combinations:

    — the distance (a) between the front of the motor vehicle and the centre of the
      coupling device (coupling hook or fifth wheel); in the case of a fifth wheel with
      several coupling points, the minimum and maximum values must be given (a_{min}
      and a_{max}),

    — the distance (b) between the centre of the coupling device of the trailer (fifth
      wheel ring) or of the semi-trailer (king-pin) and the rear of the semi-trailer, in
      the case of a device with several coupling points, the minimum and maximum
      values must be given (b_{min} and b_{max}).

The length of vehicle combinations is the length of the motor vehicle and trailer or
semi-trailer placed in a straight line behind each other.

II. The values given on the proof of compliance shall reproduce exactly the measure-
    ments carried out directly on that vehicle.

    ([1]) This information need not be repeated where the vehicle carries a single plate con-
        taining data on both weights and dimensions.

ANNEX IV

PART A

REPEALED DIRECTIVES

(referred to in Article 10)

C12.27 — Directive 85/3/EEC on the weights, dimensions and certain other technical characteristics of certain road vehicles and its successive amendments:

   — Directive 86/360/EEC

   — Directive 88/218/EEC

   — Directive 89/338/EEC

   — Directive 89/460/EEC

   — Directive 89/461/EEC

   — Directive 91/60/EEC

   — Directive 92/7/EEC

— Directive 86/364/EEC realting to proof of compliance of vehicles with Directive 85/3/EEC on the weights, dimensions and certain other technical characteristics of certain road vehicles.

PART B

C12.28 *[Deadlines for transposing Directives—Omitted.]*

ANNEX V

CORRECTION TABLE

C12.29 *[Omitted.]*

Directive 96/69/EC
of October 8, 1996

amending Directive 70/220/EEC on the approximation of the laws of the Member States relating to measures to be taken against air pollution by emissions from motor vehicles

Editorial note. The Annex to Directive 96/69/EC, although itself an amending measure, has been incorporated by reference into Table II to regulation 61 of the Road Vehicles (Construction and Use) Regulations 1986 (S.I. 1986 No. 1078).

* * *

ANNEX

Amendments to the Annexes to Directive 70/220/EEC as amended by Directive 93/59/EEC

The table in Section 5.3.1.4 is replaced by the following:

Category/class of vehicle		Reference mass RW (kg)	Limit values				
			Mass of carbon monoxide L_1 (g/km)		Combined mass of hydrocarbons and oxides of nitrogen L_2 (g/km)		Mass of particulates L_3 (g/km)
Category	Class		Petrol	Diesel	Petrol	Diesel ([1])	Diesel ([1])
M ([2])	—	all	2,2	1,0	0,5	0,7	0,08
N$_1$ ([3])	I	RW ≤ 1 250	2,2	1,0	0,5	0,7	0,08
	II	1 250 < RW ≤ 1 700	4,0	1,25	0,6	1,0	0,12
	III	1 700 < RW	5,0	1,5	0,7	1,2	0,17

([1]) Until 30 September 1999, for vehicles fitted with diesel engines of the direct injection type, the limit values L_2 and L_3 are the following:

	L_2	L_3
— category M ([2]) and N$_1$ ([3]) class I:	0,9	0,10
— category N$_1$ ([3]) class II:	1,3	0,14
— category N$_1$ ([3]) class III:	1,6	0,20

([2]) Except:
— vehicles designed to carry more than six occupants including the driver,
— vehicles whose maximum mass exceed 2 500kg.
([3]) And those category M vehicles which are specified in footnote ([2]).

[The text of the Annex is reproduced from O.J. No. L282, November 1, 1996, p. 67.]

Regulation (EC) 12/98
of December 11, 1997
laying down the conditions under which non-resident carriers may operate national road passenger transport services within a Member State

C14.01   *Editorial note.* Regulation (EC) 12/98 in effect supersedes Regulation (EEC) 2454/92 which was declared void by the European Court of Justice for a contravention of procedural rules in the course of its adoption (see Case C–388/92 *European Parliament v. EU Council* [1994] E.C.R. I–2067). The earlier Regulation was, however, continued in force by order of the court until new legislation was enacted.

For the national provisions implementing Regulation (EC) 12/98, see the Road Transport (Passenger Vehicles Cabotage) Regulations 1999 (S.I. 1999 No. 3413) above.

C14.02   *European Economic Area.* As to the Agreement on the European Economic Area generally, see the note to Regulation (EEC) 3820/85 above.

For the purposes of that agreement, Regulation (EC) 12/98 has been adapted by *ibid.*, Annex XIII, Chapter II, para.33*b*, as inserted by Decision 121/98 of the EEA Joint Committee (O.J. No. L297, November 18, 1999, p. 50).

THE COUNCIL OF THE EUROPEAN UNION,

C14.03   Having regard to the Treaty establishing the European Community, and in particular [Article 71] thereof,

Having regard to the proposal from the Commission,

Having regard to the opinion of the Economic and Social Committee,

Acting in accordance with the procedure laid down in [Article 252] of the Treaty,

(1) Whereas Council Regulation (EEC) No. 2454/92 of 23 July 1992, laying down the conditions under which non-resident carriers may operate national road passenger transport services within a Member State [*q.v.*] was declared void by the Court of Justice in its judgment of 1 June 1994 [*Case C-388/92 European Parliament v. EU Council [1994] E.C.R. I-2067*];

(2) Whereas, pursuant to [Article 71(1)(b)] of the Treaty, the establishment of a common transport policy entails, *inter alia*, laying down the conditions under which non-resident carriers may operate national transport services within a Member State;

(3) Whereas that provision entails the removal of all restrictions against carriers providing the services in question on the grounds of their nationality or the fact that they are established in a Member State other than that in which the service is to be provided;

(4) Whereas carriers providing such services should be subject to comparable systems, so as to limit inequality in the conditions of competition because of their nationality and country of establishment, and hence promote the gradual approximation of national laws;

(5) Whereas the definitions of the various coach and bus services should be the same as those adopted in the context of international transport;

(6) Whereas non-resident carriers should be allowed to operate certain forms of coach and bus services, bearing in mind the specific characteristics of each form of service;

(7) Whereas the provisions applicable to cabotage transport operations should be established;

(8) Whereas the provisions of Directive 96/71/EC of the European Parliament and of the Council of 16 December 1996 concerning the posting of workers in the framework of the provision of services [*O.J. No. L18, January 21, 1997, p. 1*] apply in cases where, for the provision of special regular services, carriers, post workers, who have an employment relationship with those carriers, from the Member State where they ordinarily work;

(9) Whereas, where regular services are concerned, only regular services provided as part of a regular international service, excluding urban and suburban services, should be opened up to cabotage, subject to certain conditions, and in particular to the legislation in force in the host Member State;

(10) Whereas provisions should be adopted so that action can be taken in the event of serious disturbance of the transport markets affected;

(11) Whereas an advisory committee should be set up with the task of assisting the Commission in drawing up documents relating to cabotage transport operations in the form of occasional services and advising the Commission on safeguard measures;

(12) Whereas it is desirable that Member States should grant each other mutual assistance with a view to the sound application of this Regulation, particularly in respect of penalties applicable in the event of infringements;

(13) Whereas it is for the Member States to adopt the measures necessary for the implementation of this Regulation;

(14) Whereas the application of this Regulation should be monitored by means of a report to be submitted by the Commission;

(15) Whereas the aforementioned judgment of the Court of Justice, which declared Regulation (EEC) No. 2454/92 void, upholds the effects of the Regulation until such time as the Council has adopted new legislation on the matter; whereas this Regulation will not be applied until eighteen months after its entry into force; whereas it must therefore be considered that the effects of the voided Regulation will persist until this Regulation has been fully implemented,

[The preamble is printed as amended by the Treaty of Amsterdam, art.12(1) and (3)] C14.04

HAS ADOPTED THIS REGULATION:

Article 1

Any carrier who operates road passenger transport services for hire or reward, and who C14.05
holds the Community licence provided for in Article 3A of Council Regulation (EEC) No. 684/92 of 16 March 1992 on common rules for the international carriage of passengers by coach and bus [*q.v.*], shall be permitted, under the conditions laid down in this Regulation and without discrimination on grounds of the carrier's nationality or place of establishment, temporarily to operate national road passenger services for hire or reward in another Member State, hereinafter referred to as the "*host Member State*", without being required to have a registered office or other establishment in that State.

Such national transport services are hereinafter referred to as "*cabotage transport operations*".

Article 2

For the purposes of this Regulation: C14.06

(1) "*Regular services*" means services which provide for the carriage of passengers at specified intervals along specified routes, passengers being taken up and set down at predetermined stopping points. Regular services shall be open to all—subject, where appropriate, to compulsory reservation.

The fact that the operating conditions of the service may be adjusted shall not affect its classification as a regular service.

(2) "*Special regular services*" means regular services which provide for the carriage of specified categories of passengers, to the exclusion of other passengers, at specified intervals along specified routes, passengers being taken up and set down at predetermined stopping points.

Special regular services shall include:

(a) the carriage of workers between home and work;

(b) carriage to and from the educational institution for school pupils and students;

(c) the carriage of soldiers and their families between their homes and the area of their barracks.

The fact that a special service may be varied according to the needs of users shall not affect its classification as a regular service.

(3) "*Occasional services*" means services which do not fall within the definition of regular services, including special regular services, and whose main characteristic is that they carry groups constituted on the initiative of a customer or of the carrier himself. These services shall not cease to be occasional services solely because they are provided at certain intervals.

(4) "*Vehicles*" means motor vehicles which, by virtue of their type of construction and equipment, are suitable for carrying more than nine persons—including the driver—and are intended for that purpose.

Article 3

C14.07   Cabotage transport operations shall be authorised for the following services:

(1) special regular services provided that they are covered by a contract concluded between the organiser and the carrier;

(2) occasional services;

(3) regular services, provided they are performed by a carrier not resident in the host Member State in the course of a regular international service in accordance with Regulation (EEC) No. 684/92.

Cabotage transport cannot be performed independently of such international service.

Urban and suburban services shall be excluded from the scope of this point.

"*Urban and suburban services*" means transport services meeting the needs of an urban centre or conurbation, and transport needs between it and the surrounding areas.

Article 4

C14.08   1. The performance of the cabotage transport operations referred to in Article 3 shall be subject, save as otherwise provided in Community legislation, to the laws, regulations and administrative provisions in force in the host Member State in relation to the following areas:

(a) rates and conditions governing the transport contract;

(b) weights and dimensions of road vehicles; such weights and dimensions may, where appropriate, exceed those applicable in the carrier's Member State of establishment, but they may under no circumstances exceed the technical standards set out in the certificate of conformity;

(c) requirements relating to the carriage of certain categories of passengers, *viz.*, schoolchildren, children and persons with reduced mobility;

(d) driving and rest time;

(e) VAT (value added tax) on transport services; in this area Article 21(1)(a) of Council Directive 77/388/EEC of 17 May 1977 on the harmonisation of the laws of the Member States relating to turnover taxes—common system of value added tax: uniform basis of assessment [*O.J. No. L145, June 13, 1977, p. 1, as last amended by Directive 96/95, O.J. No. L338, December 28, 1996, p. 89*] shall apply to the services referred to in Article 1 of this Regulation.

2. Save as otherwise provided in Community legislation, cabotage transport operations which form part of the transport services provided for in Article 3(3) shall be subject to the existing laws, regulations and administrative provisions in force in the host Member State regarding authorisations, tendering procedures, the routes to be operated and the regularity, continuity and frequency of services as well as itineraries.

3. The technical standards of construction and equipment which must be met by vehicles used to carry out cabotage transport operations shall be those laid down for vehicles put into circulation in international transport.

4. The national provisions referred to in paragraphs 1 and 2 shall be applied by the Member States to non-resident carriers on the same conditions as those imposed on their own nationals, so as effectively to prevent any open or hidden discrimination on grounds of nationality or place of establishment.

5. If it is established that, in the light of experience, the list of areas covered by the host Member State's provisions, as referred to in paragraph 1, needs to be amended, the Council shall do so by a qualified majority, on a proposal from the Commission.

Article 5

The Community licence or a certified true copy thereof shall be kept on board the vehicle and be produced when requested by an authorised inspecting officer. **C14.09**

Article 6

1. Cabotage transport operations in the form of occasional services shall be carried out under cover of a control document—*the journey form*—which must be kept on board the vehicle and be produced when requested by an authorised inspecting officer. **C14.10**

2. The journey form, the model for which shall be adopted by the Commission in accordance with the procedure laid down in Article 8, shall comprise the following information:

(a) the points of departure and destination of the service;

(b) the date of departure and the date on which the service ends.

3. The journey forms shall be supplied in books certified by the competent authority or agency in the Member State of establishment. The model for the book of journey forms shall be adopted by the Commission in accordance with the procedure laid down in Article 8.

4. In the case of special regular services, the contract concluded between the carrier and

the transport organiser, or a certified true copy of the contract, shall serve as the control document.

However, the journey form shall be completed in the form of a monthly statement.

5. The journey forms used shall be returned to the competent authority or agency in the Member State of establishment in accordance with procedures to be laid down by that authority or agency.

C14.11   **Article 7**   *[Provision of data and statistics by Member States to the Commission.]*

Article 8   *[Procedure whereby the Commission will submit draft measures to the advisory committee for its opinion.]*

Article 9

C14.12   1 In the event of serious disturbance of the internal transport market in a given geographical area due to or aggravated by cabotage, any Member State may refer the matter to the Commission with a view to the adoption of safeguard measures and shall provide the Commission with the necessary information and notify it of the measures it intends to take as regards resident carriers.

2. For the purposes of paragraph 1:

— *"serious disturbance of the internal transport market in a given geographical area"* means the occurrence on that market of problems specific to it, such that there is a serious and potentially enduring excess of supply over demand, implying a threat to the financial stability and survival of a significant number of road passenger transport undertakings.

— *"geographical area"* means an area comprising part or all of the territory of a Member State or including part or all of the territory of other Member States.

3. The Commission shall examine the situation and, after consulting the advisory committee referred to in Article 10, shall decide within one month of receipt of the relevant Member State's request whether or not safeguard measures are necessary and shall adopt them if they are necessary.

The measures introduced in accordance with this Article shall remain in force for a period not exceeding six months, renewable once for the same period.

The Commission shall without delay notify the Member States and the Council of any decision taken pursuant to this paragraph.

4. If the Commission decides to take safeguard measures concerning one or more Member States, the competent authorities of the Member States involved shall be required to take measures of equivalent scope in respect of resident carriers and shall inform the Commission thereof.

These measures shall be implemented no later than the same date as the safeguard measures decided on by the Commission.

5. Each Member State may refer a Commission decision as referred to in paragraph 3 to the Council within 30 days of its notification.

The Council, acting by a qualified majority within 30 days of referral by a Member State or, if there are referrals by more than one Member State, of the first referral, may take a different decision.

The limits of validity laid down in the second sub-paragraph of paragraph 3 shall apply to the Council's decision.

The competent authorities of the Member States concerned shall be bound to take measures of equivalent scope in respect of resident carriers and shall inform the Commission thereof.

If the Council takes no decision within the period laid down in the second sub-paragraph, the Commission decision shall become final.

6. Where the Commission considers that the measures referred to in paragraph 3 need to be prolonged, it shall submit a proposal to the Council, which shall take a decision by qualified majority.

Article 10   *[Rôle of the advisory committee.]*   **C14.13**

Article 11

1. Member States shall assist one another in applying this Regulation.   **C14.14**

2. Without prejudice to criminal prosecution, the host Member State may impose penalties on non-resident carriers who have committed infringements of this Regulation or of Community or national transport regulations within its territory on the occasion of a cabotage transport operation.

The penalties shall be imposed on a non-discriminatory basis and in accordance with paragraph 3.

3. The penalties referred to in paragraph 2 may, *inter alia*, consist of a warning or, in the event of serious or repeated infringements, a temporary ban on cabotage transport operations within the territory of the host Member State where the infringement was committed.

Where a falsified Community licence, falsified authorisation or falsified certified true copy thereof is produced, the falsified document shall be withdrawn immediately and, where appropriate, forwarded as soon as possible to the competent authority of the carrier's Member State of establishment.

4. The competent authorities of the host Member State shall inform the competent authorities of the Member State of establishment of the infringements recorded and any penalties imposed on the carrier and may, in the event of serious or repeated infringements, at the same time transmit a request that a penalty be imposed.

In the event of serious or repeated infringements, the competent authorities of the Member State of establishment shall decide whether an appropriate penalty should be imposed on the carrier concerned; these authorities shall take into account any penalty already imposed in the host Member State and ensure that the penalties already imposed on the carrier concerned are, as a whole, proportional to the infringements or infringements which gave rise to such penalties.

The penalty imposed by the competent authorities of the Member State of establishment, after consulting the competent authorities of the host Member State, may extend to withdrawal of authorisation to pursue the occupation of road passenger transport operator.

The competent authorities of the Member State of establishment may also, pursuant to its national law, arraign the carrier concerned before a competent national court or tribunal.

They shall inform the competent authorities of the host Member State of the decisions taken pursuant to this paragraph.

C14.15   *Cabotage (Passenger Services) Regulation*

Article 12

C14.15   Member States shall ensure that carriers may appeal to the courts against any administrative penalty imposed on them.

C14.16   **Article 13**   *[Reports by the Commission to the European Parliament.]*

C14.17   **Article 14**   *[Requirement for national implementing measures.]*

C14.18   **Article 15**   *[Commencement.]*

C14.19   *[This Regulation was published in O.J. No. L4, January 8, 1998, p. 10.]*

This Regulation shall be binding in its entirety and directly applicable in all Member States.

Council Act
of June 17, 1998

drawing up the Convention on Driving Disqualifications

THE COUNCIL OF THE EUROPEAN UNION,

Having regard to the Treaty on European Union, and in particular [Article 34(2)(d)] thereof,   **C15.01**

Whereas, for the purposes of achieving the objectives of the Union, the Member States regard the giving of effect to driving disqualifications as a matter of common interest coming under the cooperation provided for in Title VI of the Treaty;

HAS DECIDED that the Convention, the text of which is set out in the Annex and which is signed today by the Representatives of the Governments of the Member States of the Union, is hereby drawn up;

RECOMMENDS that it be adopted by the Member States in accordance with their respective constitutional rules.

[The text of this Act is printed as amended by the Treaty of Amsterdam, act.12(1) and (3).]   **C15.02**

Luxembourg,

17 June 1998.

Convention

on Driving Disqualifications

C16.01 THE HIGH CONTRACTING PARTIES to this Convention, Member States of the European Union,

REFERRING to the Council Act of 17 June 1998 [*see previous page*],

WHEREAS it is of the utmost importance for road safety within the European Union that a Union-wide effect be given to driving disqualifications by adequate means;

WHEREAS as a result of the free movement of persons and the increasing international road traffic, disqualifications from driving are frequently imposed by a Member State other than that in which the driver normally resides;

WHEREAS having regard to Council Directive 91/439/EEC of 29 July 1991 on driving licences [*O.J. No. L237, August 24, 1991, p. 1, as amended*], national provisions on the withdrawal, suspension and cancellation of driving licences should be applied by the Member State in whose territory the licence holder has his or her normal residence;

WHEREAS drivers disqualified from driving in a Member State other than that of their normal residence ought not to escape the effects of such measure when present in a Member State other than that of the offence;

WHEREAS the Member State of residence of the licence holder should therefore, in respect of offences considered particularly serious and under certain conditions, give effect to driving disqualifications imposed by another Member State by taking measures entailing the withdrawal, suspension or cancellation of his or her driving licence;

WHEREAS the fact that the Member State of residence has given effect to such a disqualification imposed by another Member State, should entail the consequence that the necessary measures are taken to penalise the act of driving a motor vehicle during the period of the disqualification under the laws of any Member State of the European Union in whose territory this may occur,

HAVE AGREED AS FOLLOWS:

Article 1

C16.02 For the purposes of this Convention:

(a) "*driving disqualification*" shall mean any measure related to the commission of a road traffic offence which results in withdrawal or suspension of the right to drive of a driver of a motor vehicle and which is no longer subject to a right of appeal. The measure may continue either a primary, secondary or supplementary penalty or a safety measure and may have been taken either by a judicial authority or by an administrative authority;

(b) "*State of the offence*" shall mean the Member State within the territory of which the road traffic offence that has given rise to a driving disqualification was committed;

(c) "*State of residence*" shall mean the Member State within the territory of which the person who has been disqualified from driving is normally resident within the meaning of Article 9 of Directive 91/439/EEC [*q.v.*];

(d) "*motor vehicle*" shall mean any vehicle covered by the definition in Article 3(3) of Directive 91/439/EEC [*q.v.*].

Article 2

The Member States hereby undertake to co-operate, in accordance with the provisions   **C16.03**
of this Convention, with the objective that drivers who are disqualified from driving in a
Member State other than that in which they normally reside should not escape the effects
of their disqualification when they leave the State of the offence.

Article 3

1. The State of the offence shall without delay notify the State of residence of any   **C16.04**
driving disqualification imposed for an offence arising from conduct referred to in the
Annex.

2. Each Member State may agree with other Member States that notification to it pursuant to paragraph 1 shall not take place in certain cases in which Article 6(2)(*a*) would
apply.

Article 4

1. Subject to Article 6, the State of residence which has been notified pursuant to Article   **C16.05**
3 shall without delay give effect to the decision imposing disqualification from driving taken
in the State of the offence in one of the following ways:

(a) by directly executing the decision imposing disqualification from driving, while
taking into account any part of the period of disqualification imposed by the State
of the offence which has already been served in the latter; or

(b) by executing the decision imposing disqualification from driving via a judicial or
administrative decision in accordance with the conditions laid down in paragraph
2; or

(c) by converting the decision imposing disqualification from driving into a judicial or
administrative decision of its own, thus, without prejudice to Article 11, substituting for the decision by the State of the offence a new decision in accordance
with the conditions laid down in paragraph 3.

2. If it applies the procedure laid down in paragraph 1(b) the State of residence:

(a) shall take into account any part of the period of the driving disqualification
imposed by the State of the offence which has already been served in that State;

(b) may reduce the duration of the driving disqualification but only to the maximum
term provided for acts of the same kind under its national law;

(c) shall not extend the duration of the driving disqualification imposed by the State
of the offence.

3. If it applies the procedure laid down in paragraph 1(c) the State of residence:

(a) shall be bound by the facts as established insofar as they are stated explicitly or
implicitly in the decision imposing disqualification from driving in the State of the
offence;

(b) shall take into account any part of the period of the driving disqualification
imposed by the State of the offence which has already been served in that
State;

(c) may reduce the duration of the driving disqualification to align it to the duration
which according to its national law would have been applied for the case in question;

(d) shall not extend the duration of the driving disqualification imposed by the State
of the offence;

(e) may not replace the driving disqualification by a fine or any other measure.

4. When giving effect to a driving disqualification under this Article, the State of residence shall, where necessary, determine a date from which it will enforce the driving disqualification.

5. When giving notification referred to in Article 15(2), each Member State shall indicate in a declaration which of the procedures described in paragraph 1 it intends to apply in its capacity as a State of residence. The declaration made may be replaced by a new declaration at any time.

Article 5

C16.06   Giving effect to a driving disqualification pursuant to Article 4 shall be without prejudice to any additional road safety measures that the State of residence may take under its own legislation.

Article 6

C16.07   1. The State of residence shall refuse to give effect to the driving disqualification where:

(a) the driving disqualification has already been fully enforced in the State of the offence;

(b) the offender has already had a driving disqualification imposed on him in the State of residence for the same acts and that disqualification has been or is being enforced;

(c) the offender would have benefited from a general pardon or amnesty in the State of residence if the acts had been committed within the territory of that State;

(d) the period of limitation for the measure would have expired under its own legislation;

(e) in the circumstances of the particular case, after receiving any information supplied under Article 8, it considers that the person concerned has not had an adequate opportunity to defend himself.

2. The State of residence may refuse to give effect to the driving disqualification if:

(a) the conduct for which the driving disqualification has been imposed in the State of the offence does not constitute an offence under the law of the State of residence;

(b) the remaining period of disqualification which could be enforced in the State of residence is less than one month;

(c) driving disqualification is not a measure available under the legislation of the State of residence for the acts giving rise to the driving disqualification imposed by the State of the offence.

3. When giving the notification referred to in Article 15(2) or at any other time, any Member State may declare that it will always apply paragraph 2 of this Article in part or in full. When such a declaration has been made, the other Member State shall not be obliged to communicate driving disqualifications such as referred to in that declaration pursuant to Article 3 to the Member State that has made the declaration. Any Member State may withdraw its declaration at any time.

Article 7

C16.08   1. The competent authority of the State of the offence shall forward the notification referred to in Article 3 to the central authority of the State of residence.

2. For the purposes of paragraph 1, when giving the notification referred to in Article 15(2), each Member State shall indicate:

(a) the central authority or central authorities which it designates;

(b) the competent authorities responsible for submitting the notifications referred to in Article 3.

Article 8

1. The notification referred to in Article 3 shall be accompanied by: **C16.09**

— details serving to locate the person disqualified from driving,

— the original or a certified copy of the decision imposing a driving disqualification,

— a brief statement of the circumstances and a reference to the legal provisions in the State of the offence on the basis of which the driving disqualification was imposed, if these are not given in the decision,

— an attestation that it is final,

— information regarding the enforcement of the driving disqualification in the State of the offence, including the length of the disqualification and, where known, the dates on which the disqualification starts and expires,

— the driving licence, if it has been seized.

2. Where the person on whom the driving disqualification has been imposed did not appear personally or was not represented at the proceedings, notifications pursuant to Article 3 must be accompanied by evidence that the person has been duly notified of the proceedings in accordance with the law of the State of the offence.

3. If the information communicated in accordance with paragraphs 1 and 2 is found to be insufficient to allow a decision to be taken pursuant to this Convention, in particular where, in the circumstances of the particular case, there is doubt whether the person concerned has had an adequate opportunity to defend himself, the competent authorities of the State of residence shall request the competent authorities of the State of the offence to provide the necessary supplementary information without delay.

Article 9

1. Subject to paragraphs 2 and 3, no translation of the notifications referred to in Article   **C16.10**
3 or of the accompanying material referred to in Article 8 or of any other documents relating to the application of this Convention shall be required.

2. Any Member State may, when giving the notification referred to in Article 15(2), declare that the documents referred to in paragraph 1 forwarded to it by the State of the offence must be accompanied by a translation into one of the official languages of the institutions of the European Communities indicated in its declaration.

3. Except for the document referred to in the second indent of Article 8(1) the documents referred to in paragraph 1 of this Article need not be certified.

Article 10

The State of residence shall inform the State of the offence of any decision taken in   **C16.11**
respect of a notification given pursuant to Article 3 and in respect of enforcement and, where it refuses to give effect to a driving disqualification pursuant of Article 6, of the reasons for its refusal.

Article 11

1. The right of the State of the offence to execute in its territory the full period of the   **C16.12**
driving disqualification determined by the State of the offence shall not be affected by the decision of the State of residence.

2. When giving the notification referred to in Article 15(2), any Member State may indicate that it will not apply paragraph 1 of this Article in its capacity as the State of the offence.

3. The State of the offence and the State of residence shall exercise their responsibilities under the Convention in such a way as to ensure that the total period of disqualification, taking into account any period of disqualification which is served for the offence concerned in the State of residence, does not exceed the period of disqualification originally determined by the State of the offence.

4. When notifying the person concerned of the decision to disqualify, a State of the offence which proposes to apply paragraph 1 shall at the same time inform the person of this fact, and shall confirm in the notification given in accordance with Article 3 to the State of residence that it has done so.

Article 12

C16.13   Each Member State shall adopt the measures necessary to enable it to penalise the driving of a motor vehicle in its territory when the driver is disqualified from driving by the State of residence in implementation of this Convention.

Article 13

C16.14   Costs incurred in implementing this Convention shall be borne in the Member State in which they occur.

Article 14

C16.15   1. The Court of Justice of the European Communities shall have jurisdiction to rule on any dispute between Member States regarding the interpretation or the application of this Convention whenever such dispute cannot be settled by the Council within six months of its being referred to the Council by one of its members. The Court shall also have jurisdiction to rule on any dispute between Member States and Commission regarding the interpretation or application of this Convention.

2. Any Member State shall be able to accept, through a declaration made when giving the notification referred to in Article 15(2) or at any later date, the jurisdiction of the Court of Justice to give preliminary rulings on the interpretation of this Convention.

3. A Member State making a declaration pursuant to paragraph 2 shall specify that either:

(a) any court or tribunal of that State against whose decisions there is no judicial remedy under national law may request the Court of Justice to give a preliminary ruling on a question raised in a case pending before it and concerning the interpretation of this Convention if that court or tribunal considers that a decision on the question is necessary to enable it to give judgment, or

(b) any court or tribunal of that State may request the Court of Justice to give a preliminary ruling on a question raised in a case pending before it and concerning the interpretation of this Convention if that court or tribunal considers that a decision on the question is necessary to enable it to give judgment.

4. The Statute of the Court of Justice of the European Community and its Rules of Procedure shall apply. Any Member State, whether or not it has made a declaration pursuant to paragraph 2, shall be entitled to submit statements of case or written observations to the Court in cases which arise under paragraph 3.

Article 15

1. This Convention shall be subject to adoption by the Member States in accordance with their respective constitutional requirements.

C16.16

2. Member States shall notify the Secretary-General of the Council of the European Union of the completion of their constitutional requirements for adopting this Convention.

3. This Convention shall enter into force 90 days after the notification referred to in paragraph 2 by the Member State which, being a Member of the European Union on the date of the adoption by the Council of the Act drawing up this Convention [*q.v.*], is the last to fulfil this formality.

4. Until this Convention enters into force, any Member State may, when giving the notification referred to in paragraph 2 or at any later date, declare that with respect to itself the Convention, except Article 14, shall apply to its relations with Member States that have made the same declaration. Such declarations shall apply as from 90 days after the date of their deposit.

5. This Convention and declarations made in respect of it shall be applicable only to offences committed after the entry into force of the Convention or from the date on which the Convention has become applicable between the Member States concerned.

Article 16

1. This Convention shall be open to accession by any State that becomes a member of the European Union.

C16.17

2. The text of this Convention in the language of the acceding State, drawn up by the Council of the European Union, shall be authentic.

3. Instruments of accession shall be deposited with the Secretary-General of the Council of the European Union.

4. This Convention shall enter into force with respect to any State that accedes to it 90 days after the deposit of its instrument of accession or on the date of entry into force of the Convention if it has not already entered into force at the time of expiry of those 90 days.

5. Article 15(4) shall apply to acceding Member States.

Article 17

No reservation may be entered in respect of this Convention.

C16.18

Article 18

As regards the United Kingdom, the provisions of this Convention shall apply only to the United Kingdom of Great Britain and Northern Ireland.

C16.19

Article 19　　*[Deposits of instruments of accession, etc.]*

C16.20

ANNEX

Conduct covered by Article 3 of the Convention

C16.21   1. Reckless or dangerous driving (whether or not resulting in death, injury or serious risk).

2. Wilful failure to carry out the obligations placed on drivers after being involved in road accidents (hit-and-run driving).

3. Driving a vehicle while under the influence of alcohol or other substances affecting or diminishing the mental and physical abilities of a driver.

Refusal to submit to alcohol and drug tests.

4. Driving a vehicle faster than the permitted speed.

5. Driving a vehicle whilst disqualified.

6. Other conduct constituting an offence for which a driving disqualification has been imposed by the State of the offence:

— of a duration of six months or more,

— of a duration of less than six months where that has been agreed bilaterally between the Member States concerned.

Regulation (EC) 2121/98
of October 2, 1998

laying down detailed rules for the application of Council Regulations (EC) 684/92 and (EC) 12/98 as regards documents for the carriage of passengers by coach and bus

European Economic Area. As to the Agreement on the European Economic Area generally, see the note to Regulation (EEC) 3820/85 above.   **C17.01**

For the purposes of that agreement, Regulation (EC) 2121/98 has been adapted by *ibid.*, Annex XIII, Chapter II, para.33*c*, as inserted by Decision 56/1999 of the EEA Joint Committee (O.J. No L284, November 9, 2000, p.17).

THE COMMISSION OF THE EUROPEAN COMMUNITIES

Having regard to the Treaty establishing the European Community.   **C17.02**

Having regard to Council Regulation (EEC) No. 684/92 of 16 March 1992 on common rules for the international carriage of passengers by coach and bus [*q.v.*], as amended by Regulation (EC) No. 11/98, and in particular point 3.4 of Article 2 and Articles 5(4), 6(2), 11(5) and 13(3) thereof,

Having regard to Council Regulation (EC) No. 12/98 of 11 December 1997 laying down the conditions under which non-resident carriers may operate national road passenger transport services within a Member State, and in particular Articles 6(2) and (3) and 7(1) thereof,

After consulting the committee established by Article 10 of Regulation (EC) No. 12/98,

1.   Whereas Article 4(4) of Regulation (EEC) No. 684/92 provides that regular services and certain special regular services are to be subject to authorisation;

2.   Whereas Article 11(1) of that Regulation states that occasional services are to be carried out under cover of a journey form;

3.   Whereas Article 13(1) of that Regulation provides that own-account transport operations are to be subject to a system of certificates;

4.   Whereas rules should also be laid down governing the use of the journey form referred to in Article 11 of that Regulation and the means of communicating to the Member States concerned the names of the carriers carrying out those services and of the connection points en route;

5.   Whereas the Commission adopted Regulation (EEC) No. 1839/92 of 1 July 1992 laying down detailed rules for the application of Council Regulation (EEC) No. 684/92 as regards documents for the international carriage of passengers [*q.v.*], as last amended by the Act of Accession of Austria, Finland and Sweden; whereas that Regulation has been amended by Regulation (EEC) No. 2944/93 in order to standardise, for reasons of simplicity, the control documents for shuttle services with accommodation and for occasional services;

6.   Whereas Regulation (EC) No. 11/98 abolished the concept of shuttle services and

simplified the definition of occasional services by abolishing the concept of residual occasional services;

7. Whereas it is necessary to standardise, for reasons of simplicity, the journey form for international occasional services and for occasional services in the form of cabotage provided for in Regulation (EC) No. 12/98;

8. Whereas the journey form used as a control document in the framework of special regular services in the form of cabotage must be completed in the form of a monthly statement;

9. Whereas, for reasons of transparency and simplicity, all the model documents laid down by Regulation (EEC) No. 1839/92 should be adapted to the new regulatory framework applicable to international coach and bus services and that Regulation should be replaced by the present Regulation;

10. Whereas Member States need time to have the new documents printed and distributed;

11. Whereas carriers should in the meantime be able to continue to use the documents provided for in Regulation (EEC) No. 1839/92 and Council Regulation (EEC) No. 2454/92 [*q.v.*], suitably amended where necessary to take account of Regulations (EEC) No. 684/92 and (EC) No. 12/98,

HAS ADOPTED THIS REGULATION:

CHAPTER I

CONTROL DOCUMENT — JOURNEY FORM

Article 1

C17.03

1. The control document — journey form for the occasional services referred to in point 3.1 of Article 2 of Regulation (EEC) No. 684/92 shall conform to the model in Annex I to this Regulation.

2. The control document — journey form for the occasional services referred to in point 3 of Article 2 of Regulation (EC) No. 12/98 shall conform to the model in Annex I to this Regulation.

3. The journey forms shall be in books of 25 forms in duplicate, and detachable. Each book shall bear a number. The forms shall also be numbered from 1 to 25. The cover of the book shall conform to the model in Annex II to this Regulation. Member States shall take all necessary measures to adapt these requirements to computerised processing of journey forms.

Article 2

C17.04

1. The book provided for in Article 1(3) shall be made out in the name of the carrier; it may not be transferred.

2. The journey form shall be filled in legibly in indelible letters, in duplicate, either by the carrier or by the driver for each journey prior to departure. It shall be valid for the entire journey.

3. The top copy of the journey form shall be kept on the vehicle during the whole of the journey to which it refers. A copy shall be kept at the company's base.

4. The carrier shall be responsible for keeping the journey forms.

Article 3

In the case of an international occasional service provided by a group of carriers acting on behalf of the same contractor, and which may include the travellers catching a connection en route with a different carrier of the same group, the original of the journey form shall be kept on the vehicle carrying out the service. A copy of the journey form shall be kept at the base of each carrier.

C17.05

Article 4

1. Copies of the journey forms used as control documents for occasional services in the form of cabotage pursuant to Article 6 of Regulation (EC) No. 12/98 shall be returned by the carrier to the competent authority or agency in the Member State of establishment in accordance with procedures to be laid down by that authority or agency.

C17.06

2. In the case of special regular services in the form of cabotage pursuant to Article 3 of Regulation (EC) No. 12/98, the journey form as set out in Annex I to this Regulation shall be completed in the form of a monthly statement and returned by the carrier to the competent authority or agency in the Member State of establishment in accordance with procedures to be laid down by that authority or agency.

Article 5

The journey form shall enable the holder, in the course of an international occasional service, to carry out local excursions in a Member State other than that in which the carrier is established, in accordance with the conditions laid down in the second paragraph of Article 12 of Regulation (EEC) No. 684/92. The local excursions shall be entered on the journey forms before the departure of the vehicle on the excursion concerned. The original of the journey form shall be kept on board the vehicle for the duration of the local excursion.

C17.07

Article 6

The control document shall be presented to any enforcement official on request.

C17.08

CHAPTER II

AUTHORISATIONS

Article 7   *[Applications for authorisations.]*

C17.09

Article 8

1. Authorisations shall conform to the model in Annex IV.

C17.10

2. Each vehicle carrying out a service subject to authorisation shall have on board an authorisation or a copy certified by the issuing authority.

CHAPTER III

CERTIFICATES

Article 9

1. Certificates for the own-account transport operations defined in point 4 of Article 2 of Regulation (EEC) No. 684/92 shall conform to the model in Annex V to this Regulation.

C17.11

2. Undertakings requesting a certificate shall provide the issuing authority with evidence or an assurance that the conditions laid down in point 4 of Article 2 of Regulation (EEC) No. 684/92 have been met.

3. Each vehicle carrying out a service subject to a system of certificates shall carry on board for the duration of the journey a certificate or a certified true copy, which shall be presented to enforcement officials on request.

4. Certificates shall be valid for a maximum of five years.

CHAPTER IV

COMMUNICATION OF STATISTICAL DATA

C17.12 **Article 10**   *[Provision of statistical data.]*

CHAPTER V

TRANSITIONAL AND FINAL PROVISIONS

C17.13 **Article 11**   *[Repeals Regulation (EEC) 1839/92.]*

Article 12

C17.14   Member States may authorise the use of the journey forms, applications for authorisation, authorisations and certificates drawn up in conformity with Regulation (EEC) No. 1839/92 and with Regulation (EEC) No. 2454/92 until 31 December 1999 at the latest, provided that they are amended, legibly, indelibly and appropriately in so far as is necessary, in order to conform to Regulations (EEC) No. 684/92, (EC) No. 12/98 and this Regulation.

The other Member States shall accept those documents on their territory until 31 December 1999.

C17.15 **Article 13**   *[Requirement of implementing measures.]*

C17.16 **Article 14**   *[Commencement.]*

C17.17   *[This Regulation was published in O.J. No. L268, October 3, 1998, p. 10]*

This Regulation shall be binding in its entirety and directly applicable in all Member States.

ANNEX I

EN   **JOURNEY FORM — MODEL**   **No** **C17.18**

(Light green paper — A4)

INTERNATIONAL OCCASIONAL SERVICES and OCCASIONAL SERVICES IN THE FORM OF CABOTAGE

(Each item, if necessary, can be supplemented on a separate sheet)

1	Registration number of the coach		Place, date and signature of the carrier
2	Carrier and, where appropriate, subcontractor or group of carriers		1 .... 2 .... 3 ....
3	Name of driver(s)		1 .... 2 .... 3 ....
4	Organisation or person responsible for the occasional service		1 .... 3 .... 2 .... 4 ....

5	**Type of service**	☐ International occasional service ☐ Occasional service in the form of cabotage ☐ Special regular services in the form of cabotage — monthly statement Month .... Year ....

6	Place of departure of service: .... Country: .... Place of destination of service: .... Country: ....

Journey	Route / Daily stages and/or passenger pick-up or set-down points		number of passengers	empty (mark with an X)	Planned km
Dates	from	to			
7					

8	Connection points, if any, with another carrier in the same group	Number of passengers set down	Final destination of the passengers set down	Carrier picking up the passengers	

Local excursions

9	Date	Planned km	Place of departure	Place of excursion	No of passengers

Unforeseen changes

10	

ANNEX II

Cover page

(Paper—A4)

> *To be worded in the official language(s) or one of the official languages of the carrier's Member State of establishment*

ISSUING STATE   Competent authority
—International distinguishing sign—(^{1})   ....

BOOK No. . . . .

of journey forms:

(a) **for international occasional services by coach and bus between Member States, issued on the basis of Regulation (EEC) No. 684/92**

(b) **for occasional services by coach and bus in the form of cabotage carried out in a Member State other than that in which the carrier is established, issued on the basis of Regulation (EC) No. 12/98**

to ....
(Surname and first name or trade name of carrier)

....

....
(Full address, telephone and fax number)

....
(Place and date of issue)   (Signature and stamp of issuing
                                                                                   authority or agency)

(^{1}) Austria (A), Belgium (B), Denmark (DK), Finland (FIN), France (F), Germany (D), Greece (GR), Ireland (IRL), Italy (I), Luxembourg (L), Netherlands (NL), Portugal (P), Spain (E), Sweden (S), United Kingdom (UK).

> *To be worded in the official language(s) or one of the official languages of the carrier's Member State of establishment*

Important notice

A. GENERAL PROVISIONS COMMON TO INTERNATIONAL OCCASIONAL SERVICES AND OCCASIONAL SERVICES IN THE FORM OF CABOTAGE

1. Articles 11(1) and 4(1) of Regulation (EEC) No. 684/92 and Article 6(1), (2) and (3) of Regulation (EC) No. 12/98 state that occasional services shall be carried out under cover of a control document — journey form.

2. The provisions referred to in the previous paragraph define occasional services as services "which do not fall within the definition of regular services, including special regular services, and whose main characteristic is that they carry groups constituted on the initiative of a customer or of the carrier himself".

   Regular services are "services which provide for the carriage of passengers at specified intervals along specified routes, passengers being taken up and set down at predetermined stopping points. Regular services shall be open to all, subject, where appropriate, to compulsory reservation".

   The regular nature of the service shall not be affected by any adjustment to the service operating conditions.

   Services, by whomsoever organised, which provide for the carriage of specified categories of passengers to the exclusion of other passengers, insofar as such services are operated under the conditions specified in 1.1, shall be deemed to be regular services. Such services are called "special regular services".

   Special regular services shall include:

   (a) the carriage of workers between home and work;

   (b) carriage to and from the educational institution for school pupils and students;

   (c) the carriage of soldiers and their families between their state of origin and the area of their barracks.

   The fact that a special service may be varied according to the needs of users shall not affect its classification as a "regular service".

3. The journey form shall be valid for the entire journey.

4. The Community licence and the journey form entitle the holder to carry out:

   (a) international occasional services by coach and bus between two or more Member States;

   (b) occasional services in the form of cabotage in a Member State other than that in which the carrier is established.

5. The journey form shall be completed in duplicate, either by the carrier or by the driver before the beginning of each service. The copy of the journey form shall remain in the undertaking. The driver shall keep the original on board the vehicle throughout the journey and present it on request to enforcement officials.

6. The driver shall return the journey form to the undertaking which delivered it at the end of the journey in question. The carrier shall be responsible for keeping the documents. They shall be filled in legibly and indelibly.

           Third page

B. PROVISIONS SPECIFIC TO INTERNATIONAL OCCASIONAL SERVICES

1. The second sub-paragraph of Article 2(3.1) of Regulation (EEC) No. 684/92 states that the organisation of parallel or temporary services comparable to existing regular services and serving the same clientele as the latter shall be subject to authorisation.

2. Carriers may carry out local excursions in a Member State other than that in which they are established in the case of international occasional services. Such local excursions shall be intended exclusively for non-resident passengers previously transported by the same carrier in the framework of an international occasional service. They shall be transported in the same vehicle or a vehicle belonging to the same carrier or group of carriers.

3. In the case of local excursions, the journey form must be completed before the departure of the vehicle on the excursion in question.

4. In the case of an international occasional service operated by a group of carriers acting on behalf of the same customer and possibly involving the passengers catching a connection *en route* with a different carrier of the same group, the original of the journey form shall be kept on the vehicle carrying out the service. A copy of the journey form shall be kept at the base of each carrier involved.

C. PROVISIONS SPECIFIC TO OCCASIONAL SERVICES IN THE FORM OF CABOTAGE

1. Occasional services in the form of cabotage shall be subject, save as otherwise provided in Community legislation, to the laws, regulations and administrative measures in force in the host Member State in the following areas:

    (a) rates and conditions governing the transport contract;

    (b) weights and dimensions of the road vehicles. Such weights and dimensions may, where appropriate, exceed those applicable in the carrier's Member State of establishment, but in no circumstances may they exceed the weights and dimensions set out in the certificate of conformity;

    (c) requirements relating to the carriage of certain categories of passenger, *viz.* schoolchildren, children and persons with reduced mobility;

    (d) driving and rest periods;

    (e) value added tax (VAT) on the transport services. In this area, Article 21(1)(a) of Council Directive 77/388/EEC of 17 May 1977 on the harmonisation of the laws of the Member States relating to turnover taxes — common system of value added tax: uniform basis or assessment ([1]), as last amended by Directive 96/95/EC ([2]), shall apply to the services referred to in Article 1 of this Regulation.

2. The technical standards for construction and equipment which the vehicles used to carry out the cabotage transport operations must meet shall be those laid down for vehicles put into circulation in international transport.

3. Member States shall apply the national provisions referred to in paragraphs 1 and 2 above to non-resident carriers on the same conditions as those applied to their own citizens, in order effectively to prevent any open or hidden discrimination on grounds of nationality or place of establishment.

4. In the case of an occasional service in the form of cabotage, the journey forms shall be returned by the carrier to the competent authority or agency of the Member State of establishment in accordance with procedures to be laid down by that authority or agency ([3]).

5. In the case of special regular services in the form of cabotage, the journey forms shall be completed in the form of a monthly statement and returned by the carrier to the competent authority or agency of the Member State of establishment in accordance with procedures to be laid down by that authority or agency.

[([1]) O.J. L145, 13.6.1977, p. 1.
([2]) O.J. L338, 28.12.1996, p. 89.
([3]) Member States' competent authorities may supplement point 4 with particulars of the agency responsible for collecting the journey forms and the procedure for forwarding the information.

ANNEX III

[Application for authorisation.]

ANNEX IV

(First page of the authorisation)   **C17.23**

(Pink paper—A4)

> *To be worded in the official language(s) or one of the official languages of the carrier's Member State of establishment*

ISSUING STATE
—International distinguishing sign—(^{1})   Competent authority

....

AUTHORISATION No . . . .

for a regular service (^{2})
for a non-liberalised special regular service
by coach and bus between Member States in accordance with Regulation
(EEC) No. 684/92

to: ....
(Surname, first name or trade name of carrier or of managing carrier in the case of an association of undertakings (pool))

....

Address: .... Tel. and fax: ....

Name, address, telephone and fax numbers of associates or members of the association of undertakings (pool) and sub-contractors:
(1) ....
(2) ....
(3) ....
(4) ....
(5) ....

List attached, if appropriate

Expiry date of authorisation: ....

....
(Place and date of issue)   (Signature and stamp of the issuing
                                          authority or agency)

(^{1}) Austria (A), Belgium (B), Denmark (DK), Finland (FIN), France (F), Germany (D), Greece (GR), Ireland (IRL), Italy (I), Luxembourg (L), Netherlands (NL), Portugal (P), Spain (E), Sweden (S), United Kingdom (UK).
(^{2}) Delete as appropriate.

C17.24
(Second page of authorisation No. . . . .)

1. Route:
   (a) Place of departure of service: ....
   (b) Place of destination of service: ....
   (c) Principal itinerary, with passenger pick-up and set-down points underlined: ....
   ....
   ....
   ....
   ....

2. Periods of operations: ....
   ....

3. Frequency: ....

4. Timetable: ....

5. Special regular service:
   — Category of passengers: ....

6. Other conditions or special points:
   ....
   ....
   ....
   ....
   ....
   ....

....
(Stamp of authority issuing
the authorisation)

> *To be worded in the official language(s) or one of the official languages of the carrier's Member State of establishment*

Important notice

1. This authorisation is valid for the entire journey. It may not be used except by a party whose name is indicated thereon.

2. The authorisation or a true copy certified by the issuing authority shall be kept on the vehicle for the duration of the journey and shall be presented to enforcement officials on request.

3. A true certified copy of the Community licence shall be kept on board the vehicle.

ANNEX V

C17.26

(First page of the certificate)

(Yellow paper—A4)

To be worded in the official language(s) or one of the official languages of the carrier's Member State of establishment

---

ISSUING STATE
—International distinguishing sign—(^{1})

Competent authority
....

CERTIFICATE
issued for own-account transport operations by coach and bus between Member States on the basis of Regulation (EEC) No. 684/92

(Part for the person or entity carrying out the own-account transport operations)

The undersigned ....
responsible for the undertaking, non-profit-making body or other (describe)
....
(Surname and first name or official name, full address)

certifies that:
— the transport service provided is non-profit-making and non-commercial,
— transport is only an ancillary activity for the person or entity,
— the coach or bus registration No . . . . is the property of the person or entity or has been obtained by them on deferred terms or has been subject to a long-term leasing contract,
— the coach or bus will be driven by a member of staff of the undersigned person or by the undersigned person.

....
(Signature of the person or representative of the entity)

(Part for the competent authority)

This constitutes a certificate within the meaning of Article 13 of Regulation (EEC) No. 684/92.

....
(Period of validity)

....
(Place and date of issue)

....
(Signature and stamp of the competent authority)

(^{1}) Austria (A), Belgium (B), Denmark (DK), Finland (FIN), France (F), Germany (D), Greece (GR), Ireland (IRL), Italy (I), Luxembourg (L), Netherlands (NL), Portugal (P), Spain (E), Sweden (S), United Kingdom (UK).

> *To be worded in the official language(s) or one of the official languages of the carrier's Member State of establishment*

General provisions

1. Article 2(4) of Regulation (EEC) No. 684/92 states that "own-account transport operations are transport operations carried out for non-commercial and non-profit-making purposes by a natural legal person, provided that:

   — the transport activity is only an ancillary activity for that natural or legal person;

   — the vehicles used are the property of that natural or legal person or have been obtained on deferred terms by them or have been the subject of a long-term leasing contract and are driven by a member of the staff of the natural or legal person or by the natural person himself".

2. Own-account carriers are licensed to carry out this type of transport operation without discrimination on grounds of nationality or place of establishment provided that they:

   — are authorised in the State of establishment to undertake transport by coach and bus on the conditions of access to the market laid down in national legislation;

   — meet the requirements on road safety as far as the standards for drivers and vehicles are concerned.

3. The own-account transport operations referred to in point 1 are exempt from authorisation but subject to a system of certificates.

4. The certificate entitles the holder to carry out international transport operations by coach and bus for own-account. It is issued by the competent authority of the Member State where the vehicle is registered and is valid for the entire journey, including any transit journeys.

5. The relevant parts of this certificate must be completed in indelible letters in triplicate by the person or the representative of the entity carrying out the operation and by the competent authority. One copy must be kept by the administration and one by the person or entity. The driver must keep the original or a certified true copy on board the vehicle for the entire duration of any international journeys. It must be presented to the enforcement authorities on request. The person or entity, as appropriate, is responsible for keeping the certificates.

6. The certificate is valid for a maximum of five years.

ANNEX VI

C17.28

MODEL COMMUNICATION

Referred to in Article 7(1) of Council Regulation (EC) No. 12/98 of December 11, 1997 laying down the conditions under which non-resident carriers may operate national road passenger transport services within a Member State

[Omitted.]

Regulation (EC) 2135/98
of September 24, 1998

amending Regulation (EEC) 3821/85 on recording equipment in road transport and Directive 88/599/EEC concerning the application of Regulations (EEC) 3820/85 and (EEC) 3821/85

[The text of this Regulation is printed as amended by:

Corrigendum at O.J. No. L49, February 25, 1999, p. 46.

The corrigendum noted above affected only the title to the Regulation.]

C18.01

THE COUNCIL OF THE EUROPEAN UNION,

Having regard to the Treaty establishing the European Community, and in particular [Article 71(1)(c) and (d)] thereof, C18.02

Having regard to the proposal from the Commission,

Having regard to the opinion of the Economic and Social Committee,

Acting in accordance with the procedure laid down in [Article 252] of the Treaty,

(1) Whereas Council Regulation (EEC) No. 3821/85 of 20 December 1985 on recording equipment in road transport [*q.v.*] lays down the provisions concerning the construction, installation, use and testing of recording equipment in road transport;

(2) Whereas experience has shown that the economic pressures and competition in road transport have led some drivers employed by road haulage companies to flout certain rules, particularly those concerning the driving and rest times laid down in Council Regulation (EEC) No. 3820/85 of 20 December 1985 on the harmonisation of certain social legislation relating to road transport [*q.v.*];

(3) Whereas blatant infringements and fraud present a road safety hazard and are unacceptable for reasons of competition for the individual driver who does not respect the rules;

(4) Whereas road safety would be improved by the automatic recording and regular monitoring, both by the undertaking and by the competent authorities, of details of the driver's performance and behaviour and of the vehicle's journey, such as speed and distance covered;

(5) Whereas Community social regulations contain certain requirements for limits on the daily driving and rest time and also for the total driving and rest time, for up to two weeks; whereas it is difficult to monitor compliance with these requirements given that data are recorded on several daily record sheets, out of which the record sheets for the current week and the last day of the previous week are to be stored in the cab;

(6) Whereas, to put an end to the most common abuses of the present system, it is therefore necessary to introduce new advanced equipment such as recording equipment fitted with an electronic device for storing relevant information and a personal driver card, so ensuring that the data recorded are retrievable, intelligible when printed out, and reliable, and that they provide an indisputable record of the work done by both the driver over the last few days and by the vehicle over a period of several months;

(7) Whereas the total security of the system and its components is essential if recording equipment is to function efficiently;

(8) Whereas provisions need to be established to govern the conditions under which the memory cards provided for in Annex IB may be issued and used;

(9) Whereas the data on drivers' activities must be verifiable by the drivers themselves, by the companies that employ them and by the competent authorities of the Member States; whereas, however, only data relevant to their respective activities should be accessible to the driver and his company;

(10) Whereas the recording equipment provided for in this Regulation must be installed on vehicles put into service for the first time after the publication in the *Official Journal of the European Communities* of the technical specifications some of which are defined by the Commission in accordance with the committee procedure referred to in Article 18 of Regulation (EEC) No. 3821/85; whereas a transitional period is needed to allow new recording equipment to be manufactured in accordance with those technical specifications and granted EC component type-approval;

(11) Whereas it is desirable that recording equipment complying with Annex IB should also offer the possibility of low-cost expansion of its functions for fleet management;

(12) Whereas, in accordance with the principle of subsidiarity, Community action is necessary to amend Regulation (EEC) No. 3821/85 in order to ensure that recording equipment complying with Annex IB is compatible with driver cards and that the data produced by recording equipment complying with Annexes I and IB are consistent;

(13) Whereas technical progress necessitates the prompt adoption of the technical requirements laid down in the Annexes to the Regulation; whereas, in order to facilitate the implementation of the measures needed for this purpose, provision should be made for technical adaptations of those Annexes to be approved by the Commission, acting in accordance with the committee procedure as set out in Council Decision 87/373/EEC of 13 July 1987 laying down the procedures for the exercise of implementing powers conferred on the Commission [*O.J. No. L197, July 18, 1987, p. 33*];

(14) Whereas the introduction of new recording equipment means that certain provisions of Directive 88/599/EEC [*O.J. No. L325, November 29, 1988, p. 55*] concerning the application of Regulations (EEC) No. 3820/85 and (EEC) No. 3821/85 need to be amended,

C18.03   *[The preamble is printed as amended by the Treaty of Amsterdam, art.12(1) and (3).]*

HAS ADOPTED THIS REGULATION:

C18.04   **Article 1**   *[Amends Regulation (EEC) 3821/85, q.v.]*

Article 2

C18.05   1. (a) 24 months from the date of publication in the *Official Journal of the European Communities* of the act to be adopted pursuant to Article 17(2) of Regulation (EEC) No. 3821/85, as amended by this Regulation, vehicles put into service for the first time must be fitted with recording equipment in accordance with the requirements of Annex IB to Regulation (EEC) No. 3821/85.

(b) As from the date of entry in to force of the provisions of sub-paragraph (a), vehicles used for the carriage of persons containing more than eight seats apart from the driver's seat and having a maximum weight exceeding 10 tonnes, and also vehicles used for the carriage of goods having a maximum weight exceeding 12 tonnes, registered for the first time as from 1 January 1996, shall in so far as the transmission of signals to the recording equipment with which they are fitted is exclusively electrical, satisfy the requirements of Annex IB to Regulation (EEC) No. 3821/85 when the equipment in question is replaced.

2. Member States shall take the necessary measures to ensure that they are able to issue driver cards no later than 21 months following the date of publication of the act referred to in paragraph 1(a).

3. In the event that 12 months after the date of publication of the act referred to in paragraph 1, EC type-approval has not been granted to any item of recording equipment which conforms to the requirements of Annex IB to Regulation (EEC) No. 3821/85, the Commission shall submit a proposal to the Council for an extension of the deadline laid down in paragraphs 1 and 2.

4. Drivers who, before the date laid down in paragraph 2, drive vehicles fitted with recording equipment conforming to the requirements of Annex IB to Regulation (EEC) No. 3821/85 for which the competent authorities have not yet been able to issue a driver card shall at the end of their daily work period print out the information concerning the various periods of time recorded by the recording equipment and shall indicate their identification details on the print-out (name and driving licence number), and sign it.

Article 3 *[Amends Directive 88/599/EEC (not reproduced).]* C18.06

Article 4 *[Commencement.]* C18.07

[This Regulation was published in O.J. No. L274, October 9, 1998, p. 1.] C18.08

This Regulation shall be binding in its entirety and directly applicable in all Member States.

ANNEX

[Text of Annex IB to Regulation (EEC) 3821/85, q.v.] C18.09

2/3154—4000

Section D

International Agreements

Agreement on the International Carriage of Passengers by Road by means of Occasional Coach and Bus Services (ASOR)

[THE CONTRACTING PARTIES]   **D1.01**

Desiring to promote the development of international transport and especially to facilitate the organisation and operation thereof;

Whereas some international carriage of passengers by road by means of occasional coach and bus services are liberalised as far as the European Economic Community is concerned by Council Regulation No. 117/66/EEC of 28 July 1966 on the introduction of common rules for the international carriage of passengers by coach and bus and by Regulation (EEC) No. 1016/68 of the Commission of 9 July 1968 prescribing the model control documents referred to in Articles 6 and 9 of Council Regulation No. 117/66/EEC [*O.J. No. L173, July 22, 1968, p. 8*];

Whereas in addition, the European Conference of Ministers of Transport (ECMT) adopted on 16 December 1969 resolution No. 20 concerning the formulation of general rules for international coach and bus transport [*volume of ECMT resolutions, 1969, p. 67; ibid., 1971, p. 133*] which also concerns the liberalisation of some international carriage of passengers by road by means of occasional coach and bus services;

Whereas it is desirable to provide for harmonised liberalisation measures for occasional international services for passengers by road and to simplify inspection procedures by introducing a single document;

Whereas it is desirable to assign some administrative tasks concerned with the Agreement to the Secretariat of the European Conference of Ministers of Transport;

Have decided to establish uniform rules for the international carriage of passengers by road by means of occasional coach and bus services,

AND . . . HAVE AGREED AS FOLLOWS:

[*Council Regulation 117/66/EEC (to which reference is made in the recitals) has been repealed by*   **D1.02** *Regulation (EEC) 684/92, art.21(1) (q.v.). References to the repealed Regulation should now be construed as references to Regulation (EEC) 684/92; see ibid., art.21(2). Regulation (EEC) 1016/68 (to which reference is also made) has been repealed by Regulation (EEC) 1839/92, art.10.]*

SECTION I

SCOPE AND DEFINITIONS

Article 1

1. This Agreement shall apply: **D1.03**
   (a) to the international carriage of passengers by road by means of occasional services effected:
   — between the territories of two Contracting Parties, or
   — starting and finishing in the territory of the same Contracting Party,

and, should the need arise during such services, in transit through the territory of another Contracting Party or through the territory of a non-contracting State, and

— using vehicles registered in the territory of a Contracting Party which by virtue of their construction and their equipment, are suitable for carrying more than nine persons, including the driver, and are intended for that purpose;

(b) to unladen journeys of the vehicles concerned with these services.

2. For the purpose of this Agreement, international services are understood to be services which cross the territory of at least two Contracting Parties.

3. For the purposes of this Agreement, the term *"territory of a Contracting Party"* covers, as far as the European Economic Community is concerned, those territories where the Treaty establishing that Community is applied and under the conditions laid down in that Treaty.

Article 2

D1.04   1. For the purposes of this Agreement, occasional services shall mean services falling neither within the definition of a regular service in Article 3 nor within the definition of a shuttle service in Article 4. They include:

(a) closed-door tours, that is to say services whereby the same vehicle is used to carry the same group of passengers throughout the journey and to bring them back to the place of departure;

(b) services which make the outward journey laden and the return journey unladen;

(c) all other services.

2. Save for exemptions authorised by the competent authorities of the Contracting Party concerned, in the course of occasional services no passenger may be taken up or set down during the journey. Such services may be operated with some degree of frequency without thereby ceasing to be occasional services.

Article 3

D1.05   1. For the purposes of this Agreement regular services shall mean services which provide for the carriage of passengers according to a specified frequency and along specified routes, whereby passengers may be taken up or set down at pre-determined stopping points. Regular services can be subject to the obligation to respect previously established timetables and tariffs.

2. For the purposes of this Agreement, services, by whomsoever organised, which provide for the carriage of specified categories of passengers to the exclusion of other passengers, in so far as such services are operated under the conditions set out in paragraph 1, shall also be considered to be regular services. Such services, in particular those providing for the carriage of workers to and from their place of work or of school children to and from school, are called *"special regular services"*.

3. The fact that a service may be varied according to the needs of those concerned shall not affect its classification as a regular service.

Article 4

D1.06   1. For the purposes of this Agreement, shuttle services shall mean services whereby, by means of repeated outward and return journeys, previously formed groups of passengers are carried from a single place of departure to a single destination. Each group, consisting of the passengers who made the outward journey, shall be carried back to the place of departure on a later journey.

Place of departure and destination shall mean respectively the place where the journey begins and the place where the journey ends, together with, in each case, the surrounding locality.

2. In the course of shuttle services, no passenger may be taken up or set down during the journey.

3. The first return journey and the last outward journey in a series of shuttles shall be made unladen.

4. However, the classification of a transport operation as a shuttle service shall not be affected by the fact that, with the agreement of the competent authorities in the Contracting Party or Parties concerned:

— passengers, notwithstanding the provisions of paragraph 1, make the return journey with another group,

— passengers, notwithstanding the provisions of paragraph 2, are taken up or set down along the way,

— the first outward journey and the last return journey of the series of shuttles are, notwithstanding the provisions of paragraph 3, made unladen.

SECTION II

LIBERALISATION MEASURES

Article 5

1. The occasional services referred to in Article 2(1)(a) and (b) shall be exempted from   **D1.07** the need for any transport authorisation on the territory of any Contracting Party other than that in which the vehicle is registered.

2. The occasional services referred to in Article 2(1)(c) shall be exempted from the need for any transport authorisation on the territory of any Contracting Party other than that in which the vehicle is registered where they are characterised by the following:

— the outward journey is made unladen and all the passengers are taken up in the same place, and

— the passengers:

(a) — constitute groups, in the territory of a non-Contracting Party or a Contracting Party other than that in which the vehicle is registered or that where the passengers are taken up, formed under contracts of carriage made before their arrival in the territory of the latter Contracting Party, and

— are carried in the territory of the Contracting Party in which the vehicle is registered; or

(b) — have been previously brought, by the same carrier in the circumstances provided for under Article 2(1)(b), into the territory of the Contracting Party where they are taken up again and carried into the territory of the Contracting Party in which the vehicle is registered; or

(c) — have been invited to travel into the territory of another Contracting Party, the cost of transport being borne by the person issuing the invitation. Such passengers must constitute a homogeneous group, which has not been formed solely with a view to undertaking that particular journey and which is brought into the territory of the Contracting Party where the vehicle is registered.

3. In so far as the conditions laid down in paragraph 2 are not satisfied, in the case of occasional services referred to in Article 2(1)(c), such services may be made subject to a transport authorisation in the territory of the Contracting Party concerned.

SECTION III

CONTROL DOCUMENT

Article 6

D1.08   Carriers operating occasional services within the meaning of this Agreement shall, whenever required to do so by any authorised inspecting officer, produce a passenger waybill which forms part of a control document issued by the competent authorities in the Contracting Party where the vehicle is registered or by any duly authorised agency. This control document shall replace the existing control documents.

Article 7

D1.09   1. The control document referred to in Article 6 shall consist of detachable passenger waybills in duplicate in books of 25. The control documents shall conform to the model shown in the Annex to this Agreement. This Annex shall form an integral part of the Agreement.

2. Each book and its component passenger waybills shall bear a number. The passenger waybills shall also be numbered consecutively, running from 1 to 25.

3. The wording on the cover of the book and that on the passenger waybills shall be printed in the official language or several official languages of the Member State of the European Economic Community or of any other Contracting Party in which the vehicle used is registered.

Article 8

D1.10   1. The book referred to in Article 7 shall be made out in the name of the carrier; it shall not be transferable.

2. The top copy of the passenger waybill shall be kept on the vehicle throughout the journey to which it refers.

3. The carrier shall be responsible for seeing that passenger waybills are duly and correctly completed.

Article 9

D1.11   1. The passenger waybill shall be completed in duplicate by the carrier for each journey before the start of the journey.

2. For the purpose of providing the names of passengers, the carrier may use a list already completed on a separate sheet, which shall be firmly stuck in the place provided for it under item No. 6 in the passenger waybill. The carrier's stamp or, where appropriate, the carrier's signature or that of the driver of the vehicle shall be placed across both the list and the passenger waybill.

3. For the services involving an outward journey unladen referred to in Article 5(2) of this Agreement, the list of passengers may be completed as provided in paragraph 2 at the time when the passengers are taken up.

Article 10

The competent authorities in two or more Contracting Parties may agree bilaterally or multilaterally that the list of passengers under item No. 6 of the passenger waybill need not be drawn up. In that case, the number of passengers must be shown. **D1.12**

Article 11

1. A model with stiff green covers and containing the text of the model cover page recto/verso of the control document shown in the Annex to this Agreement in each official language of all the Contracting Parties must be kept on the vehicle. **D1.13**

2. The following shall be printed on the front cover of the model in capital letters and in the official language or several official languages of the State in which the vehicle used is registered:

"Text of the model control document in Danish, Dutch, English, Finnish, French, German, Greek, Italian, Norwegian, Portuguese, Spanish, Swedish and Turkish".

3. This model shall be produced whenever required by any authorised inspecting officer.

Article 12

Notwithstanding the provisions of Article 6, control documents used for occasional services before the entry into force of this Agreement may be used for two years after the entry into force of the said Agreement pursuant to Article 18(2). **D1.14**

SECTION IV
GENERAL AND FINAL PROVISIONS

Articles 13, 14   *[Omitted.]* **D1.15**

Article 15

The provisions of Articles 5 and 6 shall not be applied to the extent that Agreements or other arrangements in force or to be concluded between two or more Contracting Parties provide for more liberal treatment. The terms "Agreements or other arrangements in force between two or more Contracting Parties" shall cover, as far as the European Economic Community is concerned, the Agreements and other arrangements which have been concluded by the Member States of that Community. **D1.16**

Articles 16, 17   *[Omitted.]* **D1.17**

Article 18

1. *[Omitted.]* **D1.18**

2. This Agreement shall enter into force, when five Contracting Parties including the European Economic Community have approved or ratified it, on the first day of the third month following the date on which the fifth instrument of approval or ratification is deposited.

3. This Agreement shall enter into force, for each Contracting Party which approves or ratifies it after the entry into force provided for under paragraph 2, on the first day of the third month following the date on which the Contracting Party concerned has deposited its instrument of approval or ratification with the ECMT Secretariat.

4. The provisions of Section II and III of this Agreement shall apply seven months after the entry into force of the Agreement as specified in paragraphs 2 and 3 respectively.

D1.19 **Articles 19–21** *[Omitted.]*

ANNEX

(green-coloured paper: DIN A4 = 29·7 x 21 cm)

(Front cover — recto)

(To be worded in the official language or several of the official
languages of the State where the vehicle is registered)

e in which the control document is issued
— Distinguishing sign of the country —

Competent authority or duly authorized
agency

Book No ....

BOOK OF PASSENGER WAYBILLS

for the international carriage of passengers by road by means of occasional coach and bus services
established pursuant to:

— **ASOR (Agreement on the International Carriage of Passengers by Road by means of
Occasional Coach and Bus Services) and**

— **Regulation No 117/66/EEC (Council Regulation on the introduction of common rules for
the international carriage of passengers by coach and bus)**

Name and first name of carrier or trade name: ....

....

Address: ....

....

....
(Place and date of issue of book)

....
(Signature and stamp of the authority or agency issuing the book)

2/4009

D1.21

(green-coloured paper: DIN A4 — 29·7 x 21 cm)

(Flyleaf of the book of waybills — recto)

> (To be worded in the official language or several of the official languages of the State where the vehicle is registered)

IMPORTANT NOTICE

I. TRANSPORT WITHIN THE JURISDICTION OF ASOR

Pursuant to Article 5 (1) and (2) of ASOR, the following shall be exempted from the need for any transport authorization on the territory of any Contracting Party other than that in which the vehicle is registered:

(a) certain occasional international services carried out by means of a vehicle registered in the territory of a Contracting Party:
— between the territories of the Contracting Parties, or
— starting and finishing in the territory of the same Contracting Party,
and, should the need arise, during such services, in transit through the territory of another Contracting Party or through the territory of a non-contracting State,

(b) unladen journeys of the vehicles concerned with these services.

The occasional services covered by the above provisions are as follows:

A. closed-door tours, i.e. services whereby the same vehicle is used to carry the same group of passengers throughout the journey and to bring them back to the place of departure, this place being situated on the territory of the Contracting Party where the vehicle is registered,

B. services which make the outward journey laden and the return journey unladen,

C. services where the outward journey is made unladen and where:
— all the passengers are taken up in the same place to be carried into the territory in which the vehicle is registered, and
— the passengers:

C.1. constitute groups in the territory either of a non-Contracting Party or of a Contracting Party other than that in which the vehicle is registered or than that where the passengers are taken up, formed under contracts of carriage made before their arrival on the territory of the latter Contracting Party, or

C.2. have been previously brought, by the same carrier, on a service referred to in B above, into the territory of the Contracting Party where they are taken up again, or

C.3. have been invited to travel into the territory of another Contracting Party, the cost of transport being borne by the person issuing the invitation. Such passengers must constitute a homogeneous group, which has not been formed solely with a view to undertaking that particular journey.

II. TRANSPORT WITHIN THE JURISDICTION OF REGULATION No 117/66/EEC

Pursuant to Article 5 (1) and (2) of Council Regulation No 117/66/EEC of 28 July 1966, certain international occasional services whose place of departure is in the territory of a Member State and whose destination is in the territory of the same or another Member State and which are operated using a vehicle registered in a Member State do not require authorization by any Member State other than the State where the vehicle is registered. For journeys in transit over the territory of an ASOR Contracting Party other than the Community, the ASOR provisions apply.

The occasional services covered by this provision are as follows:

A. closed-door tours, i.e. services whereby the same vehicle is used to carry the same group of passengers throughout the journey and to bring them back to the place of departure,

B. services which make the outward journey laden and the return journey unladen,

C. services where the outward journey is made unladen, provided that all the passengers are taken up in the same place and that the passengers:

C.1. constitute groups formed under contracts of carriage made before their arrival in the country where they are to be taken up, or

C.2. have been previously brought by the same carrier, on a service referred to in B above, into the country where such passengers are taken up again and carried out of that country, or

C.3. have been invited to travel to another Member State, the cost of transport being borne by the person issuing the invitation. Such passengers must constitute a homogeneous group, which has not been formed solely with a view to undertaking that particular journey.

III. COMMON PROVISIONS APPLICABLE TO ALL INTERNATIONAL SERVICES WITHIN THE SCOPE OF ASOR OR REGULATION No 117/66/EEC

1. For each journey carried out as an occasional service the carrier must complete a passenger waybill in duplicate, before the start of the journey.

   For the purpose of providing the names of passengers, the carrier may use a list already completed on a separate sheet, which must be firmly stuck in the place provided for it under item No 6 in the passenger waybill. The carrier's stamp or, where appropriate, the carrier's signature or that of the driver of the vehicle must be placed across both the list and the passenger waybill.

   For services where the outward journey is made unladen, the list of passengers may be completed as provided above at the time when the passengers are taken up.

   The top copy of the passenger waybill must be kept on board the vehicle throughout the journey and be produced whenever required by any authorized inspecting officer.

2. A model with stiff green covers and containing the text of the model cover page recto/verso, in each official language of all the Contracting Parties to ASOR, must be kept on the vehicle.

3. For services where the outward journey is made unladen, referred to in C, the carrier must attach the following supporting documents to the passenger waybill:
   — in cases mentioned under C.1: the copy of the contract of carriage in so far as some countries require it, or any other equivalent document which establishes the essential data of this contract (especially place, country and date of conclusion, place, country and date when passengers are taken up, place and country of destination);
   — in the case of services falling within C.2: the passenger waybill which accompanied the vehicle during the corresponding journey made by the carrier outward laden/return unladen in order to bring the passengers into the territory either of the Contracting Party or the EEC Member State where they are taken up again;
   — in the case of services falling within C.3: the letter of invitation from the person issuing the invitation or a photocopy thereof.

4. Occasional services not falling within points I and II may be made subject to transport authorization on the territory of the Contracting Party or of the Member State of the EEC concerned. For these services, a cross must be placed in the appropriate box, under point 4D of the waybill, showing whether a transport authorization is or is not required. If a transport authorization is required it must be attached to the waybill. If no transport authorization is required justification must be given.

5. In the course of occasional services no passenger may be taken up or set down during the journey, save for exemption authorized by the competent authorities. This authorization must also be attached.

6. The carrier is responsible for seeing that passenger waybills are duly and correctly completed. They shall be completed in block letters and in indelible ink.

7. The book of waybills is not transferable.

(Flyleaf of the book of waybills – verso)

(To be worded in the official language or several of the official languages of the State of registration of the vehicle)

Explanation of symbols used in the passenger waybill and instructions on how to fill it in

	Registration No	Number of passenger seats available
	Name and first name of carrier, or trade name, and address	
	Name of driver or drivers	

Type of service

A Closed-door tour

B Outward journey laden – return journey unladen
● = Locality where passengers are set down and distinguishing sign of the country

C1 Outward journey unladen in order to take up a group of passengers and transport them to the country of vehicle registration

C

● – Locality where passengers are taken up and distinguishing sign of the country

◉ – Locality where passengers are set down and distinguishing sign of the country

C2 See 'Important Notice'

C3

D Another occasional service (particulars)

⊞– The required authorization is attached

⊞– Authorization not required because ....

Itinerary

Daily stages

Dates	from	to	Use of vehicle (Indicate the number of kilometres in the relevant column)		Frontier crossing points
	Locality, and distinguishing sign of the country				
	from	to	laden	unladen	

Passenger list (surnames and initials)

1 _____	22 _____	43 _____
2 _____	23 _____	44 _____
3 _____	24 _____	45 _____
_____	_____	_____
21 _____	42 _____	63 _____

2/4011

D1.23

(Passenger waybill – recto)   (Green coloured paper – DIN A4 = 29·7 x 21 cm)

Book No ....

Waybill No ....

> (To be worded in the official language or several of the official
> languages of the State of vehicle registration)

(State in which the document is issued) — Distinguishing sign of the country

1	
2	
3	1 _____ 2 _____ 3 _____

Type of service (put a cross in the appropriate box and add the required supplementary information)

A

B

4

C	Outward journey unladen in order to take up a group of passengers and transport them to the country of vehicle registration.

C1 The passengers were assembled, under a contract of carriage made on .... with .... (travel agency, association, etc.).
They arrive(d) on ....

☐ in the territory of the Contracting Party where they are to be taken up,

☐ in the Member State of the EEC where they are to be taken up (for EEC vehicles only),

☐ copy of the contract of carriage or equivalent document (cf. Important Notice under III.3) is attached.

C2 previously brought by the same carrier on a service referred to in B, to the country where they are to be taken up again.
The passenger waybill for the previous outward laden journey and unladen return journey is attached.

C3 invited to travel to ....
Cost of transport being borne by the person issuing the invitation and the passengers constitute a homogeneous group which has not been formed solely with a view to undertaking that particular journey. The letter of invitation (or a photocopy thereof) is attached.

D Another occasional service (particulars):

☐ – The required authorization is attached

☐ – Authorization not required because ....

Itinerary

5

Dates	from	to	Km	Km	Customs
		Total	+	=	

2/4012

(Passenger waybill – verso)

1	22	43
2	23	44
3	24	45
4	25	46
5	26	47
6	27	48
7	28	49
8	29	50
9	30	51
10	31	52
11	32	53
12	33	54
13	34	55
14	35	56
15	36	57
16	37	58
17	38	59
18	39	60
19	40	61
20	41	62
21	42	63

Date of completion of waybill

Signature of carrier

Unforeseen changes

Control stamps if any

SIGNATURES

D1.24   *[The Agreement was signed in Dublin on May 26, 1982 on behalf of:*

the Council of the European Communities
Austria
Finland
Norway
Portugal
Spain
Sweden
Switzerland
Turkey.

Regulation (EEC) 56/83 imposed responsibility for the implementation of ASOR on the Member States of the European Communities. The ASOR was approved on behalf of the European Communities by Decision 82/505/EEC and entered into force within the Community on December 1, 1983; see the Road Transport (International Passenger Services) Regulations 1984 (S.I. 1984 No. 748), reg.2(1)(b) above. The ASOR entered into force for Austria on January 1, 1987.]

DECLARATION BY THE CONTRACTING PARTIES ON THE APPLICATION OF THE AGREEMENT

D1.25   The Contracting Parties agree that the liberalisation measures provided under Articles 5(2) of the Agreement shall only be enforceable between the Contracting Parties who apply the provisions of the European Agreement concerning the work of crews of vehicles engaged in International Road Transport (AETR) from 1 July 1970, or equivalent conditions to those provided under the AETR, to the occasional services governed by this Agreement.

Each Contracting Party which intends, for the reasons set out above, to adopt measures for the non-application or the suspension of the liberalisation provisions under Article 5(2) of the Agreement, declares itself ready to consult the relevant Contracting Party before the possible adoption of these measures.

DECLARATION BY THE EUROPEAN ECONOMIC COMMUNITY CONCERNING ARTICLE 5 OF THE AGREEMENT

D1.26   With regard to Article 5, the European Economic Community declares that the liberalisation measures laid down for the entry of an unladen vehicle into another Contracting Party with a view to taking up passengers for the return journey to the territory of the Contracting Party where the vehicle is registered shall only apply, where the return to the territory of the European Economic Community is concerned, to return journeys to the Member State in which the vehicle used is registered.

*   *   *

D1.27   *[This agreement is the copyright of the EC Commission and is reproduced from O.J. No. L230, August 5, 1982, pp. 39–56.]*

European Agreement concerning the Work of Crews of Vehicles engaged in International Road Transport (AETR)

(Cmnd. 7401)

[The text of this agreement has been amended by provisions published as command papers as follows: **D2.01**

Cmnd. 9037 (August 3, 1983);

Cm. 3042 (April 24, 1992); and

Cm. 3135 (February 28, 1995).

The amending provisions are referred to in the notes to the agreement by reference to the appropriate command paper. The dates referred to above are the dates on which the amendments came into force.

The text of the agreement is Crown Copyright and is reproduced with permission of the Controller of Her Majesty's Stationery Office.]

ARRANGEMENT OF ARTICLES   D2.02

IV. Record sheets
    A. General points
    B. Recording areas and their graduation
    C. Information to be printed on the record sheets
    D. Free space for hand-written insertions
V. Installation of control device
    A. General points
    B. Sealing
VI. Checks and inspections

Appendix 2. Approval Mark and Certificate
   I. Approval mark
     . . . .

THE CONTRACTING PARTIES,

D2.03   Being desirous of promoting the development and improvement of the international transport of passengers and goods by road,

Convinced of the need to increase the safety of the road traffic, to make regulations governing certain conditions of employment in international road transport in accordance with the principles of the International Labour Organisation, and jointly to adopt certain measures to ensure the observance of those regulations,

HAVE AGREED AS FOLLOWS,

Article 1: Definitions

D2.04   For the purposes of this Agreement

   (a) *"vehicle"* means any motor vehicle or trailer; this term includes any combination of vehicles;

   (b) *"motor vehicle"* means any self-propelled road vehicle which is normally used for carrying persons or goods by road or for drawing, on the road, vehicles used for the carriage of persons or goods; this term does not include agricultural tractors;

   (c) *"trailer"* means any vehicle designed to be drawn by a motor vehicle and includes semi-trailers;

   (d) *"semi-trailer"* means any trailer designed to be coupled to a motor vehicle in such a way that part of it rests on the motor vehicle and that a substantial part of its weight and of the weight of its load is borne by the motor vehicle;

   (e) *"combination of vehicles"* means coupled vehicles which travel on the road as a unit;

   (f) *"permissible maximum weight"* means the maximum weight of the laden vehicle declared permissible by the competent authority of the State in which the vehicle is registered;

   [(g) *"carriage by road"* means any journey made on roads open to the public of a vehicle, whether laden or not, used for the carriage of passengers or goods;]

   (h) *"international road transport"* [*"international carriage by road"*] means road transport which involves the crossing of at least one frontier;

   [(i) *"regular services"* means services which provide for the carriage of passengers at specified intervals along specified routes, passengers being taken up and set down at predetermined stopping points.

Rules governing the operations of services or documents taking the place thereof, approved by the competent authorities of Contracting Parties and published by the carrier before coming into operation, shall specify the conditions of carriage and in particular the frequency of services, timetables, faretables and the obligation to accept passengers for carriage, in so far as such conditions are not prescribed by any law or regulation.

Services by whomsoever organised, which provide for the carriage of specified categories of passengers to the exclusion of other passengers, in so far as such services are operated under the conditions specified in the first sub-paragraph of this definition, shall be deemed to be regular services. Such services, in particular those providing for the carriage of workers to and from their place of work or of schoolchildren to and from school, are hereinafter called "*special regular services*";]

(j) "*driver*" means any person, whether wage-earning or not, who drives the vehicle even for a short period, or who is carried on the vehicle in order to be available for driving if necessary;

(k) "*crew member*" means the driver or either of the following, whether wage-earning or not

(i) a driver's mate, *i.e.* any person accompanying the driver in order to assist him in certain manoeuvres and habitually taking an effective part in the transport operations, though not a driver in the sense of paragraph (j) of this article;

(ii) a conductor, *i.e.* any person who accompanies the driver of a vehicle engaged in the carriage of passengers and is responsible in particular for the issue or checking of tickets or other documents entitling passengers to travel on the vehicle;

[(l) "*week*" means the period between 0000 hours on Monday and 2400 hours on Sunday;]

[(m) "*rest*" means any uninterrupted period of at least one hour during which the driver may freely dispose of his time.]

(n), (o) *[repealed.]*

[Article 1 is printed as amended by Cm. 3042.   **D2.05**
In article 1, the square brackets used in the definition of "international road transport" occur in the text of the agreement and (unlike the use of square brackets elsewhere in this work) do not denote amendments to the text.
On depositing their instruments of accession to or ratification of this agreement, the governments of Belgium, Denmark, France, Luxembourg, the Netherlands and the United Kingdom each made the following declaration: "Transport operations between Member States of the European Economic Community shall be regarded as national transport operations within the meaning of the AETR in so far as such operations do not pass in transit through the territory of a third State which is a contracting party to the AETR" (cf. article 2(2) of Council Regulation (EEC) 2829/77).]

Article 2: Scope

1. This Agreement shall apply in the territory of each Contracting Party to all international road transport performed by any vehicle registered in the territory of the said Contracting Party or in the territory of any other Contracting Party.   **D2.06**

2. Nevertheless,

(a) if, in the course of an international road transport operation one or more crew members do not leave the national territory in which they normally exercise their occupational activities, the Contracting Party for that territory shall be free not to apply to him or them the provisions of this Agreement;

[(b) Unless the Contracting Parties whose territory is used agree otherwise, this Agreement shall not apply to the international road transport of goods performed by:

1. Vehicles used for the carriage of goods where the permissible maximum weight of the vehicle, including any trailer or semi-trailer, does not exceed 3.5 tonnes;

2. Vehicles used for the carriage of passengers which, by virtue of their construction and equipment are suitable for carrying not more than nine persons, including the driver, and are intended for that purpose;

3. Vehicles used for the carriage of passengers on regular services where the route covered by the service in question does not exceed 50 kilometres;

4. Vehicles with a maximum authorised speed not exceeding 30 kilometres per hour;

5. Vehicles used by or under the control of the armed services, civil defence, fire services, and forces responsible for maintaining public order;

6. Vehicles used in connection with the sewerage, flood protection, water, gas and electricity services, highway maintenance and control, refuse collection and disposal, telegraph and telephone services, carriage of postal articles, radio and television broadcasting and the detection of radio or television transmitters or receivers;

7. Vehicles used in emergencies or rescue operations;

8. Specialised vehicles used for medical purposes;

9. Vehicles transporting circus and fun-fair equipment;

10. Specialised breakdown vehicles;

11. Vehicles undergoing road tests for technical development, repair or maintenance purposes, and new or rebuilt vehicles which have not yet been put into service;

12. Vehicles used for non-commercial carriage of goods for personal use;

13. Vehicles used for milk collection from farms and the return to farms and milk containers or milk products intended for animal feed.]

(c), (d) *[repealed]*.

D2.07   *[Article 2 is printed as amended by Cm. 3042.]*

[Article 3: Application of some provisions of the Agreement to road transport performed by vehicles registered in the territories of non-Contracting States

D2.08   1. Each Contracting Party shall apply in its territory, in respect of international road transport performed by any vehicle registered in the territory of a State which is not a Contracting Party to this Agreement, provisions not less strict than those laid down in articles 5, 6, 7, 8, 9 and 10 of this Agreement.

2. It shall be open to any Contracting Party, in the case of a vehicle registered in a State which is not a Contracting Party to this Agreement, merely to require, in lieu of a control device conforming to the specifications in the annex to this Agreement, daily record sheets, completed manually by the driver.]

D2.09   *[Article 3 is printed as substituted by Cm. 3042.]*

[Article 4: General principles

D2.10   Each Contracting Party may apply higher minima or lower maxima than those laid down in articles 5 to 8 inclusive. Nevertheless, the provisions of this Agreement shall remain applicable to drivers, engaged in international road transport operations on vehicles registered in another Contracting or non-Contracting State.]

D2.11   *[Article 4 is printed as substituted by Cm. 3042.]*

[**Article 5: Crews**

1. The minimum ages for drivers engaged in the carriage of goods shall be as follows: **D2.12**

(a) for vehicles, including, where appropriate, trailers or semi-trailers, having a permissible maximum weight of not more than 7.5 tonnes, 18 years;

(b) for other vehicles:

21 years, or

18 years provided that the person concerned holds a certificate of professional competence recognised by one of the Contracting Parties confirming that he has completed a training course for drivers of vehicles intended for the carriage of goods by road. Contracting Parties shall inform one another of the prevailing national minimum training levels and other relevant conditions relating to drivers engaged in international carriage of goods under this Agreement.

2. Any driver engaged in the carriage of passengers shall have reached the age of 21 years.

Any driver engaged in the carriage of passengers on journeys beyond a 50 kilometre radius from the place where the vehicle is normally based must also fulfil one of the following conditions:

(a) he must have worked for at least one year in the carriage of goods as a driver of vehicles with a permissible maximum weight exceeding 3.5 tonnes;

(b) he must have worked for at least one year as a driver of vehicles used to provide passenger services on journeys within a 50 kilometre radius from the place where the vehicle is normally based, or other types of passenger services not subject to this Agreement provided the competent authority considers that he has by so doing acquired the necessary experience;

(c) he must hold a certificate of professional competence recognised by one of the Contracting Parties confirming that he has completed a training course for drivers of vehicles intended for the carriage of passengers by road.]

[Article 5 is printed as substituted by Cm. 3042.]   **D2.13**

[**Article 6: Driving periods**

1. The driving period between any two daily rest periods or between a daily rest period   **D2.14** and a weekly rest period, hereinafter called "*daily driving period*", shall not exceed nine hours. It may be extended twice in any one week to 10 hours.

A driver must after no more than six daily driving periods, take a weekly rest period as defined in article 8(3).

The weekly rest period may be postponed until the end of the sixth day if the total driving time over the six days does not exceed the maximum corresponding to six daily driving periods.

In the case of the international carriage of passengers, other than on regular services, the terms "six" and "sixth" in the second and third sub-paragraphs shall be replaced by "twelve" and "twelfth" respectively.

2. The total period of driving in any one fortnight shall not exceed ninety hours.]

[Article 6 is printed as substituted by Cm. 3042.]   **D2.15**

[**Article 6*bis*: Interruption of the daily rest period in the course of combined**   **D2.16**
transport operations   *[Repealed by Cm. 3042.]*

[Article 7: Breaks

D2.17   1. After four-and-a-half hours' driving, the driver shall observe a break of at least forty-five minutes, unless he begins a rest period.

2. This break may be replaced by breaks of at least fifteen minutes each distributed over the driving period or immediately after this period in such a way as to comply with the provisions of paragraph 1.

3. During these breaks, the driver may not carry out any other work. For the purposes of this article, the waiting time and time not devoted to driving spent in a vehicle in motion, a ferry, or a train shall not be regarded as "other work".

4. The breaks observed under this article may not be regarded as daily rest periods.]

D2.18   *[Article 7 is printed as substituted by Cm. 3042.]*

[Article 8: Rest periods

D2.19   1. In each period of twenty-four hours, the driver shall have a daily rest period of at least eleven consecutive hours, which may be reduced to a minimum of nine consecutive hours not more than three times in any one week, on condition that an equivalent period of rest be granted as compensation before the end of the following week.

On days when the rest is not reduced in accordance with the first sub-paragraph, it may be taken in two or three separate periods during the twenty-four hour period, one of which must be of at least eight consecutive hours. In this case the minimum length of the rest shall be increased to twelve hours.

2. During each period of thirty hours when a vehicle is manned by at least two drivers, each driver shall have a rest period of not less than eight consecutive hours.

3. In the course of each week, one of the rest periods referred to in paragraphs 1 and 2 shall be extended by way of weekly rest, to a total of forty-five consecutive hours. This rest period may be reduced to a minimum of thirty-six consecutive hours if taken at the place where the vehicle is normally based or where the driver is based, or to a minimum of twenty-four consecutive hours if taken elsewhere. Each reduction shall be compensated by an equivalent rest taken *en bloc* before the end of the third week following the week in question.

4. A weekly rest period which begins in one week and continues into the following week may be attached to either of these weeks.

5. In the case of the carriage of passengers to which article 6(1), fourth sub-paragraph, applies, the weekly rest period may be postponed until the week following that in respect of which the rest is due and added on to that second week's weekly rest.

6. Any rest taken as compensation for the reduction of the daily and/or weekly rest periods must be attached to another rest of at least eight hours and shall be granted, at the request of the person concerned, at the vehicle's parking place or driver's base.

7. The daily rest period may be taken in a vehicle, as long as it is fitted with a bunk and is stationary.

8. Notwithstanding the provisions in paragraph 1 above where a driver engaged in the carriage of goods or passengers accompanies a vehicle which is transported by ferryboat or train, the daily rest period may be interrupted not more than once, provided the following conditions are fulfilled:

> that part of the daily rest period spent on land must be able to be taken before or after the portion of the daily rest period taken on board the ferryboat or the train,

the period between the two portions of the daily rest period must be as short as possible and may on no account exceed one hour before embarkation or after disembarkation, customs formalities being included in the embarkation or disembarkation operations,

during both portions of the rest period the driver must be able to have access to a bunk or couchette.

The daily rest period, interrupted in this way, shall be increased by two hours.]

[Article 8 is printed as substituted by Cm. 3042.]

[Article 9: Exceptions

Provided that road safety is not thereby jeopardised and to enable him to reach a suitable stopping place, the driver may depart from the provisions of this Agreement to the extent necessary to ensure the safety of persons, of the vehicle or of its load. The driver shall indicate the nature of and reason for his departure from those provisions on the record sheet of the control device or in his duty roster.]   **D2.20**

[Article 9 is printed as substituted (for the original article 11) by Cm. 3042.]   **D2.21**

[Article 10: Control device

1. The Contracting Parties shall prescribe the installation and use on vehicles registered in their territory of a control device according to the following requirements: **D2.22**

   (a) The control device shall, as regards construction, installation, use and testing, comply with the requirements of this Agreement and the annex thereto, which shall form an integral part of this Agreement. [A control device which as regards construction, installation, use and testing complies with the EEC Council Regulation No. 3821.85 [*sic*] of 20 December 1985 shall be deemed to be in compliance with the requirements of this article.]

   (b) If the normal and appropriate use of a control device installed on a vehicle is not possible, each crew member shall enter by hand, using the appropriate graphic representation, the details corresponding to his occupational activities and rest periods on his record sheet.

   (c) When, by reasons of their being away from the vehicles, the crew members are unable to make use of the device, they shall insert by hand, using the appropriate graphic representation, on their record sheet the various times corresponding to their occupational activities while they were away.

   (d) The crew members must always have available, and be able to present for inspection record sheets for the current week and for the last day of the previous week on which they drove.

   (e) The crew members must ensure that the control device be activated and handled correctly and that, in case of malfunctioning, it be repaired as soon as possible.

2. The employer shall issue a sufficient number of record sheets to drivers, bearing in mind the fact that these sheets are personal in character, the length of the period of service and the possible obligation to replace sheets which are damaged, or have been taken by an authorised inspecting officer. The employer shall issue to drivers only sheets of an approved model suitable for use in the equipment installed in the vehicle.

3. Undertakings shall keep in good order the record sheets filled in as provided under (b), (c) and (d) of paragraph 1 of this article, for a period of not less than 12 months after the date of the last entry and shall produce them at the request of the control authorities.]

D2.23   *[Article 10 is printed as substituted (for article 12bis as inserted by Cm. 9037) by Cm. 3042 and as subsequently amended by Cm. 3135.]*

D2.24   **Articles 11–25**   *[Omitted.]*

*   *   *

SIGNATURES

D2.25   *[The following states have signed and ratified the agreement:*

> *Austria*
> *Belgium*
> *Federal Republic of Germany*
> *France*
> *Luxembourg*
> *the Netherlands*
> *Norway*
> *Poland*
> *Portugal*
> *Sweden*
> *Switzerland, and*
> *the United Kingdom (including the Isle of Man)*

Italy signed the agreement but has not yet ratified it.

The agreement came into operation, in accordance with the original article 16, paragraph 4, on January 5, 1976; it came into operation in the United Kingdom on August 18, 1978.

On signature of the agreement, the Contracting States agreed the following declaration which was set out in the Protocol of Signature to the agreement: "The Contracting Parties declare that this Agreement is without prejudice to such provisions as may, if appropriate, subsequently be drawn up in the matter of the duration and spread-over of work."]

ACCESSIONS

D2.26   *[The following countries have also acceded or succeeded to the agreement:*

Andorra	*Kazakhstan*
Azerbaijan	*Liechtenstein*
Belarus	*Lithuania*
Bulgaria	*Macedonia (former Yugoslav Republic)*
Croatia	*Moldavia*
Czech Republic	*Slovakia*
Denmark	*Slovenia*
Estonia	*Spain*
Finland	*Turkmenistan*
Greece	*Union of Soviet Socialist Republics*
Hungary	*Uzbekistan*
Yugoslavia	

The above statements as to ratifications and accessions set out the historical position. The exact status of all the successor states to the former USSR and Yugoslavia is not certain, although Azerbaijan, Kazakhstan, Turkmenistan, Uzbekistan and Croatia and Slovenia have formally acceded to the agreement.]

[ANNEX

CONTROL DEVICE

General Provisions

I. TYPE APPROVAL

Article 1

Applications for the approval of a type of control device or of a model record sheet shall be submitted, accompanied by the appropriate specifications, by the manufacturer or his agent to a Contracting Party. No application in respect of any one type of control device or of any one model record sheet may be submitted to more than one Contracting Party. **D2.27**

Article 2

A Contracting Party shall grant its approval to any type of control device or to any model record sheet which conforms to the requirements laid down in Appendix 1 to this Annex, provided the Contracting Party is in a position to check that production models conform to the approved prototype. **D2.28**

Any modifications or additions to an approved model must receive additional type approval from the Contracting Party which granted the original type approval.

Article 3

Contracting Parties shall issue to the applicant an approval mark, which shall conform to the model shown in Appendix 2 for each type of control device or model record sheet which they approve pursuant to article 2. **D2.29**

Article 4

The competent authorities of the Contracting Party to which the application for type approval has been submitted shall, in respect of each type of control device or model record sheet which they approve or refuse to approve, either send within one month to the authorities of the other Contracting Parties a copy of the approval certificate accompanied by copies of the relevant specifications, or, if such is the case, notify those authorities that approval has been refused; in cases of refusal they shall communicate the reasons for their decision. **D2.30**

Article 5

1. If a Contracting Party which has granted the type approval as provided for in article 2 finds that certain control device or record sheets bearing the type approval mark which it has issued do not conform to the prototype which it has approved, it shall take the necessary measures to ensure that production models conform to the approved prototype. The measures taken may, if necessary, extend to withdrawal of the type approval. **D2.31**

2. A Contracting Party which has granted the type approval shall withdraw such approval if the control device or record sheet which has been approved is not in conformity with this annex or its appendices or displays in use any general defect which makes it unsuitable for the purpose for which it is intended.

3. If a Contracting Party which has granted the type approval is notified by another Contracting Party of one of the cases referred to in paragraphs 1 and 2, it shall also, after consulting the latter Contracting Party, take the steps laid down in those paragraphs, subject to paragraph 5.

4. A Contracting Party which ascertains that one of the cases referred to in paragraph 2 has arisen may forbid until further notice the placing on the market and putting into service of the control device or record sheets. The same applies in the cases mentioned in paragraph 1 with respect to control device or record sheets which have been exempted from the initial verification, if the manufacturer, after due warning, does not bring the device into line with the approved model or with the requirements of this annex.

In any event, the competent authorities of the Contracting Parties shall notify one another within one month, of any withdrawal of the type approval or of any other measures taken pursuant to paragraphs 1, 2 and 3 and shall specify the reasons for such action.

5. If a Contracting Party which has granted the type approval disputes the existence of any of the cases specified in paragraphs 1 or 2 notified to it, the Contracting Parties concerned shall endeavour to settle the dispute.

Article 6

D2.32   1. An applicant for the type approval of a model record sheet shall state on his application the type or types of control device on which the sheet in question is designed to be used and shall provide suitable equipment of such type or types for the purpose of testing the sheet.

2. The competent authorities of each Contracting Party shall indicate on the approval certificate for the model record sheet the type or types of control device on which that model sheet may be used.

Article 7

D2.33   No Contracting Party may refuse to register any vehicle fitted with a control device, or prohibit the entry into service or use of such vehicle for any reason connected with the fact that the vehicle is fitted with such device, if the device bears the approval mark referred to in article 3 and the installation plaque referred to in article 9.

Article 8

D2.34   All decisions pursuant to this annex refusing or withdrawing approval of a type of control device or model record sheet shall specify in detail the reasons on which they are based. A decision shall be communicated to the party concerned, who shall at the same time be informed of the remedies available to him under the laws of the Contracting Party and of the time-limits for the exercise of such remedies.

II. INSTALLATION AND INSPECTION

Article 9

D2.35   1. The control device may be installed or repaired by fitters or workshops approved by the competent authorities of Contracting Parties for that purpose after the latter, should they so desire, have heard the views of the manufacturers concerned.

2. The approved fitter or workshop shall place a special mark on the seals which it affixes. The competent authorities of each Contracting Party shall maintain a register of the marks used.

3. The competent authorities of the Contracting Parties shall send each other their lists of approved fitters or workshops and also copies of the marks used.

4. For the purpose of certifying that installation of control device took place in accordance with the requirements of this annex an installation plaque affixed as provided in Appendix 1 shall be used.

III. USE OF EQUIPMENT

Article 10

The employer and drivers shall be responsible for seeing that the device functions   **D2.36**
correctly.

Article 11

1. Drivers shall not use dirty or damaged record sheets. The sheets shall be adequately   **D2.37**
protected on this account.

In case of damage to a sheet bearing recordings, drivers shall attach the damaged sheet
to the spare sheet used to replace it.

2. Drivers shall use the record sheets every day on which they are driving, starting
from the moment they take over the vehicle. The record sheet shall not be withdrawn before the end of the daily working period unless its withdrawal is otherwise
authorized. No record sheet may be used to cover a period longer than that for which it
is intended.

When, as a result of being away from the vehicle, a driver is unable to use the device
fitted to the vehicle, the periods of time shall be entered on the sheet, either manually, by
automatic recording or other means, legibly and without dirtying the sheet.

Drivers shall amend the record sheets as necessary should there be more than one driver
on board the vehicle, so that the information referred to in Chapter II (1) to (3) of Appendix
1 is recorded on the record sheet of the driver who is actually driving.

3. The control device shall be so designed that it is possible for an authorised inspecting
officer, if necessary after opening the equipment, to read the recordings relating to the nine
hours preceding the time of the check without permanently deforming, damaging or
soiling the sheet.

The control device shall, furthermore, be so designed that it is possible, without opening
the case, to verify that recordings are being made.

4. Whenever requested by an authorised inspecting officer to do so, the driver must be
able to produce record sheets for the current week, and in any case for the last day of the
previous week on which he drove.

APPENDIX 1

Requirements for Construction, Testing, Installation and Inspection

I. DEFINITIONS

In this appendix   **D2.38**

(a) *"control device"* means equipment intended for installation in road vehicles to show
and record automatically or semi-automatically details of the movement of
those vehicles and of certain working periods of their drivers;

(b) *"record sheet"* means a sheet designed to accept and retain recorded data, to be placed
in the control device and on which the marking devices of the latter inscribe a
continuous record of the information to be recorded;

(c) *"constant of the control device"* means the numerical characteristic giving the value of
the input signal required to show and record a distance travelled of 1 kilometre;
this constant must be expressed either in revolutions per kilometre (k = . . .
rev/km), or in impulses per kilometre (k = . . . imp/km);

(d) *"characteristic coefficient of the vehicle"* means the numerical characteristic giving the value of the output signal emitted by the part of the vehicle linking it with the control device (gearbox output shaft or axle) while the vehicle travels a distance of one measured kilometre under normal test conditions (see Chapter VI, paragraph 4 of this appendix). The characteristic coefficient is expressed either in revolutions per kilometre ($W = rev/km$) or in impulses per kilometre ($W = \ldots imp/km$);

(e) *"effective circumference of wheel tyres"* means the average of the distances travelled by the several wheels moving the vehicle (driving wheels) in the course of one complete rotation. The measurement of these distances must be made under normal test conditions (see Chapter VI, paragraph 4 of this appendix) and is expressed in the form: $1 = \ldots mm$.

II. GENERAL CHARACTERISTICS AND FUNCTIONS OF CONTROL DEVICE

D2.39   The control device must be able to record the following:

1. distance travelled by the vehicle;
2. speed of the vehicle;
3. driving time;
4. other periods of work or of availability;
5. breaks from work and daily rest periods;
6. opening of the case containing the record sheet;
7. for electronic control device which is device operating by signals transmitted electrically from the distance and speed sensor, any interruption exceeding 100 milliseconds in the power supply of the recording equipment (except lighting), in the power supply of the distance and speed sensor and any interruption in the signal lead to the distance and speed sensor.

For vehicles used by two drivers the control device must be capable of recording simultaneously but distinctly and on two separate sheets details of the periods listed under 3, 4 and 5.

III. CONSTRUCTION REQUIREMENTS FOR CONTROL DEVICE

A. General points

D2.40   1. Control device shall include the following:

(a) Visual instruments showing:
distance travelled (distance recorder),
speed (speedometer),
time (clock).

(b) Recording instruments comprising:
a recorder of the distance travelled,
a speed recorder,
one or more time recorders satisfying the requirements laid down in Chapter III C 4.

(c) A means of marking showing on the record sheet individually:
each opening of the case containing that sheet,
for electronic control device, as defined in point 7 of Chapter II, any interruption exceeding 100 milliseconds in the power supply of the control device (except lighting), not later than at switching-on the power supply again,
for electronic control device, as defined in point 7 of Chapter II, any interruption exceeding 100 milliseconds in the power supply of the distance and speed sensor and any interruption in the signal lead to the distance and speed sensor.

2. Any inclusion in the equipment of devices additional to those listed above must not interfere with the proper operation of the mandatory devices or with the reading of them. The control device must be submitted for approval complete with any such additional devices.

3. Materials

(a) All the constituent parts of the control device must be made of materials with sufficient stability and mechanical strength and stable electrical and magnetic characteristics.

(b) Any modification in a constituent part of the control device or in the nature of the materials used for its manufacture must, before being applied in manufacture, be submitted for approval to the authority which granted type-approval for the control device.

4. Measurement of distance travelled

The distances travelled may be measured and recorded either:

so as to include both forward and reverse movement, or
so as to include only forward movement.

Any recording of reversing movements must on no account affect the clarity and accuracy of the other recordings.

5. Measurement of speed

(a) The range of speed measurement shall be as stated in the type-approval certificate.

(b) The natural frequency and the damping of the measuring device must be such that the instruments showing and recording the speed can, within the range of measurement, follow acceleration changes of up to 2m/section 2, within the limits of accepted tolerances.

6. Measurement of time (clock)

(a) The control of the mechanism for resetting the clock must be located inside a case containing the record sheet; each opening of that case must be automatically recorded on the record sheet.

(b) If the forward movement mechanism of the record sheet is controlled by the clock, the period during which the latter will run correctly after being fully wound must be greater by at least 10 per cent than the recording period corresponding to the maximum sheet-load of the equipment.

7. Lighting and protection

(a) The visual instruments of the control device must be provided with adequate non-dazzling lighting.

(b) For normal conditions of use, all the internal parts of the control must be protected against damp and dust. In addition they must be made proof against tampering by means of casings capable of being sealed.

B. Visual instruments

1. Distance travelled indicator (distance recorder)   **D2.41**

(a) The value of the smallest grading on the control device showing distance travelled must be 0.1 kilometres. Figures showing hectometres must be clearly distinguishable from those showing whole kilometres.

(b) The figures on the distance recorder must be clearly legible and must have an apparent height of at least 4mm.

(c) The distance recorder must be capable of reading up to at least 99,999.9 kilometres.

2. Speed indicators (speedometer)

(a) Within the range of measurement, the speed scale must be uniformly graduated by 1, 2, 5 or 10 kilometres per hour. The value of a speed graduation (space between two successive marks) must not exceed 10 per cent of the maximum speed shown on the scale.

(b) The range indicated beyond that measured need not be marked by figures.

(c) The length of each space on the scale representing a speed difference of 10 kilometres per hour must not be less than 10 millimetres.

(d) On an indicator with a needle, the distance between the needle and the control device face must not exceed 3 millimetres.

3. Time indicator (clock)

The time indicator must be visible from outside the control device and give a clear, plain and unambiguous reading.

C. Recording instruments

D2.42   1. General points

(a) All equipment, whatever the form of the record sheet (strip or disc) must be provided with a mark enabling the record sheet to be inserted correctly, in such a way as to ensure that the time shown by the clock and the time-marking on the sheet correspond.

(b) The mechanism moving the record sheet must be such as to ensure that the latter moves without play and can be freely inserted and removed.

(c) For record sheets in disc form, the forward movement device must be controlled by the clock mechanism. In this case, the rotating movement of the sheet must be continuous and uniform, with a minimum speed of 7 millimetres per hour measured at the inner border of the ring marking the edge of the speed recording area.

In equipment of the strip type, where the forward movement device of the sheets is controlled by the clock mechanism the speed of rectilinear forward movement must be at least 10 millimetres per hour.

(d) Recording of the distance travelled, of the speed of the vehicle and of any opening of the case containing the record sheet or sheets must be automatic.

2. Recording distance travelled

(a) Every kilometre of distance travelled must be represented on the record by a variation of at least 1 millimetre on the corresponding co-ordinate.

(b) Even at speeds reaching the upper limit of the range of measurement, the record of distances must still be clearly legible.

3. Recording speed

(a) Whatever the form of the record sheet, the speed recording stylus must normally move in a straight line and at right angles to the direction of travel of the record sheet.

However, the movement of the stylus may be curvilinear, provided the following conditions are satisfied:

the trace drawn by the stylus must be perpendicular to the average circumference (in the case of sheets in disc form) or to the axis (in the case of sheets in strip form) of the area reserved for speed recording, the ratio between the radius of curvature of the trace drawn by the stylus and the width of the area reserved for speed recording must be not less than 2.4 to 1 whatever the form of the record sheet,

the markings on the time-scale must cross the recording area in a curve of the same radius as the trace drawn by the stylus. The spaces between the markings on the time-scale must represent a period not exceeding 1 hour.

(b) Each variation in speed of 10 kilometres per hour must be represented on the record by a variation of at least 1.5 millimetres on the corresponding co-ordinate.

4. Recording time

(a) Control device must be so constructed that the period of driving time is always recorded automatically and that it is possible, through the operation where necessary of a switch device to record separately the other periods of time as follows:

    (i) under the sign   ⊗⌒   : driving time;

    (ii) under the sign   ✗   : all other periods of work;

    (iii) under the sign   ▨   : other periods of availability, namely:

waiting time, i.e. the period during which drivers need remain at their posts only for the purpose of answering any calls to start or resume driving or to carry out other work,
time spent beside the driver while the vehicle is in motion,
time spent on a bunk while the vehicle is in motion;

    (iv) under the sign   ⊢═⊣   : breaks in work and daily rest periods.

Each contracting party may permit all the periods referred to in sub-paragraphs (ii) and (iii) above to be recorded under the sign ▨ on the record sheets used on vehicles registered in its territory.

(b) It must be possible, from the characteristics of the traces, their relative positions and if necessary the signs laid down in paragraph 4(a) to distinguish clearly between the various periods of time.

The various periods of time should be differentiated from one another on the record by differences in the thickness of the relevant traces, or by any other system of at least equal effectiveness from the point of view of legibility and ease of interpretation of the record.

(c) In the case of vehicles with a crew consisting of more than one driver, the recordings provided for in paragraph 4(a) must be made on two separate sheets, each sheet being allocated to one driver. In this case, the forward movement of the separate sheets must be effected either by a single mechanism or by separate synchronised mechanisms.

D. Closing device

1. The case containing the record sheet or sheets and the control of the mechanism for resetting the clock must be provided with a lock.   **D2.43**

2. Each opening of the case containing the record sheet or sheets and the control of the mechanism for resetting the clock must be automatically recorded on the sheet or sheets.

E. Markings

D2.44   1. The following markings must appear on the instrument face of the control device:

close to the figure shown by the distance recorder, the unit of measurement of distance, indicated by the abbreviation "km",

near the speed scale, the marking "km/h",

the measurement range of the speedometer in the form "Vmin . . . km/h, Vmax . . . km/h". This marking is not necessary if it is shown on the descriptive plaque of the equipment.

However, these requirements shall not apply to control devices approved before 10 August 1970.

2. The descriptive plaque must be built into the equipment and must show the following markings, which must be visible on the control device when installed:

name and address of the manufacturer of the equipment,

manufacturer's number and year of construction,

approval mark for the control device type,

the constant of the equipment in the form "k = . . . rev/km" or "k = . . . imp/km",

optionally, the range of speed measurement, in the form indicated in point 1,

should the sensitivity of the instrument to the angle of inclination be capable of affecting the readings given by the equipment beyond the permitted tolerances, the permissible angle expressed as:

where α is the angle measured from the horizontal position of the front face (fitted the right way up) of the equipment for which the instrument is calibrated, while β and δ represent respectively the maximum permissible upward and downward deviations from the angle of calibration α.

F. Maximum tolerances (visual and recording instruments)

D2.45   1. On the test bench before installation:

(a) distance travelled:

1 per cent more or less than the real distance, where the distance is at least 1 kilometre;

(b) speed:

3 km/h more or less than the real speed;

(c) time:

± two minutes per day with a maximum of 10 minutes per 7 days in cases where the running period of the clock after rewinding is not less than that period.

2. On installation:

(a) distance travelled:

2 per cent more or less than the real distance, where that distance is at least 1 kilometre;

(b) speed

4 km/h more or less than real speed;

(c) time

± two minutes per day, or

± 10 minutes per seven days.

3. In use:

(a) distance travelled:

4 per cent more or less than the real distance, where that distance is at least 1 kilometre;

(b) speed

6 km/h more or less than the real speed;

(c) time:

± two minutes per day, or

± 10 minutes per seven days.

4. The maximum tolerances set out in paragraphs 1, 2 and 3 are valid for temperatures between 0° and 40°C, temperatures being taken in close proximity to the equipment.

5. Measurement of the maximum tolerances set out in paragraphs 2 and 3 shall take place under the conditions laid down in Chapter VI.

IV. RECORD SHEETS

A. General points

1. The record sheets must be such that they do not impede the normal functioning of **D2.46** the instrument and that the records which they contain are indelible and easily legible and identifiable.

The record sheets must retain their dimensions and any records made on them under normal conditions of humidity and temperature.

In addition it must be possible by each crew member to enter on the sheets, without damaging them and without affecting the legibility of the recordings, the following information:

(a) on beginning to use the sheet—his surname and first name;

(b) the date and place where use of the sheet begins and the date and place where such use ends;

(c) the registration number of each vehicle to which he is assigned, both at the start of the first journey recorded on the sheet and then, in the event of a change of vehicle, during use of the sheet;

(d) the odometer reading:

at the start of the first journey recorded on the sheet,

at the end of the last journey recorded on the sheet,

in the event of a change of vehicle during a working day (reading on the vehicle to which he was assigned and reading on the vehicle to which he is to be assigned);

(e) the time of any change of vehicle.

Under normal conditions of storage, the recordings must remain clearly legible for at least one year.

2. The minimum recording capacity of the sheets, whatever their form, must be 24 hours. If several discs are linked together to increase the continuous recording capacity which can be achieved without intervention by staff, the links between the various discs must be made in such a way that there are no breaks in or overlapping of recordings at the point of transfer from one disc to another.

B. Recording areas and their graduation

D2.47   1. The record sheets shall include the following recording areas:

an area exclusively reserved for data relating to speed,

an area exclusively reserved for data relating to distance travelled,

one or more areas for data relating to driving time, to other periods of work and availability to breaks from work and to rest periods for drivers.

2. The area for recording speed must be scaled off in divisions of 20 kilometres per hour or less. The speed corresponding to each marking on the scale must be shown in figures against that marking. The symbol "km/h" must be shown at least once within the area. The last marking on the scale must coincide with the upper limit of the range of measurement.

3. The area for recording distance travelled must be set out in such a way that the number of kilometres travelled may be read without difficulty.

4. The area or areas reserved for recording the periods referred to in point 1 must be so marked that it is possible to distinguish clearly between the various periods of time.

C. Information to be printed on the record sheets

D2.48   Each sheet must bear, in printed form, the following information:

name and address or trade name of the manufacturer,

approval mark for the model of the sheet,

approval mark for the type or types of control devices in which the sheet may be used,

upper limit of the speed measurement range, printed in kilometres per hour.

By way of minimal additional requirements, each sheet must bear, in printed form a time-scale graduated in such a way that the time may be read directly at intervals of 15 minutes while each 5-minute interval may be determined without difficulty.

D. Free space for hand-written insertions

D2.49   A free space must be provided on the sheets such that drivers may as a minimum write in the following details:

surname and first name of the driver,

date and place where use of the sheet begins and date and place where such use ends,

the registration number or numbers of the vehicle or vehicles to which the driver is assigned during the use of the sheet,

odometer readings from the vehicle or vehicles to which the driver is assigned during the use of the sheet,

the time at which any change of vehicle takes place.

V. INSTALLATION OF CONTROL DEVICE

A. General points

D2.50   1. Control device must be positioned in the vehicle in such a way that the driver has a clear view from his seat of speedometer, distance recorder and clock while at the same time all parts of those instruments, including driving parts, are protected against accidental damage.

2. It must be possible to adapt the constant of the control device to the characteristic coefficient of the vehicle by means of a suitable device, to be known as an adaptor.

Vehicles with two or more axle ratios must be fitted with a switch device whereby these various ratios may be automatically brought into line with the ratio for which the control device has been adapted to the vehicle

3. After the control device has been checked on installation, an installation plaque shall be affixed to the vehicle beside the device or in the device itself and in such a way as to be clearly visible. After every inspection by an approved fitter or workshop requiring a change in the setting of the installation itself, a new plaque must be affixed in place of the previous one.

The plaque must show at least the following details:

name, address or trade name of the approved fitter or workshop,

characteristic coefficient of the vehicle, in the form "w = . . . rev/km" or "w = . . . imp/km",

effective circumference of the wheel tyres in the form "l = . . . mm",

the dates on which the characteristic coefficient of the vehicle was determined and the effective measured circumference of the wheel tyres.

B. Sealing

The following parts must be sealed: **D2.51**

(a) the installation plaque, unless it is attached in such a way that it cannot be removed without the markings thereon being destroyed;

(b) the two ends of the link between the control device proper and the vehicle;

(c) the adaptor itself and the point of its insertion into the circuit;

(d) the switch mechanism for vehicles with two or more axle ratios;

(e) the links joining the adaptor and the switch mechanism to the rest of the control device;

(f) the casings required under Chapter III A 7(b).

In particular cases, further seals may be required on approval of the control device type and a note of the positioning of these seals must be made on the approval certificate.

Only the seals mentioned in (b), (c) and (e) may be removed in cases of emergency; for each occasion that these seals are broken a written statement giving the reasons for such action must be prepared and made available to the competent authority.

VI. CHECKS AND INSPECTIONS

The Contracting Party shall nominate the bodies which shall carry out the checks and   **D2.52**
inspections.

1. Certification of new or repaired instruments

Every individual device, whether new or repaired, shall be certified in respect of its correct operation and the accuracy of its readings and recordings, within the limits laid down in Chapter III F 1, by means of sealing in accordance with Chapter V B (f).

For this purpose the Contracting Party may stipulate an initial verification, consisting of a check on and confirmation of the conformity of a new or repaired device with the type-approved model and/or with the requirements of this annex and its appendices or may delegate the power to certify to the manufacturers or to their authorised agents.

2. Installation

When being fitted to a vehicle, the control device and the whole installation must comply with the provisions relating to maximum tolerances laid down in Chapter III F 2.

The inspection tests shall be carried out by the approved fitter or workshop on his or its responsibility.

3. Periodic inspections

(a) Periodic inspections of the control device fitted to vehicles shall take place at least every two years and may be carried out in conjunction with roadworthiness tests of vehicles.

These inspections shall include the following checks:

that the control device is working correctly,

that the control device carries the type-approval mark,

that the installation plaque is affixed,

that the seals on the control device on the other parts of the installation are intact,

the actual circumference of the tyres.

(b) An inspection to ensure compliance with the provision of Chapter III F 3 on the maximum tolerances in use shall be carried out at least once every six years, although each Contracting Party may stipulate a shorter interval or such inspection in respect of vehicles registered in its territory. Such inspections must include replacement of the installation plaque.

4. Measurement of errors

The measurement of errors on installation and during use shall be carried out under the following conditions, which are to be regarded as constituting standard test conditions:

vehicle unladen, in normal running order,

tyre pressures in accordance with the manufacturer's instructions.

tyre wear within the limits allowed by law,

movement of the vehicle: the vehicle must proceed, driven by its own engine, in a straight line and on a level surface, at a speed of 50 ± 5 km/h; provided that it is of comparable accuracy, the test may also be carried out on an appropriate test bench.

APPENDIX 2

Approval Mark and Certificate

I. APPROVAL MARK

[1. The approval mark shall be made up of:

D2.53   A rectangle, within which shall be placed the letter "e" followed by a distinguishing number for the country which has issued the approval in accordance with the following conventional signs:

Germany	—	1	Austria	—	12
France	—	2	Luxembourg	—	13
Italy	—	3	Norway	—	16
Netherlands	—	4	Denmark	—	18
Sweden	—	5	Poland	—	20
Belgium	—	6	Portugal	—	21
Czech Republic	—	8	Russian Federation	—	22
Spain	—	9	Greece	—	23
Yugoslavia	—	10	Ireland	—	24
United Kingdom	—	11	Croatia	—	25

Subsequent numbers shall be assigned:

(i) To countries Contracting Parties to the 1958 Agreement Concerning the Adoption of Uniform Conditions of Approval and Reciprocal Recognition of Approval for Motor Vehicle Equipment and Parts [*Cmnd. 2535; not reproduced in this work*] the same numbers as assigned to those countries by that Agreement;

(ii) To countries non-Contracting Parties to the 1958 Agreement—in the chronological order in which they ratify or accede to this Agreement;

and

An approval number corresponding to the number of the approval certificate drawn up for the prototype of the control device or the record sheet, placed at any point within the immediate proximity of this rectangle.

Note: In order to ensure in the future conformity between conventional signs in the 1958 Agreement and those set up in the AETR Agreement new Contracting Parties should be allocated the same number in both Agreements.]

2. The approval mark shall be shown on the descriptive plaque of each set of control device and on each record sheet. It must be indelible and must always remain clearly legible.

3. The dimensions of the approval mark drawn below are expressed in millimetres, these dimensions being minima. The ratios between the dimensions must be maintained.

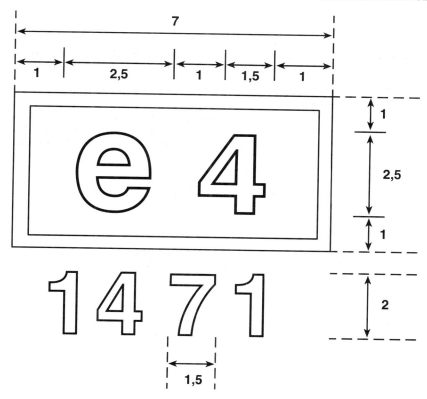

(1) These figures are shown for guidance only.

II. APPROVAL CERTIFICATE

[*Omitted.*]

D2.54   *[The Annex is printed as substituted by Cm. 3042 and as subsequently amended by Cm. 3135.
The "Note" at the end of paragraph 1 of Chapter I (approval mark) of Appendix 2 to the Annex is part
of the text of that paragraph and not an editorial comment.]*

PROTOCOL OF SIGNATURE

*   *   *

Index

All entries are to paragraph number.

Index

Index

Index

Index